The Sporting News

HOCKEY REGISTER

1997-98 EDITION

Editors/Hockey Register
MARK BONAVITA
SEAN STEWART

Contributing Editor/Hockey Register
LARRY WIGGE

The Sporting News

PUBLISHING CO.

Efrem Zimbalist III, President and Chief Executive Officer, Times Mirror Magazines; **James H. Nuckols,** President, The Sporting News; **Francis X. Farrell,** Senior Vice President, Publisher; **John D. Rawlings,** Senior Vice President, Editorial Director; **John Kastberg,** Vice President, General Manager; **Kathy Kinkeade,** Vice President, Operations; **Steve Meyerhoff,** Executive Editor; **Mike Huguenin,** Assistant Managing Editor; **Craig Carter,** Statistical Editor; **Marilyn Kasal,** Production Director; **Mike Bruner,** Prepress Director; **Chris Placzek,** Database Analyst; **Michael Behrens and Christen Webster,** Macintosh Production Artists; **Adam Bender, Brendan Roberts and Daniel Wetmore,** Editorial Assistants.

A Times Mirror Company

ON THE COVER: Detroit Red Wings' center Sergei Fedorov helped lead the Red Wings to their first Stanley Cup championship in more than 40 years. (Photo by THE SPORTING NEWS.)

Spine photo of Wayne Gretzky by Robert Seale/THE SPORTING NEWS.

Editorial assistance provided by Igor Kuperman of the Phoenix Coyotes.

Copyright © 1997 by The Sporting News Publishing Co., 10176 Corporate Square Drive, Suite 200, St. Louis, MO 63132. All rights reserved. Printed in the U.S.A.

THE SPORTING NEWS is a registered trademark of The Sporting News Publishing Co., a Times Mirror Company.

ISBN: 0-89204-581-7

10 9 8 7 6 5 4 3 2 1

CONTENTS

EXPLANATION OF AWARDS

NHL AWARDS: Alka-Seltzer Plus Award: plus/minus leader. **Art Ross Trophy:** leading scorer. **Bill Masterton Memorial Trophy:** perseverance, sportsmanship and dedication to hockey. **Bud Light/NHL Man of the Year:** service to community; called Budweiser/NHL Man of the Year prior to 1990-91. **Budweiser/NHL Man of the Year:** service to community; renamed Bud Light/NHL Man of the Year in 1990-91. **Calder Memorial Trophy:** rookie of the year. **Conn Smythe Trophy:** most valuable player in playoffs. **Dodge Performance of the Year Award:** most outstanding achievement or single-game performance. **Dodge Performer of the Year Award:** most outstanding performer in regular season. **Dodge Ram Tough Award:** highest combined total of power-play, shorthanded, game-winning and game-tying goals. **Emery Edge Award:** plus/minus leader; awarded from 1982-83 through 1987-88. **Frank J. Selke Trophy:** best defensive forward. **Hart Memorial Trophy:** most valuable player. **Jack Adams Award:** coach of the year. **James Norris Memorial Trophy:** outstanding defenseman. **King Clancy Memorial Trophy:** humanitarian contributions. **Lady Byng Memorial Trophy:** most gentlemanly player. **Lester B. Pearson Award:** outstanding player as selected by NHL Players' Association. **Lester Patrick Trophy:** outstanding service to hockey in U.S. **Trico Goaltender Award:** best save percentage. **Vezina Trophy:** best goaltender; awarded to goalkeeper(s) having played minimum of 25 games for team with fewest goals scored against prior to 1981-82. **William M. Jennings Trophy:** goalkeeper(s) having played minimum of 25 games for team with fewest goals scored against.

MINOR LEAGUE AWARDS: Baz Bastien Trophy: top goaltender (AHL). **Bobby Orr Trophy:** best defenseman (CHL); awarded prior to 1984-85. **Bob Gassoff Award:** most improved defenseman (CHL); awarded prior to 1984-85. **Commissioner's Trophy:** coach of the year (IHL). **Dudley (Red) Garrett Memorial Trophy:** rookie of the year (AHL). **Eddie Shore Plaque:** outstanding defenseman (AHL). **Fred Hunt Memorial Award:** sportsmanship, determination and dedication (AHL). **Garry F. Longman Memorial Trophy:** outstanding rookie (IHL). **Governors Trophy:** outstanding defenseman (IHL). **Harry (Hap) Holmes Memorial Trophy:** goaltender(s) having played minimum of 25 games for team with fewest goals scored against (AHL); awarded to outstanding goaltender prior to 1983-84. **Jack Butterfield Trophy:** Calder Cup playoffs MVP (AHL). **Jake Milford Trophy:** coach of the year (CHL); awarded prior to 1984-85. **James Gatschene Memorial Trophy:** most valuable player (IHL). **James Norris Memorial Trophy:** outstanding goaltender (IHL). **John B. Sollenberger Trophy:** leading scorer (AHL); originally called Wally Kilrea Trophy, later changed to Carl Liscombe Trophy until summer of 1955. **Ken McKenzie Trophy:** outstanding U.S.-born rookie (IHL). **Ken McKenzie Trophy:** top rookie (CHL); awarded to scoring leader from 1992-93. **Leo P. Lamoureux Memorial Trophy:** leading scorer (IHL); originally called George H. Wilkinson Trophy from 1946-47 through 1959-60. **Les Cunningham Plaque:** most valuable player (AHL). **Louis A.R. Pieri Memorial Award:** top coach (AHL). **Max McNab Trophy:** playoff MVP (CHL); awarded prior to 1984-85. **N.R. (Bud) Poile Trophy:** playoff MVP (IHL); originally called Turner Cup Playoff MVP from 1984-85 through 1988-89. **Phil Esposito Trophy:** leading scorer (CHL); awarded prior to 1984-85. **Terry Sawchuk Trophy:** top goaltenders (CHL); awarded prior to 1984-85. **Tommy Ivan Trophy:** most valuable player (CHL); awarded prior to 1984-85. **Turner Cup Playoff MVP:** playoff MVP (IHL); renamed N.R. (Bud) Poile Trophy in 1989-90.

MAJOR JUNIOR LEAGUE AWARDS: Association of Journalists for Major Junior League Hockey Trophy: top pro prospect (QMJHL); renamed Michael Bossy Trophy in 1983-84. **Bill Hunter Trophy:** top defenseman (WHL); called Top Defenseman Trophy prior to 1987-88 season. **Bob Brownridge Memorial Trophy:** top scorer (WHL); later renamed Bob Clarke Trophy. **Bobby Smith Trophy:** scholastic player of the year (OHL). **Bob Clarke Trophy:** top scorer (WHL); originally called Bob Brownridge Memorial Trophy. **Brad Hornung Trophy:** most sportsmanlike player (WHL); called Frank Boucher Memorial Trophy for most gentlemanly player prior to 1987-88 season. **Dave Pinkney Trophy:** top team goaltending (OHL). **Del Wilson Trophy:** top goaltender (WHL); called Top Goaltender Trophy prior to 1987-88 season. **Des Instructeurs Trophy:** rookie of the year (QMJHL); awarded to top rookie forward since 1981-82 season; renamed Michel Bergeron Trophy in 1985-86. **Dunc McCallum Memorial Trophy:** coach of the year (WHL). **Eddie Powers Memorial Trophy:** scoring champion (OHL). **Emile (Butch) Bouchard Trophy:** best defenseman (QMJHL). **Emms Family Award:** rookie of the year (OHL). **Four Broncos Memorial Trophy:** most valuable player as selected by coaches (WHL); called Most Valuable Player Trophy prior to 1987-88 season. **Frank Boucher Memorial Trophy:** most gentlemanly player (WHL); renamed Brad Hornung Trophy during 1987-88 season. **Frank J. Selke Trophy:** most gentlemanly player (QMJHL). **F.W. (Dinty) Moore Trophy:** rookie goalie with best goals-against average (OHL). **George Parsons Trophy:** sportsmanship in Memorial Cup (Can.HL). **Guy Lafleur Trophy:** most valuable player during playoffs (QMJHL). **Hap Emms Memorial Trophy:** outstanding goaltender in Memorial Cup (Can.HL). **Jacques Plante Trophy:** best goaltender (QMJHL). **Jean Beliveau Trophy:** leading point scorer (QMJHL). **Jim Mahon Memorial Trophy:** top-scoring right winger (OHL). **Jim Piggott Memorial Trophy:** rookie of the year (WHL); originally called Stewart (Butch) Paul Memorial Trophy. **Leo Lalonde Memorial Trophy:** overage player of the year (OHL). **Marcel Robert Trophy:** top scholastic/athletic performer (QMJHL). **Matt Leyden Trophy:** coach of the year (OHL). **Max Kaminsky Trophy:** outstanding defenseman (OHL); awarded to most gentlemanly player prior to 1969-70. **Michael Bossy Trophy:** top pro prospect (QMJHL); originally called Association of Journalists for Major Junior League Hockey Trophy from 1980-81 through 1982-83. **Michel Bergeron Trophy:** top rookie forward (QMJHL); awarded to rookie of the year prior to 1980-81 season. **Michel Briere Trophy:** most valuable player (QMJHL). **Most Valuable Player Trophy:** most valuable player (WHL); renamed Four Broncos Memorial Trophy during 1987-88 season. **Raymond Lagace Trophy:** top rookie defenseman or goaltender (QMJHL). **Red Tilson Trophy:** outstanding player (OHL). **Shell Cup:** awarded to offensive player of the year and defensive player of the year (QMJHL). **Stafford Smythe Memorial Trophy:** most valuable player of Memorial Cup (Can.HL). **Stewart (Butch) Paul Memorial Trophy:** rookie of the year (WHL); renamed Jim Piggott Memorial Trophy during 1987-88 season. **Top Defenseman Trophy:** top defenseman (WHL); renamed Bill Hunter Trophy during 1987-88 season. **Top Goaltender Trophy:** top goaltender (WHL); renamed Del Wilson Trophy during 1987-88 season. **William Hanley Trophy:** most gentlemanly player (OHL).

COLLEGE AWARDS: Hobey Baker Memorial Award: top college hockey player in U.S. **Senator Joseph A. Sullivan Trophy:** outstanding player in Canadian Interuniversity Athletic Union.

OTHER AWARDS: Golden Puck Award: Sweden's Player of the Year. **Golden Stick Award:** Europe's top player. **Izvestia Trophy:** leading scorer (Soviet Union).

EXPLANATION OF FOOTNOTES AND ABBREVIATIONS

*   League leader.
†   Tied for league lead.
‡   Overtime loss.
§   Led or tied for league lead, but total figure is divided between two different teams. Actual league-leading or league-tying figure is mentioned in "Statistical Notes" section.
...   Statistic unavailable, unofficial or mathematically impossible to calculate.
—   Statistic inapplicable.

POSITIONS: C: center. **D:** defenseman. **G:** goaltender. **LW:** left winger. **RW:** right winger.

STATISTICS: A: assists. **Avg.:** goals-against average. **G:** goals. **GA:** goals against. **Gms.:** games. **L:** losses. **Min.:** minutes. **PIM.:** penalties in minutes. **+/-:** plus-minus. **PP:** power-play goals. **Pts:** points. **SH:** shorthanded goals. **SO:** shutouts. **T:** ties. **W:** wins.

TEAMS: Bloom. Jefferson: Bloomington Jefferson. **Chemo. Litvinov:** Chemopetrol Litvinov. **Chemo. Litvinov Jrs.:** Chemopetrol Litvinov Juniors. **Culver Mil. Acad.:** Culver Military Academy. **Czech. Olympic team:** Czechoslovakian Olympic team. **Det. Little Caesars:** Detroit Little Caesars. **Djur. Stockholm:** Djurgarden Stockholm. **Fin. Olympic team:** Finnish Olympic team. **HC Ceske Bude.:** HC Ceske Budejovice. **HK 32 Lip. Mikulas:** HK 32 Liptovsky Mikulas. **IS Banska Byst.:** IS Banska Bystrica. **Mass.-Lowell:** Massachusetts-Lowell. **Metal. Cherepovets:** Metallurg Cherepovets. **Metal. Magnitogorsk:** Metallurg Magnitogorsk. **Metallurg-2 Novok.:** Metallurg-2 Novokuznetsk. **Motor Ceske Bude.:** Motor Ceske Budejovice. **N. Yarmouth Acad.:** North Yarmouth Academy. **N. Michigan Univ.:** Northern Michigan University. **NW Americans Jr. B:** Northwest Americans Junior B. **Poji. Pardubice Jrs.:** Pojistovna Pardubice Juniors. **Prin. Edward Island:** Prince Edward Island. **Rus. Olympic team:** Russian Olympic team. **Sault Ste. Marie:** Sault Sainte Marie. **Sever. Cherepovets:** Severstal Cherepovets. **Slov. Olympic team:** Slovakian Olympic team. **Sov. Olympic team:** Soviet Olympic team. **Std. Hradec Kralove:** Stadion Hradec Kralove. **Swed. Olympic team:** Swedish Olympic team. **Tor. Nizhny Nov.:** Torpedo Nizhny Novgorod. **Torpedo Ust-Kam.:** Torpedo Ust-Kamenogorsk. **Unif. Olympic team:** Unified Olympic team.

LEAGUES: AAHL: All American Hockey League. **ACHL:** Atlantic Coast Hockey League. **AHL:** American Hockey League. **AJHL:** Alberta Junior Hockey League. **AMHL:** Alberta Minor Hockey League. **AUAA:** Atlantic Universities Athletic Association. **BCJHL:** British Columbia Junior Hockey League. **CAHL:** Central Alberta Hockey League. **CAJHL:** Central Alberta Junior Hockey League. **Can. College:** Canadian College. **Can.HL:** Canadian Hockey League. **CCHA:** Central Collegiate Hockey Association. **CHL:** Central Hockey League. **CIS:** Commonwealth of Independent States. **CJHL:** Central Junior A Hockey League. **COJHL:** Central Ontario Junior Hockey League. **CPHL:** Central Professional Hockey League. **CWUAA:** Canada West University Athletic Association. **Conn. H.S.:** Connecticut High School. **Czech.:** Czechoslovakia. **Czech Rep.:** Czechoslovakia Republic. **ECAC:** Eastern College Athletic Conference. **ECAC-II:** Eastern College Athletic Conference, Division II. **ECHL:** East Coast Hockey League. **EHL:** Eastern Hockey League. **EURO:** Euroliga. **Fin.:** Finland. **Ger.:** Germany. **GWHC:** Great Western Hockey Conference. **Hoc. East:** Hockey East. **IHL:** International Hockey League. **III. H.S.:** Illinois High School. **Indiana H.S.:** Indiana High School. **Int'l:** International. **KIJHL:** Kootenay International Junior Hockey League. **Mass. H.S.:** Massachusetts High School. **Md. H.S.:** Maryland High School. **Met. Bos.:** Metro Boston. **Mich. H.S.:** Michigan High School. **Minn. H.S.:** Minnesota High School. **MJHL:** Manitoba Junior Hockey League. **MTHL:** Metro Toronto Hockey League. **NAHL:** North American Hockey League. **NAJHL:** North American Junior Hockey League. **N.B. H.S.:** New Brunswick High School. **NCAA-II:** National Collegiate Athletic Association, Division II. **N.D. H.S.:** North Dakota High School. **NEJHL:** New England Junior Hockey League. **NHL:** National Hockey League. **N.H. H.S.:** New Hampshire High School. **N.J. H.S.:** New Jersey High School. **Nia. D. Jr. C:** Niagara District Junior C. **NSJHL:** Nova Scotia Junior Hockey League. **N.S.Jr.A:** Nova Scotia Junior A. **N.Y. H.S.:** New York High School. **NYMJHL:** New York Major Junior Hockey League. **NYOHL:** North York Ontario Hockey League. **ODHA:** Ottawa & District Hockey Association. **OHA:** Ontario Hockey Association. **OHA Jr. A:** Ontario Hockey Association Junior A. **OHA Mjr. Jr. A:** Ontario Hockey Association Major Junior A. **OHA Senior:** Ontario Hockey Association Senior. **OHL:** Ontario Hockey League. **O.H.S.:** Ohio High School. **OJHA:** Ontario Junior Hockey Association. **OJHL:** Ontario Junior Hockey League. **OMJHL:** Ontario Major Junior Hockey League. **OPJHL:** Ontario Provincial Junior Hockey League. **OUAA:** Ontario Universities Athletic Association. **PCJHL:** Peace Caribou Junior Hockey League. **PEIHA:** Prince Edward Island Hockey Association. **PEI-JHL:** Prince Edward Island Junior Hockey League. **Penn. H.S.:** Pennsylvania High School. **QMJHL:** Quebec Major Junior Hockey League. **R.I. H.S.:** Rhode Island High School. **Rus. Div II, III:** Russian Division II, III. **SAJHL:** Southern Alberta Junior Hockey League. **SJHL:** Saskatchewan Junior Hockey League. **Sask. H.S.:** Saskatchewan High School. **SOJHL:** Southern Ontario Junior Hockey League. **Swed. Jr.:** Sweden Junior. **Switz.:** Switzerland. **TBAHA:** Thunder Bay Amateur Hockey Association. **TBJHL:** Thunder Bay Junior Hockey League. **USHL:** United States Hockey League. **USHS:** United States High School. **USSR:** Union of Soviet Socialist Republics. **Vt. H.S.:** Vermont High School. **W. Germany, W. Ger.:** West Germany. **WCHA:** Western Collegiate Hockey Association. **WCHL:** Western Canada Hockey League. **WHA:** World Hockey Association. **WHL:** Western Hockey League. **Wisc. H.S.:** Wisconsin High School. **Yukon Sr.:** Yukon Senior.

A

AALTO, ANTTI   C   MIGHTY DUCKS

PERSONAL: Born March 4, 1975, in Lappeenrana, Finland. ... 6-2/190. ... Shoots left. ... Name pronounced AN-tee AL-toh.
TRANSACTIONS/CAREER NOTES: Selected by Mighty Ducks of Anaheim in sixth round (sixth Mighty Ducks pick, 134th overall) of NHL entry draft (June 26, 1993).

		REGULAR SEASON								PLAYOFFS				
Season Team	League	Gms.	G	A	Pts.	PIM	+/-	PP	SH	Gms.	G	A	Pts.	PIM
91-92 — SaiPa Jr.	Finland	19	10	10	20	38	...	...	...	—	—	—	—	—
— SaiPa	Finland	20	6	6	12	20	...	...	...	—	—	—	—	—
92-93 — SaiPa	Finland	23	6	8	14	14	...	...	...	—	—	—	—	—
— TPS Jr.	Finland	14	6	8	14	18	...	...	...	—	—	—	—	—
— TPS Turku	Finland	1	0	0	0	0	...	...	...	—	—	—	—	—
93-94 — TPS Turku	Finland	33	5	9	14	16	...	...	...	10	1	1	2	4
94-95 — TPS Turku	Finland	44	11	7	18	18	...	...	...	5	0	1	1	2
95-96 — TPS Turku	Finland	40	15	16	31	22	...	...	...	11	3	5	8	14
— Kiekko-67	Finland Div. II	2	0	2	2	2	...	...	...	—	—	—	—	—
96-97 — TPS Turku	Finland	44	15	19	34	60	...	...	...	11	5	6	11	31

ABRAHAMSSON, ELIAS   D   BRUINS

PERSONAL: Born June 15, 1977, in Uppsala, Sweden. ... 6-3/216. ... Shoots left. ... Name pronounced AY-bruh-HAM-suhn.
TRANSACTIONS/CAREER NOTES: Selected by Boston Bruins in fifth round (sixth Bruins pick, 132nd overall) of NHL entry draft (June 22, 1996).

		REGULAR SEASON								PLAYOFFS				
Season Team	League	Gms.	G	A	Pts.	PIM	+/-	PP	SH	Gms.	G	A	Pts.	PIM
93-94 — Uppsala	Swed. Div. II	1	0	0	0	0	...	...	...	—	—	—	—	—
94-95 — Halifax	QMJHL	25	0	3	3	41	...	...	...	—	—	—	—	—
95-96 — Halifax	QMJHL	64	3	11	14	268	...	...	...	6	2	2	4	8
96-97 — Halifax	QMJHL	30	4	11	15	221	...	...	...	18	4	8	12	74

ADAMS, GREG   LW   STARS

PERSONAL: Born August 1, 1963, in Nelson, B.C. ... 6-3/198. ... Shoots left. ... Son-in-law of George Swarbrick, right winger with three NHL teams (1967-68 through 1970-71).
COLLEGE: Northern Arizona.
TRANSACTIONS/CAREER NOTES: Signed as free agent by New Jersey Devils (June 25, 1984). ... Tore tendon in right wrist (April 1986). ... Traded by Devils with G Kirk McLean to Vancouver Canucks for C Patrik Sundstrom, fourth-round pick in 1988 draft (LW Matt Ruchty) and the option to flip second-round picks in 1988 draft; Devils exercised option and selected LW Jeff Christian and Canucks selected D Leif Rohlin (September 10, 1987). ... Fractured ankle (February 1989). ... Fractured cheekbone (January 4, 1990); missed 12 games. ... Sprained left knee (October 17, 1990); missed 12 games. ... Sprained forearm, wrist and abdomen (February 27, 1991). ... Suffered concussion (October 8, 1991); missed one game. ... Suffered charley horse (January 16, 1993); missed nine games. ... Suffered charley horse (February 15, 1993); missed 22 games. ... Suffered stress fracture in hand requiring minor surgery (December 14, 1993); missed 14 games. ... Bruised foot (February 22, 1994); missed one game. ... Traded by Canucks with RW Dan Kesa and fifth-round pick (traded to Los Angeles) in 1995 draft to Dallas Stars for RW Russ Courtnall (April 7, 1995). ... Fractured hand (March 2, 1996); missed 11 games. ... Broke toe (April 7, 1996); missed final four games of season. ... Suffered herniated disc in neck (December 21, 1996); missed 30 games. ... Strained groin (April 4, 1997); missed one game.
HONORS: Played in NHL All-Star Game (1988).
STATISTICAL PLATEAUS: Three-goal games: 1991-92 (1). ... Four-goal games: 1987-88 (1). ... Total hat tricks: 2.
MISCELLANEOUS: Failed to score on a penalty shot (vs. Alain Chevrier, January 7, 1988; vs. Alan Bester, January 9, 1989; vs. Jacques Cloutier, December 10, 1989; vs. Bill Ranford, December 1, 1991; vs. Curtis Joseph, January 25, 1992).

		REGULAR SEASON								PLAYOFFS				
Season Team	League	Gms.	G	A	Pts.	PIM	+/-	PP	SH	Gms.	G	A	Pts.	PIM
80-81 — Kelowna	BCJHL	47	40	50	90	16	...	...	...	—	—	—	—	—
81-82 — Kelowna	BCJHL	45	31	42	73	24	...	...	...	—	—	—	—	—
82-83 — Northern Arizona	Indep.	29	14	21	35	46	...	...	...	—	—	—	—	—
83-84 — Northern Arizona	Indep.	47	40	50	90	16	...	...	...	—	—	—	—	—
84-85 — Maine	AHL	41	15	20	35	12	...	...	...	11	3	4	7	0
— New Jersey	NHL	36	12	9	21	14	-14	5	0	—	—	—	—	—
85-86 — New Jersey	NHL	78	35	42	77	30	-6	10	0	—	—	—	—	—
86-87 — New Jersey	NHL	72	20	27	47	19	-16	6	0	—	—	—	—	—
87-88 — Vancouver	NHL	80	36	40	76	30	-24	12	0	—	—	—	—	—
88-89 — Vancouver	NHL	61	19	14	33	24	-21	9	0	7	2	3	5	2
89-90 — Vancouver	NHL	65	30	20	50	18	-8	13	0	—	—	—	—	—
90-91 — Vancouver	NHL	55	21	24	45	10	-5	5	1	5	0	0	0	2
91-92 — Vancouver	NHL	76	30	27	57	26	8	13	1	6	0	2	2	4
92-93 — Vancouver	NHL	53	25	31	56	14	31	6	1	12	7	6	13	6
93-94 — Vancouver	NHL	68	13	24	37	20	-1	5	1	23	6	8	14	2
94-95 — Vancouver	NHL	31	5	10	15	12	1	2	2	—	—	—	—	—
— Dallas	NHL	12	3	3	6	4	-4	1	0	5	2	0	2	0
95-96 — Dallas	NHL	66	22	21	43	33	-21	11	1	—	—	—	—	—
96-97 — Dallas	NHL	50	21	15	36	2	27	5	0	3	0	1	1	0
NHL totals (13 years)		803	292	307	599	256	-53	103	7	61	17	20	37	16

ADAMS, KEVYN C MAPLE LEAFS

PERSONAL: Born October 8, 1974, in Washington, D.C. ... 6-1/192. ... Shoots right.
HIGH SCHOOL: Clarence (N.Y.).
COLLEGE: Miami of Ohio.
TRANSACTIONS/CAREER NOTES: Selected by Boston Bruins in first round (first Bruins pick, 25th overall) of NHL entry draft (June 26, 1993). ... Signed as free agent by Toronto Maple Leafs (August 1, 1997).
HONORS: Named to CCHA All-Star second team (1994-95).

			REGULAR SEASON							PLAYOFFS				
Season Team	League	Gms.	G	A	Pts.	PIM	+/-	PP	SH	Gms.	G	A	Pts.	PIM
90-91— Niagara	NAJHL	55	17	20	37	24	...	...	...	—	—	—	—	—
91-92— Niagara	NAJHL	40	25	33	58	51	...	...	...	—	—	—	—	—
92-93— Miami of Ohio	CCHA	41	17	16	33	18	...	...	...	—	—	—	—	—
93-94— Miami of Ohio	CCHA	36	15	28	43	24	...	...	...	—	—	—	—	—
94-95— Miami of Ohio	CCHA	38	20	29	49	30	...	...	...	—	—	—	—	—
95-96— Miami of Ohio	CCHA	36	17	30	47	30	...	...	...	—	—	—	—	—
96-97— Grand Rapids	IHL	82	22	25	47	47	...	...	...	5	1	1	2	4

AITKEN, JOHNATHAN D BRUINS

PERSONAL: Born May 24, 1978, in Sherwood Park, Alta. ... 6-4/190. ... Shoots left. ... Name pronounced AYT-kehn.
TRANSACTIONS/CAREER NOTES: Selected by Boston Bruins in first round (first Bruins pick, eighth overall) of NHL entry draft (June 22, 1996).

			REGULAR SEASON							PLAYOFFS				
Season Team	League	Gms.	G	A	Pts.	PIM	+/-	PP	SH	Gms.	G	A	Pts.	PIM
94-95— Medicine Hat	WHL	53	0	5	5	71	...	...	...	—	—	—	—	—
95-96— Medicine Hat	WHL	71	6	14	20	131	...	...	...	5	1	0	1	6
96-97— Brandon	WHL	65	4	18	22	211	...	...	...	6	0	0	0	4

AIVAZOFF, MICAH C RANGERS

PERSONAL: Born May 4, 1969, in Powell River, B.C. ... 6-2/195. ... Shoots left. ... Name pronounced MIGH-kuh AY-vuh-zahf.
TRANSACTIONS/CAREER NOTES: Selected by Los Angeles Kings in sixth round (sixth Kings pick, 109th overall) of NHL entry draft (June 11, 1988). ... Signed as free agent by Detroit Red Wings (July 2, 1991). ... Claimed by Pittsburgh Penguins as compensation for Red Wings claiming RW Doug Brown in 1994-95 waiver draft (January 18, 1995). ... Selected by Edmonton Oilers in 1994-95 waiver draft for cash (January 18, 1995). ... Signed as free agent by New York Islanders (September 5, 1995). ... Signed as free agent by New York Rangers (September 4, 1996).

			REGULAR SEASON							PLAYOFFS				
Season Team	League	Gms.	G	A	Pts.	PIM	+/-	PP	SH	Gms.	G	A	Pts.	PIM
85-86— Victoria	WHL	27	3	4	7	25	...	...	...	—	—	—	—	—
86-87— Victoria	WHL	72	18	39	57	112	...	...	...	5	1	0	1	2
87-88— Victoria	WHL	69	26	57	83	79	...	...	...	8	3	4	7	14
88-89— Victoria	WHL	70	35	65	100	136	...	...	...	8	5	7	12	2
89-90— New Haven	AHL	77	20	39	59	71	...	...	...	—	—	—	—	—
90-91— New Haven	AHL	79	11	29	40	84	...	...	...	—	—	—	—	—
91-92— Adirondack	AHL	61	9	20	29	50	...	...	...	19	2	8	10	25
92-93— Adirondack	AHL	79	32	53	85	100	...	...	...	11	8	6	14	10
93-94— Detroit	NHL	59	4	4	8	38	-1	0	0	—	—	—	—	—
94-95— Edmonton	NHL	21	0	1	1	2	-2	0	0	—	—	—	—	—
95-96— Utah	IHL	59	14	21	35	58	...	...	...	22	3	5	8	33
— New York Islanders	NHL	12	0	1	1	6	-6	0	0	—	—	—	—	—
96-97— Binghamton	AHL	75	12	36	48	70	...	...	...	4	1	1	2	0
NHL totals (3 years)		92	4	6	10	46	-9	0	0					

ALBELIN, TOMMY D FLAMES

PERSONAL: Born May 21, 1964, in Stockholm, Sweden. ... 6-1/190. ... Shoots left. ... Name pronounced AL-buh-leen.
TRANSACTIONS/CAREER NOTES: Selected by Quebec Nordiques in eighth round (seventh Nordiques pick, 152nd overall) of NHL entry draft (June 8, 1983). ... Traded by Nordiques to New Jersey Devils for fourth-round pick (LW Niclas Andersson) in 1989 draft (December 12, 1988). ... Injured right knee (March 2, 1990); missed two games. ... Injured groin (November 21, 1992); missed two games. ... Suffered from urinary infection (1993-94 season); missed nine games. ... Bruised thigh (December 16, 1995); missed six games. ... Traded by Devils with D Cale Hulse and RW Jocelyn Lemieux to Calgary Flames for D Phil Housley and D Dan Keczmer (February 26, 1996). ... Strained groin (November 9, 1996); missed four games. ... Reinjured groin (November 25, 1996); missed two games. ... Strained abdominal muscle (December 7, 1996); missed five games.
HONORS: Named to Swedish League All-Star team (1986-87).
MISCELLANEOUS: Member of Stanley Cup championship team (1995).

			REGULAR SEASON							PLAYOFFS				
Season Team	League	Gms.	G	A	Pts.	PIM	+/-	PP	SH	Gms.	G	A	Pts.	PIM
82-83— Djur. Stockholm	Sweden	17	2	5	7	4	...	...	...	6	1	0	1	2
83-84— Djur. Stockholm	Sweden	37	9	8	17	36	...	...	...	4	0	1	1	2
84-85— Djur. Stockholm	Sweden	32	9	8	17	22	...	...	...	8	2	1	3	4
85-86— Djur. Stockholm	Sweden	35	4	8	12	26	...	...	...	—	—	—	—	—
86-87— Djur. Stockholm	Sweden	33	7	5	12	49	...	...	...	2	0	0	0	0
87-88— Quebec	NHL	60	3	23	26	47	-7	0	0	—	—	—	—	—
88-89— Halifax	AHL	8	2	5	7	4	...	...	...	—	—	—	—	—
— Quebec	NHL	14	2	4	6	27	-6	1	0	—	—	—	—	—
— New Jersey	NHL	46	7	24	31	40	18	1	1	—	—	—	—	—

Season Team	League	REGULAR SEASON								PLAYOFFS				
		Gms.	G	A	Pts.	PIM	+/-	PP	SH	Gms.	G	A	Pts.	PIM
89-90— New Jersey	NHL	68	6	23	29	63	-1	4	0	—	—	—	—	—
90-91— Utica	AHL	14	4	2	6	10	...	...	...	—	—	—	—	—
— New Jersey	NHL	47	2	12	14	44	1	1	0	3	0	1	1	2
91-92— New Jersey	NHL	19	0	4	4	4	7	0	0	1	1	1	2	0
— Utica	AHL	11	4	6	10	4	...	...	...	—	—	—	—	—
92-93— New Jersey	NHL	36	1	5	6	14	0	1	0	5	2	0	2	0
93-94— Albany	AHL	4	0	2	2	17	...	...	...	—	—	—	—	—
— New Jersey	NHL	62	2	17	19	36	20	1	0	20	2	5	7	14
94-95— New Jersey	NHL	48	5	10	15	20	9	2	0	20	1	7	8	2
95-96— New Jersey	NHL	53	1	12	13	14	0	0	0	—	—	—	—	—
— Calgary	NHL	20	0	1	1	4	1	0	0	4	0	0	0	0
96-97— Calgary	NHL	72	4	11	15	14	-8	2	0	—	—	—	—	—
NHL totals (10 years)		545	33	146	179	327	34	13	1	53	6	14	20	18

ALFREDSSON, DANIEL   RW   SENATORS

PERSONAL: Born December 11, 1972, in Grums, Sweden. ... 5-11/200. ... Shoots right.
TRANSACTIONS/CAREER NOTES: Selected by Ottawa Senators in sixth round (fifth Senators pick, 133rd overall) of NHL entry draft (June 29, 1994). ... Strained abdominal muscle (January 29, 1997); missed six games.
HONORS: Played in NHL All-Star Game (1996 and 1997). ... Won Calder Memorial Trophy (1995-96). ... Named to NHL All-Rookie team (1995-96).
STATISTICAL PLATEAUS: Three-goal games: 1995-96 (1).

Season Team	League	REGULAR SEASON								PLAYOFFS				
		Gms.	G	A	Pts.	PIM	+/-	PP	SH	Gms.	G	A	Pts.	PIM
91-92— Molndal Hockey	Swed. Div. II	32	12	8	20	43	...	...	...	—	—	—	—	—
92-93— Vastra Frolunda	Sweden	20	1	5	6	8	...	...	...	—	—	—	—	—
93-94— Vastra Frolunda	Sweden	39	20	10	30	18	...	...	...	4	1	1	2	0
94-95— Vastra Frolunda	Sweden	22	7	11	18	22	...	...	...	—	—	—	—	—
95-96— Ottawa	NHL	82	26	35	61	28	-18	8	2	—	—	—	—	—
96-97— Ottawa	NHL	76	24	47	71	30	5	11	1	7	5	2	7	6
NHL totals (2 years)		158	50	82	132	58	-13	19	3	7	5	2	7	6

ALLEN, CHRIS   D   PANTHERS

PERSONAL: Born May 8, 1978, in Blenheim, Ont. ... 6-2/192. ... Shoots right.
TRANSACTIONS/CAREER NOTES: Selected by Florida Panthers in third round (second Panthers pick, 60th overall) of NHL entry draft (June 22, 1996).

Season Team	League	REGULAR SEASON								PLAYOFFS				
		Gms.	G	A	Pts.	PIM	+/-	PP	SH	Gms.	G	A	Pts.	PIM
92-93— Blenheim Jr. C	OHA	3	0	0	0	0	...	...	...	—	—	—	—	—
93-94— Leamington	Jr. B	52	6	20	26	38	...	...	...	—	—	—	—	—
94-95— Kingston	OHL	43	3	5	8	15	...	...	...	2	0	0	0	0
95-96— Kingston	OHL	55	21	18	39	58	...	...	...	6	0	2	2	8
96-97— Kingston	OHL	61	14	29	43	81	...	...	...	5	1	2	3	4
— Carolina	AHL	9	0	0	0	2	...	...	...	—	—	—	—	—

ALLEN, PETER   D   PENGUINS

PERSONAL: Born March 6, 1970, in Calgary. ... 6-2/185. ... Shoots right.
COLLEGE: Yale.
TRANSACTIONS/CAREER NOTES: Selected by Boston Bruins in first round (first Bruins pick, 24th overall) of NHL supplemental draft (June 21, 1991). ... Signed as free agent by Pittsburgh Penguins (August 10, 1995).

Season Team	League	REGULAR SEASON								PLAYOFFS				
		Gms.	G	A	Pts.	PIM	+/-	PP	SH	Gms.	G	A	Pts.	PIM
89-90— Yale University	ECAC	26	2	4	6	16	...	...	...	—	—	—	—	—
90-91— Yale University	ECAC	17	0	6	6	14	...	...	...	—	—	—	—	—
91-92— Yale University	ECAC	26	5	13	18	26	...	...	...	—	—	—	—	—
92-93— Yale University	ECAC	30	3	15	18	32	...	...	...	—	—	—	—	—
93-94— Richmond	ECHL	52	2	16	18	62	...	...	...	—	—	—	—	—
— Prin. Edward Island.	AHL	6	0	1	1	6	...	...	...	—	—	—	—	—
94-95— Canadian nat'l team	Int'l	52	5	15	20	36	...	...	...	—	—	—	—	—
95-96— Cleveland	IHL	65	3	45	48	55	...	...	...	3	0	0	0	2
— Pittsburgh	NHL	8	0	0	0	8	2	0	0	—	—	—	—	—
96-97— Cleveland	IHL	81	14	31	45	75	...	...	...	14	0	6	6	24
NHL totals (1 year)		8	0	0	0	8	2	0	0					

ALLISON, JAMIE   D   FLAMES

PERSONAL: Born May 13, 1975, in Lindsay, Ont. ... 6-1/190. ... Shoots left.
TRANSACTIONS/CAREER NOTES: Selected by Calgary Flames in second round (second Flames pick, 44th overall) of NHL entry draft (June 26, 1993). ... Suffered concussion (December 20, 1996); missed three games.

Season Team	League	Gms.	G	A	Pts.	PIM	+/-	PP	SH	Gms.	G	A	Pts.	PIM
		REGULAR SEASON								PLAYOFFS				
90-91 — Waterloo Jr. B	OHA	45	3	8	11	91	...	...	...	—	—	—	—	—
91-92 — Windsor	OHL	59	4	8	12	52	...	...	...	4	1	1	2	2
92-93 — Detroit	OHL	61	0	13	13	64	...	...	...	15	2	5	7	23
93-94 — Detroit	OHL	40	2	22	24	69	...	...	...	17	2	9	11	35
94-95 — Detroit	OHL	50	1	14	15	119	...	...	...	18	2	7	9	35
— Calgary	NHL	1	0	0	0	0	0	0	0	—	—	—	—	—
95-96 — Saint John	AHL	71	3	16	19	223	...	...	...	14	0	2	2	16
96-97 — Saint John	AHL	46	3	6	9	139	...	...	...	5	0	1	1	4
— Calgary	NHL	20	0	0	0	35	-4	0	0	—				
NHL totals (2 years)		21	0	0	0	35	-4	0	0					

ALLISON, JASON   C   BRUINS

PERSONAL: Born May 29, 1975, in Toronto. ... 6-3/205. ... Shoots right.
TRANSACTIONS/CAREER NOTES: Selected by Washington Capitals in first round (second Capitals pick, 17th overall) of NHL entry draft (June 26, 1993). ... Injured ankle (February 15, 1997); missed one game. ... Traded by Capitals with G Jim Carey, C Anson Carter, third-round pick (RW Lee Goren) in 1997 draft and conditional pick in 1998 draft to Boston Bruins for C Adam Oates, RW Rick Tocchet and G Bill Ranford (March 1, 1997).
HONORS: Won Can.HL Player of the Year Award (1993-94). ... Won Can.HL Top Scorer Award (1993-94). ... Won Red Tilson Trophy (1993-94). ... Won William Hanley Trophy (1993-94). ... Won Eddie Powers Memorial Trophy (1993-94). ... Named to Can.HL All-Star first team (1993-94). ... Named to OHL All-Star first team (1993-94).
MISCELLANEOUS: Failed to score on a penalty shot (vs. Dominik Hasek, April 10, 1997).

Season Team	League	Gms.	G	A	Pts.	PIM	+/-	PP	SH	Gms.	G	A	Pts.	PIM
		REGULAR SEASON								PLAYOFFS				
91-92 — London	OHL	65	11	18	29	15	...	...	...	7	0	0	0	0
92-93 — London	OHL	66	42	76	118	50	...	...	...	12	7	13	20	8
93-94 — London	OHL	56	55	87	*142	68	...	...	...	5	2	13	15	13
— Washington	NHL	2	0	1	1	0	1	0	0	—				
— Portland	AHL	6	2	1	3	0	...			—				
94-95 — London	OHL	15	15	21	36	43	...			—				
— Washington	NHL	12	2	1	3	6	-3	2	0	—				
— Portland	AHL	8	5	4	9	2	...			7	3	8	11	2
95-96 — Washington	NHL	19	0	3	3	2	-3	0	0	—				
— Portland	AHL	57	28	41	69	42	...			6	1	6	7	9
96-97 — Washington	NHL	53	5	17	22	25	-3	1	0	—				
— Boston	NHL	19	3	9	12	9	-3	1	0	—				
NHL totals (4 years)		105	10	31	41	42	-11	4	0					

ALVEY, MATT   C   BRUINS

PERSONAL: Born May 15, 1975, in Troy, N.Y. ... 6-2/210. ... Shoots right.
COLLEGE: Lake Superior State (Mich.).
TRANSACTIONS/CAREER NOTES: Selected by Boston Bruins in second round (second Bruins pick, 51st overall) of NHL entry draft (June 26, 1993).

Season Team	League	Gms.	G	A	Pts.	PIM	+/-	PP	SH	Gms.	G	A	Pts.	PIM
		REGULAR SEASON								PLAYOFFS				
90-91 — Springfield Jr. B	NEJHL	...	12	20	32	...	...	...	...	—				
91-92 — Springfield Jr. B	NEJHL	32	22	35	57	34	...			—				
92-93 — Springfield Jr. B	NEJHL	38	22	37	59	85	...			—				
93-94 — Lake Superior State	CCHA	41	6	8	14	16	...			—				
94-95 — Lake Superior State	CCHA	25	4	7	11	32	...			—				
95-96 — Lake Superior State	CCHA	38	14	8	22	40	...			—				
96-97 — Lake Superior State	CCHA	18	10	8	18	49	...			—				
— Pensacola	ECHL	7	1	2	3	0	...			3	0	0	0	4

AMONTE, TONY   RW   BLACKHAWKS

PERSONAL: Born August 2, 1970, in Weymouth, Mass. ... 6-0/190. ... Shoots left. ... Full name: Anthony Lewis Amonte. ... Name pronounced ah-MAHN-tee.
HIGH SCHOOL: Thayer Academy (Braintree, Mass.).
COLLEGE: Boston University.
TRANSACTIONS/CAREER NOTES: Selected by New York Rangers in fourth round (third Rangers pick, 68th overall) of NHL entry draft (June 11, 1988). ... Separated shoulder (December 29, 1990). ... Traded by Rangers with rights to LW Matt Oates to Chicago Blackhawks for LW Stephane Matteau and RW Brian Noonan (March 21, 1994). ... Pulled groin (1993-94 season); missed three games. ... Played in Europe during 1994-95 NHL lockout.
HONORS: Named to Hockey East All-Rookie team (1989-90). ... Named to NCAA All-Tournament team (1990-91). ... Named to Hockey East All-Star second team (1990-91). ... Named NHL Rookie of the Year by THE SPORTING NEWS (1991-92). ... Named to NHL All-Rookie team (1991-92). ... Played in NHL All-Star Game (1997).
STATISTICAL PLATEAUS: Three-goal games: 1991-92 (1), 1995-96 (1), 1996-97 (2). Total: 4.
MISCELLANEOUS: Failed to score on a penalty shot (vs. Kelly Hrudey, January 27, 1994).

Season Team	League	Gms.	G	A	Pts.	PIM	+/-	PP	SH	Gms.	G	A	Pts.	PIM
		REGULAR SEASON								PLAYOFFS				
86-87 — Thayer Academy	Mass. H.S.	25	25	32	57	...	...	...	...	—	—	—	—	—
87-88 — Thayer Academy	Mass. H.S.	28	30	38	68	...	...	...	...	—	—	—	—	—

Season Team	League	REGULAR SEASON								PLAYOFFS				
		Gms.	G	A	Pts.	PIM	+/-	PP	SH	Gms.	G	A	Pts.	PIM
88-89— Team USA Juniors	Int'l	7	1	3	4	...	...	...	...	—	—	—	—	—
89-90— Boston University	Hockey East	41	25	33	58	52	...	...	...	—	—	—	—	—
90-91— Boston University	Hockey East	38	31	37	68	82	...	...	...	—	—	—	—	—
— New York Rangers	NHL	—	—	—	—	—	—	—	—	2	0	2	2	2
91-92— New York Rangers	NHL	79	35	34	69	55	12	9	0	13	3	6	9	2
92-93— New York Rangers	NHL	83	33	43	76	49	0	13	0	—	—	—	—	—
93-94— New York Rangers	NHL	72	16	22	38	31	5	3	0	—	—	—	—	—
— Chicago	NHL	7	1	3	4	6	-5	1	0	6	4	2	6	4
94-95— Fassa	Italy	14	22	16	38	10	...	...	...	—	—	—	—	—
— Chicago	NHL	48	15	20	35	41	7	6	1	16	3	3	6	10
95-96— Chicago	NHL	81	31	32	63	62	10	5	4	7	2	4	6	6
96-97— Chicago	NHL	81	41	36	77	64	35	9	2	6	4	2	6	8
NHL totals (7 years)		451	172	190	362	308	64	46	7	50	16	19	35	32

ANDERSSON, MIKAEL — LW — LIGHTNING

PERSONAL: Born May 10, 1966, in Malmo, Sweden. ... 5-11/185. ... Shoots left. ... Full name: Bo Mikael Andersson. ... Name pronounced mih-KEHL AN-duhr-suhn.

TRANSACTIONS/CAREER NOTES: Selected by Buffalo Sabres in first round (first Sabres pick, 18th overall) of NHL entry draft (June 9, 1984). ... Sprained ankle (March 3, 1987); missed three weeks. ... Twisted ankle (March 1988). ... Sprained neck and shoulder (December 1988). ... Selected by Hartford Whalers in 1989 NHL waiver draft (October 2, 1989). ... Bruised left knee (December 13, 1989). ... Reinjured knee (February 9, 1990). ... Pulled right hamstring (March 8, 1990). ... Reinjured hamstring (March 17, 1990). ... Reinjured hamstring (April 1990). ... Underwent surgery to left knee (May 14, 1990). ... Suffered from the flu (October 4, 1990); missed two games. ... Pulled groin (January 1991). ... Injured toe (October 26, 1991); missed one game. ... Injured groin (December 17, 1991); missed three games. ... Suffered chip fracture to foot (April 12, 1992). ... Signed as free agent by Tampa Bay Lightning (July 8, 1992). ... Suffered back spasms (November 21, 1992); missed four games. ... Injured left rotator cuff (October 27, 1993); missed three games. ... Played in Europe during 1994-95 NHL lockout. ... Injured groin (March 4, 1995); missed four games. ... Sprained ankle (April 8, 1995); missed six games. ... Injured left knee (November 25, 1995); missed two games. ... Injured left knee (December 3, 1995); missed one game. ... Suffered tendinitis in left knee (December 19, 1995); missed two games. ... Pulled hamstring (November 19, 1996); missed two games. ... Bruised shoulder (December 16, 1996); missed six games. ... Injured back (April 5, 1997); missed remainder of season.

STATISTICAL PLATEAUS: Three-goal games: 1992-93 (1).

MISCELLANEOUS: Scored on a penalty shot (vs. Robb Stauber, December 15, 1992).

Season Team	League	REGULAR SEASON								PLAYOFFS				
		Gms.	G	A	Pts.	PIM	+/-	PP	SH	Gms.	G	A	Pts.	PIM
82-83— Vastra Frolunda	Sweden	1	1	0	1	...	...	...	...	—	—	—	—	—
83-84— Vastra Frolunda	Sweden	12	0	2	2	6	...	...	...	—	—	—	—	—
84-85— Vastra Frolunda	Sweden	32	16	11	27	18	...	...	...	6	3	2	5	2
85-86— Rochester	AHL	20	10	4	14	6	...	...	...	—	—	—	—	—
— Buffalo	NHL	32	1	9	10	4	0	0	0	—	—	—	—	—
86-87— Rochester	AHL	42	6	20	26	14	...	...	...	9	1	2	3	2
— Buffalo	NHL	16	0	3	3	0	-2	0	0	—	—	—	—	—
87-88— Rochester	AHL	35	12	24	36	16	...	...	...	—	—	—	—	—
— Buffalo	NHL	37	3	20	23	10	7	0	1	1	1	0	1	0
88-89— Buffalo	NHL	14	0	1	1	4	-1	0	0	—	—	—	—	—
— Rochester	AHL	56	18	33	51	12	...	...	...	—	—	—	—	—
89-90— Hartford	NHL	50	13	24	37	6	0	1	2	5	0	3	3	2
90-91— Hartford	NHL	41	4	7	11	8	0	0	0	—	—	—	—	—
— Springfield	AHL	26	7	22	29	10	...	...	...	18	†10	8	18	12
91-92— Hartford	NHL	74	18	29	47	14	18	1	3	7	0	2	2	6
92-93— Tampa Bay	NHL	77	16	11	27	14	-14	3	2	—	—	—	—	—
93-94— Tampa Bay	NHL	76	13	12	25	23	8	1	1	—	—	—	—	—
94-95— Vastra Frolunda	Sweden	7	1	0	1	31	...	...	...	—	—	—	—	—
— Tampa Bay	NHL	36	4	7	11	4	-3	0	0	—	—	—	—	—
95-96— Tampa Bay	NHL	64	8	11	19	2	0	0	0	6	1	1	2	0
96-97— Tampa Bay	NHL	70	5	14	19	8	1	0	3	—	—	—	—	—
NHL totals (12 years)		587	85	148	233	97	14	6	12	19	2	6	8	8

ANDERSSON, NIKLAS — LW — ISLANDERS

PERSONAL: Born May 20, 1971, in Kunglav, Sweden. ... 5-9/175. ... Shoots left.

TRANSACTIONS/CAREER NOTES: Selected by Quebec Nordiques in third round (fifth Nordiques pick, 68th overall) of NHL entry draft (June 17, 1989). ... Signed as free agent by New York Islanders (July 15, 1994). ... Sprained shoulder (February 5, 1997); missed two games. ... Sore foot (March 29, 1997); missed two games.

STATISTICAL PLATEAUS: Three-goal games: 1995-96 (1).

Season Team	League	REGULAR SEASON								PLAYOFFS				
		Gms.	G	A	Pts.	PIM	+/-	PP	SH	Gms.	G	A	Pts.	PIM
87-88— Frolunda	Sweden	15	5	5	10	...	...	...	...	—	—	—	—	—
88-89— Frolunda	Sweden	30	13	24	37	...	...	...	...	—	—	—	—	—
89-90— Frolunda	Sweden	38	10	21	31	14	...	...	...	—	—	—	—	—
90-91— Frolunda	Sweden	22	6	10	16	16	...	...	...	—	—	—	—	—
91-92— Halifax	AHL	57	8	26	34	41	...	...	...	—	—	—	—	—
92-93— Halifax	AHL	76	32	50	82	42	...	...	...	—	—	—	—	—
— Quebec	NHL	3	0	1	1	2	0	0	0	—	—	—	—	—
93-94— Cornwall	AHL	42	18	34	52	8	...	...	...	—	—	—	—	—
94-95— Denver	IHL	66	22	39	61	28	...	...	...	15	8	13	21	10
95-96— Utah	IHL	30	13	22	35	25	...	...	...	—	—	—	—	—
— New York Islanders....	NHL	47	14	12	26	12	-3	3	2	—	—	—	—	—
96-97— New York Islanders....	NHL	74	12	31	43	57	4	1	1	—	—	—	—	—
NHL totals (3 years)		124	26	44	70	71	1	4	3	—	—	—	—	—

ANDREYCHUK, DAVE   LW   DEVILS

A

PERSONAL: Born September 29, 1963, in Hamilton, Ont. ... 6-4/220. ... Shoots right. ... Name pronounced AN-druh-chuhk.

TRANSACTIONS/CAREER NOTES: Selected by Buffalo Sabres as underage junior in first round (third Sabres pick, 16th overall) of NHL entry draft (June 9, 1982). ... Sprained knee (March 1983). ... Fractured collarbone (March 1985). ... Twisted knee (September 1985). ... Injured right knee (September 1986). ... Strained knee ligaments in left knee (November 27, 1988). ... Broke left thumb (February 18, 1990). ... Suspended two off-days and fined $500 by NHL for cross-checking (November 16, 1992). ... Traded by Sabres with G Daren Puppa and first-round pick in 1993 draft (D Kenny Jonsson) to Toronto Maple Leafs for G Grant Fuhr and fifth-round pick (D Kevin Popp) in 1995 draft (February 2, 1993). ... Injured knee (December 27, 1993); missed one game. ... Separated shoulder (December 2, 1995); missed five games. ... Suffered from the flu (December 27, 1995); missed one game. ... Underwent thumb surgery (January 15, 1996); missed two games. Traded by Maple Leafs to New Jersey Devils for second-round pick (D Marek Posmyk) in 1996 draft and undisclosed pick in 1998 or 1999 draft (March 13, 1996). ... Fractured foot (April 13, 1997); missed remainder of regular season.

HONORS: Played in NHL All-Star Game (1990 and 1994). ... Named to THE SPORTING NEWS All-Star second team (1993-94).

STATISTICAL PLATEAUS: Three-goal games: 1987-88 (3), 1988-89 (1), 1989-90 (1), 1991-92 (1), 1992-93 (1). Total: 7. ... Four-goal games: 1991-92 (1), 1992-93 (1). Total: 2. ... Five-goal games: 1985-86 (1). ... Total hat tricks: 10.

MISCELLANEOUS: Failed to score on a penalty shot (vs. Clint Malarchuk, November 22, 1986; vs. Darcy Wakaluk, February 7, 1992; vs. Tim Cheveldae, April 8, 1995). ... Played with Team Canada in World Junior Championships (1982-83).

				REGULAR SEASON						PLAYOFFS				
Season Team	League	Gms.	G	A	Pts.	PIM	+/-	PP	SH	Gms.	G	A	Pts.	PIM
80-81— Oshawa	OMJHL	67	22	22	44	80	...	...	...	10	3	2	5	20
81-82— Oshawa	OHL	67	58	43	101	71	...	...	...	3	1	4	5	16
82-83— Oshawa	OHL	14	8	24	32	6	...	...	...	—	—	—	—	—
— Buffalo	NHL	43	14	23	37	16	6	3	0	4	1	0	1	4
83-84— Buffalo	NHL	78	38	42	80	42	20	10	0	2	0	1	1	2
84-85— Buffalo	NHL	64	31	30	61	54	-4	14	0	5	4	2	6	4
85-86— Buffalo	NHL	80	36	51	87	61	3	12	0	—	—	—	—	—
86-87— Buffalo	NHL	77	25	48	73	46	2	13	0	—	—	—	—	—
87-88— Buffalo	NHL	80	30	48	78	112	1	15	0	6	2	4	6	0
88-89— Buffalo	NHL	56	28	24	52	40	0	7	0	5	0	3	3	0
89-90— Buffalo	NHL	73	40	42	82	42	6	18	0	6	2	5	7	2
90-91— Buffalo	NHL	80	36	33	69	32	11	13	0	6	2	2	4	8
91-92— Buffalo	NHL	80	41	50	91	71	-9	*28	0	7	1	3	4	12
92-93— Buffalo	NHL	52	29	32	61	48	-8	*20	0	—	—	—	—	—
— Toronto	NHL	31	25	13	38	8	12	*12	0	21	12	7	19	35
93-94— Toronto	NHL	83	53	46	99	98	22	21	5	18	5	5	10	16
94-95— Toronto	NHL	48	22	16	38	34	-7	8	0	7	3	2	5	25
95-96— Toronto	NHL	61	20	24	44	54	-11	12	2	—	—	—	—	—
— New Jersey	NHL	15	8	5	13	10	2	2	0	—	—	—	—	—
96-97— New Jersey	NHL	82	27	34	61	48	38	4	1	1	0	0	0	0
NHL totals (15 years)		1083	503	561	1064	816	84	212	8	88	32	34	66	108

ANTOSKI, SHAWN   LW/RW   MIGHTY DUCKS

PERSONAL: Born May 25, 1970, in Brantford, Ont. ... 6-4/235. ... Shoots left. ... Name pronounced an-TAH-skee.

TRANSACTIONS/CAREER NOTES: Injured knee ligament (December 1988). ... Separated shoulder (March 1989). ... Selected by Vancouver Canucks in first round (second Canucks pick, 18th overall) of NHL entry draft (June 17, 1989). ... Suffered sore back (December 1991). ... Fractured knuckle (December 15, 1993); missed eight games. ... Sprained thumb (January 19, 1994); missed three games. ... Suffered sore hand (April 1, 1994); missed three games. ... Traded by Canucks to Philadelphia Flyers for LW Josef Beranek (February 15, 1995). ... Suffered from the flu (March 2, 1995); missed four games. ... Injured shoulder (October 22, 1995); missed one game. ... Strained hamstring (December 18, 1995); missed two games. ... Sprained right ankle (January 9, 1996); missed two games. ... Suffered from the flu (January 22, 1996); missed one game. ... Signed as free agent by Pittsburgh Penguins (July 31, 1996). ... Traded by Penguins with D Dmitri Mironov to Mighty Ducks of Anaheim for C Alex Hicks and D Fredrik Olausson (November 19, 1996). ... Strained left hip (November 20, 1996); missed 19 games. ... Strained hip (January 8, 1997); missed 10 games. ... Underwent hernia surgery (February 4, 1997); missed remainder of season.

				REGULAR SEASON						PLAYOFFS				
Season Team	League	Gms.	G	A	Pts.	PIM	+/-	PP	SH	Gms.	G	A	Pts.	PIM
87-88— North Bay	OHL	52	3	4	7	163	...	...	...	—	—	—	—	—
88-89— North Bay	OHL	57	6	21	27	201	...	...	...	9	5	3	8	24
89-90— North Bay	OHL	59	25	31	56	201	...	...	...	5	1	2	3	17
90-91— Milwaukee	IHL	62	17	7	24	330	...	...	...	5	1	2	3	10
— Vancouver	NHL	2	0	0	0	0	-2	0	0	—	—	—	—	—
91-92— Milwaukee	IHL	52	17	16	33	346	...	...	...	5	2	0	2	20
— Vancouver	NHL	4	0	0	0	29	-1	0	0	—	—	—	—	—
92-93— Hamilton	AHL	41	3	4	7	172	...	...	...	—	—	—	—	—
— Vancouver	NHL	2	0	0	0	0	0	0	0	—	—	—	—	—
93-94— Vancouver	NHL	55	1	2	3	190	-11	0	0	16	0	1	1	36
94-95— Vancouver	NHL	7	0	0	0	46	-4	0	0	—	—	—	—	—
— Philadelphia	NHL	25	0	0	0	61	0	0	0	13	0	1	1	10
95-96— Philadelphia	NHL	64	1	3	4	204	-4	0	0	7	1	1	2	28
96-97— Pittsburgh	NHL	13	0	0	0	49	0	0	0	—	—	—	—	—
— Anaheim	NHL	2	0	0	0	2	1	0	0	—	—	—	—	—
NHL totals (7 years)		174	2	5	7	581	-21	0	0	36	1	3	4	74

ARCHIBALD, DAVE   C/LW   ISLANDERS

PERSONAL: Born April 14, 1969, in Chilliwack, B.C. ... 6-1/211. ... Shoots left. ... Full name: David John Archibald.

TRANSACTIONS/CAREER NOTES: Underwent shoulder surgery (January 1984). ... Lacerated hand (October 1986). ... Selected as underage junior by Minnesota North Stars in first round (first North Stars pick, sixth overall) of NHL entry draft (June 13, 1987). ... Injured shoulder (September 1987). ... Suffered sore back (February 1989). ... Traded by North Stars to New York Rangers for D Jayson More (November 1, 1989).

... Traded by Rangers to Ottawa Senators for fifth-round pick (traded to Los Angeles) in 1993 draft (November 6, 1992). ... Injured back (January 8, 1993); missed 26 games. ... Injured groin (March 25, 1993); missed one game. ... Injured shoulder (November 13, 1993); missed 14 games. ... Injured groin (January 14, 1994); missed remainder of season. ... Sprained ankle (February 17, 1995); missed 21 games. ... Reinjured ankle (April 8, 1995); missed remainder of season. ... Sprained ankle (September 26, 1995); missed 11 games. ... Signed as free agent by New York Islanders (October 3, 1996).

		REGULAR SEASON								PLAYOFFS				
Season Team	League	Gms.	G	A	Pts.	PIM	+/-	PP	SH	Gms.	G	A	Pts.	PIM
84-85— Portland	WHL	47	7	11	18	10	...	...	...	3	0	2	2	0
85-86— Portland	WHL	70	29	35	64	56	...	...	...	15	6	7	13	11
86-87— Portland	WHL	65	50	57	107	40	...	...	...	20	10	18	28	11
87-88— Minnesota	NHL	78	13	20	33	26	-17	3	0	—	—	—	—	—
88-89— Minnesota	NHL	72	14	19	33	14	-11	7	0	5	0	1	1	0
89-90— Minnesota	NHL	12	1	5	6	6	1	1	0	—	—	—	—	—
— New York Rangers	NHL	19	2	3	5	6	0	1	0	—	—	—	—	—
— Flint	IHL	41	14	38	52	16	...	...	...	4	3	2	5	0
90-91— Canadian nat'l team	Int'l	29	19	12	31	20	...	...	...	—	—	—	—	—
91-92— Canadian nat'l team	Int'l	58	20	43	63	62	...	...	...	—	—	—	—	—
— Can. Olympic team	Int'l	8	7	1	8	18	...	...	...	—	—	—	—	—
— Bolzon	Italy	12	12	12	24	16	...	...	...	—	—	—	—	—
92-93— Binghamton	AHL	8	6	3	9	10	...	...	...	—	—	—	—	—
— Ottawa	NHL	44	9	6	15	32	-16	6	0	—	—	—	—	—
93-94— Ottawa	NHL	33	10	8	18	14	-7	2	0	—	—	—	—	—
94-95— Ottawa	NHL	14	2	2	4	19	-7	0	0	—	—	—	—	—
95-96— Ottawa	NHL	44	6	4	10	18	-14	0	0	—	—	—	—	—
— Utah	IHL	19	1	4	5	10	...	...	...	—	—	—	—	—
96-97— New York Islanders	NHL	7	0	0	0	4	-4	0	0	—	—	—	—	—
NHL totals (8 years)		323	57	67	124	139	-75	20	0	5	0	1	1	0

ARMSTRONG, CHRIS — D — PANTHERS

PERSONAL: Born June 26, 1975, in Regina, Sask. ... 6-0/184. ... Shoots left.
HIGH SCHOOL: Vanier Collegiate (Moose Jaw, Sask.).
TRANSACTIONS/CAREER NOTES: Selected by Florida Panthers in third round (third Panthers pick, 57th overall) of NHL entry draft (June 26, 1993).
HONORS: Named to Can.HL All-Star second team (1993-94). ... Named to WHL (East) All-Star first team (1993-94). ... Named to WHL (East) All-Star second team (1994-95).

		REGULAR SEASON								PLAYOFFS				
Season Team	League	Gms.	G	A	Pts.	PIM	+/-	PP	SH	Gms.	G	A	Pts.	PIM
91-92— Moose Jaw	WHL	43	2	7	9	19	...	...	...	4	0	0	0	0
92-93— Moose Jaw	WHL	67	9	35	44	104	...	...	...	—	—	—	—	—
93-94— Moose Jaw	WHL	64	13	55	68	54	...	...	...	—	—	—	—	—
— Cincinnati	IHL	1	0	0	0	0	...	...	...	10	1	3	4	2
94-95— Moose Jaw	WHL	66	17	54	71	61	...	...	...	10	2	12	14	22
— Cincinnati	IHL	—	—	—	—	—	...	...	...	9	1	3	4	10
95-96— Carolina	AHL	78	9	33	42	65	...	...	...	—	—	—	—	—
96-97— Carolina	AHL	66	9	23	32	38	...	...	...	—	—	—	—	—

ARMSTRONG, DEREK — C — SENATORS

PERSONAL: Born April 23, 1973, in Ottawa. ... 5-11/180. ... Shoots right.
HIGH SCHOOL: Lo-Ellen Park Secondary School (Sudbury, Ont.).
TRANSACTIONS/CAREER NOTES: Selected by New York Islanders in sixth round (fifth Islanders pick, 128th overall) of NHL entry draft (June 20, 1992). ... Suffered food poisoning (January 28, 1997); missed one game. ... Signed as free agent by Ottawa Senators (July 10, 1997).

		REGULAR SEASON								PLAYOFFS				
Season Team	League	Gms.	G	A	Pts.	PIM	+/-	PP	SH	Gms.	G	A	Pts.	PIM
89-90— Hawkesbury	COJHL	48	8	10	18	30	...	...	...	—	—	—	—	—
90-91— Sudbury	OHL	2	0	2	2	0	...	...	...	—	—	—	—	—
— Hawkesbury	COJHL	54	27	45	72	49	...	...	...	—	—	—	—	—
91-92— Sudbury	OHL	66	31	54	85	22	...	...	...	9	2	2	4	2
92-93— Sudbury	OHL	66	44	62	106	56	...	...	...	14	9	10	19	26
93-94— Salt Lake City	IHL	76	23	35	58	61	...	...	...	—	—	—	—	—
94-95— Denver	IHL	59	13	18	31	65	...	...	...	6	0	2	2	0
95-96— Worcester	AHL	51	11	15	26	33	...	...	...	4	2	1	3	0
— New York Islanders	NHL	19	1	3	4	14	-6	0	0	—	—	—	—	—
96-97— New York Islanders	NHL	50	6	7	13	33	-8	0	0	—	—	—	—	—
— Utah	IHL	17	4	8	12	10	...	...	...	6	0	4	4	4
NHL totals (2 years)		69	7	10	17	47	-14	0	0					

ARNOTT, JASON — C — OILERS

PERSONAL: Born October 11, 1974, in Collingworth, Ont. ... 6-3/220. ... Shoots right. ... Name pronounced AHR-niht.
HIGH SCHOOL: Henry Street (Whitby, Ont.).
TRANSACTIONS/CAREER NOTES: Selected by Edmonton Oilers in first round (first Oilers pick, seventh overall) of NHL entry draft (June 26, 1993). ... Suffered from tonsillitis (November 3, 1993); missed one game. ... Bruised sternum (November 27, 1993); missed one game. ... Sprained back (December 7, 1993); missed one game. ... Underwent appendectomy (December 28, 1993); missed three games. ... Suffered from the flu (February 22, 1995); missed one game. ... Suffered concussion (March 23, 1995); missed two games. ... Strained knee (April

19, 1995); missed two games. ... Suspended one game by NHL for game misconduct penalties (April 22, 1995). ... Suffered concussion and lacerated face (October 8, 1995); missed seven games. ... Sprained knee (February 11, 1996); missed nine games. ... Strained knee (March 19, 1996); missed one game. ... Suffered inner ear infection (April 8, 1996); missed one game. ... Fractured ankle (December 27, 1996); missed seven games. ... Injured ankle (January 22, 1997); missed two games. ... Suffered from the flu (February 12, 1997); missed two games. ... Strained lower back (March 23, 1997); missed four games.

HONORS: Named NHL Rookie of the Year by THE SPORTING NEWS (1993-94). ... Named to NHL All-Rookie team (1993-94). ... Played in NHL All-Star Game (1997).

STATISTICAL PLATEAUS: Three-goal games: 1994-95 (1), 1995-96 (1). Total: 2.

			REGULAR SEASON								PLAYOFFS				
Season Team	League	Gms.	G	A	Pts.	PIM	+/-	PP	SH		Gms.	G	A	Pts.	PIM
90-91 — Lindsay Jr. B	OHA	42	17	44	61	10	...	...	...		—	—	—	—	—
91-92 — Oshawa	OHL	57	9	15	24	12	...	...	...		—	—	—	—	—
92-93 — Oshawa	OHL	56	41	57	98	74	...	...	...		13	9	9	18	20
93-94 — Edmonton	NHL	78	33	35	68	104	1	10	0		—	—	—	—	—
94-95 — Edmonton	NHL	42	15	22	37	128	-14	7	0		—	—	—	—	—
95-96 — Edmonton	NHL	64	28	31	59	87	-6	8	0		—	—	—	—	—
96-97 — Edmonton	NHL	67	19	38	57	92	-21	10	1		12	3	6	9	18
NHL totals (4 years)		251	95	126	221	411	-40	35	1		12	3	6	9	18

ARSENAULT, DAVID — G — RED WINGS

PERSONAL: Born March 21, 1977, in Frankfurt, West Germany. ... 6-1/165. ... Catches left. ... Name pronounced AHR-sih-noh.

TRANSACTIONS/CAREER NOTES: Selected by Detroit Red Wings in fifth round (sixth Red Wings pick, 126th overall) of NHL entry draft (July 8, 1995).

			REGULAR SEASON							PLAYOFFS					
Season Team	League	Gms.	Min	W	L	T	GA	SO	Avg.	Gms.	Min.	W	L	GA	SO	Avg.
94-95 — St. Hyacinthe	QMJHL	19	862	3	10	0	75	0	5.22	—	—	—	—	—	—	—
— Drummondville	QMJHL	12	478	2	5	0	40	0	5.02	2	122	0	2	8	0	3.93
95-96 — Drummondville	QMJHL	21	1177	8	10	1	89	0	4.54	—	—	—	—	—	—	—
— Chicoutimi	QMJHL	6	207	1	1	1	14	0	4.06	5	108	0	1	10	0	5.56
96-97 — Oshawa	OHL	41	2316	24	9	5	106	2	2.75	17	1027	11	6	46	*1	*2.69

ASKEY, TOM — G — MIGHTY DUCKS

PERSONAL: Born October 4, 1974, in Kenmore, N.Y. ... 6-2/185. ... Catches left.

COLLEGE: Ohio State.

TRANSACTIONS/CAREER NOTES: Selected by Mighty Ducks of Anaheim in eighth round (eighth Ducks pick, 186th overall) of NHL entry draft (June 26, 1993).

HONORS: Named to CCHA All-Star second team (1995-96).

			REGULAR SEASON							PLAYOFFS					
Season Team	League	Gms.	Min	W	L	T	GA	SO	Avg.	Gms.	Min.	W	L	GA	SO	Avg.
92-93 — Ohio State	CCHA	25	1235	2	19	0	125	0	6.07	—	—	—	—	—	—	—
93-94 — Ohio State	CCHA	27	1488	3	19	4	103	0	4.15	—	—	—	—	—	—	—
94-95 — Ohio State	CCHA	26	1387	4	19	2	121	0	5.23	—	—	—	—	—	—	—
95-96 — Ohio State	CCHA	26	1340	8	11	4	68	0	3.04	—	—	—	—	—	—	—
96-97 — Baltimore	AHL	40	2239	17	18	2	140	1	3.75	3	138	0	3	11	0	4.78

ASTLEY, MARK — D — KINGS

PERSONAL: Born March 30, 1969, in Calgary. ... 5-11/185. ... Shoots left. ... Name pronounced AST-lee.

COLLEGE: Lake Superior State (Mich.).

TRANSACTIONS/CAREER NOTES: Selected by Buffalo Sabres in 10th round (ninth Sabres pick, 194th overall) of NHL entry draft (June 17, 1989). ... Hospitalized with strep pneumonia (March 14, 1990). ... Loaned by Sabres to Canadian Olympic team (October 15, 1993). ... Suffered from the flu (November 1, 1995); missed three games. ... Suffered inner ear problem (January 27, 1996); missed two games. ... Signed as free agent by Los Angeles Kings (September 4, 1996).

HONORS: Named to CCHA All-Star second team (1990-91). ... Named to NCAA All-America West first team (1991-92). ... Named to CCHA All-Star first team (1991-92). ... Named to NCAA All-Tournament team (1991-92).

MISCELLANEOUS: Member of silver-medal-winning Canadian Olympic team (1994).

			REGULAR SEASON								PLAYOFFS				
Season Team	League	Gms.	G	A	Pts.	PIM	+/-	PP	SH		Gms.	G	A	Pts.	PIM
87-88 — Calgary Canucks	AJHL	52	25	37	62	106	...	...	...		—	—	—	—	—
88-89 — Lake Superior State	CCHA	42	3	12	15	26	...	...	...		—	—	—	—	—
89-90 — Lake Superior State	CCHA	43	7	25	32	74	...	...	...		—	—	—	—	—
90-91 — Lake Superior State	CCHA	45	19	27	46	50	...	...	...		—	—	—	—	—
91-92 — Lake Superior State	CCHA	43	12	37	49	65	...	...	...		—	—	—	—	—
92-93 — Lugano	Switzerland	30	10	12	22	57	...	...	...		—	—	—	—	—
— Canadian nat'l team	Int'l	22	4	14	18	14	...	...	...		—	—	—	—	—
93-94 — Buffalo	NHL	1	0	0	0	0	-1	0	0		—	—	—	—	—
— Canadian nat'l team	Int'l	13	4	8	12	6	...	...	...		—	—	—	—	—
— Can. Olympic team	Int'l	8	0	1	1	4	...	...	...		—	—	—	—	—
94-95 — Rochester	AHL	46	5	24	29	49	...	...	...		3	0	2	2	2
— Buffalo	NHL	14	2	1	3	12	-2	0	0		2	0	0	0	0
95-96 — Buffalo	NHL	60	2	18	20	80	-12	0	0		—	—	—	—	—
96-97 — Phoenix	IHL	52	6	11	17	43	...	...	...		—	—	—	—	—
NHL totals (3 years)		75	4	19	23	92	-15	0	0		2	0	0	0	0

ATCHEYNUM, BLAIR RW

PERSONAL: Born April 20, 1969, in Estevan, Sask. ... 6-2/190. ... Shoots right.
TRANSACTIONS/CAREER NOTES: Selected by Swift Current Broncos in special compensation draft to replace players injured and killed in a December 30, 1986 bus crash (February 1987). ... Traded by Broncos to Moose Jaw Warriors for D Tim Logan (February 1987). ... Selected by Hartford Whalers in third round (second Whalers pick, 52nd overall) of NHL entry draft (June 17, 1989). ... Suffered concussion (January 12, 1991). ... Selected by Ottawa Senators in NHL expansion draft (June 18, 1992). ... Signed as free agent by Worcester Icecats (December 2, 1994). ... Signed as free agent by Cape Breton of AHL (September 8, 1995).
HONORS: Won Brad Hornung Trophy (1988-89). ... Named to WHL (East) All-Star first team (1988-89). ... Named to AHL All-Star first team (1996-97).

		REGULAR SEASON								PLAYOFFS				
Season Team	League	Gms.	G	A	Pts.	PIM	+/-	PP	SH	Gms.	G	A	Pts.	PIM
85-86— North Battleford	SJHL	35	25	20	45	50	...	...	...	—	—	—	—	—
86-87— Saskatoon	WHL	21	0	4	4	4	...	...	...	—	—	—	—	—
— Swift Current	WHL	5	2	1	3	0	...	...	...	—	—	—	—	—
— Moose Jaw	WHL	12	3	0	3	2	...	...	...	—	—	—	—	—
87-88— Moose Jaw	WHL	60	32	16	48	52	...	...	...	—	—	—	—	—
88-89— Moose Jaw	WHL	71	70	68	138	70	...	...	...	7	2	5	7	13
89-90— Binghamton	AHL	78	20	21	41	45	...	...	...	—	—	—	—	—
90-91— Springfield	AHL	72	25	27	52	42	...	...	...	13	0	6	6	6
91-92— Springfield	AHL	62	16	21	37	64	...	...	...	6	1	1	2	2
92-93— New Haven	AHL	51	16	18	34	47	...	...	...	—	—	—	—	—
— Ottawa	NHL	4	0	1	1	0	-3	0	0	—	—	—	—	—
93-94— Columbus	ECHL	16	15	12	27	10	...	...	...	—	—	—	—	—
— Portland	AHL	2	0	0	0	0	...	...	...	—	—	—	—	—
— Springfield	AHL	40	18	22	40	13	...	...	...	6	0	2	2	0
94-95— Minnesota	IHL	17	4	6	10	7	...	...	...	—	—	—	—	—
— Worcester	AHL	55	17	29	46	26	...	...	...	—	—	—	—	—
95-96— Cape Breton	AHL	79	30	42	72	65	...	...	...	—	—	—	—	—
96-97— Hershey	AHL	77	42	45	87	57	...	...	...	13	6	11	17	6
NHL totals (1 year)		4	0	1	1	0	-3	0	0					

AUBIN, JEAN-SEBASTIEN G PENGUINS

PERSONAL: Born July 19, 1977, in Montreal. ... 5-11/179. ... Catches right. ... Name pronounced AW-ban.
TRANSACTIONS/CAREER NOTES: Selected by Pittsburgh Penguins in third round (second Penguins pick, 76th overall) of NHL entry draft (July 8, 1995).

		REGULAR SEASON								PLAYOFFS					
Season Team	League	Gms.	Min	W	L	T	GA	SO	Avg.	Gms.	Min.	W	L	GA	SO	Avg.
94-95— Sherbrooke	QMJHL	27	1287	13	10	1	73	1	3.40	3	185	1	2	11	0	3.57
95-96— Sherbrooke	QMJHL	40	2084	18	14	2	127	1	3.66	4	174	1	3	16	0	5.52
96-97— Sherbrooke	QMJHL	4	249	3	1	0	8	0	1.93	—	—	—	—	—	—	—
— Moncton	QMJHL	23	1311	9	13	0	72	1	3.30	—	—	—	—	—	—	—
— Laval.............................	QMJHL	11	532	2	6	1	41	0	4.62	2	128	0	2	10	0	4.71

AUCOIN, ADRIAN D CANUCKS

PERSONAL: Born July 3, 1973, in London, Ont. ... 6-2/210. ... Shoots right. ... Name pronounced oh-COYN.
COLLEGE: Boston University.
TRANSACTIONS/CAREER NOTES: Selected by Vancouver Canucks in fifth round (seventh Canucks pick, 117th overall) of NHL entry draft (June 20, 1992). ... Sprained shoulder (January 10, 1997); missed six games.
MISCELLANEOUS: Member of silver-medal-winning Canadian Olympic team (1994).

		REGULAR SEASON								PLAYOFFS				
Season Team	League	Gms.	G	A	Pts.	PIM	+/-	PP	SH	Gms.	G	A	Pts.	PIM
91-92— Boston University	Hockey East	33	2	10	12	62	...	...	...	—	—	—	—	—
92-93— Canadian nat'l team ...	Int'l	42	8	10	18	71	...	...	...	—	—	—	—	—
93-94— Canadian nat'l team ...	Int'l	59	5	12	17	80	...	...	...	—	—	—	—	—
— Can. Olympic team	Int'l	4	0	0	0	2	...	...	...	—	—	—	—	—
— Hamilton	AHL	13	1	2	3	19	...	...	...	4	0	2	2	6
94-95— Syracuse	AHL	71	13	18	31	52	...	...	...	—	—	—	—	—
— Vancouver.................	NHL	1	1	0	1	0	1	0	0	4	1	0	1	0
95-96— Syracuse	AHL	29	5	13	18	47	...	...	...	—	—	—	—	—
— Vancouver.................	NHL	49	4	14	18	34	8	2	0	6	0	0	0	2
96-97— Vancouver.................	NHL	70	5	16	21	63	0	1	0	—	—	—	—	—
NHL totals (3 years)		120	10	30	40	97	9	3	0	10	1	0	1	2

AUDET, PHILIPPE LW RED WINGS

PERSONAL: Born June 4, 1977, in Ottawa. ... 6-2/175. ... Shoots left. ... Name pronounced oh-DEHT.
TRANSACTIONS/CAREER NOTES: Selected by Detroit Red Wings in second round (second Red Wings pick, 52nd overall) of NHL entry draft (July 8, 1995).
HONORS: Won Ed Chynoweth Trophy (1995-96). ... Named to Memorial Cup All-Star team (1995-96). ... Named to QMJHL All-Star first team (1996-97).

Season Team	League	Gms.	G	A	Pts.	PIM	+/-	PP	SH	Gms.	G	A	Pts.	PIM
94-95— Granby	QMJHL	62	19	17	36	93	...	...	...	7	1	3	4	4
95-96— Granby	QMJHL	67	40	43	83	162	...	...	...	21	12	18	30	32
96-97— Granby	QMJHL	67	52	56	108	150	...	...	...	4	4	1	5	25
— Adirondack	AHL	3	1	1	2	0	...	...	...	1	1	0	1	0

AUDETTE, DONALD RW SABRES

PERSONAL: Born September 23, 1969, in Laval, Que. ... 5-8/184. ... Shoots right. ... Name pronounced aw-DEHT.
TRANSACTIONS/CAREER NOTES: Selected by Buffalo Sabres in ninth round (eighth Sabres pick, 183rd overall) of NHL entry draft (June 17, 1989). ... Broke left hand (February 11, 1990); missed seven games. ... Bruised thigh (September 1990). ... Bruised thigh (October 1990); missed five games. ... Tore left knee ligaments (November 16, 1990). ... Underwent surgery to left knee (December 10, 1990). ... Sprained ankle (December 14, 1991); missed eight games. ... Injured knee (March 31, 1992). ... Underwent knee surgery prior to 1992-93 season; missed first 22 games of season. ... Tore knee cartilage (September 23, 1995); missed 11 games. ... Broke tip of right thumb (November 8, 1995); missed two games. ... Injured right knee (December 1, 1995); missed seven games. ... Underwent right knee surgery (January 26, 1996); missed remainder of season. ... Strained groin (October 26, 1996); missed five games.
HONORS: Won Guy Lafleur Trophy (1988-89). ... Named to QMJHL All-Star first team (1988-89). ... Won Dudley (Red) Garrett Memorial Trophy (1989-90). ... Named to AHL All-Star first team (1989-90).
STATISTICAL PLATEAUS: Three-goal games: 1994-95 (1), 1995-96 (1). Total: 2.
MISCELLANEOUS: Failed to score on a penalty shot (vs. Felix Potvin, November 21, 1996).

Season Team	League	Gms.	G	A	Pts.	PIM	+/-	PP	SH	Gms.	G	A	Pts.	PIM
86-87— Laval	QMJHL	66	17	22	39	36	...	...	...	14	2	6	8	10
87-88— Laval	QMJHL	63	48	61	109	56	...	...	...	14	7	12	19	20
88-89— Laval	QMJHL	70	76	85	161	123	...	...	...	17	*17	12	29	43
89-90— Rochester	AHL	70	42	46	88	78	...	...	...	15	9	8	17	29
— Buffalo	NHL	0	0	0	0	0	0	0	0	2	0	0	0	0
90-91— Rochester	AHL	5	4	0	4	2	...	...	...	—	—	—	—	—
— Buffalo	NHL	8	4	3	7	4	-1	2	0	—	—	—	—	—
91-92— Buffalo	NHL	63	31	17	48	75	-1	5	0	—	—	—	—	—
92-93— Buffalo	NHL	44	12	7	19	51	-8	2	0	8	2	2	4	6
— Rochester	AHL	6	8	4	12	10	...	...	...	—	—	—	—	—
93-94— Buffalo	NHL	77	29	30	59	41	2	16	1	7	0	1	1	6
94-95— Buffalo	NHL	46	24	13	37	27	-3	13	0	5	1	1	2	4
95-96— Buffalo	NHL	23	12	13	25	18	0	8	0	—	—	—	—	—
96-97— Buffalo	NHL	73	28	22	50	48	-6	8	0	11	4	5	9	6
NHL totals (8 years)		334	140	105	245	264	-17	54	1	33	7	9	16	22

AUGUSTA, PATRIK RW

PERSONAL: Born November 13, 1969, in Jihlava, Czechoslovakia. ... 5-10/170. ... Shoots left. ... Name pronounced pa-TREEK ah-GOOS-tuh.
TRANSACTIONS/CAREER NOTES: Selected by Toronto Maple Leafs in seventh round (eighth Maple Leafs pick, 149th overall) of NHL entry draft (June 20, 1992).
HONORS: Named to AHL All-Star second team (1993-94). ... Named to IHL All-Star second team (1996-97).

Season Team	League	Gms.	G	A	Pts.	PIM	+/-	PP	SH	Gms.	G	A	Pts.	PIM
89-90— Dukla Jihlava	Czech.	46	12	12	24	...	...	...	...	—	—	—	—	—
90-91— Dukla Jihlava	Czech.	49	20	22	42	18	...	...	...	—	—	—	—	—
91-92— Dukla Jihlava	Czech.	34	15	11	26	...	...	...	...	—	—	—	—	—
— Czec. Olympic team	Int'l	8	3	2	5	...	...	...	...	—	—	—	—	—
92-93— St. John's	AHL	75	32	45	77	74	...	...	...	8	3	3	6	23
93-94— St. John's	AHL	77	*53	43	96	105	...	...	...	11	4	8	12	4
— Toronto	NHL	2	0	0	0	0	0	0	0	—	—	—	—	—
94-95— St. John's	AHL	71	37	32	69	98	...	...	...	4	2	0	2	7
95-96— Los Angeles	IHL	79	34	51	85	83	...	...	...	—	—	—	—	—
96-97— Long Beach	IHL	82	45	42	87	96	...	...	...	18	4	4	8	33
NHL totals (1 year)		2	0	0	0	0	0	0	0					

AXELSSON, PER-JOHAN LW BRUINS

PERSONAL: Born February 26, 1975, in Kungalv, Sweden. ... 6-1/174. ... Shoots left.
TRANSACTIONS/CAREER NOTES: Selected by Boston Bruins in seventh round (seventh Bruins pick, 177th overall) of NHL entry draft (June 8, 1995).

Season Team	League	Gms.	G	A	Pts.	PIM	+/-	PP	SH	Gms.	G	A	Pts.	PIM
93-94— Frolunda	Sweden	11	0	0	0	4	...	...	...	4	0	0	0	0
94-95— Frolunda	Sweden	8	2	1	3	6	...	...	...	—	—	—	—	—
95-96— Frolunda	Sweden	36	15	5	20	10	...	...	...	13	3	0	3	10
96-97— Vastra Frolunda	Sweden	50	19	15	34	34	...	...	...	3	0	2	2	0

BABYCH, DAVE D CANUCKS

PERSONAL: Born May 23, 1961, in Edmonton. ... 6-2/215. ... Shoots left. ... Full name: David Michael Babych. ... Name pronounced BAB-ihch. ... Brother of Wayne Babych, right winger for four NHL teams (1978-79 through 1986-87).

TRANSACTIONS/CAREER NOTES: Selected by Winnipeg Jets as underage junior in first round (first Jets pick, second overall) of NHL entry draft (June 11, 1980). ... Separated shoulder (March 1984). ... Suffered back spasms (December 1984). ... Traded by Jets to Hartford Whalers for RW Ray Neufeld (November 21, 1985). ... Injured hip (January 1987); missed 12 games. ... Cut right hand (March 16, 1989); missed six games. ... Bruised neck (March 1990). ... Underwent surgery to right wrist (October 29, 1990); missed 44 games. ... Broke right thumb (February 8, 1991); missed remainder of season. ... Selected by Minnesota North Stars in NHL expansion draft (May 30, 1991). ... Traded by North Stars to Vancouver Canucks for D Craig Ludwig as part of a three-club deal in which Canucks sent D Tom Kurvers to Islanders for Ludwig (June 22, 1991). ... Suffered sore back (November 3, 1991); missed one game. ... Suffered hernia (September 22, 1992); missed 22 games. ... Sprained knee (December 7, 1992); missed 12 games. ... Suffered from the flu (March 20, 1993); missed one game. ... Suffered facial lacerations (April 4, 1993); missed three games. ... Suffered facial lacerations (December 15, 1993); missed two games. ... Bruised foot (February 13, 1994); missed one game. ... Suffered injury (February 5, 1995); missed three games. ... Injured foot (December 8, 1995); missed 23 games. ... Suffered illness (February 23, 1996); missed one game. ... Injured hand (February 29, 1996); missed one game. ... Injured ankle (April 1, 1996); missed three games. ... Strained groin (December 3, 1996); missed three games.

HONORS: Won AJHL Top Defenseman Trophy (1977-78). ... Won AJHL Rookie of the Year Trophy (1977-78). ... Named to AJHL All-Star first team (1977-78). ... Won WHL Top Defenseman Trophy (1979-80). ... Named to WHL All-Star first team (1979-80). ... Played in NHL All-Star Game (1983 and 1984).

STATISTICAL PLATEAUS: Three-goal games: 1991-92 (1).

		REGULAR SEASON								PLAYOFFS				
Season Team	League	Gms.	G	A	Pts.	PIM	+/-	PP	SH	Gms.	G	A	Pts.	PIM
77-78 — Portland	WCHL	6	1	3	4	4	...	...	...	—	—	—	—	—
— Fort Saskatchewan	AJHL	56	31	69	100	37	...	...	...	—	—	—	—	—
78-79 — Portland	WHL	67	20	59	79	63	...	...	...	25	7	22	29	22
79-80 — Portland	WHL	50	22	60	82	71	...	...	...	8	1	10	11	2
80-81 — Winnipeg	NHL	69	6	38	44	90	-61	3	0	—	—	—	—	—
81-82 — Winnipeg	NHL	79	19	49	68	92	-11	11	0	4	1	2	3	29
82-83 — Winnipeg	NHL	79	13	61	74	56	-10	7	0	3	0	0	0	0
83-84 — Winnipeg	NHL	66	18	39	57	62	-31	10	0	3	1	1	2	0
84-85 — Winnipeg	NHL	78	13	49	62	78	-16	6	0	8	2	7	9	6
85-86 — Winnipeg	NHL	19	4	12	16	14	-1	2	0	—	—	—	—	—
— Hartford	NHL	62	10	43	53	36	1	7	1	8	1	3	4	14
86-87 — Hartford	NHL	66	8	33	41	44	-16	7	0	6	1	1	2	14
87-88 — Hartford	NHL	71	14	36	50	54	-25	10	0	6	3	2	5	2
88-89 — Hartford	NHL	70	6	41	47	54	-5	4	0	4	1	5	6	2
89-90 — Hartford	NHL	72	6	37	43	62	-16	4	0	7	1	2	3	0
90-91 — Hartford	NHL	8	0	6	6	4	-4	0	0	—	—	—	—	—
91-92 — Vancouver	NHL	75	5	24	29	63	-2	4	0	13	2	6	8	10
92-93 — Vancouver	NHL	43	3	16	19	44	6	3	0	12	2	5	7	6
93-94 — Vancouver	NHL	73	4	28	32	52	0	4	0	24	3	5	8	12
94-95 — Vancouver	NHL	40	3	11	14	18	-13	1	0	11	2	2	4	14
95-96 — Vancouver	NHL	53	3	21	24	38	-5	3	0	—	—	—	—	—
96-97 — Vancouver	NHL	78	5	22	27	38	-2	2	0	—	—	—	—	—
NHL totals (17 years)		1101	140	566	706	899	-211	84	1	109	20	41	61	109

BACH, RYAN   G   RED WINGS

PERSONAL: Born October 21, 1973, in Sherwood Park, Alta. ... 6-1/195. ... Catches left. ... Full name: Ryan David Bach. ... Name pronounced BAHK.
HIGH SCHOOL: Notre Dame College (Welland, Ont.).
COLLEGE: Colorado College.
TRANSACTIONS/CAREER NOTES: Selected by Detroit Red Wings in 11th round (11th Red Wings pick, 262nd overall) of NHL entry draft (June 20, 1992).
HONORS: Named to NCAA All-America West second team (1994-95). ... Named to WCHA All-Star first team (1994-95). ... Named to NCAA All-America West first team (1995-96). ... Named to WCHA All-Star first team (1995-96).

		REGULAR SEASON								PLAYOFFS						
Season Team	League	Gms.	Min	W	L	T	GA	SO	Avg.	Gms.	Min.	W	L	GA	SO	Avg.
91-92 — Notre Dame	SJHL	33	1862	16	11	6	124	0	4.00	—	—	—	—	—	—	—
92-93 — Colorado College	WCHA	4	239	1	3	0	11	0	2.76	—	—	—	—	—	—	—
93-94 — Colorado College	WCHA	30	1733	17	7	5	105	0	3.64	—	—	—	—	—	—	—
94-95 — Colorado College	WCHA	27	1522	18	5	1	83	0	3.27	—	—	—	—	—	—	—
95-96 — Colorado College	WCHA	23	1390	17	4	2	62	2	2.68	—	—	—	—	—	—	—
96-97 — Adirondack	AHL	13	451	2	3	1	29	0	3.86	1	46	0	0	3	0	3.91
— Toledo	ECHL	20	1168	5	11	‡3	74	0	3.80	—	—	—	—	—	—	—
— Utica	Col.HL	2	119	0	1	1	8	0	4.03	—	—	—	—	—	—	—

BAILEY, SCOTT   G   BRUINS

PERSONAL: Born May 2, 1972, in Calgary. ... 6-0/183. ... Catches left.
TRANSACTIONS/CAREER NOTES: Selected by Boston Bruins in fifth round (third Bruins pick, 112th overall) of NHL entry draft (June 20, 1992). ... Suffered back spasms (January 29, 1997); missed one game.
HONORS: Won WHL (West) Rookie of the Year Award (1990-91). ... Named to WHL (West) All-Star second team (1990-91 and 1991-92).

		REGULAR SEASON								PLAYOFFS						
Season Team	League	Gms.	Min	W	L	T	GA	SO	Avg.	Gms.	Min.	W	L	GA	SO	Avg.
88-89 — Moose Jaw	WHL	2	34	...	...	...	7	0	12.35	—	—	—	—	—	—	—
89-90 —							Did not play.									
90-91 — Spokane	WHL	46	2537	33	11	0	157	4	3.71	—	—	—	—	—	—	—
91-92 — Spokane	WHL	65	3748	34	23	5	206	1	3.30	10	605	5	5	43	0	4.26
92-93 — Johnstown	ECHL	36	1750	13	15	‡3	112	1	3.84	—	—	—	—	—	—	—
93-94 — Charlotte	ECHL	36	2180	22	11	‡3	130	1	3.58	3	188	1	2	12	0	3.83
— Providence	AHL	7	377	2	2	2	24	0	3.82	—	—	—	—	—	—	—

Season Team	League	REGULAR SEASON								PLAYOFFS						
		Gms.	Min	W	L	T	GA	SO	Avg.	Gms.	Min.	W	L	GA	SO	Avg.
94-95 — Providence	AHL	52	2936	25	16	9	147	2	3.00	9	505	4	4	31	2	3.68
95-96 — Providence	AHL	37	2209	15	19	3	120	1	3.26	2	118	1	1	6	0	3.05
— Boston	NHL	11	571	5	1	2	31	0	3.26	—	—	—	—	—	—	—
96-97 — Boston	NHL	8	394	1	5	0	24	0	3.65	—	—	—	—	—	—	—
— Providence	AHL	31	1735	11	17	2	112	0	3.87	7	453	3	4	23	0	3.05
NHL totals (2 years)		19	965	6	6	2	55	0	3.42							

BAKER, AARON   G   HURRICANES

PERSONAL: Born February 17, 1978, in Eckville, Alberta. ... 6-1/174. ... Catches right.
TRANSACTIONS/CAREER NOTES: Selected by Hartford Whalers in sixth round (sixth Whalers pick, 143rd overall) of NHL entry draft (June 22, 1996). ... Whalers franchise moved to North Carolina and renamed Carolina Hurricanes for 1997-98 season; NHL approved move on June 25, 1997.

Season Team	League	REGULAR SEASON								PLAYOFFS						
		Gms.	Min	W	L	T	GA	SO	Avg.	Gms.	Min.	W	L	GA	SO	Avg.
95-96 — Tri-City	WHL	20	1082	11	6	0	61	2	3.38	1	20	0	0	1	0	3.00
96-97 — Tri-City	WHL	34	1896	11	19	1	131	1	4.15	—	—	—	—	—	—	—

BAKER, JAMIE   C   MAPLE LEAFS

PERSONAL: Born August 31, 1966, in Nepean, Ont. ... 6-0/195. ... Shoots left. ... Full name: James Paul Baker.
HIGH SCHOOL: J.S. Woodsworth (Nepean, Ont.).
COLLEGE: St. Lawrence (N.Y.).
TRANSACTIONS/CAREER NOTES: Selected by Quebec Nordiques in NHL supplemental draft (June 10, 1988). ... Broke left ankle (December 30, 1988). ... Sprained ankle (January 9, 1992); missed two games. ... Signed as free agent by Ottawa Senators (September 2, 1992). ... Sprained ankle (December 15, 1992); missed six games. ... Bruised foot (February 22, 1993); missed one game. ... Signed as free agent by San Jose Sharks (August 18, 1993). ... Suffered slight groin pull (October 16, 1993); missed 10 games. ... Suffered from the flu (February 26, 1995); missed two games. ... Injured shoulder (March 15, 1995); missed three games. ... Suffered from concussion (December 16, 1995); missed two games. ... Suffered from body aches (March 3, 1996); missed one game. ... Suffered from the flu (April 4, 1996); missed two games. ... Traded by Sharks with fifth-round pick (C Peter Cava) in 1996 draft to Toronto Maple Leafs for D Todd Gill (June 14, 1996). ... Separated shoulder (December 6, 1996); missed five games. ... Suffered head laceration (March 1, 1997); missed 12 games.
MISCELLANEOUS: Failed to score on a penalty shot (vs. Patrick Roy, March 28, 1996).

Season Team	League	REGULAR SEASON							PLAYOFFS				
		Gms.	G	A	Pts.	PIM	+/-	PP	SH	Gms.	G	A	Pts.	PIM
85-86 — St. Lawrence Univ.	ECAC	31	9	16	25	52	...	...	...	—	—	—	—	—
86-87 — St. Lawrence Univ.	ECAC	32	8	24	32	59	...	...	...	—	—	—	—	—
87-88 — St. Lawrence Univ.	ECAC	38	26	28	54	44	...	...	...	—	—	—	—	—
88-89 — St. Lawrence Univ.	ECAC	13	11	16	27	16	...	...	...	—	—	—	—	—
89-90 — Quebec	NHL	1	0	0	0	0	-1	0	0	—	—	—	—	—
— Halifax	AHL	74	17	43	60	47	...	...	...	6	0	0	0	7
90-91 — Quebec	NHL	18	2	0	2	8	-4	0	1	—	—	—	—	—
— Halifax	AHL	50	14	22	36	85	...	...	...	—	—	—	—	—
91-92 — Halifax	AHL	9	5	0	5	12	...	...	...	—	—	—	—	—
— Quebec	NHL	52	7	10	17	32	-5	3	0	—	—	—	—	—
92-93 — Ottawa	NHL	76	19	29	48	54	-20	10	0	—	—	—	—	—
93-94 — San Jose	NHL	65	12	5	17	38	2	0	0	14	3	2	5	30
94-95 — San Jose	NHL	43	7	4	11	22	-7	0	1	11	2	2	4	12
95-96 — San Jose	NHL	77	16	17	33	79	-19	2	6	—	—	—	—	—
96-97 — Toronto	NHL	58	8	8	16	28	2	1	0	—	—	—	—	—
NHL totals (8 years)		390	71	73	144	261	-52	16	8	25	5	4	9	42

BALES, MIKE   G   SENATORS

PERSONAL: Born August 6, 1971, in Saskatoon, Sask. ... 5-11/190. ... Catches left. ... Full name: Michael Raymond Bales.
COLLEGE: Ohio State.
TRANSACTIONS/CAREER NOTES: Selected by Boston Bruins in fifth round (fourth Bruins pick, 105th overall) of NHL entry draft (June 16, 1990). ... Signed as free agent by Ottawa Senators (July 4, 1994).

Season Team	League	REGULAR SEASON								PLAYOFFS						
		Gms.	Min	W	L	T	GA	SO	Avg.	Gms.	Min.	W	L	GA	SO	Avg.
88-89 — Estevan	SJHL	44	2412	...	...	...	197	1	4.90	—	—	—	—	—	—	—
89-90 — Ohio State	CCHA	21	1117	6	13	2	95	0	5.10	—	—	—	—	—	—	—
90-91 — Ohio State	CCHA	*39	*2180	11	24	3	*184	0	5.06	—	—	—	—	—	—	—
91-92 — Ohio State	CCHA	36	2061	11	20	5	*180	0	5.24	—	—	—	—	—	—	—
92-93 — Providence	AHL	44	2363	22	17	0	166	1	4.21	2	118	0	2	8	0	4.07
— Boston	NHL	1	25	0	0	0	1	0	2.40	—	—	—	—	—	—	—
93-94 — Providence	AHL	33	1757	9	15	4	130	0	4.44	—	—	—	—	—	—	—
94-95 — Prince Edward Island	AHL	45	2649	25	16	3	160	2	3.62	9	530	6	3	24	2	2.72
— Ottawa	NHL	1	3	0	0	0	0	0	0.00	—	—	—	—	—	—	—
95-96 — Prince Edward Island	AHL	2	118	0	2	0	11	0	5.59	—	—	—	—	—	—	—
— Ottawa	NHL	20	1040	2	14	1	72	0	4.15	—	—	—	—	—	—	—
96-97 — Baltimore	AHL	46	2544	13	21	8	130	3	3.07	—	—	—	—	—	—	—
— Ottawa	NHL	1	52	0	1	0	4	0	4.62	—	—	—	—	—	—	—
NHL totals (4 years)		23	1120	2	15	1	77	0	4.13							

BANHAM, FRANK　　　　　RW　　　　　MIGHTY DUCKS

PERSONAL: Born April 14, 1975, in Calahoo, Alta. ... 6-0/190. ... Shoots right.
TRANSACTIONS/CAREER NOTES: Selected by Washington Capitals in sixth round (fourth Capitals pick, 147th overall) of NHL entry draft (June 26, 1993). ... Signed as free agent by Mighty Ducks of Anaheim (January 22, 1996).
HONORS: Named to WHL (Central/East) All-Star first team (1995-96).

Season Team	League	REGULAR SEASON								PLAYOFFS				
		Gms.	G	A	Pts.	PIM	+/-	PP	SH	Gms.	G	A	Pts.	PIM
91-92— Saskatoon	WHL	71	29	33	62	55	...	...	...	9	2	7	9	8
92-93— Saskatoon	WHL	71	29	33	62	55	...	...	...	9	2	7	9	8
93-94— Saskatoon	WHL	65	28	39	67	99	...	...	...	16	8	11	19	36
94-95— Saskatoon	WHL	70	50	39	89	63	...	...	...	8	2	6	8	12
95-96— Saskatoon	WHL	72	*83	69	152	116	...	...	...	4	6	0	6	2
— Baltimore	AHL	9	1	4	5	0	...	...	...	7	1	1	2	2
96-97— Baltimore	AHL	21	11	13	24	4	...	...	...	—	—	—	—	—
— Anaheim	NHL	3	0	0	0	0	-2	0	0	—	—	—	—	—
NHL totals (1 year)		**3**	**0**	**0**	**0**	**0**	**-2**	**0**	**0**					

BANNISTER, DREW　　　　　D　　　　　OILERS

PERSONAL: Born September 4, 1974, in Belleville, Ont. ... 6-2/200. ... Shoots right.
HIGH SCHOOL: Bawating Collegiate School (Sault Ste. Marie, Ont.).
TRANSACTIONS/CAREER NOTES: Selected by Tampa Bay Lightning in second round (second Lightning pick, 26th overall) of NHL entry draft (June 20, 1992). ... Injured ribs (November 27, 1996); missed one game. ... Bruised shoulder (March 15, 1997); missed one game. ... Traded by Lightning with sixth-round pick (C Peter Sarno) in 1997 draft to Edmonton Oilers for D Jeff Norton (March 18, 1997).
HONORS: Named to Memorial Cup All-Star team (1991-92). ... Named to OHL All-Star second team (1993-94).

Season Team	League	REGULAR SEASON								PLAYOFFS				
		Gms.	G	A	Pts.	PIM	+/-	PP	SH	Gms.	G	A	Pts.	PIM
90-91— Sault Ste. Marie	OHL	41	2	8	10	51	...	...	...	4	0	0	0	0
91-92— Sault Ste. Marie	OHL	64	4	21	25	122	...	...	...	16	3	10	13	36
92-93— Sault Ste. Marie	OHL	59	5	28	33	114	...	...	...	18	2	7	9	12
93-94— Sault Ste. Marie	OHL	58	7	43	50	108	...	...	...	14	6	9	15	20
94-95— Atlanta	IHL	72	5	7	12	74	...	...	...	5	0	2	2	22
95-96— Atlanta	IHL	61	3	13	16	105	...	...	...	3	0	0	0	4
— Tampa Bay	NHL	13	0	1	1	4	-1	0	0	—	—	—	—	—
96-97— Tampa Bay	NHL	64	4	13	17	44	-21	1	0	—	—	—	—	—
— Edmonton	NHL	1	0	1	1	0	-2	0	0	12	0	0	0	30
NHL totals (2 years)		**78**	**4**	**15**	**19**	**48**	**-24**	**1**	**0**	**12**	**0**	**0**	**0**	**30**

BARNABY, MATTHEW　　　　　RW　　　　　SABRES

PERSONAL: Born May 4, 1973, in Ottawa. ... 6-0/188. ... Shoots right.
TRANSACTIONS/CAREER NOTES: Selected by Buffalo Sabres in fourth round (fifth Sabres pick, 83rd overall) of NHL entry draft (June 20, 1992). ... Suffered lower back spasms (March 24, 1995); missed one game. ... Suspended one game by NHL for accumulating three game misconduct penalties (March 31, 1996). ... Injured groin (April 3, 1996); missed five games. ... Sprained knee ligament (April 2, 1997); missed final six games of regular season and four playoff games.

Season Team	League	REGULAR SEASON								PLAYOFFS				
		Gms.	G	A	Pts.	PIM	+/-	PP	SH	Gms.	G	A	Pts.	PIM
90-91— Beauport	QMJHL	52	9	5	14	262	...	...	...	—	—	—	—	—
91-92— Beauport	QMJHL	63	29	37	66	*476	...	...	...	—	—	—	—	—
92-93— Victoriaville	QMJHL	65	44	67	111	*448	...	...	...	6	2	4	6	44
— Buffalo	NHL	2	1	0	1	10	0	1	0	1	0	1	1	4
93-94— Buffalo	NHL	35	2	4	6	106	-7	1	0	3	0	0	0	17
— Rochester	AHL	42	10	32	42	153	...	...	...	—	—	—	—	—
94-95— Rochester	AHL	56	21	29	50	274	...	...	...	—	—	—	—	—
— Buffalo	NHL	23	1	1	2	116	-2	0	0	—	—	—	—	—
95-96— Buffalo	NHL	73	15	16	31	*335	-2	0	0	—	—	—	—	—
96-97— Buffalo	NHL	68	19	24	43	249	16	2	0	8	0	4	4	36
NHL totals (5 years)		**201**	**38**	**45**	**83**	**816**	**5**	**4**	**0**	**12**	**0**	**5**	**5**	**57**

BARNES, STU　　　　　C　　　　　PENGUINS

PERSONAL: Born December 25, 1970, in Edmonton. ... 5-11/174. ... Shoots right.
TRANSACTIONS/CAREER NOTES: Selected by Winnipeg Jets in first round (first Jets pick, fourth overall) of NHL entry draft (June 17, 1989). ... Traded by Jets to Florida Panthers for C Randy Gilhen (November 26, 1993). ... Strained left calf (January 1, 1994); missed one game. ... Suffered lacerations and bruises in and around left eye (February 15, 1995); missed seven games. ... Sprained left knee (March 10, 1996); missed 10 games. ... Traded by Panthers with D Jason Woolley to Pittsburgh Penguins for C Chris Wells (November 19, 1996). ... Injured hip (April 11, 1997); missed one game.
HONORS: Won Jim Piggott Memorial Trophy (1987-88). ... Named to WHL All-Star second team (1987-88). ... Won Four Broncos Memorial Trophy (1988-89). ... Named to WHL All-Star first team (1988-89).
STATISTICAL PLATEAUS: Three-goal games: 1991-92 (1).
MISCELLANEOUS: Failed to score on a penalty shot (vs. Peter Sidorkiewicz, February 23, 1993).

Season Team	League	REGULAR SEASON								PLAYOFFS				
		Gms.	G	A	Pts.	PIM	+/-	PP	SH	Gms.	G	A	Pts.	PIM
86-87— St. Albert..................	AJHL	57	43	32	75	80	...	...	...	—	—	—	—	—
87-88— New Westminster	WHL	71	37	64	101	88	...	...	...	5	2	3	5	6
88-89— Tri-City	WHL	70	59	82	141	117	...	...	...	7	6	5	11	10
89-90— Tri-City	WHL	63	52	92	144	165	...	...	...	7	1	5	6	26
90-91— Canadian nat'l team ...	Int'l	53	22	27	49	68	...	...	...	—	—	—	—	—
91-92— Winnipeg	NHL	46	8	9	17	26	-2	4	0	—	—	—	—	—
— Moncton	AHL	30	13	19	32	10	...	...	...	11	3	9	12	6
92-93— Moncton	AHL	42	23	31	54	58	...	...	...	—	—	—	—	—
— Winnipeg	NHL	38	12	10	22	10	-3	3	0	6	1	3	4	2
93-94— Winnipeg	NHL	18	5	4	9	8	-1	2	0	—	—	—	—	—
— Florida........................	NHL	59	18	20	38	30	5	6	1	—	—	—	—	—
94-95— Florida........................	NHL	41	10	19	29	8	7	1	0	—	—	—	—	—
95-96— Florida........................	NHL	72	19	25	44	46	-12	8	0	22	6	10	16	4
96-97— Florida........................	NHL	19	2	8	10	10	-3	1	0	—	—	—	—	—
— Pittsburgh..................	NHL	62	17	22	39	16	-20	4	0	5	0	1	1	0
NHL totals (6 years)		355	91	117	208	154	-29	29	1	33	7	14	21	6

B

BARON, MURRAY   D   COYOTES

PERSONAL: Born June 1, 1967, in Prince George, B.C. ... 6-3/215. ... Shoots left.
HIGH SCHOOL: Kamloops (B.C.).
COLLEGE: North Dakota.
TRANSACTIONS/CAREER NOTES: Selected by Philadelphia Flyers as underage player in eighth round (seventh Flyers pick, 167th overall) of NHL entry draft (June 21, 1986). ... Separated left shoulder (October 5, 1989). ... Underwent surgery to have bone spur removed from foot (April 1990). ... Traded by Flyers with C Ron Sutter to St. Louis Blues for C Rod Brind'Amour and C Dan Quinn (September 22, 1991). ... Injured shoulder (December 3, 1991); missed seven games. ... Broke foot (March 22, 1993); missed remainder of regular season. ... Injured groin (December 1, 1993); missed three games. ... Injured groin (December 11, 1993); missed three games. ... Injured knee (March 7, 1994); missed one game. ... Injured knee (April 18, 1995); missed last nine games of regular season. ... Traded by Blues with LW Shayne Corson and fifth-round pick (D Gennady Razin) in 1997 draft to Montreal Canadiens for C Pierre Turgeon, C Craig Conroy and D Rory Fitzpatrick (October 29, 1996). ... Bruised eye (November 21, 1996); missed one game. ... Traded by Canadiens with RW Chris Murray to Phoenix Coyotes for D Dave Manson (March 18, 1997). ... Fractured foot (April 6, 1997); missed remainder of regular season.

Season Team	League	REGULAR SEASON								PLAYOFFS				
		Gms.	G	A	Pts.	PIM	+/-	PP	SH	Gms.	G	A	Pts.	PIM
84-85— Vernon	BCJHL	37	5	9	14	93	...	...	...	—	—	—	—	—
85-86— Vernon	BCJHL	49	15	32	47	176	...	...	...	7	1	2	3	13
86-87— North Dakota	WCHA	41	4	10	14	62	...	...	...	—	—	—	—	—
87-88— North Dakota	WCHA	41	1	10	11	95	...	...	...	—	—	—	—	—
88-89— North Dakota	WCHA	40	2	6	8	92	...	...	...	—	—	—	—	—
— Hershey	AHL	9	0	3	3	8	...	...	...	—	—	—	—	—
89-90— Hershey	AHL	50	0	10	10	101	...	...	...	—	—	—	—	—
— Philadelphia	NHL	16	2	2	4	12	-1	0	0	—	—	—	—	—
90-91— Hershey	AHL	6	2	3	5	0	...	...	...	—	—	—	—	—
— Philadelphia	NHL	67	8	8	16	74	-3	3	0	—	—	—	—	—
91-92— St. Louis	NHL	67	3	8	11	94	-3	0	0	2	0	0	0	2
92-93— St. Louis	NHL	53	2	2	4	59	-5	0	0	11	0	0	0	12
93-94— St. Louis	NHL	77	5	9	14	123	-14	0	0	4	0	0	0	10
94-95— St. Louis	NHL	39	0	5	5	93	9	0	0	7	1	1	2	2
95-96— St. Louis	NHL	82	2	9	11	190	3	0	0	13	1	0	1	20
96-97— St. Louis	NHL	11	0	2	2	11	-4	0	0	—	—	—	—	—
— Montreal	NHL	60	1	5	6	107	-16	0	0	—	—	—	—	—
— Phoenix.......................	NHL	8	0	0	0	4	0	0	0	1	0	0	0	0
NHL totals (8 years)		480	23	50	73	767	-34	3	0	38	2	1	3	46

BARRASSO, TOM   G   PENGUINS

PERSONAL: Born March 31, 1965, in Boston. ... 6-3/211. ... Catches right. ... Name pronounced buh-RAH-soh.
HIGH SCHOOL: Acton (Mass.)-Boxborough.
TRANSACTIONS/CAREER NOTES: Selected by Buffalo Sabres in first round (first Sabres pick, fifth overall) of NHL entry draft (June 8, 1983). ... Suffered chip fracture of ankle (November 1987). ... Pulled groin (April 9, 1988). ... Traded by Sabres with third-round pick in 1990 draft (RW Joe Dziedzic) to Pittsburgh Penguins for D Doug Bodger and LW Darrin Shannon (November 12, 1988). ... Pulled groin muscle (January 17, 1989). ... Injured shoulder (March 1989). ... Underwent surgery to right wrist (October 30, 1989); missed 21 games. ... Pulled groin (February 1990). ... Granted leave of absence to be with daughter as she underwent cancer treatment in Los Angeles (February 9, 1990). ... Rejoined the Penguins (March 19, 1990). ... Bruised right hand (October 29, 1991); missed two games. ... Bruised right ankle (December 26, 1991); missed three games. ... Suffered back spasms (March 1992); missed three games. ... Suffered from chicken pox (January 14, 1993); missed nine games. ... Strained groin (October 7, 1993); missed four games. ... Injured hip (November 18, 1993); missed 12 games. ... Underwent surgery on right wrist (January 20, 1995); missed first 43 games of season. ... Suffered sore wrist (May 3, 1995); missed one game. ... Pulled groin (December 7, 1995); missed eight games. ... Pulled groin and injured shoulder (February 6, 1996); missed four games. ... Suffered recurring shoulder problem (October 25, 1996); missed remainder of season.
HONORS: Won Vezina Trophy (1983-84). ... Won Calder Memorial Trophy (1983-84). ... Named to THE SPORTING NEWS All-Star second team (1983-84, 1984-85 and 1987-88). ... Named to NHL All-Star first team (1983-84). ... Named to NHL All-Rookie team (1983-84). ... Shared William M. Jennings Trophy with Bob Sauve (1984-85). ... Named to NHL All-Star second team (1984-85 and 1992-93). ... Played in NHL All-Star Game (1985). ... Named to THE SPORTING NEWS All-Star first team (1992-93).
RECORDS: Shares NHL single-season playoff records for most wins by a goaltender—16 (1992); and most consecutive wins by a goaltender—11 (1992).
MISCELLANEOUS: Member of Stanley Cup championship team (1991 and 1992). ... Holds Pittsburgh Penguins all-time records for most games played by goalie (336) and most wins (171). ... Stopped a penalty shot attempt (vs. Bryan Trottier, January 5, 1985; vs. Doug Smail, October 10, 1989). ... Allowed a penalty shot goal (vs. Marcel Dionne, March 9, 1984; vs. Scott Pearson, March 16, 1991; vs. Robert Reichel, October 24, 1996). ... Member of U.S. National Junior Team (1983).

Season Team	League	REGULAR SEASON								PLAYOFFS						
		Gms.	Min	W	L	T	GA	SO	Avg.	Gms.	Min.	W	L	GA	SO	Avg.
81-82—Acton-Boxborough	Mass. HS	23	1035	...	...	...	32	7	1.86	—	—	—	—	—	—	—
82-83—Acton-Boxborough	Mass. HS	23	1035	...	...	...	17	10	0.99	—	—	—	—	—	—	—
83-84—Buffalo	NHL	42	2475	26	12	3	117	2	2.84	3	139	0	2	8	0	3.45
84-85—Rochester	AHL	5	267	3	1	1	6	1	1.35	—	—	—	—	—	—	—
—Buffalo	NHL	54	3248	25	18	10	144	*5	*2.66	5	300	2	3	22	0	4.40
85-86—Buffalo	NHL	60	*3561	29	24	5	214	2	3.61	—	—	—	—	—	—	—
86-87—Buffalo	NHL	46	2501	17	23	2	152	2	3.65	—	—	—	—	—	—	—
87-88—Buffalo	NHL	54	3133	25	18	8	173	2	3.31	4	224	1	3	16	0	4.29
88-89—Buffalo	NHL	10	545	2	7	0	45	0	4.95	—	—	—	—	—	—	—
—Pittsburgh	NHL	44	2406	18	15	7	162	0	4.04	11	631	7	4	40	0	3.80
89-90—Pittsburgh	NHL	24	1294	7	12	3	101	0	4.68	—	—	—	—	—	—	—
90-91—Pittsburgh	NHL	48	2754	27	16	3	165	1	3.59	20	1175	12	7	51	†1	*2.60
91-92—Pittsburgh	NHL	57	3329	25	22	9	196	1	3.53	*21	*1233	*16	5	*58	1	2.82
92-93—Pittsburgh	NHL	63	3702	*43	14	5	186	4	3.01	12	722	7	5	35	2	2.91
93-94—Pittsburgh	NHL	44	2482	22	15	5	139	2	3.36	6	356	2	4	17	0	2.87
94-95—Pittsburgh	NHL	2	125	0	1	1	8	0	3.84	2	80	0	1	8	0	6.00
95-96—Pittsburgh	NHL	49	2799	29	16	2	160	2	3.43	10	558	4	5	26	1	2.80
96-97—Pittsburgh	NHL	5	270	0	5	0	26	0	5.78	—	—	—	—	—	—	—
NHL totals (14 years)		602	34624	295	218	63	1988	23	3.45	94	5418	51	39	281	5	3.11

BARRIE, LEN　　　　C　　　　PENGUINS

PERSONAL: Born June 4, 1969, in Kimberley, B.C. ... 6-0/200. ... Shoots right.

TRANSACTIONS/CAREER NOTES: Selected by Edmonton Oilers in sixth round (seventh Oilers pick, 124th overall) of NHL entry draft (June 11, 1988). ... Broke finger (March 1989). ... Traded by Victoria Cougars to Kamloops Blazers for RW Mark Cipriano (August 1989). ... Signed as free agent by Philadelphia Flyers (February 8, 1990). ... Signed as free agent by Florida Panthers (July 20, 1993). ... Signed as free agent by Pittsburgh Penguins (August 25, 1994).

HONORS: Won Can.HL Plus/Minus Award (1989-90). ... Won Bob Clarke Trophy (1989-90). ... Named to WHL (West) All-Star first team (1989-90). ... Named to IHL All-Star second team (1993-94).

Season Team	League	REGULAR SEASON								PLAYOFFS				
		Gms.	G	A	Pts.	PIM	+/-	PP	SH	Gms.	G	A	Pts.	PIM
85-86—Calgary Spurs	AJHL	23	7	14	21	86	...	...	...	—	—	—	—	—
—Calgary	WHL	32	3	0	3	18	...	...	...	—	—	—	—	—
86-87—Calgary	WHL	34	13	13	26	81	...	...	...	—	—	—	—	—
—Victoria	WHL	34	7	6	13	92	...	...	...	5	0	1	1	15
87-88—Victoria	WHL	70	37	49	86	192	...	...	...	8	2	0	2	29
88-89—Victoria	WHL	67	39	48	87	157	...	...	...	7	5	2	7	23
89-90—Philadelphia	NHL	1	0	0	0	0	-2	0	0	—	—	—	—	—
—Kamloops	WHL	70	*85	*100	*185	108	...	...	...	17	†14	23	†37	24
90-91—Hershey	AHL	63	26	32	58	60	...	...	...	7	4	0	4	12
91-92—Hershey	AHL	75	42	43	85	78	...	...	...	3	0	2	2	32
92-93—Hershey	AHL	61	31	45	76	162	...	...	...	—	—	—	—	—
—Philadelphia	NHL	8	2	2	4	9	2	0	0	—	—	—	—	—
93-94—Cincinnati	IHL	77	45	71	116	246	...	...	...	11	8	13	21	60
—Florida	NHL	2	0	0	0	0	-2	0	0	—	—	—	—	—
94-95—Cleveland	IHL	28	13	30	43	137	...	...	...	—	—	—	—	—
—Pittsburgh	NHL	48	3	11	14	66	-4	0	0	4	1	0	1	8
95-96—Cleveland	IHL	55	29	43	72	178	...	...	...	3	2	3	5	6
—Pittsburgh	NHL	5	0	0	0	18	-1	0	0	—	—	—	—	—
96-97—San Antonio	IHL	57	26	40	66	196	...	...	...	9	5	5	10	20
NHL totals (5 years)		64	5	13	18	93	-7	0	0	4	1	0	1	8

BASSEN, BOB　　　　C　　　　STARS

PERSONAL: Born May 6, 1965, in Calgary. ... 5-10/180. ... Shoots left. ... Name pronounced BA-suhn. ... Son of Hank Bassen, goaltender with three NHL teams (1954-55 through 1967-68).

HIGH SCHOOL: Sir Winston Churchill (Calgary).

TRANSACTIONS/CAREER NOTES: Signed as free agent by New York Islanders (October 19, 1984). ... Injured knee (October 12, 1985). ... Traded by Islanders with D Steve Konroyd to Chicago Blackhawks for D Gary Nylund and D Marc Bergevin (November 25, 1988). ... Selected by St. Louis Blues in 1990 waiver draft for $25,000 (October 2, 1990). ... Broke right foot (December 4, 1992); missed 22 games. ... Broke finger (January 28, 1993); missed nine games. ... Traded by Blues with C Ron Sutter and D Garth Butcher to Quebec Nordiques for D Steve Duchesne and RW Denis Chasse (January 23, 1994). ... Lacerated left eye (March 30, 1994); missed one game. ... Injured back (February 18, 1995); missed one game. ... Signed as free agent by Dallas Stars (July 18, 1995). ... Injured knee (September 30, 1995); missed first 69 games of season. ... Underwent surgery to repair herniated disc in neck (September 28, 1996); missed 36 games.

HONORS: Named to WHL (East) All-Star first team (1984-85). ... Named to IHL All-Star first team (1989-90).

Season Team	League	REGULAR SEASON								PLAYOFFS				
		Gms.	G	A	Pts.	PIM	+/-	PP	SH	Gms.	G	A	Pts.	PIM
82-83—Medicine Hat	WHL	4	3	2	5	0	...	...	...	3	0	0	0	4
83-84—Medicine Hat	WHL	72	29	29	58	93	...	...	...	14	5	11	16	12
84-85—Medicine Hat	WHL	65	32	50	82	143	...	...	...	10	2	8	10	39
85-86—New York Islanders	NHL	11	2	1	3	6	...	...	...	3	0	1	1	0
—Springfield	AHL	54	13	21	34	111	...	...	...	—	—	—	—	—
86-87—New York Islanders	NHL	77	7	10	17	89	-17	0	0	14	1	2	3	21
87-88—New York Islanders	NHL	77	6	16	22	99	8	1	0	6	0	1	1	23
88-89—New York Islanders	NHL	19	1	4	5	21	0	0	0	—	—	—	—	—
—Chicago	NHL	49	4	12	16	62	5	0	0	10	1	1	2	34

B

Season Team	League	REGULAR SEASON Gms.	G	A	Pts.	PIM	+/-	PP	SH	PLAYOFFS Gms.	G	A	Pts.	PIM
89-90— Indianapolis	IHL	73	22	32	54	179	...	...	...	12	3	8	11	33
— Chicago	NHL	6	1	1	2	8	1	0	0	—	—	—	—	—
90-91— St. Louis	NHL	79	16	18	34	183	17	0	2	13	1	3	4	24
91-92— St. Louis	NHL	79	7	25	32	167	12	0	0	6	0	2	2	4
92-93— St. Louis	NHL	53	9	10	19	63	0	0	1	11	0	0	0	10
93-94— St. Louis	NHL	46	2	7	9	44	-14	0	1	—	—	—	—	—
— Quebec	NHL	37	11	8	19	55	-3	1	0	—	—	—	—	—
94-95— Quebec	NHL	47	12	15	27	33	14	0	1	5	2	4	6	0
95-96— Michigan	IHL	1	0	0	0	4	...	...	...	—	—	—	—	—
— Dallas	NHL	13	0	1	1	15	-6	0	0	—	—	—	—	—
96-97— Dallas	NHL	46	5	7	12	41	5	0	0	7	3	1	4	4
NHL totals (12 years)		639	83	135	218	886	22	2	5	75	8	15	23	120

BATES, SHAWN   C   BRUINS

B

PERSONAL: Born April 3, 1975, in Melrose, Mass. ... 6-0/183. ... Shoots right.
HIGH SCHOOL: Medford (Mass.).
COLLEGE: Boston University.
TRANSACTIONS/CAREER NOTES: Selected by Boston Bruins in fourth round (fourth Bruins pick, 103rd overall) of NHL entry draft (June 26, 1993).
HONORS: Named to Hockey East All-Rookie team (1993-94).

Season Team	League	REGULAR SEASON Gms.	G	A	Pts.	PIM	+/-	PP	SH	PLAYOFFS Gms.	G	A	Pts.	PIM
90-91— Medford	Mass. H.S.	22	18	43	61	6	...	...	...	—	—	—	—	—
91-92— Medford	Mass. H.S.	22	38	41	79	10	...	...	...	—	—	—	—	—
92-93— Medford	Mass. H.S.	25	49	46	95	20	...	...	...	—	—	—	—	—
93-94— Boston University	Hockey East	41	10	19	29	24	...	...	...	—	—	—	—	—
94-95— Boston University	Hockey East	38	18	12	30	48	...	...	...	—	—	—	—	—
95-96— Boston University	Hockey East	40	28	22	50	54	...	...	...	—	—	—	—	—
96-97— Boston University	Hockey East	41	17	18	35	64	...	...	...	—	—	—	—	—

BATYRSHIN, RUSLAN   D   KINGS

PERSONAL: Born February 19, 1975, in Moscow, U.S.S.R. ... 6-1/180. ... Shoots left. ... Name pronounced ROOZ-lahn BAHT-uhr-shihn.
TRANSACTIONS/CAREER NOTES: Selected by Winnipeg Jets in fourth round (fourth Jets pick, 79th overall) of NHL entry draft (June 26, 1993). ... Traded by Jets with second-round pick (RW Marian Cisar) in 1996 draft to Los Angeles Kings for D Brent Thompson (August 8, 1994).

Season Team	League	REGULAR SEASON Gms.	G	A	Pts.	PIM	+/-	PP	SH	PLAYOFFS Gms.	G	A	Pts.	PIM
91-92— Dynamo Moscow	CIS Div. III	40	0	2	2	52				—	—	—	—	—
92-93— Dynamo Moscow	CIS Div. II					Statistics unavailable.								
93-94— Dynamo Moscow	CIS	19	0	0	0	10	...	...	...	3	0	0	0	22
94-95— Dynamo Moscow	CIS	36	2	2	4	65	...	...	...	12	1	1	2	6
95-96— Phoenix	IHL	71	1	9	10	144	...	...	...	2	0	0	0	2
— Los Angeles	NHL	2	0	0	0	6	0	0	0	—	—	—	—	—
96-97— Phoenix	IHL	59	3	4	7	123	...	...	...	—	—	—	—	—
NHL totals (1 year)		2	0	0	0	6	0	0	0					

BAUMGARTNER, KEN   D/LW   BRUINS

PERSONAL: Born March 11, 1966, in Flin Flon, Man. ... 6-1/205. ... Shoots left. ... Full name: Ken James Baumgartner.
TRANSACTIONS/CAREER NOTES: Selected by Buffalo Sabres as underage junior in 12th round (12th Sabres pick, 245th overall) of NHL entry draft (June 15, 1985). ... Traded by Sabres with D Larry Playfair and RW Sean McKenna to Los Angeles Kings for D Brian Engblom and C Doug Smith (January 29, 1986). ... Traded by Kings with C Hubie McDonough to New York Islanders for RW Mikko Makela (November 29, 1989). ... Suspended one game by NHL for fighting (April 5, 1990). ... Fractured right orbital bone (December 19, 1991); missed 14 games. ... Traded by Islanders with C Dave McLlwain to Toronto Maple Leafs for C Claude Loiselle and RW Daniel Marois (March 10, 1992). ... Broke bone in wrist (February 28, 1994); missed remainder of season. ... Underwent shoulder surgery (January 31, 1995); missed remainder of season. ... Traded by Maple Leafs to Mighty Ducks of Anaheim for fourth-round pick (traded to Montreal) in 1996 draft (March 20, 1996). ... Bruised shoulder (October 12, 1996); missed one game. ... Injured ankle (December 1, 1996); missed three games. ... Fractured right hand (February 9, 1997); missed 11 games. ... Signed as free agent by Boston Bruins (July 1, 1997).

Season Team	League	REGULAR SEASON Gms.	G	A	Pts.	PIM	+/-	PP	SH	PLAYOFFS Gms.	G	A	Pts.	PIM
83-84— Prince Albert	WHL	57	1	6	7	203	...	...	...	—	—	—	—	—
84-85— Prince Albert	WHL	60	3	9	12	252	...	...	...	13	1	3	4	*89
85-86— Prince Albert	WHL	70	4	23	27	277	...	...	...	20	3	9	12	112
86-87— Chur	Switzerland					Statistics unavailable.								
— New Haven	AHL	13	0	3	3	99	...	...	...	6	0	0	0	60
87-88— Los Angeles	NHL	30	2	3	5	189	5	0	0	5	0	1	1	28
— New Haven	AHL	48	1	5	6	181	...	...	...	—	—	—	—	—
88-89— Los Angeles	NHL	49	1	3	4	288	-9	0	0	5	0	0	0	8
— New Haven	AHL	10	1	3	4	26	...	...	...	—	—	—	—	—
89-90— Los Angeles	NHL	12	1	0	1	28	-10	0	0	—	—	—	—	—
— New York Islanders	NHL	53	0	5	5	194	6	0	0	4	0	0	0	27
90-91— New York Islanders	NHL	78	1	6	7	282	-14	0	0	—	—	—	—	—
91-92— New York Islanders	NHL	44	0	1	1	202	-10	0	0	—	—	—	—	—
— Toronto	NHL	11	0	0	0	23	1	0	0	—	—	—	—	—
92-93— Toronto	NHL	63	1	0	1	155	-11	0	0	7	1	0	1	0

Season Team	League	Gms.	G	A	Pts.	PIM	+/-	PP	SH	Gms.	G	A	Pts.	PIM
REGULAR SEASON										PLAYOFFS				
93-94— Toronto	NHL	64	4	4	8	185	-6	0	0	10	0	0	0	18
94-95— Toronto	NHL	2	0	0	0	5	0	0	0	—	—	—	—	—
95-96— Toronto	NHL	60	2	3	5	152	-5	0	0	—	—	—	—	—
— Anaheim	NHL	12	0	1	1	41	0	0	0	—	—	—	—	—
96-97— Anaheim	NHL	67	0	11	11	182	0	0	0	11	0	1	1	11
NHL totals (10 years)		545	12	37	49	1926	-53	0	0	42	1	2	3	92

BAUMGARTNER, NOLAN   D   CAPITALS

PERSONAL: Born March 23, 1976, in Calgary. ... 6-1/200. ... Shoots right.
HIGH SCHOOL: Norkam Secondary (Kamloops, B.C.).
TRANSACTIONS/CAREER NOTES: Selected by Washington Capitals in first round (first Capitals pick, 10th overall) of NHL entry draft (June 28, 1994). ... Injured shoulder (October 28, 1996); missed remainder of AHL season.
HONORS: Named to Memorial Cup All-Star team (1993-94 and 1994-95). ... Won Can.HL Defenseman of the Year Award (1994-95). ... Won Bill Hunter Trophy (1994-95 and 1995-96). ... Named to Can.HL All-Star first team (1994-95). ... Named to WHL (West) All-Star first team (1994-95 and 1995-96).

Season Team	League	Gms.	G	A	Pts.	PIM	+/-	PP	SH	Gms.	G	A	Pts.	PIM
REGULAR SEASON										PLAYOFFS				
92-93— Kamloops	WHL	43	0	5	5	30	...	...	...	11	1	1	2	0
93-94— Kamloops	WHL	69	13	42	55	109	...	...	...	19	3	14	17	33
94-95— Kamloops	WHL	62	8	36	44	71	...	...	...	21	4	13	17	16
95-96— Washington	NHL	1	0	0	0	0	-1	0	0	1	0	0	0	10
— Kamloops	WHL	28	13	15	28	45	...	...	...	16	1	9	10	26
96-97— Portland	AHL	8	2	2	4	4	...	...	...	—	—	—	—	—
NHL totals (1 year)		1	0	0	0	0	-1	0	0	1	0	0	0	10

BEAUFAIT, MARK   C

PERSONAL: Born May 13, 1970, in Livonia, Mich. ... 5-9/165. ... Shoots right. ... Name pronounced boh-FAY.
COLLEGE: Northern Michigan.
TRANSACTIONS/CAREER NOTES: Selected by San Jose Sharks in NHL supplemental draft (June 21, 1991). ... Signed as free agent by San Diego Gulls (August 30, 1994). ... Selected by Orlando Solar Bears in IHL expansion draft (July 13, 1995).
HONORS: Won Ken McKenzie Trophy (1992-93). ... Named to IHL All-Star second team (1996-97).

Season Team	League	Gms.	G	A	Pts.	PIM	+/-	PP	SH	Gms.	G	A	Pts.	PIM
REGULAR SEASON										PLAYOFFS				
88-89— Northern Michigan	WCHA	11	2	1	3	2	...	...	...	—	—	—	—	—
89-90— Northern Michigan	WCHA	34	10	14	24	12	...			—	—	—	—	—
90-91— Northern Michigan	WCHA	47	19	30	49	18	...			—	—	—	—	—
91-92— Northern Michigan	WCHA	41	31	50	81	47	...			—	—	—	—	—
92-93— Kansas City	IHL	66	19	40	59	22	...			9	1	1	2	8
— San Jose	NHL	5	1	0	1	0	-1	0	0	—	—	—	—	—
93-94— U.S. national team	Int'l	51	22	29	51	36	...			—	—	—	—	—
— U.S. Olympic team	Int'l	8	1	4	5	2	...			—	—	—	—	—
— Kansas City	IHL	21	12	9	21	18	...			—	—	—	—	—
94-95— San Diego	IHL	68	24	39	63	22	...			5	2	2	4	2
95-96— Orlando	IHL	77	30	79	109	87	...			22	9	*19	*28	22
96-97— Orlando	IHL	80	26	65	91	63	...			10	5	8	13	18
NHL totals (1 year)		5	1	0	1	0	-1	0	0					

BEAUPRE, DON   G   MAPLE LEAFS

PERSONAL: Born September 19, 1961, in Kitchener, Ont. ... 5-10/172. ... Catches left. ... Full name: Donald William Beaupre. ... Name pronounced boh-PRAY.
TRANSACTIONS/CAREER NOTES: Selected by Minnesota North Stars as underage junior in second round (second North Stars pick, 37th overall) of NHL entry draft (June 11, 1980). ... Bruised ribs (October 1981). ... Sprained knee (February 1985). ... Pulled groin muscle (December 1987). ... Traded by North Stars to Washington Capitals for rights to D Claudio Scremin (November 1, 1988). ... Injured ligaments in right thumb (January 31, 1990); missed nine games. ... Pulled left groin (October 30, 1990); missed 12 games. ... Pulled muscle (November 5, 1992); missed three games. ... Pulled groin (January 2, 1993); missed two games. ... Traded by Capitals to Ottawa Senators for fifth-round pick (LW Benoit Gratton) in 1995 draft (January 18, 1995). ... Suffered from the flu (March 10, 1995); missed one game. ... Traded by Senators to Toronto Maple Leafs for G Damian Rhodes (January 23, 1996).
HONORS: Named to OMJHL All-Star first team (1979-80). ... Played in NHL All-Star Game (1981 and 1992).
MISCELLANEOUS: Holds Washington Capitals all-time record for games played by a goaltender (269). ... Stopped a penalty shot attempt (vs. Miroslav Frycer, October 28, 1988; vs. Jaromir Jagr, January 26, 1993; vs. Mark Recchi, February 2, 1995; vs. Marc Bureau, November 18, 1995). ... Allowed a penalty shot goal (vs. Wayne Gretzky, April 28, 1984 (playoffs); vs. Anders Carlsson, April 2, 1989; vs. Murray Craven, March 24, 1992; vs. Eric Lindros, December 26, 1992).

Season Team	League	Gms.	Min	W	L	T	GA	SO	Avg.	Gms.	Min.	W	L	GA	SO	Avg.
REGULAR SEASON										PLAYOFFS						
78-79— Sudbury	OMJHL	54	3248	...	...	...	*259	2	4.78	10	600	...	...	44	...	4.40
79-80— Sudbury	OMJHL	59	3447	28	29	2	248	0	4.32	9	552	5	4	38	0	4.13
80-81— Minnesota	NHL	44	2585	18	14	11	138	0	3.20	6	360	4	2	26	0	4.33
81-82— Nashville	CHL	5	299	2	3	0	25	0	5.02	—	—	—	—	—	—	—
— Minnesota	NHL	29	1634	11	8	9	101	0	3.71	2	60	0	1	4	0	4.00
82-83— Birmingham	CHL	10	599	8	2	0	31	0	3.11	—	—	—	—	—	—	—
— Minnesota	NHL	36	2011	19	10	5	120	0	3.58	4	245	2	2	20	0	4.90
83-84— Salt Lake City	CHL	7	419	2	5	0	30	0	4.30	—	—	—	—	—	—	—
— Minnesota	NHL	33	1791	16	13	2	123	0	4.12	13	782	6	7	40	1	3.07

Season Team	League	REGULAR SEASON Gms.	Min	W	L	T	GA	SO	Avg.	PLAYOFFS Gms.	Min.	W	L	GA	SO	Avg.
84-85—Minnesota	NHL	31	1770	10	17	3	109	1	3.69	4	184	1	1	12	0	3.91
85-86—Minnesota	NHL	52	3073	25	20	6	182	1	3.55	5	300	2	3	17	0	3.40
86-87—Minnesota	NHL	47	2622	17	20	6	174	1	3.98	—	—	—	—	—	—	—
87-88—Minnesota	NHL	43	2288	10	22	3	161	0	4.22	—	—	—	—	—	—	—
88-89—Minnesota	NHL	1	59	0	1	0	3	0	3.05	—	—	—	—	—	—	—
—Kalamazoo	IHL	3	179	1	2	‡0	9	0	3.02	—	—	—	—	—	—	—
—Baltimore	AHL	30	1715	14	12	2	102	0	3.57	—	—	—	—	—	—	—
—Washington	NHL	11	578	5	4	0	28	1	2.91	—	—	—	—	—	—	—
89-90—Washington	NHL	48	2793	23	18	5	150	2	3.22	8	401	4	3	18	0	2.69
90-91—Baltimore	AHL	2	120	2	0	0	3	0	1.50	—	—	—	—	—	—	—
—Washington	NHL	45	2572	20	18	3	113	*5	2.64	11	624	5	5	29	†1	2.79
91-92—Baltimore	AHL	3	184	1	1	1	10	0	3.26	—	—	—	—	—	—	—
—Washington	NHL	54	3108	29	17	6	166	1	3.20	7	419	3	4	22	0	3.15
92-93—Washington	NHL	58	3282	27	23	5	181	1	3.31	2	119	1	1	9	0	4.54
93-94—Washington	NHL	53	2853	24	16	8	135	2	2.84	8	429	5	2	21	1	2.94
94-95—Ottawa	NHL	38	2161	8	25	3	121	1	3.36	—	—	—	—	—	—	—
95-96—Ottawa	NHL	33	1770	6	23	0	110	1	3.73	—	—	—	—	—	—	—
—Toronto	NHL	8	336	0	5	0	26	0	4.64	2	20	0	0	2	0	6.00
96-97—Toronto	NHL	3	110	0	3	0	10	0	5.45	—	—	—	—	—	—	—
—St. John's	AHL	47	2623	24	16	4	128	3	2.93	—	—	—	—	—	—	—
—Utah	IHL	4	238	2	2	‡0	13	0	3.28	7	438	3	4	17	1	2.33
NHL totals (18 years)		667	37396	268	277	75	2151	17	3.45	72	3943	33	31	220	3	3.35

BEDDOES, CLAYTON — C — SENATORS

PERSONAL: Born November 10, 1970, in Bentley, Alta. ... 5-11/192. ... Shoots left. ... Name pronounced BEH-dohs.
HIGH SCHOOL: Bentley (Alta.).
COLLEGE: Lake Superior State (Mich.).
TRANSACTIONS/CAREER NOTES: Signed as free agent by Boston Bruins (May 24, 1994). ... Suffered bruised ribs (December 14, 1996); missed 10 games. ... Signed as free agent by Ottawa Senators (July 17, 1997).
HONORS: Named to NCAA All-America West second team (1993-94). ... Named to CCHA All-Star second team (1993-94).

Season Team	League	REGULAR SEASON Gms.	G	A	Pts.	PIM	+/-	PP	SH	PLAYOFFS Gms.	G	A	Pts.	PIM
90-91—Lake Superior State	CCHA	45	14	28	42	26	...	...	...	—	—	—	—	—
91-92—Lake Superior State	CCHA	42	16	28	44	26	...	...	...	—	—	—	—	—
92-93—Lake Superior State	CCHA	45	18	40	58	32	...	...	...	—	—	—	—	—
93-94—Lake Superior State	CCHA	44	23	31	54	56	...	...	...	—	—	—	—	—
94-95—Providence	AHL	65	16	20	36	39	...	...	...	13	3	1	4	18
95-96—Boston	NHL	39	1	6	7	44	-5	0	0	—	—	—	—	—
—Providence	AHL	32	10	15	25	24	...	...	...	4	2	3	5	0
96-97—Boston	NHL	21	1	2	3	13	-1	0	0	—	—	—	—	—
—Providence	AHL	36	11	23	34	60	...	...	...	7	2	0	2	4
NHL totals (2 years)		60	2	8	10	57	-6	0	0					

BEERS, BOB — D — BRUINS

PERSONAL: Born May 20, 1967, in Pittsburgh. ... 6-2/200. ... Shoots right.
COLLEGE: Northern Arizona, then Maine.
TRANSACTIONS/CAREER NOTES: Selected by Boston Bruins in 11th round (10th Bruins pick, 220th overall) of NHL entry draft (June 15, 1985). ... Broke right leg (May 9, 1990). ... Underwent surgery to remove pin from right hip (December 10, 1990); missed four games. ... Suffered tendinitis in right hip (January 6, 1991). ... Traded by Bruins to Tampa Bay Lightning for D Stephane Richer (October 28, 1992). ... Traded by Lightning to Edmonton Oilers for D Chris Joseph (November 12, 1993). ... Signed as free agent by New York Islanders (August 29, 1994). ... Fractured facial bones (January 16, 1995); missed 18 games. ... Injured eye (March 5, 1995); missed one game. ... Signed as free agent by Bruins (August 5, 1996). ... Suffered from the flu (March 17, 1997); missed one game.
HONORS: Named Hockey East Tournament Most Valuable Player (1988-89). ... Named to NCAA All-America East second team (1988-89). ... Named to Hockey East All-Star second team (1988-89).

Season Team	League	REGULAR SEASON Gms.	G	A	Pts.	PIM	+/-	PP	SH	PLAYOFFS Gms.	G	A	Pts.	PIM
85-86—Northern Arizona	Indep.	28	11	39	50	96	...	...	...	—	—	—	—	—
86-87—University of Maine	Hockey East	38	0	13	13	46	...	...	...	—	—	—	—	—
87-88—University of Maine	Hockey East	41	3	11	14	72	...	...	...	—	—	—	—	—
88-89—University of Maine	Hockey East	44	10	27	37	53	...	...	...	—	—	—	—	—
89-90—Maine	AHL	74	7	36	43	63	...	...	...	—	—	—	—	—
—Boston	NHL	3	0	1	1	6	2	0	0	14	1	1	2	18
90-91—Maine	AHL	36	2	16	18	21	...	...	...	—	—	—	—	—
—Boston	NHL	16	0	1	1	10	-8	0	0	6	0	0	0	4
91-92—Boston	NHL	31	0	5	5	29	-13	0	0	1	0	0	0	0
—Maine	AHL	33	6	23	29	24	...	...	...	—	—	—	—	—
92-93—Providence	AHL	6	1	2	3	10	...	...	...	—	—	—	—	—
—Tampa Bay	NHL	64	12	24	36	70	-25	7	0	—	—	—	—	—
—Atlanta	IHL	1	0	0	0	0	...	...	...	—	—	—	—	—
93-94—Tampa Bay	NHL	16	1	5	6	12	-11	1	0	—	—	—	—	—
—Edmonton	NHL	66	10	27	37	74	-11	5	0	—	—	—	—	—
94-95—New York Islanders	NHL	22	2	7	9	6	-8	1	0	—	—	—	—	—
95-96—Utah	IHL	65	6	36	42	54	...	...	...	22	1	12	13	16
—New York Islanders	NHL	13	0	5	5	10	-2	0	0	—	—	—	—	—
96-97—Providence	AHL	45	10	12	22	18	...	...	...	—	—	—	—	—
—Boston	NHL	27	3	4	7	8	0	1	0	—	—	—	—	—
NHL totals (8 years)		258	28	79	107	225	-76	15	0	21	1	1	2	22

BELAK, WADE — D — AVALANCHE

PERSONAL: Born July 3, 1976, in North Battleford, Sask. ... 6-4/213. ... Shoots right. ... Name pronounced BEE-lak.
HIGH SCHOOL: North Battleford (Sask.) Comprehensive.
TRANSACTIONS/CAREER NOTES: Selected by Quebec Nordiques in first round (first Nordiques pick, 12th overall) of NHL entry draft (June 28, 1994). ... Nordiques franchise moved to Colorado and renamed Avalanche for 1995-96 season (June 21, 1995).

Season Team	League	REGULAR SEASON								PLAYOFFS				
		Gms.	G	A	Pts.	PIM	+/-	PP	SH	Gms.	G	A	Pts.	PIM
91-92— North Battleford	SJHL	57	6	20	26	186	...	...	...	—	—	—	—	—
92-93— North Battleford	SJHL	32	3	13	16	142	...	...	...	—	—	—	—	—
93-94— Saskatoon	WHL	69	4	13	17	226	...	...	...	16	2	2	4	43
94-95— Saskatoon	WHL	72	4	14	18	290	...	...	...	9	0	0	0	36
— Cornwall	AHL	—	—	—	—	—				11	1	2	3	40
95-96— Saskatoon	WHL	63	3	15	18	207	...	...	...	4	0	0	0	9
— Cornwall	AHL	5	0	0	0	18	...	...	...	2	0	0	0	2
96-97— Colorado	NHL	5	0	0	0	11	-1	0	0	—	—	—	—	—
— Hershey	AHL	65	1	7	8	320	...	...	...	16	0	1	1	61
NHL totals (1 year)		5	0	0	0	11	-1	0	0					

BELANGER, ERIC — C — KINGS

PERSONAL: Born December 16, 1977, in Sherbrooke, Que. ... 5-11/166. ... Shoots left. ... Name pronounced buh-LAH-zhay.
TRANSACTIONS/CAREER NOTES: Selected by Los Angeles Kings in fourth round (fifth Kings pick, 96th overall) of NHL entry draft (June 22, 1996).

Season Team	League	REGULAR SEASON								PLAYOFFS				
		Gms.	G	A	Pts.	PIM	+/-	PP	SH	Gms.	G	A	Pts.	PIM
94-95— Beauport	QMJHL	71	12	28	40	24	...	...	...	—	—	—	—	—
95-96— Rimouski	QMJHL	4	0	0	0	0	...	...	...	—	—	—	—	—
— Beauport	QMJHL	59	35	48	83	18	...	...	...	20	13	14	27	6
96-97— Beauport	QMJHL	31	13	37	50	30	...	...	...	—	—	—	—	—
— Rimouski	QMJHL	31	26	41	67	36	...	...	...	4	2	3	5	10

BELANGER, JESSE — C — OILERS

PERSONAL: Born June 15, 1969, in St. Georges Beauce, Que. ... 6-0/186. ... Shoots right. ... Name pronounced buh-LAH-zhay.
TRANSACTIONS/CAREER NOTES: Signed as free agent by Montreal Canadiens (October 3, 1990). ... Selected by Florida Panthers in NHL expansion draft (June 24, 1993). ... Strained right Achilles' tendon (October 12, 1993); missed one game. ... Broke bone in left hand (February 13, 1994); missed 12 games. ... Suffered from illness (March 24, 1995); missed one game. ... Traded by Panthers to Vancouver Canucks for future considerations (March 20, 1996). ... Signed as free agent by Edmonton Oilers (August 28, 1996).
MISCELLANEOUS: Member of Stanley Cup championship team (1993).

Season Team	League	REGULAR SEASON								PLAYOFFS				
		Gms.	G	A	Pts.	PIM	+/-	PP	SH	Gms.	G	A	Pts.	PIM
87-88— Granby	QMJHL	69	33	43	76	10	...	...	...	5	3	3	6	0
88-89— Granby	QMJHL	67	40	63	103	26	...	...	...	4	0	5	5	0
89-90— Granby	QMJHL	67	53	54	107	53	...	...	...	—	—	—	—	—
90-91— Fredericton	AHL	75	40	58	98	30	...	...	...	6	2	4	6	0
91-92— Fredericton	AHL	65	30	41	71	26	...	...	...	7	3	3	6	2
— Montreal	NHL	4	0	0	0	0	-1	0	0	—	—	—	—	—
92-93— Fredericton	AHL	39	19	32	51	24	...	...	...	—	—	—	—	—
— Montreal	NHL	19	4	2	6	4	1	0	0	9	0	1	1	0
93-94— Florida	NHL	70	17	33	50	16	-4	11	0	—	—	—	—	—
94-95— Florida	NHL	47	15	14	29	18	-5	6	0	—	—	—	—	—
95-96— Florida	NHL	63	17	21	38	10	-5	7	0	—	—	—	—	—
— Vancouver	NHL	9	3	0	3	4	0	1	0	3	0	2	2	2
96-97— Hamilton	AHL	6	4	3	7	0	...	...	...	—	—	—	—	—
— Quebec	IHL	47	34	28	62	18	...	...	...	9	3	5	8	13
— Edmonton	NHL	6	0	0	0	0	-3	0	0	—	—	—	—	—
NHL totals (6 years)		218	56	70	126	52	-17	25	0	12	0	3	3	2

BELANGER, KEN — LW — ISLANDERS

PERSONAL: Born May 14, 1974, in Sault Ste. Marie, Ont. ... 6-4/225. ... Shoots left. ... Name pronounced buh-LAH-zhay.
TRANSACTIONS/CAREER NOTES: Selected by Hartford Whalers in seventh round (seventh Whalers pick, 153rd overall) of NHL entry draft (June 20, 1992). ... Traded by Whalers to Toronto Maple Leafs for ninth-round pick (RW Matt Ball) in 1994 draft (March 18, 1994). ... Traded by Maple Leafs with G Damian Rhodes to New York Islanders for C Kirk Muller (January 23, 1996). ... Suffered concussion (February 6, 1996); missed two games. ... Suffered concussion (February 12, 1996); missed remainder of season.

Season Team	League	REGULAR SEASON								PLAYOFFS				
		Gms.	G	A	Pts.	PIM	+/-	PP	SH	Gms.	G	A	Pts.	PIM
91-92— Ottawa	OHL	51	4	4	8	174	...	...	...	11	0	0	0	24
92-93— Ottawa	OHL	34	6	12	18	139	...	...	...	—	—	—	—	—
— Guelph	OHL	29	10	14	24	86	...	...	...	5	2	1	3	14
93-94— Guelph	OHL	55	11	22	33	185	...	...	...	9	2	3	5	30
94-95— St. John's	AHL	47	5	5	10	246	...	...	...	4	0	0	0	30
— Toronto	NHL	3	0	0	0	9	0	0	0	—	—	—	—	—
95-96— St. John's	AHL	40	16	14	30	222	...	...	...	—	—	—	—	—
— New York Islanders	NHL	7	0	0	0	27	-2	0	0	—	—	—	—	—
96-97— Kentucky	AHL	38	10	12	22	164	...	...	...	4	0	1	1	27
— New York Islanders	NHL	18	0	2	2	102	-1	0	0	—	—	—	—	—
NHL totals (3 years)		28	0	2	2	138	-3	0	0					

PERSONAL: Born April 21, 1965, in Carman, Man. ... 5-11/182. ... Catches left.

COLLEGE: North Dakota.

TRANSACTIONS/CAREER NOTES: Signed as free agent by Chicago Blackhawks (June 18, 1987). ... Strained hip muscle (1993-94 season); missed four games. ... Sprained knee (January 31, 1996); missed one game. ... Injured back (February 19, 1996); missed three games. ... Traded by Blackhawks to San Jose Sharks for G Chris Terreri, D Michal Sykora, RW Ulf Dahlen and second-round pick in 1998 draft (January 25, 1997). ... Injured knee ligament (February 1, 1997); missed 13 games. ... Suffered bulging disc in back (March 1, 1997); missed seven games. ... Signed as free agent by Dallas Stars (July 2, 1997).

HONORS: Named top goaltender in MJHL (1985-86). ... Named to NCAA All-America West second team (1986-87). ... Named to NCAA All-Tournament team (1986-87). ... Named to WCHA All-Star first team (1986-87). ... Shared Garry F. Longman Memorial Trophy with John Cullen (1987-88). ... Named to IHL All-Star first team (1987-88). ... Named Rookie of the Year by THE SPORTING NEWS (1990-91). ... Won Vezina Trophy (1990-91 and 1992-93). ... Won Calder Memorial Trophy (1990-91). ... Won William M. Jennings Trophy (1990-91, 1992-93 and 1994-95). ... Won Trico Goaltender Award (1990-91). ... Named to THE SPORTING NEWS All-Star first team (1990-91). ... Named to NHL All-Star first team (1990-91 and 1992-93). ... Named to NHL All-Rookie team (1990-91). ... Played in NHL All-Star Game (1992, 1993 and 1996). ... Named to THE SPORTING NEWS All-Star second team (1992-93 and 1994-95).

RECORDS: Shares NHL single-season playoff record for most consecutive wins by goaltender—11 (1992).

MISCELLANEOUS: Stopped a penalty shot attempt (vs. Steve Maltais, February 25, 1993; vs. Roman Oksiuta, February 4, 1994; vs. Mark Howe, March 22, 1994). ... Allowed a penalty shot goal (vs. Philippe Bozon, April 3, 1993; vs. Steve Larmer, January 16, 1994).

STATISTICAL NOTES: Led NHL with .910 save percentage (1990-91).

Season Team	League	REGULAR SEASON Gms.	Min	W	L	T	GA	SO	Avg.	PLAYOFFS Gms.	Min.	W	L	GA	SO	Avg.
85-86—Winkler	MJHL	48	2880	...	...	...	124	1	2.58	—	—	—	—	—	—	—
86-87—Univ. of North Dakota	WCHA	34	2049	29	4	0	81	3	2.37	—	—	—	—	—	—	—
87-88—Saginaw	IHL	61	*3446	32	25	‡0	183	3	3.19	9	561	4	5	33	0	3.53
88-89—Chicago	NHL	23	1148	4	12	3	74	0	3.87	—	—	—	—	—	—	—
—Saginaw	IHL	29	1760	12	10	‡0	92	0	3.14	5	298	2	3	14	0	2.82
89-90—Canadian nat'l team	Int'l	33	1808	...	...	...	93	0	3.09	—	—	—	—	—	—	—
—Chicago	NHL									9	409	4	2	17	0	2.49
90-91—Chicago	NHL	*74	*4127	*43	19	7	170	4	*2.47	6	295	2	4	20	0	4.07
91-92—Chicago	NHL	52	2928	21	18	10	132	†5	2.70	18	949	12	4	39	1	*2.47
92-93—Chicago	NHL	*71	*4106	41	18	11	177	*7	2.59	4	249	0	4	13	0	3.13
93-94—Chicago	NHL	70	3998	37	24	6	178	†7	2.67	6	360	2	4	15	0	2.50
94-95—Chicago	NHL	42	2450	22	15	3	93	†5	2.28	16	1014	9	†7	37	1	2.19
95-96—Chicago	NHL	50	2956	22	17	10	135	1	2.74	9	666	6	3	23	1	*2.07
96-97—Chicago	NHL	33	1906	11	15	6	88	1	2.69	—	—	—	—	—	—	—
—San Jose	NHL	13	757	3	9	0	43	1	3.41	—	—	—	—	—	—	—
NHL totals (9 years)		428	24436	204	147	56	1090	31	2.68	68	3942	35	28	164	3	2.50

PERSONAL: Born September 1, 1964, in St. Catharines, Ont. ... 6-0/195. ... Shoots right.

TRANSACTIONS/CAREER NOTES: Separated shoulder (November 1981); coached Kitchener Rangers for two games while recovering (became the youngest coach in OHL history at 17 years old). ... Selected by Minnesota North Stars as underage junior in first round (first North Stars pick, second overall) of NHL entry draft (June 9, 1982). ... Suffered tendinitis in elbow (October 1984). ... Injured wrist (October 1986); missed 13 games. ... Strained abdominal muscles (February 1989); missed 20 games. ... Bruised left knee (September 1990). ... Strained hip and groin (December 18, 1990). ... Traded by North Stars to Montreal Canadiens for RW Russ Courtnall (August 31, 1992). ... Injured neck (December 3, 1992); missed two games. ... Injured rib cage (November 20, 1993); missed seven games. ... Separated shoulder (February 19, 1995); missed two games. ... Separated shoulder (February 25, 1995); missed five games. ... Traded by Canadiens to Tampa Bay Lightning for C Marc Bureau (June 29, 1995). ... Injured groin (January 4, 1996); missed one game. ... Suffered hip pointer (March 21, 1996); missed two games. ... Strained back (October 31, 1996); missed two games. ... Reinjured back (November 6, 1996); missed two games. ... Traded by Lightning to Mighty Ducks of Anaheim for a sixth-round pick (D Andrei Skopintsev) in 1997 draft (November 19, 1996).

HONORS: Named to Memorial Cup All-Star team (1980-81). ... Won George Parsons Trophy (1981-82). ... Named to OHL All-Star first team (1981-82). ... Played in NHL All-Star Game (1984, 1988 and 1992). ... Named to THE SPORTING NEWS All-Star second team (1989-90). ... Named to NHL All-Star second team (1989-90).

STATISTICAL PLATEAUS: Three-goal games: 1987-88 (1), 1988-89 (1), 1989-90 (1), 1990-91 (1), 1991-92 (1), 1995-96 (1). Total: 6. ... Four-goal games: 1985-86 (1), 1991-92 (1), 1992-93 (1). Total: 3. ... Total hat tricks: 9.

MISCELLANEOUS: Member of Stanley Cup championship team (1993). ... Co-captain of Minnesota North Stars (1983-84). ... Holds Dallas Stars franchise all-time record for most goals (342).

Season Team	League	REGULAR SEASON Gms.	G	A	Pts.	PIM	+/-	PP	SH	PLAYOFFS Gms.	G	A	Pts.	PIM
80-81—Kitchener	OMJHL	66	49	67	116	23	...	...	...	16	14	13	27	13
81-82—Kitchener	OHL	47	45	52	97	23	...	...	...	15	16	13	29	11
82-83—Minnesota	NHL	78	35	30	65	27	-12	15	1	9	5	4	9	18
83-84—Minnesota	NHL	78	41	42	83	66	-2	14	5	16	2	12	14	6
84-85—Minnesota	NHL	78	26	36	62	72	-18	8	1	9	2	4	6	9
85-86—Minnesota	NHL	77	31	48	79	46	16	11	0	5	5	0	5	16
86-87—Minnesota	NHL	65	26	27	53	34	-13	8	1	—	—	—	—	—
87-88—Minnesota	NHL	77	40	41	81	81	-8	21	1	—	—	—	—	—
88-89—Minnesota	NHL	60	23	27	50	55	-14	7	0	5	2	3	5	8
89-90—Minnesota	NHL	80	55	44	99	72	-3	21	1	7	4	3	7	10
90-91—Minnesota	NHL	80	35	40	75	43	-13	17	0	23	10	19	29	30
91-92—Minnesota	NHL	80	30	45	75	41	-20	12	1	7	4	4	8	14
92-93—Montreal	NHL	82	40	48	88	44	4	16	0	18	6	9	15	18
93-94—Montreal	NHL	77	33	38	71	36	9	13	0	6	1	2	3	2
94-95—Montreal	NHL	41	8	8	16	8	-7	1	0	—	—	—	—	—
95-96—Tampa Bay	NHL	79	23	26	49	39	-14	13	0	6	2	0	2	4
96-97—Tampa Bay	NHL	7	1	2	3	0	-4	0	0	—	—	—	—	—
—Anaheim	NHL	62	15	13	28	22	-11	8	0	11	2	4	6	2
NHL totals (15 years)		1101	462	515	977	686	-110	185	11	122	45	64	109	137

BENYSEK, LADISLAV — D — OILERS

PERSONAL: Born March 24, 1975, in Olomouc, Czechoslovakia. ... 6-2/200. ... Shoots left. ... Name pronounced BEHN-ih-shehk.
TRANSACTIONS/CAREER NOTES: Selected by Edmonton Oilers in 11th round (16th Oilers pick, 266th overall) of NHL entry draft (June 29, 1994).

		REGULAR SEASON							PLAYOFFS				
Season Team	League	Gms.	G	A	Pts.	PIM	+/-	PP	SH	Gms.	G	A	Pts.	PIM
93-94— HC Olomouc Jrs.	Czech Rep.						Statistics unavailable.							
94-95— Cape Breton	AHL	58	2	7	9	54	...	...	...	—	—	—	—	—
95-96— HC Olomouc	Czech Rep.	33	1	4	5	...	...	...	...	—	—	—	—	—
96-97— HC Olomouc	Czech Rep.	14	0	1	1	8	...	...	...	—	—	—	—	—

B

BERANEK, JOSEF — LW — PENGUINS

PERSONAL: Born October 25, 1969, in Litvinov, Czechoslovakia. ... 6-2/190. ... Shoots left. ... Name pronounced JOH-sehf buh-RAH-nehk.
TRANSACTIONS/CAREER NOTES: Selected by Edmonton Oilers in fourth round (third Oilers pick, 78th overall) of NHL entry draft (June 17, 1989). ... Traded by Oilers with D Greg Hawgood to Philadelphia Flyers for D Brian Benning (January 16, 1993). ... Bruised left shoulder (January 30, 1994); missed three games. ... Played in Europe during 1994-95 NHL lockout. ... Traded by Flyers to Vancouver Canucks for LW Shawn Antoski (February 15, 1995). ... Sprained thumb (February 2, 1996); missed two games. ... Injured thumb (February 17, 1996); missed one game. ... Signed as free agent by Vancouver Canucks (September 8, 1996). ... Traded by Canucks to Pittsburgh Penguins for future considerations (March 18, 1997). ... Bruised shoulder (March 24, 1997); missed one game. ... Strained groin (April 8, 1997); missed two games.
STATISTICAL PLATEAUS: Three-goal games: 1994-95 (1).

		REGULAR SEASON							PLAYOFFS				
Season Team	League	Gms.	G	A	Pts.	PIM	+/-	PP	SH	Gms.	G	A	Pts.	PIM
87-88— CHZ Litvinov	Czech.	14	7	4	11	12	...	...	...	—	—	—	—	—
88-89— CHZ Litvinov	Czech.	32	18	10	28	47	...	...	...	—	—	—	—	—
— Czechoslovakia Jr.	Czech.	5	2	7	9	2	...	...	...	—	—	—	—	—
89-90— Dukla Trencin	Czech.	49	16	21	37	...	...	...	...	—	—	—	—	—
90-91— CHZ Litvinov	Czech.	50	27	27	54	98	...	...	...	—	—	—	—	—
91-92— Edmonton	NHL	58	12	16	28	18	-2	0	0	12	2	1	3	0
92-93— Edmonton	NHL	26	2	6	8	28	-7	0	0	—	—	—	—	—
— Cape Breton	AHL	6	1	2	3	8	...	...	...	—	—	—	—	—
— Philadelphia	NHL	40	13	12	25	50	-1	1	0	—	—	—	—	—
93-94— Philadelphia	NHL	80	28	21	49	85	-2	6	0	—	—	—	—	—
94-95— Dadak Vsetin	Czech Rep.	16	7	7	14	26	...	...	...	—	—	—	—	—
— Philadelphia	NHL	14	5	5	10	2	3	1	0	—	—	—	—	—
— Vancouver	NHL	37	8	13	21	28	-10	2	0	11	1	1	2	12
95-96— Vancouver	NHL	61	6	14	20	60	-11	0	0	3	2	1	3	0
96-97— Vtesin	Czech Rep.	39	19	24	43	115	...	...	...	3	3	2	5	4
— Pittsburgh	NHL	8	3	1	4	4	-1	1	0	5	0	0	0	2
NHL totals (7 years)		324	77	88	165	275	-31	11	0	31	5	3	8	14

BERARD, BRYAN — D — ISLANDERS

PERSONAL: Born March 5, 1977, in Woonsocket, R.I. ... 6-1/190. ... Shoots left. ... Name pronounced buh-RAHRD.
HIGH SCHOOL: Mount St. Charles (Woonsocket, R.I.).
COLLEGE: University of Michigan-Dearborn.
TRANSACTIONS/CAREER NOTES: Selected by Ottawa Senators in first round (first Senators pick, first overall) of NHL entry draft (July 8, 1995). ... Traded by Senators with C Martin Straka to New York Islanders for D Wade Redden and G Damian Rhodes (January 23, 1996).
HONORS: Won Can.HL Rookie of the Year Award (1994-95). ... Won Can.HL Top Draft Prospect Award (1994-95). ... Won Emms Family Trophy (1994-95). ... Won Max Kaminsky Trophy (1994-95 and 1995-96). ... Won OHL Top Draft Prospect Award (1994-95). ... Named to Can.HL All-Star first team (1994-95 and 1995-96). ... Named to Can.HL All-Rookie team (1994-95). ... Named to OHL All-Star first team (1994-95 and 1995-96). ... Won Can.HL Defenseman of the Year Award (1995-96). ... Named NHL Rookie of the Year by THE SPORTING NEWS (1996-97). ... Won Calder Memorial Trophy (1996-97). ... Named to NHL All-Rookie team (1996-97).

		REGULAR SEASON							PLAYOFFS				
Season Team	League	Gms.	G	A	Pts.	PIM	+/-	PP	SH	Gms.	G	A	Pts.	PIM
91-92— Mount St. Charles	R.I.H.S.	32	3	15	18	10	...	...	...	—	—	—	—	—
92-93— Mount St. Charles	R.I.H.S.	32	8	12	20	18	...	...	...	—	—	—	—	—
93-94— Mount St. Charles	R.I.H.S.	32	11	36	47	5	...	...	...	—	—	—	—	—
94-95— Detroit	OHL	58	20	55	75	97	...	...	...	21	4	20	24	38
95-96— Detroit	OHL	56	31	58	89	116	...	...	...	17	7	18	25	41
96-97— New York Islanders	NHL	82	8	40	48	86	1	3	0	—	—	—	—	—
NHL totals (1 year)		82	8	40	48	86	1	3	0					

BEREHOWSKY, DRAKE — D — PENGUINS

PERSONAL: Born January 3, 1972, in Toronto. ... 6-2/211. ... Shoots right. ... Name pronounced BAIR-uh-HOW-skee.
TRANSACTIONS/CAREER NOTES: Injured knees and underwent reconstructive surgery (October 13, 1989); missed remainder of season. ... Selected by Toronto Maple Leafs in first round (first Maple Leafs pick, 10th overall) of NHL entry draft (June 16, 1990). ... Sprained knee (April 15, 1993); missed remainder of season. ... Underwent knee surgery prior to 1994-95 season; missed first four games of season. ... Traded by Maple Leafs to Pittsburgh Penguins for D Grant Jennings (April 7, 1995).
HONORS: Won Can.HL Defenseman of the Year Award (1991-92). ... Won Max Kaminsky Trophy (1991-92). ... Named to Can.HL All-Star first team (1991-92). ... Named to OHL All-Star first team (1991-92).

Season Team	League	REGULAR SEASON								PLAYOFFS				
		Gms.	G	A	Pts.	PIM	+/-	PP	SH	Gms.	G	A	Pts.	PIM
87-88— Barrie Jr. B	OHA	40	10	36	46	81	...	...	...	—	—	—	—	—
88-89— Kingston	OHL	63	7	39	46	85	...	...	...	—	—	—	—	—
89-90— Kingston	OHL	9	3	11	14	28	...	...	...	—	—	—	—	—
90-91— Toronto	NHL	8	0	1	1	25	-6	0	0	—	—	—	—	—
— Kingston	OHL	13	5	13	18	28	...	...	...	—	—	—	—	—
— North Bay	OHL	26	7	23	30	51	...	...	...	10	2	7	9	21
91-92— North Bay	OHL	62	19	63	82	147	...	...	...	21	7	24	31	22
— Toronto	NHL	1	0	0	0	0	0	0	0	—	—	—	—	—
— St. John's	AHL	—	—	—	—	—	...	...	...	6	0	5	5	21
92-93— Toronto	NHL	41	4	15	19	61	1	1	0	—	—	—	—	—
— St. John's	AHL	28	10	17	27	38	...	...	...	—	—	—	—	—
93-94— Toronto	NHL	49	2	8	10	63	-3	2	0	—	—	—	—	—
— St. John's	AHL	18	3	12	15	40	...	...	...	—	—	—	—	—
94-95— Toronto	NHL	25	0	2	2	15	-10	0	0	—	—	—	—	—
— Pittsburgh	NHL	4	0	0	0	13	1	0	0	1	0	0	0	0
95-96— Cleveland	IHL	74	6	28	34	141	...	...	...	3	0	3	3	6
— Pittsburgh	NHL	1	0	0	0	0	1	0	0	—	—	—	—	—
96-97— San Antonio	IHL	16	3	4	7	36	...	...	...	—	—	—	—	—
— Carolina	AHL	49	2	15	17	55	...	...	...	—	—	—	—	—
NHL totals (6 years)		129	6	26	32	177	-16	3	0	1	0	0	0	0

BEREZIN, SERGEI — RW — MAPLE LEAFS

PERSONAL: Born November 5, 1971, in Voskresensk, U.S.S.R. ... 5-10/187. ... Shoots right. ... Name pronounced BAIR-ih-zihn.
TRANSACTIONS/CAREER NOTES: Selected by Toronto Maple Leafs in 10th round (eighth Maple Leafs pick, 256th overall) of NHL entry draft (June 29, 1994). ... Injured hand (November 19, 1996); missed one game. ... Underwent hand surgery (December 3, 1996); missed six games. ... Strained knee (December 23, 1996); missed two games.
HONORS: Named to NHL All-Rookie team (1996-97).

Season Team	League	REGULAR SEASON								PLAYOFFS				
		Gms.	G	A	Pts.	PIM	+/-	PP	SH	Gms.	G	A	Pts.	PIM
93-94— Khimik Voskresensk	CIS	40	31	10	41	16	...	...	...	—	—	—	—	—
94-95— Koln	Germany	43	38	19	57	8	...	...	...	18	17	8	25	18
95-96— Koln	Germany	45	49	31	80	8	...	...	...	14	13	9	22	4
96-97— Toronto	NHL	73	25	16	41	2	-3	7	0	—	—	—	—	—
NHL totals (1 year)		73	25	16	41	2	-3	7	0					

BERG, AKI — D — KINGS

PERSONAL: Born July 28, 1977, in Turku, Finland. ... 6-3/196. ... Shoots left. ... Name pronounced AH-kee BUHRG.
TRANSACTIONS/CAREER NOTES: Selected by Los Angeles Kings in first round (first Kings pick, third overall) of NHL entry draft (July 8, 1995). ... Suffered charley horse (January 25, 1997); missed one game. ... Suffered concussion (February 3, 1997); missed two games. ... Sprained left ankle (April 9, 1997); missed final two games of regular season.

Season Team	League	REGULAR SEASON								PLAYOFFS				
		Gms.	G	A	Pts.	PIM	+/-	PP	SH	Gms.	G	A	Pts.	PIM
92-93— TPS Jr.	Finland	39	18	24	42	59	...	...	...	—	—	—	—	—
93-94— TPS Jr.	Finland	21	3	11	14	24	...	...	...	7	0	0	0	10
— TPS Turku	Finland	6	0	3	3	4	...	...	...	—	—	—	—	—
94-95— Kiekko-67	Finland Div. II	20	3	9	12	34	...	...	...	—	—	—	—	—
— TPS Jr.	Finland	8	1	0	1	30	...	...	...	—	—	—	—	—
— TPS Turku	Finland	5	0	0	0	4	...	...	...	—	—	—	—	—
95-96— Los Angeles	NHL	51	0	7	7	29	-13	0	0	—	—	—	—	—
— Phoenix	IHL	20	0	3	3	18	...	...	...	2	0	0	0	4
96-97— Los Angeles	NHL	41	2	6	8	24	-9	2	0	—	—	—	—	—
— Phoenix	IHL	23	1	3	4	21	...	...	...	—	—	—	—	—
NHL totals (2 years)		92	2	13	15	53	-22	2	0					

BERG, BILL — LW — RANGERS

PERSONAL: Born October 21, 1967, in St. Catharines, Ont. ... 6-1/205. ... Shoots left.
TRANSACTIONS/CAREER NOTES: Broke ankle (March 1985). ... Selected by New York Islanders as underage junior in third round (third Islanders pick, 59th overall) of NHL entry draft (June 21, 1986). ... Injured knee (October 1986). ... Separated shoulder (May 1990). ... Fractured left foot (November 9, 1991); missed 12 games. ... Claimed on waivers by Toronto Maple Leafs (December 3, 1992). ... Injured hip flexor (November 18, 1993); missed one game. ... Sprained knee (February 6, 1995); missed 16 games. ... Broke leg (October 26, 1995); missed 33 games. ... Traded by Maple Leafs with LW Sergio Momesso to New York Rangers for LW Nick Kypreos and RW Wayne Presley (February 29, 1996). ... Strained groin (November 12, 1996); missed nine games. ... Bruised foot (February 15, 1997); missed two games. ... Broke fibula (April 22, 1997); missed remainder of regular season and playoffs.
MISCELLANEOUS: Moved from defense to left wing (1990).

Season Team	League	REGULAR SEASON								PLAYOFFS				
		Gms.	G	A	Pts.	PIM	+/-	PP	SH	Gms.	G	A	Pts.	PIM
84-85— Grimsby Jr. B	OHA	42	10	22	32	153	...	...	...	—	—	—	—	—
85-86— Toronto	OHL	64	3	35	38	143	...	...	...	4	0	0	0	19
86-87— Toronto	OHL	57	3	15	18	138	...	...	...	—	—	—	—	—
— Springfield	AHL	4	1	1	2	4	...	...	...	—	—	—	—	—
87-88— Springfield	AHL	76	6	26	32	148	...	...	...	—	—	—	—	—
— Peoria	IHL	5	0	1	1	8	...	...	...	7	0	3	3	31

B

Season Team	League	REGULAR SEASON									PLAYOFFS				
		Gms.	G	A	Pts.	PIM	+/-	PP	SH		Gms.	G	A	Pts.	PIM
88-89— New York Islanders....	NHL	7	1	2	3	10	-2	1	0		—	—	—	—	—
— Springfield................	AHL	69	17	32	49	122	...	...	...		—	—	—	—	—
89-90— Springfield............	AHL	74	12	42	54	74	...	...	...		15	5	12	17	35
90-91— New York Islanders....	NHL	78	9	14	23	67	-3	0	0		—	—	—	—	—
91-92— New York Islanders....	NHL	47	5	9	14	28	-18	1	0		—	—	—	—	—
— Capital District..........	AHL	3	0	2	2	16	...	...	...		—	—	—	—	—
92-93— New York Islanders....	NHL	22	6	3	9	49	4	0	2		—	—	—	—	—
— Toronto.....................	NHL	58	7	8	15	54	-1	0	1		21	1	1	2	18
93-94— Toronto...............	NHL	83	8	11	19	93	-3	0	0		18	1	2	3	10
94-95— Toronto...............	NHL	32	5	1	6	26	-11	0	0		7	0	1	1	4
95-96— Toronto...............	NHL	23	1	1	2	33	-6	0	0		—	—	—	—	—
— New York Rangers.....	NHL	18	2	1	3	8	0	0	1		10	1	0	1	0
96-97— New York Rangers.....	NHL	67	8	6	14	37	2	0	2		3	0	0	0	2
NHL totals (8 years)...........		435	52	56	108	405	-38	2	6		59	3	4	7	34

BERGERON, J.C.　　　G　　　KINGS

PERSONAL: Born October 14, 1968, in Hauterive, Que. ... 5-9/181. ... Catches left. ... Name pronounced BUHR-zhur-ahn.

TRANSACTIONS/CAREER NOTES: Selected by Montreal Canadiens in fifth round (sixth Canadiens pick, 104th overall) of NHL entry draft (June 11, 1988). ... Traded by Canadiens to Tampa Bay Lightning for G Frederic Chabot (June 18, 1992). ... Signed as free agent by Los Angeles Kings (August 28, 1996).

HONORS: Won Aldege (Baz) Bastien Trophy (1989-90). ... Shared Harry (Hap) Holmes Memorial Trophy with Andre Racicot (1989-90). ... Named to AHL All-Star first team (1989-90). ... Shared James Norris Memorial Trophy with Mike Greenlay (1993-94).

Season Team	League	REGULAR SEASON									PLAYOFFS						
		Gms.	Min	W	L	T	GA	SO	Avg.		Gms.	Min.	W	L	GA	SO	Avg.
85-86— Shawinigan..................	QMJHL	33	1796	...	...	...	156	0	5.21		—	—	—	—	—	—	—
86-87— Verdun..........................	QMJHL	52	2991	...	...	...	*306	0	6.14		—	—	—	—	—	—	—
87-88— Verdun..........................	QMJHL	49	2715	13	31	3	*265	0	5.86		—	—	—	—	—	—	—
88-89— Verdun..........................	QMJHL	44	2417	8	34	1	199	0	4.94		—	—	—	—	—	—	—
— Sherbrooke....................	AHL	5	302	4	1	0	18	0	3.58		—	—	—	—	—	—	—
89-90— Sherbrooke................	AHL	40	2254	21	8	7	103	2	*2.74		9	497	6	2	28	0	3.38
90-91— Montreal......................	NHL	18	941	7	6	2	59	0	3.76		—	—	—	—	—	—	—
— Fredericton.................	AHL	18	1083	12	6	0	59	1	3.27		10	546	5	5	32	0	3.52
91-92— Fredericton...............	AHL	13	791	5	7	1	57	0	4.32		—	—	—	—	—	—	—
— Peoria..........................	IHL	27	1632	14	9	‡3	96	1	3.53		6	352	3	3	24	0	4.09
92-93— Atlanta.......................	IHL	31	1722	21	7	‡0	92	1	3.21		6	368	3	3	19	0	3.10
— Tampa Bay...................	NHL	21	1163	8	10	1	71	0	3.66		—	—	—	—	—	—	—
93-94— Tampa Bay.................	NHL	3	134	1	1	1	7	0	3.13		—	—	—	—	—	—	—
— Atlanta........................	IHL	48	2755	27	11	‡7	141	0	3.07		2	153	1	1	6	0	2.35
94-95— Tampa Bay.................	NHL	17	883	3	9	1	49	1	3.33		—	—	—	—	—	—	—
— Atlanta........................	IHL	6	324	3	3	‡0	24	0	4.44		—	—	—	—	—	—	—
95-96— Tampa Bay.................	NHL	12	595	2	6	2	42	0	4.24		—	—	—	—	—	—	—
— Atlanta........................	IHL	25	1326	9	10	‡3	92	0	4.16		—	—	—	—	—	—	—
96-97— Phoenix......................	IHL	42	2296	11	19	‡7	127	0	3.32		—	—	—	—	—	—	—
— Los Angeles.................	NHL	1	56	0	1	0	4	0	4.29		—	—	—	—	—	—	—
NHL totals (6 years).............		72	3772	21	33	7	232	1	3.69								

BERGEVIN, MARC　　　D　　　BLUES

PERSONAL: Born August 11, 1965, in Montreal. ... 6-1/197. ... Shoots left. ... Name pronounced BUHR-jih-vihn.

TRANSACTIONS/CAREER NOTES: Selected by Chicago Blackhawks as underage junior in third round (third Blackhawks pick, 59th overall) of NHL entry draft (June 8, 1983). ... Sprained neck (March 18, 1987). ... Traded by Blackhawks with D Gary Nylund to New York Islanders for D Steve Konroyd and C Bob Bassen (November 25, 1988). ... Bruised ribs (November 25, 1989). ... Broke hand (May 1990). ... Traded by Islanders to Hartford Whalers for future considerations; Islanders later received fifth-round pick in 1992 draft (C Ryan Duthie) to complete deal (October 31, 1990). ... Signed as free agent by Tampa Bay Lightning (July 9, 1992). ... Injured foot (March 18, 1993); missed one game. ... Bruised back (November 19, 1993); missed one game. ... Injured elbow (March 10, 1995); missed one game. ... Suffered from sore neck (April 22, 1995); missed three games. ... Traded by Lightning with RW Ben Hankinson to Detroit Red Wings for LW Shawn Burr and third-round pick (traded to Boston) in 1996 draft (August 17, 1995). ... Suffered from the flu (December 1, 1995); missed one game. ... Injured groin (April 7, 1996); missed three games. ... Signed as free agent by St. Louis Blues (July 9, 1996).

Season Team	League	REGULAR SEASON									PLAYOFFS				
		Gms.	G	A	Pts.	PIM	+/-	PP	SH		Gms.	G	A	Pts.	PIM
82-83— Chicoutimi................	QMJHL	64	3	27	30	113	...	...	...		—	—	—	—	—
83-84— Chicoutimi................	QMJHL	70	10	35	45	125	...	...	...		—	—	—	—	—
— Springfield.................	AHL	7	0	1	1	2	...	...	...		—	—	—	—	—
84-85— Chicago......................	NHL	60	0	6	6	54	-9	0	0		6	0	3	3	2
— Springfield.................	AHL	—	—	—	—	—	...	...	...		4	0	0	0	0
85-86— Chicago...................	NHL	71	7	7	14	60	0	0	0		3	0	0	0	0
86-87— Chicago...................	NHL	66	4	10	14	66	4	0	0		3	1	0	1	2
87-88— Chicago...................	NHL	58	1	6	7	85	-19	0	0		—	—	—	—	—
— Saginaw....................	IHL	10	2	7	9	20	...	...	...		—	—	—	—	—
88-89— Chicago...................	NHL	11	0	0	0	18	-3	0	0		—	—	—	—	—
— New York Islanders....	NHL	58	2	13	15	62	2	1	0		—	—	—	—	—
89-90— New York Islanders....	NHL	18	0	4	4	30	-8	0	0		—	—	—	—	—
— Springfield.................	AHL	47	7	16	23	66	...	...	...		17	2	11	13	16
90-91— Hartford....................	NHL	4	0	0	0	4	-3	0	0		—	—	—	—	—
— Capital District..........	AHL	7	0	5	5	6	...	...	...		—	—	—	—	—
— Springfield.................	AHL	58	4	23	27	85	...	...	...		18	0	7	7	26

Season Team	League	REGULAR SEASON								PLAYOFFS				
		Gms.	G	A	Pts.	PIM	+/-	PP	SH	Gms.	G	A	Pts.	PIM
91-92— Hartford	NHL	75	7	17	24	64	-13	4	1	5	0	0	0	2
92-93— Tampa Bay	NHL	78	2	12	14	66	-16	0	0	—	—	—	—	—
93-94— Tampa Bay	NHL	83	1	15	16	87	-5	0	0	—	—	—	—	—
94-95— Tampa Bay	NHL	44	2	4	6	51	-6	0	1	—	—	—	—	—
95-96— Detroit......................	NHL	70	1	9	10	33	7	0	0	17	1	0	1	14
96-97— St. Louis....................	NHL	82	0	4	4	53	-9	0	0	6	1	0	1	8
NHL totals (13 years)		778	27	107	134	733	-78	5	2	40	3	3	6	28

BERGKVIST, STEFAN   D   PENGUINS

PERSONAL: Born March 10, 1975, in Leksand, Sweden. ... 6-3/216. ... Shoots left. ... Name pronounced BURG-kuh-vihst. ... Brother of Jonas Bergqvist, right winger, Calgary Flames (1989-90).
TRANSACTIONS/CAREER NOTES: Selected by Pittsburgh Penguins in first round (first Penguins pick, 26th overall) of NHL entry draft (June 26, 1993). ... Underwent appendectomy (February 21, 1996); missed 12 games.

Season Team	League	REGULAR SEASON								PLAYOFFS				
		Gms.	G	A	Pts.	PIM	+/-	PP	SH	Gms.	G	A	Pts.	PIM
92-93— Leksand	Sweden	15	0	0	0	6	...	...	...	—	—	—	—	—
93-94— Leksand	Sweden	6	0	0	0	0	...	...	...	—	—	—	—	—
94-95— London	OHL	64	3	17	20	93	...	...	...	4	0	0	0	5
95-96— Cleveland	IHL	61	2	8	10	58	...	...	...	3	0	0	0	14
— Pittsburgh..................	NHL	2	0	0	0	2	0	0	0	4	0	0	0	2
96-97— Pittsburgh	NHL	5	0	0	0	7	-1	0	0	—	—	—	—	—
— Cleveland	IHL	33	0	1	1	54	...	...	...	4	0	0	0	0
NHL totals (2 years)		7	0	0	0	9	-1	0	0	4	0	0	0	2

BERGQVIST, PER-RAGNA   G   FLYERS

PERSONAL: Born April 11, 1976, in Leksand, Sweden. ... 5-11/183. ... Catches left.
TRANSACTIONS/CAREER NOTES: Selected by Philadelphia Flyers in fifth round (third Flyers pick, 124th overall) of NHL entry draft (June 22, 1996).

Season Team	League	REGULAR SEASON							PLAYOFFS					
		Gms.	Min	W	L	T	GA	SO	Avg.	Gms.	Min.	W	L	GA	SO	Avg.
95-96— Leksand	Swed. Jr.	3	180	...	...	...	17	0	5.67	—	—	...	...	—	—	—
— Leksand	Sweden	6	327	...	...	...	17	0	3.12	1	60	...	...	1	0	1.00
96-97— Leksand	Sweden	11	660	...	...	...	32	1	2.91	1	86	...	...	5	0	3.49

BERTUZZI, TODD   LW   ISLANDERS

PERSONAL: Born February 2, 1975, in Sudbury, Ont. ... 6-3/224. ... Shoots left. ... Name pronounced buhr-TOO-zee.
HIGH SCHOOL: Bishop MacDonnell (Guelph, Ont.).
TRANSACTIONS/CAREER NOTES: Selected by New York Islanders in first round (first Islanders pick, 23rd overall) of NHL entry draft (June 26, 1993). ... Injured eye (February 22, 1996); missed two games. ... Suspended three games by NHL for attempting to break free of a linesman (April 2, 1996). ... Bone chips in elbow (November 23, 1996); missed one game.
HONORS: Named to OHL All-Star second team (1994-95).

Season Team	League	REGULAR SEASON								PLAYOFFS				
		Gms.	G	A	Pts.	PIM	+/-	PP	SH	Gms.	G	A	Pts.	PIM
91-92— Guelph	OHL	47	7	14	21	145	...	...	...	—	—	—	—	—
92-93— Guelph	OHL	59	27	32	59	164	...	...	...	5	2	2	4	6
93-94— Guelph	OHL	61	28	54	82	165	...	...	...	9	2	6	8	30
94-95— Guelph	OHL	62	54	65	119	58	...	...	...	14	*15	18	33	41
95-96— New York Islanders....	NHL	76	18	21	39	83	-14	4	0	—	—	—	—	—
96-97— New York Islanders....	NHL	64	10	13	23	68	-3	3	0	—	—	—	—	—
— Utah	IHL	13	5	5	10	16	...	...	...	—	—	—	—	—
NHL totals (2 years)		140	28	34	62	151	-17	7	0					

BERUBE, CRAIG   LW   CAPITALS

PERSONAL: Born December 17, 1965, in Calihoo, Alta. ... 6-1/205. ... Shoots left. ... Name pronounced buh-ROO-bee.
TRANSACTIONS/CAREER NOTES: Signed as free agent by Philadelphia Flyers (March 19, 1986). ... Sprained left knee (March 1988). ... Traded by Flyers with RW Scott Mellanby and C Craig Fisher to Edmonton Oilers for RW Dave Brown, D Corey Foster and the NHL rights to RW Jari Kurri (May 30, 1991). ... Traded by Oilers with G Grant Fuhr and RW/LW Glenn Anderson to Toronto Maple Leafs for LW Vincent Damphousse, D Luke Richardson, G Peter Ing, C Scott Thornton and future considerations (September 19, 1991). ... Traded by Maple Leafs with D Alexander Godynyuk, RW Gary Leeman, D Michel Petit and G Jeff Reese to Calgary Flames for C Doug Gilmour, D Jamie Macoun, LW Kent Manderville, D Ric Nattress and G Rick Wamsley (January 2, 1992). ... Traded by Flames to Washington Capitals for fifth-round pick (C Darryl LaFrance) in 1993 draft (June 26, 1993). ... Suffered from the flu (March 31, 1995); missed three games. ... Broke jaw (September 14, 1995); missed seven games. ... Suffered mild concussion (November 10, 1995); missed four games. ... Suspended 10 games by NHL for coming off bench to fight (December 22, 1995). ... Injured right knee (March 22, 1996); missed 11 games. ... Suspended two games and fined $1,000 by NHL for slashing incident (January 19, 1997).

Season Team	League	REGULAR SEASON								PLAYOFFS				
		Gms.	G	A	Pts.	PIM	+/-	PP	SH	Gms.	G	A	Pts.	PIM
82-83— Williams Lake	PCJHL	33	9	24	33	99	...	...	...	—	—	—	—	—
— Kamloops..................	WHL	4	0	0	0	0	...	...	...	—	—	—	—	—
83-84— New Westminster	WHL	70	11	20	31	104	...	...	...	8	1	2	3	5
84-85— New Westminster	WHL	70	25	44	69	191	...	...	...	10	3	2	5	4

B

Season Team	League	REGULAR SEASON								PLAYOFFS				
		Gms.	G	A	Pts.	PIM	+/-	PP	SH	Gms.	G	A	Pts.	PIM
85-86— Kamloops	WHL	32	17	14	31	119	...	...	...	—	—	—	—	—
— Medicine Hat	WHL	34	14	16	30	95	...	...	...	25	7	8	15	102
86-87— Hershey	AHL	63	7	17	24	325	...	...	...	—	—	—	—	—
— Philadelphia	NHL	7	0	0	0	57	2	0	0	5	0	0	0	17
87-88— Hershey	AHL	31	5	9	14	119	...	...	...	—	—	—	—	—
— Philadelphia	NHL	27	3	2	5	108	1	0	0	—	—	—	—	—
88-89— Hershey	AHL	7	0	2	2	19	...	...	...	—	—	—	—	—
— Philadelphia	NHL	53	1	1	2	199	-15	0	0	16	0	0	0	56
89-90— Philadelphia	NHL	74	4	14	18	291	-7	0	0	—	—	—	—	—
90-91— Philadelphia	NHL	74	8	9	17	293	-6	0	0	—	—	—	—	—
91-92— Toronto	NHL	40	5	7	12	109	-2	1	0	—	—	—	—	—
— Calgary	NHL	36	1	4	5	155	-3	0	0	—	—	—	—	—
92-93— Calgary	NHL	77	4	8	12	209	-6	0	0	6	0	1	1	21
93-94— Washington	NHL	84	7	7	14	305	-4	0	0	8	0	0	0	21
94-95— Washington	NHL	43	2	4	6	173	-5	0	0	7	0	0	0	29
95-96— Washington	NHL	50	2	10	12	151	1	1	0	2	0	0	0	19
96-97— Washington	NHL	80	4	3	7	218	-11	0	0	—	—	—	—	—
NHL totals (11 years)		645	41	69	110	2268	-55	2	0	44	0	1	1	163

BESTER, ALLAN   G   STARS

PERSONAL: Born March 26, 1964, in Hamilton, Ont. ... 5-7/155. ... Catches left.

TRANSACTIONS/CAREER NOTES: Selected by Toronto Maple Leafs as underage junior in third round (third Maple Leafs pick, 48th overall) of NHL entry draft (June 8, 1983). ... Sprained left knee ligaments (February 1988); missed 14 games. ... Suffered phlebitis in right leg (January 1989). ... Stretched knee ligaments (April 1989). ... Suffered from bone spurs in right heel (October 1989). ... Underwent surgery for calcium deposits on his heels (October 1990). ... Traded by Maple Leafs to Detroit Red Wings for sixth-round pick (C Alexander Kuzminsky) in 1991 draft (March 5, 1991). ... Signed as free agent by Mighty Ducks of Anaheim (September 7, 1993). ... Signed as free agent by Orlando Solar Bears of IHL (July 10, 1995). ... Signed as free agent by Dallas Stars (January 20, 1996).

HONORS: Named to OHL All-Star first team (1982-83). ... Won Jack Butterfield Trophy (1991-92).

MISCELLANEOUS: Stopped a penalty shot attempt (vs. Dennis Maruk, December 23, 1986; vs. Dino Ciccarelli, November 26, 1988; vs. Michel Goulet, December 29, 1988; vs. Greg Adams, January 9, 1989; vs. Anton Stastny, March 7, 1989). ... Allowed a penalty shot goal (vs. Petr Klima, April 9, 1988 (playoffs)).

Season Team	League	REGULAR SEASON								PLAYOFFS						
		Gms.	Min	W	L	T	GA	SO	Avg.	Gms.	Min.	W	L	GA	SO	Avg.
81-82— Brantford	OHL	19	970	4	11	0	68	0	4.21	—	—	—	—	—	—	—
82-83— Brantford	OHL	56	3210	29	21	3	188	0	3.51	8	480	3	3	20	†1	*2.50
83-84— Brantford	OHL	23	1271	12	9	1	71	1	3.35	1	60	0	1	5	0	5.00
— Toronto	NHL	32	1848	11	16	4	134	0	4.35	—	—	—	—	—	—	—
84-85— St. Catharines	AHL	30	1669	9	18	1	133	0	4.78	—	—	—	—	—	—	—
— Toronto	NHL	15	767	3	9	1	54	1	4.22	—	—	—	—	—	—	—
85-86— St. Catharines	AHL	50	2855	23	23	3	173	1	3.64	11	637	7	3	27	0	2.54
— Toronto	NHL	1	20	0	0	0	2	0	6.00	—	—	—	—	—	—	—
86-87— Newmarket	AHL	3	190	1	0	0	6	0	1.89	—	—	—	—	—	—	—
— Toronto	NHL	36	1808	10	14	3	110	2	3.65	1	39	0	0	1	0	1.54
87-88— Toronto	NHL	30	1607	8	12	5	102	2	3.81	5	253	2	3	21	0	4.98
88-89— Toronto	NHL	43	2460	17	20	3	156	2	3.80	—	—	—	—	—	—	—
89-90— Newmarket	AHL	5	264	2	1	1	18	0	4.09	—	—	—	—	—	—	—
— Toronto	NHL	42	2206	20	16	0	165	0	4.49	—	—	—	—	—	—	—
90-91— Toronto	NHL	6	247	0	4	0	18	0	4.37	—	—	—	—	—	—	—
— Detroit	NHL	3	178	0	3	0	13	0	4.38	1	20	0	0	1	0	3.00
— Newmarket	AHL	19	1157	7	8	4	58	1	3.01	—	—	—	—	—	—	—
91-92— Detroit	NHL	1	31	0	0	0	2	0	3.87	—	—	—	—	—	—	—
— Adirondack	AHL	22	1268	13	8	0	78	0	3.69	†19	1174	*14	5	50	1	2.56
92-93— Adirondack	AHL	41	2268	16	15	5	133	1	3.52	10	633	7	3	26	†1	2.46
93-94— San Diego	IHL	46	2543	22	14	‡6	150	1	3.54	8	419	4	4	28	0	4.01
94-95— San Diego	IHL	58	3251	28	23	‡5	183	1	3.38	4	272	2	2	13	0	2.87
95-96— Orlando	IHL	51	2947	32	16	‡2	176	1	3.58	*23	*1343	11	12	65	2	2.90
— Dallas	NHL	10	601	4	5	1	30	0	3.00	—	—	—	—	—	—	—
96-97— Orlando	IHL	61	3115	37	13	‡3	132	2	2.54	10	512	4	4	27	0	3.16
NHL totals (10 years)		219	11773	73	99	17	786	7	4.01	7	312	2	3	23	0	4.42

BEUKEBOOM, JEFF   D   RANGERS

PERSONAL: Born March 28, 1965, in Ajax, Ont. ... 6-5/230. ... Shoots right. ... Name pronounced BOO-kuh-BOOM. ... Nephew of Ed Kea, defenseman, Atlanta Flames and St. Louis Blues (1973-74 through 1982-83); and cousin of Joe Nieuwendyk, center, Dallas Stars.

TRANSACTIONS/CAREER NOTES: Selected by Edmonton Oilers as underage junior in first round (first Oilers pick, 19th overall) of NHL entry draft (June 8,1983). ... Injured knee (December 1984). ... Lacerated knuckle (October 24, 1987). ... Suspended 10 games by NHL for leaving the bench (October 2, 1988). ... Sprained right knee (January 1989). ... Suffered hairline fracture of ankle (February 22, 1991); missed two games. ... Traded by Oilers to New York Rangers for D David Shaw (November 12, 1991), completing deal in which Oilers traded C Mark Messier with future considerations to Rangers for C Bernie Nicholls, LW Louie DeBrusk, RW Steven Rice and future considerations (October 4, 1991). ... Strained back (March 16, 1992); missed one game. ... Injured knee (December 21, 1992); missed one game. ... Bruised ankle (February 1, 1993); missed one game. ... Suspended one game by NHL for hitting from behind (May 25, 1994). ... Suffered neck spasms (March 5, 1995); missed one game. ... Bruised chest (March 18, 1995); missed three games. ... Suffered from the flu (February 15, 1997); missed two games.

HONORS: Named to OHL All-Star first team (1984-85).

MISCELLANEOUS: Member of Stanley Cup championship team (1987, 1988, 1990 and 1994). ... Failed to score on a penalty shot (vs. Richard Tabaracci, October 6, 1990).

Season Team	League	Gms.	G	A	Pts.	PIM	+/-	PP	SH	Gms.	G	A	Pts.	PIM
81-82— Newmarket................	OPJHL	49	5	30	35	218	...	...	...	—	—	—	—	—
82-83— Sault Ste. Marie	OHL	70	0	25	25	143	...	...	...	16	1	14	15	46
83-84— Sault Ste. Marie	OHL	61	6	30	36	178	...	...	...	16	1	7	8	43
84-85— Sault Ste. Marie	OHL	37	4	20	24	85	...	...	...	16	4	6	10	47
85-86— Nova Scotia	AHL	77	9	20	29	175	...	...	...	—	—	—	—	—
— Edmonton	NHL	—	—	—	—	—	...	...	...	1	0	0	0	4
86-87— Nova Scotia	AHL	14	1	7	8	35	...	...	...	—	—	—	—	—
— Edmonton	NHL	44	3	8	11	124	7	1	0	—	—	—	—	—
87-88— Edmonton	NHL	73	5	20	25	201	27	1	0	7	0	0	0	16
88-89— Cape Breton	AHL	8	0	4	4	36	...	...	...	—	—	—	—	—
— Edmonton	NHL	36	0	5	5	94	2	0	0	1	0	0	0	2
89-90— Edmonton	NHL	46	1	12	13	86	5	0	0	2	0	0	0	0
90-91— Edmonton	NHL	67	3	7	10	150	6	0	0	18	1	3	4	28
91-92— Edmonton	NHL	18	0	5	5	78	4	0	0	—	—	—	—	—
— New York Rangers	NHL	56	1	10	11	122	19	0	0	13	2	3	5	*47
92-93— New York Rangers	NHL	82	2	17	19	153	9	0	0	—	—	—	—	—
93-94— New York Rangers	NHL	68	8	8	16	170	18	1	0	22	0	6	6	50
94-95— New York Rangers	NHL	44	1	3	4	70	3	0	0	9	0	0	0	10
95-96— New York Rangers	NHL	82	3	11	14	220	19	0	0	11	0	3	3	6
96-97— New York Rangers	NHL	80	3	9	12	167	22	0	0	15	0	1	1	34
NHL totals (12 years)		696	30	115	145	1635	141	3	0	99	3	16	19	197

BICANEK, RADIM D SENATORS

PERSONAL: Born January 18, 1975, in Uherske Hradiste, Czechoslovakia. ... 6-1/205. ... Shoots left. ... Name pronounced RA-deem BEECH-ih-nehk.

TRANSACTIONS/CAREER NOTES: Selected by Ottawa Senators in second round (second Senators pick, 27th overall) of NHL entry draft (June 26, 1993).

Season Team	League	Gms.	G	A	Pts.	PIM	+/-	PP	SH	Gms.	G	A	Pts.	PIM
92-93— Jihlava.	Czech Rep.	43	2	3	5	...	...	...	...	—	—	—	—	—
93-94— Belleville...................	OHL	63	16	27	43	49	...	...	...	12	2	8	10	21
94-95— Belleville...................	OHL	49	13	26	39	61	...	...	...	16	6	5	11	30
— Ottawa	NHL	6	0	0	0	0	3	0	0	—	—	—	—	—
— Prin. Edward Island ...	AHL	—	—	—	—	—				3	0	1	1	0
95-96— Prin. Edward Island ...	AHL	74	7	19	26	87	...	...	...	5	0	2	2	6
96-97— Worcester	AHL	44	1	15	16	22	...	...	...	—	—	—	—	—
— Ottawa	NIIL	21	0	1	1	8	-4	0	0	7	0	0	0	8
NHL totals (2 years)		27	0	1	1	8	-1	0	0	7	0	0	0	8

BIERK, ZAC G LIGHTNING

PERSONAL: Born September 17, 1976, in Peterborough, Ont. ... 6-4/188. ... Catches left. ... Name pronounced BEERK.

HIGH SCHOOL: Thomas A. Stewart S.S. (Peterborough, Ont.).

TRANSACTIONS/CAREER NOTES: Selected by Tampa Bay Lightning in ninth round (eighth Lightning pick, 212th overall) of NHL entry draft (July 8, 1995).

HONORS: Won Leo Lalonde Memorial Trophy (1996-97). ... Named to Can.HL All-Star second team (1996-97). ... Named to OHL All-Star first team (1996-97).

Season Team	League	Gms.	Min	W	L	T	GA	SO	Avg.	Gms.	Min.	W	L	GA	SO	Avg.
93-94—Peterborough................	Tier II Jr. A	4	205	...	...	...	17	0	4.98	—	—	—	—	—	—	—
— Peterborough..............	OHL	9	423	0	4	2	37	0	5.25	1	33	0	0	7	0	12.73
94-95—Peterborough..............	OHL	35	1798	12	15	5	118	0	3.94	6	301	2	3	24	0	4.78
95-96—Peterborough..............	OHL	58	3292	31	16	6	174	2	3.17	*22	*1383	*14	†7	*83	0	3.60
96-97—Peterborough..............	OHL	49	2744	*28	16	0	151	2	3.30	11	666	6	5	35	0	3.15

BILLINGTON, CRAIG G AVALANCHE

PERSONAL: Born September 11, 1966, in London, Ont. ... 5-10/170. ... Catches left.

TRANSACTIONS/CAREER NOTES: Selected by New Jersey Devils as underage junior in second round (second Devils pick, 23rd overall) of NHL entry draft (June 9, 1984). ... Suffered from mononucleosis (July 1984). ... Injured hamstring (February 15, 1992); missed two games. ... Strained knee (March 11, 1992); missed six games. ... Underwent arthroscopic knee surgery (April 13, 1992). ... Suffered from sore throat (March 27, 1993); missed one game. ... Traded by Devils with C/LW Troy Mallette and fourth-round pick in 1993 draft (C Cosmo Dupaul) to Ottawa Senators for G Peter Sidorkiewicz and future considerations (June 20, 1993); Senators sent LW Mike Peluso to Devils to complete deal (June 26, 1993). ... Injured knee (January 27, 1995); missed 17 games. ... Traded by Senators to Boston Bruins for eighth-round pick (D Ray Schultz) in 1995 draft (April 7, 1995). ... Signed as free agent by Florida Panthers (September 4, 1996). ... Selected by Colorado Avalanche in NHL waiver draft for cash (September 30, 1996). ... Sprained knee ligament (November 19, 1996); missed seven games.

HONORS: Won Bobby Smith Trophy (1984-85). ... Named to OHL All-Star first team (1984-85). ... Played in NHL All-Star Game (1993).

MISCELLANEOUS: Holds Ottawa Senators all-time record for most games played by goaltender (72). ... Stopped a penalty shot attempt (vs. Rick Tocchet, January 6, 1987).

Season Team	League	Gms.	Min	W	L	T	GA	SO	Avg.	Gms.	Min.	W	L	GA	SO	Avg.
82-83—London Diamonds........	OPJHL	23	1338	...	...	...	76	0	3.41	—	—	—	—	—	—	—
83-84—Belleville	OHL	44	2335	20	19	0	162	1	4.16	1	30	0	0	3	0	6.00
84-85—Belleville	OHL	47	2544	26	19	0	180	1	4.25	14	761	7	5	47	†1	3.71

Season Team	League	REGULAR SEASON								PLAYOFFS						
		Gms.	Min	W	L	T	GA	SO	Avg.	Gms.	Min.	W	L	GA	SO	Avg.
85-86—Belleville	OHL	3	180	2	1	0	11	0	3.67	†20	1133	9	6	*68	0	3.60
—New Jersey	NHL	18	701	4	9	1	77	0	6.59	—	—	—	—	—	—	—
86-87—Maine	AHL	20	1151	9	8	2	70	0	3.65	—	—	—	—	—	—	—
—New Jersey	NHL	22	1114	4	13	2	89	0	4.79	—	—	—	—	—	—	—
87-88—Utica	AHL	*59	*3404	22	27	8	*208	1	3.67	—	—	—	—	—	—	—
88-89—New Jersey	NHL	3	140	1	1	0	11	0	4.71	—	—	—	—	—	—	—
—Utica	AHL	41	2432	17	18	6	150	2	3.70	4	219	1	3	18	0	4.93
89-90—Utica	AHL	38	2087	20	13	1	138	0	3.97	—	—	—	—	—	—	—
90-91—Can. national team	Int'l	34	1879	17	14	2	110	2	3.51	—	—	—	—	—	—	—
91-92—New Jersey	NHL	26	1363	13	7	1	69	2	3.04	—	—	—	—	—	—	—
92-93—New Jersey	NHL	42	2389	21	16	4	146	2	3.67	2	78	0	1	5	0	3.85
93-94—Ottawa	NHL	63	3319	11	*41	4	*254	0	4.59	—	—	—	—	—	—	—
94-95—Ottawa	NHL	9	472	0	6	2	32	0	4.07	—	—	—	—	—	—	—
—Boston	NHL	8	373	5	1	0	19	0	3.06	1	25	0	0	1	0	2.40
95-96—Boston	NHL	27	1380	10	13	3	79	1	3.43	1	60	0	1	6	0	6.00
96-97—Colorado	NHL	23	1200	11	8	2	53	1	2.65	1	20	0	0	1	0	3.00
NHL totals (9 years)		241	12451	80	115	19	829	6	3.99	5	183	0	2	13	0	4.26

BIRON, MARTIN   G   SABRES

PERSONAL: Born August 15, 1977, in Lac St. Charles, Que. ... 6-1/154. ... Catches left. ... Name pronounced bih-RAH.
TRANSACTIONS/CAREER NOTES: Selected by Buffalo Sabres in first round (second Sabres pick, 16th overall) of NHL entry draft (July 8, 1995).
HONORS: Won Can.HL Goaltender of the Year Award (1994-95). ... Won Raymond Lagace Trophy (1994-95). ... Won Mike Bossy Trophy (1994-95). ... Won Jacques Plante Trophy (1994-95). ... Named to Can.HL All-Star first team (1994-95). ... Named to Can.HL All-Rookie team (1994-95).

Season Team	League	REGULAR SEASON								PLAYOFFS						
		Gms.	Min	W	L	T	GA	SO	Avg.	Gms.	Min.	W	L	GA	SO	Avg.
94-95—Beauport	QMJHL	56	3193	29	16	9	132	3	2.48	16	902	8	7	37	4	2.46
95-96—Beauport	QMJHL	55	3207	29	17	7	152	1	2.84	*19	1132	*12	†8	64	0	3.39
—Buffalo	NHL	3	119	0	2	0	10	0	5.04	—	—	—	—	—	—	—
96-97—Beauport	QMJHL	18	935	6	10	1	62	1	3.98	—	—	—	—	—	—	—
—Hull	QMJHL	16	972	11	4	1	43	2	2.65	6	326	3	1	19	0	3.50
NHL totals (1 year)		3	119	0	2	0	10	0	5.04							

BLACK, JAMES   C   BLACKHAWKS

PERSONAL: Born August 15, 1969, in Regina, Sask. ... 5-11/185. ... Shoots left.
TRANSACTIONS/CAREER NOTES: Selected by Hartford Whalers in fifth round (fourth Whalers pick, 94th overall) of NHL entry draft (June 17, 1989). ... Traded by Whalers to Minnesota North Stars for C Mark Janssens (September 3, 1992). ... North Stars franchise moved from Minnesota to Dallas and renamed Stars for 1993-94 season. ... Traded by Stars with seventh-round pick in 1994 draft (RW Steve Webb) to Buffalo Sabres for RW Gord Donnelly (December 15, 1993). ... Lacerated forehead (October 27, 1993); missed five games. ... Signed as free agent by Chicago Blackhawks (August 10, 1995).

Season Team	League	REGULAR SEASON							PLAYOFFS				
		Gms.	G	A	Pts.	PIM	+/-	PP	SH	Gms.	G	A	Pts.	PIM
87-88—Portland	WHL	72	30	50	80	50	...	...	...	—	—	—	—	—
88-89—Portland	WHL	71	45	51	96	57	...	...	...	19	13	6	19	28
89-90—Hartford	NHL	1	0	0	0	0	0	0	0	—	—	—	—	—
—Binghamton	AHL	80	37	35	72	34	...	...	...	—	—	—	—	—
90-91—Hartford	NHL	1	0	0	0	0	0	0	0	—	—	—	—	—
—Springfield	AHL	79	35	61	96	34	...	...	...	18	9	9	18	6
91-92—Springfield	AHL	47	15	25	40	33	...	...	...	10	3	2	5	18
—Hartford	NHL	30	4	6	10	10	-4	1	0	—	—	—	—	—
92-93—Minnesota	NHL	10	2	1	3	4	0	0	0	—	—	—	—	—
—Kalamazoo	IHL	63	25	45	70	40	...	...	...	—	—	—	—	—
93-94—Dallas	NHL	13	2	3	5	2	-4	2	0	—	—	—	—	—
—Buffalo	NHL	2	0	0	0	0	0	0	0	—	—	—	—	—
—Rochester	AHL	45	19	32	51	28	...	...	...	4	2	3	5	0
94-95—Las Vegas	IHL	78	29	44	73	54	...	...	...	10	1	6	7	4
95-96—Indianapolis	IHL	67	32	50	82	56	...	...	...	—	—	—	—	—
—Chicago	NHL	13	3	3	6	16	1	0	0	8	1	0	1	2
96-97—Chicago	NHL	64	12	11	23	20	6	0	0	5	1	1	2	2
NHL totals (7 years)		134	23	24	47	52	-1	3	0	13	2	1	3	4

BLACK, JESSE   D   KINGS

PERSONAL: Born June 23, 1978, in Thunder Bay, Ont. ... 6-4/197. ... Shoots right.
TRANSACTIONS/CAREER NOTES: Selected by Los Angeles Kings in fifth round (sixth Kings pick, 120th overall) of NHL entry draft (June 22, 1996).

Season Team	League	REGULAR SEASON							PLAYOFFS				
		Gms.	G	A	Pts.	PIM	+/-	PP	SH	Gms.	G	A	Pts.	PIM
95-96—Niagara Falls	OHL	59	1	3	4	27	...	...	...	10	0	2	2	0
96-97—Erie	OHL	60	1	12	13	102	...	...	...	5	0	1	1	0

BLAKE, ROB   D   KINGS

PERSONAL: Born December 10, 1969, in Simcoe, Ont. ... 6-3/215. ... Shoots right. ... Full name: Robert Bowlby Blake.
COLLEGE: Bowling Green State.
TRANSACTIONS/CAREER NOTES: Dislocated shoulder (April 1987). ... Selected by Los Angeles Kings in fourth round (fourth Kings pick, 70th overall) of NHL entry draft (June 11, 1988). ... Sprained knee (April 1990). ... Injured knee (February 12, 1991); missed two games. ... Injured shoulder (October 8, 1991); missed 11 games. ... Sprained knee ligaments (November 28, 1991); missed six games. ... Suffered from the flu (January 23, 1992); missed one game. ... Suffered from the flu (February 13, 1992); missed one game. ... Strained shoulder (March 14, 1992); missed four games. ... Broke rib (December 19, 1992); missed three games. ... Bruised lower back (April 3, 1993); missed final five games of regular season and one playoff game. ... Strained groin (January 23, 1995); missed 11 games. ... Strained groin (March 11, 1995); missed 12 games. ... Strained groin (April 7, 1995); missed one game. ... Suffered partial tear of left knee ligaments (October 20, 1995); missed 76 games. ... Fractured hand (December 26, 1996); missed 11 games. ... Suspended two games and fined $1,000 by NHL for high sticking incident (February 5, 1997). ... Suffered tendinitis in left knee (February 22, 1997); missed seven games.
HONORS: Named to CCHA All-Star second team (1988-89). ... Named to NCAA All-America West first team (1989-90). ... Named to CCHA All-Star first team (1989-90). ... Named to NHL All-Rookie team (1990-91). ... Played in NHL All-Star Game (1994). ... Named to play in NHL All-Star Game (1997); replaced by LW Dimitri Khristich due to injury.
MISCELLANEOUS: Captain of Los Angeles Kings (1996-97).

			REGULAR SEASON								PLAYOFFS			
Season Team	League	Gms.	G	A	Pts.	PIM	+/-	PP	SH		Gms.	G	A	Pts.	PIM
86-87— Stratford Jr. B	OHA	31	11	20	31	115	...	...	...		—	—	—	—	—
87-88— Bowling Green	CCHA	36	5	8	13	72	...	...	...		—	—	—	—	—
88-89— Bowling Green	CCHA	46	11	21	32	140	...	...	...		—	—	—	—	—
89-90— Bowling Green	CCHA	42	23	36	59	140	...	...	...		—	—	—	—	—
— Los Angeles	NHL	4	0	0	0	4	0	0	0		8	1	3	4	4
90-91— Los Angeles	NHL	75	12	34	46	125	3	9	0		12	1	4	5	26
91-92— Los Angeles	NHL	57	7	13	20	102	-5	5	0		6	2	1	3	12
92-93— Los Angeles	NHL	76	16	43	59	152	18	10	0		23	4	6	10	46
93-94— Los Angeles	NHL	84	20	48	68	137	-7	7	0		—	—	—	—	—
94-95— Los Angeles	NHL	24	4	7	11	38	-16	4	0		—	—	—	—	—
95-96— Los Angeles	NHL	6	1	2	3	8	0	0	0		—	—	—	—	—
96-97— Los Angeles	NHL	62	8	23	31	82	-28	4	0		—	—	—	—	—
NHL totals (8 years)		388	68	170	238	648	-35	39	0		49	8	14	22	88

BLOUIN, SYLVAIN   D   RANGERS

PERSONAL: Born May 21, 1974, in Montreal. ... 6-0/210. ... Shoots left. ... Name pronounced BLOO-an.
TRANSACTIONS/CAREER NOTES: Selected by New York Rangers in fourth round (fifth Rangers pick, 104th overall) of NHL entry draft (June 29, 1994). ... Loaned by Rangers to Chicago Wolves of IHL (October 6, 1994). ... Bruised hand (February 19, 1997); missed two games. ... Suspended three games by AHL as result of match penalty (March 12, 1997).

			REGULAR SEASON								PLAYOFFS			
Season Team	League	Gms.	G	A	Pts.	PIM	+/-	PP	SH		Gms.	G	A	Pts.	PIM
91-92— Laval	QMJHL	28	0	0	0	23	...	...	...		9	0	0	0	35
92-93— Laval	QMJHL	68	0	10	10	373	...	...	...		13	1	0	1	*66
93-94— Laval	QMJHL	62	18	22	40	*492	...	...	...		21	4	13	17	*177
94-95— Binghamton	AHL	10	1	0	1	46	...	...	...		2	0	0	0	24
— Chicago	IHL	1	0	0	0	2	...	...	...		—	—	—	—	—
— Charlotte	ECHL	50	5	7	12	280	...	...	...		3	0	0	0	6
95-96— Binghamton	AHL	71	5	8	13	*352	...	...	...		4	0	3	3	4
96-97— Binghamton	AHL	62	13	17	30	301	...	...	...		4	2	1	3	16
— New York Rangers	NHL	6	0	0	0	18	-1	0	0		—	—	—	—	—
NHL totals (1 year)		6	0	0	0	18	-1	0	0						

BODGER, DOUG   D   SHARKS

PERSONAL: Born June 18, 1966, in Chemainus, B.C. ... 6-2/215. ... Shoots left. ... Name pronounced BAH-juhr.
TRANSACTIONS/CAREER NOTES: Selected by Pittsburgh Penguins as underage junior in first round (second Penguins pick, ninth overall) of NHL entry draft (June 9, 1984). ... Underwent surgery to remove bone chip on left foot (April 1985). ... Sprained knee (December 1987). ... Strained left knee (October 1988). ... Traded by Penguins with LW Darrin Shannon to Buffalo Sabres for G Tom Barrasso and third-round pick (RW Joe Dziedzic) in 1990 draft (November 12, 1988). ... Sprained left knee (October 1989); missed eight games. ... Injured shoulder (December 28, 1990); missed four games. ... Separated left shoulder (February 17, 1991); missed 18 games. ... Reinjured left shoulder (March 30, 1991). ... Injured eye (February 11, 1992); missed seven games. ... Suffered sore back (December 2, 1993); missed four games. ... Suffered from the flu (March 19, 1995); missed one game. ... Bruised shoulder (April 28, 1995); missed last three games of season. ... Traded by Sabres to San Jose Sharks for RW Martin Spanhel and first- (traded to Winnipeg) and fourth-round (traded to Buffalo) picks in 1996 draft (November 16, 1995). ... Injured knee (January 17, 1996); missed three games. ... Injured groin (February 23, 1996); missed four games.
HONORS: Named to WHL All-Star second team (1982-83). ... Named to WHL (West) All-Star first team (1983-84).

			REGULAR SEASON								PLAYOFFS			
Season Team	League	Gms.	G	A	Pts.	PIM	+/-	PP	SH		Gms.	G	A	Pts.	PIM
82-83— Kamloops	WHL	72	26	66	92	98	...	...	...		7	0	5	5	2
83-84— Kamloops	WHL	70	21	77	98	90	...	...	...		17	2	15	17	12
84-85— Pittsburgh	NHL	65	5	26	31	67	-24	3	0		—	—	—	—	—
85-86— Pittsburgh	NHL	79	4	33	37	63	3	1	0		—	—	—	—	—
86-87— Pittsburgh	NHL	76	11	38	49	52	6	5	0		—	—	—	—	—
87-88— Pittsburgh	NHL	69	14	31	45	103	-4	13	0		—	—	—	—	—
88-89— Pittsburgh	NHL	10	1	4	5	7	6	0	0		—	—	—	—	—
— Buffalo	NHL	61	7	40	47	52	9	6	0		5	1	1	2	11
89-90— Buffalo	NHL	71	12	36	48	64	0	8	0		6	1	5	6	6
90-91— Buffalo	NHL	58	5	23	28	54	-8	2	0		4	0	1	1	0
91-92— Buffalo	NHL	73	11	35	46	108	1	4	0		7	2	1	3	2

B

Season Team	League	REGULAR SEASON								PLAYOFFS				
		Gms.	G	A	Pts.	PIM	+/-	PP	SH	Gms.	G	A	Pts.	PIM
92-93— Buffalo	NHL	81	9	45	54	87	14	6	0	8	2	3	5	0
93-94— Buffalo	NHL	75	7	32	39	76	8	5	1	7	0	3	3	6
94-95— Buffalo	NHL	44	3	17	20	47	-3	2	0	5	0	4	4	0
95-96— Buffalo	NHL	16	0	5	5	18	-6	0	0	—	—	—	—	—
— San Jose	NHL	57	4	19	23	50	-18	3	0	—	—	—	—	—
96-97— San Jose	NHL	81	1	15	16	64	-14	0	0	—	—	—	—	—
NHL totals (13 years)		916	94	399	493	912	-30	58	1	42	6	18	24	25

BOHONOS, LONNY   RW   CANUCKS

PERSONAL: Born May 20, 1973, in Winnipeg. ... 5-11/190. ... Shoots right. ... Name pronounced boh-HAH-nohz.
TRANSACTIONS/CAREER NOTES: Signed as free agent by Vancouver Canucks (May 31, 1994).
HONORS: Won Bob Clarke Trophy (1993-94). ... Won Brad Hornung Trophy (1993-94). ... Named to Can.HL All-Star first team (1993-94). ... Named to WHL (West) All-Star first team (1993-94).

Season Team	League	REGULAR SEASON								PLAYOFFS				
		Gms.	G	A	Pts.	PIM	+/-	PP	SH	Gms.	G	A	Pts.	PIM
91-92— Moose Jaw	WHL	8	1	1	2	0	...	...	...	—	—	—	—	—
92-93— Seattle	WHL	46	13	13	26	27	...	...	...	—	—	—	—	—
— Portland	WHL	27	20	17	37	16	...	...	...	15	8	13	21	19
93-94— Portland	WHL	70	*62	*90	*152	80	...	...	...	10	8	11	19	13
94-95— Syracuse	AHL	67	30	45	75	71	...	...	...	—	—	—	—	—
95-96— Syracuse	AHL	74	40	39	79	82	...	...	...	16	14	8	22	16
— Vancouver	NHL	3	0	1	1	0	1	0	0	—	—	—	—	—
96-97— Syracuse	AHL	41	22	30	52	28	...	...	...	3	2	2	4	4
— Vancouver	NHL	36	11	11	22	10	-3	2	0	—	—	—	—	—
NHL totals (2 years)		39	11	12	23	10	-2	2	0					

BOIKOV, ALEXANDRE   D   SHARKS

PERSONAL: Born February 7, 1975, in Chelyabinsk, U.S.S.R. ... 6-0/190. ... Shoots left.
TRANSACTIONS/CAREER NOTES: Signed as free agent by San Jose Sharks (August 26, 1996).

Season Team	League	REGULAR SEASON								PLAYOFFS				
		Gms.	G	A	Pts.	PIM	+/-	PP	SH	Gms.	G	A	Pts.	PIM
95-96— Tri-City	WHL	71	3	49	52	230	...	...	...	11	2	4	6	28
96-97— Kentucky	AHL	76	1	19	20	182	...	...	...	4	0	1	1	4

BOILEAU, PATRICK   D   CAPITALS

PERSONAL: Born February 22, 1975, in Montreal. ... 6-0/190. ... Shoots right. ... Name pronounced BOY-loh.
HIGH SCHOOL: CEGEP Lionel-Groulx (Que.).
TRANSACTIONS/CAREER NOTES: Selected by Washington Capitals in third round (third Capitals pick, 69th overall) of NHL entry draft (June 26, 1993).
HONORS: Named to Can.HL All-Rookie team (1992-93). ... Won Marcel Robert Trophy (1993-94). ... Won Can.HL Scholastic Player of the Year Award (1993-94).

Season Team	League	REGULAR SEASON								PLAYOFFS				
		Gms.	G	A	Pts.	PIM	+/-	PP	SH	Gms.	G	A	Pts.	PIM
92-93— Laval	QMJHL	69	4	19	23	73	...	...	...	13	1	2	3	10
93-94— Laval	QMJHL	64	13	57	70	56	...	...	...	21	1	7	8	24
94-95— Laval	QMJHL	38	8	25	33	46	...	...	...	20	4	16	20	24
95-96— Portland	AHL	78	10	28	38	41	...	...	...	19	1	3	4	12
96-97— Portland	AHL	67	16	28	44	63	...	...	...	5	1	1	2	4
— Washington	NHL	1	0	0	0	0	0	0	0	—	—	—	—	—
NHL totals (1 year)		1	0	0	0	0	0	0	0					

BOMBARDIR, BRAD   D   DEVILS

PERSONAL: Born May 5, 1972, in Powell River, B.C. ... 6-2/190. ... Shoots left. ... Full name: Luke Bradley Bombardir. ... Name pronounced BAHM-bahr-deer.
COLLEGE: North Dakota.
TRANSACTIONS/CAREER NOTES: Selected by New Jersey Devils in third round (fifth Devils pick, 56th overall) of NHL entry draft (June 16, 1990).
HONORS: Named to AHL All-Star second team (1995-96).

Season Team	League	REGULAR SEASON								PLAYOFFS				
		Gms.	G	A	Pts.	PIM	+/-	PP	SH	Gms.	G	A	Pts.	PIM
88-89— Powell River	BCJHL	30	6	5	11	24	...	...	...	6	0	0	0	0
89-90— Powell River	BCJHL	60	10	35	45	93	...	...	...	8	2	3	5	4
90-91— North Dakota	WCHA	33	3	6	9	18	...	...	...	—	—	—	—	—
91-92— North Dakota	WCHA	35	3	14	17	54	...	...	...	—	—	—	—	—
92-93— North Dakota	WCHA	38	8	15	23	34	...	...	...	—	—	—	—	—
93-94— North Dakota	WCHA	38	5	17	22	38	...	...	...	—	—	—	—	—
94-95— Albany	AHL	77	5	22	27	22	...	...	...	14	0	3	3	6
95-96— Albany	AHL	80	6	25	31	63	...	...	...	3	0	1	1	4
96-97— Albany	AHL	32	0	8	8	6	...	...	...	16	1	3	4	8

BONDRA, PETER   RW   CAPITALS

PERSONAL: Born February 7, 1968, in Luck, U.S.S.R. ... 6-1/200. ... Shoots left. ... Name pronounced BAHN-druh.
TRANSACTIONS/CAREER NOTES: Selected by Washington Capitals in eighth round (ninth Capitals pick, 156th overall) of NHL entry draft (June 16, 1990). ... Dislocated left shoulder (January 17, 1991). ... Suffered recurring shoulder problems (February 13, 1991); missed 13 games. ... Injured throat (April 4, 1993); missed one game. ... Broke left hand (November 26, 1993); missed 12 games. ... Played in Europe during 1994-95 NHL lockout. ... Suffered from the flu (April 8, 1995); missed one game. ... Signed by Detroit Vipers of AHL during contract holdout (September 28, 1995); re-signed by Capitals (October 20, 1995). ... Separated shoulder (November 11, 1995); missed six games. ... Pulled groin (February 24, 1996); missed four games. ... Strained groin (December 4, 1996); missed three games. ... Suspended one game and fined $1,000 by NHL for kneeing incident (February 4, 1997). ... Suffered back spasms (April 1, 1997); missed one game.
HONORS: Played in NHL All-Star Game (1993, 1996 and 1997).
STATISTICAL PLATEAUS: Three-goal games: 1993-94 (1), 1994-95 (1), 1995-96 (2), 1996-97 (1). Total: 5. ... Four-goal games: 1995-96 (2), 1996-97 (1). Total: 3. ... Total hat tricks: 8.
MISCELLANEOUS: Failed to score on a penalty shot (vs. Mikhail Shtalenkov, December 13, 1996).

Season Team	League	REGULAR SEASON								PLAYOFFS				
		Gms.	G	A	Pts.	PIM	+/-	PP	SH	Gms.	G	A	Pts.	PIM
88-89— Kosice	Czech.	40	30	10	40	20	...	...	...	—	—	—	—	—
89-90— Kosice	Czech.	42	29	17	46	...	...	...	...	—	—	—	—	—
90-91— Washington	NHL	54	12	16	28	47	-10	4	0	4	0	1	1	2
91-92— Washington	NHL	71	28	28	56	42	16	4	0	7	6	2	8	4
92-93— Washington	NHL	83	37	48	85	70	8	10	0	6	0	6	6	0
93-94— Washington	NHL	69	24	19	43	40	22	4	0	9	2	4	6	4
94-95— HC Kosice	Slovakia	2	1	0	1	0	...	...	...	—	—	—	—	—
— Washington	NHL	47	*34	9	43	24	9	12	*6	7	5	3	8	10
95-96— Detroit	IHL	7	8	1	9	0	...	...	...	—	—	—	—	—
— Washington	NHL	67	52	28	80	40	18	11	4	6	3	2	5	8
96-97— Washington	NHL	77	46	31	77	72	7	10	4	—	—	—	—	—
NHL totals (7 years)		468	233	179	412	335	70	55	14	39	16	18	34	28

BONK, RADEK   C   SENATORS

PERSONAL: Born January 9, 1976, in Kronov, Czechoslovakia. ... 6-3/205. ... Shoots left. ... Name pronounced BAHNK.
TRANSACTIONS/CAREER NOTES: Selected by Ottawa Senators in first round (first Senators pick, third overall) of NHL entry draft (June 28, 1994). ... Injured ankle (April 26, 1995); missed last five games of season. ... Injured hand during 1995-96 season; missed one game. ... Strained abdominal muscle (November 8, 1996); missed six games. ... Broke left wrist (November 23, 1996); missed 23 games.
HONORS: Won Garry F. Longman Memorial Trophy (1993-94).
MISCELLANEOUS: Failed to score on a penalty shot (vs. Daren Puppa, January 13, 1996).

Season Team	League	REGULAR SEASON								PLAYOFFS				
		Gms.	G	A	Pts.	PIM	+/-	PP	SH	Gms.	G	A	Pts.	PIM
90-91— Opava	Czech.	35	47	42	89	25	...	...	...	—	—	—	—	—
91-92— ZPS Zlin	Czech. Div. II	45	47	36	83	30	...	...	...	—	—	—	—	—
92-93— ZPS Zlin	Czech.	30	5	5	10	10	...	...	...	—	—	—	—	—
93-94— Las Vegas	IHL	76	42	45	87	208	...	...	...	5	1	2	3	10
94-95— Las Vegas	IHL	33	7	13	20	62	...	...	...	—	—	—	—	—
— Ottawa	NHL	42	3	8	11	28	-5	1	0	—	—	—	—	—
— Prin. Edward Island	AHL	—	—	—	—	—	...	...	...	1	0	0	0	0
95-96— Ottawa	NHL	76	16	19	35	36	-5	5	0	—	—	—	—	—
96-97— Ottawa	NHL	53	5	13	18	14	-4	0	1	7	0	1	1	4
NHL totals (3 years)		171	24	40	64	78	-14	6	1	7	0	1	1	4

BONSIGNORE, JASON   C   OILERS

PERSONAL: Born April 15, 1976, in Rochester, N.Y. ... 6-4/220. ... Shoots right. ... Name pronounced BAHN-seen-yohr.
TRANSACTIONS/CAREER NOTES: Selected by Edmonton Oilers in first round (first Oilers pick, fourth overall) of NHL entry draft (June 28, 1994). ... Suffered from the flu (October 30, 1995); missed three games.

Season Team	League	REGULAR SEASON								PLAYOFFS				
		Gms.	G	A	Pts.	PIM	+/-	PP	SH	Gms.	G	A	Pts.	PIM
92-93— Newmarket	OHL	66	22	20	42	6	...	...	...	—	—	—	—	—
93-94— Newmarket	OHL	17	7	17	24	22	...	...	...	—	—	—	—	—
— Niagara Falls	OHL	41	15	47	62	41	...	...	...	—	—	—	—	—
— U.S. national team	Int'l	5	0	2	2	0	...	...	...	—	—	—	—	—
94-95— Niagara Falls	OHL	26	12	21	33	51	...	...	...	—	—	—	—	—
— Edmonton	NHL	1	1	0	1	0	-1	0	0	—	—	—	—	—
— Sudbury	OHL	23	15	14	29	45	...	...	...	17	13	10	23	12
95-96— Edmonton	NHL	20	0	2	2	4	-6	0	0	—	—	—	—	—
— Cape Breton	AHL	12	1	4	5	12	...	...	...	—	—	—	—	—
— Sudbury	OHL	18	10	16	26	37	...	...	...	—	—	—	—	—
96-97— Hamilton	AHL	78	21	33	54	78	...	...	...	7	0	0	0	4
NHL totals (2 years)		21	1	2	3	4	-7	0	0	—	—	—	—	—

BONVIE, DENNIS   D   OILERS

PERSONAL: Born July 23, 1973, in Antigonish, N.S. ... 5-11/205. ... Shoots right. ... Name pronounced BAHN-vee.
TRANSACTIONS/CAREER NOTES: Signed as free agent by Edmonton Oilers (August 26, 1994).

B

Season Team	League	REGULAR SEASON Gms.	G	A	Pts.	PIM	+/-	PP	SH	PLAYOFFS Gms.	G	A	Pts.	PIM
90-91— Antigonish..............	N.S.Jr.A					Statistics unavailable.								
91-92— Kitchener	OHL	7	1	1	2	23	...	...	...	—	—	—	—	—
— North Bay..................	OHL	49	0	12	12	261	...	...	...	21	0	1	1	91
92-93— North Bay..................	OHL	64	3	21	24	316	...	...	...	5	0	0	0	34
93-94— Cape Breton..............	AHL	63	1	10	11	278	...	...	...	4	0	0	0	11
94-95— Cape Breton..............	AHL	74	5	15	20	422	...	...	...	—	—	—	—	—
— Edmonton	NHL	2	0	0	0	0	0	0	0	—	—	—	—	—
95-96— Edmonton	NHL	8	0	0	0	47	-3	0	0	—	—	—	—	—
— Cape Breton..............	AHL	38	13	14	27	269	...	...	...	—	—	—	—	—
96-97— Hamilton	AHL	73	9	20	29	*522	...	...	...	22	3	11	14	*91
NHL totals (2 years)		10	0	0	0	47	-3	0	0					

BORDELEAU, SEBASTIEN — C — CANADIENS

PERSONAL: Born February 15, 1975, in Vancouver. ... 5-11/187. ... Shoots right. ... Name pronounced BOHR-dih-loh. ... Son of Paulin Bordeleau, head coach, Fredericton Canadiens of American Hockey League.
TRANSACTIONS/CAREER NOTES: Selected by Montreal Canadiens in third round (third Canadiens pick, 73rd overall) of NHL entry draft (June 26, 1993). ... Pulled groin (January 13, 1997); missed one game.
HONORS: Named to QMJHL All-Star first team (1994-95).

Season Team	League	REGULAR SEASON Gms.	G	A	Pts.	PIM	+/-	PP	SH	PLAYOFFS Gms.	G	A	Pts.	PIM
91-92— Hull............................	QMJHL	62	26	32	58	91	...	...	...	5	0	3	3	23
92-93— Hull............................	QMJHL	60	18	39	57	95	...	...	...	10	3	8	11	20
93-94— Hull............................	QMJHL	60	26	57	83	147	...	...	...	17	6	14	20	26
94-95— Hull............................	QMJHL	68	52	76	128	142	...	...	...	18	13	19	32	25
95-96— Fredericton.................	AHL	43	17	29	46	68	...	...	...	7	0	2	2	8
— Montreal	NHL	4	0	0	0	0	-1	0	0	—	—	—	—	—
96-97— Fredericton.................	AHL	33	17	21	38	50	...	...	...	—	—	—	—	—
— Montreal	NHL	28	2	9	11	2	-3	0	0	—	—	—	—	—
NHL totals (2 years)		32	2	9	11	2	-4	0	0					

BOTTERILL, JASON — LW — STARS

PERSONAL: Born May 19, 1976, in Edmonton. ... 6-3/205. ... Shoots left. ... Name pronounced BAH-tuhr-ihl.
HIGH SCHOOL: St. Paul's Prep (Concord, N.H.).
COLLEGE: Michigan.
TRANSACTIONS/CAREER NOTES: Selected by Dallas Stars in first round (first Stars pick, 20th overall) of NHL entry draft (June 28, 1994).
HONORS: Named to CCHA All-Rookie team (1993-94). ... Named to CCHA All-Star second team (1995-96). ... Named to NCAA All-America West second team (1996-97).

Season Team	League	REGULAR SEASON Gms.	G	A	Pts.	PIM	+/-	PP	SH	PLAYOFFS Gms.	G	A	Pts.	PIM
92-93— St. Paul......................	USHL	22	22	26	48	...	...	...	...	—	—	—	—	—
93-94— Univ. of Michigan.......	CCHA	37	21	19	40	94	...	...	...	—	—	—	—	—
94-95— Univ. of Michigan.......	CCHA	34	14	14	28	117	...	...	...	—	—	—	—	—
95-96— Univ. of Michigan.......	CCHA	37	32	25	57	143	...	...	...	—	—	—	—	—
96-97— Univ. of Michigan.......	CCHA	42	37	24	61	129	...	...	...	—	—	—	—	—

BOUCHARD, JOEL — D — FLAMES

PERSONAL: Born January 23, 1974, in Montreal. ... 6-0/196. ... Shoots left.
TRANSACTIONS/CAREER NOTES: Selected by Calgary Flames in sixth round (sixth Flames pick, 129th overall) of NHL entry draft (June 20, 1992).
HONORS: Named to QMJHL All-Star first team (1993-94).

Season Team	League	REGULAR SEASON Gms.	G	A	Pts.	PIM	+/-	PP	SH	PLAYOFFS Gms.	G	A	Pts.	PIM
90-91— Longueuil....................	QMJHL	53	3	19	22	34	...	...	...	8	0	1	1	11
91-92— Verdun	QMJHL	70	9	37	46	55	...	...	...	19	1	7	8	20
92-93— Verdun	QMJHL	60	10	49	59	126	...	...	...	4	0	2	2	4
93-94— Verdun	QMJHL	60	15	55	70	62	...	...	...	4	1	0	1	6
— Saint John	AHL	1	0	0	0	0	...	...	...	2	0	0	0	0
94-95— Saint John	AHL	77	6	25	31	63	...	...	...	5	1	0	1	4
— Calgary	NHL	2	0	0	0	0	0	0	0	—	—	—	—	—
95-96— Saint John	AHL	74	8	25	33	104	...	...	...	16	1	4	5	10
— Calgary	NHL	4	0	0	0	4	0	0	0	—	—	—	—	—
96-97— Calgary	NHL	76	4	5	9	49	-23	0	1	—	—	—	—	—
NHL totals (3 years)		82	4	5	9	53	-23	0	1					

BOUCHER, BRIAN — G — FLYERS

PERSONAL: Born August 1, 1977, in Woonsocket, R.I. ... 6-1/180. ... Catches left. ... Name pronounced boo-SHAY.
HIGH SCHOOL: Mount St. Charles (Woonsocket, R.I.), then Kamiakin (Kennewick, Wash.).
TRANSACTIONS/CAREER NOTES: Selected by Philadelphia Flyers in first round (first Flyers pick, 22nd overall) of NHL entry draft (July 8, 1995).
HONORS: Named to WHL (West) All-Star second team (1995-96). ... Named to WHL (West) All-Star first team (1996-97). ... Won Del Wilson Trophy (1996-97).

Season Team	League	REGULAR SEASON Gms.	Min	W	L	T	GA	SO	Avg.	PLAYOFFS Gms.	Min.	W	L	GA	SO	Avg.
93-94 — Mount St. Charles.........	R.I.H.S.	26	1170	...	...	...	23	12	0.87	—	—	—	—	—	—	—
94-95 — Wexford....................	Tier II Jr. A	8	425	...	...	...	23	0	3.25	—	—	—	—	—	—	—
— Tri-City....................	WHL	35	1969	17	11	2	108	1	3.29	13	795	6	5	50	0	3.77
95-96 — Tri-City....................	WHL	55	3183	33	19	2	181	1	3.41	11	653	6	5	37	†2	3.40
96-97 — Tri-City....................	WHL	41	2458	10	24	†6	149	1	3.64							

BOUCHER, PHILIPPE   D   KINGS

PERSONAL: Born March 24, 1973, in St. Apollnaire, Que. ... 6-2/188. ... Shoots right. ... Name pronounced fih-LEEP boo-SHAY.

TRANSACTIONS/CAREER NOTES: Selected by Buffalo Sabres in first round (first Sabres pick, 13th overall) of NHL entry draft (June 22, 1991). ... Traded by Sabres with G Grant Fuhr and D Denis Tsygurov to Los Angeles Kings for D Alexei Zhitnik, D Charlie Huddy, G Robb Stauber and fifth-round pick (D Marian Menhart) in 1995 draft (February 14, 1995). ... Sprained wrist (February 25, 1995); missed last 31 games of season. ... Suffered tendinitis in right wrist (October 6, 1995); missed first 25 games of season. ... Injured left hand (February 19, 1996); missed four games. ... Sprained right shoulder (October 4, 1996); missed 10 games.

HONORS: Won Can.HL Rookie of the Year Award (1990-91). ... Won Raymond Lagace Trophy (1990-91). ... Won Michael Bossy Trophy (1990-91). ... Named to QMJHL All-Star second team (1990-91 and 1991-92).

Season Team	League	REGULAR SEASON Gms.	G	A	Pts.	PIM	+/-	PP	SH	PLAYOFFS Gms.	G	A	Pts.	PIM
90-91 — Granby....................	QMJHL	69	21	46	67	92	...	...	...	—	—	—	—	—
91-92 — Granby....................	QMJHL	49	22	37	59	47	...	...	...	—	—	—	—	—
— Laval....................	QMJHL	16	7	11	18	36	...	...	...	10	5	6	11	8
92-93 — Laval....................	QMJHL	16	12	15	27	37	...	...	...	13	6	15	21	12
— Rochester................	AHL	5	4	3	7	8	...	...	...	3	0	1	1	2
— Buffalo....................	NHL	18	0	4	4	14	1	0	0	—	—	—	—	—
93-94 — Buffalo....................	NHL	38	6	8	14	29	-1	4	0	7	1	1	2	2
— Rochester................	AHL	31	10	22	32	51	...	...	...	—	—	—	—	—
94-95 — Rochester................	AHL	43	14	27	41	26	...	...	...	—	—	—	—	—
— Buffalo....................	NHL	9	1	4	5	0	6	0	0	—	—	—	—	—
— Los Angeles..............	NHL	6	1	0	1	4	-3	0	0	—	—	—	—	—
95-96 — Los Angeles..............	NHL	53	7	16	23	31	-26	5	0	—	—	—	—	—
— Phoenix....................	IHL	10	4	3	7	4	...	...	...	—	—	—	—	—
96-97 — Los Angeles..............	NHL	60	7	18	25	25	0	2	0	—	—	—	—	—
NHL totals (5 years)		184	22	50	72	103	-23	11	0	7	1	1	2	2

BOUGHNER, BOB   D   SABRES

PERSONAL: Born March 8, 1971, in Windsor, Ont. ... 6-0/206. ... Shoots right. ... Name pronounced BOOG-nuhr.

TRANSACTIONS/CAREER NOTES: Selected by Detroit Red Wings in second round (second Red Wings pick, 32nd overall) of NHL entry draft (June 17, 1989). ... Signed as free agent by Florida Panthers (August 10, 1994). ... Traded by Panthers to Buffalo Sabres for conditional pick in 1996 draft (February 1, 1996). ... Bruised left thigh (February 28, 1996); missed one game.

Season Team	League	REGULAR SEASON Gms.	G	A	Pts.	PIM	+/-	PP	SH	PLAYOFFS Gms.	G	A	Pts.	PIM
87-88 — St. Mary's Jr. B.........	OHA	36	4	18	22	177	...	...	...	—	—	—	—	—
88-89 — Sault Ste. Marie........	OHL	64	6	15	21	182	...	...	...	—	—	—	—	—
89-90 — Sault Ste. Marie........	OHL	49	7	23	30	122	...	...	...	—	—	—	—	—
90-91 — Sault Ste. Marie........	OHL	64	13	33	46	156	...	...	...	14	2	9	11	35
91-92 — Adirondack..............	AHL	1	0	0	0	7	...	...	...	—	—	—	—	—
— Toledo....................	ECHL	28	3	10	13	79	...	...	...	5	2	0	2	15
92-93 — Adirondack..............	AHL	69	1	16	17	190	...	...	...	—	—	—	—	—
93-94 — Adirondack..............	AHL	72	8	14	22	292	...	...	...	10	1	1	2	18
94-95 — Cincinnati...............	IHL	81	2	14	16	192	...	...	...	10	0	0	0	18
95-96 — Carolina....................	AHL	46	2	15	17	127	...	...	...	—	—	—	—	—
— Buffalo....................	NHL	31	0	1	1	104	3	0	0	—	—	—	—	—
96-97 — Buffalo....................	NHL	77	1	7	8	225	12	0	0	11	0	1	1	9
NHL totals (2 years)		108	1	8	9	329	15	0	0	11	0	1	1	9

BOULERICE, JESSE   D   FLYERS

PERSONAL: Born August 10, 1978, in Plattsburgh, N.Y. ... 6-1/200. ... Shoots right.

TRANSACTIONS/CAREER NOTES: Selected by Philadelphia Flyers in fifth round (fourth Flyers pick, 133rd overall) of NHL entry draft (June 22, 1996).

Season Team	League	REGULAR SEASON Gms.	G	A	Pts.	PIM	+/-	PP	SH	PLAYOFFS Gms.	G	A	Pts.	PIM
95-96 — Detroit....................	OHL	64	2	5	7	150	...	...	...	16	0	0	0	12
96-97 — Detroit....................	OHL	33	10	14	24	209	...	...	...	—	—	—	—	—

BOULIN, VLADISLAV   D   FLYERS

PERSONAL: Born May 18, 1972, in Penza, U.S.S.R. ... 6-4/196. ... Shoots right. ... Name pronounced BOH-lihn.

TRANSACTIONS/CAREER NOTES: Selected by Philadelphia Flyers in fifth round (fourth Flyers pick, 103rd overall) of NHL entry draft (June 20, 1992).

Season Team	League	REGULAR SEASON Gms.	G	A	Pts.	PIM	+/-	PP	SH	PLAYOFFS Gms.	G	A	Pts.	PIM
90-91— Dizelist Penza	USSR Div. II	68	...	...	0	...	...	...	...	—	—	—	—	—
91-92— Dizelist Penza	CIS Div. II						Statistics unavailable.							
92-93— Dynamo Moscow	CIS	32	2	1	3	55	...	...	...	4	0	0	0	2
93-94— Dynamo Moscow	CIS	43	4	2	6	36	...	...	...	7	0	1	1	16
94-95— Hershey	AHL	52	1	7	8	30	...	...	...	—	—	—	—	—
95-96— Hershey	AHL	32	1	2	3	30	...	...	...	2	0	0	0	0
96-97— Philadelphia	AHL	51	1	4	5	35	...	...	...	—	—	—	—	—

BOURQUE, RAY   D   BRUINS

B

PERSONAL: Born December 28, 1960, in Montreal. ... 5-11/215. ... Shoots left. ... Full name: Raymond Jean Bourque. ... Name pronounced BOHRK.

TRANSACTIONS/CAREER NOTES: Selected by Boston Bruins in first round (first Bruins pick, eighth overall) of NHL entry draft (August 9, 1979). ... Broke jaw (November 11, 1980). ... Injured left shoulder (October 1981). ... Fractured left wrist (April 21, 1982). ... Refractured left wrist and fractured left forearm (summer 1982). ... Broke bone over left eye (October 1982). ... Sprained left knee ligaments (December 10, 1988). ... Bruised hip (April 7, 1990). ... Bruised right shoulder (October 17, 1990); missed four games. ... Fractured finger (May 5, 1992); missed remainder of playoffs. ... Injured back (December 19, 1992); missed two games. ... Injured ankle (January 21, 1993); missed three games. ... Injured knee (March 22, 1994); missed 11 games. ... Bruised shoulder (October 20, 1996); missed nine games. ... Strained abdominal muscle (December 14, 1996); missed five games. ... Bruised ankle (March 6, 1997); missed three games. ... Injured ankle (March 17, 1997); missed three games.

HONORS: Named to QMJHL All-Star first team (1977-78 and 1978-79). ... Won Frank J. Selke Trophy (1978-79). ... Won Emile (Butch) Bouchard Trophy (1978-79). ... Named NHL Rookie of the Year by THE SPORTING NEWS (1979-80). ... Won Calder Memorial Trophy (1979-80). ... Named to NHL All-Star first team (1979-80, 1981-82, 1983-84, 1984-85, 1986-87, 1987-88, and 1989-90 through 1993-92 and 1995-96). ... Named to THE SPORTING NEWS All-Star second team (1980-81, 1982-83, 1985-86 and 1988-89). ... Named to NHL All-Star second team (1980-81, 1982-83, 1985-86, 1988-89 and 1994-95). ... Played in NHL All-Star Game (1981-1986, 1988-1994, 1996 and 1997). ... Named to THE SPORTING NEWS All-Star first team (1981-82, 1983-84, 1984-85, 1986-87, 1987-88 and 1989-90 through 1995-96). ... Won James Norris Memorial Trophy (1986-87, 1987-88, 1989-90, 1990-91 and 1993-94). ... Won King Clancy Memorial Trophy (1991-92). ... Named All-Star Game Most Valuable Player (1996).

STATISTICAL PLATEAUS: Three-goal games: 1982-83 (1).

MISCELLANEOUS: Co-captain of Boston Bruins (1985-86 through 1987-88). ... Captain of Bruins (1988-89 through 1996-97). ... Holds Boston Bruins all-time records for most assists (1,000) and most points (1,362). ... Scored on a penalty shot (vs. Chris Terreri, March 19, 1994). ... Failed to score on a penalty shot (vs. John Vanbiesbrouck, November 11, 1988).

Season Team	League	REGULAR SEASON Gms.	G	A	Pts.	PIM	+/-	PP	SH	PLAYOFFS Gms.	G	A	Pts.	PIM
76-77— Sorel	QMJHL	69	12	36	48	61	...	...	...	—	—	—	—	—
77-78— Verdun	QMJHL	72	22	57	79	90	...	...	...	4	2	1	3	0
78-79— Verdun	QMJHL	63	22	71	93	44	...	...	...	11	3	16	19	18
79-80— Boston	NHL	80	17	48	65	73	...	3	2	10	2	9	11	27
80-81— Boston	NHL	67	27	29	56	96	29	9	1	3	0	1	1	2
81-82— Boston	NHL	65	17	49	66	51	22	4	0	9	1	5	6	16
82-83— Boston	NHL	65	22	51	73	20	49	7	0	17	8	15	23	10
83-84— Boston	NHL	78	31	65	96	57	51	12	1	3	0	2	2	0
84-85— Boston	NHL	73	20	66	86	53	30	10	1	5	0	3	3	4
85-86— Boston	NHL	74	19	57	76	68	17	11	0	3	0	0	0	0
86-87— Boston	NHL	78	23	72	95	36	44	6	1	4	1	2	3	0
87-88— Boston	NHL	78	17	64	81	72	34	7	1	23	3	18	21	26
88-89— Boston	NHL	60	18	43	61	52	20	6	0	10	0	4	4	6
89-90— Boston	NHL	76	19	65	84	50	31	8	0	17	5	12	17	16
90-91— Boston	NHL	76	21	73	94	75	33	7	0	19	7	18	25	12
91-92— Boston	NHL	80	21	60	81	56	11	7	1	12	3	6	9	12
92-93— Boston	NHL	78	19	63	82	40	38	8	0	4	1	0	1	2
93-94— Boston	NHL	72	20	71	91	58	26	10	3	13	2	8	10	0
94-95— Boston	NHL	46	12	31	43	20	3	9	0	5	0	3	3	0
95-96— Boston	NHL	82	20	62	82	58	31	9	2	5	1	6	7	2
96-97— Boston	NHL	62	19	31	50	18	-11	8	1	—	—	—	—	—
NHL totals (18 years)		1290	362	1000	1362	953	...	141	14	162	34	112	146	135

BOWEN, JASON   D   FLYERS

PERSONAL: Born November 11, 1973, in Courtenay, B.C. ... 6-4/208. ... Shoots left. ... Name pronounced BOH-ihn.

TRANSACTIONS/CAREER NOTES: Selected by Philadelphia Flyers in first round (second Flyers pick, 15th overall) of NHL entry draft (June 20, 1992). ... Suffered from hyphema in left eye (November 18, 1993); missed eight games. ... Separated left shoulder (January 30, 1994); missed 14 games.

Season Team	League	REGULAR SEASON Gms.	G	A	Pts.	PIM	+/-	PP	SH	PLAYOFFS Gms.	G	A	Pts.	PIM
89-90— Tri-City	WHL	61	8	5	13	129	...	...	...	7	0	3	3	4
90-91— Tri-City	WHL	60	7	13	20	252	...	...	...	6	2	2	4	18
91-92— Tri-City	WHL	19	5	3	8	135	...	...	...	5	0	1	1	42
92-93— Tri-City	WHL	62	10	12	22	219	...	...	...	3	1	1	2	18
— Philadelphia	NHL	7	1	0	1	2	1	0	0	—	—	—	—	—
93-94— Philadelphia	NHL	56	1	5	6	87	12	0	0	—	—	—	—	—
94-95— Hershey	AHL	55	5	5	10	116	...	...	...	6	0	0	0	46
— Philadelphia	NHL	4	0	0	0	0	-2	0	0	—	—	—	—	—
95-96— Hershey	AHL	72	6	7	13	128	...	...	...	4	2	0	2	13
— Philadelphia	NHL	2	0	0	0	2	0	0	0	—	—	—	—	—
96-97— Philadelphia	AHL	61	10	12	22	160	...	...	...	6	0	1	1	10
— Philadelphia	NHL	4	0	1	1	8	1	0	0	—	—	—	—	—
NHL totals (5 years)		73	2	6	8	99	12	0	0					

BOYER, ZAC   RW

PERSONAL: Born October 25, 1971, in Inuvik, Northwest Territories. ... 6-1/199. ... Shoots right.
TRANSACTIONS/CAREER NOTES: Selected by Chicago Blackhawks in fourth round (sixth Blackhawks pick, 88th overall) of NHL entry draft (June 22, 1991). ... Signed as free agent by Dallas Stars (July 25, 1994). ... Signed as free agent by Orlando Solar Bears of IHL (September 9, 1996).

		REGULAR SEASON							PLAYOFFS				
Season Team	League	Gms.	G	A	Pts.	PIM	+/-	PP	SH	Gms.	G	A	Pts.	PIM
87-88— St. Albert	AJHL	55	16	31	47	258	...	...	...	—	—	—	—	—
88-89— Kamloops	WHL	42	10	17	27	22	...	...	...	16	9	8	17	10
89-90— Kamloops	WHL	71	24	47	71	63	...	...	...	17	4	4	8	8
90-91— Kamloops	WHL	64	45	60	105	58	...	...	...	12	6	10	16	8
91-92— Kamloops	WHL	70	40	69	109	90	...	...	...	17	9	*20	*29	16
92-93— Indianapolis	IHL	59	7	14	21	26	...	...	...	—	—	—	—	—
93-94— Indianapolis	IHL	54	13	12	25	67	...	...	...	—	—	—	—	—
94-95— Kalamazoo	IHL	22	9	7	16	22	...	...	...	15	3	9	12	8
— Dallas	NHL	1	0	0	0	0	0	0	0	2	0	0	0	0
95-96— Michigan	IHL	67	24	27	51	58	...	...	...	10	11	6	17	0
— Dallas	NHL	2	0	0	0	0	0	0	0	—	—	—	—	—
96-97— Orlando	IHL	80	25	49	74	63	...	...	...	3	0	1	1	2
NHL totals (2 years)		3	0	0	0	0	0	0	0	2	0	0	0	0

BRADLEY, BRIAN   C   LIGHTNING

PERSONAL: Born January 21, 1965, in Kitchener, Ont. ... 5-10/177. ... Shoots right. ... Full name: Brian Walter Richard Bradley.
TRANSACTIONS/CAREER NOTES: Selected by Calgary Flames as underage junior in third round (second Flames pick, 51st overall) of NHL entry draft (June 8, 1983). ... Traded by Flames with RW Peter Bakovic and future considerations to Vancouver Canucks for C Craig Coxe (March 6, 1988); Canucks received D Kevan Guy to complete deal. ... Bruised knee (January 1989). ... Broke thumb knuckle (February 1, 1990); missed seven games. ... Traded by Canucks to Toronto Maple Leafs for D Tom Kurvers (January 12, 1991). ... Sprained ankle (November 10, 1991); missed six games. ... Suffered back spasms (December 10, 1991); missed two games. ... Selected by Tampa Bay Lightning in NHL expansion draft (June 18, 1992). ... Suffered injury (October 6, 1993); missed three games. ... Injured shoulder (October 22, 1993); missed one game. ... Suffered from the flu (January 4, 1994); missed one game. ... Suffered charley horse (February 17, 1995); missed two games. ... Bruised foot (October 15, 1995); missed one game. ... Bruised right knee (October 31, 1995); missed one game. ... Suffered hip pointer (January 6, 1996); missed one game. ... Bruised left knee (March 7, 1996); missed one game. ... Injured back (March 30, 1996); missed one game. ... Injured left knee (April 6, 1996); missed one game. ... Injured left knee (April 12, 1996); missed one game. ... Sprained left knee (October 31, 1996); missed one game. ... Reinjured knee (November 4, 1996); missed four games. ... Strained left knee (November 23, 1996); missed four games. ... Injured wrist (January 9, 1997); missed 37 games.
HONORS: Played in NHL All-Star Game (1993 and 1994).
STATISTICAL PLATEAUS: Three-goal games: 1992-93 (1).
MISCELLANEOUS: Captain of Tampa Bay Lightning (1994-95). ... Holds Tampa Bay Lightning all-time records for most goals (109), most assists (184) and most points (293). ... Failed to score on a penalty shot (vs. Felix Potvin, October 22, 1992; vs. Sean Burke, April 3, 1996).

		REGULAR SEASON							PLAYOFFS				
Season Team	League	Gms.	G	A	Pts.	PIM	+/-	PP	SH	Gms.	G	A	Pts.	PIM
81-82— London	OHL	62	34	44	78	34	...	...	...	—	—	—	—	—
82-83— London	OHL	67	37	82	119	37	...	...	...	3	1	0	1	0
83-84— London	OHL	49	40	60	100	24	...	...	...	4	2	4	6	0
84-85— London	OHL	32	27	49	76	22	...	...	...	8	5	10	15	4
85-86— Calgary	NHL	5	0	1	1	0	-3	0	0	1	0	0	0	0
— Moncton	AHL	59	23	42	65	40	...	...	...	10	6	9	15	4
86-87— Moncton	AHL	20	12	16	28	8	...	...	...	—	—	—	—	—
— Calgary	NHL	40	10	18	28	16	6	2	0	—	—	—	—	—
87-88— Canadian nat'l team	Int'l	47	18	19	37	42	...	...	...	—	—	—	—	—
— Can. Olympic team	Int'l	7	0	4	4	0	...	...	...	—	—	—	—	—
— Vancouver	NHL	11	3	5	8	6	...	...	...	—	—	—	—	—
88-89— Vancouver	NHL	71	18	27	45	42	-5	6	0	7	3	4	7	10
89-90— Vancouver	NHL	67	19	29	48	65	5	2	0	—	—	—	—	—
90-91— Vancouver	NHL	44	11	20	31	42	-2	3	0	—	—	—	—	—
— Toronto	NHL	26	0	11	11	20	-7	0	0	—	—	—	—	—
91-92— Toronto	NHL	59	10	21	31	48	-3	4	0	—	—	—	—	—
92-93— Tampa Bay	NHL	80	42	44	86	92	-24	16	0	—	—	—	—	—
93-94— Tampa Bay	NHL	78	24	40	64	56	-8	6	0	—	—	—	—	—
94-95— Tampa Bay	NHL	46	13	27	40	42	-6	3	0	—	—	—	—	—
95-96— Tampa Bay	NHL	75	23	56	79	77	-11	9	0	5	0	3	3	6
96-97— Tampa Bay	NHL	35	7	17	24	16	2	1	2	—	—	—	—	—
NHL totals (12 years)		637	180	316	496	522	-56	52	2	13	3	7	10	16

BRADLEY, MATT   RW   SHARKS

PERSONAL: Born June 13, 1978, in Stittsville, Ont. ... 6-1/168. ... Shoots right.
TRANSACTIONS/CAREER NOTES: Selected by San Jose Sharks in fourth round (fourth Sharks pick, 102nd overall) of NHL entry draft (June 22, 1996).

		REGULAR SEASON							PLAYOFFS				
Season Team	League	Gms.	G	A	Pts.	PIM	+/-	PP	SH	Gms.	G	A	Pts.	PIM
94-95— Cumberland	CJHL	49	13	20	33	18	...	...	...	—	—	—	—	—
95-96— Kingston	OHL	55	10	14	24	17	...	...	...	6	0	1	1	6
96-97— Kingston	OHL	65	24	24	48	41	...	...	...	5	0	4	4	2
— Kentucky	AHL	1	0	1	1	0	...	...	...	—	—	—	—	—

B

BRASHEAR, DONALD   LW   CANUCKS

PERSONAL: Born January 7, 1972, in Bedford, Ind. ... 6-2/220. ... Shoots left. ... Name pronounced bra-SHEER.

TRANSACTIONS/CAREER NOTES: Signed as free agent by Montreal Canadiens (July 28, 1992). ... Bruised knee (November 23, 1993); missed one game. ... Injured shoulder (February 27, 1995); missed one game. ... Bruised hand (March 20, 1995); missed one game. ... Suffered cut to right thigh (December 30, 1995); missed seven games. ... Traded by Canadiens to Vancouver Canucks for D Jassen Cullimore (November 13, 1996). ... Strained back (February 8, 1997); missed three games. ... Suspended four games and fined $1,000 by NHL for fighting (February 25, 1997).

						REGULAR SEASON								PLAYOFFS		
Season Team	League	Gms.	G	A	Pts.	PIM	+/-	PP	SH		Gms.	G	A	Pts.	PIM
89-90— Longueuil	QMJHL	64	12	14	26	169	...	...	...		7	0	0	0	11
90-91— Longueuil	QMJHL	68	12	26	38	195	...	...	...		8	0	3	3	33
91-92— Verdun	QMJHL	65	18	24	42	283	...	...	...		18	4	2	6	98
92-93— Fredericton	AHL	76	11	3	14	261	...	...	...		5	0	0	0	8
93-94— Fredericton	AHL	62	38	28	66	250	...	...	...		—	—	—	—	—
— Montreal	NHL	14	2	2	4	34	0	0	0		2	0	0	0	0
94-95— Montreal	NHL	20	1	1	2	63	-5	0	0		—	—	—	—	—
— Fredericton	AHL	29	10	9	19	182	...	...	...		17	7	5	12	77
95-96— Montreal	NHL	67	0	4	4	223	-10	0	0		6	0	0	0	2
96-97— Montreal	NHL	10	0	0	0	38	-2	0	0		—	—	—	—	—
— Vancouver	NHL	59	8	5	13	207	-6	0	0		—	—	—	—	—
NHL totals (4 years)		170	11	12	23	565	-23	0	0		8	0	0	0	2

BRATHWAITE, FRED   G

PERSONAL: Born November 24, 1972, in Ottawa. ... 5-7/170. ... Catches left. ... Name pronounced BRATH-wayt.

TRANSACTIONS/CAREER NOTES: Signed as free agent by Las Vegas Thunder (August 18, 1993). ... Signed as free agent by Edmonton Oilers (October 6, 1993).

STATISTICAL NOTES: Led OHL with 3.31 goals against average and four shutouts (1991-92).

						REGULAR SEASON						PLAYOFFS					
Season Team	League	Gms.	Min	W	L	T	GA	SO	Avg.		Gms.	Min.	W	L	GA	SO	Avg.
89-90— Oshawa	OHL	20	901	11	2	1	45	1	3.00		10	451	4	2	22	0	*2.93
90-91— Oshawa	OHL	39	1986	25	6	3	112	1	3.38		13	677	*9	2	43	0	3.81
91-92— Oshawa	OHL	24	1248	12	7	2	81	0	3.89		—	—	—	—	—	—	—
— London	OHL	23	1325	23	10	4	61	§4	§2.76		10	615	5	5	36	0	3.51
92-93— Detroit	OHL	37	2192	23	10	4	134	0	3.67		15	858	9	6	48	1	3.36
93-94— Cape Breton	AHL	2	119	1	1	0	6	0	3.03		—	—	—	—	—	—	—
— Edmonton	NHL	19	982	3	10	3	58	0	3.54		—	—	—	—	—	—	—
94-95— Edmonton	NHL	14	601	2	5	1	40	0	3.99		—	—	—	—	—	—	—
95-96— Cape Breton	AHL	31	1699	12	16	0	110	1	3.88		—	—	—	—	—	—	—
— Edmonton	NHL	7	293	0	2	0	12	0	2.46		—	—	—	—	—	—	—
96-97— Manitoba	IHL	58	2945	22	22	‡5	167	1	3.40		—	—	—	—	—	—	—
NHL totals (3 years)		40	1876	5	17	4	110	0	3.52								

BRENNAN, RICH   D   SHARKS

PERSONAL: Born November 26, 1972, in Schenectady, N.Y. ... 6-2/200. ... Shoots right.

HIGH SCHOOL: Albany (N.Y.) Academy, then Tabor Academy (Marion, Mass.).

COLLEGE: Boston University.

TRANSACTIONS/CAREER NOTES: Selected by Quebec Nordiques in third round (third Nordiques pick, 56th overall) of NHL entry draft (June 22, 1991). ... Nordiques franchise moved to Colorado and renamed Avalanche for 1995-96 season (June 21, 1995). ... Signed as free agent by San Jose Sharks (July 9, 1997).

HONORS: Named to Hockey East All-Star first team (1993-94).

						REGULAR SEASON								PLAYOFFS		
Season Team	League	Gms.	G	A	Pts.	PIM	+/-	PP	SH		Gms.	G	A	Pts.	PIM
88-89— Albany Academy	N.Y. H.S.	25	17	30	47	57	...	...	...		—	—	—	—	—
89-90— Tabor Academy	Mass. H.S.	33	12	14	26	68	...	...	...		—	—	—	—	—
90-91— Tabor Academy	Mass. H.S.	34	13	37	50	91	...	...	...		—	—	—	—	—
91-92— Boston University	Hockey East	31	4	13	17	54	...	...	...		—	—	—	—	—
92-93— Boston University	Hockey East	40	9	11	20	68	...	...	...		—	—	—	—	—
93-94— Boston University	Hockey East	41	8	27	35	82	...	...	...		—	—	—	—	—
94-95— Boston University	Hockey East	31	5	23	28	56	...	...	...		—	—	—	—	—
95-96— Brantford	Col.HL	5	1	2	3	2	...	...	...		—	—	—	—	—
96-97— Hershey	AHL	74	11	45	56	88	...	...	...		23	2	†16	18	0
— Colorado	NHL	2	0	0	0	0	0	0	0		—	—	—	—	—
NHL totals (1 year)		2	0	0	0	0	0	0	0						

BRIMANIS, ARIS   D   FLYERS

PERSONAL: Born March 14, 1972, in Cleveland. ... 6-3/195. ... Shoots right. ... Full name: Aris Aldis Brimanis. ... Name pronounced AIR-ihz brih-MAN-ihz.

HIGH SCHOOL: Culver (Ind.) Military Academy.

COLLEGE: Bowling Green State.

TRANSACTIONS/CAREER NOTES: Selected by Philadelphia Flyers in fourth round (third Flyers pick, 86th overall) of NHL entry draft (June 22, 1991).

		REGULAR SEASON								PLAYOFFS				
Season Team	League	Gms.	G	A	Pts.	PIM	+/-	PP	SH	Gms.	G	A	Pts.	PIM
88-89— Culver Military	Indiana H.S.	38	10	13	23	24	...	...	...	—	—	—	—	—
89-90— Culver Military	Indiana H.S.	37	15	10	25	52	...	...	...	—	—	—	—	—
90-91— Bowling Green	CCHA	38	3	6	9	42	...	...	...	—	—	—	—	—
91-92— Bowling Green	CCHA	32	2	9	11	38	...	...	...	—	—	—	—	—
92-93— Brandon	WHL	71	8	50	58	110	...	...	...	4	2	1	3	12
93-94— Hershey	AHL	75	8	15	23	65	...	...	...	11	2	3	5	12
— Philadelphia	NHL	1	0	0	0	0	-1	0	0	—	—	—	—	—
94-95— Hershey	AHL	76	8	17	25	68	...	...	...	6	1	1	2	14
95-96— Hershey	AHL	54	9	22	31	64	...	...	...	5	1	2	3	4
— Philadelphia	NHL	17	0	2	2	12	-1	0	0	—	—	—	—	—
96-97— Philadelphia	AHL	65	14	18	32	69	...	...	...	10	2	2	4	13
— Philadelphia	NHL	3	0	1	1	0	0	0	0	—	—	—	—	—
NHL totals (3 years)		21	0	3	3	12	-2	0	0					

BRIND'AMOUR, ROD — C/LW — FLYERS

PERSONAL: Born August 9, 1970, in Ottawa. ... 6-1/200. ... Shoots left. ... Full name: Rod Jean Brind'Amour. ... Name pronounced BRIHN-duh-MOHR.
COLLEGE: Michigan State.
TRANSACTIONS/CAREER NOTES: Broke wrist (November 1985). ... Selected by St. Louis Blues in first round (first Blues pick, ninth overall) of NHL entry draft (June 11, 1988). ... Traded by Blues with C Dan Quinn to Philadelphia Flyers for C Ron Sutter and D Murray Baron (September 22, 1991). ... Lacerated elbow (November 19, 1992); missed two games. ... Bruised right hand (February 20, 1993); missed one game.
HONORS: Named CCHA Rookie of the Year (1988-89). ... Named to CCHA All-Rookie team (1988-89). ... Named to NHL All-Rookie team (1989-90). ... Played in NHL All-Star Game (1992).
STATISTICAL PLATEAUS: Three-goal games: 1992-93 (1).

		REGULAR SEASON								PLAYOFFS				
Season Team	League	Gms.	G	A	Pts.	PIM	+/-	PP	SH	Gms.	G	A	Pts.	PIM
87-88— Notre Dame	SJHL	56	46	61	107	136	...	...	...	—	—	—	—	—
88-89— Michigan State..........	CCHA	42	27	32	59	63	...	...	...	—	—	—	—	—
— St. Louis	NHL	—	—	—	—	—	—	—	—	5	2	0	2	4
89-90— St. Louis	NHL	79	26	35	61	46	23	10	0	12	5	8	13	6
90-91— St. Louis	NHL	78	17	32	49	93	2	4	0	13	2	5	7	10
91-92— Philadelphia	NHL	80	33	44	77	100	-3	8	4	—	—	—	—	—
92-93— Philadelphia	NHL	81	37	49	86	89	-8	13	4	—	—	—	—	—
93-94— Philadelphia	NHL	84	35	62	97	85	-9	14	1	—	—	—	—	—
94-95— Philadelphia	NHL	48	12	27	39	33	-4	4	1	15	6	9	15	8
95-96— Philadelphia	NHL	82	26	61	87	110	20	4	4	12	2	5	7	6
96-97— Philadelphia	NHL	82	27	32	59	41	2	8	2	19	13	8	21	10
NHL totals (9 years)		614	213	342	555	597	23	65	16	76	30	35	65	44

BRISEBOIS, PATRICE — D — CANADIENS

PERSONAL: Born January 27, 1971, in Montreal. ... 6-1/188. ... Shoots right. ... Name pronounced pa-TREEZ BREES-bwah.
TRANSACTIONS/CAREER NOTES: Underwent surgery on fractured right thumb (February 1988). ... Tore ligaments in left knee (March 1988). ... Broke left thumb (August 1988). ... Selected by Montreal Canadiens in second round (second Canadiens pick, 30th overall) of NHL entry draft (June 17, 1989). ... Traded by Laval Titans with LW Allen Kerr to Drummondville Voltigeurs for second- and third-round picks in 1990 QMJHL draft (May 26, 1990). ... Sprained right ankle (October 10, 1992); missed two games. ... Suffered charley horse (December 16, 1992); missed two games. ... Injured knee (October 30, 1993); missed 10 games. ... Suffered hairline fracture of ankle (December 1, 1993); missed 14 games. ... Sprained ankle (February 21, 1994); missed seven games. ... Suffered acute herniated disc (April 3, 1995); missed 12 games. ... Injured rib cage (November 1, 1995). ... Sprained back (February 17, 1996); missed four games. ... Suffered mild disc irritation (March 25, 1996); missed last nine games of regular season. ... Separated shoulder (January 4, 1997); missed 27 games. ... Strained shoulder (March 22, 1997); missed four games. ... Injured rib (April 10, 1997); missed remainder of regular season and two playoff games.
HONORS: Won Michael Bossy Trophy (1988-89). ... Named to QMJHL All-Star second team (1989-90). ... Won Can.HL Defenseman of the Year Award (1990-91). ... Won Emile (Butch) Bouchard Trophy (1990-91). ... Named to QMJHL All-Star first team (1990-91). ... Named to Memorial Cup All-Star team (1990-91).
MISCELLANEOUS: Member of Stanley Cup championship team (1993).

		REGULAR SEASON								PLAYOFFS				
Season Team	League	Gms.	G	A	Pts.	PIM	+/-	PP	SH	Gms.	G	A	Pts.	PIM
87-88— Laval	QMJHL	48	10	34	44	95	...	...	...	6	0	2	2	2
88-89— Laval	QMJHL	50	20	45	65	95	...	...	...	17	8	14	22	45
89-90— Laval	QMJHL	56	18	70	88	108	...	...	...	13	7	9	16	26
90-91— Montreal	NHL	10	0	2	2	4	1	0	0	—	—	—	—	—
— Drummondville	QMJHL	54	17	44	61	72	...	...	...	14	6	18	24	49
91-92— Fredericton................	AHL	53	12	27	39	51	...	...	...	—	—	—	—	—
— Montreal	NHL	26	2	8	10	20	9	0	0	11	2	4	6	6
92-93— Montreal	NHL	70	10	21	31	79	6	4	0	20	0	4	4	18
93-94— Montreal	NHL	53	2	21	23	63	5	1	0	7	0	4	4	6
94-95— Montreal	NHL	35	4	8	12	26	-2	0	0	—	—	—	—	—
95-96— Montreal	NHL	69	9	27	36	65	10	3	0	6	1	2	3	6
96-97— Montreal	NHL	49	2	13	15	24	-7	0	0	3	1	1	2	24
NHL totals (7 years)		312	29	100	129	281	22	8	0	47	4	15	19	60

BRISKE, BYRON — D — MIGHTY DUCKS

PERSONAL: Born January 23, 1976, in Humboldt, Sask. ... 6-3/195. ... Shoots right. ... Name pronounced BRIH-skee.
HIGH SCHOOL: Lindsay Thurber (Red Deer, Alta.).

TRANSACTIONS/CAREER NOTES: Selected by Mighty Ducks of Anaheim in fourth round (fourth Mighty Ducks pick, 80th overall) of NHL entry draft (June 29, 1994).

		REGULAR SEASON								PLAYOFFS				
Season Team	League	Gms.	G	A	Pts.	PIM	+/-	PP	SH	Gms.	G	A	Pts.	PIM
91-92— Victoria	WHL	1	0	0	0	0	...	...	...	—	—	—	—	—
92-93— Victoria	WHL	66	1	10	11	110	...	...	...	—	—	—	—	—
93-94— Red Deer	WHL	61	6	21	27	174	...	...	...	—	—	—	—	—
94-95— Red Deer	WHL	48	4	17	21	116	...	...	...	—	—	—	—	—
— Tri-City	WHL	15	0	1	1	22	...	...	...	13	0	0	0	18
95-96— Tri-City	WHL	72	15	38	53	189	...	...	...	11	0	5	5	36
96-97— Baltimore	AHL	69	0	6	6	131	...	...	...	1	0	0	0	0

BRODEUR, MARTIN — G — DEVILS

PERSONAL: Born May 6, 1972, in Montreal. ... 6-1/205. ... Catches left. ... Name pronounced MAHR-tai broh-DOOR.
TRANSACTIONS/CAREER NOTES: Suffered pinched nerve in elbow and slight concussion (March 9, 1990). ... Selected by New Jersey Devils in first round (first Devils pick, 20th overall) of NHL entry draft (June 16, 1990). ... Strained knee (February 24, 1994).
HONORS: Named to QMJHL All-Star second team (1991-92). ... Won Calder Memorial Trophy (1993-94). ... Named to NHL All-Rookie team (1993-94). ... Played in NHL All-Star Game (1996 and 1997). ... Named to NHL All-Star second team (1996-97). ... Shared William M. Jennings Trophy with Mike Dunham (1996 and 97).
RECORDS: Holds NHL single-season record for most minutes played by goaltender—4,434 (1995-96). ... Shares NHL single-season playoff record for most wins by goaltender—16 (1995).
MISCELLANEOUS: Member of Stanley Cup championship team (1995). ... Holds New Jersey Devils franchise all-time records for most wins (119), most shutouts (22) and goals-against average (2.25).

		REGULAR SEASON							PLAYOFFS					
Season Team	League	Gms.	Min.	W	L	T	GA	SO	Avg.	Gms.	Min.	W	L	GA	SO	Avg.
89-90— St. Hyacinthe	QMJHL	42	2333	23	13	2	156	0	4.01	12	678	5	7	46	0	4.07
90-91— St. Hyacinthe	QMJHL	52	2946	22	24	4	162	2	3.30	4	232	0	4	16	0	4.14
91-92— St. Hyacinthe	QMJHL	48	2846	27	16	4	161	2	3.39	5	317	2	3	14	0	2.65
—New Jersey	NHL	4	179	2	1	0	10	0	3.35	1	32	0	1	3	0	5.63
92-93— Utica	AHL	32	1952	14	13	5	131	0	4.03	4	258	1	3	18	0	4.19
93-94— New Jersey	NHL	47	2625	27	11	8	105	3	2.40	17	1171	8	†9	38	1	1.95
94-95— New Jersey	NHL	40	2184	19	11	6	89	3	2.45	*20	*1222	*16	4	34	*3	*1.67
95-96— New Jersey	NHL	77	*4434	34	†30	12	173	6	2.34	—	—	—	—	—	—	—
96-97— New Jersey	NHL	67	3838	37	14	13	120	*10	*1.88	10	659	5	5	19	2	1.73
NHL totals (5 years)		235	13260	119	67	39	497	22	2.25	48	3084	29	19	94	6	1.83

BROTEN, NEAL — C — STARS

PERSONAL: Born November 29, 1959, in Roseau, Minn. ... 5-9/175. ... Shoots left. ... Full name: Neal LaMoy Broten. ... Name pronounced BRAH-tuhn. ... Brother of Aaron Broten, center/left winger for six NHL teams (1980-81 through 1991-92); and brother of Paul Broten, right winger in St Louis Blues organization.
HIGH SCHOOL: Roseau (Minn.).
COLLEGE: Minnesota.
TRANSACTIONS/CAREER NOTES: Selected by Minnesota North Stars in second round (third North Stars pick, 42nd overall) of NHL entry draft (August 9, 1979). ... Fractured ankle (December 26, 1981). ... Dislocated shoulder (October 30, 1986). ... Tore shoulder ligaments (March 1987). ... Separated shoulder (November 1987). ... Underwent reconstructive shoulder surgery (February 1988). ... Suffered sterno-clavicular sprain (February 14, 1989). ... Strained groin (December 18, 1990). ... North Stars franchise moved from Minnesota to Dallas and renamed Stars for 1993-94 season. ... Pulled hip muscle (October 9, 1993); missed two games. ... Traded by Stars to New Jersey Devils for C Corey Millen (February 27, 1995). ... Bruised knee (November 11, 1995); missed one game. ... Sprained left ankle (February 16, 1996); missed 20 games. ... Traded by Devils to Los Angeles Kings for future considerations (November 22, 1996). ... Claimed on waivers by Stars (January 28, 1997). ... Strained groin (March 19, 1997); missed four games.
HONORS: Won WCHA Rookie of the Year Award (1978-79). ... Won Hobey Baker Memorial Award (1980-81). ... Named to NCAA All-America West team (1980-81). ... Named to WCHA All-Star first team (1980-81). ... Named to NCAA All-Tournament team (1980-81). ... Played in NHL All-Star Game (1983 and 1986).
STATISTICAL PLATEAUS: Three-goal games: 1983-84 (1), 1985-86 (2), 1986-87 (1), 1989-90 (1). Total: 5.
MISCELLANEOUS: Member of Stanley Cup championship team (1995). ... Member of gold-medal-winning U.S. Olympic team (1980). ... Holds Dallas Stars franchise all-time records for most games played (992), most assists (593) and most points (867). ... Failed to score on a penalty shot (vs. Rick Wamsley, March 12, 1984).

		REGULAR SEASON								PLAYOFFS				
Season Team	League	Gms.	G	A	Pts.	PIM	+/-	PP	SH	Gms.	G	A	Pts.	PIM
78-79— Univ. of Minnesota	WCHA	40	21	50	71	18	...	...	...	—	—	—	—	—
79-80— U.S. national team	Int'l	55	25	30	55	20	...	...	...	—	—	—	—	—
— U.S. Olympic team	Int'l	7	2	1	3	2	...	...	...	—	—	—	—	—
80-81— Univ. of Minnesota	WCHA	36	17	54	71	56	...	...	...	—	—	—	—	—
— Minnesota	NHL	3	2	0	2	12	1	0	0	19	1	7	8	9
81-82— Minnesota	NHL	73	38	60	98	42	14	7	2	4	0	2	2	0
82-83— Minnesota	NHL	79	32	45	77	43	24	8	2	9	1	6	7	10
83-84— Minnesota	NHL	76	28	61	89	43	16	8	3	16	5	5	10	4
84-85— Minnesota	NHL	80	19	37	56	39	-18	5	1	9	2	5	7	10
85-86— Minnesota	NHL	80	29	76	105	47	14	6	0	5	3	2	5	2
86-87— Minnesota	NHL	46	18	35	53	35	12	5	1	—	—	—	—	—
87-88— Minnesota	NHL	54	9	30	39	32	-23	4	1	—	—	—	—	—
88-89— Minnesota	NHL	68	18	38	56	57	1	4	5	5	2	2	4	4
89-90— Minnesota	NHL	80	23	62	85	45	-16	9	1	7	2	2	4	18
90-91— Minnesota	NHL	79	13	56	69	26	-3	1	2	23	9	13	22	6
91-92— Minnesota	NHL	76	8	26	34	16	-15	4	1	7	1	5	6	2
92-93— Minnesota	NHL	82	12	21	33	22	7	0	3	—	—	—	—	—
93-94— Dallas	NHL	79	17	35	52	62	10	2	1	9	2	1	3	6

Season Team	League	REGULAR SEASON Gms.	G	A	Pts.	PIM	+/-	PP	SH	PLAYOFFS Gms.	G	A	Pts.	PIM
94-95 — Dallas	NHL	17	0	4	4	4	-8	0	0	—	—	—	—	—
— New Jersey	NHL	30	8	20	28	20	9	2	0	20	7	12	19	6
95-96 — New Jersey	NHL	55	7	16	23	14	-3	1	1	—	—	—	—	—
96-97 — New Jersey	NHL	3	0	1	1	0	-1	0	0	—	—	—	—	—
— Phoenix	IHL	11	3	3	6	4	...	...	...	—	—	—	—	—
— Los Angeles	NHL	19	0	4	4	0	-9	0	0	—	—	—	—	—
— Dallas	NHL	20	8	7	15	12	6	1	1	2	0	1	1	0
NHL totals (18 years)		1099	289	634	923	571	18	67	25	135	35	63	98	77

BROTEN, PAUL — RW — BLUES

PERSONAL: Born October 27, 1965, in Roseau, Minn. ... 5-11/190. ... Shoots right. ... Name pronounced BRAH-tuhn. ... Brother of Aaron Broten, center/left winger for six NHL teams (1980-81 through 1991-92); and brother of Neal Broten, center, Dallas Stars.
HIGH SCHOOL: Roseau (Minn.).
COLLEGE: Minnesota.
TRANSACTIONS/CAREER NOTES: Selected by New York Rangers in fourth round (third Rangers pick, 77th overall) of NHL entry draft (June 9, 1984). ... Pulled thigh muscle (September 1990). ... Selected by Dallas Stars in NHL waiver draft (October 2, 1993). ... Traded by Stars to St. Louis Blues for C Guy Carbonneau (October 2, 1995).
STATISTICAL PLATEAUS: Three-goal games: 1991-92 (1).
MISCELLANEOUS: Scored on a penalty shot (vs. Mike Vernon, January 16, 1992).

Season Team	League	REGULAR SEASON Gms.	G	A	Pts.	PIM	+/-	PP	SH	PLAYOFFS Gms.	G	A	Pts.	PIM
83-84 — Roseau	Minn. H.S.	26	26	29	55	4	...	...	...	—	—	—	—	—
84-85 — Univ. of Minnesota	WCHA	44	8	8	16	26	...	...	...	—	—	—	—	—
85-86 — Univ. of Minnesota	WCHA	38	6	16	22	24	...	...	...	—	—	—	—	—
86-87 — Univ. of Minnesota	WCHA	48	17	22	39	52	...	...	...	—	—	—	—	—
87-88 — Univ. of Minnesota	WCHA	62	19	26	45	54	...	...	...	—	—	—	—	—
88-89 — Denver	IHL	77	28	31	59	133	...	...	...	4	0	2	2	6
89-90 — Flint	IHL	28	17	9	26	55	...	...	...	—	—	—	—	—
— New York Rangers	NHL	32	5	3	8	26	-4	0	0	6	1	1	2	2
90-91 — New York Rangers	NHL	28	4	6	10	18	7	0	0	5	0	0	0	2
— Binghamton	AHL	8	2	2	4	4	...	...	...	—	—	—	—	—
91-92 — New York Rangers	NHL	74	13	15	28	102	14	0	3	13	1	2	3	10
92-93 — New York Rangers	NHL	60	5	9	14	48	-6	0	1	—	—	—	—	—
93-94 — Dallas	NHL	64	12	12	24	30	18	0	0	9	1	1	2	2
94-95 — Dallas	NHL	47	7	9	16	36	-7	0	0	5	1	2	3	2
95-96 — St. Louis	NHL	17	0	1	1	4	-1	0	0	—	—	—	—	—
— Worcester	AHL	50	22	21	43	42	...	...	...	3	0	0	0	0
96-97 — Fort Wayne	IHL	59	19	28	47	82	...	...	...	—	—	—	—	—
NHL totals (7 years)		322	46	55	101	264	21	0	4	38	4	6	10	18

BROUSSEAU, PAUL — RW — LIGHTNING

PERSONAL: Born September 18, 1973, in Pierrefonds, Que. ... 6-1/203. ... Shoots right. ... Name pronounced broo-SOH.
COLLEGE: Heritage College (Fla.).
TRANSACTIONS/CAREER NOTES: Selected by Quebec Nordiques in second round (second Nordiques pick, 28th overall) of NHL entry draft (June 20, 1992). ... Nordiques franchise moved to Colorado and renamed Avalanche for 1995-96 season (June 21, 1995). ... Signed as free agent by Tampa Bay Lightning (September 5, 1996).
HONORS: Won Michael Bossy Trophy (1991-92).

Season Team	League	REGULAR SEASON Gms.	G	A	Pts.	PIM	+/-	PP	SH	PLAYOFFS Gms.	G	A	Pts.	PIM
89-90 — Chicoutimi	QMJHL	57	17	24	41	32	...	...	...	7	0	3	3	0
90-91 — Trois-Rivieres	QMJHL	67	30	66	96	48	...	...	...	6	3	2	5	2
91-92 — Hull	QMJHL	57	35	61	96	54	...	...	...	6	3	5	8	10
92-93 — Hull	QMJHL	59	27	48	75	49	...	...	...	10	7	8	15	6
93-94 — Cornwall	AHL	69	18	26	44	35	...	...	...	1	0	0	0	0
94-95 — Cornwall	AHL	57	19	17	36	29	...	...	...	7	2	1	3	10
95-96 — Cornwall	AHL	63	21	22	43	60	...	...	...	8	4	0	4	2
— Colorado	NHL	8	1	1	2	2	1	0	0	—	—	—	—	—
96-97 — Adirondack	AHL	66	35	31	66	66	...	...	...	4	1	2	3	0
— Tampa Bay	NHL	6	0	0	0	0	-4	0	0	—	—	—	—	—
NHL totals (2 years)		14	1	1	2	2	-3	0	0					

BROWN, BRAD — D — CANADIENS

PERSONAL: Born December 27, 1975, in Mississauga, Ont. ... 6-4/216. ... Shoots right.
HIGH SCHOOL: Chippewa (North Bay, Ont.).
TRANSACTIONS/CAREER NOTES: Selected by Montreal Canadiens in first round (first Canadiens pick, 18th overall) of NHL entry draft (June 28, 1994).

Season Team	League	REGULAR SEASON Gms.	G	A	Pts.	PIM	+/-	PP	SH	PLAYOFFS Gms.	G	A	Pts.	PIM
91-92 — North Bay	OHL	49	2	9	11	170	...	...	...	18	0	6	6	43
92-93 — North Bay	OHL	61	4	9	13	228	...	...	...	2	0	2	2	13
93-94 — North Bay	OHL	66	8	24	32	196	...	...	...	18	3	12	15	33

Season Team	League	Gms.	G	A	Pts.	PIM	+/-	PP	SH	Gms.	G	A	Pts.	PIM
94-95— North Bay	OHL	64	8	38	46	172	...	...	...	6	1	4	5	8
95-96— Regina	WHL	21	2	3	5	7	...	...	...	—	—	—	—	—
— Fredericton	AHL	38	0	3	3	148	...	...	...	10	2	1	3	6
96-97— Fredericton	AHL	64	3	7	10	368	...	...	...	—	—	—	—	—
— Montreal	NHL	8	0	0	0	22	-1	0	0	—	—	—	—	—
NHL totals (1 year)		8	0	0	0	22	-1	0	0					

BROWN, CURTIS C SABRES

PERSONAL: Born February 12, 1976, in Unity, Sask. ... 6-0/182. ... Shoots left.
TRANSACTIONS/CAREER NOTES: Selected by Buffalo Sabres in second round (second Sabres pick, 43rd overall) of NHL entry draft (June 28, 1994). ... Injured ankle prior to 1995-96 season; missed two games.
HONORS: Named to Can.HL All-Star second team (1994-95). ... Named to WHL (East) All-Star first team (1994-95). ... Named to WHL (Central/East) All-Star second team (1995-96).

Season Team	League	Gms.	G	A	Pts.	PIM	+/-	PP	SH	Gms.	G	A	Pts.	PIM
92-93— Moose Jaw	WHL	71	13	16	29	30	...	...	...	—	—	—	—	—
93-94— Moose Jaw	WHL	72	27	38	65	82	...	...	...	—	—	—	—	—
94-95— Moose Jaw	WHL	70	51	53	104	63	...	...	...	10	8	7	15	20
— Buffalo	NHL	1	1	1	2	2	2	0	0	—	—	—	—	—
95-96— Buffalo	NHL	4	0	0	0	0	0	0	0	—	—	—	—	—
— Moose Jaw	WHL	25	20	18	38	30	...	...	...	—	—	—	—	—
— Prince Albert	WHL	19	12	21	33	8	...	...	...	18	10	15	25	18
— Rochester	AHL	0	0	0	0	0	...	...	...	12	0	1	1	2
96-97— Buffalo	NHL	28	4	3	7	18	4	0	0	—	—	—	—	—
— Rochester	AHL	51	22	21	43	30	...	...	...	10	4	6	10	4
NHL totals (3 years)		33	5	4	9	20	6	0	0					

BROWN, DOUG RW RED WINGS

PERSONAL: Born June 12, 1964, in Southborough, Mass. ... 5-10/185. ... Shoots right. ... Full name: Douglas Allen Brown. ... Brother of Greg Brown, defenseman with three NHL teams (1990-91 and 1992-93 through 1994-95).
HIGH SCHOOL: St. Mark's (Southborough, Mass.).
COLLEGE: Boston College.
TRANSACTIONS/CAREER NOTES: Signed as free agent by New Jersey Devils (August 6, 1986). ... Broke nose (October 1988). ... Injured back (November 25, 1989). ... Bruised right foot (February 13, 1991). ... Suspended by Devils for refusing to report to Utica (November 20, 1992). ... Reinstated by Devils (November 30, 1992). ... Signed as free agent by Pittsburgh Penguins (September 29, 1993). ... Injured leg (March 26, 1994); missed seven games. ... Selected by Detroit Red Wings from Penguins in waiver draft (January 18, 1995); Penguins claimed C Micah Aivazoff as compensation (who was then claimed by Edmonton Oilers). ... Suffered from the flu (December 2, 1995); missed one game.
HONORS: Named to NCAA All-America East second team (1984-85 and 1985-86). ... Named to Hockey East All-Star second team (1984-85 and 1985-86).
MISCELLANEOUS: Member of Stanley Cup championship team (1997). ... Scored on a penalty shot (vs. Ken Wregget, November 23, 1991).

Season Team	League	Gms.	G	A	Pts.	PIM	+/-	PP	SH	Gms.	G	A	Pts.	PIM
82-83— Boston College	ECAC	22	9	8	17	0	...	...	...	—	—	—	—	—
83-84— Boston College	ECAC	38	11	10	21	6	...	...	...	—	—	—	—	—
84-85— Boston College	Hockey East	45	37	31	68	10	...	...	...	—	—	—	—	—
85-86— Boston College	Hockey East	38	16	40	56	16	...	...	...	—	—	—	—	—
86-87— Maine	AHL	73	24	34	58	15	...	...	...	—	—	—	—	—
— New Jersey	NHL	4	0	1	1	0	-4	0	0	—	—	—	—	—
87-88— New Jersey	NHL	70	14	11	25	20	7	1	4	19	5	1	6	6
— Utica	AHL	2	0	2	2	2	...	...	...	—	—	—	—	—
88-89— New Jersey	NHL	63	15	10	25	15	-7	4	0	—	—	—	—	—
— Utica	AHL	4	1	4	5	0	...	...	...	—	—	—	—	—
89-90— New Jersey	NHL	69	14	20	34	16	7	1	3	6	0	1	1	2
90-91— New Jersey	NHL	58	14	16	30	4	18	0	2	7	2	2	4	2
91-92— New Jersey	NHL	71	11	17	28	27	17	1	2	—	—	—	—	—
92-93— New Jersey	NHL	15	0	5	5	2	3	0	0	—	—	—	—	—
— Utica	AHL	25	11	17	28	8	...	...	...	—	—	—	—	—
93-94— Pittsburgh	NHL	77	18	37	55	18	19	2	0	6	0	0	0	2
94-95— Detroit	NHL	45	9	12	21	16	14	1	1	18	4	8	12	2
95-96— Detroit	NHL	62	12	15	27	4	11	0	1	13	3	3	6	4
96-97— Detroit	NHL	49	6	7	13	8	-3	1	0	14	3	3	6	2
NHL totals (11 years)		583	113	151	264	130	82	11	13	83	17	18	35	20

BROWN, JEFF D HURRICANES

PERSONAL: Born April 30, 1966, in Ottawa. ... 6-2/204. ... Shoots right. ... Full name: Jeff Randall Brown.
HIGH SCHOOL: Sudbury (Ont.).
TRANSACTIONS/CAREER NOTES: Selected by Quebec Nordiques as underage junior in second round (second Nordiques pick, 36th overall) of NHL entry draft (June 9, 1984). ... Traded by Nordiques to St. Louis Blues for G Greg Millen and C Tony Hrkac (December 13, 1989). ... Broke left ankle (February 14, 1991); missed 13 games. ... Broke foot (January 14, 1993); missed 11 games. ... Suffered from sore foot (February 11, 1993); missed two games. ... Injured hand and foot (October 30, 1993); missed three games. ... Broke thumb (January 15, 1994); missed six games. ... Traded by Blues with D Brett Hedican and C Nathan LaFayette to Vancouver Canucks for C Craig Janney (March 21, 1994). ... Cracked bone in wrist (March 6, 1995); missed 12 games. ... Sprained shoulder (April 28, 1995); missed last two games of

season. ... Traded by Canucks with third-round pick in 1998 draft to Hartford Whalers for C Jim Dowd, D Frantisek Kucera and second-round pick (D Ryan Bonni) in 1997 draft (December 19, 1995). ... Underwent lower back surgery (October 23, 1996); missed final 81 games of regular season. ... Whalers franchise moved to North Carolina and renamed Carolina Hurricanes for 1997-98 season; NHL approved move on June 25, 1997.

HONORS: Shared Max Kaminsky Trophy with Terry Carkner (1985-86). ... Named to OHL All-Star first team (1985-86).

		REGULAR SEASON								PLAYOFFS				
Season Team	League	Gms.	G	A	Pts.	PIM	+/-	PP	SH	Gms.	G	A	Pts.	PIM
81-82— Hawkesbury	COJHL	49	12	47	59	72	...	...	...	—	—	—	—	—
82-83— Sudbury	OHL	65	9	37	46	39	...	...	...	—	—	—	—	—
83-84— Sudbury	OHL	68	17	60	77	39	...	...	...	—	—	—	—	—
84-85— Sudbury	OHL	56	16	48	64	26	...	...	...	—	—	—	—	—
85-86— Sudbury	OHL	45	22	28	50	24	...	...	...	4	0	2	2	11
— Quebec	NHL	8	3	2	5	6	5	0	0	1	0	0	0	0
— Fredericton	AHL	—	—	—	—	—				1	0	1	1	0
86-87— Fredericton	AHL	26	2	14	16	16	...			—	—	—	—	—
— Quebec	NHL	44	7	22	29	16	11	3	0	13	3	3	6	2
87-88— Quebec	NHL	78	16	36	52	64	-25	9	0	—	—	—	—	—
88-89— Quebec	NHL	78	21	47	68	62	-22	13	1	—	—	—	—	—
89-90— Quebec	NHL	29	6	10	16	18	-14	2	0	—	—	—	—	—
— St. Louis	NHL	48	10	28	38	37	-12	6	1	12	2	10	12	4
90-91— St. Louis	NHL	67	12	47	59	39	4	6	1	13	3	9	12	6
91-92— St. Louis	NHL	80	20	39	59	38	8	10	0	6	2	1	3	2
92-93— St. Louis	NHL	71	25	53	78	58	-6	12	2	11	3	8	11	6
93-94— St. Louis	NHL	63	13	47	60	46	-13	7	0	—	—	—	—	—
— Vancouver	NHL	11	1	5	6	10	2	0	0	24	6	9	15	37
94-95— Vancouver	NHL	33	8	23	31	16	-2	3	0	5	1	3	4	2
95-96— Vancouver	NHL	28	1	16	17	18	6	0	0	—	—	—	—	—
— Hartford	NHL	48	7	31	38	38	2	5	0	—	—	—	—	—
96-97— Hartford	NHL	1	0	0	0	0	0	0	0	—	—	—	—	—
NHL totals (12 years)		687	150	406	556	466	-56	76	5	85	20	43	63	59

BROWN, JEFF   D   RANGERS

PERSONAL: Born April 24, 1978, in Toronto. ... 6-1/190. ... Shoots right.
TRANSACTIONS/CAREER NOTES: Selected by New York Rangers in first round (first Rangers pick, 22nd overall) of NHL entry draft (June 22, 1996).

		REGULAR SEASON								PLAYOFFS				
Season Team	League	Gms.	G	A	Pts.	PIM	+/-	PP	SH	Gms.	G	A	Pts.	PIM
93-94— Thornhill	Jr. A	47	6	18	24	90	...	...	...	—	—	—	—	—
94-95— Sarnia	OHL	58	2	14	16	52	...	...	...	—	—	—	—	—
95-96— Sarnia	OHL	65	8	20	28	111	...	...	...	10	1	2	3	12
96-97— London	OHL	63	6	31	37	92	...	...	...	—	—	—	—	—

BROWN, KEVIN   RW   HURRICANES

PERSONAL: Born May 11, 1974, in Birmingham, England. ... 6-1/212. ... Shoots right.
HIGH SCHOOL: Quinte Secondary School (Belleville, Ont.).
TRANSACTIONS/CAREER NOTES: Selected by Los Angeles Kings in fourth round (third Kings pick, 87th overall) of NHL entry draft (June 20, 1992). ... Strained knee and hip (April 12, 1995); missed two games. ... Sprained right shoulder (April 19, 1995); missed last seven games of season. ... Traded by Kings to Ottawa Senators for D Jaroslav Modry (March 20, 1996). ... Traded by Senators to Mighty Ducks of Anaheim for LW Mike Maneluk (July 1, 1996). ... Traded by Mighty Ducks to Hartford Whalers for rights to C Espen Knutsen (October 1, 1996). ... Sprained shoulder (February 16, 1997); missed seven games. ... Whalers franchise moved to North Carolina and renamed Carolina Hurricanes for 1997-98 season; NHL approved move on June 25, 1997.
HONORS: Won Jim Mahon Memorial Trophy (1992-93 and 1993-94). ... Named to OHL All-Star second team (1992-93). ... Named to Can.HL All-Star second team (1993-94). ... Named to OHL All-Star first team (1993-94).

		REGULAR SEASON								PLAYOFFS				
Season Team	League	Gms.	G	A	Pts.	PIM	+/-	PP	SH	Gms.	G	A	Pts.	PIM
89-90— Georgetown Jr. B	OHA	31	3	8	11	59	...	...	...	—	—	—	—	—
90-91— Waterloo Jr. B	OHA	46	25	33	58	116	...	...	...	—	—	—	—	—
91-92— Belleville	OHL	66	24	24	48	52	...	...	...	5	1	4	5	8
92-93— Belleville	OHL	6	2	5	7	4	...	.·..	...	—	—	—	—	—
— Detroit	OHL	56	48	86	134	76	...	...	...	15	10	18	28	18
93-94— Detroit	OHL	57	54	81	135	85	...	...	...	17	14	*26	*40	28
94-95— Phoenix	IHL	48	19	31	50	64	...	...	...	—	—	—	—	—
— Los Angeles	NHL	23	2	3	5	18	-7	0	0	—	—	—	—	—
95-96— Phoenix	IHL	45	10	16	26	39	...	...	...	—	—	—	—	—
— Los Angeles	NHL	7	1	0	1	4	-2	0	0	—	—	—	—	—
— Prince Edward Island	AHL	8	3	6	9	2	...	...	...	3	1	3	4	0
96-97— Springfield	AHL	48	32	16	48	45	...	...	...	17	†11	6	17	24
— Hartford	NHL	11	0	4	4	6	-6	0	0	—	—	—	—	—
NHL totals (3 years)		41	3	7	10	28	-15	0	0					

BROWN, ROB   LW

PERSONAL: Born April 10, 1968, in Kingston, Ont. ... 5-11/185. ... Shoots left.
TRANSACTIONS/CAREER NOTES: Selected by Pittsburgh Penguins as underage junior in fourth round (fourth Penguins pick, 67th overall) of NHL entry draft (June 21, 1986). ... Separated right shoulder (February 12, 1989); missed 12 games. ... Traded by Penguins to Hartford

Whalers for RW Scott Young (December 21, 1990). ... Injured Adam's apple (April 5, 1991); missed one playoff game. ... Traded by Whalers to Chicago Blackhawks for D Steve Konroyd (January 24, 1992). ... Signed as free agent by Dallas Stars (August 6, 1993). ... Signed as free agent by Los Angeles Kings (June 14, 1994). ... Signed as free agent by Chicago Wolves of IHL (July 17, 1995).

HONORS: Won WHL (West) Most Valuable Player Trophy (1985-86 and 1986-87). ... Won Bob Brownridge Memorial Trophy (1985-86). ... Named to WHL (West) All-Star first team (1985-86 and 1986-87). ... Won Can.HL Player of the Year Award (1986-87). ... Won Can.HL Plus/Minus Award (1986-87). ... Won WHL (West) Bob Brownridge Memorial Trophy (1986-87). ... Won WHL Player of the Year Award (1986-87). ... Played in NHL All-Star Game (1989). ... Won James Gatschene Memorial Trophy (1993-94). ... Won Leo P. Lamoureux Memorial Trophy (1993-94 and 1995-96). ... Named to IHL All-Star first team (1993-94, 1995-96 and 1996-97). ... Named to IHL All-Star second team (1994-95). ... Won Leo P. Lamoreux Memorial Trophy (1996-97).

STATISTICAL PLATEAUS: Three-goal games: 1988-89 (4), 1989-90 (3). Total: 7.

Season Team	League	REGULAR SEASON Gms.	G	A	Pts.	PIM	+/-	PP	SH	PLAYOFFS Gms.	G	A	Pts.	PIM
83-84 — Kamloops	WHL	50	16	42	58	80	...	...	...	15	1	2	3	17
84-85 — Kamloops	WHL	60	29	50	79	95	...	...	...	15	8	8	16	28
85-86 — Kamloops	WHL	69	58	*115	*173	171	...	...	...	16	*18	*28	*46	14
86-87 — Kamloops	WHL	63	*76	*136	*212	101	...	...	...	5	6	5	11	6
87-88 — Pittsburgh	NHL	51	24	20	44	56	...	...	...	—	—	—	—	—
88-89 — Pittsburgh	NHL	68	49	66	115	118	...	...	...	11	5	3	8	22
89-90 — Pittsburgh	NHL	80	33	47	80	102	-10	12	0	—	—	—	—	—
90-91 — Pittsburgh	NHL	25	6	10	16	31	...	...	...	—	—	—	—	—
— Hartford	NHL	44	18	24	42	101	...	...	...	5	1	0	1	7
91-92 — Hartford	NHL	42	16	15	31	39	...	...	...	—	—	—	—	—
— Chicago	NHL	25	5	11	16	34	...	...	...	8	2	4	6	4
92-93 — Chicago	NHL	15	1	6	7	33	6	0	0	—	—	—	—	—
— Indianapolis	IHL	19	14	19	33	32	...	...	...	2	0	1	1	2
93-94 — Kalamazoo	IHL	79	42	*113	*155	188	...	...	...	5	1	3	4	6
— Dallas	NHL	1	0	0	0	0	-1	0	0	—	—	—	—	—
94-95 — Phoenix	IHL	69	34	73	107	135	...	...	...	9	4	12	16	0
— Los Angeles	NHL	2	0	0	0	0	-2	0	0	—	—	—	—	—
95-96 — Chicago	IHL	79	52	*91	*143	100	...	...	...	9	4	11	15	6
96-97 — Chicago	IHL	76	37	*80	*117	98	...	...	...	4	2	4	6	16
NHL totals (8 years)		353	152	199	351	514	-7	12	0	24	8	7	15	33

BROWN, RYAN — D — LIGHTNING

PERSONAL: Born September 19, 1974, in Boyle, Alta. ... 6-3/215. ... Shoots right.
TRANSACTIONS/CAREER NOTES: Selected by Tampa Bay Lightning in fifth round (fifth Lightning pick, 107th overall) of NHL entry draft (June 26, 1993).

Season Team	League	REGULAR SEASON Gms.	G	A	Pts.	PIM	+/-	PP	SH	PLAYOFFS Gms.	G	A	Pts.	PIM
91-92 — Seattle	WHL	60	1	1	2	230	...	...	...	14	0	2	2	38
92-93 — Seattle	WHL	19	0	1	1	70	...	...	...	—	—	—	—	—
— Swift Current	WHL	47	1	4	5	104	...	...	...	17	0	2	2	18
93-94 — Swift Current	WHL	72	2	10	12	173	...	...	...	7	0	0	0	6
94-95 — Swift Current	WHL	7	0	1	1	28	...	...	...	—	—	—	—	—
— Prince George	WHL	32	2	7	9	103	...	...	...	—	—	—	—	—
— Tri-City	WHL	19	1	2	3	84	...	...	...	16	1	6	7	49
95-96 — Atlanta	IHL	16	0	0	0	66	...	...	...	—	—	—	—	—
— Nashville	ECHL	18	1	0	1	64	...	...	...	4	1	1	2	9
96-97 — Adirondack	AHL	6	0	0	0	39	...	...	...	—	—	—	—	—
— Raleigh	ECHL	43	7	3	10	122	...	...	...	—	—	—	—	—

BROWN, SEAN — D — OILERS

PERSONAL: Born November 5, 1976, in Oshawa, Ont. ... 6-2/205. ... Shoots left.
HIGH SCHOOL: Quinte Secondary School (Belleville, Ont.).
TRANSACTIONS/CAREER NOTES: Selected by Boston Bruins in first round (second Bruins pick, 21st overall) of NHL entry draft (July 8, 1995). ... Traded by Boston Bruins with RW Mariusz Czerkawski and first-round pick (D Matthieu Descoteaux) in 1996 draft to Edmonton Oilers for G Bill Ranford (January 11, 1996).
HONORS: Named to OHL All-Star second team (1995-96).

Season Team	League	REGULAR SEASON Gms.	G	A	Pts.	PIM	+/-	PP	SH	PLAYOFFS Gms.	G	A	Pts.	PIM
92-93 — Oshawa	Tier II Jr. A	15	0	1	1	9	...	...	...	—	—	—	—	—
93-94 — OJHL	Tier II Jr. A	32	5	14	19	165	...	...	...	—	—	—	—	—
— Belleville	OHL	28	1	2	3	53	...	...	...	8	0	0	0	17
94-95 — Belleville	OHL	58	2	16	18	200	...	...	...	16	4	2	6	67
95-96 — Belleville	OHL	37	10	23	33	150	...	...	...	—	—	—	—	—
— Sarnia	OHL	26	8	17	25	112	...	...	...	10	1	0	1	38
96-97 — Hamilton	AHL	61	1	7	8	238	...	...	...	19	1	0	1	47
— Edmonton	NHL	5	0	0	0	4	-1	0	0	—	—	—	—	—
NHL totals (1 year)		5	0	0	0	4	-1	0	0					

BROWN, TOM — D — BRUINS

PERSONAL: Born November 11, 1977, in Hamilton, Ont. ... 6-4/204. ... Shoots right.
TRANSACTIONS/CAREER NOTES: Selected by Boston Bruins in seventh round (eighth Bruins pick, 182nd overall) of NHL entry draft (June 22, 1996).

Season Team	League	Gms.	G	A	Pts.	PIM	+/-	PP	SH		Gms.	G	A	Pts.	PIM
		REGULAR SEASON									PLAYOFFS				
94-95 — Sarnia	OHL	53	0	3	3	17	...	...	...		—	—	—	—	—
95-96 — Sarnia	OHL	61	2	5	7	49	...	...	...		10	0	0	0	8
96-97 — Sarnia	OHL	1	0	0	0	4	...	...	...		—	—	—	—	—
— Sudbury	OHL	65	1	13	14	104	...	...	...		—	—	—	—	—
— Charlotte	ECHL	3	0	1	1	0	...	...	...		—	—	—	—	—
— Providence	AHL	1	0	0	0	13	...	...	...		—	—	—	—	—

BRULE, STEVE　　　　C　　　　DEVILS

PERSONAL: Born January 15, 1975, in Montreal. ... 5-11/185. ... Shoots right. ... Name pronounced broo-LAY.
TRANSACTIONS/CAREER NOTES: Selected by New Jersey Devils in sixth round (sixth Devils pick, 143rd overall) of NHL entry draft (June 26, 1993).
HONORS: Won Michel Bergeron Trophy (1992-93). ... Named to QMJHL All-Rookie team (1992-93). ... Named to QMJHL All-Star second team (1994-95).

Season Team	League	Gms.	G	A	Pts.	PIM	+/-	PP	SH		Gms.	G	A	Pts.	PIM
		REGULAR SEASON									PLAYOFFS				
92-93 — St. Jean	QMJHL	70	33	47	80	46	...	...	...		4	0	0	0	9
93-94 — St. Jean	QMJHL	66	41	64	105	46	...	...	...		5	2	1	3	0
94-95 — St. Jean	QMJHL	69	44	64	108	42	...	...	...		7	3	4	7	8
— Albany	AHL	3	1	4	5	0	...	...	...		14	9	5	14	4
95-96 — Albany	AHL	80	30	21	51	37	...	...	...		4	0	0	0	17
96-97 — Albany	AHL	79	28	48	76	27	...	...	...		16	7	7	14	12

BRUNET, BENOIT　　　　LW　　　　CANADIENS

PERSONAL: Born August 24, 1968, in Montreal. ... 5-11/195. ... Shoots left. ... Name pronounced BEHN-wah broo-NAY.
TRANSACTIONS/CAREER NOTES: Selected by Montreal Canadiens as underage junior in second round (second Canadiens pick, 27th overall) of NHL entry draft (June 21, 1986). ... Injured ankle (September 1987). ... Tore left knee ligaments (September 24, 1990); missed 24 games. ... Fractured ankle (December 4, 1991). ... Sprained left knee (November 21, 1992); missed 10 games. ... Fractured thumb (January 22, 1993); missed 14 games. ... Bruised knee (November 17, 1993); missed four games. ... Suffered mild concussion (February 2, 1994); missed six games. ... Suffered sore throat (April 8, 1994); missed three games. ... Pulled hamstring (March 18, 1995); missed two games. ... Bruised right knee (May 3, 1995); missed one game. ... Sprained wrist (November 11, 1995); missed five games. ... Reinjured wrist (November 25, 1995); missed 18 games. ... Sprained back (January 11, 1996); missed 28 games. ... Bruised thigh (October 24, 1996); missed one game. ... Fractured left leg (November 2, 1996); missed 21 games. ... Suffered from tonsillitis (December 21, 1996); missed one game. ... Fractured hand (January 20, 1997); missed 19 games.
HONORS: Named to QMJHL All-Star second team (1986-87). ... Named to AHL All-Star first team (1988-89).
MISCELLANEOUS: Member of Stanley Cup championship team (1993).

Season Team	League	Gms.	G	A	Pts.	PIM	+/-	PP	SH		Gms.	G	A	Pts.	PIM
		REGULAR SEASON									PLAYOFFS				
85-86 — Hull	QMJHL	71	33	37	70	81	...	...	...		—	—	—	—	—
86-87 — Hull	QMJHL	60	43	67	110	105	...	...	...		6	7	5	12	8
87-88 — Hull	QMJHL	62	54	89	143	131	...	...	...		10	3	10	13	11
88-89 — Montreal	NHL	2	0	1	1	0	0	0	0		—	—	—	—	—
— Sherbrooke	AHL	73	41	*76	117	95	...	...	...		6	2	0	2	4
89-90 — Sherbrooke	AHL	72	32	35	67	82	...	...	...		12	8	7	15	20
90-91 — Fredericton	AHL	24	13	18	31	16	...	...	...		6	5	6	11	2
— Montreal	NHL	17	1	3	4	0	-1	0	0		—	—	—	—	—
91-92 — Fredericton	AHL	6	7	9	16	27	...	...	...		—	—	—	—	—
— Montreal	NHL	18	4	6	10	14	4	0	0		—	—	—	—	—
92-93 — Montreal	NHL	47	10	15	25	19	13	0	0		20	2	8	10	8
93-94 — Montreal	NHL	71	10	20	30	20	14	0	3		7	1	4	5	16
94-95 — Montreal	NHL	45	7	18	25	16	7	1	1		—	—	—	—	—
95-06 — Montreal	NHL	26	7	8	15	17	-4	3	1		3	0	2	2	0
— Fredericton	AHL	3	2	1	3	6	...	...	...		—	—	—	—	—
96-97 — Montreal	NHL	39	10	13	23	14	6	2	0		4	1	3	4	4
NHL totals (8 years)		265	49	84	133	100	39	6	5		34	4	17	21	28

BRUNETTE, ANDREW　　　　LW　　　　CAPITALS

PERSONAL: Born August 24, 1973, in Sudbury, Ont. ... 6-0/212. ... Shoots left. ... Name pronounced broo-NEHT.
TRANSACTIONS/CAREER NOTES: Selected by Washington Capitals in sixth round (sixth Capitals pick, 174th overall) of NHL entry draft (June 26, 1993).
HONORS: Won Eddie Powers Memorial Trophy (1992-93). ... Named to Can.HL All-Star second team (1992-93). ... Named to OHL All-Star first team (1992-93).

Season Team	League	Gms.	G	A	Pts.	PIM	+/-	PP	SH		Gms.	G	A	Pts.	PIM
		REGULAR SEASON									PLAYOFFS				
90-91 — Owen Sound	OHL	63	15	20	35	15	...	...	...		—	—	—	—	—
91-92 — Owen Sound	OHL	66	51	47	98	42	...	...	...		5	5	0	5	8
92-93 — Owen Sound	OHL	66	*62	*100	*162	91	...	...	...		8	8	6	14	16
93-94 — Portland	AHL	23	9	11	20	10	...	...	...		2	0	1	1	0
— Hampton	ECHL	20	12	18	30	32	...	...	...		7	7	6	13	18
94-95 — Portland	AHL	79	30	50	80	53	...	...	...		7	3	3	6	10
95-96 — Portland	AHL	69	28	66	94	125	...	...	...		20	11	18	29	15
— Washington	NHL	11	3	3	6	5	0	0	0		6	1	3	4	0
96-97 — Portland	AHL	50	22	51	73	48	...	...	...		5	1	2	3	0
— Washington	NHL	23	4	7	11	12	-3	2	0		—	—	—	—	—
NHL totals (2 years)		34	7	10	17	17	-3	2	0		6	1	3	4	0

BRYLIN, SERGEI — C — DEVILS

PERSONAL: Born January 13, 1974, in Moscow, U.S.S.R. ... 5-10/190. ... Shoots left. ... Name pronounced BREE-lihn.
TRANSACTIONS/CAREER NOTES: Selected by New Jersey Devils in second round (second Devils pick, 42nd overall) of NHL entry draft (June 20, 1992). ... Suffered from tonsillitis (May 3, 1995); missed last game of season. ... Broke hand (November 16, 1995); missed 13 games.
MISCELLANEOUS: Member of Stanley Cup championship team (1995).

		REGULAR SEASON								PLAYOFFS				
Season Team	League	Gms.	G	A	Pts.	PIM	+/-	PP	SH	Gms.	G	A	Pts.	PIM
91-92— CSKA Moscow	CIS	44	1	6	7	4	...	...	...	—	—	—	—	—
92-93— CSKA Moscow	CIS	42	5	4	9	36	...	...	...	—	—	—	—	—
93-94— CSKA Moscow	CIS	39	4	6	10	36	...	...	...	3	0	1	1	0
— Russian Penguins	IHL	13	4	5	9	18	...	...	...	—	—	—	—	—
94-95— Albany	AHL	63	19	35	54	78	...	...	...	—	—	—	—	—
— New Jersey	NHL	26	6	8	14	8	12	0	0	12	1	2	3	4
95-96— New Jersey	NHL	50	4	5	9	26	-2	0	0	—	—	—	—	—
96-97— New Jersey	NHL	29	2	2	4	20	-13	0	0	—	—	—	—	—
— Albany	AHL	43	17	24	41	38	...	...	...	16	4	8	12	12
NHL totals (3 years)		105	12	15	27	54	-3	0	0	12	1	2	3	4

BUCHBERGER, KELLY — RW/LW — OILERS

PERSONAL: Born December 12, 1966, in Langenburg, Sask. ... 6-2/205. ... Shoots left. ... Full name: Kelly Michael Buchberger. ... Name pronounced BUK-buhr-guhr.
HIGH SCHOOL: Langenburg (Sask.).
TRANSACTIONS/CAREER NOTES: Selected by Edmonton Oilers as underage junior in ninth round (eighth Oilers pick, 188th overall) of NHL entry draft (June 15, 1985). ... Suspended six games by AHL for leaving bench to fight (March 30, 1988). ... Fractured right ankle (March 1989). ... Dislocated left shoulder (March 13, 1990). ... Reinjured shoulder (May 4, 1990). ... Strained shoulder (April 7, 1993); missed one game.
STATISTICAL PLATEAUS: Three-goal games: 1992-93 (1).
MISCELLANEOUS: Member of Stanley Cup championship team (1987 and 1990). ... Captain of Edmonton Oilers (1995-96). ... Holds Edmonton Oilers all-time record for most penalty minutes (1,557).

		REGULAR SEASON								PLAYOFFS				
Season Team	League	Gms.	G	A	Pts.	PIM	+/-	PP	SH	Gms.	G	A	Pts.	PIM
83-84— Melville	SAJHL	60	14	11	25	139	...	...	...	—	—	—	—	—
84-85— Moose Jaw	WHL	51	12	17	29	114	...	...	...	—	—	—	—	—
85-86— Moose Jaw	WHL	72	14	22	36	206	...	...	...	13	11	4	15	37
86-87— Nova Scotia	AHL	70	12	20	32	257	...	...	...	5	0	1	1	23
— Edmonton	NHL	—	—	—	—	—	...	...	...	3	0	1	1	5
87-88— Edmonton	NHL	19	1	0	1	81	-1	0	0	—	—	—	—	—
— Nova Scotia	AHL	49	21	23	44	206	...	...	...	2	0	0	0	11
88-89— Edmonton	NHL	66	5	9	14	234	-14	1	0	—	—	—	—	—
89-90— Edmonton	NHL	55	2	6	8	168	-8	0	0	19	0	5	5	13
90-91— Edmonton	NHL	64	3	1	4	160	-6	0	0	12	2	1	3	25
91-92— Edmonton	NHL	79	20	24	44	157	9	0	4	16	1	4	5	32
92-93— Edmonton	NHL	83	12	18	30	133	-27	1	2	—	—	—	—	—
93-94— Edmonton	NHL	84	3	18	21	199	-20	0	0	—	—	—	—	—
94-95— Edmonton	NHL	48	7	17	24	82	0	2	1	—	—	—	—	—
95-96— Edmonton	NHL	82	11	14	25	184	-20	0	2	—	—	—	—	—
96-97— Edmonton	NHL	81	8	30	38	159	4	0	0	12	5	2	7	16
NHL totals (11 years)		661	72	137	209	1557	-83	4	9	62	8	13	21	91

BUCKLEY, BRENDAN — D — MIGHTY DUCKS

PERSONAL: Born February 26, 1977, in Boston. ... 6-2/196. ... Shoots right.
HIGH SCHOOL: Belmont Hill (Boston).
COLLEGE: Boston College.
TRANSACTIONS/CAREER NOTES: Selected by Mighty Ducks of Anaheim in fifth round (third Mighty Ducks pick, 117th overall) of NHL entry draft (June 22, 1996).

		REGULAR SEASON								PLAYOFFS				
Season Team	League	Gms.	G	A	Pts.	PIM	+/-	PP	SH	Gms.	G	A	Pts.	PIM
94-95— Jr. Bruins	Jr. A	48	22	43	65	164	...	...	...	—	—	—	—	—
95-96— Boston College	Hockey East	36	0	4	4	72	...	...	...	—	—	—	—	—
96-97— Boston College	Hockey East	38	2	6	8	90	...	...	...	—	—	—	—	—

BULIS, JAN — C — CAPITALS

PERSONAL: Born March 18, 1978, in Pardubice, Czechoslovakia. ... 6-0/194. ... Shoots left. ... Name pronounced YAHN BOO-lihsh.
TRANSACTIONS/CAREER NOTES: Selected by Washington Capitals in second round (third Capitals pick, 43rd overall) of NHL entry draft (June 22, 1996).

		REGULAR SEASON								PLAYOFFS				
Season Team	League	Gms.	G	A	Pts.	PIM	+/-	PP	SH	Gms.	G	A	Pts.	PIM
94-95— Kelowna	BCJHL	51	23	25	48	36	...	...	...	17	7	9	16	0
95-96— Barrie	OHL	59	29	30	59	22	...	...	...	7	2	3	5	2
96-97— Barrie	OHL	64	42	61	103	42	...	...	...	9	3	7	10	10

BURE, PAVEL   RW/LW   CANUCKS

PERSONAL: Born March 31, 1971, in Moscow, U.S.S.R. ... 5-10/189. ... Shoots left. ... Name pronounced PA-vihl BURR-ay. ... Brother of Valeri Bure, right winger/left winger, Montreal Canadiens.
TRANSACTIONS/CAREER NOTES: Selected by Vancouver Canucks in sixth round (fourth Canucks pick, 113th overall) of NHL entry draft (June 17, 1989). ... Strained groin (October 24, 1993); missed eight games. ... Fined $500 by NHL for hitting another player with flagrant elbow (May 6, 1994). ... Played in Europe during 1994-95 NHL lockout. ... Suffered injury (March 17, 1995); missed two games. ... Tore knee ligament (November 9, 1995); missed remainder of season. ... Suspended one game and fined $1,000 by NHL for forearm blow (December 6, 1996). ... Suffered whiplash (March 3, 1997); missed remainder of season.
HONORS: Named Soviet League Rookie of the Year (1988-89). ... Won Calder Memorial Trophy (1991-92). ... Named to THE SPORTING NEWS All-Star second team (1993-94). ... Played in NHL All-Star Game (1993, 1994 and 1997). ... Named to NHL All-Star first team (1993-94). ... Named to play in NHL All-Star Game (1996); replaced due to injury.
STATISTICAL PLATEAUS: Three-goal games: 1992-93 (1), 1993-94 (3), 1994-95 (1). Total: 5. ... Four-goal games: 1992-93 (1). ... Total hat tricks: 6.
MISCELLANEOUS: Scored on a penalty shot (vs. Rick Tabaracci, February 28, 1992). ... Failed to score on a penalty shot (vs. John Vanbiesbrouck, February 17, 1992; vs. Kelly Hrudey, October 6, 1993).

					REGULAR SEASON						PLAYOFFS				
Season Team	League	Gms.	G	A	Pts.	PIM	+/-	PP	SH	Gms.	G	A	Pts.	PIM	
87-88— CSKA Moscow	USSR	5	1	1	2	0	...	...	...	—	—	—	—	—	
88-89— CSKA Moscow	USSR	32	17	9	26	8	...	...	...	—	—	—	—	—	
89-90— CSKA Moscow	USSR	46	14	11	25	22	...	...	...	—	—	—	—	—	
90-91— CSKA Moscow	USSR	46	35	12	47	24	...	...	...	—	—	—	—	—	
91-92— Vancouver	NHL	65	34	26	60	30	0	7	3	13	6	4	10	14	
92-93— Vancouver	NHL	83	60	50	110	69	35	13	†7	12	5	7	12	8	
93-94— Vancouver	NHL	76	*60	47	107	86	1	†25	4	24	*16	15	31	40	
94-95— Landshut	Germany	1	3	0	3	2	...	...	...	—	—	—	—	—	
— Spartak Moscow	CIS	1	2	0	2	2	...	...	...	—	—	—	—	—	
— Vancouver	NHL	44	20	23	43	47	-8	6	2	11	7	6	13	10	
95-96— Vancouver	NHL	15	6	7	13	8	-2	1	1	—	—	—	—	—	
96-97— Vancouver	NHL	63	23	32	55	40	-14	4	1	—	—	—	—	—	
NHL totals (6 years)		346	203	185	388	280	12	56	18	60	34	32	66	72	

BURE, VALERI   RW/LW   CANADIENS

PERSONAL: Born June 13, 1974, in Moscow, U.S.S.R. ... 5-10/168. ... Shoots right. ... Name pronounced BURR-ay. ... Brother of Pavel Bure, right winger/left winger, Vancouver Canucks.
TRANSACTIONS/CAREER NOTES: Selected by Montreal Canadiens in second round (second Canadiens pick, 33rd overall) of NHL entry draft (June 20, 1992). ... Bruised forearm (April 3, 1995); missed two games. ... Bruised kidney (October 19, 1996); missed 11 games. ... Bruised wrist (December 28, 1996); missed two games. ... Suffered concussion (January 4, 1997); missed five games.
HONORS: Named to WHL (West) All-Star first team (1992-93). ... Named to WHL (West) All-Star second team (1993-94).

					REGULAR SEASON						PLAYOFFS				
Season Team	League	Gms.	G	A	Pts.	PIM	+/-	PP	SH	Gms.	G	A	Pts.	PIM	
90-91— CSKA Moscow	USSR	3	0	0	0	0	...	...	...	—	—	—	—	—	
91-92— Spokane	WHL	53	27	22	49	78	...	...	...	10	11	6	17	10	
92-93— Spokane	WHL	66	68	79	147	49	...	...	...	9	6	11	17	14	
93-94— Spokane	WHL	59	40	62	102	48	...	...	...	3	5	3	8	2	
94-95— Fredericton	AHL	45	23	25	48	32	...	...	...	—	—	—	—	—	
— Montreal	NHL	24	3	1	4	6	-1	0	0	—	—	—	—	—	
95-96— Montreal	NHL	77	22	20	42	28	10	5	0	6	0	1	1	6	
96-97— Montreal	NHL	64	14	21	35	6	4	4	0	5	0	1	1	2	
NHL totals (3 years)		165	39	42	81	40	13	9	0	11	0	2	2	8	

BUREAU, MARC   C   CANADIENS

PERSONAL: Born May 17, 1966, in Trois-Rivieres, Que. ... 6-1/198. ... Shoots right. ... Name pronounced BYOOR-oh.
TRANSACTIONS/CAREER NOTES: Traded by Chicoutimi Sagueneens with C Stephane Roy, Lee Duhemee, Sylvain Demers and D Rene L'Ecuyer to Granby Bisons for LW Greg Choules and C Stephane Richer (January 1985). ... Signed as free agent by Calgary Flames (May 16, 1987). ... Suffered eye contusion (March 25, 1990); missed final two weeks of season. ... Traded by Flames to Minnesota North Stars for third-round pick (RW Sandy McCarthy) in 1991 draft (March 5, 1991). ... Injured shoulder (January 13, 1992); missed four games. ... Separated shoulder (February 15, 1992); missed five games. ... Separated shoulder (March 1, 1992); missed eight games. ... Claimed on waivers by Tampa Bay Lightning (October 16, 1992). ... Bruised shoulder (November 17, 1992); missed six games. ... Bruised right knee (April 3, 1993); missed remainder of season. ... Traded by Lightning to Montreal Canadiens for LW Brian Bellows (June 29, 1995). ... Broke foot (September 26, 1995); missed first eight games of season. ... Suffered sore neck (November 29, 1995); missed two games. ... Suspended five games and fined $1,000 by NHL for elbowing (February 3, 1996). ... Bruised foot (November 2, 1996); missed five games. ... Tore knee ligament (December 7, 1996); missed 26 games. ... Injured knee (February 10, 1997); missed five games. ... Suffered from the flu (April 1, 1997); missed one game. ... Broke finger (April 9, 1997); missed remainder of regular season.
HONORS: Named to IHL All-Star second team (1989-90 and 1990-91).
MISCELLANEOUS: Failed to score on a penalty shot (vs. Don Beaupre, November 18, 1995).

					REGULAR SEASON						PLAYOFFS				
Season Team	League	Gms.	G	A	Pts.	PIM	+/-	PP	SH	Gms.	G	A	Pts.	PIM	
83-84— Chicoutimi	QMJHL	56	6	16	22	14	...	...	...	—	—	—	—	—	
84-85— Granby	QMJHL	68	50	70	120	29	...	...	...	—	—	—	—	—	
85-86— Chicoutimi	QMJHL	63	36	62	98	69	...	...	...	9	3	7	10	10	
86-87— Longueuil	QMJHL	66	54	58	112	68	...	...	...	20	17	20	37	12	
87-88— Salt Lake City	IHL	69	7	20	27	86	...	...	...	7	0	3	3	8	
88-89— Salt Lake City	IHL	76	28	36	64	119	...	...	...	14	7	5	12	31	

Season Team	League	REGULAR SEASON								PLAYOFFS				
		Gms.	G	A	Pts.	PIM	+/-	PP	SH	Gms.	G	A	Pts.	PIM
89-90— Salt Lake City	IHL	67	43	48	91	173	...	...	...	11	4	8	12	0
— Calgary	NHL	5	0	0	0	4	-1	0	0	—	—	—	—	—
90-91— Calgary	NHL	5	0	0	0	2	-4	0	0	—	—	—	—	—
— Salt Lake City	IHL	54	40	48	88	101	...	...	...	—	—	—	—	—
— Minnesota	NHL	9	0	6	6	4	-3	0	0	23	3	2	5	20
91-92— Minnesota	NHL	46	6	4	10	50	-5	0	0	5	0	0	0	14
— Kalamazoo	IHL	7	2	8	10	2	...	...	...	—	—	—	—	—
92-93— Tampa Bay	NHL	63	10	21	31	111	-12	1	2	—	—	—	—	—
93-94— Tampa Bay	NHL	75	8	7	15	30	-9	0	1	—	—	—	—	—
94-95— Tampa Bay	NHL	48	2	12	14	30	-8	0	1	—	—	—	—	—
95-96— Montreal	NHL	65	3	7	10	46	-3	0	0	6	1	1	2	4
96-97— Montreal	NHL	43	6	9	15	16	4	1	1	—	—	—	—	—
NHL totals (9 years)		359	35	66	101	293	-41	2	5	34	4	3	7	38

B

BURKE, SEAN — G — HURRICANES

PERSONAL: Born January 29, 1967, in Windsor, Ont. ... 6-4/210. ... Catches left.
TRANSACTIONS/CAREER NOTES: Selected by New Jersey Devils as underage junior in second round (second Devils pick, 24th overall) of NHL entry draft (June 15, 1985). ... Injured groin (December 1988). ... Underwent arthroscopic surgery to right knee (September 5, 1989). ... Traded by Devils with D Eric Weinrich to Hartford Whalers for RW Bobby Holik, second-round pick in 1993 draft (LW Jay Pandolfo) and future considerations (August 28, 1992). ... Sprained ankle (December 27, 1992); missed seven games. ... Suffered back spasms (March 13, 1993); missed remainder of season. ... Pulled hamstring (September 29, 1993); missed seven games. ... Reinjured hamstring (October 27, 1993); missed 14 games. ... Suffered back spasms (December 23, 1993); missed one game. ... Strained groin (February 28, 1995); missed two games. ... Suffered back spasms (November 19, 1995); missed two games. ... Suffered back spasms (February 7, 1996); missed three games. ... Dislocated thumb (November 30, 1996); missed 19 games. ... Injured hip flexor (February 26, 1997); missed one game. ... Whalers franchise moved to North Carolina and renamed Carolina Hurricanes for 1997-98 season; NHL approved move on June 25, 1997.
HONORS: Played in NHL All-Star Game (1989).
MISCELLANEOUS: Member of silver-medal-winning Canadian Olympic team (1992). ... Holds Carolina Hurricanes franchise all-time records for most games played by a goaltender (256) and goals-against average (3.12). ... Stopped a penalty shot attempt (vs. Luc Robitaille, February 2, 1991; vs. Michal Pivonka, January 21, 1995; vs. Wayne Presley, March 8, 1996; vs. Brian Bradley, April 3, 1996).

Season Team	League	REGULAR SEASON							PLAYOFFS					
		Gms.	Min	W	L	T	GA	SO	Avg.	Gms.	Min.	W	L	GA	SO	Avg.
83-84— St. Michael's	MTHL	25	1482	...	...	...	120	0	4.86	—	—					—
84-85— Toronto	OHL	49	2987	25	21	3	211	0	4.24	5	266	1	3	25	0	5.64
85-86— Toronto	OHL	47	2840	16	27	3	†233	0	4.92	4	238	0	4	24	0	6.05
— Can. national team	Int'l	5	284	...	...	...	22	0	4.65	—	—					—
86-87— Can. national team	Int'l	46	2670	...	...	...	138	0	3.10	—	—					—
87-88— Can. national team	Int'l	37	1962	19	9	2	92	1	2.81	—	—					—
— Can. Olympic team	Int'l	4	238	1	2	1	12	0	3.03	—	—					—
— New Jersey	NHL	13	689	10	1	0	35	1	3.05	17	1001	9	8	*57	†1	3.42
88-89— New Jersey	NHL	62	3590	22	31	9	†230	3	3.84	—	—					—
89-90— New Jersey	NHL	52	2914	22	22	6	175	0	3.60	2	125	0	2	8	0	3.84
90-91— New Jersey	NHL	35	1870	8	12	8	112	0	3.59	—	—					—
91-92— Can. national team	Int'l	31	1721	18	6	4	75	1	2.61	—	—					—
— Can. Olympic team	Int'l	7	429	5	2	0	17	0	2.38	—	—					—
— San Diego	IHL	7	424	4	2	‡1	17	0	2.41	3	160	0	3	13	0	4.88
92-93— Hartford	NHL	50	2656	16	27	3	184	0	4.16	—	—					—
93-94— Hartford	NHL	47	2750	17	24	5	137	2	2.99	—	—					—
94-95— Hartford	NHL	42	2418	17	19	4	108	0	2.68	—	—					—
95-96— Hartford	NHL	66	3669	28	28	6	190	4	3.11	—	—					—
96-97— Hartford	NHL	51	2985	22	22	6	134	4	2.69	—	—					—
NHL totals (9 years)		418	23541	162	186	47	1305	14	3.33	19	1126	9	10	65	1	3.46

BURR, SHAWN — LW — SHARKS

PERSONAL: Born July 1, 1966, in Sarnia, Ont. ... 6-1/195. ... Shoots left.
TRANSACTIONS/CAREER NOTES: Selected by Detroit Red Wings as underage junior in first round (first Red Wings pick, seventh overall) of NHL entry draft (June 9, 1984). ... Separated left shoulder (May 1988). ... Suffered lower back spasms (October 20, 1992); missed three games. ... Underwent wrist surgery (December 8, 1993); missed 18 games. ... Injured leg (January 25, 1994); missed seven games. ... Traded by Red Wings with third-round pick (traded to Boston) in 1996 draft to Tampa Bay Lightning for D Marc Bergevin and RW Ben Hankinson (August 17, 1995). ... Injured elbow (January 15, 1996); missed one game. ... Strained lower back (October 29, 1996); missed two games. ... Cut finger (December 19, 1996); missed six games. ... Traded by Lightning to San Jose Sharks for fifth-round pick (D Mark Thompson) in 1997 draft (June 21, 1997).
HONORS: Won Emms Family Award (1983-84). ... Named to OHL All-Star second team (1985-86).
STATISTICAL PLATEAUS: Three-goal games: 1986-87 (1), 1989-90 (1). Total: 2.

Season Team	League	REGULAR SEASON								PLAYOFFS				
		Gms.	G	A	Pts.	PIM	+/-	PP	SH	Gms.	G	A	Pts.	PIM
83-84— Kitchener	OHL	68	41	44	85	50	...	...	...	16	5	12	17	22
84-85— Kitchener	OHL	38	24	42	66	50	...	...	...	4	3	3	6	2
— Detroit	NHL	9	0	0	0	2	-4	0	0	—	—	—	—	—
— Adirondack	AHL	4	0	0	0	2	...	...	...	—	—	—	—	—
85-86— Kitchener	OHL	59	60	67	127	104	...	...	...	5	2	3	5	8
— Adirondack	AHL	3	2	2	4	2	...	...	...	17	5	7	12	32
— Detroit	NHL	5	1	0	1	4	1	0	1	—	—	—	—	—
86-87— Detroit	NHL	80	22	25	47	107	2	1	2	16	7	2	9	20
87-88— Detroit	NHL	78	17	23	40	97	7	5	3	9	3	1	4	14
88-89— Detroit	NHL	79	19	27	46	78	5	1	4	6	1	2	3	6
89-90— Adirondack	AHL	3	4	2	6	2	...	...	...	—	—	—	—	—
— Detroit	NHL	76	24	32	56	82	14	4	3	—	—	—	—	—

Season Team	League	REGULAR SEASON								PLAYOFFS				
		Gms.	G	A	Pts.	PIM	+/-	PP	SH	Gms.	G	A	Pts.	PIM
90-91— Detroit......................	NHL	80	20	30	50	112	14	6	0	7	0	4	4	15
91-92— Detroit......................	NHL	79	19	32	51	118	26	2	0	11	1	5	6	10
92-93— Detroit......................	NHL	80	10	25	35	74	18	1	1	7	2	1	3	2
93-94— Detroit......................	NHL	51	10	12	22	31	12	0	1	7	2	0	2	6
94-95— Detroit......................	NHL	42	6	8	14	60	13	0	0	16	0	2	2	6
95-96— Tampa Bay..................	NHL	81	13	15	28	119	4	1	0	6	0	2	2	8
96-97— Tampa Bay..................	NHL	74	14	21	35	106	5	1	0	—	—	—	—	—
NHL totals (13 years)		814	175	250	425	990	117	22	15	85	16	19	35	87

BURRIDGE, RANDY   LW   SABRES

B

PERSONAL: Born January 7, 1966, in Fort Erie, Ont. ... 5-9/188. ... Shoots left. ... Name pronounced BUHR-ihdj.
TRANSACTIONS/CAREER NOTES: Selected by Boston Bruins in eighth round (seventh Bruins pick, 157th overall) of NHL entry draft (June 15, 1985). ... Strained groin (March 1, 1986). ... Suspended by AHL during playoffs (April 1987). ... Sprained left knee ligament (February 6, 1990); missed 18 games. ... Tore right knee ligaments (February 7, 1991). ... Underwent surgery to right knee (February 13, 1991). ... Traded by Bruins to Washington Capitals for RW Stephen Leach (June 21, 1991). ... Partially tore left knee ligament (March 1, 1992); missed 14 games. ... Underwent knee surgery (September 5, 1992); missed first 71 games of season. ... Strained groin (October 6, 1993); missed three games. ... Traded by Capitals to Los Angeles Kings for LW Warren Rychel (February 10, 1995). ... Signed as free agent by Buffalo Sabres (October 4, 1995). ... Injured shoulder (October 7, 1995); missed two games. ... Injured left knee (February 28, 1996); missed five games. ... Underwent arthroscopic knee surgery (January 28, 1997); missed 27 games.
HONORS: Played in NHL All-Star Game (1992).
STATISTICAL PLATEAUS: Three-goal games: 1988-89 (2), 1993-94 (2). Total: 4.
MISCELLANEOUS: Failed to score on a penalty shot (vs. Kay Whitmore, March 31, 1991; vs. Bill Ranford, February 3, 1996).

Season Team	League	REGULAR SEASON								PLAYOFFS				
		Gms.	G	A	Pts.	PIM	+/-	PP	SH	Gms.	G	A	Pts.	PIM
82-83— Fort Erie Jr. B.............	OHA	42	32	56	88	32	...	...	...	—	—	—	—	—
83-84— Peterborough.............	OHL	55	6	7	13	44	...	...	...	8	3	2	5	7
84-85— Peterborough.............	OHL	66	49	57	106	88	...	...	...	17	9	16	25	18
85-86— Peterborough.............	OHL	17	15	11	26	23	...	...	...	3	1	3	4	2
— Boston	NHL	52	17	25	42	28	17	1	0	3	0	4	4	12
— Moncton	AHL	—	—	—	—	—	...	...	...	3	0	2	2	2
86-87— Moncton	AHL	47	26	41	67	139	...	...	...	3	1	2	3	30
— Boston	NHL	23	1	4	5	16	-6	0	0	2	1	0	1	2
87-88— Boston	NHL	79	27	28	55	105	0	5	3	23	2	10	12	16
88-89— Boston	NHL	80	31	30	61	39	19	6	2	10	5	2	7	8
89-90— Boston	NHL	63	17	15	32	47	9	7	0	21	4	11	15	14
90-91— Boston	NHL	62	15	13	28	40	17	1	0	19	0	3	3	39
91-92— Washington	NHL	66	23	44	67	50	-4	9	0	2	0	1	1	0
92-93— Baltimore	AHL	2	0	1	1	2	...	...	...	—	—	—	—	—
— Washington	NHL	4	0	0	0	0	1	0	0	4	1	0	1	0
93-94— Washington	NHL	78	25	17	42	73	-1	8	1	11	0	2	2	12
94-95— Washington	NHL	2	0	0	0	2	0	0	0	—	—	—	—	—
— Los Angeles.................	NHL	38	4	15	19	8	-4	2	0	—	—	—	—	—
95-96— Buffalo	NHL	74	25	33	58	30	0	6	0	—	—	—	—	—
96-97— Buffalo	NHL	55	10	21	31	20	17	1	3	12	5	1	6	2
NHL totals (12 years)		676	195	245	440	458	65	46	9	107	18	34	52	105

BURT, ADAM   D   HURRICANES

PERSONAL: Born January 15, 1969, in Detroit. ... 6-1/208. ... Shoots left.
TRANSACTIONS/CAREER NOTES: Broke jaw (December 1985). ... Selected by Hartford Whalers as underage junior in second round (second Whalers pick, 39th overall) of NHL entry draft (June 13, 1987). ... Separated left shoulder (September 13, 1988). ... Bruised hip (December 1989). ... Dislocated left shoulder (January 19, 1989). ... Tore right knee ligaments (February 16, 1991); missed remainder of season. ... Sprained left wrist (January 11, 1992); missed six games. ... Broke bone in right foot (January 25, 1993); missed 13 games. ... Sprained shoulder (February 27, 1994); missed remainder of season. ... Strained groin (February 3, 1997); missed eight games. ... Sprained shoulder (March 5, 1997); missed three games. ... Whalers franchise moved to North Carolina and renamed Carolina Hurricanes for 1997-98 season; NHL approved move on June 25, 1997.
HONORS: Named to OHL All-Star second team (1987-88).
MISCELLANEOUS: Captain of Hartford Whalers (1994-95).

Season Team	League	REGULAR SEASON								PLAYOFFS				
		Gms.	G	A	Pts.	PIM	+/-	PP	SH	Gms.	G	A	Pts.	PIM
85-86— North Bay..................	OHL	49	0	11	11	81	...	...	...	10	0	0	0	24
86-87— North Bay..................	OHL	57	4	27	31	138	...	...	...	24	1	6	7	68
87-88— North Bay..................	OHL	66	17	54	71	176	...	...	...	2	0	3	3	6
— Binghamton	AHL	—	—	—	—	—	...	...	...	2	1	1	2	0
88-89— North Bay..................	OHL	23	4	11	15	45	...	...	...	12	2	12	14	12
— Team USA Juniors	Int'l	7	1	6	7	...	...	...	...	—	—	—	—	—
— Binghamton	AHL	5	0	2	2	13	...	...	...	—	—	—	—	—
— Hartford	NHL	5	0	0	0	6	...	...	...	—	—	—	—	—
89-90— Hartford	NHL	63	4	8	12	105	3	1	0	2	0	0	0	0
90-91— Springfield	AHL	9	1	3	4	22	...	...	...	—	—	—	—	—
— Hartford	NHL	42	2	7	9	63	-4	1	0	—	—	—	—	—
91-92— Hartford	NHL	66	9	15	24	93	-16	4	0	2	0	0	0	0
92-93— Hartford	NHL	65	6	14	20	116	-11	0	0	—	—	—	—	—
93-94— Hartford	NHL	63	1	17	18	75	-4	0	0	—	—	—	—	—
94-95— Hartford	NHL	46	7	11	18	65	0	3	0	—	—	—	—	—
95-96— Hartford	NHL	78	4	9	13	121	-4	0	0	—	—	—	—	—
96-97— Hartford	NHL	71	2	11	13	79	-13	0	0	—	—	—	—	—
NHL totals (9 years)		499	35	92	127	723	-49	9	0	4	0	0	0	0

BUTENSCHON, SVEN — D — PENGUINS

PERSONAL: Born March 22, 1976, in Itzehoe, West Germany. ... 6-5/201. ... Shoots left. ... Name pronounced BOO-tehn-shahn.
HIGH SCHOOL: Crocus Plains (Brandon, Man.).
TRANSACTIONS/CAREER NOTES: Selected by Pittsburgh Penguins in third round (third Penguins pick, 57th overall) of NHL entry draft (June 29, 1994).

		REGULAR SEASON								PLAYOFFS				
Season Team	League	Gms.	G	A	Pts.	PIM	+/-	PP	SH	Gms.	G	A	Pts.	PIM
93-94— Brandon	WHL	70	3	19	22	51	...	...	...	4	0	0	0	6
94-95— Brandon	WHL	21	1	5	6	44	...	...	...	18	1	2	3	11
95-96— Brandon	WHL	70	4	37	41	99	...	...	...	19	1	12	13	18
96-97— Cleveland	IHL	75	3	12	15	68	...	...	...	10	0	1	1	4

BUZAK, MIKE — G — BLUES

PERSONAL: Born February 10, 1973, in Edson, Alta. ... 6-3/197. ... Catches left. ... Name pronounced BYOO-zak.
HIGH SCHOOL: Queen Elizabeth (Edmonton).
COLLEGE: Michigan State.
TRANSACTIONS/CAREER NOTES: Selected by St. Louis Blues in seventh round (fifth Blues pick, 167th overall) of NHL entry draft (June 26, 1993).
HONORS: Named to CCHA All-Star second team (1993-94 and 1994-95).

		REGULAR SEASON								PLAYOFFS					
Season Team	League	Gms.	Min	W	L	T	GA	SO	Avg.	Gms.	Min.	W	L	GA	SO	Avg.
91-92—Michigan State	CCHA	7	311	4	0	0	22	0	4.24	—	—	—	—	—	—	—
92-93—Michigan State	CCHA	38	2090	22	10	2	102	0	2.93	—	—	—	—	—	—	—
93-94—Michigan State	CCHA	39	2297	21	12	5	104	2	2.72	—	—	—	—	—	—	—
94-95—Michigan State	CCHA	31	1797	17	10	3	94	0	3.14	—	—	—	—	—	—	—
95-96—Worcester	AHL	30	1671	9	10	5	85	0	3.05	—	—	—	—	—	—	—
96-97—Worcester	AHL	19	973	9	4	3	41	1	2.53	1	59	0	1	3	0	3.05
—Baton Rouge	ECHL	3	108	0	2	0	7	0	3.89	—	—	—	—	—	—	—

BYLSMA, DAN — LW — KINGS

PERSONAL: Born September 19, 1970, in Grand Rapids, Mich. ... 6-2/205. ... Shoots left. ... Full name: Daniel Brian Bylsma. ... Name pronounced BIGHLS-muh.
COLLEGE: Bowling Green State.
TRANSACTIONS/CAREER NOTES: Selected by Winnipeg Jets in fourth round (sixth Jets pick, 69th overall) of NHL entry draft (June 17, 1989). ... Signed as free agent by Los Angeles Kings (July 14, 1994). ... Injured knee (March 19, 1997); missed one game. ... Strained groin (April 3, 1997); missed one game.

		REGULAR SEASON								PLAYOFFS				
Season Team	League	Gms.	G	A	Pts.	PIM	+/-	PP	SH	Gms.	G	A	Pts.	PIM
87-88— St. Mary's Jr. B	OHA	40	30	39	69	33	...	...	...	—	—	—	—	—
88-89— Bowling Green	CCHA	39	4	7	11	16	...	...	...	—	—	—	—	—
89-90— Bowling Green	CCHA	44	13	17	30	32	...	...	...	—	—	—	—	—
90-91— Bowling Green	CCHA	40	9	12	21	48	...	...	...	—	—	—	—	—
91-92— Bowling Green	CCHA	34	11	14	25	24	...	...	...	—	—	—	—	—
92-93— Rochester	AHL	2	0	1	1	0	...	...	...	—	—	—	—	—
93-94— Albany	AHL	3	0	1	1	2	...	...	...	—	—	—	—	—
—Moncton	AHL	50	12	16	28	25	...	...	...	21	3	4	7	31
—Greensboro	ECHL	25	14	16	30	52	...	...	...	—	—	—	—	—
94-95— Phoenix	IHL	81	19	23	42	41	...	...	...	—	—	—	—	—
95-96— Phoenix	IHL	78	22	20	42	48	...	...	...	4	1	0	1	2
—Los Angeles	NHL	4	0	0	0	0	0	0	0	—	—	—	—	—
96-97— Los Angeles	NHL	79	3	6	9	32	-15	0	0	—	—	—	—	—
NHL totals (2 years)		83	3	6	9	32	-15	0	0					

CAIRNS, ERIC — D — RANGERS

PERSONAL: Born June 27, 1974, in Oakville, Ont. ... 6-6/230. ... Shoots left.
TRANSACTIONS/CAREER NOTES: Selected by New York Rangers in third round (third Rangers pick, 72nd overall) of NHL entry draft (June 20, 1992).

		REGULAR SEASON								PLAYOFFS				
Season Team	League	Gms.	G	A	Pts.	PIM	+/-	PP	SH	Gms.	G	A	Pts.	PIM
90-91— Burlington Jr. B	OHA	37	5	16	21	120	...	...	...	—	—	—	—	—
91-92— Detroit	OHL	64	1	11	12	237	...	...	...	7	0	0	0	31
92-93— Detroit	OHL	64	3	13	16	194	...	...	...	15	0	3	3	24
93-94— Detroit	OHL	59	7	35	42	204	...	...	...	17	0	4	4	46
94-95— Binghamton	AHL	27	0	3	3	134	...	...	...	9	1	1	2	28
—Birmingham	ECHL	11	1	3	4	49	...	...	...	—	—	—	—	—
95-96— Charlotte	ECHL	6	0	1	1	34	...	...	...	—	—	—	—	—
—Binghamton	AHL	46	1	13	14	192	...	...	...	4	0	0	0	37
96-97— New York Rangers	NHL	40	0	1	1	147	-7	0	0	3	0	0	0	0
—Binghamton	AHL	10	1	1	2	96	...	...	...	—	—	—	—	—
NHL totals (1 year)		40	0	1	1	147	-7	0	0	3	0	0	0	0

B
C

CALLAHAN, BRIAN   C   PENGUINS

PERSONAL: Born July 13, 1974, in Melrose, Mass. ... 6-0/193. ... Shoots left. ... Full name: Brian Patrick Callahan.
HIGH SCHOOL: Belmont Hill (Mass.).
COLLEGE: Boston College.
TRANSACTIONS/CAREER NOTES: Selected by Pittsburgh Penguins in 10th round (10th Penguins pick, 235th overall) of NHL entry draft (June 20, 1992).

				REGULAR SEASON								PLAYOFFS			
Season Team	League	Gms.	G	A	Pts.	PIM	+/-	PP	SH	Gms.	G	A	Pts.	PIM
91-92— Belmont Hill.	Mass. H.S.	25	20	18	38	...	...	...	...	—	—	—	—	—
92-93— Belmont Hill.	Mass. H.S.	15	19	16	35	16	...	...	...	—	—	—	—	—
93-94— Boston College..........	Hockey East	36	11	11	22	58	...	...	...	—	—	—	—	—
94-95— Boston College..........	Hockey East	34	10	1	11	58	...	...	...	—	—	—	—	—
95-96— Boston College..........	Hockey East	36	14	8	22	38	...	...	...	—	—	—	—	—
96-97— Boston College..........	Hockey East	38	19	19	38	70	...	...	...	—	—	—	—	—

CALOUN, JAN   RW   SHARKS

PERSONAL: Born December 20, 1972, in Usti-nad-Labem, Czechoslovakia. ... 5-10/190. ... Shoots right. ... Name pronounced YAHN shah-LOON.
TRANSACTIONS/CAREER NOTES: Selected by San Jose Sharks in fourth round (fourth Sharks pick, 75th overall) of NHL entry draft (June 20, 1992).
HONORS: Named to AHL All-Star second team (1996-97).

				REGULAR SEASON								PLAYOFFS			
Season Team	League	Gms.	G	A	Pts.	PIM	+/-	PP	SH	Gms.	G	A	Pts.	PIM
90-91— CHZ Litvinov	Czech.	50	28	19	47	12	...	...	...	—	—	—	—	—
91-92— Chemopetrol Litvin. ...	Czech.	46	39	13	52	...	...	...	...	—	—	—	—	—
92-93— Chemopetrol Litvin. ...	Czech.	47	45	22	67	...	...	...	...	—	—	—	—	—
93-94— Chemopetrol Litvin. ...	Czech Rep.	41	25	17	42	...	...	...	...	4	2	0	2	0
94-95— Kansas City	IHL	76	34	39	73	50	...	...	...	21	13	10	23	18
95-96— Kansas City	IHL	61	38	30	68	58	...	...	...	5	0	1	1	6
— San Jose	NHL	11	8	3	11	0	4	2	0	—	—	—	—	—
96-97— Kentucky	AHL	66	43	43	86	68	...	...	...	4	0	1	1	4
— San Jose	NHL	2	0	0	0	0	-2	0	0	—	—	—	—	—
NHL totals (2 years)		13	8	3	11	0	2	2	0					

CAMPBELL, JIM   RW   BLUES

PERSONAL: Born February 3, 1973, in Worcester, Mass. ... 6-2/190. ... Shoots right.
HIGH SCHOOL: Lawrence Academy (Groton, Mass.), then Northwood School (Lake Placid, N.Y.).
TRANSACTIONS/CAREER NOTES: Selected by Montreal Canadiens in second round (second Canadiens pick, 28th overall) of NHL entry draft (June 22, 1991). ... Loaned by Canadiens to U.S. Olympic team (September 26, 1993). ... Traded by Canadiens to Mighty Ducks of Anaheim for D Robert Dirk (January 21, 1996). ... Signed as free agent by St. Louis Blues (July 3, 1996). ... Strained thumb (February 25, 1997); missed 10 games. ... Reinjured thumb (April 6, 1997); missed remainder of regular season.
HONORS: Named to NHL All-Rookie team (1996-97).

				REGULAR SEASON								PLAYOFFS			
Season Team	League	Gms.	G	A	Pts.	PIM	+/-	PP	SH	Gms.	G	A	Pts.	PIM
88-89— Lawrence Academy....	Mass. H.S.	12	12	8	20	6	...	...	...	—	—	—	—	—
89-90— Lawrence Academy....	Mass. H.S.	8	14	7	21	8	...	...	...	—	—	—	—	—
90-91— Northwood School.....	N.Y. H.S.	26	36	47	83	36	...	...	...	—	—	—	—	—
91-92— Hull	QMJHL	64	41	44	85	51	...	...	...	6	7	3	10	8
92-93— Hull	QMJHL	50	42	29	71	66	...	...	...	8	11	4	15	43
93-94— U.S. national team	Int'l	56	24	33	57	59	...	...	...	—	—	—	—	—
— U.S. Olympic team.....	Int'l	8	0	0	0	6	...	...	...	—	—	—	—	—
— Fredericton...............	AHL	19	6	17	23	6	...	...	...	—	—	—	—	—
94-95— Fredericton...............	AHL	77	27	24	51	103	...	...	...	12	0	7	7	8
95-96— Fredericton...............	AHL	44	28	23	51	24	...	...	...	—	—	—	—	—
— Baltimore	AHL	16	13	7	20	8	...	...	...	12	7	5	12	10
— Anaheim..................	NHL	16	2	3	5	36	0	1	0	—	—	—	—	—
96-97— St. Louis	NHL	68	23	20	43	68	3	5	0	4	1	0	1	6
NHL totals (2 years)		84	25	23	48	104	3	6	0	4	1	0	1	6

CARAVAGGIO, LUCIANO   G   DEVILS

PERSONAL: Born October 3, 1975, in Toronto. ... 5-11/170. ... Catches left. ... Full name: Luciano Anthony Caravaggio.
HIGH SCHOOL: Don Bosco (Weston, Ont.).
COLLEGE: Michigan Tech.
TRANSACTIONS/CAREER NOTES: Selected by New Jersey Devils in sixth round (seventh Devils pick, 155th overall) of NHL entry draft (June 29, 1994).

					REGULAR SEASON								PLAYOFFS				
Season Team	League	Gms.	Min	W	L	T	GA	SO	Avg.	Gms.	Min.	W	L	GA	SO	Avg.
92-93— Weston	Jr. A						Statistics unavailable.									
93-94— Michigan Tech	WCHA	13	537	1	7	0	37	1	4.13	—	—	—	—	—	—	—
94-95— Michigan Tech	WCHA	31	1777	12	15	3	119	1	4.02	—	—	—	—	—	—	—
95-96— Michigan Tech	WCHA	24	1280	7	11	4	85	0	3.98	—	—	—	—	—	—	—
96-97— Michigan Tech	WCHA	28	1504	7	14	4	92	0	3.67	—	—	—	—	—	—	—

CARBONNEAU, GUY　　　　　　　C　　　　　　　STARS

PERSONAL: Born March 18, 1960, in Sept-Iles, Que. ... 5-11/184. ... Shoots right. ... Name pronounced GEE KAHR-buh-noh.
TRANSACTIONS/CAREER NOTES: Selected by Montreal Canadiens as underage junior in third round (fourth Canadiens pick, 44th overall) of NHL entry draft (August 9, 1979). ... Strained right knee ligaments (October 7, 1989); missed nine games. ... Broke nose (October 28, 1989). ... Suffered concussion (October 8, 1990). ... Fractured rib (January 13, 1992); missed six games. ... Injured elbow (March 2, 1992); missed one game. ... Suffered right knee tendinitis (October 1, 1992); missed five games. ... Broke finger (November 14, 1992); missed three games. ... Suffered knee tendinitis (February 4, 1993); missed 15 games. ... Suffered from the flu (February 11, 1994); missed one game. ... Traded by Canadiens to St. Louis Blues for C Jim Montgomery (August 19, 1994). ... Underwent knee surgery (March 31, 1995); missed six games. ... Traded by Blues to Dallas Stars for RW Paul Broten (October 2, 1995). ... Injured groin (October 17, 1995); missed five games. ... Strained groin (December 8, 1996); missed one game. ... Bruised forearm (March 31, 1997); missed two games.
HONORS: Named to QMJHL All-Star second team (1979-80). ... Won Frank J. Selke Trophy (1987-88, 1988-89 and 1991-92).
STATISTICAL PLATEAUS: Three-goal games: 1982-83 (1), 1993-94 (1). Total: 2.
MISCELLANEOUS: Member of Stanley Cup championship team (1986 and 1993). ... Co-captain of Montreal Canadiens (1989-90). ... Captain of Canadiens (1991-92 through 1993-1994).

| | | REGULAR SEASON | | | | | | | | PLAYOFFS | | | | |
Season Team	League	Gms.	G	A	Pts.	PIM	+/-	PP	SH	Gms.	G	A	Pts.	PIM
76-77 — Chicoutimi	QMJHL	59	9	20	29	8	...	...	...	4	1	0	1	0
77-78 — Chicoutimi	QMJHL	70	28	55	83	60	...	...	...	—	—	—	—	—
78-79 — Chicoutimi	QMJHL	72	62	79	141	47	...	...	...	4	2	1	3	4
79-80 — Chicoutimi	QMJHL	72	72	110	182	66	...	...	...	12	9	15	24	28
— Nova Scotia	AHL	—	—	—	—	—	...	...	...	2	1	1	2	2
80-81 — Montreal	NHL	2	0	1	1	0	0	0	0	—	—	—	—	—
— Nova Scotia	AHL	78	35	53	88	87	...	...	...	6	1	3	4	9
81-82 — Nova Scotia	AHL	77	27	67	94	124	...	...	...	9	2	7	9	8
82-83 — Montreal	NHL	77	18	29	47	68	18	0	5	3	0	0	0	2
83-84 — Montreal	NHL	78	24	30	54	75	5	3	7	15	4	3	7	12
84-85 — Montreal	NHL	79	23	34	57	43	28	0	4	12	4	3	7	8
85-86 — Montreal	NHL	80	20	36	56	57	18	1	2	20	7	5	12	35
86-87 — Montreal	NHL	79	18	27	45	68	9	0	0	17	3	8	11	20
87-88 — Montreal	NHL	80	17	21	38	61	14	0	3	11	0	4	4	2
88-89 — Montreal	NHL	79	26	30	56	44	37	1	2	21	4	5	9	10
89-90 — Montreal	NHL	68	19	36	55	37	21	1	1	11	2	3	5	6
90-91 — Montreal	NHL	78	20	24	44	63	-1	4	1	13	1	5	6	10
91-92 — Montreal	NHL	72	18	21	39	39	2	1	1	11	1	1	2	6
92-93 — Montreal	NHL	61	4	13	17	20	-9	0	1	20	3	3	6	10
93-94 — Montreal	NHL	79	14	24	38	48	16	0	0	7	1	3	4	4
94-95 — St. Louis	NHL	42	5	11	16	16	11	1	0	7	1	2	3	6
95-96 — Dallas	NHL	71	8	15	23	38	-2	0	0	—	—	—	—	—
96-97 — Dallas	NHL	73	5	16	21	36	9	0	1	7	0	1	1	6
NHL totals (16 years)		1098	239	368	607	713	176	12	30	175	31	46	77	137

CARDARELLI, JOE　　　　　　　LW　　　　　　LIGHTNING

PERSONAL: Born July 13, 1977, in Vancouver. ... 5-11/205. ... Shoots left.
HIGH SCHOOL: Joel E. Ferris (Spokane, Wash.).
TRANSACTIONS/CAREER NOTES: Selected by Tampa Bay Lightning in eighth round (seventh Lightning pick, 186th overall) of NHL entry draft (July 8, 1995).

| | | REGULAR SEASON | | | | | | | | PLAYOFFS | | | | |
Season Team	League	Gms.	G	A	Pts.	PIM	+/-	PP	SH	Gms.	G	A	Pts.	PIM
93-94 — Spokane	WHL	51	7	11	18	9	...	...	...	2	0	0	0	0
94-95 — Spokane	WHL	71	27	22	49	20	...	...	...	11	4	9	13	0
95-96 — Spokane	WHL	44	25	19	44	21	...	...	...	18	4	0	4	4
96-97 — Spokane	WHL	66	34	37	71	39	...	...	...	9	6	1	7	0

CAREY, JIM　　　　　　　G　　　　　　　BRUINS

PERSONAL: Born May 31, 1974, in Dorchester, Mass. ... 6-2/205. ... Catches left. ... Brother of Paul Carey, first baseman, Baltimore Orioles organization (1990-95).
HIGH SCHOOL: Catholic Memorial (Boston).
COLLEGE: Wisconsin.
TRANSACTIONS/CAREER NOTES: Selected by Washington Capitals in second round (second Capitals pick, 32nd overall) of NHL entry draft (June 20, 1992). ... Traded by Capitals with C Jason Allison, C Anson Carter, third-round pick (RW Lee Goren) in 1997 draft and conditional pick in 1998 draft to Boston Bruins for C Adam Oates, RW Rick Tocchet and G Bill Ranford (March 1, 1997).
HONORS: Won WCHA Rookie of the Year Award (1992-93). ... Named to WCHA All-Star second team (1992-93). ... Named to WCHA All-Rookie team (1992-93). ... Named to NHL All-Rookie team (1994-95). ... Won Dudley (Red) Garrett Memorial Trophy (1994-95). ... Won Aldege (Baz) Bastien Trophy (1994-95). ... Named to AHL All-Star first team (1994-95). ... Won Vezina Trophy (1995-96). ... Named to NHL All-Star first team (1995-96).
MISCELLANEOUS: Holds Washington Capitals all-time record for goals-against average (2.37) and shutouts (14). ... Stopped a penalty shot attempt (vs. Todd Elik, November 19, 1996). ... Allowed a penalty shot goal (vs. Jeff Friesen, December 2, 1995; vs. Sami Kapanen, March 12, 1997).

| | | REGULAR SEASON | | | | | | | | PLAYOFFS | | | | | |
Season Team	League	Gms.	Min	W	L	T	GA	SO	Avg.	Gms.	Min.	W	L	GA	SO	Avg.
89-90 — Catholic Memorial	Mass. HS	12	...	12	0	0	...	...	...	—	—	—	—	—	—	—
90-91 — Catholic Memorial	Mass. HS	14	...	13	0	0	...	6	...	—	—	—	—	—	—	—
91-92 — Catholic Memorial	Mass. HS	21	1108	19	2	0	29	6	1.57	—	—	—	—	—	—	—
92-93 — Univ. of Wisconsin	WCHA	26	1525	15	8	1	78	1	3.07	—	—	—	—	—	—	—

Season Team	League	REGULAR SEASON							PLAYOFFS						
		Gms.	Min	W	L	T	GA	SO	Avg.	Gms.	Min.	W	L	GA	SO	Avg.
93-94—Univ. of Wisconsin	WCHA	39	2247	24	13	1	114	1	3.04	—	—	—	—	—	—	—
94-95—Portland	AHL	55	3281	30	14	11	151	*6	2.76	—	—	—	—	—	—	—
—Washington	NHL	28	1604	18	6	3	57	4	2.13	7	358	2	4	25	0	4.19
95-96—Washington	NHL	71	4069	35	24	9	153	*9	2.26	3	97	0	1	10	0	6.19
96-97—Washington	NHL	40	2293	17	18	3	105	1	2.75	—	—	—	—	—	—	—
—Boston	NHL	19	1004	5	13	0	64	0	3.82	—	—	—	—	—	—	—
NHL totals (3 years)		158	8970	75	61	15	379	14	2.54	10	455	2	5	35	0	4.62

CARKNER, TERRY D PANTHERS

PERSONAL: Born March 7, 1966, in Smith Falls, Ont. ... 6-3/210. ... Shoots left.
TRANSACTIONS/CAREER NOTES: Selected by New York Rangers as underage junior in first round (first Rangers pick, 14th overall) of NHL entry draft (June 9, 1984). ... Traded by Rangers with LW Jeff Jackson to Quebec Nordiques for LW John Ogrodnick and D David Shaw (September 30, 1987). ... Suspended 10 games by NHL for leaving bench during fight (January 24, 1988). ... Traded by Nordiques to Philadelphia Flyers for D Greg Smyth and third-round pick (G John Tanner) in 1989 draft (July 25, 1988). ... Underwent surgery on left knee (September 23, 1989); missed 15 games. ... Bruised ankle (March 1990). ... Bruised foot (November 23, 1991); missed two games. ... Bruised wrist (November 19, 1992); missed one game. ... Traded by Flyers to Detroit Red Wings for D Yves Racine and fourth-round pick (LW Sebastien Vallee) in 1994 draft (October 5, 1993). ... Injured left shoulder (March 19, 1994); missed 11 games. ... Did not play due to contract dispute (February 24-March 15, 1995). ... Signed as free agent by Florida Panthers (August 17, 1995). ... Sprained ankle (November 7, 1996); missed eight games.
HONORS: Named to OHL All-Star second team (1984-85). ... Shared Max Kaminsky Trophy with Jeff Brown (1985-86). ... Named to OHL All-Star first team (1985-86).

Season Team	League	REGULAR SEASON							PLAYOFFS				
		Gms.	G	A	Pts.	PIM	+/-	PP	SH	Gms.	G	A	Pts.	PIM
82-83—Brockville	COJHL	47	8	32	40	94	...	...	...	—	—	—	—	—
83-84—Peterborough	OHL	66	4	21	25	91	...	...	...	8	0	6	6	13
84-85—Peterborough	OHL	64	14	47	61	125	...	...	...	17	2	10	12	11
85-86—Peterborough	OHL	54	12	32	44	106	...	...	...	16	1	7	8	17
86-87—New Haven	AHL	12	2	6	8	56	...	...	...	3	1	0	1	0
—New York Rangers	NHL	52	2	13	15	120	-1	0	0	1	0	0	0	0
87-88—Quebec	NHL	63	3	24	27	159	-8	2	0	—	—	—	—	—
88-89—Philadelphia	NHL	78	11	32	43	149	-6	2	1	19	1	5	6	28
89-90—Philadelphia	NHL	63	4	18	22	167	-8	1	0	—	—	—	—	—
90-91—Philadelphia	NHL	79	7	25	32	204	-15	6	0	—	—	—	—	—
91-92—Philadelphia	NHL	73	4	12	16	195	-14	0	1	—	—	—	—	—
92-93—Philadelphia	NHL	83	3	16	19	150	18	0	0	—	—	—	—	—
93-94—Detroit	NHL	68	1	6	7	130	13	0	0	7	0	0	0	4
94-95—Detroit	NHL	20	1	2	3	21	7	0	0	—	—	—	—	—
95-96—Florida	NHL	73	3	10	13	80	10	1	0	22	0	4	4	10
96-97—Florida	NHL	70	0	14	14	96	-4	0	0	5	0	0	0	6
NHL totals (11 years)		722	39	172	211	1471	-8	12	2	54	1	9	10	48

CARNEY, KEITH D BLACKHAWKS

PERSONAL: Born February 3, 1970, in Providence, R.I. ... 6-2/205. ... Shoots left. ... Full name: Keith Edward Carney.
COLLEGE: Maine.
TRANSACTIONS/CAREER NOTES: Selected by Buffalo Sabres in fourth round (third Sabres pick, 76th overall) of NHL entry draft (June 11, 1988). ... Traded by Sabres to Chicago Blackhawks for D Craig Muni (October 27, 1993).
HONORS: Named to Hockey East All-Rookie team (1988-89). ... Named to NCAA All-America East second team (1989-90). ... Named to Hockey East All-Star second team (1989-90). ... Named to NCAA All-America East first team (1990-91). ... Named to Hockey East All-Star first team (1990-91).

Season Team	League	REGULAR SEASON							PLAYOFFS				
		Gms.	G	A	Pts.	PIM	+/-	PP	SH	Gms.	G	A	Pts.	PIM
88-89—Univ. of Maine...........	Hockey East	40	4	22	26	24	...	...	...	—	—	—	—	—
89-90—Univ. of Maine...........	Hockey East	41	3	41	44	43	...	...	...	—	—	—	—	—
90-91—Univ. of Maine...........	Hockey East	40	7	49	56	38	...	...	...	—	—	—	—	—
91-92—U.S. nat'l team	Int'l	49	2	17	19	16	...	...	...	—	—	—	—	—
—Rochester	AHL	24	1	10	11	2	...	...	...	2	0	2	2	0
—Buffalo	NHL	14	1	2	3	18	-3	1	0	7	0	3	3	0
92-93—Buffalo	NHL	30	2	4	6	55	3	0	0	8	0	3	3	6
—Rochester	AHL	41	5	21	26	32	...	...	...	—	—	—	—	—
93-94—Louisville	ECHL	15	1	4	5	14	...	...	...	—	—	—	—	—
—Buffalo	NHL	7	1	3	4	4	-1	0	0	—	—	—	—	—
—Indianapolis	IHL	28	0	14	14	20	...	...	...	—	—	—	—	—
—Chicago	NHL	30	3	5	8	35	15	0	0	6	0	1	1	4
94-95—Chicago	NHL	18	1	0	1	11	-1	0	0	4	0	1	1	0
95-96—Chicago	NHL	82	5	14	19	94	31	1	0	10	0	3	3	4
96-97—Chicago	NHL	81	3	15	18	62	26	0	0	6	1	1	2	2
NHL totals (7 years)		262	16	43	59	279	70	2	0	41	1	12	13	16

CARPENTER, BOB LW DEVILS

PERSONAL: Born July 13, 1963, in Beverly, Mass. ... 6-0/200. ... Shoots left.
HIGH SCHOOL: St. John's Prep (Danvers, Mass.).

TRANSACTIONS/CAREER NOTES: Selected by Washington Capitals as underage junior in first round (first Capitals pick, third overall) of NHL entry draft (June 10, 1981). ... Traded by Capitals with second-round pick in 1989 draft (RW Jason Prosofsky) to New York Rangers for C Mike Ridley, C Kelly Miller and RW Bobby Crawford (January 1, 1987). ... Traded by Rangers with D Tom Laidlaw to Los Angeles Kings for C Marcel Dionne, C Jeff Crossman and third-round pick in 1989 draft (March 10, 1987). ... Tore rotator cuff (January 1988). ... Broke right thumb and wrist (December 31, 1988). ... Traded by Kings to Boston Bruins for C Steve Kasper and LW Jay Miller (January 23, 1989). ... Tore ligaments of right wrist (April 1989). ... Injured left knee (October 1990). ... Suffered multiple fracture of left kneecap (December 8, 1990); missed remainder of season. ... Injured left wrist and suffered stiffness in knee (April 5, 1991). ... Strained calf (March 19, 1992). ... Signed as free agent by Capitals (June 30, 1992). ... Signed as free agent by New Jersey Devils (September 30, 1993). ... Sprained ankle (February 11, 1995); missed one game. ... Suffered charley horse (April 20, 1995); missed last five games of season and first three games of playoffs. ... Suffered cut to leg (September 28, 1995); missed two games. ... Reinjured cut to leg (October 14, 1995); missed five games. ... Reinjured cut to leg (October 31, 1995); missed 16 games. ... Suffered from the flu (December 6, 1995); missed two games. ... Bruised arm (March 2, 1996); missed one game. ... Suffered from the flu (December 10, 1996); missed two games. ... Bruised shoulder (December 20, 1996); missed eight games. ... Strained neck (February 15, 1997); missed five games. ... Suffered from the flu (April 8, 1997); missed two games.
HONORS: Played in NHL All-Star Game (1985).
STATISTICAL PLATEAUS: Three-goal games: 1987-88 (1), 1989-90 (1). Total: 2. ... Four-goal games: 1981-82 (1). ... Total hat tricks: 3.
MISCELLANEOUS: Member of Stanley Cup championship team (1995). ... Failed to score on a penalty shot (vs. Billy Smith, April 14, 1985).

Season Team	League	REGULAR SEASON								PLAYOFFS				
		Gms.	G	A	Pts.	PIM	+/-	PP	SH	Gms.	G	A	Pts.	PIM
79-80— St. John's Prep	Mass. H.S.	...	28	37	65	...	...	...	...	—	—	—	—	—
80-81— St. John's Prep	Mass. H.S.	18	14	24	38	...	...	...	...	—	—	—	—	—
81-82— Washington	NHL	80	32	35	67	69	-23	7	1	—	—	—	—	—
82-83— Washington	NHL	80	32	37	69	64	0	14	0	4	1	0	1	2
83-84— Washington	NHL	80	28	40	68	51	...	...	...	8	2	1	3	25
84-85— Washington	NHL	80	53	42	95	87	20	12	0	5	1	4	5	8
85-86— Washington	NHL	80	27	29	56	105	-12	7	0	9	5	4	9	12
86-87— Washington	NHL	22	5	7	12	21	-7	4	0	—	—	—	—	—
— New York Rangers	NHL	28	2	8	10	20	-12	1	0	—	—	—	—	—
— Los Angeles	NHL	10	2	3	5	6	-8	0	0	5	1	2	3	2
87-88— Los Angeles	NHL	71	19	33	52	84	-21	10	0	5	1	1	2	0
88-89— Los Angeles	NHL	39	11	15	26	16	3	3	0	—	—	—	—	—
— Boston	NHL	18	5	9	14	10	4	1	0	8	1	1	2	4
89-90— Boston	NHL	80	25	31	56	97	-3	5	0	21	4	6	10	39
90-91— Boston	NHL	29	8	8	16	22	2	2	0	1	0	1	1	2
91-92— Boston	NHL	60	25	23	48	46	-3	6	1	8	0	1	1	6
92-93— Boston	NHL	68	11	17	28	65	-16	2	0	6	1	4	5	6
93-94— New Jersey	NHL	76	10	23	33	51	7	0	2	20	1	7	8	20
94-95— New Jersey	NHL	41	5	11	16	19	-1	0	0	17	1	4	5	6
95-96— New Jersey	NHL	52	5	5	10	14	-10	0	1	—	—	—	—	—
96-97— New Jersey	NHL	62	4	15	19	14	6	0	1	10	1	2	3	2
NHL totals (16 years)		1056	309	391	700	861	-74	74	6	127	20	38	58	134

CARTER, ANSON C BRUINS

PERSONAL: Born June 6, 1974, in Toronto. ... 6-1/175. ... Shoots right.
COLLEGE: Michigan State.
TRANSACTIONS/CAREER NOTES: Selected by Quebec Nordiques in 10th round (10th Nordiques pick, 220th overall) of NHL entry draft (June 20, 1992). ... Nordiques franchise moved to Colorado and renamed Avalanche for 1995-96 season (June 21, 1995). ... Traded by Avalanche to Washington Capitals for fourth-round pick (D Ben Storey) in 1996 entry draft (April 3, 1996). ... Signed as free agent by Washington Capitals (July 1, 1996). ... Sprained thumb (February 7, 1997); missed five games. ... Traded by Capitals with G Jim Carey, C Jason Allison, third-round pick (RW Lee Goren) in 1997 draft and conditional pick in 1998 draft to Boston Bruins for C Adam Oates, RW Rick Tocchet and G Bill Ranford (March 1, 1997).
HONORS: Named to CCHA All-Star first team (1993-94 and 1994-95). ... Named to NCAA All-America West second team (1994-95). ... Named to CCHA All-Star second team (1995-96).

Season Team	League	REGULAR SEASON								PLAYOFFS				
		Gms.	G	A	Pts.	PIM	+/-	PP	SH	Gms.	G	A	Pts.	PIM
91-92— Wexford	OHA Jr. A	42	18	22	40	24	...	...	...	—	—	—	—	—
92-93— Michigan State..........	CCHA	36	19	11	30	20	...	...	...	—	—	—	—	—
93-94— Michigan State..........	CCHA	39	30	24	54	36	...	...	...	—	—	—	—	—
94-95— Michigan State..........	CCHA	39	34	17	51	40	...	...	...	—	—	—	—	—
95-96— Michigan State..........	CCHA	42	23	20	43	36	...	...	...	—	—	—	—	—
96-97— Washington	NHL	19	3	2	5	7	0	1	0	—	—	—	—	—
— Portland	AHL	27	19	19	38	11	...	...	...	—	—	—	—	—
— Boston	NHL	19	8	5	13	2	-7	1	1	—	—	—	—	—
NHL totals (2 years)		38	11	7	18	9	-7	2	1					

CASEY, JON G

PERSONAL: Born August 29, 1962, in Grand Rapids, Minn. ... 5-10/155. ... Catches left.
HIGH SCHOOL: Grand Rapids (Minn.).
COLLEGE: North Dakota.
TRANSACTIONS/CAREER NOTES: Signed as free agent by Minnesota North Stars (April 1, 1984). ... North Stars franchise moved from Minnesota to Dallas and renamed Stars for 1993-94 season. ... Traded by Stars to Boston Bruins for G Andy Moog (June 25, 1993) to complete deal in which Bruins sent D Gord Murphy to Stars for future considerations (June 20, 1993). ... Signed as free agent by St. Louis Blues (June 30, 1994).
HONORS: Named to WCHL All-Star first team (1981-82 and 1983-84). ... Won Harry (Hap) Holmes Memorial Trophy (1984-85). ... Won Aldege (Baz) Bastien Trophy (1984-85). ... Named to AHL All-Star first team (1984-85). ... Played in NHL All-Star Game (1993).
MISCELLANEOUS: Stopped a penalty shot attempt (vs. Petr Klima, March 20, 1989; vs. Luc Robitaille, April 3, 1993; vs. Alexei Kovalev, October 5, 1993). ... Allowed a penalty shot goal (vs. Reggie Savage, November 18, 1992).

Season Team	League	REGULAR SEASON								PLAYOFFS						
		Gms.	Min	W	L	T	GA	SO	Avg.	Gms.	Min.	W	L	GA	SO	Avg.
80-81—Univ. of North Dakota...	WCHA	6	300	3	1	0	19	0	3.80	—	—	—	—	—	—	—
81-82—Univ. of North Dakota...	WCHA	18	1038	15	3	0	48	1	2.77	—	—	—	—	—	—	—
82-83—Univ. of North Dakota...	WCHA	17	1020	9	6	2	42	0	2.47	—	—	—	—	—	—	—
83-84—Univ. of North Dakota...	WCHA	37	2180	25	10	2	115	2	3.17	—	—	—	—	—	—	—
—Minnesota.................	NHL	2	84	1	0	0	6	0	4.29	—	—	—	—	—	—	—
84-85—Baltimore.................	AHL	46	2646	30	11	4	116	†4	*2.63	13	689	8	3	38	0	3.31
85-86—Springfield.................	AHL	9	464	4	3	1	30	0	3.88	—	—	—	—	—	—	—
—Minnesota.................	NHL	26	1402	11	11	1	91	0	3.89	—	—	—	—	—	—	—
86-87—Indianapolis.................	CHL	31	1794	14	15	0	133	0	4.45	—	—	—	—	—	—	—
—Springfield.................	AHL	13	770	1	8	0	56	0	4.36	—	—	—	—	—	—	—
87-88—Kalamazoo.................	IHL	42	2541	24	13	‡5	154	2	3.64	7	382	3	3	26	0	4.08
—Minnesota.................	NHL	14	663	1	7	4	41	0	3.71	—	—	—	—	—	—	—
88-89—Minnesota.................	NHL	55	2961	18	17	12	151	1	3.06	4	211	1	3	16	0	4.55
89-90—Minnesota.................	NHL	61	3407	*31	22	4	183	3	3.22	7	415	3	4	21	1	3.04
90-91—Minnesota.................	NHL	55	3185	21	20	11	158	3	2.98	*23	*1205	*14	7	*61	†1	3.04
91-92—Minnesota.................	NHL	52	2911	19	23	5	165	2	3.40	7	437	3	4	22	0	3.02
—Kalamazoo.................	IHL	4	250	2	1	‡1	11	0	2.64	—	—	—	—	—	—	—
92-93—Minnesota.................	NHL	60	3476	26	26	5	193	3	3.33	—	—	—	—	—	—	—
93-94—Boston.................	NHL	57	3192	30	15	9	153	4	2.88	11	698	5	6	34	0	2.92
94-95—St. Louis.................	NHL	19	872	7	5	4	40	0	2.75	2	30	0	1	2	0	4.00
95-96—Peoria.................	IHL	43	2514	21	19	‡2	128	3	3.05	—	—	—	—	—	—	—
—St. Louis.................	NHL	9	395	2	3	0	25	0	3.80	12	747	6	6	36	1	2.89
96-97—St. Louis.................	NHL	15	707	3	8	0	40	0	3.39	—	—	—	—	—	—	—
—Worcester.................	AHL	4	245	2	1	1	10	0	2.45	—	—	—	—	—	—	—
NHL totals (12 years)		425	23255	170	157	55	1246	16	3.21	66	3743	32	31	192	3	3.08

CASSELMAN, MIKE   C   PANTHERS

PERSONAL: Born August 23, 1968, in Morrisburg, Ont. ... 5-11/180. ... Shoots left.
COLLEGE: Clarkson (N.Y.).
TRANSACTIONS/CAREER NOTES: Selected by Detroit Red Wings in first round (first Red Wings pick, third overall) of NHL supplemental draft (June 10, 1988). ... Signed as free agent by Carolina Monarchs of AHL, Florida Panthers organization (September 20, 1995).
HONORS: Named to ECHL All-Star second team (1991-92).

Season Team	League	REGULAR SEASON							PLAYOFFS				
		Gms.	G	A	Pts.	PIM	+/-	PP	SH	Gms.	G	A	Pts.	PIM
87-88—Clarkson.................	ECAC	24	4	1	5	0	...	...	...	—	—	—	—	—
88-89—Clarkson.................	ECAC	31	3	14	17	0	...	...	...	—	—	—	—	—
89-90—Clarkson.................	ECAC	34	22	21	43	69	...	...	...	—	—	—	—	—
90-91—Clarkson.................	ECAC	40	19	35	54	44	...	...	...	—	—	—	—	—
91-92—Toledo.................	ECHL	61	39	60	99	83	...	...	...	5	0	1	1	6
—Adirondack.................	AHL	1	0	0	0	0	...	...	...	—	—	—	—	—
92-93—Toledo.................	ECHL	3	0	1	1	2	...	...	...	—	—	—	—	—
—Adirondack.................	AHL	60	12	19	31	27	...	...	...	8	3	3	6	0
93-94—Adirondack.................	AHL	77	17	38	55	34	...	...	...	12	2	4	6	10
94-95—Adirondack.................	AHL	60	17	43	60	42	...	...	...	4	0	0	0	2
95-96—Carolina	AHL	70	34	68	102	46	...	...	...	—	—	—	—	—
—Florida.................	NHL	3	0	0	0	0	-1	0	0	—	—	—	—	—
96-97—Cincinnati.................	IHL	68	30	34	64	54	...	...	...	3	1	0	1	2
NHL totals (1 year)		3	0	0	0	0	-1	0	0					

CASSELS, ANDREW   C   HURRICANES

PERSONAL: Born July 23, 1969, in Mississauga, Ont. ... 6-1/180. ... Shoots left. ... Name pronounced KAZ-uhls.
TRANSACTIONS/CAREER NOTES: Broke wrist (January 1986). ... Selected by Montreal Canadiens as underage junior in first round (first Canadiens pick, 17th overall) of NHL entry draft (June 13, 1987). ... Sprained left knee ligaments (September 1988). ... Separated right shoulder (November 22, 1989); missed 10 games. ... Traded by Canadiens to Hartford Whalers for second-round pick (RW Valeri Bure) in 1992 draft (September 17, 1991). ... Bruised kneecap (December 4, 1993); missed one game. ... Suffered facial injury (March 13, 1994); missed four games. ... Bruised forearm (December 2, 1995); missed one game. ... Suffered charley horse (March 6, 1997); missed one game. ... Whalers franchise moved to North Carolina and renamed Carolina Hurricanes for 1997-98 season; NHL approved move on June 25, 1997.
HONORS: Won Emms Family Award (1986-87). ... Won Red Tilson Trophy (1987-88). ... Won Eddie Powers Memorial Trophy (1987-88). ... Won William Hanley Trophy (1987-88). ... Named to OHL All-Star first team (1987-88 and 1988-89).
MISCELLANEOUS: Captain of Hartford Whalers (1994-95). ... Scored on a penalty shot (vs. Ron Hextall, April 6, 1994).

Season Team	League	REGULAR SEASON							PLAYOFFS				
		Gms.	G	A	Pts.	PIM	+/-	PP	SH	Gms.	G	A	Pts.	PIM
85-86—Bramalea Jr. B	OHA	33	18	25	43	26	...	...	...	—	—	—	—	—
86-87—Ottawa	OHL	66	26	66	92	28	...	...	...	11	5	9	14	7
87-88—Ottawa	OHL	61	48	*103	*151	39	...	...	...	16	8	*24	†32	13
88-89—Ottawa	OHL	56	37	97	134	66	...	...	...	12	5	10	15	10
89-90—Sherbrooke	AHL	55	22	45	67	25	...	...	...	12	2	11	13	6
—Montreal	NHL	6	2	0	2	2	1	0	0	—	—	—	—	—
90-91—Montreal	NHL	54	6	19	25	20	2	1	0	8	0	2	2	2
91-92—Hartford	NHL	67	11	30	41	18	3	2	2	7	2	4	6	6
92-93—Hartford	NHL	84	21	64	85	62	-11	8	3	—	—	—	—	—
93-94—Hartford	NHL	79	16	42	58	37	-21	8	1	—	—	—	—	—
94-95—Hartford	NHL	46	7	30	37	18	-3	1	0	—	—	—	—	—
95-96—Hartford	NHL	81	20	43	63	39	8	6	0	—	—	—	—	—
96-97—Hartford	NHL	81	22	44	66	46	-16	8	0	—	—	—	—	—
NHL totals (8 years)		498	105	272	377	242	-37	34	6	15	2	6	8	8

CASSIVI, FREDERIC   G   SENATORS

PERSONAL: Born June 12, 1975, in Sorel, Que. ... 6-4/205. ... Catches left. ... Name pronounced KA-see-vee.
TRANSACTIONS/CAREER NOTES: Selected by Ottawa Senators in ninth round (seventh Senators pick, 210th overall) of NHL entry draft (June 29, 1994).

					REGULAR SEASON							PLAYOFFS				
Season Team	League	Gms.	Min	W	L	T	GA	SO	Avg.	Gms.	Min.	W	L	GA	SO	Avg.
93-94—St. Hyacinthe	QMJHL	35	1751	15	13	3	127	1	4.35	0	0	0	0	0	0	0.00
94-95—St. Jean	QMJHL	43	2383	21	18	1	160	1	4.03	5	258	2	3	18	0	4.19
95-96—Prince Edward Island	AHL	41	2346	20	14	3	128	1	3.27	5	317	2	3	24	0	4.54
—Thunder Bay	Col.HL	12	714	6	4	2	51	0	4.29	—	—	—	—	—	—	—
96-97—Syracuse	AHL	55	3069	23	22	8	164	2	3.21	1	60	0	1	3	0	3.00

CAVICCHI, TRENT   G   CANADIENS

PERSONAL: Born March 20, 1974, in Halifax, N.S. ... 6-3/187. ... Catches left.
COLLEGE: New Hampshire.
TRANSACTIONS/CAREER NOTES: Selected by Montreal Canadiens in 10th round (12th Canadiens pick, 236th overall) of NHL entry draft (June 20, 1992).

					REGULAR SEASON							PLAYOFFS				
Season Team	League	Gms.	Min	W	L	T	GA	SO	Avg.	Gms.	Min.	W	L	GA	SO	Avg.
92-93—U. of New Hampshire	Hockey East	9	391	3	2	1	32	0	4.91	—	—	—	—	—	—	—
93-94—U. of New Hampshire	Hockey East	25	1324	14	7	1	65	1	2.95	—	—	—	—	—	—	—
94-95—U. of New Hampshire	Hockey East	23	1277	14	6	1	71	0	3.34	—	—	—	—	—	—	—
95-96—U. of New Hampshire	Hockey East	24	1340	9	12	3	95	0	4.25	—	—	—	—	—	—	—
96-97—Knoxville	ECHL	11	616	2	7	‡1	56	0	5.45	—	—	—	—	—	—	—
—Raleigh	ECHL	8	448	3	3	‡1	22	0	2.95	—	—	—	—	—	—	—

C

CHABOT, FREDERIC   G

PERSONAL: Born February 12, 1968, in Hebertville, Que. ... 5-11/175. ... Catches right. ... Name pronounced shuh-BAHT.
TRANSACTIONS/CAREER NOTES: Selected by New Jersey Devils in 10th round (10th Devils pick, 192nd overall) of NHL entry draft (June 21, 1986). ... Signed as free agent by Montreal Canadiens (January 16, 1990). ... Selected by Tampa Bay Lightning in NHL expansion draft (June 18, 1992). ... Traded by Lightning to Canadiens for G Jean-Claude Bergeron (June 18, 1992). ... Traded by Canadiens to Philadelphia Flyers for future considerations (February 21, 1994). ... Signed as free agent by Florida Panthers (August 15, 1994).
HONORS: Named to Memorial Cup All-Star team (1981-82). ... Named to WHL (East) All-Star first team (1988-89). ... Won Aldege (Baz) Bastien Trophy (1993-94). ... Named to IHL All-Star second team (1995-96). ... Won James Gatschene Memorial Trophy (1996-97). ... Named to IHL All-Star first team (1996-97).
STATISTICAL NOTES: Member of Stanley Cup championship team (1993).

					REGULAR SEASON							PLAYOFFS				
Season Team	League	Gms.	Min	W	L	T	GA	SO	Avg.	Gms.	Min.	W	L	GA	SO	Avg.
86-87—Drummondville	QMJHL	*62	*3508	31	29	0	293	1	5.01	8	481	2	6	40	0	4.99
87-88—Drummondville	QMJHL	58	3276	27	24	4	237	1	4.34	*16	1019	10	6	56	†1	*3.30
88-89—Moose Jaw	WHL	26	1385	...	...	...	114	1	4.94	—	—	—	—	—	—	—
—Prince Albert	WHL	28	1572	...	...	...	88	1	3.36	4	199	1	1	16	0	4.82
89-90—Fort Wayne	IHL	23	1208	6	13	‡3	87	1	4.32	—	—	—	—	—	—	—
—Sherbrooke	AHL	2	119	1	1	0	8	0	4.03	—	—	—	—	—	—	—
90-91—Montreal	NHL	3	108	0	0	1	6	0	3.33	—	—	—	—	—	—	—
—Fredericton	AHL	35	1800	9	15	5	122	0	4.07	—	—	—	—	—	—	—
91-92—Winston-Salem	ECHL	25	1449	15	7	‡2	71	0	*2.94	—	—	—	—	—	—	—
—Fredericton	AHL	30	1761	17	9	4	79	2	*2.69	7	457	3	4	20	0	2.63
92-93—Fredericton	AHL	45	2544	22	17	4	141	0	3.33	4	261	1	3	16	0	3.68
—Montreal	NHL	1	40	0	0	0	1	0	1.50	—	—	—	—	—	—	—
93-94—Fredericton	AHL	3	143	0	1	1	12	0	5.03	—	—	—	—	—	—	—
—Las Vegas	IHL	2	110	1	1	‡1	5	0	2.73	—	—	—	—	—	—	—
—Montreal	NHL	1	60	0	1	0	5	0	5.00	—	—	—	—	—	—	—
—Hershey	AHL	31	1607	13	6	7	75	2	*2.80	11	665	7	4	32	0	2.89
—Philadelphia	NHL	4	70	0	1	1	5	0	4.29	—	—	—	—	—	—	—
94-95—Cincinnati	IHL	48	2622	25	12	‡7	128	1	2.93	5	326	3	2	16	0	2.94
95-96—Cincinnati	IHL	38	2147	23	9	‡4	88	3	*2.46	14	854	9	5	37	1	2.60
96-97—Houston	IHL	*72	*4265	*39	26	‡7	*180	*7	2.53	13	777	8	5	34	†2	2.63
NHL totals (4 years)		9	278	0	2	2	17	0	3.67							

CHAMBERS, SHAWN   D   STARS

PERSONAL: Born October 11, 1966, in Royal Oak, Mich. ... 6-2/200. ... Shoots left. ... Full name: Shawn Randall Chambers.
COLLEGE: Alaska-Fairbanks.
TRANSACTIONS/CAREER NOTES: Selected by Minnesota North Stars in NHL supplemental draft (June 13, 1987). ... Dislocated shoulder (February 1988). ... Separated right shoulder (September 1988). ... Injured left knee (September 11, 1990); missed first 11 games of season. ... Fractured left kneecap (December 5, 1990); missed three months. ... Underwent surgery to left knee to remove piece of loose cartilage (May 1991). ... Traded by North Stars to Washington Capitals for C Trent Klatt and LW Steve Maltais (June 21, 1991). ... Suffered sore knee (October 1991); missed first 47 games of season. ... Reinjured knee (January 26, 1992); missed remainder of season. ... Underwent arthroscopic knee surgery (February 4, 1992). ... Selected by Tampa Bay Lightning in NHL expansion draft (June 18, 1992). ... Underwent arthroscopic knee surgery (October 9, 1992); missed 14 games. ... Underwent arthroscopic knee surgery (October 21, 1993); missed 14 games. ... Injured shoulder (November 13, 1993); missed two games. ... Suffered facial cuts (January 2, 1994); missed one game. ... Suffered strep throat (February 7, 1995); missed one game. ... Traded by Lightning with RW Danton Cole to New Jersey Devils for C Alexander Semak and

RW Ben Hankinson (March 14, 1995). ... Suffered charley horse (November 14, 1995); missed one game. ... Bruised shoulder (December 6, 1995); missed three games. ... Broke right hand (March 13, 1996); missed 13 games. ... Bruised right knee (November 7, 1996); missed three games. ... Injured hip (March 19, 1997); missed one game. ... Signed as free agent by Stars (July 3, 1997).
MISCELLANEOUS: Member of Stanley Cup championship team (1995).

Season Team	League	REGULAR SEASON								PLAYOFFS				
		Gms.	G	A	Pts.	PIM	+/-	PP	SH	Gms.	G	A	Pts.	PIM
85-86— Alaska-Fairbanks........	GWHC	25	15	21	36	34	...	...	...	—	—	—	—	—
86-87— Alaska-Fairbanks........	GWHC	17	11	19	30	...	...	...	...	—	—	—	—	—
— Seattle..................	WHL	28	8	25	33	58	...	...	...	—	—	—	—	—
— Fort Wayne	IHL	12	2	6	8	0	...	...	...	10	1	4	5	5
87-88— Minnesota.................	NHL	19	1	7	8	21	-6	1	0	—	—	—	—	—
— Kalamazoo	IHL	19	1	6	7	22	...	...	...	—	—	—	—	—
88-89— Minnesota.................	NHL	72	5	19	24	80	-4	1	2	3	0	2	2	0
89-90— Minnesota.................	NHL	78	8	18	26	81	-2	0	1	7	2	1	3	10
90-91— Minnesota.................	NHL	29	1	3	4	24	2	0	0	23	0	7	7	16
— Kalamazoo	IHL	3	1	1	2	0	...	...	...	—	—	—	—	—
91-92— Baltimore	AHL	5	2	3	5	9	...	...	...	—	—	—	—	—
— Washington	NHL	2	0	0	0	2	-3	0	0	—	—	—	—	—
92-93— Atlanta	IHL	6	0	2	2	18	...	...	...	—	—	—	—	—
— Tampa Bay	NHL	55	10	29	39	36	-21	5	0	—	—	—	—	—
93-94— Tampa Bay	NHL	66	11	23	34	23	-6	6	1	—	—	—	—	—
94-95— Tampa Bay	NHL	24	2	12	14	6	0	1	0	—	—	—	—	—
— New Jersey	NHL	21	2	5	7	6	2	1	0	20	4	5	9	2
95-96— New Jersey	NHL	64	2	21	23	18	1	2	0	—	—	—	—	—
96-97— New Jersey	NHL	73	4	17	21	19	17	1	0	10	1	6	7	6
NHL totals (10 years)		503	46	154	200	316	-20	18	4	63	7	21	28	34

CHARA, ZDENO   D   ISLANDERS

PERSONAL: Born March 18, 1977, in Trencin, Czechoslovakia. ... 6-8/231. ... Shoots left. ... Name pronounced zuh-DAY-yoh CHAH-ruh.
TRANSACTIONS/CAREER NOTES: Selected by New York Islanders in third round (third Islanders pick, 56th overall) of NHL entry draft (June 22, 1996).

Season Team	League	REGULAR SEASON								PLAYOFFS				
		Gms.	G	A	Pts.	PIM	+/-	PP	SH	Gms.	G	A	Pts.	PIM
94-95— Dukla Trencin Jrs.......	Slovakia	2	0	0	0	2	...	...	...	—	—	—	—	—
95-96— Dukla Trencin Jrs.......	Slovakia	22	1	13	14	80	...	...	...	—	—	—	—	—
— HC Piestany	Slovakia Dv. II	10	1	3	4	10	...	...	...	—	—	—	—	—
— Sparta Praha	Czech Rep.	15	1	2	3	42	...	...	...	—	—	—	—	—
— Sparta Praha Jrs........	Czech Rep.	1	0	0	0	0	...	...	...	—	—	—	—	—
96-97— Prince George............	WHL	49	3	19	22	120	...	...	...	15	1	7	8	45

CHARPENTIER, SEBASTIEN   G   CAPITALS

PERSONAL: Born April 18, 1977, in Drummondville, Que. ... 5-9/161. ... Catches left. ... Name pronounced SHAHR-pihnt-yay.
TRANSACTIONS/CAREER NOTES: Selected by Washington Capitals in fourth round (fourth Capitals pick, 93rd overall) of NHL entry draft (July 8, 1995).

Season Team	League	REGULAR SEASON							PLAYOFFS					
		Gms.	Min	W	L	T	GA	SO	Avg.	Gms.	Min.	W	L	GA	SO	Avg.
94-95— Laval............................	QMJHL	41	2152	25	12	1	99	2	2.76	16	886	9	4	45	0	3.05
95-96— Laval............................	QMJHL	18	938	4	10	0	97	0	6.20	—	—	—	—	—	—	—
— Val-d'Or.....................	QMJHL	33	1906	21	9	1	87	1	2.74	13	778	7	5	47	0	3.64
96-97— Shawinigan	QMJHL	*62	*3474	*37	17	4	176	1	3.04	4	105	2	1	13	0	4.00

CHARRON, ERIC   D   CAPITALS

PERSONAL: Born January 14, 1970, in Verdun, Que. ... 6-3/190. ... Shoots left. ... Name pronounced shuh-RAHN.
TRANSACTIONS/CAREER NOTES: Selected by Montreal Canadiens in first round (first Canadiens pick, 20th overall) of NHL entry draft (June 11, 1988). ... Traded by Canadiens with D Alain Cote and future considerations to Tampa Bay Lightning for D Rob Ramage (March 20, 1993); Canadiens sent D Donald Dufresne to Lightning to complete deal (June 18, 1993). ... Traded by Lightning to Washington Capitals for seventh-round pick (RW Eero Somervuori) in 1997 draft (November 17, 1995). ... Injured knee prior to 1996-97 season; missed first six games of season. ... Bruised ribs (December 13, 1996); missed one game.

Season Team	League	REGULAR SEASON								PLAYOFFS				
		Gms.	G	A	Pts.	PIM	+/-	PP	SH	Gms.	G	A	Pts.	PIM
87-88— Trois-Rivieres.............	QMJHL	67	3	13	16	135	...	...	...	—	—	—	—	—
88-89— Trois-Rivieres.............	QMJHL	38	2	16	18	111	...	...	...	—	—	—	—	—
— Verdun	QMJHL	28	2	15	17	66	...	...	...	—	—	—	—	—
— Sherbrooke	AHL	1	0	0	0	0	...	...	...	—	—	—	—	—
89-90— St. Hyacinthe	QMJHL	68	13	38	51	152	...	...	...	11	3	4	7	67
— Sherbrooke	AHL	—	—	—	—	—	...	...	...	2	0	0	0	0
90-91— Fredericton.................	AHL	71	1	11	12	108	...	...	...	2	1	0	1	29
91-92— Fredericton.................	AHL	59	2	11	13	98	...	...	...	6	1	0	1	4
92-93— Fredericton.................	AHL	54	3	13	16	93	...	...	...	—	—	—	—	—
— Montreal	NHL	3	0	0	0	2	0	0	0	—	—	—	—	—
— Atlanta	IHL	11	0	2	2	12	...	...	...	3	0	1	1	6
93-94— Atlanta	IHL	66	5	18	23	144	...	...	...	14	1	4	5	28
— Tampa Bay	NHL	4	0	0	0	2	0	0	0	—	—	—	—	—
94-95— Tampa Bay	NHL	45	1	4	5	26	1	0	0	—	—	—	—	—

Season Team	League	REGULAR SEASON								PLAYOFFS				
		Gms.	G	A	Pts.	PIM	+/-	PP	SH	Gms.	G	A	Pts.	PIM
95-96— Tampa Bay	NHL	14	0	0	0	18	-6	0	0	—	—	—	—	—
— Portland	AHL	45	0	8	8	88	...	...	...	20	1	1	2	33
— Washington	NHL	4	0	1	1	4	3	0	0	6	0	0	0	8
96-97— Washington	NHL	25	1	1	2	20	1	0	0	—	—	—	—	—
— Portland	AHL	29	6	8	14	55	...	...	...	5	0	3	3	0
NHL totals (6 years)		95	2	6	8	72	-1	0	0	6	0	0	0	8

CHASE, KELLY — RW — MAPLE LEAFS

PERSONAL: Born October 25, 1967, in Porcupine Plain, Sask. ... 6-0/199. ... Shoots right. ... Full name: Kelly Wayne Chase.
HIGH SCHOOL: Porcupine Plain (Sask.).
TRANSACTIONS/CAREER NOTES: Signed as free agent by St. Louis Blues (May 24, 1988). ... Bruised right foot (January 1990). ... Suffered back spasms (March 1990). ... Suspended 10 games by NHL for fighting (March 18, 1991). ... Injured knee (December 11, 1991); missed two games. ... Sprained left wrist (January 14, 1992); missed three games. ... Bruised thigh (February 2, 1992); missed five games. ... Injured hand (February 23, 1992); missed four games. ... Pulled groin (October 26, 1992); missed six games. ... Injured wrist (January 9, 1993); missed five games. ... Bruised lower leg (March 30, 1993); missed last six games of season. ... Suffered from the flu (December 4, 1993); missed one game. ... Injured leg (January 2, 1994); missed four games. ... Injured elbow (January 28, 1994); missed three games. ... Pulled groin (March 24, 1994); missed three games. ... Injured hand (April 5, 1994); missed one game. ... Selected by Hartford Whalers in 1994-95 waiver draft for cash (January 18, 1995). ... Suffered back spasms (February 24, 1995); missed 14 games. ... Suffered sore back (April 9, 1995); missed six games. ... Strained groin and injured neck (December 6, 1995); missed 10 games. ... Bruised hand (January 24, 1996); missed three games. ... Sprained knee (February 21, 1996); missed three games. ... Underwent arthroscopic knee surgery (December 13, 1996); missed 11 games. ... Traded by Whalers to Toronto Maple Leafs for eighth-round pick in 1998 draft (March 18, 1997). ... Suffered from tendinitis in knee (March 19, 1997); missed 10 games.

Season Team	League	REGULAR SEASON								PLAYOFFS				
		Gms.	G	A	Pts.	PIM	+/-	PP	SH	Gms.	G	A	Pts.	PIM
85-86— Saskatoon	WHL	57	7	18	25	172	...	...	...	10	3	4	7	37
86-87— Saskatoon	WHL	68	17	29	46	285	...	...	...	11	2	8	10	37
87-88— Saskatoon	WHL	70	21	34	55	*343	...	...	...	9	3	5	8	32
88-89— Peoria	IHL	38	14	7	21	278	...			—	—	—	—	—
89-90— Peoria	IHL	10	1	2	3	76	...			—	—	—	—	—
— St. Louis	NHL	43	1	3	4	244	-1	0	0	9	1	0	1	46
90-91— Peoria	IHL	61	20	34	54	406	...	...	...	10	4	3	7	61
— St. Louis	NHL	2	1	0	1	15	1	0	0	6	0	0	0	18
91-92— St. Louis	NHL	46	1	2	3	264	-6	0	0	1	0	0	0	7
92-93— St. Louis	NHL	49	2	5	7	204	-9	0	0	—	—	—	—	—
93-94— St. Louis	NHL	68	2	5	7	278	-5	0	0	4	0	1	1	6
94-95— Hartford	NHL	28	0	4	4	141	1	0	0	—	—	—	—	—
95-96— Hartford	NHL	55	2	4	6	230	-4	0	0	—	—	—	—	—
96-97— Hartford	NHL	28	1	2	3	122	2	0	0	—	—	—	—	—
— Toronto	NHL	2	0	0	0	27	0	0	0	—	—	—	—	—
NHL totals (8 years)		321	10	25	35	1525	-21	0	0	20	1	1	2	77

CHASSE, DENIS — RW — BLACKHAWKS

PERSONAL: Born February 7, 1970, in Montreal. ... 6-2/200. ... Shoots right. ... Name pronounced sha-SAY.
TRANSACTIONS/CAREER NOTES: Signed as free agent by Quebec Nordiques (May 14, 1991). ... Traded by Nordiques with D Steve Duchesne to St. Louis Blues for C Ron Sutter, C Bob Bassen and D Garth Butcher (January 23, 1994). ... Injured neck (January 29, 1993); missed remainder of season. ... Underwent neck surgery (March 9, 1994); missed remainder of season. ... Traded by Blues to Washington Capitals for RW Rob Pearson (January 29, 1996). ... Traded by Capitals to Winnipeg Jets for D Stewart Malgunas (February 15, 1996). ... Jets franchise moved to Phoenix and renamed Coyotes for 1996-97 season; NHL approved move on January 18, 1996. ... Signed as free agent by Ottawa Senators (September 5, 1996). ... Traded by Senators with D Kevin Bolibruck and sixth-round pick in 1998 draft to Chicago Blackhawks for RW Mike Prokopec (March 18, 1997). ... Strained neck and shoulder (November 13, 1996); missed seven games.

Season Team	League	REGULAR SEASON								PLAYOFFS				
		Gms.	G	A	Pts.	PIM	+/-	PP	SH	Gms.	G	A	Pts.	PIM
87-88— St. Jean	QMJHL	13	0	1	1	2	...	...	...	1	0	0	0	0
88-89— Verdun	QMJHL	38	12	12	24	61	...	...	...	—	—	—	—	—
— Drummondville	QMJHL	30	15	16	31	77	...	...	...	3	0	2	2	28
89-90— Drummondville	QMJHL	34	14	29	43	85	...	...	...	—	—	—	—	—
— Chicoutimi	QMJHL	33	19	27	46	105	...	...	...	7	7	4	11	50
90-91— Drummondville	QMJHL	62	47	54	101	246	...	...	...	13	9	11	20	56
91-92— Halifax	AHL	73	26	35	61	254	...			—	—	—	—	—
92-93— Halifax	AHL	75	35	41	76	242	...			—	—	—	—	—
93-94— Cornwall	AHL	48	27	39	66	194	...			—	—	—	—	—
— St. Louis	NHL	3	0	1	1	15	1	0	0	—	—	—	—	—
94-95— St. Louis	NHL	47	7	9	16	133	12	1	0	7	1	7	8	23
95-96— St. Louis	NHL	42	3	0	3	108	-9	1	0	—	—	—	—	—
— Worcester	AHL	3	0	0	0	6	...			—	—	—	—	—
— Washington	NHL	3	0	0	0	5	-1	0	0	—	—	—	—	—
— Winnipeg	NHL	15	0	0	0	12	-4	0	0	—	—	—	—	—
96-97— Ottawa	NHL	22	1	4	5	19	3	0	0	—	—	—	—	—
— Detroit	IHL	9	2	1	3	33	...	...	...	—	—	—	—	—
— Indianapolis	IHL	3	0	0	0	10	...			4	1	1	2	23
NHL totals (5 years)		132	11	14	25	292	2	2	0	7	1	7	8	23

CHEBATURKIN, VLADIMIR — D — ISLANDERS

PERSONAL: Born April 23, 1975, in Tyumen, U.S.S.R. ... 6-2/213. ... Shoots left. ... Name pronounced VLAD-ih-meer chuh-buh-TUHR-kihn.
TRANSACTIONS/CAREER NOTES: Selected by New York Islanders in third round (third Islanders pick, 66th overall) of NHL entry draft (June 26, 1993).

Season Team	League	REGULAR SEASON								PLAYOFFS				
		Gms.	G	A	Pts.	PIM	+/-	PP	SH	Gms.	G	A	Pts.	PIM
92-93— Kristall Elektrostal	CIS Div. II						Statistics unavailable.							
93-94— Kristall Elektrostal	CIS Div. II	42	4	4	8	38	...	...	...	—	—	—	—	—
94-95— Kristall Elektrostal	CIS	52	2	6	8	90	...	...	...	—	—	—	—	—
95-96— Kristall Elektrostal	CIS	44	1	6	7	30	...	...	...	1	0	0	0	0
96-97— Utah	IHL	68	0	4	4	34	...	...	...	—	—	—	—	—

CHELIOS, CHRIS   D   BLACKHAWKS

PERSONAL: Born January 25, 1962, in Chicago. ... 6-1/192. ... Shoots right. ... Name pronounced CHEH-lee-ohz. ... Cousin of Nikos Tselios, defenseman in Carolina Hurricanes system.

COLLEGE: Wisconsin.

TRANSACTIONS/CAREER NOTES: Selected by Montreal Canadiens as underage junior in second round (fifth Canadiens pick, 40th overall) of NHL entry draft (June 10, 1981). ... Sprained right ankle (January 1985). ... Injured left knee (April 1985). ... Sprained knee (December 19, 1985). ... Reinjured knee (January 20, 1986). ... Suffered back spasms (October 1986). ... Broke finger on left hand (December 1987). ... Bruised tailbone (February 7, 1988). ... Strained left knee ligaments (February 1990). ... Underwent surgery to repair torn abdominal muscle (April 30, 1990). ... Traded by Canadiens with second-round pick in 1991 draft (C Michael Pomichter) to Chicago Blackhawks for C Denis Savard (June 29, 1990). ... Lacerated left temple (February 9, 1991). ... Suspended four games by NHL (October 15, 1993). ... Suspended four games without pay and fined $500 by NHL for eye-scratching incident (February 5, 1994). ... Played in Europe during 1994-95 NHL lockout. ... Sprained knee (March 1, 1997); missed eight games. ... Suffered sore back (April 6, 1997); missed one game.

HONORS: Named to NCAA All-Tournament team (1982-83). ... Named to WCHA All-Star second team (1982-83). ... Named to NHL All-Rookie team (1984-85). ... Played in NHL All-Star Game (1985, 1990-1994, 1996 and 1997). ... Won James Norris Memorial Trophy (1988-89, 1992-93 and 1995-96). ... Named to THE SPORTING NEWS All-Star first team (1988-89, 1992-93 and 1995-96). ... Named to NHL All-Star first team (1988-89, 1992-93, 1994-95 and 1995-96). ... Named to THE SPORTING NEWS All-Star second team (1990-91 and 1991-92). ... Named to NHL All-Star second team (1990-91 and 1996-97). ... Named to THE SPORTING NEWS All-Star team (1996-97).

MISCELLANEOUS: Member of Stanley Cup championship team (1986). ... Captain of Chicago Blackhawks (1996-97).

Season Team	League	REGULAR SEASON								PLAYOFFS				
		Gms.	G	A	Pts.	PIM	+/-	PP	SH	Gms.	G	A	Pts.	PIM
79-80— Moose Jaw	SJHL	53	12	31	43	118	...	...	...	—	—	—	—	—
80-81— Moose Jaw	SJHL	54	23	64	87	175	...	...	...	—	—	—	—	—
81-82— Univ. of Wisconsin.....	WCHA	43	6	43	49	50	...	...	...	—	—	—	—	—
82-83— Univ. of Wisconsin.....	WCHA	45	16	32	48	62	...	...	...	—	—	—	—	—
83-84— U.S. national team	Int'l	60	14	35	49	58	...	...	...	—	—	—	—	—
— U.S. Olympic team	Int'l	6	0	3	3	8	...	...	...	—	—	—	—	—
— Montreal	NHL	12	0	2	2	12	-5	0	0	15	1	9	10	17
84-85— Montreal	NHL	74	9	55	64	87	11	2	1	9	2	8	10	17
85-86— Montreal	NHL	41	8	26	34	67	4	2	0	20	2	9	11	49
86-87— Montreal	NHL	71	11	33	44	124	-5	6	0	17	4	9	13	38
87-88— Montreal	NHL	71	20	41	61	172	15	10	1	11	3	1	4	29
88-89— Montreal	NHL	80	15	58	73	185	35	8	0	21	4	15	19	28
89-90— Montreal	NHL	53	9	22	31	136	20	1	2	5	0	1	1	8
90-91— Chicago	NHL	77	12	52	64	192	23	5	2	6	1	7	8	46
91-92— Chicago	NHL	80	9	47	56	245	24	2	2	18	6	15	21	37
92-93— Chicago	NHL	84	15	58	73	282	14	8	0	4	0	2	2	14
93-94— Chicago	NHL	76	16	44	60	212	12	7	1	6	1	1	2	8
94-95— Biel-Bienne...............	Switzerland	3	0	3	3	4	...	...	...	—	—	—	—	—
— Chicago	NHL	48	5	33	38	72	17	3	1	16	4	7	11	12
95-96— Chicago	NHL	81	14	58	72	140	25	7	0	9	0	3	3	8
96-97— Chicago	NHL	72	10	38	48	112	16	2	0	6	0	1	1	8
NHL totals (14 years)		920	153	567	720	2038	206	63	10	163	28	88	116	319

CHERVYAKOV, DENIS   D   ISLANDERS

PERSONAL: Born April 20, 1970, in St. Petersburg, U.S.S.R. ... 6-0/185. ... Shoots left. ... Name pronounced CHAIR-vuh-kahf.

TRANSACTIONS/CAREER NOTES: Selected by Boston Bruins in 11th round (ninth Bruins pick, 256th overall) of NHL entry draft (June 20, 1992). ... Loaned to Atlanta Knights (February 26, 1993). ... Returned to Providence Bruins (March 2, 1993). ... Suspended four games by AHL for a match penalty (March 22, 1995). ... Signed as free agent by New York Islanders (September 16, 1996).

Season Team	League	REGULAR SEASON								PLAYOFFS				
		Gms.	G	A	Pts.	PIM	+/-	PP	SH	Gms.	G	A	Pts.	PIM
88-89— CSKA Moscow	USSR	4	1	2	3	...	...	...	...	—	—	—	—	—
89-90— CSKA Moscow	USSR	40	4	9	13	16	...	...	...	—	—	—	—	—
90-91— CSKA Moscow	USSR	60	5	14	19	34	...	...	...	—	—	—	—	—
91-92— HC Riga	CIS	48	4	6	10	46	...	...	...	—	—	—	—	—
92-93— Boston	NHL	2	0	0	0	2	-1	0	0	—	—	—	—	—
— Providence................	AHL	48	4	12	16	99	...	...	...	—	—	—	—	—
— Atlanta	IHL	1	0	0	0	0	...	...	...	—	—	—	—	—
93-94— Providence................	AHL	58	2	16	18	128	...	...	...	—	—	—	—	—
94-95— Providence................	AHL	65	1	18	19	130	...	...	...	10	0	2	2	14
95-96— Providence................	AHL	64	3	7	10	58	...	...	...	4	1	0	1	21
96-97— Kentucky	AHL	52	2	11	13	78	...	...	...	—	—	—	—	—
NHL totals (1 year)		2	0	0	0	2	-1	0	0					

CHEVELDAE, TIM   G   BRUINS

PERSONAL: Born February 15, 1968, in Melville, Sask. ... 5-10/195. ... Catches left. ... Name pronounced SHEH-vuhl-day.

TRANSACTIONS/CAREER NOTES: Selected by Detroit Red Wings as underage junior in fourth round (fourth Red Wings pick, 64th overall) of NHL entry draft (June 21, 1986). ... Sprained right knee (October 5, 1993); missed 16 games. ... Traded by Red Wings with LW Dallas Drake

C

to Winnipeg Jets for G Bob Essensa and D Sergei Bautin (March 8, 1994). ... Traded by Jets with third-round pick (RW Chester Gallant) in 1996 draft to Philadelphia Flyers for G Dominic Roussel (February 27, 1996). ... Signed as free agent by Boston Bruins (August 21, 1996). ... Loaned by Bruins to Fort Wayne of IHL (October 7, 1996).

HONORS: Named to WHL (East) All-Star first team (1987-88). ... Played in NHL All-Star Game (1992).

MISCELLANEOUS: Stopped a penalty shot attempt (vs. Rich Sutter, November 23, 1990; vs. Ken Linseman, January 9, 1991; vs. Wes Walz, November 2, 1991; vs. Dave Andreychuk, April 8, 1995; vs. Peter Forsberg, February 1, 1996). ... Allowed a penalty shot goal (vs. Russ Courtnall, February 19, 1990; vs. Sergei Makarov, March 29, 1994).

			REGULAR SEASON								PLAYOFFS						
Season Team	League	Gms.	Min	W	L	T	GA	SO	Avg.	Gms.	Min.	W	L	GA	SO	Avg.
84-85—Melville	SAJHL	23	1167	...	...	...	98	0	5.04	—	—	—	—	—	—	—
85-86—Saskatoon	WHL	36	2030	21	10	3	165	0	4.88	8	480	6	2	29	0	3.63
86-87—Saskatoon	WHL	33	1909	20	11	0	133	2	4.18	5	308	4	1	20	0	3.90
87-88—Saskatoon	WHL	66	3798	44	19	3	235	1	3.71	6	364	4	2	27	0	4.45
88-89—Detroit	NHL	2	122	0	2	0	9	0	4.43	—	—	—	—	—	—	—
—Adirondack	AHL	30	1694	20	8	0	98	1	3.47	2	99	1	0	9	0	5.45
89-90—Detroit	AHL	31	1848	17	8	6	116	0	3.77	—	—	—	—	—	—	—
—Detroit	NHL	28	1600	10	9	8	101	0	3.79	—	—	—	—	—	—	—
90-91—Detroit	NHL	65	3615	30	26	5	*214	2	3.55	7	398	3	4	22	0	3.32
91-92—Detroit	NHL	*72	*4236	†38	23	9	226	2	3.20	11	597	3	7	25	†2	2.51
92-93—Detroit	NHL	67	3880	34	24	7	210	4	3.25	7	423	3	4	24	0	3.40
93-94—Detroit	NHL	30	1572	16	9	1	91	1	3.47	—	—	—	—	—	—	—
—Adirondack	AHL	2	125	1	0	1	7	0	3.36	—	—	—	—	—	—	—
—Winnipeg	NHL	14	788	5	8	1	52	1	3.96	—	—	—	—	—	—	—
94-95—Winnipeg	NHL	30	1571	8	16	3	97	0	3.70	—	—	—	—	—	—	—
95-96—Winnipeg	NHL	30	1695	8	18	3	111	0	3.93	—	—	—	—	—	—	—
—Hershey	AHL	8	457	4	3	0	31	0	4.07	4	250	2	2	14	0	3.36
96-97—Fort Wayne	IHL	21	1137	6	9	‡4	75	0	3.96	—	—	—	—	—	—	—
—Boston	NHL	2	93	0	1	0	5	0	3.23	—	—	—	—	—	—	—
NHL totals (10 years)		340	19172	149	136	37	1116	10	3.49	25	1418	9	15	71	2	3.00

CHIASSON, STEVE   D   HURRICANES

PERSONAL: Born April 14, 1967, in Barrie, Ont. ... 6-1/205. ... Shoots left. ... Name pronounced CHAY-sahn.

TRANSACTIONS/CAREER NOTES: Selected by Detroit Red Wings as underage junior in third round (third Red Wings pick, 50th overall) of NHL entry draft (June 15, 1985). ... Injured hand (October 1985). ... Separated right shoulder (February 1988). ... Injured foot (May 1988). ... Injured groin (October 1988). ... Bruised ribs (January 1989). ... Injured ankle (February 1989). ... Injured knee (November 29, 1990); missed three games. ... Broke right ankle (January 2, 1991). ... Reinjured right ankle (February 19, 1991); missed 26 games. ... Reinjured right ankle (March 9, 1991). ... Injured ankle (October 22, 1991); missed 14 games. ... Bruised thigh (October 25, 1992); missed three games. ... Pulled hamstring (January 21, 1993); missed one game. ... Suffered injuries (April 2, 1994); missed two games. ... Traded by Red Wings to Calgary Flames for G Mike Vernon (June 29, 1994). ... Bruised left foot (February 23, 1995); missed two games. ... Injured wrist (November 11, 1995); missed one game. ... Bruised knee (December 1, 1995); missed two games. ... Bruised hip (December 20, 1995); missed one game. ... Suffered concussion (February 9, 1996); missed two games. ... Sprained left medial collateral ligament (September 16, 1996); missed eight games. ... Reinjured left medial collateral ligament (December 3, 1996); missed 11 games. ... Traded by Flames with third-round pick (D Francis Lessard) in 1997 draft to Hartford Whalers for D Glen Featherstone, F Hnat Domenichelli, second-round pick (D Dimitri Kokorev) in 1997 draft and third-round pick in 1998 draft (March 5, 1997). ... Whalers franchise moved to North Carolina and renamed Carolina Hurricanes for 1997-98 season; NHL approved move on June 25, 1997.

HONORS: Won Stafford Smythe Memorial Trophy (1985-86). ... Named to Memorial Cup All-Star team (1985-86). ... Played in NHL All-Star Game (1993).

MISCELLANEOUS: Scored on a penalty shot (vs. Byron Dafoe, December 11, 1995).

			REGULAR SEASON							PLAYOFFS				
Season Team	League	Gms.	G	A	Pts.	PIM	+/-	PP	SH	Gms.	G	A	Pts.	PIM
83-84— Guelph	OHL	55	1	9	10	112	...	...	...	—	—	—	—	—
84-85— Guelph	OHL	61	8	22	30	139	...	...	...	—	—	—	—	—
85-86— Guelph	OHL	54	12	29	41	126	...	...	...	18	10	10	20	37
86-87— Detroit	NHL	45	1	4	5	73	-7	0	0	2	0	0	0	19
87-88— Adirondack	AHL	23	6	11	17	58	...	...	...	—	—	—	—	—
— Detroit	NHL	29	2	9	11	57	15	0	0	9	2	2	4	31
88-89— Detroit	NHL	65	12	35	47	149	-6	5	2	5	2	1	3	6
89-90— Detroit	NHL	67	14	28	42	114	-16	4	0	—	—	—	—	—
90-91— Detroit	NHL	42	3	17	20	80	0	1	0	5	3	1	4	19
91-92— Detroit	NHL	62	10	24	34	136	22	5	0	11	1	5	6	12
92-93— Detroit	NHL	79	12	50	62	155	14	6	0	7	2	2	4	19
93-94— Detroit	NHL	82	13	33	46	122	17	4	1	7	2	3	5	2
94-95— Calgary	NHL	45	2	23	25	39	10	1	0	7	1	2	3	9
95-96— Calgary	NHL	76	8	25	33	62	3	5	0	4	2	1	3	0
96-97— Calgary	NHL	47	5	11	16	32	-11	1	2	—	—	—	—	—
— Hartford	NHL	18	3	11	14	7	-10	3	0	—	—	—	—	—
NHL totals (11 years)		657	85	270	355	1026	31	35	5	57	15	17	32	117

CHORSKE, TOM   LW   SENATORS

PERSONAL: Born September 18, 1966, in Minneapolis. ... 6-1/205. ... Shoots right. ... Name pronounced CHOHR-skee.

HIGH SCHOOL: Southwest (Minneapolis).

COLLEGE: Minnesota.

TRANSACTIONS/CAREER NOTES: Selected by Montreal Canadiens in first round (second Canadiens pick, 16th overall) of NHL entry draft (June 15, 1985). ... Separated shoulder (November 18, 1988); missed 11 games. ... Suffered hip pointer (October 26, 1989). ... Sprained right shoulder (March 14, 1991). ... Traded by Canadiens with RW Stephane Richer to New Jersey Devils for LW Kirk Muller and G Roland Melanson (September 20, 1991). ... Suffered charley horse (January 14, 1993); missed two games. ... Injured elbow (April 14, 1994); missed one game. ... Played in Europe during 1994-95 NHL lockout. ... Pulled groin (April 1, 1995); missed one game. ... Bruised leg (April 20, 1995); missed two games. ... Claimed on waivers by Ottawa Senators (October 4, 1995). ... Injured back during 1995-96 season; missed two games.

... Suffered from the flu during 1995-96 season; missed one game. ... Bruised hip (October 9, 1996); missed four games. ... Injured hip flexor (October 28, 1996); missed three games. ... Underwent retinal surgery on left eye (December 15, 1996); missed six games.
HONORS: Named to WCHA All-Star first team (1988-89).
MISCELLANEOUS: Member of Stanley Cup championship team (1995).

Season Team	League		REGULAR SEASON								PLAYOFFS			
		Gms.	G	A	Pts.	PIM	+/-	PP	SH	Gms.	G	A	Pts.	PIM
84-85— Southwest	Minn. H.S.	23	44	26	70	...	...	...	...	—	—	—	—	—
85-86— Univ. of Minnesota.....	WCHA	39	6	4	10	6	...	...	...	—	—	—	—	—
86-87— Univ. of Minnesota.....	WCHA	47	20	22	42	20	...	...	...	—	—	—	—	—
87-88— U.S. national team	Int'l	36	9	16	25	24	...	...	...	—	—	—	—	—
88-89— Univ. of Minnesota.....	WCHA	37	25	24	49	28	...	...	...	—	—	—	—	—
89-90— Montreal	NHL	14	3	1	4	2	2	0	0	—	—	—	—	—
— Sherbrooke................	AHL	59	22	24	46	54	...	...	...	12	4	4	8	8
90-91— Montreal	NHL	57	9	11	20	32	-8	3	0	—	—	—	—	—
91-92— New Jersey	NHL	76	19	17	36	32	8	0	3	7	0	3	3	4
92-93— New Jersey	NHL	50	7	12	19	25	-1	0	0	1	0	0	0	0
— Utica	AHL	6	1	4	5	2	...	...	...	—	—	—	—	—
93-94— New Jersey	NHL	76	21	20	41	32	14	1	1	20	4	3	7	0
94-95— Milan...........................	Italy	7	11	5	16	6	...	...	...	—	—	—	—	—
— New Jersey	NHL	42	10	8	18	16	-4	0	0	17	1	5	6	4
95-96— Ottawa	NHL	72	15	14	29	21	-9	0	2	—	—	—	—	—
96-97— Ottawa	NHL	68	18	8	26	16	-1	1	1	5	0	1	1	2
NHL totals (8 years)		455	102	91	193	176	1	5	7	50	5	12	17	10

CHOUINARD, MARC   C   MIGHTY DUCKS   C

PERSONAL: Born May 6, 1977, in Quebec City. ... 6-5/187. ... Shoots right. ... Name pronounced shwee-NAHRD.
TRANSACTIONS/CAREER NOTES: Selected by Winnipeg Jets in second round (second Jets pick, 32nd overall) of NHL entry draft (July 8, 1995). ... Traded by Winnipeg with RW Teemu Selanne and fourth-round pick (traded to Toronto) in 1996 draft to Mighty Ducks of Anaheim for C Chad Kilger, D Oleg Tverdovsky and third-round pick (D Per-Anton Lundstrom) in 1996 draft (February 7, 1996).

Season Team	League		REGULAR SEASON								PLAYOFFS			
		Gms.	G	A	Pts.	PIM	+/-	PP	SH	Gms.	G	A	Pts.	PIM
93-94— Beauport....................	QMJHL	62	11	19	30	23	...	...	...	13	2	5	7	2
94-95— Beauport....................	QMJHL	68	24	40	64	32	...	...	...	18	1	6	7	4
95-96— Beauport....................	QMJHL	30	14	21	35	19	...	...	...	—	—	—	—	—
— Halifax........................	QMJHL	24	6	12	18	17	...	...	...	6	2	1	3	2
96-97— Halifax........................	QMJHL	63	24	49	73	52	...	...	...	18	10	16	26	12

CHRISTIAN, JEFF   LW   PENGUINS

PERSONAL: Born July 30, 1970, in Burlington, Ont. ... 6-1/210. ... Shoots left.
TRANSACTIONS/CAREER NOTES: Selected by New Jersey Devils in second round (second Devils pick, 23rd overall) of NHL entry draft (June 11, 1988). ... Traded by London Knights to Owen Sound Platers for C Todd Hlushko and D David Noseworthy (November 27, 1989). ... Suspended three games by OHL for high-sticking (March 28, 1990). ... Signed as free agent by Pittsburgh Penguins (August 2, 1994).

Season Team	League		REGULAR SEASON								PLAYOFFS			
		Gms.	G	A	Pts.	PIM	+/-	PP	SH	Gms.	G	A	Pts.	PIM
86-87— Dundas Jr. C	OHA	29	20	34	54	42	...	...	...	—	—	—	—	—
87-88— London	OHL	64	15	29	44	154	...	...	...	9	1	5	6	27
88-89— London	OHL	60	27	30	57	221	...	...	...	20	3	4	7	56
89-90— London	OHL	18	14	7	21	64	...	...	...	—	—	—	—	—
— Owen Sound	OHL	37	19	26	45	145	...	...	...	10	6	7	13	43
90-91— Utica	AHL	80	24	42	66	165	...	...	...	—	—	—	—	—
91-92— Utica	AHL	70	27	24	51	198	...	...	...	4	0	0	0	16
— New Jersey	NHL	2	0	0	0	2	0	0	0	—	—	—	—	—
92-93— Utica	AHL	22	4	6	10	39	...	...	...	—	—	—	—	—
— Cincinnati..................	IHL	36	5	12	17	113	...	...	...	—	—	—	—	—
— Hamilton....................	AHL	11	2	5	7	35	...	...	...	—	—	—	—	—
93-94— Albany	AHL	76	34	43	77	227	...	...	...	5	1	2	3	19
94-95— Cleveland	IHL	56	13	24	37	126	...	...	...	2	0	1	1	8
— Pittsburgh.................	NHL	1	0	0	0	0	0	0	0	—	—	—	—	—
95-96— Cleveland	IHL	66	23	32	55	131	...	...	...	3	0	1	1	8
— Pittsburgh.................	NHL	3	0	0	0	2	0	0	0	—	—	—	—	—
96-97— Cleveland	IHL	69	40	40	80	262	...	...	...	12	6	8	14	44
— Pittsburgh.................	NHL	11	2	2	4	13	-3	0	0	—	—	—	—	—
NHL totals (4 years)		17	2	2	4	17	-3	0	0					

CHURCH, BRAD   LW   CAPITALS

PERSONAL: Born November 14, 1976, in Dauphin, Man. ... 6-1/210. ... Shoots left.
TRANSACTIONS/CAREER NOTES: Selected by Washington Capitals in first round (first Capitals pick, 17th overall) of NHL entry draft (July 8, 1995).

Season Team	League		REGULAR SEASON								PLAYOFFS			
		Gms.	G	A	Pts.	PIM	+/-	PP	SH	Gms.	G	A	Pts.	PIM
92-93— Dauphin	MJHL	45	15	23	38	80	...	...	...	—	—	—	—	—
93-94— Prince Albert..............	WHL	71	33	20	53	197	...	...	...	—	—	—	—	—
94-95— Prince Albert..............	WHL	62	26	24	50	184	...	...	...	15	6	9	15	32
95-96— Prince Albert..............	WHL	69	42	46	88	123	...	...	...	18	15	*20	*35	74
96-97— Portland	AHL	50	4	8	12	92	...	...	...	1	0	0	0	0

CHURLA, SHANE · RW · RANGERS

PERSONAL: Born June 24, 1965, in Fernie, B.C. ... 6-1/200. ... Shoots right. ... Name pronounced CHUHR-luh. ... Cousin of Mark Rypien, quarterback, St. Louis Rams.

TRANSACTIONS/CAREER NOTES: Selected by Hartford Whalers in sixth round (fourth Whalers pick, 110th overall) of NHL entry draft (June 15, 1985). ... Pulled stomach muscles (October 1985). ... Suspended three games by AHL (October 5, 1986). ... Traded by Whalers with D Dana Murzyn to Calgary Flames for D Neil Sheehy, C Carey Wilson and the rights to LW Lane MacDonald (January 3, 1988). ... Traded by Flames with C Perry Berezan to Minnesota North Stars for LW Brian MacLellan and fourth-round pick (C Robert Reichel) in 1989 draft (March 4, 1989). ... Broke wrist (April 2, 1989). ... Bruised right hand (November 1989). ... Suspended 10 games by NHL for fighting (December 28, 1989). ... Underwent surgery to wrist (April 1990). ... Tore rib cartilage (November 17, 1990); missed five games. ... Separated shoulder (December 11, 1990); missed seven games. ... Separated right shoulder (January 17, 1991); missed 23 games. ... Selected by San Jose Sharks in dispersal draft of North Stars roster (May 30, 1991). ... Traded by Sharks to North Stars for C Kelly Kisio (June 3, 1991). ... Suffered back spasms (January 30, 1992); missed five games. ... Injured shoulder (March 19, 1992); missed five games. ... Injured shoulder (December 1, 1992); missed one game. ... Injured shoulder (December 22, 1992); missed two games. ... Strained neck (February 28, 1993); missed two games. ... Suspended three games by NHL during 1992-93 season for game misconduct penalties. ... North Stars franchise moved from Minnesota to Dallas and renamed Stars for 1993-94 season. ... Pulled groin (October 23, 1993); missed two games. ... Pulled leg muscle (November 24, 1993); missed nine games. ... Strained bicep muscle (January 9, 1994); missed one game. ... Bruised hip (April 10, 1994); missed one game. ... Bruised hand (February 4, 1995); missed one game. ... Suffered deep thigh bruise (February 15, 1995); missed one game. ... Tore knee ligament (February 24, 1995); missed 12 games. ... Suffered from the flu (April 1, 1995); missed one game. ... Suspended four games without pay and fined $500 for resisting linesman (April 17, 1995). ... Pulled stomach muscle (April 25, 1995); missed one game. ... Broke right ankle (October 26, 1995); missed nine games. ... Reinjured right ankle (January 1, 1996); missed four games. ... Injured knee (February 2, 1996); missed three games. ... Traded by Stars with D Doug Zmolek to Los Angeles Kings for Darryl Sydor and seventh-round pick (G Eoin McInerney) in 1996 draft (February 17, 1996). ... Traded by Kings with LW Jarri Kurri and D Marty McSorley to New York Rangers for C Ray Ferraro, C Nathan Lafayette, C Ian Laperriere, D Mattis Norstrom and fourth-round pick (D Sean Blanchard) in 1997 draft (March 14, 1996). ... Suspended two games and fined $1000 by NHL for slashing (November 17, 1995). ... Separated shoulder (April 4, 1996); missed four games. ... Fractured hand (September 28, 1996); missed nine games. ... Fractured orbital bone (November 16, 1996); missed 13 games. ... Sore knee (January 25, 1997); missed six games. ... Sprained finger (February 17, 1997); missed three games. ... Strained groin (March 24, 1997); missed three games.

MISCELLANEOUS: Holds Dallas Stars franchise all-time record for most penalty minutes (1,883).

			REGULAR SEASON							PLAYOFFS				
Season Team	League	Gms.	G	A	Pts.	PIM	+/-	PP	SH	Gms.	G	A	Pts.	PIM
83-84 — Medicine Hat	WHL	48	3	7	10	115	...	...	...	14	1	5	6	41
84-85 — Medicine Hat	WHL	70	14	20	34	*370	...	...	...	9	1	0	1	55
85-86 — Binghamton	AHL	52	4	10	14	306	...	...	...	3	0	0	0	22
86-87 — Binghamton	AHL	24	1	5	6	249	...	...	...	—	—	—	—	—
— Hartford	NHL	20	0	1	1	78	-2	0	0	2	0	0	0	42
87-88 — Binghamton	AHL	25	5	8	13	168	...	...	...	—	—	—	—	—
— Hartford	NHL	2	0	0	0	14	-1	0	0	—	—	—	—	—
— Calgary	NHL	29	1	5	6	132	2	0	0	7	0	1	1	17
88-89 — Calgary	NHL	5	0	0	0	25	-3	0	0	—	—	—	—	—
— Salt Lake City	IHL	32	3	13	16	278	...	...	...	—	—	—	—	—
— Minnesota	NHL	13	1	0	1	54	0	0	0	—	—	—	—	—
89-90 — Minnesota	NHL	53	2	3	5	292	-4	0	0	7	0	0	0	44
90-91 — Minnesota	NHL	40	2	2	4	286	1	0	0	22	2	1	3	90
91-92 — Minnesota	NHL	57	4	1	5	278	-12	0	0	—	—	—	—	—
92-93 — Minnesota	NHL	73	5	16	21	286	-8	1	0	—	—	—	—	—
93-94 — Dallas	NHL	69	6	7	13	333	-8	3	0	9	1	3	4	35
94-95 — Dallas	NHL	27	1	3	4	186	0	0	0	5	0	0	0	20
95-96 — Dallas	NHL	34	3	4	7	168	4	0	0	—	—	—	—	—
— Los Angeles	NHL	11	1	2	3	37	-9	0	0	—	—	—	—	—
— New York Rangers	NHL	10	0	0	0	26	-3	0	0	11	2	2	4	14
96-97 — New York Rangers	NHL	45	0	1	1	106	-10	0	0	15	0	0	0	20
NHL totals (12 years)		488	26	45	71	2301	-53	4	0	78	5	7	12	282

CHYNOWETH, DEAN · D · BRUINS

PERSONAL: Born October 30, 1968, in Saskatoon, Sask. ... 6-1/198. ... Shoots right. ... Name pronounced shih-NOWTH. ... Son of Ed Chynoweth, former president of the Western Hockey League (1972-73 through 1978-79 and 1980-81 through 1995-96).

TRANSACTIONS/CAREER NOTES: Broke hand (September 1985). ... Broke hand (April 1986). ... Broke hand (October 1986). ... Fractured rib and punctured lung (April 1987). ... Selected by New York Islanders as underage junior in first round (first Islanders pick, 13th overall) of NHL entry draft (June 13, 1987). ... Injured left eye (October 27, 1988); missed two months. ... Developed Osgood-Schlatter disease, an abnormal relationship between the muscles and the growing bones (December 1988); missed remainder of season. ... Injured ankle (October 31, 1989). ... Sprained ligaments in right thumb (November 1989). ... Strained shoulder (February 24, 1994); missed one game. ... Strained groin (March 15, 1994); missed 10 games. ... Bruised knee (February 20, 1995); missed three games. ... Injured groin (March 18, 1995); missed three games. ... Traded by Islanders to Boston Bruins for fifth-round pick (C Peter Sachl) in 1996 draft (December 9, 1995). ... Suffered pulled hamstring (March 18, 1996); missed remainder of regular season. ... Underwent offseason abdominal surgery prior to 1996-97 season; missed first seven games of season. ... Strained groin (November 19, 1996); missed three games. ... Injured back (November 30, 1996); missed two games. ... Injured eye (February 1, 1997); missed one game. ... Suffered from the flu (April 10, 1997); missed three games.

HONORS: Named to Memorial Cup All-Star team (1987-88).

			REGULAR SEASON							PLAYOFFS				
Season Team	League	Gms.	G	A	Pts.	PIM	+/-	PP	SH	Gms.	G	A	Pts.	PIM
85-86 — Medicine Hat	WHL	69	3	12	15	208	...	...	...	17	3	2	5	52
86-87 — Medicine Hat	WHL	67	3	18	21	285	...	...	...	13	4	2	6	28
87-88 — Medicine Hat	WHL	64	1	21	22	274	...	...	...	16	0	6	6	*87
88-89 — New York Islanders	NHL	6	0	0	0	48	-4	0	0	—	—	—	—	—
89-90 — New York Islanders	NHL	20	0	2	2	39	0	0	0	—	—	—	—	—
— Springfield	AHL	40	0	7	7	98	...	...	...	17	0	4	4	36
90-91 — New York Islanders	NHL	25	1	1	2	59	...	...	...	—	—	—	—	—
— Capital District	AHL	44	1	5	6	176	...	...	...	—	—	—	—	—

Season Team	League	REGULAR SEASON								PLAYOFFS				
		Gms.	G	A	Pts.	PIM	+/-	PP	SH	Gms.	G	A	Pts.	PIM
91-92— Capital District	AHL	43	4	6	10	164	...	...	...	6	1	1	2	39
— New York Islanders	NHL	11	1	0	1	23	-3	0	0	—	—	—	—	—
92-93— Capital District	AHL	52	3	10	13	197	...	...	...	4	0	1	1	9
93-94— Salt Lake City	IHL	5	0	1	1	33	...	...	...	—	—	—	—	—
— New York Islanders	NHL	39	0	4	4	122	3	0	0	2	0	0	0	2
94-95— New York Islanders	NHL	32	0	2	2	77	9	0	0	—	—	—	—	—
95-96— New York Islanders	NHL	14	0	1	1	40	-4	0	0	—	—	—	—	—
— Boston	NHL	35	2	5	7	88	-1	0	0	4	0	0	0	24
96-97— Providence	AHL	2	0	0	0	13	...	...	...	—	—	—	—	—
— Boston	NHL	57	0	3	3	171	-12	0	0	—	—	—	—	—
NHL totals (8 years)		239	4	18	22	667	-12	0	0	6	0	0	0	26

CHYZOWSKI, DAVE — LW — C

PERSONAL: Born July 11, 1971, in Edmonton. ... 6-1/190. ... Shoots left. ... Name pronounced chih-ZOW-skee.
TRANSACTIONS/CAREER NOTES: Selected by New York Islanders in first round (first Islanders pick, second overall) of NHL entry draft (June 17, 1989). ... Signed by Indianapolis of IHL (August 12, 1996).
HONORS: Named to WHL (West) All-Star first team (1988-89).

Season Team	League	REGULAR SEASON								PLAYOFFS				
		Gms.	G	A	Pts.	PIM	+/-	PP	SH	Gms.	G	A	Pts.	PIM
87-88— Kamloops	WHL	66	16	17	33	117	...	...	...	18	2	4	6	26
88-89— Kamloops	WHL	68	56	48	104	139	...	...	...	16	15	13	28	32
89-90— Kamloops	WHL	4	5	2	7	17	...	...	...	17	11	6	17	46
— Springfield	AHL	4	0	0	0	7	...	...	...	—	—	—	—	—
— New York Islanders	NHL	34	8	6	14	45	-4	3	0	—	—	—	—	—
90-91— Capital District	AHL	7	3	6	9	22	...	...	...	—	—	—	—	—
— New York Islanders	NHL	56	5	9	14	61	-19	0	0	—	—	—	—	—
91-92— New York Islanders	NHL	12	1	1	2	17	-4	0	0	—	—	—	—	—
— Capital District	AHL	55	15	18	33	121	...	...	...	6	1	1	2	23
92-93— Capital District	AHL	66	15	21	36	177	...	...	...	3	2	0	2	0
93-94— Salt Lake City	IHL	66	27	13	40	151	...	...	...	—	—	—	—	—
— New York Islanders	NHL	3	1	0	1	4	-1	0	0	?	0	0	0	0
94-95— New York Islanders	NHL	13	0	0	0	11	-2	0	0	—	—	—	—	—
— Kalamazoo	IHL	4	0	4	4	8	...	...	...	16	9	5	14	27
95-96— Adirondack	AHL	80	44	39	83	160	...	...	...	3	0	0	0	6
96-97— Indianapolis	IHL	76	34	40	74	261	...	...	...	4	0	2	2	38
— Chicago	NHL	8	0	0	0	6	1	0	0	—	—	—	—	—
NHL totals (6 years)		126	15	16	31	144	-29	3	0	2	0	0	0	0

CICCARELLI, DINO — RW — LIGHTNING

PERSONAL: Born February 8, 1960, in Sarnia, Ont. ... 5-10/185. ... Shoots right. ... Name pronounced DEE-noh SIH-sih-REHL-ee.
TRANSACTIONS/CAREER NOTES: Fractured midshaft of right femur (spring 1978). ... Signed as free agent by Minnesota North Stars (September 1979). ... Injured shoulder (November 1984). ... Broke right wrist (December 1984). ... Suspended three games by NHL for making contact with linesman (October 5, 1987). ... Suspended 10 games by NHL for stick-swinging incident (January 6, 1988). ... Suspended by North Stars for failure to report to training camp (September 10, 1988). ... Traded by North Stars with D Bob Rouse to Washington Capitals for RW Mike Gartner and D Larry Murphy (March 7, 1989). ... Suffered concussion (March 8, 1989). ... Sprained left knee (April 23, 1990). ... Fractured right hand (October 20, 1990); missed 21 games. ... Injured groin (March 24, 1991); missed five games. ... Injured eye (December 4, 1991); missed one game. ... Traded by Capitals to Detroit Red Wings for RW Kevin Miller (June 20, 1992). ... Suffered from the flu (January 30, 1993); missed two games. ... Injured foot (January 15, 1994); missed 17 games. ... Lacerated face (February 8, 1995); missed one game. ... Strained right groin (April 2, 1995); missed one game. ... Suspended three games by NHL for punching another player (April 15, 1996). ... Traded by Red Wings to Tampa Bay Lightning for conditional pick in 1998 draft (August 27, 1996). ... Injured back (December 21, 1996); missed one game. ... Suffered concussion (January 30, 1997); missed three games.
HONORS: Won Jim Mahon Memorial Trophy (1977-78). ... Named to OMJHL All-Star second team (1977-78). ... Played in NHL All-Star Game (1982, 1983, 1989 and 1997).
RECORDS: Holds NHL single-season playoff records for most points by rookie—21; and most goals by rookie—14 (1981). ... Shares NHL playoff record for most power-play goals in single-game—3 (April 29, 1993).
STATISTICAL PLATEAUS: Three-goal games: 1981-82 (3), 1982-83 (1), 1983-84 (3), 1985-86 (3), 1986-87 (1), 1988-89 (2), 1990-91 (1), 1996-97 (1). Total: 15. ... Four-goal games: 1980-81 (1), 1988-89 (1), 1988-89 (1), 1989-90 (1), 1993-94 (1). Total: 5. ... Total hat tricks: 20.
MISCELLANEOUS: Failed to score on a penalty shot (vs. Denis Herron, March 16, 1983; vs. Allan Bester, November 26, 1988).

Season Team	League	REGULAR SEASON								PLAYOFFS				
		Gms.	G	A	Pts.	PIM	+/-	PP	SH	Gms.	G	A	Pts.	PIM
76-77— London	OMJHL	66	39	43	82	45	...	...	...	—	—	—	—	—
77-78— London	OMJHL	68	*72	70	142	49	...	...	...	9	6	10	16	6
78-79— London	OMJHL	30	8	11	19	35	...	...	...	7	3	5	8	0
79-80— London	OMJHL	62	50	53	103	72	...	...	...	5	2	6	8	15
— Oklahoma City	CHL	6	3	2	5	0	...	...	...	—	—	—	—	—
80-81— Oklahoma City	CHL	48	32	25	57	45	...	...	...	—	—	—	—	—
— Minnesota	NHL	32	18	12	30	29	2	8	0	19	14	7	21	25
81-82— Minnesota	NHL	76	55	51	106	138	14	20	0	4	3	1	4	2
82-83— Minnesota	NHL	77	37	38	75	94	16	14	0	9	4	6	10	11
83-84— Minnesota	NHL	79	38	33	71	58	1	16	0	16	4	5	9	27
84-85— Minnesota	NHL	51	15	17	32	41	-10	5	0	9	3	3	6	8
85-86— Minnesota	NHL	75	44	45	89	51	12	19	0	5	0	1	1	6
86-87— Minnesota	NHL	80	52	51	103	88	10	22	0	—	—	—	—	—
87-88— Minnesota	NHL	67	41	45	86	79	...	...	...	—	—	—	—	—

Season Team	League	REGULAR SEASON								PLAYOFFS				
		Gms.	G	A	Pts.	PIM	+/-	PP	SH	Gms.	G	A	Pts.	PIM
88-89— Minnesota	NHL	65	32	27	59	64	-16	13	0	—	—	—	—	—
—Washington	NHL	11	12	3	15	12	10	3	0	6	3	3	6	12
89-90— Washington	NHL	80	41	38	79	122	-5	10	0	8	8	3	11	6
90-91— Washington	NHL	54	21	18	39	66	-17	2	0	11	5	4	9	22
91-92— Washington	NHL	78	38	38	76	78	-10	13	0	7	5	4	9	14
92-93— Detroit	NHL	82	41	56	97	81	12	21	0	7	4	2	6	16
93-94— Detroit	NHL	66	28	29	57	73	10	12	0	7	5	2	7	14
94-95— Detroit	NHL	42	16	27	43	39	12	6	0	16	9	2	11	22
95-96— Detroit	NHL	64	22	21	43	99	14	13	0	17	6	2	8	26
96-97— Tampa Bay	NHL	77	35	25	60	116	-11	12	0	—	—	—	—	—
NHL totals (17 years)		1156	586	574	1160	1328	44	209	0	141	73	45	118	211

CICCONE, ENRICO — D — HURRICANES

PERSONAL: Born April 10, 1970, in Montreal. ... 6-4/210. ... Shoots left. ... Name pronounced en-REE-koh chih-KOH-nee.
TRANSACTIONS/CAREER NOTES: Selected by Minnesota North Stars in fifth round (fifth North Stars pick, 92nd overall) of NHL entry draft (June 16, 1990). ... North Stars franchise moved from Minnesota to Dallas and renamed Stars for 1993-94 season. ... Traded by Stars to Washington Capitals (June 25, 1993) to complete deal in which Capitals sent D Paul Cavallini to Stars for future considerations (June 20, 1993). ... Pulled groin (January 25, 1994); missed seven games. ... Traded by Capitals with third-round pick (traded to Mighty Ducks of Anaheim who selected RW Craig Reichert) in 1994 draft and conditional draft pick to Tampa Bay Lightning for D Joe Reekie (March 21, 1994). ... Suffered whiplash (February 5, 1995); missed one game. ... Injured neck (March 1, 1995); missed one game. ... Injured shoulder (April 26, 1995); missed two games. ... Tore ligament in right thumb (November 18, 1995); missed 10 games. ... Sprained right knee (January 30, 1996); missed one game. ... Traded by Lightning to Chicago Blackhawks for LW Patrick Poulin, D Igor Ulanov and second-round pick (traded to New Jersey) in 1996 draft (March 20, 1996). ... Bruised ribs prior to 1996-97 season; missed first six games of season. ... Injured hip flexor (March 20, 1997); missed one game. ... Traded by Blackhawks to Carolina Hurricanes for D Ryan Risidore and fifth-round pick in 1998 draft (July 25, 1997).
MISCELLANEOUS: Holds Tampa Bay Lightning all-time record for most penalty minutes (535).

Season Team	League	REGULAR SEASON								PLAYOFFS				
		Gms.	G	A	Pts.	PIM	+/-	PP	SH	Gms.	G	A	Pts.	PIM
87-88— Shawinigan	QMJHL	61	2	12	14	324	...	...	...	—	—	—	—	—
88-89— Shawinigan	QMJHL	58	7	19	26	289	...	...	...	—	—	—	—	—
— Trois-Rivieres	QMJHL	24	0	7	7	153	...	...	...	—	—	—	—	—
89-90— Trois-Rivieres	QMJHL	40	4	24	28	227	...	...	...	3	0	0	0	15
90-91— Kalamazoo	IHL	57	4	9	13	384	...	...	...	4	0	1	1	32
91-92— Kalamazoo	IHL	53	4	16	20	406	...	...	...	10	0	1	1	58
— Minnesota	NHL	11	0	0	0	48	-2	0	0	—	—	—	—	—
92-93— Minnesota	NHL	31	0	1	1	115	2	0	0	—	—	—	—	—
— Kalamazoo	IHL	13	1	3	4	50	...	...	...	—	—	—	—	—
— Hamilton	AHL	6	1	3	4	44	...	...	...	—	—	—	—	—
93-94— Washington	NHL	46	1	1	2	174	-2	0	0	—	—	—	—	—
— Portland	AHL	6	0	0	0	27	...	...	...	—	—	—	—	—
— Tampa Bay	NHL	11	0	1	1	52	-2	0	0	—	—	—	—	—
94-95— Tampa Bay	NHL	41	2	4	6	225	3	0	0	—	—	—	—	—
95-96— Tampa Bay	NHL	55	2	3	5	258	-4	0	0	—	—	—	—	—
— Chicago	NHL	11	0	1	1	48	5	0	0	9	1	0	1	30
96-97— Chicago	NHL	67	2	2	4	233	-1	0	0	4	0	0	0	18
NHL totals (7 years)		273	7	13	20	1153	-1	0	0	13	1	0	1	48

CIERNIK, IVAN — LW — SENATORS

PERSONAL: Born October 30, 1977, in Tlmace, Slovakia. ... 6-1/198. ... Shoots left.
TRANSACTIONS/CAREER NOTES: Selected by Ottawa Senators in ninth round (sixth Senators pick, 216th overall) of NHL entry draft (June 22, 1996).

Season Team	League	REGULAR SEASON								PLAYOFFS				
		Gms.	G	A	Pts.	PIM	+/-	PP	SH	Gms.	G	A	Pts.	PIM
95-96— HC Nitra	Slovakia	35	9	7	16	36	...	...	...	—	—	—	—	—
96-97— HC Nitra	Slovakia	41	11	19	30	30	...	...	...	—	—	—	—	—

CIGER, ZDENO — LW

PERSONAL: Born October 19, 1969, in Martin, Czechoslovakia. ... 6-1/190. ... Shoots left. ... Name pronounced zuh-DAYN-yoh SEE-guhr.
TRANSACTIONS/CAREER NOTES: Selected by New Jersey Devils in third round (third Devils pick, 54th overall) of NHL entry draft (June 11, 1988). ... Bruised left shoulder (October 6, 1990). ... Injured elbow (January 24, 1991). ... Fractured right wrist (September 24, 1991); missed first 59 games of season. ... Traded by Devils with C Kevin Todd to Edmonton Oilers for C Bernie Nicholls (January 13, 1993). ... Played in Europe during 1994-95 NHL lockout. ... Injured lower right leg (December 10, 1995); missed four games.
HONORS: Named Czechoslovakian League Rookie of the Year (1988-89).

Season Team	League	REGULAR SEASON								PLAYOFFS				
		Gms.	G	A	Pts.	PIM	+/-	PP	SH	Gms.	G	A	Pts.	PIM
88-89— Dukla Trencin	Czech.	32	15	21	36	18	...	...	...	—	—	—	—	—
89-90— Dukla Trencin	Czech.	53	18	28	46	...	...	...	...	—	—	—	—	—
90-91— New Jersey	NHL	45	8	17	25	8	3	2	0	6	0	2	2	4
— Utica	AHL	8	5	4	9	2	...	...	...	—	—	—	—	—
91-92— New Jersey	NHL	20	6	5	11	10	-2	1	0	7	2	4	6	0
92-93— New Jersey	NHL	27	4	8	12	2	-8	2	0	—	—	—	—	—
— Edmonton	NHL	37	9	15	24	6	-5	0	0	—	—	—	—	—
93-94— Edmonton	NHL	84	22	35	57	8	-11	8	0	—	—	—	—	—

Season Team	League	REGULAR SEASON								PLAYOFFS				
		Gms.	G	A	Pts.	PIM	+/-	PP	SH	Gms.	G	A	Pts.	PIM
94-95— Dukla Trencin............	Slovakia	34	23	26	49	10	...	...	...	9	2	9	11	2
— Edmonton	NHL	5	2	2	4	0	-1	1	0	—	—	—	—	—
95-96— Edmonton	NHL	78	31	39	70	41	-15	12	0	—	—	—	—	—
96-97— Sparta Praha.............	Czech Rep.	44	26	27	53	...	...	...	...	2	1	3	4	...
NHL totals (6 years)		296	82	121	203	75	-39	26	0	13	2	6	8	4

CLARK, WENDEL — LW — MAPLE LEAFS

C

PERSONAL: Born October 25, 1966, in Kelvington, Sask. ... 5-10/194. ... Shoots left. ... Cousin of Joe Kocur, right winger, Detroit Red Wings.
TRANSACTIONS/CAREER NOTES: Selected by Toronto Maple Leafs as underage junior in first round (first Maple Leafs pick, first overall) of NHL entry draft (June 15, 1985). ... Suffered from virus (November 1985). ... Broke right foot (November 26, 1985); missed 14 games. ... Suffered back spasms (November 1987); missed 23 games. ... Suffered tendinitis in right shoulder (October 1987). ... Reinjured back (February 1988); missed 90 regular season games (March 1, 1989). ... Suffered recurrence of back problems (October 1989). ... Bruised muscle above left knee (November 4, 1989); missed seven games. ... Tore ligament in right knee (January 26, 1990); missed 29 games. ... Separated left shoulder (December 18, 1990). ... Pulled rib cage muscle (February 6, 1991); missed 12 games. ... Partially tore knee ligaments (October 7, 1991); missed 12 games. ... Strained knee ligaments (November 6, 1991); missed 24 games. ... Injured groin (October 24, 1992); missed four games. ... Strained rib muscle (January 17, 1993); missed 13 games. ... Strained knee (October 13, 1993); missed two games. ... Bruised foot (December 22, 1993); missed 17 games. ... Traded by Maple Leafs with D Sylvain Lefebvre, RW Landon Wilson and first-round pick in 1994 draft (D Jeffrey Kealty) to Quebec Nordiques for C Mats Sundin, D Garth Butcher, LW Todd Warriner and first-round pick (traded to Washington Capitals who selected D Nolan Baumgartner) in 1994 draft (June 28, 1994). ... Injured thigh (March 18, 1995); missed 11 games. ... Fined $1,000 by NHL for elbowing (May 10, 1995). ... Nordiques franchise moved to Colorado and renamed Avalanche for 1995-96 season (June 21, 1995). ... Traded by Avalanche to New York Islanders for RW Claude Lemieux (October 3, 1995). ... Suffered back spasms (January 30, 1996); missed eight games. ... Traded by Islanders with D Mathieu Schneider and D D.J. Smith to Toronto Maple Leafs for LW Sean Haggerty, C Darby Hendrickson, D Kenny Jonsson and first-round pick (G Roberto Luongo) in 1997 draft (March 13, 1996). ... Fractured thumb (December 10, 1996); missed 16 games. ... Bruised back (April 2, 1997); missed one game.
HONORS: Won Top Defenseman Trophy (1984-85). ... Named to WHL (East) All-Star first team (1984-85). ... Named NHL Rookie of the Year by THE SPORTING NEWS (1985-86). ... Named to NHL All-Rookie team (1985-86). ... Played in NHL All-Star Game (1986).
STATISTICAL PLATEAUS: Three-goal games: 1985-86 (1), 1989-90 (1), 1991-92 (2), 1993-94 (2), 1994-95 (1). Total: 7. ... Four-goal games: 1986-87 (1), 1996-97 (1). Total: 2. ... Total hat tricks: 9.
MISCELLANEOUS: Captain of Toronto Maple Leafs (1991-92 through 1993-94). ... Scored on a penalty shot (vs. Trevor Kidd, November 24, 1993). ... Failed to score on a penalty shot (vs. Darcy Wakaluk, December 21, 1995).

Season Team	League	REGULAR SEASON								PLAYOFFS				
		Gms.	G	A	Pts.	PIM	+/-	PP	SH	Gms.	G	A	Pts.	PIM
83-84— Saskatoon..................	WHL	72	23	45	68	225	...	...	...	—	—	—	—	—
84-85— Saskatoon..................	WHL	64	32	55	87	253	...	...	...	3	3	3	6	7
85-86— Toronto	NHL	66	34	11	45	227	-27	4	0	10	5	1	6	47
86-87— Toronto	NHL	80	37	23	60	271	-23	15	0	13	6	5	11	38
87-88— Toronto	NHL	28	12	11	23	80	-13	4	0	—	—	—	—	—
88-89— Toronto	NHL	15	7	4	11	66	-3	3	0	—	—	—	—	—
89-90— Toronto	NHL	38	18	8	26	116	2	7	0	5	1	1	2	19
90-91— Toronto	NHL	63	18	16	34	152	-5	4	0	—	—	—	—	—
91-92— Toronto	NHL	43	19	21	40	123	-14	7	0	—	—	—	—	—
92-93— Toronto	NHL	66	17	22	39	193	2	2	0	21	10	10	20	51
93-94— Toronto	NHL	64	46	30	76	115	10	21	0	18	9	7	16	24
94-95— Quebec......................	NHL	37	12	18	30	45	-1	5	0	6	1	2	3	6
95-96— New York Islanders....	NHL	58	24	19	43	60	-12	6	0	—	—	—	—	—
— Toronto	NHL	13	8	7	15	16	7	2	0	6	2	2	4	2
96-97— Toronto	NHL	65	30	19	49	75	-2	6	0	—	—	—	—	—
NHL totals (12 years)		636	282	209	491	1539	-79	86	0	79	34	28	62	187

CLOUTIER, COLIN — C — LIGHTNING

PERSONAL: Born January 27, 1976, in Winnipeg. ... 6-3/224. ... Shoots left. ... Name pronounced KAH-lihn KLOOT-yay.
HIGH SCHOOL: Crocus Plains (Brandon, Man.).
TRANSACTIONS/CAREER NOTES: Selected by Tampa Bay Lightning in second round (second Lightning pick, 34th overall) of NHL entry draft (June 28, 1994).

Season Team	League	REGULAR SEASON								PLAYOFFS				
		Gms.	G	A	Pts.	PIM	+/-	PP	SH	Gms.	G	A	Pts.	PIM
91-92— St. Boniface	MJHL	42	7	15	22	113	...	...	...	—	—	—	—	—
— Brandon	WHL	3	1	1	2	0	...	...	...	—	—	—	—	—
92-93— Brandon	WHL	60	11	15	26	138	...	...	...	4	0	0	0	18
93-94— Brandon	WHL	30	10	13	23	102	...	...	...	11	2	5	7	23
94-95— Brandon	WHL	47	16	27	43	170	...	...	...	16	5	6	11	47
95-96— Prince George...........	WHL	39	9	19	28	84	...	...	...	—	—	—	—	—
— Lethbridge	WHL	14	5	10	15	39	...	...	...	3	2	2	4	19
96-97— Adirondack...............	AHL	52	5	15	20	127	...	...	...	2	0	0	0	0

CLOUTIER, DAN — G — RANGERS

PERSONAL: Born April 22, 1976, in Mont-Laurier, Que. ... 6-2/185. ... Catches left. ... Name pronounced KLOOT-yay. ... Brother of Sylvain Cloutier, center in Detroit Red Wings system.
HIGH SCHOOL: Notre-Dame-des-Grands-Lacs (Sault Ste. Marie, Ont.).
TRANSACTIONS/CAREER NOTES: Selected by New York Rangers in first round (first Rangers pick, 26th overall) of NHL entry draft (June 28, 1994).
HONORS: Named to OHL All-Star second team (1995-96). ... Won Dave Pinkney Trophy (1995-96). ... Named to AHL All-Rooike team (1996-97).

Season Team	League	REGULAR SEASON								PLAYOFFS						
		Gms.	Min	W	L	T	GA	SO	Avg.	Gms.	Min.	W	L	GA	SO	Avg.
91-92—St. Thomas	Jr. B	14	823	...	...	...	80	...	5.83	—	—					
92-93—Sault Ste. Marie	OHL	12	572	4	6	0	44	0	4.62	4	231	1	2	12	0	3.12
93-94—Sault Ste. Marie	OHL	55	2934	28	14	6	174	†2	3.56	14	833	†10	4	52	0	3.75
94-95—Sault Ste. Marie	OHL	45	2517	15	25	2	184	1	4.39	—	—					
95-96—Sault Ste. Marie	OHL	13	641	9	3	0	43	...	4.02	—	—					
—Guelph	OHL	17	1004	12	2	2	35	2	2.09	16	993	11	5	52	*2	3.14
96-97—Binghamton	AHL	60	3367	23	†28	8	199	3	3.55	4	236	1	3	13	0	3.31

COFFEY, PAUL   D   FLYERS

PERSONAL: Born June 1, 1961, in Weston, Ont. ... 6-0/200. ... Shoots left. ... Full name: Paul Douglas Coffey.

TRANSACTIONS/CAREER NOTES: Selected by Edmonton Oilers in first round (first Oilers pick, sixth overall) of NHL entry draft (June 11, 1980). ... Suffered recurring back spasms (December 1986); missed 10 games. ... Traded by Oilers with LW Dave Hunter and RW Wayne Van Dorp to Pittsburgh Penguins for C Craig Simpson, C Dave Hannan, D Moe Mantha and D Chris Joseph (November 24, 1987). ... Tore knee cartilage (December 1987). ... Bruised right shoulder (November 16, 1988). ... Broke finger (May 1990). ... Injured back (February 27, 1991). ... Injured hip muscle (March 9, 1991). ... Scratched left eye cornea (April 9, 1991). ... Broke jaw (April 1991). ... Pulled hip muscle (February 3, 1992); missed three games. ... Traded by Penguins to Los Angeles Kings for D Brian Benning, D Jeff Chychrun and first-round pick (LW Jason Bowen) in 1992 draft (February 19, 1992). ... Suffered back spasms (March 3, 1992); missed three games. ... Fractured wrist (March 17, 1992); missed five games. ... Traded by Kings with RW Jim Hiller and C/LW Sylain Couturier to Detroit Red Wings for C Jimmy Carson, RW Marc Potvin and C Gary Shuchuk (January 29, 1993). ... Injured groin (March 18, 1993); missed one game. ... Injured groin and left knee (October 18, 1993); missed four games. ... Injured back (January 28, 1995); missed two games. ... Injured back (November 4, 1995); missed two games. ... Sprained right thumb (January 6, 1996); missed two games. ... Suffered back spasms (April 7, 1996); missed one game. ... Traded by Red Wings with C Keith Primeau and first-round pick (traded to San Jose) in 1997 draft to Hartford Whalers for LW Brendan Shanahan and D Brian Glynn (October 9, 1996). ... Injured hip flexor (October 17, 1996); missed three games. ... Suffered from the flu (November 8, 1996); missed two games. ... Injured groin (November 29, 1996); missed one game. ... Sore lower back (December 14, 1996); missed one game. ... Traded by Whalers with third-round pick (D Kris Mallette) in 1997 draft to Philadelphia Flyers for D Kevin Haller and first- (traded to San Jose) and seventh-round (C Andrew Merrick) picks in 1997 draft (December 15, 1996). ... Bruised left quadricep (December 21, 1996); missed one game. ... Suffered concussion (December 31, 1996); missed five games. ... Strained hamstring (February 4, 1997); missed two games. ... Separated left shoulder (March 25, 1997); missed three games. ... Twisted knee (April 12, 1997); missed final game of regular season.

HONORS: Named to OMJHL All-Star second team (1979-80). ... Named to NHL All-Star second team (1980-81 through 1983-84 and 1989-90). ... Named to The Sporting News All-Star second team (1981-82 through 1983-84, 1986-87 and 1989-90). ... Played in NHL All-Star Game (1982-1986, 1988-1994 and 1996-1997). ... Won James Norris Memorial Trophy (1984-85, 1985-86 and 1994-95). ... Named to The Sporting News All-Star first team (1984-85, 1985-86, 1988-89 and 1994-95). ... Named to NHL All-Star first team (1985-86, 1988-89 and 1994-95).

RECORDS: Holds NHL career records for most goals by a defenseman—381; most assists by a defenseman—1,063; and most points by a defenseman—1,444. ... Holds NHL single-season record for most goals by a defenseman—48 (1985-86). ... Shares NHL single-game records for most points by a defenseman—8; and most assists by a defenseman—6 (March 14, 1986). ... Holds NHL record for most consecutive games scoring points by a defenseman—28 (1985-86). ... Holds NHL single-season playoff records for most goals by a defenseman—12; assists by a defenseman—25; and points by a defenseman—37 (1985). ... Holds NHL single-game playoff record for most points by a defenseman—6 (May 14, 1985).

STATISTICAL PLATEAUS: Three-goal games: 1982-83 (1), 1984-85 (1), 1985-86 (1), 1987-88 (1). Total: 4. ... Four-goal games: 1984-85 (1). ... Total hat tricks: 5.

MISCELLANEOUS: Member of Stanley Cup championship team (1984, 1985, 1987 and 1991).

Season Team	League	REGULAR SEASON							PLAYOFFS				
		Gms.	G	A	Pts.	PIM	+/-	PP	SH	Gms.	G	A	Pts.	PIM
77-78—Kingston	OMJHL	8	2	2	4	11	...	...	...	—	—	—	—	—
—North York	MTHL	50	14	33	47	64	...	...	...	—	—	—	—	—
78-79—Sault Ste. Marie	OMJHL	68	17	72	89	99	...	...	...	—	—	—	—	—
79-80—Sault Ste. Marie	OMJHL	23	10	21	31	63	...	...	...	—	—	—	—	—
—Kitchener	OMJHL	52	19	52	71	130	...	...	...	—	—	—	—	—
80-81—Edmonton	NHL	74	9	23	32	130	4	2	0	9	4	3	7	22
81-82—Edmonton	NHL	80	29	60	89	106	35	13	0	5	1	1	2	6
82-83—Edmonton	NHL	80	29	67	96	87	52	9	1	16	7	7	14	14
83-84—Edmonton	NHL	80	40	86	126	104	52	14	1	19	8	14	22	21
84-85—Edmonton	NHL	80	37	84	121	97	55	12	2	18	12	25	37	44
85-86—Edmonton	NHL	79	48	90	138	120	61	9	*9	10	1	9	10	30
86-87—Edmonton	NHL	59	17	50	67	49	12	10	2	17	3	8	11	30
87-88—Pittsburgh	NHL	46	15	52	67	93	-1	6	2	—	—	—	—	—
88-89—Pittsburgh	NHL	75	30	83	113	195	-10	11	0	11	2	13	15	31
89-90—Pittsburgh	NHL	80	29	74	103	95	-25	10	0	—	—	—	—	—
90-91—Pittsburgh	NHL	76	24	69	93	128	-18	8	0	12	2	9	11	6
91-92—Pittsburgh	NHL	54	10	54	64	62	4	5	0	—	—	—	—	—
—Los Angeles	NHL	10	1	4	5	25	-3	0	0	6	4	3	7	2
92-93—Los Angeles	NHL	50	8	49	57	50	9	2	0	—	—	—	—	—
—Detroit	NHL	30	4	26	30	27	7	3	0	7	2	9	11	2
93-94—Detroit	NHL	80	14	63	77	106	28	5	0	7	1	6	7	8
94-95—Detroit	NHL	45	14	44	58	72	18	4	1	18	6	12	18	10
95-96—Detroit	NHL	76	14	60	74	90	19	3	1	17	5	9	14	30
96-97—Hartford	NHL	20	3	5	8	18	0	1	0	—	—	—	—	—
—Philadelphia	NHL	37	6	20	26	20	11	0	1	17	1	8	9	6
NHL totals (17 years)		1211	381	1063	1444	1674	310	127	20	189	59	136	195	262

COLE, DANTON   RW

PERSONAL: Born January 10, 1967, in Pontiac, Mich. ... 5-11/185. ... Shoots right. ... Full name: Danton Edward Cole.
COLLEGE: Michigan State.

TRANSACTIONS/CAREER NOTES: Selected by Winnipeg Jets in sixth round (sixth Jets pick, 123rd overall) of NHL entry draft (June 15, 1985). ... Strained knee (January 26, 1992); missed 11 games. ... Traded by Jets to Tampa Bay Lightning for future considerations (June 19, 1992). ... Tore ligament in left knee (December 15, 1992); missed 10 games. ... Injured groin (October 23, 1993); missed one game. ... Suffered cut to mouth (October 30, 1993); missed one game. ... Traded by Lightning with D Shawn Chambers to New Jersey Devils for C Alexander Semak and RW Ben Hankinson (March 14, 1995). ... Signed as free agent by New York Islanders (September 5, 1995). ... Traded by Islanders to Chicago Blackhawks for D Bob Halkidis (February 2, 1996).
MISCELLANEOUS: Member of Stanley Cup championship team (1995).

Season Team	League	Gms.	G	A	Pts.	PIM	+/-	PP	SH	Gms.	G	A	Pts.	PIM
84-85— Aurora....................	OHA	41	51	44	95	91	...	...	...	—	—	—	—	—
85-86— Michigan State...........	CCHA	43	11	10	21	22	...	...	...	—	—	—	—	—
86-87— Michigan State...........	CCHA	44	9	15	24	16	...	...	...	—	—	—	—	—
87-88— Michigan State...........	CCHA	46	20	36	56	38	...	...	...	—	—	—	—	—
88-89— Michigan State...........	CCHA	47	29	33	62	46	...	...	...	—	—	—	—	—
89-90— Winnipeg	NHL	2	1	1	2	0	-1	0	0	—	—	—	—	—
— Moncton	AHL	80	31	42	73	18	...	...	...	—	—	—	—	—
90-91— Winnipeg	NHL	66	13	11	24	24	-14	1	1	—	—	—	—	—
— Moncton	AHL	3	1	1	2	0	...	...	...	—	—	—	—	—
91-92— Winnipeg	NHL	52	7	5	12	32	-15	1	2	—	—	—	—	—
92-93— Tampa Bay	NHL	67	12	15	27	23	-2	0	1	—	—	—	—	—
— Atlanta	IHL	1	1	0	1	2	...	...	...	—	—	—	—	—
93-94— Tampa Bay	NHL	81	20	23	43	32	7	8	1	—	—	—	—	—
94-95— Tampa Bay	NHL	26	3	3	6	6	-1	1	0	—	—	—	—	—
— New Jersey	NHL	12	1	2	3	8	0	0	0	1	0	0	0	0
95-96— Utah	IHL	34	28	15	43	22	...	...	...	—	—	—	—	—
— New York Islanders....	NHL	10	1	0	1	0	0	0	0	—	—	—	—	—
— Indianapolis	IHL	32	9	12	21	20	...	...	...	5	1	5	6	8
— Chicago.....................	NHL	2	0	0	0	0	0	0	0	—	—	—	—	—
96-97— Grand Rapids.............	IHL	35	8	18	26	24	...	...	...	5	3	1	4	2
NHL totals (8 years)		318	58	60	118	125	-26	11	5	1	0	0	0	0

COLEMAN, JON — D — RED WINGS

PERSONAL: Born March 9, 1975, in Boston. ... 6-0/192. ... Shoots right.
HIGH SCHOOL: Phillips Academy (Andover, Mass.).
COLLEGE: Boston University.
TRANSACTIONS/CAREER NOTES: Selected by Detroit Red Wings in second round (second Red Wings pick, 48th overall) of NHL entry draft (June 26, 1993).
HONORS: Named to NCAA All-America East second team (1995-96). ... Named to Hockey East All-Star team (1995-96 and 1996-97). ... Named to NCAA All-America East first team (1996-97).

Season Team	League	Gms.	G	A	Pts.	PIM	+/-	PP	SH	Gms.	G	A	Pts.	PIM
89-90— Phillips Academy	Mass. H.S.	24	8	20	28	10	...	...	...	—	—	—	—	—
90-91— Phillips Academy	Mass. H.S.	24	11	25	36	18	...	...	...	—	—	—	—	—
91-92— Phillips Academy	Mass. H.S.	24	12	29	41	26	...	...	...	—	—	—	—	—
92-93— Phillips Academy	Mass. H.S.	23	14	33	47	72	...	...	...	—	—	—	—	—
93-94— Boston University	Hockey East	29	1	14	15	26	...	...	...	—	—	—	—	—
94-95— Boston University	Hockey East	40	5	23	28	42	...	...	...	—	—	—	—	—
95-96— Boston University	Hockey East	40	7	31	38	58	...	...	...	—	—	—	—	—
96-97— Boston University	Hockey East	39	5	27	32	20	...	...	...	—	—	—	—	—

CONN, ROB — LW/RW — SABRES

PERSONAL: Born September 3, 1968, in Calgary. ... 6-2/200. ... Shoots right. ... Full name: Robert Phillip Conn. ... Name pronounced KAHN.
COLLEGE: Alaska-Anchorage.
TRANSACTIONS/CAREER NOTES: Signed as free agent by Chicago Blackhawks (July 31, 1991). ... Traded by Blackhawks to New Jersey Devils for D Dean Malkoc (January 30, 1995). ... Claimed by Buffalo Sabres from Devils in waiver draft (October 2, 1995).

Season Team	League	Gms.	G	A	Pts.	PIM	+/-	PP	SH	Gms.	G	A	Pts.	PIM
88-89— Alaska-Anchorage......	Indep.	33	21	17	38	46	...	...	...	—	—	—	—	—
89-90— Alaska-Anchorage......	Indep.	34	27	21	48	46	...	...	...	—	—	—	—	—
90-91— Alaska-Anchorage......	Indep.	43	28	32	60	53	...	...	...	—	—	—	—	—
91-92— Indianapolis	IHL	72	19	16	35	100	...	...	...	—	—	—	—	—
— Chicago.....................	NHL	2	0	0	0	2	1	0	0	—	—	—	—	—
92-93— Indianapolis	IHL	75	13	14	27	81	...	...	...	5	0	1	1	6
93-94— Indianapolis	IHL	51	16	11	27	46	...	...	...	—	—	—	—	—
94-95— Indianapolis	IHL	10	4	4	8	11	...	...	...	—	—	—	—	—
— Albany.......................	AHL	68	35	32	67	76	...	...	...	14	4	6	10	16
95-96— Buffalo	NHL	28	2	5	7	18	-9	0	0	—	—	—	—	—
— Rochester	AHL	36	22	15	37	40	...	...	...	19	7	6	13	10
96-97— Indianapolis	IHL	72	25	32	57	81	...	...	...	4	0	0	0	8
NHL totals (2 years)		30	2	5	7	20	-8	0	0					

CONROY, CRAIG — C — BLUES

PERSONAL: Born September 4, 1971, in Potsdam, N.Y. ... 6-2/195. ... Shoots right.
HIGH SCHOOL: Northwood (Lake Placid, N.Y.).
COLLEGE: Clarkson (N.Y.).

TRANSACTIONS/CAREER NOTES: Selected by Montreal Canadiens in sixth round (seventh Canadiens pick, 123rd overall) of NHL entry draft (June 16, 1990). ... Traded by Canadiens with C Pierre Turgeon to St. Louis Blues for LW Shayne Corson, D Murray Baron and fifth-round pick (D Gennady Razin) in 1997 draft (October 29, 1996).
HONORS: Named to NCAA All-America East first team (1993-94). ... Named to NCAA All-Tournament team (1993-94). ... Named to ECAC All-Star first team (1993-94).

		REGULAR SEASON								PLAYOFFS				
Season Team	League	Gms.	G	A	Pts.	PIM	+/-	PP	SH	Gms.	G	A	Pts.	PIM
90-91— Clarkson..............	ECAC	40	8	21	29	24	...	...	...	—	—	—	—	—
91-92— Clarkson..............	ECAC	31	19	17	36	36	...	...	...	—	—	—	—	—
92-93— Clarkson..............	ECAC	35	10	23	33	26	...	...	...	—	—	—	—	—
93-94— Clarkson..............	ECAC	34	26	40	66	66	...	...	...	—	—	—	—	—
94-95— Fredericton...............	AHL	55	26	18	44	29	...	...	...	11	7	3	10	6
— Montreal	NHL	6	1	0	1	0	-1	0	0	—	—	—	—	—
95-96— Fredericton...............	AHL	67	31	38	69	65	...	...	...	10	5	7	12	6
— Montreal	NHL	7	0	0	0	2	-4	0	0	—	—	—	—	—
96-97— Fredericton...............	AHL	9	10	6	16	10	...	...	...	—	—	—	—	—
— St. Louis	NHL	61	6	11	17	43	0	0	0	6	0	0	0	8
— Worcester	AHL	5	5	6	11	2	...	...	...	—	—	—	—	—
NHL totals (3 years)		74	7	11	18	45	-5	0	0	6	0	0	0	8

CONVERY, BRANDON   C   MAPLE LEAFS

C

PERSONAL: Born February 4, 1974, in Kingston, Ont. ... 6-1/182. ... Shoots right. ... Name pronounced KAHN-vuhr-ee.
HIGH SCHOOL: Lasalle Secondary School (Sudbury, Ont.).
TRANSACTIONS/CAREER NOTES: Selected by Toronto Maple Leafs in first round (first Maple Leafs pick, eighth overall) of NHL entry draft (June 20, 1992). ... Broke bone in wrist (March 2, 1996); missed four games.
HONORS: Won OHL Top Prospect Award (1991-92).

		REGULAR SEASON								PLAYOFFS				
Season Team	League	Gms.	G	A	Pts.	PIM	+/-	PP	SH	Gms.	G	A	Pts.	PIM
89-90— Kingston Jr. B	OHA	42	13	25	38	4	...	...	...	—	—	—	—	—
90-91— Sudbury................	OHL	56	26	22	48	18	...	...	...	5	1	1	2	2
91-92— Sudbury................	OHL	44	40	27	67	44	...	...	...	5	3	2	5	4
92-93— Sudbury................	OHL	7	7	9	16	6	...	...	...	—	—	—	—	—
— Niagara Falls	OHL	51	38	39	77	24	...	...	...	4	1	3	4	4
— St. John's................	AHL	3	0	0	0	0	...	...	...	5	0	1	1	0
93-94— St. John's................	AHL	—	—	—	—	—	...	...	...	1	0	0	0	0
— Belleville................	OHL	23	16	19	35	22	...	...	...	12	4	10	14	13
94-95— St. John's................	AHL	76	34	37	71	43	...	...	...	5	2	2	4	4
95-96— St. John's................	AHL	57	22	23	45	28	...	...	...	—	—	—	—	—
— Toronto	NHL	11	5	2	7	4	-7	3	0	5	0	0	0	2
96-97— Toronto	NHL	39	2	8	10	20	-9	0	0	—	—	—	—	—
— St. John's................	AHL	25	14	14	28	15	...	...	...	—	—	—	—	—
NHL totals (2 years)		50	7	10	17	24	-16	3	0	5	0	0	0	2

COOPER, DAVID   D   MAPLE LEAFS

PERSONAL: Born November 2, 1973, in Ottawa. ... 6-2/204. ... Shoots left.
HIGH SCHOOL: Medicine Hat (Alta.).
TRANSACTIONS/CAREER NOTES: Selected by Buffalo Sabres in first round (first Sabres pick, 11th overall) of NHL entry draft (June 20, 1992). ... Signed as free agent by Toronto Maple Leafs (September 1996). ... Suffered from the flu (January 3, 1997); missed one game. ... Sprained knee (March 19, 1997); missed 11 games.
HONORS: Won WHL Top Prospect Award (1991-92). ... Named to WHL (East) All-Star first team (1991-92).

		REGULAR SEASON								PLAYOFFS				
Season Team	League	Gms.	G	A	Pts.	PIM	+/-	PP	SH	Gms.	G	A	Pts.	PIM
89-90— Medicine Hat.............	WHL	61	4	11	15	65	...	...	...	3	0	2	2	2
90-91— Medicine Hat.............	WHL	64	12	31	43	66	...	...	...	11	1	3	4	23
91-92— Medicine Hat.............	WHL	72	17	47	64	176	...	...	...	4	1	4	5	8
92-93— Medicine Hat.............	WHL	63	15	50	65	88	...	...	...	10	2	2	4	32
— Rochester	AHL	0	0	0	0	0	...	...	...	2	0	0	0	2
93-94— Rochester	AHL	68	10	25	35	82	...	...	...	4	1	1	2	2
94-95— Rochester	AHL	21	2	4	6	48	...	...	...	—	—	—	—	—
— South Carolina	ECHL	39	9	19	28	90	...	...	...	9	3	8	11	24
95-96— Rochester	AHL	67	9	18	27	79	...	...	...	8	0	1	1	12
96-97— St. John's................	AHL	44	16	19	35	65	...	...	...	—	—	—	—	—
— Toronto	NHL	19	3	3	6	16	-3	2	0	—	—	—	—	—
NHL totals (1 year)		19	3	3	6	16	-3	2	0	—	—	—	—	—

CORBET, RENE   LW   AVALANCHE

PERSONAL: Born June 25, 1973, in Victoriaville, Que. ... 6-0/187. ... Shoots left. ... Name pronounced ruh-NAY kohr-BAY.
TRANSACTIONS/CAREER NOTES: Selected by Quebec Nordiques in second round (second Nordiques pick, 24th overall) of NHL entry draft (June 22, 1991). ... Nordiques franchise moved to Colorado and renamed Avalanche for 1995-96 season (June 21, 1995). ... Injured shoulder (April 3, 1996); missed missed five games. ... Suffered concussion (December 17, 1996); missed three games.
HONORS: Won Michel Bergeron Trophy (1990-91). ... Named to QMJHL All-Rookie team (1990-91). ... Won Jean Beliveau Trophy (1992-93). ... Named to Can.HL All-Star first team (1992-93). ... Named to QMJHL All-Star first team (1992-93). ... Won Dudley (Red) Garrett Memorial Trophy (1993-94).
MISCELLANEOUS: Member of Stanley Cup championship team (1996).

Season Team	League	REGULAR SEASON								PLAYOFFS				
		Gms.	G	A	Pts.	PIM	+/-	PP	SH	Gms.	G	A	Pts.	PIM
90-91— Drummondville	QMJHL	45	25	40	65	34	...	...	...	14	11	6	17	15
91-92— Drummondville	QMJHL	56	46	50	96	90	...	...	...	4	1	2	3	17
92-93— Drummondville	QMJHL	63	*79	69	*148	143	...	...	...	10	7	13	20	16
93-94— Cornwall....................	AHL	68	37	40	77	56	...	...	...	13	7	2	9	18
— Quebec......................	NHL	9	1	1	2	0	1	0	0	—	—	—	—	—
94-95— Cornwall....................	AHL	65	33	24	57	79	...	...	...	12	2	8	10	27
— Quebec......................	NHL	8	0	3	3	2	3	0	0	2	0	1	1	0
95-96— Cornwall....................	AHL	9	5	6	11	10	...	...	...	—	—	—	—	—
— Colorado...................	NHL	33	3	6	9	33	10	0	0	8	3	2	5	2
96-97— Colorado...................	NHL	76	12	15	27	67	14	1	0	17	2	2	4	27
NHL totals (4 years)		126	16	25	41	102	28	1	0	27	5	5	10	29

CORCORAN, BRIAN — D — MIGHTY DUCKS

PERSONAL: Born April 23, 1972, in Baldwinsville, N.Y. ... 6-2/247. ... Shoots right.
HIGH SCHOOL: C.W. Baker (Baldwinsville, N.Y.).
COLLEGE: Massachusetts.
TRANSACTIONS/CAREER NOTES: Signed as free agent by Mighty Ducks of Anaheim (April 28, 1995).

Season Team	League	REGULAR SEASON								PLAYOFFS				
		Gms.	G	A	Pts.	PIM	+/-	PP	SH	Gms.	G	A	Pts.	PIM
93-94— Univ. of Mass.............	Hockey East	15	1	7	8	24	...	...	...	—	—	—	—	—
94-95— Univ. of Mass.............	Hockey East	20	3	3	6	40	...	...	...	—	—	—	—	—
95-96— Raleigh.......................	ECHL	56	3	13	16	165	...	...	...	—	—	—	—	—
— Baltimore	AHL	18	0	2	2	24	...	...	...	6	0	0	0	4
96-97— Baltimore	AHL	41	2	5	7	114	...	...	...	3	0	1	1	4

CORKUM, BOB — C/RW — COYOTES

PERSONAL: Born December 18, 1967, in Salisbury, Mass. ... 6-2/216. ... Shoots right. ... Full name: Robert Freeman Corkum.
HIGH SCHOOL: Triton Regional (Byfield, Mass.).
COLLEGE: Maine.
TRANSACTIONS/CAREER NOTES: Selected by Buffalo Sabres in third round (third Sabres pick, 47th overall) of NHL entry draft (June 21, 1986). ... Injured hip (March 19, 1992). ... Selected by Mighty Ducks of Anaheim in NHL expansion draft (June 24, 1993). ... Ruptured ankle tendon (March 27, 1994); missed remainder of season. ... Cut lower lip (November 24, 1995); missed two games. ... Traded by Mighty Ducks to Philadelphia Flyers for C Chris Herperger and seventh-round draft pick (LW Tony Mohagen) in 1997 draft (February 6, 1996). ... Strained right shoulder (February 17, 1996), missed three games. ... Selected by Phoenix Coyotes from Flyers in waiver draft for cash (September 30, 1996). ... Suffered from the flu (January 13, 1997); missed one game.

Season Team	League	REGULAR SEASON								PLAYOFFS				
		Gms.	G	A	Pts.	PIM	+/-	PP	SH	Gms.	G	A	Pts.	PIM
84-85— Triton Regional	Mass. H.S.	18	35	36	71	...	...	...	...	—	—	—	—	—
85-86— University of Maine.....	Hockey East	39	7	26	33	53	...	...	...	—	—	—	—	—
86-87— University of Maine....	Hockey East	35	18	11	29	24	...	...	...	—	—	—	—	—
87-88— University of Maine....	Hockey East	40	14	18	32	64	...	...	...	—	—	—	—	—
88-89— University of Maine....	Hockey East	45	17	31	48	64	...	...	...	—	—	—	—	—
89-90— Rochester	AHL	43	8	11	19	45	...	...	...	12	2	5	7	16
— Buffalo	NHL	8	2	0	2	4	2	0	0	5	1	0	1	4
90-91— Rochester	AHL	69	13	21	34	77	...	...	...	15	4	4	8	4
91-92— Rochester	AHL	52	16	12	28	47	...	...	...	8	0	6	6	8
— Buffalo	NHL	20	2	4	6	21	-9	0	0	4	1	0	1	0
92-93— Buffalo	NHL	68	6	4	10	38	-3	0	1	5	0	0	0	2
93-94— Anaheim.....................	NHL	76	23	28	51	18	4	3	3	—	—	—	—	—
94-95— Anaheim.....................	NHL	44	10	9	19	25	-7	0	0	—	—	—	—	—
95-96— Anaheim.....................	NHL	48	5	7	12	26	0	0	0	—	—	—	—	—
— Philadelphia	NHL	28	4	3	7	8	3	0	0	12	1	2	3	6
96-97— Phoenix.....................	NHL	80	9	11	20	40	-7	0	1	7	2	2	4	4
NHL totals (7 years)		372	61	66	127	180	-17	3	5	33	5	4	9	16

CORNFORTH, MARK — D — BRUINS

PERSONAL: Born November 13, 1972, in Montreal. ... 6-1/185. ... Shoots left.
COLLEGE: Merrimack (Mass.).
TRANSACTIONS/CAREER NOTES: Signed as free agent by Boston Bruins (October 5, 1995).

Season Team	League	REGULAR SEASON								PLAYOFFS				
		Gms.	G	A	Pts.	PIM	+/-	PP	SH	Gms.	G	A	Pts.	PIM
91-92— Merrimack College.....	Hockey East	23	1	9	10	20	...	...	...	—	—	—	—	—
92-93— Merrimack College.....	Hockey East	36	3	18	21	27	...	...	...	—	—	—	—	—
93-94— Merrimack College.....	Hockey East	37	5	13	18	29	...	...	...	—	—	—	—	—
94-95— Merrimack College.....	Hockey East	30	8	20	28	43	...	...	...	—	—	—	—	—
— Syracuse...................	AHL	2	0	1	1	2	...	...	...	—	—	—	—	—
95-96— Providence.................	AHL	65	5	10	15	117	...	...	...	4	0	0	0	4
— Boston	NHL	6	0	0	0	4	4	0	0	—	—	—	—	—
96-97— Providence.................	AHL	61	8	12	20	47	...	...	...	—	—	—	—	—
— Cleveland..................	IHL	13	1	4	5	25	...	...	...	14	1	3	4	29
NHL totals (1 year)		6	0	0	0	4	4	0	0					

CORSON, SHAYNE   LW/C   CANADIENS

PERSONAL: Born August 13, 1966, in Barrie, Ont. ... 6-1/200. ... Shoots left.
TRANSACTIONS/CAREER NOTES: Selected by Montreal Canadiens in first round (second Canadiens pick, eighth overall) of NHL entry draft (June 9, 1984). ... Broke jaw (January 24, 1987). ... Strained ligament in right knee (September 1987). ... Injured groin (March 1988). ... Injured knee (April 1988). ... Injured knee (April 1989). ... Bruised left shoulder (October 29, 1989). ... Broke toe on right foot (December 1989). ... Suffered hip pointer (November 10, 1990); missed seven games. ... Pulled groin (February 11, 1991). ... Traded by Canadiens with LW Vladimir Vujtek and C Brent Gilchrist to Edmonton Oilers for LW Vincent Damphousse and fourth-round pick (D Adam Wiesel) in 1993 draft (August 27, 1992). ... Fractured fibula (February 18, 1994); missed 12 games. ... Injured leg (March 23, 1994); missed remainder of season. ... Signed by St. Louis Blues to an offer sheet (July 28, 1995); Oilers received Blues first-round picks in 1996 and 1997 drafts as compensation; Oilers then traded picks to Blues for rights to G Curtis Joseph and RW Michael Grier (August 4, 1995). ... Broke jaw (March 26, 1996); missed five games. ... Traded by Blues with D Murray Baron and fifth-round pick (D Gennady Razin) in 1997 draft to Canadiens for C Pierre Turgeon, C Craig Conroy and D Rory Fitzpatrick (October 29, 1996). ... Injured knee (November 25, 1996); missed 10 games. ... Underwent arthroscopic knee surgery (December 10, 1996). ... Sprained ankle (December 26, 1996); missed 10 games. ... Injured hip flexor (February 3, 1997); missed five games.
HONORS: Played in NHL All-Star Game (1990 and 1994).
STATISTICAL PLATEAUS: Three-goal games: 1988-89 (2), 1993-94 (1). Total: 3.
MISCELLANEOUS: Captain of Edmonton Oilers (1994-95). ... Captain of St. Louis Blues (October 25, 1995 through February 24, 1996).

Season Team	League	REGULAR SEASON								PLAYOFFS				
		Gms.	G	A	Pts.	PIM	+/-	PP	SH	Gms.	G	A	Pts.	PIM
82-83— Barrie	COJHL	23	13	29	42	87	...	...	...	—	—	—	—	—
83-84— Brantford	OHL	66	25	46	71	165	...	...	...	6	4	1	5	26
84-85— Hamilton	OHL	54	27	63	90	154	...	...	...	11	3	7	10	19
85-86— Hamilton	OHL	47	41	57	98	153	...	...	...	—	—	—	—	—
— Montreal	NHL	3	0	0	0	2	-3	0	0	—	—	—	—	—
86-87— Montreal	NHL	55	12	11	23	144	10	0	1	17	6	5	11	30
87-88— Montreal	NHL	71	12	27	39	152	22	2	0	3	1	0	1	12
88-89— Montreal	NHL	80	26	24	50	193	-1	10	0	21	4	5	9	65
89-90— Montreal	NHL	76	31	44	75	144	33	7	0	11	2	8	10	20
90-91— Montreal	NHL	71	23	24	47	138	9	7	0	13	9	6	15	36
91-92— Montreal	NHL	64	17	36	53	118	15	3	0	10	2	5	7	15
92-93— Edmonton	NHL	80	16	31	47	209	-19	9	2	—	—	—	—	—
93-94— Edmonton	NHL	64	25	29	54	118	-8	11	0	—	—	—	—	—
94-95— Edmonton	NHL	48	12	24	36	86	-17	2	0	—	—	—	—	—
95-96— St. Louis	NHL	77	18	28	46	192	3	13	0	13	8	6	14	22
96-97— St. Louis	NHL	11	2	1	3	24	-4	1	0	—	—	—	—	—
— Montreal	NHL	47	6	15	21	80	-5	2	0	5	1	0	1	4
NHL totals (12 years)		747	200	294	494	1600	35	67	3	93	33	35	68	204

COTE, PATRICK   LW   STARS

PERSONAL: Born January 24, 1975, in Lasalle, Que. ... 6-3/199. ... Shoots left. ... Name pronounced koh-TAY.
TRANSACTIONS/CAREER NOTES: Selected by Dallas Stars in second round (second Stars pick, 37th overall) of NHL entry draft (July 8, 1995).

Season Team	League	REGULAR SEASON								PLAYOFFS				
		Gms.	G	A	Pts.	PIM	+/-	PP	SH	Gms.	G	A	Pts.	PIM
93-94— Beauport	QMJHL	48	2	4	6	230	...	...	...	12	1	0	1	61
94-95— Beauport	QMJHL	56	20	20	40	314	...	...	...	17	8	8	16	115
95-96— Michigan	IHL	57	4	6	10	239	...	...	...	3	0	0	0	2
— Dallas	NHL	2	0	0	0	5	-2	0	0	—	—	—	—	—
96-97— Michigan	IHL	58	14	10	24	237	...	...	...	4	2	0	2	6
— Dallas	NHL	3	0	0	0	27	0	0	0	—	—	—	—	—
NHL totals (2 years)		5	0	0	0	32	-2	0	0					

COTE, SYLVAIN   D   CAPITALS

PERSONAL: Born January 19, 1966, in Quebec City. ... 6-0/190. ... Shoots right. ... Name pronounced KOH-tay. ... Brother of Alain Cote, defenseman for five NHL teams (1985-86 through 1993-94).
TRANSACTIONS/CAREER NOTES: Selected by Hartford Whalers as underage junior in first round (first Whalers pick, 11th overall) of NHL entry draft (June 9, 1984). ... Broke toe on left foot (October 28, 1989). ... Sprained left knee (December 1989). ... Fractured right foot (January 22, 1990). ... Traded by Whalers to Washington Capitals for second-round pick (LW Andrei Nikolishin) in 1992 draft (September 8, 1991). ... Broke wrist (September 25, 1992); missed six games. ... Suffered hip pointer (January 7, 1993); missed one game. ... Injured ankle (January 16, 1996); missed one game. ... Tore right knee ligament (October 18, 1996); missed 19 games. ... Strained knee (December 6, 1996); missed five games.
HONORS: Named to QMJHL All-Star second team (1983-84). ... Won Emile (Butch) Bouchard Trophy (1985-86). ... Shared Guy Lafleur Trophy with Luc Robitaille (1985-86). ... Named to QMJHL All-Star first team (1985-86).

Season Team	League	REGULAR SEASON								PLAYOFFS				
		Gms.	G	A	Pts.	PIM	+/-	PP	SH	Gms.	G	A	Pts.	PIM
82-83— Quebec	QMJHL	66	10	24	34	50	...	...	...	—	—	—	—	—
83-84— Quebec	QMJHL	66	15	50	65	89	...	...	...	5	1	1	2	0
84-85— Hartford	NHL	67	3	9	12	17	-30	1	0	—	—	—	—	—
85-86— Hartford	NHL	2	0	0	0	0	1	0	0	—	—	—	—	—
— Hull	QMJHL	26	10	33	43	14	...	...	...	13	6	*28	34	22
86-87— Binghamton	AHL	12	2	4	6	0	...	...	...	—	—	—	—	—
— Hartford	NHL	67	2	8	10	20	10	0	0	2	0	2	2	2
87-88— Hartford	NHL	67	7	21	28	30	-8	0	1	6	1	1	2	4
88-89— Hartford	NHL	78	8	9	17	49	-7	1	0	3	0	1	1	4
89-90— Hartford	NHL	28	4	2	6	14	2	1	0	5	0	0	0	0
90-91— Hartford	NHL	73	7	12	19	17	-17	1	0	6	0	2	2	2

Season Team	League	REGULAR SEASON								PLAYOFFS				
		Gms.	G	A	Pts.	PIM	+/-	PP	SH	Gms.	G	A	Pts.	PIM
91-92— Washington	NHL	78	11	29	40	31	7	6	0	7	1	2	3	4
92-93— Washington	NHL	77	21	29	50	34	28	8	2	6	1	1	2	4
93-94— Washington	NHL	84	16	35	51	66	30	3	2	9	1	8	9	6
94-95— Washington	NHL	47	5	14	19	53	2	1	0	7	1	3	4	2
95-96— Washington	NHL	81	5	33	38	40	5	3	0	6	2	0	2	12
96-97— Washington	NHL	57	6	18	24	28	11	2	0	—	—	—	—	—
NHL totals (13 years)		806	95	219	314	399	34	27	5	57	7	20	27	40

COURTNALL, GEOFF   LW   BLUES

PERSONAL: Born August 18, 1962, in Victoria, B.C. ... 6-1/195. ... Shoots left. ... Brother of Russ Courtnall, right winger, New York Rangers.
TRANSACTIONS/CAREER NOTES: Signed as free agent by Boston Bruins (September 1983). ... Traded by Bruins with G Bill Ranford to Edmonton Oilers for G Andy Moog (March 8, 1988). ... Traded by Oilers to Washington Capitals for C Greg Adams (July 22, 1988). ... Traded by Capitals to St. Louis Blues for C Peter Zezel and D Mike Lalor (July 13, 1990). ... Traded by Blues with D Robert Dirk, C Cliff Ronning, LW Sergio Momesso and fifth-round pick in 1992 draft (RW Brian Loney) to Vancouver Canucks for C Dan Quinn and D Garth Butcher (March 5, 1991). ... Lacerated foot (February 28, 1992) and suffered from chronic fatigue (March 1992); missed nine games. ... Suspended two games by NHL (November 14, 1993). ... Suffered injury (April 20, 1995); missed three games. ... Signed as free agent by Blues (July 14, 1995). ... Broke thumb (February 18, 1996); missed 13 games.
STATISTICAL PLATEAUS: Three-goal games: 1987-88 (1), 1987-88 (1), 1988-89 (1), 1989-90 (1), 1995-96 (1). Total: 5.
MISCELLANEOUS: Member of Stanley Cup championship team (1988). ... Scored on a penalty shot (vs. Jeff Hackett, December 13, 1996). ... Failed to score on a penalty shot (vs. Alain Chevrier, February 7, 1988; vs. Damian Rhodes, March 21, 1995).
STATISTICAL NOTES: Tied for NHL lead with 11 game-winning goals (1992-93).

Season Team	League	REGULAR SEASON								PLAYOFFS				
		Gms.	G	A	Pts.	PIM	+/-	PP	SH	Gms.	G	A	Pts.	PIM
80-81— Victoria	WHL	11	3	5	8	6	...	...	...	15	2	1	3	7
81-82— Victoria	WHL	72	35	57	92	100	...	...	...	4	1	0	1	2
82-83— Victoria	WHL	71	41	73	114	186	...	...	...	12	6	7	13	42
83-84— Hershey	AHL	74	14	12	26	51	...	...	...	—	—	—	—	—
— Boston	NHL	4	0	0	0	0	-1	0	0	—	—	—	—	—
84-85— Hershey	AHL	9	8	4	12	4	...	...	...	—	—	—	—	—
— Boston	NHL	64	12	16	28	82	-3	0	0	5	0	2	2	7
85-86— Moncton	AHL	12	8	8	16	6	...	...	...	—	—	—	—	—
— Boston	NHL	64	21	16	37	61	1	2	0	3	0	0	0	2
86-87— Boston	NHL	65	13	23	36	117	-4	2	0	1	0	0	0	0
87-88— Boston	NHL	62	32	26	58	108	24	8	0	—	—	—	—	—
— Edmonton	NHL	12	4	4	8	15	1	0	0	19	0	3	3	23
88-89— Washington	NHL	79	42	38	80	112	11	16	0	6	2	5	7	12
89-90— Washington	NHL	80	35	39	74	104	27	9	0	15	4	9	13	32
90-91— St. Louis	NHL	66	27	30	57	56	19	9	0	—	—	—	—	—
— Vancouver	NHL	11	6	2	8	8	-3	3	0	6	3	5	8	4
91-92— Vancouver	NHL	70	23	34	57	116	-6	12	0	12	6	8	14	20
92-93— Vancouver	NHL	84	31	46	77	167	27	9	0	12	4	10	14	12
93-94— Vancouver	NHL	82	26	44	70	123	15	12	1	24	9	10	19	51
94-95— Vancouver	NHL	45	16	18	34	81	2	7	0	11	4	2	6	34
95-96— St. Louis	NHL	69	24	16	40	101	-9	7	1	13	0	3	3	14
96-97— St. Louis	NHL	82	17	40	57	86	3	4	0	6	3	1	4	23
NHL totals (14 years)		939	329	392	721	1337	104	100	2	133	35	58	93	234

COURTNALL, RUSS   RW   RANGERS

PERSONAL: Born June 3, 1965, in Victoria, B.C. ... 5-11/185. ... Shoots right. ... Brother of Geoff Courtnall, left winger, St. Louis Blues.
TRANSACTIONS/CAREER NOTES: Selected by Toronto Maple Leafs as underage junior in first round (first Maple Leafs pick, seventh overall) of NHL entry draft (June 8, 1983). ... Bruised knee (November 1987). ... Suffered from virus (February 1988). ... Suffered back spasms (March 1988). ... Traded by Maple Leafs to Montreal Canadiens for RW John Kordic and sixth-round pick (RW Michael Doers) in 1989 draft (November 7, 1988). ... Pulled muscle in right shoulder (October 8, 1991); missed 41 games. ... Injured hand (January 15, 1992); missed 12 games. ... Traded by Canadiens to Minnesota North Stars for LW Brian Bellows (August 31, 1992). ... North Stars franchise moved from Minnesota to Dallas and renamed Stars for 1993-94 season. ... Traded by Stars to Vancouver Canucks for LW Greg Adams, RW Dan Kesa and fifth-round pick (traded to Los Angeles) in 1995 draft (April 7, 1995). ... Injured groin (November 23, 1996); missed three games. ... Strained groin (December 3, 1996); missed 16 games. ... Traded by Canucks with LW Esa Tikkanen to Rangers for C Sergei Nemchinov and RW Brian Noonan (March 8, 1997).
HONORS: Played in NHL All-Star Game (1994).
STATISTICAL PLATEAUS: Three-goal games: 1985-86 (1), 1989-90 (1), 1992-93 (1), 1994-95 (1), 1995-96 (1). Total: 5.
MISCELLANEOUS: Scored on a penalty shot (vs. Tim Cheveldae, February 19, 1990).

Season Team	League	REGULAR SEASON								PLAYOFFS				
		Gms.	G	A	Pts.	PIM	+/-	PP	SH	Gms.	G	A	Pts.	PIM
82-83— Victoria	WHL	60	36	61	97	33	...	...	...	12	11	7	18	6
83-84— Victoria	WHL	32	29	37	66	63	...	...	...	—	—	—	—	—
— Can. Olympic team ...	Int'l	16	4	7	11	10	...	...	...	—	—	—	—	—
— Toronto	NHL	14	3	9	12	6	0	1	0	—	—	—	—	—
84-85— Toronto	NHL	69	12	10	22	44	-23	0	2	—	—	—	—	—
85-86— Toronto	NHL	73	22	38	60	52	0	3	1	10	3	6	9	8
86-87— Toronto	NHL	79	29	44	73	90	-20	3	6	13	3	4	7	11
87-88— Toronto	NHL	65	23	26	49	47	-16	6	3	6	2	1	3	0
88-89— Toronto	NHL	9	1	1	2	4	-2	0	1	—	—	—	—	—
— Montreal	NHL	64	22	17	39	15	11	7	0	21	8	5	13	18
89-90— Montreal	NHL	80	27	32	59	27	14	3	0	11	5	1	6	10
90-91— Montreal	NHL	79	26	50	76	29	5	5	1	13	8	3	11	7
91-92— Montreal	NHL	27	7	14	21	6	6	0	1	10	1	1	2	4

Season Team	League	REGULAR SEASON								PLAYOFFS				
		Gms.	G	A	Pts.	PIM	+/-	PP	SH	Gms.	G	A	Pts.	PIM
92-93—Minnesota	NHL	84	36	43	79	49	1	14	2	—	—	—	—	—
93-94—Dallas	NHL	84	23	57	80	59	6	5	0	9	1	8	9	0
94-95—Dallas	NHL	32	7	10	17	13	-8	2	0	—	—	—	—	—
—Vancouver	NHL	13	4	14	18	4	10	0	2	11	4	8	12	21
95-96—Vancouver	NHL	81	26	39	65	40	25	6	4	6	1	3	4	2
96-97—Vancouver	NHL	47	9	19	28	24	4	1	0	—	—	—	—	—
—New York Rangers	NHL	14	2	5	7	2	-3	1	1	15	3	4	7	0
NHL totals (14 years)		914	279	428	707	511	10	57	24	125	39	44	83	81

COURVILLE, LARRY — LW — CANUCKS

PERSONAL: Born April 2, 1975, in Timmins, Ont. ... 6-1/180. ... Shoots left.
HIGH SCHOOL: Huron Heights Secondary School (Newmarket, Ont.).
TRANSACTIONS/CAREER NOTES: Selected by Winnipeg Jets in fifth round (sixth Jets pick, 119th overall) of NHL entry draft (June 26, 1993). ... Returned to draft pool by Jets and selected by Vancouver Canucks in third round (second Canucks pick, 61st overall) of NHL entry draft (July 8, 1995).
HONORS: Named to OHL All-Star second team (1994-95).

Season Team	League	REGULAR SEASON								PLAYOFFS				
		Gms.	G	A	Pts.	PIM	+/-	PP	SH	Gms.	G	A	Pts.	PIM
90-91—Waterloo	USHL	48	20	18	38	144	...	...	...	—	—	—	—	—
91-92—Cornwall	OHL	60	8	12	20	80	...	...	...	6	0	0	0	8
92-93—Newmarket	OHL	64	21	18	39	181	...	...	...	7	0	6	6	14
93-94—Newmarket	OHL	39	20	19	39	134	...	...	...	—	—	—	—	—
—Moncton	AHL	8	2	0	2	37	...	...	...	10	2	2	4	27
94-95—Sarnia	OHL	16	9	9	18	58	...	...	...	—	—	—	—	—
—Oshawa	OHL	28	25	30	55	72	...	...	...	7	4	10	14	10
95-96—Syracuse	AHL	71	17	32	49	127	...	...	...	14	5	3	8	10
—Vancouver	NHL	3	1	0	1	0	1	0	0	—	—	—	—	—
96-97—Syracuse	AHL	54	20	24	44	103	...	...	...	3	0	1	1	20
—Vancouver	NHL	19	0	2	2	11	-4	0	0	—	—	—	—	—
NHL totals (2 years)		22	1	2	3	11	-3	0	0					

COUSINEAU, MARCEL — G — MAPLE LEAFS

PERSONAL: Born April 30, 1973, in Delson, Que. ... 5-9/180. ... Catches left. ... Name pronounced KOO-sih-noh.
TRANSACTIONS/CAREER NOTES: Selected by Boston Bruins in third round (third Bruins pick, 62nd overall) of NHL entry draft (June 22, 1991). ... Signed as free agent by Toronto Maple Leafs (November 13, 1993).
HONORS: Named to QMJHL All-Rookie team (1990-91).

Season Team	League	REGULAR SEASON								PLAYOFFS						
		Gms.	Min	W	L	T	GA	SO	Avg.	Gms.	Min.	W	L	GA	SO	Avg.
90-91—Beauport	QMJHL	49	2739	13	29	3	196	1	4.29	—	—	—	—	—	—	—
91-92—Beauport	QMJHL	*67	*3673	26	*32	5	*241	0	3.94	—	—	—	—	—	—	—
92-93—Drummondville	QMJHL	60	3298	20	32	2	225	0	4.09	9	498	3	6	37	1	4.46
93-94—St. John's	AHL	37	2015	13	11	9	118	0	3.51	—	—	—	—	—	—	—
94-95—St. John's	AHL	58	3342	22	27	6	171	4	3.07	3	180	0	3	9	0	3.00
95-96—St. John's	AHL	62	3629	21	26	13	192	1	3.17	4	257	1	3	11	0	2.57
96-97—St. John's	AHL	19	1053	7	8	3	58	0	3.30	11	658	6	5	28	0	2.55
—Toronto	NHL	13	566	3	5	1	31	1	3.29	—	—	—	—	—	—	—
NHL totals (1 year)		13	566	3	5	1	31	1	3.29							

CRAIG, MIKE — RW — MAPLE LEAFS

PERSONAL: Born June 6, 1971, in London, Ont. ... 6-1/180. ... Shoots right.
TRANSACTIONS/CAREER NOTES: Selected by Minnesota North Stars in second round (second North Stars pick, 28th overall) of NHL entry draft (June 17, 1989). ... Broke fibula (January 28, 1990). ... Broke right wrist (February 4, 1991); missed 17 games. ... Sprained knee (February 25, 1993); missed 12 games. ... North Stars franchise moved from Minnesota to Dallas and renamed Stars for 1993-94 season. ... Signed as free agent by Toronto Maple Leafs (July 29, 1994). ... C Peter Zezel and RW Grant Marshall awarded to Stars as compensation (August 10, 1994). ... Broke index finger (March 13, 1995); missed nine games. ... Sprained ankle (February 18, 1996); missed one game. ... Suspended two games and fined $1,000 by NHL for high-sticking incident (January 7, 1997). ... Strained groin (March 3, 1997); missed three games.
MISCELLANEOUS: Failed to score on a penalty shot (vs. Bob Essensa, January 21, 1991).

Season Team	League	REGULAR SEASON								PLAYOFFS				
		Gms.	G	A	Pts.	PIM	+/-	PP	SH	Gms.	G	A	Pts.	PIM
86-87—Woodstock Jr. C.	OHA	32	29	19	48	64	...	...	...	—	—	—	—	—
87-88—Oshawa	OHL	61	6	10	16	39	...	...	...	7	7	0	7	11
88-89—Oshawa	OHL	63	36	36	72	34	...	...	...	6	3	1	4	6
89-90—Oshawa	OHL	43	36	40	76	85	...	...	...	17	10	16	26	46
90-91—Minnesota	NHL	39	8	4	12	32	-11	1	0	10	1	1	2	20
91-92—Minnesota	NHL	67	15	16	31	155	-12	4	0	4	1	0	1	7
92-93—Minnesota	NHL	70	15	23	38	106	-11	7	0	—	—	—	—	—
93-94—Dallas	NHL	72	13	24	37	139	-14	3	0	4	0	0	0	2
94-95—Toronto	NHL	37	5	5	10	12	-21	1	0	6	0	1	1	2
95-96—Toronto	NHL	70	8	12	20	42	-8	1	0	6	0	0	0	18
96-97—Toronto	NHL	65	7	13	20	62	-20	1	0	—	—	—	—	—
NHL totals (7 years)		420	71	97	168	548	-97	18	0	26	2	2	4	49

CRAIGHEAD, JOHN   RW   MAPLE LEAFS

PERSONAL: Born November 23, 1971, in Vancouver. ... 6-0/195. ... Shoots right.
TRANSACTIONS/CAREER NOTES: Signed as free agent by Toronto Maple Leafs (July 8, 1996).

Season Team	League	Gms.	G	A	Pts.	PIM	+/-	PP	SH	Gms.	G	A	Pts.	PIM
90-91 — British Columbia	Jr. A	25	21	23	44	120	...	...	...	—	—	—	—	—
91-92 — W. Palm Beach	Sunshine	39	12	17	29	160	...	...	...	—	—	—	—	—
92-93 — British Columbia	Jr. A						Statistics unavailable.							
93-94 — Huntington	ECHL	9	4	2	6	44	...	...	...	—	—	—	—	—
— Richmond	ECHL	28	18	12	30	89	...	...	...	—	—	—	—	—
94-95 — Detroit	IHL	44	5	7	12	285	...	...	...	3	0	1	1	4
95-96 — Detroit	IHL	63	7	9	16	368	...	...	...	10	2	3	5	28
96-97 — St. John's	AHL	53	9	10	19	318	...	...	...	7	1	1	2	22
— Toronto	NHL	5	0	0	0	10	0	0	0	—	—	—	—	—
NHL totals (1 year)		**5**	**0**	**0**	**0**	**10**	**0**	**0**	**0**					

CRAVEN, MURRAY   C/LW   BLACKHAWKS

PERSONAL: Born July 20, 1964, in Medicine Hat, Alta. ... 6-2/185. ... Shoots left.
TRANSACTIONS/CAREER NOTES: Selected by Detroit Red Wings as underage junior in first round (first Red Wings pick, 17th overall) of NHL entry draft (June 9, 1982). ... Injured left knee cartilage (January 15, 1983). ... Traded by Red Wings with LW/C Joe Paterson to Philadelphia Flyers for C Darryl Sittler (October 1984). ... Broke foot (April 16, 1987). ... Hyperextended right knee and lacerated eye (November 1988). ... Bruised right foot (January 1989). ... Fractured left wrist (February 24, 1989). ... Fractured right wrist (April 5, 1989). ... Suffered back spasms (February 1990). ... Injured rotator cuff (March 24, 1990). ... Traded by Flyers with fourth-round pick (LW Kevin Smyth) in 1992 draft to Hartford Whalers for RW Kevin Dineen (November 13, 1991). ... Injured groin (January 21, 1992). ... Traded by Whalers with fifth-round pick in 1993 draft to Vancouver Canucks for LW Robert Kron, third-round pick (D Marek Malik) in 1993 draft and future considerations (March 22, 1993); Canucks sent RW Jim Sandlak to complete deal (May 17, 1993). ... Injured hip (November 2, 1993); missed three games. ... Strained groin (November 14, 1993); missed two games. ... Traded by Canucks to Chicago Blackhawks for C Christian Ruuttu (March 10, 1995). ... Suffered from sore back (1995); missed four games. ... Bruised foot (October 10, 1995); missed one game. ... Suffered charley horse (November 12, 1995); missed two games. ... Bruised knee (January 22, 1997); missed one game. ... Bruised shoulder (February 11, 1997); missed four games. ... Suffered stiff neck (March 5, 1997); missed one game.
STATISTICAL PLATEAUS: Three-goal games: 1986-87 (1), 1987-88 (1), 1991-92 (1). Total: 3.
MISCELLANEOUS: Scored on a penalty shot (vs. Don Beaupre, March 24, 1992; vs. Andre Racicot, December 23, 1990). ... Failed to score on a penalty shot (vs. Chris Terreri, October 13, 1991).

Season Team	League	Gms.	G	A	Pts.	PIM	+/-	PP	SH	Gms.	G	A	Pts.	PIM
80-81 — Medicine Hat	WHL	69	5	10	15	18	...	...	...	5	0	0	0	2
81-82 — Medicine Hat	WHL	72	35	46	81	49	...	...	...	—	—	—	—	—
82-83 — Medicine Hat	WHL	28	17	29	46	35	...	...	...	—	—	—	—	—
— Detroit	NHL	31	4	7	11	6	...	...	...	—	—	—	—	—
83-84 — Medicine Hat	WHL	48	38	56	94	53	...	...	...	4	5	3	8	4
— Detroit	NHL	15	0	4	4	6	2	0	0	—	—	—	—	—
84-85 — Philadelphia	NHL	80	26	35	61	30	45	2	2	19	4	6	10	11
85-86 — Philadelphia	NHL	78	21	33	54	34	24	2	0	5	0	3	3	4
86-87 — Philadelphia	NHL	77	19	30	49	38	1	5	3	12	3	1	4	9
87-88 — Philadelphia	NHL	72	30	46	76	58	25	6	2	7	2	5	7	4
88-89 — Philadelphia	NHL	51	9	28	37	52	4	0	0	1	0	0	0	0
89-90 — Philadelphia	NHL	76	25	50	75	42	2	7	2	—	—	—	—	—
90-91 — Philadelphia	NHL	77	19	47	66	53	-2	6	0	—	—	—	—	—
91-92 — Philadelphia	NHL	12	3	3	6	8	2	1	0	—	—	—	—	—
— Hartford	NHL	61	24	30	54	38	-4	8	4	7	3	3	6	6
92-93 — Hartford	NHL	67	25	42	67	20	-4	6	3	—	—	—	—	—
— Vancouver	NHL	10	0	10	10	12	3	0	0	12	4	6	10	4
93-94 — Vancouver	NHL	78	15	40	55	30	5	2	1	22	4	9	13	18
94-95 — Chicago	NHL	16	4	3	7	2	1	0	0	16	5	5	10	4
95-96 — Chicago	NHL	66	18	29	47	36	20	5	1	9	1	4	5	2
96-97 — Chicago	NHL	75	8	27	35	12	0	2	0	2	0	0	0	2
NHL totals (15 years)		**942**	**250**	**464**	**714**	**477**	**125**	**53**	**18**	**112**	**26**	**42**	**68**	**64**

CRAWFORD, GLENN   C   DEVILS

PERSONAL: Born February 27, 1978, in Orillia, Ont. ... 5-11/175. ... Shoots left.
TRANSACTIONS/CAREER NOTES: Selected by New Jersey Devils in fifth round (ninth Devils pick, 118th overall) of NHL entry draft (June 22, 1996).

Season Team	League	Gms.	G	A	Pts.	PIM	+/-	PP	SH	Gms.	G	A	Pts.	PIM
94-95 — Windsor	OHL	61	5	11	16	17	...	...	...	10	2	5	7	8
95-96 — Windsor	OHL	65	26	33	59	44	...	...	...	7	4	4	8	6
96-97 — Windsor	OHL	53	11	40	51	36	...	...	...	5	3	1	4	0

CREIGHTON, ADAM   C   BLACKHAWKS

PERSONAL: Born June 2, 1965, in Burlington, Ont. ... 6-5/220. ... Shoots left. ... Son of Dave Creighton, center with four NHL teams (1948-49 through 1959-60).
TRANSACTIONS/CAREER NOTES: Selected by Buffalo Sabres in first round (third Sabres pick, 11th overall) of NHL entry draft (June 8, 1983). ... Underwent knee surgery (January 1988). ... Sprained knee (September 1988). ... Traded by Sabres to Chicago Blackhawks for RW Rick

Vaive (December 2, 1988). ... Suspended five games by NHL for stick-swinging incident in preseason game (September 30, 1990). ... Sprained right hand (February 10, 1991). ... Traded by Blackhawks with LW Steve Thomas to New York Islanders for C Brent Sutter and RW Brad Lauer (October 25, 1991). ... Selected by Tampa Bay Lightning in NHL waiver draft (October 4, 1992). ... Sprained right knee ligaments (October 7, 1993); missed 14 games. ... Reinjured right knee (November 11, 1993); missed eight games. ... Injured groin (December 19, 1993); missed three games. ... Traded by Lightning to St. Louis Blues for D Tom Tilley (October 6, 1994). ... Bruised ankle (October 25, 1995); missed two games. ... Broke jaw (January 9, 1996); missed 19 games. ... Signed as free agent by Blackhawks (October 8, 1996).
HONORS: Won Stafford Smythe Memorial Cup (1983-1984). ... Named to Memorial Cup All-Star team (1983-84).
STATISTICAL PLATEAUS: Three-goal games: 1988-89 (2).

			REGULAR SEASON								PLAYOFFS				
Season Team	League	Gms.	G	A	Pts.	PIM	+/-	PP	SH		Gms.	G	A	Pts.	PIM
81-82— Ottawa	OHL	60	14	27	41	73	...	...	...		17	7	1	8	40
82-83— Ottawa	OHL	68	44	46	90	88	...	...	...		9	0	2	2	12
83-84— Ottawa	OHL	56	42	49	91	79	...	...	...		13	16	11	27	28
— Buffalo	NHL	7	2	2	4	4	0	0	0		—	—	—	—	—
84-85— Ottawa	OHL	10	4	14	18	23	...	...	...		5	6	2	8	11
— Rochester	AHL	6	5	3	8	2	...	...	...		5	2	1	3	20
— Buffalo	NHL	30	2	8	10	33	-7	1	0		—	—	—	—	—
85-86— Rochester	AHL	32	17	21	38	27	...	...	...		—	—	—	—	—
— Buffalo	NHL	19	1	1	2	2	-2	0	0		—	—	—	—	—
86-87— Buffalo	NHL	56	18	22	40	26	4	6	0		—	—	—	—	—
87-88— Buffalo	NHL	36	10	17	27	87	7	4	0		—	—	—	—	—
88-89— Buffalo	NHL	24	7	10	17	44	-5	3	0		—	—	—	—	—
— Chicago	NHL	43	15	14	29	92	-4	8	0		15	5	6	11	44
89-90— Chicago	NHL	80	34	36	70	224	4	12	0		20	3	6	9	59
90-91— Chicago	NHL	72	22	29	51	135	0	10	2		6	0	1	1	10
91-92— Chicago	NHL	11	6	6	12	16	-1	2	0		—	—	—	—	—
— New York Islanders	NHL	66	15	9	24	102	-4	2	0		—	—	—	—	—
92-93— Tampa Bay	NHL	83	19	20	39	110	-19	7	1		—	—	—	—	—
93-94— Tampa Bay	NHL	53	10	10	20	37	-7	2	0		—	—	—	—	—
94-95— St. Louis	NHL	48	14	20	34	74	17	3	0		7	2	0	2	16
95-96— St. Louis	NHL	61	11	10	21	78	0	2	0		13	1	1	2	8
96-97— Chicago	NHL	19	1	2	3	13	-2	0	0		—	—	—	—	—
— Indianapolis	IHL	6	1	7	8	11	...	...	...		—	—	—	—	—
NHL totals (14 years)		708	187	216	403	1077	-19	62	3		61	11	14	25	137

CRONAN, EARL   LW   CANADIENS

PERSONAL: Born January 2, 1973, in Warwick, R.I. ... 6-1/210. ... Shoots left.
COLLEGE: Colgate.
TRANSACTIONS/CAREER NOTES: Selected by Montreal Canadiens in ninth round (11th Canadiens pick, 212th overall) of NHL entry draft (June 20, 1992).

			REGULAR SEASON								PLAYOFFS				
Season Team	League	Gms.	G	A	Pts.	PIM	+/-	PP	SH		Gms.	G	A	Pts.	PIM
92-93— Colgate University	ECAC	33	8	9	17	40	...	...	...		—	—	—	—	—
93-94— Colgate University	ECAC	32	14	17	31	80	...	...	...		—	—	—	—	—
94-95— Colgate University	ECAC	37	21	20	41	81	...	...	...		—	—	—	—	—
95-96— Colgate University	ECAC	32	9	14	23	99	...	...	...		—	—	—	—	—
96-97— Fredericton	AHL	50	5	3	8	33	...	...	...		—	—	—	—	—

CROSS, CORY   D   LIGHTNING

PERSONAL: Born January 3, 1971, in Prince Albert, Sask. ... 6-5/212. ... Shoots left. ... Full name: Cory James Cross.
HIGH SCHOOL: Lloydminster (Alta.) Comprehensive.
COLLEGE: Alberta.
TRANSACTIONS/CAREER NOTES: Selected by Tampa Bay Lightning in NHL supplemental draft (June 19, 1992). ... Injured foot (November 3, 1995); missed one game. ... Bruised right foot (November 10, 1996); missed five games.
HONORS: Named to CWUAA All-Star second team (1992-93).

			REGULAR SEASON								PLAYOFFS				
Season Team	League	Gms.	G	A	Pts.	PIM	+/-	PP	SH		Gms.	G	A	Pts.	PIM
90-91— Univ. of Alberta	CWUAA	20	2	5	7	16	...	...	...		—	—	—	—	—
91-92— Univ. of Alberta	CWUAA	39	3	10	13	76	...	...	...		—	—	—	—	—
92-93— Univ. of Alberta	CWUAA	43	11	28	39	105	...	...	...		—	—	—	—	—
— Atlanta	IHL	7	0	1	1	2	...	...	...		4	0	0	0	6
93-94— Atlanta	IHL	70	4	14	18	72	...	...	...		9	1	2	3	14
— Tampa Bay	NHL	5	0	0	0	6	-3	0	0		—	—	—	—	—
94-95— Atlanta	IHL	41	5	10	15	67	...	...	...		—	—	—	—	—
— Tampa Bay	NHL	43	1	5	6	41	-6	0	0		—	—	—	—	—
95-96— Tampa Bay	NHL	75	2	14	16	66	4	0	0		6	0	0	0	22
96-97— Tampa Bay	NHL	72	4	5	9	95	6	0	0		—	—	—	—	—
NHL totals (4 years)		195	7	24	31	208	1	0	0		6	0	0	0	22

CROWDER, TROY   RW   CANUCKS

PERSONAL: Born May 3, 1968, in Sudbury, Ont. ... 6-4/220. ... Shoots right.
TRANSACTIONS/CAREER NOTES: Selected by New Jersey Devils as underage junior in sixth round (sixth Devils pick, 108th overall) of NHL entry draft (June 21, 1986). ... Left training camp (September 1989); returned (March 1990). ... Injured left elbow (October 4, 1990). ... Hyperextended elbow (November 1, 1990). ... Lacerated right hand and damaged ligaments (December 29, 1990). ... Signed as free agent by Detroit Red Wings (August 27, 1991); Devils received C/RW Dave Barr and RW Randy McKay as compensation. ... Strained back (October 10, 1991); missed 73 games. ... Reinjured back (May 6, 1992). ... Signed as free agent by Los Angeles Kings (September 2, 1994). ...

Sprained right wrist (January 27, 1995); missed 11 games. ... Sprained wrist (March 28, 1995); missed five games. ... Suspended 10 games by NHL for abuse of an official (September 23, 1995). ... Signed as free agent by Vancouver Canucks (October 4, 1996). ... Bruised ribs (January 25, 1997); missed 19 games. ... Injured knee (March 22, 1997); missed five games.

		REGULAR SEASON								PLAYOFFS				
Season Team	League	Gms.	G	A	Pts.	PIM	+/-	PP	SH	Gms.	G	A	Pts.	PIM
85-86— Hamilton	OHL	55	4	4	8	178	...	...	...	—	—	—	—	—
86-87— North Bay..............	OHL	35	6	11	17	90	...	...	...	23	3	9	12	99
— Belleville....................	OHL	21	5	5	10	52	...	...	...	—	—	—	—	—
87-88— North Bay..............	OHL	9	1	2	3	44	...	...	...	—	—	—	—	—
— New Jersey	NHL	—	—	—	—	—	—	—	—	1	0	0	0	12
— Belleville....................	OHL	46	12	27	39	103	...	...	...	6	2	3	5	24
— Utica	AHL	3	0	0	0	36	...	...	...	—	—	—	—	—
88-89— Utica	AHL	62	6	4	10	152	...	...	...	2	0	0	0	25
89-90— Nashville	ECHL	3	0	0	0	15	...	...	...	—	—	—	—	—
— New Jersey	NHL	10	0	0	0	23	0	0	0	2	0	0	0	10
90-91— New Jersey	NHL	59	6	3	9	182	-10	0	0	—	—	—	—	—
91-92— Detroit......................	NHL	7	0	0	0	35	0	0	0	1	0	0	0	0
92-93—					Did not play.									
93-94—					Did not play.									
94-95— Los Angeles	NHL	29	1	2	3	99	0	0	0	—	—	—	—	—
95-96— Los Angeles	NHL	15	1	0	1	42	-3	0	0	—	—	—	—	—
96-97— Vancouver	NHL	30	1	2	3	52	-6	0	0	—	—	—	—	—
— Syracuse...................	AHL	2	0	0	0	0	...	...	...	—	—	—	—	—
NHL totals (7 years)		150	9	7	16	433	-19	0	0	4	0	0	0	22

CROWE, PHIL   LW   SENATORS

PERSONAL: Born April 14, 1970, in Red Deer, Alta. ... 6-2/220. ... Shoots left.
TRANSACTIONS/CAREER NOTES: Signed as free agent by Los Angeles Kings (November 8, 1993). ... Signed as free agent by Philadelphia Flyers (July 19, 1994). ... Suffered back spasms (October 29, 1995); missed five games. ... Signed as free agent by Ottawa Senators (July 4, 1996). ... Suffered charley horse (March 25, 1997); missed two games.

		REGULAR SEASON								PLAYOFFS				
Season Team	League	Gms.	G	A	Pts.	PIM	+/-	PP	SH	Gms.	G	A	Pts.	PIM
91-92— Adirondack................	AHL	6	0	1	1	29	...	...	...	—	—	—	—	—
— Columbus	ECHL	32	4	7	11	145	...	...	...	—	—	—	—	—
92-93— Phoenix....................	IHL	53	3	3	6	190	...	...	...	—	—	—	—	—
93-94— Fort Wayne	IHL	5	0	1	1	26	...	...	...	—	—	—	—	—
— Phoenix.....................	IHL	2	0	0	0	0	...	...	...	—	—	—	—	—
— Los Angeles	NHL	31	0	2	2	77	4	0	0	—	—	—	—	—
94-95— Hershey	AHL	46	11	6	17	132	...	...	...	6	0	1	1	19
95-96— Hershey	AHL	39	6	8	14	105	...	...	...	5	1	2	3	19
— Philadelphia	NHL	16	1	1	2	28	0	0	0	—	—	—	—	—
96-97— Detroit......................	IHL	41	7	7	14	83	...	...	...	—	—	—	—	—
— Ottawa	NHL	26	0	1	1	30	0	0	0	3	0	0	0	16
NHL totals (3 years)		73	1	4	5	135	4	0	0	3	0	0	0	16

CROWLEY, MIKE   D   MIGHTY DUCKS

PERSONAL: Born July 4, 1975, in Bloomington, Minn. ... 5-11/173. ... Shoots left.
HIGH SCHOOL: Thomas Jefferson (Bloomington, Minn.).
COLLEGE: Minnesota.
TRANSACTIONS/CAREER NOTES: Selected by Philadelphia Flyers in sixth round (fifth Flyers pick, 140th overall) of NHL entry draft (June 26, 1993). ... Traded by Flyers with C Anatoli Semenov to Mighty Ducks of Anaheim for RW Brian Wesenberg (March 19, 1996).
HONORS: Named WCHA Rookie of the Year (1994-95). ... Named to NCAA All-America West first team (1995-96 and 1996-97). ... Named to WCHA All-Star first team (1995-96 and 1996-97). ... Named WCHA Player of the Year (1996-97).

		REGULAR SEASON								PLAYOFFS				
Season Team	League	Gms.	G	A	Pts.	PIM	+/-	PP	SH	Gms.	G	A	Pts.	PIM
90-91— Thomas Jefferson......	Minn. H.S.	20	3	9	12	2	...	...	...	—	—	—	—	—
91-92— Thomas Jefferson......	Minn. H.S.	28	5	18	23	8	...	...	...	—	—	—	—	—
92-93— Thomas Jefferson......	Minn. H.S.	22	10	32	42	18	...	...	...	—	—	—	—	—
93-94— Thomas Jefferson......	Minn. H.S.	28	23	54	77	26	...	...	...	—	—	—	—	—
94-95— Univ. of Minnesota.....	WCHA	41	11	27	38	60	...	...	...	—	—	—	—	—
95-96— Univ. of Minnesota.....	WCHA	42	17	46	63	28	...	...	...	—	—	—	—	—
96-97— Univ. of Minnesota.....	WCHA	42	9	47	56	24	...	...	...	—	—	—	—	—

CROZIER, GREG   LW   PENGUINS

PERSONAL: Born July 6, 1976, in Williamsville, N.Y. ... 6-4/200. ... Shoots left.
HIGH SCHOOL: Amherst (Mass.), then Lawrence Academy (Groton, Mass.).
COLLEGE: Michigan.
TRANSACTIONS/CAREER NOTES: Selected by Pittsburgh Penguins in third round (fourth Penguins pick, 73rd overall) of NHL entry draft (June 29, 1994).

		REGULAR SEASON								PLAYOFFS				
Season Team	League	Gms.	G	A	Pts.	PIM	+/-	PP	SH	Gms.	G	A	Pts.	PIM
90-91— Amherst....................	Mass. H.S.	41	52	34	86	17	...	...	...	—	—	—	—	—
91-92— Amherst....................	Mass. H.S.	46	61	47	108	47	...	...	...	—	—	—	—	—
92-93— Lawrence Academy....	Mass. H.S.	21	22	13	35	9	...	...	...	—	—	—	—	—

Season Team	League	REGULAR SEASON								PLAYOFFS				
		Gms.	G	A	Pts.	PIM	+/-	PP	SH	Gms.	G	A	Pts.	PIM
93-94— Lawrence Academy....	Mass. H.S.	19	22	26	48	10	...	...	...	—	—	—	—	—
94-95— Lawrence Academy....	Mass. H.S.	31	45	32	77	22	...	...	...	—	—	—	—	—
95-96— Univ. of Michigan.......	CCHA	42	14	10	24	46	...	...	...	—	—	—	—	—
96-97— Univ. of Michigan.......	CCHA	31	5	15	20	45	...	...	...	—	—	—	—	—

CULLEN, JOHN   C   LIGHTNING

PERSONAL: Born August 2, 1964, in Puslinch, Ont. ... 5-10/180. ... Shoots right. ... Full name: Barry John Cullen. ... Son of Barry Cullen, right winger, Toronto Maple Leafs and Detroit Red Wings (1955-56 through 1959-60); nephew of Brian Cullen, center, Toronto Maple Leafs and New York Rangers (1954-55 through 1960-61); and nephew of Ray Cullen, left winger, with four NHL teams (1965-66 through 1970-71).
COLLEGE: Boston University.
TRANSACTIONS/CAREER NOTES: Selected by Buffalo Sabres in NHL supplemental draft (September 17, 1986). ... Signed as free agent by Pittsburgh Penguins (July 1988). ... Suffered from hepatitis (October 1989); missed seven games. ... Pulled stomach muscle (November 17, 1990). ... Traded by Penguins with D Zarley Zalapski and RW Jeff Parker to Whalers for C Ron Francis, D Ulf Samuelsson and D Grant Jennings (March 4, 1991). ... Missed first three games of 1991-92 season due to contract dispute. ... Traded by Whalers to Toronto Maple Leafs for second-round pick in 1993 or 1994 draft (November 24, 1992). ... Suffered herniated disc in neck (March 2, 1993); missed 16 games. ... Sprained ankle (January 26, 1994); missed 21 games. ... Signed as free agent by Penguins (August 3, 1994). ... Suffered charley horse (March 19, 1995); missed two games. ... Signed as free agent by Tampa Bay Lightning (September 11, 1995). ... Suffered pinched nerve in neck (December 3, 1995); missed five games. ... Injured leg (March 17, 1996); missed one game. ... Pulled triceps muscle (November 29, 1996); missed one game. ... Injured ear in a car accident (January 8, 1997); missed one game. ... Strained hamstring (February 17, 1997); missed two games. ... Diagnosed with lymphoma (March 29, 1997); missed remainder of season.
HONORS: Named ECAC Rookie of the Year (1983-84). ... Named to Hockey East All-Star first team (1984-85 and 1985-86). ... Named to NCAA All-America East second team (1985-86). ... Named to Hockey East All-Star second team (1986-87). ... Won James Gatschene Memorial Trophy (1987-88). ... Won Leo P. Lamoureux Memorial Trophy (1987-88). ... Shared Garry F. Longman Memorial Trophy with Ed Belfour (1987-88). ... Named to IHL All-Star first team (1987-88). ... Played in NHL All-Star Game (1991 and 1992). ... Named to Hockey East All-Decade team (1994).
STATISTICAL PLATEAUS: Three-goal games: 1989-90 (1), 1990-91 (1), 1991-92 (1). Total: 3.
MISCELLANEOUS: Failed to score on a penalty shot (vs. Andy Moog, January 16, 1992).

Season Team	League	REGULAR SEASON								PLAYOFFS				
		Gms.	G	A	Pts.	PIM	+/-	PP	SH	Gms.	G	A	Pts.	PIM
83-84— Boston University	ECAC	40	23	33	56	28	...	...	...	—	—	—	—	—
84-85— Boston University	Hockey East	41	27	32	59	46	...	...	...	—	—	—	—	—
85-86— Boston University	Hockey East	43	25	49	74	54	...	...	...	—	—	—	—	—
86-87— Boston University	Hockey East	36	23	29	52	35	...	...	...	—	—	—	—	—
87-88— Flint..........................	IHL	81	48	*109	*157	113	...	...	...	16	11	†15	26	16
88-89— Pittsburgh	NHL	79	12	37	49	112	-25	8	0	11	3	6	9	28.
89-90— Pittsburgh	NHL	72	32	60	92	138	-13	9	0	—	—	—	—	—
90-91— Pittsburgh	NHL	65	31	63	94	83	0	10	0	—	—	—	—	—
— Hartford	NHL	13	8	8	16	18	-6	4	0	6	2	7	9	10
91-92— Hartford	NHL	77	26	51	77	141	-28	10	0	7	2	1	3	12
92-93— Hartford	NHL	19	5	4	9	58	-15	3	0	—	—	—	—	—
— Toronto	NHL	47	13	28	41	53	-8	10	0	12	2	3	5	0
93-94— Toronto	NHL	53	13	17	30	67	-2	2	0	3	0	0	0	0
94-95— Pittsburgh	NHL	46	13	24	37	66	-4	2	0	9	0	2	2	8
95-96— Tampa Bay	NHL	76	16	34	50	65	1	8	0	5	3	3	6	0
96-97— Tampa Bay	NHL	70	18	37	55	95	-14	5	0	—	—	—	—	—
NHL totals (9 years)		617	187	363	550	896	-114	71	0	53	12	22	34	58

CULLEN, MATT   C   MIGHTY DUCKS

PERSONAL: Born November 2, 1976, in Virginia, Minn. ... 6-0/195. ... Shoots left.
HIGH SCHOOL: Moorhead (Minn.) Senior.
COLLEGE: St. Cloud (Minn.) State.
TRANSACTIONS/CAREER NOTES: Selected by Mighty Ducks of Anaheim in second round (second Mighty Ducks pick, 35th overall) of NHL entry draft (June 22, 1996).
HONORS: Named to WCHA All-Rookie team (1995-96). ... Named to WCHA All-Star second team (1996-97).

Season Team	League	REGULAR SEASON								PLAYOFFS				
		Gms.	G	A	Pts.	PIM	+/-	PP	SH	Gms.	G	A	Pts.	PIM
94-95— Moorhead Senior	Minn. H.S.	28	47	42	89	78	...	...	...	—	—	—	—	—
95-96— St. Cloud State..........	WCHA	39	12	29	41	28	...	...	...	—	—	—	—	—
96-97— St. Cloud State..........	WCHA	36	15	30	45	70	...	...	...	—	—	—	—	—
— Baltimore	AHL	6	3	3	6	7	...	...	...	3	0	2	2	0

CULLIMORE, JASSEN   D   CANADIENS

PERSONAL: Born December 4, 1972, in Simcoe, Ont. ... 6-5/220. ... Shoots left. ... Name pronounced KUHL-ih-MOHR.
TRANSACTIONS/CAREER NOTES: Selected by Vancouver Canucks in second round (second Canucks pick, 29th overall) of NHL entry draft (June 22, 1991). ... Suffered injury (March 31, 1995); missed three games. ... Traded by Canucks to Montreal Canadiens for LW Donald Brashear (November 13, 1996). ... Bruised eye (March 1, 1997); missed one game.
HONORS: Named to OHL All-Star second team (1991-92).

Season Team	League	REGULAR SEASON								PLAYOFFS				
		Gms.	G	A	Pts.	PIM	+/-	PP	SH	Gms.	G	A	Pts.	PIM
88-89— Peterborough..............	Jr. B	29	11	17	28	88	...	...	...	—	—	—	—	—
89-90— Peterborough..............	OHL	59	2	6	8	61	...	...	...	11	0	2	2	8

Season Team	League	REGULAR SEASON								PLAYOFFS				
		Gms.	G	A	Pts.	PIM	+/-	PP	SH	Gms.	G	A	Pts.	PIM
90-91 — Peterborough............	OHL	62	8	16	24	74	...	...	...	4	1	0	1	7
91-92 — Peterborough............	OHL	54	9	37	46	65	...	...	...	10	3	6	9	8
92-93 — Hamilton	AHL	56	5	7	12	60	...	...	...	—	—	—	—	—
93-94 — Hamilton	AHL	71	8	20	28	86	...	...	...	3	0	1	1	2
94-95 — Syracuse....................	AHL	33	2	7	9	66	...	...	...	—	—	—	—	—
— Vancouver................	NHL	34	1	2	3	39	-2	0	0	11	0	0	0	12
95-96 — Vancouver................	NHL	27	1	1	2	21	4	0	0	—	—	—	—	—
96-97 — Vancouver................	NHL	3	0	0	0	2	-2	0	0	—	—	—	—	—
— Montreal	NHL	49	2	6	8	42	4	0	1	2	0	0	0	2
NHL totals (3 years)		113	4	9	13	104	4	0	1	13	0	0	0	14

CUMMINS, JIM   LW   BLACKHAWKS

PERSONAL: Born May 17, 1970, in Dearborn, Mich. ... 6-2/203. ... Shoots right. ... Full name: James Stephen Cummins.
COLLEGE: Michigan State.
TRANSACTIONS/CAREER NOTES: Selected by New York Rangers in fourth round (fifth Rangers pick, 67th overall) of NHL entry draft (June 17, 1989). ... Traded by Rangers with C Kevin Miller and D Dennis Vial to Detroit Red Wings for RW Joe Kocur and D Per Djoos (March 5, 1991). ... Suspended 11 games by NHL for leaving penalty box to join fight (January 23, 1993). ... Traded by Red Wings with fourth-round pick in 1993 draft (later traded to Boston which selected D Charles Paquette) to Philadelphia Flyers for rights to C Greg Johnson and future considerations (June 20, 1993). ... Suffered slightly separated shoulder during 1993-94 season. ... Traded by Flyers with fourth-round pick in 1995 draft to Tampa Bay Lightning for C Rob DiMaio (March 18, 1994). ... Traded by Lightning with D Jeff Buchanan and D Tom Tilley to Chicago Blackhawks for LW Paul Ysebaert and RW Rich Sutter (February 22, 1995). ... Sprained tricep (March 16, 1995); missed five games. ... Broke thumb (November 1, 1995); missed 16 games. ... Suspended eight games and fined $1,000 by NHL for cross checking and punching another player (March 14, 1996). ... Bruised clavicle (December 9, 1996); missed 11 games. ... Suspended one game by NHL for third game misconduct of season (January 23, 1997).
MISCELLANEOUS: Failed to score on a penalty shot (vs. Mike Vernon, April 7, 1996).

Season Team	League	REGULAR SEASON								PLAYOFFS				
		Gms.	G	A	Pts.	PIM	+/-	PP	SH	Gms.	G	A	Pts.	PIM
87-88 — Detroit Compuware......	NAJHL	31	11	15	26	146	...	...	...	—	—	—	—	—
88-89 — Michigan State...........	CCHA	36	3	9	12	100	...	...	...	—	—	—	—	—
89-90 — Michigan State...........	CCHA	41	8	7	15	94	...	...	...	—	—	—	—	—
90-91 — Michigan State...........	CCHA	34	9	6	15	110	...	...	...	—	—	—	—	—
91-92 — Adirondack................	AHL	65	7	13	20	338	...	...	...	5	0	0	0	19
— Detroit....................	NHL	1	0	0	0	7	0	0	0	—	—	—	—	—
92-93 — Adirondack................	AHL	43	16	4	20	179	...	...	...	9	3	1	4	4
— Detroit....................	NHL	7	1	1	2	58	0	0	0	—	—	—	—	—
93-94 — Philadelphia...............	NHL	22	1	2	3	71	0	0	0	—	—	—	—	—
— Hershey	AHL	17	6	6	12	70	...	...	...	—	—	—	—	—
— Atlanta	IHL	7	4	5	9	14	...	...	...	13	1	2	3	90
— Tampa Bay	NHL	4	0	0	0	13	-1	0	0	—	—	—	—	—
94-95 — Tampa Bay	NHL	10	1	0	1	41	-3	0	0	—	—	—	—	—
— Chicago..................	NHL	27	3	1	4	117	-3	0	0	14	1	1	2	4
95-96 — Chicago..................	NHL	52	2	4	6	180	-1	0	0	10	0	0	0	2
96-97 — Chicago..................	NHL	65	6	6	12	199	4	0	0	6	0	0	0	24
NHL totals (7 years)		188	14	14	28	686	-4	0	0	30	1	1	2	30

CUNNEYWORTH, RANDY   LW   SENATORS

PERSONAL: Born May 10, 1961, in Etobicoke, Ont. ... 6-0/198. ... Shoots left. ... Full name: Randolph William Cunneyworth.
TRANSACTIONS/CAREER NOTES: Selected by Buffalo Sabres as underage junior in eighth round (ninth Sabres pick, 167th overall) of NHL entry draft (June 11, 1980). ... Attended Pittsburgh Penguins training camp as unsigned free agent (summer 1985); Sabres then traded his equalization rights with RW Mike Moller to Penguins for future considerations (October 4, 1985); Penguins sent RW Pat Hughes to Sabres to complete deal (October 1985). ... Suspended three games by NHL (January 1988). ... Suspended five games by NHL (January 1988). ... Fractured right foot (January 24, 1989). ... Traded by Penguins with G Richard Tabaracci and RW Dave McLlwain to Winnipeg Jets for RW Andrew McBain, D Jim Kyte and LW Randy Gilhen (June 17, 1989). ... Broke bone in right foot (October 1989). ... Traded by Jets to Hartford Whalers for C Paul MacDermid (December 13, 1989). ... Broke tibia bone in left leg (November 28, 1990); missed 38 games. ... Strained lower back (December 1991); missed one game. ... Strained ankle (December 21, 1991); missed two games. ... Strained left ankle (January 16, 1992); missed three games. ... Reinjured ankle (February 1, 1992); missed six games. ... Bruised ribs (November 15, 1992); missed four games. ... Suffered neck spasms (December 31, 1992); missed three games. ... Traded by Whalers with D Gary Suter and undisclosed draft pick to Chicago Blackhawks for D Frantisek Kucera and LW Jocelyn Lemieux (March 11, 1994). ... Signed as free agent by Ottawa Senators (June 30, 1994). ... Suffered back spasms during 1995-96 season; missed one game. ... Suffered back spasms (February 11, 1997); missed one game. ... Fractured cheekbone (February 28, 1997); missed five games.
STATISTICAL PLATEAUS: Three-goal games: 1986-87 (1). ... Four-goal games: 1986-87 (1). ... Total hat tricks: 2.
MISCELLANEOUS: Captain of Ottawa Senators (1994-95).

Season Team	League	REGULAR SEASON								PLAYOFFS				
		Gms.	G	A	Pts.	PIM	+/-	PP	SH	Gms.	G	A	Pts.	PIM
79-80 — Ottawa	OMJHL	63	16	25	41	145	...	...	...	11	0	1	1	13
80-81 — Ottawa	OMJHL	67	54	74	128	240	...	...	...	15	5	8	13	35
— Rochester	AHL	1	0	1	1	2	...	...	...	—	—	—	—	—
— Buffalo	NHL	1	0	0	0	2	0	0	0	—	—	—	—	—
81-82 — Rochester	AHL	57	12	15	27	86	...	...	...	9	4	0	4	30
— Buffalo	NHL	20	2	4	6	47	-3	0	0	—	—	—	—	—
82-83 — Rochester	AHL	78	23	33	56	111	...	...	...	16	4	4	8	35
83-84 — Rochester	AHL	54	18	17	35	85	...	...	...	17	5	5	10	55
84-85 — Rochester	AHL	72	30	38	68	148	...	...	...	5	2	1	3	16
85-86 — Pittsburgh................	NHL	75	15	30	45	74	12	2	2					

Season Team	League	REGULAR SEASON								PLAYOFFS				
		Gms.	G	A	Pts.	PIM	+/-	PP	SH	Gms.	G	A	Pts.	PIM
86-87 — Pittsburgh	NHL	79	26	27	53	142	14	3	2	—	—	—	—	—
87-88 — Pittsburgh	NHL	71	35	39	74	141	13	14	0	—	—	—	—	—
88-89 — Pittsburgh	NHL	70	25	19	44	156	-22	10	0	11	3	5	8	26
89-90 — Winnipeg	NHL	28	5	6	11	34	-7	2	0	—	—	—	—	—
— Hartford	NHL	43	9	9	18	41	-4	2	0	4	0	0	0	2
90-91 — Springfield	AHL	2	0	0	0	5	...	...	...	—	—	—	—	—
— Hartford	NHL	32	9	5	14	49	-6	0	0	1	0	0	0	0
91-92 — Hartford	NHL	39	7	10	17	71	-5	0	0	7	3	0	3	9
92-93 — Hartford	NHL	39	5	4	9	63	-1	0	0	—	—	—	—	—
93-94 — Hartford	NHL	63	9	8	17	87	-2	0	1	—	—	—	—	—
— Chicago	NHL	16	4	3	7	13	1	0	0	6	0	0	0	8
94-95 — Ottawa	NHL	48	5	5	10	68	-19	2	0	—	—	—	—	—
95-96 — Ottawa	NHL	81	17	19	36	130	-31	4	0	—	—	—	—	—
96-97 — Ottawa	NHL	76	12	24	36	99	-7	6	0	7	1	1	2	10
NHL totals (14 years)		781	185	212	397	1217	-67	45	5	36	7	6	13	55

CYRENNE, CORY   C   SHARKS

PERSONAL: Born August 25, 1977, in Winnipeg. ... 5-9/170. ... Shoots left.
TRANSACTIONS/CAREER NOTES: Selected by San Jose Sharks in eighth round (seventh Sharks pick, 191st overall) of NHL entry draft (June 22, 1996).

Season Team	League	REGULAR SEASON								PLAYOFFS				
		Gms.	G	A	Pts.	PIM	+/-	PP	SH	Gms.	G	A	Pts.	PIM
95-96 — Brandon	WHL	69	38	59	97	58	...	...	...	19	6	14	20	18
96-97 — Brandon	WHL	55	26	56	82	23	...	...	...	6	3	3	6	0

CZERKAWSKI, MARIUSZ   LW/RW   OILERS

PERSONAL: Born April 13, 1972, in Radomski, Poland. ... 6-0/195. ... Shoots right. ... Name pronounced MAIR-ee-yuhz chuhr-KAHV-skee.
TRANSACTIONS/CAREER NOTES: Selected by Boston Bruins (fifth Bruins pick, 106th overall) of NHL entry draft (June 22, 1991). ... Played in Europe during 1994-95 NHL lockout. ... Traded by Bruins with D Sean Brown and first-round pick (D Matthieu Descoteaux) in 1996 draft to Edmonton Oilers for G Bill Ranford (January 11, 1996). ... Injured finger (March 23, 1996); missed two games. ... Suffered hip pointer (January 11, 1997); missed two games.
STATISTICAL PLATEAUS: Three-goal games: 1996-97 (2).

Season Team	League	REGULAR SEASON								PLAYOFFS				
		Gms.	G	A	Pts.	PIM	+/-	PP	SH	Gms.	G	A	Pts.	PIM
90-91 — GKS Tychy	Poland	24	25	15	40	...	...	...	...	—	—	—	—	—
91-92 — Djur. Stockholm	Sweden	39	8	5	13	4	...	...	...	3	0	0	0	2
— Polish Olympic team	Int'l	5	0	1	1	4	...	...	...	—	—	—	—	—
92-93 — Hammarby	Swed. Div. II	32	39	30	69	74	...	...	...	—	—	—	—	—
93-94 — Djur. Stockholm	Sweden	39	13	21	34	20	...	...	...	—	—	—	—	—
— Boston	NHL	4	2	1	3	0	-2	1	0	13	3	3	6	4
94-95 — Kiekko-Espoo	Finland	7	9	3	12	10	...	...	...	—	—	—	—	—
— Boston	NHL	47	12	14	26	31	4	1	0	5	1	0	1	0
95-96 — Boston	NHL	33	5	6	11	10	-11	1	0	—	—	—	—	—
— Edmonton	NHL	37	12	17	29	8	7	2	0	—	—	—	—	—
96-97 — Edmonton	NHL	76	26	21	47	16	0	4	0	12	2	1	3	10
NHL totals (4 years)		197	57	59	116	65	-2	9	0	30	6	4	10	14

DACKELL, ANDREAS   RW   SENATORS

PERSONAL: Born December 29, 1972, in Gavle, Sweden. ... 5-11/191. ... Shoots right. ... Name pronounced AHN-dray-uhz DA-kuhl.
TRANSACTIONS/CAREER NOTES: Selected by Ottawa Senators in sixth round (third Senators pick, 136th overall) of NHL entry draft (June 22, 1996).

Season Team	League	REGULAR SEASON								PLAYOFFS				
		Gms.	G	A	Pts.	PIM	+/-	PP	SH	Gms.	G	A	Pts.	PIM
90-91 — Brynas Gavle	Sweden	3	0	1	1	2	...	...	...	—	—	—	—	—
91-92 — Brynas Gavle	Sweden	4	0	0	0	2	...	...	...	2	0	1	1	4
92-93 — Brynas Gavle	Sweden	40	12	15	27	12	...	...	...	10	4	5	9	2
93-94 — Brynas Gavle	Sweden	38	12	17	29	47	...	...	...	7	2	2	4	8
94-95 — Brynas Gavle	Sweden	39	17	16	33	34	...	...	...	14	3	3	6	14
95-96 — Brynas Gavle	Sweden	22	6	6	12	8	...	...	...	—	—	—	—	—
96-97 — Ottawa	NHL	79	12	19	31	8	-6	2	0	7	1	0	1	0
NHL totals (1 year)		79	12	19	31	8	-6	2	0	7	1	0	1	0

DAFOE, BYRON   G   KINGS

PERSONAL: Born February 25, 1971, in Duncan, B.C. ... 5-11/195. ... Catches left. ... Full name: Byron Jaromir Dafoe.
TRANSACTIONS/CAREER NOTES: Selected by Washington Capitals in second round (second Capitals pick, 35th overall) of NHL entry draft (June 17, 1989). ... Underwent emergency appendectomy (December 1989). ... Traded by Capitals with LW/C Dimitri Khristich to Los Angeles Kings for first-(C Alexander Volchkov) and fourth-(RW Justin Davis) round picks in 1996 draft (July 8, 1995). ... Strained thumb (February 1, 1997); missed two games.
HONORS: Shared Harry (Hap) Holmes Memorial Trophy with Olaf Kolzig (1993-94). ... Named to AHL All-Star first team (1993-94).
MISCELLANEOUS: Allowed a penalty shot goal (vs. Steve Chiasson, December 11, 1995).

C
D

Season Team	League	REGULAR SEASON								PLAYOFFS						
		Gms.	Min	W	L	T	GA	SO	Avg.	Gms.	Min.	W	L	GA	SO	Avg.
87-88—Juan de Fuca	BCJHL	32	1716	...	...	...	129	0	4.51	—	—	—	—	—	—	—
88-89—Portland	WHL	59	3279	29	24	3	*291	1	5.32	*18	*1091	10	8	*81	*1	4.45
89-90—Portland	WHL	40	2265	14	21	3	193	0	5.11	—	—	—	—	—	—	—
90-91—Portland	WHL	8	414	1	5	1	41	0	5.94	—	—	—	—	—	—	—
—Prince Albert	WHL	32	1839	13	12	4	124	0	4.05	—	—	—	—	—	—	—
91-92—New Haven	AHL	7	364	3	2	1	22	0	3.63	—	—	—	—	—	—	—
—Baltimore	AHL	33	1847	12	16	4	119	0	3.87	—	—	—	—	—	—	—
—Hampton Roads	ECHL	10	562	6	4	‡0	26	1	2.78	—	—	—	—	—	—	—
92-93—Baltimore	AHL	48	2617	16	*20	7	191	1	4.38	5	241	2	3	22	0	5.48
—Washington	NHL	1	1	0	0	0	0	0	0.00	—	—	—	—	—	—	—
93-94—Portland	AHL	47	2662	24	16	4	148	1	3.34	1	9	0	0	1	0	6.67
—Washington	NHL	5	230	2	2	0	13	0	3.39	2	118	0	2	5	0	2.54
94-95—Baltimore	AHL	6	330	5	0	0	16	0	2.91	7	417	3	4	29	0	4.17
—Phoenix	IHL	49	2744	25	16	‡6	169	2	3.70	—	—	—	—	—	—	—
—Washington	NHL	4	187	1	1	1	11	0	3.53	1	20	0	0	1	0	3.00
95-96—Los Angeles	NHL	47	2666	14	24	8	172	1	3.87	—	—	—	—	—	—	—
96-97—Los Angeles	NHL	40	2162	13	17	5	112	0	3.11	—	—	—	—	—	—	—
NHL totals (5 years)		97	5246	30	44	14	308	1	3.52	3	138	0	2	6	0	2.61

DAGENAIS, PIERRE   LW   DEVILS

PERSONAL: Born March 4, 1978, in Blainville, Que. ... 6-3/185. ... Shoots left. ... Name pronounced da-zhih-NAY.
TRANSACTIONS/CAREER NOTES: Selected by New Jersey Devils in second round (fourth Devils pick, 47th overall) of NHL entry draft (June 22, 1996).
HONORS: Named to Can.HL All-Rookie team (1995-96). ... Named to QMJHL All-Rookie team (1995-96).

Season Team	League	REGULAR SEASON								PLAYOFFS				
		Gms.	G	A	Pts.	PIM	+/-	PP	SH	Gms.	G	A	Pts.	PIM
95-96—Moncton	QMJHL	67	43	25	68	59	...	...	...	—	—	—	—	—
96-97—Moncton	QMJHL	6	4	2	6	0	...	...	...	—	—	—	—	—
—Laval	QMJHL	37	16	14	30	22	...	...	...	—	—	—	—	—
—Rouyn-Noranda	QMJHL	27	21	8	29	22	...	...	...	—	—	—	—	—

DAHL, KEVIN   D

PERSONAL: Born December 30, 1968, in Regina, Sask. ... 5-11/190. ... Shoots right.
COLLEGE: Bowling Green State (degree in physical education).
TRANSACTIONS/CAREER NOTES: Selected by Montreal Canadiens in 11th round (12th Canadiens pick, 230th overall) of NHL entry draft (June 11, 1988). ... Signed as free agent by Calgary Flames (August 1, 1991). ... Suffered charley horse (November 2, 1992); missed two games. ... Injured heel (November 28, 1992); missed one game. ... Strained left knee (December 15, 1992); missed 18 games. ... Fractured left foot (April 9, 1993); missed one game. ... Separated left shoulder (November 6, 1993); missed nine games. ... Strained left shoulder (December 7, 1993); missed 30 games. ... Separated left shoulder (February 16, 1995); missed two games. ... Injured rib cartilage (March 31, 1995); missed seven games. ... Injured knee (November 15, 1995); missed one game. ... Injured knee (December 19, 1995); missed three games. ... Signed as free agent by Phoenix Coyotes (August 26, 1996).
MISCELLANEOUS: Member of silver-medal-winning Canadian Olympic team (1992).

Season Team	League	REGULAR SEASON								PLAYOFFS				
		Gms.	G	A	Pts.	PIM	+/-	PP	SH	Gms.	G	A	Pts.	PIM
87-88—Bowling Green	CCHA	44	2	23	25	78	...	...	...	—	—	—	—	—
88-89—Bowling Green	CCHA	46	9	26	35	51	...	...	...	—	—	—	—	—
89-90—Bowling Green	CCHA	43	8	22	30	74	...	...	...	—	—	—	—	—
90-91—Fredericton	AHL	32	1	15	16	45	...	...	...	9	0	1	1	11
—Winston-Salem	ECHL	36	7	17	24	58	...	...	...	—	—	—	—	—
91-92—Canadian nat'l team	Int'l	45	2	15	17	44	...	...	...	—	—	—	—	—
—Can. Olympic team	Int'l	8	2	0	2	6	...	...	...	—	—	—	—	—
—Salt Lake City	IHL	13	0	2	2	12	...	...	...	5	0	0	0	13
92-93—Calgary	NHL	61	2	9	11	56	9	1	0	6	0	2	2	8
93-94—Calgary	NHL	33	0	3	3	23	-2	0	0	6	0	0	0	4
—Saint John	AHL	2	0	0	0	0	...	...	...	—	—	—	—	—
94-95—Calgary	NHL	34	4	8	12	38	8	0	0	3	0	0	0	0
95-96—Calgary	NHL	32	1	1	2	26	-2	0	0	1	0	0	0	0
—Saint John	AHL	23	4	11	15	37	...	...	...	—	—	—	—	—
96-97—Las Vegas	IHL	73	10	21	31	101	...	...	...	3	0	0	0	2
—Phoenix	NHL	2	0	0	0	0	0	0	0	—	—	—	—	—
NHL totals (5 years)		162	7	21	28	143	13	1	0	16	0	2	2	12

DAHLEN, ULF   RW   BLACKHAWKS

PERSONAL: Born January 12, 1967, in Ostersund, Sweden. ... 6-2/195. ... Shoots right. ... Name pronounced DAH-lihn.
TRANSACTIONS/CAREER NOTES: Selected by New York Rangers in first round (first Rangers pick, seventh overall) of NHL entry draft (June 15, 1985). ... Bruised shin (November 1987). ... Bruised left shoulder (November 1988). ... Separated right shoulder (January 1989). ... Traded by Rangers with fourth-round pick (C Cal McGowan) in 1990 draft and future considerations to Minnesota North Stars for RW Mike Gartner (March 6, 1990). ... North Stars franchise moved from Minnesota to Dallas and renamed Stars for 1993-94 season. ... Traded by Stars with future considerations to San Jose Sharks for D Mike Lalor and D Doug Zmolek (March 19, 1994). ... Suffered from the flu (February 20, 1995); missed two games. ... Injured groin (October 28, 1995); missed three games. ... Fractured toe (January 11, 1996); missed 20 games. ... Traded by Sharks with G Chris Terreri, D Michal Sykora and second-round pick in 1998 draft to Chicago Blackhawks for G Ed Belfour (January 25, 1997). ... Suffered back spasms (March 26, 1997); missed one game.

STATISTICAL PLATEAUS: Three-goal games: 1987-88 (1), 1990-91 (1), 1992-93 (1), 1993-94 (1), 1993-94 (1). Total: 5.
MISCELLANEOUS: Failed to score on a penalty shot (vs. Daren Puppa, March 17, 1992).

		REGULAR SEASON								PLAYOFFS				
Season Team	League	Gms.	G	A	Pts.	PIM	+/-	PP	SH	Gms.	G	A	Pts.	PIM
83-84— Ostersund	Sweden	36	15	11	26	10	...	...	...	—	—	—	—	—
84-85— Ostersund	Sweden	36	33	26	59	20	...	...	...	—	—	—	—	—
85-86— Bjorkloven	Sweden	22	4	3	7	8	...	...	...	—	—	—	—	—
86-87— Bjorkloven	Sweden	31	9	12	21	20	...	...	...	6	6	2	8	4
87-88— New York Rangers	NHL	70	29	23	52	26	5	11	0	—	—	—	—	—
— Colorado	IHL	2	2	2	4	0	...	...	...	—	—	—	—	—
88-89— New York Rangers	NHL	56	24	19	43	50	-6	8	0	4	0	0	0	0
89-90— New York Rangers	NHL	63	18	18	36	30	-4	13	0	—	—	—	—	—
— Minnesota	NHL	13	2	4	6	0	1	0	0	7	1	4	5	2
90-91— Minnesota	NHL	66	21	18	39	6	7	4	0	15	2	6	8	4
91-92— Minnesota	NHL	79	36	30	66	10	-5	16	1	7	0	3	3	2
92-93— Minnesota	NHL	83	35	39	74	6	-20	13	0	—	—	—	—	—
93-94— Dallas	NHL	65	19	38	57	10	-1	12	0	—	—	—	—	—
— San Jose	NHL	13	6	6	12	0	0	3	0	14	6	2	8	0
94-95— San Jose	NHL	46	11	23	34	11	-2	4	1	11	5	4	9	0
95-96— San Jose	NHL	59	16	12	28	27	-21	5	0	—	—	—	—	—
96-97— San Jose	NHL	43	8	11	19	8	-11	3	0	—	—	—	—	—
— Chicago	NHL	30	6	8	14	10	9	1	0	5	0	1	1	0
NHL totals (10 years)		686	231	249	480	194	-48	93	2	63	14	20	34	8

DAHLQUIST, CHRIS — D — SENATORS

PERSONAL: Born December 14, 1962, in Fridley, Minn. ... 6-1/195. ... Shoots left. ... Name pronounced DAHL-KWIHST.
COLLEGE: Lake Superior State (Mich.).
TRANSACTIONS/CAREER NOTES: Signed as free agent by Pittsburgh Penguins (May 1985). ... Traded by Penguins with Jim Johnson to Minnesota North Stars for D Peter Taglianetti and D Larry Murphy (December 11, 1990). ... Broke left wrist (January 1991). ... Selected by Calgary Flames in NHL waiver draft (October 4, 1992). ... Bruised ribs (November 11, 1992); missed five games. ... Suffered charley horse (February 26, 1993); missed two games. ... Signed as free agent by Ottawa Senators (July 4, 1994). ... Loaned by Senators to Cincinnati Cyclones (October 20, 1995). ... Suffered muscle spasms (April 10, 1996).
MISCELLANEOUS: Failed to score on a penalty shot (vs. Stephane Fiset, March 21, 1992).

		REGULAR SEASON								PLAYOFFS				
Season Team	League	Gms.	G	A	Pts.	PIM	+/-	PP	SH	Gms.	G	A	Pts.	PIM
81-82— Lake Superior	CCHA	39	4	10	14	62	...	...	...	—	—	—	—	—
82-83— Lake Superior	CCHA	35	0	12	12	63	...	...	...	—	—	—	—	—
83-84— Lake Superior	CCHA	40	4	19	23	76	...	...	...	—	—	—	—	—
84-85— Lake Superior	CCHA	44	4	15	19	18	...	...	...	—	—	—	—	—
85-86— Baltimore	AHL	65	4	21	25	64	...	...	...	—	—	—	—	—
— Pittsburgh	NHL	5	1	2	3	2	...	...	...	—	—	—	—	—
86-87— Baltimore	AHL	51	1	16	17	50	...	...	...	—	—	—	—	—
— Pittsburgh	NHL	19	0	1	1	20	...	...	...	—	—	—	—	—
87-88— Pittsburgh	NHL	44	3	6	9	69	...	...	...	—	—	—	—	—
88-89— Pittsburgh	NHL	43	1	5	6	42	...	...	...	2	0	0	0	0
— Muskegon	IHL	10	3	6	9	14	...	...	...	—	—	—	—	—
89-90— Muskegon	IHL	6	1	1	2	8	...	...	...	—	—	—	—	—
— Pittsburgh	NHL	62	4	10	14	56	-2	0	0	—	—	—	—	—
90-91— Pittsburgh	NHL	22	1	2	3	30	0	0	0	—	—	—	—	—
— Minnesota	NHL	42	2	6	8	33	-1	0	0	23	1	6	7	20
91-92— Minnesota	NHL	74	1	13	14	68	-10	0	0	7	0	0	0	6
92-93— Calgary	NHL	74	3	7	10	66	0	0	0	6	3	1	4	4
93-94— Calgary	NHL	77	1	11	12	52	5	0	0	1	0	0	0	0
94-95— Ottawa	NHL	46	1	7	8	36	-30	1	0	—	—	—	—	—
95-96— Ottawa	NHL	24	1	1	2	14	-7	0	0	—	—	—	—	—
— Cincinnati	IHL	38	4	8	12	50	...	...	...	2	1	3	4	0
96-97— Las Vegas	IHL	18	1	4	5	26	...	...	...	—	—	—	—	—
NHL totals (11 years)		532	19	71	90	488	-45	1	0	39	4	7	11	30

DAIGLE, ALEXANDRE — RW — SENATORS

PERSONAL: Born February 7, 1975, in Montreal. ... 6-0/195. ... Shoots left. ... Name pronounced DAYG.
TRANSACTIONS/CAREER NOTES: Selected by Ottawa Senators in first round (first Senators pick, first overall) of NHL entry draft (June 26, 1993). ... Fractured left forearm (February 3, 1996); missed remainder of season.
HONORS: Won Can.HL Rookie of the Year Award (1991-92). ... Named QMJHL Rookie of the Year (1991-92). ... Won Michel Bergeron Trophy (1991-92). ... Named to Can.HL All-Rookie team (1991-92). ... Named to QMJHL All-Star second team (1991-92). ... Won Can.HL Top Draft Prospect Award (1992-93). ... Won QMJHL Top Draft Prospect Award (1992-93). ... Named to QMJHL All-Star first team (1992-93).
STATISTICAL PLATEAUS: Three-goal games: 1994-95 (1).
MISCELLANEOUS: Failed to score on a penalty shot attempt (vs. Guy Hebert, December 30, 1996). ... Holds Ottawa Senators all-time record for most games played (263).

		REGULAR SEASON								PLAYOFFS				
Season Team	League	Gms.	G	A	Pts.	PIM	+/-	PP	SH	Gms.	G	A	Pts.	PIM
91-92— Victoriaville	QMJHL	66	35	75	110	63	...	...	...	—	—	—	—	—
92-93— Victoriaville	QMJHL	53	45	92	137	85	...	...	...	6	5	6	11	4
93-94— Ottawa	NHL	84	20	31	51	40	-45	4	0	—	—	—	—	—
94-95— Victoriaville	QMJHL	18	14	20	34	16	...	...	...	—	—	—	—	—
— Ottawa	NHL	47	16	21	37	14	-22	4	1	—	—	—	—	—
95-96— Ottawa	NHL	50	5	12	17	24	-30	1	0	—	—	—	—	—
96-97— Ottawa	NHL	82	26	25	51	33	-33	4	0	7	0	0	0	2
NHL totals (4 years)		263	67	89	156	111	-130	13	1	7	0	0	0	2

DAIGNEAULT, J.J.　　　　　　　D　　　　　　MIGHTY DUCKS

PERSONAL: Born October 12, 1965, in Montreal. ... 5-10/186. ... Shoots left. ... Name pronounced DAYN-yoh.

TRANSACTIONS/CAREER NOTES: Underwent knee surgery (March 1984). ... Selected by Vancouver Canucks as underage junior in first round (first Canucks pick, 10th overall) of NHL entry draft (June 1984). ... Broke finger (March 19, 1986). ... Traded by Canucks with second-round pick (C Kent Hawley) in 1986 draft and fifth-round pick in 1987 draft to Philadelphia Flyers for RW Rich Sutter, D Dave Richter and third-round pick (D Don Gibson) in 1986 draft (June 1986). ... Sprained ankle (April 12, 1987). ... Traded by Flyers to Montreal Canadiens for D Scott Sandelin (November 1988). ... Bruised shoulder (December 1990). ... Suffered left hip pointer (March 16, 1991). ... Injured knee (April 7, 1991). ... Bruised left knee (November 28, 1992); missed one game. ... Injured shoulder (December 23, 1992); missed two games. ... Sprained right ankle (March 1, 1993); missed 11 games. ... Suffered injury (December 22, 1993); missed one game. ... Suspended three games and fined $500 by NHL for elbowing (January 7, 1994). ... Sprained wrist (January 10, 1994); missed six games. ... Suffered sore back (March 1, 1994); missed one game. ... Injured shoulder (February 4, 1995); missed one game. ... Suffered from cold (February 13, 1995); missed one game. ... Bruised ankle (April 12, 1995); missed one game. ... Traded by Canadiens to St. Louis Blues for G Pat Jablonski (November 7, 1995). ... Traded by Blues to Pittsburgh Penguins for sixth-round pick (C Stephen Wagner) in 1996 draft (March 20, 1996). ... Suffered back spasms (December 30, 1996); missed one game. ... Suffered back spasms (January 4, 1997); missed two games. ... Traded by Penguins to Anaheim Mighty Ducks for LW Garry Valk (February 21, 1997). ... Suspended 10 games and fined $1,000 by NHL for abusing an official (February 26, 1997).

HONORS: Won Emile (Butch) Bouchard Trophy (1982-83). ... Named to QMJHL All-Star first team (1982-83).

MISCELLANEOUS: Member of Stanley Cup championship team (1993).

				REGULAR SEASON							PLAYOFFS			
Season Team	League	Gms.	G	A	Pts.	PIM	+/-	PP	SH		Gms.	G	A	Pts.	PIM
81-82— Laval	QMJHL	64	4	25	29	41	...	...	...		18	1	3	4	2
82-83— Longueuil	QMJHL	70	26	58	84	58	...	...	...		15	4	11	15	35
83-84— Can. Olympic team	Int'l	62	6	15	21	40	...				—	—	—	—	—
— Longueuil	QMJHL	10	2	11	13	6	...	...	...		14	3	13	16	30
84-85— Vancouver	NHL	67	4	23	27	69	-14	2	0		—	—	—	—	—
85-86— Vancouver	NHL	64	5	23	28	45	-20	4	0		3	0	2	2	0
86-87— Philadelphia	NHL	77	6	16	22	56	12	0	0		9	1	0	1	0
87-88— Philadelphia	NHL	28	2	2	4	12	-8	2	0		—	—	—	—	—
— Hershey	AHL	10	1	5	6	8	...				—	—	—	—	—
88-89— Hershey	AHL	12	0	10	10	13	...				—	—	—	—	—
— Sherbrooke	AHL	63	10	33	43	48	...				6	1	3	4	2
89-90— Sherbrooke	AHL	28	8	19	27	18	...				—	—	—	—	—
— Montreal	NHL	36	2	10	12	14	11	0	0		9	0	0	0	2
90-91— Montreal	NHL	51	3	16	19	31	-2	2	0		5	0	1	1	0
91-92— Montreal	NHL	79	4	14	18	36	16	2	0		11	0	3	3	4
92-93— Montreal	NHL	66	8	10	18	57	25	0	0		20	1	3	4	22
93-94— Montreal	NHL	68	2	12	14	73	16	0	0		7	0	1	1	12
94-95— Montreal	NHL	45	3	5	8	40	2	0	0		—	—	—	—	—
95-96— Montreal	NHL	7	0	1	1	6	0	0	0		—	—	—	—	—
— St. Louis	NHL	37	1	3	4	24	-6	0	0		—	—	—	—	—
— Worcester	AHL	9	1	10	11	10	...				—	—	—	—	—
— Pittsburgh	NHL	13	3	3	6	23	0	2	0		17	1	9	10	36
96-97— Pittsburgh	NHL	53	3	14	17	36	-5	0	0		—	—	—	—	—
— Anaheim	NHL	13	2	9	11	22	5	0	0		11	2	7	9	16
NHL totals (13 years)		704	48	161	209	544	32	14	0		92	5	26	31	92

DALE, ANDREW　　　　　　　C　　　　　　　　KINGS

PERSONAL: Born February 16, 1976, in Sudbury, Ont. ... 6-1/196. ... Shoots left.

TRANSACTIONS/CAREER NOTES: Selected by Los Angeles Kings in eighth round (sixth Kings pick, 189th overall) of NHL entry draft (June 29, 1994).

				REGULAR SEASON							PLAYOFFS			
Season Team	League	Gms.	G	A	Pts.	PIM	+/-	PP	SH		Gms.	G	A	Pts.	PIM
93-94— Sudbury	OHL	53	8	13	21	21	...	...	...		9	0	3	3	4
94-95— Sudbury	OHL	65	21	30	51	99	...	...	...		18	2	9	11	37
95-96— Kitchener	OHL	64	44	45	89	75	...	...	...		12	5	5	10	25
96-97— Phoenix	IHL	32	7	6	13	19	...	...	...		—	—	—	—	—
— Mississippi	ECHL	19	6	9	15	16	...	...	...		2	0	1	1	0

DAMPHOUSSE, VINCENT　　　　　LW　　　　　CANADIENS

PERSONAL: Born December 17, 1967, in Montreal. ... 6-1/195. ... Shoots left. ... Name pronounced dahm-FOOZ.

TRANSACTIONS/CAREER NOTES: Selected by Toronto Maple Leafs as underage junior in first round (first Maple Leafs pick, sixth overall) of NHL entry draft (June 21, 1986). ... Traded by Maple Leafs with D Luke Richardson, G Peter Ing, C Scott Thornton and future considerations to Edmonton Oilers for G Grant Fuhr, LW/RW Glenn Anderson and LW Craig Berube (September 19, 1991). ... Traded by Oilers with fourth-round pick (D Adam Wiesel) in 1993 draft to Montreal Canadiens for LW Shayne Corson, LW Vladimir Vujtek and C Brent Gilchrist (August 27, 1992). ... Played in Europe during 1994-95 NHL lockout. ... Suspended two games and fined $1,000 by NHL for crosschecking (March 30, 1996).

HONORS: Named to QMJHL All-Star second team (1985-86). ... Played in NHL All-Star Game (1991 and 1992). ... Named All-Star Game Most Valuable Player (1991).

RECORDS: Shares NHL All-Star single-game record for most goals—4 (1991).

STATISTICAL PLATEAUS: Three-goal games: 1988-89 (1), 1989-90 (2), 1992-93 (2), 1993-94 (2), 1996-97 (1). Total: 8. ... Four-goal games: 1991-92 (1). ... Total hat tricks: 9.

MISCELLANEOUS: Member of Stanley Cup championship team (1993). ... Captain of Montreal Canadiens (October 29, 1996 through remainder of season). ... Failed to score on a penalty shot (vs. Dominik Hasek, March 8, 1997).

Season Team	League	REGULAR SEASON								PLAYOFFS				
		Gms.	G	A	Pts.	PIM	+/-	PP	SH	Gms.	G	A	Pts.	PIM
83-84 — Laval	QMJHL	66	29	36	65	25	...	...	...	—	—	—	—	—
84-85 — Laval	QMJHL	68	35	68	103	62	...	...	...	—	—	—	—	—
85-86 — Laval	QMJHL	69	45	110	155	70	...	...	...	14	9	27	36	12
86-87 — Toronto	NHL	80	21	25	46	26	-6	4	0	12	1	5	6	8
87-88 — Toronto	NHL	75	12	36	48	40	2	1	0	6	0	1	1	10
88-89 — Toronto	NHL	80	26	42	68	75	-8	6	0	—	—	—	—	—
89-90 — Toronto	NHL	80	33	61	94	56	2	9	0	5	0	2	2	2
90-91 — Toronto	NHL	79	26	47	73	65	-31	10	1	—	—	—	—	—
91-92 — Edmonton	NHL	80	38	51	89	53	10	12	1	16	6	8	14	8
92-93 — Montreal	NHL	84	39	58	97	98	5	9	3	20	11	12	23	16
93-94 — Montreal	NHL	84	40	51	91	75	0	13	0	7	1	2	3	8
94-95 — Ratingen	Germany	11	5	6	11	24	...	...	...	—	—	—	—	—
— Montreal	NHL	48	10	30	40	42	15	4	0	—	—	—	—	—
95-96 — Montreal	NHL	80	38	56	94	158	5	11	4	6	4	4	8	0
96-97 — Montreal	NHL	82	27	54	81	82	-6	7	2	5	0	0	0	2
NHL totals (11 years)		852	310	511	821	770	-12	86	11	77	23	34	57	54

DANDENAULT, MATHIEU D/RW RED WINGS

PERSONAL: Born February 3, 1976, in Magog, Que. ... 6-1/190. ... Shoots right. ... Name pronounced DAN-dih-noh.
HIGH SCHOOL: CEGEP de Sherbrooke (Que.).
TRANSACTIONS/CAREER NOTES: Selected by Detroit Red Wings in second round (second Red Wings pick, 49th overall) of NHL entry draft (June 28, 1994). ... Suffered from the flu (November 11, 1995); missed one game. ... Bruised ribs (March 10, 1997); missed four games.
MISCELLANEOUS: Member of Stanley Cup championship team (1997).

Season Team	League	REGULAR SEASON								PLAYOFFS				
		Gms.	G	A	Pts.	PIM	+/-	PP	SH	Gms.	G	A	Pts.	PIM
91-92 — Gloucester	OPJHL	6	3	4	7	0	...	...	...	—	—	—	—	—
92-93 — Gloucester	OPJHL	55	11	26	37	64	...	...	...	—	—	—	—	—
93-94 — Sherbrooke	QMJHL	67	17	36	53	67	...	...	...	12	4	10	14	12
94-95 — Sherbrooke	QMJHL	67	37	70	107	76	...	...	...	7	1	7	8	10
95-96 — Detroit	NHL	34	5	7	12	6	6	1	0	—	—	—	—	—
— Adirondack	AHL	4	0	0	0	0	...	...	...	—	—	—	—	—
96-97 — Detroit	NHL	65	3	9	12	28	-10	0	0	—	—	—	—	—
NHL totals (2 years)		99	8	16	24	34	-4	1	0					

DANEYKO, KEN D DEVILS

PERSONAL: Born April 17, 1964, in Windsor, Ont. ... 6-1/215. ... Shoots left. ... Name pronounced DAN-ih-koh.
TRANSACTIONS/CAREER NOTES: Selected by Seattle Breakers from Spokane Flyers in WHL dispersal draft (December 1981). ... Selected by New Jersey Devils as underage junior in first round (second Devils pick, 18th overall) of NHL entry draft (June 1982). ... Fractured right fibula (November 2, 1983). ... Suspended one game and fined $500 by NHL for playing in West Germany without permission (October 1985). ... Injured wrist (February 25, 1987). ... Broke nose (February 24, 1988). ... Injured shoulder (March 29, 1994); missed six games. ... Injured knee (March 8, 1995); missed 23 games. ... Suffered from the flu (March 9, 1996); missed two games. ... Injured hip (October 12, 1996); missed one game. ... Suffered from the flu (January 31, 1997); missed one game.
MISCELLANEOUS: Member of Stanley Cup championship team (1995). ... Holds New Jersey Devils franchise all-time record for most penalty minutes (2,121).

Season Team	League	REGULAR SEASON								PLAYOFFS				
		Gms.	G	A	Pts.	PIM	+/-	PP	SH	Gms.	G	A	Pts.	PIM
80-81 — Spokane Flyers	WHL	62	6	13	19	140	...	...	...	4	0	0	0	6
81-82 — Spokane Flyers	WHL	26	1	11	12	147	...	...	...	—	—	—	—	—
— Seattle	WHL	38	1	22	23	151	...	...	...	14	1	9	10	49
82-83 — Seattle	WHL	69	17	43	60	150	...	...	...	4	1	3	4	14
83-84 — Kamloops	WHL	19	6	28	34	52	...	...	...	17	4	9	13	28
— New Jersey	NHL	11	1	4	5	17	-1	0	0	—	—	—	—	—
84-85 — New Jersey	NHL	1	0	0	0	10	-1	0	0	—	—	—	—	—
— Maine	AHL	80	4	9	13	206	...	...	...	11	1	3	4	36
85-86 — Maine	AHL	21	3	2	5	75	...	...	...	—	—	—	—	—
— New Jersey	NHL	44	0	10	10	100	1	0	0	—	—	—	—	—
86-87 — New Jersey	NHL	79	2	12	14	183	-13	0	0	—	—	—	—	—
87-88 — New Jersey	NHL	80	5	7	12	239	-3	1	0	20	1	6	7	83
88-89 — New Jersey	NHL	80	5	5	10	283	-22	1	0	—	—	—	—	—
89-90 — New Jersey	NHL	74	6	15	21	216	15	0	1	6	2	0	2	21
90-91 — New Jersey	NHL	80	4	16	20	249	-10	1	2	7	0	1	1	10
91-92 — New Jersey	NHL	80	1	7	8	170	7	0	0	7	0	3	3	16
92-93 — New Jersey	NHL	84	2	11	13	236	4	0	0	5	0	0	0	8
93-94 — New Jersey	NHL	78	1	9	10	176	27	0	0	20	0	1	1	45
94-95 — New Jersey	NHL	25	1	2	3	54	4	0	0	20	1	0	1	22
95-96 — New Jersey	NHL	80	2	4	6	115	-10	0	0	—	—	—	—	—
96-97 — New Jersey	NHL	77	2	7	9	70	24	0	0	10	0	0	0	28
NHL totals (14 years)		873	32	109	141	2118	22	3	3	95	4	11	15	233

DANIELS, JEFF LW HURRICANES

PERSONAL: Born June 24, 1968, in Oshawa, Ont. ... 6-1/199. ... Shoots left.
TRANSACTIONS/CAREER NOTES: Selected by Pittsburgh Penguins as underage junior in sixth round (sixth Penguins pick, 109th overall) of NHL entry draft (June 21, 1986). ... Traded by Penguins to Florida Panthers for D Greg Hawgood (March 19, 1994). ... Loaned by Panthers

to Detroit Vipers of IHL (February 14, 1995). ... Signed as free agent by Hartford Whalers (July 18, 1995). ... Tore knee ligament (December 20, 1996); missed 25 games. ... Whalers franchise moved to North Carolina and renamed Carolina Hurricanes for 1997-98 season; NHL approved move on June 25, 1997.
MISCELLANEOUS: Member of Stanley Cup championship team (1992).

Season Team	League	REGULAR SEASON								PLAYOFFS				
		Gms.	G	A	Pts.	PIM	+/-	PP	SH	Gms.	G	A	Pts.	PIM
84-85— Oshawa	OHL	59	7	11	18	16	...	...	...	—	—	—	—	—
85-86— Oshawa	OHL	62	13	19	32	23	...	...	...	6	0	1	1	0
86-87— Oshawa	OHL	54	14	9	23	22	...	...	...	15	3	2	5	5
87-88— Oshawa	OHL	64	29	39	68	59	...	...	...	4	2	3	5	0
88-89— Muskegon	IHL	58	21	21	42	58	...	...	...	11	3	5	8	11
89-90— Muskegon	IHL	80	30	47	77	39	...	...	...	6	1	1	2	7
90-91— Pittsburgh	NHL	11	0	2	2	2	0	0	0	—	—	—	—	—
— Muskegon	IHL	62	23	29	52	18	...	...	...	5	1	3	4	2
91-92— Pittsburgh	NHL	2	0	0	0	0	0	0	0	—	—	—	—	—
— Muskegon	IHL	44	19	16	35	38	...	...	...	10	5	4	9	9
92-93— Pittsburgh	NHL	58	5	4	9	14	-5	0	0	12	3	2	5	0
— Cleveland	IHL	3	2	1	3	0	...	...	...	—	—	—	—	—
93-94— Pittsburgh	NHL	63	3	5	8	20	-1	0	0	—	—	—	—	—
— Florida	NHL	7	0	0	0	0	0	0	0	—	—	—	—	—
94-95— Florida	NHL	3	0	0	0	0	0	0	0	—	—	—	—	—
— Detroit	IHL	25	8	12	20	6	...	...	...	5	1	0	1	0
95-96— Springfield	AHL	72	22	20	42	32	...	...	...	10	3	0	3	2
96-97— Springfield	AHL	38	18	14	32	19	...	...	...	16	7	3	10	4
— Hartford	NHL	10	0	2	2	0	2	0	0	—	—	—	—	—
NHL totals (6 years)		154	8	13	21	36	-4	0	0	12	3	2	5	0

DANIELS, SCOTT   LW   FLYERS

PERSONAL: Born September 19, 1969, in Prince Albert, Sask. ... 6-3/200. ... Shoots left.
TRANSACTIONS/CAREER NOTES: Traded by Kamloops Blazers with C Mario Desjardins, Wayne MacDonald, Jason Bennings and future considerations to New Westminster Bruins for C Glenn Mulvenna and D Garth Premak (February 1987). ... Selected by Hartford Whalers in seventh round (sixth Whalers pick, 136th overall) of NHL entry draft (June 17, 1989). ... Injured knee (March 25, 1995); missed seven games. ... Suffered mild concussion (February 21, 1996); missed two games. ... Signed as free agent by Philadelphia Flyers (June 18, 1996). ... Fined $1,000 by NHL for fighting (November 13, 1996). ... Strained left buttock (November 4, 1996); missed two games. ... Bruised right quadricep (December 21, 1996); missed ten games. ... Bruised wrist (February 15, 1997); missed three games. ... Suffered from tonsillitis (March 1, 1997); missed two games. ... Strained rib muscle (March 22, 1997); missed seven games. ... Suffered charley horse (April 12, 1997); missed final game of regular season.

Season Team	League	REGULAR SEASON								PLAYOFFS				
		Gms.	G	A	Pts.	PIM	+/-	PP	SH	Gms.	G	A	Pts.	PIM
86-87— Kamloops	WHL	43	6	4	10	66	...	...	...	—	—	—	—	—
— New Westminster	WHL	19	4	7	11	30	...	...	...	—	—	—	—	—
87-88— New Westminster	WHL	37	6	11	17	157	...	...	...	—	—	—	—	—
— Regina	WHL	19	2	3	5	83	...	...	...	—	—	—	—	—
88-89— Regina	WHL	64	21	26	47	241	...	...	...	—	—	—	—	—
89-90— Regina	WHL	53	28	31	59	171	...	...	...	—	—	—	—	—
90-91— Springfield	AHL	40	2	6	8	121	...	...	...	—	—	—	—	—
— Louisville	ECHL	9	5	3	8	34	...	...	...	1	0	2	2	0
91-92— Springfield	AHL	54	7	15	22	213	...	...	...	10	0	0	0	32
92-93— Hartford	NHL	1	0	0	0	19	0	0	0	—	—	—	—	—
— Springfield	AHL	60	11	12	23	181	...	...	...	12	2	7	9	12
93-94— Springfield	AHL	52	9	11	20	185	...	...	...	6	0	1	1	53
94-95— Springfield	AHL	48	9	5	14	277	...	...	...	—	—	—	—	—
— Hartford	NHL	12	0	2	2	55	1	0	0	—	—	—	—	—
95-96— Hartford	NHL	53	3	4	7	254	-4	0	0	—	—	—	—	—
— Springfield	AHL	6	4	1	5	17	...	...	...	—	—	—	—	—
96-97— Philadelphia	NHL	56	5	3	8	237	2	0	0	—	—	—	—	—
NHL totals (4 years)		122	8	9	17	565	-1	0	0					

DARBY, CRAIG   C   FLYERS

PERSONAL: Born September 26, 1972, in Oneida, N.Y. ... 6-3/180. ... Shoots right.
HIGH SCHOOL: Albany (N.Y.) Academy.
COLLEGE: Providence.
TRANSACTIONS/CAREER NOTES: Selected by Montreal Canadiens in second round (third Canadiens pick, 43rd overall) of NHL entry draft (June 22, 1991). ... Traded by Canadiens with LW Kirk Muller and D Mathieu Schneider to New York Islanders for D Vladimir Malakhov and C Pierre Turgeon (April 5, 1995). ... Claimed on waivers by Philadelphia Flyers (June 4, 1996).
HONORS: Named Hockey East co-Rookie of the Year with Ian Moran (1991-92). ... Named to Hockey East All-Rookie team (1991-92).

Season Team	League	REGULAR SEASON								PLAYOFFS				
		Gms.	G	A	Pts.	PIM	+/-	PP	SH	Gms.	G	A	Pts.	PIM
89-90— Albany Academy	N.Y. H.S.	29	32	53	85	...	...	...	...	—	—	—	—	—
90-91— Albany Academy	N.Y. H.S.	27	33	61	94	53	...	...	...	—	—	—	—	—
91-92— Providence College	Hockey East	35	17	24	41	47	...	...	...	—	—	—	—	—
92-93— Providence College	Hockey East	35	11	21	32	62	...	...	...	—	—	—	—	—
93-94— Fredericton	AHL	66	23	33	56	51	...	...	...	—	—	—	—	—
94-95— Fredericton	AHL	64	21	47	68	82	...	...	...	—	—	—	—	—
— Montreal	NHL	10	0	2	2	0	-5	0	0	—	—	—	—	—
— New York Islanders	NHL	3	0	0	0	0	-1	0	0	—	—	—	—	—

Season Team	League	REGULAR SEASON								PLAYOFFS				
		Gms.	G	A	Pts.	PIM	+/-	PP	SH	Gms.	G	A	Pts.	PIM
95-96— Worcester	AHL	68	22	28	50	47	...	...	...	4	1	1	2	2
— New York Islanders....	NHL	10	0	2	2	0	-1	0	0	—	—	—	—	—
96-97— Philadelphia	AHL	59	26	33	59	24	...	...	...	10	3	6	9	0
— Philadelphia	NHL	9	1	4	5	2	2	0	1	—	—	—	—	—
NHL totals (3 years)		32	1	8	9	2	-5	0	1					

DARLING, DION   D   CANADIENS

PERSONAL: Born October 22, 1974, in Edmonton. ... 6-3/205. ... Shoots left.
TRANSACTIONS/CAREER NOTES: Selected by Montreal Canadiens in fifth round (seventh Canadiens pick, 125th overall) of NHL entry draft (June 26, 1993).

Season Team	League	REGULAR SEASON								PLAYOFFS				
		Gms.	G	A	Pts.	PIM	+/-	PP	SH	Gms.	G	A	Pts.	PIM
91-92— St. Albert...................	AJHL	29	5	15	20	101	...	...	...	—	—	—	—	—
92-93— Spokane......................	WHL	68	1	4	5	168	...	...	...	9	0	1	1	14
93-94— Moose Jaw	WHL	23	4	6	10	96	...	...	...	—	—	—	—	—
— Spokane......................	WHL	45	1	8	9	190	...	...	...	—	—	—	—	—
— Wheeling....................	ECHL	3	0	1	1	7	...	...	...	9	0	1	1	14
94-95— Wheeling....................	ECHL	4	0	0	0	24	...	...	...	—	—	—	—	—
— Fredericton................	AHL	51	0	2	2	153	...	...	...	—	—	—	—	—
95-96— Fredericton................	AHL	74	3	2	5	215	...	...	...	6	0	0	0	5
96-97— Fredericton................	AHL	58	2	6	8	150	...	...	...	—	—	—	—	—

DAVIDSSON, JOHAN   C   MIGHTY DUCKS

PERSONAL: Born January 6, 1976, in Jonkoping, Sweden. ... 5-11/170. ... Shoots left.
TRANSACTIONS/CAREER NOTES: Selected by Mighty Ducks of Anaheim in second round (second Mighty Ducks pick, 28th overall) of NHL entry draft (June 28, 1994).

Season Team	League	REGULAR SEASON								PLAYOFFS				
		Gms.	G	A	Pts.	PIM	+/-	PP	SH	Gms.	G	A	Pts.	PIM
92-93— HV 71 Jonkoping	Sweden	8	1	0	1	0	...	...	...	—	—	—	—	—
93-94— HV 71 Jonkoping	Sweden	38	2	5	7	4	...	...	...	—	—	—	—	—
94-95— HV 71 Jonkoping	Sweden	37	4	7	11	20	...	...	...	13	3	2	5	0
95-96— HV 71 Jonkoping	Sweden	39	7	11	18	20	...	...	...	4	0	2	2	0
96-97— HV 71 Jonkoping	Sweden	50	18	21	39	18	...	...	...	5	0	3	3	2

DAVIS, CHRIS   G   SABRES

PERSONAL: Born December 1, 1974, in Calgary. ... 6-3/165. ... Catches left.
HIGH SCHOOL: Lord Beaverbrook Secondary (Calgary).
COLLEGE: Alaska-Anchorage.
TRANSACTIONS/CAREER NOTES: Selected by Buffalo Sabres in 10th round (eighth Sabres pick, 246th overall) of NHL entry draft (June 26, 1993).

Season Team	League	REGULAR SEASON							PLAYOFFS					
		Gms.	Min	W	L	T	GA	SO	Avg.	Gms.	Min.	W	L	GA	SO	Avg.
92-93— Calgary Royals	AJHL	42	2374	22	17	...	134	3	3.39	—	—	—	—	—	—	—
93-94— Alaska-Anchorage.........	WCHA	9	390	2	4	0	27	0	4.15	—	—	—	—	—	—	—
94-95— Alaska-Anchorage.........	WCHA	14	671	4	6	0	49	0	4.38	—	—	—	—	—	—	—
95-96— Alaska-Anchorage.........	WCHA	22	1146	6	10	3	80	1	4.19	—	—	—	—	—	—	—
96-97— Alaska-Anchorage.........	WCHA	9	365	1	6	0	22	0	3.62	—	—	—	—	—	—	—

DAW, JEFF   C   OILERS

PERSONAL: Born February 28, 1972, in Carlisle, Ont. ... 6-3/195. ... Shoots right.
COLLEGE: Massachusetts-Lowell.
TRANSACTIONS/CAREER NOTES: Signed as free agent by Edmonton Oilers (June 12, 1996).

Season Team	League	REGULAR SEASON								PLAYOFFS				
		Gms.	G	A	Pts.	PIM	+/-	PP	SH	Gms.	G	A	Pts.	PIM
92-93— Mass.-Lowell	Hockey East	37	12	18	30	14	...	...	...	—	—	—	—	—
93-94— Mass.-Lowell	Hockey East	40	6	12	18	12	...	...	...	—	—	—	—	—
94-95— Mass.-Lowell	Hockey East	40	27	15	42	24	...	...	...	—	—	—	—	—
95-96— Mass.-Lowell	Hockey East	40	23	28	51	10	...	...	...	—	—	—	—	—
96-97— Hamilton	AHL	56	11	8	19	39	...	...	...	19	4	5	9	0

DAWE, JASON   RW   SABRES

PERSONAL: Born May 29, 1973, in North York, Ont. ... 5-10/189. ... Shoots left. ... Name pronounced DAW.
TRANSACTIONS/CAREER NOTES: Tore ankle ligaments (September 1989). ... Selected by Buffalo Sabres in second round (second Sabres pick, 35th overall) of NHL entry draft (June 22, 1991). ... Slightly sprained knee (February 11, 1995); missed three games. ... Fractured ribs (February 21, 1996); missed six games.
HONORS: Won George Parsons Trophy (1992-93). ... Named to Can.HL All-Star second team (1992-93). ... Named to OHL All-Star first team (1992-93).
STATISTICAL PLATEAUS: Three-goal games: 1995-96 (1).

Season Team	League	REGULAR SEASON								PLAYOFFS				
		Gms.	G	A	Pts.	PIM	+/-	PP	SH	Gms.	G	A	Pts.	PIM
89-90— Peterborough.............	OHL	50	15	18	33	19	...	...	...	12	4	7	11	4
90-91— Peterborough.............	OHL	66	43	27	70	43	...	...	...	4	3	1	4	0
91-92— Peterborough.............	OHL	66	53	55	108	55	...	...	...	4	5	0	5	0
92-93— Peterborough.............	OHL	59	58	68	126	80	...	...	...	21	18	33	51	18
— Rochester.................	AHL	0	0	0	0	0				3	1	0	1	0
93-94— Rochester.................	AHL	48	22	14	36	44	...	...	...	—	—	—	—	—
— Buffalo	NHL	32	6	7	13	12	1	3	0	6	0	1	1	6
94-95— Rochester.................	AHL	44	27	19	46	24	...	...	...	—	—	—	—	—
— Buffalo	NHL	42	7	4	11	19	-6	0	1	5	2	1	3	6
95-96— Buffalo	NHL	67	25	25	50	33	-8	8	1	—	—	—	—	—
— Rochester.................	AHL	7	5	4	9	2	...	...	...	—	—	—	—	—
96-97— Buffalo	NHL	81	22	26	48	32	14	4	1	11	2	1	3	6
NHL totals (4 years)		222	60	62	122	96	1	15	3	22	4	3	7	18

DAZE, ERIC   LW   BLACKHAWKS

PERSONAL: Born July 2, 1975, in Montreal. ... 6-4/215. ... Shoots left. ... Name pronounced dah-ZAY.
TRANSACTIONS/CAREER NOTES: Selected by Chicago Blackhawks in fourth round (fifth Blackhawks pick, 90th overall) of NHL entry draft (June 26, 1993). ... Sprained left ankle (preseason, 1996-97 season); missed eight games. ... Suffered from the flu (January 20, 1997); missed one game.
HONORS: Named to QMJHL All-Star first team (1993-94 and 1994-95). ... Won Can.HL Most Sportsmanlike Player of the Year Award (1994-95). ... Won Frank J. Selke Trophy (1994-95). ... Named NHL Rookie of the Year by The Sporting News (1995-96). ... Named to NHL All-Rookie team (1995-96).
STATISTICAL PLATEAUS: Three-goal games: 1996-97 (1).

Season Team	League	REGULAR SEASON								PLAYOFFS				
		Gms.	G	A	Pts.	PIM	+/-	PP	SH	Gms.	G	A	Pts.	PIM
92-93— Beauport	QMJHL	68	19	36	55	24	...	...	...	—	—	—	—	—
93-94— Beauport	QMJHL	66	59	48	107	31	...	...	...	15	16	8	24	2
94-95— Beauport	QMJHL	57	54	45	99	20	...	...	...	16	9	12	21	23
— Chicago......................	NHL	4	1	1	2	2	2	0	0	16	0	1	1	4
95-96— Chicago......................	NHL	80	30	23	53	18	16	2	0	10	3	5	8	0
96-97— Chicago......................	NHL	71	22	19	41	16	-4	11	0	6	2	1	3	2
NHL totals (3 years)		155	53	43	96	36	14	13	0	32	5	7	12	6

DEADMARSH, ADAM   RW   AVALANCHE

PERSONAL: Born May 10, 1975, in Trail, B.C. ... 6-0/195. ... Shoots right. ... Cousin of Butch Deadmarsh, left winger with three NHL teams (1970-71 through 1974-75).
HIGH SCHOOL: Lakeridge (Fruitvale, B.C.).
TRANSACTIONS/CAREER NOTES: Selected by Quebec Nordiques in first round (second Nordiques pick, 14th overall) of NHL entry draft (June 26, 1993). ... Nordiques franchise moved to Colorado and renamed Avalanche for 1995-96 season (June 21, 1995). ... Strained groin (April 3, 1996); missed four games.
MISCELLANEOUS: Member of Stanley Cup championship team (1996). ... Scored on a penalty shot (vs. Jeff Hackett, March 1, 1997).

Season Team	League	REGULAR SEASON								PLAYOFFS				
		Gms.	G	A	Pts.	PIM	+/-	PP	SH	Gms.	G	A	Pts.	PIM
91-92— Portland	WHL	68	30	30	60	81	...	...	...	6	3	3	6	13
92-93— Portland	WHL	58	33	36	69	126	...	...	...	16	7	8	15	29
93-94— Portland	WHL	65	43	56	99	212	...	...	...	10	9	8	17	33
94-95— Portland	WHL	29	28	20	48	129	...	...	...	—	—	—	—	—
— Quebec......................	NHL	48	9	8	17	56	16	0	0	6	0	1	1	0
95-96— Colorado	NHL	78	21	27	48	142	20	3	0	22	5	12	17	25
96-97— Colorado	NHL	78	33	27	60	136	8	10	3	17	3	6	9	24
NHL totals (3 years)		204	63	62	125	334	44	13	3	45	8	19	27	49

DEAN, KEVIN   D   DEVILS

PERSONAL: Born April 1, 1969, in Madison, Wis. ... 6-3/200. ... Shoots left.
HIGH SCHOOL: Culver (Ind.) Military Academy.
COLLEGE: New Hampshire.
TRANSACTIONS/CAREER NOTES: Selected by New Jersey Devils in fourth round (fourth Devils pick, 86th overall) of NHL entry draft (June 13, 1987). ... Suffered rib injury (September 19, 1996); missed three games.
HONORS: Named to AHL All-Star first team (1994-95).
MISCELLANEOUS: Member of Stanley Cup championship team (1995).

Season Team	League	REGULAR SEASON								PLAYOFFS				
		Gms.	G	A	Pts.	PIM	+/-	PP	SH	Gms.	G	A	Pts.	PIM
85-86— Culver Military	Indiana H.S.	35	28	44	72	48	...	...	...	—	—	—	—	—
86-87— Culver Military	Indiana H.S.	25	19	25	44	30	...	...	...	—	—	—	—	—
87-88— New Hampshire	Hockey East	27	1	6	7	34	...	...	...	—	—	—	—	—
88-89— New Hampshire	Hockey East	34	1	12	13	28	...	...	...	—	—	—	—	—
89-90— New Hampshire	Hockey East	39	2	6	8	42	...	...	...	—	—	—	—	—
90-91— New Hampshire	Hockey East	31	10	12	22	22	...	...	...	—	—	—	—	—
— Utica	AHL	7	0	1	1	2	...	...	...	—	—	—	—	—
91-92— Utica	AHL	23	0	3	3	6	...	...	...	—	—	—	—	—
— Cincinnati..................	ECHL	30	3	22	25	43	...	...	...	9	1	6	7	8

D

Season Team	League	REGULAR SEASON								PLAYOFFS				
		Gms.	G	A	Pts.	PIM	+/-	PP	SH	Gms.	G	A	Pts.	PIM
92-93— Utica	AHL	57	2	16	18	76	...	...	...	5	1	0	1	8
— Cincinnati	IHL	13	2	1	3	15	...	...	...	—	—	—	—	—
93-94— Albany	AHL	70	9	33	42	92	...	...	...	5	0	2	2	7
94-95— Albany	AHL	68	5	37	42	66	...	...	...	8	0	4	4	4
— New Jersey	NHL	17	0	1	1	4	6	0	0	3	0	2	2	0
95-96— New Jersey	NHL	41	0	6	6	28	4	0	0	—	—	—	—	—
— Albany	AHL	1	1	0	1	2	...	...	...	—	—	—	—	—
96-97— New Jersey	NHL	28	2	4	6	6	2	0	0	1	1	0	1	0
— Albany	AHL	2	0	1	1	4	...	...	...	—	—	—	—	—
NHL totals (3 years)		86	2	11	13	38	12	0	0	4	1	2	3	0

DeBRUSK, LOUIE   LW   OILERS

PERSONAL: Born March 19, 1971, in Cambridge, Ont. ... 6-2/230. ... Shoots left. ... Full name: Dennis Louis DeBrusk. ... Name pronounced duh-BRUHSK.
HIGH SCHOOL: Saugeen (Port Elgin, Ont.).
TRANSACTIONS/CAREER NOTES: Selected by New York Rangers in third round (fourth Rangers pick, 49th overall) of NHL entry draft (June 17, 1989). ... Traded by Rangers with C Bernie Nicholls, RW Steven Rice and future considerations to Edmonton Oilers for C Mark Messier and future considerations (October 4, 1991); Rangers traded D David Shaw to Oilers for D Jeff Beukeboom to complete deal (November 12, 1991). ... Separated shoulder (January 28, 1992); missed four games. ... Strained groin (January 1993); missed five games. ... Strained abdominal muscle (January 1993); missed 11 games. ... Underwent blood tests (April 17, 1995); missed one game. ... Suspended two games by NHL for headbutting an opponent (October 6, 1995). ... Injured elbow (November 26, 1995); missed 14 games. ... Suspended four games and fined $1,000 by NHL for slashing (October 9, 1996).

Season Team	League	REGULAR SEASON								PLAYOFFS				
		Gms.	G	A	Pts.	PIM	+/-	PP	SH	Gms.	G	A	Pts.	PIM
87-88— Stratford Jr. B	OHA	43	13	14	27	205	...	...	...	—	—	—	—	—
88-89— London	OHL	59	11	11	22	149	...	...	...	19	1	1	2	43
89-90— London	OHL	61	21	19	40	198	...	...	...	6	2	2	4	24
90-91— London	OHL	61	31	33	64	*223	...	...	...	7	2	2	4	14
— Binghamton	AHL	2	0	0	0	7	...	...	...	2	0	0	0	9
91-92— Edmonton	NHL	25	2	1	3	124	4	0	0	—	—	—	—	—
— Cape Breton	AHL	28	2	2	4	73	...	...	...	—	—	—	—	—
92-93— Edmonton	NHL	51	8	2	10	205	-16	0	0	—	—	—	—	—
93-94— Edmonton	NHL	48	4	6	10	185	-9	0	0	—	—	—	—	—
— Cape Breton	AHL	5	3	1	4	58	...	...	...	—	—	—	—	—
94-95— Edmonton	NHL	34	2	0	2	93	-4	0	0	—	—	—	—	—
95-96— Edmonton	NHL	38	1	3	4	96	-7	0	0	—	—	—	—	—
96-97— Edmonton	NHL	32	2	0	2	94	-6	0	0	6	0	0	0	4
NHL totals (6 years)		228	19	12	31	797	-38	0	0	6	0	0	0	4

DELISLE, JONATHAN   RW   CANADIENS

PERSONAL: Born June 30, 1977, in Montreal. ... 5-10/186. ... Shoots right. ... Name pronounced duh-LIHL.
TRANSACTIONS/CAREER NOTES: Selected by Montreal Canadiens in fourth round (fourth Canadiens pick, 86th overall) of NHL entry draft (July 8, 1995).

Season Team	League	REGULAR SEASON								PLAYOFFS				
		Gms.	G	A	Pts.	PIM	+/-	PP	SH	Gms.	G	A	Pts.	PIM
93-94— Verdun	QMJHL	61	16	17	33	130	...	...	...	4	0	1	1	14
94-95— Hull	QMJHL	60	21	38	59	218	...	...	...	19	11	8	19	43
95-96— Hull	QMJHL	62	31	57	88	193	...	...	...	18	6	13	19	64
96-97— Hull	QMJHL	61	35	53	88	210	...	...	...	14	11	13	24	48

DELISLE, XAVIER   RW   LIGHTNING

PERSONAL: Born May 24, 1977, in Quebec City. ... 5-11/184. ... Shoots right. ... Name pronounced ZAYV-yoor dih LIGHL.
TRANSACTIONS/CAREER NOTES: Selected by Tampa Bay Lightning in sixth round (fifth Lightning pick, 157th overall) of NHL entry draft (June 22, 1996).
HONORS: Named to QMJHL All-Star second team (1995-96). ... Named to Memorial Cup All-Star team (1995-96).

Season Team	League	REGULAR SEASON								PLAYOFFS				
		Gms.	G	A	Pts.	PIM	+/-	PP	SH	Gms.	G	A	Pts.	PIM
93-94— Granby	QMJHL	46	11	22	33	25	...	...	...	7	2	0	2	0
94-95— Granby	QMJHL	72	18	36	54	48	...	...	...	13	2	6	8	4
95-96— Granby	QMJHL	67	45	75	120	45	...	...	...	20	13	*27	*40	12
96-97— Granby	QMJHL	59	36	56	92	20	...	...	...	5	1	4	5	6

DEMITRA, PAVOL   RW   BLUES

PERSONAL: Born November 29, 1974, in Dubnica, Czechoslovakia. ... 6-0/189. ... Shoots left. ... Name pronounced PA-vuhl dih-MEE-truh.
TRANSACTIONS/CAREER NOTES: Selected by Ottawa Senators in ninth round (ninth Senators pick, 227th overall) of NHL entry draft (June 26,1993). ... Broke ankle (October 14, 1993); missed 23 games. ... Rights traded by Senators to St. Louis Blues for D Christer Olsson (November 27, 1996).

Season Team	League	REGULAR SEASON								PLAYOFFS				
		Gms.	G	A	Pts.	PIM	+/-	PP	SH	Gms.	G	A	Pts.	PIM
91-92— Sparta Dubnica	Czech Div. II	28	13	10	23	12	...	...	...	—	—	—	—	—
92-93— Dukla Trencin	Czech.	46	11	17	28	0	...	...	...	—	—	—	—	—
— CAPEH Dubnica	Czech Div. II	4	3	0	3	...	...	...	...	—	—	—	—	—
93-94— Ottawa	NHL	12	1	1	2	4	-7	1	0	—	—	—	—	—
— Prin. Edward Island ...	AHL	41	18	23	41	8	...	...	...	—	—	—	—	—
94-95— Prin. Edward Island ...	AHL	61	26	48	74	23	...	...	...	5	0	7	7	0
— Ottawa	NHL	16	4	3	7	0	-4	1	0	—	—	—	—	—
95-96— Prin. Edward Island ...	AHL	48	28	53	81	44	...	...	...	—	—	—	—	—
— Ottawa	NHL	31	7	10	17	6	-3	2	0	—	—	—	—	—
96-97— Las Vegas	IHL	22	8	13	21	10	...	...	...	—	—	—	—	—
— Grand Rapids	IHL	42	20	30	50	24	...	...	...	—	—	—	—	—
— St. Louis	NHL	8	3	0	3	2	0	2	0	6	1	3	4	6
NHL totals (4 years)		67	15	14	29	12	-14	6	0	6	1	3	4	6

DEMPSEY, NATHAN — D — MAPLE LEAFS

PERSONAL: Born July 14, 1974, in Spruce Grove, Alta. ... 6-0/170. ... Shoots left.
TRANSACTIONS/CAREER NOTES: Selected by Toronto Maple Leafs in 11th round (11th Leafs pick, 245th overall) of NHL entry draft (June 20, 1992).

Season Team	League	REGULAR SEASON								PLAYOFFS				
		Gms.	G	A	Pts.	PIM	+/-	PP	SH	Gms.	G	A	Pts.	PIM
91-92— Regina	WHL	70	4	22	26	72	...	...	...	—	—	—	—	—
92-93— St. John's	AHL	0	0	0	0	0	...	...	...	2	0	0	0	0
— Regina	WHL	72	12	29	41	95	...	...	...	13	3	8	11	14
93-94— Regina	WHL	56	14	36	50	100	...	...	...	4	0	0	0	4
94-95— St. John's	AHL	74	7	30	37	91	...	...	...	5	1	0	1	11
95-96— St. John's	AHL	73	5	15	20	103	...	...	...	4	1	0	1	9
96-97— St. John's	AHL	52	8	18	26	108	...	...	...	6	1	0	1	4
— Toronto	NHL	14	1	1	2	2	-2	0	0	—	—	—	—	—
NHL totals (1 year)		14	1	1	2	2	-2	0	0	—	—	—	—	—

DENIS, MARC — G — AVALANCHE

PERSONAL: Born August 1, 1977, in Montreal. ... 6-0/188. ... Catches left. ... Name pronounced deh-NEE.
TRANSACTIONS/CAREER NOTES: Selected by Colorado Avalanche in first round (first Avalanche pick, 25th overall) of NHL entry draft (July 8, 1995).
HONORS: Won Marcel Robert Trophy (1995-96). ... Won Can.HL Goaltender of the Year Award (1996-97). ... Won Jacques Plante Trophy (1996-97). ... Named to Can.HL All-Star first team (1996-97). ... Named to QMJHL All-Star first team (1996-97).

Season Team	League	REGULAR SEASON								PLAYOFFS						
		Gms.	Min.	W	L	T	GA	SO	Avg.	Gms.	Min.	W	L	GA	SO	Avg.
94-95—Chicoutimi	QMJHL	32	1688	17	9	1	98	0	3.48	6	374	4	2	19	1	3.05
95-96—Chicoutimi	QMJHL	51	2895	23	21	4	157	2	3.25	16	917	8	†8	66	0	4.32
96-97—Chicoutimi	QMJHL	41	2317	22	15	2	104	4	*2.69	*21	*1226	*11	*10	*70	*1	3.43
—Colorado......................	NHL	1	60	0	1	0	3	0	3.00	—	—	—	—	—	—	—
—Hershey	AHL	—	—	—	—	—	—	—	—	4	56	1	0	1	0	*1.07
NHL totals (1 year)		1	60	0	1	0	3	0	3.00							

DERKSEN, DUANE — G — CAPITALS

PERSONAL: Born July 7, 1968, in St. Boniface, Man. ... 6-1/180. ... Catches left. ... Full name: Duane Edward Derksen.
COLLEGE: Wisconsin.
TRANSACTIONS/CAREER NOTES: Selected by Washington Capitals in third round (fourth Capitals pick, 57th overall) of NHL entry draft (June 11, 1988).
HONORS: Named NCAA Tournament Most Outstanding Goalie (1989-90). ... Named to NCAA All-Tournament team (1989-90). ... Named to WCHA All-Star second team (1989-90 and 1990-91). ... Won WCHA Most Valuable Player Award (1991-92). ... Named to NCAA All-America West second team (1991-92). ... Named to WCHA All-Star first team (1991-92).

Season Team	League	REGULAR SEASON								PLAYOFFS						
		Gms.	Min	W	L	T	GA	SO	Avg.	Gms.	Min.	W	L	GA	SO	Avg.
86-87—Winkler	SOJHL	48	2140	...	...	...	171	1	4.79	—	—	—	—	—	—	—
87-88—Winkler	SOJHL	38	2294	...	...	...	198	0	5.18	—	—	—	—	—	—	—
88-89—Univ. of Wisconsin	WCHA	11	561	4	5	0	37	0	3.96	—	—	—	—	—	—	—
89-90—Univ. of Wisconsin	WCHA	41	2345	31	8	1	133	2	3.40	—	—	—	—	—	—	—
90-91—Univ. of Wisconsin	WCHA	42	2474	24	15	3	133	3	3.23	—	—	—	—	—	—	—
91-92—Univ. of Wisconsin	WCHA	35	2064	21	12	2	110	0	3.20	—	—	—	—	—	—	—
92-93—Baltimore	AHL	26	1247	6	13	3	86	0	4.14	4	188	1	1	7	0	2.23
—Hampton Roads...........	ECHL	13	747	7	5	‡0	48	0	3.86	—	—	—	—	—	—	—
93-94—Adirondack	AHL	11	600	4	6	0	37	0	3.70	—	—	—	—	—	—	—
—Rochester	AHL	6	235	2	1	0	14	0	3.57	—	—	—	—	—	—	—
—Milwaukee	IHL	9	490	4	2	‡2	28	0	3.43	—	—	—	—	—	—	—
94-95—Richmond....................	ECHL	27	1558	15	8	‡0	83	0	3.20	4	99	1	0	6	0	3.62
—Minnesota	IHL	7	251	1	3	‡3	21	0	5.02	—	—	—	—	—	—	—
95-96—Madison	Col.HL	40	2209	19	15	3	128	1	3.48	6	362	2	4	27	0	4.48
—Milwaukee	IHL	1	33	0	0	‡0	1	0	1.82	—	—	—	—	—	—	—
—Fort Wayne	IHL	1	22	0	0	‡0	3	0	8.18	—	—	—	—	—	—	—
96-97—Madison	Col.HL	59	3364	36	17	5	190	0	3.39	5	278	2	3	17	0	3.67
—Milwaukee	IHL	1	60	0	0	‡1	2	0	2.00	—	—	—	—	—	—	—

DEROUVILLE, PHILIPPE — G — PENGUINS

PERSONAL: Born August 7, 1974, in Arthabaska, Que. ... 6-1/185. ... Catches left. ... Name pronounced fih-LEEP duh-ROO-vihl.
TRANSACTIONS/CAREER NOTES: Selected by Pittsburgh Penguins in fifth round (fifth Penguins pick, 115th overall) of NHL entry draft (June 20, 1992). ... Suffered from mild case of mononucleosis (February 16, 1995); missed seven games.
HONORS: Won Raymond Lagace Trophy (1991-92). ... Named to QMJHL All-Star second team (1992-93 and 1993-94). ... Won Jacques Plante Trophy (1993-94).

			REGULAR SEASON								PLAYOFFS					
Season Team	League	Gms.	Min	W	L	T	GA	SO	Avg.	Gms.	Min.	W	L	GA	SO	Avg.
90-91—Longueuil	QMJHL	20	1030	13	6	0	50	0	2.91	—	—	—	—	—	—	—
91-92—Longueuil	QMJHL	34	1854	20	6	3	99	2	3.20	11	593	†7	2	28	†1	2.83
92-93—Verdun	QMJHL	*61	*3491	30	27	2	210	1	3.61	4	257	0	4	18	0	4.20
93-94—Verdun	QMJHL	51	2845	28	22	0	145	1	*3.06	4	210	0	4	14	0	4.00
94-95—Verdun	QMJHL	1	60	1	0	0	3	0	3.00	—	—	—	—	—	—	—
—Cleveland	IHL	41	2369	24	10	‡5	131	1	3.32	—	—	—	—	—	—	—
95-96—Cleveland	IHL	38	2008	19	11	‡3	129	1	3.86	—	—	—	—	—	—	—
96-97—Kansas City	IHL	26	1470	11	11	‡4	69	2	2.82	2	32	0	1	4	0	7.35
—Pittsburgh	NHL	2	77	0	0	0	6	0	4.68	—	—	—	—	—	—	—
NHL totals (1 year)		2	77	0	0	0	6	0	4.68							

DESCOTEAUX, MATHIEU — D — OILERS

PERSONAL: Born September 23, 1977, in Pierreville, Que. ... 6-3/200. ... Shoots left. ... Name pronounced day-koh-TOH.
TRANSACTIONS/CAREER NOTES: Selected by Edmonton Oilers in first round (second Oilers pick, 19th overall) of NHL entry draft (June 22, 1996).

			REGULAR SEASON							PLAYOFFS			
Season Team	League	Gms.	G	A	Pts.	PIM	+/-	PP	SH	Gms.	G	A	Pts.	PIM
94-95 — Shawinigan	QMJHL	50	3	2	5	28	...	...	...	—	—	—	—	—
95-96 — Shawinigan	QMJHL	69	2	13	15	129	...	...	...	6	0	0	0	6
96-97 — Shawinigan	QMJHL	38	6	18	24	103	...	...	...	—	—	—	—	—
— Hull	QMJHL	32	6	19	25	34	...	...	...	14	2	5	7	20

D

DESJARDINS, ERIC — D — FLYERS

PERSONAL: Born June 14, 1969, in Rouyn, Que. ... 6-1/200. ... Shoots right. ... Name pronounced day-zhar-DAN.
TRANSACTIONS/CAREER NOTES: Selected by Montreal Canadiens as underage junior in second round (third Canadiens pick, 38th overall) of NHL entry draft (June 13, 1987). ... Suffered from the flu (January 1989). ... Pulled groin (November 2, 1989); missed seven games. ... Sprained left ankle (January 26, 1991); missed 16 games. ... Fractured right thumb (December 8, 1991); missed two games. ... Traded by Canadiens with LW Gilbert Dionne and C John LeClair to Philadelphia Flyers for RW Mark Recchi and third-round pick (C Martin Hohenberger) in 1995 draft (February 9, 1995). ... Slightly strained groin (March 28, 1995); missed one game. ... Reinjured groin (April 1, 1995); missed three games. ... Suffered from the flu (December 26, 1995); missed one game.
HONORS: Named to QMJHL All-Star second team (1986-87). ... Won Emile (Butch) Bouchard Trophy (1987-88). ... Named to QMJHL All-Star first team (1987-88). ... Played in NHL All-Star Game (1992 and 1996).
RECORDS: Shares NHL single-game playoff record for most goals by defensemen—3 (June 3, 1993).
MISCELLANEOUS: Member of Stanley Cup championship team (1993).

			REGULAR SEASON							PLAYOFFS			
Season Team	League	Gms.	G	A	Pts.	PIM	+/-	PP	SH	Gms.	G	A	Pts.	PIM
86-87 — Granby	QMJHL	66	14	24	38	75	...	...	...	8	3	2	5	10
87-88 — Granby	QMJHL	62	18	49	67	138	...	...	...	5	0	3	3	10
— Sherbrooke	AHL	3	0	0	0	6	...	...	...	4	0	2	2	2
88-89 — Montreal	NHL	36	2	12	14	26	9	1	0	14	1	1	2	6
89-90 — Montreal	NHL	55	3	13	16	51	1	1	0	6	0	0	0	10
90-91 — Montreal	NHL	62	7	18	25	27	7	0	0	13	1	4	5	8
91-92 — Montreal	NHL	77	6	32	38	50	17	4	0	11	3	3	6	4
92-93 — Montreal	NHL	82	13	32	45	98	20	7	0	20	4	10	14	23
93-94 — Montreal	NHL	84	12	23	35	97	-1	6	1	7	0	2	2	4
94-95 — Montreal	NHL	9	0	6	6	2	2	0	0	—	—	—	—	—
— Philadelphia	NHL	34	5	18	23	12	10	1	0	15	4	4	8	10
95-96 — Philadelphia	NHL	80	7	40	47	45	19	5	0	12	0	6	6	2
96-97 — Philadelphia	NHL	82	12	34	46	50	25	5	1	19	2	8	10	12
NHL totals (9 years)		601	67	228	295	458	109	30	2	117	15	38	53	79

DEULING, JARRETT — LW — ISLANDERS

PERSONAL: Born March 4, 1974, in Vernon, B.C. ... 5-11/194. ... Shoots left. ... Name pronounced DOO-lihng.
HIGH SCHOOL: Norkam Secondary (Kamloops, B.C.).
TRANSACTIONS/CAREER NOTES: Selected by New York Islanders in third round (second Islanders pick, 56th overall) of NHL entry draft (June 20, 1992). ... Sprained left ankle (April 2, 1996); missed four games.
HONORS: Won WHL Playoff Most Valuable Player Award (1991-92).

			REGULAR SEASON							PLAYOFFS			
Season Team	League	Gms.	G	A	Pts.	PIM	+/-	PP	SH	Gms.	G	A	Pts.	PIM
90-91 — Kamloops	WHL	48	4	12	16	43	...	...	...	12	5	2	7	7
91-92 — Kamloops	WHL	68	28	26	54	79	...	...	...	17	10	6	16	18
92-93 — Kamloops	WHL	68	31	32	63	93	...	...	...	13	6	7	13	14
93-94 — Kamloops	WHL	70	44	59	103	171	...	...	...	18	*13	8	21	43
94-95 — Worcester	AHL	63	11	8	19	37	...	...	...	—	—	—	—	—

Season Team	League	REGULAR SEASON								PLAYOFFS				
		Gms.	G	A	Pts.	PIM	+/-	PP	SH	Gms.	G	A	Pts.	PIM
95-96— New York Islanders....	NHL	14	0	1	1	11	-1	0	0	—	—	—	—	—
— Worcester	AHL	57	16	7	23	57	...	...	...	4	1	2	3	2
96-97— Kentucky	AHL	58	15	31	46	57	...	...	...	4	3	0	3	8
— New York Islanders....	NHL	1	0	0	0	0	0	0	0	—	—	—	—	—
NHL totals (2 years)		15	0	1	1	11	-1	0	0					

DEVEREAUX, BOYD — LW — OILERS

PERSONAL: Born April 16, 1978, in Seaforth, Ont. ... 6-2/195. ... Shoots left. ... Name pronounced DEH-vuh-roh.
TRANSACTIONS/CAREER NOTES: Selected by Edmonton Oilers in first round (first Oilers pick, sixth overall) of NHL entry draft (June 22, 1996).
HONORS: Won Can.HL Scholastic Player of the Year Award (1995-96). ... Named to OHL All-Rookie second team (1995-96). ... Won Bobby Smith Trophy (1995-96).

Season Team	League	REGULAR SEASON								PLAYOFFS				
		Gms.	G	A	Pts.	PIM	+/-	PP	SH	Gms.	G	A	Pts.	PIM
93-94— Stratford	OPJHL	46	12	27	39	8	...	...	...	—	—	—	—	—
94-95— Stratford	OPJHL	45	31	74	105	21	...	...	...	—	—	—	—	—
95-96— Kitchener	OHL	66	20	38	58	35	...	...	...	12	3	7	10	4
96-97— Kitchener	OHL	54	28	41	69	37	...	...	...	13	4	11	15	8
— Hamilton	AHL	—	—	—	—	—	...	...	...	1	0	1	1	0

De VRIES, GREG — D — OILERS

PERSONAL: Born January 4, 1973, in Sundridge, Ont. ... 6-3/218. ... Shoots left. ... Name pronounced duh-VREES.
COLLEGE: Bowling Green State.
TRANSACTIONS/CAREER NOTES: Signed as free agent by Edmonton Oilers (March 28, 1994). ... Sprained ankle (January 26, 1997); missed four games.

Season Team	League	REGULAR SEASON								PLAYOFFS				
		Gms.	G	A	Pts.	PIM	+/-	PP	SH	Gms.	G	A	Pts.	PIM
91-92— Bowling Green	CCHA	24	0	3	3	20	...	...	...	—	—	—	—	—
92-93— Niagara Falls	OHL	62	3	23	26	86	...	...	...	4	0	1	1	6
93-94— Niagara Falls	OHL	64	5	40	45	135	...	...	...	—	—	—	—	—
— Cape Breton	AHL	9	0	0	0	11	...	...	...	1	0	0	0	0
94-95— Cape Breton	AHL	77	5	19	24	68	...	...	...	—	—	—	—	—
95-96— Cape Breton	AHL	58	9	30	39	174	...	...	...	—	—	—	—	—
— Edmonton	NHL	13	1	1	2	12	-2	0	0	—	—	—	—	—
96-97— Hamilton	AHL	34	4	14	18	26	...	...	...	—	—	—	—	—
— Edmonton	NHL	37	0	4	4	52	-2	0	0	12	0	1	1	8
NHL totals (2 years)		50	1	5	6	64	-4	0	0	12	0	1	1	8

DEWOLF, JOSHUA — D — DEVILS

PERSONAL: Born July 25, 1977, in Bloomington, Minn. ... 6-2/190. ... Shoots left.
HIGH SCHOOL: Twin Cities (Bloomington, Minn.).
COLLEGE: St. Cloud (Minn.) State.
TRANSACTIONS/CAREER NOTES: Selected by New Jersey Devils in second round (third Devils pick, 41st overall) of NHL entry draft (June 22, 1996).

Season Team	League	REGULAR SEASON								PLAYOFFS				
		Gms.	G	A	Pts.	PIM	+/-	PP	SH	Gms.	G	A	Pts.	PIM
93-94— Bloom. Jefferson	USHL	25	1	14	15	32	...	...	...	—	—	—	—	—
94-95— Bloom. Jefferson	USHL	28	6	22	28	52	...	...	...	—	—	—	—	—
95-96— Twin Cities	Tier II	40	11	15	26	38	...	...	...	—	—	—	—	—
96-97— St. Cloud State..........	WCHA	31	3	11	14	62	...	...	...	—	—	—	—	—

DIDUCK, GERALD — D — COYOTES

PERSONAL: Born April 6, 1965, in Edmonton. ... 6-2/217. ... Shoots right. ... Name pronounced DIH-dihk.
TRANSACTIONS/CAREER NOTES: Selected by New York Islanders as underage junior in first round (second Islanders pick, 16th overall) of NHL entry draft (June 8, 1983). ... Fractured left foot (November 1987). ... Fractured right hand (November 1988). ... Injured knee (January 1989). ... Traded by Islanders to Montreal Canadiens for D Craig Ludwig (September 4, 1990). ... Traded by Canadiens to Vancouver Canucks for fourth-round pick (LW Vladimir Vujtek) in 1991 draft (January 12, 1991). ... Bruised knee (March 16, 1991). ... Strained groin (January 4, 1993); missed three games. ... Suffered stress fracture in ankle (January 1, 1994); missed 14 games. ... Bruised foot (February 17, 1994); missed six games. ... Suffered eye contusion (March 31, 1994); missed five games. ... Traded by Canucks to Chicago Blackhawks for RW Bogdan Savenko and third-round pick (LW Larry Courville) in 1995 draft (April 7, 1995). ... Signed as free agent by Hartford Whalers (August 1, 1995). ... Strained hamstring (November 4, 1996); missed four games. ... Suffered hernia (December 16, 1996); missed nine games. ... Traded by Whalers to Phoenix Coyotes for RW Chris Murray (March 18, 1997).

Season Team	League	REGULAR SEASON								PLAYOFFS				
		Gms.	G	A	Pts.	PIM	+/-	PP	SH	Gms.	G	A	Pts.	PIM
81-82— Lethbridge	WHL	71	1	15	16	81	...	...	...	12	0	3	3	27
82-83— Lethbridge	WHL	67	8	16	24	151	...	...	...	20	3	12	15	49
83-84— Lethbridge	WHL	65	10	24	34	133	...	...	...	5	1	4	5	27
— Indianapolis	IHL	—	—	—	—	—	...	...	...	10	1	6	7	19
84-85— New York Islanders....	NHL	65	2	8	10	80	2	0	0	—	—	—	—	—
85-86— New York Islanders....	NHL	10	1	2	3	2	5	0	0	—	—	—	—	—
— Springfield	AHL	61	6	14	20	175	...	...	...	—	—	—	—	—

Season Team	League	REGULAR SEASON Gms.	G	A	Pts.	PIM	+/-	PP	SH	PLAYOFFS Gms.	G	A	Pts.	PIM
86-87— Springfield	AHL	45	6	8	14	120	...	...	...	—	—	—	—	—
— New York Islanders....	NHL	30	2	3	5	67	-3	0	0	14	0	1	1	35
87-88— New York Islanders....	NHL	68	7	12	19	113	22	4	0	6	1	0	1	42
88-89— New York Islanders....	NHL	65	11	21	32	155	9	6	0	—	—	—	—	—
89-90— New York Islanders....	NHL	76	3	17	20	163	2	1	0	5	0	0	0	12
90-91— Montreal	NHL	32	1	2	3	39	3	0	0	—	—	—	—	—
— Vancouver	NHL	31	3	7	10	66	-8	0	0	6	1	0	1	11
91-92— Vancouver	NHL	77	6	21	27	229	-3	2	0	5	0	0	0	10
92-93— Vancouver	NHL	80	6	14	20	171	32	0	1	12	4	2	6	12
93-94— Vancouver	NHL	55	1	10	11	72	2	0	0	24	1	7	8	22
94-95— Vancouver	NHL	22	1	3	4	15	-8	1	0	—	—	—	—	—
— Chicago	NHL	13	1	0	1	48	3	0	0	16	1	3	4	22
95-96— Hartford	NHL	79	1	9	10	88	7	0	0	—	—	—	—	—
96-97— Hartford	NHL	56	1	10	11	40	-9	0	0	—	—	—	—	—
— Phoenix	NHL	11	1	2	3	23	2	1	0	7	0	0	0	10
NHL totals (13 years)		770	48	141	189	1371	58	15	1	95	8	13	21	176

DiMAIO, ROB — LW — BRUINS

PERSONAL: Born February 19, 1968, in Calgary. ... 5-10/190. ... Shoots right. ... Name pronounced duh-MIGH-oh.

TRANSACTIONS/CAREER NOTES: Traded by Kamloops Blazers with LW Dave Mackey and C Kalvin Knibbs to Medicine Hat Tigers for LW Doug Pickel and LW Sean Pass (December 1985). ... Selected by New York Islanders in sixth round (sixth Islanders pick, 118th overall) of NHL entry draft (June 13, 1987). ... Suspended two games by WHL for leaving bench during fight (January 28, 1988). ... Bruised left hand (February 1989). ... Sprained clavicle (November 1989). ... Sprained wrist (February 20, 1992); missed four games. ... Reinjured wrist (February 29, 1992); missed final 17 games of season. ... Underwent surgery to repair torn ligaments in wrist (March 11, 1992). ... Selected by Tampa Bay Lightning in NHL expansion draft (June 18, 1992). ... Bruised wrist (November 28, 1992); missed four games. ... Sprained ankle (February 14, 1993); missed nine games. ... Reinjured right ankle (March 20, 1993); missed three games. ... Reinjured right ankle (April 1, 1993); missed remainder of season. ... Broke left leg (October 16, 1993); missed 27 games. ... Traded by Lightning to Philadelphia Flyers for RW Jim Cummins and fourth-round pick in 1995 draft (March 18, 1994). ... Bruised foot (February 28, 1995); missed two games. ... Suffered from the flu (April 16, 1995); missed one game. ... Suffered bone bruise in left leg (December 16, 1995); missed 14 games. ... Sprained right knee (March 29, 1996); missed final eight games of regular season. ... Selected by San Jose Sharks from Flyers in waiver draft for cash (September 30, 1996). ... Traded by Sharks to Boston Bruins for fifth-round pick (RW Adam Nittel) in 1997 draft (September 30, 1996). ... Strained knee (November 6, 1996); missed five games. ... Suffered from the flu (December 17, 1996); missed one game. ... Sprained knee (March 8, 1997); missed two games. ... Injured hip (April 5, 1997); missed two games.

HONORS: Won Stafford Smythe Memorial Trophy (1987-88). ... Named to Memorial Cup All-Star team (1987-88).

Season Team	League	REGULAR SEASON Gms.	G	A	Pts.	PIM	+/-	PP	SH	PLAYOFFS Gms.	G	A	Pts.	PIM
84-85— Kamloops	WHL	55	9	18	27	29	...	...	...	—	—	—	—	—
85-86— Kamloops	WHL	6	1	0	1	0	...	...	...	—	—	—	—	—
— Medicine Hat	WHL	55	20	30	50	82	...	...	...	—	—	—	—	—
86-87— Medicine Hat	WHL	70	27	43	70	130	...	...	...	20	7	11	18	46
87-88— Medicine Hat	WHL	54	47	43	90	120	...	...	...	14	12	19	†31	59
88-89— New York Islanders....	NHL	16	1	0	1	30	-6	0	0	—	—	—	—	—
— Springfield	AHL	40	13	18	31	67	...	...	...	—	—	—	—	—
89-90— New York Islanders....	NHL	7	0	0	0	2	0	0	0	1	1	0	1	4
— Springfield	AHL	54	25	27	52	69	...	...	...	16	4	7	11	45
90-91— New York Islanders....	NHL	1	0	0	0	0	0	0	0	—	—	—	—	—
— Capital District	AHL	12	3	4	7	22	...	...	...	—	—	—	—	—
91-92— New York Islanders....	NHL	50	5	2	7	43	-23	0	2	—	—	—	—	—
92-93— Tampa Bay	NHL	54	9	15	24	62	0	2	0	—	—	—	—	—
93-94— Tampa Bay	NHL	39	8	7	15	40	-5	2	0	—	—	—	—	—
— Philadelphia	NHL	14	3	5	8	6	1	0	0	—	—	—	—	—
94-95— Philadelphia	NHL	36	3	1	4	53	8	0	0	15	2	4	6	4
95-96— Philadelphia	NHL	59	6	15	21	58	0	1	1	3	0	0	0	0
96-97— Boston	NHL	72	13	15	28	82	-21	0	3	—	—	—	—	—
NHL totals (9 years)		348	48	60	108	376	-46	5	6	19	3	4	7	8

DINEEN, KEVIN — RW — HURRICANES

PERSONAL: Born October 28, 1963, in Quebec City. ... 5-11/190. ... Shoots right. ... Son of Bill Dineen, right winger, Detroit Red Wings and Chicago Blackhawks (1953-54 through 1957-58) and former head coach, Philadelphia Flyers (1992-93); brother of Gord Dineen, defenseman for four NHL teams (1982-83 through 1994-95); and brother of Peter Dineen, defenseman, Los Angeles Kings and Red Wings (1986-87 and 1989-90).

COLLEGE: Denver.

TRANSACTIONS/CAREER NOTES: Selected by Hartford Whalers as underage junior in third round (third Whalers pick, 56th overall) of NHL entry draft (June 9, 1982). ... Sprained left shoulder (October 24, 1985); missed nine games. ... Broke knuckle (January 12, 1986); missed seven games. ... Sprained knee (February 14, 1986). ... Suffered shoulder tendinitis (September 1988). ... Underwent surgery to right knee cartilage (August 1, 1990). ... Suffered hip pointer (November 28, 1990). ... Hospitalized due to complications caused by Crohn's disease (January 1, 1991); missed eight games. ... Injured groin (March 1991). ... Traded by Whalers to Philadelphia Flyers for C/LW Murray Craven and fourth-round pick (LW Kevin Smyth) in 1992 draft (November 13, 1991). ... Sprained wrist (February 4, 1992); missed one game. ... Strained right rotator cuff (December 3, 1992); missed one game. ... Suffered injury (October 9, 1993); missed one game. ... Bruised right shoulder (November 13, 1993); missed two games. ... Suffered recurrence of Crohn's disease (February 10, 1994); missed five games. ... Separated shoulder (March 8, 1994); missed three games. ... Strained left shoulder (January 31, 1995); missed three games. ... Reinjured left shoulder (February 11, 1995); missed three games. ... Traded by Flyers to Whalers for future considerations (December 28, 1995). ... Broke bone in wrist (February 9, 1996); missed 27 games. ... Strained abdominal muscle (March 13, 1997); missed one game. ... Whalers franchise moved to North Carolina and renamed Carolina Hurricanes for 1997-98 season; NHL approved move on June 25, 1997.

HONORS: Named to THE SPORTING NEWS All-Star second team (1986-87). ... Played in NHL All-Star Game (1988 and 1989). ... Named Bud Light/NHL Man of the Year (1990-91).

1989-90 (2), 1992-93 (3), 1993-94 (1). Total: 9. ... Four-

Whalers (1996-97). ... Failed to score on a penalty shot

PP	SH		Gms.	G	A	Pts.	PIM
...	...		—	—	—	—	—
...	...		—	—	—	—	—
...	...		—	—	—	—	—
...	...		—	—	—	—	—
...	...		—	—	—	—	—
8	4		—	—	—	—	—
6	0		10	6	7	13	18
11	0		6	2	1	3	31
5	0		6	4	4	8	8
20	1		4	1	0	1	10
8	2		6	3	2	5	18
4	0		6	1	0	1	16
1	0		—	—	—	—	—
5	3		—	—	—	—	—
6	3		—	—	—	—	—
5	1		—	—	—	—	—
...	...		—	—	—	—	—
4	0		15	6	4	10	18
0	0		—	—	—	—	—
0	0		—	—	—	—	—
8	0		—	—	—	—	—
91	14		53	23	18	41	119

FLAMES

es pick, 19th overall) of NHL entry draft (June 28, 1994).

PP	SH		Gms.	G	A	Pts.	PIM
...	...		4	0	0	0	0
...	...		13	1	7	8	39
...	...		3	1	0	1	9
...	...		19	12	11	23	60
...	...		1	0	0	0	0

hoots left. ... Name pronounced zhil-BAIR dee-AHN. ...
gs and New York Rangers (1971-72 through 1988-89).
d (fifth Canadiens pick, 81st overall) of NHL entry draft
roin (December 18, 1993); missed eight games. ... Traded
s for RW Mark Recchi and third-round pick (C Martin
, 1995); missed two games. ... Signed as free agent by

ond team (1995-96).

PP	SH		Gms.	G	A	Pts.	PIM
...	...		—	—	—	—	—
...	...		5	1	1	2	4
...	...		17	13	10	23	22
...	...		9	6	5	11	8
0	0		—	—	—	—	—
			—	—	—	—	—
7	0		11	3	4	7	10
6	1		20	6	6	12	20
			—	—	—	—	—
3	0		5	1	2	3	0
0	0		—	—	—	—	—
0	0		3	0	0	0	4
0	0		—	—	—	—	—
			—	—	—	—	—
0	0		—	—	—	—	—
...	...		—	—	—	—	—
16	1		39	10	12	22	34

D

DiPIETRO, PAUL   C   KINGS

PERSONAL: Born September 8, 1970, in Sault Ste. Marie, Ont. ... 5-8/179. ... Shoots right. ... Name pronounced dee-pee-EH-troh.
TRANSACTIONS/CAREER NOTES: Selected by Montreal Canadiens in fifth round (sixth Canadiens pick, 102nd overall) of NHL entry draft (June 16, 1990). ... Strained hip flexor (February 12, 1992). ... Bruised thumb (November 24, 1993). ... Suffered contusion (January 4, 1994); missed two games. ... Separated shoulder (January 15, 1994); missed six games. ... Traded by Canadiens to Toronto Maple Leafs for conditional fourth-round draft pick (April 6, 1995). ... Signed as free agent by Los Angeles Kings (July 10, 1996). ... Loaned by Phoenix of the IHL to Cincinnati of the AHL (January 20, 1997).
MISCELLANEOUS: Member of Stanley Cup championship team (1993).

		REGULAR SEASON								PLAYOFFS				
Season Team	League	Gms.	G	A	Pts.	PIM	+/-	PP	SH	Gms.	G	A	Pts.	PIM
86-87— Sudbury	OHL	49	5	11	16	13	...	...	...	—	—	—	—	—
87-88— Sudbury	OHL	63	25	42	67	27	...	...	...	—	—	—	—	—
88-89— Sudbury	OHL	57	31	48	79	27	...	...	...	—	—	—	—	—
89-90— Sudbury	OHL	66	56	63	119	57	...	...	...	7	3	6	9	7
90-91— Fredericton	AHL	78	39	31	70	38	...	...	...	9	5	6	11	2
91-92— Fredericton	AHL	43	26	31	57	52	...	...	...	7	3	4	7	8
— Montreal	NHL	33	4	6	10	25	5	0	0	—	—	—	—	—
92-93— Fredericton	AHL	26	8	16	24	16	...	...	...	—	—	—	—	—
— Montreal	NHL	29	4	13	17	14	11	0	0	17	8	5	13	8
93-94— Montreal	NHL	70	13	20	33	37	-2	2	0	7	2	4	6	2
94-95— Montreal	NHL	22	4	5	9	4	-3	0	0	—	—	—	—	—
— Toronto	NHL	12	1	1	2	6	-6	0	0	7	1	1	2	0
95-96— St. John's	AHL	2	2	2	4	0	...	...	...	—	—	—	—	—
— Houston	IHL	36	18	23	41	44	...	...	...	—	—	—	—	—
— Toronto	NHL	20	4	4	8	4	-3	1	0	—	—	—	—	—
— Las Vegas	IHL	13	5	6	11	10	...	...	...	13	4	8	12	16
96-97— Phoenix	IHL	33	9	20	29	32	...	...	...	—	—	—	—	—
— Los Angeles	NHL	6	1	0	1	6	-2	0	0	—	—	—	—	—
— Cincinnati	IHL	32	15	14	29	28	...	...	...	3	1	1	2	2
NHL totals (6 years)		192	31	49	80	96	0	3	0	31	11	10	21	10

D

DIRK, ROBERT   D   CANADIENS

PERSONAL: Born August 20, 1966, in Regina, Sask. ... 6-4/210. ... Shoots left.
TRANSACTIONS/CAREER NOTES: Selected by St. Louis Blues as underage junior in third round (fourth Blues pick, 53rd overall) of NHL entry draft (June 9, 1984). ... Traded by Blues with LW Geoff Courtnall, C Cliff Ronning, LW Sergio Momesso and fifth-round pick in 1992 draft (RW Brian Loney) to Vancouver Canucks for C Dan Quinn and D Garth Butcher (March 5, 1991). ... Sprained ankle (November 26, 1991); missed three games. ... Sprained knee (February 1, 1992); missed four games. ... Bruised ribs (March 6, 1993); missed four games. ... Injured shoulder (September 22, 1992); missed two games. ... Pulled groin (February 12, 1993); missed six games. ... Traded by Canucks to Chicago Blackhawks for fourth-round pick (RW Mike Dubinsky) in 1994 draft (March 21, 1994). ... Suffered from sore shoulder (1994); missed four games. ... Traded by Blackhawks to Mighty Ducks of Anaheim for fourth-round pick (D Chris Van Dyk) in 1995 draft (July 12, 1994). ... Lacerated chin (April 13, 1995); missed seven games. ... Traded by Mighty Ducks to Montreal Canadiens for C Jim Campbell (January 21, 1996). ... Fractured scapula (January 22, 1996); missed 13 games.
HONORS: Named to WHL All-Star second team (1985-86).

		REGULAR SEASON								PLAYOFFS				
Season Team	League	Gms.	G	A	Pts.	PIM	+/-	PP	SH	Gms.	G	A	Pts.	PIM
82-83— Regina	WHL	1	0	0	0	0	...	...	...	—	—	—	—	—
— Kelowna	BCJHL	40	8	23	31	87	...	...	...	—	—	—	—	—
83-84— Regina	WHL	62	2	10	12	64	...	...	...	23	1	12	13	24
84-85— Regina	WHL	69	10	34	44	97	...	...	...	8	0	0	0	4
85-86— Regina	WHL	72	19	60	79	140	...	...	...	10	3	5	8	8
86-87— Peoria	IHL	76	5	17	22	155	...	...	...	—	—	—	—	—
87-88— St. Louis	NHL	7	0	1	1	16	...	...	...	6	0	1	1	2
— Peoria	IHL	54	4	21	25	126	...	...	...	—	—	—	—	—
88-89— St. Louis	NHL	9	0	1	1	11	...	...	...	—	—	—	—	—
— Peoria	IHL	22	0	2	2	54	...	...	...	—	—	—	—	—
89-90— Peoria	IHL	24	1	2	3	79	...	...	...	3	0	0	0	0
— St. Louis	NHL	37	1	1	2	128	9	0	0	9	0	1	1	2
90-91— Peoria	IHL	3	0	0	0	2	...	...	...	—	—	—	—	—
— St. Louis	NHL	41	1	3	4	100	2	0	0	—	—	—	—	—
— Vancouver	NHL	11	1	0	1	20	-7	0	0	6	0	0	0	13
91-92— Vancouver	NHL	72	2	7	9	126	6	0	0	13	0	0	0	20
92-93— Vancouver	NHL	69	4	8	12	150	25	0	0	9	0	0	0	6
93-94— Vancouver	NHL	65	2	3	5	105	18	0	0	—	—	—	—	—
— Chicago	NHL	6	0	0	0	26	0	0	0	2	0	0	0	15
94-95— Anaheim	NHL	38	1	3	4	56	-3	0	0	—	—	—	—	—
95-96— Anaheim	NHL	44	1	2	3	42	8	0	0	—	—	—	—	—
— Montreal	NHL	3	0	0	0	6	0	0	0	—	—	—	—	—
96-97— Detroit	IHL	48	2	8	10	36	...	...	...	—	—	—	—	—
— Chicago	IHL	31	1	5	6	26	...	...	...	3	0	0	0	0
NHL totals (9 years)		402	13	29	42	786	58	0	0	45	0	2	2	58

DOAN, SHANE   RW   COYOTES

PERSONAL: Born October 10, 1976, in Eston, Sask. ... 6-1/215. ... Shoots right. ... Name pronounced dohn.
TRANSACTIONS/CAREER NOTES: Selected by Winnipeg Jets in first round (first Jets pick, seventh overall) of NHL entry draft (July 8, 1995). ... Suffered from the flu (January 8, 1996); missed one game. ... Bruised ribs (January 14, 1996); missed two games. ... Strained back (February 23, 1996); missed two games. ... Jets franchise moved to Phoenix and renamed Coyotes for 1996-97 season; NHL approved move

on January 18, 1996. ... Sprained ankle (October 14, 1996); missed two games. ... Strained ligament in foot (November 8, 1996); missed eight games. ... Bruised hand (February 22, 1997); missed four games.
HONORS: Won Stafford Smyth Memorial Trophy (1994-95). ... Named to Memorial Cup All-Star team (1994-95).

			REGULAR SEASON							PLAYOFFS				
Season Team	League	Gms.	G	A	Pts.	PIM	+/-	PP	SH	Gms.	G	A	Pts.	PIM
92-93— Kamloops..................	WHL	51	7	12	19	55	...	...	...	13	0	1	1	8
93-94— Kamloops..................	WHL	52	24	24	48	88	...	...	...	—	—	—	—	—
94-95— Kamloops..................	WHL	71	37	57	94	106	...	...	...	21	6	10	16	16
95-96— Winnipeg	NHL	74	7	10	17	101	-9	1	0	6	0	0	0	6
96-97— Phoenix....................	NHL	63	4	8	12	49	-3	0	0	4	0	0	0	2
NHL totals (2 years)		137	11	18	29	150	-12	1	0	10	0	0	0	8

DOIG, JASON   D   COYOTES

PERSONAL: Born January 29, 1977, in Montreal. ... 6-3/216. ... Shoots right. ... Name pronounced DOYG.
TRANSACTIONS/CAREER NOTES: Selected by Winnipeg Jets in second round (third Jets pick, 34th overall) of NHL entry draft (July 8, 1995). ... Suffered irregular heart beat (November 17, 1995); missed four games. ... Jets franchise moved to Phoenix and renamed Coyotes for 1996-97 season; NHL approved move on January 18, 1996. ... Hyperextended elbow prior to 1996-97 season; missed first five games of season.
HONORS: Won Guy Lafleur Trophy (1995-96). ... Named to Memorial Cup All-Star team (1995-96).

			REGULAR SEASON							PLAYOFFS				
Season Team	League	Gms.	G	A	Pts.	PIM	+/-	PP	SH	Gms.	G	A	Pts.	PIM
93-94— St. Jean..................	QMJHL	63	8	17	25	65	...	...	...	5	0	2	2	2
94-95— Laval	QMJHL	55	13	42	55	259	...	...	...	20	4	13	17	39
95-96— Winnipeg	NHL	15	1	1	2	28	-2	0	0	—	—	—	—	—
— Springfield	AHL	5	0	0	0	28				—	—	—	—	—
— Laval	QMJHL	2	1	1	2	*6	...	...	...	—	—	—	—	—
— Granby	QMJHL	27	6	35	41	*105	...	...	...	20	10	22	32	110
96-97— Las Vegas	IHL	6	0	1	1	19	...	...	...	—	—	—	—	—
— Granby	QMJHL	39	14	33	47	197	...	...	...	5	0	4	4	27
— Springfield	AHL	5	0	3	3	2	...	...	...	17	1	4	5	37
NHL totals (1 year)		15	1	1	2	28	-2	0	0					

DOLLAS, BOBBY   D   MIGHTY DUCKS   D

PERSONAL: Born January 31, 1965, in Montreal. ... 6-2/212. ... Shoots left. ... Name pronounced DAH-lihz.
TRANSACTIONS/CAREER NOTES: Selected by Winnipeg Jets as underage junior in first round (second Jets pick, 14th overall) of NHL entry draft (June 8, 1983). ... Traded by Jets to Quebec Nordiques for RW Stu Kulak (December 17, 1987). ... Signed as free agent by Detroit Red Wings (October 18, 1990). ... Suffered from the flu (December 15, 1990); missed two games. ... Injured leg (January 9, 1991). ... Strained abdomen (November 7, 1991); missed 15 games. ... Selected by Mighty Ducks of Anaheim in NHL expansion draft (June 24, 1993). ... Sprained left thumb (October 1, 1993); missed five games. ... Suffered from chicken pox (March 30, 1997); missed three games.
HONORS: Won Raymond Lagace Trophy (1982-83). ... Named to QMJHL All-Star second team (1982-83). ... Won Eddie Shore Plaque (1992-93). ... Named to AHL All-Star first team (1992-93).
MISCELLANEOUS: Holds Mighty Ducks of Anaheim all-time record for most games played (283).

			REGULAR SEASON							PLAYOFFS				
Season Team	League	Gms.	G	A	Pts.	PIM	+/-	PP	SH	Gms.	G	A	Pts.	PIM
82-83— Laval	QMJHL	63	16	45	61	144	...	...	...	11	5	5	10	23
83-84— Laval	QMJHL	54	12	33	45	80	...	...	...	14	1	8	9	23
— Winnipeg	NHL	1	0	0	0	0	-2	0	0	—	—	—	—	—
84-85— Winnipeg	NHL	9	0	0	0	0	3	0	0	—	—	—	—	—
— Sherbrooke	AHL	8	1	3	4	4	...	...	...	17	3	6	9	17
85-86— Sherbrooke	AHL	25	4	7	11	29	...	...	...	—	—	—	—	—
— Winnipeg	NHL	46	0	5	5	66	-3	0	0	3	0	0	0	2
86-87— Sherbrooke	AHL	75	6	18	24	87	...	...	...	16	2	4	6	13
87-88— Quebec.....................	NHL	9	0	0	0	2	-4	0	0	—	—	—	—	—
— Moncton	AHL	26	4	10	14	20	...	...	...	—	—	—	—	—
— Fredericton	AHL	33	4	8	12	27	...	...	...	15	2	2	4	24
88-89— Halifax.....................	AHL	57	5	19	24	65	...	...	...	4	1	0	1	14
— Quebec.......................	NHL	16	0	3	3	16	-11	0	0	—	—	—	—	—
89-90— Canadian nat'l team ...	Int'l	68	8	29	37	60	...	...	...	—	—	—	—	—
90-91— Detroit......................	NHL	56	3	5	8	20	6	0	0	7	1	0	1	13
91-92— Detroit......................	NHL	27	3	1	4	20	4	0	1	2	0	1	1	0
— Adirondack................	AHL	19	1	6	7	33	...	...	...	18	7	4	11	22
92-93— Adirondack................	AHL	64	7	36	43	54	...	...	...	11	3	8	11	8
— Detroit........................	NHL	6	0	0	0	2	-1	0	0	—	—	—	—	—
93-94— Anaheim...................	NHL	77	9	11	20	55	20	1	0	—	—	—	—	—
94-95— Anaheim...................	NHL	45	7	13	20	12	-3	3	1	—	—	—	—	—
95-96— Anaheim...................	NHL	82	8	22	30	64	9	0	1	—	—	—	—	—
96-97— Anaheim...................	NHL	79	4	14	18	55	17	1	0	11	0	0	0	4
NHL totals (12 years)		453	34	74	108	312	35	5	3	23	1	1	2	19

DOMENICHELLI, HNAT   C   FLAMES

PERSONAL: Born February 17, 1976, in Edmonton. ... 6-0/180. ... Shoots left. ... Name pronounced NAT doh-mih-KEHL-ee.
TRANSACTIONS/CAREER NOTES: Selected by Hartford Whalers in fourth round (second Whalers pick, 83rd overall) of NHL entry draft (June 29, 1994). ... Traded by Whalers with D Glen Featherstone, second-round pick (D Dimitri Kokorev) in 1997 draft and third-round pick in 1998 draft to Calgary Flames for D Steve Chiasson and third-round pick (D Francis Lessard) in 1997 draft (March 5, 1997).

Season Team	League	REGULAR SEASON								PLAYOFFS				
		Gms.	G	A	Pts.	PIM	+/-	PP	SH	Gms.	G	A	Pts.	PIM
92-93— Kamloops..................	WHL	45	12	8	20	15	...	...	...	11	1	1	2	2
93-94— Kamloops..................	WHL	69	27	40	67	31	...	...	...	19	10	12	22	0
94-95— Kamloops..................	WHL	72	52	62	114	34	...	...	...	19	9	9	18	9
95-96— Kamloops..................	WHL	62	59	89	148	37	...	...	...	16	7	9	16	29
96-97— Hartford	NHL	13	2	1	3	7	-4	1	0	—	—	—	—	—
— Springfield	AHL	39	24	24	48	12	...	...	...	—	—	—	—	—
— Calgary	NHL	10	1	2	3	2	1	0	0	—	—	—	—	—
— Saint John	AHL	1	1	1	2	0	...	...	...	5	5	0	5	2
NHL totals (2 years)		23	3	3	6	9	-3	1	0					

DOMI, TIE RW MAPLE LEAFS

PERSONAL: Born November 1, 1969, in Windsor, Ont. ... 5-10/200. ... Shoots right. ... Name pronounced TIGH DOH-mee.

TRANSACTIONS/CAREER NOTES: Suspended indefinitely by OHL for leaving the bench during fight (November 2, 1986). ... Selected by Toronto Maple Leafs in second round (second Maple Leafs pick, 27th overall) of NHL entry draft (June 11, 1988). ... Traded by Maple Leafs with G Mark Laforest to New York Rangers for RW Greg Johnston (June 28, 1990). ... Suspended six games by AHL for pre-game fighting (November 25, 1990). ... Sprained right knee (March 11, 1992); missed eight games. ... Traded by Rangers with LW Kris King to Winnipeg Jets for C Ed Olczyk (December 28, 1992). ... Fined $500 by NHL for premeditated fight (January 4, 1993). ... Sprained knee (January 25, 1994); missed three games. ... Traded by Jets to Toronto Maple Leafs for C Mike Eastwood and third-round pick (RW Brad Isbister) in 1995 draft (April 7, 1995). ... Strained groin (April 8, 1995); missed two games. ... Suffered from the flu (April 19, 1995); missed one game. ... Suspended eight games by NHL for fighting (October 17, 1995). ... Sprained knee (December 2, 1995); missed two games. ... Fined $1,000 by NHL for fighting (November 13, 1996). ... Sprained ankle (April 2, 1997); missed two games.

Season Team	League	REGULAR SEASON								PLAYOFFS				
		Gms.	G	A	Pts.	PIM	+/-	PP	SH	Gms.	G	A	Pts.	PIM
85-86— Windsor Jr. B............	OHA	32	8	17	25	346	...	...	...	—	—	—	—	—
86-87— Peterborough.............	OHL	18	1	1	2	79	...	...	...	—	—	—	—	—
87-88— Peterborough.............	OHL	60	22	21	43	*292	...	...	...	12	3	9	12	24
88-89— Peterborough.............	OHL	43	14	16	30	175	...	...	...	17	10	9	19	*70
89-90— Newmarket................	AHL	57	14	11	25	285	...	...	...	—	—	—	—	—
— Toronto	NHL	2	0	0	0	42	0	0	0	—	—	—	—	—
90-91— New York Rangers	NHL	28	1	0	1	185	-5	0	0	—	—	—	—	—
— Binghamton	AHL	25	11	6	17	219	...	...	...	7	3	2	5	16
91-92— New York Rangers	NHL	42	2	4	6	246	-4	0	0	6	1	1	2	32
92-93— New York Rangers	NHL	12	2	0	2	95	-1	0	0	—	—	—	—	—
— Winnipeg	NHL	49	3	10	13	249	2	0	0	6	1	0	1	23
93-94— Winnipeg	NHL	81	8	11	19	*347	-8	0	0	—	—	—	—	—
94-95— Winnipeg	NHL	31	4	4	8	128	-6	0	0	—	—	—	—	—
— Toronto	NHL	9	0	1	1	31	1	0	0	7	1	0	1	0
95-96— Toronto	NHL	72	7	6	13	297	-3	0	0	6	0	2	2	4
96-97— Toronto	NHL	80	11	17	28	275	-17	2	0	—	—	—	—	—
NHL totals (8 years)		406	38	53	91	1895	-41	2	0	25	3	3	6	59

DONATO, TED C/LW BRUINS

PERSONAL: Born April 28, 1968, in Dedham, Mass. ... 5-10/181. ... Shoots left. ... Full name: Edward Paul Donato. ... Name pronounced duh-NAH-toh. ... Brother of Dan Donato, infielder, New York Yankees organization.

HIGH SCHOOL: Catholic Memorial (Boston).

COLLEGE: Harvard (degree in history).

TRANSACTIONS/CAREER NOTES: Selected by Boston Bruins in sixth round (sixth Bruins pick, 98th overall) of NHL entry draft (June 13, 1987). ... Broke collarbone (November 18, 1989). ... Played in Europe during 1994-95 NHL lockout. ... Injured groin (November 21, 1996); missed two games. ... Fractured finger (March 9, 1997); missed 13 games.

Season Team	League	REGULAR SEASON								PLAYOFFS				
		Gms.	G	A	Pts.	PIM	+/-	PP	SH	Gms.	G	A	Pts.	PIM
86-87— Catholic Memorial......	Mass. H.S.	22	29	34	63	30	...	...	...	—	—	—	—	—
87-88— Harvard University	ECAC	28	12	14	26	24	...	...	...	—	—	—	—	—
88-89— Harvard University	ECAC	34	14	37	51	30	...	...	...	—	—	—	—	—
89-90— Harvard University	ECAC	16	5	6	11	34	...	...	...	—	—	—	—	—
90-91— Harvard University	ECAC	28	19	37	56	26	...	...	...	—	—	—	—	—
91-92— U.S. national team	Int'l	52	11	22	33	24	...	...	...	—	—	—	—	—
— U.S. Olympic team......	Int'l	8	4	3	7	8	...	...	...	—	—	—	—	—
— Boston	NHL	10	1	2	3	8	-1	0	0	15	3	4	7	4
92-93— Boston	NHL	82	15	20	35	61	2	3	2	4	0	1	1	0
93-94— Boston	NHL	84	22	32	54	59	0	9	2	13	4	2	6	10
94-95— TuTo Turku	Finland	14	5	5	10	47	...	...	...	—	—	—	—	—
— Boston	NHL	47	10	10	20	10	3	1	0	5	0	0	0	4
95-96— Boston	NHL	82	23	26	49	46	6	7	0	5	1	2	3	2
96-97— Boston	NHL	67	25	26	51	37	-9	6	2	—	—	—	—	—
NHL totals (6 years)		372	96	116	212	221	1	26	6	42	8	9	17	20

DONNELLY, MIKE   LW   ISLANDERS

PERSONAL: Born October 10, 1963, in Livonia, Mich. ... 5-11/185. ... Shoots left. ... Full name: Michael Chene Donnelly.
HIGH SCHOOL: Franklin (Livonia, Mich.).
COLLEGE: Michigan State.
TRANSACTIONS/CAREER NOTES: Signed as free agent by New York Rangers (August 1986). ... Dislocated and fractured right index finger (November 1987). ... Traded by Rangers with fifth-round pick (RW Alexander Mogilny) in 1988 draft to Buffalo Sabres for LW Paul Cyr and 10th-round pick (C Eric Fenton) in 1988 draft (December 1987). ... Traded by Sabres to Los Angeles Kings for LW Mikko Makela (October 1, 1990). ... Traded by Kings to Dallas Stars for fourth-round pick (traded to Washington) in 1996 draft (February 17, 1995). ... Suffered concussion (March 8, 1995); missed one game. ... Suffered intestinal disorder (November 14, 1995); missed 12 games. ... Signed as free agent by New York Islanders (July 25, 1996).
HONORS: Named NCAA Tournament Most Valuable Player (1985-86). ... Named to NCAA All-America West first team (1985-86). ... Named to NCAA All-Tournament team (1985-86). ... Named to CCHA All-Star first team (1985-86).
STATISTICAL PLATEAUS: Three-goal games: 1992-93 (1), 1993-94 (1). Total: 2.
MISCELLANEOUS: Scored on a penalty shot (vs. Kirk McLean, November 11, 1992). ... Failed to score on a penalty shot (vs. Curtis Joseph, April 7, 1994).

Season Team	League	REGULAR SEASON								PLAYOFFS				
		Gms.	G	A	Pts.	PIM	+/-	PP	SH	Gms.	G	A	Pts.	PIM
82-83— Michigan State..........	CCHA	24	7	13	20	8	...	...	...	—	—	—	—	—
83-84— Michigan State..........	CCHA	44	18	14	32	40	...	...	...	—	—	—	—	—
84-85— Michigan State..........	CCHA	44	26	21	47	48	...	...	...	—	—	—	—	—
85-86— Michigan State..........	CCHA	44	59	38	97	65	...	...	...	—	—	—	—	—
86-87— New York Rangers	NHL	5	1	1	2	0	0	0	0	—	—	—	—	—
— New Haven.................	AHL	58	27	34	61	52	...	...	...	7	2	0	2	9
87-88— Colorado	IHL	8	7	11	18	15	...	...	...	—	—	—	—	—
— New York Rangers	NHL	17	2	2	4	8	-5	0	0	—	—	—	—	—
— Buffalo	NHL	40	6	8	14	44	-1	0	0	—	—	—	—	—
88-89— Buffalo	NHL	22	4	6	10	10	-1	0	0	—	—	—	—	—
— Rochester	AHL	53	32	37	69	53	...	...	...	—	—	—	—	—
89-90— Rochester	AHL	68	43	55	98	71	...	...	...	16	*12	7	19	9
— Buffalo	NHL	12	1	2	3	8	-4	0	0	—	—	—	—	—
90-91— Los Angeles..............	NHL	53	7	5	12	41	3	0	0	12	5	4	9	6
— New Haven.................	AHL	18	10	6	16	2	...	...	...	—	—	—	—	—
91-92— Los Angeles..............	NHL	80	29	16	45	20	5	0	1	6	1	0	1	4
92-93— Los Angeles..............	NHL	84	29	40	69	45	17	8	1	24	6	7	13	14
93-94— Los Angeles..............	NHL	81	21	21	42	34	2	4	2	—	—	—	—	—
94-95— Los Angeles..............	NHL	9	1	1	2	4	-7	0	0	—	—	—	—	—
— Dallas........................	NHL	35	11	14	25	29	3	3	0	5	0	1	1	6
95-96— Dallas........................	NHL	24	2	5	7	10	-2	0	0	—	—	—	—	—
— Michigan....................	IHL	21	8	15	23	20	...	...	...	8	3	0	3	10
96-97— New York Islanders....	NHL	3	0	0	0	2	0	0	0	—	—	—	—	—
— Utah	IHL	14	7	2	9	33	...	...	...	—	—	—	—	—
— Detroit.......................	IIHL	19	4	4	8	12	...	...	...	—	—	—	—	—
NHL totals (11 years)		465	114	121	235	255	10	15	4	47	12	12	24	30

DONOVAN, SHEAN   RW   SHARKS

PERSONAL: Born January 22, 1975, in Timmins, Ont. ... 6-3/210. ... Shoots right. ... Name pronounced SHAWN DAHN-ih-vihn.
TRANSACTIONS/CAREER NOTES: Selected by San Jose Sharks in second round (second Sharks pick, 28th overall) of NHL entry draft (June 26, 1993). ... Suffered a concussion (October 5, 1996); missed two games. ... Sore knee (December 21, 1996); missed two games.

Season Team	League	REGULAR SEASON								PLAYOFFS				
		Gms.	G	A	Pts.	PIM	+/-	PP	SH	Gms.	G	A	Pts.	PIM
91-92— Ottawa	OHL	58	11	8	19	14	...	...	...	11	1	0	1	5
92-93— Ottawa	OHL	66	29	23	52	33	...	...	...	—	—	—	—	—
93-94— Ottawa	OHL	62	35	49	84	63	...	...	...	17	10	11	21	14
94-95— Ottawa	OHL	29	22	19	41	41	...	...	...	—	—	—	—	—
— San Jose....................	NHL	14	0	0	0	6	-6	0	0	7	0	1	1	6
— Kansas City...............	IHL	5	0	2	2	7	...	...	...	14	5	3	8	23
95-96— Kansas City...............	IHL	4	0	0	0	8	...	...	...	5	0	0	0	8
— San Jose....................	NHL	74	13	8	21	39	-17	0	1	—	—	—	—	—
96-97— San Jose....................	NHL	73	9	6	15	42	-18	0	1	—	—	—	—	—
— Kentucky...................	AHL	3	1	3	4	18	...	...	...	—	—	—	—	—
NHL totals (3 years)		161	22	14	36	87	-41	0	2	7	0	1	1	6

DOWD, JIM   C   ISLANDERS

PERSONAL: Born December 25, 1968, in Brick, N.J. ... 6-1/190. ... Shoots right.
HIGH SCHOOL: Brick (N.J.) Township.
COLLEGE: Lake Superior State (Mich.).
TRANSACTIONS/CAREER NOTES: Selected by New Jersey Devils in eighth round (seventh Devils pick, 149th overall) of NHL entry draft (June 13, 1987). ... Injured shoulder (February 2, 1995) and underwent shoulder surgery (February 15, 1995); missed 35 games. ... Traded by Devils with second-round pick in 1997 draft to Hartford Whalers for RW Jocelyn Lemieux and second-round pick in 1998 draft (December 19, 1995). ... Traded by Whalers with D Frantisek Kucera and second-round pick (D Ryan Bonni) in 1997 draft to Vancouver Canucks for D Jeff Brown and third-round pick in 1998 draft (December 19, 1995). ... Selected by New York Islanders from Canucks in waiver draft for cash (September 30, 1996).
HONORS: Named to NCAA All-America West second team (1989-90). ... Named to CCHA All-Star second team (1989-90). ... Named to NCAA All-America West first team (1990-91). ... Named CCHA Player of the Year (1990-91). ... Named to CCHA All-Star first team (1990-91).
MISCELLANEOUS: Member of Stanley Cup championship team (1995).

Season Team	League	Gms.	G	A	Pts.	PIM	+/-	PP	SH	Gms.	G	A	Pts.	PIM
83-84— Brick Township	N.J. H.S.	...	19	30	49	...	...	...	...	—	—	—	—	—
84-85— Brick Township	N.J. H.S.	...	58	55	113	...	...	...	...	—	—	—	—	—
85-86— Brick Township	N.J. H.S.	...	47	51	98	...	...	...	...	—	—	—	—	—
86-87— Brick Township	N.J. H.S.	20	62	53	115	...	...	...	...	—	—	—	—	—
87-88— Lake Superior	CCHA	45	18	27	45	16	...	...	...	—	—	—	—	—
88-89— Lake Superior	CCHA	46	24	35	59	40	...	...	...	—	—	—	—	—
89-90— Lake Superior	CCHA	46	25	67	92	30	...	...	...	—	—	—	—	—
90-91— Lake Superior	CCHA	44	24	54	78	53	...	...	...	—	—	—	—	—
91-92— Utica	AHL	78	17	42	59	47	...	...	...	4	2	2	4	4
— New Jersey	NHL	1	0	0	0	0	0	0	0	—	—	—	—	—
92-93— Utica	AHL	78	27	45	72	62	...	...	...	5	1	7	8	10
— New Jersey	NHL	1	0	0	0	0	-1	0	0	—	—	—	—	—
93-94— New Jersey	NHL	15	5	10	15	0	8	2	0	19	2	6	8	8
— Albany......................	AHL	58	26	37	63	76	...	...	...	—	—	—	—	—
94-95— New Jersey	NHL	10	1	4	5	0	-5	1	0	11	2	1	3	8
95-96— New Jersey	NHL	28	4	9	13	17	-1	0	0	—	—	—	—	—
— Vancouver...............	NHL	38	1	6	7	6	-8	0	0	1	0	0	0	0
96-97— New York Islanders....	NHL	3	0	0	0	0	-1	0	0	—	—	—	—	—
— Utah........................	IHL	48	10	21	31	27	...	...	...	—	—	—	—	—
— Saint John	AHL	24	5	11	16	18	...	...	...	5	1	2	3	0
NHL totals (6 years)		96	11	29	40	23	-8	3	0	31	4	7	11	16

DOYLE, JASON   RW   BRUINS

PERSONAL: Born April 15, 1977, in Toronto. ... 6-1/203. ... Shoots right.
TRANSACTIONS/CAREER NOTES: Selected by Boston Bruins in third round (fourth Bruins pick, 80th overall) of NHL entry draft (June 22, 1996).

Season Team	League	Gms.	G	A	Pts.	PIM	+/-	PP	SH	Gms.	G	A	Pts.	PIM
94-95— London	OHL	45	4	10	14	7	...	...	...	4	1	1	2	0
95-96— London	OHL	21	11	5	16	24	...	...	...	—	—	—	—	—
— Sault Ste. Marie	OHL	44	17	17	34	30	...	...	...	4	1	1	2	6
96-97— Owen Sound	OHL	63	13	16	29	38	...	...	...	4	1	1	2	4

DRAKE, DALLAS   RW   COYOTES

PERSONAL: Born February 4, 1969, in Trail, B.C. ... 6-0/180. ... Shoots left. ... Full name: Dallas James Drake.
COLLEGE: Northern Michigan.
TRANSACTIONS/CAREER NOTES: Selected by Detroit Red Wings in sixth round (sixth Red Wings pick, 116th overall) of NHL entry draft (June 17, 1989). ... Bruised left leg (November 27, 1992); missed three games. ... Suffered back spasms (December 28, 1992); missed one game. ... Bruised kneecap (January 23, 1993); missed three games. ... Suffered concussion (February 13, 1993); missed one game. ... Injured right wrist (October 16, 1993); missed three games. ... Injured tendon in right hand (December 14, 1993); missed 16 games. ... Traded by Detroit Red Wings with G Tim Cheveldae to Winnipeg Jets for G Bob Essensa and D Sergei Bautin (March 8, 1994). ... Suffered back spasms (March 17, 1995); missed four games. ... Bruised right shoulder (October 22, 1995); missed seven games. ... Suffered ear infection (November 21, 1995); missed two games. ... Strained Achilles' tendon (December 28, 1995); missed two games. ... Jets franchise moved to Phoenix and renamed Coyotes for 1996-97 season; NHL approved move on January 18, 1996. ... Sprained ankle (November 16, 1996); missed eight games. ... Sprained knee (January 29, 1997); missed 10 games.
HONORS: Named to NCAA All-America West first team (1991-92). ... Won WCHA Player of the Year Award (1991-92). ... Named to WCHA All-Star first team (1991-92).

Season Team	League	Gms.	G	A	Pts.	PIM	+/-	PP	SH	Gms.	G	A	Pts.	PIM
84-85— Rossland....................	KIJHL	30	13	37	50	...	...	...	...	—	—	—	—	—
85-86— Rossland....................	KIJHL	41	53	73	126	...	...	...	...	—	—	—	—	—
86-87— Rossland....................	KIJHL	40	55	80	135	...	...	...	...	—	—	—	—	—
87-88— Vernon	BCJHL	47	39	85	124	50	...	...	...	11	9	17	26	30
88-89— N. Michigan Univ.	WCHA	45	18	24	42	26	...	...	...	—	—	—	—	—
89-90— N. Michigan Univ.	WCHA	36	13	24	37	42	...	...	...	—	—	—	—	—
90-91— N. Michigan Univ.	WCHA	44	22	36	58	89	...	...	...	—	—	—	—	—
91-92— N. Michigan Univ.	WCHA	40	*39	44	83	58	...	...	...	—	—	—	—	—
92-93— Detroit.......................	NHL	72	18	26	44	93	15	3	2	7	3	3	6	6
93-94— Detroit.......................	NHL	47	10	22	32	37	5	0	1	—	—	—	—	—
— Adirondack...............	AHL	1	2	0	2	0	...	...	...	—	—	—	—	—
— Winnipeg.................	NHL	15	3	5	8	12	-6	1	1	—	—	—	—	—
94-95— Winnipeg..................	NHL	43	8	18	26	30	-6	0	0	—	—	—	—	—
95-96— Winnipeg..................	NHL	69	19	20	39	36	-7	4	4	3	0	0	0	0
96-97— Phoenix.....................	NHL	63	17	19	36	52	-11	5	1	7	0	1	1	2
NHL totals (6 years)		309	75	110	185	260	-10	13	9	17	3	4	7	8

DRAPER, KRIS   C   RED WINGS

PERSONAL: Born May 24, 1971, in Toronto. ... 5-11/184. ... Shoots left. ... Full name: Kris Bruce Draper.
TRANSACTIONS/CAREER NOTES: Selected by Winnipeg Jets in third round (fourth Jets pick, 62nd overall) of NHL entry draft (June 17, 1989). ... Traded by Jets to Detroit Red Wings for future considerations (June 30, 1993). ... Sprained right knee ligament (February 4, 1995); missed eight games. ... Suffered from the flu (January 5, 1996); missed one game. ... Injured right knee (February 15, 1996); missed 12 games. ... Reinjured right knee (March 25, 1996); missed three games.
MISCELLANEOUS: Member of Stanley Cup championship team (1997).

Season Team	League	REGULAR SEASON								PLAYOFFS				
		Gms.	G	A	Pts.	PIM	+/-	PP	SH	Gms.	G	A	Pts.	PIM
88-89— Canadian nat'l team ...	Int'l	60	11	15	26	16	...	...	...	—	—	—	—	—
89-90— Canadian nat'l team ...	Int'l	61	12	22	34	44	...	...	...	—	—	—	—	—
90-91— Winnipeg	NHL	3	1	0	1	5	0	0	0	—	—	—	—	—
— Moncton	AHL	7	2	1	3	2	...	...	...	—	—	—	—	—
— Ottawa	OHL	39	19	42	61	35	...	...	...	17	8	11	19	20
91-92— Moncton	AHL	61	11	18	29	113	...	...	...	4	0	1	1	6
— Winnipeg	NHL	10	2	0	2	2	0	0	0	2	0	0	0	0
92-93— Winnipeg	NHL	7	0	0	0	2	-6	0	0	—	—	—	—	—
— Moncton	AHL	67	12	23	35	40	...	...	...	5	2	2	4	18
93-94— Adirondack	AHL	46	20	23	43	49	...	...	...	—	—	—	—	—
— Detroit	NHL	39	5	8	13	31	11	0	1	7	2	2	4	4
94-95— Detroit	NHL	36	2	6	8	22	1	0	0	18	4	1	5	12
95-96— Detroit	NHL	52	7	9	16	32	2	0	1	18	4	2	6	18
96-97— Detroit	NHL	76	8	5	13	73	-11	1	0	20	2	4	6	12
NHL totals (7 years)		223	25	28	53	167	-3	1	2	65	12	9	21	46

DRAPER, TOM — G

PERSONAL: Born November 20, 1966, in Outremont, Que. ... 5-11/185. ... Catches left. ... Full name: Thomas Edward Draper.
COLLEGE: Vermont.
TRANSACTIONS/CAREER NOTES: Selected by Winnipeg Jets in eighth round (eighth Jets pick, 165th overall) of NHL entry draft (June 15, 1985). ... Traded by Jets to St. Louis Blues for future considerations (February 28, 1991); C Jim Vesey sent to Jets by Blues to complete deal (May 24, 1991). ... Traded by Blues to Jets for future considerations (May 24, 1991). ... Traded by Jets to Buffalo Sabres for future considerations; Jets later received seventh-round pick in 1992 draft (D Artur Oktyabrev) to complete deal (June 22, 1991). ... Traded by Sabres to New York Islanders for seventh-round pick (G Steve Plouffe) in 1994 draft (September 30, 1993). ... Signed as a free agent by Winnipeg Jets (December 14, 1995). ... Jets franchise moved to Phoenix and renamed Coyotes for 1996-97 season; NHL approved move on January 18, 1996.
HONORS: Named to ECAC All-Star first team (1985-86). ... Named to AHL All-Star second team (1988-89).
MISCELLANEOUS: Stopped a penalty shot attempt (vs. Marty McInnis, March 8, 1992). ... Allowed a penalty shot goal (vs. Mats Sundin, March 3, 1992).

Season Team	League	REGULAR SEASON								PLAYOFFS						
		Gms.	Min	W	L	T	GA	SO	Avg.	Gms.	Min.	W	L	GA	SO	Avg.
83-84— Univ. of Vermont	ECAC	20	1205	8	12	0	82	0	4.08	—	—	—	—	—	—	—
84-85— Univ. of Vermont	ECAC	24	1316	5	17	0	90	0	4.10	—	—	—	—	—	—	—
85-86— Univ. of Vermont	ECAC	29	1697	15	12	1	87	1	3.08	—	—	—	—	—	—	—
86-87— Univ. of Vermont	ECAC	29	1662	16	13	0	96	2	3.47	—	—	—	—	—	—	—
87-88— Tappara........................	Finland	28	1619	16	3	9	87	0	3.22	—	—	—	—	—	—	—
88-89— Moncton	AHL	54	2962	27	17	5	171	2	3.46	7	419	5	2	24	0	3.44
— Winnipeg	NHL	2	120	1	1	0	12	0	6.00	—	—	—	—	—	—	—
89-90— Moncton	AHL	51	2844	20	24	3	167	1	3.52	—	—	—	—	—	—	—
— Winnipeg	NHL	6	359	2	4	0	26	0	4.35	—	—	—	—	—	—	—
90-91— Fort Wayne	IHL	10	564	5	3	‡1	32	0	3.40	—	—	—	—	—	—	—
— Moncton	AHL	30	1779	15	13	2	95	1	3.20	—	—	—	—	—	—	—
— Peoria	IHL	10	584	6	3	‡1	36	0	3.70	4	214	2	1	10	0	2.80
91-92— Rochester	AHL	9	531	4	3	2	28	0	3.16	—	—	—	—	—	—	—
— Buffalo	NHL	26	1403	10	9	5	75	1	3.21	7	433	3	4	19	1	2.63
92-93— Buffalo	NHL	11	664	5	6	0	41	0	3.70	—	—	—	—	—	—	—
— Rochester	AHL	5	303	3	2	0	22	0	4.36	—	—	—	—	—	—	—
93-94— New York Islanders	NHL	7	227	1	3	0	16	0	4.23	—	—	—	—	—	—	—
— Salt Lake City	IHL	35	1929	7	23	‡3	140	0	4.35	—	—	—	—	—	—	—
94-95— Minnesota	IHL	59	3063	25	20	‡6	187	1	3.66	2	118	0	2	10	0	5.08
95-96— Milwaukee	IHL	31	1793	14	12	‡3	101	1	3.38	—	—	—	—	—	—	—
— Winnipeg	NHL	1	34	0	0	0	3	0	5.29	—	—	—	—	—	—	—
96-97— Long Beach	IHL	39	2267	28	7	‡3	87	2	2.30	*18	*1096	*13	5	41	†2	2.24
NHL totals (6 years)		53	2807	19	23	5	173	1	3.70	7	433	3	4	19	1	2.63

DRIVER, BRUCE — D — RANGERS

PERSONAL: Born April 29, 1962, in Toronto. ... 6-0/185. ... Shoots left. ... Full name: Bruce Douglas Driver.
COLLEGE: Wisconsin.
TRANSACTIONS/CAREER NOTES: Selected by Colorado Rockies as underage junior in sixth round (sixth Rockies pick, 108th overall) of NHL entry draft (June 10, 1981). ... Rockies franchise moved from Colorado to New Jersey and renamed Devils for 1982-83 season. ... Underwent surgery to left knee (February 1985). ... Reinjured knee (April 2, 1985). ... Bruised shoulder (March 9, 1986). ... Sprained ankle (February 1988). ... Broke right leg in three places (December 7, 1988). ... Broke rib (January 8, 1991); missed three games. ... Reinjured rib (January 22, 1991); missed four games. ... Injured shoulder (December 5, 1993); missed 14 games. ... Dislocated shoulder (February 20, 1995); missed three games. ... Suffered stiff neck (April 16, 1995); missed one game. ... Signed as free agent by New York Rangers (August 24, 1995). ... Underwent shoulder surgery prior to 1995-96 season; missed first 13 games of season. ... Suffered from the flu (March 9, 1996); missed two games. ... Suffered from the flu (April 12, 1996); missed one game. ... Suffered from the flu (December 18, 1996); missed one game. ... Suffered from the flu (January 8, 1997); missed two games.
HONORS: Named to NCAA All-America West team (1981-82). ... Named to NCAA All-Tournament team (1981-82). ... Named to WCHA All-Star first team (1981-82). ... Named to WCHA All-Star second team (1982-83).
MISCELLANEOUS: Member of Stanley Cup championship team (1995). ... Captain of New Jersey Devils (1991-92).

Season Team	League	REGULAR SEASON								PLAYOFFS				
		Gms.	G	A	Pts.	PIM	+/-	PP	SH	Gms.	G	A	Pts.	PIM
78-79— Royal York Royals	OPJHL	45	13	36	49	...	...	...	...	—	—	—	—	—
79-80— Royal York Royals	OPJHL	43	13	57	70	102	...	...	...	—	—	—	—	—
80-81— Univ. of Wisconsin.....	WCHA	42	5	15	20	42	...	...	...	—	—	—	—	—
81-82— Univ. of Wisconsin.....	WCHA	46	7	37	44	84	...	...	...	—	—	—	—	—

Season Team	League	REGULAR SEASON								PLAYOFFS				
		Gms.	G	A	Pts.	PIM	+/-	PP	SH	Gms.	G	A	Pts.	PIM
82-83— Univ. of Wisconsin.....	WCHA	39	16	34	50	50	...			—	—	—	—	—
83-84— Can. Olympic team	Int'l	61	11	17	28	44	...			—	—	—	—	—
— Maine...............	AHL	12	2	6	8	15	...		...	16	0	10	10	8
— New Jersey	NHL	4	0	2	2	0	...		...	—	—	—	—	—
84-85— New Jersey	NHL	67	9	23	32	36	...		...	—	—	—	—	—
85-86— Maine...............	AHL	15	4	7	11	16	...		...	—	—	—	—	—
— New Jersey	NHL	40	3	15	18	32	...		...	—	—	—	—	—
86-87— New Jersey	NHL	74	6	28	34	36	...		...	—	—	—	—	—
87-88— New Jersey	NHL	74	15	40	55	68	...		...	20	3	7	10	14
88-89— New Jersey	NHL	27	1	15	16	24	...		...	—	—	—	—	—
89-90— New Jersey	NHL	75	7	46	53	63	6	1	0	6	1	5	6	6
90-91— New Jersey	NHL	73	9	36	45	62	...		...	7	1	2	3	12
91-92— New Jersey	NHL	78	7	35	42	66	...		...	7	0	4	4	2
92-93— New Jersey	NHL	83	14	40	54	66	-10	6	0	5	1	3	4	4
93-94— New Jersey	NHL	66	8	24	32	63	29	3	1	20	3	5	8	12
94-95— New Jersey	NHL	41	4	12	16	18	-1	1	0	17	1	6	7	8
95-96— New York Rangers	NHL	66	3	34	37	42	2	3	0	11	0	7	7	4
96-97— New York Rangers	NHL	79	5	25	30	48	8	2	1	15	0	1	1	2
NHL totals (14 years)		847	91	375	466	624	34	16	2	108	10	40	50	64

DROLET, JIMMY — D — CANADIENS

PERSONAL: Born February 19, 1976, in Vanier, Que. ... 6-0/187. ... Shoots left. ... Name pronounced droo-LEHT.
TRANSACTIONS/CAREER NOTES: Selected by Montreal Canadiens in fifth round (seventh Canadiens pick, 122nd overall) of NHL entry draft (June 29, 1994).
HONORS: Won Raymond Lagace Trophy (1993-94). ... Named to QMJHL All-Rookie team (1993-94).

Season Team	League	REGULAR SEASON								PLAYOFFS				
		Gms.	G	A	Pts.	PIM	+/-	PP	SH	Gms.	G	A	Pts.	PIM
93-94— St. Hyacinthe	QMJHL	72	10	46	56	93	...	...	...	7	1	7	8	10
94-95— St. Hyacinthe	QMJHL	68	9	27	36	126	...	...	...	5	0	2	2	12
95-96— Granby	QMJHL	62	8	53	61	135	...	...	...	21	7	18	25	28
96-97— Fredericton................	AHL	57	3	2	5	43	...	...	...	—	—	—	—	—

DROPPA, IVAN — D — PANTHERS

PERSONAL: Born February 1, 1972, in Liptovsky Mikulas, Czechoslovakia. ... 6-2/209. ... Shoots left. ... Name pronounced IGH-vihn DROH-puh.
TRANSACTIONS/CAREER NOTES: Selected by Chicago Blackhawks in second round (second Blackhawks pick, 37th overall) of NHL entry draft (June 16, 1990). ... Traded by Blackhawks to Florida Panthers for D Alain Nasreddine and conditional pick in 1999 draft (December 18, 1996).

Season Team	League	REGULAR SEASON								PLAYOFFS				
		Gms.	G	A	Pts.	PIM	+/-	PP	SH	Gms.	G	A	Pts.	PIM
89-90— Liptovsky Mikulas	Czech.					Statistics unavailable.								
90-91— VSZ Kosice	Czech.	49	1	7	8	12	...	...		—	—	—	—	—
91-92— VSZ Kosice	Czech.	43	4	9	13		...	...		—	—	—	—	—
92-93— Indianapolis	IHL	77	14	29	43	92	...	...		5	0	1	1	2
93-94— Indianapolis	IHL	55	9	10	19	71	...	...		—	—	—	—	—
— Chicago......................	NHL	12	0	1	1	12	2	0	0	—	—	—	—	—
94-95— Indianapolis	IHL	67	5	28	33	91	...	...		—	—	—	—	—
95-96— Indianapolis	IHL	72	6	30	36	71	...	...		3	0	1	1	2
— Chicago......................	NHL	7	0	0	0	2	2	0	0	—	—	—	—	—
96-97— Indianapolis	IHL	26	1	13	14	44	...	...		—	—	—	—	—
— Carolina	AHL	47	4	22	26	48	...	...		—	—	—	—	—
NHL totals (2 years)		19	0	1	1	14	4	0	0					

DROUIN, P.C. — LW — BRUINS

PERSONAL: Born April 22, 1974, in St. Lambert, Que. ... 6-2/208. ... Name pronounced droo-AN. ... Full name: Pierre Claude Drouin.
TRANSACTIONS/CAREER NOTES: Signed as free agent by Boston Bruins (October 14, 1996).

Season Team	League	REGULAR SEASON								PLAYOFFS				
		Gms.	G	A	Pts.	PIM	+/-	PP	SH	Gms.	G	A	Pts.	PIM
93-94— Cornell	ECAC	26	4	16	20	48	...	...	...	—	—	—	—	—
94-95— Cornell	ECAC	21	6	13	19	32	...	...	...	—	—	—	—	—
95-96— Cornell	ECAC	31	18	14	32	60	...	...	...	—	—	—	—	—
96-97— Providence.................	AHL	42	12	11	23	10	...	...	...	—	—	—	—	—
— Boston	NHL	3	0	0	0	0	1	0	0	—	—	—	—	—
NHL totals (1 year)		3	0	0	0	0	1	0	0					

DRUCE, JOHN — RW — FLYERS

PERSONAL: Born February 23, 1966, in Peterborough, Ont. ... 6-2/195. ... Shoots right. ... Name pronounced DROOZ.
TRANSACTIONS/CAREER NOTES: Broke collarbone (October 1983). ... Tore ligaments in ankle (December 1984). ... Selected by Washington Capitals in second round (second Capitals pick, 40th overall) of NHL entry draft (June 15, 1985). ... Tore thumb ligaments (October 1985). ... Fractured wrist (October 18, 1992); missed 18 games. ... Traded by Capitals to Winnipeg Jets with conditional pick in 1993 draft for RW Pat Elynuik (October 1, 1992). ... Signed as free agent by Los Angeles Kings (August 2, 1993). ... Strained groin (April 7, 1995); missed two

games. ... Traded by Kings with seventh-round pick (LW Todd Fedoruk) in 1997 draft to Philadelphia Flyers for fourth-round pick (C Mikael Simons) in 1996 draft (March 19, 1996). ... Sprained left knee (April 18, 1996); missed 10 playoff games. ... Strained neck (November 13, 1996); missed three games. ... Sprained shoulder (December 10, 1996); missed five games. ... Suffered lacerated leg (March 2, 1997); missed seven games.

STATISTICAL PLATEAUS: Three-goal games: 1991-92 (1), 1993-94 (1). Total: 2.

		REGULAR SEASON								PLAYOFFS				
Season Team	League	Gms.	G	A	Pts.	PIM	+/-	PP	SH	Gms.	G	A	Pts.	PIM
83-84— Peterborough Jr. B.....	OHA	40	15	18	33	69	...	...	...	—	—	—	—	—
84-85— Peterborough............	OHL	54	12	14	26	90	...	...	...	17	6	2	8	21
85-86— Peterborough............	OHL	49	22	24	46	84	...	...	...	16	0	5	5	34
86-87— Binghamton	AHL	7	13	9	22	131	...	...	...	12	0	3	3	28
87-88— Binghamton	AHL	68	32	29	61	82	...	...	...	1	0	0	0	0
88-89— Washington	NHL	48	8	7	15	62	7	0	0	1	0	0	0	0
— Baltimore	AHL	16	2	11	13	10	...	...	...	—	—	—	—	—
89-90— Washington	NHL	45	8	3	11	52	-3	1	0	15	14	3	17	23
— Baltimore	AHL	26	15	16	31	38	...	...	...	—	—	—	—	—
90-91— Washington	NHL	80	22	36	58	46	4	7	1	11	1	1	2	7
91-92— Washington	NHL	67	19	18	37	39	14	1	0	7	1	0	1	2
92-93— Winnipeg	NHL	50	6	14	20	37	-4	0	0	2	0	0	0	0
93-94— Phoenix....................	IHL	8	5	6	11	9	...	...	...	—	—	—	—	—
— Los Angeles	NHL	55	14	17	31	50	16	1	1	—	—	—	—	—
94-95— Los Angeles	NHL	43	15	5	20	20	-3	3	0	—	—	—	—	—
95-96— Los Angeles	NHL	64	9	12	21	14	-26	0	0	—	—	—	—	—
— Philadelphia	NHL	13	4	4	8	13	6	0	0	2	0	2	2	2
96-97— Philadelphia	NHL	43	7	8	15	12	-5	1	0	13	1	0	1	2
NHL totals (9 years)		508	112	124	236	345	6	14	2	51	17	6	23	36

DRURY, TED   C   MIGHTY DUCKS

PERSONAL: Born September 13, 1971, in Boston. ... 6-0/185. ... Shoots left. ... Full name: Theodore Evans Drury. ... Name pronounced DROO-ree. ... Brother of Chris Drury, center in Colorado Avalanche system.
HIGH SCHOOL: Fairfield (Conn.) College Prep School.
COLLEGE: Harvard.
TRANSACTIONS/CAREER NOTES: Broke ankle (January 1988). ... Selected by Calgary Flames in second round (second Flames pick, 42nd overall) of NHL entry draft (June 17, 1989). ... Fractured kneecap (December 22, 1993); missed 15 games. ... Traded by Flames with D Gary Suter and LW Paul Ranheim to Hartford Whalers for C Mikael Nylander, D Zarley Zalapski and D James Patrick (March 10, 1994). ... Strained back (March 9, 1995); missed three games. ... Injured shoulder (November 4, 1995); missed three games. ... Suffered slight concussion (January 22, 1996); missed two games. ... Injured wrist (January 29, 1996). ... Signed as free agent by Ottawa Senators for 1995-96 season. ... Traded by Senators with rights to D Marc Moro to Mighty Ducks of Anaheim for C Shaun Van Allen and D Jason York (October 1, 1996). ... Fractured wrist (January 31, 1997); missed five games.
HONORS: Named to NCAA All-America East first team (1992-93). ... Named ECAC Player of the Year (1992-93). ... Named to ECAC All-Star first team (1992-93).

		REGULAR SEASON								PLAYOFFS				
Season Team	League	Gms.	G	A	Pts.	PIM	+/-	PP	SH	Gms.	G	A	Pts.	PIM
87-88— Fairfield Coll. Prep	Conn. H.S.	—	21	28	49	...	...	...	...	—	—	—	—	—
88-89— Fairfield Coll. Prep	Conn. H.S.	...	35	31	66	...	...	...	...	—	—	—	—	—
89-90— Harvard University.....	ECAC	17	9	13	22	10	...	...	...	—	—	—	—	—
90-91— Harvard University.....	ECAC	26	18	18	36	22	...	...	...	—	—	—	—	—
91-92— U.S. national team	Int'l	53	11	23	34	30	...	...	...	—	—	—	—	—
— U.S. Olympic team.....	Int'l	7	1	1	2	0	...	...	...	—	—	—	—	—
92-93— Harvard University.....	ECAC	31	22	41	*63	26	...	...	...	—	—	—	—	—
93-94— Calgary	NHL	34	5	7	12	26	-5	0	1	—	—	—	—	—
— U.S. national team	Int'l	11	1	4	5	11	...	...	...	—	—	—	—	—
— U.S. Olympic team.....	Int'l	7	1	2	3	2	...	...	...	—	—	—	—	—
— Hartford	NHL	16	1	5	6	10	-10	0	0	—	—	—	—	—
94-95— Hartford	NHL	34	3	6	9	21	-3	0	0	—	—	—	—	—
— Springfield	AHL	2	0	1	1	0	...	...	...	—	—	—	—	—
95-96— Ottawa	NHL	42	9	7	16	54	-19	1	0	—	—	—	—	—
96-97— Anaheim....................	NHL	73	9	9	18	54	-9	1	0	10	1	0	1	4
NHL totals (5 years)		199	27	34	61	165	-46	2	1	10	1	0	1	4

DUBE, CHRISTIAN   C   RANGERS

PERSONAL: Born April 25, 1977, in Quebec City. ... 6-0/183. ... Shoots right. ... Name pronounced doo-BAY.
TRANSACTIONS/CAREER NOTES: Selected by New York Rangers in second round (first Rangers pick, 39th overall) of NHL entry draft (July 8, 1995). ... Injured right shoulder (September 28, 1996); missed two games.
HONORS: Won Michael Bergeron Trophy (1993-94). ... Won Can.HL Player of the Year Award (1995-96). ... Named to Can.HL All-Star first team (1995-96). ... Won Frank Selke Trophy (1995-96). ... Won Michel Briere Trophy (1995-96). ... Named to QMJHL All-Star first team (1995-96). ... Won Stafford Smythe Memorial Trophy (1996-97). ... Named to Memorial Cup All-Star Team (1996-97).

		REGULAR SEASON								PLAYOFFS				
Season Team	League	Gms.	G	A	Pts.	PIM	+/-	PP	SH	Gms.	G	A	Pts.	PIM
93-94— Sherbrooke................	QMJHL	72	31	41	72	22	...	...	...	11	3	2	5	6
94-95— Sherbrooke................	QMJHL	71	36	65	101	43	...	...	...	7	1	7	8	8
95-96— Sherbrooke................	QMJHL	62	52	93	145	105	...	...	...	7	5	5	10	6
96-97— New York Rangers	NHL	27	1	1	2	4	-4	1	0	3	0	0	0	0
— Hull	QMJHL	19	15	22	37	27	...	...	...	14	7	16	23	14
NHL totals (1 year)		27	1	1	2	4	-4	1	0	3	0	0	0	0

D

DUBINSKY, STEVE — C — BLACKHAWKS

PERSONAL: Born July 9, 1970, in Montreal. ... 6-0/190. ... Shoots left. ... Name pronounced doo-BIHN-skee.
COLLEGE: Clarkson (N.Y.).
TRANSACTIONS/CAREER NOTES: Selected by Chicago Blackhawks in 11th round (11th Blackhawks pick, 226th overall) of NHL entry draft (June 16, 1990).

Season Team	League	REGULAR SEASON								PLAYOFFS				
		Gms.	G	A	Pts.	PIM	+/-	PP	SH	Gms.	G	A	Pts.	PIM
89-90— Clarkson	ECAC	35	7	10	17	24	...	...	...	—	—	—	—	—
90-91— Clarkson	ECAC	38	15	23	38	26	...	...	...	—	—	—	—	—
91-92— Clarkson	ECAC	33	21	34	55	40	...	...	...	—	—	—	—	—
92-93— Clarkson	ECAC	35	18	26	44	58	...	...	...	—	—	—	—	—
93-94— Chicago	NHL	27	2	6	8	16	1	0	0	6	0	0	0	10
— Indianapolis	IHL	54	15	25	40	63	...	...	...	—	—	—	—	—
94-95— Indianapolis	IHL	62	16	11	27	29	...	...	...	—	—	—	—	—
— Chicago	NHL	16	0	0	0	8	-5	0	0	—	—	—	—	—
95-96— Indianapolis	IHL	16	8	8	16	10	...	...	...	—	—	—	—	—
— Chicago	NHL	43	2	3	5	14	3	0	0	—	—	—	—	—
96-97— Indianapolis	IHL	77	32	40	72	53	...	...	...	1	3	1	4	0
— Chicago	NHL	5	0	0	0	0	2	0	0	4	1	0	1	4
NHL totals (4 years)		91	4	9	13	38	1	0	0	10	1	0	1	14

DUCHESNE, STEVE — D — SENATORS

PERSONAL: Born June 30, 1965, in Sept-Iles, Que. ... 5-11/195. ... Shoots left. ... Name pronounced doo-SHAYN.
TRANSACTIONS/CAREER NOTES: Signed as free agent by Los Angeles Kings (October 1, 1984). ... Strained left knee (January 26, 1988). ... Separated left shoulder (November 1988). ... Traded by Kings with fourth-round pick in 1991 draft (D Aris Brimanis) to Philadelphia Flyers for D Jeff Chychrun and rights to RW Jari Kurri (May 30, 1991). ... Traded by Flyers with G Ron Hextall, C Mike Ricci, C Peter Forsberg, D Kerry Huffman, first-round pick (G Jocelyn Thibault) in 1993 draft, cash and future considerations to Quebec Nordiques for C Eric Lindros (June 20, 1992). ... Flyers sent LW Chris Simon and first-round pick (traded to Toronto) in 1994 draft to Nordiques to complete deal (July 21, 1992). ... Suffered a concussion (January 2, 1993); missed one game. ... Suffered from the flu (March 20, 1993); missed one game. ... Refused to report to Nordiques in 1993-94 due to contract dispute. ... Traded by Nordiques with RW Denis Chasse to St. Louis Blues for C Ron Sutter, C Bob Bassen and D Garth Butcher (January 23, 1994). ... Injured back (March 30, 1994); missed one game. ... Injured shoulder (March 31, 1995); missed one game. ... Traded by Blues to Ottawa Senators for second-round pick (traded to Buffalo) in 1996 draft (August 4, 1995). ... Sprained ankle (November 18, 1995); missed 20 games. ... Bruised hand (October 9, 1996); missed two games. ... Suffered sore back (March 4, 1997); missed two games.
HONORS: Named to QMJHL All-Star first team (1984-85). ... Named to NHL All-Rookie team (1986-87). ... Played in NHL All-Star Game (1989, 1990 and 1993).
STATISTICAL PLATEAUS: Three-goal games: 1988-89 (1), 1991-92 (1), 1993-94 (1). Total: 3.

Season Team	League	REGULAR SEASON								PLAYOFFS				
		Gms.	G	A	Pts.	PIM	+/-	PP	SH	Gms.	G	A	Pts.	PIM
83-84— Drummondville	QMJHL	67	1	34	35	79	...	...	...	—	—	—	—	—
84-85— Drummondville	QMJHL	65	22	54	76	94	...	...	...	5	4	7	11	8
85-86— New Haven	AHL	75	14	35	49	76	...	...	...	5	0	2	2	9
86-87— Los Angeles	NHL	75	13	25	38	74	8	5	0	5	2	2	4	4
87-88— Los Angeles	NHL	71	16	39	55	109	0	5	0	5	1	3	4	14
88-89— Los Angeles	NHL	79	25	50	75	92	31	8	5	11	4	4	8	12
89-90— Los Angeles	NHL	79	20	42	62	36	-3	6	0	10	2	9	11	6
90-91— Los Angeles	NHL	78	21	41	62	66	19	8	0	12	4	8	12	8
91-92— Philadelphia	NHL	78	18	38	56	86	-7	7	2	—	—	—	—	—
92-93— Quebec	NHL	82	20	62	82	57	15	8	0	6	0	5	5	6
93-94— St. Louis	NHL	36	12	19	31	14	1	8	0	4	0	2	2	2
94-95— St. Louis	NHL	47	12	26	38	36	29	1	0	7	0	4	4	2
95-96— Ottawa	NHL	62	12	24	36	42	-23	7	0	—	—	—	—	—
96-97— Ottawa	NHL	78	19	28	47	38	-9	10	2	7	1	4	5	0
NHL totals (11 years)		765	188	394	582	650	61	73	9	67	14	41	55	54

DUERDEN, DAVE — LW — PANTHERS

PERSONAL: Born April 11, 1977, in Oshawa, Ont. ... 6-2/182. ... Shoots left. ... Name pronounced DEER-dihn.
HIGH SCHOOL: Thomas A. Stewart (Peterborough, Ont.).
TRANSACTIONS/CAREER NOTES: Selected by Florida Panthers in fourth round (fourth Panthers pick, 80th overall) of NHL entry draft (July 8, 1995).
HONORS: Named to OHL All-Star second team (1996-97).

Season Team	League	REGULAR SEASON								PLAYOFFS				
		Gms.	G	A	Pts.	PIM	+/-	PP	SH	Gms.	G	A	Pts.	PIM
93-94— Wexford	Tier II Jr. A	47	17	24	41	26	...	...	...	—	—	—	—	—
94-95— Peterborough	OHL	66	20	33	53	21	...	...	...	11	6	2	8	6
95-96— Peterborough	OHL	66	35	35	70	47	...	...	...	24	14	13	27	16
96-97— Peterborough	OHL	66	36	48	84	34	...	...	...	4	2	4	6	0

DUFFUS, PARRIS — G — COYOTES

PERSONAL: Born January 27, 1970, in Denver. ... 6-2/192. ... Catches left. ... Name pronounced PAIR-ihz DUH-fihz.
COLLEGE: Cornell.
TRANSACTIONS/CAREER NOTES: Selected by St. Louis Blues in ninth round (sixth Blues pick, 180th overall) of NHL entry draft (June 16, 1990). ... Signed as free agent by Winnipeg Jets (July 21, 1995). ... Jets franchise moved to Phoenix and renamed Coyotes for 1996-97 season; NHL approved move on January 18, 1996.
HONORS: Named to NCAA All-America East first team (1991-92). ... Named to ECAC All-Star second team (1991-92).

		REGULAR SEASON								PLAYOFFS						
Season Team	League	Gms.	Min	W	L	T	GA	SO	Avg.	Gms.	Min.	W	L	GA	SO	Avg.
88-89—Melfort	SJHL	39	2207	5	28	3	227	1	6.17	—	—	—	—	—	—	—
89-90—Melfort	SJHL	51	2828	17	26	3	226	2	4.79	—	—	—	—	—	—	—
90-91—Cornell University	ECAC	4	37	0	0	0	3	0	4.86	—	—	—	—	—	—	—
91-92—Cornell University	ECAC	28	1677	14	11	3	74	1	2.65	—	—	—	—	—	—	—
92-93—Hampton Roads	ECHL	4	245	3	1	‡0	13	0	3.18	—	—	—	—	—	—	—
—Peoria	IHL	37	2149	16	15	‡0	142	0	3.96	1	59	0	1	5	0	5.08
93-94—Peoria	IHL	36	1845	19	10	‡3	141	0	4.59	2	92	0	1	6	0	3.91
94-95—Peoria	IHL	29	1581	17	7	‡3	71	3	2.69	7	410	4	2	17	0	2.49
95-96—Minnesota	IHL	35	1812	10	17	‡2	100	1	3.31	—	—	—	—	—	—	—
96-97—Las Vegas	IHL	58	3266	28	19	‡6	176	3	3.23	3	175	0	3	8	0	2.74
—Phoenix	NHL	1	29	0	0	0	1	0	2.07	—	—	—	—	—	—	—
NHL totals (1 year)		1	29	0	0	0	1	0	2.07							

DUFRESNE, DONALD — D — OILERS

PERSONAL: Born April 10, 1967, in Quebec City. ... 6-1/206. ... Shoots left. ... Name pronounced DOH-nal doo-FRAYN.

TRANSACTIONS/CAREER NOTES: Suffered from pneumonia (November 1984). ... Selected by Montreal Canadiens in sixth round (eighth Canadiens pick, 117th overall) of NHL entry draft (June 15, 1985). ... Dislocated shoulder (January 8, 1988). ... Sprained ankle (February 1989). ... Separated shoulder (October 5, 1989); missed 15 games. ... Reinjured shoulder (December 9, 1989). ... Tore ligaments in right knee (December 9, 1991); missed 15 games. ... Sprained knee (February 20, 1993); missed three games. ... Strained rib cage muscles (March 3, 1993); missed three games. ... Traded by Canadiens to Tampa Bay Lightning (June 18, 1993) to complete deal in which Canadiens sent D Eric Charron, D Alain Cote and future considerations to Lightning for D Rob Ramage (March 20, 1993). ... Suffered knee ligament sprain (January 26, 1994); missed eight games. ... Reinjured knee (February 17, 1994); missed seven games. ... Traded by Lightning to Los Angeles Kings for sixth-round pick (C Daniel Juden) in 1994 draft (March 19, 1994). ... Selected by St. Louis Blues from Kings in waiver draft for cash (January 18, 1995). ... Traded by Blues with D Jeff Norton to Edmonton Oilers for D Igor Kravchuk and D Ken Sutton (January 4, 1996). ... Tore knee cartilage (October 26, 1996); missed 12 games. ... Fractured foot (February 17, 1997); missed 17 games.

HONORS: Named to QMJHL All-Star second team (1985-86 and 1986-87).

MISCELLANEOUS: Member of Stanley Cup championship team (1993).

		REGULAR SEASON							PLAYOFFS				
Season Team	League	Gms.	G	A	Pts.	PIM	+/-	PP	SH	Gms.	G	A	Pts.	PIM
83-84—Trois-Rivieres	QMJHL	67	7	12	19	97	...	...	...	—	—	—	—	—
84-85—Trois-Rivieres	QMJHL	65	5	30	35	112	...	...	...	7	1	3	4	12
85-86—Trois-Rivieres	QMJHL	63	8	32	40	160	...	...	...	1	0	0	0	0
86-87—Longueuil	QMJHL	67	5	29	34	97	...	...	...	20	1	8	9	38
87-88—Sherbrooke	AHL	47	1	8	9	107	...	...	...	6	1	1	2	34
88-89—Montreal	NHL	13	0	1	1	43	3	0	0	6	1	1	2	4
—Sherbrooke	AHL	47	0	12	12	170	...	...	...	—	—	—	—	—
89-90—Montreal	NHL	18	0	4	4	23	1	0	0	10	0	1	1	18
—Sherbrooke	AHL	38	2	11	13	104	...	...	...	0	0	0	0	0
90-91—Fredericton	AHL	10	1	4	5	35	...	...	...	1	0	0	0	0
—Montreal	NHL	53	2	13	15	55	5	0	0	10	0	1	1	21
91-92—Montreal	NHL	3	0	0	0	2	2	0	0	—	—	—	—	—
—Fredericton	AHL	31	8	12	20	60	...	...	...	7	0	0	0	10
92-93—Montreal	NHL	32	1	2	3	32	0	0	0	2	0	0	0	0
93-94—Tampa Bay	NHL	51	2	6	8	48	-2	0	0	—	—	—	—	—
—Los Angeles	NHL	9	0	0	0	10	-5	0	0	—	—	—	—	—
94-95—St. Louis	NHL	22	0	3	3	10	2	0	0	3	0	0	0	4
95-96—St. Louis	NHL	3	0	0	0	4	-2	0	0	—	—	—	—	—
—Worcester	AHL	13	1	1	2	14	...	...	...	—	—	—	—	—
—Edmonton	NHL	42	1	6	7	16	-2	0	0	—	—	—	—	—
96-97—Edmonton	NHL	22	0	1	1	15	-1	0	0	3	0	0	0	0
NHL totals (10 years)		268	6	36	42	258	1	0	0	34	1	3	4	47

DUMONT, JEAN-PIERRE — LW — ISLANDERS

PERSONAL: Born May 1, 1978, in Montreal. ... 6-1/187. ... Shoots left.

TRANSACTIONS/CAREER NOTES: Selected by New York Islanders in first round (first Islanders pick, third overall) of NHL entry draft (June 22, 1996).

HONORS: Won Mike Bossy Trophy (1995-96). ... Named to QMJHL All-Star second team (1996-97).

		REGULAR SEASON							PLAYOFFS				
Season Team	League	Gms.	G	A	Pts.	PIM	+/-	PP	SH	Gms.	G	A	Pts.	PIM
93-94—Val-d'Or	QMJHL	25	9	11	20	10	...	...	...	—	—	—	—	—
94-95—Val-d'Or	QMJHL	48	5	14	19	24	...	...	...	—	—	—	—	—
95-96—Val-d'Or	QMJHL	66	48	57	105	109	...	...	...	13	12	8	20	22
96-97—Val-d'Or	QMJHL	62	44	64	108	88	...	...	...	13	9	7	16	12

DUNHAM, MIKE — G — DEVILS

PERSONAL: Born June 1, 1972, in Johnson City, N.Y. ... 6-3/200. ... Catches left. ... Full name: Michael Francis Dunham.

HIGH SCHOOL: Canterbury (New Milford, Conn.).

COLLEGE: Maine.

TRANSACTIONS/CAREER NOTES: Selected by New Jersey Devils in third round (fourth Devils pick, 53rd overall) of NHL entry draft (June 16, 1990).

HONORS: Named to NCAA All-America East first team (1992-93). ... Named to Hockey East All-Star first team (1992-93). ... Shared Harry (Hap) Holmes Memorial Trophy with Corey Schwab (1994-95). ... Shared Jack Butterfield Trophy with Corey Schwab (1994-95). ... Named to AHL All-Star second team (1995-96). ... Shared William M. Jennings Trophy with Martin Brodeur (1996-97).

		REGULAR SEASON								PLAYOFFS					
Season Team	League	Gms.	Min	W	L	T	GA	SO	Avg.	Gms.	Min.	W	L	GA	SO	Avg.
87-88—Canterbury School........	Conn. HS	29	...	...	...	...	...	4	2.37	—	—	—	—	—	—	—
88-89—Canterbury School........	Conn. HS	25	...	...	...	...	63	2	...	—	—	—	—	—	—	—
89-90—Canterbury School........	Conn. HS	32	1558	...	...	...	55	...	2.12	—	—	—	—	—	—	—
90-91—University of Maine	Hockey East	23	1275	14	5	2	63	2	*2.96	—	—	—	—	—	—	—
91-92—University of Maine	Hockey East	7	382	6	0	0	14	1	2.20	—	—	—	—	—	—	—
—U.S. national team........	Int'l	3	157	0	1	1	10	0	3.82	—	—	—	—	—	—	—
—U.S. Olympic team........	Int'l							Did not play.		—	—	—	—	—	—	—
92-93—University of Maine	Hockey East	25	1429	21	1	1	63	...	2.65	—	—	—	—	—	—	—
93-94—U.S. national team........	Int'l	33	1983	...	...	...	125	4	3.78	—	—	—	—	—	—	—
—U.S. Olympic team........	Int'l	3	179	...	...	...	15	0	5.03	—	—	—	—	—	—	—
—Albany	AHL	5	305	2	2	1	26	0	5.11	—	—	—	—	—	—	—
94-95—Albany	AHL	35	2120	20	7	8	99	1	2.80	7	420	6	1	20	1	2.86
95-96—Albany	AHL	44	2591	30	10	2	109	1	2.52	3	181	1	2	5	1	1.66
96-97—Albany	AHL	3	184	1	1	1	12	0	3.91	—	—	—	—	—	—	—
—New Jersey	NHL	26	1013	8	7	1	43	2	2.55	—	—	—	—	—	—	—
NHL totals (1 year)..............		26	1013	8	7	1	43	2	2.55							

DVORAK, RADEK   RW   PANTHERS

PERSONAL: Born March 9, 1977, in Ceske Budejovice, Czechoslovakia. ... 6-2/185. ... Shoots right. ... Name pronounced duh-VOHR-ak.
TRANSACTIONS/CAREER NOTES: Selected by Florida Panthers in first round (first Panthers pick, 10th overall) of NHL entry draft (July 8, 1995).

		REGULAR SEASON							PLAYOFFS				
Season Team	League	Gms.	G	A	Pts.	PIM	+/-	PP	SH	Gms.	G	A	Pts.	PIM
92-93— Motor Ceske-Bude.....	Czech.	35	44	46	90	...	...	...	...	—	—	—	—	—
93-94— HC Ceske Bude..........	Czech Rep.	8	0	0	0	...	...	...	...	—	—	—	—	—
— Motor Ceske-Bude.....	Czech Rep.	20	17	18	35	...	...	...	...	—	—	—	—	—
94-95— HC Ceske Bude..........	Czech Rep.	10	3	5	8	...	...	...	...	9	5	1	6	0
95-96— Florida......................	NHL	77	13	14	27	20	5	0	0	16	1	3	4	0
96-97— Florida......................	NHL	78	18	21	39	30	-2	2	0	3	0	0	0	0
NHL totals (2 years)		155	31	35	66	50	3	2	0	19	1	3	4	0

DWYER, GORDIE   LW   BLUES

PERSONAL: Born January 25, 1978, in Drummondville, Que. ... 6-2/198. ... Shoots left.
TRANSACTIONS/CAREER NOTES: Selected by St. Louis Blues in third round (second Blues pick, 67th overall) of NHL entry draft (June 22, 1996).

		REGULAR SEASON							PLAYOFFS				
Season Team	League	Gms.	G	A	Pts.	PIM	+/-	PP	SH	Gms.	G	A	Pts.	PIM
94-95— Hull	QMJHL	57	3	7	10	204	...	...	...	17	1	3	4	54
95-96— Hull	QMJHL	25	5	9	14	199	...	...	...	—	—	—	—	—
— Laval	QMJHL	22	5	17	22	72	...	...	...	—	—	—	—	—
— Beauport....................	QMJHL	22	4	9	13	87	...	...	...	20	3	5	8	104
96-97— Drummondville	QMJHL	66	21	48	69	391	...	...	...	8	6	1	7	39

DYKHUIS, KARL   D   FLYERS

PERSONAL: Born July 8, 1972, in Sept-Iles, Que. ... 6-3/205. ... Shoots left. ... Name pronounced DIGHK-howz.
TRANSACTIONS/CAREER NOTES: Selected by Chicago Blackhawks in first round (first Blackhawks pick, 16th overall) of NHL entry draft (June 16, 1990). ... QMJHL rights traded by Hull Olympiques to Longueuil College Francais for first- and sixth-round draft picks (January 10, 1991). ... Traded by Blackhawks to Philadelphia Flyers for D Bob Wilkie (February 16, 1995). ... Sprained knee (November 26, 1996); missed two games. ... Suffered facial lacerations (December 31, 1996); missed two games. ... Dislocated shoulder (January 28, 1997); missed 13 games.
HONORS: Won Raymond Lagace Trophy (1988-89). ... Won Michael Bossy Trophy (1989-90). ... Named to QMJHL All-Star first team (1989-90).

		REGULAR SEASON							PLAYOFFS				
Season Team	League	Gms.	G	A	Pts.	PIM	+/-	PP	SH	Gms.	G	A	Pts.	PIM
88-89— Hull	QMJHL	63	2	29	31	59	...	...	...	9	1	9	10	6
89-90— Hull	QMJHL	69	10	45	55	119	...	...	...	11	2	5	7	2
90-91— Longueuil..................	QMJHL	3	1	4	5	6	...	...	...	—	—	—	—	—
— Canadian nat'l team ...	Int'l	37	2	9	11	16	...	...	...	—	—	—	—	—
91-92— Longueuil..................	QMJHL	29	5	19	24	55	...	...	...	17	0	12	12	14
— Chicago......................	NHL	6	1	3	4	4	-1	1	0	—	—	—	—	—
92-93— Indianapolis	IHL	59	5	18	23	76	...	...	...	5	1	1	2	8
— Chicago......................	NHL	12	0	5	5	0	2	0	0	—	—	—	—	—
93-94— Indianapolis	IHL	73	7	25	32	132	...	...	...	—	—	—	—	—
94-95— Indianapolis	IHL	52	2	21	23	63	...	...	...	—	—	—	—	—
— Hershey	AHL	1	0	0	0	0	...	...	...	—	—	—	—	—
— Philadelphia	NHL	33	2	6	8	37	7	1	0	15	4	4	8	14
95-96— Philadelphia	NHL	82	5	15	20	101	12	1	0	12	2	2	4	22
96-97— Philadelphia	NHL	62	4	15	19	35	6	2	0	18	0	3	3	2
NHL totals (5 years)		195	12	44	56	177	26	5	0	45	6	9	15	38

DZIEDZIC, JOE   LW   PENGUINS

PERSONAL: Born December 18, 1971, in Minneapolis. ... 6-3/227. ... Shoots left. ... Full name: Joseph Walter Dziedzic. ... Name pronounced DEED-zihk.
HIGH SCHOOL: Edison (Minneapolis).
COLLEGE: Minnesota.
TRANSACTIONS/CAREER NOTES: Selected by Pittsburgh Penguins in third round (second Penguins pick, 61st overall) of NHL entry draft (June 16, 1990). ... Suffered stiff neck (November 8, 1995); missed four games. ... Suffered back spasms (October 11, 1996); missed three games. ... Separated shoulder (January 25, 1997); missed two games. ... Injured groin (March 18, 1997); missed two games.

		REGULAR SEASON								PLAYOFFS				
Season Team	League	Gms.	G	A	Pts.	PIM	+/-	PP	SH	Gms.	G	A	Pts.	PIM
88-89 — Minneapolis Edison ...	Minn. H.S.	25	47	27	74	34	...	...	...	—	—	—	—	—
89-90 — Minneapolis Edison ...	Minn. H.S.	17	29	19	48	0	...	...	...	—	—	—	—	—
90-91 — Univ. of Minnesota.....	WCHA	20	6	4	10	26	...	...	...	—	—	—	—	—
91-92 — Univ. of Minnesota.....	WCHA	37	9	10	19	68	...	...	...	—	—	—	—	—
92-93 — Univ. of Minnesota.....	WCHA	41	11	14	25	62	...	...	...	—	—	—	—	—
93-94 — Univ. of Minnesota.....	WCHA	18	7	10	17	48	...	...	...	—	—	—	—	—
94-95 — Cleveland ...	IHL	68	15	15	30	74	...	...	...	4	1	0	1	10
95-96 — Pittsburgh ...	NHL	69	5	5	10	68	-5	0	0	16	1	2	3	19
96-97 — Pittsburgh ...	NHL	59	9	9	18	63	-4	0	0	5	0	1	1	4
NHL totals (2 years)		128	14	14	28	131	-9	0	0	21	1	3	4	23

EAGLES, MIKE   C   CAPITALS

PERSONAL: Born March 7, 1963, in Sussex, N.B. ... 5-10/190. ... Shoots left. ... Full name: Michael Bryant Eagles.
TRANSACTIONS/CAREER NOTES: Selected by Quebec Nordiques as underage junior in sixth round (fifth Nordiques pick, 116th overall) of NHL entry draft (June 10, 1981). ... Broke hand (October 1984). ... Injured ribs (February 21, 1986). ... Traded by Nordiques to Chicago Blackhawks for G Bob Mason (July 1988). ... Broke left hand (February 1989). ... Bruised kidney (January 15, 1990); missed eight games. ... Traded by Blackhawks to Winnipeg Jets for fourth-round pick (D Igor Kravchuk) in 1991 draft (December 14, 1990). ... Fractured thumb (February 17, 1992); missed 14 games. ... Suffered concussion (November 30, 1993); missed one game. ... Strained shoulder (March 7, 1994); missed one game. ... Bruised kidneys (March 27, 1994); missed remainder of season. ... Traded by Jets with D Igor Ulanov to Washington Capitals for third-(traded to Dallas) and fifth-(G Brian Elder) round picks in 1995 draft (April 7, 1995). ... Suffered broken finger (January 1, 1996); missed 11 games.
MISCELLANEOUS: Scored on a penalty shot (vs. Doug Keans, November 9, 1987).

		REGULAR SEASON								PLAYOFFS				
Season Team	League	Gms.	G	A	Pts.	PIM	+/-	PP	SH	Gms.	G	A	Pts.	PIM
79-80 — Melville	SJHL	55	46	30	76	77	...	...	...	—	—	—	—	—
80-81 — Kitchener	OMJHL	56	11	27	38	64	...	...	...	18	4	2	6	36
81-82 — Kitchener	OHL	62	26	40	66	148	...	...	...	15	3	11	14	27
82-83 — Kitchener	OHL	58	26	36	62	133	...	...	...	12	5	7	12	27
— Quebec................	NHL	2	0	0	0	2	-1	0	0	—	—	—	—	—
83-84 — Fredericton................	AHL	68	13	29	42	85	...	...	...	4	0	0	0	5
84-85 — Fredericton................	AHL	36	4	20	24	80	...	...	...	3	0	0	0	2
85-86 — Quebec................	NHL	73	11	12	23	49	3	1	0	3	0	0	0	2
86-87 — Quebec................	NHL	73	13	19	32	55	-15	0	2	4	1	0	1	10
87-88 — Quebec................	NHL	76	10	10	20	74	-18	1	2	—	—	—	—	—
88-89 — Chicago................	NHL	47	5	11	16	44	-8	0	0	—	—	—	—	—
89-90 — Indianapolis	IHL	24	11	13	24	47	...	...	...	13	*10	10	20	34
— Chicago................	NHL	23	1	2	3	34	-4	0	0	—	—	—	—	—
90-91 — Indianapolis	IHL	25	15	14	29	47	...	...	...	—	—	—	—	—
— Winnipeg	NHL	44	0	9	9	79	-10	0	0	—	—	—	—	—
91-92 — Winnipeg	NHL	65	7	10	17	118	-17	0	1	7	0	0	0	8
92-93 — Winnipeg	NHL	84	8	18	26	131	-1	1	0	5	0	1	1	6
93-94 — Winnipeg	NHL	73	4	8	12	96	-20	0	1	—	—	—	—	—
94-95 — Winnipeg	NHL	27	2	1	3	40	-13	0	0	—	—	—	—	—
— Washington	NHL	13	1	3	4	8	2	0	0	7	0	2	2	4
95-96 — Washington	NHL	70	4	7	11	75	-1	0	0	6	1	1	2	2
96-97 — Washington	NHL	70	1	7	8	42	-4	0	0	—	—	—	—	—
NHL totals (13 years)		740	67	117	184	847	-107	3	6	32	2	4	6	32

EAKINS, DALLAS   D   PANTHERS

PERSONAL: Born January 20, 1967, in Dade City, Fla. ... 6-2/195. ... Shoots left. ... Name pronounced EE-kihns.
TRANSACTIONS/CAREER NOTES: Selected by Washington Capitals as underage junior in 10th round (11th Capitals pick, 208th overall) of NHL entry draft (June 15, 1985). ... Injured back (October 1988). ... Signed as free agent by Winnipeg Jets (September 1989). ... Signed as free agent by Florida Panthers (July 14, 1993). ... Traded by Panthers to St. Louis Blues for fourth-round draft pick (RW Ivan Novoseltsev) in 1997 draft (September 28, 1995). ... Broke wrist (December 8, 1995); missed 29 games. ... Claimed on waivers by Winnipeg Jets (March 20, 1996). ... Jets franchise moved to Phoenix and renamed Coyotes for 1996-97 season; NHL approved move on January 18, 1996. ... Suffered back spasms (November 26, 1996); missed three games. ... Traded by Coyotes with C Mike Eastwood to New York Rangers for D Jay More (February 6, 1997). ... Signed as free agent by Florida Panthers (July 7, 1997).

		REGULAR SEASON								PLAYOFFS				
Season Team	League	Gms.	G	A	Pts.	PIM	+/-	PP	SH	Gms.	G	A	Pts.	PIM
84-85 — Peterborough............	OHL	48	0	8	8	96	...	...	...	7	0	0	0	18
85-86 — Peterborough............	OHL	60	6	16	22	134	...	...	...	16	0	1	1	30
86-87 — Peterborough............	OHL	54	3	11	14	145	...	...	...	12	1	4	5	37
87-88 — Peterborough............	OHL	64	11	27	38	129	...	...	...	12	3	12	15	16
88-89 — Baltimore	AHL	62	0	10	10	139	...	...	...	—	—	—	—	—
89-90 — Moncton	AHL	75	2	11	13	189	...	...	...					

D

E

Season Team	League	REGULAR SEASON Gms.	G	A	Pts.	PIM	+/-	PP	SH	PLAYOFFS Gms.	G	A	Pts.	PIM
90-91— Moncton	AHL	75	1	12	13	132	...	...	...	9	0	1	1	44
91-92— Moncton	AHL	67	3	13	16	136	...	...	...	11	2	1	3	16
92-93— Moncton	AHL	55	4	6	10	132	...	...	...	—	—	—	—	—
— Winnipeg	NHL	14	0	2	2	38	2	0	0	—	—	—	—	—
93-94— Cincinnati	IHL	80	1	18	19	143	...	...	...	8	0	1	1	41
— Florida	NHL	1	0	0	0	0	0	0	0	—	—	—	—	—
94-95— Cincinnati	IHL	59	6	12	18	69	...	...	...	—	—	—	—	—
— Florida	NHL	17	0	1	1	35	2	0	0	—	—	—	—	—
95-96— St. Louis	NHL	16	0	1	1	34	-2	0	0	—	—	—	—	—
— Worcester	AHL	4	0	0	0	12	...	...	...	—	—	—	—	—
— Winnipeg	NHL	2	0	0	0	0	1	0	0	—	—	—	—	—
96-97— Phoenix	NHL	4	0	0	0	10	-3	0	0	—	—	—	—	—
— Springfield	AHL	38	6	7	13	63	...	...	...	—	—	—	—	—
— Binghamton	AHL	19	1	7	8	15	...	...	...	—	—	—	—	—
— New York Rangers	NHL	3	0	0	0	6	-1	0	0	4	0	0	0	4
NHL totals (7 years)		57	0	4	4	123	-1	0	0	4	0	0	0	4

EASTWOOD, MIKE　　　　　C　　　　　RANGERS

PERSONAL: Born July 1, 1967, in Cornwall, Ont. ... 6-3/205. ... Shoots right.
COLLEGE: Western Michigan.
TRANSACTIONS/CAREER NOTES: Selected by Toronto Maple Leafs in fifth round (fifth Maple Leafs pick, 91st overall) of NHL entry draft (June 13, 1987). ... Traded by Maple Leafs with third-round pick (RW Brad Isbister) in 1995 draft to Winnipeg Jets for RW Tie Domi (April 7, 1995). ... Jets franchise moved to Phoenix and renamed Coyotes for 1996-97 season; NHL approved move on January 18, 1996. ... Fractured wrist (October 28, 1996); missed eight games. ... Traded by Coyotes with D Dallas Eakins to New York Rangers for D Jay More (February 6, 1997).
HONORS: Named to CCHA All-Star second team (1990-91).

Season Team	League	REGULAR SEASON Gms.	G	A	Pts.	PIM	+/-	PP	SH	PLAYOFFS Gms.	G	A	Pts.	PIM
86-87— Pembroke	COJHL					Statistics unavailable.								
87-88— Western Michigan	CCHA	42	5	8	13	14	...	...	...	—	—	—	—	—
88-89— Western Michigan	CCHA	40	10	13	23	87	...	...	...	—	—	—	—	—
89-90— Western Michigan	CCHA	40	25	27	52	36	...	...	...	—	—	—	—	—
90-91— Western Michigan	CCHA	42	29	32	61	84	...	...	...	—	—	—	—	—
91-92— St. John's	AHL	61	18	25	43	28	...	...	...	16	9	10	19	16
— Toronto	NHL	9	0	2	2	4	-4	0	0	—	—	—	—	—
92-93— St. John's	AHL	60	24	35	59	32	...	...	...	—	—	—	—	—
— Toronto	NHL	12	1	6	7	21	-2	0	0	10	1	2	3	8
93-94— Toronto	NHL	54	8	10	18	28	2	1	0	18	3	2	5	12
94-95— Toronto	NHL	36	5	5	10	32	-12	0	0	—	—	—	—	—
— Winnipeg	NHL	13	3	6	9	4	3	0	0	—	—	—	—	—
95-96— Winnipeg	NHL	80	14	14	28	20	-14	2	0	6	0	1	1	2
96-97— Phoenix	NHL	33	1	3	4	4	-3	0	0	—	—	—	—	—
— New York Rangers	NHL	27	1	7	8	10	2	0	0	15	1	2	3	22
NHL totals (6 years)		264	33	53	86	123	-28	3	0	49	5	7	12	44

EGELAND, ALLAN　　　　　C　　　　　LIGHTNING

PERSONAL: Born January 31, 1973, in Lethbridge, Alta. ... 6-0/184. ... Shoots left. ... Name pronounced EHG-uh-luhnd.
TRANSACTIONS/CAREER NOTES: Selected by Tampa Bay Lightning in third round (third Lightning pick, 55th overall) of NHL entry draft (June 26, 1993).
HONORS: Named to WHL (West) All-Star first team (1992-93). ... Named to WHL (West) All-Star second team (1993-94).

Season Team	League	REGULAR SEASON Gms.	G	A	Pts.	PIM	+/-	PP	SH	PLAYOFFS Gms.	G	A	Pts.	PIM
90-91— Lethbridge	WHL	67	2	16	18	57	...	...	...	9	0	0	0	0
91-92— Tacoma	WHL	72	35	39	74	115	...	...	...	4	0	1	1	18
92-93— Tacoma	WHL	71	56	57	113	119	...	...	...	7	9	7	16	18
93-94— Tacoma	WHL	70	47	76	123	204	...	...	...	8	5	3	8	26
94-95— Atlanta	IHL	60	8	16	24	112	...	...	...	5	0	1	1	16
95-96— Tampa Bay	NHL	5	0	0	0	2	...	...	...	—	—	—	—	—
— Atlanta	IHL	68	22	22	44	182	...	...	...	3	0	1	1	0
96-97— Adirondack	AHL	52	18	32	50	184	...	...	...	2	0	1	1	4
— Tampa Bay	NHL	4	0	0	0	5	-3	0	0	—	—	—	—	—
NHL totals (2 years)		9	0	0	0	7	-3	0	0	—	—	—	—	—

ELDER, BRIAN　　　　　G　　　　　COYOTES

PERSONAL: Born June 8, 1976, in Oak Lake, Man. ... 6-0/175. ... Catches left.
TRANSACTIONS/CAREER NOTES: Selected by Winnipeg Jets in fifth round (sixth Jets pick, 121st overall) of NHL entry draft (July 8, 1995). ... Jets franchise moved to Phoenix and renamed Coyotes for 1996-97 season; NHL approved move on January 18, 1996.
HONORS: Named to WHL (East) All-Star second team (1996-97).

Season Team	League	REGULAR SEASON Gms.	Min.	W	L	T	GA	SO	Avg.	PLAYOFFS Gms.	Min.	W	L	GA	SO	Avg.
94-95— Brandon	WHL	23	1325	16	5	1	69	0	3.12	13	756	6	7	38	1	3.02
95-96— Brandon	WHL	34	1962	23	9	1	113	3	3.46	—	—	—	—	—	—	—
96-97— Brandon	WHL	52	2928	32	15	0	132	2	*2.70	6	374	2	4	0	20	0.00

E

ELIAS, PATRIK　　　　　　　LW　　　　　　　DEVILS

PERSONAL: Born April 13, 1976, in Trebic, Czechoslovakia. ... 6-0/175. ... Shoots left. ... Name pronounced EH-lee-ahsh.
TRANSACTIONS/CAREER NOTES: Selected by New Jersey Devils in second round (second Devils pick, 51st overall) of NHL entry draft (June 28, 1994).

		REGULAR SEASON								PLAYOFFS				
Season Team	League	Gms.	G	A	Pts.	PIM	+/-	PP	SH	Gms.	G	A	Pts.	PIM
92-93— HC Kladno	Czech.	2	0	0	0	...	...	...	...	—	—	—	—	—
93-94— HC Kladno	Czech Rep.	15	1	2	3	...	...	...	...	11	2	2	4	0
— Czech Rep. Olympic...	Int'l	5	2	5	7	...	...	...	...					
94-95— HC Kladno	Czech Rep.	28	4	3	7	...	...	...	...	7	1	2	3	0
95-96— Albany	AHL	74	27	36	63	83	...	...	...	4	1	1	2	2
— New Jersey	NHL	1	0	0	0	0	-1	0	0					
96-97— Albany	AHL	57	24	43	67	76	...	...	...	6	1	2	3	8
— New Jersey	NHL	17	2	3	5	2	-4	0	0	8	2	3	5	4
NHL totals (2 years)		18	2	3	5	2	-5	0	0	8	2	3	5	4

ELIK, TODD　　　　　　　C　　　　　　　BRUINS

PERSONAL: Born April 15, 1966, in Brampton, Ont. ... 6-2/195. ... Shoots left. ... Name pronounced EHL-ihk.
COLLEGE: Regina (Sask.).
TRANSACTIONS/CAREER NOTES: Signed as free agent by New York Rangers (February 26, 1988). ... Traded by Rangers with LW Igor Liba, D Michael Boyce and future considerations to Los Angeles Kings for D Dean Kennedy and D Denis Larocque (December 12, 1988). ... Suffered lacerations near right eye (January 1991). ... Injured thigh (February 26, 1991); missed one game. ... Traded by Kings to Minnesota North Stars for D Charlie Huddy, LW Randy Gilhen, RW Jim Thomson and fourth-round pick (D Alexei Zhitnik) in 1991 draft (June 22, 1991). ... Broke foot (November 14, 1992); missed five games. ... Suffered head injury (January 23, 1993); missed six games. ... Traded by North Stars to Edmonton Oilers for C Brent Gilchrist (March 5, 1993). ... Injured shoulder (April 6, 1993); missed remainder of season. ... Claimed on waivers by San Jose Sharks (October 26, 1993). ... Injured hip (February 6, 1995); missed four games. ... Traded by Sharks to St. Louis Blues for LW Kevin Miller (March 23, 1995). ... Signed as free agent by Boston Bruins (July 31, 1995). ... Fractured wrist (April 3, 1996); missed remainder of regular season. ... Strained shoulder (January 2, 1997); missed three games.
HONORS: Named to CWUAA All-Star second team (1986-87).
MISCELLANEOUS: Failed to score on a penalty shot (vs. Curtis Joseph, April 16, 1992; vs. Jim Carey, November 19, 1996).

		REGULAR SEASON								PLAYOFFS				
Season Team	League	Gms.	G	A	Pts.	PIM	+/-	PP	SH	Gms.	G	A	Pts.	PIM
83-84— Kingston	OHL	64	5	16	21	17	...	...	...	—	—	—	—	—
84-85— Kingston	OHL	34	14	11	25	6	...	...	...	—	—	—	—	—
— North Bay	OHL	23	4	6	10	2	...	...	...	4	2	0	2	0
85-86— North Bay	OHL	40	12	34	46	20	...	...	...	10	7	6	13	0
86-87— Univ. of Regina	CWUAA	27	26	34	60	137	...	...	...	—	—	—	—	—
87-88— Denver	IHL	81	44	56	100	83	...	...	...	12	8	12	20	9
88-89— Denver	IHL	28	20	15	35	22	...	...	...	—	—	—	—	—
— New Haven	AHL	43	11	25	36	31	...	...	...	17	10	12	22	44
89-90— Los Angeles	NHL	48	10	23	33	41	4	1	0	10	3	9	12	10
— New Haven	AHL	32	20	23	43	42	...	...	...	—	—	—	—	—
90-91— Los Angeles	NHL	74	21	37	58	58	20	2	0	12	2	7	9	6
91-92— Minnesota	NHL	62	14	32	46	125	0	4	3	5	1	1	2	2
92-93— Minnesota	NHL	46	13	18	31	48	-5	4	0	—	—	—	—	—
— Edmonton	NHL	14	1	9	10	8	1	0	0	—	—	—	—	—
93-94— Edmonton	NHL	4	0	0	0	6	0	0	0	—	—	—	—	—
— San Jose	NHL	75	25	41	66	89	-3	9	0	14	5	5	10	12
94-95— San Jose	NHL	22	7	10	17	18	3	4	0	—	—	—	—	—
— St. Louis	NHL	13	2	4	6	4	5	0	0	7	4	3	7	2
95-96— Boston	NHL	59	13	33	46	40	2	6	0	4	0	2	2	16
— Providence	AHL	7	2	7	9	10	...	...	...	—	—	—	—	—
96-97— Boston	NHL	31	4	12	16	16	-12	1	0	—	—	—	—	—
— Providence	AHL	37	16	29	45	63	...	...	...	10	1	6	7	33
NHL totals (8 years)		448	110	219	329	453	15	31	3	52	15	27	42	48

ELLETT, DAVE　　　　　　　D　　　　　　　BRUINS

PERSONAL: Born March 30, 1964, in Cleveland. ... 6-2/205. ... Shoots left.
COLLEGE: Bowling Green State.
TRANSACTIONS/CAREER NOTES: Selected by Winnipeg Jets as underage junior in fourth round (third Jets pick, 75th overall) of NHL entry draft (June 9, 1982). ... Bruised thigh (March 6, 1988); missed 10 games. ... Sprained ankle (November 16, 1988). ... Traded by Jets with C Paul Fenton to Toronto Maple Leafs for C Ed Olczyk and LW Mark Osborne (November 10, 1990). ... Separated shoulder (March 2, 1993); missed 14 games. ... Suffered rib strain (December 11, 1993); missed 10 games. ... Separated shoulder (March 31, 1994); missed remainder of season. ... Cracked bone in foot (February 27, 1995); missed 15 games. ... Sprained knee (October 4, 1995); missed one game. ... Suffered from the flu (January 1, 1996). ... Scratched eye (December 27, 1996); missed one game. ... Bruised rib (January 31, 1997); missed four games. ... Traded by Maple Leafs with C Doug Gilmour and third-round pick in 1999 draft to New Jersey Devils for D Jason Smith, C Steve Sullivan and C Alyn McCauley (February 25, 1997). ... Signed as free agent by Boston Bruins (July 2, 1997).
HONORS: Named to NCAA All-Tournament team (1983-84). ... Played in NHL All-Star Game (1989 and 1992). ... Named to CCHA All-Star second team (1983-84).

		REGULAR SEASON								PLAYOFFS				
Season Team	League	Gms.	G	A	Pts.	PIM	+/-	PP	SH	Gms.	G	A	Pts.	PIM
81-82— Ottawa	COJHL	50	9	35	44	...	...	...	...	—	—	—	—	—
82-83— Bowling Green	CCHA	40	4	13	17	34	...	...	...	—	—	—	—	—
83-84— Bowling Green	CCHA	43	15	39	54	9	...	...	...	—	—	—	—	—
84-85— Winnipeg	NHL	80	11	27	38	85	20	3	0	8	1	5	6	4

E

Season Team	League	REGULAR SEASON Gms.	G	A	Pts.	PIM	+/-	PP	SH		PLAYOFFS Gms.	G	A	Pts.	PIM
85-86— Winnipeg	NHL	80	15	31	46	96	-38	2	0		3	0	1	1	0
86-87— Winnipeg	NHL	78	13	31	44	53	19	5	0		10	0	8	8	2
87-88— Winnipeg	NHL	68	13	45	58	106	-8	5	0		5	1	2	3	10
88-89— Winnipeg	NHL	75	22	34	56	62	-18	9	2		—	—	—	—	—
89-90— Winnipeg	NHL	77	17	29	46	96	-15	8	0		7	2	0	2	6
90-91— Winnipeg	NHL	17	4	7	11	6	-4	1	1		—	—	—	—	—
— Toronto	NHL	60	8	30	38	69	-4	5	0		—	—	—	—	—
91-92— Toronto	NHL	79	18	33	51	95	-13	9	1		—	—	—	—	—
92-93— Toronto	NHL	70	6	34	40	46	19	4	0		21	4	8	12	8
93-94— Toronto	NHL	68	7	36	43	42	6	5	0		18	3	15	18	31
94-95— Toronto	NHL	33	5	10	15	26	-6	3	0		7	0	2	2	0
95-96— Toronto	NHL	80	3	19	22	59	-10	1	1		6	0	0	0	4
96-97— Toronto	NHL	56	4	10	14	34	-8	0	0		—	—	—	—	—
— New Jersey	NHL	20	2	5	7	6	2	1	0		10	0	3	3	10
NHL totals (13 years)		941	148	381	529	881	-58	61	5		95	11	44	55	75

ELLIOTT, JASON — G — RED WINGS

PERSONAL: Born October 11, 1975, in Chapman, Australia. ... 6-2/183. ... Catches left.
COLLEGE: Cornell.
TRANSACTIONS/CAREER NOTES: Selected by Detroit Red Wings in eighth round (eighth Red Wings pick, 205th overall) of NHL entry draft (June 29, 1994).
HONORS: Named ECAC Playoff Most Valuable Player (1996-97).

Season Team	League	REGULAR SEASON Gms.	Min	W	L	T	GA	SO	Avg.		PLAYOFFS Gms.	Min.	W	L	GA	SO	Avg.
93-94— Kimberley	RMJHL	0	0	0	0	0	0	0	...		—	—	—	—	—	—	—
94-95— Cornell University	ECAC	16	877	16	5	1	62	0	4.24		—	—	—	—	—	—	—
95-96— Cornell University	ECAC	19	971	12	2	1	38	2	2.35		—	—	—	—	—	—	—
96-97— Cornell University	ECAC	27	1475	16	7	2	67	0	2.73		—	—	—	—	—	—	—

ELOMO, MIIKKA — LW — CAPITALS

PERSONAL: Born April 21, 1977, in Turku, Finland. ... 6-0/183. ... Shoots left. ... Name pronounced EHL-uh-moh.
TRANSACTIONS/CAREER NOTES: Selected by Washington Capitals in first round (second Capitals pick, 23rd overall) of NHL entry draft (July 8, 1995).

Season Team	League	REGULAR SEASON Gms.	G	A	Pts.	PIM	+/-	PP	SH		PLAYOFFS Gms.	G	A	Pts.	PIM
93-94— TPS Jr.	Finland	30	8	5	13	24	...	...	...		5	1	1	2	2
94-95— Kiekko-67	Finland Dv.II	14	9	2	11	39	...	...	...		—	—	—	—	—
— TPS Jr.	Finland	14	3	8	11	24	...	...	...		—	—	—	—	—
95-96— Kiekko-67	Finland Dv.II	21	9	6	15	100	...	...	...		—	—	—	—	—
— TPS Jr.	Finland	6	0	2	2	18	...	...	...		—	—	—	—	—
— TPS Turku	Finland	10	1	1	2	8	...	...	...		3	0	0	0	2
96-97— Portland	AHL	52	8	9	17	37	...	...	...		—	—	—	—	—

ELYNUIK, PAT — RW — STARS

PERSONAL: Born October 30, 1967, in Foam Lake, Sask. ... 6-1/192. ... Shoots right. ... Full name: Pat Gerald Elynuik. ... Name pronounced EHL-ih-nuhk.
TRANSACTIONS/CAREER NOTES: Selected by Winnipeg Jets as underage junior in first round (first Jets pick, eighth overall) of NHL entry draft (June 21, 1986). ... Separated left shoulder (March 7, 1989). ... Strained groin (December 14, 1991); missed six games. ... Sprained knee (February 2, 1992); missed three games. ... Injured eye (March 17, 1992); missed five games. ... Traded by Jets to Washington Capitals for RW John Druce and conditional pick in 1993 draft (October 1, 1992). ... Traded by Capitals to Tampa Bay Lightning for fifth-round pick in 1995 draft (October 22, 1993). ... Signed as free agent by Ottawa Senators (June 21, 1994). ... Bruised ribs (April 22, 1995); missed three games. ... Signed as free agent by Dallas Stars (August 6, 1996).
HONORS: Named to WHL (East) All-Star first team (1985-86 and 1986-87).

Season Team	League	REGULAR SEASON Gms.	G	A	Pts.	PIM	+/-	PP	SH		PLAYOFFS Gms.	G	A	Pts.	PIM
84-85— Prince Albert	WHL	70	23	20	43	54	...	...	...		13	9	3	12	7
85-86— Prince Albert	WHL	68	53	53	106	62	...	...	...		20	7	9	16	17
86-87— Prince Albert	WHL	64	51	62	113	40	...	...	...		8	5	5	10	12
87-88— Winnipeg	NHL	13	1	3	4	12	...	...	...		—	—	—	—	—
— Moncton	AHL	30	11	18	29	35	...	...	...		—	—	—	—	—
88-89— Winnipeg	NHL	56	26	25	51	29	...	...	...		—	—	—	—	—
— Moncton	AHL	7	8	2	10	2	...	...	...		—	—	—	—	—
89-90— Winnipeg	NHL	80	32	42	74	83	2	14	0		7	2	4	6	2
90-91— Winnipeg	NHL	80	31	34	65	73	-13	16	0		—	—	—	—	—
91-92— Winnipeg	NHL	60	25	25	50	65	-2	9	0		7	2	2	4	4
92-93— Washington	NHL	80	22	35	57	66	3	8	0		6	2	3	5	19
93-94— Washington	NHL	4	1	1	2	0	-3	1	0		—	—	—	—	—
— Tampa Bay	NHL	63	12	14	26	64	-18	3	1		—	—	—	—	—
94-95— Ottawa	NHL	41	3	7	10	51	-11	0	0		—	—	—	—	—
95-96— Ottawa	NHL	29	1	2	3	16	2	0	0		—	—	—	—	—
— Fort Wayne	IHL	42	22	28	50	43	...	...	...		—	—	—	—	—
96-97— Michigan	IHL	81	24	34	58	62	...	...	...		4	1	0	1	0
NHL totals (9 years)		506	154	188	342	459	-40	51	1		20	6	9	15	25

E

EMERSON, NELSON   C   HURRICANES

PERSONAL: Born August 17, 1967, in Hamilton, Ont. ... 5-11/175. ... Shoots right. ... Full name: Nelson Donald Emerson.
COLLEGE: Bowling Green State.
TRANSACTIONS/CAREER NOTES: Selected by St. Louis Blues in third round (second Blues pick, 44th overall) of NHL entry draft (June 15, 1985). ... Fractured bone under his eye (December 28, 1991). ... Injured leg (April 3, 1993); missed one game. ... Traded by Blues with D Stephane Quintal to Winnipeg Jets for D Phil Housley (September 24, 1993). ... Sprained neck (January 25, 1994); missed one game. ... Traded by Jets to Hartford Whalers for C Darren Turcotte (October 6, 1995). ... Suffered mild concussion (February 17, 1996); missed one game. ... Fractured ankle prior to 1996-97 season; missed five games. ... Fractured ankle (November 4, 1996); missed six games. ... Strained groin (January 1, 1997); missed three games. ... Whalers franchise moved to North Carolina and renamed Carolina Hurricanes for 1997-98 season; NHL approved move on June 25, 1997.
HONORS: Named CCHA Rookie of the Year (1986-87). ... Named to NCAA All-America West second team (1987-88). ... Named to CCHA All-Star first team (1987-88 and 1989-90). ... Named to NCAA All-America West first team (1989-90). ... Named to CCHA All-Star second team (1988-89). ... Won Garry F. Longman Memorial Trophy (1990-91). ... Named to IHL All-Star first team (1990-91).
STATISTICAL PLATEAUS: Three-goal games: 1994-95 (1).

				REGULAR SEASON								PLAYOFFS			
Season Team	League	Gms.	G	A	Pts.	PIM	+/-	PP	SH		Gms.	G	A	Pts.	PIM
84-85 — Stratford Jr. B	OHA	40	23	38	61	70	...	...	...		—	—	—	—	—
85-86 — Stratford Jr. B	OHA	39	54	58	112	91	...	...	...		—	—	—	—	—
86-87 — Bowling Green	CCHA	45	26	35	61	28	...	...	...		—	—	—	—	—
87-88 — Bowling Green	CCHA	45	34	49	83	54	...	...	...		—	—	—	—	—
88-89 — Bowling Green	CCHA	44	22	46	68	46	...	...	...		—	—	—	—	—
89-90 — Bowling Green	CCHA	44	30	52	82	42	...	...	...		—	—	—	—	—
— Peoria	IHL	3	1	1	2	0	...	...	...		—	—	—	—	—
90-91 — St. Louis	NHL	4	0	3	3	2	-2	0	0		—	—	—	—	—
— Peoria	IHL	73	36	79	115	91	...	...	...		17	9	12	21	16
91-92 — St. Louis	NHL	79	23	36	59	66	-5	3	0		6	3	3	6	21
92-93 — St. Louis	NHL	82	22	51	73	62	2	5	2		11	1	6	7	6
93-94 — Winnipeg	NHL	83	33	41	74	80	-38	4	5		—	—	—	—	—
94-95 — Winnipeg	NHL	48	14	23	37	26	-12	4	1		—	—	—	—	—
95-96 — Hartford	NHL	81	29	29	58	78	-7	12	2		—	—	—	—	—
96-97 — Hartford	NHL	66	9	29	38	34	-21	2	1		—	—	—	—	—
NHL totals (7 years)		443	130	212	342	348	-83	30	11		17	4	9	13	27

EMMA, DAVID   C/RW   BRUINS

PERSONAL: Born January 14, 1969, in Cranston, R.I. ... 5-11/187. ... Shoots left. ... Full name: David Anaclethe Emma.
HIGH SCHOOL: Bishop Hendricken (Warwick, R.I.).
COLLEGE: Boston College.
TRANSACTIONS/CAREER NOTES: Selected by New Jersey Devils in sixth round (sixth Devils pick, 110th overall) of NHL entry draft (June 17, 1989). ... Refused assignment and left team (March 15, 1995). ... Loaned by Devils to Detroit Vipers (October 6, 1995). ... Signed as free agent by Boston Bruins (August 27, 1996). ... Loaned by Bruins to Phoenix Roadrunners for remainder of season (March 18, 1997).
HONORS: Named to Hockey East All-Freshman team (1987-88). ... Named to Hockey East All-Star second team (1988-89). ... Named to Hockey East All-Star first team (1989-90 and 1990-91). ... Won Hobey Baker Memorial Award (1990-91). ... Named Hockey East Player of the Year (1990-91). ... Named to NCAA All-America East first team (1989-90 and 1990-91). ... Named to Hockey East All-Decade team (1994).

				REGULAR SEASON								PLAYOFFS			
Season Team	League	Gms.	G	A	Pts.	PIM	+/-	PP	SH		Gms.	G	A	Pts.	PIM
86-87 — Bishop Hendricken	R.I.H.S.						Statistics unavailable.								
87-88 — Boston College	Hockey East	30	19	16	35	30	...	...	...		—	—	—	—	—
88-89 — Boston College	Hockey East	36	20	31	51	36	...	...	...		—	—	—	—	—
89-90 — Boston College	Hockey East	42	38	34	*72	46	...	...	...		—	—	—	—	—
90-91 — Boston College	Hockey East	39	35	46	81	44	...	...	...		—	—	—	—	—
91-92 — U.S. national team	Int'l	55	15	16	31	32	...	...	...		—	—	—	—	—
— U.S. Olympic team	Int'l	6	0	1	1	6	...	...	...		—	—	—	—	—
— Utica	AHL	15	4	7	11	12	...	...	...		4	1	1	2	2
92-93 — Utica	AHL	61	21	40	61	47	...	...	...		5	2	1	3	6
— New Jersey	NHL	2	0	0	0	0	0	0	0		—	—	—	—	—
93-94 — New Jersey	NHL	15	5	5	10	2	0	1	0		—	—	—	—	—
— Albany	AHL	56	26	29	55	53	...	...	...		5	1	2	3	8
94-95 — New Jersey	NHL	6	0	1	1	0	-2	0	0		—	—	—	—	—
— Albany	AHL	1	0	0	0	0	...	...	...		—	—	—	—	—
95-96 — Detroit	IHL	79	30	32	62	75	...	...	...		11	5	2	7	2
96-97 — Boston	NHL	5	0	0	0	0	-1	0	0		—	—	—	—	—
— Providence	AHL	53	10	18	28	24	...	...	...		—	—	—	—	—
— Phoenix	IHL	8	0	4	4	4	...	...	...		—	—	—	—	—
NHL totals (4 years)		28	5	6	11	2	-3	1	0						

ERIKSSON, ANDERS   D   RED WINGS

PERSONAL: Born January 9, 1975, in Bollnas, Sweden. ... 6-3/218. ... Shoots left.
TRANSACTIONS/CAREER NOTES: Selected by Detroit Red Wings in first round (first Red Wings pick, 22nd overall) of NHL entry draft (June 26, 1993).

				REGULAR SEASON								PLAYOFFS			
Season Team	League	Gms.	G	A	Pts.	PIM	+/-	PP	SH		Gms.	G	A	Pts.	PIM
92-93 — MoDo Ornskoldvik	Sweden	20	0	2	2	2	...	...	...		—	—	—	—	—
93-94 — MoDo Ornskoldvik	Sweden	38	2	8	10	42	...	...	...		11	0	0	0	8
94-95 — MoDo Ornskoldvik	Sweden	39	3	6	9	54	...	...	...		—	—	—	—	—

E

Season Team	League	REGULAR SEASON								PLAYOFFS				
		Gms.	G	A	Pts.	PIM	+/-	PP	SH	Gms.	G	A	Pts.	PIM
95-96 — Adirondack..................	AHL	75	6	36	42	64	...	...	...	3	0	0	0	0
— Detroit....................	NHL	1	0	0	0	2	1	0	0	3	0	0	0	0
96-97 — Detroit....................	NHL	23	0	6	6	10	5	0	0	—	—	—	—	—
— Adirondack..................	AHL	44	3	25	28	36	...	...	...	4	0	1	1	4
NHL totals (2 years)		24	0	6	6	12	6	0	0	3	0	0	0	0

ERREY, BOB   LW   STARS

PERSONAL: Born September 21, 1964, in Montreal. ... 5-11/175. ... Shoots left. ... Name pronounced AIR-ee. ... Cousin of Ted Lindsay, Hall of Fame left winger, Detroit Red Wings and Chicago Blackhawks (1944-45 through 1959-60 and 1964-65).

TRANSACTIONS/CAREER NOTES: Selected by Pittsburgh Penguins as underage junior in first round (first Penguins pick, 15th overall) of NHL entry draft (June 8, 1983). ... Sprained right knee (March 18, 1987). ... Broke right wrist (October 1987). ... Injured shoulder (May 9, 1992). ... Sprained ankle (September 29, 1992); missed 14 games. ... Bruised tailbone (February 27, 1993); missed two games. ... Traded by Penguins to Buffalo Sabres for D Mike Ramsey (March 22, 1993). ... Sprained ankle (April 4, 1993); missed four games. ... Injured hip (April 18, 1993); missed two games. ... Signed as free agent by San Jose Sharks (August 17, 1993). ... Injured rib (October 10, 1993); missed three games. ... Suffered from the flu (October 26, 1993); missed three games. ... Suspended two games by NHL for checking from behind (December 31, 1993). ... Suffered hyperextended knee (February 1, 1994); missed two games. ... Sprained knee (March 22, 1994); missed five games. ... Injured ankle (February 6, 1995); missed two games. ... Reinjured ankle (February 17, 1995); missed two games. ... Traded by Sharks to Detroit Red Wings for fifth-round pick (C Michal Bros) in 1995 draft (February 27, 1995). ... Bruised sternum (January 30, 1996); missed two games. ... Injured right foot (March 12, 1996); missed two games. ... Broke foot (March 22, 1996); missed four games. ... Suspended two games and fined $1000 by NHL for slashing (April 14, 1996). ... Claimed on waivers by Sharks (February 8, 1997). ... Signed as free agent by Dallas Stars (July 17, 1997).

HONORS: Named to OHL All-Star first team (1982-83).

STATISTICAL PLATEAUS: Three-goal games: 1991-92 (1).

MISCELLANEOUS: Member of Stanley Cup championship team (1991 and 1992). ... Captain of San Jose Sharks (1993-94). ... Scored on a penalty shot (vs. Chris Terreri, January 5, 1991; vs. Darcy Wakaluk, October 31, 1991). ... Failed to score on a penalty shot (vs. Nikolai Khabiblulin, March 22, 1995).

Season Team	League	REGULAR SEASON								PLAYOFFS				
		Gms.	G	A	Pts.	PIM	+/-	PP	SH	Gms.	G	A	Pts.	PIM
81-82 — Peterborough.............	OHL	68	29	31	60	39	...	...	...	9	3	1	4	9
82-83 — Peterborough.............	OHL	67	53	47	100	74	...	...	...	4	1	3	4	7
83-84 — Pittsburgh.................	NHL	65	9	13	22	29	-20	1	0	—	—	—	—	—
84-85 — Baltimore.................	AHL	59	17	24	41	14	...	...	...	8	3	4	7	11
— Pittsburgh.................	NHL	16	0	2	2	7	-8	0	0	—	—	—	—	—
85-86 — Baltimore.................	AHL	18	8	7	15	28	...	...	...	—	—	—	—	—
— Pittsburgh.................	NHL	37	11	6	17	8	1	0	1	—	—	—	—	—
86-87 — Pittsburgh.................	NHL	72	16	18	34	46	-5	2	1	—	—	—	—	—
87-88 — Pittsburgh.................	NHL	17	3	6	9	18	6	0	0	—	—	—	—	—
88-89 — Pittsburgh.................	NHL	76	26	32	58	124	40	0	3	11	1	2	3	12
89-90 — Pittsburgh.................	NHL	78	20	19	39	109	3	0	1	—	—	—	—	—
90-91 — Pittsburgh.................	NHL	79	20	22	42	115	11	0	1	24	5	2	7	29
91-92 — Pittsburgh.................	NHL	78	19	16	35	119	1	0	3	14	3	0	3	10
92-93 — Pittsburgh.................	NHL	54	8	6	14	76	-2	0	0	—	—	—	—	—
— Buffalo......................	NHL	8	1	3	4	4	2	0	0	4	0	1	1	10
93-94 — San Jose....................	NHL	64	12	18	30	126	-11	5	0	14	3	2	5	10
94-95 — San Jose....................	NHL	13	2	2	4	27	4	0	0	—	—	—	—	—
— Detroit......................	NHL	30	6	11	17	31	9	0	0	18	1	5	6	30
95-96 — Detroit......................	NHL	71	11	21	32	66	30	2	2	14	0	4	4	8
96-97 — Detroit......................	NHL	36	1	2	3	27	-3	0	0	—	—	—	—	—
— San Jose....................	NHL	30	3	6	9	20	-2	0	0	—	—	—	—	—
NHL totals (14 years)		824	168	203	371	952	56	10	12	99	13	16	29	109

ESCHE, ROBERT   G   COYOTES

PERSONAL: Born January 22, 1978, in Utica, N.Y. ... 6-0/188. ... Catches left.

TRANSACTIONS/CAREER NOTES: Selected by Phoenix Coyotes in sixth round (fifth Coyotes pick, 139th overall) of NHL entry draft (June 22, 1996).

Season Team	League	REGULAR SEASON							PLAYOFFS					
		Gms.	Min	W	L	T	GA	SO	Avg.	Gms.	Min.	W	L	GA	SO	Avg.
95-96 — Detroit	OHL	23	1219	13	6	0	76	1	3.74	3	105	0	2	4	0	2.29
96-97 — Detroit	OHL	58	3241	24	28	2	206	2	3.81	5	317	1	4	19	0	3.60

ESSENSA, BOB   G   OILERS

PERSONAL: Born January 14, 1965, in Toronto. ... 6-0/185. ... Catches left. ... Full name: Robert Earle Essensa. ... Name pronounced EH-sihn-zuh.

HIGH SCHOOL: Henry Carr (Rexdale, Ont.).

COLLEGE: Michigan State.

TRANSACTIONS/CAREER NOTES: Selected by Winnipeg Jets in fourth round (fifth Jets pick, 69th overall) of NHL entry draft (June 8, 1983). ... Suffered severe lacerations to both hands and wrist (February 1985). ... Injured groin (September 1990); missed three weeks. ... Sprained knee (October 12, 1991); missed four games. ... Injured left hamstring (December 8, 1991); missed four games. ... Sprained knee (March 6, 1992); missed seven games. ... Strained knee (March 6, 1992); missed two games. ... Traded by Jets with D Sergei Bautin to Detroit Red Wings for G Tim Cheveldae and LW Dallas Drake (March 8, 1994). ... Loaned by Red Wings to San Diego Gulls (January 27, 1995). ... Traded by Red Wings to Edmonton Oilers for future considerations (June 14, 1996).

HONORS: Named to CCHA All-Star first team (1984-85). ... Named to CCHA All-Star second team (1985-86). ... Named to NHL All-Rookie team (1989-90).

MISCELLANEOUS: Holds Poenix Coyotes franchise all-time records for games played by goaltender (281), most wins (116) and most shutouts (14). ... Stopped a penalty shot attempt (Philippe Bozon, November 3, 1993). ... Allowed a penalty shot goal (vs. Steve Yzerman, February 13, 1989; vs. Mike Craig, January 21, 1991; vs. Paul Ranheim, October 31, 1993).

		REGULAR SEASON								PLAYOFFS						
Season Team	League	Gms.	Min	W	L	T	GA	SO	Avg.	Gms.	Min.	W	L	GA	SO	Avg.
81-82—Henry Carr	MTHL	17	948	...	...	...	79	...	5.00	—	—	—	—	—	—	—
82-83—Henry Carr	MTHL	31	1840	...	...	...	98	2	3.20	—	—	—	—	—	—	—
83-84—Michigan State	CCHA	17	947	11	4	0	44	2	2.79	—	—	—	—	—	—	—
84-85—Michigan State	CCHA	18	1059	15	2	0	29	2	1.64	—	—	—	—	—	—	—
85-86—Michigan State	CCHA	23	1333	17	4	1	74	1	3.33	—	—	—	—	—	—	—
86-87—Michigan State	CCHA	25	1383	19	3	1	64	*2	*2.78	—	—	—	—	—	—	—
87-88—Moncton	AHL	27	1287	7	11	1	100	1	4.66	—	—	—	—	—	—	—
88-89—Winnipeg	NHL	20	1102	6	8	3	68	1	3.70	—	—	—	—	—	—	—
—Fort Wayne	IHL	22	1287	14	7	‡0	70	0	3.26	—	—	—	—	—	—	—
89-90—Moncton	AHL	6	358	3	3	0	15	0	2.51	—	—	—	—	—	—	—
—Winnipeg	NHL	36	2035	18	9	5	107	1	3.15	4	206	2	1	12	0	3.50
90-91—Moncton	AHL	2	125	1	0	1	6	0	2.88	—	—	—	—	—	—	—
—Winnipeg	NHL	55	2916	19	24	6	153	4	3.15	—	—	—	—	—	—	—
91-92—Winnipeg	NHL	47	2627	21	17	6	126	†5	2.88	1	33	0	0	3	0	5.45
92-93—Winnipeg	NHL	67	3855	33	26	6	227	2	3.53	6	367	2	4	20	0	3.27
93-94—Winnipeg	NHL	56	3136	19	30	6	201	1	3.85	—	—	—	—	—	—	—
—Detroit	NHL	13	778	4	7	2	34	1	2.62	2	109	0	2	9	0	4.95
94-95—San Diego	IHL	16	919	6	8	‡1	52	0	3.39	1	59	0	1	3	0	3.05
95-96—Adirondack	AHL	3	178	1	2	0	11	0	3.71	—	—	—	—	—	—	—
—Fort Wayne	IHL	45	2529	24	14	‡5	122	1	2.89	5	298	2	3	12	0	2.42
96-97—Edmonton	NHL	19	868	4	8	0	41	1	2.83	—	—	—	—	—	—	—
NHL totals (7 years)		313	17317	124	129	34	957	16	3.32	13	715	4	7	44	0	3.69

EWEN, TODD   RW   SHARKS

PERSONAL: Born March 22, 1966, in Saskatoon, Sask. ... 6-3/230. ... Shoots right. ... Name pronounced YOO-ihn.

TRANSACTIONS/CAREER NOTES: Selected by Edmonton Oilers as underage junior in eighth round (eighth Oilers pick, 168th overall) of NHL entry draft (June 9, 1984). ... Traded by Oilers to St. Louis Blues for D Shawn Evans (October 15, 1986). ... Sprained ankle (October 1987). ... Suspended one game by NHL for third game misconduct of season (January 1988). ... Pulled groin (October 1988). ... Tore right eye muscle (December 1988). ... Pulled left hamstring and bruised shoulder (February 1989). ... Suspended 10 games by NHL for coming off bench to instigate fight during playoff game (April 18, 1989; missed three playoff games and first seven games of 1989-90 season. ... Broke right hand (October 28, 1989). ... Traded by Blues to Montreal Canadiens for the return of a draft pick dealt to Montreal for D Mike Lalor (December 12, 1989) ... Strained knee ligaments and underwent surgery (November 19, 1990); missed 24 games. ... Fractured right hand at home (February 14, 1991); missed remainder of season. ... Separated shoulder (February 12, 1992); missed two games. ... Injured hand (January 10, 1993); missed two games. ... Pulled muscle in back (February 20, 1993); missed three games. ... Traded by Canadiens with C Patrik Carnback to Mighty Ducks of Anaheim for third-round pick (RW Chris Murray) in 1994 draft (August 10, 1993). ... Broke nose (October 19, 1993); missed one game. ... Sprained shoulder (April 2, 1994); missed five games. ... Suffered hip pointer (January 20, 1995); missed four games. ... Suffered slightly pulled groin (February 24, 1995); missed three games. ... Sprained thumb (March 31, 1995); missed five games. ... Suffered charley horse (April 21, 1995); missed six games. ... Injured left hand (November 7, 1995); missed 19 games. ... Lacerated right hand (March 10, 1996); missed two games. ... Signed as free agent by San Jose Sharks (July 25, 1996). ... Injured knee (October 8, 1996); missed 14 games. ... Injured groin (December 11, 1996); missed four games. ... Reinjured groin (December 26, 1996); missed four games. ... Injured hand (January 13, 1997); missed one game. ... Injured knee (February 23, 1997); missed four games. ... Reinjured knee (March 11, 1997); missed four games.

MISCELLANEOUS: Member of Stanley Cup championship team (1993). ... Holds Mighty Ducks of Anaheim all-time record for most penalty minutes (650).

		REGULAR SEASON							PLAYOFFS				
Season Team	League	Gms.	G	A	Pts.	PIM	+/-	PP	SH	Gms.	G	A	Pts.	PIM
82-83—Vernon	BCJHL	42	20	23	43	195	...	...	...	—	—	—	—	—
—Kamloops	WHL	3	0	0	0	2	...	...	...	2	0	0	0	0
83-84—New Westminster	WHL	68	11	13	24	176	...	...	...	7	2	1	3	15
84-85—New Westminster	WHL	56	11	20	31	304	...	...	...	10	1	8	9	60
85-86—New Westminster	WHL	60	28	24	52	289	...	...	...	—	—	—	—	—
—Maine	AHL	—	—	—	—	—	...	...	...	3	0	0	0	7
86-87—Peoria	IHL	16	3	3	6	110	...	...	...	—	—	—	—	—
—St. Louis	NHL	23	2	0	2	84	-1	0	0	4	0	0	0	23
87-88—St. Louis	NHL	64	4	2	6	227	-5	0	0	6	0	0	0	21
88-89—St. Louis	NHL	34	4	5	9	171	4	0	0	2	0	0	0	21
89-90—Peoria	IHL	2	0	0	0	12	...	...	...	—	—	—	—	—
—St. Louis	NHL	3	0	0	0	11	-2	0	0	—	—	—	—	—
—Montreal	NHL	41	4	6	10	158	1	0	0	10	0	0	0	4
90-91—Montreal	NHL	28	3	2	5	128	4	0	0	—	—	—	—	—
91-92—Montreal	NHL	46	1	2	3	130	3	0	0	3	0	0	0	18
92-93—Montreal	NHL	75	5	9	14	193	6	0	0	1	0	0	0	0
93-94—Anaheim	NHL	76	9	9	18	272	-7	0	0	—	—	—	—	—
94-95—Anaheim	NHL	24	0	0	0	90	-2	0	0	—	—	—	—	—
95-96—Anaheim	NHL	53	4	3	7	285	-5	0	0	—	—	—	—	—
96-97—San Jose	NHL	51	0	2	2	162	-5	0	0	—	—	—	—	—
NHL totals (11 years)		518	36	40	76	1911	-9	0	0	26	0	0	0	87

E
F

FAIRCHILD, KELLY   C   MAPLE LEAFS

PERSONAL: Born April 9, 1973, in Hibbing, Minn. ... 5-11/180. ... Shoots left.
COLLEGE: Wisconsin.

TRANSACTIONS/CAREER NOTES: Selected by Los Angeles Kings in seventh round (seventh Kings pick, 152nd overall) of NHL entry draft (June 22, 1991). ... Traded by Kings with RW Dixon Ward, C Guy Leveque and RW Shayne Toporowski to Toronto Maple Leafs for LW Eric Lacroix, D Chris Snell and fourth-round pick (C Eric Belanger) in 1996 draft (October 3, 1994). ... Loaned by Maple Leafs to Orlando Solar Bears (February 10, 1997).

HONORS: Named to WCHA All-Star first team (1993-94).

		REGULAR SEASON								PLAYOFFS				
Season Team	League	Gms.	G	A	Pts.	PIM	+/-	PP	SH	Gms.	G	A	Pts.	PIM
91-92— Univ. of Wisconsin.....	WCHA	37	11	10	21	45	...	...	...	—	—	—	—	—
92-93— Univ. of Wisconsin.....	WCHA	42	25	29	54	54	...	...	...	—	—	—	—	—
93-94— Univ. of Wisconsin.....	WCHA	42	20	44	64	81	...	...	...	—	—	—	—	—
94-95— St. John's................	AHL	53	27	23	50	51	...	...	...	4	0	2	2	4
95-96— St. John's................	AHL	78	29	49	78	85	...	...	...	2	0	1	1	4
— Toronto	NHL	1	0	1	1	2	1	0	0	—	—	—	—	—
96-97— St. John's................	AHL	29	9	22	31	36	...	...	...	—	—	—	—	—
— Toronto	NHL	22	0	2	2	2	-5	0	0	—	—	—	—	—
— Orlando	IHL	25	9	6	15	20	...	...	...	9	6	5	11	16
NHL totals (2 years)		23	0	3	3	4	-4	0	0					

FALLOON, PAT   RW   FLYERS

PERSONAL: Born September 22, 1972, in Foxwarren, Man. ... 5-11/190. ... Shoots right. ... Name pronounced fuh-LOON.

TRANSACTIONS/CAREER NOTES: WHL rights traded with future considerations by Regina Pats to Spokane Chiefs for RW Jamie Heward (October 1987). ... Tore right knee cartilage and underwent surgery (July 24, 1990). ... Selected by San Jose Sharks in first round (first Sharks pick, second overall) of NHL entry draft (June 22, 1991). ... Bruised shoulder (November 19, 1992); missed one game. ... Dislocated right shoulder (January 10, 1993) and underwent arthroscopic surgery (January 15, 1993); missed remainder of season. ... Injured hamstring (March 2, 1995); missed one game. ... Traded by Sharks to Philadelphia Flyers for LW Martin Spanhel and first-(traded to Winnipeg) and fourth-(traded to Buffalo) round picks in 1996 draft (November 16, 1995). ... Pulled left groin (December 21, 1996); missed seven games. ... Reinjured left groin (January 13, 1997); missed three games.

HONORS: Named WHL (West) Division Rookie of the Year (1988-89). ... Named to WHL All-Star second team (1988-89). ... Won WHL (West) Division Most Sportsmanlike Player Award (1989-90). ... Named to WHL (West) All-Star first team (1989-90 and 1990-91). ... Won Can.HL Most Sportsmanlike Player of the Year Award (1990-91). ... Won Brad Hornung Trophy (1990-91). ... Won Stafford Smythe Memorial Trophy (1990-91). ... Named to Memorial Cup All-Star team (1990-91).

MISCELLANEOUS: Holds San Jose Sharks all-time records for most goals (76), most assists (86) and most points (162).

		REGULAR SEASON								PLAYOFFS				
Season Team	League	Gms.	G	A	Pts.	PIM	+/-	PP	SH	Gms.	G	A	Pts.	PIM
87-88— Yellowbeard	Tier II	52	74	69	143	50	...	...	...	—	—	—	—	—
88-89— Spokane....................	WHL	72	22	56	78	41	...	...	...	5	5	8	13	4
89-90— Spokane....................	WHL	71	60	64	124	48	...	...	...	6	5	8	13	4
90-91— Spokane....................	WHL	61	64	74	138	33	...	...	...	15	10	14	24	10
91-92— San Jose	NHL	79	25	34	59	16	-32	5	0	—	—	—	—	—
92-93— San Jose	NHL	41	14	14	28	12	-25	5	1	—	—	—	—	—
93-94— San Jose	NHL	83	22	31	53	18	-3	6	0	14	1	2	3	6
94-95— San Jose	NHL	46	12	7	19	25	-4	0	0	11	3	1	4	0
95-96— San Jose	NHL	9	3	0	3	4	-1	0	0	—	—	—	—	—
— Philadelphia	NHL	62	22	26	48	6	15	9	0	12	3	2	5	2
96-97— Philadelphia	NHL	52	11	12	23	10	-8	2	0	14	3	1	4	2
NHL totals (6 years)		372	109	124	233	91	-58	27	1	51	10	6	16	10

FEATHERSTONE, GLEN   D   FLAMES

PERSONAL: Born July 8, 1968, in Toronto. ... 6-4/215. ... Shoots left.

TRANSACTIONS/CAREER NOTES: Selected by St. Louis Blues as underage junior in fourth round (fourth Blues pick, 73rd overall) of NHL entry draft (June 21, 1986). ... Suffered sore back (March 7, 1991); missed two games. ... Signed as free agent by Boston Bruins (July 25, 1991); Bruins and Blues later arranged a trade in which Bruins received Featherstone and LW Dave Thomlinson, whom they had also previously signed as free agent, for RW Dave Christian, whom the Blues had previously signed as free agent, third-round (LW Vitali Prokhorov) and either seventh-round pick in 1992 draft or sixth-round pick in 1993 draft; Blues used seventh-round pick in 1992 draft to select C Lance Burns. ... Suffered hip pointer (October 5, 1991); missed three games. ... Strained back (November 1991); missed remainder of season. ... Underwent back surgery (November 15, 1991). ... Injured groin (December 31, 1992); missed seven games. ... Injured knee and thigh (March 1, 1993); missed remainder of season. ... Injured shoulder (November 18, 1993); missed five games. ... Suffered sore shoulder (January 24, 1994); missed four games. ... Injured knee (February 12, 1994); missed four games. ... Reinjured knee (March 8, 1994); missed two games. ... Suffered from the flu (April 1, 1994); missed one game. ... Traded by Bruins to New York Rangers for C Daniel Lacroix (August 19, 1994). ... Traded by Rangers with D Michael Stewart, first-round pick (G Jean-Sebastien Giguere) in 1995 draft and fourth-round pick (C Steve Wasylko) in 1996 draft to Hartford Whalers for RW Pat Verbeek (March 23, 1995). ... Suspended four games without pay by NHL for engaging in verbal confrontation with fans and throwing helmet into stands and injuring usher (April 4, 1995). ... Bruised shin (November 15, 1995); missed four games. ... Suspended one game by NHL after collecting third game misconduct penalty of season (November 28, 1995). ... Bruised foot (January 16, 1996); missed one game. ... Injured lower back (February 25, 1996); missed three games. ... Suspended two games by NHL after collecting fourth game misconduct penalty of season (March 17, 1996). ... Bruised foot (April 4, 1996); missed remainder of season. ... Injured elbow (October 2, 1996); missed three games. ... Suffered back spasms (December 11, 1996); missed two games. ... Fractured foot (December 21, 1996); missed 11 games. ... Underwent elbow surgery (January 21, 1997); missed five games. ... Traded by Whalers with F Hnat Domenichelli, second-round pick (D Dimitri Kokorev) in 1997 draft and third-round pick in 1998 draft to Calgary Flames for D Steve Chiasson and third-round pick (D Francis Lessard) in 1997 draft (March 5, 1997). ... Injured shoulder (March 29, 1997); missed one game.

		REGULAR SEASON								PLAYOFFS				
Season Team	League	Gms.	G	A	Pts.	PIM	+/-	PP	SH	Gms.	G	A	Pts.	PIM
85-86— Windsor....................	OHL	49	0	6	6	135	...	...	...	14	1	1	2	23
86-87— Windsor....................	OHL	47	6	11	17	154	...	...	...	14	2	6	8	19
87-88— Windsor....................	OHL	53	7	27	34	201	...	...	...	12	6	9	15	47
88-89— Peoria	IHL	37	5	19	24	97	...	...	...	—	—	—	—	—
— St. Louis	NHL	18	0	2	2	22	-3	0	0	6	0	0	0	0

Season Team	League	Gms.	G	A	Pts.	PIM	+/-	PP	SH	Gms.	G	A	Pts.	PIM
		REGULAR SEASON								**PLAYOFFS**				
89-90— Peoria	IHL	15	1	4	5	43	...	...	...	—	—	—	—	—
— St. Louis	NHL	58	0	12	12	145	-1	0	0	12	0	2	2	47
90-91— St. Louis	NHL	68	5	15	20	204	19	1	0	9	0	0	0	31
91-92— Boston	NHL	7	1	0	1	20	-2	0	0	—	—	—	—	—
92-93— Providence	AHL	8	3	4	7	60	...	...	...	—	—	—	—	—
— Boston	NHL	34	5	5	10	102	6	1	0	—	—	—	—	—
93-94— Boston	NHL	58	1	8	9	152	-5	0	0	1	0	0	0	0
94-95— New York Rangers	NHL	6	1	0	1	18	0	0	0	—	—	—	—	—
— Hartford	NHL	13	1	1	2	32	-7	0	0	—	—	—	—	—
95-96— Hartford	NHL	68	2	10	12	138	10	0	0	—	—	—	—	—
96-97— Hartford	NHL	41	2	5	7	87	0	0	0	—	—	—	—	—
— Calgary	NHL	13	1	3	4	19	-1	0	0	—	—	—	—	—
NHL totals (9 years)		384	19	61	80	939	16	2	0	28	0	2	2	78

FEDOROV, SERGEI　　　　C　　　　RED WINGS

PERSONAL: Born December 13, 1969, in Minsk, U.S.S.R. ... 6-1/200. ... Shoots left. ... Name pronounced SAIR-gay FEH-duh-rahf.
TRANSACTIONS/CAREER NOTES: Selected by Detroit Red Wings in fourth round (fourth Red Wings pick, 74th overall) of NHL entry draft (June 17, 1989). ... Bruised left shoulder (October 1990). ... Reinjured left shoulder (January 16, 1991). ... Sprained left shoulder (November 27, 1992); missed seven games. ... Suffered from the flu (January 30, 1993); missed two games. ... Suffered charley horse (February 11, 1993); missed one game. ... Suffered concussion (April 5, 1994); missed two games. ... Suspended four games without pay and fined $500 by NHL for high-sticking incident in playoff game (May 17, 1994); suspension reduced to three games due to abbreviated 1994-95 season. ... Suffered from the flu (February 7, 1995); missed one game. ... Bruised right hamstring (April 9, 1995); missed one game. ... Suffered from tonsillitis (October 6, 1995); missed three games. ... Sprained left wrist (December 15, 1995); missed one game. ... Strained groin (January 9, 1997); missed two games. ... Reinjured groin (January 20, 1997); missed six games.
HONORS: Named to NHL All-Rookie team (1990-91). ... Played in NHL All-Star Game (1992, 1994 and 1996). ... Named NHL Player of the Year by The Sporting News (1993-94). ... Named to The Sporting News All-Star first team (1993-94). ... Won Hart Memorial Trophy (1993-94). ... Won Frank J. Selke Trophy (1993-94 and 1995-96). ... Won Lester B. Pearson Award (1993-94). ... Named to NHL All-Star first team (1993-94).
STATISTICAL PLATEAUS: Three-goal games: 1993-94 (1). ... Four-goal games: 1994-95 (1). ... Five-goal games: 1996-97 (1). ... Total hat tricks: 3.
MISCELLANEOUS: Member of Stanley Cup championship team (1997). ... Scored on a penalty shot (vs. Andy Moog, December 27, 1993). ... Failed to score on a penalty shot (vs. Kelly Hrudey, February 12, 1995).

Season Team	League	Gms.	G	A	Pts.	PIM	+/-	PP	SH	Gms.	G	A	Pts.	PIM
		REGULAR SEASON								**PLAYOFFS**				
85-86— Dynamo Minsk	USSR	15	6	1	7	10	...	...	...	—	—	—	—	—
86-87— CSKA Moscow	USSR	29	6	6	12	12	...	...	...	—	—	—	—	—
87-88— CSKA Moscow	USSR	48	7	9	16	20	...	...	...	—	—	—	—	—
88-89— CSKA Moscow	USSR	44	9	8	17	35	...	...	...	—	—	—	—	—
89-90— CSKA Moscow	USSR	48	19	10	29	20	...	...	...	—	—	—	—	—
90-91— Detroit	NHL	77	31	48	79	66	11	11	3	7	1	5	6	4
91-92— Detroit	NHL	80	32	54	86	72	26	7	2	11	5	5	10	8
92-93— Detroit	NHL	73	34	53	87	72	33	13	4	7	3	6	9	23
93-94— Detroit	NHL	82	56	64	120	34	48	13	4	7	1	7	8	6
94-95— Detroit	NHL	42	20	30	50	24	6	7	3	17	7	*17	*24	6
95-96— Detroit	NHL	78	39	68	107	48	49	11	3	19	2	*18	20	10
96-97— Detroit	NHL	74	30	33	63	30	29	9	2	20	8	12	20	12
NHL totals (7 years)		506	242	350	592	346	202	71	21	88	27	70	97	69

FEDYK, BRENT　　　　LW　　　　STARS

PERSONAL: Born March 8, 1967, in Yorkton, Sask. ... 6-0/196. ... Shoots right. ... Name pronounced FEH-dihk.
TRANSACTIONS/CAREER NOTES: Selected by Detroit Red Wings as underage junior in first round (first Red Wings pick, eighth overall) of NHL entry draft (June 15, 1985). ... Strained hip in training camp (September 1985); missed three weeks. ... Traded by Regina Pats with RW Ken McIntyre, LW Grant Kazuik, D Gerald Bzdel and the WHL rights to LW Kevin Kowalchuk to Seattle Thunderbirds for RW Craig Endean, C Ray Savard, Grant Chorney, C Erin Ginnell and WHL rights to LW Frank Kovacs (November 1986). ... Traded by Thunderbirds to Portland Winter Hawks for future considerations (February 1987). ... Injured knee (December 22, 1990); missed one game. ... Suffered deep shin bruise (January 26, 1991); missed five games. ... Suffered concussion (March 1991). ... Traded by Red Wings to Philadelphia Flyers for fourth-round pick (later traded to Boston which selected D Charles Paquette) in 1993 draft (October 1, 1992). ... Strained right shoulder (December 11, 1992); missed three games. ... Fractured thumb (January 31, 1993); missed one game. ... Sprained left ankle (March 11, 1993); missed one game. ... Fractured toe (April 6, 1993); missed remainder of season. ... Strained left wrist (February 24, 1994); missed three games. ... Suspended one game by NHL for second stick-related game misconduct (March 24, 1994). ... Pulled right hamstring (February 16, 1995); missed three games. ... Strained neck (March 7, 1995); missed 13 games. ... Suffered chip fracture in first vertebrae of neck (May 26, 1995); missed remainder of playoffs. ... Traded by Flyers to Dallas Stars for RW Trent Klatt (December 13, 1995). ... Strained hamstring (February 18, 1996); missed six games. ... Left Michigan K-Wings due to recurring back injuries (December 26, 1996).
HONORS: Named to WHL All-Star second team (1985-86).
MISCELLANEOUS: Failed to score on a penalty shot (vs. Vince Riendeau, January 25, 1991).

Season Team	League	Gms.	G	A	Pts.	PIM	+/-	PP	SH	Gms.	G	A	Pts.	PIM
		REGULAR SEASON								**PLAYOFFS**				
82-83— Regina	WHL	1	0	0	0	0	...	...	...	—	—	—	—	—
83-84— Regina	WHL	63	15	28	43	30	...	...	...	23	8	7	15	6
84-85— Regina	WHL	66	35	35	70	48	...	...	...	8	5	4	9	0
85-86— Regina	WHL	50	43	34	77	47	...	...	...	5	0	1	1	0
86-87— Regina	WHL	12	9	6	15	9	...	...	...	—	—	—	—	—
— Seattle	WHL	13	5	11	16	9	...	...	...	—	—	—	—	—
— Portland	WHL	11	5	4	9	6	...	...	...	14	5	6	11	0
87-88— Detroit	NHL	2	0	1	1	2	...	...	...	—	—	—	—	—
— Adirondack	AHL	34	9	11	20	22	...	...	...	5	0	2	2	6

F

Season Team	League	REGULAR SEASON								PLAYOFFS				
		Gms.	G	A	Pts.	PIM	+/-	PP	SH	Gms.	G	A	Pts.	PIM
88-89 — Detroit	NHL	5	2	0	2	0	...	...	...	—	—	—	—	—
— Adirondack	AHL	66	40	28	68	33	...	...	...	15	7	8	15	23
89-90 — Detroit	NHL	27	1	4	5	6	-1	0	0	—	—	—	—	—
— Adirondack	AHL	33	14	15	29	24	...	...	...	6	2	1	3	4
90-91 — Detroit	NHL	67	16	19	35	38	20	0	0	6	1	0	1	2
91-92 — Adirondack	AHL	1	0	2	2	0	...	...	...	—	—	—	—	—
— Detroit	NHL	61	5	8	13	42	-5	0	0	1	0	0	0	2
92-93 — Philadelphia	NHL	74	21	38	59	48	14	4	1	—	—	—	—	—
93-94 — Philadelphia	NHL	72	20	18	38	74	-14	5	0	—	—	—	—	—
94-95 — Philadelphia	NHL	30	8	4	12	14	-2	3	0	9	2	2	4	8
95-96 — Philadelphia	NHL	24	10	5	15	24	1	4	0	—	—	—	—	—
— Dallas	NHL	41	10	9	19	30	-17	4	0	—	—	—	—	—
96-97 — Michigan	IHL	9	1	2	3	4	...	...	...	—	—	—	—	—
NHL totals (9 years)		403	93	106	199	278	-4	20	1	16	3	2	5	12

FERGUSON, CRAIG — RW — PANTHERS

PERSONAL: Born April 8, 1970, in Castro Valley, Calif. ... 5-11/190. ... Shoots left.
COLLEGE: Yale.
TRANSACTIONS/CAREER NOTES: Selected by Montreal Canadiens in seventh round (seventh Canadiens pick, 146th overall) of NHL entry draft (June 22, 1991). ... Traded by Canadiens with LW Yves Sarault to Calgary Flames for eighth-round pick (D Petr Kubos) in 1997 draft (November 25, 1995). ... Traded by Flames to Los Angeles Kings for LW Pat Conacher (February 10, 1996). ... Signed as free agent by Florida Panthers (August 6, 1996).

Season Team	League	REGULAR SEASON								PLAYOFFS				
		Gms.	G	A	Pts.	PIM	+/-	PP	SH	Gms.	G	A	Pts.	PIM
88-89 — Yale University	ECAC	24	11	6	17	20	...	...	...	—	—	—	—	—
89-90 — Yale University	ECAC	35	6	15	21	38	...	...	...	—	—	—	—	—
90-91 — Yale University	ECAC	29	11	10	21	34	...	...	...	—	—	—	—	—
91-92 — Yale University	ECAC	27	9	16	25	28	...	...	...	—	—	—	—	—
92-93 — Wheeling	ECHL	9	6	5	11	24	...	...	...	—	—	—	—	—
— Fredericton	AHL	55	15	13	28	20	...	...	...	5	0	1	1	2
93-94 — Fredericton	AHL	57	29	32	61	60	...	...	...	17	6	2	8	6
— Montreal	NHL	2	0	1	1	0	1	0	0	—	—	—	—	—
94-95 — Fredericton	AHL	80	27	35	62	62	...	...	...	17	6	2	8	6
— Montreal	NHL	1	0	0	0	0	0	0	0	—	—	—	—	—
95-96 — Montreal	NHL	10	1	0	1	2	-5	0	0	—	—	—	—	—
— Calgary	NHL	8	0	0	0	4	-4	0	0	—	—	—	—	—
— Saint John	AHL	18	5	13	18	8	...	...	...	—	—	—	—	—
— Phoenix	IHL	31	6	9	15	25	...	...	...	4	0	2	2	6
96-97 — Carolina	AHL	74	29	41	70	57	...	...	...	—	—	—	—	—
— Florida	NHL	3	0	0	0	0	-1	0	0	—	—	—	—	—
NHL totals (4 years)		24	1	1	2	6	-9	0	0					

FERGUSON, SCOTT — D — OILERS

PERSONAL: Born January 6, 1973, in Camrose, Alta. ... 6-1/195. ... Shoots left.
TRANSACTIONS/CAREER NOTES: Signed as free agent by Edmonton Oilers (June 2, 1994).

Season Team	League	REGULAR SEASON								PLAYOFFS				
		Gms.	G	A	Pts.	PIM	+/-	PP	SH	Gms.	G	A	Pts.	PIM
90-91 — Kamloops	WHL	4	0	0	0	0	...	...	...	—	—	—	—	—
91-92 — Kamloops	WHL	62	4	10	14	148	...	...	...	12	0	2	2	21
92-93 — Kamloops	WHL	71	4	19	23	206	...	...	...	13	0	2	2	24
93-94 — Kamloops	WHL	68	5	49	54	180	...	...	...	19	5	11	16	48
94-95 — Wheeling	ECHL	5	1	5	6	16	...	...	...	—	—	—	—	—
— Cape Breton	AHL	58	4	6	10	103	...	...	...	—	—	—	—	—
95-96 — Cape Breton	AHL	80	5	16	21	196	...	...	...	—	—	—	—	—
96-97 — Hamilton	AHL	74	6	14	20	115	...	...	...	21	5	7	12	59

FERNANDEZ, MANNY — G — STARS

PERSONAL: Born August 27, 1974, in Etobicoke, Ont. ... 6-0/185. ... Catches left. ... Nephew of Jacques Lemaire, Hall of Fame center, Montreal Canadiens (1967-68 through 1978-79) and current coach of New Jersey Devils.
TRANSACTIONS/CAREER NOTES: Selected by Quebec Nordiques in third round (fourth Nordiques pick, 52nd overall) of NHL entry draft (June 20, 1992). ... Traded by Nordiques to Dallas Stars for D Tommy Sjodin and undisclosed draft pick (February 13, 1994).
HONORS: Won Guy Lafleur Trophy (1992-93). ... Won Michel Briere Trophy (1993-94). ... Named to QMJHL All-Star first team (1993-94). ... Named to Can.HL All-Star second team (1993-94). ... Named to IHL All-Star second team (1994-95).

Season Team	League	REGULAR SEASON							PLAYOFFS					
		Gms.	Min.	W	L	T	GA	SO	Avg.	Gms.	Min.	W	L	GA	SO	Avg.
91-92 — Laval	QMJHL	31	1593	14	13	2	99	1	3.73	9	468	3	5	†39	0	5.00
92-93 — Laval	QMJHL	43	2348	26	14	2	141	1	3.60	13	818	12	1	42	0	3.08
93-94 — Laval	QMJHL	51	2776	29	14	1	143	*5	3.09	19	1116	14	5	49	†1	*2.63
94-95 — Kalamazoo	IHL	46	2470	21	10	‡9	115	2	2.79	12	655	9	1	†30	1	2.75
— Dallas	NHL	1	59	0	1	0	3	0	3.05	—	—	—	—	—	—	—
95-96 — Michigan	IHL	47	2663	22	15	‡9	133	†4	3.00	6	372	5	1	14	0	*2.26
— Dallas	NHL	5	249	0	1	1	19	0	4.58	—	—	—	—	—	—	—
96-97 — Michigan	IHL	48	2721	20	24	‡2	142	1	3.13	4	277	1	3	15	0	3.25
NHL totals (2 years)		6	308	0	2	1	22	0	4.29							

- 114 -

FERRARO, CHRIS   C   RANGERS

PERSONAL: Born January 24, 1973, in Port Jefferson, N.Y. ... 5-10/175. ... Shoots right. ... Name pronounced fuh-RAH-roh. ... Twin brother of Peter Ferraro, center in New York Rangers system.
COLLEGE: Maine.
TRANSACTIONS/CAREER NOTES: Selected by New York Rangers in fourth round (fourth Rangers pick, 85th overall) of NHL entry draft (June 20, 1992).
HONORS: Named to Hockey East Rookie All-Star team (1992-93).

Season Team	League	REGULAR SEASON								PLAYOFFS				
		Gms.	G	A	Pts.	PIM	+/-	PP	SH	Gms.	G	A	Pts.	PIM
90-91— Dubuque	USHL	45	53	44	97	...	...	...	...	—	—	—	—	—
91-92— Waterloo	USHL	38	49	50	99	106	...	...	...	—	—	—	—	—
92-93— University of Maine	Hockey East	39	25	26	51	46	...	...	...	—	—	—	—	—
93-94— U.S. national team	Int'l	48	8	34	42	58	...	...	...	—	—	—	—	—
— University of Maine	Hockey East	4	0	1	1	8	...	...	...	—	—	—	—	—
94-95— Atlanta	IHL	54	13	14	27	72	...	...	...	—	—	—	—	—
— Binghamton	AHL	13	6	4	10	38	...	...	...	10	2	3	5	16
95-96— Binghamton	AHL	77	32	67	99	208	...	...	...	4	4	2	6	13
— New York Rangers	NHL	2	1	0	1	0	-3	1	0	—	—	—	—	—
96-97— Binghamton	AHL	53	29	34	63	94	...	...	...	—	—	—	—	—
— New York Rangers	NHL	12	1	1	2	6	1	0	0	—	—	—	—	—
NHL totals (2 years)		**14**	**2**	**1**	**3**	**6**	**-2**	**1**	**0**					

FERRARO, PETER   RW   RANGERS

PERSONAL: Born January 24, 1973, in Port Jefferson, N.Y. ... 5-10/190. ... Shoots right. ... Name pronounced fuh-RAH-roh. ... Twin brother of Chris Ferraro, right winger, New York Rangers.
COLLEGE: Maine.
TRANSACTIONS/CAREER NOTES: Selected by New York Rangers in first round (first Rangers pick, 24th overall) of NHL entry draft (June 20, 1992).
HONORS: Named to AHL All-Star first team (1995-96).

Season Team	League	REGULAR SEASON								PLAYOFFS				
		Gms.	G	A	Pts.	PIM	+/-	PP	SH	Gms.	G	A	Pts.	PIM
90-91— Dubuque	USHL	29	21	31	52	83	...	...	...	—	—	—	—	—
91-92— Waterloo	USHL	42	48	53	101	168	...	...	...	—	—	—	—	—
92-93— University of Maine	Hockey East	36	18	32	50	106	...	...	...	—	—	—	—	—
93-94— U.S. national team	Int'l	59	28	39	67	48	...	...	...	—	—	—	—	—
— U.S. Olympic team	Int'l	8	6	0	6	6	...	...	...	—	—	—	—	—
— University of Maine	Hockey East	4	3	6	9	16	...	...	...	—	—	—	—	—
94-95— Atlanta	IHL	61	15	24	39	118	...	...	...	11	4	3	7	51
— Binghamton	AHL	12	2	6	8	67	...	...	...	4	1	6	7	22
95-96— Binghamton	AHL	68	48	53	101	157	...	...	...	—	—	—	—	—
— New York Rangers	NHL	5	0	1	1	0	-5	0	0	—	—	—	—	—
96-97— Binghamton	AHL	75	38	39	77	171	...	...	...	4	3	1	4	18
— New York Rangers	NHL	2	0	0	0	0	0	0	0	2	0	0	0	0
NHL totals (2 years)		**7**	**0**	**1**	**1**	**0**	**-5**	**0**	**0**	**2**	**0**	**0**	**0**	**0**

FERRARO, RAY   C   KINGS

PERSONAL: Born August 23, 1964, in Trail, B.C. ... 5-10/186. ... Shoots left. ... Name pronounced fuh-RAH-roh.
TRANSACTIONS/CAREER NOTES: Selected by Hartford Whalers as underage junior in fifth round (fifth Whalers pick, 88th overall) of NHL entry draft (June 9, 1982). ... Traded by Whalers to New York Islanders for D Doug Crossman (November 13, 1990). ... Fractured right fibula (December 10, 1992); missed 36 games. ... Suffered from the flu (March 25, 1993); missed one game. ... Injured knee (March 9, 1995); missed one game. ... Signed as free agent by New York Rangers (July 19, 1995). ... Traded by Rangers with C Nathan Lafayette, C Ian Laperriere, D Mattias Norstrom and fourth-round pick (D Sean Blanchard) in 1997 draft to Los Angeles Kings for RW Shane Churla, LW Jari Kurri and D Marty McSorley (March 14, 1996). ... Strained neck (February 1, 1997); missed one game.
HONORS: Won WHL Most Valuable Player Trophy (1983-84). ... Won Bob Brownridge Memorial Trophy (1983-84). ... Won WHL Player of the Year Award (1983-84). ... Named to WHL (East) All-Star first team (1983-84). ... Played in NHL All-Star Game (1992).
STATISTICAL PLATEAUS: Three-goal games: 1984-85 (2), 1986-87 (1), 1988-89 (1), 1989-90 (1), 1991-92 (1), 1995-96 (1). Total: 7. ... Four-goal games: 1991-92 (1). ... Total hat tricks: 8.

Season Team	League	REGULAR SEASON								PLAYOFFS				
		Gms.	G	A	Pts.	PIM	+/-	PP	SH	Gms.	G	A	Pts.	PIM
81-82— Penticton	BCJHL	48	65	70	135	50	...	...	...	—	—	—	—	—
82-83— Portland	WHL	50	41	49	90	39	...	...	...	14	14	10	24	13
83-84— Brandon	WHL	72	*108	84	*192	84	...	...	...	11	13	15	28	20
84-85— Binghamton	AHL	37	20	13	33	29	...	...	...	—	—	—	—	—
— Hartford	NHL	44	11	17	28	40	-1	6	0	—	—	—	—	—
85-86— Hartford	NHL	76	30	47	77	57	12	14	0	10	3	6	9	4
86-87— Hartford	NHL	80	27	32	59	42	-9	14	0	6	1	1	2	8
87-88— Hartford	NHL	68	21	29	50	81	1	6	0	6	1	1	2	6
88-89— Hartford	NHL	80	41	35	76	86	1	11	0	4	2	0	2	4
89-90— Hartford	NHL	79	25	29	54	109	-15	7	0	7	0	3	3	2
90-91— Hartford	NHL	15	2	5	7	18	-1	1	0	—	—	—	—	—
— New York Islanders	NHL	61	19	16	35	52	-11	5	0	—	—	—	—	—
91-92— New York Islanders	NHL	80	40	40	80	92	25	7	0	—	—	—	—	—
92-93— New York Islanders	NHL	46	14	13	27	40	0	3	0	18	13	7	20	18
— Capital District	AHL	1	0	2	2	2	...	...	...	—	—	—	—	—

F

Season Team	League	Gms.	G	A	Pts.	PIM	+/-	PP	SH	Gms.	G	A	Pts.	PIM
93-94— New York Islanders....	NHL	82	21	32	53	83	1	5	0	4	1	0	1	6
94-95— New York Islanders....	NHL	47	22	21	43	30	1	2	0	—	—	—	—	—
95-96— New York Rangers.....	NHL	65	25	29	54	82	13	8	0	—	—	—	—	—
— Los Angeles................	NHL	11	4	2	6	10	-13	1	0	—	—	—	—	—
96-97— Los Angeles.............	NHL	81	25	21	46	112	-22	11	0	—	—	—	—	—
NHL totals (13 years)		915	327	368	695	934	-18	101	0	55	21	18	39	48

FETISOV, SLAVA   D   RED WINGS

PERSONAL: Born May 20, 1958, in Moscow, U.S.S.R. ... 6-1/215. ... Shoots left. ... Name pronounced SLAH-vuh fuh-TEE-sahf.

TRANSACTIONS/CAREER NOTES: Selected by Montreal Canadiens in 12th round (14th Canadiens pick, 201st overall) of NHL entry draft (June 15, 1978). ... Selected by New Jersey Devils in eighth round (sixth Devils pick, 150th overall) of NHL entry draft (June 8, 1983). ... Tore cartilage in left knee (November 22, 1989); missed six games. ... Suffered bronchial pneumonia and hospitalized twice (November 28, 1990); missed 10 games. ... Suffered from the flu (October 14, 1992); missed one game. ... Sprained knee (November 30, 1993); missed four games. ... Played in Europe during 1994-95 NHL lockout. ... Bruised leg (February 25, 1995); missed six games. ... Traded by Devils to Detroit Red Wings for third-round pick (RW David Gosselin) in 1995 draft (April 3, 1995). ... Injured groin (November 2, 1995); missed two games. ... Suspended two games by NHL for high-sticking (January 10, 1996). ... Underwent arthroscopic knee surgery (prior to 1996-97 season); missed first five games of season. ... Suffered from the flu (January 14, 1997); missed one game.

HONORS: Named to Soviet League All-Star team (1977-78 and 1981-82 through 1987-88). ... Won Soviet Player of the Year Award (1981-82 and 1985-86). ... Won Golden Stick Award (1983-84, 1987-88 and 1988-89). ... Played in NHL All-Star Game (1997).

MISCELLANEOUS: Member of Stanley Cup championship team (1997). ... Member of silver-medal-winning (1980) and gold-medal-winning U.S.S.R. Olympic team (1984 and 1988).

Season Team	League	Gms.	G	A	Pts.	PIM	+/-	PP	SH	Gms.	G	A	Pts.	PIM
76-77— CSKA Moscow..........	USSR	28	3	4	7	14	...	...	...	—	—	—	—	—
77-78— CSKA Moscow..........	USSR	35	9	18	27	46	...	...	...	—	—	—	—	—
78-79— CSKA Moscow..........	USSR	29	10	19	29	40	...	...	...	—	—	—	—	—
79-80— CSKA Moscow..........	USSR	37	10	14	24	46	...	...	...	—	—	—	—	—
— Sov. Olympic team..........	Int'l	7	5	4	9	10	...	...	...	—	—	—	—	—
80-81— CSKA Moscow..........	USSR	48	13	16	29	44	...	...	...	—	—	—	—	—
81-82— CSKA Moscow..........	USSR	46	15	26	41	20	...	...	...	—	—	—	—	—
82-83— CSKA Moscow..........	USSR	43	6	17	23	46	...	...	...	—	—	—	—	—
83-84— CSKA Moscow..........	USSR	44	19	30	49	38	...	...	...	—	—	—	—	—
— Sov. Olympic team..........	Int'l	7	3	8	11	8	...	...	...	—	—	—	—	—
84-85— CSKA Moscow..........	USSR	20	13	12	25	6	...	...	...	—	—	—	—	—
85-86— CSKA Moscow..........	USSR	40	15	19	34	12	...	...	...	—	—	—	—	—
86-87— CSKA Moscow..........	USSR	39	13	20	33	18	...	...	...	—	—	—	—	—
87-88— CSKA Moscow..........	USSR	46	18	17	35	26	...	...	...	—	—	—	—	—
— Sov. Olympic team..........	Int'l	8	4	9	13	6	...	...	...	—	—	—	—	—
88-89— CSKA Moscow..........	USSR	23	9	8	17	18	...	...	...	—	—	—	—	—
89-90— New Jersey.............	NHL	72	8	34	42	52	9	2	0	6	0	2	2	10
90-91— New Jersey.............	NHL	67	3	16	19	62	5	1	0	7	0	0	0	17
— Utica........................	AHL	1	1	1	2	0	...	...	...	—	—	—	—	—
91-92— New Jersey.............	NHL	70	3	23	26	108	11	0	0	6	0	3	3	8
92-93— New Jersey.............	NHL	76	4	23	27	158	7	1	1	5	0	2	2	4
93-94— New Jersey.............	NHL	52	1	14	15	30	14	0	0	14	1	0	1	8
94-95— Spartak Moscow.......	CIS	1	0	1	1	4	...	...	...	—	—	—	—	—
— New Jersey.................	NHL	4	0	1	1	0	-2	0	0	—	—	—	—	—
— Detroit......................	NHL	14	3	11	14	2	3	3	0	18	0	8	8	14
95-96— Detroit.................	NHL	69	7	35	42	96	37	1	1	19	1	4	5	34
96-97— Detroit.................	NHL	64	5	23	28	76	26	0	0	20	0	4	4	42
NHL totals (8 years)		488	34	180	214	584	110	8	2	95	2	23	25	137

FICHAUD, ERIC   G   ISLANDERS

PERSONAL: Born November 4, 1975, in Montreal. ... 5-11/171. ... Catches left. ... Name pronounced FEE-shoh.

HIGH SCHOOL: CEGEP de Chicoutimi (Que.).

TRANSACTIONS/CAREER NOTES: Selected by Toronto Maple Leafs in first round (first Maple Leafs pick, 16th overall) of NHL entry draft (June 28, 1994). ... Traded by Maple Leafs to New York Islanders for C Benoit Hogue, third-round pick (RW Ryan Pepperall) in 1995 draft and fifth-round pick (D Brandon Sugden) in 1996 draft (April 6, 1995). ... Strained abdominal muscle (October 12, 1996); missed two games.

HONORS: Named to Memorial Cup All-Star team (1993-94). ... Won Hap Emms Memorial Trophy (1993-94). ... Won QMJHL Top Draft Prospect Award (1993-94). ... Won Guy Lafleur Award (1993-94). ... Named to QMJHL All-Star first team (1994-95).

Season Team	League	Gms.	Min	W	L	T	GA	SO	Avg.	Gms.	Min.	W	L	GA	SO	Avg.
92-93—Chicoutimi	QMJHL	43	2040	18	13	1	149	0	4.38	—	—	—	—	—	—	—
93-94—Chicoutimi	QMJHL	63	3493	37	21	3	192	4	3.30	26	1560	16	10	86	†1	3.31
94-95—Chicoutimi	QMJHL	46	2637	21	19	4	151	4	3.44	7	430	2	5	20	0	2.79
95-96—Worcester	AHL	34	1988	13	15	6	97	1	2.93	2	127	1	1	7	0	3.31
—New York Islanders	NHL	24	1234	7	12	2	68	1	3.31	—	—	—	—	—	—	—
96-97—New York Islanders	NHL	34	1759	9	14	4	91	0	3.10	—	—	—	—	—	—	—
NHL totals (2 years)		58	2993	16	26	6	159	1	3.19							

FINLEY, JEFF   D   RANGERS

PERSONAL: Born April 14, 1967, in Edmonton. ... 6-0/205. ... Shoots left.

TRANSACTIONS/CAREER NOTES: Selected by New York Islanders as underage junior in third round (fourth Islanders pick, 55th overall) of NHL entry draft (June 15, 1985). ... Suffered swollen left knee (September 1988). ... Traded by Islanders to Ottawa Senators for D Chris

Luongo (June 30, 1993). ... Signed as free agent by Philadelphia Flyers (August 2, 1993). ... Traded by Flyers to Winnipeg Jets for LW Russ Romaniuk (June 26, 1995). ... Separated shoulder (December 10, 1995); missed one game. ... Jets franchise moved to Phoenix and renamed Coyotes for 1996-97 season; NHL approved move on January 18, 1996. ... Suffered from the flu (December 7, 1996); missed two games. ... Injured hip flexor (December 30, 1996); missed one game. ... Sprained ankle (March 27, 1997); missed remainder of regular season. ... Signed as free agent by New York Rangers (July 16, 1997).

			REGULAR SEASON							PLAYOFFS				
Season Team	League	Gms.	G	A	Pts.	PIM	+/-	PP	SH	Gms.	G	A	Pts.	PIM
83-84— Portland	WHL	5	0	0	0	0	...	...	...	5	0	1	1	4
— Summerland	BCJHL	49	0	21	21	14	...	...	...	—	—	—	—	—
84-85— Portland	WHL	69	6	44	50	57	...	...	...	6	1	2	3	2
85-86— Portland	WHL	70	11	59	70	83	...	...	...	15	1	7	8	16
86-87— Portland	WHL	72	13	53	66	113	...	...	...	20	1	†21	22	27
87-88— Springfield	AHL	52	5	18	23	50	...	...	...	—	—	—	—	—
— New York Islanders	NHL	10	0	5	5	15	5	0	0	1	0	0	0	2
88-89— New York Islanders	NHL	4	0	0	0	6	1	0	0	—	—	—	—	—
— Springfield	AHL	65	3	16	19	55	...	...	...	—	—	—	—	—
89-90— New York Islanders	NHL	11	0	1	1	0	0	0	0	5	0	2	2	2
— Springfield	AHL	57	1	15	16	41	...	...	...	13	1	4	5	23
90-91— Capital District	AHL	67	10	34	44	34	...	...	...	—	—	—	—	—
— New York Islanders	NHL	11	0	0	0	4	-1	0	0	—	—	—	—	—
91-92— Capital District	AHL	20	1	9	10	6	...	...	...	—	—	—	—	—
— New York Islanders	NHL	51	1	10	11	26	-6	0	0	—	—	—	—	—
92-93— Capital District	AHL	61	6	29	35	34	...	...	...	4	0	1	1	0
93-94— Philadelphia	NHL	55	1	8	9	24	16	0	0	—	—	—	—	—
94-95— Hershey	AHL	36	2	9	11	33	...	...	...	6	0	1	1	8
95-96— Springfield	AHL	14	3	12	15	22	...	...	...	—	—	—	—	—
— Winnipeg	NHL	65	1	5	6	81	-2	0	0	6	0	0	0	4
96-97— Phoenix	NHL	65	3	7	10	40	-8	1	0	1	0	0	0	2
NHL totals (8 years)		272	6	36	42	196	5	1	0	13	0	2	2	10

FINN, STEVEN   D   KINGS

PERSONAL: Born August 20, 1966, in Laval, Que. ... 6-0/191. ... Shoots left.

TRANSACTIONS/CAREER NOTES: Selected by Quebec Nordiques as underage junior in third round (third Nordiques pick, 57th overall) of NHL entry draft (June 9, 1984). ... Separated left shoulder (January 31, 1990). ... Lacerated right index finger (October 25, 1990); missed five games. ... Sprained wrist (November 25, 1991); missed six games. ... Sprained right wrist (February 15, 1992); missed seven games. ... Injured eye (January 22, 1993); missed one game. ... Bruised left arm (March 8, 1993); missed one game. ... Suffered from stomach virus (December 17, 1993); missed one game. ... Bruised knee (March 22, 1995); missed three games. ... Nordiques franchise moved to Colorado and renamed Avalanche for 1995-96 season (June 21, 1995). ... Traded by Avalanche to Tampa Bay Lightning for fourth-round pick (LW Brad Larsen) in 1997 draft (October 5, 1995). ... Traded by Lightning to Los Angeles Kings for D Michel Petit (November 13, 1995). ... Injured groin (December 11, 1995); missed four games. ... Injured left eye (February 17, 1996); missed three games. ... Broke left foot (March 25, 1996); missed remainder of season. ... Bruised right knee (prior to 1996-97 season); missed first seven games of season. ... Strained lower back (January 2, 1997); missed four games. ... Sprained right shoulder (January 14, 1997); missed one game. ... Sprained ankle (February 20, 1997); missed one game. ... Sprained left shoulder (March 4, 1997); missed three games.

HONORS: Named to QMJHL All-Star first team (1983-84). ... Named to QMJHL All-Star second team (1984-85).

MISCELLANEOUS: Captain of Quebec Nordiques (1990-91).

			REGULAR SEASON							PLAYOFFS				
Season Team	League	Gms.	G	A	Pts.	PIM	+/-	PP	SH	Gms.	G	A	Pts.	PIM
82-83— Laval	QMJHL	69	7	30	37	108	...	...	...	6	0	2	2	6
83-84— Laval	QMJHL	68	7	39	46	159	...	...	...	14	1	6	7	27
84-85— Laval	QMJHL	61	20	33	53	169	...	...	...	—	—	—	—	—
— Fredericton	AHL	4	0	0	0	14	...	...	...	6	1	1	2	4
85-86— Laval	QMJHL	29	4	15	19	111	...	...	...	14	6	16	22	57
— Quebec	NHL	17	0	1	1	28	...	...	...	—	—	—	—	—
86-87— Fredericton	AHL	38	7	19	26	73	...	...	...	—	—	—	—	—
— Quebec	NHL	36	2	5	7	40	-8	0	0	13	0	2	2	29
87-88— Quebec	NHL	75	3	7	10	198	-4	1	0	—	—	—	—	—
88-89— Quebec	NHL	77	2	6	8	235	-21	0	1	—	—	—	—	—
89-90— Quebec	NHL	64	3	9	12	208	-33	1	0	—	—	—	—	—
90-91— Quebec	NHL	71	6	13	19	228	-26	0	0	—	—	—	—	—
91-92— Quebec	NHL	65	4	7	11	194	-9	0	0	—	—	—	—	—
92-93— Quebec	NHL	80	5	9	14	160	-3	0	0	6	0	1	1	8
93-94— Quebec	NHL	80	4	13	17	159	-9	0	0	—	—	—	—	—
94-95— Quebec	NHL	40	0	3	3	64	1	0	0	4	0	1	1	2
95-96— Tampa Bay	NHL	16	0	0	0	24	-6	0	0	—	—	—	—	—
— Los Angeles	NHL	50	3	2	5	102	-6	0	0	—	—	—	—	—
96-97— Los Angeles	NHL	54	2	3	5	84	-8	0	0	—	—	—	—	—
NHL totals (12 years)		725	34	78	112	1724	-132	2	1	23	0	4	4	39

FISET, STEPHANE   G   KINGS

PERSONAL: Born June 17, 1970, in Montreal. ... 6-1/195. ... Catches left. ... Name pronounced FEE-seh.

TRANSACTIONS/CAREER NOTES: Selected by Quebec Nordiques in second round (third Nordiques pick, 24th overall) of NHL entry draft (June 13, 1987). ... Underwent shoulder surgery (May 1989). ... Twisted knee (December 9, 1990). ... Sprained left knee (January 14, 1992); missed 12 games. ... Suffered slipped disc (November 4, 1993); missed 18 games. ... Injured groin (February 28, 1995); missed two games. ... Nordiques franchise moved to Colorado and renamed Avalanche for 1995-96 season (June 21, 1995). ... Traded by Avalanche with first-round pick in 1998 draft to Los Angeles Kings for LW Eric Lacroix and first-round pick in 1998 draft (June 20, 1996). ... Strained abdominal muscle (December 3, 1996); missed one game. ... Strained groin and abdominal muscles (March 5, 1997); missed 13 games.

HONORS: Won Can.HL Goaltender of the Year Award (1988-89). ... Won Jacques Plante Trophy (1988-89). ... Named to QMJHL All-Star first team (1988-89).

F

MISCELLANEOUS: Member of Stanley Cup championship team (1996). ... Holds Colorado Avalanche franchise all-time record for most shutouts (6) and goals-against average (2.96). ... Stopped a penalty shot attempt (vs. Craig Janney, January 9, 1992; vs. Chris Dahlquist, March 21, 1992). ... Allowed a penalty shot goal (vs. Kevin Miller, December 5, 1995).

				REGULAR SEASON								PLAYOFFS				
Season Team	League	Gms.	Min	W	L	T	GA	SO	Avg.	Gms.	Min.	W	L	GA	SO	Avg.
87-88—Victoriaville	QMJHL	40	2221	14	17	4	146	1	3.94	2	163	0	2	10	0	3.68
88-89—Victoriaville	QMJHL	43	2401	25	14	0	138	1	*3.45	12	711	9	2	33	0	*2.78
89-90—Victoriaville	QMJHL	24	1383	14	6	3	63	1	2.73	*14	*790	7	6	*49	0	3.72
—Quebec	NHL	6	342	0	5	1	34	0	5.96	—	—	—	—	—	—	—
90-91—Quebec	NHL	3	186	0	2	1	12	0	3.87	—	—	—	—	—	—	—
—Halifax	AHL	36	1902	10	15	8	131	0	4.13	—	—	—	—	—	—	—
91-92—Halifax	AHL	29	1675	8	14	6	110	†3	3.94	—	—	—	—	—	—	—
—Quebec	NHL	23	1133	7	10	2	71	1	3.76	—	—	—	—	—	—	—
92-93—Quebec	NHL	37	1939	18	9	4	110	1	3.40	1	21	0	0	1	0	2.86
—Halifax	AHL	3	180	2	1	0	11	0	3.67	—	—	—	—	—	—	—
93-94—Cornwall	AHL	1	60	0	1	0	4	0	4.00	—	—	—	—	—	—	—
—Quebec	NHL	50	2798	20	25	4	158	2	3.39	—	—	—	—	—	—	—
94-95—Quebec	NHL	32	1879	17	10	3	87	2	2.78	4	209	1	2	16	0	4.59
95-96—Colorado	NHL	37	2107	22	6	7	103	1	2.93	1	1	0	0	0	0	0.00
96-97—Los Angeles	NHL	44	2482	13	24	5	132	4	3.19	—	—	—	—	—	—	—
NHL totals (8 years)		232	12866	97	91	27	707	10	3.30	6	231	1	2	17	0	4.42

FISHER, CRAIG   C   PANTHERS

PERSONAL: Born June 30, 1970, in Oshawa, Ont. ... 6-3/180. ... Shoots left. ... Full name: Craig Francis Fisher.
COLLEGE: Miami of Ohio.
TRANSACTIONS/CAREER NOTES: Suffered concussion (October 1987). ... Selected by Philadelphia Flyers in third round (third Flyers pick, 56th overall) of NHL entry draft (June 11, 1988). ... Traded by Flyers with RW Scott Mellanby and LW Craig Berube to Edmonton Oilers for RW Dave Brown, D Corey Foster and the NHL rights to RW Jari Kurri (May 30, 1991). ... Traded by Oilers to Winnipeg Jets for future considerations (December 9, 1993). ... Signed as free agent by Chicago Blackhawks (June 23, 1994). ... Traded to Indianapolis Ice with D Bob Kellogg to Orlando Solar Bears for C James Black (August 11, 1995). ... Signed as free agent by New York Islanders (July 25, 1996). ... Traded by Islanders to Florida Panthers for cash (December 7, 1996).
HONORS: Named to CCHA All-Rookie team (1988-89). ... Named to CCHA All-Star first team (1989-90). ... Named to IHL All-Star first team (1995-96).

				REGULAR SEASON							PLAYOFFS			
Season Team	League	Gms.	G	A	Pts.	PIM	+/-	PP	SH	Gms.	G	A	Pts.	PIM
86-87—Oshawa Jr. B	OHA	34	22	26	48	18	...			—	—	—	—	—
87-88—Oshawa Jr. B	OHA	36	42	34	76	48	...			—	—	—	—	—
88-89—Miami of Ohio	CCHA	37	22	20	42	37	...			—	—	—	—	—
89-90—Miami of Ohio	CCHA	39	37	29	66	38	...			—	—	—	—	—
—Philadelphia	NHL	2	0	0	0	0	0	0	0	—	—	—	—	—
90-91—Hershey	AHL	77	43	36	79	46	...			7	5	3	8	2
—Philadelphia	NHL	2	0	0	0	0	0	0	0	—	—	—	—	—
91-92—Cape Breton	AHL	60	20	25	45	28	...			1	0	0	0	0
92-93—Cape Breton	AHL	75	32	29	61	74	...			1	0	0	0	2
93-94—Cape Breton	AHL	16	5	5	10	11	...			—	—	—	—	—
—Moncton	AHL	46	26	35	61	36	...			21	11	11	22	28
—Winnipeg	NHL	4	0	0	0	2	-1	0	0	—	—	—	—	—
94-95—Indianapolis	IHL	77	53	40	93	65	...			—	—	—	—	—
95-96—Orlando	IHL	82	*74	56	130	81	...			14	10	7	17	6
96-97—Utah	IHL	15	6	7	13	4	...			—	—	—	—	—
—Carolina	AHL	42	33	29	62	16	...			—	—	—	—	—
—Florida	NHL	4	0	0	0	0	-2	0	0	—	—	—	—	—
NHL totals (4 years)		12	0	0	0	2	-3	0	0					

FITZGERALD, TOM   RW/C   PANTHERS

PERSONAL: Born August 28, 1968, in Melrose, Mass. ... 6-1/195. ... Shoots right. ... Full name: Thomas James Fitzgerald.
HIGH SCHOOL: Austin Prep (Reading, Mass.).
COLLEGE: Providence.
TRANSACTIONS/CAREER NOTES: Selected by New York Islanders in first round (first Islanders pick, 17th overall) of NHL entry draft (June 21, 1986). ... Bruised left knee (November 7, 1990). ... Strained abdominal muscle (October 22, 1991); missed 16 games. ... Tore rib cage muscle (October 24, 1992); missed four games. ... Selected by Florida Panthers in NHL expansion draft (June 24, 1993). ... Sore hip (March 18, 1994); missed one game. ... Bruised eye (November 13, 1996); missed one game. ... Suffered from the flu (December 29, 1996); missed one game. ... Strained abdominal muscle (January 25, 1997); missed three games. ... Strained abdominal muscle (February 22, 1997); missed five games.
RECORDS: Shares NHL single-game playoff record for most shorthanded goals—2 (May 8, 1993).
MISCELLANEOUS: Holds Florida Panthers all-time record for most games played (213).

				REGULAR SEASON							PLAYOFFS			
Season Team	League	Gms.	G	A	Pts.	PIM	+/-	PP	SH	Gms.	G	A	Pts.	PIM
84-85—Austin Prep	Mass. H.S.	18	20	21	41	...	...	...	...	—	—	—	—	—
85-86—Austin Prep	Mass. H.S.	24	35	38	73	...	...	...	...	—	—	—	—	—
86-87—Providence College	Hockey East	27	8	14	22	22	...	..	...	—	—	—	—	—
87-88—Providence College	Hockey East	36	19	15	34	50	...	...	...	—	—	—	—	—
88-89—Springfield	AHL	61	24	18	42	43	...	...	...	—	—	—	—	—
—New York Islanders	NHL	23	3	5	8	10	1	0	0	—	—	—	—	—
89-90—Springfield	AHL	53	30	23	53	32	...	...	...	14	2	9	11	13
—New York Islanders	NHL	19	2	5	7	4	-3	0	0	4	1	0	1	4
90-91—New York Islanders	NHL	41	5	5	10	24	-9	0	0	—	—	—	—	—
—Capital District	AHL	27	7	7	14	50	...	...	...					

Season Team	League	Gms.	G	A	Pts.	PIM	+/-	PP	SH	Gms.	G	A	Pts.	PIM
91-92 — New York Islanders....	NHL	45	6	11	17	28	-3	0	2	—	—	—	—	—
— Capital District..........	AHL	4	1	1	2	4	...	...	...	—	—	—	—	—
92-93 — New York Islanders....	NHL	77	9	18	27	34	-2	0	3	18	2	5	7	18
93-94 — Florida................	NHL	83	18	14	32	54	-3	0	3	—	—	—	—	—
94-95 — Florida................	NHL	48	3	13	16	31	-3	0	0	—	—	—	—	—
95-96 — Florida................	NHL	82	13	21	34	75	-3	1	6	22	4	4	8	34
96-97 — Florida................	NHL	71	10	14	24	64	7	0	2	5	0	1	1	0
NHL totals (9 years)		489	69	106	175	324	-18	1	16	49	7	10	17	56

FITZPATRICK, MARK   G   PANTHERS

PERSONAL: Born November 13, 1968, in Toronto. ... 6-2/198. ... Catches left.

TRANSACTIONS/CAREER NOTES: Injured knee (February 1987). ... Selected by Los Angeles Kings as underage junior in second round (second Kings pick, 27th overall) of NHL entry draft (June 13, 1987). ... Traded by Kings with D Wayne McBean and future considerations to New York Islanders for G Kelly Hrudey (February 22, 1989); Kings sent D Doug Crossman to Islanders to complete deal (May 23, 1989). ... Developed Eosinophilic Myalgia Syndrome (EMS) after a reaction to L-Trytophan, an ingredient in a vitamin supplement (September 1990); returned to play (March 1991). ... Suffered recurrence of EMS and underwent biopsy on right thigh (October 22, 1991); missed 10 games. ... Strained abdominal muscle (December 15, 1992); missed five games. ... Traded by Islanders with first-round pick (C Adam Deadmarsh) in 1993 draft to Quebec Nordiques for G Ron Hextall and first-round pick (C/RW Todd Bertuzzi) in 1993 draft (June 20, 1993). ... Selected by Florida Panthers in NHL expansion draft (June 24, 1993). ... Suspended two games without pay and fined $500 by NHL for high-sticking incident (February 16, 1994). ... Sprained lower back (April 22, 1995); missed one game. ... Suffered recurring back spasms (April 26, 1995); missed last four games of season.

HONORS: Won Top Goaltender Trophy (1985-86). ... Named to WHL All-Star second team (1985-86 and 1987-88). ... Named to Memorial Cup All-Star team (1986-87 and 1987-88). ... Won Bill Masterton Memorial Trophy (1991-92).

MISCELLANEOUS: Stopped a penalty shot attempt (vs. Doug Gilmour, October 7, 1989; vs. Dean McAmmond, January 5, 1996; vs. Jaromir Jagr, November 9, 1996). ... Failed to stop a penalty shot attempt (vs. Mike Sillinger, January 14, 1997).

		REGULAR SEASON								PLAYOFFS						
Season Team	League	Gms.	Min	W	L	T	GA	SO	Avg.	Gms.	Min.	W	L	GA	SO	Avg.
83-84 — Revelstoke..............	BCJHL	21	1019	...	...	...	90	0	5.30	—	—	—	—	—	—	—
84-85 — Medicine Hat............	WHL	3	180	...	...	...	9	0	3.00	—	—	—	—	—	—	—
85-86 — Medicine Hat............	WHL	41	2074	26	6	1	99	1	*2.86	*19	986	12	5	*58	0	3.53
86-87 — Medicine Hat............	WHL	50	2844	31	11	4	159	*4	3.35	*20	*1224	12	8	71	†1	3.48
87-88 — Medicine Hat............	WHL	63	3600	36	15	6	194	†2	*3.23	16	959	12	4	52	†1	*3.25
88-89 — New Haven..............	AHL	18	980	10	5	1	54	1	3.31	—	—	—	—	—	—	—
— Los Angeles..............	NHL	17	957	6	7	3	64	0	4.01	—	—	—	—	—	—	—
— New York Islanders	NHL	11	627	3	5	2	41	0	3.92	—	—	—	—	—	—	—
89-90 — New York Islanders	NHL	47	2653	19	19	5	150	3	3.39	1	152	0	2	13	0	5.13
90-91 — Capital District..........	AHL	12	734	3	7	2	47	0	3.84	—	—	—	—	—	—	—
— New York Islanders	NHL	2	120	1	1	0	6	0	3.00	—	—	—	—	—	—	—
91-92 — Capital District..........	AHL	14	782	6	5	1	39	0	2.99	—	—	—	—	—	—	—
— New York Islanders	NHL	30	1743	11	13	5	93	0	3.20	—	—	—	—	—	—	—
92-93 — New York Islanders	NHL	39	2253	17	15	5	130	0	3.46	3	77	0	1	4	0	3.12
— Capital District..........	AHL	5	284	1	3	1	18	0	3.80	—	—	—	—	—	—	—
93-94 — Florida................	NHL	28	1603	12	8	6	73	1	2.73	—	—	—	—	—	—	—
94-95 — Florida................	NHL	15	819	6	7	2	36	2	2.64	—	—	—	—	—	—	—
95-96 — Florida................	NHL	34	1786	15	11	3	88	0	2.96	2	60	0	0	6	0	6.00
96-97 — Florida................	NHL	30	1680	8	9	9	66	0	2.36	—	—	—	—	—	—	—
NHL totals (9 years)		253	14241	98	95	40	747	6	3.15	9	289	0	3	23	0	4.78

FITZPATRICK, RORY   D   BLUES

PERSONAL: Born January 11, 1975, in Rochester, N.Y. ... 6-1/195. ... Shoots right.

TRANSACTIONS/CAREER NOTES: Selected by Montreal Canadiens in second round (second Canadiens pick, 47th overall) of NHL entry draft (June 26, 1993). ... Traded by Canadiens with C Pierre Turgeon and C Craig Conroy to St. Louis Blues for LW Shayne Corson, D Murray Baron and fifth-round pick (D Gennady Razin) in 1997 draft (October 29, 1996).

HONORS: Named to OHL All-Rookie team (1992-93).

		REGULAR SEASON							PLAYOFFS				
Season Team	League	Gms.	G	A	Pts.	PIM	+/-	PP	SH	Gms.	G	A	Pts.	PIM
90-91 — Rochester Jr. B	OHA	40	0	5	5	...	...	...	...	—	—	—	—	—
91-92 — Rochester Jr. B	OHA	28	8	28	36	141	...	...	...	—	—	—	—	—
92-93 — Sudbury................	OHL	58	4	20	24	68	...	...	...	14	0	0	0	17
93-94 — Sudbury................	OHL	65	12	34	46	112	...	...	...	10	2	5	7	10
94-95 — Sudbury................	OHL	56	12	36	48	72	...	...	...	18	3	15	18	21
— Fredericton..............	AHL	—	—	—	—	—	...	...	...	10	1	2	3	5
95-96 — Fredericton............	AHL	18	4	6	10	36	...	...	...	—	—	—	—	—
— Montreal................	NHL	42	0	2	2	18	-7	0	0	6	1	1	2	0
96-97 — Montreal..............	NHL	6	0	1	1	6	-2	0	0	—	—	—	—	—
— Worcester..............	AHL	49	4	13	17	78	...	...	...	5	1	2	3	0
— St. Louis..............	NHL	2	0	0	0	2	-2	0	0	—	—	—	—	—
NHL totals (3 years)		50	0	3	3	26	-11	0	0	6	1	1	2	0

FLAHERTY, WADE   G   ISLANDERS

PERSONAL: Born January 11, 1968, in Terrace, B.C. ... 6-0/200. ... Catches right.

TRANSACTIONS/CAREER NOTES: Selected by Buffalo Sabres in ninth round (10th Sabres pick, 181st overall) of NHL entry draft (June 11, 1988). ... Signed as free agent by San Jose Sharks (September 3, 1991). ... Injured ribs (February 28, 1995); missed three games. ... Strained groin (February 1, 1996); missed two games. ... Suffered back spasms (March 8, 1996); missed six games. ... Suffered back spasms (March 31, 1996); missed seven games. ... Broke collarbone (September 12, 1996); missed 23 games. ... Signed as free agent by New York Islanders (July 1, 1997).

F

HONORS: Named to WHL All-Star second team (1987-88). ... Won ECHL Playoff Most Valuable Player Award (1989-90). ... Shared James Norris Memorial Trophy with Arturs Irbe (1991-92). ... Named to IHL All-Star second team (1992-93 and 1993-94).

Season Team	League	REGULAR SEASON								PLAYOFFS						
		Gms.	Min	W	L	T	GA	SO	Avg.	Gms.	Min.	W	L	GA	SO	Avg.
84-85—Kelowna	WHL	1	55	0	0	0	5	0	5.45	—	—	—	—	—	—	—
85-86—Seattle	WHL	9	271	1	3	0	36	0	7.97	—	—	—	—	—	—	—
—Spokane	WHL	5	161	0	3	0	21	0	7.83	—	—	—	—	—	—	—
86-87—Nanaimo	BCJHL	15	830	...	...	...	53	0	3.83	—	—	—	—	—	—	—
—Victoria	WHL	3	127	0	2	0	16	0	7.56	—	—	—	—	—	—	—
87-88—Victoria	WHL	36	2052	20	15	0	135	0	3.95	5	300	2	3	18	0	3.60
88-89—Victoria	WHL	42	2408	21	19	0	180	0	4.49	8	480	3	5	35	0	4.38
89-90—Kalamazoo	IHL	1	13	0	0	‡0	0	0	0.00	—	—	—	—	—	—	—
—Greensboro	ECHL	27	1308	12	10	‡0	96	—	4.40	†9	567	*8	1	21	0	*2.22
90-91—Kansas City	IHL	†56	2990	16	31	‡4	*224	0	4.49	—	—	—	—	—	—	—
91-92—Kansas City	IHL	43	2603	26	14	‡3	140	1	3.23	1	1	0	0	0	0	0.00
—San Jose	NHL	3	178	0	3	0	13	0	4.38	—	—	—	—	—	—	—
92-93—Kansas City	IHL	61	*3642	*34	19	‡0	*195	2	3.21	12	*733	6	*5	†34	*1	2.78
—San Jose	NHL	1	60	0	1	0	5	0	5.00	—	—	—	—	—	—	—
93-94—Kansas City	IHL	60	*3564	32	19	‡9	202	0	3.40	—	—	—	—	—	—	—
94-95—San Jose	NHL	18	852	5	6	1	44	1	3.10	7	377	2	3	31	0	4.93
95-96—San Jose	NHL	24	1137	3	12	1	92	0	4.85	—	—	—	—	—	—	—
96-97—Kentucky	AHL	19	1032	8	6	2	54	1	3.14	3	200	1	2	11	0	3.30
—San Jose	NHL	7	359	2	4	0	31	0	5.18	—	—	—	—	—	—	—
NHL totals (5 years)		53	2586	10	26	2	185	1	4.29	7	377	2	3	31	0	4.93

FLATLEY, PATRICK   RW   RANGERS

PERSONAL: Born October 3, 1963, in Toronto. ... 6-2/205. ... Shoots right. ... Full name: Patrick William Flatley.
HIGH SCHOOL: Henry Carr (Rexdale, Ont.).
COLLEGE: Wisconsin.
TRANSACTIONS/CAREER NOTES: Selected by New York Islanders as underage junior in first round (first Islanders pick, 21st overall) of NHL entry draft (June 9, 1982). ... Broke bone in left hand (April 1985). ... Strained left knee ligaments (February 4, 1987). ... Separated right shoulder (November 1987). ... Injured right knee (January 1988). ... Underwent reconstructive knee surgery (February 1988). ... Injured right knee (December 1988). ... Suffered sore right ankle (February 1989). ... Reinjured right knee (March 1989). ... Bruised right ankle (October 1989). ... Pulled groin muscle (February 13, 1990). ... Reinjured groin (March 2, 1990); missed six games. ... Sprained right knee (October 13, 1990). ... Bruised left knee (November 30, 1990). ... Fractured finger on left hand (February 16, 1991). ... Fractured right thumb (December 19, 1991); missed 42 games. ... Broke ribs (January 5, 1993); missed four games. ... Broke jaw (October 22, 1993); missed eight games. ... Suffered sore foot (January 8, 1994); missed one game. ... Pulled abdominal muscle (March 27, 1994); missed 10 games. ... Injured hip flexor (March 26, 1995); missed two games. ... Pulled groin (October 17, 1995); missed eight games. ... Pulled groin (November 11, 1995); missed three games. ... Injured knee (December 27, 1995); missed one game. ... Pulled groin (January 22, 1996); missed nine games. ... Sprained right knee (April 2, 1996); missed two games. ... Injured groin (March 7, 1996); missed one game. ... Injured knee (April 2, 1996); missed two games. ... Injured knee (April 10, 1996); missed two games. ... Signed as free agent by New York Rangers (September 8, 1996). ... Strained groin (January 20, 1997); missed three games. ... Strained groin (February 15, 1997); missed three games.
HONORS: Named to NCAA All-America West team (1982-83). ... Named to NCAA All-Tournament team (1982-83). ... Named to WCHA All-Star first team (1982-83).
STATISTICAL PLATEAUS: Three-goal games: 1990-91 (1). ... Four-goal games: 1985-86 (1). ... Total hat tricks: 2.
MISCELLANEOUS: Captain of New York Islanders (1991-92 through 1995-96).

Season Team	League	REGULAR SEASON								PLAYOFFS				
		Gms.	G	A	Pts.	PIM	+/-	PP	SH	Gms.	G	A	Pts.	PIM
80-81—Henry Carr	MTHL	42	30	61	91	122	...	...	...	—	—	—	—	—
81-82—Univ. of Wisconsin	WCHA	33	17	20	37	65	...	...	...	—	—	—	—	—
82-83—Univ. of Wisconsin	WCHA	43	25	44	69	76	...	...	...	—	—	—	—	—
83-84—Can. Olympic team	Int'l	57	33	17	50	136	...	...	...	—	—	—	—	—
—New York Islanders	NHL	16	2	7	9	6	3	1	0	21	9	6	15	14
84-85—New York Islanders	NHL	78	20	31	51	106	-8	2	0	4	1	0	1	6
85-86—New York Islanders	NHL	73	18	34	52	66	20	6	0	3	0	0	0	21
86-87—New York Islanders	NHL	63	16	35	51	81	17	6	0	11	3	2	5	6
87-88—New York Islanders	NHL	40	9	15	24	28	7	5	1	—	—	—	—	—
88-89—New York Islanders	NHL	41	10	15	25	31	-5	2	1	—	—	—	—	—
—Springfield	AHL	2	1	1	2	2	...	...	...	—	—	—	—	—
89-90—New York Islanders	NHL	62	17	32	49	101	10	4	0	5	3	0	3	2
90-91—New York Islanders	NHL	56	20	25	45	74	-2	8	0	—	—	—	—	—
91-92—New York Islanders	NHL	38	8	28	36	31	14	4	1	—	—	—	—	—
92-93—New York Islanders	NHL	80	13	47	60	63	5	1	2	15	2	7	9	12
93-94—New York Islanders	NHL	64	12	30	42	40	12	2	1	—	—	—	—	—
94-95—New York Islanders	NHL	45	7	20	27	12	9	1	0	—	—	—	—	—
95-96—New York Islanders	NHL	56	8	9	17	21	-24	0	0	—	—	—	—	—
96-97—New York Rangers	NHL	68	10	12	22	26	6	0	0	11	0	0	0	14
NHL totals (14 years)		780	170	340	510	686	64	42	6	70	18	15	33	75

FLEURY, THEO   RW   FLAMES

PERSONAL: Born June 29, 1968, in Oxbow, Sask. ... 5-6/172. ... Shoots right. ... Name pronounced FLUH-ree.
TRANSACTIONS/CAREER NOTES: Selected by Calgary Flames in eighth round (ninth Flames pick, 166th overall) of NHL entry draft (June 13, 1987). ... Played in Europe during 1994-95 NHL lockout. ... Injured eye (April 6, 1996); missed two games. ... Injured knee (April 6, 1997); missed one game.
HONORS: Named to WHL (East) All-Star first team (1986-87). ... Shared Bob Clarke Trophy with Joe Sakic (1987-88). ... Named to WHL All-Star second team (1987-88). ... Shared Alka-Seltzer Plus Award with Marty McSorley (1990-91). ... Played in NHL All-Star Game (1991, 1992, 1996 and 1997). ... Named to NHL All-Star second team (1994-95).
RECORDS: Holds NHL single-game record for highest plus-minus rating—9 (February 10, 1993).

F

STATISTICAL PLATEAUS: Three-goal games: 1990-91 (5), 1992-93 (1), 1993-94 (1), 1995-96 (3), 1996-97 (1). Total: 11.
MISCELLANEOUS: Member of Stanley Cup championship team (1989). ... Captain of Calgary Flames (1995-96 and 1996-97). ... Scored on a penalty shot (vs. Jacques Cloutier, February 23, 1991; vs. Rick Wamsley, December 11, 1992; vs. Patrick Roy, October 22, 1996).

		REGULAR SEASON							PLAYOFFS				
Season Team	League	Gms.	G	A	Pts.	PIM	+/-	PP	SH	Gms.	G	A	Pts.	PIM
84-85— Moose Jaw	WHL	71	29	46	75	82	...	...	...	—	—	—	—	—
85-86— Moose Jaw	WHL	72	43	65	108	124	...	...	...	—	—	—	—	—
86-87— Moose Jaw	WHL	66	61	68	129	110	...	...	...	9	7	9	16	34
87-88— Moose Jaw	WHL	65	68	92	†160	235	...	...	...	—	—	—	—	—
— Salt Lake City	IHL	2	3	4	7	7	...	...	...	8	11	5	16	16
88-89— Salt Lake City	IHL	40	37	37	74	81	...	...	...	—	—	—	—	—
— Calgary	NHL	36	14	20	34	46	5	5	0	22	5	6	11	24
89-90— Calgary	NHL	80	31	35	66	157	22	9	3	6	2	3	5	10
90-91— Calgary	NHL	79	51	53	104	136	†48	9	7	7	2	5	7	14
91-92— Calgary	NHL	80	33	40	73	133	0	11	1	—	—	—	—	—
92-93— Calgary	NHL	83	34	66	100	88	14	12	2	6	5	7	12	27
93-94— Calgary	NHL	83	40	45	85	186	30	16	1	7	6	4	10	5
94-95— Tappara	Finland	10	8	9	17	22	...	...	...	—	—	—	—	—
— Calgary	NHL	47	29	29	58	112	6	9	2	7	7	7	14	2
95-96— Calgary	NHL	80	46	50	96	112	17	17	5	4	2	1	3	14
96-97— Calgary	NHL	81	29	38	67	104	-12	9	2	—	—	—	—	—
NHL totals (9 years)		649	307	376	683	1074	130	97	23	59	29	33	62	96

FOOTE, ADAM   D   AVALANCHE

PERSONAL: Born July 10, 1971, in Toronto. ... 6-1/202. ... Shoots right. ... Full name: Adam David Vernon Foote. ... Name pronounced FUT.
TRANSACTIONS/CAREER NOTES: Selected by Quebec Nordiques in second round (second Nordiques pick, 22nd overall) of NHL entry draft (June 17, 1989). ... Fractured right thumb (February 1992); missed remainder of season. ... Injured knee (October 21, 1992); missed one game. ... Suffered from the flu (January 28, 1993); missed two games. ... Injured groin (January 18, 1994); missed eight games. ... Suffered herniated disc (February 11, 1994); underwent surgery and missed remainder of season. ... Injured back (February 9, 1995); missed two games. ... Injured groin (February 28, 1995); missed two games. ... Injured groin (March 26, 1995); missed four games. ... Reinjured groin (April 6, 1995); missed five games. ... Nordiques franchise moved to Colorado and renamed Avalanche for 1995-96 season (June 21, 1995). ... Broke wrist prior to 1995-96 season; missed first two games of season. ... Separated left shoulder (January 6, 1996); missed five games. ... Bruised left knee (February 8, 1997); missed two games.
HONORS: Named to OHL All-Star first team (1990-91).
MISCELLANEOUS: Member of Stanley Cup championship team (1996).

		REGULAR SEASON							PLAYOFFS				
Season Team	League	Gms.	G	A	Pts.	PIM	+/-	PP	SH	Gms.	G	A	Pts.	PIM
88-89— Sault Ste. Marie	OHL	66	7	32	39	120	...	...	...	—	—	—	—	—
89-90— Sault Ste. Marie	OHL	61	12	43	55	199	...	...	...	—	—	—	—	—
90-91— Sault Ste. Marie	OHL	59	18	51	69	93	...	...	...	14	5	12	17	28
91-92— Quebec	NHL	46	2	5	7	44	-4	0	0	—	—	—	—	—
— Halifax	AHL	6	0	1	1	2	...	...	...	—	—	—	—	—
92-93— Quebec	NHL	81	4	12	16	168	6	0	1	6	0	1	1	2
93-94— Quebec	NHL	45	2	6	8	67	3	0	0	—	—	—	—	—
94-95— Quebec	NHL	35	0	7	7	52	17	0	0	6	0	1	1	14
95-96— Colorado	NHL	73	5	11	16	88	27	1	0	22	1	3	4	36
96-97— Colorado	NHL	78	2	19	21	135	16	0	0	17	0	4	4	62
NHL totals (6 years)		358	15	60	75	554	65	1	1	51	1	9	10	114

FORBES, COLIN   C   FLYERS

PERSONAL: Born February 16, 1976, in New Westminister, B.C. ... 6-3/190. ... Shoots left.
TRANSACTIONS/CAREER NOTES: Selected by Philadelphia Flyers in seventh round (fifth Flyers pick, 166th overall) of NHL entry draft (June 29, 1994).

		REGULAR SEASON							PLAYOFFS				
Season Team	League	Gms.	G	A	Pts.	PIM	+/-	PP	SH	Gms.	G	A	Pts.	PIM
93-94— Sherwood Park	AJHL	47	18	22	40	76	...	...	...	—	—	—	—	—
94-95— Portland	WHL	72	24	31	55	108	...	...	...	9	1	3	4	10
95-96— Portland	WHL	72	33	44	77	137	...	...	...	7	2	5	7	14
— Hershey	AHL	2	1	0	1	2	...	...	...	4	0	2	2	2
96-97— Philadelphia	AHL	74	21	28	49	108	...	...	...	10	5	5	10	33
— Philadelphia	NHL	3	1	0	1	0	0	0	0	3	0	0	0	0
NHL totals (1 year)		3	1	0	1	0	0	0	0	3	0	0	0	0

FORSBERG, JONAS   G   SHARKS

PERSONAL: Born June 15, 1975, in Stockholm, Sweden. ... 5-10/154. ... Catches left.
TRANSACTIONS/CAREER NOTES: Selected by San Jose Sharks in ninth round (11th Sharks pick, 210th overall) of NHL entry draft (June 26, 1993).

		REGULAR SEASON								PLAYOFFS						
Season Team	League	Gms.	Min	W	L	T	GA	SO	Avg.	Gms.	Min.	W	L	GA	SO	Avg.
92-93— Djur. Stockholm	Sweden							Statistics unavailable.								
93-94— Djur. Stockholm	Sweden	1	60	...	...	...	4	0	4.00	—	—	—	—	—	—	—
94-95— Djur. Stockholm	Sweden	1	60	...	...	...	6	0	6.00	—	—	—	—	—	—	—
95-96— Djur. Stockholm	Sweden							Did not play—injured.								
96-97— Manglerud Star	Norway							Statistics unavailable.								

FORSBERG, PETER   C   AVALANCHE

PERSONAL: Born July 20, 1973, in Ornskoldsvik, Sweden. ... 6-0/190. ... Shoots left.
TRANSACTIONS/CAREER NOTES: Selected by Philadelphia Flyers in first round (first Flyers pick, sixth overall) of NHL entry draft (June 22, 1991). ... Traded by Flyers with G Ron Hextall, C Mike Ricci, D Steve Duchesne, D Kerry Huffman, first-round pick (G Jocelyn Thibault) in 1993 draft, cash and future considerations to Quebec Nordiques for C Eric Lindros (June 20, 1992); Flyers sent LW Chris Simon and first-round pick (traded to Toronto) in 1994 draft to Nordiques to complete deal (July 21, 1992). ... Played in Europe during 1994-95 NHL lock-out. ... Suffered from the flu (March 1, 1995); missed one game. ... Nordiques franchise moved to Colorado and renamed Avalanche for 1995-96 season (June 21, 1995). ... Bruised thigh (December 14, 1996); missed 17 games.
HONORS: Named to Swedish League All-Star team (1991-92). ... Named Swedish League Player of the Year (1993-94). ... Named NHL Rookie of the Year by THE SPORTING NEWS (1994-95). ... Won Calder Memorial Trophy (1994-95). ... Named to NHL All-Rookie team (1994-95). ... Played in NHL All-Star Game (1996). ... Named to play in NHL All-Star Game (1997); replaced by LW Brendan Shanahan due to injury.
STATISTICAL PLATEAUS: Three-goal games: 1995-96 (2), 1996-97 (1). Total: 3.
MISCELLANEOUS: Member of Stanley Cup championship team (1996). ... Member of gold-medal-winning Swedish Olympic team (1994). ... Failed to score on a penalty shot (vs. Tim Cheveldae, February 1, 1996; vs. Grant Fuhr, December 6, 1996).

Season Team	League	REGULAR SEASON Gms.	G	A	Pts.	PIM	+/-	PP	SH	PLAYOFFS Gms.	G	A	Pts.	PIM
89-90 — MoDo Hockey Jrs.	Sweden Jr.	30	15	12	27	42	...	...	...	—	—	—	—	—
90-91 — MoDo Ornskoldvik	Sweden	23	7	10	17	22	...	...	...	—	—	—	—	—
91-92 — MoDo Ornskoldvik	Sweden	39	9	19	28	78	...	...	...	—	—	—	—	—
92-93 — MoDo Ornskoldvik	Sweden	39	23	24	47	92	...	...	...	3	4	1	5	0
93-94 — MoDo Ornskoldvik	Sweden	39	18	26	44	82	...	...	...	11	9	7	16	14
— Swe. Olympic team	Int'l	8	2	6	8	6	...	...	...	—	—	—	—	—
94-95 — MoDo Ornskoldvik	Sweden	11	5	9	14	20	...	...	...	—	—	—	—	—
— Quebec	NHL	47	15	35	50	16	17	3	0	6	2	4	6	4
95-96 — Colorado	NHL	82	30	86	116	47	26	7	3	22	10	11	21	18
96-97 — Colorado	NHL	65	28	58	86	73	31	5	4	14	5	12	17	10
NHL totals (3 years)		**194**	**73**	**179**	**252**	**136**	**74**	**15**	**7**	**42**	**17**	**27**	**44**	**32**

FOSTER, COREY   D   ISLANDERS

PERSONAL: Born October 27, 1969, in Ottawa. ... 6-3/204. ... Shoots left.
TRANSACTIONS/CAREER NOTES: Selected by New Jersey Devils in first round (first Devils pick, 12th overall) of NHL entry draft (June 11, 1988). ... Traded by Devils to Edmonton Oilers for first-round pick (C Jason Miller) in 1989 draft (June 17, 1989). ... Traded by Oilers with RW Dave Brown and rights to RW Jari Kurri to Philadelphia Flyers for RW Scott Mellanby, LW Craig Berube and C Craig Fisher (May 30, 1991). ... Fractured collarbone during preseason (September 1991); missed first 14 games of season. ... Signed as free agent by Ottawa Senators (June 20, 1994). ... Signed as a free agent by Pittsburgh Penguins (August 8, 1995). ... Selected by New York Islanders from Penguins in waiver draft for cash (September 30, 1996).

Season Team	League	REGULAR SEASON Gms.	G	A	Pts.	PIM	+/-	PP	SH	PLAYOFFS Gms.	G	A	Pts.	PIM
86-87 — Peterborough	OHL	30	3	4	7	4	...	...	...	1	0	0	0	0
87-88 — Peterborough	OHL	66	13	31	44	58	...	...	...	11	5	9	14	13
88-89 — Peterborough	OHL	55	14	42	56	42	...	...	...	17	1	17	18	12
— New Jersey	NHL	2	0	0	0	0	-2	0	0	—	—	—	—	—
89-90 — Cape Breton	AHL	54	7	17	24	32	...	...	...	1	0	0	0	0
90-91 — Cape Breton	AHL	67	14	11	25	51	...	...	...	4	2	4	6	4
91-92 — Philadelphia	NHL	25	3	4	7	20	-14	1	0	—	—	—	—	—
— Hershey	AHL	19	5	9	14	26	...	...	...	6	1	1	2	5
92-93 — Hershey	AHL	80	9	25	34	102	...	...	...	—	—	—	—	—
93-94 — Hershey	AHL	66	21	37	58	96	...	...	...	9	2	5	7	10
94-95 — Prin. Edward Island	AHL	78	13	34	47	61	...	...	...	11	2	5	7	12
95-96 — Cleveland	IHL	61	10	36	46	93	...	...	...	—	—	—	—	—
— Pittsburgh	NHL	11	2	2	4	2	-2	1	0	3	0	0	0	4
96-97 — New York Islanders	NHL	7	0	0	0	2	-2	0	0	—	—	—	—	—
— Cleveland	IHL	51	5	29	34	71	...	...	...	14	0	9	9	22
NHL totals (4 years)		**45**	**5**	**6**	**11**	**24**	**-20**	**2**	**0**	**3**	**0**	**0**	**0**	**4**

FOUNTAIN, MIKE   G

PERSONAL: Born January 26, 1972, in Gravenhurst, Ont. ... 6-1/176. ... Catches left. ... Name pronounced FOWN-tihn.
COLLEGE: Trent (Ont.).
TRANSACTIONS/CAREER NOTES: Selected by Vancouver Canucks in second round (third Canucks pick, 45th overall) of NHL entry draft (June 20, 1992).
HONORS: Named to Can.HL All-Star second team (1991-92). ... Named to OHL All-Star first team (1991-92). ... Named to AHL All-Star second team (1993-94).

Season Team	League	REGULAR SEASON Gms.	Min.	W	L	T	GA	SO	Avg.	PLAYOFFS Gms.	Min.	W	L	GA	SO	Avg.
88-89 — Huntsville Jr. C	OHA	22	1306	...	...	...	82	0	3.77	—	—	—	—	—	—	—
89-90 — Chatham Jr. B	OHA	21	1249	...	...	...	76	0	3.65	—	—	—	—	—	—	—
90-91 — Sault Ste. Marie	OHL	7	380	5	2	0	19	0	3.00	—	—	—	—	—	—	—
— Oshawa	OHL	30	1483	17	5	1	84	0	3.40	8	292	1	4	26	0	5.34
91-92 — Oshawa	OHL	40	2260	18	13	6	149	1	3.96	7	428	3	4	26	0	3.64
92-93 — Can. national team	Int'l	13	...	7	5	1	37	1	2.98	—	—	—	—	—	—	—
— Hamilton	AHL	12	618	2	8	0	46	0	4.47	—	—	—	—	—	—	—
93-94 — Hamilton	AHL	70	*4005	*34	28	6	241	*4	3.61	3	146	0	2	12	0	4.93
94-95 — Syracuse	AHL	61	*3618	25	*29	7	225	2	3.73	—	—	—	—	—	—	—
95-96 — Syracuse	AHL	54	3060	21	27	3	184	1	3.61	15	915	8	*7	57	†2	3.74
96-97 — Vancouver	NHL	6	245	2	2	0	14	1	3.43	—	—	—	—	—	—	—
— Syracuse	AHL	25	1462	8	14	2	78	1	3.20	2	120	0	2	12	0	6.00
NHL totals (1 year)		**6**	**245**	**2**	**2**	**0**	**14**	**1**	**3.43**							

FRANCIS, RON   C   PENGUINS

PERSONAL: Born March 1, 1963, in Sault Ste. Marie, Ont. ... 6-2/202. ... Shoots left. ... Cousin of Mike Liut, goaltender with three NHL teams (1979-80 through 1991-92) and Cincinnati Stingers of WHA (1977-78 and 1978-79).
TRANSACTIONS/CAREER NOTES: Selected by Hartford Whalers as underage junior in first round (first Whalers pick, fourth overall) of NHL entry draft (June 10, 1981). ... Injured eye (January 27, 1982); missed three weeks. ... Strained ligaments in right knee (November 30, 1983). ... Broke left ankle (January 18, 1986); missed 27 games. ... Broke left index finger (January 28, 1989); missed 11 games. ... Broke nose (November 24, 1990). ... Traded by Whalers with D Ulf Samuelsson and D Grant Jennings to Pittsburgh Penguins for C John Cullen, D Zarley Zalapski and RW Jeff Parker (March 4, 1991). ... Suffered from the flu (February 19, 1995); missed one game. ... Suffered back spasms (February 21, 1995); missed three games. ... Injured hip flexor (January 5, 1996); missed two games. ... Suspended two games and fined $1000 by NHL for checking player from behind (February 27, 1996). ... Broke left foot (May 11, 1996); missed remainder of playoffs. ... Injured groin (February 22, 1997); missed one game.
HONORS: Played in NHL All-Star Game (1983, 1985, 1990 and 1996). ... Won Lady Byng Memorial Trophy (1994-95). ... Won Frank J. Selke Trophy (1994-95). ... Won NHL Alka-Seltzer Plus award (1994-95).
STATISTICAL PLATEAUS: Three-goal games: 1982-83 (1), 1984-85 (1), 1985-86 (2), 1987-88 (1), 1988-89 (1), 1989-90 (1), 1990-91 (1), 1995-96 (1). Total: 9. ... Four-goal games: 1983-84 (1). ... Total hat tricks: 10.
MISCELLANEOUS: Member of Stanley Cup championship team (1991 and 1992). ... Captain of Hartford Whalers (1984-85 through 1990-1991). ... Captain of Pittsburgh Penguins (1994-95 and 1995-96). ... Holds Carolina Hurricanes franchise all-time records for most games played (714), most goals (264), most assists (557) and most points (821).. ... Scored on a penalty shot (vs. Richard Sevigny, January 17, 1986).

				REGULAR SEASON							PLAYOFFS			
Season Team	League	Gms.	G	A	Pts.	PIM	+/-	PP	SH	Gms.	G	A	Pts.	PIM
80-81— Sault Ste. Marie	OMJHL	64	26	43	69	33	...			19	7	8	15	34
81-82— Sault Ste. Marie	OHL	25	18	30	48	46	...			—	—	—	—	—
— Hartford	NHL	59	25	43	68	51	-13	12	0	—	—	—	—	—
82-83— Hartford	NHL	79	31	59	90	60	-25	4	2	—	—	—	—	—
83-84— Hartford	NHL	72	23	60	83	45	-10	5	0	—	—	—	—	—
84-85— Hartford	NHL	80	24	57	81	66	-23	4	0	—	—	—	—	—
85-86— Hartford	NHL	53	24	53	77	24	8	7	1	10	1	2	3	4
86-87— Hartford	NHL	75	30	63	93	45	10	7	0	6	2	2	4	6
87-88— Hartford	NHL	80	25	50	75	87	-8	11	1	6	2	5	7	2
88-89— Hartford	NHL	69	29	48	77	36	4	8	0	4	0	2	2	0
89-90— Hartford	NHL	80	32	69	101	73	13	15	1	7	3	3	6	8
90-91— Hartford	NHL	67	21	55	76	51	-2	10	1	—	—	—	—	—
— Pittsburgh	NHL	14	2	9	11	21	0	0	0	24	7	10	17	24
91-92— Pittsburgh	NHL	70	21	33	54	30	-7	5	1	21	8	*19	27	6
92-93— Pittsburgh	NHL	84	24	76	100	68	6	9	2	12	6	11	17	19
93-94— Pittsburgh	NHL	82	27	66	93	62	-3	8	0	6	0	2	2	6
94-95— Pittsburgh	NHL	44	11	*48	59	18	*30	3	0	12	6	13	19	4
95-96— Pittsburgh	NHL	77	27	92	119	56	25	12	1	11	3	6	9	4
96-97— Pittsburgh	NHL	81	27	63	90	20	7	10	1	5	1	2	3	2
NHL totals (16 years)		1166	403	944	1347	813	12	130	11	124	39	77	116	85

FRANEK, PETR   G   AVALANCHE

PERSONAL: Born April 6, 1975, in Most, Czechoslovakia. ... 5-11/187. ... Catches left. ... Name pronounced FRAN-nehk.
TRANSACTIONS/CAREER NOTES: Selected by Quebec Nordiques in eighth round (10th Nordiques pick, 205th overall) of NHL entry draft (June 29, 1993). ... Nordiques franchise moved to Colorado and renamed Avalanche for 1995-96 season (June 21, 1995).

			REGULAR SEASON								PLAYOFFS					
Season Team	League	Gms.	Min	W	L	T	GA	SO	Avg.	Gms.	Min.	W	L	GA	SO	Avg.
92-93— Litvinov	Czech.	5	273	...	...	...	15	...	3.30	—	—	—	—	—	—	—
93-94— Litvinov	Czech Rep.	11	535	...	...	...	34	...	3.81	2	61	...	...	10	...	9.84
94-95— Litvinov	Czech Rep.	12	657	...	...	...	47	...	4.29	1	16	...	...	0	...	0.00
95-96— Litvinov	Czech Rep.	36	2089	...	...	...	94	3	2.70	16	948	...	...	47	...	2.97
96-97— Hershey	AHL	15	457	4	1	0	23	3	3.02	—	—	—	—	—	—	—
— Brantford	Col.HL	6	321	4	1	0	14	0	2.62	—	—	—	—	—	—	—
— Quebec	IHL	6	357	3	3	‡0	18	0	3.03	1	40	0	1	4	0	6.00

FRASER, IAIN   C   SHARKS

PERSONAL: Born August 10, 1969, in Scarborough, Ont. ... 5-10/175. ... Shoots left.
TRANSACTIONS/CAREER NOTES: Selected by New York Islanders in 12th round (14th Islanders pick, 233rd overall) of NHL entry draft (June 17, 1989). ... Signed as free agent by Quebec Nordiques (August 3, 1993). ... Injured mouth (October 15, 1993); missed one game. ... Suffered from the flu (November 22, 1993); missed one game. ... Bruised left foot (December 28, 1993); missed three games. ... Bruised right knee (January 26, 1994); missed one game. ... Injured back (February 21, 1994); missed six games. ... Traded by Nordiques to Dallas Stars for undisclosed pick in 1996 draft (January 31, 1995). ... Claimed on waivers by Edmonton Oilers (March 3, 1995). ... Loaned by Oilers to Denver Grizzlies of IHL (April 10, 1995). ... Signed as free agent by Winnipeg Jets (October 13, 1995). ... Bruised hand (April 6, 1996); missed two games. ... Signed as free agent by San Jose Sharks (August 26, 1996).
HONORS: Won Leo LaLonde Memorial Trophy (1989-90). ... Won Stafford Smythe Memorial Trophy (1989-90). ... Named to Memorial Cup All-Star team (1989-90). ... Named to AHL All-Star second team (1992-93).

				REGULAR SEASON							PLAYOFFS			
Season Team	League	Gms.	G	A	Pts.	PIM	+/-	PP	SH	Gms.	G	A	Pts.	PIM
86-87— Oshawa Jr. B.............	OHA	31	18	22	40	119	...	...	...	—	—	—	—	—
87-88— Oshawa	OHL	16	4	4	8	22	...	...	...	6	2	3	5	2
88-89— Oshawa	OHL	62	33	57	90	87	...	...	...	6	2	8	10	12
89-90— Oshawa	OHL	56	40	65	105	75	...	...	...	17	10	*22	32	8
90-91— Richmond	ECHL	3	1	1	2	0	...	...	...	—	—	—	—	—
— Capital District	AHL	32	5	13	18	16	...	...	...	—	—	—	—	—

Season Team	League	Gms.	G	A	Pts.	PIM	+/-	PP	SH	Gms.	G	A	Pts.	PIM
91-92— Capital District	AHL	45	9	11	20	24	...	...	...	—	—	—	—	—
92-93— Capital District	AHL	74	41	69	110	16	...	...	...	4	0	1	1	0
— New York Islanders....	NHL	7	2	2	4	2	-1	1	0	—	—	—	—	—
93-94— Quebec....................	NHL	60	17	20	37	23	-5	2	0	—	—	—	—	—
— Canadian nat'l team ...	Int'l	4	0	1	1	4	...	...	...	—	—	—	—	—
94-95— Dallas......................	NHL	4	0	0	0	0	-3	0	0	—	—	—	—	—
— Edmonton..................	NHL	9	3	0	3	0	3	0	0	—	—	—	—	—
— Denver	IHL	1	0	0	0	0	...	...	...	—	—	—	—	—
95-96— Springfield	AHL	53	24	47	71	27	...	...	...	6	0	6	6	2
— Winnipeg..................	NHL	12	1	1	2	4	1	0	0	4	0	0	0	0
96-97— Kentucky..................	AHL	57	27	33	60	24	...	...	...	—	—	—	—	—
— San Jose..................	NHL	2	0	0	0	2	-1	0	0	—	—	—	—	—
NHL totals (5 years)		94	23	23	46	31	-6	3	0	4	0	0	0	0

FRASER, SCOTT   C   FLAMES

PERSONAL: Born May 3, 1972, in Moncton, New Brunswick. ... 6-1/178. ... Shoots right.
COLLEGE: Dartmouth.
TRANSACTIONS/CAREER NOTES: Selected by Montreal Canadiens in ninth round (12th Canadiens pick, 193rd overall) of NHL entry draft (June 22, 1991). ... Traded by Canadiens to Calgary Flames for RW David Ling and sixth-round pick in 1998 draft (October 24, 1996).
HONORS: Named to ECAC All-Star second team (1992-93).

		REGULAR SEASON								PLAYOFFS				
Season Team	League	Gms.	G	A	Pts.	PIM	+/-	PP	SH	Gms.	G	A	Pts.	PIM
90-91— Dartmouth College.....	ECAC	24	10	10	20	30	...	...	...	—	—	—	—	—
91-92— Dartmouth College.....	ECAC	24	11	7	18	60	...	...	...	—	—	—	—	—
92-93— Canadian nat'l team ...	Int'l	5	1	0	1	0	...	...	...	—	—	—	—	—
— Dartmouth College.....	ECAC	26	21	23	44	13	...	...	...	—	—	—	—	—
93-94— Dartmouth College.....	ECAC	24	17	13	30	34	...	...	...	—	—	—	—	—
— Canadian nat'l team ...	Int'l	4	0	1	1	4	...	...	...	—	—	—	—	—
94-95— Wheeling.................	ECHL	8	4	2	6	8	...	...	...	—	—	—	—	—
— Fredericton................	AHL	65	23	25	48	36	...	...	...	16	3	5	8	14
95-96— Fredericton................	AHL	58	37	37	74	43	...	...	...	10	9	7	16	2
— Montreal	NHL	14	2	0	2	4	-1	0	0	—	—	—	—	—
96-97— Saint John	AHL	37	22	10	32	24	...	...	...	—	—	—	—	—
— Fredericton................	AHL	7	3	8	11	0	...	...	...	—	—	—	—	—
— San Antonio	IHL	8	0	1	1	2	...	...	...	—	—	—	—	—
— Carolina	AHL	18	9	19	28	12	...	...	...	—	—	—	—	—
NHL totals (1 year)		14	2	0	2	4	-1	0	0	—	—	—	—	—

FRIESEN, JEFF   LW/C   SHARKS

PERSONAL: Born August 5, 1976, in Meadow Lake, Sask. ... 6-0/200. ... Shoots left. ... Name pronounced FREE-sihn.
HIGH SCHOOL: Robert Usher (Regina, Sask.).
TRANSACTIONS/CAREER NOTES: Selected by San Jose Sharks in first round (first Sharks pick, 11th overall) of NHL entry draft (June 28, 1994). ... Injured hand (October 18, 1996); missed two games.
HONORS: Won Can.HL Rookie of the Year Award (1992-93). ... Won Jim Piggott Memorial Trophy (1992-93). ... Named to NHL All-Rookie team (1994-95).
STATISTICAL PLATEAUS: Three-goal games: 1995-96 (1).
MISCELLANEOUS: Scored on a penalty shot (vs. Jim Carey, December 2, 1995).

		REGULAR SEASON								PLAYOFFS				
Season Team	League	Gms.	G	A	Pts.	PIM	+/-	PP	SH	Gms.	G	A	Pts.	PIM
91-92— Regina	WHL	4	3	1	4	2	...	...	...	—	—	—	—	—
92-93— Regina	WHL	70	45	38	83	23	...	...	...	13	7	10	17	8
93-94— Regina	WHL	66	51	67	118	48	...	...	...	4	3	2	5	2
94-95— Regina	WHL	25	21	23	44	22	...	...	...	—	—	—	—	—
— San Jose..................	NHL	48	15	10	25	14	-8	5	1	11	1	5	6	4
95-96— San Jose..................	NHL	79	15	31	46	42	-19	2	0	—	—	—	—	—
96-97— San Jose..................	NHL	82	28	34	62	75	-8	6	2	—	—	—	—	—
NHL totals (3 years)		209	58	75	133	131	-35	13	3	11	1	5	6	4

FRYLEN, EDVIN   D   BLUES

PERSONAL: Born December 23, 1975, in Jarfalla, Sweden. ... 6-0/211. ... Shoots left.
TRANSACTIONS/CAREER NOTES: Selected by St. Louis Blues in fifth round (third Blues pick, 120th overall) of NHL entry draft (June 29, 1994).

		REGULAR SEASON								PLAYOFFS				
Season Team	League	Gms.	G	A	Pts.	PIM	+/-	PP	SH	Gms.	G	A	Pts.	PIM
91-92— Vasteras....................	Sweden	2	0	0	0	0	...	...	...	—	—	—	—	—
92-93— Vasteras....................	Sweden	29	0	2	2	14	...	...	...	3	0	0	0	0
93-94— Vasteras....................	Sweden	32	1	0	1	26	...	...	...	—	—	—	—	—
94-95— Vasteras....................	Sweden	25	2	1	3	14	...	...	...	4	0	0	0	4
95-96— Vasteras....................	Sweden	39	8	5	13	16	...	...	...	—	—	—	—	—
96-97— Vasteras....................	Sweden	47	8	3	11	32	...	...	...	—	—	—	—	—

F

FUHR, GRANT　　　　　　　　　G　　　　　　　　　BLUES

PERSONAL: Born September 28, 1962, in Spruce Grove, Alta. ... 5-9/188. ... Catches right. ... Name pronounced FYOOR.

TRANSACTIONS/CAREER NOTES: Selected by Edmonton Oilers in first round (first Oilers pick, eighth overall) of NHL entry draft (June 10, 1981). ... Suffered partial separation of right shoulder (December 1981). ... Strained left knee ligaments and underwent surgery (December 13, 1983). ... Separated shoulder (February 1985). ... Bruised left shoulder (November 3, 1985); missed 10 games. ... Bruised left shoulder (November 1987). ... Injured right knee (November 1987). ... Suffered cervical neck strain (January 18, 1989). ... Underwent appendectomy (September 14, 1989); missed first six games of season. ... Underwent reconstructive surgery to left shoulder (December 27, 1989). ... Tore adhesions in left shoulder (March 13, 1990). ... Suspended six months by NHL for admitting to using drugs earlier in career (September 27, 1990). ... Traded by Oilers with RW/LW Glenn Anderson and LW Craig Berube to Toronto Maple Leafs for LW Vincent Damphousse, D Luke Richardson, G Peter Ing, C Scott Thornton and future considerations (September 19, 1991). ... Sprained thumb (October 17, 1991); missed two games. ... Pulled groin (November 12, 1991); missed three games. ... Sprained knee (February 11, 1992); missed four games. ... Sprained knee (October 20, 1992); missed 10 games. ... Strained shoulder (December 5, 1992); missed three games. ... Bruised shoulder muscle (January 17, 1993); missed four games. ... Traded by Maple Leafs with fifth-round pick (D Kevin Popp) in 1995 draft to Buffalo Sabres for LW Dave Andreychuk, G Daren Puppa and first-round pick (D Kenny Jonsson) in 1993 draft (February 2, 1993). ... Injured knee (November 24, 1993); missed 24 games. ... Traded by Sabres with D Philippe Boucher and D Denis Tsygurov to Los Angeles Kings for D Alexei Zhitnik, D Charlie Huddy, G Robb Stauber and fifth-round pick (D Marian Menhart) in 1995 draft (February 14, 1995). ... Signed as free agent by St. Louis Blues (July 11, 1995). ... Injured knee (March 31, 1996); missed three games. ... Underwent knee surgery due to injury suffered in play-offs (April 27, 1996); missed remainder of playoffs.

HONORS: Won Stewart (Butch) Paul Memorial Trophy (1979-80). ... Named to WHL All-Star first team (1979-80 and 1980-81). ... Won WHL Top Goaltender Trophy (1980-81). ... Named to THE SPORTING NEWS All-Star second team (1981-82 and 1985-86). ... Named to NHL All-Star second team (1981-82). ... Played in NHL All-Star Game (1982, 1984-1986, 1988 and 1989). ... Named All-Star Game Most Valuable Player (1986). ... Won Vezina Trophy (1987-88). ... Named to THE SPORTING NEWS All-Star first team (1987-88). ... Named to NHL All-Star first team (1987-88). ... Shared William M. Jennings Trophy with Dominik Hasek (1993-94).

RECORDS: Holds NHL single-season records for most points by a goaltender—14 (1983-84); and most games by a goaltender—79 (1995-96); and most consecutive appearances—76 (1995-96). ... Shares NHL single-season playoff record for most wins by a goaltender—16 (1987-88).

MISCELLANEOUS: Member of Stanley Cup championship team (1984, 1985, 1987, 1988 and 1990). ... Stopped a penalty shot attempt (vs. Ron Duguay, January 9, 1984; vs. Brent Peterson, January 13, 1984; vs. Ron Sutter, May 28, 1985 (playoffs); vs. Dave Poulin, May 30, 1985 (playoffs); vs. Brendan Shanahan, December 27, 1992; vs. Dave Hannan, October 22, 1995; vs. Peter Forsberg, December 6, 1996). ... Allowed a penalty shot goal (vs. Steve Yzerman, January 3, 1992; vs. Alexei Gusarov, March 10, 1993).

Season Team	League	Gms.	Min	W	L	T	GA	SO	Avg.	Gms.	Min.	W	L	GA	SO	Avg.
79-80—Victoria	WHL	43	2488	30	12	0	130	2	3.14	8	465	5	3	22	0	2.84
80-81—Victoria	WHL	59	*3448	48	9	1	160	†4	*2.78	15	899	12	3	45	1	3.00
81-82—Edmonton	NHL	48	2847	28	5	14	157	0	3.31	5	309	2	3	26	0	5.05
82-83—Moncton	AHL	10	604	4	5	1	40	0	3.97	—	—	—	—	—	—	—
—Edmonton	NHL	32	1803	13	12	5	129	0	4.29	1	11	0	0	0	0	0.00
83-84—Edmonton	NHL	45	2625	30	10	4	171	1	3.91	16	883	11	4	44	1	2.99
84-85—Edmonton	NHL	46	2559	26	8	7	165	1	3.87	†18	*1064	*15	3	55	0	3.10
85-86—Edmonton	NHL	40	2184	29	8	0	143	0	3.93	9	541	5	4	28	0	3.11
86-87—Edmonton	NHL	44	2388	22	13	3	137	0	3.44	19	1148	14	5	47	0	2.46
87-88—Edmonton	NHL	*75	*4304	40	24	9	*246	†4	3.43	*19	*1136	*16	2	55	0	2.90
88-89—Edmonton	NHL	59	3341	23	26	6	213	1	3.83	7	417	3	4	24	1	3.45
89-90—Cape Breton	AHL	2	120	2	0	0	6	0	3.00	—	—	—	—	—	—	—
—Edmonton	NHL	21	1081	9	7	3	70	1	3.89	—	—	—	—	—	—	—
90-91—Cape Breton	AHL	4	240	2	2	0	17	0	4.25	—	—	—	—	—	—	—
—Edmonton	NHL	13	778	6	4	3	39	1	3.01	17	1019	8	7	51	0	3.00
91-92—Toronto	NHL	65	3774	25	*33	5	*230	2	3.66	—	—	—	—	—	—	—
92-93—Toronto	NHL	29	1665	13	9	4	87	1	3.14	—	—	—	—	—	—	—
—Buffalo	NHL	29	1694	11	15	2	98	0	3.47	8	474	3	4	27	1	3.42
93-94—Buffalo	NHL	32	1726	13	12	3	106	2	3.68	—	—	—	—	—	—	—
—Rochester	AHL	5	310	3	0	2	10	0	1.94	—	—	—	—	—	—	—
94-95—Buffalo	NHL	3	180	1	2	0	12	0	4.00	—	—	—	—	—	—	—
—Los Angeles	NHL	14	698	1	7	3	47	0	4.04	—	—	—	—	—	—	—
95-96—St. Louis	NHL	*79	4365	30	28	*16	*209	3	2.87	2	69	1	0	1	0	0.87
96-97—St. Louis	NHL	73	4261	33	27	11	193	2	2.72	6	357	2	4	13	2	2.18
NHL totals (16 years)		747	42273	353	250	98	2452	20	3.48	127	7428	80	40	371	5	3.00

GAGE, JOAQUIN　　　　　　　　G　　　　　　　　OILERS

PERSONAL: Born October 19, 1973, in Vancouver. ... 6-0/200. ... Catches left. ... Name pronounced wah-KEEN GAYJ.
COLLEGE: Portland (Ore.) Community College.
TRANSACTIONS/CAREER NOTES: Selected by Edmonton Oilers in fifth round (sixth Oilers pick, 109th overall) of NHL entry draft (June 20, 1992).

Season Team	League	Gms.	Min	W	L	T	GA	SO	Avg.	Gms.	Min.	W	L	GA	SO	Avg.
90-91—Bellingham Jr. A	BCJHL	16	751	...	...	...	64	0	5.11	—	—	—	—	—	—	—
—Portland	WHL	3	180	0	3	0	17	0	5.67	—	—	—	—	—	—	—
91-92—Portland	WHL	63	3635	27	30	4	269	2	4.44	6	366	2	4	28	0	4.59
92-93—Portland	WHL	38	2302	21	16	1	153	2	3.99	8	427	5	2	30	0	4.22
93-94—Prince Albert	WHL	53	3041	24	25	3	212	1	4.18	—	—	—	—	—	—	—
94-95—Cape Breton	AHL	54	3010	17	28	5	207	0	4.13	—	—	—	—	—	—	—
—Edmonton	NHL	2	99	0	2	0	7	0	4.24	—	—	—	—	—	—	—
95-96—Edmonton	NHL	16	717	2	8	1	45	0	3.77	—	—	—	—	—	—	—
—Cape Breton	AHL	21	1161	8	11	0	80	0	4.13	—	—	—	—	—	—	—
96-97—Hamilton	AHL	29	1558	7	14	4	91	0	3.50	—	—	—	—	—	—	—
—Wheeling	ECHL	3	120	1	0	‡0	8	0	4.00	—	—	—	—	—	—	—
NHL totals (2 years)		18	816	2	10	1	52	0	3.82							

F

G

GAGNER, DAVE   C   PANTHERS

PERSONAL: Born December 11, 1964, in Chatham, Ont. ... 5-10/185. ... Shoots left. ... Name pronounced GAHN-yay.
TRANSACTIONS/CAREER NOTES: Selected by New York Rangers as underage junior in first round (first Rangers pick, 12th overall) of NHL entry draft (June 8, 1983). ... Fractured ankle (February 5, 1986). ... Underwent emergency appendectomy (December 1986). ... Traded by Rangers with RW Jay Caufield to Minnesota North Stars for D Jari Gronstrand and D Paul Boutilier (October 8, 1987). ... Broke kneecap (March 31, 1989). ... Underwent surgery to left knee cartilage (November 11, 1990). ... Underwent arthroscopic knee surgery (December 18, 1991); missed one game. ... Hyperextended knee (March 17, 1992); missed one game. ... North Stars franchise moved from Minnesota to Dallas and renamed Stars for 1993-94 season. ... Separated shoulder (November 1, 1993); missed seven games. ... Played in Europe during 1994-95 NHL lockout. ... Traded by Stars to Toronto Maple Leafs for LW Benoit Hogue and LW Randy Wood (January 28, 1996). ... Sprained shoulder (February 28, 1996); missed three games. ... Suffered concussion (March 30, 1996); missed three games. ... Traded by Maple Leafs to Calgary Flames for third-round pick (D Mike Lankshear) in 1996 draft (June 22, 1996). ... Signed as free agent by Florida Panthers (July 4, 1997).
HONORS: Won Bobby Smith Trophy (1982-83). ... Named to OHL All-Star second team (1982-83). ... Played in NHL All-Star Game (1991).
RECORDS: Shares NHL single-game playoff record for most points in one period—4 (April 8, 1991, first period).
STATISTICAL PLATEAUS: Three-goal games: 1988-89 (2), 1990-91 (1). Total: 3. ... Four-goal games: 1993-94 (1). ... Total hat tricks: 4.
MISCELLANEOUS: Failed to score on a penalty shot (vs. Bill Ranford, October 28, 1992; vs. Chris Osgood, April 1, 1995).

Season Team	League	REGULAR SEASON								PLAYOFFS				
		Gms.	G	A	Pts.	PIM	+/-	PP	SH	Gms.	G	A	Pts.	PIM
81-82— Brantford	OHL	68	30	46	76	31	...	...	...	11	3	6	9	6
82-83— Brantford	OHL	70	55	66	121	57	...	...	...	8	5	5	10	4
83-84— Can. Olympic team	Int'l	50	19	18	37	26	...	...	...	—	—	—	—	—
— Brantford	OHL	12	7	13	20	4	...	...	...	6	0	4	4	6
84-85— New Haven	AHL	38	13	20	33	23	...	...	...	—	—	—	—	—
— New York Rangers	NHL	38	6	6	12	16	-16	0	1	—	—	—	—	—
85-86— New York Rangers	NHL	32	4	6	10	19	1	0	0	—	—	—	—	—
— New Haven	AHL	16	10	11	21	11	...	...	...	4	1	2	3	2
86-87— New York Rangers	NHL	10	1	4	5	12	-1	0	0	—	—	—	—	—
— New Haven	AHL	56	22	41	63	50	...	...	...	7	1	5	6	18
87-88— Kalamazoo	IHL	14	16	10	26	26	...	...	...	—	—	—	—	—
— Minnesota	NHL	51	8	11	19	55	-14	0	2	—	—	—	—	—
88-89— Minnesota	NHL	75	35	43	78	104	13	11	3	—	—	—	—	—
— Kalamazoo	IHL	1	0	1	1	4	...	...	...	—	—	—	—	—
89-90— Minnesota	NHL	79	40	38	78	54	-1	10	0	7	2	3	5	16
90-91— Minnesota	NHL	73	40	42	82	114	9	20	0	23	12	15	27	28
91-92— Minnesota	NHL	78	31	40	71	107	-4	17	0	7	2	4	6	8
92-93— Minnesota	NHL	84	33	43	76	143	-13	17	0	—	—	—	—	—
93-94— Dallas	NHL	76	32	29	61	83	13	10	0	9	5	1	6	2
94-95— Courmaosta	Italy	1	0	4	4	0	...	...	...	—	—	—	—	—
— Dallas	NHL	48	14	28	42	42	2	7	0	5	1	1	2	4
95-96— Dallas	NHL	45	14	13	27	44	-17	6	0	—	—	—	—	—
— Toronto	NHL	28	7	15	22	59	-2	1	0	6	0	2	2	6
96-97— Calgary	NHL	82	27	33	60	48	2	9	0	—	—	—	—	—
NHL totals (13 years)		799	292	351	643	900	-28	108	6	57	22	26	48	64

GALLANT, CHESTER   RW   FLYERS

PERSONAL: Born December 22, 1977, in Thunder Bay, Ont. ... 6-1/184. ... Shoots right.
TRANSACTIONS/CAREER NOTES: Selected by Philadelphia Flyers in third round (second Flyers pick, 64th overall) of NHL entry draft (June 22, 1996).

Season Team	League	REGULAR SEASON								PLAYOFFS				
		Gms.	G	A	Pts.	PIM	+/-	PP	SH	Gms.	G	A	Pts.	PIM
94-95— Sudbury	OHL	37	3	5	8	63	...	...	...	—	—	—	—	—
— Niagara Falls	OHL	26	3	5	8	70	...	...	...	6	1	0	1	19
95-96— Niagara Falls	OHL	66	10	20	30	178	...	...	...	10	2	0	2	18
96-97— Erie	OHL	56	7	15	22	183	...	...	...	5	1	0	1	8

GALLEY, GARRY   D   KINGS

PERSONAL: Born April 16, 1963, in Ottawa. ... 6-0/204. ... Shoots left.
COLLEGE: Bowling Green State.
TRANSACTIONS/CAREER NOTES: Selected by Los Angeles Kings in fifth round (fourth Kings pick, 100th overall) of NHL entry draft (June 8, 1983). ... Injured knee (December 8, 1985). ... Traded by Kings to Washington Capitals for G Al Jensen (February 14, 1987). ... Signed as free agent by Boston Bruins; third-round pick in 1989 draft awarded to Capitals as compensation (July 8, 1988). ... Sprained left shoulder (September 30, 1989); missed first nine games of season. ... Suffered lacerations to cheek, both lips and part of neck (October 6, 1990). ... Dislocated right shoulder (December 22, 1990). ... Bruised left kneecap (March 23, 1991); missed two games. ... Pulled hamstring (April 17, 1991); missed three playoff games. ... Traded by Bruins with C Wes Walz and future considerations to Philadelphia Flyers for D Gord Murphy, RW Brian Dobbin and third-round pick (LW Sergei Zholtok) in 1992 draft (January 2, 1992). ... Bruised ribs (January 9, 1992); missed one game. ... Fractured foot (March 3, 1992); missed two games. ... Bruised jaw (February 24, 1993); missed one game. ... Strained shoulder (March 6, 1994); missed three games. ... Sprained wrist (February 13, 1995); missed three games. ... Traded by Flyers to Buffalo Sabres for D Petr Svoboda (April 7, 1995). ... Injured shoulder (November 12, 1995); missed three games. ... Injured knee (February 14, 1996); missed one game. ... Strained right shoulder (November 7, 1996); missed four games. ... Suffered concussion (December 4, 1996); missed two games. ... Tore abdominal muscle (February 9, 1997); missed one game. ... Fractured jaw (February 23, 1997); missed two games. ... Signed as free agent by Kings (July 5, 1997).
HONORS: Named to CCHA All-Star first team (1982-83 and 1983-84). ... Named to NCAA All-Tournament team (1983-84). ... Played in NHL All-Star Game (1991 and 1994).

G

Season Team	League	REGULAR SEASON Gms.	G	A	Pts.	PIM	+/-	PP	SH	PLAYOFFS Gms.	G	A	Pts.	PIM
81-82— Bowling Green	CCHA	42	3	36	39	48	...	...	...	—	—	—	—	—
82-83— Bowling Green	CCHA	40	17	29	46	40	...	...	...	—	—	—	—	—
83-84— Bowling Green	CCHA	44	15	52	67	61	...	...	...	—	—	—	—	—
84-85— Los Angeles	NHL	78	8	30	38	82	3	1	1	3	1	0	1	2
85-86— Los Angeles	NHL	49	9	13	22	46	-9	1	0	—	—	—	—	—
— New Haven	AHL	4	2	6	8	6	...	...	...	—	—	—	—	—
86-87— Los Angeles	NHL	30	5	11	16	57	-9	2	0	—	—	—	—	—
— Washington	NHL	18	1	10	11	10	3	1	0	2	0	0	0	0
87-88— Washington	NHL	58	7	23	30	44	11	3	0	13	2	4	6	13
88-89— Boston	NHL	78	8	21	29	80	-7	2	1	9	0	1	1	33
89-90— Boston	NHL	71	8	27	35	75	2	1	0	21	3	3	6	34
90-91— Boston	NHL	70	6	21	27	84	0	1	0	16	1	5	6	17
91-92— Boston	NHL	38	2	12	14	83	-3	1	0	—	—	—	—	—
— Philadelphia	NHL	39	3	15	18	34	1	2	0	—	—	—	—	—
92-93— Philadelphia	NHL	83	13	49	62	115	18	4	1	—	—	—	—	—
93-94— Philadelphia	NHL	81	10	60	70	91	-11	5	1	—	—	—	—	—
94-95— Philadelphia	NHL	33	2	20	22	20	0	1	0	—	—	—	—	—
— Buffalo	NHL	14	1	9	10	10	4	1	0	5	0	3	3	4
95-96— Buffalo	NHL	78	10	44	54	81	-2	7	1	—	—	—	—	—
96-97— Buffalo	NHL	71	4	34	38	102	10	1	1	12	0	6	6	14
NHL totals (13 years)		**889**	**97**	**399**	**496**	**1014**	**11**	**34**	**6**	**81**	**7**	**22**	**29**	**117**

GARDINER, BRUCE　　　　　C　　　　　SENATORS

PERSONAL: Born February 11, 1971, in Barrie, Ont. ... 6-1/193. ... Shoots right.
COLLEGE: Colgate.
TRANSACTIONS/CAREER NOTES: Selected by St. Louis Blues in sixth round (sixth Blues pick, 131st overall) of NHL entry draft (June 22, 1991). ... Signed as free agent by Ottawa Senators (June 14, 1994). ... Suffered broken leg (September 23, 1995). ... Bruised left foot (November 27, 1996); missed two games. ... Separated left shoulder (February 1, 1997); missed 10 games.
HONORS: Named to ECAC All-Star second team (1993-94).

Season Team	League	REGULAR SEASON Gms.	G	A	Pts.	PIM	+/-	PP	SH	PLAYOFFS Gms.	G	A	Pts.	PIM
90-91— Colgate University	ECAC	27	4	9	13	72	...	...	...	—	—	—	—	—
91-92— Colgate University	ECAC	23	7	8	15	77	...	...	...	—	—	—	—	—
92-93— Colgate University	ECAC	33	17	12	29	64	...	...	...	—	—	—	—	—
93-94— Colgate University	ECAC	33	23	23	46	68	...	...	...	—	—	—	—	—
— Peoria	IHL	3	0	0	0	0	...	...	...	—	—	—	—	—
94-95— Prin. Edward Island ...	AHL	72	17	20	37	132	...	...	...	7	4	1	5	4
95-96— Prin. Edward Island ...	AHL	38	11	13	24	87	...	...	...	5	2	4	6	4
96-97— Ottawa	NHL	67	11	10	21	49	4	0	1	7	0	1	1	2
NHL totals (1 year)		**67**	**11**	**10**	**21**	**49**	**4**	**0**	**1**	**7**	**0**	**1**	**1**	**2**

GARON, MATHIEU　　　　　G　　　　　CANADIENS

PERSONAL: Born January 9, 1978, in Chandler, Que. ... 6-1/175. ... Catches right.
TRANSACTIONS/CAREER NOTES: Selected by Montreal Canadiens in second round (second Canadiens pick, 44th overall) of NHL entry draft (June 22, 1996).
HONORS: Won Raymond Lagace Trophy (1995-96). ... Named to QMJHL All-Rookie team (1995-96).

Season Team	League	REGULAR SEASON Gms.	Min.	W	L	T	GA	SO	Avg.	PLAYOFFS Gms.	Min.	W	L	GA	SO	Avg.
95-96— Victoriaville	QMJHL	51	2709	18	27	0	189	1	4.19	12	676	7	4	38	1	3.37
96-97— Victoriaville	QMJHL	53	3026	29	18	3	148	*6	2.93	6	330	2	4	23	0	4.18

GARPENLOV, JOHAN　　　　　LW　　　　　PANTHERS

PERSONAL: Born March 21, 1968, in Stockholm, Sweden. ... 5-11/185. ... Shoots left. ... Name pronounced YO-hahn GAHR-pihn-LAHV.
TRANSACTIONS/CAREER NOTES: Selected by Detroit Red Wings in fifth round (fifth Red Wings pick, 85th overall) of NHL entry draft (June 9, 1984). ... Traded by Red Wings to San Jose Sharks for D Bob McGill and eighth-round pick (G C.J. Denomme) in 1992 draft (March 10, 1992). ... Strained back (October 20, 1992); missed three games. ... Suffered from the flu (March 25, 1993); missed one game. ... Injured thigh (October 10, 1993); missed one game. ... Sprained groin (January 30, 1995); missed six games. ... Traded by Sharks to Florida Panthers for conditional fifth-round pick in 1998 draft (March 3, 1995). ... Sprained knee ligament (November 18, 1996); missed 13 games. ... Sprained knee ligament (February 22, 1997); missed 16 games.
STATISTICAL PLATEAUS: Three-goal games: 1990-91 (1), 1992-93 (1), 1995-96 (1). Total: 3. ... Four-goal games: 1990-91 (1). ... Total hat tricks: 4.

Season Team	League	REGULAR SEASON Gms.	G	A	Pts.	PIM	+/-	PP	SH	PLAYOFFS Gms.	G	A	Pts.	PIM
86-87— Djur. Stockholm	Sweden	29	5	8	13	20	...	...	...	—	—	—	—	—
87-88— Djur. Stockholm	Sweden	30	7	10	17	12	...	...	...	—	—	—	—	—
88-89— Djur. Stockholm	Sweden	36	12	19	31	20	...	...	...	—	—	—	—	—
89-90— Djur. Stockholm	Sweden	39	20	13	33	36	...	...	...	8	2	4	6	4
90-91— Detroit......................	NHL	71	18	22	40	18	-4	2	0	6	0	1	1	4
91-92— Detroit......................	NHL	16	1	1	2	4	2	0	0	—	—	—	—	—
— Adirondack.................	AHL	9	3	3	6	6	...	...	...	—	—	—	—	—
— San Jose....................	NHL	12	5	6	11	4	-2	1	0	—	—	—	—	—
92-93— San Jose....................	NHL	79	22	44	66	56	-26	14	0	—	—	—	—	—

G

Season Team	League	REGULAR SEASON								PLAYOFFS				
		Gms.	G	A	Pts.	PIM	+/-	PP	SH	Gms.	G	A	Pts.	PIM
93-94— San Jose..................	NHL	80	18	35	53	28	9	7	0	14	4	6	10	6
94-95— San Jose..................	NHL	13	1	1	2	2	-3	0	0	—	—	—	—	—
— Florida..........................	NHL	27	3	9	12	0	4	0	0	—	—	—	—	—
95-96— Florida....................	NHL	82	23	28	51	36	-10	8	0	20	4	2	6	8
96-97— Florida....................	NHL	53	11	25	36	47	10	1	0	4	2	0	2	4
NHL totals (8 years)		433	102	171	273	195	-20	33	0	44	10	9	19	22

GARTNER, MIKE RW COYOTES

PERSONAL: Born October 29, 1959, in Ottawa. ... 6-0/188. ... Shoots right. ... Full name: Michael Alfred Gartner.

TRANSACTIONS/CAREER NOTES: Signed as underage junior by Cincinnati Stingers (August 1978). ... Selected by Washington Capitals in first round (first Capitals pick, fourth overall) of NHL entry draft (August 9, 1979). ... Injured eye (February 1983). ... Underwent arthroscopic surgery to repair torn cartilage in left knee (March 1986). ... Sprained right knee (November 1988). ... Traded by Capitals with D Larry Murphy to Minnesota North Stars for RW Dino Ciccarelli and D Bob Rouse (March 7, 1989). ... Underwent surgery to repair cartilage in left knee (April 14, 1989). ... Traded by North Stars to New York Rangers for C Ulf Dahlen, fourth-round pick (C Cal McGowan) in 1990 draft and future considerations (March 6, 1990). ... Underwent arthroscopic surgery to repair elbow (January 27, 1994); missed one game. ... Traded by Rangers to Toronto Maple Leafs for RW Glenn Anderson, rights to D Scott Malone and fourth-round pick (D Alexander Korobolin) in 1994 draft (March 21, 1994). ... Suffered partially collapsed lung (February 3, 1995); missed seven games. ... Suffered hairline fracture in foot (March 17, 1995); missed three games. ... Traded by Maple Leafs to Phoenix Coyotes for fourth-round pick (LW Vladimir Antipov) in 1996 draft (June 22, 1996).

HONORS: Won Emms Family Award (1976-77). ... Named to OMJHL All-Star first team (1977-78). ... Played in NHL All-Star Game (1980, 1985, 1986, 1988, 1990, 1993 and 1996). ... Named All-Star Game Most Valuable Player (1993).

RECORDS: Holds NHL career record for most consecutive 30-goal seasons—15 (1979-80 through 1993-94); and most 30-or-more goal seasons—17. ... Holds NHL All-Star Game records for fastest two goals from start of game—3:37 (1993); and fastest two goals from start of period—3:37 (1993). ... Shares NHL All-Star Game record for most goals—4 (1991).

STATISTICAL PLATEAUS: Three-goal games: 1979-80 (2), 1980-81 (1), 1981-82 (1), 1982-83 (1), 1983-84 (1), 1984-85 (1), 1985-86 (3), 1987-88 (1), 1989-90 (2), 1991-92 (1), 1996-97 (1). Total: 15. ... Four-goal games: 1980-81 (1), 1986-87 (1). Total: 2. ... Total hat tricks: 17.

MISCELLANEOUS: Holds Washington Capitals all-time records for most goals (397) and most points (789). ... Scored on a penalty shot (vs. Wayne Thomas, December 20, 1980; vs. Mike Liut, January 17, 1987; vs. Glenn Resch, April 4, 1987).

Season Team	League	REGULAR SEASON								PLAYOFFS				
		Gms.	G	A	Pts.	PIM	+/-	PP	SH	Gms.	G	A	Pts.	PIM
75-76— St. Catharines	OHA Mj. Jr. A	3	1	3	4	0	...	...	...	—	—	—	—	—
76-77— Niagara Falls	OMJHL	62	33	42	75	125	...	...	...	—	—	—	—	—
77-78— Niagara Falls	OMJHL	64	41	49	90	56	...	...	...	—	—	—	—	—
78-79— Cincinnati...................	WHA	78	27	25	52	123	...	...	...	3	0	2	2	2
79-80— Washington	NHL	77	36	32	68	66	...	4	0	—	—	—	—	—
80-81— Washington	NHL	80	48	46	94	100	-5	13	0	—	—	—	—	—
81-82— Washington	NHL	80	35	45	80	121	-11	5	2	—	—	—	—	—
82-83— Washington	NHL	73	38	38	76	54	-2	10	1	4	0	0	0	4
83-84— Washington	NHL	80	40	45	85	90	22	8	0	8	3	7	10	16
84-85— Washington	NHL	80	50	52	102	71	17	17	0	5	4	3	7	9
85-86— Washington	NHL	74	35	40	75	63	-5	11	2	9	2	10	12	4
86-87— Washington	NHL	78	41	32	73	61	1	5	6	7	4	3	7	14
87-88— Washington	NHL	80	48	33	81	73	20	19	0	14	3	4	7	14
88-89— Washington	NHL	56	26	29	55	71	8	6	0	—	—	—	—	—
— Minnesota	NHL	13	7	7	14	6	3	3	0	5	0	0	0	0
89-90— Minnesota	NHL	67	34	36	70	32	-8	15	4	—	—	—	—	—
— New York Rangers.....	NHL	12	11	5	16	6	4	6	0	10	5	3	8	12
90-91— New York Rangers.....	NHL	79	49	20	69	53	-9	22	1	6	1	1	2	0
91-92— New York Rangers.....	NHL	76	40	41	81	55	11	15	0	13	8	8	16	4
92-93— New York Rangers.....	NHL	84	45	23	68	59	-4	13	0	—	—	—	—	—
93-94— New York Rangers.....	NHL	71	28	24	52	58	11	10	5	—	—	—	—	—
— Toronto	NHL	10	6	6	12	4	9	1	0	18	5	6	11	14
94-95— Toronto	NHL	38	12	8	20	6	0	2	1	5	2	2	4	2
95-96— Toronto	NHL	82	35	19	54	52	5	15	0	6	4	1	5	4
96-97— Phoenix....................	NHL	82	32	31	63	38	-11	13	1	7	1	2	3	4
WHA totals (1 year)............		78	27	25	52	123	...	...	...	3	0	2	2	2
NHL totals (18 years)		1372	696	612	1308	1139	...	213	23	117	42	50	92	101

GAUDREAU, ROB RW

PERSONAL: Born January 20, 1970, in Cranston, R.I. ... 5-11/185. ... Shoots right. ... Full name: Robert Rene Gaudreau. ... Name pronounced guh-DROH. ... Son of Bob Gaudreau, member of 1968 U.S. Olympic hockey team.

HIGH SCHOOL: Bishop Hendricken (Warwick, R.I.).

COLLEGE: Providence.

TRANSACTIONS/CAREER NOTES: Separated shoulder (February 1987). ... Selected by Pittsburgh Penguins in ninth round (eighth Penguins pick, 127th overall) of NHL entry draft (June 11, 1988). ... Traded by Penguins to Minnesota North Stars for C Richard Zemlak (November 1, 1988). ... Selected by San Jose Sharks in NHL dispersal draft (May 30, 1991). ... Bruised hand (March 21, 1993); missed one game. ... Selected by Ottawa Senators in 1994-95 waiver draft for cash (January 18, 1995). ... Injured knee (April 10, 1995); missed remainder of season.

HONORS: Named Hockey East co-Rookie of the Year with Scott Pellerin (1988-89). ... Named to Hockey East All-Rookie team (1988-89). ... Named to Hockey East All-Star second team (1990-91). ... Named to NCAA All-America East second team (1991-92). ... Named to Hockey East All-Star first team (1991-92). ... Named to Hockey East All-Decade team (1994).

STATISTICAL PLATEAUS: Three-goal games: 1992-93 (2), 1993-94 (1). Total: 3.

Season Team	League	REGULAR SEASON								PLAYOFFS				
		Gms.	G	A	Pts.	PIM	+/-	PP	SH	Gms.	G	A	Pts.	PIM
86-87— Bishop Hendricken.....	R.I.H.S.	33	41	39	80	...	...	...	...	—	—	—	—	—
87-88— Bishop Hendricken.....	R.I.H.S.	...	52	60	112	...	...	...	...	—	—	—	—	—
88-89— Providence College	Hockey East	42	28	29	57	32	...	...	...	—	—	—	—	—

Season Team	League	REGULAR SEASON Gms.	G	A	Pts.	PIM	+/-	PP	SH	PLAYOFFS Gms.	G	A	Pts.	PIM
89-90— Providence College	Hockey East	32	20	18	38	12	...	...	...	—	—	—	—	—
90-91— Providence College	Hockey East	36	34	27	61	20	...	...	...	—	—	—	—	—
91-92— Providence College	Hockey East	36	21	34	55	22	...	...	...	—	—	—	—	—
92-93— Kansas City................	IHL	19	8	6	14	6	...	...	...	—	—	—	—	—
— San Jose....................	NHL	59	23	20	43	18	-18	5	2	—	—	—	—	—
93-94— San Jose....................	NHL	84	15	20	35	28	-10	6	0	14	2	0	2	0
94-95— Ottawa	NHL	36	5	9	14	8	-16	0	0	—	—	—	—	—
95-96— Prin. Edward Island ...	AHL	3	2	0	2	4	...	...	...	—	—	—	—	—
— Ottawa	NHL	52	8	5	13	15	-19	1	1	—	—	—	—	—
96-97—							Did not play.							
NHL totals (4 years)		231	51	54	105	69	-63	12	3	14	2	0	2	0

GAUTHIER, DENIS — D — FLAMES

PERSONAL: Born October 1, 1976, in Montreal. ... 6-1/195. ... Shoots left. ... Name pronounced GO-chay.
TRANSACTIONS/CAREER NOTES: Selected by Calgary Flames in first round (first Flames pick, 20th overall) of NHL entry draft (July 8, 1995).
HONORS: Named to Can.HL All-Star first team (1995-96). ... Won Emile Bouchard Trophy (1995-96). ... Named to QMJHL All-Star first team (1995-96).

Season Team	League	REGULAR SEASON Gms.	G	A	Pts.	PIM	+/-	PP	SH	PLAYOFFS Gms.	G	A	Pts.	PIM
92-93— Drummondville	QMJHL	61	1	7	8	136	...	...	...	10	0	5	5	40
93-94— Drummondville	QMJHL	60	0	7	7	176	...	...	...	9	2	0	2	41
94-95— Drummondville	QMJHL	64	9	31	40	190	...	...	...	4	0	5	5	12
95-96— Drummondville	QMJHL	53	25	49	74	140	...	...	...	6	4	4	8	32
— Saint John	AHL	5	2	0	2	8	...	...	...	16	1	6	7	20
96-97— Saint John	AHL	73	3	28	31	74	...	...	...	5	0	0	0	6

GAVEY, AARON — C — FLAMES

PERSONAL: Born February 22, 1974, in Sudbury, Ont. ... 6-2/194. ... Shoots left. ... Name pronounced GAY-vee.
TRANSACTIONS/CAREER NOTES: Selected by Tampa Bay Lightning in fourth round (fourth Lightning pick, 74th overall) of NHL entry draft (June 20, 1992). ... Bruised left ankle (January 3, 1996); missed one game. ... Suffered facial laceration (February 4, 1996); missed eight games. ... Traded by Lightning to Calgary Flames for G Rick Tabaracci (November 19, 1996). ... Strained neck (February 28, 1997); missed 14 games.

Season Team	League	REGULAR SEASON Gms.	G	A	Pts.	PIM	+/-	PP	SH	PLAYOFFS Gms.	G	A	Pts.	PIM
90-91— Peterborough Jr. B.....	OHA	42	26	30	56	68	...	...	...	—	—	—	—	—
91-92— Sault Ste. Marie	OHL	48	7	11	18	27	...	...	...	19	5	1	6	10
92-93— Sault Ste. Marie	OHL	62	45	39	84	114	...	...	...	18	5	9	14	36
93-94— Sault Ste. Marie	OHL	60	42	60	102	116	...	...	...	14	11	10	21	22
94-95— Atlanta	IHL	66	18	17	35	85	...	...	...	5	0	1	1	9
95-96— Tampa Bay	NHL	73	8	4	12	56	-6	1	1	6	0	0	0	4
96-97— Tampa Bay	NHL	16	1	2	3	12	-1	0	0	—	—	—	—	—
— Calgary	NHL	41	7	9	16	34	-11	3	0	—	—	—	—	—
NHL totals (2 years)		130	16	15	31	102	-18	4	1	6	0	0	0	4

GELINAS, MARTIN — LW — CANUCKS

PERSONAL: Born June 5, 1970, in Shawinigan, Que. ... 5-11/195. ... Shoots left. ... Name pronounced MAHR-tai ZHEHL-ih-nuh.
HIGH SCHOOL: Polyvalente Val- Maurice (Shawinigan, Que.).
TRANSACTIONS/CAREER NOTES: Broke left clavicle (November 1983). ... Suffered hairline fracture of clavicle (July 1986). ... Selected by Los Angeles Kings in first round (first Kings pick, seventh overall) of NHL entry draft (June 11, 1988). ... Traded by Kings with C Jimmy Carson, first-round picks in 1989 (traded to New Jersey), 1991 (LW Martin Rucinsky) and 1993 (D Nick Stajduhar) drafts and cash to Edmonton Oilers for C Wayne Gretzky, RW/D Marty McSorley and LW/C Mike Krushelnyski (August 9, 1988). ... Suspended five games by NHL (March 9, 1990). ... Underwent shoulder surgery (June 1990). ... Traded by Oilers with sixth-round pick (C Nicholas Checco) in 1993 draft to Quebec Nordiques for LW Scott Pearson (June 20, 1993). ... Injured thigh (October 20, 1993); missed one game. ... Separated left shoulder (November 25, 1993); missed 10 games. ... Claimed on waivers by Vancouver Canucks (January 15, 1994). ... Suffered charley horse (March 27, 1994); missed six games. ... Injured knee (April 30, 1995); missed last game of season and eight playoff games. ... Fractured rib (November 2, 1996); missed eight games.
HONORS: Won Can.HL Rookie of the Year Award (1987-88). ... Won Michel Bergeron Trophy (1987-88). ... Named to QMJHL All-Star first team (1987-88).
STATISTICAL PLATEAUS: Three-goal games: 1989-90 (1), 1996-97 (1). Total: 2. ... Four-goal games: 1996-97 (1). ... Total hat tricks: 3.
MISCELLANEOUS: Member of Stanley Cup championship team (1990).

Season Team	League	REGULAR SEASON Gms.	G	A	Pts.	PIM	+/-	PP	SH	PLAYOFFS Gms.	G	A	Pts.	PIM
87-88— Hull	QMJHL	65	63	68	131	74	...	...	...	17	15	18	33	32
88-89— Edmonton	NHL	6	1	2	3	0	-1	0	0	—	—	—	—	—
— Hull	QMJHL	41	38	39	77	31	...	...	...	9	5	4	9	14
89-90— Edmonton	NHL	46	17	8	25	30	0	5	0	20	2	3	5	6
90-91— Edmonton	NHL	73	20	20	40	34	-7	4	0	18	3	6	9	25
91-92— Edmonton	NHL	68	11	18	29	62	14	1	0	15	1	3	4	10
92-93— Edmonton	NHL	65	11	12	23	30	3	0	0	—	—	—	—	—
93-94— Quebec	NHL	31	6	6	12	8	-2	0	0	—	—	—	—	—
— Vancouver	NHL	33	8	8	16	26	-6	3	0	24	5	4	9	14
94-95— Vancouver	NHL	46	13	10	23	36	8	1	0	3	0	1	1	0
95-96— Vancouver	NHL	81	30	26	56	59	8	3	4	6	1	1	2	12
96-97— Vancouver	NHL	74	35	33	68	42	6	6	1	—	—	—	—	—
NHL totals (9 years)		523	152	143	295	327	23	23	5	86	12	18	30	67

G

GENDRON, MARTIN   RW   CAPITALS

PERSONAL: Born February 15, 1974, in Valleyfield, Que. ... 5-9/190. ... Shoots right. ... Name pronounced MAHR-tai ZHEHN-drah.
TRANSACTIONS/CAREER NOTES: Selected by Washington Capitals in third round (fourth Capitals pick, 71st overall) of NHL entry draft (June 20, 1992).
HONORS: Named to QMJHL All-Rookie team (1990-91). ... Won Can.HL Most Sportsmanlike Player of the Year Award (1991-92). ... Won Shell Cup (1991-92). ... Won Frank J. Selke Trophy (1991-92 and 1992-93). ... Named to QMJHL All-Star first team (1991-92). ... Named to Can.HL All-Star first team (1992-93). ... Named to QMJHL All-Star second team (1992-93).

				REGULAR SEASON							PLAYOFFS				
Season Team	League	Gms.	G	A	Pts.	PIM	+/-	PP	SH		Gms.	G	A	Pts.	PIM
90-91 — St. Hyacinthe	QMJHL	55	34	23	57	33	...	...	...		4	1	2	3	0
91-92 — St. Hyacinthe	QMJHL	69	*71	66	137	45	...	...	...		6	7	4	11	14
92-93 — St. Hyacinthe	QMJHL	63	73	61	134	44	...	...	...		—	—	—	—	—
— Baltimore	AHL	10	1	2	3	2	...	...	...		3	0	0	0	0
93-94 — Canadian nat'l team	Int'l	19	4	5	9	2	...	...	...		—	—	—	—	—
— Hull	QMJHL	37	39	36	75	18	...	...	...		20	*21	17	38	8
94-95 — Portland	AHL	72	36	32	68	54	...	...	...		4	5	1	6	2
— Washington	NHL	8	2	1	3	2	3	0	0		—	—	—	—	—
95-96 — Washington	NHL	20	2	1	3	8	-5	0	0		—	—	—	—	—
— Portland	AHL	48	38	29	67	39	...	...	...		22	*15	18	33	8
96-97 — Las Vegas	IHL	81	51	39	90	20	...	...	...		3	2	1	3	0
NHL totals (2 years)		**28**	**4**	**2**	**6**	**10**	**-2**	**0**	**0**						

GERNANDER, KEN   C/LW   RANGERS

PERSONAL: Born June 30, 1969, in Grand Rapids, Minn. ... 5-10/180. ... Shoots left. ... Full name: Kenneth Robert Gernander. ... Name pronounced juhr-NAN-duhr.
HIGH SCHOOL: Greenway (Coleraine, Minn.).
COLLEGE: Minnesota.
TRANSACTIONS/CAREER NOTES: Selected by Winnipeg Jets in fifth round (fourth Jets pick, 96th overall) of NHL entry draft (June 13, 1987). ... Signed as free agent by New York Rangers (September 9, 1994).
HONORS: Won Fred Hunt Memorial Award (1995-96).

				REGULAR SEASON							PLAYOFFS				
Season Team	League	Gms.	G	A	Pts.	PIM	+/-	PP	SH		Gms.	G	A	Pts.	PIM
85-86 — Greenway	Minn. H.S.	23	14	23	37	...	...	...	...		—	—	—	—	—
86-87 — Greenway	Minn. H.S.	26	35	34	69	...	...	...	...		—	—	—	—	—
87-88 — Univ. of Minnesota	WCHA	44	14	14	28	14	...	...	...		—	—	—	—	—
88-89 — Univ. of Minnesota	WCHA	44	9	11	20	2	...	...	...		—	—	—	—	—
89-90 — Univ. of Minnesota	WCHA	44	32	17	49	24	...	...	...		—	—	—	—	—
90-91 — Univ. of Minnesota	WCHA	44	23	20	43	24	...	...	...		—	—	—	—	—
91-92 — Moncton	AHL	43	8	18	26	9	...	...	...		8	1	1	2	2
— Fort Wayne	IHL	13	7	6	13	2	...	...	...		—	—	—	—	—
92-93 — Moncton	AHL	71	18	29	47	20	...	...	...		5	1	4	5	0
93-94 — Moncton	AHL	71	22	25	47	12	...	...	...		19	6	1	7	0
94-95 — Binghamton	AHL	80	28	25	53	24	...	...	...		11	2	2	4	6
95-96 — Binghamton	AHL	63	44	29	73	38	...	...	...		—	—	—	—	—
— New York Rangers	NHL	10	2	3	5	4	-3	2	0		6	0	0	0	0
96-97 — Binghamton	AHL	46	13	18	31	30	...	...	...		2	0	1	1	0
— New York Rangers	NHL	—	—	—	—	—	...	...	...		9	0	0	0	0
NHL totals (2 years)		**10**	**2**	**3**	**5**	**4**	**-3**	**2**	**0**		**15**	**0**	**0**	**0**	**0**

GIGUERE, JEAN-SEBASTIEN   G   HURRICANES

PERSONAL: Born May 16, 1977, in Montreal. ... 6-0/175. ... Catches left. ... Name pronounced zhee-GAIR.
TRANSACTIONS/CAREER NOTES: Selected by Hartford Whalers in first round (first Whalers pick, 13th overall) of NHL entry draft (July 8, 1995). ... Whalers franchise moved to North Carolina and renamed Carolina Hurricanes for 1997-98 season; NHL approved move on June 25, 1997.
HONORS: Named to QMJHL All-Star second team (1996-97).

				REGULAR SEASON							PLAYOFFS					
Season Team	League	Gms.	Min	W	L	T	GA	SO	Avg.		Gms.	Min.	W	L	GA	SO	Avg.
93-94 — Verdun	QMJHL	25	1234	13	5	2	66	0	3.21		—	—	—	—	—	—	—
94-95 — Halifax	QMJHL	47	2755	14	27	5	181	2	3.94		7	417	3	4	17	1	2.45
95-96 — Verdun	QMJHL	55	3228	26	23	2	185	1	3.44		6	356	1	5	24	0	4.04
96-97 — Halifax	QMJHL	50	3009	28	19	3	169	2	3.37		16	954	9	7	58	0	3.65
— Hartford	NHL	8	394	1	4	0	24	0	3.65		—	—	—	—	—	—	—
NHL totals (1 year)		**8**	**394**	**1**	**4**	**0**	**24**	**0**	**3.65**								

GILCHRIST, BRENT   LW   RED WINGS

PERSONAL: Born April 3, 1967, in Moose Jaw, Sask. ... 5-11/185. ... Shoots left.
TRANSACTIONS/CAREER NOTES: Strained medial collateral ligament (January 1985). ... Selected by Montreal Canadiens as underage junior in sixth round (sixth Canadiens pick, 79th overall) of NHL entry draft (June 15, 1985). ... Injured knee (January 1987). ... Broke right index finger (November 17, 1990); missed 19 games. ... Separated left shoulder (February 6, 1991); missed two games. ... Reinjured left shoulder (February 13, 1991); missed five games. ... Traded by Canadiens with LW Shayne Corson and LW Vladimir Vujtek to Edmonton Oilers for LW Vincent Damphousse and fourth-round pick (D Adam Wiesel) in 1993 draft (August 27, 1992). ... Suffered concussion (October 1992); missed two games. ... Fractured nose (December 21, 1992); missed two games. ... Traded by Oilers to Minnesota North Stars for C Todd Elik (March 5, 1993). ... Separated shoulder (March 18, 1993); missed remainder of season. ... North Stars franchise moved from Minnesota to

Dallas and renamed Stars for 1993-94 season. ... Strained shoulder (October 27, 1993); missed four games. ... Pulled groin (November 21, 1993); missed four games. ... Underwent oral surgery (February 2, 1995); missed no games. ... Strained groin (February 20, 1995); missed two games. ... Strained groin and sprained wrist (February 26, 1995); missed 13 games. ... Suffered from sore wrist (April 11, 1995); missed one game. ... Injured groin (October 14, 1995); missed four games. ... Injured hip flexor (November 6, 1996); missed two games. ... Strained groin (December 21, 1996); missed three games. ... Strained groin (March 5, 1997); missed two games. ... Strained groin (March 16, 1997); missed seven games. ... Signed as free agent by Detroit Red Wings (July 8, 1997).
STATISTICAL PLATEAUS: Three-goal games: 1991-92 (1).
MISCELLANEOUS: Failed to score on a penalty shot (vs. Kirk McLean, January 27, 1994).

		REGULAR SEASON								PLAYOFFS				
Season Team	League	Gms.	G	A	Pts.	PIM	+/-	PP	SH	Gms.	G	A	Pts.	PIM
83-84— Kelowna	WHL	69	16	11	27	16	...	...	...	—	—	—	—	—
84-85— Kelowna	WHL	51	35	38	73	58	...	...	...	6	5	2	7	8
85-86— Spokane	WHL	52	45	45	90	57	...	...	...	9	6	7	13	19
86-87— Spokane	WHL	46	45	55	100	71	...	...	...	5	2	7	9	6
— Sherbrooke	AHL	—	—	—	—	—	...	...	...	10	2	7	9	2
87-88— Sherbrooke	AHL	77	26	48	74	83	...	...	...	6	1	3	4	6
88-89— Montreal	NHL	49	8	16	24	16	9	0	0	9	1	1	2	10
— Sherbrooke	AHL	7	6	5	11	7	...	...	...	—	—	—	—	—
89-90— Montreal	NHL	57	9	15	24	28	3	1	0	8	2	0	2	2
90-91— Montreal	NHL	51	6	9	15	10	-3	1	0	13	5	3	8	6
91-92— Montreal	NHL	79	23	27	50	57	29	2	0	11	2	4	6	6
92-93— Edmonton	NHL	60	10	10	20	47	-10	2	0	—	—	—	—	—
— Minnesota	NHL	8	0	1	1	2	-2	0	0	—	—	—	—	—
93-94— Dallas	NHL	76	17	14	31	31	0	3	1	9	3	1	4	2
94-95— Dallas	NHL	32	9	4	13	16	-3	1	3	5	0	1	1	2
95-96— Dallas	NHL	77	20	22	42	36	-11	6	1	—	—	—	—	—
96-97— Dallas	NHL	67	10	20	30	24	6	2	0	6	2	2	4	2
NHL totals (9 years)		556	112	138	250	267	18	18	5	61	15	12	27	30

GILHEN, RANDY C COYOTES

PERSONAL: Born June 13, 1963, in Zweibrucken, West Germany. ... 6-0/190. ... Shoots left. ... Name pronounced GIHL-ihn.
TRANSACTIONS/CAREER NOTES: Selected by Hartford Whalers as underage junior in sixth round (sixth Whalers pick, 109th overall) of NHL entry draft (June 9, 1982). ... Signed as free agent by Winnipeg Jets (August 1985). ... Separated shoulder (November 16, 1988). ... Traded by Jets with RW Andrew McBain and D Jim Kyte to Pittsburgh Penguins for C/LW Randy Cunneyworth, G Richard Tabaracci and RW Dave McLlwain (June 17, 1989). ... Sprained knee (November 2, 1989). ... Selected by Minnesota North Stars in NHL expansion draft (May 30, 1991). ... Traded by North Stars with D Charlie Huddy, RW Jim Thomson and fourth-round pick (D Alexei Zhitnik) in 1991 draft to Los Angeles Kings for C Todd Elik (June 22, 1991). ... Traded by Kings to New York Rangers for C Corey Millen (December 23, 1991). ... Sprained right knee (January 30, 1993); missed seven games. ... Traded by Rangers to Tampa Bay Lightning for LW Mike Hartman (March 22, 1993). ... Selected by Florida Panthers in NHL expansion draft (June 24, 1993). ... Traded by Panthers to Jets for C Stu Barnes (November 26, 1993). ... Underwent elbow surgery (January 16, 1994); missed four games. ... Dislocated shoulder (March 7, 1994); missed 15 games. ... Injured knee (February 4, 1996); missed remainder of season. ... Jets franchise moved to Phoenix and renamed Coyotes for 1996-97 season; NHL approved move on January 18, 1996.
MISCELLANEOUS: Member of Stanley Cup championship team (1991).

		REGULAR SEASON								PLAYOFFS				
Season Team	League	Gms.	G	A	Pts.	PIM	+/-	PP	SH	Gms.	G	A	Pts.	PIM
79-80— Saskatoon	SJHL	55	18	34	52	112	...	...	...	—	—	—	—	—
— Saskatoon	WHL	9	2	2	4	20	...	...	...	—	—	—	—	—
80-81— Saskatoon	WHL	68	10	5	15	154	...	...	...	—	—	—	—	—
81-82— Winnipeg	WHL	61	41	37	78	87	...	...	...	—	—	—	—	—
82-83— Winnipeg	WHL	71	57	44	101	84	...	...	...	3	2	2	4	0
— Hartford	NHL	2	0	1	1	0	...	...	...	—	—	—	—	—
— Binghamton	AHL	—	—	—	—	—	...	...	...	5	2	0	2	2
83-84— Binghamton	AHL	73	8	12	20	72	...	...	...	—	—	—	—	—
84-85— Salt Lake City	IHL	57	20	20	40	28	...	...	...	—	—	—	—	—
— Binghamton	AHL	18	3	3	6	9	...	...	...	8	4	1	5	16
85-86— Fort Wayne	IHL	82	44	40	84	48	...	...	...	15	10	8	18	6
86-87— Winnipeg	NHL	2	0	0	0	0	...	...	...	—	—	—	—	—
— Sherbrooke	AHL	75	36	29	65	44	...	...	...	17	7	13	20	10
87-88— Winnipeg	NHL	13	3	2	5	15	...	...	...	4	1	0	1	10
— Moncton	AHL	68	40	47	87	51	...	...	...	—	—	—	—	—
88-89— Winnipeg	NHL	64	5	3	8	38	...	...	...	—	—	—	—	—
89-90— Pittsburgh	NHL	61	5	11	16	54	-8	0	0	—	—	—	—	—
90-91— Pittsburgh	NHL	72	15	10	25	51	3	1	2	16	1	0	1	14
91-92— Los Angeles	NHL	33	3	6	9	14	-3	0	1	—	—	—	—	—
— New York Rangers	NHL	40	7	7	14	14	5	0	0	13	1	2	3	2
92-93— New York Rangers	NHL	33	3	2	5	8	-8	0	1	—	—	—	—	—
— Tampa Bay	NHL	11	0	2	2	6	-6	0	0	—	—	—	—	—
93-94— Florida	NHL	20	4	4	8	16	1	0	0	—	—	—	—	—
— Winnipeg	NHL	40	3	3	6	34	-13	0	0	—	—	—	—	—
94-95— Winnipeg	NHL	44	5	6	11	52	-17	0	1	—	—	—	—	—
95-96— Winnipeg	NHL	22	2	3	5	12	1	0	0	—	—	—	—	—
96-97— Manitoba	IHL	79	21	24	45	101	...	...	...	—	—	—	—	—
NHL totals (11 years)		457	55	60	115	314	-45	1	5	33	3	2	5	26

G

GILL, HAL D BRUINS

PERSONAL: Born April 6, 1975, in Concord, Mass. ... 6-6/222. ... Shoots left.
HIGH SCHOOL: Nashoba Regional (Bolton, Mass.).

COLLEGE: Providence.
TRANSACTIONS/CAREER NOTES: Selected by Boston Bruins in eighth round (eighth Bruins pick, 207th overall) of NHL entry draft (June 26, 1993).

		REGULAR SEASON								PLAYOFFS				
Season Team	League	Gms.	G	A	Pts.	PIM	+/-	PP	SH	Gms.	G	A	Pts.	PIM
93-94 — Providence College	Hockey East	31	1	2	3	26	...	...	...	—	—	—	—	—
94-95 — Providence College	Hockey East	26	1	3	4	22	...	...	...	—	—	—	—	—
95-96 — Providence College	Hockey East	39	5	12	17	54	...	...	...	—	—	—	—	—
96-97 — Providence College	Hockey East	35	5	16	21	52	...	...	...	—	—	—	—	—

GILL, TODD — D — SHARKS

PERSONAL: Born November 9, 1965, in Brockville, Ont. ... 6-0/180. ... Shoots left.
TRANSACTIONS/CAREER NOTES: Selected by Toronto Maple Leafs as underage junior in second round (second Maple Leafs pick, 25th overall) of NHL entry draft (June 9, 1984). ... Broke bone in right foot (October 1987). ... Bruised shoulder (March 1989). ... Fractured finger (October 15, 1991); missed three games. ... Strained back (February 8, 1992); missed three games. ... Injured back prior to 1992-93 season; missed first two games of season. ... Bruised foot (November 14, 1992); missed 11 games. ... Strained groin (November 1, 1993); missed 26 games. ... Suffered back spasms (February 24, 1994); missed 13 games. ... Injured shoulder (March 17, 1995); missed one game. ... Pulled hamstring (November 10, 1995); missed four games. ... Suffered back spasms (February 7, 1996); missed four games. ... Traded by Maple Leafs to San Jose Sharks for C Jamie Baker and fifth-round pick (C Peter Cava) in 1996 draft (June 14, 1996). ... Sore knee (April 9, 1997); missed three games.
MISCELLANEOUS: Captain of San Jose Sharks (1996-97).

		REGULAR SEASON								PLAYOFFS				
Season Team	League	Gms.	G	A	Pts.	PIM	+/-	PP	SH	Gms.	G	A	Pts.	PIM
82-83 — Windsor	OHL	70	12	24	36	108	...	...	...	3	0	0	0	11
83-84 — Windsor	OHL	68	9	48	57	184	...	...	...	3	1	1	2	10
84-85 — Toronto	NHL	10	1	0	1	13	-1	0	0	—	—	—	—	—
— Windsor	OHL	53	17	40	57	148	...	...	...	4	0	1	1	14
85-86 — St. Catharines	AHL	58	8	25	33	90	...	...	...	10	1	6	7	17
— Toronto	NHL	15	1	2	3	28	0	0	0	1	0	0	0	0
86-87 — Newmarket...............	AHL	11	1	8	9	33	...	...	...	—	—	—	—	—
— Toronto	NHL	61	4	27	31	92	-3	1	0	13	2	2	4	42
87-88 — Newmarket...............	AHL	2	0	1	1	2	...	...	...	—	—	—	—	—
— Toronto	NHL	65	8	17	25	131	-20	1	0	6	1	3	4	20
88-89 — Toronto	NHL	59	11	14	25	72	-3	0	0	—	—	—	—	—
89-90 — Toronto	NHL	48	1	14	15	92	-8	0	0	5	0	3	3	16
90-91 — Toronto	NHL	72	2	22	24	113	-4	0	0	—	—	—	—	—
91-92 — Toronto	NHL	74	2	15	17	91	-22	1	0	—	—	—	—	—
92-93 — Toronto	NHL	69	11	32	43	66	4	5	0	21	1	10	11	26
93-94 — Toronto	NHL	45	4	24	28	44	8	2	0	18	1	5	6	37
94-95 — Toronto	NHL	47	7	25	32	64	-8	3	1	7	0	3	3	6
95-96 — Toronto	NHL	74	7	18	25	116	-15	1	0	6	0	0	0	24
96-97 — San Jose	NHL	79	0	21	21	101	-20	0	0	—	—	—	—	—
NHL totals (13 years)		718	59	231	290	1023	-92	14	1	77	5	26	31	171

GILLAM, SEAN — D — RED WINGS

PERSONAL: Born May 7, 1976, in Lethbridge, Alta. ... 6-2/187. ... Shoots right. ... Name pronounced GIHL-uhm.
HIGH SCHOOL: Spokane (Wash.).
TRANSACTIONS/CAREER NOTES: Selected by Detroit Red Wings in third round (third Red Wings pick, 75th overall) of NHL entry draft (June 29, 1994).
HONORS: Named to WHL (West) All-Star second team (1994-95 and 1995-96).

		REGULAR SEASON								PLAYOFFS				
Season Team	League	Gms.	G	A	Pts.	PIM	+/-	PP	SH	Gms.	G	A	Pts.	PIM
92-93 — Spokane....................	WHL	70	6	27	33	121	...	...	...	10	0	2	2	10
93-94 — Spokane....................	WHL	70	7	17	24	106	...	...	...	3	0	0	0	6
94-95 — Spokane....................	WHL	72	16	40	56	192	...	...	...	11	0	3	3	33
95-96 — Spokane....................	WHL	69	11	58	69	123	...	...	...	18	2	12	14	26
96-97 — Adirondack................	AHL	64	1	7	8	50	...	...	...	—	—	—	—	—

G

GILMOUR, DOUG — C — DEVILS

PERSONAL: Born June 25, 1963, in Kingston, Ont. ... 5-11/170. ... Shoots left.
TRANSACTIONS/CAREER NOTES: Selected by St. Louis Blues as underage junior in seventh round (fourth Blues pick, 134th overall) of NHL entry draft (June 9, 1982). ... Sprained ankle (October 7, 1985); missed four games. ... Suffered concussion (January 1988). ... Bruised shoulder (March 1988). ... Traded by Blues with RW Mark Hunter, LW Steve Bozek and D/RW Michael Dark to Calgary Flames for C Mike Bullard, C Craig Coxe and D Tim Corkery (September 5, 1988). ... Suffered abscessed jaw (March 1989); missed six games. ... Broke bone in right foot (August 12, 1989). ... Traded by Flames with D Ric Nattress, D Jamie Macoun, LW Kent Manderville and G Rick Wamsley to Toronto Maple Leafs for LW Craig Berube, D Alexander Godynyuk, LW Gary Leeman, D Michel Petit and G Jeff Reese (January 2, 1992). ... Suspended eight off-days and fined $500 by NHL for slashing (November 27, 1992). ... Suspended one preseason game and fined $500 by NHL for head-butting (September 26, 1993). ... Played in Europe during 1994-95 NHL lockout. ... Pinched nerve in neck (February 8, 1995); missed one game. ... Broke nose (April 7, 1995); missed three games. ... Bruised ribs (March 19, 1996); missed one game. ... Traded by Maple Leafs with D Dave Ellett and third-round pick in 1999 draft to New Jersey Devils for D Jason Smith, C Steve Sullivan and C Alyn McCauley (February 25, 1997). ... Bruised eye (March 5, 1997); missed three games.
HONORS: Won Red Tilson Trophy (1982-83). ... Won Eddie Powers Memorial Trophy (1982-83). ... Named to OHL All-Star first team (1982-83). ... Won Frank J. Selke Trophy (1992-93). ... Named to THE SPORTING NEWS All-Star second team (1992-93). ... Played in NHL All-Star Game (1993 and 1994).
STATISTICAL PLATEAUS: Three-goal games: 1985-86 (1), 1987-88 (1), 1993-94 (1). Total: 3.

MISCELLANEOUS: Member of Stanley Cup championship team (1989). ... Captain of Toronto Maple Leafs (1994-95 through February 25, 1997). ... Failed to score on a penalty shot (vs. Gilles Meloche, February 3, 1985; vs. Pat Riggin, March 1, 1987; vs. Mark Fitzpatrick, October 7, 1989).

Season Team	League	REGULAR SEASON								PLAYOFFS				
		Gms.	G	A	Pts.	PIM	+/-	PP	SH	Gms.	G	A	Pts.	PIM
80-81— Cornwall	QMJHL	51	12	23	35	35	...	...	...	—	—	—	—	—
81-82— Cornwall	OHL	67	46	73	119	42	...	...	...	5	6	9	15	2
82-83— Cornwall	OHL	68	*70	*107	*177	62	...	...	...	8	8	10	18	16
83-84— St. Louis	NHL	80	25	28	53	57	6	3	1	11	2	9	11	10
84-85— St. Louis	NHL	78	21	36	57	49	3	3	1	3	1	1	2	2
85-86— St. Louis	NHL	74	25	28	53	41	-3	2	1	19	9	12	†21	25
86-87— St. Louis	NHL	80	42	63	105	58	-2	17	1	6	2	2	4	16
87-88— St. Louis	NHL	72	36	50	86	59	-13	19	2	10	3	14	17	18
88-89— Calgary	NHL	72	26	59	85	44	45	11	0	22	11	11	22	20
89-90— Calgary	NHL	78	24	67	91	54	20	12	1	6	3	1	4	8
90-91— Calgary	NHL	78	20	61	81	144	27	2	2	7	1	1	2	0
91-92— Calgary	NHL	38	11	27	38	46	12	4	1	—	—	—	—	—
— Toronto	NHL	40	15	34	49	32	13	6	0	—	—	—	—	—
92-93— Toronto	NHL	83	32	95	127	100	32	15	3	21	10	†25	35	30
93-94— Toronto	NHL	83	27	84	111	105	25	10	1	18	6	22	28	42
94-95— Rapperswil	Switz. Div. II	9	2	13	15	16	...	...	...	—	—	—	—	—
— Toronto	NHL	44	10	23	33	26	-5	3	0	7	0	6	6	6
95-96— Toronto	NHL	81	32	40	72	77	-5	10	2	6	1	7	8	12
96-97— Toronto	NHL	61	15	45	60	46	-5	2	1	—	—	—	—	—
— New Jersey	NHL	20	7	15	22	22	7	2	0	10	0	4	4	14
NHL totals (14 years)		1062	368	755	1123	960	157	121	17	146	49	115	164	203

GLYNN, BRIAN   D   RED WINGS

PERSONAL: Born November 23, 1967, in Iserlohn, West Germany. ... 6-4/224. ... Shoots left. ... Full name: Brian Thomas Glynn.
TRANSACTIONS/CAREER NOTES: Selected by Calgary Flames in second round (second Flames pick, 37th overall) of NHL entry draft (June 21, 1986). ... Traded by Flames to Minnesota North Stars for D Frantisek Musil (October 26, 1990). ... Traded by North Stars to Edmonton Oilers for D David Shaw (January 21, 1992). ... Injured knee (March 15, 1992); missed seven games. ... Injured knee (November 4, 1992); missed two games. ... Traded by Oilers to Ottawa Senators for eighth-round pick (D Rob Guinn) in 1994 draft (September 14, 1993). ... Claimed on waivers by Vancouver Canucks (February 5, 1994). ... Selected by Hartford Whalers from Canucks in waiver draft for cash (January 18, 1995). ... Pulled groin (October 11, 1995); missed two games. ... Bruised foot (October 21, 1995); missed two games. ... Bruised knee (January 24, 1996); missed one game. ... Traded by Whalers with LW Brendan Shanahan to Detroit Red Wings for C Keith Primeau, D Paul Coffey and first-round pick (traded to San Jose) in 1997 draft (October 9, 1996).
HONORS: Won Governors Trophy (1989-90). ... Named to IHL All-Star first team (1989-90).

Season Team	League	REGULAR SEASON								PLAYOFFS				
		Gms.	G	A	Pts.	PIM	+/-	PP	SH	Gms.	G	A	Pts.	PIM
84-85— Saskatoon	SJHL	12	1	0	1	2	...	...	...	3	0	0	0	0
85-86— Saskatoon	WHL	66	7	25	32	131	...	...	...	13	0	3	3	30
86-87— Saskatoon	WHL	44	2	26	28	163	...	...	...	11	1	3	4	19
87-88— Calgary	NHL	67	5	14	19	87	-2	4	0	1	0	0	0	0
88-89— Salt Lake City	IHL	31	3	10	13	105	...	...	...	14	3	7	10	31
— Calgary	NHL	9	0	1	1	19	1	0	0	—	—	—	—	—
89-90— Calgary	NHL	1	0	0	0	0	-1	0	0	—	—	—	—	—
— Salt Lake City	IHL	80	17	44	61	164	...	...	...	—	—	—	—	—
90-91— Salt Lake City	IHL	8	1	3	4	18	...	...	...	—	—	—	—	—
— Minnesota	NHL	66	8	11	19	83	-5	3	0	23	2	6	8	18
91-92— Minnesota	NHL	37	2	12	14	24	-16	0	0	—	—	—	—	—
— Edmonton	NHL	25	2	6	8	6	11	0	1	16	4	1	5	12
92-93— Edmonton	NHL	64	4	12	16	60	-13	2	0	—	—	—	—	—
93-94— Ottawa	NHL	48	2	13	15	41	-15	1	0	—	—	—	—	—
— Vancouver	NHL	16	0	0	0	12	-4	0	0	17	0	3	3	10
94-95— Hartford	NHL	43	1	6	7	32	-2	0	0	—	—	—	—	—
95-96— Hartford	NHL	54	0	4	4	44	-15	0	0	—	—	—	—	—
96-97— Hartford	NHL	1	1	0	1	2	2	0	0	—	—	—	—	—
— San Antonio	IHL	62	13	11	24	46	...	...	...	9	2	6	8	4
NHL totals (10 years)		431	25	79	104	410	-59	10	1	57	6	10	16	40

GODYNYUK, ALEXANDER   D   BLUES

G

PERSONAL: Born January 27, 1970, in Kiev, U.S.S.R. ... 6-1/210. ... Shoots left. ... Name pronounced goh-DIHN-yuhk.
TRANSACTIONS/CAREER NOTES: Selected by Toronto Maple Leafs in sixth round (fifth Maple Leafs pick, 115th overall) of NHL entry draft (June 16, 1990). ... Traded by Maple Leafs with LW Craig Berube, RW Gary Leeman, D Michel Petit and G Jeff Reese to Calgary Flames for C Doug Gilmour, D Jamie Macoun, LW Kent Manderville, D Ric Nattress and G Rick Wamsley (January 2, 1992). ... Injured shoulder (February 23, 1993); missed one game. ... Selected by Florida Panthers in NHL expansion draft (June 24, 1993). ... Strained stomach muscle (November 14, 1993); missed two games. ... Traded by Panthers to Hartford Whalers for D Jim McKenzie (December 16, 1993). ... Bruised knee (December 28, 1993); missed one game. ... Injured knee (March 25, 1994); missed remainder of season. ... Injured groin (March 7, 1995); missed four games. ... Sore back (October 22, 1996); missed four games. ... Strained groin (November 23, 1996); missed five games. ... Whalers franchise moved to North Carolina and renamed Carolina Hurricanes for 1997-98 season; NHL approved move on June 25, 1997. ... Traded by Hurricanes with sixth-round draft pick in 1998 draft to St. Louis Blues for RW Steve Leach (June 27, 1997).

Season Team	League	REGULAR SEASON								PLAYOFFS				
		Gms.	G	A	Pts.	PIM	+/-	PP	SH	Gms.	G	A	Pts.	PIM
86-87— Sokol Kiev	USSR	9	0	1	1	2	...	...	...	—	—	—	—	—
87-88— Sokol Kiev	USSR	2	0	0	0	2	...	...	...	—	—	—	—	—

Season Team	League	REGULAR SEASON								PLAYOFFS				
		Gms.	G	A	Pts.	PIM	+/-	PP	SH	Gms.	G	A	Pts.	PIM
88-89— Sokol Kiev	USSR	30	3	3	6	12	...	...	...	—	—	—	—	—
89-90— Sokol Kiev	USSR	37	3	2	5	31	...	...	...	—	—	—	—	—
90-91— Sokol Kiev	USSR	19	3	1	4	20	...	...	...	—	—	—	—	—
— Toronto	NHL	18	0	3	3	16	-3	0	0	—	—	—	—	—
— Newmarket	AHL	11	0	1	1	29	...	...	...	—	—	—	—	—
91-92— Toronto	NHL	31	3	6	9	59	-12	1	0	—	—	—	—	—
— Calgary	NHL	6	0	1	1	4	-2	0	0	—	—	—	—	—
— Salt Lake City	IHL	17	2	1	3	24	...	...	...	—	—	—	—	—
92-93— Calgary	NHL	27	3	4	7	19	6	0	0	—	—	—	—	—
93-94— Florida	NHL	26	0	10	10	35	5	0	0	—	—	—	—	—
— Hartford	NHL	43	3	9	12	40	8	0	0	—	—	—	—	—
94-95— Hartford	NHL	14	0	0	0	8	1	0	0	—	—	—	—	—
95-96— Hartford	NHL	3	0	0	0	2	-1	0	0	—	—	—	—	—
— Detroit	IHL	7	0	3	3	12	...	...	...	—	—	—	—	—
— Minnesota	IHL	45	9	17	26	81	...	...	...	—	—	—	—	—
— Springfield	AHL	14	1	3	4	19	...	...	...	—	—	—	—	—
96-97— Hartford	NHL	55	1	6	7	41	-10	0	0	—	—	—	—	—
NHL totals (7 years)		223	10	39	49	224	-8	1	0					

GOLDMANN, ERICH   D   SENATORS

PERSONAL: Born April 7, 1976, in Dingolfing, West Germany. ... 6-3/196. ... Shoots left.
TRANSACTIONS/CAREER NOTES: Selected by Ottawa Senators in eighth round (fifth Senators pick, 212th overall) of NHL entry draft (June 22, 1996).

Season Team	League	REGULAR SEASON								PLAYOFFS				
		Gms.	G	A	Pts.	PIM	+/-	PP	SH	Gms.	G	A	Pts.	PIM
95-96— Mannheim	Germany	47	0	3	3	40	...	...	...	8	0	0	0	2
96-97— Kaufbeuren	Germany	44	2	4	6	58	...	...	...	6	1	0	1	2

GOLUBOVSKY, YAN   D   RED WINGS

PERSONAL: Born March 9, 1976, in Novosibirsk, U.S.S.R. ... 6-3/185. ... Shoots right. ... Name pronounced YAN goh-loo-BAHV-skee.
TRANSACTIONS/CAREER NOTES: Selected by Detroit Red Wings in first round (first Red Wings pick, 23rd overall) of NHL entry draft (June 28, 1994).

Season Team	League	REGULAR SEASON								PLAYOFFS				
		Gms.	G	A	Pts.	PIM	+/-	PP	SH	Gms.	G	A	Pts.	PIM
93-94— Dynamo-2 Moscow	CIS Div. III	10	0	1	1	...	...	...	...	—	—	—	—	—
— Russian Penguins	IHL	8	0	0	0	23	...	...	...	—	—	—	—	—
94-95— Adirondack	AHL	57	4	2	6	39	...	...	...	—	—	—	—	—
95-96— Adirondack	AHL	71	5	16	21	97	...	...	...	3	0	0	0	2
96-97— Adirondack	AHL	62	2	11	13	67	...	...	...	4	0	0	0	0

GONCHAR, SERGEI   D   CAPITALS

PERSONAL: Born April 13, 1974, in Chelyabinsk, U.S.S.R. ... 6-2/212. ... Shoots left. ... Name pronounced GAHN-chahr.
TRANSACTIONS/CAREER NOTES: Selected by Washington Capitals in first round (first Capitals pick, 14th overall) of NHL entry draft (June 20, 1992). ... Injured groin (November 30, 1995); missed two games. ... Suffered from the flu (December 13, 1995); missed one game. ... Suffered from the flu (November 7, 1996); missed one game. ... Hyperextended elbow (November 18, 1996); missed one game. ... Suffered back spasms (December 28, 1996); missed eight games. ... Bruised knee (January 29, 1997); missed two games. ... Sprained knee (February 26, 1997); missed 12 games.

Season Team	League	REGULAR SEASON								PLAYOFFS				
		Gms.	G	A	Pts.	PIM	+/-	PP	SH	Gms.	G	A	Pts.	PIM
90-91— Mechel Chelyabinsk	USSR	2	0	0	0	0	...	...	...	—	—	—	—	—
91-92— Traktor Chelyabinsk	CIS	31	1	0	1	6	...	...	...	—	—	—	—	—
92-93— Dynamo Moscow	CIS	31	1	3	4	70	...	...	...	10	0	0	0	12
93-94— Dynamo Moscow	CIS	44	4	5	9	36	...	...	...	10	0	3	3	14
— Portland	AHL	—	—	—	—	—	...	...	...	2	0	0	0	0
94-95— Portland	AHL	61	10	32	42	67	...	...	...	—	—	—	—	—
— Washington	NHL	31	2	5	7	22	4	0	0	7	2	2	4	2
95-96— Washington	NHL	78	15	26	41	60	25	4	0	6	2	4	6	4
96-97— Washington	NHL	57	13	17	30	36	-11	3	0	—	—	—	—	—
NHL totals (3 years)		166	30	48	78	118	18	7	0	13	4	6	10	6

GONEAU, DANIEL   LW   RANGERS

PERSONAL: Born January 16, 1976, in Lachine, Que. ... 6-0/190. ... Shoots left. ... Name pronounced guh-NOH.
TRANSACTIONS/CAREER NOTES: Selected by Boston Bruins in second round (second Bruins pick, 48th overall) of NHL entry draft (June 28, 1994). ... Returned to draft pool by Bruins and selected by New York Rangers in second round (second Rangers pick, 48th overall) of NHL entry draft (June 22, 1996).
HONORS: Won Can.HL Plus/Minus Award (1995-96). ... Named to QMJHL All-Star first team (1995-96).

Season Team	League	REGULAR SEASON								PLAYOFFS				
		Gms.	G	A	Pts.	PIM	+/-	PP	SH	Gms.	G	A	Pts.	PIM
92-93— Laval	QMJHL	62	16	25	41	44	...	...	...	13	0	4	4	4
93-94— Laval	QMJHL	68	29	57	86	81	...	...	...	19	8	21	29	45
94-95— Laval	QMJHL	56	16	31	47	78	...	...	...	20	5	10	15	33

G

Season Team	League	Gms.	G	A	Pts.	PIM	+/-	PP	SH	Gms.	G	A	Pts.	PIM
95-96 — Granby	QMJHL	67	54	51	105	115	...	...	...	21	11	22	33	40
96-97 — New York Rangers	NHL	41	10	3	13	10	-5	3	0	—	—	—	—	—
— Binghamton	AHL	39	15	15	30	10	...	...	...					
NHL totals (1 year)		41	10	3	13	10	-5	3	0					

GORDON, ROBB   C/LW   CANUCKS

PERSONAL: Born January 13, 1976, in Surrey, B.C. ... 6-0/179. ... Shoots right.
HIGH SCHOOL: Max Cameron (Powell River, B.C.).
COLLEGE: Michigan.
TRANSACTIONS/CAREER NOTES: Selected by Vancouver Canucks in second round (second Canucks pick, 39th overall) of NHL entry draft (June 28, 1994).
HONORS: Named to WHL (West) All-Star first team (1995-96).

		REGULAR SEASON								PLAYOFFS				
Season Team	League	Gms.	G	A	Pts.	PIM	+/-	PP	SH	Gms.	G	A	Pts.	PIM
92-93 — Powell River	BCJHL	60	55	38	93	76	...	...	...	18	8	10	18	24
93-94 — Powell River	BCJHL	60	69	89	158	141	...	...	...	10	11	14	25	29
94-95 — Univ. of Michigan	CCHA	39	15	26	41	72	...	...	...	—	—	—	—	—
95-96 — Kelowna	WHL	58	51	63	114	84	...	...	...	6	3	6	9	19
96-97 — Syracuse	AHL	63	11	14	25	72	...	...	...	3	0	0	0	7

GRAHAME, JOHN   G   BRUINS

PERSONAL: Born August 31, 1975, in Denver. ... 6-2/195. ... Catches left.
COLLEGE: Lake Superior State.
TRANSACTIONS/CAREER NOTES: Selected by Boston Bruins in ninth round (seventh Bruins pick, 229th overall) of NHL entry draft (June 29, 1994).

		REGULAR SEASON							PLAYOFFS					
Season Team	League	Gms.	Min	W	L	T	GA	SO	Avg.	Gms.	Min.	W	L	GA	SO	Avg.
93-94 — Sioux City	USHL	20	1136	...	...	...	72	0	3.80	—	—	—	—	—	—	—
94-95 — Lake Superior State	CCHA	28	1616	16	7	3	75	1	2.78	—	—	—	—	—	—	—
95-96 — Lake Superior State	CCHA	29	1658	21	4	2	67	2	2.42	—	—	—	—	—	—	—
96-97 — Lake Superior State	CCHA	37	2197	19	13	4	134	3	3.66	—	—	—	—	—	—	—

GRANATO, TONY   LW   SHARKS

PERSONAL: Born July 25, 1964, in Downers Grove, Ill. ... 5-10/185. ... Shoots right. ... Full name: Anthony Lewis Granato. ... Name pronounced gruh-NAH-toh.
HIGH SCHOOL: Northwood School (Lake Placid, N.Y.).
COLLEGE: Wisconsin.
TRANSACTIONS/CAREER NOTES: Selected by New York Rangers in sixth round (fifth Rangers pick, 120th overall) of NHL entry draft (June 9, 1982). ... Bruised foot (February 1989). ... Traded by Rangers with RW Tomas Sandstrom to Los Angeles Kings for C Bernie Nicholls (January 20, 1990). ... Pulled groin (January 25, 1990); missed 12 games. ... Injured knee (March 20, 1990). ... Tore rib cartilage (December 18, 1990); missed 10 games. ... Strained back (October 6, 1992); missed three games. ... Strained back (December 4, 1993); missed one game. ... Strained lower back (December 13, 1993); missed nine games. ... Suspended 15 games without pay and fined $500 by NHL for slashing incident (February 16, 1994). ... Strained back (April 3, 1994); missed remainder of season. ... Strained hip flexor (March 13, 1995); missed one game. ... Broke bone in foot (April 6, 1995); missed 13 games. ... Underwent brain surgery (February 14, 1996); missed remainder of season. ... Signed as free agent by San Jose Sharks (August 15, 1996). ... Sore back (December 21, 1996); missed one game. ... Sore back (January 29, 1997); missed two games. ... Suspended three games and fined $1,000 by NHL for cross-checking incident (February 5, 1997).
HONORS: Named to NCAA All-America West second team (1984-85 and 1986-87). ... Named to WCHA All-Star second team (1986-87). ... Named to NHL All-Rookie team (1988-89). ... Played in NHL All-Star Game (1997). ... Won Bill Masterton Memorial Trophy (1996-97).
STATISTICAL PLATEAUS: Three-goal games: 1988-89 (2), 1991-92 (1), 1994-95 (1), 1996-97 (2). Total: 6. ... Four-goal games: 1988-89 (1). ... Total hat tricks: 7.
MISCELLANEOUS: Failed to score on a penalty shot (vs. Jocelyn Thibault, November 25, 1993).

		REGULAR SEASON								PLAYOFFS				
Season Team	League	Gms.	G	A	Pts.	PIM	+/-	PP	SH	Gms.	G	A	Pts.	PIM
81-82 — Northwood School	N.Y. H.S.						Statistics unavailable.							
82-83 — Northwood School	N.Y. H.S.						Statistics unavailable.							
83-84 — Univ. of Wisconsin	WCHA	35	14	17	31	48	...	...	...	—	—	—	—	—
84-85 — Univ. of Wisconsin	WCHA	42	33	34	67	94	...	...	...	—	—	—	—	—
85-86 — Univ. of Wisconsin	WCHA	32	25	24	49	36	...	...	...	—	—	—	—	—
86-87 — Univ. of Wisconsin	WCHA	42	28	45	73	64	...	...	...	—	—	—	—	—
87-88 — U.S. national team	Int'l	49	40	31	71	55	...	...	...	—	—	—	—	—
— U.S. Olympic team	Int'l	6	1	7	8	4	...	...	...	—	—	—	—	—
— Denver	IHL	22	13	14	27	36	...	...	...	8	9	4	13	16
88-89 — New York Rangers	NHL	78	36	27	63	140	17	4	4	4	1	1	2	21
89-90 — New York Rangers	NHL	37	7	18	25	77	1	1	0	—	—	—	—	—
— Los Angeles	NHL	19	5	6	11	45	-2	1	0	10	5	4	9	12
90-91 — Los Angeles	NHL	68	30	34	64	154	22	11	1	12	1	4	5	28
91-92 — Los Angeles	NHL	80	39	29	68	187	4	7	2	6	1	5	6	10
92-93 — Los Angeles	NHL	81	37	45	82	171	-1	14	2	24	6	11	17	50
93-94 — Los Angeles	NHL	50	7	14	21	150	-2	2	0	—	—	—	—	—
94-95 — Los Angeles	NHL	33	13	11	24	68	9	2	0	—	—	—	—	—
95-96 — Los Angeles	NHL	49	17	18	35	46	-5	5	0	—	—	—	—	—
96-97 — San Jose	NHL	76	25	15	40	159	-7	5	1	—	—	—	—	—
NHL totals (9 years)		571	216	217	433	1197	36	52	10	56	14	25	39	121

G

GRAND-PIERRE, JEAN-LUC   D   SABRES

PERSONAL: Born February 2, 1977, in Montreal. ... 6-2/187. ... Shoots right. ... Name pronounced zhah-LOOK GRAHN-pee-AIR.
HIGH SCHOOL: CEGEP de Val d'Or (Que.).
TRANSACTIONS/CAREER NOTES: Selected by St. Louis Blues in seventh round (sixth Blues pick, 179th overall) of NHL entry draft (July 8, 1995). ... Traded by Blues with second-round pick (D Cory Sarich) in 1996 draft and third-round pick (RW Maxim Afinogenov) in 1997 draft to Buffalo Sabres for LW Yuri Khmylev and eighth-round pick (C Andrei Podkowicky) in 1996 draft (March 20, 1996).

		REGULAR SEASON							PLAYOFFS				
Season Team	League	Gms.	G	A	Pts.	PIM	+/-	PP	SH	Gms.	G	A	Pts.	PIM
93-94— Beauport	QMJHL	46	1	4	5	27	...	...	...	1	0	0	0	0
94-95— Val-d'Or	QMJHL	59	10	13	23	126	...	...	...	—	—	—	—	—
95-96— Val-d'Or	QMJHL	67	13	21	34	209	...	...	...	13	1	4	5	47
96-97— Val-d'Or	QMJHL	58	9	24	33	196	...	...	...	13	5	8	13	46

GRATTON, CHRIS   C   LIGHTNING

PERSONAL: Born July 5, 1975, in Brantford, Ont. ... 6-3/212. ... Shoots left. ... Name pronounced GRAT-ihn.
HIGH SCHOOL: Loyalist Collegiate (Brantford, Ont.).
TRANSACTIONS/CAREER NOTES: Selected by Tampa Bay Lightning in first round (first Lightning pick, third overall) of NHL entry draft (June 26, 1993). ... Bruised shoulder (April 2, 1995); missed two games.
HONORS: Won Emms Family Award (1991-92). ... Named to OHL Rookie All-Star team (1991-92). ... Won OHL Top Draft Prospect Award (1992-93).
STATISTICAL PLATEAUS: Three-goal games: 1996-97 (1).

		REGULAR SEASON							PLAYOFFS				
Season Team	League	Gms.	G	A	Pts.	PIM	+/-	PP	SH	Gms.	G	A	Pts.	PIM
90-91— Brantford Jr. B	OHA	31	30	30	60	28	...	...	...	—	—	—	—	—
91-92— Kingston	OHL	62	27	39	66	35	...	...	...	—	—	—	—	—
92-93— Kingston	OHL	58	55	54	109	125	...	...	...	16	11	18	29	42
93-94— Tampa Bay	NHL	84	13	29	42	123	-25	5	1	—	—	—	—	—
94-95— Tampa Bay	NHL	46	7	20	27	89	-2	2	0	—	—	—	—	—
95-96— Tampa Bay	NHL	82	17	21	38	105	-13	7	0	6	0	2	2	27
96-97— Tampa Bay	NHL	82	30	32	62	201	-28	9	0	—	—	—	—	—
NHL totals (4 years)		**294**	**67**	**102**	**169**	**518**	**-68**	**23**	**1**	**6**	**0**	**2**	**2**	**27**

GRAVES, ADAM   LW   RANGERS

PERSONAL: Born April 12, 1968, in Toronto. ... 6-0/205. ... Shoots left.
TRANSACTIONS/CAREER NOTES: Bruised shoulder (February 1986). ... Selected by Detroit Red Wings as underage junior in second round (second Red Wings pick, 22nd overall) of NHL entry draft (June 21, 1986). ... Traded by Red Wings with C/RW Joe Murphy, LW Petr Klima and D Jeff Sharples to Edmonton Oilers for C Jimmy Carson, C Kevin McClelland and fifth-round pick (traded to Montreal Canadiens who selected D Brad Layzell) in 1991 draft (November 2, 1989). ... Signed as free agent by New York Rangers (September 2, 1991); Oilers received C/LW Troy Mallette as compensation (September 9, 1991). ... Suffered from infected elbow (February 11, 1995); missed one game.
HONORS: Won King Clancy Memorial Trophy (1993-94). ... Named to THE SPORTING NEWS All-Star first team (1993-94). ... Named to NHL All-Star second team (1993-94). ... Played in NHL All-Star Game (1994).
STATISTICAL PLATEAUS: Three-goal games: 1989-90 (1), 1991-92 (1), 1992-93 (1), 1993-94 (1), 1994-95 (1), 1996-97 (1). Total: 6.
MISCELLANEOUS: Member of Stanley Cup championship team (1990 and 1994). ... Captain of New York Rangers (1995-96).

		REGULAR SEASON							PLAYOFFS				
Season Team	League	Gms.	G	A	Pts.	PIM	+/-	PP	SH	Gms.	G	A	Pts.	PIM
84-85— King City Jr. B	OHA	25	23	33	56	29	...	...	...	—	—	—	—	—
85-86— Windsor	OHL	62	27	37	64	35	...	...	...	16	5	11	16	10
86-87— Windsor	OHL	66	45	55	100	70	...	...	...	14	9	8	17	32
— Adirondack	AHL	—	—	—	—	—	...	...	...	5	0	1	1	0
87-88— Detroit	NHL	9	0	1	1	8	-2	0	0	—	—	—	—	—
— Windsor	OHL	37	28	32	60	107	...	...	...	12	14	18	†32	16
88-89— Detroit	NHL	56	7	5	12	60	-5	0	0	5	0	0	0	4
— Adirondack	AHL	14	10	11	21	28	...	...	...	14	11	7	18	17
89-90— Detroit	NHL	13	0	1	1	13	-5	0	0	—	—	—	—	—
— Edmonton	NHL	63	9	12	21	123	5	1	0	22	5	6	11	17
90-91— Edmonton	NHL	76	7	18	25	127	-21	2	0	18	2	4	6	22
91-92— New York Rangers	NHL	80	26	33	59	139	19	4	4	10	5	3	8	22
92-93— New York Rangers	NHL	84	36	29	65	148	-4	12	1	—	—	—	—	—
93-94— New York Rangers	NHL	84	52	27	79	127	27	20	4	23	10	7	17	24
94-95— New York Rangers	NHL	47	17	14	31	51	9	9	0	10	4	4	8	8
95-96— New York Rangers	NHL	82	22	36	58	100	18	9	1	10	7	1	8	4
96-97— New York Rangers	NHL	82	33	28	61	66	10	10	4	15	2	1	3	12
NHL totals (10 years)		**676**	**209**	**204**	**413**	**962**	**51**	**67**	**14**	**113**	**35**	**26**	**61**	**113**

G

GREEN, JOSH   LW   KINGS

PERSONAL: Born November 16, 1977, in Camrose, Alta. ... 6-3/180. ... Shoots left.
TRANSACTIONS/CAREER NOTES: Selected by Los Angeles Kings in second round (first Kings pick, 30th overall) of NHL entry draft (June 22, 1996).

		REGULAR SEASON							PLAYOFFS				
Season Team	League	Gms.	G	A	Pts.	PIM	+/-	PP	SH	Gms.	G	A	Pts.	PIM
93-94— Medicine Hat	WHL	63	22	22	44	43	...	...	...	3	0	0	0	4
94-95— Medicine Hat	WHL	68	32	23	55	64	...	...	...	5	5	1	6	2
95-96— Medicine Hat	WHL	46	18	25	43	55	...	...	...	5	2	2	4	4
96-97— Medicine Hat	WHL	51	25	32	57	61	...	...	...	—	—	—	—	—
— Swift Current	WHL	23	10	15	25	33	...	...	...	10	9	7	16	19

GREEN, TRAVIS   C   ISLANDERS

PERSONAL: Born December 20, 1970, in Castlegar, B.C. ... 6-1/193. ... Shoots right.

TRANSACTIONS/CAREER NOTES: Selected by New York Islanders in second round (second Islanders pick, 23rd overall) of NHL entry draft (June 17, 1989). ... Traded by Spokane Chiefs to Medicine Hat Tigers for RW Mark Woolf, D/LW Chris Lafreniere and C Frank Esposito (January 26, 1990). ... Suffered sore groin (November 30, 1995); missed four games. ... Sprained knee (February 8, 1996); missed nine games.

STATISTICAL PLATEAUS: Three-goal games: 1993-94 (1).

		REGULAR SEASON							PLAYOFFS				
Season Team	League	Gms.	G	A	Pts.	PIM	+/-	PP	SH	Gms.	G	A	Pts.	PIM
85-86 — Castlegar	KIJHL	35	30	40	70	41	...	...	...	—	—	—	—	—
86-87 — Spokane	WHL	64	8	17	25	27	...	...	...	3	0	0	0	0
87-88 — Spokane	WHL	72	33	53	86	42	...	...	...	15	10	10	20	13
88-89 — Spokane	WHL	72	51	51	102	79	...	...	...	—	—	—	—	—
89-90 — Spokane	WHL	50	45	44	89	80	...	...	...	—	—	—	—	—
— Medicine Hat	WHL	25	15	24	39	19	...	...	...	3	0	0	0	2
90-91 — Capital District	AHL	73	21	34	55	26	...	...	...	—	—	—	—	—
91-92 — Capital District	AHL	71	23	27	50	10	...	...	...	7	0	4	4	21
92-93 — Capital District	AHL	20	12	11	23	39	...	...	...	—	—	—	—	—
— New York Islanders	NHL	61	7	18	25	43	4	1	0	12	3	1	4	6
93-94 — New York Islanders	NHL	83	18	22	40	44	16	1	0	4	0	0	0	2
94-95 — New York Islanders	NHL	42	5	7	12	25	-10	0	0	—	—	—	—	—
95-96 — New York Islanders	NHL	69	25	45	70	42	-20	14	1	—	—	—	—	—
96-97 — New York Islanders	NHL	79	23	41	64	38	-5	10	0	—	—	—	—	—
NHL totals (5 years)		**334**	**78**	**133**	**211**	**192**	**-15**	**26**	**1**	**16**	**3**	**1**	**4**	**8**

GRETZKY, WAYNE   C   RANGERS

PERSONAL: Born January 26, 1961, in Brantford, Ont. ... 6-0/180. ... Shoots left. ... Full name: Wayne Douglas Gretzky. ... Brother of Brent Gretzky, center for Tampa Bay Lightning (1993-94 and 1994-95).

TRANSACTIONS/CAREER NOTES: Signed as underage junior by Indianapolis Racers to multi-year contract (May 1978). ... Traded by Racers with LW Peter Driscoll and G Ed Mio to Edmonton Oilers for cash and future considerations (November 1978). ... Bruised right shoulder (January 28, 1984). ... Underwent surgery on left ankle to remove benign growth (June 1984). ... Twisted right knee (December 30, 1987). ... Suffered corneal abrasion to left eye (February 19, 1988); missed three games. ... Traded by Oilers with RW/D Marty McSorley and LW/C Mike Krushelnyski to Los Angeles Kings for C Jimmy Carson, LW Martin Gelinas, first-round picks in 1989 (traded to New Jersey), 1991 (LW Martin Rucinsky) and 1993 (D Nick Stajduhar) drafts and cash (August 9, 1988). ... Injured groin (March 17, 1990). ... Strained lower back (March 22, 1990); missed five regular-season games and two playoff games. ... Missed five games due to personal reasons (October 1991). ... Sprained knee (February 25, 1992); missed one game. ... Suffered herniated thoracic disc prior to 1992-93 season; missed first 39 games of season. ... Sprained left knee (April 9, 1994). ... Traded by Kings to St. Louis Blues for LW Craig Johnson, C Patrice Tardiff, C Roman Vopat, fifth-round pick (D Peter Hogan) in 1996 draft and first-round pick (LW Matt Zultek) in 1997 draft (February 27, 1996). ... Bruised lower back (April 4, 1996); missed three games. ... Signed as free agent by New York Rangers (July 21, 1996).

HONORS: Won William Hanley Trophy (1977-78). ... Won Emms Family Award (1977-78). ... Named to OMJHL All-Star second team (1977-78). ... Named WHA Rookie of the Year by THE SPORTING NEWS (1978-79). ... Won WHA Rookie of the Year Award (1978-79). ... Named to WHA All-Star second team (1978-79). ... Won Hart Memorial Trophy (1979-80 through 1986-87 and 1988-89). ... Won Lady Byng Memorial Trophy (1979-80, 1990-91, 1991-92 and 1993-94). ... Named to THE SPORTING NEWS All-Star second team (1979-80, 1987-88, 1988-89, 1991-92 and 1993-94). ... Named to NHL All-Star second team (1979-80, 1987-88 through 1989-90, 1993-94 and 1996-97). ... Named NHL Player of Year by THE SPORTING NEWS (1980-81 through 1986-87). ... Won Art Ross Memorial Trophy (1980-81 through 1986-87, 1989-90, 1990-91 and 1993-94). ... Named to THE SPORTING NEWS All-Star first team (1980-81 through 1986-87 and 1990-91) ... Named to NHL All-Star first team (1980-81 through 1986-87 and 1990-91). ... Played in NHL All-Star Game (1980-1986, 1988-1994 and 1996-1997). ... Named Man of the Year by THE SPORTING NEWS (1981). ... Won Lester B. Pearson Award (1981-82 through 1984-85 and 1986-87). ... Won Emery Edge Award (1983-84, 1984-85 and 1986-87). ... Named All-Star Game Most Valuable Player (1983 and 1989). ... Named Canadian Athlete of the Year (1985). ... Won Conn Smythe Trophy (1984-85 and 1987-88). ... Won Dodge Performer of the Year Award (1984-85 through 1986-87). ... Won Dodge Performance of the Year Award (1988-89). ... Won Lester Patrick Trophy (1993-94).

RECORDS: Holds NHL career records for points—2,705; goals—862; assists—1,843; overtime assists—15; points by a center—2,705; goals by a center—862; assists by a center—1,843; most points including playoffs—3,087; most goals including playoffs—984; most assists including playoffs—2,103; most games with three or more goals—49; most 40-or-more goal seasons—12; most consecutive 40-or-more goal seasons—12 (1979-80 through 1990-91); most consecutive 60-or-more goal seasons—4 (1981-82 through 1984-85); most 100-or-more point seasons—15; most consecutive 100-or-more point seasons—13 (1979-80 through 1991-92); highest assist-per-game average—1.381; and highest points-per-game average—2.026. ... Shares NHL career records for most 50-or-more goal seasons—9; and most 60-or-more goal seasons—5. ... Holds NHL single-season records for most goals—92 (1981-82); assists—163 (1985-86); points—215 (1985-86); games with three or more goals—10 (1981-82 and 1983-84); highest goals-per-game average—1.18 (1983-84); highest assists-per-game average—2.04 (1985-86); highest points-per-game average—2.77 (1983-84); most points including playoffs—255 (1984-85); most goals including playoffs—100 (1983-84); most assists including playoffs—174 (1985-86); most points by a center—215 (1985-86); most goals by a center—92 (1981-82); most assists by a center—163 (1985-86); and most goals, 50 games from start of season—61 (1981-82 and 1983-84). ... Shares NHL single-game records for most assists—7 (January 15, 1980; December 11, 1985; and February 14, 1986); most assists for road games—7(December 11, 1985); and most goals in one period—4 (February 18, 1981). ... Holds NHL records for most consecutive games scoring points—51 (October 5, 1983 through January 28, 1984); longest point-scoring streak from start of season—51 (1983-84); most consecutive games with an assist—23 (1990-91); and most assists in game by rookie—7 (February 15, 1980). ... Holds NHL career playoff records for most points—382; most goals—122; most assists—260; most games with three-or-more goals—10; and most game-winning goals—23. ... Holds NHL single-season playoff records for most assists—31 (1988); and most points—47 (1985). ... Shares NHL single-season playoff record for most shorthanded goals—3 (1983). ... Holds NHL final-series playoff records for most assists—10 (1988); and most points—13 (1988). ... Shares NHL single-series playoff record for most assists—14 (1985). ... Shares NHL single-game playoff records for most assists—6 (April 9, 1987); most shorthanded goals—2 (April 6, 1983); most assists in one period—3 (done five times); and most points in one period—4 (April 12, 1987). ... Holds NHL career All-Star Game record for most goals—12. ... Holds NHL All-Star Game records for most goals in one period—4 (1983); and most points in one period—4 (1983). ... Shares NHL All-Star Game record for most goals—4 (February 8, 1983).

STATISTICAL PLATEAUS: Three-goal games: 1979-80 (2), 1980-81 (2), 1981-82 (6), 1982-83 (2), 1983-84 (6), 1984-85 (5), 1985-86 (3), 1986-87 (3), 1987-88 (1), 1988-89 (2), 1989-90 (1), 1990-91 (2), 1991-92 (1). Total: 36. ... Four-goal games: 1980-81 (1), 1981-82 (3), 1983-84 (4), 1986-87 (1). Total: 9. ... Five-goal games: 1980-81 (1), 1981-82 (1), 1984-85 (1), 1987-88 (1). Total: 4. ... Total hat tricks: 49.

G

MISCELLANEOUS: Member of Stanley Cup championship team (1984, 1985, 1987 and 1988). ... Captain of Edmonton Oilers (1983-84 through 1987-88). ... Captain of Los Angeles Kings (1989-90 through February 26, 1996). ... Captain of St. Louis Blues (February 27, 1996 through remainder of season). ... Holds Edmonton Oilers all-time records for most points (1,669), most goals (583) and most assists (1,086). ... Scored on a penalty shot (vs. Pierre Hamel, February 6, 1981; vs. Michel Larocque, January 16, 1982; vs. Pat Riggin, November 24, 1982; vs. Richard Brodeur, January 19, 1983; vs. Don Beaupre, April 28, 1984 (playoffs)). ... Failed to score on a penalty shot (vs. Pat Riggin, November 24, 1982; vs. Peter Ing, January 5, 1991).

		REGULAR SEASON								PLAYOFFS				
Season Team	League	Gms.	G	A	Pts.	PIM	+/-	PP	SH		Gms.	G	A	Pts.	PIM
76-77 — Peterborough	OMJHL	3	0	3	3	0	...	...	...		—	—	—	—	—
77-78 — Sault Ste. Marie	OMJHL	64	70	112	182	14	...	...	...		13	6	20	26	0
78-79 — Indianapolis	WHA	8	3	3	6	0	...	...	...		—	—	—	—	—
— Edmonton	WHA	72	43	61	104	19	...	...	...		13	†10	10	*20	2
79-80 — Edmonton	NHL	79	51	*86	†137	21	...	13	1		3	2	1	3	0
80-81 — Edmonton	NHL	80	55	*109	*164	28	41	15	4		9	7	14	21	4
81-82 — Edmonton	NHL	80	*92	*120	*212	26	*81	18	†6		5	5	7	12	8
82-83 — Edmonton	NHL	80	*71	*125	*196	59	60	18	*6		16	12	*26	*38	4
83-84 — Edmonton	NHL	74	*87	*118	*205	39	*76	*20	*12		19	13	*22	*35	12
84-85 — Edmonton	NHL	80	*73	*135	*208	52	*98	8	*11		18	17	*30	*47	4
85-86 — Edmonton	NHL	80	52	*163	*215	46	71	11	3		10	8	11	19	2
86-87 — Edmonton	NHL	79	*62	*121	*183	28	*70	13	*7		21	5	*29	*34	6
87-88 — Edmonton	NHL	64	40	*109	149	24	39	9	5		19	12	*31	*43	16
88-89 — Los Angeles	NHL	78	54	†114	168	26	15	11	5		11	5	17	22	0
89-90 — Los Angeles	NHL	73	40	*102	*142	42	8	10	4		7	3	7	10	0
90-91 — Los Angeles	NHL	78	41	*122	*163	16	30	8	0		12	4	11	15	2
91-92 — Los Angeles	NHL	74	31	*90	121	34	-12	12	2		6	2	5	7	2
92-93 — Los Angeles	NHL	45	16	49	65	6	6	0	2		24	15	†25	*40	4
93-94 — Los Angeles	NHL	81	38	*92	*130	20	-25	14	4		—	—	—	—	—
94-95 — Los Angeles	NHL	48	11	37	48	6	-20	3	0		—	—	—	—	—
95-96 — Los Angeles	NHL	62	15	66	81	32	-7	5	0		—	—	—	—	—
— St. Louis	NHL	18	8	13	21	2	-6	1	1		13	2	14	16	0
96-97 — New York Rangers	NHL	82	25	†72	97	28	12	6	0		15	10	10	20	2
WHA totals (1 year)		80	46	64	110	19	...	...	...		13	10	10	20	2
NHL totals (18 years)		1335	862	1843	2705	535		195	73		208	122	260	382	66

GRIER, MIKE — RW — OILERS

PERSONAL: Born January 5, 1975, in Detroit. ... 6-1/225. ... Shoots right.
HIGH SCHOOL: St. Sebastian's (Needham, Mass.).
COLLEGE: Boston University.
TRANSACTIONS/CAREER NOTES: Selected by St. Louis Blues in ninth round (seventh Blues pick, 219th overall) of NHL entry draft (June 26, 1993). ... Rights traded by Blues with rights to G Curtis Joseph to Edmonton Oilers for first-round picks in 1996 (C Marty Reasoner) and 1997 (traded to Los Angeles) drafts (August 4, 1995); picks had been awarded earlier to Oilers as compensation for Blues signing free agent LW Shayne Corson (July 28, 1995).
HONORS: Named to NCAA All-America East first team (1994-95). ... Named to Hockey East All-Star first team (1994-95).

		REGULAR SEASON								PLAYOFFS				
Season Team	League	Gms.	G	A	Pts.	PIM	+/-	PP	SH		Gms.	G	A	Pts.	PIM
92-93 — St. Sebastian's	Mass. H.S.	22	16	27	43	32	...	...	...		—	—	—	—	—
93-94 — Boston University	Hockey East	39	9	9	18	56	...	...	...		—	—	—	—	—
94-95 — Boston University	Hockey East	37	29	26	55	85	...	...	...		—	—	—	—	—
95-96 — Boston University	Hockey East	38	21	25	46	82	...	...	...		—	—	—	—	—
96-97 — Edmonton	NHL	79	15	17	32	45	7	4	0		12	3	1	4	4
NHL totals (1 year)		79	15	17	32	45	7	4	0		12	3	1	4	4

GRIEVE, BRENT — LW

PERSONAL: Born May 9, 1969, in Oshawa, Ont. ... 6-1/205. ... Shoots left. ... Name pronounced GREEV.
TRANSACTIONS/CAREER NOTES: Selected by New York Islanders in fourth round (fourth Islanders pick, 65th overall) of NHL entry draft (June 17, 1989). ... Traded by Islanders to Edmonton Oilers for D Marc Laforge (December 15, 1993). ... Signed as free agent by Chicago Blackhawks (July 6, 1994). ... Tore knee ligaments (February 28, 1995); missed 18 games.
STATISTICAL PLATEAUS: Three-goal games: 1993-94 (1).

		REGULAR SEASON								PLAYOFFS				
Season Team	League	Gms.	G	A	Pts.	PIM	+/-	PP	SH		Gms.	G	A	Pts.	PIM
86-87 — Oshawa	OHL	60	9	19	28	102	...	...	...		24	3	8	11	22
87-88 — Oshawa	OHL	56	19	20	39	122	...	...	...		7	0	1	1	8
88-89 — Oshawa	OHL	49	34	33	67	105	...	...	...		6	4	3	7	4
89-90 — Oshawa	OHL	62	46	47	93	125	...	...	...		17	10	10	20	26
90-91 — Kansas City	IHL	5	2	2	4	2	...	...	...		—	—	—	—	—
— Capital District	AHL	61	14	13	27	80	...	...	...		—	—	—	—	—
91-92 — Capital District	AHL	74	34	32	66	84	...	...	...		7	3	1	4	16
92-93 — Capital District	AHL	79	34	28	62	122	...	...	...		4	1	1	2	10
93-94 — Salt Lake City	IHL	22	9	5	14	30	...	...	...		—	—	—	—	—
— New York Islanders	NHL	3	0	0	0	7	0	0	0		—	—	—	—	—
— Cape Breton	AHL	20	10	11	21	14	...	...	...		4	2	4	6	16
— Edmonton	NHL	24	13	5	18	14	4	4	0		—	—	—	—	—
94-95 — Chicago	NHL	24	1	5	6	23	2	0	0		—	—	—	—	—
95-96 — Indianapolis	IHL	24	9	10	19	16	...	...	...		—	—	—	—	—
— Chicago	NHL	28	2	4	6	28	5	0	0		—	—	—	—	—
— Phoenix	IHL	13	8	11	19	14	...	...	...		—	—	—	—	—
96-97 — Los Angeles	NHL	18	4	2	6	15	-2	0	0		—	—	—	—	—
— Phoenix	IHL	31	10	14	24	51	...	...	...		—	—	—	—	—
NHL totals (5 years)		97	20	16	36	87	9	4	0		—	—	—	—	—

G

GRIMSON, STU   LW   HURRICANES

PERSONAL: Born May 20, 1965, in Kamloops, B.C. ... 6-6/226. ... Shoots left.
COLLEGE: Manitoba.
TRANSACTIONS/CAREER NOTES: Fractured forearm (February 1983). ... Selected by Detroit Red Wings in 10th round (11th Red Wings pick, 186th overall) of NHL entry draft (June 8, 1983). ... Returned to draft pool and selected by Calgary Flames in seventh round (eighth Flames pick, 143rd overall) of NHL entry draft (June 15, 1985). ... Broke cheekbone (January 9, 1990). ... Claimed on waivers by Chicago Blackhawks (October 1, 1990). ... Injured eye (February 3, 1993). ... Selected by Mighty Ducks of Anaheim in NHL expansion draft (June 24, 1993). ... Lacerated hand (January 16, 1994); missed one game. ... Lacerated hand (March 9, 1994); missed one game. ... Lacerated hand (March 26, 1994); missed five games. ... Traded by Mighty Ducks with D Mark Ferner and sixth-round pick (LW Magnus Nilsson) in 1996 draft to Red Wings for C/RW Mike Sillinger and D Jason York (April 4, 1995). ... Signed by New York Rangers to offer sheet (August 18, 1995); Red Wings matched offer (August 24, 1995). ... Suffered from the flu (December 12, 1995); missed two games. ... Suspended two games and fined $1,000 by NHL for striking another player with a gloved hand (January 12, 1996). ... Claimed on waivers by Hartford Whalers (October 12, 1996). ... Whalers franchise moved to North Carolina and renamed Carolina Hurricanes for 1997-98 season; NHL approved move on June 25, 1997.

Season Team	League	REGULAR SEASON								PLAYOFFS				
		Gms.	G	A	Pts.	PIM	+/-	PP	SH	Gms.	G	A	Pts.	PIM
82-83— Regina	WHL	48	0	1	1	144	...	...	...	5	0	0	0	14
83-84— Regina	WHL	63	8	8	16	131	...	...	...	21	0	1	1	29
84-85— Regina	WHL	71	24	32	56	248	...	...	...	8	1	2	3	14
85-86— Univ. of Manitoba	CWUAA	12	7	4	11	113	...	...	...	3	1	1	2	20
86-87— Univ. of Manitoba	CWUAA	29	8	8	16	67	...	...	...	14	4	2	6	28
87-88— Salt Lake City	IHL	38	9	5	14	268	...	...	...	—	—	—	—	—
88-89— Calgary	NHL	1	0	0	0	5	0	0	0	—	—	—	—	—
— Salt Lake City	IHL	72	9	18	27	*397	...	...	...	15	2	3	5	*86
89-90— Salt Lake City	IHL	62	8	8	16	319	...	...	...	4	0	0	0	8
— Calgary	NHL	3	0	0	0	17	-1	0	0	—	—	—	—	—
90-91— Chicago	NHL	35	0	1	1	183	-3	0	0	5	0	0	0	46
91-92— Chicago	NHL	54	2	2	4	234	-2	0	0	14	0	1	1	10
— Indianapolis	IHL	5	1	1	2	17	...	...	...	—	—	—	—	—
92-93— Chicago	NHL	78	1	1	2	193	2	1	0	2	0	0	0	4
93-94— Anaheim	NHL	77	1	5	6	199	-6	0	0	—	—	—	—	—
94-95— Anaheim	NHL	31	0	1	1	110	-7	0	0	—	—	—	—	—
— Detroit	NHL	11	0	0	0	37	-4	0	0	11	1	0	1	26
95-96— Detroit	NHL	56	0	1	1	128	-10	0	0	2	0	0	0	0
96-97— Detroit	NHL	1	0	0	0	0	-1	0	0	—	—	—	—	—
— Hartford	NHL	75	2	2	4	218	-7	0	0	—	—	—	—	—
NHL totals (9 years)		422	6	13	19	1324	-39	1	0	34	1	1	2	86

GROLEAU, FRANCOIS   D   CANADIENS

PERSONAL: Born January 23, 1973, in Longueuil, Que. ... 6-0/200. ... Shoots left. ... Name pronounced FRAN-swah GROO-loh.
TRANSACTIONS/CAREER NOTES: Selected by Calgary Flames in second round (second Flames pick, 41st overall) of NHL entry draft (June 22, 1991). ... Traded by Flames to Quebec Nordiques for D Ed Ward (March 24, 1995). ... Signed as free agent by Montreal Canadiens (March 14, 1996).
HONORS: Won Raymond Lagace Trophy (1989-90). ... Named to QMJHL All-Star second team (1989-90). ... Won Emile (Butch) Bouchard Trophy (1991-92). ... Named to QMJHL All-Star first team (1991-92).

Season Team	League	REGULAR SEASON								PLAYOFFS				
		Gms.	G	A	Pts.	PIM	+/-	PP	SH	Gms.	G	A	Pts.	PIM
89-90— Shawinigan	QMJHL	60	11	54	65	80	...	...	...	6	0	1	1	12
90-91— Shawinigan	QMJHL	70	9	60	69	70	...	...	...	6	0	3	3	2
91-92— Shawinigan	QMJHL	65	8	70	78	74	...	...	...	10	5	15	20	8
92-93— St. Jean	QMJHL	48	7	38	45	66	...	...	...	4	0	1	1	14
93-94— Saint John	AHL	73	8	14	22	49	...	...	...	7	0	1	1	2
94-95— Saint John	AHL	65	6	34	40	28	...	...	...	—	—	—	—	—
— Cornwall	AHL	8	1	2	3	7	...	...	...	14	2	7	9	16
95-96— San Francisco	IHL	63	6	26	32	60	...	...	...	—	—	—	—	—
— Fredericton	AHL	12	3	5	8	10	...	...	...	10	1	6	7	14
— Montreal	NHL	2	0	1	1	2	2	0	0	—	—	—	—	—
96-97— Fredericton	AHL	47	8	24	32	43	...	...	...	—	—	—	—	—
— Montreal	NHL	5	0	0	0	4	0	0	0	—	—	—	—	—
NHL totals (2 years)		7	0	1	1	6	2	0	0					

GRONMAN, TUOMAS   D   BLACKHAWKS

PERSONAL: Born March 22, 1974, in Vitasaari, Finland. ... 6-3/202. ... Shoots left. ... Name pronounced GRAHN-muhn.
TRANSACTIONS/CAREER NOTES: Selected by Quebec Nordiques in second round (third Nordiques pick, 29th overall) of NHL entry draft (June 20, 1992). ... Nordiques franchise moved to Colorado and renamed Avalanche for 1995-96 season (June 21, 1995). ... Traded by Avalanche to Chicago Blackhawks for second-round pick in 1998 draft (July 10, 1996). ... Dislocated elbow (October 15, 1996); missed 12 games.

Season Team	League	REGULAR SEASON								PLAYOFFS				
		Gms.	G	A	Pts.	PIM	+/-	PP	SH	Gms.	G	A	Pts.	PIM
90-91— Rauman Lukko	Finland	40	15	20	35	60	...	...	...	—	—	—	—	—
91-92— Tacoma	WHL	61	5	18	23	102	...	...	...	4	0	1	1	2
92-93— Rauman Lukko	Finland	45	2	11	13	46	...	...	...	—	—	—	—	—
93-94— Lukko	Finland	44	4	12	16	40	...	...	...	9	0	1	1	14
94-95— TPS Turku	Finland	47	4	20	24	66	...	...	...	13	2	2	4	43
95-96— TPS Turku	Finland	32	5	7	12	85	...	...	...	11	1	4	5	16
96-97— Chicago	NHL	16	0	1	1	13	-4	0	0	—	—	—	—	—
— Indianapolis	IHL	51	5	16	21	89	...	...	...	4	1	1	2	6
NHL totals (1 year)		16	0	1	1	13	-4	0	0					

GROSEK, MICHAL — LW — SABRES

PERSONAL: Born June 1, 1975, in Gottwaldov, Czechoslovakia. ... 6-2/207. ... Shoots right. ... Name pronounced GROH-shehk.
TRANSACTIONS/CAREER NOTES: Selected by Winnipeg Jets in sixth round (seventh Jets pick, 145th overall) of NHL entry draft (June 26, 1993). ... Sprained knee ligaments (February 15, 1995); missed four games. ... Fractured foot (April 5, 1995); missed remainder of season. ... Traded by Jets with D Darryl Shannon to Buffalo Sabres for D Craig Muni (February 15, 1996).
STATISTICAL PLATEAUS: Three-goal games: 1996-97 (1).

Season Team	League	REGULAR SEASON								PLAYOFFS				
		Gms.	G	A	Pts.	PIM	+/-	PP	SH	Gms.	G	A	Pts.	PIM
92-93 — ZPS Zlin	Czech.	17	1	3	4	0	...	...	...	—	—	—	—	—
93-94 — Moncton	AHL	20	1	2	3	47	...	...	...	2	0	0	0	0
— Tacoma	WHL	30	25	20	45	106	...	...	...	7	2	2	4	30
— Winnipeg	NHL	3	1	0	1	0	-1	0	0	—	—	—	—	—
94-95 — Springfield	AHL	45	10	22	32	98	...	...	...	—	—	—	—	—
— Winnipeg	NHL	24	2	2	4	21	-3	0	0	—	—	—	—	—
95-96 — Springfield	AHL	39	16	19	35	68	...	...	...	—	—	—	—	—
— Winnipeg	NHL	1	0	0	0	0	-1	0	0	—	—	—	—	—
— Buffalo	NHL	22	6	4	10	31	0	2	0	—	—	—	—	—
96-97 — Buffalo	NHL	82	15	21	36	71	25	1	0	12	3	3	6	8
NHL totals (4 years)		132	24	27	51	123	20	3	0	12	3	3	6	8

GROSS, PAVEL — RW — ISLANDERS

PERSONAL: Born May 11, 1968, in Ustin Ogroh, Czechoslovakia. ... 6-3/195. ... Shoots right.
TRANSACTIONS/CAREER NOTES: Selected by New York Islanders in sixth round (seventh Islanders pick, 111th overall) of NHL entry draft (June 11, 1988).

Season Team	League	REGULAR SEASON								PLAYOFFS				
		Gms.	G	A	Pts.	PIM	+/-	PP	SH	Gms.	G	A	Pts.	PIM
87-88 — Sparta Prague	Czech.	29	4	6	10	10	...	...	...	—	—	—	—	—
88-89 — Sparta Prague	Czech.	39	13	9	22	22	...	...	...	—	—	—	—	—
89-90 — Sparta Prague	Czech.	36	10	9	19	...	...	...	...	—	—	—	—	—
90-91 — Freiburg	Germany	32	11	24	35	66	...	...	...	—	—	—	—	—
91-92 — Freiburg	Germany	43	15	22	37	59	...	...	...	—	—	—	—	—
92-93 — Freiburg	Germany	41	11	20	31	62	...	...	...	8	5	5	10	6
93-94 — Mannheim	Germany	42	14	24	38	30	...	...	...	—	—	—	—	—
94-95 — Mannheim	Germany	42	21	40	61	99	...	...	...	6	4	3	7	0
95-96 — Mannheim	Germany	49	29	43	72	81	...	...	...	8	4	2	6	14
96-97 — Mannheim	Germany	50	14	46	60	67	...	...	...	9	6	9	15	0

GRUDEN, JOHN — D — BRUINS

PERSONAL: Born April 6, 1970, in Hastings, Minn. ... 6-0/180. ... Shoots left. ... Name pronounced GROO-dihn.
COLLEGE: Ferris State (Mich.).
TRANSACTIONS/CAREER NOTES: Selected by Boston Bruins in seventh round (seventh Bruins pick, 168th overall) of NHL entry draft (June 16, 1990). ... Suffered back spasms (March 15, 1995); missed two games.
HONORS: Named to NCAA All-America first team (1993-94). ... Named to CCHA All-Star first team (1993-94).

Season Team	League	REGULAR SEASON								PLAYOFFS				
		Gms.	G	A	Pts.	PIM	+/-	PP	SH	Gms.	G	A	Pts.	PIM
90-91 — Ferris State	CCHA	37	4	11	15	27	...	...	...	—	—	—	—	—
91-92 — Ferris State	CCHA	37	9	14	23	24	...	...	...	—	—	—	—	—
92-93 — Ferris State	CCHA	41	16	14	30	58	...	...	...	—	—	—	—	—
93-94 — Ferris State	CCHA	38	11	25	36	52	...	...	...	—	—	—	—	—
— Boston	NHL	7	0	1	1	2	-3	0	0	—	—	—	—	—
94-95 — Boston	NHL	38	0	6	6	22	3	0	0	—	—	—	—	—
— Providence	AHL	1	0	1	1	0	...	...	...	—	—	—	—	—
95-96 — Boston	NHL	14	0	0	0	4	-3	0	0	3	0	1	1	0
— Providence	AHL	39	5	19	24	29	...	...	...	—	—	—	—	—
96-97 — Providence	AHL	78	18	27	45	52	...	...	...	10	3	6	9	4
NHL totals (3 years)		59	0	7	7	28	-3	0	0	3	0	1	1	0

GUERARD, DANIEL — RW — SENATORS

PERSONAL: Born April 9, 1974, in La Salle, Que. ... 6-3/222. ... Shoots right. ... Name pronounced gair-AHR.
TRANSACTIONS/CAREER NOTES: Selected by Ottawa Senators in fifth round (fifth Senators pick, 98th overall) of NHL entry draft (June 20, 1992).

Season Team	League	REGULAR SEASON								PLAYOFFS				
		Gms.	G	A	Pts.	PIM	+/-	PP	SH	Gms.	G	A	Pts.	PIM
91-92 — Victoriaville	QMJHL	31	5	16	21	66	...	...	...	—	—	—	—	—
92-93 — Verdun	QMJHL	58	31	26	57	131	...	...	...	4	1	1	2	17
— New Haven	AHL	2	2	1	3	0	...	...	...	—	—	—	—	—
93-94 — Verdun	QMJHL	53	31	34	65	169	...	...	...	4	3	1	4	4
— Prin. Edward Island	AHL	3	0	0	0	17	...	...	...	—	—	—	—	—
94-95 — Prin. Edward Island	AHL	68	20	22	42	95	...	...	...	8	0	1	1	16
— Ottawa	NHL	2	0	0	0	0	0	0	0	—	—	—	—	—
95-96 — Prin. Edward Island	AHL	42	3	7	10	56	...	...	...	—	—	—	—	—
96-97 — Worcester	AHL	49	8	8	16	50	...	...	...	—	—	—	—	—
NHL totals (1 year)		2	0	0	0	0	0	0	0	—	—	—	—	—

G

GUERIN, BILL — RW/C — DEVILS

PERSONAL: Born November 9, 1970, in Wilbraham, Mass. ... 6-2/210. ... Shoots right. ... Full name: William Robert Guerin. ... Name pronounced GAIR-ihn.
COLLEGE: Boston College.
TRANSACTIONS/CAREER NOTES: Selected by New Jersey Devils in first round (first Devils pick, fifth overall) of NHL entry draft (June 17, 1989). ... Suffered from the flu (February 1992); missed three games. ... Suffered from sore leg (March 19, 1994); missed two games. ... Suffered from the flu (December 6, 1995); missed two games.
STATISTICAL PLATEAUS: Three-goal games: 1996-97 (1).
MISCELLANEOUS: Member of Stanley Cup championship team (1995).

		REGULAR SEASON									PLAYOFFS				
Season Team	League	Gms.	G	A	Pts.	PIM	+/-	PP	SH		Gms.	G	A	Pts.	PIM
85-86 — Springfield Jr. B	NEJHL	48	26	19	45	71	...	...	...		—	—	—	—	—
86-87 — Springfield Jr. B	NEJHL	32	34	20	54	40	...	...	...		—	—	—	—	—
87-88 — Springfield Jr. B	NEJHL	38	31	44	75	146	...	...	...		—	—	—	—	—
88-89 — Springfield Jr. B	NEJHL	31	32	37	69	90	...	...	...		—	—	—	—	—
89-90 — Boston College..........	Hockey East	39	14	11	25	64	...	...	...		—	—	—	—	—
90-91 — Boston College..........	Hockey East	38	26	19	45	102	...	...	...		—	—	—	—	—
91-92 — U.S. national team	Int'l	46	12	15	27	67	...	...	...		—	—	—	—	—
— Utica	AHL	22	13	10	23	6	...	...	...		4	1	3	4	14
— New Jersey	NHL	5	0	1	1	9	1	0	0		6	3	0	3	4
92-93 — New Jersey	NHL	65	14	20	34	63	14	0	0		5	1	1	2	4
— Utica	AHL	18	10	7	17	47	...	...	...		—	—	—	—	—
93-94 — New Jersey	NHL	81	25	19	44	101	14	2	0		17	2	1	3	35
94-95 — New Jersey	NHL	48	12	13	25	72	6	4	0		20	3	8	11	30
95-96 — New Jersey	NHL	80	23	30	53	116	7	8	0		—	—	—	—	—
96-97 — New Jersey	NHL	82	29	18	47	95	-2	7	0		8	2	1	3	18
NHL totals (6 years)		**361**	**103**	**101**	**204**	**456**	**40**	**21**	**0**		**56**	**11**	**11**	**22**	**91**

GUOLLA, STEVE — LW — SHARKS

PERSONAL: Born March 15, 1973, in Scarborough, Ont. ... 6-0/190. ... Shoots left. ... Name pronounced guh-WAH-luh.
HIGH SCHOOL: Stephen Leacock (Agincourt, Ont.).
COLLEGE: Michigan State.
TRANSACTIONS/CAREER NOTES: Sprained knee (December 1991); missed eight games. ... Selected by Ottawa Senators (first Senators pick, third overall) in NHL supplemental draft (June 28, 1994). ... Signed as free agent by San Jose Sharks (August 26, 1996).
HONORS: Named to NCCA All-America West second team (1993-94). ... Named to CCHA All-Star second team (1993-94).

		REGULAR SEASON									PLAYOFFS				
Season Team	League	Gms.	G	A	Pts.	PIM	+/-	PP	SH		Gms.	G	A	Pts.	PIM
90-91 — Wexford Jr. B	MTHL	...	37	42	79	...	...	...	...		—	—	—	—	—
91-92 — Michigan State..........	CCHA	33	4	9	13	8	...	...	...		—	—	—	—	—
92-93 — Michigan State..........	CCHA	39	19	35	54	6	...	...	...		—	—	—	—	—
93-94 — Michigan State..........	CCHA	41	23	46	69	16	...	...	...		—	—	—	—	—
94-95 — Michigan State..........	CCHA	40	16	35	51	16	...	...	...		—	—	—	—	—
95-96 — Prin. Edward Island ...	AHL	72	32	48	80	28	...	...	...		3	0	0	0	0
96-97 — Kentucky	AHL	34	22	22	44	10	...	...	...		4	2	1	3	0
— San Jose	NHL	43	13	8	21	14	-10	2	0		—	—	—	—	—
NHL totals (1 year)		**43**	**13**	**8**	**21**	**14**	**-10**	**2**	**0**						

GUREN, MILOSLAV — D — CANADIENS

PERSONAL: Born September 24, 1976, in Gottwaldov, Czechoslovakia. ... 6-2/215. ... Shoots left.
TRANSACTIONS/CAREER NOTES: Selected by Montreal Canadiens in third round (second Canadiens pick, 60th overall) of NHL entry draft (July 8, 1995).

		REGULAR SEASON									PLAYOFFS				
Season Team	League	Gms.	G	A	Pts.	PIM	+/-	PP	SH		Gms.	G	A	Pts.	PIM
93-94 — ZPS Zlin	Czech Rep.	22	1	5	6	...	...	...	...		3	0	0	0	...
94-95 — ZPS Zlin	Czech Rep.	32	3	7	10	10	...	...	...		12	1	0	1	6
95-96 — ZPS Zlin	Czech Rep.	28	1	2	3	...	...	...	...		7	1	0	1	0
96-97 — Fredericton..................	AHL	79	6	26	32	26	...	...	...		—	—	—	—	—

GUSAROV, ALEXEI — D — AVALANCHE

PERSONAL: Born July 8, 1964, in Leningrad, U.S.S.R. ... 6-3/185. ... Shoots left. ... Name pronounced GOO-sah-rahv.
TRANSACTIONS/CAREER NOTES: Selected by Quebec Nordiques in 11th round (11th Nordiques pick, 213th overall) in the NHL entry draft (June 11, 1988). ... Suffered hairline fracture of left ankle (December 15, 1990); missed seven games. ... Hyperextended right knee (February 28, 1991). ... Fractured finger (October 13, 1991); missed four games. ... Suffered from the flu (February 9, 1993); missed two games. ... Suffered concussion (March 31, 1993); missed two games. ... Bruised left thumb (November 13, 1993); missed one game. ... Suffered from the flu (January 11, 1994); missed two games. ... Suffered from inflammation of sinuses (March 30, 1994); missed two games. ... Injured foot (January 21, 1995); missed nine games. ... Reinjured foot (February 11, 1995); missed six games. ... Injured knee (March 26, 1995); missed last 17 games of season and entire playoffs. ... Nordiques franchise moved to Colorado and renamed Avalanche for 1995-96 season (June 21, 1995). ... Suffered concussion (December 13, 1995); missed two games. ... Suffered from the flu (November 11, 1996); missed three games. ... Scratched cornea (November 30, 1996); missed three games. ... Suffered concussion (December 17, 1996); missed 13 games.
MISCELLANEOUS: Member of Stanley Cup championship team (1996). ... Member of gold-medal-winning U.S.S.R. Olympic team (1988). ... Scored on a penalty shot (vs. Grant Fuhr, March 10, 1993).

G

Season Team	League	Gms.	G	A	Pts.	PIM	+/-	PP	SH	Gms.	G	A	Pts.	PIM
				REGULAR SEASON								PLAYOFFS		
81-82 — SKA Leningrad	USSR	20	1	2	3	16	...	...	...	—	—	—	—	—
82-83 — SKA Leningrad	USSR	42	2	1	3	32	...	...	...	—	—	—	—	—
83-84 — SKA Leningrad	USSR	43	2	3	5	32	...	...	...	—	—	—	—	—
84-85 — CSKA Moscow	USSR	36	3	2	5	26	...	...	...	—	—	—	—	—
85-86 — CSKA Moscow	USSR	40	3	5	8	30	...	...	...	—	—	—	—	—
86-87 — CSKA Moscow	USSR	38	4	7	11	24	...	...	...	—	—	—	—	—
87-88 — CSKA Moscow	USSR	39	3	2	5	28	...	...	...	—	—	—	—	—
88-89 — CSKA Moscow	USSR	42	5	4	9	37	...	...	...	—	—	—	—	—
89-90 — CSKA Moscow	USSR	42	4	7	11	42	...	...	...	—	—	—	—	—
90-91 — CSKA Moscow	USSR	15	0	0	0	12	...	...	...	—	—	—	—	—
— Quebec	NHL	36	3	9	12	12	-4	1	0	—	—	—	—	—
— Halifax	AHL	2	0	3	3	2	...	...	...	—	—	—	—	—
91-92 — Quebec	NHL	68	5	18	23	22	-9	3	0	—	—	—	—	—
— Halifax	AHL	3	0	0	0	0	...	...	...	—	—	—	—	—
92-93 — Quebec	NHL	79	8	22	30	57	18	0	2	5	0	1	1	0
93-94 — Quebec	NHL	76	5	20	25	38	3	0	1	—	—	—	—	—
94-95 — Quebec	NHL	14	1	2	3	6	-1	0	0	—	—	—	—	—
95-96 — Colorado	NHL	65	5	15	20	56	29	0	0	21	0	9	9	12
96-97 — Colorado	NHL	58	2	12	14	28	4	0	0	17	0	3	3	14
NHL totals (7 years)		396	29	98	127	219	40	4	3	43	0	13	13	26

GUSEV, SERGEI — D — STARS

PERSONAL: Born July 31, 1975, in Nizhny Tagil, U.S.S.R. ... 6-1/195. ... Shoots left. ... Name pronounced GOO-sehf.
TRANSACTIONS/CAREER NOTES: Selected by Dallas Stars in third round (fourth Stars pick, 69th overall) of NHL entry draft (July 8, 1995).

Season Team	League	Gms.	G	A	Pts.	PIM	+/-	PP	SH	Gms.	G	A	Pts.	PIM
				REGULAR SEASON								PLAYOFFS		
94-95 — CSK VVS Samara	CIS	50	3	5	8	58	...	...	...	—	—	—	—	—
95-96 — Michigan	IHL	73	11	17	28	76	...	...	...	—	—	—	—	—
96-97 — Michigan	IHL	51	7	8	15	44	...	...	...	4	0	4	4	6

GUSMANOV, RAVIL — RW/LW — FLAMES

PERSONAL: Born July 22, 1972, in Naberezhnye Chelny, U.S.S.R. ... 6-3/185. ... Shoots left. ... Name pronounced RAH-vihl GOOS-mah-nahv.
TRANSACTIONS/CAREER NOTES: Selected by Winnipeg Jets in fourth round (fifth Jets pick, 93rd overall) of NHL entry draft (June 26, 1993). ... Traded by Jets to Chicago Blackhawks for fourth-round pick (traded to Toronto) in 1996 draft (March 20, 1996); Maple Leafs then traded pick to Phoenix Coyotes (Coyotes selected LW Vladimir Antipov) for RW Mike Gartner. ... Traded by Blackhawks to Calgary Flames for D Marc Hussey (March 18, 1997).

Season Team	League	Gms.	G	A	Pts.	PIM	+/-	PP	SH	Gms.	G	A	Pts.	PIM
				REGULAR SEASON								PLAYOFFS		
90-91 — Traktor Chelyabinsk	USSR	15	0	0	0	10	...	...	...	—	—	—	—	—
91-92 — Traktor Chelyabinsk	CIS	38	4	4	8	20	...	...	...	—	—	—	—	—
92-93 — Traktor Chelyabinsk	CIS	39	15	8	23	30	...	...	...	—	—	—	—	—
93-94 — Traktor Chelyabinsk	CIS	43	18	9	27	51	...	...	...	8	4	0	4	2
— Rus. Olympic team	Int'l	8	3	1	4	0	...	...	...	6	4	3	7	10
94-95 — Springfield	AHL	72	18	15	33	14	...	...	...	—	—	—	—	—
95-96 — Springfield	AHL	60	36	32	68	20	...	...	...	—	—	—	—	—
— Winnipeg	NHL	4	0	0	0	0	-3	0	0	—	—	—	—	—
— Indianapolis	IHL	11	6	10	16	4	...	...	...	5	2	3	5	4
96-97 — Indianapolis	IHL	60	21	27	48	14	...	...	...	—	—	—	—	—
— Saint John	AHL	12	4	4	8	2	...	...	...	3	0	1	1	2
NHL totals (1 year)		4	0	0	0	0	-3	0	0					

GUSTAFSSON, PER — D — MAPLE LEAFS

PERSONAL: Born April 6, 1970, in Jonkoping, Sweden. ... 6-2/190. ... Shoots left. ... Name pronounced PAIR GUZ-tuhv-suhn.
TRANSACTIONS/CAREER NOTES: Selected by Florida Panthers in 11th round (10th Panthers pick, 261st overall) of NHL entry draft (June 29, 1994). ... Traded by Panthers to Toronto Maple Leafs for D Mike Lankshear (June 12, 1997).

Season Team	League	Gms.	G	A	Pts.	PIM	+/-	PP	SH	Gms.	G	A	Pts.	PIM
				REGULAR SEASON								PLAYOFFS		
93-94 — HV 71 Jonkoping	Sweden	34	9	7	16	10	...	...	...	—	—	—	—	—
94-95 — HV 71 Jonkoping	Sweden	38	10	6	16	14	...	...	...	13	7	5	12	8
95-96 — HV 71 Jonkoping	Sweden	34	8	13	21	12	...	...	...	4	3	1	4	2
96-97 — Florida	NHL	58	7	22	29	22	11	2	0	—	—	—	—	—
NHL totals (1 year)		58	7	22	29	22	11	2	0					

GUZDA, BRAD — G — KINGS

PERSONAL: Born April 28, 1973, in Banff, Alta. ... 6-3/180. ... Catches left.
TRANSACTIONS/CAREER NOTES: Signed as free agent by Los Angeles Kings (May 29, 1996).

Season Team	League	Gms.	Min	W	L	T	GA	SO	Avg.	Gms.	Min.	W	L	GA	SO	Avg.
					REGULAR SEASON								PLAYOFFS			
95-96 — Knoxville	ECHL	19	1083	16	1	‡0	69	0	3.82	7	433	3	4	24	0	3.33
— Muskegon	Col.HL	2	12	0	0	0	5	0	25.00	—	—	—	—	—	—	—
96-97 — Knoxville	ECHL	35	1852	12	18	‡2	166	1	5.38	—	—	—	—	—	—	—
— Phoenix	IHL	5	164	0	1	‡2	12	0	4.37	—	—	—	—	—	—	—

G

HACKETT, JEFF　　　　　　　　G　　　　　　　BLACKHAWKS

PERSONAL: Born June 1, 1968, in London, Ont. ... 6-1/185. ... Catches left.
TRANSACTIONS/CAREER NOTES: Selected by New York Islanders as underage junior in second round (second Islanders pick, 34th overall) of NHL entry draft (June 13, 1987). ... Strained groin (May 13, 1990). ... Selected by San Jose Sharks in NHL expansion draft (May 30, 1991). ... Injured groin and hamstring (December 3, 1991); missed nine games. ... Injured knee (March 23, 1992). ... Injured groin (October 30, 1992); missed 12 games. ... Suffered from the flu (February 20, 1993); missed five games. ... Traded by Sharks to Chicago Blackhawks for third-round pick (C Alexei Yegorov) in 1994 draft (July 13, 1993). ... Pulled groin (October 17, 1995); missed three games. ... Broke finger (March 22, 1996); missed three games. ... Broke finger (October 6, 1996); missed 12 games. ... Pulled groin (March 18, 1997); missed two games.
HONORS: Won F.W. (Dinty) Moore Trophy (1986-87). ... Shared Dave Pinkney Trophy with Sean Evoy (1986-87). ... Won Jack Butterfield Trophy (1989-90).
MISCELLANEOUS: Stopped a penalty shot attempt (vs. Brett Hull, January 4, 1996). ... Allowed a penalty shot goal (vs. Randy Wood, January 11, 1994; vs. Geoff Courtnall, December 13, 1996; vs. Adam Deadmarsh, March 1, 1997).

		REGULAR SEASON								PLAYOFFS						
Season Team	League	Gms.	Min	W	L	T	GA	SO	Avg.	Gms.	Min.	W	L	GA	SO	Avg.
85-86—London Jr. B	OHA	19	1150	...	...	...	66	0	3.44	—	—	—	—	—	—	—
86-87—Oshawa	OHL	31	1672	18	9	2	85	2	3.05	15	895	8	7	40	0	2.68
87-88—Oshawa	OHL	53	3165	30	21	2	205	0	3.89	7	438	3	4	31	0	4.25
88-89—New York Islanders	NHL	13	662	4	7	0	39	0	3.53	—	—	—	—	—	—	—
—Springfield	AHL	29	1677	12	14	2	116	0	4.15	—	—	—	—	—	—	—
89-90—Springfield	AHL	54	3045	24	25	3	187	1	3.68	†17	934	10	5	*60	0	3.85
90-91—New York Islanders	NHL	30	1508	5	18	1	91	0	3.62	—	—	—	—	—	—	—
91-92—San Jose	NHL	42	2314	11	27	1	148	0	3.84	—	—	—	—	—	—	—
92-93—San Jose	NHL	36	2000	2	30	1	176	0	5.28	—	—	—	—	—	—	—
93-94—Chicago	NHL	22	1084	2	12	3	62	0	3.43	—	—	—	—	—	—	—
94-95—Chicago	NHL	7	328	1	3	2	13	0	2.38	2	26	0	0	1	0	2.31
95-96—Chicago	NHL	35	2000	18	11	4	80	4	2.40	1	60	0	1	5	0	5.00
96-97—Chicago	NHL	41	2473	19	18	4	89	2	2.16	6	345	2	4	25	0	4.35
NHL totals (8 years)		226	12369	62	126	16	698	6	3.39	9	431	2	5	31	0	4.32

HAGGERTY, RYAN　　　　　　　C　　　　　　　OILERS

PERSONAL: Born May 2, 1973, in Rye, N.Y. ... 6-1/195. ... Shoots left. ... Full name: Ryan O'Neil Haggerty. ... Brother of Sean Haggerty, left winger in New York Islanders system.
HIGH SCHOOL: Westminster (Conn.) School.
COLLEGE: Boston College.
TRANSACTIONS/CAREER NOTES: Selected by Edmonton Oilers in fifth round (sixth Oilers pick, 93rd overall) of NHL entry draft (June 22, 1991).

		REGULAR SEASON								PLAYOFFS				
Season Team	League	Gms.	G	A	Pts.	PIM	+/-	PP	SH	Gms.	G	A	Pts.	PIM
90-91—Westminster	Conn. H.S.	25	34	38	72	...	...	...	...	—	—	—	—	—
91-92—Boston College	Hockey East	34	12	5	17	16	...	...	...	—	—	—	—	—
92-93—Boston College	Hockey East	32	6	5	11	12	...	...	...	—	—	—	—	—
93-94—Boston College	Hockey East	36	17	23	40	16	...	...	...	—	—	—	—	—
94-95—Boston College	Hockey East	35	23	22	45	20	...	...	...	—	—	—	—	—
95-96—Cape Breton	AHL	29	5	6	11	12	...	...	...	—	—	—	—	—
—Wheeling	ECHL	4	0	2	2	0	...	...	...	—	—	—	—	—
96-97—Wheeling	ECHL	67	17	31	48	22	...	...	...	3	1	2	3	0

HAGGERTY, SEAN　　　　　　　LW　　　　　　　ISLANDERS

PERSONAL: Born February 11, 1976, in Rye, N.Y. ... 6-1/186. ... Shoots left. ... Brother of Ryan Haggerty, center in Edmonton Oilers system.
HIGH SCHOOL: Westminster School (Simsbury, Conn.).
TRANSACTIONS/CAREER NOTES: Selected by Toronto Maple Leafs in second round (second Maple Leafs pick, 48th overall) of NHL entry draft (June 28, 1994). ... Traded by Maple Leafs with C Darby Hendrickson, D Kenny Jonsson and first-round pick (G Roberto Luongo) in 1997 draft to New York Islanders for LW Wendel Clark, D Mathieu Schneider and D D.J. Smith (March 13, 1996).
HONORS: Named to OHL All-Rookie team (1993-94). ... Named to Memorial Cup All-Star team (1994-95). ... Named to OHL All-Star second team (1995-96).

		REGULAR SEASON								PLAYOFFS				
Season Team	League	Gms.	G	A	Pts.	PIM	+/-	PP	SH	Gms.	G	A	Pts.	PIM
90-91—Westminster Prep	USHS (East)	25	20	22	42	...	...	...	...	—	—	—	—	—
91-92—Westminster Prep	USHS (East)	25	24	36	60	...	...	...	...	—	—	—	—	—
92-93—Boston	NEJHL	72	70	111	181	80	...	...	...	—	—	—	—	—
93-94—Detroit	OHL	60	31	32	63	21	...	...	...	17	9	10	19	11
94-95—Detroit	OHL	61	40	49	89	37	...	...	...	21	13	24	37	18
95-96—Detroit	OHL	66	*60	51	111	78	...	...	...	17	15	9	24	30
—Toronto	NHL	1	0	0	0	0	0	0	0	—	—	—	—	—
—Worcester	AHL	0	...	...	...	...	...	...	...	1	0	0	0	2
96-97—Kentucky	AHL	77	13	22	35	60	...	...	...	4	1	0	1	4
NHL totals (1 year)		1	0	0	0	0	0	0	0					

HAJT, CHRIS　　　　　　　D　　　　　　　OILERS

PERSONAL: Born July 5, 1978, in Amherst, N.Y. ... 6-3/210. ... Shoots left. ... Name pronounced HIGHT. ... Son of Bill Hajt, defenseman, Buffalo Sabres (1973-74 through 1986-87).

H

TRANSACTIONS/CAREER NOTES: Selected by Edmonton Oilers in second round (third Oilers pick, 32nd overall) of NHL entry draft (June 22, 1996).

Season Team	League	REGULAR SEASON								PLAYOFFS				
		Gms.	G	A	Pts.	PIM	+/-	PP	SH	Gms.	G	A	Pts.	PIM
94-95 — Guelph	OHL	57	1	7	8	35	...	...	...	14	0	2	2	9
95-96 — Guelph	OHL	63	8	27	35	69	...	...	...	16	0	6	6	13
96-97 — Guelph	OHL	58	11	15	26	62	...	...	...	18	0	8	8	25

HALLER, KEVIN D HURRICANES

PERSONAL: Born December 5, 1970, in Trochu, Alta. ... 6-2/192. ... Shoots left. ... Name pronounced HAW-luhr.

TRANSACTIONS/CAREER NOTES: Broke leg (October 1986). ... Broke leg (May 1987). ... Selected by Buffalo Sabres in first round (first Sabres pick, 14th overall) of NHL entry draft (June 17, 1989). ... Separated shoulder (May 7, 1991); missed seven games. ... Traded by Sabres to Montreal Canadiens for D Petr Svoboda (March 10, 1992). ... Suspended four games and fined $500 by NHL for slashing (November 2, 1993). ... Traded by Canadiens to Philadelphia Flyers for D Yves Racine (June 29, 1994). ... Pulled right groin (January 26, 1995); missed four games. ... Suffered from the flu (March 2, 1995); missed two games. ... Strained groin (March 15, 1995); missed six games. ... Suffered sprain in chest (December 16, 1995); missed 13 games. ... Broke thumb (April 27, 1996); missed remainder of playoffs. ... Traded by Flyers with first- (traded to San Jose) and seventh-round (C Andrew Merrick) picks in 1997 draft to Hartford Whalers for D Paul Coffey and third-round pick (D Kris Mallette) in 1997 draft (December 15, 1996). ... Suffered from the flu (December 20, 1996); missed one game. ... Strained groin (January 1, 1997); missed 13 games. ... Sprained shoulder (March 5, 1997); missed six games. ... Whalers franchise moved to North Carolina and renamed Carolina Hurricanes for 1997-98 season; NHL approved move on June 25, 1997.

HONORS: Won Bill Hunter Trophy (1989-90). ... Named to WHL (East) All-Star first team (1989-90).

MISCELLANEOUS: Member of Stanley Cup championship team (1993).

Season Team	League	REGULAR SEASON								PLAYOFFS				
		Gms.	G	A	Pts.	PIM	+/-	PP	SH	Gms.	G	A	Pts.	PIM
87-88 — Olds	AJHL	54	13	31	44	58	...	...	...	—	—	—	—	—
88-89 — Regina	WHL	72	10	31	41	99	...	...	...	—	—	—	—	—
89-90 — Regina	WHL	58	16	37	53	93	...	...	...	11	2	9	11	16
— Buffalo	NHL	2	0	0	0	0	0	0	0	—	—	—	—	—
90-91 — Rochester	AHL	52	2	8	10	53	...	...	...	10	2	1	3	6
— Buffalo	NHL	21	1	8	9	20	9	1	0	6	1	4	5	10
91-92 — Buffalo	NHL	58	6	15	21	75	-13	2	0	—	—	—	—	—
— Rochester	AHL	4	0	0	0	18	...	...	...	—	—	—	—	—
— Montreal	NHL	8	2	2	4	17	4	1	0	9	0	0	0	6
92-93 — Montreal	NHL	73	11	14	25	117	7	6	0	17	1	6	7	16
93-94 — Montreal	NHL	68	4	9	13	118	3	0	0	7	1	1	2	19
94-95 — Philadelphia	NHL	36	2	8	10	48	16	0	0	15	4	4	8	10
95-96 — Philadelphia	NHL	69	5	9	14	92	18	0	2	6	0	1	1	8
96-97 — Philadelphia	NHL	27	0	5	5	37	-1	0	0	—	—	—	—	—
— Hartford	NHL	35	2	6	8	48	-11	0	0	—	—	—	—	—
NHL totals (9 years)		397	33	76	109	572	32	10	2	60	7	16	23	69

HAMEL, DENIS LW SABRES

PERSONAL: Born May 10, 1977, in Lachute, Que. ... 6-2/175. ... Shoots left. ... Name pronounced uh-MEHL.

TRANSACTIONS/CAREER NOTES: Selected by St. Louis Blues in sixth round (fifth Blues pick, 153rd overall) of NHL entry draft (July 8, 1995). ... Traded by Blues to Buffalo Sabres for D Charlie Huddy (March 19, 1996).

Season Team	League	REGULAR SEASON								PLAYOFFS				
		Gms.	G	A	Pts.	PIM	+/-	PP	SH	Gms.	G	A	Pts.	PIM
94-95 — Chicoutimi	QMJHL	66	15	12	27	155	...	...	...	13	2	0	2	29
95-96 — Chicoutimi	QMJHL	65	40	49	89	199	...	...	...	17	10	14	24	64
96-97 — Chicoutimi	QMJHL	70	50	50	100	339	...	...	...	20	15	10	25	65

HAMRLIK, ROMAN D LIGHTNING

PERSONAL: Born April 12, 1974, in Gottwaldov, Czechoslovakia. ... 6-2/202. ... Shoots left. ... Name pronounced ROH-muhn HAM-uhr-lihk. ... Brother of Martin Hamrlik, defenseman in St. Louis Blues system.

TRANSACTIONS/CAREER NOTES: Selected by Tampa Bay Lightning in first round (first Lightning pick, first overall) of NHL entry draft (June 20, 1992). ... Bruised shoulder (November 3, 1993); missed six games. ... Bruised shoulder (March 1, 1994); missed seven games. ... Played in Europe during 1994-95 NHL lockout. ... Suffered back spasms (January 9, 1997); missed two games.

HONORS: Played in NHL All-Star Game (1996).

MISCELLANEOUS: Shares Tampa Bay Lightning all-time record for most games played (340).

Season Team	League	REGULAR SEASON								PLAYOFFS				
		Gms.	G	A	Pts.	PIM	+/-	PP	SH	Gms.	G	A	Pts.	PIM
90-91 — TJ Zlin	Czech.	14	2	2	4	18	...	...	...	—	—	—	—	—
91-92 — ZPS Zlin	Czech.	34	5	5	10	34	...	...	...	—	—	—	—	—
92-93 — Tampa Bay	NHL	67	6	15	21	71	-21	1	0	—	—	—	—	—
— Atlanta	IHL	2	1	1	2	2	...	...	...	—	—	—	—	—
93-94 — Tampa Bay	NHL	64	3	18	21	135	-14	0	0	—	—	—	—	—
94-95 — ZPS Zlin	Czech Rep.	2	1	0	1	10	...	...	...	—	—	—	—	—
— Tampa Bay	NHL	48	12	11	23	86	-18	7	1	—	—	—	—	—
95-96 — Tampa Bay	NHL	82	16	49	65	103	-24	12	0	5	0	1	1	4
96-97 — Tampa Bay	NHL	79	12	28	40	57	-29	6	0	—	—	—	—	—
NHL totals (5 years)		340	49	121	170	452	-106	26	1	5	0	1	1	4

H

HANDZUS, MICHAL   C   BLUES

PERSONAL: Born March 11, 1977, in Banska Bystrica, Czechoslovakia. ... 6-3/191. ... Shoots left. ... Name pronounced han-ZOOZ.
TRANSACTIONS/CAREER NOTES: Selected by St. Louis Blues in fourth round (third Blues pick, 101st overall) of NHL entry draft (July 8, 1995).

		REGULAR SEASON								PLAYOFFS				
Season Team	League	Gms.	G	A	Pts.	PIM	+/-	PP	SH	Gms.	G	A	Pts.	PIM
93-94— IS Banska Byst. Jrs....	Slovakia	40	23	36	59	...	...	...	...	—	—	—	—	—
94-95— IS Banska Bystrica.....	Slovakia Dv.II	22	15	14	29	10	...	...	...	—	—	—	—	—
95-96— IS Banska Bystrica.....	Slovakia Dv.II	19	3	1	4	8	...	...	...	—	—	—	—	—
96-97— Poprad	Slovakia	44	15	18	33	...	...	...	...	—	—	—	—	—

HANKINSON, CASEY   LW   BLACKHAWKS

PERSONAL: Born May 8, 1976, in Edina, Minn. ... 6-1/187. ... Shoots left. ... Brother of Ben Hankinson, right winger in Detroit Red Wings system.
HIGH SCHOOL: Edina (Minn.).
COLLEGE: Minnesota.
TRANSACTIONS/CAREER NOTES: Selected by Chicago Blackhawks in eighth round (ninth Blackhawks pick, 201st overall) of NHL entry draft (July 8, 1995).

		REGULAR SEASON								PLAYOFFS				
Season Team	League	Gms.	G	A	Pts.	PIM	+/-	PP	SH	Gms.	G	A	Pts.	PIM
92-93— Edina........................	Minn. H.S.	25	20	26	46	...	...	...	...	—	—	—	—	—
93-94— Edina........................	Minn. H.S.	24	21	20	41	50	...	...	...	—	—	—	—	—
94-95— Univ. of Minnesota.....	WCHA	33	7	1	8	86	...	...	...	—	—	—	—	—
95-96— Univ. of Minnesota.....	WCHA	39	16	19	35	101	...	...	...	—	—	—	—	—
96-97— Univ. of Minnesota.....	WCHA	42	17	24	41	79	...	...	...	—	—	—	—	—

HANNAN, DAVE   C   AVALANCHE

PERSONAL: Born November 26, 1961, in Sudbury, Ont. ... 5-10/180. ... Shoots left.
TRANSACTIONS/CAREER NOTES: Bruised shoulder; missed part of 1980-81 season. ... Selected by Pittsburgh Penguins in 10th round (ninth Penguins pick, 196th overall) of NHL entry draft (June 10, 1981). ... Injured knee and underwent surgery (January 9, 1987). ... Traded by Penguins with C Craig Simpson, D Chris Joseph and D Moe Mantha to Edmonton Oilers for D Paul Coffey, LW Dave Hunter and RW Wayne Van Dorp (November 24, 1987). ... Selected by Penguins in NHL waiver draft (October 3, 1988); LW Dave Hunter was taken by Oilers as compensation. ... Suffered hip pointer (October 1988). ... Sprained knee (March 1989). ... Selected by Toronto Maple Leafs in NHL waiver draft for $7,500 (October 2, 1989). ... Injured left knee ligaments (November 22, 1989). ... Underwent surgery to left knee (December 18, 1989); missed 23 games. ... Traded by Maple Leafs to Buffalo Sabres for fifth-round pick (RW Chris de Ruiter) in 1992 draft (March 10, 1992). ... Injured shoulder (April 12, 1992). ... Broke toe (January 19, 1993); missed three games. ... Strained back (March 13, 1995); missed four games. ... Suffered sore groin (April 9, 1995); missed one game. ... Strained left hip (February 25, 1996); missed two games. ... Traded by Sabres to Colorado Avalanche for sixth-round pick (C Darren Mortier) in 1996 draft (March 20, 1996). ... Injured rotator cuff (February 3, 1997); missed three games.
STATISTICAL PLATEAUS: Three-goal games: 1987-88 (1).
MISCELLANEOUS: Member of Stanley Cup championship team (1988 and 1996). ... Member of silver-medal-winning Canadian Olympic team (1992). ... Scored on a penalty shot (vs. Pat Riggin, October 14, 1983). ... Failed to score on a penalty shot (vs. Grant Fuhr, October 22, 1995).

		REGULAR SEASON								PLAYOFFS				
Season Team	League	Gms.	G	A	Pts.	PIM	+/-	PP	SH	Gms.	G	A	Pts.	PIM
77-78— Windsor	OMJHL	68	14	16	30	43	...	...	...	—	—	—	—	—
78-79— Sault Ste. Marie	OMJHL	26	7	8	15	13	...	...	...	—	—	—	—	—
79-80— Sault Ste. Marie	OMJHL	28	11	10	21	31	...	...	...	—	—	—	—	—
— Brantford	OMJHL	25	5	10	15	26	...	...	...	—	—	—	—	—
80-81— Brantford	OMJHL	56	46	35	81	155	...	...	...	6	2	4	6	20
81-82— Erie	AHL	76	33	37	70	129	...	...	...	—	—	—	—	—
— Pittsburgh	NHL	1	0	0	0	0	-2	0	0	—	—	—	—	—
82-83— Baltimore	AHL	5	2	2	4	13	...	...	...	—	—	—	—	—
— Pittsburgh	NHL	74	11	22	33	127	-28	2	0	—	—	—	—	—
83-84— Baltimore	AHL	47	18	24	42	98	...	...	...	10	2	6	8	27
— Pittsburgh	NHL	24	2	3	5	33	-2	0	1	—	—	—	—	—
84-85— Baltimore	AHL	49	20	25	45	91	...	...	...	—	—	—	—	—
— Pittsburgh	NHL	30	6	7	13	43	-8	0	1	—	—	—	—	—
85-86— Pittsburgh	NHL	75	17	18	35	91	-4	0	3	—	—	—	—	—
86-87— Pittsburgh	NHL	58	10	15	25	56	-2	0	1	—	—	—	—	—
87-88— Pittsburgh	NHL	21	4	3	7	23	-2	0	1	—	—	—	—	—
— Edmonton	NHL	51	9	11	20	43	12	0	2	12	1	1	2	8
88-89— Pittsburgh	NHL	72	10	20	30	157	-12	2	1	8	0	1	1	4
89-90— Toronto	NHL	39	6	9	15	55	-12	0	1	3	1	0	1	4
90-91— Toronto	NHL	74	11	23	34	82	-9	0	1	—	—	—	—	—
91-92— Toronto	NHL	35	2	2	4	16	-10	0	1	—	—	—	—	—
— Can. nat'l team...........	Int'l	3	0	0	0	2	...	...	...	—	—	—	—	—
— Can. Olympic team	Int'l	8	3	5	8	8	...	...	...	—	—	—	—	—
— Buffalo	NHL	12	2	4	6	48	1	0	2	7	2	0	2	2
92-93— Buffalo	NHL	55	5	15	20	43	8	0	0	8	1	1	2	18
93-94— Buffalo	NHL	83	6	15	21	53	10	0	3	7	1	0	1	6
94-95— Buffalo	NHL	42	4	12	16	32	3	0	2	5	0	2	2	2
95-96— Buffalo	NHL	57	6	10	16	30	2	1	1	—	—	—	—	—
— Colorado	NHL	4	1	0	1	2	1	0	0	13	0	2	2	2
96-97— Ottawa	NHL	34	2	2	4	8	-1	0	1	—	—	—	—	—
NHL totals (17 years)		841	114	191	305	942	-55	5	22	63	6	7	13	46

H

HANSEN, TAVIS — C/RW — COYOTES

PERSONAL: Born June 17, 1975, in Prince Albert, Sask. ... 6-1/180. ... Shoots right.
TRANSACTIONS/CAREER NOTES: Selected by Winnipeg Jets in third round (third Jets pick, 58th overall) of NHL entry draft (June 29, 1994). ... Jets franchise moved to Phoenix and renamed Coyotes for 1996-97 season; NHL approved move on January 18, 1996.

Season Team	League	Gms.	G	A	Pts.	PIM	+/-	PP	SH	Gms.	G	A	Pts.	PIM
			REGULAR SEASON								PLAYOFFS			
93-94— Tacoma	WHL	71	23	31	54	122	...	...	...	8	1	3	4	17
94-95— Tacoma	WHL	71	32	41	73	142	...	...	...	4	1	1	2	8
95-96— Springfield	AHL	67	6	16	22	85	...	...	...	5	1	2	3	2
96-97— Springfield	AHL	12	3	1	4	23	...	...	...	—	—	—	—	—
— Phoenix	NHL	1	0	0	0	0	0	0	0	—	—	—	—	—
NHL totals (1 year)		**1**	**0**	**0**	**0**	**0**	**0**	**0**	**0**					

HARDY, FRANCOIS — D — SENATORS

PERSONAL: Born July 6, 1978, in Les Saules, Que. ... 6-2/185. ... Shoots left.
TRANSACTIONS/CAREER NOTES: Selected by Ottawa Senators in seventh round (fourth Senators pick, 163rd overall) of NHL entry draft (June 22, 1996).

Season Team	League	Gms.	G	A	Pts.	PIM	+/-	PP	SH	Gms.	G	A	Pts.	PIM
			REGULAR SEASON								PLAYOFFS			
95-96— Val-d'Or	QMJHL	55	2	3	5	93	...	...	...	3	0	0	0	4
96-97— Val-d'Or	QMJHL	57	2	10	12	130	...	...	...	13	1	1	2	20

HARKINS, BRETT — LW — BRUINS

PERSONAL: Born July 2, 1970, in North Ridgefield, Ohio. ... 6-1/185. ... Shoots left. ... Full name: Brett Alan Harkins. ... Brother of Todd Harkins, right winger, Calgary Flames (1991-92 and 1992-93) and Hartford Whalers (1993-94).
COLLEGE: Bowling Green State.
TRANSACTIONS/CAREER NOTES: Selected by New York Islanders in seventh round (ninth Islanders pick, 133rd overall) of NHL entry draft (June 17, 1989). ... Signed as free agent by Adirondack Red Wings (1993). ... Signed as free agent by Boston Bruins (July 6, 1994). ... Signed as free agent by Florida Panthers (July 19, 1995). ... Signed as free agent by Boston Bruins (September 5, 1996). ... Suffered back spasms (March 27, 1997); missed five games.
HONORS: Named to CCHA All-Rookie team (1989-90).
MISCELLANEOUS: Failed to score on a penalty shot (vs. Ron Tugnutt, March 22, 1997).

Season Team	League	Gms.	G	A	Pts.	PIM	+/-	PP	SH	Gms.	G	A	Pts.	PIM
			REGULAR SEASON								PLAYOFFS			
87-88— Brockville	COJHL	55	21	55	76	36	...	...	...	—	—	—	—	—
88-89— Detroit Compuware	NAJHL	38	23	46	69	94	...	...	...	—	—	—	—	—
89-90— Bowling Green	CCHA	41	11	43	54	45	...	...	...	—	—	—	—	—
90-91— Bowling Green	CCHA	40	22	38	60	30	...	...	...	—	—	—	—	—
91-92— Bowling Green	CCHA	34	8	39	47	32	...	...	...	—	—	—	—	—
92-93— Bowling Green	CCHA	35	19	28	47	28	...	...	...	—	—	—	—	—
93-94— Adirondack	AHL	80	22	47	69	23	...	...	...	10	1	5	6	4
94-95— Providence	AHL	80	23	†69	92	32	...	...	...	13	8	14	22	4
— Boston	NHL	1	0	1	1	0	0	0	0	—	—	—	—	—
95-96— Carolina	AHL	55	23	†71	94	44	...	...	...	—	—	—	—	—
— Florida	NHL	8	0	3	3	6	-2	0	0	—	—	—	—	—
96-97— Providence	AHL	28	9	31	40	32	...	...	...	10	2	10	12	0
— Boston	NHL	44	4	14	18	8	-3	3	0	—	—	—	—	—
NHL totals (3 years)		**53**	**4**	**18**	**22**	**14**	**-5**	**3**	**0**					

HARLOCK, DAVID — D — MAPLE LEAFS

PERSONAL: Born March 16, 1971, in Toronto. ... 6-2/205. ... Shoots left. ... Full name: David Alan Harlock.
COLLEGE: Michigan.
TRANSACTIONS/CAREER NOTES: Injured knee (October 1988). ... Selected by New Jersey Devils in second round (second Devils pick, 24th overall) of NHL entry draft (June 16, 1990). ... Signed as free agent by Toronto Maple Leafs (August 20, 1993). ... Loaned by Maple Leafs to Canadian Olympic team (October 3, 1993).
MISCELLANEOUS: Member of silver-medal-winning Canadian Olympic team (1994).

Season Team	League	Gms.	G	A	Pts.	PIM	+/-	PP	SH	Gms.	G	A	Pts.	PIM
			REGULAR SEASON								PLAYOFFS			
86-87— Toronto Red Wings	MTHL	86	17	55	72	60	...	...	...	—	—	—	—	—
87-88— Toronto Red Wings	MTHL	70	16	56	72	100	...	...	...	—	—	—	—	—
88-89— St. Michael's Jr. B	ODHA	25	4	15	19	34	...	...	...	—	—	—	—	—
89-90— Univ. of Michigan	CCHA	42	2	13	15	44	...	...	...	—	—	—	—	—
90-91— Univ. of Michigan	CCHA	39	2	8	10	70	...	...	...	—	—	—	—	—
91-92— Univ. of Michigan	CCHA	44	1	6	7	80	...	...	...	—	—	—	—	—
92-93— Univ. of Michigan	CCHA	38	3	9	12	58	...	...	...	—	—	—	—	—
93-94— Can. nat'l team	Int'l	41	0	3	3	28	...	...	...	—	—	—	—	—
— Can. Olympic team	Int'l	8	0	0	0	8	...	...	...	—	—	—	—	—
— Toronto	NHL	6	0	0	0	0	-2	0	0	—	—	—	—	—
— St. John's	AHL	10	0	3	3	2	...	...	...	9	0	0	0	6
94-95— St. John's	AHL	58	0	6	6	44	...	...	...	5	0	0	0	0
— Toronto	NHL	1	0	0	0	0	-1	0	0	—	—	—	—	—
95-96— St. John's	AHL	77	0	12	12	92	...	...	...	4	0	1	1	2
— Toronto	NHL	1	0	0	0	0	0	0	0	—	—	—	—	—
96-97— San Antonio	IHL	69	3	10	13	82	...	...	...	9	0	0	0	10
NHL totals (3 years)		**8**	**0**	**0**	**0**	**0**	**-3**	**0**	**0**					

H

HARVEY, TODD — RW/C — STARS

PERSONAL: Born February 17, 1975, in Hamilton, Ont. ... 6-0/195. ... Shoots right.
TRANSACTIONS/CAREER NOTES: Selected by Dallas Stars in first round (first Stars pick, ninth overall) of NHL entry draft (June 26, 1993). ... Strained back (March 13, 1995); missed one game. ... Sprained knee (October 30, 1995); missed two games. ... Pulled groin (November 3, 1996); missed one game. ... Sprained knee (November 19, 1996); missed five games. ... Suffered from the flu (December 29, 1996); missed one game. ... Suspended two games and fined $1,000 by NHL for elbowing incident (February 2, 1997). ... Bruised hand (April 4, 1997); missed one game.
HONORS: Named to Can.HL All-Rookie team (1991-92). ... Named to OHL Rookie All-Star team (1991-92).
STATISTICAL PLATEAUS: Three-goal games: 1994-95 (1).

		REGULAR SEASON								PLAYOFFS				
Season Team	League	Gms.	G	A	Pts.	PIM	+/-	PP	SH	Gms.	G	A	Pts.	PIM
89-90 — Cambridge Jr. B	OHA	41	35	27	62	213	...	...	...	—	—	—	—	—
90-91 — Cambridge Jr. B	OHA	35	32	39	71	174	...	...	...	—	—	—	—	—
91-92 — Detroit	OHL	58	21	43	64	141	...	...	...	7	3	5	8	32
92-93 — Detroit	OHL	55	50	50	100	83	...	...	...	15	9	12	21	39
93-94 — Detroit	OHL	49	34	51	85	75	...	...	...	17	10	12	22	26
94-95 — Detroit	OHL	11	8	14	22	12	...	...	...	—	—	—	—	—
— Dallas	NHL	40	11	9	20	67	-3	2	0	5	0	0	0	8
95-96 — Dallas	NHL	69	9	20	29	136	-13	3	0	—	—	—	—	—
— Michigan	IHL	5	1	3	4	8	...	...	...	0	0	0	0	0
96-97 — Dallas	NHL	71	9	22	31	142	19	1	0	7	0	1	1	10
NHL totals (3 years)		180	29	51	80	345	3	6	0	12	0	1	1	18

HASEK, DOMINIK — G — SABRES

PERSONAL: Born January 29, 1965, in Pardubice, Czechoslovakia. ... 5-11/168. ... Catches left. ... Name pronounced HA-shehk.
TRANSACTIONS/CAREER NOTES: Selected by Chicago Blackhawks in 10th round (11th Blackhawks pick, 199th overall) of NHL entry draft (June 8, 1983). ... Traded by Blackhawks to Buffalo Sabres for G Stephane Beauregard and future considerations (August 7, 1992). ... Injured groin (November 25, 1992); missed three games. ... Pulled stomach muscle (January 6, 1993); missed six games. ... Played in Europe during 1994-95 NHL lockout. ... Strained rotator cuff (March 16, 1995); missed three games. ... Injured abdominals (December 15, 1995); missed 10 games. ... Sprained left knee (April 6, 1996); missed last two games of regular season. ... Fractured rib (March 19, 1997); missed five games. ... Sprained knee ligament (April 21, 1997); missed six playoff games. ... Suspended three playoff games and fined $10,000 by NHL for grabbing a reporter who had written a critical column (May 1, 1997).
HONORS: Named Czechoslovakian League Player of the Year (1986-87, 1988-89 and 1989-90). ... Named to Czechoslovakian League All-Star team (1988-89 and 1989-90). ... Named to IHL All-Star first team (1990-91). ... Named to NHL All-Rookie team (1991-92). ... Won Vezina Trophy (1993-94, 1994-95 and 1996-97). ... Shared William M. Jennings Trophy with Grant Fuhr (1993-94). ... Named to THE SPORTING NEWS All-Star second team (1993-94). ... Named to NHL All-Star first team (1993-94, 1994-95 and 1996-97). ... Named to THE SPORTING NEWS All-Star first team (1994-95). ... Played in NHL All-Star Game (1996 and 1997). ... Named NHL Player of the Year by THE SPORTING NEWS (1996-97). ... Named to THE SPORTING NEWS All-Star team (1996-97). ... Won Hart Memorial Trophy (1996-97).
MISCELLANEOUS: Stopped a penalty shot attempt (vs. Mark Recchi, March 8, 1995; vs. Marlo Lemieux, March 23, 1996; vs. Vincent Damphousse, March 8, 1997; vs. Jason Allison, April 10, 1997). ... Holds Buffalo Sabres all-time records for goals-against average (2.39) and most shutouts (19). ... Allowed a penalty shot goal (vs. John MacLean, February 27, 1997).
STATISTICAL NOTES: Led NHL in save percentage with .930 in 1993-94, .930 in 1994-95, .920 in 1995-96 and .930 in 1996-97.

		REGULAR SEASON								PLAYOFFS						
Season Team	League	Gms.	Min	W	L	T	GA	SO	Avg.	Gms.	Min.	W	L	GA	SO	Avg.
81-82 — Pardubice	Czech.	12	661	...	...	...	34	0	3.09	—						
82-83 — Pardubice	Czech.	42	2358	...	...	...	105	0	2.67	—						
83-84 — Pardubice	Czech.	40	2304	...	...	...	108	0	2.81	—						
84-85 — Pardubice	Czech.	42	2419	...	...	...	131	0	3.25	—						
85-86 — Pardubice	Czech.	45	2689	...	...	...	138	0	3.08	—						
86-87 — Pardubice	Czech.	23	2515	...	...	...	103	0	2.46	—						
87-88 — Pardubice	Czech.	31	2265	...	...	...	98	0	2.60	—						
— Czech. Olympic team	Int'l	8	217	...	...	...	18	...	4.98	—						
88-89 — Pardubice	Czech.	42	2507	...	...	...	114	0	2.73	—						
89-90 — Dukla Jihlava	Czech.	40	2251	...	...	...	80	0	2.13	—						
90-91 — Chicago	NHL	5	195	3	0	1	8	0	2.46	3	69	0	0	3	0	2.61
— Indianapolis	IHL	33	1903	20	11	‡4	80	*5	*2.52	1	60	1	0	3	0	3.00
91-92 — Indianapolis	IHL	20	1162	7	10	‡3	69	1	3.56	—						
— Chicago	NHL	20	1014	10	4	1	44	1	2.60	3	158	0	2	8	0	3.04
92-93 — Buffalo	NHL	28	1429	11	10	4	75	0	3.15	1	45	1	0	1	0	1.33
93-94 — Buffalo	NHL	58	3358	30	20	6	109	†7	*1.95	7	484	3	4	13	2	*1.61
94-95 — HC Pardubice	Czech. Rep.	2	125	...	...	...	6	...	2.88	—						
— Buffalo	NHL	41	2416	19	14	7	85	†5	*2.11	5	309	1	4	18	0	3.50
95-96 — Buffalo	NHL	59	3417	22	†30	6	161	2	2.83	—						
96-97 — Buffalo	NHL	67	4037	37	20	10	153	5	2.27	3	153	1	1	5	0	1.96
NHL totals (7 years)		278	15866	132	98	35	635	20	2.40	22	1218	6	11	48	2	2.36

HATCHER, DERIAN — D — STARS

PERSONAL: Born June 4, 1972, in Sterling Heights, Mich. ... 6-5/225. ... Shoots left. ... Brother of Kevin Hatcher, defenseman, Pittsburgh Penguins.
TRANSACTIONS/CAREER NOTES: Underwent knee surgery (January 1989). ... Selected by Minnesota North Stars in first round (first North Stars pick, eighth overall) of NHL entry draft (June 16, 1990). ... Suspended 10 games by NHL (December 1991). ... Fractured ankle in off-ice incident (January 19, 1992); missed 21 games. ... Sprained knee (January 6, 1993); missed 14 games. ... Suspended one game by NHL for game misconduct penalties (March 9, 1993). ... North Stars franchise moved from Minnesota to Dallas and renamed Stars for 1993-94 season. ... Sprained ankle (February 2, 1995); missed one game. ... Suffered staph infection on little finger (February 14, 1995); missed four games. ... Injured right knee ligament (May 1, 1995); missed entire playoffs. ... Injured shoulder (November 14, 1995); missed three games.

H

... Strained knee (December 8, 1996); missed 14 games. ... Underwent arthroscopic knee surgery (March 19, 1997); missed five games.
HONORS: Played in NHL All-Star Game (1997).
MISCELLANEOUS: Captain of Dallas Stars (1995-96 and 1996-97).

Season Team	League	REGULAR SEASON								PLAYOFFS				
		Gms.	G	A	Pts.	PIM	+/-	PP	SH	Gms.	G	A	Pts.	PIM
88-89— Detroit G.P.D.	MNHL	51	19	35	54	100	...	...	...	—	—	—	—	—
89-90— North Bay	OHL	64	14	38	52	81	...	...	...	5	2	3	5	8
90-91— North Bay	OHL	64	13	50	63	163	...	...	...	10	2	10	12	28
91-92— Minnesota	NHL	43	8	4	12	88	7	0	0	5	0	2	2	8
92-93— Minnesota	NHL	67	4	15	19	178	-27	0	0	—	—	—	—	—
— Kalamazoo	IHL	2	1	2	3	21	...	...	...	—	—	—	—	—
93-94— Dallas	NHL	83	12	19	31	211	19	2	1	9	0	2	2	14
94-95— Dallas	NHL	43	5	11	16	105	3	2	0	—	—	—	—	—
95-96— Dallas	NHL	79	8	23	31	129	-12	2	0	—	—	—	—	—
96-97— Dallas	NHL	63	3	19	22	97	8	0	0	7	0	2	2	20
NHL totals (6 years)		378	40	91	131	808	-2	6	1	21	0	6	6	42

HATCHER, KEVIN   D   PENGUINS

PERSONAL: Born September 9, 1966, in Detroit. ... 6-4/225. ... Shoots right. ... Full name: Kevin John Hatcher. ... Brother of Derian Hatcher, defenseman, Dallas Stars.

TRANSACTIONS/CAREER NOTES: Selected by Washington Capitals as underage junior in first round (first Capitals pick, 17th overall) of NHL entry draft (June 9, 1984). ... Tore left knee cartilage (October 1987). ... Pulled groin (January 1989). ... Fractured two metatarsal bones in left foot (February 5, 1989); missed 15 games. ... Sprained left knee (April 27, 1990). ... Did not attend Capitals training camp due to contract dispute (September 1990). ... Injured right knee (November 10, 1990). ... Suspended one game by NHL for game misconduct penalties (February 2, 1993). ... Fractured right hand (December 23, 1993); missed 10 games. ... Suffered from the flu (March 29, 1994); missed one game. ... Pulled thigh (April 9, 1994); missed one game. ... Traded by Capitals to Dallas Stars for D Mark Tinordi and rights to D Rick Mrozik (January 18, 1995). ... Injured shoulder (October 17, 1995). ... Suspended three games. ... Suspended four games and fined $1,000 by NHL for slashing (December 5, 1995). ... Traded by Stars to Pittsburgh Penguins for D Sergei Zubov (June 22, 1996). ... Stiff neck (February 5, 1997); missed two games.

HONORS: Named to OHL All-Star second team (1984-85). ... Played in NHL All-Star Game (1990-1992 and 1996 and 1997).

STATISTICAL PLATEAUS: Three-goal games: 1992-93 (1), 1995-96 (1). Total: 2.

Season Team	League	REGULAR SEASON								PLAYOFFS				
		Gms.	G	A	Pts.	PIM	+/-	PP	SH	Gms.	G	A	Pts.	PIM
83-84— North Bay	OHL	67	10	39	49	61	...	...	...	4	2	2	4	11
84-85— North Bay	OHL	58	26	37	63	75	...	...	...	8	5	8	13	9
— Washington	NHL	2	1	0	1	0	1	0	1	1	0	0	0	0
85-86— Washington	NHL	79	9	10	19	119	6	1	0	9	1	1	2	19
86-87— Washington	NHL	78	8	16	24	144	-29	1	0	7	1	0	1	20
87-88— Washington	NHL	71	14	27	41	137	1	5	0	14	5	7	12	55
88-89— Washington	NHL	62	13	27	40	101	19	3	0	6	1	4	5	20
89-90— Washington	NHL	80	13	41	54	102	4	4	0	11	0	8	8	32
90-91— Washington	NHL	79	24	50	74	69	-10	9	2	11	3	3	6	8
91-92— Washington	NHL	79	17	37	54	105	18	8	1	7	2	4	6	19
92-93— Washington	NHL	83	34	45	79	114	-7	13	1	6	0	1	1	14
93-94— Washington	NHL	72	16	24	40	108	-13	6	0	11	3	4	7	37
94-95— Dallas	NHL	47	10	19	29	66	-4	3	0	5	2	1	3	2
95-96— Dallas	NHL	74	15	26	41	58	-24	7	0	—	—	—	—	—
96-97— Pittsburgh	NHL	80	15	39	54	103	11	9	0	5	1	1	2	4
NHL totals (13 years)		886	189	361	550	1226	-27	69	5	93	19	34	53	230

HAUER, BRETT   D   OILERS

PERSONAL: Born July 11, 1971, in Edina, Minn. ... 6-2/180. ... Shoots right. ... Full name: Brett Timothy Hauer. ... Name pronounced HOW-uhr. ... Cousin of Don Jackson, defenseman with three NHL teams (1977-78 through 1986-87).

HIGH SCHOOL: Richfield (Minn.).

COLLEGE: Minnesota-Duluth.

TRANSACTIONS/CAREER NOTES: Selected by Vancouver Canucks in fourth round (third Canucks pick, 71st overall) of NHL entry draft (June 17, 1989). ... Separated shoulder (December 1990). ... Traded by Canucks to Edmonton Oilers for sixth-round pick (D Larry Shapley) in 1997 draft (August 24, 1995).

HONORS: Named WCHA Student-Athlete of the Year (1992-93). ... Named to NCAA All-America West first team (1992-93). ... Named to WCHA All-Star first team (1992-93).

Season Team	League	REGULAR SEASON								PLAYOFFS				
		Gms.	G	A	Pts.	PIM	+/-	PP	SH	Gms.	G	A	Pts.	PIM
87-88— Richfield	Minn. H.S.	24	3	3	6	...	...	...	...	—	—	—	—	—
88-89— Richfield	Minn. H.S.	24	8	15	23	70	...	...	...	—	—	—	—	—
89-90— Minnesota-Duluth	WCHA	37	2	6	8	44	...	...	...	—	—	—	—	—
90-91— Minnesota-Duluth	WCHA	30	1	7	8	54	...	...	...	—	—	—	—	—
91-92— Minnesota-Duluth	WCHA	33	8	14	22	40	...	...	...	—	—	—	—	—
92-93— Minnesota-Duluth	WCHA	40	10	46	56	54	...	...	...	—	—	—	—	—
93-94— U.S. national team	Int'l	57	6	14	20	88	...	...	...	—	—	—	—	—
— U.S. Olympic team	Int'l	8	0	0	0	10	...	...	...	—	—	—	—	—
— Las Vegas	IHL	21	0	7	7	8	...	...	...	1	0	0	0	0
94-95— AIK	Sweden	37	1	3	4	38	...	...	...	—	—	—	—	—
95-96— Cape Breton	AHL	17	3	5	8	29	...	...	...	—	—	—	—	—
— Edmonton	NHL	29	4	2	6	30	-11	2	0	—	—	—	—	—
96-97— Chicago	IHL	81	10	30	40	50	...	...	...	4	2	0	2	4
NHL totals (1 year)		29	4	2	6	30	-11	2	0	—	—	—	—	—

H

HAWERCHUK, DALE   C   FLYERS

PERSONAL: Born April 4, 1963, in Toronto. ... 5-11/190. ... Shoots left. ... Name pronounced HOW-uhr-chuhk.

TRANSACTIONS/CAREER NOTES: Selected by Winnipeg Jets as underage junior in first round (first Jets pick, first overall) of NHL entry draft (June 10, 1981). ... Broke rib (April 13, 1985). ... Fractured cheekbone (February 1, 1989). ... Traded by Jets with first-round pick in 1990 draft (LW Brad May) to Buffalo Sabres for D Phil Housley, LW Scott Arniel, RW Jeff Parker and first-round pick (C Keith Tkachuk) in 1990 draft (June 16, 1990). ... Injured hip (March 8, 1992); missed one game. ... Sprained right knee (February 12, 1993); missed three games. ... Pulled groin (February 25, 1995); missed six games. ... Suffered partial groin tear (March 14, 1995); missed nine games. ... Strained hip (April 14, 1995); missed last 10 games of regular season and three playoff games. ... Signed as free agent by St. Louis Blues (July 8, 1995). ... Traded by Blues to Philadelphia Flyers for C Craig MacTavish (March 15, 1996). ... Strained hip (October 16, 1996); missed six games. ... Pulled rib cage muscle (January 25, 1997); missed three games. ... Strained groin (February 13, 1997); missed four games. ... Pulled groin (March 2, 1997); missed 14 games.

HONORS: Won Instructeurs Trophy (1979-80). ... Won Guy Lafleur Trophy (1979-80). ... Named to Memorial Cup All-Star team (1979-80 and 1980-81). ... Won Can.HL Player of the Year Award (1980-81). ... Won Michel Briere Trophy (1980-81). ... Won Jean Beliveau Trophy (1980-81). ... Won Association of Journalists for Major Junior League Hockey Trophy (1980-81). ... Won CCM Trophy (1980-81). ... Named to QMJHL All-Star first team (1980-81). ... Named NHL Rookie of the Year by THE SPORTING NEWS (1981-82). ... Won Calder Memorial Trophy (1981-82). ... Played in NHL All-Star Game (1982, 1985, 1986, 1988 and 1997). ... Named to The Sporting News All-Star second team (1984-85). ... Named to NHL All-Star second team (1984-85).

RECORDS: Holds NHL single-game record for most assists in one period—5 (March 6, 1984).

STATISTICAL PLATEAUS: Three-goal games: 1981-82 (2), 1982-83 (3), 1983-84 (1), 1984-85 (3), 1988-89 (2), 1990-91 (1), 1991-92 (1), 1996-97 (1). Total: 14.

MISCELLANEOUS: Captain of Winnipeg Jets (1984-85 through 1989-90). ... Holds Phoenix Coyotes franchise all-time records for most goals (379) and most points (929). ... Failed to score on a penalty shot (vs. Clint Malarchuk, December 17, 1988).

STATISTICAL NOTES: Youngest player in NHL history to have 100-point season (18 years, 351 days; 1981-82 season).

Season Team	League	REGULAR SEASON								PLAYOFFS				
		Gms.	G	A	Pts.	PIM	+/-	PP	SH	Gms.	G	A	Pts.	PIM
79-80— Cornwall	QMJHL	72	37	66	103	21	...	...	...	18	20	25	45	0
80-81— Cornwall	QMJHL	72	*81	*102	*183	69	...	...	...	19	15	20	35	8
81-82— Winnipeg	NHL	80	45	58	103	47	-4	12	0	4	1	7	8	5
82-83— Winnipeg	NHL	79	40	51	91	31	-17	13	1	3	1	4	5	8
83-84— Winnipeg	NHL	80	37	65	102	73	-14	10	0	3	1	1	2	0
84-85— Winnipeg	NHL	80	53	77	130	74	22	17	3	3	2	1	3	4
85-86— Winnipeg	NHL	80	46	59	105	44	-27	18	2	3	0	3	3	0
86-87— Winnipeg	NHL	80	47	53	100	54	3	10	0	10	5	8	13	4
87-88— Winnipeg	NHL	80	44	77	121	59	-9	20	3	5	3	4	7	16
88-89— Winnipeg	NHL	75	41	55	96	28	-30	14	3	—	—	—	—	—
89-90— Winnipeg	NHL	79	26	55	81	60	-11	8	0	7	3	5	8	2
90-91— Buffalo	NHL	80	31	58	89	32	2	12	0	6	2	4	6	10
91-92— Buffalo	NHL	77	23	75	98	27	-22	13	0	7	2	5	7	0
92-93— Buffalo	NHL	81	16	80	96	52	-17	8	0	8	5	9	14	2
93-94— Buffalo	NHL	81	35	51	86	91	10	13	1	7	0	7	7	4
94-95— Buffalo	NHL	23	5	11	16	2	-2	2	0	2	0	0	0	0
95-96— St. Louis	NHL	66	13	28	41	22	5	5	0	—	—	—	—	—
— Philadelphia	NHL	16	4	16	20	4	10	1	0	12	3	6	9	12
96-97— Philadelphia	NHL	51	12	22	34	32	9	6	0	17	2	5	7	0
NHL totals (16 years)		1188	518	891	1409	732	-92	182	13	97	30	69	99	67

HAWGOOD, GREG   D   SHARKS

PERSONAL: Born August 10, 1968, in St. Albert, Alta. ... 5-10/190. ... Shoots left. ... Full name: Gregory William Hawgood.

TRANSACTIONS/CAREER NOTES: Selected by Boston Bruins as underage junior in 10th round (ninth Bruins pick, 202nd overall) of NHL entry draft (June 21, 1986). ... Announced that he would play in Italy for 1990-91 season (July 1990). ... Traded by Bruins to Edmonton Oilers for C Vladimir Ruzicka (October 22, 1990). ... Traded by Oilers with C Josef Beranek to Philadelphia Flyers for D Brian Benning (January 16, 1993). ... Traded by Flyers to Florida Panthers for future considerations (November 28, 1993). ... Bruised left thumb (January 13, 1994); missed seven games. ... Traded by Panthers to Pittsburgh Penguins for LW Jeff Daniels (March 19, 1994). ... Dislocated left shoulder (February 14, 1995); missed eight games. ... Signed as free agent by San Jose Sharks (September 8, 1996). ... Suspended two games and fined $1,000 by NHL for slashing incident (December 31, 1996).

HONORS: Named to WHL (West) All-Star first team (1985-86 through 1987-88). ... Won Can.HL Defenseman of the Year Award (1987-88). ... Won Bill Hunter Trophy (1987-88). ... Won Eddie Shore Plaque (1991-92). ... Named to AHL All-Star first team (1991-92). ... Named to IHL All-Star first team (1995-96). ... Won James Norris Memorial Trophy (1995-96). ... Won Governors Trophy (1995-96).

Season Team	League	REGULAR SEASON								PLAYOFFS				
		Gms.	G	A	Pts.	PIM	+/-	PP	SH	Gms.	G	A	Pts.	PIM
83-84— Kamloops	WHL	49	10	23	33	39	...	...	...	—	—	—	—	—
84-85— Kamloops	WHL	66	25	40	65	72	...	...	...	—	—	—	—	—
85-86— Kamloops	WHL	71	34	85	119	86	...	...	...	16	9	22	31	16
86-87— Kamloops	WHL	61	30	93	123	139	...	...	...	—	—	—	—	—
87-88— Boston	NHL	1	0	0	0	0	-1	0	0	3	1	0	1	0
— Kamloops	WHL	63	48	85	133	142	...	...	...	16	10	16	26	33
88-89— Boston	NHL	56	16	24	40	84	4	5	0	10	0	2	2	2
— Maine	AHL	21	2	9	11	41	...	...	...	—	—	—	—	—
89-90— Boston	NHL	77	11	27	38	76	12	2	0	15	1	3	4	12
90-91— Asiago	Italy	2	3	0	3	9	...	...	...	—	—	—	—	—
— Maine	AHL	5	0	1	1	13	...	...	...	—	—	—	—	—
— Cape Breton	AHL	55	10	32	42	73	...	...	...	4	0	3	3	23
— Edmonton	NHL	6	0	1	1	6	-2	0	0	—	—	—	—	—
91-92— Cape Breton	AHL	56	20	55	75	26	...	...	...	3	2	2	4	0
— Edmonton	NHL	20	2	11	13	22	19	0	0	13	0	3	3	23
92-93— Edmonton	NHL	29	5	13	18	35	-1	2	0	—	—	—	—	—
— Philadelphia	NHL	40	6	22	28	39	-7	5	0	—	—	—	—	—

H

Season Team	League	Gms.	G	A	Pts.	PIM	+/-	PP	SH		Gms.	G	A	Pts.	PIM
		REGULAR SEASON									PLAYOFFS				
93-94 — Philadelphia	NHL	19	3	12	15	19	2	3	0		—	—	—	—	—
— Florida	NHL	33	2	14	16	9	8	0	0		—	—	—	—	—
— Pittsburgh	NHL	12	1	2	3	8	-1	1	0		1	0	0	0	0
94-95 — Cleveland	IHL	—	—	—	—	—	...	...	...		3	1	0	1	4
95-96 — Las Vegas	IHL	78	20	65	85	101	...	...	...		15	5	11	16	24
96-97 — San Jose	NHL	63	6	12	18	69	-22	3	0		—	—	—	—	—
NHL totals (8 years)		356	52	138	190	367	11	21	0		42	2	8	10	37

HAY, DWAYNE LW CAPITALS

PERSONAL: Born February 11, 1977, in London, Ont. ... 6-1/183. ... Shoots left.
HIGH SCHOOL: Bishop MacDonnell (Guelph, Ont.).
TRANSACTIONS/CAREER NOTES: Selected by Washington Capitals in second round (third Capitals pick, 43rd overall) of NHL entry draft (July 8, 1995).

Season Team	League	Gms.	G	A	Pts.	PIM	+/-	PP	SH		Gms.	G	A	Pts.	PIM
		REGULAR SEASON									PLAYOFFS				
93-94 — Listowel Jr. B	OHA	48	10	24	34	56	...	...	...		—	—	—	—	—
94-95 — Guelph	OHL	65	26	28	54	37	...	...	...		14	5	7	12	6
95-96 — Guelph	OHL	60	28	30	58	49	...	...	...		16	4	9	13	18
96-97 — Guelph	OHL	32	17	17	34	21	...	...	...		11	4	6	10	0

HEALEY, PAUL RW FLYERS

PERSONAL: Born March 20, 1975, in Edmonton. ... 6-2/185. ... Shoots right.
TRANSACTIONS/CAREER NOTES: Selected by Philadelphia Flyers in eighth round (seventh Flyers pick, 192nd overall) of NHL entry draft (June 26, 1993).
HONORS: Named to WHL (East) All-Star second team (1994-95).

Season Team	League	Gms.	G	A	Pts.	PIM	+/-	PP	SH		Gms.	G	A	Pts.	PIM
		REGULAR SEASON									PLAYOFFS				
92-93 — Prince Albert	WHL	72	12	20	32	66	...	...	...		—	—	—	—	—
93-94 — Prince Albert	WHL	63	23	26	49	70	...	...	...		—	—	—	—	—
94-95 — Prince Albert	WHL	71	43	50	93	67	...	...	...		12	3	4	7	2
95-96 — Hershey	AHL	61	7	15	22	35	...	...	...		—	—	—	—	—
96-97 — Philadelphia	AHL	64	21	19	40	56	...	...	...		10	4	1	5	10
— Philadelphia	NHL	2	0	0	0	0	0	0	0		—	—	—	—	—
NHL totals (1 year)		2	0	0	0	0	0	0	0						

HEALY, GLENN G MAPLE LEAFS

PERSONAL: Born August 23, 1962, in Pickering, Ont. ... 5-10/190. ... Catches left.
COLLEGE: Western Michigan.
TRANSACTIONS/CAREER NOTES: Signed as free agent by Los Angeles Kings (June 13, 1985). ... Signed as free agent by New York Islanders (August 16, 1989); Kings received fourth-round pick (traded to Minnesota) in 1990 draft as compensation. ... Strained left ankle ligaments (October 13, 1990); missed eight games. ... Fractured right index finger (November 10, 1991); missed five games. ... Fractured right thumb (January 3, 1992); missed 10 games. ... Severed tip of finger in practice and underwent reconstructive surgery (March 2, 1992); missed 13 games. ... Suffered from tendinitis in right wrist (January 9, 1993); missed four games. ... Selected by Mighty Ducks of Anaheim in NHL expansion draft (June 24, 1993). ... Selected by Tampa Bay Lightning in Phase II of NHL expansion draft (June 25, 1993). ... Traded by Lightning to New York Rangers for third-round pick in 1993 draft; Lightning reacquired their original pick which they had traded away earlier (June 25, 1993). ... Signed as free agent by Toronto Maple Leafs (July 8, 1997).
HONORS: Named to NCAA All-America West second team (1984-85). ... Named to CCHA All-Star second team (1984-85).
MISCELLANEOUS: Member of Stanley Cup championship team (1994).

Season Team	League	Gms.	Min	W	L	T	GA	SO	Avg.		Gms.	Min.	W	L	GA	SO	Avg.
		REGULAR SEASON									PLAYOFFS						
81-82 — Western Michigan U.	CCHA	27	1569	7	19	1	116	0	4.44		—	—	—	—	—	—	—
82-83 — Western Michigan U.	CCHA	30	1733	8	19	2	116	0	4.02		—	—	—	—	—	—	—
83-84 — Western Michigan U.	CCHA	38	2242	19	16	3	146	0	3.91		—	—	—	—	—	—	—
84-85 — Western Michigan U.	CCHA	37	2172	21	14	2	118	0	3.26		—	—	—	—	—	—	—
85-86 — Toledo	IHL	7	402	...	...	...	28	0	4.18		—	—	—	—	—	—	—
— New Haven	AHL	43	2410	21	15	4	160	0	3.98		2	119	0	2	11	0	5.55
— Los Angeles	NHL	1	51	0	0	0	6	0	7.06		—	—	—	—	—	—	—
86-87 — New Haven	AHL	47	2828	21	15	0	173	1	3.67		7	427	3	4	19	0	2.67
87-88 — Los Angeles	NHL	34	1869	12	18	1	135	1	4.33		4	240	1	3	20	0	5.00
88-89 — Los Angeles	NHL	48	2699	25	19	2	192	0	4.27		3	97	0	1	6	0	3.71
89-90 — New York Islanders	NHL	39	2197	12	19	6	128	2	3.50		4	166	1	2	9	0	3.25
90-91 — New York Islanders	NHL	53	2999	18	24	9	166	0	3.32		—	—	—	—	—	—	—
91-92 — New York Islanders	NHL	37	1960	14	16	4	124	1	3.80		—	—	—	—	—	—	—
92-93 — New York Islanders	NHL	47	2655	22	20	2	146	1	3.30		18	1109	9	8	59	0	3.19
93-94 — New York Rangers	NHL	29	1368	10	12	2	69	2	3.03		2	68	0	0	1	0	0.88
94-95 — New York Rangers	NHL	17	888	8	6	1	35	1	2.36		5	230	2	1	13	0	3.39
95-96 — New York Rangers	NHL	44	2564	17	14	11	124	2	2.90		—	—	—	—	—	—	—
96-97 — New York Rangers	NHL	23	1357	5	12	4	59	1	2.61		—	—	—	—	—	—	—
NHL totals (11 years)		372	20607	143	160	42	1184	11	3.45		36	1910	13	15	108	0	3.39

H

HEBERT, GUY   G   MIGHTY DUCKS

PERSONAL: Born January 7, 1967, in Troy, N.Y. ... 5-11/185. ... Catches left. ... Full name: Guy Andrew Hebert. ... Name pronounced GEE ay-BAIR.
HIGH SCHOOL: LaSalle Institute (Troy, N.Y.).
COLLEGE: Hamilton (N.Y.).
TRANSACTIONS/CAREER NOTES: Selected by St. Louis Blues in eighth round (eighth Blues pick, 159th overall) of NHL entry draft (June 13, 1987). ... Selected by Mighty Ducks of Anaheim in NHL expansion draft (June 24, 1993). ... Suffered concussion (April 30, 1995); missed one game. ... Suffered concussion (December 9, 1996); missed two games.
HONORS: Shared James Norris Memorial Trophy with Pat Jablonski (1990-91). ... Named to IHL All-Star second team (1990-91). ... Played in NHL All-Star Game (1997).
MISCELLANEOUS: Holds Mighty Ducks of Anaheim all-time records for most games played by a goaltender (217), most wins (89), most shutouts (12) and goals-against average (2.83). ... Stopped a penalty shot attempt (vs. Alexandre Daigle, December 30, 1996).

			REGULAR SEASON							PLAYOFFS						
Season Team	League	Gms.	Min	W	L	T	GA	SO	Avg.	Gms.	Min.	W	L	GA	SO	Avg.
85-86—Hamilton College	Div. II	18	1011	4	12	2	69	2	4.09	—	—	—	—	—	—	—
86-87—Hamilton College	Div. II	18	1070	12	5	0	40	0	2.24	—	—	—	—	—	—	—
87-88—Hamilton College	Div. II	8	450	5	3	0	19	0	2.53	—	—	—	—	—	—	—
88-89—Hamilton College	Div. II	25	1453	18	7	0	62	0	2.56	—	—	—	—	—	—	—
89-90—Peoria	IHL	30	1706	7	13	‡7	124	1	4.36	2	76	0	1	5	0	3.95
90-91—Peoria	IHL	36	2093	24	10	‡1	100	2	*2.87	8	458	3	4	32	0	4.19
91-92—Peoria	IHL	29	1731	20	9	‡0	98	0	3.40	4	239	3	1	9	0	*2.26
—St. Louis	NHL	13	738	5	5	1	36	0	2.93	—	—	—	—	—	—	—
92-93—St. Louis	NHL	24	1210	8	8	2	74	1	3.67	1	2	0	0	0	0	0.00
93-94—Anaheim	NHL	52	2991	20	27	3	141	2	2.83	—	—	—	—	—	—	—
94-95—Anaheim	NHL	39	2092	12	20	4	109	2	3.13	—	—	—	—	—	—	—
95-96—Anaheim	NHL	59	3326	28	23	5	157	4	2.83	—	—	—	—	—	—	—
96-97—Anaheim	NHL	67	3863	29	25	12	172	4	2.67	9	534	4	4	18	1	2.02
NHL totals (6 years)		254	14220	102	108	27	689	13	2.91	10	536	4	4	18	1	2.01

HECHT, JOCHEN   C   BLUES

PERSONAL: Born June 21, 1977, in Mannheim, West Germany. ... 6-1/180. ... Shoots left.
TRANSACTIONS/CAREER NOTES: Selected by St. Louis Blues in second round (first Blues pick, 49th overall) of NHL entry draft (July 8, 1995).

			REGULAR SEASON							PLAYOFFS				
Season Team	League	Gms.	G	A	Pts.	PIM	+/-	PP	SH	Gms.	G	A	Pts.	PIM
94-95—Mannheim	Germany	43	11	12	23	68	...	...	...	10	5	4	9	12
95-96—Mannheim	Germany	44	12	16	28	68	...	...	...	8	3	2	5	6
96-97—Mannheim	Germany	46	21	21	42	36	...	...	...	9	3	3	6	4

HEDBERG, JOHAN   G   FLYERS

PERSONAL: Born May 5, 1973, in Leksand, Sweden. ... 5-11/180. ... Catches left.
TRANSACTIONS/CAREER NOTES: Selected by Philadelphia Flyers in ninth round (eighth Flyers pick, 218th overall) of NHL entry draft (June 29, 1994).

			REGULAR SEASON							PLAYOFFS						
Season Team	League	Gms.	Min	W	L	T	GA	SO	Avg.	Gms.	Min.	W	L	GA	SO	Avg.
92-93—Leksand	Sweden	10	600	...	...	...	24	...	2.40	—	—	—	—	—	—	—
93-94—Leksand	Sweden	17	1020	...	...	...	48	...	2.81	—	—	—	—	—	—	—
94-95—Leksand	Sweden	17	986	...	...	...	58	...	3.53	—	—	—	—	—	—	—
95-96—Leksand	Sweden	34	2013	...	...	...	95	...	2.83	4	240	...	...	13	...	3.25
96-97—Leksand	Sweden	38	2260	...	...	...	95	3	2.52	8	581	...	...	18	1	1.86

HEDICAN, BRET   D   CANUCKS

PERSONAL: Born August 10, 1970, in St. Paul, Minn. ... 6-2/205. ... Shoots left. ... Full name: Bret Michael Hedican. ... Name pronounced HEHD-ih-kuhn.
HIGH SCHOOL: North St. Paul (Minn.).
COLLEGE: St. Cloud (Minn.) State.
TRANSACTIONS/CAREER NOTES: Selected by St. Louis Blues in 10th round (10th Blues pick, 198th overall) of NHL entry draft (June 11, 1988). ... Sprained knee ligaments (September 27, 1992); missed first 15 games of season. ... Injured shoulder (October 24, 1993); missed three games. ... Injured groin (January 18, 1994); missed six games. ... Traded by Blues with D Jeff Brown and C Nathan LaFayette to Vancouver Canucks for C Craig Janney (March 21, 1994). ... Strained groin (March 27, 1994); missed three games. ... Injured back (February 1, 1996); missed three games. ... Strained back (October 5, 1996); missed six games. ... Strained groin (December 4, 1996); missed five games. ... Strained groin (December 26, 1996); missed four games.
HONORS: Named to WCHA All-Star first team (1990-91).

			REGULAR SEASON							PLAYOFFS				
Season Team	League	Gms.	G	A	Pts.	PIM	+/-	PP	SH	Gms.	G	A	Pts.	PIM
88-89—St. Cloud State	WCHA	28	5	3	8	28	...	...	...	—	—	—	—	—
89-90—St. Cloud State	WCHA	36	4	17	21	37	...	...	...	—	—	—	—	—
90-91—St. Cloud State	WCHA	41	18	30	48	52	...	...	...	—	—	—	—	—
91-92—U.S. national team	Int'l	54	1	8	9	59	...	...	...	—	—	—	—	—
—U.S. Olympic team	Int'l	8	0	0	0	4	...	...	...	—	—	—	—	—
—St. Louis	NHL	4	1	0	1	0	1	0	0	5	0	0	0	0
92-93—Peoria	IHL	19	0	8	8	10	...	...	...	—	—	—	—	—
—St. Louis	NHL	42	0	8	8	30	-2	0	0	10	0	0	0	14

H

Season Team	League	REGULAR SEASON								PLAYOFFS				
		Gms.	G	A	Pts.	PIM	+/-	PP	SH	Gms.	G	A	Pts.	PIM
93-94 — St. Louis	NHL	61	0	11	11	64	-8	0	0	—	—	—	—	—
— Vancouver	NHL	8	0	1	1	0	1	0	0	24	1	6	7	16
94-95 — Vancouver	NHL	45	2	11	13	34	-3	0	0	11	0	2	2	6
95-96 — Vancouver	NHL	77	6	23	29	83	8	1	0	6	0	1	1	10
96-97 — Vancouver	NHL	67	4	15	19	51	-3	2	0	—	—	—	—	—
NHL totals (6 years)		304	13	69	82	262	-6	3	0	56	1	9	10	46

HEINZE, STEVE RW BRUINS

PERSONAL: Born January 30, 1970, in Lawrence, Mass. ... 5-11/193. ... Shoots right. ... Full name: Stephen Herbert Heinze. ... Name pronounced HIGHNS.

HIGH SCHOOL: Lawrence Academy (Groton, Mass.).

COLLEGE: Boston College.

TRANSACTIONS/CAREER NOTES: Selected by Boston Bruins in second round (second Bruins pick, 60th overall) of NHL entry draft (June 11, 1988). ... Injured shoulder (May 1, 1992). ... Injured shoulder (March 20, 1993); missed 11 games. ... Injured knee (February 18, 1994); missed five games. ... Reinjured knee (March 26, 1994); missed two games. ... Strained abdominal muscle (December 5, 1996); missed one game. ... Strained hip and groin and tore knee ligament (December 17, 1996); missed remainder of season.

HONORS: Named to Hockey East All-Rookie team (1988-89). ... Named to NCAA All-America East first team (1989-90). ... Named to Hockey East All-Star first team (1989-90).

STATISTICAL PLATEAUS: Three-goal games: 1992-93 (1), 1995-96 (1). Total: 2.

Season Team	League	REGULAR SEASON								PLAYOFFS				
		Gms.	G	A	Pts.	PIM	+/-	PP	SH	Gms.	G	A	Pts.	PIM
86-87 — Lawrence Academy	Mass. H.S.	23	26	24	50	...	...	...	...	—	—	—	—	—
87-88 — Lawrence Academy	Mass. H.S.	23	30	25	55	...	...	...	...	—	—	—	—	—
88-89 — Boston College	Hockey East	36	26	23	49	26	...	...	...	—	—	—	—	—
89-90 — Boston College	Hockey East	40	27	36	63	41	...	...	...	—	—	—	—	—
90-91 — Boston College	Hockey East	35	21	26	47	35	...	...	...	—	—	—	—	—
91-92 — U.S. national team	Int'l	49	18	15	33	38	...	...	...	—	—	—	—	—
— U.S. Olympic team	Int'l	8	1	3	4	8	...	...	...	—	—	—	—	—
— Boston	NHL	14	3	4	7	6	-1	0	0	7	0	3	3	17
92-93 — Boston	NHL	73	18	13	31	24	20	0	2	4	1	1	2	2
93-94 — Boston	NHL	77	10	11	21	32	-2	0	2	13	2	3	5	7
94-95 — Boston	NHL	36	7	9	16	23	0	0	1	5	0	0	0	0
95-96 — Boston	NHL	76	16	12	28	43	-3	0	1	5	1	1	2	4
96-97 — Boston	NHL	30	17	8	25	27	-8	4	2	—	—	—	—	—
NHL totals (6 years)		306	71	57	128	155	6	4	8	34	4	8	12	30

HELENIUS, SAMI D FLAMES

PERSONAL: Born January 22, 1974, in Helsinki, Finland. ... 6-5/220. ... Shoots left. ... Name pronounced huh-LEH-nee-uhz.

TRANSACTIONS/CAREER NOTES: Selected by Calgary Flames in fifth round (fifth Flames pick, 102nd overall) of NHL entry draft (June 20, 1992).

Season Team	League	REGULAR SEASON								PLAYOFFS				
		Gms.	G	A	Pts.	PIM	+/-	PP	SH	Gms.	G	A	Pts.	PIM
91-92 — Jokerit Helsinki Jrs.	Finland					Statistics unavailable.				—	—	—	—	—
92-93 — Vantaa HT	Finland Dv.II	21	3	2	5	60	...	...	...	—	—	—	—	—
— Jokerit Helsinki Jrs.	Finland	1	0	0	0	0	...	...	...	—	—	—	—	—
93-94 — Reipas Lahti	Finland	37	2	3	5	46	...	...	...	—	—	—	—	—
94-95 — Saint John	AHL	69	2	5	7	217	...	...	...	—	—	—	—	—
95-96 — Saint John	AHL	68	0	3	3	231	...	...	...	10	0	0	0	9
96-97 — Saint John	AHL	72	5	10	15	218	...	...	...	2	0	0	0	0
— Calgary	NHL	3	0	1	1	0	1	0	0	—	—	—	—	—
NHL totals (1 year)		3	0	1	1	0	1	0	0					

HELMER, BRYAN D DEVILS

PERSONAL: Born July 15, 1972, in Sault Ste. Marie, Ont. ... 6-1/200. ... Shoots right.

TRANSACTIONS/CAREER NOTES: Signed as free agent by New Jersey Devils (October 1, 1993).

Season Team	League	REGULAR SEASON								PLAYOFFS				
		Gms.	G	A	Pts.	PIM	+/-	PP	SH	Gms.	G	A	Pts.	PIM
89-90 — Wellington	OJHL	51	6	22	28	204	...			—	—	—	—	—
— Belleville	OHL	6	0	1	1	0	...			—	—	—	—	—
90-91 — Wellington	OJHL	50	11	14	25	109	...			—	—	—	—	—
91-92 — Wellington	OJHL	45	19	32	51	66	...			—	—	—	—	—
92-93 — Wellington	OJHL	57	25	62	87	62	...			—	—	—	—	—
93-94 — Albany	AHL	65	4	19	23	79	...			5	0	0	0	9
94-95 — Albany	AHL	77	7	36	43	101	...			7	1	0	1	9
95-96 — Albany	AHL	80	14	30	44	107	...			4	2	0	2	6
96-97 — Albany	AHL	77	12	27	39	113	...			16	1	7	8	10

H

HENDRICKSON, DARBY C MAPLE LEAFS

PERSONAL: Born August 28, 1972, in Richfield, Minn. ... 6-0/185. ... Shoots left.
HIGH SCHOOL: Richfield (Minn.).
COLLEGE: Minnesota.

TRANSACTIONS/CAREER NOTES: Selected by Toronto Maple Leafs in fourth round (third Maple Leafs pick, 73rd overall) of NHL entry draft (June 16, 1990). ... Suspended for three games by NHL for kneeing incident (October 26, 1995). ... Suffered from the flu (December 30, 1995); missed one game. ... Traded by Maple Leafs with LW Sean Haggerty, D Kenny Jonsson and first-round pick (G Roberto Luongo) in 1997 draft to New York Islanders for LW Wendel Clark, D Mathieu Schneider and D D.J. Smith (March 13, 1996). ... Traded by Islanders to Maple Leafs for conditional pick in 1998 draft (October 11, 1996). ... Strained back (January 27, 1997); missed five games.
HONORS: Won WCHA Rookie of the Year Award (1991-92). ... Named to WCHA All-Rookie team (1991-92).

Season Team	League	Gms.	G	A	Pts.	PIM	+/-	PP	SH	Gms.	G	A	Pts.	PIM
87-88— Richfield	Minn. H.S.	22	12	9	21	10	...	...	...	—	—	—	—	—
88-89— Richfield	Minn. H.S.	22	22	20	42	12	...	...	...	—	—	—	—	—
89-90— Richfield	Minn. H.S.	24	23	27	50	49	...	...	...	—	—	—	—	—
90-91— Richfield	Minn. H.S.	27	32	29	61	...	...	...	...	—	—	—	—	—
91-92— Univ. of Minnesota	WCHA	41	25	28	53	61	...	...	...	—	—	—	—	—
92-93— Univ. of Minnesota	WCHA	31	12	15	27	35	...	...	...	—	—	—	—	—
93-94— U.S. national team	Int'l	59	12	16	28	30	...	...	...	—	—	—	—	—
— U.S. Olympic team	Int'l	8	0	0	0	6	...	...	...	—	—	—	—	—
— St. John's	AHL	6	4	1	5	4	...	...	...	3	1	1	2	0
— Toronto	NHL	—	—	—	—	—	—	—	—	2	0	0	0	0
94-95— St. John's	AHL	59	16	20	36	48	...	...	...	—	—	—	—	—
— Toronto	NHL	8	0	1	1	4	0	0	0	—	—	—	—	—
95-96— Toronto	NHL	46	6	6	12	47	-2	0	0	—	—	—	—	—
— New York Islanders	NHL	16	1	4	5	33	-6	0	0	—	—	—	—	—
96-97— St. John's	AHL	12	5	4	9	21	...	...	...	—	—	—	—	—
— Toronto	NHL	64	11	6	17	47	-20	0	1	—	—	—	—	—
NHL totals (4 years)		134	18	17	35	131	-28	0	1	2	0	0	0	0

HENRY, FREDERIC   G   DEVILS

PERSONAL: Born August 9, 1977, in Cap Rouge, Que. ... 5-11/155. ... Catches left.
TRANSACTIONS/CAREER NOTES: Selected by New Jersey Devils in eighth round (10th Devils pick, 200th overall) of NHL entry draft (July 8, 1995).

Season Team	League	Gms.	Min	W	L	T	GA	SO	Avg.	Gms.	Min.	W	L	GA	SO	Avg.
94-95— Granby	QMJHL	15	866	8	5	0	47	0	3.26	6	232	1	2	21	0	5.43
95-96— Granby	QMJHL	28	1533	19	5	2	69	†3	2.70	12	607	9	2	21	*2	*2.08
96-97— Granby	QMJHL	57	3327	33	16	*6	161	4	2.90	5	301	1	4	20	0	3.99
— Albany	AHL	1	60	1	0	0	3	0	3.00	—	—	—	—	—	—	—

HERPERGER, CHRIS   LW   MIGHTY DUCKS

PERSONAL: Born February 24, 1974, in Esterhazy, Sask. ... 6-0/190. ... Shoots left. ... Name pronounced HUHR-puhr-guhr.
TRANSACTIONS/CAREER NOTES: Signed by Philadelphia Flyers in 10th round (10th Flyers pick, 223rd overall) of NHL entry draft (June 20, 1992). ... Traded by Flyers with seventh-round pick (LW Tony Mohagen) in 1997 draft to Mighty Ducks of Anaheim for C Bob Corkum (February 6, 1996).
HONORS: Named to WHL (West) All-Star second team (1994-95).

Season Team	League	Gms.	G	A	Pts.	PIM	+/-	PP	SH	Gms.	G	A	Pts.	PIM
90-91— Swift Current	WHL	10	0	1	1	5	...	...	...	—	—	—	—	—
91-92— Swift Current	WHL	72	14	19	33	44	...	...	...	8	0	1	1	9
92-93— Seattle	WHL	66	29	18	47	61	...	...	...	5	1	1	2	6
93-94— Seattle	WHL	71	44	51	95	110	...	...	...	9	12	10	22	12
94-95— Seattle	WHL	59	49	52	101	106	...	...	...	4	4	0	4	6
— Hershey	AHL	4	0	0	0	0	...	...	...	—	—	—	—	—
95-96— Hershey	AHL	46	8	12	20	36	...	...	...	0	0	0	0	0
— Baltimore	AHL	21	2	3	5	17	...	...	...	9	2	3	5	6
96-97— Baltimore	AHL	67	19	22	41	88	...	...	...	3	0	0	0	0

HEWARD, JAMIE   D   FLYERS

PERSONAL: Born March 30, 1971, in Regina, Sask. ... 6-2/207. ... Shoots right. ... Name pronounced HYOO-uhrd.
TRANSACTIONS/CAREER NOTES: Traded by Spokane Chiefs to Regina Pats for RW Pat Falloon and future considerations (October 1987). ... Broke jaw (November 1988). ... Selected by Pittsburgh Penguins in first round (first Penguins pick, 16th overall) of NHL entry draft (June 17, 1989). ... Suffered from mononucleosis (September 1989). ... Signed as free agent by Toronto Maple Leafs (May 4, 1995). ... Signed as free agent by Philadelphia Flyers (July 10, 1997).
HONORS: Named to WHL (East) All-Star first team (1990-91). ... Named to AHL All-Star first team (1995-96).

Season Team	League	Gms.	G	A	Pts.	PIM	+/-	PP	SH	Gms.	G	A	Pts.	PIM
87-88— Regina	WHL	68	10	17	27	17	...	...	...	4	1	1	2	2
88-89— Regina	WHL	52	31	28	59	29	...	...	...	—	—	—	—	—
89-90— Regina	WHL	72	14	44	58	42	...	...	...	11	2	2	4	10
90-91— Regina	WHL	71	23	61	84	41	...	...	...	8	2	9	11	6
91-92— Muskegon	IHL	54	6	21	27	37	...	...	...	14	1	4	5	4
92-93— Cleveland	IHL	58	9	18	27	64	...	...	...	—	—	—	—	—
93-94— Cleveland	IHL	73	8	16	24	72	...	...	...	—	—	—	—	—
94-95— Canadian nat'l team	Int'l	51	11	35	46	32	...	...	...	—	—	—	—	—
95-96— St. John's	AHL	73	22	34	56	33	...	...	...	3	1	1	2	6
— Toronto	NHL	5	0	0	0	0	-1	0	0	—	—	—	—	—
96-97— Toronto	NHL	20	1	4	5	6	-6	0	0	—	—	—	—	—
— St. John's	AHL	27	8	19	27	26	...	...	...	9	1	3	4	6
NHL totals (2 years)		25	1	4	5	6	-7	0	0					

H

HEXTALL, RON   G   FLYERS

PERSONAL: Born May 3, 1964, in Winnipeg. ... 6-3/200. ... Catches left.

TRANSACTIONS/CAREER NOTES: Selected by Philadelphia Flyers as underage junior in sixth round (sixth Flyers pick, 119th overall) of NHL entry draft (June 9, 1982). ... Suspended eight games by NHL for slashing (May 1987). ... Pulled hamstring (March 7, 1989). ... Suspended first 12 games of 1989-90 season by NHL for attacking opposing player in final playoff game (May 11, 1989). ... Did not attend training camp due to a contract dispute (September 1989). ... Pulled groin (November 4, 1989). ... Pulled hamstring (November 15, 1989). ... Tore right groin muscle (December 13, 1989); missed 29 games. ... Injured left groin (March 8, 1990). ... Pulled groin (October 11, 1990); missed five games. ... Sprained left knee ligament (October 27, 1990); missed five weeks. ... Tore groin muscle (March 12, 1991); missed nine games. ... Suffered from the flu (November 14, 1991); missed one game. ... Developed shoulder tendinitis (November 27, 1991); missed nine games. ... Traded by Flyers with C Mike Ricci, C Peter Forsberg, D Steve Duchesne, D Kerry Huffman, first-round pick (Jocelyn Thibault) in 1993 draft, cash and future considerations to Quebec Nordiques for C Eric Lindros (June 20, 1992); Flyers sent LW Chris Simon and first-round pick in 1994 draft (traded to Toronto) to Nordiques to complete deal (July 21, 1992). ... Strained muscle in left thigh (February 20, 1993); missed 14 games. ... Traded by Nordiques with first-round pick (LW Todd Bertuzzi) in 1993 draft to New York Islanders for G Mark Fitzpatrick and first-round pick (C Adam Deadmarsh) in 1993 draft (June 20, 1993). ... Traded by Islanders with sixth-round pick (D Dimitri Tertyshny) in 1995 draft to Flyers for G Tommy Soderstrom (September 22, 1994). ... Injured groin (February 3, 1995); missed three games. ... Strained hamstring (October 20, 1995); missed nine games. ... Injured buttocks (November 20, 1995); missed two games. ... Suffered from the flu (October 10, 1996); missed one game. ... Strained hamstring (March 1, 1997); missed one game.

HONORS: Won Dudley (Red) Garrett Memorial Trophy (1985-86). ... Named to AHL All-Star first team (1985-86). ... Named NHL Rookie of the Year by THE SPORTING NEWS (1986-87). ... Won Vezina Trophy (1986-87). ... Won Conn Smythe Trophy (1986-87). ... Named to THE SPORTING NEWS All-Star second team (1986-87). ... Named to NHL All-Star first team (1986-87). ... Named to NHL All-Rookie team (1986-87). ... Played in NHL All-Star Game (1988).

MISCELLANEOUS: Allowed a penalty shot goal (vs. Dave Tippett, October 31, 1987; vs. Mark Johnson, March 12, 1988; vs. Andrew Cassels, April 6, 1994; vs. Benoit Hogue, January 24, 1995). ... Scored a goal into Washington Capitals empty net, becoming the first goaltender to score a goal in Stanley Cup playoffs (April 11, 1989).

Season Team	League	Gms.	Min	W	L	T	GA	SO	Avg.	Gms.	Min.	W	L	GA	SO	Avg.
80-81—Melville	SJHL	42	2127	...	...	...	254	0	7.17	—	—	—	—	—	—	—
81-82—Brandon	WHL	30	1398	12	11	0	133	0	5.71	3	103	0	2	16	0	9.32
82-83—Brandon	WHL	44	2589	13	30	0	249	0	5.77	—	—	—	—	—	—	—
83-84—Brandon	WHL	46	2670	29	13	2	190	0	4.27	10	592	5	5	37	0	3.75
84-85—Kalamazoo	IHL	19	1103	6	11	‡1	80	0	4.35	—	—	—	—	—	—	—
—Hershey	AHL	11	555	4	6	0	34	0	3.68	—	—	—	—	—	—	—
85-86—Hershey	AHL	*53	*3061	30	19	2	174	*5	3.41	13	780	5	7	42	*1	3.23
86-87—Philadelphia	NHL	*66	*3799	37	21	6	190	1	3.00	*26	*1540	15	11	*71	†2	2.77
87-88—Philadelphia	NHL	62	3561	30	22	7	208	0	3.50	7	379	2	4	30	0	4.75
88-89—Philadelphia	NHL	64	3756	30	28	6	202	0	3.23	15	886	8	7	49	0	3.32
89-90—Philadelphia	NHL	8	419	4	2	1	29	0	4.15	—	—	—	—	—	—	—
—Hershey	AHL	1	49	1	0	0	3	0	3.67	—	—	—	—	—	—	—
90-91—Philadelphia	NHL	36	2035	13	16	5	106	0	3.13	—	—	—	—	—	—	—
91-92—Philadelphia	NHL	45	2668	16	21	6	151	3	3.40	—	—	—	—	—	—	—
92-93—Quebec	NHL	54	2988	29	16	5	172	0	3.45	6	372	2	4	18	0	2.90
93-94—New York Islanders	NHL	65	3581	27	26	6	184	5	3.08	3	158	0	3	16	0	6.08
94-95—Philadelphia	NHL	31	1824	17	9	4	88	1	2.89	15	897	10	5	*42	0	2.81
95-96—Philadelphia	NHL	53	3102	31	13	7	112	4	*2.17	12	760	6	6	27	0	2.13
96-97—Philadelphia	NHL	55	3094	31	16	5	132	5	2.56	8	444	4	3	22	0	2.97
NHL totals (11 years)		539	30827	265	190	58	1574	19	3.06	92	5436	47	43	275	2	3.04

HICKS, ALEX   C   PENGUINS

PERSONAL: Born September 4, 1969, in Calgary. ... 6-1/195. ... Shoots left.

TRANSACTIONS/CAREER NOTES: Signed as free agent by Mighty Ducks of Anaheim (August 23, 1995). ... Traded by Mighty Ducks with D Fredrik Olausson to Pittsburgh Penguins for LW Shawn Antoski and D Dmitri Mironov (November 19, 1996). ... Suffered hip pointer (December 15, 1996); missed four games. ... Bruised leg (February 5, 1997); missed one game. ... Strained groin (February 18, 1997); missed two games. ... Strained groin (March 24, 1997); missed one game.

Season Team	League	Gms.	G	A	Pts.	PIM	+/-	PP	SH	Gms.	G	A	Pts.	PIM
92-93—Toledo	ECHL	52	26	34	60	100	...	...	...	16	6	10	16	79
93-94—Toledo	ECHL	60	31	49	80	240	...	...	...	14	10	10	20	56
94-95—Las Vegas	IHL	78	24	42	66	212	...	...	...	9	2	4	6	47
95-96—Baltimore	AHL	13	2	10	12	23	...	...	...	—	—	—	—	—
—Anaheim	NHL	64	10	11	21	37	11	0	0	—	—	—	—	—
96-97—Anaheim	NHL	18	2	6	8	14	1	0	0	—	—	—	—	—
—Pittsburgh	NHL	55	5	15	20	76	-6	0	0	5	0	1	1	2
NHL totals (2 years)		137	17	32	49	127	6	0	0	5	0	1	1	2

HIGGINS, MATT   C   CANADIENS

PERSONAL: Born October 29, 1977, in Vernon, B.C. ... 6-2/168. ... Shoots left.

TRANSACTIONS/CAREER NOTES: Selected by Montreal Canadiens in first round (first Canadiens pick, 18th overall) of NHL entry draft (June 22, 1996).

Season Team	League	Gms.	G	A	Pts.	PIM	+/-	PP	SH	Gms.	G	A	Pts.	PIM
93-94—Moose Jaw	WHL	64	6	10	16	10	...	...	...	—	—	—	—	—
94-95—Moose Jaw	WHL	72	36	34	70	26	...	...	...	10	1	2	3	2
95-96—Moose Jaw	WHL	67	30	33	63	43	...	...	...	—	—	—	—	—
96-97—Moose Jaw	WHL	71	33	57	90	51	...	...	...	12	3	5	8	2

H

HILL, SEAN   D   SENATORS

PERSONAL: Born February 14, 1970, in Duluth, Minn. ... 6-0/203. ... Shoots right. ... Full name: Sean Ronald Hill.
COLLEGE: Wisconsin.
TRANSACTIONS/CAREER NOTES: Selected by Montreal Canadiens in eighth round (ninth Canadiens pick, 167th overall) of NHL entry draft (June 11, 1988). ... Injured knee (December 29, 1990). ... Suspended two games by WCHA for elbowing (January 18, 1991). ... Strained abdominal muscle (October 13, 1992); missed 14 games. ... Selected by Mighty Ducks of Anaheim in NHL expansion draft (June 24, 1993). ... Sprained shoulder (January 6, 1994); missed nine games. ... Traded by Mighty Ducks with ninth-round pick (G Frederic Cassivi) in 1994 draft to Ottawa Senators for third-round pick (traded to Tampa Bay) in 1994 draft (June 29, 1994). ... Strained abdominal muscle during 1995-96 season; missed two games. ... Tore left knee ligament (October 18, 1996); missed remainder of season.
HONORS: Named to WCHA All-Star second team (1989-90 and 1990-91). ... Named to NCAA All-America West second team (1990-91).
MISCELLANEOUS: Member of Stanley Cup championship team (1993).

			REGULAR SEASON							PLAYOFFS				
Season Team	League	Gms.	G	A	Pts.	PIM	+/-	PP	SH	Gms.	G	A	Pts.	PIM
88-89— Univ. of Wisconsin.....	WCHA	45	2	23	25	69	...	...	...	—	—	—	—	—
89-90— Univ. of Wisconsin.....	WCHA	42	14	39	53	78	...	...	...	—	—	—	—	—
90-91— Univ. of Wisconsin.....	WCHA	37	19	32	51	122	...	...	...	—	—	—	—	—
— Fredericton............	AHL	—	—	—	—	—	...	...	...	3	0	2	2	2
— Montreal	NHL	—	—	—	—	—	...	...	...	1	0	0	0	0
91-92— Fredericton............	AHL	42	7	20	27	65	...	...	...	7	1	3	4	6
—U.S. national team	Int'l	12	4	3	7	16	...	...	...	—	—	—	—	—
— U.S. Olympic team	Int'l	8	2	0	2	6	...	...	...	—	—	—	—	—
— Montreal	NHL	—	—	—	—	—	...	...	...	4	1	0	1	2
92-93— Montreal	NHL	31	2	6	8	54	-5	1	0	3	0	0	0	4
— Fredericton............	AHL	6	1	3	4	10	...	...	...	—	—	—	—	—
93-94— Anaheim	NHL	68	7	20	27	78	-12	2	1	—	—	—	—	—
94-95— Ottawa	NHL	45	1	14	15	30	-11	0	0	—	—	—	—	—
95-96— Ottawa	NHL	80	7	14	21	94	-26	2	0	—	—	—	—	—
96-97— Ottawa	NHL	5	0	0	0	4	1	0	0	—	—	—	—	—
NHL totals (7 years)		229	17	54	71	260	-53	5	1	8	1	0	1	6

HILLIER, CRAIG   G   PENGUINS

PERSONAL: Born February 28, 1978, in Cole Harbour, Nova Scotia. ... 6-1/174. ... Catches left.
TRANSACTIONS/CAREER NOTES: Selected by Pittsburgh Penguins in first round (first Penguins pick, 23rd overall) of NHL entry draft (June 22, 1996).
HONORS: Named to OHL All-Star first team (1995-96).

			REGULAR SEASON							PLAYOFFS				
Season Team	League	Gms.	Min	W	L	T	GA	SO	Avg.	Gms.	Min.	W	L	GA	SO	Avg.
94-95— Ottawa	OHL	24	1078	6	7	2	69	1	3.84	—	—	—	—	—	—	—
95-96— Ottawa	OHL	44	2439	24	14	3	117	2	2.88	3	130	0	2	12	0	5.54
96-97— Ottawa	OHL	36	2007	23	6	4	89	2	2.66	10	540	4	5	33	0	3.67

HIRSCH, COREY   G   CANUCKS

PERSONAL: Born July 1, 1972, in Medicine Hat, Alta. ... 5-10/160. ... Catches left.
TRANSACTIONS/CAREER NOTES: Selected by New York Rangers in eighth round (seventh Rangers pick, 169th overall) of NHL entry draft (June 22, 1991). ... Loaned by Rangers to Canadian Olympic team (October 1, 1993). ... Returned to Rangers (March 8, 1994). ... Traded by Rangers to Vancouver Canucks for C Nathan LaFayette (April 7, 1995). ... Bruised ribs (October 6, 1996); missed five games.
HONORS: Named to WHL (West) All-Star second team (1989-90). ... Won Can.HL Goaltender of the Year Award (1991-92). ... Won Hap Emms Memorial Trophy (1991-92). ... Won Del Wilson Trophy (1991-92). ... Won WHL Player of the Year Award (1991-92). ... Named to Can.HL All-Star first team (1991-92). ... Named to Memorial Cup All-Star team (1991-92). ... Named to WHL (West) All-Star first team (1991-92). ... Won Aldege (Baz) Bastien Trophy (1992-93). ... Won Dudley (Red) Garrett Memorial Trophy (1992-93). ... Shared Harry (Hap) Holmes Memorial Trophy with Boris Rousson (1992-93). ... Named to AHL All-Star first team (1992-93). ... Named to NHL All-Rookie team (1995-96).
MISCELLANEOUS: Member of silver-medal-winning Canadian Olympic team (1994).

			REGULAR SEASON							PLAYOFFS				
Season Team	League	Gms.	Min	W	L	T	GA	SO	Avg.	Gms.	Min.	W	L	GA	SO	Avg.
88-89—Kamloops	WHL	32	1516	11	12	2	106	2	4.20	5	245	3	2	19	0	4.65
89-90—Kamloops	WHL	63	3608	48	13	0	230	3	3.82	17	1043	14	3	60	0	3.45
90-91—Kamloops	WHL	38	1970	26	7	1	100	3	3.05	11	623	5	6	42	0	4.04
91-92—Kamloops	WHL	48	2732	35	10	2	124	*5	*2.72	*16	*954	*11	5	35	*2	*2.20
92-93—Binghamton	AHL	46	2692	*35	4	5	125	1	*2.79	14	831	7	7	46	0	3.32
—New York Rangers	NHL	4	224	1	2	1	14	0	3.75	—	—	—	—	—	—	—
93-94—Can. national team	Int'l	37	2158	19	15	2	107	0	2.97	—	—	—	—	—	—	—
—Can. Olympic team	Int'l	8	495	5	2	1	17	0	2.06	—	—	—	—	—	—	—
—Binghamton	AHL	10	611	5	4	1	38	0	3.73	—	—	—	—	—	—	—
94-95—Binghamton	AHL	57	3371	31	20	5	175	0	3.11	—	—	—	—	—	—	—
95-96—Vancouver	NHL	41	2338	17	14	6	114	1	2.93	6	338	2	3	21	0	3.73
96-97—Vancouver	NHL	39	2127	12	20	4	116	2	3.27	—	—	—	—	—	—	—
NHL totals (3 years)		84	4689	30	36	11	244	3	3.12	6	338	2	3	21	0	3.73

HITCHEN, ALLEN   G   CANUCKS

PERSONAL: Born March 6, 1978, in Scarbourough, Ont. ... 6-1/190. ... Catches left.
TRANSACTIONS/CAREER NOTES: Signed as free agent by Vancouver Canucks (October 7, 1996).

H

Season Team	League	REGULAR SEASON Gms.	Min	W	L	T	GA	SO	Avg.	PLAYOFFS Gms.	Min.	W	L	GA	SO	Avg.
95-96 — Peterborough...............	OHL	17	727	4	6	3	60	0	4.95	3	126	2	1	9	0	4.29
96-97 — Peterborough...............	OHL	5	186	2	2	0	16	0	5.16	—	—	—	—	—	—	—

HLAVAC, JAN   LW   ISLANDERS

PERSONAL: Born September 20, 1976, in Prague, Czechoslovakia. ... 6-0/183. ... Shoots left. ... Name pronounced YAHN luh-VAHCH.
TRANSACTIONS/CAREER NOTES: Selected by New York Islanders in second round (second Islanders pick, 28th overall) of NHL entry draft (July 8, 1995).

Season Team	League	REGULAR SEASON Gms.	G	A	Pts.	PIM	+/-	PP	SH	PLAYOFFS Gms.	G	A	Pts.	PIM
93-94 — Sparta Prague Jr.	Czech Rep.	27	12	15	27	...	...	...	...	—	—	—	—	—
— Sparta Prague...........	Czech Rep.	9	1	1	2	...	...	...	...	—	—	—	—	—
94-95 — Sparta Prague...........	Czech Rep.	38	7	6	13	...	...	...	...	5	0	2	2	0
95-96 — Sparta Prague...........	Czech Rep.	34	8	5	13	...	...	...	...	12	1	2	3	0
96-97 — Sparta Prague...........	Czech Rep.	38	8	13	21	24	...	...	...	10	5	2	7	2

HLUSHKO, TODD   LW   FLAMES

PERSONAL: Born February 7, 1970, in Toronto. ... 5-11/200. ... Shoots left. ... Name pronounced huh-LOOSH-koh.
TRANSACTIONS/CAREER NOTES: Selected by Washington Capitals in 14th round (14th Capitals pick, 240th overall) of NHL entry draft (June 16, 1990). ... Signed as free agent by Philadelphia Flyers (March 6, 1994). ... Signed as free agent by Calgary Flames (June 27, 1994). ... Separated shoulder (February 11, 1995); missed 25 games. ... Suffered concussion (March 9, 1997); missed last 13 games of regular season.

Season Team	League	REGULAR SEASON Gms.	G	A	Pts.	PIM	+/-	PP	SH	PLAYOFFS Gms.	G	A	Pts.	PIM
88-89 — Guelph	OHL	66	28	18	46	71	...	...	...	7	5	3	8	18
89-90 — Owen Sound	OHL	25	9	17	26	31	...	...	...	—	—	—	—	—
— London	OHL	40	27	17	44	39	...	...	...	6	2	4	6	10
90-91 — Baltimore	AHL	66	9	14	23	55	...	...	...	—	—	—	—	—
91-92 — Baltimore	AHL	74	16	35	51	113	...	...	...	—	—	—	—	—
92-93 — Canadian nat'l team ...	Int'l	58	22	26	48	10	...	...	...	—	—	—	—	—
93-94 — Canadian nat'l team ...	Int'l	55	22	6	28	61	...	...	...	—	—	—	—	—
— Can. Olympic team ...	Int'l	8	5	0	5	6	...	...	...	—	—	—	—	—
— Philadelphia	NHL	2	1	0	1	0	1	0	0	—	—	—	—	—
— Hershey	AHL	9	6	0	6	4	...	...	...	6	2	1	3	4
94-95 — Saint John	AHL	46	22	10	32	36	...	...	...	4	2	2	4	22
— Calgary	NHL	2	0	1	1	2	1	0	0	1	0	0	0	2
95-96 — Saint John	AHL	35	14	13	27	70	...	...	...	16	8	1	9	26
— Calgary	NHL	4	0	0	0	6	0	0	0	—	—	—	—	—
96-97 — Calgary	NHL	58	7	11	18	49	-2	0	0	—	—	—	—	—
NHL totals (4 years)		66	8	12	20	57	0	0	0	1	0	0	0	2

HOCKING, JUSTIN   D   SENATORS

PERSONAL: Born January 9, 1974, in Stettler, Alta. ... 6-4/206. ... Shoots right. ... Name pronounced HAH-kihng.
COLLEGE: Spokane (Wash.) Falls Community College.
TRANSACTIONS/CAREER NOTES: Selected by Los Angeles Kings in second round (first Kings pick, 39th overall) of NHL entry draft (June 20, 1992). ... Signed as free aegnt by Ottawa Senators (July 31, 1997).
HONORS: Named to WHL (East) All-Star second team (1993-94).

Season Team	League	REGULAR SEASON Gms.	G	A	Pts.	PIM	+/-	PP	SH	PLAYOFFS Gms.	G	A	Pts.	PIM
90-91 — Fort Saskatchewan......	AJHL	38	4	6	10	84	...	...	...	—	—	—	—	—
91-92 — Spokane....................	WHL	71	4	6	10	309	...	...	...	10	0	3	3	28
92-93 — Spokane....................	WHL	16	0	1	1	75	...	...	...	—	—	—	—	—
— Medicine Hat..............	WHL	54	1	9	10	119	...	...	...	10	0	1	1	75
93-94 — Medicine Hat..............	WHL	68	7	26	33	236	...	...	...	3	0	0	0	6
— Phoenix.....................	IHL	3	0	0	0	15	...	...	...	—	—	—	—	—
— Los Angeles	NHL	1	0	0	0	0	0	0	0	—	—	—	—	—
94-95 — Phoenix.....................	IHL	20	1	1	2	50	...	...	...	1	0	0	0	0
— Syracuse...................	AHL	7	0	0	0	24	...	...	...	—	—	—	—	—
— Portland....................	AHL	9	0	1	1	34	...	...	...	—	—	—	—	—
— Knoxville...................	ECHL	20	0	6	6	70	...	...	...	4	0	0	0	26
95-96 — Prin. Edward Island ...	AHL	74	4	8	12	251	...	...	...	4	0	2	2	5
96-97 — Worcester	AHL	68	1	10	11	198	...	...	...	5	0	3	3	2
NHL totals (1 year)		1	0	0	0	0	0	0	0	—	—	—	—	—

HODSON, KEVIN   G   RED WINGS

PERSONAL: Born March 27, 1972, in Winnipeg. ... 6-0/175. ... Catches left.
TRANSACTIONS/CAREER NOTES: Signed as free agent by Chicago Blackhawks (August 27, 1992). ... Signed as free agent by Detroit Red Wings (May 3, 1993).
HONORS: Won Hap Emms Memorial Trophy (1992-93).

Season Team	League	REGULAR SEASON Gms.	Min	W	L	T	GA	SO	Avg.	PLAYOFFS Gms.	Min.	W	L	GA	SO	Avg.
90-91 — Sault Ste. Marie............	OHL	30	1638	18	11	0	88	2	*3.22	10	600	*9	1	28	0	2.80
91-92 — Sault Ste. Marie............	OHL	50	2722	28	12	4	151	0	3.33	18	1116	12	6	59	1	3.17

H

Season Team	League	Gms.	Min	W	L	T	GA	SO	Avg.	Gms.	Min.	W	L	GA	SO	Avg.
									REGULAR SEASON					PLAYOFFS		
92-93—Sault Ste. Marie............	OHL	26	1470	18	5	2	76	1	*3.10	8	448	8	0	17	0	2.28
—Indianapolis.................	IHL	14	777	5	9	‡0	53	0	4.09	—	—	—	—	—	—	—
93-94—Adirondack	AHL	37	2083	20	10	5	102	2	2.94	3	89	0	2	10	0	6.74
94-95—Adirondack	AHL	51	2731	19	22	8	161	1	3.54	4	238	0	4	14	0	3.53
95-96—Adirondack	AHL	32	1654	13	13	2	87	0	3.16	3	149	0	2	8	0	3.22
—Detroit	NHL	4	163	2	0	0	3	1	1.10	—	—	—	—	—	—	—
96-97—Detroit	NHL	6	294	2	2	1	8	1	1.63	—	—	—	—	—	—	—
—Quebec	IHL	2	118	1	1	‡0	7	0	3.56	—	—	—	—	—	—	—
NHL totals (2 years)		10	457	4	2	1	11	2	1.44							

HOGAN, PETER — D — KINGS

PERSONAL: Born January 10, 1978, in Scarborough, Ont. ... 6-2/167. ... Shoots right.
TRANSACTIONS/CAREER NOTES: Selected by Los Angeles Kings in fifth round (seventh Kings pick, 123rd overall) of NHL entry draft (June 22, 1996).

Season Team	League	Gms.	G	A	Pts.	PIM	+/-	PP	SH	Gms.	G	A	Pts.	PIM
				REGULAR SEASON							PLAYOFFS			
95-96—Oshawa..................	OHL	66	3	25	28	54	...	...	...	5	2	0	2	2
96-97—Oshawa..................	OHL	65	13	37	50	56	...	...	...	18	1	11	12	22

HOGLUND, JONAS — LW — FLAMES

PERSONAL: Born August 29, 1972, in Hammaro, Sweden. ... 6-3/213. ... Shoots right. ... Name pronounced HOHG-luhnd.
TRANSACTIONS/CAREER NOTES: Selected by Calgary Flames in 10th round (11th Flames pick, 222nd overall) of NHL entry draft (June 20, 1992).

Season Team	League	Gms.	G	A	Pts.	PIM	+/-	PP	SH	Gms.	G	A	Pts.	PIM
				REGULAR SEASON							PLAYOFFS			
88-89—Farjestad Karlstad	Sweden	1	0	0	0	0	...	...	...	—	—	—	—	—
89-90—Farjestad Karlstad	Sweden	1	0	0	0	0	...	...	...	—	—	—	—	—
90-91—Farjestad Karlstad	Sweden	40	5	5	10	4	...	...	...	8	1	0	1	0
91-92—Farjestad Karlstad	Sweden	40	14	11	25	6	...	...	...	6	2	4	6	2
92-93—Farjestad Karlstad	Sweden	40	13	13	26	14	...	...	...	3	1	0	1	0
93-94—Farjestad Karlstad	Sweden	22	7	2	9	10	...	...	...	—	—	—	—	—
94-95—Farjestad Karlstad	Sweden	40	14	12	26	16	...	...	...	4	3	2	5	0
95-96—Farjestad Karlstad	Sweden	40	32	11	43	18	...	...	...	8	2	1	3	6
96-97—Calgary	NHL	68	19	16	35	12	-4	3	0	—	—	—	—	—
NHL totals (1 year)		68	19	16	35	12	-4	3	0					

HOGUE, BENOIT — LW — STARS

PERSONAL: Born October 28, 1966, in Repentigny, Que. ... 5-10/194. ... Shoots left. ... Name pronounced BEHN-wah HOHG.
TRANSACTIONS/CAREER NOTES: Selected by Buffalo Sabres as underage junior in second round (second Sabres pick, 35th overall) of NHL entry draft (June 15, 1985). ... Suspended six games by AHL for fighting (October 1987). ... Suffered sore back (March 1988). ... Broke left cheekbone (October 11, 1989); missed 20 games. ... Sprained left ankle (March 14, 1990). ... Traded by Sabres with C Pierre Turgeon, D Uwe Krupp and C Dave McLlwain to New York Islanders for C Pat LaFontaine, LW Randy Wood, D Randy Hillier and future considerations; Sabres later received fourth-round pick (D Dean Melanson) in 1992 draft (October 25, 1991). ... Suffered stiff neck (December 7, 1992); missed five games. ... Suffered sore hand and foot (January 14, 1993); missed three games. ... Sprained knee ligament (March 14, 1993); missed six games. ... Injured shoulder (February 4, 1995); missed one game. ... Traded by Islanders with third-round pick (RW Ryan Pepperall) in 1995 draft and fifth-round pick (D Brandon Sugden) in 1996 draft to Toronto Maple Leafs for G Eric Fichaud (April 6, 1995). ... Sprained wrist (December 27, 1995); missed four games. ... Traded by Maple Leafs with LW Randy Wood to Dallas Stars for C Dave Gagner (January 28, 1996). ... Sprained neck (November 27, 1996); missed one game. ... Injured elbow (February 2, 1997); missed two games. ... Reinjured elbow (February 23, 1997); missed four games.
STATISTICAL PLATEAUS: Three-goal games: 1992-93 (1).
MISCELLANEOUS: Scored on a penalty shot (vs. Ron Tugnutt, February, 16, 1993; vs. Ron Hextall, January 24, 1995).

Season Team	League	Gms.	G	A	Pts.	PIM	+/-	PP	SH	Gms.	G	A	Pts.	PIM
				REGULAR SEASON							PLAYOFFS			
83-84—St. Jean.....................	QMJHL	59	14	11	25	42	...	...	...	—	—	—	—	—
84-85—St. Jean.....................	QMJHL	63	46	44	90	92	...	...	...	—	—	—	—	—
85-86—St. Jean.....................	QMJHL	65	54	54	108	115	...	...	...	9	6	4	10	26
86-87—Rochester	AHL	52	14	20	34	52	...	...	...	12	5	4	9	8
87-88—Buffalo	NHL	3	1	1	2	0	3	0	0	—	—	—	—	—
—Rochester	AHL	62	24	31	55	141	...	...	...	7	6	1	7	46
88-89—Buffalo	NHL	69	14	30	44	120	-5	1	2	5	0	0	0	17
89-90—Buffalo	NHL	45	11	7	18	79	0	1	0	3	0	0	0	10
90-91—Buffalo	NHL	76	19	28	47	76	-8	1	0	5	3	1	4	10
91-92—Buffalo	NHL	3	0	1	1	0	0	0	0	—	—	—	—	—
—New York Islanders....	NHL	72	30	45	75	67	30	8	0	—	—	—	—	—
92-93—New York Islanders....	NHL	70	33	42	75	108	13	5	3	18	6	6	12	31
93-94—New York Islanders....	NHL	83	36	33	69	73	-7	9	5	4	0	1	1	4
94-95—New York Islanders....	NHL	33	6	4	10	34	0	1	0	—	—	—	—	—
—Toronto	NHL	12	3	3	6	0	0	1	0	7	0	0	0	6
95-96—Toronto	NHL	44	12	25	37	68	6	3	0	—	—	—	—	—
—Dallas........................	NHL	34	7	20	27	36	4	2	0	—	—	—	—	—
96-97—Dallas........................	NHL	73	19	24	43	54	8	5	0	7	2	2	4	6
NHL totals (10 years)		617	191	263	454	715	44	37	10	49	11	10	21	84

H

HOHENBERGER, MARTIN — LW — CANADIENS

PERSONAL: Born January 29, 1977, in Villach, Austria. ... 6-1/205. ... Shoots left. ... Name pronounced HOH-ihn-BUHR-guhr.
TRANSACTIONS/CAREER NOTES: Selected by Montreal Canadiens in third round (third Canadiens pick, 74th overall) of NHL entry draft (July 8, 1995).

		REGULAR SEASON								PLAYOFFS				
Season Team	League	Gms.	G	A	Pts.	PIM	+/-	PP	SH	Gms.	G	A	Pts.	PIM
93-94— Victoria	WHL	61	3	13	16	28	...	...	...	—	—	—	—	—
94-95— Prince George	WHL	47	10	21	31	81	...	...	...	—	—	—	—	—
95-96— Prince George	WHL	37	10	19	29	19	...	...	...	—	—	—	—	—
— Lethbridge	WHL	20	5	1	6	21	...	...	...	4	0	3	3	4
96-97— Lethbridge	WHL	57	26	33	59	74	...	...	...	19	7	13	20	15

HOLDEN, JOSH — C — CANUCKS

PERSONAL: Born January 18, 1978, in Calgary. ... 6-0/170. ... Shoots left.
TRANSACTIONS/CAREER NOTES: Selected by Vancouver Canucks in first round (first Canucks pick, 12th overall) of NHL entry draft (June 22, 1996).

		REGULAR SEASON								PLAYOFFS				
Season Team	League	Gms.	G	A	Pts.	PIM	+/-	PP	SH	Gms.	G	A	Pts.	PIM
94-95— Regina	WHL	62	20	23	43	45	...	...	...	4	3	1	4	0
95-96— Regina	WHL	70	57	55	112	105	...	...	...	11	4	5	9	23
96-97— Regina	WHL	58	49	49	98	148	...	...	...	5	3	2	5	10

HOLIK, BOBBY — RW — DEVILS

PERSONAL: Born January 1, 1971, in Jihlava, Czechoslovakia. ... 6-3/22. ... Shoots right. ... Name pronounced hoh-LEEK.
TRANSACTIONS/CAREER NOTES: Selected by Hartford Whalers in first round (first Whalers pick, 10th overall) of NHL entry draft (June 17, 1989). ... Broke right thumb (February 1990). ... Traded by Whalers with second-round pick (LW Jay Pandolfo) in 1993 draft and future considerations to New Jersey Devils for G Sean Burke and D Eric Weinrich (August 28, 1992). ... Fractured right thumb (January 22, 1993); missed 22 games. ... Bruised left shoulder (December 8, 1993); missed 11 games. ... Broke left index finger (October 7, 1995); missed 13 games. ... Sprained left ankle (February 28, 1996); missed six games.
STATISTICAL PLATEAUS: Three-goal games: 1992-93 (2).
MISCELLANEOUS: Member of Stanley Cup championship team (1995).

		REGULAR SEASON								PLAYOFFS				
Season Team	League	Gms.	G	A	Pts.	PIM	+/-	PP	SH	Gms.	G	A	Pts.	PIM
87-88— Dukla Jihlava	Czech.	31	5	9	14	...	...	...	...	—	—	—	—	—
88-89— Dukla Jihlava	Czech.	24	7	10	17	...	...	...	...	—	—	—	—	—
89-90— Czech. nat'l team	Int'l	10	1	5	6	0	...	...	...	—	—	—	—	—
— Dukla Jihlava	Czech.	42	15	26	41	...	...	...	...	—	—	—	—	—
90-91— Hartford	NHL	78	21	22	43	113	-3	8	0	6	0	0	0	7
91-92— Hartford	NHL	76	21	24	45	44	4	1	0	7	0	1	1	6
92-93— Utica	AHL	1	0	0	0	2	...	...	...	—	—	—	—	—
— New Jersey	NHL	61	20	19	39	76	-6	7	0	5	1	1	2	6
93-94— New Jersey	NHL	70	13	20	33	72	28	2	0	20	0	3	3	6
94-95— New Jersey	NHL	48	10	10	20	18	9	0	0	20	4	4	8	22
95-96— New Jersey	NHL	63	13	17	30	58	9	1	0	—	—	—	—	—
96-97— New Jersey	NHL	82	23	39	62	54	24	5	0	10	2	3	5	4
NHL totals (7 years)		478	121	151	272	435	65	24	0	68	7	12	19	51

HOLLAND, JASON — D — ISLANDERS

PERSONAL: Born April 30, 1976, in Morinville, Alta. ... 6-3/195. ... Shoots right.
HIGH SCHOOL: Norkam (Kamloops, B.C.).
TRANSACTIONS/CAREER NOTES: Selected by New York Islanders in second round (second Islanders pick, 38th overall) of NHL entry draft (June 28, 1994).
HONORS: Named to Can.HL All-Star second team (1995-96). ... Named to WHL (West) All-Star first team (1995-96). ... Named to AHL All-Rookie team (1996-97).

		REGULAR SEASON								PLAYOFFS				
Season Team	League	Gms.	G	A	Pts.	PIM	+/-	PP	SH	Gms.	G	A	Pts.	PIM
92-93— Kamloops	WHL	4	0	0	0	2	...	...	...	—	—	—	—	—
93-94— Kamloops	WHL	59	14	15	29	80	...	...	...	18	2	3	5	4
94-95— Kamloops	WHL	71	9	32	41	65	...	...	...	21	2	7	9	9
95-96— Kamloops	WHL	63	24	33	57	98	...	...	...	16	4	9	13	22
96-97— Kentucky	AHL	72	14	25	39	46	...	...	...	4	0	2	2	0
— New York Islanders	NHL	4	1	0	1	0	1	0	0	—	—	—	—	—
NHL totals (1 year)		4	1	0	1	0	1	0	0					

HOLLINGER, TERRY — D — SABRES

PERSONAL: Born February 24, 1971, in Regina, Sask. ... 6-1/200. ... Shoots left. ... Name pronounced HAHL-ihn-juhr.
TRANSACTIONS/CAREER NOTES: Selected by St. Louis Blues in sixth round (sixth Blues pick, 153rd overall) of NHL entry draft (June 22, 1991). ... Signed as free agent by Buffalo Sabres (August 16, 1995).
HONORS: Named to AHL All-Star second team (1995-96). ... Named to AHL All-Star first team (1996-97).

Season Team	League	REGULAR SEASON								PLAYOFFS				
		Gms.	G	A	Pts.	PIM	+/-	PP	SH	Gms.	G	A	Pts.	PIM
87-88— Regina	WHL	7	1	1	2	4	...	...	...	—	—	—	—	—
88-89— Regina	WHL	65	2	27	29	49	...	...	...	—	—	—	—	—
89-90— Regina	WHL	70	14	43	57	40	...	...	...	11	1	3	4	10
90-91— Regina	WHL	8	1	6	7	6	...	...	...	—	—	—	—	—
— Lethbridge	WHL	62	9	32	41	113	...	...	...	16	3	14	17	22
91-92— Lethbridge	WHL	65	23	62	85	155	...	...	...	5	1	2	3	13
— Peoria	IHL	1	0	2	2	0	...	...	...	5	0	1	1	0
92-93— Peoria	IHL	72	2	28	30	67	...	...	...	4	1	1	2	0
93-94— Peoria	IHL	78	12	31	43	96	...	...	...	6	0	3	3	31
— St. Louis	NHL	2	0	0	0	0	1	0	0	—	—	—	—	—
94-95— Peoria	IHL	69	7	25	32	137	...	...	...	4	2	4	6	8
— St. Louis	NHL	5	0	0	0	2	-1	0	0	—	—	—	—	—
95-96— Rochester	AHL	62	5	50	55	71	...	...	...	19	3	11	14	12
96-97— Rochester	AHL	73	12	51	63	54	...	...	...	10	2	7	9	27
NHL totals (2 years)		7	0	0	0	2	0	0	0					

HOLMSTROM, TOMAS   LW   RED WINGS

PERSONAL: Born January 23, 1973, in Pitea, Sweden. ... 6-0/200. ... Shoots left.
TRANSACTIONS/CAREER NOTES: Selected by Detroit Red Wings in 10th round (ninth Red Wings pick, 257th overall) of NHL entry draft (June 29, 1994). ... Sprained knee (October 30, 1996); missed seven games. ... Bruised shoulder (March 28, 1997); missed one game.
MISCELLANEOUS: Member of Stanley Cup championship team (1997).

Season Team	League	REGULAR SEASON								PLAYOFFS				
		Gms.	G	A	Pts.	PIM	+/-	PP	SH	Gms.	G	A	Pts.	PIM
94-95— Lulea	Sweden	40	14	14	28	56	...	...	...	8	1	2	3	20
95-96— Lulea	Sweden	34	12	11	23	78	...	...	...	11	6	2	8	22
96-97— Detroit	NHL	47	6	3	9	33	-10	3	0	1	0	0	0	0
— Adirondack	AHL	6	3	1	4	7	...	...	...	—	—	—	—	—
NHL totals (1 year)		47	6	3	9	33	-10	3	0	1	0	0	0	0

HOLZINGER, BRIAN   C   SABRES

PERSONAL: Born October 10, 1972, in Parma, Ohio. ... 5-11/190. ... Shoots right. ... Full name: Brian Alan Holzinger. ... Name pronounced HOHL-zihng-uhr.
HIGH SCHOOL: Parma (Ohio).
COLLEGE: Bowling Green State.
TRANSACTIONS/CAREER NOTES: Selected by Buffalo Sabres in sixth round (seventh Sabres pick, 124th overall) of NHL entry draft (June 22, 1991).
HONORS: Named to CCHA All-Star second team (1993-94). ... Won Hobey Baker Memorial Award (1994-95). ... Named to NCAA All-America West first team (1994-95). ... Named CCHA Player of the Year (1994-95). ... Named to CCHA All-Star first team (1994-95).

Season Team	League	REGULAR SEASON								PLAYOFFS				
		Gms.	G	A	Pts.	PIM	+/-	PP	SH	Gms.	G	A	Pts.	PIM
90-91— Det. Jr. Red Wings	NAJHL	37	45	41	86	16	...	...	...	—	—	—	—	—
91-92— Bowling Green	CCHA	30	14	8	22	36	...	...	...	—	—	—	—	—
92-93— Bowling Green	CCHA	41	31	26	57	44	...	...	...	—	—	—	—	—
93-94— Bowling Green	CCHA	38	22	15	37	24	...	...	...	—	—	—	—	—
94-95— Bowling Green	CCHA	38	35	34	69	42	...	...	...	—	—	—	—	—
— Buffalo	NHL	4	0	3	3	0	2	0	0	4	2	1	3	2
95-96— Buffalo	NHL	58	10	10	20	37	-21	5	0	—	—	—	—	—
— Rochester	AHL	17	10	11	21	14	...	...	...	19	10	14	24	10
96-97— Buffalo	NHL	81	22	29	51	54	9	2	2	12	2	5	7	8
NHL totals (3 years)		143	32	42	74	91	-10	7	2	16	4	6	10	10

HOUDA, DOUG   D   ISLANDERS

PERSONAL: Born June 3, 1966, in Blairmore, Alta. ... 6-2/190. ... Shoots right. ... Name pronounced HOO-duh.
TRANSACTIONS/CAREER NOTES: Selected by Detroit Red Wings as underage junior in second round (second Red Wings pick, 28th overall) of NHL entry draft (June 9, 1984). ... Fractured left cheekbone (September 23, 1988). ... Injured knee and underwent surgery (November 21, 1989). ... Traded by Red Wings to Hartford Whalers for D Doug Crossman (February 20, 1991). ... Separated shoulder (February 28, 1994); missed three games. ... Strained shoulder (March 15, 1994); missed two games. ... Traded by Whalers to Los Angeles Kings for RW Marc Potvin (November 3, 1993). ... Traded by Kings to Buffalo Sabres for D Sean O'Donnell (July 26, 1994). ... Severed tendon in hand (February 11, 1995); missed 12 games. ... Signed as free agent by New York Islanders (October 23, 1996).
HONORS: Named to WHL All-Star second team (1984-85). ... Named to AHL All-Star first team (1987-88).

Season Team	League	REGULAR SEASON								PLAYOFFS				
		Gms.	G	A	Pts.	PIM	+/-	PP	SH	Gms.	G	A	Pts.	PIM
81-82— Calgary	WHL	3	0	0	0	0	...	...	...	—	—	—	—	—
82-83— Calgary	WHL	71	5	23	28	99	...	...	...	16	1	3	4	44
83-84— Calgary	WHL	69	6	30	36	195	...	...	...	4	0	0	0	7
84-85— Calgary	WHL	65	20	54	74	182	...	...	...	8	3	4	7	29
— Kalamazoo	IHL	—	—	—	—	—	...	...	...	7	0	2	2	10
85-86— Calgary	WHL	16	4	10	14	60	...	...	...	—	—	—	—	—
— Medicine Hat	WHL	35	9	23	32	80	...	...	...	25	4	19	23	64
— Detroit	NHL	6	0	0	0	4	-7	0	0	—	—	—	—	—
86-87— Adirondack	AHL	77	6	23	29	142	...	...	...	11	1	8	9	50
87-88— Detroit	NHL	11	1	1	2	10	0	0	0	—	—	—	—	—
— Adirondack	AHL	71	10	32	42	169	...	...	...	11	0	3	3	44

H

REGULAR SEASON									PLAYOFFS				
Season Team	League	Gms.	G	A	Pts.	PIM	+/-	PP	SH	Gms.	G	A	Pts.	PIM
88-89— Adirondack.................	AHL	7	0	3	3	8	...	...	...	—	—	—	—	—
—Detroit......................	NHL	57	2	11	13	67	17	0	0	6	0	1	1	0
89-90— Detroit....................	NHL	73	2	9	11	127	-5	0	0	—	—	—	—	—
90-91— Adirondack.................	AHL	38	9	17	26	67	...	...	...	—	—	—	—	—
—Detroit......................	NHL	22	0	4	4	43	-2	0	0	—	—	—	—	—
—Hartford....................	NHL	19	1	2	3	41	-3	0	0	6	0	0	0	8
91-92— Hartford....................	NHL	56	3	6	9	125	-2	1	0	6	0	2	2	13
92-93— Hartford....................	NHL	60	2	6	8	167	-19	0	0	—	—	—	—	—
93-94— Hartford....................	NHL	7	0	0	0	23	-4	0	0	—	—	—	—	—
—Los Angeles..............	NHL	54	2	6	8	165	-15	0	0	—	—	—	—	—
94-95— Buffalo....................	NHL	28	1	2	3	68	1	0	0	—	—	—	—	—
95-96— Buffalo....................	NHL	38	1	3	4	52	3	0	0	—	—	—	—	—
—Rochester................	AHL	21	1	6	7	41	...	...	...	19	3	5	8	30
96-97— Utah......................	IHL	3	0	0	0	7	...	...	...	—	—	—	—	—
—New York Islanders....	NHL	70	2	8	10	99	1	0	0	—	—	—	—	—
NHL totals (11 years)		501	17	58	75	991	-35	1	0	18	0	3	3	21

HOUDE, ERIC   C   CANADIENS

PERSONAL: Born December 9, 1976, in Montreal. ... 5-11/185. ... Shoots left. ... Name pronounced UD.
COLLEGE: Saint Mary's (Halifax, Nova Scotia).
TRANSACTIONS/CAREER NOTES: Selected by Montreal Canadiens in ninth round (ninth Canadiens pick, 216th overall) of NHL entry draft (July 8, 1995).
HONORS: Named to AHL All-Rookie team (1996-97).

REGULAR SEASON									PLAYOFFS				
Season Team	League	Gms.	G	A	Pts.	PIM	+/-	PP	SH	Gms.	G	A	Pts.	PIM
93-94— St. Jean......................	QMJHL	71	16	16	32	14	...	...	...	5	1	1	2	4
94-95— St. Jean......................	QMJHL	40	10	13	23	23	...	...	...	—	—	—	—	—
—Halifax....................	QMJHL	28	13	23	36	8	...	...	...	3	2	1	3	4
95-96— Halifax....................	QMJHL	69	40	48	88	35	...	...	...	6	3	4	7	2
96-97— Fredericton..............	AHL	66	30	36	66	20	...	...	...	—	—	—	—	—
—Montreal	NHL	13	0	2	2	2	1	0	0	—	—	—	—	—
NHL totals (1 year)		13	0	2	2	2	1	0	0					

HOUGH, MIKE   LW   ISLANDERS

PERSONAL: Born February 6, 1963, in Montreal. ... 6-1/197. ... Shoots left. ... Name pronounced HUHF.
TRANSACTIONS/CAREER NOTES: Selected by Quebec Nordiques as underage junior in ninth round (seventh Nordiques pick, 181st overall) of NHL entry draft (June 9, 1982). ... Sprained left shoulder and developed tendinitis (November 5, 1989); missed 14 games. ... Broke right thumb (January 23, 1990); missed 12 games. ... Injured back (November 8, 1990); missed nine games. ... Separated left shoulder (January 15, 1991); missed three games. ... Suffered concussion (February 10, 1991). ... Injured knee (December 28, 1991); missed three games. ... Fractured left thumb (February 15, 1992); missed 14 games. ... Suffered concussion prior to 1992-93 season; missed first two games of season. ... Sprained right shoulder (April 6, 1993); missed four games. ... Traded by Nordiques to Washington Capitals for RW Paul MacDermid and RW Reggie Savage (June 20, 1993). ... Selected by Florida Panthers in NHL expansion draft (June 24, 1993). ... Hyperextended left knee (October 30, 1993); missed five games. ... Broke finger (January 22, 1996); missed five games. ... Bruised thigh (April 8, 1996); missed three games. ... Sprained knee (February 6, 1997); missed five games. ... Signed as free agent by New York Islanders (July 1, 1997).
MISCELLANEOUS: Captain of Quebec Nordiques (1991-92). ... Failed to score on a penalty shot (vs. Olaf Kolzig, February 29, 1996).

REGULAR SEASON									PLAYOFFS				
Season Team	League	Gms.	G	A	Pts.	PIM	+/-	PP	SH	Gms.	G	A	Pts.	PIM
80-81— Dixie......................	OPJHL	24	15	20	35	84	...	...	...	—	—	—	—	—
81-82— Kitchener	OHL	58	14	34	48	172	...	...	...	14	1	5	6	16
82-83— Kitchener	OHL	61	17	27	44	156	...	...	...	12	5	4	9	30
83-84— Fredericton.............	AHL	69	11	16	27	142	...	...	...	1	0	0	0	7
84-85— Fredericton.............	AHL	76	21	27	48	49	...	...	...	6	1	1	2	2
85-86— Fredericton.............	AHL	74	21	33	54	68	...	...	...	6	0	3	3	8
86-87— Quebec..................	NHL	56	6	8	14	79	-8	1	1	9	0	3	3	26
—Fredericton.............	AHL	10	1	3	4	20	...	...	...	—	—	—	—	—
87-88— Fredericton.............	AHL	46	16	25	41	133	...	...	...	15	4	8	12	55
—Quebec..................	NHL	17	3	2	5	2	-8	0	0	—	—	—	—	—
88-89— Halifax....................	AHL	22	11	10	21	87	...	...	...	—	—	—	—	—
—Quebec..................	NHL	46	9	10	19	39	-7	1	3	—	—	—	—	—
89-90— Quebec..................	NHL	43	13	13	26	84	-24	3	1	—	—	—	—	—
90-91— Quebec..................	NHL	63	13	20	33	111	-7	1	1	—	—	—	—	—
91-92— Quebec..................	NHL	61	16	22	38	77	-1	6	2	—	—	—	—	—
92-93— Quebec..................	NHL	77	8	22	30	69	-11	2	1	6	0	1	1	2
93-94— Florida....................	NHL	78	6	23	29	62	3	0	1	—	—	—	—	—
94-95— Florida....................	NHL	48	6	7	13	38	1	0	0	—	—	—	—	—
95-96— Florida....................	NHL	64	7	16	23	37	4	0	1	22	4	1	5	8
96-97— Florida....................	NHL	69	8	6	14	48	12	0	0	5	1	0	1	2
NHL totals (11 years)		622	95	149	244	646	-46	14	11	42	5	5	10	38

H

HOULDER, BILL   D   SHARKS

PERSONAL: Born March 11, 1967, in Thunder Bay, Ont. ... 6-3/218. ... Shoots left.
TRANSACTIONS/CAREER NOTES: Selected by Washington Capitals as underage junior in fourth round (fourth Capitals pick, 82nd overall) of NHL entry draft (June 15, 1985). ... Pulled groin (January 1989). ... Traded by Capitals to Buffalo Sabres for D Shawn Anderson (September

30, 1990). ... Selected by Mighty Ducks of Anaheim in NHL expansion draft (June 24, 1993). ... Traded by Mighty Ducks to St. Louis Blues for D Jason Marshall (August 29, 1994). ... Signed as free agent by Tampa Bay Lightning (August 1, 1995). ... Pulled groin (October 7, 1995); missed two games. ... Injured ribs (November 8, 1995); missed four games. ... Pulled groin (February 3, 1996); missed three games. ... Reinjured groin (March 5, 1996); missed six games. ... Reinjured groin (March 26, 1996); missed five games. ... Bruised wrist (November 4, 1996); missed three games. ... Signed as free agent by San Jose Sharks (July 9, 1997).

HONORS: Named to AHL All-Star first team (1990-91). ... Won Governors Trophy (1992-93). ... Named to IHL All-Star first team (1992-93).

Season Team	League	REGULAR SEASON								PLAYOFFS				
		Gms.	G	A	Pts.	PIM	+/-	PP	SH	Gms.	G	A	Pts.	PIM
83-84— Thunder Bay	TBAHA	23	4	18	22	37	...	...	...	—	—	—	—	—
84-85— North Bay	OHL	66	4	20	24	37	...	...	...	8	0	0	0	2
85-86— North Bay	OHL	59	5	30	35	97	...	...	...	10	1	6	7	12
86-87— North Bay	OHL	62	17	51	68	68	...	...	...	22	4	19	23	20
87-88— Washington	NHL	30	1	2	3	10	-2	0	0	—	—	—	—	—
— Fort Wayne	IHL	43	10	14	24	32	...			—	—	—	—	—
88-89— Baltimore	AHL	65	10	36	46	50	...			—	—	—	—	—
— Washington	NHL	8	0	3	3	4	7	0	0	—	—	—	—	—
89-90— Baltimore	AHL	26	3	7	10	12	...			7	0	2	2	2
— Washington	NHL	41	1	11	12	28	8	0	0	—	—	—	—	—
90-91— Rochester	AHL	69	13	53	66	28	...			15	5	13	18	4
— Buffalo	NHL	7	0	2	2	4	-2	0	0	—	—	—	—	—
91-92— Rochester	AHL	42	8	26	34	16	...			16	5	6	11	4
— Buffalo	NHL	10	1	0	1	8	-2	0	0	—	—	—	—	—
92-93— San Diego	IHL	64	24	48	72	39	...			—	—	—	—	—
— Buffalo	NHL	15	3	5	8	6	5	0	0	8	0	2	2	4
93-94— Anaheim	NHL	80	14	25	39	40	-18	3	0	—	—	—	—	—
94-95— St. Louis	NHL	41	5	13	18	20	16	1	0	4	1	1	2	0
95-96— Tampa Bay	NHL	61	5	23	28	22	1	3	0	6	0	1	1	4
96-97— Tampa Bay	NHL	79	4	21	25	30	16	0	0	—	—	—	—	—
NHL totals (10 years)		372	34	105	139	172	29	7	0	18	1	4	5	8

HOULE, JEAN-FRANCOIS   LW   CANADIENS

PERSONAL: Born January 14, 1975, in La Salle, Que. ... 5-9/180. ... Shoots left. ... Son of Rejean Houle, left winger/right winger, Montreal Canadiens (1969-70 through 1972-73 and 1976-77 through 1982-83) and Quebec Nordiques of WHA (1973-74 through 1975-76).
HIGH SCHOOL: Northwood (Lake Placid, N.Y.).
COLLEGE: Clarkson (N.Y.).
TRANSACTIONS/CAREER NOTES: Selected by Montreal Canadiens in fourth round (fifth Canadiens pick, 99th overall) of NHL entry draft (June 26, 1993).

Season Team	League	REGULAR SEASON								PLAYOFFS				
		Gms.	G	A	Pts.	PIM	+/-	PP	SH	Gms.	G	A	Pts.	PIM
92-93— Northwood School	N.Y. H.S.	28	37	45	82	...	...	...	...	—	—	—	—	—
93-94— Clarkson	ECAC	34	6	19	25	18	...			—	—	—	—	—
94-95— Clarkson	ECAC	34	8	11	19	42	...			—	—	—	—	—
95-96— Clarkson	ECAC	38	14	15	29	46	...			—	—	—	—	—
96-97— Clarkson	ECAC	37	21	37	58	40	...			—	—	—	—	—

HOUSE, BOBBY   RW   DEVILS

PERSONAL: Born January 7, 1973, in Whitehorse, Yukon. ... 6-1/200. ... Shoots right. ... Name pronounced HOUZ.
TRANSACTIONS/CAREER NOTES: Traded by Spokane Chiefs with Marty Murray and G Don Blishen to Brandon Wheat Kings for G Trevor Kidd and Bart Cote (January 21, 1991). ... Selected by Chicago Blackhawks in third round (fourth Blackhawks pick, 66th overall) of NHL entry draft (June 22, 1991). ... Traded by Blackhawks to New Jersey Devils (February 15, 1995).
HONORS: Named to WHL (East) All-Star second team (1992-93).

Season Team	League	REGULAR SEASON								PLAYOFFS				
		Gms.	G	A	Pts.	PIM	+/-	PP	SH	Gms.	G	A	Pts.	PIM
88-89— Houjens	Yukon Sr.	28	36	27	63	28	...	...	...	—	—	—	—	—
89-90— Spokane	WHL	64	18	16	34	74	...			5	0	0	0	6
90-91— Spokane	WHL	38	11	19	30	63	...			—	—	—	—	—
— Brandon	WHL	23	18	7	25	14	...			—	—	—	—	—
91-92— Brandon	WHL	71	35	42	77	133	...			—	—	—	—	—
92-93— Brandon	WHL	61	57	39	96	87	...			4	2	2	4	0
93-94— Indianapolis	IHL	42	10	8	18	51	...			—	—	—	—	—
— Flint	Col.HL	4	3	3	6	0	...			—	—	—	—	—
94-95— Indianapolis	IHL	26	2	3	5	26	...			—	—	—	—	—
— Columbus	ECHL	9	11	6	17	2	...			—	—	—	—	—
— Albany	AHL	26	4	7	11	12	...			8	1	1	2	0
95-96— Albany	AHL	77	37	49	86	57	...			4	0	0	0	4
96-97— Albany	AHL	68	18	16	34	65	...			16	3	2	5	23

HOUSLEY, PHIL   D   CAPITALS

PERSONAL: Born March 9, 1964, in St. Paul, Minn. ... 5-10/185. ... Shoots left.
HIGH SCHOOL: South St. Paul (Minn.).
TRANSACTIONS/CAREER NOTES: Selected by Buffalo Sabres as underage player in first round (first Sabres pick, sixth overall) of NHL entry draft (June 9, 1982). ... Bruised shoulder (January 1984). ... Suspended three games by NHL (October 1984). ... Injured back (November 1987). ... Bruised back (January 12, 1989). ... Suffered hip pointer and bruised back (March 18, 1989). ... Pulled shoulder ligaments while playing at World Cup Tournament (April 1989). ... Traded by Sabres with LW Scott Arniel, RW Jeff Parker and first-round pick (C Keith

H

Tkachuk) in 1990 draft to Winnipeg Jets for C Dale Hawerchuk and first-round pick (LW Brad May) in 1990 draft (June 16, 1990). ... Strained abdomen (February 26, 1992); missed five games. ... Strained groin (October 31, 1992); missed two games. ... Sprained wrist (January 19, 1993); missed two games. ... Traded by Jets to St. Louis Blues for RW Nelson Emerson and D Stephane Quintal (September 24, 1993). ... Suffered back spasms (October 26, 1993); missed five games. ... Suffered sore back (November 18, 1993). ... Underwent back surgery (January 4, 1994); missed 53 games. ... Traded by Blues with second-round picks in 1996 (C Steve Begin) and 1997 (RW John Tripp) drafts to Calgary Flames for free-agent rights to D Al MacInnis and fourth-round pick (D Didier Tremblay) in 1997 draft (July 4, 1994). ... Played in Europe during 1994-95 NHL lockout. ... Crushed right pinky (February 9, 1995); missed five games. ... Suffered from the flu (January 10, 1996); missed two games. ... Suffered from the flu (January 17, 1996); missed one game. ... Traded by Flames with D Dan Keczmer to New Jersey Devils for D Tommy Albelin, D Cale Hulse and LW Jocelyn Lemieux (February 26, 1996). ... Signed as free agent by Washington Capitals (July 22, 1996). ... Strained groin (March 16, 1997); missed five games.
HONORS: Named to NHL All-Rookie team (1982-83). ... Played in NHL All-Star Game (1984 and 1989-1993). ... Named to THE SPORTING NEWS All-Star second team (1991-92). ... Named to NHL All-Star second team (1991-92).
STATISTICAL PLATEAUS: Three-goal games: 1982-83 (1), 1987-88 (1). Total: 2.
MISCELLANEOUS: Failed to score on a penalty shot (vs. Curtis Joseph, December 19, 1992). ... Member of Team U.S.A. at World Junior Championships and World Cup Tournament (1982).

		REGULAR SEASON								PLAYOFFS				
Season Team	League	Gms.	G	A	Pts.	PIM	+/-	PP	SH	Gms.	G	A	Pts.	PIM
80-81— St. Paul	USHL	6	7	7	14	6	...	...	...	—	—	—	—	—
81-82— South St. Paul	Minn. H.S.	22	31	34	65	18	...	...	...	—	—	—	—	—
82-83— Buffalo	NHL	77	19	47	66	39	-4	11	0	10	3	4	7	2
83-84— Buffalo	NHL	75	31	46	77	33	4	13	2	3	0	0	0	6
84-85— Buffalo	NHL	73	16	53	69	28	15	3	0	5	3	2	5	2
85-86— Buffalo	NHL	79	15	47	62	54	-9	7	0	—	—	—	—	—
86-87— Buffalo	NHL	78	21	46	67	57	-2	8	1	—	—	—	—	—
87-88— Buffalo	NHL	74	29	37	66	96	-17	6	0	6	2	4	6	6
88-89— Buffalo	NHL	72	26	44	70	47	6	5	0	5	1	3	4	2
89-90— Buffalo	NHL	80	21	60	81	32	11	8	1	6	1	4	5	4
90-91— Winnipeg	NHL	78	23	53	76	24	-13	12	1	—	—	—	—	—
91-92— Winnipeg	NHL	74	23	63	86	92	-5	11	0	7	1	4	5	0
92-93— Winnipeg	NHL	80	18	79	97	52	-14	6	0	6	0	7	7	2
93-94— St. Louis	NHL	26	7	15	22	12	-5	4	0	4	2	1	3	4
94-95— Grasshoppers	Switz. Div. II	10	6	8	14	34	...	...	...	—	—	—	—	—
—Calgary	NHL	43	8	35	43	18	17	3	0	7	0	9	9	0
95-96— Calgary	NHL	59	16	36	52	22	-2	6	0	—	—	—	—	—
—New Jersey	NHL	22	1	15	16	8	-4	0	0	—	—	—	—	—
96-97— Washington	NHL	77	11	29	40	24	-10	3	1	—	—	—	—	—
NHL totals (15 years)		1067	285	705	990	638	-32	106	6	59	13	38	51	28

HRDINA, JAN   RW   PENGUINS

PERSONAL: Born February 5, 1976, in Hradec Kralove, Czechoslovakia. ... 5-11/180. ... Shoots right. ... Name pronounced YAHN huhr-DEE-nuh.
TRANSACTIONS/CAREER NOTES: Selected by Pittsburgh Penguins in fifth round (fourth Penguins pick, 128th overall) of NHL entry draft (July 8, 1995).

		REGULAR SEASON								PLAYOFFS				
Season Team	League	Gms.	G	A	Pts.	PIM	+/-	PP	SH	Gms.	G	A	Pts.	PIM
93-94— Std. Hradec Kralove...	Czech Rep.	21	1	5	6	...	...	...	...	—	—	—	—	—
94-95— Seattle	WHL	69	41	59	100	79	...	...	...	4	0	1	1	8
95-96— Seattle	WHL	30	19	28	47	37	...	...	...	—	—	—	—	—
—Spokane	WHL	18	10	16	26	25	...	...	...	18	5	14	19	49
96-97— Cleveland	IHL	68	23	31	54	82	...	...	...	13	1	2	3	8

HRUDEY, KELLY   G   SHARKS

PERSONAL: Born January 13, 1961, in Edmonton. ... 5-10/190. ... Catches left. ... Full name: Kelly Stephen Hrudey. ... Name pronounced ROO-dee.
TRANSACTIONS/CAREER NOTES: Selected by New York Islanders as underage junior in second round (second Islanders pick, 38th overall) of NHL entry draft (June 11, 1980). ... Traded by Islanders to Los Angeles Kings for D Wayne McBean, G Mark Fitzpatrick and future considerations (February 27, 1989); Kings sent D Doug Crossman to Islanders to complete deal (May 23, 1989). ... Suffered from the flu (April 1989). ... Suffered from mononucleosis (February 1990); missed 14 games. ... Bruised ribs (April 20, 1990). ... Suffered from the flu (March 11, 1993); missed one game. ... Suffered from the flu (March 26, 1993); missed one game. ... Bruised right kneecap (January 22, 1995); missed four games. ... Sprained ankle during 1995-96 season; missed first 20 games of season. ... Signed as free agent by San Jose Sharks (July 18, 1996).
HONORS: Named to WHL All-Star second team (1980-81). ... Shared Terry Sawchuk Trophy with Robert Holland (1981-82 and 1982-83). ... Won Max McNab Trophy (1981-82). ... Named to CHL All-Star first team (1981-82 and 1982-83). ... Won Tommy Ivan Trophy (1982-83).
MISCELLANEOUS: Stopped a penalty shot attempt (vs. Ron Sutter, November 18, 1984; vs. Mats Sundin, February 2, 1993; vs. Pavel Bure, October 6, 1993; vs. Tony Amonte, January 27, 1994; vs. Sergei Fedorov, February 12, 1995; vs. Dirk Graham, March 9, 1995). ... Allowed a penalty shot goal (vs. Michel Goulet, January 26, 1984; vs. Bill Gardner, October 13, 1984; vs. Joe Mullen, December 2, 1986; vs. Mario Lemieux, January 19, 1988 and March 7, 1989; vs. Al MacInnis, April 4, 1990 (playoffs); vs. Norman Lacombe, February 5, 1991).

		REGULAR SEASON							PLAYOFFS					
Season Team	League	Gms.	Min	W	L	T	GA	SO	Avg.	Gms.	Min.	W	L	GA	SO	Avg.
78-79—Medicine Hat	WHL	57	3093	12	34	7	*318	0	6.17	—	—	—	—	—	—	—
79-80—Medicine Hat	WHL	57	3049	25	23	4	212	1	4.17	13	638	6	6	48	0	4.51
80-81—Medicine Hat	WHL	55	3023	32	19	1	200	†4	3.97	4	244	...	...	17	0	4.18
—Indianapolis	CHL	—	—	—	—	—	—	—	—	2	135	...	...	8	0	3.56
81-82—Indianapolis	CHL	51	3033	27	19	4	149	1	*2.95	13	842	11	2	34	*1	*2.42
82-83—Indianapolis	CHL	47	2744	26	17	1	139	2	3.04	10	†637	*7	3	28	0	*2.64
83-84—Indianapolis	CHL	6	370	3	2	1	21	0	3.41	—	—	—	—	—	—	—
—New York Islanders	NHL	12	535	7	2	0	28	0	3.14	—	—	—	—	—	—	—

		REGULAR SEASON								PLAYOFFS						
Season Team	League	Gms.	Min	W	L	T	GA	SO	Avg.	Gms.	Min.	W	L	GA	SO	Avg.
84-85 — New York Islanders	NHL	41	2335	19	17	3	141	2	3.62	5	281	1	3	8	0	1.71
85-86 — New York Islanders	NHL	45	2563	19	15	8	137	1	3.21	2	120	0	2	6	0	3.00
86-87 — New York Islanders	NHL	46	2634	21	15	7	145	0	3.30	14	842	7	7	38	0	2.71
87-88 — New York Islanders	NHL	47	2751	22	17	5	153	3	3.34	6	381	2	4	23	0	3.62
88-89 — New York Islanders	NHL	50	2800	18	24	3	183	0	3.92	—	—	—	—	—	—	—
— Los Angeles..................	NHL	16	974	10	4	2	47	1	2.90	10	566	4	6	35	0	3.71
89-90 — Los Angeles..................	NHL	52	2860	22	21	6	194	2	4.07	9	539	4	4	39	0	4.34
90-91 — Los Angeles..................	NHL	47	2730	26	13	6	132	3	2.90	12	798	6	6	37	0	2.78
91-92 — Los Angeles..................	NHL	60	3509	26	17	*13	197	1	3.37	6	355	2	4	22	0	3.72
92-93 — Los Angeles..................	NHL	50	2718	18	21	6	175	2	3.86	20	1261	10	10	74	0	3.52
93-94 — Los Angeles..................	NHL	64	3713	22	31	7	228	1	3.68	—	—	—	—	—	—	—
94-95 — Los Angeles..................	NHL	35	1894	14	13	5	99	0	3.14	—	—	—	—	—	—	—
95-96 — Los Angeles..................	NHL	36	2077	7	15	10	113	0	3.26	—	—	—	—	—	—	—
— Phoenix..................	IHL	1	50	0	1	0	5	0	6.00	—	—	—	—	—	—	—
96-97 — San Jose..................	NHL	48	2631	16	24	5	140	0	3.19	—	—	—	—	—	—	—
NHL totals (14 years)		649	36724	267	249	86	2112	16	3.45	84	5143	36	46	282	0	3.29

HUARD, BILL　　　　LW　　　　OILERS

PERSONAL: Born June 24, 1967, in Alland, Ont. ... 6-1/215. ... Shoots left. ... Name pronounced HYOO-uhrd.

TRANSACTIONS/CAREER NOTES: Signed as free agent by New Jersey Devils (October 1, 1989). ... Signed as free agent by Boston Bruins (December 4, 1992). ... Signed as free agent by Ottawa Senators (July 20, 1993). ... Injured hip (December 9, 1993); missed three games. ... Strained back (February 23, 1994); missed nine games. ... Strained groin (March 29, 1995); missed five games. ... Traded by Senators to Quebec Nordiques for rights to D Mika Stromberg and fourth-round pick (LW Kevin Boyd) in 1995 draft (April 7, 1995). ... Nordiques franchise moved to Colorado and renamed Avalanche for 1995-96 season (June 21, 1995). ... Claimed by Dallas Stars from Nordiques in NHL waiver draft (October 2, 1995). ... Separated shoulder (October 10, 1996); missed 11 games. ... Strained shoulder (November 20, 1996); missed three games. ... Signed as free agent by Edmonton Oilers (July 3, 1997).

		REGULAR SEASON							PLAYOFFS				
Season Team	League	Gms.	G	A	Pts.	PIM	+/-	PP	SH	Gms.	G	A	Pts.	PIM
86-87 — Peterborough.............	OHL	61	14	11	25	61	...	...	...	12	5	2	7	19
87-88 — Peterborough.............	OHL	66	28	33	61	132	...	...	...	12	7	8	15	33
88-89 — Carolina..................	ECHL	40	27	21	48	177	...	...	...	10	7	2	9	70
89-90 — Utica	AHL	27	1	7	8	67	...	...	...	5	0	1	1	33
— Nashville..................	ECHL	34	24	27	51	212	...	...	...	—	—	—	—	—
90-91 — Utica	AHL	72	11	16	27	359	...	...	...	—	—	—	—	—
91-92 — Utica	AHL	62	9	11	20	233	...	...	...	4	1	1	2	4
92-93 — Providence...............	AHL	72	18	19	37	302	...	...	...	6	3	0	3	9
— Boston..................	NHL	2	0	0	0	0	0	0	0	—	—	—	—	—
93-94 — Ottawa	NHL	63	2	2	4	162	-19	0	0	—	—	—	—	—
94-95 — Ottawa	NHL	26	1	1	2	64	-2	0	0	—	—	—	—	—
— Quebec..................	NHL	7	2	2	4	13	2	0	0	1	0	0	0	0
95-96 — Dallas..................	NHL	51	6	6	12	176	3	0	0	—	—	—	—	—
— Michigan..................	IHL	12	1	1	2	74	...	...	...	—	—	—	—	—
96-97 — Dallas..................	NHL	40	5	6	11	105	5	0	0	—	—	—	—	—
NHL totals (5 years)		189	16	17	33	520	-11	0	0	1	0	0	0	0

HUDDY, CHARLIE　　　　D

PERSONAL: Born June 2, 1959, in Oshawa, Ont. ... 6-0/210. ... Shoots left. ... Full name: Charles William Huddy. ... Name pronounced HUH-dee.

TRANSACTIONS/CAREER NOTES: Signed as free agent by Edmonton Oilers (September 14, 1979). ... Injured shoulder (November 10, 1980). ... Suffered back spasms (February 1986); missed three games. ... Broke finger (April 1986). ... Suffered hematoma of left thigh and underwent surgery (May 7, 1988); missed six playoff games. ... Strained hamstring (January 2, 1989). ... Sprained right ankle (December 22, 1990); missed 17 games. ... Broke left toe (February 16, 1991); missed nine games. ... Twisted back (March 1991). ... Selected by Minnesota North Stars in NHL expansion draft (May 30, 1991). ... Traded by North Stars with LW Randy Gilhen, RW Jim Thomson and fourth-round pick (D Alexei Zhitnik) in 1991 draft to Los Angeles Kings for C Todd Elik (June 22, 1991). ... Injured groin (October 10, 1991); missed seven games. ... Strained groin (November 7, 1991); missed five games. ... Bruised chest (February 1, 1992); missed seven games. ... Bruised chest (March 3, 1992); missed five games. ... Suffered from the flu (January 14, 1993); missed one game. ... Strained groin (October 27, 1993); missed five games. ... Traded by Kings with D Alexei Zhitnik, G Robb Stauber and fifth-round pick (D Marian Menhart) in 1995 draft to Buffalo Sabres for G Grant Fuhr, D Philippe Boucher and D Denis Tsygurov (February 14, 1995). ... Sprained knee (December 31, 1995); missed six games. ... Traded by Sabres with seventh-round pick in 1997 draft to St. Louis Blues for rights to LW Denis Hamel (March 19, 1996). ... Named player/assistant coach for Rochester of AHL (September 16, 1996); called up by Sabres on February 26, 1997.

HONORS: Won Emery Edge Award (1982-83).

MISCELLANEOUS: Member of Stanley Cup championship team (1984, 1985, 1987, 1988 and 1990).

		REGULAR SEASON							PLAYOFFS				
Season Team	League	Gms.	G	A	Pts.	PIM	+/-	PP	SH	Gms.	G	A	Pts.	PIM
77-78 — Oshawa..................	OMJHL	59	17	18	35	81	...	...	...	6	2	1	3	10
78-79 — Oshawa..................	OMJHL	64	20	38	58	108	...	...	...	5	3	4	7	12
79-80 — Houston..................	CHL	79	14	34	48	46	...	...	...	6	1	0	1	2
80-81 — Edmonton	NHL	12	2	5	7	6	-1	1	0	—	—	—	—	—
— Wichita..................	CHL	47	8	36	44	71	...	...	...	17	3	11	14	10
81-82 — Wichita..................	CHL	32	7	19	26	51	...	...	...	—	—	—	—	—
— Edmonton	NHL	41	4	11	15	46	17	0	0	5	1	2	3	14
82-83 — Edmonton	NHL	76	20	37	57	58	*62	7	0	15	1	6	7	10
83-84 — Edmonton	NHL	75	8	34	42	43	50	3	0	12	1	9	10	8
84-85 — Edmonton	NHL	80	7	44	51	46	50	3	0	18	3	17	20	17
85-86 — Edmonton	NHL	76	6	35	41	55	30	1	0	7	0	2	2	0

H

Season Team	League	REGULAR SEASON								PLAYOFFS				
		Gms.	G	A	Pts.	PIM	+/-	PP	SH	Gms.	G	A	Pts.	PIM
86-87— Edmonton	NHL	58	4	15	19	35	27	0	0	21	1	7	8	21
87-88— Edmonton	NHL	77	13	28	41	71	23	2	0	13	4	5	9	10
88-89— Edmonton	NHL	76	11	33	44	52	0	5	2	7	2	0	2	4
89-90— Edmonton	NHL	70	1	23	24	56	-13	1	0	22	0	6	6	11
90-91— Edmonton	NHL	53	5	22	27	32	4	2	0	18	3	7	10	10
91-92— Los Angeles	NHL	56	4	19	23	43	-10	2	1	6	1	1	2	10
92-93— Los Angeles	NHL	82	2	25	27	64	16	0	0	23	1	4	5	12
93-94— Los Angeles	NHL	79	5	13	18	71	4	1	0	—	—	—	—	—
94-95— Los Angeles	NHL	9	0	1	1	6	-6	0	0					
— Buffalo	NHL	32	2	4	6	36	-1	1	0	3	0	0	0	0
95-96— Buffalo	NHL	52	5	5	10	59	-5	2	0					
— St. Louis	NHL	12	0	0	0	6	-7	0	0	13	1	0	1	8
96-97— Rochester	AHL	63	6	8	14	36	...	...	...	4	0	0	0	0
— Buffalo	NHL	1	0	0	0	0	-1	0	0					
NHL totals (17 years)		1017	99	354	453	785	239	31	3	183	19	66	85	135

HUDSON, MIKE   C   COYOTES

PERSONAL: Born February 6, 1967, in Guelph, Ont. ... 6-1/205. ... Shoots left.

TRANSACTIONS/CAREER NOTES: Traded by Hamilton Steelhawks with D Keith Vanrooyen to Sudbury Wolves for C Brad Belland (October 1985). ... Selected by Chicago Blackhawks as underage junior in seventh round (sixth Blackhawks pick, 140th overall) of NHL entry draft (June 21, 1986). ... Cut right hand (December 21, 1989); missed 12 games. ... Suffered elbow tendinitis (September 1990). ... Underwent elbow surgery (May 1991). ... Suffered viral infection (December 20, 1992); missed 21 games. ... Traded by Blackhawks to Edmonton Oilers for D Craig Muni (March 22, 1993). ... Suffered nerve disorder in left shoulder (March 1993); missed two games. ... Fractured left hand (October 9, 1993); missed 16 games. ... Selected by New York Rangers in 1993 waiver draft (October 3, 1993). ... Suspended one game for high-sticking incident (March 13, 1994). ... Suspended 10 games and fined $500 by NHL for hitting another player with a two-handed swing (March 16, 1994). ... Selected by Pittsburgh Penguins in 1994-95 waiver draft for cash (January 18, 1995). ... Strained upper back (April 11, 1995); missed three games. ... Suffered stiff neck (April 22, 1995); missed three games. ... Suffered stiff neck (May 2, 1995); missed last two games of season. ... Signed as free agent by Toronto Maple Leafs (August 28, 1995). ... Sprained shoulder (September 30, 1995); missed two games. ... Bruised ankle (November 24, 1995); missed two games. ... Claimed on waivers by St. Louis Blues (January 4, 1996). ... Bruised thigh (February 16, 1996); missed four games. ... Injured neck (April 3, 1996); missed five games. ... Signed as free agent by Phoenix Coyotes (November 12, 1996).

MISCELLANEOUS: Member of Stanley Cup championship team (1994). ... Failed to score on a penalty shot (vs. Chris Osgood, November 18, 1996).

Season Team	League	REGULAR SEASON								PLAYOFFS				
		Gms.	G	A	Pts.	PIM	+/-	PP	SH	Gms.	G	A	Pts.	PIM
84-85— Hamilton	OHL	50	10	12	22	13	...	...	...	—	—	—	—	—
85-86— Hamilton	OHL	7	3	2	5	4	...	...	...	—	—	—	—	—
— Sudbury	OHL	59	35	42	77	20	...	...	...	4	2	5	7	7
86-87— Sudbury	OHL	63	40	57	97	18	...	...	...	—	—	—	—	—
87-88— Saginaw	IHL	75	18	30	48	44	...	...	...	10	2	3	5	20
88-89— Chicago	NHL	41	7	16	23	20	-12	0	1	10	1	2	3	18
— Saginaw	IHL	30	15	17	32	10	...	...	...					
89-90— Chicago	NHL	49	9	12	21	56	-3	0	0	4	0	0	0	2
90-91— Chicago	NHL	55	7	9	16	62	5	0	0	6	0	2	2	8
— Indianapolis	IHL	3	1	2	3	0	...	...	...					
91-92— Chicago	NHL	76	14	15	29	92	-11	2	1	16	3	5	8	26
92-93— Chicago	NHL	36	1	6	7	44	-6	0	0	—	—	—	—	—
— Edmonton	NHL	5	0	1	1	2	-1	0	0					
93-94— New York Rangers	NHL	48	4	7	11	47	-5	0	0	—	—	—	—	—
94-95— Pittsburgh	NHL	40	2	9	11	34	-1	0	0	11	0	0	0	6
95-96— Toronto	NHL	27	2	0	2	29	-5	0	0	—	—	—	—	—
— St. Louis	NHL	32	3	12	15	26	7	0	0	2	0	1	1	4
96-97— Phoenix	NHL	7	0	0	0	2	-4	0	0	—	—	—	—	—
— Phoenix	IHL	33	6	9	15	10	...	...	...					
NHL totals (9 years)		416	49	87	136	414	-36	2	2	49	4	10	14	64

HUFFMAN, KERRY   D

PERSONAL: Born January 3, 1968, in Peterborough, Ont. ... 6-2/214. ... Shoots left. ... Brother-in-law of Mike Posavad, defenseman, St. Louis Blues (1985-86 and 1986-87).

TRANSACTIONS/CAREER NOTES: Selected by Philadelphia Flyers as underage junior in first round (first Flyers pick, 20th overall) of NHL entry draft (June 21, 1986). ... Sprained ankle (November 1987). ... Suffered calcium deposits in thigh (January 1988); missed 22 games. ... Bruised right knee (March 15, 1990). ... Suspended by Flyers after leaving team in dispute over ice time (November 16, 1990). ... Returned to Flyers (December 10, 1990). ... Suffered from tonsillitis (October 1991); missed one game. ... Traded by Flyers with G Ron Hextall, C Mike Ricci, C Peter Forsberg, D Steve Duchesne, first-round pick (Jocelyn Thibault) in 1993 draft, cash and future considerations to Quebec Nordiques for C Eric Lindros (June 20, 1992); Flyers sent LW Chris Simon and first-round pick (traded to Toronto) in 1994 draft to Nordiques to complete deal (July 21, 1992). ... Broke ribs (October 17, 1992); missed three games. ... Injured shoulder (November 28, 1992); missed 14 games. ... Fractured finger (March 8, 1993); missed 10 games. ... Claimed on waivers by Ottawa Senators (January 15, 1994). ... Suffered back spasms (March 23, 1994); missed two games. ... Injured groin (February 1, 1995); missed two games. ... Injured shoulder (April 24, 1995); missed remainder of season. ... Injured left knee (December 26, 1995); missed seven games. ... Fractured left wrist (February 3, 1996); missed 25 games. ... Traded by Senators to Philadelphia Flyers for future considerations (March 19, 1996).

HONORS: Won Max Kaminsky Trophy (1986-87). ... Named to OHL All-Star first team (1986-87).

H

Season Team	League	REGULAR SEASON								PLAYOFFS				
		Gms.	G	A	Pts.	PIM	+/-	PP	SH	Gms.	G	A	Pts.	PIM
84-85— Peterborough Jr. B	OHA	24	2	5	7	53	...	...	...	—	—	—	—	—
85-86— Guelph	OHL	56	3	24	27	35	...	...	...	20	1	10	11	10
86-87— Guelph	OHL	44	4	31	35	20	...	...	...	5	0	2	2	8
— Hershey	AHL	3	0	1	1	0	...	...	...	4	0	0	0	0
— Philadelphia	NHL	9	0	0	0	2	...	...	...	—	—	—	—	—

Season Team	League	REGULAR SEASON								PLAYOFFS				
		Gms.	G	A	Pts.	PIM	+/-	PP	SH	Gms.	G	A	Pts.	PIM
87-88— Philadelphia	NHL	52	6	17	23	34	...	...	...	2	0	0	0	0
88-89— Hershey	AHL	29	2	13	15	16	...	...	...	—	—	—	—	—
— Philadelphia	NHL	29	0	11	11	31	...	...	...	—	—	—	—	—
89-90— Philadelphia	NHL	43	1	12	13	34	-3	0	0	—	—	—	—	—
90-91— Hershey	AHL	45	5	29	34	20	...	...	...	7	1	2	3	0
— Philadelphia	NHL	10	1	2	3	10	1	0	0	—	—	—	—	—
91-92— Philadelphia	NHL	60	14	18	32	41	1	4	0	—	—	—	—	—
92-93— Quebec.....................	NHL	52	4	18	22	54	0	3	0	3	0	0	0	0
93-94— Quebec.....................	NHL	28	0	6	6	28	2	0	0	—	—	—	—	—
— Ottawa....................	NHL	34	4	8	12	12	-30	2	1	—	—	—	—	—
94-95— Ottawa....................	NHL	37	2	4	6	46	-17	2	0	—	—	—	—	—
95-96— Ottawa....................	NHL	43	4	11	15	63	-18	3	0	—	—	—	—	—
— Philadelphia	NHL	4	1	1	2	6	0	0	0	6	0	0	0	2
96-97— Las Vegas	IHL	44	5	19	24	38	...	...	...	3	0	0	0	2
NHL totals (10 years)		**401**	**37**	**108**	**145**	**361**	**-64**	**14**	**1**	**11**	**0**	**0**	**0**	**2**

HUGHES, BRENT — LW — ISLANDERS

PERSONAL: Born April 5, 1966, in New Westminster, B.C. ... 5-11/180. ... Shoots left. ... Full name: Brent Allen Hughes.
TRANSACTIONS/CAREER NOTES: Traded by New Westminster Bruins to Victoria Cougars for future considerations (October 1986). ... Signed as free agent by Winnipeg Jets (July 1987). ... Traded by Jets with LW Craig Duncanson and C Simon Wheeldon to Washington Capitals for LW Bob Joyce, D Kent Paynter and C Tyler Larter (May 21, 1991). ... Traded by Capitals with future considerations to Boston Bruins for RW John Byce and D Dennis Smith (February 24, 1992). ... Separated shoulder (November 28, 1992); missed 11 games. ... Claimed by Buffalo Sabres from Bruins in waiver draft (October 2, 1995). ... Signed as free agent by New York Islanders (July 25, 1996).
HONORS: Named to WHL (West) All-Star first team (1986-87).

Season Team	League	REGULAR SEASON								PLAYOFFS				
		Gms.	G	A	Pts.	PIM	+/-	PP	SH	Gms.	G	A	Pts.	PIM
83-84— New Westminster	WHL	67	21	18	39	133	...	...	...	9	2	2	4	27
84-85— New Westminster	WHL	64	25	32	57	135	...	...	...	11	2	1	3	37
85-86— New Westminster	WHL	71	28	52	80	180	...	...	...	—	—	—	—	—
86-87— New Westminster	WHL	8	5	4	9	22	...	...	...	—	—	—	—	—
— Victoria	WHL	61	38	61	99	146	...	...	...	5	4	1	5	8
87-88— Moncton	AHL	77	13	19	32	206	...	...	...	—	—	—	—	—
88-89— Winnipeg	NHL	28	3	2	5	82	-7	0	1	—	—	—	—	—
— Moncton	AHL	54	34	34	68	286	...	...	...	10	9	4	13	40
89-90— Moncton	AHL	65	31	29	60	277	...	...	...	—	—	—	—	—
— Winnipeg	NHL	11	1	2	3	33	-4	0	0	—	—	—	—	—
90-91— Moncton	AHL	63	21	22	43	144	...	...	...	3	0	0	0	7
91-92— Baltimore	AHL	55	25	29	54	190	...	...	...	—	—	—	—	—
— Maine	AHL	12	6	4	10	34	...	...	...	—	—	—	—	—
— Boston	NHL	8	1	1	2	38	1	0	0	10	2	0	2	20
92-93— Boston	NHL	62	5	4	9	191	-4	0	0	1	0	0	0	2
93-94— Providence	AHL	6	2	5	7	4	...	...	...	—	—	—	—	—
— Boston	NHL	77	13	11	24	143	10	1	0	13	2	1	3	27
94-95— Boston	NHL	44	6	6	12	139	6	0	0	5	0	0	0	4
95-96— Buffalo	NHL	76	5	10	15	148	-9	0	0	—	—	—	—	—
96-97— New York Islanders....	NHL	51	7	3	10	57	-4	0	0	—	—	—	—	—
— Utah	IHL	5	2	2	4	11	...	...	...	—	—	—	—	—
NHL totals (8 years)		**357**	**41**	**39**	**80**	**831**	**-11**	**1**	**1**	**29**	**4**	**1**	**5**	**53**

HUGHES, RYAN — C

PERSONAL: Born January 17, 1972, in Montreal. ... 6-2/196. ... Shoots left. ... Full name: Ryan Laine Hughes.
COLLEGE: Cornell.
TRANSACTIONS/CAREER NOTES: Selected by Quebec Nordiques in second round (second Nordiques pick, 22nd overall) of NHL entry draft (June 16, 1990). ... Signed as free agent by Boston Bruins (October 6, 1995).

Season Team	League	REGULAR SEASON								PLAYOFFS				
		Gms.	G	A	Pts.	PIM	+/-	PP	SH	Gms.	G	A	Pts.	PIM
89-90— Cornell University	ECAC	28	7	16	23	35	...	...	...	—	—	—	—	—
90-91— Cornell University	ECAC	32	18	34	52	28	...	...	...	—	—	—	—	—
— Victoria	WHL	1	0	1	1	2	...	...	...	—	—	—	—	—
91-92— Cornell University	ECAC	27	8	13	21	36	...	...	...	—	—	—	—	—
92-93— Cornell University	ECAC	26	8	14	22	30	...	...	...	—	—	—	—	—
93-94— Cornwall..................	AHL	54	17	12	29	24	...	...	...	13	2	4	6	6
94-95— Cornwall..................	AHL	72	15	24	39	48	...	...	...	14	0	7	7	10
95-96— Providence...............	AHL	78	22	52	74	89	...	...	...	4	1	2	3	20
— Boston	NHL	3	0	0	0	0	0	0	0	—	—	—	—	—
96-97— Chicago...................	IHL	14	2	6	8	12	...	...	...	—	—	—	—	—
— Quebec....................	IHL	30	2	3	5	24	...	...	...	8	1	1	2	4
NHL totals (1 year)		**3**	**0**	**0**	**0**	**0**	**0**	**0**	**0**					

HULBIG, JOE — LW — OILERS

PERSONAL: Born September 29, 1973, in Wrentham, Mass. ... 6-3/215. ... Shoots left. ... Name pronounced HUHL-bihg.
HIGH SCHOOL: St. Sebastian's Country Day (Needham, Mass.).
COLLEGE: Providence.
TRANSACTIONS/CAREER NOTES: Selected by Edmonton Oilers in first round (first Oilers pick, 13th overall) of NHL entry draft (June 20, 1992).

H

Season Team	League	REGULAR SEASON								PLAYOFFS				
		Gms.	G	A	Pts.	PIM	+/-	PP	SH	Gms.	G	A	Pts.	PIM
89-90— St. Sebastian's	Mass. H.S.	30	13	12	25	...	...	...	...	—	—	—	—	—
90-91— St. Sebastian's	Mass. H.S.	...	23	19	42	...	...	...	...	—	—	—	—	—
91-92— St. Sebastian's	Mass. H.S.	17	19	24	43	30	...	...	...	—	—	—	—	—
92-93— Providence College	Hockey East	26	3	13	16	22	...	...	...	—	—	—	—	—
93-94— Providence College	Hockey East	28	6	4	10	36	...	...	...	—	—	—	—	—
94-95— Providence College	Hockey East	37	14	21	35	36	...	...	...	—	—	—	—	—
95-96— Providence College	Hockey East	31	14	22	36	56	...	...	...	—	—	—	—	—
96-97— Hamilton	AHL	73	18	28	46	59	...	...	...	16	6	10	16	6
— Edmonton	NHL	6	0	0	0	0	-1	0	0	6	0	1	1	2
NHL totals (1 year)		6	0	0	0	0	-1	0	0	6	0	1	1	2

HULL, BRETT   RW   BLUES

PERSONAL: Born August 9, 1964, in Belleville, Ont. ... 5-10/201. ... Shoots right. ... Son of Bobby Hull, Hall of Fame left winger with three NHL teams (1957-58 through 1971-72 and 1979-80) and Winnipeg Jets of WHA (1972-73 through 1978-79); and nephew of Dennis Hull, left winger, Chicago Blackhawks and Detroit Red Wings (1964-65 through 1977-78).

COLLEGE: Minnesota-Duluth.

TRANSACTIONS/CAREER NOTES: Selected by Calgary Flames in sixth round (sixth Flames pick, 117th overall) of NHL entry draft (June 9, 1984). ... Traded by Flames with LW Steve Bozek to St. Louis Blues for D Rob Ramage and G Rick Wamsley (March 7, 1988). ... Sprained left ankle (January 15, 1991); missed two regular-season games and All-Star Game. ... Suffered back spasms (March 12, 1992); missed seven games. ... Suffered sore wrist (March 20, 1993); missed four games. ... Injured abdominal muscle (October 7, 1993); missed three games. ... Pulled groin (November 1, 1995); missed two games. ... Pulled groin (November 10, 1995); missed five games. ... Pulled hamstring (March 28, 1996); missed four games. ... Strained groin (March 30, 1997); missed four games.

HONORS: Won WCHA Freshman of the Year Award (1984-85). ... Named to WCHA All-Star first team (1985-86). ... Won Dudley (Red) Garrett Memorial Trophy (1986-87). ... Named to AHL All-Star first team (1986-87). ... Won Lady Byng Memorial Trophy (1989-90). ... Won Dodge Ram Tough Award (1989-90 and 1990-91). ... Named to THE SPORTING NEWS All-Star first team (1989-90 through 1991-92). ... Named to NHL All-Star first team (1989-90 through 1991-92). ... Played in NHL All-Star Game (1989, 1990, 1992-1994, 1996 and 1997). ... Named NHL Player of the Year by THE SPORTING NEWS (1990-91). ... Won Hart Memorial Trophy (1990-91). ... Won Lester B. Pearson Award (1990-91). ... Won Pro Set NHL Player of the Year Award (1990-91). ... Named All-Star Game Most Valuable Player (1992).

RECORDS: Holds NHL single-season record for most goals by a right winger—86 (1990-91).

STATISTICAL PLATEAUS: Three-goal games: 1987-88 (1), 1989-90 (5), 1990-91 (4), 1991-92 (8), 1993-94 (3), 1994-95 (1), 1995-96 (1), 1996-97 (2). Total: 25. ... Four-goal games: 1994-95 (1), 1995-96 (1). Total: 2. ... Total hat tricks: 27.

MISCELLANEOUS: Captain of St. Louis Blues (1992-93 through October 22, 1995). ... Holds St. Louis Blues all-time record for most goals (500). ... Failed to score on a penalty shot (vs. Glen Healy, December 31, 1992; vs. Bill Ranford, March 26, 1995; vs. Jeff Hackett, January 4, 1996). ... Shares distinction with Bobby Hull of being the first father-son duo to win the same NHL trophy (both the Lady Byng Memorial and Hart Memorial trophies).

STATISTICAL NOTES: Became the first son of an NHL 50-goal scorer to score 50 goals in one season (1989-90). ... Tied for NHL lead with 12 game-winning goals (1989-90). ... Led NHL in game-winning goals with 11 (1990-91).

Season Team	League	REGULAR SEASON								PLAYOFFS				
		Gms.	G	A	Pts.	PIM	+/-	PP	SH	Gms.	G	A	Pts.	PIM
82-83— Penticton	BCJHL	50	48	56	104	27	...	...	...	—	—	—	—	—
83-84— Penticton	BCJHL	56	*105	83	*188	20	...	...	...	—	—	—	—	—
84-85— Minnesota-Duluth	WCHA	48	32	28	60	24	...	...	...	—	—	—	—	—
85-86— Minnesota-Duluth	WCHA	42	*52	32	84	46	...	...	...	—	—	—	—	—
— Calgary	NHL	—	—	—	—	—				2	0	0	0	0
86-87— Moncton	AHL	67	50	42	92	16	...	...	...	3	2	2	4	2
— Calgary	NHL	5	1	0	1	0	-1	0	0	4	2	1	3	0
87-88— Calgary	NHL	52	26	24	50	12	10	4	0	—	—	—	—	—
— St. Louis	NHL	13	6	8	14	4	4	2	0	10	7	2	9	4
88-89— St. Louis	NHL	78	41	43	84	33	-17	16	0	10	5	5	10	6
89-90— St. Louis	NHL	80	*72	41	113	24	-1	*27	0	12	13	8	21	17
90-91— St. Louis	NHL	78	*86	45	131	22	23	*29	0	13	11	8	19	4
91-92— St. Louis	NHL	73	*70	39	109	48	-2	20	5	6	4	4	8	4
92-93— St. Louis	NHL	80	54	47	101	41	-27	29	0	11	8	5	13	2
93-94— St. Louis	NHL	81	57	40	97	38	-3	†25	3	4	2	1	3	0
94-95— St. Louis	NHL	48	29	21	50	10	13	9	3	7	6	2	8	0
95-96— St. Louis	NHL	70	43	40	83	30	4	16	5	13	6	5	11	10
96-97— St. Louis	NHL	77	42	40	82	10	-9	12	2	6	2	7	9	2
NHL totals (12 years)		735	527	388	915	272	-6	189	18	98	66	48	114	49

HULL, JODY   RW   PANTHERS

PERSONAL: Born February 2, 1969, in Petrolia, Ont. ... 6-2/200. ... Shoots right.

HIGH SCHOOL: Thomas A. Stewart (Peterborough, Ont.).

TRANSACTIONS/CAREER NOTES: Strained ankle ligaments (September 1986). ... Pulled groin (February 1987). ... Selected by Hartford Whalers as underage junior in first round (first Whalers pick, 18th overall) of NHL entry draft (June 13, 1987). ... Pulled hamstring (March 1989). ... Traded by Whalers to New York Rangers for C Carey Wilson and third-round pick (C Mikael Nylander) in 1991 draft (July 9, 1990). ... Sprained muscle in right hand (October 6, 1990). ... Bruised left big toe (November 19, 1990); missed six games. ... Injured knee (March 13, 1991). ... Traded by Rangers to Ottawa Senators for future considerations (July 28, 1992). ... Injured groin (December 7, 1992); missed three games. ... Suffered concussion (January 10, 1993); missed one game. ... Sprained ankle (January 19, 1993); missed eight games. ... Sprained left ankle (April 1, 1993); missed two games. ... Signed as free agent by Florida Panthers (August 10, 1993). ... Bruised right shoulder (February 1, 1994); missed one game. ... Separated right shoulder (March 4, 1994); missed three games. ... Separated right shoulder (March 18, 1994); missed six games. ... Suffered viral illness (February 1, 1995); missed two games. ... Broke rib (October 28, 1995); missed four games. ... Suffered back spasms (May 5, 1996); missed four playoff games.

HONORS: Named to OHL All-Star second team (1987-88).

STATISTICAL PLATEAUS: Three-goal games: 1988-89 (1).

H

		REGULAR SEASON								PLAYOFFS				
Season Team	League	Gms.	G	A	Pts.	PIM	+/-	PP	SH	Gms.	G	A	Pts.	PIM
84-85— Cambridge Jr. B	OHA	38	13	17	30	39	...	...	...	—	—	—	—	—
85-86— Peterborough............	OHL	61	20	22	42	29	...	...	...	16	1	5	6	4
86-87— Peterborough............	OHL	49	18	34	52	22	...	...	...	12	4	9	13	14
87-88— Peterborough............	OHL	60	50	44	94	33	...	...	...	12	10	8	18	8
88-89— Hartford.................	NHL	60	16	18	34	10	6	6	0	1	0	0	0	2
89-90— Binghamton	AHL	21	7	10	17	6	...	...	...	—	—	—	—	—
— Hartford.................	NHL	38	7	10	17	21	-6	2	0	5	0	1	1	2
90-91— New York Rangers	NHL	47	5	8	13	10	2	0	0	—	—	—	—	—
91-92— New York Rangers	NHL	3	0	0	0	2	-4	0	0	—	—	—	—	—
— Binghamton	AHL	69	34	31	65	28	...	...	...	11	5	2	7	4
92-93— Ottawa...................	NHL	69	13	21	34	14	-24	5	1	—	—	—	—	—
93-94— Florida..................	NHL	69	13	13	26	8	6	0	1	—	—	—	—	—
94-95— Florida..................	NHL	46	11	8	19	8	-1	0	0	—	—	—	—	—
95-96— Florida..................	NHL	78	20	17	37	25	5	2	0	14	3	2	5	0
96-97— Florida..................	NHL	67	10	6	16	4	1	0	1	5	0	0	0	0
NHL totals (9 years)		477	95	101	196	102	-15	15	3	25	3	3	6	4

HULSE, CALE   D   FLAMES

PERSONAL: Born November 10, 1973, in Edmonton. ... 6-3/215. ... Shoots right. ... Name pronounced HUHLZ.
COLLEGE: Portland.
TRANSACTIONS/CAREER NOTES: Selected by New Jersey Devils in third round (third Devils pick, 66th overall) of NHL entry draft (June 20, 1992). ... Traded by Devils with D Tommy Albelin and RW Jocelyn Lemieux to Calgary Flames for D Phil Housley and D Dan Keczmer (February 26, 1996). ... Bruised ankle (February 28, 1997); missed four games. ... Reinjured ankle (March 7, 1997); missed one game. ... Reinjured ankle (March 21, 1997); missed one game.

		REGULAR SEASON								PLAYOFFS				
Season Team	League	Gms.	G	A	Pts.	PIM	+/-	PP	SH	Gms.	G	A	Pts.	PIM
90-91— Calgary Royals..........	AJHL	49	3	23	26	220	...	...	...	—	—	—	—	—
91-92— Portland	WHL	70	4	18	22	250	...	...	...	6	0	2	2	27
92-93— Portland	WHL	72	10	26	36	284	...	...	...	16	4	4	8	*65
93-94— Albany	AHL	79	7	14	21	186	...	...	...	5	0	3	3	11
94-95— Albany	AHL	77	5	13	18	215	...	...	...	12	1	1	2	17
95-96— Albany	AHL	42	4	23	27	107	...	...	...	0	0	0	0	
— New Jersey	NHL	8	0	0	0	15	-2	0	0	—	—	—	—	—
— Saint John	AHL	13	2	7	9	39	...	...	...	0	0	0	0	0
— Calgary	NHL	3	0	0	0	5	3	0	0	1	0	0	0	0
96-97— Calgary	NHL	63	1	6	7	91	-2	0	1	—	—	—	—	—
NHL totals (3 years)		74	1	6	7	111	-1	0	1	1	0	0	0	0

HULST, KENT   C

PERSONAL: Born April 8, 1968, in St. Thomas, Ont. ... 6-0/200. ... Shoots left.
TRANSACTIONS/CAREER NOTES: Selected by Toronto Maple Leafs as underage junior in fourth round (fourth Maple Leafs pick, 69th overall) of NHL entry draft (June 21, 1986). ... Separated shoulder (September 1988). ... Signed as free agent by Quebec Nordiques (September 20, 1991). ... Signed as free agent by Portland of AHL (1993).

		REGULAR SEASON								PLAYOFFS				
Season Team	League	Gms.	G	A	Pts.	PIM	+/-	PP	SH	Gms.	G	A	Pts.	PIM
84-85— St. Thomas Jr. B	OHA	47	21	25	46	29	...	...	...	—	—	—	—	—
85-86— Belleville..................	OHL	43	6	17	23	20	...	...	...	—	—	—	—	—
— Windsor	OHL	17	6	10	16	9	...	...	...	—	—	—	—	—
86-87— Windsor	OHL	37	18	20	38	49	...	...	...	—	—	—	—	—
— Belleville..................	OHL	27	13	10	23	17	...	...	...	6	1	1	2	0
87-88— Belleville..................	OHL	66	42	43	85	48	...	...	...	6	3	1	4	7
88-89— Belleville..................	OHL	45	21	41	62	43	...	...	...	—	—	—	—	—
— Flint.......................	IHL	7	0	1	1	4	...	...	...	—	—	—	—	—
— Newmarket.................	AHL	—	—	—	—	—	...	...	...	2	1	1	2	2
89-90— Newmarket.................	AHL	80	26	34	60	29	...	...	...	—	—	—	—	—
90-91— Newmarket.................	AHL	79	28	37	65	57	...	...	...	—	—	—	—	—
91-92— New Haven...............	AHL	†80	21	39	60	59	...	...	...	5	2	2	4	0
92-93— Lyss	Switz.	30	10	20	30	...	...	...	...	—	—	—	—	—
93-94— Portland	AHL	72	34	33	67	68	...	...	...	17	4	6	10	14
94-95— Portland	AHL	29	10	17	27	80	...	...	...	7	3	1	4	2
95-96— Portland	AHL	75	25	47	72	122	...	...	...	24	11	16	27	30
96-97— Portland	AHL	48	19	31	50	60	...	...	...	5	1	2	3	4

HULTBERG, JOHN   G   OILERS

PERSONAL: Born April 25, 1977, in Streamwood, Ill. ... 6-0/185. ... Catches left.
TRANSACTIONS/CAREER NOTES: Selected by Edmonton Oilers in ninth round (10th Oilers pick, 221st overall) of NHL entry draft (June 22, 1996).
HONORS: Named to OHL All-Rookie second team (1995-96).

		REGULAR SEASON							PLAYOFFS					
Season Team	League	Gms.	Min	W	L	T	GA	SO	Avg.	Gms.	Min.	W	L	GA	SO	Avg.
95-96—Kingston	OHL	40	2036	13	15	4	125	1	3.68	3	206	1	2	17	0	4.95
96-97—Barrie......................	OHL	27	1354	14	4	3	74	0	3.28	2	120	1	1	8	0	4.00

H

HUNTER, DALE   C   CAPITALS

PERSONAL: Born July 31, 1960, in Petrolia, Ont. ... 5-10/200. ... Shoots left. ... Full name: Dale Robert Hunter. ... Brother of Mark Hunter, right winger for four NHL teams (1981-82 through 1992-93); and brother of Dave Hunter, left winger, Edmonton Oilers of WHA (1978-79); and three NHL teams (1979-80 through 1988-89).

TRANSACTIONS/CAREER NOTES: Selected by Quebec Nordiques as underage junior in second round (second Nordiques pick, 41st overall) of NHL entry draft (August 9, 1979). ... Suspended three games by NHL (March 1984). ... Suffered hand infection (April 21, 1985). ... Broke lower fibula of left leg (November 25, 1986). ... Traded by Nordiques with G Clint Malarchuk to Washington Capitals for C Alan Haworth, LW Gaetan Duchesne and first-round pick (C Joe Sakic) in 1987 draft (June 13, 1987). ... Broke thumb (September 1988). ... Suspended four games by NHL for elbowing (February 10, 1991). ... Suspended first 21 games of 1993-94 season by NHL for blindside check on player (May 4, 1993). ... Injured knee ligament (November 26, 1993); missed 10 games. ... Bruised left knee (February 13, 1995); missed three games.

HONORS: Played in NHL All-Star Game (1997).

RECORDS: Holds NHL career playoff record for most penalty minutes—661.

STATISTICAL PLATEAUS: Three-goal games: 1981-82 (2), 1983-84 (1), 1991-92 (1). Total: 4.

MISCELLANEOUS: Captain of Washington Capitals (1994-95 through 1996-97). ... Holds Colorado Avalanche franchise all-time record for most penalty minutes (1,545). ... Holds Washington Capitals all-time record for most penalty minutes (1,798). ... Scored on a penalty shot (vs. Rejean Lemelin, December 6, 1983). ... Failed to score on a penalty shot (vs. Wendell Young, December 6, 1989).

Season Team	League	REGULAR SEASON								PLAYOFFS				
		Gms.	G	A	Pts.	PIM	+/-	PP	SH	Gms.	G	A	Pts.	PIM
77-78 — Kitchener	OMJHL	68	22	42	64	115	...	...	...	—	—	—	—	—
78-79 — Sudbury	OMJHL	59	42	68	110	188	...	...	...	10	4	12	16	47
79-80 — Sudbury	OMJHL	61	34	51	85	189	...	...	...	9	6	9	15	45
80-81 — Quebec	NHL	80	19	44	63	226	5	2	0	5	4	2	6	34
81-82 — Quebec	NHL	80	22	50	72	272	26	0	2	16	3	7	10	52
82-83 — Quebec	NHL	80	17	46	63	206	10	1	2	4	2	1	3	24
83-84 — Quebec	NHL	77	24	55	79	232	35	7	2	9	2	3	5	41
84-85 — Quebec	NHL	80	20	52	72	209	23	3	3	17	4	6	10	*97
85-86 — Quebec	NHL	80	28	42	70	265	37	0	0	3	0	0	0	15
86-87 — Quebec	NHL	46	10	29	39	135	4	0	0	13	1	7	8	56
87-88 — Washington	NHL	79	22	37	59	240	7	11	0	14	7	5	12	98
88-89 — Washington	NHL	80	20	37	57	219	-3	9	0	6	0	4	4	29
89-90 — Washington	NHL	80	23	39	62	233	17	9	1	15	4	8	12	61
90-91 — Washington	NHL	76	16	30	46	234	-22	9	0	11	1	9	10	41
91-92 — Washington	NHL	80	28	50	78	205	-2	13	0	7	1	4	5	16
92-93 — Washington	NHL	84	20	59	79	198	3	10	0	6	7	1	8	35
93-94 — Washington	NHL	52	9	29	38	131	-4	1	0	7	0	3	3	14
94-95 — Washington	NHL	45	8	15	23	101	-4	3	0	7	4	4	8	24
95-96 — Washington	NHL	82	13	24	37	112	5	4	0	6	1	5	6	24
96-97 — Washington	NHL	82	14	32	46	125	-2	3	0	—	—	—	—	—
NHL totals (17 years)		**1263**	**313**	**670**	**983**	**3343**	**135**	**85**	**10**	**146**	**41**	**69**	**110**	**661**

HUNTER, TIM   RW   SHARKS

PERSONAL: Born September 10, 1960, in Calgary. ... 6-2/200. ... Shoots right. ... Full name: Timothy Robert Hunter.

TRANSACTIONS/CAREER NOTES: Selected by Atlanta Flames in third round (fourth Flames pick, 54th overall) of NHL entry draft (August 9, 1979). ... Flames franchise moved to Calgary (May 21, 1980). ... Bruised hand (October 1987). ... Injured right eye (October 17, 1988). ... Suspended 10 games and fined $500 by NHL for leaving bench to fight (November 1, 1989). ... Tore shoulder muscles (October 6, 1990); missed four games. ... Reinjured shoulder (October 18, 1990); missed 21 games. ... Reinjured shoulder (December 2, 1990); missed 20 games. ... Suffered back spasms (October 1991); missed one game. ... Fractured left ankle (December 8, 1991); missed 39 games. ... Selected by Tampa Bay Lightning in NHL expansion draft (June 18, 1992). ... Traded by Lightning to Quebec Nordiques for future considerations (June 22, 1992); Nordiques sent RW Martin Simard to Lightning to complete deal (September 14, 1992). ... Bruised knee (December 29, 1992); missed one game. ... Suffered back spasms (January 28, 1993); missed three games. ... Claimed on waivers by Vancouver Canucks (February 12, 1993). ... Sprained knee (November 2, 1993); missed 14 games. ... Suffered back spasms (March 3, 1994); missed seven games. ... Suspended three games by NHL for wrestling with linesman (March 26, 1994). ... Injured shoulder (April 9, 1995); missed remainder of season. ... Signed as free agent by San Jose Sharks (July 25, 1996). ... Injured back (December 20, 1996); missed 10 games.

MISCELLANEOUS: Member of Stanley Cup championship team (1989). ... Co-captain of Calgary Flames (1988-89).

Season Team	League	REGULAR SEASON								PLAYOFFS				
		Gms.	G	A	Pts.	PIM	+/-	PP	SH	Gms.	G	A	Pts.	PIM
77-78 — Kamloops	BCJHL	51	9	28	37	266	...	...	...	—	—	—	—	—
— Seattle	WCHL	3	1	2	3	4	...	...	...	—	—	—	—	—
78-79 — Seattle	WHL	70	8	41	49	300	...	...	...	—	—	—	—	—
79-80 — Seattle	WHL	72	14	53	67	311	...	...	...	12	1	2	3	41
80-81 — Birmingham	CHL	58	3	5	8	*236	...	...	...	—	—	—	—	—
— Nova Scotia	AHL	17	0	0	0	62	...	...	...	6	0	1	1	45
81-82 — Oklahoma City	CHL	55	4	12	16	222	...	...	...	—	—	—	—	—
— Calgary	NHL	2	0	0	0	9	0	0	0	—	—	—	—	—
82-83 — Calgary	NHL	16	1	0	1	54	-2	0	0	9	1	0	1	*70
— Colorado	CHL	46	5	12	17	225	...	...	...	—	—	—	—	—
83-84 — Calgary	NHL	43	4	4	8	130	0	0	0	7	0	0	0	21
84-85 — Calgary	NHL	71	11	11	22	259	14	1	0	4	0	0	0	24
85-86 — Calgary	NHL	66	8	7	15	291	-9	2	0	19	0	3	3	108
86-87 — Calgary	NHL	73	6	15	21	361	-1	0	0	6	0	0	0	51
87-88 — Calgary	NHL	68	8	5	13	337	-8	0	0	9	4	0	4	32
88-89 — Calgary	NHL	75	3	9	12	*375	22	0	0	19	0	4	4	32
89-90 — Calgary	NHL	67	2	3	5	279	-9	0	0	6	0	0	0	4
90-91 — Calgary	NHL	34	5	2	7	143	1	0	0	7	0	0	0	10
91-92 — Calgary	NHL	30	1	3	4	167	2	0	0	—	—	—	—	—
92-93 — Quebec	NHL	48	5	3	8	94	-4	0	0	—	—	—	—	—
— Vancouver	NHL	26	0	4	4	99	1	0	0	11	0	0	0	26
93-94 — Vancouver	NHL	56	3	4	7	171	-7	0	1	24	0	0	0	26

H

Season Team	League	REGULAR SEASON Gms.	G	A	Pts.	PIM	+/-	PP	SH	PLAYOFFS Gms.	G	A	Pts.	PIM
94-95 — Vancouver	NHL	34	3	2	5	120	1	0	0	11	0	0	0	22
95-96 — Vancouver	NHL	60	2	0	2	122	-8	0	0	—	—	—	—	—
96-97 — San Jose	NHL	46	0	4	4	135	0	0	0	—	—	—	—	—
NHL totals (16 years)		815	62	76	138	3146	-7	3	1	132	5	7	12	426

HUSCROFT, JAMIE — D — LIGHTNING

PERSONAL: Born January 9, 1967, in Creston, B.C. ... 6-2/200. ... Shoots right. ... Name pronounced HUZ-krawft.

TRANSACTIONS/CAREER NOTES: Selected by New Jersey Devils as underage junior in ninth round (ninth Devils pick, 171st overall) of NHL entry draft (June 15, 1985). ... Fractured arm (October 1986); missed eight weeks. ... Traded by Seattle Thunderbirds to Medicine Hat Tigers for C Mike Schwengler (February 1987). ... Fractured right wrist (October 1988). ... Signed as free agent by Boston Bruins (July 16, 1992). ... Signed as free agent by Calgary Flames (July 27, 1995). ... Strained back prior to 1995-96 season; missed one game. ... Bruised foot (October 27, 1995); missed one game. ... Suffered from the flu (December 11, 1995); missed three games. ... Injured groin (April 1, 1996); missed three games. ... Cut forearm (March 4, 1997); missed three games. ... Traded by Flames to Tampa Bay Lightning for G Tyler Moss (March 18, 1997).

Season Team	League	REGULAR SEASON Gms.	G	A	Pts.	PIM	+/-	PP	SH	PLAYOFFS Gms.	G	A	Pts.	PIM
83-84 — Portland	WHL	63	0	12	12	77	...	...	...	5	0	0	0	15
84-85 — Seattle	WHL	69	3	13	16	273	...	...	...	—	—	—	—	—
85-86 — Seattle	WHL	66	6	20	26	394	...	...	...	5	0	1	1	18
86-87 — Seattle	WHL	21	1	18	19	99	...	...	...	20	0	3	3	0
— Medicine Hat	WHL	35	4	21	25	170	...	...	...	20	0	3	3	*125
87-88 — Flint	IHL	3	1	0	1	2	...	...	...	16	0	1	1	110
— Utica	AHL	71	5	7	12	316	...	...	...	—	—	—	—	—
88-89 — Utica	AHL	41	2	10	12	215	...	...	...	5	0	0	0	40
— New Jersey	NHL	15	0	2	2	51	-3	0	0	—	—	—	—	—
89-90 — New Jersey	NHL	42	2	3	5	149	-2	0	0	5	0	0	0	16
— Utica	AHL	22	3	6	9	122	...	...	...	—	—	—	—	—
90-91 — New Jersey	NHL	8	0	1	1	27	1	0	0	3	0	0	0	6
— Utica	AHL	59	3	15	18	339	...	...	...	—	—	—	—	—
91-92 — Utica	AHL	50	4	7	11	224	...	...	...	—	—	—	—	—
92-93 — Providence	AHL	69	2	15	17	257	...	...	...	2	0	1	1	6
93-94 — Providence	AHL	32	1	10	11	157	...	...	...	—	—	—	—	—
— Boston	NHL	36	0	1	1	144	-2	0	0	4	0	0	0	9
94-95 — Boston	NHL	34	0	6	6	103	-3	0	0	5	0	0	0	11
95-96 — Calgary	NHL	70	3	9	12	162	14	0	0	4	0	1	1	4
96-97 — Calgary	NHL	39	0	4	4	117	2	0	0	—	—	—	—	—
— Tampa Bay	NHL	13	0	1	1	34	-4	0	0	—	—	—	—	—
NHL totals (7 years)		257	5	27	32	787	3	0	0	21	0	1	1	46

HUSKA, RYAN — LW — BLACKHAWKS

PERSONAL: Born July 2, 1975, in Cranbrook, B.C. ... 6-2/194. ... Shoots left. ... Name pronounced HUHZ-kuh.

HIGH SCHOOL: Norkam Secondary (Kamloops, B.C.).

TRANSACTIONS/CAREER NOTES: Selected by Chicago Blackhawks in third round (fourth Blackhawks pick, 76th overall) of NHL entry draft (June 26, 1993).

Season Team	League	REGULAR SEASON Gms.	G	A	Pts.	PIM	+/-	PP	SH	PLAYOFFS Gms.	G	A	Pts.	PIM
91-92 — Kamloops	WHL	44	4	5	9	23	...	...	...	6	0	1	1	0
92-93 — Kamloops	WHL	68	17	15	32	50	...	...	...	13	2	6	8	4
93-94 — Kamloops	WHL	69	23	31	54	66	...	...	...	19	9	5	14	23
94-95 — Kamloops	WHL	66	27	40	67	78	...	...	...	17	7	8	15	12
95-96 — Indianapolis	IHL	28	2	3	5	15	...	...	...	5	1	1	2	27
96-97 — Indianapolis	IHL	80	18	12	30	100	...	...	...	4	0	0	0	4

HUSSEY, MARC — D — BLACKHAWKS

PERSONAL: Born January 22, 1974, in Chatham, N.B. ... 6-4/210. ... Shoots right. ... Name pronounced HUH-see.

HIGH SCHOOL: Vanier Collegiate (Moose Jaw, Sask.).

TRANSACTIONS/CAREER NOTES: Selected by Pittsburgh Penguins in second round (second Penguins pick, 43rd overall) of NHL entry draft (June 20, 1992). ... Signed as free agent by Calgary Flames (September 1995). ... Traded by Flames to Chicago Blackhawks for LW Ravil Gusmanov (March 18, 1997).

Season Team	League	REGULAR SEASON Gms.	G	A	Pts.	PIM	+/-	PP	SH	PLAYOFFS Gms.	G	A	Pts.	PIM
90-91 — Moose Jaw	WHL	68	5	8	13	67	...	...	...	8	2	2	4	7
91-92 — Moose Jaw	WHL	72	7	27	34	203	...	...	...	4	1	1	2	0
92-93 — Moose Jaw	WHL	68	12	28	40	121	...	...	...	—	—	—	—	—
93-94 — Moose Jaw	WHL	17	4	5	9	33	...	...	...	—	—	—	—	—
— Tri-City	WHL	16	3	6	9	26	...	...	...	—	—	—	—	—
— Medicine Hat	WHL	41	6	24	30	90	...	...	...	3	0	1	1	4
94-95 — Canadian nat'l team	Int'l	36	2	7	9	42	...	...	...	—	—	—	—	—
— St. John's	AHL	11	0	1	1	20	...	...	...	—	—	—	—	—
95-96 — Saint John	AHL	68	10	21	31	120	...	...	...	5	0	0	0	8
96-97 — Utah	IHL	8	0	1	1	6	...	...	...	—	—	—	—	—
— Indianapolis	IHL	14	0	2	2	17	...	...	...	4	0	1	1	10
— Saint John	AHL	46	6	18	24	62	...	...	...	—	—	—	—	—

H

IAFRATE, AL   D   SHARKS

PERSONAL: Born March 21, 1966, in Dearborn, Mich. ... 6-2/240. ... Shoots left. ... Full name: Al Anthony Iafrate. ... Name pronounced igh-uh-FRAY-tee.

TRANSACTIONS/CAREER NOTES: Selected by Toronto Maple Leafs as underage junior in first round (first Maple Leafs pick, fourth overall) of NHL entry draft (June 9, 1984). ... Bruised knee (February 1985). ... Broke nose (October 2, 1985); missed five games. ... Strained neck (January 29, 1986); missed six games. ... Suffered stiff back (January 1988). ... Broke back (October 22, 1988). ... Cut hand (December 9, 1988). ... Tore right knee ligament (March 24, 1990). ... Underwent knee surgery (April 9, 1990). ... Traded by Maple Leafs to Washington Capitals for D Bob Rouse and C Peter Zezel (January 16, 1991). ... Took a leave of absence due to mental exhaustion (March 30, 1991). ... Injured eye (February 19, 1992); missed one game. ... Pulled hamstring (April 10, 1993); missed three games. ... Sprained right knee (December 21, 1993); missed four games. ... Sore knee (January 2, 1994); missed one game. ... Traded by Capitals to Boston Bruins for LW Joe Juneau (March 21, 1994). ... Underwent offseason knee surgery; missed entire 1994-95 season. ... Missed entire 1995-96 season with knee injury. ... Traded by Bruins to San Jose Sharks for RW Jeff Odgers and fifth-round pick (D Elias Abrahamsson) in 1996 draft (June 21, 1996). ... Broke toe (November 12, 1996); missed eight games. ... Reinjured toe (December 7, 1996); missed four games. ... Sore back (January 24, 1997); missed two games. ... Underwent back surgery (March 5, 1997); missed remainder of season.

HONORS: Played in NHL All-Star Game (1988, 1990, 1993 and 1994). ... Named to The Sporting News All-Star second team (1992-93). ... Named to NHL All-Star second team (1992-93).

RECORDS: Shares NHL single-game playoff record for most goals by defenseman—3 (April 26, 1993).

Season Team	League	Gms.	G	A	Pts.	PIM	+/-	PP	SH	Gms.	G	A	Pts.	PIM
83-84 — U.S. national team	Int'l	55	4	17	21	26	...	...	...	—	—	—	—	—
— U.S. Olympic team	Int'l	6	0	0	0	2	...	...	...	—	—	—	—	—
— Belleville	OHL	10	2	4	6	2	...	...	...	3	0	1	1	2
84-85 — Toronto	NHL	68	5	16	21	51	-19	3	0	—	—	—	—	—
85-86 — Toronto	NHL	65	8	25	33	40	-10	2	0	10	0	3	3	4
86-87 — Toronto	NHL	80	9	21	30	55	-18	0	0	13	1	3	4	11
87-88 — Toronto	NHL	77	22	30	52	80	-21	4	3	6	3	4	7	6
88-89 — Toronto	NHL	65	13	20	33	72	3	1	2	—	—	—	—	—
89-90 — Toronto	NHL	75	21	42	63	135	-4	6	1	—	—	—	—	—
90-91 — Toronto	NHL	42	3	15	18	113	-15	2	0	—	—	—	—	—
— Washington	NHL	30	6	8	14	124	-1	0	1	10	1	3	4	22
91-92 — Washington	NHL	78	17	34	51	180	1	6	0	7	4	2	6	14
92-93 — Washington	NHL	81	25	41	66	169	15	11	1	6	6	0	6	4
93-94 — Washington	NHL	67	10	35	45	143	10	4	0	—	—	—	—	—
— Boston	NHL	12	5	8	13	20	6	2	0	13	3	1	4	6
94-95 — Boston	NHL					Did not play—injured.								
95-96 — Boston	NHL					Did not play—injured.								
96-97 — San Jose	NHL	38	6	9	15	91	-10	3	0	—	—	—	—	—
NHL totals (13 years)		**778**	**150**	**304**	**454**	**1273**	**-63**	**44**	**8**	**65**	**18**	**16**	**34**	**67**

IGINLA, JAROME   RW   FLAMES

PERSONAL: Born July 1, 1977, in Edmonton. ... 6-1/202. ... Shoots right. ... Name pronounced igh-GIHN-luh.

TRANSACTIONS/CAREER NOTES: Selected by Dallas Stars in first round (first Stars pick, 11th overall) of NHL entry draft (July 8, 1995). ... Traded by Stars with C Corey Millen to Calgary Flames for C Joe Nieuwendyk (December 19, 1995).

HONORS: Won George Parsons Trophy (1994-95). ... Won Four Broncos Memorial Trophy (1995-96). ... Named to Can.HL All-Star first team (1995-96). ... Named to WHL (West) All-Star first team (1995-96). ... Named to NHL All-Rookie team (1996-97).

Season Team	League	Gms.	G	A	Pts.	PIM	+/-	PP	SH	Gms.	G	A	Pts.	PIM
93-94 — Kamloops	WHL	48	6	23	29	33	...	...	...	19	3	6	9	10
94-95 — Kamloops	WHL	72	33	38	71	111	...	...	...	21	7	11	18	34
95-96 — Kamloops	WHL	63	63	73	136	120	...	...	...	16	16	13	29	44
— Calgary	NHL	—	—	—	—	—				2	1	1	2	0
96-97 — Calgary	NHL	82	21	29	50	37	-4	8	1	—	—	—	—	—
NHL totals (2 years)		**82**	**21**	**29**	**50**	**37**	**-4**	**8**	**1**	**2**	**1**	**1**	**2**	**0**

INTRANUOVO, RALPH   C/RW   OILERS

PERSONAL: Born December 11, 1973, in Scarborough, Ont. ... 5-8/185. ... Shoots left. ... Name pronounced ihn-trah-NOO-voh.

TRANSACTIONS/CAREER NOTES: Selected by Edmonton Oilers in fourth round (fifth Oilers pick, 96th overall) of NHL entry draft (June 20, 1992). ... Bruised left wrist (February 27, 1996); missed 10 games. ... Selected by Toronto Maple Leafs in NHL waiver draft for cash (September 30, 1996). ... Claimed on waivers by Oilers (October 25, 1996).

HONORS: Won Stafford Smythe Memorial Trophy (1992-93). ... Named to AHL All-Star second team (1994-95 and 1996-97).

Season Team	League	Gms.	G	A	Pts.	PIM	+/-	PP	SH	Gms.	G	A	Pts.	PIM
90-91 — Sault Ste. Marie	OHL	63	25	42	67	22	...	...	...	14	7	13	20	17
91-92 — Sault Ste. Marie	OHL	65	50	63	113	44	...	...	...	18	10	14	24	12
92-93 — Sault Ste. Marie	OHL	54	31	47	78	61	...	...	...	18	10	16	26	30
93-94 — Cape Breton	AHL	66	21	31	52	39	...	...	...	4	1	2	3	2
94-95 — Cape Breton	AHL	70	46	47	93	62	...	...	...	—	—	—	—	—
— Edmonton	NHL	1	0	1	1	0	1	0	0	—	—	—	—	—
95-96 — Cape Breton	AHL	52	34	39	73	84	...	...	...	—	—	—	—	—
— Edmonton	NHL	13	1	2	3	4	-3	0	0	—	—	—	—	—
96-97 — Toronto	NHL	3	0	1	1	0	-1	0	0	—	—	—	—	—
— Hamilton	AHL	68	36	40	76	88	...	...	...	22	8	4	12	30
— Edmonton	NHL	5	1	0	1	0	0	0	0	—	—	—	—	—
NHL totals (4 years)		**22**	**2**	**4**	**6**	**4**	**-3**	**0**	**0**					

IRBE, ARTURS   G   STARS

PERSONAL: Born February 2, 1967, in Riga, U.S.S.R. ... 5-8/175. ... Catches left. ... Name pronounced AHR-tuhrs UHR-bay.
TRANSACTIONS/CAREER NOTES: Selected by Minnesota North Stars in 10th round (11th North Stars pick, 196th overall) of NHL entry draft (June 17, 1989). ... Selected by San Jose Sharks in NHL dispersal draft (May 30, 1991). ... Sprained knee (November 27, 1992); missed 19 games. ... Injured foot (February 15, 1995); missed one game. ... Injured knee (January 17, 1996); remainder of season. ... Signed as free agent by Dallas Stars (July 22, 1996). ... Strained groin (November 8, 1996); missed six games.
HONORS: Named Soviet League Rookie of the Year (1987-88). ... Shared James Norris Memorial Trophy with Wade Flaherty (1991-92). ... Named to IHL All-Star first team (1991-92). ... Played in NHL All-Star Game (1994).
MISCELLANEOUS: Holds San Jose Sharks all-time records for most games played by goalie (183), most wins (57), most shutouts (8) and goals-against average (3.47). ... Allowed a penalty shot goal (vs. Mats Sundin, March 15, 1995; vs. Igor Larionov, November 22, 1995).

			REGULAR SEASON								PLAYOFFS						
Season Team	League	Gms.	Min	W	L	T	GA	SO	Avg.	Gms.	Min.	W	L	GA	SO	Avg.
86-87—Dynamo Riga	USSR	2	27	...	...	...	1	0	2.22	—	—	—	—	—	—	—
87-88—Dynamo Riga	USSR	34	1870	...	...	...	84	0	2.70	—	—	—	—	—	—	—
88-89—Dynamo Riga	USSR	41	2460	...	...	...	117	0	2.85	—	—	—	—	—	—	—
89-90—Dynamo Riga	USSR	48	2880	...	...	...	116	0	2.42	—	—	—	—	—	—	—
90-91—Dynamo Riga	USSR	46	2713	...	...	...	133	0	2.94	—	—	—	—	—	—	—
91-92—Kansas City	IHL	32	1955	24	7	‡1	80	0	*2.46	15	914	12	3	44	0	2.89
—San Jose	NHL	13	645	2	6	3	48	0	4.47	—	—	—	—	—	—	—
92-93—Kansas City	IHL	6	364	3	3	‡0	20	0	3.30	—	—	—	—	—	—	—
—San Jose	NHL	36	2074	7	26	0	142	1	4.11	—	—	—	—	—	—	—
93-94—San Jose	NHL	*74	*4412	30	28	*16	209	3	2.84	14	806	7	7	50	0	3.72
94-95—San Jose	NHL	38	2043	14	19	3	111	4	3.26	6	316	2	4	27	0	5.13
95-96—San Jose	NHL	22	1112	4	12	4	85	0	4.59	—	—	—	—	—	—	—
—Kansas City	IHL	4	226	1	2	1	16	0	4.25	—	—	—	—	—	—	—
96-97—Dallas	NHL	35	1965	17	12	3	88	3	2.69	1	13	0	0	0	0	0.00
NHL totals (6 years)		218	12251	74	103	29	683	11	3.35	21	1135	9	11	77	0	4.07

ISBISTER, BRAD   RW   COYOTES

PERSONAL: Born March 7, 1977, in Edmonton. ... 6-2/198. ... Shoots right. ... Name pronounced ihs-BIH-stuhr.
HIGH SCHOOL: Milwaukie (Ore.).
TRANSACTIONS/CAREER NOTES: Selected by Winnipeg Jets in third round (fourth Jets pick, 67th overall) of NHL entry draft (July 8, 1995). ... Jets franchise moved to Phoenix and renamed Coyotes for 1996-97 season; NHL approved move on January 18, 1996.
HONORS: Named to WHL (West) All-Star second team (1996-97).

			REGULAR SEASON							PLAYOFFS			
Season Team	League	Gms.	G	A	Pts.	PIM	+/-	PP	SH	Gms.	G	A	Pts.	PIM
93-94—Portland	WHL	64	7	10	17	45	...	...	...	10	0	2	2	0
94-95—Portland	WHL	67	16	20	36	123	...	...	...	—	—	—	—	—
95-96—Portland	WHL	71	45	44	89	184	...	...	...	7	2	4	6	20
96-97—Springfield	AHL	7	3	1	4	14	...	...	...	9	1	2	3	10
—Portland	WHL	24	15	18	33	45	...	...	...	6	2	1	3	16

IVANKOVIC, FRANK   G   PENGUINS

PERSONAL: Born October 7, 1976, in Toronto. ... 6-4/194. ... Catches left.
HIGH SCHOOL: Henry Street (Whitby, Ont.).
TRANSACTIONS/CAREER NOTES: Selected by Pittsburgh Penguins in ninth round (eighth Penguins pick, 232nd overall) of NHL entry draft (July 8, 1995).

			REGULAR SEASON							PLAYOFFS						
Season Team	League	Gms.	Min	W	L	T	GA	SO	Avg.	Gms.	Min.	W	L	GA	SO	Avg.
93-94—Oakville	Tier II Jr. A	20	1031	...	...	...	76	0	4.42	—	—	—	—	—	—	—
—Oshawa	OHL	8	253	1	2	0	21	0	4.98	—	—	—	—	—	—	—
94-95—Oshawa	OHL	19	805	10	3	0	61	0	4.55	3	121	2	0	5	0	2.48
95-96—London	OHL	18	885	0	18	0	112	0	7.59	—	—	—	—	—	—	—
—Oshawa	OHL	10	547	4	4	0	42	0	4.61	—	—	—	—	—	—	—
96-97—Columbus	CHL	2	120	1	1	0	0	9	0.00	—	—	—	—	—	—	—

JABLONSKI, PAT   G   COYOTES

PERSONAL: Born June 20, 1967, in Toledo, Ohio. ... 6-0/180. ... Catches right.
TRANSACTIONS/CAREER NOTES: Selected by St. Louis Blues in seventh round (sixth Blues pick, 138th overall) of NHL entry draft (June 15, 1985). ... Pulled groin (December 7, 1991); missed 26 games. ... Traded by Blues with D Rob Robinson, RW Darin Kimble and RW Steve Tuttle to Tampa Bay Lightning for future considerations (June 19, 1992). ... Traded by Lightning to Toronto Maple Leafs for future considerations (February 21, 1994). ... Loaned by Maple Leafs to Chicago Wolves of IHL (February 17, 1995). ... Returned to Maple Leafs (March 6, 1995). ... Loaned by Maple Leafs to Houston Aeros of IHL (March 29, 1995). ... Returned to Maple Leafs (April 7, 1995). ... Signed as free agent by Blues (October 2, 1995). ... Traded by Blues to Montreal Canadiens for D J.J. Daigneault (November 7, 1995). ... Traded by Canadiens to Phoenix Coyotes for D Steve Cheredaryk (March 18, 1997).
HONORS: Shared James Norris Memorial Trophy with Guy Hebert (1990-91).
MISCELLANEOUS: Stopped a penalty shot attempt (vs. Michel Goulet, March 26, 1991; vs. Bryan Marchment, December 31, 1992). ... Allowed a penalty shot goal (vs. Pierre Turgeon, November 7, 1992).

			REGULAR SEASON							PLAYOFFS						
Season Team	League	Gms.	Min	W	L	T	GA	SO	Avg.	Gms.	Min.	W	L	GA	SO	Avg.
84-85—Detroit Compuware	NAJHL	29	1483	...	...	...	95	0	3.84	—	—	—	—	—	—	—
85-86—Windsor	OHL	29	1600	6	16	4	119	1	4.46	6	263	0	3	20	0	4.56

I

J

Season Team	League	Gms.	Min	W	L	T	GA	SO	Avg.	Gms.	Min.	W	L	GA	SO	Avg.
				REGULAR SEASON								**PLAYOFFS**				
86-87—Windsor	OHL	41	2328	22	14	2	128	†3	3.30	12	710	8	4	38	0	3.21
87-88—Windsor	OHL	18	994	14	3	0	48	2	*2.90	9	537	8	0	28	0	3.13
—Peoria	IHL	5	285	2	2	†1	17	0	3.58	—	—	—	—	—	—	—
88-89—Peoria	IHL	35	2051	11	20	†3	163	1	4.77	3	130	0	2	13	0	6.00
89-90—St. Louis	NHL	4	208	0	3	0	17	0	4.90	—	—	—	—	—	—	—
—Peoria	IHL	36	2043	14	17	†4	165	0	4.85	4	223	1	3	19	0	5.11
90-91—St. Louis	NHL	8	492	2	3	3	25	0	3.05	3	90	0	0	5	0	3.33
—Peoria	IHL	29	1738	23	3	†2	87	0	3.00	10	532	7	2	23	0	*2.59
91-92—St. Louis	NHL	10	468	3	6	0	38	0	4.87	—	—	—	—	—	—	—
—Peoria	IHL	8	493	6	1	†1	29	1	3.53	—	—	—	—	—	—	—
92-93—Tampa Bay	NHL	43	2268	8	24	4	150	1	3.97	—	—	—	—	—	—	—
93-94—Tampa Bay	NHL	15	834	5	6	3	54	0	3.88	—	—	—	—	—	—	—
—St. John's	AHL	16	963	12	3	1	49	1	3.05	—	—	—	—	—	—	—
94-95—Chicago	IHL	4	217	0	4	†0	17	0	4.70	—	—	—	—	—	—	—
—Houston	IHL	3	179	1	1	†1	9	0	3.02	—	—	—	—	—	—	—
95-96—St. Louis	NHL	1	8	0	0	0	1	0	7.50	—	—	—	—	—	—	—
—Montreal	NHL	23	1264	5	9	6	62	0	2.94	1	49	0	0	1	0	1.22
96-97—Montreal	NHL	17	754	4	6	2	50	0	3.98	—	—	—	—	—	—	—
—Phoenix	NHL	2	59	0	1	0	2	0	2.03	—	—	—	—	—	—	—
NHL totals (7 years)		123	6355	27	58	18	399	1	3.77	4	139	0	0	6	0	2.59

JACKMAN, RICHARD D STARS

PERSONAL: Born June 28, 1978, in Toronto. ... 6-2/170. ... Shoots right.
TRANSACTIONS/CAREER NOTES: Selected by Dallas Stars in first round (first Stars pick, fifth overall) of NHL entry draft (June 22, 1996).
HONORS: Named to Can.HL All-Rookie team (1995-96). ... Named to OHL All-Rookie first team (1995-96).

Season Team	League	Gms.	G	A	Pts.	PIM	+/-	PP	SH	Gms.	G	A	Pts.	PIM
				REGULAR SEASON							**PLAYOFFS**			
95-96—Sault Ste. Marie	OHL	66	13	29	42	97	...	...	...	4	1	0	1	15
96-97—Sault Ste. Marie	OHL	53	13	34	47	116	...	...	...	10	2	6	8	24

JACKSON, DANE RW ISLANDERS

PERSONAL: Born May 17, 1970, in Winnipeg. ... 6-1/200. ... Shoots right.
COLLEGE: North Dakota.
TRANSACTIONS/CAREER NOTES: Selected by Vancouver Canucks in third round (third Canucks pick, 44th overall) of NHL entry draft (June 11, 1988). ... Bruised shoulder (January 9, 1994); missed two games. ... Signed as free agent by Buffalo Sabres (August 16, 1995). ... Signed as free agent by New York Islanders (July 21, 1997).

Season Team	League	Gms.	G	A	Pts.	PIM	+/-	PP	SH	Gms.	G	A	Pts.	PIM
				REGULAR SEASON							**PLAYOFFS**			
87-88—Vernon	BCJHL	50	28	32	60	99	...	...	...	13	7	10	17	49
88-89—North Dakota	WCHA	30	4	5	9	33	...	...	...	—	—	—	—	—
89-90—North Dakota	WCHA	44	15	11	26	56	...	...	...	—	—	—	—	—
90-91—North Dakota	WCHA	37	17	9	26	79	...	...	...	—	—	—	—	—
91-92—North Dakota	WCHA	39	23	19	42	81	...	...	...	—	—	—	—	—
92-93—Hamilton	AHL	68	23	20	43	59	...	...	...	—	—	—	—	—
93-94—Hamilton	AHL	60	25	35	60	75	...	...	...	4	2	2	4	16
—Vancouver	NHL	12	5	1	6	9	3	0	0	—	—	—	—	—
94-95—Syracuse	AHL	78	30	28	58	162	...	...	...	—	—	—	—	—
—Vancouver	NHL	3	1	0	1	4	0	0	0	6	0	0	0	10
95-96—Rochester	AHL	50	27	19	46	132	...	...	...	19	4	6	10	53
—Buffalo	NHL	22	5	4	9	41	3	0	0	—	—	—	—	—
96-97—Rochester	AHL	78	24	34	58	111	...	...	...	10	7	4	11	14
NHL totals (3 years)		37	11	5	16	54	6	0	0	6	0	0	0	10

JAGR, JAROMIR RW PENGUINS

PERSONAL: Born February 15, 1972, in Kladno, Czechoslovakia. ... 6-2/216. ... Shoots left. ... Name pronounced YAHR-oh-meer YAH-guhr.
TRANSACTIONS/CAREER NOTES: Selected by Pittsburgh Penguins in first round (first Penguins pick, fifth overall) of NHL entry draft (June 16, 1990). ... Separated shoulder (February 23, 1993); missed three games. ... Strained groin (January 21, 1994); missed four games. ... Played in Europe during 1994-95 NHL lockout. ... Suffered from the flu (January 11, 1997); missed one game. ... Strained groin (February 16, 1997); missed three games. ... Pulled groin (February 27, 1997); missed 13 games. ... Strained groin (April 10, 1997); missed two games.
HONORS: Named to Czechoslovakian League All-Star team (1989-90). ... Named to NHL All-Rookie team (1990-91). ... Played in NHL All-Star Game (1992, 1993 and 1996). ... Won Art Ross Trophy (1994-95). ... Named to THE SPORTING NEWS All-Star first team (1994-95 and 1995-96). ... Named to NHL All-Star first team (1994-95 and 1995-96). ... Played in NHL All-Star Game (1988 and 1990-1994). ... Named to play in NHL All-Star Game (1997); replaced by C Adam Oates due to injury. ... Named to NHL All-Star second team (1996-97).
RECORDS: Holds NHL single-season records for most points by a right winger—149; and most assists by a right winger—87.
STATISTICAL PLATEAUS: Three-goal games: 1990-91 (1), 1994-95 (1), 1996-97 (2). Total: 4.
MISCELLANEOUS: Member of Stanley Cup championship team (1991 and 1992). ... Captain of Pittsburgh Penguins (1995-96). ... Failed to score on a penalty shot (vs. Don Beaupre, January 26, 1993; vs. Mark Fitzpatrick, November 9, 1996).
STATISTICAL NOTES: Led NHL with 12 game-winning goals (1995-96).

Season Team	League	Gms.	G	A	Pts.	PIM	+/-	PP	SH	Gms.	G	A	Pts.	PIM
				REGULAR SEASON							**PLAYOFFS**			
88-89—Poldi Kladno	Czech Rep.	39	8	10	18	...	...	...	...	—	—	—	—	—
89-90—Poldi Kladno	Czech Rep.	51	30	30	60	...	...	...	...	—	—	—	—	—

Season Team	League	REGULAR SEASON								PLAYOFFS				
		Gms.	G	A	Pts.	PIM	+/-	PP	SH	Gms.	G	A	Pts.	PIM
90-91 — Pittsburgh................	NHL	80	27	30	57	42	-4	7	0	24	3	10	13	6
91-92 — Pittsburgh................	NHL	70	32	37	69	34	12	4	0	†21	11	13	24	6
92-93 — Pittsburgh................	NHL	81	34	60	94	61	30	10	1	12	5	4	9	23
93-94 — Pittsburgh................	NHL	80	32	67	99	61	15	9	0	6	2	4	6	16
94-95 — HC Kladno................	Czech Rep.	11	8	14	22	10	...	...	...	—	—	—	—	—
— HC Bolzano................	Euro	5	8	8	16	4	...	...	...	—	—	—	—	—
— HC Bolzano................	Italy	1	0	0	0	0	...	...	...	—	—	—	—	—
— Schalker Haie.............	Ger. Div. II	1	1	10	11	0	...	...	...	—	—	—	—	—
— Pittsburgh................	NHL	48	32	38	†70	37	23	8	3	12	10	5	15	6
95-96 — Pittsburgh................	NHL	82	62	87	149	96	31	20	1	18	11	12	23	18
96-97 — Pittsburgh................	NHL	63	47	48	95	40	22	11	2	5	4	4	8	4
NHL totals (7 years)		504	266	367	633	371	129	69	7	98	46	52	98	79

JAKOPIN, JOHN   LW   PANTHERS

PERSONAL: Born May 16, 1975, in Toronto. ... 6-5/225. ... Shoots left. ... Name pronounced jack-oh-pin.
COLLEGE: Merrimack (Mass.).
TRANSACTIONS/CAREER NOTES: Selected by Detroit Red Wings in fourth round (fourth Red Wings pick, 97th overall) of NHL entry draft (June 26, 1993). ... Signed as free agent by Florida Panthers (June 4, 1997).
HONORS: Named to Hockey East All-Rookie team (1993-94).

Season Team	League	REGULAR SEASON								PLAYOFFS				
		Gms.	G	A	Pts.	PIM	+/-	PP	SH	Gms.	G	A	Pts.	PIM
92-93 — St. Michaels Tier II.....	Jr. A	45	9	21	30	42	...	...	...	—	—	—	—	—
93-94 — Merrimack College.....	Hockey East	36	2	8	10	64	...	...	...	—	—	—	—	—
94-95 — Merrimack College.....	Hockey East	37	4	10	14	42	...	...	...	—	—	—	—	—
95-96 — Merrimack College.....	Hockey East	32	10	15	25	68	...	...	...	—	—	—	—	—
96-97 — Merrimack College.....	Hockey East	31	4	12	16	68	...	...	...	—	—	—	—	—
— Adirondack................	AHL	3	0	0	0	9	...	...	...	—	—	—	—	—

JANNEY, CRAIG   C   COYOTES

PERSONAL: Born September 26, 1967, in Hartford, Conn. ... 6-1/195. ... Shoots left. ... Full name: Craig Harlan Janney.
HIGH SCHOOL: Deerfield (Mass.) Academy.
COLLEGE: Boston College.
TRANSACTIONS/CAREER NOTES: Broke collarbone (December 1985). ... Selected by Boston Bruins in first round (first Bruins pick, 13th overall) of NHL entry draft (June 21, 1986). ... Suffered from mononucleosis (December 1986). ... Pulled right groin (December 1988); missed seven games. ... Tore right groin muscle (October 26, 1989); missed 21 games. ... Strained left shoulder (April 5, 1990). ... Sprained left shoulder (December 13, 1990). ... Sprained right ankle (March 30, 1991). ... Traded by Bruins with D Stephane Quintal to St. Louis Blues for C Adam Oates (February 7, 1992). ... Cut leg (December 1, 1993); missed one game. ... Strained knee (February 20, 1994); missed 11 games. ... Awarded to Vancouver Canucks with second-round pick (C Dave Scatchard) in 1994 draft as compensation for Blues signing free agent C Petr Nedved (March 14, 1994). ... Traded by Canucks to Blues for D Jeff Brown, D Bret Hedican and C Nathan LaFayette (March 21, 1994). ... Left Blues for personal reasons (February 17-March 6, 1995). ... Traded by Blues to San Jose Sharks for D Jeff Norton, third-round pick (traded to Colorado) in 1997 draft and future considerations (March 6, 1995). ... Traded by Sharks to Winnipeg Jets for C Darren Turcotte and second-round pick (traded to Chicago) in 1996 draft (March 18, 1996). ... Jets franchise moved to Phoenix and renamed Coyotes for 1996-97 season; NHL approved move on January 18, 1996.
HONORS: Named to NCAA All-America East first team (1986-87). ... Named to Hockey East All-Star first team (1986-87). ... Named to Hockey East All-Decade team (1994).
STATISTICAL PLATEAUS: Three-goal games: 1987-88 (1), 1991-92 (1), 1992-93 (1). Total: 3.
MISCELLANEOUS: Failed to score on a penalty shot (vs. Stephane Fiset, January 9, 1992; vs. Robb Stauber, March 20, 1993).

Season Team	League	REGULAR SEASON								PLAYOFFS				
		Gms.	G	A	Pts.	PIM	+/-	PP	SH	Gms.	G	A	Pts.	PIM
84-85 — Deerfield Academy.....	Mass. H.S.	17	33	35	68	6	...	...	...	—	—	—	—	—
85-86 — Boston College..........	Hockey East	34	13	14	27	8	...	...	...	—	—	—	—	—
86-87 — Boston College..........	Hockey East	37	28	*55	*83	6	...	...	...	—	—	—	—	—
87-88 — U.S. national team	Int'l	52	26	44	70	6	...	...	...	—	—	—	—	—
— U.S. Olympic team	Int'l	5	3	1	4	2	...	...	...	—	—	—	—	—
— Boston	NHL	15	7	9	16	0	6	1	0	23	6	10	16	11
88-89 — Boston	NHL	62	16	46	62	12	20	2	0	10	4	9	13	21
89-90 — Boston	NHL	55	24	38	62	4	3	11	0	18	3	19	22	2
90-91 — Boston	NHL	77	26	66	92	8	15	9	1	18	4	18	22	11
91-92 — Boston	NHL	53	12	39	51	20	1	3	0	—	—	—	—	—
— St. Louis	NHL	25	6	30	36	2	5	3	0	6	0	6	6	0
92-93 — St. Louis	NHL	84	24	82	106	12	-4	8	0	11	2	9	11	0
93-94 — St. Louis	NHL	69	16	68	84	24	-14	8	0	4	1	3	4	0
94-95 — St. Louis	NHL	8	2	5	7	0	3	1	0	—	—	—	—	—
— San Jose...................	NHL	27	5	15	20	10	-4	2	0	11	3	4	7	4
95-96 — San Jose...................	NHL	71	13	49	62	26	-35	5	0	—	—	—	—	—
— Winnipeg	NHL	13	7	13	20	0	2	2	0	6	1	2	3	0
96-97 — Phoenix..................	NHL	77	15	38	53	26	-1	5	0	7	0	3	3	4
NHL totals (10 years)		636	173	498	671	144	-3	60	1	114	24	83	107	53

JANSSENS, MARK   C   MIGHTY DUCKS

PERSONAL: Born May 19, 1968, in Surrey, B.C. ... 6-3/212. ... Shoots left.
TRANSACTIONS/CAREER NOTES: Selected by New York Rangers as underage junior in fourth round (fourth Rangers pick, 72nd overall) of NHL entry draft (June 21, 1986). ... Fractured skull and suffered cerebral concussion (December 10, 1988). ... Traded by Rangers to

Minnesota North Stars for C Mario Thyer and third-round pick (D Maxim Galanov) in 1993 draft (March 10, 1992). ... Traded by North Stars to Hartford Whalers for C James Black (September 3, 1992). ... Separated shoulder (December 26, 1992); missed five games. ... Fined $500 by Whalers for involvement in bar brawl (April 1, 1994). ... Suffered slight concussion (February 4, 1995); missed two games. ... Sprained knee (January 22, 1997); missed 14 games. ... Traded by Whalers to Mighty Ducks of Anaheim for LW Jon Battaglia and fourth-round pick in 1998 draft (March 18, 1997).

			REGULAR SEASON							PLAYOFFS				
Season Team	League	Gms.	G	A	Pts.	PIM	+/-	PP	SH	Gms.	G	A	Pts.	PIM
84-85— Regina	WHL	70	8	22	30	51	...	...	...	5	1	1	2	0
85-86— Regina	WHL	71	25	38	63	146	...	...	...	9	0	2	2	17
86-87— Regina	WHL	68	24	38	62	209	...	...	...	3	0	1	1	14
87-88— Regina	WHL	71	39	51	90	202	...	...	...	4	3	4	7	6
— New York Rangers	NHL	1	0	0	0	0	0	0	0	—	—	—	—	—
— Colorado	IHL	6	2	2	4	24	...	...	...	12	3	2	5	20
88-89— New York Rangers	NHL	5	0	0	0	0	-4	0	0	—	—	—	—	—
— Denver	IHL	38	19	19	38	104	...	...	...	4	3	0	3	18
89-90— New York Rangers	NHL	80	5	8	13	161	-26	0	0	9	2	1	3	10
90-91— New York Rangers	NHL	67	9	7	16	172	-1	0	0	6	3	0	3	6
91-92— New York Rangers	NHL	4	0	0	0	5	-1	0	0	—	—	—	—	—
— Binghamton	AHL	55	10	23	33	109	...	...	...	—	—	—	—	—
— Minnesota	NHL	3	0	0	0	0	-1	0	0	—	—	—	—	—
— Kalamazoo	IHL	2	0	0	0	2	...	...	...	11	1	2	3	22
92-93— Hartford	NHL	76	12	17	29	237	-15	0	0	—	—	—	—	—
93-94— Hartford	NHL	84	2	10	12	137	-13	0	0	—	—	—	—	—
94-95— Hartford	NHL	46	2	5	7	93	-8	0	0	—	—	—	—	—
95-96— Hartford	NHL	81	2	7	9	155	-13	0	0	—	—	—	—	—
96-97— Hartford	NHL	54	2	4	6	90	-10	0	0	—	—	—	—	—
— Anaheim	NHL	12	0	2	2	47	-3	0	0	11	0	0	0	15
NHL totals (11 years)		513	34	60	94	1097	-95	0	0	26	5	1	6	31

JANTUNEN, MARKO — C — FLAMES

PERSONAL: Born February 14, 1971, in Lahti, Finland. ... 5-10/185. ... Shoots left. ... Name pronounced YAHN-too-nehn.
TRANSACTIONS/CAREER NOTES: Selected by Calgary Flames in 11th round (12th Flames pick, 239th overall) of NHL entry draft (June 22, 1991).

			REGULAR SEASON							PLAYOFFS				
Season Team	League	Gms.	G	A	Pts.	PIM	+/-	PP	SH	Gms.	G	A	Pts.	PIM
90-91— Reipas	Finland	39	9	20	29	20	...	...	...	—	—	—	—	—
91-92— Reipas	Finland	42	10	14	24	46	...	...	...	—	—	—	—	—
92-93— KalPa Kuopio	Finland	48	21	27	48	63	...	...	...	—	—	—	—	—
93-94— TPS Turku	Finland	48	29	29	58	22	...	...	...	11	2	6	8	12
94-95— Vastra Frolunda	Sweden	22	15	8	23	22	...	...	...	—	—	—	—	—
95-96— Vastra Frolunda	Sweden	40	17	14	31	66	...	...	...	13	8	8	16	10
96-97— Calgary	NHL	3	0	0	0	0	-1	0	0	—	—	—	—	—
— Saint John	AHL	23	8	16	24	18	...	...	...	—	—	—	—	—
— Vastra Frolunda	Sweden	13	4	7	11	16	...	...	...	3	2	0	2	6
NHL totals (1 year)		3	0	0	0	0	-1	0	0					

JENNINGS, GRANT — D

PERSONAL: Born May 5, 1965, in Hudson Bay, Sask. ... 6-3/200. ... Shoots left.
TRANSACTIONS/CAREER NOTES: Injured shoulder (1984-85). ... Signed as free agent by Washington Capitals (June 25, 1985). ... Injured knee (October 1986). ... Traded by Capitals with RW Ed Kastelic to Hartford Whalers for D Neil Sheehy and RW Mike Millar (July 6, 1988). ... Broke left hand (October 6, 1988). ... Bruised right foot (October 1988). ... Sprained left shoulder (December 1988). ... Underwent surgery to left shoulder (April 14, 1989). ... Sprained left knee (February 7, 1990). ... Twisted knee (March 14, 1990). ... Strained left ankle (September 1990). ... Bruised shoulder (December 1, 1990); missed six games. ... Injured shoulder (February 13, 1991). ... Traded by Whalers with C Ron Francis and D Ulf Samuelsson to Pittsburgh Penguins for C John Cullen, D Zarley Zalapski and RW Jeff Parker (March 4, 1991). ... Separated left shoulder (March 1991). ... Bruised hand (February 15, 1992); missed seven games. ... Bruised right hand (March 15, 1992); missed one game. ... Bruised left foot (March 11, 1993); missed one game. ... Injured groin (December 11, 1993); missed two games. ... Sprained knee (December 28, 1993); missed 14 games. ... Bruised shoulder (January 31, 1994); missed one game. ... Injured hand (March 8, 1994); missed one game. ... Injured groin (January 25, 1995); missed three games. ... Reinjured groin (February 7, 1995); missed three games. ... Reinjured groin (February 25, 1995); missed three games. ... Traded by Penguins to Toronto Maple Leafs for D Drake Berehowsky (April 7, 1995). ... Injured groin (April 21, 1995); missed one game. ... Signed as free agent by Buffalo Sabres (August 25, 1995). ... Pulled right groin (December 29, 1995); missed four games.
MISCELLANEOUS: Member of Stanley Cup championship team (1991 and 1992).

			REGULAR SEASON							PLAYOFFS				
Season Team	League	Gms.	G	A	Pts.	PIM	+/-	PP	SH	Gms.	G	A	Pts.	PIM
83-84— Saskatoon	WHL	64	5	13	18	102	...	...	...	—	—	—	—	—
84-85— Saskatoon	WHL	47	10	24	34	134	...	...	...	2	1	0	1	2
85-86— Binghamton	AHL	51	0	4	4	109	...	...	...	—	—	—	—	—
86-87— Fort Wayne	IHL	3	0	0	0	0	...	...	...	—	—	—	—	—
— Binghamton	AHL	47	1	5	6	125	...	...	...	13	0	2	2	17
87-88— Binghamton	AHL	56	2	12	14	195	...	...	...	3	1	0	1	15
— Washington	NHL	—				—	...	...	...	1	0	0	0	0
88-89— Hartford	NHL	55	3	10	13	159	...	...	...	4	1	0	1	17
— Binghamton	AHL	2	0	0	0	2	...	...	...	—	—	—	—	—
89-90— Hartford	NHL	64	3	6	9	171	-4	0	0	7	0	0	0	13
90-91— Hartford	NHL	44	1	4	5	82	-13	0	0	—	—	—	—	—
— Pittsburgh	NHL	13	1	3	4	26	2	0	0	13	1	1	2	16
91-92— Pittsburgh	NHL	53	4	5	9	104	-1	0	2	10	0	0	0	12
92-93— Pittsburgh	NHL	58	0	5	5	65	6	0	0	12	0	0	0	8

Season Team	League	Gms.	G	A	Pts.	PIM	+/-	PP	SH	Gms.	G	A	Pts.	PIM
93-94— Pittsburgh	NHL	61	2	4	6	126	-10	0	1	3	0	0	0	2
94-95— Pittsburgh	NHL	25	0	4	4	36	2	0	0	—				
— Toronto	NHL	10	0	2	2	7	-6	0	0	4	0	0	0	0
95-96— Rochester	AHL	9	0	1	1	28	...	0	0	0	0	0	0	
— Buffalo	NHL	6	0	0	0	28	1	0	0	—				
— Atlanta	IHL	3	0	0	0	19	...	...	...	3	0	0	0	20
96-97— Quebec	IHL	42	2	10	12	79	...	...	...	—				
NHL totals (9 years)		389	14	43	57	804	-23	0	3	54	2	1	3	68

JINMAN, LEE   C   STARS

PERSONAL: Born January 10, 1976, in Scarborough, Ont. ... 5-10/160. ... Shoots right. ... Name pronounced JIHN-muhn.
HIGH SCHOOL: Chippewa (North Bay, Ont.).
TRANSACTIONS/CAREER NOTES: Selected by Dallas Stars in second round (second Stars pick, 46th overall) of NHL entry draft (June 28, 1994).
HONORS: Named to Can.HL All-Rookie team (1993-94). ... Named to OHL All-Rookie team (1993-94).

		REGULAR SEASON								PLAYOFFS				
Season Team	League	Gms.	G	A	Pts.	PIM	+/-	PP	SH	Gms.	G	A	Pts.	PIM
92-93— Wexford	Tier II Jr. A	42	37	53	90	14	...	...	...	—				
93-94— North Bay	OHL	66	31	66	97	33	...	...	...	18	*18	19	37	8
94-95— North Bay	OHL	63	39	65	104	41	...	...	...	6	5	5	10	4
95-96— North Bay	OHL	38	19	33	52	23	...	...	...	3	0	0	0	20
— Detroit	OHL	26	10	35	45	26	...	...	...	17	6	15	21	16
96-97— Michigan	IHL	81	17	40	57	65	...	...	...	4	1	1	2	2

JOHANSSON, ANDREAS   C   PENGUINS

PERSONAL: Born May 19, 1973, in Hofors, Sweden. ... 5-10/198. ... Shoots left. ... Name pronounced joh-HAN-suhn.
TRANSACTIONS/CAREER NOTES: Selected by New York Islanders in seventh round (seventh Islanders pick, 136th overall) of NHL entry draft (June 22, 1991). ... Injured back (April 5, 1996); missed three games. ... Traded by Islanders with D Darius Kasparaitis to Pittsburgh Penguins for C Bryan Smolinski (November 17, 1996). ... Bruised shoulder (December 10, 1996); missed 12 games. ... Suffered from the flu (January 26, 1997); missed one game. ... Suffered back spasms (February 15, 1997); missed one game.

		REGULAR SEASON								PLAYOFFS				
Season Team	League	Gms.	G	A	Pts.	PIM	+/-	PP	SH	Gms.	G	A	Pts.	PIM
90-91— Falun	Sweden	31	12	10	22	38	...	...	...	—				
91-92— Farjestad Karlstad	Sweden	30	3	1	4	4	...	...	...	6	0	0	0	4
92-93— Farjestad Karlstad	Sweden	38	4	7	11	38	...	...	...	2	0	0	0	0
93-94— Farjestad Karlstad	Sweden	20	3	6	9	6	...	...	...	—				
94-95— Farjestad Karlstad	Sweden	36	9	10	19	42	...	...	...	4	0	0	0	10
95-96— Worcester	AHL	29	5	5	10	32	...	...	...	0	0	0	0	
— Utah	IHL	22	4	13	17	28	...	...	...	12	0	5	5	6
— New York Islanders	NHL	3	0	1	1	0	1	0	0	—				
96-97— New York Islanders	NHL	15	2	2	4	0	-6	1	0	—				
— Pittsburgh	NHL	27	2	7	9	20	-6	0	0	—				
— Cleveland	IHL	10	2	4	6	42	...	...	...	11	1	5	6	8
NHL totals (2 years)		45	4	10	14	20	-11	1	0					

JOHANSSON, CALLE   D   CAPITALS

PERSONAL: Born February 14, 1967, in Goteborg, Sweden. ... 5-11/200. ... Shoots left. ... Name pronounced KAL-ee yoh-HAHN-sehn.
TRANSACTIONS/CAREER NOTES: Selected by Buffalo Sabres in first round (first Sabres pick, 14th overall) of NHL entry draft (June 15, 1985). ... Dislocated thumb (October 9, 1988). ... Traded by Sabres with second-round pick (G Byron Dafoe) in 1989 draft to Washington Capitals for D Grant Ledyard, G Clint Malarchuk and sixth-round pick (C Brian Holzinger) in 1991 draft (March 6, 1989). ... Injured back (October 7, 1989); missed 10 games. ... Bruised ribs (January 9, 1993); missed seven games. ... Played in Europe during 1994-95 NHL lockout. ... Suffered from the flu (March 25, 1995); missed two games. ... Broke hand (April 4, 1996); missed remainder of season. ... Broke jaw (November 12, 1996); missed 16 games. ... Bruised foot (February 14, 1997); missed one game.
HONORS: Named to NHL All-Rookie team (1987-88).

		REGULAR SEASON								PLAYOFFS				
Season Team	League	Gms.	G	A	Pts.	PIM	+/-	PP	SH	Gms.	G	A	Pts.	PIM
83-84— Vastra Frolunda	Sweden	34	5	10	15	20	...	...	...	—				
84-85— Vastra Frolunda	Sweden	36	14	15	29	20	...	...	...	6	1	2	3	4
85-86— Bjorkloven	Sweden	17	1	1	2	14	...	...	...	—				
86-87— Bjorkloven	Sweden	30	2	13	15	18	...	...	...	6	1	3	4	6
87-88— Buffalo	NHL	71	4	38	42	37	12	2	0	6	0	1	1	0
88-89— Buffalo	NHL	47	2	11	13	33	-7	0	0	—				
— Washington	NHL	12	1	7	8	4	1	1	0	6	1	2	3	0
89-90— Washington	NHL	70	8	31	39	25	7	4	0	15	1	6	7	4
90-91— Washington	NHL	80	11	41	52	23	-2	2	1	10	2	7	9	8
91-92— Washington	NHL	80	14	42	56	49	2	5	2	7	0	5	5	4
92-93— Washington	NHL	77	7	38	45	56	3	6	0	6	0	5	5	4
93-94— Washington	NHL	84	9	33	42	59	3	4	0	6	1	3	4	4
94-95— Kloten	Switzerland	5	1	2	3	8	...	...	...	—				
— Washington	NHL	46	5	26	31	35	-6	4	0	7	3	1	4	0
95-96— Washington	NHL	78	10	25	35	50	13	4	0	—				
96-97— Washington	NHL	65	6	11	17	16	-2	2	0	—				
NHL totals (10 years)		710	77	303	380	387	24	34	3	63	8	30	38	24

JOHNSON, BRENT   G   BLUES

PERSONAL: Born March 12, 1977, in Farmington, Mich. ... 6-2/185. ... Catches left.
TRANSACTIONS/CAREER NOTES: Selected by Colorado Avalanche in fifth round (fifth Avalanche pick, 129th overall) of NHL entry draft (July 8, 1995). ... Rights traded by Avalanche to St. Louis Blues for third-round pick (RW Ville Nieminen) in 1997 draft and conditional third-round pick in 2000 draft (May 30, 1997).

			REGULAR SEASON							PLAYOFFS						
Season Team	League	Gms.	Min	W	L	T	GA	SO	Avg.	Gms.	Min.	W	L	GA	SO	Avg.
94-95—Owen Sound	OHL	18	904	3	9	1	75	0	4.98	4	253	0	4	24	0	5.69
95-96—Owen Sound	OHL	58	3211	24	28	1	243	1	4.54	6	371	2	4	29	0	4.69
96-97—Owen Sound	OHL	50	2798	20	28	1	201	1	4.31	4	253	0	4	24	0	5.69

JOHNSON, CRAIG   LW   KINGS

PERSONAL: Born March 18, 1972, in St. Paul, Minn. ... 6-2/185. ... Shoots left.
HIGH SCHOOL: Hill-Murray (St. Paul, Minn.).
COLLEGE: Minnesota.
TRANSACTIONS/CAREER NOTES: Suffered stress fracture of vertebrae (February 1987). ... Selected by St. Louis Blues in second round (first Blues pick, 33rd overall) of NHL entry draft (June 16, 1990). ... Separated shoulder (December 1990). ... Traded by Blues with C Patrice Tardiff, C Roman Vopat, fifth-round pick (D Peter Hogan) in 1996 draft and first-round pick (LW Matt Zultek) in 1997 draft to Los Angeles Kings for C Wayne Gretzky (February 27, 1996). ... Sprained left shoulder (March 13, 1996); missed seven games. ... Strained abdominal muscle prior to 1996-97 season; missed first seven games of season. ... Strained groin (November 2, 1996); missed one game. ... Strained abdominal muscle (November 30, 1996); missed 36 games. ... Strained groin (March 29, 1997); missed six games.
HONORS: Named to WCHA All-Rookie Team (1990-91).

			REGULAR SEASON							PLAYOFFS				
Season Team	League	Gms.	G	A	Pts.	PIM	+/-	PP	SH		Gms.	G	A	Pts.	PIM
87-88—Hill Murray	Minn. H.S.	28	14	20	34	4	...	...	...	—	—	—	—	—
88-89—Hill Murray	Minn. H.S.	24	22	30	52	10	...	...	...	—	—	—	—	—
89-90—Hill Murray	Minn. H.S.	23	15	36	51	...	...	...	...	—	—	—	—	—
90-91—Univ. of Minnesota	WCHA	33	13	18	31	34	...	...	...	—	—	—	—	—
91-92—Univ. of Minnesota	WCHA	44	19	39	58	70	...	...	...	—	—	—	—	—
92-93—Univ. of Minnesota	WCHA	42	22	24	46	70	...	...	...	—	—	—	—	—
93-94—U.S. national team	Int'l	54	25	26	51	64	...	...	...	—	—	—	—	—
—U.S. Olympic team	Int'l	8	0	4	4	4	...	...	...	—	—	—	—	—
94-95—Peoria	IHL	16	2	6	8	25	...	...	...	9	0	4	4	10
—St. Louis	NHL	15	3	3	6	6	4	0	0	1	0	0	0	2
95-96—Worcester	AHL	5	3	0	3	2	...	...	...	—	—	—	—	—
—St. Louis	NHL	49	8	7	15	30	-4	1	0	—	—	—	—	—
—Los Angeles	NHL	11	5	4	9	6	-4	3	0	—	—	—	—	—
96-97—Los Angeles	NHL	31	4	3	7	26	-7	1	0	—	—	—	—	—
NHL totals (3 years)		106	20	17	37	68	-11	5	0	1	0	0	0	2

JOHNSON, GREG   C   PENGUINS

PERSONAL: Born March 16, 1971, in Thunder Bay, Ont. ... 5-11/185. ... Shoots left.
COLLEGE: North Dakota.
TRANSACTIONS/CAREER NOTES: Selected by Philadelphia Flyers in second round (first Flyers pick, 33rd overall) of NHL entry draft (June 17, 1989). ... Separated right shoulder (November 24, 1990). ... Rights traded by Flyers with future considerations to Detroit Red Wings for RW Jim Cummins and fourth-round pick (traded to Boston) in 1993 draft (June 20, 1993). ... Loaned to Canadian Olympic team (January 19, 1994). ... Returned to Red Wings (March 1, 1994). ... Sprained left ankle (April 14, 1995); missed last nine games of season. ... Injured left hand (October 8, 1995); missed two games. ... Injured knee (March 19, 1996); missed 12 games. ... Traded by Red Wings to Pittsburgh Penguins for RW Tomas Sandstrom (January 27, 1997). ... Bruised shoulder (April 3, 1997); missed one game.
HONORS: Named to USHL All-Star first team (1988-89). ... Named Canadian Junior A Player of the Year (1989). ... Named to Centennial Cup All-Star first team (1989). ... Named to NCAA All-America West first team (1990-91 and 1992-93). ... Named to WCHA All-Star first team (1990-91 through 1992-93). ... Named to NCAA West All-America second team (1991-92).
MISCELLANEOUS: Member of silver-medal-winning Canadian Olympic team (1994).

			REGULAR SEASON							PLAYOFFS				
Season Team	League	Gms.	G	A	Pts.	PIM	+/-	PP	SH		Gms.	G	A	Pts.	PIM
88-89—Thunder Bay Jrs.	USHL	47	32	64	96	4	...	...	...	12	5	13	18	0
89-90—North Dakota	WCHA	44	17	38	55	11	...	...	...	—	—	—	—	—
90-91—North Dakota	WCHA	38	18	*61	79	6	...	...	...	—	—	—	—	—
91-92—North Dakota	WCHA	39	20	54	74	8	...	...	...	—	—	—	—	—
92-93—Canadian nat'l team	Int'l	23	6	14	20	2	...	...	...	—	—	—	—	—
—North Dakota	WCHA	34	19	45	64	18	...	...	...	—	—	—	—	—
93-94—Detroit	NHL	52	6	11	17	22	-7	1	1	7	2	2	4	2
—Canadian nat'l team	Int'l	6	2	6	8	4	...	...	...	—	—	—	—	—
—Can. Olympic team	Int'l	8	0	3	3	0	...	...	...	—	—	—	—	—
—Adirondack	AHL	3	2	4	6	0	...	...	...	4	0	4	4	2
94-95—Detroit	NHL	22	3	5	8	14	1	2	0	1	0	0	0	0
95-96—Detroit	NHL	60	18	22	40	30	6	5	0	13	3	1	4	8
96-97—Detroit	NHL	43	6	10	16	12	-5	0	0	—	—	—	—	—
—Pittsburgh	NHL	32	7	9	16	14	-13	1	0	5	1	0	1	2
NHL totals (4 years)		209	40	57	97	92	-18	9	1	26	6	3	9	12

JOHNSON, JIM   D   COYOTES

PERSONAL: Born August 9, 1962, in New Hope, Minn. ... 6-1/190. ... Shoots left. ... Full name: James Erik Johnson.
HIGH SCHOOL: Cooper (New Hope, Minn.).
COLLEGE: Minnesota-Duluth.
TRANSACTIONS/CAREER NOTES: Signed as free agent by Pittsburgh Penguins (June 9, 1985). ... Tore cartilage in right knee (January 1988). ... Suffered back pain (October 1990). ... Injured neck (November 12, 1990); missed three games. ... Traded by Penguins with D Chris Dahlquist to Minnesota North Stars for D Peter Taglianetti and D Larry Murphy (December 11, 1990). ... Sprained back (February 12, 1991); missed two games. ... Bruised hip (April 1991). ... Injured groin (December 7, 1991); missed five games. ... Strained hamstring (March 10, 1992); missed two games. ... Cut face (November 14, 1992); missed two games. ... Broke finger (January 3, 1993); missed one game. ... Sprained knee (April 14, 1993); missed final two games of season. ... North Stars franchise moved from Minnesota to Dallas and renamed Stars for 1993-94 season. ... Sprained knee (October 23, 1993); missed three games. ... Injured neck (January 18, 1994); missed 14 games. ... Traded by Stars to Washington Capitals for LW Alan May and seventh-round pick (RW Jeff Dewar) in 1995 draft (March 21, 1994). ... Tore knee ligament (April 5, 1994); missed remainder of season. ... Bruised arm (February 13, 1995); missed one game. ... Suffered partial tear of ligament in left wrist (November 3, 1995); missed five games. ... Strained shoulder (January 1, 1996); missed five games. ... Signed as free agent by Phoenix Coyotes (July 15, 1996). ... Bruised heel (October 8, 1996); missed one game. ... Strained neck (November 16, 1996); missed six games. ... Suffered back spasms (February 26, 1997); missed two games. ... Sprained thumb (March 17, 1997); missed seven games.

		REGULAR SEASON							PLAYOFFS				
Season Team	League	Gms.	G	A	Pts.	PIM	+/-	PP	SH	Gms.	G	A	Pts.	PIM
81-82— Minnesota-Duluth	WCHA	40	0	10	10	62	...	...	...	—	—	—	—	—
82-83— Minnesota-Duluth	WCHA	44	3	18	21	118	...	...	...	—	—	—	—	—
83-84— Minnesota-Duluth	WCHA	43	3	13	16	116	...	...	...	—	—	—	—	—
84-85— Minnesota-Duluth	WCHA	47	7	29	36	49	...	...	...	—	—	—	—	—
85-86— Pittsburgh	NHL	80	3	26	29	115	12	0	0	—	—	—	—	—
86-87— Pittsburgh	NHL	80	5	25	30	116	-6	0	0	—	—	—	—	—
87-88— Pittsburgh	NHL	55	1	12	13	87	-4	0	0	—	—	—	—	—
88-89— Pittsburgh	NHL	76	2	14	16	163	7	1	0	11	0	5	5	44
89-90— Pittsburgh	NHL	75	3	13	16	154	-20	1	0	—	—	—	—	—
90-91— Pittsburgh	NHL	24	0	5	5	23	-3	0	0	—	—	—	—	—
— Minnesota	NHL	44	1	9	10	100	9	0	0	14	0	1	1	52
91-92— Minnesota	NHL	71	4	10	14	102	11	0	0	7	1	3	4	18
92-93— Minnesota	NHL	79	3	20	23	105	9	1	0	—	—	—	—	—
93-94— Dallas	NHL	53	0	7	7	51	-6	0	0	—	—	—	—	—
— Washington	NHL	8	0	0	0	12	-1	0	0	—	—	—	—	—
94-95— Washington	NHL	47	0	13	13	43	6	0	0	7	0	2	2	8
95-96— Washington	NHL	66	2	4	6	34	-3	0	0	6	0	0	0	6
96-97— Phoenix	NHL	55	3	7	10	74	5	0	0	6	0	0	0	4
NHL totals (12 years)		813	27	165	192	1179	16	3	0	51	1	11	12	132

JOHNSON, MATT   LW   KINGS

PERSONAL: Born November 23, 1975, in Pelham, Ont. ... 6-5/223. ... Shoots left.
TRANSACTIONS/CAREER NOTES: Selected by Los Angeles Kings in second round (second Kings pick, 33rd overall) of NHL entry draft (June 28, 1994). ... Suffered from the flu (February 25, 1995); missed one game. ... Bruised right hand (April 3, 1995); missed four games. ... Strained shoulder (December 18, 1996); missed six games. ... Suffered concussion (February 1, 1997); missed one game. ... Suspended four games and fined $1,000 by NHL for elbowing incident (February 5, 1997). ... Strained back (March 10, 1997); missed final 13 games of regular season.

		REGULAR SEASON							PLAYOFFS				
Season Team	League	Gms.	G	A	Pts.	PIM	+/-	PP	SH	Gms.	G	A	Pts.	PIM
91-92— Welland	Jr. B	38	6	19	25	214	...	...	...	—	—	—	—	—
92-93— Peterborough	OHL	66	8	17	25	211	...	...	...	16	1	1	2	54
93-94— Peterborough	OHL	50	13	24	37	233	...	...	...	—	—	—	—	—
94-95— Peterborough	OHL	14	1	2	3	43	...	...	...	—	—	—	—	—
— Los Angeles	NHL	14	1	0	1	102	0	0	0	—	—	—	—	—
95-96— Los Angeles	NHL	1	0	0	0	5	0	0	0	—	—	—	—	—
— Phoenix	IHL	29	4	4	8	87	...	...	...	—	—	—	—	—
96-97— Los Angeles	NHL	52	1	3	4	194	-4	0	0	—	—	—	—	—
NHL totals (3 years)		67	2	3	5	301	-4	0	0					

JOHNSON, MIKE   RW   MAPLE LEAFS

PERSONAL: Born October 3, 1974, in Scarborough, Ont. ... 6-3/190. ... Shoots right.
COLLEGE: Bowling Green State.
TRANSACTIONS/CAREER NOTES: Signed as free agent by Toronto Maple Leafs (March 16, 1997).

		REGULAR SEASON							PLAYOFFS				
Season Team	League	Gms.	G	A	Pts.	PIM	+/-	PP	SH	Gms.	G	A	Pts.	PIM
93-94— Bowling Green	CCHA	38	6	14	20	18	...	...	...	—	—	—	—	—
94-95— Bowling Green	CCHA	37	16	33	49	35	...	...	...	—	—	—	—	—
95-96— Bowling Green	CCHA	30	12	19	31	22	...	...	...	—	—	—	—	—
96-97— Bowling Green	CCHA	35	26	29	55	42	...	...	...	3	4	3	7	4
— Toronto	NHL	13	2	2	4	4	-2	0	1	—	—	—	—	—
NHL totals (1 year)		13	2	2	4	4	-2	0	1					

JOMPHE, JEAN-FRANCOIS   C   MIGHTY DUCKS

PERSONAL: Born December 28, 1972, in Harve St. Pierre, Que. ... 6-1/195. ... Shoots left. ... Name pronounced ZHAHMF.
TRANSACTIONS/CAREER NOTES: Signed as free agent by Mighty Ducks of Anaheim (September 7, 1993). ... Loaned by Mighty Ducks to Canadian national team (September 28, 1994). ... Strained abdominal muscle (March 7, 1997); missed final 16 games of regular season.

Season Team	League	Gms.	G	A	Pts.	PIM	+/-	PP	SH	Gms.	G	A	Pts.	PIM
90-91 — Shawinigan	QMJHL	42	17	22	39	14	...	...	...	6	2	1	3	2
91-92 — Shawinigan	QMJHL	44	28	33	61	69	...	...	...	10	6	10	16	10
92-93 — Sherbrooke	QMJHL	60	43	43	86	86	...	...	...	15	10	13	23	18
93-94 — San Diego	IHL	29	2	3	5	12	...	...	...	—	—	—	—	—
— Greensboro	ECHL	25	9	9	18	41	...	...	...	1	1	0	1	0
94-95 — Canadian nat'l team ...	Int'l	52	33	25	58	85	...	...	...	—	—	—	—	—
95-96 — Baltimore	AHL	47	21	34	55	75	...	...	...	—	—	—	—	—
— Anaheim	NHL	31	2	12	14	39	7	2	0	—	—	—	—	—
96-97 — Anaheim	NHL	64	7	14	21	53	-9	0	1	—	—	—	—	—
NHL totals (2 years)		95	9	26	35	92	-2	2	1					

JONES, KEITH   RW   AVALANCHE

PERSONAL: Born November 8, 1968, in Brantford, Ont. ... 6-2/200. ... Shoots left.

COLLEGE: Western Michigan.

TRANSACTIONS/CAREER NOTES: Selected by Washington Capitals in seventh round (seventh Capitals pick, 141st overall) of NHL entry draft (June 11, 1988). ... Suffered from the flu (January 21, 1993); missed two games. ... Sprained wrist (January 25, 1994); missed six games. ... Injured foot (March 16, 1995); missed one game. ... Separated ribs and bruised foot (March 29, 1995); missed six games. ... Pulled groin (March 12, 1996); missed seven games. ... Reinjured groin (March 29, 1996); missed seven games. ... Traded by Capitals with first-round pick in 1998 draft and fourth-round pick in 1997 or 1998 draft to Colorado Avalanche for D Curtis Leschyshyn and LW Chris Simon (November 2, 1996). ... Injured knee (April 26, 1997); missed remainder of playoffs.

HONORS: Named to CCHA All-Star first team (1991-92).

MISCELLANEOUS: Failed to score on a penalty shot (vs. Patrick Labrecque, November 1, 1995).

Season Team	League	Gms.	G	A	Pts.	PIM	+/-	PP	SH	Gms.	G	A	Pts.	PIM
87-88 — Niagara Falls	OHA	40	50	80	130	...	...	...	...	—	—	—	—	—
88-89 — Western Michigan.....	CCHA	37	9	12	21	51	...	...	...	—	—	—	—	—
89-90 — Western Michigan.....	CCHA	40	19	18	37	82	...	...	...	—	—	—	—	—
90-91 — Western Michigan.....	CCHA	41	30	19	49	106	...	...	...	—	—	—	—	—
91-92 — Western Michigan.....	CCHA	35	25	31	56	77	...	...	...	—	—	—	—	—
— Baltimore	AHL	6	2	4	6	0	...	...	...	—	—	—	—	—
92-93 — Baltimore	AHL	8	7	3	10	4	...	...	...	—	—	—	—	—
— Washington	NHL	71	12	14	26	124	18	0	0	6	0	0	0	10
93-94 — Washington	NHL	68	16	19	35	149	4	5	0	11	0	1	1	36
— Portland	AHL	6	5	7	12	4	...	...	...	—	—	—	—	—
94-95 — Washington	NHL	40	14	6	20	65	-2	1	0	7	4	4	8	22
95-96 — Washington	NHL	68	18	23	41	103	8	5	0	2	0	0	0	7
96-97 — Washington	NHL	11	2	3	5	13	-2	1	0	—	—	—	—	—
— Colorado	NHL	67	23	20	43	105	5	13	1	6	3	3	6	4
NHL totals (5 years)		325	85	85	170	559	31	25	1	32	7	8	15	79

JONSSON, KENNY   D   ISLANDERS

PERSONAL: Born October 5, 1974, in Angelholm, Sweden. ... 6-3/195. ... Shoots left. ... Name pronounced YAHN-suhn.

TRANSACTIONS/CAREER NOTES: Selected by Toronto Maple Leafs in first round (first Maple Leafs pick, 12th overall) of NHL entry draft (June 26, 1993). ... Played in Europe during 1994-95 NHL lockout. ... Suffered from the flu (February 13, 1995); missed two games. ... Strained hip flexor (February 27, 1995); missed one game. ... Suffered hip pointer (April 7, 1995); missed one game. ... Suffered from the flu (April 19, 1995); missed one game. ... Strained back (December 9, 1995); missed one game. ... Separated shoulder (January 30, 1996); missed 17 games. ... Traded by Maple Leafs with C Darby Hendrickson, LW Sean Haggerty and first-round pick (G Robert Luongo) in 1997 draft to New York Islanders for LW Wendal Clark, D Mathieu Schneider and D D.J. Smith (March 13, 1996). ... Suffered from the flu (December 23, 1996); missed one game.

HONORS: Named Swedish League Rookie of the Year (1992-93). ... Named to NHL All-Rookie team (1994-95).

Season Team	League	Gms.	G	A	Pts.	PIM	+/-	PP	SH	Gms.	G	A	Pts.	PIM
91-92 — Rogle Angelholm	Sweden	30	4	11	15	24	...	...	...	—	—	—	—	—
92-93 — Rogle Angelholm	Sweden	39	3	10	13	42	...	...	...	—	—	—	—	—
93-94 — Rogle Angelholm	Sweden	36	4	13	17	40	...	...	...	3	1	1	2	0
— Swed. Olympic team..	Int'l	3	1	0	1	0	...	...	...	—	—	—	—	—
94-95 — Rogle Angelholm	Sweden	8	3	1	4	20	...	...	...	—	—	—	—	—
— St. John's...................	AHL	10	2	5	7	2	...	...	...	—	—	—	—	—
— Toronto	NHL	39	2	7	9	16	-8	0	0	4	0	0	0	0
95-96 — Toronto	NHL	50	4	22	26	22	12	3	0	—	—	—	—	—
— New York Islanders....	NHL	16	0	4	4	10	-5	0	0	—	—	—	—	—
96-97 — New York Islanders....	NHL	81	3	18	21	24	10	1	0	—	—	—	—	—
NHL totals (3 years)		186	9	51	60	72	9	4	0	4	0	0	0	0

JOSEPH, CHRIS   D   CANUCKS

PERSONAL: Born September 10, 1969, in Burnaby, B.C. ... 6-2/202. ... Shoots right. ... Full name: Robin Christopher Joseph.

HIGH SCHOOL: Alpha (Burnaby, B.C.).

TRANSACTIONS/CAREER NOTES: Selected by Pittsburgh Penguins in first round (first Penguins pick, fifth overall) of NHL entry draft (June 13, 1987). ... Traded by Penguins with C Craig Simpson, C Dave Hannan and D Moe Mantha to Edmonton Oilers for D Paul Coffey, LW Dave Hunter and RW Wayne Van Dorp (November 24, 1987). ... Strained knee ligaments (January 1989). ... Traded by Oilers to Tampa Bay Lightning for D Bob Beers (November 12, 1993). ... Selected by Pittsburgh Penguins from Lightning in waiver draft for cash (January 18, 1995). ... Injured knee (March 2, 1995); missed 14 games. ... Injured knee (March 7, 1996); missed four games. ... Selected by Vancouver Canucks from Penguins in waiver draft for cash (September 30, 1996). ... Injured groin (December 18, 1996); missed seven games. ... Suffered from the flu (February 27, 1997); missed two games.

Season Team	League	REGULAR SEASON								PLAYOFFS				
		Gms.	G	A	Pts.	PIM	+/-	PP	SH	Gms.	G	A	Pts.	PIM
85-86— Seattle..............	WHL	72	4	8	12	50	...	...	...	5	0	3	3	12
86-87— Seattle..............	WHL	67	13	45	58	155	...	...	...	—	—	—	—	—
87-88— Pittsburgh................	NHL	17	0	4	4	12	2	0	0	—	—	—	—	—
— Edmonton...............	NHL	7	0	4	4	6	-3	0	0	—	—	—	—	—
— Nova Scotia	AHL	8	0	2	2	8	...	...	...	4	0	0	0	9
— Seattle.............	WHL	23	5	14	19	49	...	...	...	—	—	—	—	—
88-89— Cape Breton	AHL	5	1	1	2	18	...	...	...	—	—	—	—	—
— Edmonton...............	NHL	44	4	5	9	54	-9	0	0	—	—	—	—	—
89-90— Edmonton...............	NHL	4	0	2	2	2	-2	0	0	—	—	—	—	—
— Cape Breton	AHL	61	10	20	30	69	...	...	...	6	2	1	3	4
90-91— Edmonton...............	NHL	49	5	17	22	59	3	2	0	—	—	—	—	—
91-92— Edmonton...............	NHL	7	0	0	0	8	-1	0	0	5	1	3	4	2
— Cape Breton	AHL	63	14	29	43	72	...	...	...	5	0	2	2	8
92-93— Edmonton...............	NHL	33	2	10	12	48	-9	1	0	—	—	—	—	—
93-94— Edmonton...............	NHL	10	1	1	2	28	-8	1	0	—	—	—	—	—
— Tampa Bay	NHL	66	10	19	29	108	-13	7	0	—	—	—	—	—
94-95— Pittsburgh................	NHL	33	5	10	15	46	3	3	0	10	1	1	2	12
95-96— Pittsburgh................	NHL	70	5	14	19	71	6	0	0	15	1	0	1	8
96-97— Vancouver................	NHL	63	3	13	16	62	-21	2	0	—	—	—	—	—
NHL totals (10 years)		403	35	99	134	504	-52	16	0	30	3	4	7	22

JOSEPH, CURTIS   G   OILERS

PERSONAL: Born April 29, 1967, in Keswick, Ont. ... 5-10/182. ... Catches left. ... Full name: Curtis Shayne Joseph.
HIGH SCHOOL: Huron Heights (Newmarket, Ont.).
COLLEGE: Wisconsin.
TRANSACTIONS/CAREER NOTES: Signed as free agent by St. Louis Blues (June 16, 1989). ... Dislocated left shoulder (April 11, 1990). ... Underwent surgery to left shoulder (May 10, 1990). ... Sprained right knee (February 26, 1991); missed remainder of season. ... Injured ankle (March 12, 1992); missed seven games. ... Suffered sore knee (January 2, 1993); missed three games. ... Suffered from the flu (February 9, 1993); missed one game. ... Slightly strained groin (January 26, 1995); missed three games. ... Pulled hamstring (April 16, 1995); missed four games. ... Rights traded by Blues with rights to RW Michael Grier to Edmonton Oilers for first-round picks in 1996 (C Marty Reasoner) and 1997 (traded to Los Angeles) drafts (August 4, 1995); picks had been awarded to Oilers as compensation for Blues signing free agent LW Shayne Corson (July 28, 1995). ... Injured right knee (March 30, 1996); missed three games. ... Strained groin (December 18, 1996); missed seven games.
HONORS: Named OHA Most Valuable Player (1986-87). ... Won WCHA Most Valuable Player Award (1988-89). ... Won WCHA Rookie of the Year Award (1988-89). ... Named to NCAA All-America West second team (1988-89). ... Named to WCHA All-Star first team (1988-89). ... Played in NHL All-Star Game (1994).
MISCELLANEOUS: Stopped a penalty shot attempt (vs. Greg Adams, January 25, 1992; vs. Todd Elik, April 16, 1992; vs. Phil Housley, December 19, 1992; vs. Mike Donnelly, April 7, 1994). ... Allowed a penalty shot goal (vs. Curtis Joseph, October 26, 1996). ... Holds Edmonton Oilers all-time record for goals-against average (3.09).
STATISTICAL NOTES: Led NHL with .911 save percentage (1992-93).

Season Team	League	REGULAR SEASON							PLAYOFFS						
		Gms.	Min	W	L	T	GA	SO	Avg.	Gms.	Min.	W	L	GA	SO	Avg.
86-87— Richmond Hill..............	OHA					Statistics unavailable.									
87-88— Notre Dame	SCMHL	36	2174	25	4	7	94	1	2.59	—	—	—	—	—	—	—
88-89— Univ. of Wisconsin	WCHA	38	2267	21	11	5	94	1	2.49	—	—	—	—	—	—	—
89-90— Peoria	IHL	23	1241	10	8	‡2	80	0	3.87	—	—	—	—	—	—	—
— St. Louis	NHL	15	852	9	5	1	48	0	3.38	6	327	4	1	18	0	3.30
90-91— St. Louis	NHL	30	1710	16	10	2	89	0	3.12	—	—	—	—	—	—	—
91-92— St. Louis	NHL	60	3494	27	20	10	175	2	3.01	6	379	2	4	23	0	3.64
92-93— St. Louis	NHL	68	3890	29	28	9	196	1	3.02	11	715	7	4	27	2	2.27
93-94— St. Louis	NHL	71	4127	36	23	11	213	1	3.10	4	246	0	4	15	0	3.66
94-95— St. Louis	NHL	36	1914	20	10	1	89	1	2.79	7	392	3	3	24	0	3.67
95-96— Las Vegas	IHL	15	873	12	2	1	29	1	1.99	—	—	—	—	—	—	—
— Edmonton	NHL	34	1936	15	16	2	111	0	3.44	—	—	—	—	—	—	—
96-97— Edmonton	NHL	72	4100	32	29	9	200	6	2.93	12	767	5	7	36	2	2.82
NHL totals (8 years)		386	22023	184	141	45	1121	11	3.05	46	2826	21	23	143	4	3.04

JOVANOVSKI, ED   D   PANTHERS

PERSONAL: Born June 26, 1976, in Windsor, Ont. ... 6-2/210. ... Shoots left. ... Name pronounced joh-vuh-NAHV-skee.
HIGH SCHOOL: Riverside Secondary (Windsor, Ont.).
TRANSACTIONS/CAREER NOTES: Selected by Florida Panthers in first round (first Panthers pick, first overall) of NHL entry draft (June 28, 1994). ... Broke right index finger (September 29, 1995); missed first 11 games of season. ... Sprained knee (January 15, 1997); missed 16 games.
HONORS: Named to Can.HL All-Rookie team (1993-94). ... Named to OHL All-Star second team (1993-94). ... Named to OHL All-Rookie team (1993-94). ... Named to Can.HL All-Star second team (1994-95). ... Named to OHL All-Star first team (1994-95). ... Named to NHL All-Rookie team (1995-96).

Season Team	League	REGULAR SEASON								PLAYOFFS				
		Gms.	G	A	Pts.	PIM	+/-	PP	SH	Gms.	G	A	Pts.	PIM
92-93— Windsor	OHL Jr. B	48	7	46	53	88	...	...	...	—	—	—	—	—
93-94— Windsor	OHL	62	15	35	50	221	...	...	...	4	0	0	0	15
94-95— Windsor	OHL	50	23	42	65	198	...	...	...	9	2	7	9	39
95-96— Florida	NHL	70	10	11	21	137	-3	2	0	22	1	8	9	52
96-97— Florida	NHL	61	7	16	23	172	-1	3	0	5	0	0	0	4
NHL totals (2 years)		131	17	27	44	309	-4	5	0	27	1	8	9	56

JUHLIN, PATRIK   LW   FLYERS

PERSONAL: Born April 24, 1970, in Huddinge, Sweden. ... 6-0/187. ... Shoots left. ... Name pronounced yoo-LEEN.
TRANSACTIONS/CAREER NOTES: Selected by Philadelphia Flyers in second round (second Flyers pick, 34th overall) of NHL entry draft (June 17, 1989). ... Played in Europe during 1994-95 NHL lockout. ... Sprained left knee (April 26, 1995); missed last three games of season. ... Injured groin (December 23, 1995); missed nine games. ... Reinjured groin (February 3, 1996); missed 18 games.
HONORS: Named to AHL All-Star first team (1996-97).
MISCELLANEOUS: Member of gold-medal-winning Swedish Olympic team (1994).

		REGULAR SEASON								PLAYOFFS				
Season Team	League	Gms.	G	A	Pts.	PIM	+/-	PP	SH	Gms.	G	A	Pts.	PIM
87-88— Vasteras....................	Sweden	28	25	10	35	...	...	...	...	—	—	—	—	—
88-89— Vasteras....................	Sweden	30	29	13	42	...	...	...	...	—	—	—	—	—
89-90— Vasteras....................	Sweden	35	10	13	23	18	...	...	...	2	0	0	0	0
90-91— Vasteras....................	Sweden	40	13	9	22	24	...	...	...	—	—	—	—	—
91-92— Vasteras....................	Sweden	39	15	12	27	40	...	...	...	—	—	—	—	—
92-93— Vasteras....................	Sweden	34	14	12	26	22	...	...	...	3	0	1	1	0
93-94— Vasteras....................	Sweden	40	15	16	31	20	...	...	...	4	1	1	2	0
— Swe. Olympic team....	Int'l	8	7	1	8	16	...	...	...	—	—	—	—	—
94-95— Vasteras....................	Sweden	11	5	9	14	8	...	...	...	—	—	—	—	—
— Philadelphia	NHL	42	4	3	7	6	-13	0	0	13	1	0	1	2
95-96— Hershey	AHL	14	5	2	7	8	...	...	...	1	0	0	0	0
96-97— Philadelphia	AHL	78	31	60	91	24	...	...	...	9	7	6	13	4
NHL totals (1 year)		42	4	3	7	6	-13	0	0	13	1	0	1	2

JUNEAU, JOE   C   CAPITALS

PERSONAL: Born January 5, 1968, in Pont-Rouge, Que. ... 6-0/195. ... Shoots left. ... Name pronounced zhoh-AY ZHOO-noh.
COLLEGE: Rensselaer Polytechnic Institute (N.Y.).
TRANSACTIONS/CAREER NOTES: Selected by Boston Bruins in fourth round (third Bruins pick, 81st overall) of NHL entry draft (June 11, 1988). ... Suffered ligament problem in back (November 1990). ... Broke jaw (November 7, 1993); missed seven games. ... Reinjured jaw (February 18, 1994); missed two games. ... Traded by Bruins to Washington Capitals for D Al Iafrate (March 21, 1994). ... Strained hip flexor (January 29, 1995); missed one game. ... Strained back (February 15, 1995); missed one game. ... Bruised arm (April 11, 1995); missed one game. ... Injured leg (April 30, 1995); missed one game. ... Suffered from the flu (January 17, 1996); missed two games. ... Pulled hamstring (November 19, 1996); missed eight games. ... Bruised back and shoulder (January 1, 1997); missed two games. ... Sprained shoulder (February 7, 1997); missed four games. ... Sprained shoulder (February 18, 1997); missed five games. ... Strained hip (March 26, 1997); missed four games. ... Strained hip (April 12, 1997); missed one game.
HONORS: Named to NCAA All-America East first team (1989-90). ... Named to ECAC All-Star first team (1989-90). ... Named to NCAA All-America East second team (1990-91). ... Named to ECAC All-Star second team (1990-91). ... Named to NHL All-Rookie team (1992-93).
RECORDS: Holds NHL single-season record for most assists by a left winger—70 (1992-93). ... Holds NHL single-season record for most assists by a rookie—70 (1992-93).
STATISTICAL PLATEAUS: Three-goal games: 1992-93 (1), 1996-97 (1). Total: 2.
MISCELLANEOUS: Member of silver-medal-winning Canadian Olympic team (1992).

		REGULAR SEASON								PLAYOFFS				
Season Team	League	Gms.	G	A	Pts.	PIM	+/-	PP	SH	Gms.	G	A	Pts.	PIM
87-88— R.P.I.	ECAC	31	16	29	45	18	...	...	...	—	—	—	—	—
88-89— R.P.I.	ECAC	30	12	23	35	40	...	...	...	—	—	—	—	—
89-90— R.P.I.	ECAC	34	18	*52	*70	31	...	...	...	—	—	—	—	—
90-91— R.P.I.	ECAC	29	23	40	63	70	...	...	...	—	—	—	—	—
91-92— Canadian nat'l team ...	Int'l	60	20	49	69	35	...	...	...	—	—	—	—	—
— Can. Olympic team	Int'l	8	6	9	15	4	...	...	...	—	—	—	—	—
— Boston	NHL	14	5	14	19	4	6	2	0	15	4	8	12	21
92-93— Boston	NHL	84	32	70	102	33	23	9	0	4	2	4	6	6
93-94— Boston	NHL	63	14	58	72	35	11	4	0	—	—	—	—	—
— Washington	NHL	11	5	8	13	6	0	2	0	11	4	5	9	6
94-95— Washington	NHL	44	5	38	43	8	-1	3	0	7	2	6	8	2
95-96— Washington	NHL	80	14	50	64	30	-3	7	2	5	0	7	7	6
96-97— Washington	NHL	58	15	27	42	8	-11	9	1	—	—	—	—	—
NHL totals (6 years)		354	90	265	355	124	25	36	3	42	12	30	42	41

KAMENSKY, VALERI   LW   AVALANCHE

PERSONAL: Born April 18, 1966, in Voskresensk, U.S.S.R. ... 6-2/198. ... Shoots right. ... Name pronounced kuh-MEHN-skee.
TRANSACTIONS/CAREER NOTES: Selected by Quebec Nordiques in seventh round (eighth Nordiques pick, 129th overall) of NHL entry draft (June 11, 1988). ... Fractured leg (October 1991); missed 57 games. ... Broke left thumb (October 17, 1992); missed three games. ... Broke right ankle (October 27, 1992); missed 47 games. ... Bruised left foot (October 21, 1993); missed two games. ... Bruised right foot (December 21, 1993); missed one game. ... Played in Europe during 1994-95 NHL lockout. ... Suffered kidney infection (February 26, 1995); missed eight games. ... Nordiques franchise moved to Colorado and renamed Avalanche for 1995-96 season (June 21, 1995). ... Bruised ribs (January 3, 1996); missed one game. ... Separated shoulder (December 31, 1996); missed six games. ... Injured shoulder (February 25, 1997); missed three games.
HONORS: Won Soviet Player of the Year Award (1990-91).
STATISTICAL PLATEAUS: Three-goal games: 1995-96 (2), 1996-97 (1). Total: 3.
MISCELLANEOUS: Member of Stanley Cup championship team (1996). ... Member of gold-medal-winning U.S.S.R. Olympic team (1988). ... Scored on a penalty shot (vs. Curtis Joseph, October 26, 1996).

		REGULAR SEASON								PLAYOFFS				
Season Team	League	Gms.	G	A	Pts.	PIM	+/-	PP	SH	Gms.	G	A	Pts.	PIM
82-83— Khimik	USSR	5	0	0	0	0	...	...	...	—	—	—	—	—
83-84— Khimik	USSR	20	2	2	4	6	...	...	...	—	—	—	—	—

J
K

Season Team	League	REGULAR SEASON								PLAYOFFS				
		Gms.	G	A	Pts.	PIM	+/-	PP	SH	Gms.	G	A	Pts.	PIM
84-85— Khimik	USSR	45	9	3	12	24	...	...	...	—	—	—	—	—
85-86— CSKA Moscow	USSR	40	15	9	24	8	...	...	...	—	—	—	—	—
86-87— CSKA Moscow	USSR	37	13	8	21	16	...	...	...	—	—	—	—	—
87-88— CSKA Moscow	USSR	51	26	20	46	40	...	...	...	—	—	—	—	—
— Sov. Olympic team	Int'l	8	4	2	6	4	...	...	...	—	—	—	—	—
88-89— CSKA Moscow	USSR	40	18	10	28	30	...	...	...	—	—	—	—	—
89-90— CSKA Moscow	USSR	45	19	18	37	38	...	...	...	—	—	—	—	—
90-91— CSKA Moscow	USSR	46	20	26	46	66	...	...	...	—	—	—	—	—
91-92— Quebec	NHL	23	7	14	21	14	-1	2	0	—	—	—	—	—
92-93— Quebec	NHL	32	15	22	37	14	13	2	3	6	0	1	1	6
93-94— Quebec	NHL	76	28	37	65	42	12	6	0	—	—	—	—	—
94-95— Ambri Piotta	Switzerland	12	13	6	19	2	...	...	...	—	—	—	—	—
— Quebec	NHL	40	10	20	30	22	3	5	1	2	1	0	1	0
95-96— Colorado	NHL	81	38	47	85	85	14	18	1	22	10	12	22	28
96-97— Colorado	NHL	68	28	38	66	38	5	8	0	17	8	14	22	16
NHL totals (6 years)		320	126	178	304	215	46	41	5	47	19	27	46	50

KAMINSKI, KEVIN   C   CAPITALS

PERSONAL: Born March 13, 1969, in Churchbridge, Sask. ... 5-10/190. ... Shoots left.
TRANSACTIONS/CAREER NOTES: Selected by Minnesota North Stars as underage junior in third round (third North Stars pick, 48th overall) of NHL entry draft (June 13, 1987). ... Suspended 12 games by WHL for cross-checking (November 4, 1987). ... Traded by North Stars to Quebec Nordiques for LW Gaetan Duchesne (June 18, 1989). ... Separated shoulder in training camp (September 1989). ... Suspended two games by AHL for head-butting (January 26, 1990). ... Traded by Nordiques to Washington Capitals for D Mark Matier (June 15, 1993). ... Suspended three games by AHL for postgame altercation (November 30, 1994). ... Separated ribs (October 18, 1995); missed six games. ... Injured groin (January 30, 1996); missed two games. ... Tore calf muscle (September 27, 1996); missed 15 games. ... Suffered from the flu (December 21, 1996); missed two games. ... Injured knee (February 7, 1997); missed two games. ... Strained groin (March 10, 1997); missed four games.

Season Team	League	REGULAR SEASON								PLAYOFFS				
		Gms.	G	A	Pts.	PIM	+/-	PP	SH	Gms.	G	A	Pts.	PIM
84-85— Saskatoon	WHL	5	0	1	1	17	...	...	...	—	—	—	—	—
85-86— Saskatoon	WHL	4	1	1	2	35	...	...	...	—	—	—	—	—
86-87— Saskatoon	WHL	67	26	44	70	235	...	...	...	11	5	6	11	45
87-88— Saskatoon	WHL	55	38	61	99	247	...	...	...	10	5	7	12	37
88-89— Saskatoon	WHL	52	25	43	68	199	...	...	...	8	4	9	13	25
— Minnesota	NHL	1	0	0	0	0	0	0	0	—	—	—	—	—
89-90— Quebec	NHL	1	0	0	0	0	-1	0	0	—	—	—	—	—
— Halifax	AHL	19	3	4	7	128	...	...	...	2	0	0	0	5
90-91— Halifax	AHL	7	1	0	1	44	...	...	...	—	—	—	—	—
— Fort Wayne	IHL	56	9	15	24	*455	...	...	...	19	4	2	6	*169
91-92— Halifax	AHL	63	18	27	45	329	...	...	...	—	—	—	—	—
— Quebec	NHL	5	0	0	0	45	-2	0	0	—	—	—	—	—
92-93— Halifax	AHL	79	27	37	64	*345	...	...	...	—	—	—	—	—
93-94— Portland	AHL	39	10	22	32	263	...	...	...	16	4	5	9	*91
— Washington	NHL	13	0	5	5	87	2	0	0	—	—	—	—	—
94-95— Portland	AHL	34	15	20	35	292	...	...	...	—	—	—	—	—
— Washington	NHL	27	1	1	2	102	-6	0	0	5	0	0	0	36
95-96— Washington	NHL	54	1	2	3	164	-1	0	0	3	0	0	0	16
96-97— Washington	NHL	38	1	2	3	130	0	0	0	—	—	—	—	—
NHL totals (7 years)		139	3	10	13	528	-8	0	0	8	0	0	0	52

KANE, BOYD   LW   PENGUINS

PERSONAL: Born April 18, 1978, in Swift Current, Sask. ... 6-2/200. ... Shoots left.
TRANSACTIONS/CAREER NOTES: Selected by Pittsburgh Penguins in third round (third Penguins pick, 72nd overall) of NHL entry draft (June 22, 1996).

Season Team	League	REGULAR SEASON								PLAYOFFS				
		Gms.	G	A	Pts.	PIM	+/-	PP	SH	Gms.	G	A	Pts.	PIM
95-96— Regina	WHL	72	21	42	63	155	...	...	...	11	5	7	12	12
96-97— Regina	WHL	66	25	50	75	154	...	...	...	5	1	1	2	15

KAPANEN, SAMI   RW   HURRICANES

PERSONAL: Born June 14, 1973, in Vantaa, Finland. ... 5-10/173. ... Shoots left. ... Name pronounced KAP-ih-nehn.
TRANSACTIONS/CAREER NOTES: Selected by Hartford Whalers in fourth round (fourth Whalers pick, 87th overall) of NHL entry draft (July 8, 1995). ... Suffered from the flu (October 20, 1996); missed two games. ... Sprained knee (November 30, 1996); missed 16 games. ... Sprained knee (January 10, 1997); missed nine games. ... Sprained knee (February 26, 1997); missed three games. ... Sprained knee (March 15, 1997); missed six games. ... Suffered from the flu (April 5, 1997); missed one game. ... Whalers franchise moved to North Carolina and renamed Carolina Hurricanes for 1997-98 season; NHL approved move on June 25, 1997.
MISCELLANEOUS: Scored on a a penalty shot (vs. Jim Carey, March 12, 1997).

Season Team	League	REGULAR SEASON								PLAYOFFS				
		Gms.	G	A	Pts.	PIM	+/-	PP	SH	Gms.	G	A	Pts.	PIM
90-91— KalPa Kuopio	Finland	14	1	2	3	2	...	...	...	8	2	1	3	2
91-92— KalPa Kuopio	Finland	42	15	10	25	8	...	...	...	—	—	—	—	—
92-93— KalPa Kuopio	Finland	37	4	17	21	12	...	...	...	—	—	—	—	—
93-94— KalPa Kuopio	Finland	48	23	32	55	16	...	...	...	—	—	—	—	—

Season Team	League	Gms.	G	A	Pts.	PIM	+/-	PP	SH	Gms.	G	A	Pts.	PIM
		REGULAR SEASON								**PLAYOFFS**				
94-95— HIFK Helsinki	Finland	49	14	28	42	42	...	...	...	3	0	0	0	0
95-96— Springfield	AHL	28	14	17	31	4	...	...	...	3	1	2	3	0
— Hartford	NHL	35	5	4	9	6	0	0	0	—	—	—	—	—
96-97— Hartford	NHL	45	13	12	25	2	6	3	0	—	—	—	—	—
NHL totals (2 years)		80	18	16	34	8	6	3	0					

KARIYA, PAUL   LW   MIGHTY DUCKS

PERSONAL: Born October 16, 1974, in Vancouver. ... 5-11/175. ... Shoots left. ... Name pronounced kuh-REE-uh.
COLLEGE: Maine.
TRANSACTIONS/CAREER NOTES: Selected by Mighty Ducks of Anaheim in first round (first Mighty Ducks pick, fourth overall) of NHL entry draft (June 26, 1993). ... Suffered lower back spasms (February 12, 1995); missed one game. ... Strained abdominal muscle prior to 1996-97 season; missed first 11 games of season. ... Suffered mild concussion (November 13, 1996); missed two games.
HONORS: Won Hobey Baker Memorial Award (1992-93). ... Named Hockey East Player of the Year (1992-93). ... Named Hockey East Rookie of the Year (1992-93). ... Named to NCAA All-America East first team (1992-93). ... Named to NCAA All-Tournament team (1992-93). ... Named to Hockey East All-Star first team (1992-93). ... Named to Hockey East All-Rookie team (1992-93). ... Named to Hockey East All-Decade team (1994). ... Named to NHL All-Rookie team (1994-95). ... Played in NHL All-Star Game (1996 and 1997). ... Won Lady Byng Memorial Trophy (1995-96 and 1996-97). ... Named to NHL All-Star first team (1995-96 and 1996-97).
STATISTICAL NOTES: Led NHL with 10 game-winning goals (1996-97).
STATISTICAL PLATEAUS: Three-goal games: 1996-97 (2).
MISCELLANEOUS: Member of silver-medal-winning Canadian Olympic team (1994). ... Captain of Mighty Ducks of Anaheim (1996-97). ... Holds Mighty Ducks of Anaheim all-time records for most goals (112), most assists (134) and most points (246).

Season Team	League	Gms.	G	A	Pts.	PIM	+/-	PP	SH	Gms.	G	A	Pts.	PIM
		REGULAR SEASON								**PLAYOFFS**				
90-91— Penticton	BCJHL	54	45	67	112	8	...	...	...	—	—	—	—	—
91-92— Penticton	BCJHL	40	46	86	132	16	...	...	...	—	—	—	—	—
92-93— University of Maine	Hockey East	39	25	*75	*100	12	...	...	...	—	—	—	—	—
93-94— Canadian nat'l team	Int'l	23	7	34	41	2	...	...	...	—	—	—	—	—
— Can. Olympic team	Int'l	8	3	4	7	2	...	...	...	—	—	—	—	—
— University of Maine	Hockey East	12	8	16	24	4	...	...	...	—	—	—	—	—
94-95— Anaheim	NHL	47	18	21	39	4	-17	7	1	—	—	—	—	—
95-96— Anaheim	NHL	82	50	58	108	20	9	20	3	—	—	—	—	—
96-97— Anaheim	NHL	69	44	55	99	6	36	15	3	11	7	6	13	4
NHL totals (3 years)		198	112	134	246	30	28	42	7	11	7	6	13	4

KARPA, DAVE   D   MIGHTY DUCKS

PERSONAL: Born May 7, 1971, in Regina, Sask. ... 6-1/210. ... Shoots right. ... Full name: David James Karpa.
COLLEGE: Ferris State (Mich.).
TRANSACTIONS/CAREER NOTES: Selected by Quebec Nordiques in fourth round (fourth Nordiques pick, 68th overall) of NHL entry draft (June 22, 1991). ... Broke right wrist (January 26, 1994); missed 18 games. ... Traded by Nordiques to Los Angeles Kings for fourth-round pick in 1995 or 1996 draft (February 28, 1995); trade invalidated by NHL because Karpa failed his physical examination (March 3, 1995). ... Traded by Nordiques to Mighty Ducks of Anaheim for fourth-round pick (traded to St. Louis) in 1997 draft (March 8, 1995). ... Underwent right wrist surgery (May 9, 1995). ... Bruised right knee (November 24, 1995); missed eight games. ... Fractured right hand (February 4, 1997); missed 13 games.

Season Team	League	Gms.	G	A	Pts.	PIM	+/-	PP	SH	Gms.	G	A	Pts.	PIM
		REGULAR SEASON								**PLAYOFFS**				
88-89— Notre Dame	SCMHL	...	16	37	53	...	...	...	...	—	—	—	—	—
89-90— Notre Dame	SCMHL	43	9	19	28	271	...	...	...	—	—	—	—	—
90-91— Ferris State	CCHA	41	6	19	25	109	...	...	...	—	—	—	—	—
91-92— Ferris State	CCHA	34	7	12	19	124	...	...	...	—	—	—	—	—
— Halifax	AHL	2	0	0	0	4	...	...	...	—	—	—	—	—
— Quebec	NHL	4	0	0	0	14	2	0	0	—	—	—	—	—
92-93— Halifax	AHL	71	4	27	31	167	...	...	...	—	—	—	—	—
— Quebec	NHL	12	0	1	1	13	-6	0	0	3	0	0	0	0
93-94— Quebec	NHL	60	5	12	17	148	0	2	0	—	—	—	—	—
— Cornwall	AHL	1	0	0	0	0	...	...	...	12	2	2	4	27
94-95— Cornwall	AHL	6	0	2	2	19	...	...	...	—	—	—	—	—
— Quebec	NHL	2	0	0	0	0	-1	0	0	—	—	—	—	—
— Anaheim	NHL	28	1	5	6	91	0	0	0	—	—	—	—	—
95-96— Anaheim	NHL	72	3	16	19	270	-3	0	1	—	—	—	—	—
96-97— Anaheim	NHL	69	2	11	13	210	11	0	0	8	1	1	2	20
NHL totals (6 years)		247	11	45	56	746	3	2	1	11	1	1	2	20

KARPENKO, IGOR   G   MIGHTY DUCKS

PERSONAL: Born July 23, 1976, in Kiev, U.S.S.R. ... 5-8/158. ... Catches left.
TRANSACTIONS/CAREER NOTES: Selected by Mighty Ducks of Anaheim in eighth round (seventh Mighty Ducks pick, 185th overall) of NHL entry draft (July 8, 1995).

Season Team	League	Gms.	Min	W	L	T	GA	SO	Avg.	Gms.	Min.	W	L	GA	SO	Avg.
		REGULAR SEASON								**PLAYOFFS**						
93-94— Sokol Kiev	CIS	5	63	...	...	...	3	...	2.86	—	—	—	—	—	—	—
94-95— Sokol Kiev	CIS	23	1292	...	...	...	67	...	3.11	—	—	—	—	—	—	—
95-96— Sokol Kiev	CIS	23	1269	...	...	...	62	...	2.93	—	—	—	—	—	—	—
96-97— Las Vegas	IHL	3	133	0	2	‡0	12	0	5.41	—	—	—	—	—	—	—
— Port Huron	Col.HL	23	1148	9	9	1	67	0	3.50	3	179	1	2	16	0	5.36

K

KARPOV, VALERI   RW/LW   MIGHTY DUCKS

PERSONAL: Born August 5, 1971, in Chelyabinsk, U.S.S.R. ... 5-10/195. ... Shoots left. ... Name pronounced vuh-LAIR-ee KAHR-pahv.
TRANSACTIONS/CAREER NOTES: Selected by Mighty Ducks of Anaheim in third round (third Mighty Ducks pick, 56th overall) of NHL entry draft (June 26, 1993). ... Played in Europe during 1994-95 NHL lockout. ... Broke wrist (October 23, 1995); missed 29 games. ... Suffered concussion (October 24, 1996); missed eight games.
HONORS: Named to CIS All-Star team (1992-93 and 1993-94).

Season Team	League	REGULAR SEASON								PLAYOFFS				
		Gms.	G	A	Pts.	PIM	+/-	PP	SH	Gms.	G	A	Pts.	PIM
88-89— Traktor Chelyabinsk ...	USSR	5	0	0	0	0	...	...	...	—	—	—	—	—
89-90— Traktor Chelyabinsk ...	USSR	24	1	2	3	6	...	...	...	—	—	—	—	—
90-91— Traktor Chelyabinsk ...	USSR	25	8	4	12	15	...	...	...	—	—	—	—	—
91-92— Traktor Chelyabinsk ...	CIS	44	16	10	26	34	...	...	...	—	—	—	—	—
92-93— CSKA Moscow	CIS	9	2	6	8	0	...	...	...	—	—	—	—	—
— Traktor Chelyabinsk ...	CIS	38	12	21	33	6	...	...	...	8	0	1	1	10
93-94— Traktor Chelyabinsk ...	CIS	32	11	19	30	18	...	...	...	6	2	5	7	2
— Rus. Olympic team	Int'l	8	3	1	4	2	...	...	...	—	—	—	—	—
94-95— Traktor Chelyabinsk ...	CIS	10	6	8	14	8	...	...	...	—	—	—	—	—
— Anaheim	NHL	30	4	7	11	6	-4	0	0	—	—	—	—	—
— San Diego	IHL	5	3	3	6	0	...	...	...	—	—	—	—	—
95-96— Anaheim	NHL	37	9	8	17	10	-1	0	0	—	—	—	—	—
96-97— Anaheim	NHL	9	1	0	1	16	-2	0	0	—	—	—	—	—
— Baltimore	AHL	10	4	8	12	8	...	...	...	—	—	—	—	—
— Long Beach................	IHL	30	18	17	35	19	...	...	...	18	8	7	15	18
NHL totals (3 years)		76	14	15	29	32	-7	0	0					

KARPOVTSEV, ALEXANDER   D   RANGERS

PERSONAL: Born April 7, 1970, in Moscow, U.S.S.R. ... 6-1/200. ... Shoots right. ... Name pronounced KAHR-piht-sehf.
TRANSACTIONS/CAREER NOTES: Selected by Quebec Nordiques in seventh round (seventh Nordiques pick, 158th overall) of NHL entry draft (June 16, 1990). ... Traded by Nordiques to New York Rangers for D Mike Hurlbut (September 9, 1993). ... Bruised buttocks (October 9, 1993); missed one game. ... Bruised hip (November 3, 1993); missed six games. ... Reinjured hip (November 23, 1993); missed one game. ... Injured face (February 28, 1994); missed two games. ... Suffered injury (March 14, 1994); missed two games. ... Played in Europe during 1994-95 NHL lockout. ... Suffered sore ankle (April 14, 1995); missed one game. ... Hyperextended elbow (October 29, 1995); missed one game. ... Suffered back spasms (February 10, 1996); missed one game. ... Suffered back spasms (February 18, 1996); missed two games. ... Bruised thumb (March 13, 1996); missed two games. ... Suffered back spasms (March 27, 1996); missed six games. ... Bruised toe (April 3, 1997); missed one game. ... Hyperextended elbow (April 10, 1997); missed one game.
MISCELLANEOUS: Member of Stanley Cup championship team (1994).

Season Team	League	REGULAR SEASON								PLAYOFFS				
		Gms.	G	A	Pts.	PIM	+/-	PP	SH	Gms.	G	A	Pts.	PIM
89-90— Dynamo Moscow.......	USSR	35	1	1	2	27	...	...	...	—	—	—	—	—
90-91— Dynamo Moscow.......	USSR	40	0	5	5	15	...	...	...	—	—	—	—	—
91-92— Dynamo Moscow.......	CIS	28	3	2	5	22	...	...	...	—	—	—	—	—
92-93— Dynamo Moscow.......	CIS	40	3	11	14	100	...	...	...	—	—	—	—	—
93-94— New York Rangers.....	NHL	67	3	15	18	58	12	1	0	17	0	4	4	12
94-95— Dynamo Moscow.......	CIS	13	0	2	2	10	...	...	...	—	—	—	—	—
— New York Rangers.....	NHL	47	4	8	12	30	-4	1	0	8	1	0	1	0
95-96— New York Rangers.....	NHL	40	2	16	18	26	12	1	0	6	0	1	1	4
96-97— New York Rangers.....	NHL	77	9	29	38	59	1	6	1	13	1	3	4	20
NHL totals (4 years)		231	18	68	86	173	21	9	1	44	2	8	10	36

KASPARAITIS, DARIUS   D   PENGUINS

PERSONAL: Born October 16, 1972, in Elektrenai, U.S.S.R. ... 5-11/190. ... Shoots left. ... Name pronounced KAZ-puhr-IGH-tihz.
TRANSACTIONS/CAREER NOTES: Selected by New York Islanders in first round (first Islanders pick, fifth overall) of NHL entry draft (June 20, 1992). ... Suffered back spasms (February 12, 1993); missed two games. ... Strained back (April 15, 1993); missed one game. ... Strained lower back (November 10, 1993); missed two games. ... Jammed wrist (March 5, 1994); missed four games. ... Tore knee ligament (February 20, 1995); missed remainder of season and first 15 games of 1995-96 season. ... Suffered from the flu (December 2, 1995); missed two games. ... Severed two tendons in right hand (December 9, 1995); missed 16 games. ... Injured groin (February 8, 1996); missed two games. ... Traded by Islanders with C Andreas Johansson to Pittsburgh Penguins for C Bryan Smolinski (November 17, 1996). ... Suffered concussion (December 23, 1996); missed two games. ... Cut face (January 2, 1997); missed one game. ... Twisted ankle (January 23, 1997); missed one game. ... Suffered slight concussion (March 18, 1997); missed three games.
MISCELLANEOUS: Member of gold-medal-winning Unified Olympic team (1992).

Season Team	League	REGULAR SEASON								PLAYOFFS				
		Gms.	G	A	Pts.	PIM	+/-	PP	SH	Gms.	G	A	Pts.	PIM
88-89— Dynamo Moscow.......	USSR	3	0	0	0	0	...	...	...	—	—	—	—	—
89-90— Dynamo Moscow......	USSR	1	0	0	0	0	...	...	...	—	—	—	—	—
90-91— Dynamo Moscow......	USSR	17	0	1	1	10	...	...	...	—	—	—	—	—
91-92— Dynamo Moscow......	CIS	31	2	10	12	14	...	...	...	—	—	—	—	—
— Unif. Olympic team....	Int'l	8	0	2	2	2	...	...	...	—	—	—	—	—
92-93— Dynamo Moscow......	CIS	7	1	3	4	8	...	...	...	—	—	—	—	—
— New York Islanders....	NHL	79	4	17	21	166	15	0	0	18	0	5	5	31
93-94— New York Islanders....	NHL	76	1	10	11	142	-6	0	0	4	0	0	0	8
94-95— New York Islanders....	NHL	13	0	1	1	22	-11	0	0	—	—	—	—	—
95-96— New York Islanders....	NHL	46	1	7	8	93	-12	0	0	—	—	—	—	—
96-97— New York Islanders....	NHL	18	0	5	5	16	-7	0	0	—	—	—	—	—
— Pittsburgh.................	NHL	57	2	16	18	84	24	0	0	5	0	0	0	6
NHL totals (5 years)		289	8	56	64	523	3	0	0	27	0	5	5	45

KEANE, MIKE RW RANGERS

PERSONAL: Born May 29, 1967, in Winnipeg. ... 5-10/185. ... Shoots right. ... Name pronounced KEEN.
TRANSACTIONS/CAREER NOTES: Signed as free agent by Montreal Canadiens (March 1987). ... Separated right shoulder (December 21, 1988). ... Cut left kneecap (October 31, 1990); missed seven games. ... Injured neck (March 1991). ... Sprained ankle (January 16, 1992); missed four games. ... Re-sprained ankle (February 1, 1992); missed 10 games. ... Bruised ankle (March 11, 1992); missed one game. ... Suspended four off-days and fined $500 by NHL for swinging stick in preseason game (October 13, 1992). ... Suffered wrist tendinitis (January 26, 1993); missed three games. ... Suffered back spasms (February 12, 1993); missed two games. ... Fractured toe (February 27, 1993); missed two games. ... Suffered back spasms (October 16, 1993); missed one game. ... Suffered back spasms (January 12, 1994); missed three games. ... Injured groin (November 1, 1995); missed one game. ... Injured neck (November 18, 1995); missed three games. ... Injured groin (November 25, 1995); missed two games. ... Traded by Canadiens with G Patrick Roy to Colorado Avalanche for G Jocelyn Thibault, LW Martin Rucinsky and RW Andrei Kovalenko (December 6, 1995). ... Signed as free agent by New York Rangers (July 7, 1997).
MISCELLANEOUS: Member of Stanley Cup championship team (1993 and 1996). ... Captain of Montreal Canadiens (1994-95 through December 6, 1995).

		REGULAR SEASON								PLAYOFFS				
Season Team	League	Gms.	G	A	Pts.	PIM	+/-	PP	SH	Gms.	G	A	Pts.	PIM
83-84— Winnipeg	WHL	1	0	0	0	0	...	...	...	—	—	—	—	—
84-85— Moose Jaw	WHL	65	17	26	43	141	...	...	...	—	—	—	—	—
85-86— Moose Jaw	WHL	67	34	49	83	162	...	...	...	13	6	8	14	9
86-87— Moose Jaw	WHL	53	25	45	70	107	...	...	...	9	3	9	12	11
— Sherbrooke	AHL	—	—	—	—	—	...	...	...	9	2	2	4	16
87-88— Sherbrooke	AHL	78	25	43	68	70	...	...	...	6	1	1	2	18
88-89— Montreal	NHL	69	16	19	35	69	9	5	0	21	4	3	7	17
89-90— Montreal	NHL	74	9	15	24	78	0	1	0	11	0	1	1	8
90-91— Montreal	NHL	73	13	23	36	50	6	2	1	12	3	2	5	6
91-92— Montreal	NHL	67	11	30	41	64	16	2	0	8	1	1	2	16
92-93— Montreal	NHL	77	15	45	60	95	29	0	0	19	2	13	15	6
93-94— Montreal	NHL	80	16	30	46	119	6	6	2	6	3	1	4	4
94-95— Montreal	NHL	48	10	10	20	15	5	1	0	—	—	—	—	—
95-96— Montreal	NHL	18	0	7	7	6	-6	0	0	—	—	—	—	—
— Colorado	NHL	55	10	10	20	40	1	0	2	22	3	2	5	16
96-97— Colorado	NHL	81	10	17	27	63	2	0	1	17	3	1	4	24
NHL totals (9 years)		642	110	206	316	599	68	17	6	116	19	24	43	97

KECZMER, DAN D STARS

PERSONAL: Born May 25, 1968, in Mt. Clemens, Mich. ... 6-1/190. ... Shoots left. ... Full name: Daniel Leonard Keczmer. ... Name pronounced KEHZ-muhr.
COLLEGE: Lake Superior State (Mich.).
TRANSACTIONS/CAREER NOTES: Selected by Minnesota North Stars in 10th round (11th North Stars pick, 201st overall) of NHL entry draft (June 21, 1986). ... Injured shoulder (February 2, 1990). ... Claimed by San Jose Sharks as part of ownership change with North Stars (October 1990). ... Traded by Sharks to Hartford Whalers for C Dean Evason (October 2, 1991). ... Released by U.S. National team prior to Olympics (January 1992). ... Bruised right leg (February 8, 1993); missed three games. ... Traded by Whalers to Calgary Flames for G Jeff Reese and future considerations (November 19, 1993). ... Separated right shoulder (February 16, 1995); missed 10 games. ... Traded by Flames with D Phil Housley to New Jersey Devils for D Tommy Albelin, D Cale Hulse and RW Jocelyn Lemieux (February 26, 1996). ... Signed as free agent by Dallas Stars (August 7, 1996).
HONORS: Named to CCHA All-Star second team (1989-90).

		REGULAR SEASON								PLAYOFFS				
Season Team	League	Gms.	G	A	Pts.	PIM	+/-	PP	SH	Gms.	G	A	Pts.	PIM
86-87— Lake Superior State	CCHA	38	3	5	8	28	...	...	...	—	—	—	—	—
87-88— Lake Superior State	CCHA	41	2	15	17	34	...	...	...	—	—	—	—	—
88-89— Lake Superior State	CCHA	46	3	26	29	70	...	...	...	—	—	—	—	—
89-90— Lake Superior State	CCHA	43	13	23	36	48	...	...	...	—	—	—	—	—
90-91— Minnesota	NHL	9	0	1	1	6	0	0	0	—	—	—	—	—
— Kalamazoo	IHL	60	4	20	24	60	...	...	...	9	1	2	3	10
91-92— U.S. national team	Int'l	51	3	11	14	56	...	...	...	—	—	—	—	—
— Springfield	AHL	18	3	4	7	10	...	...	...	4	0	0	0	6
— Hartford	NHL	1	0	0	0	0	-1	0	0	—	—	—	—	—
92-93— Springfield	AHL	37	1	13	14	38	...	...	...	12	0	4	4	14
— Hartford	NHL	23	4	4	8	28	-3	2	0	—	—	—	—	—
93-94— Hartford	NHL	12	0	1	1	12	-6	0	0	—	—	—	—	—
— Springfield	AHL	7	0	1	1	4	...	...	...	—	—	—	—	—
— Calgary	NHL	57	1	20	21	48	-2	0	0	3	0	0	0	4
94-95— Calgary	NHL	28	2	3	5	10	7	0	0	7	0	1	1	2
95-96— Saint John	AHL	22	3	11	14	14	...	...	...	—	—	—	—	—
— Calgary	NHL	13	0	0	0	14	-6	0	0	—	—	—	—	—
— Albany	AHL	17	0	4	4	4	...	...	...	1	0	0	0	0
96-97— Michigan	IHL	42	3	17	20	24	...	...	...	—	—	—	—	—
— Dallas	NHL	13	0	1	1	6	3	0	0	—	—	—	—	—
NHL totals (8 years)		156	7	30	37	124	-8	2	0	10	0	1	1	6

KELLEHER, CHRIS D PENGUINS

PERSONAL: Born March 23, 1975, in Cambridge, Mass. ... 6-1/215. ... Shoots left.
HIGH SCHOOL: Belmont (Mass.) Hill, then St. Sebastian's (Needham, Mass.).
COLLEGE: Boston University.
TRANSACTIONS/CAREER NOTES: Selected by Pittsburgh Penguins in fifth round (fifth Penguins pick, 130th overall) of NHL entry draft (June 26, 1993).
HONORS: Named to NCAA All-America East second team (1996-97).

Season Team	League	REGULAR SEASON								PLAYOFFS				
		Gms.	G	A	Pts.	PIM	+/-	PP	SH	Gms.	G	A	Pts.	PIM
90-91— Belmont Hill...............	Mass. H.S.	20	4	23	27	14	...	...	...	—	—	—	—	—
91-92— St. Sebastian's...........	Mass. H.S.	28	7	27	34	12	...	...	...	—	—	—	—	—
92-93— St. Sebastian's...........	Mass. H.S.	25	8	30	38	16	...	...	...	—	—	—	—	—
93-94— St. Sebastian's...........	Mass. H.S.	24	10	21	31	...	...	...	...	—	—	—	—	—
94-95— Boston University	Hockey East	35	3	17	20	62	...	...	...	—	—	—	—	—
95-96— Boston University	Hockey East	37	7	18	25	43	...	...	...	—	—	—	—	—
96-97— Boston University	Hockey East	39	10	24	34	54	...	...	...	—	—	—	—	—

KELLY, STEVE   C   OILERS

PERSONAL: Born October 26, 1976, in Vancouver. ... 6-1/190. ... Shoots left.
TRANSACTIONS/CAREER NOTES: Selected by Edmonton Oilers in first round (first Oilers pick, sixth overall) of NHL entry draft (July 8, 1995).

Season Team	League	REGULAR SEASON								PLAYOFFS				
		Gms.	G	A	Pts.	PIM	+/-	PP	SH	Gms.	G	A	Pts.	PIM
92-93— Prince Albert.............	WHL	65	11	9	20	75	...	...	...	—	—	—	—	—
93-94— Prince Albert.............	WHL	65	19	42	61	106	...	...	...	—	—	—	—	—
94-95— Prince Albert.............	WHL	68	31	41	72	153	...	...	...	15	7	9	16	35
95-96— Prince Albert.............	WHL	70	27	74	101	203	...	...	...	18	13	18	31	47
96-97— Hamilton..................	AHL	48	9	29	38	111	...	...	...	11	3	3	6	24
— Edmonton	NHL	8	1	0	1	6	-1	0	0	6	0	0	0	2
NHL totals (1 year)		**8**	**1**	**0**	**1**	**6**	**-1**	**0**	**0**	**6**	**0**	**0**	**0**	**2**

KENADY, CHRIS   RW   BLUES

PERSONAL: Born April 10, 1973, in Mound, Minn. ... 6-2/195. ... Shoots right. ... Name pronounced KEHN-ih-dee.
HIGH SCHOOL: Mound (Minn.) Westonka.
COLLEGE: Denver.
TRANSACTIONS/CAREER NOTES: Selected by St. Louis Blues in eighth round (eighth Blues pick, 175th overall) of NHL entry draft (June 22, 1991).

Season Team	League	REGULAR SEASON								PLAYOFFS				
		Gms.	G	A	Pts.	PIM	+/-	PP	SH	Gms.	G	A	Pts.	PIM
90-91— St. Paul	USHL	45	16	20	36	57	...	...	...	—	—	—	—	—
91-92— Univ. of Denver..........	WCHA	36	8	5	13	56	...	...	...	—	—	—	—	—
92-93— Univ. of Denver..........	WCHA	38	8	16	24	95	...	...	...	—	—	—	—	—
93-94— Univ. of Denver..........	WCHA	37	14	11	25	125	...	...	...	—	—	—	—	—
94-95— Univ. of Denver..........	WCHA	39	21	17	38	113	...	...	...	—	—	—	—	—
95-96— Worcester	AHL	43	9	10	19	58	...	...	...	2	0	0	0	0
96-97— Worcester	AHL	73	23	26	49	131	...	...	...	5	0	1	1	2

KENNEDY, MIKE   LW   MAPLE LEAFS

PERSONAL: Born April 3, 1972, in Vancouver. ... 6-1/195. ... Shoots right.
COLLEGE: British Columbia.
TRANSACTIONS/CAREER NOTES: Selected by Minnesota North Stars in fifth round (third North Stars pick, 97th overall) of NHL entry draft (June 22, 1991). ... North Stars franchise moved from Minnesota to Dallas and renamed Stars for 1993-94 season. ... Signed as free agent by Toronto Maple Leafs (July 3, 1997).

Season Team	League	REGULAR SEASON								PLAYOFFS				
		Gms.	G	A	Pts.	PIM	+/-	PP	SH	Gms.	G	A	Pts.	PIM
89-90— British Columbia........	CWUAA	9	5	7	12	0	...	...	...	—	—	—	—	—
90-91— British Columbia........	CWUAA	28	17	17	34	18	...	...	...	—	—	—	—	—
91-92— Seattle........................	WHL	71	42	47	89	134	...	...	...	15	11	6	17	20
92-93— Kalamazoo	IHL	77	21	30	51	39	...	...	...	—	—	—	—	—
93-94— Kalamazoo	IHL	63	20	18	38	42	...	...	...	—	—	—	—	—
94-95— Kalamazoo	IHL	42	20	28	48	29	...	...	...	—	—	—	—	—
— Dallas.........................	NHL	44	6	12	18	33	4	2	0	5	0	0	0	9
95-96— Dallas.........................	NHL	61	9	17	26	48	-7	4	0	—	—	—	—	—
96-97— Dallas.........................	NHL	24	1	6	7	13	3	0	0	—	—	—	—	—
— Michigan	IHL	2	0	1	1	2	...	...	...	—	—	—	—	—
NHL totals (3 years)		**129**	**16**	**35**	**51**	**94**	**0**	**6**	**0**	**5**	**0**	**0**	**0**	**9**

KENNEDY, SHELDON   RW

PERSONAL: Born June 15, 1969, in Brandon, Man. ... 5-10/180. ... Shoots right.
TRANSACTIONS/CAREER NOTES: Broke ankle (January 18, 1987); missed six weeks. ... Selected by Detroit Red Wings in fourth round (fifth Red Wings pick, 80th overall) of NHL entry draft (June 11, 1988). ... Separated shoulder (December 5, 1989). ... Injured thumb (March 2, 1990). ... Took leave of absence to attend alcohol treatment program (March 21, 1990). ... Injured left arm in automobile accident (summer 1990); missed 48 games. ... Suffered from tonsillitis (February 8, 1991); missed two games. ... Suffered from food poisoning (February 19, 1991). ... Sent to alcohol treatment center for evaluation (March 27, 1991). ... Bruised ribs (November 27, 1993); missed two games. ... Injured sternum (March 22, 1994); missed five games. ... Traded by Red Wings to Winnipeg Jets for third-round pick (C Darryl Laplante) in 1995 draft (May 25, 1994). ... Selected by Calgary Flames from Jets in waiver draft for cash (January 18, 1995). ... Sprained left shoulder (January 26, 1995); missed one game. ... Suffered charley horse (January 28, 1995); missed 10 games. ... Suffered from the flu (February 28, 1995); missed one game. ... Sprained left shoulder (April 8, 1995); missed six games. ... Fined $1,000 by NHL for high-sticking (May 10, 1995). ... Strained abdominal muscle (October 5, 1995); missed 12 games. ... Strained abdominal muscle (November 4, 1995); missed one

K

game. ... Strained abdominal muscle (November 8, 1995); missed 12 games. ... Signed as free agent by Boston Bruins (July 17, 1996). ... Suffered from the flu (November 29, 1996); missed two games. ... Suffered neck spasms (December 29, 1996); missed three games. ... Injured chest (February 4, 1997); missed one game.

HONORS: Named to Memorial Cup All-Star team (1988-89).

Season Team	League	REGULAR SEASON								PLAYOFFS				
		Gms.	G	A	Pts.	PIM	+/-	PP	SH	Gms.	G	A	Pts.	PIM
86-87— Swift Current	WHL	49	23	41	64	64	...	...	...	4	0	3	3	4
87-88— Swift Current	WHL	59	53	64	117	45	...	...	...	10	8	9	17	12
88-89— Swift Current	WHL	51	58	48	106	92	...	...	...	—	—	—	—	—
89-90— Detroit	NHL	20	2	7	9	10	0	0	0	—	—	—	—	—
— Adirondack	AHL	26	11	15	26	35	...	...	...	—	—	—	—	—
90-91— Adirondack	AHL	11	1	3	4	8	...	...	...	—	—	—	—	—
— Detroit	NHL	7	1	0	1	12	-1	0	0	—	—	—	—	—
91-92— Adirondack	AHL	46	25	24	49	56	...	...	...	16	5	9	14	12
— Detroit	NHL	27	3	8	11	24	-2	0	0	—	—	—	—	—
92-93— Detroit	NHL	68	19	11	30	46	-1	1	0	7	1	1	2	2
93-94— Detroit	NHL	61	6	7	13	30	-2	0	1	7	1	2	3	0
94-95— Calgary	NHL	30	7	8	15	45	5	1	0	7	3	1	4	16
95-96— Calgary	NHL	41	3	7	10	36	3	0	0	3	1	0	1	2
— Saint John	AHL	3	4	0	4	8	...	...	...	—	—	—	—	—0
96-97— Boston	NHL	56	8	10	18	30	-17	0	4	—	—	—	—	—
— Providence	AHL	3	0	1	1	2	...	...	...	—	—	—	—	—
NHL totals (8 years)		310	49	58	107	233	-15	2	5	24	6	4	10	20

K

KESA, DAN — RW — HURRICANES

PERSONAL: Born November 23, 1971, in Vancouver. ... 6-0/198. ... Shoots right. ... Name pronounced KEH-suh.
TRANSACTIONS/CAREER NOTES: Selected by Vancouver Canucks in fifth round (fifth Canucks pick, 95th overall) of NHL entry draft (June 22, 1991). ... Loaned by Syracuse Crunch to Canadian national team (April 6, 1995). ... Traded by Canucks with LW Greg Adams and fifth-round pick (traded to Los Angeles Kings) in 1995 draft to Dallas Stars for RW Russ Courtnall (April 7, 1995). ... Traded by Stars to Hartford Whalers for C Robert Petrovicky (November 29, 1995). ... Whalers franchise moved to North Carolina and renamed Carolina Hurricanes for 1997-98 season; NHL approved move on June 25, 1997.

Season Team	League	REGULAR SEASON								PLAYOFFS				
		Gms.	G	A	Pts.	PIM	+/-	PP	SH	Gms.	G	A	Pts.	PIM
88-89— Richmond	BCJHL	44	21	21	42	71	...	...	...	—	—	—	—	—
89-90— Richmond	BCJHL	54	39	38	77	103	...	...	...	—	—	—	—	—
90-91— Prince Albert	WHL	69	30	23	53	116	...	...	...	3	1	1	2	0
91-92— Prince Albert	WHL	62	46	51	97	201	...	...	...	10	9	10	19	27
92-93— Hamilton	AHL	62	16	24	40	76	...	...	...	—	—	—	—	—
93-94— Hamilton	AHL	53	37	33	70	33	...	...	...	4	1	4	5	4
— Vancouver	NHL	19	2	4	6	18	-3	1	0	—	—	—	—	—
94-95— Syracuse	AHL	70	34	44	78	81	...	...	...	—	—	—	—	—
95-96— Detroit	IHL	27	9	6	15	22	...	...	...	12	6	4	10	4
— Springfield	AHL	22	10	5	15	13	...	...	...	—	—	—	—	—0
— Michigan	IHL	15	4	11	15	33	...	...	...	—	—	—	—	—
— Dallas	NHL	3	0	0	0	0	-1	0	0	—	—	—	—	—
96-97— Detroit	IHL	60	22	21	43	19	...	...	...	20	7	5	12	20
NHL totals (2 years)		22	2	4	6	18	-4	1	0					

KHABIBULIN, NIKOLAI — G — COYOTES

PERSONAL: Born January 13, 1973, in Sverdlovsk, U.S.S.R. ... 6-1/180. ... Catches left. ... Name pronounced hah-bee-BOO-lihn.
TRANSACTIONS/CAREER NOTES: Selected by Winnipeg Jets in ninth round (eighth Jets pick, 204th overall) of NHL entry draft (June 20, 1992). ... Sprained knee (November 30, 1995); missed 20 games. ... Jets franchise moved to Phoenix and renamed Coyotes for 1996-97 season; NHL approved move on January 18, 1996.
MISCELLANEOUS: Stopped a penalty shot attempt (vs. Bob Errey, March 22, 1995; vs. Kevin Stevens, February 26, 1996). ... Holds Phoenix Coyotes franchise all-time record for goals-against average (3.03).

Season Team	League	REGULAR SEASON								PLAYOFFS						
		Gms.	Min	W	L	T	GA	SO	Avg.	Gms.	Min.	W	L	GA	SO	Avg.
88-89—Avtomo. Sverdlovsk	USSR	1	3	0	0	0	0	0	0.00	—	—	—	—	—	—	—
89-90—Avtomo. Sverd. Jr.	USSR						Statistics unavailable.									
90-91—Sputnik Nizhny Tagil	USSR Div. 3						Statistics unavailable.									
91-92—CSKA Moscow	CIS	2	34	...	...	...	2	...	3.53	—	—	—	—	—	—	—
92-93—CSKA Moscow	CIS	13	491	...	...	...	27	...	3.30	—	—	—	—	—	—	—
93-94—CSKA Moscow	CIS	46	2625	...	...	...	116	5	2.65	3	193	1	2	11	0	3.42
— Russian Penguins	IHL	12	639	2	7	‡2	47	0	4.41	—	—	—	—	—	—	—
94-95—Springfield	AHL	23	1240	9	9	4	80	0	3.87	—	—	—	—	—	—	—
— Winnipeg	NHL	26	1339	8	9	4	76	0	3.41	—	—	—	—	—	—	—
95-96— Winnipeg	NHL	53	2914	26	20	3	152	2	3.13	6	359	2	4	19	0	3.18
96-97— Phoenix	NHL	72	4091	30	33	6	193	7	2.83	7	426	3	4	15	1	2.11
NHL totals (3 years)		151	8344	64	62	13	421	9	3.03	13	785	5	8	34	1	2.60

KHLOPOTNOV, DENIS — G — PANTHERS

PERSONAL: Born January 27, 1978, in Moscow, U.S.S.R. ... 6-3/187. ... Catches left.
TRANSACTIONS/CAREER NOTES: Selected by Florida Panthers in eighth round (eighth Panthers pick, 209th overall) of NHL entry draft (June 22, 1996).

Season Team	League	REGULAR SEASON								PLAYOFFS					
		Gms.	Min	W	L	T	GA	SO	Avg.	Gms.	Min.	W	L	GA	SO	Avg.
95-96—CSKA-2 Moscow	CIS Div. II						Statistics unavailable.									
96-97—CSKA-2 Moscow	Rus. Div. II	21	...	...	...	...	42	...	...	—	—	—	—	—	—	—

KHMYLEV, YURI — LW — BLUES

PERSONAL: Born August 9, 1964, in Moscow, U.S.S.R. ... 6-1/190. ... Shoots right. ... Name pronounced HIHM-ih-lehv.

TRANSACTIONS/CAREER NOTES: Selected by Buffalo Sabres in fifth round (seventh Sabres pick, 108th overall) of NHL entry draft (June 20, 1992). ... Strained right shoulder (November 2, 1992); missed two games. ... Strained neck (September 19, 1993); missed six games. ... Suffered hairline fracture of left fibula (March 27, 1994); missed six games. ... Bruised ankle (December 16, 1995); missed one game. ... Suffered from the flu (December 27, 1995); missed one game. ... Traded by Sabres with eighth-round pick (C Andrei Podkowicky) in 1996 draft to St. Louis Blues for D Jean-Luc Grand Pierre, second-round pick (D Cory Sarich) in 1996 draft and third-round pick (RW Maxim Afinogenov) in 1997 draft (March 20, 1996). ... Injured groin (March 31, 1996); missed two games.

STATISTICAL PLATEAUS: Three-goal games: 1992-93 (1).

MISCELLANEOUS: Member of gold-medal-winning Unified Olympic team (1992).

Season Team	League	REGULAR SEASON								PLAYOFFS				
		Gms.	G	A	Pts.	PIM	+/-	PP	SH	Gms.	G	A	Pts.	PIM
81-82— Soviet Wings	USSR	8	2	2	4	2	...	...	...	—	—	—	—	—
82-83— Soviet Wings	USSR	51	9	7	16	14	...	...	...	—	—	—	—	—
83-84— Soviet Wings	USSR	43	7	8	15	10	...	...	...	—	—	—	—	—
84-85— Soviet Wings	USSR	30	11	4	15	24	...	...	...	—	—	—	—	—
85-86— Soviet Wings	USSR	40	24	9	33	22	...	...	...	—	—	—	—	—
86-87— Soviet Wings	USSR	40	15	15	30	48	...	...	...	—	—	—	—	—
87-88— Soviet Wings	USSR	48	21	8	29	46	...	...	...	—	—	—	—	—
88-89— Soviet Wings	USSR	44	16	18	34	38	...	...	...	—	—	—	—	—
89-90— Soviet Wings	USSR	44	14	13	27	30	...	...	...	—	—	—	—	—
90-91— Soviet Wings	USSR	45	25	14	39	26	...	...	...	—	—	—	—	—
91-92— Soviet Wings	CIS	42	19	17	36	20	...	...	...	—	—	—	—	—
— Unif. Olympic team	Int'l	8	4	6	10	...	...	...	...	—	—	—	—	—
92-93— Buffalo	NHL	68	20	19	39	28	6	0	3	8	4	3	7	4
93-94— Buffalo	NHL	72	27	31	58	49	13	11	0	7	3	1	4	8
94-95— Buffalo	NHL	48	8	17	25	14	8	2	1	5	0	1	1	8
95-96— Buffalo	NHL	66	8	20	28	40	-12	5	1	—	—	—	—	—
— St. Louis	NHL	7	0	1	1	0	-5	0	0	6	1	1	2	4
96-97— St. Louis	NHL	2	1	0	1	2	-1	0	0	—	—	—	—	—
— Quebec	IHL	15	1	7	8	4	...	...	...	—	—	—	—	—
— Hamilton	AHL	52	5	19	24	43	...	...	...	22	6	7	13	12
NHL totals (5 years)		263	64	88	152	133	9	18	5	26	8	6	14	24

KHRISTICH, DIMITRI — LW — KINGS

PERSONAL: Born July 23, 1969, in Kiev, U.S.S.R. ... 6-2/200. ... Shoots right. ... Name pronounced KRIH-stihch.

TRANSACTIONS/CAREER NOTES: Selected by Washington Capitals in sixth round (sixth Capitals pick, 120th overall) of NHL entry draft (June 11, 1988). ... Injured hip (February 16, 1990); missed six games. ... Broke foot (October 3, 1992); missed 20 games. ... Traded by Capitals with G Byron Dafoe to Los Angeles Kings for first-(C Alexander Volchkov) and fourth-(RW Justin Davis) round picks in 1996 draft (July 8, 1995). ... Suffered concussion (December 21, 1995); missed three games. ... Sprained right knee (February 23, 1996); missed three games. ... Suffered cut near right eye (February 7, 1997); missed seven games.

HONORS: Played in NHL All-Star Game (1997).

STATISTICAL PLATEAUS: Three-goal games: 1992-93 (2).

MISCELLANEOUS: Scored on a penalty shot (vs. Darcy Wakaluk, January 7, 1992).

Season Team	League	REGULAR SEASON								PLAYOFFS				
		Gms.	G	A	Pts.	PIM	+/-	PP	SH	Gms.	G	A	Pts.	PIM
88-89— Sokol Kiev................	USSR	42	17	8	25	15	...	...	...	—	—	—	—	—
89-90— Sokol Kiev................	USSR	47	14	22	36	32	...	...	...	—	—	—	—	—
90-91— Sokol Kiev................	USSR	28	10	12	22	20	...	...	...	—	—	—	—	—
— Baltimore	AHL	3	0	0	0	0	...	1	...	—	—	—	—	—
— Washington	NHL	40	13	14	27	21	-1	1	0	11	1	3	4	6
91-92— Washington	NHL	80	36	37	73	35	24	14	1	7	3	2	5	15
92-93— Washington	NHL	64	31	35	66	28	29	9	1	6	2	5	7	2
93-94— Washington	NHL	83	29	29	58	73	-2	10	0	11	2	3	5	10
94-95— Washington	NHL	48	12	14	26	41	0	8	0	7	1	4	5	0
95-96— Los Angeles..............	NHL	76	27	37	64	44	0	12	0	—	—	—	—	—
96-97— Los Angeles..............	NHL	75	19	37	56	38	8	3	0	—	—	—	—	—
NHL totals (7 years)		466	167	203	370	280	58	57	2	42	9	17	26	33

KIDD, TREVOR — G — FLAMES

PERSONAL: Born March 29, 1972, in St. Boniface, Man. ... 6-2/194. ... Catches left.

TRANSACTIONS/CAREER NOTES: Broke finger (December 1987). ... Selected by Calgary Flames in first round (first Flames pick, 11th overall) of NHL entry draft (June 16, 1990). ... Traded by Brandon Wheat Kings with D Bart Cote to Spokane Chiefs for RW Bobby House, C Marty Murray and G Don Blishen (January 21, 1991). ... Sprained left ankle (October 18, 1993); missed one game.

HONORS: Won Del Wilson Trophy (1989-90). ... Named to WHL (West) All-Star first team (1989-90).

MISCELLANEOUS: Member of silver-medal-winning Canadian Olympic team (1992). ... Holds Calgary Flames all-time record for goals-against average (2.83). ... Stopped a penalty shot attempt (vs. Teemu Selanne, February 6, 1995). ... Allowed a penalty shot goal (vs. Wendel Clark, November 24, 1993; vs. Joe Sakic, January 14, 1996).

K

Season Team	League	REGULAR SEASON								PLAYOFFS						
		Gms.	Min	W	L	T	GA	SO	Avg.	Gms.	Min.	W	L	GA	SO	Avg.
88-89 —Brandon	WHL	32	1509	...	...	...	102	0	4.06	—	—	—	—	—	—	—
89-90 —Brandon	WHL	*63	*3676	24	32	2	254	2	4.15	—	—	—	—	—	—	—
90-91 —Brandon	WHL	30	1730	10	19	1	117	0	4.06	—	—	—	—	—	—	—
—Spokane	WHL	14	749	8	3	0	44	0	3.52	15	926	*14	1	32	*2	*2.07
91-92 —Canadian nat'l team	Int'l	28	1349	18	4	4	79	2	3.51	—	—	—	—	—	—	—
—Can. Olympic team	Int'l	1	60	1	0	0	0	1	0.00	—	—	—	—	—	—	—
—Calgary	NHL	2	120	1	1	0	8	0	4.00	—	—	—	—	—	—	—
92-93 —Salt Lake City	IHL	30	1696	10	16	‡0	111	1	3.93	—	—	—	—	—	—	—
93-94 —Calgary	NHL	31	1614	13	7	6	85	0	3.16	—	—	—	—	—	—	—
94-95 —Calgary	NHL	†43	2463	22	14	6	107	3	2.61	7	434	3	4	26	1	3.59
95-96 —Calgary	NHL	47	2570	15	21	8	119	3	2.78	2	83	0	1	9	0	6.51
96-97 —Calgary	NHL	55	2979	21	23	6	141	4	2.84	—	—	—	—	—	—	—
NHL totals (5 years)		178	9746	72	66	26	460	10	2.83	9	517	3	5	35	1	4.06

KILGER, CHAD   C   COYOTES

PERSONAL: Born November 27, 1976, in Cornwall, Ont. ... 6-3/204. ... Shoots left. ... Son of Bob Kilger, former NHL referee (1970-71 through 1979-80) and current deputy speaker in House of Commons in Canadian Parliament.

TRANSACTIONS/CAREER NOTES: Selected by Mighty Ducks of Anaheim in first round (first Mighty Ducks pick, fourth overall) of NHL entry draft (July 8, 1995). ... Traded by Mighty Ducks with D Oleg Tverdovsky and third-round pick (D Per-Anton Lundstrom) in 1996 draft to Winnipeg Jets for C Marc Chouinard, RW Teemu Selanne and fourth-round pick (traded to Toronto) in 1996 draft (February 7, 1996). ... Suffered from the flu (February 21, 1996); missed one game. ... Jets franchise moved to Phoenix and renamed Coyotes for 1996-97 season; NHL approved move on January 18, 1996. ... Bruised thigh (October 7, 1996); missed one game.

Season Team	League	REGULAR SEASON							PLAYOFFS				
		Gms.	G	A	Pts.	PIM	+/-	PP	SH	Gms.	G	A	Pts.	PIM
92-93 —Cornwall	CJHL	55	30	36	66	26	...	...	...	6	0	0	0	0
93-94 —Kingston	OHL	66	17	35	52	23	...	...	...	6	7	2	9	8
94-95 —Kingston	OHL	65	42	53	95	95	...	...	...	6	5	2	7	10
95-96 —Anaheim	NHL	45	5	7	12	22	-2	0	0	—	—	—	—	—
—Winnipeg	NHL	29	2	3	5	12	-2	0	0	4	1	0	1	0
96-97 —Phoenix	NHL	24	4	3	7	13	-5	1	0	—	—	—	—	—
—Springfield	AHL	52	17	28	45	36	...	...	...	16	5	7	12	56
NHL totals (2 years)		98	11	13	24	47	-9	1	0	4	1	0	1	0

KING, DEREK   LW   MAPLE LEAFS

PERSONAL: Born February 11, 1967, in Hamilton, Ont. ... 6-0/212. ... Shoots left.

TRANSACTIONS/CAREER NOTES: Selected by New York Islanders as underage junior in first round (second Islanders pick, 13th overall) of NHL entry draft (June 15, 1985). ... Sprained right knee (September 1985). ... Fractured left wrist (December 12, 1987). ... Separated shoulder (November 23, 1988). ... Suffered concussion (November 2, 1990). ... Separated right shoulder (February 14, 1991). ... Bruised hip (November 27, 1992); missed two games. ... Suffered hip pointer (December 26, 1992); missed four games. ... Broke finger on left hand (April 3, 1993); missed one game. ... Suffered hip pointer (January 8, 1994); missed two games. ... Injured knee (March 9, 1995); missed one game. ... Injured elbow (April 28, 1995); missed two games. ... Injured foot (November 24, 1995); missed one game. ... Broke jaw and suffered mild concussion (March 3, 1996); missed remainder of season. ... Traded by Islanders to Hartford Whalers for fifth-round pick (C Adam Edinger) in 1997 draft (March 18, 1997). ... Signed as free agent by Toronto Maple Leafs (July 3, 1997).

HONORS: Won Emms Family Award (1984-85). ... Named to OHL All-Star first team (1986-87).

STATISTICAL PLATEAUS: Three-goal games: 1989-90 (1), 1991-92 (2), 1993-94 (1), 1996-97 (1). Total: 5. ... Four-goal games: 1990-91 (1). ... Total hat tricks: 6.

Season Team	League	REGULAR SEASON							PLAYOFFS				
		Gms.	G	A	Pts.	PIM	+/-	PP	SH	Gms.	G	A	Pts.	PIM
83-84 —Hamilton Jr. A.	OHA	37	10	14	24	142	...	...	...	—	—	—	—	—
84-85 —Sault Ste. Marie	OHL	63	35	38	73	106	...	...	...	16	3	13	16	11
85-86 —Sault Ste. Marie	OHL	25	12	17	29	33	...	...	...	—	—	—	—	—
—Oshawa	OHL	19	8	13	21	15	...	...	...	6	3	2	5	13
86-87 —Oshawa	OHL	57	53	53	106	74	...	...	...	17	14	10	24	40
—New York Islanders	NHL	2	0	0	0	0	0	0	0	—	—	—	—	—
87-88 —New York Islanders	NHL	55	12	24	36	30	7	1	0	5	0	2	2	2
—Springfield	AHL	10	7	6	13	6	...	...	...	—	—	—	—	—
88-89 —Springfield	AHL	4	4	0	4	0	...	...	...	—	—	—	—	—
—New York Islanders	NHL	60	14	29	43	14	10	4	0	—	—	—	—	—
89-90 —Springfield	AHL	21	11	12	23	33	...	...	...	—	—	—	—	—
—New York Islanders	NHL	46	13	27	40	20	2	5	0	4	0	0	0	4
90-91 —New York Islanders	NHL	66	19	26	45	44	1	2	0	—	—	—	—	—
91-92 —New York Islanders	NHL	80	40	38	78	46	-10	21	0	—	—	—	—	—
92-93 —New York Islanders	NHL	77	38	38	76	47	-4	21	0	18	3	11	14	14
93-94 —New York Islanders	IHL	78	30	40	70	59	18	10	0	4	0	1	1	0
94-95 —New York Islanders	NHL	43	10	16	26	41	-5	7	0	—	—	—	—	—
95-96 —New York Islanders	NHL	61	12	20	32	23	-10	5	1	—	—	—	—	—
96-97 —New York Islanders	NHL	70	23	30	53	20	-6	5	0	—	—	—	—	—
—Hartford	NHL	12	3	3	6	2	0	1	0	—	—	—	—	—
NHL totals (11 years)		650	214	291	505	346	3	82	1	31	3	14	17	20

KING, KRIS   LW   MAPLE LEAFS

PERSONAL: Born February 18, 1966, in Bracebridge, Ont. ... 5-11/205. ... Shoots left.

TRANSACTIONS/CAREER NOTES: Selected by Washington Capitals as underage junior in fourth round (fourth Capitals pick, 80th overall) of NHL entry draft (June 9, 1984). ... Signed as free agent by Detroit Red Wings (June 1987). ... Traded by Red Wings to New York Rangers for

K

LW Chris McRae and fifth-round pick (D Tony Burns) in 1990 draft (September 7, 1989). ... Sprained knee (January 7, 1991); missed six games. ... Traded by Rangers with RW Tie Domi to Winnipeg Jets for C Ed Olczyk (December 28, 1992). ... Suffered abdominal injury (February 13, 1996); missed one game. ... Jets franchise moved to Phoenix and renamed Coyotes for 1996-97 season; NHL approved move on January 18, 1996. ... Signed as free agent by Toronto Maple Leafs (July 7, 1997).
HONORS: Won King Clancy Trophy (1995-96).

Season Team	League	REGULAR SEASON								PLAYOFFS				
		Gms.	G	A	Pts.	PIM	+/-	PP	SH	Gms.	G	A	Pts.	PIM
82-83— Gravenhurst..............	SOJHL	32	72	53	125	115	...	...	...	—	—	—	—	—
83-84— Peterborough.............	OHL	62	13	18	31	168	...	...	...	8	3	3	6	14
84-85— Peterborough.............	OHL	61	18	35	53	222	...	...	...	16	2	8	10	28
85-86— Peterborough.............	OHL	58	19	40	59	254	...	...	...	8	4	0	4	21
86-87— Peterborough.............	OHL	46	23	33	56	160	...	...	...	12	5	8	13	41
— Binghamton	AHL	7	0	0	0	18	...	...	...	—	—	—	—	—
87-88— Adirondack.................	AHL	78	21	32	53	337	...	...	...	10	4	4	8	53
— Detroit........................	NHL	3	1	0	1	2	1	0	0	—	—	—	—	—
88-89— Detroit........................	NHL	55	2	3	5	168	-7	0	0	2	0	0	0	2
89-90— New York Rangers	NHL	68	6	7	13	286	2	0	0	10	0	1	1	38
90-91— New York Rangers	NHL	72	11	14	25	154	-1	0	0	6	2	0	2	36
91-92— New York Rangers	NHL	79	10	9	19	224	13	0	0	13	4	1	5	14
92-93— New York Rangers	NHL	30	0	3	3	67	-1	0	0	—	—	—	—	—
— Winnipeg	NHL	48	8	8	16	136	5	0	0	6	1	1	2	4
93-94— Winnipeg	NHL	83	4	8	12	205	-22	0	0	—	—	—	—	—
94-95— Winnipeg	NHL	48	4	2	6	85	0	0	0	—	—	—	—	—
95-96— Winnipeg	NHL	81	9	11	20	151	-7	0	1	5	0	1	1	4
96-97— Phoenix.....................	NHL	81	3	11	14	185	-7	0	0	7	0	0	0	17
NHL totals (10 years)		648	58	76	134	1663	-24	0	1	49	7	4	11	115

KING, STEVEN — LW/RW — FLYERS

PERSONAL: Born July 22, 1969, in East Greenwich, R.I. ... 6-0/195. ... Shoots right.
COLLEGE: Brown.
TRANSACTIONS/CAREER NOTES: Selected by New York Rangers in NHL supplemental draft (June 21, 1991). ... Selected by Mighty Ducks of Anaheim in NHL expansion draft (June 24, 1993). ... Sprained shoulder (January 1, 1994); missed six games. ... Underwent reconstructive shoulder surgery (February 3, 1994); missed remainder of season. ... Underwent shoulder surgery (January 5, 1995); missed entire 1994-95 season. ... Signed as free agent by Philadelphia Flyers (July 23, 1996).

Season Team	League	REGULAR SEASON								PLAYOFFS				
		Gms.	G	A	Pts.	PIM	+/-	PP	SH	Gms.	G	A	Pts.	PIM
87-88— Brown University	ECAC	24	10	5	15	30	...	...	...	—	—	—	—	—
88-89— Brown University	ECAC	26	8	5	13	73	...	...	...	—	—	—	—	—
89-90— Brown University	ECAC	27	19	8	27	53	...	...	...	—	—	—	—	—
90-91— Brown University	ECAC	27	19	15	34	76	...	...	...	—	—	—	—	—
91-92— Binghamton	AHL	66	27	15	42	56	...	...	...	10	2	0	2	14
92-93— Binghamton	AHL	53	35	33	68	100	...	...	...	14	7	9	16	26
— New York Rangers	NHL	24	7	5	12	16	4	5	0	—	—	—	—	—
93-94— Anaheim.....................	NHL	36	8	3	11	44	-7	3	0	—	—	—	—	—
94-95— Anaheim.....................	NHL					Did not play—injured.								
95-96— Baltimore	AHL	68	40	21	61	95	...	...	...	12	7	5	12	20
— Anaheim.....................	NHL	7	2	0	2	15	-1	1	0	—	—	—	—	—
96-97— Philadelphia	AHL	39	17	10	27	47	...	...	...	—	—	—	—	—
— Michigan....................	IHL	39	15	11	26	39	...	...	...	4	1	2	3	12
NHL totals (4 years)		67	17	8	25	75	-4	9	0					

KINNEAR, GEORDIE — D — DEVILS

PERSONAL: Born July 9, 1973, in Simcoe, Ont. ... 6-1/200. ... Shoots left. ... Name pronounced JOHR-dee kuh-NEER.
TRANSACTIONS/CAREER NOTES: Selected by New Jersey Devils in seventh round (seventh Devils pick, 162nd overall) of NHL entry draft (June 20, 1992).

Season Team	League	REGULAR SEASON								PLAYOFFS				
		Gms.	G	A	Pts.	PIM	+/-	PP	SH	Gms.	G	A	Pts.	PIM
90-91— Peterborough.............	Jr. B	6	0	6	6	51	...	...	...	—	—	—	—	—
— Peterborough.............	OHL	37	1	0	1	76	...	...	...	2	0	0	0	10
91-92— Peterborough.............	OHL	63	5	16	21	195	...	...	...	10	0	2	2	36
92-93— Peterborough.............	OHL	58	6	22	28	161	...	...	...	19	1	5	6	43
93-94— Albany.......................	AHL	59	3	12	15	197	...	...	...	5	0	0	0	21
94-95— Albany.......................	AHL	68	5	11	16	136	...	...	...	9	1	1	2	7
95-96— Albany.......................	AHL	73	4	7	11	170	...	...	...	4	0	1	1	2
96-97— Albany.......................	AHL	59	2	9	11	175	...	...	...	10	0	1	1	15

KIPRUSOFF, MARKO — D — CANADIENS

PERSONAL: Born June 6, 1972, in Turku, Finland. ... 6-0/194. ... Shoots right. ... Name pronounced KIHP-roo-sahf.
TRANSACTIONS/CAREER NOTES: Selected by Montreal Canadiens in fourth round (fourth Canadiens pick, 70th overall) of NHL entry draft (June 29, 1994). ... Suffered concussion (December 15, 1995); missed two games.
HONORS: Named to Finnish League All-Star team (1993-94).

Season Team	League	REGULAR SEASON								PLAYOFFS				
		Gms.	G	A	Pts.	PIM	+/-	PP	SH	Gms.	G	A	Pts.	PIM
90-91— TPS Turku..................	Finland	3	0	0	0	0	...	...	...	—	—	—	—	—
91-92— TPS Turku..................	Finland	23	0	2	2	0	...	...	...	—	—	—	—	—

Season Team	League	REGULAR SEASON Gms.	G	A	Pts.	PIM	+/-	PP	SH	PLAYOFFS Gms.	G	A	Pts.	PIM
— HPK Hameenlinna	Finland	3	0	0	0	0	...	...	...	—	—	—	—	—
92-93— TPS Turku	Finland	43	3	7	10	14	...	...	...	12	2	3	5	6
93-94— TPS Turku	Finland	48	5	19	24	8	...	...	...	11	0	6	6	4
94-95— TPS Turku	Finland	50	10	21	31	16	...	...	...	13	0	9	9	2
95-96— Montreal	NHL	24	0	4	4	8	-3	0	0	—	—	—	—	—
— Fredericton	AHL	28	4	10	14	2	...	...	...	10	2	5	7	2
96-97— Kiekko-67	Finland Dv.II	21	6	2	8	98	...	...	...	6	2	2	4	6
— TPS Jr.	Finland	11	5	1	6	28	...	...	...	—	—	—	—	—
NHL totals (1 year)		24	0	4	4	8	-3	0	0	—	—	—	—	—

KIPRUSOFF, MIIKKA   G   SHARKS

PERSONAL: Born October 26, 1976, in Turku, Finland. ... 6-0/176. ... Catches left.

TRANSACTIONS/CAREER NOTES: Selected by San Jose Sharks in fifth round (fifth Sharks pick, 115 overall) of NHL entry draft (July 8, 1995).

Season Team	League	REGULAR SEASON Gms.	Min	W	L	T	GA	SO	Avg.	PLAYOFFS Gms.	Min.	W	L	GA	SO	Avg.
93-94— TPS Jr.	Finland	35	...	...	...	...	...	...	2.88	6	...	...	...	...	...	4.23
94-95— TPS Jr.	Finland	31	1880	...	...	...	93	...	2.97	—	...	...	...	...	...	—
— TPS Turku	Finland	4	240	...	...	...	12	0	3.00	2	120	...	...	7	...	3.50
95-96— TPS Turku	Finland	12	550	...	...	...	38	...	4.15	4	114	...	...	4	...	2.11
— Kiekko	Finland	5	300	...	...	...	7	...	1.40	—	...	...	...	...	...	—
— TPS Jr.	Finland	3	180	...	...	...	9	...	3.00	—	...	...	...	...	...	—
96-97— AIK	Sweden	42	2466	...	...	...	104	3	2.53	4	420	...	...	23	0	3.28

KLATT, TRENT   RW   FLYERS

PERSONAL: Born January 30, 1971, in Robbinsdale, Minn. ... 6-1/205. ... Shoots right. ... Full name: Trent Thomas Klatt. ... Name pronounced KLAT.

HIGH SCHOOL: Osseo (Minn.).

COLLEGE: Minnesota.

TRANSACTIONS/CAREER NOTES: Selected by Washington Capitals in fourth round (fifth Capitals pick, 82nd overall) of NHL entry draft (June 17, 1989). ... Rights traded by Capitals with LW Steve Maltais to Minnesota North Stars for D Sean Chambers (June 21, 1991). ... Injured finger (January 7, 1993); missed three games. ... North Stars franchise moved from Minnesota to Dallas and renamed Stars for 1993-94 season. ... Strained back (November 9, 1993); missed one game. ... Sprained knee (November 11, 1993); missed two games. ... Sprained knee (February 6, 1994); missed three games. ... Traded by Stars to Philadelphia Flyers for LW Brent Fedyk (December 13, 1995). ... Suffered concussion (March 9, 1997); missed two games.

STATISTICAL PLATEAUS: Three-goal games: 1996-97 (1).

Season Team	League	REGULAR SEASON Gms.	G	A	Pts.	PIM	+/-	PP	SH	PLAYOFFS Gms.	G	A	Pts.	PIM
87-88— Osseo	Minn. H.S.	22	19	17	36	...	...	...	...	—	—	—	—	—
88-89— Osseo	Minn. H.S.	22	24	39	63	...	...	...	...	—	—	—	—	—
89-90— Univ. of Minnesota	WCHA	38	22	14	36	16	...	...	...	—	—	—	—	—
90-91— Univ. of Minnesota	WCHA	39	16	28	44	58	...	...	...	—	—	—	—	—
91-92— Univ. of Minnesota	WCHA	44	30	36	66	78	...	...	...	—	—	—	—	—
— Minnesota	NHL	1	0	0	0	0	0	0	0	6	0	0	0	2
92-93— Kalamazoo	IHL	31	8	11	19	18	...	...	...	—	—	—	—	—
— Minnesota	NHL	47	4	19	23	38	2	1	0	—	—	—	—	—
93-94— Dallas	NHL	61	14	24	38	30	13	3	0	9	2	1	3	4
— Kalamazoo	IHL	6	3	2	5	4	...	...	...	—	—	—	—	—
94-95— Dallas	NHL	47	12	10	22	26	-2	5	0	5	1	0	1	0
95-96— Dallas	NHL	22	4	4	8	23	0	0	0	—	—	—	—	—
— Michigan	IHL	2	1	2	3	5	...	...	...	—	—	—	—	—
— Philadelphia	NHL	49	3	8	11	21	2	0	0	12	4	1	5	0
96-97— Philadelphia	NHL	76	24	21	45	20	9	5	5	19	4	3	7	12
NHL totals (7 years)		303	61	86	147	158	24	14	5	51	11	5	16	18

KLEE, KEN   D   CAPITALS

PERSONAL: Born April 24, 1971, in Indianapolis. ... 6-1/205. ... Shoots right. ... Full name: Kenneth William Klee.

HIGH SCHOOL: Rockhurst (Kansas City, Mo.).

COLLEGE: St. Michael's College (Vt.), then Bowling Green State.

TRANSACTIONS/CAREER NOTES: Selected by Washington Capitals in ninth round (11th Capitals pick, 177th overall) of NHL entry draft (June 16, 1990). ... Injured foot (January 27, 1995); missed six games. ... Pulled groin (March 12, 1996); missed 13 games. ... Sprained knee (April 10, 1996); missed two games.

MISCELLANEOUS: Failed to score on a penalty shot (vs. Mike Richter, March 12, 1997).

Season Team	League	REGULAR SEASON Gms.	G	A	Pts.	PIM	+/-	PP	SH	PLAYOFFS Gms.	G	A	Pts.	PIM
89-90— Bowling Green	CCHA	39	0	5	5	52	...	...	...	—	—	—	—	—
90-91— Bowling Green	CCHA	37	7	28	35	50	...	...	...	—	—	—	—	—
91-92— Bowling Green	CCHA	10	0	1	1	14	...	...	...	—	—	—	—	—
92-93— Baltimore	AHL	77	4	14	18	68	...	...	...	7	0	1	1	15
93-94— Portland	AHL	65	2	9	11	87	...	...	...	17	1	2	3	14
94-95— Portland	AHL	49	5	7	12	89	...	...	...	—	—	—	—	—
— Washington	NHL	23	3	1	4	41	2	0	0	7	0	0	0	4
95-96— Washington	NHL	66	8	3	11	60	-1	0	1	1	0	0	0	0
96-97— Washington	NHL	80	3	8	11	115	-5	0	0	—	—	—	—	—
NHL totals (3 years)		169	14	12	26	216	-4	0	1	8	0	0	0	4

KLEMM, JON — D — AVALANCHE

PERSONAL: Born January 8, 1970, in Cranbrook, B.C. ... 6-2/197. ... Shoots right. ... Full name: Jonathan Darryl Klemm.
TRANSACTIONS/CAREER NOTES: Signed as free agent by Quebec Nordiques (May 1991). ... Injured abdomen (March 28, 1995); missed five games. ... Reinjured abdomen (April 8, 1995); missed remainder of season. ... Nordiques franchise moved to Colorado and renamed Avalanche for 1995-96 season (June 21, 1995). ... Injured groin (January 27, 1996); missed one game.
HONORS: Named to WHL (West) All-Star second team (1990-91).
MISCELLANEOUS: Member of Stanley Cup championship team (1996).

		REGULAR SEASON								PLAYOFFS				
Season Team	League	Gms.	G	A	Pts.	PIM	+/-	PP	SH	Gms.	G	A	Pts.	PIM
87-88— Seattle	WHL	68	6	7	13	24	...	...	...	—	—	—	—	—
88-89— Seattle	WHL	2	1	1	2	0	...	...	...	—	—	—	—	—
— Spokane	WHL	66	6	34	40	42	...	...	...	—	—	—	—	—
89-90— Spokane	WHL	66	3	28	31	100	...	...	...	6	1	1	2	5
90-91— Spokane	WHL	72	7	58	65	65	...	...	...	15	3	6	9	8
91-92— Halifax	AHL	70	6	13	19	40	...	...	...	—	—	—	—	—
— Quebec	NHL	4	0	1	1	0	2	0	0	—	—	—	—	—
92-93— Halifax	AHL	80	3	20	23	32	...	...	...	—	—	—	—	—
93-94— Cornwall	AHL	66	4	26	30	78	...	...	...	13	1	2	3	6
— Quebec	NHL	7	0	0	0	4	-1	0	0	—	—	—	—	—
94-95— Cornwall	AHL	65	6	13	19	84	...	...	...	—	—	—	—	—
— Quebec	NHL	4	1	0	1	2	3	0	0	—	—	—	—	—
95-96— Colorado	NHL	56	3	12	15	20	12	0	1	15	2	1	3	0
96-97— Colorado	NHL	80	9	15	24	37	12	1	2	17	1	1	2	6
NHL totals (5 years)		151	13	28	41	63	28	1	3	32	3	2	5	6

KLIMA, PETR — RW/LW — OILERS

PERSONAL: Born December 23, 1964, in Chaomutov, Czechoslovakia. ... 6-0/190. ... Shoots right. ... Name pronounced KLEE-muh.
TRANSACTIONS/CAREER NOTES: Selected by Detroit Red Wings in fifth round (fifth Red Wings pick, 88th overall) of NHL entry draft (June 8, 1983). ... Broke right thumb (May 1988). ... Sprained right ankle (November 12, 1988). ... Pulled groin (December 1988). ... Injured back (February 1989). ... Traded by Red Wings with C/RW Joe Murphy, C/LW Adam Graves and D Jeff Sharples to Edmonton Oilers for C Jimmy Carson, C Kevin McClelland and fifth-round pick (traded to Montreal) in 1991 draft (November 2, 1989). ... Suspended four games by NHL for butt-ending player (October 25, 1990). ... Pulled groin (March 15, 1991). ... Scratched cornea in right eye (November 18, 1991); missed one game. ... Strained groin (February 2, 1992); missed six games. ... Strained left knee ligaments (October 14, 1992); missed six games. ... Strained groin (January 7, 1993); missed eight games. ... Traded by Oilers to Tampa Bay Lightning for future considerations (June 16, 1993). ... Separated shoulder (February 27, 1994); missed eight games. ... Played in Europe during 1994-95 NHL lockout. ... Separated left shoulder (February 23, 1996); missed seven games. ... Bruised knee (April 8, 1996); missed three games. ... Traded by Lightning to Los Angeles Kings for fifth-round pick (C Jan Sulc) in 1997 draft (August 22, 1996). ... Traded by Kings to Pittsburgh Penguins for conditional pick in 1997 draft (October 25, 1996); Klima did not meet conditions for the pick and the draft choice was forfeited. ... Signed as free agent by Edmonton Oilers (February 26, 1997).
STATISTICAL PLATEAUS: Three-goal games: 1985-86 (2), 1986-87 (1), 1990-91 (3). Total: 6.
MISCELLANEOUS: Member of Stanley Cup championship team (1990). ... Scored on a penalty shot (vs. Alan Bester, April 9, 1988 (playoffs)). ... Failed to score on a penalty shot (vs. John Vanbiesbrouck, February 17, 1987; vs. Jon Casey, March 20, 1989; vs. Rejean Lemelin, May 18, 1990 (playoffs)).

		REGULAR SEASON								PLAYOFFS				
Season Team	League	Gms.	G	A	Pts.	PIM	+/-	PP	SH	Gms.	G	A	Pts.	PIM
82-83— Czec. national team	Int'l	44	19	17	36	74	...	...	...	—	—	—	—	—
83-84— Dukla Jihlava	Czech.	41	20	16	36	46	...	...	...	—	—	—	—	—
— Czec. national team	Int'l	7	6	5	11	...	...	...	...	—	—	—	—	—
84-85— Dukla Jihlava	Czech.	35	23	22	45	...	...	...	...	—	—	—	—	—
85-86— Detroit	NHL	74	32	24	56	16	-39	8	0	—	—	—	—	—
86-87— Detroit	NHL	77	30	23	53	42	-9	6	0	13	1	2	3	4
87-88— Detroit	NHL	78	37	25	62	46	4	6	5	12	10	8	18	10
88-89— Adirondack	AHL	5	5	1	6	4	...	...	...	—	—	—	—	—
— Detroit	NHL	51	25	16	41	44	5	1	0	6	2	4	6	19
89-90— Detroit	NHL	13	5	5	10	6	-8	2	0	—	—	—	—	—
— Edmonton	NHL	63	25	28	53	66	-1	7	0	21	5	0	5	8
90-91— Edmonton	NHL	70	40	28	68	113	24	7	1	18	7	6	13	16
91-92— Edmonton	NHL	57	21	13	34	52	-18	5	0	15	1	4	5	8
92-93— Edmonton	NHL	68	32	16	48	100	-15	13	0	—	—	—	—	—
93-94— Tampa Bay	NHL	75	28	27	55	76	-15	10	0	—	—	—	—	—
94-95— Wolfsburg	Ger. Div. II	12	27	11	38	28	...	...	...	—	—	—	—	—
— ZPS Zlin	Czech Rep.	1	1	0	1	...	...	...	...	—	—	—	—	—
— Tampa Bay	NHL	47	13	13	26	26	-13	4	0	—	—	—	—	—
95-96— Tampa Bay	NHL	67	22	30	52	68	-25	8	0	4	2	0	2	14
96-97— Los Angeles	NHL	8	0	4	4	2	-7	0	0	—	—	—	—	—
— Pittsburgh	NHL	9	1	3	4	4	-4	0	0	—	—	—	—	—
— Cleveland	IHL	19	7	14	21	6	...	...	...	—	—	—	—	—
— Edmonton	NHL	16	1	5	6	6	-1	0	0	6	0	0	0	4
NHL totals (13 years)		773	312	260	572	667	-122	77	6	95	28	24	52	83

KLIMENTIEV, SERGEI — D — SABRES

PERSONAL: Born April 5, 1975, in Kiev, U.S.S.R. ... 5-11/200. ... Shoots left. ... Name pronounced klih-MEHN-tee-ehv.
TRANSACTIONS/CAREER NOTES: Selected by Buffalo Sabres in fifth round (fourth Sabres pick, 121st overall) of NHL entry draft (June 29, 1994).

Season Team	League	Gms.	G	A	Pts.	PIM	+/-	PP	SH	Gms.	G	A	Pts.	PIM
91-92 — SVSM Kiev	CIS Div. III	42	4	15	19	...	...	...	...	—	—	—	—	—
92-93 — Sokol-Eskulap Kiev	CIS	3	0	0	0	4	...	...	...	1	0	0	0	0
93-94 — Medicine Hat	WHL	72	16	26	42	165	...	...	...	3	0	0	0	4
94-95 — Medicine Hat	WHL	71	19	45	64	146	...	...	...	5	4	2	6	14
— Rochester	AHL	7	0	0	0	8	...	...	...	1	0	0	0	0
95-96 — Rochester	AHL	70	7	29	36	74	...	...	...	19	2	8	10	16
96-97 — Rochester	AHL	77	14	28	42	114	...	...	...	10	1	4	5	28

KLIMOVICH, SERGEI   C   BLACKHAWKS

PERSONAL: Born May 8, 1974, in Novosibirsk, U.S.S.R. ... 6-2/189. ... Shoots right. ... Name pronounced SAIR-gay KLEE-muh-vihch.
TRANSACTIONS/CAREER NOTES: Selected by Chicago Blackhawks in second round (third Blackhawks pick, 41st overall) of NHL entry draft (June 20, 1992).

Season Team	League	Gms.	G	A	Pts.	PIM	+/-	PP	SH	Gms.	G	A	Pts.	PIM
91-92 — Dynamo Moscow	CIS	3	0	0	0	0	...	...	...	—	—	—	—	—
92-93 — Dynamo Moscow	CIS	30	4	1	5	14	...	...	...	10	1	0	1	2
93-94 — Dynamo Moscow	CIS	39	7	4	11	14	...	...	...	12	2	3	5	6
94-95 — Dynamo Moscow	CIS	4	1	0	1	2	...	...	...	—	—	—	—	—
— Indianapolis	IHL	71	14	30	44	20	...	...	...	—	—	—	—	—
95-96 — Indianapolis	IHL	68	17	21	38	28	...	...	...	5	1	1	2	6
96-97 — Indianapolis	IHL	75	20	37	57	98	...	...	...	3	1	2	3	0
— Chicago	NHL	1	0	0	0	2	0	0	0	—	—	—	—	—
NHL totals (1 year)		**1**	**0**	**0**	**0**	**2**	**0**	**0**	**0**					

KNIPSCHEER, FRED   C   BLUES

PERSONAL: Born September 3, 1969, in Fort Wayne, Ind. ... 5-11/187. ... Shoots left. ... Name pronounced kuh-NIHP-sheer.
COLLEGE: St. Cloud (Minn.) State.
TRANSACTIONS/CAREER NOTES: Signed as free agent by Boston Bruins (April 30, 1993). ... Injured shoulder (April 2, 1995); missed four games. ... Traded by Bruins to St. Louis Blues for D Rick Zombo (October 2, 1995).

Season Team	League	Gms.	G	A	Pts.	PIM	+/-	PP	SH	Gms.	G	A	Pts.	PIM
90-91 — St. Cloud State	WCHA	40	9	10	19	57	...	...	...	—	—	—	—	—
91-92 — St. Cloud State	WCHA	33	15	17	32	48	...	...	...	—	—	—	—	—
92-93 — St. Cloud State	WCHA	36	34	26	60	68	...	...	...	—	—	—	—	—
93-94 — Boston	NHL	11	3	2	5	14	3	0	0	12	2	1	3	6
— Providence	AHL	62	26	13	39	50	...	...	...	—	—	—	—	—
94-95 — Providence	AHL	71	29	34	63	81	...	...	...	—	—	—	—	—
— Boston	NHL	16	3	1	4	2	1	0	0	4	0	0	0	0
95-96 — Worcester	AHL	68	36	37	73	93	...	...	...	3	0	0	0	2
— St. Louis	NHL	1	0	0	0	2	0	0	0	—	—	—	—	—
96-97 — Indianapolis	IHL	41	10	9	19	46	...	...	...	4	0	2	2	10
— Phoenix	IHL	24	5	11	16	19	...	...	...	—	—	—	—	—
NHL totals (3 years)		**28**	**6**	**3**	**9**	**18**	**4**	**0**	**0**	**16**	**2**	**1**	**3**	**6**

KNUBLE, MICHAEL   RW   RED WINGS

PERSONAL: Born July 4, 1972, in Toronto. ... 6-3/215. ... Shoots right. ... Name pronounced kuh-NOO-buhl.
HIGH SCHOOL: East Kentwood (Mich.).
COLLEGE: Michigan.
TRANSACTIONS/CAREER NOTES: Selected by Detroit Red Wings in fourth round (fourth Red Wings pick, 76th overall) of NHL entry draft (June 22, 1991).
HONORS: Named to CCHA All-Star first team (1993-94). ... Named to NCAA All-America West second team (1994-95). ... Named to CCHA All-Star second team (1994-95).

Season Team	League	Gms.	G	A	Pts.	PIM	+/-	PP	SH	Gms.	G	A	Pts.	PIM
88-89 — East Kentwood	Mich. H.S.	28	52	37	89	60	...	...	...	—	—	—	—	—
89-90 — East Kentwood	Mich. H.S.	29	63	40	103	40	...	...	...	—	—	—	—	—
90-91 — Kalamazoo	NAJHL	36	18	24	42	30	...	...	...	—	—	—	—	—
91-92 — Univ. of Michigan	CCHA	43	7	8	15	48	...	...	...	—	—	—	—	—
92-93 — Univ. of Michigan	CCHA	39	26	16	42	57	...	...	...	—	—	—	—	—
93-94 — Univ. of Michigan	CCHA	41	32	26	58	71	...	...	...	—	—	—	—	—
94-95 — Univ. of Michigan	CCHA	34	38	22	60	62	...	...	...	—	—	—	—	—
— Adirondack	AHL	—	—	—	—	—	...	...	...	3	0	0	0	0
95-96 — Adirondack	AHL	80	22	23	45	59	...	...	...	3	1	0	1	0
96-97 — Adirondack	AHL	68	28	35	63	54	...	...	...	—	—	—	—	—
— Detroit	NHL	9	1	0	1	0	-1	0	0	—	—	—	—	—
NHL totals (1 year)		**9**	**1**	**0**	**1**	**0**	**-1**	**0**	**0**					

KNUTSEN, ESPEN   C   MIGHTY DUCKS

PERSONAL: Born January 12, 1972, in Oslo, Norway. ... 5-11/172. ... Shoots left.
TRANSACTIONS/CAREER NOTES: Selected by Hartford Whalers in 10th round (ninth Whalers pick, 204th overall) of NHL entry draft (June 16, 1990). ... Rights traded by Whalers to Mighty Ducks of Anaheim for RW Kevin Brown (October 1, 1996).

Season Team	League	REGULAR SEASON								PLAYOFFS				
		Gms.	G	A	Pts.	PIM	+/-	PP	SH	Gms.	G	A	Pts.	PIM
89-90— Valerengen..................	Knutsen	34	22	26	48		...	...	...	—	—	—	—	—
90-91— Valerengen..................	Knutsen	31	30	24	54	42	...	...	...	5	3	4	7	0
91-92— Valerengen..................	Knutsen	30	28	26	54	37	...	...	...	8	7	8	15	15
92-93— Valerengen..................	Knutsen	13	11	13	24	4	...	...	...	—	—	—	—	—
93-94— Valerengen..................	Knutsen	38	32	26	58	20	...	...	...	—	—	—	—	—
94-95— Djur. Stockholm.........	Sweden	30	6	14	20	18	...	...	...	3	0	1	1	0
95-96— Djur. Stockholm.........	Sweden	32	10	23	33	50	...	...	...	4	1	0	1	2
96-97— Djur. Stockholm.........	Sweden	39	16	33	49	20	...	...	...	4	2	4	6	6

KOCHAN, DIETER   G   CANUCKS

PERSONAL: Born November 5, 1974, in Saskatoon, Sask. ... 6-1/171. ... Catches left.
HIGH SCHOOL: North (Sioux City, Iowa).
COLLEGE: Northern Michigan.
TRANSACTIONS/CAREER NOTES: Selected by Vancouver Canucks in fourth round (third Canucks pick, 98th overall) of NHL entry draft (June 26, 1993).

Season Team	League	REGULAR SEASON								PLAYOFFS					
		Gms.	Min	W	L	T	GA	SO	Avg.	Gms.	Min.	W	L	GA	SO	Avg.
91-92—Sioux City	USHL	23	1131	7	10	0	100	...	5.31	—	—	—	—	—	—
92-93—Kelowna.......................	BCJHL	44	2582	34	8	0	137	1	*3.18	—	—	—	—	—	—
93-94—Northern Michigan.......	WCHA	16	984	9	7	0	57	2	3.48	—	—	—	—	—	—
94-95—Northern Michigan.......	WCHA	29	1512	8	17	3	107	0	4.25	—	—	—	—	—	—
95-96—Northern Michigan.......	WCHA	31	1627	7	21	2	123	0	4.54	—	—	—	—	—	—
96-97—Northern Michigan.......	WCHA	26	1528	8	15	2	99	0	3.89	—	—	—	—	—	—

KOCUR, JOEY   RW   RED WINGS

PERSONAL: Born December 21, 1964, in Calgary. ... 6-0/205. ... Shoots right. ... Name pronounced KOH-suhr. ... Cousin of Wendel Clark, left winger, Toronto Maple Leafs.
TRANSACTIONS/CAREER NOTES: Stretched knee ligaments (December 1981). ... Selected by Detroit Red Wings as underage junior in fifth round (sixth Red Wings pick, 88th overall) of NHL entry draft (June 8, 1983). ... Cut right hand (January 1985). ... Sprained thumb (December 11, 1985). ... Strained ligaments (March 26, 1986). ... Suffered sore right elbow (October 1987). ... Strained sternum and collarbone (November 1987). ... Injured shoulder (December 1987). ... Separated shoulder (May 1988). ... Injured knee (November 1988). ... Injured back (February 1989). ... Bruised right foot (February 16, 1990). ... Strained right knee ligaments (March 1990). ... Injured right hand and arm (December 1, 1990); missed three weeks. ... Traded by Red Wings with D Per Djoos to New York Rangers for C Kevin Miller, D Dennis Vial and RW Jim Cummins (March 5, 1991). ... Suspended four games by NHL for high-sticking (March 10, 1991). ... Suspended additional four games by NHL for high-sticking during appeal of March 10 incident (March 14, 1991); missed final seven games of 1990-91 season and first game of 1991-92 season. ... Underwent surgery to middle knuckle of right hand (May 10, 1991). ... Injured hip flexor (October 1991); missed first five games of season. ... Separated shoulder (January 28, 1992); missed 13 games. ... Slightly sprained right knee (March 5, 1992); missed six games. ... Sprained leg (November 21, 1992); missed one game. ... Injured back (February 10, 1993); missed two games. ... Injured back (February 20, 1993); missed two games. ... Pulled groin (April 9, 1993); missed three games. ... Bruised hand (January 28, 1994); missed three games. ... Reinjured hand (February 9, 1994); missed four games. ... Suffered back spasms (April 4, 1994); missed two games. ... Traded by Rangers to Vancouver Canucks for G Kay Whitmore (March 20, 1996). ... Suffered back spasms (April 1, 1996); missed three games. ... Signed as free agent by Red Wings (December 26, 1996). ... Injured hip flexor (January 9, 1997). ... Suffered from the flu (March 26, 1997); missed one game. ... Strained lower back (April 9, 1997); missed two games.
MISCELLANEOUS: Member of Stanley Cup championship team (1994 and 1997). ... Scored on a penalty shot (vs. Jacques Cloutier, November 29, 1990).

Season Team	League	REGULAR SEASON								PLAYOFFS				
		Gms.	G	A	Pts.	PIM	+/-	PP	SH	Gms.	G	A	Pts.	PIM
80-81— Yorkton	SJHL	48	6	9	15	307	...	...	...	—	—	—	—	—
81-82— Yorkton	SJHL	47	20	21	41	199	...	...	...	—	—	—	—	—
82-83— Saskatoon	WHL	62	23	17	40	289	...	...	...	6	2	3	5	25
83-84— Saskatoon	WHL	69	40	41	81	258	...	...	...	—	—	—	—	—
84-85— Detroit.......................	NHL	17	1	0	1	64	-4	0	0	3	1	0	1	5
— Adirondack..............	AHL	47	12	7	19	171	...	...	...	—	—	—	—	—
85-86— Adirondack..............	AHL	9	6	2	8	34	...	...	...	—	—	—	—	—
— Detroit.......................	NHL	59	9	6	15	*377	-24	2	0	—	—	—	—	—
86-87— Detroit.......................	NHL	77	9	9	18	276	-10	2	0	16	2	3	5	71
87-88— Detroit.......................	NHL	64	7	7	14	263	-11	0	0	10	0	1	1	13
88-89— Detroit.......................	NHL	60	9	9	18	213	-4	1	0	3	0	1	1	6
89-90— Detroit.......................	NHL	71	16	20	36	268	-4	1	0	—	—	—	—	—
90-91— Detroit.......................	NHL	52	5	4	9	253	-6	0	0	—	—	—	—	—
— New York Rangers.....	NHL	5	0	0	0	36	-1	0	0	6	0	2	2	21
91-92— New York Rangers.....	NHL	51	7	4	11	121	-4	0	0	12	1	1	2	38
92-93— New York Rangers.....	NHL	65	3	6	9	131	-9	2	0	—	—	—	—	—
93-94— New York Rangers.....	NHL	71	2	1	3	129	-9	0	0	20	1	1	2	17
94-95— New York Rangers.....	NHL	48	1	2	3	71	-4	0	0	10	0	0	0	8
95-96— New York Rangers.....	NHL	38	1	2	3	49	-4	0	0	—	—	—	—	—
— Vancouver..................	NHL	7	0	1	1	19	-3	0	0	1	0	0	0	0
96-97— San Antonio	IHL	5	1	1	2	24	...	...	...	—	—	—	—	—
— Detroit.......................	NHL	34	2	1	3	70	-7	0	0	19	1	3	4	22
NHL totals (13 years)		719	72	72	144	2340	-104	8	0	100	6	12	18	201

KOHN, LADISLAV   RW   FLAMES

PERSONAL: Born March 4, 1975, in Uherske Hradiste, Czechoslovakia. ... 5-10/175. ... Shoots left. ... Name pronounced KOHN.
TRANSACTIONS/CAREER NOTES: Selected by Calgary Flames in seventh round (ninth Flames pick, 175th overall) in NHL entry draft (June 29, 1994).

K

			REGULAR SEASON								PLAYOFFS				
Season Team	League	Gms.	G	A	Pts.	PIM	+/-	PP	SH		Gms.	G	A	Pts.	PIM
93-94 — Brandon	WHL	2	0	0	0	0	...	...	...		—	—	—	—	—
— Swift Current	WHL	69	33	35	68	68	...	...	...		7	5	4	9	8
94-95 — Swift Current	WHL	65	32	60	92	122	...	...	...		6	2	6	8	14
— Saint John	AHL	1	0	0	0	0	...	...	...		—	—	—	—	—
95-96 — Saint John	AHL	73	28	45	73	97	...	...	...		16	6	5	11	12
— Calgary	NHL	5	1	0	1	2	-1	0	0		—	—	—	—	—
96-97 — Saint John	AHL	76	28	29	57	81	...	...	...		5	0	0	0	0
NHL totals (1 year)		5	1	0	1	2	-1	0	0						

KOIVU, SAKU   C   CANADIENS

PERSONAL: Born November 23, 1974, in Turku, Finland. ... 5-9/175. ... Shoots left. ... Name pronounced KOY-voo.
TRANSACTIONS/CAREER NOTES: Selected by Montreal Canadiens in first round (first Canadiens pick, 21st overall) of NHL entry draft (June 26, 1993). ... Tore knee ligament (December 7, 1996); missed 26 games. ... Sprained shoulder (March 10, 1997); missed five games. ... Suffered from tonsillitis (March 29, 1997); missed one game.
MISCELLANEOUS: Member of bronze-medal-winning Finnish Olympic team (1994).

			REGULAR SEASON								PLAYOFFS				
Season Team	League	Gms.	G	A	Pts.	PIM	+/-	PP	SH		Gms.	G	A	Pts.	PIM
91-92 — TPS Jr.	Finland	42	30	37	67	63	...	...	...		—	—	—	—	—
92-93 — TPS Turku	Finland	46	3	7	10	28	...	...	...		—	—	—	—	—
93-94 — TPS Turku	Finland	47	23	30	53	42	...	...	...		11	4	8	12	16
— Fin. Olympic team	Int'l	8	4	3	7	12	...	...	...		—	—	—	—	—
94-95 — TPS Turku	Finland	45	27	47	74	73	...	...	...		13	7	10	17	16
95-96 — Montreal	NHL	82	20	25	45	40	-7	8	3		6	3	1	4	8
96-97 — Montreal	NHL	50	17	39	56	38	7	5	0		5	1	3	4	10
NHL totals (2 years)		132	37	64	101	78	0	13	3		11	4	4	8	18

KOLESAR, MARK   LW   MAPLE LEAFS

PERSONAL: Born January 23, 1973, in Brampton, Ont. ... 6-1/188. ... Shoots right. ... Name pronounced KOH-lih-sahr.
TRANSACTIONS/CAREER NOTES: Signed as free agent by Toronto Maple Leafs (May 24, 1994).

			REGULAR SEASON								PLAYOFFS				
Season Team	League	Gms.	G	A	Pts.	PIM	+/-	PP	SH		Gms.	G	A	Pts.	PIM
91-92 — Brandon	WHL	56	6	7	13	36	...	...	...		—	—	—	—	—
92-93 — Brandon	WHL	68	27	33	60	110	...	...	...		4	0	0	0	4
93-94 — Brandon	WHL	59	29	37	66	131	...	...	...		14	8	3	11	48
94-95 — St. John's	AHL	65	12	18	30	62	...	...	...		5	1	0	1	2
95-96 — St. John's	AHL	52	22	13	35	47	...	...	...		—	—	—	—	—
— Toronto	NHL	21	2	2	4	14	0	0	0		3	1	0	1	2
96-97 — St. John's	AHL	62	22	28	50	64	...	...	...		10	1	3	4	6
— Toronto	NHL	7	0	0	0	0	-3	0	0		—	—	—	—	—
NHL totals (2 years)		28	2	2	4	14	-3	0	0		3	1	0	1	2

KOLKUNOV, ALEXEI   C   PENGUINS

PERSONAL: Born February 3, 1977, in Belgorod, U.S.S.R. ... 6-0/185. ... Shoots right.
TRANSACTIONS/CAREER NOTES: Selected by Pittsburgh Penguins in sixth round (fifth Penguins pick, 154th overall) of NHL entry draft (July 8, 1995).

			REGULAR SEASON								PLAYOFFS				
Season Team	League	Gms.	G	A	Pts.	PIM	+/-	PP	SH		Gms.	G	A	Pts.	PIM
94-95 — Soviet Wings	CIS	7	0	0	0	0	...	...	...		4	1	0	1	0
95-96 — Krylja Sovetov	CIS	43	9	3	12	35	...	...	...		—	—	—	—	—
96-97 — Krylja Sovetov	Russian	44	9	16	25	36	...	...	...		2	0	0	0	4

KOLZIG, OLAF   G   CAPITALS

PERSONAL: Born April 6, 1970, in Johannesburg, South Africa. ... 6-3/225. ... Catches left. ... Name pronounced OH-lahf KOHL-zihg.
TRANSACTIONS/CAREER NOTES: Underwent surgery to right knee (November 1988). ... Selected by Washington Capitals in first round (first Capitals pick, 19th overall) of NHL entry draft (June 17, 1989). ... Loaned by Capitals to Rochester Americans (October 2, 1992). ... Dislocated kneecap (October 13, 1993); missed 14 games. ... Suffered from mononucleosis (October 8, 1996); missed three games.
HONORS: Shared Harry (Hap) Holmes Memorial Trophy with Byron Dafoe (1993-94). ... Won Jack Butterfield Trophy (1993-94).
MISCELLANEOUS: Stopped a penalty shot attempt (vs. Mike Hough, February 29, 1996; vs. Todd Marchant, January, 26, 1997).

			REGULAR SEASON								PLAYOFFS					
Season Team	League	Gms.	Min	W	L	T	GA	SO	Avg.		Gms.	Min.	W	L	GA	SO	Avg.
87-88 — New Westminster	WHL	15	650	6	5	0	48	1	4.43		3	149	0	0	11	0	4.43
88-89 — Tri-City	WHL	30	1671	16	10	2	97	1	*3.48		—	—	—	—	—	—	—
89-90 — Washington	NHL	2	120	0	2	0	12	0	6.00		—	—	—	—	—	—	—
— Tri-City	WHL	48	2504	27	27	3	187	1	4.48		6	318	4	0	27	0	5.09
90-91 — Baltimore	AHL	26	1367	10	12	1	72	0	3.16		—	—	—	—	—	—	—
— Hampton Roads	ECHL	21	1248	11	9	‡1	71	2	3.41		3	180	1	2	14	0	4.67
91-92 — Baltimore	AHL	28	1503	5	17	2	105	1	4.19		—	—	—	—	—	—	—
— Hampton Roads	ECHL	14	847	11	3	‡0	41	0	2.90		—	—	—	—	—	—	—
92-93 — Rochester	AHL	49	2737	25	16	4	168	0	3.68		17	*1040	9	*8	61	0	3.52
— Washington	NHL	1	20	0	0	0	2	0	6.00		—	—	—	—	—	—	—

Season Team	League	REGULAR SEASON								PLAYOFFS						
		Gms.	Min	W	L	T	GA	SO	Avg.	Gms.	Min.	W	L	GA	SO	Avg.
93-94—Portland	AHL	29	1726	16	8	5	88	3	3.06	17	1035	†12	5	44	0	*2.55
—Washington	NHL	7	224	0	3	0	20	0	5.36	—	—	—	—	—	—	—
94-95—Washington	NHL	14	724	2	8	2	30	0	2.49	2	44	1	0	1	0	1.36
—Portland	AHL	2	125	1	0	1	3	0	1.44	—	—	—	—	—	—	—
95-96—Washington	NHL	18	897	4	8	2	46	0	3.08	5	341	2	3	11	0	1.94
—Portland	AHL	5	300	5	0	0	7	1	1.40	—	—	—	—	—	—	—
96-97—Washington	NHL	29	1644	8	15	4	71	2	2.59	—	—	—	—	—	—	—
NHL totals (6 years)		71	3629	14	36	8	181	2	2.99	7	385	3	3	12	0	1.87

KOMARNISKI, ZENITH   D   CANUCKS

PERSONAL: Born August 13, 1978, in Edmonton. ... 6-0/190. ... Shoots left. ... Name pronounced ZEH-nihth koh-mahr-NIH-skee.
TRANSACTIONS/CAREER NOTES: Selected by Vancouver Canucks in third round (second Canucks pick, 75th overall) of NHL entry draft (June 22, 1996).
HONORS: Named to WHL (West) All-Star first team (1996-97).

Season Team	League	REGULAR SEASON								PLAYOFFS				
		Gms.	G	A	Pts.	PIM	+/-	PP	SH	Gms.	G	A	Pts.	PIM
94-95—Tri-City	WHL	66	5	19	24	110	...	...	...	17	1	2	3	47
95-96—Tri-City	WHL	42	5	21	26	85	...	...	...	—	—	—	—	—
96-97—Tri-City	WHL	58	12	44	56	112	...	...	...	—	—	—	—	—

KONOWALCHUK, STEVE   LW   CAPITALS

PERSONAL: Born November 11, 1972, in Salt Lake City. ... 6-1/195. ... Shoots left. ... Full name: Steven Reed Konowalchuk. ... Name pronounced kah-nah-WAHL-chuhk.
TRANSACTIONS/CAREER NOTES: Selected by Washington Capitals in third round (fifth Capitals pick, 58th overall) of NHL entry draft (June 22, 1991). ... Separated shoulder (October 13, 1995); missed four games. ... Injured left hand (March 26, 1996); missed eight games. ... Separated rib cartilage prior to 1996-97 season; missed four games.
HONORS: Won Four Broncos Memorial Trophy (1991-92). ... Named to Can.HL All-Star second team (1991-92). ... Named to WHL (West) All-Star first team (1991-92).
STATISTICAL PLATEAUS: Three-goal games: 1995-96 (2).
MISCELLANEOUS: Failed to score on a penalty shot (vs. Mike Richter, March 5, 1995).

Season Team	League	REGULAR SEASON								PLAYOFFS				
		Gms.	G	A	Pts.	PIM	+/-	PP	SH	Gms.	G	A	Pts.	PIM
90-91—Portland	WHL	72	43	49	92	78	...	...	...	—	—	—	—	—
91-92—Portland	WHL	64	51	53	104	95	...	...	...	6	3	6	9	12
—Baltimore	AHL	3	1	1	2	0	...	...	...	—	—	—	—	—
—Washington	NHL	1	0	0	0	0	0	0	0	—	—	—	—	—
92-93—Baltimore	AHl	37	18	28	46	74	...	...	...	—	—	—	—	—
—Washington	NHL	36	4	7	11	16	4	1	0	2	0	1	1	0
93-94—Portland	AHL	8	11	4	15	4	...	...	...	—	—	—	—	—
—Washington	NHL	62	12	14	26	33	9	0	0	11	0	1	1	10
94-95—Washington	NHL	46	11	14	25	44	7	3	3	7	2	5	7	12
95-96—Washington	NHL	70	23	22	45	92	13	7	1	2	0	2	2	0
96-97—Washington	NHL	78	17	25	42	67	-3	2	1	—	—	—	—	—
NHL totals (6 years)		293	67	82	149	252	30	13	5	22	2	9	11	22

KONSTANTINOV, VLADIMIR   D   RED WINGS

PERSONAL: Born March 19, 1967, in Murmansk, U.S.S.R. ... 6-0/195. ... Shoots right. ... Name pronounced KAHN-stan-TEE-nahf.
TRANSACTIONS/CAREER NOTES: Selected by Detroit Red Wings in 11th round (12th Red Wings pick, 221st overall) of NHL entry draft (June 17, 1989). ... Injured groin (December 3, 1992); missed two games. ... Sprained knee (October 27, 1993); missed four games. ... Played in Europe during 1994-95 NHL lockout. ... Injured Achilles' tendon prior to 1996-97 season; missed first two games of season. ... Bruised sternum (November 2, 1996); missed one game.
HONORS: Named to NHL All-Rookie team (1991-92). ... Won Alka-Seltzer Plus award (1995-96). ... Named to NHL All-Star second team (1995-96).
MISCELLANEOUS: Member of Stanley Cup championship team (1997).

Season Team	League	REGULAR SEASON								PLAYOFFS				
		Gms.	G	A	Pts.	PIM	+/-	PP	SH	Gms.	G	A	Pts.	PIM
84-85—CSKA Moscow	USSR	40	1	4	5	10	...	...	...	—	—	—	—	—
85-86—CSKA Moscow	USSR	26	4	3	7	12	...	...	...	—	—	—	—	—
86-87—CSKA Moscow	USSR	35	2	2	4	19	...	...	...	—	—	—	—	—
87-88—CSKA Moscow	USSR	50	3	6	9	32	...	...	...	—	—	—	—	—
88-89—CSKA Moscow	USSR	37	7	8	15	20	...	...	...	—	—	—	—	—
89-90—CSKA Moscow	USSR	47	14	13	27	44	...	...	...	—	—	—	—	—
90-91—CSKA Moscow	USSR	45	5	12	17	42	...	...	...	—	—	—	—	—
91-92—Detroit	NHL	79	8	26	34	172	25	1	0	11	0	1	1	16
92-93—Detroit	NHL	82	5	17	22	137	22	0	0	7	0	1	1	8
93-94—Detroit	NHL	80	12	21	33	138	30	1	3	7	0	2	2	4
94-95—Wedemark	Ger. Div. II	15	13	17	30	51	...	...	...	—	—	—	—	—
—Detroit	NHL	47	3	11	14	101	10	0	0	18	1	1	2	22
95-96—Detroit	NHL	81	14	20	34	139	*60	3	1	19	4	5	9	28
96-97—Detroit	NHL	77	5	33	38	151	38	0	0	20	0	4	4	29
NHL totals (6 years)		446	47	128	175	838	185	5	4	82	5	14	19	107

KORDIC, DAN D FLYERS

PERSONAL: Born April 18, 1971, in Edmonton. ... 6-5/227. ... Shoots left. ... Name pronounced KOHR-dihk. ... Brother of John Kordic, right winger for four NHL teams (1985-86 through 1991-92).
TRANSACTIONS/CAREER NOTES: Selected by Philadelphia Flyers in fifth round (eighth Flyers pick, 88th overall) of NHL entry draft (June 16, 1990). ... Suffered from the flu (January 1992); missed five games. ... Underwent knee surgery prior to 1992-93 season; missed 63 games. ... Sprained left knee (February 26, 1997); missed two games.

		REGULAR SEASON								PLAYOFFS				
Season Team	League	Gms.	G	A	Pts.	PIM	+/-	PP	SH	Gms.	G	A	Pts.	PIM
87-88— Medicine Hat............	WHL	63	1	5	6	75	...	...	...	—	—	—	—	—
88-89— Medicine Hat............	WHL	70	1	13	14	190	...	...	...	—	—	—	—	—
89-90— Medicine Hat............	WHL	59	4	12	16	182	...	...	...	3	0	0	0	9
90-91— Medicine Hat............	WHL	67	8	15	23	150	...	...	...	12	2	6	8	42
91-92— Philadelphia	NHL	46	1	3	4	126	1	0	0	—	—	—	—	—
92-93— Hershey	AHL	14	0	2	2	17	...	...	...	—	—	—	—	—
93-94— Hershey	AHL	64	0	4	4	164	...	...	...	11	0	3	3	26
— Philadelphia	NHL	4	0	0	0	5	0	0	0	—	—	—	—	—
94-95— Hershey	AHL	37	0	2	2	121	...	...	...	6	0	1	1	21
95-96— Hershey	AHL	52	2	6	8	101	...	...	...	—	—	—	—	—
— Philadelphia	NHL	9	1	0	1	31	1	0	0	—	—	—	—	—
96-97— Philadelphia	NHL	75	1	4	5	210	-1	0	0	12	1	0	1	22
NHL totals (4 years)		134	3	7	10	372	1	0	0	12	1	0	1	22

K

KOROBOLIN, ALEXANDER D RANGERS

PERSONAL: Born March 12, 1976, in Chelyabinsk, U.S.S.R. ... 6-2/189. ... Shoots left. ... Name pronounced KOH-ruh-BOH-lihn.
TRANSACTIONS/CAREER NOTES: Selected by New York Rangers in fourth round (fourth Rangers pick, 100th overall) of NHL entry draft (June 29, 1994).

		REGULAR SEASON								PLAYOFFS				
Season Team	League	Gms.	G	A	Pts.	PIM	+/-	PP	SH	Gms.	G	A	Pts.	PIM
93-94— Mechel Chelyabinsk ...	CIS Div. II	32	0	0	0	30	...	...	...	—	—	—	—	—
94-95— Mechel Chelyabinsk ...	CIS Div. II						Statistics unavailable.							
95-96— Mechel Chelyabinsk ...	CIS Div. II						Statistics unavailable.							
96-97— Mechel Chelyabinsk ...	Rus. Div. II	60	2	7	9	54	...	...	...	—	—	—	—	—

KOROLEV, IGOR LW COYOTES

PERSONAL: Born September 6, 1970, in Moscow, U.S.S.R. ... 6-1/187. ... Shoots left. ... Name pronounced EE-gohr KOHR-ih-lehv.
TRANSACTIONS/CAREER NOTES: Selected by St. Louis Blues in second round (first Blues pick, 38th overall) of NHL entry draft (June 20, 1992). ... Suffered from the flu (March 3, 1994); missed one game. ... Injured hip (March 12, 1994); missed three games. ... Selected by Winnipeg Jets in 1994-95 waiver draft for cash (January 18, 1995). ... Played in Europe during 1994-95 NHL lockout. ... Broke wrist (December 10, 1995); missed two games. ... Jets franchise moved to Phoenix and renamed Coyotes for 1996-97 season; NHL approved move on January 18, 1996. ... Suffered hip pointer (February 1, 1996); missed three games.
STATISTICAL PLATEAUS: Three-goal games: 1995-96 (1).

		REGULAR SEASON								PLAYOFFS				
Season Team	League	Gms.	G	A	Pts.	PIM	+/-	PP	SH	Gms.	G	A	Pts.	PIM
88-89— Dynamo Moscow.......	USSR	1	0	0	0	2	...	...	...	—	—	—	—	—
89-90— Dynamo Moscow.......	USSR	17	3	2	5	2	...	...	...	—	—	—	—	—
90-91— Dynamo Moscow.......	USSR	38	12	4	16	12	...	...	...	—	—	—	—	—
91-92— Dynamo Moscow.......	CIS	39	15	12	27	16	...	...	...	—	—	—	—	—
92-93— Dynamo Moscow.......	CIS	5	1	2	3	4	...	...	...	—	—	—	—	—
— St. Louis	NHL	74	4	23	27	20	-1	2	0	3	0	0	0	0
93-94— St. Louis	NHL	73	6	10	16	40	-12	0	0	2	0	0	0	0
94-95— Dynamo Moscow.......	CIS	13	4	6	10	18	...	...	...	—	—	—	—	—
— Winnipeg	NHL	45	8	22	30	10	1	1	0	—	—	—	—	—
95-96— Winnipeg	NHL	73	22	29	51	42	1	8	0	6	0	3	3	0
96-97— Michigan....................	IHL	4	2	2	4	0	...	...	...	—	—	—	—	—
— Phoenix.....................	IHL	4	2	6	8	4	...	...	...	—	—	—	—	—
— Phoenix.....................	NHL	41	3	7	10	28	-5	2	0	1	0	0	0	0
NHL totals (5 years)		306	43	91	134	140	-16	13	0	12	0	3	3	0

KOROLYUK, ALEXANDER RW SHARKS

PERSONAL: Born January 15, 1976, in Moscow, U.S.S.R. ... 5-9/165. ... Shoots left. ... Name pronounced KOHR-uhl-yook.
TRANSACTIONS/CAREER NOTES: Selected by San Jose Sharks in sixth round (sixth Sharks pick, 141st overall) of NHL entry draft (June 29, 1994).

		REGULAR SEASON								PLAYOFFS				
Season Team	League	Gms.	G	A	Pts.	PIM	+/-	PP	SH	Gms.	G	A	Pts.	PIM
93-94— Soviet Wings	CIS	22	4	4	8	20	...	...	...	3	1	0	1	4
94-95— Soviet Wings	CIS	52	16	13	29	62	...	...	...	4	1	2	3	4
95-96— Soviet Wings	CIS	50	30	19	49	77	...	...	...	—	—	—	—	—
96-97— Manitoba....................	IHL	42	20	16	36	71	...	...	...	—	—	—	—	—

KOVALENKO, ANDREI RW OILERS

PERSONAL: Born July 7, 1970, in Gorky, U.S.S.R. ... 5-10/215. ... Shoots left. ... Name pronounced koh-vuh-LEHN-koh.
TRANSACTIONS/CAREER NOTES: Selected by Quebec Nordiques in eighth round (sixth Nordiques pick, 148th overall) of NHL entry draft (June 16, 1990). ... Suffered from tonsillitis (December 22, 1992); missed two games. ... Suffered from the flu (March 15, 1993); missed one

game. ... Suffered concussion (November 4, 1993); missed five games. ... Bruised ribs (January 11, 1994); missed two games. ... Injured shoulder (January 25, 1994); missed 14 games. ... Suffered from tonsillitis (April 3, 1994); missed two games. ... Played in Europe during 1994-95 NHL lockout. ... Pulled groin (March 9, 1995); missed one game. ... Injured neck (April 5, 1995); missed one game. ... Injured thumb (April 20, 1995); missed one game. ... Nordiques franchise moved to Colorado and renamed Avalanche for 1995-96 season (June 21, 1995). ... Traded by Avalanche with G Jocelyn Thibault and LW Martin Rucinsky to Montreal Canadiens for G Patrick Roy and RW Mike Keane (December 6, 1995). ... Broke nose (December 16, 1995); missed five games. ... Strained left rotator cuff (February 15, 1996); missed two games. ... Traded by Canadiens to Edmonton Oilers for C Scott Thornton (September 6, 1996). ... Suffered back spasms (February 17, 1997); missed two games. ... Suffered hip pointer (March 1, 1997); missed five games.
STATISTICAL PLATEAUS: Three-goal games: 1992-93 (1).
MISCELLANEOUS: Member of gold-medal-winning Unified Olympic team (1992). ... Scored on a penalty shot (vs. Kirk McLean, December 4, 1993).

Season Team	League	REGULAR SEASON								PLAYOFFS				
		Gms.	G	A	Pts.	PIM	+/-	PP	SH	Gms.	G	A	Pts.	PIM
88-89— CSKA Moscow..........	USSR	10	1	0	1	0	...	...	...	—	—	—	—	—
89-90— CSKA Moscow..........	USSR	48	8	5	13	18	...	...	...	—	—	—	—	—
90-91— CSKA Moscow..........	USSR	45	13	8	21	26	...	...	...	—	—	—	—	—
91-92— CSKA Moscow..........	CIS	44	19	13	32	32	...	...	...	—	—	—	—	—
— Unif. Olympic team	Int'l	8	1	1	2	2	...	...	...	—	—	—	—	—
92-93— CSKA Moscow..........	CIS	3	3	1	4	4	...	...	...	—	—	—	—	—
— Quebec..................	NHL	81	27	41	68	57	13	8	1	4	1	0	1	2
93-94— Quebec..................	NHL	58	16	17	33	46	-5	5	0	—	—	—	—	—
94-95— Lada Togliatti	CIS	11	9	2	11	14	...	...	...	—	—	—	—	—
— Quebec..................	NHL	45	14	10	24	31	-4	1	0	6	0	1	1	2
95-96— Colorado	NHL	26	11	11	22	16	11	3	0	—	—	—	—	—
— Montreal	NHL	51	17	17	34	33	9	3	0	6	0	0	0	6
96-97— Edmonton	NHL	74	32	27	59	81	-5	14	0	12	4	3	7	6
NHL totals (5 years)		**335**	**117**	**123**	**240**	**264**	**19**	**34**	**1**	**28**	**5**	**4**	**9**	**16**

KOVALEV, ALEXEI   RW   RANGERS

PERSONAL: Born February 24, 1973, in Moscow, U.S.S.R. ... 6-2/210. ... Shoots left. ... Name pronounced KOH-vuh-lahf.
TRANSACTIONS/CAREER NOTES: Selected by New York Rangers in first round (first Rangers pick, 15th overall) of NHL entry draft (June 22, 1991). ... Suffered back spasms (January 16, 1993); missed one game. ... Suspended one game by NHL (November 10, 1993). ... Suspended five games by NHL for tripping (November 30, 1993). ... Suspended two games by NHL (February 12, 1994). ... Played in Europe during 1994-95 NHL lockout. ... Suffered from the flu (December 2, 1995); missed one game. ... Tore knee ligament (January 8, 1997); missed remainder of season.
STATISTICAL PLATEAUS: Three-goal games: 1992-93 (1), 1996-97 (1). Total: 2.
MISCELLANEOUS: Member of Stanley Cup championship team (1994). ... Member of gold-medal-winning Unified Olympic team (1992). ... Failed to score on a penalty shot (vs. Jon Casey, October 5, 1993).

Season Team	League	REGULAR SEASON								PLAYOFFS				
		Gms.	G	A	Pts.	PIM	+/-	PP	SH	Gms.	G	A	Pts.	PIM
89-90— Dynamo Moscow.......	USSR	1	0	0	0	0	...	...	...	—	—	—	—	—
90-91— Dynamo Moscow.......	USSR	18	1	2	3	4	...	...	...	—	—	—	—	—
91-92— Dynamo Moscow.......	CIS	33	16	9	25	20	...	...	...	—	—	—	—	—
— Unif. Olympic team	Int'l	8	1	2	3	14	...	...	...	—	—	—	—	—
92-93— New York Rangers	NHL	65	20	18	38	79	-10	3	0	—	—	—	—	—
— Binghamton	AHL	13	13	11	24	35	...	...	...	9	3	5	8	14
93-94— New York Rangers	NHL	76	23	33	56	154	18	7	0	23	9	12	21	18
94-95— Lada Togliatti	CIS	12	8	8	16	49	...	...	...	—	—	—	—	—
— New York Rangers	NHL	48	13	15	28	30	-6	1	1	10	4	7	11	10
95-96— New York Rangers	NHL	81	24	34	58	98	5	8	1	11	3	4	7	14
96-97— New York Rangers	NHL	45	13	22	35	42	11	1	0	—	—	—	—	—
NHL totals (5 years)		**315**	**93**	**122**	**215**	**403**	**18**	**20**	**2**	**44**	**16**	**23**	**39**	**42**

KOZLOV, SLAVA   LW   RED WINGS

PERSONAL: Born May 3, 1972, in Voskresensk, U.S.S.R. ... 5-10/185. ... Shoots left. ... Name pronounced VYACH-ih-slav KAHS-lahf.
TRANSACTIONS/CAREER NOTES: Selected by Detroit Red Wings in third round (second Red Wings pick, 45th overall) of NHL entry draft (June 16, 1990). ... Played in Europe during 1994-95 NHL lockout. ... Bruised left foot (April 16, 1995); missed one game.
HONORS: Named Soviet League Rookie of the Year (1989-90).
STATISTICAL PLATEAUS: Three-goal games: 1993-94 (1). ... Four-goal games: 1995-96 (1). ... Total hat tricks: 2.
MISCELLANEOUS: Member of Stanley Cup championship team (1997).

Season Team	League	REGULAR SEASON								PLAYOFFS				
		Gms.	G	A	Pts.	PIM	+/-	PP	SH	Gms.	G	A	Pts.	PIM
89-90— Khimik	USSR	45	14	12	26	38	...	...	...	—	—	—	—	—
90-91— Khimik	USSR	45	11	13	24	46	...	...	...	—	—	—	—	—
91-92— CSKA Moscow..........	CIS	11	6	5	11	12	...	...	...	—	—	—	—	—
— Detroit......................	NHL	7	0	2	2	2	-2	0	0	—	—	—	—	—
92-93— Detroit......................	NHL	17	4	1	5	14	-1	0	0	4	0	2	2	2
— Adirondack.................	AHL	45	23	36	59	54	...	...	...	4	1	1	2	4
93-94— Detroit......................	NHL	77	34	39	73	50	27	8	2	7	2	5	7	12
— Adirondack.................	AHL	3	0	1	1	15	...	...	...	—	—	—	—	—
94-95— CSKA Moscow..........	CIS	10	3	4	7	14	...	...	...	—	—	—	—	—
— Detroit......................	NHL	46	13	20	33	45	12	5	0	18	9	7	16	10
95-96— Detroit......................	NHL	82	36	37	73	70	33	9	0	19	5	7	12	10
96-97— Detroit......................	NHL	75	23	22	45	46	21	3	0	20	8	5	13	14
NHL totals (6 years)		**304**	**110**	**121**	**231**	**227**	**90**	**25**	**2**	**68**	**24**	**26**	**50**	**48**

KOZLOV, VIKTOR   LW   SHARKS

PERSONAL: Born February 14, 1975, in Togliatti, U.S.S.R. ... 6-4/225. ... Shoots right. ... Name pronounced KAHZ-lahv.
TRANSACTIONS/CAREER NOTES: Selected by San Jose Sharks in first round (first Sharks pick, sixth overall) of NHL entry draft (June 26, 1993). ... Suffered displaced ankle fracture (November 27, 1994); missed 13 games. ... Played in Europe during 1994-95 NHL lockout. ... Bruised ankle (March 26, 1997); missed four games.

Season Team	League	REGULAR SEASON								PLAYOFFS				
		Gms.	G	A	Pts.	PIM	+/-	PP	SH	Gms.	G	A	Pts.	PIM
90-91— Lada Togliatti	USSR Div. II	2	2	0	2	0	...	...	...	—	—	—	—	—
91-92— Lada Togliatti	CIS	3	0	0	0	0	...	...	...	—	—	—	—	—
92-93— Dynamo Moscow	CIS	30	6	5	11	4	...	...	...	10	3	0	3	0
93-94— Dynamo Moscow	CIS	42	16	9	25	14	...	...	...	7	3	2	5	0
94-95— Dynamo Moscow	CIS	3	1	1	2	2	...	...	...	—	—	—	—	—
— San Jose	NHL	16	2	0	2	2	-5	0	0	—	—	—	—	—
— Kansas City	IHL	—	—	—	—	—				13	4	5	9	12
95-96— Kansas City	IHL	15	4	7	11	12	...	...	...	—	—	—	—	—
— San Jose	NHL	62	6	13	19	6	-15	1	0	—	—	—	—	—
96-97— San Jose	NHL	78	16	25	41	40	-16	4	0	—	—	—	—	—
NHL totals (3 years)		156	24	38	62	48	-36	5	0					

KRAVCHUK, IGOR   D   BLUES

PERSONAL: Born September 13, 1966, in Ufa, U.S.S.R. ... 6-1/205. ... Shoots left. ... Name pronounced EE-gohr KRAV-chuhk.
TRANSACTIONS/CAREER NOTES: Selected by Chicago Blackhawks in fourth round (fifth Blackhawks pick, 71st overall) of NHL entry draft (June 22, 1991). ... Sprained knee (October 25, 1992); missed four games. ... Sprained left ankle (December 29, 1992); missed 18 games. ... Traded by Blackhawks with C Dean McAmmond to Edmonton Oilers for RW Joe Murphy (February 25, 1993). ... Sprained left knee (April 6, 1993); missed remainder of season. ... Strained groin (November 15, 1993); missed three games. ... Injured left knee (January 30, 1995) and underwent surgery (February 6, 1995); missed 12 games. ... Suffered deep bone bruise to left leg (October 21, 1995); missed six games. ... Injured knee (November 20, 1995); missed four games. ... Traded by Oilers with D Ken Sutton to St. Louis Blues for D Donald Dufresne and D Jeff Norton (January 4, 1996).
MISCELLANEOUS: Member of gold-medal-winning U.S.S.R. Olympic team (1988) and gold-medal-winning Unified Olympic team (1992).

Season Team	League	REGULAR SEASON								PLAYOFFS				
		Gms.	G	A	Pts.	PIM	+/-	PP	SH	Gms.	G	A	Pts.	PIM
87-88— CSKA Moscow	USSR	47	1	8	9	12	...	...	...	—	—	—	—	—
88-89— CSKA Moscow	USSR	27	3	4	7	2	...	...	...	—	—	—	—	—
89-90— CSKA Moscow	USSR	48	1	3	4	16	...	...	...	—	—	—	—	—
90-91— CSKA Moscow	USSR	41	6	5	11	16	...	...	...	—	—	—	—	—
91-92— CSKA Moscow	CIS	30	3	7	10	2	...	...	...	—	—	—	—	—
— Unif. Olympic team	Int'l	8	3	2	5	...				—	—	—	—	—
— Chicago	NHL	18	1	8	9	4	-3	0	0	18	2	6	8	8
92-93— Chicago	NHL	38	6	9	15	30	11	3	0	—	—	—	—	—
— Edmonton	NHL	17	4	8	12	2	-8	1	0	—	—	—	—	—
93-94— Edmonton	NHL	81	12	38	50	16	-12	5	0	—	—	—	—	—
94-95— Edmonton	NHL	36	7	11	18	29	-15	3	1	—	—	—	—	—
95-96— Edmonton	NHL	26	4	4	8	10	-13	3	0	—	—	—	—	—
— St. Louis	NHL	40	3	12	15	24	-6	0	0	10	1	5	6	4
96-97— St. Louis	NHL	82	4	24	28	35	7	1	0	2	0	0	0	2
NHL totals (6 years)		338	41	114	155	150	-39	16	1	30	3	11	14	14

KRIVOKRASOV, SERGEI   RW   BLACKHAWKS

PERSONAL: Born April 15, 1974, in Angarsk, U.S.S.R. ... 5-11/185. ... Shoots left. ... Name pronounced SAIR-gay kree-voh-KRAS-ahv.
TRANSACTIONS/CAREER NOTES: Selected by Chicago Blackhawks in first round (first Blackhawks pick, 12th overall) of NHL entry draft (June 20, 1992). ... Sprained knee (January 31, 1996); missed 14 games. ... Sprained knee (March 14, 1996); missed 13 games.

Season Team	League	REGULAR SEASON								PLAYOFFS				
		Gms.	G	A	Pts.	PIM	+/-	PP	SH	Gms.	G	A	Pts.	PIM
90-91— CSKA Moscow	USSR	41	4	0	4	8	...	...	...	—	—	—	—	—
91-92— CSKA Moscow	CIS	42	10	8	18	35	...	...	...	—	—	—	—	—
92-93— Chicago	NHL	4	0	0	0	2	-2	0	0	—	—	—	—	—
— Indianapolis	IHL	78	36	33	69	157	...	...	...	5	3	1	4	2
93-94— Indianapolis	IHL	53	19	26	45	145	...	...	...	—	—	—	—	—
— Chicago	NHL	9	1	0	1	4	-2	0	0	—	—	—	—	—
94-95— Indianapolis	IHL	29	12	15	27	41	...	...	...	—	—	—	—	—
— Chicago	NHL	41	12	7	19	33	9	6	0	10	0	0	0	8
95-96— Indianapolis	IHL	9	4	5	9	28	...	...	...	—	—	—	—	—
— Chicago	NHL	46	6	10	16	32	10	0	0	5	1	0	1	2
96-97— Chicago	NHL	67	13	11	24	42	-1	2	0	6	1	0	1	4
NHL totals (5 years)		167	32	28	60	113	14	8	0	21	2	0	2	14

KRIZ, PAVEL   D   BLACKHAWKS

PERSONAL: Born January 2, 1977, in Kladno, Czechoslovakia. ... 6-2/205. ... Shoots right.
TRANSACTIONS/CAREER NOTES: Selected by Chicago Blackhawks in fourth round (fifth Blackhawks pick, 97th overall) of NHL entry draft (July 8, 1995).

Season Team	League	Gms.	G	A	Pts.	PIM	+/-	PP	SH	Gms.	G	A	Pts.	PIM
92-93— Kladno	Czech. Jrs.	30	10	14	24	50	...	...	...	—	—	—	—	—
93-94— Kladno	Czech. Jrs.	45	20	25	45	52	...	...	...	—	—	—	—	—
94-95— Tri-City	WHL	68	6	34	40	47	...	...	...	17	5	12	17	6
95-96— Saskatoon	WHL	71	11	52	63	96	...	...	...	4	0	2	2	0
96-97— Pardubice	Czech.	37	0	7	7	63	...	...	...	8	0	1	1	8

KRON, ROBERT   RW   HURRICANES

PERSONAL: Born February 27, 1967, in Brno, Czechoslovakia. ... 5-11/182. ... Shoots right. ... Name pronounced KRAHN.

TRANSACTIONS/CAREER NOTES: Selected by Vancouver Canucks in fourth round (fifth Canucks pick, 88th overall) of NHL entry draft (June 15, 1985). ... Played entire season with a broken bone in left wrist (1990-91). ... Underwent surgery to repair torn knee ligaments and wrist fracture (March 22, 1991). ... Fractured ankle (January 28, 1992); missed 22 games. ... Traded by Canucks with third-round pick (D Marek Malik) in 1993 draft and future considerations to Hartford Whalers for C/LW Murray Craven and fifth-round pick (D Scott Walker) in 1993 draft (March 22, 1993); Canucks sent RW Jim Sandlak to Whalers to complete deal (May 17, 1993). ... Sprained shoulder (February 26, 1994); missed seven games. ... Broke thumb (March 29, 1995); missed 11 games. ... Injured groin (March 27, 1996); missed one game. ... Strained abdominal muscle (April 8, 1996); missed three games. ... Sprained knee (January 25, 1997); missed 12 games. ... Whalers franchise moved to North Carolina and renamed Carolina Hurricanes for 1997-98 season; NHL approved move on June 25, 1997.

Season Team	League	Gms.	G	A	Pts.	PIM	+/-	PP	SH	Gms.	G	A	Pts.	PIM
86-87— Zetor Brno	Czech.	28	14	11	25	...	...	...	...	—	—	—	—	—
87-88— Zetor Brno	Czech.	32	12	6	18	...	...	...	...	—	—	—	—	—
88-89— Zetor Brno	Czech.	43	28	19	47	...	...	...	...	—	—	—	—	—
89-90— Dukla Trencin ...	Czech.	39	22	22	44	...	...	...	...	—	—	—	—	—
90-91— Vancouver	NHL	76	12	20	32	21	-11	2	3	—	—	—	—	—
91-92— Vancouver	NHL	36	2	2	4	2	-9	0	0	11	1	2	3	2
92-93— Vancouver	NHL	32	10	11	21	14	10	2	2	—	—	—	—	—
—Hartford	NHL	13	4	2	6	4	-5	2	0	—	—	—	—	—
93-94— Hartford	NHL	77	24	26	50	8	0	2	1	—	—	—	—	—
94-95— Hartford	NHL	37	10	8	18	10	-3	3	1	—	—	—	—	—
95-96— Hartford	NHL	77	22	28	50	6	-1	8	1	—	—	—	—	—
96-97— Hartford	NHL	68	10	12	22	10	-18	2	0	—	—	—	—	—
NHL totals (7 years)		416	94	109	203	75	-37	21	8	11	1	2	3	2

KROUPA, VLASTIMIL   D   SHARKS

PERSONAL: Born April 27, 1975, in Most, Czechoslovakia. ... 6-3/210. ... Shoots left. ... Name pronounced VLAS-tih-mihl KROO-puh.

TRANSACTIONS/CAREER NOTES: Selected by San Jose Sharks in second round (third Sharks pick, 45th overall) of NHL entry draft (June 26, 1993). ... Injured back (November 17, 1995); missed two games.

Season Team	League	Gms.	G	A	Pts.	PIM	+/-	PP	SH	Gms.	G	A	Pts.	PIM
91-92— Litvinov	Czech. Jrs.	37	9	16	25	...	...	...	...	—	—	—	—	—
92-93— Chemopetrol Litvin. ...	Czech.	9	0	1	1	...	...	...	...	—	—	—	—	—
93-94— San Jose	NHL	27	1	3	4	20	-6	0	0	14	1	2	3	21
—Kansas City	IHL	39	3	12	15	12	...	...	...	—	—	—	—	—
94-95— Kansas City	IHL	51	4	8	12	49	...	...	...	12	2	4	6	22
—San Jose	NHL	14	0	2	2	16	-7	0	0	6	0	0	0	4
95-96— Kansas City	IHL	39	5	22	27	44	...	...	...	5	0	1	1	6
—San Jose	NHL	27	1	7	8	18	-17	0	0	—	—	—	—	—
96-97— Kentucky	AHL	5	0	3	3	0	...	...	...	—	—	—	—	—
—San Jose	NHL	35	2	6	8	12	-17	2	0	—	—	—	—	—
NHL totals (4 years)		103	4	18	22	66	-47	2	0	20	1	2	3	25

KRUPP, UWE   D   AVALANCHE

PERSONAL: Born June 24, 1965, in Cologne, West Germany. ... 6-6/235. ... Shoots right. ... Name pronounced YOO-ee KROOP.

TRANSACTIONS/CAREER NOTES: Selected by Buffalo Sabres in 11th round (13th Sabres pick, 214th overall) of NHL entry draft (June 8, 1983). ... Bruised hip (November 1987). ... Injured head (April 1988). ... Broke rib (January 6, 1989). ... Banned from international competition for 18 months by IIHF after failing random substance test (April 20, 1990). ... Suffered from cyst on foot (January 2, 1991). ... Traded by Sabres with C Pierre Turgeon, RW Benoit Hogue and C Dave McLlwain to New York Islanders for C Pat LaFontaine, LW Randy Wood, D Randy Hillier and future considerations; Sabres received fourth-round pick (D Dean Melanson) in 1992 draft to complete deal (October 25, 1991). ... Sprained left knee (December 28, 1991); missed five games. ... Bruised thigh (February 7, 1992). ... Suffered from the flu (March 2, 1993); missed one game. ... Suffered sore shoulder (April 10, 1993); missed three games. ... Broke toe (October 10, 1993); missed three games. ... Fractured sinus bone (October 26, 1993); missed 17 games. ... Suffered severely sprained hamstring (December 19, 1993); missed nine games. ... Suffered from the flu, bruised jaw and sprained wrist (February 27, 1994); missed four games. ... Sprained wrist (March 5, 1994); missed nine games. ... Traded by Islanders with first-round pick (D Wade Belak) in 1994 draft to Quebec Nordiques for C Ron Sutter and first-round pick (RW Brett Lindros) in 1994 draft (June 28, 1994). ... Played in Europe during 1994-95 NHL lockout. ... Injured hip (February 23, 1995); missed two games. ... Injured hip flexor (April 18, 1995); missed two games. ... Nordiques franchise moved to Colorado and renamed Avalanche for 1995-96 season (June 21, 1995). ... Tore knee ligaments (October 6, 1995); missed first 76 games of season. ... Separated shoulder (November 8, 1996); missed five games. ... Suffered tendinitis in elbow (February 18, 1997); missed eight games. ... Suffered sore back (March 26, 1997); missed remainder of season.

HONORS: Played in NHL All-Star Game (1991).

STATISTICAL PLATEAUS: Three-goal games: 1994-95 (1).

MISCELLANEOUS: Member of Stanley Cup championship team (1996).

Season Team	League	REGULAR SEASON								PLAYOFFS				
		Gms.	G	A	Pts.	PIM	+/-	PP	SH	Gms.	G	A	Pts.	PIM
83-84—KEC	Germany	40	0	4	4	22	...	...	...	—	—	—	—	—
84-85—KEC	Germany	39	11	8	19	36	...	...	...	—	—	—	—	—
85-86—KEC	Germany	45	10	21	31	83	...	...	...	—	—	—	—	—
86-87—Rochester	AHL	42	3	19	22	50	...	...	...	17	1	11	12	16
—Buffalo	NHL	26	1	4	5	23	-9	0	0	—	—	—	—	—
87-88—Buffalo	NHL	75	2	9	11	151	-1	0	0	6	0	0	0	15
88-89—Buffalo	NHL	70	5	13	18	55	0	0	1	5	0	1	1	4
89-90—Buffalo	NHL	74	3	20	23	85	15	0	1	6	0	0	0	4
90-91—Buffalo	NHL	74	12	32	44	66	14	6	0	6	1	1	2	6
91-92—Buffalo	NHL	8	2	0	2	6	0	0	0	—	—	—	—	—
—New York Islanders	NHL	59	6	29	35	43	13	2	0	—	—	—	—	—
92-93—New York Islanders	NHL	80	9	29	38	67	6	2	0	18	1	5	6	12
93-94—New York Islanders	NHL	41	7	14	21	30	11	3	0	4	0	1	1	4
94-95—Landshut	Germany	5	1	2	3	6	...	...	...	—	—	—	—	—
—Quebec	NHL	44	6	17	23	20	14	3	0	5	0	2	2	2
95-96—Colorado	NHL	6	0	3	3	4	4	0	0	22	4	12	16	33
96-97—Colorado	NHL	60	4	17	21	48	12	2	0	—	—	—	—	—
NHL totals (11 years)		617	57	187	244	598	79	18	2	72	6	22	28	80

KRUSE, PAUL — LW — ISLANDERS

PERSONAL: Born March 15, 1970, in Merritt, B.C. ... 6-0/202. ... Shoots left. ... Name pronounced KROOS.

TRANSACTIONS/CAREER NOTES: Selected by Calgary Flames in fourth round (sixth Flames pick, 83rd overall) of NHL entry draft (June 16, 1990). ... Injured eye (March 8, 1992); missed four games. ... Suffered hip pointer (March 21, 1993); missed one game. ... Broke toe on right foot (September 27, 1993); missed 12 games. ... Bruised left foot (March 2, 1995); missed one game. ... Bruised left knee (April 29, 1995); missed one game. ... Bruised ribs (February 13, 1996); missed three games. ... Cut wrist (April 9, 1996); missed two games. ... Traded by Flames to New York Islanders for third-round pick (traded to Hartford) in 1997 draft (November 27, 1996). ... Strained abdominal muscle (March 16, 1997); missed 12 games.

Season Team	League	REGULAR SEASON								PLAYOFFS				
		Gms.	G	A	Pts.	PIM	+/-	PP	SH	Gms.	G	A	Pts.	PIM
86-87—Merritt	BCJHL	35	8	15	23	120	...	...	...	—	—	—	—	—
87-88—Merritt	BCJHL	44	12	32	44	227	...	...	...	4	1	4	5	18
—Moose Jaw	WHL	1	0	0	0	0	...	...	...	—	—	—	—	—
88-89—Kamloops	WHL	68	8	15	23	209	...	...	...	—	—	—	—	—
89-90—Kamloops	WHL	67	22	23	45	291	...	...	...	17	3	5	8	†79
90-91—Salt Lake City	IHL	83	24	20	44	313	...	...	...	4	1	1	2	4
—Calgary	NHL	1	0	0	0	7	-1	0	0	—	—	—	—	—
91-92—Salt Lake City	IHL	57	14	15	29	267	...	...	...	5	1	2	3	19
—Calgary	NHL	16	3	1	4	65	1	0	0	—	—	—	—	—
92-93—Salt Lake City	IHL	35	1	4	5	206	...	...	...	—	—	—	—	—
—Calgary	NHL	27	2	3	5	41	2	0	0	—	—	—	—	—
93-94—Calgary	NHL	68	3	8	11	185	-6	0	0	7	0	0	0	14
94-95—Calgary	NHL	45	11	5	16	141	13	0	0	7	4	2	6	10
95-96—Calgary	NHL	75	3	12	15	145	-5	0	0	3	0	0	0	4
96-97—Calgary	NHL	14	2	0	2	30	-4	0	0	—	—	—	—	—
—New York Islanders	NHL	48	4	2	6	111	-5	0	0	—	—	—	—	—
NHL totals (7 years)		294	28	31	59	725	-5	0	0	17	4	2	6	28

KRYGIER, TODD — LW — CAPITALS

PERSONAL: Born October 12, 1965, in Northville, Mich. ... 6-0/193. ... Shoots left. ... Full name: Todd Andrew Krygier. ... Name pronounced KREE-guhr.

COLLEGE: Connecticut.

TRANSACTIONS/CAREER NOTES: Selected by Hartford Whalers in NHL supplemental draft (June 10, 1988). ... Bruised heel (March 13, 1990). ... Traded by Whalers to Washington Capitals for fourth-round pick (traded to Calgary) in 1993 draft (October 3, 1991). ... Separated right shoulder (December 28, 1993); missed seven games. ... Traded by Capitals to Mighty Ducks of Anaheim for fourth-round pick (traded to Dallas) in 1996 draft (February 2, 1995). ... Slightly strained groin (March 11, 1995); missed three games. ... Strained groin (March 30, 1995); missed three games. ... Traded by Mighty Ducks to Washington Capitals for G Mike Torchia (March 8, 1996). ... Suffered from the flu (April 11, 1996); missed one game. ... Injured wrist (November 6, 1996); missed one game. ... Sprained left wrist (December 20, 1996); missed 17 games. ... Reinjured left wrist (March 10, 1997); missed six games.

STATISTICAL PLATEAUS: Three-goal games: 1993-94 (1).

Season Team	League	REGULAR SEASON								PLAYOFFS				
		Gms.	G	A	Pts.	PIM	+/-	PP	SH	Gms.	G	A	Pts.	PIM
84-85—Univ. of Connecticut	ECAC-II	14	14	11	25	12	...	...	...	—	—	—	—	—
85-86—Univ. of Connecticut	ECAC-II	32	29	27	56	46	...	...	...	—	—	—	—	—
86-87—Univ. of Connecticut	ECAC-II	28	24	24	48	44	...	...	...	—	—	—	—	—
87-88—Univ. of Connecticut	ECAC-II	27	32	39	71	38	...	...	...	—	—	—	—	—
—New Haven	AHL	13	1	5	6	34	...	...	...	—	—	—	—	—
88-89—Binghamton	AHL	76	26	42	68	77	...	...	...	—	—	—	—	—
89-90—Binghamton	AHL	12	1	9	10	16	...	...	...	—	—	—	—	—
—Hartford	NHL	58	18	12	30	52	4	5	1	7	2	1	3	4
90-91—Hartford	NHL	72	13	17	30	95	1	3	0	6	0	2	2	0
91-92—Washington	NHL	67	13	17	30	107	-1	1	0	5	2	1	3	4
92-93—Washington	NHL	77	11	12	23	60	-13	0	2	6	1	1	2	4
93-94—Washington	NHL	66	12	18	30	60	-4	0	1	5	2	0	2	10
94-95—Anaheim	NHL	35	11	11	22	10	1	1	0	—	—	—	—	—
95-96—Anaheim	NHL	60	9	28	37	70	-9	2	1	—	—	—	—	—
—Washington	NHL	16	6	5	11	12	8	1	0	6	2	0	2	12
96-97—Washington	NHL	47	5	11	16	37	-10	1	0	—	—	—	—	—
NHL totals (8 years)		498	98	131	229	503	-23	14	5	35	9	5	14	34

K

KUCERA, FRANTISEK   D   FLYERS

PERSONAL: Born February 3, 1968, in Prague, Czechoslovakia. ... 6-2/205. ... Shoots right. ... Name pronounced koo-CHAIR-uh.

TRANSACTIONS/CAREER NOTES: Selected by Chicago Blackhawks in fourth round (third Blackhawks pick, 77th overall) of NHL entry draft (June 21, 1986). ... Pulled groin (March 20, 1993); missed 11 games. ... Pulled groin (1993-94 season); missed five games. ... Traded by Blackhawks with LW Jocelyn Lemieux to Hartford Whalers for LW Randy Cunneyworth and D Gary Suter (March 11, 1994). ... Played in Europe during 1994-95 NHL lockout. ... Injured hip flexor (November 5, 1995); missed one game. ... Traded by Whalers with C Jim Dowd and second-round pick (D Ryan Bonni) in 1997 draft to Vancouver Canucks for D Jeff Brown and third-round pick in 1998 draft (December 19, 1995). ... Separated shoulder (January 8, 1996); missed 19 games. ... Traded by Canucks to Philadelphia Flyers for future considerations (March 18, 1997).

		REGULAR SEASON								PLAYOFFS				
Season Team	League	Gms.	G	A	Pts.	PIM	+/-	PP	SH	Gms.	G	A	Pts.	PIM
85-86 — Sparta Prague	Czech.	15	0	0	0	...	...	...	...	—	—	—	—	—
86-87 — Sparta Prague	Czech.	33	7	2	9	14	...	...	...	—	—	—	—	—
87-88 — Sparta Prague	Czech.	34	4	2	6	30	...	...	...	—	—	—	—	—
88-89 — Dukla Jihlava	Czech.	45	10	9	19	28	...	...	...	—	—	—	—	—
89-90 — Dukla Jihlava	Czech.	43	9	10	19	...	...	...	...	—	—	—	—	—
90-91 — Chicago	NHL	40	2	12	14	32	3	1	0	—	—	—	—	—
— Indianapolis	IHL	35	8	19	27	23	...	...	...	7	0	1	1	15
91-92 — Chicago	NHL	61	3	10	13	36	3	1	0	6	0	0	0	0
— Indianapolis	IHL	7	1	2	3	4	...	...	...	—	—	—	—	—
92-93 — Chicago	NHL	71	5	14	19	59	7	1	0	—	—	—	—	—
93-94 — Chicago	NHL	60	4	13	17	34	9	2	0	—	—	—	—	—
— Hartford	NHL	16	1	3	4	14	-12	1	0	—	—	—	—	—
94-95 — Sparta Prague	Czech Rep.	16	1	2	3	14	...	...	...	—	—	—	—	—
— Hartford	NHL	48	3	17	20	30	3	0	0	—	—	—	—	—
95-96 — Hartford	NHL	30	2	6	8	10	-3	0	0	—	—	—	—	—
— Vancouver	NHL	24	1	0	1	10	5	0	0	6	0	1	1	0
96-97 — Vancouver	NHL	2	0	0	0	0	0	0	0	—	—	—	—	—
— Houston	IHL	12	0	3	3	20	...	...	...	—	—	—	—	—
— Syracuse	AHL	42	6	29	35	36	...	...	...	—	—	—	—	—
— Philadelphia	AHL	9	1	5	6	2	...	...	...	10	1	6	7	20
— Philadelphia	NHL	2	0	0	0	2	-2	0	0	—	—	—	—	—
NHL totals (8 years)		354	21	75	96	227	13	6	0	12	0	1	1	0

KURRI, JARI   RW   AVALANCHE

PERSONAL: Born May 18, 1960, in Helsinki, Finland. ... 6-1/195. ... Shoots right. ... Name pronounced YAH-ree KUHR-ee.
TRANSACTIONS/CAREER NOTES: Selected by Edmonton Oilers in fourth round (third Oilers pick, 69th overall) of NHL entry draft (June 11, 1980). ... Pulled groin (November 24, 1981). ... Pulled groin (January 1984); missed 16 games. ... Sprained left knee ligament (February 12, 1989). ... Signed two-year contract with Milan Devils of Italian Hockey League (July 30, 1990). ... Injured knee (January 1991). ... Rights traded by Oilers with RW Dave Brown and D Corey Foster to Philadelphia Flyers for RW Scott Mellanby, LW Craig Berube and C Craig Fisher (May 30, 1991). ... Rights traded by Flyers to Los Angeles Kings for D Steve Duchesne, C Steve Kasper and fourth-round pick (D Aris Brimanis) in 1991 draft (May 30, 1991). ... Sprained shoulder (November 12, 1991); missed three games. ... Suffered from the flu (January 1992); missed two games. ... Bruised knee (November 6, 1993); missed two games. ... Strained hip flexor (March 11, 1995); missed two games. ... Strained groin (March 20, 1995); missed two games. ... Strained groin (March 26, 1995); missed five games. ... Strained groin (April 7, 1995); missed one game. ... Broke right thumb (December 21, 1995); missed 11 games. ... Traded by Kings with RW Shane Churla and D Marty McSorley to New York Rangers for C Ray Ferraro, C Ian Laperriere, C Nathan Lafayette, D Mattias Norstrom and fourth-round pick (D Sean Blanchard) in 1997 draft (March 14, 1996). ... Signed as free agent by Mighty Ducks of Anaheim (August 14, 1996). ... Signed as free agent by Colorado Avalanche (July 11, 1997).
HONORS: Named to NHL All-Star second team (1983-84, 1985-86 and 1988-89). ... Played in NHL All-Star Game (1983, 1985, 1986, 1988-1990 and 1993). ... Won Lady Byng Memorial Trophy (1984-85). ... Named to THE SPORTING NEWS All-Star first team (1984-85). ... Named to NHL All-Star first team (1984-85 and 1986-87). ... Named to THE SPORTING NEWS All-Star second team (1985-86 and 1988-89).
RECORDS: Holds NHL single-season playoff record for most three-or-more-goal games—4 (1985). ... Shares NHL single-season playoff records for most goals—19 (1985); and most game-winning goals—5 (1987). ... Holds NHL single-series playoff records for most goals—12 (1985); and most three-or-more-goal games—3 (1985). ... Shares NHL single-game playoff records for most shorthanded goals—2 (April 24, 1983); most shorthanded goals in one period—2 (April 24, 1983); and most power-play goals—3 (April 9, 1987).
STATISTICAL PLATEAUS: Three-goal games: 1980-81 (3), 1982-83 (2), 1983-84 (3), 1984-85 (5), 1985-86 (2), 1986-87 (1), 1988-89 (2), 1991-92 (1), 1992-93 (1), 1995-96 (1). Total: 21. ... Four-goal games: 1985-86 (1). ... Five-goal games: 1983-84 (1). ... Total hat tricks: 23.
MISCELLANEOUS: Member of Stanley Cup championship team (1984, 1985, 1987, 1988 and 1990).
STATISTICAL NOTES: Tied for NHL lead with nine game-winning goals (1985-86).

		REGULAR SEASON								PLAYOFFS				
Season Team	League	Gms.	G	A	Pts.	PIM	+/-	PP	SH	Gms.	G	A	Pts.	PIM
77-78 — Jokerit	Finland	29	2	9	11	12	...	...	...	—	—	—	—	—
78-79 — Jokerit	Finland	33	16	14	30	12	...	...	...	—	—	—	—	—
79-80 — Jokerit	Finland	33	23	16	39	22	...	...	...	6	7	2	9	13
— Fin. Olympic team	Int'l	7	2	1	3	6	...	...	...	—	—	—	—	—
80-81 — Edmonton	NHL	75	32	43	75	40	26	9	0	9	5	7	12	4
81-82 — Edmonton	NHL	71	32	54	86	32	38	6	1	5	2	5	7	10
82-83 — Edmonton	NHL	80	45	59	104	22	47	10	1	16	8	15	23	8
83-84 — Edmonton	NHL	64	52	61	113	14	38	10	5	19	*14	14	28	13
84-85 — Edmonton	NHL	73	71	64	135	30	76	14	3	18	*19	12	31	6
85-86 — Edmonton	NHL	78	*68	63	131	22	45	16	6	10	2	10	12	4
86-87 — Edmonton	NHL	79	54	54	108	41	-9	0	0	21	*15	10	25	20
87-88 — Edmonton	NHL	80	43	53	96	30	25	10	3	19	*14	17	31	12
88-89 — Edmonton	NHL	76	44	58	102	69	19	10	5	7	3	5	8	6
89-90 — Edmonton	NHL	78	33	60	93	48	18	10	2	22	10	15	25	18
90-91 — Milan	Italy	40	37	60	97	8	...	...	...	10	10	12	22	2
91-92 — Los Angeles	NHL	73	23	37	60	24	-24	10	1	4	1	2	3	4
92-93 — Los Angeles	NHL	82	27	60	87	38	19	12	2	24	9	8	17	12

Season Team	League	REGULAR SEASON								PLAYOFFS				
		Gms.	G	A	Pts.	PIM	+/-	PP	SH	Gms.	G	A	Pts.	PIM
93-94— Los Angeles	NHL	81	31	46	77	48	-24	14	4	—	—	—	—	—
94-95— Jokerit Helsinki	Finland	20	10	9	19	10	...	...	...	—	—	—	—	—
— Los Angeles	NHL	38	10	19	29	24	-17	2	0	—	—	—	—	—
95-96— Los Angeles	NHL	57	17	23	40	37	-12	5	1	—	—	—	—	—
— New York Rangers	NHL	14	1	4	5	2	-4	0	0	11	3	5	8	2
96-97— Anaheim	NHL	82	13	22	35	12	-13	3	0	11	1	2	3	4
NHL totals (16 years)		1181	596	780	1376	533	248	141	34	196	106	127	233	123

KUSTER, HENRY   RW   BRUINS

PERSONAL: Born November 11, 1977, in Edmonton. ... 6-2/195. ... Shoots right. ... Name pronounced KOO-stuhr.
TRANSACTIONS/CAREER NOTES: Selected by Boston Bruins in second round (second Bruins pick, 45th overall) of NHL entry draft (June 22, 1996).

Season Team	League	REGULAR SEASON								PLAYOFFS				
		Gms.	G	A	Pts.	PIM	+/-	PP	SH	Gms.	G	A	Pts.	PIM
93-94— Medicine Hat	WHL	71	28	27	55	60	...	...	...	—	—	—	—	—
94-95— Medicine Hat	WHL	67	14	28	42	54	...	...	...	5	1	3	4	6
95-96— Medicine Hat	WHL	72	35	43	78	54	...	...	...	1	0	0	0	0
96-97— Medicine Hat	WHL	72	26	35	61	47	...	...	...	4	0	1	1	4

K

KUZNETSOV, MAXIM   D   RED WINGS

PERSONAL: Born March 24, 1977, in Pavlodar, U.S.S.R. ... 6-5/198. ... Shoots left.
TRANSACTIONS/CAREER NOTES: Selected by Detroit Red Wings in first round (first Red Wings pick, 26th overall) of NHL entry draft (July 8, 1995).

Season Team	League	REGULAR SEASON								PLAYOFFS				
		Gms.	G	A	Pts.	PIM	+/-	PP	SH	Gms.	G	A	Pts.	PIM
94-95— Dynamo Moscow	CIS	11	0	0	0	8	...	...	...	—	—	—	—	—
95-96— Dynamo Moscow	CIS	9	1	1	2	22	...	...	...	4	0	0	0	0
96-97— Dynamo Moscow	Russian	23	0	2	2	16	...	...	...	—	—	—	—	—
— Adirondack	AHL	2	0	1	1	6	...	...	...	2	0	0	0	0

KVALEVOG, TOBY   G   SENATORS

PERSONAL: Born December 22, 1974, in Fargo, N.D. ... 5-11/170. ... Catches left.
HIGH SCHOOL: Bemidji (Minn.).
COLLEGE: North Dakota.
TRANSACTIONS/CAREER NOTES: Selected by Ottawa Senators in ninth round (eighth Senators pick, 209th overall) of NHL entry draft (June 29, 1993).

Season Team	League	REGULAR SEASON							PLAYOFFS					
		Gms.	Min	W	L	T	GA	SO	Avg.	Gms.	Min.	W	L	GA	SO	Avg.
92-93— Bemidji	Minn. HS	21	945	...	...	...	60	0	3.81	—	—	—	—	—	—	—
93-94— Univ. of North Dakota	WCHA	32	1813	11	17	3	120	0	3.97	—	—	—	—	—	—	—
94-95— Univ. of North Dakota	WCHA	32	1829	14	13	4	120	1	3.94	—	—	—	—	—	—	—
95-96— Univ. of North Dakota	WCHA	35	1890	15	15	1	123	0	3.90	—	—	—	—	—	—	—
96-97— Univ. of North Dakota	WCHA	22	1132	12	5	2	61	1	3.23	—	—	—	—	—	—	—

KVASHA, OLEG   LW   PANTHERS

PERSONAL: Born July 26, 1978, in Moscow, U.S.S.R. ... 6-5/205. ... Shoots right. ... Name pronounced kuh-VAH-shuh.
TRANSACTIONS/CAREER NOTES: Selected by Florida Panthers in third round (third Panthers pick, 65th overall) of NHL entry draft (June 22, 1996).

Season Team	League	REGULAR SEASON								PLAYOFFS				
		Gms.	G	A	Pts.	PIM	+/-	PP	SH	Gms.	G	A	Pts.	PIM
95-96— CSKA Moscow	CIS	38	2	3	5	14	...	...	...	2	0	0	0	0
96-97— CSKA Moscow	Russian	44	20	22	42	115	...	...	...	—	—	—	—	—

KYPREOS, NICK   LW   MAPLE LEAFS

PERSONAL: Born June 4, 1966, in Toronto. ... 6-0/207. ... Shoots left. ... Full name: Nicholas George Kypreos. ... Name pronounced KIHP-ree-ohz.
TRANSACTIONS/CAREER NOTES: Signed as free agent by Philadelphia Flyers (September 30, 1984). ... Underwent surgery to right knee (summer 1988); missed first 52 games of 1988-89 season. ... Selected by Washington Capitals in NHL waiver draft for $20,000 (October 2, 1989). ... Underwent surgery to right knee (February 8, 1990). ... Traded by Capitals to Hartford Whalers for RW Mark Hunter and future considerations (June 15, 1992); Whalers sent LW Yvon Corriveau to Capitals to complete deal (August 20, 1992). ... Suspended two games by NHL for game misconduct penalties (February 3,1993). ... Injured abdominal muscle (April 3, 1993); missed remainder of season. ... Traded by Whalers with RW Steve Larmer, D Barry Richter and sixth-round pick (C Yuri Litvinov) in 1994 draft to New York Rangers for D James Patrick and C Darren Turcotte (November 2, 1993). ... Suspended five games and fined $500 by NHL for deliberately injuring player with late hit (November 2, 1993). ... Underwent root canal surgery (April 1, 1994); missed one game. ... Traded by Rangers with RW Wayne Presley to Toronto Maple Leafs for LW Bill Berg and LW Sergio Momesso (February 29, 1996). ... Suspended one playoff game by NHL for interfering with opposing goaltender (April 21, 1996). ... Fractured bone in ankle (November 19, 1996); missed 35 games.
HONORS: Named to OHL All-Star first team (1985-86). ... Named to OHL All-Star second team (1986-87).
MISCELLANEOUS: Member of Stanley Cup championship team (1994).

Season Team	League	REGULAR SEASON Gms.	G	A	Pts.	PIM	+/-	PP	SH	PLAYOFFS Gms.	G	A	Pts.	PIM
83-84— North Bay..........	OHL	51	12	11	23	36	...	...	...	4	3	2	5	9
84-85— North Bay..........	OHL	64	41	36	77	71	...	...	...	8	2	2	4	15
85-86— North Bay..........	OHL	64	62	35	97	112	...	...	...	—	—	—	—	—
86-87— North Bay..........	OHL	46	49	41	90	54	...	...	...	24	11	5	16	78
— Hershey	AHL	10	0	1	1	4	...	...	...	—	—	—	—	—
87-88— Hershey	AHL	71	24	20	44	101	...	...	...	12	0	2	2	17
88-89— Hershey	AHL	28	12	15	27	19	...	...	...	12	4	5	9	11
89-90— Washington	NHL	31	5	4	9	82	2	0	0	7	1	0	1	15
— Baltimore	AHL	14	6	5	11	6	...	...	...	7	4	1	5	17
90-91— Washington	NHL	79	9	9	18	196	-4	0	0	9	0	1	1	38
91-92— Washington	NHL	65	4	6	10	206	-3	0	0	—	—	—	—	—
92-93— Hartford	NHL	75	17	10	27	325	-5	0	0	—	—	—	—	—
93-94— Hartford	NHL	10	0	0	0	37	-8	0	0	—	—	—	—	—
— New York Rangers.....	NHL	46	3	5	8	102	-8	0	0	3	0	0	0	2
94-95— New York Rangers.....	NHL	40	1	3	4	93	0	0	0	10	0	2	2	6
95-96— New York Rangers.....	NHL	42	3	4	7	77	1	0	0	—	—	—	—	—
— Toronto	NHL	19	1	1	2	30	0	0	0	5	0	0	0	4
96-97— Toronto	NHL	35	3	2	5	62	1	0	0	—	—	—	—	—
— St. John's..........	AHL	4	0	0	0	4	...	...	...	—	—	—	—	—
NHL totals (8 years)		**442**	**46**	**44**	**90**	**1210**	**-24**	**0**	**0**	**34**	**1**	**3**	**4**	**65**

KYTE, JIM   D   SHARKS

PERSONAL: Born March 21, 1964, in Ottawa. ... 6-5/220. ... Shoots left.
TRANSACTIONS/CAREER NOTES: Broke left wrist (March 1980). ... Selected by Winnipeg Jets as underage junior in first round (first Jets pick, 12th overall) of NHL entry draft (June 9, 1982). ... Suffered stress fracture in lower back (February 1988). ... Sprained shoulder (March 1989). ... Traded by Jets with RW Andrew McBain and LW Randy Gilhen to Pittsburgh Penguins for C/LW Randy Cunneyworth, G Richard Tabaracci and RW Dave McLlwain (June 17, 1989). ... Traded by Penguins to Calgary Flames for C Jiri Hrdina (December 13, 1990). ... Fractured bone in left hand during preseason (September 1991). ... Fractured right ankle (January 27, 1991); missed remainder of season. ... Signed as free agent by Ottawa Senators (September 10, 1992). ... Signed as free agent by San Jose Sharks (March 30, 1995). ... Injured knee (October 7, 1995); missed three games.

Season Team	League	REGULAR SEASON Gms.	G	A	Pts.	PIM	+/-	PP	SH	PLAYOFFS Gms.	G	A	Pts.	PIM
80-81— Hawkesbury	COJHL	42	2	24	26	133	...	...	...	—	—	—	—	—
81-82— Cornwall..........	OHL	52	4	13	17	148	...	...	...	5	0	0	0	10
82-83— Cornwall..........	OHL	65	6	30	36	195	...	...	...	8	0	2	2	24
— Winnipeg	NHL	2	0	0	0	0	...	...	...	—	—	—	—	—
83-84— Winnipeg	NHL	58	1	2	3	55	...	...	...	3	0	0	0	11
84-85— Winnipeg	NHL	71	0	3	3	111	...	...	...	8	0	0	0	14
85-86— Winnipeg	NHL	71	1	3	4	126	...	...	...	3	0	0	0	12
86-87— Winnipeg	NHL	72	5	5	10	162	...	...	...	10	0	4	4	36
87-88— Winnipeg	NHL	51	1	3	4	128	...	...	...	—	—	—	—	—
88-89— Winnipeg	NHL	74	3	9	12	190	...	...	...	—	—	—	—	—
89-90— Pittsburgh	NHL	56	3	1	4	125	-10	0	0	—	—	—	—	—
90-91— Muskegon	IHL	25	2	5	7	157	...	...	...	—	—	—	—	—
— Pittsburgh	NHL	1	0	0	0	2	0	0	0	—	—	—	—	—
— Calgary	NHL	42	0	9	9	153	10	0	0	7	0	0	0	7
91-92— Calgary	NHL	21	0	1	1	107	2	0	0	—	—	—	—	—
— Salt Lake City..........	IHL	6	0	1	1	9	...	...	...	—	—	—	—	—
92-93— New Haven	AHL	63	6	18	24	163	...	...	...	—	—	—	—	—
— Ottawa	NHL	4	0	1	1	4	0	0	0	—	—	—	—	—
93-94— Las Vegas	IHL	75	2	16	18	246	...	...	...	4	0	1	1	51
94-95— Las Vegas	IHL	76	3	17	20	195	...	...	...	—	—	—	—	—
— San Jose	NHL	18	2	5	7	33	-7	0	0	11	0	2	2	14
95-96— San Jose	NHL	57	1	7	8	146	-12	0	0	—	—	—	—	—
96-97— Kansas City	IHL	76	3	8	11	259	...	...	...	3	0	0	0	2
NHL totals (13 years)		**598**	**17**	**49**	**66**	**1342**	**-17**	**0**	**0**	**42**	**0**	**6**	**6**	**94**

LABBE, JEAN-FRANCOIS   G   AVALANCHE

PERSONAL: Born June 15, 1972, in Sherbrooke, Quebec. ... 5-9/170. ... Catches left. ... Name pronounced lah-BAY.
TRANSACTIONS/CAREER NOTES: Signed as free agent by Ottawa Senators (1993). ... Nordiques franchise moved to Colorado and renamed Avalanche for 1995-96 season (June 21, 1995). ... Traded by Senators to Colorado Avalanche for conditional draft pick (September 20, 1995).
HONORS: Won Jacques Plante Trophy (1991-92). ... Named to QMJHL All-Star first team (1991-92). ... Named Col.HL Rookie of the Year (1993-94). ... Named Col.HL Playoff Most Valuable Player (1993-94). ... Named to Col.HL All-Star first team (1993-94). ... Won Les Cunningham Award (1996-97). ... Won Baz Batien Trophy (1996-97). ... Won Harry (Hap) Holmes Memorial Trophy (1996-97). ... Named to AHL All-Star first team (1996-97).

Season Team	League	REGULAR SEASON Gms.	Min	W	L	T	GA	SO	Avg.	PLAYOFFS Gms.	Min.	W	L	GA	SO	Avg.
89-90— Trois-Rivieres	QMJHL	28	1499	13	10	0	106	1	4.24	3	132	1	1	8	0	3.64
90-91— Trois-Rivieres	QMJHL	54	2870	35	14	0	158	5	3.30	5	230	1	4	19	0	4.96
91-92— Trois-Rivieres	QMJHL	48	2749	31	13	3	142	3	*3.10	15	791	10	3	33	†1	*2.50
92-93— Hull	QMJHL	46	2701	25	16	2	155	2	3.44	10	518	6	3	24	†1	*2.78
93-94— Prince Edward Island..........	AHL	7	390	4	3	0	22	0	3.38	—	—	—	—	—	—	—
— Thunder Bay	Col.HL	52	*2900	*35	11	4	150	*2	*3.10	8	493	7	1	18	*2	*2.19
94-95— Prince Edward Island..........	AHL	32	1817	13	14	3	94	2	3.10	—	—	—	—	—	—	—
95-96— Cornwall	AHL	55	2971	25	21	5	144	3	2.91	8	470	3	5	21	1	2.68
96-97— Hershey	AHL	66	3811	†34	22	9	160	*6	*2.52	*23	*1364	*14	8	59	1	2.60

K
L

LABELLE, MARC   LW   SENATORS

PERSONAL: Born December 20, 1969, in Maniwaki, Que. ... 6-1/215. ... Shoots left. ... Name pronounced la-BEHL.

TRANSACTIONS/CAREER NOTES: Signed as free agent by Montreal Canadiens (January 21, 1991). ... Signed as free agent by Ottawa Senators (August 6, 1992). ... Selected by Florida Panthers in NHL expansion draft (June 24, 1993). ... Signed as free agent by Dallas Stars (April 15, 1996). ... Signed as free agent by Senators (July 3, 1997).

				REGULAR	SEASON								PLAYOFFS		
Season Team	League	Gms.	G	A	Pts.	PIM	+/-	PP	SH		Gms.	G	A	Pts.	PIM
87-88— Victoriaville	QMJHL	63	11	14	25	236	...	...	...		5	2	4	6	20
88-89— Victoriaville	QMJHL	62	9	26	35	202	...	...	...		5	6	3	9	30
89-90— Victoriaville	QMJHL	56	18	21	39	192	...	...	...		6	4	8	12	42
90-91— Fredericton	AHL	25	1	4	5	95	...	...	...		4	0	2	2	25
— Richmond	ECHL	5	1	1	2	37	...	...	...		—	—	—	—	—
91-92— Fredericton	AHL	62	7	10	17	238	...	...	...		3	0	0	0	6
92-93— New Haven	AHL	31	5	4	9	124	...	...	...		—	—	—	—	—
— San Diego	IHL	5	0	2	2	5	...	...	...		—	—	—	—	—
— Thunder Bay	Col.HL	9	0	5	5	17	...	...	...		7	0	1	1	11
93-94— Cincinnati	IHL	37	2	1	3	133	...	...	...		4	0	1	1	6
94-95— Cincinnati	IHL	54	3	4	7	173	...	...	...		8	0	0	0	7
95-96— Cincinnati	IHL	57	6	11	17	218	...	...	...		0	0	0	0	0
— Milwaukee	IHL	20	5	3	8	50	...	...	...		5	1	1	2	4
96-97— Dallas	NHL	9	0	0	0	46	-4	0	0		—	—	—	—	—
— Michigan	IHL	46	4	7	11	148	...	...	...		3	0	0	0	6
— Milwaukee	IHL	14	1	1	2	33	...	...	...		—	—	—	—	—
NHL totals (1 year)		**9**	**0**	**0**	**0**	**46**	**-4**	**0**	**0**						

LABRECQUE, PATRICK   G   CANADIENS

PERSONAL: Born March 6, 1971, in Laval, Que. ... 6-0/187. ... Catches left. ... Name pronounced luh-BREHK.

TRANSACTIONS/CAREER NOTES: Selected by Quebec Nordiques in fifth round (fifth Nordiques pick, 90th overall) of NHL entry draft (June 22, 1991). ... Signed as free agent by Montreal Canadiens (June 21, 1994).

MISCELLANEOUS: Stopped a penalty shot attempt (vs. Keith Jones, November 1, 1995).

				REGULAR	SEASON							PLAYOFFS					
Season Team	League	Gms.	Min	W	L	T	GA	SO	Avg.		Gms.	Min.	W	L	GA	SO	Avg.
89-90—St. Jean	QMJHL	48	2630	...	...	...	196	0	4.47		—	—	—	—	—	—	—
90-91—St. Jean	QMJHL	59	3375	17	34	6	216	1	3.84		—	—	—	—	—	—	—
91-92—Halifax	AHL	29	1570	5	12	8	114	0	4.36		—	—	—	—	—	—	—
92-93—Halifax	AHL	20	914	3	12	2	76	0	4.99		—	—	—	—	—	—	—
— Greensboro	ECHL	11	650	6	3	‡2	31	0	2.86		1	59	0	1	5	0	5.08
93-94—Cornwall	AHL	4	198	1	2	0	8	1	2.42		—	—	—	—	—	—	—
— Greensboro	ECHL	29	1609	17	8	‡2	89	0	3.32		1	22	0	0	4	0	10.91
94-95—Wheeling	ECHL	5	281	2	3	‡0	22	0	4.70		—	—	—	—	—	—	—
— Fredericton	AHL	35	1913	15	17	1	104	1	3.26		16	*968	*10	*6	40	1	2.48
95-96—Montreal	NHL	2	98	0	1	0	7	0	4.29		—	—	—	—	—	—	—
— Fredericton	AHL	48	2686	23	18	6	153	3	3.42		7	405	3	3	31	0	4.59
96-97—Fredericton	AHL	12	602	1	7	1	31	0	3.09		—	—	—	—	—	—	—
NHL totals (1 year)		**2**	**98**	**0**	**1**	**0**	**7**	**0**	**4.29**								

LACHANCE, BOB   RW   BLUES

PERSONAL: Born February 1, 1974, in Northampton, Mass. ... 5-11/180. ... Shoots right. ... Brother of Scott Lachance, defenseman, New York Islanders.

COLLEGE: Boston University.

TRANSACTIONS/CAREER NOTES: Selected by St. Louis Blues in sixth round (fifth Blues pick, 134th overall) of NHL entry draft (June 20, 1992).

				REGULAR	SEASON							PLAYOFFS		
Season Team	League	Gms.	G	A	Pts.	PIM	+/-	PP	SH		Gms.	G	A	Pts.	PIM
91-92— Springfield Jr. B	NEJHL	46	40	98	138	87	...	...	...		—	—	—	—	—
92-93— Boston University	Hockey East	33	4	10	14	24	...	...	...		—	—	—	—	—
93-94— Boston University	Hockey East	32	13	19	32	42	...	...	...		—	—	—	—	—
94-95— Boston University	Hockey East	37	12	29	41	51	...	...	...		—	—	—	—	—
95-96— Boston University	Hockey East	39	15	37	52	67	...	...	...		—	—	—	—	—
— Worcester	AHL	7	1	0	1	6	...	...	...		—	—	—	—	—
96-97— Worcester	AHL	74	21	35	56	66	...	...	...		5	0	2	2	4

LACHANCE, SCOTT   D   ISLANDERS

PERSONAL: Born October 22, 1972, in Charlottesville, Va. ... 6-1/196. ... Shoots left. ... Full name: Scott Joseph Lachance. ... Brother of Bob Lachance, right winger, St. Louis Blues system.

COLLEGE: Boston University.

TRANSACTIONS/CAREER NOTES: Selected by New York Islanders in first round (first Islanders pick, fourth overall) of NHL entry draft (June 22, 1991). ... Sprained wrist (April 13, 1993); missed remainder of season. ... Underwent wrist surgery (April 30, 1993). ... Suffered mild separation of right shoulder (October 8, 1993); missed four games. ... Broke ankle (February 25, 1995); missed 22 games. ... Injured groin (October 31, 1995); missed 27 games.

HONORS: Named to Hockey East All-Rookie team (1990-91). ... Played in NHL All-Star Game (1997).

Season Team	League	REGULAR SEASON								PLAYOFFS				
		Gms.	G	A	Pts.	PIM	+/-	PP	SH	Gms.	G	A	Pts.	PIM
88-89— Springfield Jr. B........	NEJHL	36	8	28	36	20	...	...	...	—	—	—	—	—
89-90— Springfield Jr. B........	NEJHL	34	25	41	66	62	...	...	...	—	—	—	—	—
90-91— Boston University	Hockey East	31	5	19	24	48	...	...	...	—	—	—	—	—
91-92— U.S. national team	Int'l	36	1	10	11	34	...	...	...	—	—	—	—	—
— U.S. Olympic team.....	Int'l	8	0	1	1	6	...	...	...	—	—	—	—	—
— New York Islanders....	NHL	17	1	4	5	9	13	0	0	—	—	—	—	—
92-93— New York Islanders....	NHL	75	7	17	24	67	-1	0	1	—	—	—	—	—
93-94— New York Islanders....	NHL	74	3	11	14	70	-5	0	0	3	0	0	0	0
94-95— New York Islanders....	NHL	26	6	7	13	26	2	3	0	—	—	—	—	—
95-96— New York Islanders....	NHL	55	3	10	13	54	-19	1	0	—	—	—	—	—
96-97— New York Islanders....	NHL	81	3	11	14	47	-7	1	0	—	—	—	—	—
NHL totals (6 years)		328	23	60	83	273	-17	5	1	3	0	0	0	0

LACROIX, DAN   C   FLYERS

PERSONAL: Born March 11, 1969, in Montreal. ... 6-2/205. ... Shoots left. ... Name pronounced luh-KWAH.

TRANSACTIONS/CAREER NOTES: Selected as underage junior by New York Rangers in second round (second Rangers pick, 31st overall) of NHL entry draft (June 13, 1987). ... Traded by Rangers to Boston Bruins for D Glen Featherstone (August 19, 1994). ... Claimed on waivers by Rangers (March 23, 1995). ... Signed as free agent by Philadelphia Flyers (July 15, 1996). ... Bruised ribs (September 25, 1996); missed first five games of season. ... Suspended two games and fined $1,000 by NHL for throwing flagrant elbow (October 17, 1996).

HONORS: Won Marcel Robert Trophy (1988-89).

Season Team	League	REGULAR SEASON								PLAYOFFS				
		Gms.	G	A	Pts.	PIM	+/-	PP	SH	Gms.	G	A	Pts.	PIM
86-87— Granby	QMJHL	54	9	16	25	311	...	...	...	8	1	2	3	22
87-88— Granby	QMJHL	58	24	50	74	468	...	...	...	5	0	4	4	12
88-89— Granby	QMJHL	70	45	49	94	320	...	...	...	4	1	1	2	57
— Denver	IHL	2	0	1	1	0	...	...	...	2	0	1	1	0
89-90— Flint......................	IHL	61	12	16	28	128	...	...	...	4	2	0	2	24
90-91— Binghamton	AHL	54	7	12	19	237	...	...	...	5	1	0	1	24
91-92— Binghamton	AHL	52	12	20	32	149	...	...	...	11	2	4	6	28
92-93— Binghamton	AHL	73	21	22	43	255	...	...	...	—	—	—	—	—
93-94— New York Rangers	NHL	4	0	0	0	0	0	0	0	—	—	—	—	—
— Binghamton	AHL	59	20	23	43	278	...	...	...	—	—	—	—	—
94-95— Providence................	AHL	40	15	11	26	266	...	...	...	—	—	—	—	—
— Boston	NHL	23	1	0	1	38	-2	0	0	—	—	—	—	—
— New York Rangers	NHL	1	0	0	0	0	0	0	0	—	—	—	—	—
95-96— Binghamton	AHL	26	12	15	27	155	...	...	...	—	—	—	—	—
— New York Rangers	NHL	25	2	2	4	30	-1	0	0	—	—	—	—	—
96-97— Philadelphia	NHL	74	7	1	8	163	-1	1	0	12	0	1	1	22
NHL totals (4 years)		127	10	3	13	231	-4	1	0	12	0	1	1	22

LACROIX, ERIC   LW   AVALANCHE

PERSONAL: Born July 15, 1971, in Montreal. ... 6-1/205. ... Shoots left. ... Name pronounced luh-KWAH.

HIGH SCHOOL: Governor Dummer (Byfield, Mass.).

COLLEGE: St. Lawrence (N.Y.).

TRANSACTIONS/CAREER NOTES: Selected by Toronto Maple Leafs in seventh round (sixth Maple Leafs pick, 136th overall) of NHL entry draft (June 16, 1990). ... Separated shoulder (November 27, 1993); missed eight games. ... Traded by Maple Leafs with D Chris Snell and fourth-round pick (C Eric Belanger) in 1996 draft to Los Angeles Kings for RW Dixon Ward, C Guy Leveque, RW Shayne Toporowski and C Kelly Fairchild (October 3, 1994). ... Sprained knee (February 4, 1995); missed one game. ... Sprained knee (February 23, 1995); missed two games. ... Suspended three games by NHL for unnecessary contact with an official (October 16, 1995). ... Suspended five games by NHL for checking from behind (November 22, 1995). ... Traded by Kings with first-round pick in 1998 draft to Colorado Avalanche for G Stephane Fiset and first-round pick in 1998 draft (June 20, 1996).

STATISTICAL PLATEAUS: Three-goal games: 1996-97 (1).

Season Team	League	REGULAR SEASON								PLAYOFFS				
		Gms.	G	A	Pts.	PIM	+/-	PP	SH	Gms.	G	A	Pts.	PIM
89-90— Governor Dummer.....	Mass. H.S.	...	23	18	41	...	...	...	...	—	—	—	—	—
90-91— St. Lawrence Univ.....	ECAC	35	13	11	24	35	...	...	...	—	—	—	—	—
91-92— St. Lawrence Univ.....	ECAC	34	11	20	31	40	...	...	...	—	—	—	—	—
92-93— St. John's................	AHL	76	15	19	34	59	...	...	...	9	5	3	8	4
93-94— St. John's................	AHL	59	17	22	39	69	...	...	...	11	5	3	8	6
— Toronto	NHL	3	0	0	0	2	0	0	0	2	0	0	0	0
94-95— St. John's................	AHL	1	0	0	0	2	...	...	...	—	—	—	—	—
— Phoenix.................	IHL	25	7	1	8	31	...	...	...	—	—	—	—	—
— Los Angeles.............	NHL	45	9	7	16	54	2	2	1	—	—	—	—	—
95-96— Los Angeles.............	NHL	72	16	16	32	110	-11	3	0	—	—	—	—	—
96-97— Colorado	NHL	81	18	18	36	26	16	2	0	17	1	4	5	19
NHL totals (4 years)		201	43	41	84	192	7	7	1	19	1	4	5	19

LaFAYETTE, NATHAN   C   KINGS

PERSONAL: Born February 17, 1973, in New Westminster, B.C. ... 6-1/195. ... Shoots right. ... Name pronounced LAH-fay-eht.

TRANSACTIONS/CAREER NOTES: Traded by Kingston Frontenacs with Joel Sandie to Cornwall Royals for D Rod Pasma and Shawn Caplice (January 6, 1991). ... Selected by St. Louis Blues in third round (third Blues pick, 65th overall) of NHL entry draft (June 22, 1991). ... Traded by Blues with D Jeff Brown and D Bret Hedican to Vancouver Canucks for C Craig Janney (March 21, 1994). ... Traded by Canucks to New York Rangers for G Corey Hirsch (April 7, 1995). ... Traded by Rangers with C Ray Ferraro, C Ian Laperiere, D Mattis Norstrom and fourth-round pick (D Sean Blanchard) in 1997 draft to Los Angeles Kings for RW Shane Churla, LW Jari Kurri and D/RW Marty McSorley (March 14, 1996). ... Loaned by Kings to Syracuse of the AHL (December 27, 1996).

HONORS: Won Bobby Smith Trophy (1990-91 and 1991-92). ... Won Can.HL Scholastic Player of the Year Award (1991-92).

			REGULAR SEASON								PLAYOFFS				
Season Team	League	Gms.	G	A	Pts.	PIM	+/-	PP	SH		Gms.	G	A	Pts.	PIM
89-90— Kingston	OHL	53	6	8	14	14	...	...	...		7	0	1	1	0
90-91— Kingston	OHL	35	13	13	26	10	...	...	...		—	—	—	—	—
— Cornwall..................	OHL	28	16	22	38	25	...	...	...		—	—	—	—	—
91-92— Cornwall..................	OHL	66	28	45	73	26	...	...	...		6	2	5	7	16
92-93— Newmarket..............	OHL	58	49	38	87	26	...	...	...		7	4	6	10	19
93-94— Peoria....................	IHL	27	13	11	24	20	...	...	...		—	—	—	—	—
— St. Louis...............	NHL	38	2	3	5	14	-9	0	0		—	—	—	—	—
— Vancouver............	NHL	11	1	1	2	4	2	0	0		20	2	7	9	4
94-95— Syracuse..............	AHL	27	9	9	18	10	...	...	...		—	—	—	—	—
— Vancouver............	NHL	27	4	4	8	2	2	0	1		—	—	—	—	—
— New York Rangers.....	NHL	12	0	0	0	0	1	0	0		—	—	—	—	—
95-96— Binghamton...........	AHL	57	21	27	48	32	...	...	...		—	—	—	—	—
— New York Rangers.....	NHL	5	0	0	0	2	-1	0	0		—	—	—	—	—
— Los Angeles.............	NHL	12	2	4	6	6	-3	1	0		—	—	—	—	—
96-97— Phoenix..................	IHL	31	2	5	7	16	...	...	...		—	—	—	—	—
— Syracuse..............	AHL	26	14	11	25	18	...	...	...		3	1	0	1	2
— Los Angeles.............	NHL	15	1	3	4	8	-8	0	1		—	—	—	—	—
NHL totals (4 years)		120	10	15	25	36	-16	1	2		20	2	7	9	4

LAFLAMME, CHRISTIAN   D   BLACKHAWKS

PERSONAL: Born November 24, 1976, in St. Charles, Que. ... 6-1/195. ... Shoots right. ... Name pronounced lah-FLAHM.
TRANSACTIONS/CAREER NOTES: Selected by Chicago Blackhawks in second round (second Blackhawks pick, 45th overall) of NHL entry draft (July 8, 1995).
HONORS: Named to QMJHL All-Rookie team (1992-93). ... Named to QMJHL All-Star second team (1994-95).

			REGULAR SEASON								PLAYOFFS				
Season Team	League	Gms.	G	A	Pts.	PIM	+/-	PP	SH		Gms.	G	A	Pts.	PIM
92-93— Verdun.....................	QMJHL	69	2	17	19	70	...	...	...		3	0	2	2	6
93-94— Verdun.....................	QMJHL	72	4	34	38	85	...	...	...		4	0	3	3	4
94-95— Beauport...............	QMJHL	67	6	41	47	82	...	...	...		8	1	4	5	6
95-96— Beauport...............	QMJHL	41	13	23	36	63	...	...	...		20	7	17	24	32
96-97— Indianapolis	IHL	62	5	15	20	60	...	...	...		4	1	1	2	16
— Chicago.................	NHL	4	0	1	1	2	3	0	0		—	—	—	—	—
NHL totals (1 year)		4	0	1	1	2	3	0	0						

LaFONTAINE, PAT   C   SABRES

PERSONAL: Born February 22, 1965, in St. Louis. ... 5-10/182. ... Shoots right. ... Name pronounced luh-FAHN-tayn.
TRANSACTIONS/CAREER NOTES: Selected by New York Islanders as underage junior in first round (first Islanders pick, third overall) of NHL entry draft (June 8, 1983). ... Damaged ligaments in left knee (August 16, 1984). ... Suffered from mononucleosis (January 1985). ... Separated right shoulder (January 25, 1986). ... Bruised knee (March 1988). ... Broke nose (October 7, 1988); played entire season with injury. ... Sprained ligaments in right wrist (November 5, 1988). ... Strained left hamstring (October 13, 1990); missed three games. ... Traded by Islanders with LW Randy Wood, D Randy Hillier and future considerations to Buffalo Sabres for C Pierre Turgeon, RW Benoit Hogue, D Uwe Krupp and C Dave McLlwain; Sabres later received fourth-round pick (D Dean Melanson) in 1992 draft (October 25, 1991). ... Fractured jaw (November 16, 1991); missed 13 games. ... Injured knee (November 13, 1993); missed remainder of season and first 24 games of 1994-95 season. ... Suffered mild concussion (December 27, 1995); missed two games. ... Suffered concussion (October 17, 1996); missed remainder of season.
HONORS: Won Can.HL Player of the Year Award (1982-83). ... Won Michel Briere Trophy (1982-83). ... Won Jean Beliveau Trophy (1982-83). ... Won Frank J. Selke Trophy (1982-83). ... Won Des Instructeurs Trophy (1982-83). ... Won Guy Lafleur Trophy (1982-83). ... Named to QMJHL All-Star first team (1982-83). ... Played in NHL All-Star Game (1988-1991 and 1993). ... Won Dodge Performer of the Year Award (1989-90). ... Named to THE SPORTING NEWS All-Star second team (1989-90). ... Named to NHL All-Star second team (1992-93). ... Won Bill Masterton Memorial Trophy (1994-95).
RECORDS: Holds NHL playoff record for fastest two goals from the start of a period—35 seconds (May 19, 1984).
STATISTICAL PLATEAUS: Three-goal games: 1983-84 (1), 1987-88 (1), 1988-89 (2), 1989-90 (2), 1990-91 (1), 1991-92 (4), 1992-93 (1), 1995-96 (1). Total: 13.
MISCELLANEOUS: Captain of Buffalo Sabres (1992-93 through 1996-97). ... Scored on a penalty shot (vs. Peter Sidorkiewicz, November 29, 1992).

			REGULAR SEASON								PLAYOFFS				
Season Team	League	Gms.	G	A	Pts.	PIM	+/-	PP	SH		Gms.	G	A	Pts.	PIM
82-83— Verdun	QMJHL	70	*104	*130	*234	10	...	...	...		15	11	*24	*35	4
83-84— U.S. national team	Int'l	58	56	55	111	22	...	...	...		—	—	—	—	—
— U.S. Olympic team	Int'l	6	5	3	8	0	...	...	...		—	—	—	—	—
— New York Islanders....	NHL	15	13	6	19	6	9	1	0		16	3	6	9	8
84-85— New York Islanders....	NHL	67	19	35	54	32	9	1	0		9	1	2	3	4
85-86— New York Islanders....	NHL	65	30	23	53	43	16	2	0		3	1	0	1	0
86-87— New York Islanders....	NHL	80	38	32	70	70	-10	19	1		14	5	7	12	10
87-88— New York Islanders....	NHL	75	47	45	92	52	15	15	0		6	4	5	9	8
88-89— New York Islanders....	NHL	79	45	43	88	26	-8	16	0		—	—	—	—	—
89-90— New York Islanders....	NHL	74	54	51	105	38	-13	13	2		2	0	1	1	0
90-91— New York Islanders....	NHL	75	41	44	85	42	-6	12	2		—	—	—	—	—
91-92— Buffalo	NHL	57	46	47	93	98	10	23	0		7	8	3	11	4
92-93— Buffalo	NHL	84	53	95	148	63	11	20	2		7	2	10	12	0

Season Team	League	REGULAR SEASON								PLAYOFFS				
		Gms.	G	A	Pts.	PIM	+/-	PP	SH	Gms.	G	A	Pts.	PIM
93-94— Buffalo	NHL	16	5	13	18	2	-4	1	0	—	—	—	—	—
94-95— Buffalo	NHL	22	12	15	27	4	2	6	1	5	2	2	4	2
95-96— Buffalo	NHL	76	40	51	91	36	-8	15	3	—	—	—	—	—
96-97— Buffalo	NHL	13	2	6	8	4	-8	1	0	—	—	—	—	—
NHL totals (14 years)		798	445	506	951	516	12	145	11	69	26	36	62	36

LAKOVIC, SASHA   LW   FLAMES

PERSONAL: Born September 7, 1971, in Vancouver. ... 6-0/207. ... Shoots left.
TRANSACTIONS/CAREER NOTES: Traded by Saginaw of Col.HL with RW Jamie Allen to Brantford of Col.HL for C Jamey Hicks (July 27, 1994). ... Traded by Saint John of AHL to Las Vegas of IHL for D Ryan Best and future considerations (March 20, 1997). ... Signed as free agent by Calgary Flames (October 15, 1996). ... Suspended two games by NHL for attacking a fan (November 26, 1996).

Season Team	League	REGULAR SEASON								PLAYOFFS				
		Gms.	G	A	Pts.	PIM	+/-	PP	SH	Gms.	G	A	Pts.	PIM
95-96— Las Vegas	IHL	49	1	2	3	416	...	...	...	13	1	1	2	57
96-97— Saint John	AHL	18	1	8	9	182	...	...	...	—	—	—	—	—
—Calgary	NHL	19	0	1	1	54	-1	0	0	—	—	—	—	—
—Las Vegas	IHL	10	0	0	0	81	...	...	...	2	0	0	0	14
NHL totals (1 year)		19	0	1	1	54	-1	0	0					

LALIME, PATRICK   G   PENGUINS

PERSONAL: Born July 7, 1974, in St. Bonaventure, Que. ... 6-2/170. ... Catches left. ... Name pronounced luh-LEEM.
TRANSACTIONS/CAREER NOTES: Selected by Pittsburgh Penguins in sixth round (sixth Penguins pick, 156th overall) of NHL entry draft (June 26, 1993).
HONORS: Named to NHL All-Rookie team (1996-97).

Season Team	League	REGULAR SEASON								PLAYOFFS					
		Gms.	Min	W	L	T	GA	SO	Avg.	Gms.	Min.	W	L	GA	SO	Avg.
92-93—Shawinigan	QMJHL	44	2467	10	24	4	192	0	4.67	—	—	—	—	—	—	—
93-94—Shawinigan	QMJHL	48	2733	22	20	2	192	1	4.22	5	223	1	3	25	0	6.73
94-95—Hampton Roads	ECHL	26	1471	15	7	‡3	82	2	3.34	—	—	—	—	—	—	—
—Cleveland	IHL	23	1230	7	10	‡4	91	0	4.44	—	—	—	—	—	—	—
95-96—Cleveland	IHL	41	2314	20	12	‡7	149	0	3.86	—	—	—	—	—	—	—
96-97—Cleveland	IHL	14	834	6	6	‡2	45	1	3.24	—	—	—	—	—	—	—
—Pittsburgh	NHI	39	2058	21	12	3	101	3	2.94	—	—	—	—	—	—	—
NHL totals (1 year)		39	2058	21	12	3	101	3	2.94							

LALOR, MIKE   D   STARS

PERSONAL: Born March 8, 1963, in Fort Erie, Ont. ... 6-0/200. ... Shoots left. ... Full name: John Michael Lalor. ... Name pronounced LAH-luhr.
TRANSACTIONS/CAREER NOTES: Signed as free agent by Montreal Canadiens (September 1983). ... Suffered from bursitis in right ankle (September 1987). ... Suffered stress fracture of left ankle (November 1, 1988). ... Traded by Canadiens to St. Louis Blues for option to flip first-round picks in 1990 draft and second- or third-round picks in 1991 draft; Canadiens exercised option (January 16, 1989). ... Traded by Blues with C Peter Zezel to Washington Capitals for LW Geoff Courtnall (July 13, 1990). ... Traded by Capitals to Winnipeg Jets for RW Paul MacDermid (March 2, 1992). ... Broke finger (November 12, 1992); missed 13 games. ... Strained neck (January 8, 1993); missed one game. ... Suffered rib contusion (March 23, 1993); missed two games. ... Strained knee ligaments (October 26, 1993); missed 22 games. ... Traded by San Jose Sharks with D Doug Zmolek to Dallas Stars for LW Ulf Dahlen and future considerations (March 19, 1994). ... Strained shoulder (October 5, 1996); missed seven games. ... Bruised shoulder (March 5, 1997); missed two games. ... Bruised shoulder (March 16, 1997); missed two games.
MISCELLANEOUS: Member of Stanley Cup championship team (1986).

Season Team	League	REGULAR SEASON								PLAYOFFS				
		Gms.	G	A	Pts.	PIM	+/-	PP	SH	Gms.	G	A	Pts.	PIM
81-82— Brantford	OHL	64	3	13	16	114	...	...	...	11	0	6	6	11
82-83— Brantford	OHL	65	10	30	40	113	...	...	...	6	1	3	4	20
83-84— Nova Scotia	AHL	67	5	11	16	80	...	...	...	12	0	2	2	13
84-85— Sherbrooke	AHL	79	9	23	32	114	...	...	...	17	3	5	8	36
85-86— Montreal	NHL	62	3	5	8	56	-4	0	0	17	1	2	3	29
86-87— Montreal	NHL	57	0	10	10	47	5	0	0	13	2	1	3	29
87-88— Montreal	NHL	66	1	10	11	113	4	0	0	11	0	0	0	11
88-89— Montreal	NHL	12	1	4	5	15	-1	0	0	—	—	—	—	—
—St. Louis	NHL	36	1	14	15	54	15	0	0	10	1	1	2	14
89-90— St. Louis	NHL	78	0	16	16	81	-6	0	0	12	0	2	2	31
90-91— Washington	NHL	68	1	5	6	61	-23	0	0	10	1	2	3	22
91-92— Washington	NHL	64	5	7	12	64	14	0	0	—	—	—	—	—
—Winnipeg	NHL	15	2	3	5	14	11	0	0	7	0	0	0	19
92-93— Winnipeg	NHL	64	1	8	9	76	-10	0	0	4	0	2	2	4
93-94— San Jose	NHL	23	0	2	2	8	-5	0	0	—	—	—	—	—
—Dallas	NHL	12	0	1	1	6	-5	0	0	5	0	0	0	6
94-95— Dallas	NHL	12	0	0	0	9	0	0	0	3	0	0	0	2
—Kalamazoo	IHL	5	0	1	1	11	...	...	...	—	—	—	—	—
95-96— San Francisco	IHL	12	2	2	4	6	...	...	...	—	—	—	—	—
—Dallas	NHL	63	1	2	3	31	-10	0	0	—	—	—	—	—
96-97— Dallas	NHL	55	1	1	2	42	3	0	0	—	—	—	—	—
NHL totals (12 years)		687	17	88	105	677	-12	0	0	92	5	10	15	167

LAMB, MARK — C

PERSONAL: Born August 3, 1964, in Swift Current, Sask. ... 5-9/180. ... Shoots left.
HIGH SCHOOL: Swift Current (Sask.).
TRANSACTIONS/CAREER NOTES: Selected by Calgary Flames as underage junior in fourth round (fifth Flames pick, 72nd overall) of NHL entry draft (June 9, 1982). ... Refused to dress for a game after Nanaimo Islanders released coach Les Calder; asked to be traded (December 1982). ... Traded by Islanders to Medicine Hat Tigers for Glen Kulka and G Daryl Reaugh (December 1982). ... Signed as free agent by Detroit Red Wings (July 1, 1986). ... Selected by Edmonton Oilers in NHL waiver draft (October 5, 1987). ... Pinched nerve in neck (October 21, 1990). ... Selected by Ottawa Senators in NHL expansion draft (June 18, 1992). ... Suffered sore foot (October 24, 1992); missed two games. ... Injured neck (December 17, 1992); missed 10 games. ... Traded by Senators to Philadelphia Flyers for LW Claude Boivin and G Kirk Daubenspeck (March 5, 1994). ... Traded by Flyers to Montreal Canadiens for cash (February 10, 1995). ... Signed as free agent by Houston of IHL (September 13, 1996).
HONORS: Won Frank Boucher Memorial Trophy (1983-84). ... Named to WHL (East) All-Star first team (1983-84).
MISCELLANEOUS: Member of Stanley Cup championship team (1990). ... Captain of Ottawa Senators (1993-94).

		REGULAR SEASON								PLAYOFFS				
Season Team	League	Gms.	G	A	Pts.	PIM	+/-	PP	SH	Gms.	G	A	Pts.	PIM
80-81— Billings	WHL	24	1	8	9	12	...	...	...	—	—	—	—	—
81-82— Billings	WHL	72	45	56	101	46	...	...	...	5	4	6	10	4
82-83— Nanaimo	WHL	30	14	37	51	16	...	...	...	—	—	—	—	—
— Medicine Hat	WHL	46	22	43	65	33	...	...	...	5	3	2	5	4
— Colorado	CHL	—	—	—	—	31	...	...	...	6	0	2	2	0
83-84— Medicine Hat	WHL	72	59	77	136	30	...	...	...	14	12	11	23	6
84-85— Medicine Hat	WHL	—	—	—	—	—	...	...	...	6	3	2	5	2
— Moncton	AHL	80	23	49	72	53	...	...	...	—	—	—	—	—
85-86— Calgary	NHL	1	0	0	0	0	...	...	...	—	—	—	—	—
— Moncton	AHL	79	26	50	76	51	...	...	...	10	2	6	8	17
86-87— Detroit	NHL	22	2	1	3	8	...	...	...	11	0	0	0	11
— Adirondack	AHL	49	14	36	50	45	...	...	...	—	—	—	—	—
87-88— Nova Scotia	AHL	69	27	61	88	45	...	...	...	5	0	5	5	6
— Edmonton	NHL	2	0	0	0	0	...	...	...	—	—	—	—	—
88-89— Cape Breton	AHL	54	33	49	82	29	...	...	...	—	—	—	—	—
— Edmonton	NHL	20	2	8	10	14	...	...	...	6	0	2	2	8
89-90— Edmonton	NHL	58	12	16	28	42	10	2	0	22	6	11	17	2
90-91— Edmonton	NHL	37	4	8	12	25	-2	1	0	15	0	5	5	20
91-92— Edmonton	NHL	59	6	22	28	46	4	2	0	16	1	1	2	10
92-93— Ottawa	NHL	71	7	19	26	64	-40	1	0	—	—	—	—	—
93-94— Ottawa	NHL	66	11	18	29	56	-41	4	1	—	—	—	—	—
— Philadelphia	NHL	19	1	6	7	16	-3	0	0	—	—	—	—	—
94-95— Philadelphia	NHL	8	0	2	2	2	1	0	0	—	—	—	—	—
— Montreal	NHL	39	1	0	1	18	-13	0	0	—	—	—	—	—
95-96— Montreal	NHL	1	0	0	0	0	0	0	0	—	—	—	—	—
— Houston	IHL	67	17	60	77	65	...	...	...	—	—	—	—	—
96-97— Houston	IHL	81	25	53	78	83	...	...	...	13	3	12	15	10
NHL totals (11 years)		**403**	**46**	**100**	**146**	**291**	**-84**	**10**	**1**	**70**	**7**	**19**	**26**	**51**

LAMBERT, DENNY — LW — SENATORS

PERSONAL: Born January 7, 1970, in Wawa, Ont. ... 5-11/200. ... Shoots left. ... Name pronounced lam-BAIR.
TRANSACTIONS/CAREER NOTES: Signed as free agent by Mighty Ducks of Anaheim (August 16, 1993). ... Signed as free agent by Ottawa Senators (July 8, 1996).

		REGULAR SEASON								PLAYOFFS				
Season Team	League	Gms.	G	A	Pts.	PIM	+/-	PP	SH	Gms.	G	A	Pts.	PIM
88-89— Sault Ste. Marie	OHL	61	14	15	29	203	...	...	...	—	—	—	—	—
89-90— Sault Ste. Marie	OHL	61	23	29	52	*276	...	...	...	—	—	—	—	—
90-91— Sault Ste. Marie	OHL	59	28	39	67	169	...	...	...	14	7	9	16	48
91-92— San Diego	IHL	71	17	14	31	229	...	...	...	3	0	0	0	10
92-93— St. Thomas	Col.HL	5	2	6	8	9	...	...	...	—	—	—	—	—
— San Diego	IHL	56	18	12	30	277	...	...	...	14	1	1	2	44
93-94— San Diego	IHL	79	13	14	27	314	...	...	...	6	1	0	1	45
94-95— San Diego	IHL	75	25	35	60	222	...	...	...	—	—	—	—	—
— Anaheim	NHL	13	1	3	4	4	3	0	0	—	—	—	—	—
95-96— Anaheim	NHL	33	0	8	8	55	-2	0	0	—	—	—	—	—
— Baltimore	AHL	44	14	28	42	126	...	...	...	12	3	9	12	39
96-97— Ottawa	NHL	80	4	16	20	217	-4	0	0	6	0	1	1	9
NHL totals (3 years)		**126**	**5**	**27**	**32**	**276**	**-3**	**0**	**0**	**6**	**0**	**1**	**1**	**9**

LAMBERT, JUDD — G — DEVILS

PERSONAL: Born June 3, 1974, in Richmond, B.C. ... 6-1/175. ... Catches left.
COLLEGE: Colorado College.
TRANSACTIONS/CAREER NOTES: Selected by New Jersey Devils in ninth round (ninth Devils pick, 221st overall) of NHL entry draft (June 29, 1993).
HONORS: Named to WCHA All-Star second team (1995-96).

		REGULAR SEASON							PLAYOFFS					
Season Team	League	Gms.	Min	W	L	T	GA	SO	Avg.	Gms.	Min.	W	L	GA	SO	Avg.
92-93— Chilliwack	BCJHL	50	2488	...	...	...	234	...	5.64	—	—	—	—	—	—	—
93-94— Colorado College	WCHA	11	620	6	4	0	33	0	3.19	—	—	—	—	—	—	—
94-95— Colorado College	WCHA	21	1060	12	7	0	57	1	3.23	—	—	—	—	—	—	—
95-96— Colorado College	WCHA	19	1179	16	1	2	42	1	2.14	—	—	—	—	—	—	—
96-97— Colorado College	WCHA	34	1993	19	12	1	101	3	3.04	—	—	—	—	—	—	—

LAMOTHE, MARC   G   BLACKHAWKS

PERSONAL: Born February 27, 1974, in New Liskeard, Ont. ... 6-1/204. ... Catches left. ... Name pronounced luh-MAHT.
TRANSACTIONS/CAREER NOTES: Selected by Montreal Canadiens in fourth round (sixth Canadiens pick, 92nd overall) of NHL entry draft (June 20, 1992). ... Signed as free agent by Chicago Blackhawks (August 21, 1996).

		REGULAR SEASON								PLAYOFFS					
Season Team	League	Gms.	Min	W	L	T	GA	SO	Avg.	Gms.	Min.	W	L	GA	SO	Avg.
90-91—Ottawa	OHA Mj Jr.A	25	1220	...	...	...	82	1	4.03	—	—	—	—	—	—	—
91-92—Kingston	OHL	42	2378	10	25	2	189	1	4.77	—	—	—	—	—	—	—
92-93—Kingston	OHL	45	2489	23	12	6	162	†1	3.91	15	733	8	5	46	†1	3.77
93-94—Kingston	OHL	48	2828	23	20	5	177	†2	3.76	6	224	2	2	12	0	3.21
94-95—Fredericton	AHL	9	428	2	5	0	32	0	4.49	—	—	—	—	—	—	—
—Wheeling	ECHL	13	737	9	2	‡1	38	0	3.09	—	—	—	—	—	—	—
95-96—Fredericton	AHL	23	1165	5	9	3	73	1	3.76	3	160	1	2	9	0	3.38
96-97—Indianapolis	IHL	38	2271	20	14	‡4	100	1	2.64	1	20	0	0	1	0	3.00

LANDRY, ERIC   C/LW   OILERS

PERSONAL: Born January 20, 1975, in Gatineaux, Que. ... 5-11/185. ... Shoots left.
TRANSACTIONS/CAREER NOTES: Signed as free agent by Cape Breton of AHL prior to 1995-96 season.

		REGULAR SEASON							PLAYOFFS				
Season Team	League	Gms.	G	A	Pts.	PIM	+/-	PP	SH	Gms.	G	A	Pts.	PIM
93-94— St. Hyacinthe	QMJHL	69	42	34	76	128	...	...	...	7	4	2	6	13
94-95— St. Hyacinthe	QMJHL	68	38	36	74	249	...	...	...	5	2	1	3	10
95-96— Cape Breton	AHL	74	19	33	52	187	...	...	...	—	—	—	—	—
96-97— Hamilton	AHL	74	15	17	32	139	...	...	...	22	6	7	13	43

LANG, ROBERT   C   OILERS

L

PERSONAL: Born December 19, 1970, in Teplice, Czechoslovakia. ... 6-2/180. ... Shoots right. ... Name pronounced LUHNG.
TRANSACTIONS/CAREER NOTES: Selected by Los Angeles Kings in seventh round (sixth Kings pick, 133rd overall) of NHL entry draft (June 16, 1990). ... Dislocated shoulder (April 3, 1994); missed remainder of season. ... Played in Europe during 1994-95 NHL lockout. ... Strained left shoulder (March 26, 1995); missed one game. ... Strained back (November 20, 1995); missed seven games. ... Signed as free agent by Edmonton Oilers (October 19, 1996). ... Loaned by Oilers to Sparta Praha of Czech Republic League (October 19, 1996).

		REGULAR SEASON							PLAYOFFS				
Season Team	League	Gms.	G	A	Pts.	PIM	+/-	PP	SH	Gms.	G	A	Pts.	PIM
88-89—Litvinov	Czech.	7	3	2	5	0	...	...	...	—	—	—	—	—
89-90—Litvinov	Czech.	39	11	10	21	20	...	...	...	—	—	—	—	—
90-91—Litvinov	Czech.	56	26	26	52	38	...	...	...	—	—	—	—	—
91-92—Litvinov	Czech.	43	12	31	43	34	...	...	...	—	—	—	—	—
—Czech. nat'l team	Int'l	8	5	8	13	8	...	...	...	—	—	—	—	—
—Czec. Olympic team	Int'l	8	5	8	13	8	...	...	...	—	—	—	—	—
92-93— Los Angeles	NHL	11	0	5	5	2	-3	0	0	—	—	—	—	—
—Phoenix	IHL	38	9	21	30	20	...	...	...	—	—	—	—	—
93-94— Phoenix	IHL	44	11	24	35	34	...	...	...	—	—	—	—	—
—Los Angeles	NHL	32	9	10	19	10	7	0	0	—	—	—	—	—
94-95— Chemo. Litvinov	Czech Rep.	16	4	19	23	28	...	...	...	—	—	—	—	—
—Los Angeles	NHL	36	4	8	12	4	-7	0	0	—	—	—	—	—
95-96— Los Angeles	NHL	68	6	16	22	10	-15	0	2	—	—	—	—	—
96-97— Sparta Praha	Czech Rep.	38	14	27	41	30	...	...	...	5	1	2	3	4
NHL totals (4 years)		147	19	39	58	26	-18	0	2					

LANGDON, DARREN   LW   RANGERS

PERSONAL: Born January 8, 1971, in Deer Lake, Nfld. ... 6-1/205. ... Shoots left.
TRANSACTIONS/CAREER NOTES: Signed as free agent by New York Rangers (August 16, 1993). ... Suspended three games by NHL for abuse of an official in preseason game (September 23, 1995). ... Sprained right knee (December 13, 1996); missed 13 games. ... Suspended two games by NHL for initiating an altercation (March 7, 1997).

		REGULAR SEASON							PLAYOFFS				
Season Team	League	Gms.	G	A	Pts.	PIM	+/-	PP	SH	Gms.	G	A	Pts.	PIM
91-92— Summerside	MJHL	44	34	49	83	441	...	...	...	—	—	—	—	—
92-93— Binghamton	AHL	18	3	4	7	115	...	...	...	8	0	1	1	14
—Dayton	ECHL	54	23	22	45	429	...	...	...	3	0	1	1	40
93-94— Binghamton	AHL	54	2	7	9	327	...	...	...	11	1	3	4	*84
94-95— Binghamton	AHL	55	6	14	20	296	...	...	...	11	1	3	4	84
—New York Rangers	NHL	18	1	1	2	62	0	0	0	—	—	—	—	—
95-96— New York Rangers	NHL	64	7	4	11	175	2	0	0	2	0	0	0	0
—Binghamton	AHL	1	0	0	0	12	...	...	...	—	—	—	—	—
96-97— New York Rangers	NHL	60	3	6	9	195	-1	0	0	10	0	0	0	2
NHL totals (3 years)		142	11	11	22	432	1	0	0	12	0	0	0	2

LANGENBRUNNER, JAMIE   C   STARS

PERSONAL: Born April 21, 1975, in Edmonton. ... 5-11/185. ... Shoots right. ... Name pronounced LANG-ihn-BROO-nuhr.
HIGH SCHOOL: Cloquet (Minn.).

TRANSACTIONS/CAREER NOTES: Selected by Dallas Stars in second round (second Stars pick, 35th overall) of NHL entry draft (June 26, 1993). ... Suffered back spasms (February 21, 1997); missed one game.

		REGULAR SEASON								PLAYOFFS				
Season Team	League	Gms.	G	A	Pts.	PIM	+/-	PP	SH	Gms.	G	A	Pts.	PIM
90-91— Cloquet	Minn. H.S.	20	6	16	22	8	...	...	...	—	—	—	—	—
91-92— Cloquet	Minn. H.S.	23	16	23	39	24	...	...	...	—	—	—	—	—
92-93— Cloquet	Minn. H.S.	27	27	62	89	18	...	...	...	—	—	—	—	—
93-94— Peterborough	OHL	62	33	58	91	53	...	...	...	7	4	6	10	2
94-95— Peterborough	OHL	62	42	57	99	84	...	...	...	11	8	14	22	12
— Dallas	NHL	2	0	0	0	2	0	0	0	—	—	—	—	—
— Kalamazoo	IHL	—	—	—	—	—	...	...	...	11	1	3	4	2
95-96— Michigan	IHL	59	25	40	65	129	...	...	...	10	3	10	13	8
— Dallas	NHL	12	2	2	4	6	-2	1	0	—	—	—	—	—
96-97— Dallas	NHL	76	13	26	39	51	-2	3	0	5	1	1	2	14
NHL totals (3 years)		90	15	28	43	59	-4	4	0	5	1	1	2	14

LANGKOW, DAYMOND   C   LIGHTNING

PERSONAL: Born September 27, 1976, in Edmonton. ... 5-10/170. ... Shoots left. ... Name pronounced LANG-kow.
TRANSACTIONS/CAREER NOTES: Selected by Tampa Bay Lightning in first round (first Lightning pick, fifth overall) of NHL entry draft (July 8, 1995).
HONORS: Won Bob Clarke Trophy (1994-95). ... Named to Can.HL All-Star first team (1994-95). ... Named to WHL (West) All-Star first team (1994-95). ... Named to WHL (West) All-Star second team (1995-96).

		REGULAR SEASON								PLAYOFFS				
Season Team	League	Gms.	G	A	Pts.	PIM	+/-	PP	SH	Gms.	G	A	Pts.	PIM
91-92— Tri-City	WHL	1	0	0	0	0	...	...	...	4	2	2	4	15
92-93— Tri-City	WHL	65	22	42	64	96	...	...	...	4	1	0	1	4
93-94— Tri-City	WHL	61	40	43	83	174	...	...	...	4	2	2	4	15
94-95— Tri-City	WHL	72	67	73	140	142	...	...	...	17	12	15	27	52
95-96— Tampa Bay	NHL	4	0	1	1	0	-1	0	0	—	—	—	—	—
— Tri-City	WHL	48	30	61	91	103	...	...	...	11	14	13	27	20
96-97— Adirondack	AHL	2	1	1	2	0	...	...	...	—	—	—	—	—
— Tampa Bay	NHL	79	15	13	28	35	1	3	1	—	—	—	—	—
NHL totals (2 years)		83	15	14	29	35	0	3	1	—	—	—	—	—

LANGKOW, SCOTT   G   COYOTES

PERSONAL: Born April 21, 1975, in Edmonton. ... 5-11/190. ... Catches left. ... Name pronounced LANG-koh.
HIGH SCHOOL: Aloha (Beaverton, Ore.).
TRANSACTIONS/CAREER NOTES: Selected by Winnipeg Jets in second round (second Jets pick, 31st overall) of NHL entry draft (June 26, 1993). ... Jets franchise moved to Phoenix and renamed Coyotes for 1996-97 season; NHL approved move on January 18, 1996.
HONORS: Named to WHL (West) All-Star second team (1993-94 and 1994-95). ... Won Harry (Hap) Holmes Memorial Trophy (1995-96).

		REGULAR SEASON								PLAYOFFS					
Season Team	League	Gms.	Min	W	L	T	GA	SO	Avg.	Gms.	Min.	W	L	GA	SO	Avg.
91-92— Portland	WHL	1	33	0	0	0	2	0	3.64	—	—	—	—	—	—	—
92-93— Portland	WHL	34	2064	24	8	2	119	2	3.46	9	535	6	3	31	0	3.48
93-94— Portland	WHL	39	2302	27	9	1	121	2	3.15	10	600	6	4	34	0	3.40
94-95— Portland	WHL	63	3638	20	36	5	240	1	3.96	8	510	3	5	30	0	3.53
95-96— Springfield	AHL	39	2329	18	15	6	116	3	2.99	7	392	4	2	23	0	3.52
— Winnipeg	NHL	1	6	0	0	0	0	0	0.00	—	—	—	—	—	—	—
96-97— Springfield	AHL	33	1929	15	9	7	85	0	2.64							
NHL totals (1 year)		1	6	0	0	0	0	0	0.00							

LANK, JEFF   D   FLYERS

PERSONAL: Born March 1, 1975, in Indianhead, Sask. ... 6-3/185. ... Shoots left.
HIGH SCHOOL: Carlton Comprehensive (Prince Albert, Sask.).
TRANSACTIONS/CAREER NOTES: Selected by Montreal Canadiens in fifth round (sixth Canadiens pick, 113th overall) of NHL entry draft (June 26, 1993). ... Returned to draft pool by Canadiens and selected by Philadelphia Flyers in ninth round (ninth Flyers pick, 230th overall) of entry draft (July 8, 1995).

		REGULAR SEASON								PLAYOFFS				
Season Team	League	Gms.	G	A	Pts.	PIM	+/-	PP	SH	Gms.	G	A	Pts.	PIM
90-91— Columbia Valley	KIJHL	36	4	28	32	40	...	...	...	—	—	—	—	—
91-92— Prince Albert	WHL	56	2	8	10	26	...	...	...	9	0	0	0	2
92-93— Prince Albert	WHL	63	1	11	12	60	...	...	...	—	—	—	—	—
93-94— Prince Albert	WHL	72	9	38	47	62	...	...	...	—	—	—	—	—
94-95— Prince Albert	WHL	68	12	25	37	60	...	...	...	13	2	10	12	8
95-96— Hershey	AHL	72	7	13	20	70	...	...	...	5	0	0	0	8
96-97— Philadelphia	AHL	44	2	12	14	49	...	...	...	7	2	1	3	4

LAPERRIERE, DAN   D   CAPITALS

PERSONAL: Born March 28, 1969, in Laval, Que. ... 6-1/180. ... Shoots left. ... Full name: Daniel Jacques Laperriere. ... Name pronounced luh-PAIR-ee-AIR. ... Son of Jacques Laperriere, assistant coach, Montreal Canadiens and Hall of Fame defenseman, Canadiens (1962-63 through 1973-74).

COLLEGE: St. Lawrence (N.Y.).

TRANSACTIONS/CAREER NOTES: Selected by St. Louis Blues in fifth round (fourth Blues pick, 93rd overall) of NHL entry draft (June 17, 1989). ... Suffered from the flu (October 9, 1992); missed two games. ... Traded by Blues with ninth-round pick (D Libor Zabransky) in 1995 draft to Ottawa Senators for ninth-round pick (RW Eric Kasminski) in 1995 draft (April 7, 1995). ... Signed as free agent by Washington Capitals (July 1, 1996).

HONORS: Named to ECAC All-Star second team (1990-91). ... Named to NCAA All-America East first team (1991-92). ... Named ECAC Player of the Year (1991-92). ... Named ECAC Playoff Most Valuable Player (1991-92). ... Named to ECAC All-Star first team (1991-92).

		REGULAR SEASON								PLAYOFFS				
Season Team	League	Gms.	G	A	Pts.	PIM	+/-	PP	SH	Gms.	G	A	Pts.	PIM
88-89— St. Lawrence Univ......	ECAC	34	1	11	12	14	...	...	...	—	—	—	—	—
89-90— St. Lawrence Univ......	ECAC	29	6	19	25	16	...	...	...	—	—	—	—	—
90-91— St. Lawrence Univ......	ECAC	34	7	32	39	18	...	...	...	—	—	—	—	—
91-92— St. Lawrence Univ......	ECAC	32	8	*45	53	36	...	...	...	—	—	—	—	—
92-93— St. Louis	NHL	5	0	1	1	0	-3	0	0	—	—	—	—	—
— Peoria	IHL	54	4	20	24	28	...	...	...	—	—	—	—	—
93-94— Peoria	IHL	56	10	37	47	16	...	...	...	6	0	2	2	2
— St. Louis	NHL	20	1	3	4	8	-1	1	0	—	—	—	—	—
94-95— Peoria	IHL	65	19	33	52	42	...	...	...	—	—	—	—	—
— St. Louis	NHL	4	0	0	0	15	1	0	0	—	—	—	—	—
— Ottawa	NHL	13	1	1	2	0	-4	1	0	—	—	—	—	—
95-96— Prin. Edward Island ...	AHL	15	2	7	9	4	...	...	...	—	—	—	—	—
— Atlanta	IHL	15	4	9	13	4	...	...	...	—	—	—	—	—
— Kansas City...............	IHL	23	2	6	8	11	...	...	...	5	0	1	1	0
— Ottawa	NHL	6	0	0	0	4	2	0	0	—	—	—	—	—
96-97— Portland..................	AHL	69	14	26	40	33	...	...	...	5	0	2	2	2
NHL totals (4 years)		48	2	5	7	27	-5	2	0					

LAPERRIERE, IAN   C   KINGS

PERSONAL: Born January 19, 1974, in Montreal. ... 6-1/195. ... Shoots right. ... Name pronounced EE-ihn luh-PAIR-ee-AIR.

TRANSACTIONS/CAREER NOTES: Selected by St. Louis Blues in seventh round (sixth Blues pick, 158th overall) of NHL entry draft (June 20, 1992). ... Suffered concussion (March 26, 1995); missed three games. ... Traded by Blues to New York Rangers for LW Stephane Matteau (December 28, 1995). ... Traded by Rangers with C Ray Ferraro, C Nathan Lafayette, D Matis Norstrom and fourth-round pick (D Sean Blanchard) in 1997 draft to Los Angeles Kings for RW Shane Churla, LW Jari Kurri and D/RW Marty McSorley (March 14, 1996). ... Sprained left shoulder (March 16, 1996); missed two games. ... Strained shoulder (October 29, 1996); missed three games. ... Strained hip flexor (February 1, 1997); missed three games. ... Suffered concussion (February 25, 1997); missed two games. ... Underwent shoulder surgery (March 17, 1997); missed final 11 games of regular season.

HONORS: Named to QMJHL All-Star second team (1992-93).

		REGULAR SEASON								PLAYOFFS				
Season Team	League	Gms.	G	A	Pts.	PIM	+/-	PP	SH	Gms.	G	A	Pts.	PIM
90-91— Drummondville	QMJHL	65	19	29	48	117	...	...	...	—	—	—	—	—
91-92— Drummondville	QMJHL	70	28	49	77	160	...	...	...	—	—	—	—	—
92-93— Drummondville	QMJHL	60	44	†96	140	188	...	...	...	10	6	13	19	20
93-94— Drummondville	QMJHL	62	41	72	113	150	...	...	...	9	4	6	10	35
— St. Louis	NHL	1	0	0	0	0	0	0	0	—	—	—	—	—
— Peoria	IHL	—	—	—	—	—				5	1	3	4	2
94-95— Peoria	IHL	51	16	32	48	111	...	...	...	—	—	—	—	—
— St. Louis	NHL	37	13	14	27	85	12	1	0	7	0	4	4	21
95-96— St. Louis	NHL	33	3	6	9	87	-4	1	0	—	—	—	—	—
— Worcester	AHL	3	2	1	3	22	...	...	...	—	—	—	—	—
— New York Rangers..........	NHL	28	1	2	3	53	-5	0	0	—	—	—	—	—
— Los Angeles	NHL	10	2	3	5	15	-2	0	0	—	—	—	—	—
96-97— Los Angeles	NHL	62	8	15	23	102	-25	0	1	—	—	—	—	—
NHL totals (5 years)		171	27	40	67	342	-24	2	1	7	0	4	4	21

LAPLANTE, DARRYL   C   RED WINGS

PERSONAL: Born March 28, 1977, in Calgary. ... 6-1/177. ... Shoots right. ... Name pronounced luh-PLANT.

COLLEGE: Vanier (Edson, Alta.).

TRANSACTIONS/CAREER NOTES: Selected by Detroit Red Wings in third round (third Red Wings pick, 58th overall) of NHL entry draft (July 8, 1995).

		REGULAR SEASON								PLAYOFFS				
Season Team	League	Gms.	G	A	Pts.	PIM	+/-	PP	SH	Gms.	G	A	Pts.	PIM
94-95— Moose Jaw	WHL	71	22	24	46	66	...	...	...	10	2	2	4	7
95-96— Moose Jaw	WHL	72	42	40	82	76	...	...	...	—	—	—	—	—
96-97— Moose Jaw	WHL	69	38	42	80	79	...	...	...	12	2	4	6	15

LAPOINTE, CLAUDE   C   ISLANDERS

PERSONAL: Born October 11, 1968, in Lachine, Que. ... 5-9/181. ... Shoots left. ... Name pronounced KLOHD luh-pwah.

TRANSACTIONS/CAREER NOTES: Traded by Trois-Rivieres Draveurs with G Alain Dubeau and third-round pick (D Patrice Brisebois) in QMJHL draft to Laval Titans for D Raymond Saumier, LW Mike Gober, D Eric Gobeil and second-round pick (D Eric Charron) in QMJHL draft (May 1987). ... Selected by Quebec Nordiques in 12th round (12th Nordiques pick, 234th overall) of NHL entry draft (June 11, 1988). ... Tore groin muscle (February 9, 1991). ... Injured groin (October 23, 1991); missed one game. ... Injured back in training camp (September 1992); missed five games. ... Bruised hip (April 6, 1993); missed two games. ... Sprained left knee (October 18, 1993); missed 13 games. ... Sprained back (February 1, 1994); missed nine games. ... Injured back (March 19, 1994); missed three games. ... Suffered lower back pain (January 21, 1995); missed 16 games. ... Suffered from the flu (April 16, 1995); missed one game. ... Injured hip (April 30, 1995); missed one game.

... Nordiques franchise moved to Colorado and renamed Avalanche for 1995-96 season (June 21, 1995). ... Traded by Avalanche to Calgary Flames for seventh-round pick (C Samuel Pahlsson) in 1996 draft (November 1, 1995). ... Pulled groin (December 20, 1995); missed one game. ... Reinjured groin (December 27, 1995); missed three games. ... Reinjured groin (January 5, 1996); missed three games. ... Injured hip (January 26, 1996); missed 17 games. ... Signed as free agent by New York Islanders (August 22, 1996). ... Hyperextended ankle (January 2, 1997); missed one game. ... Suffered sore ankle (January 25, 1997); missed one game.

Season Team	League	REGULAR SEASON								PLAYOFFS				
		Gms.	G	A	Pts.	PIM	+/-	PP	SH	Gms.	G	A	Pts.	PIM
85-86— Trois-Rivieres............	QMJHL	72	19	38	57	74	...	...	...	—	—	—	—	—
86-87— Trois-Rivieres............	QMJHL	70	47	57	104	123	...	...	...	—	—	—	—	—
87-88— Laval	QMJHL	69	37	83	120	143	...	...	...	13	2	17	19	53
88-89— Laval	QMJHL	63	32	72	104	158	...	...	...	17	5	14	19	66
89-90— Halifax......................	AHL	63	18	19	37	51	...	...	...	6	1	1	2	34
90-91— Quebec.....................	NHL	13	2	2	4	4	3	0	0	—	—	—	—	—
— Halifax......................	AHL	43	17	17	34	46	...	...	...	—	—	—	—	—
91-92— Quebec.....................	NHL	78	13	20	33	86	-8	0	2	—	—	—	—	—
92-93— Quebec.....................	NHL	74	10	26	36	98	5	0	0	6	2	4	6	8
93-94— Quebec.....................	NHL	59	11	17	28	70	2	1	1	—	—	—	—	—
94-95— Quebec.....................	NHL	29	4	8	12	41	5	0	0	5	0	0	0	8
95-96— Colorado	NHL	3	0	0	0	0	-1	0	0	—	—	—	—	—
— Calgary	NHL	32	4	5	9	20	2	0	2	2	0	0	0	0
— Saint John	AHL	12	5	3	8	10	...	...	...	—	—	—	—	—
96-97— Utah	IHL	9	7	6	13	14	...	...	...	—	—	—	—	—
— New York Islanders....	NHL	73	13	5	18	49	-12	0	3	—	—	—	—	—
NHL totals (7 years)		361	57	83	140	368	-4	1	8	13	2	4	6	16

LAPOINTE, MARTIN   RW   RED WINGS

PERSONAL: Born September 12, 1973, in Lachine, Que. ... 5-11/200. ... Shoots right. ... Name pronounced MAHR-tai luh-POYNT.
TRANSACTIONS/CAREER NOTES: Selected by Detroit Red Wings in first round (first Red Wings pick, 10th overall) of NHL entry draft (June 22, 1991). ... Fractured wrist (October 9, 1991); missed 22 games. ... Injured left knee (February 29, 1996); missed eight games. ... Injured leg (April 10, 1996); missed two games. ... Fractured finger (December 1, 1996); missed four games.
HONORS: Won Michel Bergeron Trophy (1989-90). ... Named to QMJHL All-Star first team (1989-90 and 1992-93). ... Named to QMJHL All-Star second team (1990-91).
MISCELLANEOUS: Member of Stanley Cup championship team (1997).

Season Team	League	REGULAR SEASON								PLAYOFFS				
		Gms.	G	A	Pts.	PIM	+/-	PP	SH	Gms.	G	A	Pts.	PIM
89-90— Laval	QMJHL	65	42	54	96	77	...	...	...	14	8	17	25	54
90-91— Laval	QMJHL	64	44	54	98	66	...	...	...	13	7	14	21	26
91-92— Detroit......................	NHL	4	0	1	1	5	2	0	0	3	0	1	1	4
— Laval	QMJHL	31	25	30	55	84	...	...	...	10	4	10	14	32
— Adirondack..............	AHL	—	—	—	—	—	...	...	...	8	2	2	4	4
92-93— Adirondack..............	AHL	8	1	2	3	9	...	...	...	—	—	—	—	—
— Detroit......................	NHL	3	0	0	0	0	-2	0	0	—	—	—	—	—
— Laval	QMJHL	35	38	51	89	41	...	...	...	13	*13	*17	*30	22
93-94— Adirondack..............	AHL	28	25	21	46	47	...	...	...	4	1	1	2	8
— Detroit......................	NHL	50	8	8	16	55	7	2	0	4	0	0	0	6
94-95— Adirondack..............	AHL	39	29	16	45	80	...	...	...	—	—	—	—	—
— Detroit......................	NHL	39	4	6	10	73	1	0	0	2	0	1	1	8
95-96— Detroit......................	NHL	58	6	3	9	93	0	1	0	11	1	2	3	12
96-97— Detroit......................	NHL	78	16	17	33	167	-14	5	1	20	4	8	12	60
NHL totals (6 years)		232	34	35	69	393	-6	8	1	40	5	12	17	90

LARAQUE, GEORGES   RW   OILERS

PERSONAL: Born December 7, 1976, in Montreal. ... 6-3/235. ... Shoots right. ... Name pronounced luh-RAHK.
TRANSACTIONS/CAREER NOTES: Selected by Edmonton Oilers in second round (second Oilers pick, 31st overall) of NHL entry draft (July 8, 1995).

Season Team	League	REGULAR SEASON								PLAYOFFS				
		Gms.	G	A	Pts.	PIM	+/-	PP	SH	Gms.	G	A	Pts.	PIM
93-94— St. Jean....................	QMJHL	70	11	11	22	142	...	...	...	4	0	0	0	7
94-95— St. Jean....................	QMJHL	62	19	22	41	259	...	...	...	7	1	1	2	42
95-96— Laval	QMJHL	11	8	13	21	76	...	...	...	—	—	—	—	—
— St. Hyacinthe	QMJHL	8	3	4	7	59	...	...	...	—	—	—	—	—
— Granby	QMJHL	22	9	7	16	125	...	...	...	18	7	6	13	104
96-97— Hamilton...................	AHL	73	14	20	34	179	...	...	...	15	1	3	4	12

LARIONOV, IGOR   C   RED WINGS

PERSONAL: Born December 3, 1960, in Voskresensk, U.S.S.R. ... 5-9/170. ... Shoots left. ... Name pronounced EE-gohr LAIR-ee-AH-nahf.
TRANSACTIONS/CAREER NOTES: Selected by Vancouver Canucks in 11th round (11th Canucks pick, 214th overall) of NHL entry draft (June 15, 1985). ... Injured groin (October 25, 1990); missed four games. ... Sprained ankle (January 8, 1991). ... Reinjured ankle (January 30, 1991); missed seven games. ... Signed to play with Lugano of Switzerland (July 14, 1992). ... Selected by San Jose Sharks in NHL waiver draft (October 4, 1992). ... Injured shoulder (September 30, 1993); missed four games. ... Reinjured shoulder (October 16, 1993); missed four games. ... Suffered from the flu (November 7, 1993); missed two games. ... Sprained knee (December 12, 1993); missed 10 games. ... Suffered from respiratory infection (February 11, 1994); missed one game. ... Suffered from the flu (February 26, 1994); missed two games. ... Injured groin (February 15, 1995); missed three games. ... Injured foot (February 26, 1995); missed 12 games. ... Traded by Sharks with a conditional pick in 1998 draft to Detroit Red Wings for RW Ray Sheppard (October 25, 1995). ... Suffered from the flu (December 29, 1995); missed two games. ... Pulled groin (October 15, 1996); missed four games. ... Bruised wrist (October 30, 1996); missed seven games. ...

Suffered from the flu (March 21, 1997); missed one game. ... Bruised back (April 8, 1997); missed three games.
HONORS: Named to Soviet League All-Star team (1982-83 and 1985-86 through 1987-88). ... Won Soviet Player of the Year Award (1987-88).
STATISTICAL PLATEAUS: Three-goal games: 1991-92 (2), 1993-94 (2). Total: 4.
MISCELLANEOUS: Member of Stanley Cup championship team (1997). ... Member of gold-medal-winning U.S.S.R. Olympic team (1984 and 1988). ... Scored on a penalty shot (vs. Arturs Irbe, November 22, 1995).

		REGULAR SEASON								PLAYOFFS				
Season Team	League	Gms.	G	A	Pts.	PIM	+/-	PP	SH	Gms.	G	A	Pts.	PIM
77-78— Khimik Voskresensk ..	USSR	6	3	0	3	4	...	...	...	—	—	—	—	—
78-79— Khimik Voskresensk ..	USSR	25	3	4	7	12	...	...	...	—	—	—	—	—
79-80— Khimik Voskresensk ..	USSR	42	11	7	18	24	...	...	...	—	—	—	—	—
80-81— Khimik Voskresensk ..	USSR	56	22	23	45	36	...	...	...	—	—	—	—	—
81-82— CSKA Moscow..........	USSR	46	31	22	53	6	...	...	...	—	—	—	—	—
82-83— CSKA Moscow..........	USSR	44	20	19	39	20	...	...	...	—	—	—	—	—
83-84— CSKA Moscow..........	USSR	43	15	26	41	30	...	...	...	—	—	—	—	—
— Sov. Olympic team.....	Int'l	7	1	4	5	6	...	...	...	—	—	—	—	—
84-85— CSKA Moscow..........	USSR	40	18	28	46	20	...	...	...	—	—	—	—	—
85-86— CSKA Moscow..........	USSR	40	21	31	52	33	...	...	...	—	—	—	—	—
86-87— CSKA Moscow..........	USSR	39	20	26	46	34	...	...	...	—	—	—	—	—
87-88— CSKA Moscow..........	USSR	51	25	32	57	54	...	...	...	—	—	—	—	—
— Sov. Olympic team.....	Int'l	8	4	9	13	4	...	...	...	—	—	—	—	—
88-89— CSKA Moscow..........	USSR	31	15	12	27	22	...	...	...	—	—	—	—	—
89-90— Vancouver................	NHL	74	17	27	44	20	-5	8	0	—	—	—	—	—
90-91— Vancouver................	NHL	64	13	21	34	14	-3	1	1	6	1	0	1	6
91-92— Vancouver................	NHL	72	21	44	65	54	7	10	3	13	3	7	10	4
92-93— Lugano....................	Switzerland	24	10	19	29	44	...	...	...	—	—	—	—	—
93-94— San Jose.................	NHL	60	18	38	56	40	20	3	2	14	5	13	18	10
94-95— San Jose.................	NHL	33	4	20	24	14	-3	0	0	11	1	8	9	2
95-96— San Jose.................	NHL	4	1	1	2	0	-6	1	0	—	—	—	—	—
— Detroit.......................	NHL	69	21	50	71	34	37	9	1	19	6	7	13	6
96-97— Detroit.......................	NHL	64	12	42	54	26	31	2	1	20	4	8	12	8
NHL totals (7 years)		440	107	243	350	202	78	34	8	83	20	43	63	36

LARIVEE, FRANCIS   G   MAPLE LEAFS

PERSONAL: Born November 8, 1977, in Verdun, Que. ... 6-2/198. ... Catches left.
TRANSACTIONS/CAREER NOTES: Selected by Toronto Maple Leafs in second round (second Maple Leafs pick, 50th overall) of NHL entry draft (June 22, 1996).

		REGULAR SEASON								PLAYOFFS					
Season Team	League	Gms.	Min	W	L	T	GA	SO	Avg.	Gms.	Min.	W	L	GA	SO	Avg.
93-94— Val-d'Or	QMJHL	36	1706	5	20	1	162	3	5.70	—	—	—	—	—	—	—
94-95— Val-d'Or	QMJHL	38	1795	9	21	1	132	0	4.41	—	—	—	—	—	—	—
95-96— Val-d'Or	QMJII IL	22	1162	12	4	2	73	0	3.77	—	—	—	—	—	—	—
— Laval..............................	QMJHL	39	2085	9	24	1	178	0	5.12	—	—	—	—	—	—	—
96-97— Laval..........................	QMJHL	21	1069	6	11	1	79	1	4.44	—	—	—	—	—	—	—
— Granby...........................	QMJHL	3	135	2	0	0	7	0	3.11	1	1	0	0	1	0	60.00
— St. John's	AHL	4	244	3	1	0	9	0	2.21	2	1	0	0	0	0	0.00

LAROCQUE, MARIO   D   LIGHTNING

PERSONAL: Born April 24, 1978, in Montreal. ... 6-3/172. ... Shoots left.
TRANSACTIONS/CAREER NOTES: Selected by Tampa Bay Lightning in first round (first Lightning pick, 16th overall) of NHL entry draft (June 22, 1996).
HONORS: Named to QMJHL All-Rookie team (1995-96).

		REGULAR SEASON								PLAYOFFS				
Season Team	League	Gms.	G	A	Pts.	PIM	+/-	PP	SH	Gms.	G	A	Pts.	PIM
95-96— Hull	QMJHL	68	7	19	26	196	...	...	...	14	2	5	7	16
96-97— Hull	QMJHL	64	13	37	50	160	...	...	...	14	2	5	7	34

LAROUCHE, STEVE   C   KINGS

PERSONAL: Born April 14, 1971, in Rouyn, Que. ... 6-0/184. ... Shoots right. ... Name pronounced luh-ROOSH.
TRANSACTIONS/CAREER NOTES: Selected by Montreal Canadiens in second round (third Canadiens pick, 41st overall) of NHL entry draft (June 17, 1989). ... Injured shoulder (October 8, 1989). ... QMJHL rights traded by Trois-Rivieres Draveurs with C Sabastien Parent and sixth-round pick in 1990 QMJHL draft to Chicoutimi Sagueneens for Paul Brosseau and Jasmin Ouellet (May 26, 1990). ... Tore left knee ligaments (October 5, 1990); missed two months. ... Sent home by Chicoutimi coach Joe Canale for indifferent play (January 1991). ... Signed as free agent by Ottawa Senators (September 3, 1994). ... Traded by Senators to New York Rangers for RW Jean-Yves Roy (October 6, 1995). ... Traded by Rangers to Los Angeles Kings for D Chris Snell (January 14, 1996).
HONORS: Named to QMJHL All-Star second team (1989-90). ... Won Les Cunningham Plaque (1994-95). ... Won Fred Hunt Memorial Award (1994-95). ... Named to AHL All-Star first team (1994-95). ... Named to IHL All-Star first team (1996-97).
STATISTICAL PLATEAUS: Three-goal games: 1994-95 (1).

		REGULAR SEASON								PLAYOFFS				
Season Team	League	Gms.	G	A	Pts.	PIM	+/-	PP	SH	Gms.	G	A	Pts.	PIM
87-88— Trois-Rivieres.............	QMJHL	66	11	29	40	25	...	...	...	—	—	—	—	—
88-89— Trois-Rivieres.............	QMJHL	70	51	102	153	53	...	...	...	4	4	2	6	6
89-90— Trois-Rivieres.............	QMJHL	60	55	90	145	40	...	...	...	7	3	5	8	8
90-91— Chicoutimi................	QMJHL	45	35	41	76	64	...	...	...	17	†13	*20	*33	20
91-92— Fredericton.................	AHL	74	21	35	56	41	...	...	...	7	1	0	1	0

Season Team	League	REGULAR SEASON Gms.	G	A	Pts.	PIM	+/-	PP	SH	PLAYOFFS Gms.	G	A	Pts.	PIM
92-93— Fredericton...............	AHL	77	27	65	92	52	...	...	...	5	2	5	7	6
93-94— Atlanta...................	IHL	80	43	53	96	73	...	...	...	14	*16	10	*26	16
94-95— Prin. Edward Island ...	AHL	70	*53	48	101	54	...	...	...	2	1	0	1	0
— Ottawa	NHL	18	8	7	15	6	-5	2	0	—	—	—	—	—
95-96— Binghamton	AHL	39	20	46	66	47	...	...	...	—	—	—	—	—
— New York Rangers.....	NHL	1	0	0	0	0	0	0	0	—	—	—	—	—
— Phoenix.................	IHL	33	19	17	36	14	...	...	...	4	0	1	1	8
— Los Angeles...............	NHL	7	1	2	3	4	0	1	0	—	—	—	—	—
96-97— Quebec...............	IHL	79	49	53	102	78	...	...	...	9	3	10	13	18
NHL totals (3 years)		26	9	9	18	10	-5	3	0					

LAUER, BRAD   LW   PENGUINS

PERSONAL: Born October 27, 1966, in Humboldt, Sask. ... 6-0/195. ... Shoots left. ... Name pronounced LOW-uhr.

TRANSACTIONS/CAREER NOTES: Selected by New York Islanders as underage junior in second round (third Islanders pick, 34th overall) of NHL entry draft (June 15, 1985). ... Fractured left kneecap (October 1988). ... Reinjured left knee (March 1989). ... Strained abdomen (February 1990). ... Bruised right quadricep (April 1990). ... Traded by Islanders with C Brent Sutter to Chicago Blackhawks for C Adam Creighton and LW Steve Thomas (October 25, 1991). ... Signed as free agent by Las Vegas Thunder (July 19, 1993). ... Signed as free agent by Ottawa Senators (January 1, 1994). ... Injured hip flexor (March 13, 1994); missed three games. ... Suspended by Las Vegas Thunder for failing to report from Senators (March 26, 1994). ... Signed as free agent by Pittsburgh Penguins (September 6, 1994).

HONORS: Named to IHL All-Star first team (1992-93).

Season Team	League	REGULAR SEASON Gms.	G	A	Pts.	PIM	+/-	PP	SH	PLAYOFFS Gms.	G	A	Pts.	PIM
83-84— Regina	WHL	60	5	7	12	51	...	...	...	16	0	1	1	24
84-85— Regina	WHL	72	33	46	79	57	...	...	...	8	6	6	12	9
85-86— Regina	WHL	57	36	38	74	69	...	...	...	10	4	5	9	2
86-87— New York Islanders....	NHL	61	7	14	21	65	...	...	...	6	2	0	2	4
87-88— New York Islanders....	NHL	69	17	18	35	67	...	...	...	5	3	1	4	4
88-89— Springfield	AHL	8	1	5	6	0	...	...	...	—	—	—	—	—
— New York Islanders....	NHL	14	3	2	5	2	...	...	...	—	—	—	—	—
89-90— New York Islanders....	NHL	63	6	18	24	19	5	0	0	4	0	2	2	10
— Springfield	AHL	7	4	2	6	0	...	...	...	—	—	—	—	—
90-91— New York Islanders....	NHL	44	4	8	12	45	-6	0	1	—	—	—	—	—
— Capital District	AHL	11	5	11	16	14	...	...	...	—	—	—	—	—
91-92— New York Islanders....	NHL	8	1	0	1	2	-2	0	1	—	—	—	—	—
— Indianapolis	IHL	57	24	30	54	46	...	...	...	—	—	—	—	—
— Chicago	NHL	6	0	0	0	4	-3	0	0	7	1	1	2	2
92-93— Indianapolis	IHL	62	*50	41	91	80	...	...	...	5	3	1	4	6
— Chicago	NHL	7	0	1	1	2	-1	0	0	—	—	—	—	—
93-94— Ottawa	NHL	30	2	5	7	6	-15	0	1	—	—	—	—	—
— Las Vegas	IHL	32	21	21	42	30	...	...	...	4	1	0	1	2
94-95— Cleveland	IHL	51	32	27	59	48	...	...	...	4	4	2	6	6
95-96— Cleveland	IHL	53	25	27	52	44	...	...	...	—	—	—	—	—
— Pittsburgh................	NHL	21	4	1	5	6	-5	1	0	12	1	1	2	4
96-97— Cleveland	IHL	64	27	21	48	61	...	...	...	14	4	6	10	8
NHL totals (10 years)		323	44	67	111	218	-27	1	3	34	7	5	12	24

LAUKKANEN, JANNE   D   SENATORS

PERSONAL: Born March 19, 1970, in Lahti, Finland. ... 6-0/180. ... Shoots left. ... Name pronounced YAH-nee LOW-kih-nehn.

TRANSACTIONS/CAREER NOTES: Selected by Quebec Nordiques in eighth round (eighth Nordiques pick, 156th overall) of NHL entry draft (June 22, 1991). ... Injured groin (April 14, 1995); missed four games. ... Reinjured groin (April 30, 1995); missed last game of season. ... Nordiques franchise moved to Colorado and renamed Avalanche for 1995-96 season (June 21, 1995). ... Traded by Avalanche to Ottawa Senators for LW Brad Larsen (January 25, 1996). ... Injured hip flexor during 1995-96 season; missed five games. ... Sprained left knee (March 25, 1996); missed two games. ... Bruised finger (November 15, 1996); missed one game. ... Suffered from the flu (December 10, 1996); missed two games. ... Suffered from the flu (March 17, 1997); missed one game. ... Injured knee (March 25, 1997); missed two games.

MISCELLANEOUS: Member of bronze-medal-winning Finnish Olympic team (1994).

Season Team	League	REGULAR SEASON Gms.	G	A	Pts.	PIM	+/-	PP	SH	PLAYOFFS Gms.	G	A	Pts.	PIM
89-90— Ilves Tampere	Finland	39	5	6	11	10	...	...	...	—	—	—	—	—
90-91— Reipas......................	Finland	44	8	14	22	56	...	...	...	—	—	—	—	—
91-92— Helsinki HPK	Finland	43	5	14	19	62	...	...	...	—	—	—	—	—
— Fin. Olympic team......	Int'l	8	0	1	1	6	...	...	...	—	—	—	—	—
92-93— HPK Hameenlinna......	Finland	47	8	21	29	76	...	...	...	12	1	4	5	10
93-94— HPK Hameenlinna......	Finland	48	5	24	29	46	...	...	...	—	—	—	—	—
— Fin. Olympic team......	Int'l	8	0	2	2	12	...	...	...	—	—	—	—	—
94-95— Cornwall....................	AHL	55	8	26	34	41	...	...	...	—	—	—	—	—
— Quebec....................	NHL	11	0	3	3	4	3	0	0	6	1	0	1	2
95-96— Cornwall....................	AHL	35	7	20	27	60	...	...	...	—	—	—	—	—
— Colorado	NHL	3	0	1	1	0	-1	1	0	—	—	—	—	—
— Ottawa	NHL	20	0	2	2	14	0	0	0	—	—	—	—	—
96-97— Ottawa	NHL	76	3	18	21	76	-14	2	0	7	0	1	1	6
NHL totals (3 years)		110	4	23	27	94	-12	3	0	13	1	1	2	8

LAUS, PAUL   D   PANTHERS

PERSONAL: Born September 26, 1970, in Beamsville, Ont. ... 6-1/216. ... Shoots right. ... Name pronounced LAWS.

TRANSACTIONS/CAREER NOTES: Suffered inflamed knuckles (September 1988). ... Suspended three playoff games by OHL for spearing (April 28, 1989). ... Selected by Pittsburgh Penguins in second round (second Penguins pick, 37th overall) of NHL entry draft (June 17, 1989).

... Selected by Florida Panthers in NHL expansion draft (June 24, 1993). ... Strained groin (February 19, 1995); missed six games. ... Separated left shoulder (April 16, 1995); missed two games. ... Bruised left ankle (October 16, 1996); missed two games. ... Sprained ankle (March 5, 1997); missed one game. ... Bruised hand (March 19, 1997); missed two games.
MISCELLANEOUS: Holds Florida Panthers all-time record for most penalty minutes (796).

Season Team	League	REGULAR SEASON								PLAYOFFS				
		Gms.	G	A	Pts.	PIM	+/-	PP	SH	Gms.	G	A	Pts.	PIM
86-87— St. Catharines Jr. B	OHA	40	1	8	9	56	...	...	...	—	—	—	—	—
87-88— Hamilton	OHL	56	1	9	10	171	...	...	...	14	0	0	0	28
88-89— Niagara Falls	OHL	49	1	10	11	225	...	...	...	15	0	5	5	56
89-90— Niagara Falls	OHL	60	13	35	48	231	...	...	...	16	6	16	22	71
90-91— Muskegon	IHL	35	3	4	7	103	...	...	...	4	0	0	0	13
—Albany......................	IHL	7	0	0	0	7	...	...	...	—	—	—	—	—
—Knoxville	ECHL	20	6	12	18	83	...	...	...	—	—	—	—	—
91-92— Muskegon	IHL	75	0	21	21	248	...	...	...	14	2	5	7	70
92-93— Cleveland	IHL	76	8	18	26	427	...	...	...	4	1	0	1	27
93-94— Florida....................	NHL	39	2	0	2	109	9	0	0	—	—	—	—	—
94-95— Florida....................	NHL	37	0	7	7	138	12	0	0	—	—	—	—	—
95-96— Florida....................	NHL	78	3	6	9	236	-2	0	0	21	2	6	8	*62
96-97— Florida....................	NHL	77	0	12	12	313	13	0	0	5	0	1	1	4
NHL totals (4 years)		231	5	25	30	796	32	0	0	26	2	7	9	66

LAWRENCE, MARK — RW — ISLANDERS

PERSONAL: Born January 27, 1972, in Burlington, Ont. ... 6-4/215. ... Shoots right.
TRANSACTIONS/CAREER NOTES: Selected by Dallas Stars in sixth round (fourth Stars pick, 118th overall) of NHL entry draft (June 22, 1991). ... Signed as free agent by New York Islanders (July 29, 1997).

Season Team	League	REGULAR SEASON								PLAYOFFS				
		Gms.	G	A	Pts.	PIM	+/-	PP	SH	Gms.	G	A	Pts.	PIM
87-88— Burlington Jr. B...........	OHA	40	11	12	23	90	...	...	...	—	—	—	—	—
88-89— Niagara Falls	OHL	63	9	27	36	142	...	...	...	—	—	—	—	—
89-90— Niagara Falls	OHL	54	15	18	33	123	...	...	...	16	2	5	7	42
90-91— Detroit...................	OHL	66	27	38	65	53	...	...	...	—	—	—	—	—
91-92— Detroit...................	OHL	28	19	26	45	54	...	...	...	—	—	—	—	—
—North Bay	OHL	24	13	14	27	21	...	...	...	21	*23	12	35	36
92-93— Dayton....................	ECHL	20	8	14	22	46	...	...	...	—	—	—	—	—
—Kalamazoo	IHL	57	22	13	35	47	...	...	...	—	—	—	—	—
93-94— Kalamazoo	IHL	64	17	20	37	90	...	...	...	—	—	—	—	—
94-95— Kalamazoo	IHL	77	21	29	50	92	...	...	...	16	3	7	10	28
—Dallas......................	NHL	2	0	0	0	0	0	0	0	—	—	—	—	—
95-96— Michigan..................	IHL	55	15	14	29	92	...	...	...	10	3	4	7	30
—Dallas......................	NHL	13	0	1	1	17	0	0	0	—	—	—	—	—
96-97— Michigan..................	IHL	68	15	21	36	141	...	...	...	4	0	0	0	18
NHL totals (2 years)		15	0	1	1	17	0	0	0					

LEACH, STEVE — RW — HURRICANES

PERSONAL: Born January 16, 1966, in Cambridge, Mass. ... 5-11/200. ... Shoots right. ... Full name: Stephen Morgan Leach.
HIGH SCHOOL: Matignon (Cambridge, Mass.).
COLLEGE: New Hampshire.
TRANSACTIONS/CAREER NOTES: Selected by Washington Capitals in second round (second Capitals pick, 34th overall) of NHL entry draft (June 9, 1984). ... Strained left knee (February 1989). ... Injured thumb (March 1990). ... Suffered concussion (October 10, 1990). ... Separated right shoulder (February 2, 1991); missed four games. ... Traded by Capitals to Boston Bruins for LW Randy Burridge (June 21, 1991). ... Injured thigh (October 1992); missed one game. ... Injured ribs (January 1993); missed four games. ... Injured knee (January 8, 1994); missed 25 games. ... Reinjured knee (March 7, 1994); missed 15 games. ... Broke foot (April 8, 1995). ... Traded by Bruins to St. Louis Blues for F Kevin Sawyer and D Steve Staios (March 7, 1996). ... Injured ankle (November 3, 1996); missed 59 games. ... Traded by Blues to Carolina Hurricanes for D Alexander Godynyuk and sixth-round pick in 1998 draft (June 27, 1997).
HONORS: Named to Hockey East All-Freshman team (1984-85).

Season Team	League	REGULAR SEASON								PLAYOFFS				
		Gms.	G	A	Pts.	PIM	+/-	PP	SH	Gms.	G	A	Pts.	PIM
83-84— Matignon	Mass. H.S.	21	27	22	49	49	...	...	...	—	—	—	—	—
84-85— New Hampshire	Hockey East	41	12	25	37	53	...	...	...	—	—	—	—	—
85-86— New Hampshire	Hockey East	25	22	6	28	30	...	...	...	—	—	—	—	—
—Washington	NHL	11	1	1	2	2	0	0	0	6	0	1	1	0
86-87— Binghamton	AHL	54	18	21	39	39	...	...	...	13	3	1	4	6
—Washington	NHL	15	1	0	1	6	-4	0	0	—	—	—	—	—
87-88— U.S. national team	Int'l	53	26	20	46	...	...	...	...	—	—	—	—	—
—U.S. Olympic team	Int'l	6	1	2	3	0	...	...	...	—	—	—	—	—
—Washington	NHL	8	1	1	2	17	2	0	0	9	2	1	3	0
88-89— Washington	NHL	74	11	19	30	94	-4	4	0	6	1	0	1	12
89-90— Washington	NHL	70	18	14	32	104	10	0	0	14	2	2	4	6
90-91— Washington	NHL	68	11	19	30	99	-9	4	0	9	1	2	3	8
91-92— Boston	NHL	78	31	29	60	147	-8	12	0	15	4	0	4	10
92-93— Boston	NHL	79	26	25	51	126	-6	9	0	4	1	1	2	2
93-94— Boston	NHL	42	5	10	15	74	-10	1	0	5	0	1	1	2
94-95— Boston	NHL	35	5	6	11	68	-3	1	0	—	—	—	—	—
95-96— Boston	NHL	59	9	13	22	86	-4	1	0	—	—	—	—	—
—St. Louis	NHL	14	2	4	6	22	-3	0	0	11	3	2	5	10
96-97— St. Louis	NHL	17	2	1	3	24	-2	0	0	6	0	0	0	33
NHL totals (12 years)		570	123	142	265	869	-41	32	0	85	14	10	24	83

LeBOUTILLIER, PETER   RW   MIGHTY DUCKS

PERSONAL: Born January 11, 1975, in Minnedosa, Man. ... 6-1/198. ... Shoots right. ... Name pronounced luh-BOO-tih-YAY.
HIGH SCHOOL: Lindsay Thurber (Red Deer, Alta.).
TRANSACTIONS/CAREER NOTES: Selected by New York Islanders in sixth round (sixth Islanders pick, 144th overall) of NHL entry draft (June 26, 1993). ... Returned to draft pool by Islanders and selected by Mighty Ducks of Anaheim in sixth round (fifth Mighty Ducks pick, 133rd overall) of entry draft (July 8, 1995). ... Strained knee (March 14, 1997); missed five games. ... Strained knee (March 26, 1997); missed final seven games of regular season.

		REGULAR SEASON								PLAYOFFS				
Season Team	League	Gms.	G	A	Pts.	PIM	+/-	PP	SH	Gms.	G	A	Pts.	PIM
91-92— Neepawa	Jr. A	35	11	14	25	99	...	...	...	—	—	—	—	—
92-93— Red Deer	WHL	67	8	26	34	284	...	...	...	2	0	1	1	5
93-94— Red Deer	WHL	66	19	20	39	300	...	...	...	2	0	1	1	4
94-95— Red Deer	WHL	59	27	16	43	159	...	...	...	—	—	—	—	—
95-96— Baltimore	AHL	68	7	9	16	228	...	...	...	11	0	0	0	33
96-97— Baltimore	AHL	47	6	12	18	175	...	...	...	—	—	—	—	—
— Anaheim	NHL	23	1	0	1	121	0	0	0	—	—	—	—	—
NHL totals (1 year)		23	1	0	1	121	0	0	0					

LeCLAIR, JOHN   LW   FLYERS

PERSONAL: Born July 5, 1969, in St. Albans, Vt. ... 6-2/220. ... Shoots left. ... Full name: John Clark LeClair.
HIGH SCHOOL: Bellows Free Academy (St. Albans, Vt.).
COLLEGE: Vermont.
TRANSACTIONS/CAREER NOTES: Selected by Montreal Canadiens in second round (second Canadiens pick, 33rd overall) of NHL entry draft (June 13, 1987). ... Injured thigh; missed 16 games during 1988-89 season. ... Injured knee and underwent surgery (January 20, 1990); missed remainder of season. ... Injured shoulder (January 15, 1992); missed four games. ... Suffered charley horse (January 20, 1993); missed four games. ... Sprained knee (October 2, 1993); missed eight games. ... Bruised sternum (March 28, 1994); missed two games. ... Traded by Canadiens with LW Gilbert Dionne and D Eric Desjardins to Philadelphia Flyers for RW Mark Recchi and third-round pick (C Martin Hohenberger) in 1995 draft (February 9, 1995). ... Strained right hip (April 18, 1995); missed one playoff game.
HONORS: Named to ECAC All-Star second team (1990-91). ... Named to THE SPORTING NEWS All-Star first team (1994-95). ... Named to NHL All-Star first team (1994-95). ... Played in NHL All-Star Game (1996 and 1997). ... Named to NHL All-Star second team (1995-96 and 1996-97). ... Named to THE SPORTING NEWS All-Star team (1996-97).
STATISTICAL PLATEAUS: Three-goal games: 1994-95 (2), 1995-96 (2), 1996-97 (1). Total: 5. ... Four-goal games: 1996-97 (1). ... Total hat tricks: 6.
MISCELLANEOUS: Member of Stanley Cup championship team (1993).

		REGULAR SEASON								PLAYOFFS				
Season Team	League	Gms.	G	A	Pts.	PIM	+/-	PP	SH	Gms.	G	A	Pts.	PIM
85-86— Bellows Free Acad.	Vt. H.S.	22	41	28	69	14	...	...	...	—	—	—	—	—
86-87— Bellows Free Acad.	Vt. H.S.	23	44	40	84	25	...	...	...	—	—	—	—	—
87-88— Univ. of Vermont	ECAC	31	12	22	34	62	...	...	...	—	—	—	—	—
88-89— Univ. of Vermont	ECAC	19	9	12	21	40	...	...	...	—	—	—	—	—
89-90— Univ. of Vermont	ECAC	10	10	6	16	38	...	...	...	—	—	—	—	—
90-91— Univ. of Vermont	ECAC	33	25	20	45	58	...	...	...	—	—	—	—	—
— Montreal	NHL	10	2	5	7	2	1	0	0	3	0	0	0	0
91-92— Montreal	NHL	59	8	11	19	14	5	3	0	8	1	1	2	4
— Fredericton	AHL	8	7	7	14	10	...	...	...	2	0	0	0	4
92-93— Montreal	NHL	72	19	25	44	33	11	2	0	20	4	6	10	14
93-94— Montreal	NHL	74	19	24	43	32	17	1	0	7	2	1	3	8
94-95— Montreal	NHL	9	1	4	5	10	-1	1	0	—	—	—	—	—
— Philadelphia	NHL	37	25	24	49	20	21	5	0	15	5	7	12	4
95-96— Philadelphia	NHL	82	51	46	97	64	21	19	0	11	6	5	11	6
96-97— Philadelphia	NHL	82	50	47	97	58	*44	10	0	19	9	12	21	10
NHL totals (7 years)		425	175	186	361	233	119	41	0	83	27	32	59	46

LECLERC, MIKE   LW   MIGHTY DUCKS

PERSONAL: Born November 10, 1976, in Winnipeg. ... 6-1/205. ... Shoots left. ... Name pronounced luh-KLAIR.
TRANSACTIONS/CAREER NOTES: Selected by Mighty Ducks of Anaheim in third round (third Mighty Ducks pick, 55th overall) of NHL entry draft (July 8, 1995).
HONORS: Named to WHL (Central/East) All-Star second team (1995-96). ... Named to AHL All-Rookie team (1996-97).

		REGULAR SEASON								PLAYOFFS				
Season Team	League	Gms.	G	A	Pts.	PIM	+/-	PP	SH	Gms.	G	A	Pts.	PIM
91-92— St. Boniface	Tier II Jr. A	43	16	12	28	25	...	...	...	—	—	—	—	—
— Victoria	WHL	2	0	0	0	0	...	...	...	—	—	—	—	—
92-93— Victoria	WHL	70	4	11	15	118	...	...	...	—	—	—	—	—
93-94— Victoria	WHL	68	29	11	40	112	...	...	...	—	—	—	—	—
94-95— Prince George	WHL	43	20	36	56	78	...	...	...	—	—	—	—	—
— Brandon	WHL	23	5	8	13	50	...	...	...	18	10	6	16	33
95-96— Brandon	WHL	71	58	53	111	161	...	...	...	19	6	19	25	25
96-97— Baltimore	AHL	71	29	27	56	134	...	...	...	—	—	—	—	—
— Anaheim	NHL	5	1	1	2	0	2	0	0	1	0	0	0	0
NHL totals (1 year)		5	1	1	2	0	2	0	0	1	0	0	0	0

LECOMPTE, ERIC   LW   BLACKHAWKS

PERSONAL: Born April 4, 1975, in Montreal. ... 6-4/190. ... Shoots left. ... Name pronounced luh-KAHMT.
TRANSACTIONS/CAREER NOTES: Selected by Chicago Blackhawks in first round (first Blackhawks pick, 24th overall) of NHL entry draft (June 26, 1993).

Season Team	League	REGULAR SEASON Gms.	G	A	Pts.	PIM	+/-	PP	SH	PLAYOFFS Gms.	G	A	Pts.	PIM
91-92 — Hull	QMJHL	60	16	17	33	138	...	...	...	6	1	0	1	4
92-93 — Hull	QMJHL	66	33	38	71	149	...	...	...	10	4	4	8	52
93-94 — Hull	QMJHL	62	39	49	88	171	...	...	...	20	10	10	20	68
94-95 — Hull	QMJHL	12	11	9	20	58	...	...	...	—	—	—	—	—
— St. Jean	QMJHL	18	9	10	19	54	...	...	...	—	—	—	—	—
— Sherbrooke	QMJHL	34	22	29	51	111	...	...	...	4	2	2	4	4
— Indianapolis	IHL	3	2	0	2	2	...	...	...	—	—	—	—	—
95-96 — Indianapolis	IHL	79	24	20	44	131	...	...	...	—	—	—	—	0
96-97 — Indianapolis	IHL	35	2	3	5	74	...	...	...	—	—	—	—	—
— Fort Wayne	IHL	14	1	2	3	62	...	...	...	—	—	—	—	—
— Worcester	AHL	8	0	1	1	4	...	...	...	—	—	—	—	—

LEDYARD, GRANT — D — CANUCKS

PERSONAL: Born November 19, 1961, in Winnipeg. ... 6-2/195. ... Shoots left.

TRANSACTIONS/CAREER NOTES: Signed as free agent by New York Rangers (July 7, 1982). ... Injured hip (October 1984). ... Traded by Rangers to Los Angeles Kings for LW Brian MacLellan and fourth-round pick (C Michael Sullivan) in 1987 draft; Rangers also sent second-round pick (D Neil Wilkinson) in 1986 draft and fourth-round pick (RW John Weisbrod) in 1987 draft to Minnesota North Stars and the North Stars sent G Roland Melanson to the Kings as part of the same deal (December 1986). ... Sprained ankle (October 1987). ... Traded by Kings to Washington Capitals for RW Craig Laughlin (February 9, 1988). ... Traded by Capitals with G Clint Malarchuk and sixth-round pick (C Brian Holzinger) in 1991 draft to Buffalo Sabres for D Calle Johansson and second-round pick (G Byron Dafoe) in 1989 draft (March 6, 1989). ... Injured knee (February 12, 1991). ... Injured shoulder (March 2, 1991). ... Bruised ankle (March 14, 1992); missed four games. ... Broke finger (October 28, 1992); missed 25 games. ... Injured eye (March 7, 1993); missed three games. ... Signed as free agent by Dallas Stars (August 13, 1993). ... Sprained ankle (February 13, 1995); missed two games. ... Fractured ankle (April 16, 1995); missed last eight games of season and first game of playoffs. ... Suffered from the flu (May 14, 1995); missed one game. ... Fractured orbital bone prior to 1996-97 season; missed first game of season. ... Suspended two games and fined $1,000 by NHL for kneeing incident (November 26, 1996). ... Suffered from the flu (February 2, 1997); missed two games. ... Signed as free agent by Vancouver Canucks (July 14, 1997).

HONORS: Named MJHL Most Valuable Player (1981-82). ... Named to MJHL All-Star first team (1981-82). ... Won Bob Gassoff Award (1983-84). ... Won Max McNab Trophy (1983-84).

Season Team	League	REGULAR SEASON Gms.	G	A	Pts.	PIM	+/-	PP	SH	PLAYOFFS Gms.	G	A	Pts.	PIM
79-80 — Fort Garry	MJHL	49	13	24	37	90	...	...	...	—	—	—	—	—
80-81 — Saskatoon	WHL	71	9	28	37	148	...	...	...	—	—	—	—	—
81-82 — Fort Garry	MJHL	63	25	45	70	150	...	...	...	—	—	—	—	—
82-83 — Tulsa	CHL	80	13	29	42	115	...	...	...	—	—	—	—	—
83-84 — Tulsa	CHL	58	9	17	26	71	...	...	...	9	5	4	9	10
84-85 — New Haven	AHL	36	6	20	26	18	...	...	...	—	—	—	—	—
— New York Rangers	NHL	42	8	12	20	53	8	1	0	3	0	2	2	4
85-86 — New York Rangers	NHL	27	2	9	11	20	-7	0	0	—	—	—	—	—
— Los Angeles	NHL	52	7	18	25	78	-22	4	0	—	—	—	—	—
86-87 — Los Angeles	NHL	67	14	23	37	93	-40	5	0	5	0	0	0	10
87-88 — New Haven	AHL	3	2	1	3	4	...	...	...	—	—	—	—	—
— Los Angeles	NHL	23	1	7	8	52	-7	1	0	—	—	—	—	—
— Washington	NHL	21	4	3	7	14	-4	1	0	14	1	0	1	30
88-89 — Washington	NHL	61	3	11	14	43	1	1	0	—	—	—	—	—
— Buffalo	NHL	13	1	5	6	8	1	0	0	5	1	2	3	2
89-90 — Buffalo	NHL	67	2	13	15	37	2	0	0	—	—	—	—	—
90-91 — Buffalo	NHL	60	8	23	31	46	13	2	1	6	3	3	6	10
91-92 — Buffalo	NHL	50	5	16	21	45	-4	0	0	—	—	—	—	—
92-93 — Buffalo	NHL	50	2	14	16	45	-2	1	0	8	0	0	0	8
— Rochester	AHL	5	0	2	2	8	...	...	...	—	—	—	—	—
93-94 — Dallas	NHL	84	9	37	46	42	7	6	0	9	1	2	3	6
94-95 — Dallas	NHL	38	5	13	18	20	6	4	0	3	0	0	0	2
95-96 — Dallas	NHL	73	5	19	24	20	-15	2	0	—	—	—	—	—
96-97 — Dallas	NHL	67	1	15	16	61	31	0	0	7	0	2	2	0
NHL totals (13 years)		795	77	238	315	677	-32	28	1	60	6	11	17	72

LEEMAN, GARY — RW

PERSONAL: Born February 19, 1964, in Toronto. ... 5-11/186. ... Shoots right.

TRANSACTIONS/CAREER NOTES: Selected by Toronto Maple Leafs as underage junior in second round (second Maple Leafs pick, 24th overall) of NHL entry draft (June 9, 1982). ... Broke finger (January 1984). ... Broke wrist (March 1984). ... Separated shoulder (March 1985). ... Cracked kneecap (April 14, 1987). ... Cracked bone in right hand (April 1988). ... Fractured bone behind left ear (October 22, 1988). ... Injured back (January 1988). ... Separated right shoulder (November 10, 1990); missed 21 games. ... Suffered back spasms (November 18, 1991); missed one game. ... Traded by Maple Leafs with D Alexander Godynyuk, LW Craig Berube, D Michel Petit and G Jeff Reese to Calgary Flames for C Doug Gilmour, D Jamie Macoun, LW Kent Manderville, D Ric Nattress and G Rick Wamsley (January 2, 1992). ... Bruised thigh (February 1992). ... Sprained ankle (February 21, 1992); missed eight games. ... Traded by Flames to Montreal Canadiens for C Brian Skrudland (January 28, 1993). ... Bruised lower back (February 3, 1993); missed four games. ... Injured ankle (April 2, 1993); missed five games. ... Injured shoulder (January 12, 1994); missed two games. ... Fractured forearm (April 11, 1994); missed remainder of season. ... Signed as free agent by Vancouver Canucks (January 14, 1995). ... Signed as free agent by St. Louis Blues (September 26, 1996).

HONORS: Won Top Defenseman Trophy (1982-83). ... Named to WHL All-Star first team (1982-83). ... Played in NHL All-Star Game (1989).

STATISTICAL PLATEAUS: Three-goal games: 1986-87 (1), 1988-89 (1), 1989-90 (2), 1992-93 (2). Total: 6.

MISCELLANEOUS: Failed to score on a penalty shot (vs. Pete Peeters, November 4, 1990). ... Member of Stanley Cup championship team (1993).

Season Team	League	REGULAR SEASON Gms.	G	A	Pts.	PIM	+/-	PP	SH	PLAYOFFS Gms.	G	A	Pts.	PIM
81-82 — Regina	WHL	72	19	41	60	112	...	...	...	3	2	2	4	0
82-83 — Regina	WHL	63	24	62	86	88	...	...	...	5	1	5	6	4

Season Team	League	REGULAR SEASON								PLAYOFFS				
		Gms.	G	A	Pts.	PIM	+/-	PP	SH	Gms.	G	A	Pts.	PIM
— Toronto	NHL	—	—	—	—	—				2	0	0	0	0
83-84 — Toronto	NHL	52	4	8	12	31	...	...	...	—	—	—	—	—
84-85 — St. Catharines	AHL	7	2	2	4	11				—	—	—	—	—
— Toronto	NHL	53	5	26	31	72	-12	3	0	—	—	—	—	—
85-86 — St. Catharines	AHL	25	15	13	28	6				—	—	—	—	—
— Toronto	NHL	53	9	23	32	20	-1	1	1	10	2	10	12	2
86-87 — Toronto	NHL	80	21	31	52	66	-26	4	3	5	0	1	1	14
87-88 — Toronto	NHL	80	30	31	61	62	-6	6	0	2	2	0	2	2
88-89 — Toronto	NHL	61	32	43	75	66	5	7	1	—	—	—	—	—
89-90 — Toronto	NHL	80	51	44	95	63	4	14	1	5	3	3	6	16
90-91 — Toronto	NHL	52	17	12	29	39	-25	4	0	—	—	—	—	—
91-92 — Toronto	NHL	34	7	13	20	44	-1	3	0	—	—	—	—	—
— Calgary	NHL	29	2	7	9	27	-11	1	0	—	—	—	—	—
92-93 — Calgary	NHL	30	9	5	14	10	5	0	0	—	—	—	—	—
— Montreal	NHL	20	6	12	18	14	9	1	0	11	1	2	3	2
93-94 — Montreal	NHL	31	4	11	15	17	5	0	0	1	0	0	0	0
— Fredericton	AHL	23	18	8	26	16	...	...	...	—	—	—	—	—
94-95 — Vancouver	NHL	10	2	0	2	0	-3	0	0	—	—	—	—	—
95-96 —		German League statistics unavailable.												
96-97 — Worcester	AHL	24	9	7	16	41	...	...	...	—	—	—	—	—
— St. Louis	NHL	2	0	1	1	0	0	0	0	—	—	—	—	—
— Utah	IHL	15	6	1	7	20	...	...	...	4	0	3	3	4
NHL totals (14 years)		667	199	267	466	531	-57	44	6	36	8	16	24	36

LEETCH, BRIAN   D   RANGERS

PERSONAL: Born March 3, 1968, in Corpus Christi, Texas. ... 5-11/190. ... Shoots left. ... Full name: Brian Joseph Leetch.
HIGH SCHOOL: Avon (Conn.) Old Farms School for Boys.
COLLEGE: Boston College.
TRANSACTIONS/CAREER NOTES: Selected by New York Rangers in first round (first Rangers pick, ninth overall) of NHL entry draft (June 21, 1986). ... Fractured left knee at U.S. Olympic Festival (July 1987). ... Fractured bone in left foot (December 1988). ... Suffered hip pointer (March 15, 1989). ... Fractured left ankle (March 14, 1990). ... Injured ankle (November 21, 1992); missed one game. ... Suffered stretched nerve in neck (December 17, 1992); missed 34 games. ... Broke ankle (March 19, 1993) and underwent ankle surgery (March 31, 1993); missed remainder of season.
HONORS: Named Hockey East Player of the Year (1986-87). ... Named Hockey East Rookie of the Year (1986-87). ... Named Hockey East Tournament Most Valuable Player (1986-87). ... Named to NCAA All-America East first team (1986-87). ... Named to Hockey East All-Star first team (1986-87). ... Named to Hockey East All-Freshman team (1986-87). ... Named NHL Rookie of the Year by THE SPORTING NEWS (1988-89). ... Won Calder Memorial Trophy (1988-89). ... Named to NHL All-Rookie team (1988-89). ... Named to THE SPORTING NEWS All-Star second team (1990-91 and 1993-94). ... Named to NHL All-Star second team (1990-91, 1993-94 and 1995-96). ... Played in NHL All-Star Game (1990-1992, 1994, 1996 and 1997). ... Won James Norris Memorial Trophy (1991-92 and 1996-97). ... Named to THE SPORTING NEWS All-Star first team (1991-92). ... Named to NHL All-Star first team (1991-92). ... Won Conn Smythe Trophy (1993-94). ... Named to Hockey East All-Decade team (1994). ... Named to NHL All-Star team (1996 and 1997). ... Named to THE SPORTING NEWS All-Star team (1996-97).
RECORDS: Holds NHL single-season record for most goals by a rookie defenseman—23 (1988-89).
MISCELLANEOUS: Member of Stanley Cup championship team (1994).

Season Team	League	REGULAR SEASON								PLAYOFFS				
		Gms.	G	A	Pts.	PIM	+/-	PP	SH	Gms.	G	A	Pts.	PIM
84-85 — Avon Old Farms	Conn. H.S.	26	30	46	76	15	...	...	...	—	—	—	—	—
85-86 — Avon Old Farms	Conn. H.S.	28	40	44	84	18	...	...	...	—	—	—	—	—
86-87 — Boston College	Hockey East	37	9	38	47	10	...	...	...	—	—	—	—	—
87-88 — U.S. national team	Int'l	60	13	61	74	38	...	...	...	—	—	—	—	—
— U.S. Olympic team	Int'l	6	1	5	6	4	...	...	...	—	—	—	—	—
— New York Rangers	NHL	17	2	12	14	0	5	1	0	—	—	—	—	—
88-89 — New York Rangers	NHL	68	23	48	71	50	8	8	3	4	3	2	5	2
89-90 — New York Rangers	NHL	72	11	45	56	26	-18	5	0	—	—	—	—	—
90-91 — New York Rangers	NHL	80	16	72	88	42	2	6	0	6	1	3	4	0
91-92 — New York Rangers	NHL	80	22	80	102	26	25	10	1	13	4	11	15	4
92-93 — New York Rangers	NHL	36	6	30	36	26	2	2	1	—	—	—	—	—
93-94 — New York Rangers	NHL	84	23	56	79	67	28	17	1	23	11	*23	*34	6
94-95 — New York Rangers	NHL	48	9	32	41	18	0	3	0	10	6	8	14	8
95-96 — New York Rangers	NHL	82	15	70	85	30	12	7	0	11	1	6	7	4
96-97 — New York Rangers	NHL	82	20	58	78	40	31	9	0	15	2	8	10	6
NHL totals (10 years)		649	147	503	650	325	95	68	6	82	28	61	89	30

LEFEBVRE, SYLVAIN   D   AVALANCHE

PERSONAL: Born October 14, 1967, in Richmond, Que. ... 6-2/205. ... Shoots left. ... Name pronounced luh-FAYV.
TRANSACTIONS/CAREER NOTES: Signed as free agent by Montreal Canadiens (September 24, 1986). ... Traded by Canadiens to Toronto Maple Leafs for third-round pick (D Martin Belanger) in 1994 draft (August 20, 1992). ... Traded by Maple Leafs with LW Wendel Clark, RW Landon Wilson and first-round pick (D Jeffrey Kealty) in 1994 draft to Quebec Nordiques for C Mats Sundin, D Garth Butcher, LW Todd Warriner and first-round pick (traded to Washington) in 1994 draft (June 28, 1994). ... Nordiques franchise moved to Colorado and renamed Avalanche for 1995-96 season (June 21, 1995). ... Sprained right ankle (November 29, 1995); missed six games. ... Fractured forearm (December 18, 1996); missed 10 games.
HONORS: Named to AHL All-Star second team (1988-89).
MISCELLANEOUS: Member of Stanley Cup championship team (1996).

Season Team	League	REGULAR SEASON								PLAYOFFS				
		Gms.	G	A	Pts.	PIM	+/-	PP	SH	Gms.	G	A	Pts.	PIM
84-85 — Laval	QMJHL	66	7	5	12	31	...	...	...	—	—	—	—	—
85-86 — Laval	QMJHL	71	8	17	25	48	...	...	...	14	1	0	1	25

Season Team	League	Gms.	G	A	Pts.	PIM	+/-	PP	SH		Gms.	G	A	Pts.	PIM
		REGULAR SEASON									PLAYOFFS				
86-87— Laval	QMJHL	70	10	36	46	44	...	...	...		15	1	6	7	12
87-88— Sherbrooke	AHL	79	3	24	27	73	...	...	...		6	2	3	5	4
88-89— Sherbrooke	AHL	77	15	32	47	119	...	...	...		6	1	3	4	4
89-90— Montreal	NHL	68	3	10	13	61	18	0	0		6	0	0	0	2
90-91— Montreal	NHL	63	5	18	23	30	-11	1	0		11	1	0	1	6
91-92— Montreal	NHL	69	3	14	17	91	9	0	0		2	0	0	0	2
92-93— Toronto	NHL	81	2	12	14	90	8	0	0		21	3	3	6	20
93-94— Toronto	NHL	84	2	9	11	79	33	0	0		18	0	3	3	16
94-95— Quebec	NHL	48	2	11	13	17	13	0	0		6	0	2	2	2
95-96— Colorado	NHL	75	5	11	16	49	26	2	0		22	0	5	5	12
96-97— Colorado	NHL	71	2	11	13	30	12	1	0		17	0	0	0	25
NHL totals (8 years)		559	24	96	120	447	108	4	0		103	4	13	17	85

LEHTINEN, JERE   RW   STARS

PERSONAL: Born June 24, 1973, in Espoo, Finland. ... 6-0/185. ... Shoots right. ... Name pronounced YAIR-ee LEH-tih-nehn.
TRANSACTIONS/CAREER NOTES: Selected by Minnesota North Stars in fourth round (third North Stars pick, 88th overall) of NHL entry draft (June 20, 1992). ... North Stars franchise moved from Minnesota to Dallas and renamed Stars for 1993-94 season. ... Strained groin (December 21, 1995); missed six games. ... Reaggravated groin (January 10, 1996); missed one game. ... Sprained ankle (March 20, 1996); missed remainder of season. ... Sprained knee (January 31, 1997); missed 13 games. ... Sprained knee (March 5, 1997); missed five games.
MISCELLANEOUS: Member of bronze-medal-winning Finnish Olympic team (1994).

Season Team	League	Gms.	G	A	Pts.	PIM	+/-	PP	SH		Gms.	G	A	Pts.	PIM
		REGULAR SEASON									PLAYOFFS				
90-91— Kiekko-Espoo	Finland	32	15	9	24	12	...	...	...		—	—	—	—	—
91-92— Kiekko-Espoo	Finland	43	32	17	49	6	...	...	...		—	—	—	—	—
92-93— Kiekko-Espoo	Finland	45	13	14	27	6	...	...	...		—	—	—	—	—
93-94— TPS Turku	Finland	42	19	20	39	6	...	...	...		11	11	2	13	2
— Fin. Olympic team	Int'l	8	3	0	3	11	...	...	...		—	—	—	—	—
94-95— TPS Turku	Finland	39	19	23	42	33	...	...	...		13	8	6	14	4
95-96— Dallas	NHL	57	6	22	28	16	5	0	0		—	—	—	—	—
— Michigan	IHL	1	1	0	1	0	...	...	...		—	—	—	—	—
96-97— Dallas	NHL	63	16	27	43	2	26	3	1		7	2	2	4	0
NHL totals (2 years)		120	22	49	71	18	31	3	1		7	2	2	4	0

LEITZA, BRIAN   G   PENGUINS

PERSONAL: Born March 16, 1974, in Lake Villa, Ill. ... 6-2/185. ... Catches left. ... Name pronounced LEET-suh.
HIGH SCHOOL: Antioch (Ill.) Community.
COLLEGE: St. Cloud (Minn.) State.
TRANSACTIONS/CAREER NOTES: Selected by Pittsburgh Penguins in 11th round (14th Penguins pick, 284th overall) of NHL entry draft (June 29, 1994).
HONORS: Named to WCHA All-Rookie team (1994-95).

Season Team	League	Gms.	Min	W	L	T	GA	SO	Avg.		Gms.	Min.	W	L	GA	SO	Avg.
		REGULAR SEASON									PLAYOFFS						
93-94— Sioux City	USHL	32	1793	18	10	1	98	0	3.28		—	—	—	—	—	—	—
94-95— St. Cloud State	WCHA	30	1625	13	15	0	93	2	3.43		—	—	—	—	—	—	—
95-96— St. Cloud State	WCHA	35	2064	12	19	4	131	2	3.81		—	—	—	—	—	—	—
96-97— St. Cloud State	WCHA	30	1738	19	8	1	93	...	3.21		—	—	—	—	—	—	—

LEMANOWICZ, DAVID   G   PANTHERS

PERSONAL: Born March 8, 1976, in Edmonton. ... 6-2/190. ... Catches left. ... Name pronounced luh-MAHN-ih-wihts.
TRANSACTIONS/CAREER NOTES: Selected by Florida Panthers in ninth round (ninth Panthers pick, 218th overall) of NHL entry draft (July 8, 1995).

Season Team	League	Gms.	Min	W	L	T	GA	SO	Avg.		Gms.	Min.	W	L	GA	SO	Avg.
		REGULAR SEASON									PLAYOFFS						
92-93— Spokane	WHL	16	738	3	11	0	61	1	4.96		—	—	—	—	—	—	—
93-94— Spokane	WHL	6	256	1	2	0	21	0	4.92		—	—	—	—	—	—	—
94-95— Spokane	WHL	16	761	5	5	1	41	2	3.23		1	1	...	...	0	0	0.00
95-96— Spokane	WHL	62	3362	42	10	2	162	*4	*2.89		18	1036	9	†6	59	†2	3.42
96-97— Carolina	AHL	33	1796	11	18	0	117	2	3.91		—	—	—	—	—	—	—
— Port Huron	Col.HL	3	167	1	2	0	11	0	3.95		—	—	—	—	—	—	—

LEMIEUX, CLAUDE   RW   AVALANCHE

PERSONAL: Born July 16, 1965, in Buckingham, Que. ... 6-1/215. ... Shoots right. ... Name pronounced luh-MYOO. ... Brother of Jocelyn Lemieux, right winger, Phoenix Coyotes.
TRANSACTIONS/CAREER NOTES: Selected by Montreal Canadiens as underage junior in second round (second Canadiens pick, 26th overall) of NHL entry draft (June 8, 1983). ... Tore ankle ligaments (October 1987). ... Fractured orbital bone above right eye (January 14, 1988). ... Pulled groin (March 1989). ... Underwent surgery to repair torn stomach muscle (November 1, 1989); missed 41 games. ... Traded by Canadiens to New Jersey Devils for LW Sylvain Turgeon (September 4, 1990). ... Bruised retina right eye (February 25, 1991). ... Suffered sore back (November 27, 1991); missed four games. ... Injured ankle (March 11, 1992); missed two games. ... Suffered back spasms (October 24, 1992); missed three games. ... Injured right elbow (March 21, 1993); missed one game. ... Suspended three games and fined $500 by NHL for altercation with opponent's bench (March 28, 1995). ... Traded by Devils to New York Islanders for RW Steve Thomas

(October 3, 1995). ... Traded by Islanders to Colorado Avalanche for LW Wendel Clark (October 3, 1995). ... Broke finger (December 3, 1995); missed two games. ... Suspended one playoff game and fined $1000 by NHL for punching another player (May 24, 1996). ... Suspended two games in Stanley Cup finals and fined $1,000 by NHL for checking from behind (June 2, 1996). ... Tore abdominal muscle (October 30, 1996); missed 37 games.

HONORS: Named to QMJHL All-Star second team (1983-84). ... Won Guy Lafleur Trophy (1984-85). ... Named to QMJHL All-Star first team (1984-85). ... Won Conn Smythe Trophy (1994-95).

STATISTICAL PLATEAUS: Three-goal games: 1988-89 (1), 1990-91 (2), 1992-93 (1), 1995-96 (2). Total: 6.

MISCELLANEOUS: Member of Stanley Cup championship team (1986, 1995 and 1996).

Season Team	League	REGULAR SEASON								PLAYOFFS				
		Gms.	G	A	Pts.	PIM	+/-	PP	SH	Gms.	G	A	Pts.	PIM
82-83— Trois-Rivieres............	QMJHL	62	28	38	66	187	...	...	...	4	1	0	1	30
83-84— Verdun	QMJHL	51	41	45	86	225	...	...	...	9	8	12	20	63
— Montreal	NHL	8	1	1	2	12	-2	0	0	—	—	—	—	—
— Nova Scotia	AHL	—	—	—	—	—				2	1	0	1	0
84-85— Verdun	QMJHL	52	58	66	124	152	...	...	...	14	*23	17	*40	38
— Montreal	NHL	1	0	1	1	7	1	0	0	—	—	—	—	—
85-86— Sherbrooke	AHL	58	21	32	53	145	...			—	—	—	—	—
— Montreal	NHL	10	1	2	3	22	-6	1	0	20	10	6	16	68
86-87— Montreal	NHL	76	27	26	53	156	0	5	0	17	4	9	13	41
87-88— Montreal	NHL	78	31	30	61	137	16	6	0	11	3	2	5	20
88-89— Montreal	NHL	69	29	22	51	136	14	7	0	18	4	3	7	58
89-90— Montreal	NHL	39	8	10	18	106	-8	3	0	11	1	3	4	38
90-91— New Jersey	NHL	78	30	17	47	105	-8	10	0	7	4	0	4	34
91-92— New Jersey	NHL	74	41	27	68	109	9	13	1	7	4	3	7	26
92-93— New Jersey	NHL	77	30	51	81	155	3	13	0	5	2	0	2	19
93-94— New Jersey	NHL	79	18	26	44	86	13	5	0	20	7	11	18	44
94-95— New Jersey	NHL	45	6	13	19	86	2	1	0	20	*13	3	16	20
95-96— Colorado	NHL	79	39	32	71	117	14	9	2	19	5	7	12	55
96-97— Colorado	NHL	45	11	17	28	43	-4	5	0	17	13	10	23	32
NHL totals (14 years)		758	272	275	547	1277	44	78	3	172	70	57	127	455

LEMIEUX, JOCELYN   RW   COYOTES

PERSONAL: Born November 18, 1967, in Mont-Laurier, Que. ... 5-10/200. ... Shoots left. ... Name pronounced luh-MYOO. ... Brother of Claude Lemieux, right winger, Colorado Avalanche.

TRANSACTIONS/CAREER NOTES: Selected by St. Louis Blues as underage junior in first round (first Blues pick, 10th overall) of NHL entry draft (June 21, 1986). ... Severed tendon in left pinkie (December 1986). ... Broke left leg and tore ligaments (January 1988). ... Traded by Blues with G Darrell May and second-round pick (D Patrice Brisebois) in 1989 draft to Montreal Canadiens for LW Sergio Momesso and G Vincent Riendeau (August 9, 1988). ... Traded by Canadiens to Chicago Blackhawks for third-round pick (D Charles Poulin) in 1990 draft (January 5, 1990). ... Suffered concussion and cracked orbital bone above right eye (February 26, 1991); missed a month. ... Traded by Blackhawks with D Frantisek Kucera to Hartford Whalers for LW Randy Cunneyworth and D Gary Suter (March 11, 1994). ... Injured shoulder (March 14, 1995); missed seven games. ... Traded by Whalers with second-round pick in 1998 draft to New Jersey Devils for C Jim Dowd and second-round pick (traded to Calgary) in 1997 draft (December 19, 1995). ... Injured shoulder (December 26, 1995); missed two games. ... Traded by Devils with D Tommy Albelin and D Cal Hulse to Calgary Flames for D Phil Housley and D Dan Keczmer (February 26, 1996). ... Signed as free agent by Phoenix Coyotes (March 17, 1997). ... Fractured arm (March 22, 1997); missed remainder of regular season.

HONORS: Named to QMJHL All-Star first team (1985-86).

STATISTICAL PLATEAUS: Three-goal games: 1989-90 (1), 1993-94 (1). Total: 2.

Season Team	League	REGULAR SEASON								PLAYOFFS				
		Gms.	G	A	Pts.	PIM	+/-	PP	SH	Gms.	G	A	Pts.	PIM
84-85— Laval	QMJHL	68	13	19	32	92	...	...	...	—	—	—	—	—
85-86— Laval	QMJHL	71	57	68	125	131	...	...	...	14	9	15	24	37
86-87— St. Louis	NHL	53	10	8	18	94	1	1	0	5	0	1	1	6
87-88— Peoria	IHL	8	0	5	5	35	...			—	—	—	—	—
— St. Louis	NHL	23	1	0	1	42	-5	0	0	5	0	0	0	0
88-89— Montreal	NHL	1	0	1	1	0	-1	0	0	—	—	—	—	—
— Sherbrooke	AHL	73	25	28	53	134	...			4	3	1	4	6
89-90— Montreal	NHL	34	4	2	6	61	-1	0	0	—	—	—	—	—
— Chicago...................	NHL	39	10	11	21	47	0	1	0	18	1	8	9	28
90-91— Chicago...................	NHL	67	6	7	13	119	-7	1	1	4	0	0	0	0
91-92— Chicago...................	NHL	78	6	10	16	80	-2	0	0	18	3	1	4	33
92-93— Chicago...................	NHL	81	10	21	31	111	5	1	0	4	1	0	1	2
93-94— Chicago...................	NHL	66	12	8	20	63	5	0	0	—	—	—	—	—
— Hartford	NHL	16	6	1	7	19	-8	0	0	—	—	—	—	—
94-95— Hartford	NHL	41	6	5	11	32	-7	0	0	—	—	—	—	—
95-96— Hartford	NHL	29	1	2	3	31	-11	0	0	—	—	—	—	—
— New Jersey	NHL	18	0	1	1	4	-7	0	0	—	—	—	—	—
— Calgary...................	NHL	20	4	4	8	10	-1	0	0	4	0	0	0	0
96-97— Long Beach	IHL	28	4	10	14	54	...	...	...	—	—	—	—	—
— Phoenix...................	NHL	2	1	0	1	0	0	0	0	2	0	0	0	4
NHL totals (11 years)		568	77	81	158	713	-39	4	1	60	5	10	15	73

LEMIEUX, MARIO   C

PERSONAL: Born October 5, 1965, in Montreal. ... 6-4/220. ... Shoots right. ... Name pronounced luh-MYOO. ... Brother of Alain Lemieux, center for three NHL teams (1981-82 through 1986-87).

TRANSACTIONS/CAREER NOTES: Selected by Pittsburgh Penguins as underage junior in first round (first Penguins pick, first overall) of NHL entry draft (June 9, 1984). ... Sprained left knee (September 1984). ... Reinjured knee (December 2, 1984). ... Sprained right knee (December

20, 1986). ... Bruised right shoulder (November 1987). ... Sprained right wrist (November 3, 1988). ... Suffered herniated disk (February 14, 1990); missed 21 games. ... Underwent surgery to remove part of herniated disk (July 11, 1990); missed first 50 games of season. ... Suffered back spasms (October 1991); missed three games. ... Suffered back spasms (January 4, 1992); missed three games. ... Injured back (January 29, 1992); missed six games. ... Suffered from the flu (February 1992); missed one game. ... Fractured bone in hand (May 5, 1992). ... Injured heel (December 1992); missed one game. ... Injured back (January 5, 1993); missed three games. ... Diagnosed with Hodgkin's Disease (January 12, 1993) and underwent radiation treatment (February 1-March 2); missed 20 games. ... Injured back prior to 1993-94 season; missed first 10 games of season. ... Injured back (October 28, 1993); missed one game. ... Injured back (November 2, 1993); missed one game. ... Suffered from the flu (November 9, 1993); missed one game. ... Injured back (November 11, 1993); missed 38 games. ... Injured back (February 13, 1994); missed two games. ... Injured back (February 19, 1994); missed two games. ... Injured back (March 12, 1994); missed four games. ... Fined $500 by NHL for charging at a referee (April 6, 1994). ... On medical leave of absence during entire 1994-95 season. ... Suffered back spasms (November 9, 1996); missed one game. ... Suffered back spasms (January 21, 1997); missed one game. ... Suffered back spasms (February 4, 1997); missed one game. ... Injured hip flexor (March 4, 1997); missed one game. ... Injured hip flexor (March 14, 1997); missed two games.

HONORS: Named to QMJHL All-Star second team (1982-83). ... Won Can.HL Player of the Year Award (1983-84). ... Won Michel Briere Trophy (1983-84). ... Won Jean Beliveau Trophy (1983-84). ... Won Michael Bossy Trophy (1983-84). ... Won Guy Lafleur Trophy (1983-84). ... Named to QMJHL All-Star first team (1983-84). ... Named NHL Rookie of the Year by THE SPORTING NEWS (1984-85). ... Won Calder Memorial Trophy (1984-85). ... Named to NHL All-Rookie team (1984-85). ... Won Lester B. Pearson Award (1985-86, 1987-88, 1992-93 and 1995-96). ... Named to THE SPORTING NEWS All-Star second team (1985-86). ... Named to NHL All-Star second team (1985-86, 1986-87 and 1991-92). ... Played in NHL All-Star Game (1985, 1986, 1988-1990, 1992, 1996 and 1997). ... Named All-Star Game Most Valuable Player (1985, 1988 and 1990). ... Named NHL Player of the Year by THE SPORTING NEWS (1987-1988, 1988-89, 1992-93 and 1995-96). ... Won Hart Memorial Trophy (1987-88, 1992-93 and 1995-96). ... Won Art Ross Memorial Trophy (1987-88, 1988-89, 1991-92, 1992-93, 1995-96 and 1996-97). ... Won Dodge Performance of the Year Award (1987-88). ... Won Dodge Performer of the Year Award (1987-88 and 1988-89). ... Named to THE SPORTING NEWS All-Star first team (1987-88, 1988-89, 1992-93 and 1995-96). ... Named to NHL All-Star first team (1987-88, 1988-89, 1992-93, 1995-96 and 1996-97). ... Won Dodge Ram Tough Award (1988-89). ... Won Conn Smythe Trophy (1990-91 and 1991-92). ... Won Pro Set NHL Player of the Year Award (1991-92). ... Won Bill Masterton Memorial Trophy (1992-93). ... Named to THE SPORTING NEWS All-Star team (1996-97).

RECORDS: Holds NHL career records for highest goals-per-game average—.823; most overtime points—19; and most overtime goals—9. ... Holds NHL single-season record for most shorthanded goals—13 (1988-89). ... Shares NHL single-game playoff records for most goals— 5 (April 25, 1989); most single-season playoff game-winning goals—5 (1992); most points—8 (April 25, 1989); most goals in one period— 4 (April 25, 1989); and most points in one period—4 (April 25, 1989 and April 23, 1992). ... Holds NHL All-Star single-game record for most points—6 (1988). ... Shares NHL All-Star single-game record for most goals—4 (1990).

STATISTICAL PLATEAUS: Three-goal games: 1986-87 (5), 1987-88 (3), 1988-89 (7), 1989-90 (3), 1990-91 (1), 1991-92 (1), 1992-93 (1), 1995-96 (4), 1996-97 (1). Total: 26. ... Four-goal games: 1985-86 (1), 1986-87 (1), 1987-88 (2), 1988-89 (1), 1989-90 (1), 1992-93 (2), 1995-96 (1), 1996-97 (1). Total: 10. ... Five-goal games: 1988-89 (1), 1992-93 (1), 1995-96 (1). Total: 3. ... Total hat tricks: 39.

MISCELLANEOUS: Member of Stanley Cup championship team (1991 and 1992). ... Captain of Pittsburgh Penguins (1987-88 through 1993-94 and 1996-97). ... Holds Pittsburgh Penguins all-time records for most goals (613), most assists (881) and most points (1,494). ... Scored on a penalty shot vs. Mario Gosselin, December 29, 1984; vs. Kelly Hrudey January 19, 1988; vs. Chris Terreri, December 31, 1988; vs. Kelly Hrudey, March 7, 1989; vs. Bob Mason, November 24, 1989; vs. John Vanbiesbrouck, April 11, 1997). ... Failed to score on a penalty shot (vs. Bill Ranford, March 17, 1992; vs. Dominik Hasek, March 23, 1996).

Season Team	League	REGULAR SEASON								PLAYOFFS				
		Gms.	G	A	Pts.	PIM	+/-	PP	SH	Gms.	G	A	Pts.	PIM
81-82— Laval	QMJHL	64	30	66	96	22	...	...	...	18	5	9	14	31
82-83— Laval	QMJHL	66	84	100	184	76	...	...	...	12	†14	18	32	18
83-84— Laval	QMJHL	70	*133	*149	*282	92	...	...	...	14	*29	*23	*52	29
84-85— Pittsburgh	NHL	73	43	57	100	54	-35	11	0	—	—	—	—	—
85-86— Pittsburgh	NHL	79	48	93	141	43	-6	17	0	—	—	—	—	—
86-87— Pittsburgh	NHL	63	54	53	107	57	13	19	0	—	—	—	—	—
87-88— Pittsburgh	NHL	77	*70	98	*168	92	23	22	*10	—	—	—	—	—
88-89— Pittsburgh	NHL	76	*85	†114	*199	100	41	*31	*13	11	12	7	19	16
89-90— Pittsburgh	NHL	59	45	78	123	78	-18	14	3	—	—	—	—	—
90-91— Pittsburgh	NHL	26	19	26	45	30	8	6	1	23	16	*28	*44	16
91-92— Pittsburgh	NHL	64	44	87	*131	94	27	12	4	15	*16	18	*34	2
92-93— Pittsburgh	NHL	60	69	91	*160	38	*55	16	6	11	8	10	18	10
93-94— Pittsburgh	NHL	22	17	20	37	32	-2	7	0	6	4	3	7	2
94-95— Pittsburgh	NHL						Did not play.			—	—	—	—	—
95-96— Pittsburgh	NHL	70	*69	†92	*161	54	10	*31	*8	18	11	16	27	33
96-97— Pittsburgh	NHL	76	50	†72	*122	65	27	15	3	5	3	3	6	4
NHL totals (13 years)		745	613	881	1494	737	143	201	48	89	70	85	155	83

LEROUX, FRANCOIS   D   PENGUINS

PERSONAL: Born April 18, 1970, in St. Adele, Que. ... 6-6/236. ... Shoots left. ... Name pronounced FRAN-swah luh-ROO.

TRANSACTIONS/CAREER NOTES: Selected by Edmonton Oilers in first round (first Oilers pick, 19th overall) of NHL entry draft (June 11, 1988). ... Separated shoulder (March 20, 1989). ... Traded by St. Jean Lynx with LW Patrick Lebeau and LW Jean Blouin to Victoriaville Tigres for RW Trevor Duhaime, second- and third-round draft picks and future considerations (February 15, 1990). ... Tore left knee ligaments (March 18, 1990). ... Underwent surgery to left knee (March 22, 1990). ... Claimed on waivers by Ottawa Senators (October 6, 1993). ... Fractured left thumb (December 6, 1993); missed 16 games. ... Selected by Pittsburgh Penguins from Senators in waiver draft for cash (January 18, 1995). ... Suffered from the flu (February 16, 1995); missed one game. ... Twisted knee (March 9, 1995); missed two games. ... Suffered back spasms (April 23, 1995); missed one game. ... Suffered back spasms (October 12, 1995); missed one game. ... Suffered back spasms (December 30, 1995); missed eight games. ... Cracked thumb (February 12, 1996); missed one game. ... Suffered hip pointer (December 15, 1996); missed two games. ... Suffered back spasms (January 7, 1997); missed three games. ... Suffered from the flu (February 1, 1997); missed one game. ... Suffered from the flu (March 14, 1997); missed two games.

Season Team	League	REGULAR SEASON								PLAYOFFS				
		Gms.	G	A	Pts.	PIM	+/-	PP	SH	Gms.	G	A	Pts.	PIM
87-88— St. Jean	QMJHL	58	3	8	11	143	...	...	...	7	2	0	2	21
88-89— Edmonton	NHL	2	0	0	0	0	1	0	0	—	—	—	—	—
— St. Jean	QMJHL	57	8	34	42	185	...	...	...	—	—	—	—	—
89-90— Edmonton	NHL	3	0	1	1	0	-2	0	0	—	—	—	—	—
— St. Jean/Victoriaville ..	QMJHL	54	4	33	37	160	...	...	...	—	—	—	—	—

Season Team	League	Gms.	G	A	Pts.	PIM	+/-	PP	SH	Gms.	G	A	Pts.	PIM
90-91— Cape Breton	AHL	71	2	7	9	124	...	...	...	4	0	1	1	19
—Edmonton	NHL	1	0	2	2	0	1	0	0	—	—	—	—	—
91-92— Cape Breton	AHL	61	7	22	29	114	...	...	...	5	0	0	0	8
—Edmonton	NHL	4	0	0	0	7	-1	0	0	—	—	—	—	—
92-93— Cape Breton	AHL	55	10	24	34	139	...	...	...	16	0	5	5	29
—Edmonton	NHL	1	0	0	0	4	0	0	0	—	—	—	—	—
93-94— Ottawa	NHL	23	0	1	1	70	-4	0	0	—	—	—	—	—
—Prin. Edward Island ...	AHL	25	4	6	10	52	...	...	...	—	—	—	—	—
94-95— Prin. Edward Island ...	AHL	45	4	14	18	137	...	...	...	—	—	—	—	—
—Pittsburgh	NHL	40	0	2	2	114	7	0	0	12	0	2	2	14
95-96— Pittsburgh	NHL	66	2	9	11	161	2	0	0	18	1	1	2	20
96-97— Pittsburgh	NHL	59	0	3	3	81	-3	0	0	3	0	0	0	0
NHL totals (9 years)		199	2	18	20	437	1	0	0	33	1	3	4	34

LEROUX, JEAN-YVES   LW   BLACKHAWKS

PERSONAL: Born June 24, 1976, in Montreal. ... 6-2/193. ... Shoots left. ... Name pronounced zhahn-eev luh-ROO.

TRANSACTIONS/CAREER NOTES: Selected by Chicago Blackhawks in second round (second Blackhawks pick, 40th overall) of NHL entry draft (June 28, 1994).

Season Team	League	Gms.	G	A	Pts.	PIM	+/-	PP	SH	Gms.	G	A	Pts.	PIM
92-93— Beauport	QMJHL	62	20	25	45	33	...	...	...	—	—	—	—	—
93-94— Beauport	QMJHL	45	14	25	39	43	...	...	...	15	7	6	13	33
94-95— Beauport	QMJHL	59	19	33	52	125	...	...	...	17	4	6	10	39
95-96— Beauport	QMJHL	54	41	41	82	176	...	...	...	20	5	18	23	20
96-97— Indianapolis	IHL	69	14	17	31	112	...	...	...	4	1	0	1	2
—Chicago.....................	NHL	1	0	1	1	5	1	0	0	—	—	—	—	—
NHL totals (1 year)		1	0	1	1	5	1	0	0					

LESCHYSHYN, CURTIS   D   HURRICANES

L

PERSONAL: Born September 21, 1969, in Thompson, Man. ... 6-1/205. ... Shoots left. ... Full name: Curtis Michael Leschyshyn. ... Name pronounced luh-SIH-shuhn.

TRANSACTIONS/CAREER NOTES: Selected by Quebec Nordiques in first round (first Nordiques pick, third overall) of NHL entry draft (June 11, 1988). ... Separated shoulder (January 10, 1989). ... Sprained left knee (November 1989). ... Damaged knee ligaments (February 18, 1991) and underwent surgery (February 20, 1991); missed final 19 games of 1990-91 season and first 30 games of 1991-92 season. ... Strained back (October 13, 1992); missed two games. ... Strained right collarbone (December 30, 1994); missed two games. ... Pulled thigh muscle (March 19, 1994); missed two games. ... Injured groin (March 31, 1994); missed remainder of season. ... Lacerated groin (April 22, 1995); missed last four games of season. ... Nordiques franchise moved to Colorado and renamed Avalanche for 1995-96 season (June 21, 1995). ... Injured hip flexor (January 17, 1996); missed three games. ... Traded by Avalanche with LW Chris Simon to Washington Capitals for RW Keith Jones, first-round pick in 1998 draft and fourth-round pick in 1997 or 1998 draft (November 2, 1996). ... Traded by Capitals to Hartford Whalers for C Andrei Nikolishin (November 9, 1996). ... Injured abdominal muscle (March 7, 1997); missed five games. ... Whalers franchise moved to North Carolina and renamed Carolina Hurricanes for 1997-98 season; NHL approved move on June 25, 1997.

HONORS: Named to WHL (East) All-Star first team (1987-88).

MISCELLANEOUS: Member of Stanley Cup championship team (1996).

Season Team	League	Gms.	G	A	Pts.	PIM	+/-	PP	SH	Gms.	G	A	Pts.	PIM
85-86— Saskatoon...................	WHL	1	0	0	0	0	...	...	...	—	—	—	—	—
86-87— Saskatoon...................	WHL	70	14	26	40	107	...	...	...	11	1	5	6	14
87-88— Saskatoon...................	WHL	56	14	41	55	86	...	...	...	10	2	5	7	16
88-89— Quebec......................	NHL	71	4	9	13	71	-32	1	1	—	—	—	—	—
89-90— Quebec......................	NHL	68	2	6	8	44	-41	1	0	—	—	—	—	—
90-91— Quebec......................	NHL	55	3	7	10	49	-19	2	0	—	—	—	—	—
91-92— Quebec......................	NHL	42	5	12	17	42	-28	3	0	—	—	—	—	—
—Halifax......................	AHL	6	0	2	2	4	...	...	...	—	—	—	—	—
92-93— Quebec......................	NHL	82	9	23	32	61	25	4	0	6	1	1	2	6
93-94— Quebec......................	NHL	72	5	17	22	65	-2	3	0	—	—	—	—	—
94-95— Quebec......................	NHL	44	2	13	15	20	29	0	0	3	0	1	1	4
95-96— Colorado	NHL	77	4	15	19	73	32	0	0	17	1	2	3	6
96-97— Colorado	NHL	11	0	5	5	6	1	0	0	—	—	—	—	—
—Washington	NHL	2	0	0	0	2	0	0	0	—	—	—	—	—
—Hartford	NHL	64	4	13	17	30	-19	1	1	—	—	—	—	—
NHL totals (9 years)		588	38	120	158	463	-54	15	2	26	2	4	6	18

LEVINS, SCOTT   C/RW   COYOTES

PERSONAL: Born January 30, 1970, in Portland, Ore. ... 6-4/216. ... Shoots right. ... Name pronounced LEH-vihns.

TRANSACTIONS/CAREER NOTES: Selected by Winnipeg Jets in fourth round (fourth Jets pick, 75th overall) of NHL entry draft (June 16, 1990). ... Bruised shoulder (November 17, 1992); missed four games. ... Selected by Florida Panthers in NHL expansion draft (June 24, 1993). ... Fractured hip bone (October 17, 1993); missed eight games. ... Traded by Panthers with LW Evgeny Davydov and sixth-round pick (D Mike Gaffney) in 1994 draft to Ottawa Senators for RW Bob Kudelski (January 6, 1994). ... Injured eye (January 10, 1994); missed one game. ... Injured left knee (February 12, 1994); missed one game. ... Injured back (March 15, 1994); missed four games. ... Suffered ear infection (April 12, 1995); missed two games. ... Suffered concussion during 1995-96 season; missed three games. ... Signed as free agent by Phoenix Coyotes (July 31, 1997).

HONORS: Named to WHL All-Star second team (1989-90).

Season Team	League	REGULAR SEASON								PLAYOFFS				
		Gms.	G	A	Pts.	PIM	+/-	PP	SH	Gms.	G	A	Pts.	PIM
88-89— Penticton	BCJHL	50	27	58	85	154	...	...	...	—	—	—	—	—
89-90— Tri-City	WHL	71	25	37	62	132	...	...	...	6	2	3	5	18
90-91— Moncton	AHL	74	12	26	38	133	...	...	...	4	0	0	0	4
91-92— Moncton	AHL	69	15	18	33	271	...	...	...	11	3	4	7	30
92-93— Moncton	AHL	54	22	26	48	158	...	...	...	5	1	3	4	14
— Winnipeg	NHL	9	0	1	1	18	-2	0	0	—	—	—	—	—
93-94— Florida	NHL	29	5	6	11	69	0	2	0	—	—	—	—	—
— Ottawa	NHL	33	3	5	8	93	-26	2	0	—	—	—	—	—
94-95— Ottawa	NHL	24	5	6	11	51	4	0	0	—	—	—	—	—
— Prin. Edward Island ...	AHL	6	0	4	4	14	...	...	...	—	—	—	—	—
95-96— Ottawa	NHL	27	0	2	2	80	-3	0	0	—	—	—	—	—
— Detroit.....................	IHL	9	0	0	0	9	...	...	...	—	—	—	—	—
96-97— Springfield	AHL	68	24	23	47	267	...	...	...	11	5	4	9	37
NHL totals (4 years)		122	13	20	33	311	-27	4	0					

LIBBY, JEFF D ISLANDERS

PERSONAL: Born March 1, 1974, in Nurnberg, West Germany. ... 6-3/215. ... Shoots left.
COLLEGE: University of Maine.
TRANSACTIONS/CAREER NOTES: Signed as free agent by New York Islanders (April 14, 1997).

Season Team	League	REGULAR SEASON								PLAYOFFS				
		Gms.	G	A	Pts.	PIM	+/-	PP	SH	Gms.	G	A	Pts.	PIM
94-95— University of Maine....	Hockey East	22	2	4	6	6	...	...	...	—	—	—	—	—
95-96— University of Maine....	Hockey East	39	0	9	9	42	...	...	...	—	—	—	—	—
96-97— University of Maine....	Hockey East	34	6	25	31	41	...	...	...	—	—	—	—	—

LIDSTER, DOUG D RANGERS

PERSONAL: Born October 18, 1960, in Kamloops, B.C. ... 6-1/190. ... Shoots right. ... Full name: John Douglas Andrew Lidster.
COLLEGE: Colorado College.
TRANSACTIONS/CAREER NOTES: Selected by Vancouver Canucks in seventh round (sixth Canucks pick, 133rd overall) of NHL entry draft (June 11, 1980). ... Strained left knee (January 1988). ... Hyperextended elbow (October 1988). ... Broke hand (November 13, 1988). ... Fractured cheekbone (March 1989). ... Separated shoulder (March 1, 1992); missed 13 games. ... Sprained knee (December 13, 1992); missed nine games. ... Suffered from the flu (February 24, 1993); missed one game. ... Traded by Canucks to New York Rangers (June 25, 1993) to complete deal in which Rangers sent G John Vanbiesbrouck to Canucks for future considerations (June 20, 1993). ... Traded by Rangers with LW Esa Tikkanen to St. Louis Blues for C Petr Nedved (July 24, 1994); trade arranged as compensation for Blues signing Coach Mike Keenan. ... Broke nose (April 27, 1995); missed two games. ... Traded by Blues to Rangers for D Jay Wells (July 31, 1995). ... Suffered from the flu (December 30, 1995); missed one game. ... Suffered facial fracture (January 5, 1996); missed 12 games. ... Suffered back spasms (October 24, 1996); missed two games.
HONORS: Named to WCHA All-Star first team (1981-82 and 1982-83). ... Named to NCAA All-America West team (1982-83).
MISCELLANEOUS: Member of Stanley Cup championship team (1994). ... Captain of Vancouver Canucks (1990-91).

Season Team	League	REGULAR SEASON								PLAYOFFS				
		Gms.	G	A	Pts.	PIM	+/-	PP	SH	Gms.	G	A	Pts.	PIM
77-78— Seattle........................	WHL	2	0	0	0	0	...	...	...	—	—	—	—	—
78-79— Kamloops.................	BCJHL	59	36	47	83	50	...	...	...	—	—	—	—	—
79-80— Colorado College	WCHA	39	18	25	43	52	...	...	...	—	—	—	—	—
80-81— Colorado College	WCHA	36	10	30	40	54	...	...	...	—	—	—	—	—
81-82— Colorado College	WCHA	36	13	22	35	32	...	...	...	—	—	—	—	—
82-83— Colorado College	WCHA	34	15	41	56	30	...	...	...	—	—	—	—	—
83-84— Can. Olympic team	Int'l	59	6	20	26	28	...	...	...	—	—	—	—	—
— Vancouver.................	NHL	8	0	0	0	4	-7	0	0	2	0	1	1	0
84-85— Vancouver.................	NHL	78	6	24	30	55	-11	2	0	—	—	—	—	—
85-86— Vancouver.................	NHL	78	12	16	28	56	-12	1	1	3	0	1	1	2
86-87— Vancouver.................	NHL	80	12	51	63	40	-35	3	0	—	—	—	—	—
87-88— Vancouver.................	NHL	64	4	32	36	105	-19	2	1	—	—	—	—	—
88-89— Vancouver.................	NHL	63	5	17	22	78	-4	3	0	7	1	1	2	9
89-90— Vancouver.................	NHL	80	8	28	36	36	-16	1	0	—	—	—	—	—
90-91— Vancouver.................	NHL	78	6	32	38	77	-6	4	0	6	0	2	2	6
91-92— Vancouver.................	NHL	66	6	23	29	39	9	3	0	11	1	2	3	11
92-93— Vancouver.................	NHL	71	6	19	25	36	9	3	0	12	0	3	3	8
93-94— New York Rangers	NHL	34	0	2	2	33	-12	0	0	9	2	0	2	10
94-95— St. Louis...................	NHL	37	2	7	9	12	9	1	0	4	0	0	0	2
95-96— New York Rangers	NHL	59	5	9	14	50	11	0	0	7	1	0	1	6
96-97— New York Rangers	NHL	48	3	4	7	24	10	0	0	15	1	5	6	8
NHL totals (14 years)		844	75	264	339	645	-74	23	2	76	6	15	21	62

LIDSTROM, NICKLAS D RED WINGS

PERSONAL: Born April 28, 1970, in Vasteras, Sweden. ... 6-2/190. ... Shoots left. ... Name pronounced NIHK-luhs LIHD-struhm.
TRANSACTIONS/CAREER NOTES: Selected by Detroit Red Wings in third round (third Red Wings pick, 53rd overall) of NHL entry draft (June 17, 1989). ... Played in Europe during 1994-95 NHL lockout. ... Suffered back spasms (April 9, 1995); missed five games. ... Suffered from the flu (April 14, 1996); missed one game. ... Suffered from the flu (January 20, 1997); missed one game.
HONORS: Named to Swedish League All-Star team (1990-91). ... Named to NHL All-Rookie team (1991-92). ... Played in NHL All-Star Game (1996).
MISCELLANEOUS: Member of Stanley Cup championship team (1997).

Season Team	League	REGULAR SEASON								PLAYOFFS				
		Gms.	G	A	Pts.	PIM	+/-	PP	SH	Gms.	G	A	Pts.	PIM
88-89— Vasteras....................	Sweden	19	0	2	2	4	...	...	...	—	—	—	—	—
89-90— Vasteras....................	Sweden	39	8	8	16	14	...	...	...	—	—	—	—	—
90-91— Vasteras....................	Sweden	20	2	12	14	14	...	...	...	—	—	—	—	—
91-92— Detroit...................	NHL	80	11	49	60	22	36	5	0	11	1	2	3	0
92-93— Detroit...................	NHL	84	7	34	41	28	7	3	0	7	1	0	1	0
93-94— Detroit...................	NHL	84	10	46	56	26	43	4	0	7	3	2	5	0
94-95— Vasteras................	Sweden	13	2	10	12	4	...	...	...	—	—	—	—	—
— Detroit....................	NHL	43	10	16	26	6	15	7	0	18	4	12	16	8
95-96— Detroit...................	NHL	81	17	50	67	20	29	8	1	19	5	9	14	10
96-97— Detroit...................	NHL	79	15	42	57	30	11	8	0	20	2	6	8	2
NHL totals (6 years)		451	70	237	307	132	141	35	1	82	16	31	47	20

LIEVERS, BRETT   C   SENATORS

PERSONAL: Born June 18, 1971, in Syracuse, N.Y. ... 6-1/180. ... Shoots right. ... Name pronounced LEE-vuhrs.
HIGH SCHOOL: Wayzata (Minn.).
COLLEGE: St. Cloud (Minn.) State.
TRANSACTIONS/CAREER NOTES: Selected by New York Rangers in 11th round (13th Rangers pick, 223rd overall) of NHL entry draft (June 16, 1990). ... Missed 1992-93 season due to injuries. ... Injured knee (October 30, 1993); missed six games. ... Signed as free agent by Ottawa Senators (July 12, 1996).
HONORS: Won Ken McKenzie Trophy (1995-96).

Season Team	League	REGULAR SEASON								PLAYOFFS				
		Gms.	G	A	Pts.	PIM	+/-	PP	SH	Gms.	G	A	Pts.	PIM
90-91— St. Cloud State...........	WCHA	40	14	18	32	4	...	...	...	—	—	—	—	—
91-92— St. Cloud State...........	WCHA	16	2	10	12	2	...	...	...	—	—	—	—	—
92-93— St. Cloud State...........	WCHA						Did not play—redshirted.							
93-94— St. Cloud State...........	WCHA	32	16	16	32	2	...	...	...	—	—	—	—	—
94-95— St. Cloud State...........	WCHA	38	21	27	48	8	...	...	...	—	—	—	—	—
95-96— Utah......................	IHL	79	36	27	63	42	...	...	...	20	10	3	13	6
96-97— Utah......................	IHL	74	22	26	48	11	...	...	...	7	2	0	2	0

LIND, JUHA   C   STARS

PERSONAL: Born January 2, 1974, in Helsinki, Finland. ... 5-11/160. ... Shoots left. ... Name pronounced YOO-hah LEEND.
TRANSACTIONS/CAREER NOTES: Selected by Minnesota North Stars in eighth round (sixth North Stars pick, 178th overall) of NHL entry draft (June 26, 1992). ... North Stars franchise moved from Minnesota to Dallas and renamed Stars for 1993-94 season.

Season Team	League	REGULAR SEASON								PLAYOFFS				
		Gms.	G	A	Pts.	PIM	+/-	PP	SH	Gms.	G	A	Pts.	PIM
91-92— Jokerit Helsinki Jrs.	Finland	28	16	24	40	10	...	...	...	—	—	—	—	—
92-93— Vantaa HT	Finland Dv.II	25	8	12	20	8	...	...	...	—	—	—	—	—
— Jokerit Helsinki	Finland	6	0	0	0	2	...	...	...	1	0	0	0	0
93-94— Jokerit Helsinki	Finland	47	17	11	28	37	...	...	...	11	2	5	7	4
94-95— Jokerit Helsinki	Finland	50	10	8	18	12	...	...	...	11	1	2	3	6
95-96— Jokerit Helsinki	Finland	50	15	22	37	32	...	...	...	11	4	5	9	4
96-97— Jokerit...................	Finland	50	16	22	38	28	...	...	...	9	5	3	8	0

LINDEN, TREVOR   RW   CANUCKS

PERSONAL: Born April 11, 1970, in Medicine Hat, Alta. ... 6-4/210. ... Shoots right. ... Brother of Jamie Linden, right winger in Florida Panthers system.
TRANSACTIONS/CAREER NOTES: Selected by Vancouver Canucks in first round (first Canucks pick, second overall) of NHL entry draft (June 11, 1988). ... Hyperextended elbow (October 1989). ... Separated shoulder (March 17, 1990). ... Sprained knee ligament (December 1, 1996); missed 24 games. ... Bruised ribs (March 8, 1997); missed eight games. ... Injured knee (April 5, 1997); missed one game.
HONORS: Named to WHL All-Star second team (1987-88). ... Named to Memorial Cup All-Star team (1987-88). ... Named to NHL All-Rookie team (1988-89). ... Played in NHL All-Star Game (1991 and 1992). ... Won King Clancy Memorial Trophy (1996-97).
STATISTICAL PLATEAUS: Three-goal games: 1988-89 (2), 1990-91 (1), 1995-96 (1). Total: 4.
MISCELLANEOUS: Captain of Vancouver Canucks (1990-91 through 1996-97).

Season Team	League	REGULAR SEASON								PLAYOFFS				
		Gms.	G	A	Pts.	PIM	+/-	PP	SH	Gms.	G	A	Pts.	PIM
85-86— Medicine Hat..............	WHL	5	2	0	2	0	...	...	...	—	—	—	—	—
86-87— Medicine Hat..............	WHL	72	14	22	36	59	...	...	...	20	5	4	9	17
87-88— Medicine Hat..............	WHL	67	46	64	110	76	...	...	...	16	†13	12	25	19
88-89— Vancouver.................	NHL	80	30	29	59	41	-10	10	1	7	3	4	7	8
89-90— Vancouver.................	NHL	73	21	30	51	43	-17	6	2	—	—	—	—	—
90-91— Vancouver.................	NHL	80	33	37	70	65	-25	16	2	6	0	7	7	2
91-92— Vancouver.................	NHL	80	31	44	75	101	3	6	1	13	4	8	12	6
92-93— Vancouver.................	NHL	84	33	39	72	64	19	8	0	12	5	8	13	16
93-94— Vancouver.................	NHL	84	32	29	61	73	6	10	2	24	12	13	25	18
94-95— Vancouver.................	NHL	48	18	22	40	40	-5	9	0	11	2	6	8	12
95-96— Vancouver.................	NHL	82	33	47	80	42	6	12	1	6	4	4	8	6
96-97— Vancouver.................	NHL	49	9	31	40	27	5	2	2	—	—	—	—	—
NHL totals (9 years)		660	240	308	548	496	-18	79	11	79	30	50	80	68

L

LINDGREN, MATS   LW   OILERS

PERSONAL: Born October 1, 1974, in Skelleftea, Sweden. ... 6-2/200. ... Shoots left.
HIGH SCHOOL: Lindsay Thurber (Red Deer, Alta.).
TRANSACTIONS/CAREER NOTES: Selected by Winnipeg Jets in first round (first Jets pick, 15th overall) of NHL entry draft (June 26, 1993). ... Traded by Jets with D Boris Mironov and first-(C Jason Bonsignore) and fourth-(RW Adam Copeland) round picks in 1994 draft to Edmonton Oilers for D Dave Manson and sixth-round pick (traded to New Jersey) in 1994 draft (March 15, 1994). ... Strained lower back (March 17, 1995); missed 23 games.
HONORS: Named Swedish League Rookie of the Year (1993-94).

		REGULAR SEASON							PLAYOFFS				
Season Team	League	Gms.	G	A	Pts.	PIM	+/-	PP	SH	Gms.	G	A	Pts.	PIM
90-91— Skelleftea	Swed. Dv.II	1	0	0	0	0	...	...	...	—	—	—	—	—
91-92— Skelleftea	Swed. Dv.II	29	14	8	22	14	...	...	...	—	—	—	—	—
92-93— Skelleftea	Swed. Dv.II	32	20	14	34	18	...	...	...	—	—	—	—	—
93-94— Farjestad Karlstad	Sweden	22	11	6	17	26	...	...	...	—	—	—	—	—
94-95— Farjestad Karlstad	Sweden	37	17	15	32	20	...	...	...	3	0	0	0	4
95-96— Cape Breton	AHL	13	7	5	12	6	...	...	...	—	—	—	—	—
96-97— Hamilton	AHL	9	6	7	13	6	...	...	...	—	—	—	—	—
— Edmonton	NHL	69	11	14	25	12	-7	2	3	12	0	4	4	0
NHL totals (1 year)		69	11	14	25	12	-7	2	3	12	0	4	4	0

LINDROS, ERIC   C   FLYERS

PERSONAL: Born February 28, 1973, in London, Ont. ... 6-4/229. ... Shoots right. ... Name pronounced LIHND-rahz. ... Brother of Brett Lindros, right winger, New York Islanders (1994-95 and 1995-96).
TRANSACTIONS/CAREER NOTES: Selected by Sault Ste. Marie Greyhounds in OHL priority draft; refused to report (August 30, 1989); played for Detroit Compuware. ... Rights traded by Greyhounds to Oshawa Generals for RW Mike DeCoff, RW Jason Denomme, G Mike Lenarduzzi, second-round picks in 1991 and 1992 drafts and cash (December 17, 1989). ... Suspended two games by OHL for fighting (February 7, 1990). ... Selected by Quebec Nordiques in first round (first Nordiques pick, first overall) of NHL entry draft (June 22, 1991); refused to report. ... Traded by Nordiques to Philadelphia Flyers for G Ron Hextall, C Mike Ricci, C Peter Forsberg, D Steve Duchesne, D Kerry Huffman, first-round pick (G Jocelyn Thibault) in 1993 draft, cash and future considerations (June 20, 1992); Flyers sent LW Chris Simon and first-round pick (traded to Toronto Maple Leafs) in 1994 draft to Nordiques to complete deal (July 21, 1992). ... Sprained knee ligament (November 22, 1992); missed nine games. ... Injured knee (December 29, 1992); missed two games. ... Reinjured knee (January 10, 1993); missed 12 games. ... Tore ligament in right knee (November 12, 1993); missed 14 games. ... Suffered back spasms (March 6, 1994); missed one game. ... Sprained shoulder (April 4, 1994); missed remainder of season. ... Suffered from the flu (January 29, 1995); missed one game. ... Bruised eye (April 30, 1995); missed last game of season and first three playoff games. ... Bruised left knee (November 2, 1995); missed seven games. ... Injured knee (April 5, 1996); missed two games. ... Pulled right groin (October 1, 1996); missed 23 games. ... Bruised bone in back (February 13, 1997); missed two games. ... Suffered charley horse (March 2, 1997); missed one game. ... Bruised calf (March 22, 1997); missed two games. ... Suspended two games and fined $2,000 by NHL for two high-sticking incidents (April 9, 1997).
HONORS: Named to Memorial Cup All-Star Team (1989-90). ... Won Can.HL Player of the Year Award (1990-91). ... Won Can.HL Plus/Minus Award (1990-91). ... Won Can.HL Top Draft Prospect Award (1990-91). ... Won Red Tilson Trophy (1990-91). ... Won Eddie Powers Memorial Trophy (1990-91). ... Named to OHL All-Star first team (1990-91). ... Named to NHL All-Rookie team (1992-93). ... Played in NHL All-Star Game (1994, 1996 and 1997). ... Named NHL Player of the Year by The Sporting News (1994-95). ... Won Hart Memorial Trophy (1994-95). ... Named to The Sporting News All-Star first team (1994-95). ... Named to NHL All-Star first team (1994-95). ... Named to NHL All-Star second team (1995-96).
STATISTICAL PLATEAUS: Three-goal games: 1992-93 (3), 1993-94 (1), 1994-95 (3), 1995-96 (1). Total: 8. ... Four-goal games: 1996-97 (1). ... Total hat tricks: 9.
MISCELLANEOUS: Member of silver-medal-winning Canadian Olympic team (1992). ... Captain of Philadelphia Flyers (1994-95 through 1996-97). ... Scored on a penalty shot (vs. Don Beaupre, December 26, 1992; vs. Steve Shields, May 11, 1997 (playoffs)).

		REGULAR SEASON							PLAYOFFS				
Season Team	League	Gms.	G	A	Pts.	PIM	+/-	PP	SH	Gms.	G	A	Pts.	PIM
88-89— St. Michaels	MTHL	37	24	43	67	193	...	...	...	—	—	—	—	—
89-90— Detroit Compuware	NAJHL	14	23	29	52	123	...	...	...	—	—	—	—	—
— Oshawa	OHL	25	17	19	36	61	...	...	...	17	*18	18	36	*76
90-91— Oshawa	OHL	57	*71	78	*149	189	...	...	...	16	*18	20	*38	*93
91-92— Oshawa	OHL	13	9	22	31	54	...	...	...	—	—	—	—	—
— Canadian nat'l team	Int'l	24	19	16	35	34	...	...	...	—	—	—	—	—
— Can. Olympic team	Int'l	8	5	6	11	6	...	...	...	—	—	—	—	—
92-93— Philadelphia	NHL	61	41	34	75	147	28	8	1	—	—	—	—	—
93-94— Philadelphia	NHL	65	44	53	97	103	16	13	2	—	—	—	—	—
94-95— Philadelphia	NHL	46	29	41	†70	60	27	7	0	12	4	11	15	18
95-96— Philadelphia	NHL	73	47	68	115	163	26	15	0	12	6	6	12	43
96-97— Philadelphia	NHL	52	32	47	79	136	31	9	0	19	12	14	26	40
NHL totals (5 years)		297	193	243	436	609	128	52	3	43	22	31	53	101

LINDSAY, BILL   LW   PANTHERS

PERSONAL: Born May 17, 1971, in Big Fork, Mont. ... 5-11/185. ... Shoots left. ... Full name: William Hamilton Lindsay.
TRANSACTIONS/CAREER NOTES: Selected by Quebec Nordiques in fifth round (sixth Nordiques pick, 103rd overall) of NHL entry draft (June 22, 1991). ... Separated right shoulder (December 26, 1992); missed four games. ... Selected by Florida Panthers in NHL expansion draft (June 24, 1993). ... Cut left hand (February 22, 1996); missed seven games. ... Injured hip flexor (April 1, 1996); missed three games.
HONORS: Named to WHL (West) All-Star second team (1991-92).

		REGULAR SEASON							PLAYOFFS				
Season Team	League	Gms.	G	A	Pts.	PIM	+/-	PP	SH	Gms.	G	A	Pts.	PIM
89-90— Tri-City	WHL	72	40	45	85	84	...	...	...	—	—	—	—	—
90-91— Tri-City	WHL	63	46	47	93	151	...	...	...	—	—	—	—	—

L

Season Team	League	REGULAR SEASON							PLAYOFFS				
		Gms.	G	A	Pts.	PIM	+/-	PP	SH	Gms.	G	A	Pts.	PIM
91-92— Tri-City	WHL	42	34	59	93	111	...	...	...	3	2	3	5	16
— Quebec	NHL	23	2	4	6	14	-6	0	0	—	—	—	—	—
92-93— Quebec	NHL	44	4	9	13	16	0	0	0	—	—	—	—	—
— Halifax	AHL	20	11	13	24	18	...	...	...	—	—	—	—	—
93-94— Florida	NHL	84	6	6	12	97	-2	0	0	—	—	—	—	—
94-95— Florida	NHL	48	10	9	19	46	1	0	1	—	—	—	—	—
95-96— Florida	NHL	73	12	22	34	57	13	0	3	22	5	5	10	18
96-97— Florida	NHL	81	11	23	34	120	1	0	1	3	0	1	1	8
NHL totals (6 years)		353	45	73	118	350	7	0	5	25	5	6	11	26

LING, DAVID — RW — CANADIENS

PERSONAL: Born January 9, 1975, in Halifax, N.S. ... 5-9/185. ... Shoots right.
TRANSACTIONS/CAREER NOTES: Selected by Quebec Nordiques in seventh round (ninth Nordiques pick, 179th overall) of NHL entry draft (June 29, 1993). ... Nordiques franchise moved to Colorado and renamed Avalanche for 1995-96 season (June 21, 1995). ... Traded by Avalanche with ninth-round pick (D Steve Shirreffs) to Calgary Flames for ninth-round pick (RW Chris George) in 1995 draft (July 7, 1995). ... Traded by Flames with sixth-round pick in 1998 draft to Montreal Canadiens for C Scott Fraser (October 24, 1996).
HONORS: Won Can.HL Player of the Year Award (1994-95). ... Won Jim Mahon Memorial Trophy (1994-95). ... Won Red Tilson Trophy (1994-95). ... Named to Can.HL All-Star first team (1994-95). ... Named to OHL All-Star first team (1994-95).

Season Team	League	REGULAR SEASON							PLAYOFFS				
		Gms.	G	A	Pts.	PIM	+/-	PP	SH	Gms.	G	A	Pts.	PIM
92-93— Kingston	OHL	64	17	46	63	275	...	...	...	16	3	12	15	72
93-94— Kingston	OHL	61	37	40	77	254	...	...	...	6	4	2	6	16
94-95— Kingston	OHL	62	*61	74	135	136	...	...	...	6	7	8	15	12
95-96— Saint John	AHL	75	24	32	56	179	...	...	...	9	0	5	5	12
96-97— Fredericton	AHL	48	22	36	58	229	...	...	...	—	—	—	—	—
— Montreal	NHL	2	0	0	0	0	0	0	0	—	—	—	—	—
— Saint John	AHL	5	0	2	2	19	...	...	...	—	—	—	—	—
NHL totals (1 year)		2	0	0	0	0	0	0	0	—	—	—	—	—

LiPUMA, CHRIS — D — SHARKS

PERSONAL: Born March 23, 1971, in Chicago. ... 6-1/210. ... Shoots left. ... Name pronounced lih-POO-muh.
TRANSACTIONS/CAREER NOTES: Signed as free agent by Tampa Bay Lightning (August 24, 1992). ... Sprained left knee (February 7, 1995); missed nine games. ... Signed as free agent by San Jose Sharks (August 26, 1996). ... Claimed on waivers by New Jersey Devils (March 15, 1997). ... Claimed on waivers by Sharks (March 18, 1997).

Season Team	League	REGULAR SEASON							PLAYOFFS				
		Gms.	G	A	Pts.	PIM	+/-	PP	SH	Gms.	G	A	Pts.	PIM
88-89— Kitchener	OHL	59	7	13	20	101	...	...	...	—	—	—	—	—
89-90— Kitchener	OHL	63	11	26	37	125	...	...	...	17	1	4	5	6
90-91— Kitchener	OHL	61	6	30	36	145	...	...	...	4	0	1	1	4
91-92— Kitchener	OHL	61	13	59	72	115	...	...	...	14	4	9	13	34
92-93— Atlanta	IHL	66	4	14	18	379	...	...	...	9	1	1	2	35
— Tampa Bay	NHL	15	0	5	5	34	1	0	0	—	—	—	—	—
93-94— Tampa Bay	NHL	27	0	4	4	77	1	0	0	—	—	—	—	—
— Atlanta	IHL	42	2	10	12	254	...	...	...	11	1	1	2	28
94-95— Atlanta	IHL	41	5	12	17	191	...	...	...	—	—	—	—	—
— Tampa Bay	NHL	1	0	0	0	0	2	0	0	—	—	—	—	—
— Nashville	ECHL	1	0	0	0	0	...	...	...	—	—	—	—	—
95-96— Atlanta	IHL	48	5	11	16	146	...	...	...	—	—	—	—	—
— Tampa Bay	NHL	21	0	0	0	13	-7	0	0	—	—	—	—	—
96-97— Kentucky	AHL	48	6	17	23	93	...	...	...	4	0	3	3	6
— San Jose	NHL	8	0	0	0	22	-2	0	0	—	—	—	—	—
NHL totals (5 years)		72	0	9	9	146	-5	0	0					

LOJKIN, ALEXEI — LW — CANADIENS

PERSONAL: Born February 21, 1974, in Minsk, U.S.S.R. ... 5-9/178. ... Shoots left.
TRANSACTIONS/CAREER NOTES: Signed as free agent by Montreal Canadiens (October 21, 1995).

Season Team	League	REGULAR SEASON							PLAYOFFS				
		Gms.	G	A	Pts.	PIM	+/-	PP	SH	Gms.	G	A	Pts.	PIM
93-94— Chicoutimi	QMJHL	66	40	67	107	68	...	...	...	27	9	34	43	15
94-95— Chicoutimi	QMJHL	57	43	58	101	26	...	...	...	11	6	5	11	2
95-96— Fredericton	AHL	73	24	33	57	16	...	...	...	7	1	3	4	0
96-97— Fredericton	AHL	79	33	56	89	41	...	...	...	—	—	—	—	—

LONEY, BRIAN — RW — CANUCKS

PERSONAL: Born August 9, 1972, in Winnipeg. ... 6-2/195. ... Shoots right.
COLLEGE: Ohio State.
TRANSACTIONS/CAREER NOTES: Selected by Vancouver Canucks in fifth round (sixth Canucks pick, 110th overall) of NHL entry draft (June 20, 1992).
HONORS: Named CCHA Rookie of the Year (1991-92).

Season Team	League	REGULAR SEASON Gms.	G	A	Pts.	PIM	+/-	PP	SH	PLAYOFFS Gms.	G	A	Pts.	PIM
91-92— Ohio State	CCHA	37	21	34	55	109	...	...	...	—	—	—	—	—
92-93— Red Deer	WHL	66	39	36	75	147	...	...	...	4	1	1	2	19
—Canadian nat'l team	Int'l	1	0	1	1	0	...	...	...	—	—	—	—	—
—Hamilton	AHL	3	0	2	2	0	...	...	...	—	—	—	—	—
93-94— Hamilton	AHL	67	18	16	34	76	...	...	...	4	0	0	0	8
94-95— Syracuse	AHL	67	23	17	40	98	...	...	...	—	—	—	—	—
95-96— Syracuse	AHL	48	34	17	51	157	...	...	...	14	3	8	11	20
—Vancouver	NHL	12	2	3	5	6	2	0	0	—	—	—	—	—
96-97— Syracuse	AHL	76	19	39	58	123	...	...	...	3	0	0	0	0
NHL totals (1 year)		12	2	3	5	6	2	0	0					

LONG, ANDREW   RW   PANTHERS

PERSONAL: Born August 10, 1978, in Toronto. ... 6-2/181. ... Shoots right.
TRANSACTIONS/CAREER NOTES: Selected by Florida Panthers in fifth round (fifth Panthers pick, 129th overall) of NHL entry draft (June 22, 1996).

Season Team	League	REGULAR SEASON Gms.	G	A	Pts.	PIM	+/-	PP	SH	PLAYOFFS Gms.	G	A	Pts.	PIM
94-95— Guelph	OHL	36	1	6	7	9	...	...	...	—	—	—	—	—
95-96— Guelph	OHL	49	8	10	18	16	...	...	...	10	0	1	1	4
96-97— Guelph	OHL	42	10	36	46	30	...	...	...	13	2	10	12	6

LOWE, KEVIN   D   OILERS

PERSONAL: Born April 15, 1959, in Lachute, Que. ... 6-2/200. ... Shoots left. ... Full name: Kevin Hugh Lowe. ... Name pronounced LOH. ... Husband of Karen Percy, Canadian Olympic bronze-medal-winning downhill skier (1988); and brother of Ken Lowe, trainer for Edmonton Oilers.
TRANSACTIONS/CAREER NOTES: Selected by Edmonton Oilers in first round (first Oilers pick, 21st overall) of NHL entry draft (August 9, 1979). ... Broke index finger (March 7, 1986); missed six games. ... Broke left wrist (March 9, 1988). ... Pulled rib muscle (September 1988). ... Suffered concussion (October 14, 1988). ... Suffered back spasms (April 8, 1990). ... Bruised back (December 28, 1991); missed one game. ... Strained rotator cuff (January 28, 1992); missed three games. ... Re-strained rotator cuff (February 5, 1992); missed 21 games. ... Strained groin (April 12, 1992); missed playoffs. ... Did not report to Oilers in 1992-93 season because of contract dispute; missed 30 games. ... Traded by Oilers to New York Rangers for RW Roman Oksiuta and third-round pick (RW Alexander Kerch) in 1993 draft (December 11, 1992). ... Suffered stiff neck (December 19, 1992); missed one game. ... Suffered from the flu (December 23, 1992); missed one game. ... Injured back (February 15, 1993); missed one game. ... Injured back (February 24, 1993); missed one game. ... Suspended three preseason games and fined $500 by NHL for high-sticking incident (September 28, 1993). ... Bruised right foot (October 9, 1993); missed two games. ... Bruised thigh (October 15, 1993); missed one game. ... Suffered from the flu (December 31, 1993); missed one game. ... Injured back (February 28, 1994); missed one game. ... Reinjured back (March 10, 1994); missed one game. ... Reinjured back (March 14, 1994); missed two games. ... Sprained wrist (April 2, 1994); missed five games. ... Suffered from the flu (March 18, 1995); missed one game. ... Pinched nerve in neck (April 23, 1995); missed two games. ... Suffered sore hand (October 11, 1995); missed one game. ... Suffered from the flu (October 21, 1995); missed two games. ... Bruised foot (January 24, 1996); missed one game. ... Strained groin (February 27, 1996); missed 17 games. ... Signed as free agent by Oilers (September 19, 1996). ... Strained neck (October 4, 1996); missed six games. ... Strained neck (October 22, 1996); missed two games. ... Strained neck (January 21, 1997); missed one game. ... Suffered from the flu (February 12, 1997); missed one game. ... Injured ankle (April 11, 1997); missed last game of regular season and 11 playoff games.
HONORS: Named to QMJHL All-Star second team (1977-78 and 1978-79). ... Played in NHL All-Star Game (1984-1986, 1988-1990 and 1993). ... Won King Clancy Memorial Trophy (1989-90). ... Named Budweiser/NHL Man of the Year (1989-90).
MISCELLANEOUS: Member of Stanley Cup championship team (1984, 1985, 1987, 1988, 1990 and 1994). ... Captain of Edmonton Oilers (1991-92). ... Holds Edmonton Oilers record for most games played (1,030).

Season Team	League	REGULAR SEASON Gms.	G	A	Pts.	PIM	+/-	PP	SH	PLAYOFFS Gms.	G	A	Pts.	PIM
76-77— Quebec	QMJHL	69	3	19	22	39	...	...	...	—	—	—	—	—
77-78— Quebec	QMJHL	64	13	52	65	86	...	...	...	4	1	2	3	6
78-79— Quebec	QMJHL	68	26	60	86	120	...	...	...	6	1	7	8	36
79-80— Edmonton	NHL	64	2	19	21	70	...	2	0	3	0	1	1	0
80-81— Edmonton	NHL	79	10	24	34	94	-7	4	0	9	0	2	2	11
81-82— Edmonton	NHL	80	9	31	40	63	46	1	1	5	0	3	3	0
82-83— Edmonton	NHL	80	6	34	40	43	39	1	0	16	1	8	9	10
83-84— Edmonton	NHL	80	4	42	46	59	37	1	0	19	3	7	10	16
84-85— Edmonton	NHL	80	4	22	26	104	9	1	0	16	0	5	5	8
85-86— Edmonton	NHL	74	2	16	18	90	24	0	0	10	1	3	4	15
86-87— Edmonton	NHL	77	8	29	37	94	41	2	2	21	2	4	6	22
87-88— Edmonton	NHL	70	9	15	24	89	18	2	1	19	0	2	2	26
88-89— Edmonton	NHL	76	7	18	25	98	26	0	0	7	1	2	3	4
89-90— Edmonton	NHL	78	7	26	33	140	18	2	1	20	0	2	2	10
90-91— Edmonton	NHL	73	3	13	16	113	-9	0	0	14	1	1	2	14
91-92— Edmonton	NHL	55	2	8	10	107	-4	0	0	11	0	3	3	16
92-93— New York Rangers	NHL	49	3	12	15	58	-2	0	0	—	—	—	—	—
93-94— New York Rangers	NHL	71	5	14	19	70	4	0	0	22	1	0	1	20
94-95— New York Rangers	NHL	44	1	7	8	58	-2	1	0	10	0	1	1	12
95-96— New York Rangers	NHL	53	1	5	6	76	20	0	0	10	0	4	4	4
96-97— Edmonton	NHL	64	1	13	14	50	-1	0	0	1	0	0	0	0
NHL totals (18 years)		1247	84	348	432	1476	...	17	5	213	10	48	58	188

LOWRY, DAVE   LW   PANTHERS

PERSONAL: Born January 14, 1965, in Sudbury, Ont. ... 6-1/195. ... Shoots left. ... Name pronounced LOW-ree.
HIGH SCHOOL: Sir Wilfrid Laurier (London, Ont.).

TRANSACTIONS/CAREER NOTES: Underwent arthroscopic knee surgery (December 1982). ... Selected as underage junior by Vancouver Canucks in sixth round (fourth Canucks pick, 110th overall) of NHL entry draft (June 8, 1983). ... Traded by Canucks to St. Louis Blues for C Ernie Vargas (September 29, 1988). ... Injured groin (March 1990). ... Sprained shoulder (October 1991); missed two games. ... Injured knee (October 26, 1992); missed 26 games. ... Selected by Florida Panthers in NHL expansion draft (June 24, 1993). ... Fractured cheekbone (November 26, 1993); missed three games. ... Injured knee (December 12, 1993); missed one game. ... Suffered abrasion to right cornea (April 28, 1995); missed three games. ... Sprained left knee (October 24, 1995); missed 18 games. ... Sprained knee ligament (February 9, 1997); missed three games.

HONORS: Named to OHL All-Star first team (1984-85).

		REGULAR SEASON									PLAYOFFS				
Season Team	League	Gms.	G	A	Pts.	PIM	+/-	PP	SH		Gms.	G	A	Pts.	PIM
82-83 — London	OHL	42	11	16	27	48	...	...	...		3	0	0	0	14
83-84 — London	OHL	66	29	47	76	125	...	...	...		8	6	6	12	41
84-85 — London	OHL	61	60	60	120	94	...	...	...		8	6	5	11	10
85-86 — Vancouver	NHL	73	10	8	18	143	-21	1	0		3	0	0	0	0
86-87 — Vancouver	NHL	70	8	10	18	176	-23	0	0		—	—	—	—	—
87-88 — Fredericton	AHL	46	18	27	45	59	...	...	...		14	7	3	10	72
— Vancouver	NHL	22	1	3	4	38	-2	0	0		—	—	—	—	—
88-89 — Peoria	IHL	58	31	35	66	45	...	...	...		—	—	—	—	—
— St. Louis	NHL	21	3	3	6	11	1	0	1		10	0	5	5	4
89-90 — St. Louis	NHL	78	19	6	25	75	1	0	2		12	2	1	3	39
90-91 — St. Louis	NHL	79	19	21	40	168	19	0	2		13	1	4	5	35
91-92 — St. Louis	NHL	75	7	13	20	77	-11	0	0		6	0	1	1	20
92-93 — St. Louis	NHL	58	5	8	13	101	-18	0	0		11	2	0	2	14
93-94 — Florida	NHL	80	15	22	37	64	-4	3	0		—	—	—	—	—
94-95 — Florida	NHL	45	10	10	20	25	-3	2	0		—	—	—	—	—
95-96 — Florida	NHL	63	10	14	24	36	-2	0	0		22	10	7	17	39
96-97 — Florida	NHL	77	15	14	29	51	2	2	0		5	0	0	0	0
NHL totals (12 years)		741	122	132	254	965	-61	8	5		82	15	18	33	151

LUDWIG, CRAIG   D   STARS

PERSONAL: Born March 15, 1961, in Rhinelander, Wis. ... 6-3/217. ... Shoots left. ... Full name: Craig Lee Ludwig. ... Name pronounced LUHD-wihg.

COLLEGE: North Dakota.

TRANSACTIONS/CAREER NOTES: Selected by Montreal Canadiens in third round (fifth Canadiens pick, 61st overall) of NHL entry draft (June 11, 1980). ... Fractured knuckle in left hand (October 1984). ... Broke hand (December 2, 1985); missed nine games. ... Broke right facial bone (January 1988); missed five games. ... Suspended five games by NHL for elbowing (November 19, 1988). ... Separated right shoulder (March 21, 1990). ... Traded by Canadiens to New York Islanders for D Gerald Diduck (September 4, 1990). ... Traded by Islanders to Minnesota North Stars as part of a three-way deal in which North Stars sent D Dave Babych to Vancouver Canucks and Canucks sent D Tom Kurvers to Islanders (June 22, 1991). ... Injured foot (December 8, 1991); missed six games. ... Injured foot (January 30, 1993); missed two games. ... Pinched nerve in neck (March 18, 1993); missed two games. ... North Stars franchise moved from Minnesota to Dallas and renamed Stars for 1993-94 season. ... Suffered sore back (April 2, 1995); missed one game. ... Broke finger (December 23, 1995); missed 12 games. ... Sprained knee (February 4, 1996); missed four games. ... Injured hip flexor (February 23, 1997); missed three games.

HONORS: Named to WCHA All-Star second team (1981-82).

MISCELLANEOUS: Member of Stanley Cup championship team (1986).

		REGULAR SEASON									PLAYOFFS				
Season Team	League	Gms.	G	A	Pts.	PIM	+/-	PP	SH		Gms.	G	A	Pts.	PIM
79-80 — North Dakota	WCHA	33	1	8	9	32	...	...	...		—	—	—	—	—
80-81 — North Dakota	WCHA	34	4	8	12	48	...	...	...		—	—	—	—	—
81-82 — North Dakota	WCHA	47	5	26	31	70	...	...	...		—	—	—	—	—
82-83 — Montreal	NHL	80	0	25	25	59	4	0	0		3	0	0	0	2
83-84 — Montreal	NHL	80	7	18	25	52	-10	0	0		15	0	3	3	23
84-85 — Montreal	NHL	72	5	14	19	90	5	1	0		12	0	2	2	6
85-86 — Montreal	NHL	69	2	4	6	63	7	0	0		20	0	1	1	48
86-87 — Montreal	NHL	75	4	12	16	105	3	0	0		17	2	3	5	30
87-88 — Montreal	NHL	74	4	10	14	69	17	0	0		11	1	1	2	6
88-89 — Montreal	NHL	74	3	13	16	73	33	0	1		21	0	2	2	24
89-90 — Montreal	NHL	73	1	15	16	108	24	0	0		11	0	1	1	16
90-91 — New York Islanders	NHL	75	1	8	9	77	-24	0	0		—	—	—	—	—
91-92 — Minnesota	NHL	73	2	9	11	54	0	0	0		7	0	1	1	19
92-93 — Minnesota	NHL	78	1	10	11	153	1	0	0		—	—	—	—	—
93-94 — Dallas	NHL	84	1	13	14	123	-1	1	0		9	0	3	3	8
94-95 — Dallas	NHL	47	2	7	9	61	-6	0	0		4	0	1	1	2
95-96 — Dallas	NHL	65	1	2	3	70	-17	0	0		—	—	—	—	—
96-97 — Dallas	NHL	77	2	11	13	62	17	0	0		7	0	2	2	18
NHL totals (15 years)		1096	36	171	207	1219	53	2	1		137	3	20	23	202

LUHNING, WARREN   RW   ISLANDERS

PERSONAL: Born July 3, 1975, in Edmonton. ... 6-2/195. ... Shoots right.

COLLEGE: Michigan.

TRANSACTIONS/CAREER NOTES: Selected by New York Islanders in fourth round (fourth Islanders pick, 92nd overall) of NHL entry draft (June 26, 1993).

		REGULAR SEASON									PLAYOFFS				
Season Team	League	Gms.	G	A	Pts.	PIM	+/-	PP	SH		Gms.	G	A	Pts.	PIM
92-93 — Calgary Royals	AJHL	46	18	25	43	287	...	...	...		—	—	—	—	—
93-94 — Univ. of Michigan	CCHA	38	13	6	19	83	...	...	...		—	—	—	—	—
94-95 — Univ. of Michigan	CCHA	36	17	24	41	80	...	...	...		—	—	—	—	—
95-96 — Univ. of Michigan	CCHA	40	20	32	52	123	...	...	...		—	—	—	—	—
96-97 — Univ. of Michigan	CCHA	43	22	23	45	106	...	...	...		—	—	—	—	—

LUKOWICH, BRAD   D   STARS

PERSONAL: Born August 12, 1976, in Surrey, B.C. ... 6-1/170. ... Shoots left.
HIGH SCHOOL: Norkam Secondary (Kamloops, B.C.).
TRANSACTIONS/CAREER NOTES: Selected by New York Islanders in fourth round (fourth Islanders pick, 90th overall) of NHL entry draft (June 29, 1994). ... Traded by Islanders to Dallas Stars for third-round pick (D Robert Schnabel) in 1997 draft (June 1, 1996).

Season Team	League	REGULAR SEASON								PLAYOFFS				
		Gms.	G	A	Pts.	PIM	+/-	PP	SH	Gms.	G	A	Pts.	PIM
92-93— Cranbook	Tier II Jr. A	54	21	41	62	162	...	...	...	—	—	—	—	—
— Kamloops	WHL	1	0	0	0	0	...	...	...	—	—	—	—	—
93-94— Kamloops	WHL	42	5	11	16	166	...	...	...	16	0	1	1	35
94-95— Kamloops	WHL	63	10	35	45	125	...	...	...	18	0	7	7	21
95-96— Kamloops	WHL	65	14	55	69	114	...	...	...	13	2	10	12	29
96-97— Michigan	IHL	69	2	6	8	77	...	...	...	4	0	1	1	2

LUMME, JYRKI   D   CANUCKS

PERSONAL: Born July 16, 1966, in Tampere, Finland. ... 6-1/205. ... Shoots left. ... Name pronounced YUHR-kee LOO-mee.
TRANSACTIONS/CAREER NOTES: Selected by Montreal Canadiens in third round (third Canadiens pick, 57th overall) of NHL entry draft (June 21, 1986). ... Strained left knee ligaments (December 1988). ... Stretched knee ligaments (February 21, 1989). ... Bruised right foot (November 1989). ... Traded by Canadiens to Vancouver Canucks for second-round pick (C Craig Darby) in 1991 draft (March 6, 1990). ... Cut eye (November 19, 1991); missed three games. ... Sprained knee (January 19, 1993); missed nine games. ... Played in Europe during 1994-95 NHL lockout. ... Injured knee (February 15, 1995); missed six games. ... Bruised ribs (March 1, 1995); missed five games. ... Sprained ankle (November 13, 1996); missed two games. ... Strained shoulder (December 23, 1996); missed 11 games. ... Suffered charley horse (March 13, 1997); missed three games.
MISCELLANEOUS: Member of silver-medal-winning Finnish Olympic team (1988).

Season Team	League	REGULAR SEASON								PLAYOFFS				
		Gms.	G	A	Pts.	PIM	+/-	PP	SH	Gms.	G	A	Pts.	PIM
84-85— Koo Vee	Finland	30	6	4	10	44	...	...	...	—	—	—	—	—
85-86— Ilves Tampere	Finland	31	1	5	6	4	...	...	...	—	—	—	—	—
86-87— Ilves Tampere	Finland	43	12	12	24	52	...	...	...	4	0	1	1	0
87-88— Ilves Tampere	Finland	43	8	22	30	75	...	...	...	—	—	—	—	—
— Fin. Olympic team	Int'l	6	0	1	1	2	...	...	...	—	—	—	—	—
88-89— Montreal	NHL	21	1	3	4	10	3	1	0	—	—	—	—	—
— Sherbrooke	AHL	26	4	11	15	10	...	...	...	6	1	3	4	4
89-90— Montreal	NHL	54	1	19	20	41	17	0	0	—	—	—	—	—
— Vancouver	NHL	11	3	7	10	8	0	0	0	—	—	—	—	—
90-91— Vancouver	NHL	80	5	27	32	59	-15	1	0	6	2	3	5	0
91-92— Vancouver	NHL	75	12	32	44	65	25	3	1	13	2	3	5	4
92-93— Vancouver	NHL	74	8	36	44	55	30	3	2	12	0	5	5	6
93-94— Vancouver	NHL	83	13	42	55	50	3	1	3	24	2	11	13	16
94-95— Ilves Tampere	Finland	12	4	4	8	24	...	...	...	—	—	—	—	—
— Vancouver	NHL	36	5	12	17	26	4	3	0	11	2	6	8	8
95-96— Vancouver	NHL	80	17	37	54	50	-9	8	0	6	1	3	4	2
96-97— Vancouver	NHL	66	11	24	35	32	8	5	0	—	—	—	—	—
NHL totals (9 years)		**580**	**76**	**239**	**315**	**396**	**66**	**25**	**6**	**72**	**9**	**31**	**40**	**36**

LUONGO, CHRIS   D

PERSONAL: Born March 17, 1967, in Detroit. ... 6-0/199. ... Shoots right. ... Full name: Christopher John Luongo. ... Name pronounced loo-WAHN-goh.
HIGH SCHOOL: Notre Dame (Harper Woods, Mich.).
COLLEGE: Michigan State.
TRANSACTIONS/CAREER NOTES: Selected by Detroit Red Wings in fifth round (fifth Red Wings pick, 92nd overall) of NHL entry draft (June 15, 1985). ... Signed as free agent by Ottawa Senators (September 9, 1992). ... Traded by Senators to New York Islanders for D Jeff Finley (June 30, 1993).
HONORS: Named to NCAA All-Tournament team (1986-87). ... Named to CCHA All-Star second team (1988-89).

Season Team	League	REGULAR SEASON								PLAYOFFS				
		Gms.	G	A	Pts.	PIM	+/-	PP	SH	Gms.	G	A	Pts.	PIM
84-85— St. Clair Shores	NAJHL	41	2	25	27	...	...	...	...	—	—	—	—	—
85-86— Michigan State	CCHA	38	1	5	6	29	...	...	...	—	—	—	—	—
86-87— Michigan State	CCHA	27	4	16	20	38	...	...	...	—	—	—	—	—
87-88— Michigan State	CCHA	45	3	15	18	49	...	...	...	—	—	—	—	—
88-89— Michigan State	CCHA	47	4	21	25	42	...	...	...	—	—	—	—	—
89-90— Adirondack	AHL	53	9	14	23	37	...	...	...	3	0	0	0	0
— Phoenix	IHL	23	5	9	14	41	...	...	...	—	—	—	—	—
90-91— Detroit	NHL	4	0	1	1	4	0	0	0	—	—	—	—	—
— Adirondack	AHL	76	14	25	39	71	...	...	...	2	0	0	0	7
91-92— Adirondack	AHL	80	6	20	26	60	...	...	...	19	3	5	8	10
92-93— Ottawa	NHL	76	3	9	12	68	-47	1	0	—	—	—	—	—
— New Haven	AHL	7	0	2	2	2	...	...	...	—	—	—	—	—
93-94— Salt Lake City	IHL	51	9	31	40	54	...	...	...	—	—	—	—	—
— New York Islanders	NHL	17	1	3	4	13	-1	0	0	—	—	—	—	—
94-95— Denver	IHL	41	1	14	15	26	...	...	...	—	—	—	—	—
— New York Islanders	NHL	47	1	3	4	36	-2	0	0	—	—	—	—	—
95-96— New York Islanders	NHL	74	3	7	10	55	-23	1	0	—	—	—	—	—
96-97— Milwaukee	IHL	81	10	35	45	69	...	...	...	2	0	0	0	0
NHL totals (5 years)		**218**	**8**	**23**	**31**	**176**	**-73**	**2**	**0**					

MacDONALD, AARON   G   PANTHERS

PERSONAL: Born August 29, 1977, in Grande Prairie, Alta. ... 6-1/186. ... Catches left.
TRANSACTIONS/CAREER NOTES: Selected by Florida Panthers in second round (second Panthers pick, 36th overall) of NHL entry draft (July 8, 1995).

		REGULAR SEASON								PLAYOFFS						
Season Team	League	Gms.	Min	W	L	T	GA	SO	Avg.	Gms.	Min.	W	L	GA	SO	Avg.
93-94 —Swift Current	WHL	18	710	6	6	...	48	0	4.06	1	1	0	0	0	0	0.00
94-95 —Swift Current	WHL	53	2957	24	20	6	177	4	3.59	6	393	2	4	18	0	2.75
95-96 —Swift Current	WHL	29	1657	14	12	2	98	0	3.55	—	—	—	—	—	—	—
—Calgary	WHL	19	1025	2	14	1	84	0	4.92	—	—	—	—	—	—	—
96-97 —Calgary	WHL	30	1679	6	19	3	112	0	4.00	—	—	—	—	—	—	—
—Kelowna	WHL	23	1364	17	6	0	76	0	3.34	6	360	2	4	24	0	4.00

MacDONALD, DAVID   G   ISLANDERS

PERSONAL: Born September 23, 1976, in St. Thomas, Ont. ... 5-10/185. ... Catches left.
HIGH SCHOOL: Sudbury (Ont.).
TRANSACTIONS/CAREER NOTES: Selected by New York Islanders in ninth round (sixth Islanders pick, 210th overall) of NHL entry draft (July 8, 1995).
HONORS: Won F.W. (Dinty) Moore Trophy (1994-95).

		REGULAR SEASON								PLAYOFFS						
Season Team	League	Gms.	Min	W	L	T	GA	SO	Avg.	Gms.	Min.	W	L	GA	SO	Avg.
93-94 —Petrolia Jr. B	OHA	24	1227	...	...	...	118	0	5.77	—	—	—	—	—	—	—
—Sudbury	OHL	1	60	0	1	0	6	0	6.00	—	—	—	—	—	—	—
94-95 —Sudbury	OHL	26	1327	14	7	2	68	1	3.07	4	117	1	0	9	0	4.62
95-96 —Sudbury	OHL	40	2093	14	20	1	162	0	4.64	—	—	—	—	—	—	—
96-97 —Guelph	OHL	19	1088	6	9	2	63	0	3.97	18	1028	10	6	63	†1	3.68

MacDONALD, TODD   G   PANTHERS

PERSONAL: Born July 5, 1975, in Charlottetown, P.E.I. ... 6-0/155. ... Catches left.
TRANSACTIONS/CAREER NOTES: Selected by Florida Panthers in fifth round (seventh Panthers pick, 109th overall) of NHL entry draft (June 26, 1993).
HONORS: Named to WHL (West) All-Star first team (1994-95).

		REGULAR SEASON								PLAYOFFS						
Season Team	League	Gms.	Min	W	L	T	GA	SO	Avg.	Gms.	Min.	W	L	GA	SO	Avg.
91-92 —Kingston	OHA Mj Jr.	28	1680	...	...	...	84	0	3.00	—	—	—	—	—	—	—
92-93 —Tacoma	WHL	19	823	6	6	0	59	0	4.30	—	—	—	—	—	—	—
93-94 —Tacoma	WHL	29	1606	13	10	2	109	1	4.07	—	—	—	—	—	—	—
94-95 —Tacoma	WHL	60	3433	35	21	2	179	3	3.13	4	255	1	3	13	0	3.06
95-96 —Carolina	AHL	18	979	3	12	2	78	0	4.78	—	—	—	—	—	—	—
—Detroit	Col.HL	2	119	1	1	0	8	0	4.03	2	132	1	1	3	0	1.36
96-97 —Carolina	AHL	1	58	0	1	0	4	0	4.14	—	—	—	—	—	—	—
—Cincinnati	IHL	31	1616	11	9	‡5	73	2	2.71	1	20	0	0	1	0	3.00

MacINNIS, AL   D   BLUES

PERSONAL: Born July 11, 1963, in Inverness, N.S. ... 6-2/200. ... Shoots right. ... Name pronounced muh-KIHN-ihz.
TRANSACTIONS/CAREER NOTES: Selected by Calgary Flames as underage junior in first round (first Flames pick, 15th overall) of NHL entry draft (June 10, 1981). ... Twisted knee (February 1985). ... Lacerated hand (March 23, 1986). ... Stretched ligaments of knee (April 8, 1990). ... Separated shoulder (November 22, 1991); missed eight games. ... Dislocated left hip (November 12, 1992); missed 34 games. ... Strained shoulder (December 22, 1993); missed one game. ... Strained shoulder (January 2, 1994); missed four games. ... Bruised knee (February 24, 1994); missed four games. ... Traded by Flames with fourth-round pick (D Didier Tremblay) in 1997 draft to St. Louis Blues for D Phil Housley and second-round pick in 1996 (C Steve Begin) and 1997 (RW John Tripp) drafts (July 4, 1994). ... Injured shoulder (January 31, 1995); missed eight games. ... Suffered from the flu (April 9, 1995); missed three games. ... Injured shoulder (April 25, 1995); missed last five games of season. ... Dislocated shoulder (February 4, 1997); missed nine games.
HONORS: Named to OHL All-Star first team (1981-82 and 1982-83). ... Named to Memorial Cup All-Star team (1981-82). ... Won Max Kaminsky Trophy (1982-83). ... Played in NHL All-Star Game (1985, 1988, 1990-1992, 1994, 1996 and 1997). ... Named to NHL All-Star second team (1986-87, 1988-89 and 1993-94). ... Won Conn Smythe Trophy (1988-89). ... Named to THE SPORTING NEWS All-Star first team (1989-90 and 1990-91). ... Named to THE SPORTING NEWS All-Star second team (1993-94). ... Named to NHL All-Star first team (1989-90 and 1990-91).
STATISTICAL PLATEAUS: Three-goal games: 1991-92 (1), 1996-97 (1). Total: 2.
MISCELLANEOUS: Member of Stanley Cup championship team (1989). ... Holds Calgary Flames all-time records for most games played (803), most points (822) and most assists (609). ... Scored on a penalty shot (vs. Kelly Hrudey, April 4, 1990 (playoffs)).

		REGULAR SEASON								PLAYOFFS				
Season Team	League	Gms.	G	A	Pts.	PIM	+/-	PP	SH	Gms.	G	A	Pts.	PIM
79-80 —Regina Blues	SJHL	59	20	28	48	110	...	...	...	—	—	—	—	—
80-81 —Kitchener	OMJHL	47	11	28	39	59	...	...	...	18	4	12	16	20
81-82 —Kitchener	OHL	59	25	50	75	145	...	...	...	15	5	10	15	44
—Calgary	NHL	2	0	0	0	0	...	...	...	—	—	—	—	—
82-83 —Kitchener	OHL	51	38	46	84	67	...	...	...	8	3	8	11	9
—Calgary	NHL	14	1	3	4	9	0	0	0	—	—	—	—	—
83-84 —Colorado	CHL	19	5	14	19	22	...	...	...	—	—	—	—	—
—Calgary	NHL	51	11	34	45	42	...	...	...	11	2	12	14	13
84-85 —Calgary	NHL	67	14	52	66	75	7	8	0	4	1	2	3	8
85-86 —Calgary	NHL	77	11	57	68	76	39	4	0	21	4	*15	19	30
86-87 —Calgary	NHL	79	20	56	76	97	20	7	0	4	1	0	1	0

M

Season Team	League	REGULAR SEASON Gms.	G	A	Pts.	PIM	+/-	PP	SH	PLAYOFFS Gms.	G	A	Pts.	PIM
87-88— Calgary	NHL	80	25	58	83	114	13	7	2	7	3	6	9	18
88-89— Calgary	NHL	79	16	58	74	126	38	8	0	22	7	*24	*31	46
89-90— Calgary	NHL	79	28	62	90	82	20	14	1	6	2	3	5	8
90-91— Calgary	NHL	78	28	75	103	90	42	17	0	7	2	3	5	8
91-92— Calgary	NHL	72	20	57	77	83	13	11	0	—	—	—	—	—
92-93— Calgary	NHL	50	11	43	54	61	15	7	0	6	1	6	7	10
93-94— Calgary	NHL	75	28	54	82	95	35	12	1	7	2	6	8	12
94-95— St. Louis	NHL	32	8	20	28	43	19	2	0	7	1	5	6	10
95-96— St. Louis	NHL	82	17	44	61	88	5	9	1	13	3	4	7	20
96-97— St. Louis	NHL	72	13	30	43	65	2	6	1	6	1	2	3	4
NHL totals (16 years)		989	251	703	954	1146	268	112	6	121	30	88	118	187

MacINTYRE, ANDY — LW — BLACKHAWKS

PERSONAL: Born April 16, 1974, in Thunder Bay, Ont. ... 6-1/190. ... Shoots left.
HIGH SCHOOL: Marion Graham (Saskatoon, Sask.).
TRANSACTIONS/CAREER NOTES: Selected by Chicago Blackhawks in fourth round (fourth Blackhawks pick, 89th overall) of NHL entry draft (June 20, 1992).
HONORS: Named to WHL (East) All-Star second team (1993-94).

Season Team	League	REGULAR SEASON Gms.	G	A	Pts.	PIM	+/-	PP	SH	PLAYOFFS Gms.	G	A	Pts.	PIM
89-90— Elk Valley	BCJHL	40	24	22	46	14	...	...	...	—	—	—	—	—
90-91— Seattle	WHL	71	16	13	29	52	...	...	...	6	0	0	0	2
91-92— Seattle	WHL	12	6	2	8	18	...	...	...	—	—	—	—	—
— Saskatoon	WHL	55	22	13	35	66	...	...	...	22	10	2	12	17
92-93— Saskatoon	WHL	72	35	29	64	82	...	...	...	9	3	2	5	2
93-94— Saskatoon	WHL	72	54	35	89	58	...	...	...	16	6	6	12	16
94-95— Indianapolis	IHL	51	9	8	17	17	...	...	...	—	—	—	—	—
— Columbus	ECHL	22	7	8	15	5	...	...	...	—	—	—	—	—
95-96— Indianapolis	IHL	21	2	7	9	11	...	...	...	—	—	—	—	—
— Columbus	ECHL	27	5	7	12	31	...	...	...	2	0	1	1	0
96-97— Indianapolis	IHL	22	2	4	6	26	...	...	...	—	—	—	—	—
— Jacksonville	ECHL	37	13	13	26	17	...	...	...	—	—	—	—	—

MacIVER, NORM — D — COYOTES

PERSONAL: Born September 8, 1964, in Thunder Bay, Ont. ... 5-11/180. ... Shoots left. ... Full name: Norman Steven Maciver.
HIGH SCHOOL: Sir Winston Churchill (Thunder Bay, Ont.).
COLLEGE: Minnesota-Duluth.
TRANSACTIONS/CAREER NOTES: Signed as free agent by New York Rangers (September 8, 1986). ... Dislocated right shoulder (March 1988). ... Suffered hip pointer (November 1988). ... Traded by Rangers with LW Don Maloney and C Brian Lawton to Hartford Whalers for C Carey Wilson and fifth-round pick (C Lubos Rob) in 1990 draft (December 26, 1988). ... Traded by Whalers to Edmonton Oilers for D Jim Ennis (October 9, 1989). ... Selected by Ottawa Senators in NHL waiver draft (October 4, 1992). ... Suffered sore back (December 9, 1992); missed one game. ... Injured back (January 19, 1993); missed one game. ... Injured wrist (January 28, 1993); missed two games. ... Suffered chest contusion (October 26, 1993); missed 10 games. ... Injured left knee (January 13, 1994); missed three games. ... Injured ankle (March 2, 1994); missed 15 games. ... Broke leg (April 10, 1994); missed three games. ... Pulled groin (1995); missed one game. ... Bruised ribs (1995); missed three games. ... Suffered slight concussion (March 29, 1995); missed one game. ... Traded by Senators with C Troy Murray to Pittsburgh Penguins for C Martin Straka (April 7, 1995). ... Traded by Penguins to Winnipeg Jets for D Neil Wilkinson (December 28, 1995). ... Pulled groin (March 3, 1996); missed seven games. ... Pulled groin (March 23, 1996); missed one game. ... Jets franchise moved to Phoenix and renamed Coyotes for 1996-97 season; NHL approved move on January 18, 1996. ... Sprained neck (October 22, 1996); missed seven games. ... Underwent neck surgery (November 22, 1996); missed 27 games. ... Bruised foot (March 10, 1997); missed seven games. ... Sprained thumb (April 1, 1997); missed remainder of season.
HONORS: Named to WCHA All-Star second team (1983-84). ... Named to NCAA All-America West first team (1984-85 and 1985-86). ... Named to WCHA All-Star first team (1984-85 and 1985-86). ... Won Eddie Shore Plaque (1990-91). ... Named to AHL All-Star first team (1990-91).

Season Team	League	REGULAR SEASON Gms.	G	A	Pts.	PIM	+/-	PP	SH	PLAYOFFS Gms.	G	A	Pts.	PIM
82-83— Minnesota-Duluth	WCHA	45	1	26	27	40	...	...	...	6	0	2	2	2
83-84— Minnesota-Duluth	WCHA	31	13	28	41	28	...	...	...	8	1	10	11	8
84-85— Minnesota-Duluth	WCHA	47	14	47	61	63	...	...	...	10	3	3	6	6
85-86— Minnesota-Duluth	WCHA	42	11	51	62	36	...	...	...	4	2	3	5	2
86-87— New Haven	AHL	71	6	30	36	73	...	...	...	7	0	0	0	9
— New York Rangers	NHL	3	0	1	1	0	-5	0	0	—	—	—	—	—
87-88— Colorado	IHL	27	6	20	26	22	...	...	...	—	—	—	—	—
— New York Rangers	NHL	37	9	15	24	14	...	...	...	—	—	—	—	—
88-89— New York Rangers	NHL	26	0	10	10	14	-3	0	0	—	—	—	—	—
— Hartford	NHL	37	1	22	23	24	0	1	0	1	0	0	0	2
89-90— Binghamton	AHL	2	0	0	0	0	...	...	...	—	—	—	—	—
— Cape Breton	AHL	68	13	37	50	55	...	...	...	6	0	7	7	10
— Edmonton	NHL	1	0	0	0	0	-1	0	0	—	—	—	—	—
90-91— Cape Breton	AHL	56	13	46	59	60	...	...	...	18	0	4	4	8
— Edmonton	NHL	21	2	5	7	14	1	1	0	13	1	2	3	10
91-92— Edmonton	NHL	57	6	34	40	38	20	2	0	—	—	—	—	—
92-93— Ottawa	NHL	80	17	46	63	84	-46	7	1	—	—	—	—	—
93-94— Ottawa	NHL	53	3	20	23	26	-26	0	0	—	—	—	—	—
94-95— Ottawa	NHL	28	4	7	11	10	-9	2	0	—	—	—	—	—
— Pittsburgh	NHL	13	0	9	9	6	7	0	0	12	1	4	5	8
95-96— Pittsburgh	NHL	32	2	21	23	32	12	1	0	—	—	—	—	—
— Winnipeg	NHL	39	5	25	30	26	-6	2	0	6	1	0	1	2
96-97— Phoenix	NHL	32	4	9	13	24	-11	1	0	—	—	—	—	—
NHL totals (11 years)		459	53	224	277	312	-67	17	1	50	3	10	13	30

M

MacLEAN, DONALD   C   KINGS

PERSONAL: Born January 14, 1977, in Sydney, Nova Scotia. ... 6-2/174. ... Shoots left.
TRANSACTIONS/CAREER NOTES: Selected by Los Angeles Kings in second round (second Kings pick, 33rd overall) of NHL entry draft (July 8, 1995).

		REGULAR SEASON								PLAYOFFS				
Season Team	League	Gms.	G	A	Pts.	PIM	+/-	PP	SH	Gms.	G	A	Pts.	PIM
94-95— Beauport	QMJHL	64	15	27	42	37	...	...	...	17	4	4	8	6
95-96— Beauport	QMJHL	1	0	1	1	0	...	...	...	—	—	—	—	—
— Laval	QMJHL	21	17	11	28	29	...	...	...	—	—	—	—	—
— Hull	QMJHL	39	26	34	60	44	...	...	...	17	6	7	13	14
96-97— Hull	QMJHL	69	34	47	81	67	...	...	...	14	11	10	21	29

MacLEAN, JOHN   RW   DEVILS

PERSONAL: Born November 20, 1964, in Oshawa, Ont. ... 6-0/210. ... Shoots right. ... Name pronounced muh-KLAYN.
TRANSACTIONS/CAREER NOTES: Selected by New Jersey Devils as underage junior in first round (first Devils pick, sixth overall) of NHL entry draft (June 8, 1983). ... Bruised shoulder (November 1984). ... Injured right knee (January 25, 1985). ... Reinjured knee and underwent arthroscopic surgery (January 31, 1985). ... Bruised ankle (November 2, 1986). ... Sprained right elbow (December 1988). ... Bruised ribs (March 1, 1989). ... Suffered concussion and stomach contusions (October 1990). ... Suffered concussion (December 11, 1990). ... Tore ligament in right knee (September 30, 1991); missed entire 1991-92 season. ... Underwent surgery to right knee (November 23, 1991). ... Injured forearm (November 3, 1993); missed two games. ... Lacerated eye (February 24, 1994); missed one game. ... Bruised foot (April 9, 1995); missed one game. ... Injured knee (March 10, 1996); missed six games.
HONORS: Named to Memorial Cup All-Star team (1982-83). ... Played in NHL All-Star Game (1989 and 1991).
STATISTICAL PLATEAUS: Three-goal games: 1987-88 (1), 1988-89 (3), 1990-91 (2). Total: 6.
MISCELLANEOUS: Member of Stanley Cup championship team (1995). ... Scored on a penalty shot attempt (vs. Dominik Hasek, February 27, 1997). ... Holds New Jersey Devils franchise all-time records for most games played (908), most goals (344), most assists (346), and most points (690).

		REGULAR SEASON								PLAYOFFS				
Season Team	League	Gms.	G	A	Pts.	PIM	+/-	PP	SH	Gms.	G	A	Pts.	PIM
81-82— Oshawa	OHL	67	17	22	39	197	...	...	...	12	3	6	9	63
82-83— Oshawa	OHL	66	47	51	98	138	...	...	...	17	*18	20	†38	35
83-84— New Jersey	NHL	23	1	0	1	10	-7	0	0	—	—	—	—	—
— Oshawa	OHL	30	23	36	59	58	...	...	...	7	2	5	7	18
84-85— New Jersey	NHL	61	13	20	33	44	-11	1	0	—	—	—	—	—
85-86— New Jersey	NHL	74	21	36	57	112	-2	1	0	—	—	—	—	—
86-87— New Jersey	NHL	80	31	36	67	120	-23	9	0	—	—	—	—	—
87-88— New Jersey	NHL	76	23	16	39	147	-10	12	0	20	7	11	18	60
88-89— New Jersey	NHL	74	42	45	87	122	26	14	0	—	—	—	—	—
89-90— New Jersey	NHL	80	41	38	79	80	17	10	3	6	4	1	5	12
90-91— New Jersey	NHL	78	45	33	78	150	8	19	2	7	5	3	8	20
91-92— New Jersey	NHL	Did not play—injured.												
92-93— New Jersey	NHL	80	24	24	48	102	-6	7	1	5	0	1	1	10
93-94— New Jersey	NHL	80	37	33	70	95	30	8	0	20	6	10	16	22
94-95— New Jersey	NHL	46	17	12	29	32	13	2	1	20	5	13	18	14
95-96— New Jersey	NHL	76	20	28	48	91	3	3	3	—	—	—	—	—
96-97— New Jersey	NHL	80	29	25	54	49	11	5	0	10	4	5	9	4
NHL totals (14 years)		908	344	346	690	1154	49	91	10	88	31	44	75	142

MacLEOD, PAT   D   STARS

PERSONAL: Born June 15, 1969, in Melfort, Sask. ... 5-11/190. ... Shoots left. ... Name pronounced muh-KLOWD.
TRANSACTIONS/CAREER NOTES: Injured knee (March 1989). ... Selected by Minnesota North Stars in fifth round (fifth North Stars pick, 87th overall) of NHL entry draft (June 17, 1989). ... Selected by San Jose Sharks in NHL dispersal draft (May 30, 1991). ... Sprained shoulder (December 30, 1992); missed 21 games. ... Signed as free agent by Milwaukee Admirals (September 10, 1993). ... Signed as free agent by Dallas Stars (July 31, 1995).
HONORS: Named to WHL All-Star first team (1988-89). ... Named to IHL All-Star second team (1991-92). ... Named to IHL All-Star first team (1993-94).

		REGULAR SEASON								PLAYOFFS				
Season Team	League	Gms.	G	A	Pts.	PIM	+/-	PP	SH	Gms.	G	A	Pts.	PIM
87-88— Kamloops	WHL	50	13	33	46	27	...	...	...	18	2	7	9	6
88-89— Kamloops	WHL	37	11	34	45	14	...	...	...	15	7	18	25	24
89-90— Kalamazoo	IHL	82	9	38	47	27	...	...	...	10	1	6	7	2
90-91— Kalamazoo	IHL	59	10	30	40	16	...	...	...	11	1	2	3	5
— Minnesota	NHL	1	0	1	1	0	1	0	0	—	—	—	—	—
91-92— San Jose	NHL	37	5	11	16	4	-32	3	0	—	—	—	—	—
— Kansas City	IHL	45	9	21	30	19	...	...	...	11	1	4	5	4
92-93— San Jose	NHL	13	0	1	1	10	-19	0	0	—	—	—	—	—
— Kansas City	IHL	18	8	8	16	14	...	...	...	10	2	4	6	7
93-94— Milwaukee	IHL	73	21	52	73	18	...	...	...	3	1	2	3	0
94-95— Milwaukee	IHL	69	11	36	47	16	...	...	...	15	3	6	9	8
95-96— Michigan	IHL	50	3	23	26	18	...	...	...	7	0	3	3	0
— Dallas	NHL	2	0	0	0	0	0	0	0	—	—	—	—	—
96-97— Cincinnati	IHL	41	5	8	13	8	...	...	...	3	2	0	2	0
NHL totals (4 years)		53	5	13	18	14	-50	3	0					

M

MACOUN, JAMIE — D — MAPLE LEAFS

PERSONAL: Born August 17, 1961, in Newmarket, Ont. ... 6-2/200. ... Shoots left. ... Name pronounced muh-KOW-ihn.
COLLEGE: Ohio State.
TRANSACTIONS/CAREER NOTES: Signed as free agent by Calgary Flames (January 30, 1983). ... Fractured cheekbone (December 26, 1984). ... Suffered nerve damage to left arm in automobile accident (May 1987). ... Suffered concussion (January 23, 1989). ... Traded by Flames with C Doug Gilmour, LW Kent Manderville, D Ric Nattress and G Rick Wamsley to Toronto Maple Leafs for LW Craig Berube, D Alexander Godynyuk, LW Gary Leeman, D Michel Petit and G Jeff Reese (January 2, 1992). ... Pulled groin (February 27, 1993); missed four games. ... Suspended for one game for two stick-related game misconducts (March 9, 1994). ... Suffered from the flu (March 10, 1994); missed one game. ... Strained hip muscle (April 2, 1995); missed two games. ... Injured rib (December 3, 1996); missed seven games. ... Strained rib (January 3, 1997); missed two games.
HONORS: Named to NHL All-Rookie team (1983-84).
MISCELLANEOUS: Member of Stanley Cup championship team (1989).

		REGULAR SEASON								PLAYOFFS				
Season Team	League	Gms.	G	A	Pts.	PIM	+/-	PP	SH	Gms.	G	A	Pts.	PIM
80-81 — Ohio State	CCHA	38	9	20	29	83	...	...	...	—	—	—	—	—
81-82 — Ohio State	CCHA	25	2	18	20	89	...	...	...	—	—	—	—	—
82-83 — Ohio State	CCHA	19	6	21	27	54	...	...	...	—	—	—	—	—
— Calgary	NHL	22	1	4	5	25	3	0	0	9	0	2	2	8
83-84 — Calgary	NHL	72	9	23	32	97	3	0	1	11	1	0	1	0
84-85 — Calgary	NHL	70	9	30	39	67	44	0	0	4	1	0	1	4
85-86 — Calgary	NHL	77	11	21	32	81	14	0	2	22	1	6	7	23
86-87 — Calgary	NHL	79	7	33	40	111	33	1	0	3	0	1	1	8
87-88 — Calgary	NHL	Did not play—injured.												
88-89 — Calgary	NHL	72	8	19	27	76	40	0	0	22	3	6	9	30
89-90 — Calgary	NHL	78	8	27	35	70	34	1	0	6	0	3	3	10
90-91 — Calgary	NHL	79	7	15	22	84	29	1	1	7	0	1	1	4
91-92 — Calgary	NHL	37	2	12	14	53	10	1	0	—	—	—	—	—
— Toronto	NHL	39	3	13	16	18	0	2	0	—	—	—	—	—
92-93 — Toronto	NHL	77	4	15	19	55	3	2	0	21	0	6	6	36
93-94 — Toronto	NHL	82	3	27	30	115	-5	1	0	18	1	1	2	12
94-95 — Toronto	NHL	46	2	8	10	75	-6	1	0	7	1	2	3	8
95-96 — Toronto	NHL	82	0	8	8	87	2	0	0	6	0	2	2	8
96-97 — Toronto	NHL	73	1	10	11	93	-14	0	0	—	—	—	—	—
NHL totals (15 years)		985	75	265	340	1107	190	10	4	136	8	30	38	151

MacTAVISH, CRAIG — C

PERSONAL: Born August 15, 1958, in London, Ont. ... 6-1/195. ... Shoots left.
HIGH SCHOOL: Westminster (London, Ont.).
COLLEGE: Lowell (Mass.).
TRANSACTIONS/CAREER NOTES: Selected by Boston Bruins in ninth round (ninth Bruins pick, 153rd overall) of NHL amateur draft (June 15, 1978). ... Involved in automobile accident in which another driver was killed (January 25, 1984); pleaded guilty to vehicular homicide, driving while under the influence of alcohol and reckless driving and sentenced to a year in prison (May 1984); missed 1984-85 season. ... Signed as free agent by Edmonton Oilers (February 1, 1985). ... Strained lower back (January 1993); missed one game. ... Suffered concussion (March 10, 1993); missed one game. ... Strained wrist (October 18, 1993); missed one game. ... Reinjured wrist (December 7, 1993); missed one game. ... Suffered whiplash (December 15, 1993); missed four games. ... Bruised foot (December 30, 1993); missed one game. ... Traded by Oilers to New York Rangers for C Todd Marchant (March 21, 1994). ... Signed as free agent by Philadelphia Flyers (July 6, 1994). ... Injured foot (January 24, 1995); missed one game. ... Bruised foot (April 14, 1995); missed two games. ... Underwent knee surgery (September 25, 1995); missed first eight games of season. ... Traded by Flyers to St. Louis Blues for C Dale Hawerchuk (March 15, 1996). ... Announced retirement (April 29, 1997).
HONORS: Named ECAC Division II Rookie of the Year (1977-78). ... Named to ECAC Division II All-Star second team (1977-78). ... Named to NCAA All-America East (College Division) first team (1978-79). ... Named ECAC Division II Player of the Year (1978-79). ... Named to ECAC Division II All-Star first team (1978-79). ... Played in NHL All-Star Game (1996).
STATISTICAL PLATEAUS: Three-goal games: 1985-86 (1), 1990-91 (1). Total: 2.
MISCELLANEOUS: Member of Stanley Cup championship team (1987, 1988, 1990 and 1994). ... Captain of Edmonton Oilers (1992-93 and 1993-94). ... Scored on a penalty shot (vs. Mike Vernon, December 23, 1988). ... Does not wear a helmet.

		REGULAR SEASON								PLAYOFFS				
Season Team	League	Gms.	G	A	Pts.	PIM	+/-	PP	SH	Gms.	G	A	Pts.	PIM
77-78 — University of Lowell	ECAC-II	24	26	19	45	...	...	...	...	—	—	—	—	—
78-79 — University of Lowell	ECAC-II	31	36	52	88	...	...	...	...	—	—	—	—	—
79-80 — Binghamton	AHL	34	17	15	32	20	...	...	...	—	—	—	—	—
— Boston	NHL	46	11	17	28	8		0	0	10	2	3	5	7
80-81 — Boston	NHL	24	3	5	8	13	-1	0	0	—	—	—	—	—
— Springfield	AHL	53	19	24	43	89	...	...	...	7	5	4	9	8
81-82 — Erie	AHL	72	32	32	55	37	...	...	...	—	—	—	—	—
— Boston	NHL	2	0	1	1	0	...	...	...	—	—	—	—	—
82-83 — Boston	NHL	75	10	20	30	18	15	0	0	17	3	1	4	18
83-84 — Boston	NHL	70	20	23	43	35	9	7	0	1	0	0	0	0
84-85 — Boston	NHL	Did not play.												
85-86 — Edmonton	NHL	74	23	24	47	70	17	4	1	10	4	4	8	11
86-87 — Edmonton	NHL	79	20	19	39	55	9	1	4	21	1	9	10	16
87-88 — Edmonton	NHL	80	15	17	32	47	-3	0	3	19	0	1	1	31
88-89 — Edmonton	NHL	80	21	31	52	55	10	2	4	7	0	1	1	8
89-90 — Edmonton	NHL	80	21	22	43	89	13	1	6	22	2	6	8	29
90-91 — Edmonton	NHL	80	17	15	32	76	-1	2	6	18	3	3	6	20
91-92 — Edmonton	NHL	80	12	18	30	98	-1	0	2	16	3	0	3	28
92-93 — Edmonton	NHL	82	10	20	30	110	-16	0	0	—	—	—	—	—

M

Season Team	League	REGULAR SEASON								PLAYOFFS				
		Gms.	G	A	Pts.	PIM	+/-	PP	SH	Gms.	G	A	Pts.	PIM
93-94— Edmonton	NHL	66	16	10	26	80	-20	0	0	—	—	—	—	—
— New York Rangers	NHL	12	4	2	6	11	6	1	0	23	1	4	5	22
94-95— Philadelphia	NHL	45	3	9	12	23	2	0	0	15	1	4	5	20
95-96— Philadelphia	NHL	55	5	8	13	62	-3	0	0	—	—	—	—	—
— St. Louis	NHL	13	0	1	1	8	-6	0	0	13	0	2	2	6
96-97— St. Louis	NHL	50	2	5	7	33	-12	0	0	1	0	0	0	2
NHL totals (18 years)		1093	213	267	480	891	...	18	29	193	20	38	58	218

MADDEN, JOHN   DEVILS

PERSONAL: Born May 4, 1973, in Barrie, Ont. ... 5-11/185. ... Shoots left.
COLLEGE: Michigan
TRANSACTIONS/CAREER NOTES: Signed as free agent by New Jersey Devils (June 26, 1997).
HONORS: Named CCHA Tournament Most Valuable Player (1995-96). ... Named to NCAA All-America West first team (1996-97).

Season Team	League	REGULAR SEASON								PLAYOFFS				
		Gms.	G	A	Pts.	PIM	+/-	PP	SH	Gms.	G	A	Pts.	PIM
92-93— Barrie	COJHL	62	...	...	162	...	...	...	...	18	...	...	38	...
93-94— Univ. of Michigan	CCHA	36	6	11	17	14	...	...	...	—	—	—	—	—
94-95— Univ. of Michigan	CCHA	39	21	22	43	8	...	...	...	—	—	—	—	—
95-96— Univ. of Michigan	CCHA	43	27	30	57	45	...	...	...	—	—	—	—	—
96-97— Univ. of Michigan	CCHA	42	26	37	63	56	...	...	...	—	—	—	—	—

MAGLIARDITI, MARC   G   BLACKHAWKS

PERSONAL: Born July 9, 1976, in Niagara Falls, N.Y. ... 5-11/170. ... Catches left.
COLLEGE: Western Michigan.
TRANSACTIONS/CAREER NOTES: Selected by Chicago Blackhawks in sixth round (sixth Blackhawk pick, 146th overall) of NHL entry draft (July 8, 1995).
HONORS: Named to NCAA All-America West second team (1995-96). ... Named to CCHA All-Star first team (1995-96). ... Named CCHA Rookie of the Year (1995-96). ... Named to CCHA All-Rookie team (1995-96).

Season Team	League	REGULAR SEASON								PLAYOFFS						
		Gms.	Min	W	L	T	GA	SO	Avg.	Gms.	Min.	W	L	GA	SO	Avg.
94-95—Des Moines	USHL	29	1727	...	...	...	82	0	2.85	—	—	—	—	—	—	—
95-96—Western Michigan	CCHA	36	2111	23	11	2	92	5	2.61	—	—	—	—	—	—	—
96-97—Spokane	WHL	29	1456	12	13	1	74	0	3.05	—	—	—	—	—	—	—
—Red Deer	WHL	13	653	8	3	0	41	0	3.77	*16	*945	9	†7	*54	0	3.43

MAJOR, MARK   LW   BRUINS

PERSONAL: Born March 20, 1970, in Toronto. ... 6-4/216. ... Shoots left.
TRANSACTIONS/CAREER NOTES: Selected by Pittsburgh Penguins in second round (second Penguins pick, 25th overall) of NHL entry draft (June 11, 1988). ... Broke hand (September 1989); missed training camp. ... Signed as free agent by Boston Bruins (July 22, 1993).

Season Team	League	REGULAR SEASON								PLAYOFFS				
		Gms.	G	A	Pts.	PIM	+/-	PP	SH	Gms.	G	A	Pts.	PIM
87-88— North Bay	OHL	57	16	17	33	272	...	...	...	4	0	2	2	8
88-89— North Bay	OHL	11	3	2	5	58	...	...	...	—	—	—	—	—
— Kingston	OHL	53	22	29	51	193	...	...	...					
89-90— Kingston	OHL	62	29	32	61	168	...	...	...	6	3	3	6	12
90-91— Muskegon	IHL	60	8	10	18	160	...	...	...	5	0	0	0	0
91-92— Muskegon	IHL	80	13	18	31	302	...	...	...	12	1	3	4	29
92-93— Cleveland	IHL	82	13	15	28	155	...	...	...	3	0	0	0	0
93-94— Providence	AHL	61	17	9	26	176	...	...	...	—	—	—	—	—
94-95— Detroit	IHL	78	17	19	36	229	...	...	...	5	0	1	1	23
95-96— Adirondack	AHL	78	10	19	29	234	...	...	...	3	0	0	0	21
96-97— Adirondack	AHL	78	17	18	35	213	...	...	...	4	0	0	0	13
— Detroit	NHL	2	0	0	0	5	0	0	0					
NHL totals (1 year)		2	0	0	0	5	0	0	0					

MAKAROV, SERGEI   RW

PERSONAL: Born June 19, 1958, in Chelyabinsk, U.S.S.R. ... 5-11/195. ... Shoots left. ... Name pronounced SAIR-gay muh-kah-rahf.
TRANSACTIONS/CAREER NOTES: Selected by Calgary Flames in 12th round (14th Flames pick, 231st overall) of NHL entry draft (June 8, 1983). ... Traded by Flames to Hartford Whalers for future considerations (June 20, 1993). ... Traded by Whalers with first-round (RW Victor Kozlov), second-round (D Vlastimil Kroupa) and third-round (LW Ville Peltonen) picks in 1993 draft to San Jose Sharks for first-round pick (D Chris Pronger) in 1993 draft (June 26, 1993). ... Bruised big toe (March 22, 1994); missed one game. ... Suspended one game by NHL for spearing (March 8, 1995). ... Retired prior to 1995-96 season. ... Signed as free agent by Dallas Stars (October 18, 1996).
HONORS: Won Golden Stick Award (1979-80 and 1985-86). ... Won Soviet Player of the Year Award (1979-80, 1984-85 and 1988-89). ... Won Izvestia Trophy (1979-80 through 1981-82 and 1983-84 through 1988-89). ... Named to Soviet League All-Star team (1978-79 and 1980-81 through 1987-88). ... Won Calder Memorial Trophy (1989-90). ... Named to NHL All-Rookie team (1989-90).
STATISTICAL PLATEAUS: Three-goal games: 1990-91 (2), 1992-93 (1), 1993-94 (1). Total: 4.
MISCELLANEOUS: Member of silver-medal-winning U.S.S.R. Olympic team (1980) and gold-medal-winning U.S.S.R. Olympic team (1984 and 1988). ... Scored on a penalty shot (vs. Tim Cheveldae, March 29, 1994).

Season Team	League	REGULAR SEASON								PLAYOFFS				
		Gms.	G	A	Pts.	PIM	+/-	PP	SH	Gms.	G	A	Pts.	PIM
76-77— Traktor Chelyabinsk ...	USSR	11	1	0	1	4	...	...	...	—	—	—	—	—
77-78— Traktor Chelyabinsk ...	USSR	36	18	13	31	10	...	...	...	—	—	—	—	—
78-79— CSKA Moscow ...	USSR	44	18	21	39	12	...	...	...	—	—	—	—	—
79-80— CSKA Moscow ...	USSR	44	29	39	*68	16	...	...	...	—	—	—	—	—
— Sov. Olympic team.....	Int'l	7	5	6	11	2	...	...	...	—	—	—	—	—
80-81— CSKA Moscow ...	USSR	49	42	37	*79	22	...	...	...	—	—	—	—	—
81-82— CSKA Moscow ...	USSR	46	32	43	*75	18	...	...	...	—	—	—	—	—
82-83— CSKA Moscow ...	USSR	30	25	17	42	6	...	...	...	—	—	—	—	—
83-84— CSKA Moscow ...	USSR	44	36	37	*73	28	...	...	...	—	—	—	—	—
— Sov. Olympic team.....	Int'l	7	3	3	6	6	...	...	...	—	—	—	—	—
84-85— CSKA Moscow ...	USSR	40	26	39	*65	28	...	...	...	—	—	—	—	—
85-86— CSKA Moscow ...	USSR	40	30	32	*62	28	...	...	...	—	—	—	—	—
86-87— CSKA Moscow ...	USSR	40	21	32	*53	26	...	...	...	—	—	—	—	—
87-88— CSKA Moscow ...	USSR	51	23	45	*68	50	...	...	...	—	—	—	—	—
— Sov. Olympic team.....	Int'l	8	3	8	11	10	...	...	...	—	—	—	—	—
88-89— CSKA Moscow ...	USSR	44	21	33	*54	42	...	...	...	—	—	—	—	—
89-90— Calgary	NHL	80	24	62	86	55	33	6	0	6	0	6	6	0
90-91— Calgary	NHL	78	30	49	79	44	15	9	0	3	1	0	1	0
91-92— Calgary	NHL	68	22	48	70	60	14	6	0	—	—	—	—	—
92-93— Calgary	NHL	71	18	39	57	40	0	5	0	—	—	—	—	—
93-94— San Jose..................	NHL	80	30	38	68	78	11	10	0	14	8	2	10	4
94-95— San Jose..................	NHL	43	10	14	24	40	-4	1	0	11	3	3	6	4
95-96—						Did not play—retired.								
96-97— Dallas......................	NHL	4	0	0	0	0	-2	0	0	—	—	—	—	—
NHL totals (7 years)		424	134	250	384	317	67	37	0	34	12	11	23	8

MALAKHOV, VLADIMIR   D   CANADIENS

PERSONAL: Born August 30, 1968, in Sverdlovsk, U.S.S.R. ... 6-3/220. ... Shoots left. ... Name pronounced MAL-uh-kahv.
TRANSACTIONS/CAREER NOTES: Selected by New York Islanders in 10th round (12th Islanders pick, 191st overall) of NHL entry draft (June 17, 1989). ... Suffered sore groin prior to 1992-93 season; missed first two games of season. ... Injured right shoulder (January 16, 1993); missed eight games. ... Sprained shoulder (March 14, 1993); missed five games. ... Suffered concussion (December 7, 1993); missed one game. ... Strained lower back (December 28, 1993); missed six games. ... Injured hip flexor (February 9, 1995); missed five games. ... Suffered charley horse (March 14, 1995); missed two games. ... Traded by Islanders with C Pierre Turgeon to Montreal Canadiens for LW Kirk Muller, D Mathieu Schneider and C Craig Darby (April 5, 1995). ... Injured hip flexor (April 24, 1995); missed one game. ... Suffered from stomach flu (October 25, 1995); missed two games. ... Bruised right leg (December 12, 1995); missed two games. ... Bruised ribs (October 24, 1996); missed one game. ... Fractured thumb (December 23, 1996); missed 16 games.
HONORS: Named to NHL All-Rookie team (1992-93).
MISCELLANEOUS: Member of gold-medal-winning Unified Olympic team (1992).

Season Team	League	REGULAR SEASON								PLAYOFFS				
		Gms.	G	A	Pts.	PIM	+/-	PP	SH	Gms.	G	A	Pts.	PIM
86-87— Spartak Moscow........	USSR	22	0	1	1	12	...	...	...	—	—	—	—	—
87-88— Spartak Moscow........	USSR	28	2	2	4	26	...	...	...	—	—	—	—	—
88-89— CSKA Moscow	USSR	34	6	2	8	16	...	...	...	—	—	—	—	—
89-90— CSKA Moscow	USSR	48	2	10	12	34	...	...	...	—	—	—	—	—
90-91— CSKA Moscow	USSR	46	5	13	18	22	...	...	...	—	—	—	—	—
91-92— Unif. Olympic team	Int'l	8	3	0	3	4	...	...	...	—	—	—	—	—
— CSKA Moscow	CIS	40	1	9	10	12	...	...	...	—	—	—	—	—
92-93— Capital District	AHL	3	2	1	3	11	...	...	...	—	—	—	—	—
— New York Islanders....	NHL	64	14	38	52	59	14	7	0	17	3	6	9	12
93-94— New York Islanders....	NHL	76	10	47	57	80	29	4	0	4	0	0	0	6
94-95— New York Islanders....	NHL	26	3	13	16	32	-1	1	0	—	—	—	—	—
— Montreal	NHL	14	1	4	5	14	-2	0	0	—	—	—	—	—
95-96— Montreal	NHL	61	5	23	28	79	7	2	0	—	—	—	—	—
96-97— Montreal	NHL	65	10	20	30	43	3	5	0	5	0	0	0	6
NHL totals (5 years)		306	43	145	188	307	50	19	0	26	3	6	9	24

MALGUNAS, STEWART   D   CAPITALS

PERSONAL: Born April 21, 1970, in Prince George, B.C. ... 6-0/200. ... Shoots left. ... Name pronounced mal-GOO-nuhz.
TRANSACTIONS/CAREER NOTES: Selected by Detroit Red Wings in fourth round (third Red Wings pick, 66th overall) of NHL entry draft (June 16, 1990). ... Injured knee (September 26, 1992); missed first 10 games of season. ... Traded by Red Wings to Philadelphia Flyers for fifth-round pick (G Frederic Deschenes) in 1994 draft (September 8, 1993). ... Sprained medial collateral ligament in left knee (February 5, 1994); missed 12 games. ... Signed as free agent by Winnipeg Jets (August 8, 1995). ... Traded by Jets to Washington Capitals for RW Denis Chasse (February 15, 1996). ... Injured shoulder (April 6, 1996); missed three games.
HONORS: Named to WHL (West) All-Star first team (1989-90).

Season Team	League	REGULAR SEASON								PLAYOFFS				
		Gms.	G	A	Pts.	PIM	+/-	PP	SH	Gms.	G	A	Pts.	PIM
87-88— Prince George............	BCJHL	54	12	34	46	99	...	...	...	—	—	—	—	—
— New Westminster	WHL	6	0	0	0	0	...	...	...	—	—	—	—	—
88-89— Seattle........................	WHL	72	11	41	52	51	...	...	...	—	—	—	—	—
89-90— Seattle........................	WHL	63	15	48	63	116	...	...	...	13	2	9	11	32
90-91— Adirondack................	AHL	78	5	19	24	70	...	...	...	2	0	0	0	4
91-92— Adirondack................	AHL	69	4	28	32	82	...	...	...	18	2	6	8	28
92-93— Adirondack................	AHL	45	3	12	15	39	...	...	...	11	3	3	6	8
93-94— Philadelphia	NHL	67	1	3	4	86	2	0	0	—	—	—	—	—
94-95— Hershey	AHL	32	3	5	8	28	...	...	...	6	2	1	3	31
— Philadelphia	NHL	4	0	0	0	4	-1	0	0	—	—	—	—	—

M

Season Team	League	REGULAR SEASON								PLAYOFFS				
		Gms.	G	A	Pts.	PIM	+/-	PP	SH	Gms.	G	A	Pts.	PIM
95-96— Winnipeg	NHL	29	0	1	1	32	-10	0	0	—	—	—	—	—
— Portland	AHL	16	2	5	7	18	...	...	...	13	1	3	4	19
— Washington	NHL	1	0	0	0	0	0	0	0	—	—	—	—	—
96-97— Portland	AHL	68	6	12	18	59	...	...	...	5	0	0	0	8
— Washington	NHL	6	0	0	0	2	2	0	0	—	—	—	—	—
NHL totals (5 years)		107	1	4	5	124	-7	0	0					

MALIK, MAREK   D   HURRICANES

PERSONAL: Born June 24, 1975, in Ostrava, Czechoslovakia. ... 6-6/220. ... Shoots left. ... Name pronounced muh-REHK muh-LEEK.
TRANSACTIONS/CAREER NOTES: Selected by Hartford Whalers in third round (second Whalers pick, 72nd overall) of NHL entry draft (June 26, 1993). ... Suffered from the flu (January 20, 1997); missed three games. ... Bruised shin (March 20, 1997); missed four games. ... Whalers franchise moved to North Carolina and renamed Carolina Hurricanes for 1997-98 season; NHL approved move on June 25, 1997.

Season Team	League	REGULAR SEASON								PLAYOFFS				
		Gms.	G	A	Pts.	PIM	+/-	PP	SH	Gms.	G	A	Pts.	PIM
91-92— TJ Vitkovice Jrs	Czech. Jrs.						Statistics unavailable.							
92-93— TJ Vitkovice	Czech.	20	5	10	15	16	...	...	...	—	—	—	—	—
93-94— HC Vitkovice	Czech. Rep.	38	3	3	6	...	...	...	...	3	0	1	1	0
94-95— Springfield	AHL	58	11	30	41	91	...	...	...	—	—	—	—	—
— Hartford	NHL	1	0	1	1	0	1	0	0	—	—	—	—	—
95-96— Springfield	AHL	68	8	14	22	135	...	...	...	8	1	3	4	20
— Hartford	NHL	7	0	0	0	4	-3	0	0	—	—	—	—	—
96-97— Springfield	AHL	3	0	3	3	4	...	...	...	—	—	—	—	—
— Hartford	NHL	47	1	5	6	50	5	0	0	—	—	—	—	—
NHL totals (3 years)		55	1	6	7	54	3	0	0					

MALKOC, DEAN   D   BRUINS

PERSONAL: Born January 26, 1970, in Vancouver. ... 6-3/200. ... Shoots left. ... Name pronounced MAL-kahk.
TRANSACTIONS/CAREER NOTES: Selected by New Jersey Devils in fifth round (seventh Devils pick, 95th overall) of NHL entry draft (June 16, 1990). ... Traded by Kamloops Blazers with LW Todd Esselmont to Swift Current Broncos for RW Eddie Patterson (October 17, 1990). ... Signed as free agent by Vancouver Canucks (August 9, 1995). ... Selected by Boston Bruins from Canucks in waiver draft for cash (September 30, 1996). ... Injured left wrist and underwent arthroscopic surgery (October 5, 1996); missed 35 games.

Season Team	League	REGULAR SEASON								PLAYOFFS				
		Gms.	G	A	Pts.	PIM	+/-	PP	SH	Gms.	G	A	Pts.	PIM
87-88— Williams Lake	PCJHL	...	6	32	38	215	...	...	...	—	—	—	—	—
88-89— Powell River	BCJHL	55	10	32	42	370	...	...	...	—	—	—	—	—
89-90— Kamloops	WHL	48	3	18	21	209	...	...	...	17	0	3	3	56
90-91— Kamloops	WHL	8	1	4	5	47	...	...	...	—	—	—	—	—
— Swift Current	WHL	56	10	23	33	248	...	...	...	3	0	2	2	5
— Utica	AHL	1	0	0	0	0	...	...	...	—	—	—	—	—
91-92— Utica	AHL	66	1	11	12	274	...	...	...	4	0	2	2	6
92-93— Utica	AHL	73	5	19	24	255	...	...	...	5	0	1	1	8
93-94— Albany	AHL	79	0	9	9	296	...	...	...	5	0	0	0	21
94-95— Albany	AHL	9	0	1	1	52	...	...	...	—	—	—	—	—
— Indianapolis	IHL	62	1	3	4	193	...	...	...	—	—	—	—	—
95-96— Vancouver	NHL	41	0	2	2	136	-10	0	0	—	—	—	—	—
96-97— Boston	NHL	33	0	0	0	70	-14	0	0	—	—	—	—	—
— Providence	AHL	4	0	2	2	28	...	...	...	—	—	—	—	—
NHL totals (2 years)		74	0	2	2	206	-24	0	0					

MALLETTE, TROY   LW   BRUINS

PERSONAL: Born February 25, 1970, in Sudbury, Ont. ... 6-3/219. ... Shoots left. ... Full name: Troy Matthew Mallette. ... Name pronounced muh-LEHT.
TRANSACTIONS/CAREER NOTES: Selected by New York Rangers in second round (first Rangers pick, 22nd overall) of NHL entry draft (June 11, 1988). ... Fined $500 by NHL for head-butting (March 19, 1990). ... Sprained left knee ligaments (September 1990). ... Fined $500 by NHL for attempting to injure another player (October 28, 1990). ... Reinjured knee (October 29, 1990). ... Injured shoulder (January 13, 1991). ... Awarded to Edmonton Oilers as compensation for Rangers signing free agent C/LW Adam Graves (September 9, 1991). ... Strained knee ligament (November 1991); missed two games. ... Traded by Oilers to New Jersey Devils for LW David Maley (January 12, 1992). ... Sprained right ankle (January 24, 1992); missed four games. ... Suffered pinched nerve in neck (January 2, 1993); missed one game. ... Traded by Devils with G Craig Billington and fourth-round pick (C Cosmo Dupaul) in 1993 draft to Ottawa Senators for G Peter Sidorkiewicz and future considerations (June 20, 1993). ... Senators sent LW Mike Peluso to Devils to complete deal (June 26, 1993). ... Bruised ribs (February 24, 1995); missed five games. ... Injured hip flexor (November 4, 1995); missed 11 games. ... Reinjured hip flexor (December 2, 1995); missed three games. ... Signed as free agent by Boston Bruins (July 17, 1996). ... Injured hip (preseason, 1996-97 season); missed two games. ... Suffered back spasms (October 24, 1996); missed one game. ... Suffered back spasms (November 26, 1996); missed four games. ... Suspended two games and fined $1,000 by NHL for elbowing incident (January 7, 1997). ... Injured neck (March 22, 1997); missed two games.

Season Team	League	REGULAR SEASON								PLAYOFFS				
		Gms.	G	A	Pts.	PIM	+/-	PP	SH	Gms.	G	A	Pts.	PIM
86-87— Sault Ste. Marie	OHL	65	20	25	45	157	...	...	...	4	0	2	2	2
87-88— Sault Ste. Marie	OHL	62	18	30	48	186	...	...	...	6	1	3	4	12
88-89— Sault Ste. Marie	OHL	64	39	37	76	172	...	...	...	—	—	—	—	—
89-90— New York Rangers	NHL	79	13	16	29	305	-8	4	0	10	2	2	4	81
90-91— New York Rangers	NHL	71	12	10	22	252	-8	0	0	5	0	0	0	18
91-92— Edmonton	NHL	15	1	3	4	36	-1	0	0	—	—	—	—	—
— New Jersey	NHL	17	3	4	7	43	7	0	0	—	—	—	—	—

M

		REGULAR SEASON								PLAYOFFS				
Season Team	League	Gms.	G	A	Pts.	PIM	+/-	PP	SH	Gms.	G	A	Pts.	PIM
92-93— New Jersey	NHL	34	4	3	7	56	3	0	0	—	—	—	—	—
— Utica	AHL	5	3	3	6	17	...	...	...	—	—	—	—	—
93-94— Ottawa	NHL	82	7	16	23	166	-33	0	0	—	—	—	—	—
94-95— Ottawa	NHL	23	3	5	8	35	6	0	0	—	—	—	—	—
— Prin. Edward Island	AHL	5	1	5	6	9	...	...	...	—	—	—	—	—
95-96— Ottawa	NHL	64	2	3	5	171	-7	0	0	—	—	—	—	—
96-97— Boston	NHL	68	6	8	14	155	-8	0	0	—	—	—	—	—
NHL totals (8 years)		453	51	68	119	1219	-49	4	0	15	2	2	4	99

MALTAIS, STEVE — LW

PERSONAL: Born January 25, 1969, in Arvida, Ont. ... 6-2/210. ... Shoots left. ... Name pronounced MAHL-tay.

TRANSACTIONS/CAREER NOTES: Selected by Washington Capitals as underage junior in third round (second Capitals pick, 57th overall) of NHL entry draft (June 13, 1987). ... Traded by Capitals with C Trent Klatt to Minnesota North Stars for D Shawn Chambers (June 21, 1991). ... Traded by North Stars to Quebec Nordiques for C Kip Miller (March 8, 1992). ... Selected by Tampa Bay Lightning in NHL expansion draft (June 18, 1992). ... Traded by Lightning to Detroit Red Wings for D Dennis Vial (June 8, 1993). ... Signed as free agent by Chicago Wolves (September 8, 1994).

HONORS: Named to OHL All-Star second team (1988-89). ... Named to IHL All-Star first team (1994-95). ... Named to IHL All-Star second team (1995-96 and 1996-97).

MISCELLANEOUS: Failed to score on a penalty shot (vs. Ed Belfour, February 25, 1993).

		REGULAR SEASON								PLAYOFFS				
Season Team	League	Gms.	G	A	Pts.	PIM	+/-	PP	SH	Gms.	G	A	Pts.	PIM
85-86— Wexford Jr. B	MTHL	33	35	19	54	38	...	...	...	—	—	—	—	—
86-87— Cornwall	OHL	65	32	12	44	29	...	...	...	5	0	0	0	2
87-88— Cornwall	OHL	59	39	46	85	30	...	...	...	11	9	6	15	33
88-89— Cornwall	OHL	58	53	70	123	67	...	...	...	18	14	16	30	16
— Fort Wayne	IHL	—	—	—	—	—	—	—	—	4	2	1	3	0
89-90— Washington	NHL	8	0	0	0	2	-2	0	0	1	0	0	0	0
— Baltimore	AHL	67	29	37	66	54	...	...	...	12	6	10	16	6
90-91— Baltimore	AHL	73	36	43	79	97	...	...	...	6	1	4	5	10
— Washington	NHL	7	0	0	0	2	...	...	...	—	—	—	—	—
91-92— Kalamazoo	IHL	48	25	31	56	51	...	...	...	—	—	—	—	—
— Minnesota	NHL	12	2	1	3	2	...	...	...	—	—	—	—	—
— Halifax	AHL	10	3	3	6	0	...	...	...	—	—	—	—	—
92-93— Atlanta	IHL	16	14	10	24	22	...	...	...	—	—	—	—	—
— Tampa Bay	NHL	63	7	13	20	35	-20	4	0	—	—	—	—	—
93-94— Adirondack	AHL	73	35	49	84	79	...	...	...	12	5	11	16	14
— Detroit	NHL	4	0	1	1	0	-1	0	0	—	—	—	—	—
94-95— Chicago	IHL	79	*57	40	97	145	...	...	...	3	1	1	2	0
95-96— Chicago	IHL	81	56	66	122	161	...	...	...	9	7	7	14	20
96-97— Chicago	IHL	81	*60	54	114	62	...	...	...	4	2	0	2	4
NHL totals (5 years)		94	9	15	24	41	-23	4	0	1	0	0	0	0

MALTBY, KIRK — LW — RED WINGS

PERSONAL: Born December 22, 1972, in Guelph, Ont. ... 6-0/186. ... Shoots right.

COLLEGE: Georgian (Ont.).

TRANSACTIONS/CAREER NOTES: Selected by Edmonton Oilers in third round (fourth Oilers pick, 65th overall) of NHL entry draft (June 20, 1992). ... Suffered chip fracture of ankle bone (February 2, 1994); missed 13 games. ... Lacerated right eye (March 1, 1995); missed last game of season. ... Scratched left cornea (February 1, 1996); missed 16 games. ... Traded by Oilers to Detroit Red Wings for D Dan McGillis (March 20, 1996).

MISCELLANEOUS: Member of Stanley Cup championship team (1997).

		REGULAR SEASON								PLAYOFFS				
Season Team	League	Gms.	G	A	Pts.	PIM	+/-	PP	SH	Gms.	G	A	Pts.	PIM
88-89— Cambridge Jr. B	OHA	48	28	18	46	138	...	...	...	—	—	—	—	—
89-90— Owen Sound	OHL	61	12	15	27	90	...	...	...	12	1	6	7	15
90-91— Owen Sound	OHL	66	34	32	66	100	...	...	...	—	—	—	—	—
91-92— Owen Sound	OHL	64	50	41	91	99	...	...	...	5	3	3	6	18
92-93— Cape Breton	AHL	73	22	23	45	130	...	...	...	16	3	3	6	45
93-94— Edmonton	NHL	68	11	8	19	74	-2	0	1	—	—	—	—	—
94-95— Edmonton	NHL	47	8	3	11	49	-11	0	2	—	—	—	—	—
95-96— Edmonton	NHL	49	2	6	8	61	-16	0	0	—	—	—	—	—
— Cape Breton	AHL	4	1	2	3	6	...	...	...	—	—	—	—	—
— Detroit	NHL	6	1	0	1	6	0	0	0	8	0	1	1	4
96-97— Detroit	NHL	66	3	5	8	75	3	0	0	20	5	2	7	24
NHL totals (5 years)		236	25	22	47	265	-26	0	3	28	5	3	8	28

MANDERVILLE, KENT — C — HURRICANES

PERSONAL: Born April 12, 1971, in Edmonton. ... 6-3/200. ... Shoots left. ... Full name: Kent Stephen Manderville.

COLLEGE: Cornell.

TRANSACTIONS/CAREER NOTES: Selected by Calgary Flames in second round (first Flames pick, 24th overall) of NHL entry draft (June 17, 1989). ... Traded by Flames with C Doug Gilmour, D Jamie Macoun, D Ric Nattress and G Rick Wamsley to Toronto Maple Leafs for LW Craig Berube, D Alexander Godynyuk, RW Gary Leeman, D Michel Petit and G Jeff Reese (January 2, 1992). ... Bruised hand (October 5, 1993); missed one game. ... Suffered from the flu (December 17, 1993); missed two games. ... Sprained ankle (January 30, 1995); missed one game. ... Traded by Maple Leafs to Edmonton Oilers for C Peter White and fourth-round pick (RW Jason Sessa) in 1996 draft (December 4, 1995).

M

... Sprained left wrist (February 18, 1996); missed nine games. ... Signed as free agent by Hartford Whalers (October 1, 1996). ... Whalers franchise moved to North Carolina and renamed Carolina Hurricanes for 1997-98 season; NHL approved move on June 25, 1997.
HONORS: Named ECAC Rookie of the Year (1989-90). ... Named to ECAC All-Rookie team (1989-90).
STATISTICAL PLATEAUS: Three-goal games: 1996-97 (1).
MISCELLANEOUS: Member of silver-medal-winning Canadian Olympic team (1992).

Season Team	League	REGULAR SEASON								PLAYOFFS				
		Gms.	G	A	Pts.	PIM	+/-	PP	SH	Gms.	G	A	Pts.	PIM
88-89— Notre Dame	SJHL	58	39	36	75	165	...	...	...	—	—	—	—	—
89-90— Cornell University	ECAC	26	11	15	26	28	...	...	...	—	—	—	—	—
90-91— Cornell University	ECAC	28	17	14	31	60	...	...	...	—	—	—	—	—
— Canadian nat'l team	Int'l	3	1	2	3	0	...	...	...	—	—	—	—	—
91-92— Canadian nat'l team	Int'l	63	16	23	39	75	...	...	...	—	—	—	—	—
— Can. Olympic team	Int'l	8	1	2	3	0	...	...	...	—	—	—	—	—
— Toronto	NHL	15	0	4	4	0	1	0	0	—	—	—	—	—
— St. John's	AHL	—	—	—	—	—	...	...	...	12	5	9	14	14
92-93— Toronto	NHL	18	1	1	2	17	-9	0	0	18	1	0	1	8
— St. John's	AHL	56	19	28	47	86	...	...	...	2	0	2	2	0
93-94— Toronto	NHL	67	7	9	16	63	5	0	0	12	1	0	1	4
94-95— Toronto	NHL	36	0	1	1	22	-2	0	0	7	0	0	0	6
95-96— St. John's	AHL	27	16	12	28	26	...	...	...	—	—	—	—	—
— Edmonton	NHL	37	3	5	8	38	-5	0	2	—	—	—	—	—
96-97— Springfield	AHL	23	5	20	25	18	...	...	...	—	—	—	—	—
— Hartford	NHL	44	6	5	11	18	3	0	0	—	—	—	—	—
NHL totals (6 years)		217	17	25	42	158	-7	0	2	37	2	0	2	18

MANELUK, MIKE — LW — SENATORS

PERSONAL: Born October 1, 1973, in Winnipeg. ... 5-11/188. ... Shoots right. ... Name pronounced MAN-ih-luhk.
TRANSACTIONS/CAREER NOTES: Signed as free agent by Mighty Ducks of Anaheim (January 28, 1994). ... Traded by Mighty Ducks to Ottawa Senators for RW Kevin Brown (July 1, 1996).

Season Team	League	REGULAR SEASON								PLAYOFFS				
		Gms.	G	A	Pts.	PIM	+/-	PP	SH	Gms.	G	A	Pts.	PIM
90-91— St. Boniface	MJHL	45	29	41	70	199	...	...	...	—	—	—	—	—
91-92— Brandon	WHL	68	23	30	53	102	...	...	...	—	—	—	—	—
92-93— Brandon	WHL	72	36	51	87	75	...	...	...	4	2	1	3	2
93-94— Brandon	WHL	63	50	47	97	112	...	...	...	13	11	3	14	23
— San Diego	IHL	—	—	—	—	—	...	...	...	1	0	0	0	0
94-95— San Diego	IHL	10	0	1	1	4	...	...	...	—	—	—	—	—
— Canadian nat'l team	Int'l	44	36	24	60	34	...	...	...	—	—	—	—	—
95-96— Baltimore	AHL	74	33	38	71	73	...	...	...	6	4	3	7	14
96-97— Worcester	AHL	70	27	27	54	89	...	...	...	5	1	2	3	14

MANLOW, ERIC — C — BLACKHAWKS

PERSONAL: Born April 7, 1975, in Belleville, Ont. ... 6-0/190. ... Shoots left.
TRANSACTIONS/CAREER NOTES: Selected by Chicago Blackhawks in second round (second Blackhawks pick, 50th overall) of NHL entry draft (June 26, 1993).

Season Team	League	REGULAR SEASON								PLAYOFFS				
		Gms.	G	A	Pts.	PIM	+/-	PP	SH	Gms.	G	A	Pts.	PIM
91-92— Kitchener	OHL	59	12	20	32	17	...	...	...	14	2	5	7	8
92-93— Kitchener	OHL	53	26	21	47	31	...	...	...	4	0	1	1	2
93-94— Kitchener	OHL	49	28	32	60	25	...	...	...	3	0	1	1	4
94-95— Kitchener	OHL	44	25	29	54	26	...	...	...	—	—	—	—	—
— Detroit	OHL	16	4	16	20	11	...	...	...	21	11	10	21	18
95-96— Indianapolis	IHL	75	6	11	17	32	...	...	...	4	0	1	1	4
96-97— Columbus	ECHL	32	18	18	36	20	...	...	...	—	—	—	—	—
— Baltimore	AHL	36	6	6	12	13	...	...	...	3	0	0	0	0

MANN, CAMERON — RW — BRUINS

PERSONAL: Born April 20, 1977, in Thompson, Man. ... 5-11/185. ... Shoots right. ... Name pronounced MAN.
HIGH SCHOOL: Thomas A. Stewart (Peterborough, Ont.).
TRANSACTIONS/CAREER NOTES: Selected by Boston Bruins in fourth round (fifth Bruins pick, 99th overall) of NHL entry draft (July 8, 1995).
HONORS: Named to OHL All-Star first team (1995-96 and 1996-97). ... Won Jim Mahon Memorial Trophy (1995-96). ... Won Stafford Smythe Memorial Trophy (May 1996). ... Named to Memorial Cup All-Star team (1995-96). ... Named to OHL All-Star first team (1996-97).

Season Team	League	REGULAR SEASON								PLAYOFFS				
		Gms.	G	A	Pts.	PIM	+/-	PP	SH	Gms.	G	A	Pts.	PIM
93-94— Peterborough	Tier II Jr. A	16	3	14	17	23	...	...	...	—	—	—	—	—
— Peterborough	OHL	49	8	17	25	18	...	...	...	7	1	1	2	2
94-95— Peterborough	OHL	64	18	25	43	40	...	...	...	11	3	8	11	4
95-96— Peterborough	OHL	66	42	60	102	108	...	...	...	24	*27	16	*43	33
96-97— Peterborough	OHL	51	33	50	83	91	...	...	...	11	10	18	28	16

MANSON, DAVE — D — CANADIENS

PERSONAL: Born January 27, 1967, in Prince Albert, Sask. ... 6-2/202. ... Shoots left.
HIGH SCHOOL: Carleton (Prince Albert, Sask.).

TRANSACTIONS/CAREER NOTES: Selected by Chicago Blackhawks as underage junior in first round (first Blackhawks pick, 11th overall) of NHL entry draft (June 15, 1985). ... Suspended three games by NHL for pushing linesman (October 8, 1989). ... Bruised right thigh (December 8, 1989). ... Suspended 13 games by NHL for abusing linesman and returning to ice to fight (December 23, 1989). ... Suspended three games by NHL for biting (February 27, 1990). ... Suspended four games by NHL for attempting to injure another player (October 20, 1990). ... Traded by Blackhawks with third-round pick (RW Kirk Maltby) in 1992 draft to Edmonton Oilers for D Steve Smith (October 2, 1991). ... Suspended five off-days and fined $500 by NHL for spearing (October 19, 1992). ... Strained ligaments in left knee (December 7, 1992); missed one game. ... Separated shoulder (October 22, 1993); missed 13 games. ... Traded by Oilers with sixth-round pick in 1994 draft to Winnipeg Jets for C Mats Lindgren, D Boris Mironov and first-(C Jason Bonsignore) and fourth-(RW Adam Copeland) round picks in 1994 draft (March 15, 1994). ... Bruised kidneys (January 21, 1995); missed one game. ... Bruised hand (April 19, 1995); missed two games. ... Jets franchise moved to Phoenix and renamed Coyotes for 1996-97 season; NHL approved move on January 18, 1996. ... Broke toe (November 8, 1996); missed five games. ... Traded by Coyotes to Montreal Canadiens for D Murray Baron and RW Chris Murray (March 18, 1997). ... Fined $1,000 by NHL for criticizing a referee (April 21, 1997).

HONORS: Named to WHL All-Star second team (1985-86). ... Played in NHL All-Star Game (1989 and 1993).

MISCELLANEOUS: Failed to score on a penalty shot (vs. Darcy Wakaluk, January 24, 1991).

Season Team	League	Gms.	G	A	Pts.	PIM	+/-	PP	SH	Gms.	G	A	Pts.	PIM
83-84— Prince Albert	WHL	70	2	7	9	233	...	...	...	5	0	0	0	4
84-85— Prince Albert	WHL	72	8	30	38	247	...	...	...	13	1	0	1	34
85-86— Prince Albert	WHL	70	14	34	48	177	...	...	...	20	1	8	9	63
86-87— Chicago	NHL	63	1	8	9	146	-2	0	0	3	0	0	0	10
87-88— Saginaw	IHL	6	0	3	3	37	...	...	...	—	—	—	—	—
— Chicago	NHL	54	1	6	7	185	-12	0	0	5	0	0	0	27
88-89— Chicago	NHL	79	18	36	54	352	5	8	1	16	0	8	8	*84
89-90— Chicago	NHL	59	5	23	28	301	4	1	0	20	2	4	6	46
90-91— Chicago	NHL	75	14	15	29	191	20	6	1	6	0	1	1	36
91-92— Edmonton	NHL	79	15	32	47	220	9	7	0	16	3	9	12	44
92-93— Edmonton	NHL	83	15	30	45	210	-28	9	1	—	—	—	—	—
93-94— Edmonton	NHL	57	3	13	16	140	-4	0	0	—	—	—	—	—
— Winnipeg	NHL	13	1	4	5	51	-10	1	0	—	—	—	—	—
94-95— Winnipeg	NHL	44	3	15	18	139	-20	2	0	—	—	—	—	—
95-96— Winnipeg	NHL	82	7	23	30	205	8	3	0	6	2	1	3	30
96-97— Phoenix	NHL	66	3	17	20	164	-23	2	0	—	—	—	—	—
— Montreal	NHL	9	1	1	2	23	-1	0	0	—	—	—	—	—
NHL totals (11 years)		763	87	223	310	2327	-56	39	3	72	7	23	30	277

MARA, ROB   RW   BLACKHAWKS

PERSONAL: Born September 25, 1975, in Boston. ... 6-1/175. ... Shoots right.
HIGH SCHOOL: Belmont Hill (Mass.).
COLLEGE: Colgate.
TRANSACTIONS/CAREER NOTES: Selected by Chicago Blackhawks in 11th round (10th Blackhawks pick, 263rd overall) of NHL entry draft (June 29, 1994).

Season Team	League	Gms.	G	A	Pts.	PIM	+/-	PP	SH	Gms.	G	A	Pts.	PIM
93-94— Belmont Hill	Mass. H.S.	28	18	28	46	...	...	...	...	—	—	—	—	—
94-95— Colgate University	ECAC	33	6	8	14	30	...	...	...	—	—	—	—	—
95-96— Colgate University	ECAC	33	8	6	14	36	...	...	...	—	—	—	—	—
96-97— Colgate University	ECAC	32	18	15	33	44	...	...	...	—	—	—	—	—

MARACLE, NORM   G   RED WINGS

PERSONAL: Born October 2, 1974, in Belleville, Ont. ... 5-9/175. ... Catches left. ... Name pronounced MAIR-ih-kuhl.
HIGH SCHOOL: Marion Graham (Regina, Sask.).
TRANSACTIONS/CAREER NOTES: Selected by Detroit Red Wings in fifth round (sixth Red Wings pick, 126th overall) of NHL entry draft (June 26, 1993).
HONORS: Named to Can.HL All-Rookie team (1991-92). ... Named to WHL (East) All-Star second team (1992-93). ... Won Can.HL Goaltender-of-the-Year Award (1993-94). ... Won Del Wilson Trophy (1993-94). ... Named to Can.HL All-Star first team (1993-94). ... Named to WHL (East) All-Star first team (1993-94). ... Named to AHL All-Star second team (1996-97).

Season Team	League	Gms.	Min	W	L	T	GA	SO	Avg.	Gms.	Min.	W	L	GA	SO	Avg.
91-92—Saskatoon	WHL	29	1529	13	6	3	87	1	3.41	15	860	9	5	37	0	2.58
92-93—Saskatoon	WHL	53	2939	27	18	3	160	1	3.27	9	569	4	5	33	0	3.48
93-94—Saskatoon	WHL	56	3219	*41	13	1	148	2	2.76	16	939	†11	5	48	†1	3.07
94-95—Adirondack	AHL	39	1997	12	15	2	119	0	3.58	—	—	—	—	—	—	—
95-96—Adirondack	AHL	54	2949	24	18	6	135	2	2.75	1	29	0	1	4	0	8.28
96-97—Adirondack	AHL	*68	*3843	†34	22	9	*173	5	2.70	4	192	1	3	10	1	3.13

MARCHANT, TODD   C   OILERS

PERSONAL: Born August 12, 1973, in Buffalo, N.Y. ... 5-10/180. ... Shoots left. ... Name pronounced MAHR-shahnt.
COLLEGE: Clarkson (N.Y.).
TRANSACTIONS/CAREER NOTES: Selected by New York Rangers in seventh round (eighth Rangers pick, 164th overall) of NHL entry draft (June 26, 1993). ... Traded by Rangers to Edmonton Oilers for C Craig MacTavish (March 21, 1994). ... Suffered concussion (March 9, 1997); missed three games.
MISCELLANEOUS: Failed to score on a penalty shot (vs. Damian Rhodes, November 13, 1996; vs. Olaf Kolzig, January 26, 1997).

M

Season Team	League	REGULAR SEASON								PLAYOFFS				
		Gms.	G	A	Pts.	PIM	+/-	PP	SH	Gms.	G	A	Pts.	PIM
91-92— Clarkson....................	ECAC	33	20	12	32	32	...	...	...	—	—	—	—	—
92-93— Clarkson....................	ECAC	33	18	28	46	38	...	...	...	—	—	—	—	—
93-94— U.S. national team	Int'l	59	28	39	67	48	...	...	...	—	—	—	—	—
— U.S. Olympic team.....	Int'l	8	1	1	2	6	...	...	...	—	—	—	—	—
— Binghamton	AHL	8	2	7	9	6	...	...	...	—	—	—	—	—
— New York Rangers.....	NHL	1	0	0	0	0	-1	0	0	—	—	—	—	—
— Edmonton	NHL	3	0	1	1	2	-1	0	0	—	—	—	—	—
— Cape Breton	AHL	3	1	4	5	2	...	...	...	5	1	1	2	0
94-95— Cape Breton	AHL	38	22	25	47	25	...	...	...	—	—	—	—	—
— Edmonton	NHL	45	13	14	27	32	-3	3	2	—	—	—	—	—
95-96— Edmonton	NHL	81	19	19	38	66	-19	2	3	—	—	—	—	—
96-97— Edmonton	NHL	79	14	19	33	44	11	0	4	12	4	2	6	12
NHL totals (4 years)		209	46	53	99	144	-13	5	9	12	4	2	6	12

MARCHMENT, BRYAN — D — OILERS

PERSONAL: Born May 1, 1969, in Scarborough, Ont. ... 6-1/205. ... Shoots left.

TRANSACTIONS/CAREER NOTES: Suspended three games by OHL (October 1, 1986). ... Selected by Winnipeg Jets as underage junior in first round (first Jets pick, 16th overall) of NHL entry draft (June 13, 1987). ... Suspended six games by AHL for fighting (December 10, 1989). ... Sprained shoulder (March 1990). ... Suffered back spasms (March 13, 1991). ... Traded by Jets with D Chris Norton to Chicago Blackhawks for C Troy Murray and LW Warren Rychel (July 22, 1991). ... Fractured cheekbone (December 12, 1991); missed 12 games. ... Suspended one preseason game and fined $500 by NHL for headbutting (September 30, 1993). ... Traded with RW Steve Larmer by Blackhawks to Hartford Whalers for LW Patrick Poulin and D Eric Weinrich (November 2, 1993). ... Suspended two games and fined $500 by NHL for illegal check (December 21, 1993). ... Sprained ankle (January 14, 1994); missed three games. ... Sprained ankle (February 19, 1994); missed remainder of season. ... Awarded to Edmonton Oilers as compensation for Whalers signing free agent RW Steven Rice (August 30, 1994). ... Suspended one game by NHL for game misconduct penalties (March 22, 1995). ... Suspended two games by NHL for game misconduct penalties (March 27, 1995). ... Strained lower back (April 15, 1995); missed two games. ... Suspended three games and fined $500 by NHL for leaving bench to fight (April 29, 1995). ... Suspended five games by NHL for kneeing player in preseason game (September 25, 1995). ... Injured ribs (October 22, 1996); missed two games. ... Suffered from the flu (January 28, 1997); missed one game. ... Cracked ribs (February 13, 1997); missed eight games. ... Suffered concussion (April 18, 1997); missed remainder of season.

HONORS: Named to OHL All-Star second team (1988-89).

MISCELLANEOUS: Failed to score on a penalty shot (vs. Pat Jablonski, December 31, 1992).

Season Team	League	REGULAR SEASON								PLAYOFFS				
		Gms.	G	A	Pts.	PIM	+/-	PP	SH	Gms.	G	A	Pts.	PIM
84-85— Toronto Nationals	MTHL	...	14	35	49	229	...	...	...	—	—	—	—	—
85-86— Belleville....................	OHL	57	5	15	20	225	...	...	...	21	0	7	7	*83
86-87— Belleville....................	OHL	52	6	38	44	238	...	...	...	6	0	4	4	17
87-88— Belleville....................	OHL	56	7	51	58	200	...	...	...	6	1	3	4	19
88-89— Belleville....................	OHL	43	14	36	50	198	...	...	...	5	0	1	1	12
— Winnipeg	NHL	2	0	0	0	2	0	0	0	—	—	—	—	—
89-90— Winnipeg	NHL	7	0	2	2	28	0	0	0	—	—	—	—	—
— Moncton	AHL	56	4	19	23	217	...	...	...	—	—	—	—	—
90-91— Winnipeg	NHL	28	2	2	4	91	-5	0	0	—	—	—	—	—
— Moncton	AHL	33	2	11	13	101	...	...	...	—	—	—	—	—
91-92— Chicago...................	NHL	58	5	10	15	168	-4	2	0	16	1	0	1	36
92-93— Chicago...................	NHL	78	5	15	20	313	15	1	0	4	0	0	0	12
93-94— Chicago...................	NHL	13	1	4	5	42	-2	0	0	—	—	—	—	—
— Hartford	NHL	42	3	7	10	124	-12	0	1	—	—	—	—	—
94-95— Edmonton	NHL	40	1	5	6	184	-11	0	0	—	—	—	—	—
95-96— Edmonton	NHL	78	3	15	18	202	-7	0	0	—	—	—	—	—
96-97— Edmonton	NHL	71	3	13	16	132	13	1	0	3	0	0	0	4
NHL totals (9 years)		417	23	73	96	1286	-13	4	1	23	1	0	1	52

MARHA, JOSEF — C — AVALANCHE

PERSONAL: Born June 2, 1976, in Havl. Brod, Czechoslovakia. ... 6-0/176. ... Shoots left. ... Name pronounced MAHR-hah.

TRANSACTIONS/CAREER NOTES: Selected by Quebec Nordiques in second round (third Nordiques pick, 35th overall) of NHL entry draft (June 28, 1994). ... Nordiques franchise moved to Colorado and renamed Avalanche for 1995-96 season (June 21, 1995).

Season Team	League	REGULAR SEASON								PLAYOFFS				
		Gms.	G	A	Pts.	PIM	+/-	PP	SH	Gms.	G	A	Pts.	PIM
91-92— Jihlava.	Czech.	25	12	13	25	0	...	...	...	—	—	—	—	—
92-93— Dukla Jihlava	Czech.	7	2	2	4	4	...	...	...	—	—	—	—	—
93-94— Dukla Jihlava	Czech Rep.	41	7	2	9	...	...	...	...	3	0	1	1	0
94-95— Dukla Jihlava	Czech Rep.	35	3	7	10	...	...	...	...	—	—	—	—	—
95-96— Cornwall....................	AHL	74	18	30	48	30	...	...	...	8	1	2	3	10
— Colorado	NHL	2	0	1	1	0	1	0	0	—	—	—	—	—
96-97— Hershey	AHL	67	23	49	72	44	...	...	...	19	6	†16	*22	10
— Colorado	NHL	6	0	1	1	0	0	0	0	—	—	—	—	—
NHL totals (2 years)		8	0	2	2	0	1	0	0					

MARINUCCI, CHRIS — LW — KINGS

PERSONAL: Born December 29, 1971, in Grand Rapids, Minn. ... 6-0/175. ... Shoots left. ... Full name: Christopher Jon Marinucci. ... Name pronounced mair-ih-NOO-chee.

HIGH SCHOOL: Grand Rapids (Minn.).

M

COLLEGE: Minnesota-Duluth.
TRANSACTIONS/CAREER NOTES: Selected by New York Islanders in fifth round (fourth Islanders pick, 90th overall) of NHL entry draft (June 16, 1990). ... Traded by Islanders to Los Angeles Kings for C Nicholas Vachon (November 19, 1996).
HONORS: Named to WCHA All-Star second team (1992-93). ... Won Hobey Baker Memorial Award (1993-94). ... Named WCHA Player of the Year (1993-94). ... Named to WCHA All-Star first team (1993-94). ... Won Ken McKenzie Trophy (1994-95).

Season Team	League	Gms.	G	A	Pts.	PIM	+/-	PP	SH	Gms.	G	A	Pts.	PIM
		REGULAR SEASON								PLAYOFFS				
88-89— Grand Rapids............	Minn. H.S.	25	24	18	42	...	...	...	...	—	—	—	—	—
89-90— Grand Rapids............	Minn. H.S.	28	24	39	63	0	...	...	...	—	—	—	—	—
90-91— Minnesota-Duluth......	WCHA	36	6	10	16	20	...	...	...	—	—	—	—	—
91-92— Minnesota-Duluth......	WCHA	37	6	13	19	41	...	...	...	—	—	—	—	—
92-93— Minnesota-Duluth......	WCHA	40	35	42	77	52	...	...	...	—	—	—	—	—
93-94— Minnesota-Duluth......	WCHA	38	*30	31	61	65	...	...	...	—	—	—	—	—
94-95— Denver	IHL	74	29	40	69	42	...	...	...	14	3	4	7	12
— New York Islanders....	NHL	12	1	4	5	2	-1	0	0	—	—	—	—	—
95-96— Utah	IHL	8	3	5	8	8	...	...	...	—	—	—	—	—
96-97— Utah	IHL	21	3	13	16	6	...	...	...	—	—	—	—	—
— Phoenix.....................	IHL	62	23	29	52	26	...	...	...	—	—	—	—	—
— Los Angeles	NHL	1	0	0	0	0	-2	0	0	—	—	—	—	—
NHL totals (2 years)		13	1	4	5	2	-3	0	0					

MAROIS, DAN   RW   STARS

PERSONAL: Born October 3, 1968, in Montreal. ... 6-0/190. ... Shoots right. ... Name pronounced MAIR-wah.
TRANSACTIONS/CAREER NOTES: Selected by Toronto Maple Leafs as underage junior in second round (second Maple Leafs pick, 28th overall) of NHL entry draft (June 13, 1987). ... Suffered from the flu (January 1989). ... Damaged ligaments in right knee and underwent surgery (April 2, 1989). ... Bruised left shoulder (November 12, 1989); missed 11 games. ... Injured wrist (October 25, 1991); missed two games. ... Traded by Maple Leafs with C Claude Loiselle to New York Islanders for LW Ken Baumgartner and C Dave McLlwain (March 10, 1992). ... Strained lower back (December 23, 1992); missed three games. ... Strained lower back (March 7, 1993); missed five games. ... Traded by Islanders to Boston Bruins for eighth-round pick (C Peter Hogardh) in 1994 draft (March 18, 1993). ... Underwent back surgery (April 1, 1993). ... Injured shoulder (October 22, 1993); missed 54 games. ... Underwent back surgery (December 1994); missed entire season. ... Signed as free agent by Dallas Stars (January 26, 1996).
STATISTICAL PLATEAUS: Three-goal games: 1988-89 (2), 1989-90 (1). Total: 3.

Season Team	League	Gms.	G	A	Pts.	PIM	+/-	PP	SH	Gms.	G	A	Pts.	PIM
		REGULAR SEASON								PLAYOFFS				
85-86— Verdun	QMJHL	58	42	35	77	110	...	...	...	5	4	2	6	6
86-87— Chicoutimi	QMJHL	40	22	26	48	143	...	...	...	16	7	14	21	25
87-88— Verdun	QMJHL	67	52	36	88	153	...	...	...	—	—	—	—	—
— Newmarket...............	AHL	8	4	4	8	4	...	...	...	—	—	—	—	—
— Toronto	NHL	—	—	—	—	—	...	...	...	3	1	0	1	0
88-89— Toronto	NHL	76	31	23	54	76	...	...	...	—	—	—	—	—
89-90— Toronto	NHL	68	39	37	76	82	1	14	0	5	2	2	4	12
90-91— Toronto	NHL	78	21	9	30	112	-16	6	0	—	—	—	—	—
91-92— Toronto	NHL	63	15	11	26	76	-36	4	0	—	—	—	—	—
— New York Islanders....	NHL	12	2	5	7	18	2	0	0	—	—	—	—	—
92-93— New York Islanders....	NHL	28	2	5	7	35	-3	0	0	—	—	—	—	—
— Capital District	AHL	4	2	0	2	0	...	...	...	—	—	—	—	—
93-94— Boston	NHL	22	7	3	10	18	-4	3	0	11	0	1	1	16
— Providence.................	AHL	6	1	2	3	6	...	...	...	—	—	—	—	—
94-95— Boston	NHL				Did not play—injured.					—	—	—	—	—
95-96— Michigan	IHL	61	28	28	56	105	...	...	...	—	—	—	—	—
— Dallas........................	NHL	3	0	0	0	2	0	0	0	—	—	—	—	—
— Minnesota.................	IHL	13	4	3	7	20	0	0	0	—	—	—	—	—
96-97— Quebec	IHL	7	1	1	2	12	...	...	...	—	—	—	—	—
— Utah..........................	IHL	29	7	9	16	58	...	...	...	—	—	—	—	—
NHL totals (9 years)		350	117	93	210	419	-56	27	0	19	3	3	6	28

MARSHALL, GRANT   RW   STARS

PERSONAL: Born June 9, 1973, in Toronto. ... 6-1/185. ... Shoots right.
HIGH SCHOOL: Hillcrest (Thunder Bay, Ont.).
TRANSACTIONS/CAREER NOTES: Selected by Toronto Maple Leafs in first round (second Maple Leafs pick, 23rd overall) of NHL entry draft (June 20, 1992). ... Awarded to Dallas Stars with C Peter Zezel as compensation for Maple Leafs signing free-agent RW Mike Craig (August 10, 1994). ... Strained muscle (November 15, 1996); missed four games. ... Sprained shoulder (December 8, 1996); missed four games. ... Suffered concussion (January 4, 1997); missed two games.

Season Team	League	Gms.	G	A	Pts.	PIM	+/-	PP	SH	Gms.	G	A	Pts.	PIM
		REGULAR SEASON								PLAYOFFS				
90-91— Ottawa	OHL	26	6	11	17	25	...	...	...	1	0	0	0	0
91-92— Ottawa	OHL	61	32	51	83	132	...	...	...	11	6	11	17	11
92-93— Newmarket................	OHL	31	12	25	37	85	...	...	...	7	4	7	11	20
— Ottawa	OHL	30	14	28	42	83	...	...	...	—	—	—	—	—
— St. John's..................	AHL	2	0	0	0	0	...	...	...	2	0	0	0	2
93-94— St. John's..................	AHL	67	11	29	40	155	...	...	...	11	1	5	6	17
94-95— Kalamazoo	IHL	61	17	29	46	96	...	...	...	16	9	3	12	27
— Dallas........................	NHL	2	0	1	1	0	1	0	0	—	—	—	—	—
95-96— Dallas.......................	NHL	70	9	19	28	111	0	0	0	—	—	—	—	—
96-97— Dallas.......................	NHL	56	6	4	10	98	5	0	0	5	0	2	2	8
NHL totals (3 years)		128	15	24	39	209	6	0	0	5	0	2	2	8

MARSHALL, JASON   D   MIGHTY DUCKS

PERSONAL: Born February 22, 1971, in Cranbrook, B.C. ... 6-2/200. ... Shoots right.

TRANSACTIONS/CAREER NOTES: WHL rights traded by Regina Pats with RW Devin Derksen to Tri-City Americans for RW Mark Cipriano (August 1988). ... Selected by St. Louis Blues in first round (first Blues pick, ninth overall) of NHL entry draft (June 17, 1989). ... Traded by Blues to Mighty Ducks of Anaheim for D Bill Houlder (August 29, 1994). ... Cut finger (November 24, 1996); missed two games. ... Bruised hand (March 19, 1997); missed five games.

Season Team	League				REGULAR SEASON								PLAYOFFS		
		Gms.	G	A	Pts.	PIM	+/-	PP	SH	Gms.	G	A	Pts.	PIM
87-88— Columbia Valley	KIJHL	40	4	28	32	150	—	...	...	—	—	—	—	—
88-89— Vernon	BCJHL	48	10	30	40	197	...	...	...	31	6	6	12	141
— Canadian nat'l team	Int'l	2	0	1	1	0	...	...	...	—	—	—	—	—
89-90— Canadian nat'l team	Int'l	72	1	11	12	57	...	...	...	—	—	—	—	—
90-91— Tri-City	WHL	59	10	34	44	236	...	...	...	7	1	2	3	20
— Peoria	IHL	—					...	...	...	18	0	1	1	48
91-92— Peoria	IHL	78	4	18	22	178	...	...	...	10	0	1	1	16
— St. Louis	NHL	2	1	0	1	4	0	0	0	—	—	—	—	—
92-93— Peoria	IHL	77	4	16	20	229	...	...	...	4	0	0	0	20
93-94— Peoria	IHL	20	1	1	2	72	...	...	...	3	2	0	2	2
— Canadian nat'l team	Int'l	41	3	10	13	60	...	...	...	—	—	—	—	—
94-95— San Diego	IHL	80	7	18	25	218	...	...	...	5	0	1	1	8
— Anaheim	NHL	1	0	0	0	0	-2	0	0	—	—	—	—	—
95-96— Baltimore	AHL	57	1	13	14	150	...	...	...	—	—	—	—	—
— Anaheim	NHL	24	0	1	1	42	3	0	0	—	—	—	—	—
96-97— Anaheim	NHL	73	1	9	10	140	6	0	0	7	0	1	1	4
NHL totals (4 years)		100	2	10	12	186	7	0	0	7	0	1	1	4

MARTIN, CRAIG   RW   COYOTES

PERSONAL: Born January 21, 1971, in Amherst, N.S. ... 6-2/215. ... Shoots right.

TRANSACTIONS/CAREER NOTES: Suspended by QMJHL for opening game of 1990-91 season for fighting in a playoff game (April 14, 1990). ... Selected by Winnipeg Jets in fifth round (sixth Jets pick, 98th overall) of NHL entry draft (June 16, 1990). ... Suspended by QMJHL for striking referee with stick (December 9, 1990). ... Signed as free agent by Detroit Red Wings (July 28, 1993). ... Selected by Jets in 1994-95 NHL waiver draft for cash (January 18, 1995). ... Jets franchise moved to Phoenix and renamed Coyotes for 1996-97 season; NHL approved move on January 18, 1996.

Season Team	League				REGULAR SEASON								PLAYOFFS		
		Gms.	G	A	Pts.	PIM	+/-	PP	SH	Gms.	G	A	Pts.	PIM
87-88— Hull	QMJHL	66	5	5	10	137	...	...	...	—	—	—	—	—
88-89— Hull	QMJHL	70	14	29	43	260	...	...	...	—	—	—	—	—
89-90— Hull	QMJHL	66	14	31	45	299	...	...	...	11	2	1	3	65
90-91— Hull	QMJHL	18	5	6	11	166	...	...	...	—	—	—	—	—
— St. Hyacinthe	QMJHL	36	8	9	17	87	...	...	...	—	—	—	—	—
91-92— Fort Wayne	IHL	24	0	0	0	115	...	...	...	—	—	—	—	—
— Moncton	AHL	11	1	1	2	70	...	...	...	—	—	—	—	—
92-93— Moncton	AHL	64	5	13	18	198	...	...	...	5	0	1	1	22
93-94— Adirondack	AHL	76	15	24	39	297	...	...	...	12	2	2	4	63
94-95— Winnipeg	NHL	20	0	1	1	19	-4	0	0	—	—	—	—	—
— Springfield	AHL	6	0	1	1	21	...	...	...	—	—	—	—	—
95-96— Springfield	AHL	48	6	5	11	245	...	...	...	8	0	1	1	34
96-97— Carolina	AHL	44	1	2	3	239	...	...	...	—	—	—	—	—
— Florida	NHL	1	0	0	0	5	0	0	0	—	—	—	—	—
— San Antonio	IHL	15	3	3	6	99	...	...	...	6	0	1	1	25
NHL totals (2 years)		21	0	1	1	24	-4	0	0	—	—	—	—	—

MARTIN, MATT   D   MAPLE LEAFS

PERSONAL: Born April 30, 1971, in Hamden, Conn. ... 6-3/205. ... Shoots left.

HIGH SCHOOL: Avon (Conn.) Old Farms School for Boys.

COLLEGE: Maine.

TRANSACTIONS/CAREER NOTES: Selected by Toronto Maple Leafs in fourth round (fourth Maple Leaf pick, 66th overall) of 1989 NHL entry draft (June 17, 1989). ... Loaned to U.S. Olympic team (October 5, 1993). ... Returned to Maple Leafs (October 19, 1993). ... Loaned to U.S. Olympic team (October 28, 1993). ... Returned to Maple Leafs (November 3, 1993). ... Loaned to U.S. Olympic team (November 15, 1993). ... Returned to Maple Leafs (March 1, 1994). ... Suffered hip pointer (April 8, 1995); missed three games. ... Broke ankle (January 6, 1996); missed 30 games.

Season Team	League				REGULAR SEASON								PLAYOFFS		
		Gms.	G	A	Pts.	PIM	+/-	PP	SH	Gms.	G	A	Pts.	PIM
88-89— Avon Old Farms	Conn. H.S.	...	9	23	32	...	...	...	...	—	—	—	—	—
89-90—						Statistics unavailable.								
90-91— University of Maine	Hockey East	35	3	12	15	48	...	...	...	—	—	—	—	—
91-92— University of Maine	Hockey East	30	4	14	18	46	...	...	...	—	—	—	—	—
92-93— University of Maine	Hockey East	44	6	26	32	88	...	...	...	—	—	—	—	—
— St. John's	AHL	2	0	0	0	2	...	...	...	9	1	5	6	4
93-94— U.S. national team	Int'l	39	7	8	15	127	...	...	...	—	—	—	—	—
— Toronto	NHL	12	0	1	1	6	0	0	0	—	—	—	—	—
— U.S. Olympic team	Int'l	8	0	2	2	8	...	...	...	—	—	—	—	—
— St. John's	AHL	12	1	5	6	9	...	...	...	11	1	5	6	33
94-95— St. John's	AHL	49	2	16	18	54	...	...	...	—	—	—	—	—
— Toronto	NHL	15	0	0	0	13	2	0	0	—	—	—	—	—
95-96— Toronto	NHL	13	0	0	0	14	-1	0	0	—	—	—	—	—

M

Season Team	League	REGULAR SEASON								PLAYOFFS				
		Gms.	G	A	Pts.	PIM	+/-	PP	SH	Gms.	G	A	Pts.	PIM
96-97— Toronto	NHL	36	0	4	4	38	-12	0	0	—	—	—	—	—
— St. John's...................	AHL	12	1	3	4	4	...	...	...	—	—	—	—	—
NHL totals (4 years)		76	0	5	5	71	-11	0	0	—	—	—	—	—

MARTIN, MIKE — D — RANGERS

PERSONAL: Born October 27, 1976, in Stratford, Ont. ... 6-3/205. ... Shoots right.
TRANSACTIONS/CAREER NOTES: Selected by New York Rangers in third round (second Rangers pick, 65th overall) of NHL entry draft (July 8, 1995).

Season Team	League	REGULAR SEASON								PLAYOFFS				
		Gms.	G	A	Pts.	PIM	+/-	PP	SH	Gms.	G	A	Pts.	PIM
91-92— Stratford	OPJHL	16	2	3	5	14	...	...	...	—	—	—	—	—
92-93— Windsor	OHL	61	2	7	9	80	...	...	...	4	1	2	3	4
93-94— Windsor	OHL	64	2	29	31	94	...	...	...	4	1	2	3	4
94-95— Windsor	OHL	53	9	28	37	79	...	...	...	10	1	3	4	21
95-96— Windsor	OHL	65	19	48	67	128	...	...	...	7	0	6	6	14
96-97— Binghamton	AHL	62	2	7	9	45	...	...	...	3	0	1	1	2

MARTINS, STEVE — C — HURRICANES

PERSONAL: Born April 13, 1972, in Gatineau, Que. ... 5-9/180. ... Shoots left.
HIGH SCHOOL: Choate Rosemary Hall (Wallingford, Conn.).
COLLEGE: Harvard.
TRANSACTIONS/CAREER NOTES: Injured ankle (1992); missed first 11 games of 1992-93 season. ... Selected by Hartford Whalers in first round (first Whalers pick, fifth overall) of NHL supplemental draft (June 24, 1994). ... Whalers franchise moved to North Carolina and renamed Carolina Hurricanes for 1997-98 season; NHL approved move on June 25, 1997.
HONORS: Named to NCAA All-America East first team (1993-94). ... Named ECAC Player of the Year (1993-94). ... Named to NCAA All-Tournament team (1993-94). ... Named to ECAC All-Star first team (1993-94).

Season Team	League	REGULAR SEASON								PLAYOFFS				
		Gms.	G	A	Pts.	PIM	+/-	PP	SH	Gms.	G	A	Pts.	PIM
91-92— Harvard University	ECAC	20	13	14	27	26	...	...	...	—	—	—	—	—
92-93— Harvard University	ECAC	18	6	8	14	40	...	...	...	—	—	—	—	—
93-94— Harvard University	ECAC	32	25	35	60	93	...	...	...	—	—	—	—	—
94-95— Harvard University	ECAC	28	15	23	38	93	...	...	...	—	—	—	—	—
95-96— Springfield	AHL	30	9	20	29	10	...	...	...	—	—	—	—	—
— Hartford	NHL	23	1	3	4	8	-3	0	0	—	—	—	—	—
96-97— Springfield	AHL	63	12	31	43	78	...	...	...	17	1	3	4	26
— Hartford	NHL	2	0	1	1	0	0	0	0	—	—	—	—	—
NHL totals (2 years)		25	1	4	5	8	-3	0	0	—	—	—	—	—

MASON, CHRIS — G — MIGHTY DUCKS

PERSONAL: Born April 20, 1976, in Red Deer, Alta. ... 5-11/180. ... Catches left.
TRANSACTIONS/CAREER NOTES: Selected by New Jersey Devils in fifth round (seventh Devils pick, 122nd overall) of NHL entry draft (July 8, 1995). ... Signed as free agent by Mighty Ducks of Anaheim (May 31, 1997).

Season Team	League	REGULAR SEASON								PLAYOFFS						
		Gms.	Min.	W	L	T	GA	SO	Avg.	Gms.	Min.	W	L	GA	SO	Avg.
94-95— Prince George	WHL	44	2288	8	30	1	192	1	5.03	—	—	—	—	—	—	—
95-96— Prince George	WHL	59	3289	16	37	1	236	1	4.31	—	—	—	—	—	—	—
96-07— Prince George	WHL	50	2851	19	24	4	172	2	3.62	15	938	9	6	44	†1	2.81

MASON, WESLEY — LW — DEVILS

PERSONAL: Born December 12, 1977, in Sault Ste. Marie, Ont. ... 6-2/180. ... Shoots right.
TRANSACTIONS/CAREER NOTES: Selected by New Jersey Devils in second round (second Devils pick, 38th overall) of NHL entry draft (June 22, 1996).

Season Team	League	REGULAR SEASON								PLAYOFFS				
		Gms.	G	A	Pts.	PIM	+/-	PP	SH	Gms.	G	A	Pts.	PIM
94-95— Sarnia	OHL	38	1	8	9	50	...	...	...	2	0	0	0	9
95-96— Sarnia	OHL	63	23	45	68	97	...	...	...	10	3	2	5	16
96-97— Sarnia	OHL	66	45	46	91	72	...	...	...	12	7	11	18	10

MASTAD, MILT — D — BRUINS

PERSONAL: Born March 5, 1975, in Regina, Sask. ... 6-3/205. ... Shoots left. ... Name pronounced muh-STAD.
HIGH SCHOOL: Meadowdale (Lynnwood, Wash.).
TRANSACTIONS/CAREER NOTES: Selected by Boston Bruins in sixth round (sixth Bruins pick, 155th overall) of NHL entry draft (June 26, 1993).

Season Team	League	REGULAR SEASON								PLAYOFFS				
		Gms.	G	A	Pts.	PIM	+/-	PP	SH	Gms.	G	A	Pts.	PIM
91-92— Surrey Jr. A	BCJHL	55	1	13	14	122	...	...	...	—	—	—	—	—
92-93— Seattle........................	WHL	60	1	1	2	123	...	...	...	5	0	1	1	14

M

Season Team	League	REGULAR SEASON								PLAYOFFS				
		Gms.	G	A	Pts.	PIM	+/-	PP	SH	Gms.	G	A	Pts.	PIM
93-94 — Seattle	WHL	29	1	3	4	59	...	...	...	—	—	—	—	—
— Moose Jaw	WHL	41	2	8	10	74	...	...	...	—	—	—	—	—
94-95 — Moose Jaw	WHL	68	1	8	9	155	...	...	...	5	0	0	0	6
95-96 — Providence	AHL	18	0	2	2	52	...	...	...	—	—	—	—	—
96-97 — Providence	AHL	33	0	2	2	106	...	...	...	—	—	—	—	—
— Charlotte	ECHL	9	0	0	0	25	...	...	...	3	0	1	1	4

MATTE, CHRISTIAN — RW — AVALANCHE

PERSONAL: Born January 20, 1975, in Hull, Que. ... 5-11/166. ... Shoots right. ... Name pronounced MAT.

TRANSACTIONS/CAREER NOTES: Selected by Quebec Nordiques in sixth round (eighth Nordiques pick, 153rd overall) of NHL entry draft (June 26, 1993). ... Nordiques franchise moved to Colorado and renamed Avalanche for 1995-96 season (June 21, 1995). ... Broke hand (January 2, 1997); missed six games.

HONORS: Named to QMJHL All-Star second team (1993-94).

Season Team	League	REGULAR SEASON								PLAYOFFS				
		Gms.	G	A	Pts.	PIM	+/-	PP	SH	Gms.	G	A	Pts.	PIM
92-93 — Granby	QMJHL	68	17	36	53	56	...	...	...	—	—	—	—	—
93-94 — Granby	QMJHL	59	50	47	97	103	...	...	...	7	5	5	10	12
— Cornwall	AHL	1	0	0	0	0	...	...	...	—	—	—	—	—
94-95 — Granby	QMJHL	66	50	66	116	86	...	...	...	13	11	7	18	12
— Cornwall	AHL	—	—	—	—	—	...	...	...	3	0	1	1	2
95-96 — Cornwall	AHL	64	20	32	52	51	...	...	...	7	1	1	2	6
96-97 — Hershey	AHL	49	18	18	36	78	...	...	...	22	8	3	11	25
— Colorado	NHL	5	1	1	2	0	1	0	0	—	—	—	—	—
NHL totals (1 year)		5	1	1	2	0	1	0	0					

MATTEAU, STEPHANE — LW — SHARKS

PERSONAL: Born September 2, 1969, in Rouyn, Que. ... 6-3/215. ... Shoots left. ... Name pronounced muh-TOH.

TRANSACTIONS/CAREER NOTES: Selected by Calgary Flames as underage junior in second round (second Flames pick, 25th overall) of NHL entry draft (June 13, 1987). ... Bruised thigh (October 10, 1991); missed 43 games. ... Traded by Flames to Chicago Blackhawks for D Trent Yawney (December 16, 1991). ... Fractured left foot (January 27, 1992); missed 12 games. ... Suffered tonsillitis (September 1992); missed first three games of 1992-93 season. ... Pulled groin (December 17, 1993); missed three games. ... Traded by Blackhawks with RW Brian Noonan to New York Rangers for RW Tony Amonte and rights to LW Matt Oates (March 21, 1994). ... Suffered from the flu (February 1, 1995); missed one game. ... Suffered back spasms (April 24, 1995); missed two games. ... Broke hand (September 24, 1995); missed six games. ... Traded by Rangers to St. Louis Blues for C Ian Laperriere (December 28, 1995). ... Traded by Blues to San Jose Sharks for C Darren Turcotte (July 25, 1997).

MISCELLANEOUS: Member of Stanley Cup championship team (1994).

Season Team	League	REGULAR SEASON								PLAYOFFS				
		Gms.	G	A	Pts.	PIM	+/-	PP	SH	Gms.	G	A	Pts.	PIM
85-86 — Hull	QMJHL	60	6	8	14	19	...	...	...	4	0	0	0	0
86-87 — Hull	QMJHL	69	27	48	75	113	...	...	...	8	3	7	10	8
87-88 — Hull	QMJHL	57	17	40	57	179	...	...	...	18	5	14	19	84
88-89 — Hull	QMJHL	59	44	45	89	202	...	...	...	9	8	6	14	30
— Salt Lake City	IHL	—	—	—	—	—	...	...	...	9	0	4	4	13
89-90 — Salt Lake City	IHL	81	23	35	58	130	...	...	...	10	6	3	9	38
90-91 — Calgary	NHL	78	15	19	34	93	17	0	1	5	0	1	1	0
91-92 — Calgary	NHL	4	1	0	1	19	2	0	0	—	—	—	—	—
— Chicago	NHL	20	5	8	13	45	3	1	0	18	4	6	10	24
92-93 — Chicago	NHL	79	15	18	33	98	6	2	0	3	0	1	1	2
93-94 — Chicago	NHL	65	15	16	31	55	10	2	0	—	—	—	—	—
— New York Rangers	NHL	12	4	3	7	2	5	1	0	23	6	3	9	20
94-95 — New York Rangers	NHL	41	3	5	8	25	-8	0	0	9	0	1	1	10
95-96 — New York Rangers	NHL	32	4	2	6	22	-4	1	0	—	—	—	—	—
— St. Louis	NHL	46	7	13	20	65	-4	3	0	11	0	2	2	8
96-97 — St. Louis	NHL	74	16	20	36	50	11	1	2	5	0	0	0	0
NHL totals (7 years)		451	85	104	189	474	38	11	3	74	10	14	24	64

MATTSSON, JESPER — C — FLAMES

PERSONAL: Born May 13, 1975, in Malmo, Sweden. ... 6-0/173. ... Shoots right.

TRANSACTIONS/CAREER NOTES: Selected by Calgary Flames in first round (first Flames pick, 18th overall) of NHL entry draft (June 26, 1993).

Season Team	League	REGULAR SEASON								PLAYOFFS				
		Gms.	G	A	Pts.	PIM	+/-	PP	SH	Gms.	G	A	Pts.	PIM
91-92 — Malmo	Sweden	24	0	1	1	2	...	...	...	5	0	0	0	0
92-93 — Malmo	Sweden	40	9	8	17	14	...	...	...	5	0	0	0	0
93-94 — Malmo	Sweden	40	3	6	9	14	...	...	...	9	1	2	3	2
94-95 — Malmo	Sweden	37	9	6	15	18	...	...	...	9	2	0	2	18
95-96 — Saint John	AHL	73	12	26	38	18	...	...	...	9	1	1	2	2
96-97 — Saint John	AHL	72	22	18	40	32	...	...	...	3	1	1	2	0

MATVICHUK, RICHARD — D — STARS

PERSONAL: Born February 5, 1973, in Edmonton. ... 6-2/190. ... Shoots left. ... Name pronounced MAT-vih-chuhk.

TRANSACTIONS/CAREER NOTES: Selected by Minnesota North Stars in first round (first North Stars pick, eighth overall) of 1991 NHL entry draft (June 22, 1991). ... Strained lower back (November 9, 1992); missed two games. ... Sprained ankle (December 27, 1992); missed 10 games. ... North Stars franchise moved from Minnesota to Dallas and renamed Stars for 1993-94 season. ... Bruised shoulder (April 5, 1994); missed one game. ... Tore knee ligaments and underwent knee surgery (September 20, 1994); missed first 16 games of season. ... Suffered concussion (March 13, 1996); missed five games. ... Bruised shoulder (October 26, 1996); missed two games. ... Strained groin (February 18, 1997); missed 19 games.

HONORS: Won Bill Hunter Trophy (1991-92). ... Named to Can.HL All-Star second team (1991-92). ... Named to WHL (East) All-Star first team (1991-92).

		REGULAR SEASON								PLAYOFFS				
Season Team	League	Gms.	G	A	Pts.	PIM	+/-	PP	SH	Gms.	G	A	Pts.	PIM
88-89— Fort Saskatchewan.....	AJHL	58	7	36	43	147	...	...	...	—	—	—	—	—
89-90— Saskatoon................	WHL	56	8	24	32	126	...	...	...	10	2	8	10	16
90-91— Saskatoon................	WHL	68	13	36	49	117	...	...	...	—	—	—	—	—
91-92— Saskatoon................	WHL	58	14	40	54	126	...	...	...	22	1	9	10	61
92-93— Minnesota................	NHL	53	2	3	5	26	-8	1	0	—	—	—	—	—
— Kalamazoo	IHL	3	0	1	1	6	...	...	...	—	—	—	—	—
93-94— Kalamazoo	IHL	43	8	17	25	84	...	...	...	—	—	—	—	—
— Dallas...................	NHL	25	0	3	3	22	1	0	0	7	1	1	2	12
94-95— Dallas...................	NHL	14	0	2	2	14	-7	0	0	5	0	2	2	4
— Kalamazoo	IHL	17	0	6	6	16	...	...	...	—	—	—	—	—
95-96— Dallas...................	NHL	73	6	16	22	71	4	0	0	—	—	—	—	—
96-97— Dallas...................	NHL	57	5	7	12	87	1	0	2	7	0	1	1	20
NHL totals (5 years)		222	13	31	44	220	-9	1	2	19	1	4	5	36

MAY, BRAD   LW   SABRES

PERSONAL: Born November 29, 1971, in Toronto. ... 6-1/206. ... Shoots left.

TRANSACTIONS/CAREER NOTES: Selected by Buffalo Sabres in first round (first Sabres pick, 14th overall) of NHL entry draft (June 16, 1990). ... Injured knee (August 1990). ... Injured left knee ligaments (November 1990). ... Broke bone in hand (March 11, 1995); missed 15 games. ... Injured left arm (March 3, 1996); missed one game. ... Suspended one game for accumulating three game misconduct penalties (March 31, 1996). ... Underwent right shoulder surgery (October 14, 1996); missed 27 games. ... Broken right hand (December 20, 1996); missed nine games. ... Fractured thumb (March 1, 1997); missed four games.

HONORS: Named to OHL All-Star second team (1989-90 and 1990-91).

MISCELLANEOUS: Scored on a penalty shot (vs. Andy Moog, November, 11, 1992).

		REGULAR SEASON								PLAYOFFS				
Season Team	League	Gms.	G	A	Pts.	PIM	+/-	PP	SH	Gms.	G	A	Pts.	PIM
07-08— Markham Jr. B	OHA	6	1	1	2	21	...	...	...	—	—	—	—	—
88-89— Niagara Falls	OHL	65	8	14	22	304	...	...	...	17	0	1	1	55
89-90— Niagara Falls	OHL	61	33	58	91	223	...	...	...	16	9	13	22	64
90-91— Niagara Falls	OHL	34	37	32	69	93	...	...	...	14	11	14	25	53
91-92— Buffalo	NHL	69	11	6	17	309	-12	1	0	7	1	4	5	2
92-93— Buffalo	NHL	82	13	13	26	242	3	0	0	8	1	1	2	14
93-94— Buffalo	NHL	84	18	27	45	171	-6	3	0	7	0	2	2	9
94-95— Buffalo	NHL	33	3	3	6	87	5	1	0	4	0	0	0	2
95-96— Buffalo	NHL	79	15	29	44	295	6	3	0	—	—	—	—	—
96-97— Buffalo	NHL	42	3	4	7	106	-8	1	0	10	1	1	2	32
NHL totals (6 years)		389	63	82	145	1210	-12	9	0	36	3	8	11	59

MAYERS, JAMAL   C   BLUES

PERSONAL: Born October 24, 1974, in Toronto. ... 6-0/190. ... Shoots right. ... Name pronounced MIGHRS.

HIGH SCHOOL: Erindale Secondary (Mississauga, Ont.).

COLLEGE: Western Michigan.

TRANSACTIONS/CAREER NOTES: Selected by St. Louis Blues in fourth round (third Blues pick, 89th overall) of NHL entry draft (June 26, 1993).

		REGULAR SEASON								PLAYOFFS				
Season Team	League	Gms.	G	A	Pts.	PIM	+/-	PP	SH	Gms.	G	A	Pts.	PIM
90-91— Thornhill	Jr. A	44	12	24	36	78	...	...	...	—	—	—	—	—
91-92— Thornhill	Jr. A	56	38	69	107	36	...	...	...	—	—	—	—	—
92-93— Western Michigan......	CCHA	38	8	17	25	26	...	...	...	—	—	—	—	—
93-94— Western Michigan......	CCHA	40	17	32	49	40	...	...	...	—	—	—	—	—
94-95— Western Michigan......	CCHA	39	13	33	46	40	...	...	...	—	—	—	—	—
95-96— Western Michigan......	CCHA	38	17	22	39	75	...	...	...	—	—	—	—	—
96-97— Worcester	AHL	62	12	14	26	104	...	...	...	5	4	4	8	4
— St. Louis	NHL	6	0	1	1	2	-3	0	0	—	—	—	—	—
NHL totals (1 year)		6	0	1	1	2	-3	0	0					

McALLISTER, CHRIS   D   CANUCKS

PERSONAL: Born June 16, 1975, in Saskatoon, Sask. ... 6-7/236. ... Shoots left.

TRANSACTIONS/CAREER NOTES: Selected by Vancouver Canucks in second round (first Canucks pick, 40th overall) of NHL entry draft (July 8, 1995).

		REGULAR SEASON								PLAYOFFS				
Season Team	League	Gms.	G	A	Pts.	PIM	+/-	PP	SH	Gms.	G	A	Pts.	PIM
93-94— Humboldt..................	SJHL	50	3	5	8	150	...	...	...	—	—	—	—	—
— Saskatoon................	WHL	2	0	0	0	5	...	...	...	—	—	—	—	—
94-95— Saskatoon................	WHL	65	2	8	10	134	...	...	...	10	0	0	0	28
95-96— Syracuse	AHL	68	0	2	2	142	...	...	...	16	0	0	0	34
96-97— Syracuse	AHL	43	3	1	4	108	...	...	...	3	0	0	0	6

M

McALPINE, CHRIS   D   BLUES

PERSONAL: Born December 1, 1971, in Roseville, Minn. ... 6-0/190. ... Shoots right. ... Name pronounced muh-KAL-pighn.
HIGH SCHOOL: Roseville (Minn.).
COLLEGE: Minnesota.
TRANSACTIONS/CAREER NOTES: Selected by New Jersey Devils in seventh round (seventh Devils pick, 137th overall) of NHL entry draft (June 16, 1990). ... Injured thumb (March 26, 1995); missed four games. ... Traded by Devils with ninth-round pick in 1999 draft to St. Louis Blues for C Peter Zezel (February 11, 1997).
HONORS: Named to NCCA All-America West second team (1993-94). ... Named to WCHA All-Star first team (1993-94).
MISCELLANEOUS: Member of Stanley Cup championship team (1995).

Season Team	League	REGULAR SEASON Gms.	G	A	Pts.	PIM	+/-	PP	SH	PLAYOFFS Gms.	G	A	Pts.	PIM
89-90 — Roseville	Minn. H.S.	25	15	13	28	...	...	...	...	—	—	—	—	—
90-91 — Univ. of Minnesota	WCHA	38	7	9	16	112	...	...	...	—	—	—	—	—
91-92 — Univ. of Minnesota	WCHA	39	3	9	12	126	...	...	...	—	—	—	—	—
92-93 — Univ. of Minnesota	WCHA	41	14	9	23	82	...	...	...	—	—	—	—	—
93-94 — Univ. of Minnesota	WCHA	36	12	18	30	121	...	...	...	—	—	—	—	—
94-95 — Albany	AHL	48	4	18	22	49	...	...	...	—	—	—	—	—
— New Jersey	NHL	24	0	3	3	17	4	0	0	—	—	—	—	—
95-96 — Albany	AHL	57	5	14	19	72	...	...	...	4	0	0	0	13
96-97 — Albany	AHL	44	1	9	10	48	...	...	...	—	—	—	—	—
— St. Louis	NHL	15	0	0	0	24	-2	0	0	4	0	1	1	0
NHL totals (2 years)		39	0	3	3	41	2	0	0	4	0	1	1	0

McAMMOND, DEAN   LW   OILERS

PERSONAL: Born June 15, 1973, in Grand Cache, Alta. ... 5-11/195. ... Shoots left.
TRANSACTIONS/CAREER NOTES: Selected by Chicago Blackhawks in first round (first Blackhawks pick, 22nd overall) of NHL entry draft (June 22, 1991). ... Traded by Blackhawks with D Igor Kravchuk to Edmonton Oilers for RW Joe Murphy (February 25, 1993). ... Severed left Achilles' tendon (February 1, 1995); missed last 41 games of season. ... Fractured nose (November 11, 1996); missed two games. ... Suffered from the flu (January 21, 1997); missed two games. ... Suffered back spasms (March 1, 1997); missed remainder of season.
HONORS: Won Can.HL Plus/Minus Award (1991-92).
MISCELLANEOUS: Failed to score on a penalty shot (vs. Mark Fitzpatrick, January 5, 1996).

Season Team	League	REGULAR SEASON Gms.	G	A	Pts.	PIM	+/-	PP	SH	PLAYOFFS Gms.	G	A	Pts.	PIM
89-90 — Prince Albert	WHL	53	11	11	22	49	...	...	...	14	2	3	5	18
90-91 — Prince Albert	WHL	71	33	35	68	108	...	...	...	2	0	1	1	6
91-92 — Prince Albert	WHL	63	37	54	91	189	...	...	...	10	12	11	23	26
— Chicago	NHL	5	0	2	2	0	-2	0	0	3	0	0	0	2
92-93 — Prince Albert	WHL	30	19	29	48	44	...	...	...	—	—	—	—	—
— Swift Current	WHL	18	10	13	23	29	...	...	...	17	*16	19	35	20
93-94 — Edmonton	NHL	45	6	21	27	16	12	2	0	—	—	—	—	—
— Cape Breton	AHL	28	9	12	21	38	...	...	...	—	—	—	—	—
94-95 — Edmonton	NHL	6	0	0	0	0	-1	0	0	—	—	—	—	—
95-96 — Edmonton	NHL	53	15	15	30	23	6	4	0	—	—	—	—	—
— Cape Breton	AHL	22	9	15	24	55	...	...	...	—	—	—	—	—
96-97 — Edmonton	NHL	57	12	17	29	28	-15	4	0	—	—	—	—	—
NHL totals (5 years)		166	33	55	88	67	0	10	0	3	0	0	0	2

McARTHUR, MARK   G   ISLANDERS

PERSONAL: Born November 16, 1975, in East York, Ont. ... 5-10/175. ... Catches left.
HIGH SCHOOL: Bishop MacDonnell (Guelph, Ont.).
TRANSACTIONS/CAREER NOTES: Selected by New York Islanders in fifth round (fifth Islanders pick, 112th overall) of NHL entry draft (June 29, 1994).
HONORS: Shared Dave Pinkney Trophy with Andy Adams (1994-95). ... Named to OHL All-Star second team (1994-95). ... Won James Norris Memorial Trophy (1995-96).

Season Team	League	REGULAR SEASON Gms.	Min	W	L	T	GA	SO	Avg.	PLAYOFFS Gms.	Min.	W	L	GA	SO	Avg.
91-92 — Peterborough	Jr. B	25	1198	...	...	...	98	0	4.91	—	—	—	—	—	—	—
92-93 — Guelph	OHL	35	1853	14	14	3	180	0	5.83	—	—	—	—	—	—	—
93-94 — Guelph	OHL	51	2936	25	18	5	201	0	4.11	9	561	4	5	38	0	4.06
94-95 — Guelph	OHL	48	2776	34	8	4	130	1	*2.81	13	797	9	4	44	0	3.31
95-96 — Utah	IHL	26	1482	12	12	‡0	77	0	3.12	—	—	—	—	—	—	—
96-97 — Utah	IHL	56	3111	28	20	‡6	155	3	2.99	—	—	—	—	—	—	—

McBAIN, JASON   D   HURRICANES

PERSONAL: Born April 12, 1974, in Ilion, N.Y. ... 6-3/205. ... Shoots right.
TRANSACTIONS/CAREER NOTES: Selected by Hartford Whalers in fourth round (fifth Whalers pick, 81st overall) of NHL entry draft (June 20, 1992). ... Whalers franchise moved to North Carolina and renamed Carolina Hurricanes for 1997-98 season; NHL approved move on June 25, 1997.

Season Team	League	REGULAR SEASON Gms.	G	A	Pts.	PIM	+/-	PP	SH	PLAYOFFS Gms.	G	A	Pts.	PIM
90-91 — Lethbridge	WHL	52	2	7	9	39	...	...	...	1	0	0	0	0
91-92 — Lethbridge	WHL	13	0	1	1	12	...	...	...	—	—	—	—	—
— Portland	WHL	54	9	23	32	95	...	...	...	6	1	0	1	13

Season Team	League	Gms.	G	A	Pts.	PIM	+/-	PP	SH	Gms.	G	A	Pts.	PIM
		REGULAR SEASON								PLAYOFFS				
92-93 — Portland	WHL	71	9	35	44	76	...	...	...	16	2	12	14	14
93-94 — Portland	WHL	63	15	51	66	86	...	...	...	10	2	7	9	14
94-95 — Springfield	AHL	77	16	28	44	92	...	...	...	—	—	—	—	—
95-96 — Springfield	AHL	73	11	33	44	43	...	...	...	8	1	1	2	2
— Hartford	NHL	3	0	0	0	0	-1	0	0	—	—	—	—	—
96-97 — Springfield	AHL	58	8	26	34	40	...	...	...	16	0	8	8	12
— Hartford	NHL	6	0	0	0	0	-4	0	0	—	—	—	—	—
NHL totals (2 years)		9	0	0	0	0	-5	0	0					

McBAIN, MIKE — D — LIGHTNING

PERSONAL: Born January 12, 1977, in Kimberley, B.C. ... 6-0/191. ... Shoots left. ... Brother of Jason McBain, defenseman in Carolina Hurricanes system.
TRANSACTIONS/CAREER NOTES: Selected by Tampa Bay Lightning in second round (second Lightning pick, 30th overall) of NHL entry draft (July 8, 1995).

Season Team	League	Gms.	G	A	Pts.	PIM	+/-	PP	SH	Gms.	G	A	Pts.	PIM
		REGULAR SEASON								PLAYOFFS				
92-93 — Kimberley	RMJHL	35	0	4	4	38	...	...	...	—	—	—	—	—
93-94 — Red Deer	WHL	58	4	13	17	41	...	...	...	4	0	0	0	0
94-95 — Red Deer	WHL	68	6	28	34	55	...	...	...	—	—	—	—	—
95-96 — Red Deer	WHL	68	7	34	41	68	...	...	...	10	1	7	8	10
96-97 — Red Deer	WHL	59	14	35	49	55	...	...	...	15	1	6	7	9

McCABE, BRYAN — D — ISLANDERS

PERSONAL: Born June 8, 1975, in St. Catharines, Ont. ... 6-1/204. ... Shoots left.
HIGH SCHOOL: Joel E. Ferris (Spokane, Wash.).
TRANSACTIONS/CAREER NOTES: Selected by New York Islanders in second round (second Islanders pick, 40th overall) of NHL entry draft (June 26, 1993).
HONORS: Named to WHL (West) All-Star second team (1992-93). ... Named to WHL (West) All-Star first team (1993-94). ... Named to WHL (East) All-Star first team (1994-95). ... Named to Memorial Cup All-Star team (1994-95).

Season Team	League	Gms.	G	A	Pts.	PIM	+/-	PP	SH	Gms.	G	A	Pts.	PIM
		REGULAR SEASON								PLAYOFFS				
91-92 — Medicine Hat	WHL	68	6	24	30	157	...	...	...	4	0	0	0	6
92-93 — Medicine Hat	WHL	14	0	13	13	83	...	...	...	—	—	—	—	—
— Spokane	WHL	46	3	44	47	134	...	...	...	10	1	5	6	28
93-94 — Spokane	WHL	64	22	62	84	218	...	...	...	3	0	4	4	4
94-95 — Spokane	WHL	42	14	39	53	115	...	...	...	—	—	—	—	—
— Brandon	WHL	20	6	10	16	38	...	...	...	18	4	13	17	59
95-96 — New York Islanders	NHL	82	7	16	23	156	-24	3	0	—	—	—	—	—
96-97 — New York Islanders	NHL	82	8	20	28	165	-2	2	1	—	—	—	—	—
NHL totals (2 years)		164	15	36	51	321	-26	5	1					

McCARTHY, SANDY — RW — FLAMES

PERSONAL: Born June 15, 1972, in Toronto. ... 6-3/225. ... Shoots right.
TRANSACTIONS/CAREER NOTES: Suspended one game by QMJHL for attempting to injure another player (October 2, 1989). ... Suspended one playoff game by QMJHL for pre-game fight (March 19, 1990). ... Selected by Calgary Flames in third round (third Flames pick, 52nd overall) of NHL entry draft (June 22, 1991). ... Strained right shoulder (December 18, 1993); missed two games. ... Strained right shoulder (December 27, 1993); missed one game. ... Strained right knee (January 20, 1995); missed five games. ... Suffered hernia (February 3, 1995); missed six games. ... Injured ribs (December 16, 1995); missed seven games. ... Fractured ankle (October 9, 1996); missed 25 games. ... Reinjured left ankle (January 9, 1997); underwent ankle surgery (January 24, 1997) and missed 23 games.

Season Team	League	Gms.	G	A	Pts.	PIM	+/-	PP	SH	Gms.	G	A	Pts.	PIM
		REGULAR SEASON								PLAYOFFS				
89-90 — Laval	QMJHL	65	10	11	21	269	...	...	...	—	—	—	—	—
90-91 — Laval	QMJHL	68	21	19	40	297	...	...	...	—	—	—	—	—
91-92 — Laval	QMJHL	62	39	51	90	326	...	...	...	8	4	5	9	81
92-93 — Salt Lake City	IHL	77	18	20	38	220	...	...	...	—	—	—	—	—
93-94 — Calgary	NHL	79	5	5	10	173	-3	0	0	7	0	0	0	34
94-95 — Calgary	NHL	37	5	3	8	101	1	0	0	6	0	1	1	17
95-96 — Calgary	NHL	75	9	7	16	173	-8	3	0	4	0	0	0	10
96-97 — Calgary	NHL	33	3	5	8	113	-8	1	0	—	—	—	—	—
NHL totals (4 years)		224	22	20	42	560	-18	4	0	17	0	1	1	61

McCARTY, DARREN — RW — RED WINGS

PERSONAL: Born April 1, 1972, in Burnaby, B.C. ... 6-1/215. ... Shoots right.
HIGH SCHOOL: Quinte Secondary School (Belleville, Ont.).
TRANSACTIONS/CAREER NOTES: Selected by Detroit Red Wings in second round (second Red Wings pick, 46th overall) of NHL entry draft (June 20, 1992). ... Injured groin (January 29, 1994); missed five games. ... Injured shoulder (March 23, 1994); missed five games. ... Separated right shoulder (February 7, 1995); missed eight games. ... Injured right hand (March 30, 1995); missed two games. ... Injured left knee (April 9, 1995); missed five games. ... Injured right heel (November 7, 1995); missed one game ... Separated shoulder (December 2, 1995); missed six games. ... Lacerated right forearm (January 12, 1996); missed three games. ... Injured left hand (February 15, 1996); missed seven games. ... Injured hand (January 3, 1997); missed seven games. ... Bruised thigh (January 29, 1997); missed four games. ... Injured groin (April 5, 1997); missed two games.

M

HONORS: Won Jim Mahon Memorial Trophy (1991-92). ... Named to Can.HL All-Star first team (1991-92). ... Named to OHL All-Star first team (1991-92).
MISCELLANEOUS: Member of Stanley Cup championship team (1997).

Season Team	League	REGULAR SEASON								PLAYOFFS				
		Gms.	G	A	Pts.	PIM	+/-	PP	SH	Gms.	G	A	Pts.	PIM
88-89 — Peterborough Jr. B.....	OHA	34	18	17	35	135	...	...	...	—	—	—	—	—
89-90 — Belleville..................	OHL	63	12	15	27	142	...	...	...	11	1	1	2	21
90-91 — Belleville..................	OHL	60	30	37	67	151	...	...	...	6	2	2	4	13
91-92 — Belleville..................	OHL	65	*55	72	127	177	...	...	...	5	1	4	5	13
92-93 — Adirondack...............	AHL	73	17	19	36	278	...	...	...	11	0	1	1	33
93-94 — Detroit....................	NHL	67	9	17	26	181	12	0	0	7	2	2	4	8
94-95 — Detroit....................	NHL	31	5	8	13	88	5	1	0	18	3	2	5	14
95-96 — Detroit....................	NHL	63	15	14	29	158	14	8	0	19	3	2	5	20
96-97 — Detroit....................	NHL	68	19	30	49	126	14	5	0	20	3	4	7	34
NHL totals (4 years)		229	48	69	117	553	45	14	0	64	11	10	21	76

McCLEARY, TRENT   C   BRUINS

PERSONAL: Born October 10, 1972, in Swift Current, Sask. ... 6-0/180. ... Shoots right.
TRANSACTIONS/CAREER NOTES: Signed as free agent by Ottawa Senators (October 9, 1992). ... Bruised foot during 1995-96 season; missed two games. ... Injured right thumb (April 1, 1996); missed two games. ... Traded by Senators with third-round pick (LW Eric Naud) in 1996 draft to Boston Bruins for C Shawn McEachern (June 22, 1996). ... Strained abdominal muscle (January 4, 1997); missed one game. ... Sprained knee (February 11, 1997); missed 18 games.

Season Team	League	REGULAR SEASON								PLAYOFFS				
		Gms.	G	A	Pts.	PIM	+/-	PP	SH	Gms.	G	A	Pts.	PIM
91-92 — Swift Current	WHL	72	23	22	45	240	...	...	...	8	1	2	3	16
92-93 — Swift Current	WHL	63	17	33	50	138	...	...	...	17	5	4	9	16
— New Haven..............	AHL	2	1	0	1	6	...	...	...	—	—	—	—	—
93-94 — Prin. Edward Island ...	AHL	4	0	0	0	6	...	...	...	—	—	—	—	—
— Thunder Bay	Col.HL	51	23	17	40	123	...	...	...	9	2	11	13	15
94-95 — Prin. Edward Island ...	AHL	51	9	20	29	60	...	...	...	9	2	3	5	26
95-96 — Ottawa	NHL	75	4	10	14	68	-15	0	1	—	—	—	—	—
96-97 — Boston	NHL	59	3	5	8	33	-16	0	0	—	—	—	—	—
NHL totals (2 years)		134	7	15	22	101	-31	0	1					

McCOSH, SHAWN   C   FLYERS

PERSONAL: Born June 5, 1969, in Oshawa, Ont. ... 6-0/188. ... Shoots right.
TRANSACTIONS/CAREER NOTES: Selected by Detroit Red Wings in fifth round (fifth Red Wings pick, 95th overall) of NHL entry draft (June 17, 1989). ... Traded by Red Wings to Los Angeles Kings for eighth-round pick (D Justin Krall) in 1992 draft (August 15, 1990). ... Traded by Kings with RW Bob Kudelski to Ottawa Senators for RW Jim Thomson and C Marc Fortier (December 20, 1992). ... Signed as free agent by New York Rangers (August 17, 1993). ... Signed as free agent by Philadelphia Flyers (July 31, 1995).

Season Team	League	REGULAR SEASON								PLAYOFFS				
		Gms.	G	A	Pts.	PIM	+/-	PP	SH	Gms.	G	A	Pts.	PIM
86-87 — Hamilton	OHL	50	11	17	28	49	...	...	...	6	1	0	1	2
87-88 — Hamilton	OHL	64	17	36	53	96	...	...	...	14	6	8	14	14
88-89 — Niagara Falls	OHL	56	41	62	103	75	...	...	...	14	4	13	17	23
89-90 — Niagara Falls	OHL	9	6	10	16	24	...	...	...	—	—	—	—	—
— Dukes of Hamilton ...	OHL	39	24	28	52	65	...	...	...	—	—	—	—	—
90-91 — New Haven	AHL	66	16	21	37	104	...	...	...	—	—	—	—	—
91-92 — Los Angeles	NHL	4	0	0	0	4	0	0	0	—	—	—	—	—
— Phoenix......................	IHL	71	21	32	53	118	...	...	...	—	—	—	—	—
— New Haven......................	AHL	—	—	—	—	—				5	0	1	1	0
92-93 — Phoenix......................	IHL	22	9	8	17	36	...	...	...	—	—	—	—	—
— New Haven......................	AHL	46	22	32	54	54	...	...	...	—	—	—	—	—
93-94 — Binghamton	AHL	75	31	44	75	68	...	...	...	—	—	—	—	—
94-95 — Binghamton	AHL	67	23	60	83	73	...	...	...	8	3	9	12	6
— New York Rangers	NHL	5	1	0	1	2	1	0	0	—	—	—	—	—
95-96 — Hershey	AHL	71	31	52	83	82	...	...	...	5	1	5	6	8
96-97 — Philadelphia	AHL	79	30	51	81	110	...	...	...	10	3	9	12	23
NHL totals (2 years)		9	1	0	1	6	1	0	0					

McCRIMMON, BRAD   D   COYOTES

PERSONAL: Born March 29, 1959, in Dodsland, Sask. ... 5-11/205. ... Shoots left. ... Full name: Byron Brad McCrimmon.
TRANSACTIONS/CAREER NOTES: Traded by Bruins to Philadelphia Flyers for G Pete Peeters (June 1982). ... Broke bone in right hand (February 2, 1985); missed 13 games. ... Separated left shoulder and underwent surgery (May 9, 1985). ... Missed start of 1986-87 season due to contract dispute. ... Traded by Flyers to Calgary Flames for third-round pick (G Dominic Roussel) in 1988 draft and first-round pick in 1989 draft (August 1987). ... Suffered from skin rash (February 1989). ... Fractured ankle (March 1989). ... Traded by Flames to Detroit Red Wings for second-round pick (traded to New Jersey Devils who selected D David Harlock) in 1990 draft (June 16, 1990). ... Fractured right ankle (January 12, 1991); missed 16 games. ... Suffered from the flu (October 24, 1992); missed one game. ... Traded by Red Wings to Hartford Whalers for sixth-round pick in 1993 draft (June 1, 1993). ... Bruised back (December 10, 1995); missed two games. ... Signed as free agent by Phoenix Coyotes (July 3, 1996). ... Sprained wrist (January 23, 1997); missed 22 games.
HONORS: Named to WCHL All-Star second team (1976-77). ... Won Top Defenseman Trophy (1977-78). ... Named to WCHL All-Star first team (1977-78). ... Named to WHL All-Star first team (1978-79). ... Named to Memorial Cup All-Star team (1978-79). ... Won Emery Edge Award (1987-88). ... Named to THE SPORTING NEWS All-Star second team (1987-88). ... Named to NHL All-Star second team (1987-88). ... Played in NHL All-Star Game (1988).
MISCELLANEOUS: Member of Stanley Cup championship team (1989). ... Captain of Calgary Flames (1989-90).

Season Team	League	REGULAR SEASON								PLAYOFFS				
		Gms.	G	A	Pts.	PIM	+/-	PP	SH	Gms.	G	A	Pts.	PIM
76-77— Brandon	WCHL	72	18	66	84	96	...	...	...	—	—	—	—	—
77-78— Brandon	WCHL	65	19	78	97	245	...	...	...	8	2	11	13	20
78-79— Brandon	WHL	66	24	74	98	139	...	...	...	22	9	19	28	34
79-80— Boston	NHL	72	5	11	16	94	...	1	0	10	1	1	2	28
80-81— Boston	NHL	78	11	18	29	148	27	1	0	3	0	1	1	2
81-82— Boston	NHL	78	1	8	9	83	4	0	0	2	0	0	0	2
82-83— Philadelphia	NHL	79	4	21	25	61	24	1	0	3	0	0	0	4
83-84— Philadelphia	NHL	71	0	24	24	76	19	0	0	1	0	0	0	4
84-85— Philadelphia	NHL	66	8	35	43	81	52	1	0	11	2	1	3	15
85-86— Philadelphia	NHL	80	13	42	55	85	83	2	0	5	2	0	2	2
86-87— Philadelphia	NHL	71	10	29	39	52	45	3	2	26	3	5	8	30
87-88— Calgary	NHL	80	7	43	50	98	*48	1	3	9	2	3	5	22
88-89— Calgary	NHL	72	5	17	22	96	43	2	1	22	0	3	3	30
89-90— Calgary	NHL	79	4	15	19	78	18	0	0	6	0	2	2	8
90-91— Detroit	NHL	64	0	13	13	81	7	0	0	7	1	1	2	21
91-92— Detroit	NHL	79	7	22	29	118	39	2	1	11	0	1	1	8
92-93— Detroit	NHL	60	1	14	15	71	21	1	0	—	—	—	—	—
93-94— Hartford	NHL	65	1	5	6	72	-7	0	0	—	—	—	—	—
94-95— Hartford	NHL	33	0	1	1	42	7	0	0	—	—	—	—	—
95-96— Hartford	NHL	58	3	6	9	62	15	0	1	—	—	—	—	—
96-97— Phoenix	NHL	37	1	5	6	18	2	0	0	—	—	—	—	—
NHL totals (18 years)		1222	81	329	410	1416	...	15	8	116	11	18	29	176

McEACHERN, SHAWN — LW — SENATORS

PERSONAL: Born February 28, 1969, in Waltham, Mass. ... 5-11/195. ... Shoots left. ... Name pronounced muh-GEHK-rihn.
HIGH SCHOOL: Matignon (Cambridge, Mass.).
COLLEGE: Boston University.
TRANSACTIONS/CAREER NOTES: Selected by Pittsburgh Penguins in sixth round (sixth Penguins pick, 110th overall) of NHL entry draft (June 13, 1987). ... Traded by Penguins to Los Angeles Kings for D Marty McSorley (August 27, 1993). ... Traded by Kings to Penguins for D Marty McSorley and D Jim Paek (February 15, 1994). ... Played in Europe during 1994-95 NHL lockout. ... Suspended for first three games of 1994-95 season and fined $500 by NHL for slashing (September 21, 1994); suspension reduced to two games due to abbreviated 1994-95 season. ... Traded by Penguins with LW Kevin Stevens to Boston Bruins for C Bryan Smolinski and RW Glen Murray (August 2, 1995). ... Traded by Bruins to Ottawa Senators for RW Trent McCleary and third-round pick (LW Eric Naud) in 1996 draft (June 22, 1996). ... Fractured jaw (December 6, 1996); missed 17 games.
HONORS: Named to Hockey East All-Star second team (1989-90). ... Named Hockey East Tournament Most Valuable Player (1990-91). ... Named to NCAA All-America East first team (1990-91). ... Named to Hockey East All-Star first team (1990-91).
MISCELLANEOUS: Member of Stanley Cup championship team (1992).

Season Team	League	REGULAR SEASON								PLAYOFFS				
		Gms.	G	A	Pts.	PIM	+/-	PP	SH	Gms.	G	A	Pts.	PIM
85-86— Matignon	Mass. H.S.	20	32	20	52		...	...	...	—	—	—	—	—
86-87— Matignon	Mass. H.S.	16	29	28	57		...	...	...	—	—	—	—	—
87-88— Matignon	Mass. H.S.		52	40	92		...	...	...	—	—	—	—	—
88-89— Boston University	Hockey East	36	20	28	48	32	...	...	...	—	—	—	—	—
89-90— Boston University	Hockey East	43	25	31	56	78	...	...	...	—	—	—	—	—
90-91— Boston University	Hockey East	41	34	48	82	43	...	...	...	—	—	—	—	—
91-92— U.S. national team	Int'l	57	26	23	49	38	...	...	...	—	—	—	—	—
—U.S. Olympic team	Int'l	8	1	0	1	10	...	...	...	—	—	—	—	—
—Pittsburgh	NHL	15	0	4	4	0	1	0	0	19	2	7	9	4
92-93— Pittsburgh	NHL	84	28	33	61	46	21	7	0	12	3	2	5	10
93-94— Los Angeles	NHL	49	8	13	21	24	1	0	3	—	—	—	—	—
—Pittsburgh	NHL	27	12	9	21	10	13	0	2	6	1	0	1	2
94-95— Kiekko-Espoo	Finland	8	1	3	4	6	...	...	...	—	—	—	—	—
—Pittsburgh	NHL	44	13	13	26	22	4	1	2	11	0	2	2	8
95-96— Boston	NHL	82	24	29	53	34	-5	3	2	5	2	1	3	8
96-97— Ottawa	NHL	65	11	20	31	18	-5	0	1	7	2	0	2	8
NHL totals (6 years)		366	96	121	217	154	30	11	10	60	10	12	22	40

McGILLIS, DAN — D — OILERS

PERSONAL: Born July 1, 1972, in Hawkesbury, Ont. ... 6-2/225. ... Shoots left.
COLLEGE: Northeastern.
TRANSACTIONS/CAREER NOTES: Selected by Detroit Red Wings in 10th round (10th Red Wings pick, 238th overall) of NHL entry draft (June 20, 1992). ... Signed as free agent by Edmonton Oilers (September 6, 1996).
HONORS: Named to Hockey East All-Star first team (1994-95). ... Named to NCAA All-America East first team (1995-96). ... Named to Hockey East All-Star team (1995-96).

Season Team	League	REGULAR SEASON								PLAYOFFS				
		Gms.	G	A	Pts.	PIM	+/-	PP	SH	Gms.	G	A	Pts.	PIM
91-92— Hawkesbury	Tier II Jr. A	36	5	19	24	106	...	...	...	—	—	—	—	—
92-93— Northeastern Univ.	Hockey East	35	5	12	17	42	...	...	...	—	—	—	—	—
93-94— Northeastern Univ.	Hockey East	38	4	25	29	82	...	...	...	—	—	—	—	—
94-95— Northeastern Univ.	Hockey East	34	9	22	31	70	...	...	...	—	—	—	—	—
95-96— Northeastern Univ.	Hockey East	34	12	24	36	50	...	...	...	—	—	—	—	—
96-97— Edmonton	NHL	73	6	16	22	52	2	2	1	12	0	5	5	24
NHL totals (1 year)		73	6	16	22	52	2	2	1	12	0	5	5	24

M

McHUGH, MIKE   LW   FLYERS

PERSONAL: Born August 16, 1965, in Bowdoin, Mass. ... 5-10/190. ... Shoots left.
COLLEGE: Maine.
TRANSACTIONS/CAREER NOTES: Selected by Minnesota North Stars in NHL supplemental draft (June 10, 1988). ... Selected by San Jose Sharks in NHL dispersal draft (May 30, 1991). ... Traded by Sharks to Hartford Whalers for LW Paul Fenton (October 18, 1991). ... Signed as free agent by Hershey of AHL (1993).
HONORS: Named Hockey East Player of the Year (1987-88). ... Named to NCAA All-America East second team (1987-88). ... Named to Hockey East All-Rookie team (1987-88). ... Won Jack Butterfield Trophy (1996-97).

Season Team	League	REGULAR SEASON								PLAYOFFS				
		Gms.	G	A	Pts.	PIM	+/-	PP	SH	Gms.	G	A	Pts.	PIM
84-85— University of Maine....	Hockey East	25	9	8	17	9	...	...	...	—	—	—	—	—
85-86— University of Maine....	Hockey East	38	9	10	19	24	...	...	...	—	—	—	—	—
86-87— University of Maine....	Hockey East	42	21	29	50	40	...	...	...	—	—	—	—	—
87-88— University of Maine....	Hockey East	44	29	37	66	90	...	...	...	—	—	—	—	—
88-89— Kalamazoo	IHL	70	17	29	46	89	...	...	...	6	3	1	4	17
— Minnesota	NHL	3	0	0	0	2	-1	0	0	—	—	—	—	—
89-90— Kalamazoo	IHL	73	14	17	31	96	...	...	...	10	0	6	6	16
— Minnesota	NHL	3	0	0	0	0	-1	0	0	—	—	—	—	—
90-91— Kalamazoo	IHL	69	27	38	65	82	...	...	...	11	3	8	11	6
— Minnesota	NHL	6	0	0	0	0	-3	0	0	—	—	—	—	—
91-92— San Jose	NHL	8	1	0	1	14	-3	0	0	—	—	—	—	—
— Springfield	AHL	70	23	31	54	51	...	...	...	11	4	7	11	25
92-93— Springfield	AHL	67	19	27	46	111	...	...	...	11	5	2	7	12
93-94— Hershey	AHL	80	27	43	70	58	...	...	...	11	9	3	12	14
94-95— Hershey	AHL	68	24	26	50	102	...	...	...	6	3	2	5	6
95-96— Hershey	AHL	75	15	42	57	118	...	...	...	5	2	2	4	2
96-97— Hershey	AHL	77	23	45	68	135	...	...	...	23	9	7	16	33
NHL totals (4 years)		20	1	0	1	16	-8	0	0					

McINNIS, MARTY   C/LW   FLAMES

PERSONAL: Born June 2, 1970, in Weymouth, Mass. ... 5-11/183. ... Shoots right. ... Full name: Martin Edward McInnis. ... Name pronounced muh-KIH-nihz.
HIGH SCHOOL: Milton (Mass.) Academy.
COLLEGE: Boston College.
TRANSACTIONS/CAREER NOTES: Selected by New York Islanders in eighth round (10th Islanders pick, 163rd overall) of NHL entry draft (June 11, 1988). ... Injured eye (March 9, 1993); missed two games. ... Fractured patella (March 27, 1993); missed remainder of regular season and 14 playoff games. ... Sprained wrist (April 18, 1995); missed one game. ... Injured ribs (March 7, 1996); missed one game. ... Injured ribs (March 16, 1996); missed six games. ... Traded by Islanders with G Tyrone Garner and sixth-round pick (D Ilja Demidov) in 1997 draft to Calgary Flames for C Robert Reichel (March 18, 1997).
MISCELLANEOUS: Scored on a penalty shot (vs. Kelly Hrudey, April 4, 1990). ... Failed to score on a penalty shot (vs. Tom Draper, March 8, 1992).

Season Team	League	REGULAR SEASON								PLAYOFFS				
		Gms.	G	A	Pts.	PIM	+/-	PP	SH	Gms.	G	A	Pts.	PIM
86-87— Milton Academy........	Mass. H.S.	...	21	19	40	...	...	...	...	—	—	—	—	—
87-88— Milton Academy........	Mass. H.S.	...	26	25	51	...	...	...	...	—	—	—	—	—
88-89— Boston College..........	Hockey East	39	13	19	32	8	...	...	...	—	—	—	—	—
89-90— Boston College..........	Hockey East	41	24	29	53	43	...	...	...	—	—	—	—	—
90-91— Boston College..........	Hockey East	38	21	36	57	40	...	...	...	—	—	—	—	—
91-92— U.S. national team.....	Int'l	54	15	19	34	20	...	...	...	—	—	—	—	—
— U.S. Olympic team.....	Int'l	8	5	2	7	4	...	...	...	—	—	—	—	—
— New York Islanders.....	NHL	15	3	5	8	0	6	0	0	—	—	—	—	—
92-93— New York Islanders....	NHL	56	10	20	30	24	7	0	1	3	0	1	1	0
— Capital District	AHL	10	4	12	16	2	...	...	...	—	—	—	—	—
93-94— New York Islanders....	NHL	81	25	31	56	24	31	3	5	4	0	0	0	0
94-95— New York Islanders....	NHL	41	9	7	16	8	-1	0	0	—	—	—	—	—
95-96— New York Islanders....	NHL	74	12	34	46	39	-11	2	0	—	—	—	—	—
96-97— New York Islanders....	NHL	70	20	22	42	20	-7	4	1	—	—	—	—	—
— Calgary	NHL	10	3	4	7	2	-1	1	0	—	—	—	—	—
NHL totals (6 years)		347	82	123	205	117	24	10	7	7	0	1	1	0

McKAY, RANDY   RW   DEVILS

PERSONAL: Born January 25, 1967, in Montreal. ... 6-2/210. ... Shoots right. ... Full name: Hugh Randall McKay.
COLLEGE: Michigan Tech.
TRANSACTIONS/CAREER NOTES: Selected by Detroit Red Wings in sixth round (sixth Red Wings pick, 113th overall) of NHL entry draft (June 15, 1985). ... Injured knee (February 1989). ... Lacerated forearm (February 23, 1991). ... Sent by Red Wings with C Dave Barr to New Jersey Devils as compensation for Red Wings signing free agent RW Troy Crowder (September 9,1991). ... Sprained knee (January 16, 1993); missed nine games. ... Bruised shoulder (November 3, 1993); missed three games. ... Bruised shoulder (January 24, 1994); missed three games. ... Injured groin (February 24, 1995); missed nine games. ... Reinjured groin (March 18, 1995); missed six games. ... Suffered charley horse (May 26, 1995); missed one playoff game. ... Suffered slight concussion (December 31, 1995); missed five games. ... Bruised eye (February 27, 1997); missed five games.
STATISTICAL PLATEAUS: Three-goal games: 1996-97 (1).
MISCELLANEOUS: Member of Stanley Cup championship team (1995).

Season Team	League	REGULAR SEASON								PLAYOFFS				
		Gms.	G	A	Pts.	PIM	+/-	PP	SH	Gms.	G	A	Pts.	PIM
84-85— Michigan Tech	WCHA	25	4	5	9	32	...	...	...	—	—	—	—	—
85-86— Michigan Tech	WCHA	40	12	22	34	46	...	...	...	—	—	—	—	—
86-87— Michigan Tech	WCHA	39	5	11	16	46	...	...	...	—	—	—	—	—
87-88— Michigan Tech	WCHA	41	17	24	41	70	...	...	...	—	—	—	—	—
— Adirondack................	AHL	10	0	3	3	12	...	...	...	6	0	4	4	0
88-89— Adirondack................	AHL	58	29	34	63	170	...	...	...	14	4	7	11	60
— Detroit.......................	NHL	3	0	0	0	0	-1	0	0	2	0	0	0	2
89-90— Detroit.......................	NHL	33	3	6	9	51	1	0	0	—	—	—	—	—
— Adirondack................	AHL	36	16	23	39	99	...	...	...	6	3	0	3	35
90-91— Detroit.......................	NHL	47	1	7	8	183	-15	0	0	5	0	1	1	41
91-92— New Jersey	NHL	80	17	16	33	246	6	2	0	7	1	3	4	10
92-93— New Jersey	NHL	73	11	11	22	206	0	1	0	5	0	0	0	16
93-94— New Jersey	NHL	78	12	15	27	244	24	0	0	20	1	2	3	24
94-95— New Jersey	NHL	33	5	7	12	44	10	0	0	19	8	4	12	11
95-96— New Jersey	NHL	76	11	10	21	145	7	3	0	—	—	—	—	—
96-97— New Jersey	NHL	77	9	18	27	109	15	0	0	10	1	1	2	0
NHL totals (9 years)		500	69	90	159	1228	47	6	0	68	11	11	22	104

McKEE, JAY — D — SABRES

PERSONAL: Born September 8, 1977, in Kingston, Ont. ... 6-3/195. ... Shoots left.
HIGH SCHOOL: Stamford (Niagara Falls, Ont.).
TRANSACTIONS/CAREER NOTES: Selected by Buffalo Sabres in first round (first Sabres pick, 14th overall) of NHL entry draft (July 8, 1995).
HONORS: Named to OHL All-Star second team (1995-96).

Season Team	League	REGULAR SEASON								PLAYOFFS				
		Gms.	G	A	Pts.	PIM	+/-	PP	SH	Gms.	G	A	Pts.	PIM
92-93— Ernestown..................	Jr. C	36	0	17	17	37	...	...	...	—	—	—	—	—
93-94— Sudbury	OHL	51	0	1	1	51	...	...	...	3	0	0	0	0
94-95— Sudbury	OHL	39	6	6	12	91	...	...	...	—	—	—	—	—
— Niagara Falls	OHL	26	3	13	16	60	...	...	...	6	2	3	5	10
95-96— Buffalo	NHL	1	0	1	1	2	1	0	0	—	—	—	—	—
— Rochester	AHL	4	0	1	1	15	...	...	...	—	—	—	—	—
— Niagara Falls	OHL	64	5	41	46	129	...	...	...	10	1	5	6	16
96-97— Buffalo	NHL	43	1	9	10	35	3	0	0	3	0	0	0	0
— Rochester	AHL	7	2	5	7	4	...	...	...	—	—	—	—	—
NHL totals (2 years)		44	1	10	11	37	4	0	0	3	0	0	0	0

McKENNA, STEVE — D — KINGS

PERSONAL: Born August 21, 1973, in Hespeler, Ont. ... 6-8/245. ... Shoots left.
COLLEGE: Merrimack (Mass.).
TRANSACTIONS/CAREER NOTES: Signed as free agent by Los Angeles Kings (May 17, 1996).

Season Team	League	REGULAR SEASON								PLAYOFFS				
		Gms.	G	A	Pts.	PIM	+/-	PP	SH	Gms.	G	A	Pts.	PIM
93-94— Merrimack College.....	Hockey East	37	1	2	3	74	...	...	...	—	—	—	—	—
94-95— Merrimack College.....	Hockey East	37	1	9	10	74	...	...	...	—	—	—	—	—
95-96— Merrimack College.....	Hockey East	33	3	11	14	67	...	...	...	—	—	—	—	—
96-97— Phoenix......................	IHL	66	6	5	11	187	...	...	...	—	—	—	—	—
— Los Angeles	NHL	9	0	0	0	37	1	0	0	—	—	—	—	—
NHL totals (1 year)		9	0	0	0	37	1	0	0					

McKENZIE, JIM — LW — COYOTES

PERSONAL: Born November 3, 1969, in Gull Lake, Sask. ... 6-3/215. ... Shoots left.
TRANSACTIONS/CAREER NOTES: Selected by Hartford Whalers in fourth round (third Whalers pick, 73rd overall) of NHL entry draft (June 17, 1989). ... Injured elbow (January 31, 1992); missed two games. ... Injured hip flexor (November 11, 1992); missed three games. ... Injured hip flexor (December 5, 1992); missed four games. ... Suffered back spasms (January 24, 1993); missed three games. ... Suspended two games by NHL for game misconduct penalties (April 3, 1993). ... Suspended three games by NHL for game misconduct penalties (April 10, 1993). ... Traded by Whalers to Florida Panthers for D Alexander Godynyuk (December 16, 1993). ... Traded by Panthers to Dallas Stars for fourth-round pick (LW Jamie Wright) in 1994 draft (December 16, 1993). ... Traded by Stars to Pittsburgh Penguins for RW Mike Needham (March 21, 1994). ... Broke toe (November 24, 1993); missed four games. ... Bruised hand (March 11, 1995); missed one game. ... Sprained wrist (April 5, 1995); missed seven games. ... Signed as free agent by New York Islanders (July 31, 1995). ... Claimed by Winnipeg Jets in NHL waiver draft (October 2, 1995). ... Jets franchise moved to Phoenix and renamed Coyotes for 1996-97 season; NHL approved move on January 18, 1996. ... Fractured leg (November 8, 1996); missed five games. ... Suffered from the flu (January 27, 1997); missed one game.
STATISTICAL PLATEAUS: Three-goal games: 1996-97 (1).

Season Team	League	REGULAR SEASON								PLAYOFFS				
		Gms.	G	A	Pts.	PIM	+/-	PP	SH	Gms.	G	A	Pts.	PIM
85-86— Moose Jaw	WHL	3	0	2	2	0	...	...	...	—	—	—	—	—
86-87— Moose Jaw	WHL	65	5	3	8	125	...	...	...	9	0	0	0	7
87-88— Moose Jaw	WHL	62	1	17	18	134	...	...	...	—	—	—	—	—
88-89— Victoria	WHL	67	15	27	42	176	...	...	...	8	1	4	5	30
89-90— Binghamton	AHL	56	4	12	16	149	...	...	...	—	—	—	—	—
— Hartford	NHL	5	0	0	0	4	0	0	0	—	—	—	—	—
90-91— Springfield	AHL	24	3	4	7	102	...	...	...	—	—	—	—	—
— Hartford	NHL	41	4	3	7	108	-7	0	0	6	0	0	0	8
91-92— Hartford	NHL	67	5	1	6	87	-6	0	0	—	—	—	—	—

Season Team	League	REGULAR SEASON									PLAYOFFS				
		Gms.	G	A	Pts.	PIM	+/-	PP	SH		Gms.	G	A	Pts.	PIM
92-93— Hartford	NHL	64	3	6	9	202	-10	0	0		—	—	—	—	—
93-94— Hartford	NHL	26	1	2	3	67	-6	0	0		—	—	—	—	—
—Dallas	NHL	34	2	3	5	63	4	0	0		—	—	—	—	—
—Pittsburgh	NHL	11	0	0	0	16	-5	0	0		3	0	0	0	0
94-95— Pittsburgh	NHL	39	2	1	3	63	-7	0	0		5	0	0	0	4
95-96— Winnipeg	NHL	73	4	2	6	202	-4	0	0		1	0	0	0	2
96-97— Phoenix	NHL	65	5	3	8	200	-5	0	0		7	0	0	0	2
NHL totals (8 years)		425	26	21	47	1012	-46	0	0		22	0	0	0	16

McLAREN, KYLE   D   BRUINS

PERSONAL: Born June 18, 1977, in Humboldt, Sask. ... 6-4/219. ... Shoots left.
TRANSACTIONS/CAREER NOTES: Selected by Boston Bruins in first round (first Bruins pick, ninth overall) of NHL entry draft (July 8, 1995). ... Injured back (November 21, 1995); missed one game. ... Injured knee (November 25, 1995); missed five games. ... Suffered from the flu (January 3, 1996); missed one game. ... Suffered concussion (March 10, 1996); missed one game. ... Suffered from charley horse (October 26, 1996); missed two games. ... Strained shoulder (February 2, 1997); missed 13 games. ... Injured foot (March 15, 1997); missed one game. ... Sprained thumb (March 27, 1997); missed final seven games of regular season.
HONORS: Named to NHL All-Rookie team (1995-96).

Season Team	League	REGULAR SEASON									PLAYOFFS				
		Gms.	G	A	Pts.	PIM	+/-	PP	SH		Gms.	G	A	Pts.	PIM
93-94— Tacoma	WHL	62	1	9	10	53	...	...	...		6	1	4	5	6
94-95— Tacoma	WHL	47	13	19	32	68	...	...	...		4	1	1	2	4
95-96— Boston	NHL	74	5	12	17	73	16	0	0		5	0	0	0	14
96-97— Boston	NHL	58	5	9	14	54	-9	0	0		—	—	—	—	—
NHL totals (2 years)		132	10	21	31	127	7	0	0		5	0	0	0	14

McLAREN, STEVE   D   BLACKHAWKS

PERSONAL: Born February 3, 1975, in Owen Sound, Ont. ... 6-0/194. ... Shoots left.
HIGH SCHOOL: Widdlifield (North Bay, Ont.).
TRANSACTIONS/CAREER NOTES: Selected by Chicago Blackhawks in fourth round (third Blackhawks pick, 85th overall) of NHL entry draft (June 29, 1994).

Season Team	League	REGULAR SEASON									PLAYOFFS				
		Gms.	G	A	Pts.	PIM	+/-	PP	SH		Gms.	G	A	Pts.	PIM
93-94— North Bay	OHL	55	2	15	17	130	...	...	...		18	0	3	3	50
94-95— North Bay	OHL	27	3	10	13	119	...	...	...		6	2	1	3	23
95-96— Indianapolis	IHL	54	1	2	3	170	...	...	...		3	0	0	0	2
96-97— Indianapolis	IHL	63	2	5	7	309	...	...	...		4	0	0	0	10

M

McLEAN, KIRK   G   CANUCKS

PERSONAL: Born June 26, 1966, in Willowdale, Ont. ... 6-0/192. ... Catches left. ... Name pronounced muh-KLAYN.
TRANSACTIONS/CAREER NOTES: Selected by New Jersey Devils as underage junior in sixth round (sixth Devils pick, 107th overall) of NHL entry draft (June 9, 1984). ... Traded by Devils with C Greg Adams and second-round pick (D Leif Rohlin) to Vancouver Canucks for C Patrik Sundstrom, second- (LW Jeff Christian) and fourth- (LW Matt Ruchty) round picks in 1988 draft (September 15, 1987). ... Suffered tendinitis in left wrist (February 25, 1991). ... Injured knee (January 13, 1996); missed 18 games. ... Injured knee (November 11, 1996); missed 19 games. ... Injured finger (March 5, 1997); missed nine games.
HONORS: Played in NHL All-Star Game (1990 and 1992). ... Named to THE SPORTING NEWS All-Star second team (1991-92). ... Named to NHL All-Star second team (1991-92).
RECORDS: Holds NHL single-season playoff record for most minutes played by a goaltender—1,544 (1994).
MISCELLANEOUS: Holds Vancouver Canucks all-time record for most games played by goalie (487), most wins (205), goals-against average (3.25) and most shutouts (19). ... Stopped a penalty shot attempt (vs. Brent Gilchrist, January 27, 1994). ... Allowed a penalty shot goal (vs. Brent Ashton, December 11, 1988; vs. Mike Donnelly, November 12, 1992; vs. Andrei Kovalenko, December 4, 1993).

Season Team	League	REGULAR SEASON								PLAYOFFS						
		Gms.	Min	W	L	T	GA	SO	Avg.		Gms.	Min.	W	L	GA	SO	Avg.
83-84— Oshawa	OHL	17	940	5	9	0	67	0	4.28		—	—	—	—	—	—	—
84-85— Oshawa	OHL	47	2581	23	17	2	143	1	*3.32		5	271	1	3	21	0	4.65
85-86— Oshawa	OHL	51	2830	24	21	2	169	1	3.58		4	201	1	2	18	0	5.37
—New Jersey	NHL	2	111	1	1	0	11	0	5.95		—	—	—	—	—	—	—
86-87— New Jersey	NHL	4	160	1	1	0	10	0	3.75		—	—	—	—	—	—	—
—Maine	AHL	45	2606	15	23	4	140	1	3.22		—	—	—	—	—	—	—
87-88— Vancouver	NHL	41	2380	11	27	3	147	1	3.71		—	—	—	—	—	—	—
88-89— Vancouver	NHL	42	2477	20	17	3	127	4	3.08		5	302	2	3	18	0	3.58
89-90— Vancouver	NHL	*63	*3739	21	30	10	*216	0	3.47		—	—	—	—	—	—	—
90-91— Vancouver	NHL	41	1969	10	22	3	131	0	3.99		2	123	1	1	7	0	3.41
91-92— Vancouver	NHL	65	3852	†38	17	9	176	†5	2.74		13	785	6	7	33	†2	2.52
92-93— Vancouver	NHL	54	3261	28	21	5	184	3	3.39		12	754	6	6	42	0	3.34
93-94— Vancouver	NHL	52	3128	23	26	3	156	3	2.99		24	*1544	15	†9	59	†4	2.29
94-95— Vancouver	NHL	40	2374	18	12	10	109	1	2.75		11	660	4	†7	36	0	3.27
95-96— Vancouver	NHL	45	2645	15	21	9	156	2	3.54		1	21	0	1	3	0	8.57
96-97— Vancouver	NHL	44	2581	21	18	3	138	0	3.21		—	—	—	—	—	—	—
NHL totals (12 years)		493	28677	207	213	58	1561	19	3.27		68	4189	34	34	198	6	2.84

McLENNAN, JAMIE　　　　　　G　　　　　　BLUES

PERSONAL: Born June 30, 1971, in Edmonton. ... 6-0/190. ... Catches left.
TRANSACTIONS/CAREER NOTES: Selected by New York Islanders in third round (third Islanders pick, 48th overall) of NHL entry draft (June 22, 1991). ... Signed as free agent by St. Louis Blues (July 3, 1996).
HONORS: Won Del Wilson Trophy (1990-91). ... Named to WHL (East) All-Star first team (1990-91).

Season Team	League	REGULAR SEASON								PLAYOFFS						
		Gms.	Min	W	L	T	GA	SO	Avg.	Gms.	Min.	W	L	GA	SO	Avg.
88-89—Spokane	WHL	11	578	...	...	...	63	0	6.54	—	—	—	—	—	—	—
—Lethbridge	WHL	7	368	...	...	...	22	0	3.59	—	—	—	—	—	—	—
89-90—Lethbridge	WHL	34	1690	20	...	2	110	1	3.91	13	677	6	5	44	0	3.90
90-91—Lethbridge	WHL	56	3230	32	18	4	205	0	3.81	*16	*970	8	8	*56	0	3.46
91-92—Capital District	AHL	18	952	4	10	2	60	1	3.78	—	—	—	—	—	—	—
—Richmond	ECHL	32	1837	16	12	‡2	114	0	3.72	—	—	—	—	—	—	—
92-93—Capital District	AHL	38	2171	17	14	6	117	1	3.23	1	20	0	1	5	0	15.00
93-94—Salt Lake City	IHL	24	1320	8	12	‡2	80	0	3.64	—	—	—	—	—	—	—
—New York Islanders	NHL	22	1287	8	7	6	61	0	2.84	2	82	0	1	6	0	4.39
94-95—New York Islanders	NHL	21	1185	6	11	2	67	0	3.39	—	—	—	—	—	—	—
—Denver	IHL	4	240	3	0	‡1	12	0	3.00	11	641	8	2	23	1	*2.15
95-96—Utah	IHL	14	728	9	2	2	29	0	2.39	—	—	—	—	—	—	—
—New York Islanders	NHL	13	636	3	9	1	39	0	3.68	—	—	—	—	—	—	—
—Worcester	AHL	22	1215	14	7	1	57	0	2.81	2	118	0	2	8	0	4.07
96-97—Worcester	AHL	39	2152	18	13	4	100	2	2.79	4	262	2	2	16	0	3.66
NHL totals (3 years)		56	3108	17	27	9	167	0	3.22	2	82	0	1	6	0	4.39

McLLWAIN, DAVE　　　　　　C/RW　　　　　　ISLANDERS

PERSONAL: Born January 9, 1967, in Seaforth, Ont. ... 6-0/185. ... Shoots right. ... Name pronounced MA-kuhl-wayn.
TRANSACTIONS/CAREER NOTES: Traded by Kitchener Rangers with D John Keller and RW Todd Stromback to North Bay Centennials for RW Ron Sanko, RW Peter Lisy, Richard Hawkins and D Brett MacDonald (November 1985). ... Selected by Pittsburgh Penguins as underage junior in ninth round (ninth Penguins pick, 172nd overall) of NHL entry draft (June 21, 1986). ... Traded by Penguins with C/LW Randy Cunneyworth and G Richard Tabaracci to Winnipeg Jets for RW Andrew McBain, D Jim Kyte and LW Randy Gilhen (June 17, 1989). ... Injured wrist (October 28, 1990). ... Tore medial collateral ligament of right knee (December 3, 1990); missed 16 games. ... Traded by Jets with D Gord Donnelly, fifth-round pick (LW Yuri Khmylev) in 1992 draft and future considerations to Buffalo Sabres for LW Darrin Shannon, LW Mike Hartman and D Dean Kennedy (October 11, 1991). ... Traded by Sabres with C Pierre Turgeon, RW Benoit Hogue and D Uwe Krupp to New York Islanders for C Pat LaFontaine, LW Randy Wood, D Randy Hillier and future considerations (October 25, 1991); Sabres received fourth-round pick (D Dean Melanson) in 1992 draft to complete deal. ... Traded by Islanders with LW Ken Baumgartner to Toronto Maple Leafs for C Claude Loiselle and RW Daniel Marois (March 10, 1992). ... Selected by Ottawa Senators in 1993 waiver draft (October 3, 1993). ... Separated left shoulder (December 30, 1993); missed 17 games. ... Suffered charley horse (April 7, 1994); missed one game. ... Bruised ribs (February 6, 1995); missed two games. ... Injured knee (April 10, 1995); missed one game. ... Traded by Senators to Pittsburgh Penguins for eighth-round pick (D Erich Goldmann) in 1996 draft (March 1, 1996). ... Signed as free agent by Islanders (July 25, 1996).
HONORS: Named to OHL All-Star second team (1986-87).
MISCELLANEOUS: Failed to score on a penalty shot (vs. Ron Tugnutt, October 12, 1991).

Season Team	League	REGULAR SEASON								PLAYOFFS				
		Gms.	G	A	Pts.	PIM	+/-	PP	SH	Gms.	G	A	Pts.	PIM
84-85—Kitchener	OHL	61	13	21	34	29	...	...	...	—	—	—	—	—
85-86—Kitchener	OHL	13	7	7	14	12	...	...	...	—	—	—	—	—
—North Bay	OHL	51	30	28	58	25	...	...	...	10	4	4	8	2
86-87—North Bay	OHL	60	46	73	119	35	...	...	...	24	7	18	25	40
87-88—Muskegon	IHL	9	4	6	10	23	...	...	...	6	2	3	5	8
—Pittsburgh	NHL	66	11	8	19	40	-1	1	0	—	—	—	—	—
88-89—Muskegon	IHL	46	37	35	72	51	...	...	...	7	8	2	10	6
—Pittsburgh	NHL	24	1	2	3	4	11	0	0	3	0	1	1	0
89-90—Winnipeg	NHL	80	25	26	51	60	-1	1	†7	7	0	1	1	2
90-91—Winnipeg	NHL	60	14	11	25	46	-13	2	2	—	—	—	—	—
91-92—Winnipeg	NHL	3	1	1	2	2	1	0	0	—	—	—	—	—
—Buffalo	NHL	5	0	0	0	2	-3	0	0	—	—	—	—	—
—New York Islanders	NHL	54	8	15	23	28	-8	1	1	—	—	—	—	—
—Toronto	NHL	11	1	2	3	4	1	0	0	—	—	—	—	—
92-93—Toronto	NHL	66	14	4	18	30	-18	1	1	4	0	0	0	0
93-94—Ottawa	NHL	66	17	26	43	48	-40	1	1	—	—	—	—	—
94-95—Ottawa	NHL	43	5	6	11	22	-26	1	0	—	—	—	—	—
95-96—Cleveland	AHL	60	30	45	75	80	...	...	...	—	—	—	—	—
—Ottawa	NHL	1	0	1	1	2	0	0	0	—	—	—	—	—
—Pittsburgh	NHL	18	2	4	6	4	-5	0	0	—	—	—	—	—
96-97—Cleveland	IHL	63	29	46	75	85	...	...	...	14	8	15	23	6
—New York Islanders	NHL	4	1	1	2	0	-2	1	0	—	—	—	—	—
NHL totals (10 years)		501	100	107	207	292	-126	9	12	14	0	2	2	2

M

McRAE, BASIL　　　　　　LW

PERSONAL: Born January 5, 1961, in Beaverton, Ont. ... 6-2/210. ... Shoots left. ... Full name: Basil Paul McRae. ... Name pronounced BA-zihl muh-KRAY. ... Brother of Chris McRae, left winger, Toronto Maple Leafs (1987-88 and 1988-89) and Detroit Red Wings (1989-90).
TRANSACTIONS/CAREER NOTES: Selected by Quebec Nordiques as underage junior in fifth round (third Nordiques pick, 87th overall) of NHL entry draft (June 11, 1980). ... Traded by Nordiques to Toronto Maple Leafs for D Richard Turmel (August 12, 1983). ... Signed as free agent by Detroit Red Wings (August 1985). ... Traded by Red Wings with LW John Ogrodnick and RW Doug Shedden to Nordiques for LW Brent Ashton, RW Mark Kumpel and D Gilbert Delorme (January 17, 1987). ... Signed as free agent by Minnesota North Stars (July 1987). ...

Strained right knee ligaments (October 10, 1989); missed nine games. ... Suspended five games and fined $500 by NHL for fighting (December 28, 1989). ... Strained abdominal muscle (October 1990). ... Underwent abdominal surgery (November 29, 1990); missed 35 games. ... Severed tendon (February 29, 1992); missed final 17 games of regular season. ... Selected by Tampa Bay Lightning in NHL expansion draft (June 18, 1992). ... Fractured bone in lower leg (October 11, 1992); missed 35 games. ... Traded by Lightning with D Doug Crossman and fourth-round pick (LW Andrei Petrakov) in 1996 draft to St. Louis Blues for LW Jason Ruff (January 28, 1993). ... Suffered allergic reaction (November 16, 1993); missed two games. ... Pulled abdominal muscle (January 3, 1994); missed seven games. ... Underwent abdominal surgery (February 10, 1994); missed 18 games. ... Injured abdomen (March 22, 1994); missed three games. ... Injured rib (April 1, 1994); missed remainder of season. ... Injured back (February 13, 1995); missed nine games. ... Strained shoulder (November 7, 1995); missed 60 games. ... Signed as free agent by Chicago Blackhawks (October 7, 1996). ... Announced retirement (December 3, 1996).

Season Team	League	REGULAR SEASON								PLAYOFFS				
		Gms.	G	A	Pts.	PIM	+/-	PP	SH	Gms.	G	A	Pts.	PIM
77-78— Seneca Jr. B	OHA	36	21	38	59	80	...	...	...	—	—	—	—	—
78-79— London	OMJHL	66	13	28	41	79				—	—	—	—	—
79-80— London	OMJHL	67	23	35	58	116	...	...	...	5	0	0	0	18
80-81— London	OMJHL	65	29	23	52	266	...	...	...	—	—	—	—	—
81-82— Fredericton	AHL	47	11	15	26	175	...	...	...	—	—	—	—	—
— Quebec	NHL	20	4	3	7	69	-3	0	0	9	1	0	1	34
82-83— Fredericton	AHL	53	22	19	41	146	...	...	...	12	1	5	6	75
— Quebec	NHL	22	1	1	2	59	-1	0	0	—	—	—	—	—
83-84— Toronto	NHL	3	0	0	0	19	-3	0	0	—	—	—	—	—
— St. Catharines	AHL	78	14	25	39	187	...	...	...	6	0	0	0	40
84-85— St. Catharines	AHL	72	30	25	55	186	...	...	...	—	—	—	—	—
— Toronto	NHL	1	0	0	0	0	0	0	0	—	—	—	—	—
85-86— Detroit	NHL	4	0	0	0	5	-4	0	0	—	—	—	—	—
— Adirondack	AHL	69	22	30	52	259	...	...	...	17	5	4	9	101
86-87— Detroit	NHL	36	2	2	4	193	-3	1	0	—	—	—	—	—
— Quebec	NHL	33	9	5	14	149	1	3	0	13	3	1	4	*99
87-88— Minnesota	NHL	80	5	11	16	382	-28	0	0	—	—	—	—	—
88-89— Minnesota	NHL	78	12	19	31	365	-8	4	0	5	0	0	0	58
89-90— Minnesota	NHL	66	9	17	26	*351	-5	2	0	7	1	0	1	24
90-91— Minnesota	NHL	40	1	3	4	224	-8	0	0	22	1	1	2	*94
91-92— Minnesota	NHL	59	5	8	13	245	-14	0	0	—	—	—	—	—
92-93— Tampa Bay	NHL	14	2	3	5	71	-3	1	0	—	—	—	—	—
— St. Louis	NHL	33	1	3	4	98	-13	1	0	11	0	1	1	24
93-94— St. Louis	NHL	40	1	2	3	103	-7	0	0	2	0	0	0	12
94-95— St. Louis	NHL	21	0	5	5	72	4	0	0	7	2	1	3	4
— Peoria	IHL	2	0	0	0	12	...	...	...	—	—	—	—	—
95-96— St. Louis	NHL	18	1	1	2	40	-5	0	0	2	0	0	0	0
96-97— Chicago	NHL	8	0	0	0	12	-2	0	0	—	—	—	—	—
NHL totals (16 years)		576	53	83	136	2457	-102	12	0	78	8	4	12	349

McSORLEY, MARTY   D/RW   SHARKS

M

PERSONAL: Born May 18, 1963, in Hamilton, Ont. ... 6-1/230. ... Shoots right. ... Full name: Martin James McSorley.

TRANSACTIONS/CAREER NOTES: Signed as free agent by Pittsburgh Penguins (April 1983). ... Traded by Penguins with C Tim Hrynewich to Edmonton Oilers for G Gilles Meloche (August 1985). ... Suspended by NHL for AHL incident (March 1987). ... Sprained knee (November 1987). ... Suspended three playoff games by NHL for spearing (April 23, 1988). ... Traded by Oilers with C Wayne Gretzky and LW/C Mike Krushelnyski to Los Angeles Kings for C Jimmy Carson, LW Martin Gelinas, first-round picks in 1989 (traded to New Jersey), 1991 (LW Martin Rucinsky) and 1993 (D Nick Stajduhar) drafts and cash (August 9, 1988). ... Injured shoulder (December 31, 1988). ... Sprained knee (February 1989). ... Suspended four games by NHL for game-misconduct penalties (1989-90). ... Twisted right knee (October 14, 1990); missed four games. ... Twisted ankle (February 9, 1991). ... Suspended three games by NHL for striking another player with a gloved hand (March 2, 1991). ... Suffered from throat virus (November 23, 1991); missed six games. ... Sprained shoulder (February 19, 1992); missed three games. ... Suspended six off-days and fined $500 by NHL for cross-checking (October 31, 1992). ... Suspended one game by NHL for game misconduct penalties (November 27, 1992). ... Traded by Kings to Pittsburgh Penguins for C Shawn McEachern (August 27, 1993). ... Sprained ankle (November 16, 1993); missed eight games. ... Traded by Penguins with D Jim Paek to Los Angeles Kings for RW Thomas Sandstrom and C Shawn McEachern (February 15, 1993). ... Suspended four games without pay and fined $500 for eye-gouging incident (February 23, 1994). ... Sprained abdomen (April 7, 1994); missed remainder of season. ... Strained groin (February 12, 1995); missed seven games. ... Strained groin (January 5, 1996); missed six games. ... Bruised left thigh (February 28, 1996); missed 11 games. ... Traded by Kings with RW Shane Churla and LW Jari Kurri to New York Rangers for C Ray Ferraro, C Nathan Lafayette, C Ian Laperriere, D Mattias Norstrom and fourth-round pick (D Sean Blanchard) in 1997 draft (March 14, 1996). ... Injured groin (April 4, 1996); missed four games. ... Injured groin (April 12, 1996); missed one game. ... Traded by Rangers to San Jose Sharks for D Jayson More, C Brian Swanson and fourth-round pick in 1998 draft (August 20, 1996). ... Underwent hip surgery (September 10, 1996); missed 17 games. ... Injured groin (November 16, 1996); missed five games. ... Reinjured groin (January 2, 1997); missed three games.

HONORS: Shared Alka-Seltzer Plus Award with Theoren Fleury (1990-91).

MISCELLANEOUS: Member of Stanley Cup championship team (1987 and 1988). ... Holds Los Angeles Kings all-time record for penalty minutes (1,846).

Season Team	League	REGULAR SEASON								PLAYOFFS				
		Gms.	G	A	Pts.	PIM	+/-	PP	SH	Gms.	G	A	Pts.	PIM
81-82— Belleville	OHL	58	6	13	19	234	...	...	...	—	—	—	—	—
82-83— Belleville	OHL	70	10	41	51	183	...	...	...	4	0	0	0	7
— Baltimore	AHL	2	0	0	0	22	...	...	...	—	—	—	—	—
83-84— Pittsburgh	NHL	72	2	7	9	224	-39	0	0	—	—	—	—	—
84-85— Baltimore	AHL	58	6	24	30	154	...	...	...	14	0	7	7	47
— Pittsburgh	NHL	15	0	0	0	15	-3	0	0	—	—	—	—	—
85-86— Edmonton	NHL	59	11	12	23	265	9	0	0	8	0	2	2	50
— Nova Scotia	AHL	9	2	4	6	34	...	...	...	—	—	—	—	—
86-87— Edmonton	NHL	41	2	4	6	159	-4	0	0	21	4	3	7	65
— Nova Scotia	AHL	7	2	2	4	48	...	...	...	—	—	—	—	—
87-88— Edmonton	NHL	60	9	17	26	223	23	0	0	16	0	3	3	67
88-89— Los Angeles	NHL	66	10	17	27	350	3	2	0	11	0	2	2	33

Season Team	League	REGULAR SEASON								PLAYOFFS				
		Gms.	G	A	Pts.	PIM	+/-	PP	SH	Gms.	G	A	Pts.	PIM
89-90— Los Angeles	NHL	75	15	21	36	322	2	2	1	10	1	3	4	18
90-91— Los Angeles	NHL	61	7	32	39	221	†48	1	1	12	0	0	0	58
91-92— Los Angeles	NHL	71	7	22	29	268	-13	2	1	6	1	0	1	21
92-93— Los Angeles	NHL	81	15	26	41	*399	1	3	3	24	4	6	10	60
93-94— Pittsburgh	NHL	47	3	18	21	139	-9	0	0	—	—	—	—	—
— Los Angeles	NHL	18	4	6	10	55	-3	1	0	—	—	—	—	—
94-95— Los Angeles	NHL	41	3	18	21	83	-14	1	0	—	—	—	—	—
95-96— Los Angeles	NHL	59	10	21	31	148	-14	1	1	—	—	—	—	—
— New York Rangers	NHL	9	0	2	2	21	-6	0	0	4	0	0	0	0
96-97— San Jose	NHL	57	4	12	16	186	-6	0	1	—	—	—	—	—
NHL totals (14 years)		832	102	235	337	3078	-25	13	8	112	10	19	29	372

McSWEEN, DON — D — MIGHTY DUCKS

PERSONAL: Born June 9, 1964, in Detroit. ... 5-11/197. ... Shoots left. ... Full name: Donald Kennedy McSween.
COLLEGE: Michigan State.
TRANSACTIONS/CAREER NOTES: Selected by Buffalo Sabres in eighth round (10th Sabres pick, 154th overall) of NHL entry draft (June 8, 1983). ... Signed as free agent by Detroit Red Wings (August 29, 1992). ... Loaned to San Diego Gulls (October 6, 1992). ... Signed as free agent by Mighty Ducks of Anaheim (January 12, 1994). ... Suffered from chicken pox (March 7, 1994); missed seven games. ... Lacerated right forearm (January 21, 1995); missed last 48 games of 1994-95 season and first 50 games of 1995-96 season.
HONORS: Named to NCAA All-America West second team (1985-86 and 1986-87). ... Named to CCHA All-Star first team (1985-86 and 1986-87). ... Named to NCAA All-Tournament team (1986-87). ... Named to AHL All-Star first team (1989-90).

Season Team	League	REGULAR SEASON								PLAYOFFS				
		Gms.	G	A	Pts.	PIM	+/-	PP	SH	Gms.	G	A	Pts.	PIM
83-84— Michigan State	CCHA	46	10	26	36	30	...	...	...	—	—	—	—	—
84-85— Michigan State	CCHA	44	2	23	25	52	...	...	...	—	—	—	—	—
85-86— Michigan State	CCHA	45	9	29	38	18	...	...	...	—	—	—	—	—
86-87— Michigan State	CCHA	45	7	23	30	34	...	...	...	—	—	—	—	—
87-88— Rochester	AHL	63	9	29	38	108	...	...	...	6	0	1	1	15
— Buffalo	NHL	5	0	1	1	6	...	...	...	—	—	—	—	—
88-89— Rochester	AHL	66	7	22	29	45	...	...	...	—	—	—	—	—
89-90— Buffalo	NHL	4	0	0	0	6	-3	0	0	—	—	—	—	—
— Rochester	AHL	70	16	43	59	43	...	...	...	17	3	10	13	12
90-91— Rochester	AHL	74	7	44	51	57	...	...	...	15	2	5	7	8
91-92— Rochester	AHL	75	6	32	38	60	...	...	...	16	5	6	11	18
92-93— San Diego	IHL	80	15	40	55	85	...	...	...	14	1	2	3	10
93-94— San Diego	IHL	38	5	13	18	36	...	...	...	—	—	—	—	—
— Anaheim	NHL	32	3	9	12	39	4	1	0	—	—	—	—	—
94-95— Anaheim	NHL	2	0	0	0	0	4	0	0	—	—	—	—	—
95-96— Anaheim	NHL	4	0	0	0	4	0	0	0	—	—	—	—	—
— Baltimore	AHL	12	1	9	10	2	...	...	...	—	—	—	—	—
96-97— Grand Rapids	IHL	75	7	20	27	66	...	...	...	3	0	1	1	8
NHL totals (5 years)		47	3	10	13	55	1	1	0					

McTAVISH, DALE — C — FLAMES

PERSONAL: Born February 28, 1972, in Eganville, Ont. ... 6-1/200. ... Shoots left.
COLLEGE: St. Francis Xavier (Antigonish, Nova Scotia).
TRANSACTIONS/CAREER NOTES: Signed as free agent by Calgary Flames (March 18, 1997).

Season Team	League	REGULAR SEASON								PLAYOFFS				
		Gms.	G	A	Pts.	PIM	+/-	PP	SH	Gms.	G	A	Pts.	PIM
89-90— Peterborough	OHL	66	21	27	48	44	...	...	...	4	1	0	1	0
90-91— Peterborough	OHL	66	26	35	61	34	...	...	...	12	1	5	6	2
91-92— Peterborough	OHL	60	25	31	56	59	...	...	...	10	2	5	7	11
92-93— Peterborough	OHL	66	31	50	81	98	...	...	...	21	9	8	17	22
93-94— St. Francis Xavier	CIAU	25	29	24	53	...				—	—	—	—	—
94-95— St. Francis Xavier	CIAU	25	25	27	52	...				—	—	—	—	—
95-96— Canadian nat'l team	Int'l	53	24	32	56	91	...	...	...	—	—	—	—	—
— Saint John	AHL	4	2	3	5	5	...	...	...	15	5	4	9	15
96-97— Saint John	AHL	53	16	21	37	65	...	...	...	3	0	1	1	0
— Calgary	NHL	9	1	2	3	2	-4	0	0	—	—	—	—	—
NHL totals (1 year)		9	1	2	3	2	-4	0	0					

MELLANBY, SCOTT — RW — PANTHERS

PERSONAL: Born June 11, 1966, in Montreal. ... 6-1/199. ... Shoots right. ... Full name: Scott Edgar Mellanby.
HIGH SCHOOL: Henry Carr (Rexdale, Ont.).
COLLEGE: Wisconsin.
TRANSACTIONS/CAREER NOTES: Selected by Philadelphia Flyers as underage junior in second round (first Flyers pick, 27th overall) of NHL entry draft (June 9, 1984). ... Lacerated right index finger (October 1987). ... Severed nerve and damaged tendon in left forearm (August 1989); missed first 20 games of season. ... Suffered viral infection (November 1989). ... Traded by Flyers with LW Craig Berube and C Craig Fisher to Edmonton Oilers for RW Dave Brown, D Corey Foster and rights to RW Jari Kurri (May 30, 1991). ... Injured shoulder (February 14, 1993); missed 15 games. ... Selected by Florida Panthers in NHL expansion draft (June 24, 1993). ... Fractured nose and lacerated face (February 1, 1994); missed four games. ... Fractured finger (March 7, 1996); missed three games.
HONORS: Played in NHL All-Star Game (1996).
MISCELLANEOUS: Holds Florida Panthers all-time records for most goals (102), most assists (109), most points (211), and most games played (289).

M

Season Team	League	REGULAR SEASON								PLAYOFFS				
		Gms.	G	A	Pts.	PIM	+/-	PP	SH	Gms.	G	A	Pts.	PIM
83-84— Henry Carr	MTHL	39	37	37	74	97	...	...	...	—	—	—	—	—
84-85— Univ. of Wisconsin	WCHA	40	14	24	38	60	...	...	...	—	—	—	—	—
85-86— Univ. of Wisconsin	WCHA	32	21	23	44	89	...	...	...	—	—	—	—	—
—Philadelphia	NHL	2	0	0	0	0	-1	0	0	—	—	—	—	—
86-87— Philadelphia	NHL	71	11	21	32	94	8	1	0	24	5	5	10	46
87-88— Philadelphia	NHL	75	25	26	51	185	-7	7	0	7	0	1	1	16
88-89— Philadelphia	NHL	76	21	29	50	183	-13	11	0	19	4	5	9	28
89-90— Philadelphia	NHL	57	6	17	23	77	-4	0	0	—	—	—	—	—
90-91— Philadelphia	NHL	74	20	21	41	155	8	5	0	—	—	—	—	—
91-92— Edmonton	NHL	80	23	27	50	197	5	7	0	16	2	1	3	29
92-93— Edmonton	NHL	69	15	17	32	147	-4	6	0	—	—	—	—	—
93-94— Florida	NHL	80	30	30	60	149	0	17	0	—	—	—	—	—
94-95— Florida	NHL	48	13	12	25	90	-16	4	0	—	—	—	—	—
95-96— Florida	NHL	79	32	38	70	160	4	19	0	22	3	6	9	44
96-97— Florida	NHL	82	27	29	56	170	7	9	1	5	0	2	2	4
NHL totals (12 years)		793	223	267	490	1607	-13	86	1	93	14	20	34	167

MESSIER, ERIC   D   AVALANCHE

PERSONAL: Born October 29, 1973, in Drummondville, Que. ... 6-2/200. ... Shoots left.
TRANSACTIONS/CAREER NOTES: Signed as free agent by Colorado Avalanche (October 1, 1995).

Season Team	League	REGULAR SEASON								PLAYOFFS				
		Gms.	G	A	Pts.	PIM	+/-	PP	SH	Gms.	G	A	Pts.	PIM
91-92— Trois-Rivieres	QMJHL	58	2	10	12	28	...	...	...	15	2	2	4	13
92-93— Sherbrooke	QMJHL	51	4	17	21	82	...	...	...	15	0	4	4	18
93-94— Sherbrooke	QMJHL	67	4	24	28	69	...	...	...	12	1	7	8	14
94-95—						Statistics unavailable.								
95-96— Cornwall	AHL	72	5	9	14	111	...	...	...	8	1	1	2	20
96-97— Hershey	AHL	55	16	26	42	69	...	...	...	9	3	8	11	14
—Colorado	NHL	21	0	0	0	4	7	0	0	—	—	—	—	—

MESSIER, MARK   C   CANUCKS

PERSONAL: Born January 18, 1961, in Edmonton. ... 6-1/205. ... Shoots left. ... Full name: Mark Douglas Messier. ... Name pronounced MEHZ-yay. ... Brother of Paul Messier, center, Colorado Rockies (1978-79); cousin of Mitch Messier, center/right winger in Dallas Stars system; cousin of Joby Messier, defenseman with New York Rangers (1992-93 through 1994-95); and brother-in-law of John Blum, defenseman for four NHL teams (1982-83 through 1989-90).
TRANSACTIONS/CAREER NOTES: Given five-game trial by Indianapolis Racers (November 1978). ... Signed as free agent by Cincinnati Stingers (January 1979). ... Selected by Edmonton Oilers in third round (second Oilers pick, 48th overall) of NHL entry draft (August 9, 1979). ... Injured ankle (November 7, 1981). ... Chipped bone in wrist (March 1983). ... Suspended six games by NHL for hitting another player with stick (January 18, 1984). ... Sprained knee ligaments (November 1984). ... Suspended 10 games by NHL for injuring another player (December 26, 1984). ... Bruised left foot (December 3, 1985); missed 17 games. ... Suspended and fined by Oilers after refusing to report to training camp (October 1987); missed three weeks of camp. ... Suspended six games by NHL for injuring another player with his stick (October 23, 1988). ... Twisted left knee (January 28, 1989). ... Strained right knee (February 3, 1989). ... Bruised left knee (February 12, 1989). ... Sprained left knee ligaments (October 16, 1990); missed 10 games. ... Reinjured left knee (December 12, 1990); missed three games. ... Reinjured knee (December 22, 1990); missed nine games. ... Broke left thumb (February 11, 1991); missed eight games. ... Missed one game due to contract dispute (October 1991). ... Traded by Oilers with future considerations to New York Rangers for C Bernie Nicholls, LW Louie DeBrusk, RW Steven Rice and future considerations (October 4, 1991); Oilers traded D Jeff Beukeboom to Rangers for D David Shaw to complete deal (November 12, 1991). ... Sprained ligament in wrist (January 19, 1993); missed six games. ... Strained rib cage muscle (February 27, 1993); missed two games. ... Strained rib cage muscle (March 11, 1993); missed one game. ... Suspended three off-days and fined $500 by NHL for stick-swinging incident (March 18, 1993). ... Sprained wrist (December 22, 1993); missed six games. ... Bruised thigh (March 16, 1994); missed two games. ... Suffered back spasms (April 30, 1995); missed two games. ... Bruised shoulder (February 27, 1996); missed two games. ... Bruised ribs (April 4, 1996); missed six games. ... Suspended two games and fined $1,000 by NHL for checking opponent from behind (October 8, 1996). ... Hyperextended elbow (December 7, 1996); missed four games. ... Suffered back spasms (February 23, 1997); missed two games. ... Suffered charley horse (March 27, 1997); missed two games. ... Signed as free agent by Vancouver Canucks (July 28, 1997).
HONORS: Named to The Sporting News All-Star first team (1981-82, 1982-83, 1989-90 and 1991-92). ... Named to NHL All-Star first team (1981-82, 1982-83, 1989-90 and 1991-92). ... Played in NHL All-Star Game (1982-1984, 1986, 1988-1992, 1994, 1996 and 1997). ... Won Conn Smythe Trophy (1983-84). ... Named to NHL All-Star second team (1983-84). ... Named to The Sporting News All-Star second team (1986-87). ... Named NHL Player of the Year by The Sporting News (1989-90 and 1991-92). ... Won Hart Memorial Trophy (1989-90 and 1991-92). ... Won Lester B. Pearson Award (1989-90 and 1991-92).
RECORDS: Holds NHL career playoff record for most shorthanded goals—11; and most games—236.. ... Shares NHL single-game playoff record for most shorthanded goals—2 (April 21, 1992).
STATISTICAL PLATEAUS: Three-goal games: 1980-81 (1), 1981-82 (2), 1982-83 (1), 1983-84 (2), 1985-86 (1), 1987-88 (1), 1989-90 (2), 1991-92 (2), 1995-96 (1), 1996-97 (2). Total: 15. ... Four-goal games: 1982-83 (1), 1988-89 (1), 1989-90 (1), 1991-92 (1). Total: 4. ... Total hat tricks: 19.
MISCELLANEOUS: Member of Stanley Cup championship team (1984, 1985, 1987, 1988, 1990 and 1994). ... Captain of Edmonton Oilers (1988-89 through 1990-91). ... Captain of New York Rangers (1991-92 through 1996-97).

Season Team	League	REGULAR SEASON								PLAYOFFS				
		Gms.	G	A	Pts.	PIM	+/-	PP	SH	Gms.	G	A	Pts.	PIM
76-77— Spruce Grove	AJHL	57	27	39	66	91	...	...	...	—	—	—	—	—
77-78— St. Albert	AJHL					Statistics unavailable.								
—Portland	WHL	—	—	—	—	—	...	...	...	7	4	1	5	2
78-79— Indianapolis	WHA	5	0	0	0	0	...	...	...	—	—	—	—	—
—Cincinnati	WHA	47	1	10	11	58	...	...	...	—	—	—	—	—
79-80— Houston	CHL	4	0	3	3	4	...	...	...	—	—	—	—	—
—Edmonton	NHL	75	12	21	33	120	...	1	1	3	1	2	3	2

M

Season Team	League	REGULAR SEASON								PLAYOFFS				
		Gms.	G	A	Pts.	PIM	+/-	PP	SH	Gms.	G	A	Pts.	PIM
80-81 — Edmonton	NHL	72	23	40	63	102	-12	4	0	9	2	5	7	13
81-82 — Edmonton	NHL	78	50	38	88	119	21	10	0	5	1	2	3	8
82-83 — Edmonton	NHL	77	48	58	106	72	19	12	1	15	15	6	21	14
83-84 — Edmonton	NHL	73	37	64	101	165	40	7	4	19	8	18	26	19
84-85 — Edmonton	NHL	55	23	31	54	57	8	4	5	18	12	13	25	12
85-86 — Edmonton	NHL	63	35	49	84	68	36	10	5	10	4	6	10	18
86-87 — Edmonton	NHL	77	37	70	107	73	21	7	4	21	12	16	28	16
87-88 — Edmonton	NHL	77	37	74	111	103	21	12	3	19	11	23	34	29
88-89 — Edmonton	NHL	72	33	61	94	130	-5	6	6	7	1	11	12	8
89-90 — Edmonton	NHL	79	45	84	129	79	19	13	6	22	9	*22	†31	20
90-91 — Edmonton	NHL	53	12	52	64	34	15	3	1	18	4	11	15	16
91-92 — New York Rangers	NHL	79	35	72	107	76	31	12	4	11	7	7	14	6
92-93 — New York Rangers	NHL	75	25	66	91	72	-6	7	2	—	—	—	—	—
93-94 — New York Rangers	NHL	76	26	58	84	76	25	6	2	23	12	18	30	33
94-95 — New York Rangers	NHL	46	14	39	53	40	8	3	3	10	3	10	13	8
95-96 — New York Rangers	NHL	74	47	52	99	122	29	14	1	11	4	7	11	16
96-97 — New York Rangers	NHL	71	36	48	84	88	12	7	5	15	3	9	12	6
WHA totals (1 year)		52	1	10	11	58	...							
NHL totals (18 years)		1272	575	977	1552	1596	...	138	53	236	109	186	295	244

MIETTINEN, TOMMI — C/LW — MIGHTY DUCKS

PERSONAL: Born December 3, 1975, in Kuopio, Finland. ... 5-10/165. ... Shoots left.
TRANSACTIONS/CAREER NOTES: Selected by Mighty Ducks of Anaheim in 10th round (10th Mighty Ducks pick, 236th overall) of NHL entry draft (June 29, 1994).

Season Team	League	REGULAR SEASON								PLAYOFFS				
		Gms.	G	A	Pts.	PIM	+/-	PP	SH	Gms.	G	A	Pts.	PIM
92-93 — KalPa Juniors	Finland Jrs.	26	16	27	43	14	...	...	...	—	—	—	—	—
— KalPa Kuopio	Finland	14	0	0	0	0	...	...	...	—	—	—	—	—
93-94 — KalPa Kuopio	Finland	47	5	7	12	14	...	...	...	—	—	—	—	—
94-95 — KalPa Kuopio	Finland	48	13	16	29	26	...	...	...	3	1	1	2	2
95-96 — TPS Turku	Finland	36	3	10	13	10	...	...	...	10	2	1	3	29
96-97 — TPS Turku	Finland	41	6	15	21	6	...	...	...	12	3	4	7	8

MILLAR, CRAIG — D — OILERS

PERSONAL: Born July 12, 1976, in Winnipeg, Man. ... 6-2/200. ... Shoots left.
TRANSACTIONS/CAREER NOTES: Selected by Buffalo Sabres in ninth round (10th Sabres pick, 225th overall) of NHL entry draft (June 29, 1994). ... Traded by Sabres with LW Barrie Moore to Edmonton Oilers for F Miroslav Satan (March 18, 1997).
HONORS: Named to WHL (Central/East) All-Star first team (1995-96). ... Named to AHL All-Rookie team (1996-97).

M

Season Team	League	REGULAR SEASON								PLAYOFFS				
		Gms.	G	A	Pts.	PIM	+/-	PP	SH	Gms.	G	A	Pts.	PIM
92-93 — Swift Current	WHL	43	2	1	3	8	...	...	...	—	—	—	—	—
93-94 — Swift Current	WHL	66	2	9	11	53	...	...	...	—	—	—	—	—
94-95 — Swift Current	WHL	72	8	42	50	80	...	...	...	6	1	1	2	10
95-96 — Swift Current	WHL	72	31	46	77	151	...	...	...	6	1	0	1	22
96-97 — Rochester	AHL	64	7	18	25	65	...	...	...	—	—	—	—	—
— Edmonton	NHL	1	0	0	0	2	0	0	0	—	—	—	—	—
— Hamilton	AHL	10	1	3	4	10	...	...	...	22	4	4	8	21
NHL totals (1 year)		1	0	0	0	2	0	0	0					

MILLEN, COREY — C — FLAMES

PERSONAL: Born April 29, 1964, in Cloquet, Minn. ... 5-7/170. ... Shoots right.
HIGH SCHOOL: Cloquet (Minn.).
COLLEGE: Minnesota.
TRANSACTIONS/CAREER NOTES: Selected by New York Rangers as underage player in third round (third Rangers pick, 57th overall) of NHL entry draft (June 9, 1982). ... Injured knee and underwent surgery (November 1982). ... Injured shoulder (October 1984). ... Tested positive for a non-anabolic steroid in a random test at World Cup Tournament and was banned from play (April 1989). ... Sprained left knee ligaments and underwent surgery (September 18, 1989); missed four months. ... Underwent surgery to left knee (August 1990); missed four months. ... Traded by Rangers to Los Angeles Kings for C Randy Gilhen (December 23, 1991). ... Suffered shoulder contusion (February 29, 1992); missed one game. ... Strained back (October 13, 1992); missed four games. ... Strained groin (December 22, 1992); missed 38 games. ... Traded by Kings to New Jersey Devils for fifth-round pick (G Jason Saal) in 1993 draft (June 26, 1993). ... Traded by Devils to Dallas Stars for C Neal Broten (February 27, 1995). ... Bruised foot (April 17, 1995); missed one game. ... Traded by Stars with rights to C/RW Jarome Iginla to Calgary Flames for C Joe Nieuwendyk (December 19, 1995). ... Suffered back spasms (February 8, 1996); missed one game. ... Suffered back spasms (February 11, 1996); missed one game. ... Pulled groin (March 12, 1996); missed 15 games. ... Fractured jaw (December 23, 1996); missed five games. ... Bruised hip (March 4, 1997); missed one game.
HONORS: Named to WCHA All-Star second team (1984-85 through 1986-87). ... Named to NCAA All-America West second team (1985-86). ... Named to NCAA All-Tournament team (1986-87).

Season Team	League	REGULAR SEASON								PLAYOFFS				
		Gms.	G	A	Pts.	PIM	+/-	PP	SH	Gms.	G	A	Pts.	PIM
81-82 — Cloquet	Minn. H.S.	18	46	35	81	...	...	...	...	—	—	—	—	—
82-83 — Univ. of Minnesota	WCHA	21	14	15	29	18	...	...	...	—	—	—	—	—
83-84 — U.S. national team	Int'l	45	15	11	26	10	...	...	...	—	—	—	—	—
— U.S. Olympic team	Int'l	6	0	0	0	2	...	...	...	—	—	—	—	—

Season Team	League	REGULAR SEASON								PLAYOFFS				
		Gms.	G	A	Pts.	PIM	+/-	PP	SH	Gms.	G	A	Pts.	PIM
84-85— Univ. of Minnesota.....	WCHA	38	28	36	64	60	...	...	...	—	—	—	—	—
85-86— Univ. of Minnesota.....	WCHA	48	41	42	83	64	...	...	...	—	—	—	—	—
86-87— Univ. of Minnesota.....	WCHA	42	36	29	65	62	...	...	...	—	—	—	—	—
87-88— U.S. national team	Int'l	47	41	43	84	26	...	...	...	—	—	—	—	—
— U.S. Olympic team.....	Int'l	6	6	5	11	4	...	...	...	—	—	—	—	—
88-89— Ambri Piotta..............	Switz.	36	32	22	54	18	...	...	...	6	4	3	7	0
89-90— New York Rangers	NHL	4	0	0	0	2	-2	0	0	—	—	—	—	—
— Flint............................	IHL	11	4	5	9	2	...	...	...	—	—	—	—	—
90-91— Binghamton	AHL	40	19	37	56	68	...	...	...	6	0	7	7	8
— New York Rangers	NHL	4	3	1	4	0	1	2	0	6	1	2	3	0
91-92— New York Rangers	NHL	11	1	4	5	10	-1	0	0	—	—	—	—	—
— Binghamton	AHL	15	8	7	15	44	...	...	...	—	—	—	—	—
— Los Angeles	NHL	46	20	21	41	44	3	8	1	6	0	1	1	6
92-93— Los Angeles	NHL	42	23	16	39	42	16	9	2	23	2	4	6	12
93-94— New Jersey	NHL	78	20	30	50	52	24	4	0	7	1	0	1	2
94-95— New Jersey	NHL	17	2	3	5	8	2	0	0	—	—	—	—	—
— Dallas	NHL	28	3	15	18	28	4	1	0	5	1	0	1	2
95-96— Michigan	IHL	11	8	11	19	14	...	...	...	—	—	—	—	—
— Dallas	NHL	13	3	4	7	8	0	1	0	—	—	—	—	—
— Calgary	NHL	31	4	10	14	10	8	1	0	—	—	—	—	—
96-97— Calgary	NHL	61	11	15	26	32	-19	1	0	—	—	—	—	—
NHL totals (9 years)		335	90	119	209	236	36	27	3	47	5	7	12	22

MILLER, AARON — D — AVALANCHE

PERSONAL: Born August 11, 1971, in Buffalo. ... 6-3/205. ... Shoots right. ... Full name: Aaron Michael Miller.
COLLEGE: Vermont.
TRANSACTIONS/CAREER NOTES: Selected by New York Rangers in fifth round (sixth Rangers pick, 88th overall) of NHL entry draft (June 17, 1989). ... Traded by Rangers with fifth-round pick (LW Bill Lindsay) in 1991 draft to Quebec Nordiques for D Joe Cirella (January 17, 1991). ... Nordiques franchise moved to Colorado and renamed Avalanche for 1995-96 season (June 21, 1995).
HONORS: Named to ECAC All-Rookie team (1989-90). ... Named to NCAA All-America East second team (1992-93). ... Named to ECAC All-Star first team (1992-93).

Season Team	League	REGULAR SEASON								PLAYOFFS				
		Gms.	G	A	Pts.	PIM	+/-	PP	SH	Gms.	G	A	Pts.	PIM
87-88— Niagara	NAJHL	30	4	9	13	2	...	...	...	—	—	—	—	—
88-89— Niagara	NAJHL	59	24	38	62	60	...	...	...	—	—	—	—	—
89-90— Univ. of Vermont.......	ECAC	31	1	15	16	24	...	...	...	—	—	—	—	—
90-91— Univ. of Vermont.......	ECAC	30	3	7	10	22	...	...	...	—	—	—	—	—
91-92— Univ. of Vermont.......	ECAC	31	3	16	19	36	...	...	...	—	—	—	—	—
92-93— Univ. of Vermont.......	ECAC	30	4	13	17	16	...	...	...	—	—	—	—	—
93-94— Cornwall....................	AHL	64	4	10	14	49	...	...	...	13	0	2	2	10
— Quebec	NHL	1	0	0	0	0	-1	0	0	—	—	—	—	—
94-95— Cornwall....................	AHL	76	4	18	22	69	...	...	...	—	—	—	—	—
— Quebec	NHL	9	0	3	3	6	2	0	0	—	—	—	—	—
95-96— Cornwall....................	AHL	62	4	23	27	77	...	...	...	8	0	1	1	6
— Colorado	NHL	5	0	0	0	0	0	0	0	—	—	—	—	—
96-97— Colorado	NHL	56	5	12	17	15	15	0	0	17	1	2	3	10
NHL totals (4 years)		71	5	15	20	21	16	0	0	17	1	2	3	10

MILLER, AREN — G — RED WINGS

PERSONAL: Born January 13, 1978, in Oxbow, Sask. ... 6-3/208. ... Catches left.
TRANSACTIONS/CAREER NOTES: Selected by Detroit Red Wings in second round (second Red Wings pick, 52nd overall) of NHL entry draft (June 22, 1996).

Season Team	League	REGULAR SEASON							PLAYOFFS					
		Gms.	Min	W	L	T	GA	SO	Avg.	Gms.	Min.	W	L	GA	SO	Avg.
95-96— Spokane......................	WHL	23	965	8	7	2	50	1	3.11	3	81	0	3	8	0	5.93
96-97— Spokane......................	WHL	52	2834	22	20	3	151	3	3.20	9	555	4	5	28	†1	3.03

MILLER, KELLY — LW — CAPITALS

PERSONAL: Born March 3, 1963, in Lansing, Mich. ... 5-11/195. ... Shoots left. ... Full name: Kelly David Miller. ... Brother of Kevin Miller, left winger, Chicago Blackhawks; and brother of Kip Miller, center for five NHL teams (1990-91, 1991-92 and 1993-94 through 1995-96).
HIGH SCHOOL: Eastern (Lansing, Mich.).
COLLEGE: Michigan State.
TRANSACTIONS/CAREER NOTES: Selected by New York Rangers in ninth round (ninth Rangers pick, 183rd overall) of NHL entry draft (June 9, 1982). ... Injured ankle (September 1985). ... Sprained knee (January 27, 1986); missed five games. ... Traded by Rangers with C Mike Ridley and RW Bobby Crawford to Washington Capitals for C Bobby Carpenter and second-round pick (RW Jason Prosofsky) in 1989 draft (January 1, 1987). ... Pulled groin (November 1988). ... Sprained knee (September 22, 1990). ... Strained abdominal muscle and groin (December 14, 1995); missed eight games. ... Sprained knee (March 6, 1997); missed one game. ... Sprained shoulder (March 11, 1997); missed three games. ... Injured knee and shoulder (April 12, 1997); missed one game.
HONORS: Named to NCAA All-America West first team (1984-85). ... Named to CCHA All-Star first team (1984-85).
MISCELLANEOUS: Holds Washington Capitals all-time record for games played (802).

Season Team	League	REGULAR SEASON								PLAYOFFS				
		Gms.	G	A	Pts.	PIM	+/-	PP	SH	Gms.	G	A	Pts.	PIM
81-82— Michigan State...........	CCHA	40	11	19	30	21	...	...	...	—	—	—	—	—
82-83— Michigan State...........	CCHA	36	16	19	35	12	...	...	...	—	—	—	—	—

M

Season Team	League	REGULAR SEASON								PLAYOFFS				
		Gms.	G	A	Pts.	PIM	+/-	PP	SH	Gms.	G	A	Pts.	PIM
83-84— Michigan State..........	CCHA	46	28	21	49	12	...	...	...	—	—	—	—	—
84-85— Michigan State..........	CCHA	43	27	23	50	21	...	...	...	—	—	—	—	—
— New York Rangers.....	NHL	5	0	2	2	2	-2	0	0	3	0	0	0	2
85-86— New York Rangers.....	NHL	74	13	20	33	52	3	0	1	16	3	4	7	4
86-87— New York Rangers.....	NHL	38	6	14	20	22	-5	2	0	—	—	—	—	—
— Washington	NHL	39	10	12	22	26	10	3	1	7	2	2	4	0
87-88— Washington	NHL	80	9	23	32	35	9	0	1	14	4	4	8	10
88-89— Washington	NHL	78	19	21	40	45	13	2	1	6	1	0	1	2
89-90— Washington	NHL	80	18	22	40	49	-2	3	2	15	3	5	8	23
90-91— Washington	NHL	80	24	26	50	29	10	4	2	11	4	2	6	6
91-92— Washington	NHL	78	14	38	52	49	20	0	1	7	1	2	3	4
92-93— Washington	NHL	84	18	27	45	32	-2	3	0	6	0	3	3	2
93-94— Washington	NHL	84	14	25	39	32	8	0	1	11	2	7	9	0
94-95— Washington	NHL	48	10	13	23	6	5	2	0	7	0	3	3	4
95-96— Washington	NHL	74	7	13	20	30	7	0	2	6	0	1	1	4
96-97— Washington	NHL	77	10	14	24	33	4	0	1	—	—	—	—	—
NHL totals (13 years)		919	172	270	442	442	78	19	13	109	20	33	53	61

MILLER, KEVIN — LW — BLACKHAWKS

PERSONAL: Born August 9, 1965, in Lansing, Mich. ... 5-11/190. ... Shoots right. ... Full name: Kevin Bradley Miller. ... Brother of Kelly Miller, left winger, Washington Capitals; and brother of Kip Miller, center for five NHL teams (1990-91, 1991-92 and 1993-94 through 1995-96).

HIGH SCHOOL: Eastern (Lansing, Mich.).

COLLEGE: Michigan State.

TRANSACTIONS/CAREER NOTES: Selected by New York Rangers in 10th round (10th Rangers pick, 202nd overall) of NHL entry draft (June 9, 1984). ... Pulled groin (September 1990). ... Sprained shoulder (December 1990). ... Traded by Rangers with D Dennis Vial and RW Jim Cummings to Detroit Red Wings for RW Joe Kocur and D Per Djoos (March 5, 1991). ... Traded by Red Wings to Washington Capitals for RW Dino Ciccarelli (June 20, 1992). ... Traded by Capitals to St. Louis Blues for D Paul Cavallini (November 1, 1992). ... Suffered sore knee (November 3, 1993); missed two games. ... Injured knee (November 24, 1993); missed two games. ... Injured hip (March 30, 1994); missed one game. ... Suffered sore groin (April 8, 1994); missed three games. ... Traded by Blues to San Jose Sharks for C Todd Elik (March 23, 1995). ... Injured knee (March 15, 1996); missed two games. ... Traded by Sharks to Pittsburgh Penguins for fifth-round pick in 1996 draft (March 20, 1996). ... Signed as free agent by Chicago Blackhawks (July 17, 1996). ... Suffered from the flu (November 22, 1996); missed one game. ... Pulled groin (January 10, 1997); missed two games.

STATISTICAL PLATEAUS: Three-goal games: 1991-92 (1), 1992-93 (1), 1993-94 (1), 1995-96 (1). Total: 4.

MISCELLANEOUS: Scored on a penalty shot (vs. Patrick Roy, October 30, 1991; vs. Stephane Fiset, December 5, 1995). ... Failed to score on a penalty shot (vs. Mike Vernon, December 17, 1993).

Season Team	League	REGULAR SEASON								PLAYOFFS				
		Gms.	G	A	Pts.	PIM	+/-	PP	SH	Gms.	G	A	Pts.	PIM
84-85— Michigan State..........	CCHA	44	11	29	40	84	...			—	—	—	—	—
85-86— Michigan State..........	CCHA	45	19	52	71	112	...			—	—	—	—	—
86-87— Michigan State..........	CCHA	42	25	56	81	63	...			—	—	—	—	—
87-88— Michigan State..........	CCHA	9	6	3	9	18	...			—	—	—	—	—
— U.S. Olympic team......	Int'l	50	32	34	66	...				—	—	—	—	—
88-89— New York Rangers.....	NHL	24	3	5	8	2	-1	0	0	—	—	—	—	—
— Denver	IHL	55	29	47	76	19	...			4	2	1	3	2
89-90— New York Rangers.....	NHL	16	0	5	5	2	-1	0	0	1	0	0	0	0
— Flint............................	IHL	48	19	23	42	41	...			—	—	—	—	—
90-91— New York Rangers.....	NHL	63	17	27	44	63	1	1	2	—	—	—	—	—
— Detroit........................	NHL	11	5	2	7	4	-4	0	1	7	3	2	5	20
91-92— Detroit........................	NHL	80	20	26	46	53	6	3	1	9	0	2	2	4
92-93— Washington	NHL	10	0	3	3	35	-4	0	0	—	—	—	—	—
— St. Louis	NHL	72	24	22	46	65	6	8	3	10	0	3	3	11
93-94— St. Louis	NHL	75	23	25	48	83	6	6	3	3	1	0	1	4
94-95— St. Louis	NHL	15	2	5	7	0	4	0	0	—	—	—	—	—
— San Jose	NHL	21	6	7	13	13	0	1	1	6	0	0	0	2
95-96— San Jose	NHL	68	22	20	42	41	-8	2	2	—	—	—	—	—
— Pittsburgh..................	NHL	13	6	5	11	4	4	1	0	18	3	2	5	8
96-97— Chicago......................	NHL	69	14	17	31	41	-10	5	1	6	0	1	1	0
NHL totals (9 years)		537	142	169	311	406	-1	27	14	60	7	10	17	49

MILLER, KIP — C — BLACKHAWKS

PERSONAL: Born June 11, 1969, in Lansing, Mich. ... 5-10/185. ... Shoots left. ... Full name: Kip Charles Miller. ... Brother of Kelly Miller, left winger, Washington Capitals; and brother of Kevin Miller, left winger, Chicago Blackhawks.

HIGH SCHOOL: Eastern (Lansing, Mich.).

COLLEGE: Michigan State.

TRANSACTIONS/CAREER NOTES: Selected by Quebec Nordiques in fourth round (fourth Nordiques pick, 72nd overall) of NHL entry draft (June 13, 1987). ... Injured hand and forearm in off-ice accident (November 1987). ... Traded by Nordiques to Minnesota North Stars for LW Steve Maltais (March 8, 1992). ... North Stars franchise moved from Minnesota to Dallas and renamed Stars for 1993-94 season. ... Signed as free agent by San Jose Sharks (August 10, 1993). ... Signed as free agent by New York Islanders (August 2, 1994). ... Signed as free agent by Chicago Blackhawks (August 10, 1995). ... Loaned by Blackhawks to Chicago Wolves of IHL (September 17, 1996).

HONORS: Named to NCAA All-America West first team (1988-89 and 1989-90). ... Named to CCHA All-Star first team (1988-89 and 1989-90). ... Won Hobey Baker Memorial Award (1989-90). ... Named CCHA Player of the Year (1989-90). ... Won N.R. (Bud) Poile Trophy (1994-95).

Season Team	League	REGULAR SEASON								PLAYOFFS				
		Gms.	G	A	Pts.	PIM	+/-	PP	SH	Gms.	G	A	Pts.	PIM
86-87— Michigan State..........	CCHA	41	20	19	39	92	...	...	...	—	—	—	—	—
87-88— Michigan State..........	CCHA	39	16	25	41	51	...	...	...	—	—	—	—	—

Season Team	League	REGULAR SEASON								PLAYOFFS				
		Gms.	G	A	Pts.	PIM	+/-	PP	SH	Gms.	G	A	Pts.	PIM
88-89— Michigan State...........	CCHA	47	32	45	77	94	...	...	...	—	—	—	—	—
89-90— Michigan State...........	CCHA	45	*48	53	*101	60	...	...	...	—	—	—	—	—
90-91— Quebec.....................	NHL	13	4	3	7	7	-1	0	0	—	—	—	—	—
— Halifax.....................	AHL	66	36	33	69	40	...	...	...	—	—	—	—	—
91-92— Quebec.....................	NHL	36	5	10	15	12	-21	1	0	—	—	—	—	—
— Halifax.....................	AHL	24	9	17	26	8	...	...	...	—	—	—	—	—
— Minnesota.................	NHL	3	1	2	3	2	-1	1	0	—	—	—	—	—
— Kalamazoo	IHL	6	1	8	9	4	...	...	...	12	3	9	12	12
92-93— Kalamazoo	IHL	61	17	39	56	59	...	...	...	—	—	—	—	—
93-94— San Jose...................	NHL	11	2	2	4	6	-1	0	0	—	—	—	—	—
— Kansas City.............	IHL	71	38	54	92	51	...	...	...	—	—	—	—	—
94-95— Denver.....................	IHL	71	46	60	106	54	...	...	...	17	*15	14	29	8
— New York Islanders....	NHL	8	0	1	1	0	1	0	0	—	—	—	—	—
95-96— Indianapolis	IHL	73	32	59	91	46	...	...	...	5	2	6	8	2
— Chicago....................	NHL	10	1	4	5	2	1	0	0	—	—	—	—	—
96-97— Chicago....................	IHL	43	11	41	52	32	...	...	...	—	—	—	—	—
— Indianapolis	IHL	37	17	24	41	18	...	...	...	4	2	2	4	2
NHL totals (6 years)		81	13	22	35	29	-22	2	0					

MILLER, TODD   C   ISLANDERS

PERSONAL: Born May 24, 1978, in Elliot Lake, Ont. ... 6-0/174. ... Shoots right.
TRANSACTIONS/CAREER NOTES: Selected by New York Islanders in sixth round (seventh Islanders pick, 138th overall) of NHL entry draft (June 22, 1996).

Season Team	League	REGULAR SEASON								PLAYOFFS				
		Gms.	G	A	Pts.	PIM	+/-	PP	SH	Gms.	G	A	Pts.	PIM
95-96— Sarnia	OHL	62	12	16	28	44	...	...	...	1	0	0	0	0
96-97— Owen Sound	OHL	36	8	19	27	24	...	...	...	—	—	—	—	—

MILLS, CRAIG   RW   BLACKHAWKS

PERSONAL: Born August 27, 1976, in Toronto. ... 5-11/190. ... Shoots right.
TRANSACTIONS/CAREER NOTES: Selected by Winnipeg Jets in fifth round (fifth Jets pick, 108th overall) of NHL entry draft (June 29, 1994). ... Jets franchise moved to Phoenix and renamed Coyotes for 1996-97 season; NHL approved move on January 18, 1996. ... Traded by Coyotes with C Alexei Zhamnov and first-round pick (RW Ty Jones) in 1997 draft to Chicago Blackhawks for C Jeremy Roenick (August 16, 1996).
HONORS: Won Can.HL Humanitarian Award (1995-96).

Season Team	League	REGULAR SEASON								PLAYOFFS				
		Gms.	G	A	Pts.	PIM	+/-	PP	SH	Gms.	G	A	Pts.	PIM
92-93— St. Michaels Tier II.....	Jr. A	44	8	12	20	51	...	...	...	—	—	—	—	—
93-94— Belleville....................	OHL	63	15	18	33	88	...	...	...	12	2	1	3	11
94-95— Belleville....................	OHL	62	39	41	80	104	...	...	...	13	7	9	16	8
95-96— Belleville....................	OHL	48	10	19	29	113	...	...	...	14	4	5	9	32
— Winnipeg	NHL	4	0	2	2	0	0	0	0	1	0	0	0	0
— Springfield	AHL	0	0	0	0	0	0	0	0	2	0	0	0	0
96-97— Indianapolis	IHL	80	12	7	19	199	...	...	...	4	0	0	0	4
NHL totals (1 year)		4	0	2	2	0	0	0	0	1	0	0	0	0

MINARD, MIKE   G   OILERS

PERSONAL: Born January 11, 1976, in Owen Sound, Ont. ... 6-3/205. ... Catches left.
TRANSACTIONS/CAREER NOTES: Selected by Edmonton Oilers in fourth round (fourth Oilers pick, 83rd overall) of NHL entry draft (July 8, 1995).

Season Team	League	REGULAR SEASON							PLAYOFFS					
		Gms.	Min	W	L	T	GA	SO	Avg.	Gms.	Min.	W	L	GA	SO	Avg.
94-95—Chilliwack	BCJHL	40	2330	...	...	...	136	0	3.50	—	—	—	—	—	—	—
95-96— Barrie..........................	OHL	1	52	0	1	0	8	0	9.23	—	—	—	—	—	—	—
— Detroit	OHL	42	2314	25	10	4	128	2	3.32	17	922	9	6	55	1	3.58
96-97— Hamilton......................	AHL	3	100	1	1	0	7	0	4.20	—	—	—	—	—	—	—
— Wheeling	ECHL	23	899	3	7	‡1	69	0	4.61	3	148	0	2	16	0	6.49

MIRONOV, BORIS   D   OILERS

PERSONAL: Born March 21, 1972, in Moscow, U.S.S.R. ... 6-3/215. ... Shoots right. ... Name pronounced MIH-rin-nahv. ... Brother of Dmitri Mironov, defenseman, Pittsburgh Penguins.
TRANSACTIONS/CAREER NOTES: Selected by Winnipeg Jets in second round (second Jets pick, 27th overall) of NHL entry draft (June 20, 1992). ... Traded by Jets with C Mats Lindgren and first- (C Jason Bonsignore) and fourth- (RW Adam Copeland) round picks in 1994 draft to Edmonton Oilers for D Dave Manson and sixth-round pick in 1994 draft (March 15, 1994). ... Bruised ankle (April 3, 1995); missed one game. ... Strained lower back (April 13, 1995); missed 10 games. ... Strained abdominal muscle (January 21, 1997); missed 12 games. ... Strained groin (February 19, 1997); missed five games. ... Strained groin (March 7, 1997); missed five games.
HONORS: Named to NHL All-Rookie team (1993-94).

Season Team	League	REGULAR SEASON								PLAYOFFS				
		Gms.	G	A	Pts.	PIM	+/-	PP	SH	Gms.	G	A	Pts.	PIM
88-89— CSKA Moscow...........	USSR	1	0	0	0	0	...	...	...	—	—	—	—	—
89-90— CSKA Moscow...........	USSR	7	0	0	0	0	...	...	...	—	—	—	—	—
90-91— CSKA Moscow...........	USSR	36	1	5	6	16	...	...	...	—	—	—	—	—
91-92— CSKA Moscow...........	CIS	36	2	1	3	22	...	...	...	—	—	—	—	—

M

Season Team	League	REGULAR SEASON								PLAYOFFS				
		Gms.	G	A	Pts.	PIM	+/-	PP	SH	Gms.	G	A	Pts.	PIM
92-93 — CSKA Moscow	CIS	19	0	5	5	20	...	...	...	—	—	—	—	—
93-94 — Winnipeg	NHL	65	7	22	29	96	-29	5	0	—	—	—	—	—
— Edmonton	NHL	14	0	2	2	14	-4	0	0	—	—	—	—	—
94-95 — Cape Breton	AHL	4	2	5	7	23	...	...	...	—	—	—	—	—
— Edmonton	NHL	29	1	7	8	40	-9	0	0	—	—	—	—	—
95-96 — Edmonton	NHL	78	8	24	32	101	-23	7	0	—	—	—	—	—
96-97 — Edmonton	NHL	55	6	26	32	85	2	2	0	12	2	8	10	16
NHL totals (4 years)		241	22	81	103	336	-63	14	0	12	2	8	10	16

MIRONOV, DMITRI — D — MIGHTY DUCKS

PERSONAL: Born December 25, 1965, in Moscow, U.S.S.R. ... 6-3/215. ... Shoots right. ... Name pronounced MIHR-ih-hanv. ... Brother of Boris Mironov, defenseman, Edmonton Oilers.

TRANSACTIONS/CAREER NOTES: Selected by Toronto Maple Leafs in eighth round (seventh Maple Leafs pick, 160th overall) of NHL entry draft (June 22, 1991). ... Broke nose (March 23, 1992). ... Suffered infected tooth (March 18, 1993); missed 10 games. ... Suffered quad contusion (December 28, 1993); missed one game. ... Lacerated lip (March 7, 1994); missed two games. ... Suffered rib and muscle strain (April 2, 1994); missed remainder of season. ... Bruised thigh (February 18, 1995); missed one game. ... Separated shoulder (March 27, 1995); missed 14 games. ... Traded by Maple Leafs with second-round pick (traded to New Jersey) in 1996 draft to Pittsburgh Penguins for D Larry Murphy (July 8, 1995). ... Bruised shoulder (March 14, 1996); missed eight games. ... Traded by Penguins with LW Shawn Antoski to Mighty Ducks of Anaheim for C Alex Hicks and D Fredrik Olausson (November 19, 1996).

MISCELLANEOUS: Member of gold-medal-winning Unified Olympic team (1992).

Season Team	League	REGULAR SEASON								PLAYOFFS				
		Gms.	G	A	Pts.	PIM	+/-	PP	SH	Gms.	G	A	Pts.	PIM
90-91 — Soviet Wings	USSR	45	16	12	28	22	...	...	...	—	—	—	—	—
91-92 — Soviet Wings	USSR	35	15	16	31	62	...	...	...	—	—	—	—	—
— Unif. Olympic team	Int'l	8	3	1	4	4	...	...	...	—	—	—	—	—
— Toronto	NHL	7	1	0	1	0	-4	0	0	—	—	—	—	—
92-93 — Toronto	NHL	59	7	24	31	40	-1	4	0	14	1	2	3	2
93-94 — Toronto	NHL	76	9	27	36	78	5	3	0	18	6	9	15	6
94-95 — Toronto	NHL	33	5	12	17	28	6	2	0	6	2	1	3	2
95-96 — Pittsburgh	NHL	72	3	31	34	88	19	1	0	15	0	1	1	10
96-97 — Pittsburgh	NHL	15	1	5	6	24	-4	0	0	—	—	—	—	—
— Anaheim	NHL	62	12	34	46	77	20	3	1	11	1	10	11	10
NHL totals (6 years)		324	38	133	171	335	41	13	1	64	10	23	33	30

MITCHELL, JEFF — RW — STARS

PERSONAL: Born May 16, 1975, in Wayne, Ind. ... 6-1/190. ... Shoots right.

TRANSACTIONS/CAREER NOTES: Selected by Los Angeles Kings in third round (third Kings pick, 68th overall) of NHL entry draft (June 26, 1993). ... Traded by Kings to Dallas Stars for fifth-round pick (C Jason Morgan) in 1995 draft (June 6, 1995).

Season Team	League	REGULAR SEASON								PLAYOFFS				
		Gms.	G	A	Pts.	PIM	+/-	PP	SH	Gms.	G	A	Pts.	PIM
92-93 — Detroit	OHL	62	10	15	25	100	...	...	...	15	3	3	6	16
93-94 — Detroit	OHL	59	25	18	43	99	...	...	...	17	3	5	8	22
94-95 — Detroit	OHL	61	30	30	60	121	...	...	...	21	9	12	21	48
95-96 — Michigan	IHL	50	5	4	9	119	...	...	...	—	—	—	—	—
96-97 — Michigan	IHL	24	0	3	3	40	...	...	...	—	—	—	—	—
— Philadelphia	AHL	31	7	5	12	103	...	...	...	10	1	1	2	20

M

MODANO, MIKE — C — STARS

PERSONAL: Born June 7, 1970, in Livonia, Mich. ... 6-3/190. ... Shoots left. ... Name pronounced muh-DAH-noh.

TRANSACTIONS/CAREER NOTES: Selected by Minnesota North Stars in first round (first North Stars pick, first overall) of NHL entry draft (June 11, 1988). ... Fractured scaphoid bone in left wrist (January 24, 1989). ... Broke nose (March 4, 1990). ... Pulled groin (November 30, 1992); missed two games. ... North Stars franchise moved from Minnesota to Dallas and renamed Stars for 1993-94 season. ... Strained medial collateral knee ligament (January 6, 1994); missed six games. ... Suffered concussion (February 26, 1994); missed two games. ... Bruised ankle (March 12, 1995); missed four games. ... Ruptured tendons in ankle (April 4, 1995) and underwent surgery (April 11, 1995); missed last 14 games of season and entire playoffs. ... Injured stomach muscle (November 9, 1995); missed four games. ... Suffered from the flu (February 9, 1997); missed one game.

HONORS: Named to WHL (East) All-Star first team (1988-89). ... Named to NHL All-Rookie team (1989-90). ... Played in NHL All-Star Game (1993). ... Named to play in NHL All-Star Game (1997); replaced by LW Keith Tkachuk due to injury.

STATISTICAL PLATEAUS: Three-goal games: 1989-90 (1), 1993-94 (1). Total: 2. ... Four-goal games: 1995-96 (1). ... Total hat tricks: 3.

Season Team	League	REGULAR SEASON								PLAYOFFS				
		Gms.	G	A	Pts.	PIM	+/-	PP	SH	Gms.	G	A	Pts.	PIM
86-87 — Prince Albert	WHL	70	32	30	62	96	...	...	...	8	1	4	5	4
87-88 — Prince Albert	WHL	65	47	80	127	80	...	...	...	9	7	11	18	18
88-89 — Prince Albert	WHL	41	39	66	105	74	...	...	...	—	—	—	—	—
— Minnesota	NHL	—	—	—	—	—	...	...	...	2	0	0	0	0
89-90 — Minnesota	NHL	80	29	46	75	63	-7	12	0	7	1	1	2	12
90-91 — Minnesota	NHL	79	28	36	64	61	2	9	0	23	8	12	20	16
91-92 — Minnesota	NHL	76	33	44	77	46	-9	5	0	7	3	2	5	4
92-93 — Minnesota	NHL	82	33	60	93	83	-7	9	0	—	—	—	—	—
93-94 — Dallas	NHL	76	50	43	93	54	-8	18	0	9	7	3	10	16
94-95 — Dallas	NHL	30	12	17	29	8	7	4	1	—	—	—	—	—
95-96 — Dallas	NHL	78	36	45	81	63	-12	8	4	—	—	—	—	—
96-97 — Dallas	NHL	80	35	48	83	42	43	9	5	7	4	1	5	0
NHL totals (9 years)		581	256	339	595	420	9	74	10	55	23	19	42	48

MODIN, FREDRIK   LW   MAPLE LEAFS

PERSONAL: Born October 8, 1974, in Jonkoping, Sweden. ... 6-3/222. ... Shoots left. ... Name pronounced moh-DEEN.
TRANSACTIONS/CAREER NOTES: Selected by Toronto Maple Leafs in third round (third Maple Leafs pick, 64th overall) of NHL entry draft (June 29, 1994). ... Suffered concussion (October 22, 1996); missed three games. ... Suffered from the flu (March 10, 1997); missed one game.

				REGULAR SEASON						PLAYOFFS				
Season Team	League	Gms.	G	A	Pts.	PIM	+/-	PP	SH	Gms.	G	A	Pts.	PIM
91-92— Sundsvall Timra........	Swed. Div. II	11	1	0	1	0	...	...	...	—	—	—	—	—
92-93— Sundsvall Timra........	Swed. Div. II	30	5	7	12	12	...	...	...	—	—	—	—	—
93-94— Sundsvall Timra........	Swed. Div. II	30	16	15	31	36	...	...	...	—	—	—	—	—
94-95— Brynas Gavle.............	Sweden	38	9	10	19	33	...	...	...	14	4	4	8	6
95-96— Brynas Gavle.............	Sweden	22	4	8	12	22	...	...	...	—	—	—	—	—
96-97— Toronto	NHL	76	6	7	13	24	-14	0	0	—	—	—	—	—
NHL totals (1 year)		76	6	7	13	24	-14	0	0					

MODRY, JAROSLAV   D   KINGS

PERSONAL: Born February 27, 1971, in Ceske-Budejovice, Czechoslovakia. ... 6-2/195. ... Shoots left. ... Name pronounced MOH-dree.
TRANSACTIONS/CAREER NOTES: Selected by New Jersey Devils in ninth round (10th Devils pick, 179th overall) of NHL entry draft (June 16, 1990). ... Played in Europe during 1994-95 NHL lockout. ... Injured ankle (January 31, 1995); missed two games. ... Reinjured ankle (February 18, 1995); missed three games. ... Traded by Devils to Ottawa Senators for fourth-round pick (C Alyn McCauley) in 1995 draft (July 8, 1995). ... Suffered ruptured eardrum (December 27, 1995). ... Traded by Senators to Los Angeles Kings for RW Kevin Brown (March 20, 1996). ... Sprained left knee (January 14, 1997); missed one game.

				REGULAR SEASON						PLAYOFFS				
Season Team	League	Gms.	G	A	Pts.	PIM	+/-	PP	SH	Gms.	G	A	Pts.	PIM
88-89— Budejovice	Czech.	28	0	1	1	...	...	...	...	—	—	—	—	—
89-90— Budejovice	Czech.	41	2	2	4	...	...	...	...	—	—	—	—	—
90-91— Dukla Trencin............	Czech.	33	1	9	10	6	...	...	...	—	—	—	—	—
91-92— Dukla Trencin............	Czech.	18	0	4	4	...	...	...	...	—	—	—	—	—
— Budejovice	Czech Div. II	14	4	10	14	...	...	...	...	—	—	—	—	—
92-93— Utica	AHL	80	7	35	42	62	...	...	...	5	0	2	2	2
93-94— New Jersey	NHL	41	2	15	17	18	10	2	0	—	—	—	—	—
— Albany	AHL	19	1	5	6	25	...	...	...	—	—	—	—	—
94-95— HC Ceske Budejov.....	Czech Rep.	19	1	3	4	30	...	...	...	—	—	—	—	—
— New Jersey	NHL	11	0	0	0	0	-1	0	0	—	—	—	—	—
— Albany	AHL	18	5	6	11	14	...	...	...	14	3	3	6	4
95-96— Ottawa	NHL	64	4	14	18	38	-17	1	0	—	—	—	—	—
— Los Angeles	NHL	9	0	3	3	6	-4	0	0	—	—	—	—	—
96-97— Los Angeles	NHL	30	3	3	6	25	-13	1	1	—	—	—	—	—
— Phoenix	IHL	23	3	12	15	17	...	...	...	—	—	—	—	—
— Utah	IHL	11	1	4	5	20	...	...	...	7	0	1	1	6
NHL totals (4 years)		155	9	35	44	87	-25	4	1					

M

MOGER, SANDY   RW   BRUINS

PERSONAL: Born March 21, 1969, in 100 Mile House, B.C. ... 6-3/208. ... Shoots right. ... Full name: Alexander Sandy Moger. ... Name pronounced MOH-guhr.
COLLEGE: Lake Superior State (Mich.).
TRANSACTIONS/CAREER NOTES: Broke wrist (September 1988). ... Selected by Vancouver Canucks in ninth round (seventh Canucks pick, 176th overall) of NHL entry draft (June 17, 1989). ... Signed as free agent by Boston Bruins (July 6, 1994). ... Broke arm (April 28, 1995); missed remainder of season and entire playoffs. ... Broke foot (preseason, 1996-97 season); missed first seven games of season. ... Fractured elbow (December 14, 1996); missed 25 games. ... Fractured finger (March 12, 1997); missed remainder of season.
HONORS: Named to CCHA All-Star second team (1991-92).

				REGULAR SEASON						PLAYOFFS				
Season Team	League	Gms.	G	A	Pts.	PIM	+/-	PP	SH	Gms.	G	A	Pts.	PIM
86-87— Vernon	BCJHL	13	5	4	9	10	...	...	...	—	—	—	—	—
87-88— Yorkton	SJHL	60	39	41	80	144	...	...	...	—	—	—	—	—
88-89— Lake Superior	CCHA	31	4	6	10	28	...	...	...	—	—	—	—	—
89-90— Lake Superior	CCHA	46	17	15	32	76	...	...	...	—	—	—	—	—
90-91— Lake Superior	CCHA	45	27	21	48	*172	...	...	...	—	—	—	—	—
91-92— Lake Superior	CCHA	42	26	25	51	111	...	...	...	—	—	—	—	—
92-93— Hamilton	AHL	78	23	26	49	57	...	...	...	—	—	—	—	—
93-94— Hamilton	AHL	29	9	8	17	41	...	...	...	—	—	—	—	—
94-95— Providence................	AHL	63	32	29	61	105	...	...	...	—	—	—	—	—
— Boston	NHL	18	2	6	8	6	-1	2	0	—	—	—	—	—
95-96— Boston	NHL	80	15	14	29	65	-9	4	0	5	2	2	4	12
96-97— Providence................	AHL	3	0	2	2	19	...	...	...	—	—	—	—	—
— Boston	NHL	34	10	3	13	45	-12	3	0	—	—	—	—	—
NHL totals (3 years)		132	27	23	50	116	-22	9	0	5	2	2	4	12

MOGILNY, ALEXANDER   RW   CANUCKS

PERSONAL: Born February 18, 1969, in Khabarovsk, U.S.S.R. ... 5-11/192. ... Shoots left. ... Name pronounced moh-GIHL-nee.
TRANSACTIONS/CAREER NOTES: Selected by Buffalo Sabres in fifth round (fourth Sabres pick, 89th overall) of NHL entry draft (June 11, 1988). ... Suffered from the flu (November 26, 1989). ... Missed games due to fear of flying (January 22, 1990); spent remainder of season traveling on ground. ... Separated shoulder (February 8, 1991); missed six games. ... Suffered from the flu (November 1991); missed two

games. ... Suffered from the flu (December 18, 1991); missed one game. ... Bruised shoulder (October 10, 1992); missed six games. ... Broke fibula and tore ankle ligaments (May 6, 1993); missed remainder of 1992-93 playoffs and first nine games of 1993-94 season. ... Suffered sore ankle (February 2, 1994); missed four games. ... Suffered inflamed tendon in ankle (February 15, 1994); missed four games. ... Played in Europe during 1994-95 NHL lockout. ... Pinched nerve in neck (April 9, 1995); missed three games. ... Traded by Sabres with fifth-round pick (LW Todd Norman) in 1995 draft to Vancouver Canucks for RW Mike Peca, D Mike Wilson and first-round pick (D Jay McKee) in 1995 draft (July 8, 1995). ... Pulled hamstring (October 28, 1995); missed three games. ... Suffered from the flu (December 3, 1996); missed two games. ... Strained groin (April 4, 1997); missed remainder of season.

HONORS: Played in NHL All-Star Game (1992-1994 and 1996). ... Named to The Sporting News All-Star second team (1992-93). ... Named to NHL All-Star second team (1992-93 and 1995-96).
RECORDS: Shares NHL record for fastest goal from start of a game—5 seconds (December 21, 1991).
STATISTICAL PLATEAUS: Three-goal games: 1990-91 (1), 1991-92 (1), 1992-93 (5), 1993-94 (1), 1995-96 (3), 1996-97 (1). Total: 12. ... Four-goal games: 1992-93 (2). ... Total hat tricks: 14.
MISCELLANEOUS: Member of gold-medal-winning U.S.S.R. Olympic team (1988). ... Captain of Buffalo Sabres (1993-94 and 1994-95). ... Failed to score on a penalty shot (vs. Bill Ranford, January 10, 1992; vs. Robb Stauber, December 17, 1993).
STATISTICAL NOTES: Led NHL with 11 game-winning goals (1992-93).

		REGULAR SEASON									PLAYOFFS				
Season Team	League	Gms.	G	A	Pts.	PIM	+/-	PP	SH		Gms.	G	A	Pts.	PIM
86-87 — CSKA Moscow	USSR	28	15	1	16	4	...	...	...		—	—	—	—	—
87-88 — CSKA Moscow	USSR	39	12	8	20	20	...	...	...		—	—	—	—	—
88-89 — CSKA Moscow	USSR	31	11	11	22	24	...	...	...		—	—	—	—	—
89-90 — Buffalo	NHL	65	15	28	43	16	8	4	0		4	0	1	1	2
90-91 — Buffalo	NHL	62	30	34	64	16	14	3	3		6	0	6	6	2
91-92 — Buffalo	NHL	67	39	45	84	73	7	15	0		2	0	2	2	0
92-93 — Buffalo	NHL	77	†76	51	127	40	7	27	0		7	7	3	10	6
93-94 — Buffalo	NHL	66	32	47	79	22	8	17	0		7	4	2	6	6
94-95 — Spartak Moscow	CIS	1	0	1	1	0	...	...	...		—	—	—	—	—
— Buffalo	NHL	44	19	28	47	36	0	12	0		5	3	2	5	2
95-96 — Vancouver	NHL	79	55	52	107	16	14	10	5		6	1	8	9	8
96-97 — Vancouver	NHL	76	31	42	73	18	9	7	1		—	—	—	—	—
NHL totals (8 years)		536	297	327	624	237	67	95	9		37	15	24	39	26

MOMESSO, SERGIO   LW

PERSONAL: Born September 4, 1965, in Montreal. ... 6-3/215. ... Shoots left. ... Name pronounced moh-MEH-soh.
TRANSACTIONS/CAREER NOTES: Selected by Montreal Canadiens as underage junior in second round (third Canadiens pick, 27th overall) of NHL entry draft (June 8, 1983). ... Tore cruciate ligament in left knee and underwent surgery (December 5, 1985); missed remainder of season. ... Tore ligaments, injured cartilage and fractured left knee (December 5, 1986). ... Lacerated leg (February 1988). ... Traded by Canadiens with G Vincent Riendeau to St. Louis Blues for LW Jocelyn Lemieux, G Darrell May and second-round pick (D Patrice Brisebois) in 1989 draft (August 9, 1988). ... Fractured right ankle (November 12, 1988). ... Traded by Blues with LW Geoff Courtnall, D Robert Dirk, C Cliff Ronning and fifth-round pick (RW Brian Loney) in 1992 draft to Vancouver Canucks for C Dan Quinn and D Garth Butcher (March 5, 1991). ... Separated shoulder (December 3, 1991); missed 22 games. ... Sprained knee (November 30, 1993); missed 11 games. ... Suspended two games and fined $500 by NHL for stick-swinging incident (March 28, 1994). ... Played in Europe during 1994-95 NHL lockout. ... Traded by Canucks to Toronto Maple Leafs for C Mike Ridley (July 8, 1995). ... Traded by Maple Leafs with LW Bill Berg to New York Rangers for LW Nick Kypreos and RW Wayne Presley (February 29, 1996). ... Traded by Rangers to Blues for RW Brian Noonan (November 13, 1996).
HONORS: Named to QMJHL All-Star first team (1984-85).
STATISTICAL PLATEAUS: Three-goal games: 1987-88 (1).
MISCELLANEOUS: Member of Stanley Cup championship team (1987).

		REGULAR SEASON									PLAYOFFS				
Season Team	League	Gms.	G	A	Pts.	PIM	+/-	PP	SH		Gms.	G	A	Pts.	PIM
82-83 — Shawinigan	QMJHL	70	27	42	69	93	...	...	...		10	5	4	9	55
83-84 — Nova Scotia	AHL	—	—	—	—	—	...	...	...		8	0	2	2	4
— Shawinigan	QMJHL	68	42	88	130	235	...	...	...		6	4	4	8	13
— Montreal	NHL	1	0	0	0	0	1	0	0		—	—	—	—	—
84-85 — Shawinigan	QMJHL	64	56	90	146	216	...	...	...		8	7	8	15	17
85-86 — Montreal	NHL	24	8	7	15	46	-4	3	0		—	—	—	—	—
86-87 — Montreal	NHL	59	14	17	31	96	0	3	0		11	1	3	4	31
— Sherbrooke	AHL	6	1	6	7	10	...	...	...		—	—	—	—	—
87-88 — Montreal	NHL	53	7	14	21	101	9	1	0		6	0	2	2	16
88-89 — St. Louis	NHL	53	9	17	26	139	-1	0	0		10	2	5	7	24
89-90 — St. Louis	NHL	79	24	32	56	199	-15	4	0		12	3	2	5	63
90-91 — St. Louis	NHL	59	10	18	28	131	12	0	0		—	—	—	—	—
— Vancouver	NHL	11	6	2	8	43	1	3	0		6	0	3	3	25
91-92 — Vancouver	NHL	58	20	23	43	198	16	2	0		13	0	5	5	30
92-93 — Vancouver	NHL	84	18	20	38	200	11	4	0		12	3	0	3	30
93-94 — Vancouver	NHL	68	14	13	27	149	-2	4	0		24	3	4	7	56
94-95 — Milan	Italy	2	1	4	5	2	...	...	...		—	—	—	—	—
— Vancouver	NHL	48	10	15	25	65	-2	6	0		11	3	1	4	16
95-96 — Toronto	NHL	54	7	8	15	112	-11	4	0		—	—	—	—	—
— New York Rangers	NHL	19	4	4	8	30	-2	2	0		11	3	1	4	14
96-97 — New York Rangers	NHL	9	0	0	0	11	-2	0	0		—	—	—	—	—
— St. Louis	NHL	31	1	3	4	37	-4	0	0		3	0	0	0	6
NHL totals (13 years)		710	152	193	345	1557	7	36	0		119	18	26	44	311

MONTGOMERY, JIM   C   FLYERS

PERSONAL: Born June 30, 1969, in Montreal. ... 5-9/180. ... Shoots right.
COLLEGE: Maine.

M

TRANSACTIONS/CAREER NOTES: Signed as free agent by St. Louis Blues (June 2, 1993). ... Suspended four games and fined $500 by NHL for high-sticking incident (October 4, 1993). ... Traded by Blues to Montreal Canadiens for C Guy Carbonneau (August 19, 1994). ... Claimed on waivers by Philadelphia Flyers (February 10, 1995).

HONORS: Named to NCAA All-America East second team (1990-91 and 1992-93). ... Named to Hockey East All-Star second team (1990-91 and 1991-92). ... Named NCAA Tournament Most Valuable Player (1992-93). ... Named Hockey East Tournament Most Valuable Player (1992-93). ... Named to NCAA All-Tournament team (1992-93). ... Named to Hockey East All-Star first team (1992-93). ... Named to Hockey East All-Decade team (1994). ... Named to AHL All-Star second team (1995-96).

		REGULAR SEASON								PLAYOFFS				
Season Team	League	Gms.	G	A	Pts.	PIM	+/-	PP	SH	Gms.	G	A	Pts.	PIM
89-90— University of Maine....	Hockey East	45	26	34	60	35	...	...	...	—	—	—	—	—
90-91— University of Maine....	Hockey East	43	24	57	81	44	...	...	...	—	—	—	—	—
91-92— University of Maine....	Hockey East	37	21	44	65	46	...	...	...	—	—	—	—	—
92-93— University of Maine....	Hockey East	45	32	63	95	40	...	...	...	—	—	—	—	—
93-94— St. Louis	NHL	67	6	14	20	44	-1	0	0	—	—	—	—	—
— Peoria	IHL	12	7	8	15	10	...	...	...	—	—	—	—	—
94-95— Montreal	NHL	5	0	0	0	2	-2	0	0	—	—	—	—	—
— Philadelphia	NHL	8	1	1	2	6	-2	0	0	7	1	0	1	2
— Hershey	AHL	16	8	6	14	14	...	...	...	6	3	2	5	25
95-96— Hershey	AHL	78	34	†71	105	95	...	...	...	4	3	2	5	6
— Philadelphia	NHL	5	1	2	3	9	1	0	0	1	0	0	0	0
96-97— Kolner Haie	Germany	50	12	35	47	111	...	...	...	—	—	—	—	—
NHL totals (3 years)		85	8	17	25	61	-4	0	0	8	1	0	1	2

MOOG, ANDY   G   CANADIENS

PERSONAL: Born February 18, 1960, in Penticton, B.C. ... 5-8/170. ... Catches left. ... Full name: Donald Andrew Moog. ... Name pronounced MOHG.

TRANSACTIONS/CAREER NOTES: Selected by Edmonton Oilers in seventh round (sixth Oilers pick, 132nd overall) of NHL entry draft (June 11, 1980). ... Suffered viral infection (December 1983). ... Injured ligaments in both knees (March 1, 1985). ... Traded by Oilers to Boston Bruins for LW Geoff Courtnall and G Bill Ranford (March 1988). ... Hyperextended right knee (January 31, 1991); missed three weeks. ... Injured back (January 1993); missed three games. ... Injured hamstring (February 1993); missed four games. ... Traded by Bruins to Dallas Stars for G Jon Casey (June 25, 1993) to complete deal in which Bruins sent D Gord Murphy to Stars for future considerations (June 20, 1993). ... Strained groin (November 24, 1993); missed five games. ... Strained hip muscle (March 30, 1995); missed two games. ... Strained hamstring (April 11, 1995); missed one game. ... Reinjured hamstring (April 19, 1995); missed five games. ... Bruised knee (January 3, 1996); missed 18 games. ... Sprained knee (December 30, 1996); missed three games. ... Strained back and ankle (March 7, 1997); missed eight games. ... Signed as free agent by Montreal Canadiens (July 17, 1997).

HONORS: Named to WHL All-Star second team (1979-80). ... Named to CHL All-Star second team (1981-82). ... Named to THE SPORTING NEWS All-Star second team (1982-83). ... Played in NHL All-Star Game (1985, 1986, 1991 and 1997). ... Shared William M. Jennings Trophy with Rejean Lemelin (1989-90).

MISCELLANEOUS: Member of Stanley Cup championship team (1984, 1985 and 1987). ... Stopped a penalty shot attempt (vs. John Cullen, January 16, 1992). ... Allowed a penalty shot goal (vs. Rocky Trottier, December 17, 1984; vs. John Tucker, April 9, 1988; vs. Brad May, November, 11, 1992; Sergei Fedorov, December 27, 1993).

		REGULAR SEASON							PLAYOFFS						
Season Team	League	Gms.	Min	W	L	T	GA	SO	Avg.	Gms.	Min.	W	L	GA	SO	Avg.
76-77— Kamloops	BCJHL	44	2735	...	...	...	173	0	*3.80	—	—	—	—	—	—	—
— Kamloops	WCHL	1	35	...	...	...	6	0	10.29	—	—	—	—	—	—	—
77-78— Penticton	BCJHL	39	2243	...	...	...	191	0	5.11	—	—	—	—	—	—	—
78-79— Billings...................	WHL	26	1306	13	5	4	90	*3	4.13	5	229	1	3	21	0	5.50
79-80— Billings...................	WHL	46	2435	23	14	1	149	1	3.67	3	190	2	1	10	0	3.16
80-81— Wichita	CHL	29	1602	14	13	1	89	0	3.33	5	300	3	2	16	0	3.20
— Edmonton	NHL	7	313	3	3	0	20	0	3.83	9	526	5	4	32	0	3.65
81-82— Edmonton	NHL	8	399	3	5	0	32	0	4.81	—	—	—	—	—	—	—
— Wichita	CHL	40	2391	23	13	3	119	1	2.99	7	434	3	4	23	0	3.18
82-83— Edmonton	NHL	50	2833	33	8	7	167	1	3.54	16	949	11	5	48	0	3.03
83-84— Edmonton	NHL	38	2212	27	8	1	139	1	3.77	7	263	4	0	12	0	2.74
84-85— Edmonton	NHL	39	2019	22	9	3	111	1	3.30	2	20	0	0	0	0	0.00
85-86— Edmonton	NHL	47	2664	27	9	7	164	1	3.69	1	60	1	0	1	0	1.00
86-87— Edmonton	NHL	46	2461	28	11	3	144	0	3.51	2	120	2	0	8	0	4.00
87-88— Canadian nat'l team	Int'l	27	1438	10	7	5	86	0	3.59	—	—	—	—	—	—	—
— Can. Olympic team	Int'l	4	240	4	0	0	9	1	2.25	—	—	—	—	—	—	—
— Boston	NHL	6	360	4	2	0	17	1	2.83	7	354	1	4	25	0	4.24
88-89— Boston	NHL	41	2482	18	14	8	133	1	3.22	6	359	4	2	14	0	2.34
89-90— Boston	NHL	46	2536	24	10	7	122	3	2.89	20	1195	13	7	44	*2	*2.21
90-91— Boston	NHL	51	2844	25	13	9	136	4	2.87	19	1133	10	9	60	0	3.18
91-92— Boston	NHL	62	3640	28	22	9	196	1	3.23	15	866	8	7	46	1	3.19
92-93— Boston	NHL	55	3194	37	14	3	168	3	3.16	3	161	0	3	14	0	5.22
93-94— Dallas....................	NHL	55	3121	24	20	7	170	2	3.27	4	246	1	3	12	0	2.93
94-95— Dallas....................	NHL	31	1770	10	12	7	72	2	2.44	5	277	1	4	16	0	3.47
95-96— Dallas....................	NHL	41	2228	13	19	7	111	1	2.99	—	—	—	—	—	—	—
96-97— Dallas....................	NHL	48	2738	28	13	5	98	3	2.15	7	449	3	4	21	0	2.81
NHL totals (17 years)		671	37814	354	192	83	2000	25	3.17	123	6978	64	52	353	3	3.04

MOORE, BARRIE   LW   OILERS

PERSONAL: Born May 22, 1975, in London, Ont. ... 5-11/175. ... Shoots left.

HIGH SCHOOL: Lo-Ellen Park Secondary School (Sudbury, Ont.).

TRANSACTIONS/CAREER NOTES: Selected by Buffalo Sabres in eighth round (sixth Sabres pick, 194th overall) of NHL entry draft (June 26, 1993). ... Traded by Sabres with D Craig Millar to Edmonton Oilers for F Miroslav Satan (March 18, 1997).

Season Team	League	REGULAR SEASON								PLAYOFFS				
		Gms.	G	A	Pts.	PIM	+/-	PP	SH	Gms.	G	A	Pts.	PIM
90-91— Strathroy Jr. B	OHA	19	9	10	19	30	...	...	...	—	—	—	—	—
91-92— Sudbury	OHL	62	15	38	53	57	...	...	...	11	0	7	7	12
92-93— Sudbury	OHL	57	13	26	39	71	...	...	...	14	4	3	7	19
93-94— Sudbury	OHL	65	36	49	85	69	...	...	...	10	3	5	8	14
94-95— Sudbury	OHL	60	47	42	89	67	...	...	...	18	15	14	29	24
95-96— Rochester	AHL	64	26	29	55	40	...	...	...	18	3	6	9	18
— Buffalo	NHL	3	0	0	0	0	0	0	0	—	—	—	—	—
96-97— Rochester	AHL	32	14	15	29	14	...	...	...	—	—	—	—	—
— Buffalo	NHL	31	2	6	8	18	1	1	0	—	—	—	—	—
— Hamilton	AHL	9	5	2	7	0	...	...	...	22	2	6	8	15
— Edmonton	NHL	4	0	0	0	0	0	0	0	—	—	—	—	—
NHL totals (3 years)		38	2	6	8	18	1	1	0					

MORAN, IAN — D — PENGUINS

PERSONAL: Born August 24, 1972, in Cleveland. ... 5-11/195. ... Shoots right. ... Name pronounced muh-RAN.
HIGH SCHOOL: Belmont Hill (Mass.).
COLLEGE: Boston College.
TRANSACTIONS/CAREER NOTES: Underwent knee surgery (June 1988). ... Separated shoulder (March 1989). ... Selected by Pittsburgh Penguins in sixth round (fifth Penguins pick, 107th overall) of NHL entry draft (June 16, 1990). ... Bruised shoulder (November 22, 1995); missed nine games. ... Injured shoulder (February 21, 1996); missed one game. ... Underwent shoulder surgery (March 21, 1996); missed remainder of season. ... Injured back and neck (April 10, 1997); missed two games.
HONORS: Named Hockey East co-Rookie of the Year with Craig Darby (1991-92). ... Named to Hockey East All-Rookie team (1991-92).

Season Team	League	REGULAR SEASON								PLAYOFFS				
		Gms.	G	A	Pts.	PIM	+/-	PP	SH	Gms.	G	A	Pts.	PIM
87-88— Belmont Hill	Mass. H.S.	25	3	13	16	15	...	...	...	—	—	—	—	—
88-89— Belmont Hill	Mass. H.S.	23	7	25	32	8	...	...	...	—	—	—	—	—
89-90— Belmont Hill	Mass. H.S.	...	10	36	46	0	...	...	...	—	—	—	—	—
90-91— Belmont Hill	Mass. H.S.	23	7	44	51	12	...	...	...	—	—	—	—	—
91-92— Boston College..........	Hockey East	30	2	16	18	44	...	...	...	—	—	—	—	—
92-93— Boston College..........	Hockey East	31	8	12	20	32	...	...	...	—	—	—	—	—
93-94— U.S. national team	Int'l	50	8	15	23	69	...	...	...	—	—	—	—	—
— Cleveland	IHL	33	5	13	18	39	...	...	...	—	—	—	—	—
94-95— Cleveland	IHL	64	7	31	38	94	...	...	...	4	0	1	1	2
— Pittsburgh...................	NHL	—	—	—	—	—	...	...	...	8	0	0	0	0
95-96— Pittsburgh.................	NHL	51	1	1	2	47	-1	0	0	—	—	—	—	—
96-97— Cleveland	IHL	36	6	23	29	26	...	...	...	—	—	—	—	—
— Pittsburgh...................	NHL	36	4	5	9	22	-11	0	0	5	1	2	3	4
NHL totals (3 years)		87	5	6	11	69	-12	0	0	13	1	2	3	4

MORE, JAY — D — COYOTES

M

PERSONAL: Born January 12, 1969, in Souris, Man. ... 6-3/215. ... Shoots right. ... Name pronounced MOHR.
TRANSACTIONS/CAREER NOTES: Selected by New York Rangers as underage junior in first round (first Rangers pick, 10th overall) of NHL entry draft (June 13, 1987). ... Traded by Rangers to Minnesota North Stars for C Dave Archibald (November 1, 1989). ... Traded by North Stars to Montreal Canadiens for G Brian Hayward (November 7, 1990). ... Selected by San Jose Sharks in NHL expansion draft (May 30, 1991). ... Injured foot during preseason (September 1991); missed 16 games. ... Injured knee (March 1992). ... Pulled groin (December 9, 1992); missed four games. ... Reaggravated groin injury (December 23, 1992); missed four games. ... Suspended one game by NHL for accumulating three game misconduct penalties (January 27, 1993). ... Strained hip (March 7, 1993); missed one game. ... Suspended for last game of season and first game of 1993-94 season for accumulating four game misconduct penalties (April 11, 1993). ... Fractured wrist (October 23, 1993); missed 25 games. ... Bruised hand (February 18, 1995); missed two games. ... Injured leg (April 7, 1995); missed one game. ... Injured jaw (November 7, 1995); missed one game. ... Injured groin (November 21, 1995); missed one game. ... Injured abdomen (January 5, 1996); missed two games. ... Injured hand (March 20, 1996); missed one game. ... Injured back (April 4, 1996); missed three games. ... Traded by Sharks with C Brian Swanson and fourth-round draft pick in 1998 draft to New York Rangers for D Marty McSorley (August 20, 1996). ... Traded by Rangers to Phoenix Coyotes for C Mike Eastwood and D Dallas Eakins (February 6, 1997). ... Suffered concussion (February 10, 1997); missed two games.
HONORS: Named to WHL (West) All-Star first team (1987-88).

Season Team	League	REGULAR SEASON								PLAYOFFS				
		Gms.	G	A	Pts.	PIM	+/-	PP	SH	Gms.	G	A	Pts.	PIM
84-85— Lethbridge	WHL	71	3	9	12	101	...	...	...	4	1	0	1	7
85-86— Lethbridge	WHL	61	7	18	25	155	...	...	...	9	0	2	2	36
86-87— New Westminster	WHL	64	8	29	37	217	...	...	...	—	—	—	—	—
87-88— New Westminster	WHL	70	13	47	60	270	...	...	...	5	0	2	2	26
88-89— Denver	IHL	62	7	15	22	138	...	...	...	3	0	1	1	26
— New York Rangers	NHL	1	0	0	0	0	-1	0	0	—	—	—	—	—
89-90— Flint	IHL	9	1	5	6	41	...	...	...	—	—	—	—	—
— Kalamazoo	IHL	64	9	25	34	216	...	...	...	10	0	3	3	13
— Minnesota..................	NHL	5	0	0	0	16	1	0	0	—	—	—	—	—
90-91— Kalamazoo	IHL	10	0	5	5	46	...	...	...	—	—	—	—	—
— Fredericton................	AHL	57	7	17	24	152	...	...	...	9	1	1	2	34
91-92— San Jose..................	NHL	46	4	13	17	85	-32	1	0	—	—	—	—	—
— Kansas City	IHL	2	0	2	2	4	...	...	...	—	—	—	—	—
92-93— San Jose..................	NHL	73	5	6	11	179	-35	0	1	—	—	—	—	—
93-94— San Jose..................	NHL	49	1	6	7	63	-5	0	0	13	0	2	2	32
— Kansas City	IHL	2	1	0	1	25	...	...	...	—	—	—	—	—
94-95— San Jose..................	NHL	45	0	6	6	71	7	0	0	11	0	4	4	6
95-96— San Jose..................	NHL	74	2	7	9	147	-32	0	0	—	—	—	—	—
96-97— New York Rangers	NHL	14	0	1	1	25	0	0	0	—	—	—	—	—
— Phoenix......................	NHL	23	1	6	7	37	10	0	0	7	0	0	0	7
NHL totals (8 years)		330	13	45	58	623	-87	1	1	31	0	6	6	45

MOREAU, ETHAN — LW — BLACKHAWKS

PERSONAL: Born September 22, 1975, in Orillia, Ont. ... 6-2/205. ... Shoots left. ... Name pronounced muh-ROH.
TRANSACTIONS/CAREER NOTES: Selected by Chicago Blackhawks in first round (first Blackhawks pick, 14th overall) of NHL entry draft (June 28, 1994).
HONORS: Won Bobby Smith Trophy (1993-94).

Season Team	League	REGULAR SEASON								PLAYOFFS				
		Gms.	G	A	Pts.	PIM	+/-	PP	SH	Gms.	G	A	Pts.	PIM
90-91 — Orillia	OHA	42	17	22	39	26	...	...	...	—	—	—	—	—
91-92 — Niagara Falls	OHL	62	20	35	55	39	...	...	...	17	4	6	10	4
92-93 — Niagara Falls	OHL	65	32	41	73	69	...	...	...	4	0	3	3	4
93-94 — Niagara Falls	OHL	59	44	54	98	100	...	...	...	—	—	—	—	—
94-95 — Niagara Falls	OHL	39	25	41	66	69	...	...	...	—	—	—	—	—
— Sudbury	OHL	23	13	17	30	22	...	...	...	18	6	12	18	26
95-96 — Indianapolis	IHL	71	21	20	41	126	...	...	...	5	4	0	4	8
— Chicago	NHL	8	0	1	1	4	1	0	0	—	—	—	—	—
96-97 — Chicago	NHL	82	15	16	31	123	13	0	0	6	1	0	1	9
NHL totals (2 years)		90	15	17	32	127	14	0	0	6	1	0	1	9

MORGAN, JASON — C — KINGS

PERSONAL: Born October 9, 1976, in Kitchener, Ont. ... 6-1/199. ... Shoots left.
HIGH SCHOOL: Loyalist C & VI (Kingston, Ont.).
TRANSACTIONS/CAREER NOTES: Selected by Los Angeles Kings in fifth round (fifth Kings pick, 118th overall) of NHL entry draft (July 8, 1995).

Season Team	League	REGULAR SEASON								PLAYOFFS				
		Gms.	G	A	Pts.	PIM	+/-	PP	SH	Gms.	G	A	Pts.	PIM
93-94 — Kitchener	OHL	65	6	15	21	16	...	...	...	5	1	0	1	0
94-95 — Kitchener	OHL	35	3	15	18	25	...	...	...	—	—	—	—	—
— Kingston	OHL	20	0	3	3	14	...	...	...	6	0	2	2	0
95-96 — Kingston	OHL	66	16	38	54	50	...	...	...	6	1	2	3	0
96-97 — Phoenix	IHL	57	3	6	9	29	...	...	...	—	—	—	—	—
— Mississippi	ECHL	6	3	0	3	0	...	...	...	3	1	1	2	6
— Los Angeles	NHL	3	0	0	0	0	-3	0	0	—	—	—	—	—
NHL totals (1 year)		3	0	0	0	0	-3	0	0					

MORO, MARC — D — MIGHTY DUCKS

PERSONAL: Born July 17, 1977, in Toronto. ... 6-0/209. ... Shoots left. ... Name pronounced muh-ROH.
HIGH SCHOOL: Loyalist C & VI (Kingston, Ont.).
TRANSACTIONS/CAREER NOTES: Selected by Ottawa Senators in second round (second Senators pick, 27th overall) of NHL entry draft (July 8, 1995). ... Rights traded by Senators with C Ted Drury to Mighty Ducks of Anaheim for C Shaun Van Allen and D Jason York (October 1, 1996).

Season Team	League	REGULAR SEASON								PLAYOFFS				
		Gms.	G	A	Pts.	PIM	+/-	PP	SH	Gms.	G	A	Pts.	PIM
92-93 — Mississauga	Jr. A	2	0	0	0	0	...	...	...	—	—	—	—	—
93-94 — Kingston	Tier II Jr. A	12	0	2	2	20	...	...	...	—	—	—	—	—
— Kingston	OHL	43	0	3	3	81	...	...	...	—	—	—	—	—
94-95 — Kingston	OHL	64	4	12	16	255	...	...	...	6	0	0	0	23
95-96 — Kingston	OHL	66	4	17	21	261	...	...	...	6	0	0	0	12
— Prin. Edward Island	AHL	2	0	0	0	7	...	...	...	2	0	0	0	4
96-97 — Sault Ste. Marie	OHL	63	4	13	17	171	...	...	...	11	1	6	7	38

MOROZOV, ALEXEI — RW — PENGUINS

PERSONAL: Born February 16, 1977, in Moscow, U.S.S.R. ... 6-1/178. ... Shoots left.
TRANSACTIONS/CAREER NOTES: Selected by Pittsburgh Penguins in first round (first Penguins pick, 24th overall) of NHL entry draft (July 8, 1995).

Season Team	League	REGULAR SEASON								PLAYOFFS				
		Gms.	G	A	Pts.	PIM	+/-	PP	SH	Gms.	G	A	Pts.	PIM
93-94 — Soviet Wings	CIS	7	0	0	0	0	...	...	...	3	0	0	0	2
94-95 — Soviet Wings	CIS	48	15	12	27	53	...	...	...	4	0	3	3	0
95-96 — Soviet Wings	CIS	47	12	9	21	26	...	...	...	—	—	—	—	—
96-97 — Krylja Sovetov	Russian	44	21	11	32	32	...	...	...	2	0	1	1	2

MOROZOV, VALENTIN — C — PENGUINS

PERSONAL: Born June 1, 1975, in Moscow, U.S.S.R. ... 5-11/176. ... Shoots left.
TRANSACTIONS/CAREER NOTES: Selected by Pittsburgh Penguins in sixth round (eighth Penguins pick, 154th overall) of NHL entry draft (June 29, 1994).

Season Team	League	REGULAR SEASON								PLAYOFFS				
		Gms.	G	A	Pts.	PIM	+/-	PP	SH	Gms.	G	A	Pts.	PIM
92-93 — CSKA Moscow	CIS	17	0	0	0	6	...	...	...	—	—	—	—	—
93-94 — CSKA Moscow	CIS	18	4	1	5	8	...	...	...	3	0	1	1	0
94-95 — CSKA Moscow	CIS	47	9	4	13	10	...	...	...	2	2	0	2	0
95-96 — CSKA Moscow	CIS	51	30	11	41	28	...	...	...	—	—	—	—	—
96-97 — CSKA Moscow	Russian II	4	2	1	3	0	...	...	...	—	—	—	—	—
— HC CSKA Moscow	Russian	22	8	5	13	8	...	...	...	—	—	—	—	—

M

MORRIS, DEREK   D   FLAMES

PERSONAL: Born August 24, 1978, in Edmonton. ... 6-0/180. ... Shoots right.
TRANSACTIONS/CAREER NOTES: Selected by Calgary Flames in first round (first Flames pick, 13th overall) of NHL entry draft (June 22, 1996).
HONORS: Named to Can.HL All-Star second team (1996-97). ... Named to WHL (East) All-Star first team (1996-97).

| | | REGULAR SEASON | | | | | | | PLAYOFFS | | | | |
Season Team	League	Gms.	G	A	Pts.	PIM	+/-	PP	SH	Gms.	G	A	Pts.	PIM
95-96— Regina	WHL	67	8	44	52	70	...	...	...	11	1	7	8	26
96-97— Regina	WHL	67	18	57	75	180	...	...	...	5	0	3	3	9
— Saint John	AHL	7	0	3	3	7	...	...	...	5	0	3	3	7

MORRISON, BRENDAN   C   DEVILS

PERSONAL: Born August 12, 1975, in North Vancouver. ... 5-11/176. ... Shoots left.
HIGH SCHOOL: Pitt Meadows (B.C.) Secondary.
COLLEGE: Michigan.
TRANSACTIONS/CAREER NOTES: Selected by New Jersey Devils in second round (third Devils pick, 39th overall) of NHL entry draft (June 26, 1993).
HONORS: Won CCHA Rookie of the Year Award (1993-94). ... Named to CCHA All-Rookie team (1993-94). ... Named to NCAA All-America West first team (1994-95, 1995-96 and 1996-97). ... Named to CCHA All-Star first team (1994-95, 1995-96 and 1996-97). ... Named CCHA Player of the Year (1995-96 and 1996-97). ... Named to NCAA All-Tournament team (1995-96). ... Won Hobey Baker Memorial Award (1996-97). ... Named CCHA Tournament Most Valuable Player (1996-97).

| | | REGULAR SEASON | | | | | | | | PLAYOFFS | | | | |
Season Team	League	Gms.	G	A	Pts.	PIM	+/-	PP	SH	Gms.	G	A	Pts.	PIM
92-93 — Penticton	BCJHL	56	35	59	94	45	...	...	...	—	—	—	—	—
93-94 — Univ. of Michigan.......	CCHA	38	20	28	48	24	...	...	...	—	—	—	—	—
94-95 — Univ. of Michigan.......	CCHA	39	23	53	76	42	...	...	...	—	—	—	—	—
95-96 — Univ. of Michigan.......	CCHA	35	28	44	72	41	...	...	...	—	—	—	—	—
96-97 — Univ. of Michigan.......	CCHA	43	31	57	88	52	...	...	...	—	—	—	—	—

MOSS, TYLER   G   FLAMES

PERSONAL: Born June 29, 1975, in Ottawa. ... 6-0/168. ... Catches right.
TRANSACTIONS/CAREER NOTES: Selected by Tampa Bay Lightning in second round (second Lightning pick, 29th overall) of NHL entry draft (June 26, 1993). ... Traded by Lightning to Calgary Flames for D Jamie Huscroft (March 18, 1997).
HONORS: Named to OHL All-Rookie team (1992-93). ... Named to OHL All-Star first team (1994-95).

| | | REGULAR SEASON | | | | | | | PLAYOFFS | | | | | |
Season Team	League	Gms.	Min	W	L	T	GA	SO	Avg.	Gms.	Min.	W	L	GA	SO	Avg.
91-92 — Nepean	COJIIL	26	1335	...	...	...	109	0	4.90	—	—	—	—	—	—	—
92-93 — Kingston	OHL	31	1537	13	7	5	97	0	3.79	6	228	1	2	19	0	5.00
93-94 — Kingston	OHL	13	795	6	4	3	42	1	3.17	3	136	0	2	8	0	3.53
94-95 — Kingston	OHL	57	3249	33	17	5	164	1	3.03	6	333	2	4	27	0	4.86
95-96 — Atlanta	IHL	40	2030	11	19	‡4	138	1	4.08	3	213	0	3	11	0	3.10
96-97 —Adirondack	AHL	11	507	1	5	2	42	1	4.97	—	—	—	—	—	—	—
—Grand Rapids...............	IHL	15	715	5	6	‡1	35	0	2.94	—	—	—	—	—	—	—
—Saint John	AHL	9	534	6	1	1	17	0	1.91	5	242	2	3	15	0	3.72
—Muskegon.....................	Col.HL	2	119	1	1	0	5	0	2.52	—	—	—	—	—	—	—

MUIR, BRYAN   D   OILERS

PERSONAL: Born June 8, 1973, in Winnipeg. ... 6-4/220. ... Shoots left.
COLLEGE: New Hampshire.
TRANSACTIONS/CAREER NOTES: Signed to five-game amateur tryout from the Canadian national team (February 29, 1996). ... Signed as free agent by Edmonton Oilers (April 1996).

| | | REGULAR SEASON | | | | | | | PLAYOFFS | | | | |
Season Team	League	Gms.	G	A	Pts.	PIM	+/-	PP	SH	Gms.	G	A	Pts.	PIM
92-93 — New Hampshire	Hockey East	26	1	2	3	24	...	...	...	—	—	—	—	—
93-94 — New Hampshire	Hockey East	36	0	4	4	48	...	...	...	—	—	—	—	—
94-95 — New Hampshire	Hockey East	28	9	9	18	48	...	...	...	—	—	—	—	—
95-96 — Canadian nat'l team ...	Int'l	42	6	12	18	36	...	...	...	—	—	—	—	—
— Edmonton	NHL	5	0	0	0	6	-4	0	0	—	—	—	—	—
96-97 — Hamilton	AHL	75	8	16	24	80	...	...	...	14	0	5	5	12
— Edmonton	NHL	—	—	—	—	—	...	...	...	5	0	0	0	4
NHL totals (2 years)		5	0	0	0	6	-4	0	0	5	0	0	0	4

MULLEN, JOE   RW   BRUINS

PERSONAL: Born February 26, 1957, in New York. ... 5-9/180. ... Shoots right. ... Full name: Joseph Patrick Mullen. ... Brother of Brian Mullen, right winger for four NHL teams (1982-83 through 1993-94) and current NHL director of off-ice programs.
COLLEGE: Boston College.
TRANSACTIONS/CAREER NOTES: Signed as free agent by St. Louis Blues (August 16, 1979). ... Injured leg (October 18, 1982). ... Tore ligaments in left knee and underwent surgery (January 29, 1983); missed remainder of season. ... Traded by Blues with D Terry Johnson and D Rik Wilson to Calgary Flames for LW Eddy Beers, LW Gino Cavallini and D Charles Bourgeois (February 1, 1986). ... Bruised knee (April 1988). ... Suffered from the flu (April 1989). ... Traded by Flames to Pittsburgh Penguins for second-round pick (D Nicolas Perreault) in 1990

M

draft (June 16, 1990). ... Injured neck (January 22, 1991). ... Underwent neck surgery for herniated disk (February 6, 1991); missed remainder of season. ... Damaged ligament in knee (May 5, 1992); missed remainder of playoffs and first 11 games of 1992-93 season. ... Strained muscle in upper back (March 28, 1995); missed three games. ... Signed as free agent by Boston Bruins (September 8, 1995). ... Suffered herniated disk in neck (November 25, 1995); missed 32 games. ... Sprained knee (March 21, 1996); missed remainder of season. ... Signed as free agent by Pittsburgh Penguins (September 4, 1996).

HONORS: Named NYMJHL Most Valuable Player (1974-75). ... Named to NCAA All-America East (University Division) first team (1977-78 and 1978-79). ... Named to ECAC All-Star first team (1977-78 and 1978-79). ... Won Ken McKenzie Trophy (1979-80). ... Named to CHL All-Star second team (1979-80). ... Won Tommy Ivan Trophy (1980-81). ... Won Phil Esposito Trophy (1980-81). ... Named to CHL All-Star first team (1980-81). ... Won Lady Byng Memorial Trophy (1986-87 and 1988-89). ... Named to THE SPORTING NEWS All-Star first team (1988-89). ... Named to NHL All-Star first team (1988-89). ... Played in NHL All-Star Game (1989, 1990 and 1994). ... Named to THE SPORTING NEWS All-Star second team (1991-92).

STATISTICAL PLATEAUS: Three-goal games: 1983-84 (1), 1984-85 (1), 1988-89 (2), 1989-90 (1), 1991-92 (1), 1992-93 (1). Total: 7. ... Four-goal games: 1988-89 (2), 1991-92 (2). Total: 4. ... Total hat tricks: 11.

MISCELLANEOUS: Member of Stanley Cup championship team (1989, 1991 and 1992). ... Scored on a penalty shot (vs. Roland Melanson, February 16, 1985; vs. Kelly Hrudey, December 2, 1986; vs. Kari Takko, February 14, 1987).

STATISTICAL NOTES: Led NHL with 12 game-winning goals (1986-87).

Season Team	League	REGULAR SEASON								PLAYOFFS				
		Gms.	G	A	Pts.	PIM	+/-	PP	SH	Gms.	G	A	Pts.	PIM
71-72— N.Y. 14th Precinct......	NYMJHL	30	13	11	24	2	...	...	...	—	—	—	—	—
72-73— N.Y. Westsiders	NYMJHL	40	14	28	42	8	...	...	...	—	—	—	—	—
73-74— N.Y. Westsiders	NYMJHL	†42	71	49	120	41	...	...	...	7	9	9	18	0
74-75— N.Y. Westsiders	NYMJHL	40	*110	72	*182	20	...	...	...	13	*24	13	*37	2
75-76— Boston College..........	ECAC	24	16	18	34	4	...	...	...	—	—	—	—	—
76-77— Boston College..........	ECAC	28	28	26	54	8	...	...	...	—	—	—	—	—
77-78— Boston College..........	ECAC	34	34	34	68	12	...	...	...	—	—	—	—	—
78-79— Boston College..........	ECAC	25	32	24	56	8	...	...	...	—	—	—	—	—
79-80— Salt Lake City............	IHL	75	40	32	72	21	...	...	...	13	†9	11	20	0
— St. Louis	NHL	—	—	—	—	—	—	—	—	1	0	0	0	0
80-81— Salt Lake City............	IHL	80	59	58	*117	8	...	...	...	17	11	9	20	0
81-82— Salt Lake City............	IHL	27	21	27	48	12	...	...	...	—	—	—	—	—
— St. Louis	NHL	45	25	34	59	4	11	10	0	10	7	11	18	4
82-83— St. Louis	NHL	49	17	30	47	6	-5	5	0	—	—	—	—	—
83-84— St. Louis	NHL	80	41	44	85	19	-8	13	0	6	2	0	2	0
84-85— St. Louis	NHL	79	40	52	92	6	5	13	0	3	0	0	0	0
85-86— St. Louis	NHL	48	28	24	52	10	-7	9	0	—	—	—	—	—
— Calgary	NHL	29	16	22	38	11	3	5	0	21	*12	7	19	4
86-87— Calgary	NHL	79	47	40	87	14	18	15	0	6	2	1	3	0
87-88— Calgary	NHL	80	40	44	84	30	28	12	0	7	2	4	6	10
88-89— Calgary	NHL	79	51	59	110	16	*51	13	1	21	*16	8	24	4
89-90— Calgary	NHL	78	36	33	69	24	6	8	3	6	3	0	3	0
90-91— Pittsburgh	NHL	47	17	22	39	6	9	8	0	22	8	9	17	4
91-92— Pittsburgh	NHL	77	42	45	87	30	12	14	0	9	3	1	4	4
92-93— Pittsburgh	NHL	72	33	37	70	14	19	9	3	12	4	2	6	6
93-94— Pittsburgh	NHL	84	38	32	70	41	9	6	2	6	1	0	1	2
94-95— Pittsburgh	NHL	45	16	21	37	6	15	5	2	12	0	3	3	4
95-96— Boston	NHL	37	8	7	15	0	-2	4	0	—	—	—	—	—
96-97— Pittsburgh	NHL	54	7	15	22	4	0	1	0	1	0	0	0	0
NHL totals (17 years)		1062	502	561	1063	241	164	150	11	143	60	46	106	42

M

MULLER, KIRK   LW/C   PANTHERS

PERSONAL: Born February 8, 1966, in Kingston, Ont. ... 6-0/205. ... Shoots left. ... Name pronounced MUH-luhr.

TRANSACTIONS/CAREER NOTES: Selected by New Jersey Devils as underage junior in first round (first Devils pick, second overall) of NHL entry draft (June 9, 1984). ... Strained knee (January 13, 1986). ... Fractured ribs (April 1986). ... Traded by Devils with G Roland Melanson to Montreal Canadiens for RW Stephane Richer and RW Tom Chorske (September 1991). ... Injured eye (January 21, 1992); missed one game. ... Bruised ribs (November 7, 1992); missed one game. ... Sprained wrist (March 6, 1993); missed two games. ... Injured shoulder (October 11, 1993); missed eight games. ... Traded by Canadiens with D Mathieu Schneider and C Craig Darby to New York Islanders for C Pierre Turgeon and D Vladimir Malakhov (April 5, 1995). ... Traded by Islanders to Toronto Maple Leafs for LW Ken Belanger and G Damian Rhodes (January 23, 1996). ... Separated shoulder (January 3, 1997); missed two games. ... Bruised ankle (March 8, 1997); missed two games. ... Traded by Maple Leafs to Florida Panthers for RW Jason Podollan (March 18, 1997).

HONORS: Won William Hanley Trophy (1982-83). ... Played in NHL All-Star Game (1985, 1986, 1988, 1990, 1992 and 1993).

STATISTICAL PLATEAUS: Three-goal games: 1986-87 (1), 1987-88 (3), 1991-92 (2), 1995-96 (1). Total: 7.

MISCELLANEOUS: Member of Stanley Cup championship team (1993). ... Captain of New Jersey Devils (1987-88 through 1990-91). ... Captain of Montreal Canadiens (1994-95). ... Scored on a penalty shot (vs. Greg Millen, March 21, 1987). ... Failed to score on a penalty shot (vs. Mike Vernon, March 14, 1989).

Season Team	League	REGULAR SEASON								PLAYOFFS				
		Gms.	G	A	Pts.	PIM	+/-	PP	SH	Gms.	G	A	Pts.	PIM
80-81— Kingston	OMJHL	2	0	0	0	0	...	...	...	—	—	—	—	—
81-82— Kingston	OHL	67	12	39	51	27	...	...	...	4	5	1	6	4
82-83— Guelph	OHL	66	52	60	112	41	...	...	...	—	—	—	—	—
83-84— Can. Olympic team	Int'l	15	2	2	4	6	...	...	...	—	—	—	—	—
— Guelph	OHL	49	31	63	94	27	...	...	...	—	—	—	—	—
84-85— New Jersey	NHL	80	17	37	54	69	-31	9	1	—	—	—	—	—
85-86— New Jersey	NHL	77	25	41	66	45	-19	5	1	—	—	—	—	—
86-87— New Jersey	NHL	79	26	50	76	75	-7	10	1	—	—	—	—	—
87-88— New Jersey	NHL	80	37	57	94	114	19	17	2	20	4	8	12	37
88-89— New Jersey	NHL	80	31	43	74	119	-23	12	1	—	—	—	—	—
89-90— New Jersey	NHL	80	30	56	86	74	-1	9	0	6	1	3	4	11
90-91— New Jersey	NHL	80	19	51	70	76	1	7	0	7	0	2	2	10

Season Team	League	REGULAR SEASON								PLAYOFFS				
		Gms.	G	A	Pts.	PIM	+/-	PP	SH	Gms.	G	A	Pts.	PIM
91-92— Montreal	NHL	78	36	41	77	86	15	15	1	11	4	3	7	31
92-93— Montreal	NHL	80	37	57	94	77	8	12	0	20	10	7	17	18
93-94— Montreal	NHL	76	23	34	57	96	-1	9	2	7	6	2	8	4
94-95— Montreal	NHL	33	8	11	19	33	-21	3	0	—	—	—	—	—
— New York Islanders....	NHL	12	3	5	8	14	3	1	1	—	—	—	—	—
95-96— New York Islanders....	NHL	15	4	3	7	15	-10	0	0	—	—	—	—	—
— Toronto	NHL	36	9	16	25	42	-3	7	0	6	3	2	5	0
96-97— Toronto	NHL	66	20	17	37	85	-23	9	1	—	—	—	—	—
— Florida	NHL	10	1	2	3	4	-2	1	0	5	1	2	3	4
NHL totals (13 years)		962	326	521	847	1024	-95	126	11	82	29	29	58	115

MUNI, CRAIG   D

PERSONAL: Born July 19, 1962, in Toronto. ... 6-3/208. ... Shoots left. ... Full name: Craig Douglas Muni. ... Name pronounced MYOO-nee.
TRANSACTIONS/CAREER NOTES: Selected by Toronto Maple Leafs as underage junior in second round (first Maple Leafs pick, 25th overall) of NHL entry draft (June 11, 1980). ... Tore left knee ligaments (September 1981). ... Broke ankle (January 1983). ... Signed as free agent by Edmonton Oilers (August 18, 1986). ... Traded by Oilers to Buffalo Sabres for cash (October 2, 1986). ... Traded by Sabres to Pittsburgh Penguins for future considerations (October 3, 1986). ... Traded by Penguins to Oilers to complete earlier trade for G Gilles Meloche (October 6, 1986). ... Bruised kidney (May 1987). ... Bruised ankle (January 1988). ... Bruised ankle (December 17, 1988). ... Strained right shoulder (January 1989). ... Broke little finger of right hand (January 27, 1990); missed eight games. ... Suffered pinched nerve (January 15, 1992); missed 17 games. ... Injured knee (March 19, 1992); missed eight games. ... Suspended two games by NHL during playoffs for kneeing (May 22, 1992); missed final 1992 playoff game and first game of 1992-93 regular season. ... Suffered from the flu (December 1992); missed one game. ... Injured eye (February 18, 1993); missed two games. ... Traded by Oilers to Chicago Blackhawks for C Mike Hudson (March 22, 1993). ... Traded by Blackhawks to Buffalo Sabres for D Keith Carney (October 27, 1993). ... Pulled left hamstring (February 15, 1995); missed six games. ... Injured left knee (March 16, 1995); missed two games. ... Traded by Sabres to Winnipeg Jets for LW Michael Grosek and D Darryl Shannon (February 15, 1996). ... Strained groin (March 13, 1996); missed three games. ... Signed as free agent by Pittsburgh Penguins (October 1, 1996). ... Bruised leg (December 10, 1996); missed three games. ... Suffered from the flu (January 14, 1997); missed two games. ... Injured jaw (February 8, 1997); missed six games.
MISCELLANEOUS: Member of Stanley Cup championship team (1987, 1988 and 1990).

Season Team	League	REGULAR SEASON								PLAYOFFS				
		Gms.	G	A	Pts.	PIM	+/-	PP	SH	Gms.	G	A	Pts.	PIM
79-80— Kingston	OMJHL	66	6	28	34	114	...	...	...	—	—	—	—	—
80-81— Kingston	OMJHL	38	2	14	16	65	...	...	...	—	—	—	—	—
— Windsor	OMJHL	25	5	11	16	41	...	...	...	11	1	4	5	14
— New Brunswick..........	AHL	—	—	—	—	—	...	...	...	2	0	1	1	10
81-82— Toronto	NHL	3	0	0	0	2	-4	0	0	—	—	—	—	—
— Windsor	OHL	49	5	32	37	92	...	...	...	9	2	3	5	16
— Cincinnati	CHL	—	—	—	—	—	...	...	...	3	0	2	2	2
82-83— Toronto	NHL	2	0	1	1	0	-3	0	0	—	—	—	—	—
— St. Catharines	AHL	64	6	32	38	52	...	...	...	—	—	—	—	—
83-84— St. Catharines	AHL	64	4	16	20	79	...	...	...	7	0	1	1	0
84-85— St. Catharines	AHL	68	7	17	24	54	...	...	...	—	—	—	—	—
— Toronto	NHL	8	0	0	0	0	0	0	0	—	—	—	—	—
85-86— Toronto	NHL	6	0	1	1	4	-3	0	0	—	—	—	—	—
— St. Catharines	AHL	73	3	34	37	91	...	...	...	13	0	5	5	16
86-87— Edmonton	NHL	79	7	22	29	85	45	0	0	14	0	2	2	17
87-88— Edmonton	NHL	72	4	15	19	77	32	0	1	19	0	4	4	31
88-89— Edmonton	NHL	69	5	13	18	71	43	0	0	7	0	3	3	8
89-90— Edmonton	NHL	71	5	12	17	81	22	0	2	22	0	3	3	16
90-91— Edmonton	NHL	76	1	9	10	77	10	0	0	18	0	3	3	20
91-92— Edmonton	NHL	54	2	5	7	34	11	0	0	3	0	0	0	2
92-93— Edmonton	NHL	72	0	11	11	67	-15	0	0	—	—	—	—	—
— Chicago....................	NHL	9	0	0	0	8	1	0	0	4	0	0	0	2
93-94— Chicago....................	NHL	9	0	4	4	4	3	0	0	—	—	—	—	—
— Buffalo	NHL	73	2	8	10	62	28	0	1	7	0	0	0	4
94-95— Buffalo	NHL	40	0	6	6	36	-4	0	0	5	0	1	1	2
95-96— Buffalo	NHL	47	0	4	4	69	-12	0	0	—	—	—	—	—
— Winnipeg	NHL	25	1	3	4	37	6	0	0	6	0	1	1	2
96-97— Pittsburgh	NHL	64	0	4	4	36	-6	0	0	3	0	0	0	0
NHL totals (15 years)		779	27	118	145	750	154	0	4	108	0	17	17	104

M

MURPHY, BURKE   LW   FLAMES

PERSONAL: Born June 5, 1973, in Gloucester, Ont. ... 6-2/195. ... Shoots left.
COLLEGE: St. Lawrence (N.Y.).
TRANSACTIONS/CAREER NOTES: Selected by Calgary Flames in 11th round (11th Flames pick, 278th overall) in NHL entry draft (June 29, 1993).
HONORS: Named to ECAC All-Star second team (1994-95). ... Named to NCAA All-America East second team (1995-96). ... Named to ECAC All-Star first team (1995-96).

Season Team	League	REGULAR SEASON								PLAYOFFS				
		Gms.	G	A	Pts.	PIM	+/-	PP	SH	Gms.	G	A	Pts.	PIM
92-93— St. Lawrence Univ......	ECAC	32	19	10	29	32	...	...	...	—	—	—	—	—
93-94— St. Lawrence Univ......	ECAC	30	20	17	37	42	...	...	...	—	—	—	—	—
94-95— St. Lawrence Univ......	ECAC	33	27	23	50	51	...	...	...	—	—	—	—	—
95-96— St. Lawrence Univ......	ECAC	35	33	25	58	37	...	...	...	—	—	—	—	—
96-97— Saint John	AHL	54	8	18	26	20	...	...	...	—	—	—	—	—

MURPHY, GORD   D   PANTHERS

PERSONAL: Born February 23, 1967, in Willowdale, Ont. ... 6-2/198. ... Shoots right.
TRANSACTIONS/CAREER NOTES: Injured clavicle (January 1985). ... Selected by Philadelphia Flyers as underage junior in ninth round (10th Flyers pick, 189th overall) of NHL entry draft (June 15, 1985). ... Injured left foot and suffered hip pointer (March 24, 1990). ... Traded by Flyers with RW Brian Dobbin and third-round pick (LW Sergei Zholtok) in 1992 draft to Boston Bruins for D Garry Galley, C Wes Walz and future considerations (January 2, 1992). ... Injured ankle (January 1993); missed 16 games. ... Traded by Bruins to Dallas Stars for future considerations (June 20, 1993); Bruins sent G Andy Moog to Stars for G Jon Casey to complete deal (June 25, 1993). ... Selected by Florida Panthers in NHL expansion draft (June 24, 1993). ... Suffered illness (March 26, 1995); missed one game. ... Sprained left ankle (April 5, 1995); missed one game. ... Sprained right ankle (January 29, 1996); missed nine games. ... Injured toe (April 8, 1996); missed three games.
HONORS: Named to Memorial Cup All-Star team (1986-87).

		REGULAR SEASON								PLAYOFFS				
Season Team	League	Gms.	G	A	Pts.	PIM	+/-	PP	SH	Gms.	G	A	Pts.	PIM
83-84 — Don Mills Flyers.........	MTHL	65	24	42	66	130	...	...	...	—	—	—	—	—
84-85 — Oshawa................	OHL	59	3	12	15	25	...	...	...	—	—	—	—	—
85-86 — Oshawa................	OHL	64	7	15	22	56	...	...	...	6	1	1	2	6
86-87 — Oshawa................	OHL	56	7	30	37	95	...	...	...	24	6	16	22	22
87-88 — Hershey................	AHL	62	8	20	28	44	...	...	...	12	0	8	8	12
88-89 — Philadelphia............	NHL	75	4	31	35	68	-3	3	0	19	2	7	9	13
89-90 — Philadelphia............	NHL	75	14	27	41	95	-7	4	0	—	—	—	—	—
90-91 — Philadelphia............	NHL	80	11	31	42	58	-7	6	0	—	—	—	—	—
91-92 — Philadelphia............	NHL	31	2	8	10	33	-4	0	0	—	—	—	—	—
— Boston	NHL	42	3	6	9	51	2	0	0	15	1	0	1	12
92-93 — Boston	NHL	49	5	12	17	62	-13	3	0	—	—	—	—	—
— Providence..............	AHL	2	1	3	4	2	...	...	...	—	—	—	—	—
93-94 — Florida................	NHL	84	14	29	43	71	-11	9	0	—	—	—	—	—
94-95 — Florida................	NHL	46	6	16	22	24	-14	5	0	—	—	—	—	—
95-96 — Florida................	NHL	70	8	22	30	30	5	4	0	14	0	4	4	6
96-97 — Florida................	NHL	80	8	15	23	51	3	2	0	5	0	5	5	4
NHL totals (9 years)		632	75	197	272	543	-49	36	0	53	3	16	19	35

MURPHY, JOE   RW   BLUES

PERSONAL: Born October 16, 1967, in London, Ont. ... 6-1/190. ... Shoots left. ... Full name: Joseph Patrick Murphy.
COLLEGE: Michigan State.
TRANSACTIONS/CAREER NOTES: Selected by Detroit Red Wings in first round (first Red Wings pick, first overall) of NHL entry draft (June 21, 1986). ... Sprained right ankle (January 1988). ... Traded by Red Wings with C/LW Adam Graves, LW Petr Klima and D Jeff Sharples to Edmonton Oilers for C Jimmy Carson, C Kevin McClelland and fifth-round pick (traded to Montreal Canadiens who selected D Brad Layzell) in 1991 draft (November 2, 1989). ... Bruised both thighs (March 1990). ... Did not report to Oilers in 1992-93 season because of contract dispute; missed 63 games. ... Traded by Oilers to Chicago Blackhawks for D Igor Kravchuk and C Dean McAmmond (February 25, 1993). ... Pulled groin (February 3, 1995); missed three games. ... Reinjured groin (March 6, 1995); missed four games. ... Sprained knee (March 21, 1995); missed one game. ... Suspended 10 games by NHL for being third man in fight (September 20, 1995). ... Strained back (December 28, 1995); missed four games. ... Strained back (January 6, 1996). ... Signed as free agent by St. Louis Blues (July 3, 1996). ... Suffered from a virus (October 31, 1996); missed five games. ... Strained groin (January 30, 1997); missed one game.
HONORS: Named BCJHL Rookie of the Year (1984-85). ... Named CCHA Rookie of the Year (1985-86).
MISCELLANEOUS: Member of Stanley Cup championship team (1990).

		REGULAR SEASON								PLAYOFFS				
Season Team	League	Gms.	G	A	Pts.	PIM	+/-	PP	SH	Gms.	G	A	Pts.	PIM
84-85 — Penticton	BCJHL	51	68	84	*152	92	...	...	...	—	—	—	—	—
85-86 — Michigan State..........	CCHA	35	24	37	61	50	...	...	...	—	—	—	—	—
— Canadian nat'l team ...	Int'l	8	3	3	6	2	...	...	...	—	—	—	—	—
86-87 — Adirondack..............	AHL	71	21	38	59	61	...	...	...	10	2	1	3	33
— Detroit..................	NHL	5	0	1	1	2	0	0	0	—	—	—	—	—
87-88 — Adirondack..............	AHL	6	5	6	11	4	...	...	...	—	—	—	—	—
— Detroit..................	NHL	50	10	9	19	37	-4	1	0	8	0	1	1	6
88-89 — Detroit..................	NHL	26	1	7	8	28	-7	0	0	—	—	—	—	—
— Adirondack..............	AHL	47	31	35	66	66	...	...	...	16	6	11	17	17
89-90 — Detroit..................	NHL	9	3	1	4	4	4	0	0	—	—	—	—	—
— Edmonton..............	NHL	62	7	18	25	56	1	2	0	22	6	8	14	16
90-91 — Edmonton..............	NHL	80	27	35	62	35	2	4	1	15	2	5	7	14
91-92 — Edmonton..............	NHL	80	35	47	82	52	17	10	2	16	8	16	24	12
92-93 — Chicago................	NHL	19	7	10	17	18	-3	5	0	4	0	0	0	8
93-94 — Chicago................	NHL	81	31	39	70	111	1	7	4	6	1	3	4	25
94-95 — Chicago................	NHL	40	23	18	41	89	7	7	0	16	9	3	12	29
95-96 — Chicago................	NHL	70	22	29	51	86	-3	8	0	10	6	2	8	33
96-97 — St. Louis	NHL	75	20	25	45	69	-1	4	1	6	1	1	2	10
NHL totals (11 years)		597	186	239	425	587	14	48	8	103	33	39	72	153

MURPHY, LARRY   D   RED WINGS

PERSONAL: Born March 8, 1961, in Scarborough, Ont. ... 6-2/210. ... Shoots right. ... Full name: Lawrence Thomas Murphy.
TRANSACTIONS/CAREER NOTES: Selected by Los Angeles Kings as underage junior in first round (first Kings pick, fourth overall) of NHL entry draft (June 11, 1980). ... Traded by Kings to Washington Capitals for D Brian Engblom and RW Ken Houston (October 18, 1983). ... Injured foot (October 29, 1985). ... Broke ankle (May 1988). ... Traded by Capitals with RW Mike Gartner to Minnesota North Stars for RW Dino Ciccarelli and D Bob Rouse (March 7, 1989). ... Traded by North Stars with D Peter Taglianetti to Pittsburgh Penguins for D Jim Johnson and D Chris Dahlquist (December 11, 1990). ... Fractured right foot (February 22, 1991); played until March 5 then missed five games. ... Suffered back spasms (March 28, 1993); missed one game. ... Traded by Penguins to Toronto Maple Leafs for D Dmitri Mironov and second-

M

round pick (traded to New Jersey) in 1996 draft (July 8, 1995). ... Traded by Maple Leafs to Detroit Red Wings for future considerations (March 18, 1997).
HONORS: Won Max Kaminsky Trophy (1979-80). ... Named to OMJHL All-Star first team (1979-80). ... Named to Memorial Cup All-Star team (1979-80). ... Named to THE SPORTING NEWS All-Star second team (1986-87 and 1992-93). ... Named to NHL All-Star second team (1986-87, 1992-93 and 1994-95). ... Played in NHL All-Star Game (1994 and 1996).
RECORDS: Holds NHL rookie-season records for most points by a defenseman—76; and most assists by a defenseman—60 (1980-81).
MISCELLANEOUS: Member of Stanley Cup championship team (1991, 1992 and 1997).

		REGULAR SEASON								PLAYOFFS				
Season Team	League	Gms.	G	A	Pts.	PIM	+/-	PP	SH	Gms.	G	A	Pts.	PIM
78-79— Peterborough	OMJHL	66	6	21	27	82	...	...	...	19	1	9	10	42
79-80— Peterborough	OMJHL	68	21	68	89	88	...	...	...	14	4	13	17	20
80-81— Los Angeles	NHL	80	16	60	76	79	17	5	1	4	3	0	3	2
81-82— Los Angeles	NHL	79	22	44	66	95	-13	8	1	10	2	8	10	12
82-83— Los Angeles	NHL	77	14	48	62	81	2	9	0	—	—	—	—	—
83-84— Los Angeles	NHL	6	0	3	3	0	-4	0	0	—	—	—	—	—
— Washington	NHL	72	13	33	46	50	12	2	0	8	0	3	3	6
84-85— Washington	NHL	79	13	42	55	51	21	3	0	5	2	3	5	0
85-86— Washington	NHL	78	21	44	65	50	3	8	1	9	1	5	6	6
86-87— Washington	NHL	80	23	58	81	39	25	8	0	7	2	2	4	6
87-88— Washington	NHL	79	8	53	61	72	2	7	0	13	4	4	8	33
88-89— Washington	NHL	65	7	29	36	70	-5	3	0	—	—	—	—	—
— Minnesota	NHL	13	4	6	10	12	5	3	0	5	0	2	2	8
89-90— Minnesota	NHL	77	10	58	68	44	-13	4	0	7	1	2	3	31
90-91— Minnesota	NHL	31	4	11	15	38	-8	1	0	—	—	—	—	—
— Pittsburgh	NHL	44	5	23	28	30	2	2	0	23	5	18	23	44
91-92— Pittsburgh	NHL	77	21	56	77	48	33	7	2	21	6	10	16	19
92-93— Pittsburgh	NHL	83	22	63	85	73	45	6	2	12	2	11	13	10
93-94— Pittsburgh	NHL	84	17	56	73	44	10	7	0	6	0	5	5	0
94-95— Pittsburgh	NHL	48	13	25	38	18	12	4	0	12	2	13	15	0
95-96— Toronto	NHL	82	12	49	61	34	-2	8	0	6	0	2	2	4
96-97— Toronto	NHL	69	7	32	39	20	1	4	0	—	—	—	—	—
— Detroit	NHL	12	2	4	6	0	2	1	0	20	2	9	11	8
NHL totals (17 years)		1315	254	797	1051	948	147	100	7	168	32	97	129	189

MURRAY, CHRIS   RW   HURRICANES

PERSONAL: Born October 25, 1974, in Port Hardy, B.C. ... 6-2/210. ... Shoots right.
TRANSACTIONS/CAREER NOTES: Selected by Montreal Canadiens in third round (third Canadiens pick, 54th overall) of NHL entry draft (June 29, 1994). ... Suspended three games without pay and fined $1000 by NHL for cross-checking (April 3, 1996). ... Fractured hand (October 3, 1996); missed 10 games. ... Traded by Canadiens with D Murray Baron to Phoenix Coyotes for D Dave Manson (March 18, 1997). ... Traded by Coyotes to Hartford Whalers for D Gerald Diduck (March 18, 1997). ... Suffered from the flu (March 27, 1997); missed two games. ... Whalers franchise moved to North Carolina and renamed Carolina Hurricanes for 1997-98 season; NHL approved move on June 25, 1997.

		REGULAR SEASON								PLAYOFFS				
Season Team	League	Gms.	G	A	Pts.	PIM	+/-	PP	SH	Gms.	G	A	Pts.	PIM
90-91— Bellingham Jr. A	BCJHL	54	5	8	13	150	...	...	...	—	—	—	—	—
91-92— Kamloops	WHL	33	1	1	2	168	...	...	...	5	0	0	0	10
92-93— Kamloops	WHL	62	6	10	16	217	...	...	...	13	0	4	4	34
93-94— Kamloops	WHL	59	14	16	30	260	...	...	...	15	4	2	6	107
94-95— Fredericton	AHL	55	6	12	18	234	...	...	...	12	1	1	2	50
— Montreal	NHL	3	0	0	0	4	0	0	0	—	—	—	—	—
95-96— Fredericton	AHL	30	13	13	26	217	...	...	...	—	—	—	—	—
— Montreal	NHL	48	3	4	7	163	5	0	0	4	0	0	0	4
96-97— Montreal	NHL	56	4	2	6	114	-8	0	0	—	—	—	—	—
— Hartford	NHL	8	1	1	2	10	1	0	0	—	—	—	—	—
NHL totals (3 years)		115	8	7	15	291	-2	0	0	4	0	0	0	4

MURRAY, GLEN   RW   KINGS

PERSONAL: Born November 1, 1972, in Halifax, Nova Scotia. ... 6-2/200. ... Shoots right.
TRANSACTIONS/CAREER NOTES: Selected by Boston Bruins in first round (first Bruins pick, 18th overall) of NHL entry draft (June 22, 1991). ... Injured elbow (December 15, 1993); missed two games. ... Traded by Bruins with C Bryan Smolinski to Pittsburgh Penguins for LW Kevin Stevens and C Shawn McEachern (August 2, 1995). ... Separated shoulder (January 1, 1996); missed 10 games. ... Suffered concussion (April 11, 1996); missed one game. ... Traded by Penguins to Los Angeles Kings for C Ed Olczyk (March 18, 1997).

		REGULAR SEASON								PLAYOFFS				
Season Team	League	Gms.	G	A	Pts.	PIM	+/-	PP	SH	Gms.	G	A	Pts.	PIM
89-90— Sudbury	OHL	62	8	28	36	17	...	...	...	7	0	0	0	4
90-91— Sudbury	OHL	66	27	38	65	82	...	...	...	5	8	4	12	10
91-92— Sudbury	OHL	54	37	47	84	93	...	...	...	11	7	4	11	18
— Boston	NHL	5	3	1	4	0	2	1	0	15	4	2	6	10
92-93— Providence	AHL	48	30	26	56	42	...	...	...	6	1	4	5	4
— Boston	NHL	27	3	4	7	8	-6	2	0	—	—	—	—	—
93-94— Boston	NHL	81	18	13	31	48	-1	0	0	13	4	5	9	14
94-95— Boston	NHL	35	5	2	7	46	-11	0	0	2	0	0	0	2
95-96— Pittsburgh	NHL	69	14	15	29	57	4	0	0	18	2	6	8	10
96-97— Pittsburgh	NHL	66	11	11	22	24	-19	3	0	—	—	—	—	—
— Los Angeles	NHL	11	5	3	8	8	-2	0	0	—	—	—	—	—
NHL totals (6 years)		294	59	49	108	191	-33	6	0	48	10	13	23	36

M

MURRAY, MARTY   C   FLAMES

PERSONAL: Born February 16, 1975, in Deloraine, Man. ... 5-9/170. ... Shoots left.
TRANSACTIONS/CAREER NOTES: Selected by Calgary Flames in fourth round (fifth Flames pick, 96th overall) of NHL entry draft (June 26, 1993). ... Bruised foot (April 8, 1996); missed three games.
HONORS: Named to Can.HL All-Star second team (1993-94). ... Named to WHL (East) All-Star first team (1993-94 and 1994-95). ... Won Four Broncos Memorial Trophy (1994-95).

		REGULAR SEASON								PLAYOFFS				
Season Team	League	Gms.	G	A	Pts.	PIM	+/-	PP	SH	Gms.	G	A	Pts.	PIM
91-92— Brandon	WHL	68	20	36	56	12	...	...	...	—	—	—	—	—
92-93— Brandon	WHL	67	29	65	94	50	...	...	...	4	1	3	4	0
93-94— Brandon	WHL	64	43	71	114	33	...	...	...	14	6	14	20	14
94-95— Brandon	WHL	65	40	88	128	53	...	...	...	18	9	20	29	16
95-96— Calgary	NHL	15	3	3	6	0	-4	2	0	—	—	—	—	—
— Saint John	AHL	58	25	31	56	20	...	...	...	14	2	4	6	4
96-97— Saint John	AHL	67	19	39	58	40	...	...	...	5	2	3	5	4
— Calgary	NHL	2	0	0	0	4	0	0	0	—	—	—	—	—
NHL totals (2 years)		17	3	3	6	4	-4	2	0					

MURRAY, REM   C/LW   KINGS

PERSONAL: Born October 9, 1972, in Stratford, Ont. ... 6-2/195. ... Shoots left.
COLLEGE: Michigan State.
TRANSACTIONS/CAREER NOTES: Selected by Los Angeles Kings in sixth round (fifth Kings pick, 135th overall) of NHL entry draft (June 20, 1992).
HONORS: Named to CCHA All-Star second team (1994-95).
STATISTICAL PLATEAUS: Three-goal games: 1996-97 (1).

		REGULAR SEASON								PLAYOFFS				
Season Team	League	Gms.	G	A	Pts.	PIM	+/-	PP	SH	Gms.	G	A	Pts.	PIM
90-91— Stratford Jr. B	OHA	48	39	59	98	22	...	...	...	—	—	—	—	—
91-92— Michigan State	CCHA	44	12	36	48	16	...	...	...	—	—	—	—	—
92-93— Michigan State	CCHA	40	22	35	57	24	...	...	...	—	—	—	—	—
93-94— Michigan State	CCHA	41	16	38	54	18	...	...	...	—	—	—	—	—
94-95— Michigan State	CCHA	40	20	36	56	21	...	...	...	—	—	—	—	—
95-96— Cape Breton	AHL	79	31	59	90	40	...	...	...	—	—	—	—	—
96-97— Edmonton	NHL	82	11	20	31	16	9	1	0	12	1	2	3	4
NHL totals (1 year)		82	11	20	31	16	9	1	0	12	1	2	3	4

M

MURRAY, ROB   C   COYOTES

PERSONAL: Born April 4, 1967, in Toronto. ... 6-1/180. ... Shoots right.
TRANSACTIONS/CAREER NOTES: Selected by Washington Capitals as underage junior in third round (third Capitals pick, 61st overall) of NHL entry draft (June 15, 1985). ... Suspended two games by OHL (November 2, 1986). ... Injured right hip (December 21, 1989); missed 10 games. ... Selected by Minnesota North Stars in NHL expansion draft (May 30, 1991). ... Traded by North Stars with future considerations to Winnipeg Jets for seventh-round pick (G Geoff Finch) in 1991 draft and future considerations (May 30, 1991). ... Strained groin (November 2, 1992); missed three games. ... Suffered back spasms (December 15, 1992); missed six games. ... Jets franchise moved to Phoenix and renamed Coyotes for 1996-97; NHL approved move on January 18, 1996.

		REGULAR SEASON								PLAYOFFS				
Season Team	League	Gms.	G	A	Pts.	PIM	+/-	PP	SH	Gms.	G	A	Pts.	PIM
83-84— Mississauga	OHA	35	18	36	54	32	...	...	...	—	—	—	—	—
84-85— Peterborough	OHL	63	12	9	21	155	...	...	...	17	2	7	9	45
85-86— Peterborough	OHL	52	14	18	32	125	...	...	...	16	1	2	3	50
86-87— Peterborough	OHL	62	17	37	54	204	...	...	...	3	1	4	5	8
87-88— Fort Wayne	IHL	80	12	21	33	139	...	...	...	6	0	2	2	16
88-89— Baltimore	AHL	80	11	23	34	235	...	...	...	—	—	—	—	—
89-90— Baltimore	AHL	23	5	4	9	63	...	...	...	—	—	—	—	—
— Washington	NHL	41	2	7	9	58	-10	0	0	9	0	0	0	18
90-91— Baltimore	AHL	48	6	20	26	177	...	...	...	4	0	0	0	12
— Washington	NHL	17	0	3	3	19	0	0	0	—	—	—	—	—
91-92— Moncton	AHL	60	16	15	31	247	...	...	...	8	0	1	1	56
— Winnipeg	NHL	9	0	1	1	18	-2	0	0	—	—	—	—	—
92-93— Moncton	AHL	56	16	21	37	147	...	...	...	3	0	0	0	6
— Winnipeg	NHL	10	1	0	1	6	0	0	0	—	—	—	—	—
93-94— Moncton	AHL	69	25	32	57	280	...	...	...	21	2	3	5	60
— Winnipeg	NHL	6	0	0	0	2	0	0	0	—	—	—	—	—
94-95— Springfield	AHL	78	16	38	54	373	...	...	...	—	—	—	—	—
— Winnipeg	NHL	10	0	2	2	2	1	0	0	—	—	—	—	—
95-96— Springfield	AHL	74	10	28	38	263	...	...	...	10	1	6	7	32
— Winnipeg	NHL	1	0	0	0	2	-1	0	0	—	—	—	—	—
96-97— Springfield	AHL	78	16	27	43	234	...	...	...	17	2	3	5	66
NHL totals (7 years)		94	3	13	16	107	-12	0	0	9	0	0	0	18

MURRAY, TROY   C

PERSONAL: Born July 31, 1962, in Winnipeg. ... 6-1/195. ... Shoots right. ... Full name: Troy Norman Murray.
COLLEGE: North Dakota.

TRANSACTIONS/CAREER NOTES: Selected by Chicago Blackhawks in third round (sixth Blackhawks pick, 57th overall) of NHL entry draft (June 11, 1980). ... Injured knee ligaments (November 1983). ... Lacerated face (December 1988). ... Injured right elbow and underwent surgery (December 26, 1989); missed 11 games. ... Developed bursitis on right elbow and hospitalized (February 8, 1990). ... Traded by Blackhawks with LW Warren Rychel to Winnipeg Jets for D Bryan Marchment and D Chris Norton (July 22, 1991). ... Separated shoulder (October 23, 1991); missed four games. ... Lacerated knee (December 14, 1991); missed three games. ... Separated shoulder (October 7, 1992); missed five games. ... Suffered hip pointer (November 10, 1992); missed two games. ... Fractured foot (December 19, 1992); missed 22 games. ... Traded by Jets to Chicago Blackhawks for D Steve Bancroft and undisclosed pick in 1993 draft (February 21, 1993). ... Traded by Blackhawks to Ottawa Senators for future considerations (March 11, 1994). ... Bruised ribs (February 8, 1995); missed one game. ... Traded by Senators with D Norm Maciver to Pittsburgh Penguins for C Martin Straka (April 7, 1995). ... Signed as free agent by Colorado Avalanche (August 8, 1995). ... Sprained right knee (November 28, 1995); missed 11 games. ... Sprained right knee (January 9, 1996); missed three games. ... Injured finger (March 9, 1996); missed one game.

HONORS: Won WCHA Freshman of the Year Award (1980-81). ... Named to WCHA All-Star second team (1980-81 and 1981-82). ... Won Frank J. Selke Trophy (1985-86).

STATISTICAL PLATEAUS: Three-goal games: 1985-86 (3), 1989-90 (1). Total: 4.

MISCELLANEOUS: Member of Stanley Cup championship team (1996). ... Co-captain of Chicago Blackhawks (1987-88). ... Captain of Winnipeg Jets (1991-92 and 1992-93). ... Scored on a penalty shot (vs. Kari Takko, December 30, 1987). ... Failed to score on a penalty shot (vs. Mike Richter, November 27, 1991).

		REGULAR SEASON								PLAYOFFS				
Season Team	League	Gms.	G	A	Pts.	PIM	+/-	PP	SH	Gms.	G	A	Pts.	PIM
79-80 — St. Albert	AJHL	60	53	47	100	101	...	...	...	—	—	—	—	—
80-81 — North Dakota	WCHA	38	33	45	78	28	...	...	...	—	—	—	—	—
81-82 — North Dakota	WCHA	42	22	29	51	62	...	...	...	—	—	—	—	—
— Chicago	NHL	1	0	0	0	0	...	...	...	7	1	0	1	5
82-83 — Chicago	NHL	54	8	8	16	27	...	...	...	2	0	0	0	0
83-84 — Chicago	NHL	61	15	15	30	45	...	...	...	5	1	0	1	7
84-85 — Chicago	NHL	80	26	40	66	82	...	...	...	15	5	14	19	24
85-86 — Chicago	NHL	80	45	54	99	94	...	...	...	2	0	0	0	2
86-87 — Chicago	NHL	77	28	43	71	59	...	...	...	4	0	0	0	5
87-88 — Chicago	NHL	79	22	36	58	96	...	...	...	5	1	0	1	8
88-89 — Chicago	NHL	79	21	30	51	113	...	...	...	16	3	6	9	25
89-90 — Chicago	NHL	68	17	38	55	86	-2	3	1	20	4	4	8	2
90-91 — Chicago	NHL	75	14	23	37	74	13	4	0	6	0	1	1	12
91-92 — Winnipeg	NHL	74	17	30	47	69	-13	5	2	7	0	0	0	2
92-93 — Winnipeg	NHL	29	3	4	7	34	-15	1	0	—	—	—	—	—
— Chicago	NHL	22	1	3	4	25	0	1	0	4	0	0	0	2
93-94 — Chicago	NHL	12	0	1	1	6	1	0	0	—	—	—	—	—
— Indianapolis	IHL	8	3	3	6	12	...	...	...					
— Ottawa	NHL	15	2	3	5	4	1	0	1	—	—	—	—	—
94-95 — Ottawa	NHL	33	4	10	14	16	-1	0	0	—	—	—	—	—
— Pittsburgh	NHL	13	0	2	2	23	-1	0	0	12	2	1	3	12
95-96 — Colorado	NHL	63	7	14	21	22	15	0	0	8	0	0	0	19
96-97 — Chicago	IHL	81	21	29	50	63	...	...	...	4	0	2	2	2
NHL totals (16 years)		915	230	354	584	875	-2	14	4	113	17	26	43	125

MURZYN, DANA — D — CANUCKS

M

PERSONAL: Born December 9, 1966, in Regina, Sask. ... 6-2/208. ... Shoots left. ... Name pronounced MUHR-zihn.

TRANSACTIONS/CAREER NOTES: Selected by Hartford Whalers as underage junior in first round (first Whalers pick, fifth overall) of NHL entry draft (June 15, 1985). ... Traded by Whalers with RW Shane Churla to Calgary Flames for C Carey Wilson, D Neil Sheehy and LW Lane MacDonald (January 3, 1988). ... Strained knee (March 13, 1989). ... Pulled groin (February 4, 1990). ... Bruised hip (October 25, 1990); missed 14 games. ... Separated shoulder (December 1, 1990); missed 34 games. ... Traded by Flames to Vancouver Canucks for RW Ron Stern, D Kevan Guy and option to switch fourth-round picks in 1992 draft; Flames did not exercise option (March 5, 1991). ... Suffered from the flu (February 26, 1993); missed two games. ... Underwent minor knee surgery (January 21, 1995); missed five games. ... Sprained knee (April 30, 1995); missed last game of season. ... Underwent knee surgery (November 8, 1995); missed 12 games. ... Sprained wrist (October 17, 1996); missed 14 games. ... Injured shoulder (December 1, 1996); missed four games.

HONORS: Named to WHL (East) All-Star first team (1984-85). ... Named to NHL All-Rookie team (1985-86).

STATISTICAL PLATEAUS: Three-goal games: 1989-90 (1).

MISCELLANEOUS: Member of Stanley Cup championship team (1989).

		REGULAR SEASON								PLAYOFFS				
Season Team	League	Gms.	G	A	Pts.	PIM	+/-	PP	SH	Gms.	G	A	Pts.	PIM
83-84 — Calgary	WHL	65	11	20	31	135	...	...	...	2	0	0	0	0
84-85 — Calgary	WHL	72	32	60	92	233	...	...	...	8	1	11	12	16
85-86 — Hartford	NHL	78	3	23	26	125	1	0	0	4	0	0	0	10
86-87 — Hartford	NHL	74	9	19	28	95	18	1	0	6	2	1	3	29
87-88 — Hartford	NHL	33	1	6	7	45	-8	1	0	—	—	—	—	—
— Calgary	NHL	41	6	5	11	94	9	0	0	5	2	0	2	13
88-89 — Calgary	NHL	63	3	19	22	142	26	0	1	21	0	3	3	20
89-90 — Calgary	NHL	78	7	13	20	140	19	1	0	6	2	2	4	2
90-91 — Calgary	NHL	19	0	2	2	30	-4	0	0	—	—	—	—	—
— Vancouver	NHL	10	1	0	1	8	-3	0	0	6	0	1	1	8
91-92 — Vancouver	NHL	70	3	11	14	147	15	0	1	1	0	0	0	15
92-93 — Vancouver	NHL	79	5	11	16	196	34	0	0	12	3	2	5	18
93-94 — Vancouver	NHL	80	6	14	20	109	4	0	1	7	0	0	0	4
94-95 — Vancouver	NHL	40	0	8	8	129	14	0	0	8	0	1	1	22
95-96 — Vancouver	NHL	69	2	10	12	130	9	0	0	6	0	0	0	25
96-97 — Vancouver	NHL	61	1	7	8	118	7	0	0	—	—	—	—	—
NHL totals (12 years)		795	47	148	195	1508	141	3	3	82	9	10	19	166

MUSIL, FRANK   D   SENATORS

PERSONAL: Born December 17, 1964, in Pardubice, Czechoslovakia. ... 6-3/215. ... Shoots left. ... Name pronounced moo-SIHL.
TRANSACTIONS/CAREER NOTES: Selected by Minnesota North Stars in second round (third North Stars pick, 38th overall) of NHL entry draft (June 8, 1983). ... Separated shoulder (December 9, 1986). ... Fractured foot (December 17, 1988). ... Suffered concussion (February 9, 1989). ... Strained lower back muscles (February 18, 1989). ... Suffered back spasms (November 2, 1989); missed 10 games. ... Separated right shoulder (April 1990). ... Traded by North Stars to Calgary Flames for D Brian Glynn (October 26, 1990). ... Suffered back spasms (November 8, 1993); missed one game. ... Strained neck (December 28, 1993); missed four games. ... Hyperextended elbow (March 22, 1994); missed four games. ... Played in Europe during 1994-95 NHL lockout. ... Bruised right knee (January 24, 1995); missed one game. ... Sprained right knee (February 9, 1995); missed three games. ... Suffered back spasms (February 28, 1995); missed one game. ... Sprained right knee (April 7, 1995); missed seven games. ... Traded by Flames to Ottawa Senators for fourth-round pick (D Chris St. Croix) in 1997 draft (October 7, 1995). ... Suffered concussion during 1995-96 season; missed one game. ... Lacerated neck (January 21, 1996); missed six games. ... Bruised right foot (February 3, 1996); missed seven games.

			REGULAR SEASON								PLAYOFFS				
Season Team	League	Gms.	G	A	Pts.	PIM	+/-	PP	SH		Gms.	G	A	Pts.	PIM
85-86— Dukla Jihlava	Czech.	35	3	7	10	85	...	...	...		—	—	—	—	—
86-87— Minnesota	NHL	72	2	9	11	148	0	0	0		—	—	—	—	—
87-88— Minnesota	NHL	80	9	8	17	213	-2	1	1		—	—	—	—	—
88-89— Minnesota	NHL	55	1	19	20	54	4	0	0		5	1	1	2	4
89-90— Minnesota	NHL	56	2	8	10	109	0	0	0		4	0	0	0	14
90-91— Minnesota	NHL	8	0	2	2	23	0	0	0		—	—	—	—	—
—Calgary	NHL	67	7	14	21	160	12	2	0		7	0	0	0	10
91-92— Calgary	NHL	78	4	8	12	103	12	1	1		—	—	—	—	—
92-93— Calgary	NHL	80	6	10	16	131	28	0	0		6	1	1	2	7
93-94— Calgary	NHL	75	1	8	9	50	38	0	0		7	0	1	1	4
94-95— Sparta Prague	Czech Rep.	19	1	4	5	30	...	...	...		—	—	—	—	—
—Sachsen	Germany	1	0	0	0	2	...	...	...		—	—	—	—	—
—Calgary	NHL	35	0	5	5	61	6	0	0		5	0	1	1	0
95-96— Ottawa	NHL	65	1	3	4	85	-10	0	0		—	—	—	—	—
96-97— Ottawa	NHL	57	0	5	5	58	6	0	0		—	—	—	—	—
NHL totals (11 years)		728	33	99	132	1195	94	4	2		34	2	4	6	39

MUZECHKA, MIKE   D   ISLANDERS

PERSONAL: Born February 1, 1978, in Edmonton. ... 6-2/200. ... Shoots left.
TRANSACTIONS/CAREER NOTES: Selected by New York Islanders in ninth round (10th Islanders choice, 218th overall) of NHL entry draft (June 22, 1996).

			REGULAR SEASON								PLAYOFFS				
Season Team	League	Gms.	G	A	Pts.	PIM	+/-	PP	SH		Gms.	G	A	Pts.	PIM
95-96— Calgary	WHL	69	1	8	9	91	...	...	...		—	—	—	—	—
96-97— Portland	WHL	65	1	8	9	74	...	...	...		6	1	1	2	4

MUZZATTI, JASON   G   HURRICANES

PERSONAL: Born February 3, 1970, in Toronto. ... 6-2/214. ... Catches left. ... Full name: Jason Mark Muzzatti. ... Name pronounced moo-ZAH-tee.
COLLEGE: Michigan State.
TRANSACTIONS/CAREER NOTES: Selected by Calgary Flames in first round (first Flames pick, 21st overall) of NHL entry draft (June 11, 1988). ... Loaned to Indianapolis Ice of IHL (January 11, 1993). ... Suffered from the flu (November 4, 1993); missed four games. ... Claimed on waivers by Hartford Whalers (June 1995). ... Whalers franchise moved to North Carolina and renamed Carolina Hurricanes for 1997-98 season; NHL approved move on June 25, 1997.
HONORS: Named to CCHA All-Star second team (1987-88). ... Named to NCAA All-America West second team (1989-90). ... Named to CCHA All-Star first team (1989-90). ... Named to CCHA All-Tournament team (1989-90).

			REGULAR SEASON								PLAYOFFS					
Season Team	League	Gms.	Min	W	L	T	GA	SO	Avg.		Gms.	Min.	W	L	GA	SO	Avg.
86-87— St. Mikes Jr. B	MTHL	20	1054	...	...	...	69	1	3.93		—	—	—	—	—	—	—
87-88— Michigan State	CCHA	33	1916	19	9	3	109	1	3.41		—	—	—	—	—	—	—
88-89— Michigan State	CCHA	42	2515	32	9	1	127	3	3.03		—	—	—	—	—	—	—
89-90— Michigan State	CCHA	33	1976	24	6	0	99	0	3.01		—	—	—	—	—	—	—
90-91— Michigan State	CCHA	22	1204	8	10	2	75	0	3.74		—	—	—	—	—	—	—
91-92— Salt Lake City	IHL	52	3033	24	22	‡5	167	2	3.30		4	247	1	3	18	0	4.37
92-93— Salt Lake City	IHL	13	747	5	6	‡0	52	0	4.18		—	—	—	—	—	—	—
—Canadian nat'l team	Int'l	16	880	6	9	0	53	0	3.61		—	—	—	—	—	—	—
—Indianapolis	IHL	12	707	5	6	‡0	48	0	4.07		—	—	—	—	—	—	—
93-94— Calgary	NHL	1	60	0	1	0	8	0	8.00		—	—	—	—	—	—	—
—Saint John	AHL	51	2939	26	21	3	183	2	3.74		7	415	3	4	19	0	2.75
94-95— Saint John	AHL	31	1741	10	14	4	101	2	3.48		—	—	—	—	—	—	—
—Calgary	NHL	1	10	0	0	0	0	0	0.00		—	—	—	—	—	—	—
95-96— Springfield	AHL	5	300	4	0	1	12	1	2.40		—	—	—	—	—	—	—
—Hartford	NHL	22	1013	4	8	3	49	1	2.90		—	—	—	—	—	—	—
96-97— Hartford	NHL	31	1591	9	13	5	91	0	3.43		—	—	—	—	—	—	—
NHL totals (4 years)		55	2674	13	22	8	148	1	3.32								

MYHRES, BRANTT   RW   OILERS

PERSONAL: Born March 18, 1974, in Edmonton. ... 6-3/220. ... Shoots right. ... Name pronounced MIGHRS.
HIGH SCHOOL: Sir Winston Churchill (Calgary).

TRANSACTIONS/CAREER NOTES: Selected by Tampa Bay Lightning in fifth round (fifth Lightning pick, 97th overall) of NHL entry draft (June 20, 1992). ... Injured shoulder (April 11, 1995); missed one game. ... Injured hip (February 1, 1997); missed one game. ... Sprained ankle (February 23, 1997); missed three games. ... Suffered from the flu (April 4, 1997); missed three games. ... Traded by Lightning with conditional draft pick to Edmonton Oilers for C Vladimir Vujtek (July 16, 1997).

		REGULAR SEASON								PLAYOFFS				
Season Team	League	Gms.	G	A	Pts.	PIM	+/-	PP	SH	Gms.	G	A	Pts.	PIM
90-91— Portland	WHL	59	2	7	9	125	...	...	...	—	—	—	—	—
91-92— Portland	WHL	4	0	2	2	22	...	...	...	—	—	—	—	—
— Lethbridge	WHL	53	4	11	15	359	...	...	...	5	0	0	0	36
92-93— Lethbridge	WHL	64	13	35	48	277	...	...	...	3	0	0	0	11
93-94— Atlanta	IHL	2	0	0	0	17	...	...	...	—	—	—	—	—
— Lethbridge	WHL	34	10	21	31	103	...	...	...	—	—	—	—	—
— Spokane	WHL	27	10	22	32	139	...	...	...	3	1	4	5	7
94-95— Atlanta	NHL	40	5	5	10	213	...	...	...	—	—	—	—	—
— Tampa Bay	NHL	15	2	0	2	81	-2	0	0	—	—	—	—	—
95-96— Atlanta	IHL	12	0	2	2	58	...	...	...	—	—	—	—	—
96-97— San Antonio	IHL	12	0	0	0	98	...	...	...	—	—	—	—	—
— Tampa Bay	NHL	47	3	1	4	136	1	0	0	—	—	—	—	—
NHL totals (2 years)		102	10	6	16	430	-1	0	0					

MYRVOLD, ANDERS   D   BRUINS

PERSONAL: Born August 12, 1975, in Lorenskog, Norway. ... 6-2/200. ... Shoots left. ... Name pronounced MIHR-vohld.
TRANSACTIONS/CAREER NOTES: Selected by Quebec Nordiques in fifth round (sixth Nordiques pick, 127th overall) of NHL entry draft (June 26, 1993). ... Nordiques franchise moved to Colorado and renamed Avalanche for 1995-96 season (June 21, 1995). ... Traded by Avalanche with RW Landon Wilson to Boston Bruins for first-round pick in 1998 draft (November 22, 1996).
HONORS: Named to Can.HL All-Rookie team (1994-95).

		REGULAR SEASON								PLAYOFFS				
Season Team	League	Gms.	G	A	Pts.	PIM	+/-	PP	SH	Gms.	G	A	Pts.	PIM
92-93— Farjestad Karlstad	Sweden	2	0	0	0	0	...	...	...	—	—	—	—	—
93-94— Grums	Swed. Div. II	24	1	0	1	59	...	...	...	—	—	—	—	—
94-95— Laval	QMJHL	64	14	50	64	173	...	...	...	20	4	10	14	68
— Cornwall	AHL	—	—	—	—	—	...	...	...	3	0	1	1	2
95-96— Colorado	NHL	4	0	1	1	6	-2	0	0	—	—	—	—	—
— Cornwall	AHL	70	5	24	29	125	...	...	...	5	1	0	1	19
96-97— Hershey	AHL	20	0	3	3	16	...	...	...	—	—	—	—	—
— Providence	AHL	53	6	15	21	107	...	...	...	10	0	1	1	6
— Boston	NHL	9	0	2	2	4	-1	0	0	—	—	—	—	—
NHL totals (2 years)		13	0	3	3	10	-3	0	0					

NABOKOV, DIMITRI   C/LW   BLACKHAWKS

PERSONAL: Born January 4, 1977, in Novosibirsk, U.S.S.R. ... 6-2/209. ... Shoots right.
TRANSACTIONS/CAREER NOTES: Selected by Chicago Blackhawks in first round (first Blackhawks pick, 19th overall) of NHL entry draft (July 8, 1995).
HONORS: Named to WHL (East) All-Star second team (1996-97).

		REGULAR SEASON								PLAYOFFS				
Season Team	League	Gms.	G	A	Pts.	PIM	+/-	PP	SH	Gms.	G	A	Pts.	PIM
93-94— Soviet Wings	CIS	17	0	2	2	6	...	...	...	3	0	0	0	0
94-95— Soviet Wings	CIS	49	15	12	27	32	...	...	...	4	5	0	5	6
95-96— Soviet Wings	CIS	50	12	14	26	51	...	...	...	—	—	—	—	—
96-97— Regina	WHL	50	39	56	95	61	...	...	...	5	2	3	5	2
— Soviet Wings	Russian	1	0	0	0	0	...	...	...	—	—	—	—	—

NABOKOV, YEVGENY   G   SHARKS

PERSONAL: Born July 25, 1975, in Ust-Kamenogorsk, U.S.S.R. ... 6-0/180. ... Catches left. ... Name pronounced ehv-GEH-nee.
TRANSACTIONS/CAREER NOTES: Selected by San Jose Sharks in ninth round (ninth Sharks pick, 219th overall) of NHL entry draft (June 29, 1994).

		REGULAR SEASON							PLAYOFFS					
Season Team	League	Gms.	Min	W	L	T	GA	SO	Avg.	Gms.	Min.	W	L	GA	SO	Avg.
92-93— Torpedo Ust-Kam.	CIS	4	109	...	...	...	5	...	2.75	—	—	—	—	—	—	—
93-94— Torpedo Ust-Kam.	CIS	11	539	...	...	...	29	0	3.23	—	—	—	—	—	—	—
94-95— Dynamo Moscow	CIS	37	2075	...	...	...	70	...	2.02	—	—	—	—	—	—	—
95-96— Dynamo Moscow	CIS	37	1948	...	...	...	70	...	2.16	6	298	...	...	7	...	1.41
96-97— Dynamo Moscow	Russian	27	1588	...	...	...	56	2	2.11	4	245	...	...	12	0	2.82

NAMESTNIKOV, JOHN   D   CANUCKS

PERSONAL: Born October 9, 1971, in Novgorod, U.S.S.R. ... 5-11/190. ... Shoots right. ... Name pronounced nuh-MEHZ-nih-kahf.
TRANSACTIONS/CAREER NOTES: Selected by Vancouver Canucks in sixth round (fifth Canucks pick, 117th overall) of NHL entry draft (June 22, 1991). ... Sprained ankle (May 7, 1995); missed 10 playoff games.

		REGULAR SEASON								PLAYOFFS				
Season Team	League	Gms.	G	A	Pts.	PIM	+/-	PP	SH	Gms.	G	A	Pts.	PIM
88-89— Torpedo Gorky	USSR	2	0	0	0	2	...	...	...	—	—	—	—	—
89-90— Torpedo Gorky	USSR	23	0	0	0	25	...	...	...	—	—	—	—	—

Season Team	League	REGULAR SEASON								PLAYOFFS				
		Gms.	G	A	Pts.	PIM	+/-	PP	SH	Gms.	G	A	Pts.	PIM
90-91— Torp. Nizhny Nov.	USSR	45	1	2	3	49	...	...	...	—	—	—	—	—
91-92— CSKA Moscow..........	CIS	42	1	1	2	47	...	...	...	—	—	—	—	—
92-93— CSKA Moscow..........	CIS	42	5	5	10	68	...	...	...	—	—	—	—	—
93-94— Hamilton..............	AHL	59	7	27	34	97	...	...	...	4	0	2	2	19
—Vancouver................	NHL	17	0	5	5	10	-2	0	0	—	—	—	—	—
94-95— Syracuse..............	AHL	59	11	22	33	59	...	...	...	—	—	—	—	—
—Syracuse................	NHL	16	0	3	3	4	2	0	0	1	0	0	0	2
95-96— Syracuse..............	AHL	59	13	34	47	85	...	...	...	15	1	8	9	16
—Vancouver................	NHL	—	—	—	—	—				1	0	0	0	0
96-97— Syracuse..............	AHL	55	9	37	46	73	...	...	...	3	2	0	2	0
—Vancouver................	NHL	2	0	0	0	4	-1	0	0	—	—	—	—	—
NHL totals (4 years)		35	0	8	8	18	-1	0	0	2	0	0	0	2

NASH, TYSON   LW   CANUCKS

PERSONAL: Born March 11, 1975, in Edmonton. ... 6-0/180. ... Shoots left.
TRANSACTIONS/CAREER NOTES: Selected by Vancouver Canucks in 10th round (eighth Canucks pick, 247th overall) of NHL entry draft (June 29, 1994).

Season Team	League	REGULAR SEASON								PLAYOFFS				
		Gms.	G	A	Pts.	PIM	+/-	PP	SH	Gms.	G	A	Pts.	PIM
90-91— Kamloops..................	WHL	3	0	0	0	0	...	...	...	—	—	—	—	—
91-92— Kamloops..................	WHL	33	1	6	7	32	...	...	...	4	0	0	0	0
92-93— Kamloops..................	WHL	61	10	16	26	78	...	...	...	13	3	2	5	32
93-94— Kamloops..................	WHL	65	20	36	56	137	...	...	...	16	3	3	6	12
94-95— Kamloops..................	WHL	63	34	41	75	70	...	...	...	21	10	7	17	30
95-96— Syracuse..................	AHL	50	4	7	11	58	...	...	...	4	0	0	0	11
—Raleigh..................	ECHL	6	1	1	2	8	...	...	...	—	—	—	—	—
96-97— Syracuse..................	AHL	77	17	17	34	105	...	...	...	3	0	2	2	0

NASLUND, MARKUS   LW   CANUCKS

PERSONAL: Born July 30, 1973, in Harnosand, Sweden. ... 5-11/185. ... Shoots left. ... Name pronounced NAZ-luhnd.
TRANSACTIONS/CAREER NOTES: Selected by Pittsburgh Penguins in first round (first Penguins pick, 16th overall) of NHL entry draft (June 22, 1991). ... Traded by Penguins to Vancouver Canucks for LW Alex Stojanov (March 20, 1996). ... Suffered from the flu (November 26, 1996); missed one game.
STATISTICAL PLATEAUS: Three-goal games: 1995-96 (1).

Season Team	League	REGULAR SEASON								PLAYOFFS				
		Gms.	G	A	Pts.	PIM	+/-	PP	SH	Gms.	G	A	Pts.	PIM
89-90— MoDo Hockey Jrs.	Sweden Jr.	33	43	35	78	20	...	...	...	—	—	—	—	—
90-91— MoDo Ornskoldvik.....	Sweden	32	10	9	19	14	...	...	...	—	—	—	—	—
91-92— MoDo Ornskoldvik.....	Sweden	39	22	18	40	54	...	...	...	—	—	—	—	—
92-93— MoDo Ornskoldvik.....	Sweden	39	22	17	39	67	...	...	...	3	3	2	5	0
93-94— Pittsburgh..............	NHL	71	4	7	11	27	-3	1	0	—	—	—	—	—
—Cleveland	IHL	5	1	6	7	4	...	...	...	—	—	—	—	—
94-95— Pittsburgh..............	NHL	14	2	2	4	2	0	0	0	—	—	—	—	—
—Cleveland	IHL	7	3	4	7	6	...	...	...	4	1	3	4	8
95-96— Pittsburgh..............	NHL	66	19	33	52	36	17	3	0	—	—	—	—	—
—Vancouver................	NHL	10	3	0	3	6	1	0	0	6	1	2	3	8
96-97— Vancouver................	NHL	78	21	20	41	30	-15	4	0	—	—	—	—	—
NHL totals (4 years)		239	49	62	111	101	2	9	0	6	1	2	3	8

NAUD, ERIC   LW   BRUINS

PERSONAL: Born October 2, 1977, in La Sarre, Que. ... 6-1/187. ... Shoots left. ... Name pronounced NOHD.
TRANSACTIONS/CAREER NOTES: Selected by Boston Bruins in third round (third Bruins pick, 53rd overall) of NHL entry draft (June 22, 1996).

Season Team	League	REGULAR SEASON								PLAYOFFS				
		Gms.	G	A	Pts.	PIM	+/-	PP	SH	Gms.	G	A	Pts.	PIM
95-96— St. Hyacinthe	QMJHL	63	11	21	32	230	...	...	...	12	1	2	3	19
96-97— Rouyn-Noranda	QMJHL	34	8	11	19	147	...	...	...	—	—	—	—	—
—Hull..........................	QMJHL	2	0	0	0	15	...	...	...	12	4	2	6	63

NAUMENKO, NICK   D   BLUES

PERSONAL: Born July 7, 1974, in Chicago. ... 5-11/180. ... Shoots right. ... Name pronounced nah-MEHN-koh.
COLLEGE: North Dakota.
TRANSACTIONS/CAREER NOTES: Selected by St. Louis Blues in eighth round (ninth Blues pick, 182nd overall) of NHL entry draft (June 20, 1992).
HONORS: Named to WCHA All-Star first team (1994-95). ... Named to WCHA All-Star first team (1995-96).

Season Team	League	REGULAR SEASON								PLAYOFFS				
		Gms.	G	A	Pts.	PIM	+/-	PP	SH	Gms.	G	A	Pts.	PIM
91-92— Dubuque	USHL	24	6	19	25	4	...	...	...	—	—	—	—	—
92-93— North Dakota	WCHA	38	10	24	34	26	...	...	...	—	—	—	—	—
93-94— North Dakota	WCHA	32	4	22	26	22	...	...	...	—	—	—	—	—
94-95— North Dakota	WCHA	39	13	26	39	78	...	...	...	—	—	—	—	—
95-96— North Dakota	WCHA	37	11	30	41	52	...	...	...	—	—	—	—	—
96-97— Worcester	AHL	54	6	22	28	72	...	...	...	1	0	0	0	0

NAZAROV, ANDREI — LW — SHARKS

PERSONAL: Born March 21, 1972, in Chelyabinsk, U.S.S.R. ... 6-5/230. ... Shoots right. ... Name pronounced nuh-ZAH-rahv.
TRANSACTIONS/CAREER NOTES: Selected by San Jose Sharks in first round (second Sharks pick, 10th overall) of NHL entry draft (June 20, 1992). ... Suspended four games and fined $500 by NHL for head-butting (March 8, 1995). ... Suffered facial fracture (February 5, 1997); missed 14 games. ... Suspended 13 games by NHL for physical abuse of officials (March 25, 1997).

Season Team	League		REGULAR SEASON									PLAYOFFS			
		Gms.	G	A	Pts.	PIM	+/-	PP	SH		Gms.	G	A	Pts.	PIM
90-91— Mechel Chelyabinsk...	USSR	2	0	0	0	0	...	...	...		—	—	—	—	—
91-92— Dynamo Moscow......	CIS	2	1	0	1	2	...	...	...		—	—	—	—	—
92-93— Dynamo Moscow......	CIS	42	8	2	10	79	...	...	...		10	1	1	2	8
93-94— Kansas City..............	IHL	71	15	18	33	64	...	...	...		—	—	—	—	—
— San Jose..................	NHL	1	0	0	0	0	0	0	0		—	—	—	—	—
94-95— Kansas City..............	IHL	43	15	10	25	55	...	...	...		—	—	—	—	—
— San Jose..................	NHL	26	3	5	8	94	-1	0	0		6	0	0	0	9
95-96— San Jose..................	NHL	42	7	7	14	62	-15	2	0		—	—	—	—	—
— Kansas City..............	IHL	27	4	6	10	118	...	...	...		2	0	0	0	2
96-97— San Jose..................	NHL	60	12	15	27	222	-4	1	0		—	—	—	—	—
— Kentucky..................	AHL	3	1	2	3	4	...	...	...		—	—	—	—	—
NHL totals (4 years)		129	22	27	49	378	-20	3	0		6	0	0	0	9

NDUR, RUMUN — D — SABRES

PERSONAL: Born July 7, 1975, in Zaria, Nigeria. ... 6-2/200. ... Shoots left. ... Name pronounced ruh-MOHN EHN-duhr.
HIGH SCHOOL: Bishop MacDonnell (Guelph, Ont.).
TRANSACTIONS/CAREER NOTES: Selected by Buffalo Sabres in third round (third Sabres pick, 69th overall) of NHL entry draft (June 29, 1994).

Season Team	League		REGULAR SEASON									PLAYOFFS			
		Gms.	G	A	Pts.	PIM	+/-	PP	SH		Gms.	G	A	Pts.	PIM
91-92— Clearwater..................	Jr. C	4	0	4	4	4	...	...	...		—	—	—	—	—
— Sarnia	Jr. B	30	2	5	7	46	...	...	...		—	—	—	—	—
92-93— Guelph	Jr. B	24	7	8	15	202	...	...	...		—	—	—	—	—
— Guelph	OHL	22	1	3	4	30	...	...	...		4	0	1	1	4
93-94— Guelph	OHL	61	6	33	39	176	...	...	...		9	4	1	5	24
94-95— Guelph	OHL	63	10	21	31	187	...	...	...		14	0	4	4	28
95-96— Rochester	AHL	73	2	12	14	306	...	...	...		17	1	2	3	33
96-97— Rochester	AHL	68	5	11	16	282	...	...	...		10	3	1	4	21
— Buffalo	NHL	2	0	0	0	2	1	0	0		—	—	—	—	—
NHL totals (1 year)		2	0	0	0	2	1	0	0						

NECKAR, STANISLAV — D — SENATORS

PERSONAL: Born December 22, 1975, in Ceske Budejovice, Czechoslovakia. ... 6-1/212. ... Shoots left. ... Name pronounced NEHTS-kash.
TRANSACTIONS/CAREER NOTES: Selected by Ottawa Senators in second round (second Senators pick, 29th overall) of NHL entry draft (June 28, 1994). ... Partially tore knee ligament (October 18, 1996); missed remainder of season.

Season Team	League		REGULAR SEASON									PLAYOFFS			
		Gms.	G	A	Pts.	PIM	+/-	PP	SH		Gms.	G	A	Pts.	PIM
91-92— Budejovice	Czech Div. II	18	1	3	4	...	...	...	...		—	—	—	—	—
92-93— Motor Ceske-Bude....	Czech.	42	2	9	11	12	...	...	...		—	—	—	—	—
93-94— HC Ceske Bude.	Czech Rep.	12	3	2	5	2	...	...	...		3	0	0	0	0
94-95— Detroit......................	IHL	15	2	2	4	15	...	...	...		—	—	—	—	—
— Ottawa	NHL	48	1	3	4	37	-20	0	0		—	—	—	—	—
95-96— Ottawa	NHL	82	3	9	12	54	-16	1	0		—	—	—	—	—
96-97— Ottawa	NHL	5	0	0	0	2	2	0	0		—	—	—	—	—
NHL totals (3 years)		135	4	12	16	93	-34	1	0						

N

NEDVED, PETR — C — PENGUINS

PERSONAL: Born December 9, 1971, in Liberec, Czechoslovakia. ... 6-3/195. ... Shoots left. ... Name pronounced NEHD-vehd.
TRANSACTIONS/CAREER NOTES: Defected from Czechoslovakia to Canada when Czechoslovakian midget team was playing in Calgary (January 1989). ... WHL rights traded by Moose Jaw Warriors with D Brian Ilkuf to Seattle Thunderbirds for D Corey Beaulieu (February 3, 1989). ... Selected by Vancouver Canucks in first round (first Canucks pick, second overall) of NHL entry draft (June 16, 1990). ... Signed as free agent by St. Louis Blues (March 4, 1994). ... C Craig Janney and second-round pick (C Dave Scatchard) in 1994 draft awarded to Canucks as compensation (March 14, 1994). ... Traded by Blues to New York Rangers for LW Esa Tikkanen and D Doug Lidster (July 24, 1994); trade arranged as compensation for Blues signing coach Mike Keenan. ... Strained abdomen (February 27, 1995); missed two games. ... Traded by Rangers with D Sergei Zubov to Pittsburgh Penguins for LW Luc Robitaille and D Ulf Samuelsson (August 31, 1995). ... Bruised thigh (November 18, 1995); missed two games. ... Bruised tailbone (December 19, 1996); missed two games. ... Sprained wrist (January 14, 1997); missed two games. ... Suffered charley horse (February 8, 1997); missed one game. ... Sprained wrist (March 20, 1997); missed three games.
HONORS: Won Can.HL Rookie of the Year Award (1989-90). ... Won Jim Piggott Memorial Trophy (1989-90).
STATISTICAL PLATEAUS: Four-goal games: 1995-96 (1).
MISCELLANEOUS: Member of silver-medal-winning Canadian Olympic team (1994).

Season Team	League		REGULAR SEASON									PLAYOFFS			
		Gms.	G	A	Pts.	PIM	+/-	PP	SH		Gms.	G	A	Pts.	PIM
88-89— Litvinov......................	Czech. Jrs.	20	32	19	51	12	...	...	...		—	—	—	—	—
89-90— Seattle......................	WHL	71	65	80	145	80	...	...	...		11	4	9	13	2

Season Team	League	REGULAR SEASON							PLAYOFFS				
		Gms.	G	A	Pts.	PIM	+/-	PP	SH	Gms.	G	A	Pts.	PIM
90-91 — Vancouver	NHL	61	10	6	16	20	-21	1	0	6	0	1	1	0
91-92 — Vancouver	NHL	77	15	22	37	36	-3	5	0	10	1	4	5	16
92-93 — Vancouver	NHL	84	38	33	71	96	20	2	1	12	2	3	5	2
93-94 — Canadian nat'l team	Int'l	17	19	12	31	16	...	...	...	—	—	—	—	—
— Can. Olympic team	Int'l	8	5	1	6	6	...	...	...	—	—	—	—	—
— St. Louis	NHL	19	6	14	20	8	2	2	0	4	0	1	1	4
94-95 — New York Rangers	NHL	46	11	12	23	26	-1	1	0	10	3	2	5	6
95-96 — Pittsburgh	NHL	80	45	54	99	68	37	8	1	18	10	10	20	16
96-97 — Pittsburgh	NHL	74	33	38	71	66	-2	12	3	5	1	2	3	12
NHL totals (7 years)		441	158	179	337	320	32	31	5	65	17	23	40	56

NEDVED, ZDENEK   RW   MAPLE LEAFS

PERSONAL: Born March 3, 1975, in Lany, Czechoslovakia. ... 6-0/180. ... Shoots left. ... Name pronounced NEHD-vehd.

TRANSACTIONS/CAREER NOTES: Selected by Toronto Maple Leafs in fifth round (third Maple Leafs pick, 123rd overall) of NHL entry draft (June 26, 1993).

Season Team	League	REGULAR SEASON							PLAYOFFS				
		Gms.	G	A	Pts.	PIM	+/-	PP	SH	Gms.	G	A	Pts.	PIM
91-92 — PZ Kladno	Czech.	19	15	12	27	22	...	...	...	—	—	—	—	—
92-93 — Sudbury	OHL	18	3	9	12	6	...	...	...	—	—	—	—	—
93-94 — Sudbury	OHL	60	50	50	100	42	...	...	...	10	7	8	15	10
94-95 — Sudbury	OHL	59	47	51	98	36	...	...	...	18	12	16	28	16
— Toronto	NHL	1	0	0	0	2	0	0	0	—	—	—	—	—
95-96 — Toronto	NHL	7	1	1	2	6	-1	0	0	—	—	—	—	—
— St. John's	AHL	41	13	14	27	22	...	...	...	4	2	0	2	0
96-97 — St. John's	AHL	51	9	25	34	34	...	...	...	7	2	2	4	6
— Toronto	NHL	23	3	5	8	6	4	1	0	—	—	—	—	—
NHL totals (3 years)		31	4	6	10	14	3	1	0					

NELSON, JEFF   C

PERSONAL: Born December 18, 1972, in Prince Albert, Sask. ... 6-0/190. ... Shoots left. ... Full name: Jeffrey Arthur Nelson. ... Brother of Todd Nelson, defenseman in Washington Capitals system.

TRANSACTIONS/CAREER NOTES: Selected by Washington Capitals in second round (fourth Capitals pick, 36th overall) of NHL entry draft (June 22, 1991). ... Signed as free agent by Grand Rapids of IHL (September 9, 1996).

HONORS: Won Can.HL Scholastic Player of the Year Award (1988-89 and 1989-90). ... Named WHL Scholastic Player of the Year (1988-89 and 1989-90). ... Named WHL (East) Player of the Year (1990-91). ... Named to WHL All-Star second team (1990-91). ... Named to WHL (East) All-Star second team (1991-92).

Season Team	League	REGULAR SEASON							PLAYOFFS				
		Gms.	G	A	Pts.	PIM	+/-	PP	SH	Gms.	G	A	Pts.	PIM
88-89 — Prince Albert	WHL	71	30	57	87	74	...	...	...	4	0	3	3	4
89-90 — Prince Albert	WHL	72	28	69	97	79	...	...	...	14	2	11	13	10
90-91 — Prince Albert	WHL	72	46	74	120	58	...	...	...	3	1	1	2	4
91-92 — Prince Albert	WHL	64	48	65	113	84	...	...	...	9	7	14	21	18
92-93 — Baltimore	AHL	72	14	38	52	12	...	...	...	7	1	3	4	2
93-94 — Portland	AHL	80	34	73	107	92	...	...	...	17	10	5	15	20
94-95 — Portland	AHL	64	33	50	83	57	...	...	...	7	1	4	5	8
— Washington	NHL	10	1	0	1	2	-2	0	0	—	—	—	—	—
95-96 — Portland	AHL	39	15	32	47	62	...	...	...	—	—	—	—	—
— Washington	NHL	33	0	7	7	16	3	0	0	3	0	0	0	4
96-97 — Grand Rapids	IHL	82	34	55	89	85	...	...	...	5	0	4	4	4
NHL totals (2 years)		43	1	7	8	18	1	0	0	3	0	0	0	4

NEMCHINOV, SERGEI   C   ISLANDERS

PERSONAL: Born January 14, 1964, in Moscow, U.S.S.R. ... 6-0/205. ... Shoots left. ... Name pronounced SAIR-gay nehm-CHEE-nahf.

TRANSACTIONS/CAREER NOTES: Selected by New York Rangers in 12th round (14th Rangers pick, 244th overall) of NHL entry draft (June 16, 1990). ... Sprained knee (November 4, 1991); missed seven games. ... Strained buttocks (April 4, 1993); missed three games. ... Suspended eight games and fined $500 by NHL for hitting another player (March 16, 1994). ... Bruised Achilles' tendon (January 30, 1995); missed one game. ... Suffered mild concussion (December 13, 1995); missed one game. ... Bruised elbow (April 7, 1996); missed two games. ... Traded by Rangers with RW Brian Noonan to Vancouver Canucks for LW Esa Tikkanen and RW Russ Courtnall (March 8, 1997). ... Strained rib muscle (February 28, 1997); missed 11 games. ... Injured foot (April 4, 1997); missed three games. ... Signed as free agent by New York Islanders (July 2, 1997).

STATISTICAL PLATEAUS: Three-goal games: 1992-93 (1).

MISCELLANEOUS: Member of Stanley Cup championship team (1994).

Season Team	League	REGULAR SEASON							PLAYOFFS				
		Gms.	G	A	Pts.	PIM	+/-	PP	SH	Gms.	G	A	Pts.	PIM
81-82 — Soviet Wings	USSR	15	1	0	1	0	...	...	...	—	—	—	—	—
82-83 — CSKA Moscow	USSR	11	0	0	0	2	...	...	...	—	—	—	—	—
83-84 — CSKA Moscow	USSR	20	6	5	11	4	...	...	...	—	—	—	—	—
84-85 — CSKA Moscow	USSR	31	2	4	6	4	...	...	...	—	—	—	—	—
85-86 — Soviet Wings	USSR	39	7	12	19	28	...	...	...	—	—	—	—	—
86-87 — Soviet Wings	USSR	40	13	9	22	24	...	...	...	—	—	—	—	—
87-88 — Soviet Wings	USSR	48	17	11	28	26	...	...	...	—	—	—	—	—
88-89 — Soviet Wings	USSR	43	15	14	29	28	...	...	...	—	—	—	—	—
89-90 — Soviet Wings	USSR	48	17	16	33	34	...	...	...	—	—	—	—	—

N

Season Team	League	REGULAR SEASON								PLAYOFFS				
		Gms.	G	A	Pts.	PIM	+/-	PP	SH	Gms.	G	A	Pts.	PIM
90-91— Soviet Wings	USSR	46	21	24	45	30	...			—	—	—	—	—
91-92— New York Rangers	NHL	73	30	28	58	15	19	2	0	13	1	4	5	8
92-93— New York Rangers	NHL	81	23	31	54	34	15	0	1	—	—	—	—	—
93-94— New York Rangers	NHL	76	22	27	49	36	13	4	0	23	2	5	7	6
94-95— New York Rangers	NHL	47	7	6	13	16	-6	0	0	10	4	5	9	2
95-96— New York Rangers	NHL	78	17	15	32	38	9	0	0	6	0	1	1	2
96-97— New York Rangers	NHL	63	6	13	19	12	5	1	0	—	—	—	—	—
— Vancouver.................	NHL	6	2	3	5	4	4	0	0	—	—	—	—	—
NHL totals (6 years)		424	107	123	230	155	59	7	1	52	7	15	22	18

NEMECEK, JAN   D   KINGS

PERSONAL: Born February 14, 1976, in Pisek, Czechoslovakia. ... 6-1/194. ... Shoots right. ... Name pronounced YAHN NEHM-ih-chehk.
TRANSACTIONS/CAREER NOTES: Selected by Los Angeles Kings in ninth round (seventh Kings pick, 215th overall) of NHL entry draft (June 29, 1994).
HONORS: Named to QMJHL All-Star second team (1995-96).

Season Team	League	REGULAR SEASON								PLAYOFFS				
		Gms.	G	A	Pts.	PIM	+/-	PP	SH	Gms.	G	A	Pts.	PIM
92-93— Budejovice	Czech.	15	0	0	0	...	...	...	...	—	—	—	—	—
93-94— Budejovice	Czech.	16	0	1	1	16	...	...	...	—	—	—	—	—
94-95— Hull	QMJHL	49	10	16	26	48	...	...	...	21	5	9	14	10
95-96— Hull	QMJHL	57	17	49	66	58	...	...	...	17	2	13	15	10
96-97— Phoenix....................	IHL	24	1	1	2	2	...	...	...	—	—	—	—	—
— Mississippi...................	ECHL	20	3	9	12	16	...	...	...	3	0	0	0	4

NEMIROVSKY, DAVID   RW   PANTHERS

PERSONAL: Born August 1, 1976, in Toronto. ... 6-1/192. ... Shoots right. ... Name pronounced nehm-uh-RAHV-skee.
TRANSACTIONS/CAREER NOTES: Selected by Florida Panthers in fourth round (fifth Panthers pick, 84th overall) of NHL entry draft (June 29, 1994).

Season Team	League	REGULAR SEASON								PLAYOFFS				
		Gms.	G	A	Pts.	PIM	+/-	PP	SH	Gms.	G	A	Pts.	PIM
91-92— Pickering-Weston	Jr. A	38	27	23	50	70	...	...	...	—	—	—	—	—
92-93— Weston-North York....	MTHL	40	19	23	42	27	...	...	...	—	—	—	—	—
93-94— Ottawa	OHL	64	21	31	52	18	...	...	...	17	10	10	20	2
94-95— Ottawa	OHL	59	27	29	56	25	...	...	...	—	—	—	—	—
95-96— Florida....................	NHL	9	0	2	2	2	-1	0	0	—	—	—	—	—
— Sarnia	OHL	26	18	27	45	14	...	...	...	10	8	8	16	6
— Carolina	AHL	5	1	2	3	0	...	...	...	—	—	—	—	—
96-97— Carolina	AHL	34	21	21	42	18	...	...	...	—	—	—	—	—
— Florida......................	NHL	39	7	7	14	32	1	1	0	3	1	0	1	0
NHL totals (2 years)		48	7	9	16	34	0	1	0	3	1	0	1	0

NICHOL, SCOTT   C   SABRES

PERSONAL: Born December 31, 1974, in Calgary. ... 5-8/160. ... Shoots right.
TRANSACTIONS/CAREER NOTES: Selected by Buffalo Sabres in 11th round (ninth Sabres pick, 272nd overall) of NHL entry draft (June 26, 1993).

Season Team	League	REGULAR SEASON								PLAYOFFS				
		Gms.	G	A	Pts.	PIM	+/-	PP	SH	Gms.	G	A	Pts.	PIM
92-93— Portland....................	WHL	67	31	33	64	146	...	...	...	—	—	—	—	—
93-94— Portland....................	WHL	65	40	53	93	144	...	...	...	—	—	—	—	—
94-95— Rochester	AHL	71	11	16	27	136	...	...	...	5	0	3	3	14
95-96— Rochester	AHL	62	14	17	31	170	...	...	...	19	7	6	13	36
— Buffalo	NHL	2	0	0	0	10	0	0	0	—	—	—	—	—
96-97— Rochester	AHL	68	22	21	43	133	...	...	...	10	2	1	3	26
NHL totals (1 year)		2	0	0	0	10	0	0	0					

N

NICHOLLS, BERNIE   C   SHARKS

PERSONAL: Born June 24, 1961, in Haliburton, Ont. ... 6-0/190. ... Shoots right. ... Full name: Bernard Irvine Nicholls.
TRANSACTIONS/CAREER NOTES: Selected by Los Angeles Kings as underage junior in fourth round (fourth Kings pick, 73rd overall) of NHL entry draft (June 11, 1980). ... Partially tore right knee ligament (November 18, 1982). ... Broke jaw (February 1984); missed two games. ... Fractured left index finger in three places (October 8, 1987). ... Traded by Kings to New York Rangers for RW Tomas Sandstrom and LW Tony Granato (January 20, 1990). ... Separated left shoulder (January 22, 1991); missed five games. ... Suspended three games by NHL for stick-swinging incident (February 14, 1991). ... Traded by Rangers with LW Louie DeBrusk, RW Steven Rice and future considerations to Edmonton Oilers for C Mark Messier and future considerations (October 4, 1991); Rangers traded D David Shaw to Oilers for D Jeff Beukeboom to complete the deal (November 12, 1991). ... Did not report to Oilers to be with his wife for the birth of their child (October 4, 1991); missed 27 games. ... Reported to Oilers (December 6, 1991). ... Strained abdominal muscle (February 16, 1992); missed two games. ... Suspended seven off-days and fined $500 by NHL for swinging stick in preseason game (October 13, 1992). ... Traded by Oilers to New Jersey Devils for C Kevin Todd and LW Zdeno Ciger (January 13, 1993). ... Fractured left foot (February 27, 1993); missed 13 games. ... Sprained left knee (December 4, 1993); missed nine games. ... Injured hand (April 10, 1994); missed one game. ... Suspended one game by NHL for cross-check to neck (May 21, 1994). ... Signed as free agent by Chicago Blackhawks (July 14, 1994). ... Bruised spleen (November 5, 1995); missed 23 games. ... Signed as free agent by San Jose Sharks (July 30, 1996). ... Suspended two games and fined $1,000 by NHL for deliberate-injury penalty (February 28, 1997). ... Underwent hernia surgery (March 11, 1997); missed final 15 games of regular season.

STATISTICAL PLATEAUS: Three-goal games: 1981-82 (3), 1983-84 (1), 1984-85 (1), 1985-86 (1), 1986-87 (1), 1987-88 (1), 1988-89 (4), 1993-94 (1), 1994-95 (1). Total: 14. ... Four-goal games: 1983-84 (1), 1984-85 (1), 1994-95 (2). Total: 4. ... Total hat tricks: 18.

Season Team	League	REGULAR SEASON								PLAYOFFS				
		Gms.	G	A	Pts.	PIM	+/-	PP	SH	Gms.	G	A	Pts.	PIM
78-79— Kingston	OMJHL	2	0	1	1	0	...	...	...	—	—	—	—	—
79-80— Kingston	OMJHL	68	36	43	79	85	...	...	...	3	1	0	1	10
80-81— Kingston	OMJHL	65	63	89	152	109	...	...	...	14	8	10	18	17
81-82— New Haven	AHL	55	41	30	71	31	...	...	...	—	—	—	—	—
— Los Angeles	NHL	22	14	18	32	27	2	8	1	10	4	0	4	23
82-83— Los Angeles	NHL	71	28	22	50	124	-23	12	0	—	—	—	—	—
83-84— Los Angeles	NHL	78	41	54	95	83	-21	8	4	—	—	—	—	—
84-85— Los Angeles	NHL	80	46	54	100	76	-4	15	0	3	1	1	2	9
85-86— Los Angeles	NHL	80	36	61	97	78	-5	10	4	—	—	—	—	—
86-87— Los Angeles	NHL	80	33	48	81	101	-16	10	1	5	2	5	7	6
87-88— Los Angeles	NHL	65	32	46	78	114	2	8	7	5	2	6	8	11
88-89— Los Angeles	NHL	79	70	80	150	96	30	21	8	11	7	9	16	12
89-90— Los Angeles	NHL	47	27	48	75	66	-6	8	0	—	—	—	—	—
— New York Rangers	NHL	32	12	25	37	20	-3	7	0	10	7	5	12	16
90-91— New York Rangers	NHL	71	25	48	73	96	5	8	0	5	4	3	7	8
91-92— New York Rangers	NHL	1	0	0	0	0	-1	0	0	—	—	—	—	—
— Edmonton	NHL	49	20	29	49	60	5	7	0	16	8	11	19	25
92-93— Edmonton	NHL	46	8	32	40	40	-16	4	0	—	—	—	—	—
— New Jersey	NHL	23	5	15	20	40	3	1	0	5	0	0	0	6
93-94— New Jersey	NHL	61	19	27	46	86	24	3	0	16	4	9	13	28
94-95— Chicago	NHL	48	22	29	51	32	4	11	2	16	1	11	12	8
95-96— Chicago	NHL	59	19	41	60	60	11	6	0	10	2	7	9	4
96-97— San Jose	NHL	65	12	33	45	63	-21	2	1	—	—	—	—	—
NHL totals (16 years)		1057	469	710	1179	1262	-30	149	28	112	42	67	109	156

NICKULAS, ERIC   C   BRUINS

PERSONAL: Born March 25, 1975, in Cape Cod, Mass. ... 5-11/190. ... Shoots right.
HIGH SCHOOL: Barnstable (Hyannis, Mass.), then Tabor (Marion, Mass.), then Cushing Academy (Ashburnham, Mass.).
COLLEGE: New Hampshire.
TRANSACTIONS/CAREER NOTES: Selected by Boston Bruins in fourth round (third Bruins pick, 99th overall) of NHL entry draft (June 29, 1994).

Season Team	League	REGULAR SEASON								PLAYOFFS				
		Gms.	G	A	Pts.	PIM	+/-	PP	SH	Gms.	G	A	Pts.	PIM
91-92— Barnstable	Mass. Jr. A	24	30	25	55		...	...	...	—	—	—	—	—
92-93— Tabor Academy	Mass. H.S.	28	25	25	50		...	...	...	—	—	—	—	—
93-94— Cushing Academy	Mass. H.S.	25	46	36	82		...	...	...	—	—	—	—	—
94-95— New Hampshire	Hockey East	33	15	9	24	32	...	...	...	—	—	—	—	—
95-96— New Hampshire	Hockey East	34	26	12	38	66	...	...	...	—	—	—	—	—
96-97— New Hampshire	Hockey East	39	29	22	51	80	...	...	...	—	—	—	—	—

NIECKAR, BARRY   LW   MIGHTY DUCKS

PERSONAL: Born December 16, 1967, in Rama, Sask. ... 6-3/205. ... Shoots left. ... Name pronounced NIGH-kahr.
TRANSACTIONS/CAREER NOTES: Signed as free agent by Hartford Whalers (September 1992). ... Signed as free agent by Calgary Flames (February 10, 1995). ... Signed as free agent by New York Islanders (July 25, 1995). ... Signed as free agent by Mighty Ducks of Anaheim (October 2, 1996).

Season Team	League	REGULAR SEASON								PLAYOFFS				
		Gms.	G	A	Pts.	PIM	+/-	PP	SH	Gms.	G	A	Pts.	PIM
91-92— Phoenix	IHL	5	0	0	0	9	...	...	...	—	—	—	—	—
— Raleigh	ECHL	46	10	18	28	229	...	...	...	4	4	0	4	22
92-93— Springfield	AHL	21	2	4	6	65	...	...	...	6	1	0	1	14
— Hartford	NHL	2	0	0	0	2	-2	0	0	—	—	—	—	—
93-94— Springfield	AHL	30	0	2	2	67	...	...	...	—	—	—	—	—
94-95— Saint John	AHL	65	8	7	15	*491	...	...	...	4	0	0	0	22
— Calgary	NHL	3	0	0	0	12	0	0	0	—	—	—	—	—
95-96— Utah	IHL	53	9	15	24	194	...	...	...	—	—	—	—	—
— Peoria	IHL	10	3	3	6	72	...	...	...	12	4	6	10	48
96-97— Long Beach	IHL	63	3	10	13	386	...	...	...	5	0	0	0	22
— Anaheim	NHL	2	0	0	0	5	0	0	0	—	—	—	—	—
NHL totals (3 years)		7	0	0	0	19	-2	0	0					

NIEDERMAYER, ROB   C   PANTHERS

PERSONAL: Born December 28, 1974, in Cassiar, B.C. ... 6-2/200. ... Shoots left. ... Name pronounced NEE-duhr-MIGH-uhr. ... Brother of Scott Niedermayer, defenseman, New Jersey Devils.
COLLEGE: Medicine Hat.
TRANSACTIONS/CAREER NOTES: Selected by Florida Panthers in first round (first Panthers pick, fifth overall) of NHL entry draft (June 26, 1993). ... Separated right shoulder (November 18, 1993); missed 17 games. ... Sprained knee ligament (November 22, 1996); missed 17 games. ... Strained groin (March 5, 1997); missed two games. ... Sprained wrist (March 20, 1997); missed three games.
HONORS: Won WHL Top Draft Prospect Award (1992-93). ... Named to WHL (East) All-Star first team (1992-93).
MISCELLANEOUS: Failed to score on a penalty shot (vs. Corey Hirsch, March 13, 1997).

Season Team	League	REGULAR SEASON								PLAYOFFS				
		Gms.	G	A	Pts.	PIM	+/-	PP	SH	Gms.	G	A	Pts.	PIM
90-91— Medicine Hat.............	WHL	71	24	26	50	8	...	...	...	12	3	7	10	2
91-92— Medicine Hat.............	WHL	71	32	46	78	77	...	...	...	4	2	3	5	2
92-93— Medicine Hat.............	WHL	52	43	34	77	67	...	...	...	—	—	—	—	—
93-94— Florida.....................	NHL	65	9	17	26	51	-11	3	0	—	—	—	—	—
94-95— Medicine Hat.............	WHL	13	9	15	24	14	...	...	...	—	—	—	—	—
— Florida.....................	NHL	48	4	6	10	36	-13	1	0	—	—	—	—	—
95-96— Florida.....................	NHL	82	26	35	61	107	1	11	0	22	5	3	8	12
96-97— Florida.....................	NHL	60	14	24	38	54	4	3	0	5	2	1	3	6
NHL totals (4 years)		255	53	82	135	248	-19	18	0	27	7	4	11	18

NIEDERMAYER, SCOTT D DEVILS

PERSONAL: Born August 31, 1973, in Edmonton. ... 6-0/200. ... Shoots left. ... Name pronounced NEE-duhr-MIGH-uhr. ... Brother of Rob Niedermayer, center, Florida Panthers.

TRANSACTIONS/CAREER NOTES: Stretched left knee ligaments (March 12, 1991); missed nine games. ... Selected by New Jersey Devils in first round (first Devils pick, third overall) of NHL entry draft (June 22, 1991). ... Suffered sore back (December 9, 1992); missed four games. ... Injured knee (December 19, 1995); missed three games. ... Strained groin (February 12, 1997); missed one game.

HONORS: Won Can.HL Scholastic Player of the Year Award (1990-91). ... Named WHL Scholastic Player of the Year (1990-91). ... Named to WHL (West) All-Star first team (1990-91 and 1991-92). ... Won Stafford Smythe Memorial Trophy (1991-92). ... Named to Can.HL All-Star first team (1991-92). ... Named to Memorial Cup All-Star team (1991-92). ... Named to NHL All-Rookie team (1992-93).

MISCELLANEOUS: Member of Stanley Cup championship team (1995). ... Failed to score on a penalty shot (vs. Ken Wregget, February 7, 1996).

Season Team	League	REGULAR SEASON								PLAYOFFS				
		Gms.	G	A	Pts.	PIM	+/-	PP	SH	Gms.	G	A	Pts.	PIM
89-90— Kamloops...................	WHL	64	14	55	69	64	...	...	...	17	2	14	16	35
90-91— Kamloops...................	WHL	57	26	56	82	52	...	...	...	—	—	—	—	—
91-92— New Jersey.................	NHL	4	0	1	1	2	1	0	0	—	—	—	—	—
— Kamloops...................	WHL	35	7	32	39	61	...	...	...	17	9	14	23	28
92-93— New Jersey.................	NHL	80	11	29	40	47	8	5	0	5	0	3	3	2
93-94— New Jersey.................	NHL	81	10	36	46	42	34	5	0	20	2	2	4	8
94-95— New Jersey.................	NHL	48	4	15	19	18	19	4	0	20	4	7	11	10
95-96— New Jersey.................	NHL	79	8	25	33	46	5	6	0	—	—	—	—	—
96-97— New Jersey.................	NHL	81	5	30	35	64	-4	3	0	10	2	4	6	6
NHL totals (6 years)		373	38	136	174	219	63	23	0	55	8	16	24	26

NIELSEN, JEFF RW RANGERS

PERSONAL: Born September 20, 1971, in Grand Rapids, Minn. ... 6-0/195. ... Shoots right. ... Full name: Jeffrey Michael Nielsen.

HIGH SCHOOL: Grand Rapids (Minn.).

COLLEGE: Minnesota.

TRANSACTIONS/CAREER NOTES: Selected by New York Rangers in fourth round (fourth Rangers pick, 69th overall) of NHL entry draft (June 16, 1990).

HONORS: Named to WCHA All-Star second team (1993-94).

Season Team	League	REGULAR SEASON								PLAYOFFS				
		Gms.	G	A	Pts.	PIM	+/-	PP	SH	Gms.	G	A	Pts.	PIM
87-88— Grand Rapids.............	Minn. H.S.	21	9	11	20	14	...	...	...	—	—	—	—	—
88-89— Grand Rapids.............	Minn. H.S.	25	13	17	30	26	...	...	...	—	—	—	—	—
89-90— Grand Rapids.............	Minn. H.S.	28	32	25	57		...	...	...	—	—	—	—	—
90-91— Univ. of Minnesota.....	WCHA	45	11	14	25	50	...	...	...	—	—	—	—	—
91-92— Univ. of Minnesota.....	WCHA	44	15	15	30	74	...	...	...	—	—	—	—	—
92-93— Univ. of Minnesota.....	WCHA	42	21	20	41	80	...	...	...	—	—	—	—	—
93-94— Univ. of Minnesota.....	WCHA	41	29	16	45	94	...	...	...	—	—	—	—	—
94-95— Binghamton	AHL	76	24	13	37	139	...	...	...	7	0	0	0	22
95-96— Binghamton	AHL	64	22	20	42	56	...	...	...	4	1	1	2	4
96-97— Binghamton	AHL	76	27	26	53	71	...	...	...	4	0	0	0	7
— New York Rangers.....	NHL	2	0	0	0	2	-1	0	0	—	—	—	—	—
NHL totals (1 year)		2	0	0	0	2	-1	0	0	—	—	—	—	—

NIEUWENDYK, JOE C STARS

PERSONAL: Born September 10, 1966, in Oshawa, Ont. ... 6-1/195. ... Shoots left. ... Name pronounced NOO-ihn-dighk. ... Cousin of Jeff Beukeboom, defenseman, New York Rangers.

COLLEGE: Cornell.

TRANSACTIONS/CAREER NOTES: Selected by Calgary Flames in second round (second Flames pick, 27th overall) of NHL entry draft (June 15, 1985). ... Suffered concussion (November 1987). ... Bruised ribs (May 25, 1989). ... Tore left knee ligament (April 17, 1990). ... Underwent arthroscopic knee surgery (September 28, 1991); missed 12 games. ... Suffered from the flu (November 19, 1992); missed one game. ... Strained right knee (March 26, 1993); missed four games. ... Suffered from charley horse (November 13, 1993); missed three games. ... Strained right knee ligaments (February 24, 1994); missed 17 games. ... Strained back (April 29, 1995); missed two games. ... Traded by Flames to Dallas Stars for C Corey Millen and rights to C/RW Jarome Iginla (December 19, 1995). ... Bruised chest (October 5, 1996); missed 12 games.

HONORS: Won Ivy League Rookie of the Year Trophy (1984-85). ... Named to NCAA All-America East first team (1985-86 and 1986-87). ... Named to ECAC All-Star first team (1985-86 and 1986-87). ... Named ECAC Player of the Year (1986-87). ... Named NHL Rookie of the Year by THE SPORTING NEWS (1987-88). ... Won Calder Memorial Trophy (1987-88). ... Won Dodge Ram Tough Award (1987-88). ... Named to NHL All-Rookie team (1987-88). ... Played in NHL All-Star Game (1988-1990 and 1994). ... Won King Clancy Trophy (1994-95).

RECORDS: Shares NHL single-game record for most goals in one period—4 (January 11, 1989).

STATISTICAL PLATEAUS: Three-goal games: 1987-88 (2), 1988-89 (1), 1989-90 (1), 1992-93 (1), 1993-94 (1), 1994-95 (1). Total: 7. ... Four-goal games: 1987-88 (2). ... Five-goal games: 1988-89 (1). ... Total hat tricks: 10.
MISCELLANEOUS: Member of Stanley Cup championship team (1989). ... Captain of Calgary Flames (1991-92 through 1994-95). ... Holds Calgary Flames all-time record for most goals (314). ... Scored on a penalty shot (vs. Steve Weeks, December 16, 1988). ... Failed to score on a penalty shot (vs. Jeff Reese, December 12, 1988; vs. Ken Wregget, January 23, 1993).
STATISTICAL NOTES: Third player in NHL history to score 50 goals in each of his first two seasons. ... Led NHL with 11 game-winning goals (1988-89).

Season Team	League	REGULAR SEASON Gms.	G	A	Pts.	PIM	+/-	PP	SH	PLAYOFFS Gms.	G	A	Pts.	PIM
83-84— Pickering Jr. B	MTHL	38	30	28	58	35	...	...	...	—	*	—	—	—
84-85— Cornell University	ECAC	23	18	21	39	20	...	...	...	—	—	—	—	—
85-86— Cornell University	ECAC	21	21	21	42	45	...	...	...	—	—	—	—	—
86-87— Cornell University	ECAC	23	26	26	52	26	...	...	...	—	—	—	—	—
— Calgary	NHL	9	5	1	6	0	0	2	0	6	2	2	4	0
87-88— Calgary	NHL	75	51	41	92	23	20	*31	3	8	3	4	7	2
88-89— Calgary	NHL	77	51	31	82	40	26	19	3	22	10	4	14	10
89-90— Calgary	NHL	79	45	50	95	40	32	18	0	6	4	6	10	4
90-91— Calgary	NHL	79	45	40	85	36	19	22	4	7	4	1	5	10
91-92— Calgary	NHL	69	22	34	56	55	-1	7	0	—	—	—	—	—
92-93— Calgary	NHL	79	38	37	75	52	9	14	0	6	3	6	9	10
93-94— Calgary	NHL	64	36	39	75	51	19	14	1	6	2	2	4	0
94-95— Calgary	NHL	46	21	29	50	33	11	3	0	5	4	3	7	0
95-96— Dallas	NHL	52	14	18	32	41	-17	8	0	—	—	—	—	—
96-97— Dallas	NHL	66	30	21	51	32	-5	8	0	7	2	2	4	6
NHL totals (11 years)		695	358	341	699	403	113	146	11	73	34	30	64	42

NIINIMAA, JANNE   D   FLYERS

PERSONAL: Born May 22, 1975, in Raahe, Finland. ... 6-1/200. ... Shoots left. ... Name pronounced YAH-nee NEE-nuh-muh.
TRANSACTIONS/CAREER NOTES: Selected by Philadelphia Flyers in second round (first Flyers pick, 36th overall) of NHL entry draft (June 26, 1993).
HONORS: Named to NHL All-Rookie team (1996-97).

Season Team	League	REGULAR SEASON Gms.	G	A	Pts.	PIM	+/-	PP	SH	PLAYOFFS Gms.	G	A	Pts.	PIM
91-92— Karpat Oulu	Finland Dv.II	41	2	11	13	49	...	...	...	—	—	—	—	—
92-93— Karpat Oulu	Finland Dv.II	29	2	3	5	14	...	...	...	—	—	—	—	—
— Karpat Jr.	Finland	10	3	9	12	16	...	...	...	—	—	—	—	—
93-94— Jokerit Helsinki	Finland	45	3	8	11	24	...	...	...	12	1	1	2	4
94-95— Jokerit Helsinki	Finland	42	7	10	17	36	...	...	...	10	1	4	5	35
95-96— Jokerit Helsinki	Finland	49	5	15	20	79	...	...	...	11	0	2	2	12
96-97— Philadelphia	NHL	77	4	40	44	58	12	1	0	19	1	12	13	16
NHL totals (1 year)		77	4	40	44	58	12	1	0	19	1	12	13	16

NIKOLISHIN, ANDREI   C   CAPITALS

PERSONAL: Born March 25, 1973, in Vorkuta, U.S.S.R. ... 5-11/204. ... Shoots left. ... Name pronounced nih-koh-LEE-shuhn.
TRANSACTIONS/CAREER NOTES: Selected by Hartford Whalers in second round (second Whalers pick, 47th overall) of NHL entry draft (June 20, 1992). ... Played in Europe during 1994-95 NHL lockout. ... Sprained ankle (October 21, 1995); missed one game. ... Injured back (November 15, 1995); missed five games. ... Strained back (December 2, 1995); missed 15 games. ... Traded by Whalers to Washington Capitals for D Curtis Leschyshyn (November 9, 1996). ... Suffered bulging disc in back (February 2, 1997); missed eight games.
HONORS: Named to CIS All-Star team (1993-94). ... Named CIS Player of the Year (1993-94).

Season Team	League	REGULAR SEASON Gms.	G	A	Pts.	PIM	+/-	PP	SH	PLAYOFFS Gms.	G	A	Pts.	PIM
90-91— Dynamo Moscow	USSR	2	0	0	0	0	...	...	...	—	—	—	—	—
91-92— Dynamo Moscow	CIS	18	1	0	1	4	...	...	...	—	—	—	—	—
92-93— Dynamo Moscow	CIS	42	5	7	12	30	...	...	...	10	2	1	3	8
93-94— Dynamo Moscow	CIS	41	8	12	20	30	...	...	...	9	1	3	4	4
— Rus. Olympic team	Int'l	8	2	5	7	6	...	...	...	—	—	—	—	—
94-95— Dynamo Moscow	CIS	12	7	2	9	6	...	...	...	—	—	—	—	—
— Hartford	NHL	39	8	10	18	10	7	1	1	—	—	—	—	—
95-96— Hartford	NHL	61	14	37	51	34	-2	4	1	—	—	—	—	—
96-97— Hartford	NHL	12	2	5	7	2	-2	0	0	—	—	—	—	—
— Washington	NHL	59	7	14	21	30	5	1	0	—	—	—	—	—
NHL totals (3 years)		171	31	66	97	76	8	6	2					

NIKOLOV, ANGEL   D   SHARKS

PERSONAL: Born November 18, 1975, in Most, Czechoslovakia. ... 6-1/176. ... Shoots left. ... Name pronounced NIHK-uh-lahv.
TRANSACTIONS/CAREER NOTES: Selected by San Jose Sharks in second round (second Sharks pick, 37th overall) of NHL entry draft (June 28, 1994).

Season Team	League	REGULAR SEASON Gms.	G	A	Pts.	PIM	+/-	PP	SH	PLAYOFFS Gms.	G	A	Pts.	PIM
93-94— Litvinov	Czech.	10	2	2	4	0	...	...	...	—	—	—	—	—
94-95— Litvinov	Czech.	41	1	4	5		...	...	...	—	—	—	—	—
95-96— Litvinov	Czech.	40	1	7	8		...	...	...	10	0	1	1	0
96-97— Litvinov	Czech.	47	0	9	9	44	...	...	...	—	—	—	—	—

NIKULIN, IGOR   RW   MIGHTY DUCKS

PERSONAL: Born August 26, 1972, in Cherepovets, U.S.S.R. ... 6-1/200. ... Shoots left. ... Name pronounced nih-KOO-lihn.
TRANSACTIONS/CAREER NOTES: Selected by Mighty Ducks of Anaheim in fifth round (fourth Mighty Ducks pick, 107th overall) of NHL entry draft (July 8, 1995).

				REGULAR SEASON						PLAYOFFS			
Season Team	League	Gms.	G	A	Pts.	PIM	+/-	PP	SH	Gms.	G	A	Pts.	PIM
92-93— Metal. Cherepovets	CIS	42	11	11	22	22	...	...	...	—	—	—	—	—
93-94— Metal. Cherepovets	CIS	44	14	15	29	52	...	...	...	2	1	0	1	0
94-95— Sever. Cherepovets	CIS	52	14	12	26	28	...	...	...	—	—	—	—	—
95-96— Sever. Cherepovets	CIS	47	20	13	33	28	...	...	...	3	0	1	1	2
— Baltimore	AHL	4	2	2	4	2	...	...	...	—	—	—	—	—
96-97— Fort Wayne	IHL	10	1	2	3	4	...	...	...	—	—	—	—	—
— Baltimore	AHL	61	27	25	52	14	...	...	...	3	2	1	3	2
— Anaheim	NHL	—	—	—	—	—	...	...	...	1	0	0	0	0
NHL totals (1 year)										1	0	0	0	0

NILSON, MARCUS   C   PANTHERS

PERSONAL: Born March 1, 1978, in Stockholm, Sweden. ... 6-1/183. ... Shoots right.
TRANSACTIONS/CAREER NOTES: Selected by Florida Panthers in first round (first Panthers pick, 20th overall) of NHL entry draft (June 22, 1996).

				REGULAR SEASON						PLAYOFFS			
Season Team	League	Gms.	G	A	Pts.	PIM	+/-	PP	SH	Gms.	G	A	Pts.	PIM
94-95— Djurgarden Jrs...........	Sweden	24	7	8	15	22	...	...	...	—	—	—	—	—
95-96— Djurgarden Jrs...........	Sweden	25	19	17	36	46	...	...	...	2	1	1	2	12
— Djur. Stockholm........	Sweden	12	0	0	0	0	...	...	...	1	0	0	0	0
96-97— Djur. Stockholm........	Sweden	37	0	3	3	33	...	...	...	4	0	0	0	0

NILSSON, MAGNUS   RW   RED WINGS

PERSONAL: Born February 1, 1978, in Finspang, Sweden. ... 6-1/187. ... Shoots left.
TRANSACTIONS/CAREER NOTES: Selected by Detroit Red Wings in sixth round (fifth Red Wings pick, 144th overall) of NHL entry draft (June 22, 1996).

				REGULAR SEASON						PLAYOFFS			
Season Team	League	Gms.	G	A	Pts.	PIM	+/-	PP	SH	Gms.	G	A	Pts.	PIM
95-96— V. H. Norrkoping........	Swed. Div. II	28	3	3	6	16	...	...	...	—	—	—	—	—
96-97— Malmo................	Sweden	12	0	0	0	0	...	...	...	—	—	—	—	—
— Malmo Jrs.	Sweden Jr.	14	10	9	19	45	...	...	...	—	—	—	—	—

NOBLE, TOM   G   BLACKHAWKS

PERSONAL: Born March 21, 1975, in Quincy, Mass. ... 5-10/165. ... Catches left.
HIGH SCHOOL: Catholic Memorial (Boston).
COLLEGE: Boston University.
TRANSACTIONS/CAREER NOTES: Selected by Chicago Blackhawks in 11th round (12th Blackhawks pick, 284th overall) of NHL entry draft (June 26, 1993).
HONORS: Named to Hockey East All-Star team (1996-97).

				REGULAR SEASON						PLAYOFFS				
Season Team	League	Gms.	Min	W	L	T	GA	SO	Avg.	Gms.	Min.	W	L	GA	SO	Avg.
92-93—Catholic Memorial	Mass. H.S.	21	1475	...	...	...	31	4	1.26	—	—	—	—	—	—	—
93-94—Catholic Memorial	Mass. H.S.	24	1080	...	...	...	22	1	1.22	—	—	—	—	—	—	—
94-95—Boston University	Hockey East	18	1003	15	2	0	46	0	2.75	—	—	—	—	—	—	—
95-96—Boston University	Hockey East	28	1536	19	5	2	77	0	3.01	—	—	—	—	—	—	—
96-97—Boston University	Hockey East	17	1017	10	5	2	53	0	3.13	—	—	—	—	—	—	—

N

NOLAN, OWEN   RW   SHARKS

PERSONAL: Born February 12, 1972, in Belfast, Northern Ireland. ... 6-1/215. ... Shoots right.
TRANSACTIONS/CAREER NOTES: Separated shoulder (February 22, 1990); missed eight games. ... Selected by Quebec Nordiques in first round (first Nordiques pick, first overall) of NHL entry draft (June 16, 1990). ... Suffered concussion, sore knee and sore back (October 1990). ... Suspended four off-days by NHL for cross-checking (December 7, 1992). ... Bruised hand (March 2, 1993); missed three games. ... Bruised shoulder (March 15, 1993); eight games. ... Injured right shoulder (October 19, 1993); missed 11 games. ... Dislocated left shoulder (November 12, 1993); missed remainder of season. ... Bruised shoulder (April 16, 1995); missed two games. ... Nordiques franchise moved to Colorado and renamed Avalanche for 1995-96 season (June 21, 1995). ... Traded by Avalanche to San Jose Sharks for D Sandis Ozolinsh (October 26, 1995). ... Suffered from the flu (March 5, 1996); missed two games. ... Suffered from an illness (November 27, 1996); missed one game. ... Bruised shoulder (January 9, 1997); missed two games. ... Sore ankle (March 20, 1997); missed four games. ... Strained groin (April 7, 1997); missed three games.
HONORS: Won Emms Family Award (1988-89). ... Won Jim Mahon Memorial Trophy (1989-90). ... Named to OHL All-Star first team (1989-90). ... Played in NHL All-Star Game (1992, 1996 and 1997).
STATISTICAL PLATEAUS: Three-goal games: 1991-92 (2), 1992-93 (2), 1994-95 (3), 1996-97 (1). Total: 8. ... Four-goal games: 1995-96 (1). ... Total hat tricks: 9.
STATISTICAL NOTES: Led NHL with eight game-winning goals (1994-95).

Season Team	League	REGULAR SEASON								PLAYOFFS				
		Gms.	G	A	Pts.	PIM	+/-	PP	SH	Gms.	G	A	Pts.	PIM
88-89— Cornwall	OHL	62	34	25	59	213	...	...	...	18	5	11	16	41
89-90— Cornwall	OHL	58	51	59	110	240	...	...	...	6	7	5	12	26
90-91— Quebec	NHL	59	3	10	13	109	-19	0	0	—	—	—	—	—
— Halifax	AHL	6	4	4	8	11	...	...	...	—	—	—	—	—
91-92— Quebec	NHL	75	42	31	73	183	-9	17	0	—	—	—	—	—
92-93— Quebec	NHL	73	36	41	77	185	-1	15	0	5	1	0	1	2
93-94— Quebec	NHL	6	2	2	4	8	2	0	0	—	—	—	—	—
94-95— Quebec	NHL	46	30	19	49	46	21	13	2	6	2	3	5	6
95-96— Colorado	NHL	9	4	4	8	9	-3	4	0	—	—	—	—	—
— San Jose	NHL	72	29	32	61	137	-30	12	1	—	—	—	—	—
96-97— San Jose	NHL	72	31	32	63	155	-19	10	0	—	—	—	—	—
NHL totals (7 years)		412	177	171	348	832	-58	71	3	11	3	3	6	8

NOONAN, BRIAN   RW   CANUCKS

PERSONAL: Born May 29, 1965, in Boston. ... 6-1/200. ... Shoots right.

HIGH SCHOOL: Archbishop Williams (Braintree, Mass.).

TRANSACTIONS/CAREER NOTES: Selected by Chicago Blackhawks in ninth round (10th Blackhawks pick, 179th overall) of NHL entry draft (June 8, 1983). ... Separated shoulder (April 3, 1988). ... Refused to report to Indianapolis (October 18, 1990); suspended without pay by Blackhawks. ... Suffered death in family (February 28, 1991); missed six games. ... Damaged left knee ligaments (January 30, 1992); missed 12 games. ... Bruised shoulder (October 31, 1992); missed four games. ... Suspended one game by NHL for accumulating three game misconduct penalties (January 21, 1993). ... Suffered from the flu (February 25, 1993); missed three games. ... Traded by Blackhawks with LW Stephane Matteau to New York Rangers for RW Tony Amonte and rights to LW Matt Oates (March 21, 1994). ... Sprained right knee (April 2, 1995); missed three games. ... Strained groin (May 6, 1995); missed five playoff games. ... Signed as free agent by St. Louis Blues (July 11, 1995). ... Injured knee (November 3, 1996); missed four games. ... Traded by Blues to Rangers for LW Sergio Momesso (November 13, 1996). ... Traded by Rangers with C Sergei Nemchinov to Vancouver Canucks for LW Esa Tikkanen and RW Russ Courtnall (March 8, 1997).

HONORS: Won Ken McKenzie Trophy (1985-86). ... Named to IHL All-Star second team (1989-90). ... Named to IHL All-Star first team (1990-91).

STATISTICAL PLATEAUS: Three-goal games: 1991-92 (2), 1994-95 (1). Total: 3. ... Four-goal games: 1991-92 (1). ... Total hat tricks: 4.

MISCELLANEOUS: Member of Stanley Cup championship team (1994).

Season Team	League	REGULAR SEASON								PLAYOFFS				
		Gms.	G	A	Pts.	PIM	+/-	PP	SH	Gms.	G	A	Pts.	PIM
82-83— Archbishop Williams	Mass. H.S.	21	26	17	43	...	...	...	...	—	—	—	—	—
83-84— Archbishop Williams	Mass. H.S.	17	14	23	37	...	...	...	...	—	—	—	—	—
84-85— New Westminster	WHL	72	50	66	116	76	...	...	...	11	8	7	15	4
85-86— Saginaw	IHL	76	39	39	78	69	...	...	...	11	6	3	9	6
— Nova Scotia	AHL	2	0	0	0	0	...	...	...	—	—	—	—	—
86-87— Nova Scotia	AHL	70	25	26	51	30	...	...	...	5	3	1	4	4
87-88— Chicago	NHL	77	10	20	30	44	-27	3	0	3	0	0	0	4
88-89— Chicago	NHL	45	4	12	16	28	-2	2	0	1	0	0	0	0
— Saginaw	IHL	19	18	13	31	36	...	...	...	1	0	0	0	0
89-90— Chicago	NHL	8	0	2	2	6	0	0	0	—	—	—	—	—
— Indianapolis	IHL	56	40	36	76	85	...	...	...	14	6	9	15	20
90-91— Indianapolis	IHL	59	38	53	91	67	...	...	...	7	6	4	10	18
— Chicago	NHL	7	0	4	4	2	-1	0	0	—	—	—	—	—
91-92— Chicago	NHL	65	19	12	31	81	9	4	0	18	6	9	15	30
92-93— Chicago	NHL	63	16	14	30	82	3	5	0	4	3	0	3	4
93-94— Chicago	NHL	64	14	21	35	57	2	8	0	—	—	—	—	—
— New York Rangers	NHL	12	4	2	6	12	5	2	0	22	4	7	11	17
94-95— New York Rangers	NHL	45	14	13	27	26	-3	7	0	5	0	0	0	8
95-96— St. Louis	NHL	81	13	22	35	84	2	3	1	13	4	1	5	10
96-97— St. Louis	NHL	13	2	5	7	0	2	0	0	—	—	—	—	—
— New York Rangers	NHL	44	6	9	15	28	-7	3	0	—	—	—	—	—
— Vancouver	NHL	16	4	8	12	6	2	0	1	—	—	—	—	—
NHL totals (10 years)		540	106	144	250	456	-15	37	2	66	17	17	34	73

NORSTROM, MATTIAS   D   KINGS

PERSONAL: Born January 2, 1972, in Stockholm, Sweden. ... 6-1/205. ... Shoots left. ... Name pronounced muh-TEE-uhz NOHR-struhm.

TRANSACTIONS/CAREER NOTES: Selected by New York Rangers in second round (second Rangers pick, 48th overall) of NHL entry draft (June 20, 1992). ... Suffered from the flu (April 28, 1995); missed two games. ... Separated shoulder (December 30, 1995); missed six games. ... Traded by Rangers with C Ray Ferraro, C Ian Laperriere, C Nathan Lafayette and fourth-round pick (D Sean Blanchard) in 1997 draft to Los Angeles Kings for RW Shane Churla, LW Jari Kurri and D Marty McSorley (March 14, 1996). ... Bruised left wrist (November 7, 1996); missed one game.

MISCELLANEOUS: Member of Stanley Cup championship team (1994).

Season Team	League	REGULAR SEASON								PLAYOFFS				
		Gms.	G	A	Pts.	PIM	+/-	PP	SH	Gms.	G	A	Pts.	PIM
91-92— AIK Solna	Sweden	39	4	4	8	28	...	...	...	—	—	—	—	—
92-93— AIK Solna	Sweden	22	0	1	1	16	...	...	...	—	—	—	—	—
93-94— New York Rangers	NHL	9	0	2	2	6	0	0	0	—	—	—	—	—
— Binghamton	AHL	55	1	9	10	70	...	...	...	—	—	—	—	—
94-95— Binghamton	AHL	63	9	10	19	91	...	...	...	—	—	—	—	—
— New York Rangers	NHL	9	0	3	3	2	2	0	0	3	0	0	0	0
95-96— New York Rangers	NHL	25	2	1	3	22	5	0	0	—	—	—	—	—
— Los Angeles	NHL	11	0	1	1	18	-8	0	0	—	—	—	—	—
96-97— Los Angeles	NHL	80	1	21	22	84	-4	0	0	—	—	—	—	—
NHL totals (4 years)		134	3	28	31	132	-5	0	0	3	0	0	0	0

NORTON, JEFF — D — LIGHTNING

PERSONAL: Born November 25, 1965, in Cambridge, Mass. ... 6-2/200. ... Shoots left. ... Full name: Jeffrey Zaccari Norton.
HIGH SCHOOL: Cushing Academy (Ashburnham, Mass.).
COLLEGE: Michigan.
TRANSACTIONS/CAREER NOTES: Selected by New York Islanders in third round (third Islanders pick, 62nd overall) of NHL entry draft (June 9, 1984). ... Bruised ribs (November 16, 1988). ... Injured groin (February 1990). ... Strained groin and abdominal muscles (March 2, 1990); missed games. ... Suffered concussion (April 9, 1990). ... Suspended eight games by NHL for intentionally injuring another player in preseason game (September 30, 1990). ... Dislocated right shoulder (November 3, 1990); missed four games. ... Reinjured shoulder (December 27, 1990); missed five games. ... Reinjured shoulder and underwent surgery (February 23, 1991); missed remainder of season. ... Suffered concussion (October 26, 1991); missed one game. ... Tore ligaments in left wrist (January 3, 1992); missed final 42 games of season. ... Underwent surgery to left wrist (January 8, 1992). ... Injured hip flexor (October 23, 1992); missed five games. ... Suffered sore shoulder (December 31, 1992); missed one game. ... Pulled groin (February 25, 1993); missed two games. ... Traded by Islanders to San Jose Sharks for third-round pick (D Jason Strudwick) in 1994 draft (June 20, 1993). ... Sprained ankle (December 11, 1993); missed nine games. ... Reinjured ankle (January 4, 1994); missed five games. ... Sprained ankle (February 19, 1994); missed five games. ... Suffered from the flu (January 28, 1995); missed one game. ... Traded by Sharks with third-round pick (traded to Colorado) in 1997 draft and future considerations to St. Louis Blues for C Craig Janney (March 6, 1995). ... Injured hand (March 7, 1995); missed one game. ... Traded by Blues with D Donald Dufresne to Edmonton Oilers for D Igor Kravchuck and D Ken Sutton (January 4, 1996). ... Fractured thumb (February 9, 1996); missed two games. ... Suffered back spasms (March 17, 1996); missed one game. ... Sprained left knee (March 24, 1996); missed nine games. ... Sprained ankle (October 15, 1996); missed six games. ... Strained groin (January 7, 1997); missed one game. ... Traded by Oilers to Tampa Bay Lightning for D Drew Bannister and sixth-round draft pick in 1997 (March 18, 1997).
HONORS: Named to CCHA All-Star second team (1986-87).

Season Team	League	REGULAR SEASON								PLAYOFFS				
		Gms.	G	A	Pts.	PIM	+/-	PP	SH	Gms.	G	A	Pts.	PIM
83-84— Cushing Academy	Mass. H.S.	21	22	33	55	...	...	...	...	—	—	—	—	—
84-85— Univ. of Michigan	CCHA	37	8	16	24	103	...	...	...	—	—	—	—	—
85-86— Univ. of Michigan	CCHA	37	15	30	45	99	...	...	...	—	—	—	—	—
86-87— Univ. of Michigan	CCHA	39	12	37	49	92	...	...	...	—	—	—	—	—
87-88— U.S. national team	Int'l	57	7	25	32	...	...	...	...	—	—	—	—	—
— U.S. Olympic team	Int'l	6	0	4	4	4	...	...	...	—	—	—	—	—
— New York Islanders	NHL	15	1	6	7	14	3	1	0	3	0	2	2	13
88-89— New York Islanders	NHL	69	1	30	31	74	-24	1	0	—	—	—	—	—
89-90— New York Islanders	NHL	60	4	49	53	65	-9	4	0	4	1	3	4	17
90-91— New York Islanders	NHL	44	3	25	28	16	-13	2	1	—	—	—	—	—
91-92— New York Islanders	NHL	28	1	18	19	18	2	0	1	—	—	—	—	—
92-93— New York Islanders	NHL	66	12	38	50	45	-3	5	0	10	1	1	2	4
93-94— San Jose	NHL	64	7	33	40	36	16	1	0	14	1	5	6	20
94-95— San Jose	NHL	20	1	9	10	39	1	0	0	—	—	—	—	—
— St. Louis	NHL	28	2	18	20	33	21	0	0	7	1	1	2	11
95-96— St. Louis	NHL	36	4	7	11	26	4	0	0	—	—	—	—	—
— Edmonton	NHL	30	4	16	20	18	5	1	0	—	—	—	—	—
96-97— Edmonton	NHL	62	2	11	13	42	-7	0	0	—	—	—	—	—
— Tampa Bay	NHL	13	0	5	5	16	0	0	0	—	—	—	—	—
NHL totals (10 years)		535	42	265	307	440	-4	15	2	38	4	12	16	65

NUMMINEN, TEPPO — D — COYOTES

PERSONAL: Born July 3, 1968, in Tampere, Finland. ... 6-1/195. ... Shoots right. ... Full name: Teppo Kalevi Numminen. ... Name pronounced TEH-poh NOO-mih-nehn.
TRANSACTIONS/CAREER NOTES: Selected by Winnipeg Jets in second round (second Jets pick, 29th overall) of NHL entry draft (June 21, 1986). ... Separated shoulder (March 5, 1989). ... Broke thumb (April 14, 1990). ... Fractured foot (January 28, 1993); missed 17 games. ... Dislocated thumb (February 9, 1994); missed remainder of season. ... Played in Europe during 1994-95 NHL lockout. ... Suffered from stomach flu (January 23, 1995); missed one game. ... Suffered surface stress fracture in right knee (February 22, 1995); missed five games. ... Separated shoulder (November 30, 1995); missed eight games. ... Jets franchise moved to Phoenix and renamed Coyotes for 1996-97 season; NHL approved move on January 18, 1996.
MISCELLANEOUS: Member of silver-medal-winning Finnish Olympic team (1988).

N

Season Team	League	REGULAR SEASON								PLAYOFFS				
		Gms.	G	A	Pts.	PIM	+/-	PP	SH	Gms.	G	A	Pts.	PIM
84-85— Tappara	Finland	30	14	17	31	10	...	...	...	—	—	—	—	—
85-86— Tappara	Finland	39	2	4	6	6	...	...	...	8	0	0	0	0
86-87— Tappara	Finland	44	9	9	18	16	...	...	...	9	4	1	5	4
87-88— Tappara	Finland	44	10	10	20	29	...	...	...	10	6	6	12	6
— Fin. Olympic team	Int'l	6	1	4	5	0	...	...	...	—	—	—	—	—
88-89— Winnipeg	NHL	69	1	14	15	36	-11	0	1	—	—	—	—	—
89-90— Winnipeg	NHL	79	11	32	43	20	-4	1	0	7	1	2	3	10
90-91— Winnipeg	NHL	80	8	25	33	28	-15	3	0	—	—	—	—	—
91-92— Winnipeg	NHL	80	5	34	39	32	15	4	0	7	0	0	0	0
92-93— Winnipeg	NHL	66	7	30	37	33	4	3	1	6	1	1	2	2
93-94— Winnipeg	NHL	57	5	18	23	28	-23	4	0	—	—	—	—	—
94-95— TuTo Turku	Finland	12	3	8	11	4	...	...	...	—	—	—	—	—
— Winnipeg	NHL	42	5	16	21	16	12	2	0	—	—	—	—	—
95-96— Winnipeg	NHL	74	11	43	54	22	-4	6	0	6	0	0	0	2
96-97— Phoenix	NHL	82	2	25	27	28	-3	0	0	7	3	3	6	0
NHL totals (9 years)		629	55	237	292	243	-29	23	2	33	5	6	11	14

NURMINEN, KAI — LW — KINGS

PERSONAL: Born March 29, 1969, in Turku, Finland. ... 6-1/198. ... Shoots left. ... Name pronounced KIGH NUHR-mih-nehn.
TRANSACTIONS/CAREER NOTES: Selected by Los Angeles Kings in eighth round (ninth Kings pick, 193rd overall) in NHL entry draft (June 22, 1996). ... Bruised thigh (January 15, 1997); missed two games. ... Bruised thigh (February 5, 1997); missed two games.

Season Team	League	Gms.	G	A	Pts.	PIM	+/-	PP	SH		Gms.	G	A	Pts.	PIM
89-90 — TPS Jr.	Finland Jr.	35	28	17	45	32	...	...	...		—	—	—	—	—
90-91 — Tuto.	Finland Dv. II	33	26	20	46	14	...	...	...		—	—	—	—	—
91-92 — Kiekko-67	Finland Dv. II	44	44	19	63	34	...	...	...		—	—	—	—	—
92-93 — TPS	Finland	31	4	6	10	13	...	...	...		7	1	2	3	0
— Kiekko-67	Finland Dv. II	8	6	4	10	2	...	...	...		—	—	—	—	—
93-94 — TPS	Finland	45	23	12	35	20	...	...	...		11	0	3	3	4
94-95 — HPK	Finland	49	30	25	55	40	...	...	...		—	—	—	—	—
95-96 — HV 71 Jonkoping	Sweden	40	31	24	55	30	...	...	...		4	3	1	4	8
96-97 — Los Angeles	NHL	67	16	11	27	22	-3	4	0		—	—	—	—	—
NHL totals (1 year)		67	16	11	27	22	-3	4	0						

NYLANDER, MICHAEL   C   FLAMES

PERSONAL: Born October 3, 1972, in Stockholm, Sweden. ... 5-11/190. ... Shoots left. ... Name pronounced NEE-lan-duhr.

TRANSACTIONS/CAREER NOTES: Selected by Hartford Whalers in third round (fourth Whalers pick, 59th overall) of NHL entry draft (June 22, 1991). ... Broke jaw (January 23, 1993); missed 15 games. ... Traded by Whalers with D Zarley Zalapski and D James Patrick to Calgary Flames for D Gary Suter, LW Paul Ranheim and C Ted Drury (March 10, 1994). ... Played in Europe during 1994-95 NHL lockout. ... Broke left wrist and forearm (January 24, 1995); missed 42 games. ... Injured wrist (January 16, 1996); missed three games.

HONORS: Named Swedish League Rookie of the Year (1991-92).

STATISTICAL PLATEAUS: Three-goal games: 1992-93 (1).

		REGULAR SEASON									PLAYOFFS				
Season Team	League	Gms.	G	A	Pts.	PIM	+/-	PP	SH		Gms.	G	A	Pts.	PIM
89-90 — Huddinge	Sweden	31	7	15	22	4	...	...	...		—	—	—	—	—
90-91 — Huddinge	Sweden	33	14	20	34	10	...	...	...		—	—	—	—	—
91-92 — AIK Solna	Sweden	40	11	17	28	30	...	...	...		—	—	—	—	—
— Swedish nat'l team	Int'l	6	0	1	1	0	...	...	...		—	—	—	—	—
92-93 — Hartford	NHL	59	11	22	33	36	-7	3	0		—	—	—	—	—
93-94 — Hartford	NHL	58	11	33	44	24	-2	4	0		—	—	—	—	—
— Springfield	AHL	4	0	9	9	0	...	...	...		—	—	—	—	—
— Calgary	NHL	15	2	9	11	6	10	0	0		3	0	0	0	0
94-95 — JyP HT	Finland	16	11	19	30	63	...	...	...		—	—	—	—	—
— Calgary	NHL	6	0	1	1	2	1	0	0		6	0	6	6	2
95-96 — Calgary	NHL	73	17	38	55	20	0	4	0		4	0	0	0	0
96-97 — Lugano	Switzerland	36	12	43	55	...	...	...	...		—	—	—	—	—
NHL totals (5 years)		211	41	103	144	88	2	11	0		13	0	6	6	2

OATES, ADAM   C   CAPITALS

PERSONAL: Born August 27, 1962, in Weston, Ont. ... 5-11/185. ... Shoots right. ... Name pronounced OHTS.

COLLEGE: Rensselaer Polytechnic Institute (N.Y.).

TRANSACTIONS/CAREER NOTES: Signed as free agent by Detroit Red Wings (June 28, 1985). ... Pulled abdominal muscle (October 1987). ... Suffered from chicken pox (November 1988). ... Bruised thigh (December 1988). ... Traded by Red Wings with RW Paul MacLean to St. Louis Blues for LW Tony McKegney and C Bernie Federko (June 15, 1989). ... Tore rib and abdominal muscles (November 5, 1990); missed 18 games. ... Traded by Blues to Boston Bruins for C Craig Janney and D Stephane Quintal (February 7, 1992). ... Injured groin (January 6, 1994); missed seven games. ... Injured knee (October 28, 1995); missed 12 games. ... Traded by Bruins with RW Rick Tocchet and G Bill Ranford to Washington Capitals for G Jim Carey, C Jason Allison, C Anson Carter, third-round pick (RW Lee Goren) in 1997 draft and conditional pick in 1998 draft (March 1, 1997). ... Injured back (April 10, 1997); missed two games.

HONORS: Named to ECAC All-Star second team (1983-84). ... Named to NCAA All-America East first team (1984-85). ... Named to NCAA All-Tournament team (1984-85). ... Named to ECAC All-Star first team (1984-85). ... Named to THE SPORTING NEWS All-Star second team (1990-91). ... Named to NHL All-Star second team (1990-91). ... Played in NHL All-Star Game (1991-1994 and 1997).

RECORDS: Holds NHL All-Star Game record for most assists in one period—4 (first period, 1993).

STATISTICAL PLATEAUS: Three-goal games: 1992-93 (2), 1993-94 (2). Total: 5. ... Four-goal games: 1995-96 (1). ... Total hat tricks: 6.

STATISTICAL NOTES: Tied for NHL lead with 11 game-winning goals (1992-93).

		REGULAR SEASON									PLAYOFFS				
Season Team	League	Gms.	G	A	Pts.	PIM	+/-	PP	SH		Gms.	G	A	Pts.	PIM
82-83 — R.P.I.	ECAC	22	9	33	42	8	...	...	...		—	—	—	—	—
83-84 — R.P.I.	ECAC	38	26	57	83	15	...	...	...		—	—	—	—	—
84-85 — R.P.I.	ECAC	38	31	60	91	29	...	...	...		—	—	—	—	—
85-86 — Adirondack	AHL	34	18	28	46	4	...	...	...		17	7	14	21	4
— Detroit	NHL	38	9	11	20	10	1	0	-24		—	—	—	—	—
86-87 — Detroit	NHL	76	15	32	47	21	0	4	0		16	4	7	11	6
87-88 — Detroit	NHL	63	14	40	54	20	16	3	0		16	8	12	20	6
88-89 — Detroit	NHL	69	16	62	78	14	-1	2	0		6	0	8	8	2
89-90 — St. Louis	NHL	80	23	79	102	30	9	6	2		12	2	12	14	4
90-91 — St. Louis	NHL	61	25	90	115	29	15	3	1		13	7	13	20	10
91-92 — St. Louis	NHL	54	10	59	69	12	-4	3	0		—	—	—	—	—
— Boston	NHL	26	10	20	30	10	-5	3	0		15	5	14	19	4
92-93 — Boston	NHL	84	45	*97	142	32	15	24	1		4	0	9	9	4
93-94 — Boston	NHL	77	32	80	112	45	10	16	2		13	3	9	12	8
94-95 — Boston	NHL	48	12	41	53	8	-11	4	1		5	1	0	1	2
95-96 — Boston	NHL	70	25	67	92	18	16	7	1		5	2	5	7	2
96-97 — Boston	NHL	63	18	52	70	10	-3	2	2		—	—	—	—	—
— Washington	NHL	17	4	8	12	4	-2	1	0		—	—	—	—	—
NHL totals (12 years)		826	258	738	996	263	56	78	-14		105	32	89	121	48

N
O

O'CONNELL, ALBIE   LW   ISLANDERS

PERSONAL: Born May 20, 1976, in Cambridge, Mass. ... 6-0/188. ... Shoots left.
HIGH SCHOOL: St. Sebastian's Country Day (Needham, Mass.).
TRANSACTIONS/CAREER NOTES: Selected by New York Islanders in fifth round (sixth Islanders pick, 116th overall) of NHL entry draft (June 29, 1994).

		REGULAR SEASON								PLAYOFFS				
Season Team	League	Gms.	G	A	Pts.	PIM	+/-	PP	SH	Gms.	G	A	Pts.	PIM
91-92— St. Sebastian's	Mass. H.S.	16	4	9	13	10	...	...	...	—	—	—	—	—
92-93— St. Sebastian's	Mass. H.S.	23	7	15	22	15	...	...	...	—	—	—	—	—
93-94— St. Sebastian's	Mass. H.S.	24	16	23	39	26	...	...	...	—	—	—	—	—
94-95— St. Sebastian's	Mass. H.S.	26	19	25	44	...	...	...	...	—	—	—	—	—
95-96— Boston University	Hockey East	38	9	8	17	34	...	...	...	—	—	—	—	—
96-97— Boston University	Hockey East	41	12	12	24	72	...	...	...	—	—	—	—	—

ODELEIN, LYLE   D   DEVILS

PERSONAL: Born July 21, 1968, in Quill Lake, Sask. ... 5-11/210. ... Shoots right. ... Name pronounced OH-duh-lighn.
TRANSACTIONS/CAREER NOTES: Selected by Montreal Canadiens as underage junior in seventh round (eighth Canadiens pick, 141st overall) of NHL entry draft (June 21, 1986). ... Bruised right ankle (January 22, 1991); missed five games. ... Twisted right ankle (February 9, 1991). ... Suspended one game by NHL for game misconduct penalties (March 1, 1993). ... Bruised shoulder (January 24, 1994); missed three games. ... Suspended two games without pay and fined $1000 by NHL for shooting puck into the opposing team's bench (April 3, 1996). ... Traded by Canadiens to New Jersey Devils for RW Stephane Richer (August 22, 1996). ... Bruised knee (January 21, 1997); missed three games.
STATISTICAL PLATEAUS: Three-goal games: 1993-94 (1).
MISCELLANEOUS: Member of Stanley Cup championship team (1993).

		REGULAR SEASON								PLAYOFFS				
Season Team	League	Gms.	G	A	Pts.	PIM	+/-	PP	SH	Gms.	G	A	Pts.	PIM
85-86— Moose Jaw	WHL	67	9	37	46	117	...	...	...	13	1	6	7	34
86-87— Moose Jaw	WHL	59	9	50	59	70	...	...	...	9	2	5	7	26
87-88— Moose Jaw	WHL	63	15	43	58	166	...	...	...	—	—	—	—	—
88-89— Sherbrooke	AHL	33	3	4	7	120	...	...	...	3	0	2	2	5
— Peoria	IHL	36	2	8	10	116	...			—	—	—	—	—
89-90— Sherbrooke	AHL	68	7	24	31	265	...	...	...	12	6	5	11	79
— Montreal	NHL	8	0	2	2	33	...	...	...	—	—	—	—	—
90-91— Montreal	NHL	52	0	2	2	259	7	0	0	12	0	0	0	54
91-92— Montreal	NHL	71	1	7	8	212	15	0	0	7	0	0	0	11
92-93— Montreal	NHL	83	2	14	16	205	35	0	0	20	1	5	6	30
93-94— Montreal	NHL	79	11	29	40	276	8	6	0	7	0	0	0	17
94-95— Montreal	NHL	48	3	7	10	152	-13	0	0	—	—	—	—	—
95-96— Montreal	NHL	79	3	14	17	230	8	0	1	6	1	1	2	6
96-97— New Jersey	NHL	79	3	13	16	110	16	1	0	10	2	2	4	19
NHL totals (8 years)		499	23	88	111	1477	76	7	1	62	4	8	12	137

ODGERS, JEFF   RW   BRUINS

PERSONAL: Born May 31, 1969, in Spy Hill, Sask. ... 6-0/195. ... Shoots right. ... Name pronounced AH-juhrs.
TRANSACTIONS/CAREER NOTES: Signed as free agent by San Jose Sharks (September 3, 1991). ... Injured hand (December 21, 1991); missed four games. ... Broke hand (November 5, 1992); missed 15 games. ... Suspended one game by NHL for accumulating three game misconduct penalties (January 29, 1993). ... Suspended two games by NHL for accumulating four game misconduct penalties (February 19, 1993). ... Traded by Sharks with fifth-round pick (D Elias Abrahamsson) in 1996 draft to Boston Bruins for D Al Iafrate (June 21, 1996). ... Injured neck (January 9, 1997); missed one game.
MISCELLANEOUS: Captain of San Jose Sharks (1994-95 and 1995-96). ... Holds San Jose Sharks all-time records for most games played (334) and most penalty minutes (1,001).

		REGULAR SEASON								PLAYOFFS				
Season Team	League	Gms.	G	A	Pts.	PIM	+/-	PP	SH	Gms.	G	A	Pts.	PIM
86-87— Brandon	WHL	70	7	14	21	150	...	...	...	—	—	—	—	—
87-88— Brandon	WHL	70	17	18	35	202	...	...	...	4	1	1	2	14
88-89— Brandon	WHL	71	31	29	60	277	...	...	...	—	—	—	—	—
89-90— Brandon	WHL	64	37	28	65	209	...	...	...	—	—	—	—	—
90-91— Kansas City...............	IHL	77	12	19	31	*318	...	...	...	—	—	—	—	—
91-92— Kansas City...............	IHL	12	2	2	4	56	...	...	...	9	3	0	3	13
— San Jose	NHL	61	7	4	11	217	-21	0	0	—	—	—	—	—
92-93— San Jose	NHL	66	12	15	27	253	-26	6	0	—	—	—	—	—
93-94— San Jose	NHL	81	13	8	21	222	-13	7	0	11	0	0	0	11
94-95— San Jose	NHL	48	4	3	7	117	-8	0	0	11	1	1	2	23
95-96— San Jose	NHL	78	12	4	16	192	-4	0	0	—	—	—	—	—
96-97— Boston	NHL	80	7	8	15	197	-15	1	0	—	—	—	—	—
NHL totals (6 years)		414	55	42	97	1198	-87	14	0	22	1	1	2	34

ODJICK, GINO   LW   CANUCKS

PERSONAL: Born September 7, 1970, in Maniwaki, Que. ... 6-3/210. ... Shoots left. ... Name pronounced OH-jihk.
TRANSACTIONS/CAREER NOTES: Suspended five games by QMJHL for attempting to attack another player (May 1, 1989). ... Suspended one game by QMJHL for fighting (March 19, 1990). ... Suspended one game by QMJHL for fighting (April 14, 1990). ... Selected by Vancouver Canucks in fifth round (fifth Canucks pick, 86th overall) of NHL entry draft (June 16, 1990). ... Broke cheekbone (February 27, 1991). ...

O

Suspended six games by NHL for stick foul (November 26, 1991). ... Underwent arthroscopic knee surgery (February 11, 1993); missed five games. ... Suspended one game by NHL for accumulating three game misconduct penalties (January 27, 1993). ... Suspended one game by NHL for accumulating four game misconduct penalties (March 26, 1993). ... Suspended two games by NHL for stick incident (April 8, 1993). ... Separated shoulder (November 27, 1993); missed two games. ... Suspended by NHL for 10 games (September 1994); NHL reduced suspension to six games due to abbreviated 1994-95 season (January 19, 1995). ... Strained groin (March 10, 1995); missed six games. ... Strained abdomen (April 7, 1995); missed last 13 games of season. ... Injured knee (October 10, 1995); missed one game. ... Strained abdominal muscle (November 22, 1995); missed 24 games. ... Suspended four games and fined $1,000 by NHL for striking opposing player (November 29, 1995). ... Strained groin (January 20, 1997); missed five games. ... Fractured finger (April 4, 1997); missed remainder of season.

MISCELLANEOUS: Scored on a penalty shot (vs. Mike Vernon, October 19, 1991). ... Holds Vancouver Canucks all-time record for most penalty minutes (1,946).

		REGULAR SEASON								PLAYOFFS				
Season Team	League	Gms.	G	A	Pts.	PIM	+/-	PP	SH	Gms.	G	A	Pts.	PIM
88-89— Laval	QMJHL	50	9	15	24	278	...	...	...	16	0	9	9	*129
89-90— Laval	QMJHL	51	12	26	38	280	...	...	...	13	6	5	11	*110
90-91— Milwaukee	IHL	17	7	3	10	102	...	...	...	—	—	—	—	—
— Vancouver	NHL	45	7	1	8	296	-6	0	0	6	0	0	0	18
91-92— Vancouver	NHL	65	4	6	10	348	-1	0	0	4	0	0	0	6
92-93— Vancouver	NHL	75	4	13	17	370	3	0	0	1	0	0	0	0
93-94— Vancouver	NHL	76	16	13	29	271	13	4	0	10	0	0	0	18
94-95— Vancouver	NHL	23	4	5	9	109	-3	0	0	5	0	0	0	47
95-96— Vancouver	NHL	55	3	4	7	181	-16	0	0	6	3	1	4	6
96-97— Vancouver	NHL	70	5	8	13	371	-5	1	0	—	—	—	—	—
NHL totals (7 years)		409	43	50	93	1946	-15	5	0	32	3	1	4	95

O'DONNELL, SEAN   D   KINGS

PERSONAL: Born September 13, 1971, in Ottawa. ... 6-3/225. ... Shoots left.
TRANSACTIONS/CAREER NOTES: Selected by Buffalo Sabres in sixth round (sixth Sabres pick, 123rd overall) of NHL entry draft (June 22, 1991). ... Traded by Sabres to Los Angeles Kings for D Doug Houda (July 26, 1994). ... Bruised sternum (February 4, 1995); missed two games. ... Sprained left wrist (January 27, 1996); missed eight games. ... Sprained wrist (December 26, 1996); missed nine games. ... Suspended one game by NHL for an altercation while on the bench (January 30, 1997). ... Strained back (March 1, 1997); missed two games.

		REGULAR SEASON								PLAYOFFS				
Season Team	League	Gms.	G	A	Pts.	PIM	+/-	PP	SH	Gms.	G	A	Pts.	PIM
90-91— Sudbury	OHL	66	8	23	31	114	...	...	...	5	1	4	5	10
91-92— Rochester	AHL	73	4	9	13	193	...	...	...	16	1	2	3	21
92-93— Rochester	AHL	74	3	18	21	203	...	...	...	17	1	6	7	38
93-94— Rochester	AHL	64	2	10	12	242	...	...	...	4	0	1	1	21
94-95— Phoenix	IHL	61	2	18	20	132	...	...	...	9	0	1	1	21
— Los Angeles	NHL	15	0	2	2	49	-2	0	0	—	—	—	—	—
95-96— Los Angeles	NHL	71	2	5	7	127	3	0	0	—	—	—	—	—
96-97— Los Angeles	NHL	55	5	12	17	144	-13	2	0	—	—	—	—	—
NHL totals (3 years)		141	7	19	26	320	-12	2	0					

ODUYA, FREDRIK   D   SHARKS

PERSONAL: Born May 31, 1975, in Stockholm, Sweden. ... 6-2/185. ... Shoots left. ... Name pronounced oh-DOO-yuh.
TRANSACTIONS/CAREER NOTES: Selected by San Jose Sharks in sixth round (eighth Sharks pick, 154th overall) of NHL entry draft (June 26, 1993).

		REGULAR SEASON								PLAYOFFS				
Season Team	League	Gms.	G	A	Pts.	PIM	+/-	PP	SH	Gms.	G	A	Pts.	PIM
91-92— Windsor	OHL Jr. B	43	2	8	10	24	...	...	...	—	—	—	—	—
92-93— Guelph	OHL	23	2	4	6	29	...	...	...	—	—	—	—	—
— Ottawa	OHL	17	0	3	3	70	...	...	...	—	—	—	—	—
93-94— Ottawa	OHL	51	11	12	23	181	...	...	...	17	0	3	3	22
94-95— Ottawa	OHL	61	2	13	15	175	...	...	...	—	—	—	—	—
95-96— Kansas City	IHL	56	2	6	8	235	...	...	...	3	0	0	0	2
96-97— Kentucky	AHL	69	2	9	11	241	...	...	...	—	—	—	—	—

O'GRADY, MIKE   D   PANTHERS

PERSONAL: Born March 22, 1977, in Neilburg, Sask. ... 6-3/200. ... Shoots left.
TRANSACTIONS/CAREER NOTES: Selected by Florida Panthers in third round (third Panthers pick, 62nd overall) of NHL entry draft (July 8, 1995).

		REGULAR SEASON								PLAYOFFS				
Season Team	League	Gms.	G	A	Pts.	PIM	+/-	PP	SH	Gms.	G	A	Pts.	PIM
93-94— Saskatoon	WHL	13	0	1	1	29	...	...	...	—	—	—	—	—
94-95— Saskatoon	WHL	39	0	7	7	157	...	...	...	—	—	—	—	—
— Lethbridge	WHL	21	1	2	3	124	...	...	...	—	—	—	—	—
95-96— Lethbridge	WHL	61	2	9	11	242	...	...	...	4	1	0	1	8
96-97— Lethbridge	WHL	61	8	25	33	262	...	...	...	18	1	5	6	41

OHLUND, MATTIAS   D   CANUCKS

PERSONAL: Born September 9, 1976, in Pitea, Sweden. ... 6-3/209. ... Shoots left. ... Name pronounced muh-TIGH-uhz OH-luhnd.
TRANSACTIONS/CAREER NOTES: Selected by Vancouver Canucks in first round (first Canucks pick, 13th overall) of NHL entry draft (June 28, 1994).

O

Season Team	League	REGULAR SEASON Gms.	G	A	Pts.	PIM	+/-	PP	SH		PLAYOFFS Gms.	G	A	Pts.	PIM
92-93— Pitea	Swed. Div. II	22	0	6	6	16	...	...	...		—	—	—	—	—
93-94— Pitea	Swed. Div. II	28	7	10	17	62	...	...	...		—	—	—	—	—
94-95— Lulea	Sweden	34	6	10	16	34	...	...	...		9	4	0	4	16
95-96— Lulea	Sweden	38	4	10	14	26	...	...	...		13	0	1	1	47
96-97— Lulea	Sweden	47	7	9	16	38	...	...	...		10	1	2	3	8

OKSIUTA, ROMAN   RW   PENGUINS

PERSONAL: Born August 21, 1970, in Murmansk, U.S.S.R. ... 6-3/230. ... Shoots left. ... Name pronounced ROH-muhn ahks-YOO-tuh.
TRANSACTIONS/CAREER NOTES: Selected by New York Rangers in 10th round (11th Rangers pick, 202nd overall) of NHL entry draft (June 17, 1989). ... Traded by Rangers with third-round draft pick (RW Alexander Kerch) in 1993 draft to Edmonton Oilers for D Kevin Lowe (December 11, 1992). ... Traded by Oilers to Vancouver Canucks for D Jiri Slegr (April 7, 1995). ... Strained groin (February 6, 1996); missed four games. ... Traded by Canucks to Mighty Ducks of Anaheim for C Mike Sillinger (March 15, 1996). ... Strained groin (January 23, 1997); missed six games. ... Traded by Mighty Ducks to Pittsburgh Penguins for C Richard Park (March 18, 1997).
MISCELLANEOUS: Failed to score on a penalty shot (vs. Ed Belfour, February 4, 1994).

Season Team	League	REGULAR SEASON Gms.	G	A	Pts.	PIM	+/-	PP	SH		PLAYOFFS Gms.	G	A	Pts.	PIM
87-88— Khim. Voskresensk	USSR	11	1	0	1	4	...	...	...		—	—	—	—	—
88-89— Khim. Voskresensk	USSR	34	13	3	16	14	...	...	...		—	—	—	—	—
89-90— Khim. Voskresensk	USSR	37	13	6	19	16	...	...	...		—	—	—	—	—
90-91— Khim. Voskresensk	USSR	41	12	8	20	24	...	...	...		—	—	—	—	—
91-92— Khim. Voskresensk	CIS	42	24	20	*44	28	...	...	...		—	—	—	—	—
92-93— Cape Breton	AHL	43	26	25	51	22	...	...	...		16	9	19	28	12
93-94— Edmonton	NHL	10	1	2	3	4	-1	0	0		—	—	—	—	—
— Cape Breton	AHL	47	31	22	53	90	...	...	...		4	2	2	4	22
94-95— Cape Breton	AHL	25	9	7	16	20	...	...	...		—	—	—	—	—
— Edmonton	NHL	26	11	2	13	8	-14	5	0		—	—	—	—	—
— Vancouver	NHL	12	5	2	7	2	2	1	0		10	2	3	5	0
95-96— Vancouver	NHL	56	16	23	39	42	2	5	0		—	—	—	—	—
— Anaheim	NHL	14	7	5	12	18	2	6	0		—	—	—	—	—
96-97— Anaheim	NHL	28	6	7	13	22	-12	2	0		—	—	—	—	—
— Pittsburgh	NHL	7	0	0	0	4	-4	0	0		—	—	—	—	—
NHL totals (4 years)		153	46	41	87	100	-25	19	0		10	2	3	5	0

OLAUSSON, FREDRIK   D   PENGUINS

PERSONAL: Born October 5, 1966, in Vaxsjo, Sweden. ... 6-2/195. ... Shoots right. ... Name pronounced OH-luh-suhn.
TRANSACTIONS/CAREER NOTES: Selected by Winnipeg Jets in fourth round (fourth Jets pick, 81st overall) of NHL entry draft (June 15, 1985). ... Dislocated shoulder (August 1987). ... Underwent shoulder surgery (November 1987). ... Signed five-year contract with Farjestad, Sweden (June 19, 1989); Farjestad agreed to allow Olausson to remain in Winnipeg. ... Sprained knee (January 22, 1993); missed 11 games. ... Lacerated ankle (November 8, 1993); missed two games. ... Suffered from the flu (January 18, 1993); missed one game. ... Sprained knee (January 23, 1993); missed 11 games. ... Suffered from the flu (March 4, 1993); missed one game. ... Traded by Jets with seventh-round pick (LW Curtis Sheptak) in 1994 draft to Edmonton Oilers for third-round pick (C Tavis Hansen) in 1994 draft (December 5, 1993). ... Strained knee (January 11, 1994). ... Played in Europe during 1994-95 NHL lockout. ... Suffered from the flu (February 17, 1995); missed one game. ... Suffered colitis (March 3, 1995); missed 10 games. ... Cracked ribs (November 4, 1995); missed 14 games. ... Suffered irregular heart beat (December 6, 1995); missed five games. ... Claimed on waivers by Mighty Ducks of Anaheim (January 16, 1996) ... Traded by Mighty Ducks with C Alex Hicks to Pittsburgh Penguins for LW Shawn Antoski and D Dmitri Mironov (November 19, 1996). ... Fractured cheekbone (January 26, 1997); missed nine games. ... Strained groin (February 27, 1997); missed three games.
HONORS: Named to Swedish League All-Star team (1985-86).

Season Team	League	REGULAR SEASON Gms.	G	A	Pts.	PIM	+/-	PP	SH		PLAYOFFS Gms.	G	A	Pts.	PIM
83-84— Nybro	Sweden	28	8	14	22	32	...	...	...		—	—	—	—	—
84-85— Farjestad Karlstad	Sweden	34	6	12	18	24	...	...	...		3	1	0	1	0
85-86— Farjestad Karlstad	Sweden	33	5	12	17	14	...	...	...		8	3	2	5	6
86-87— Winnipeg	NHL	72	7	29	36	24	-3	1	0		10	2	3	5	4
87-88— Winnipeg	NHL	38	5	10	15	18	3	2	0		5	1	1	2	0
88-89— Winnipeg	NHL	75	15	47	62	32	6	4	0		—	—	—	—	—
89-90— Winnipeg	NHL	77	9	46	55	32	-1	3	0		7	0	2	2	2
90-91— Winnipeg	NHL	71	12	29	41	24	-22	5	0		—	—	—	—	—
91-92— Winnipeg	NHL	77	20	42	62	34	-31	13	1		7	1	5	6	4
92-93— Winnipeg	NHL	68	16	41	57	22	-4	11	0		6	0	2	2	2
93-94— Winnipeg	NHL	18	2	5	7	10	-3	1	0		—	—	—	—	—
— Edmonton	NHL	55	9	19	28	20	-4	6	0		—	—	—	—	—
94-95— Ehrwald	Austria	10	4	3	7	8	...	...	...		—	—	—	—	—
— Edmonton	NHL	33	0	10	10	20	-4	0	0		—	—	—	—	—
95-96— Edmonton	NHL	20	0	6	6	14	-14	0	0		—	—	—	—	—
— Anaheim	NHL	36	2	16	18	24	7	1	0		—	—	—	—	—
96-97— Anaheim	NHL	20	2	9	11	8	-5	1	0		—	—	—	—	—
— Pittsburgh	NHL	51	7	20	27	24	21	2	0		4	0	1	1	0
NHL totals (11 years)		711	106	329	435	306	-54	50	1		39	4	14	18	12

OLCZYK, EDDIE   LW   PENGUINS

PERSONAL: Born August 16, 1966, in Chicago. ... 6-1/205. ... Shoots left. ... Name pronounced OHL-chehk.
TRANSACTIONS/CAREER NOTES: Selected by Chicago Blackhawks in first round (first Blackhawks pick, third overall) of NHL entry draft (June 9, 1984). ... Hyperextended knee (September 3, 1984). ... Broke bone in left foot (December 16, 1984). ... Traded by Blackhawks with LW Al Secord to Toronto Maple Leafs for RW Rick Vaive, LW Steve Thomas and D Bob McGill (September 1987). ... Pinched nerve in left

knee (January 3, 1990). ... Traded by Maple Leafs with LW Mark Osborne to Winnipeg Jets for D Dave Ellett and LW Paul Fenton (November 10, 1990). ... Dislocated elbow and sprained ankle (January 8, 1992); missed 15 games. ... Sprained knee (November 24, 1992); missed nine games. ... Traded by Jets to New York Rangers for LW Kris King and RW Tie Domi (December 28, 1992). ... Fractured right thumb (January 31, 1994); missed 24 games. ... Suffered from kidney stones (January 24, 1995); missed six games. ... Suffered back spasms (March 3, 1995); missed three games. ... Traded by Rangers to Jets for fifth-round pick (D Alexei Vasiljev) in 1995 draft (April 7, 1995). ... Strained rib cage (October 28, 1995); missed four games. ... Strained back (January 3, 1996); missed four games. ... Sprained knee (March 7, 1996); missed 13 games. ... Signed as free agent by Los Angeles Kings (July 8, 1996). ... Suffered from the flu (December 12, 1996); missed two games. ... Traded by Kings to Pittsburgh Penguins for RW Glen Murray (March 18, 1997).
STATISTICAL PLATEAUS: Three-goal games: 1988-89 (1), 1989-90 (1), 1992-93 (1), 1995-96 (1), 1996-97 (1). Total: 5.
MISCELLANEOUS: Member of Stanley Cup championship team (1994).

		REGULAR SEASON								PLAYOFFS				
Season Team	League	Gms.	G	A	Pts.	PIM	+/-	PP	SH	Gms.	G	A	Pts.	PIM
83-84 — U.S. national team	Int'l	56	19	40	59	36	...	...	...	—	—	—	—	—
— U.S. Olympic team.....	Int'l	6	2	6	8	0	...	...	...	—	—	—	—	—
84-85 — Chicago.....................	NHL	70	20	30	50	67	11	1	1	15	6	5	11	11
85-86 — Chicago.....................	NHL	79	29	50	79	47	2	8	1	3	0	0	0	0
86-87 — Chicago.....................	NHL	79	16	35	51	119	-4	2	1	4	1	1	2	4
87-88 — Toronto	NHL	80	42	33	75	55	-22	14	4	6	5	4	9	2
88-89 — Toronto	NHL	80	38	52	90	75	0	11	2	—	—	—	—	—
89-90 — Toronto	NHL	79	32	56	88	78	0	6	0	5	1	2	3	14
90-91 — Toronto	NHL	18	4	10	14	13	-7	0	0	—	—	—	—	—
— Winnipeg	NHL	61	26	31	57	69	-20	14	0	—	—	—	—	—
91-92 — Winnipeg	NHL	64	32	33	65	67	11	12	0	6	2	1	3	4
92-93 — Winnipeg	NHL	25	8	12	20	26	-11	2	0	—	—	—	—	—
— New York Rangers	NHL	46	13	16	29	26	9	0	0	—	—	—	—	—
93-94 — New York Rangers	NHL	37	3	5	8	28	-1	0	0	1	0	0	0	0
94-95 — New York Rangers	NHL	20	2	1	3	4	-2	1	0	—	—	—	—	—
— Winnipeg	NHL	13	2	8	10	8	1	1	0	—	—	—	—	—
95-96 — Winnipeg	NHL	51	27	22	49	65	0	16	0	6	1	2	3	6
96-97 — Los Angeles	NHL	67	21	23	44	45	-22	5	1	—	—	—	—	—
— Pittsburgh.................	NHL	12	4	7	11	6	8	0	0	5	1	0	1	12
NHL totals (13 years)		**881**	**319**	**424**	**743**	**798**	**-47**	**93**	**10**	**51**	**17**	**15**	**32**	**53**

OLIVER, DAVID   RW   RANGERS

PERSONAL: Born April 17, 1971, in Sechelt, B.C. ... 6-0/190. ... Shoots right.
COLLEGE: Michigan.
TRANSACTIONS/CAREER NOTES: Selected by Edmonton Oilers in seventh round (seventh Oilers pick, 144th overall) of NHL entry draft (June 22, 1991). ... Suffered hip pointer (January 24, 1997); missed one game. ... Claimed on waivers by New York Rangers (February 22, 1997).
HONORS: Named to CCHA All-Star second team (1992-93). ... Named to NCAA All-America West first team (1993-94). ... Named CCHA Player of the Year (1993-94). ... Named to CCHA All-Star first team (1993-94).
STATISTICAL PLATEAUS: Three-goal games: 1994-95 (1).

		REGULAR SEASON								PLAYOFFS				
Season Team	League	Gms.	G	A	Pts.	PIM	+/-	PP	SH	Gms.	G	A	Pts.	PIM
90-91 — Univ. of Michigan.......	CCHA	27	13	11	24	34	...	...	...	—	—	—	—	—
91-92 — Univ. of Michigan.......	CCHA	44	31	27	58	32	...	...	...	—	—	—	—	—
92-93 — Univ. of Michigan.......	CCHA	40	35	20	55	18	...	...	...	—	—	—	—	—
93-94 — Univ. of Michigan.......	CCHA	41	28	40	68	16	...	...	...	—	—	—	—	—
94-95 — Cape Breton	AHL	32	11	18	29	8	...	...	...	—	—	—	—	—
— Edmonton	NHL	44	16	14	30	20	-11	10	0	—	—	—	—	—
95-96 — Edmonton	NHL	80	20	19	39	34	-22	14	0	—	—	—	—	—
96-97 — Edmonton	NHL	17	1	2	3	4	-8	0	0	—	—	—	—	—
— New York Rangers	NHL	14	2	1	3	4	3	0	0	3	0	0	0	0
NHL totals (3 years)		**155**	**39**	**36**	**75**	**62**	**-38**	**24**	**0**	**3**	**0**	**0**	**0**	**0**

OLIWA, KRZYSZTOF   LW   DEVILS

PERSONAL: Born April 12, 1973, in Tychy, Poland. ... 6-5/235. ... Shoots left. ... Name pronounced KRIH-stahf OH-lee-wah.
TRANSACTIONS/CAREER NOTES: Selected by New Jersey Devils in third round (fourth Devils pick, 65th overall) of NHL entry draft (June 26, 1993). ... Loaned by Devils to Detroit Vipers of IHL (January 31, 1995). ... Returned by Vipers to Albany (February 9, 1995). ... Loaned by Devils to Saint John of AHL (February 17, 1995).

		REGULAR SEASON								PLAYOFFS				
Season Team	League	Gms.	G	A	Pts.	PIM	+/-	PP	SH	Gms.	G	A	Pts.	PIM
90-91 — GKS Katowice	Poland Jrs.	5	4	4	8	10	...	...	...	—	—	—	—	—
91-92 — GKS Tychy	Poland	10	3	7	10	6	...	...	...	—	—	—	—	—
92-93 — Welland Jr. B	OHA	30	13	21	34	127	...	...	...	—	—	—	—	—
93-94 — Albany......................	AHL	33	2	4	6	151	...	...	...	—	—	—	—	—
— Raleigh.......................	ECHL	15	0	2	2	65	...	...	...	9	0	0	0	35
94-95 — Albany......................	AHL	20	1	1	2	77	...	...	...	—	—	—	—	—
— Detroit.......................	IHL	4	0	1	1	24	...	...	...	—	—	—	—	—
— Saint John	AHL	14	1	4	5	79	...	...	...	—	—	—	—	—
— Raleigh.......................	ECHL	5	0	2	2	32	...	...	...	—	—	—	—	—
95-96 — Albany......................	AHL	51	5	11	16	217	...	...	...	—	—	—	—	—
— Raleigh.......................	ECHL	9	1	0	1	53	...	...	...	—	—	—	—	—
96-97 — Albany......................	AHL	60	13	14	27	322	...	...	...	15	7	1	8	49
— New Jersey	NHL	1	0	0	0	5	-1	0	0	—	—	—	—	—
NHL totals (1 year)		**1**	**0**	**0**	**0**	**5**	**-1**	**0**	**0**					

OLSON, BOYD   C   CANADIENS

PERSONAL: Born April 4, 1976, in Edmonton. ... 6-1/173. ... Shoots left.
TRANSACTIONS/CAREER NOTES: Selected by Montreal Canadiens in sixth round (sixth Canadiens pick, 138th overall) of NHL entry draft (July 8, 1995).

		REGULAR SEASON								PLAYOFFS				
Season Team	League	Gms.	G	A	Pts.	PIM	+/-	PP	SH	Gms.	G	A	Pts.	PIM
93-94 — Tri-City	WHL	2	0	1	1	0	...	...	...	—	—	—	—	—
94-95 — Tri-City	WHL	69	16	16	32	87	...	...	...	17	6	2	8	22
95-96 — Tri-City	WHL	62	13	12	25	105	...	...	...	11	1	4	5	16
— Fredericton	AHL	0	0	0	0	0	...	...	...	2	1	0	1	0
96-97 — Fredericton	AHL	74	8	12	20	43	...	...	...	—	—	—	—	—

OLSSON, CHRISTER   D   SENATORS

PERSONAL: Born July 24, 1970, in Arboga, Sweden. ... 5-11/195. ... Shoots left.
TRANSACTIONS/CAREER NOTES: Selected by St. Louis Blues in 11th round (10th Blues pick, 275th overall) of NHL entry Draft (June 29, 1993). ... Traded by Blues to Ottawa Senators for LW Pavol Demitra (November 27, 1996). ... Bruised ribs (February 1, 1997); missed four games.

		REGULAR SEASON								PLAYOFFS				
Season Team	League	Gms.	G	A	Pts.	PIM	+/-	PP	SH	Gms.	G	A	Pts.	PIM
91-92 — Mora	Swed. Div. II	36	6	10	16	38	...	...	...	—	—	—	—	—
92-93 — Brynas Gavle	Sweden	22	4	4	8	18	...	...	...	—	—	—	—	—
93-94 — Brynas Gavle	Sweden	38	7	3	10	50	...	...	...	7	0	3	3	6
94-95 — Brynas Gavle	Sweden	39	6	5	11	18	...	...	...	14	1	3	4	8
95-96 — Worcester	AHL	39	7	7	14	22	...	...	...	—	—	—	—	—
— St. Louis	NHL	26	2	8	10	14	-6	2	0	3	0	0	0	0
96-97 — Worcester	AHL	2	0	0	0	0	...	...	...	—	—	—	—	—
— St. Louis	NHL	5	0	1	1	0	1	0	0	—	—	—	—	—
— Ottawa	NHL	25	2	3	5	10	-5	1	0	—	—	—	—	—
NHL totals (2 years)		56	4	12	16	24	-10	3	0	3	0	0	0	0

O'NEILL, JEFF   C   HURRICANES

PERSONAL: Born February 23, 1976, in Richmond Hill, Ont. ... 6-0/195. ... Shoots right.
HIGH SCHOOL: Bishop MacDonnell (Guelph, Ont.).
TRANSACTIONS/CAREER NOTES: Selected by Hartford Whalers in first round (first Whalers pick, fifth overall) of NHL entry draft (June 28, 1994). ... Bruised foot (December 30, 1995); missed four games. ... Reinjured foot (January 10, 1996); missed four games. ... Injured shoulder (February 17, 1996); missed four games. ... Injured groin (January 2, 1997); missed one game. ... Sprained wrist (April 2, 1997); missed four games. ... Whalers franchise moved to North Carolina and renamed Carolina Hurricanes for 1997-98 season; NHL approved move on June 25, 1997.
HONORS: Won Emms Family Award (1992-93). ... Named to Can.HL All-Rookie team (1992-93). ... Named to OHL All-Rookie team (1992-93). ... Won Can.HL Top Draft Prospect Award (1993-94). ... Named to Can.HL All-Star second team (1994-95). ... Named to OHL All-Star first team (1994-95).
STATISTICAL PLATEAUS: Three-goal games: 1996-97 (1).

		REGULAR SEASON								PLAYOFFS				
Season Team	League	Gms.	G	A	Pts.	PIM	+/-	PP	SH	Gms.	G	A	Pts.	PIM
91-92 — Thornhill	Tier II Jr. A	43	27	53	80	48	...	...	...	—	—	—	—	—
92-93 — Guelph	OHL	65	32	47	79	88	...	...	...	5	2	2	4	6
93-94 — Guelph	OHL	66	45	81	126	95	...	...	...	9	2	11	13	31
94-95 — Guelph	OHL	57	43	81	124	56	...	...	...	14	8	18	26	34
95-96 — Hartford	NHL	65	8	19	27	40	-3	1	0	—	—	—	—	—
96-97 — Hartford	NHL	72	14	16	30	40	-24	2	1	—	—	—	—	—
— Springfield	AHL	1	0	0	0	0	...	...	...	—	—	—	—	—
NHL totals (2 years)		137	22	35	57	80	-27	3	1					

O'NEILL, MIKE   G   MIGHTY DUCKS

PERSONAL: Born November 3, 1967, in LaSalle, Que. ... 5-7/160. ... Catches left. ... Full name: Michael Anthony O'Neill Jr.
COLLEGE: Yale.
TRANSACTIONS/CAREER NOTES: Selected by Winnipeg Jets in NHL supplemental draft (June 10, 1988). ... Dislocated shoulder (April 8, 1991); missed remainder of playoffs. ... Dislocated shoulder (February 1, 1993); missed two games. ... Underwent shoulder surgery (February 12, 1993); missed remainder of season. ... Injured knee (March 16, 1994); missed one game. ... Signed as free agent by Mighty Ducks of Anaheim (July 28, 1995).
HONORS: Named to ECAC All-Star first team (1986-87 and 1988-89). ... Named to NCAA All-America East first team (1988-89).
MISCELLANEOUS: Allowed a penalty shot goal (vs. Laurie Boschman, February 1, 1993).

		REGULAR SEASON							PLAYOFFS					
Season Team	League	Gms.	Min	W	L	T	GA	SO	Avg.	Gms.	Min.	W	L	GA	SO	Avg.
85-86 — Yale University	ECAC	6	389	3	1	0	17	0	2.62	—	—	—	—	—	—	—
86-87 — Yale University	ECAC	16	964	9	6	1	55	2	3.42	—	—	—	—	—	—	—
87-88 — Yale University	ECAC	24	1385	6	17	0	101	0	4.38	—	—	—	—	—	—	—
88-89 — Yale University	ECAC	25	1490	10	14	1	93	0	3.74	—	—	—	—	—	—	—
89-90 — Tappara	Finland	41	2369	23	13	5	127	2	3.22	—	—	—	—	—	—	—
90-91 — Fort Wayne	IHL	8	490	5	2	‡1	31	0	3.80	—	—	—	—	—	—	—
— Moncton	AHL	30	1613	13	7	6	84	0	3.12	8	435	3	4	29	0	4.00

O

Season Team	League	REGULAR SEASON								PLAYOFFS						
		Gms.	Min	W	L	T	GA	SO	Avg.	Gms.	Min.	W	L	GA	SO	Avg.
91-92 — Fort Wayne	IHL	33	1858	22	6	‡3	97	†4	3.13	—	—	—	—	—	—	—
— Moncton	AHL	32	1902	14	16	2	108	1	3.41	11	670	4	†7	43	1	3.85
— Winnipeg	NHL	1	13	0	0	0	1	0	4.62	—	—	—	—	—	—	—
92-93 — Moncton	AHL	30	1649	13	10	4	88	1	3.20	—	—	—	—	—	—	—
— Winnipeg	NHL	2	73	0	0	1	6	0	4.93	—	—	—	—	—	—	—
93-94 — Moncton	AHL	12	717	8	4	0	33	1	2.76	—	—	—	—	—	—	—
— Fort Wayne	IHL	11	642	4	4	‡3	38	0	3.55	—	—	—	—	—	—	—
— Winnipeg	NHL	17	738	0	9	1	51	0	4.15	—	—	—	—	—	—	—
94-95 — Fort Wayne	IHL	28	1603	11	12	‡4	109	0	4.08	—	—	—	—	—	—	—
— Phoenix	IHL	21	1257	13	4	‡4	64	1	3.05	9	536	4	5	33	0	3.69
95-96 — Baltimore	AHL	74	4250	31	31	7	250	2	3.53	12	688	6	6	43	0	3.75
96-97 — Long Beach	IHL	45	2644	26	12	‡6	145	1	3.29	1	7	0	0	0	0	0.00
— Anaheim	NHL	1	31	0	0	0	3	0	5.81	—	—	—	—	—	—	—
NHL totals (4 years)		21	855	0	9	2	61	0	4.28							

ORSZAGH, VLADIMIR — LW — ISLANDERS

PERSONAL: Born May 24, 1977, in Banska Bystrica, Czechoslovakia. ... 5-11/173. ... Shoots left. ... Name pronounced OHR-sahg.
TRANSACTIONS/CAREER NOTES: Selected by New York Islanders in fifth round (fourth Islanders pick, 106th overall) of NHL entry draft (July 8, 1995).

Season Team	League	REGULAR SEASON							PLAYOFFS				
		Gms.	G	A	Pts.	PIM	+/-	PP	SH	Gms.	G	A	Pts.	PIM
93-94 — IS Banska Bys. Jrs.	Slovakia	...	38	27	65	...	...	...	...	—	—	—	—	—
94-95 — Banska Bystrica	Slov. Div. II	38	18	12	30	...	...	...	...	—	—	—	—	—
— Martim. ZTS Martin	Slovakia	1	0	0	0	0	...	...	...	—	—	—	—	—
95-96 — Banska Bystrica	Slovakia	31	9	5	14	22	...	...	...	—	—	—	—	—
96-97 — Utah	IHL	68	12	15	27	30	...	...	...	3	0	1	1	4

OSGOOD, CHRIS — G — RED WINGS

PERSONAL: Born November 26, 1972, in Peace River, Alta. ... 5-11/175. ... Catches left.
TRANSACTIONS/CAREER NOTES: Selected by Detroit Red Wings in third round (third Red Wings pick, 54th overall) of NHL entry draft (June 22, 1991). ... Strained hamstring (January 14, 1997); missed five games.
HONORS: Named to WHL (East) All-Star second team (1990-91). ... Played in NHL All-Star Game (1996). ... Named to THE SPORTING NEWS All-Star first team (1995-96). ... Shared William M. Jennings Trophy with Mike Vernon (1995-96). ... Named to NHL All-Star second team (1995-96). ... Named to play in NHL All-Star Game (1997); replaced by G Guy Hebert due to injury.
MISCELLANEOUS: Member of Stanley Cup championship team (1997). ... Stopped a penalty shot attempt (vs. Peter Zezel, March 4, 1994; vs. Dave Gagner, April 1, 1995; vs. Mike Hudson, November 18, 1996).

Season Team	League	REGULAR SEASON								PLAYOFFS						
		Gms.	Min	W	L	T	GA	SO	Avg.	Gms.	Min.	W	L	GA	SO	Avg.
89-90 — Medicine Hat	WHL	57	3094	24	28	2	228	0	4.42	3	173	3	4	17	0	5.90
90-91 — Medicine Hat	WHL	46	2630	23	18	3	173	2	3.95	12	714	7	5	42	0	3.53
91-92 — Medicine Hat	WHL	15	819	10	3	0	44	0	3.22	—	—	—	—	—	—	—
— Brandon	WHL	16	890	3	10	1	60	1	4.04	—	—	—	—	—	—	—
— Seattle	WHL	21	1217	12	7	1	65	1	3.20	15	904	9	6	51	0	3.38
92-93 — Adirondack	AHL	45	2438	19	19	2	159	0	3.91	1	59	0	1	2	0	2.03
93-94 — Adirondack	AHL	4	240	3	1	0	13	0	3.25	—	—	—	—	—	—	—
— Detroit	NHL	41	2286	23	8	5	105	2	2.76	6	307	3	2	12	1	2.35
94-95 — Adirondack	AHL	2	120	1	1	0	6	0	3.00	—	—	—	—	—	—	—
— Detroit	NHL	19	1087	14	5	0	41	1	2.26	2	68	0	0	2	0	1.76
95-96 — Detroit	NHL	50	2933	*39	6	5	106	5	2.17	15	936	8	7	33	2	2.12
96-97 — Detroit	NHL	47	2769	23	13	9	106	6	2.30	2	47	0	0	2	0	2.55
NHL totals (4 years)		157	9075	99	32	19	358	14	2.37	25	1358	11	9	49	3	2.16

O'SULLIVAN, CHRIS — D — FLAMES

PERSONAL: Born May 15, 1974, in Dorchester, Mass. ... 6-3/199. ... Shoots left.
HIGH SCHOOL: Catholic Memorial (Boston).
COLLEGE: Boston University.
TRANSACTIONS/CAREER NOTES: Selected by Calgary Flames in second round (second Flames pick, 30th overall) of NHL entry draft (June 20, 1992).
HONORS: Named to NCAA All-America second team (1994-95).

Season Team	League	REGULAR SEASON							PLAYOFFS				
		Gms.	G	A	Pts.	PIM	+/-	PP	SH	Gms.	G	A	Pts.	PIM
91-92 — Catholic Memorial	Mass. H.S.	26	26	23	49	65	...	...	...	—	—	—	—	—
92-93 — Boston University	Hockey East	5	0	2	2	4	...	...	...	—	—	—	—	—
93-94 — Boston University	Hockey East	32	5	18	23	25	...	...	...	—	—	—	—	—
94-95 — Boston University	Hockey East	40	23	33	56	48	...	...	...	—	—	—	—	—
95-96 — Boston University	Hockey East	37	12	35	47	50	...	...	...	—	—	—	—	—
96-97 — Calgary	NHL	27	2	8	10	2	0	1	0	—	—	—	—	—
— Saint John	AHL	29	3	8	11	17	...	...	...	5	0	4	4	0
NHL totals (1 year)		27	2	8	10	2	0	1	0					

PERSONAL: Born October 29, 1961, in Elk River, Minn. ... 6-4/225. ... Shoots right. ... Full name: Joel Stuart Otto.
COLLEGE: Bemidji (Minn.) State.
TRANSACTIONS/CAREER NOTES: Signed as free agent by Calgary Flames (September 11, 1984). ... Tore right knee cartilage (March 10, 1987). ... Strained right knee ligaments (October 8, 1987). ... Bruised ribs (November 1989). ... Hospitalized after being crosschecked from behind (January 13, 1990). ... Injured ankle (March 10, 1992); missed two games. ... Injured rib (January 5, 1993); missed eight games. ... Bruised foot (February 2, 1993); missed one game. ... Signed as free agent by Philadelphia Flyers (July 20, 1995). ... Sprained right knee (November 2, 1995); missed two games. ... Sprained left knee (February 14, 1996); missed six games. ... Sprained left knee (March 8, 1996); missed two games. ... Reinjured left knee (March 19, 1996); missed five games. ... Bruised ribs (October 10, 1996); missed four games.
STATISTICAL PLATEAUS: Three-goal games: 1986-87 (1), 1993-94 (1). Total: 2.
MISCELLANEOUS: Member of Stanley Cup championship team (1989).

		REGULAR SEASON							PLAYOFFS				
Season Team	League	Gms.	G	A	Pts.	PIM	+/-	PP	SH	Gms.	G	A	Pts.	PIM
80-81— Bemidji State	NCAA-II	23	5	11	16	10	...	...	...	—	—	—	—	—
81-82— Bemidji State	NCAA-II	31	19	33	52	24	...	...	...	—	—	—	—	—
82-83— Bemidji State	NCAA-II	37	33	28	61	68	...	...	...	—	—	—	—	—
83-84— Bemidji State	NCAA-II	31	32	43	75	32	...	...	...	—	—	—	—	—
84-85— Moncton	AHL	56	27	36	63	89	...	...	...	—	—	—	—	—
— Calgary	NHL	17	4	8	12	30	3	1	0	3	2	1	3	10
85-86— Calgary	NHL	79	25	34	59	188	22	9	1	22	5	10	15	80
86-87— Calgary	NHL	68	19	31	50	185	8	5	0	2	0	2	2	6
87-88— Calgary	NHL	62	13	39	52	194	16	4	1	9	3	2	5	26
88-89— Calgary	NHL	72	23	30	53	213	12	10	2	22	6	13	19	46
89-90— Calgary	NHL	75	13	20	33	116	4	7	0	6	2	2	4	2
90-91— Calgary	NHL	76	19	20	39	183	-4	7	1	7	1	2	3	8
91-92— Calgary	NHL	78	13	21	34	161	-10	5	1	—	—	—	—	—
92-93— Calgary	NHL	75	19	33	52	150	2	6	1	6	4	2	6	4
93-94— Calgary	NHL	81	11	12	23	92	-17	3	1	3	0	1	1	4
94-95— Calgary	NHL	47	8	13	21	130	8	0	2	7	0	3	3	2
95-96— Philadelphia	NHL	67	12	29	41	115	11	6	1	12	3	4	7	11
96-97— Philadelphia	NHL	78	13	19	32	99	12	0	1	18	1	5	6	8
NHL totals (13 years)		875	192	309	501	1856	67	63	12	117	27	47	74	207

PERSONAL: Born August 3, 1972, in Riga, U.S.S.R. ... 6-3/205. ... Shoots left. ... Name pronounced SAN-diz OH-zoh-linsh.
TRANSACTIONS/CAREER NOTES: Selected by San Jose Sharks in second round (third Sharks pick, 30th overall) of NHL entry draft (June 22, 1991). ... Strained back (November 7, 1992); missed one game. ... Tore knee ligaments (December 30, 1992) and underwent surgery to repair anterior cruciate ligament; missed remainder of season. ... Injured knee (December 11, 1993); missed one game. ... Traded by Sharks to Colorado Avalanche for RW Owen Nolan (October 26, 1995). ... Separated left shoulder (December 7, 1995); missed four games. ... Broke finger (February 23, 1996); missed two games. ... Suffered back spasms (March 9, 1997); missed two games.
HONORS: Played in NHL All-Star Game (1994 and 1997). ... Named to NHL All-Star first team (1996-97).
MISCELLANEOUS: Member of Stanley Cup championship team (1996).

		REGULAR SEASON							PLAYOFFS				
Season Team	League	Gms.	G	A	Pts.	PIM	+/-	PP	SH	Gms.	G	A	Pts.	PIM
90-91— Dynamo Riga	USSR	44	0	3	3	49	...	...	...	—	—	—	—	—
91-92— HC Riga	CIS	30	5	0	5	42	...	...	...	—	—	—	—	—
— Kansas City	IHL	34	6	9	15	20	...	...	...	15	2	5	7	22
92-93— San Jose	NHL	37	7	16	23	40	-9	2	0	—	—	—	—	—
93-94— San Jose	NHL	81	26	38	64	24	16	4	0	14	0	10	10	8
94-95— San Jose	NHL	48	9	16	25	30	-6	3	1	11	3	2	5	6
95-96— San Francisco	IHL	2	1	0	1	0	...	...	...	—	—	—	—	—
— San Jose	NHL	7	1	3	4	4	2	1	0	—	—	—	—	—
— Colorado	NHL	66	13	37	50	50	0	7	1	22	5	14	19	16
96-97— Colorado	NHL	80	23	45	68	88	4	13	0	17	4	13	17	24
NHL totals (5 years)		319	79	155	234	236	7	30	2	64	12	39	51	54

PERSONAL: Born May 5, 1972, in Skalica, Czechoslovakia. ... 5-10/183. ... Shoots left. ... Name pronounced PAHL-fee.
TRANSACTIONS/CAREER NOTES: Selected by New York Islanders in second round (second Islanders pick, 26th overall) of NHL entry draft (June 22, 1991). ... Loaned to Slovak Olympic team (January 31, 1994). ... Suffered concussion (February 17, 1996); missed one game. ... Sprained shoulder (January 13, 1997); missed two games.
HONORS: Named Czechoslovakian League Rookie of the Year (1990-91). ... Named to Czechoslovakian League All-Star team (1991-92). ... Named to play in NHL All-Star Game (1997); replaced by D Scott Lachance due to injury.
STATISTICAL PLATEAUS: Three-goal games: 1995-96 (2), 1996-97 (1). Total: 3.

		REGULAR SEASON							PLAYOFFS				
Season Team	League	Gms.	G	A	Pts.	PIM	+/-	PP	SH	Gms.	G	A	Pts.	PIM
90-91— Nitra	Czech.	50	34	16	50	18	...	...	...	—	—	—	—	—
91-92— Dukla Trencin	Czech.	32	23	25	*48		...	...	...	—	—	—	—	—
92-93— Dukla Trencin	Czech.	43	38	41	79		...	...	...	—	—	—	—	—
93-94— Salt Lake City	IHL	57	25	32	57	83	...	...	...	—	—	—	—	—
— Slov. Olympic team	Int'l	8	3	7	10	8	...	...	...	—	—	—	—	—
— New York Islanders	NHL	5	0	0	0	0	-6	0	0	—	—	—	—	—

O
P

Season Team	League	REGULAR SEASON								PLAYOFFS				
		Gms.	G	A	Pts.	PIM	+/-	PP	SH	Gms.	G	A	Pts.	PIM
94-95— Denver	IHL	33	20	23	43	40	...	...	...	—	—	—	—	—
— New York Islanders....	NHL	33	10	7	17	6	3	1	0	—	—	—	—	—
95-96— New York Islanders....	NHL	81	43	44	87	56	-17	17	1	—	—	—	—	—
96-97— New York Islanders....	NHL	80	48	42	90	43	21	6	4	—	—	—	—	—
NHL totals (4 years)		199	101	93	194	105	1	24	5					

PANDOLFO, JAY — LW — DEVILS

PERSONAL: Born December 27, 1974, in Winchester, Mass. ... 6-1/195. ... Shoots left.
HIGH SCHOOL: Burlington (Mass.).
COLLEGE: Boston University.
TRANSACTIONS/CAREER NOTES: Selected by New Jersey Devils in second round (second Devils pick, 32nd overall) of NHL entry draft (June 26, 1993).
HONORS: Named to NCAA All-America East first team (1995-96). ... Named Hockey East Player of the Year (1995-96). ... Named to Hockey East All-Star team (1995-96).

Season Team	League	REGULAR SEASON								PLAYOFFS				
		Gms.	G	A	Pts.	PIM	+/-	PP	SH	Gms.	G	A	Pts.	PIM
90-91— Burlington	Mass. H.S.	20	19	27	46	10	...	...	...	—	—	—	—	—
91-92— Burlington	Mass. H.S.	20	35	34	69	14	...	...	...	—	—	—	—	—
92-93— Boston University	Hockey East	37	16	22	38	16	...	...	...	—	—	—	—	—
93-94— Boston University	Hockey East	37	17	25	42	27	...	...	...	—	—	—	—	—
94-95— Boston University	Hockey East	20	7	13	20	6	...	...	...	—	—	—	—	—
95-96— Boston University	Hockey East	39	38	29	67	6	...	...	...	—	—	—	—	—
— Albany	AHL	5	3	1	4	0	...	...	...	3	0	0	0	0
96-97— Albany	AHL	12	3	9	12	0	...	...	...	—	—	—	—	—
— New Jersey	NHL	46	6	8	14	6	-1	0	0	6	0	1	1	0
NHL totals (1 year)		46	6	8	14	6	-1	0	0	6	0	1	1	0

PAQUETTE, CHARLES — D — BRUINS

PERSONAL: Born June 17, 1975, in Lachute, Que. ... 6-1/193. ... Shoots left. ... Name pronounced pa-KEHT.
TRANSACTIONS/CAREER NOTES: Selected by Boston Bruins in fourth round (third Bruins pick, 88th overall) of NHL entry draft (June 26, 1993).
HONORS: Named to QMJHL All-Star first team (1994-95).

Season Team	League	REGULAR SEASON								PLAYOFFS				
		Gms.	G	A	Pts.	PIM	+/-	PP	SH	Gms.	G	A	Pts.	PIM
91-92— Trois-Rivieres	QMJHL	60	1	7	8	101	...	...	...	6	0	0	0	2
92-93— Sherbrooke	QMJHL	54	2	5	7	104	...	...	...	15	0	0	0	33
93-94— Sherbrooke	QMJHL	63	5	14	19	165	...	...	...	8	0	2	2	15
94-95— Sherbrooke	QMJHL	53	15	26	41	186	...	...	...	5	1	1	2	18
95-96— Providence	AHL	11	0	1	1	8	...	...	...	4	0	1	1	4
— Charlotte	ECHL	45	4	5	9	114	...	...	...	3	0	1	1	6
96-97— Providence	AHL	18	0	3	3	25	...	...	...	6	0	0	0	8

PARENT, RICH — G — BLUES

PERSONAL: Born January 12, 1973, in Montreal. ... 6-3/195. ... Catches left.
TRANSACTIONS/CAREER NOTES: Signed as free agent by St. Louis Blues (July 17, 1997).
HONORS: Won Norris Trophy (1996-97). ... Named Colonial Hockey League Goaltender of the year (1994-95 and 1995-96).

Season Team	League	REGULAR SEASON							PLAYOFFS					
		Gms.	Min	W	L	T	GA	SO	Avg.	Gms.	Min.	W	L	GA	SO	Avg.
94-95— Muskegon	Col.HL	35	1867	17	11	3	112	1	3.60	13	725	7	3	47	1	3.89
95-96— Muskegon	Col.HL	36	2086	23	7	4	85	2	2.44	—	—	—	—	—	—	—
— Detroit	IHL	19	1040	16	0	‡1	48	2	2.77	7	362	3	3	22	0	3.64
96-97— Detroit	IHL	53	2815	31	13	‡4	104	4	2.22	15	786	8	3	0	1	*1.60

PARK, RICHARD — C — MIGHTY DUCKS

PERSONAL: Born May 27, 1976, in Seoul, South Korea. ... 5-11/189. ... Shoots right.
TRANSACTIONS/CAREER NOTES: Selected by Pittsburgh Penguins in second round (second Penguins pick, 50th overall) of NHL entry draft (June 28, 1994). ... Traded by Penguins to Mighty Ducks of Anaheim for RW Roman Oksiuta (March 18, 1997).

Season Team	League	REGULAR SEASON								PLAYOFFS				
		Gms.	G	A	Pts.	PIM	+/-	PP	SH	Gms.	G	A	Pts.	PIM
91-92— Williams Lake	PCJHL	76	49	58	107	91	...	...	...	—	—	—	—	—
92-93— Belleville	OHL	66	23	38	61	38	...	...	...	5	0	0	0	14
93-94— Belleville	OHL	59	27	49	76	70	...	...	...	12	3	5	8	18
94-95— Belleville	OHL	45	28	51	79	35	...	...	...	16	9	18	27	12
— Pittsburgh	NHL	1	0	1	1	2	1	0	0	3	0	0	0	2
95-96— Belleville	OHL	6	7	6	13	2	...	...	...	14	18	12	30	10
— Pittsburgh	NHL	56	4	6	10	36	3	0	1	1	0	0	0	0
96-97— Cleveland	IHL	50	12	15	27	30	...	...	...	—	—	—	—	—
— Pittsburgh	NHL	1	0	0	0	0	-1	0	0	—	—	—	—	—
— Anaheim	NHL	11	1	1	2	10	0	0	0	11	0	1	1	2
NHL totals (3 years)		69	5	8	13	48	3	0	1	15	0	1	1	4

P

PASSMORE, STEVE   G   OILERS

PERSONAL: Born January 29, 1973, in Thunder Bay, Ont. ... 5-9/165. ... Catches left.
TRANSACTIONS/CAREER NOTES: Selected by Quebec Nordiques in ninth round (10th Nordiques pick, 196th overall) of NHL entry draft (June 20, 1992). ... Traded by Nordiques to Edmonton Oilers for D Brad Werenka (March 21, 1994).
HONORS: Named to WHL (West) All-Star first team (1992-93 and 1993-94). ... Won Fred Hunt Memorial Award (1996-97).

Season Team	League	Gms.	Min	W	L	T	GA	SO	Avg.	Gms.	Min.	W	L	GA	SO	Avg.
88-89—Tri-City	WHL	1	60	...	...	...	6	0	6.00	—	—	—	—	—	—	—
89-90—Tri-City	WHL	4	215	...	...	...	17	0	4.74	—	—	—	—	—	—	—
90-91—Victoria	WHL	35	1838	3	25	1	190	0	6.20	—	—	—	—	—	—	—
91-92—Victoria	WHL	*71	*4228	15	50	7	347	0	4.92	—	—	—	—	—	—	—
92-93—Victoria	WHL	43	2402	14	24	2	150	1	3.75	—	—	—	—	—	—	—
—Kamloops	WHL	25	1479	19	6	0	69	1	2.80	7	401	4	2	22	1	3.29
93-94—Kamloops	WHL	36	1927	22	9	2	88	1	*2.74	18	1099	†11	7	60	0	3.28
94-95—Cape Breton	AHL	25	1455	8	13	3	93	0	3.84	—	—	—	—	—	—	—
95-96—Cape Breton	AHL	2	90	1	0	0	2	0	1.33	—	—	—	—	—	—	—
96-97—Raleigh	ECHL	2	118	1	1	‡0	13	0	6.61	—	—	—	—	—	—	—
—Hamilton	AHL	27	1568	12	12	3	70	1	2.68	22	1325	12	*10	*61	†2	2.76

PATRICK, JAMES   D   FLAMES

PERSONAL: Born June 14, 1963, in Winnipeg. ... 6-2/200. ... Shoots right. ... Brother of Steve Patrick, right winger for three NHL teams (1980-81 through 1985-86).
COLLEGE: North Dakota.
TRANSACTIONS/CAREER NOTES: Selected by New York Rangers as underage junior in first round (first Rangers pick, ninth overall) of NHL entry draft (June 10, 1981). ... Injured groin (October 1984). ... Pinched nerve (December 15, 1985). ... Strained left knee ligaments (March 1988). ... Bruised shoulder and chest (December 1988). ... Pulled groin (March 13, 1989). ... Sprained shoulder (November 4, 1992); missed three games. ... Bruised right shoulder (November 27, 1992); missed three games. ... Sprained left knee (January 27, 1993); missed four games. ... Suffered herniated disc (February 24, 1993); missed two games. ... Suffered herniated disc (March 28, 1993); missed remainder of season. ... Traded by Rangers with C Darren Turcotte to Hartford Whalers for RW Steve Larmer, LW Nick Kypreos and sixth-round pick (C Yuri Litvinov) in 1994 draft (November 2, 1993). ... Suffered herniated disc (December 7, 1993); missed five games. ... Traded by Whalers with C Mikael Nylander and D Zarley Zalapski to Calgary Flames for D Gary Suter, LW Paul Ranheim and C Ted Drury (March 10, 1994). ... Strained left hip (March 10, 1995); missed five games. ... Suffered concussion (April 9, 1996); missed two games. ... Sore back (October 16, 1996); missed one game. ... Strained knee (October 24, 1996); missed five games. ... Suffered concussion (November 20, 1996); missed two games. ... Underwent knee surgery (December 12, 1996); missed remainder of season.
HONORS: Named SJHL Player of the Year (1980-81). ... Named to SJHL All-Star first team (1980-81). ... Won WCHA Rookie of the Year Award (1981-82). ... Named to WCHA All-Star second team (1981-82). ... Named to NCAA All-Tournament team (1981-82). ... Named to NCAA All-America West team (1982-83). ... Named to WCHA All-Star first team (1982-83).

Season Team	League	Gms.	G	A	Pts.	PIM	+/-	PP	SH	Gms.	G	A	Pts.	PIM
80-81—Prince Albert	SJHL	59	21	61	82	162	...	...	...	4	1	6	7	0
81-82—North Dakota	WCHA	42	5	24	29	26	...	...	...	—	—	—	—	—
82-83—North Dakota	WCHA	36	12	36	48	29	...	...	...	—	—	—	—	—
83-84—Can. Olympic team	Int'l	63	7	24	31	52	...	...	...					
—New York Rangers	NHL	12	1	7	8	2	6	0	0	5	0	3	3	2
84-85—New York Rangers	NHL	75	8	28	36	71	-17	4	1	3	0	0	0	4
85-86—New York Rangers	NHL	75	14	29	43	88	14	2	1	16	1	5	6	34
86-87—New York Rangers	NHL	78	10	45	55	62	13	5	0	6	1	2	3	2
87-88—New York Rangers	NHL	70	17	45	62	52	16	9	0	—	—	—	—	—
88-89—New York Rangers	NHL	68	11	36	47	41	3	6	0	4	0	1	1	2
89-90—New York Rangers	NHL	73	14	43	57	50	4	9	0	10	3	8	11	0
90-91—New York Rangers	NHL	74	10	49	59	58	-5	6	0	6	0	0	0	6
91-92—New York Rangers	NHL	80	14	57	71	54	34	6	0	13	0	7	7	12
92-93—New York Rangers	NHL	60	5	21	26	61	1	3	0	—	—	—	—	—
93-94—New York Rangers	NHL	6	0	3	3	2	1	0	0	—	—	—	—	—
—Hartford	NHL	47	8	20	28	32	-12	4	1	—	—	—	—	—
—Calgary	NHL	15	2	2	4	6	6	1	0	7	0	1	1	6
94-95—Calgary	NHL	43	0	10	10	14	-3	0	0	5	0	1	1	0
95-96—Calgary	NHL	80	3	32	35	30	3	1	0	4	0	0	0	2
96-97—Calgary	NHL	19	3	1	4	6	2	1	0	—	—	—	—	—
NHL totals (14 years)		875	120	428	548	629	66	57	3	79	5	28	33	70

PATTERSON, ED   RW   PENGUINS

PERSONAL: Born November 14, 1972, in Delta, B.C. ... 6-2/210. ... Shoots right.
TRANSACTIONS/CAREER NOTES: Selected by Pittsburgh Penguins in seventh round (seventh Penguins pick, 148th overall) of NHL entry draft (June 22, 1991). ... Underwent minor surgery on left leg (November 3, 1995); missed nine games. ... Suffered back spasms (January 3, 1996); missed 14 games. ... Underwent back surgery (March 8, 1996); missed 17 games.

Season Team	League	Gms.	G	A	Pts.	PIM	+/-	PP	SH	Gms.	G	A	Pts.	PIM
90-91—Swift Current	WHL	7	2	7	9	0	...	...	...	—	—	—	—	—
—Kamloops	WHL	55	14	33	47	134	...	...	...	5	0	0	0	7
91-92—Kamloops	WHL	38	19	25	44	120	...	...	...	1	0	0	0	0
92-93—Cleveland	IHL	63	4	16	20	131	...	...	...	3	1	1	2	2
93-94—Cleveland	IHL	55	21	32	53	73	...	...	...					
—Pittsburgh	NHL	27	3	1	4	10	-5	0	0	—	—	—	—	—

P

Season Team	League	REGULAR SEASON							PLAYOFFS				
		Gms.	G	A	Pts.	PIM	+/-	PP	SH	Gms.	G	A	Pts.	PIM
94-95— Cleveland	IHL	58	13	17	30	93	...	...	...	4	1	2	3	6
95-96— Pittsburgh..................	NHL	35	0	2	2	38	-5	0	0	—	—	—	—	—
96-97— Pittsburgh..................	NHL	6	0	0	0	8	0	0	0	—	—	—	—	—
— Cleveland	IHL	40	6	12	18	75	...	...	...	13	2	4	6	61
NHL totals (3 years)		68	3	3	6	56	-10	0	0					

PATTISON, ROB   RW   DEVILS

PERSONAL: Born September 18, 1971, in Sherborn, Mass. ... 6-0/195. ... Shoots left.
TRANSACTIONS/CAREER NOTES: Signed as free agent by New Jersey Devils (October 1, 1995).

Season Team	League	REGULAR SEASON							PLAYOFFS				
		Gms.	G	A	Pts.	PIM	+/-	PP	SH	Gms.	G	A	Pts.	PIM
90-91— Univ. of Vermont.......	ECAC	24	7	3	10	14	...	...	...	—	—	—	—	—
91-92— Univ. of Vermont.......	ECAC	25	6	12	18	8	...	...	...	—	—	—	—	—
92-93— Univ. of Vermont.......	ECAC						Did not play.			—	—	—	—	—
93-94— Univ. of Vermont.......	ECAC	32	8	19	27	14	...	...	...	—	—	—	—	—
94-95— Univ. of Vermont.......	ECAC	8	8	6	14	8	...	...	...	—	—	—	—	—
95-96— Raleigh......................	ECHL	67	14	23	37	122	...	...	...	4	1	2	3	0
— Albany......................	AHL	5	4	3	7	0	...	...	...	2	0	0	0	0
96-97— Albany......................	AHL	61	24	15	39	31	...	...	...	16	5	1	6	20

PAUL, JEFF   RW   BLACKHAWKS

PERSONAL: Born March 1, 1978, in London, Ont. ... 6-3/196. ... Shoots right.
TRANSACTIONS/CAREER NOTES: Selected by Chicago Blackhawks in second round (second Blackhawks pick, 42nd overall) of NHL entry draft (June 22, 1996).

Season Team	League	REGULAR SEASON							PLAYOFFS				
		Gms.	G	A	Pts.	PIM	+/-	PP	SH	Gms.	G	A	Pts.	PIM
94-95— Niagara Falls	OHL	57	3	10	13	64	...	...	...	6	0	2	2	0
95-96— Niagara Falls	OHL	48	1	7	8	81	...	...	...	10	0	4	4	37
96-97— Erie	OHL	60	4	23	27	152	...	...	...	5	2	0	2	12

PAYETTE, ANDRE   C   FLYERS

PERSONAL: Born July 29, 1976, in Cornwall, Ont. ... 6-2/182. ... Shoots left. ... Name pronounced pigh-YEHT.
TRANSACTIONS/CAREER NOTES: Selected by Philadelphia Flyers in 10th round (ninth Flyers pick, 244th overall) of NHL entry draft (June 29, 1994).

Season Team	League	REGULAR SEASON							PLAYOFFS				
		Gms.	G	A	Pts.	PIM	+/-	PP	SH	Gms.	G	A	Pts.	PIM
93-94— Sault Ste. Marie	OHL	40	2	3	5	98	...	...	...	—	—	—	—	—
94-95— Sault Ste. Marie	OHL	50	15	15	30	177	...	...	...	—	—	—	—	—
95-96— S.S. Marie.................	OHL	57	20	19	39	257	...	...	...	4	0	0	0	5
96-97— Kingston	OHL	33	13	13	26	162	...	...	...	2	0	0	0	2

PAYNE, DAVIS   LW   BRUINS

PERSONAL: Born October 24, 1970, in King City, Ont. ... 6-2/205. ... Shoots left.
COLLEGE: Michigan Tech.
TRANSACTIONS/CAREER NOTES: Selected by Edmonton Oilers in seventh round (sixth Oilers pick, 140th overall) of NHL entry draft (June 17, 1989). ... Lacerated tendons in index and middle fingers of right hand (February 9, 1990); missed remainder of season. ... Signed as free agent by Boston Bruins (October 6, 1995). ... Separated right shoulder (February 28, 1996); missed seven games.

Season Team	League	REGULAR SEASON							PLAYOFFS				
		Gms.	G	A	Pts.	PIM	+/-	PP	SH	Gms.	G	A	Pts.	PIM
88-89— Michigan Tech	WCHA	35	5	3	8	39	...	...	...	—	—	—	—	—
89-90— Michigan Tech	WCHA	30	11	10	21	81	...	...	...	—	—	—	—	—
90-91— Michigan Tech	WCHA	41	15	20	35	82	...	...	...	—	—	—	—	—
91-92— Michigan Tech	WCHA	24	6	1	7	71	...	...	...	—	—	—	—	—
92-93— Greensboro	ECHL	57	15	20	35	178	...	...	...	1	0	0	0	4
93-94— Phoenix	IHL	22	6	3	9	51	...	...	...	—	—	—	—	—
— Greensboro	ECHL	36	17	17	34	139	...	...	...	8	2	1	3	27
— Rochester	AHL	2	0	0	0	5	...	...	...	3	0	2	2	0
94-95— Greensboro	ECHL	62	25	36	61	195	...	...	...	17	7	10	17	38
— Providence................	AHL	2	1	0	1	0	...	...	...	—	—	—	—	—
95-96— Providence................	AHL	51	17	22	39	72	...	...	...	4	1	4	5	2
— Boston	NHL	7	0	0	0	7	0	0	0	—	—	—	—	—
96-97— Providence................	AHL	57	18	15	33	104	...	...	...	—	—	—	—	—
— Boston	NHL	15	0	1	1	7	-4	0	0	—	—	—	—	—
NHL totals (2 years)		22	0	1	1	14	-4	0	0					

P

PEAKE, PAT   C   CAPITALS

PERSONAL: Born May 28, 1973, in Detroit. ... 6-1/195. ... Shoots right. ... Full name: Patrick Michael Peake. ... Name pronounced PEEK.
TRANSACTIONS/CAREER NOTES: Injured wrist (August 31, 1990). ... Selected by Washington Capitals in first round (first Capitals pick, 14th overall) of NHL entry draft (June 22, 1991). ... Suffered sore ankle (October 30, 1993); missed two games. ... Suffered sore shoulder

(December 23, 1993); missed six games. ... Suffered from the flu (February 2, 1994); missed two games. ... Bruised ribs (February 21, 1994); missed 14 games. ... Suffered from the flu (February 15, 1995); missed one game. ... Suffered from mononeucleosis (March 2, 1995); missed nine games. ... Broke thyroid cartilage (October 29, 1995); missed 10 games. ... Injured shoulder (January 28, 1996); missed three games. ... Injured kidney (March 9, 1996); missed one game. ... Bruised knee (April 3, 1996); missed five games. ... Fractured heel (April 26, 1996); missed one playoff game and first 67 games of 1996-97 season. ... Suffered concussion (April 10, 1997); missed three games.

HONORS: Won Can.HL Player of the Year Award (1992-93). ... Won Red Tilson Trophy (1992-93). ... Won William Hanley Trophy (1992-93). ... Named to Can.HL All-Star first team (1992-93). ... Named to OHL All-Star first team (1992-93).

Season Team	League	REGULAR SEASON								PLAYOFFS				
		Gms.	G	A	Pts.	PIM	+/-	PP	SH	Gms.	G	A	Pts.	PIM
89-90— Detroit Compuware....	NAJHL	40	36	37	73	57	...	...	...	—	—	—	—	—
90-91— Detroit......................	OHL	63	39	51	90	54	...	...	...	—	—	—	—	—
91-92— Detroit......................	OHL	53	41	52	93	44	...	...	...	7	8	9	17	10
— Baltimore.....................	AHL	3	1	0	1	4	...	...	...	—	—	—	—	—
92-93— Detroit......................	OHL	46	58	78	136	64	...	...	...	2	1	3	4	2
93-94— Portland	AHL	4	0	5	5	2	...	...	...	—	—	—	—	—
— Washington	NHL	49	11	18	29	39	1	3	0	8	0	1	1	8
94-95— Washington	NHL	18	0	4	4	12	-6	0	0	—	—	—	—	—
— Portland	AHL	5	1	3	4	2	...	...	...	4	0	3	3	6
95-96— Washington	NHL	62	17	19	36	46	7	8	0	5	2	1	3	12
96-97— Portland	AHL	3	0	2	2	0	...	...	...	—	—	—	—	—
— Washington	NHL	4	0	0	0	4	1	0	0	—	—	—	—	—
NHL totals (4 years)		133	28	41	69	101	3	11	0	13	2	2	4	20

PEARSON, ROB   RW

PERSONAL: Born August 3, 1971, in Oshawa, Ont. ... 6-3/200. ... Shoots right.
TRANSACTIONS/CAREER NOTES: Broke wrist (November 13, 1988). ... Selected by Toronto Maple Leafs in first round (second Maple Leafs pick, 12th overall) of NHL entry draft (June 17, 1989). ... Dislocated right knee (August 15, 1989). ... Suspended five games by OHL for checking from behind (February 7, 1990). ... Broke collarbone (August 1990). ... Traded by Belleville Bulls to Oshawa Generals for C Jarrod Skalde (November 18, 1990). ... Partially tore knee ligament (October 23, 1993); missed 13 games. ... Traded by Maple Leafs with first-round pick (D Nolan Baumgartner) in 1994 draft to Washington Capitals for C Mike Ridley and first-round pick (G Eric Fichaud) in 1994 draft (June 28, 1994). ... Traded by Capitals to St. Louis Blues for RW Denis Chasse (January 29, 1996). ... Injured neck (March 31, 1996); missed five games.
HONORS: Won Jim Mahon Memorial Trophy (1990-91). ... Named to OHL All-Star first team (1990-91).

Season Team	League	REGULAR SEASON								PLAYOFFS				
		Gms.	G	A	Pts.	PIM	+/-	PP	SH	Gms.	G	A	Pts.	PIM
88-89— Belleville....................	OHL	26	8	12	20	51	...	...	...	—	—	—	—	—
89-90— Belleville....................	OHL	58	48	40	88	174	...	...	...	11	5	5	10	26
90-91— Belleville....................	OHL	10	6	3	9	27	...	...	...	—	—	—	—	—
— Oshawa......................	OHL	41	57	52	109	76	...	...	...	16	16	17	33	39
— Newmarket.................	AHL	3	0	0	0	29	...	...	...	—	—	—	—	—
91-92— Toronto	NHL	47	14	10	24	58	-16	6	0	—	—	—	—	—
— St. John's..................	AHL	27	15	14	29	107	...	...	...	13	5	4	9	40
92-93— Toronto	NHL	78	23	14	37	211	-2	8	0	14	2	2	4	31
93-94— Toronto	NHL	67	12	18	30	189	-6	1	0	14	1	0	1	32
94-95— Washington	NHL	32	0	6	6	96	-6	0	0	3	1	0	1	17
95-96— Portland	AHL	44	18	24	42	143	...	...	...	—	—	—	—	—
— St. Louis	NHL	27	6	4	10	54	4	1	0	2	0	0	0	14
96-97— Worcester	AHL	46	11	16	27	199	...	...	...	5	3	0	3	16
— St. Louis	NHL	18	1	2	3	37	-5	0	0	—	—	—	—	—
NHL totals (6 years)		269	56	54	110	645	-31	16	0	33	4	2	6	94

PEARSON, SCOTT   LW   MAPLE LEAFS

PERSONAL: Born December 19, 1969, in Cornwall, Ont. ... 6-1/205. ... Shoots left.
TRANSACTIONS/CAREER NOTES: Underwent surgery to left wrist (May 1988). ... Selected by Toronto Maple Leafs in first round (first Maple Leafs pick, sixth overall) of NHL entry draft (June 11, 1988). ... Traded by Maple Leafs with second-round picks in 1991 draft (D Eric Lavigne) and 1992 draft (D Tuomas Gronman) to Quebec Nordiques for C/LW Aaron Broten, D Michel Petit and RW Lucien Deblois (November 17, 1990). ... Sprained left knee (September 27, 1992); missed first 22 games of season. ... Traded by Nordiques to Edmonton Oilers for LW Martin Gelinas and sixth-round pick (C Nicholas Checco) in 1993 draft (June 20, 1993). ... Sprained knee ligament (February 2, 1994); missed 11 games. ... Traded by Oilers to Buffalo Sabres for D Ken Sutton (April 7, 1995). ... Signed as free agent by Maple Leafs (July 8, 1996). ... Strained groin and abdominal muscle (October 19, 1996); missed 60 games.
MISCELLANEOUS: Scored on a penalty shot (vs. Tom Barrasso, March 16, 1991). ... Failed to score on a penalty shot (vs. Damian Rhodes, November 20, 1993).

Season Team	League	REGULAR SEASON								PLAYOFFS				
		Gms.	G	A	Pts.	PIM	+/-	PP	SH	Gms.	G	A	Pts.	PIM
85-86— Kingston	OHL	63	16	23	39	56	...	...	...	—	—	—	—	—
86-87— Kingston	OHL	62	30	24	54	101	...	...	...	9	3	3	6	42
87-88— Kingston	OHL	46	26	32	58	118	...	...	...	—	—	—	—	—
88-89— Kingston	OHL	13	9	8	17	34	...	...	...	—	—	—	—	—
— Niagara Falls.............	OHL	32	26	34	60	90	...	...	...	17	14	10	24	53
— Toronto	NHL	9	0	1	1	2	0	0	0	—	—	—	—	—
89-90— Newmarket................	AHL	18	12	11	23	64	...	...	...	—	—	—	—	—
— Toronto	NHL	41	5	10	15	90	-7	0	0	2	2	0	2	10
90-91— Toronto	NHL	12	0	0	0	20	-5	0	0	—	—	—	—	—
— Quebec......................	NHL	35	11	4	15	86	-4	0	0	—	—	—	—	—
— Halifax.......................	AHL	24	12	15	27	44	...	...	...	—	—	—	—	—
91-92— Quebec......................	NHL	10	1	2	3	14	-5	0	0	—	—	—	—	—
— Halifax.......................	AHL	5	2	1	3	4	...	...	...	—	—	—	—	—

Season Team	League	REGULAR SEASON								PLAYOFFS				
		Gms.	G	A	Pts.	PIM	+/-	PP	SH	Gms.	G	A	Pts.	PIM
92-93 — Halifax	AHL	5	3	1	4	25	...	...	...	—	—	—	—	—
— Quebec	NHL	41	13	1	14	95	3	0	0	3	0	0	0	0
93-94 — Edmonton	NHL	72	19	18	37	165	-4	3	0	—	—	—	—	—
94-95 — Edmonton	NHL	28	1	4	5	54	-11	0	0	—	—	—	—	—
— Buffalo	NHL	14	2	1	3	20	-3	0	0	5	0	0	0	4
95-96 — Rochester	AHL	26	8	8	16	113	...	...	...	—	—	—	—	—
— Buffalo	NHL	27	4	0	4	67	-4	0	0	—	—	—	—	—
96-97 — Toronto	NHL	1	0	0	0	2	0	0	0	—	—	—	—	—
— St. John's	AHL	14	5	2	7	26	...	...	...	9	5	2	7	14
NHL totals (9 years)		290	56	41	97	615	-40	3	0	10	2	0	2	14

PECA, MIKE C SABRES

PERSONAL: Born March 26, 1974, in Toronto. ... 5-11/181. ... Shoots right. ... Name pronounced PEH-kuh.
HIGH SCHOOL: LaSalle Secondary (Kinston, Ont.).
TRANSACTIONS/CAREER NOTES: Selected by Vancouver Canucks in second round (second Canucks pick, 40th overall) of NHL entry draft (June 20, 1992). ... Cracked cheek bone (February 9, 1995); missed 12 games. ... Injured wrist (April 26, 1995); missed one game. ... Traded by Canucks with D Mike Wilson and first-round pick (D Jay McKee) in 1995 draft to Buffalo Sabres for RW Alexander Mogilny and fifth-round pick (LW Todd Norman) in 1995 draft (July 8, 1995). ... Strained back (October 29, 1995); missed six games. ... Bruised sternum (December 2, 1995); missed one game. ... Sprained right knee (March 18, 1996); missed seven games. ... Injured shoulder (November 27, 1996); missed three games.
HONORS: Won Frank J. Selke Trophy (1996-97).

Season Team	League	REGULAR SEASON								PLAYOFFS				
		Gms.	G	A	Pts.	PIM	+/-	PP	SH	Gms.	G	A	Pts.	PIM
90-91 — Sudbury	OHL	62	14	27	41	24	...	...	...	5	1	0	1	7
91-92 — Sudbury	OHL	39	16	34	50	61	...	...	...	—	—	—	—	—
— Ottawa	OHL	27	8	17	25	32	...	...	...	11	6	10	16	6
92-93 — Ottawa	OHL	55	38	64	102	80	...	...	...	—	—	—	—	—
— Hamilton	AHL	9	6	3	9	11	...	...	...	—	—	—	—	—
93-94 — Ottawa	OHL	55	50	63	113	101	...	...	...	17	7	22	29	30
— Vancouver	NHL	4	0	0	0	2	-1	0	0	—	—	—	—	—
94-95 — Syracuse	AHL	35	10	24	34	75	...	...	...	—	—	—	—	—
— Vancouver	NHL	33	6	6	12	30	-6	2	0	5	0	1	1	8
95-96 — Buffalo	NHL	68	11	20	31	67	-1	4	3	—	—	—	—	—
96-97 — Buffalo	NHL	79	20	29	49	80	26	5	*6	10	0	2	2	8
NHL totals (4 years)		184	37	55	92	179	18	11	9	15	0	3	3	16

PEDERSON, DENIS C DEVILS

PERSONAL: Born September 10, 1975, in Prince Albert, Sask. ... 6-2/190. ... Shoots right. ... Name pronounced PEE-duhr-suhn.
HIGH SCHOOL: Carlton Comprehensive (Prince Albert, Sask.).
TRANSACTIONS/CAREER NOTES: Selected by New Jersey Devils in first round (first Devils pick, 13th overall) of NHL entry draft (June 26, 1993). ... Bruised thigh (December 31, 1996); missed one game. ... Sore head (February 19, 1997); missed one game. ... Suffered from the flu (March 11, 1997); missed one game.
HONORS: Named to WHL All-Rookie team (1992-93). ... Named to WHL (East) All-Star second team (1993-94).

Season Team	League	REGULAR SEASON								PLAYOFFS				
		Gms.	G	A	Pts.	PIM	+/-	PP	SH	Gms.	G	A	Pts.	PIM
91-92 — Prince Albert	WHL	10	0	0	0	6	...	...	...	7	0	1	1	13
92-93 — Prince Albert	WHL	72	33	40	73	134	...	...	...	—	—	—	—	—
93-94 — Prince Albert	WHL	71	53	45	98	157	...	...	...	—	—	—	—	—
94-95 — Prince Albert	WHL	63	30	38	68	122	...	...	...	15	11	14	25	14
— Albany	AHL	—	—	—	—	—	—	—	—	3	0	0	0	2
95-96 — Albany	AHL	68	28	43	71	104	...	...	...	4	1	2	3	0
— New Jersey	NHL	10	3	1	4	0	-1	1	0	—	—	—	—	—
96-97 — Albany	AHL	3	1	3	4	7	...	...	...	—	—	—	—	—
— New Jersey	NHL	70	12	20	32	62	7	3	0	9	0	0	0	2
NHL totals (2 years)		80	15	21	36	62	6	4	0	9	0	0	0	2

PEDERSON, TOM D MAPLE LEAFS

PERSONAL: Born January 14, 1970, in Bloomington, Minn. ... 5-9/180. ... Shoots right. ... Full name: Thomas Stuart Pederson.
HIGH SCHOOL: Thomas Jefferson (Bloomington, Minn.).
COLLEGE: Minnesota.
TRANSACTIONS/CAREER NOTES: Selected by Minnesota North Stars in 11th round (12th North Stars pick, 217th overall) of NHL entry draft (June 17, 1989). ... Selected by San Jose Sharks in NHL dispersal draft (May 30, 1991). ... Strained back (January 8, 1993); missed one game. ... Injured shoulder (January 30, 1993); missed four games. ... Strained groin (February 22, 1993); missed five games. ... Injured thigh (October 20, 1995); missed eight games. ... Pinched nerve (December 16, 1995); missed one game. ... Suffered sore neck (December 23, 1995); missed four games. ... Strained groin (January 24, 1996); missed six games. ... Injured neck (March 6, 1996); missed three games. ... Signed as free agent by Toronto Maple Leafs (December 13, 1996).

P

Season Team	League	REGULAR SEASON								PLAYOFFS				
		Gms.	G	A	Pts.	PIM	+/-	PP	SH	Gms.	G	A	Pts.	PIM
87-88 — Thomas Jefferson	Minn. H.S.	22	16	27	43		...	...	...	—	—	—	—	—
88-89 — Univ. of Minnesota	WCHA	42	5	24	29	46	...	...	...	—	—	—	—	—
89-90 — Univ. of Minnesota	WCHA	43	8	30	38	58	...	...	...	—	—	—	—	—
90-91 — Univ. of Minnesota	WCHA	36	12	20	32	46	...	...	...	—	—	—	—	—

Season Team	League	REGULAR SEASON									PLAYOFFS				
		Gms.	G	A	Pts.	PIM	+/-	PP	SH		Gms.	G	A	Pts.	PIM
91-92— U.S. national team	Int'l	44	3	11	14	41	...	...	...		—	—	—	—	—
— Kansas City	IHL	20	6	9	15	16	...	...	...		13	1	6	7	14
92-93— Kansas City	IHL	26	6	15	21	10	...	...	...		12	1	6	7	2
— San Jose	NHL	44	7	13	20	31	-16	2	0		—	—	—	—	—
93-94— Kansas City	IHL	7	3	1	4	0	...	...	...		—	—	—	—	—
— San Jose	NHL	74	6	19	25	31	3	3	0		14	1	6	7	2
94-95— San Jose	NHL	47	5	11	16	31	-14	0	0		10	0	5	5	8
95-96— San Jose	NHL	60	1	4	5	40	-9	1	0		—	—	—	—	—
96-97— Toronto	NHL	15	1	2	3	9	0	1	0		—	—	—	—	—
— St. John's	AHL	1	0	4	4	2	...	...	...		—	—	—	—	—
— Utah	IHL	10	1	2	3	8	...	...	...		7	1	3	4	4
NHL totals (5 years)		240	20	49	69	142	-36	7	0		24	1	11	12	10

PELLERIN, SCOTT   RW   BLUES

PERSONAL: Born January 9, 1970, in Shediac, N.B. ... 5-11/180. ... Shoots left. ... Full name: Jaque-Frederick Scott Pellerin. ... Name pronounced PEHL-ih-rihn.

COLLEGE: Maine.

TRANSACTIONS/CAREER NOTES: Selected by New Jersey Devils in third round (fourth Devils pick, 47th overall) of NHL entry draft (June 17, 1989). ... Signed as free agent by St. Louis Blues (July 3, 1996).

HONORS: Named Hockey East co-Rookie of the Year with Rob Gaudreau (1988-89). ... Named to Hockey East All-Rookie team (1988-89). ... Won Hobey Baker Memorial Award (1991-92). ... Named to NCAA All-America East first team (1991-92). ... Named Hockey East Player of the Year (1991-92). ... Named Hockey East Tournament Most Valuable Player (1991-92). ... Named to Hockey East All-Star first team (1991-92). ... Named to Hockey East All-Decade team (1994).

Season Team	League	REGULAR SEASON									PLAYOFFS				
		Gms.	G	A	Pts.	PIM	+/-	PP	SH		Gms.	G	A	Pts.	PIM
87-88— Notre Dame	SJHL	57	37	49	86	139	...	...	...		—	—	—	—	—
88-89— University of Maine	Hockey East	45	29	33	62	92	...	...	...		—	—	—	—	—
89-90— University of Maine	Hockey East	42	22	34	56	68	...	...	...		—	—	—	—	—
90-91— University of Maine	Hockey East	43	23	25	48	60	...	...	...		—	—	—	—	—
91-92— University of Maine	Hockey East	37	32	25	57	54	...	...	...		3	1	0	1	0
— Utica	AHL	—	—	—	—	—	—	—	—		2	0	1	1	0
92-93— Utica	AHL	27	15	18	33	33	...	...	...		—	—	—	—	—
— New Jersey	NHL	45	10	11	21	41	-1	1	2		—	—	—	—	—
93-94— Albany	IHL	73	28	46	74	84	...	...	...		5	2	1	3	11
— New Jersey	NHL	1	0	0	0	2	0	0	0		—	—	—	—	—
94-95— Albany	AHL	74	23	33	56	95	...	...	...		14	6	4	10	8
95-96— Albany	AHL	75	35	47	82	142	...	...	...		4	0	3	3	10
— New Jersey	NHL	6	2	1	3	0	1	0	0		—	—	—	—	—
96-97— Worcester	AHL	24	10	16	26	37	...	...	...		—	—	—	—	—
— St. Louis	NHL	54	8	10	18	35	12	0	2		6	0	0	0	6
NHL totals (4 years)		106	20	22	42	78	12	1	4		6	0	0	0	6

PELTONEN, VILLE   LW   SHARKS

PERSONAL: Born May 24, 1973, in Vantaa, Finland. ... 5-10/180. ... Shoots left. ... Name pronounced VIHL-lay PEHL-tuh-nehn.

TRANSACTIONS/CAREER NOTES: Selected by San Jose Sharks in third round (fourth Sharks pick, 58th overall) of NHL entry draft (June 26, 1993). ... Injured knee (October 15, 1996); missed 10 games.

MISCELLANEOUS: Member of bronze-medal-winning Finnish Olympic team (1994). ... Failed to score on a penalty shot (vs. Patrick Roy, March 5, 1996).

Season Team	League	REGULAR SEASON									PLAYOFFS				
		Gms.	G	A	Pts.	PIM	+/-	PP	SH		Gms.	G	A	Pts.	PIM
91-92— HIFK Helsinki	Finland	6	0	0	0	0	...	...	...		—	—	—	—	—
92-93— HIFK Helsinki	Finland	46	13	24	37	16	...	...	...		4	0	2	2	2
93-94— HIFK Helsinki	Finland	43	16	22	38	14	...	...	...		3	0	0	0	2
— Fin. Olympic team	Int'l	8	4	3	7	0	...	...	...		—	—	—	—	—
94-95— HIFK Helsinki	Finland	45	20	16	36	16	...	...	...		3	0	0	0	0
95-96— Kansas City	IHL	29	5	13	18	8	...	...	...		—	—	—	—	—
— San Jose	NHL	31	2	11	13	14	-7	0	0		—	—	—	—	—
96-97— San Jose	NHL	28	2	3	5	0	-8	1	0		—	—	—	—	—
— Kentucky	AHL	40	22	30	52	21	...	...	...		—	—	—	—	—
NHL totals (2 years)		59	4	14	18	14	-15	1	0						

PELUSO, MIKE   LW   RANGERS

PERSONAL: Born November 8, 1965, in Hibbing, Minn. ... 6-4/200. ... Shoots left. ... Full name: Michael David Peluso. ... Name pronounced puh-LOO-soh.

HIGH SCHOOL: Greenway (Coleraine, Minn.).

COLLEGE: Alaska-Anchorage.

TRANSACTIONS/CAREER NOTES: Selected by New Jersey Devils in 10th round (10th Devils pick, 190th overall) of NHL entry draft (June 15, 1985). ... Signed as free agent by Chicago Blackhawks (September 7, 1989). ... Bruised jaw and cheek (November 8, 1990); missed five games. ... Suspended 10 games by NHL for fighting (March 17, 1991). ... Selected by Ottawa Senators in NHL expansion draft (June 18, 1992). ... Suspended one game by NHL for accumulating three game misconduct penalties (February 1, 1993). ... Pinched nerve in neck (March 27, 1993); missed two games. ... Traded by Senators to Devils (June 26, 1993) to complete deal in which Devils sent G Craig Billington, C/LW Troy Mallette and fourth-round pick (C Cosmo Dupaul) in 1993 draft to Senators for G Peter Sidorkiewicz and future considerations (June 20, 1993). ... Suffered concussion (December 18, 1993); missed two games. ... Suspended one game by NHL for non-stick

P

related game misconduct (January 7, 1994). ... Suspended two games by NHL for non-stick related game misconduct (February 4, 1994). ... Suspended three games by NHL for non-stick related game misconduct (March 7, 1994). ... Suffered sore neck (March 8, 1995); missed one game. ... Suffered from the flu (April 5, 1995); missed one game. ... Fined $1,000 by NHL for throwing an elbow (May 12, 1995). ... Bruised shoulder (October 12, 1995); missed three games. ... Injured neck (February 1, 1996); missed one game. ... Injured leg (February 21, 1996); missed two games. ... Injured knee (February 22, 1996); missed 16 games. ... Traded by Devils with D Ricard Persson to St. Louis Blues for D Ken Sutton and second-round pick in 1999 draft (November 26, 1996). ... Injured shoulder (December 22, 1996); missed nine games. ... Traded by Blues to New York Rangers as compensation for Blues hiring Larry Pleau as general manager (June 21, 1997).

MISCELLANEOUS: Member of Stanley Cup championship team (1995).

			REGULAR SEASON								PLAYOFFS				
Season Team	League	Gms.	G	A	Pts.	PIM	+/-	PP	SH		Gms.	G	A	Pts.	PIM
83-84— Greenway	Minn. H.S.	12	5	15	20	30	...	...	...		—	—	—	—	—
84-85— Stratford	OPJHL	52	11	45	56	114	...	...	...		—	—	—	—	—
85-86— Alaska-Anchorage	Indep.	32	2	11	13	59	...	...	...		—	—	—	—	—
86-87— Alaska-Anchorage	Indep.	30	5	21	26	68	...	...	...		—	—	—	—	—
87-88— Alaska-Anchorage	Indep.	35	4	33	37	76	...	...	...		—	—	—	—	—
88-89— Alaska-Anchorage	Indep.	33	10	27	37	75	...	...	...		—	—	—	—	—
89-90— Indianapolis	IHL	75	7	10	17	279	...	...	...		14	0	1	1	58
— Chicago	NHL	2	0	0	0	15	0	0	0		—	—	—	—	—
90-91— Indianapolis	IHL	6	2	1	3	21	...	...	...		5	0	2	2	40
— Chicago	NHL	53	6	1	7	320	-3	2	0		3	0	0	0	2
91-92— Chicago	NHL	63	6	3	9	*408	1	2	0		17	1	2	3	8
— Indianapolis	IHL	4	0	1	1	15	...	...	...		—	—	—	—	—
92-93— Ottawa	NHL	81	15	10	25	318	-35	2	0		—	—	—	—	—
93-94— New Jersey	NHL	69	4	16	20	238	19	0	0		17	1	0	1	*64
94-95— New Jersey	NHL	46	2	9	11	167	5	0	0		20	1	2	3	8
95-96— New Jersey	NHL	57	3	8	11	146	4	0	0		—	—	—	—	—
96-97— New Jersey	NHL	20	0	2	2	68	0	0	0		—	—	—	—	—
— St. Louis	NHL	44	2	3	5	158	0	0	0		5	0	0	0	25
NHL totals (8 years)		435	38	52	90	1838	-9	6	0		62	3	4	7	107

PEPPERALL, COLIN   LW   RANGERS

PERSONAL: Born April 28, 1978, in Niagara Falls, Ont. ... 5-10/155. ... Shoots left.
TRANSACTIONS/CAREER NOTES: Selected by New York Rangers in fifth round (fourth Rangers pick, 131st overall) of NHL entry draft (June 22, 1996).

			REGULAR SEASON								PLAYOFFS				
Season Team	League	Gms.	G	A	Pts.	PIM	+/-	PP	SH		Gms.	G	A	Pts.	PIM
95-96— Niagara Falls	OHL	66	26	26	52	47	...	...	...		10	3	4	7	8
96-97— Erie	OHL	66	36	36	72	39	...	...	...		5	3	2	5	2

PERREAULT, YANIC   C   KINGS

PERSONAL: Born April 4, 1971, in Sherbrooke, Que. ... 5-11/182. ... Shoots left. ... Name pronounced YAH-nihk puh-ROH.
TRANSACTIONS/CAREER NOTES: Selected by Toronto Maple Leafs in third round (first Maple Leafs pick, 47th overall) of NHL entry draft (June 22, 1991). ... Signed as free agent by Los Angeles Kings (July 14, 1994). ... Strained abdominal muscle (December 13, 1996); missed 11 games. ... Underwent kidney surgery (February 3, 1997); missed remainder of season.
HONORS: Won Can.HL Rookie of the Year Award (1988-89). ... Won Michel Bergeron Trophy (1988-89). ... Won Marcel Robert Trophy (1989-90). ... Won Michel Briere Trophy (1990-91). ... Won Jean Beliveau Trophy (1990-91). ... Won Frank J. Selke Trophy (1990-91). ... Won Shell Cup (1990-91). ... Named to QMJHL All-Star first team (1990-91).

			REGULAR SEASON								PLAYOFFS				
Season Team	League	Gms.	G	A	Pts.	PIM	+/-	PP	SH		Gms.	G	A	Pts.	PIM
88-89— Trois-Rivieres	QMJHL	70	53	55	108	48	...	...	...		—	—	—	—	—
89-90— Trois-Rivieres	QMJHL	63	51	63	114	75	...	...	...		7	6	5	11	19
90-91— Trois-Rivieres	QMJHL	67	*87	98	*185	103	...	...	...		6	4	7	11	6
91-92— St. John's	AHL	62	38	38	76	19	...	...	...		16	7	8	15	4
92-93— St. John's	AHL	79	49	46	95	56	...	...	...		9	4	5	9	2
93-94— St. John's	AHL	62	45	60	105	38	...	...	...		11	*12	6	18	14
— Toronto	NHL	13	3	3	6	0	1	2	0		—	—	—	—	—
94-95— Phoenix	IHL	68	51	48	99	52	...	...	...		—	—	—	—	—
— Los Angeles	NHL	26	2	5	7	20	3	0	0		—	—	—	—	—
95-96— Los Angeles	NHL	78	25	24	49	16	-11	8	3		—	—	—	—	—
96-97— Los Angeles	NHL	41	11	14	25	20	0	1	1		—	—	—	—	—
NHL totals (4 years)		158	41	46	87	56	-7	11	4						

PERSSON, RICARD   D   BLUES

PERSONAL: Born August 24, 1969, in Ostersund, Sweden. ... 6-2/205. ... Shoots left. ... Name pronounced RIH-kahrd PEER-suhn.
TRANSACTIONS/CAREER NOTES: Selected by New Jersey Devils in second round (second Devils pick, 23rd overall) of NHL entry draft (June 13, 1987). ... Traded by Devils with LW Mike Peluso to St. Louis Blues for D Ken Sutton and second-round pick in 1999 draft (November 26, 1996).

			REGULAR SEASON								PLAYOFFS				
Season Team	League	Gms.	G	A	Pts.	PIM	+/-	PP	SH		Gms.	G	A	Pts.	PIM
85-86— Ostersund	Swed. Div. II	24	2	2	4	16	...	...	...		—	—	—	—	—
86-87— Ostersund	Swed. Div. II	31	10	11	21	28	...	...	...		—	—	—	—	—
87-88— Leksand	Sweden	31	2	0	2	8	...	...	...		2	0	1	1	2
88-89— Leksand	Sweden	33	2	4	6	28	...	...	...		9	0	1	1	6
89-90— Leksand	Sweden	43	9	10	19	62	...	...	...		3	0	0	0	6
90-91— Leksand	Sweden	37	6	9	15	42	...	...	...						

P

Season Team	League	REGULAR SEASON								PLAYOFFS				
		Gms.	G	A	Pts.	PIM	+/-	PP	SH	Gms.	G	A	Pts.	PIM
91-92— Leksand	Sweden	21	0	7	7	28	...	...	...	—	—	—	—	—
92-93— Leksand	Sweden	36	7	15	22	63	...	...	...	2	0	2	2	0
93-94— Malmo	Sweden	40	11	9	20	38	...	...	...	11	2	0	2	12
94-95— Malmo	Sweden	31	3	13	16	38	...	...	...	9	0	2	2	8
— Albany	AHL	—					...	...	...	9	3	5	8	7
95-96— New Jersey	NHL	12	2	1	3	8	5	1	0	—	—	—	—	—
— Albany	AHL	67	15	31	46	59	...	...	...	4	0	0	0	7
96-97— New Jersey	NHL	1	0	0	0	0	0	0	0	—	—	—	—	—
— Albany	AHL	13	1	4	5	8	...	...	...	—	—	—	—	—
— St. Louis	NHL	54	4	8	12	45	-2	1	0	6	0	0	0	27
NHL totals (3 years)		67	6	9	15	53	3	2	0	6	0	0	0	27

PETERS, GEOFF   C   BLACKHAWKS

PERSONAL: Born April 30, 1978, in Hamilton, Ont. ... 6-0/174. ... Shoots left.
TRANSACTIONS/CAREER NOTES: Selected by Chicago Blackhawks in second round (third Blackhawks pick, 46th overall) of NHL entry draft (June 22, 1996).

Season Team	League	REGULAR SEASON								PLAYOFFS				
		Gms.	G	A	Pts.	PIM	+/-	PP	SH	Gms.	G	A	Pts.	PIM
94-95— Niagara Falls	OHL	57	11	9	20	37	...	...	...	6	2	0	2	4
95-96— Niagara Falls	OHL	64	25	34	59	51	...	...	...	10	4	4	8	8
96-97— Erie	OHL	28	12	10	22	39	...	...	...	5	1	3	4	7

PETERSON, BRENT   LW   LIGHTNING

PERSONAL: Born July 20, 1972, in Calgary. ... 6-3/195. ... Shoots left. ... Name pronounced PEE-tuhr-suhn.
COLLEGE: Michigan Tech.
TRANSACTIONS/CAREER NOTES: Selected by Tampa Bay Lightning in NHL supplemental draft (June 25, 1993). ... Sprained wrist (December 4, 1996); missed four games.

Season Team	League	REGULAR SEASON								PLAYOFFS				
		Gms.	G	A	Pts.	PIM	+/-	PP	SH	Gms.	G	A	Pts.	PIM
91-92— Michigan Tech	WCHA	39	11	9	20	18	...	...	...	—	—	—	—	—
92-93— Michigan Tech	WCHA	37	24	18	42	32	...	...	...	—	—	—	—	—
93-94— Michigan Tech	WCHA	43	25	21	46	30	...	...	...	—	—	—	—	—
94-95— Michigan Tech	WCHA	39	20	16	36	27	...	...	...	—	—	—	—	—
95-96— Atlanta	IHL	69	9	19	28	33	...	...	...	3	0	0	0	0
96-97— Adirondack	AHL	52	22	23	45	56	...	...	...	4	3	1	4	2
— Tampa Bay	NHL	17	2	0	2	4	-4	0	0	—	—	—	—	—
NHL totals (1 year)		17	2	0	2	4	-4	0	0	—	—	—	—	—

PETIT, MICHEL   D   FLYERS

PERSONAL: Born February 12, 1964, in St. Malo, Que. ... 6-1/205. ... Shoots right. ... Name pronounced puh-TEE.
TRANSACTIONS/CAREER NOTES: Selected by Vancouver Canucks as underage junior in first round (first Canucks pick, 11th overall) of NHL entry draft (June 9, 1982). ... Separated shoulder (March 1984). ... Injured knee (February 1987). ... Traded by Canucks to New York Rangers for D Willie Huber and D Larry Melnyk (November 1987). ... Pulled groin (December 1987). ... Fractured right collarbone (December 27, 1988); missed 11 games. ... Traded by Rangers to Quebec Nordiques for D Randy Moller (October 5, 1989). ... Traded by Nordiques with C/LW Aaron Broten and RW Lucien DeBlois to Toronto Maple Leafs for LW Scott Pearson and second-round picks in 1991 draft (D Eric Lavigne) and 1992 draft (D Tuomas Gronman) (November 17, 1990). ... Sprained knee (February 4, 1991); missed five games. ... Sprained thumb (November 9, 1991); missed six games. ... Traded by Maple Leafs with D Alexander Godynyuk, RW Gary Leeman, LW Craig Berube and G Jeff Reese to Calgary Flames for C Doug Gilmour, D Jamie Macoun, LW Kent Manderville, D Ric Nattress and G Rick Wamsley (January 2, 1992). ... Suffered back spasms (March 3, 1992); missed four games. ... Pulled groin prior to 1992-93 season; missed first four games of season. ... Dislocated right shoulder (October 22, 1992); missed 29 games. ... Suffered hip pointer (October 21, 1993); missed one game. ... Suffered concussion (January 15, 1994); missed two games. ... Pulled groin (February 2, 1994); missed four games. ... Signed as free agent by Los Angeles Kings (June 16, 1994). ... Strained groin (February 2, 1995); missed three games. ... Strained groin (February 15, 1995); missed four games. ... Sprained knee (April 17, 1995); missed one game. ... Suspended 10 games by NHL for abusing official (September 28, 1995). ... Traded by Kings to Tampa Bay Lightning for D Steven Finn (November 27, 1995). ... Bruised ribs (November 27, 1995); missed one game. ... Bruised ribs (December 19, 1995); missed two games. ... Injured right hip flexor and suffered lower back strain (February 15, 1996); missed two games. ... Sprained back (February 21, 1996); missed 15 games. ... Signed as free agent by Edmonton Oilers (October 24, 1996). ... Bruised hand (November 9, 1996); missed two games. ... Claimed on waivers by Philadelphia Flyers (January 17, 1997). ... Suspended two games by NHL for kneeing penalty (February 25, 1997).
HONORS: Won Raymond Lagace Trophy (1981-82). ... Won Association of Journalists of Hockey Trophy (1981-82). ... Named to QMJHL All-Star first team (1981-82 and 1982-83).

Season Team	League	REGULAR SEASON								PLAYOFFS				
		Gms.	G	A	Pts.	PIM	+/-	PP	SH	Gms.	G	A	Pts.	PIM
81-82— Sherbrooke	QMJHL	63	10	39	49	106	...	...	...	22	5	20	25	24
82-83— St. Jean	QMJHL	62	19	67	86	196	...	...	...	3	0	0	0	35
— Vancouver	NHL	2	0	0	0	0	-4	0	0	—	—	—	—	—
83-84— Can. Olympic team	Int'l	19	3	10	13	58	...	...	...	—	—	—	—	—
— Vancouver	NHL	44	6	9	15	53	-6	5	0	1	0	0	0	0
84-85— Vancouver	NHL	69	5	26	31	127	-26	1	1	—	—	—	—	—
85-86— Fredericton	AHL	25	0	13	13	79	...	...	...	—	—	—	—	—
— Vancouver	NHL	32	1	6	7	27	-6	1	0	—	—	—	—	—
86-87— Vancouver	NHL	69	12	13	25	131	-5	4	0	—	—	—	—	—
87-88— Vancouver	NHL	10	0	3	3	35	-4	0	0	—	—	—	—	—
— New York Rangers	NHL	64	9	24	33	223	3	2	0	—	—	—	—	—

P

Season Team	League	REGULAR SEASON								PLAYOFFS				
		Gms.	G	A	Pts.	PIM	+/-	PP	SH	Gms.	G	A	Pts.	PIM
88-89— New York Rangers.....	NHL	69	8	25	33	154	-15	5	0	4	0	2	2	27
89-90— Quebec....................	NHL	63	12	24	36	215	-38	5	0	—	—	—	—	—
90-91— Quebec....................	NHL	19	4	7	11	47	-15	3	0	—	—	—	—	—
— Toronto	NHL	54	9	19	28	132	-19	3	1	—	—	—	—	—
91-92— Toronto	NHL	34	1	13	14	85	-17	1	0	—	—	—	—	—
— Calgary	NHL	36	3	10	13	79	2	3	0	—	—	—	—	—
92-93— Calgary	NHL	35	3	9	12	54	-5	2	0	—	—	—	—	—
93-94— Calgary	NHL	63	2	21	23	110	5	0	0	—	—	—	—	—
94-95— Los Angeles..............	NHL	40	5	12	17	84	4	2	0	—	—	—	—	—
95-96— Los Angeles..............	NHL	9	0	1	1	27	-1	0	0	—	—	—	—	—
— Tampa Bay	NHL	45	4	7	11	108	-10	0	0	6	0	0	0	20
96-97— Edmonton	NHL	18	2	4	6	20	-13	0	0	—	—	—	—	—
— Philadelphia...............	NHL	20	0	3	3	51	2	0	0	3	0	0	0	6
NHL totals (15 years)		795	86	236	322	1762	-168	37	2	14	0	2	2	53

PETRAKOV, ANDREI   RW   BLUES

PERSONAL: Born April 26, 1976, in Sverdlovsk, U.S.S.R. ... 6-0/198. ... Shoots left. ... Name pronounced PEHT-ruh-kahv.
TRANSACTIONS/CAREER NOTES: Selected by St. Louis Blues in fourth round (fourth Blues pick, 97th overall) of NHL entry draft (June 22, 1996).

Season Team	League	REGULAR SEASON								PLAYOFFS				
		Gms.	G	A	Pts.	PIM	+/-	PP	SH	Gms.	G	A	Pts.	PIM
92-93— Avtomobilist Yek.......	CIS	5	0	0	0	0	...	...	...	1	0	0	0	0
93-94— Avtomobilist Yek.......	CIS	35	4	2	6	10	...	...	...	—	—	—	—	—
94-95— Avtomobilist Yek.......	CIS	11	1	1	2	6	...	...	...	1	0	0	0	0
95-96— Avtomobilist Yek.......	CIS	52	17	6	23	14	...	...	...	—	—	—	—	—
96-97— Spartak Yek.............	Russian	14	6	1	7	6	...	...	...	—	—	—	—	—
— Metal. Magnitogorsk..	Russian	18	4	0	4	8	...	...	...	9	0	0	0	0

PETROV, SERGEI   RW/LW   BLACKHAWKS

PERSONAL: Born January 22, 1975, in St. Petersburg, U.S.S.R. ... 5-11/185. ... Shoots left. ... Full name: Sergei Alexander Petrov.
HIGH SCHOOL: Cloquet (Minn.).
COLLEGE: Minnesota-Duluth.
TRANSACTIONS/CAREER NOTES: Selected by Chicago Blackhawks in eighth round (ninth Blackhawks pick, 206th overall) of NHL entry draft (June 26, 1993). ... Injured wrist (1993-94 season); missed last four games of season.

Season Team	League	REGULAR SEASON								PLAYOFFS				
		Gms.	G	A	Pts.	PIM	+/-	PP	SH	Gms.	G	A	Pts.	PIM
92-93— Cloquet	Minn. H.S.	28	37	32	69	...	...	...	...	—	—	—	—	—
93-94— Minnesota-Duluth	WCHA	28	2	4	6	26	...	...	...	—	—	—	—	—
94-95— Minnesota-Duluth	WCHA	30	6	6	12	46	...	...	...	—	—	—	—	—
95-96—					Statistics unavailable.					—	—	—	—	—
96-97— Minnesota-Duluth	WCHA	35	5	12	17	26	...	...	...	—	—	—	—	—

PETROVICKY, ROBERT   C   BLUES

PERSONAL: Born October 26, 1973, in Kosice, Czechoslovakia. ... 5-11/172. ... Shoots left. ... Name pronounced peht-roh-VEETS-kee.
TRANSACTIONS/CAREER NOTES: Selected by Hartford Whalers in first round (first Whalers pick, ninth overall) of NHL entry draft (June 20, 1992). ... Sprained left ankle (February 28, 1993); missed five games. ... Loaned to Slovakian Olympic team (February 11, 1994). ... Returned to Whalers (February 28, 1994). ... Traded by Whalers to Dallas Stars for Dan Kesa (November 29, 1995). ... Signed as free agent by St. Louis Blues (September 6, 1996).
HONORS: Named to Czechoslovakian League All-Star team (1991-92).

Season Team	League	REGULAR SEASON								PLAYOFFS				
		Gms.	G	A	Pts.	PIM	+/-	PP	SH	Gms.	G	A	Pts.	PIM
90-91— Dukla Trencin.............	Czech.	33	9	14	23	12	...	...	...	—	—	—	—	—
91-92— Dukla Trencin.............	Czech.	46	25	36	61	...	...	...	...	—	—	—	—	—
92-93— Hartford	NHL	42	3	6	9	45	-10	0	0	—	—	—	—	—
— Springfield	AHL	16	5	3	8	39	...	...	...	15	5	6	11	14
93-94— Hartford	NHL	33	6	5	11	39	-1	1	0	—	—	—	—	—
— Springfield	AHL	30	16	8	24	39	...	...	...	4	0	2	2	4
— Slov. Olympic team....	Int'l	8	1	6	7	18	...	...	...	—	—	—	—	—
94-95— Springfield	AHL	74	30	52	82	121	...	...	...	—	—	—	—	—
— Hartford	NHL	2	0	0	0	0	0	0	0	—	—	—	—	—
95-96— Springfield	AHL	9	4	8	12	18	...	...	...	—	—	—	—	—
— Detroit....................	IHL	12	5	3	8	16	...	...	...	—	—	—	—	—
— Michigan..................	IHL	50	23	23	46	63	...	...	...	7	3	1	4	16
— Dallas......................	NHL	5	1	1	2	0	1	1	0	—	—	—	—	—
96-97— Worcester	AHL	12	5	4	9	19	...	...	...	—	—	—	—	—
— St. Louis	NHL	44	7	12	19	10	2	0	0	2	0	0	0	0
NHL totals (5 years)		126	17	24	41	94	-8	2	0	2	0	0	0	0

P

PETRUK, RANDY   G   AVALANCHE

PERSONAL: Born April 23, 1978, in Cranbrooke, B.C. ... 5-9/178. ... Catches right.
TRANSACTIONS/CAREER NOTES: Selected by Colorado Avalanche in fourth round (fifth Avalanche pick, 107th overall) of NHL entry draft (June 22, 1996).

			REGULAR SEASON							PLAYOFFS					
Season Team	League	Gms.	Min	W	L	T	GA	SO	Avg.	Gms.	Min.	W	L	GA	SO	Avg.
94-95—Kamloops	WHL	27	1462	16	3	4	71	1	2.91	7	423	5	2	19	0	2.70
95-96—Kamloops	WHL	52	3071	34	15	1	181	1	3.54	16	990	9	†6	58	0	3.52
96-97—Kamloops	WHL	*60	*3475	25	28	5	210	0	3.63	—	—	—	—	—	—	—

PHILLIPS, CHRIS   D   SENATORS

PERSONAL: Born March 9, 1978, in Calgary. ... 6-2/200. ... Shoots left. ... Nephew of Rod Phillips, Edmonton Oilers play-by-play announcer.
TRANSACTIONS/CAREER NOTES: Selected by Ottawa Senators in first round (first Senators pick, first overall) of NHL entry draft (June 22, 1996).
HONORS: Won Can.HL Top Draft Prospect Award (1995-96). ... Won Jim Piggott Memorial Trophy (1995-96). ... Named to Can.HL All-Rookie team (1995-96). ... Named to Memorial Cup All-Star Team (1996-97). ... Named to Can.HL All-Star first team (1996-97). ... Named to WHL (East) All-Star first team (1996-97). ... Won Bill Hunter Trophy (1996-97).

			REGULAR SEASON							PLAYOFFS				
Season Team	League	Gms.	G	A	Pts.	PIM	+/-	PP	SH	Gms.	G	A	Pts.	PIM
93-94— Fort McMurray..........	AJHL	56	6	16	22	72	...	...	...	—	—	—	—	—
94-95— Fort McMurray..........	AJHL	48	16	32	48	127	...	...	...	—	—	—	—	—
95-96— Prince Albert............	WHL	61	10	30	40	97	...	...	...	18	2	12	14	30
96-97— Prince Albert............	WHL	32	3	23	26	58	...	...	...	—	—	—	—	—
— Lethbridge	WHL	26	4	18	22	28	...	...	...	19	4	*21	25	20

PHILLIPS, GREG   D   KINGS

PERSONAL: Born March 27, 1978, in Winnipeg. ... 6-2/190. ... Shoots right.
TRANSACTIONS/CAREER NOTES: Selected by Los Angeles Kings in third round (third Kings pick, 57th overall) of NHL entry draft (June 22, 1996).

			REGULAR SEASON							PLAYOFFS				
Season Team	League	Gms.	G	A	Pts.	PIM	+/-	PP	SH	Gms.	G	A	Pts.	PIM
94-95— Saskatoon.................	WHL	64	3	5	8	94	...	...	...	10	0	0	0	4
95-96— Saskatoon.................	WHL	67	21	24	45	132	...	...	...	4	1	2	3	2
96-97— Saskatoon.................	WHL	34	17	19	36	64	...	...	...	—	—	—	—	—

PICARD, MICHEL   LW   CAPITALS

PERSONAL: Born November 7, 1969, in Beauport, Que. ... 5-11/190. ... Shoots left. ... Name pronounced pih-KAHRD.
TRANSACTIONS/CAREER NOTES: Selected by Hartford Whalers in ninth round (eighth Whalers pick, 178th overall) of NHL entry draft (June 17, 1989). ... Separated shoulder (November 14, 1991); missed seven games. ... Traded by Whalers to San Jose Sharks for future considerations (October 9, 1992); Sharks sent LW Yvon Corriveau to Whalers to complete deal (January 21, 1993). ... Signed as free agent by Portland of AHL (1993). ... Signed as free agent by Ottawa Senators (June 23, 1994). ... Suspended two games and fined $1,000 by NHL for cross-checking (March 16, 1996). ... Traded by Senators to Washington Capitals for cash (May 21, 1996).
HONORS: Named to QMJHL All-Star second team (1988-89). ... Named to AHL All-Star first team (1990-91 and 1994-95). ... Named to AHL All-Star second team (1993-94). ... Named to IHL All-Star first team (1996-97).

			REGULAR SEASON							PLAYOFFS				
Season Team	League	Gms.	G	A	Pts.	PIM	+/-	PP	SH	Gms.	G	A	Pts.	PIM
86-87— Trois-Rivieres............	QMJHL	66	33	35	68	53	...	...	...	—	—	—	—	—
87-88— Trois-Rivieres............	QMJHL	69	40	55	95	71	...	...	...	—	—	—	—	—
88-89— Trois-Rivieres............	QMJHL	66	59	81	140	107	...	...	...	4	1	3	4	2
89-90— Binghamton	AHL	67	16	24	40	98	...	...	...	—	—	—	—	—
90-91— Hartford	NHL	5	1	0	1	2	-2	0	0	—	—	—	—	—
— Springfield	AHL	77	*56	40	96	61	...	...	...	18	8	13	21	18
91-92— Hartford	NHL	25	3	5	8	6	-2	1	0	—	—	—	—	—
— Springfield	AHL	40	21	17	38	44	...	...	...	11	2	0	2	34
92-93— Kansas City...............	IHL	33	7	10	17	51	...	...	...	12	3	2	5	20
— San Jose	NHL	25	4	0	4	24	-17	2	0	—	—	—	—	—
93-94— Portland	AHL	61	41	44	85	99	...	...	...	17	11	10	21	22
94-95— Prin. Edward Island ...	AHL	57	32	57	89	58	...	...	...	8	4	4	8	6
— Ottawa	NHL	24	5	8	13	14	-1	1	0	—	—	—	—	—
95-96— Prin. Edward Island ...	AHL	55	37	45	82	79	...	...	...	5	5	1	6	2
— Ottawa	NHL	17	2	6	8	10	-1	0	0	—	—	—	—	—
96-97— Grand Rapids............	IHL	82	46	55	101	58	...	...	...	5	2	0	2	10
NHL totals (5 years)		96	15	19	34	56	-23	4	0					

PILON, RICH   D   ISLANDERS

PERSONAL: Born April 30, 1968, in Saskatoon, Sask. ... 6-0/205. ... Shoots left. ... Name pronounced PEE-lahn.
TRANSACTIONS/CAREER NOTES: Selected by New York Islanders as underage junior in seventh round (ninth Islanders pick, 143rd overall) of NHL entry draft (June 21, 1986). ... Injured right leg (December 1988). ... Injured right eye (November 4, 1989); missed remainder of season. ... Injured left knee ligament (February 23, 1991). ... Suffered sore left shoulder (January 9, 1992); missed three games. ... Lacerated finger (January 30, 1992); missed four games. ... Bruised hand (October 31, 1992); missed two games. ... Bruised hand (November 22, 1992); missed four games. ... Sprained left knee (December 10, 1992); missed eight games. ... Injured lower back (January 10, 1993); missed 11 games. ... Injured left shoulder (November 13, 1993); missed seven games. ... Reinjured left shoulder (December 3, 1993); missed 32 games. ... Reinjured left shoulder (March 17, 1994); missed 14 games. ... Suffered sore groin (February 22, 1995); missed four games. ... Sprained ankle (March 5, 1995); missed 17 games. ... Broke wrist (April 18, 1995); missed last seven games of season. ... Injured wrist prior to 1995-96 season; missed first 26 games of season. ... Injured groin (December 12, 1995); missed four games. ... Injured wrist (January 9,

P

1996); missed one game. ... Strained hip flexor (February 4, 1996); missed four games. ... Strained hip flexor (March 3, 1996); missed last 18 games of regular season. ... Aggravated groin (October 9, 1996); missed 20 games. ... Suspended two games and fined $1,000 by NHL for slashing incident (January 11, 1997). ... Sprained knee ligament (February 11, 1997); missed three games. ... Injured foot (March 26, 1997); missed four games. ... Bruised knee (April 2, 1997); missed one game.

HONORS: Named to WHL All-Star second team (1987-88).

				REGULAR SEASON							PLAYOFFS				
Season Team	League	Gms.	G	A	Pts.	PIM	+/-	PP	SH		Gms.	G	A	Pts.	PIM
85-86— Prince Albert..............	WHL	6	0	0	0	0	...	...	...		—	—	—	—	—
86-87— Prince Albert..............	WHL	68	4	21	25	192	...	...	...		7	1	6	7	17
87-88— Prince Albert..............	WHL	65	13	34	47	177	...	...	...		9	0	6	6	38
88-89— New York Islanders....	NHL	62	0	14	14	242	-9	0	0		—	—	—	—	—
89-90— New York Islanders....	NHL	14	0	2	2	31	2	0	0		—	—	—	—	—
90-91— New York Islanders....	NHL	60	1	4	5	126	-12	0	0		—	—	—	—	—
91-92— New York Islanders....	NHL	65	1	6	7	183	-1	0	0		—	—	—	—	—
92-93— New York Islanders....	NHL	44	1	3	4	164	-4	0	0		15	0	0	0	50
— Capital District	AHL	6	0	1	1	8	...	...	...		—	—	—	—	—
93-94— New York Islanders....	NHL	28	1	4	5	75	-4	0	0		—	—	—	—	—
— Salt Lake City............	IHL	2	0	0	0	8	...	...	...		—	—	—	—	—
94-95— New York Islanders....	NHL	20	1	1	2	40	-3	0	0		—	—	—	—	—
— Chicago....................	IHL	2	0	0	0	0	...	...	...		—	—	—	—	—
95-96— New York Islanders....	NHL	27	0	3	3	72	-9	0	0		—	—	—	—	—
96-97— New York Islanders....	NHL	52	1	4	5	179	4	0	0		—	—	—	—	—
NHL totals (9 years)		372	6	41	47	1112	-36	0	0		15	0	0	0	50

PITLICK, LANCE — D — SENATORS

PERSONAL: Born November 5, 1967, in Fridley, Minn. ... 6-0/203. ... Shoots right.
HIGH SCHOOL: Cooper (New Hope, Minn.).
COLLEGE: Minnesota.
TRANSACTIONS/CAREER NOTES: Selected by Minnesota North Stars in ninth round (10th North Stars pick, 180th overall) of NHL entry draft (June 21, 1986). ... Severely pulled lower abdominal muscles (December 1, 1989). ... Underwent surgery to have tendons sewn onto his abdominal muscle for reinforcement (January 18, 1990). ... Signed as free agent by Philadelphia Flyers (September 5, 1990). ... Signed as free agent by Ottawa Senators (June 22, 1994). ... Bruised ribs (March 27, 1995); missed two games. ... Injured groin (January 5, 1996); missed one game. ... Injured groin during 1995-96 season; missed four games. ... Strained abdominal muscle (April 1, 1996); missed four games. ... Injured left knee (January 9, 1997); missed nine games. ... Strained groin (February 16, 1997); missed one game.

				REGULAR SEASON							PLAYOFFS				
Season Team	League	Gms.	G	A	Pts.	PIM	+/-	PP	SH		Gms.	G	A	Pts.	PIM
84-85— Cooper.....................	Minn. H.S.	23	8	4	12	...	...	...	...		—	—	—	—	—
85-86— Cooper.....................	Minn. H.S.	21	17	8	25	...	...	...	...		—	—	—	—	—
86-87— Univ. of Minnesota.....	WCHA	45	0	9	9	88	...	...	...		10	0	2	2	4
87-88— Univ. of Minnesota.....	WCHA	38	3	9	12	76	...	...	...		8	1	1	2	14
88-89— Univ. of Minnesota.....	WCHA	47	4	9	13	95	...	...	...		8	2	1	3	95
89-90— Univ. of Minnesota.....	WCHA	14	3	2	5	26	...	...	...		—	—	—	—	—
90-91— Hershey	AHL	64	6	15	21	75	...	...	...		3	0	0	0	9
91-92— U.S. national team ...	Int'l	19	0	1	1	38	...	...	...		—	—	—	—	—
— Hershey	AHL	4	0	0	0	6	...	...	...		3	0	0	0	4
92-93— Hershey	AHL	53	5	10	15	77	...	...	...		—	—	—	—	—
93-94— Hershey	AHL	58	4	13	17	93	...	...	...		11	1	0	1	11
94-95— Prin. Edward Island ...	AHL	61	8	19	27	55	...	...	...		11	1	4	5	10
— Ottawa	NHL	15	0	1	1	6	-5	0	0		—	—	—	—	—
95-96— Prin. Edward Island ...	AHL	29	4	10	14	39	...	...	...		5	0	0	0	0
— Ottawa	NHL	28	1	6	7	20	-8	0	0		—	—	—	—	—
96-97— Ottawa	NHL	66	5	5	10	91	2	0	0		7	0	0	0	4
NHL totals (3 years)		109	6	12	18	117	-11	0	0		7	0	0	0	4

PITTIS, DOMENIC — C — PENGUINS

PERSONAL: Born October 1, 1974, in Calgary. ... 5-11/180. ... Shoots left. ... Name pronounced PIH-tihz.
HIGH SCHOOL: Catholic Central (Lethbridge, Alta).
TRANSACTIONS/CAREER NOTES: Selected by Pittsburgh Penguins in second round (second Penguins pick, 52nd overall) of NHL entry draft (June 26, 1993).
HONORS: Named to WHL (East) All-Star second team (1993-94).

				REGULAR SEASON							PLAYOFFS				
Season Team	League	Gms.	G	A	Pts.	PIM	+/-	PP	SH		Gms.	G	A	Pts.	PIM
91-92— Lethbridge	WHL	65	6	17	23	48	...	...	...		5	0	2	2	4
92-93— Lethbridge	WHL	66	46	73	119	69	...	...	...		4	3	3	6	8
93-94— Lethbridge	WHL	72	58	69	127	93	...	...	...		8	4	11	15	16
94-95— Cleveland	IHL	62	18	32	50	66	...	...	...		3	0	2	2	2
95-96— Cleveland	IHL	74	10	28	38	100	...	...	...		3	0	0	0	2
96-97— Pittsburgh	NHL	1	0	0	0	0	-1	0	0		—	—	—	—	—
— Long Beach.................	IHL	65	23	43	66	91	...	...	...		18	5	9	14	26
NHL totals (1 year)		1	0	0	0	0	-1	0	0						

PIVONKA, MICHAL — C — CAPITALS

PERSONAL: Born January 28, 1966, in Kladno, Czechoslovakia. ... 6-2/195. ... Shoots left. ... Name pronounced pih-VAHN-kuh.
TRANSACTIONS/CAREER NOTES: Selected by Washington Capitals in third round (third Capitals pick, 59th overall) of NHL entry draft (June 9, 1984). ... Strained ankle ligaments (March 1987). ... Sprained right wrist (October 1987). ... Sprained left ankle (March 1988). ... Sprained

left knee (March 9, 1990). ... Pulled groin (October 10, 1992); missed three games. ... Pulled groin (October 21, 1992); missed 12 games. ... Suffered concussion (March 25, 1994); missed one game. ... Played in Europe during 1994-95 NHL lockout. ... Injured leg (April 30, 1995); missed one game. ... Missed first nine games of 1995-96 season due to contract dispute. ... Tore knee cartilage (October 26, 1996); missed 20 games. ... Suffered from the flu (March 2, 1997); missed one game. ... Suffered concussion (March 26, 1997); missed seven games.
STATISTICAL PLATEAUS: Three-goal games: 1991-92 (1).
MISCELLANEOUS: Holds Washington Capitals all-time record for most assists (406).

		REGULAR SEASON								PLAYOFFS				
Season Team	League	Gms.	G	A	Pts.	PIM	+/-	PP	SH	Gms.	G	A	Pts.	PIM
85-86— Dukla Jihlava	Czech.	42	5	13	18	...	...	...	...	—	—	—	—	—
86-87— Washington	NHL	73	18	25	43	41	-19	4	0	7	1	1	2	2
87-88— Washington	NHL	71	11	23	34	28	1	3	0	14	4	9	13	4
88-89— Baltimore	AHL	31	12	24	36	19	...	...	...	—	—	—	—	—
— Washington	NHL	52	8	19	27	30	9	1	0	6	3	1	4	10
89-90— Washington	NHL	77	25	39	64	54	-7	10	3	11	0	2	2	6
90-91— Washington	NHL	79	20	50	70	34	3	6	0	11	2	3	5	8
91-92— Washington	NHL	80	23	57	80	47	10	7	4	7	1	5	6	13
92-93— Washington	NHL	69	21	53	74	66	14	6	1	6	0	2	2	0
93-94— Washington	NHL	82	14	36	50	38	2	5	0	7	4	4	8	4
94-95— Klagenfurt	Austria	7	2	4	6	4	...	...	...	—	—	—	—	—
— Washington	NHL	46	10	23	33	50	3	4	2	7	1	4	5	21
95-96— Detroit.......................	IHL	7	1	9	10	19	...	...	...	—	—	—	—	—
— Washington	NHL	73	16	65	81	36	18	6	2	6	3	2	5	18
96-97— Washington	NHL	54	7	16	23	22	-15	2	0	—	—	—	—	—
NHL totals (11 years)		756	173	406	579	446	19	54	12	82	19	33	52	86

PLANTE, DAN — RW — ISLANDERS

PERSONAL: Born October 5, 1971, in Hayward, Wis. ... 5-11/202. ... Shoots right. ... Full name: Daniel Leon Plante. ... Name pronounced PLAHNT.
HIGH SCHOOL: Edina (Minn.).
COLLEGE: Wisconsin.
TRANSACTIONS/CAREER NOTES: Selected by New York Islanders in third round (third Islanders pick, 48th overall) of NHL entry draft (June 16, 1990). ... Injured knee (September 1994). ... Injured shoulder (February 10, 1996); missed one game. ... Bruised right knee (February 23, 1996); missed five games.

		REGULAR SEASON								PLAYOFFS				
Season Team	League	Gms.	G	A	Pts.	PIM	+/-	PP	SH	Gms.	G	A	Pts.	PIM
88-89— Edina........................	Minn. H.S.	27	10	26	36	12	...	...	...	—	—	—	—	—
89-90— Edina........................	Minn. H.S.	24	8	18	26	...	...	...	...	—	—	—	—	—
90-91— Univ. of Wisconsin.....	WCHA	33	1	2	3	54	...	...	...	—	—	—	—	—
91-92— Univ. of Wisconsin.....	WCHA	40	15	16	31	113	...	...	...	—	—	—	—	—
92-93— Univ. of Wisconsin.....	WCHA	42	26	31	57	142	...	...	...	—	—	—	—	—
93-94— Salt Lake City	IHL	66	7	17	24	148	...	...	...	—	—	—	—	—
— New York Islanders....	NHL	12	0	1	1	4	-2	0	0	1	1	0	1	2
94-95— Denver	IHL	2	0	0	0	4	...	...	...	—	—	—	—	—
95-96— New York Islanders....	NHL	73	5	3	8	50	-22	0	2	—	—	—	—	—
96-97— New York Islanders....	NHL	67	4	9	13	75	-6	0	2	—	—	—	—	—
NHL totals (3 years)		152	9	13	22	129	-30	0	4	1	1	0	1	2

PLANTE, DEREK — C — SABRES

PERSONAL: Born January 17, 1971, in Cloquet, Minn. ... 5-11/181. ... Shoots left. ... Full name: Derek John Plante. ... Name pronounced PLANT.
HIGH SCHOOL: Cloquet (Minn.).
COLLEGE: Minnesota-Duluth.
TRANSACTIONS/CAREER NOTES: Broke arm (March 1988). ... Selected by Buffalo Sabres in eighth round (seventh Sabres pick, 161st overall) of NHL entry draft (June 17, 1989). ... Injured collarbone (December 15, 1989). ... Reinjured collarbone (January 20, 1990). ... Bruised left shoulder (March 8, 1994); missed two games. ... Strained back (December 15, 1995); missed three games.
HONORS: Named to NCAA All-America West first team (1992-93). ... Named WCHA Player of the Year (1992-93). ... Named to WCHA All-Star first team (1992-93).
STATISTICAL PLATEAUS: Three-goal games: 1993-94 (1).

		REGULAR SEASON								PLAYOFFS				
Season Team	League	Gms.	G	A	Pts.	PIM	+/-	PP	SH	Gms.	G	A	Pts.	PIM
87-88— Cloquet	Minn. H.S.	23	16	25	41	...	...	...	...	—	—	—	—	—
88-89— Cloquet	Minn. H.S.	24	30	33	63	...	...	...	...	—	—	—	—	—
89-90— Minnesota-Duluth	WCHA	28	10	11	21	12	...	...	...	—	—	—	—	—
90-91— Minnesota-Duluth	WCHA	36	23	20	43	6	...	...	...	—	—	—	—	—
91-92— Minnesota-Duluth	WCHA	37	27	36	63	28	...	...	...	—	—	—	—	—
92-93— Minnesota-Duluth	WCHA	37	*36	*56	*92	30	...	...	...	—	—	—	—	—
93-94— U.S. national team	Int'l	2	...	1	1	...	...	...	...	—	—	—	—	—
— Buffalo	NHL	77	21	35	56	24	4	8	1	7	1	0	1	0
94-95— Buffalo	NHL	47	3	19	22	12	-4	2	0	—	—	—	—	—
95-96— Buffalo	NHL	76	23	33	56	28	-4	4	0	—	—	—	—	—
96-97— Buffalo	NHL	82	27	26	53	24	14	5	0	12	4	6	10	4
NHL totals (4 years)		282	74	113	187	88	10	19	1	19	5	6	11	4

P

PLAVSIC, ADRIEN — D — MIGHTY DUCKS

PERSONAL: Born January 13, 1970, in Montreal. ... 6-1/195. ... Shoots left. ... Name pronounced PLAV-sihk.
COLLEGE: New Hampshire.
TRANSACTIONS/CAREER NOTES: Selected by St. Louis Blues in second round (second Blues pick, 30th overall) of NHL entry draft (June 11, 1988). ... Suffered concussion (September 25, 1989). ... Traded by Blues with first-round pick (LW/RW Shawn Antoski) in 1990 draft and second-round pick in 1991 draft to Vancouver Canucks for RW Rich Sutter, D Harold Snepsts and second-round pick (LW Craig Johnson) in 1990 draft that had been traded to Canucks in an earlier deal (March 6, 1990). ... Sprained knee (November 9, 1990); missed 15 games. ... Suffered from the flu (February 22, 1993); missed one game. ... Suffered concussion (December 4, 1993); missed four games. ... Traded by Canucks to Tampa Bay Lightning for fifth-round pick (LW David Darguzas) in 1997 draft (March 22, 1995). ... Signed as free agent by Mighty Ducks of Anaheim (August 27, 1996).
MISCELLANEOUS: Member of silver-medal-winning Canadian Olympic team (1992).

		REGULAR SEASON								PLAYOFFS				
Season Team	League	Gms.	G	A	Pts.	PIM	+/-	PP	SH	Gms.	G	A	Pts.	PIM
87-88— New Hampshire	Hockey East	30	5	6	11	45	...	...	...	—	—	—	—	—
88-89— Canadian nat'l team ...	Int'l	62	5	10	15	25	...	...	...	—	—	—	—	—
89-90— Peoria	IHL	51	7	14	21	87	...	...	...	—	—	—	—	—
— St. Louis	NHL	4	0	1	1	2	3	0	0	—	—	—	—	—
— Vancouver.................	NHL	11	3	2	5	8	-2	2	0	—	—	—	—	—
— Milwaukee.................	IHL	3	1	2	3	14	...	...	...	6	1	3	4	6
90-91— Vancouver.................	NHL	48	2	10	12	62	-23	0	0	—	—	—	—	—
91-92— Canadian nat'l team ...	Int'l	38	6	9	15	29	...	...	...	—	—	—	—	—
— Can. Olympic team ...	Int'l	8	0	2	2	0	...	...	...	—	—	—	—	—
— Vancouver.................	NHL	16	1	9	10	14	4	0	0	13	1	7	8	4
92-93— Vancouver.................	NHL	57	6	21	27	53	28	5	0	—	—	—	—	—
93-94— Vancouver.................	NHL	47	1	9	10	6	-5	0	0	—	—	—	—	—
— Hamilton...................	AHL	2	0	0	0	0	...	...	...	—	—	—	—	—
94-95— Vancouver.................	NHL	3	0	1	1	4	3	0	0	—	—	—	—	—
— Tampa Bay...............	NHL	15	2	1	3	4	5	0	0	—	—	—	—	—
95-96— Atlanta.....................	IHL	68	5	34	39	32	...	...	...	3	0	1	1	4
— Tampa Bay...............	NHL	7	1	2	3	6	5	0	0	—	—	—	—	—
96-97— Anaheim....................	NHL	6	0	0	0	2	-5	0	0	—	—	—	—	—
— Long Beach..............	IHL	69	7	28	35	86	...	...	...	18	0	9	9	10
NHL totals (8 years)		214	16	56	72	161	13	7	0	13	1	7	8	4

PLOUFFE, STEVE — G — SABRES

PERSONAL: Born November 23, 1975, in Laval, Que. ... 5-11/167. ... Catches left. ... Name pronounced Ploof.
HIGH SCHOOL: Cegep (Saint-Georges, Que.).
TRANSACTIONS/CAREER NOTES: Selected by Buffalo Sabres in seventh round (sixth Sabres pick, 168th overall) of NHL entry draft (June 29, 1994).

		REGULAR SEASON								PLAYOFFS					
Season Team	League	Gms.	Min	W	L	T	GA	SO	Avg.	Gms.	Min.	W	L	GA	SO	Avg.
92-93— Granby.........................	QMJHL	52	2678	...	...	...	240	0	5.38	—	—	—	—	—	—	—
93-94— Granby.........................	QMJHL	46	2492	16	25	1	172	1	4.14	—	—	—	—	—	—	—
94-95— Shawinigan.................	QMJHL	32	1702	12	11	5	113	0	3.98	2	79	1	1	6	0	4.56
95-96— Fort Worth	CHL	30	1581	10	13	4	110	0	4.17	—	—	—	—	—	—	—
96-97— Fort Worth	CHL	52	2983	*38	9	5	143	*2	2.88	*17	*1021	*11	†6	*53	†1	3.11

POAPST, STEVE — D — CAPITALS

PERSONAL: Born January 3, 1969, in Cornwall, Ont. ... 6-0/180. ... Shoots left. ... Name pronounced PAHPS.
COLLEGE: Colgate.
TRANSACTIONS/CAREER NOTES: Signed as free agent by Portland of AHL (July 1993). ... Signed as free agent by Washington Capitals (February 4, 1995).

		REGULAR SEASON								PLAYOFFS				
Season Team	League	Gms.	G	A	Pts.	PIM	+/-	PP	SH	Gms.	G	A	Pts.	PIM
89-90— Colgate University......	ECAC	38	4	15	19	54	...	...	...	—	—	—	—	—
90-91— Colgate University......	ECAC	32	6	15	21	43	...	...	...	—	—	—	—	—
91-92— Hampton Roads.........	ECHL	55	8	20	28	29	...	...	...	14	1	4	5	12
92-93— Hampton Roads.........	ECHL	63	10	35	45	57	...	...	...	4	0	1	1	4
— Baltimore.................	AHL	7	0	1	1	4	...	...	...	7	0	3	3	6
93-94— Portland....................	AHL	78	14	21	35	47	...	...	...	12	0	3	3	8
94-95— Portland....................	AHL	71	8	22	30	60	...	...	...	7	0	1	1	16
95-96— Portland....................	AHL	70	10	24	34	79	...	...	...	20	2	6	8	16
— Washington	NHL	3	1	0	1	0	-1	0	0	6	0	0	0	0
96-97— Portland....................	AHL	47	1	20	21	34	...	...	...	5	0	1	1	6
NHL totals (1 year)		3	1	0	1	0	-1	0	0	6	0	0	0	0

PODEIN, SHJON — LW — FLYERS

PERSONAL: Born March 5, 1968, in Rochester, Minn. ... 6-2/200. ... Shoots left. ... Name pronounced SHAWN poh-DEEN.
COLLEGE: Minnesota-Duluth.
TRANSACTIONS/CAREER NOTES: Selected by Edmonton Oilers in eighth round (ninth Oilers pick, 166th overall) of NHL entry draft (June 11, 1988). ... Injured knee (March 9, 1994); missed five games. ... Signed as free agent by Philadelphia Flyers (July 27, 1994). ... Bruised right foot (February 22, 1996); missed three games.

P

Season Team	League	REGULAR SEASON								PLAYOFFS				
		Gms.	G	A	Pts.	PIM	+/-	PP	SH	Gms.	G	A	Pts.	PIM
87-88— Minnesota-Duluth	WCHA	30	4	4	8	48	...	...	...	—	—	—	—	—
88-89— Minnesota-Duluth	WCHA	36	7	5	12	46	...	...	...	—	—	—	—	—
89-90— Minnesota-Duluth	WCHA	35	21	18	39	36	...	...	...	—	—	—	—	—
90-91— Cape Breton	AHL	63	14	15	29	65	...	...	...	4	0	0	0	5
91-92— Cape Breton	AHL	80	30	24	54	46	...	...	...	5	3	1	4	2
92-93— Cape Breton	AHL	38	18	21	39	32	...	...	...	9	2	2	4	29
— Edmonton	NHL	40	13	6	19	25	-2	2	1	—	—	—	—	—
93-94— Edmonton	NHL	28	3	5	8	8	3	0	0	—	—	—	—	—
— Cape Breton	AHL	5	4	4	8	4	...	...	...	—	—	—	—	—
94-95— Philadelphia	NHL	44	3	7	10	33	-2	0	0	15	1	3	4	10
95-96— Philadelphia	NHL	79	15	10	25	89	25	0	4	12	1	2	3	50
96-97— Philadelphia	NHL	82	14	18	32	41	7	0	0	19	4	3	7	16
NHL totals (5 years)		273	48	46	94	196	31	2	5	46	6	8	14	76

PODOLKA, MICHAEL   G   RED WINGS

PERSONAL: Born August 11, 1977, in Most, Czechoslovakia. ... 5-11/146. ... Catches left. ... Name pronounced puh-DOHL-kuh.
TRANSACTIONS/CAREER NOTES: Selected by Detroit Red Wings in fifth round (fourth Red Wings pick, 135th overall) of NHL entry draft (June 22, 1996).

Season Team	League	REGULAR SEASON								PLAYOFFS						
		Gms.	Min	W	L	T	GA	SO	Avg.	Gms.	Min.	W	L	GA	SO	Avg.
95-96—Sault Ste. Marie............	OHL	44	2391	20	15	4	149	1	3.74	1	60	0	1	6	0	6.00
96-97—Sault Ste. Marie............	OHL	47	2626	26	14	4	134	1	3.06	11	662	6	4	35	†1	3.17

PODOLLAN, JASON   RW/C   MAPLE LEAFS

PERSONAL: Born February 18, 1976, in Vernon, B.C. ... 6-1/192. ... Shoots right. ... Name pronounced puh-DOH-lihn.
HIGH SCHOOL: University (Spokane, Wash.).
TRANSACTIONS/CAREER NOTES: Selected by Florida Panthers in second round (third Panthers pick, 31st overall) of NHL entry draft (June 28, 1994). ... Traded by Panthers to Toronto Maple Leafs for C Kirk Muller (March 18, 1997). ... Strained shoulder (March 19, 1997); missed two games.
HONORS: Named to WHL (West) All-Star second team (1995-96).

Season Team	League	REGULAR SEASON								PLAYOFFS				
		Gms.	G	A	Pts.	PIM	+/-	PP	SH	Gms.	G	A	Pts.	PIM
91-92— Penticton	Jr. A	59	20	26	46	66	...	...	...	—	—	—	—	—
— Spokane....................	WHL	2	0	0	0	2	...	...	...	10	3	1	4	16
92-93— Spokane....................	WHL	72	36	33	69	108	...	...	...	10	4	4	8	14
93-94— Spokane....................	WHL	69	29	37	66	108	...	...	...	3	3	0	3	2
94-95— Spokane....................	WHL	72	43	41	84	102	...	...	...	11	5	7	12	18
— Cincinnati..................	IHL	—	—	—	—	—				3	0	0	0	2
95-96— Spokane....................	WHL	56	37	25	62	103	...	...	...	18	*21	12	33	28
96-97— Carolina	AHL	39	21	25	46	36	...	...	...	—	—	—	—	—
— Florida......................	NHL	19	1	1	2	4	-3	1	0	—	—	—	—	—
— St. John's..................	AHL	—	—	—	—	—				11	2	3	5	6
— Toronto	NHL	10	0	3	3	6	-2	0	0	—	—	—	—	—
NHL totals (2 years)		29	1	4	5	10	-5	1	0					

POESCHEK, RUDY   D   BLUES

PERSONAL: Born September 29, 1966, in Terrace, B.C. ... 6-2/210. ... Shoots right. ... Full name: Rudolph Leopold Poeschek. ... Name pronounced POH-shehk.
TRANSACTIONS/CAREER NOTES: Injured knee (December 1984). ... Selected by New York Rangers as underage junior in 12th round (12th Rangers pick, 238th overall) of NHL entry draft (June 15, 1985). ... Injured shoulder (November 1986). ... Bruised right hand (February 1989). ... Suspended six games by AHL for pre-game fight (November 25, 1990). ... Traded by Rangers to Winnipeg Jets for C Guy Larose (January 22, 1991). ... Signed as free agent by Tampa Bay Lightning (August 13, 1993). ... Sprained ankle (February 7, 1995); missed two games. ... Reinjured ankle (February 14, 1995); missed nine games. ... Broke thumb (April 16, 1995); missed last eight games of season. ... Injured knee (October 20, 1995); missed one game. ... Sprained left knee (October 22, 1996); missed 12 games. ... Signed as free agent by St. Louis Blues (July 7, 1997).

Season Team	League	REGULAR SEASON								PLAYOFFS				
		Gms.	G	A	Pts.	PIM	+/-	PP	SH	Gms.	G	A	Pts.	PIM
83-84— Kamloops..................	WHL	47	3	9	12	93	...	...	...	8	0	2	2	7
84-85— Kamloops..................	WHL	34	6	7	13	100	...	...	...	15	0	3	3	56
85-86— Kamloops..................	WHL	32	3	13	16	92	...	...	...	16	3	7	10	40
86-87— Kamloops..................	WHL	54	13	18	31	153	...	...	...	15	2	4	6	37
87-88— New York Rangers	NHL	1	0	0	0	2	0	0	0	—	—	—	—	—
— Colorado	IHL	82	7	31	38	210	...	...	...	12	2	2	4	31
88-89— Denver	IHL	2	0	0	0	6	...	...	...	—	—	—	—	—
— New York Rangers	NHL	52	0	2	2	199	-8	0	0	—	—	—	—	—
89-90— Flint	IHL	38	8	13	21	109	...	...	...	4	0	0	0	16
— New York Rangers	NHL	15	0	0	0	55	-1	0	0	—	—	—	—	—
90-91— Binghamton	AHL	38	1	3	4	162	...	...	...	—	—	—	—	—
— Moncton	AHL	23	2	4	6	67	...	...	...	9	1	1	2	41
— Winnipeg	NHL	1	0	0	0	5	0	0	0	—	—	—	—	—
91-92— Moncton	AHL	63	4	18	22	170	...	...	...	11	0	2	2	46
— Winnipeg	NHL	4	0	0	0	17	-5	0	0	—	—	—	—	—

P

Season Team	League	REGULAR SEASON								PLAYOFFS				
		Gms.	G	A	Pts.	PIM	+/-	PP	SH	Gms.	G	A	Pts.	PIM
92-93 — St. John's	AHL	78	7	24	31	189	...	...	...	9	0	4	4	13
93-94 — Tampa Bay	NHL	71	3	6	9	118	3	0	0	—	—	—	—	—
94-95 — Tampa Bay	NHL	25	1	1	2	92	0	0	0	—	—	—	—	—
95-96 — Tampa Bay	NHL	57	1	3	4	88	-2	0	0	3	0	0	0	12
96-97 — Tampa Bay	NHL	60	0	6	6	120	-3	0	0	—	—	—	—	—
NHL totals (9 years)		286	5	18	23	696	-16	0	0	3	0	0	0	12

POPOVIC, PETER — D — CANADIENS

PERSONAL: Born February 10, 1968, in Koping, Sweden. ... 6-6/235. ... Shoots right. ... Name pronounced PAH-poh-vihk.
TRANSACTIONS/CAREER NOTES: Selected by Montreal Canadiens in fifth round (fifth Canadiens pick, 93rd overall) of NHL entry draft (June 11, 1988). ... Injured knee (November 20, 1993); missed six games. ... Bruised shoulder (December 22, 1993); missed seven games. ... Played in Europe during 1994-95 NHL lockout. ... Cut face (March 11, 1995); missed six games. ... Broke finger on right hand (December 23, 1995); missed six games. ... Bruised foot (February 17, 1997); missed one game. ... Injured rib (April 7, 1997); missed remainder of regular season and two playoff games.

Season Team	League	REGULAR SEASON								PLAYOFFS				
		Gms.	G	A	Pts.	PIM	+/-	PP	SH	Gms.	G	A	Pts.	PIM
86-87 — Vasteras	Sweden	24	1	2	3	10	...			—	—	—	—	—
87-88 — Vasteras	Sweden	28	3	17	20	16	...			—	—	—	—	—
88-89 — Vasteras	Sweden	22	1	4	5	32	...			—	—	—	—	—
89-90 — Vasteras	Sweden	30	2	10	12	24	...			2	0	1	1	2
90-91 — Vasteras	Sweden	40	3	2	5	62	...			4	0	0	0	4
91-92 — Vasteras	Sweden	34	7	10	17	30	...			—	—	—	—	—
92-93 — Vasteras	Sweden	39	6	12	18	46	...			3	0	1	1	2
93-94 — Montreal	NHL	47	2	12	14	26	10	1	0	6	0	1	1	0
94-95 — Vasteras	Sweden	11	0	3	3	10	...			—	—	—	—	—
— Montreal	NHL	33	0	5	5	8	-10	0	0	—	—	—	—	—
95-96 — Montreal	NHL	76	2	12	14	69	21	0	0	6	0	2	2	4
96-97 — Montreal	NHL	78	1	13	14	32	9	0	0	3	0	0	0	2
NHL totals (4 years)		234	5	42	47	135	30	1	0	15	0	3	3	6

POTI, TOM — D — OILERS

PERSONAL: Born March 22, 1977, in Worcester, Mass. ... 6-3/180. ... Shoots left.
HIGH SCHOOL: Cushing Academy (Ashburnham, Mass.).
COLLEGE: Boston University.
TRANSACTIONS/CAREER NOTES: Selected by Edmonton Oilers in third round (fourth Oilers pick, 59th overall) of NHL entry draft (June 22, 1996).
HONORS: Named to NCAA All-Tournament team (1996-97). ... Named to Hockey East All-Rookie team (1996-97).

Season Team	League	REGULAR SEASON								PLAYOFFS				
		Gms.	G	A	Pts.	PIM	+/-	PP	SH	Gms.	G	A	Pts.	PIM
94-95 — Cushing Academy	Mass. H.S.	36	16	47	63	35	...	...	...	—	—	—	—	—
95-96 — Cushing Academy	Mass. H.S.	29	14	59	73	18	...	...	...	—	—	—	—	—
96-97 — Boston University	Hockey East	38	4	17	21	54	...	...	...	—	—	—	—	—

POTOMSKI, BARRY — LW — KINGS

PERSONAL: Born November 24, 1972, in Windsor, Ont. ... 6-2/215. ... Shoots left.
TRANSACTIONS/CAREER NOTES: Signed as free agent by Los Angeles Kings (July 7, 1994). ... Sprained left shoulder (March 25, 1996); missed seven games. ... Suffered herniated disc (October 17, 1996); missed 24 games.

Season Team	League	REGULAR SEASON								PLAYOFFS				
		Gms.	G	A	Pts.	PIM	+/-	PP	SH	Gms.	G	A	Pts.	PIM
90-91 — London	OHL	65	14	17	31	202	...	...	...	7	0	2	2	10
91-92 — London	OHL	61	19	32	51	224	...	...	...	10	5	1	6	22
92-93 — Toledo	ECHL	43	5	18	23	184	...	...	...	14	5	2	7	73
— Erie	ECHL	5	1	1	2	31	...	...	...	—	—	—	—	—
93-94 — Toledo	ECHL	13	9	4	13	81	...	...	...	—	—	—	—	—
— Adirondack	AHL	50	9	5	14	224	...	...	...	11	1	1	2	44
94-95 — Phoenix	IHL	42	5	6	11	171	...	...	...	—	—	—	—	—
95-96 — Phoenix	IHL	24	5	2	7	74	...	...	...	3	1	0	1	8
— Los Angeles	NHL	33	3	2	5	104	-7	1	0	—	—	—	—	—
96-97 — Los Angeles	NHL	26	3	2	5	93	-8	0	0	—	—	—	—	—
— Phoenix	IHL	28	2	11	13	58	...	...	...	—	—	—	—	—
NHL totals (2 years)		59	6	4	10	197	-15	1	0	—	—	—	—	—

POTVIN, FELIX — G — MAPLE LEAFS

PERSONAL: Born June 23, 1971, in Anjou, Que. ... 6-0/190. ... Catches left. ... Name pronounced PAHT-va.
TRANSACTIONS/CAREER NOTES: Selected by Toronto Maple Leafs in second round (second Maple Leafs pick, 31st overall) of NHL entry draft (June 16, 1990).
HONORS: Named to QMJHL All-Star second team (1989-90). ... Won Can.HL Goaltender of the Year Award (1990-91). ... Won Hap Emms Memorial Trophy (1990-91). ... Won Jacques Plante Trophy (1990-91). ... Won Shell Cup (1990-91). ... Won Guy Lafleur Trophy (1990-91). ... Named to Memorial Cup All-Star team (1990-91). ... Named to QMJHL All-Star first team (1990-91). ... Won Aldege (Baz) Bastien Trophy

P

(1991-92). ... Won Dudley (Red) Garrett Memorial Trophy (1991-92). ... Named to AHL All-Star first team (1991-92). ... Named to NHL All-Rookie team (1992-93). ... Played in NHL All-Star Game (1994 and 1996).
MISCELLANEOUS: Stopped a penalty shot attempt (vs. Brian Bradley, October 22, 1992; vs. Donald Audette, November 21, 1996).

			REGULAR SEASON								PLAYOFFS					
Season Team	League	Gms.	Min	W	L	T	GA	SO	Avg.	Gms.	Min.	W	L	GA	SO	Avg.
88-89—Chicoutimi	QMJHL	*65	*3489	25	31	1	*271	†2	4.66	—	—	—	—	—	—	—
89-90—Chicoutimi	QMJHL	*62	*3478	31	26	2	231	†2	3.99	—	—	—	—	—	—	—
90-91—Chicoutimi	QMJHL	54	3216	33	15	4	145	*6	†2.71	*16	*992	*11	5	46	0	*2.78
91-92—St. John's	AHL	35	2070	18	10	6	101	2	2.93	11	642	7	4	41	0	3.83
—Toronto	NHL	4	210	0	2	1	8	0	2.29	—	—	—	—	—	—	—
92-93—Toronto	NHL	48	2781	25	15	7	116	2	*2.50	21	1308	11	10	62	1	2.84
—St. John's	AHL	5	309	3	0	2	18	0	3.50	—	—	—	—	—	—	—
93-94—Toronto	NHL	66	3883	34	22	9	187	3	2.89	18	1124	9	†9	46	3	2.46
94-95—Toronto	NHL	36	2144	15	13	7	104	0	2.91	7	424	3	4	20	1	2.83
95-96—Toronto	NHL	69	4009	30	26	11	192	2	2.87	6	350	2	4	19	0	3.26
96-97—Toronto	NHL	*74	*4271	27	*36	7	*224	0	3.15	—	—	—	—	—	—	—
NHL totals (6 years)		297	17298	131	114	42	831	7	2.88	52	3206	25	27	147	5	2.75

POTVIN, MARC — RW

PERSONAL: Born January 29, 1967, in Ottawa. ... 6-1/215. ... Shoots right. ... Full name: Marc Richard Potvin. ... Name pronounced PAHT-vihn. ... Cousin of Denis Potvin, defenseman, New York Islanders (1973-74 through 1987-88).
COLLEGE: Bowling Green State.
TRANSACTIONS/CAREER NOTES: Selected by Detroit Red Wings in ninth round (ninth Red Wings pick, 169th overall) of NHL entry draft (June 21, 1986). ... Traded by Red Wings with C Jimmy Carson and C Gary Shuchuk to Los Angeles Kings for D Paul Coffey, RW Jim Hiller and C/LW Sylvain Couturier (January 29, 1993). ... Broke nose (February 18, 1993); missed one game. ... Traded by Kings to Hartford Whalers for D Doug Houda (November 3, 1993). ... Suffered from post-concussion syndrome (March 9, 1994); missed six games. ... Fined $500 by Whalers for involvement in bar brawl (April 1, 1994). ... Signed as free agent by Boston Bruins (June 28, 1994).

			REGULAR SEASON							PLAYOFFS			
Season Team	League	Gms.	G	A	Pts.	PIM	+/-	PP	SH	Gms.	G	A	Pts.	PIM
85-86—Stratford	OPJHL	63	5	6	11	117	...	...	...	—	—	—	—	—
86-87—Bowling Green	CCHA	43	5	15	20	74	...	...	...	—	—	—	—	—
87-88—Bowling Green	CCHA	45	15	21	36	80	...	...	...	—	—	—	—	—
88-89—Bowling Green	CCHA	46	23	12	35	63	...	...	...	—	—	—	—	—
89-90—Bowling Green	CCHA	40	19	17	36	72	...	...	...	—	—	—	—	—
—Adirondack.................	AHL	5	2	1	3	9	...	...	...	4	0	1	1	23
90-91—Adirondack.................	AHL	63	9	13	22	†365	...	...	...	—	—	—	—	—
—Detroit........................	NHL	9	0	0	0	55	-4	0	0	6	0	0	0	32
91-92—Adirondack.................	AHL	51	13	16	29	314	...	...	...	19	5	4	9	57
—Detroit........................	NHL	5	1	0	1	52	-2	0	0	1	0	0	0	0
92-93—Adirondack.................	AHL	37	8	12	20	109	...	...	...	—	—	—	—	—
—Los Angeles..............	NHL	20	0	1	1	61	-10	0	0	1	0	0	0	0
93-94—Los Angeles..............	NHL	3	0	0	0	26	-3	0	0	—	—	—	—	—
—Hartford	NHL	51	2	3	5	246	-5	0	0	—	—	—	—	—
94-95—Boston	NHL	6	0	1	1	4	1	0	0	—	—	—	—	—
—Providence.................	AHL	21	4	14	18	84	...	...	...	12	2	4	6	25
95-96—Providence.................	AHL	48	9	9	18	118	...	...	...	—	—	—	—	—
—Boston	NHL	27	0	0	0	12	-2	0	0	5	0	1	1	18
96-97—Portland	AHL	71	17	15	32	222	...	...	...	5	0	0	0	12
NHL totals (6 years)		121	3	5	8	456	-25	0	0	13	0	1	1	50

POULIN, PATRICK — LW — LIGHTNING

PERSONAL: Born April 23, 1973, in Vanier, Que. ... 6-1/208. ... Shoots left. ... Name pronounced POO-lai.
TRANSACTIONS/CAREER NOTES: Broke wrist (January 15, 1991). ... Selected by Hartford Whalers in first round (first Whalers pick, ninth overall) of NHL entry draft (June 22, 1991). ... Traded by Whalers with D Eric Weinrich to Chicago Blackhawks for RW Steve Larmer and D Bryan Marchment (November 2, 1993). ... Sprained ankle (December 28, 1995); missed 19 games. ... Suffered back spasms (March 5, 1996); missed two games. ... Traded by Blackhawks with D Igor Ulanov and second-round pick (traded to New Jersey) to Tampa Bay Lightning for D Enrico Ciccone (March 20, 1996). ... Injured knee (January 13, 1997); missed one game. ... Injured knee (March 6, 1997); missed six games.
HONORS: Won Jean Beliveau Trophy (1991-92). ... Named to Can.HL All-Star first team (1991-92). ... Named to QMJHL All-Star first team (1991-92).

			REGULAR SEASON							PLAYOFFS			
Season Team	League	Gms.	G	A	Pts.	PIM	+/-	PP	SH	Gms.	G	A	Pts.	PIM
89-90—St. Hyacinthe	QMJHL	60	25	26	51	55	...	...	...	12	1	9	10	5
90-91—St. Hyacinthe	QMJHL	56	32	38	70	82	...	...	...	4	0	2	2	23
91-92—St. Hyacinthe	QMJHL	56	52	86	*138	58	...	...	...	5	2	2	4	4
—Springfield	AHL	—	—	—	—	—				1	0	0	0	0
—Hartford	NHL	1	0	0	0	2	-1	0	0	7	2	1	3	0
92-93—Hartford	NHL	81	20	31	51	37	-19	4	0	—	—	—	—	—
93-94—Hartford	NHL	9	2	1	3	11	-8	1	0	—	—	—	—	—
—Chicago.....................	NHL	58	12	13	25	40	0	1	0	4	0	0	0	0
94-95—Chicago.....................	NHL	45	15	15	30	53	13	4	0	16	4	1	5	8
95-96—Chicago.....................	NHL	38	7	8	15	16	7	1	0	—	—	—	—	—
—Indianapolis	IHL	1	0	1	1	0	...	...	...	—	—	—	—	—
—Tampa Bay	NHL	8	0	1	1	0	0	0	0	2	0	0	0	0
96-97—Tampa Bay	NHL	73	12	14	26	56	-16	2	3	—	—	—	—	—
NHL totals (7 years)		313	68	83	151	215	-24	13	3	29	6	2	8	8

P

PRATT, NOLAN   D   HURRICANES

PERSONAL: Born August 14, 1975, in Fort McMurray, Alta. ... 6-2/208. ... Shoots left.
HIGH SCHOOL: Sunset (Beaverton, Ore.).
TRANSACTIONS/CAREER NOTES: Selected by Hartford Whalers in fifth round (fourth Whalers pick, 115th overall) of NHL entry draft (June 26, 1993). ... Whalers franchise moved to North Carolina and renamed Carolina Hurricanes for 1997-98 season; NHL approved move on June 25, 1997.

		REGULAR SEASON								PLAYOFFS				
Season Team	League	Gms.	G	A	Pts.	PIM	+/-	PP	SH	Gms.	G	A	Pts.	PIM
91-92— Portland	WHL	22	2	9	11	13	...	...	...	6	1	3	4	12
92-93— Portland	WHL	70	4	19	23	97	...	...	...	16	2	7	9	31
93-94— Portland	WHL	72	4	32	36	105	...	...	...	10	1	2	3	14
94-95— Portland	WHL	72	6	37	43	196	...	...	...	9	1	6	7	10
95-96— Springfield	AHL	62	2	6	8	72	...	...	...	2	0	0	0	0
— Richmond	ECHL	4	1	0	1	2	...	...	...	—	—	—	—	—
96-97— Hartford	NHL	9	0	2	2	6	0	0	0	—	—	—	—	—
— Springfield	AHL	66	1	18	19	127	...	...	...	17	0	3	3	18
NHL totals (1 year)		9	0	2	2	6	0	0	0					

PRESLEY, WAYNE   RW   MAPLE LEAFS

PERSONAL: Born March 23, 1965, in Dearborn, Mich. ... 5-11/180. ... Shoots right.
TRANSACTIONS/CAREER NOTES: Selected by Chicago Blackhawks as an underage junior in second round (second Blackhawks pick, 39th overall) of NHL entry draft (June 8, 1983). ... Traded by Kitchener Rangers to Sault Ste. Marie Greyhounds for RW Shawn Tyers (January 1985). ... Underwent surgery to repair ligaments and cartilage in right knee (November 1987); missed 36 games. ... Dislocated shoulder (May 6, 1989). ... Traded by Blackhawks to San Jose Sharks for third-round pick (RW Bogdan Savenko) in 1993 draft (September 20, 1991). ... Injured knee (November 17, 1991). ... Injured hand (December 3, 1991); missed eight games. ... Traded by Sharks to Buffalo Sabres for C Dave Snuggerud (March 9, 1992). ... Bruised foot (October 8, 1992); missed one game. ... Injured knee (October 1993); missed four games. ... Pulled groin (April 18, 1995); missed one game. ... Signed as free agent by New York Rangers (August 2, 1995). ... Traded by Rangers with LW Nick Kypreos to Toronto Maple Leafs for LW Bill Berg and LW Sergio Momesso (February 29, 1996).
HONORS: Won Jim Mahon Memorial Trophy (1983-84). ... Named to OHL All-Star first team (1983-84).
RECORDS: Shares NHL single-season and single-series playoff records for most shorthanded goals—3 (1989).
STATISTICAL PLATEAUS: Three-goal games: 1987-88 (1).
MISCELLANEOUS: Scored on a penalty shot (vs. Reggie Lemelin, February 9, 1991). ... Failed to score on a penalty shot (vs. Vincent Riendeau, February 10, 1994; vs. Sean Burke, March 8, 1996).

		REGULAR SEASON								PLAYOFFS				
Season Team	League	Gms.	G	A	Pts.	PIM	+/-	PP	SH	Gms.	G	A	Pts.	PIM
82-83— Kitchener	OHL	70	39	48	87	99	...	...	...	12	1	4	5	9
83-84— Kitchener	OHL	70	63	76	139	156	...	...	...	16	12	16	28	38
84-85— Kitchener	OHL	31	25	21	46	77	...	...	...					
— Sault Ste. Marie	OHL	11	5	9	14	14	...	...	...	16	13	9	22	13
— Chicago	NHL	3	0	1	1	0	...	...	...	—	—	—	—	—
85-86— Nova Scotia	AHL	29	6	9	15	22	...	...	...	—	—	—	—	—
— Chicago	NHL	38	7	8	15	38	...	...	...	3	0	0	0	0
86-87— Chicago	NHL	80	32	29	61	114	...	...	...	4	1	0	1	9
87-88— Chicago	NHL	42	12	10	22	52	...	...	...	5	0	0	0	4
88-89— Chicago	NHL	72	21	19	40	100	...	...	...	14	7	5	12	18
89-90— Chicago	NHL	49	6	7	13	69	-19	1	0	19	9	6	15	29
90-91— Chicago	NHL	71	15	19	34	122	11	1	0	6	0	1	1	38
91-92— San Jose	NHL	47	8	14	22	76	-29	3	0	—	—	—	—	—
— Buffalo	NHL	12	2	2	4	57	2	0	0	7	3	3	6	14
92-93— Buffalo	NHL	79	15	17	32	96	5	0	1	8	1	0	1	6
93-94— Buffalo	NHL	65	17	8	25	103	18	1	5	7	2	1	3	14
94-95— Buffalo	NHL	46	14	5	19	41	5	0	5	5	3	1	4	8
95-96— New York Rangers	NHL	61	4	6	10	71	7	0	1	—	—	—	—	—
— Toronto	NHL	19	2	2	4	14	-4	1	0	5	0	0	0	2
96-97— St. John's	AHL	2	0	0	0	0	...	...	...	—	—	—	—	—
— Detroit	IHL	42	7	16	23	80	...	...	...	18	0	4	4	50
NHL totals (12 years)		684	155	147	302	953	-4	7	12	83	26	17	43	142

PRESTIFILIPPO, J.R.   G   ISLANDERS

PERSONAL: Born March 23, 1977, in Newark, N.J. ... 5-10/170. ... Catches left. ... Full name: Joseph Robert Prestifilippo. ... Name pronounced pres-tah-fuh-LEE-poh.
HIGH SCHOOL: Hotchkiss School (Lakeville, Conn.).
COLLEGE: Harvard.
TRANSACTIONS/CAREER NOTES: Selected by New York Islanders in seventh round (eighth Islanders pick, 165th overall) of NHL entry draft (June 22, 1996).
HONORS: Named ECAC Rookie of the Year (1996-97).

		REGULAR SEASON							PLAYOFFS					
Season Team	League	Gms.	Min	W	L	T	GA	SO	Avg.	Gms.	Min.	W	L	GA	SO	Avg.
95-96—Hotchkiss	Conn. H.S.	24	1440	...	...	...	56	3	2.33	—	—	—	—	—	—	—
96-97—Harvard	ECAC	31	1866	10	18	3	99	1	3.18	—	—	—	—	—	—	—

P

PRIMEAU, KEITH   C   HURRICANES

PERSONAL: Born November 24, 1971, in Toronto. ... 6-5/220. ... Shoots left. ... Name pronounced PREE-moh. ... Brother of Wayne Primeau, center, Buffalo Sabres.

TRANSACTIONS/CAREER NOTES: Selected by Detroit Red Wings in first round (first Red Wings pick, third overall) of NHL entry draft (June 16, 1990). ... Suffered from the flu (January 13, 1993); missed two games. ... Sprained right shoulder (February 9, 1993); missed one game. ... Sprained right knee (March 2, 1993); missed two games. ... Sprained right knee (April 1, 1993); missed four games. ... Injured right thumb (February 10, 1995); missed one game. ... Suffered from the flu (February 25, 1995); missed one game. ... Reinjured thumb (March 2, 1995); missed one game. ... Injured ribs (November 1, 1995); missed eight games. ... Injured left knee (January 13, 1996); missed one game. ... Traded by Red Wings with D Paul Coffey and first-round pick (traded to San Jose) in 1997 draft to Hartford Whalers for LW Brendan Shanahan and D Brian Glynn (October 9, 1996). ... Suffered from the flu (December 3, 1996); missed one game. ... Suffered concussion (December 21, 1996); missed one game. ... Suspended two games by NHL for slashing incident (January 3, 1997). ... Suffered from asthma (February 12, 1997); missed one game. ... Whalers franchise moved to North Carolina and renamed Carolina Hurricanes for 1997-98 season; NHL approved move on June 25, 1997.

HONORS: Won Eddie Powers Memorial Trophy (1989-90). ... Named to OHL All-Star second team (1989-90).

		REGULAR SEASON								PLAYOFFS				
Season Team	League	Gms.	G	A	Pts.	PIM	+/-	PP	SH	Gms.	G	A	Pts.	PIM
87-88— Hamilton	OHL	47	6	6	12	69	...	...	...	11	0	2	2	2
88-89— Niagara Falls	OHL	48	20	35	55	56	...	...	...	17	9	6	15	12
89-90— Niagara Falls	OHL	65	*57	70	*127	97	...	...	...	16	*16	17	*33	49
90-91— Detroit	NHL	58	3	12	15	106	-12	0	0	5	1	1	2	25
— Adirondack	AHL	6	3	5	8	8	...	...	...	—	—	—	—	—
91-92— Detroit	NHL	35	6	10	16	83	9	0	0	11	0	0	0	14
— Adirondack	AHL	42	21	24	45	89	...	...	...	9	1	7	8	27
92-93— Detroit	NHL	73	15	17	32	152	-6	4	1	7	0	2	2	26
93-94— Detroit	NHL	78	31	42	73	173	34	7	3	7	0	2	2	6
94-95— Detroit	NHL	45	15	27	42	99	17	1	0	17	4	5	9	45
95-96— Detroit	NHL	74	27	25	52	168	19	6	2	17	1	4	5	28
96-97— Hartford	NHL	75	26	25	51	161	-3	6	3	—	—	—	—	—
NHL totals (7 years)		438	123	158	281	942	58	24	9	64	6	14	20	144

PRIMEAU, WAYNE   C   SABRES

PERSONAL: Born June 4, 1976, in Scarborough, Ont. ... 6-3/193. ... Shoots left. ... Name pronounced PREE-moh. ... Brother of Keith Primeau, center, Hartford Whalers.

HIGH SCHOOL: St. Mary's (Owen Sound, Ont.).

TRANSACTIONS/CAREER NOTES: Selected by Buffalo Sabres in first round (first Sabres pick, 17th overall) of NHL entry draft (June 28, 1994).

		REGULAR SEASON								PLAYOFFS				
Season Team	League	Gms.	G	A	Pts.	PIM	+/-	PP	SH	Gms.	G	A	Pts.	PIM
92-93— Owen Sound	OHL	66	10	27	37	110	...	...	...	8	1	4	5	0
93-94— Owen Sound	OHL	65	25	50	75	75	...	...	...	9	1	6	7	8
94-95— Owen Sound	OHL	66	34	62	96	84	...	...	...	10	4	9	13	15
— Buffalo	NHL	1	1	0	1	0	-2	0	0	—	—	—	—	—
95-96— Buffalo	NHL	2	0	0	0	0	0	0	0	—	—	—	—	—
— Owen Sound	OHL	28	15	29	44	52	...	...	...	—	—	—	—	—
— Oshawa	OHL	24	12	13	25	33	...	...	...	3	2	3	5	2
— Rochester	AHL	8	2	3	5	6	...	...	...	17	3	1	4	11
96-97— Rochester	AHL	24	9	5	14	27	...	...	...	1	0	0	0	0
— Buffalo	NHL	45	2	4	6	64	-2	1	0	9	0	0	0	6
NHL totals (3 years)		48	3	4	7	64	-4	1	0	9	0	0	0	6

PROBERT, BOB   LW   BLACKHAWKS

PERSONAL: Born June 5, 1965, in Windsor, Ont. ... 6-3/225. ... Shoots left. ... Name pronounced PROH-buhrt.

TRANSACTIONS/CAREER NOTES: Selected by Detroit Red Wings as underage junior in third round (third Red Wings pick, 46th overall) of NHL entry draft (June 8, 1983). ... Entered in-patient alcohol abuse treatment center (July 22, 1986). ... Suspended six games by NHL during the 1987-88 season for game misconduct penalties. ... Suspended without pay by Red Wings for skipping practice and missing team buses, flights and curfews (September 23, 1988). ... Reactivated by Red Wings (November 23, 1988). ... Suspended three games by NHL for hitting another player (December 10, 1988). ... Removed from team after showing up late for a game (January 26, 1989). ... Reactivated by Red Wings (February 15, 1989). ... Charged with smuggling cocaine into the United States (March 2, 1989). ... Expelled from the NHL (March 4, 1989). ... Reinstated by NHL (March 14, 1990). ... Unable to play any games in Canada while appealing deportation order by U.S. Immigration Department during 1990-91 and 1991-92 seasons. ... Fractured left wrist (December 1, 1990); missed 12 games. ... Suspended one game by NHL for game misconduct penalties (February 9, 1993). ... Bruised tailbone (November 20, 1993); missed eight games. ... Suspended four games by NHL for stick-swinging incident (October 16, 1993). ... Suspended two games and fined $500 by NHL for head-butting (April 7, 1994). ... Signed as free agent by Chicago Blackhawks (July 23, 1994). ... Placed on inactive status by NHL for violating substance abuse policies (September 2, 1994). ... Reinstated by NHL and declared eligible for 1995-96 season (April 28, 1995). ... Sprained knee (December 26, 1995); missed three games. ... Suspended one game by NHL for elbowing (February 10, 1996).

HONORS: Played in NHL All-Star Game (1988).

STATISTICAL PLATEAUS: Three-goal games: 1987-88 (1).

MISCELLANEOUS: Holds Detroit Red Wings all-time record for most penalty minutes (2,090). ... Scored on a penalty shot (vs. Kari Takko, March 5, 1987).

		REGULAR SEASON								PLAYOFFS				
Season Team	League	Gms.	G	A	Pts.	PIM	+/-	PP	SH	Gms.	G	A	Pts.	PIM
82-83— Brantford	OHL	51	12	16	28	133	...	...	...	8	2	2	4	23
83-84— Brantford	OHL	65	35	38	73	189	...	...	...	6	0	3	3	16

P

Season Team	League	REGULAR SEASON Gms.	G	A	Pts.	PIM	+/-	PP	SH	PLAYOFFS Gms.	G	A	Pts.	PIM
84-85— Hamilton	OHL	4	0	1	1	21	...	...	...	—	—	—	—	—
— Sault Ste. Marie	OHL	44	20	52	72	172	...	...	...	15	6	11	17	*60
85-86— Adirondack	AHL	32	12	15	27	152	...	...	...	10	2	3	5	68
— Detroit	NHL	44	8	13	21	186	-14	3	0	—	—	—	—	—
86-87— Detroit	NHL	63	13	11	24	221	-6	2	0	16	3	4	7	63
— Adirondack	AHL	7	1	4	5	15	...	...	...	—	—	—	—	—
87-88— Detroit	NHL	74	29	33	62	*398	16	15	0	16	8	13	21	51
88-89— Detroit	NHL	25	4	2	6	106	-11	1	0	—	—	—	—	—
89-90— Detroit	NHL	4	3	0	3	21	0	0	0	—	—	—	—	—
90-91— Detroit	NHL	55	16	23	39	315	-3	4	0	6	1	2	3	50
91-92— Detroit	NHL	63	20	24	44	276	16	8	0	11	1	6	7	28
92-93— Detroit	NHL	80	14	29	43	292	-9	6	0	7	0	3	3	10
93-94— Detroit	NHL	66	7	10	17	275	-1	1	0	7	1	1	2	8
94-95— Chicago	NHL						Did not play.							
95-96— Chicago	NHL	78	19	21	40	237	15	1	0	10	0	2	2	23
96-97— Chicago	NHL	82	9	14	23	326	-3	1	0	6	2	1	3	41
NHL totals (12 years)		634	142	180	322	2653	0	42	0	79	16	32	48	274

PROKOPEC, MIKE   RW   SENATORS

PERSONAL: Born May 17, 1974, in Toronto. ... 6-2/190. ... Shoots right. ... Name pronounced PROH-koh-pehk.

TRANSACTIONS/CAREER NOTES: Selected by Chicago Blackhawks in seventh round (seventh Blackhawks pick, 161st overall) of NHL entry draft (June 20, 1992). ... Traded by Blackhawks to Ottawa Senators for RW Denis Chaase, D Kevin Bolibruck and sixth-round pick in 1998 draft (March 18, 1997).

Season Team	League	REGULAR SEASON Gms.	G	A	Pts.	PIM	+/-	PP	SH	PLAYOFFS Gms.	G	A	Pts.	PIM
91-92— Cornwall	OHL	59	12	15	27	75	...	...	...	6	0	0	0	0
92-93— Newmarket	OHL	40	6	14	20	70	...	...	...	—	—	—	—	—
— Guelph	OHL	28	10	14	24	27	...	...	...	5	1	0	1	14
93-94— Guelph	OHL	66	52	58	110	93	...	...	...	9	12	4	16	17
94-95— Indianapolis	IHL	70	21	12	33	80	...	...	...	—	—	—	—	—
95-96— Indianapolis	IHL	67	18	22	40	131	...	...	...	5	2	0	2	4
— Chicago	NHL	9	0	0	0	5	-4	0	0	—	—	—	—	—
96-97— Indianapolis	IHL	57	13	18	31	143	...	...	...	—	—	—	—	—
— Chicago	NHL	6	0	0	0	6	-1	0	0	—	—	—	—	—
— Detroit	IHL	3	2	0	2	4	...	...	...	8	2	1	3	14
NHL totals (2 years)		15	0	0	0	11	-5	0	0					

PRONGER, CHRIS   D   BLUES

PERSONAL: Born October 10, 1974, in Dryden, Ont. ... 6-6/205. ... Shoots left. ... Brother of Sean Pronger, center, Mighty Ducks of Anaheim.
COLLEGE: Trent (Ont.).
TRANSACTIONS/CAREER NOTES: Selected by Hartford Whalers in first round (first Whalers pick, second overall) of NHL entry draft (June 26, 1993). ... Bruised left wrist (March 29, 1994); missed three games. ... Fined $500 by Whalers for involvement in bar brawl (April 1, 1994). ... Injured left shoulder (January 21, 1995); missed five games. ... Traded by Whalers to St. Louis Blues for LW Brendan Shanahan (July 27, 1995). ... Suspended four games by NHL for slashing (November 1, 1995). ... Injured hand (February 15, 1997); missed one game.
HONORS: Named to Can.HL All-Rookie team (1991-92). ... Named to OHL Rookie All-Star team (1991-92). ... Won Can.HL Plus/Minus Award (1992-93). ... Won Can.HL Top Defenseman Award (1992-93). ... Won Max Kaminsky Award (1992-93). ... Named to Can.HL All-Star first team (1992-93). ... Named to OHL All-Star first team (1992-93). ... Named to NHL All-Rookie team (1993-94).

Season Team	League	REGULAR SEASON Gms.	G	A	Pts.	PIM	+/-	PP	SH	PLAYOFFS Gms.	G	A	Pts.	PIM
90-91— Stratford	OPJHL	48	15	37	52	132	...	...	...	—	—	—	—	—
91-92— Peterborough	OHL	63	17	45	62	90	...	...	...	10	1	8	9	28
92-93— Peterborough	OHL	61	15	62	77	108	...	...	...	21	15	25	40	51
93-94— Hartford	NHL	81	5	25	30	113	-3	2	0	—	—	—	—	—
94-95— Hartford	NHL	43	5	9	14	54	-12	3	0	—	—	—	—	—
95-96— St. Louis	NHL	78	7	18	25	110	-18	3	1	13	1	5	6	16
96-97— St. Louis	NHL	79	11	24	35	143	15	4	0	6	1	1	2	22
NHL totals (4 years)		281	28	76	104	420	-18	12	1	19	2	6	8	38

PRONGER, SEAN   C   MIGHTY DUCKS

PERSONAL: Born November 30, 1972, in Dryden, Ont. ... 6-2/205. ... Shoots left. ... Full name: Sean James Pronger. ... Brother of Chris Pronger, defenseman, St. Louis Blues.
COLLEGE: Bowling Green State.
TRANSACTIONS/CAREER NOTES: Selected by Vancouver Canucks in third round (third Canucks pick, 51st overall) of NHL entry draft (June 22, 1991). ... Signed as free agent by Mighty Ducks of Anaheim (February 14, 1995). ... Strained abdominal muscle (February 17, 1997); missed two games.

P

Season Team	League	REGULAR SEASON Gms.	G	A	Pts.	PIM	+/-	PP	SH	PLAYOFFS Gms.	G	A	Pts.	PIM
89-90— Thunder Bay Flyers	USHL	48	18	34	52	61	...	...	...	—	—	—	—	—
90-91— Bowling Green	CCHA	40	3	7	10	30	...	...	...	—	—	—	—	—
91-92— Bowling Green	CCHA	34	9	7	16	28	...	...	...	—	—	—	—	—
92-93— Bowling Green	CCHA	39	23	23	46	35	...	...	...	—	—	—	—	—
93-94— Bowling Green	CCHA	38	17	17	34	38	...	...	...	—	—	—	—	—

Season Team	League	REGULAR SEASON								PLAYOFFS				
		Gms.	G	A	Pts.	PIM	+/-	PP	SH	Gms.	G	A	Pts.	PIM
94-95— Knoxville	ECHL	34	18	23	41	55	...	...	...	—	—	—	—	—
— Greensboro	ECHL	2	0	2	2	0	...	...	...	—	—	—	—	—
— San Diego	IHL	8	0	0	0	2	...	...	...	—	—	—	—	—
95-96— Baltimore	AHL	72	16	17	33	61	...	...	...	12	3	7	10	16
— Anaheim	NHL	7	0	1	1	6	0	0	0	—	—	—	—	—
96-97— Baltimore	AHL	41	26	17	43	17	...	...	...	—	—	—	—	—
— Anaheim	NHL	39	7	7	14	20	6	1	0	9	0	2	2	4
NHL totals (2 years)		46	7	8	15	26	6	1	0	9	0	2	2	4

PROSOFSKY, TYLER   C   CANUCKS

PERSONAL: Born February 19, 1976, in Saskatoon, Sask. ... 5-11/175. ... Shoots left. ... Name pronounced proh-SAHF-skee.
TRANSACTIONS/CAREER NOTES: Selected by Chicago Blackhawks in seventh round (seventh Blackhawks pick, 170th overall) of NHL entry draft (June 29, 1994). ... Returned to draft pool by Blackhawks and selected by Vancouver Canucks in fifth round (fourth Canucks pick, 121st overall) of NHL entry draft (June 22, 1996).

Season Team	League	REGULAR SEASON								PLAYOFFS				
		Gms.	G	A	Pts.	PIM	+/-	PP	SH	Gms.	G	A	Pts.	PIM
92-93— Tacoma	WHL	62	10	9	19	79	...	...	...	7	0	0	0	5
93-94— Tacoma	WHL	70	20	22	42	132	...	...	...	8	1	1	2	23
94-95— Tacoma	WHL	71	20	27	47	161	...	...	...	4	0	1	1	21
95-96— Kelowna	WHL	63	35	40	75	148	...	...	...	6	4	3	7	30
96-97— Kelowna	WHL	3	2	2	4	11	...	...	...	6	5	2	7	24

PROSPAL, VACLAV   C   FLYERS

PERSONAL: Born February 17, 1975, in Ceske-Budejovice, Czechoslovakia. ... 6-2/185. ... Shoots left. ... Name pronounced VA-slav PRAHS-puhl.
TRANSACTIONS/CAREER NOTES: Selected by Philadelphia Flyers in third round (second Flyers pick, 71st overall) of NHL entry draft (June 26, 1993).
HONORS: Named to AHL All-Star first team (1996-97).

Season Team	League	REGULAR SEASON								PLAYOFFS				
		Gms.	G	A	Pts.	PIM	+/-	PP	SH	Gms.	G	A	Pts.	PIM
91-92— M. C.-Budejovice	Czech. Jrs.	36	16	16	32	12	...	...	...	—	—	—	—	—
92-93— M. C.-Budejovice	Czech. Jrs.	36	26	31	57	24	...	...	...	—	—	—	—	—
93-94— Hershey	AHL	55	14	21	35	38	...	...	...	2	0	0	0	2
94-95— Hershey	AHL	69	13	32	45	36	...	...	...	2	1	0	1	4
95-96— Hershey	AHL	68	15	36	51	59	...	...	...	5	2	4	6	2
96-97— Philadelphia	AHL	63	32	63	95	70	...	...	...	—	—	—	—	—
— Philadelphia	NHL	18	5	10	15	4	3	0	0	5	1	3	4	4
NHL totals (1 year)		18	5	10	15	4	3	0	0	5	1	3	4	4

PROTSENKO, BORIS   RW   PENGUINS

PERSONAL: Born August 21, 1978, in Kherson, U.S.S.R. ... 6-0/185. ... Shoots right.
TRANSACTIONS/CAREER NOTES: Selected by Pittsburgh Penguins in third round (fourth Penguins pick, 77th overall) of NHL entry draft (June 22, 1996).

Season Team	League	REGULAR SEASON								PLAYOFFS				
		Gms.	G	A	Pts.	PIM	+/-	PP	SH	Gms.	G	A	Pts.	PIM
94-95— Fernie	Tier II Jr. A	47	27	25	52	199	...	...	...	—	—	—	—	—
95-96— Calgary	WHL	71	46	29	75	68	...	...	...	—	—	—	—	—
96-97— Calgary	WHL	67	35	32	67	136	...	...	...	—	—	—	—	—

PRPIC, JOEL   C   BRUINS

PERSONAL: Born September 25, 1974, in Sudbury, Ont. ... 6-6/200. ... Shoots left. ... Name pronounced PUHR-pihk.
COLLEGE: St. Lawrence.
TRANSACTIONS/CAREER NOTES: Selected by Boston Bruins in ninth round (ninth Bruins pick, 233rd overall) of NHL entry draft (June 26, 1993).

Season Team	League	REGULAR SEASON								PLAYOFFS				
		Gms.	G	A	Pts.	PIM	+/-	PP	SH	Gms.	G	A	Pts.	PIM
92-93— Waterloo Jr. B	OHA	45	17	43	60	160	...	...	...	—	—	—	—	—
93-94— St. Lawrence Univ.	ECAC	31	2	4	6	90	...	...	...	—	—	—	—	—
94-95— St. Lawrence Univ.	ECAC	32	7	10	17	62	...	...	...	—	—	—	—	—
95-96— St. Lawrence Univ.	ECAC	32	3	10	13	77	...	...	...	—	—	—	—	—
96-97— St. Lawrence Univ.	ECAC	34	10	8	18	57	...	...	...	—	—	—	—	—

PUPPA, DAREN   G   LIGHTNING   P

PERSONAL: Born March 23, 1965, in Kirkland Lake, Ont. ... 6-3/205. ... Catches right. ... Full name: Daren James Puppa. ... Name pronounced POO-puh.
COLLEGE: Rensselaer Polytechnic Institute (N.Y.).

TRANSACTIONS/CAREER NOTES: Selected by Buffalo Sabres in fourth round (sixth Sabres pick, 74th overall) of NHL entry draft (June 8, 1983). ... Injured knee (February 1986). ... Fractured left index finger (October 1987). ... Sprained right wrist (January 14, 1989). ... Broke right arm (January 27, 1989). ... Injured back (November 21, 1990); missed nine games. ... Pulled groin and stomach muscles (February 19, 1991). ... Fractured arm (November 12, 1991); missed 16 games. ... Suffered sore knee (January 21, 1993); missed seven games. ... Traded by Sabres with LW Dave Andreychuk and first-round pick (D Kenny Jonsson) in 1993 draft to Toronto Maple Leafs for G Grant Fuhr and fifth-round pick (D Kevin Popp) in 1995 draft (February 2, 1993). ... Selected by Florida Panthers in NHL expansion draft (June 24, 1993). ... Selected by Tampa Bay Lightning in Phase II of NHL expansion draft (June 25, 1993). ... Suffered from tonsillitis (December 11, 1993); missed two games. ... Sprained lower back (February 5, 1994); missed two games. ... Injured hand (April 2, 1995); missed two games. ... Injured right forearm (November 5, 1995); missed one game. ... Injured right knee (November 29, 1995) and underwent surgery (December 8, 1995); missed 12 games. ... Strained groin (January 6, 1996); missed one game. ... Suffered back spasms (February 10, 1996); missed two games. ... Suffered back spasms (February 13, 1996); missed two games. ... Suffered back spasms (February 23, 1996); missed one game. ... Injured back (April 12, 1996); missed one game. ... Injured groin (October 5, 1996); missed nine games. ... Underwent back surgery (November 6, 1996); missed 41 games. ... Suffered sore back (April 5, 1997); missed one game.

HONORS: Named to AHL All-Star first team (1986-87). ... Named to THE SPORTING NEWS All-Star second team (1989-90). ... Named to NHL All-Star second team (1989-90). ... Played in NHL All-Star Game (1990).

MISCELLANEOUS: Holds Tampa Bay Lightning all-time records for most games played by goaltender (162), most wins (66), most shutouts (10) and goals-against average (2.60). ... Stopped a penalty shot attempt (vs. Ulf Dahlen, March 17, 1992; vs. Doug Weight, January 3, 1996; vs. Radek Bonk, January 13, 1996). ... Allowed a penalty shot goal (vs. Steve Yzerman, January 29, 1992).

			REGULAR SEASON								PLAYOFFS						
Season Team	League	Gms.	Min	W	L	T	GA	SO	Avg.	Gms.	Min.	W	L	GA	SO	Avg.
83-84—R.P.I.	ECAC	32	1816	24	6	0	89	0	2.94	—	—	—	—	—	—	—
84-85—R.P.I.	ECAC	32	1830	31	1	0	78	0	2.56	—	—	—	—	—	—	—
85-86—Buffalo	NHL	7	401	3	4	0	21	1	3.14	—	—	—	—	—	—	—
—Rochester	AHL	20	1092	8	11	0	79	0	4.34	—	—	—	—	—	—	—
86-87—Buffalo	NHL	3	185	0	2	1	13	0	4.22	—	—	—	—	—	—	—
—Rochester	AHL	57	3129	33	14	0	146	1	*2.80	*16	*944	10	6	*48	*1	3.05
87-88—Rochester	AHL	26	1415	14	8	2	65	2	2.76	2	108	0	1	5	0	2.78
—Buffalo	NHL	17	874	8	6	1	61	0	4.19	3	142	1	1	11	0	4.65
88-89—Buffalo	NHL	37	1908	17	10	6	107	1	3.36	—	—	—	—	—	—	—
89-90—Buffalo	NHL	56	3241	31	16	6	156	1	2.89	6	370	2	4	15	0	2.43
90-91—Buffalo	NHL	38	2092	15	11	6	118	2	3.38	2	81	0	1	10	0	7.41
91-92—Buffalo	NHL	33	1757	11	14	4	114	0	3.89	—	—	—	—	—	—	—
—Rochester	AHL	2	119	0	2	0	9	0	4.54	—	—	—	—	—	—	—
92-93—Buffalo	NHL	24	1306	11	5	4	78	0	3.58	—	—	—	—	—	—	—
—Toronto	NHL	8	479	6	2	0	18	2	2.25	1	20	0	0	1	0	3.00
93-94—Tampa Bay	NHL	63	3653	22	33	6	165	4	2.71	—	—	—	—	—	—	—
94-95—Tampa Bay	NHL	36	2013	14	19	2	90	1	2.68	—	—	—	—	—	—	—
95-96—Tampa Bay	NHL	57	3189	29	16	9	131	5	2.46	4	173	1	3	14	0	4.86
96-97—Tampa Bay	NHL	6	325	1	1	2	14	0	2.58	—	—	—	—	—	—	—
—Adirondack	AHL	1	62	1	0	0	3	0	2.90	—	—	—	—	—	—	—
NHL totals (12 years)		385	21423	168	139	47	1086	17	3.04	16	786	4	9	51	0	3.89

PURINTON, DALE   D   RANGERS

PERSONAL: Born October 11, 1976, in Fort Wayne, Ind. ... 6-1/201. ... Shoots left.

TRANSACTIONS/CAREER NOTES: Selected by New York Rangers in fifth round (fourth Ranger pick, 117th overall) of NHL entry draft (July 8, 1995).

			REGULAR SEASON							PLAYOFFS			
Season Team	League	Gms.	G	A	Pts.	PIM	+/-	PP	SH	Gms.	G	A	Pts.	PIM
93-94—Vernon	Tier II Jr. A	42	1	6	7	194	...	...	...	—	—	—	—	—
94-95—Tacoma	WHL	65	0	8	8	291	...	...	...	3	0	0	0	13
95-96—Kelowna	WHL	22	1	4	5	88	...	...	...	—	—	—	—	—
—Lethbridge	WHL	37	3	6	9	144	...	...	...	4	1	1	2	25
96-97—Lethbridge	WHL	51	6	26	32	254	...	...	...	18	3	5	8	*88

PUSHOR, JAMIE   D   RED WINGS

PERSONAL: Born February 11, 1973, in Lethbridge, Alta. ... 6-3/212. ... Shoots right. ... Name pronounced PUSH-uhr.

TRANSACTIONS/CAREER NOTES: Selected by Detroit Red Wings in second round (second Red Wings pick, 32nd overall) of NHL entry draft (June 22, 1991).

MISCELLANEOUS: Member of Stanley Cup championship team (1997).

			REGULAR SEASON							PLAYOFFS			
Season Team	League	Gms.	G	A	Pts.	PIM	+/-	PP	SH	Gms.	G	A	Pts.	PIM
89-90—Lethbridge	WHL	10	0	2	2	2	...	...	...	—	—	—	—	—
90-91—Lethbridge	WHL	71	1	13	14	193	...	...	...	—	—	—	—	—
91-92—Lethbridge	WHL	49	2	15	17	232	...	...	...	5	0	0	0	33
92-93—Lethbridge	WHL	72	6	22	28	200	...	...	...	4	0	1	1	9
93-94—Adirondack	AHL	73	1	17	18	124	...	...	...	12	0	0	0	22
94-95—Adirondack	AHL	58	2	11	13	129	...	...	...	4	0	1	1	0
95-96—Detroit	NHL	5	0	1	1	17	2	0	0	—	—	—	—	—
—Adirondack	AHL	65	2	16	18	126	...	...	...	3	0	0	0	5
96-97—Detroit	NHL	75	4	7	11	129	1	0	0	5	0	1	1	5
NHL totals (2 years)		80	4	8	12	146	3	0	0	5	0	1	1	5

P

PYSZ, PATRIK   C   BLACKHAWKS

PERSONAL: Born January 15, 1975, in Zakopane, Poland. ... 5-11/187. ... Shoots left.
TRANSACTIONS/CAREER NOTES: Selected by Chicago Blackhawks in fourth round (sixth Blackhawks pick, 102nd overall) of NHL entry draft (June 26, 1993).

		REGULAR SEASON							PLAYOFFS				
Season Team	League	Gms.	G	A	Pts.	PIM	+/-	PP	SH	Gms.	G	A	Pts.	PIM
91-92— Podhale Nowy Targ....	Poland						Statistics unavailable.							
92-93— Augsburg..................	Ger. Div. II	36	7	5	12	12	...	...	...	8	2	1	3	0
93-94— Augsburg..................	Ger. Div. II	41	4	17	21	26	...	...	...	9	5	5	10	8
94-95— Augsburg..................	Germany	41	5	13	18	61	...	...	...	5	0	2	2	6
95-96— Mannheim.................	Germany	50	14	24	38	50	...	...	...	8	0	2	2	26
96-97— Columbus.................	ECHL	36	7	9	16	29	...	...	...	2	0	0	0	0

QUINN, DAN   C/RW

PERSONAL: Born June 1, 1965, in Ottawa. ... 5-11/182. ... Shoots left.
TRANSACTIONS/CAREER NOTES: Selected by Calgary Flames as underage junior in first round (first Flames pick, 13th overall) of NHL entry draft (June 8, 1983). ... Traded by Flames to Pittsburgh Penguins for C Mike Bullard (November 1986). ... Broke left wrist (October 1987). ... Traded by Penguins with RW Andrew McBain and C Dave Capuano to Vancouver Canucks for RW Tony Tanti, C Barry Pederson and D Rod Buskas (January 8, 1990). ... Bruised shoulder (January 1991). ... Traded by Canucks with D Garth Butcher to St. Louis Blues for LW Geoff Courtnall, D Robert Dirk, C Cliff Ronning, LW Sergio Momesso and fifth-round pick (RW Brian Loney) in 1992 draft (March 5, 1991). ... Traded by Blues with C Rod Brind'Amour to Philadelphia Flyers for C Ron Sutter and D Murray Baron (September 22, 1991). ... Signed as free agent by Minnesota North Stars (October 5, 1992). ... Signed as free agent by Ottawa Senators (March 15, 1993). ... Signed as free agent by Los Angeles Kings (September 2, 1994). ... Played in Europe during 1994-95 NHL lockout. ... Strained groin (February 18, 1995); missed one game. ... Signed as free agent by Senators (July 20, 1995). ... Broke left hand (November 2, 1995); missed eight games. ... Loaned by Senators to Detroit Vipers of IHL (January 8, 1996). ... Traded by Senators to Philadelphia Flyers for cash (January 23, 1996). ... Signed as free agent by Penguins (July 31, 1996). ... Leg injury (October 22, 1996); missed two games. ... Announced retirement during 1996-97 season.
STATISTICAL PLATEAUS: Three-goal games: 1987-88 (3), 1989-90 (1), 1995-96 (1). Total: 5.
MISCELLANEOUS: Captain of Vancouver Canucks (1990-91). ... Scored on a penalty shot (vs. Mikhail Shtalenkov, March 21, 1995).

		REGULAR SEASON							PLAYOFFS				
Season Team	League	Gms.	G	A	Pts.	PIM	+/-	PP	SH	Gms.	G	A	Pts.	PIM
81-82— Belleville....................	OHL	67	19	32	51	41	...	...	...	—	—	—	—	—
82-83— Belleville....................	OHL	70	59	88	147	27	...	...	...	4	2	6	8	2
83-84— Belleville....................	OHL	24	23	36	59	12	...	...	...	—	—	—	—	—
— Calgary	NHL	54	19	33	52	20	...	...	...	8	3	5	8	4
84-85— Calgary	NHL	74	20	38	58	22	9	7	0	3	0	0	0	0
85-86— Calgary	NHL	78	30	42	72	44	-12	17	3	18	8	7	15	10
86-87— Calgary	NHL	16	3	6	9	14	-6	1	0	—	—	—	—	—
— Pittsburgh	NHL	64	28	43	71	40	14	10	3	—	—	—	—	—
87-88— Pittsburgh	NHL	70	40	39	79	50	8	21	1	—	—	—	—	—
88-89— Pittsburgh	NHL	79	34	60	94	102	-37	16	0	11	6	3	9	10
89-90— Pittsburgh	NHL	41	9	20	29	22	-15	5	0	—	—	—	—	—
— Vancouver................	NHL	37	16	18	34	27	-2	6	0	—	—	—	—	—
90-91— Vancouver................	NHL	64	18	31	49	46	-28	8	0	—	—	—	—	—
— St. Louis	NHL	14	4	7	11	20	-5	4	0	13	4	7	11	32
91-92— Philadelphia	NHL	67	11	26	37	26	-13	6	0	—	—	—	—	—
92-93— Minnesota	NHL	11	0	4	4	6	-4	0	0	—	—	—	—	—
93-94— Ottawa	NHL	13	7	0	7	6	0	2	0	—	—	—	—	—
— Bern.........................	Switzerland	25	12	22	34	50	...	...	...	—	—	—	—	—
94-95— Zug	Switzerland	7	7	6	13	26	...	...	...	—	—	—	—	—
— Los Angeles..............	NHL	44	14	17	31	32	-3	2	0	—	—	—	—	—
95-96— Ottawa	NHL	28	6	18	24	24	-8	4	0	—	—	—	—	—
— Detroit......................	IHL	4	0	5	5	2	...	...	...	0	0	0	0	0
— Philadelphia	NHL	35	7	14	21	22	2	3	0	12	1	4	5	6
96-97— Pittsburgh	NHL	16	0	3	3	10	-6	0	0	—	—	—	—	—
NHL totals (15 years)		805	266	419	685	533	-106	112	7	65	22	26	48	62

QUINT, DERON   D   COYOTES

PERSONAL: Born March 12, 1976, in Dover, N.H. ... 6-1/185. ... Shoots left.
HIGH SCHOOL: Meadowdale (Lynnwood, Wash.).
TRANSACTIONS/CAREER NOTES: Selected by Winnipeg Jets in second round (first Jets pick, 30th overall) of NHL entry draft (June 28, 1994). ... Suffered from the flu (January 29, 1996); missed two games. ... Jets franchise moved to Phoenix and renamed Coyotes for 1996-97 season; NHL approved move on January 18, 1996.
HONORS: Won WHL Top Draft Choice Award (1993-94). ... Named to Can.HL All-Rookie team (1993-94). ... Named to WHL (West) All-Star first team (1994-95).

		REGULAR SEASON							PLAYOFFS				
Season Team	League	Gms.	G	A	Pts.	PIM	+/-	PP	SH	Gms.	G	A	Pts.	PIM
90-91— Cardigan Prep............	USHS (East)	31	67	54	121	...	...	...	...	—	—	—	—	—
91-92— Cardigan Prep............	USHS (East)	32	111	68	179	...	...	...	...	—	—	—	—	—
92-93— Tabor Academy..........	Mass. H.S.	28	15	26	41	30	...	...	...	1	0	2	2	0
93-94— Seattle......................	WHL	63	15	29	44	47	...	...	...	9	4	12	16	8
94-95— Seattle......................	WHL	65	29	60	89	82	...	...	...	3	1	2	3	6
95-96— Winnipeg	NHL	51	5	13	18	22	-2	2	0	—	—	—	—	—

Season Team	League	REGULAR SEASON								PLAYOFFS				
		Gms.	G	A	Pts.	PIM	+/-	PP	SH	Gms.	G	A	Pts.	PIM
— Springfield	AHL	11	2	3	5	4	...	...	...	10	2	3	5	6
— Seattle......................	WHL	0	0	0	0	0	...	...	...	5	4	1	5	6
96-97 — Springfield	AHL	43	6	18	24	20	...	...	...	12	2	7	9	4
— Phoenix....................	NHL	27	3	11	14	4	-4	1	0	7	0	2	2	0
NHL totals (2 years)		78	8	24	32	26	-6	3	0	7	0	2	2	0

QUINTAL, STEPHANE   D   CANADIENS

PERSONAL: Born October 22, 1968, in Boucherville, Que. ... 6-3/225. ... Shoots right. ... Name pronounced steh-FAN kay-TAL.

HIGH SCHOOL: Polyvalente de Mortagne (Boucherville, Que.).

TRANSACTIONS/CAREER NOTES: Broke wrist (December 1985). ... Selected by Boston Bruins as underage junior in first round (second Bruins pick, 14th overall) of NHL entry draft (June 13, 1987). ... Injured knee (October 1988). ... Injured knee (January 1989). ... Sprained right knee (October 17, 1989); missed eight games. ... Fractured left ankle (April 9, 1991); missed remainder of playoffs. ... Traded by Bruins with C Craig Janney to St. Louis Blues for C Adam Oates (February 7, 1992). ... Traded by Blues with RW Nelson Emerson to Winnipeg Jets for D Phil Housley (September 24, 1993). ... Sprained wrist (January 16, 1994); missed two games. ... Sprained neck (April 6, 1994); missed one game. ... Sprained ankle (February 6, 1995); missed five games. ... Traded by Jets to Montreal Canadiens for second-round pick (D Jason Doig) in 1995 draft (July 8, 1995). ... Suffered concussion (November 11, 1995); missed one game. ... Sprained right Knee (February 7, 1996); missed seven games. ... Underwent knee surgery (March 19, 1996); missed five games. ... Bruised foot (December 21, 1996); missed two games. ... Injured collarbone (January 1, 1997); missed two games. ... Sprained left knee (February 6, 1997); missed seven games.

HONORS: Named to QMJHL All-Star first team (1986-87).

Season Team	League	REGULAR SEASON								PLAYOFFS				
		Gms.	G	A	Pts.	PIM	+/-	PP	SH	Gms.	G	A	Pts.	PIM
85-86 — Granby	QMJHL	67	2	17	19	144	...	...	...	—	—	—	—	—
86-87 — Granby	QMJHL	67	13	41	54	178	...	...	...	8	0	9	9	10
87-88 — Hull	QMJHL	38	13	23	36	138	...	...	...	19	7	12	19	30
88-89 — Maine	AHL	16	4	10	14	28	...	...	...	—	—	—	—	—
— Boston	NHL	26	0	1	1	29	-5	0	0	—	—	—	—	—
89-90 — Boston	NHL	38	2	2	4	22	-11	0	0	—	—	—	—	—
— Maine	AHL	37	4	16	20	27	...	...	...	—	—	—	—	—
90-91 — Maine	AHL	23	1	5	6	30	...	...	...	—	—	—	—	—
— Boston	NHL	45	2	6	8	89	2	1	0	3	0	1	1	7
91-92 — Boston	NHL	49	4	10	14	77	-8	0	0	—	—	—	—	—
— St. Louis	NHL	26	0	6	6	32	-3	0	0	4	1	2	3	6
92-93 — St. Louis	NHL	75	1	10	11	100	-6	0	1	9	0	0	0	8
93-94 — Winnipeg	NHL	81	8	18	26	119	-25	1	1	—	—	—	—	—
94-95 — Winnipeg	NHL	43	6	17	23	78	0	3	0	—	—	—	—	—
95-96 — Montreal	NHL	68	2	14	16	117	-4	0	1	6	0	1	1	6
96-97 — Montreal	NHL	71	7	15	22	100	1	1	0	5	0	1	1	6
NHL totals (9 years)		522	32	99	131	763	-59	6	3	27	1	5	6	33

RACINE, BRUCE   G   BLUES

PERSONAL: Born August 9, 1966, in Cornwall, Ont. ... 6-0/178. ... Catches left. ... Full name: Bruce Michael Racine. ... Name pronounced ruh-SEEN.

HIGH SCHOOL: St. Pius X (Ottawa).

COLLEGE: Northeastern.

TRANSACTIONS/CAREER NOTES: Selected by Pittsburgh Penguins in third round (third Penguins pick, 58th overall) of NHL entry draft (June 15, 1985). ... Signed as free agent by Toronto Maple Leafs (August 3, 1993). ... Signed as free agent by St. Louis Blues (August 10, 1995).

HONORS: Named to Hockey East All-Star second team (1984-85). ... Named to Hockey East All-Freshman team (1984-85). ... Named to NCAA All-America East first team (1986-87 and 1987-88). ... Named to Hockey East All-Star first team (1986-87). ... Named Hockey East Tournament Most Valuable Player (1987-88). ... Named to Hockey East All-Decade team (1994).

Season Team	League	REGULAR SEASON							PLAYOFFS					
		Gms.	Min	W	L	T	GA	SO	Avg.	Gms.	Min.	W	L	GA	SO	Avg.
84-85 — Northeastern Univ........	Hoc. East	26	1615	11	14	1	103	1	3.83	—	—	—	—	—	—	—
85-86 — Northeastern Univ........	Hoc. East	37	2212	17	14	1	171	0	4.64	—	—	—	—	—	—	—
86-87 — Northeastern Univ........	Hoc. East	33	1966	12	18	3	133	0	4.06	—	—	—	—	—	—	—
87-88 — Northeastern Univ........	Hoc. East	30	1809	15	11	4	108	1	3.58	—	—	—	—	—	—	—
88-89 — Muskegon	IHL	51	*3039	37	11	‡0	184	*3	3.63	5	300	4	1	15	0	3.00
89-90 — Muskegon	IHL	49	2911	29	15	‡4	182	1	3.75	—	—	—	—	—	—	—
90-91 — Albany	IHL	29	1567	7	18	‡1	104	0	3.98	—	—	—	—	—	—	—
— Muskegon	IHL	9	516	4	4	‡1	40	0	4.65	—	—	—	—	—	—	—
91-92 — Muskegon	IHL	27	1559	13	10	‡3	91	1	3.50	1	60	0	1	6	0	6.00
92-93 — Cleveland	IHL	35	1949	13	16	‡0	140	1	4.31	2	37	0	0	2	0	3.24
93-94 — St. John's	AHL	37	1875	20	9	2	116	0	3.71	—	—	—	—	—	—	—
94-95 — St. John's	AHL	27	1492	11	10	4	85	1	3.42	2	119	1	1	3	0	1.51
95-96 — Peoria	IHL	22	1228	11	10	‡1	69	1	3.37	1	58	0	1	3	0	3.10
— St. Louis	NHL	11	230	0	3	0	12	0	3.13	1	1	0	0	0	0	0.00
96-97 — San Antonio	IHL	44	2426	25	14	‡2	122	6	3.02	6	325	3	2	17	0	3.14
NHL totals (1 year)		11	230	0	3	0	12	0	3.13	1	1	0	0	0	0	

RACINE, YVES   D   LIGHTNING

PERSONAL: Born February 7, 1969, in Matane, Que. ... 6-0/200. ... Shoots left. ... Name pronounced EEV ruh-SEEN.

TRANSACTIONS/CAREER NOTES: Selected by Detroit Red Wings as underage junior in first round (first Red Wings pick, 11th overall) of NHL entry draft (June 13, 1987). ... Injured shoulder (March 22, 1991); missed four games. ... Sprained left shoulder (November 11, 1992); missed four games. ... Traded by Red Wings with fourth-round pick (LW Sebastien Vallee) in 1994 draft to Philadelphia Flyers for D Terry Carkner (October 5, 1993). ... Tore knee ligament (October 16, 1993); missed 15 games. ... Traded by Flyers to Montreal Canadiens for D Kevin Haller (June 29, 1994). ... Suffered from the flu (March 8, 1995); missed one game. ... Separated shoulder (December 2, 1995); missed 11 games. ... Claimed on waivers by San Jose Sharks (January 23, 1996). ... Injured knee (April 4, 1996); missed four games. ... Traded by San Jose Sharks to Calgary Flames for cash (December 17, 1996). ... Signed as free agent by Tampa Bay Lightning (July 16, 1997).

HONORS: Named to QMJHL All-Star first team (1987-88 and 1988-89). ... Won Emile (Butch) Bouchard Trophy (1988-89).

		REGULAR SEASON								PLAYOFFS				
Season Team	League	Gms.	G	A	Pts.	PIM	+/-	PP	SH	Gms.	G	A	Pts.	PIM
86-87— Longueuil..................	QMJHL	70	7	43	50	50	...	...	...	20	3	11	14	14
87-88— Victoriaville..............	QMJHL	69	10	84	94	150	...	...	...	5	0	0	0	13
— Adirondack................	AHL	—	—	—	—	—	—	—	—	9	4	2	6	2
88-89— Victoriaville..............	QMJHL	63	23	85	108	95	...	...	...	18	3	*30	*33	41
— Adirondack................	AHL	—	—	—	—	—	—	—	—	2	1	1	2	0
89-90— Detroit....................	NHL	28	4	9	13	23	-3	1	0	—	—	—	—	—
— Adirondack................	AHL	46	8	27	35	31	...	...	...	—	—	—	—	—
90-91— Adirondack................	AHL	16	3	9	12	10	...	...	...	—	—	—	—	—
— Detroit....................	NHL	62	7	40	47	33	1	2	0	7	2	0	2	0
91-92— Detroit....................	NHL	61	2	22	24	94	-6	1	0	11	2	1	3	10
92-93— Detroit....................	NHL	80	9	31	40	80	10	5	0	7	1	3	4	27
93-94— Philadelphia	NHL	67	9	43	52	48	-11	5	1	—	—	—	—	—
94-95— Montreal	NHL	47	4	7	11	42	-1	2	0	—	—	—	—	—
95-96— Montreal	NHL	25	0	3	3	26	-7	0	0	—	—	—	—	—
— San Jose....................	NHL	32	1	16	17	28	-3	0	0	—	—	—	—	—
96-97— Kentucky..................	AHL	4	0	1	1	2	...	...	...	—	—	—	—	—
— Quebec....................	IHL	6	0	4	4	4	...	...	...	—	—	—	—	—
— Calgary....................	NHL	46	1	15	16	24	4	1	0	—	—	—	—	—
NHL totals (8 years)		448	37	186	223	398	-16	17	1	25	5	4	9	37

RAGNARSSON, MARCUS   D   SHARKS

PERSONAL: Born August 13, 1971, in Ostervala, Sweden. ... 6-1/220. ... Shoots left. ... Name pronounced RAG-nuhr-suhn.
TRANSACTIONS/CAREER NOTES: Selected by San Jose Sharks in fifth round (fifth Sharks pick, 99th overall) of NHL entry draft (June 20, 1992). ... Injured foot (November 8, 1995); missed two games. ... Injured head (December 5, 1995); missed two games. ... Injured knee (January 10, 1996); missed one game. ... Suffered from the flu (January 16, 1996); missed one game. ... Injured hamstring (February 10, 1996); missed four games. ... Injured back (March 22, 1996); missed one game. ... Injured leg (November 1, 1996); missed two games. ... Broke toe (December 9, 1996); missed two games.

		REGULAR SEASON								PLAYOFFS				
Season Team	League	Gms.	G	A	Pts.	PIM	+/-	PP	SH	Gms.	G	A	Pts.	PIM
89-90— Djur. Stockholm........	Sweden	13	0	2	2	0	...	...	...	1	0	0	0	0
90-91— Djur. Stockholm........	Sweden	35	4	1	5	12	...	...	...	7	0	0	0	6
91-92— Djur. Stockholm........	Sweden	40	8	5	13	14	...	...	...	—	—	—	—	—
92-93— Djur. Stockholm........	Sweden	35	3	3	6	53	...	...	...	6	0	2	2	0
93-94— Djur. Stockholm........	Sweden	19	0	4	4	24	...	...	...	—	—	—	—	—
94-95— Djur. Stockholm........	Sweden	38	7	9	16	20	...	...	...	3	0	0	0	4
95-96— San Jose..................	NHL	71	8	31	39	42	-24	4	0	—	—	—	—	—
96-97— San Jose..................	NHL	69	3	14	17	63	-18	2	0	—	—	—	—	—
NHL totals (2 years)		140	11	45	56	105	-42	6	0					

RAM, JAMIE   G   RANGERS

PERSONAL: Born January 18, 1971, in Scarborough, Ont. ... 5-11/180. ... Catches left.
COLLEGE: Michigan Tech.
TRANSACTIONS/CAREER NOTES: Selected by New York Rangers in 10th round (ninth Rangers pick, 213th overall) of NHL entry draft (June 22, 1991).
HONORS: Named to NCAA All-America West first team (1992-93 and 1993-94). ... Named to WCHA All-Star first team (1992-93 and 1993-94).

		REGULAR SEASON							PLAYOFFS					
Season Team	League	Gms.	Min	W	L	T	GA	SO	Avg.	Gms.	Min.	W	L	GA	SO	Avg.
90-91—Michigan Tech	WCHA	14	826	5	9	0	57	0	4.14	—	—	—	—	—	—	—
91-92—Michigan Tech	WCHA	23	1144	9	9	1	83	0	4.35	—	—	—	—	—	—	—
92-93—Michigan Tech	WCHA	36	2078	16	14	5	115	0	3.32	—	—	—	—	—	—	—
93-94—Michigan Tech	WCHA	39	2192	12	20	5	117	1	3.20	—	—	—	—	—	—	—
94-95—Binghamton	AHL	26	1472	12	10	2	81	1	3.30	11	664	6	5	29	1	2.62
95-96—Binghamton	AHL	40	2262	18	16	3	151	1	4.01	1	34	0	0	1	0	1.76
—New York Rangers........	NHL	1	27	0	0	0	0	0	0.00	—	—	—	—	—	—	—
96-97—Kentucky..................	AHL	50	2937	25	19	5	161	4	3.29	1	60	0	1	3	0	3.00
NHL totals (1 year)		1	27	0	0	0	0	0								

RAMSEY, MIKE   D

PERSONAL: Born December 3, 1960, in Minneapolis. ... 6-3/195. ... Shoots left. ... Full name: Michael Allen Ramsey.
COLLEGE: Minnesota.
TRANSACTIONS/CAREER NOTES: Selected by Buffalo Sabres in first round (first Sabres pick, 11th overall) of NHL entry draft (August 9, 1979). ... Dislocated thumb (December 4, 1983). ... Injured groin (October 1987). ... Fractured bone in right hand (November 2, 1988). ... Pulled groin (January 12, 1989). ... Pulled rib cage muscle (November 26, 1990); missed seven games. ... Injured groin (November 22, 1991); missed five games. ... Injured groin (January 31, 1992); missed three games. ... Injured groin (March 8, 1992); missed three games. ...

Injured leg (April 12, 1992). ... Underwent shoulder surgery (August 8, 1992); missed first nine games of season. ... Strained groin (November 7, 1992); missed four games. ... Bruised hand (November 18, 1992); missed six games. ... Sprained knee (January 29, 1993); missed four games. ... Traded by Sabres to Pittsburgh Penguins for LW Bob Errey (March 22, 1993). ... Broke toe (November 11, 1993); missed nine games. ... Signed as free agent by Detroit Red Wings (August 3, 1994). ... Injured groin (January 24, 1995); missed one game. ... Strained left hip flexor (March 6, 1995); missed five games. ... Injured groin (November 17, 1995); missed four games. ... Broke left foot (January 12, 1996); missed nine games. ... Bruised knee (April 10, 1996); missed one game. ... Announced retirement (March 18, 1997).
HONORS: Played in NHL All-Star Game (1982, 1983, 1985 and 1986).
MISCELLANEOUS: Member of gold-medal-winning U.S. Olympic team (1980). ... Captain of Buffalo Sabres (1990-91 through 1992-93).

		REGULAR SEASON								PLAYOFFS				
Season Team	League	Gms.	G	A	Pts.	PIM	+/-	PP	SH	Gms.	G	A	Pts.	PIM
78-79— Univ. of Minnesota.....	WCHA	26	6	11	17	30	...	...	...	—	—	—	—	—
79-80— U.S. national team.....	Int'l	56	11	22	33	55	...	...	...	—	—	—	—	—
— U.S. Olympic team.....	Int'l	7	0	2	2	8	...	...	...	—	—	—	—	—
— Buffalo........	NHL	13	1	6	7	6	...	0	0	13	1	2	3	12
80-81— Buffalo........	NHL	72	3	14	17	56	3	0	0	8	0	3	3	20
81-82— Buffalo........	NHL	80	7	23	30	56	18	2	0	4	1	1	2	14
82-83— Buffalo........	NHL	77	8	30	38	55	19	1	1	10	4	4	8	15
83-84— Buffalo........	NHL	72	9	22	31	82	26	1	0	3	0	1	1	6
84-85— Buffalo........	NHL	79	8	22	30	102	31	3	0	5	0	1	1	23
85-86— Buffalo........	NHL	76	7	21	28	117	1	1	0	—	—	—	—	—
86-87— Buffalo........	NHL	80	8	31	39	109	1	2	1	—	—	—	—	—
87-88— Buffalo........	NHL	63	5	16	21	77	6	1	0	6	0	3	3	29
88-89— Buffalo........	NHL	56	2	14	16	84	5	0	0	5	1	0	1	11
89-90— Buffalo........	NHL	73	4	21	25	47	21	1	0	6	0	1	1	8
90-91— Buffalo........	NHL	71	6	14	20	46	14	0	0	5	1	0	1	12
91-92— Buffalo........	NHL	66	3	14	17	67	8	0	0	7	0	2	2	8
92-93— Buffalo........	NHL	33	2	8	10	20	4	0	0	—	—	—	—	—
— Pittsburgh........	NHL	12	1	2	3	8	13	0	0	12	0	6	6	4
93-94— Pittsburgh........	NHL	65	2	2	4	22	-4	0	0	1	0	0	0	0
94-95— Detroit........	NHL	33	1	2	3	23	11	0	0	15	0	1	1	4
95-96— Detroit........	NHL	47	2	4	6	35	17	0	0	15	0	4	4	10
96-97— Detroit........	NHL	2	0	0	0	0	0	0	0	—	—	—	—	—
NHL totals (18 years)		1070	79	266	345	1012	...	12	2	115	8	29	37	176

RANFORD, BILL   G   CAPITALS

PERSONAL: Born December 14, 1966, in Brandon, Man. ... 5-11/185. ... Catches left.
HIGH SCHOOL: New Westminster (B.C.).
TRANSACTIONS/CAREER NOTES: Selected by Boston Bruins as underage junior in third round (second Bruins pick, 52nd overall) of NHL entry draft (June 15, 1985). ... Traded by Bruins with LW Geoff Courtnall and second-round pick (C Petro Koivunen) in 1988 draft to Edmonton Oilers for G Andy Moog (March 1988). ... Sprained ankle (February 14, 1990); missed six games. ... Strained groin (January 4, 1992); missed two games. ... Strained hamstring (January 29, 1992); missed five games. ... Strained right quadriceps (November 12, 1992); missed two games. ... Strained left hamstring (April 7, 1993); missed two games. ... Bruised hand (March 23, 1993); missed one game. ... Strained hamstring (April 5, 1994); missed three games. ... Suffered back spasms (April 29, 1995); missed three games. ... Sprained ankle (January 3, 1996); missed two games. ... Traded by Oilers to Boston Bruins for D Sean Brown, RW Mariusz Czerkawski and first-round pick (D Matthieu Descoteaux) in 1996 draft (January 11, 1996). ... Suffered tendinitis in shoulder (December 29, 1996); missed 20 games. ... Traded by Bruins with C Adam Oates and RW Rick Tocchet to Washington Capitals for G Jim Carey, C Jason Allison, C Anson Carter, third-round pick (RW Lee Goren) in 1997 draft and conditional pick in 1998 draft (March 1, 1997).
HONORS: Named to WHL All-Star second team (1985-86). ... Won Conn Smythe Trophy (1989-90). ... Played in NHL All-Star Game (1991).
RECORDS: Shares NHL single-season playoff record for most wins by a goaltender—16 (1990).
MISCELLANEOUS: Member of Stanley Cup championship team (1988 and 1990). ... Holds Edmonton Oilers all-time record for most games played by a goaltender (433). ... Stopped a penalty shot attempt (vs. Claude Loiselle, October 28, 1989; vs. Tom Kurvers, March 10, 1990; vs. Greg Adams, December 1, 1991; vs. Alexander Mogilny, January 10, 1992; vs. Mario Lemieux, March 17, 1992; vs. Dave Gagner, October 28, 1992; vs. C.J. Young, December 27, 1992; vs. Brett Hull, March 26, 1995; vs. Randy Burridge, February 3, 1996). ... Allowed a penalty shot goal (vs. Robert Reichel, February 7, 1994).
STATISTICAL NOTES: Tied for NHL lead with 30 regular-season losses (1995-96).

		REGULAR SEASON								PLAYOFFS						
Season Team	League	Gms.	Min	W	L	T	GA	SO	Avg.	Gms.	Min.	W	L	GA	SO	Avg.
83-84— New Westminster.........	WHL	27	1450	10	14	0	130	0	5.38	1	27	0	0	2	0	4.44
84-85— New Westminster.........	WHL	38	2034	19	17	0	142	0	4.19	7	309	2	3	26	0	5.05
85-86— New Westminster.........	WHL	53	2791	17	29	1	225	1	4.84	—	—	—	—	—	—	—
— Boston.........	NHL	4	240	3	1	0	10	0	2.50	2	120	0	2	7	0	3.50
86-87— Moncton.........	AHL	3	180	3	0	0	6	0	2.00	—	—	—	—	—	—	—
— Boston.........	NHL	41	2234	16	20	2	124	3	3.33	2	123	0	2	8	0	3.90
87-88— Maine.........	AHL	51	2856	27	16	6	165	1	3.47	—	—	—	—	—	—	—
— Edmonton.........	NHL	6	325	3	0	2	16	0	2.95	—	—	—	—	—	—	—
88-89— Edmonton.........	NHL	29	1509	15	8	2	88	1	3.50	—	—	—	—	—	—	—
89-90— Edmonton.........	NHL	56	3107	24	16	9	165	1	3.19	*22	*1401	*16	6	*59	1	2.53
90-91— Edmonton.........	NHL	60	3415	27	27	3	182	0	3.20	3	135	1	2	8	0	3.56
91-92— Edmonton.........	NHL	67	3822	27	26	10	228	1	3.58	16	909	8	*8	51	†2	3.37
92-93— Edmonton.........	NHL	67	3753	17	38	6	240	1	3.84	—	—	—	—	—	—	—
93-94— Edmonton.........	NHL	71	4070	22	34	11	236	1	3.48	—	—	—	—	—	—	—
94-95— Edmonton.........	NHL	40	2203	15	20	3	133	2	3.62	—	—	—	—	—	—	—
95-96— Edmonton.........	NHL	37	2015	13	†18	5	128	1	3.81	—	—	—	—	—	—	—
— Boston.........	NHL	40	2307	21	†12	4	109	1	2.83	4	239	1	3	16	0	4.02
96-97— Boston.........	NHL	37	2147	12	16	8	125	2	3.49	—	—	—	—	—	—	—
— Washington.........	NHL	18	1010	8	7	2	46	0	2.73	—	—	—	—	—	—	—
NHL totals (12 years)		573	32157	223	243	67	1830	14	3.41	49	2927	26	23	149	3	3.05

RANHEIM, PAUL — LW — HURRICANES

PERSONAL: Born January 25, 1966, in St. Louis. ... 6-1/210. ... Shoots right. ... Full name: Paul Stephen Ranheim. ... Name pronounced RAN-HIGHM.
HIGH SCHOOL: Edina (Minn.).
COLLEGE: Wisconsin.
TRANSACTIONS/CAREER NOTES: Selected by Calgary Flames in second round (third Flames pick, 38th overall) of NHL entry draft (June 8, 1983). ... Broke right ankle (December 11, 1990); missed 41 games. ... Traded by Flames with D Gary Suter and C Ted Drury to Hartford Whalers for C Michael Nylander, D Zarley Zalapski and D James Patrick (March 10, 1994). ... Suffered finger infection on left hand (November 28, 1995); missed six games. ... Suffered abdominal strain (October 27, 1996); missed five games. ... Sore groin (November 11, 1996); missed one game. ... Whalers franchise moved to North Carolina and renamed Carolina Hurricanes for 1997-98 season; NHL approved move on June 25, 1997.
HONORS: Named to WCHA All-Star second team (1986-87). ... Named to NCAA All-America West first team (1987-88). ... Named to WCHA All-Star first team (1987-88). ... Won Garry F. Longman Memorial Trophy (1988-89). ... Won Ken McKenzie Trophy (1988-89). ... Named to IHL All-Star second team (1988-89).
STATISTICAL PLATEAUS: Three-goal games: 1991-92 (1).
MISCELLANEOUS: Scored on a penalty shot (vs. Bob Essensa, October 31, 1993).

		REGULAR SEASON								PLAYOFFS				
Season Team	League	Gms.	G	A	Pts.	PIM	+/-	PP	SH	Gms.	G	A	Pts.	PIM
82-83 — Edina High School	Minn. H.S.	26	12	25	37	4	...	...	...	—	—	—	—	—
83-84 — Edina High School	Minn. H.S.	26	16	24	40	6	...	...	...	—	—	—	—	—
84-85 — Univ. of Wisconsin.....	WCHA	42	11	11	22	40	...	...	...	—	—	—	—	—
85-86 — Univ. of Wisconsin.....	WCHA	33	17	17	34	34	...	...	...	—	—	—	—	—
86-87 — Univ. of Wisconsin.....	WCHA	42	24	35	59	54	...	...	...	—	—	—	—	—
87-88 — Univ. of Wisconsin.....	WCHA	44	36	26	62	63	...	...	...	—	—	—	—	—
88-89 — Calgary	NHL	5	0	0	0	0	-3	0	0	—	—	—	—	—
— Salt Lake City.............	IHL	75	*68	29	97	16	...	...	...	14	5	5	10	8
89-90 — Calgary	NHL	80	26	28	54	23	27	1	3	6	1	3	4	2
90-91 — Calgary	NHL	39	14	16	30	4	20	2	0	7	2	2	4	0
91-92 — Calgary	NHL	80	23	20	43	32	16	1	3	—	—	—	—	—
92-93 — Calgary	NHL	83	21	22	43	26	-4	3	4	6	0	1	1	0
93-94 — Calgary	NHL	67	10	14	24	20	-7	0	2	—	—	—	—	—
— Hartford	NHL	15	0	3	3	2	-11	0	0	—	—	—	—	—
94-95 — Hartford	NHL	47	6	14	20	10	-3	0	0	—	—	—	—	—
95-96 — Hartford	NHL	73	10	20	30	14	-2	0	1	—	—	—	—	—
96-97 — Hartford	NHL	67	10	11	21	18	-13	0	3	—	—	—	—	—
NHL totals (9 years)		556	120	148	268	149	20	7	16	19	3	6	9	2

RASMUSSEN, ERIK — C — SABRES

PERSONAL: Born March 28, 1977, in Minneapolis. ... 6-1/193. ... Shoots left. ... Name pronounced RAS-muh-suhn.
HIGH SCHOOL: Saint Louis (Minn.) Park.
COLLEGE: Minnesota.
TRANSACTIONS/CAREER NOTES: Selected by Buffalo Sabres in first round (first Sabres pick, seventh overall) of NHL entry draft (June 22, 1996).
HONORS: Named to WCHA All-Rookie team (1995-96).

		REGULAR SEASON								PLAYOFFS				
Season Team	League	Gms.	G	A	Pts.	PIM	+/-	PP	SH	Gms.	G	A	Pts.	PIM
92-93 — Saint Louis Park	Minn. H.S.	23	16	24	40	50	...	...	...	—	—	—	—	—
93-94 — Saint Louis Park	Minn. H.S.	18	25	18	43	60	...	...	...	—	—	—	—	—
94-95 — Saint Louis Park	Minn. H.S.	23	19	33	52	80	...	...	...	—	—	—	—	—
95-96 — Univ. of Minnesota.....	WCHA	31	13	28	41	51	...	...	...	—	—	—	—	—
96-97 — Univ. of Minnesota.....	WCHA	34	15	12	27	123	...	...	...	—	—	—	—	—

RATHJE, MIKE — D — SHARKS

PERSONAL: Born May 11, 1974, in Manville, Alta. ... 6-5/230. ... Shoots left. ... Name pronounced RATH-jee.
HIGH SCHOOL: Medicine Hat (Alta.).
TRANSACTIONS/CAREER NOTES: Selected by San Jose Sharks in first round (first Sharks pick, third overall) of NHL entry draft (June 20, 1992). ... Strained abdomen (February 19, 1994); missed three games. ... Sprained knee (February 26, 1994); missed four games. ... Sprained knee (February 2, 1995); missed three games. ... Injured foot (February 15, 1995); missed one game. ... Injured hip flexor (April 25, 1995); missed two games. ... Strained abdomen (October 6, 1995); missed first two games of season. ... Injured shoulder (November 14, 1995); missed 12 games. ... Strained groin (November 8, 1996); missed 50 games.
HONORS: Named to Can.HL All-Star second team (1992-93). ... Named to WHL (East) All-Star second team (1991-92 and 1992-93).

		REGULAR SEASON								PLAYOFFS				
Season Team	League	Gms.	G	A	Pts.	PIM	+/-	PP	SH	Gms.	G	A	Pts.	PIM
90-91 — Medicine Hat..............	WHL	64	1	16	17	28	...	...	...	12	0	4	4	2
91-92 — Medicine Hat..............	WHL	67	11	23	34	109	...	...	...	4	0	1	1	2
92-93 — Medicine Hat..............	WHL	57	12	37	49	103	...	...	...	10	3	3	6	12
— Kansas City................	IHL	—	—	—	—	—	...	...	...	5	0	0	0	12
93-94 — San Jose...................	NHL	47	1	9	10	59	-9	1	0	1	0	0	0	0
— Kansas City................	IHL	6	0	2	2	0	...	...	...	—	—	—	—	—
94-95 — Kansas City................	IHL	6	0	1	1	7	...	...	...	—	—	—	—	—
— San Jose...................	NHL	42	2	7	9	29	-1	0	0	11	5	2	7	4
95-96 — Kansas City................	IHL	36	6	11	17	34	...	...	...	—	—	—	—	—
— San Jose...................	NHL	27	0	7	7	14	-16	0	0	—	—	—	—	—
96-97 — San Jose...................	NHL	31	0	8	8	21	-1	0	0	—	—	—	—	—
NHL totals (4 years)		147	3	31	34	123	-27	1	0	12	5	2	7	4

R

RAY, ROB — RW — SABRES

PERSONAL: Born June 8, 1968, in Stirling, Ont. ... 6-0/203. ... Shoots left.
TRANSACTIONS/CAREER NOTES: Broke jaw (January 1987). ... Selected by Buffalo Sabres in fifth round (fifth Sabres pick, 97th overall) of NHL entry draft (June 11, 1988). ... Tore right knee ligament (April 11, 1993); missed remainder of season. ... Suffered from the flu (March 11, 1995); missed one game. ... Broke right cheekbone (November 27, 1995); missed eight games.
MISCELLANEOUS: Holds Buffalo Sabres all-time record for most penalty minutes (2,034).

Season Team	League	Gms.	G	A	Pts.	PIM	+/-	PP	SH	Gms.	G	A	Pts.	PIM
84-85— Whitby Lawmen	OPJHL	35	5	10	15	318	...	...	...	—	—	—	—	—
85-86— Cornwall	OHL	53	6	13	19	253	...	...	...	6	0	0	0	26
86-87— Cornwall	OHL	46	17	20	37	158	...	...	...	5	1	1	2	16
87-88— Cornwall	OHL	61	11	41	52	179	...	...	...	11	2	3	5	33
88-89— Rochester	AHL	74	11	18	29	*446	...	...	...	—	—	—	—	—
89-90— Buffalo	NHL	27	2	1	3	99	-2	0	0	—	—	—	—	—
— Rochester	AHL	43	2	13	15	335	...	...	...	17	1	3	4	*115
90-91— Rochester	AHL	8	1	1	2	15	...	...	...	—	—	—	—	—
— Buffalo	NHL	66	8	8	16	*350	-11	0	0	6	1	1	2	56
91-92— Buffalo	NHL	63	5	3	8	354	-9	0	0	7	0	0	0	2
92-93— Buffalo	NHL	68	3	2	5	211	-3	1	0	—	—	—	—	—
93-94— Buffalo	NHL	82	3	4	7	274	2	0	0	7	1	0	1	43
94-95— Buffalo	NHL	47	0	3	3	173	-4	0	0	5	0	0	0	14
95-96— Buffalo	NHL	71	3	6	9	287	-8	0	0	—	—	—	—	—
96-97— Buffalo	NHL	82	7	3	10	286	3	0	0	12	0	1	1	28
NHL totals (8 years)		506	31	30	61	2034	-32	1	0	37	2	2	4	143

REASONER, MARTY — C — BLUES

PERSONAL: Born February 26, 1977, in Rochester, N.Y. ... 6-1/188. ... Shoots left.
HIGH SCHOOL: Deerfield Academy (Mass.).
COLLEGE: Boston College.
TRANSACTIONS/CAREER NOTES: Selected by St. Louis Blues in first round (first Blues pick, 14th overall) of NHL entry draft (June 22, 1996).
HONORS: Named to Hockey East All-Rookie team (1995-96). ... Named Hockey East Rookie of the Year (1995-96). ... Named to Hockey East All-Star team (1996-97).

Season Team	League	Gms.	G	A	Pts.	PIM	+/-	PP	SH	Gms.	G	A	Pts.	PIM
93-94— Deerfield Academy	Mass. H.S.	22	27	24	51	...	...	...	...	—	—	—	—	—
94-95— Deerfield Academy	Mass. H.S.	26	25	32	57	14	...	...	...	—	—	—	—	—
95-96— Boston College	Hockey East	34	16	29	45	32	...	...	...	—	—	—	—	—
96-97— Boston College	Hockey East	35	20	24	44	31	...	...	...	—	—	—	—	—

RECCHI, MARK — RW — CANADIENS

PERSONAL: Born February 1, 1968, in Kamloops, B.C. ... 5-10/180. ... Shoots left. ... Name pronounced REH-kee.
TRANSACTIONS/CAREER NOTES: Broke ankle (January 1987). ... Selected by Pittsburgh Penguins in fourth round (fourth Penguins pick, 67th overall) of NHL entry draft (June 11, 1988). ... Injured left shoulder (December 23, 1990). ... Sprained right knee (March 30, 1991). ... Traded by Penguins with D Brian Benning and first-round pick (LW Jason Bowen) in 1992 draft to Philadelphia Flyers for RW Rick Tocchet, D Kjell Samuelsson, G Ken Wregget and third-round pick (February 19, 1992). ... Traded by Flyers with third-round pick (C Martin Hohenberger) in 1995 draft to Montreal Canadiens for D Eric Desjardins, LW Gilbert Dionne and LW John LeClair (February 9, 1995).
HONORS: Named to WHL (West) All-Star team (1987-88). ... Named to IHL All-Star second team (1988-89). ... Named to NHL All-Star second team (1991-92). ... Played in NHL All-Star Game (1991, 1993, 1994 and 1997). ... Named All-Star Game Most Valuable Player (1997).
STATISTICAL PLATEAUS: Three-goal games: 1991-92 (1), 1996-97 (1). Total: 2.
MISCELLANEOUS: Member of Stanley Cup championship team (1991). ... Failed to score on a penalty shot (vs. Don Beaupre, February 6, 1995; vs. Dominik Hasek, March 8, 1995).

Season Team	League	Gms.	G	A	Pts.	PIM	+/-	PP	SH	Gms.	G	A	Pts.	PIM
84-85— Langley Eagles	BCJHL	51	26	39	65	39	...	...	...	—	—	—	—	—
85-86— New Westminster	WHL	72	21	40	61	55	...	...	...	—	—	—	—	—
86-87— Kamloops	WHL	40	26	50	76	63	...	...	...	13	3	16	19	17
87-88— Kamloops	WHL	62	61	*93	154	75	...	...	...	17	10	*21	†31	18
88-89— Pittsburgh	NHL	15	1	1	2	0	-2	0	0	—	—	—	—	—
— Muskegon	IHL	63	50	49	99	86	...	...	...	14	7	*14	†21	28
89-90— Muskegon	IHL	4	7	4	11	2	...	...	...	—	—	—	—	—
— Pittsburgh	NHL	74	30	37	67	44	6	6	2	—	—	—	—	—
90-91— Pittsburgh	NHL	78	40	73	113	48	0	12	0	24	10	24	34	33
91-92— Pittsburgh	NHL	58	33	37	70	78	-16	16	1	—	—	—	—	—
— Philadelphia	NHL	22	10	17	27	18	-5	4	0	—	—	—	—	—
92-93— Philadelphia	NHL	84	53	70	123	95	1	15	4	—	—	—	—	—
93-94— Philadelphia	NHL	84	40	67	107	46	-2	11	0	—	—	—	—	—
94-95— Philadelphia	NHL	10	2	3	5	12	-6	1	0	—	—	—	—	—
— Montreal	NHL	39	14	29	43	16	-3	8	0	—	—	—	—	—
95-96— Montreal	NHL	82	28	50	78	69	20	11	2	6	3	3	6	0
96-97— Montreal	NHL	82	34	46	80	58	-1	7	2	5	4	2	6	2
NHL totals (9 years)		628	285	430	715	484	-8	91	11	35	17	29	46	35

REDDEN, WADE   D   SENATORS

PERSONAL: Born June 12, 1977, in Lloydminster, Sask. ... 6-2/193. ... Shoots left.
HIGH SCHOOL: Crocus Plaines (Brandon, Man.).
TRANSACTIONS/CAREER NOTES: Selected by New York Islanders in first round (first Islanders pick, second overall) of NHL entry draft (July 8, 1995). ... Traded by Islanders with G Damian Rhodes to Ottawa Senators for G Don Beaupre, D Bryan Berard and C Martin Straka (January 23, 1996).
HONORS: Won Jim Piggott Memorial Trophy (1993-94). ... Won WHL Top Draft Prospect Award (1994-95). ... Named to Can.HL All-Star second team (1994-95 and 1995-96). ... Named to WHL (East) All-Star second team (1994-95). ... Named to WHL (Central/East) All-Star first team (1995-96). ... Named to Memorial Cup All-Star team (1995-96).

Season Team	League	REGULAR SEASON								PLAYOFFS				
		Gms.	G	A	Pts.	PIM	+/-	PP	SH	Gms.	G	A	Pts.	PIM
92-93— Lloydminster.............	SJHL	34	4	11	15	64	...	...	...	—	—	—	—	—
93-94— Brandon...................	WHL	64	4	35	39	98	...	...	...	14	2	4	6	10
94-95— Brandon...................	WHL	64	14	46	60	83	...	...	...	18	5	10	15	8
95-96— Brandon...................	WHL	51	9	45	54	55	...	...	...	19	5	10	15	19
96-97— Ottawa	NHL	82	6	24	30	41	1	2	0	7	1	3	4	2
NHL totals (1 year)		82	6	24	30	41	1	2	0	7	1	3	4	2

REEKIE, JOE   D   CAPITALS

PERSONAL: Born February 22, 1965, in Victoria, B.C. ... 6-3/220. ... Shoots left. ... Full name: Joseph James Reekie.
TRANSACTIONS/CAREER NOTES: Selected by Hartford Whalers as underage junior in seventh round (eighth Whalers pick, 124th overall) of NHL entry draft (June 8, 1983). ... Selected by Buffalo Sabres in sixth round (sixth Sabres pick, 119th overall) of NHL entry draft (June 15, 1985). ... Injured ankle (March 14, 1987). ... Injured shoulder (October 1987). ... Broke kneecap (November 15, 1987). ... Underwent surgery to left knee (September 1988). ... Traded by Sabres to New York Islanders for sixth-round pick (G Bill Pye) in 1989 draft (June 17, 1989). ... Sprained right knee (November 1989). ... Broke two bones in left hand and suffered facial cuts in automobile accident and underwent surgery (December 7, 1989). ... Broke left middle finger (March 21, 1990). ... Injured eye (January 12, 1991); missed six games. ... Fractured knuckle on left hand (January 3, 1992); missed 22 games. ... Selected by Tampa Bay Lightning in NHL expansion draft (June 18, 1992). ... Broke left leg (January 16, 1993); missed remainder of season. ... Traded by Lightning to Washington Capitals for D Enrico Ciccone, third-round pick (RW Craig Reichert) in 1994 draft and conditional draft pick (March 21, 1994). ... Bruised foot (April 4, 1996); missed four games. ... Fractured heel (February 14, 1997); missed 17 games.

Season Team	League	REGULAR SEASON								PLAYOFFS				
		Gms.	G	A	Pts.	PIM	+/-	PP	SH	Gms.	G	A	Pts.	PIM
81-82— Nepean......................	COJHL	16	2	5	7	4	...	...	...	—	—	—	—	—
82-83— North Bay.................	OHL	59	2	9	11	49	...	...	...	8	0	1	1	11
83-84— North Bay.................	OHL	9	1	0	1	18	...	...	...	—	—	—	—	—
— Cornwall..................	OHL	53	6	27	33	166	...	...	...	3	0	0	0	4
84-85— Cornwall..................	OHL	65	19	63	82	134	...	...	...	9	4	13	17	18
85-86— Rochester..................	AHL	77	3	25	28	178	...	...	...	—	—	—	—	—
— Buffalo	NHL	3	0	0	0	14	-2	0	0	—	—	—	—	—
86-87— Buffalo	NHL	56	1	8	9	82	6	0	0	—	—	—	—	—
— Rochester...............	AHL	22	0	6	6	52	...	...	...	—	—	—	—	—
87-88— Buffalo	NHL	30	1	4	5	68	-3	0	0	2	0	0	0	4
88-89— Rochester..................	AHL	21	1	2	3	56	...	...	...	—	—	—	—	—
— Buffalo	NHL	15	1	3	4	26	6	1	0	—	—	—	—	—
89-90— New York Islanders....	NHL	31	1	8	9	43	13	0	0	—	—	—	—	—
— Springfield.............	AHL	15	1	4	5	24	...	...	...	—	—	—	—	—
90-91— Capital District	AHL	2	1	0	1	0	...	...	...	—	—	—	—	—
— New York Islanders....	NHL	66	3	16	19	96	17	0	0	—	—	—	—	—
91-92— New York Islanders....	NHL	54	4	12	16	85	15	0	0	—	—	—	—	—
— Capital District	AHL	3	2	2	4	2	...	...	...	—	—	—	—	—
92-93— Tampa Bay	NHL	42	2	11	13	69	2	0	0	—	—	—	—	—
93-94— Tampa Bay	NHL	73	1	11	12	127	8	0	0	—	—	—	—	—
— Washington	NHL	12	0	5	5	29	7	0	0	11	2	1	3	29
94-95— Washington	NHL	48	1	6	7	97	10	0	0	7	0	0	0	2
95-96— Washington	NHL	78	3	7	10	149	7	0	0	—	—	—	—	—
96-97— Washington	NHL	65	1	8	9	107	8	0	0	—	—	—	—	—
NHL totals (12 years)		573	19	99	118	992	94	1	0	20	2	1	3	35

REESE, JEFF   G   DEVILS

PERSONAL: Born March 24, 1966, in Brantford, Ont. ... 5-9/175. ... Catches left.
TRANSACTIONS/CAREER NOTES: Selected by Toronto Maple Leafs as underage junior in fourth round (third Maple Leafs pick, 67th overall) of NHL entry draft (June 9, 1984). ... Broke left kneecap (October 23, 1989); missed two months. ... Bruised left kneecap (April 12, 1990). ... Broke transverse processes (March 23, 1991); missed remainder of season. ... Traded by Maple Leafs with D Alexander Godynyuk, RW Gary Leeman, D Michel Petit and LW Craig Berube to Calgary Flames for C Doug Gilmour, D Jamie Macoun, LW Kent Manderville, D Ric Nattress and G Rick Wamsley (January 2, 1992). ... Cut hand prior to 1992-93 season; missed first three games of season. ... Strained shoulder (October 31, 1993); missed three games. ... Traded by Flames with future considerations to Hartford Whalers for D Dan Keczmer (November 19, 1993). ... Strained hip flexor (December 23, 1993); missed six games. ... Traded by Whalers to Tampa Bay Lightning for undisclosed draft pick (December 1, 1995). ... Suffered from dehydration (December 3, 1995); missed one game. ... Suffered sprained right knee and ankle (December 28, 1995); missed three games. ... Traded by Lightning with second-(LW Pierre Dagenais) and eighth-(RW Jason Bertsch) round picks in 1996 draft to New Jersey Devils for G Corey Schwab (June 22, 1996).
HONORS: Shared James Norris Memorial Trophy with Rich Parent (1996-97). ... Named to IHL All-Star second team (1996-97).
RECORDS: Holds NHL single-game record for most assists by a goaltender—3 (February 10, 1993).
MISCELLANEOUS: Stopped a penalty shot attempt (vs. Joe Nieuwendyk, December 12, 1988; vs. Hakan Loob, February 22, 1989).

Season Team	League	REGULAR SEASON							PLAYOFFS						
		Gms.	Min	W	L	T	GA	SO	Avg.	Gms.	Min.	W	L	GA	SO	Avg.
82-83—Hamilton A's	OJHL	40	2380	...	...	...	176	0	4.44	—	—	—	—	—	—	—
83-84—London	OHL	43	2308	18	19	0	173	0	4.50	6	327	3	3	27	0	4.95
84-85—London	OHL	50	2878	31	15	1	186	1	3.88	8	440	5	2	20	†1	*2.73
85-86—London	OHL	*57	*3281	25	26	3	215	0	3.93	5	299	0	4	25	0	5.02
86-87—Newmarket	AHL	50	2822	11	29	0	193	1	4.10	—	—	—	—	—	—	—
87-88—Newmarket	AHL	28	1587	10	14	3	103	0	3.89	—	—	—	—	—	—	—
—Toronto...................	NHL	5	249	1	2	1	17	0	4.10	—	—	—	—	—	—	—
88-89—Toronto	NHL	10	486	2	6	1	40	0	4.94	—	—	—	—	—	—	—
—Newmarket	AHL	37	2072	17	14	3	132	0	3.82	—	—	—	—	—	—	—
89-90—Newmarket	AHL	7	431	3	2	2	29	0	4.04	—	—	—	—	—	—	—
—Toronto...................	NHL	21	1101	9	6	3	81	0	4.41	2	108	1	1	6	0	3.33
90-91—Toronto	NHL	30	1430	6	13	3	92	1	3.86	—	—	—	—	—	—	—
—Newmarket	AHL	3	180	2	1	0	7	0	2.33	—	—	—	—	—	—	—
91-92—Toronto	NHL	8	413	1	5	1	20	1	2.91	—	—	—	—	—	—	—
—Calgary	NHL	12	587	3	2	2	37	0	3.78	—	—	—	—	—	—	—
92-93—Calgary	NHL	26	1311	14	4	1	70	1	3.20	4	209	1	3	17	0	4.88
93-94—Calgary	NHL	1	13	0	0	0	1	0	4.62	—	—	—	—	—	—	—
—Hartford	NHL	19	1086	5	9	3	56	1	3.09	—	—	—	—	—	—	—
94-95—Hartford	NHL	11	477	2	5	1	26	0	3.27	—	—	—	—	—	—	—
95-96—Hartford	NHL	7	275	2	3	0	14	1	3.05	—	—	—	—	—	—	—
—Tampa Bay............	NHL	19	994	7	7	1	54	0	3.26	5	198	1	1	12	0	3.64
96-97—Detroit	IHL	32	1763	23	4	†3	55	4	*1.87	11	518	7	3	22	0	2.55
—New Jersey	NHL	3	139	0	2	0	13	0	5.61	—	—	—	—	—	—	—
NHL totals (10 years)		172	8561	52	64	17	521	5	3.65	11	515	3	5	35	0	4.08

REGAN, BRIAN   G   WHALERS

PERSONAL: Born September 23, 1975, in New Haven, Conn. ... 6-0/175. ... Catches left. ... Full name: Brian Christopher Regan.
HIGH SCHOOL: Westminster (Conn.).
COLLEGE: Massachusetts.
TRANSACTIONS/CAREER NOTES: Selected by Hartford Whalers in 10th round (seventh Whalers pick, 239th overall) of NHL entry draft (June 29, 1994).

Season Team	League	REGULAR SEASON							PLAYOFFS						
		Gms.	Min	W	L	T	GA	SO	Avg.	Gms.	Min.	W	L	GA	SO	Avg.
93-94—Westminster	Conn. HS	16	...	...	...	...	...	...	2.90	—	—	—	—	—	—	—
94-95—Univ. of Mass.	Hockey East	22	1139	3	14	2	92	0	4.85	—	—	—	—	—	—	—
95-96—Univ. of Mass.	Hockey East	28	1616	7	16	4	121	0	4.49	—	—	—	—	—	—	—
96-97—Univ. of Mass.	Hockey East	31	1692	10	19	0	127	1	4.50	—	—	—	—	—	—	—

REICHEL, ROBERT   C   ISLANDERS

PERSONAL: Born June 25, 1971, in Litvinov, Czechoslovakia. ... 5-10/185. ... Shoots right. ... Name pronounced RIGH-kuhl.
TRANSACTIONS/CAREER NOTES: Selected by Calgary Flames in fourth round (fifth Flames pick, 70th overall) of NHL entry draft (June 17, 1989). ... Strained right knee (March 16, 1993); missed three games. ... Played in Europe during 1994-95 NHL lockout. ... Traded by Flames to New York Islanders for LW Marty McInnis, G Tyrone Garner and sixth-round pick (D Ilja Demidov) in 1997 draft (March 18, 1997).
HONORS: Named to Czechoslovakian League All-Star team (1989-90).
STATISTICAL PLATEAUS: Three-goal games: 1992-93 (2), 1993-94 (2). Total: 4.
MISCELLANEOUS: Scored on a penalty shot (vs. Bill Ranford, February 7, 1994; vs. Tom Barrasso, October 24, 1996).

Season Team	League	REGULAR SEASON							PLAYOFFS				
		Gms.	G	A	Pts.	PIM	+/-	PP	SH	Gms.	G	A	Pts.	PIM
88-89—Litvinov.....................	Czech.	...	20	31	51	...	...	...	...	—	—	—	—	—
89-90—Litvinov.....................	Czech.	52	49	34	*83	...	...	...	...	—	—	—	—	—
90-91—Calgary	NHL	66	19	22	41	22	17	3	0	6	1	1	2	0
91-92—Calgary	NHL	77	20	34	54	32	1	8	0	—	—	—	—	—
92-93—Calgary	NHL	80	40	48	88	54	25	12	0	6	2	4	6	2
93-94—Calgary	NHL	84	40	53	93	58	20	14	0	7	0	5	5	0
94-95—Frankfurt	Germany	21	19	24	43	41	...	...	...	—	—	—	—	—
—Calgary	NHL	48	18	17	35	28	-2	5	0	7	2	4	6	4
95-96—Frankfurt	Germany	46	47	54	101	84	...	...	...	3	1	3	4	0
96-97—Calgary	NHL	70	16	27	43	22	-2	6	0	—	—	—	—	—
—New York Islanders....	NHL	12	5	14	19	4	7	0	1	—	—	—	—	—
NHL totals (6 years)		437	158	215	373	220	66	48	1	26	5	14	19	6

REICHERT, CRAIG   RW   MIGHTY DUCKS

PERSONAL: Born May 11, 1974, in Winnipeg. ... 6-1/200. ... Shoots right. ... Name pronounced RIGH-kuhrt.
HIGH SCHOOL: Dr. E.P. Scarlett (Calgary).
TRANSACTIONS/CAREER NOTES: Selected by Mighty Ducks of Anaheim in third round (third Mighty Ducks pick, 67th overall) of NHL entry draft (June 29, 1994).

Season Team	League	REGULAR SEASON							PLAYOFFS				
		Gms.	G	A	Pts.	PIM	+/-	PP	SH	Gms.	G	A	Pts.	PIM
91-92— Spokane....................	WHL	68	14	30	44	86	...	...	...	4	1	0	1	4
92-93— Red Deer..................	WHL	66	32	33	65	62	...	...	...	4	3	1	4	2
93-94— Red Deer..................	WHL	72	52	67	119	153	...	...	...	4	2	2	4	8

Season Team	League	REGULAR SEASON								PLAYOFFS				
		Gms.	G	A	Pts.	PIM	+/-	PP	SH	Gms.	G	A	Pts.	PIM
94-95 — San Diego	IHL	49	4	12	16	28	...	...	...	—	—	—	—	—
95-96 — Baltimore	AHL	68	10	17	27	50	...	...	...	1	0	0	0	0
96-97 — Baltimore	AHL	77	22	53	75	54	...	...	...	3	0	2	2	0
— Anaheim	NHL	3	0	0	0	0	-2	0	0	—	—	—	—	—
NHL totals (1 year)		3	0	0	0	0	-2	0	0					

REID, DAVE   LW   STARS

PERSONAL: Born May 15, 1964, in Toronto. ... 6-1/217. ... Shoots left.
TRANSACTIONS/CAREER NOTES: Selected by Boston Bruins as underage junior in third round (fourth Bruins pick, 60th overall) of NHL entry draft (June 9, 1982). ... Underwent knee surgery (December 1986). ... Separated shoulder (November 1987); missed 10 games. ... Signed as free agent by Toronto Maple Leafs (August 1988). ... Suffered from pneumonia (March 1992); missed 10 games. ... Injured knee (March 25, 1993); missed remainder of season. ... Signed as free agent by Bruins (November 22, 1991). ... Injured hip (April 1995); missed two games. ... Fractured index finger (February 1, 1996); missed 16 games. ... Signed as free agent by Dallas Stars (July 3, 1996).
STATISTICAL PLATEAUS: Three-goal games: 1995-96 (1), 1996-97 (1). Total: 2.

Season Team	League	REGULAR SEASON								PLAYOFFS				
		Gms.	G	A	Pts.	PIM	+/-	PP	SH	Gms.	G	A	Pts.	PIM
81-82 — Peterborough	OHL	68	10	32	42	41	...	...	...	9	2	3	5	11
82-83 — Peterborough	OHL	70	23	34	57	33	...	...	...	4	3	1	4	0
83-84 — Peterborough	OHL	60	33	64	97	12	...	...	...	—	—	—	—	—
— Boston	NHL	8	1	0	1	2	1	0	0	—	—	—	—	—
84-85 — Hershey	AHL	43	10	14	24	6	...	...	...	—	—	—	—	—
— Boston	NHL	35	14	13	27	27	-1	2	0	5	1	0	1	0
85-86 — Moncton	AHL	26	14	18	32	4	...	...	...	—	—	—	—	—
— Boston	NHL	37	10	10	20	10	2	4	0	—	—	—	—	—
86-87 — Boston	NHL	12	3	3	6	0	-1	0	0	2	0	0	0	0
— Moncton	AHL	40	12	22	34	23	...	...	...	5	0	1	1	0
87-88 — Maine	AHL	63	21	37	58	40	...	...	...	10	6	7	13	0
— Boston	NHL	3	0	0	0	0	0	0	0	—	—	—	—	—
88-89 — Toronto	NHL	77	9	21	30	22	12	1	1	—	—	—	—	—
89-90 — Toronto	NHL	70	9	19	28	9	-8	0	4	3	0	0	0	0
90-91 — Toronto	NHL	69	15	13	28	18	-10	1	*8	—	—	—	—	—
91-92 — Maine	AHL	12	1	5	6	4	...	...	...	—	—	—	—	—
— Boston	NHL	43	7	7	14	27	5	2	1	15	2	5	7	4
92-93 — Boston	NHL	65	20	16	36	10	12	1	5	—	—	—	—	—
93-94 — Boston	NHL	83	6	17	23	25	10	0	2	13	2	1	3	2
94-95 — Boston	NHL	38	5	5	10	10	8	0	0	5	0	0	0	0
95-96 — Boston	NHL	63	23	21	44	4	14	1	6	5	0	2	2	2
96-97 — Dallas	NHL	82	19	20	39	10	12	1	1	7	1	0	1	4
NHL totals (14 years)		685	141	165	306	174	56	13	28	55	6	8	14	12

RENBERG, MIKAEL   LW   FLYERS

PERSONAL: Born May 5, 1972, in Pitea, Sweden. ... 6-2/218. ... Shoots left.
TRANSACTIONS/CAREER NOTES: Selected by Philadelphia Flyers in second round (third Flyers pick, 40th overall) of NHL entry draft (June 16, 1990). ... Played in Europe during 1994-95 NHL lockout. ... Suffered sore shoulder (March 25, 1995); missed one game. ... Strained abdominal muscles (December 30, 1995); missed one game. ... Strained lower abdominal muscles (January 22, 1996); missed 17 games. ... Strained lower abdominal muscles (March 12, 1996); missed one game. ... Strained lower abdominal muscles (March 16, 1996); missed one game. ... Reinjured lower abdominal muscle (March 19, 1996); missed 11 games. ... Underwent abdominal surgery (May 1996). ... Strained groin (March 8, 1997); missed one game. ... Cut face (April 6, 1997); missed remainder of regular season.
HONORS: Named to NHL All-Rookie team (1993-94).
STATISTICAL PLATEAUS: Three-goal games: 1993-94 (1).

Season Team	League	REGULAR SEASON								PLAYOFFS				
		Gms.	G	A	Pts.	PIM	+/-	PP	SH	Gms.	G	A	Pts.	PIM
88-89 — Pitea	Sweden	12	6	3	9	...	...	...	...	—	—	—	—	—
89-90 — Pitea	Sweden	29	15	19	34	...	...	...	...	—	—	—	—	—
90-91 — Lulea	Sweden	29	11	6	17	12	...	...	...	5	1	1	2	4
91-92 — Lulea	Sweden	38	8	15	23	20	...	...	...	2	0	0	0	0
92-93 — Lulea	Sweden	39	19	13	32	61	...	...	...	11	4	4	8	0
93-94 — Philadelphia	NHL	83	38	44	82	36	8	9	0	—	—	—	—	—
94-95 — Lulea	Sweden	10	9	4	13	16	...	...	...	—	—	—	—	—
— Philadelphia	NHL	47	26	31	57	20	20	8	0	15	6	7	13	6
95-96 — Philadelphia	NHL	51	23	20	43	45	8	9	0	11	3	6	9	14
96-97 — Philadelphia	NHL	77	22	37	59	65	36	1	0	18	5	6	11	4
NHL totals (4 years)		258	109	132	241	166	72	27	0	44	14	19	33	24

RHEAUME, PASCAL   C   DEVILS

PERSONAL: Born June 21, 1973, in Quebec City. ... 6-1/200. ... Shoots left. ... Name pronounced ray-OHM.
TRANSACTIONS/CAREER NOTES: Signed as free agent by New Jersey Devils (October 1, 1992).

Season Team	League	REGULAR SEASON								PLAYOFFS				
		Gms.	G	A	Pts.	PIM	+/-	PP	SH	Gms.	G	A	Pts.	PIM
91-92 — Trois-Rivieres	QMJHL	65	17	20	37	84	...	...	...	14	5	4	9	23
92-93 — Sherbrooke	QMJHL	65	28	34	62	88	...	...	...	14	6	5	11	31

R

Season Team	League	REGULAR SEASON								PLAYOFFS				
		Gms.	G	A	Pts.	PIM	+/-	PP	SH	Gms.	G	A	Pts.	PIM
93-94 — Albany...............	AHL	55	17	18	35	43	...	...	...	5	0	1	1	0
94-95 — Albany...............	AHL	78	19	25	44	46	...	...	...	14	3	6	9	19
95-96 — Albany...............	AHL	68	26	42	68	50	...	...	...	4	1	2	3	2
96-97 — Albany...............	AHL	51	22	23	45	40	...	...	...	16	2	8	10	16
— New Jersey...............	NHL	2	1	0	1	0	1	0	0	—	—	—	—	—
NHL totals (1 year)............		2	1	0	1	0	1	0	0					

RHODES, DAMIAN   G   SENATORS

PERSONAL: Born May 28, 1969, in St. Paul, Minn. ... 6-0/180. ... Catches left.
HIGH SCHOOL: Richfield (Minn.).
COLLEGE: Michigan Tech.
TRANSACTIONS/CAREER NOTES: Selected by Toronto Maple Leafs in sixth round (sixth Maple Leafs pick, 112th overall) of NHL entry draft (June 13, 1987). ... Traded by Maple Leafs with LW Ken Belanger to New York Islanders for LW Kirk Muller (January 23, 1996). ... Traded by Islanders with D Wade Redden to Ottawa Senators for D Bryan Berard and C Martin Straka (January 23, 1996). ... Bruised calf (February 23, 1997); missed 10 games.
MISCELLANEOUS: Stopped a penalty shot attempt (vs. Scott Pearson, November 20, 1993; vs. Geoff Courtnall, March 21, 1995; vs. Martin Straka, April 3, 1996; vs. Todd Marchant, November 13, 1996). ... Holds Ottawa Senators all-time records for games played by a goaltender (86), most wins (24), goals-against average (2.74) and shares record for most shutouts (3).

Season Team	League	REGULAR SEASON								PLAYOFFS						
		Gms.	Min	W	L	T	GA	SO	Avg.	Gms.	Min.	W	L	GA	SO	Avg.
85-86 — Richfield.	Minn. HS	16	720	...	...	...	56	0	4.67	—	—	—	—	—	—	—
86-87 — Richfield.	Minn. HS	19	673	...	...	...	51	1	4.55	—	—	—	—	—	—	—
87-88 — Michigan Tech	WCHA	29	1623	16	10	1	114	0	4.21	—	—	—	—	—	—	—
88-89 — Michigan Tech	WCHA	37	2216	15	22	0	163	0	4.41	—	—	—	—	—	—	—
89-90 — Michigan Tech	WCHA	25	1358	6	17	0	119	0	5.26	—	—	—	—	—	—	—
90-91 — Toronto	NHL	1	60	1	0	0	1	0	1.00	—	—	—	—	—	—	—
— Newmarket	AHL	38	2154	8	24	3	144	1	4.01	—	—	—	—	—	—	—
91-92 — St. John's	AHL	43	2454	20	16	5	148	0	3.62	6	331	4	1	16	0	2.90
92-93 — St. John's	AHL	52	*3074	27	16	8	184	1	3.59	9	538	4	5	37	0	4.13
93-94 — Toronto	NHL	22	1213	9	7	3	53	0	2.62	1	0	0	0	0	0	0.00
94-95 — Toronto	NHL	13	760	6	6	1	34	0	2.68	—	—	—	—	—	—	—
95-96 — Toronto	NHL	11	624	4	5	1	29	0	2.79	—	—	—	—	—	—	—
— Ottawa	NHL	36	2123	10	22	4	98	2	2.77	—	—	—	—	—	—	—
96-97 — Ottawa	NHL	50	2934	14	20	*14	133	1	2.72	—	—	—	—	—	—	—
NHL totals (5 years)		133	7714	44	60	23	348	3	2.71	1	0	0	0	0	0	0.00

RICCI, MIKE   C   AVALANCHE

PERSONAL: Born October 27, 1971, in Scarborough, Ont. ... 6-0/190. ... Shoots left. ... Name pronounced REE-chee.
TRANSACTIONS/CAREER NOTES: Separated right shoulder (December 1989). ... Selected by Philadelphia Flyers in first round (first Flyers pick, fourth overall) of NHL entry draft (June 16, 1990). ... Broke right index finger and thumb (October 4, 1990); missed nine games. ... Traded by Flyers with G Ron Hextall, C Peter Forsberg, D Steve Duchesne, D Kerry Huffman, first-round pick (G Jocelyn Thibault) in 1993 draft, cash and future considerations to Quebec Nordiques for C Eric Lindros (June 20, 1992); Flyers sent LW Chris Simon and first-round pick (traded to Toronto) in 1994 draft to Nordiques to complete deal (July 21, 1992). ... Sprained left wrist (November 3, 1992); missed four games. ... Suffered from the flu (January 5, 1993); missed two games. ... Nordiques franchise moved to Colorado and renamed Avalanche for 1995-96 season (July 21, 1995). ... Underwent sinus surgery (October 15, 1995); missed one game. ... Injured ankle (November 5, 1995); missed one game. ... Sprained left ankle (December 11, 1995); missed two games. ... Suffered back spasms (January 4, 1996); missed 16 games. ... Strained shoulder (October 30, 1996); missed 11 games. ... Broke thumb (January 6, 1997); missed four games.
HONORS: Named to OHL All-Star second team (1988-89). ... Won Can.HL Player of the Year Award (1989-90). ... Won Red Tilson Trophy (1989-90). ... Won William Hanley Trophy (1989-90). ... Named to OHL All-Star first team (1989-90).
STATISTICAL PLATEAUS: Five-goal games: 1993-94 (1).
MISCELLANEOUS: Member of Stanley Cup championship team (1996). ... Failed to score on a penalty shot (vs. Chris Terreri, November 17, 1990).

Season Team	League	REGULAR SEASON								PLAYOFFS				
		Gms.	G	A	Pts.	PIM	+/-	PP	SH	Gms.	G	A	Pts.	PIM
87-88 — Peterborough.............	OHL	41	24	37	61	20	...	...	...	8	5	5	10	4
88-89 — Peterborough.............	OHL	60	54	52	106	43	...	...	...	17	19	16	35	18
89-90 — Peterborough.............	OHL	60	52	64	116	39	...	...	...	12	5	7	12	26
90-91 — Philadelphia	NHL	68	21	20	41	64	-8	9	0	—	—	—	—	—
91-92 — Philadelphia	NHL	78	20	36	56	93	-10	11	2	—	—	—	—	—
92-93 — Quebec......................	NHL	77	27	51	78	123	8	12	1	6	0	6	6	8
93-94 — Quebec......................	NHL	83	30	21	51	113	-9	13	3	—	—	—	—	—
94-95 — Quebec......................	NHL	48	15	21	36	40	5	9	0	6	1	3	4	8
95-96 — Colorado	NHL	62	6	21	27	52	1	3	0	22	6	11	17	18
96-97 — Colorado	NHL	63	13	19	32	59	-3	5	0	17	2	4	6	17
NHL totals (7 years)		479	132	189	321	544	-16	62	6	51	9	24	33	51

RICE, STEVE   RW   HURRICANES

PERSONAL: Born May 26, 1971, in Waterloo, Ont. ... 6-0/223. ... Shoots right.
TRANSACTIONS/CAREER NOTES: Underwent knee surgery (October 1986). ... Selected by New York Rangers in first round (first Rangers pick, 20th overall) of NHL entry draft (June 17, 1989). ... Suffered back spasms (September 14, 1989). ... Injured left shoulder (October 1990). ... Traded by Rangers with C Bernie Nicholls, LW Louie DeBrusk and future considerations to Edmonton Oilers for C Mark Messier and future considerations (October 4, 1991); Rangers later traded D David Shaw to Oilers for D Jeff Beukeboom to complete deal (November 12,

1991). ... Bruised right hip (March 1993); missed two games. ... Fractured hand (February 12, 1994); missed 16 games. ... Signed as free agent by Hartford Whalers (August 18, 1994); D Bryan Marchment awarded to Oilers as compensation (August 30, 1994). ... Injured shoulder (April 4, 1995); missed three games. ... Suffered concussion (April 26, 1995); missed three games. ... Bruised shoulder (December 10, 1995); missed four games. ... Injured shoulder (December 29, 1995); missed 11 games. ... Suffered back spasms (February 8, 1997); missed two games. ... Whalers franchise moved to North Carolina and renamed Carolina Hurricanes for 1997-98 season; NHL approved move on June 25, 1997.
HONORS: Named to Memorial Cup All-Star team (1989-90). ... Named to OHL All-Star second team (1990-91). ... Named to AHL All-Star second team (1992-93).
STATISTICAL PLATEAUS: Three-goal games: 1994-95 (1).

		REGULAR SEASON								PLAYOFFS				
Season Team	League	Gms.	G	A	Pts.	PIM	+/-	PP	SH	Gms.	G	A	Pts.	PIM
87-88— Kitchener	OHL	59	11	14	25	43	...	...	...	4	0	1	1	0
88-89— Kitchener	OHL	64	36	31	67	42	...	...	...	5	2	1	3	8
89-90— Kitchener	OHL	58	39	37	76	102	...	...	...	16	4	8	12	24
90-91— New York Rangers	NHL	11	1	1	2	4	2	0	0	2	2	1	3	6
— Binghamton	AHL	8	4	1	5	12	...	...	...	5	2	0	2	2
— Kitchener	OHL	29	30	30	60	43	...	...	...	6	5	6	11	2
91-92— Edmonton	NHL	3	0	0	0	2	-2	0	0	—	—	—	—	—
— Cape Breton	AHL	45	32	20	52	38	...	...	...	5	4	4	8	10
92-93— Cape Breton	AHL	51	34	28	62	63	...	...	...	14	4	6	10	22
— Edmonton	NHL	28	2	5	7	28	-4	0	0	—	—	—	—	—
93-94— Edmonton	NHL	63	17	15	32	36	-10	6	0	—	—	—	—	—
94-95— Hartford	NHL	40	11	10	21	61	2	4	0	—	—	—	—	—
95-96— Hartford	NHL	59	10	12	22	47	-4	1	0	—	—	—	—	—
96-97— Hartford	NHL	78	21	14	35	59	-11	5	0	—	—	—	—	—
NHL totals (7 years)		282	62	57	119	237	-27	16	0	2	2	1	3	6

RICHARDS, TRAVIS — D — STARS

PERSONAL: Born March 22, 1970, in Crystal, Minn. ... 6-1/185. ... Shoots right.
HIGH SCHOOL: Armstrong (Plymouth, Minn.).
COLLEGE: Minnesota.
TRANSACTIONS/CAREER NOTES: Selected by Minnesota North Stars in ninth round (ninth North Stars pick, 169th overall) of NHL entry draft (June 11, 1988). ... North Stars franchise moved from Minnesota to Dallas and renamed Stars for 1993-94 season.

		REGULAR SEASON								PLAYOFFS				
Season Team	League	Gms.	G	A	Pts.	PIM	+/-	PP	SH	Gms.	G	A	Pts.	PIM
87-88— Armstrong	Minn. H.S.	24	14	14	28	...	...	...	...	—	—	—	—	—
88-89— Univ. of Minnesota.....	WCHA							Did not play.						
89-90— Univ. of Minnesota.....	WCHA	45	4	24	28	38	...	...	...	—	—	—	—	—
90-91— Univ. of Minnesota.....	WCHA	45	9	25	34	28	...	...	...	—	—	—	—	—
91-92— Univ. of Minnesota.....	WCHA	44	10	23	33	65	...	...	...	—	—	—	—	—
92-93— Univ. of Minnesota.....	WCHA	42	12	26	38	54	...	...	...	—	—	—	—	—
93-94— U.S. national team	Int'l	51	1	11	12	12	...	...	...	—	—	—	—	—
— U.S. Olympic team	Int'l	8	0	0	0	2	...	...	...	—	—	—	—	—
— Kalamazoo	IHL	19	2	10	12	20	...	...	...	4	1	1	2	0
94-95— Kalamazoo	IHL	63	4	16	20	53	...	...	...	15	1	5	6	12
— Dallas........................	NHL	2	0	0	0	0	0	0	0	—	—	—	—	—
95-96— Michigan....................	IHL	65	8	15	23	55	...	...	...	9	2	2	4	4
— Dallas........................	NHL	1	0	0	0	2	-1	0	0	—	—	—	—	—
96-97— Grand Rapids.............	IHL	77	10	13	23	83	...	...	...	5	1	3	4	2
NHL totals (2 years)		3	0	0	0	2	-1	0	0	—	—	—	—	—

RICHARDSON, LUKE — D — FLYERS

PERSONAL: Born March 26, 1969, in Ottawa. ... 6-4/210. ... Shoots left. ... Full name: Luke Glen Richardson.
TRANSACTIONS/CAREER NOTES: Selected by Toronto Maple Leafs as underage junior in first round (first Maple Leafs pick, seventh overall) of NHL entry draft (June 13, 1987). ... Traded by Maple Leafs with LW Vincent Damphousse, G Peter Ing, C Scott Thornton and future considerations to Edmonton Oilers for G Grant Fuhr, LW Glenn Anderson and LW Craig Berube (September 19, 1991). ... Strained clavicular joint (February 11, 1992); missed three games. ... Suffered from the flu (March 1993); missed one game. ... Fractured cheekbone (January 7, 1994); missed 15 games. ... Suffered from the flu (February 28, 1995); missed two games. ... Signed as free agent by Philadelphia Flyers (July 14, 1997).

		REGULAR SEASON								PLAYOFFS				
Season Team	League	Gms.	G	A	Pts.	PIM	+/-	PP	SH	Gms.	G	A	Pts.	PIM
84-85— Ottawa Jr. B	ODHA	35	5	26	31	72	...	...	...	—	—	—	—	—
85-86— Peterborough.............	OHL	63	6	18	24	57	...	...	...	16	2	1	3	50
86-87— Peterborough.............	OHL	59	13	32	45	70	...	...	...	12	0	5	5	24
87-88— Toronto	NHL	78	4	6	10	90	-25	0	0	2	0	0	0	0
88-89— Toronto	NHL	55	2	7	9	106	-15	0	0	—	—	—	—	—
89-90— Toronto	NHL	67	4	14	18	122	-1	0	0	5	0	0	0	22
90-91— Toronto	NHL	78	1	9	10	238	-28	0	0	—	—	—	—	—
91-92— Edmonton	NHL	75	2	19	21	118	-9	0	0	16	0	5	5	45
92-93— Edmonton	NHL	82	3	10	13	142	-18	0	2	—	—	—	—	—
93-94— Edmonton	NHL	69	2	6	8	131	-13	0	0	—	—	—	—	—
94-95— Edmonton	NHL	46	3	10	13	40	-6	1	1	—	—	—	—	—
95-96— Edmonton	NHL	82	2	9	11	108	-27	0	0	—	—	—	—	—
96-97— Edmonton	NHL	82	1	11	12	91	9	0	0	12	0	2	2	14
NHL totals (10 years)		714	24	101	125	1186	-133	1	3	35	0	7	7	81

R

RICHER, STEPHANE   RW   CANADIENS

PERSONAL: Born June 7, 1966, in Buckingham, Que. ... 6-2/215. ... Shoots right. ... Full name: Stephane Joseph Jean Richer. ... Name pronounced REE-shay.

TRANSACTIONS/CAREER NOTES: Selected by Montreal Canadiens as underage junior in second round (third Canadiens pick, 29th overall) of NHL entry draft (June 9, 1984). ... Traded by Granby Bisons with LW Greg Choules to Chicoutimi Sagueneens for C Stephane Roy, RW Marc Bureau, Lee Duhemee, Sylvain Demers and D Rene L'Ecuyer (January 1985). ... Sprained ankle (November 18, 1985); missed 13 games. ... Bruised right hand (March 12, 1988). ... Broke right thumb (April 1988). ... Sprained right thumb (September 1988). ... Suspended 10 games by NHL for slashing (November 16, 1988). ... Suffered from the flu (March 15, 1989). ... Bruised right shoulder (September 1989). ... Bruised left foot (February 1990). ... Injured left ankle (April 21, 1990). ... Injured knee (December 12, 1990). ... Traded by Canadiens with RW Tom Chorske to New Jersey Devils for LW Kirk Muller and G Roland Melanson (September 20, 1991). ... Injured groin (October 22, 1991); missed two games. ... Injured left knee (March 24, 1992); missed three games. ... Injured back (December 6, 1992); missed two games. ... Pulled groin (March 14, 1995); missed two games. ... Reinjured groin (March 22, 1995); missed one game. ... Injured groin (October 17, 1995); missed one game. ... Bruised wrist (December 6, 1995); missed seven games. ... Suffered from the flu (February 11, 1996); missed one game. ... Traded by Devils to Canadiens for D Lyle Odelein (August 22, 1996). ... Suffered back spasms (November 25, 1996); missed six games. ... Bruised foot (January 20, 1997); missed five games. ... Suffered hairline fracture in foot (February 17, 1997); missed four games. ... Suffered back spasms (April 5, 1997); missed four games.

HONORS: Named QMJHL Rookie of the Year (1983-84). ... Named to QMJHL All-Star second team (1984-85). ... Played in NHL All-Star Game (1990).

STATISTICAL PLATEAUS: Three-goal games: 1987-88 (1), 1989-90 (2), 1990-91 (1), 1991-92 (1), 1992-93 (1), 1995-96 (1). Total: 7. ... Four-goal games: 1985-86 (1), 1987-88 (1). Total: 2. ... Total hat tricks: 9.

MISCELLANEOUS: Member of Stanley Cup championship team (1986 and 1995).

STATISTICAL NOTES: Led NHL with 11 game-winning goals (1987-88).

Season Team	League	REGULAR SEASON								PLAYOFFS				
		Gms.	G	A	Pts.	PIM	+/-	PP	SH	Gms.	G	A	Pts.	PIM
83-84— Granby	QMJHL	67	39	37	76	58	...	...	...	3	1	1	2	4
84-85— Granby/Chicoutimi	QMJHL	57	61	59	120	71	...	...	...	12	13	13	26	25
— Montreal	NHL	1	0	0	0	0	0	0	0	—	—	—	—	—
— Sherbrooke	AHL	—	—	—	—	—	—	—	—	9	6	3	9	10
85-86— Montreal	NHL	65	21	16	37	50	1	5	0	16	4	1	5	23
86-87— Sherbrooke	AHL	12	10	4	14	11	...	...	...	—	—	—	—	—
— Montreal	NHL	57	20	19	39	80	11	4	0	5	3	2	5	0
87-88— Montreal	NHL	72	50	28	78	72	12	16	0	8	7	5	12	6
88-89— Montreal	NHL	68	25	35	60	61	4	11	0	21	6	5	11	14
89-90— Montreal	NHL	75	51	40	91	46	35	9	0	9	7	3	10	2
90-91— Montreal	NHL	75	31	30	61	53	0	9	0	13	9	5	14	6
91-92— New Jersey	NHL	74	29	35	64	25	-1	5	1	7	1	2	3	0
92-93— New Jersey	NHL	78	38	35	73	44	-1	7	1	5	2	2	4	2
93-94— New Jersey	NHL	80	36	36	72	16	31	7	3	20	7	5	12	6
94-95— New Jersey	NHL	45	23	16	39	10	8	1	2	19	6	15	21	2
95-96— New Jersey	NHL	73	20	12	32	30	-8	3	4	—	—	—	—	—
96-97— Montreal	NHL	63	22	24	46	32	0	2	0	5	0	0	0	0
NHL totals (13 years)		826	366	326	692	519	92	79	11	128	52	45	97	61

RICHTER, BARRY   D   BRUINS

PERSONAL: Born September 11, 1970, in Madison, Wis. ... 6-0/200. ... Shoots left. ... Full name: Barron Patrick Richter. ... Name pronounced RIHK-tuhr. ... Son of Pat Richter, tight end, Washington Redskins (1963-1970).

HIGH SCHOOL: Culver (Ind.) Military Academy.

COLLEGE: Wisconsin.

TRANSACTIONS/CAREER NOTES: Selected by Hartford Whalers in second round (second Whalers pick, 32nd overall) of NHL entry draft (June 11, 1988). ... Traded by Whalers with RW Steve Larmer, LW Nick Kypreos and sixth-round pick (C Yuri Litvinov) in 1994 draft to New York Rangers for D James Patrick and C Darren Turcotte (November 2, 1993). ... Signed as free agent by Boston Bruins (July 17, 1996). ... Strained groin (November 4, 1996); missed four games.

HONORS: Named to NCAA All-Tournament team (1991-92). ... Named to NCAA All-America West first team (1992-93). ... Named to WCHA All-Star first team (1992-93). ... Named to AHL All-Star first team (1995-96). ... Won Eddie Shore Plaque (1995-96).

Season Team	League	REGULAR SEASON								PLAYOFFS				
		Gms.	G	A	Pts.	PIM	+/-	PP	SH	Gms.	G	A	Pts.	PIM
86-87— Culver Military	Indiana H.S.	35	19	26	45	...	...	...	...	—	—	—	—	—
87-88— Culver Military	Indiana H.S.	35	24	29	53	18	...	...	...	—	—	—	—	—
88-89— Culver Military	Indiana H.S.	19	21	29	50	16	...	...	...	—	—	—	—	—
89-90— Univ. of Wisconsin	WCHA	42	13	23	36	26	...	...	...	—	—	—	—	—
90-91— Univ. of Wisconsin	WCHA	43	15	20	35	42	...	...	...	—	—	—	—	—
91-92— Univ. of Wisconsin	WCHA	39	10	25	35	62	...	...	...	—	—	—	—	—
92-93— Univ. of Wisconsin	WCHA	42	14	32	46	74	...	...	...	—	—	—	—	—
93-94— U.S. national team	Int'l	56	7	16	23	50	...	...	...	—	—	—	—	—
— U.S. Olympic team	Int'l	8	0	3	3	4	...	...	...	—	—	—	—	—
— Binghamton	AHL	21	0	9	9	12	...	...	...	—	—	—	—	—
94-95— Binghamton	AHL	73	15	41	56	54	...	...	...	11	4	5	9	12
95-96— Binghamton	AHL	69	20	61	81	64	...	...	...	3	0	3	3	0
— New York Rangers	NHL	4	0	1	1	0	2	0	0	—	—	—	—	—
96-97— Boston	NHL	50	5	13	18	32	-7	1	0	—	—	—	—	—
— Providence	AHL	19	2	6	8	4	...	...	...	10	4	4	8	4
NHL totals (2 years)		54	5	14	19	32	-5	1	0					

RICHTER, MIKE   G   RANGERS

PERSONAL: Born September 22, 1966, in Philadelphia. ... 5-11/185. ... Catches left. ... Full name: Michael Thomas Richter. ... Name pronounced RIHK-tuhr.
HIGH SCHOOL: Northwood School (Lake Placid, N.Y.).
COLLEGE: Wisconsin.
TRANSACTIONS/CAREER NOTES: Selected by New York Rangers in second round (second Rangers pick, 28th overall) of NHL entry draft (June 15, 1985). ... Bruised thigh (January 30, 1992); missed 12 games. ... Injured groin (December 30, 1995); missed 15 games. ... Reinjured groin (February 18, 1996); missed eight games. ... Separated left shoulder (January 19, 1997); missed two games.
HONORS: Won WCHA Rookie of the Year Award (1985-86). ... Named to WCHA All-Star second team (1985-86 and 1986-87). ... Played in NHL All-Star Game (1992 and 1994). ... Named All-Star Game Most Valuable Player (1994).
RECORDS: Shares NHL single-season playoff record for most wins by goaltender—16 (1994).
MISCELLANEOUS: Member of Stanley Cup championship team (1994). ... Stopped a penalty shot attempt (vs. Kevin Dineen, October 19, 1989; vs. Pelle Eklund, January 14, 1990; vs. Troy Murray, November 27, 1991; vs. Steve Konowalchuk, March 5, 1995; vs. Ken Klee, March 12, 1997).

				REGULAR SEASON								PLAYOFFS					
Season Team	League	Gms.	Min	W	L	T	GA	SO	Avg.	Gms.	Min.	W	L	GA	SO	Avg.
84-85—Northwood School........	N.Y. H.S.	24	1374	...	...	...	52	2	2.27	—	—	—	—	—	—	—
85-86—Univ. of Wisconsin	WCHA	24	1394	14	9	0	92	1	3.96	—	—	—	—	—	—	—
86-87—Univ. of Wisconsin	WCHA	36	2136	19	16	1	126	0	3.54	—	—	—	—	—	—	—
87-88—U.S. national team........	Int'l	29	1559	17	7	2	86	0	3.31	—	—	—	—	—	—	—
—U.S. Olympic team........	Int'l	4	230	2	2	0	15	0	3.91	—	—	—	—	—	—	—
—Colorado.....................	IHL	22	1298	16	5	‡0	68	1	3.14	10	536	5	3	35	0	3.92
88-89—Denver...................	IHL	*57	3031	23	26	‡0	*217	1	4.30	4	210	0	4	21	0	6.00
—New York Rangers........	NHL	—	—	—	—	—	—	—	—	1	58	0	1	4	0	4.14
89-90—New York Rangers........	NHL	23	1320	12	5	5	66	0	3.00	6	330	3	2	19	0	3.45
—Flint.....................	IHL	13	782	7	4	‡2	49	0	3.76	—	—	—	—	—	—	—
90-91—New York Rangers........	NHL	45	2596	21	13	7	135	0	3.12	6	313	2	4	14	†1	2.68
91-92—New York Rangers........	NHL	41	2298	23	12	2	119	3	3.11	7	412	4	2	24	1	3.50
92-93—New York Rangers........	NHL	38	2105	13	19	3	134	1	3.82	—	—	—	—	—	—	—
—Binghamton..................	AHL	5	305	4	0	1	6	0	1.18	—	—	—	—	—	—	—
93-94—New York Rangers........	NHL	68	3710	*42	12	6	159	5	2.57	23	1417	*16	7	49	†4	2.07
94-95—New York Rangers........	NHL	35	1993	14	17	2	97	2	2.92	7	384	2	5	23	0	3.59
95-96—New York Rangers........	NHL	41	2396	24	13	3	107	3	2.68	11	661	5	6	36	0	3.27
96-97—New York Rangers........	NHL	61	3598	33	22	6	161	4	2.68	15	939	9	6	33	3	2.11
NHL totals (9 years)		352	20016	182	113	34	978	18	2.93	76	4514	41	33	202	9	2.68

RIDLEY, MIKE   C   CANUCKS

PERSONAL: Born July 8, 1963, in Winnipeg. ... 6-0/195. ... Shoots left.
COLLEGE: Manitoba.
TRANSACTIONS/CAREER NOTES: Signed as free agent by New York Rangers (September 1985). ... Traded by Rangers with LW Kelly Miller and RW Bobby Crawford to Washington Capitals for C Bobby Carpenter and second-round pick (RW Jason Prosofsky) in 1989 draft (January 1987). ... Suffered collapsed left lung (March 9, 1990); missed six games. ... Bruised ribs (April 5, 1990). ... Suffered from stomach flu (February 21, 1994); missed one game. ... Traded by Capitals with first-round pick (G Eric Fichaud) in 1994 draft to Toronto Maple Leafs for RW Rob Pearson and first-round pick (D Nolan Baumgartner) in 1994 draft (June 28, 1994). ... Traded by Maple Leafs to Vancouver Canucks for LW Sergio Momesso (July 8, 1995). ... Injured back (December 9, 1995); missed 40 games. ... Injured back (January 14, 1997); missed four games. ... Injured back (March 8, 1997); missed three games.
HONORS: Won Senator Joseph A. Sullivan Trophy (1983-84). ... Named to CIAU All-Canadian team (1983-84 and 1984-85). ... Named to NHL All-Rookie team (1985-86). ... Played in NHL All-Star Game (1989).
STATISTICAL PLATEAUS: Three-goal games: 1986-87 (1), 1988-89 (1), 1990-91 (1). Total: 3. ... Four-goal games: 1988-89 (1). ... Total hat tricks: 4.
MISCELLANEOUS: Failed to score on a penalty shot (vs. Corrado Micalef, February 16, 1986).

				REGULAR SEASON						PLAYOFFS			
Season Team	League	Gms.	G	A	Pts.	PIM	+/-	PP	SH	Gms.	G	A	Pts.	PIM
83-84—Univ. of Manitoba	CWUAA	46	39	41	80	...	...	...	...	—	—	—	—	—
84-85—Univ. of Manitoba	CWUAA	30	29	38	67	48	...	...	...	—	—	—	—	—
85-86—New York Rangers	NHL	80	22	43	65	69	0	7	0	16	6	8	14	26
86-87—New York Rangers	NHL	38	16	20	36	20	-10	4	0	—	—	—	—	—
—Washington	NHL	40	15	19	34	20	-1	6	0	7	2	1	3	6
87-88—Washington	NHL	70	28	31	59	22	1	12	0	14	6	5	11	10
88-89—Washington	NHL	80	41	48	89	49	17	16	0	6	0	5	5	2
89-90—Washington	NHL	74	30	43	73	27	0	8	3	14	3	4	7	8
90-91—Washington	NHL	79	23	48	71	26	9	6	5	11	3	4	7	8
91-92—Washington	NHL	80	29	40	69	38	3	5	5	7	0	11	11	0
92-93—Washington	NHL	84	26	56	82	44	5	6	2	6	1	5	6	0
93-94—Washington	NHL	81	26	44	70	24	15	10	2	11	4	6	10	6
94-95—Toronto	NHL	48	10	27	37	14	1	2	2	7	3	1	4	2
95-96—Vancouver.................	NHL	37	6	15	21	29	-3	2	0	5	0	0	0	2
96-97—Vancouver.................	NHL	75	20	32	52	42	0	3	0	—	—	—	—	—
NHL totals (12 years)		866	292	466	758	424	37	87	19	104	28	50	78	70

RIIHIJARVI, TEEMU   RW   SHARKS

PERSONAL: Born March 1, 1977, in Espoo, Finland. ... 6-6/202. ... Shoots left.
TRANSACTIONS/CAREER NOTES: Selected by San Jose Sharks in first round (first Sharks pick, 12th overall) of NHL entry draft (July 8, 1995).

Season Team	League	REGULAR SEASON								PLAYOFFS				
		Gms.	G	A	Pts.	PIM	+/-	PP	SH	Gms.	G	A	Pts.	PIM
93-94— Kiekko-Espoo Jrs.......	Finland	29	8	5	13	22	...	...	...	—	—	—	—	—
— Kiekko-Espoo............	Finland	13	1	1	2	6	...	...	...	—	—	—	—	—
94-95— Kiekko-Espoo Jrs.......	Finland	30	10	4	14	50	...	...	...	—	—	—	—	—
— Kiekko-Espoo............	Finland	13	1	0	1	4	...	...	...	—	—	—	—	—
95-96— Kiekko-Espoo............	Finland	2	0	0	0	0	...	...	...	—	—	—	—	—
— Haukat	Finland Dv.II	4	0	0	0	2	...	...	...	—	—	—	—	—
— Kiekko-Espoo Jrs.......	Finland	19	2	4	6	46	...	...	...	—	—	—	—	—
96-97— Kiekko-Espoo............	Finland	47	3	1	4	8	...	...	...	4	0	0	0	2

R

RIVERS, JAMIE — D — BLUES

PERSONAL: Born March 16, 1975, in Ottawa. ... 6-0/190. ... Shoots left. ... Brother of Shawn Rivers, defenseman with Tampa Bay Lightning (1992-93).
HIGH SCHOOL: Lasalle Secondary (Sudbury, Ont.).
TRANSACTIONS/CAREER NOTES: Selected by St. Louis Blues in third round (second Blues pick, 63rd overall) of NHL entry draft (June 26, 1993).
HONORS: Won Max Kaminsky Award (1993-94). ... Named to OHL All-Star first team (1993-94). ... Named to Can.HL All-Star second team (1993-94). ... Named to OHL All-Star second team (1994-95). ... Named to AHL All-Star second team (1996-97).

Season Team	League	REGULAR SEASON								PLAYOFFS				
		Gms.	G	A	Pts.	PIM	+/-	PP	SH	Gms.	G	A	Pts.	PIM
90-91— Ottawa	OHA Jr. A	55	4	30	34	74	...	...	...	—	—	—	—	—
91-92— Sudbury....................	OHL	55	3	13	16	20	...	...	...	8	0	0	0	0
92-93— Sudbury....................	OHL	62	12	43	55	20	...	...	...	14	7	19	26	4
93-94— Sudbury....................	OHL	65	32	*89	121	58	...	...	...	10	1	9	10	14
94-95— Sudbury....................	OHL	46	9	56	65	30	...	...	...	18	7	26	33	22
95-96— St. Louis	NHL	3	0	0	0	2	-1	0	0	—	—	—	—	—
— Worcester	AHL	75	7	45	52	130	...	...	...	4	0	1	1	4
96-97— Worcester	AHL	63	8	35	43	83	...	...	...	5	1	2	3	14
— St. Louis	NHL	15	2	5	7	6	-4	1	0	—	—	—	—	—
NHL totals (2 years)		18	2	5	7	8	-5	1	0					

RIVET, CRAIG — D — CANADIENS

PERSONAL: Born September 13, 1974, in North Bay, Ont. ... 6-1/190. ... Shoots right. ... Name pronounced REE-vay.
TRANSACTIONS/CAREER NOTES: Selected by Montreal Canadiens in third round (fourth Canadiens pick, 68th overall) of NHL entry draft (June 20, 1992). ... Separated shoulder (January 20, 1997); missed six games.

Season Team	League	REGULAR SEASON								PLAYOFFS				
		Gms.	G	A	Pts.	PIM	+/-	PP	SH	Gms.	G	A	Pts.	PIM
90-91— Barrie Jr. B...............	OHA	42	9	17	26	55	...	...	...	—	—	—	—	—
91-92— Kingston	OHL	66	5	21	26	97	...	...	...	—	—	—	—	—
92-93— Kingston	OHL	64	19	55	74	117	...	...	...	16	5	7	12	39
93-94— Fredericton................	AHL	4	0	2	2	2	...	...	...	—	—	—	—	—
— Kingston	OHL	61	12	52	64	100	...	...	...	6	0	3	3	6
94-95— Fredericton................	AHL	78	5	27	32	126	...	...	...	12	0	4	4	17
— Montreal	NHL	5	0	1	1	5	2	0	0	—	—	—	—	—
95-96— Fredericton................	AHL	49	5	18	23	189	...	...	...	6	0	0	0	12
— Montreal	NHL	19	1	4	5	54	4	0	0	—	—	—	—	—
96-97— Montreal	NHL	35	0	4	4	54	7	0	0	5	0	1	1	14
— Fredericton................	AHL	23	3	12	15	99	...	...	...	—	—	—	—	—
NHL totals (3 years)		59	1	9	10	113	13	0	0	5	0	1	1	14

ROBERTS, DAVE — LW — CANUCKS

PERSONAL: Born May 28, 1970, in Alameda, Calif. ... 6-0/185. ... Shoots left. ... Full name: David Lance Roberts. ... Son of Doug Roberts, defenseman for four NHL teams (1965-66 through 1974-75) and New England Whalers of WHA (1975-76 and 1976-77); and nephew of Gord Roberts, defenseman for New England Whalers of WHA (1975-76 through 1978-79) and seven NHL teams (1979-80 through 1994-95).
HIGH SCHOOL: Avon (Conn.) Old Farms School for Boys.
COLLEGE: Michigan.
TRANSACTIONS/CAREER NOTES: Selected by St. Louis Blues in sixth round (fifth Blues pick, 114th overall) of NHL entry draft (June 17, 1989). ... Injured elbow (March 7, 1995); missed one game. ... Suffered illness (April 9, 1995); missed one game. ... Traded by Blues to Edmonton Oilers for future considerations (March 12, 1996). ... Fractured cheekbone (March 19, 1996); missed 10 games. ... Signed as free agent by Vancouver Canucks (July 10, 1996). ... Suffered from the flu (December 11, 1996); missed one game. ... Injured hip flexor and strained groin (February 8, 1997); missed 12 games. ... Injured hip flexor (March 11, 1997); missed seven games.
HONORS: Named CCHA Rookie of the Year (1989-90). ... Named to CCHA All-Rookie team (1989-90). ... Named to NCAA All-America West second team (1990-91). ... Named to CCHA All-Star second team (1990-91 and 1992-93).

Season Team	League	REGULAR SEASON								PLAYOFFS				
		Gms.	G	A	Pts.	PIM	+/-	PP	SH	Gms.	G	A	Pts.	PIM
87-88— Avon Old Farms........	Conn. H.S.	...	18	39	57	...	...	...	...	—	—	—	—	—
88-89— Avon Old Farms........	Conn. H.S.	...	28	48	76	...	...	...	...	—	—	—	—	—
89-90— Univ. of Michigan.......	CCHA	42	21	32	53	46	...	...	...	—	—	—	—	—
90-91— Univ. of Michigan.......	CCHA	43	40	35	75	58	...	...	...	—	—	—	—	—
91-92— Univ. of Michigan.......	CCHA	44	16	42	58	68	...	...	...	—	—	—	—	—
92-93— Univ. of Michigan.......	CCHA	40	27	38	65	40	...	...	...	—	—	—	—	—

Season Team	League	Gms.	G	A	Pts.	PIM	+/-	PP	SH		Gms.	G	A	Pts.	PIM
93-94— U.S. national team	Int'l	49	17	28	45	68	...	...	...		—	—	—	—	—
— U.S. Olympic team.....	Int'l	8	1	5	6	4	...	...	...		—	—	—	—	—
— Peoria	IHL	10	4	6	10	4	...	...	...		—	—	—	—	—
— St. Louis	NHL	1	0	0	0	2	0	0	0		3	0	0	0	12
94-95— Peoria	IHL	65	30	38	68	65	...	...	...		—	—	—	—	—
— St. Louis	NHL	19	6	5	11	10	2	3	0		6	0	0	0	4
95-96— Worcester	AHL	22	8	17	25	46	...	...	...		—	—	—	—	—
— St. Louis	NHL	28	1	6	7	12	-7	1	0		—	—	—	—	—
— Edmonton	NHL	6	2	4	6	6	0	0	0		—	—	—	—	—
96-97— Vancouver..................	NHL	58	10	17	27	51	11	1	1		—	—	—	—	—
NHL totals (4 years)		112	19	32	51	81	6	5	1		9	0	0	0	16

ROBERTS, GARY LW R

PERSONAL: Born May 23, 1966, in North York, Ont. ... 6-1/190. ... Shoots left.

TRANSACTIONS/CAREER NOTES: Selected by Calgary Flames as underage junior in first round (first Flames pick, 12th overall) of NHL entry draft (June 9, 1984). ... Injured back (January 1989). ... Suffered whiplash (November 9, 1991); missed one game. ... Suffered from the flu (January 19, 1993); missed one game. ... Suffered left quadricep hematoma (February 16, 1993); missed 25 games. ... Suspended one game by NHL for high-sticking (November 19, 1993). ... Suspended four games and fined $500 by NHL for two slashing incidents and fined $500 for high-sticking (January 7, 1994). ... Fractured thumb (March 20, 1994); missed one game. ... Fractured thumb (April 3, 1994); missed last five games of season. ... Suffered neck and spinal injury (February 4, 1995); underwent surgery and missed last 40 games of 1994-95 season and first 42 games of 1995-96 season. ... Injured neck (April 3, 1996); missed five games. ... Announced retirement (June 17, 1996); expected to play hockey in 1997-98 season.

HONORS: Named to OHL All-Star second team (1984-85 and 1985-86). ... Played in NHL All-Star Game (1992 and 1993). ... Won Bill Masterton Memorial Trophy (1995-96).

STATISTICAL PLATEAUS: Three-goal games: 1989-90 (1), 1991-92 (2), 1992-93 (2), 1993-94 (1), 1995-96 (3). Total: 9. ... Four-goal games: 1993-94 (1). ... Total hat tricks: 10.

MISCELLANEOUS: Member of Stanley Cup championship team (1989).

Season Team	League	Gms.	G	A	Pts.	PIM	+/-	PP	SH		Gms.	G	A	Pts.	PIM
82-83— Ottawa	OHL	53	12	8	20	83	...	...			5	1	0	1	19
83-84— Ottawa	OHL	48	27	30	57	144	...	...			13	10	7	17	*62
84-85— Ottawa	OHL	59	44	62	106	186	...	...			5	2	8	10	10
— Moncton	AHL	7	4	2	6	7	...	...			—	—	—	—	—
85-86— Ottawa	OHL	24	26	25	51	83	...	...			—	—	—	—	—
— Guelph	OHL	23	18	15	33	65	...	...			20	18	13	31	43
86-87— Moncton	AHL	38	20	18	38	72	...	...			—	—	—	—	—
— Calgary	NHL	32	5	10	15	85	...	...			2	0	0	0	4
87-88— Calgary	NHL	74	13	15	28	282	...	...			9	2	3	5	29
88-89— Calgary	NHL	71	22	16	38	250	...	...			22	5	7	12	57
89-90— Calgary	NHL	78	39	33	72	222	31	5	0		6	2	5	7	41
90-91— Calgary	NHL	80	22	31	53	252	15	0	0		7	1	3	4	18
91-92— Calgary	NHL	76	53	37	90	207	32	15	0		—	—	—	—	—
92-93— Calgary	NHL	58	38	41	79	172	32	8	3		5	1	6	7	43
93-94— Calgary	NHL	73	41	43	84	145	37	12	3		7	2	6	8	24
94-95— Calgary	NHL	8	2	2	4	43	1	2	0		—	—	—	—	—
95-96— Calgary	NHL	35	22	20	42	78	15	9	0		—	—	—	—	—
96-97—							Did not play.								
NHL totals (10 years)		585	257	248	505	1736	163	51	6		58	13	30	43	216

ROBERTSSON, BERT D CANUCKS

PERSONAL: Born June 30, 1974, in Sodertalje, Sweden. ... 6-2/198. ... Shoots left. ... Name pronounced ROH-behrt-suhn.

TRANSACTIONS/CAREER NOTES: Selected by Vancouver Canucks in 10th round (eighth Canucks pick, 254th overall) of NHL entry draft (June 29, 1993).

Season Team	League	Gms.	G	A	Pts.	PIM	+/-	PP	SH		Gms.	G	A	Pts.	PIM
92-93— Sodertalje..................	Swed. Div. II	23	1	2	3	24	...	...	...		—	—	—	—	—
93-94— Sodertalje..................	Swed. Div. II	28	0	1	1	12	...	...	...		—	—	—	—	—
94-95— Sodertalje..................	Swed. Div. II	23	1	2	3	24	...	...	...		—	—	—	—	—
95-96— Syracuse....................	AHL	65	1	7	8	109	...	...	...		16	0	1	1	26
96-97— Syracuse....................	AHL	†80	4	9	13	132	...	...	...		3	1	0	1	4

ROBIDAS, STEPHANE D CANADIENS

PERSONAL: Born March 3, 1973, in Sherbrooke, Que. ... 5-11/192. ... Shoots right.

TRANSACTIONS/CAREER NOTES: Selected by Montreal Canadiens in seventh round (Canadiens seventh pick, 164th overall) of NHL entry draft (June 26, 1993).

HONORS: Won Emile Bouchard Trophy (1996-97). ... Named to Can.HL All-Star second team (1996-97). ... Named to QMJHL All-Star first team (1996-97).

Season Team	League	Gms.	G	A	Pts.	PIM	+/-	PP	SH		Gms.	G	A	Pts.	PIM
93-94— Shawinigan	QMJHL	67	3	18	21	33	...	...	...		1	0	0	0	0
94-95— Shawinigan	QMJHL	71	13	56	69	44	...	...	...		15	7	12	19	4
95-96— Shawinigan	QMJHL	67	23	56	79	53	...	...	...		6	1	5	6	10
96-97— Shawinigan	QMJHL	67	24	51	75	59	...	...	...		7	4	6	10	14

ROBITAILLE, LUC   LW   RANGERS

PERSONAL: Born February 17, 1966, in Montreal. ... 6-1/195. ... Shoots left. ... Name pronounced LOOK ROH-bih-tigh.

TRANSACTIONS/CAREER NOTES: Selected by Los Angeles Kings as underage junior in ninth round (ninth Kings pick, 171st overall) of NHL entry draft (June 9, 1984). ... Suspended four games by NHL for crosschecking from behind (November 10, 1990). ... Underwent surgery to repair slight fracture of right ankle (June 15, 1994). ... Traded by Kings to Pittsburgh Penguins for RW Rick Tocchet and second-round pick (RW Pavel Rosa) in 1995 draft (July 29, 1994). ... Suspended by NHL for two games for high-sticking (February 7, 1995). ... Traded by Penguins with D Ulf Samuelsson to New York Rangers for D Sergei Zubov and C Petr Nedved (August 31, 1995). ... Suffered stress fracture in ankle (December 15, 1995); missed five games. ... Fractured foot (March 12, 1997); missed remaining 13 games of regular season.

HONORS: Named to QMJHL All-Star second team (1984-85). ... Won Can.HL Player of the Year Award (1985-86). ... Shared Guy Lafleur Trophy with Sylvain Cote (1985-86). ... Named to QMJHL All-Star first team (1985-86). ... Named to Memorial Cup All-Star team (1985-86). ... Won Calder Memorial Trophy (1986-87). ... Named to THE SPORTING NEWS All-Star second team (1986-87 and 1991-92). ... Named to NHL All-Star second team (1986-87 and 1991-92). ... Named to NHL All-Rookie team (1986-87). ... Named to THE SPORTING NEWS All-Star first team (1987-88 through 1990-91 and 1992-93). ... Played in NHL All-Star Game (1988-1993). ... Named to NHL All-Star first team (1987-88 through 1990-91 and 1992-93).

RECORDS: Holds NHL single-season records for most points by a left-winger—125 (1992-93); and most goals by a left-winger—63 (1992-93).

STATISTICAL PLATEAUS: Three-goal games: 1986-87 (1), 1987-88 (3), 1988-89 (1), 1989-90 (2), 1992-93 (2). Total: 9. ... Four-goal games: 1991-92 (1), 1993-94 (1), 1994-95 (1). Total: 3. ... Total hat tricks: 12.

MISCELLANEOUS: Scored on a penalty shot (vs. Eldon Reddick, October 25, 1987; vs. Kay Whitmore, February 6, 1992). ... Failed to score on a penalty shot (vs. Sean Burke, February 2, 1989; vs. Jon Casey, April 3, 1993).

		REGULAR SEASON								PLAYOFFS				
Season Team	League	Gms.	G	A	Pts.	PIM	+/-	PP	SH	Gms.	G	A	Pts.	PIM
83-84— Hull	QMJHL	70	32	53	85	48	...	...	...					
84-85— Hull	QMJHL	64	55	94	149	115	...	...	...	5	4	2	6	27
85-86— Hull	QMJHL	63	68	*123	†191		...	...	...	15	17	27	*44	28
86-87— Los Angeles	NHL	79	45	39	84	28	-18	18	0	5	1	4	5	2
87-88— Los Angeles	NHL	80	53	58	111	82	-9	17	0	5	2	5	7	18
88-89— Los Angeles	NHL	78	46	52	98	65	5	10	0	11	2	6	8	10
89-90— Los Angeles	NHL	80	52	49	101	38	8	20	0	10	5	5	10	10
90-91— Los Angeles	NHL	76	45	46	91	68	28	11	0	12	12	4	16	22
91-92— Los Angeles	NHL	80	44	63	107	95	-4	26	0	6	3	4	7	12
92-93— Los Angeles	NHL	84	63	62	125	100	18	24	2	24	9	13	22	28
93-94— Los Angeles	NHL	83	44	42	86	86	-20	24	0	—	—	—	—	—
94-95— Pittsburgh	NHL	46	23	19	42	37	10	5	0	12	7	4	11	26
95-96— New York Rangers	NHL	77	23	46	69	80	13	11	0	11	1	5	6	8
96-97— New York Rangers	NHL	69	24	24	48	48	16	5	0	15	4	7	11	4
NHL totals (11 years)		832	462	500	962	727	47	171	2	111	46	57	103	140

ROBITAILLE, RANDY   C   BRUINS

PERSONAL: Born October 12, 1975, in Ottawa. ... 5-11/190. ... Shoots left.

COLLEGE: Miami of Ohio.

TRANSACTIONS/CAREER NOTES: Signed as free agent by Boston Bruins (March 27, 1997). ... Injured shoulder (March 27, 1997); missed final seven games of regular season.

HONORS: Named to CCHA All-Rookie team (1995-96). ... Named to CCHA All-Star first team (1996-97). ... Named to NCAA All-America West first team (1996-97).

		REGULAR SEASON								PLAYOFFS				
Season Team	League	Gms.	G	A	Pts.	PIM	+/-	PP	SH	Gms.	G	A	Pts.	PIM
94-95— Ottawa	CJHL	54	48	77	125	111	...	...	...	—	—	—	—	—
95-96— Miami of Ohio	CCHA	36	14	31	45	26	...	...	...	—	—	—	—	—
96-97— Miami of Ohio	CCHA	39	27	34	61	44	...	...	...	—	—	—	—	—
— Boston	NHL	1	0	0	0	0	0	0	0	—	—	—	—	—
NHL totals (1 year)		1	0	0	0	0	0	0	0	—	—	—	—	—

ROCHE, DAVE   LW   PENGUINS

PERSONAL: Born June 13, 1975, in Lindsay, Ont. ... 6-4/224. ... Shoots left. ... Name pronounced ROHSH. ... Brother of Scott Roche, goaltender in St. Louis Blues system.

TRANSACTIONS/CAREER NOTES: Selected by Pittsburgh Penguins in third round (third Penguins pick, 62nd overall) of NHL entry draft (June 26, 1993). ... Sprained ankle (November 21, 1995); missed three games. ... Injured shoulder (April 10, 1996); missed eight games. ... Suspended one playoff game and fined $1,000 by NHL for butt-ending (May 26, 1996).

		REGULAR SEASON								PLAYOFFS				
Season Team	League	Gms.	G	A	Pts.	PIM	+/-	PP	SH	Gms.	G	A	Pts.	PIM
90-91— Peterborough Jr. B	OHA	40	22	17	39	85	...	...	...	—	—	—	—	—
91-92— Peterborough	OHL	62	10	17	27	105	...	...	...	10	0	0	0	34
92-93— Peterborough	OHL	56	40	60	100	105	...	...	...	21	14	15	29	42
93-94— Peterborough	OHL	34	15	22	37	127	...	...	...	—	—	—	—	—
— Windsor	OHL	29	14	20	34	73	...	...	...	4	1	1	2	15
94-95— Windsor	OHL	66	55	59	114	180	...	...	...	10	9	6	15	16
95-96— Pittsburgh	NHL	71	7	7	14	130	-5	0	0	16	2	7	9	26
96-97— Pittsburgh	NHL	61	5	5	10	155	-13	2	0	—	—	—	—	—
— Cleveland	IHL	18	5	5	10	25	...	...	...	13	6	3	9	*87
NHL totals (2 years)		132	12	12	24	285	-18	2	0	16	2	7	9	26

ROCHE, SCOTT   G   BLUES

PERSONAL: Born March 19, 1977, in Peterborough, Ont. ... 6-4/220. ... Catches left. ... Name pronounced ROHCH. ... Brother of Dave Roche, left winger, Pittsburgh Penguins.
HIGH SCHOOL: Chippewa (North Bay, Ont.).
TRANSACTIONS/CAREER NOTES: Selected by St. Louis Blues in third round (second Blues pick, 75th overall) of NHL entry draft (July 8, 1995).
HONORS: Shared Dave Pinkney Trophy with Sandy Allan (1993-94). ... Won F.W. (Dinty) Moore Trophy (1993-94). ... Named to OHL All-Star first team (1994-95).

		REGULAR SEASON								PLAYOFFS					
Season Team	League	Gms.	Min	W	L	T	GA	SO	Avg.	Gms.	Min.	W	L	GA	SO	Avg.
93-94—North Bay	OHL	32	1587	15	5	4	93	0	3.52	5	191	2	1	9	0	2.83
94-95—North Bay	OHL	47	2599	24	17	2	167	2	3.86	6	348	2	4	30	0	5.17
95-96—North Bay	OHL	53	2859	12	29	5	232	1	4.87	—	—	—	—	—	—	—
96-97—Windsor	OHL	47	2496	20	16	4	152	1	3.65	5	267	1	4	26	0	5.84

ROCHEFORT, RICHARD   C   DEVILS

PERSONAL: Born January 7, 1977, in North Bay, Ont. ... 5-9/180. ... Shoots right.
TRANSACTIONS/CAREER NOTES: Selected by New Jersey Devils in seventh round (ninth Devils pick, 174th overall) of NHL entry draft (July 8, 1995).

		REGULAR SEASON							PLAYOFFS				
Season Team	League	Gms.	G	A	Pts.	PIM	+/-	PP	SH	Gms.	G	A	Pts.	PIM
93-94—Waterloo Jr. B	OHA	45	21	32	53	41	...	...	...	—	—	—	—	—
94-95—Sudbury	OHL	57	21	44	65	26	...	...	...	13	3	7	10	6
95-96—Sudbury	OHL	56	25	40	65	38	...	...	...	—	—	—	—	—
96-97—Sarnia	OHL	46	23	47	70	63	...	...	...	12	3	9	12	8

ROENICK, JEREMY   C/RW   COYOTES

PERSONAL: Born January 17, 1970, in Boston. ... 6-0/195. ... Shoots right. ... Name pronounced ROH-nihk.
HIGH SCHOOL: Thayer Academy (Braintree, Mass.).
TRANSACTIONS/CAREER NOTES: Selected by Chicago Blackhawks in first round (first Blackhawks pick, eighth overall) of NHL entry draft (June 11, 1988). ... Sprained knee ligaments (January 9, 1989); missed one month. ... Played in Europe during 1994-95 NHL lockout. ... Sprained knee ligament (April 2, 1995); missed remainder of season and first eight games of playoffs. ... Pulled thigh muscle (March 4, 1996); missed three games. ... Sprained ankle (March 17, 1996); missed 12 games. ... Traded by Blackhawks to Phoenix Coyotes for C Alexei Zhamnov, RW Craig Mills and first-round pick (RW Ty Jones) in 1997 draft (August 16, 1996). ... Missed first four games of 1996-97 season due to contract dispute. ... Sprained knee (November 23, 1996); missed six games.
HONORS: Named to QMJHL All-Star second team (1988-89). ... Named NHL Rookie of the Year by THE SPORTING NEWS (1989-90). ... Played in NHL All-Star Game (1991-1994).
STATISTICAL PLATEAUS: Three-goal games: 1989-90 (1), 1990-91 (2), 1992-93 (1). Total: 4. ... Four-goal games: 1991-92 (1), 1993-94 (1). Total: 2. ... Total hat tricks: 6.
MISCELLANEOUS: Failed to score on a penalty shot (vs. Andrei Trefilov, March 7, 1995).
STATISTICAL NOTES: Led NHL with 13 game-winning goals (1991-92).

		REGULAR SEASON								PLAYOFFS				
Season Team	League	Gms.	G	A	Pts.	PIM	+/-	PP	SH	Gms.	G	A	Pts.	PIM
86-87—Thayer Academy	Mass. H.S.	24	31	34	65	...	...	...	...	—	—	—	—	—
87-88—Thayer Academy	Mass. H.S.	24	34	50	84	...	...	...	...	—	—	—	—	—
88-89—U.S. national team	Int'l	11	8	8	16	0	...	...	...	—	—	—	—	—
—Chicago	NHL	20	9	9	18	4	4	2	0	10	1	3	4	7
—Hull	QMJHL	28	34	36	70	14	...	...	...	—	—	—	—	—
89-90—Chicago	NHL	78	26	40	66	54	2	6	0	20	11	7	18	8
90-91—Chicago	NHL	79	41	53	94	80	38	15	4	6	3	5	8	4
91-92—Chicago	NHL	80	53	50	103	98	23	22	3	18	12	10	22	12
92-93—Chicago	NHL	84	50	57	107	86	15	22	3	4	1	2	3	2
93-94—Chicago	NHL	84	46	61	107	125	21	24	5	6	1	6	7	2
94-95—Koln	Germany	3	3	1	4	2	...	...	...	—	—	—	—	—
—Chicago	NHL	33	10	24	34	14	5	5	0	8	1	2	3	16
95-96—Chicago	NHL	66	32	35	67	109	9	12	4	10	5	7	12	2
96-97—Phoenix	NHL	72	29	40	69	115	-7	10	3	6	2	4	6	4
NHL totals (9 years)		596	296	369	665	685	110	118	22	88	37	46	83	57

ROHLIN, LEIF   D   CANUCKS

PERSONAL: Born February 26, 1968, in Vasteras, Sweden. ... 6-1/198. ... Shoots left. ... Name pronounced LEEF roh-LEEN.
TRANSACTIONS/CAREER NOTES: Selected by Vancouver Canucks in second round (second Canucks pick, 33rd overall) of NHL entry draft (June 11, 1988).

		REGULAR SEASON							PLAYOFFS				
Season Team	League	Gms.	G	A	Pts.	PIM	+/-	PP	SH	Gms.	G	A	Pts.	PIM
86-87—Vasteras	Swed. Div. II	27	2	5	7	12	...	...	...	12	0	2	2	8
87-88—Vasteras	Swed. Div. II	30	2	15	17	46	...	...	...	7	0	4	4	8
88-89—Vasteras	Sweden	22	3	7	10	18	...	...	...	—	—	—	—	—
89-90—Vasteras	Sweden	32	3	6	9	40	...	...	...	2	0	0	0	2
90-91—Vasteras	Sweden	40	4	10	14	46	...	...	...	4	0	1	1	8
91-92—Vasteras	Sweden	39	4	6	10	52	...	...	...					

Season Team	League	REGULAR SEASON								PLAYOFFS				
		Gms.	G	A	Pts.	PIM	+/-	PP	SH	Gms.	G	A	Pts.	PIM
92-93— Vasteras	Sweden	37	5	7	12	24	...	...	...	2	0	0	0	0
93-94— Vasteras	Sweden	40	6	14	20	26	...	...	...	4	0	1	1	6
94-95— Vasteras	Sweden	39	15	15	30	46	...	...	...	4	2	0	2	2
95-96— Vancouver	NHL	56	6	16	22	32	0	1	0	5	0	0	0	0
96-97— Vancouver	NHL	40	2	8	10	8	4	0	0	—	—	—	—	—
NHL totals (2 years)		96	8	24	32	40	4	1	0	5	0	0	0	0

ROHLOFF, JON　　　D　　　BRUINS

PERSONAL: Born October 3, 1969, in Mankato, Minn. ... 5-11/220. ... Shoots right. ... Full name: Jon Richard Rohloff. ... Name pronounced ROH-lawf.
HIGH SCHOOL: Grand Rapids (Minn.).
COLLEGE: Minnesota-Duluth.
TRANSACTIONS/CAREER NOTES: Selected by Boston Bruins in ninth round (seventh Bruins pick, 186th overall) of NHL entry draft (June 11, 1988). ... Sprained ankle prior to 1996-97 season; missed 17 games. ... Strained groin (January 9, 1997); missed 23 games.
HONORS: Named to WCHA All-Star second team (1992-93).

Season Team	League	REGULAR SEASON								PLAYOFFS				
		Gms.	G	A	Pts.	PIM	+/-	PP	SH	Gms.	G	A	Pts.	PIM
86-87— Grand Rapids	Minn. H.S.	21	12	23	35	16	...	...	...	—	—	—	—	—
87-88— Grand Rapids	Minn. H.S.	23	10	13	23	...	...	...	...	—	—	—	—	—
88-89— Minnesota-Duluth	WCHA	39	1	2	3	44	...	...	...	—	—	—	—	—
89-90— Minnesota-Duluth	WCHA	5	0	1	1	6	...	...	...	—	—	—	—	—
90-91— Minnesota-Duluth	WCHA	32	6	11	17	38	...	...	...	—	—	—	—	—
91-92— Minnesota-Duluth	WCHA	27	9	9	18	48	...	...	...	—	—	—	—	—
92-93— Minnesota-Duluth	WCHA	36	15	19	34	87	...	...	...	—	—	—	—	—
93-94— Providence	AHL	55	12	23	35	59	...	...	...	—	—	—	—	—
94-95— Boston	NHL	34	3	8	11	39	1	0	0	5	0	0	0	6
— Providence	AHL	4	2	1	3	6	...	...	...	—	—	—	—	—
95-96— Boston	NHL	79	1	12	13	59	-8	1	0	5	1	2	3	2
96-97— Providence	AHL	3	1	1	2	0	...	...	...	—	—	—	—	—
— Boston	NHL	37	3	5	8	31	-14	1	0	—	—	—	—	—
NHL totals (3 years)		150	7	25	32	129	-21	2	0	10	1	2	3	8

ROLOSON, DWAYNE　　　G　　　FLAMES

PERSONAL: Born October 12, 1969, in Simcoe, Ont. ... 6-1/180. ... Catches left. ... Name pronounced ROH-luh-suhn.
COLLEGE: Massachusetts-Lowell.
TRANSACTIONS/CAREER NOTES: Signed as free agent by Calgary Flames (July 4, 1994).
HONORS: Named Hockey East Tournament Most Valuable Player (1993-94).

Season Team	League	REGULAR SEASON								PLAYOFFS						
		Gms.	Min	W	L	T	GA	SO	Avg.	Gms.	Min.	W	L	GA	SO	Avg.
90-91— Mass.-Lowell	Hoc. East	15	823	5	9	0	63	0	4.59	—	—	—	—	—	—	—
91-92— Mass.-Lowell	Hoc. East	12	660	3	8	0	52	0	4.73	—	—	—	—	—	—	—
92-93— Mass.-Lowell	Hoc. East	39	2342	20	17	2	150	0	3.84	—	—	—	—	—	—	—
93-94— Mass.-Lowell	Hoc. East	40	2305	23	10	7	106	0	2.76	—	—	—	—	—	—	—
94-95— Saint John	AHL	46	2734	16	21	8	156	1	3.42	5	299	1	4	13	0	2.61
95-96— Saint John	AHL	67	4026	33	22	11	190	1	2.83	16	1027	10	6	49	1	2.86
96-97— Calgary	NHL	31	1618	9	14	3	78	1	2.89	—	—	—	—	—	—	—
— Saint John	AHL	8	481	6	2	0	22	1	2.74	—	—	—	—	—	—	—
NHL totals (1 year)		31	1618	9	14	3	78	1	2.89							

ROLSTON, BRIAN　　　LW　　　DEVILS

PERSONAL: Born February 21, 1973, in Flint, Mich. ... 6-2/200. ... Shoots left.
COLLEGE: Lake Superior State (Mich.).
TRANSACTIONS/CAREER NOTES: Selected by New Jersey Devils in first round (second Devils pick, 11th overall) of NHL entry draft (June 22, 1991). ... Loaned by Devils to U.S. Olympic team (November 2, 1993). ... Broke foot (October 17, 1995); missed 11 games.
HONORS: Named to NCAA All-Tournament team (1991-92 and 1992-93). ... Named to NCAA All-America West second team (1992-93). ... Named to CCHA All-Star first team (1992-93).
STATISTICAL PLATEAUS: Three-goal games: 1996-97 (1).
MISCELLANEOUS: Member of Stanley Cup championship team (1995).

Season Team	League	REGULAR SEASON								PLAYOFFS				
		Gms.	G	A	Pts.	PIM	+/-	PP	SH	Gms.	G	A	Pts.	PIM
89-90— Detroit Compuware	NAJHL	40	36	37	73	57	...	...	...	—	—	—	—	—
90-91— Detroit Compuware	NAJHL	36	49	46	95	14	...	...	...	—	—	—	—	—
91-92— Lake Superior State	CCHA	41	18	28	46	16	...	...	...	—	—	—	—	—
92-93— Lake Superior State	CCHA	39	33	31	64	20	...	...	...	—	—	—	—	—
93-94— U.S. national team	Int'l	41	20	28	48	36	...	...	...	—	—	—	—	—
— U.S. Olympic team	Int'l	8	7	0	7	8	...	...	...	—	—	—	—	—
— Albany	AHL	17	5	5	10	8	...	...	...	5	1	2	3	0
94-95— Albany	AHL	18	9	11	20	10	...	...	...	—	—	—	—	—
— New Jersey	NHL	40	7	11	18	17	5	2	0	6	2	1	3	4
95-96— New Jersey	NHL	58	13	11	24	8	9	3	1	—	—	—	—	—
96-97— New Jersey	NHL	81	18	27	45	20	6	2	2	10	4	1	5	6
NHL totals (3 years)		179	38	49	87	45	20	7	3	16	6	2	8	10

RONAN, ED   RW   SABRES

PERSONAL: Born March 21, 1968, in Quincy, Mass. ... 6-0/197. ... Shoots right. ... Name pronounced ROH-nuhn.
COLLEGE: Boston University.
TRANSACTIONS/CAREER NOTES: Selected by Montreal Canadiens in 11th round (13th Canadiens pick, 227th overall) of NHL entry draft (June 13, 1987). ... Suffered concussion (October 6, 1993); missed four games. ... Suffered from the flu (March 6, 1994); missed one game. ... Signed as free agent by Winnipeg Jets (October 13, 1995). ... Signed as free agent by Buffalo Sabres (September 5, 1996).
MISCELLANEOUS: Member of Stanley Cup championship team (1993).

Season Team	League	Gms.	G	A	Pts.	PIM	+/-	PP	SH	Gms.	G	A	Pts.	PIM
87-88 — Boston University	Hockey East	31	2	5	7	20	...	...	...	—	—	—	—	—
88-89 — Boston University	Hockey East	36	4	11	15	34	...	...	...	—	—	—	—	—
89-90 — Boston University	Hockey East	44	17	23	40	50	...	...	...	—	—	—	—	—
90-91 — Boston University	Hockey East	41	16	19	35	38	...	...	...	—	—	—	—	—
91-92 — Fredericton.................	AHL	78	25	34	59	82	...	...	...	7	5	1	6	6
— Montreal	NHL	3	0	0	0	0	0	0	0	—	—	—	—	—
92-93 — Montreal	NHL	53	5	7	12	20	6	0	0	14	2	3	5	10
— Fredericton.................	AHL	16	10	5	15	15	...	...	...	5	2	4	6	6
93-94 — Montreal	NHL	61	6	8	14	42	3	0	0	7	1	0	1	0
94-95 — Montreal	NHL	30	1	4	5	12	-7	0	0	—	—	—	—	—
95-96 — Winnipeg	NHL	17	0	0	0	16	-3	0	0	—	—	—	—	—
— Springfield	AHL	31	8	16	24	50	...	...	...	10	7	6	13	4
96-97 — Rochester	AHL	47	13	21	34	62	...	...	...	—	—	—	—	—
— Buffalo	NHL	18	1	4	5	11	4	0	0	6	1	0	1	6
NHL totals (6 years)		182	13	23	36	101	3	0	0	27	4	3	7	16

R

RONNING, CLIFF   C   COYOTES

PERSONAL: Born October 1, 1965, in Vancouver. ... 5-8/170. ... Shoots left.
HIGH SCHOOL: Burnaby North (B.C.).
TRANSACTIONS/CAREER NOTES: Selected by St. Louis Blues as underage junior in seventh round (ninth Blues pick, 134th overall) of NHL entry draft (June 9, 1984). ... Injured groin (November 1988). ... Agreed to play in Italy for 1989-90 season (August 1989). ... Fractured right index finger (November 12, 1990); missed 12 games. ... Traded by Blues with LW Geoff Courtnall, D Robert Dirk, LW Sergio Momesso and fifth-round pick (RW Brian Loney) in 1992 draft to Vancouver Canucks for C Dan Quinn and D Garth Butcher (March 5, 1991). ... Sprained hand (January 4, 1993). ... Separated shoulder (January 8, 1994); missed eight games. ... Strained groin (February 9, 1995); missed four games. ... Injured groin (October 8, 1995); missed two games. ... Signed as free agent by Phoenix Coyotes (July 2, 1996). ... Fractured hand (October 10, 1996); missed 12 games. ... Suffered from the flu (December 17, 1996); missed one game.
HONORS: Won Stewart (Butch) Paul Memorial Trophy (1983-84). ... Named to WHL All-Star second team (1983-84). ... Won WHL Most Valuable Player Trophy (1984-85). ... Won Bob Brownridge Memorial Trophy (1984-85). ... Won Frank Boucher Memorial Trophy (1984-85). ... Named to WHL (West) All-Star first team (1984-85).
STATISTICAL PLATEAUS: Three-goal games: 1986-87 (1), 1992-93 (1), 1995-96 (1). Total: 3.

Season Team	League	Gms.	G	A	Pts.	PIM	+/-	PP	SH	Gms.	G	A	Pts.	PIM
82-83 — New Westminster	BCJHL	52	82	68	150	42	...	...	...	—	—	—	—	—
83-84 — New Westminster	WHL	71	69	67	136	10	...	...	...	9	8	13	21	10
84-85 — New Westminster	WHL	70	*89	108	*197	20	...	...	...	11	10	14	24	4
85-86 — Canadian nat'l team ...	Int'l	71	55	63	118	53	...	...	...	—	—	—	—	—
— St. Louis	NHL	—	—	—	—	—	...	...	...	5	1	1	2	2
86-87 — Canadian nat'l team ...	Int'l	26	16	16	32	12	...	...	...	—	—	—	—	—
— St. Louis	NHL	42	11	14	25	6	-1	2	0	4	0	1	1	0
87-88 — St. Louis	NHL	26	5	8	13	12	6	1	0	—	—	—	—	—
88-89 — St. Louis	NHL	64	24	31	55	18	3	16	0	7	1	3	4	0
— Peoria	IHL	12	11	20	31	8	...	...	...	—	—	—	—	—
89-90 — Asiago......................	Italy	42	76	60	136	30	...	...	...	6	7	12	19	4
90-91 — St. Louis	NHL	48	14	18	32	10	2	5	0	—	—	—	—	—
— Vancouver..................	NHL	11	6	6	12	0	-2	2	0	6	6	3	9	12
91-92 — Vancouver..................	NHL	80	24	47	71	42	18	6	0	13	8	5	13	6
92-93 — Vancouver..................	NHL	79	29	56	85	30	19	10	0	12	2	9	11	6
93-94 — Vancouver..................	NHL	76	25	43	68	42	7	10	0	24	5	10	15	16
94-95 — Vancouver..................	NHL	41	6	19	25	27	-4	3	0	11	3	5	8	2
95-96 — Vancouver..................	NHL	79	22	45	67	42	16	5	0	6	0	2	2	6
96-97 — Phoenix......................	NHL	69	19	32	51	26	-9	8	0	7	0	7	7	12
NHL totals (11 years)		615	185	319	504	255	55	68	0	95	26	46	72	62

ROSA, PAVEL   RW   KINGS

PERSONAL: Born June 7, 1977, in Most, Czechoslovakia. ... 5-11/178. ... Shoots right.
TRANSACTIONS/CAREER NOTES: Selected by Los Angeles Kings in second round (third Kings pick, 50th overall) of NHL entry draft (July 8, 1995).
HONORS: Won Michel Bergeron Trophy (1995-96). ... Named to QMJHL All-Rookie team (1995-96). ... Won Can.HL Top Scorer Award (1996-97). ... Won Jean Beliveau Trophy (1996-97). ... Named to Can.HL All-Star first team (1996-97). ... Named to QMJHL All-Star first team (1996-97).

Season Team	League	Gms.	G	A	Pts.	PIM	+/-	PP	SH	Gms.	G	A	Pts.	PIM
94-95 — Chemo. Litvinov Jrs...	Czech Rep.	40	56	42	98	...	...	...	...	—	—	—	—	—
— Chemo. Litvinov.........	Czech Rep.	—	—	—	—	—	...	...	...	1	0	0	0	0
95-96 — Hull	QMJHL	61	46	70	116	39	...	...	...	18	14	22	36	25
96-97 — Hull	QMJHL	68	*63	*89	*152	56	...	...	...	14	18	13	31	16

ROUSE, BOB — D — RED WINGS

PERSONAL: Born June 18, 1964, in Surrey, B.C. ... 6-2/210. ... Shoots right. ... Name pronounced ROWZ.
TRANSACTIONS/CAREER NOTES: Selected by Minnesota North Stars as underage junior in fourth round (third North Stars pick, 80th overall) of NHL entry draft (June 9, 1982). ... Suffered hip contusions (January 1988). ... Traded by North Stars with RW Dino Ciccarelli to Washington Capitals for RW Mike Gartner and D Larry Murphy (March 7, 1989). ... Sprained right knee (December 12, 1989); missed eight games. ... Traded by Capitals with C Peter Zezel to Toronto Maple Leafs for D Al Iafrate (January 16, 1991). ... Broke collarbone (February 16, 1991). ... Suspended four games by NHL for stick-swinging incident (October 14, 1993). ... Strained knee (December 29, 1993); missed three games. ... Tore knee cartilage (January 29, 1994); missed 14 games. ... Signed as free agent by Detroit Red Wings (August 5, 1994). ... Underwent hernia surgery (September 9, 1995); missed five games. ... Suffered from the flu (March 26, 1997); missed two games.
HONORS: Won Top Defenseman Trophy (1983-84). ... Named to WHL (East) All-Star first team (1983-84).
MISCELLANEOUS: Member of Stanley Cup championship team (1997). ... Captain of Minnesota North Stars (1988-89).

| | | REGULAR SEASON | | | | | | | | | PLAYOFFS | | | | |
Season Team	League	Gms.	G	A	Pts.	PIM	+/-	PP	SH	Gms.	G	A	Pts.	PIM
80-81 — Billings	WHL	70	0	13	13	116	...	...	...	5	0	0	0	2
81-82 — Billings	WHL	71	7	22	29	209	...	...	...	5	0	2	2	10
82-83 — Nanaimo	WHL	29	7	20	27	86	...	...	...	—	—	—	—	—
— Lethbridge	WHL	42	8	30	38	82	...	...	...	20	2	13	15	55
83-84 — Lethbridge	WHL	71	18	42	60	101	...	...	...	5	0	1	1	28
— Minnesota	NHL	1	0	0	0	0	0	0	0	—	—	—	—	—
84-85 — Springfield	AHL	8	0	3	3	6	...	...	...	—	—	—	—	—
— Minnesota	NHL	63	2	9	11	113	-14	0	0	—	—	—	—	—
85-86 — Minnesota	NHL	75	1	14	15	151	15	0	0	3	0	0	0	2
86-87 — Minnesota	NHL	72	2	10	12	179	6	0	0	—	—	—	—	—
87-88 — Minnesota	NHL	74	0	12	12	168	-30	0	0	—	—	—	—	—
88-89 — Minnesota	NHL	66	4	13	17	124	-5	0	1	—	—	—	—	—
— Washington	NHL	13	0	2	2	36	2	0	0	6	2	0	2	4
89-90 — Washington	NHL	70	4	16	20	123	-2	0	0	15	2	3	5	47
90-91 — Washington	NHL	47	5	15	20	65	-7	1	0	—	—	—	—	—
— Toronto	NHL	13	2	4	6	10	-11	1	0	—	—	—	—	—
91-92 — Toronto	NHL	79	3	19	22	97	-20	1	0	—	—	—	—	—
92-93 — Toronto	NHL	82	3	11	14	130	7	0	1	21	3	8	11	29
93-94 — Toronto	NHL	63	5	11	16	101	8	1	1	18	0	3	3	29
94-95 — Detroit	NHL	48	1	7	8	36	14	0	0	18	0	3	3	8
95-96 — Detroit	NHL	58	0	6	6	48	5	0	0	7	0	1	1	4
96-97 — Detroit	NHL	70	4	9	13	58	8	0	2	20	0	0	0	55
NHL totals (14 years)		894	36	158	194	1439	-24	4	5	108	7	18	25	178

ROUSSEL, DOMINIC — G — FLYERS

PERSONAL: Born February 22, 1970, in Hull, Que. ... 6-1/190. ... Catches left. ... Name pronounced roo-SEHL.
TRANSACTIONS/CAREER NOTES: Selected by Philadelphia Flyers as underage junior in third round (fourth Flyers pick, 63rd overall) of NHL entry draft (June 11, 1988). ... Pulled groin (November 29, 1992); missed three games. ... Reinjured groin (December 11, 1992); missed 11 games. ... Suffered from the flu (March 24, 1994); missed three games. ... Suffered inner ear infection (March 2, 1995); missed five games. ... Traded by Flyers to Winnipeg Jets for G Tim Cheveldae and third-round pick (RW Chester Gallant) in 1996 draft (February 27, 1996). ... Signed as free agent by Flyers (July 10, 1996).

| | | REGULAR SEASON | | | | | | | PLAYOFFS | | | | | |
Season Team	League	Gms.	Min	W	L	T	GA	SO	Avg.	Gms.	Min.	W	L	GA	SO	Avg.
87-88 — Trois-Rivieres	QMJHL	51	2905	18	25	4	251	0	5.18	—	—	—	—	—	—	—
88-89 — Shawinigan	QMJHL	46	2555	24	15	2	171	0	4.02	10	638	6	4	36	0	3.39
89-90 — Shawinigan	QMJHL	37	1985	20	14	1	133	0	4.02	2	120	1	1	12	0	6.00
90-91 — Hershey	AHL	45	2507	20	14	7	151	1	3.61	7	366	3	4	21	0	3.44
91-92 — Hershey	AHL	35	2040	15	11	6	121	1	3.56	—	—	—	—	—	—	—
— Philadelphia	NHL	17	922	7	8	2	40	1	2.60	—	—	—	—	—	—	—
92-93 — Philadelphia	NHL	34	1769	13	11	5	111	1	3.76	—	—	—	—	—	—	—
— Hershey	AHL	6	372	0	3	3	23	0	3.71	—	—	—	—	—	—	—
93-94 — Philadelphia	NHL	60	3285	29	20	5	183	1	3.34	—	—	—	—	—	—	—
94-95 — Philadelphia	NHL	19	1075	11	7	0	42	1	2.34	1	23	0	0	0	0	0.00
— Hershey	AHL	1	59	0	1	0	5	0	5.08	—	—	—	—	—	—	—
95-96 — Philadelphia	NHL	9	456	2	3	2	22	1	2.89	—	—	—	—	—	—	—
— Hershey	AHL	12	689	4	4	3	32	0	2.79	—	—	—	—	—	—	—
— Winnipeg	NHL	7	285	2	2	0	16	0	3.37	—	—	—	—	—	—	—
96-97 — Philadelphia	AHL	36	1852	18	9	3	82	2	2.66	1	26	0	0	3	0	6.92
NHL totals (6 years)		146	7792	64	51	14	414	5	3.19	1	23	0	0	0	0	0.00

ROY, ANDRE — LW — BRUINS

PERSONAL: Born February 8, 1975, in Port Chester, N.Y. ... 6-3/202. ... Shoots left. ... Name pronounced WAH.
TRANSACTIONS/CAREER NOTES: Selected by Boston Bruins in sixth round (fifth Bruins pick, 151st overall) of NHL entry draft (June 29, 1994).

| | | REGULAR SEASON | | | | | | | | PLAYOFFS | | | | |
Season Team	League	Gms.	G	A	Pts.	PIM	+/-	PP	SH	Gms.	G	A	Pts.	PIM
93-94 — Beauport	QMJHL	33	6	7	13	125	...	...	...	—	—	—	—	—
— Chicoutimi	QMJHL	32	4	14	18	152	...	...	...	25	3	6	9	94
94-95 — Chicoutimi	QMJHL	20	15	8	23	90	...	...	...	—	—	—	—	—
— Drummondville	QMJHL	34	18	13	31	233	...	...	...	4	2	0	2	34
95-96 — Providence	AHL	58	7	8	15	167	...	...	...	1	0	0	0	10

Season Team	League	REGULAR SEASON								PLAYOFFS				
		Gms.	G	A	Pts.	PIM	+/-	PP	SH	Gms.	G	A	Pts.	PIM
— Boston	NHL	3	0	0	0	0	0	0	0	—	—	—	—	—
96-97— Providence	AHL	50	17	11	28	234	...	...	...	—	—	—	—	—
— Boston	NHL	10	0	2	2	12	-5	0	0	—	—	—	—	—
NHL totals (2 years)		13	0	2	2	12	-5	0	0					

ROY, JEAN-YVES   RW   BRUINS

PERSONAL: Born February 17, 1969, in Rosemere, Que. ... 5-10/180. ... Shoots left. ... Name pronounced ZHAHN-eev WAH.
COLLEGE: Maine.
TRANSACTIONS/CAREER NOTES: Signed as free agent by New York Rangers (July 20, 1992). ... Traded by Rangers to Ottawa Senators for C Steve Larouche (October 6, 1995). ... Signed as free agent by Boston Bruins (July 9, 1996).
HONORS: Named to NCAA All-America East second team (1989-90). ... Named to Hockey East All-Rookie team (1989-90). ... Named to NCAA All-America East first team (1990-91 and 1991-92). ... Named to NCAA All-Tournament team (1990-91). ... Named to Hockey East All-Star first team (1990-91). ... Named to Hockey East All-Star second team (1991-92).
MISCELLANEOUS: Member of silver-medal-winning Canadian Olympic team (1994).

Season Team	League	REGULAR SEASON								PLAYOFFS				
		Gms.	G	A	Pts.	PIM	+/-	PP	SH	Gms.	G	A	Pts.	PIM
89-90— University of Maine	Hockey East	46	39	26	65	52	...	...	...	—	—	—	—	—
90-91— University of Maine	Hockey East	43	37	45	82	26	...	...	...	—	—	—	—	—
91-92— University of Maine	Hockey East	35	32	24	56	62	...	...	...	—	—	—	—	—
92-93— Canadian nat'l team	Int'l	23	9	6	15	35	...	...	...	—	—	—	—	—
— Binghamton	AHL	49	13	15	28	21	...	...	...	14	5	2	7	4
93-94— Binghamton	AHL	65	41	24	65	33	...	...	...	—	—	—	—	—
— Canadian nat'l team	Int'l	6	3	2	5	2	...	...	...	—	—	—	—	—
— Can. Olympic team	Int'l	8	1	0	1	19	...	...	...	—	—	—	—	—
94-95— Binghamton	AHL	67	41	36	77	28	...	...	...	11	4	6	10	12
— New York Rangers	NHL	3	1	0	1	2	-1	0	0	—	—	—	—	—
95-96— Prin. Edward Island	AHL	67	40	55	95	64	...	...	...	5	4	9	13	6
— Ottawa	NHL	4	1	1	2	2	3	0	0	—	—	—	—	—
96-97— Providence	AHL	27	9	16	25	30	...	...	...	10	2	7	9	2
— Boston	NHL	52	10	15	25	22	-8	2	0	—	—	—	—	—
NHL totals (3 years)		59	12	16	28	26	-6	2	0					

ROY, PATRICK   G   AVALANCHE

PERSONAL: Born October 5, 1965, in Quebec City. ... 6-0/192. ... Catches left. ... Name pronounced WAH.
TRANSACTIONS/CAREER NOTES: Selected by Montreal Canadiens as underage junior in third round (fourth Canadiens pick, 51st overall) of NHL entry draft (June 9, 1984). ... Suspended eight games by NHL for slashing (October 19, 1987). ... Sprained left knee ligaments (December 12, 1990); missed nine games. ... Tore left ankle ligaments (January 27, 1991); missed 14 games. ... Reinjured left ankle (March 16, 1991). ... Strained hip flexor (March 6, 1993); missed two games. ... Suffered stiff neck (December 11, 1993); missed two games. ... Strained neck (December 22, 1993); missed four games. ... Traded by Canadiens with RW Mike Keane to Colorado Avalanche for G Jocelyn Thibault, LW Martin Rucinsky and RW Andrei Kovalenko (December 6, 1995). ... Sprained thumb (January 23, 1997); missed two games. ... Injured shoulder (March 26, 1997); missed two games.
HONORS: Won Conn Smythe Trophy (1985-86 and 1992-93). ... Named to NHL All-Rookie team (1985-86). ... Shared William M. Jennings Trophy with Brian Hayward (1986-87 through 1988-89). ... Named to NHL All-Star second team (1987-88 and 1990-91). ... Named to THE SPORTING NEWS All-Star first team (1988-89, 1989-90 and 1991-92). ... Won Trico Goaltender Award (1988-89 and 1989-90). ... Named to NHL All-Star first team (1988-89, 1989-90 and 1991-92). ... Won Vezina Trophy (1988-89, 1989-90 and 1991-92). ... Played in NHL All-Star Game (1988, 1990-1994 and 1997). ... Named to THE SPORTING NEWS All-Star second team (1990-91). ... Won William M. Jennings Trophy (1991-92).
RECORDS: Holds NHL career playoff record for most games played by goaltender—153. ... Shares NHL single-season playoff records for most wins by goaltender—16 (1993 and 1996); and most consecutive wins by goaltender—11 (1993).
MISCELLANEOUS: Member of Stanley Cup championship team (1986, 1993 and 1996). ... Holds Colorado Avalanche franchise all-time records for most shutouts (8) and goals-against average (2.46). ... Stopped a penalty shot attempt (vs. Dan Daoust, January 1, 1986; vs. Ville Peltonen, March 5, 1996; vs. Jamie Baker, March 28, 1996). ... Allowed a penalty shot goal (vs. Michel Goulet, January 10, 1987; vs. Jock Callender, March 18, 1989; vs. Pierre Turgeon, October 17, 1990; vs. Kevin Miller, October 10, 1991; vs. Theoren Fleury, October 22, 1996).
STATISTICAL NOTES: Led NHL in save percentage with .900 in 1987-88, .908 in 1988-89, .912 in 1989-90 and .914 in 1991-92.

Season Team	League	REGULAR SEASON								PLAYOFFS						
		Gms.	Min	W	L	T	GA	SO	Avg.	Gms.	Min.	W	L	GA	SO	Avg.
82-83— Granby	QMJHL	54	2808	...	...	...	293	0	6.26	—	—	—	—	—	—	—
83-84— Granby	QMJHL	61	3585	29	29	1	265	0	4.44	4	244	0	4	22	0	5.41
84-85— Granby	QMJHL	44	2463	16	25	1	228	0	5.55	—	—	—	—	—	—	—
—Montreal	NHL	1	20	1	0	0	0	0	0.00	—	—	—	—	—	—	—
—Sherbrooke	AHL	1	60	1	0	0	4	0	4.00	*13	*769	10	3	37	0	*2.89
85-86— Montreal	NHL	47	2651	23	18	3	148	1	3.35	20	1218	*15	5	39	†1	1.92
86-87— Montreal	NHL	46	2686	22	16	6	131	1	2.93	6	330	4	2	22	0	4.00
87-88— Montreal	NHL	45	2586	23	12	9	125	3	2.90	8	430	3	4	24	0	3.35
88-89— Montreal	NHL	48	2744	33	5	6	113	4	*2.47	19	1206	13	6	42	2	*2.09
89-90— Montreal	NHL	54	3173	31	16	5	134	3	2.53	11	641	5	6	26	1	2.43
90-91— Montreal	NHL	48	2835	25	15	6	128	1	2.71	13	785	7	5	40	0	3.06
91-92— Montreal	NHL	67	3935	36	22	8	155	†5	*2.36	11	686	4	7	30	1	2.62
92-93— Montreal	NHL	62	3595	31	25	5	192	2	3.20	20	1293	*16	4	46	0	*2.13
93-94— Montreal	NHL	68	3867	35	17	11	161	†7	2.50	6	375	3	3	16	0	2.56
94-95— Montreal	NHL	†43	2566	17	20	6	127	1	2.97	—	—	—	—	—	—	—
95-96— Montreal	NHL	22	1260	12	9	1	62	1	2.95	—	—	—	—	—	—	—
— Colorado	NHL	39	2305	22	15	1	103	1	2.68	22	*1454	*16	6	*51	*3	2.10
96-97— Colorado	NHL	62	3698	*38	15	7	143	7	2.32	17	1034	10	7	38	3	2.21
NHL totals (13 years)		652	37921	349	205	74	1722	37	2.72	153	9452	96	55	374	11	2.37

ROY, STEPHANE   C   BLUES

PERSONAL: Born January 26, 1976, in Ste.-Martine, Que. ... 6-0/190. ... Shoots left. ... Name pronounced WAH.
TRANSACTIONS/CAREER NOTES: Selected by St. Louis Blues in third round (first Blues pick, 68th overall) of NHL entry draft (June 29, 1994).

Season Team	League	REGULAR SEASON								PLAYOFFS				
		Gms.	G	A	Pts.	PIM	+/-	PP	SH	Gms.	G	A	Pts.	PIM
93-94— Val-d'Or	QMJHL	72	25	28	53	116	...	...	...	—	—	—	—	—
94-95— St. Jean	QMJHL	68	19	52	71	113	...	...	...	—	—	—	—	—
95-96— Val-d'Or	QMJHL	62	43	72	115	89	...	...	...	13	9	15	24	10
— Worcester	AHL	1	0	0	0	2	...	...	...	0	0	0	0	0
96-97— Worcester	AHL	66	24	23	47	57	...	...	...	5	2	0	2	4

ROYER, REMI   D   BLACKHAWKS

PERSONAL: Born February 12, 1978, in Donnacona, Que. ... 6-1/183. ... Shoots right. ... Brother of Gaetan Royer, right winger in Chicago Blackhawks system.
TRANSACTIONS/CAREER NOTES: Selected by Chicago Blackhawks in second round (first Blackhawks pick, 31st overall) of NHL entry draft (June 22, 1996).

Season Team	League	REGULAR SEASON								PLAYOFFS				
		Gms.	G	A	Pts.	PIM	+/-	PP	SH	Gms.	G	A	Pts.	PIM
94-95— Victoriaville	QMJHL	57	3	17	20	144	...	...	...	4	0	1	1	7
95-96— Victoriaville	QMJHL	43	12	14	26	209	...	...	...	—	—	—	—	—
— St. Hyacinthe	QMJHL	19	10	9	19	80	...	...	...	12	1	4	5	29
96-97— Rouyn-Noranda	QMJHL	29	3	12	15	87	...	...	...	—	—	—	—	—
— Indianapolis	IHL	10	0	1	1	17	...	...	...	—	—	—	—	—

ROZSIVAL, MICHAL   D   PENGUINS

PERSONAL: Born September 3, 1978, in Vlasim, Czechoslovakia. ... 6-1/189. ... Shoots right. ... Name pronounced ROH-sih-vahl.
TRANSACTIONS/CAREER NOTES: Selected by Pittsburgh Penguins in fourth round (fifth Penguins pick, 105th overall) of NHL entry draft (June 22, 1996).

Season Team	League	REGULAR SEASON								PLAYOFFS				
		Gms.	G	A	Pts.	PIM	+/-	PP	SH	Gms.	G	A	Pts.	PIM
94-95— Dukla Jihlava Jrs.	Czech Rep.	31	8	13	21		...	...	...	—	—	—	—	—
95-96— Dukla Jihlava Jrs.	Czech Rep.	36	3	4	7		...	...	...	—	—	—	—	—
96-97— Swift Current	WHL	63	8	31	39	80	...	...	...	10	0	6	6	15

RUCCHIN, STEVE   C   MIGHTY DUCKS

PERSONAL: Born July 4, 1971, in Thunder Bay, Ont. ... 6-3/215. ... Shoots left. ... Name pronounced ROO-shihn.
COLLEGE: Western Ontario.
TRANSACTIONS/CAREER NOTES: Selected by Mighty Ducks of Anaheim in first round (first Mighty Ducks pick, second overall) of NHL supplemental draft (June 28, 1994). ... Suffered from the flu (March 7, 1995); missed two games. ... Sprained left knee (November 27, 1995); missed 18 games.
HONORS: Named OUAA Player of the Year (1993-94). ... Named to CIAU All-Star first team (1993-94).

Season Team	League	REGULAR SEASON								PLAYOFFS				
		Gms.	G	A	Pts.	PIM	+/-	PP	SH	Gms.	G	A	Pts.	PIM
90-91— Univ. of W. Ontario	OUAA	34	13	16	29	14	...	...	...	—	—	—	—	—
91-92— Univ. of W. Ontario	OUAA	37	28	34	62	36	...	...	...	—	—	—	—	—
92-93— Univ. of W. Ontario	OUAA	34	22	26	48	16	...	...	...	—	—	—	—	—
93-94— Univ. of W. Ontario	OUAA	35	30	23	53	30	...	...	...	—	—	—	—	—
94-95— San Diego	IHL	41	11	15	26	14	...	...	...	—	—	—	—	—
— Anaheim	NHL	43	6	11	17	23	7	0	0	—	—	—	—	—
95-96— Anaheim	NHL	64	19	25	44	12	3	8	1	—	—	—	—	—
96-97— Anaheim	NHL	79	19	48	67	24	26	6	1	8	1	2	3	10
NHL totals (3 years)		186	44	84	128	59	36	14	2	8	1	2	3	10

RUCINSKY, MARTIN   LW   CANADIENS

PERSONAL: Born March 11, 1971, in Most, Czechoslovakia. ... 6-0/198. ... Shoots left. ... Name pronounced roo-SHIHN-skee.
TRANSACTIONS/CAREER NOTES: Selected by Edmonton Oilers in first round (second Oilers pick, 20th overall) of NHL entry draft (June 22, 1991). ... Traded by Oilers to Quebec Nordiques for G Ron Tugnutt and LW Brad Zavisha (March 10, 1992). ... Suffered from the flu (February 28, 1993); missed one game. ... Bruised buttocks (December 3, 1994); missed one game. ... Sprained right wrist (January 11, 1994); missed one game. ... Broke left cheek (January 30, 1994); missed four games. ... Suffered hairline fracture of right wrist (March 7, 1994); missed one game. ... Suffered hairline fracture of right wrist (March 21, 1994); missed six games. ... Suffered hairline fracture of right wrist (April 5, 1994); missed one game. ... Played in Europe during 1994-95 NHL lockout. ... Separated shoulder (February 25, 1995); missed 17 games. ... Reinjured shoulder (April 6, 1995); missed last 11 games of season and playoffs. ... Nordiques franchise moved to Colorado and renamed Avalanche for 1995-96 season (June 21, 1995). ... Traded by Avalanche with G Jocelyn Thibault and RW Andrei Kovalenko to Montreal Canadiens for G Patrick Roy and RW Mike Keane (December 6, 1995). ... Sprained right knee (April 6, 1996); missed two games. ... Injured hand (October 19, 1996); missed one game. ... Strained knee (November 25, 1996); missed one game. ... Separated shoulder (December 28, 1996); missed 10 games.
STATISTICAL PLATEAUS: Three-goal games: 1995-96 (1), 1996-97 (1). Total: 2.

Season Team	League	Gms.	G	A	Pts.	PIM	+/-	PP	SH	Gms.	G	A	Pts.	PIM
88-89— CHZ Litvinov	Czech.	3	1	0	1	2	...	...	...	—	—	—	—	—
89-90— CHZ Litvinov	Czech.	47	12	6	18	...	...	...	...	—	—	—	—	—
90-91— CHZ Litvinov	Czech.	49	23	18	41	79	...	...	...	—	—	—	—	—
— Czechoslovakia Jr.	Czech.	7	9	5	14	2	...	...	...	—	—	—	—	—
91-92— Cape Breton	AHL	35	11	12	23	34	...	...	...	—	—	—	—	—
— Edmonton	NHL	2	0	0	0	0	-3	0	0	—	—	—	—	—
— Halifax	AHL	7	1	1	2	6	...	...	...	—	—	—	—	—
— Quebec	NHL	4	1	1	2	2	1	0	0	—	—	—	—	—
92-93— Quebec	NHL	77	18	30	48	51	16	4	0	6	1	1	2	4
93-94— Quebec	NHL	60	9	23	32	58	4	4	0	—	—	—	—	—
94-95— Chemo. Litvinov	Czech Rep.	13	12	10	22	34	...	...	...	—	—	—	—	—
— Quebec	NHL	20	3	6	9	14	5	0	0	—	—	—	—	—
95-96— Colorado	NHL	22	4	11	15	14	10	0	0	—	—	—	—	—
— Montreal	NHL	56	25	35	60	54	8	9	2	—	—	—	—	—
96-97— Montreal	NHL	70	28	27	55	62	1	6	3	5	0	0	0	4
NHL totals (7 years)		311	88	133	221	255	42	23	5	11	1	1	2	8

RUMBLE, DARREN — D — FLYERS

PERSONAL: Born January 23, 1969, in Barrie, Ont. ... 6-1/200. ... Shoots left. ... Full name: Darren William Rumble.
HIGH SCHOOL: Eastview (Barrie, Ont.).
TRANSACTIONS/CAREER NOTES: Selected by Philadelphia Flyers as underage junior in first round (first Flyers pick, 20th overall) of NHL entry draft (June 13, 1987). ... Stretched knee ligaments (November 27, 1988). ... Selected by Ottawa Senators in NHL expansion draft (June 18, 1992). ... Bruised thigh (November 29, 1993); missed four games. ... Injured thumb (March 5, 1994); missed one game. ... Signed as free agent by Flyers (July 31, 1995).
HONORS: Named to AHL All-Star second team (1994-95). ... Won Eddie Shore Award (1996-97). ... Named to AHL All-Star first team (1996-97).

		REGULAR SEASON								PLAYOFFS				
Season Team	League	Gms.	G	A	Pts.	PIM	+/-	PP	SH	Gms.	G	A	Pts.	PIM
85-86— Barrie Jr. B	OHA	46	14	32	46	91	...	...	...	—	—	—	—	—
86-87— Kitchener	OHL	64	11	32	43	44	...	...	...	4	0	1	1	9
87-88— Kitchener	OHL	55	15	50	65	64	...	...	...	—	—	—	—	—
88-89— Kitchener	OHL	46	11	28	39	25	...	...	...	5	1	0	1	2
89-90— Hershey	AHL	57	2	13	15	31	...	...	...	—	—	—	—	—
90-91— Philadelphia	NHL	3	1	0	1	0	1	0	0	—	—	—	—	—
— Hershey	AHL	73	6	35	41	48	...	...	...	3	0	5	5	2
91-92— Hershey	AHL	79	12	54	66	118	...	...	...	6	0	3	3	2
92-93— Ottawa	NHL	69	3	13	16	61	-24	0	0	—	—	—	—	—
— New Haven	AHL	2	1	0	1	0	...	...	...	—	—	—	—	—
93-94— Ottawa	NHL	70	6	9	15	116	-50	0	0	—	—	—	—	—
— Prin. Edward Island ...	AHL	3	2	0	2	0	...	...	...	—	—	—	—	—
94-95— Prin. Edward Island ...	AHL	70	7	46	53	77	...	...	...	11	0	6	6	4
95-96— Philadelphia	NHL	5	0	0	0	4	0	0	0	—	—	—	—	—
— Hershey	AHL	58	13	37	50	83	...	...	...	5	0	0	0	6
96-97— Philadelphia	AHL	72	18	44	62	83	...	...	...	7	0	3	3	19
— Philadelphia	NHL	10	0	0	0	0	-2	0	0	—	—	—	—	—
NHL totals (5 years)		157	10	22	32	181	-75	0	0	—	—	—	—	—

RUSSELL, BLAINE — G — MIGHTY DUCKS

PERSONAL: Born January 11, 1977, in Wetaskiwin, Alta. ... 6-0/180. ... Catches left.
TRANSACTIONS/CAREER NOTES: Selected by the Mighty Ducks of Anaheim in sixth round (fourth Mighty Ducks pick, 149th overall) of NHL entry draft (June 22, 1996).

		REGULAR SEASON							PLAYOFFS					
Season Team	League	Gms.	Min	W	L	T	GA	SO	Avg.	Gms.	Min.	W	L	GA	SO	Avg.
95-96— Spokane	WHL	1	37	0	1	0	5	0	8.11	—	—	—	—	—	—	—
— Prince Albert	WHL	34	1920	25	5	2	98	2	3.06	7	380	4	2	20	0	3.16
96-97— Prince Albert	WHL	29	1690	9	15	3	99	2	3.51	—	—	—	—	—	—	—
— Lethbridge	WHL	6	370	4	1	1	17	0	2.76	14	817	*13	1	29	0	*2.13

RUSSELL, CAM — D — BLACKHAWKS

PERSONAL: Born January 12, 1969, in Halifax, N.S. ... 6-4/195. ... Shoots left.
TRANSACTIONS/CAREER NOTES: Selected by Chicago Blackhawks as underage junior in third round (third Blackhawks pick, 50th overall) of NHL entry draft (June 13, 1987). ... Suffered from the flu (December 26, 1992); missed one game. ... Suspended one game by NHL for accumulating three game misconduct penalties (February 11, 1993). ... Underwent surgery for a herniated disc in neck (March 18, 1994); missed remainder of season. ... Broke bone in hand (April 2, 1995); missed remainder of season. ... Bruised shoulder (November 22, 1995); missed five games. ... Broke left orbital bone (December 23, 1995); missed five games. ... Suffered concussion (January 10, 1997); missed two games.

		REGULAR SEASON							PLAYOFFS				
Season Team	League	Gms.	G	A	Pts.	PIM	+/-	PP	SH	Gms.	G	A	Pts.	PIM
85-86— Hull	QMJHL	56	3	4	7	24	...	...	...	15	0	2	2	4
86-87— Hull	QMJHL	66	3	16	19	119	...	...	...	8	0	1	1	16
87-88— Hull	QMJHL	53	9	18	27	141	...	...	...	19	2	5	7	39
88-89— Hull	QMJHL	66	8	32	40	109	...	...	...	9	2	6	8	6

Season Team	League	REGULAR SEASON								PLAYOFFS				
		Gms.	G	A	Pts.	PIM	+/-	PP	SH	Gms.	G	A	Pts.	PIM
89-90 — Indianapolis	IHL	46	3	15	18	114	...	...	...	9	0	1	1	24
— Chicago	NHL	19	0	1	1	27	-3	0	0	1	0	0	0	0
90-91 — Indianapolis	IHL	53	5	9	14	125	...	...	...	6	0	2	2	30
— Chicago	NHL	3	0	0	0	5	1	0	0	1	0	0	0	0
91-92 — Indianapolis	IHL	41	4	9	13	78	...	...	...	—	—	—	—	—
— Chicago	NHL	19	0	0	0	34	-8	0	0	12	0	2	2	2
92-93 — Chicago	NHL	67	2	4	6	151	5	0	0	4	0	0	0	0
93-94 — Chicago	NHL	67	1	7	8	200	10	0	0	—	—	—	—	—
94-95 — Chicago	NHL	33	1	3	4	88	4	0	0	16	0	3	3	8
95-96 — Chicago	NHL	61	2	2	4	129	8	0	0	6	0	0	0	2
96-97 — Chicago	NHL	44	1	1	2	65	-8	0	0	4	0	0	0	4
NHL totals (8 years)		**313**	**7**	**18**	**25**	**699**	**9**	**0**	**0**	**44**	**0**	**5**	**5**	**16**

RYAN, TERRY LW CANADIENS

PERSONAL: Born January 14, 1977, in St. John's, Nfld. ... 6-2/198. ... Shoots left.
TRANSACTIONS/CAREER NOTES: Selected by Montreal Canadiens in first round (first Canadiens pick, eighth overall) of NHL entry draft (July 8, 1995). ... Suffered post-concussion headaches (November 6, 1996); missed 37 games.
HONORS: Named to WHL (West) All-Star second team (1994-95).

Season Team	League	REGULAR SEASON								PLAYOFFS				
		Gms.	G	A	Pts.	PIM	+/-	PP	SH	Gms.	G	A	Pts.	PIM
91-92 — Quesnel	PCJHL	65	35	40	75	260	...	...	...	—	—	—	—	—
92-93 — Quesnel	PCJHL	46	45	40	85	222	...	...	...	—	—	—	—	—
— Tri-City	WHL	1	0	0	0	0	...	...	...	1	0	1	1	5
93-94 — Tri-City	WHL	61	16	17	33	176	...	...	...	4	0	1	1	25
94-95 — Tri-City	WHL	70	50	60	110	207	...	...	...	17	12	15	27	36
95-96 — Tri-City	WHL	59	32	37	69	133	...	...	...	5	0	0	0	4
— Fredericton	AHL	0	0	0	0	0	...	...	...	3	0	0	0	2
96-97 — Montreal	NHL	3	0	0	0	0	0	0	0	—	—	—	—	—
— Red Deer	WHL	16	13	22	35	10	...	...	...	16	*18	6	24	32
NHL totals (1 year)		**3**	**0**	**0**	**0**	**0**	**0**	**0**	**0**					

RYCHEL, WARREN LW MIGHTY DUCKS

PERSONAL: Born May 12, 1967, in Tecumseh, Ont. ... 6-0/205. ... Shoots left. ... Full name: Warren Stanley Rychel. ... Name pronounced RIGH-kuhl.
TRANSACTIONS/CAREER NOTES: Signed as free agent by Chicago Blackhawks (September 19, 1986). ... Hyperextended left knee (February 1989). ... Traded by Blackhawks with C Troy Murray to Winnipeg Jets for D Bryan Marchment and D Chris Norton (July 22, 1991). ... Traded by Jets to Minnesota North Stars for RW Tony Joseph and future considerations (December 30, 1991). ... Signed as free agent by San Diego Gulls (August 11, 1992). ... Signed as free agent by Los Angeles Kings (October 3, 1992). ... Bruised ankle (December 1, 1992); missed 14 games. ... Traded by Kings to Washington Capitals for LW Randy Burridge (February 10, 1995). ... Traded by Capitals to Toronto Maple Leafs for fourth-round pick (G Sebastien Charpentier) in 1995 draft (February 10, 1995). ... Suspended two games and fined $500 by NHL for spearing (March 2, 1995). ... Strained groin (April 17, 1995); missed three games. ... Traded by Maple Leafs to Colorado Avalanche for cash (October 2, 1995). ... Suffered back spasms (January 14, 1996); missed two games. ... Signed as free agent by Mighty Ducks of Anaheim (July 23, 1996). ... Suffered back spasms (January 22, 1997); missed four games. ... Suffered back spasms (February 8, 1997); missed four games.
MISCELLANEOUS: Member of Stanley Cup championship team (1996).

Season Team	League	REGULAR SEASON								PLAYOFFS				
		Gms.	G	A	Pts.	PIM	+/-	PP	SH	Gms.	G	A	Pts.	PIM
83-84 — Essex Jr. C	OHA	24	11	16	27	86	...	...	...	—	—	—	—	—
84-85 — Sudbury	OHL	35	5	8	13	74	...	...	...	—	—	—	—	—
— Guelph	OHL	29	1	3	4	48	...	...	...	—	—	—	—	—
85-86 — Guelph	OHL	38	14	5	19	119	...	...	...	—	—	—	—	—
— Ottawa	OHL	29	11	18	29	54	...	...	...	—	—	—	—	—
86-87 — Ottawa	OHL	28	11	7	18	57	...	...	...	—	—	—	—	—
— Kitchener	OHL	21	5	5	10	39	...	...	...	4	0	0	0	9
87-88 — Saginaw	IHL	51	2	7	9	113	...	...	...	1	0	0	0	0
— Peoria	IHL	7	2	1	3	7	...	...	...	—	—	—	—	—
88-89 — Saginaw	IHL	50	15	14	29	226	...	...	...	6	0	0	0	51
— Chicago	NHL	2	0	0	0	17	-1	0	0	—	—	—	—	—
89-90 — Indianapolis	IHL	77	23	16	39	374	...	...	...	14	1	3	4	64
90-91 — Indianapolis	IHL	68	33	30	63	338	...	...	...	5	2	1	3	30
— Chicago	NHL	—	—	—	—	—	—	—	—	3	1	3	4	2
91-92 — Moncton	AHL	36	14	15	29	211	...	...	...	—	—	—	—	—
— Kalamazoo	IHL	45	15	20	35	165	...	...	...	8	0	3	3	51
92-93 — Los Angeles	NHL	70	6	7	13	314	-15	0	0	23	6	7	13	39
93-94 — Los Angeles	NHL	80	10	9	19	322	-19	0	0	—	—	—	—	—
94-95 — Los Angeles	NHL	7	0	0	0	19	-5	0	0	—	—	—	—	—
— Toronto	NHL	26	1	6	7	101	1	0	0	3	0	0	0	0
95-96 — Colorado	NHL	52	6	2	8	147	6	0	0	12	1	0	1	23
96-97 — Anaheim	NHL	70	10	7	17	218	6	1	1	11	0	2	2	9
NHL totals (7 years)		**307**	**33**	**31**	**64**	**1138**	**-27**	**1**	**1**	**52**	**8**	**12**	**20**	**83**

RYDER, DAN   G

PERSONAL: Born October 24, 1972, in Kitchener, Ont. ... 6-1/200. ... Catches left.
TRANSACTIONS/CAREER NOTES: Selected by San Jose Sharks in fifth round (fifth Sharks pick, 89th overall) of NHL entry draft (June 22, 1991).

Season Team	League	Gms.	Min	W	L	T	GA	SO	Avg.	Gms.	Min.	W	L	GA	SO	Avg.
90-91—Sudbury	OHL	37	2089	18	9	4	126	...	3.62	2	26	...	...	1	0	2.31
—Hamilton	OHL	1	40	...	...	...	1	0	1.50	—	—	—	—	—	—	—
91-92—Sudbury	OHL	23	1157	9	11	1	91	0	4.72	—	—	—	—	—	—	—
—Ottawa	OHL	24	1380	24	16	0	55	3	2.39	11	625	5	6	38	0	3.65
92-93—Columbus	ECHL	1	60	0	1	‡0	6	0	6.00	—	—	—	—	—	—	—
—Kansas City	IHL	10	514	3	3	‡2	35	0	4.09	—	—	—	—	—	—	—
—Johnstown	ECHL	4	214	1	1	‡1	15	...	4.21	—	—	—	—	—	—	—
93-94—Roanoke	ECHL	42	1946	22	13	‡0	129	0	3.98	—	—	—	—	—	—	—
—Kansas City	IHL	3	139	1	1	‡0	11	0	4.75	—	—	—	—	—	—	—
94-95—Kansas City	IHL	3	140	1	2	‡0	11	0	4.71	—	—	—	—	—	—	—
—Roanoke	ECHL	21	1008	7	6	‡2	66	1	3.93	1	20	0	0	1	0	3.00
95-96—Detroit	Col.HL	28	1424	11	12	1	87	0	3.67	5	247	3	1	16	0	3.89
96-97—Port Huron	Col.HL	1	60	0	1	0	8	0	8.00	—	—	—	—	—	—	—
—Saginaw	Col.HL	46	2273	12	§24	3	§186	0	4.91	—	—	—	—	—	—	—

SACCO, DAVID   LW   MIGHTY DUCKS

PERSONAL: Born July 31, 1970, in Medford, Mass. ... 6-0/180. ... Shoots right. ... Full name: David Anthony Sacco. ... Name pronounced SA-koh. ... Brother of Joe Sacco, right winger, Mighty Ducks of Anaheim.
HIGH SCHOOL: Medford (Mass.).
COLLEGE: Boston University.
TRANSACTIONS/CAREER NOTES: Selected by Toronto Maple Leafs in 10th round (ninth Maple Leafs pick, 195th overall) of NHL entry draft (June 11, 1988). ... Loaned to U.S. Olympic team (February 27, 1994). ... Returned to Maple Leafs (March 1, 1994). ... Traded by Maple Leafs to Mighty Ducks of Anaheim for RW Terry Yake (September 28, 1994). ... Underwent knee surgery (December 19, 1995); missed nine games.
HONORS: Named to NCAA All-America East first team (1991-92 and 1992-93). ... Named to Hockey East All-Star first team (1991-92 and 1992-93).

Season Team	League	Gms.	G	A	Pts.	PIM	+/-	PP	SH	Gms.	G	A	Pts.	PIM
88-89—Boston University	Hockey East	35	14	29	43	40	...	...	...	—	—	—	—	—
89-90—Boston University	Hockey East	3	0	4	4	2	...	...	...	—	—	—	—	—
90-91—Boston University	Hockey East	40	21	40	61	24	...	...	...	—	—	—	—	—
91-92—Boston University	Hockey East	35	14	33	47	30	...	...	...	—	—	—	—	—
92-93—Boston University	Hockey East	40	25	37	62	86	...	...	...	—	—	—	—	—
93-94—U.S. national team	Int'l	32	8	20	28	88	...	...	...	—	—	—	—	—
—U.S. Olympic team	Int'l	8	3	5	8	12	...	...	...	—	—	—	—	—
—Toronto	NHL	4	1	1	2	4	-2	1	0	—	—	—	—	—
—St. John's	AHL	5	3	1	4	2	...	...	...	—	—	—	—	—
94-95—San Diego	IHL	45	11	25	36	57	...	...	...	4	3	1	4	0
—Anaheim	NHL	8	0	2	2	0	-3	0	0	—	—	—	—	—
95-96—Baltimore	AHL	25	14	16	30	18	...	...	...	2	0	1	1	4
—Anaheim	NHL	23	4	10	14	18	1	2	0	—	—	—	—	—
96-97—Baltimore	AHL	51	18	38	56	30	...	...	...	1	0	2	2	0
NHL totals (3 years)		35	5	13	18	22	-4	3	0					

SACCO, JOE   RW   MIGHTY DUCKS

PERSONAL: Born February 4, 1969, in Medford, Mass. ... 6-1/195. ... Shoots left. ... Full name: Joseph William Sacco. ... Name pronounced SA-koh. ... Brother of David Sacco, left winger in Mighty Ducks of Anaheim system.
HIGH SCHOOL: Medford (Mass.).
COLLEGE: Boston University.
TRANSACTIONS/CAREER NOTES: Selected by Toronto Maple Leafs in fourth round (fourth Maple Leafs pick, 71st overall) of NHL entry draft (June 13, 1987). ... Selected by Mighty Ducks of Anaheim in NHL expansion draft (June 24, 1993). ... Bruised left thumb (February 5, 1995); missed seven games. ... Strained chest muscle (January 22, 1997); missed five games.

Season Team	League	Gms.	G	A	Pts.	PIM	+/-	PP	SH	Gms.	G	A	Pts.	PIM
85-86—Medford	Mass. H.S.	20	30	30	60	...	...	...	...	—	—	—	—	—
86-87—Medford	Mass. H.S.	21	22	32	54	...	...	...	...	—	—	—	—	—
87-88—Boston University	Hockey East	34	14	22	36	38	...	...	...	—	—	—	—	—
88-89—Boston University	Hockey East	33	21	19	40	66	...	...	...	—	—	—	—	—
89-90—Boston University	Hockey East	44	28	24	52	70	...	...	...	—	—	—	—	—
90-91—Newmarket	AHL	49	18	17	35	24	...	...	...	—	—	—	—	—
—Toronto	NHL	20	0	5	5	2	-5	0	0	—	—	—	—	—
91-92—U.S. national team	Int'l	50	11	26	37	51	...	...	...	—	—	—	—	—
—U.S. Olympic team	Int'l	8	0	2	2	0	...	...	...	—	—	—	—	—
—Toronto	NHL	17	7	4	11	4	8	0	0	—	—	—	—	—
—St. John's	AHL	—	...	...	...	...	...	...	...	1	1	1	2	0
92-93—Toronto	NHL	23	4	4	8	8	-4	0	0	—	—	—	—	—
—St. John's	AHL	37	14	16	30	45	...	...	...	7	6	4	10	2
93-94—Anaheim	NHL	84	19	18	37	61	-11	3	1	—	—	—	—	—
94-95—Anaheim	NHL	41	10	8	18	23	-8	2	0	—	—	—	—	—
95-96—Anaheim	NHL	76	13	14	27	40	1	1	2	—	—	—	—	—
96-97—Anaheim	NHL	77	12	17	29	35	1	1	1	11	2	0	2	2
NHL totals (7 years)		338	65	70	135	173	-18	7	4	11	2	0	2	2

R
S

SAKIC, JOE   C   AVALANCHE

PERSONAL: Born July 7, 1969, in Burnaby, B.C. ... 5-11/185. ... Shoots left. ... Full name: Joseph Steve Sakic. ... Name pronounced SAK-ihk.
TRANSACTIONS/CAREER NOTES: Selected by Quebec Nordiques as underage junior in first round (second Nordiques pick, 15th overall) of NHL entry draft (June 13, 1987). ... Sprained right ankle (November 28, 1988). ... Developed bursitis in left ankle (January 21, 1992); missed three games. ... Suffered recurrence of bursitis in left ankle (January 30, 1992); missed eight games. ... Injured eye (January 2, 1993); missed six games. ... Nordiques franchise moved to Colorado and renamed Avalanche for 1995-96 season (June 21, 1995). ... Cut calf (January 4, 1997); missed 17 games.
HONORS: Won WHL (East) Most Valuable Player Trophy (1986-87). ... Won WHL (East) Stewart (Butch) Paul Memorial Trophy (1986-87). ... Named to WHL All-Star second team (1986-87). ... Won Can.HL Player of the Year Award (1987-88). ... Won Four Broncos Memorial Trophy (1987-88). ... Shared Bob Clarke Trophy with Theoren Fleury (1987-88). ... Won WHL Player of the Year Award (1987-88). ... Named to WHL (East) All-Star first team (1987-88). ... Played in NHL All-Star Game (1990-1994 and 1996). ... Won Conn Smythe Trophy (1995-96). ... Named to play in NHL All-Star Game (1997); replaced by RW Teemu Selanne due to injury.
STATISTICAL PLATEAUS: Three-goal games: 1988-89 (2), 1989-90 (1), 1990-91 (1), 1996-97 (1). Total: 5. ... Four-goal games: 1991-92 (1). ... Total hat tricks: 6.
MISCELLANEOUS: Member of Stanley Cup championship team (1996). ... Captain of Quebec Nordiques (1990-91 through 1994-95). ... Scored on a penalty shot (vs. Ken Wregget, December 9, 1989; vs. Trevor Kidd, January 14, 1996).

				REGULAR SEASON							PLAYOFFS				
Season Team	League	Gms.	G	A	Pts.	PIM	+/-	PP	SH		Gms.	G	A	Pts.	PIM
86-87— Swift Current	WHL	72	60	73	133	31	...	...	...		4	0	1	1	0
87-88— Swift Current	WHL	64	†78	82	†160	64	...	...	...		10	11	13	24	12
88-89— Quebec	NHL	70	23	39	62	24	-36	10	0		—	—	—	—	—
89-90— Quebec	NHL	80	39	63	102	27	-40	8	1		—	—	—	—	—
90-91— Quebec	NHL	80	48	61	109	24	-26	12	3		—	—	—	—	—
91-92— Quebec	NHL	69	29	65	94	20	5	6	3		—	—	—	—	—
92-93— Quebec	NHL	78	48	57	105	40	-3	20	2		6	3	3	6	2
93-94— Quebec	NHL	84	28	64	92	18	-8	10	1		—	—	—	—	—
94-95— Quebec	NHL	47	19	43	62	30	7	3	2		6	4	1	5	0
95-96— Colorado	NHL	82	51	69	120	44	14	17	6		22	*18	16	*34	14
96-97— Colorado	NHL	65	22	52	74	34	-10	10	2		17	8	17	25	14
NHL totals (9 years)		655	307	513	820	261	-97	96	20		51	33	37	70	30

SALEI, RUSLAN   D   MIGHTY DUCKS

PERSONAL: Born November 2, 1974, in Minsk, U.S.S.R. ... 6-2/200. ... Shoots left. ... Name pronounced ROO-sluhn suh-LAY.
TRANSACTIONS/CAREER NOTES: Selected by Mighty Ducks of Anaheim in first round (first Mighty Ducks pick, ninth overall) of NHL entry draft (June 22, 1996).

				REGULAR SEASON							PLAYOFFS				
Season Team	League	Gms.	G	A	Pts.	PIM	+/-	PP	SH		Gms.	G	A	Pts.	PIM
92-93— Dynamo Minsk	CIS	9	1	0	1	10	...	...	...		—	—	—	—	—
93-94— Tivali Minsk	CIS	39	2	3	5	50	...	...	...		—	—	—	—	—
94-95— Tivali Minsk	CIS	51	4	2	6	44	...	...	...		—	—	—	—	—
95-96— Las Vegas	IHL	76	7	23	30	123	...	...	...		15	3	7	10	18
96-97— Anaheim	NHL	30	0	1	1	37	-8	0	0		—	—	—	—	—
— Baltimore	AHL	12	1	4	5	12	...	...	...		—	—	—	—	—
— Las Vegas	IHL	8	0	2	2	24	...	...	...		3	2	1	3	6
NHL totals (1 year)		30	0	1	1	37	-8	0	0						

SALO, SAMI   D   SENATORS

PERSONAL: Born September 2, 1974, in Turku, Finland. ... 6-3/189. ... Shoots right.
TRANSACTIONS/CAREER NOTES: Selected by Ottawa Senators in ninth round (seventh Senators pick, 239th overall) of NHL entry draft (June 22, 1996).

				REGULAR SEASON							PLAYOFFS				
Season Team	League	Gms.	G	A	Pts.	PIM	+/-	PP	SH		Gms.	G	A	Pts.	PIM
94-95— Turku	Finland	7	1	2	3	6	...	...	...		—	—	—	—	—
— Kiekko-67	Finland II	19	4	2	6	4	...	...	...		—	—	—	—	—
95-96— TPS Turku	Finland	47	7	14	21	32	...	...	...		11	1	3	4	8
96-97— TPS Turku	Finland	48	9	6	15	10	...	...	...		10	2	3	5	4

SALO, TOMMY   G   ISLANDERS

PERSONAL: Born February 1, 1971, in Surahammar, Sweden. ... 5-11/173. ... Catches left. ... Name pronounced SAH-loh.
TRANSACTIONS/CAREER NOTES: Selected by New York Islanders in fifth round (fifth Islanders pick, 118th overall) of NHL entry draft (June 26, 1993). ... Suffered from tonsillitis (February 8, 1997); missed one game.
HONORS: Won James Gatchene Memorial Trophy (1994-95). ... Won James Norris Memorial Trophy (1994-95). ... Won Garry F. Longman Memorial Trophy (1994-95). ... Named to IHL All-Star first team (1994-95). ... Won N.R. (Bud) Poile Trophy (1995-96).
MISCELLANEOUS: Member of gold-medal-winning Swedish Olympic team (1994). ... Allowed a penalty shot goal (vs. Rob Zamuner January 11, 1997).

				REGULAR SEASON							PLAYOFFS				
Season Team	League	Gms.	Min	W	L	T	GA	SO	Avg.		Gms.	Min.	W	L	GA	SO	Avg.
90-91— Vasteras	Sweden	2	100	...	...	...	11	0	6.60		—	—	—	—	—	—	—
91-92— Vasteras	Sweden								Did not play.								
92-93— Vasteras	Sweden	24	1431	...	...	...	59	2	2.47		—	—	—	—	—	—	—

Season Team	League	REGULAR SEASON								PLAYOFFS						
		Gms.	Min	W	L	T	GA	SO	Avg.	Gms.	Min.	W	L	GA	SO	Avg.
93-94—Vasteras	Sweden	32	1896	...	...	...	106	...	3.35	—	—	—	—	—	—	—
—Swed. Olympic team	Int'l	6	370	...	...	...	13	1	2.11	—	—	—	—	—	—	—
94-95—Denver	IHL	65	*3810	*45	14	‡4	165	†3	*2.60	8	390	7	0	20	0	3.08
—New York Islanders	NHL	6	358	1	5	0	18	0	3.02	—	—	—	—	—	—	—
95-96—New York Islanders	NHL	10	523	1	7	1	35	0	4.02	—	—	—	—	—	—	—
—Utah	IHL	45	2695	28	15	‡2	119	†4	2.65	22	1341	*15	7	51	*3	2.28
96-97—New York Islanders	NHL	58	3208	20	27	8	151	5	2.82	—	—	—	—	—	—	—
NHL totals (3 years)		74	4089	22	39	9	204	5	2.99							

SAMUELSSON, KJELL D FLYERS

PERSONAL: Born October 18, 1958, in Tyngsryd, Sweden. ... 6-6/235. ... Shoots right. ... Name pronounced SHEHL SAM-yuhl-suhn.

TRANSACTIONS/CAREER NOTES: Selected by New York Rangers in sixth round (fifth Rangers pick, 119th overall) of NHL entry draft (June 9, 1984). ... Traded by Rangers with second-round pick (LW Patrik Juhlin) in 1989 draft to Philadelphia Flyers for G Bob Froese (December 18, 1986). ... Pulled groin (February 1988). ... Suffered herniated disc (October 1988). ... Bruised hand (March 1989). ... Bruised right shoulder (November 22, 1989); missed 13 games. ... Underwent shoulder surgery (March 1990). ... Traded by Flyers with RW Rick Tocchet, G Ken Wregget and third-round pick in 1992 draft to Pittsburgh Penguins for RW Mark Recchi, D Brian Benning and first-round pick (LW Jason Bowen) in 1992 draft (February 19, 1992). ... Bruised knee (November 27, 1992); missed one game. ... Broke bone in foot (December 1, 1992); missed nine games. ... Fractured cheekbone (December 27, 1992); missed nine games. ... Suffered from the flu (March 18, 1993); missed one game. ... Injured groin (October 19, 1993); missed nine games. ... Injured groin (December 28, 1993); missed 13 games. ... Suffered from the flu (February 27, 1995); missed four games. ... Injured groin (April 8, 1995); missed one game. ... Suffered from the flu (April 28, 1995); missed two games. ... Signed as free agent by Flyers (July 7, 1995). ... Suffered from the flu (November 10, 1995); missed one game. ... Sprained right thumb (December 22, 1995); missed one game. ... Strained neck (February 22, 1996); missed one game. ... Suffered from the flu (March 26, 1996); missed two games. ... Suffered from the flu (April 3, 1996); missed two games. ... Suffered from a virus (October 26, 1996); missed one game. ... Sore back (November 7, 1996); missed four games. ... Sore ribs (November 16, 1996); missed three games. ... Strained neck (January 9, 1997); missed final 39 games of regular season.

HONORS: Played in NHL All-Star Game (1988).

MISCELLANEOUS: Member of Stanley Cup championship team (1992).

Season Team	League	REGULAR SEASON							PLAYOFFS				
		Gms.	G	A	Pts.	PIM	+/-	PP	SH	Gms.	G	A	Pts.	PIM
82-83—Tyngsryd	Sweden	32	11	6	17	57	...	...	...	—	—	—	—	—
83-84—Leksand	Sweden	36	6	7	13	59	...	...	...	—	—	—	—	—
84-85—Leksand	Sweden	35	9	5	14	34	...	...	...	—	—	—	—	—
85-86—New York Rangers	NHL	9	0	0	0	10	-1	0	0	9	0	1	1	8
—New Haven	AHL	56	6	21	27	87	...	...	...	3	0	0	0	10
86-87—New York Rangers	NHL	30	2	6	8	50	-2	0	0	—	—	—	—	—
—Philadelphia	NHL	46	1	6	7	86	-9	0	0	26	0	4	4	25
87-88—Philadelphia	NHL	74	6	24	30	184	28	3	0	7	2	5	7	23
88-89—Philadelphia	NHL	69	3	14	17	140	13	0	1	19	1	3	4	24
89-90—Philadelphia	NHL	66	5	17	22	91	20	0	0	—	—	—	—	—
90-91—Philadelphia	NHL	78	9	19	28	82	4	1	0	—	—	—	—	—
91-92—Philadelphia	NHL	54	4	9	13	76	1	0	0	—	—	—	—	—
—Pittsburgh	NHL	20	1	2	3	34	0	0	0	15	0	3	3	12
92-93—Pittsburgh	NHL	63	3	6	9	106	25	0	0	12	0	3	3	2
93-94—Pittsburgh	NHL	59	5	8	13	118	18	1	0	6	0	0	0	26
94-95—Pittsburgh	NHL	41	1	6	7	54	8	0	0	11	0	1	1	32
95-96—Philadelphia	NHL	75	3	11	14	81	20	0	0	12	1	0	1	24
96-97—Philadelphia	NHL	34	4	3	7	47	17	0	0	5	0	0	0	2
NHL totals (12 years)		718	47	131	178	1159	142	5	1	122	4	20	24	178

SAMUELSSON, ULF D RANGERS

PERSONAL: Born March 26, 1964, in Fagersta, Sweden. ... 6-1/205. ... Shoots left. ... Name pronounced UHLF SAM-yuhl-suhn.

TRANSACTIONS/CAREER NOTES: Selected by Hartford Whalers in fourth round (fourth Whalers pick, 67th overall) of NHL entry draft (June 9, 1982). ... Suffered from the flu (December 1988); missed nine games. ... Tore ligaments in right knee and underwent surgery (August 1989); missed part of 1989-90 season. ... Traded by Whalers with C Ron Francis and D Grant Jennings to Pittsburgh Penguins for C John Cullen, D Zarley Zalapski and RW Jeff Parker (March 4, 1991). ... Injured hip flexor (October 29, 1991); missed six games. ... Underwent surgery to right elbow (December 1991); missed four games. ... Bruised left hand (February 8, 1992); missed one game. ... Suffered from the flu (February 1992); missed one game. ... Strained shoulder (November 10, 1992); missed two games. ... Broke cheekbone (November 27, 1992); missed two games. ... Bruised knee (January 1993); missed one game. ... Suspended one game by NHL (February 1993). ... Suspended three off-days by NHL for stick-swinging incident (March 18, 1993). ... Suffered back spasms (April 4, 1993); missed one game. ... Injured knee (November 2, 1993); missed one game. ... Bruised foot (December 14, 1993); missed two games. ... Played in Europe during 1994-95 NHL lockout. ... Strained right elbow (March 21, 1995) and underwent elbow surgery (March 23, 1995); missed three games. ... Bruised knee (April 28, 1995); missed one game. ... Traded by Penguins with LW Luc Robitaille to New York Rangers for D Sergei Zubov and C Petr Nedved (August 31, 1995). ... Suffered mild concussion (October 14, 1995); missed two games. ... Separated shoulder (October 22, 1995); missed two games. ... Underwent elbow surgery (December 28, 1995); missed four games. ... Sprained knee (October 25, 1996); missed nine games.

MISCELLANEOUS: Member of Stanley Cup championship team (1991 and 1992).

Season Team	League	REGULAR SEASON							PLAYOFFS				
		Gms.	G	A	Pts.	PIM	+/-	PP	SH	Gms.	G	A	Pts.	PIM
83-84—Leksand	Sweden	36	5	10	15	53	...	...	...	—	—	—	—	—
84-85—Binghamton	AHL	36	5	11	16	92	...	...	...	—	—	—	—	—
—Hartford	NHL	41	2	6	8	83	-6	0	0	—	—	—	—	—
85-86—Hartford	NHL	80	5	19	24	174	8	0	1	10	1	2	3	38
86-87—Hartford	NHL	78	2	31	33	162	29	0	0	5	0	1	1	41
87-88—Hartford	NHL	76	8	33	41	159	-10	3	0	5	0	0	0	8
88-89—Hartford	NHL	71	9	26	35	181	23	3	0	4	0	2	2	4
89-90—Hartford	NHL	55	2	11	13	177	15	0	0	7	1	0	1	2

Season Team	League	REGULAR SEASON								PLAYOFFS				
		Gms.	G	A	Pts.	PIM	+/-	PP	SH	Gms.	G	A	Pts.	PIM
90-91 — Hartford	NHL	62	3	18	21	174	13	0	0	—	—	—	—	—
— Pittsburgh	NHL	14	1	4	5	37	4	0	0	20	3	2	5	34
91-92 — Pittsburgh	NHL	62	1	14	15	206	2	1	0	21	0	2	2	39
92-93 — Pittsburgh	NHL	77	3	26	29	249	36	0	0	12	1	5	6	24
93-94 — Pittsburgh	NHL	80	5	24	29	199	23	1	0	6	0	1	1	18
94-95 — Leksand	Sweden	2	0	0	0	8	...	...	...	—	—	—	—	—
— Pittsburgh	NHL	44	1	15	16	113	11	0	0	7	0	2	2	8
95-96 — New York Rangers	NHL	74	1	18	19	122	9	0	0	11	1	5	6	16
96-97 — New York Rangers	NHL	73	6	11	17	138	3	1	0	15	0	2	2	30
NHL totals (13 years)		887	49	256	305	2174	160	9	1	123	7	24	31	262

SANDERSON, GEOFF   LW   HURRICANES

PERSONAL: Born February 1, 1972, in Hay River, Northwest Territories. ... 6-0/190. ... Shoots left.

TRANSACTIONS/CAREER NOTES: Selected by Hartford Whalers in second round (second Whalers pick, 36th overall) of NHL entry draft (June 16, 1990). ... Bruised shoulder (October 14, 1991); missed one game. ... Injured groin (November 13, 1991); missed three games. ... Bruised knee (December 7, 1991); missed five games. ... Suffered from the flu (February 1, 1994). ... Fined $500 by Whalers for involvement in bar brawl (April 1, 1994). ... Played in Europe during 1994-95 NHL lockout. ... Whalers franchise moved to North Carolina and renamed Carolina Hurricanes for 1997-98 season; NHL approved move on June 25, 1997.

HONORS: Played in NHL All-Star Game (1994 and 1997).

STATISTICAL PLATEAUS: Three-goal games: 1992-93 (2), 1994-95 (1), 1995-96 (2). Total: 5.

Season Team	League	REGULAR SEASON								PLAYOFFS				
		Gms.	G	A	Pts.	PIM	+/-	PP	SH	Gms.	G	A	Pts.	PIM
88-89 — Swift Current	WHL	58	17	11	28	16	...	...	...	12	3	5	8	6
89-90 — Swift Current	WHL	70	32	62	94	56	...	...	...	4	1	4	5	8
90-91 — Swift Current	WHL	70	62	50	112	57	...	...	...	3	1	2	3	4
— Hartford	NHL	2	1	0	1	0	-2	0	0	3	0	0	0	0
— Springfield	AHL	—	—	—	—	—	...	...	...	1	0	0	0	2
91-92 — Hartford	NHL	64	13	18	31	18	5	2	0	7	1	0	1	2
92-93 — Hartford	NHL	82	46	43	89	28	-21	21	2	—	—	—	—	—
93-94 — Hartford	NHL	82	41	26	67	42	-13	15	1	—	—	—	—	—
94-95 — HPK Hameenlinna	Finland	12	6	4	10	24	...	...	...	—	—	—	—	—
— Hartford	NHL	46	18	14	32	24	-10	4	0	—	—	—	—	—
95-96 — Hartford	NHL	81	34	31	65	40	0	6	0	—	—	—	—	—
96-97 — Hartford	NHL	82	36	31	67	29	-9	12	1	—	—	—	—	—
NHL totals (7 years)		439	189	163	352	181	-50	60	4	10	1	0	1	2

SANDSTROM, TOMAS   RW   MIGHTY DUCKS

PERSONAL: Born September 4, 1964, in Jakobstad, Finland. ... 6-2/207. ... Shoots left.

TRANSACTIONS/CAREER NOTES: Selected by New York Rangers in second round (second Rangers pick, 36th overall) of NHL entry draft (June 9, 1982). ... Suffered concussion (February 24, 1986). ... Fractured right ankle (February 11, 1987). ... Fractured right index finger (November 1987). ... Traded by Rangers with LW Tony Granato to Los Angeles Kings for C Bernie Nicholls (January 20, 1990). ... Fractured vertebrae (November 29, 1990); missed 10 games. ... Partially dislocated shoulder (December 28, 1991); missed 26 games. ... Fractured left forearm (November 21, 1992); missed 24 games. ... Fractured jaw (February 28, 1993); missed 21 games. ... Pulled hamstring (October 26, 1993); missed four games. ... Traded by Kings to Pittsburgh Penguins for D Marty McSorley and D Jim Peak (February 15, 1994). ... Played in Europe during 1994-95 NHL lockout. ... Sprained foot (January 22, 1995); missed one game. ... Underwent ankle surgery (February 20, 1996); missed nine games. ... Injured shoulder (March 13, 1996); missed 15 games. ... Pulled groin (October 11, 1996); missed seven games. ... Traded by Penguins to Detroit Red Wings for C Greg Johnson (January 27, 1997). ... Signed as free agent by Mighty Ducks of Anaheim (August 1, 1997).

HONORS: Named to NHL All-Rookie team (1984-85). ... Played in NHL All-Star Game (1988 and 1991).

STATISTICAL PLATEAUS: Three-goal games: 1986-87 (3), 1990-91 (3), 1992-93 (1). Total: 7. ... Four-goal games: 1986-87 (1). ... Total hat tricks: 8.

MISCELLANEOUS: Member of Stanley Cup championship team (1997). ... Scored on a penalty shot (vs. Wendell Young, February 10, 1990).

Season Team	League	REGULAR SEASON								PLAYOFFS				
		Gms.	G	A	Pts.	PIM	+/-	PP	SH	Gms.	G	A	Pts.	PIM
81-82 — Fagersta	Swed. Div. II	32	28	11	39	74	...	...	...	—	—	—	—	—
82-83 — Brynas Gavle	Sweden	36	22	14	36	36	...	...	...	—	—	—	—	—
83-84 — Brynas Gavle	Sweden	34	20	10	30		...	...	...	—	—	—	—	—
— Swe. Olympic team	Int'l	7	2	1	3	6	...	...	...	—	—	—	—	—
84-85 — New York Rangers	NHL	74	29	29	58	51	3	5	0	3	0	2	2	0
85-86 — New York Rangers	NHL	73	25	29	54	109	-4	8	2	16	4	6	10	20
86-87 — New York Rangers	NHL	64	40	34	74	60	8	13	0	6	1	2	3	20
87-88 — New York Rangers	NHL	69	28	40	68	95	-6	11	0	—	—	—	—	—
88-89 — New York Rangers	NHL	79	32	56	88	148	5	11	2	4	3	2	5	12
89-90 — New York Rangers	NHL	48	19	19	38	100	-10	6	0	—	—	—	—	—
— Los Angeles	NHL	28	13	20	33	28	-1	1	1	10	5	4	9	19
90-91 — Los Angeles	NHL	68	45	44	89	106	27	16	0	10	4	4	8	14
91-92 — Los Angeles	NHL	49	17	22	39	70	-2	5	0	6	0	3	3	8
92-93 — Los Angeles	NHL	39	25	27	52	57	12	8	0	24	8	17	25	12
93-94 — Los Angeles	NHL	51	17	24	41	59	-12	4	0	—	—	—	—	—
— Pittsburgh	NHL	27	6	11	17	24	5	0	0	6	0	0	0	4
94-95 — Malmo	Sweden	12	10	5	15	14	...	...	...	—	—	—	—	—
— Pittsburgh	NHL	47	21	23	44	42	1	4	1	12	3	3	6	16
95-96 — Pittsburgh	NHL	58	35	35	70	69	4	17	1	18	4	2	6	30
96-97 — Pittsburgh	NHL	40	9	15	24	33	4	1	1	20	0	4	4	24
— Detroit	NHL	34	9	9	18	36	2	0	1	—	—	—	—	—
NHL totals (13 years)		848	370	437	807	1087	36	110	9	135	32	49	81	179

SANDWITH, TERRAN   D   FLYERS

PERSONAL: Born April 17, 1972, in Edmonton. ... 6-4/220. ... Shoots left.
TRANSACTIONS/CAREER NOTES: Selected by Philadelphia Flyers in second round (fourth Flyers pick, 42nd overall) of NHL entry draft (June 16, 1990). ... Suffered blood disorder (September 1990). ... Loaned to Canadian national team prior to 1995-96 season.

Season Team	League	Gms.	G	A	Pts.	PIM	+/-	PP	SH	Gms.	G	A	Pts.	PIM
				REGULAR SEASON								PLAYOFFS		
87-88— Hobbema	AJHL	58	5	8	13	106	...	...	...	—	—	—	—	—
88-89— Tri-City	WHL	31	0	0	0	29	...	...	...	6	0	0	0	4
89-90— Tri-City	WHL	70	4	14	18	92	...	...	...	7	0	2	2	14
90-91— Tri-City	WHL	46	5	17	22	132	...	...	...	7	1	0	1	14
91-92— Brandon	WHL	41	6	14	20	145	...	...	...	—	—	—	—	—
— Saskatoon	WHL	18	2	5	7	53	...	...	...	18	2	1	3	28
92-93— Hershey	AHL	61	1	12	13	140	...	...	...	—	—	—	—	—
93-94— Hershey	AHL	62	3	5	8	169	...	...	...	2	0	1	1	4
94-95— Hershey	AHL	11	1	1	2	32	...	...	...	—	—	—	—	—
— Kansas City	IHL	25	0	3	3	73	...	...	...	—	—	—	—	—
95-96— Canadian nat'l team	Int'l	47	3	12	15	63	...	...	...	—	—	—	—	—
— Cape Breton	AHL	5	0	2	2	4	...	...	...	—	—	—	—	—
96-97— Hamilton	AHL	78	3	6	9	213	...	...	...	22	0	2	2	27

SARAULT, YVES   LW   AVALANCHE

S

PERSONAL: Born December 23, 1972, in Valleyfield, Que. ... 6-1/183. ... Shoots left. ... Name pronounced EEV SA-roh.
TRANSACTIONS/CAREER NOTES: Traded by Victoriaville Tigers with D Jason Downey to St. Jean Lynx for D Sylvain Bourgeois (May 26, 1990). ... Selected by Montreal Canadiens in third round (third Canadiens pick, 61st overall) of NHL entry draft (June 22, 1991). ... Traded by Canadiens with RW Craig Ferguson to Calgary Flames for eighth-round pick (D Petr Kubos) in 1997 draft (November 25, 1995). ... Signed as free agent by Colorado Avalanche (September 7, 1996).
HONORS: Named to QMJHL All-Star second team (1991-92).

Season Team	League	Gms.	G	A	Pts.	PIM	+/-	PP	SH	Gms.	G	A	Pts.	PIM
				REGULAR SEASON								PLAYOFFS		
89-90— Victoriaville	QMJHL	70	12	28	40	140	...	...	...	16	0	3	3	26
90-91— St. Jean	QMJHL	56	22	24	46	113	...	...	...	—	—	—	—	—
91-92— St. Jean	QMJHL	50	28	38	66	96	...	...	...	—	—	—	—	—
— Trois-Rivieres	QMJHL	18	16	14	30	10	...	...	...	15	10	10	20	18
92-93— Fredericton	AHL	59	14	17	31	41	...	...	...	3	0	1	1	2
— Wheeling	ECHL	2	1	3	4	0	...	...	...	—	—	—	—	—
93-94— Fredericton	AHL	60	13	14	27	72	...	...	...	—	—	—	—	—
94-95— Fredericton	AHL	69	24	21	45	96	...	...	...	13	2	1	3	33
— Montreal	NHL	8	0	1	1	0	-1	0	0	—	—	—	—	—
95-96— Montreal	NHL	14	0	0	0	4	-7	0	0	—	—	—	—	—
— Calgary	NHL	11	2	1	3	4	-2	0	0	—	—	—	—	—
— Saint John	AHL	26	10	12	22	34	...	...	...	16	6	2	8	33
96-97— Colorado	NHL	28	2	1	3	6	0	0	0	5	0	0	0	2
— Hershey	AHL	6	2	3	5	8	...	...	...	—	—	—	—	—
NHL totals (3 years)		61	4	3	7	14	-10	0	0	5	0	0	0	2

SARICH, COREY   D   SABRES

PERSONAL: Born August 16, 1978, in Saskatoon, Sask. ... 6-3/175. ... Shoots right. ... Name pronounced SAIRCH.
TRANSACTIONS/CAREER NOTES: Selected by Buffalo Sabres in second round (second Sabres pick, 27th overall) of NHL entry draft (June 22, 1996).

Season Team	League	Gms.	G	A	Pts.	PIM	+/-	PP	SH	Gms.	G	A	Pts.	PIM
				REGULAR SEASON								PLAYOFFS		
94-95— Saskatoon	WHL	6	0	0	0	4	...	...	...	3	0	1	1	0
95-96— Saskatoon	WHL	59	5	18	23	54	...	...	...	3	0	0	0	4
96-97— Saskatoon	WHL	58	6	27	33	158	...	...	...	—	—	—	—	—

SATAN, MIROSLAV   LW   SABRES

PERSONAL: Born October 22, 1974, in Topolcany, Czechoslovakia. ... 6-1/195. ... Shoots left. ... Name pronounced shuh-TAN.
TRANSACTIONS/CAREER NOTES: Selected by Edmonton Oilers in fifth round (sixth Oilers pick, 111th overall) of NHL entry draft (June 26, 1993). ... Suffered collapsed lung (October 1, 1995); missed two games. ... Separated right shoulder (January 13, 1996); missed four games. ... Suffered from the flu (March 9, 1997); missed one game. ... Traded by Oilers to Buffalo Sabres for D Craig Millar and LW Barrie Moore (March 18, 1997).
STATISTICAL NOTES: Led NHL with 21.0 shooting percentage (1996-97).
STATISTICAL PLATEAUS: Three-goal games: 1996-97 (1).

Season Team	League	Gms.	G	A	Pts.	PIM	+/-	PP	SH	Gms.	G	A	Pts.	PIM
				REGULAR SEASON								PLAYOFFS		
91-92— VTJ Topolcany	Czech. Div. II	9	2	1	3	6	...	...	...	—	—	—	—	—
— VTJ Topolcany Jrs	Czech. Jrs.	31	30	22	52		...	...	...	—	—	—	—	—
92-93— Dukla Trencin	Czech.	38	11	6	17		...	...	...	—	—	—	—	—
93-94— Dukla Trencin	Slovakia	30	32	16	48	16	...	...	...	—	—	—	—	—
— Slov. Olympic team	Int'l	8	9	0	9	0	...	...	...	—	—	—	—	—
94-95— Detroit	IHL	8	1	3	4	4	...	...	...	—	—	—	—	—
— San Diego	IHL	6	0	2	2	6	...	...	...	—	—	—	—	—
— Cape Breton	AHL	25	24	16	40	15	...	...	...	—	—	—	—	—

Season Team	League	REGULAR SEASON								PLAYOFFS				
		Gms.	G	A	Pts.	PIM	+/-	PP	SH	Gms.	G	A	Pts.	PIM
95-96— Edmonton	NHL	62	18	17	35	22	0	6	0	—	—	—	—	—
96-97— Edmonton	NHL	64	17	11	28	22	-4	5	0	—	—	—	—	—
— Buffalo	NHL	12	8	2	10	4	1	2	0	7	0	0	0	0
NHL totals (2 years)		138	43	30	73	48	-3	13	0	7	0	0	0	0

SAVAGE, BRIAN   C   CANADIENS

PERSONAL: Born February 24, 1971, in Sudbury, Ont. ... 6-1/190. ... Shoots left.
HIGH SCHOOL: Lo-Ellen Park Secondary (Sudbury, Ont.).
COLLEGE: Miami of Ohio.
TRANSACTIONS/CAREER NOTES: Selected by Montreal Canadiens in eighth round (11th Canadiens pick, 171st overall) of NHL entry draft (June 22, 1991). ... Bruised knee (February 4, 1995); missed 10 games. ... Bruised knee (April 5, 1995); missed one game. ... Suffered hip pointer (February 17, 1996); missed six games. ... Suffered from the flu (April 1, 1996); missed one game. ... Injured groin (October 26, 1996); missed one game.
HONORS: Named to NCAA All-America West second team (1992-93). ... Named CCHA Player of the Year (1992-93). ... Named to CCHA All-Star first team (1992-93).
STATISTICAL PLATEAUS: Three-goal games: 1995-96 (1), 1996-97 (1). Total: 2.
MISCELLANEOUS: Member of silver-medal-winning Canadian Olympic team (1994).

Season Team	League	REGULAR SEASON								PLAYOFFS				
		Gms.	G	A	Pts.	PIM	+/-	PP	SH	Gms.	G	A	Pts.	PIM
90-91— Miami of Ohio	CCHA	28	5	6	11	26	...	...	...	—	—	—	—	—
91-92— Miami of Ohio	CCHA	40	24	16	40	43	...	...	...	—	—	—	—	—
92-93— Miami of Ohio	CCHA	38	37	21	58	44	...	...	...	—	—	—	—	—
— Canadian nat'l team	Int'l	9	3	0	3	12	...	...	...	—	—	—	—	—
93-94— Canadian nat'l team	Int'l	51	20	26	46	38	...	...	...	—	—	—	—	—
— Can. Olympic team	Int'l	8	2	2	4	6	...	...	...	—	—	—	—	—
— Fredericton	AHL	17	12	15	27	4	...	...	...	—	—	—	—	—
— Montreal	NHL	3	1	0	1	0	0	0	0	3	0	2	2	0
94-95— Montreal	NHL	37	12	7	19	27	5	0	0	—	—	—	—	—
95-96— Montreal	NHL	75	25	8	33	28	-8	4	0	6	0	2	2	2
96-97— Montreal	NHL	81	23	37	60	39	-14	5	0	5	1	1	2	0
NHL totals (4 years)		196	61	52	113	94	-17	9	0	14	1	5	6	2

SAVARD, DENIS   C

PERSONAL: Born February 4, 1961, in Pointe Gatineau, Que. ... 5-10/175. ... Shoots right. ... Full name: Denis Joseph Savard. ... Name pronounced suh-VAHRD.
TRANSACTIONS/CAREER NOTES: Selected by Chicago Blackhawks as underage junior in first round (first Blackhawks pick, third overall) of NHL entry draft (June 11, 1980). ... Strained knee (October 15, 1980). ... Broke nose (January 7, 1984). ... Injured ankle (October 13, 1984). ... Bruised ribs (March 22, 1987). ... Broke right ankle (January 21, 1989); missed 19 games. ... Sprained left ankle (January 17, 1990). ... Broke left index finger (January 26, 1990); missed 17 games. ... Traded by Blackhawks to Montreal Canadiens for D Chris Chelios and second-round pick (C Michael Pomichter) in 1991 draft (June 29, 1990). ... Suffered sinus infection (January 17, 1991); missed five games. ... Injured right thumb (March 16, 1991). ... Injured eye (October 30, 1991); missed two games. ... Suffered from the flu (November 22, 1992); missed two games. ... Sprained knee (January 2, 1993); missed four games. ... Suspended one game by NHL for game misconduct penalties (January 23, 1993). ... Separated shoulder (February 17, 1993); missed 10 games. ... Signed as free agent by Tampa Bay Lightning (July 29, 1993). ... Suspended four games and fined $500 by NHL for slashing (November 22, 1993). ... Bruised shoulder (March 7, 1995); missed three games. ... Traded by Lightning to Blackhawks for sixth-round pick (C Xavier Delisle) in 1996 draft (April 6, 1995). ... Sore hand (November 29, 1996); missed two games. ... Sore hand (December 9, 1996); missed one game. ... Suffered charley horse (December 15, 1996); missed one game. ... Sprained thumb (April 6, 1997); missed three games. ... Announced retirement (June 26, 1997).
HONORS: Won Michel Briere Trophy (1979-80). ... Named to QMJHL All-Star first team (1979-80). ... Named to The Sporting News All-Star second team (1982-83). ... Named to NHL All-Star second team (1982-83). ... Played in NHL All-Star Game (1982-1984, 1986, 1988, 1991 and 1996).
RECORDS: Shares NHL record for fastest goal from start of period—4 seconds (January 12, 1986).
STATISTICAL PLATEAUS: Three-goal games: 1983-84 (1), 1984-85 (3), 1985-86 (1), 1986-87 (3), 1987-88 (2), 1989-90 (1), 1991-92 (1). Total: 12.
MISCELLANEOUS: Member of Stanley Cup championship team (1993). ... Co-captain of Chicago Blackhawks (1987-88). ... Scored on a penalty shot (vs. Mike Liut, January 4, 1983; vs. Roland Melanson, March 10, 1985; vs. Greg Stefan, December 15, 1985; vs. Glen Hanlon, February 3, 1988). ... Failed to score on a penalty shot (vs. Richard Brodeur, January 10, 1982; vs. Don Edwards, October 23, 1983; vs. John Blue, January 25, 1993).

Season Team	League	REGULAR SEASON								PLAYOFFS				
		Gms.	G	A	Pts.	PIM	+/-	PP	SH	Gms.	G	A	Pts.	PIM
77-78— Montreal	QMJHL	72	37	79	116	22	...	...	...	—	—	—	—	—
78-79— Montreal	QMJHL	70	46	*112	158	88	...	...	...	11	5	6	11	46
79-80— Montreal	QMJHL	72	63	118	181	93	...	...	...	10	7	16	23	8
80-81— Chicago	NHL	76	28	47	75	47	27	4	0	3	0	0	0	0
81-82— Chicago	NHL	80	32	87	119	82	0	8	0	15	11	7	18	52
82-83— Chicago	NHL	78	35	86	121	99	26	13	0	13	8	9	17	22
83-84— Chicago	NHL	75	37	57	94	71	-13	12	0	5	1	3	4	9
84-85— Chicago	NHL	79	38	67	105	56	16	7	0	15	9	20	29	20
85-86— Chicago	NHL	80	47	69	116	111	7	14	1	3	4	1	5	6
86-87— Chicago	NHL	70	40	50	90	108	15	7	0	4	1	0	1	12
87-88— Chicago	NHL	80	44	87	131	95	4	14	7	5	4	3	7	10
88-89— Chicago	NHL	58	23	59	82	110	-5	7	5	16	8	11	19	10
89-90— Chicago	NHL	60	27	53	80	56	8	10	2	20	7	15	22	41
90-91— Montreal	NHL	70	28	31	59	52	-1	7	2	13	2	11	13	35
91-92— Montreal	NHL	77	28	42	70	73	6	12	1	11	3	9	12	8

Season Team	League	REGULAR SEASON Gms.	G	A	Pts.	PIM	+/-	PP	SH	PLAYOFFS Gms.	G	A	Pts.	PIM
92-93— Montreal	NHL	63	16	34	50	90	1	4	1	14	0	5	5	4
93-94— Tampa Bay	NHL	74	18	28	46	106	-1	2	1	—	—	—	—	—
94-95— Tampa Bay	NHL	31	6	11	17	10	-6	1	0	—	—	—	—	—
— Chicago	NHL	12	4	4	8	8	3	1	0	16	7	11	18	10
95-96— Chicago	NHL	69	13	35	48	102	20	2	0	10	1	2	3	8
96-97— Chicago	NHL	64	9	18	27	60	-10	2	0	6	0	2	2	2
NHL totals (17 years)		1196	473	865	1338	1336	97	127	20	169	66	109	175	256

SAVARD, MARC   C   RANGERS

PERSONAL: Born July 17, 1977, in Ottawa. ... 5-10/177. ... Shoots left.
HIGH SCHOOL: Henry Street (Whitby, Ont.).
TRANSACTIONS/CAREER NOTES: Selected by New York Rangers in fourth round (third Rangers pick, 91st overall) of NHL entry draft (July 8, 1995).
HONORS: Won Can.HL Top Scorer Award (1994-95). ... Won Eddie Powers Memorial Trophy (1994-95). ... Named to OHL All-Star second team (1994-95).

Season Team	League	REGULAR SEASON Gms.	G	A	Pts.	PIM	+/-	PP	SH	PLAYOFFS Gms.	G	A	Pts.	PIM
92-93— Metcalfe	Jr. B	31	46	53	99	26	...	...	...	—	—	—	—	—
93-94— Oshawa	OHL	61	18	39	57	24	...	...	...	5	4	3	7	8
94-95— Oshawa	OHL	66	43	96	*139	78	...	...	...	7	5	6	11	8
95-96— Oshawa	OHL	48	28	59	87	77	...	...	...	5	4	5	9	6
96-97— Oshawa	OHL	64	43	*87	*130	94	...	...	...	18	13	†24	*37	20

SAVARY, NEIL   G   BRUINS

PERSONAL: Born April 3, 1976, in Halifax, N.E. ... 6-0/169. ... Catches left. ... Name pronounced SAY-vuh-ree.
TRANSACTIONS/CAREER NOTES: Selected by Boston Bruins in 10th round (eighth Bruins pick, 255th overall) of NHL entry draft (June 29, 1994).

Season Team	League	REGULAR SEASON Gms.	Min	W	L	T	GA	SO	Avg.	PLAYOFFS Gms.	Min.	W	L	GA	SO	Avg.
93-94— Hull	QMJHL	32	1708	15	14	0	118	2	4.15	6	158	0	2	14	0	5.32
94-95— Hull	QMJHL	30	1525	14	12	1	118	0	4.64	—	—	—	—	—	—	—
95-96— Halifax	QMJHL	23	1188	10	13	0	78	0	3.94	1	0	0	0	0	0	0.00
96-97— Halifax	QMJHL	1	60	0	1	0	8	0	8.00	—	—	—	—	—	—	—

SAWYER, KEVIN   LW   STARS

PERSONAL: Born February 18, 1974, in Christina Lake, B.C. ... 6-2/205. ... Shoots left.
TRANSACTIONS/CAREER NOTES: Signed as free agent by St. Louis Blues (February 16, 1995). ... Traded by Blues with D Steve Staios to Boston Bruins for RW Steve Leach (March 8, 1996). ... Signed as free agent by Dallas Stars (July 25, 1997).

Season Team	League	REGULAR SEASON Gms.	G	A	Pts.	PIM	+/-	PP	SH	PLAYOFFS Gms.	G	A	Pts.	PIM
92-93— Spokane	WHL	62	4	3	7	274	...	...	...	—	—	—	—	—
93-94— Spokane	WHL	60	10	15	25	350	...	...	...	3	0	1	1	6
94-95— Spokane	WHL	54	7	9	16	365	...	...	...	11	2	0	2	58
— Peoria	IHL	—	—	—	—	—	...	...	...	2	0	0	0	12
95-96— Worcester	AHL	41	3	4	7	268	...	...	...	—	—	—	—	—
— St. Louis	NHL	6	0	0	0	23	-2	0	0	—	—	—	—	—
— Providence	AHL	4	0	0	0	29	...	...	...	4	0	1	1	9
— Boston	NHL	2	0	0	0	5	1	0	0	—	—	—	—	—
96-97— Providence	AHL	60	8	9	17	367	...	...	...	6	0	0	0	32
— Boston	NHL	2	0	0	0	0	0	0	0	—	—	—	—	—
NHL totals (3 years)		10	0	0	0	28	-1	0	0					

SCATCHARD, DAVE   C   CANUCKS

PERSONAL: Born February 20, 1976, in Hinton, Alta. ... 6-2/185. ... Shoots right.
TRANSACTIONS/CAREER NOTES: Selected by Vancouver Canucks in second round (third Canucks pick, 42nd overall) of NHL entry draft (June 28, 1994).

Season Team	League	REGULAR SEASON Gms.	G	A	Pts.	PIM	+/-	PP	SH	PLAYOFFS Gms.	G	A	Pts.	PIM
92-93— Kimberley	RMJHL	51	20	23	43	61	...	...	...	—	—	—	—	—
93-94— Portland	WHL	47	9	11	20	46	...	...	...	10	2	1	3	4
94-95— Portland	WHL	71	20	30	50	148	...	...	...	8	0	3	3	21
95-96— Portland	WHL	59	19	28	47	146	...	...	...	7	1	8	9	14
— Syracuse	AHL	1	0	0	0	0	...	...	...	15	2	5	7	29
96-97— Syracuse	AHL	26	8	7	15	65	...	...	...	—	—	—	—	—

SCHAEFER, PETER   LW   CANUCKS

PERSONAL: Born July 12, 1977, in Yellow Grass, Sask. ... 5-11/178. ... Shoots left.
HIGH SCHOOL: Crocus Plains (Brandon, Man.).

TRANSACTIONS/CAREER NOTES: Selected by Vancouver Canucks in third round (third Canucks pick, 66th overall) of NHL entry draft (July 8, 1995).
HONORS: Named to WHL (East) All-Star first team (1995-96 and 1996-97). ... Won Four Broncos Memorial Trophy (1996-97). ... Named to Can.HL All-Star first team (1996-97).

Season Team	League	REGULAR SEASON								PLAYOFFS				
		Gms.	G	A	Pts.	PIM	+/-	PP	SH	Gms.	G	A	Pts.	PIM
93-94 — Brandon	WHL	2	1	0	1	0	...	...	...	—	—	—	—	—
94-95 — Brandon	WHL	68	27	32	59	34	...	...	...	18	5	3	8	18
95-96 — Brandon	WHL	69	47	61	108	53	...	...	...	19	10	13	23	5
96-97 — Brandon	WHL	61	49	74	123	85	...	...	...	6	1	4	5	4
— Syracuse	AHL	5	0	3	3	0	...	...	...	3	1	3	4	14

SCHAFER, PAXTON — G — BRUINS

PERSONAL: Born February 26, 1976, in Medicine Hat, Alta. ... 5-9/164. ... Catches left.
COLLEGE: Medicine Hat (Alta.).
TRANSACTIONS/CAREER NOTES: Selected by Boston Bruins in second round (third Bruins pick, 47th overall) of NHL entry draft (July 8, 1995).
HONORS: Won Del Wilson Trophy (1994-95). ... Named to Can.HL All-Star first team (1994-95). ... Named to WHL (East) All-Star first team (1994-95).

Season Team	League	REGULAR SEASON								PLAYOFFS					
		Gms.	Min	W	L	T	GA	SO	Avg.	Gms.	Min.	W	L	GA	SO	Avg.
93-94 — Medicine Hat	WHL	19	909	6	9	1	67	0	4.42	—	—	—	—	—	—	—
94-95 — Medicine Hat	WHL	61	3519	32	26	2	185	0	3.15	5	339	1	4	18	0	3.19
95-96 — Medicine Hat	WHL	60	3256	24	30	3	200	1	3.69	5	251	1	4	25	0	5.98
96-97 — Providence	AHL	22	1206	9	10	0	75	1	3.73	—	—	—	—	—	—	—
— Charlotte	ECHL	4	239	3	1	‡0	7	0	1.76	—	—	—	—	—	—	—

SCHMIDT, CHRIS — LW — KINGS

PERSONAL: Born March 1, 1976, in Beaverlodge, Alta. ... 6-3/193. ... Shoots left.
HIGH SCHOOL: Meadowdale (Lynwood, Wash.).
TRANSACTIONS/CAREER NOTES: Selected by Los Angeles Kings in fifth round (fourth Kings pick, 111th overall) of NHL entry draft (June 29, 1994).

Season Team	League	REGULAR SEASON								PLAYOFFS				
		Gms.	G	A	Pts.	PIM	+/-	PP	SH	Gms.	G	A	Pts.	PIM
92-93 — Seattle	WHL	61	6	7	13	17	...	...	...	5	0	1	1	0
93-94 — Seattle	WHL	68	7	17	24	26	...	...	...	9	3	1	4	2
94-95 — Seattle	WHL	61	21	11	32	31	...	...	...	3	0	0	0	0
95-96 — Seattle	WHL	61	39	23	62	135	...	...	...	5	1	5	6	9
96-97 — Mississippi	ECHL	18	7	7	14	35	...	...	...	—	—	—	—	—
— Phoenix	IHL	37	3	6	9	60	...	...	...	—	—	—	—	—

SCHMIDT, COLIN — LW — OILERS

PERSONAL: Born February 3, 1974, in Regina, Sask. ... 5-11/190. ... Shoots left.
HIGH SCHOOL: Archbishop M.C. O'Neill (Regina, Sask.).
COLLEGE: Colorado College.
TRANSACTIONS/CAREER NOTES: Selected by Edmonton Oilers in eighth round (ninth Oilers pick, 190th overall) of NHL entry draft (June 20, 1992).
HONORS: Named to WCHA All-Star second team (1994-95). ... Named to WCHA All-Star second team (1995-96).

Season Team	League	REGULAR SEASON								PLAYOFFS				
		Gms.	G	A	Pts.	PIM	+/-	PP	SH	Gms.	G	A	Pts.	PIM
92-93 — Colorado College	WCHA	27	8	13	21	26	...	...	...	—	—	—	—	—
93-94 — Colorado College	WCHA	38	14	22	36	49	...	...	...	—	—	—	—	—
94-95 — Colorado College	WCHA	43	26	31	57	61	...	...	...	—	—	—	—	—
95-96 — Colorado College	WCHA	42	21	37	58	101	...	...	...	—	—	—	—	—
96-97 — Hamilton	AHL	15	2	2	4	2	...	...	...	—	—	—	—	—
— Wheeling	ECHL	37	9	19	28	25	...	...	...	—	—	—	—	—

SCHNEIDER, MATHIEU — D — MAPLE LEAFS

PERSONAL: Born June 12, 1969, in New York. ... 5-10/192. ... Shoots left.
HIGH SCHOOL: Mount St. Charles Academy (Woonsocket, R.I.).
TRANSACTIONS/CAREER NOTES: Selected by Montreal Canadiens in third round (fourth Canadiens pick, 44th overall) of NHL entry draft (June 13, 1987). ... Bruised left shoulder (February 1990). ... Sprained left ankle (January 26, 1991); missed nine games. ... Sprained ankle (January 27, 1993); missed 24 games. ... Separated shoulder (April 18, 1993); missed seven playoff games. ... Injured ankle (December 6, 1993); missed two games. ... Underwent arthroscopic elbow surgery (March 29, 1994); missed five games. ... Suffered from cold (February 27, 1995); missed one game. ... Traded by Canadiens with LW Kirk Muller and C Craig Darby to New York Islanders for D Vladimir Malakhov and C Pierre Turgeon (April 5, 1995). ... Bruised ribs (October 28, 1995); missed one game. ... Traded by Islanders with LW Wendel Clark and D D.J. Smith to Toronto Maple Leafs for LW Sean Haggerty, C Darby Hendrickson, D Kenny Jonsson and first-round pick (G Roberto Luongo) in 1997 draft (March 13, 1996). ... Suspended three games by NHL for elbowing incident (November 14, 1996). ... Strained groin (December 12, 1996); missed 27 games. ... Reinjured groin (February 12, 1997); underwent surgery (March 7, 1997) and missed remainder of season.
HONORS: Named to OHL All-Star first team (1987-88 and 1988-89). ... Played in NHL All-Star Game (1996).
MISCELLANEOUS: Member of Stanley Cup championship team (1993). ... Captain of New York Islanders (1995-96).

Season Team	League	REGULAR SEASON								PLAYOFFS				
		Gms.	G	A	Pts.	PIM	+/-	PP	SH	Gms.	G	A	Pts.	PIM
85-86— Mount St. Charles......	R.I.H.S.	19	3	27	30	...				—	—	—	—	—
86-87— Cornwall....................	OHL	63	7	29	36	75	...	...	...	5	0	0	0	22
87-88— Montreal..................	NHL	4	0	0	0	2	-2	0	0	—	—	—	—	—
— Cornwall....................	OHL	48	21	40	61	85	...	...	...	11	2	6	8	14
— Sherbrooke................	AHL	—	—	—	—	—				3	0	3	3	12
88-89— Cornwall....................	OHL	59	16	57	73	96	...	...	...	18	7	20	27	30
89-90— Sherbrooke................	AHL	28	6	13	19	20	...	...	...	—	—	—	—	—
— Montreal..................	NHL	44	7	14	21	25	2	5	0	9	1	3	4	31
90-91— Montreal..................	NHL	69	10	20	30	63	7	5	0	13	2	7	9	18
91-92— Montreal..................	NHL	78	8	24	32	72	10	2	0	10	1	4	5	6
92-93— Montreal..................	NHL	60	13	31	44	91	8	3	0	11	1	2	3	16
93-94— Montreal..................	NHL	75	20	32	52	62	15	11	0	1	0	0	0	0
94-95— Montreal..................	NHL	30	5	15	20	49	-3	2	0	—	—	—	—	—
— New York Islanders....	NHL	13	3	6	9	30	-5	1	0	—	—	—	—	—
95-96— New York Islanders....	NHL	65	11	36	47	93	-18	7	0	—	—	—	—	—
— Toronto....................	NHL	13	2	5	7	10	-2	0	0	6	0	4	4	8
96-97— Toronto....................	NHL	26	5	7	12	20	3	1	0	—	—	—	—	—
NHL totals (9 years)		477	84	190	274	517	15	37	0	50	5	20	25	79

SCHULTE, PAXTON — LW — FLAMES

PERSONAL: Born July 16, 1972, in Edmonton. ... 6-2/217. ... Shoots left. ... Name pronounced SHOOL-tee.
COLLEGE: North Dakota, then Spokane (Wash.) Falls.
TRANSACTIONS/CAREER NOTES: Selected by Quebec Nordiques in sixth round (seventh Nordiques pick, 124th overall) of NHL entry draft (June 20, 1992). ... Nordiques franchise moved to Colorado and renamed Avalanche for 1995-96 season (June 21, 1995). ... Traded by Avalanche to Calgary Flames for LW Vesa Viitakoski (March 19, 1996).

Season Team	League	REGULAR SEASON								PLAYOFFS				
		Gms.	G	A	Pts.	PIM	+/-	PP	SH	Gms.	G	A	Pts.	PIM
89-90— Sherwood Park..........	AJHL	56	28	38	66	151	...	...	...	—	—	—	—	—
90-91— North Dakota	WCHA	38	2	4	6	32	...	...	...	—	—	—	—	—
91-92— Spokane....................	WHL	70	42	42	84	222	...	...	...	10	2	8	10	48
92-93— Spokane....................	WHL	45	38	35	73	142	...	...	...	10	5	6	11	12
93-94— Cornwall....................	AHL	56	15	15	30	102	...	...	...	—	—	—	—	—
— Quebec....................	NHL	1	0	0	0	2	0	0	0	—	—	—	—	—
94-95— Cornwall....................	AHL	74	14	22	36	217	...	...	...	14	3	3	6	29
95-96— Cornwall....................	AHL	69	25	31	56	171	...	...	...	—	—	—	—	—
— Saint John	AHL	14	4	5	9	25	...	...	...	14	4	7	11	40
96-97— Saint John	AHL	71	14	23	37	274	...	...	...	4	2	0	2	35
— Calgary	NHL	1	0	0	0	2	1	0	0	—	—	—	—	—
NHL totals (2 years)		2	0	0	0	4	1	0	0					

SCHWAB, COREY — G — LIGHTNING

PERSONAL: Born November 4, 1970, in Battleford, Sask. ... 6-0/180. ... Catches left. ... Name pronounced SHWAHB.
TRANSACTIONS/CAREER NOTES: Selected by New Jersey Devils in 10th round (12th Devils pick, 200th overall) of NHL entry draft (June 16, 1990). ... Injured groin (October 12, 1995); missed six games. ... Traded by Devils to Tampa Bay Lightning for G Jeff Reese and second- (LW Pierre Dagenais) and eighth-(RW Jason Bertsch) round picks in 1996 draft (June 22, 1996). ... Injured groin (January 9, 1997); missed one game.
HONORS: Shared Harry (Hap) Holmes Memorial Trophy with Mike Dunham (1994-95). ... Shared Jack Butterfield Trophy with Mike Dunham (1994-95). ... Named to AHL All-Star second team (1994-95).

Season Team	League	REGULAR SEASON							PLAYOFFS					
		Gms.	Min	W	L	T	GA	SO	Avg.	Gms.	Min.	W	L	GA	SO	Avg.
88-89— Seattle	WHL	10	386	2	2	0	31	0	4.82	—	—	—	—	—	—	—
89-90— Seattle	WHL	27	1150	15	2	1	69	0	3.60	3	49	0	0	2	0	2.45
90-91— Seattle	WHL	58	3289	32	18	3	224	1	4.09	6	382	1	5	25	0	3.93
91-92— Utica............................	AHL	24	1322	9	12	1	95	1	4.31	—	—	—	—	—	—	—
— Cincinnati...................	AHL	8	450	6	0	1	31	0	4.13	9	540	6	3	29	0	3.22
92-93— Utica............................	AHL	40	2387	18	16	5	169	2	4.25	1	59	0	1	6	0	6.10
— Cincinnati...................	IHL	3	185	1	2	‡0	17	0	5.51							
93-94— Albany......................	AHL	51	3059	27	21	3	184	0	3.61	5	298	1	4	20	0	4.03
94-95— Albany......................	AHL	45	2711	25	10	9	117	3	*2.59	7	425	6	1	19	0	2.68
95-96— Albany......................	AHL	5	298	3	2	0	13	0	2.62	—	—	—	—	—	—	—
— New Jersey................	NHL	10	331	0	3	0	12	0	2.18	—	—	—	—	—	—	—
96-97— Tampa Bay..................	NHL	31	1462	11	12	1	74	2	3.04	—	—	—	—	—	—	—
NHL totals (2 years)		41	1793	11	15	1	86	2	2.88							

SCOTT, TRAVIS — G

PERSONAL: Born September 14, 1975, in Ottawa. ... 6-2/185. ... Catches left.
TRANSACTIONS/CAREER NOTES: Signed as free agent by St. Louis Blues prior to 1996-97 season.

Season Team	League	REGULAR SEASON							PLAYOFFS					
		Gms.	Min	W	L	T	GA	SO	Avg.	Gms.	Min.	W	L	GA	SO	Avg.
91-92— Smiths Falls-Nepean.....	Jr. A	22	1151	...	...	...	90	1	4.69	—	—	—	—	—	—	—
92-93— Nepean	COJHL	36	1968	...	...	...	133	0	4.05	—	—	—	—	—	—	—
93-94— Windsor.......................	OHL	45	2312	20	18	0	158	1	4.10	4	240	0	4	16	0	4.00

Season Team	League	Gms.	Min	W	L	T	GA	SO	Avg.	Gms.	Min.	W	L	GA	SO	Avg.
94-95—Windsor	OHL	48	2644	26	14	3	147	*3	3.34	3	94	0	1	6	1	3.83
95-96—Oshawa	OHL	31	1763	15	9	4	78	†3	*2.65	5	315	1	4	23	0	4.38
96-97—Baton Rouge	ECHL	10	501	5	2	‡1	22	0	2.63	—	—	—	—	—	—	—
—Worcester	AHL	29	1482	14	10	1	75	1	3.04	—	—	—	—	—	—	—

SELANNE, TEEMU   RW   MIGHTY DUCKS

PERSONAL: Born July 3, 1970, in Helsinki, Finland. ... 6-0/200. ... Shoots right. ... Name pronounced TAY-moo suh-LAH-nee.

TRANSACTIONS/CAREER NOTES: Selected by Winnipeg Jets in first round (first Jets pick, 10th overall) of NHL entry draft (June 11, 1988). ... Broke left leg (October 19, 1989). ... Severed Achilles' tendon (January 26, 1994); missed 33 games. ... Played in Europe during 1994-95 NHL lockout. ... Suffered from patella tendinitis (February 28, 1995); missed one game. ... Suspended two games and fined $500 by NHL (March 28, 1995). ... Traded by Jets with C Marc Chouinard and fourth-round pick (traded to Toronto) in 1996 draft to Mighty Ducks of Anaheim for C Chad Kilger, D Oleg Tverdovsky and third-round pick (D Per-Anton Lundstrom) in 1996 draft (February 7, 1996). ... Strained abdominal muscle (March 23, 1997); missed four games.

HONORS: Named to Finnish League All-Star team (1990-91 and 1991-92). ... Named NHL Rookie of the Year by THE SPORTING NEWS (1992-93). ... Won Calder Memorial Trophy (1992-93). ... Named to THE SPORTING NEWS All-Star first team (1992-93). ... Named to NHL All-Star first team (1992-93 and 1996-97). ... Named to NHL All-Rookie team (1992-93). ... Played in NHL All-Star Game (1993, 1994, 1996 and 1997). ... Named to THE SPORTING NEWS All-Star team (1996-97).

RECORDS: Holds NHL rookie-season records for most points—132; and goals—76 (1993).

STATISTICAL PLATEAUS: Three-goal games: 1992-93 (4), 1993-94 (2), 1995-96 (2), 1996-97 (1). Total: 9. ... Four-goal games: 1992-93 (1), 1995-96 (1). Total: 2. ... Total hat tricks: 11.

MISCELLANEOUS: Scored on a penalty shot (vs. Wendell Young, March 9, 1993). ... Failed to score on a penalty shot (vs. Trevor Kidd, February 6, 1995).

Season Team	League	Gms.	G	A	Pts.	PIM	+/-	PP	SH	Gms.	G	A	Pts.	PIM
87-88—Jokerit Helsinki	Finland	33	42	23	65	18	...	...	...	5	4	3	7	2
88-89—Jokerit Helsinki	Finland	34	35	33	68	12	...	...	...	5	7	3	10	4
89-90—Jokerit Helsinki	Finland	11	4	8	12	0	...	...	...	—	—	—	—	—
90-91—Jokerit Helsinki	Finland	42	*33	25	58	12	...	...	...	—	—	—	—	—
91-92—Fin. Olympic team	Int'l	8	7	4	11	...	...	...	...	—	—	—	—	—
—Jokerit Helsinki	Finland	44	39	23	62	20	...	...	...	—	—	—	—	—
92-93—Winnipeg	NHL	84	†76	56	132	45	8	24	0	6	4	2	6	2
93-94—Winnipeg	NHL	51	25	29	54	22	-23	11	0	—	—	—	—	—
94-95—Jokerit Helsinki	Finland	20	7	12	19	6	...	...	...	—	—	—	—	—
—Winnipeg	NHL	45	22	26	48	2	1	8	2	—	—	—	—	—
95-96—Winnipeg	NHL	51	24	48	72	18	3	6	1	—	—	—	—	—
—Anaheim	NHL	28	16	20	36	4	2	3	0	—	—	—	—	—
96-97—Anaheim	NHL	78	51	58	109	34	28	11	1	11	7	3	10	4
NHL totals (5 years)		337	214	237	451	125	19	63	4	17	11	5	16	6

SELIVANOV, ALEXANDER   RW   LIGHTNING

PERSONAL: Born March 23, 1971, in Moscow, U.S.S.R. ... 6-1/187. ... Shoots left. ... Name pronounced sehl-ih-VAH-nahv.

TRANSACTIONS/CAREER NOTES: Selected by Philadelphia Flyers in sixth round (sixth Flyers pick, 140th overall) of NHL entry draft (June 29, 1994). ... Rights traded by Flyers to Tampa Bay Lightning for fourth-round pick in 1995 draft (September 6, 1994). ... Loaned by Lightning to Chicago Wolves (December 14, 1994). ... Sprained ankle (February 10, 1996); missed two games. ... Injured back (November 25, 1996); missed one game. ... Injured wrist (December 14, 1996); missed one game. ... Sprained knee (February 4, 1997); missed one game. ... Underwent knee surgery (February 25, 1997); missed eight games.

Season Team	League	Gms.	G	A	Pts.	PIM	+/-	PP	SH	Gms.	G	A	Pts.	PIM
88-89—Spartak Moscow	USSR	1	0	0	0	0	...	...	...	—	—	—	—	—
89-90—Spartak Moscow	USSR	4	0	0	0	0	...	...	...	—	—	—	—	—
90-91—Spartak Moscow	USSR	21	3	1	4	6	...	...	...	—	—	—	—	—
91-92—Spartak Moscow	CIS	31	6	7	13	16	...	...	...	—	—	—	—	—
92-93—Spartak Moscow	CIS	42	12	19	31	16	...	...	...	3	2	0	2	2
93-94—Spartak Moscow	CIS	45	30	11	41	50	...	...	...	6	5	1	6	2
94-95—Atlanta	IHL	4	0	3	3	2	...	...	...	—	—	—	—	—
—Chicago	IHL	14	4	1	5	8	...	...	...	—	—	—	—	—
—Tampa Bay	NHL	43	10	6	16	14	-2	4	0	—	—	—	—	—
95-96—Tampa Bay	NHL	79	31	21	52	93	3	13	0	6	2	2	4	6
96-97—Tampa Bay	NHL	69	15	18	33	61	-3	3	0	—	—	—	—	—
NHL totals (3 years)		191	56	45	101	168	-2	20	0	6	2	2	4	6

SEMAK, ALEXANDER   C   CANUCKS

PERSONAL: Born February 11, 1966, in Ufa, U.S.S.R. ... 5-10/185. ... Shoots left. ... Name pronounced SEE-mahk.

TRANSACTIONS/CAREER NOTES: Selected by New Jersey Devils in 10th round (12th Devils pick, 207th overall) of NHL entry draft (June 11, 1988). ... Injured shoulder (February 8, 1992); missed seven games. ... Suffered injury (November 30, 1993); missed two games. ... Strained knee (December 11, 1993); missed 17 games. ... Played in Europe during 1994-95 NHL lockout. ... Traded by Devils with RW Ben Hankinson to Tampa Bay Lightning for D Shawn Chambers and RW Danton Cole (March 14, 1995). ... Traded by Lightning to New York Islanders for fifth-round pick (D Karel Betik) in 1997 draft (September 14, 1995). ... Bruised right knee (March 30, 1996); missed eight games. ... Selected by Vancouver Canucks from Islanders in waiver draft for cash (September 30, 1996).

STATISTICAL PLATEAUS: Three-goal games: 1993-94 (1).

Season Team	League	REGULAR SEASON								PLAYOFFS				
		Gms.	G	A	Pts.	PIM	+/-	PP	SH	Gms.	G	A	Pts.	PIM
82-83— Salavet Yulayev Ufa ...	USSR	13	2	1	3	4	...	...	...	—	—	—	—	—
83-84— Salavet Yulayev Ufa....	USSR					Statistics unavailable.								
84-85— Salavet Yulayev Ufa ...	USSR	47	19	17	36	64	...	...	...	—	—	—	—	—
85-86— Salavet Yulayev Ufa ...	USSR	22	9	7	16	22	...	...	...	—	—	—	—	—
86-87— Dynamo Moscow	USSR	40	20	8	28	32	...	...	...	—	—	—	—	—
87-88— Dynamo Moscow	USSR	47	21	14	35	40	...	...	...	—	—	—	—	—
88-89— Dynamo Moscow	USSR	44	18	10	28	22	...	...	...	—	—	—	—	—
89-90— Dynamo Moscow	USSR	43	23	11	34	33	...	...	...	—	—	—	—	—
90-91— Dynamo Moscow	USSR	46	17	21	38	48	...	...	...	—	—	—	—	—
91-92— Dynamo Moscow	CIS	18	6	11	17	18	...	...	...	—	—	—	—	—
— Utica	AHL	7	3	2	5	0	...	...	...	—	—	—	—	—
— New Jersey	NHL	25	5	6	11	0	5	0	0	1	0	0	0	0
92-93— New Jersey	NHL	82	37	42	79	70	24	4	1	5	1	1	2	0
93-94— New Jersey	NHL	54	12	17	29	22	6	2	2	2	0	0	0	0
94-95— Salavat Yulayev Ufa ...	CIS	9	9	6	15	4	...	...	...	—	—	—	—	—
— New Jersey	NHL	19	2	6	8	13	-4	0	0	—	—	—	—	—
— Tampa Bay	NHL	22	5	5	10	12	-3	0	0	—	—	—	—	—
95-96— New York Islanders	NHL	69	20	14	34	68	-4	6	0	—	—	—	—	—
96-97— Vancouver	NHL	18	2	1	3	2	-2	1	0	—	—	—	—	—
— Syracuse	AHL	23	10	14	24	12	...	...	...	—	—	—	—	—
— Las Vegas	IHL	13	11	13	24	10	...	...	...	3	0	4	4	4
NHL totals (6 years)		289	83	91	174	187	22	13	3	8	1	1	2	0

SEMENOV, ANATOLI   C/LW   SABRES

S

PERSONAL: Born March 5, 1962, in Moscow, U.S.S.R. ... 6-2/200. ... Shoots left. ... Name pronounced AN-uh-TOH-lee SEH-mih-nahf.

TRANSACTIONS/CAREER NOTES: Selected by Edmonton Oilers in sixth round (fifth Oilers pick, 120th overall) of NHL entry draft (June 17, 1989). ... Bruised ribs (March 1, 1991); missed five games. ... Suffered hairline fracture in left foot (October 1991); missed four games. ... Suffered concussion (November 1991); missed two games. ... Injured shoulder (January 4, 1992); missed six games. ... Sprained ankle (February 28, 1992); missed one game. ... Selected by Tampa Bay Lightning in NHL expansion draft (June 18, 1992). ... Traded by Lightning to Vancouver Canucks for C Dave Capuano and fourth-round pick (traded to New Jersey Devils) in 1994 draft (November 3, 1992). ... Strained knee (January 9, 1993); missed six games. ... Selected by Mighty Ducks of Anaheim in NHL expansion draft (June 24, 1993). ... Dislocated elbow (December 7, 1993); missed 21 games. ... Aggravated elbow injury (January 28, 1994); missed two games. ... Traded by Mighty Ducks to Philadelphia Flyers for D Milos Holan (March 8, 1995). ... Bruised ribs (December 21, 1995); missed six games. ... Traded by Flyers with D Mike Crowley to Mighty Ducks for RW Brian Wesenberg (March 19, 1996). ... Signed as free agent by Buffalo Sabres (September 5, 1996). ... Tore rotator cuff (December 28, 1996); missed remainder of season.

HONORS: Named to Soviet League All-Star team (1984-85).

MISCELLANEOUS: Member of gold-medal-winning U.S.S.R. Olympic team (1988).

Season Team	League	REGULAR SEASON								PLAYOFFS				
		Gms.	G	A	Pts.	PIM	+/-	PP	SH	Gms.	G	A	Pts.	PIM
79-80— Dynamo Moscow	USSR	8	3	0	3	2	...	...	...	—	—	—	—	—
80-81— Dynamo Moscow	USSR	47	18	14	32	18	...	...	...	—	—	—	—	—
81-82— Dynamo Moscow	USSR	44	12	14	26	28	...	...	...	—	—	—	—	—
82-83— Dynamo Moscow	USSR	44	22	18	40	26	...	...	...	—	—	—	—	—
83-84— Dynamo Moscow	USSR	19	10	5	15	14	...	...	...	—	—	—	—	—
84-85— Dynamo Moscow	USSR	30	17	12	29	32	...	...	...	—	—	—	—	—
85-86— Dynamo Moscow	USSR	32	18	17	35	19	...	...	...	—	—	—	—	—
86-87— Dynamo Moscow	USSR	40	15	29	44	32	...	...	...	—	—	—	—	—
87-88— Dynamo Moscow	USSR	32	17	8	25	22	...	...	...	—	—	—	—	—
88-89— Dynamo Moscow	USSR	31	9	12	21	24	...	...	...	—	—	—	—	—
89-90— Dynamo Moscow	USSR	48	13	20	33	16	...	...	...	—	—	—	—	—
— Edmonton	NHL	—	—	—	—	—				2	0	0	0	0
90-91— Edmonton	NHL	57	15	16	31	26	17	3	1	12	5	5	10	6
91-92— Edmonton	NHL	59	20	22	42	16	12	3	0	8	1	1	2	6
92-93— Tampa Bay	NHL	13	2	3	5	4	-5	0	0	—	—	—	—	—
— Vancouver	NHL	62	10	34	44	28	21	3	2	12	1	3	4	0
93-94— Anaheim	NHL	49	11	19	30	12	-4	4	0	—	—	—	—	—
94-95— Anaheim	NHL	15	3	4	7	4	-10	2	0	—	—	—	—	—
— Philadelphia	NHL	26	1	2	3	6	-2	0	0	15	2	4	6	0
95-96— Philadelphia	NHL	44	3	13	16	14	3	0	0	—	—	—	—	—
— Anaheim	NHL	12	1	9	10	10	-4	0	0	—	—	—	—	—
96-97— Buffalo	NHL	25	2	4	6	2	-3	1	0	—	—	—	—	—
NHL totals (8 years)		362	68	126	194	122	25	16	3	49	9	13	22	12

SEVERYN, BRENT   D/LW   AVALANCHE

PERSONAL: Born February 22, 1966, in Vegreville, Alta. ... 6-2/211. ... Shoots left. ... Full name: Brent Leonard Severyn. ... Name pronounced SEHV-rihn.

COLLEGE: Alberta.

TRANSACTIONS/CAREER NOTES: Selected by Winnipeg Jets in fifth round (fifth Jets pick, 99th overall) of NHL entry draft (June 9, 1984). ... Injured knee (October 1985). ... Signed as free agent by Quebec Nordiques (July 15, 1988). ... Traded by Nordiques to New Jersey Devils for D Dave Marcinyshyn (June 3, 1991). ... Traded by Devils to Jets for sixth-round pick (C Ryan Smart) in 1994 draft (September 30, 1993). ... Traded by Jets to Florida Panthers for D Milan Tichy (October 3, 1993). ... Suffered left eye abrasion (November 23, 1993); missed one game. ... Traded by Panthers to New York Islanders for fourth-round pick (LW Dave Duerden) in 1995 draft (March 3, 1995). ... Suspended three games by NHL for shoving a linesman (October 26, 1995). ... Injured back (February 15, 1996); missed six games. ... Injured neck (March 16, 1996); missed two games. ... Traded by Islanders to Colorado Avalanche for third-round pick (traded to Calgary) in 1997 draft (September 4, 1996). ... Suspended two games by NHL for initiating an altercation (February 18, 1997).

HONORS: Named to CWUAA All-Star team (1987-88). ... Named to AHL All-Star first team (1992-93).

Season Team	League	Gms.	G	A	Pts.	PIM	+/-	PP	SH	Gms.	G	A	Pts.	PIM
82-83— Vegreville	CAJHL	21	20	22	42	10	...	...	...	—	—	—	—	—
83-84— Seattle	WHL	72	14	22	36	49	...	...	...	5	2	1	3	2
84-85— Seattle	WHL	38	8	32	40	54	...	...	...	—	—	—	—	—
— Brandon	WHL	26	7	16	23	57	...	...	...	—	—	—	—	—
85-86— Seattle	WHL	33	11	20	31	164	...	...	...	5	0	4	4	4
— Saskatoon	WHL	9	1	4	5	38	...	...	...	—	—	—	—	—
86-87— Univ. of Alberta	CWUAA	43	7	19	26	171	...	...	...	—	—	—	—	—
87-88— Univ. of Alberta	CWUAA	46	21	29	50	178	...	...	...	—	—	—	—	—
88-89— Halifax	AHL	47	2	12	14	141	...	...	...	—	—	—	—	—
89-90— Quebec	NHL	35	0	2	2	42	-19	0	0	—	—	—	—	—
— Halifax	AHL	43	6	9	15	105	...	...	...	6	1	2	3	49
90-91— Halifax	AHL	50	7	26	33	202	...	...	...	—	—	—	—	—
91-92— Utica	AHL	80	11	33	44	211	...	...	...	4	0	1	1	4
92-93— Utica	AHL	77	20	32	52	240	...	...	...	5	0	0	0	35
93-94— Florida	NHL	67	4	7	11	156	-1	1	0	—	—	—	—	—
94-95— Florida	NHL	9	1	1	2	37	-3	1	0	—	—	—	—	—
— New York Islanders....	NHL	19	1	3	4	34	1	0	0	—	—	—	—	—
95-96— New York Islanders....	NHL	65	1	8	9	180	3	0	0	—	—	—	—	—
96-97— Colorado	NHL	66	1	4	5	193	-6	0	0	8	0	0	0	12
NHL totals (5 years)		261	8	25	33	642	-25	2	0	8	0	0	0	12

SEVIGNY, PIERRE   LW   CANADIENS

PERSONAL: Born September 8, 1971, in Trois-Rivieres, Que. ... 6-0/189. ... Shoots left. ... Name pronounced SAY-vuhn-yee.
TRANSACTIONS/CAREER NOTES: Selected by Montreal Canadiens in third round (fourth Canadiens pick, 51st overall) of NHL entry draft (June 17, 1989). ... Severed knee ligament in off-ice accident (March 25, 1991). ... Tore knee ligaments (December 6, 1993); missed 23 games. ... Cut elbow (January 9, 1997); missed nine games.
HONORS: Named to QMJHL All-Star second team (1989-90 and 1990-91).

Season Team	League	Gms.	G	A	Pts.	PIM	+/-	PP	SH	Gms.	G	A	Pts.	PIM
88-89— Verdun	QMJHL	67	27	43	70	88	...	...	...	—	—	—	—	—
89-90— St. Hyacinthe	QMJHL	67	47	72	119	205	...	...	...	12	8	8	16	42
90-91— St. Hyacinthe	QMJHL	60	36	46	82	203	...	...	...	—	—	—	—	—
91-92— Fredericton	AHL	74	22	37	59	145	...	...	...	7	1	1	2	26
92-93— Fredericton	AHL	80	36	40	76	113	...	...	...	5	1	1	2	2
93-94— Montreal	NHL	43	4	5	9	42	6	1	0	3	0	1	1	0
94-95— Montreal	NHL	19	0	0	0	15	-5	0	0	—	—	—	—	—
95-96— Fredericton	AHL	76	39	42	81	188	...	...	...	10	5	9	14	20
96-97— Fredericton	AHL	32	9	17	26	58	...	...	...	—	—	—	—	—
— Montreal	NHL	13	0	0	0	5	0	0	0	—	—	—	—	—
NHL totals (3 years)		75	4	5	9	62	1	1	0	3	0	1	1	0

SHAFRANOV, KONSTANTIN   RW   BLUES

PERSONAL: Born September 11, 1968, in Magnitogorsk, U.S.S.R. ... 5-11/176. ... Shoots left. ... Name pronounced shuh-FRAH-nahv.
TRANSACTIONS/CAREER NOTES: Selected by St. Louis Blues in ninth round (10th Blues pick, 229th overall) of NHL entry draft (June 22, 1996).

Season Team	League	Gms.	G	A	Pts.	PIM	+/-	PP	SH	Gms.	G	A	Pts.	PIM
86-87—Torpedo Ust-Kam.	USSR Div. II	6	0	0	0	2	...	...	...	...	...	...	...	...
87-88—Torpedo Ust-Kam.	USSR Div. II	...	7	...	...	...	...	...	...	...	...	...	...	...
— SKA Novofibirsk.	USSR Div. III	...	1	0	0	...	...	...	...	...	...	...	...	...
88-89— SKA Novofibirsk.	USSR Div. II							Statistics available.						
89-90— Torpedo Ust-Kam.	USSR	28	6	8	14	16	...	...	...	...	...	...	...	...
90-91— Torpedo Ust-Kam.	USSR	40	16	6	22	32	...	...	...	...	...	...	...	...
91-92— Torpedo Ust-Kam.	CIS	36	10	6	16	40	...	...	...	...	...	...	...	...
92-93— Torpedo Ust-Kam.	CIS	42	19	19	38	26	...	...	...	1	0	1	1	0
93-94— Detroit	Col.HL	4	3	2	5	0	...	...	...	—	—	—	—	—
— Torpedo Ust-Kam.	CIS	28	18	21	39	6	...	...	...	—	—	—	—	—
94-95— Metallurg Magn.	CIS	47	21	30	51	24	...	...	...	7	5	4	9	12
95-96— Metallurg Magn.	CIS	6	3	3	6	0	...	...	...	—	—	—	—	—
— Fort Wayne	IHL	74	46	28	74	26	...	...	...	5	1	2	3	4
96-97— Worcester	AHL	62	23	25	48	16	...	...	...	5	0	2	2	0
— St. Louis	NHL	5	2	1	3	0	1	0	0	—	—	—	—	—
NHL totals (1 year)		5	2	1	3	0	1	0	0					

SHALDYBIN, YEVGENY   D   BRUINS

PERSONAL: Born July 29, 1975, in Novosibirsk, U.S.S.R. ... 6-2/198. ... Shoots left. ... Name pronounced ev-GEH-nee SHALD-yoo-bihn.
TRANSACTIONS/CAREER NOTES: Selected by Boston Bruins in sixth round (fifth Bruin pick, 151st overall) of NHL entry draft (July 8, 1995).

Season Team	League	Gms.	G	A	Pts.	PIM	+/-	PP	SH	Gms.	G	A	Pts.	PIM
93-94— Torpedo Yaroslavl	CIS	14	0	0	0	0	...	...	...	—	—	—	—	—
94-95— Torpedo Yaroslavl	CIS	42	2	5	7	10	...	...	...	4	0	1	1	0
95-96— Torpedo Yaroslavl	CIS	41	0	2	2	10	...	...	...	—	—	—	—	—
96-97— Providence	AHL	65	4	13	17	28	...	...	...	3	0	0	0	0
— Boston	NHL	3	1	0	1	0	-2	0	0	—	—	—	—	—
NHL totals (1 year)		3	1	0	1	0	-2	0	0					

PERSONAL: Born January 23, 1969, in Mimico, Ont. ... 6-3/218. ... Shoots right. ... Full name: Brendan Frederick Shanahan.
HIGH SCHOOL: Michael Power/St. Joseph's (Islington, Ont.).
TRANSACTIONS/CAREER NOTES: Bruised tendons in shoulder (January 1987). ... Selected by New Jersey Devils as underage junior in first round (first Devils pick, second overall) of NHL entry draft (June 13, 1987). ... Broke nose (December 1987). ... Suffered back spasms (March 1989). ... Suspended five games by NHL for stick-fighting (January 13, 1990). ... Suffered lower abdominal strain (February 1990). ... Suffered lacerations to lower right side of face and underwent surgery (January 8, 1991); missed five games. ... Signed as free agent by St. Louis Blues (July 25, 1991); D Scott Stevens awarded to Devils as compensation (September 3, 1991). ... Pulled groin (October 24, 1992); missed 12 games. ... Suspended six off-days and fined $500 by NHL for hitting another player in face with his stick (January 7, 1993). ... Suspended one game by NHL for high-sticking incident (February 23, 1993). ... Suffered viral infection (November 18, 1993); missed one game. ... Injured hamstring (March 22, 1994); missed two games. ... Played in Europe during 1994-95 NHL lockout. ... Suffered viral infection (January 20, 1995); missed three games. ... Broke ankle (May 15, 1995); missed last two games of playoffs. ... Traded by Blues to Hartford Whalers for D Chris Pronger (July 27, 1995). ... Sprained wrist (November 11, 1995); missed eight games. ... Traded by Whalers with D Brian Glynn to Detroit Red Wings for C Keith Primeau, D Paul Coffey and first-round pick (traded to San Jose) in 1997 draft (October 9, 1996). ... Suspended one game and fined $1,000 by NHL for crosschecking (October 11, 1996). ... Pulled groin (October 30, 1996); missed one game.
HONORS: Played in NHL All-Star Game (1994, 1996 and 1997). ... Named to NHL All-Star first team (1993-94).
STATISTICAL PLATEAUS: Three-goal games: 1992-93 (1), 1993-94 (4), 1995-96 (1), 1996-97 (3). Total: 9.
MISCELLANEOUS: Member of Stanley Cup championship team (1997). ... Captain of Hartford Whalers (1995-96). ... Failed to score on a penalty shot (vs. Grant Fuhr, December 27, 1992).

Season Team	League	Gms.	G	A	Pts.	PIM	+/-	PP	SH	Gms.	G	A	Pts.	PIM
				REGULAR SEASON								PLAYOFFS		
84-85 — Mississauga	MTHL	36	20	21	41	26	...	...	...	—	—	—	—	—
85-86 — London	OHL	59	28	34	62	70	...	...	...	5	5	5	10	5
86-87 — London	OHL	56	39	53	92	128	...	...	...	—	—	—	—	—
87-88 — New Jersey	NHL	65	7	19	26	131	-20	2	0	12	2	1	3	44
88-89 — New Jersey	NHL	68	22	28	50	115	2	9	0	—	—	—	—	—
89-90 — New Jersey	NHL	73	30	42	72	137	15	8	0	6	3	3	6	20
90-91 — New Jersey	NHL	75	29	37	66	141	4	7	0	7	3	5	8	12
91-92 — St. Louis	NHL	80	33	36	69	171	-3	13	0	6	2	3	5	14
92-93 — St. Louis	NHL	71	51	43	94	174	10	18	0	11	4	3	7	18
93-94 — St. Louis	NHL	81	52	50	102	211	-9	15	*7	4	2	5	7	4
94-95 — Dusseldorf	Germany	3	5	3	8	4	...	...	...	—	—	—	—	—
— St. Louis	NHL	45	20	21	41	136	7	6	2	5	4	5	9	14
95-96 — Hartford	NHL	74	44	34	78	125	2	17	2	—	—	—	—	—
96-97 — Hartford	NHL	2	1	0	1	0	1	0	1	—	—	—	—	—
— Detroit	NHL	79	46	41	87	131	31	†20	2	20	9	8	17	43
NHL totals (10 years)		713	335	351	686	1472	40	115	14	71	29	33	62	169

PERSONAL: Born December 8, 1969, in Barrie, Ont. ... 6-2/205. ... Shoots left. ... Brother of Darryl Shannon, defenseman, Buffalo Sabres.
TRANSACTIONS/CAREER NOTES: Separated right shoulder (November 1986). ... Dislocated left elbow (November 1987). ... Separated left shoulder (January 1988). ... Selected by Pittsburgh Penguins in first round (first Penguins pick, fourth overall) of NHL entry draft (June 11, 1988). ... Traded by Penguins with D Doug Bodger to Buffalo Sabres for G Tom Barrasso and third-round pick (LW Joe Dziedzic) in 1990 draft (November 12, 1988). ... Strained knee ligaments (May 1990). ... Injured jaw (January 8, 1991); missed five games. ... Traded by Sabres with LW Mike Hartman and D Dean Kennedy to Winnipeg Jets for RW Dave McLlwain, D Gordon Donnelly, fifth-round pick (LW Yuri Khmylev) in 1992 draft and future considerations (October 11, 1991). ... Injured knee (November 20, 1991). ... Injured eye (November 25, 1991); missed one game. ... Sprained leg (December 31, 1991); missed seven games. ... Strained calf (October 12, 1993); missed five games. ... Fractured rib (February 4, 1995); missed seven games. ... Strained abdomen (March 11, 1995); missed one game. ... Strained left groin (March 20, 1995); missed remainder of season. ... Sprained knee (December 6, 1995); missed four games. ... Strained groin (January 8, 1996); missed five games. ... Injured ribs (March 7, 1996); missed two games. ... Jets franchise moved to Phoenix and renamed Coyotes for 1996-97 season; NHL approved move on January 18, 1996.
HONORS: Named to OHL All-Scholastic team (1986-87). ... Won Bobby Smith Trophy (1987-88). ... Named to Memorial Cup All-Star team (1987-88).

Season Team	League	Gms.	G	A	Pts.	PIM	+/-	PP	SH	Gms.	G	A	Pts.	PIM
				REGULAR SEASON								PLAYOFFS		
85-86 — Barrie Jr. B	OHA	40	13	22	35	21	...	...	...	—	—	—	—	—
86-87 — Windsor	OHL	60	16	67	83	116	...	...	...	14	4	6	10	8
87-88 — Windsor	OHL	43	33	41	74	49	...	...	...	12	6	12	18	9
88-89 — Windsor	OHL	54	33	48	81	47	...	...	...	4	1	6	7	2
— Buffalo	NHL	3	0	0	0	0	-2	0	0	2	0	0	0	0
89-90 — Buffalo	NHL	17	2	7	9	4	6	0	0	6	0	1	1	4
— Rochester	AHL	50	20	23	43	25	...	...	...	9	4	1	5	2
90-91 — Rochester	AHL	49	26	34	60	56	...	...	...	10	3	5	8	22
— Buffalo	NHL	34	8	6	14	12	-11	1	0	6	1	2	3	4
91-92 — Buffalo	NHL	1	0	1	1	0	1	0	0	—	—	—	—	—
— Winnipeg	NHL	68	13	26	39	41	5	3	0	7	0	1	1	10
92-93 — Winnipeg	NHL	84	20	40	60	91	-4	12	0	6	2	4	6	6
93-94 — Winnipeg	NHL	77	21	37	58	87	-18	9	0	—	—	—	—	—
94-95 — Winnipeg	NHL	19	5	3	8	14	-6	3	0	—	—	—	—	—
95-96 — Winnipeg	NHL	63	5	18	23	28	-5	0	0	6	1	0	1	6
96-97 — Phoenix	NHL	82	11	13	24	41	4	1	0	7	3	1	4	4
NHL totals (9 years)		448	85	151	236	318	-30	29	0	40	7	9	16	34

SHANNON, DARRYL   D   SABRES

PERSONAL: Born June 21, 1968, in Barrie, Ont. ... 6-2/208. ... Shoots left. ... Brother of Darrin Shannon, left winger, Phoenix Coyotes.
TRANSACTIONS/CAREER NOTES: Selected by Toronto Maple Leafs in second round (second Maple Leafs pick, 36th overall) of NHL entry draft (June 21, 1986). ... Broke right leg and right thumb, bruised chest and suffered slipped disk in automobile accident (June 20, 1990). ... Signed as free agent with Winnipeg Jets (July 8, 1993). ... Traded by Jets with LW Michael Grosek to Buffalo Sabres for D Craig Muni (February 15, 1996). ... Injured right knee (April 10, 1996); missed one game.
HONORS: Named to OHL All-Star second team (1986-87). ... Won Max Kaminsky Trophy (1987-88). ... Named to OHL All-Star first team (1987-88). ... Named to Memorial Cup All-Star team (1987-88).

		REGULAR SEASON								PLAYOFFS				
Season Team	League	Gms.	G	A	Pts.	PIM	+/-	PP	SH	Gms.	G	A	Pts.	PIM
84-85— Barrie Jr. B	OHA	39	5	23	28	50	...	...	...	—	—	—	—	—
85-86— Windsor	OHL	57	6	21	27	52	...	...	...	16	5	6	11	22
86-87— Windsor	OHL	64	23	27	50	83	...	...	...	14	4	8	12	18
87-88— Windsor	OHL	60	16	70	86	116	...	...	...	12	3	8	11	17
88-89— Toronto	NHL	14	1	3	4	6	5	0	0	—	—	—	—	—
—Newmarket	AHL	61	5	24	29	37	...	...	...	5	0	3	3	10
89-90— Newmarket	AHL	47	4	15	19	58	...	...	...	—	—	—	—	—
—Toronto	NHL	10	0	1	1	12	-10	0	0	—	—	—	—	—
90-91— Toronto	NHL	10	0	1	1	0	1	0	0	—	—	—	—	—
—Newmarket	AHL	47	2	14	16	51	...	...	...	—	—	—	—	—
91-92— Toronto	NHL	48	2	8	10	23	-17	1	0	—	—	—	—	—
92-93— Toronto	NHL	16	0	0	0	11	-5	0	0	—	—	—	—	—
—St. John's	AHL	7	1	1	2	4	...	...	...	—	—	—	—	—
93-94— Moncton	AHL	37	1	10	11	62	...	...	...	20	1	7	8	32
—Winnipeg	NHL	20	0	4	4	18	-6	0	0	—	—	—	—	—
94-95— Winnipeg	NHL	40	5	9	14	48	1	0	1	—	—	—	—	—
95-96— Winnipeg	NHL	48	2	7	9	72	5	0	0	—	—	—	—	—
—Buffalo	NHL	26	2	6	8	20	10	0	0	—	—	—	—	—
96-97— Buffalo	NHL	82	4	19	23	112	23	1	0	12	2	3	5	8
NHL totals (9 years)		314	16	58	74	322	7	2	1	12	2	3	5	8

SHANTZ, JEFF   C   BLACKHAWKS

PERSONAL: Born October 10, 1973, in Edmonton. ... 6-0/184. ... Shoots right.
HIGH SCHOOL: Robert Usher (Regina, Sask.).
TRANSACTIONS/CAREER NOTES: Selected by Chicago Blackhawks in second round (second Blackhawks pick, 36th overall) of NHL entry draft (June 20, 1992). ... Bruised right shoulder (1993-94 season); missed six games. ... Suffered swollen eye (November 30, 1996); missed one game. ... Sprained knee (February 25, 1997); missed 10 games.
HONORS: Named to WHL (East) All-Star first team (1992-93).

		REGULAR SEASON								PLAYOFFS				
Season Team	League	Gms.	G	A	Pts.	PIM	+/-	PP	SH	Gms.	G	A	Pts.	PIM
89-90— Regina	WHL	1	0	0	0	0	...	...	...	—	—	—	—	—
90-91— Regina	WHL	69	16	21	37	22	...	...	...	8	2	2	4	2
91-92— Regina	WHL	72	39	50	89	75	...	...	...	—	—	—	—	—
92-93— Regina	WHL	64	29	54	83	75	...	...	...	13	2	12	14	14
93-94— Chicago	NHL	52	3	13	16	30	-14	0	0	6	0	0	0	6
—Indianapolis	IHL	19	5	9	14	20	...	...	...	—	—	—	—	—
94-95— Indianapolis	IHL	32	9	15	24	20	...	...	...	—	—	—	—	—
—Chicago	NHL	45	6	12	18	33	11	0	2	16	3	1	4	2
95-96— Chicago	NHL	78	6	14	20	24	12	1	2	10	2	3	5	6
96-97— Chicago	NHL	69	9	21	30	28	11	0	1	6	0	4	4	6
NHL totals (4 years)		244	24	60	84	115	20	1	5	38	5	8	13	20

SHARIFIJANOV, VADIM   RW   DEVILS

PERSONAL: Born December 23, 1975, in Ufa, U.S.S.R. ... 5-11/210. ... Shoots left. ... Name pronounced vah-DEEM shair-eef-YAH-nahf.
TRANSACTIONS/CAREER NOTES: Selected by New Jersey Devils in first round (first Devils pick, 25th overall) of NHL entry draft (June 28, 1994).

		REGULAR SEASON								PLAYOFFS				
Season Team	League	Gms.	G	A	Pts.	PIM	+/-	PP	SH	Gms.	G	A	Pts.	PIM
92-93— Salavat Yulayev Ufa ...	CIS	37	6	4	10	16	...	...	...	2	1	0	1	0
93-94— Salavat Yulayev Ufa ...	CIS	46	10	6	16	36	...	...	...	5	3	0	3	4
94-95— CSKA Moscow	CIS	34	7	3	10	26	...	...	...	2	0	0	0	0
—Albany	AHL	1	1	1	2	0	...	...	...	9	3	3	6	10
95-96— Albany	AHL	69	14	28	42	28	...	...	...	—	—	—	—	—
96-97— Albany	AHL	70	14	27	41	89	...	...	...	10	3	3	6	6
—New Jersey	NHL	2	0	0	0	0	0	0	0	—	—	—	—	—
NHL totals (1 year)		2	0	0	0	0	0	0	0					

SHAW, BRAD   D

PERSONAL: Born April 28, 1964, in Cambridge, Ont. ... 6-0/190. ... Shoots right. ... Full name: Bradley William Shaw.
HIGH SCHOOL: Canterbury (Ottawa), then Eastwood (Kitchener, Ont.).
TRANSACTIONS/CAREER NOTES: Selected by Detroit Red Wings as underage junior in fifth round (fifth Red Wings pick, 86th overall) of NHL entry draft (June 9, 1982). ... Traded by Red Wings to Hartford Whalers for eighth-round pick (LW Lars Karlsson) in 1984 draft (May 29, 1984). ... Fractured finger on left hand (February 1988). ... Broke nose (October 21, 1989). ... Suffered back spasms (November 12, 1989). ... Bruised right foot (February 28, 1990). ... Injured groin (October 28, 1991); missed two games. ... Injured knee (January 31, 1992); missed

four games. ... Bruised knee (February 29, 1992); missed four games. ... Injured groin (March 14, 1992); missed three games. ... Traded by Whalers to New Jersey Devils for future considerations (June 15, 1992). ... Selected by Ottawa Senators in NHL expansion draft (June 18, 1992). ... Suffered slight concussion (October 8, 1992); missed two games. ... Suffered back spasms (December 22, 1993); missed five games. ... Suffered back spasms (March 4, 1994); missed nine games. ... Pulled abdominal muscle (September 1994); missed first 10 games of season. ... Loaned by Senators to Atlanta of IHL (February 10, 1995).

HONORS: Won Max Kaminsky Trophy (1983-84). ... Named to OHL All-Star first team (1983-84). ... Won Eddie Shore Plaque (1986-87). ... Named to AHL All-Star first team (1986-87 and 1987-88). ... Named to NHL All-Rookie team (1989-90). ... Named to IHL All-Star first team (1996-97).

MISCELLANEOUS: Captain of Ottawa Senators (1993-94).

		REGULAR SEASON							PLAYOFFS				
Season Team	League	Gms.	G	A	Pts.	PIM	+/-	PP	SH	Gms.	G	A	Pts.	PIM
81-82— Ottawa	OHL	68	13	59	72	24	...	...	...	15	1	13	14	4
82-83— Ottawa	OHL	63	12	66	78	24	...	...	...	9	2	9	11	4
83-84— Ottawa	OHL	68	11	71	82	75	...	...	...	13	2	*27	29	9
84-85— Salt Lake City	IHL	44	3	29	32	25	...	...	...	—	—	—	—	—
— Binghamton	AHL	24	1	10	11	4	...	...	...	8	1	8	9	6
85-86— Hartford	NHL	8	0	2	2	4	...	...	...	—	—	—	—	—
— Binghamton	AHL	64	10	44	54	33	...	...	...	5	0	2	2	6
86-87— Hartford	NHL	2	0	0	0	0	...	...	...	—	—	—	—	—
— Binghamton	AHL	77	9	30	39	43	...	...	...	12	1	8	9	2
87-88— Binghamton	AHL	73	12	50	62	50	...	...	...	4	0	5	5	4
— Hartford	NHL	1	0	0	0	0	...	...	...	—	—	—	—	—
88-89— Verice	Italy	35	10	30	40	44	...	...	...	11	4	8	12	13
— Hartford	NHL	3	1	0	1	0	...	...	...	3	1	0	1	0
— Canadian nat'l team	Int'l	4	1	0	1	2	...	...	...	—	—	—	—	—
89-90— Hartford	NHL	64	3	32	35	30	2	3	0	7	2	5	7	0
90-91— Hartford	NHL	72	4	28	32	29	...	...	...	6	1	2	3	2
91-92— Hartford	NHL	62	3	22	25	44	...	...	...	3	0	1	1	4
92-93— Ottawa	NHL	81	7	34	41	34	-47	4	0	—	—	—	—	—
93-94— Ottawa	NHL	66	4	19	23	59	-41	1	0	—	—	—	—	—
94-95— Ottawa	NHL	2	0	0	0	0	3	0	0	—	—	—	—	—
— Atlanta	IHL	26	1	18	19	17	...	...	...	5	3	4	7	9
95-96— Detroit	IHL	79	7	54	61	46	...	...	...	8	2	3	5	8
96-97— Detroit	IHL	59	6	32	38	30	...	...	...	21	2	9	11	10
NHL totals (10 years)		361	22	137	159	200	-83	8	0	19	4	8	12	6

SHAW, DAVID — D — LIGHTNING

PERSONAL: Born May 25, 1964, in St. Thomas, Ont. ... 6-2/204. ... Shoots right.

TRANSACTIONS/CAREER NOTES: Selected by Quebec Nordiques as underage junior in first round (first Nordiques pick, 13th overall) of NHL entry draft (June 9, 1982). ... Sprained wrist (December 18, 1985). ... Traded by Nordiques with LW John Ogrodnick to New York Rangers for LW Jeff Jackson and D Terry Carkner (September 30, 1987). ... Separated shoulder (October 1987). ... Suspended 12 games by NHL for slashing (October 27, 1988). ... Bruised shoulder (March 15, 1989). ... Dislocated right shoulder (November 2, 1989). ... Reinjured right shoulder (November 22, 1989); missed 10 games. ... Underwent surgery to right shoulder (February 7, 1990). ... Bruised finger (September 1990). ... Bruised left big toe (October 31, 1990). ... Sprained knee (October 20, 1991). ... Traded by Rangers to Edmonton Oilers for D Jeff Beukeboom (November 12, 1991) to complete deal in which Rangers traded C Bernie Nicholls, LW Louie DeBrusk, RW Steven Rice and future considerations to Oilers for C Mark Messier and future considerations (October 4, 1991). ... Traded by Oilers to Minnesota North Stars for D Brian Glynn (January 21, 1992). ... Traded by North Stars to Boston Bruins for future considerations (September 2, 1992). ... Injured thigh (October 1992); missed one game. ... Injured foot (December 1992); missed one game. ... Injured ribs (March 1993); missed five games. ... Suffered pinched nerve (December 26, 1993); missed three games. ... Suffered charley horse (January 6, 1994); missed seven games. ... Injured knee (January 28, 1994); missed 17 games. ... Injured shoulder (April 1995); missed three games. ... Traded by Bruins to Tampa Bay Lightning for third-round pick (RW Jason Doyle) in 1996 draft (August 17, 1995). ... Injured left shoulder prior to 1995-96 season; missed one game. ... Injured shoulder (October 21, 1995); missed five games. ... Suffered bruised left shoulder (January 2, 1996); missed one game. ... Sprained left knee (February 19, 1996); missed seven games. ... Injured back (October 12, 1996); missed one game. ... Injured left knee (November 27, 1996); missed three games.

HONORS: Named to OHL All-Star first team (1983-84). ... Named to Memorial Cup All-Star team (1983-84).

		REGULAR SEASON							PLAYOFFS				
Season Team	League	Gms.	G	A	Pts.	PIM	+/-	PP	SH	Gms.	G	A	Pts.	PIM
80-81— Stratford Jr. B	OHA	41	12	19	31	30	...	...	...	—	—	—	—	—
81-82— Kitchener	OHL	68	6	25	31	99	...	...	...	15	2	2	4	51
82-83— Kitchener	OHL	57	18	56	74	78	...	...	...	12	2	10	12	18
— Quebec	NHL	2	0	0	0	0	-1	0	0	—	—	—	—	—
83-84— Kitchener	OHL	58	14	34	48	73	...	...	...	16	4	9	13	12
— Quebec	NHL	3	0	0	0	0	2	0	0	—	—	—	—	—
84-85— Guelph	OHL	2	0	0	0	0	...	...	...	—	—	—	—	—
— Fredericton	AHL	48	7	6	13	73	...	...	...	2	0	0	0	7
— Quebec	NHL	14	0	0	0	11	-5	0	0	—	—	—	—	—
85-86— Quebec	NHL	73	7	19	26	78	14	2	0	—	—	—	—	—
86-87— Quebec	NHL	75	0	19	19	69	-35	0	0	—	—	—	—	—
87-88— New York Rangers	NHL	68	7	25	32	100	-8	5	0	—	—	—	—	—
88-89— New York Rangers	NHL	63	6	11	17	88	14	3	1	4	0	2	2	30
89-90— New York Rangers	NHL	22	2	10	12	22	-3	1	1	—	—	—	—	—
90-91— New York Rangers	NHL	77	2	10	12	89	8	0	0	6	0	0	0	11
91-92— New York Rangers	NHL	10	0	1	1	15	1	0	0	—	—	—	—	—
— Edmonton	NHL	12	1	1	2	8	-8	0	0	—	—	—	—	—
— Minnesota	NHL	37	0	7	7	49	-5	0	0	7	2	2	4	10
92-93— Boston	NHL	77	10	14	24	108	10	1	1	4	0	1	1	6
93-94— Boston	NHL	55	1	9	10	85	-11	0	0	13	1	2	3	16
94-95— Boston	NHL	44	3	4	7	36	-9	1	0	5	0	1	1	4
95-96— Tampa Bay	NHL	66	1	11	12	64	5	0	0	6	0	1	1	4
96-97— Tampa Bay	NHL	57	1	10	11	72	1	0	0	—	—	—	—	—
NHL totals (15 years)		755	41	151	192	894	-30	13	3	45	3	9	12	81

SHAW, LLOYD — D — MIGHTY DUCKS

PERSONAL: Born September 26, 1976, in Regina, Sask. ... 6-3/220. ... Shoots right.
HIGH SCHOOL: Lake Washington Senior (Kirkland, Wash.).
TRANSACTIONS/CAREER NOTES: Selected by Vancouver Canucks in fourth round (fourth Canucks pick, 92nd overall) of NHL entry draft (July 8, 1995). ... Signed as free agent by Mighty Ducks of Anaheim (June 25, 1997).

		REGULAR SEASON								PLAYOFFS				
Season Team	League	Gms.	G	A	Pts.	PIM	+/-	PP	SH	Gms.	G	A	Pts.	PIM
93-94— Seattle	WHL	47	0	4	4	107	...	...	...	8	0	0	0	23
94-95— Seattle	WHL	66	3	12	15	313	...	...	...	3	0	0	0	13
95-96— Seattle	WHL	27	0	1	1	92	...	...	...	—	—	—	—	—
— Red Deer	WHL	37	2	4	6	120	...	...	...	10	0	2	2	25
96-97— Red Deer	WHL	66	8	16	24	257	...	...	...	16	0	6	6	60

SHEPPARD, RAY — RW — PANTHERS

PERSONAL: Born May 27, 1966, in Pembroke, Ont. ... 6-1/195. ... Shoots right.
TRANSACTIONS/CAREER NOTES: Selected by Buffalo Sabres as underage junior in third round (third Sabres pick, 60th overall) of NHL entry draft (June 9, 1984). ... Injured left knee (September 1986); missed Sabres training camp. ... Bruised back during training camp (September 1988). ... Suffered facial lacerations (November 25, 1988). ... Suffered facial lacerations (November 27, 1988). ... Suffered from the flu (December 1988). ... Sprained ankle (January 30, 1989). ... Injured left knee (March 16, 1990). ... Traded by Sabres to New York Rangers for future considerations and cash (July 10, 1990). ... Sprained medial collateral ligaments of right knee (February 18, 1991); missed 13 games. ... Dislocated left shoulder (March 24, 1991). ... Signed as free agent by Detroit Red Wings (August 5, 1991). ... Strained lower abdomen (March 20, 1992); missed five games. ... Injured knee (October 8, 1992); missed five games. ... Reinjured knee (October 28, 1992); missed two games. ... Suffered back spasms (February 13, 1993); missed three games. ... Strained back (March 2, 1993); missed two games. ... Injured left knee (October 6, 1995); missed two games. ... Injured back (February 22, 1995); missed two games. ... Traded by Red Wings to San Jose Sharks for C Igor Larionov and conditional draft pick in 1998 (October 25, 1995). ... Injured groin (November 2, 1995); missed one game. ... Injured knee (December 16, 1995); missed two games. ... Injured shoulder (February 5, 1996); missed nine games. ... Traded by Sharks with fourth-round pick (D Joey Tetarenko) in 1996 draft to Florida Panthers for second-(traded to Chicago) and fourth-(RW Matt Bradley) round picks in 1996 draft (March 16, 1996). ... Sprained right shoulder (September 27, 1996); missed two games. ... Sprained knee ligament (February 1, 1997); missed 11 games.
HONORS: Won Red Tilson Trophy (1985-86). ... Won Eddie Powers Memorial Trophy (1985-86). ... Won Jim Mahon Memorial Trophy (1985-86). ... Named to OHL All-Star first team (1985-86). ... Named to NHL All-Rookie team (1987-88).
STATISTICAL PLATEAUS: Three-goal games: 1987-88 (2), 1991-92 (1), 1993-94 (2), 1994-95 (1), 1995-96 (1), 1995-96 (1), 1996-97 (3). Total: 11.

		REGULAR SEASON								PLAYOFFS				
Season Team	League	Gms.	G	A	Pts.	PIM	+/-	PP	SH	Gms.	G	A	Pts.	PIM
82-83— Brockville	COJHL	48	27	36	63	81	...	...	...	—	—	—	—	—
83-84— Cornwall	OHL	68	44	36	80	69	...	...	...	—	—	—	—	—
84-85— Cornwall	OHL	49	25	33	58	51	...	...	...	9	2	12	14	4
85-86— Cornwall	OHL	63	*81	61	*142	25	...	...	...	6	7	4	11	0
86-87— Rochester	AHL	55	18	13	31	11	...	...	...	15	12	3	15	2
87-88— Buffalo	NHL	74	38	27	65	14	-6	15	0	6	1	1	2	2
88-89— Buffalo	NHL	67	22	21	43	15	-7	7	0	1	0	1	1	0
89-90— Buffalo	NHL	18	4	2	6	0	3	1	0	—	—	—	—	—
— Rochester	AHL	5	3	5	8	2	...	...	...	17	8	7	15	9
90-91— New York Rangers	NHL	59	24	23	47	21	8	7	0	—	—	—	—	—
91-92— Detroit	NHL	74	36	26	62	27	7	11	1	11	6	2	8	4
92-93— Detroit	NHL	70	32	34	66	29	7	10	0	7	2	3	5	0
93-94— Detroit	NHL	82	52	41	93	26	13	19	0	7	2	1	3	4
94-95— Detroit	NHL	43	30	10	40	17	11	11	0	17	4	3	7	5
95-96— Detroit	NHL	5	2	2	4	2	0	0	0	—	—	—	—	—
— San Jose	NHL	51	27	19	46	10	-19	12	0	—	—	—	—	—
— Florida	NHL	14	8	2	10	4	0	2	0	21	8	8	16	0
96-97— Florida	NHL	68	29	31	60	4	4	13	0	5	2	0	2	0
NHL totals (10 years)		625	304	238	542	169	21	108	1	75	25	19	44	15

SHEVALIER, JEFF — LW/C — KINGS

PERSONAL: Born March 14, 1974, in Mississauga, Ont. ... 5-11/180. ... Shoots left. ... Name pronounced shuh-VAHL-yay.
HIGH SCHOOL: Chippewa Secondary (North Bay, Ont.).
TRANSACTIONS/CAREER NOTES: Selected by Los Angeles Kings in fifth round (fourth Kings pick, 111th overall) of NHL entry draft (June 20, 1992). ... Suffered concussion (March 24, 1997); missed one game. ... Strained groin (April 7, 1997); missed three games.
HONORS: Named to OHL All-Star first team (1993-94).

		REGULAR SEASON								PLAYOFFS				
Season Team	League	Gms.	G	A	Pts.	PIM	+/-	PP	SH	Gms.	G	A	Pts.	PIM
90-91— Oakville Jr.B	OHA	5	1	4	5	0	...	...	...	—	—	—	—	—
— Georgetown Jr. B	OHA	12	11	11	22	8	...	...	...	—	—	—	—	—
— Acton Jr. C	OHA	28	29	31	60	62	...	...	...	—	—	—	—	—
91-92— North Bay	OHL	64	28	29	57	26	...	...	...	21	5	11	16	25
92-93— North Bay	OHL	62	59	54	113	46	...	...	...	2	1	2	3	4
93-94— North Bay	OHL	64	52	49	101	52	...	...	...	17	8	14	22	18
94-95— Phoenix	IHL	68	31	39	70	44	...	...	...	9	5	4	9	0
— Los Angeles	NHL	1	1	0	1	0	1	0	0	—	—	—	—	—
95-96— Phoenix	IHL	79	29	38	67	72	...	...	...	4	2	2	4	2
96-97— Phoenix	IHL	46	16	21	37	26	...	...	...	—	—	—	—	—
— Los Angeles	NHL	26	4	9	13	6	-6	1	0	—	—	—	—	—
NHL totals (2 years)		27	5	9	14	6	-5	1	0					

S

SHIELDS, STEVE   G   SABRES

PERSONAL: Born July 19, 1972, in Toronto. ... 6-3/210. ... Catches left.
COLLEGE: Michigan.
TRANSACTIONS/CAREER NOTES: Selected by Buffalo Sabres in fifth round (fifth Sabres pick, 101st overall) of NHL entry draft (June 22, 1991).
HONORS: Named to NCAA All-America West second team (1992-93 and 1993-94). ... Named to CCHA All-Star first team (1992-93 and 1993-94).
MISCELLANEOUS: Allowed a penalty shot goal (vs. Eric Lindros, May 11, 1997 (playoffs)).

			REGULAR SEASON							PLAYOFFS						
Season Team	League	Gms.	Min	W	L	T	GA	SO	Avg.	Gms.	Min.	W	L	GA	SO	Avg.
90-91—Univ. of Michigan	CCHA	37	1963	26	6	3	106	0	3.24	—	—	—	—	—	—	—
91-92—Univ. of Michigan	CCHA	37	2091	27	7	2	98	1	2.81	—	—	—	—	—	—	—
92-93—Univ. of Michigan	CCHA	39	2027	30	6	2	75	...	2.22	—	—	—	—	—	—	—
93-94—Univ. of Michigan	CCHA	36	1961	28	6	1	87	2	2.66	—	—	—	—	—	—	—
94-95—South Carolina..............	ECHL	21	1158	11	5	‡2	52	2	2.69	3	144	0	2	11	0	4.58
—Rochester	AHL	13	673	3	8	0	53	0	4.73	1	20	0	0	3	0	9.00
95-96—Rochester	AHL	43	2356	20	17	2	140	1	3.57	*19	*1126	*15	3	47	1	2.50
—Buffalo	NHL	2	75	1	0	0	4	0	3.20	—	—	—	—	—	—	—
96-97—Rochester	AHL	23	1331	14	6	2	60	1	2.70	—	—	—	—	—	—	—
—Buffalo	NHL	13	789	3	8	2	39	0	2.97	10	570	4	6	26	1	2.74
NHL totals (2 years)		15	864	4	8	2	43	0	2.99	10	570	4	6	26	1	2.74

SHTALENKOV, MIKHAIL   G   MIGHTY DUCKS

S

PERSONAL: Born October 20, 1965, in Moscow, U.S.S.R. ... 6-2/185. ... Catches left. ... Name pronounced mih-KIGHL shtuh-LEHN-kahf.
TRANSACTIONS/CAREER NOTES: Selected by Mighty Ducks of Anaheim in fifth round (fifth Mighty Ducks pick, 108th overall) of NHL entry draft (June 26, 1993).
HONORS: Named Soviet League Rookie of the Year (1986-87). ... Won Garry F. Longman Memorial Trophy (1992-93).
MISCELLANEOUS: Stopped a penalty shot attempt (vs. Peter Bondra, December 13, 1996). ... Allowed a penalty shot goal (vs. Dan Quinn, March 21, 1995).

			REGULAR SEASON							PLAYOFFS						
Season Team	League	Gms.	Min	W	L	T	GA	SO	Avg.	Gms.	Min.	W	L	GA	SO	Avg.
86-87—Dynamo Moscow...........	USSR	17	893	...	...	...	36	1	2.42	—	—	—	—	—	—	—
87-88—Dynamo Moscow...........	USSR	25	1302	...	...	...	72	1	3.32	—	—	—	—	—	—	—
88-89—Dynamo Moscow...........	USSR	4	80	...	...	...	3	0	2.25	—	—	—	—	—	—	—
89-90—Dynamo Moscow...........	USSR	6	20	...	...	...	1	0	3.00	—	—	—	—	—	—	—
90-91—Dynamo Moscow...........	USSR	31	1568	...	...	...	56	2	2.14	—	—	—	—	—	—	—
91-92—Dynamo Moscow...........	CIS	27	1268	...	...	...	45	1	2.13	—	—	—	—	—	—	—
—Unif. Olympic team....	Int'l	8	440	...	...	...	12	3	1.64	—	—	—	—	—	—	—
92-93—Milwaukee	IHL	47	2669	26	14	‡5	135	2	3.03	3	209	1	1	11	0	3.16
93-94—San Diego....................	IHL	28	1616	15	11	‡2	93	0	3.45	—	—	—	—	—	—	—
—Anaheim	NHL	10	543	3	4	1	24	0	2.65	—	—	—	—	—	—	—
94-95—Anaheim	NHL	18	810	4	7	1	49	0	3.63	—	—	—	—	—	—	—
95-96—Anaheim	NHL	30	1637	7	16	3	85	0	3.12	—	—	—	—	—	—	—
96-97—Anaheim	NHL	24	1079	7	8	1	52	2	2.89	4	211	0	3	10	0	2.84
NHL totals (4 years)		82	4069	21	35	6	210	2	3.10	4	211	0	3	10	0	2.84

SHUCHUK, GARY   RW/C   KINGS

PERSONAL: Born February 17, 1967, in Edmonton. ... 5-10/185. ... Shoots right. ... Full name: Gary Robert Shuchuk. ... Name pronounced SHOO-chuhk.
COLLEGE: Wisconsin.
TRANSACTIONS/CAREER NOTES: Selected by Detroit Red Wings in NHL supplemental draft (June 10, 1988). ... Traded by Red Wings with C Jimmy Carson and RW Marc Potvin to Los Angeles Kings for D Paul Coffey, RW Jim Hiller and C/LW Sylvain Couturier (January 29, 1993). ... Hyperextended right elbow (February 20, 1993); missed four games. ... Sprained knee (January 29, 1994); missed 10 games.
HONORS: Named to NCAA All-America West first team (1989-90). ... Won WCHA Most Valuable Player Award (1989-90). ... Named to WCHA All-Star first team (1989-90).

			REGULAR SEASON							PLAYOFFS				
Season Team	League	Gms.	G	A	Pts.	PIM	+/-	PP	SH	Gms.	G	A	Pts.	PIM
86-87— Univ. of Wisconsin.....	WCHA	42	19	11	30	72	...	...	...	—	—	—	—	—
87-88— Univ. of Wisconsin.....	WCHA	44	7	22	29	70	...	...	...	—	—	—	—	—
88-89— Univ. of Wisconsin.....	WCHA	46	18	19	37	102	...	...	...	—	—	—	—	—
89-90— Univ. of Wisconsin.....	WCHA	45	41	39	80	70	...	...	...	—	—	—	—	—
90-91— Detroit........................	NHL	6	1	2	3	6	1	0	0	3	0	0	0	0
— Adirondack..................	AHL	59	23	24	47	32	...	...	...	—	—	—	—	—
91-92— Adirondack..................	AHL	79	32	48	80	48	...	...	...	19	4	9	13	18
92-93— Adirondack..................	AHL	47	24	53	77	66	...	...	...	—	—	—	—	—
— Los Angeles...............	NHL	25	2	4	6	16	0	0	0	17	2	2	4	12
93-94— Los Angeles...............	NHL	56	3	4	7	30	-8	0	0	—	—	—	—	—
94-95— Los Angeles...............	NHL	22	3	6	9	6	-2	0	0	—	—	—	—	—
— Phoenix......................	IHL	13	8	7	15	12	...	...	...	—	—	—	—	—
95-96— Phoenix......................	IHL	33	8	21	29	76	...	...	...	4	1	0	1	4
— Los Angeles...............	NHL	33	4	10	14	12	3	0	0	—	—	—	—	—
96-97— Houston	IHL	55	18	23	41	48	...	...	...	13	5	2	7	18
NHL totals (5 years)		142	13	26	39	70	-6	0	0	20	2	2	4	12

SIDORKIEWICZ, PETER   G   DEVILS

PERSONAL: Born June 29, 1963, in Dabrown Bialostocka, Poland. ... 5-9/180. ... Catches left. ... Full name: Peter Paul Sidorkiewicz. ... Name pronounced sih-DOHR-kuh-VIHCH.
HIGH SCHOOL: O'Neill (Oshawa, Ont.).
TRANSACTIONS/CAREER NOTES: Selected by Washington Capitals as underage junior in fifth round (fifth Capitals pick, 91st overall) of NHL entry draft (June 10, 1981). ... Sprained right ankle (March 3, 1991). ... Traded by Capitals with C Dean Evason to Hartford Whalers for LW David Jensen (March 1985). ... Selected by Ottawa Senators in NHL expansion draft (June 18, 1992). ... Traded by Senators with future considerations to New Jersey Devils for G Craig Billington and C/LW Troy Mallette and fourth-round pick (C Cosmo Dupaul) in 1993 draft (June 20, 1993); Senators sent LW Mike Peluso to Devils to complete deal (June 26, 1993). ... Loaned to Fort Wayne Komets of IHL (February 2, 1995).
HONORS: Shared Dave Pinkney Trophy with Jeff Hogg (1982-83). ... Named to Memorial Cup All-Star team (1982-83). ... Named to AHL All-Star second team (1986-87). ... Named to NHL All-Rookie team (1988-89). ... Played in NHL All-Star Game (1993).
MISCELLANEOUS: Allowed a penalty shot goal (vs. Bob Sweeney, December 12, 1990; vs. Pat LaFontaine, November 29, 1992). ... Stopped a penalty shot attempt (vs. Stu Barnes, February 23, 1993).

		REGULAR SEASON								PLAYOFFS						
Season Team	League	Gms.	Min	W	L	T	GA	SO	Avg.	Gms.	Min.	W	L	GA	SO	Avg.
80-81 —Oshawa	OMJHL	7	308	3	3	0	24	0	4.68	5	266	2	2	20	0	4.51
81-82 —Oshawa	OHL	29	1553	14	11	1	123	*2	4.75	1	13	0	0	1	0	4.62
82-83 —Oshawa	OHL	60	3536	36	20	3	213	0	3.61	*17	*1020	15	1	*60	0	3.53
83-84 —Oshawa	OHL	52	2966	28	21	1	205	1	4.15	7	420	3	4	27	†1	3.86
84-85 —Fort Wayne	IHL	10	590	4	4	‡2	43	0	4.37	—	—	—	—	—	—	—
—Binghamton	AHL	45	2691	31	9	5	137	3	3.05	8	481	4	4	31	0	3.87
85-86 —Binghamton	AHL	49	2819	21	22	3	150	2	*3.19	4	235	1	3	12	0	3.06
86-87 —Binghamton	AHL	57	3304	23	16	0	161	4	2.92	13	794	6	7	36	0	*2.72
87-88 —Hartford	NHL	1	60	0	1	0	6	0	6.00	—	—	—	—	—	—	—
—Binghamton	AHL	42	2346	19	17	3	144	0	3.68	3	147	0	2	8	0	3.27
88-89 —Hartford	NHL	44	2635	22	18	4	133	4	3.03	2	124	0	2	8	0	3.87
89-90 —Hartford	NHL	46	2703	19	19	7	161	1	3.57	7	429	3	4	23	0	3.22
90-91 —Hartford	NHL	52	2953	21	22	7	164	1	3.33	6	359	2	4	24	0	4.01
91-92 —Hartford	NHL	35	1995	9	19	6	111	2	3.34	—	—	—	—	—	—	—
92-93 —Ottawa	NHL	64	3388	8	*46	3	*250	0	4.43	—	—	—	—	—	—	—
93-94 —New Jersey	NHL	3	130	0	3	0	6	0	2.77	—	—	—	—	—	—	—
—Albany	AHL	15	908	6	7	2	60	0	3.96	—	—	—	—	—	—	—
—Fort Wayne	IHL	11	591	6	3	‡0	27	†2	2.74	18	*1054	10	*6	59	†1	3.36
94-95 —Fort Wayne	IHL	16	942	8	6	‡1	58	1	3.69	3	144	1	2	12	0	5.00
95-96 —Albany	AHL	32	1809	19	7	5	89	3	2.95	1	58	0	1	3	0	3.10
96-97 —Albany	AHL	62	3539	31	23	6	171	2	2.90	16	921	7	8	48	0	3.13
NHL totals (7 years)		245	13864	79	128	27	831	8	3.60	15	912	5	10	55	0	3.62

SILLINGER, MIKE   RW   CANUCKS

PERSONAL: Born June 29, 1971, in Regina, Sask. ... 5-10/190. ... Shoots right. ... Name pronounced SIHL-ihn-juhr.
TRANSACTIONS/CAREER NOTES: Selected by Detroit Red Wings in first round (first Red Wings pick, 11th overall) of NHL entry draft (June 17, 1989). ... Fractured rib in training camp (September 1990). ... Suffered from the flu (March 5, 1993); missed three games. ... Strained rotator cuff (October 9, 1993); missed four games. ... Played in Europe during 1994-95 NHL lockout. ... Injured eye (January 17, 1995); missed four games. ... Traded by Red Wings with D Jason York to Mighty Ducks of Anaheim for LW Stu Grimson, D Mark Ferner and sixth-round pick (LW Magnus Nilsson) in 1996 draft (April 4, 1995). ... Traded by Mighty Ducks to Vancouver Canucks for RW Roman Oksuita (March 15, 1996). ... Suffered concussion (March 26, 1997); missed two games.
HONORS: Named to WHL All-Star second team (1989-90). ... Named to WHL (East) All-Star first team (1990-91).
MISCELLANEOUS: Scored on a penalty shot (vs. Mark Fitzpatrick, January 14, 1997).

		REGULAR SEASON							PLAYOFFS				
Season Team	League	Gms.	G	A	Pts.	PIM	+/-	PP	SH	Gms.	G	A	Pts.	PIM
87-88 — Regina	WHL	67	18	25	43	17	...	...	...	4	2	2	4	0
88-89 — Regina	WHL	72	53	78	131	52	...	...	...	—	—	—	—	—
89-90 — Regina	WHL	70	57	72	129	41	...	...	...	11	12	10	22	2
— Adirondack	AHL	—	—	—	—	—	—	—	—	1	0	0	0	0
90-91 — Regina	WHL	57	50	66	116	42	...	...	...	8	6	9	15	4
— Detroit	NHL	3	0	1	1	0	-2	0	0	3	0	1	1	0
91-92 — Adirondack	AHL	64	25	41	66	26	...	...	...	15	9	*19	*28	12
— Detroit	NHL	—	—	—	—	—	—	—	—	8	2	2	4	2
92-93 — Detroit	NHL	51	4	17	21	16	0	0	0	—	—	—	—	—
— Adirondack	AHL	15	10	20	30	31	...	...	...	11	5	13	18	10
93-94 — Detroit	NHL	62	8	21	29	10	2	0	1	—	—	—	—	—
94-95 — Wien	Austria	13	13	14	27	10	...	...	...	—	—	—	—	—
— Detroit	NHL	13	2	6	8	2	3	0	0	—	—	—	—	—
— Anaheim	NHL	15	2	5	7	6	1	2	0	—	—	—	—	—
95-96 — Anaheim	NHL	62	13	21	34	32	-20	7	0	—	—	—	—	—
— Vancouver	NHL	12	1	3	4	6	2	0	1	6	0	0	0	2
96-97 — Vancouver	NHL	78	17	20	37	25	-3	3	3	—	—	—	—	—
NHL totals (7 years)		296	47	94	141	97	-17	12	5	17	2	3	5	4

SIM, JON   C   STARS

PERSONAL: Born September 29, 1977, in New Glasgow, Nova Scotia. ... 5-9/175. ... Shoots left.
TRANSACTIONS/CAREER NOTES: Selected by Dallas Stars in third round (fifth Capitals pick, 70th overall) of NHL entry draft (June 22, 1996).

Season Team	League	REGULAR SEASON								PLAYOFFS				
		Gms.	G	A	Pts.	PIM	+/-	PP	SH	Gms.	G	A	Pts.	PIM
94-95— Sarnia	OHL	25	9	12	21	19	...	...	...	4	3	2	5	2
95-96— Sarnia	OHL	63	56	46	102	130	...	...	...	10	8	7	15	26
96-97— Sarnia	OHL	64	†56	39	95	109	...	...	...	12	9	5	14	32

SIMON, CHRIS — LW — CAPITALS

PERSONAL: Born January 30, 1972, in Wawa, Ont. ... 6-3/219. ... Shoots left. ... Name pronounced SIGH-muhn.

TRANSACTIONS/CAREER NOTES: Suspended six games by OHL for shooting the puck in frustration and striking another player (January 20, 1990). ... Selected by Philadelphia Flyers in second round (second Flyers pick, 25th overall) of NHL entry draft (June 16, 1990). ... Underwent surgery to repair left rotator cuff and torn muscle (September 1990). ... Traded by Flyers with first-round pick (traded to Toronto) in 1994 draft to Quebec Nordiques (July 21, 1992) to complete deal in which Flyers sent G Ron Hextall, C Mike Ricci, C Peter Forsberg, D Steve Duchesne, first-round pick (G Jocelyn Thibault) in 1993 draft and cash to Nordiques for C Eric Lindros (June 20, 1992). ... Suffered from the flu (March 13, 1993); missed one game. ... Injured back (December 1, 1993); missed 31 games. ... Injured back (February 16, 1994); missed one game. ... Injured back (March 6, 1994); missed one game. ... Injured back (March 18, 1994); missed remainder of season. ... Injured back (January 31, 1995); missed six games. ... Injured shoulder (March 22, 1995); missed 13 games. ... Nordiques franchise moved to Colorado and renamed Avalanche for 1995-96 season (June 21, 1995). ... Suffered back spasms (January 6, 1996); missed two games. ... Injured shoulder (February 5, 1996); missed four games. ... Traded by Avalanche with D Curtis Leschyshyn to Washington Capitals for RW Keith Jones, first-round pick in 1998 draft and fourth-round pick in 1998 draft (November 2, 1996). ... Injured arm (December 20, 1996); missed two games. ... Suffered back spasms (January 24, 1997); missed 17 games. ... Suffered back spasms (March 22, 1997); missed one game. ... Strained shoulder (March 29, 1997); missed six games.

MISCELLANEOUS: Member of Stanley Cup championship team (1996).

Season Team	League	REGULAR SEASON								PLAYOFFS				
		Gms.	G	A	Pts.	PIM	+/-	PP	SH	Gms.	G	A	Pts.	PIM
87-88— Sault Ste. Marie	OHA	55	42	36	78	172	...			—	—	—	—	—
88-89— Ottawa	OHL	36	4	2	6	31	...			—	—	—	—	—
89-90— Ottawa	OHL	57	36	38	74	146	...			3	2	1	3	4
90-91— Ottawa	OHL	20	16	6	22	69	...			17	5	9	14	59
91-92— Ottawa	OHL	2	1	1	2	24	...			—	—	—	—	—
— Sault Ste. Marie	OHL	31	19	25	44	143	...			11	5	8	13	49
92-93— Halifax	AHL	36	12	6	18	131	...			—	—	—	—	—
— Quebec	NHL	16	1	1	2	67	-2	0	0	5	0	0	0	26
93-94— Quebec	NHL	37	4	4	8	132	-2	0	0	—	—	—	—	—
94-95— Quebec	NHL	29	3	9	12	106	14	0	0	6	1	1	2	19
95-96— Colorado	NHL	64	16	18	34	250	10	4	0	12	1	2	3	11
96-97— Washington	NHL	42	9	13	22	165	-1	3	0	—	—	—	—	—
NHL totals (5 years)		188	33	45	78	720	19	7	0	23	2	3	5	56

SIMON, JASON — LW — COYOTES

PERSONAL: Born March 21, 1969, in Sarnia, Ont. ... 6-1/190. ... Shoots left.

TRANSACTIONS/CAREER NOTES: Selected by New Jersey Devils in ninth round (ninth Devils pick, 215th overall) of NHL entry draft (June 26, 1993). ... Signed as free agent by New York Islanders (January 6, 1994). ... Signed as free agent by Winnipeg Jets (July 21, 1995). ... Jets franchise moved to Phoenix and renamed Coyotes for 1996-97 season; NHL approved move on January 18, 1996.

Season Team	League	REGULAR SEASON								PLAYOFFS				
		Gms.	G	A	Pts.	PIM	+/-	PP	SH	Gms.	G	A	Pts.	PIM
86-87— London	OHL	33	1	2	3	33	...			—	—	—	—	—
— Sudbury	OHL	26	2	3	5	50	...			—	—	—	—	—
87-88— Sudbury	OHL	26	5	7	12	35	...			—	—	—	—	—
— Hamilton	OHL	29	5	13	18	124	...			11	0	2	2	15
88-89— Windsor	OHL	62	23	39	62	193	...			4	1	4	5	13
89-90— Utica	AHL	16	3	4	7	28	...			2	0	0	0	12
— Nashville	ECHL	13	4	3	7	81	...			5	1	3	4	17
90-91— Johnstown	ECHL	22	11	9	20	55	...			—	—	—	—	—
— Utica	AHL	50	2	12	14	189	...			—	—	—	—	—
91-92— Utica	AHL	1	0	0	0	12	...			—	—	—	—	—
— San Diego	IHL	13	1	4	5	45	...			3	0	1	1	9
92-93— Flint	Col.HL	44	17	32	49	202	...			—	—	—	—	—
— Detroit	Col.HL	11	7	13	20	38	...			6	1	2	3	40
93-94— Detroit	Col.HL	13	9	16	25	87	...			—	—	—	—	—
— Salt Lake City	IHL	50	7	7	14	*323	...			—	—	—	—	—
— New York Islanders	NHL	4	0	0	0	34	0	0	0	—	—	—	—	—
94-95— Denver	IHL	61	3	6	9	300	...			1	0	0	0	12
95-96— Springfield	AHL	18	2	2	4	90	...			7	1	0	1	26
96-97— Las Vegas	IHL	64	4	3	7	402	...			3	0	0	0	0
— Phoenix	NHL	1	0	0	0	0	-1	0	0	—	—	—	—	—
NHL totals (2 years)		5	0	0	0	34	-1	0	0					

SIMONS, MIKAEL — C — KINGS

PERSONAL: Born January 15, 1978, in Falun, Sweden. ... 6-2/187. ... Shoots left. ... Name pronounced see-MOHNS.

TRANSACTIONS/CAREER NOTES: Selected by Los Angeles Kings in fourth round (fourth Kings pick, 84th overall) of NHL entry draft (June 22, 1996).

Season Team	League	REGULAR SEASON								PLAYOFFS				
		Gms.	G	A	Pts.	PIM	+/-	PP	SH	Gms.	G	A	Pts.	PIM
94-95— Mora Jrs.	Sweden Jr.	26	5	3	8	57	...	...	...	—	—	—	—	—
95-96— Mora Jrs.	Sweden Jr.	10	4	4	8	12	...	...	...	—	—	—	—	—
— Mora	Swed. Div. II	33	6	3	9	22	...	...	...	6	0	2	2	2
96-97— Mora	Swed. Div. II	29	11	8	19	38	...	...	...	—	—	—	—	—

S

SIMPSON, REID   LW   DEVILS

PERSONAL: Born May 21, 1969, in Flin Flon, Man. ... 6-2/220. ... Shoots left.
TRANSACTIONS/CAREER NOTES: Selected by Philadelphia Flyers in fourth round (third Flyers pick, 72nd overall) of NHL entry draft (June 17, 1989). ... Signed as free agent by Minnesota North Stars (December 13, 1992). ... North Stars franchise moved from Minnesota to Dallas and renamed Stars for 1993-94 season. ... Traded by Stars with D Roy Mitchell to New Jersey Devils for future considerations (March 21, 1994). ... Bruised right shoulder (November 27, 1995); missed six games. ... Strained groin (September 9, 1996); missed first two games of season. ... Reinjured groin (October 16, 1996); underwent second groin surgery (November 22, 1996) and missed 38 games.

Season Team	League	Gms.	G	A	Pts.	PIM	+/-	PP	SH		Gms.	G	A	Pts.	PIM
85-86— Flin Flon	MJHL	40	20	21	41	200	...	...	.....		—	—	—	—	—
— New Westminster	WHL	2	0	0	0	0	...	...	...		—	—	—	—	—
86-87— Prince Albert	WHL	47	3	8	11	105	...	...	...		—	—	—	—	—
87-88— Prince Albert	WHL	72	13	14	27	164	...	...	...		10	1	0	1	43
88-89— Prince Albert	WHL	59	26	29	55	264	...	...	...		4	2	1	3	30
89-90— Prince Albert	WHL	29	15	17	32	121	...	...	...		14	4	7	11	34
— Hershey	AHL	28	2	2	4	175	...	...	...		—	—	—	—	—
90-91— Hershey	AHL	54	9	15	24	183	...	...	...		1	0	0	0	0
91-92— Hershey	AHL	60	11	7	18	145	...	...	...		—	—	—	—	—
— Philadelphia	NHL	1	0	0	0	0	0	0	0		—	—	—	—	—
92-93— Kalamazoo	IHL	45	5	5	10	193	...	...	...		—	—	—	—	—
— Minnesota	NHL	1	0	0	0	5	0	0	0		—	—	—	—	—
93-94— Albany	AHL	37	9	5	14	135	...	...	...		5	1	1	2	18
— Kalamazoo	IHL	5	0	0	0	16	...	...	...		—	—	—	—	—
94-95— Albany	AHL	70	18	25	43	268	...	...	...		14	1	8	9	13
— New Jersey	NHL	9	0	0	0	27	-1	0	0		—	—	—	—	—
95-96— New Jersey	NHL	23	1	5	6	79	2	0	0		—	—	—	—	—
— Albany	AHL	6	1	3	4	17	...	...	...		—	—	—	—	—
96-97— Albany	AHL	3	0	0	0	10	...	...	...		—	—	—	—	—
— New Jersey	NHL	27	0	4	4	60	0	0	0		5	0	0	0	29
NHL totals (5 years)		61	1	9	10	171	1	0	0		5	0	0	0	29

SIMPSON, TODD   D   FLAMES

PERSONAL: Born May 28, 1973, in Edmonton. ... 6-3/215. ... Shoots left.
TRANSACTIONS/CAREER NOTES: Signed as free agent by Calgary Flames (July 6, 1994).

Season Team	League	Gms.	G	A	Pts.	PIM	+/-	PP	SH		Gms.	G	A	Pts.	PIM
92-93— Tri-City	WHL	69	5	18	23	196	...	...	...		4	0	0	0	13
93-94— Tri-City	WHL	12	2	3	5	32	...	...	...		—	—	—	—	—
— Saskatoon	WHL	51	7	19	26	175	...	...	...		16	1	5	6	42
94-95— Saint John	AHL	80	3	10	13	321	...	...	...		5	0	0	0	4
95-96— Calgary	NHL	6	0	0	0	32	0	0	0		—	—	—	—	—
— Saint John	AHL	66	4	13	17	277	...	...	...		16	2	3	5	32
96-97— Calgary	NHL	82	1	13	14	208	-14	0	0		—	—	—	—	—
NHL totals (2 years)		88	1	13	14	240	-14	0	0						

SKALDE, JARROD   C   FLAMES

PERSONAL: Born February 26, 1971, in Niagara Falls, Ont. ... 6-0/170. ... Shoots left. ... Name pronounced SKAHL-dee.
TRANSACTIONS/CAREER NOTES: Selected by New Jersey Devils in second round (third Devils pick, 26th overall) of NHL entry draft (June 17, 1989). ... Traded by Oshawa Generals to Belleville Bulls for RW Rob Pearson (November 18, 1990). ... Selected by Mighty Ducks of Anaheim in NHL expansion draft (June 24, 1993). ... Signed as free agent by Las Vegas Thunder (August 18, 1994). ... Signed as free agent by Mighty Ducks (May 31, 1995). ... Traded by Mighty Ducks to Calgary Flames for D Bobby Marshall (October 30, 1995).
HONORS: Named to OHL All-Star second team (1990-91).

Season Team	League	Gms.	G	A	Pts.	PIM	+/-	PP	SH		Gms.	G	A	Pts.	PIM
86-87— Fort Erie Jr. B	OHA	41	27	34	61	36	...	...	...		—	—	—	—	—
87-88— Oshawa	OHL	60	12	16	28	24	...	...	...		7	2	1	3	2
88-89— Oshawa	OHL	65	38	38	76	36	...	...	...		6	1	5	6	2
89-90— Oshawa	OHL	62	40	52	92	66	...	...	...		17	10	7	17	6
90-91— New Jersey	NHL	1	0	1	1	0	0	0	0		—	—	—	—	—
— Utica	AHL	3	3	2	5	0	...	...	...		—	—	—	—	—
— Oshawa	OHL	15	8	14	22	14	...	...	...		—	—	—	—	—
— Belleville	OHL	40	30	52	82	21	...	...	...		6	9	6	15	10
91-92— Utica	AHL	62	20	20	40	56	...	...	...		4	3	1	4	8
— New Jersey	NHL	15	2	4	6	4	-1	0	0		—	—	—	—	—
92-93— Cincinnati	IHL	4	1	2	3	4	...	...	...		—	—	—	—	—
— Utica	AHL	59	21	39	60	76	...	...	...		5	0	2	2	19
— New Jersey	NHL	11	0	2	2	4	-3	0	0		—	—	—	—	—
93-94— San Diego	IHL	57	25	38	63	79	...	...	...		9	3	12	15	10
— Anaheim	NHL	20	5	4	9	10	-3	2	0		—	—	—	—	—
94-95— Las Vegas	IHL	74	34	41	75	103	...	...	...		9	2	4	6	8
95-96— Baltimore	AHL	11	2	6	8	55	...	...	...		—	—	—	—	—
— Saint John	AHL	68	27	40	67	98	...	...	...		16	4	9	13	6
— Calgary	NHL	1	0	0	0	0	0	0	0		—	—	—	—	—
96-97— Saint John	AHL	65	32	36	68	94	...	...	...		3	0	0	0	14
NHL totals (5 years)		48	7	11	18	18	-7	2	0						

S

SKOREPA, ZDENEK   RW   DEVILS

PERSONAL: Born August 10, 1976, in Duchcov, Czechoslovakia. ... 6-0/185. ... Shoots left.
TRANSACTIONS/CAREER NOTES: Selected by New Jersey Devils in fourth round (fourth Devils pick, 103rd overall) of NHL entry draft (June 29, 1994).

		REGULAR SEASON								PLAYOFFS				
Season Team	League	Gms.	G	A	Pts.	PIM	+/-	PP	SH	Gms.	G	A	Pts.	PIM
93-94— Chemo. Litvinov........	Czech Rep.	20	4	7	11	...	...	...	...	4	0	0	0	0
94-95— Chemo. Litvinov........	Czech Rep.	28	3	3	6	20	...	...	...	3	0	0	0	2
95-96— Kingston	OHL	37	21	18	39	13	...	...	...	6	5	2	7	5
96-97— Albany......................	AHL	60	12	12	24	38	...	...	...	13	3	2	5	14

SKRBEK, PAVEL   D   PENGUINS

PERSONAL: Born August 9, 1978, in Kladno, Czechoslovakia. ... 6-3/191. ... Shoots left.
TRANSACTIONS/CAREER NOTES: Selected by Pittsburgh Penguins in second round (second Penguins pick, 28th overall) of NHL entry draft (June 22, 1996).

		REGULAR SEASON								PLAYOFFS				
Season Team	League	Gms.	G	A	Pts.	PIM	+/-	PP	SH	Gms.	G	A	Pts.	PIM
94-95— HC Kladno Jrs............	Czech Rep.	29	7	6	13	...	...	...	...	—	—	—	—	—
95-96— HC Kladno Jrs............	Czech Rep.	29	10	12	22	...	...	...	...	—	—	—	—	—
— HC Kladno.................	Czech Rep.	13	0	1	1	...	...	...	...	5	0	0	0	0
96-97— HC Kladno.................	Czech Rep.	35	1	5	6	26	...	...	...	3	0	0	0	4

S

SKRUDLAND, BRIAN   C   RANGERS

PERSONAL: Born July 31, 1963, in Peace River, Alta. ... 6-0/195. ... Shoots left. ... Name pronounced SKROOD-luhnd. ... Cousin of Barry Pederson, center for four NHL teams (1980-81 through 1991-92).
TRANSACTIONS/CAREER NOTES: Signed as free agent by Montreal Canadiens (August 1983). ... Injured groin (February 1988). ... Strained left knee ligaments (December 27, 1988). ... Bruised right foot (January 1989). ... Sprained right ankle (October 7, 1989); missed 21 games. ... Pulled hip muscle (November 4, 1990); missed six games. ... Broke foot (January 17, 1991); missed 14 games including All-Star Game. ... Broke left thumb (October 5, 1991); missed five games. ... Sprained knee (October 26, 1991); missed 25 games. ... Broke nose (January 25, 1992); missed eight games. ... Tore right knee ligaments (October 6, 1992); missed 27 games. ... Injured shoulder (January 14, 1993); missed one game. ... Traded by Canadiens to Calgary Flames for RW Gary Leeman (January 28, 1993). ... Sprained ankle (February 16, 1993); missed four games. ... Broke thumb (March 2, 1993); missed 12 games. ... Lacerated right ear (April 11, 1993); missed one game. ... Selected by Florida Panthers in NHL expansion draft (June 24, 1993). ... Sprained right ankle (April 4, 1994); missed five games. ... Injured left hip flexor (March 22, 1995); missed one game. ... Suspended one game for high-sticking (February 13, 1996). ... Injured left hip flexor (April 12, 1996); missed one game. ... Cracked rib (October 30, 1996); missed three games. ... Suffered from the flu (December 10, 1996); missed one game. ... Bruised right shoulder (January 23, 1997); missed five games. ... Fractured ribs (February 7, 1997); missed six games. ... Sprained knee ligament (March 7, 1997); missed remainder of season. ... Signed as free agent by New York Rangers (July 7, 1997).
HONORS: Won Jack Butterfield Trophy (1984-85).
MISCELLANEOUS: Member of Stanley Cup championship team (1986). ... Captain of Florida Panthers (1994-95 and 1996-97).

		REGULAR SEASON								PLAYOFFS				
Season Team	League	Gms.	G	A	Pts.	PIM	+/-	PP	SH	Gms.	G	A	Pts.	PIM
80-81— Saskatoon.................	WHL	66	15	27	42	97	...	...	...	—	—	—	—	—
81-82— Saskatoon.................	WHL	71	27	29	56	135	...	...	...	5	0	1	1	2
82-83— Saskatoon.................	WHL	71	35	59	94	42	...	...	...	6	1	3	4	19
83-84— Nova Scotia	AHL	56	13	12	25	55	...	...	...	12	2	8	10	14
84-85— Sherbrooke	AHL	70	22	28	50	109	...	...	...	17	9	8	17	23
85-86— Montreal	NHL	65	9	13	22	57	3	2	0	20	2	4	6	76
86-87— Montreal	NHL	79	11	17	28	107	18	0	1	14	1	5	6	29
87-88— Montreal	NHL	79	12	24	36	112	44	0	1	11	1	5	6	24
88-89— Montreal	NHL	71	12	29	41	84	22	1	1	21	3	7	10	40
89-90— Montreal	NHL	59	11	31	42	56	21	4	0	11	3	5	8	30
90-91— Montreal	NHL	57	15	19	34	85	12	1	1	13	3	10	13	42
91-92— Montreal	NHL	42	3	3	6	36	-4	0	0	11	1	1	2	20
92-93— Montreal	NHL	23	5	3	8	55	1	0	2	—	—	—	—	—
— Calgary	NHL	16	2	4	6	10	3	0	0	6	0	3	3	12
93-94— Florida.....................	NHL	79	15	25	40	136	13	0	2	—	—	—	—	—
94-95— Florida.....................	NHL	47	5	9	14	88	0	1	0	—	—	—	—	—
95-96— Florida.....................	NHL	79	7	20	27	129	6	0	1	21	1	3	4	18
96-97— Florida.....................	NHL	51	5	13	18	48	4	0	0	—	—	—	—	—
NHL totals (12 years)		747	112	210	322	1003	143	9	9	128	15	43	58	291

SLANEY, JOHN   D   KINGS

PERSONAL: Born February 7, 1972, in St. John's, Nfld. ... 6-0/195. ... Shoots left.
TRANSACTIONS/CAREER NOTES: Selected by Washington Capitals in first round (first Capitals pick, ninth overall) of NHL entry draft (June 16, 1990). ... Sprained right ankle (March 9, 1994); missed six games. ... Traded by Capitals to Colorado Avalanche for third-round pick (C Shawn McNeil) in 1996 draft (July 12, 1995). ... Traded by Avalanche to Los Angeles Kings for sixth-round pick (RW Brian Willsie) in 1996 draft (December 28, 1995). ... Broke right hand (March 6, 1996); missed 12 games. ... Suffered concussion (November 17, 1996); missed one game.
HONORS: Won Max Kaminsky Trophy (1989-90). ... Named to OHL All-Star first team (1989-90). ... Named to OHL All-Star second team (1990-91).

Season Team	League	REGULAR SEASON Gms.	G	A	Pts.	PIM	+/-	PP	SH	PLAYOFFS Gms.	G	A	Pts.	PIM
88-89 — Cornwall	OHL	66	16	43	59	23	...	...	...	18	8	16	24	10
89-90 — Cornwall	OHL	64	38	59	97	60	...	...	...	6	0	8	8	11
90-91 — Cornwall	OHL	34	21	25	46	28	...	...	...	—	—	—	—	—
91-92 — Cornwall	OHL	34	19	41	60	43	...	...	...	6	3	8	11	0
— Baltimore	AHL	6	2	4	6	0	...	...	...	—	—	—	—	—
92-93 — Baltimore	AHL	79	20	46	66	60	...	...	...	7	0	7	7	8
93-94 — Portland	AHL	29	14	13	27	17	...	...	...	—	—	—	—	—
— Washington	NHL	47	7	9	16	27	3	3	0	11	1	1	2	2
94-95 — Washington	NHL	16	0	3	3	6	-3	0	0	—	—	—	—	—
— Portland	AHL	8	3	10	13	4	...	...	...	7	1	3	4	4
95-96 — Colorado	NHL	7	0	3	3	4	2	0	0	—	—	—	—	—
— Cornwall	AHL	5	0	4	4	2	...	...	...	—	—	—	—	—
— Los Angeles	NHL	31	6	11	17	10	5	3	1	—	—	—	—	—
96-97 — Los Angeles	NHL	32	3	11	14	4	-10	1	0	—	—	—	—	—
— Phoenix	IHL	35	9	25	34	8	...	...	...	—	—	—	—	—
NHL totals (5 years)		133	16	37	53	51	-3	7	1	11	1	1	2	2

SLEGR, JIRI — D — OILERS

PERSONAL: Born May 30, 1971, in Litvinov, Czechoslovakia. ... 6-1/205. ... Shoots left. ... Name pronounced YIH-ree SLAY-guhr. ... Son of Jiri Bubla, defenseman, Vancouver Canucks (1981-82 through 1985-86).

TRANSACTIONS/CAREER NOTES: Selected by Vancouver Canucks in second round (third Canucks pick, 23rd overall) of NHL entry draft (June 16, 1990). ... Played in Europe during 1994-95 NHL lockout. ... Traded by Canucks to Edmonton Oilers for RW Roman Oksiuta (April 7, 1995). ... Sprained ligaments in left knee (December 27, 1995); missed 19 games.

HONORS: Named to Czechoslovakian League All-Star team (1990-91).

Season Team	League	REGULAR SEASON Gms.	G	A	Pts.	PIM	+/-	PP	SH	PLAYOFFS Gms.	G	A	Pts.	PIM
88-89 — Litvinov	Czech.	8	0	0	0	...	...	...	...	—	—	—	—	—
89-90 — Litvinov	Czech.	51	4	15	19	...	...	...	...	—	—	—	—	—
90-91 — Litvinov	Czech.	39	10	33	43	26	...	...	...	—	—	—	—	—
91-92 — Litvinov	Czech.	38	7	22	29	30	...	...	...	—	—	—	—	—
— Czech. Olympic team	Int'l	8	1	1	2	...	...	...	...	—	—	—	—	—
92-93 — Vancouver	NHL	41	4	22	26	109	16	2	0	5	0	3	3	4
— Hamilton	AHL	21	4	14	18	42	...	...	...	—	—	—	—	—
93-94 — Vancouver	NHL	78	5	33	38	86	0	1	0	—	—	—	—	—
94-95 — Chemopetrol Litvin.	Czech Rep.	11	3	10	13	43	...	...	...	—	—	—	—	—
— Vancouver	NHL	19	1	5	6	32	0	0	0	—	—	—	—	—
— Edmonton	NHL	12	1	5	6	14	-5	1	0	—	—	—	—	—
95-96 — Edmonton	NHL	57	4	13	17	74	-1	0	1	—	—	—	—	—
— Cape Breton	AHL	4	1	2	3	4	...	...	...	—	—	—	—	—
NHL totals (4 years)		207	15	78	93	315	10	4	1	5	0	3	3	4

SMEHLIK, RICHARD — D — SABRES

PERSONAL: Born January 23, 1970, in Ostrava, Czechoslovakia. ... 6-3/222. ... Shoots left. ... Name pronounced SHMEHL-ihk.

TRANSACTIONS/CAREER NOTES: Selected by Buffalo Sabres in fifth round (third Sabres pick, 97th overall) of NHL entry draft (June 16, 1990). ... Injured hip (October 30, 1992); missed two games. ... Played in Europe during 1994-95 NHL lockout. ... Bruised shoulder (January 27, 1995); missed six games. ... Tore knee ligaments (August 15, 1995); missed entire season. ... Suffered tendinitis in knee (January 12, 1996); missed five games. ... Suffered sore knee (November 19, 1996); missed six games. ... Suffered sore knee (February 23, 1997); missed one game. ... Strained groin (March 30, 1997); missed three games.

Season Team	League	REGULAR SEASON Gms.	G	A	Pts.	PIM	+/-	PP	SH	PLAYOFFS Gms.	G	A	Pts.	PIM
88-89 — Vitkovice	Czech.	38	2	5	7	12	...	...	...	—	—	—	—	—
89-90 — Vitkovice	Czech.	43	4	3	7	...	...	...	...	—	—	—	—	—
90-91 — Dukla Jihlava	Czech.	51	4	2	6	22	...	...	...	—	—	—	—	—
91-92 — Vitkovice	Czech.	47	9	10	19	...	...	...	...	—	—	—	—	—
— Czec. Olympic team	Int'l	8	0	1	1	2	...	...	...	—	—	—	—	—
92-93 — Buffalo	NHL	80	4	27	31	59	9	0	0	8	0	4	4	2
93-94 — Buffalo	NHL	84	14	27	41	69	22	3	3	7	0	2	2	10
94-95 — HC Vitkovice	Czech Rep.	13	5	2	7	12	...	...	...	—	—	—	—	—
— Buffalo	NHL	39	4	7	11	46	5	0	1	5	0	0	0	2
95-96 — Buffalo	NHL	Did not play—injured.												
96-97 — Buffalo	NHL	62	11	19	30	43	19	2	0	12	0	2	2	4
NHL totals (4 years)		265	33	80	113	217	55	5	4	32	0	8	8	18

SMITH, D.J. — D — MAPLE LEAFS

PERSONAL: Born May 13, 1977, in Windsor, Ont. ... 6-1/200. ... Shoots left.

HIGH SCHOOL: Holy Names (Windsor, Ont.).

TRANSACTIONS/CAREER NOTES: Selected by New York Islanders in second round (third Islanders pick, 41st overall) of NHL entry draft (July 8, 1995). ... Traded by Islanders with LW Wendel Clark and D Mathieu Schneider to Toronto Maple Leafs for LW Sean Haggerty, C Darby Hendrickson, D Kenny Jonsson and first-round pick (G Roberto Luongo) in 1997 draft (March 13, 1996).

HONORS: Named to OHL All-Star second team (1996-97).

Season Team	League	REGULAR SEASON Gms.	G	A	Pts.	PIM	+/-	PP	SH	PLAYOFFS Gms.	G	A	Pts.	PIM
92-93 — Belle River	Jr. C	50	11	29	40	101	...	...	...	—	—	—	—	—
93-94 — Windsor	Jr. B	51	8	34	42	267	...	...	...	—	—	—	—	—

Season Team	League	REGULAR SEASON								PLAYOFFS				
		Gms.	G	A	Pts.	PIM	+/-	PP	SH	Gms.	G	A	Pts.	PIM
94-95—Windsor	OHL	61	4	13	17	201	...	...	...	10	1	3	4	41
95-96—Windsor	OHL	64	14	45	59	260	...	...	...	7	1	7	8	23
96-97—Windsor	OHL	63	15	52	67	190	...	...	...	5	1	7	8	11
—Toronto	NHL	8	0	1	1	7	-5	0	0	—	—	—	—	—
—St. John's	AHL	—	—	—	—	—	—	—	—	1	0	0	0	0
NHL totals (1 year)		8	0	1	1	7	-5	0	0					

SMITH, GEOFF   D   PANTHERS

PERSONAL: Born March 7, 1969, in Edmonton. ... 6-3/200. ... Shoots left. ... Full name: Geoff Arthur Smith.
HIGH SCHOOL: Harry Ainlay (Edmonton).
COLLEGE: North Dakota.
TRANSACTIONS/CAREER NOTES: Selected by Edmonton Oilers in third round (third Oilers pick, 63rd overall) of NHL entry draft (June 13, 1987). ... Fractured ankle (October 1988); missed first 10 games of season. ... Left University of North Dakota and signed to play with Kamloops Blazers (January 1989). ... Broke jaw (March 1989). ... Pulled back muscle (February 8, 1991); missed eight games. ... Bruised shoulder (April 26, 1992). ... Traded by Oilers to Florida Panthers for third-(D Corey Neilson) and sixth-round picks in 1994 draft (December 6, 1993). ... Lacerated left leg (December 10, 1993); missed two games. ... Separated left shoulder (February 15, 1997); missed 23 games.
HONORS: Named to WHL All-Star first team (1988-89). ... Named to NHL All-Rookie team (1989-90).
MISCELLANEOUS: Member of Stanley Cup championship team (1990).

Season Team	League	REGULAR SEASON								PLAYOFFS				
		Gms.	G	A	Pts.	PIM	+/-	PP	SH	Gms.	G	A	Pts.	PIM
86-87—St. Albert	AJHL	57	7	28	35	101	...	...	...	—	—	—	—	—
87-88—North Dakota	WCHA	9	0	1	1	8	...	...	...	—	—	—	—	—
88-89—Kamloops	WHL	32	4	31	35	29	...	...	...	6	1	3	4	12
89-90—Edmonton	NHL	74	4	11	15	52	13	1	0	3	0	0	0	0
90-91—Edmonton	NHL	59	1	12	13	55	13	0	0	4	0	0	0	0
91-92—Edmonton	NHL	74	2	16	18	43	-5	0	0	5	0	1	1	6
92-93—Edmonton	NHL	78	4	14	18	30	-11	0	1	—	—	—	—	—
93-94—Edmonton	NHL	21	0	3	3	12	-10	0	0	—	—	—	—	—
—Florida	NHL	56	1	5	6	38	-3	0	0	—	—	—	—	—
94-95—Florida	NHL	47	2	4	6	22	-5	0	0	—	—	—	—	—
95-96—Florida	NHL	31	3	7	10	20	-4	2	0	1	0	0	0	2
96-97—Carolina	AHL	27	3	4	7	20	...	...	...	—	—	—	—	—
—Florida	NHL	3	0	0	0	2	1	0	0	—	—	—	—	—
NHL totals (8 years)		443	17	72	89	274	-11	3	1	13	0	1	1	8

SMITH, JASON   D   MAPLE LEAFS

PERSONAL: Born November 2, 1973, in Calgary. ... 6-3/205. ... Shoots right.
TRANSACTIONS/CAREER NOTES: Selected by New Jersey Devils in first round (first Devils pick, 18th overall) of NHL entry draft (June 20, 1992). ... Injured right knee (November 5, 1994); missed 37 games. ... Bruised hand (November 5, 1995); missed 15 games. ... Traded by Devils with C Steve Sullivan and C Alyn McCauley to Toronto Maple Leafs for C Doug Gilmour, D Dave Ellett and third-round pick in 1999 draft (February 25, 1997).
HONORS: Named to Can.HL All-Rookie team (1991-92). ... Won Bill Hunter Trophy (1992-93). ... Named to Can.HL All-Star first team (1992-93). ... Named to WHL (East) All-Star first team (1992-93).

Season Team	League	REGULAR SEASON								PLAYOFFS				
		Gms.	G	A	Pts.	PIM	+/-	PP	SH	Gms.	G	A	Pts.	PIM
90-91—Calgary Canucks	AJHL	45	3	15	18	69	...	...	...	—	—	—	—	—
—Regina	WHL	2	0	0	0	7	...	...	...	—	—	—	—	—
91-92—Regina	WHL	62	9	29	38	168	...	...	...	—	—	—	—	—
92-93—Regina	WHL	64	14	52	66	175	...	...	...	13	4	8	12	39
—Utica	AHL	—	—	—	—	—	—	—	—	1	0	0	0	2
93-94—New Jersey	NHL	41	0	5	5	43	7	0	0	6	0	0	0	7
—Albany	AHL	20	6	3	9	31	...	...	...	—	—	—	—	—
94-95—Albany	AHL	7	0	2	2	15	...	...	...	11	2	2	4	19
—New Jersey	NHL	2	0	0	0	0	-3	0	0	—	—	—	—	—
95-96—New Jersey	NHL	64	2	1	3	86	5	0	0	—	—	—	—	—
96-97—New Jersey	NHL	57	1	2	3	38	-8	0	0	—	—	—	—	—
—Toronto	NHL	21	0	5	5	16	-4	0	0	—	—	—	—	—
NHL totals (4 years)		185	3	13	16	183	-3	0	0	6	0	0	0	7

SMITH, STEVE   D   BLACKHAWKS

PERSONAL: Born April 30, 1963, in Glasgow, Scotland. ... 6-4/215. ... Shoots left. ... Full name: James Stephen Smith.
TRANSACTIONS/CAREER NOTES: Selected by Edmonton Oilers as underage junior in sixth round (fifth Oilers pick, 111th overall) of NHL entry draft (June 10, 1981). ... Strained right shoulder (November 1, 1985). ... Pulled stomach muscle (February 1986). ... Separated left shoulder (September 20, 1988). ... Aggravated shoulder injury (October 1988). ... Dislocated left shoulder and tore cartilage (January 2, 1989). ... Underwent surgery to left shoulder (January 23, 1989); missed 45 games. ... Traded by Oilers to Chicago Blackhawks for D Dave Manson and third-round pick in either 1992 or 1993 draft; Oilers used third-round pick in 1992 draft to select RW Kirk Maltby (September 26, 1991). ... Pulled rib-cage muscle (December 31, 1991); missed three games. ... Strained back muscle (December 27, 1992); missed four games. ... Suspended four games and fined $500 by NHL for slashing (November 22, 1993). ... Broke left leg (February 24, 1994); missed remainder of season. ... Suffered back spasms (October 5, 1995); missed 14 games. ... Suffered sore back (November 22, 1995); missed 11 games. ... Suffered sore back (January 2, 1996); missed 11 games. ... Suffered sore back (January 28, 1996); missed six games. ... Fractured left fibula (April 7, 1996); missed seven games. ... Injured nerve in leg (October 5, 1996); missed 10 games. ... Suffered sore back (November 17, 1996), missed three games. ... Suffered sore back (November 27, 1996); missed 13 games. ... Suffered sore back (December 31, 1996); missed 28 games.

HONORS: Played in NHL All-Star Game (1991).
MISCELLANEOUS: Member of Stanley Cup championship team (1987, 1988 and 1990).

Season Team	League	REGULAR SEASON								PLAYOFFS				
		Gms.	G	A	Pts.	PIM	+/-	PP	SH	Gms.	G	A	Pts.	PIM
80-81 — London	OMJHL	62	4	12	16	141	...	...	...	—	—	—	—	—
81-82 — London	OHL	58	10	36	46	207	...	...	...	4	1	2	3	13
82-83 — London	OHL	50	6	35	41	133	...	...	...	3	1	0	1	10
— Moncton	AHL	2	0	0	0	0	...	...	...	—	—	—	—	—
83-84 — Moncton	AHL	64	1	8	9	176	...	...	...	—	—	—	—	—
84-85 — Nova Scotia	AHL	68	2	28	30	161	...	...	...	5	0	3	3	40
— Edmonton	NHL	2	0	0	0	2	...	...	...	—	—	—	—	—
85-86 — Nova Scotia	AHL	4	0	2	2	11	...	...	...	—	—	—	—	—
— Edmonton	NHL	55	4	20	24	166	...	...	...	6	0	1	1	14
86-87 — Edmonton	NHL	62	7	15	22	165	...	...	...	15	1	3	4	45
87-88 — Edmonton	NHL	79	12	43	55	286	...	...	...	19	1	11	12	55
88-89 — Edmonton	NHL	35	3	19	22	97	5	0	0	7	2	2	4	20
89-90 — Edmonton	NHL	75	7	34	41	171	6	3	0	22	5	10	15	37
90-91 — Edmonton	NHL	77	13	41	54	193	14	4	0	18	1	2	3	45
91-92 — Chicago	NHL	76	9	21	30	304	23	3	0	18	1	11	12	16
92-93 — Chicago	NHL	78	10	47	57	214	12	7	1	4	0	0	0	10
93-94 — Chicago	NHL	57	5	22	27	174	-5	1	0	—	—	—	—	—
94-95 — Chicago	NHL	48	1	12	13	128	6	0	0	16	0	1	1	26
95-96 — Chicago	NHL	37	0	9	9	71	12	0	0	6	0	0	0	16
96-97 — Chicago	NHL	21	0	0	0	29	4	0	0	3	0	0	0	4
NHL totals (13 years)		702	71	283	354	2000	77	18	1	134	11	41	52	288

SMOLINSKI, BRYAN　　　　C　　　　ISLANDERS

PERSONAL: Born December 27, 1971, in Toledo, Ohio. ... 6-1/202. ... Shoots right. ... Full name: Bryan Anthony Smolinski.
COLLEGE: Michigan State.
TRANSACTIONS/CAREER NOTES: Selected by Boston Bruins in first round (first Bruins pick, 21st overall) of NHL entry draft (June 16, 1990). ... Injured knee (April 14, 1994); missed one game. ... Suffered charley horse (April 1995); missed four games. ... Traded by Bruins with RW Glen Murray to Pittsburgh Penguins for LW Kevin Stevens and C Shawn McEachern (August 2, 1995). ... Bruised knee (January 16, 1996); missed one game. ... Traded by Penguins to New York Islanders for D Darius Kasparaitis and C Andreas Johansson (November 17, 1996).
HONORS: Named to CCHA All-Rookie team (1989-90). ... Named to NCAA All-America West first team (1992-93). ... Named to CCHA All-Star first team (1992-93).
STATISTICAL PLATEAUS: Three-goal games: 1994-95 (1).

Season Team	League	REGULAR SEASON								PLAYOFFS				
		Gms.	G	A	Pts.	PIM	+/-	PP	SH	Gms.	G	A	Pts.	PIM
87-88 — Det. Little Caesars	MNHL	80	43	77	120	...	...	...	...	—	—	—	—	—
88-89 — Stratford Jr. B	OHA	46	32	62	94	132	...	...	...	—	—	—	—	—
89-90 — Michigan State	CCHA	39	10	17	27	45	...	...	...	—	—	—	—	—
90-91 — Michigan State	CCHA	35	9	12	21	24	...	...	...	—	—	—	—	—
91-92 — Michigan State	CCHA	44	30	35	65	59	...	...	...	—	—	—	—	—
92-93 — Michigan State	CCHA	40	31	37	68	93	...	...	...	—	—	—	—	—
— Boston	NHL	9	1	3	4	0	3	0	0	4	1	0	1	2
93-94 — Boston	NHL	83	31	20	51	82	4	4	3	13	5	4	9	4
94-95 — Boston	NHL	44	18	13	31	31	-3	6	0	5	0	1	1	4
95-96 — Pittsburgh	NHL	81	24	40	64	69	6	8	2	18	5	4	9	10
96-97 — Detroit	IHL	6	5	7	12	10	...	...	...	—	—	—	—	—
— New York Islanders	NHL	64	28	28	56	25	9	9	0	—	—	—	—	—
NHL totals (5 years)		281	102	104	206	207	19	27	5	40	11	9	20	20

SMYTH, BRAD　　　　RW　　　　KINGS

PERSONAL: Born March 13, 1973, in Ottawa. ... 6-0/200. ... Shoots right. ... Name pronounced SMIHTH.
TRANSACTIONS/CAREER NOTES: Signed as free agent by Florida Panthers (October 4, 1993). ... Traded by Panthers to Los Angeles Kings for third-round pick (D Vratislav Cech) in 1997 draft (November 28, 1996).
HONORS: Named to AHL All-Star first team (1995-96). ... Won John B. Sollenberger Trophy (1995-96). ... Won Les Cunningham Plaque (1995-96).

Season Team	League	REGULAR SEASON								PLAYOFFS				
		Gms.	G	A	Pts.	PIM	+/-	PP	SH	Gms.	G	A	Pts.	PIM
90-91 — London	OHL	29	2	6	8	22	...	...	...	—	—	—	—	—
91-92 — London	OHL	58	17	18	35	93	...	...	...	10	2	0	2	8
92-93 — London	OHL	66	54	55	109	118	...	...	...	12	7	8	15	25
93-94 — Cincinnati	IHL	30	7	3	10	54	...	...	...	10	8	8	16	19
— Birmingham	ECHL	29	26	30	56	38	...	...	...	—	—	—	—	—
94-95 — Cincinnati	IHL	26	2	11	13	34	...	...	...	1	0	0	0	2
— Birmingham	ECHL	36	33	35	68	52	...	...	...	3	5	2	7	0
— Springfield	AHL	3	0	0	0	7	...	...	...	—	—	—	—	—
95-96 — Carolina	AHL	68	*68	58	*126	80	...	...	...	—	—	—	—	—
— Florida	NHL	7	1	1	2	4	-3	1	0	—	—	—	—	—
96-97 — Florida	NHL	8	1	0	1	2	-3	0	0	—	—	—	—	—
— Los Angeles	NHL	44	8	8	16	74	-7	0	0	—	—	—	—	—
— Phoenix	IHL	3	5	2	7	0	...	...	...	—	—	—	—	—
NHL totals (2 years)		59	10	9	19	80	-13	1	0					

SMYTH, GREG   D   MAPLE LEAFS

PERSONAL: Born April 23, 1966, in Oakville, Ont. ... 6-3/212. ... Shoots right. ... Name pronounced SMIHTH.
TRANSACTIONS/CAREER NOTES: Selected by Philadelphia Flyers as underage junior in second round (first Flyers pick, 22nd overall) of NHL entry draft (June 9, 1984). ... Suspended 10 games by OHL for fighting with fans (December 1984). ... Suspended by London Knights (October 1985). ... Suspended eight games by OHL (November 7, 1985). ... Traded by Flyers with third-round pick in 1989 draft (G John Tanner) to Quebec Nordiques for D Terry Carkner (July 25, 1988). ... Broke two bones in right hand during training camp (September 1988). ... Suspended eight games by AHL for fighting (December 17, 1988). ... Injured back (February 15, 1990). ... Recalled from Halifax by Quebec and refused to report (February 10, 1991). ... Traded by Nordiques to Calgary Flames for RW Martin Simard (March 10, 1992). ... Strained stomach (October 6, 1992); missed first four games of season. ... Injured ribs (December 4, 1992); missed four games. ... Signed as free agent by Florida Panthers (July 14, 1993). ... Underwent surgery to right elbow (October 6, 1993); missed five games. ... Traded by Panthers to Toronto Maple Leafs for future considerations (December 7, 1993). ... Claimed on waivers by Chicago Blackhawks (January 9, 1994). ... Pulled rib cage muscle (January 27, 1994); missed four games. ... Signed as free agent by Chicago of IHL (September 5, 1995). ... Signed as free agent by Toronto Maple Leafs (August 22, 1996).
HONORS: Named to OHL All-Star second team (1985-86).

| | | REGULAR SEASON | | | | | | | | | PLAYOFFS | | | | |
Season Team	League	Gms.	G	A	Pts.	PIM	+/-	PP	SH		Gms.	G	A	Pts.	PIM
83-84— London	OHL	64	4	21	25	*252	...	...	...		6	1	0	1	24
84-85— London	OHL	47	7	16	23	188	...	...	...		8	2	2	4	27
85-86— Hershey	AHL	2	0	1	1	5	...	...	...		8	0	0	0	60
— London	OHL	46	12	42	54	197	...	...	...		4	1	2	3	28
86-87— Hershey	AHL	35	0	2	2	158	...	...	...		2	0	0	0	19
— Philadelphia	NHL	1	0	0	0	0	-2	0	0		1	0	0	0	2
87-88— Hershey	AHL	21	0	10	10	102	...	...	...		—	—	—	—	—
— Philadelphia	NHL	48	1	6	7	192	-2	0	0		5	0	0	0	38
88-89— Halifax	AHL	43	3	9	12	310	...	...	...		4	0	1	1	35
— Quebec	NHL	10	0	1	1	70	-9	0	0		—	—	—	—	—
89-90— Quebec	NHL	13	0	0	0	57	-8	0	0		—	—	—	—	—
— Halifax	AHL	49	5	14	19	235	...	...	...		6	1	0	1	52
90-91— Quebec	NHL	1	0	0	0	0	0	0	0		—	—	—	—	—
— Halifax	AHL	56	6	23	29	340	...	...	...		—	—	—	—	—
91-92— Quebec	NHL	29	0	2	2	138	-10	0	0		—	—	—	—	—
— Halifax	AHL	9	1	3	4	35	...	...	...		—	—	—	—	—
— Calgary	NHL	7	1	1	2	15	7	0	0		—	—	—	—	—
92-93— Calgary	NHL	35	1	2	3	95	2	1	0		—	—	—	—	—
— Salt Lake City	IHL	5	0	1	1	31	...	...	...		—	—	—	—	—
93-94— Florida	NHL	12	1	0	1	37	0	0	0		—	—	—	—	—
— Toronto	NHL	11	0	1	1	38	-2	0	0		—	—	—	—	—
— Chicago	NHL	38	0	0	0	108	-2	0	0		6	0	0	0	0
94-95— Chicago	NHL	22	0	3	3	33	2	0	0		—	—	—	—	—
— Indianapolis	IHL	2	0	0	0	0	...	...	...		—	—	—	—	—
95-96— Chicago	IHL	15	1	3	4	53	...	...	...		—	—	—	—	—
— Los Angeles	IHL	41	2	7	9	231	...	...	...		—	—	—	—	—
96-97— St. John's	AHL	43	2	4	6	273	...	...	...		5	0	1	1	14
— Toronto	NHL	2	0	0	0	0	0	0	0		—	—	—	—	—
NHL totals (11 years)		229	4	16	20	783	-24	1	0		12	0	0	0	40

SMYTH, KEVIN   LW

PERSONAL: Born November 22, 1973, in Banff, Alta. ... 6-2/217. ... Shoots left. ... Name pronounced SMIHTH. ... Brother of Ryan Smyth, left winger, Edmonton Oilers.
TRANSACTIONS/CAREER NOTES: Selected by Hartford Whalers in fourth round (fourth Whalers pick, 79th overall) of NHL entry draft (June 20, 1992). ... Bruised spleen (February 11, 1994); missed six games. ... Injured shoulder (March 22, 1994); missed four games. ... Sprained knee (December 15, 1995), missed seven games.

| | | REGULAR SEASON | | | | | | | | | PLAYOFFS | | | | |
Season Team	League	Gms.	G	A	Pts.	PIM	+/-	PP	SH		Gms.	G	A	Pts.	PIM
90-91— Moose Jaw	WHL	66	30	45	75	96	...	...	...		6	1	1	2	0
91-92— Moose Jaw	WHL	71	30	55	85	114	...	...	...		4	1	3	4	6
92-93— Moose Jaw	WHL	64	44	38	82	111	...	...	...		—	—	—	—	—
93-94— Springfield	AHL	42	22	27	49	72	...	...	...		6	4	5	9	0
— Hartford	NHL	21	3	2	5	10	-1	0	0		—	—	—	—	—
94-95— Springfield	AHL	57	17	22	39	72	...	...	...		—	—	—	—	—
— Hartford	NHL	16	1	5	6	13	-3	0	0		—	—	—	—	—
95-96— Hartford	NHL	21	2	1	3	8	-5	1	0		—	—	—	—	—
— Springfield	AHL	47	15	33	48	87	...	...	...		10	5	5	10	8
96-97— Orlando	IHL	38	14	17	31	49	...	...	...		10	1	2	3	6
NHL totals (3 years)		58	6	8	14	31	-9	1	0						

SMYTH, RYAN   LW   OILERS

PERSONAL: Born February 21, 1976, in Banff, Alta. ... 6-1/195. ... Shoots left. ... Name pronounced SMIHTH. ... Brother of Kevin Smyth, left winger with Hartford Whalers (1993-94 through 1995-96).
HIGH SCHOOL: Vanier Comm. Catholic (Edson, Alta.).
TRANSACTIONS/CAREER NOTES: Selected by Edmonton Oilers in first round (second Oilers pick, sixth overall) of NHL entry draft (June 28, 1994).
HONORS: Named to Can.HL All-Star first team (1994-95). ... Named to WHL (East) All-Star second team (1994-95).
STATISTICAL PLATEAUS: Three-goal games: 1996-97 (1).

Season Team	League	REGULAR SEASON								PLAYOFFS				
		Gms.	G	A	Pts.	PIM	+/-	PP	SH	Gms.	G	A	Pts.	PIM
91-92— Moose Jaw	WHL	2	0	0	0	0	...	...	...	—	—	—	—	—
92-93— Moose Jaw	WHL	64	19	14	33	59	...	...	...	—	—	—	—	—
93-94— Moose Jaw	WHL	72	50	55	105	88	...	...	...	—	—	—	—	—
94-95— Moose Jaw	WHL	50	41	45	86	66	...	...	...	10	6	9	15	22
— Edmonton	NHL	3	0	0	0	0	-1	0	0	—	—	—	—	—
95-96— Edmonton	NHL	48	2	9	11	28	-10	1	0	—	—	—	—	—
— Cape Breton	AHL	9	6	5	11	4	...	...	...	—	—	—	—	—
96-97— Edmonton	NHL	82	39	22	61	76	-7	†20	0	12	5	5	10	12
NHL totals (3 years)		133	41	31	72	104	-18	21	0	12	5	5	10	12

SNELL, CHRIS — D — BLACKHAWKS

PERSONAL: Born May 12, 1971, in Regina, Sask. ... 5-10/200. ... Shoots left.
TRANSACTIONS/CAREER NOTES: Signed as free agent by Toronto Maple Leafs (August 3, 1993). ... Traded by Maple Leafs with LW Eric Lacroix and fourth-round pick (C Eric Belanger) in 1996 draft to Los Angeles Kings for RW Dixon Ward, C Guy Leveque, RW Shayne Toporowski and C Kelly Fairchild (October 3, 1994). ... Suffered from the flu (April 23, 1995); missed one game. ... Traded by Kings to New York Rangers for C Steve Larouche (January 15, 1996). ... Signed as free agent by Chicago Blackhawks (August 16, 1996).
HONORS: Named to OHL All-Star first team (1989-90). ... Won Eddie Shore Plaque (1993-94). ... Named to AHL All-Star first team (1993-94). ... Named to IHL All-Star first team (1994-95). ... Named to IHL All-Star second team (1996-97).

Season Team	League	REGULAR SEASON								PLAYOFFS				
		Gms.	G	A	Pts.	PIM	+/-	PP	SH	Gms.	G	A	Pts.	PIM
89-90— Ottawa	OHL	63	18	62	80	36	...	...	...	3	2	4	6	4
90-91— Ottawa	OHL	54	23	59	82	58	...	...	...	17	3	14	17	8
91-92— Rochester	AHL	65	5	27	32	66	...	...	...	10	2	1	3	6
92-93— Rochester	AHL	76	14	57	71	83	...	...	...	17	5	8	13	39
93-94— St. John's	AHL	75	22	74	96	92	...	...	...	11	1	15	16	10
— Toronto	NHL	2	0	0	0	2	-1	0	0	—	—	—	—	—
94-95— Phoenix	IHL	57	15	49	64	122	...	...	...	—	—	—	—	—
— Los Angeles	NHL	32	2	7	9	22	-7	0	2	—	—	—	—	—
95-96— Phoenix	IHL	40	9	22	31	113	...	...	...	—	—	—	—	—
— Binghamton	AHL	32	7	25	32	48	...	...	...	4	2	2	4	6
96-97— Indianapolis	IHL	73	22	45	67	130	...	...	...	2	0	0	0	2
NHL totals (2 years)		34	2	7	9	24	-8	0	2					

SNOPEK, JAN — D — OILERS

PERSONAL: Born June 22, 1976, in Prague, Czechoslovakia. ... 6-3/215. ... Shoots right.
HIGH SCHOOL: Henry Street (Whitby, Ont.).
TRANSACTIONS/CAREER NOTES: Selected by Edmonton Oilers in fifth round (fifth Oilers pick, 109th overall) of NHL entry draft (July 8, 1995).
HONORS: Named to Memorial Cup All-Star Team (1996-97).

Season Team	League	REGULAR SEASON								PLAYOFFS				
		Gms.	G	A	Pts.	PIM	+/-	PP	SH	Gms.	G	A	Pts.	PIM
92-93— Sparta Prague	Czech.	40	3	8	11	80	...	...	...	—	—	—	—	—
93-94— Oshawa	OHL	52	0	5	5	51	...	...	...	—	—	—	—	—
94-95— Oshawa	OHL	64	14	30	44	97	...	...	...	7	0	1	1	4
95-96— Oshawa	OHL	64	7	28	35	79	...	...	...	5	0	0	0	2
96-97— Oshawa	OHL	57	10	32	42	103	...	...	...	15	2	7	9	24

SNOW, GARTH — G — FLYERS

PERSONAL: Born July 28, 1969, in Wrentham, Mass. ... 6-3/200. ... Catches left.
HIGH SCHOOL: Mount St. Charles Academy (Woonsocket, R.I.).
COLLEGE: Maine.
TRANSACTIONS/CAREER NOTES: Selected by Quebec Nordiques in sixth round (sixth Nordiques pick, 114th overall) of NHL entry draft (June 13, 1987). ... Nordiques franchise moved to Colorado and renamed Avalanche for 1995-96 season (June 21, 1995). ... Rights traded by Avalanche to Philadelphia Flyers for third-(traded to Washington) and sixth-(G Kai Fischer) round picks in 1996 draft (July 12, 1995). ... Pulled groin (March 27, 1997); missed three games.
HONORS: Named to NCAA All-Tournament team (1992-93). ... Named to Hockey East All-Star second team (1992-93).

Season Team	League	REGULAR SEASON								PLAYOFFS						
		Gms.	Min	W	L	T	GA	SO	Avg.	Gms.	Min.	W	L	GA	SO	Avg.
88-89— University of Maine	Hoc. East	5	241	2	2	0	14	1	3.49	—	—	—	—	—	—	—
89-90— University of Maine	Hoc. East								Did not play.							
90-91— University of Maine	Hoc. East	25	1290	18	4	0	64	0	2.98	—	—	—	—	—	—	—
91-92— University of Maine	Hoc. East	31	1792	25	4	2	73	2	2.44	—	—	—	—	—	—	—
92-93— University of Maine	Hoc. East	23	1210	21	0	1	42	1	2.08	—	—	—	—	—	—	—
93-94— U.S. national team	Int'l	23	1324	...	...	...	71	...	3.22	—	—	—	—	—	—	—
— Quebec	NHL	5	279	3	2	0	16	0	3.44	—	—	—	—	—	—	—
— U.S. Olympic team	Int'l	5	299	...	...	...	17	0	3.41	—	—	—	—	—	—	—
— Cornwall	AHL	16	927	6	5	3	51	0	3.30	13	790	8	5	42	0	3.19
94-95— Cornwall	AHL	62	3558	*32	20	7	162	3	2.73	8	402	4	3	14	†2	*2.09
— Quebec	NHL	2	119	1	1	0	11	0	5.55	1	9	0	0	1	0	6.67
95-96— Philadelphia	NHL	26	1437	12	8	4	69	0	2.88	1	1	0	0	0	0	0.00
96-97— Philadelphia	NHL	35	1884	14	8	8	79	2	2.52	12	699	8	4	33	0	2.83
NHL totals (4 years)		68	3719	30	19	12	175	2	2.82	14	709	8	4	34	0	2.88

SODERSTROM, TOMMY   G   ISLANDERS

PERSONAL: Born July 17, 1969, in Stockholm, Sweden. ... 5-9/156. ... Catches left. ... Name pronounced SAH-duhr-struhm.
TRANSACTIONS/CAREER NOTES: Selected by Philadelphia Flyers in 11th round (14th Flyers pick, 214th overall) of NHL entry draft (June 16, 1990). ... Underwent procedure to correct Wolff-Parkinson-White syndrome (November 3, 1993); missed six games. ... Traded by Flyers to New York Islanders for G Ron Hextall and sixth-round pick (D Dmitri Tertyshny) in 1995 draft (September 22, 1994).
HONORS: Named Swedish League Rookie of the Year (1990-91). ... Named to Swedish League All-Star team (1991-92).

			REGULAR SEASON								PLAYOFFS					
Season Team	League	Gms.	Min	W	L	T	GA	SO	Avg.	Gms.	Min.	W	L	GA	SO	Avg.
89-90—Djur. Stockholm...........	Sweden	4	240	...	...	...	14	0	3.50	—	—	—	—	—	—	—
90-91—Djur. Stockholm...........	Sweden	39	2340	22	12	6	104	3	2.67	7	423	...	...	10	2	1.42
91-92—Djur. Stockholm...........	Sweden	31	2357	15	8	11	112	0	2.85	10	635	...	...	28	0	2.65
—Swed. Olympic team....	Int'l	5	296	...	...	...	13	0	2.64	—	—	—	—	—	—	—
92-93—Hershey	AHL	7	373	4	1	0	15	0	2.41	—	—	—	—	—	—	—
—Philadelphia	NHL	44	2512	20	17	6	143	5	3.42	—	—	—	—	—	—	—
93-94—Philadelphia	NHL	34	1736	6	18	4	116	2	4.01	—	—	—	—	—	—	—
—Hershey	AHL	9	462	3	4	1	37	0	4.81	—	—	—	—	—	—	—
94-95—New York Islanders	NHL	26	1350	8	12	3	70	1	3.11	—	—	—	—	—	—	—
95-96—New York Islanders	NHL	51	2590	11	22	6	167	2	3.87	—	—	—	—	—	—	—
96-97—New York Islanders	NHL	1	0	0	0	0	0	0	0.00	—	—	—	—	—	—	—
—Utah	IHL	26	1463	12	11	‡0	76	0	3.12	—	—	—	—	—	—	—
—Rochester	AHL	2	120	2	0	0	8	0	4.00	—	—	—	—	—	—	—
NHL totals (5 years)		156	8188	45	69	19	496	10	3.63							

SOLING, JONAS   RW   CANUCKS

PERSONAL: Born September 7, 1978, in Stockholm, Sweden. ... 6-4/187. ... Shoots left. ... Name pronounced YOH-nuhz SOH-lihng.
TRANSACTIONS/CAREER NOTES: Selected by Vancouver Canucks in fourth round (third Canucks pick, 93rd overall) of NHL entry draft (June 22, 1996).

			REGULAR SEASON							PLAYOFFS			
Season Team	League	Gms.	G	A	Pts.	PIM	+/-	PP	SH	Gms.	G	A	Pts.	PIM
94-95—Huddinge Jrs.	Sweden	1	3	1	4	6	...	...	...	—	—	—	—	—
95-96—Huddinge Jrs.	Sweden	24	8	4	12	18	...	...	...	—	—	—	—	—
—Huddinge	Swed. Div. II	5	0	0	0	0	...	...	...	—	—	—	—	—
96-97—Sudbury....................	OHL	66	18	22	40	60	...	...	...	—	—	—	—	—

SOROCHAN, LEE   D   RANGERS

PERSONAL: Born September 9, 1975, in Edmonton. ... 6-1/210. ... Shoots left. ... Name pronounced SOHR-ih-kihn.
HIGH SCHOOL: Gibbons (Alta.).
TRANSACTIONS/CAREER NOTES: Selected by New York Rangers in second round (second Rangers pick, 34th overall) of NHL entry draft (June 26, 1993).

			REGULAR SEASON							PLAYOFFS			
Season Team	League	Gms.	G	A	Pts.	PIM	+/-	PP	SH	Gms.	G	A	Pts.	PIM
91-92—Lethbridge	WHL	67	2	9	11	105	...	...	...	5	0	2	2	6
92-93—Lethbridge	WHL	69	8	32	40	208	...	...	...	4	0	1	1	12
93-94—Lethbridge	WHL	46	5	27	32	123	...	...	...	9	4	3	7	16
94-95—Lethbridge	WHL	29	4	15	19	93	...	...	...	—	—	—	—	—
—Saskatoon	WHL	24	5	13	18	63	...	...	...	10	3	6	9	34
—Binghamton	AHL	—	—	—	—	—	...	...	...	8	0	0	0	11
95-96—Binghamton	AHL	45	2	8	10	26	...	...	...	1	0	0	0	0
96-97—Binghamton	AHL	77	4	27	31	160	...	...	...	4	0	2	2	18

SOURAY, SHELDON   D   DEVILS

PERSONAL: Born July 13, 1976, in Elk Point, Alta. ... 6-2/210. ... Shoots left. ... Name pronounced SOOR-ay.
TRANSACTIONS/CAREER NOTES: Selected by New Jersey Devils in third round (third Devils pick, 71st overall) of NHL entry draft (June 29, 1994).
HONORS: Named to WHL (West) All-Star second team (1995-96).

			REGULAR SEASON							PLAYOFFS			
Season Team	League	Gms.	G	A	Pts.	PIM	+/-	PP	SH	Gms.	G	A	Pts.	PIM
92-93—Fort Saskatchewan.....	AJHL	35	0	12	12	125	...	...	...	—	—	—	—	—
—Tri-City	WHL	2	0	0	0	0	...	...	...	—	—	—	—	—
93-94—Tri-City	WHL	42	3	6	9	122	...	...	...	—	—	—	—	—
94-95—Tri-City	WHL	40	2	24	26	140	...	...	...	—	—	—	—	—
—Prince George...........	WHL	11	2	3	5	23	...	...	...	—	—	—	—	—
—Albany.......................	AHL	7	0	2	2	8	...	...	...	—	—	—	—	—
95-96—Prince George...........	WHL	32	9	18	27	91	...	...	...	—	—	—	—	—
—Kelowna....................	WHL	27	7	20	27	94	...	...	...	6	0	5	5	2
—Albany.......................	AHL	6	0	2	2	12	...	...	...	4	0	1	1	4
96-97—Albany.......................	AHL	70	2	11	13	160	...	...	...	16	2	3	5	47

S

PERSONAL: Born July 28, 1973, in Hamilton, Ont. ... 6-1/205. ... Shoots right. ... Name pronounced STAY-ohz.
TRANSACTIONS/CAREER NOTES: Selected by St. Louis Blues in second round (first Blues pick, 27th overall) of NHL entry draft (June 22, 1991). ... Traded by Blues with LW Kevin Sawyer to Boston Bruins for RW Steve Leach (March 8, 1996). ... Strained groin (November 6, 1996); missed 13 games. ... Claimed on waivers by Vancouver Canucks (March 18, 1997).

		REGULAR SEASON								PLAYOFFS				
Season Team	League	Gms.	G	A	Pts.	PIM	+/-	PP	SH	Gms.	G	A	Pts.	PIM
89-90— Hamilton Jr. B	OHA	40	9	27	36	66	...	...	...	—	—	—	—	—
90-91— Niagara Falls	OHL	66	17	29	46	115	...	...	...	12	2	3	5	10
91-92— Niagara Falls	OHL	65	11	42	53	122	...	...	...	17	7	8	15	27
92-93— Niagara Falls	OHL	12	4	14	18	30	...	...	...	—	—	—	—	—
— Sudbury	OHL	53	13	44	57	67	...	...	...	11	5	6	11	22
93-94— Peoria	IHL	38	3	9	12	42	...	...	...	—	—	—	—	—
94-95— Peoria	IHL	60	3	13	16	64	...	...	...	6	0	0	0	10
95-96— Peoria	IHL	6	0	1	1	14	...	...	...	—	—	—	—	—
— Worcester	AHL	57	1	11	12	114	...	...	...	—	—	—	—	—
— Providence	AHL	7	1	4	5	8	...	...	...	—	—	—	—	—
— Boston	NHL	12	0	0	4	-5	0	0		3	0	0	0	0
96-97— Boston	NHL	54	3	8	11	71	-26	0	0	—	—	—	—	—
— Vancouver	NHL	9	0	6	6	20	2	0	0	—	—	—	—	—
NHL totals (2 years)		**75**	**3**	**14**	**17**	**95**	**-29**	**0**	**0**	**3**	**0**	**0**	**0**	**0**

PERSONAL: Born December 6, 1974, in Kitchener, Ont. ... 6-2/195. ... Shoots left. ... Name pronounced STAJ-doo-hahr.
TRANSACTIONS/CAREER NOTES: Selected by Edmonton Oilers in first round (second Oilers pick, 16th overall) of NHL entry draft (June 26, 1993). ... Loaned to Canadian national team prior to 1995-96 season. ... Injured toe (January 3, 1996); missed three games.
HONORS: Named to OHL All-Star first team (1993-94).

		REGULAR SEASON								PLAYOFFS				
Season Team	League	Gms.	G	A	Pts.	PIM	+/-	PP	SH	Gms.	G	A	Pts.	PIM
90-91— London	OHL	66	3	12	15	39	...	...	...	7	0	0	0	2
91-92— London	OHL	66	6	15	21	62	...	...	...	10	1	4	5	10
92-93— London	OHL	49	15	46	61	58	...	...	...	12	4	11	15	10
93-94— London	OHL	52	34	52	86	58	...	...	...	5	0	2	2	8
94-95— Cape Breton	AHL	54	12	26	38	55	...	...	...	—	—	—	—	—
95-96— Canadian nat'l team	Int'l	46	7	21	28	60	...	...	...	—	—	—	—	—
— Cape Breton	AHL	8	2	0	2	11	...	...	...	—	—	—	—	—
— Edmonton	NHL	2	0	0	0	4	2	0	0	—	—	—	—	—
96-97— Hamilton	AHL	11	1	2	3	2	...	...	...	—	—	—	—	—
— Quebec	IHL	7	1	3	4	2	...	...	...	—	—	—	—	—
— Pensacola	ECHL	30	9	15	24	32	...	...	...	12	1	6	7	34
NHL totals (1 year)		**2**	**0**	**0**	**0**	**4**	**2**	**0**	**0**					

PERSONAL: Born May 5, 1966, in Sarnia, Ont. ... 5-10/185. ... Shoots right. ... Son of Pat Stapleton, defenseman, Boston Bruins and Chicago Blackhawks (1961-62 through 1972-73); and Chicago Cougars, Indianapolis Racers and Cincinnati Stingers of WHA (1973-74 through 1977-78).
TRANSACTIONS/CAREER NOTES: Selected by Chicago Blackhawks in seventh round (seventh Blackhawks pick, 132nd overall) of NHL entry draft (June 9, 1984). ... Signed as free agent by Pittsburgh Penguins (September 4, 1992). ... Claimed on waivers by Edmonton Oilers (February 19, 1994). ... Signed as free agent by Winnipeg Jets (August 9, 1995). ... Suffered charley horse (October 12, 1995); missed one game. ... Broke jaw (November 1, 1995); missed 16 games. ... Strained groin (March 27, 1996); missed five games. ... Jets franchise moved to Phoenix and renamed Coyotes for 1996-97 season; NHL approved move on January 18, 1996.

		REGULAR SEASON								PLAYOFFS				
Season Team	League	Gms.	G	A	Pts.	PIM	+/-	PP	SH	Gms.	G	A	Pts.	PIM
82-83— Strathroy Jr. B	OHA	40	39	38	77	99	...	...	...	—	—	—	—	—
83-84— Cornwall	OHL	70	24	45	69	94	...	...	...	3	1	2	3	4
84-85— Cornwall	OHL	56	41	44	85	68	...	...	...	9	2	4	6	23
85-86— Cornwall	OHL	56	39	65	104	74	...	...	...	6	2	3	5	2
86-87— Canadian nat'l team	Int'l	21	2	4	6	4	...	...	...	—	—	—	—	—
— Chicago	NHL	39	3	6	9	6	-9	0	0	4	0	0	0	2
87-88— Saginaw	IHL	31	11	19	30	52	...	...	...	10	5	6	11	10
— Chicago	NHL	53	2	9	11	59	-10	0	0	—	—	—	—	—
88-89— Chicago	NHL	7	0	1	1	7	-1	0	0	—	—	—	—	—
— Saginaw	IHL	69	21	47	68	162	...	...	...	6	1	3	4	4
89-90— Arvika	Sweden	30	15	18	33	...	...	...	...	—	—	—	—	—
— Indianapolis	IHL	16	5	10	15	6	...	...	...	13	9	10	19	38
90-91— Chicago	NHL	7	0	1	1	2	0	0	0	—	—	—	—	—
— Indianapolis	IHL	75	29	52	81	76	...	...	...	7	1	4	5	0
91-92— Indianapolis	IHL	59	18	40	58	65	...	...	...	—	—	—	—	—
— Chicago	NHL	19	4	4	8	8	0	1	0	—	—	—	—	—
92-93— Pittsburgh	NHL	78	4	9	13	10	-8	0	1	4	0	0	0	0
93-94— Pittsburgh	NHL	58	7	4	11	18	-4	3	0	—	—	—	—	—
— Edmonton	NHL	23	5	9	14	28	-1	1	0	—	—	—	—	—
94-95— Edmonton	NHL	46	6	11	17	21	-12	3	0	—	—	—	—	—
95-96— Winnipeg	NHL	58	10	14	24	37	-4	3	1	6	0	0	0	21
96-97— Phoenix	NHL	55	4	11	15	36	-4	2	0	7	0	0	0	14
NHL totals (10 years)		**443**	**45**	**79**	**124**	**232**	**-53**	**13**	**2**	**21**	**0**	**0**	**0**	**37**

STERN, RONNIE   RW   FLAMES

PERSONAL: Born January 11, 1967, in Ste. Agatha Des Mont, Que. ... 6-0/201. ... Shoots right.
TRANSACTIONS/CAREER NOTES: Selected by Vancouver Canucks as underage junior in fourth round (third Canucks pick, 70th overall) of NHL entry draft (June 21, 1986). ... Bruised shoulder (April 1989). ... Suffered laceration near eye and dislocated shoulder (March 19, 1990). ... Fractured wrist (October 30, 1990); missed 10 weeks. ... Traded by Canucks with D Kevan Guy and option to switch fourth-round picks in 1992 draft to Calgary Flames for D Dana Murzyn; Flames did not exercise option (March 5, 1991). ... Suffered back spasms (October 15, 1992); missed 11 games. ... Broke bone in right foot (October 11, 1993); missed three games. ... Bruised shoulder (December 7, 1993); missed one game. ... Bruised shoulder (December 28, 1993); missed six games. ... Sprained left ankle (February 6, 1995); missed four games. ... Strained thigh (April 25, 1995); missed three games. ... Suspended two games by NHL for accumulating four game misconduct penalties (March 22, 1995). ... Suspended four games by NHL for slashing (December 19, 1995). ... Suffered back spasms (December 27, 1995); missed five games. ... Suspended four games and fined $1,000 by NHL for slashing (December 19, 1995). ... Injured neck and shoulder (January 14, 1996); missed 21 games. ... Sore lower back (October 19, 1996); missed three games.
STATISTICAL PLATEAUS: Three-goal games: 1991-92 (1), 1992-93 (1), 1994-95 (1). Total: 3.

		REGULAR SEASON								PLAYOFFS				
Season Team	League	Gms.	G	A	Pts.	PIM	+/-	PP	SH	Gms.	G	A	Pts.	PIM
84-85 — Longueuil	QMJHL	67	6	14	20	176	...	...	...	—	—	—	—	—
85-86 — Longueuil	QMJHL	70	39	33	72	317	...	...	...	—	—	—	—	—
86-87 — Longueuil	QMJHL	56	32	39	71	266	...	...	...	19	11	9	20	55
87-88 — Fredericton	AHL	2	1	0	1	4	...	...	...	—	—	—	—	—
— Flint	IHL	55	14	19	33	294	...	...	...	16	8	8	16	94
— Vancouver	NHL	15	0	0	0	52	-7	0	0	—	—	—	—	—
88-89 — Milwaukee	IHL	45	19	23	42	280	...	...	...	5	1	0	1	11
— Vancouver	NHL	17	1	0	1	49	-6	0	0	3	0	1	1	17
89-90 — Milwaukee	IHL	26	8	9	17	165	...	...	...	—	—	—	—	—
— Vancouver	NHL	34	2	3	5	208	-17	0	0	—	—	—	—	—
90-91 — Milwaukee	IHL	7	2	2	4	81	...	...	...	—	—	—	—	—
— Vancouver	NHL	31	2	3	5	171	-14	0	0	—	—	—	—	—
— Calgary	NHL	13	1	3	4	69	0	0	0	7	1	3	4	14
91-92 — Calgary	NHL	72	13	9	22	338	0	0	1	—	—	—	—	—
92-93 — Calgary	NHL	70	10	15	25	207	4	0	0	6	0	0	0	43
93-94 — Calgary	NHL	71	9	20	29	243	6	0	1	7	2	0	2	12
94-95 — Calgary	NHL	39	9	4	13	163	4	1	0	7	3	1	4	8
95-96 — Calgary	NHL	52	10	5	15	111	2	0	0	4	0	2	2	8
96-97 — Calgary	NHL	79	7	10	17	157	-4	0	1	—	—	—	—	—
NHL totals (10 years)		493	64	72	136	1768	-32	1	3	34	6	7	13	102

STEVENS, KEVIN   LW   KINGS

PERSONAL: Born April 15, 1965, in Brockton, Mass. ... 6-3/217. ... Shoots left. ... Full name: Kevin Michael Stevens.
HIGH SCHOOL: Silver Lake (Mass.).
COLLEGE: Boston College.
TRANSACTIONS/CAREER NOTES: Selected by Los Angeles Kings in sixth round (sixth Kings pick, 108th overall) of NHL entry draft (June 8, 1983). ... Traded by Kings to Pittsburgh Penguins for LW Anders Hakansson (September 9, 1983). ... Damaged cartilage in left knee (November 5, 1992) and underwent arthroscopic surgery (November 6, 1992); missed nine games. ... Suspended one game by NHL (March 1993). ... Suffered from bronchitis (April 3, 1993); missed two games. ... Fractured left ankle (February 4, 1995); missed 21 games. ... Traded by Penguins with C Shawn McEachern to Boston Bruins for C Bryan Smolinski and RW Glen Murray (August 2, 1995). ... Traded by Bruins to Los Angeles Kings for RW Rick Tocchet (January 25, 1996). ... Fractured left fibula (February 29, 1996); missed 10 games. ... Suffered concussion (October 15, 1996); missed one game. ... Suffered back spasms (November 27, 1996); missed one game. ... Bruised ankle (February 20, 1997); missed seven games. ... Injured knee (April 9, 1997); missed two games.
HONORS: Named to NCAA All-America East second team (1986-87). ... Named to Hockey East All-Star first team (1986-87). ... Named to THE SPORTING NEWS All-Star second team (1990-91 and 1992-93). ... Named to NHL All-Star second team (1990-91 and 1992-93). ... Named to THE SPORTING NEWS All-Star first team (1991-92). ... Named to NHL All-Star first team (1991-92). ... Played in NHL All-Star Game (1991-1993).
STATISTICAL PLATEAUS: Three-goal games: 1989-90 (1), 1990-91 (1), 1991-92 (3), 1992-93 (2), 1993-94 (1). Total: 8. ... Four-goal games: 1991-92 (1), 1992-93 (1). Total: 2. ... Total hat tricks: 10.
MISCELLANEOUS: Member of Stanley Cup championship team (1991 and 1992). ... Failed to score on a penalty shot (vs. Nikolai Khabibulin, February 26, 1996).

		REGULAR SEASON								PLAYOFFS				
Season Team	League	Gms.	G	A	Pts.	PIM	+/-	PP	SH	Gms.	G	A	Pts.	PIM
82-83 — Silver Lake	Minn. H.S.	18	24	27	51		...	...	...	—	—	—	—	—
83-84 — Boston College	ECAC	37	6	14	20	36	...	...	...	—	—	—	—	—
84-85 — Boston College	Hockey East	40	13	23	36	36	...	...	...	—	—	—	—	—
85-86 — Boston College	Hockey East	42	17	27	44	56	...	...	...	—	—	—	—	—
86-87 — Boston College	Hockey East	39	*35	35	70	54	...	...	...	—	—	—	—	—
87-88 — U.S. national team	Int'l	44	22	23	45	52	...	...	...	—	—	—	—	—
— U.S. Olympic team	Int'l	5	1	3	4	2	...	...	...	—	—	—	—	—
— Pittsburgh	NHL	16	5	2	7	8	-6	2	0	—	—	—	—	—
88-89 — Pittsburgh	NHL	24	12	3	15	19	-8	4	0	11	3	7	10	16
— Muskegon	IHL	45	24	41	65	113	...	...	...	—	—	—	—	—
89-90 — Pittsburgh	NHL	76	29	41	70	171	-13	12	0	—	—	—	—	—
90-91 — Pittsburgh	NHL	80	40	46	86	133	-1	18	0	24	*17	16	33	53
91-92 — Pittsburgh	NHL	80	54	69	123	254	8	19	0	21	13	15	28	28
92-93 — Pittsburgh	NHL	72	55	56	111	177	17	26	0	12	5	11	16	22
93-94 — Pittsburgh	NHL	83	41	47	88	155	-24	21	0	6	1	1	2	10
94-95 — Pittsburgh	NHL	27	15	12	27	51	0	6	0	12	4	7	11	21
95-96 — Boston	NHL	41	10	13	23	49	1	3	0	—	—	—	—	—
— Los Angeles	NHL	20	3	10	13	22	-11	3	0	—	—	—	—	—
96-97 — Los Angeles	NHL	69	14	20	34	96	-27	4	0	—	—	—	—	—
NHL totals (10 years)		588	278	319	597	1135	-64	118	0	86	43	57	100	150

S

PERSONAL: Born April 1, 1964, in Kitchener, Ont. ... 6-2/215. ... Shoots left. ... Brother of Mike Stevens, center/left winger for four NHL teams (1984-85 and 1987-88 through 1989-90)..

TRANSACTIONS/CAREER NOTES: Selected by Washington Capitals as underage junior in first round (first Capitals pick, fifth overall) of NHL entry draft (June 9, 1982). ... Bruised right knee (November 6, 1985); missed seven games. ... Broke right index finger (December 14, 1986). ... Bruised shoulder (April 1988). ... Suffered from poison oak (November 1988). ... Lacerated face during World Cup (April 21, 1989). ... Broke left foot (December 29, 1989); missed 17 games. ... Suspended three games by NHL for scratching (February 27, 1990). ... Suspended left shoulder (March 27, 1990). ... Dislocated left shoulder (May 3, 1990). ... Signed as free agent by St. Louis Blues (July 9, 1990); Blues owed Capitals two first-round draft picks among the top seven over next two years and $100,000 cash; upon failing to get a pick in the top seven in 1991, Blues forfeited their first-round pick in 1991 (LW Trevor Halverson), 1992 (D Sergei Gonchar), 1993 (D Brendan Witt), 1994 (traded to Toronto Maple Leafs) and 1995 (LW Miikka Elomo) drafts to Capitals (July 9, 1990). ... Awarded to New Jersey Devils as compensation for Blues signing free agent RW/LW Brendan Shanahan (September 3, 1991). ... Strained right knee (February 20, 1992); missed 12 games. ... Suffered concussion (December 27, 1992); missed three games. ... Strained knee (November 19, 1993); missed one game. ... Suspended one game by NHL for highsticking incident (October 7, 1996). ... Suffered from the flu (December 23, 1996); missed one game.

HONORS: Named to NHL All-Rookie team (1982-83). ... Named to THE SPORTING NEWS All-Star second team (1987-88). ... Named to NHL All-Star first team (1987-88 and 1993-94). ... Named to NHL All-Star second team (1991-92 and 1996-97). ... Played in NHL All-Star Game (1985, 1989, 1991-1994 and 1996-1997). ... Named to THE SPORTING NEWS All-Star first team (1993-94).

MISCELLANEOUS: Member of Stanley Cup championship team (1995). ... Captain of St. Louis Blues (1990-91). ... Captain of New Jersey Devils (1992-93, 1995-96 and 1996-97). ... Holds Washington Capitals all-time record for most penalty minutes (1,630).

		REGULAR SEASON							PLAYOFFS				
Season Team	League	Gms.	G	A	Pts.	PIM	+/-	PP	SH	Gms.	G	A	Pts.	PIM
80-81 — Kitchener Jr. B	OHA	39	7	33	40	82	...	...	...	—	—	—	—	—
— Kitchener	OHL	1	0	0	0	0	...	...	...	—	—	—	—	—
81-82 — Kitchener	OHL	68	6	36	42	158	...	...	...	15	1	10	11	71
82-83 — Washington	NHL	77	9	16	25	195	15	0	0	4	1	0	1	26
83-84 — Washington	NHL	78	13	32	45	201	26	7	0	8	1	8	9	21
84-85 — Washington	NHL	80	21	44	65	221	19	16	0	5	0	1	1	20
85-86 — Washington	NHL	73	15	38	53	165	0	3	0	9	3	8	11	12
86-87 — Washington	NHL	77	10	51	61	283	13	2	0	7	0	5	5	19
87-88 — Washington	NHL	80	12	60	72	184	14	5	1	13	1	11	12	46
88-89 — Washington	NHL	80	7	61	68	225	1	6	0	6	1	4	5	11
89-90 — Washington	NHL	56	11	29	40	154	1	7	0	15	2	7	9	25
90-91 — St. Louis	NHL	78	5	44	49	150	23	1	0	13	0	3	3	36
91-92 — New Jersey	NHL	68	17	42	59	124	24	7	1	7	2	1	3	29
92-93 — New Jersey	NHL	81	12	45	57	120	14	8	0	5	2	2	4	10
93-94 — New Jersey	NHL	83	18	60	78	112	*53	5	1	20	2	9	11	42
94-95 — New Jersey	NHL	48	2	20	22	56	4	1	0	20	1	7	8	24
95-96 — New Jersey	NHL	82	5	23	28	100	7	2	1	—	—	—	—	—
96-97 — New Jersey	NHL	79	5	19	24	70	26	0	0	10	0	4	4	2
NHL totals (15 years)		1120	162	584	746	2360	240	70	4	142	16	70	86	323

PERSONAL: Born July 28, 1974, in San Bernardino, Calif. ... 6-1/220. ... Shoots left. ... Full name: Jeremy Joseph Stevenson.
HIGH SCHOOL: St. Lawrence (Cornwall, Ont.).
TRANSACTIONS/CAREER NOTES: Selected by Winnipeg Jets in third round (third Jets pick, 60th overall) of NHL entry draft (June 20, 1992). ... Returned to draft pool by Jets and selected by Mighty Ducks of Anaheim in 11th round (10th Mighty Ducks pick, 262nd overall) of NHL entry draft (June 28, 1994). ... Fractured ankle (October 24, 1996); missed 33 games.

		REGULAR SEASON							PLAYOFFS				
Season Team	League	Gms.	G	A	Pts.	PIM	+/-	PP	SH	Gms.	G	A	Pts.	PIM
90-91 — Cornwall	OHL	58	13	20	33	124	...	...	...	—	—	—	—	—
91-92 — Cornwall	OHL	63	15	23	38	176	...	...	...	6	3	1	4	4
92-93 — Newmarket	OHL	54	28	28	56	144	...	...	...	5	5	1	6	28
93-94 — Newmarket	OHL	9	2	4	6	27	...	...	...	—	—	—	—	—
— Sault Ste. Marie	OHL	48	18	19	37	183	...	...	...	14	1	1	2	23
94-95 — Greensboro	ECHL	43	14	13	27	231	...	...	...	17	6	11	17	64
95-96 — Baltimore	AHL	60	11	10	21	295	...	...	...	12	4	2	6	23
— Anaheim	NHL	3	0	1	1	12	1	0	0	—	—	—	—	—
96-97 — Baltimore	AHL	25	8	8	16	125	...	...	...	3	0	0	0	8
— Anaheim	NHL	5	0	0	0	14	-1	0	0	—	—	—	—	—
NHL totals (2 years)		8	0	1	1	26	0	0	0					

PERSONAL: Born May 18, 1972, in Port Alberni, B.C. ... 6-3/215. ... Shoots right.
TRANSACTIONS/CAREER NOTES: Underwent surgery to remove growth in chest (August 1987). ... Injured shoulder (December 1987). ... Selected by Montreal Canadiens in first round (first Canadiens pick, 12th overall) of NHL entry draft (June 16, 1990). ... Suffered from the flu (October 21, 1995); missed two games. ... Sprained knee (October 7, 1996); missed five games. ... Sprained knee (October 26, 1996); missed four games. ... Sprained knee (November 11, 1996); missed seven games.
HONORS: Named to Can.HL All-Star second team (1991-92). ... Named to Memorial Cup All-Star team (1991-92). ... Named to WHL (West) All-Star first team (1991-92).

		REGULAR SEASON							PLAYOFFS				
Season Team	League	Gms.	G	A	Pts.	PIM	+/-	PP	SH	Gms.	G	A	Pts.	PIM
88-89 — Seattle	WHL	69	15	12	27	84	...	...	...	—	—	—	—	—
89-90 — Seattle	WHL	62	29	32	61	276	...	...	...	13	3	2	5	35
90-91 — Seattle	WHL	57	36	27	63	222	...	...	...	6	1	5	6	15
— Fredericton	AHL	—	—	—	—	—				4	0	0	0	5

Season Team	League	REGULAR SEASON								PLAYOFFS				
		Gms.	G	A	Pts.	PIM	+/-	PP	SH	Gms.	G	A	Pts.	PIM
91-92 — Seattle	WHL	58	20	32	52	264	...	...	...	15	9	3	12	55
92-93 — Fredericton	AHL	79	25	34	59	102	...	...	...	5	2	3	5	11
— Montreal	NHL	1	0	0	0	0	-1	0	0	—	—	—	—	—
93-94 — Fredericton	AHL	66	19	28	47	155	...	...	...	—	—	—	—	—
— Montreal	NHL	2	0	0	0	2	-2	0	0	3	0	2	2	0
94-95 — Fredericton	AHL	37	12	12	24	109	...	...	...	—	—	—	—	—
— Montreal	NHL	41	6	1	7	86	0	0	0	—	—	—	—	—
95-96 — Montreal	NHL	80	9	16	25	167	-2	0	0	6	0	1	1	2
96-97 — Montreal	NHL	65	8	13	21	97	-14	1	0	5	1	1	2	2
NHL totals (5 years)		189	23	30	53	352	-19	1	0	14	1	4	5	4

STEWART, CAM — LW — BRUINS

PERSONAL: Born September 18, 1971, in Kitchener, Ont. ... 5-11/199. ... Shoots left.
COLLEGE: Michigan.
TRANSACTIONS/CAREER NOTES: Strained knee ligaments (June 1989). ... Selected by Boston Bruins in third round (second Bruins pick, 63rd overall) of NHL entry draft (June 16, 1990). ... Fractured finger (November 13, 1993); missed seven games. ... Injured neck (January 11, 1997); missed two games. ... Suffered back spasms (January 20, 1997); missed six games.

S

Season Team	League	REGULAR SEASON								PLAYOFFS				
		Gms.	G	A	Pts.	PIM	+/-	PP	SH	Gms.	G	A	Pts.	PIM
88-89 — Elmira Jr. B	OHA	43	38	50	88	138	...	...	...	—	—	—	—	—
89-90 — Elmira Jr. B	OHA	46	44	95	139	172	...	...	...	—	—	—	—	—
90-91 — Univ. of Michigan	CCHA	44	8	24	32	122	...	...	...	—	—	—	—	—
91-92 — Univ. of Michigan	CCHA	44	13	15	28	106	...	...	...	—	—	—	—	—
92-93 — Univ. of Michigan	CCHA	39	20	39	59	69	...	...	...	—	—	—	—	—
93-94 — Boston	NHL	57	3	6	9	66	-6	0	0	8	0	3	3	7
— Providence	AHL	14	3	2	5	5	...	...	...	—	—	—	—	—
94-95 — Boston	NHL	5	0	0	0	2	0	0	0	—	—	—	—	—
— Providence	AHL	31	13	11	24	38	...	...	...	9	2	5	7	0
95-96 — Providence	AHL	54	17	25	42	39	...	...	...	—	—	—	—	—
— Boston	NHL	6	0	0	0	0	-2	0	0	5	1	0	1	2
96-97 — Boston	NHL	15	0	1	1	4	-2	0	0	—	—	—	—	—
— Providence	AHL	18	4	3	7	37	...	...	...	—	—	—	—	—
— Cincinnati	IHL	7	3	2	5	8	...	...	...	1	0	0	0	0
NHL totals (4 years)		83	3	7	10	72	-10	0	0	13	1	3	4	9

STEWART, JASON — D — ISLANDERS

PERSONAL: Born April 30, 1976, in St. Paul, Minn. ... 5-11/185. ... Shoots right.
HIGH SCHOOL: Simley (Inver Groves Heights, Minn.).
COLLEGE: St. Cloud (Minn.) State.
TRANSACTIONS/CAREER NOTES: Selected by New York Islanders in sixth round (seventh Islanders pick, 142nd overall) of NHL entry draft (June 29, 1994).

Season Team	League	REGULAR SEASON								PLAYOFFS				
		Gms.	G	A	Pts.	PIM	+/-	PP	SH	Gms.	G	A	Pts.	PIM
90-91 — Simley	Minn. H.S.	26	2	5	7	4	...	...	...	—	—	—	—	—
91-92 — Simley	Minn. H.S.	23	7	5	12	10	...	...	...	—	—	—	—	—
92-93 — Simley	Minn. H.S.	23	19	15	34	20	...	...	...	—	—	—	—	—
93-94 — Simley	Minn. H.S.	23	15	15	30	32	...	...	...	—	—	—	—	—
94-95 — St. Cloud State	WCHA	28	1	3	4	16	...	...	...	—	—	—	—	—
95-96 — St. Cloud State	WCHA	39	4	7	11	40	...	...	...	—	—	—	—	—
96-97 — St. Cloud State	WCHA	40	6	5	11	32	...	...	...	—	—	—	—	—

STILLMAN, CORY — C — FLAMES

PERSONAL: Born December 20, 1973, in Peterborough, Ont. ... 6-0/185. ... Shoots left.
HIGH SCHOOL: Herman E. Fawcett (Brantford, Ont.).
TRANSACTIONS/CAREER NOTES: Selected by Calgary Flames in first round (first Flames pick, sixth overall) of NHL entry draft (June 20, 1992). ... Suspended four games by AHL for incident involving on-ice official (March 29, 1995). ... Suffered from the flu (October 8, 1995); missed one game. ... Bruised knee (January 14, 1996); missed two games. ... Injured shoulder (December 16, 1996); missed five games.
HONORS: Won Emms Family Award (1990-91).

Season Team	League	REGULAR SEASON								PLAYOFFS				
		Gms.	G	A	Pts.	PIM	+/-	PP	SH	Gms.	G	A	Pts.	PIM
89-90 — Peterborough Jr. B	OHA	41	30	54	84	76	...	...	...	—	—	—	—	—
90-91 — Windsor	OHL	64	31	70	101	31	...	...	...	11	3	6	9	8
91-92 — Windsor	OHL	53	29	61	90	59	...	...	...	7	2	4	6	8
92-93 — Peterborough	OHL	61	25	55	80	55	...	...	...	18	3	8	11	18
— Canadian nat'l team	Int'l	1	0	0	0	0	...	...	...	—	—	—	—	—
93-94 — Saint John	AHL	79	35	48	83	52	...	...	...	7	2	4	6	16
94-95 — Saint John	AHL	63	28	53	81	70	...	...	...	5	0	2	2	2
— Calgary	NHL	10	0	2	2	2	1	0	0	—	—	—	—	—
95-96 — Calgary	NHL	74	16	19	35	41	-5	4	1	2	1	1	2	0
96-97 — Calgary	NHL	58	6	20	26	14	-6	2	0	—	—	—	—	—
NHL totals (3 years)		142	22	41	63	57	-10	6	1	2	1	1	2	0

STOJANOV, ALEK   LW   PENGUINS

PERSONAL: Born April 25, 1973, in Windsor, Ont. ... 6-4/225. ... Shoots left. ... Name pronounced stoy-YAH-nahf.
TRANSACTIONS/CAREER NOTES: Dislocated shoulder (July 1989). ... Selected by Vancouver Canucks in first round (first Canucks pick, seventh overall) of NHL entry draft (June 22, 1991). ... Strained neck (December 8, 1995); missed two games. ... Traded by Canucks to Pittsburgh Penguins for RW Markus Naslund (March 20, 1996). ... Suffered concussion (April 11, 1996); missed one game. ... Cracked rib prior to 1996-97 season; missed first two games of season. ... Suffered from the flu (November 12, 1996); missed three games. ... Suffered head and shoulder injuries in an auto accident (December 28, 1996); missed 21 games. ... Strained groin (March 5, 1997); missed 18 games.

				REGULAR SEASON								PLAYOFFS			
Season Team	League	Gms.	G	A	Pts.	PIM	+/-	PP	SH		Gms.	G	A	Pts.	PIM
89-90— Dukes of Hamilton	OHL	37	4	4	8	91	...	...	...		—	—	—	—	—
90-91— Dukes of Hamilton	OHL	62	25	20	45	179	...	...	...		4	1	1	2	14
91-92— Guelph	OHL	33	12	15	27	91	...	...	...		—	—	—	—	—
92-93— Guelph	OHL	35	27	28	55	11	...	...	...		—	—	—	—	—
— Newmarket	OHL	14	9	7	16	21	...	...	...		7	1	3	4	26
— Hamilton	AHL	4	4	0	4	0	...	...	...		—	—	—	—	—
93-94— Hamilton	AHL	4	0	1	1	5	...	...	...		—	—	—	—	—
94-95— Syracuse	AHL	73	18	12	30	270	...	...	...		—	—	—	—	—
— Vancouver..................	NHL	4	0	0	0	13	-2	0	0		5	0	0	0	2
95-96— Pittsburgh..............	NHL	68	1	1	2	130	-13	0	0		9	0	0	0	19
96-97— Pittsburgh..............	NHL	35	1	4	5	79	3	0	0		—	—	—	—	—
NHL totals (3 years)		107	2	5	7	222	-12	0	0		14	0	0	0	21

S

STORM, JIM   LW   ISLANDERS

PERSONAL: Born February 5, 1971, in Milford, Mich. ... 6-2/200. ... Shoots left. ... Full name: James David Storm.
COLLEGE: Michigan Tech.
TRANSACTIONS/CAREER NOTES: Selected by Hartford Whalers in fourth round (fifth Whalers pick, 75th overall) of NHL entry draft (June 22, 1991). ... Joined U.S. national team (October 6-November 6, 1993). ... Signed as free agent by Dallas Stars (August 24, 1995). ... Signed as free agent by New York Islanders (July 1, 1997).

				REGULAR SEASON								PLAYOFFS			
Season Team	League	Gms.	G	A	Pts.	PIM	+/-	PP	SH		Gms.	G	A	Pts.	PIM
88-89— Detroit Compuware....	NAJHL	60	30	45	75	50	...	...	...		—	—	—	—	—
89-90— Detroit Compuware....	NAJHL	55	38	73	111	58	...	...	...		—	—	—	—	—
90-91— Michigan Tech	WCHA	36	16	17	33	46	...	...	...		—	—	—	—	—
91-92— Michigan Tech	WCHA	39	25	33	58	12	...	...	...		—	—	—	—	—
92-93— Michigan Tech	WCHA	33	22	32	54	30	...	...	...		—	—	—	—	—
93-94— Hartford	NHL	68	6	10	16	27	4	1	0		—	—	—	—	—
— U.S. national team	Int'l	28	8	12	20	14	...	...	...		—	—	—	—	—
94-95— Springfield	AHL	33	11	11	22	29	...	...	...		—	—	—	—	—
— Hartford	NHL	6	0	3	3	0	2	0	0		—	—	—	—	—
95-96— Michigan................	IHL	60	18	33	51	27	...	...	...		10	4	8	12	2
— Dallas....................	NHL	10	1	2	3	17	-1	0	0		—	—	—	—	—
96-97— Michigan................	IHL	75	25	24	49	27	...	...	...		4	0	1	1	4
NHL totals (3 years)		84	7	15	22	44	5	1	0						

STORR, JAMIE   G   KINGS

PERSONAL: Born December 28, 1975, in Brampton, Ont. ... 6-2/192. ... Catches left.
HIGH SCHOOL: West Hill (Owen Sound, Ont.).
TRANSACTIONS/CAREER NOTES: Selected by Los Angeles Kings in first round (first Kings pick, seventh overall) of NHL entry draft (June 28, 1994).
HONORS: Named to OHL All-Star first team (1993-94).

				REGULAR SEASON							PLAYOFFS				
Season Team	League	Gms.	Min	W	L	T	GA	SO	Avg.		Gms.	Min.	W	L	GA	SO	Avg.
90-91— Brampton......................	Jr. B	24	1145	...	...	...	91	0	4.77		—	—	—	—	—	—	—
91-92— Owen Sound................	OHL	34	1733	11	16	1	128	0	4.43		5	299	1	4	28	0	5.62
92-93— Owen Sound................	OHL	41	2362	20	17	3	180	0	4.57		8	454	4	4	35	0	4.63
93-94— Owen Sound................	OHL	35	2004	21	11	1	120	1	3.59		9	547	4	5	44	0	4.83
94-95— Owen Sound................	OHL	17	977	5	9	2	64	0	3.93		—	—	—	—	—	—	—
— Los Angeles	NHL	5	263	1	3	1	17	0	3.88		—	—	—	—	—	—	—
— Windsor	OHL	4	241	3	1	0	8	1	1.99		10	520	6	3	34	1	3.92
95-96— Los Angeles	NHL	5	262	3	1	0	12	0	2.75		—	—	—	—	—	—	—
— Phoenix	IHL	48	2711	22	20	‡4	139	2	3.08		2	118	1	1	4	1	2.03
96-97— Phoenix	IHL	44	2441	16	22	‡4	147	0	3.61		—	—	—	—	—	—	—
— Los Angeles	NHL	5	265	2	1	1	11	0	2.49		—	—	—	—	—	—	—
NHL totals (3 years)		15	790	6	5	2	40	0	3.04								

STRAKA, MARTIN   C   PANTHERS

PERSONAL: Born September 3, 1972, in Plzen, Czechoslovakia. ... 5-10/178. ... Shoots left. ... Name pronounced STRAH-kuh.
TRANSACTIONS/CAREER NOTES: Selected by Pittsburgh Penguins in first round (first Penguins pick, 19th overall) of NHL entry draft (June 20, 1992). ... Played in Europe during 1994-95 NHL lockout. ... Suffered from the flu (February 14, 1995); missed four games. ... Traded by Penguins to Ottawa Senators for D Norm Maciver and C Troy Murray (April 7, 1995). ... Strained knee (April 19, 1995); missed remainder of season. ... Injured hamstring (November 11, 1995); missed one game. ... Traded by Senators with D Bryan Berard to New York Islanders for D Wade Redden and G Damian Rhodes (January 23, 1996). ... Claimed on waivers by Florida Panthers (March 15, 1996). ... Bruised buttocks

(April 10, 1996); missed last two games of season. ... Strained groin (January 1, 1997); missed one game. ... Strained groin (January 8, 1997); missed two games. ... Strained groin (January 22, 1997); missed four games. ... Strained groin (March 5, 1997); missed nine games.
HONORS: Named to Czechoslovakian League All-Star team (1991-92).
STATISTICAL PLATEAUS: Three-goal games: 1993-94 (1).
MISCELLANEOUS: Failed to score on a penalty shot (vs. Jocelyn Thibault, March 16, 1995; vs. Damian Rhodes, April 3, 1996).

Season Team	League		REGULAR SEASON							PLAYOFFS			
		Gms.	G	A	Pts.	PIM	+/-	PP	SH	Gms.	G	A	Pts.	PIM
89-90— Skoda Plzen..............	Czech.	1	0	3	3	...	...	...	...	—	—	—	—	—
90-91— Skoda Plzen..............	Czech.	47	7	24	31	6	...	...	...	—	—	—	—	—
91-92— Skoda Plzen..............	Czech.	50	27	28	55	20	...	...	...	—	—	—	—	—
92-93— Pittsburgh.................	NHL	42	3	13	16	29	2	0	0	11	2	1	3	2
— Cleveland	IHL	4	4	3	7	0	...	...	...	—	—	—	—	—
93-94— Pittsburgh.................	NHL	84	30	34	64	24	24	2	0	6	1	0	1	2
94-95— Interconex Plzen	Czech Rep.	19	10	11	21	18	...	...	...	—	—	—	—	—
— Pittsburgh.................	NHL	31	4	12	16	16	0	0	0	—	—	—	—	—
— Ottawa	NHL	6	1	1	2	0	-1	0	0	—	—	—	—	—
95-96— Ottawa	NHL	43	9	16	25	29	-14	5	0	—	—	—	—	—
— New York Islanders....	NHL	22	2	10	12	6	-6	0	0	—	—	—	—	—
— Florida......................	NHL	12	2	4	6	6	1	1	0	13	2	2	4	2
96-97— Florida......................	NHL	55	7	22	29	12	9	2	0	4	0	0	0	0
NHL totals (5 years)		295	58	112	170	122	15	10	0	34	5	3	8	6

STROBEL, MARK   D   DEVILS   S

PERSONAL: Born August 15, 1973, in St. Paul, Minn. ... 6-0/200. ... Shoots left.
TRANSACTIONS/CAREER NOTES: Signed as free agent by New Jersey Devils (October 1, 1995).

Season Team	League		REGULAR SEASON							PLAYOFFS			
		Gms.	G	A	Pts.	PIM	+/-	PP	SH	Gms.	G	A	Pts.	PIM
91-92— Univ. of Wisconsin.....	WCHA	37	1	2	3	48	...	...	...	—	—	—	—	—
92-93— Univ. of Wisconsin.....	WCHA	36	4	9	13	73	...	...	...	—	—	—	—	—
93-94— Univ. of Wisconsin.....	WCHA	41	7	12	19	57	...	...	...	—	—	—	—	—
94-95— Univ. of Wisconsin.....	WCHA	37	9	18	27	74	...	...	...	—	—	—	—	—
95-96— Albany......................	AHL	28	1	1	2	36	...	...	...	—	—	—	—	—
— Raleigh.....................	ECHL	26	1	5	6	18	...	...	...	—	—	—	—	—
96-97— Albany......................	AHL	60	3	10	13	65	...	...	...	8	1	1	2	2

STRUDWICK, JASON   D   ISLANDERS

PERSONAL: Born July 17, 1975, in Edmonton. ... 6-3/207. ... Shoots left.
COLLEGE: University College of the Cariboo (Kamloops, B.C.).
TRANSACTIONS/CAREER NOTES: Selected by New York Islanders in third round (third Islanders pick, 63rd overall) of NHL entry draft (June 29, 1994).

Season Team	League		REGULAR SEASON							PLAYOFFS			
		Gms.	G	A	Pts.	PIM	+/-	PP	SH	Gms.	G	A	Pts.	PIM
93-94— Kamloops..................	WHL	61	6	8	14	118	...	...	...	19	0	4	4	24
94-95— Kamloops..................	WHL	72	3	11	14	183	...	...	...	21	1	1	2	39
95-96— Worcester	AHL	60	2	7	9	119	...	...	...	4	0	1	1	0
— New York Islanders....	NHL	1	0	0	0	7	0	0	0	—	—	—	—	—
96-97— Kentucky...................	AHL	80	1	9	10	198	...	...	...	4	0	0	0	0
NHL totals (1 year)		1	0	0	0	7	0	0	0					

STUMPEL, JOZEF   C   BRUINS

PERSONAL: Born June 20, 1972, in Nitra, Czechoslovakia. ... 6-2/211. ... Shoots right. ... Name pronounced JOH-sehf STUHM-puhl.
TRANSACTIONS/CAREER NOTES: Selected by Boston Bruins in second round (second Bruins pick, 40th overall) of NHL entry draft (June 22, 1991). ... Injured shoulder (December 1992); missed nine games. ... Injured knee (March 17, 1994); missed nine games. ... Played in Europe during 1994-95 NHL lockout. ... Injured knee (April 1995). ... Fractured cheek bone (February 27, 1996); missed three games. ... Suffered back spasms (January 4, 1997); missed one game. ... Suffered back spasms (February 1, 1997); missed three games.
STATISTICAL PLATEAUS: Three-goal games: 1995-96 (1).

Season Team	League		REGULAR SEASON							PLAYOFFS			
		Gms.	G	A	Pts.	PIM	+/-	PP	SH	Gms.	G	A	Pts.	PIM
89-90— Nitra.........................	Czech.	38	12	11	23	0	...	...	...	—	—	—	—	—
90-91— Nitra.........................	Czech.	49	23	22	45	14	...	...	...	—	—	—	—	—
91-92— Boston	NHL	4	1	0	1	0	1	0	0	—	—	—	—	—
— Koln	Germany	33	19	18	37	35	...	...	...	—	—	—	—	—
92-93— Providence................	AHL	56	31	61	92	26	...	...	...	6	4	4	8	0
— Boston	NHL	13	1	3	4	4	-3	0	0	—	—	—	—	—
93-94— Boston	NHL	59	8	15	23	14	4	0	0	13	1	7	8	4
— Providence................	AHL	17	5	12	17	4	...	...	...	—	—	—	—	—
94-95— Koln	Germany	25	16	23	39	18	...	...	...	—	—	—	—	—
— Boston	NHL	44	5	13	18	8	4	1	0	5	0	0	0	0
95-96— Boston	NHL	76	18	36	54	14	-8	5	0	5	1	2	3	0
96-97— Boston	NHL	78	21	55	76	14	-22	6	0	—	—	—	—	—
NHL totals (6 years)		274	54	122	176	54	-24	12	0	23	2	9	11	4

STURM, MARCO   C   SHARKS

PERSONAL: Born September 8, 1978, in Dingolfing, West Germany. ... 5-11/178. ... Shoots left.
TRANSACTIONS/CAREER NOTES: Selected by San Jose Sharks in first round (second Sharks pick, 21st overall) of NHL entry draft (June 22, 1996).

		REGULAR SEASON								PLAYOFFS				
Season Team	League	Gms.	G	A	Pts.	PIM	+/-	PP	SH	Gms.	G	A	Pts.	PIM
95-96 — Landshut..............	Germany	47	12	20	32	50	...	...	...	—	—	—	—	—
96-97 — Landshut..............	Germany	46	16	27	43	40	...	...	...	7	1	4	5	6

SULLIVAN, MIKE   LW   FLAMES

PERSONAL: Born February 28, 1968, in Marshfield, Mass. ... 6-2/202. ... Shoots left. ... Full name: Michael Barry Sullivan.
HIGH SCHOOL: Boston College.
COLLEGE: Boston University.
TRANSACTIONS/CAREER NOTES: Selected by New York Rangers in fourth round (fourth Rangers pick, 69th overall) of NHL entry draft (June 13, 1987). ... Traded by Rangers with D Mark Tinordi, D Paul Jerrard, RW Brett Barnett and third-round pick (C Murray Garbutt) in 1989 draft to Minnesota North Stars for LW Igor Liba, C Brian Lawton and rights to LW Eric Bennett (October 11, 1988). ... Signed as free agent by San Jose Sharks (August 9, 1991). ... Sprained left knee (April 6, 1993); missed remainder of season. ... Claimed on waivers by Calgary Flames (January 6, 1994). ... Pulled groin (January 29, 1994); missed 13 games. ... Bruised knee (April 6, 1994); missed one game. ... Bruised left foot (March 17, 1995); missed two games. ... Sprained right ankle (April 13, 1995); missed last eight games of season. ... Suffered concussion (February 15, 1997); missed two games. ... Suffered back spasms (March 16, 1997); missed two games.

		REGULAR SEASON								PLAYOFFS				
Season Team	League	Gms.	G	A	Pts.	PIM	+/-	PP	SH	Gms.	G	A	Pts.	PIM
85-86 — Boston College...........	Mass. H.S.	22	26	33	59	...	...	...	...	—	—	—	—	—
86-87 — Boston University	Hockey East	37	13	18	31	18	...	...	...	—	—	—	—	—
87-88 — Boston University	Hockey East	30	18	22	40	30	...	...	...	—	—	—	—	—
88-89 — Boston University	Hockey East	36	19	17	36	30	...	...	...	—	—	—	—	—
— Virginia	ECHL	2	0	0	0	0	...	...	...	—	—	—	—	—
89-90 — Boston University	Hockey East	38	11	20	31	26	...	...	...	—	—	—	—	—
90-91 — San Diego	IHL	74	12	23	35	27	...	...	...	—	—	—	—	—
91-92 — Kansas City	IHL	10	2	8	10	8	...	...	...	—	—	—	—	—
— San Jose.....................	NHL	64	8	11	19	15	-18	1	0	—	—	—	—	—
92-93 — San Jose	NHL	81	6	8	14	30	-42	0	2	—	—	—	—	—
93-94 — San Jose	NHL	26	2	2	4	4	-3	0	2	—	—	—	—	—
— Kansas City	IHL	6	3	3	6	0	...	...	...	—	—	—	—	—
— Saint John	AHL	5	2	0	2	4	...	...	...	—	—	—	—	—
— Calgary.....................	NHL	19	2	3	5	6	2	0	0	7	1	1	2	8
94-95 — Calgary..................	NHL	38	4	7	11	14	-2	0	0	7	3	5	8	2
95-96 — Calgary..................	NHL	81	9	12	21	24	-6	0	1	4	0	0	0	0
96-97 — Calgary..................	NHL	67	5	6	11	10	-11	0	3	—	—	—	—	—
NHL totals (7 years)		376	36	49	85	103	-80	1	8	18	4	6	10	10

SULLIVAN, MIKE   C   RED WINGS

PERSONAL: Born October 16, 1973, in Woburn, Mass. ... 6-1/200. ... Shoots left.
HIGH SCHOOL: Reading (Mass.) Memorial.
COLLEGE: New Hampshire.
TRANSACTIONS/CAREER NOTES: Selected by Detroit Red Wings in fifth round (fourth Red Wings pick, 118th overall) of NHL entry draft (June 20, 1992).

		REGULAR SEASON								PLAYOFFS				
Season Team	League	Gms.	G	A	Pts.	PIM	+/-	PP	SH	Gms.	G	A	Pts.	PIM
91-92 — Reading	Mass. H.S.	24	39	41	80	...	...	...	...	—	—	—	—	—
92-93 — New Hampshire	Hockey East	36	5	5	10	12	...	...	...	—	—	—	—	—
93-94 — New Hampshire	Hockey East	40	13	14	27	30	...	...	...	—	—	—	—	—
94-95 — New Hampshire	Hockey East	36	13	26	39	14	...	...	...	—	—	—	—	—
95-96 — Hampshire	Hockey East	34	9	17	26	28	...	...	...	—	—	—	—	—
96-97 — Adirondack................	AHL	17	1	3	4	2	...	...	...	—	—	—	—	—
— Toledo........................	ECHL	36	9	23	32	18	...	...	...	—	—	—	—	—

SULLIVAN, STEVE   C   MAPLE LEAFS

PERSONAL: Born July 6, 1974, in Timmins, Ont. ... 5-9/155. ... Shoots right.
TRANSACTIONS/CAREER NOTES: Selected by New Jersey Devils in ninth round (10th Devils pick, 233rd overall) of NHL entry draft (June 29, 1994). ... Traded by Devils with D Jason Smith and C Alyn McCauley to Toronto Maple Leafs for C Doug Gilmour, D Dave Ellett and third-round pick in 1999 draft (February 25, 1997).
HONORS: Named to AHL All-Star first team (1995-96).

		REGULAR SEASON								PLAYOFFS				
Season Team	League	Gms.	G	A	Pts.	PIM	+/-	PP	SH	Gms.	G	A	Pts.	PIM
92-93 — Timmins....................	USHL	47	66	55	121	141	...	...	...	—	—	—	—	—
93-94 — Sault Ste. Marie	OHL	63	51	62	113	82	...	...	...	14	9	16	25	22
94-95 — Albany......................	AHL	75	31	50	81	124	...	...	...	14	4	7	11	10
95-96 — Albany......................	AHL	53	33	42	75	127	...	...	...	4	3	0	3	6
— New Jersey	NHL	16	5	4	9	8	3	2	0	—	—	—	—	—
96-97 — Albany......................	AHL	15	8	7	15	16	...	...	...	—	—	—	—	—
— New Jersey	NHL	33	8	14	22	14	9	2	0	—	—	—	—	—
— Toronto	NHL	21	5	11	16	23	5	1	0	—	—	—	—	—
NHL totals (2 years)		70	18	29	47	45	17	5	0					

SUNDIN, MATS   RW   MAPLE LEAFS

PERSONAL: Born February 13, 1971, in Sollentuna, Sweden. ... 6-4/215. ... Shoots right. ... Full name: Mats Johan Sundin. ... Name pronounced suhn-DEEN.

TRANSACTIONS/CAREER NOTES: Selected by Quebec Nordiques in first round (first Nordiques pick, first overall) of NHL entry draft (June 17, 1989). ... Separated right shoulder (January 2, 1993); missed three games. ... Suspended one game by NHL for second stick-related infraction (March 2, 1993). ... Traded by Nordiques with D Garth Butcher, LW Todd Warriner and first-round pick (traded to Washington Capitals who selected D Nolan Baumgartner) in 1994 draft to Toronto Maple Leafs for LW Wendel Clark, D Sylvain Lefebvre, RW Landon Wilson and first-round pick (D Jeffrey Kealty) in 1994 draft (June 28, 1994). ... Played in Europe during 1994-95 NHL lockout. ... Sprained shoulder (March 25, 1995); missed one game. ... Suffered slight tear of knee cartilage (October 24, 1995); missed four games.

HONORS: Named to Swedish League All-Star team (1990-91 and 1991-92). ... Played in NHL All-Star Game (1996 and 1997).

STATISTICAL PLATEAUS: Three-goal games: 1990-91 (2), 1992-93 (1), 1996-97 (1). Total: 4. ... Five-goal games: 1991-92 (1). ... Total hat tricks: 5.

MISCELLANEOUS: Scored on a penalty shot (vs. Tom Draper, March 3, 1992; vs. Arturs Irbe, March 15, 1995). ... Failed to score on a penalty shot (vs. Kelly Hrudey, February 2, 1993).

Season Team	League	REGULAR SEASON								PLAYOFFS				
		Gms.	G	A	Pts.	PIM	+/-	PP	SH	Gms.	G	A	Pts.	PIM
88-89 — Nacka	Sweden	25	10	8	18	18	...	...	...	—	—	—	—	—
89-90 — Djur. Stockholm	Sweden	34	10	8	18	16	...	...	...	8	7	0	7	4
90-91 — Quebec	NHL	80	23	36	59	58	-24	4	0	—	—	—	—	—
91-92 — Quebec	NHL	80	33	43	76	103	-19	8	2	—	—	—	—	—
92-93 — Quebec	NHL	80	47	67	114	96	21	13	4	6	3	1	4	6
93-94 — Quebec	NHL	84	32	53	85	60	1	6	2	—	—	—	—	—
94-95 — Djur. Stockholm	Sweden	12	7	2	9	14	...	...	...	—	—	—	—	—
— Toronto	NHL	47	23	24	47	14	-5	9	0	7	5	4	9	4
95-96 — Toronto	NHL	76	33	50	83	46	8	7	6	6	3	1	4	4
96-97 — Toronto	NHL	82	41	53	94	59	6	7	4	—	—	—	—	—
NHL totals (7 years)		529	232	326	558	436	-12	54	18	19	11	6	17	14

SUNDIN, RONNIE   D   RANGERS

PERSONAL: Born March 10, 1970, in Frolunda, Sweden. ... 6-1/220. ... Shoots left. ... Name pronounced suhn-DEEN.

TRANSACTIONS/CAREER NOTES: Selected by New York Rangers in ninth round (eighth Rangers pick, 237th overall) of NHL entry draft (June 22, 1996).

Season Team	League	REGULAR SEASON								PLAYOFFS				
		Gms.	G	A	Pts.	PIM	+/-	PP	SH	Gms.	G	A	Pts.	PIM
91-92 — Mora	Sweden II	35	2	5	7	18	...	...	...	2	0	0	0	0
92-93 — Vastra Frolunda	Sweden	17	2	3	5	12	...	...	...	—	—	—	—	—
93-94 — Vastra Frolunda	Sweden	38	0	9	9	42	...	...	...	4	0	0	0	0
94-95 — Vastra Frolunda	Sweden	11	3	4	7	6	...	...	...	—	—	—	—	—
95-96 — Vastra Frolunda	Sweden	40	3	6	9	18	...	...	...	13	1	4	5	10
96-97 — Vastra Frolunda	Sweden	47	3	14	17	24	...	...	...	3	1	0	1	2

SUNDSTROM, NIKLAS   RW   RANGERS

PERSONAL: Born June 6, 1975, in Ornskoldsvik, Sweden. ... 6-0/185. ... Shoots left.

TRANSACTIONS/CAREER NOTES: Selected by New York Rangers in first round (first Rangers pick, eighth overall) of NHL entry draft (June 26, 1993).

Season Team	League	REGULAR SEASON								PLAYOFFS				
		Gms.	G	A	Pts.	PIM	+/-	PP	SH	Gms.	G	A	Pts.	PIM
91-92 — MoDo Ornskoldvik	Sweden	9	1	3	4	0	...	...	...	—	—	—	—	—
92-93 — MoDo Ornskoldvik	Sweden	40	7	11	18	18	...	...	...	—	—	—	—	—
93-94 — MoDo Ornskoldvik	Sweden	37	7	12	19	28	...	...	...	11	4	3	7	2
94-95 — MoDo Ornskoldvik	Sweden	33	8	13	21	30	...	...	...	—	—	—	—	—
95-96 — New York Rangers	NHL	82	9	12	21	14	2	1	1	11	4	3	7	4
96-97 — New York Rangers	NHL	82	24	28	52	20	23	5	1	9	0	5	5	2
NHL totals (2 years)		164	33	40	73	34	25	6	2	20	4	8	12	6

SUTER, GARY   D   BLACKHAWKS

PERSONAL: Born June 24, 1964, in Madison, Wis. ... 6-0/200. ... Shoots left. ... Full name: Gary Lee Suter. ... Name pronounced SOO-tuhr.

COLLEGE: Wisconsin.

TRANSACTIONS/CAREER NOTES: Selected by Calgary Flames in ninth round (ninth Flames pick, 180th overall) of NHL entry draft (June 9, 1984). ... Stretched knee ligament (December 1986). ... Suspended first four games of regular season and next six international games in which NHL participates for high-sticking during Canada Cup (September 4, 1987). ... Injured left knee (February 1988). ... Pulled hamstring (February 1989). ... Ruptured appendix (February 22, 1989); missed 16 games. ... Broke jaw (April 11, 1989). ... Bruised knee (December 12, 1991); missed 10 games. ... Injured ribs (March 16, 1993); missed one game. ... Suffered from the flu (March 30, 1993); missed one game. ... Tore left knee ligaments (November 4, 1993); missed 33 games. ... Strained left leg muscle (January 24, 1994); missed 10 games. ... Traded by Flames with LW Paul Ranheim and C Ted Drury to Hartford Whalers for C Michael Nylander, D Zarley Zalapski and D James Patrick (March 10, 1994). ... Traded by Hartford with LW Randy Cunneyworth and third-round pick (traded to Vancouver) in 1995 draft to Chicago Blackhawks for D Frantisek Kucera and LW Jocelyn Lemieux (March 11, 1994). ... Cracked bone in hand (May 25, 1995); missed four playoff games.

HONORS: Named USHL Top Defenseman (1982-83). ... Named to USHL All-Star first team (1982-83). ... Won Calder Memorial Trophy (1985-86). ... Named to NHL All-Rookie team (1985-86). ... Played in NHL All-Star Game (1986, 1988, 1989 and 1991). ... Named to THE SPORTING NEWS All-Star first team (1987-88). ... Named to NHL All-Star second team (1987-88). ... Named to THE SPORTING NEWS All-Star second team (1988-89). ... Named to play in NHL All-Star Game (1996); replaced by D Larry Murphy due to injury.

S

RECORDS: Shares NHL single-game record for most assists by a defenseman—6 (April 4, 1986).
MISCELLANEOUS: Member of Stanley Cup championship team (1989).

Season Team	League	REGULAR SEASON Gms.	G	A	Pts.	PIM	+/-	PP	SH	PLAYOFFS Gms.	G	A	Pts.	PIM
81-82— Dubuque	USHL	18	3	4	7	32	...	...	...	—	—	—	—	—
82-83— Dubuque	USHL	41	9	10	19	112	...	...	...	—	—	—	—	—
83-84— Univ. of Wisconsin	WCHA	35	4	18	22	68	...	...	...	—	—	—	—	—
84-85— Univ. of Wisconsin	WCHA	39	12	39	51	110	...	...	...	—	—	—	—	—
85-86— Calgary	NHL	80	18	50	68	141	11	9	0	10	2	8	10	8
86-87— Calgary	NHL	68	9	40	49	70	-10	4	0	6	0	3	3	10
87-88— Calgary	NHL	75	21	70	91	124	39	6	1	9	1	9	10	6
88-89— Calgary	NHL	63	13	49	62	78	26	8	0	5	0	3	3	10
89-90— Calgary	NHL	76	16	60	76	97	4	5	0	6	0	1	1	14
90-91— Calgary	NHL	79	12	58	70	102	26	6	0	7	1	6	7	12
91-92— Calgary	NHL	70	12	43	55	128	1	4	0	—	—	—	—	—
92-93— Calgary	NHL	81	23	58	81	112	-1	10	1	6	2	3	5	8
93-94— Calgary	NHL	25	4	9	13	20	-3	2	1	—	—	—	—	—
— Chicago	NHL	16	2	3	5	18	-9	2	0	6	3	2	5	6
94-95— Chicago	NHL	48	10	27	37	42	14	5	0	12	2	5	7	10
95-96— Chicago	NHL	82	20	47	67	80	3	12	2	10	3	3	6	8
96-97— Chicago	NHL	82	7	21	28	70	-4	3	0	6	1	4	5	8
NHL totals (12 years)		845	167	535	702	1082	97	76	5	83	15	47	62	100

SUTTER, BRENT   C   BLACKHAWKS

PERSONAL: Born June 10, 1962, in Viking, Alta. ... 5-11/187. ... Shoots right. ... Full name: Brent Colin Sutter. ... Name pronounced SUH-tuhr. ... Brother of Brian Sutter, head coach, Calgary Flames and left winger, St. Louis Blues (1976-77 through 1987-88); brother of Darryl Sutter, head coach, San Jose Sharks and left winger, Chicago Blackhawks (1979-80 through 1986-87); brother of Duane Sutter, right winger, New York Islanders and Blackhawks (1979-80 through 1989-90); brother of Rich Sutter, right winger with seven NHL teams (1982-83 through 1994-95) and brother of Ron Sutter, center, San Jose Sharks.
TRANSACTIONS/CAREER NOTES: Selected by New York Islanders as underage junior in first round (first Islanders pick, 17th overall) of NHL entry draft (June 11, 1980). ... Damaged tendon and developed infection in right hand (January 1984); missed 11 games. ... Separated shoulder (March 1985). ... Bruised left shoulder (October 19, 1985); missed 12 games. ... Bruised shoulder (December 21, 1985); missed seven games. ... Strained abductor muscle in right leg (March 1987). ... Suffered non-displaced fracture of right thumb (December 1987). ... Lacerated right leg (January 19, 1990). ... Hospitalized with an infection in right leg after stitches were removed (January 28, 1990); missed seven games. ... Traded by Islanders with RW Brad Lauer to Chicago Blackhawks for C Adam Creighton and LW Steve Thomas (October 25, 1991). ... Injured abdomen (March 11, 1992). ... Broke foot (September 25, 1992); missed 14 games. ... Bruised index finger (January 19, 1993); missed three games. ... Injured ear (March 9, 1993); missed two games. ... Strained back (February 1994); missed five games. ... Pulled groin (October 30, 1996); missed 36 games. ... Sprained knee (March 26, 1997); missed six games.
HONORS: Played in NHL All-Star Game (1985).
STATISTICAL PLATEAUS: Three-goal games: 1981-82 (1), 1983-84 (1), 1984-85 (2), 1986-87 (1), 1989-90 (1). Total: 6.
MISCELLANEOUS: Member of Stanley Cup championship team (1982 and 1983). ... Captain of New York Islanders (1987-88 through 1991-92). ... Failed to score on a penalty shot (vs. Al Jensen, December 26, 1986).

Season Team	League	REGULAR SEASON Gms.	G	A	Pts.	PIM	+/-	PP	SH	PLAYOFFS Gms.	G	A	Pts.	PIM
77-78— Red Deer	AJHL	60	12	18	30	33	...	...	...	—	—	—	—	—
78-79— Red Deer	AJHL	60	42	42	84	79	...	...	...	—	—	—	—	—
79-80— Red Deer	AJHL	59	70	101	171	131	...	...	...	—	—	—	—	—
— Lethbridge	WHL	5	1	0	1	2	...	...	...	—	—	—	—	—
80-81— New York Islanders	NHL	3	2	2	4	0	2	1	0	—	—	—	—	—
— Lethbridge	WHL	68	54	54	108	116	...	...	...	9	6	4	10	51
81-82— Lethbridge	WHL	34	46	34	80	162	...	...	...	—	—	—	—	—
— New York Islanders	NHL	43	21	22	43	114	28	3	0	19	2	6	8	36
82-83— New York Islanders	NHL	80	21	19	40	128	14	1	0	20	10	11	21	26
83-84— New York Islanders	NHL	69	34	15	49	69	4	7	0	20	4	10	14	18
84-85— New York Islanders	NHL	72	42	60	102	51	42	12	0	10	3	3	6	14
85-86— New York Islanders	NHL	61	24	31	55	74	11	10	0	3	0	1	1	2
86-87— New York Islanders	NHL	69	27	36	63	73	23	6	3	5	1	0	1	4
87-88— New York Islanders	NHL	70	29	31	60	55	13	11	2	6	2	1	3	18
88-89— New York Islanders	NHL	77	29	34	63	77	-12	17	2	—	—	—	—	—
89-90— New York Islanders	NHL	67	33	35	68	65	9	17	3	5	2	3	5	2
90-91— New York Islanders	NHL	75	21	32	53	49	-8	6	2	—	—	—	—	—
91-92— New York Islanders	NHL	8	4	6	10	6	-5	1	0	—	—	—	—	—
— Chicago	NHL	61	18	32	50	30	-5	7	1	18	3	5	8	22
92-93— Chicago	NHL	65	20	34	54	67	10	8	2	4	1	1	2	4
93-94— Chicago	NHL	73	9	29	38	43	17	3	2	6	0	0	0	2
94-95— Chicago	NHL	47	7	8	15	51	6	1	0	16	1	2	3	4
95-96— Chicago	NHL	80	13	27	40	56	14	0	0	10	1	1	2	6
96-97— Chicago	NHL	39	7	7	14	18	10	0	0	2	0	0	0	6
NHL totals (17 years)		1059	361	460	821	1026	173	111	17	144	30	44	74	164

SUTTER, RON   C   SHARKS

PERSONAL: Born December 2, 1963, in Viking, Alta. ... 6-0/180. ... Shoots right. ... Name pronounced SUH-tuhr. ... Brother of Brian Sutter, head coach, Calgary Flames and left winger, St. Louis Blues (1976-77 through 1987-88); brother of Darryl Sutter, head coach, San Jose Sharks and left winger, Chicago Blackhawks (1979-80 through 1986-87); brother of Duane Sutter, right winger, New York Islanders and Blackhawks (1979-80 through 1989-90); brother of Rich Sutter, right winger with seven NHL teams (1982-83 through 1994-95) and brother of Ron Sutter, center, San Jose Sharks.

HIGH SCHOOL: Winston Churchill (Lethbridge, Ont.).

TRANSACTIONS/CAREER NOTES: Selected by Philadelphia Flyers as underage junior in first round (first Flyers pick, fourth overall) of NHL entry draft (June 9, 1982). ... Broke ankle (November 27, 1981). ... Bruised ribs (March 1985). ... Suffered stress fracture in lower back (January 1987). ... Tore rib cartilage (March 1988). ... Fractured jaw (October 29, 1988). ... Pulled groin (March 1989). ... Traded by Flyers with D Murray Baron to St. Louis Blues for C Rod Brind'Amour and C Dan Quinn (September 22, 1991). ... Strained ligament in right knee (February 1, 1992); missed 10 games. ... Suffered abdominal pull (September 1992); missed first 18 games of season. ... Separated shoulder (March 30, 1993); missed remainder of season. ... Underwent abdominal surgery during off-season; missed nine games. ... Traded by Blues with C Bob Bassen and D Garth Butcher to Quebec Nordiques for D Steve Duchesne and RW Denis Chasse (January 23, 1994). ... Suffered sore neck (November 16, 1993); missed two games. ... Traded by Nordiques with first-round pick (RW Brett Lindros) in 1994 draft to New York Islanders for D Uwe Krupp and first-round pick (D Wade Belak) in 1994 draft (June 28, 1994). ... Sprained right ankle (February 7, 1995); missed 18 games. ... Signed as free agent by Boston Bruins (March 8, 1996). ... Signed as free agent by San Jose Sharks (October 12, 1996).

MISCELLANEOUS: Captain of Philadelphia Flyers (1989-90 and 1990-91). ... Failed to score on a penalty shot (vs. Kelly Hrudey, November 18, 1984; vs. Grant Fuhr, May 28, 1985 (playoffs)).

			REGULAR SEASON							PLAYOFFS				
Season Team	League	Gms.	G	A	Pts.	PIM	+/-	PP	SH	Gms.	G	A	Pts.	PIM
79-80— Red Deer..................	AJHL	60	12	33	45	44	...	...	...	—	—	—	—	—
80-81— Lethbridge	WHL	72	13	32	45	152	...	...	...	9	2	5	7	29
81-82— Lethbridge	WHL	59	38	54	92	207	...	...	...	12	6	5	11	28
82-83— Lethbridge	WHL	58	35	48	83	98	...	...	...	20	*22	†19	*41	45
— Philadelphia	NHL	10	1	1	2	9	0	0	0	—	—	—	—	—
83-84— Philadelphia	NHL	79	19	32	51	101	4	5	3	3	0	0	0	22
84-85— Philadelphia	NHL	73	16	29	45	94	13	2	0	19	4	8	12	28
85-86— Philadelphia	NHL	75	18	42	60	159	26	0	0	5	0	2	2	10
86-87— Philadelphia	NHL	39	10	17	27	69	10	0	0	16	1	7	8	12
87-88— Philadelphia	NHL	69	8	25	33	146	-9	1	0	7	0	1	1	26
88-89— Philadelphia	NHL	55	26	22	48	80	25	4	1	19	1	9	10	51
89-90— Philadelphia	NHL	75	22	26	48	104	2	0	2	—	—	—	—	—
90-91— Philadelphia	NHL	80	17	28	45	92	2	2	0	—	—	—	—	—
91-92— St. Louis	NHL	68	19	27	46	91	9	5	4	6	1	3	4	8
92-93— St. Louis	NHL	59	12	15	27	99	-11	4	0	—	—	—	—	—
93-94— St. Louis	NHL	36	6	12	18	46	-1	1	0	—	—	—	—	—
— Quebec	NHL	37	9	13	22	44	3	4	0	—	—	—	—	—
94-95— New York Islanders....	NHL	27	1	4	5	21	-8	0	0	—	—	—	—	—
95-96— Phoenix	IHL	25	6	13	19	28	...	...	...	—	—	—	—	—
— Boston	NHL	18	5	7	12	24	10	0	1	5	0	0	0	8
96-97— San Jose	NHL	78	5	7	12	65	-8	1	2	—	—	—	—	—
NHL totals (15 years)		878	194	307	501	1244	67	29	13	80	7	30	37	165

SUTTON, KEN — D — DEVILS

PERSONAL: Born November 5, 1969, in Edmonton. ... 6-0/200. ... Shoots left.

TRANSACTIONS/CAREER NOTES: Selected by Buffalo Sabres in fifth round (fourth Sabres pick, 98th overall) of NHL entry draft (June 17, 1989). ... Separated shoulder (March 3, 1992); missed six games. ... Broke ankle (September 15, 1992); missed first 19 games of season. ... Broke finger (February 15, 1995); missed 10 games. ... Traded by Sabres to Edmonton Oilers for LW Scott Pearson (April 7, 1995). ... Traded by Oilers with D Igor Kravchuk to St. Louis Blues for D Donald Dufresne and D Jeff Norton (January 4, 1996). ... Loaned by Blues to Manitoba Moose of IHL (September 11-November 26, 1996). ... Traded by Blues with second-round pick in 1999 draft to New Jersey Devils for LW Mike Peluso and D Ricard Persson (November 26, 1996).

HONORS: Named to Memorial Cup All-Star team (1988-89).

			REGULAR SEASON							PLAYOFFS				
Season Team	League	Gms.	G	A	Pts.	PIM	+/-	PP	SH	Gms.	G	A	Pts.	PIM
87-88— Calgary Canucks	AJHL	53	13	43	56	228	...	...	...	—	—	—	—	—
88-89— Saskatoon	WHL	71	22	31	53	104	...	...	...	8	2	5	7	12
89-90— Rochester	AHL	57	5	14	19	83	...	...	...	11	1	6	7	15
90-91— Buffalo	NHL	15	3	6	9	13	2	2	0	6	0	1	1	2
— Rochester	AHL	62	7	24	31	65	...	...	...	3	1	1	2	14
91-92— Buffalo	NHL	64	2	18	20	71	5	0	0	7	0	2	2	4
92-93— Buffalo	NHL	63	8	14	22	30	-3	1	0	8	3	1	4	8
93-94— Buffalo	NHL	78	4	20	24	71	-6	1	0	4	0	0	0	2
94-95— Buffalo	NHL	12	1	2	3	30	-2	0	0	—	—	—	—	—
— Edmonton	NHL	12	3	1	4	12	-1	0	0	—	—	—	—	—
95-96— Edmonton	NHL	32	0	8	8	39	-12	0	0	—	—	—	—	—
— St. Louis	NHL	6	0	0	0	4	-1	0	0	1	0	0	0	0
— Worcester	AHL	32	4	16	20	60	...	...	...	4	0	2	2	21
96-97— Manitoba.................	IHL	20	3	10	13	48	...	...	...	—	—	—	—	—
— Albany.....................	AHL	61	6	13	19	79	...	...	...	16	4	8	12	55
NHL totals (6 years)		282	21	69	90	270	-18	4	0	26	3	4	7	16

SVEHLA, ROBERT — D — PANTHERS

PERSONAL: Born January 2, 1969, in Martin, Czechoslovakia. ... 6-1/190. ... Shoots left. ... Name pronounced SHVAY-luh.

TRANSACTIONS/CAREER NOTES: Selected by Calgary Flames in fourth round (fourth Flames pick, 78th overall) of NHL entry draft (June 20, 1992). ... Traded by Flames with D Magnus Svensson to Florida Panthers for third-round pick (LW Dmitri Vlasenkov) in 1996 draft and future considerations (September 29, 1994). ... Sprained left rotator cuff (April 22, 1995); missed two games. ... Reinjured left rotator cuff (April 28, 1995); missed one game.

HONORS: Named Czechoslovakian League Player of the Year (1991-92). ... Named to Czechoslovakian League All-Star team (1991-92). ... Played in NHL All-Star Game (1997).

MISCELLANEOUS: Member of bronze-medal-winning Czechoslovakian Olympic team (1992).

Season Team	League	REGULAR SEASON								PLAYOFFS				
		Gms.	G	A	Pts.	PIM	+/-	PP	SH	Gms.	G	A	Pts.	PIM
89-90— Dukla Trencin	Czech.	29	4	3	7	...	...	...	...	—	—	—	—	—
90-91— Dukla Trencin	Czech.	58	16	9	25	...	...	...	...	—	—	—	—	—
91-92— Dukla Trencin	Czech.	51	23	28	51	0	...	...	...	—	—	—	—	—
—Czec. Olympic team...	Int'l	8	2	1	3	...	...	...	...	—	—	—	—	—
92-93— Malmo	Sweden	40	19	10	29	86	...	...	...	6	0	1	1	0
93-94— Malmo	Sweden	37	14	25	39	*127	...	...	...	10	5	1	6	23
—Slov. Olympic team...	Int'l	8	2	4	6	26	...	...	...	—	—	—	—	—
94-95— Malmo	Sweden	32	11	13	24	83	...	...	...	9	2	3	5	6
—Florida	NHL	5	1	1	2	0	3	1	0	—	—	—	—	—
95-96— Florida	NHL	81	8	49	57	94	-3	7	0	22	0	6	6	32
96-97— Florida	NHL	82	13	32	45	86	2	5	0	5	1	4	5	4
NHL totals (3 years)		168	22	82	104	180	2	13	0	27	1	10	11	36

SVEJKOVSKY, JAROSLAV   LW   CAPITALS

PERSONAL: Born October 1, 1976, in Plzen, Czechoslovakia. ... 6-0/186. ... Shoots right. ... Name pronounced svay-KOH-skee.
TRANSACTIONS/CAREER NOTES: Selected by Washington Capitals in first round (second Capitals pick, 17th overall) of NHL entry draft (June 22, 1996).
HONORS: Named to WHL (West) All-Star second team (1995-96). ... Won Dudley (Red) Garrett Memorial Trophy (1996-97). ... Named to AHL All-Rookie team (1996-97).
STATISTICAL PLATEAUS: Four-goal games: 1996-97 (1).

Season Team	League	REGULAR SEASON								PLAYOFFS				
		Gms.	G	A	Pts.	PIM	+/-	PP	SH	Gms.	G	A	Pts.	PIM
93-94— Plzen Juniors	Czech Rep.	8	0	0	0	8	...	...	...	—	—	—	—	—
94-95— Plzen Juniors	Czech Rep.	25	18	19	37	30	...	...	...	—	—	—	—	—
95-96— Tri-City	WHL	70	58	43	101	118	...	...	...	11	10	9	19	8
96-97— Portland	AHL	54	38	28	66	56	...	...	...	5	2	0	2	6
—Washington	NHL	19	7	3	10	4	-1	2	0	—	—	—	—	—
NHL totals (1 year)		19	7	3	10	4	-1	2	0					

SVOBODA, PETR   D   FLYERS

PERSONAL: Born February 14, 1966, in Most, Czechoslovakia. ... 6-1/190. ... Shoots left. ... Name pronounced svuh-BOH-duh.
TRANSACTIONS/CAREER NOTES: Selected by Montreal Canadiens in first round (first Canadiens pick, fifth overall) of NHL entry draft (June 9, 1984). ... Suffered back spasms (January 1988). ... Suffered hip pointer (March 1988). ... Sprained right wrist (November 21, 1988); missed five games. ... Injured back (March 1989). ... Separated shoulder (November 1989). ... Pulled groin (November 22, 1989). ... Aggravated groin injury (December 11, 1989); missed 15 games. ... Bruised left foot (March 11, 1990). ... Suffered stomach disorder (November 28, 1990); missed five games. ... Broke left foot (January 15, 1991); missed 15 games. ... Injured mouth (December 14, 1991). ... Sprained ankle (February 17, 1992); missed seven games. ... Traded by Canadiens to Buffalo Sabres for D Kevin Haller (March 10, 1992). ... Bruised knee (October 28, 1992); missed four games. ... Tore ligament in right knee (January 17, 1993); missed remainder of season. ... Injured knee (October 12, 1993); missed three games. ... Suffered knee inflammation (October 16, 1993); missed seven games. ... Sprained left knee (March 17, 1994); missed 12 games. ... Played in Europe during 1994-95 NHL lockout. ... Separated shoulder (March 2, 1995); missed two games. ... Fractured jaw (March 16, 1995); missed one game. ... Traded by Sabres to Philadelphia Flyers for D Garry Galley (April 7, 1995). ... Strained neck (April 26, 1995); missed one game. ... Injured groin (October 31, 1995); missed one game. ... Suffered pinched nerve in neck (November 16, 1995); missed three games. ... Pulled hamstring (January 11, 1996); missed two games. ... Suffered concussion (February 2, 1996); missed one game. ... Strained shoulder (April 4, 1996); missed two games. ... Separated left shoulder (October 15, 1996); missed six games. ... Strained groin (December 31, 1996); missed four games. ... Suffered pinched nerve in neck (January 28, 1997); missed three games. ... Strained groin (March 13, 1997); missed two games.
MISCELLANEOUS: Member of Stanley Cup championship team (1986).

Season Team	League	REGULAR SEASON								PLAYOFFS				
		Gms.	G	A	Pts.	PIM	+/-	PP	SH	Gms.	G	A	Pts.	PIM
83-84— Czechoslovakia Jr.	Czech.	40	15	21	36	14	...	...	...	—	—	—	—	—
84-85— Montreal	NHL	73	4	27	31	65	16	0	0	7	1	1	2	12
85-86— Montreal	NHL	73	1	18	19	93	24	0	0	8	0	0	0	21
86-87— Montreal	NHL	70	5	17	22	63	14	1	0	14	0	5	5	10
87-88— Montreal	NHL	69	7	22	29	149	46	2	0	10	0	5	5	12
88-89— Montreal	NHL	71	8	37	45	147	28	4	0	21	1	11	12	16
89-90— Montreal	NHL	60	5	31	36	98	20	2	0	10	0	5	5	2
90-91— Montreal	NHL	60	4	22	26	52	5	3	0	2	0	1	1	2
91-92— Montreal	NHL	58	5	16	21	94	9	1	0	—	—	—	—	—
—Buffalo	NHL	13	1	6	7	52	-8	0	0	7	1	4	5	6
92-93— Buffalo	NHL	40	2	24	26	59	3	1	0	—	—	—	—	—
93-94— Buffalo	NHL	60	2	14	16	89	11	1	0	3	0	0	0	4
94-95— Chemopetrol Litvin...	Czech Rep.	8	2	0	2	40	...	...	...	—	—	—	—	—
—Buffalo	NHL	26	0	5	5	60	-5	0	0	—	—	—	—	—
—Philadelphia	NHL	11	0	3	3	10	0	0	0	14	0	4	4	8
95-96— Philadelphia	NHL	73	1	28	29	105	28	0	0	12	0	6	6	22
96-97— Philadelphia	NHL	67	2	12	14	94	10	1	0	16	1	2	3	16
NHL totals (13 years)		824	47	282	329	1230	201	16	0	124	4	44	48	131

SWANSON, BRIAN   C   RANGERS

PERSONAL: Born March 24, 1976, in Eagle River, Alaska. ... 5-10/180. ... Shoots left.
COLLEGE: Colorado College.
TRANSACTIONS/CAREER NOTES: Selected by San Jose Sharks in fifth round (fifth Sharks pick, 115th overall) of NHL entry draft (June 29, 1994). ... Traded by Sharks with D Jayson More and fourth-round pick in 1998 draft to New York Rangers for D Marty McSorley (August 20, 1996).

Season Team	League	REGULAR SEASON								PLAYOFFS				
		Gms.	G	A	Pts.	PIM	+/-	PP	SH	Gms.	G	A	Pts.	PIM
93-94— Omaha	USHL	47	38	42	80	40	...	...	...	—	—	—	—	—
94-95— Portland	WHL	65	3	18	21	91	...	...	...	9	2	1	3	18
95-96— Colorado College	WCHA	40	26	33	59	24	...	...	...	—	—	—	—	—
96-97— Colorado College	WCHA	43	19	32	51	47	...	...	...	—	—	—	—	—

SWEENEY, BOB   C   FLAMES

PERSONAL: Born January 25, 1964, in Boxborough, Mass. ... 6-3/200. ... Shoots right. ... Full name: Robert Emmett Sweeney. ... Brother of Tim Sweeney, center, Boston Bruins.
HIGH SCHOOL: Acton (Mass.)-Boxborough.
COLLEGE: Boston College.
TRANSACTIONS/CAREER NOTES: Selected by Boston Bruins in sixth round (sixth Bruins pick, 123rd overall) of NHL entry draft (June 9, 1982). ... Pulled rib muscle (November 1989); missed six games. ... Injured left shoulder (April 23, 1991). ... Sprained knee (February 4, 1992); missed 11 games. ... Claimed on waivers by Buffalo Sabres and Calgary Flames; NHL awarded rights to Sabres (October 9, 1992). ... Injured rib (November 7, 1993); missed five games. ... Injured right knee (March 9, 1994); missed 14 games. ... Suspended three games by NHL for fighting (October 11, 1993). ... Bruised shoulder (January 25, 1995); missed two games. ... Claimed by New York Islanders in NHL waiver draft (October 2, 1995). ... Traded by Islanders to Calgary Flames for LW Pat Conacher and sixth-round pick (traded to Calgary) in 1997 draft (March 20, 1996).
HONORS: Named to NCAA All-America East second team (1984-85). ... Named to Hockey East All-Star second team (1984-85).
STATISTICAL PLATEAUS: Three-goal games: 1989-90 (1).
MISCELLANEOUS: Scored on a penalty shot (vs. Peter Sidorkiewicz, December 12, 1990).

S

Season Team	League	REGULAR SEASON								PLAYOFFS				
		Gms.	G	A	Pts.	PIM	+/-	PP	SH	Gms.	G	A	Pts.	PIM
82-83— Boston College	ECAC	30	17	11	28	10	...	...	...	—	—	—	—	—
83-84— Boston College	ECAC	23	14	7	21	10	...	...	...	—	—	—	—	—
84-85— Boston College	Hockey East	44	32	32	64	43	...	...	...	—	—	—	—	—
85-86— Boston College	Hockey East	41	15	24	39	52	...	...	...	—	—	—	—	—
86-87— Boston	NHL	14	2	4	6	21	...	...	...	3	0	0	0	0
— Moncton	AHL	58	29	26	55	81	...	...	...	4	0	2	2	13
87-88— Boston	NHL	80	22	23	45	73	...	...	...	23	6	8	14	66
88-89— Boston	NHL	75	14	14	28	99	...	...	...	10	2	4	6	19
89-90— Boston	NHL	70	22	24	46	93	2	5	2	20	0	2	2	30
90-91— Boston	NHL	80	15	33	48	115	12	0	1	17	4	2	6	45
91-92— Boston	NHL	63	6	14	20	103	-9	0	1	14	1	0	1	25
— Maine	AHL	1	1	0	1	0	...	...	...	—	—	—	—	—
92-93— Buffalo	NHL	80	21	26	47	118	2	4	3	8	2	2	4	8
93-94— Buffalo	NHL	60	11	14	25	94	3	3	3	1	0	0	0	0
94-95— Buffalo	NHL	45	5	4	9	18	-6	1	2	5	0	0	0	4
95-96— New York Islanders	NHL	66	6	6	12	59	-23	0	1	—	—	—	—	—
— Calgary	NHL	6	1	1	2	6	3	0	0	2	0	0	0	0
96-97— Quebec	IHL	69	10	21	31	120	...	...	...	9	2	0	2	8
NHL totals (10 years)		639	125	163	288	799	-16	13	13	103	15	18	33	197

SWEENEY, DON   D   BRUINS

PERSONAL: Born August 17, 1966, in St. Stephen, N.B. ... 5-10/184. ... Shoots left. ... Full name: Donald Clark Sweeney.
HIGH SCHOOL: St. Paul (N.B.).
COLLEGE: Harvard.
TRANSACTIONS/CAREER NOTES: Selected by Boston Bruins in eighth round (eighth Bruins pick, 166th overall) of NHL entry draft (June 9, 1984). ... Bruised left heel (February 22, 1990). ... Injured knee (October 12, 1991); missed four games. ... Sprained knee (October 5, 1993); missed six games. ... Injured ribs (December 15, 1993); missed three games. ... Injured shoulder (October 17, 1995); missed three games. ... Injured shoulder (October 31, 1995); missed two games.
HONORS: Named to NCAA All-America East second team (1987-88). ... Named to ECAC All-Star first team (1987-88).

Season Team	League	REGULAR SEASON								PLAYOFFS				
		Gms.	G	A	Pts.	PIM	+/-	PP	SH	Gms.	G	A	Pts.	PIM
83-84— St. Paul N.B.	N.B. H.S.	22	33	26	59	...	...	...	...	—	—	—	—	—
84-85— Harvard University	ECAC	29	3	7	10	30	...	...	...	—	—	—	—	—
85-86— Harvard University	ECAC	31	4	5	9	29	...	...	...	—	—	—	—	—
86-87— Harvard University	ECAC	34	7	14	21	22	...	...	...	—	—	—	—	—
87-88— Harvard University	ECAC	30	6	23	29	37	...	...	...	—	—	—	—	—
— Maine	AHL	—	—	—	—	—	...	...	...	6	1	3	4	0
88-89— Maine	AHL	42	8	17	25	24	...	...	...	—	—	—	—	—
— Boston	NHL	36	3	5	8	20	-6	0	0	—	—	—	—	—
89-90— Boston	NHL	58	3	5	8	58	11	0	0	21	1	5	6	18
— Maine	AHL	11	0	8	8	8	...	...	...	—	—	—	—	—
90-91— Boston	NHL	77	8	13	21	67	2	0	1	19	3	0	3	25
91-92— Boston	NHL	75	3	11	14	74	-9	0	0	15	0	0	0	10
92-93— Boston	NHL	84	7	27	34	68	34	0	1	4	0	0	0	4
93-94— Boston	NHL	75	6	15	21	50	29	1	2	12	2	1	3	4
94-95— Boston	NHL	47	3	19	22	24	6	1	0	5	0	0	0	4
95-96— Boston	NHL	77	4	24	28	42	-4	2	0	5	0	2	2	6
96-97— Boston	NHL	82	3	23	26	39	-5	0	0	—	—	—	—	—
NHL totals (9 years)		611	40	142	182	442	58	4	4	81	6	8	14	71

SWEENEY, TIM   LW   BRUINS

PERSONAL: Born April 12, 1967, in Boston. ... 5-11/185. ... Shoots left. ... Full name: Timothy Paul Sweeney. ... Brother of Bob Sweeney, center for four NHL teams (1986-87 through 1995-96).
HIGH SCHOOL: Weymouth (Mass.).
COLLEGE: Boston College.
TRANSACTIONS/CAREER NOTES: Selected by Calgary Flames in sixth round (seventh Flames pick, 122nd overall) of NHL entry draft (June 15, 1985). ... Fractured index finger (January 26, 1988). ... Bruised ankle (May 1990). ... Signed as free agent by Boston Bruins (September 1992). ... Selected by Mighty Ducks of Anaheim in NHL expansion draft (June 24, 1993). ... Suffered injury (November 26, 1993); missed four games. ... Signed as free agent by Providence Bruins of AHL, Boston Bruins organization (April 9, 1995). ... Fractured foot (December 27, 1996); missed 15 games. ... Strained abdominal muscle (February 23, 1997); missed one game.
HONORS: Named to NCAA All-America East second team (1988-89). ... Named to Hockey East All-Star first team (1988-89). ... Won Ken McKenzie Trophy (1989-90). ... Named to IHL All-Star second team (1989-90). ... Named to AHL All-Star second team (1992-93).

		REGULAR SEASON								PLAYOFFS				
Season Team	League	Gms.	G	A	Pts.	PIM	+/-	PP	SH	Gms.	G	A	Pts.	PIM
83-84— Weymouth North	Mass. H.S.	23	33	26	59	...	...	...	...	—	—	—	—	—
84-85— Weymouth North	Mass. H.S.	22	32	56	88	...	...	...	...	—	—	—	—	—
85-86— Boston College..........	Hockey East	32	8	4	12	8	...	...	...	—	—	—	—	—
86-87— Boston College..........	Hockey East	38	31	16	47	28	...	...	...	—	—	—	—	—
87-88— Boston College..........	Hockey East	18	9	11	20	18	...	...	...	—	—	—	—	—
88-89— Boston College..........	Hockey East	39	29	44	73	26	...	...	...	—	—	—	—	—
89-90— Salt Lake City............	IHL	81	46	51	97	32	...	...	...	11	5	4	9	4
90-91— Calgary	NHL	42	7	9	16	8	1	0	0	—	—	—	—	—
— Salt Lake City............	IHL	31	19	16	35	8	...	...	...	4	3	3	6	0
91-92— Calgary	NHL	11	1	2	3	4	0	0	0	—	—	—	—	—
— U.S. national team	Int'l	21	9	11	20	10	...	...	...	—	—	—	—	—
— U.S. Olympic team	Int'l	8	3	4	7	6	...	...	...	—	—	—	—	—
92-93— Providence................	AHL	60	41	55	96	32	...	...	...	3	2	2	4	0
— Boston	NHL	14	1	7	8	6	1	0	0	3	0	0	0	0
93-94— Anaheim....................	NHL	78	16	27	43	49	3	6	1	—	—	—	—	—
94-95— Anaheim....................	NHL	13	1	1	2	2	-3	0	0	—	—	—	—	—
— Providence................	AHL	2	2	2	4	0	...	...	...	13	8	*17	*25	6
95-96— Boston	NHL	41	8	8	16	14	4	1	0	1	0	0	0	2
— Providence................	AHL	34	17	22	39	12	...	...	...	—	—	—	—	—
96-97— Providence................	AHL	23	11	22	33	6	...	...	...	—	—	—	—	—
— Boston	NHL	36	10	11	21	14	0	2	0	—	—	—	—	—
NHL totals (7 years)		235	44	65	109	97	6	9	1	4	0	0	0	2

SYDOR, DARRYL   D   STARS

PERSONAL: Born May 13, 1972, in Edmonton. ... 6-0/200. ... Shoots left. ... Full name: Darryl Marion Sydor. ... Name pronounced sih-DOHR.
TRANSACTIONS/CAREER NOTES: Selected by Los Angeles Kings in first round (first Kings pick, seventh overall) of NHL entry draft (June 16, 1990). ... Bruised hip (November 27, 1992); missed two games. ... Sprained right shoulder (March 15, 1993); missed two games. ... Traded by Kings with seventh-round pick (G Eoin McInerney) in 1996 draft to Dallas Stars for RW Shane Churla and D Doug Zmolek (February 17, 1996).
HONORS: Named to WHL (West) All-Star first team (1989-90 through 1991-92). ... Won Bill Hunter Trophy (1990-91). ... Named to Can.HL All-Star second team (1991-92)

		REGULAR SEASON								PLAYOFFS				
Season Team	League	Gms.	G	A	Pts.	PIM	+/-	PP	SH	Gms.	G	A	Pts.	PIM
88-89— Kamloops...................	WHL	65	12	14	26	86	...	...	...	15	1	4	5	19
89-90— Kamloops...................	WHL	67	29	66	95	129	...	...	...	17	2	9	11	28
90-91— Kamloops...................	WHL	66	27	78	105	88	...	...	...	12	3	*22	25	10
91-92— Kamloops...................	WHL	29	9	39	48	43	...	...	...	17	3	15	18	18
— Los Angeles	NHL	18	1	5	6	22	-3	0	0	—	—	—	—	—
92-93— Los Angeles	NHL	80	6	23	29	63	-2	0	0	24	3	8	11	16
93-94— Los Angeles	NHL	84	8	27	35	94	-9	1	0	—	—	—	—	—
94-95— Los Angeles	NHL	48	4	19	23	36	-2	3	0	—	—	—	—	—
95-96— Los Angeles	NHL	58	1	11	12	34	-11	1	0	—	—	—	—	—
— Dallas........................	NHL	26	2	6	8	41	-1	1	0	—	—	—	—	—
96-97— Dallas........................	NHL	82	8	40	48	51	37	2	0	7	0	2	2	0
NHL totals (6 years)		396	30	131	161	341	9	8	0	31	3	10	13	16

SYKORA, MICHAL   D   BLACKHAWKS

PERSONAL: Born July 5, 1973, in Pardubice, Czechoslovakia. ... 6-5/225. ... Shoots left. ... Name pronounced sih-KOHR-uh.
TRANSACTIONS/CAREER NOTES: Selected by San Jose Sharks in sixth round (sixth Sharks pick, 123rd overall) of NHL entry draft (June 20, 1992). ... Strained knee (November 11, 1993); missed four games. ... Injured shoulder (February 24, 1995); missed remainder of season. ... Injured foot (February 17, 1996); missed one game. ... Traded by Sharks with G Chris Terreri, F Ulf Dahlen and second-round pick in 1998 draft to Chicago Blackhawks for G Ed Belfour (January 25, 1997). ... Bruised left shoulder (March 10, 1997); missed three games.
HONORS: Named to Can.HL All-Star second team (1992-93). ... Named to WHL (West) All-Star first team (1992-93).

		REGULAR SEASON								PLAYOFFS				
Season Team	League	Gms.	G	A	Pts.	PIM	+/-	PP	SH	Gms.	G	A	Pts.	PIM
90-91— Pardubice....................	Czech.	2	0	0	0	...	...	...	...	—	—	—	—	—
91-92— Tacoma	WHL	61	13	23	36	66	...	...	...	4	0	2	2	2
92-93— Tacoma	WHL	70	23	50	73	73	...	...	...	7	4	8	12	2
93-94— San Jose	NHL	22	1	4	5	14	-4	0	0	—	—	—	—	—
— Kansas City	IHL	47	5	11	16	30	...	...	...	—	—	—	—	—

S

Season Team	League	REGULAR SEASON Gms.	G	A	Pts.	PIM	+/-	PP	SH	PLAYOFFS Gms.	G	A	Pts.	PIM
94-95— Kansas City	IHL	36	1	10	11	30	...	...	...	—	—	—	—	—
— San Jose	NHL	16	0	4	4	10	6	0	0	—	—	—	—	—
95-96— San Jose	NHL	79	4	16	20	54	-14	1	0	—	—	—	—	—
96-97— San Jose	NHL	35	2	5	7	59	0	1	0	—	—	—	—	—
— Chicago	NHL	28	1	9	10	10	4	0	0	1	0	0	0	0
NHL totals (4 years)		180	8	38	46	147	-8	2	0	1	0	0	0	0

SYKORA, PETR — C — DEVILS

PERSONAL: Born November 19, 1976, in Plzen, Czechoslovakia. ... 6-0/190. ... Shoots left. ... Name pronounced sih-KOHR-uh.
TRANSACTIONS/CAREER NOTES: Signed as free agent by Cleveland Lumberjacks (January 31, 1994). ... Rights traded by Lumberjacks to Detroit Vipers for cash and future considerations (July 27, 1994). ... Injured shoulder (1995); missed remainder of season. ... Selected by New Jersey Devils in first round (first Devils pick, 18th overall) of NHL entry draft (July 8, 1995). ... Injured back (February 21, 1996); missed two games. ... Sore groin (October 5, 1996); missed two games. ... Reinjured groin (November 9, 1996); missed four games. ... Reinjured groin (November 30, 1996); missed three games.
HONORS: Named to NHL All-Rookie team (1995-96).

Season Team	League	REGULAR SEASON Gms.	G	A	Pts.	PIM	+/-	PP	SH	PLAYOFFS Gms.	G	A	Pts.	PIM
91-92— Skoda Plzen	Czech.	30	50	50	100	...	...	...	...	—	—	—	—	—
92-93— Skoda Plzen	Czech.	19	12	5	17	...	...	...	...	—	—	—	—	—
93-94— Skoda Plzen	Czech Rep.	37	10	16	26	...	...	...	...	4	0	1	1	0
— Cleveland	AHL	13	4	5	9	8	...	...	...	—	—	—	—	—
94-95— Detroit	IHL	29	12	17	29	16	...	...	...	—	—	—	—	—
95-96— Albany	AHL	5	4	1	5	0	...	...	...	—	—	—	—	—
— New Jersey	NHL	63	18	24	42	32	7	8	0	—	—	—	—	—
96-97— New Jersey	NHL	19	1	2	3	4	-8	0	0	2	0	0	0	2
— Albany	AHL	43	20	25	45	48	...	...	...	4	1	4	5	2
NHL totals (2 years)		82	19	26	45	36	-1	8	0	2	0	0	0	2

SYMES, BRAD — D — OILERS

PERSONAL: Born April 26, 1976, in Edmonton. ... 6-2/210. ... Shoots left. ... Name pronounced SIGHMS.
TRANSACTIONS/CAREER NOTES: Selected by Edmonton Oilers in third round (fifth Oilers pick, 60th overall) of NHL entry draft (June 29, 1994).

Season Team	League	REGULAR SEASON Gms.	G	A	Pts.	PIM	+/-	PP	SH	PLAYOFFS Gms.	G	A	Pts.	PIM
91-92— Sherwood Park	AJHL	17	3	7	10	92	...	...	...	—	—	—	—	—
92-93— Portland	WHL	68	4	2	6	107	...	...	...	16	0	1	1	7
93-94— Portland	WHL	71	7	15	22	170	...	...	...	7	0	0	0	21
94-95— Portland	WHL	70	8	16	24	134	...	...	...	9	0	2	2	27
95-96— Portland	WHL	62	9	12	21	118	...	...	...	7	1	2	3	14
96-97— Hamilton	AHL	5	0	0	0	7	...	...	...	—	—	—	—	—
— Wheeling	ECHL	51	6	17	23	63	...	...	...	1	0	0	0	0

TABARACCI, RICK — G — FLAMES

PERSONAL: Born January 2, 1969, in Toronto. ... 5-11/180. ... Catches right. ... Full name: Richard Stephen Tabaracci. ... Name pronounced TA-buh-RA-chee.
TRANSACTIONS/CAREER NOTES: Selected by Pittsburgh Penguins as underage junior in second round (second Penguins pick, 26th overall) of NHL entry draft (June 13, 1987). ... Traded by Penguins with C/LW Randy Cunneyworth and RW Dave McLlwain to Winnipeg Jets for RW Andrew McBain, D Jim Kyte and LW Randy Gilhen (June 17, 1989). ... Pulled right hamstring (December 11, 1990); missed seven games. ... Strained back (October 10, 1992); missed one game. ... Suffered back spasms (December 1, 1992); missed one game. ... Suffered back spasms (January 19, 1993); missed seven games. ... Traded by Jets to Washington Capitals for G Jim Hrivnak and future considerations (March 22, 1993). ... Tore knee ligaments (September 16, 1993); missed seven games. ... Sprained knee (February 20, 1994); missed 21 games. ... Strained hamstring (February 13, 1995). ... Loaned by Capitals to Chicago Wolves (March 27, 1995). ... Traded by Capitals to Calgary Flames for fifth-round pick (D Joel Cort) in 1995 draft (April 7, 1995). ... Traded by Flames to Tampa Bay Lightning for C Aaron Gavey (November 19, 1996). ... Bruised sternum (January 8, 1997); missed one game. ... Traded by Lightning to Flames for fourth-round pick in 1998 draft (June 21, 1997).
HONORS: Named to OHL All-Star first team (1987-88). ... Named to OHL All-Star second team (1988-89).
MISCELLANEOUS: Stopped a penalty shot attempt (vs. Jeff Beukeboom, October 6, 1990). ... Allowed a penalty shot goal (vs. Pavel Bure, February 28, 1992).

Season Team	League	REGULAR SEASON Gms.	Min	W	L	T	GA	SO	Avg.	PLAYOFFS Gms.	Min.	W	L	GA	SO	Avg.
85-86— Markham Jr. B	OHA	40	2176	...	...	...	188	1	5.18	—	—	—	—	—	—	—
86-87— Cornwall	OHL	*59	*3347	23	32	3	*290	1	5.20	5	303	1	4	26	0	5.15
87-88— Cornwall	OHL	58	3448	33	18	6	200	†3	3.48	11	642	5	6	37	0	3.46
— Muskegon	IHL	—	—	—	—	—	—	—	—	1	13	0	0	1	0	4.62
88-89— Cornwall	OHL	50	2974	24	20	5	*210	1	4.24	18	1080	10	8	65	†1	3.61
— Pittsburgh	NHL	1	33	0	0	0	4	0	7.27	—	—	—	—	—	—	—
89-90— Moncton	AHL	27	1580	10	15	2	107	2	4.06	—	—	—	—	—	—	—
— Fort Wayne	IHL	22	1064	8	9	‡1	73	0	4.12	3	159	1	2	19	0	7.17
90-91— Moncton	AHL	11	645	4	5	2	41	0	3.81	—	—	—	—	—	—	—
— Winnipeg	NHL	24	1093	4	9	4	71	1	3.90	—	—	—	—	—	—	—
91-92— Moncton	AHL	23	1313	10	11	1	80	0	3.66	—	—	—	—	—	—	—
— Winnipeg	NHL	18	966	6	7	3	52	0	3.23	7	387	3	4	26	0	4.03

Season Team	League	\multicolumn{9}{c}{REGULAR SEASON}									\multicolumn{7}{c}{PLAYOFFS}						
		Gms.	Min	W	L	T	GA	SO	Avg.	Gms.	Min.	W	L	GA	SO	Avg.
92-93—Winnipeg	NHL	19	959	5	10	0	70	0	4.38	—	—	—	—	—	—	—
—Moncton	AHL	5	290	2	1	2	18	0	3.72	—	—	—	—	—	—	—
—Washington	NHL	6	343	3	2	0	10	2	1.75	4	304	1	3	14	0	2.76
93-94—Portland	AHL	3	177	3	0	0	8	0	2.71	—	—	—	—	—	—	—
—Washington	NHL	32	1770	13	14	2	91	2	3.08	2	111	0	2	6	0	3.24
94-95—Washington	NHL	8	394	1	3	2	16	0	2.44	—	—	—	—	—	—	—
—Chicago	IHL	2	120	1	1	‡0	9	0	4.50	—	—	—	—	—	—	—
—Calgary	NHL	5	202	2	0	1	5	0	1.49	1	19	0	0	0	0	0.00
95-96—Calgary	NHL	43	2391	19	16	3	117	3	2.94	3	204	0	3	7	0	2.06
96-97—Calgary	NHL	7	361	2	4	0	14	1	2.33	—	—	—	—	—	—	—
—Tampa Bay	NHL	55	3012	20	25	6	138	4	2.75	—	—	—	—	—	—	—
NHL totals (10 years)		218	11524	75	90	21	588	13	3.06	17	1025	4	12	53	0	3.10

TALLAS, ROB   G   BRUINS

PERSONAL: Born March 20, 1973, in Edmonton. ... 6-0/178. ... Catches left.

TRANSACTIONS/CAREER NOTES: Attended Boston Bruins training camp on tryout basis prior to 1995-96 season. ... Signed as free agent by Boston Bruins (September 13, 1995). ... Injured ankle (March 24, 1997); missed eight games.

Season Team	League	\multicolumn{9}{c}{REGULAR SEASON}									\multicolumn{7}{c}{PLAYOFFS}						
		Gms.	Min	W	L	T	GA	SO	Avg.	Gms.	Min.	W	L	GA	SO	Avg.
92-93—Seattle	WHL	52	3151	24	23	3	194	2	3.69	5	333	1	4	18	0	3.24
93-94—Seattle	WHL	51	2849	23	21	3	188	0	3.96	9	567	5	4	40	0	4.23
94-95—Charlotte	ECHL	36	2011	21	9	‡3	114	0	3.40	—	—	—	—	—	—	—
—Providence	AHL	2	82	1	0	0	4	1	2.93	—	—	—	—	—	—	—
95-96—Boston	NHL	1	60	1	0	0	3	0	3.00	—	—	—	—	—	—	—
—Providence	AHL	37	2136	12	16	7	117	1	3.29	2	135	0	2	9	0	4.00
96-97—Providence	AHL	24	1423	9	14	1	83	0	3.50	—	—	—	—	—	—	—
—Boston	NHL	28	1244	8	12	1	69	1	3.33	—	—	—	—	—	—	—
NHL totals (2 years)		29	1304	9	12	1	72	1	3.31							

TAMER, CHRIS   D   PENGUINS

PERSONAL: Born November 17, 1970, in Dearborn, Mich. ... 6-2/212. ... Shoots left. ... Full name: Chris Thomas Tamer. ... Name pronounced TAY-muhr.

COLLEGE: Michigan.

TRANSACTIONS/CAREER NOTES: Selected by Pittsburgh Penguins in fourth round (third Penguins pick, 68th overall) of NHL entry draft (June 16, 1990). ... Injured shoulder (March 27, 1994); missed four games. ... Fractured ankle (May 6, 1995); missed eight playoff games. ... Pulled abdominal muscle (December 17, 1995); missed five games. ... Sprained wrist (December 30, 1995); missed five games. ... Fractured jaw (January 17, 1996); missed two games. ... Pulled abdominal muscle (November 22, 1996); missed 20 games. ... Injured hip flexor (January 4, 1997); missed 13 games. ... Injured hip flexor (March 4, 1997); missed four games.

Season Team	League	\multicolumn{9}{c}{REGULAR SEASON}									\multicolumn{5}{c}{PLAYOFFS}				
		Gms.	G	A	Pts.	PIM	+/-	PP	SH	Gms.	G	A	Pts.	PIM
87-88—Redford	NAJHL	40	10	20	30	217	...	...	...	—	—	—	—	—
88-89—Redford	NAJHL	31	6	13	19	79	...	...	...	—	—	—	—	—
89-90—Univ. of Michigan	CCHA	42	2	7	9	147	...	...	...	—	—	—	—	—
90-91—Univ. of Michigan	CCHA	45	8	19	27	130	...	...	...	—	—	—	—	—
91-92—Univ. of Michigan	CCHA	43	4	15	19	125	...	...	...	—	—	—	—	—
92-93—Univ. of Michigan	CCHA	39	5	18	23	113	...	...	...	—	—	—	—	—
93-94—Cleveland	IHL	53	1	2	3	160	...	...	...	—	—	—	—	—
—Pittsburgh	NHL	12	0	0	0	9	3	0	0	5	0	0	0	2
94-95—Cleveland	IHL	48	4	10	14	204	...	...	...	—	—	—	—	—
—Pittsburgh	NHL	36	2	0	2	82	0	0	0	4	0	0	0	18
95-96—Pittsburgh	NHL	70	4	10	14	153	20	0	0	18	0	7	7	24
96-97—Pittsburgh	NHL	45	2	4	6	131	-25	0	1	4	0	0	0	4
NHL totals (4 years)		163	8	14	22	375	-2	0	1	31	0	7	7	48

TANCILL, CHRIS   RW   STARS

PERSONAL: Born February 7, 1968, in Livonia, Mich. ... 5-10/185. ... Shoots left. ... Full name: Christopher William Tancill.

COLLEGE: Wisconsin.

TRANSACTIONS/CAREER NOTES: Selected by Hartford Whalers in NHL supplemental draft (June 16, 1989). ... Traded by Whalers to Detroit Red Wings for RW Daniel Shank (December 18, 1991). ... Signed as free agent by Dallas Stars (August 27, 1993). ... Signed as free agent by San Jose Sharks (August 31, 1994). ... Injured toe (January 9, 1996); missed one game. ... Injured foot (February 17, 1996); missed four games. ... Signed as free agent by Stars (July 25, 1997).

HONORS: Named NCAA Tournament Most Valuable Player (1989-90). ... Named to NCAA All-Tournament team (1989-90). ... Named to AHL All-Star first team (1991-92 and 1992-93).

Season Team	League	\multicolumn{9}{c}{REGULAR SEASON}									\multicolumn{5}{c}{PLAYOFFS}				
		Gms.	G	A	Pts.	PIM	+/-	PP	SH	Gms.	G	A	Pts.	PIM
86-87—Univ. of Wisconsin	WCHA	40	9	23	32	26	...	...	...	—	—	—	—	—
87-88—Univ. of Wisconsin	WCHA	44	13	14	27	48	...	...	...	—	—	—	—	—
88-89—Univ. of Wisconsin	WCHA	44	20	23	43	50	...	...	...	—	—	—	—	—
89-90—Univ. of Wisconsin	WCHA	45	39	32	71	44	...	...	...	—	—	—	—	—
90-91—Hartford	NHL	9	1	1	2	4	2	0	1	—	—	—	—	—
—Springfield	AHL	72	37	35	72	46	...	...	...	17	8	4	12	32

Season Team	League	Gms.	G	A	Pts.	PIM	+/-	PP	SH	Gms.	G	A	Pts.	PIM
				REGULAR SEASON								PLAYOFFS		
91-92 — Springfield	AHL	17	12	7	19	20	...	...	...	—	—	—	—	—
— Hartford	NHL	10	0	0	0	2	-6	0	0	—	—	—	—	—
— Adirondack	AHL	50	36	34	70	42	...	...	...	19	7	9	16	31
— Detroit	NHL	1	0	0	0	0	0	0	0	—	—	—	—	—
92-93 — Adirondack	AHL	68	*59	43	102	62	...	...	...	10	7	7	14	10
— Detroit	NHL	4	1	0	1	2	-2	0	0	—	—	—	—	—
93-94 — Dallas	NHL	12	1	3	4	8	-7	0	0	—	—	—	—	—
— Kalamazoo	IHL	60	41	54	95	55	...	...	...	5	0	2	2	8
94-95 — San Jose	NHL	26	3	11	14	10	1	0	1	11	1	1	2	8
— Kansas City	IHL	64	31	28	59	40	...	...	...	—	—	—	—	—
95-96 — Kansas City	IHL	27	12	16	28	18	...	...	...	—	—	—	—	—
— San Jose	NHL	45	7	16	23	20	-12	0	1	—	—	—	—	—
96-97 — San Jose	NHL	25	4	0	4	8	-5	1	0	—	—	—	—	—
— Kentucky	AHL	42	19	26	45	31	...	...	...	4	2	0	2	2
NHL totals (8 years)		132	17	31	48	54	-29	1	3	11	1	1	2	8

TARDIF, PATRICE   RW/C   KINGS

PERSONAL: Born October 30, 1970, in Thetford Mines, Que. ... 6-2/202. ... Shoots left. ... Name pronounced pah-TREEZ TAHR-deef.
COLLEGE: Champlain Regional (Que.), then Maine.
TRANSACTIONS/CAREER NOTES: Selected by St. Louis Blues in third round (second Blues pick, 54th overall) of NHL entry draft (June 16, 1990). ... Traded by Blues with LW Craig Johnson, C Roman Vopat, fifth-round pick (D Peter Hogan) in 1996 draft and first-round pick (LW Matt Zultek) in 1997 draft to Los Angeles Kings for C Wayne Gretzky (February 27, 1996).
HONORS: Named to Hockey East All-Rookie team (1990-91).

Season Team	League	Gms.	G	A	Pts.	PIM	+/-	PP	SH	Gms.	G	A	Pts.	PIM
				REGULAR SEASON								PLAYOFFS		
89-90 — Champlain J.C.	Can. Coll.	27	58	36	94	36	...	...	...	—	—	—	—	—
90-91 — University of Maine	Hockey East	36	13	12	25	18	...	...	...	—	—	—	—	—
91-92 — University of Maine	Hockey East	31	18	20	38	14	...	...	...	—	—	—	—	—
92-93 — University of Maine	Hockey East	45	23	25	48	22	...	...	...	—	—	—	—	—
93-94 — University of Maine	Hockey East	34	18	15	33	42	...	...	...	—	—	—	—	—
— Peoria	IHL	11	4	4	8	21	...	...	...	4	2	0	2	4
94-95 — Peoria	IHL	53	27	18	45	83	...	...	...	—	—	—	—	—
— St. Louis	NHL	27	3	10	13	29	4	1	0	—	—	—	—	—
95-96 — Worcester	AHL	30	13	13	26	69	...	...	...	—	—	—	—	—
— St. Louis	NHL	23	3	0	3	12	-2	0	0	—	—	—	—	—
— Los Angeles	NHL	15	1	1	2	37	-9	1	0	—	—	—	—	—
96-97 — Phoenix	IHL	9	0	3	3	13	...	...	...	—	—	—	—	—
— Detroit	IHL	66	24	23	47	70	...	...	...	11	0	1	1	8
NHL totals (2 years)		65	7	11	18	78	-7	2	0					

TARDIF, STEVE   C   BLACKHAWKS

PERSONAL: Born March 29, 1977, in St. Anges, Que. ... 5-11/178. ... Shoots left.
TRANSACTIONS/CAREER NOTES: Selected by Chicago Blackhawks in seventh round (eighth Blackhawks pick, 175th overall) of NHL entry draft (July 8, 1995).

Season Team	League	Gms.	G	A	Pts.	PIM	+/-	PP	SH	Gms.	G	A	Pts.	PIM
				REGULAR SEASON								PLAYOFFS		
93-94 — Drummondville	QMJHL	71	5	16	21	117	...	...	...	10	0	1	1	19
94-95 — Drummondville	QMJHL	64	10	33	43	313	...	...	...	4	1	2	3	9
95-96 — Drummondville	QMJHL	54	17	33	50	291	...	...	...	6	2	3	5	58
96-97 — Drummondville	QMJHL	65	24	40	64	357	...	...	...	6	1	5	6	52

TAYLOR, ANDREW   LW   ISLANDERS

PERSONAL: Born January 17, 1977, in Stratford, Ont. ... 6-2/193. ... Shoots left.
COLLEGE: Assumption College (Worcester, Mass.).
TRANSACTIONS/CAREER NOTES: Selected by New York Islanders in seventh round (fifth Islanders pick, 158th overall) of NHL entry draft (July 8, 1995).

Season Team	League	Gms.	G	A	Pts.	PIM	+/-	PP	SH	Gms.	G	A	Pts.	PIM
				REGULAR SEASON								PLAYOFFS		
92-93 — Stratford Jr. B	OHA	40	11	17	28	117	...	...	...	—	—	—	—	—
93-94 — Kitchener	OHL	62	1	8	9	60	...	...	...	5	0	1	1	6
94-95 — Kitchener	OHL	42	4	5	9	65	...	...	...	—	—	—	—	—
— Detroit	OHL	18	2	2	4	11	...	...	...	9	0	0	0	7
95-96 — Detroit	OHL	63	14	24	38	82	...	...	...	17	2	5	7	13
96-97 — Detroit	OHL	66	32	39	71	106	...	...	...	5	3	0	3	8

TAYLOR, CHRIS   C   KINGS

PERSONAL: Born March 6, 1972, in Stratford, Ont. ... 6-1/198. ... Shoots left. ... Brother of Tim Taylor, left winger, Detroit Red Wings.
TRANSACTIONS/CAREER NOTES: Tore knee ligaments (March 1989). ... Selected by New York Islanders in second round (second Islanders pick, 27th overall) of NHL entry draft (June 16, 1990). ... Signed as free agent by Los Angeles Kings (August 1, 1997).

T

Season Team	League	REGULAR SEASON								PLAYOFFS				
		Gms.	G	A	Pts.	PIM	+/-	PP	SH	Gms.	G	A	Pts.	PIM
88-89— London	OHL	62	7	16	23	52	...	...	...	15	0	2	2	15
89-90— London	OHL	66	45	60	105	60	...	...	...	6	3	2	5	6
90-91— London	OHL	65	50	78	128	50	...	...	...	7	4	8	12	6
91-92— London	OHL	66	48	74	122	57	...	...	...	10	8	16	24	9
92-93— Roanoke	ECHL	5	2	1	3	0	...	...	...	—	—	—	—	—
—Capital District	AHL	77	19	43	62	32	...	...	...	4	0	1	1	2
93-94— Raleigh	ECHL	2	0	0	0	0	...	...	...	—	—	—	—	—
—Salt Lake City	IHL	79	21	20	41	38	...	...	...	—	—	—	—	—
94-95— Denver	IHL	78	38	48	86	47	...	...	...	14	7	6	13	10
—Roanoke	ECHL	1	0	0	0	2	...	...	...	—	—	—	—	—
—New York Islanders	NHL	10	0	3	3	2	1	0	0	—	—	—	—	—
95-96— Utah	IHL	50	18	23	41	60	...	...	...	22	5	11	16	26
—New York Islanders	NHL	11	0	1	1	2	1	0	0	—	—	—	—	—
96-97— Utah	IHL	71	27	40	67	24	...	...	...	7	1	2	3	0
—New York Islanders	NHL	1	0	0	0	0	0	0	0	—	—	—	—	—
NHL totals (3 years)		22	0	4	4	4	2	0	0					

TAYLOR, TIM   C   RED WINGS

PERSONAL: Born February 6, 1969, in Stratford, Ont. ... 6-1/190. ... Shoots left. ... Full name: Tim Robertson Taylor. ... Brother of Chris Taylor, center in New York Islanders system.

TRANSACTIONS/CAREER NOTES: Suffered from mononucleosis (October 1986). ... Selected by Washington Capitals in second round (second Capitals pick, 36th overall) of NHL entry draft (June 11, 1988). ... Traded by Capitals to Vancouver Canucks for C Eric Murano (January 29, 1991). ... Signed as free agent by Detroit Red Wings (July 28, 1993). ... Injured right shoulder (April 5, 1996); missed three games. ... Sprained shoulder (October 15, 1996); missed 16 games. ... Suffered from an illness (April 9, 1997); missed two games.

HONORS: Won John B. Sollenberger Trophy (1993-94). ... Named to AHL All-Star first team (1993-94).

MISCELLANEOUS: Member of Stanley Cup championship team (1997).

Season Team	League	REGULAR SEASON								PLAYOFFS				
		Gms.	G	A	Pts.	PIM	+/-	PP	SH	Gms.	G	A	Pts.	PIM
86-87— London	OHL	34	7	9	16	11	...	...	...	—	—	—	—	—
87-88— London	OHL	64	46	50	96	66	...	...	...	12	9	9	18	26
88-89— London	OHL	61	34	80	114	93	...	...	...	21	*21	25	*46	58
89-90— Baltimore	AHL	74	22	21	43	63	...	...	...	9	2	2	4	13
90-91— Baltimore	AHL	79	25	42	67	75	...	...	...	5	0	1	1	4
91-92— Baltimore	AHL	65	9	18	27	131	...	...	...	—	—	—	—	—
92-93— Baltimore	AHL	41	15	16	31	49	...	...	...	—	—	—	—	—
—Hamilton	AHL	36	15	22	37	37	...	...	...	—	—	—	—	—
93-94— Adirondack	AHL	79	36	*81	117	86	...	...	...	12	2	10	12	12
—Detroit	NHL	1	1	0	1	0	-1	0	0	—	—	—	—	—
94-95— Detroit	NHL	22	0	4	4	16	3	0	0	6	0	1	1	12
95-96— Detroit	NHL	72	11	14	25	39	11	1	1	18	0	4	4	4
96-97— Detroit	NHL	44	3	4	7	52	-6	0	1	2	0	0	0	0
NHL totals (4 years)		139	15	22	37	107	7	1	2	26	0	5	5	16

TERRERI, CHRIS   G   BLACKHAWKS

PERSONAL: Born November 15, 1964, in Warwick, R.I. ... 5-8/160. ... Catches left. ... Full name: Christopher Arnold Terreri. ... Name pronounced tuh-RAIR-ee.

COLLEGE: Providence.

TRANSACTIONS/CAREER NOTES: Selected by New Jersey Devils in fifth round (third Devils pick, 87th overall) of NHL entry draft (June 8, 1983). ... Strained knee (October 1986). ... Strained lower back (March 21, 1992); missed five games. ... Traded by Devils to San Jose Sharks for second-round pick (traded to Pittsburgh) in 1996 draft (November 14, 1995). ... Injured elbow (March 15, 1996); missed 12 games. ... Injured wrist (October 20, 1996); missed 12 games. ... Traded by Sharks with D Michal Sykora, RW Ulf Dahlen and second-round pick in 1998 draft to Chicago Blackhawks for G Ed Belfour (January 25, 1997).

HONORS: Named NCAA Tournament Most Valuable Player (1984-85). ... Named Hockey East Player of the Year (1984-85). ... Named Hockey East Tournament Most Valuable Player (1984-85). ... Named to NCAA All-Tournament team (1984-85). ... Named to NCAA All-America East first team (1984-85). ... Named to Hockey East All-Star first team (1984-85). ... Named to NCAA All-America East second team (1985-86). ... Named to Hockey East All-Decade team (1994).

MISCELLANEOUS: Member of Stanley Cup championship team (1995). ... Holds New Jersey Devils franchise all-time records for most games played by goaltender (268). ... Stopped a penalty shot attempt (vs. Mike Ricci, November 17, 1990; vs. Murray Craven, October 13, 1991). ... Allowed a penalty shot goal (vs. Mario Lemieux, December 31, 1988; vs. Bob Errey, January 5, 1991; vs. Ray Bourque, March 19, 1994).

Season Team	League	REGULAR SEASON							PLAYOFFS					
		Gms.	Min	W	L	T	GA	SO	Avg.	Gms.	Min.	W	L	GA	SO	Avg.
82-83— Providence College	ECAC	11	529	7	1	0	17	2	1.93	—	—	—	—	—	—	—
83-84— Providence College	ECAC	10	391	4	2	0	20	0	3.07	—	—	—	—	—	—	—
84-85— Providence College	Hockey East	41	2515	15	13	5	131	1	3.13	—	—	—	—	—	—	—
85-86— Providence College	Hockey East	27	1540	6	16	0	96	0	3.74	—	—	—	—	—	—	—
86-87— Maine	AHL	14	765	4	9	1	57	0	4.47	—	—	—	—	—	—	—
—New Jersey	NHL	7	286	0	3	1	21	0	4.41	—	—	—	—	—	—	—
87-88— U.S. national team	Int'l	26	1430	17	7	2	81	0	3.40	—	—	—	—	—	—	—
—U.S. Olympic team	Int'l	3	128	1	1	0	14	0	6.56	—	—	—	—	—	—	—
—Utica	AHL	7	399	5	1	0	18	0	2.71	—	—	—	—	—	—	—
88-89— New Jersey	NHL	8	402	0	4	2	18	0	2.69	—	—	—	—	—	—	—
—Utica	AHL	39	2314	20	15	3	132	0	3.42	2	80	0	1	6	0	4.50
89-90— New Jersey	NHL	35	1931	15	12	3	110	0	3.42	4	238	2	2	13	0	3.28
90-91— New Jersey	NHL	53	2970	24	21	7	144	1	2.91	7	428	3	4	21	0	2.94

Season Team	League	REGULAR SEASON								PLAYOFFS					
		Gms.	Min	W	L	T	GA	SO	Avg.	Gms.	Min.	W	L	GA	SO	Avg.
91-92—New Jersey	NHL	54	3186	22	22	10	169	1	3.18	7	386	3	3	23	0	3.58
92-93—New Jersey	NHL	48	2672	19	21	3	151	2	3.39	4	219	1	3	17	0	4.66
93-94—New Jersey	NHL	44	2340	20	11	4	106	2	2.72	4	200	3	0	9	0	2.70
94-95—New Jersey	NHL	15	734	3	7	2	31	0	2.53	1	8	0	0	0	0	0.00
95-96—New Jersey	NHL	4	210	3	0	0	9	0	2.57	—	—	—	—	—	—	—
—San Jose	NHL	46	2516	13	29	1	155	0	3.70	—	—	—	—	—	—	—
96-97—San Jose	NHL	22	1200	6	10	3	55	0	2.75	—	—	—	—	—	—	—
—Chicago	NHL	7	429	4	1	2	19	0	2.66	2	44	0	0	3	0	4.09
NHL totals (10 years)		343	18876	129	141	38	988	6	3.14	29	1523	12	12	86	0	3.39

TETARENKO, JOEY   D   PANTHERS

PERSONAL: Born March 3, 1978, in Prince Albert, Sask. ... 6-1/202. ... Shoots right.

TRANSACTIONS/CAREER NOTES: Selected by Florida Panthers in fourth round (fourth Panthers pick, 82nd overall) of NHL entry draft (June 22, 1996).

Season Team	League	REGULAR SEASON							PLAYOFFS				
		Gms.	G	A	Pts.	PIM	+/-	PP	SH	Gms.	G	A	Pts.	PIM
94-95— Portland	WHL	59	0	1	1	134	...	...	...	9	0	0	0	8
95-96— Portland	WHL	71	4	11	15	190	...	...	...	7	0	1	1	17
96-97— Portland	WHL	68	8	18	26	182	...	...	...	2	0	0	0	2

THEODORE, JOSE   G   CANADIENS

PERSONAL: Born September 13, 1976, in Laval, Que. ... 5-11/181. ... Catches right. ... Name pronounced ZOH-zhay TAY-uh-dohr.

TRANSACTIONS/CAREER NOTES: Selected by Montreal Canadiens in second round (second Canadiens pick, 44th overall) of NHL entry draft (June 28, 1994).

HONORS: Named to QMJHL All-Star second team (1994-95 and 1995-96).

Season Team	League	REGULAR SEASON								PLAYOFFS					
		Gms.	Min	W	L	T	GA	SO	Avg.	Gms.	Min.	W	L	GA	SO	Avg.
92-93—St. Jean	QMJHL	34	1776	12	16	2	112	0	3.78	3	175	0	2	11	0	3.77
93-94—St. Jean	QMJHL	57	3225	20	29	6	194	0	3.61	5	296	1	4	18	1	3.65
94-95—Hull	QMJHL	58	3348	32	22	2	193	5	3.46	21	1263	15	6	59	1	2.80
—Fredericton	AHL	—	—	—	—	—	—	—	—	1	60	0	1	3	0	3.00
95-96—Hull	QMJHL	48	2803	33	11	2	158	0	3.38	5	300	2	3	20	0	4.00
—Montreal	NHL	1	9	0	0	0	1	0	6.67	—	—	—	—	—	—	—
96-97—Fredericton	AHL	26	1469	12	12	0	87	0	3.55	—	—	—	—	—	—	—
—Montreal	NHL	16	821	5	6	2	53	0	3.87	2	168	1	1	7	0	2.50
NHL totals (2 years)		17	830	5	6	2	54	0	3.90	2	168	1	1	7	0	2.50

THERIEN, CHRIS   D   FLYERS

PERSONAL: Born December 14, 1971, in Ottawa. ... 6-5/230. ... Shoots left. ... Name pronounced TAIR-ee-uhn.

HIGH SCHOOL: Northwood School (Lake Placid, N.Y.).

COLLEGE: Providence.

TRANSACTIONS/CAREER NOTES: Selected by Philadelphia Flyers in third round (seventh Flyers pick, 47th overall) of NHL entry draft (June 16, 1990).

HONORS: Named to Hockey East All-Rookie Team (1990-91). ... Named to Hockey East All-Star second team (1992-93). ... Named to NHL All-Rookie team (1994-95).

Season Team	League	REGULAR SEASON							PLAYOFFS				
		Gms.	G	A	Pts.	PIM	+/-	PP	SH	Gms.	G	A	Pts.	PIM
89-90— Northwood School	N.Y. H.S.	31	35	37	72	54	...	...	...	—	—	—	—	—
90-91— Providence College	Hockey East	36	4	18	22	36	...	...	...	—	—	—	—	—
91-92— Providence College	Hockey East	36	16	25	41	38	...	...	...	—	—	—	—	—
92-93— Providence College	Hockey East	33	8	11	19	52	...	...	...	—	—	—	—	—
—Canadian nat'l team	Int'l	8	1	4	5	8	...	...	...	—	—	—	—	—
93-94— Canadian nat'l team	Int'l	59	7	15	22	46	...	...	...	—	—	—	—	—
—Can. Olympic team	Int'l	4	0	0	0	4	...	...	...	—	—	—	—	—
—Hershey	AHL	6	0	0	0	2	...	...	...	—	—	—	—	—
94-95— Hershey	AHL	34	3	13	16	27	...	...	...	—	—	—	—	—
—Philadelphia	NHL	48	3	10	13	38	8	1	0	15	0	0	0	10
95-96— Philadelphia	NHL	82	6	17	23	89	16	3	0	12	0	0	0	18
96-97— Philadelphia	NHL	71	2	22	24	64	27	0	0	19	1	6	7	6
NHL totals (3 years)		201	11	49	60	191	51	4	0	46	1	6	7	34

THIBAULT, JOCELYN   G   CANADIENS

PERSONAL: Born January 12, 1975, in Montreal. ... 5-11/170. ... Catches left. ... Name pronounced TEE-boh.

TRANSACTIONS/CAREER NOTES: Selected by Quebec Nordiques in first round (first Nordiques pick, 10th overall) of NHL entry draft (June 26, 1993). ... Sprained shoulder (March 28, 1995); missed 10 games. ... Nordiques franchise moved to Colorado and renamed Avalanche for 1995-96 season (June 21, 1995). ... Traded by Avalanche with LW Martin Rucinsky and RW Andrei Kovalenko to Montreal Canadiens for G Patrick Roy and RW Mike Keane (December 6, 1995). ... Bruised right hand (February 21, 1996); missed two games. ... Fractured finger (October 24, 1996); missed nine games. ... Suffered from the flu (February 3, 1997); missed two games.

HONORS: Named to QMJHL All-Rookie team (1991-92). ... Won Can.HL Goaltender-of-the-Year Award (1992-93). ... Won Jacques Plante Trophy (1992-93). ... Won Michel Briere Trophy (1992-93). ... Won Marcel Robert Trophy (1992-93). ... Named to Can.HL All-Star first team (1992-93). ... Named to QMJHL All-Star first team (1992-93).
MISCELLANEOUS: Stopped a penalty shot attempt (vs. Tony Granato, November 25, 1993; vs. Martin Straka, March 16, 1995).

			REGULAR SEASON							PLAYOFFS					
Season Team	League	Gms.	Min	W	L	T	GA	SO	Avg.	Gms.	Min.	W	L	GA	SO	Avg.
91-92—Trois-Rivieres	QMJHL	30	1497	14	7	1	77	0	3.09	3	300	...	...	20	0	4.00
92-93—Sherbrooke	QMJHL	56	3190	34	14	5	159	*3	*2.99	15	883	9	6	57	0	3.87
93-94—Cornwall	AHL	4	240	4	0	0	9	1	2.25	—	—	—	—	—	—	—
—Quebec	NHL	29	1504	8	13	3	83	0	3.31	—	—	—	—	—	—	—
94-95—Sherbrooke	QMJHL	13	776	6	6	1	38	1	2.94	—	—	—	—	—	—	—
—Quebec	NHL	18	898	12	2	2	35	1	2.34	3	148	1	2	8	0	3.24
95-96—Colorado	NHL	10	558	3	4	2	28	0	3.01	—	—	—	—	—	—	—
—Montreal	NHL	40	2334	23	13	3	110	3	2.83	6	311	2	4	18	0	3.47
96-97—Montreal	NHL	61	3397	22	24	11	164	1	2.90	3	179	0	3	13	0	4.36
NHL totals (4 years)		158	8691	68	56	21	420	5	2.90	12	638	3	9	39	0	3.67

THIBEAULT, DAVID LW SHARKS

PERSONAL: Born May 12, 1978, in Trois-Rivieres, Que. ... 6-1/190. ... Shoots left. ... Name pronounced TEE-bow.
TRANSACTIONS/CAREER NOTES: Selected by San Jose Sharks in ninth round (eighth Sharks pick, 217th overall) of NHL entry draft (June 22, 1996).

			REGULAR SEASON							PLAYOFFS			
Season Team	League	Gms.	G	A	Pts.	PIM	+/-	PP	SH	Gms.	G	A	Pts.	PIM
94-95—Drummondville	QMJHL	61	10	19	29	101	...	...	...	4	0	0	0	0
95-96—Drummondville	QMJHL	57	23	35	58	99	...	...	...	6	0	3	3	12
96-97—Laval	QMJHL	8	3	1	4	48	...	...	...	—	—	—	—	—
—Victoriaville	QMJHL	58	39	38	77	35	...	...	...	6	3	3	6	4
—Kentucky....................	AHL	1	0	0	0	0	...	...	...	—	—	—	—	—

THOMAS, STEVE LW DEVILS

PERSONAL: Born July 15, 1963, in Stockport, England. ... 5-11/190. ... Shoots left.
TRANSACTIONS/CAREER NOTES: Signed as free agent by Toronto Maple Leafs (June 1984). ... Broke wrist during training camp (September 1984). ... Traded by Maple Leafs with RW Rick Vaive and D Bob McGill to Chicago Blackhawks for LW Al Secord and RW Ed Olczyk (September 3, 1987). ... Pulled stomach muscle (October 1987). ... Separated left shoulder (February 20, 1988); underwent surgery (May 1988). ... Pulled back muscle (October 18, 1988). ... Separated right shoulder (December 21, 1988). ... Underwent surgery to repair chronic shoulder separation problem (January 25, 1989). ... Strained knee ligaments during training camp (September 1990); missed first 11 games of season. ... Traded by Blackhawks with C Adam Creighton to New York Islanders for C Brent Sutter and RW Brad Lauer (October 25, 1991). ... Bruised ribs (March 10, 1992); missed one game. ... Bruised ribs (November 21, 1992); missed three games. ... Suffered neck muscle spasms (January 4, 1994); missed five games. ... Injured back and thumb (January 24, 1995); missed one game. ... Traded by Islanders to New Jersey Devils for RW Claude Lemieux (October 3, 1995). ... Injured head (February 1, 1996); missed one game. ... Suffered from the flu (October 24, 1996); missed two games. ... Strained ankle (November 30, 1996); missed 10 games. ... Strained knee (December 31, 1996); missed 12 games.
HONORS: Won Dudley (Red) Garrett Memorial Trophy (1984-85). ... Named to AHL All-Star first team (1984-85).
STATISTICAL PLATEAUS: Three-goal games: 1987-88 (1), 1989-90 (1), 1990-91 (1), 1993-94 (1). Total: 4. ... Four-goal games: 1989-90 (1), 1991-92 (1). Total: 2. ... Total hat tricks: 6.

			REGULAR SEASON							PLAYOFFS			
Season Team	League	Gms.	G	A	Pts.	PIM	+/-	PP	SH	Gms.	G	A	Pts.	PIM
81-82—Markham	OHA	48	68	57	125	113	...	...	...	—	—	—	—	—
82-83—Toronto	OHL	61	18	20	38	42	...	...	...	—	—	—	—	—
83-84—Toronto	OHL	70	51	54	105	77	...	...	...	—	—	—	—	—
84-85—Toronto	NHL	18	1	1	2	2	-13	0	0	—	—	—	—	—
—St. Catharines	AHL	64	42	48	90	56	...	...	...	—	—	—	—	—
85-86—St. Catharines	AHL	19	18	14	32	35	...	...	...	—	—	—	—	—
—Toronto	NHL	65	20	37	57	36	-15	5	0	10	6	8	14	9
86-87—Toronto	NHL	78	35	27	62	114	-3	3	0	13	2	3	5	13
87-88—Chicago......................	NHL	30	13	13	26	40	1	5	0	3	1	2	3	6
88-89—Chicago......................	NHL	45	21	19	40	69	-2	8	0	12	3	5	8	10
89-90—Chicago......................	NHL	76	40	30	70	91	-3	13	0	20	7	6	13	33
90-91—Chicago......................	NHL	69	19	35	54	129	8	2	0	6	1	2	3	15
91-92—Chicago......................	NHL	11	2	6	8	26	-3	0	0	—	—	—	—	—
—New York Islanders....	NHL	71	28	42	70	71	11	3	0	—	—	—	—	—
92-93—New York Islanders....	NHL	79	37	50	87	111	3	12	0	18	9	8	17	37
93-94—New York Islanders....	NHL	78	42	33	75	139	-9	17	0	4	1	0	1	8
94-95—New York Islanders....	NHL	47	11	15	26	60	-14	3	0	—	—	—	—	—
95-96—New Jersey	NHL	81	26	35	61	98	-2	6	0	—	—	—	—	—
96-97—New Jersey	NHL	57	15	19	34	46	9	1	0	10	1	1	2	18
NHL totals (13 years)		805	310	362	672	1032	-32	78	0	96	31	35	66	149

THOMAS, TIM G AVALANCHE

PERSONAL: Born April 15, 1974, in Flint, Mich. ... 5-11/182. ... Catches left.
COLLEGE: Vermont.
TRANSACTIONS/CAREER NOTES: Selected by Quebec Nordiques in ninth round (11th Nordiques pick, 217th overall) of NHL entry draft (June 29, 1994). ... Nordiques franchise moved to Colorado and renamed Avalanche for 1995-96 season (June 21, 1995).
HONORS: Named to NCAA All-America East second team (1994-95 and 1995-96). ... Named to ECAC All-Star first team (1994-95). ... Named to ECAC All-Star first team (1995-96).

		REGULAR SEASON								PLAYOFFS						
Season Team	League	Gms.	Min	W	L	T	GA	SO	Avg.	Gms.	Min.	W	L	GA	SO	Avg.
92-93 — Lakeland	Tier II	27	1580	...	...		87	...	3.30	—	—	—	—	—	—	—
93-94 — University of Vermont	ECAC	33	1863	15	11	6	95	1	3.06	—	—	—	—	—	—	—
94-95 — University of Vermont	ECAC	34	2011	18	14	2	90	3	2.69	—	—	—	—	—	—	—
95-96 — University of Vermont	ECAC	37	2254	26	7	4	88	3	2.34	—	—	—	—	—	—	—
96-97 — University of Vermont	ECAC	36	2158	22	11	3	101	2	2.81	—	—	—	—	—	—	—

THOMPSON, BRENT   D   COYOTES

PERSONAL: Born January 9, 1971, in Calgary. ... 6-2/200. ... Shoots left. ... Full name: Brenton Keith Thompson.

TRANSACTIONS/CAREER NOTES: Stretched knee ligaments and separated shoulder (September 1987). ... Selected by Los Angeles Kings in second round (first Kings pick, 39th overall) of NHL entry draft (June 17, 1989). ... Strained hip flexor prior to 1992-93 season; missed first six games of season. ... Strained abdominal muscles (January 23, 1992); missed 17 games. ... Traded by Kings to Winnipeg Jets for D Ruslan Batyrshin and second-round pick (RW Marian Cisar) in 1996 draft (August 8, 1994). ... Jets franchise moved to Phoenix and renamed Coyotes for 1996-97 season; NHL approved move on January 18, 1996.

HONORS: Named to WHL (East) All-Star second team (1990-91).

		REGULAR SEASON								PLAYOFFS				
Season Team	League	Gms.	G	A	Pts.	PIM	+/-	PP	SH	Gms.	G	A	Pts.	PIM
88-89 — Medicine Hat	WHL	72	3	10	13	160	...	...	...	3	0	0	0	2
89-90 — Medicine Hat	WHL	68	10	35	45	167	...	...	...	3	0	1	1	14
90-91 — Medicine Hat	WHL	51	5	40	45	87	...	...	...	12	1	7	8	16
— Phoenix	IHL	—								4	0	1	1	6
91-92 — Phoenix	IHL	42	4	13	17	139	...	...	...	—	—	—	—	—
— Los Angeles	NHL	27	0	5	5	89	-7	0	0	4	0	0	0	4
92-93 — Phoenix	IHL	22	0	5	5	112	...	...	...	—	—	—	—	—
— Los Angeles	NHL	30	0	4	4	76	-4	0	0	—	—	—	—	—
93-94 — Phoenix	IHL	26	1	11	12	118	...	...	...	—	—	—	—	—
— Los Angeles	NHL	24	1	0	1	81	-1	0	0	—	—	—	—	—
94-95 — Winnipeg	NHL	29	0	0	0	78	-17	0	0	—	—	—	—	—
95-96 — Winnipeg	NHL	10	0	1	1	21	-2	0	0	—	—	—	—	—
— Springfield	AHL	58	2	10	12	203	...	...	...	10	1	4	5	*55
96-97 — Phoenix	IHL	12	0	1	1	67	...	...	...	—	—	—	—	—
— Springfield	AHL	64	2	15	17	215	...	...	...	17	0	2	2	31
— Phoenix	NHL	1	0	0	0	7	-1	0	0	—	—	—	—	—
NHL totals (6 years)		121	1	10	11	352	-32	0	0	4	0	0	0	4

THORNTON, SCOTT   C   CANADIENS

PERSONAL: Born January 9, 1971, in London, Ont. ... 6-3/210. ... Shoots left. ... Cousin of Joe Thornton, center, Boston Bruins organization.

TRANSACTIONS/CAREER NOTES: Selected by Toronto Maple Leafs in first round (first Maple Leafs pick, third overall) of NHL entry draft (June 17, 1989). ... Suspended 12 games by OHL for refusing to leave ice following penalty (February 7, 1990). ... Separated shoulder (January 24, 1991); missed eight games. ... Traded by Maple Leafs with LW Vincent Damphousse, D Luke Richardson, G Peter Ing and future considerations to Edmonton Oilers for G Grant Fuhr, RW/LW Glenn Anderson and LW Craig Berube (September 19, 1991). ... Suffered concussion (November 23, 1991); missed one game. ... Sprained ankle (October 6, 1993); missed 13 games. ... Suffered back spasms (November 21, 1993); missed one game. ... Suffered wrist contusion (April 14, 1994); missed one game. ... Suffered from Cytomegalo virus (January 9, 1996); missed three games. ... Traded by Oilers to Montreal Canadiens for RW Andrei Kovalenko (September 6, 1996). ... Bruised hand (December 28, 1996); missed three games. ... Suffered from the flu (February 10, 1997); missed one game. ... Underwent arthroscopic knee surgery (March 6, 1997); missed five games.

		REGULAR SEASON								PLAYOFFS				
Season Team	League	Gms.	G	A	Pts.	PIM	+/-	PP	SH	Gms.	G	A	Pts.	PIM
86-87 — London Diamonds	OPJHL	31	10	7	17	10	...	...	...	—	—	—	—	—
87-88 — Belleville	OHL	62	11	19	30	54	...	...	...	6	0	1	1	2
88-89 — Belleville	OHL	59	28	34	62	103	...	...	...	5	1	1	2	6
89-90 — Belleville	OHL	47	21	28	49	91	...	...	...	11	2	10	12	15
90-91 — Belleville	OHL	3	2	1	3	2	...	...	...	6	0	7	7	14
— Newmarket	AHL	5	1	0	1	4	...	...	...	—	—	—	—	—
— Toronto	NHL	33	1	3	4	30	-15	0	0	—	—	—	—	—
91-92 — Edmonton	NHL	15	0	1	1	43	-6	0	0	1	0	0	0	0
— Cape Breton	AHL	49	9	14	23	40	...	...	...	5	1	0	1	8
92-93 — Cape Breton	AHL	58	23	27	50	102	...	...	...	16	1	2	3	35
— Edmonton	NHL	9	0	1	1	0	-4	0	0	—	—	—	—	—
93-94 — Edmonton	NHL	61	4	7	11	104	-15	0	0	—	—	—	—	—
— Cape Breton	AHL	2	1	1	2	31	...	...	...	—	—	—	—	—
94-95 — Edmonton	NHL	47	10	12	22	89	-4	0	1	—	—	—	—	—
95-96 — Edmonton	NHL	77	9	9	18	149	-25	0	2	—	—	—	—	—
96-97 — Montreal	NHL	73	10	10	20	128	-19	1	1	5	1	0	1	2
NHL totals (7 years)		315	34	43	77	543	-88	1	4	6	1	0	1	2

TICHY, MILAN   D

PERSONAL: Born September 22, 1969, in Plzen, Czechoslovakia. ... 6-3/198. ... Shoots left. ... Name pronounced tee-SHEE.

TRANSACTIONS/CAREER NOTES: Selected by Chicago Blackhawks in eighth round (sixth Blackhawks pick, 153rd overall) of NHL entry draft (June 17, 1989). ... Selected by Florida Panthers in NHL expansion draft (June 24, 1993). ... Traded by Panthers to Winnipeg Jets for D Brent Severyn (October 3, 1993). ... Signed as free agent by New York Islanders (August 2, 1994). ... Injured back (January 9, 1996); missed remainder of season.

Season Team	League	REGULAR SEASON								PLAYOFFS				
		Gms.	G	A	Pts.	PIM	+/-	PP	SH	Gms.	G	A	Pts.	PIM
87-88 — Skoda Plzen	Czech.	30	1	3	4	20	...	...	...	—	—	—	—	—
88-89 — Skoda Plzen	Czech.	36	1	12	13	44	...	...	...	—	—	—	—	—
89-90 — Dukla Trencin	Czech.	51	14	8	22	87	...	...	...	—	—	—	—	—
90-91 — Dukla Trencin	Czech.	39	9	11	20	72	...	...	...	—	—	—	—	—
91-92 — Indianapolis	IHL	49	6	23	29	28	...	...	...	—	—	—	—	—
92-93 — Indianapolis	IHL	49	7	32	39	62	...	...	...	4	0	5	5	14
— Chicago	NHL	13	0	1	1	30	7	0	0	—	—	—	—	—
93-94 — Moncton	AHL	48	1	20	21	103	...	...	...	20	3	3	6	12
94-95 — Denver	IHL	71	18	36	54	90	...	...	...	17	4	9	13	12
— New York Islanders	NHL	2	0	0	0	2	-1	0	0	—	—	—	—	—
95-96 — Utah	IHL	21	1	12	13	26	...	...	...	—	—	—	—	—
— New York Islanders	NHL	8	0	4	4	8	3	0	0	—	—	—	—	—
— ZPS Zlin	Czech. Rep.	8	0	3	3	...	...	...	...	4	0	0	0	...
96-97 —						Statistics unavailable.								
NHL totals (3 years)		23	0	5	5	40	9	0	0					

TIKKANEN, ESA   LW   RANGERS

PERSONAL: Born January 25, 1968, in Helsinki, Finland. ... 6-1/200. ... Shoots left. ... Full name: Esa Kalervo Tikkanen. ... Name pronounced EH-suh TEE-kuh-nehn.

TRANSACTIONS/CAREER NOTES: Selected by Edmonton Oilers in fourth round (fourth Oilers pick, 82nd overall) of NHL entry draft (August 8, 1983). ... Broke foot (December 10, 1985). ... Lacerated elbow, developed bursitis and underwent surgery (December 9, 1986). ... Fractured left wrist (January 1989). ... Injured right knee (October 28, 1989). ... Underwent left knee surgery (August 1990); missed first 10 days of training camp. ... Sprained wrist (December 1, 1991); missed one game. ... Sprained wrist (December 20, 1991); missed two games. ... Fractured shoulder (January 4, 1992); missed 37 games. ... Suffered from the flu (December 1992); missed one game. ... Suffered elbow infection (February 1993); missed two games. ... Traded by Oilers to New York Rangers for C Doug Weight (March 17, 1993). ... Bruised knee (January 14, 1994); missed one game. ... Traded by Rangers with D Doug Lidster to St. Louis Blues for C Petr Nedved (July 24, 1994); trade arranged as compensation for Blues signing Coach Mike Keenan. ... Played in Europe during 1994-95 NHL lockout. ... Injured shoulder (April 3, 1995); missed one game. ... Suffered illness (April 28, 1995); missed two games. ... Injured leg (May 1, 1995); missed two games. ... Traded by Blues to New Jersey Devils for third-round pick (traded to Colorado) in 1997 draft (November 1, 1995). ... Injured knee (November 23, 1995); missed 15 games. ... Traded by Devils to Vancouver Canucks for second-round pick (LW Wesley Mason) in 1996 draft (November 23, 1995). ... Traded by Canucks with RW Russ Courtnall to Rangers for C Sergei Nemchinov and RW Brian Noonan (March 8, 1997).

STATISTICAL PLATEAUS: Three-goal games: 1986-87 (2), 1987-88 (1), 1988-89 (1), 1990-91 (1). Total: 5.

MISCELLANEOUS: Member of Stanley Cup championship team (1985, 1987, 1988, 1990 and 1994).

Season Team	League	REGULAR SEASON								PLAYOFFS				
		Gms.	G	A	Pts.	PIM	+/-	PP	SH	Gms.	G	A	Pts.	PIM
81-82 — Regina	WHL	2	0	0	0	0	...	...	...	—	—	—	—	—
82-83 — Helsinki Junior IFK	Finland	30	34	31	65	104	...	...	...	4	4	3	7	10
— Helsinki IFK	Finland	—	—	—	—	—	...	...	...	1	0	0	0	2
83-84 — Helsinki IFK	Finland	36	19	11	30	30	...	...	...	2	0	0	0	0
— Helsinki Junior IFK	Finland	6	5	9	14	13	...	...	...	4	4	3	7	8
84-85 — Helsinki IFK	Finland	36	21	33	54	42	...	...	...	—	—	—	—	—
— Edmonton	NHL	—	—	—	—	—	...	...	...	3	0	0	0	2
85-86 — Nova Scotia	AHL	15	4	8	12	17	...	...	...	—	—	—	—	—
— Edmonton	NHL	35	7	6	13	28	5	0	0	8	3	2	5	7
86-87 — Edmonton	NHL	76	34	44	78	120	44	6	0	21	7	2	9	22
87-88 — Edmonton	NHL	80	23	51	74	153	21	6	1	19	10	17	27	72
88-89 — Edmonton	NHL	67	31	47	78	92	10	6	8	7	1	3	4	12
89-90 — Edmonton	NHL	79	30	33	63	161	17	6	4	22	13	11	24	26
90-91 — Edmonton	NHL	79	27	42	69	85	22	3	2	18	12	8	20	24
91-92 — Edmonton	NHL	40	12	16	28	44	-8	6	2	16	5	3	8	8
92-93 — Edmonton	NHL	66	14	19	33	76	-11	2	4	—	—	—	—	—
— New York Rangers	NHL	15	2	5	7	18	-13	0	0	—	—	—	—	—
93-94 — New York Rangers	NHL	83	22	32	54	114	5	5	3	23	4	4	8	34
94-95 — HIFK Helsinki	Finland	19	2	11	13	16	...	...	...	—	—	—	—	—
— St. Louis	NHL	43	12	23	35	22	13	5	2	7	2	2	4	20
95-96 — St. Louis	NHL	11	1	4	5	18	1	0	1	—	—	—	—	—
— New Jersey	NHL	9	0	2	2	4	-6	0	0	—	—	—	—	—
— Vancouver	NHL	38	13	24	37	14	6	8	0	6	3	2	5	2
96-97 — Vancouver	NHL	62	12	15	27	66	-9	4	1	—	—	—	—	—
— New York Rangers	NHL	14	1	2	3	6	0	0	1	15	9	3	12	26
NHL totals (13 years)		797	241	365	606	1021	97	57	29	165	69	57	126	255

TIMANDER, MATTIAS   D   BRUINS

PERSONAL: Born April 16, 1974, In Solleftea, Sweden. ... 6-3/215. ... Shoots left. ... Name pronounced tih-MAN-duhr.

TRANSACTIONS/CAREER NOTES: Selected by Boston Bruins in seventh round (seventh Bruins pick, 208th overall) of NHL entry draft (June 21, 1992). ... Injured shoulder (November 26, 1996); missed four games.

Season Team	League	REGULAR SEASON								PLAYOFFS				
		Gms.	G	A	Pts.	PIM	+/-	PP	SH	Gms.	G	A	Pts.	PIM
92-93 — MoDo Ornskoldvik	Sweden	1	0	0	0	0	...	...	...	—	—	—	—	—
93-94 — MoDo Ornskoldvik	Sweden	23	2	2	4	6	...	...	...	11	2	0	2	10
94-95 — MoDo Ornskoldvik	Sweden	39	8	9	17	24	...	...	...	—	—	—	—	—
95-96 — MoDo Ornskoldvik	Sweden	37	4	10	14	34	...	...	...	7	1	1	2	8
96-97 — Boston	NHL	41	1	8	9	14	-9	0	0	—	—	—	—	—
— Providence	AHL	32	3	11	14	20	...	...	...	10	1	1	2	12
NHL totals (1 year)		41	1	8	9	14	-9	0	0					

TIMONEN, KIMMO　　　　　　　　　　D　　　　　　　　　　KINGS

PERSONAL: Born March 18, 1975, in Kuopio, Finland. ... 5-10/180. ... Shoots left. ... Name pronounced KEE-moh TEE-muh-nehn.
TRANSACTIONS/CAREER NOTES: Selected by Los Angeles Kings in 10th round (11th Kings pick, 250th overall) of NHL entry draft (June 26, 1993).

		REGULAR SEASON							PLAYOFFS				
Season Team	League	Gms.	G	A	Pts.	PIM	+/-	PP	SH	Gms.	G	A	Pts.	PIM
91-92— KalPa Kuopio	Finland	5	0	0	0	0	...	...	...	—	—	—	—	—
92-93— KalPa Kuopio	Finland	33	0	2	2	4	...	...	...	—	—	—	—	—
93-94— KalPa Kuopio	Finland	46	6	7	13	55	...	...	...	—	—	—	—	—
94-95— TPS Turku	Finland	45	3	4	7	10	...	...	...	13	0	1	1	6
95-96— TPS Turku	Finland	48	3	21	24	22	...	...	...	9	1	2	3	12
96-97— TPS Turku	Finland	50	10	14	24	18	...	...	...	12	2	7	9	8

TINORDI, MARK　　　　　　　　　　D　　　　　　　　　　CAPITALS

PERSONAL: Born May 9, 1966, in Red Deer, Alta. ... 6-4/213. ... Shoots left. ... Name pronounced tuh-NOHR-dee.
TRANSACTIONS/CAREER NOTES: Signed as free agent by New York Rangers (January 4, 1987). ... Suffered abdominal pains (January 1988). ... Underwent left knee surgery (October 6, 1988). ... Traded by Rangers with D Paul Jerrard, C Mike Sullivan, RW Brett Barnett and third-round pick (C Murray Garbutt) in 1989 draft to Minnesota North Stars for LW Igor Liba, C Brian Lawton and rights to LW Eric Bennett (October 11, 1988). ... Bruised ribs (December 1988). ... Underwent knee surgery (April 1989). ... Suspended four games by NHL for cross-checking in a preseason game (September 27, 1989). ... Bruised shoulder (December 1989). ... Fined $500 by NHL for fighting (December 28, 1989). ... Suffered concussion (January 17, 1990); missed six games. ... Suspended 10 games by NHL for leaving penalty box to fight during a pre-season game (September 26, 1990). ... Suffered from foot palsy (October 15, 1991); missed 17 games. ... Sprained knee (January 19, 1993); missed four games. ... Broke collarbone (March 16, 1993); missed remainder of season. ... North Stars franchise moved from Minnesota to Dallas and renamed Stars for 1993-94 season. ... Suffered from the flu (December 27, 1993); missed one game. ... Fractured femur (February 23, 1994); missed 22 games. ... Traded by Stars with rights to D Rick Mrozik to Washington Capitals for D Kevin Hatcher (January 18, 1995). ... Bruised ribs (February 24, 1995); missed two games. ... Sprained knee (April 24, 1995); missed last four games of season. ... Suffered concussion (February 8, 1996); missed three games. ... Suffered concussion (February 15, 1996); missed eight games. ... Suffered from the flu (November 27, 1996); missed one game. ... Fractured ankle (January 9, 1997); missed 20 games. ... Strained hip (March 18, 1997); missed five games.
HONORS: Named to WHL (East) All-Star first team (1986-87). ... Played in NHL All-Star Game (1992).
MISCELLANEOUS: Captain of Minnesota North Stars (1991-92 and 1992-93). ... Captain of Dallas Stars (1993-94).

		REGULAR SEASON							PLAYOFFS				
Season Team	League	Gms.	G	A	Pts.	PIM	+/-	PP	SH	Gms.	G	A	Pts.	PIM
82-83— Lethbridge	WHL	64	0	4	4	50	...	...	...	20	1	1	2	6
83-84— Lethbridge	WHL	72	5	14	19	53	...	...	...	5	0	1	1	7
84-85— Lethbridge	WHL	58	10	15	25	134	...	...	...	4	0	2	2	12
85-86— Lethbridge	WHL	58	8	30	38	139	...	...	...	8	1	3	4	15
86-87— Calgary	WHL	61	29	37	66	148	...	...	...	—	—	—	—	—
— New Haven	AHL	2	0	0	0	2	...	...	...	2	0	0	0	0
87-88— New York Rangers	NHL	24	1	2	3	50	-5	0	0	—	—	—	—	—
— Colorado	IHL	41	8	19	27	150	...	...	...	11	1	5	6	31
88-89— Minnesota	NHL	47	2	3	5	107	-9	0	0	5	0	0	0	0
— Kalamazoo	IHL	10	0	0	0	35	...	...	...	—	—	—	—	—
89-90— Minnesota	NHL	66	3	7	10	240	0	1	0	7	0	1	1	16
90-91— Minnesota	NHL	69	5	27	32	189	1	1	0	23	5	6	11	78
91-92— Minnesota	NHL	63	4	24	28	179	-13	4	0	7	1	2	3	11
92-93— Minnesota	NHL	69	15	27	42	157	-1	7	0	—	—	—	—	—
93-94— Dallas	NHL	61	6	18	24	143	6	1	0	—	—	—	—	—
94-95— Washington	NHL	42	3	9	12	71	-5	2	0	1	0	0	0	2
95-96— Washington	NHL	71	3	10	13	113	26	2	0	6	0	0	0	16
96-97— Washington	NHL	56	2	6	8	118	3	0	0	—	—	—	—	—
NHL totals (10 years)		568	44	133	177	1367	3	18	0	49	6	9	15	123

TITOV, GERMAN　　　　　　　　　　C　　　　　　　　　　FLAMES

PERSONAL: Born October 16, 1965, in Borovsk, U.S.S.R. ... 6-1/201. ... Shoots left. ... Name pronounced GUHR-muhn TEE-tahv.
TRANSACTIONS/CAREER NOTES: Selected by Calgary Flames in 10th round (10th Flames pick, 252nd overall) of NHL entry draft (June 26, 1993). ... Fractured hand (December 31, 1993); missed four games. ... Bruised hand (February 18, 1994); missed two games. ... Bruised hand (April 2, 1994); missed one game. ... Played in Europe during 1994-95 NHL lockout. ... Pulled groin (March 28, 1995); missed eight games. ... Sore lower back (October 13, 1996); missed one game. ... Injured ankle (January 22, 1997); missed one game. ... Reinjured ankle (March 7, 1997); missed one game.
STATISTICAL PLATEAUS: Three-goal games: 1994-95 (1), 1996-97 (1). Total: 2.

		REGULAR SEASON							PLAYOFFS				
Season Team	League	Gms.	G	A	Pts.	PIM	+/-	PP	SH	Gms.	G	A	Pts.	PIM
82-83— Khimik	USSR	16	0	2	2	4	...	...	...	—	—	—	—	—
83-84— Khimik	USSR							Did not play.						
84-85— Khimik	USSR							Did not play.						
85-86— Khimik	USSR							Did not play.						
86-87— Khimik	USSR	23	1	0	1	10	...	...	...	—	—	—	—	—
87-88— Khimik	USSR	39	6	5	11	10	...	...	...	—	—	—	—	—
88-89— Khimik	USSR	44	10	3	13	24	...	...	...	—	—	—	—	—
89-90— Khimik	USSR	44	6	14	20	19	...	...	...	—	—	—	—	—
90-91— Khimik	USSR	45	13	11	24	28	...	...	...	—	—	—	—	—
91-92— Khimik	CIS	42	18	13	31	35	...	...	...	—	—	—	—	—
92-93— TPS Turku	Finland	47	25	19	44	49	...	...	...	—	—	—	—	—

T

Season Team	League	REGULAR SEASON								PLAYOFFS				
		Gms.	G	A	Pts.	PIM	+/-	PP	SH	Gms.	G	A	Pts.	PIM
93-94— Calgary	NHL	76	27	18	45	28	20	8	3	7	2	1	3	4
94-95— TPS Turku..................	Finland	14	6	6	12	20	...	...	...	—	—	—	—	—
— Calgary	NHL	40	12	12	24	16	6	3	2	7	5	3	8	10
95-96— Calgary	NHL	82	28	39	67	24	9	13	2	4	0	2	2	0
96-97— Calgary	NHL	79	22	30	52	36	-12	12	0	—	—	—	—	—
NHL totals (4 years)		277	89	99	188	104	23	36	7	18	7	6	13	14

TJARNQVIST, DANIEL   D   PANTHERS

PERSONAL: Born October 14, 1976, in Umea, Sweden. ... 6-2/176. ... Shoots left. ... Name pronounced TAHRN-kuh-vihst.
TRANSACTIONS/CAREER NOTES: Selected by Florida Panthers in fourth round (fifth Panthers pick, 88th overall) of NHL entry draft (July 8, 1995).

Season Team	League	REGULAR SEASON								PLAYOFFS				
		Gms.	G	A	Pts.	PIM	+/-	PP	SH	Gms.	G	A	Pts.	PIM
94-95— Rogle Angelholm	Sweden	33	2	4	6	2	...	...	...	—	—	—	—	—
95-96— Rogle Angelholm	Sweden	22	1	7	8	6	...	...	...	—	—	—	—	—
96-97— Jokerit Helsinki	Finland	44	3	8	11	4	...	...	...	9	0	3	3	4

TKACHUK, KEITH   LW   COYOTES

PERSONAL: Born March 28, 1972, in Melrose, Mass. ... 6-2/215. ... Shoots left. ... Full name: Keith Matthew Tkachuk. ... Name pronounced kuh-CHUHK.
HIGH SCHOOL: Malden (Mass.) Catholic.
COLLEGE: Boston University.
TRANSACTIONS/CAREER NOTES: Selected by Winnipeg Jets in first round (first Jets pick, 19th overall) of NHL entry draft (June 16, 1990). ... Lacerated forearm (November 12, 1993); missed one game. ... Strained groin (October 9, 1995); missed three games. ... Suffered concussion (November 26, 1995); missed one game. ... Suspended two games and fined $1000 by NHL for stick-swinging incident (March 16, 1996). ... Jets franchise moved to Phoenix and renamed Coyotes for 1996-97 season; NHL approved move on January 18, 1996. ... Suffered from the flu (March 5, 1997); missed one game.
HONORS: Named to Hockey East All-Rookie team (1990-91). ... Named to NHL All-Star second team (1994-95). ... Named to THE SPORTING NEWS All-Star first team (1995-96). ... Played in NHL All-Star Game (1997).
STATISTICAL PLATEAUS: Three-goal games: 1993-94 (1), 1996-97 (1). Total: 2. ... Four-goal games: 1995-96 (1), 1996-97 (1). Total: 2. ... Total hat tricks: 4.
MISCELLANEOUS: Captain of Winnipeg Jets (1993-94 and 1994-95). ... Captain of Phoenix Coyotes (1996-97).

Season Team	League	REGULAR SEASON								PLAYOFFS				
		Gms.	G	A	Pts.	PIM	+/-	PP	SH	Gms.	G	A	Pts.	PIM
88-89— Malden Catholic.........	Mass. H.S.	21	30	16	46	...	...	...	...	—	—	—	—	—
89-90— Malden Catholic.........	Mass. H.S.	6	12	14	26	...	...	...	...	—	—	—	—	—
90-91— Boston University	Hockey East	36	17	23	40	70	...	...	...	—	—	—	—	—
91-92— U.S. national team	Int'l	45	10	10	20	141	...	...	...	—	—	—	—	—
— U.S. Olympic team.....	Int'l	8	1	1	2	12	...	...	...	—	—	—	—	—
— Winnipeg	NHL	17	3	5	8	28	0	2	0	7	3	0	3	30
92-93— Winnipeg	NHL	83	28	23	51	201	-13	12	0	6	4	0	4	14
93-94— Winnipeg	NHL	84	41	40	81	255	-12	22	3	—	—	—	—	—
94-95— Winnipeg	NHL	48	22	29	51	152	-4	7	2	—	—	—	—	—
95-96— Winnipeg	NHL	76	50	48	98	156	11	20	2	6	1	2	3	22
96-97— Phoenix....................	NHL	81	*52	34	86	228	-1	9	2	7	6	0	6	7
NHL totals (6 years)		389	196	179	375	1020	-19	72	9	26	14	2	16	73

TOCCHET, RICK   RW   COYOTES

PERSONAL: Born April 9, 1964, in Scarborough, Ont. ... 6-0/210. ... Shoots right. ... Name pronounced TAH-keht.
TRANSACTIONS/CAREER NOTES: Selected by Philadelphia Flyers as underage junior in sixth round (fifth Flyers pick, 121st overall) of NHL entry draft (June 8, 1983). ... Bruised right knee (November 23, 1985); missed seven games. ... Separated left shoulder (February 1988). ... Suspended 10 games by NHL for injuring an opposing player during a fight (October 27, 1988). ... Hyperextended right knee (April 21, 1989). ... Suffered viral infection (November 1989). ... Tore tendon in left groin area (January 26, 1991); missed five games. ... Reinjured groin (March 1991); missed five games. ... Sprained knee (November 29, 1991); missed five games. ... Bruised heel (January 18, 1991); missed 10 games. ... Traded by Flyers with G Ken Wregget, D Kjell Samuelsson and third-round pick in 1992 draft to Pittsburgh Penguins for RW Mark Recchi, D Brian Benning and first-round pick (LW Jason Bowen) in 1992 draft (February 19, 1992). ... Fractured jaw (March 15, 1992); missed three games. ... Bruised left foot (October 10, 1992); missed two games. ... Bruised foot (February 8, 1993); missed one game. ... Bruised ribs (November 13, 1993); missed two games. ... Suffered back spasms (December 2, 1993); missed two games. ... Suffered back spasms (December 31, 1993); missed 12 games. ... Injured back (February 21, 1994); missed one game. ... Injured back (February 28, 1994); missed 10 games. ... Underwent back surgery (June 8, 1994). ... Traded by Penguins with second-round pick (RW Pavel Rosa) in 1995 draft to Los Angeles Kings for LW Luc Robitaille (July 29, 1994). ... Strained lower back (April 1, 1995); missed five games. ... Suffered back spasms (April 17, 1995); missed six games. ... Suffered back spasms (May 3, 1995); missed one game. ... Traded by Kings to Boston Bruins for LW Kevin Stevens (January 25, 1996). ... Bruised shoulder (November 7, 1996); missed two games. ... Strained knee (November 29, 1996); missed 17 games. ... Traded by Bruins with C Adam Oates and G Bill Ranford to Washington Capitals for G Jim Carey, C Jason Allison, C Anson Carter, third-round pick (RW Lee Goren) in 1997 draft and conditional pick in 1998 draft (March 1, 1997). ... Bruised foot (March 1, 1997); missed three games. ... Strained back (April 6, 1997); missed four games. ... Signed as free agent by Phoenix Coyotes (July 8, 1997).
HONORS: Played in NHL All-Star Game (1989-1991 and 1993).
RECORDS: Shares NHL All-Star Game record for fastest goal from start of period—19 seconds (1993, second period).
STATISTICAL PLATEAUS: Three-goal games: 1987-88 (2), 1988-89 (2), 1989-90 (1), 1990-91 (1), 1991-92 (1), 1992-93 (2), 1994-95 (1), 1995-96 (2). Total: 12. ... Four-goal games: 1987-88 (1), 1989-90 (1). Total: 2. ... Total hat tricks: 14.
MISCELLANEOUS: Member of Stanley Cup championship team (1992). ... Captain of Philadelphia Flyers (1991-92). ... Holds Philadelphia

Flyers all-time record for most penalty minutes (1,683). ... Failed to score on a penalty shot (vs. Craig Billington, January 6, 1987; vs. Geoff Sarjeant, March 18, 1996).

Season Team	League	REGULAR SEASON								PLAYOFFS				
		Gms.	G	A	Pts.	PIM	+/-	PP	SH	Gms.	G	A	Pts.	PIM
81-82— Sault Ste. Marie	OHL	59	7	15	22	184	...	...	...	11	1	1	2	28
82-83— Sault Ste. Marie	OHL	66	32	34	66	146	...	...	...	16	4	13	17	*67
83-84— Sault Ste. Marie	OHL	64	44	64	108	209	...	...	...	16	*22	14	†36	41
84-85— Philadelphia	NHL	75	14	25	39	181	6	0	0	19	3	4	7	72
85-86— Philadelphia	NHL	69	14	21	35	284	12	3	0	5	1	2	3	26
86-87— Philadelphia	NHL	69	21	26	47	288	16	1	1	26	11	10	21	72
87-88— Philadelphia	NHL	65	31	33	64	301	3	10	2	5	1	4	5	55
88-89— Philadelphia	NHL	66	45	36	81	183	-1	16	1	16	6	6	12	69
89-90— Philadelphia	NHL	75	37	59	96	196	4	15	1	—	—	—	—	—
90-91— Philadelphia	NHL	70	40	31	71	150	2	8	0	—	—	—	—	—
91-92— Philadelphia	NHL	42	13	16	29	102	3	4	0	—	—	—	—	—
— Pittsburgh	NHL	19	14	16	30	49	12	4	1	14	6	13	19	24
92-93— Pittsburgh	NHL	80	48	61	109	252	28	20	4	12	7	6	13	24
93-94— Pittsburgh	NHL	51	14	26	40	134	-15	5	1	6	2	3	5	20
94-95— Los Angeles	NHL	36	18	17	35	70	-8	7	1	—	—	—	—	—
95-96— Los Angeles	NHL	44	13	23	36	117	3	4	0	—	—	—	—	—
— Boston	NHL	27	16	8	24	64	7	6	0	5	4	0	4	21
96-97— Boston	NHL	40	16	14	30	67	-3	3	0	—	—	—	—	—
— Washington	NHL	13	5	5	10	31	0	1	0	—	—	—	—	—
NHL totals (13 years)		841	359	417	776	2469	69	107	12	108	41	48	89	383

TODD, KEVIN — C — MIGHTY DUCKS

PERSONAL: Born May 4, 1968, in Winnipeg. ... 5-10/180. ... Shoots left. ... Full name: Kevin Lee Todd.
HIGH SCHOOL: Tec Voc (Winnipeg).
TRANSACTIONS/CAREER NOTES: Stretched knee ligaments (December 1985). ... Selected by New Jersey Devils as underage junior in seventh round (seventh Devils pick, 129th overall) of NHL entry draft (June 21, 1986). ... Injured thigh (October 31, 1992); missed one game. ... Reinjured thigh (November 13, 1992); missed three games. ... Bruised shoulder (December 15, 1992); missed five games. ... Traded by Devils with LW Zdeno Ciger to Edmonton Oilers for C Bernie Nicholls (January 13, 1993). ... Separated left shoulder (March 14, 1993); missed remainder of season. ... Traded by Oilers to Chicago Blackhawks for D Adam Bennett (October 7, 1993). ... Injured knee (November 18, 1993); missed 12 games. ... Traded by Blackhawks to Los Angeles Kings for fourth-round pick (D Steve McLaren) in 1994 draft (March 21, 1994). ... Tore cartilage in knee (March 9, 1995); missed 15 games. ... Sprained left ankle (January 22, 1996); missed three games. ... Injured back (April 3, 1996); missed two games. ... Signed as free agent by Pittsburgh Penguins (July 10, 1996). ... Claimed on waivers by Mighty Ducks of Anaheim (October 4, 1996). ... Suffered tendinitis in elbow (January 31, 1997); missed seven games.
HONORS: Won Les Cunningham Plaque (1990-91). ... Won John B. Sollenberger Trophy (1990-91). ... Named to AHL All-Star first team (1990-91). ... Named to NHL All-Rookie team (1991-92).

Season Team	League	REGULAR SEASON								PLAYOFFS				
		Gms.	G	A	Pts.	PIM	+/-	PP	SH	Gms.	G	A	Pts.	PIM
85-86— Prince Albert	WHL	55	14	25	39	19	...	...	...	20	7	6	13	29
86-87— Prince Albert	WHL	71	39	46	85	92	...	...	...	8	2	5	7	17
87-88— Prince Albert	WHL	72	49	72	121	83	...	...	...	10	8	11	19	27
88-89— New Jersey	NHL	1	0	0	0	0	-1	0	0	—	—	—	—	—
— Utica	AHL	78	26	45	71	62	...	...	...	4	2	0	2	6
89-90— Utica	AHL	71	18	36	54	72	...	...	...	5	2	4	6	2
90-91— Utica	AHL	75	37	*81	*118	75	...	...	...	—	—	—	—	—
— New Jersey	NHL	1	0	0	0	0	-1	0	0	1	0	0	0	6
91-92— New Jersey	NHL	80	21	42	63	69	8	2	0	7	3	2	5	8
92-93— New Jersey	NHL	30	5	5	10	16	-4	0	0	—	—	—	—	—
— Utica	AHL	2	2	1	3	0	...	...	...	—	—	—	—	—
— Edmonton	NHL	25	4	9	13	10	-5	0	0	—	—	—	—	—
93-94— Chicago	NHL	35	5	6	11	16	-2	1	0	—	—	—	—	—
— Los Angeles	NHL	12	3	8	11	8	-1	3	0	—	—	—	—	—
94-95— Los Angeles	NHL	33	3	8	11	12	-5	0	0	—	—	—	—	—
95-96— Los Angeles	NHL	74	16	27	43	38	6	0	2	—	—	—	—	—
96-97— Anaheim	NHL	65	9	21	30	44	-7	0	0	4	0	0	0	2
NHL totals (9 years)		356	66	126	192	213	-12	6	2	12	3	2	5	16

TOMS, JEFF — C — LIGHTNING

PERSONAL: Born June 4, 1974, in Swift Current, Sask. ... 6-5/200. ... Shoots left.
TRANSACTIONS/CAREER NOTES: Selected by New Jersey Devils in ninth round (10th Devils pick, 210th overall) of NHL entry draft (June 26, 1993). ... Traded by Devils to Tampa Bay Lightning for fourth-round pick (traded to Calgary) in 1994 draft (May 31, 1994).

Season Team	League	REGULAR SEASON								PLAYOFFS				
		Gms.	G	A	Pts.	PIM	+/-	PP	SH	Gms.	G	A	Pts.	PIM
91-92— Sault Ste. Marie	OHL	36	9	5	14	0	...	...	...	16	0	1	1	2
92-93— Sault Ste. Marie	OHL	59	16	23	39	20	...	...	...	16	4	4	8	7
93-94— Sault Ste. Marie	OHL	64	52	45	97	19	...	...	...	14	11	4	15	2
94-95— Atlanta	IHL	40	7	8	15	10	...	...	...	4	0	0	0	4
95-96— Atlanta	IHL	68	16	18	34	18	...	...	...	1	0	0	0	0
— Tampa Bay	NHL	1	0	0	0	0	0	0	0	—	—	—	—	—
96-97— Adirondack	AHL	37	11	16	27	8	...	...	...	4	1	2	3	0
— Tampa Bay	NHL	34	2	8	10	10	2	0	0	—	—	—	—	—
NHL totals (2 years)		35	2	8	10	10	2	0	0					

T

TOPOROWSKI, SHAYNE RW MAPLE LEAFS

PERSONAL: Born August 6, 1975, in Prince Albert, Sask. ... 6-2/210. ... Shoots right. ... Name pronounced TAHP-uhr-OW-skee.
HIGH SCHOOL: Carlton Comprehensive (Paddockwood, Sask.).
TRANSACTIONS/CAREER NOTES: Selected by Los Angeles Kings in second round (first Kings pick, 42nd overall) of NHL entry draft (June 26, 1993). ... Traded by Kings with RW Dixon Ward, C Guy Leveque and C Kelly Fairchild to Toronto Maple Leafs for LW Eric Lacroix, D Chris Snell and fourth-round pick (C Eric Belanger) in 1996 draft (October 3, 1994).

					REGULAR SEASON						PLAYOFFS			
Season Team	League	Gms.	G	A	Pts.	PIM	+/-	PP	SH	Gms.	G	A	Pts.	PIM
91-92— Prince Albert.............	WHL	6	2	0	2	2	...	...	...	7	2	1	3	6
92-93— Prince Albert.............	WHL	72	25	32	57	235	...	...	...	—	—	—	—	—
93-94— Prince Albert.............	WHL	68	37	45	82	183	...	...	...	—	—	—	—	—
94-95— Prince Albert.............	WHL	72	36	38	74	151	...	...	...	15	10	8	18	25
95-96— St. John's.................	AHL	72	11	26	37	216	...	...	...	4	1	1	2	4
96-97— St. John's.................	AHL	72	20	17	37	210	...	...	...	11	3	2	5	16
— Toronto	NHL	3	0	0	0	7	0	0	0	—	—	—	—	—
NHL totals (1 year)		3	0	0	0	7	0	0	0					

TORCHIA, MIKE G MIGHTY DUCKS

PERSONAL: Born February 23, 1972, in Toronto. ... 5-11/225. ... Catches left. ... Name pronounced TOHRK-yuh.
TRANSACTIONS/CAREER NOTES: Broke ankle (July 1989). ... Selected by Minnesota North Stars in fourth round (second North Stars pick, 74th overall) of NHL entry draft (June 22, 1991). ... North Stars franchise moved from Minnesota to Dallas and renamed Stars for 1993-94 season. ... Traded by Stars to Washington Capitals for cash (July 14, 1995). ... Traded by Capitals to Mighty Ducks of Anaheim for LW Todd Krygier (March 8, 1996).
HONORS: Won Hap Emms Memorial Trophy (1989-90). ... Named to Memorial Cup All-Star team (1989-90). ... Named to OHL All-Star first team (1990-91).

				REGULAR SEASON							PLAYOFFS					
Season Team	League	Gms.	Min	W	L	T	GA	SO	Avg.	Gms.	Min.	W	L	GA	SO	Avg.
88-89—Kitchener	OHL	30	1672	14	9	4	112	0	4.02	2	126	0	2	8	0	3.81
89-90—Kitchener	OHL	40	2280	25	11	2	136	1	3.58	*17	*1023	*11	6	60	0	3.52
90-91—Kitchener	OHL	57	*3317	25	24	7	219	0	3.96	6	382	2	4	30	0	4.71
91-92—Kitchener	OHL	55	3042	25	24	3	203	1	4.00	14	900	7	7	47	0	3.13
92-93—Can. national team....	Int'l	5	300	5	0	0	11	1	2.20	—	—	—	—	—	—	—
—Kalamazoo....................	IHL	48	2729	19	17	‡9	173	0	3.80	—	—	—	—	—	—	—
93-94—Kalamazoo.................	IHL	43	2168	23	12	‡2	133	0	3.68	4	221	1	2	14	†1	3.80
94-95—Kalamazoo.................	IHL	41	2140	19	14	‡5	106	†3	2.97	6	257	0	4	17	0	3.97
—Dallas.........................	NHL	6	327	3	2	1	18	0	3.30	—	—	—	—	—	—	—
95-96—Portland......................	AHL	12	576	2	6	2	46	0	4.79	—	—	—	—	—	—	—
—Hampton Roads............	ECHL	5	260	2	2	‡0	17	0	3.92	—	—	—	—	—	—	—
—Michigan......................	IHL	1	60	1	0	‡0	1	0	1.00	—	—	—	—	—	—	—
—Orlando........................	IHL	7	341	3	1	‡1	17	0	2.99	—	—	—	—	—	—	—
—Baltimore.....................	AHL	5	256	2	1	1	18	0	4.22	1	40	0	0	0	0	0.00
96-97—Fort Wayne.................	IHL	57	2970	20	*31	‡3	172	1	3.47	—	—	—	—	—	—	—
—Baltimore.....................	AHL	—	—	—	—	—	—	—	—	1	40	0	0	4	0	6.00
NHL totals (1 year)		6	327	3	2	1	18	0	3.30							

TRAVERSE, PATRICK D SENATORS

PERSONAL: Born March 14, 1974, in Montreal. ... 6-3/190. ... Shoots left.
TRANSACTIONS/CAREER NOTES: Selected by Ottawa Senators in third round (third Senators pick, 50th overall) of NHL entry draft (June 20, 1992).

					REGULAR SEASON						PLAYOFFS			
Season Team	League	Gms.	G	A	Pts.	PIM	+/-	PP	SH	Gms.	G	A	Pts.	PIM
91-92— Shawinigan	QMJHL	59	3	11	14	12	...	...	...	10	0	0	0	4
92-93— St. Jean.....................	QMJHL	68	6	30	36	24	...	...	...	4	0	1	1	2
— New Haven................	AHL	2	0	0	0	2	...	...	...	—	—	—	—	—
93-94— Prin. Edward Island ...	AHL	3	0	1	1	2	...	...	...	—	—	—	—	—
— St. Jean....................	QMJHL	66	15	37	52	30	...	...	...	5	0	4	4	4
94-95— Prin. Edward Island ...	AHL	70	5	13	18	19	...	...	...	7	0	2	2	0
95-96— Prin. Edward Island ...	AHL	55	4	21	25	32	...	...	...	5	1	2	3	2
— Ottawa	NHL	5	0	0	0	2	-1	0	0	—	—	—	—	—
96-97— Worcester	AHL	24	0	4	4	23	...	...	...	—	—	—	—	—
— Grand Rapids............	IHL	10	2	1	3	10	...	...	...	2	0	1	1	2
NHL totals (1 year)		5	0	0	0	2	-1	0	0					

TREBIL, DAN D MIGHTY DUCKS

PERSONAL: Born April 10, 1974, in Bloomington, Minn. ... 6-2/210. ... Shoots right. ... Name pronounced TREH-bihl.
HIGH SCHOOL: Thomas Jefferson (Bloomington, Minn.).
COLLEGE: Minnesota.
TRANSACTIONS/CAREER NOTES: Selected by New Jersey Devils in sixth round (seventh Devils pick, 138th overall) of NHL entry draft (June 20, 1992). ... Signed as free agent by Mighty Ducks of Anaheim (May 30, 1996).
HONORS: Named to NCAA All-America West second team (1995-96). ... Named to WCHA All-Star second team (1995-96).

Season Team	League	Gms.	G	A	Pts.	PIM	+/-	PP	SH	Gms.	G	A	Pts.	PIM
89-90— Thomas Jefferson	Minn. H.S.	22	3	6	9	10	...	...	...	—	—	—	—	—
90-91— Thomas Jefferson	Minn. H.S.	23	4	12	16	8	...	...	...	—	—	—	—	—
91-92— Thomas Jefferson	Minn. H.S.	28	7	26	33	6	...	...	...	—	—	—	—	—
92-93— Univ. of Minnesota	WCHA	36	2	11	13	16	...	...	...	—	—	—	—	—
93-94— Univ. of Minnesota	WCHA	42	1	21	22	24	...	...	...	—	—	—	—	—
94-95— Univ. of Minnesota	WCHA	44	10	33	43	10	...	...	...	—	—	—	—	—
95-96— Univ. of Minnesota	WCHA	42	11	35	46	36	...	...	...	—	—	—	—	—
96-97— Baltimore	AHL	49	4	20	24	38	...	...	...	—	—	—	—	—
— Anaheim	NHL	29	3	3	6	23	5	0	0	9	0	1	1	6
NHL totals (1 year)		29	3	3	6	23	5	0	0	9	0	1	1	6

TREFILOV, ANDREI   G   SABRES

PERSONAL: Born August 31, 1969, in Moscow, U.S.S.R. ... 6-0/190. ... Catches left. ... Name pronounced AHN-dray TREH-fih-lahf.

TRANSACTIONS/CAREER NOTES: Selected by Calgary Flames in 12th round (14th Flames pick, 261st overall) of NHL entry draft (June 22, 1991). ... Twisted right knee ligament (February 2, 1994); missed 23 games. ... Signed as free agent by Buffalo Sabres (July 13, 1995). ... Sprained right knee (December 23, 1995); missed 18 games. ... Suffered labrum tear in right shoulder (December 18, 1996); underwent arthroscopic surgery on right shoulder (December 21, 1996) and missed remainder of regular season.

MISCELLANEOUS: Member of gold-medal-winning Unified Olympic team (1992). ... Stopped a penalty shot attempt (vs. Jeremy Roenick, March 7, 1995).

Season Team	League	Gms.	Min	W	L	T	GA	SO	Avg.	Gms.	Min.	W	L	GA	SO	Avg.
90-91— Dynamo Moscow	USSR	20	1070	...	...	...	36	0	2.02	—	—	—	—	—	—	—
91-92— Dynamo Moscow	CIS	28	1326	...	...	...	35	0	1.58	—	—	—	—	—	—	—
— Unified Olympic team	Int'l	4	38	...	...	...	2	2	3.16	—	—	—	—	—	—	—
92-93— Salt Lake City	IHL	44	2536	23	17	‡0	135	0	3.19	—	—	—	—	—	—	—
— Calgary	NHL	1	65	0	0	1	5	0	4.62	—	—	—	—	—	—	—
93-94— Saint John	AHL	28	1629	10	10	7	93	0	3.43	—	—	—	—	—	—	—
— Calgary	NHL	11	623	3	4	2	26	2	2.50	—	—	—	—	—	—	—
94-95— Saint John	AHL	7	383	1	5	1	20	0	3.13	—	—	—	—	—	—	—
— Calgary	NHL	6	236	0	3	0	16	0	4.07	—	—	—	—	—	—	—
95-96— Buffalo	NHL	22	1094	8	8	1	64	0	3.51	—	—	—	—	—	—	—
— Rochester	AHL	5	299	4	1	0	13	0	2.61	—	—	—	—	—	—	—
96-97— Buffalo	NHL	3	159	0	2	0	10	0	3.77	1	5	0	0	0	0	0.00
NHL totals (5 years)		43	2177	11	17	4	121	2	3.33	1	5	0	0	0	0	0.00

TREMBLAY, YANNICK   D   MAPLE LEAFS

PERSONAL: Born November 15, 1975, in Pointe-aux-Trembles, Que. ... 6-2/185. ... Shoots right.

COLLEGE: St. Thomas (N.B.).

TRANSACTIONS/CAREER NOTES: Selected by Toronto Maple Leafs in sixth round (fourth Maple Leafs pick, 145th overall) of NHL entry draft (July 8, 1995).

Season Team	League	Gms.	G	A	Pts.	PIM	+/-	PP	SH	Gms.	G	A	Pts.	PIM
93-94— St. Thomas Univ.	AUAA	25	2	3	5	10	...	...	...	—	—	—	—	—
94-95— Beauport	QMJHL	70	10	32	42	22	...	...	...	17	6	8	14	6
95-96— Beauport	QMJHL	61	12	33	45	42	...	...	...	20	3	16	19	18
— St. John's	AHL	3	0	1	1	0	...	...	...	—	—	—	—	—
96-97— Sherbrooke	QMJHL	42	21	25	46	212	...	...	...	—	—	—	—	—
— Saint John	AHL	3	0	1	1	0	...	...	...	—	—	—	—	—
— Toronto	NHL	5	0	0	0	0	-4	0	0	—	—	—	—	—
NHL totals (1 year)		5	0	0	0	0	-4	0	0					

TREPANIER, PASCAL   AVALANCHE

PERSONAL: Born April 9, 1973, in Gaspe, Que. ... 6-0/205. ... Shoots right. ... Name pronounced TREH-puhn-yeh.

TRANSACTIONS/CAREER NOTES: Loaned by Kalamazoo of IHL to Dayton of ECHL (December 6, 1994). ... Returned by Dayton to Kalamazoo (December 12, 1994). ... Loaned by Dayton of ECHL to Cornwall of AHL (February 28, 1995). ... Signed as free agent by Colorado Avalanche (August 30, 1996).

HONORS: Named to AHL All-Star second team (1996-97).

Season Team	League	Gms.	G	A	Pts.	PIM	+/-	PP	SH	Gms.	G	A	Pts.	PIM
90-91— Hull	QMJHL	46	3	3	6	56	...	...	...	4	0	2	2	7
91-92— Trois-Rivieres	QMJHL	53	4	18	22	125	...	...	...	15	3	5	8	21
92-93— Sherbrooke	QMJHL	59	15	33	48	130	...	...	...	15	5	7	12	36
93-94— Sherbrooke	QMJHL	48	16	41	57	67	...	...	...	12	1	8	9	14
94-95— Cornwall	AHL	4	0	0	0	9	...	...	...	—	—	—	—	—
— Dayton	ECHL	36	16	28	44	113	...	...	...	—	—	—	—	—
— Kalamazoo	IHL	14	1	2	3	47	...	...	...	—	—	—	—	—
95-96— Cornwall	AHL	70	13	20	33	142	...	...	...	8	1	2	3	24
96-97— Hershey	AHL	73	14	39	53	151	...	...	...	23	6	13	19	59

TRNKA, PAVEL   D   MIGHTY DUCKS

PERSONAL: Born July 27, 1976, in Plzen, Czechoslovakia. ... 6-3/200. ... Shoots left. ... Name pronounced TRIHN-kuh.

TRANSACTIONS/CAREER NOTES: Selected by Mighty Ducks of Anaheim in fifth round (fifth Mighty Ducks pick, 106th overall) of NHL entry draft (June 29, 1994).

T

Season Team	League	Gms.	G	A	Pts.	PIM	+/-	PP	SH		Gms.	G	A	Pts.	PIM
92-93 — Skoda Plzen	Czech. Jrs.				Statistics unavailable.										
93-94 — Skoda Plzen	Czech Rep.	12	0	1	1	...	...	...			—	—	—	—	—
94-95 — HC Kladno	Czech Rep.	28	0	5	5	...	...	...			—	—	—	—	—
— Skoda Plzen	Czech Rep.	6	0	0	0	...	...	...			6	0	0	0	0
95-96 — Baltimore	AHL	69	2	6	8	44	...	...			6	0	0	0	2
96-97 — Baltimore	AHL	69	6	14	20	86	...	...			3	0	0	0	2

TSULYGIN, NIKOLAI   D   MIGHTY DUCKS

PERSONAL: Born May 29, 1975, in Ufa, U.S.S.R. ... 6-3/210. ... Shoots right. ... Name pronounced tsoo-LEE-gihn.
TRANSACTIONS/CAREER NOTES: Selected by Mighty Ducks of Anaheim in second round (second Mighty Ducks pick, 30th overall) of NHL entry draft (June 26, 1993).

		REGULAR SEASON									PLAYOFFS				
Season Team	League	Gms.	G	A	Pts.	PIM	+/-	PP	SH		Gms.	G	A	Pts.	PIM
92-93 — Salavat Yulayev Ufa	CIS	42	5	4	9	21	...	...	...		2	0	0	0	0
93-94 — Salavat Yulayev Ufa	CIS	43	0	14	14	24	...	...	...		5	0	1	1	0
94-95 — CSKA Moscow	CIS	16	0	0	0	12	...	...	...		—	—	—	—	—
— Salavat Yulayev Ufa	CIS	13	2	2	4	10	...	...	...		7	0	0	0	4
95-96 — Baltimore	AHL	78	3	18	21	109	...	...	...		12	0	5	5	18
96-97 — Fort Wayne	IHL	5	2	1	3	8	...	...	...		—	—	—	—	—
— Anaheim	NHL	22	0	1	1	8	-5	0	0		—	—	—	—	—
— Baltimore	AHL	17	4	13	17	8	...	...	...		3	0	0	0	0
NHL totals (1 year)		22	0	1	1	8	-5	0	0						

TSYPLAKOV, VLADIMIR   LW   KINGS

PERSONAL: Born April 18, 1969, in Inta, U.S.S.R. ... 6-2/194. ... Shoots left. ... Name pronounced SIHP-luh-kahf.
TRANSACTIONS/CAREER NOTES: Selected by Los Angeles Kings in third round (fourth Kings pick, 59th overall) of NHL entry draft (July 8, 1995). ... Underwent reconstructive surgery on right shoulder (December 14, 1995); missed 45 games. ... Strained abdominal muscle prior to 1996-97 season; missed first nine games of season. ... Strained groin (February 13, 1997); missed three games.

		REGULAR SEASON									PLAYOFFS				
Season Team	League	Gms.	G	A	Pts.	PIM	+/-	PP	SH		Gms.	G	A	Pts.	PIM
88-89 — Dynamo Minsk	USSR	19	6	1	7	4	...	...	...		—	—	—	—	—
89-90 — Dynamo Minsk	USSR	47	11	6	17	20	...	...	...		—	—	—	—	—
90-91 — Dynamo Minsk	USSR	28	6	5	11	14	...	...	...		—	—	—	—	—
91-92 — Dynamo Minsk	CIS	29	10	9	19	16	...	...	...		—	—	—	—	—
92-93 — Detroit	Col.HL	44	33	43	76	20	...	...	...		6	5	4	9	6
— Indianapolis	IHL	11	6	7	13	4	...	...	...		5	1	1	2	2
93-94 — Fort Wayne	IHL	63	31	32	63	51	...	...	...		14	6	8	14	16
94-95 — Fort Wayne	IHL	79	38	40	78	39	...	...	...		4	2	4	6	2
95-96 — Las Vegas	IHL	9	5	6	11	4	...	...	...		—	—	—	—	—
— Los Angeles	NHL	23	5	5	10	4	1	0	0		—	—	—	—	—
96-97 — Los Angeles	NHL	67	16	23	39	12	8	1	0		—	—	—	—	—
NHL totals (2 years)		90	21	28	49	16	9	1	0						

TUCKER, DARCY   C   CANADIENS

PERSONAL: Born March 15, 1975, in Castor, Alta. ... 5-10/179. ... Shoots left.
TRANSACTIONS/CAREER NOTES: Selected by Montreal Canadiens in sixth round (eighth Canadiens pick, 151st overall) of NHL entry draft (June 26, 1993). ... Bruised knee (December 16, 1996); missed one game.
HONORS: Won Stafford Smythe Memorial Trophy (1993-94). ... Named to Can.HL All-Star first team (1993-94). ... Named to WHL (West) All-Star first team (1993-94 and 1994-95). ... Named to Memorial Cup All-Star team (1993-94 and 1994-95). ... Won Dudley (Red) Garrett Memorial Trophy (1995-96).

		REGULAR SEASON									PLAYOFFS				
Season Team	League	Gms.	G	A	Pts.	PIM	+/-	PP	SH		Gms.	G	A	Pts.	PIM
91-92 — Kamloops	WHL	26	3	10	13	42	...	...	...		9	0	1	1	16
92-93 — Kamloops	WHL	67	31	58	89	155	...	...	...		13	7	6	13	34
93-94 — Kamloops	WHL	66	52	88	140	143	...	...	...		19	9	*18	*27	43
94-95 — Kamloops	WHL	64	64	73	137	94	...	...	...		21	16	15	31	19
95-96 — Fredericton	AHL	74	29	64	93	174	...	...	...		7	7	3	10	14
— Montreal	NHL	3	0	0	0	0	-1	0	0		—	—	—	—	—
96-97 — Montreal	NHL	73	7	13	20	110	-5	1	0		4	0	0	0	0
NHL totals (2 years)		76	7	13	20	110	-6	1	0		4	0	0	0	0

TUGNUTT, RON   G   SENATORS

PERSONAL: Born October 22, 1967, in Scarborough, Ont. ... 5-11/155. ... Catches left. ... Full name: Ronald Frederick Bradley Tugnutt.
TRANSACTIONS/CAREER NOTES: Selected by Quebec Nordiques as underage junior in fourth round (fourth Nordiques pick, 81st overall) of NHL entry draft (June 21, 1986). ... Sprained ankle (March 1989). ... Sprained knee (January 13, 1990). ... Injured hamstring (January 29, 1991); missed 11 games. ... Traded by Nordiques with LW Brad Zavisha to Edmonton Oilers for LW Martin Rucinsky (March 10, 1992). ... Selected by Mighty Ducks of Anaheim in NHL expansion draft (June 24, 1993). ... Traded by Mighty Ducks to Montreal Canadiens for C Stephan Lebeau (February 20, 1994). ... Strained knee (January 28, 1995); missed five games. ... Signed as free agent Washington Capitals prior to 1995-96 season. ... Signed as free agent by Ottawa Senators (July 17, 1996).

HONORS: Won F.W. (Dinty) Moore Trophy (1984-85). ... Shared Dave Pinkney Trophy with Kay Whitmore (1985-86). ... Named to OHL All-Star first team (1986-87).
MISCELLANEOUS: Stopped a penalty shot attempt (vs. Dave McLlwain, October 12, 1991; vs. Cam Neely, October 15, 1993; vs. Brett Harkins, March 22, 1997). ... Allowed a penalty shot goal (vs. Benoit Hogue, February 16, 1993). ... Shares Ottawa Senators all-time record for shutouts (3).

			REGULAR SEASON							PLAYOFFS						
Season Team	League	Gms.	Min	W	L	T	GA	SO	Avg.	Gms.	Min.	W	L	GA	SO	Avg.
84-85—Peterborough...............	OHL	18	938	7	4	2	59	0	3.77	—	—	—	—	—	—	—
85-86—Peterborough...............	OHL	26	1543	18	7	0	74	1	2.88	3	133	2	0	6	0	2.71
86-87—Peterborough...............	OHL	31	1891	21	7	2	88	2	*2.79	6	374	3	3	21	1	3.37
87-88—Quebec	NHL	6	284	2	3	0	16	0	3.38	—	—	—	—	—	—	—
—Fredericton	AHL	34	1962	20	9	4	118	1	3.61	4	204	1	2	11	0	3.24
88-89—Quebec	NHL	26	1367	10	10	3	82	0	3.60	—	—	—	—	—	—	—
—Halifax	AHL	24	1368	14	7	2	79	1	3.46	—	—	—	—	—	—	—
89-90—Quebec	NHL	35	1978	5	24	3	152	0	4.61	—	—	—	—	—	—	—
—Halifax	AHL	6	366	1	5	0	23	0	3.77	—	—	—	—	—	—	—
90-91—Halifax	AHL	2	100	0	1	0	8	0	4.80	—	—	—	—	—	—	—
—Quebec	NHL	56	3144	12	†29	10	212	0	4.05	—	—	—	—	—	—	—
91-92—Quebec	NHL	30	1583	6	17	3	106	1	4.02	—	—	—	—	—	—	—
—Halifax	AHL	8	447	3	3	1	30	0	4.03	—	—	—	—	—	—	—
—Edmonton	NHL	3	124	1	1	0	10	0	4.84	2	60	0	0	3	0	3.00
92-93—Edmonton	NHL	26	1338	9	12	2	93	0	4.17	—	—	—	—	—	—	—
93-94—Anaheim	NHL	28	1520	10	15	1	76	1	3.00	—	—	—	—	—	—	—
—Montreal	NHL	8	378	2	3	1	24	0	3.81	1	59	0	1	5	0	5.08
94-95—Montreal	NHL	7	346	1	3	1	18	0	3.12	—	—	—	—	—	—	—
95-96—Portland......................	AHL	58	3067	21	23	6	171	2	3.35	13	781	7	6	36	1	2.77
96-97—Ottawa	NHL	37	1991	17	15	1	93	3	2.80	7	425	3	4	14	1	1.98
NHL totals (10 years)		262	14053	75	132	25	882	5	3.77	10	544	3	5	22	1	2.43

TUOMAINEN, MARKO   RW   OILERS

PERSONAL: Born April 25, 1972, in Kuopio, Finland. ... 6-3/203. ... Shoots right. ... Name pronounced too-oh-MIGH-nehn.
COLLEGE: Clarkson (N.Y.).
TRANSACTIONS/CAREER NOTES: Selected by Edmonton Oilers in ninth round (10th Oilers pick, 205th overall) of NHL entry draft (June 20, 1992).
HONORS: Named to ECAC All-Star first team (1992-93 and 1994-95). ... Named to NCAA All-America East second team (1994-95).

			REGULAR SEASON							PLAYOFFS			
Season Team	League	Gms.	G	A	Pts.	PIM	+/-	PP	SH	Gms.	G	A	Pts.	PIM
89-90—KalPa Kuopio	Finland	5	0	0	0	0	...	...	...	—	—	—	—	—
90-91—KalPa Kuopio	Finland	30	2	1	3	2	...	...	...	8	0	0	0	6
91-92—Clarkson......................	ECAC	29	11	13	24	34	...	...	...	—	—	—	—	—
92-93—Clarkson......................	ECAC	35	25	30	55	26	...	...	...	—	—	—	—	—
93-94—Clarkson......................	ECAC	34	23	29	52	60	...	...	...	—	—	—	—	—
94-95—Clarkson......................	ECAC	37	23	37	60	34	...	...	...	—	—	—	—	—
—Edmonton	NHL	4	0	0	0	0	0	0	0	—	—	—	—	—
95-96—Cape Breton	AHL	58	25	35	60	71	...	...	...	—	—	—	—	—
96-97—Hamilton	AHL	79	31	21	52	130	...	...	...	22	7	5	12	4
NHL totals (1 year)		4	0	0	0	0	0	0	0	—	—	—	—	—

TURCO, MARTY   G   STARS

PERSONAL: Born August 13, 1975, in Sault Ste. Marie, Ont. ... 5-11/160. ... Catches left.
HIGH SCHOOL: St. Mary's College (Sault Ste. Marie, Ont.).
COLLEGE: Michigan.
TRANSACTIONS/CAREER NOTES: Selected by Dallas Stars in fifth round (fourth Stars pick, 124th overall) of NHL entry draft (June 29, 1994).
HONORS: Named CCHA Rookie of the Year (1994-95). ... Named to NCAA All-Tournament team (1995-96). ... Named to CCHA All-Star first team (1996-1997). ... Named to NCAA All-America West first team (1996-97).

			REGULAR SEASON							PLAYOFFS						
Season Team	League	Gms.	Min	W	L	T	GA	SO	Avg.	Gms.	Min.	W	L	GA	SO	Avg.
93-94—Cambridge Jr. B............	OHA	34	1937	...	...	...	114	0	3.53	—	—	—	—	—	—	—
94-95—Univ. of Michigan	CCHA	37	2064	27	7	1	95	1	2.76	—	—	—	—	—	—	—
95-96—Univ. of Michigan	CCHA	42	2334	34	7	1	84	5	2.16	—	—	—	—	—	—	—
96-97—Univ. of Michigan	CCHA	41	2296	33	4	4	87	4	2.27	—	—	—	—	—	—	—

TURCOTTE, DARREN   C   BLUES

PERSONAL: Born March 2, 1968, in Boston. ... 6-0/190. ... Shoots left. ... Name pronounced TUHR-kaht.
TRANSACTIONS/CAREER NOTES: Selected by New York Rangers as underage junior in sixth round (sixth Rangers pick, 114th overall) of NHL entry draft (June 21, 1986). ... Separated shoulder (October 1987); missed 34 games. ... Suffered concussion (March 1989). ... Sprained left ankle (October 1989). ... Injured knee (April 11, 1990). ... Broke left foot (April 27, 1990). ... Suffered contusion above left ankle (November 13, 1991); missed two games. ... Bruised right foot (March 4, 1992); missed one game. ... Reinjured right foot (March 9, 1992); missed two games. ... Sprained ankle (January 2, 1993); missed one game. ... Suffered hairline fracture in foot (February 10, 1993); missed 11 games. ... Traded by Rangers with D James Patrick to Hartford Whalers for RW Steve Larmer, LW Nick Kypreos and sixth-round pick (C Yuri Litvinov) in 1994 draft (November 2, 1993). ... Underwent medial collateral ligament surgery (December 9, 1993); missed 50 games. ... Traded by Whalers to Winnipeg Jets for RW Nelson Emerson (October 6, 1995). ... Injured hand (December 19, 1995); missed one game. ... Strained right thumb (February 13, 1996); missed six games. ... Traded by Jets with second-round pick (traded to Chicago) in 1996 draft to

San Jose Sharks for C Craig Janney (March 18, 1996). ... Injured back (April 6, 1996); missed one game. ... Strained knee (October 5, 1996); missed three games. ... Injured ear (January 24, 1997); missed 13 games. ... Suffered from an illness (March 11, 1997); missed one game. ... Traded by Sharks to St. Louis Blues for LW Stephane Matteau (July 25, 1997).

HONORS: Played in NHL All-Star Game (1991).

STATISTICAL PLATEAUS: Three-goal games: 1988-89 (1), 1989-90 (1), 1990-91 (1), 1991-92 (1). Total: 4.

MISCELLANEOUS: Failed to score on a penalty shot (vs. Wendell Young, December 29, 1991).

			REGULAR SEASON								PLAYOFFS			
Season Team	League	Gms.	G	A	Pts.	PIM	+/-	PP	SH	Gms.	G	A	Pts.	PIM
84-85— North Bay	OHL	62	33	32	65	28	...	...	...	8	0	2	2	0
85-86— North Bay	OHL	62	35	37	72	35	...	...	...	10	3	4	7	8
86-87— North Bay	OHL	55	30	48	78	20	...	...	...	18	12	8	20	6
87-88— Colorado	IHL	8	4	3	7	9	...	...	...	6	2	6	8	8
— North Bay	OHL	32	30	33	63	16	...	...	...	4	3	0	3	4
88-89— Denver	IHL	40	21	28	49	32	...	...	...	—	—	—	—	—
— New York Rangers	NHL	20	7	3	10	4	0	2	0	1	0	0	0	0
89-90— New York Rangers	NHL	76	32	34	66	32	3	10	1	10	1	6	7	4
90-91— New York Rangers	NHL	74	26	41	67	37	-5	15	2	6	1	2	3	0
91-92— New York Rangers	NHL	71	30	23	53	57	11	13	1	8	4	0	4	6
92-93— New York Rangers	NHL	71	25	28	53	40	-3	7	3	—	—	—	—	—
93-94— New York Rangers	NHL	13	2	4	6	13	-2	0	0	—	—	—	—	—
— Hartford	NHL	19	2	11	13	4	-11	0	0	—	—	—	—	—
94-95— Hartford	NHL	47	17	18	35	22	1	3	1	—	—	—	—	—
95-96— Winnipeg	NHL	59	16	16	32	26	-3	2	0	—	—	—	—	—
— San Jose	NHL	9	6	5	11	4	8	0	1	—	—	—	—	—
96-97— San Jose	NHL	65	16	21	37	16	-8	3	1	—	—	—	—	—
NHL totals (9 years)		524	179	204	383	255	-9	55	10	25	6	8	14	10

TUREK, ROMAN — G — STARS

PERSONAL: Born May 21, 1970, in Strakonice, Czechoslovakia. ... 6-3/190. ... Catches right. ... Name pronounced ROH-mahn TOOR-ihk.

TRANSACTIONS/CAREER NOTES: Selected by Minnesota North Stars in sixth round (North Stars 6th pick, 113th overall) of NHL entry draft (June 16, 1990). ... Strained groin (January 8, 1997); missed three games. ... Injured knee (March 31, 1997); missed seven games.

			REGULAR SEASON							PLAYOFFS					
Season Team	League	Gms.	Min	W	L	T	GA	SO	Avg.	Gms.	Min.	W	L	GA	SO	Avg.
90-91— Budejovice	Czech.	26	1244	...	...	...	98	0	4.73	—	—	...	...	—	...	—
91-92— Budejovice	Czech Div. II								Did not play.							
92-93— Budejovice	Czech.	43	2555	...	...	...	121	0	2.84	—	—	...	...	—	...	—
93-94— Budejovice	Czech. Rep.	44	2584	...	...	...	111	0	2.58	3	180	...	...	12	...	4.00
—Czech Olympic team	Int'l	2	120	2	0	0	4	2	2.00	—	—	...	...	—	...	—
94-95— Budejovice	Czech. Rep.	44	2587	...	...	...	119	0	2.76	9	498	...	...	25	...	3.01
95-96— Nurnberg	Germany	48	2787	...	...	...	154	0	3.32	5	338	...	...	14	...	2.49
96-97— Michigan	IHL	29	1555	8	13	4	77	0	2.97	—	—	...	...	—	...	—
—Dallas	NHL	6	263	3	1	0	9	0	2.05	—	—	...	...	—	...	—
NHL totals (1 year)		6	263	3	1	0	9	0	2.05							

TURGEON, PIERRE — C — BLUES

PERSONAL: Born August 29, 1969, in Rouyn, Que. ... 6-1/202. ... Shoots left. ... Name pronounced TUHR-zhaw. ... Brother of Sylvain Turgeon, left winger with four NHL teams (1983-84 through 1994-95).

TRANSACTIONS/CAREER NOTES: Underwent knee surgery (June 1985). ... Selected by Buffalo Sabres as underage junior in first round (first Sabres pick, first overall) of NHL entry draft (June 13, 1987). ... Traded by Sabres with RW Benoit Hogue, D Uwe Krupp and C Dave McLlwain to New York Islanders for C Pat LaFontaine, LW Randy Wood, D Randy Hillier and future considerations; Sabres later received fourth-round pick (D Dean Melanson) in 1992 draft to complete deal (October 25, 1991). ... Injured right knee (January 3, 1992); missed three games. ... Separated shoulder (April 28, 1993); missed six playoff games. ... Suffered from tendinitis in right wrist (October 5, 1993); missed one game. ... Suffered from the flu (December 29, 1993); missed one game. ... Fractured cheekbone (January 26, 1994); missed 12 games. ... Traded by Islanders with D Vladimir Malakhov to Montreal Canadiens for LW Kirk Muller, D Mathieu Schneider and C Craig Darby (April 5, 1995). ... Strained shoulder (November 8, 1995); missed two games. ... Bruised thigh (October 24, 1996); missed one game. ... Traded by Canadiens with C Craig Conroy and D Rory Fitzpatrick to St. Louis Blues for LW Shayne Corson, D Murray Baron and fifth-round pick (D Gennady Razin) in 1997 draft (October 29, 1996).

HONORS: Won Michel Bergeron Trophy (1985-86). ... Won Michael Bossy Trophy (1986-87). ... Played in NHL All-Star Game (1990, 1993, 1994 and 1996). ... Won Lady Byng Memorial Trophy (1992-93).

STATISTICAL PLATEAUS: Three-goal games: 1989-90 (1), 1990-91 (1), 1991-92 (2), 1992-93 (4), 1993-94 (2), 1994-95 (1), 1995-96 (1). Total: 12.

MISCELLANEOUS: Captain of Montreal Canadiens (1995-96 through October 29, 1996). ... Scored on a penalty shot (vs. Patrick Roy, October 17, 1990; vs. Pat Jablonski, November 7, 1992).

			REGULAR SEASON							PLAYOFFS				
Season Team	League	Gms.	G	A	Pts.	PIM	+/-	PP	SH	Gms.	G	A	Pts.	PIM
85-86— Granby	QMJHL	69	47	67	114	31	...	...	...	—	—	—	—	—
86-87— Granby	QMJHL	58	69	85	154	8	...	...	...	7	9	6	15	15
87-88— Buffalo	NHL	76	14	28	42	34	...	...	...	6	4	3	7	4
88-89— Buffalo	NHL	80	34	54	88	26	-2	19	0	5	3	5	8	2
89-90— Buffalo	NHL	80	40	66	106	29	10	17	1	6	2	4	6	2
90-91— Buffalo	NHL	78	32	47	79	26	14	13	2	6	3	1	4	6
91-92— Buffalo	NHL	8	2	6	8	4	-1	0	0	—	—	—	—	—
— New York Islanders	NHL	69	38	49	87	16	8	13	0	—	—	—	—	—
92-93— New York Islanders	NHL	83	58	74	132	26	-1	24	0	11	6	7	13	0
93-94— New York Islanders	NHL	69	38	56	94	18	14	10	4	4	0	1	1	0

Season Team	League	REGULAR SEASON								PLAYOFFS				
		Gms.	G	A	Pts.	PIM	+/-	PP	SH	Gms.	G	A	Pts.	PIM
94-95 — New York Islanders....	NHL	34	13	14	27	10	-12	3	2	—	—	—	—	—
— Montreal	NHL	15	11	9	20	4	12	2	0	—	—	—	—	—
95-96 — Montreal	NHL	80	38	58	96	44	19	17	1	6	2	4	6	2
96-97 — Montreal	NHL	9	1	10	11	2	4	0	0	—	—	—	—	—
— St. Louis	NHL	69	25	49	74	12	4	5	0	5	1	1	2	2
NHL totals (10 years)		750	344	520	864	251	69	123	10	49	21	26	47	18

TUZZOLINO, TONY — RW — ISLANDERS

PERSONAL: Born October 9, 1975, in Buffalo, N.Y. ... 6-2/200. ... Shoots right. ... Name pronounced TUZZ-oh-LEEN-oh.
COLLEGE: Michigan State.
TRANSACTIONS/CAREER NOTES: Selected by Quebec Nordiques in fifth round (seventh Nordiques pick, 113th overall) of NHL entry draft (June 29, 1994). ... Nordiques franchise moved to Colorado and renamed Avalanche for 1995-96 season (June 21, 1995). ... Signed as free agent by New York Islanders (April 23, 1997).

Season Team	League	REGULAR SEASON								PLAYOFFS				
		Gms.	G	A	Pts.	PIM	+/-	PP	SH	Gms.	G	A	Pts.	PIM
91-92 — Niagara	NAJHL	45	19	27	46	82	...	...	...	—	—	—	—	—
92-93 — Niagara	NAJHL	50	36	41	77	134	...	...	...	—	—	—	—	—
93-94 — Michigan State...........	CCHA	38	4	3	7	50	...	...	...	—	—	—	—	—
94-95 — Michigan State...........	CCHA	39	9	19	28	81	...	...	...	—	—	—	—	—
95-96 — Michigan State...........	CCHA	41	12	17	29	120	...	...	...	—	—	—	—	—
96-97 — Michigan State...........	CCHA	39	14	18	32	45	...	...	...	—	—	—	—	—

TVERDOVSKY, OLEG — D — COYOTES

PERSONAL: Born May 18, 1976, in Donetsk, U.S.S.R. ... 6-1/200. ... Shoots left. ... Name pronounced OH-lehg teh-vuhr-DAHV-skee.
TRANSACTIONS/CAREER NOTES: Selected by Mighty Ducks of Anaheim in first round (first Mighty Ducks pick, second overall) of NHL entry draft (June 28, 1994). ... Suffered from pink eye (March 15, 1995); missed two games. ... Traded by Mighty Ducks with C Chad Kilger and third-round pick (D Per-Anton Lundstrom) in 1996 draft to Winnipeg Jets for C Marc Chouinard, RW Teemu Selanne and fourth-round pick (traded to Toronto) in 1996 draft (February 7, 1996). ... Jets franchise moved to Phoenix and renamed Coyotes for 1996-97 season; NHL approved move on January 18, 1996.
HONORS: Played in NHL All-Star Game (1997).

Season Team	League	REGULAR SEASON								PLAYOFFS				
		Gms.	G	A	Pts.	PIM	+/-	PP	SH	Gms.	G	A	Pts.	PIM
92-93 — Soviet Wings	CIS	21	0	1	1	6	...	...	...	6	0	0	0	0
93-94 — Soviet Wings	CIS	46	4	10	14	22	...	...	...	3	1	0	1	2
94-95 — Brandon	WHL	7	1	4	5	4	...	...	...	—	—	—	—	—
— Anaheim.....................	NHL	36	3	9	12	14	-6	1	1	—	—	—	—	—
95-96 — Anaheim.....................	NHL	51	7	15	22	35	0	2	0	—	—	—	—	—
— Winnipeg...................	NHL	31	0	8	8	6	-7	0	0	6	0	1	1	0
96-97 — Phoenix.....................	NHL	82	10	45	55	30	-5	3	1	7	0	1	1	0
NHL totals (3 years)		200	20	77	97	85	-18	6	2	13	0	2	2	0

TWIST, TONY — LW — BLUES

PERSONAL: Born May 9, 1968, in Sherwood Park, Alta. ... 6-1/230. ... Shoots left. ... Full name: Anthony Rory Twist.
TRANSACTIONS/CAREER NOTES: Suspended three games and fined $250 by WHL for leaving the penalty box to fight (January 28, 1988). ... Selected by St. Louis Blues in ninth round (ninth Blues pick, 177th overall) of NHL entry draft (June 11, 1988). ... Suspended 13 games by IHL for checking goaltender after play stopped (December 15, 1990). ... Traded by Blues with RW Herb Raglan and LW Andy Rymsha to Quebec Nordiques for RW Darin Kimble (February 4, 1991). ... Injured shoulder (December 18, 1993); missed six games. ... Hyperextended right elbow (March 30, 1994); missed five games. ... Signed as free agent by Blues (August 3, 1994). ... Injured shoulder (March 26, 1995); missed last 20 games of season. ... Underwent bicep surgery (September 22, 1995); missed 21 games. ... Bruised knee (January 16, 1996); missed one game. ... Sprained ankle (March 26, 1996); missed seven games. ... Suffered back spasms (December 18, 1996); missed nine games. ... Suffered from a virus (February 20, 1997); missed four games.

Season Team	League	REGULAR SEASON								PLAYOFFS				
		Gms.	G	A	Pts.	PIM	+/-	PP	SH	Gms.	G	A	Pts.	PIM
86-87 — Saskatoon..................	WHL	64	0	8	8	181	...	...	...	—	—	—	—	—
87-88 — Saskatoon..................	WHL	55	1	8	9	226	...	...	...	10	1	1	2	6
88-89 — Peoria	IHL	67	3	8	11	312	...	...	...	—	—	—	—	—
89-90 — St. Louis	NHL	28	0	0	0	124	-2	0	0	—	—	—	—	—
— Peoria	IHL	36	1	5	6	200	...	...	...	5	0	1	1	8
90-91 — Peoria	IHL	38	2	10	12	244	...	...	...	—	—	—	—	—
— Quebec.....................	NHL	24	0	0	0	104	-4	0	0	—	—	—	—	—
91-92 — Quebec.....................	NHL	44	0	1	1	164	-3	0	0	—	—	—	—	—
92-93 — Quebec.....................	NHL	34	0	2	2	64	0	0	0	—	—	—	—	—
93-94 — Quebec.....................	NHL	49	0	4	4	101	-1	0	0	—	—	—	—	—
94-95 — St. Louis	NHL	28	3	0	3	89	0	0	0	1	0	0	0	6
95-96 — St. Louis	NHL	51	3	2	5	100	-1	0	0	10	1	1	2	16
96-97 — St. Louis	NHL	64	1	2	3	121	-8	0	0	6	0	0	0	0
NHL totals (8 years)		322	7	11	18	867	-19	0	0	17	1	1	2	22

T

ULANOV, IGOR   D   LIGHTNING

PERSONAL: Born October 1, 1969, in Kraskokamsk, U.S.S.R. ... 6-5/205. ... Shoots right. ... Name pronounced EE-gohr yoo-LAH-nahv.
TRANSACTIONS/CAREER NOTES: Selected by Winnipeg Jets in 10th round (eighth Jets pick, 203rd overall) of NHL entry draft (June 22, 1991). ... Suffered back spasms (March 7, 1992); missed five games. ... Fractured foot (March 16, 1995); missed 19 games. ... Traded by Jets with C Mike Eagles to Washington Capitals for third-round (traded to Dallas Stars) and fifth-round (G Brian Elder) picks in 1995 draft (April 7, 1995). ... Traded by Capitals to Chicago Blackhawks for third-round pick (G Dave Weninger) in 1996 draft (October 17, 1995). ... Traded by Blackhawks with LW Patrick Poulin and second-round pick (D Jeff Paul) in 1996 draft to Tampa Bay Lightning for D Enrico Ciccone (March 20, 1996). ... Injured ribs (October 5, 1996); missed three games. ... Strained groin (February 14, 1997); missed six games.

		REGULAR SEASON								PLAYOFFS				
Season Team	League	Gms.	G	A	Pts.	PIM	+/-	PP	SH	Gms.	G	A	Pts.	PIM
90-91— Khimik	USSR	41	2	2	4	52	...	...	...	—	—	—	—	—
91-92— Khimik	CIS	27	1	4	5	24	...	...	...	—	—	—	—	—
— Winnipeg	NHL	27	2	9	11	67	5	0	0	7	0	0	0	39
— Moncton	AHL	3	0	1	1	16	...	...	...	—	—	—	—	—
92-93— Moncton	AHL	9	1	3	4	26	...	...	...	—	—	—	—	—
— Fort Wayne	IHL	3	0	1	1	29	...	...	...	—	—	—	—	—
— Winnipeg	NHL	56	2	14	16	124	6	0	0	4	0	0	0	4
93-94— Winnipeg	NHL	74	0	17	17	165	-11	0	0	—	—	—	—	—
94-95— Winnipeg	NHL	19	1	3	4	27	-2	0	0	—	—	—	—	—
— Washington	NHL	3	0	1	1	2	3	0	0	2	0	0	0	4
95-96— Indianapolis	IHL	1	0	0	0	0	...	...	...	—	—	—	—	—
— Chicago	NHL	53	1	8	9	92	12	0	0	—	—	—	—	—
— Tampa Bay	NHL	11	2	1	3	24	-1	0	0	5	0	0	0	15
96-97— Tampa Bay	NHL	59	1	7	8	108	2	0	0	—	—	—	—	—
NHL totals (6 years)		302	9	60	69	609	14	0	0	18	0	0	0	62

USTORF, STEFAN   C   CAPITALS

PERSONAL: Born January 3, 1974, in Kaufbeuren, West Germany. ... 6-0/185. ... Shoots left. ... Name pronounced OOS-tohrf.
TRANSACTIONS/CAREER NOTES: Selected by Washington Capitals in third round (third Capitals pick, 53rd overall) of NHL entry draft (June 20, 1992). ... Suffered from the flu (December 23, 1995); missed three games. ... Pulled hamstring (January 5, 1996); missed one game. ... Separated shoulder (February 10, 1996); missed 11 games. ... Suffered concussion (March 8, 1996); missed one game.

		REGULAR SEASON								PLAYOFFS				
Season Team	League	Gms.	G	A	Pts.	PIM	+/-	PP	SH	Gms.	G	A	Pts.	PIM
91-92— Kaufbeuren	Germany	41	2	22	24	46	...	...	...	—	—	—	—	—
92-93— Kaufbeuren	Germany	37	14	18	32	32	...	...	...	3	1	0	1	10
93-94— Kaufbeuren	Germany	38	10	20	30	21	...	...	...	3	0	0	0	4
— Ger. Olympic team	Int'l	8	1	2	3	2	...	...	...	—	—	—	—	—
94-95— Portland	AHL	63	21	38	59	51	...	...	...	7	1	6	7	7
95-96— Washington	NHL	48	7	10	17	14	8	0	0	5	0	0	0	0
— Portland	AHL	8	1	4	5	6	...	...	...	—	—	—	—	—
96-97— Washington	NHL	6	0	0	0	2	-3	0	0	—	—	—	—	—
— Portland	AHL	36	7	17	24	27	...	...	...	—	—	—	—	—
NHL totals (2 years)		54	7	10	17	16	5	0	0	5	0	0	0	0

VACHON, NICK   C   ISLANDERS

PERSONAL: Born July 20, 1972, in Montreal. ... 5-10/190. ... Shoots left.
COLLEGE: Boston University
TRANSACTIONS/CAREER NOTES: Selected by Toronto Maple Leafs in 12th round (11th Maple Leafs pick, 241st overall) of NHL entry draft (June 16, 1990). ... Signed as free agent by Los Angeles Kings (September 12, 1995). ... Traded by Kings to New York Islanders for C Chris Marinucci (November 19, 1996).

		REGULAR SEASON								PLAYOFFS				
Season Team	League	Gms.	G	A	Pts.	PIM	+/-	PP	SH	Gms.	G	A	Pts.	PIM
90-91— Boston University	Hockey East	8	0	1	1	4	...	...	...	—	—	—	—	—
91-92— Boston University	Hockey East	16	6	7	13	10	...	...	...	—	—	—	—	—
— Portland	WHL	25	9	19	28	46	...	...	...	6	0	3	3	14
92-93— Portland	WHL	66	33	58	91	100	...	...	...	16	11	7	18	34
93-94— Atlanta	IHL	3	1	1	2	0	...	...	...	—	—	—	—	—
— Knoxville	ECHL	61	29	57	86	139	...	...	...	3	0	0	0	2
94-95— Phoenix	IHL	64	13	26	39	137	...	...	...	9	1	2	3	24
95-96— Phoenix	IHL	73	13	17	30	168	...	...	...	1	0	0	0	2
96-97— Phoenix	IHL	16	3	3	6	18	...	...	...	—	—	—	—	—
— Utah	IHL	33	3	5	8	110	...	...	...	—	—	—	—	—
— New York Islanders	NHL	1	0	0	0	0	-1	0	0	—	—	—	—	—
— Long Beach	IHL	13	1	2	3	42	...	...	...	18	1	2	3	43
NHL totals (1 year)		1	0	0	0	0	-1	0	0					

VALIQUETTE, STEPHEN   G   KINGS

PERSONAL: Born August 20, 1977, in Etobicoke, Ont. ... 6-5/205. ... Catches left.
TRANSACTIONS/CAREER NOTES: Selected by Los Angeles Kings in eighth round (14th Kings pick, 190th overall) of NHL entry draft (June 22, 1996).

Season Team	League	REGULAR SEASON								PLAYOFFS					
		Gms.	Min	W	L	T	GA	SO	Avg.	Gms.	Min.	W	L	GA	SO	Avg.
94-95—Sudbury	OHL	4	138	2	0	0	6	0	2.61	—	—	—	—	—	—	—
95-96—Sudbury	OHL	39	1887	13	16	2	123	0	3.91	—	—	—	—	—	—	—
96-97—Sudbury	OHL	61	3311	21	29	7	*232	1	4.20	—	—	—	—	—	—	—

VALK, GARRY   LW   PENGUINS

PERSONAL: Born November 27, 1967, in Edmonton. ... 6-1/205. ... Shoots left. ... Name pronounced VAHLK.
COLLEGE: North Dakota.
TRANSACTIONS/CAREER NOTES: Selected by Vancouver Canucks in sixth round (fifth Canucks pick, 108th overall) of NHL entry draft (June 13, 1987). ... Sprained thumb (November 24, 1991); missed one game. ... Sprained shoulder (January 21, 1992); missed eight games. ... Sprained knee (February 26, 1993); missed 12 games. ... Selected by Mighty Ducks of Anaheim in NHL waiver draft (October 3, 1993). ... Suffered concussion (December 5, 1993); missed one game. ... Suffered post-concussion syndrome (December 5, 1993); missed four games. ... Sprained left knee (January 16, 1995); missed 10 games. ... Injured right eye (December 7, 1995); missed one game. ... Injured ear (December 22, 1995); missed one game. ... Traded by Mighty Ducks to Pittsburgh Penguins for D J.J. Daigneault (February 21, 1997). ... Bruised ribs (March 16, 1997); missed five games. ... Injured knee (April 11, 1997); missed one game.
STATISTICAL PLATEAUS: Three-goal games: 1995-96 (1).

Season Team	League	REGULAR SEASON								PLAYOFFS				
		Gms.	G	A	Pts.	PIM	+/-	PP	SH	Gms.	G	A	Pts.	PIM
85-86— Sherwood Park	AJHL	40	20	26	46	116	...	...	...	—	—	—	—	—
86-87— Sherwood Park	AJHL	59	42	44	86	204	...	...	...	—	—	—	—	—
87-88— North Dakota	WCHA	38	23	12	35	64	...	...	...	—	—	—	—	—
88-89— North Dakota	WCHA	40	14	17	31	71	...	...	...	—	—	—	—	—
89-90— North Dakota	WCHA	43	22	17	39	92	...	...	...	—	—	—	—	—
90-91— Vancouver	NHL	59	10	11	21	67	-23	1	0	5	0	0	0	20
— Milwaukee	IHL	10	12	4	16	13	...	...	...	3	0	0	0	2
91-92— Vancouver	NHL	65	8	17	25	56	3	2	1	4	0	0	0	5
92-93— Vancouver	NHL	48	6	7	13	77	6	0	0	7	0	1	1	12
— Hamilton	AHL	7	3	6	9	6	...	...	...	—	—	—	—	—
93-94— Anaheim	NHL	78	18	27	45	100	8	4	1	—	—	—	—	—
94-95— Anaheim	NHL	36	3	6	9	34	-4	0	0	—	—	—	—	—
95-96— Anaheim	NHL	79	12	12	24	125	8	1	1	—	—	—	—	—
96-97— Anaheim	NHL	53	7	7	14	53	-2	0	0	—	—	—	—	—
— Pittsburgh	NHL	17	3	4	7	25	-6	0	0	—	—	—	—	—
NHL totals (7 years)		435	67	91	158	537	-10	8	3	16	0	1	1	37

VAN ALLEN, SHAUN   C   SENATORS

PERSONAL: Born August 29, 1967, in Shaunavon, Sask. ... 6-2/205. ... Shoots left. ... Full name: Shaun Kelly Van Allen.
HIGH SCHOOL: Walter Murray (Saskatoon, Sask.).
TRANSACTIONS/CAREER NOTES: Selected by Edmonton Oilers in fifth round (fifth Oilers pick, 105th overall) of NHL entry draft (June 13, 1987). ... Suffered concussion (January 9, 1993); missed 11 games. ... Signed as free agent by Mighty Ducks of Anaheim (July 22, 1993). ... Suffered back spasms (February 7, 1995); missed two games. ... Suffered from the flu (May 1, 1995); missed one game. ... Dislocated right thumb (November 15, 1995); missed 21 games. ... Suffered back spasms (February 7, 1996); missed four games. ... Traded by Mighty Ducks with D Jason York to Ottawa Senators for C Ted Drury and rights to D Marc Moro (October 1, 1996).
HONORS: Named to AHL All-Star second team (1990-91). ... Won John B. Sollenberger Trophy (1991-92). ... Named to AHL All-Star first team (1991-92).

Season Team	League	REGULAR SEASON								PLAYOFFS				
		Gms.	G	A	Pts.	PIM	+/-	PP	SH	Gms.	G	A	Pts.	PIM
84-85— Swift Current	SAJHL	61	12	20	32	136	...	...	...	—	—	—	—	—
85-86— Saskatoon	WHL	55	12	11	23	43	...	...	...	13	4	8	12	28
86-87— Saskatoon	WHL	72	38	59	97	116	...	...	...	11	4	6	10	24
87-88— Nova Scotia	AHL	19	4	10	14	17	...	...	...	4	1	1	2	4
— Milwaukee	IHL	40	14	28	42	34	...	...	...	—	—	—	—	—
88-89— Cape Breton	AHL	76	32	42	74	81	...	...	...	—	—	—	—	—
89-90— Cape Breton	AHL	61	25	44	69	83	...	...	...	4	0	2	2	8
90-91— Edmonton	NHL	2	0	0	0	0	0	0	0	—	—	—	—	—
— Cape Breton	AHL	76	25	75	100	182	...	...	...	4	0	1	1	8
91-92— Cape Breton	AHL	77	29	*84	*113	80	...	...	...	5	3	7	10	14
92-93— Cape Breton	AHL	43	14	62	76	68	...	...	...	15	8	9	17	18
— Edmonton	NHL	21	1	4	5	6	-2	0	0	—	—	—	—	—
93-94— Anaheim	NHL	80	8	25	33	64	0	2	2	—	—	—	—	—
94-95— Anaheim	NHL	45	8	21	29	32	-4	1	1	—	—	—	—	—
95-96— Anaheim	NHL	49	8	17	25	41	13	0	0	—	—	—	—	—
96-97— Ottawa	NHL	80	11	14	25	35	-8	1	1	7	0	1	1	4
NHL totals (6 years)		277	36	81	117	178	-1	4	4	7	0	1	1	4

VANBIESBROUCK, JOHN   G   PANTHERS

PERSONAL: Born September 4, 1963, in Detroit. ... 5-8/176. ... Catches left. ... Name pronounced van-BEES-bruk.
TRANSACTIONS/CAREER NOTES: Selected by New York Rangers in fourth round (fifth Rangers pick, 72nd overall) of NHL entry draft (June 10, 1981). ... Fractured jaw (October 1987). ... Severely lacerated wrist (June 1988). ... Underwent knee surgery (May 11, 1990). ... Suffered lower back spasms (February 25, 1992); missed 11 games. ... Pulled groin (November 2, 1992); missed four games. ... Traded by Rangers to Vancouver Canucks for future considerations (June 20, 1993); Canucks sent D Doug Lidster to Rangers to complete deal (June 25, 1993).

V

... Selected by Florida Panthers in NHL expansion draft (June 24, 1993). ... Lacerated hand (February 1, 1994); missed seven games.
HONORS: Won F.W. (Dinty) Moore Trophy (1980-81). ... Shared Dave Pinkney Trophy with Marc D'Amour (1981-82). ... Named to OHL All-Star second team (1982-83). ... Shared Tommy Ivan Trophy with D Bruce Affleck (1983-84). ... Shared Terry Sawchuk Trophy with Ron Scott (1983-84). ... Named to CHL All-Star first team (1983-84). ... Won Vezina Trophy (1985-86). ... Named to THE SPORTING NEWS All-Star first team (1985-86 and 1993-94). ... Named to NHL All-Star first team (1985-86). ... Played in NHL All-Star Game (1994, 1996 and 1997). ... Named to NHL All-Star second team (1993-94).
MISCELLANEOUS: Holds Florida Panthers all-time records for most games played by goalie (208), most wins (88), most shutouts (9) and goals-against average (2.49). ... Stopped a penalty shot attempt (vs. Petr Klima, February 17, 1987; vs. Ray Bourque, November 11, 1988; vs. Pavel Bure, February 17, 1992). ... Allowed a penalty shot goal (vs. Pat Verbeek, March 27, 1988; vs. Keith Acton, March 25, 1990; vs. Mario Lemieux, April 11, 1997).

Season Team	League	REGULAR SEASON							PLAYOFFS					
		Gms.	Min	W	L	T	GA	SO	Avg.	Gms.	Min.	W	L	GA	SO	Avg.
80-81—Sault Ste. Marie	OMJHL	56	2941	31	16	1	203	0	4.14	11	457	3	3	24	1	3.15
81-82—Sault Ste. Marie	OHL	31	1686	12	12	2	102	0	3.63	7	276	1	4	20	0	4.35
—New York Rangers	NHL	1	60	1	0	0	1	0	1.00	—	—	—	—	—	—	—
82-83—Sault Ste. Marie	OHL	*62	3471	39	21	1	209	0	3.61	16	944	7	6	56	*1	3.56
83-84—New York Rangers	NHL	3	180	2	1	0	10	0	3.33	1	1	0	0	0	0	0.00
—Tulsa	CHL	37	2153	20	13	2	124	*3	3.46	4	240	4	0	10	0	*2.50
84-85—New York Rangers	NHL	42	2358	12	24	3	166	1	4.22	1	20	0	0	0	0	0.00
85-86—New York Rangers	NHL	61	3326	31	21	5	184	3	3.32	16	899	8	8	49	*1	3.27
86-87—New York Rangers	NHL	50	2656	18	20	5	161	0	3.64	4	195	1	3	11	1	3.38
87-88—New York Rangers	NHL	56	3319	27	22	7	187	2	3.38	—	—	—	—	—	—	—
88-89—New York Rangers	NHL	56	3207	28	21	4	197	0	3.69	2	107	0	1	6	0	3.36
89-90—New York Rangers	NHL	47	2734	19	19	7	154	1	3.38	6	298	2	3	15	0	3.02
90-91—New York Rangers	NHL	40	2257	15	18	6	126	3	3.35	1	52	0	0	1	0	1.15
91-92—New York Rangers	NHL	45	2526	27	13	3	120	2	2.85	7	368	2	5	23	0	3.75
92-93—New York Rangers	NHL	48	2757	20	18	7	152	4	3.31	—	—	—	—	—	—	—
93-94—Florida	NHL	57	3440	21	25	11	145	1	2.53	—	—	—	—	—	—	—
94-95—Florida	NHL	37	2087	14	15	4	86	4	2.47	—	—	—	—	—	—	—
95-96—Florida	NHL	57	3178	26	20	7	142	2	2.68	22	1332	12	*10	50	1	2.25
96-97—Florida	NHL	57	3347	27	19	10	128	2	2.29	5	328	1	4	13	1	2.38
NHL totals (15 years)		657	37432	288	256	79	1959	25	3.14	65	3600	26	34	168	4	2.80

VANDENBUSSCHE, RYAN   RW   RANGERS

PERSONAL: Born February 28, 1973, in Simcoe, Ontario. ... 6-0/195. ... Shoots right.
TRANSACTIONS/CAREER NOTES: Selected by Toronto Maple Leafs in eighth round (173rd overall) of NHL entry draft (June 20, 1992). ... Signed as free agent by New York Rangers (August 22, 1995).

Season Team	League	REGULAR SEASON								PLAYOFFS				
		Gms.	G	A	Pts.	PIM	+/-	PP	SH	Gms.	G	A	Pts.	PIM
90-91—Cornwall	OHL	49	3	8	11	139	...	...	...	—	—	—	—	—
91-92—Cornwall	OHL	61	13	15	28	232	...	...	...	6	0	2	2	9
92-93—Newmarket	OHL	30	15	12	27	161	...	...	...	—	—	—	—	—
—Guelph	OHL	29	3	14	17	99	...	...	...	5	1	3	4	13
—St. John's	AHL	1	0	0	0	0	...	...	...	—	—	—	—	—
93-94—St. John's	AHL	44	4	10	14	124	...	...	...	—	—	—	—	—
—Springfield	AHL	9	1	2	3	29	...	...	...	5	0	0	0	16
94-95—St. John's	AHL	53	2	13	15	239	...	...	...	—	—	—	—	—
95-96—Binghamton	AHL	68	3	17	20	240	...	...	...	4	0	0	0	9
96-97—Binghamton	AHL	38	8	11	19	133	...	...	...	—	—	—	—	—
—New York Rangers	NHL	11	1	0	1	30	-2	0	0	—	—	—	—	—
NHL totals (1 year)		11	1	0	1	30	-2	0	0	—	—	—	—	—

V

VAN IMPE, DARREN   D   MIGHTY DUCKS

PERSONAL: Born May 18, 1973, in Saskatoon, Sask. ... 6-1/205. ... Shoots left. ... Name pronounced VAN-IHMP.
TRANSACTIONS/CAREER NOTES: Selected by New York Islanders in seventh round (seventh Islanders pick, 170th overall) of NHL entry draft (June 26, 1993). ... Traded by Islanders to Mighty Ducks of Anaheim for ninth-round pick (LW Mike Broda) in 1995 draft (September 2, 1994).
HONORS: Named to WHL (East) All-Star first team (1992-93 and 1993-94).

Season Team	League	REGULAR SEASON								PLAYOFFS				
		Gms.	G	A	Pts.	PIM	+/-	PP	SH	Gms.	G	A	Pts.	PIM
92-93—Red Deer	WHL	54	23	47	70	118	...	...	...	4	2	5	7	16
93-94—Red Deer	WHL	58	20	64	84	125	...	...	...	4	2	4	6	6
94-95—San Diego	IHL	76	6	17	23	74	...	...	...	5	0	0	0	0
—Anaheim	NHL	1	0	1	1	4	0	0	0	—	—	—	—	—
95-96—Baltimore	AHL	63	11	47	58	79	...	...	...	—	—	—	—	—
—Anaheim	NHL	16	1	2	3	14	8	0	0	—	—	—	—	—
96-97—Anaheim	NHL	74	4	19	23	90	3	2	0	9	0	2	2	16
NHL totals (3 years)		91	5	22	27	108	11	2	0	9	0	2	2	16

VAN OENE, DARREN   LW   SABRES

PERSONAL: Born January 18, 1978, in Edmonton. ... 6-3/207. ... Shoots left. ... Name pronounced van OH-ihn.
TRANSACTIONS/CAREER NOTES: Selected by Buffalo Sabres in second round (third Sabres pick, 33rd overall) of NHL entry draft (June 22, 1996).

Season Team	League	REGULAR SEASON								PLAYOFFS				
		Gms.	G	A	Pts.	PIM	+/-	PP	SH	Gms.	G	A	Pts.	PIM
94-95— Brandon	WHL	59	5	13	18	108	...	...	...	18	1	1	2	34
95-96— Brandon	WHL	47	10	18	28	126	...	...	...	18	1	6	7	*78
96-97— Brandon	WHL	56	21	27	48	139	...	...	...	6	2	3	5	19

VARADA, VACLAV   LW   SABRES

PERSONAL: Born April 26, 1976, in Valasske Mezirici, Czechoslovakia. ... 6-0/198. ... Shoots left. ... Name pronounced vuh-RAH-duh.

TRANSACTIONS/CAREER NOTES: Selected by San Jose Sharks in fourth round (fourth Sharks pick, 89th overall) of NHL entry draft (June 29, 1994). ... Traded by Sharks with LW Martin Spahnel and fourth-round pick (D Mike Martone) in 1996 draft to Buffalo Sabres for D Doug Bodger (November 16, 1995). ... Fractured left hand (February 2, 1997); missed 15 games.

Season Team	League	REGULAR SEASON								PLAYOFFS				
		Gms.	G	A	Pts.	PIM	+/-	PP	SH	Gms.	G	A	Pts.	PIM
92-93— TJ Vitkovice	Czech.	1	0	0	0	...	...	...	...	—	—	—	—	—
93-94— HC Vitkovice	Czech Rep.	24	6	7	13	...	...	...	...	5	1	1	2	0
94-95— Tacoma	WHL	68	50	38	88	108	...	...	...	4	4	3	7	11
95-96— Kelowna	WHL	59	39	46	85	100	...	...	...	6	3	3	6	16
— Rochester	AHL	5	3	0	3	4	...	...	...	—	—	—	—	—
— Buffalo	NHL	1	0	0	0	0	0	0	0	—	—	—	—	—
96-97— Rochester	AHL	53	23	25	48	81	...	...	...	10	1	6	7	27
— Buffalo	NHL	5	0	0	0	2	0	0	0	—	—	—	—	—
NHL totals (2 years)		6	0	0	0	2	0	0	0					

VARLAMOV, SERGEI   LW   FLAMES

PERSONAL: Born July 21, 1978, in Kiev, Ukraine. ... 5-11/176. ... Shoots left.
TRANSACTIONS/CAREER NOTES: Signed as free agent by Calgary Flames (September 18, 1996).

Season Team	League	REGULAR SEASON								PLAYOFFS				
		Gms.	G	A	Pts.	PIM	+/-	PP	SH	Gms.	G	A	Pts.	PIM
95-96— Swift Current	WHL	55	23	21	44	65	...	...	...	—	—	—	—	—
96-97— Swift Current	WHL	72	46	39	85	94	...	...	...	—	—	—	—	—
— Saint John	AHL	1	0	0	0	2	...	...	...	—	—	—	—	—

VASILEVSKI, ALEXANDER   RW   BLUES

PERSONAL: Born January 8, 1975, in Kiev, U.S.S.R. ... 5-11/190. ... Shoots left. ... Name pronounced vas-ih-LEHV-skee.
TRANSACTIONS/CAREER NOTES: Selected by St. Louis Blues in 11th round (ninth Blues pick, 271st overall) of NHL entry draft (June 26, 1993).

Season Team	League	REGULAR SEASON								PLAYOFFS				
		Gms.	G	A	Pts.	PIM	+/-	PP	SH	Gms.	G	A	Pts.	PIM
92-93— Victoria	WHL	71	27	25	52	52	...	...	...	—	—	—	—	—
93-94— Victoria	WHL	69	34	51	85	78	...	...	...	—	—	—	—	—
94-95— Prince George	WHL	48	32	34	66	52	...	...	...	—	—	—	—	—
— Brandon	WHL	23	6	11	17	39	...	...	...	18	3	6	9	34
95-96— Worcester	AHL	69	18	21	39	112	...	...	...	4	2	1	3	10
— St. Louis	NHL	1	0	0	0	0	-1	0	0	—	—	—	—	—
96-97— Worcester	AHL	61	9	23	32	100	...	...	...	—	—	—	—	—
— St. Louis	NHL	3	0	0	0	2	-1	0	0	—	—	—	—	—
— Grand Rapids	IHL	10	1	5	6	43	...	...	...	5	0	1	1	19
NHL totals (2 years)		4	0	0	0	2	-2	0	0					

VASILYEV, ANDREI   LW   ISLANDERS

PERSONAL: Born March 30, 1972, in Voskresensk, U.S.S.R. ... 5-9/180. ... Shoots right. ... Name pronounced AHN-dray vuh-SIHL-ee-yehv.
TRANSACTIONS/CAREER NOTES: Selected by New York Islanders in 11th round (11th Islanders pick, 248th overall) of NHL entry draft (June 26, 1993). ... Selected by Orlando Solar Bears in IHL expansion draft (July 13, 1995). ... Separated right shoulder and broke collarbone (December 12, 1995); missed 12 games.

Season Team	League	REGULAR SEASON								PLAYOFFS				
		Gms.	G	A	Pts.	PIM	+/-	PP	SH	Gms.	G	A	Pts.	PIM
91-92— CSKA Moscow	CIS	28	7	2	9	2	...	...	...	—	—	—	—	—
92-93— Khimik	CIS	34	4	8	12	20	...	...	...	—	—	—	—	—
93-94— CSKA Moscow	CIS	46	17	6	23	8	...	...	...	3	1	0	1	0
94-95— Denver	IHL	74	28	37	65	48	...	...	...	13	9	4	13	22
— New York Islanders....	NHL	2	0	0	0	2	0	0	0	—	—	—	—	—
95-96— Utah	IHL	43	26	20	46	34	...	...	...	22	12	4	16	18
— New York Islanders....	NHL	10	2	5	7	2	4	0	0	—	—	—	—	—
96-97— Utah	IHL	56	16	18	34	42	...	...	...	7	4	1	5	0
— New York Islanders....	NHL	3	0	0	0	2	-3	0	0	—	—	—	—	—
NHL totals (3 years)		15	2	5	7	6	1	0	0					

V

VASILJEV, ALEXEI   D   RANGERS

PERSONAL: Born September 1, 1977, in Yaroslavl, U.S.S.R. ... 6-0/185. ... Shoots left.
TRANSACTIONS/CAREER NOTES: Selected by New York Rangers in fifth round (fourth Rangers pick, 110th overall) of NHL entry draft (July 8, 1995).

		REGULAR SEASON								PLAYOFFS				
Season Team	League	Gms.	G	A	Pts.	PIM	+/-	PP	SH	Gms.	G	A	Pts.	PIM
93-94 — Yaroslavl	CIS	2	0	1	1	4	...	...	...	—	—	—	—	—
94-95 — Torpedo-2 Yaroslavl	CIS Div. II						Statistics unavailable.							
95-96 — Yaroslavl	CIS	40	4	7	11	4	...	...	...	—	—	—	—	—
96-97 — Yaroslavl	Russian	44	2	8	10	10	...	...	...	9	1	1	2	8

VASKE, DENNIS   D   ISLANDERS

PERSONAL: Born October 11, 1967, in Rockford, Ill. ... 6-2/210. ... Shoots left. ... Full name: Dennis James Vaske. ... Name pronounced VAS-kee.
HIGH SCHOOL: Armstrong (Plymouth, Minn.).
COLLEGE: Minnesota-Duluth.
TRANSACTIONS/CAREER NOTES: Selected by New York Islanders in second round (second Islanders pick, 38th overall) of NHL entry draft (June 21, 1986). ... Lacerated forehead (April 8, 1993); missed three games. ... Broke foot (December 19, 1993); missed 13 games. ... Broke ankle (April 18, 1995); missed last seven games of season. ... Suffered concussion and lacerated face (November 22, 1995); missed remainder of season. ... Separated shoulder (September 17, 1996); missed 18 games. ... Suffered mild concussion (November 29, 1996); missed 48 games.

		REGULAR SEASON								PLAYOFFS				
Season Team	League	Gms.	G	A	Pts.	PIM	+/-	PP	SH	Gms.	G	A	Pts.	PIM
84-85 — Armstrong.	Minn. H.S.	22	5	18	23	...	...	...	...	—	—	—	—	—
85-86 — Armstrong.	Minn. H.S.	20	9	13	22	...	...	...	...	—	—	—	—	—
86-87 — Minnesota-Duluth	WCHA	33	0	2	2	40	...	...	...	—	—	—	—	—
87-88 — Minnesota-Duluth	WCHA	39	1	6	7	90	...	...	...	—	—	—	—	—
88-89 — Minnesota-Duluth	WCHA	37	9	19	28	86	...	...	...	—	—	—	—	—
89-90 — Minnesota-Duluth	WCHA	37	5	24	29	72	...	...	...	—	—	—	—	—
90-91 — New York Islanders	NHL	5	0	0	0	2	4	0	0	—	—	—	—	—
— Capital District	AHL	67	10	10	20	65	...	...	...	—	—	—	—	—
91-92 — Capital District	AHL	31	1	11	12	59	...	...	...	—	—	—	—	—
— New York Islanders	NHL	39	0	1	1	39	5	0	0	—	—	—	—	—
92-93 — Capital District	AHL	42	4	15	19	70	...	...	...	—	—	—	—	—
— New York Islanders	NHL	27	1	5	6	32	9	0	0	18	0	6	6	14
93-94 — New York Islanders	NHL	65	2	11	13	76	21	0	0	4	0	1	1	2
94-95 — New York Islanders	NHL	41	1	11	12	53	3	0	0	—	—	—	—	—
95-96 — New York Islanders	NHL	19	1	6	7	21	-13	1	0	—	—	—	—	—
96-97 — New York Islanders	NHL	17	0	4	4	12	3	0	0	—	—	—	—	—
NHL totals (7 years)		213	5	38	43	235	32	1	0	22	0	7	7	16

VELLINGA, MIKE   D   BLACKHAWKS

PERSONAL: Born August 19, 1978, in Chatham, Ont. ... 6-1/218. ... Shoots right.
TRANSACTIONS/CAREER NOTES: Selected by Chicago Blackhawks in seventh round (fifth Blackhawks pick, 184th overall) of the NHL entry draft (June 22, 1996).

		REGULAR SEASON								PLAYOFFS				
Season Team	League	Gms.	G	A	Pts.	PIM	+/-	PP	SH	Gms.	G	A	Pts.	PIM
95-96 — Guelph	OHL	57	3	8	11	32	...	...	...	16	2	6	8	6
96-97 — Guelph	OHL	66	6	30	36	73	...	...	...	18	1	9	10	34

VERBEEK, PAT   RW   STARS

PERSONAL: Born May 24, 1964, in Sarnia, Ont. ... 5-9/190. ... Shoots right.
TRANSACTIONS/CAREER NOTES: Selected by New Jersey Devils as underage junior in third round (third Devils pick, 43rd overall) of NHL entry draft (June 9, 1982). ... Suffered severed left thumb between knuckles in a corn-planting machine on his farm and underwent surgery to have thumb reconnected (May 15, 1985). ... Pulled side muscle (March 1987). ... Bruised chest (October 28, 1988). ... Traded by Devils to Hartford Whalers for LW Sylvain Turgeon (June 17, 1989). ... Missed first three games of 1991-92 season due to contract dispute. ... Fined $500 by Whalers for involvement in bar brawl (April 1, 1994). ... Traded by Whalers to New York Rangers for D Glen Featherstone, D Michael Stewart, first-round pick (G Jean-Sebastien Giguere) in 1995 draft and fourth-round pick (C Steve Wasylko) in 1996 draft (March 23, 1995). ... Injured knee (February 17, 1996); missed two games. ... Separated shoulder (March 1, 1996); missed nine games. ... Suffered back spasms (April 7, 1996); missed two games. ... Signed as free agent by Dallas Stars (July 3, 1996). ... Sprained knee (January 4, 1997); missed one game.
HONORS: Won Emms Family Award (1981-82). ... Played in NHL All-Star Game (1991 and 1996).
STATISTICAL PLATEAUS: Three-goal games: 1985-86 (1), 1986-87 (1), 1987-88 (1), 1988-89 (1), 1992-93 (2), 1993-94 (2), 1995-96 (2). Total: 10. ... Four-goal games: 1987-88 (1). ... Total hat tricks: 11.
MISCELLANEOUS: Scored on a penalty shot (vs. John Vanbiesbrouck, March 27, 1988).
STATISTICAL NOTES: Only player in NHL history to lead team in goals scored and penalty minutes (1989-90 and 1990-91). ... Captain of Hartford Whalers (1992-93 through 1993-94).

		REGULAR SEASON								PLAYOFFS				
Season Team	League	Gms.	G	A	Pts.	PIM	+/-	PP	SH	Gms.	G	A	Pts.	PIM
80-81 — Petrolia Jr. B.	OPJHL	42	44	44	88	155	...	...	...	—	—	—	—	—
81-82 — Sudbury	OHL	66	37	51	88	180	...	...	...	—	—	—	—	—

Season Team	League	REGULAR SEASON Gms.	G	A	Pts.	PIM	+/-	PP	SH	PLAYOFFS Gms.	G	A	Pts.	PIM
82-83— Sudbury	OHL	61	40	67	107	184	...	...	...	—	—	—	—	—
— New Jersey	NHL	6	3	2	5	8	-2	0	0	—	—	—	—	—
83-84— New Jersey	NHL	79	20	27	47	158	-19	5	1	—	—	—	—	—
84-85— New Jersey	NHL	78	15	18	33	162	-24	5	1	—	—	—	—	—
85-86— New Jersey	NHL	76	25	28	53	79	-25	4	1	—	—	—	—	—
86-87— New Jersey	NHL	74	35	24	59	120	-23	17	0	—	—	—	—	—
87-88— New Jersey	NHL	73	46	31	77	227	29	13	0	20	4	8	12	51
88-89— New Jersey	NHL	77	26	21	47	189	-18	9	0	—	—	—	—	—
89-90— Hartford	NHL	80	44	45	89	228	1	14	0	7	2	2	4	26
90-91— Hartford	NHL	80	43	39	82	246	0	15	0	6	3	2	5	40
91-92— Hartford	NHL	76	22	35	57	243	-16	10	0	7	0	2	2	12
92-93— Hartford	NHL	84	39	43	82	197	-7	16	0	—	—	—	—	—
93-94— Hartford	NHL	84	37	38	75	177	-15	15	1	—	—	—	—	—
94-95— Hartford	NHL	29	7	11	18	53	0	3	0	—	—	—	—	—
— New York Rangers	NHL	19	10	5	15	18	-2	4	0	10	4	6	10	20
95-96— New York Rangers	NHL	69	41	41	82	129	29	17	0	11	3	6	9	12
96-97— Dallas	NHL	81	17	36	53	128	3	5	0	7	1	3	4	16
NHL totals (15 years)		1065	430	444	874	2362	-89	152	4	68	17	29	46	177

VERCIK, RUDOLF — LW — RANGERS

PERSONAL: Born March 19, 1976, in Bratislava, Czechoslovakia. ... 6-1/189. ... Shoots left. ... Name pronounced VAIR-chihk.

TRANSACTIONS/CAREER NOTES: Selected by New York Rangers in second round (second Rangers pick, 52nd overall) of NHL entry draft (June 28, 1994).

Season Team	League	REGULAR SEASON Gms.	G	A	Pts.	PIM	+/-	PP	SH	PLAYOFFS Gms.	G	A	Pts.	PIM
93-94— Slovan Bratislava	Slovakia	17	1	4	5	14	...	...	...	—	—	—	—	—
94-95— Slovan Bratislava	Slovakia	33	14	9	23	??	...	...	...	—	—	—	—	—
95-96— Slovan Bratislava	Slovakia	28	7	3	10	61	...	...	...	—	—	—	—	—
96-97— Slovan Bratislava	Slovakia	40	8	3	11	...	...	...	...	2	0	0	0	0

VERNON, MIKE — G — RED WINGS

PERSONAL: Born February 24, 1963, in Calgary. ... 5-9/175. ... Catches left.

TRANSACTIONS/CAREER NOTES: Selected by Calgary Flames in third round (second Flames pick, 56th overall) of NHL entry draft (June 10, 1981). ... Injured hip (March 2, 1988). ... Suffered back spasms (February 1989). ... Suffered back spasms (March 1990); missed 10 games. ... Suffered lacerated forehead (October 25, 1992); missed five games. ... Suffered from the flu (November 15, 1993); missed two games. ... Twisted knee (December 30, 1993); missed 14 games. ... Traded by Flames to Detroit Red Wings for D Steve Chiasson (June 29, 1994). ... Pulled groin (December 29, 1995); missed 12 games. ... Suffered from the flu (October 23, 1996); missed three games. ... Injured knee (March 12, 1997); missed three games.

HONORS: Won WHL Most Valuable Player Trophy (1981-82 and 1982-83). ... Won WHL Top Goaltender Trophy (1981-82 and 1982-83). ... Won WHL Player of the Year Award (1981-82). ... Named to WHL All-Star first team (1981-82 and 1982-83). ... Named to CHL All-Star second team (1983-84). ... Named to THE SPORTING NEWS All-Star second team (1988-89). ... Named to NHL All-Star second team (1988-89). ... Played in NHL All-Star Game (1988-1991 and 1993). ... Shared William M. Jennings Trophy with Chris Osgood (1995-96). ... Won Conn Smythe Trophy (1996-97).

RECORDS: Shares NHL single-season playoff record for most wins by a goaltender—16 (1989).

MISCELLANEOUS: Member of Stanley Cup championship team (1989 and 1997). ... Stopped a penalty shot attempt (vs. Kirk Muller, March 14, 1989; vs. Jim Cummins, April 7, 1996). ... Allowed a penalty shot goal (vs. Stan Smyl, January 16, 1987; vs. Craig MacTavish, December 23, 1988; vs. Gino Odjick, October 19, 1991; vs. Paul Broten, January 16, 1992). ... Holds Calgary Flames all-time records for games played by a goaltender (467) and most wins (225)..

Season Team	League	REGULAR SEASON Gms.	Min.	W	L	T	GA	SO	Avg.	PLAYOFFS Gms.	Min.	W	L	GA	SO	Avg.
80-81— Calgary	WHL	59	3154	33	17	1	198	1	3.77	22	1271	...	...	82	1	3.87
81-82— Calgary	WHL	42	2329	22	14	2	143	*3	*3.68	9	527	...	...	30	0	*3.42
— Oklahoma City	CHL	—	—	—	—	—	—	—	—	1	70	0	1	4	0	3.43
82-83— Calgary	WHL	50	2856	19	18	2	155	*3	*3.26	16	925	9	7	60	0	3.89
— Calgary	NHL	2	100	0	2	0	11	0	6.60	—	—	—	—	—	—	—
83-84— Calgary	NHL	1	11	0	1	0	4	0	21.82	—	—	—	—	—	—	—
— Colorado	CHL	*46	*2648	30	13	2	148	1	*3.35	6	347	2	4	21	0	3.63
84-85— Moncton	AHL	41	2050	10	20	4	134	0	3.92	—	—	—	—	—	—	—
85-86— Salt Lake City	IHL	10	601	...	...	...	34	1	3.39	—	—	—	—	—	—	—
— Moncton	AHL	6	374	3	1	2	21	0	3.37	—	—	—	—	—	—	—
— Calgary	NHL	18	921	9	3	3	52	1	3.39	*21	*1229	12	*9	*60	0	2.93
86-87— Calgary	NHL	54	2957	30	21	1	178	1	3.61	5	263	2	3	16	0	3.65
87-88— Calgary	NHL	64	3565	39	16	7	210	1	3.53	9	515	4	4	34	0	3.96
88-89— Calgary	NHL	52	2938	*37	6	5	130	0	2.65	*22	*1381	*16	5	*52	*3	2.26
89-90— Calgary	NHL	47	2795	23	14	9	146	0	3.13	6	342	2	3	19	0	3.33
90-91— Calgary	NHL	54	3121	31	19	3	172	1	3.31	7	427	3	4	21	0	2.95
91-92— Calgary	NHL	63	3640	24	30	9	217	0	3.58	—	—	—	—	—	—	—
92-93— Calgary	NHL	64	3732	29	26	9	203	2	3.26	4	150	1	1	15	0	6.00
93-94— Calgary	NHL	48	2798	26	17	5	131	3	2.81	7	466	3	4	23	0	2.96
94-95— Detroit	NHL	30	1807	19	6	4	76	1	2.52	18	1063	12	6	41	1	2.31
95-96— Detroit	NHL	32	1855	21	7	2	70	3	2.26	4	243	2	2	11	0	2.72
96-97— Detroit	NHL	33	1952	13	11	8	79	0	2.43	20	1229	16	4	36	1	1.76
NHL totals (14 years)		562	32192	301	179	65	1679	13	3.13	123	7308	73	45	328	5	2.69

V

VIAL, DENNIS   D   SENATORS

PERSONAL: Born April 10, 1969, in Sault Ste. Marie, Ont. ... 6-1/225. ... Shoots left. ... Name pronounced vee-AL.
TRANSACTIONS/CAREER NOTES: Suspended three games by OHL for spearing (October 1986). ... Selected by New York Rangers in sixth round (fifth Rangers pick, 110th overall) of NHL entry draft (June 11, 1988). ... Suspended indefinitely by OHL for leaving the bench to fight (March 23, 1989). ... Traded by Rangers with C Kevin Miller and RW Jim Cummins to Detroit Red Wings for RW Joe Kocur and D Per Djoos (March 5, 1991). ... Injured right knee and ankle (December 7, 1991); missed two games. ... Traded by Red Wings with D Doug Crossman to Quebec Nordiques for cash (June 15, 1992). ... Traded by Nordiques to Red Wings for cash (September 9, 1992). ... Separated right shoulder (January 19, 1993); missed 15 games. ... Traded by Red Wings to Tampa Bay Lightning for LW Steve Maltais (June 8, 1993). ... Selected by Mighty Ducks of Anaheim in NHL expansion draft (June 24, 1993). ... Selected by Ottawa Senators in Phase II of NHL expansion draft (June 25, 1993). ... Injured left foot (November 10, 1993); missed 12 games. ... Fractured left hand (December 21, 1993); missed 13 games. ... Suspended one game and fined $500 by NHL for shooting a puck into opposing team's bench (March 23, 1994). ... Suffered ankle contusion (March 27, 1995); missed one game. ... Broke thumb (September 18, 1995); missed 11 games. ... Suffered from the flu during 1995-96 season; missed two games. ... Bruised right ankle (March 6, 1996); missed one game. ... Sprained right ankle (September 15, 1996); missed one game. ... Suffered bone chip in right hand (October 19, 1996); missed 15 games. ... Broke finger (November 30, 1996); missed 12 games. ... Underwent finger surgery (January 20, 1997); missed remainder of the season.
MISCELLANEOUS: Holds Ottawa Senators all-time record for most penalty minutes (580).

Season Team	League	REGULAR SEASON								PLAYOFFS				
		Gms.	G	A	Pts.	PIM	+/-	PP	SH	Gms.	G	A	Pts.	PIM
85-86 — Hamilton	OHL	31	1	1	2	66	...	...	...	—	—	—	—	—
86-87 — Hamilton	OHL	53	1	8	9	194	...	...	...	8	0	0	0	8
87-88 — Hamilton	OHL	52	3	17	20	229	...	...	...	13	2	2	4	49
88-89 — Niagara Falls	OHL	50	10	27	37	227	...	...	...	15	1	7	8	44
89-90 — Flint	IHL	79	6	29	35	351	...	...	...	4	0	0	0	10
90-91 — Binghamton	AHL	40	2	7	9	250	...	...	...	—	—	—	—	—
— New York Rangers	NHL	21	0	0	0	61	-4	0	0	—	—	—	—	—
— Detroit	NHL	9	0	0	0	16	...	...	...	—	—	—	—	—
91-92 — Detroit	NHL	27	1	0	1	72	1	0	0	—	—	—	—	—
— Adirondack	AHL	20	2	4	6	107	...	...	...	17	1	3	4	43
92-93 — Detroit	NHL	9	0	1	1	20	1	0	0	—	—	—	—	—
— Adirondack	AHL	30	2	11	13	177	...	...	...	11	1	1	2	14
93-94 — Ottawa	NHL	55	2	5	7	214	-9	0	0	—	—	—	—	—
94-95 — Ottawa	NHL	27	0	4	4	65	0	0	0	—	—	—	—	—
95-96 — Ottawa	NHL	64	1	4	5	276	-13	0	0	—	—	—	—	—
96-97 — Ottawa	NHL	11	0	1	1	25	0	0	0	—	—	—	—	—
NHL totals (7 years)		223	4	15	19	749	-24	0	0					

VIRTUE, TERRY   D   BLUES

PERSONAL: Born August 12, 1970, in Scarborough, Ont. ... 6-0/200. ... Shoots right.
TRANSACTIONS/CAREER NOTES: Signed as free agent by St. Louis Blues (January 29, 1996).

Season Team	League	REGULAR SEASON								PLAYOFFS				
		Gms.	G	A	Pts.	PIM	+/-	PP	SH	Gms.	G	A	Pts.	PIM
88-89 — Victoria	WHL	8	1	1	2	13	...	...	...	—	—	—	—	—
89-90 — Tri-City	WHL	58	2	19	21	167	...	...	...	—	—	—	—	—
90-91 — Tri-City	WHL	11	1	8	9	24	...	...	...	—	—	—	—	—
— Portland	WHL	59	9	44	53	127	...	...	...	—	—	—	—	—
91-92 — Roanoke	ECHL	38	4	22	26	165	...	...	...	—	—	—	—	—
— Louisville	ECHL	23	1	15	16	58	...	...	...	13	0	8	8	49
92-93 — Louisville	ECHL	28	0	17	17	84	...	...	...	—	—	—	—	—
— Wheeling	ECHL	31	3	15	18	86	...	...	...	16	3	5	8	18
93-94 — Wheeling	ECHL	34	5	28	33	61	...	...	...	6	2	2	4	4
— Cape Breton	AHL	26	4	6	10	10	...	...	...	6	0	0	0	17
94-95 — Worcester	AHL	73	14	25	39	183	...	...	...	—	—	—	—	—
95-96 — Worcester	AHL	76	7	31	38	234	...	...	...	4	0	0	0	4
96-97 — Worcester	AHL	80	16	26	42	220	...	...	...	5	0	4	4	8

VOKOUN, TOMAS   G   CANADIENS

PERSONAL: Born July 2, 1976, in Karlovy Vary, Czechoslovakia. ... 5-11/208. ... Catches right. ... Name pronounced TOH-mahz voh-KOON.
TRANSACTIONS/CAREER NOTES: Selected by Montreal Canadiens in ninth round (11th Canadiens pick, 226th overall) of NHL entry draft (June 29, 1994).

Season Team	League	REGULAR SEASON								PLAYOFFS						
		Gms.	Min	W	L	T	GA	SO	Avg.	Gms.	Min.	W	L	GA	SO	Avg.
93-94 — Poldi Kladno	Czech Rep.	1	20	...	...	...	2	0	6.00	—	—	—	—	—	—	—
94-95 — Poldi Kladno	Czech Rep.	26	1368	...	...	...	70	...	3.07	5	240	...	...	19	...	4.75
95-96 — Wheeling	ECHL	35	1911	20	10	‡2	117	0	3.67	7	436	4	3	19	0	2.61
— Fredericton	AHL	0	0	0	0	0	0	.	0.00	1	59	0	1	4	0	4.09
96-97 — Fredericton	AHL	47	2645	12	26	7	154	2	3.49	—	—	—	—	—	—	—
— Montreal	NHL	1	20	0	0	0	4	0	12.00	—	—	—	—	—	—	—
NHL totals (1 year)		1	20	0	0	0	4	0	12.00							

VOLCHKOV, ALEXANDRE   LW   CAPITALS

PERSONAL: Born September 15, 1977, in Moscow, U.S.S.R. ... 6-2/214. ... Shoots left. ... Name pronounced VOHLCH-kahv.
TRANSACTIONS/CAREER NOTES: Selected by Washington Capitals in first round (first Capitals pick, fourth overall) of NHL entry draft (June 22, 1996).

V

HONORS: Named to Can.HL All-Rookie team (1995-96). ... Named to OHL All-Rookie first team (1995-96). ... Named to OHL All-Star second team (1996-97).

		REGULAR SEASON							PLAYOFFS				
Season Team	League	Gms.	G	A	Pts.	PIM	+/-	PP	SH	Gms.	G	A	Pts.	PIM
94-95— CSKA Moscow Jrs.....	CIS	50	20	30	50	20	...	...	...	—	—	—	—	—
95-96— Barrie........................	OHL	47	37	27	64	36	...	...	...	7	2	3	5	12
96-97— Barrie........................	OHL	56	29	53	82	76	...	...	...	9	6	9	15	12
— Portland...................	AHL	—	—	—	—	—				4	0	0	0	0

VON STEFENELLI, PHIL   D   SENATORS

PERSONAL: Born April 10, 1969, in Vancouver. ... 6-0/201. ... Shoots left. ... Name pronounced VAHN stehf-ih-NEHL-ee.
COLLEGE: Boston University.
TRANSACTIONS/CAREER NOTES: Selected by Vancouver Canucks in sixth round (fifth Canucks pick, 122nd overall) of NHL entry draft (June 11, 1988). ... Signed as free agent by Boston Bruins (July 6, 1993). ... Signed as free agent by Ottawa Senators (July 12, 1996).

		REGULAR SEASON							PLAYOFFS				
Season Team	League	Gms.	G	A	Pts.	PIM	+/-	PP	SH	Gms.	G	A	Pts.	PIM
85-86— Richmond..................	BCJHL	41	6	11	17	28	...	...	...	12	1	1	2	14
86-87— Richmond..................	BCJHL	52	5	32	37	51	...	...	...	—	—	—	—	—
87-88— Boston University	Hockey East	34	3	13	16	38	...	...	...	—	—	—	—	—
88-89— Boston University	Hockey East	33	2	6	8	34	...	...	...	—	—	—	—	—
89-90— Boston University	Hockey East	44	8	20	28	40	...	...	...	—	—	—	—	—
90-91— Boston University	Hockey East	41	7	23	30	32	...	...	...	—	—	—	—	—
91-92— Milwaukee.................	IHL	80	2	34	36	40	...	...	...	5	1	2	3	2
92-93— Hamilton....................	AHL	78	11	20	31	75	...	...	...	—	—	—	—	—
93-94— Hamilton....................	AHL	80	10	31	41	89	...	...	...	4	1	0	1	2
94-95— Providence................	AHL	75	6	13	19	93	...	...	...	13	2	4	6	6
95-96— Providence................	AHL	42	9	21	30	52	...	...	...	—	—	—	—	—
— Boston	NHL	27	0	4	4	16	2	0	0	—	—	—	—	—
96-97— Detroit......................	IHL	67	14	26	40	86	...	...	...	21	2	4	6	20
— Ottawa	NHL	6	0	1	1	7	-3	0	0	—	—	—	—	—
NHL totals (2 years)		33	0	5	5	23	-1	0	0					

VOPAT, JAN   D   KINGS

PERSONAL: Born March 22, 1973, in Most, Czechoslovakia. ... 6-0/198. ... Shoots left. ... Name pronounced YAHN VOH-paht.
TRANSACTIONS/CAREER NOTES: Selected by Hartford Whalers in third round (third Whalers pick, 57th overall) of NHL entry draft (June 20, 1992). ... Traded by Whalers to Los Angeles Kings for fourth-round pick (C Ian MacNeil) in 1995 draft (May 31, 1995). ... Underwent back surgery (October 22, 1996); missed 30 games. ... Sprained ankle (January 24, 1997); missed six games. ... Sprained ankle (February 15, 1997); missed one game. ... Bruised thigh (April 7, 1997); missed one game.

		REGULAR SEASON							PLAYOFFS				
Season Team	League	Gms.	G	A	Pts.	PIM	+/-	PP	SH	Gms.	G	A	Pts.	PIM
90-91— CHZ Litvinov..............	Czech.	25	1	4	5	4	...	...	...	—	—	—	—	—
91-92— Chemo. Litvinov........	Czech.	46	4	2	6	6	...	...	...	—	—	—	—	—
92-93— Chemo. Litvinov........	Czech.	45	12	10	22	...	...	...	...	—	—	—	—	—
93-94— Chemo. Litvinov........	Czech Rep.	41	9	19	28	...	...	...	...	4	1	1	2	0
— Czech Rep. Olympic...	Int'l	8	0	1	1	8	...	...	...	—	—	—	—	—
94-95— Chemo. Litvinov........	Czech Rep.	42	7	18	25	...	...	...	...	4	0	2	2	0
95-96— Phoenix....................	IHL	47	0	9	9	34	...	...	...	4	0	2	2	4
— Los Angeles..............	NHL	11	1	4	5	4	3	0	0	—	—	—	—	—
96-97— Los Angeles	NHL	33	4	5	9	22	3	0	0	—	—	—	—	—
— Phoenix....................	IHL	4	0	6	6	6	...	...	...	—	—	—	—	—
NHL totals (2 years)		44	5	9	14	26	6	0	0					

VOPAT, ROMAN   C   KINGS

PERSONAL: Born April 21, 1976, in Litvinov, Czechoslovakia. ... 6-3/216. ... Shoots left. ... Name pronounced ROH-muhn VOH-paht.
TRANSACTIONS/CAREER NOTES: Selected by St. Louis Blues in seventh round (fourth Blues pick, 172nd overall) of NHL entry draft (June 29, 1994). ... Traded by Blues with LW Craig Johnson, RW/C Patrice Tardiff, fifth-round pick (D Peter Hogan) in 1996 draft and first-round pick (LW Matt Zultek) in 1997 draft to Los Angeles Kings for C Wayne Gretzky (February 27, 1996). ... Suffered concussion (March 22, 1997); missed one game.

		REGULAR SEASON							PLAYOFFS				
Season Team	League	Gms.	G	A	Pts.	PIM	+/-	PP	SH	Gms.	G	A	Pts.	PIM
93-94— Chemopetrol Litvinov.	Czech Rep.	7	0	0	0	...	...	...	...	—	—	—	—	—
94-95— Moose Jaw	WHL	72	23	20	43	141	...	...	...	10	4	1	5	28
— Peoria	IHL	—	—	—	—	—	...	...	...	6	0	2	2	2
95-96— St. Louis	NHL	25	2	3	5	48	-8	1	0	—	—	—	—	—
— Worcester	AHL	5	2	0	2	14	...	...	...	—	—	—	—	—
— Moose Jaw	WHL	7	0	4	4	34	...	...	...	—	—	—	—	—
— Prince Albert.............	WHL	22	15	5	20	81	...	...	...	18	9	8	17	57
96-97— Phoenix.....................	IHL	50	8	8	16	139	...	...	...	—	—	—	—	—
— Los Angeles..............	NHL	29	4	5	9	60	-7	1	0	—	—	—	—	—
NHL totals (2 years)		54	6	8	14	108	-15	2	0					

VOROBIEV, VLADIMIR   LW   RANGERS

PERSONAL: Born October 2, 1972, in Cherepovets, U.S.S.R. ... 6-3/205. ... Shoots right. ... Name pronounced vuh-ROH-bee-yehf.
TRANSACTIONS/CAREER NOTES: Selected by New York Rangers in 10th round (10th Rangers pick, 240th overall) of NHL entry draft (June 20, 1992).

		REGULAR SEASON								PLAYOFFS				
Season Team	League	Gms.	G	A	Pts.	PIM	+/-	PP	SH	Gms.	G	A	Pts.	PIM
92-93— Metal. Cherepovets....	CIS	42	18	5	23	18	...	...	...	—	—	—	—	—
93-94— Dynamo Moscow.......	CIS	11	3	1	4	2	...	...	...	—	—	—	—	—
94-95— Dynamo Moscow.......	CIS	48	9	20	29	28	...	...	...	14	1	7	8	2
95-96— Dynamo Moscow.......	CIS	42	19	9	28	49	...	...	...	9	2	8	10	2
96-97— Binghamton	AHL	61	22	27	49	6	...	...	...	4	1	1	2	2
— New York Rangers	NHL	16	5	5	10	6	4	2	0	—	—	—	—	—
NHL totals (1 year)		16	5	5	10	6	4	2	0					

VUKOTA, MICK   RW   ISLANDERS

PERSONAL: Born September 14, 1966, in Saskatoon, Sask. ... 6-1/225. ... Shoots right. ... Name pronounced vuh-KOH-tuh.
TRANSACTIONS/CAREER NOTES: Signed as free agent by New York Islanders (September 1987). ... Suspended six games by AHL for returning from locker room to fight (November 20, 1987). ... Suffered sore back (February 1990). ... Separated left shoulder (March 18, 1990). ... Suspended 10 games by NHL for fighting (April 5, 1990); missed final four games of 1989-90 season and first six games of 1990-91 season. ... Injured shoulder prior to 1992-93 season; missed first two games of season. ... Bruised left hand (October 26, 1993); missed two games. ... Suspended 10 games and fined $10,000 by NHL for leaving bench to fight (January 7, 1994). ... Suspended two games without pay and fined $500 by NHL for improper conduct in playoff game (May 17, 1994). ... Injured knee (November 28, 1995); missed one game. ... Fractured right thumb (December 23, 1995); missed 43 games.
STATISTICAL PLATEAUS: Three-goal games: 1989-90 (1).
MISCELLANEOUS: Holds New York Islanders all-time record for most penalty minutes (1,879).

		REGULAR SEASON								PLAYOFFS				
Season Team	League	Gms.	G	A	Pts.	PIM	+/-	PP	SH	Gms.	G	A	Pts.	PIM
83-84— Winnipeg	WHL	3	1	1	2	10	...	...	...	—	—	—	—	—
84-85— Kelowna.....................	WHL	66	10	6	16	247	...	...	...	—	—	—	—	—
85-86— Spokane....................	WHL	64	19	14	33	369	...	...	...	9	6	4	10	68
86-87— Spokane....................	WHL	61	25	28	53	*337	...	...	...	4	0	0	0	40
87-88— New York Islanders....	NHL	17	1	0	1	82	1	0	0	2	0	0	0	23
— Springfield	AHL	52	7	9	16	372	...	...	...	—	—	—	—	—
88-89— Springfield	AHL	3	1	0	1	33	...	...	...	—	—	—	—	—
— New York Islanders....	NHL	48	2	2	4	237	-17	0	0	—	—	—	—	—
89-90— New York Islanders....	NHL	76	4	8	12	290	10	0	0	1	0	0	0	17
90-91— Capital District	AHL	2	0	0	0	9	...	...	...	—	—	—	—	—
— New York Islanders....	NHL	60	2	4	6	238	-13	0	0	—	—	—	—	—
91-92— New York Islanders....	NHL	74	0	6	6	293	-6	0	0	—	—	—	—	—
92-93— New York Islanders....	NHL	74	2	5	7	216	3	0	0	15	0	0	0	16
93-94— New York Islanders....	NHL	72	3	1	4	237	-5	0	0	4	0	0	0	17
94-95— New York Islanders....	NHL	40	0	2	2	109	1	0	0	—	—	—	—	—
95-96— New York Islanders....	NHL	32	1	1	2	106	-3	0	0	—	—	—	—	—
96-97— New York Islanders....	NHL	17	1	0	1	71	-2	0	0	—	—	—	—	—
— Utah..........................	IHL	43	11	11	22	185	...	...	...	7	1	2	3	20
NHL totals (10 years)		510	16	29	45	1879	-31	0	0	22	0	0	0	73

VYSHEDKEVICH, SERGEI   D   DEVILS

PERSONAL: Born January 3, 1975, in Moscow, U.S.S.R. ... 6-0/185. ... Shoots left. ... Name pronounced vih-SHEHD-keh-vihch.
TRANSACTIONS/CAREER NOTES: Selected by New Jersey Devils in third round (third Devils pick, 70th overall) of NHL entry draft (July 8, 1995).

		REGULAR SEASON								PLAYOFFS				
Season Team	League	Gms.	G	A	Pts.	PIM	+/-	PP	SH	Gms.	G	A	Pts.	PIM
94-95— Dynamo Moscow.......	CIS	49	6	7	13	67	...	...	...	14	2	0	2	12
95-96— Dynamo Moscow.......	CIS	49	5	4	9	12	...	...	...	13	1	1	2	6
96-97— Albany......................	AHL	65	8	27	35	16	...	...	...	12	0	6	6	0

WAGNER, STEPHEN   G   BLUES

PERSONAL: Born January 17, 1977, in Red Deer, Alta. ... 6-2/200. ... Catches left.
COLLEGE: Denver.
TRANSACTIONS/CAREER NOTES: Selected by St. Louis Blues in sixth round (fifth Blues pick, 159th overall) of NHL entry draft (June 22, 1996).

		REGULAR SEASON							PLAYOFFS					
Season Team	League	Gms.	Min	W	L	T	GA	SO	Avg.	Gms.	Min.	W	L	GA	SO	Avg.
95-96— Olds..........................	AJHL	47	2787	...	...	...	139	2	2.99	—	—	—	—	—	—	—
96-97— University of Denver.....	WCHA	22	1202	13	6	0	57	...	2.85	—	—	—	—	—	—	—

V
W

WAITE, JIM — G — BLACKHAWKS

PERSONAL: Born April 15, 1969, in Sherbrooke, Que. ... 6-1/180. ... Catches left. ... Name pronounced WAYT.

TRANSACTIONS/CAREER NOTES: Selected by Chicago Blackhawks as underage junior in first round (first Blackhawks pick, eighth overall) of NHL entry draft (June 13, 1987). ... Broke collarbone (December 6, 1988). ... Sprained ankle (October 12, 1991); missed one game. ... Loaned to Hershey Bears for part of 1991-92 season. ... Traded by Blackhawks to San Jose Sharks for future considerations (June 18, 1993); Sharks sent D Neil Wilkinson to Blackhawks to complete deal (July 9, 1993). ... Sprained knee (January 11, 1994); missed two games. ... Underwent arthroscopic knee surgery (March 7, 1994); missed eight games. ... Traded by Sharks to Blackhawks for fourth-round pick (traded to New York Rangers) in 1997 draft (February 6, 1995).

HONORS: Won Raymond Lagace Trophy (1986-87). ... Named to QMJHL All-Star second team (1986-87). ... Won James Norris Memorial Trophy (1989-90). ... Named to IHL All-Star first team (1989-90).

| | | REGULAR SEASON | | | | | | | | PLAYOFFS | | | | | | |
Season Team	League	Gms.	Min	W	L	T	GA	SO	Avg.	Gms.	Min.	W	L	GA	SO	Avg.
86-87—Chicoutimi	QMJHL	50	2569	23	17	3	209	†2	4.88	11	576	4	6	54	*1	5.63
87-88—Chicoutimi	QMJHL	36	2000	17	16	1	150	0	4.50	4	222	1	2	17	0	4.59
88-89—Chicago	NHL	11	494	0	7	1	43	0	5.22	—	—	—	—	—	—	—
—Saginaw	IHL	5	304	3	1	‡0	10	0	1.97	—	—	—	—	—	—	—
89-90—Indianapolis	IHL	54	*3207	34	14	‡5	135	*5	*2.53	†10	*602	9	1	19	†1	*1.89
—Chicago	NHL	4	183	2	0	0	14	0	4.59	—	—	—	—	—	—	—
90-91—Indianapolis	IHL	49	2888	26	18	‡4	167	3	3.47	6	369	2	4	20	0	3.25
—Chicago	NHL	1	60	1	0	0	2	0	2.00	—	—	—	—	—	—	—
91-92—Chicago	NHL	17	877	4	7	4	54	0	3.69	—	—	—	—	—	—	—
—Indianapolis	IHL	13	702	4	7	‡1	53	0	4.53	—	—	—	—	—	—	—
—Hershey	AHL	11	631	6	4	1	44	0	4.18	6	360	2	4	19	0	3.17
92-93—Chicago	NHL	20	996	6	7	1	49	2	2.95	—	—	—	—	—	—	—
93-94—San Jose	NHL	15	697	3	7	0	50	0	4.30	2	40	0	0	3	0	4.50
94-95—Chicago	NHL	2	119	1	1	0	5	0	2.52	—	—	—	—	—	—	—
—Indianapolis	IHL	4	239	2	1	‡1	13	0	3.26	—	—	—	—	—	—	—
95-96—Indianapolis	IHL	56	3157	28	18	‡6	179	0	3.40	5	297	2	3	15	1	3.03
—Chicago	NHL	1	31	0	0	0	0	0	0.00	—	—	—	—	—	—	—
96-97—Chicago	NHL	2	105	0	1	1	7	0	4.00	—	—	—	—	—	—	—
—Indianapolis	IHL	41	2450	22	15	‡4	112	4	2.74	4	222	1	3	13	0	3.51
NHL totals (9 years)		73	3562	17	30	7	224	2	3.77	2	40	0	0	3	0	4.50

WAKALUK, DARCY — G — COYOTES

PERSONAL: Born March 14, 1966, in Pincher Creek, Alta. ... 5-11/180. ... Catches left. ... Name pronounced WAHK-ih-luhk.

TRANSACTIONS/CAREER NOTES: Selected by Buffalo Sabres as underage junior in seventh round (seventh Sabres pick, 144th overall) of NHL entry draft (June 9, 1984). ... Traded by Sabres to Minnesota North Stars for eighth-round pick (D Jiri Kuntos) in 1991 draft and future considerations (May 26, 1991). ... Hyperextended knee (February 17, 1993); missed two games. ... North Stars franchise moved from Minnesota to Dallas and renamed Stars for 1993-94 season. ... Broke hand (March 16, 1995); missed nine games. ... Strained back (April 14, 1995); missed three games. ... Pulled hamstring (January 15, 1996); missed five games. ... Signed as free agent by Phoenix Coyotes (July 2, 1996). ... Underwent arthoscopic knee surgery (January 5, 1997); missed remainder of season.

HONORS: Shared Harry (Hap) Holmes Memorial Trophy with David Littman (1990-91).

MISCELLANEOUS: Stopped a penalty shot attempt (vs. Dave Manson, January 24, 1991; vs. Dave Andreychuk, February 7, 1992; vs. Steve Yzerman, March 19, 1993; vs. Wendel Clark, December 21, 1995). ... Allowed a penalty shot goal (vs. Bob Errey, October 31, 1991; vs. Dimitri Kristich, January 7, 1992; vs. Bob Kudelski, October 30, 1993). ... First goaltender in AHL history to score goal (vs. Utica, December 5, 1987).

| | | REGULAR SEASON | | | | | | | | PLAYOFFS | | | | | | |
Season Team	League	Gms.	Min	W	L	T	GA	SO	Avg.	Gms.	Min.	W	L	GA	SO	Avg.
83-84—Kelowna	WHL	31	1555	...	...	...	163	0	6.29	—	—	—	—	—	—	—
84-85—Kelowna	WHL	54	3094	19	30	4	244	0	4.73	5	282	1	4	22	0	4.68
85-86—Spokane	WHL	47	2562	21	22	1	224	1	5.25	7	419	3	4	37	0	5.30
86-87—Rochester	AHL	11	545	2	2	0	26	0	2.86	5	141	2	0	11	0	4.68
87-88—Rochester	AHL	55	2763	27	16	3	159	0	3.45	6	328	3	3	22	0	4.02
88-89—Buffalo	NHL	6	214	1	3	0	15	0	4.21	—	—	—	—	—	—	—
—Rochester	AHL	33	1566	11	14	0	97	1	3.72	—	—	—	—	—	—	—
89-90—Rochester	AHL	56	3095	31	16	4	173	2	3.35	†17	*1001	10	6	50	0	*3.00
90-91—Buffalo	NHL	16	630	4	5	3	35	0	3.33	2	37	0	1	2	0	3.24
—Rochester	AHL	26	1363	10	10	3	68	*4	*2.99	9	544	6	3	30	0	3.31
91-92—Minnesota	NHL	36	1905	13	19	1	104	1	3.28	—	—	—	—	—	—	—
—Kalamazoo	IHL	1	60	1	0	‡0	7	0	7.00	—	—	—	—	—	—	—
92-93—Minnesota	NHL	29	1596	10	12	5	97	1	3.65	—	—	—	—	—	—	—
93-94—Dallas	NHL	36	2000	18	9	6	88	3	2.64	5	307	4	1	15	0	2.93
94-95—Dallas	NHL	15	754	4	8	0	40	2	3.18	1	20	0	0	1	0	3.00
95-96—Dallas	NHL	37	1875	9	16	5	106	1	3.39	—	—	—	—	—	—	—
96-97—Phoenix	NHL	16	782	8	3	1	39	1	2.99	—	—	—	—	—	—	—
NHL totals (8 years)		191	9756	67	75	21	524	9	3.22	8	364	4	2	18	0	2.97

WALKER, SCOTT — C — CANUCKS

PERSONAL: Born July 19, 1973, in Montreal. ... 5-9/180. ... Shoots right.

TRANSACTIONS/CAREER NOTES: Selected by Vancouver Canucks in fifth round (fourth Canucks pick, 124th overall) of NHL entry draft (June 26, 1993). ... Strained abdominal muscle (October 12, 1996); missed eight games. ... Strained groin (December 13, 1996); missed six games.

HONORS: Named to OHL All-Star second team (1992-93).

| | | REGULAR SEASON | | | | | | | PLAYOFFS | | | | |
Season Team	League	Gms.	G	A	Pts.	PIM	+/-	PP	SH	Gms.	G	A	Pts.	PIM
89-90—Kit.-Cambridge Jr. B	OHA	33	7	27	34	91	...	...	...	—	—	—	—	—
90-91—Cambridge Jr. B	OHA	45	10	27	37	241	...	...	...	—	—	—	—	—

W

Season Team	League	REGULAR SEASON								PLAYOFFS				
		Gms.	G	A	Pts.	PIM	+/-	PP	SH	Gms.	G	A	Pts.	PIM
91-92— Owen Sound	OHL	53	7	31	38	128	...	...	...	5	0	7	7	8
92-93— Owen Sound	OHL	57	23	68	91	110	...	...	...	8	1	5	6	16
— Canadian nat'l team	Int'l	2	3	0	3	0	...	...	...	—	—	—	—	—
93-94— Hamilton	AHL	77	10	29	39	272	...	...	...	4	0	1	1	25
94-95— Syracuse	AHL	74	14	38	52	334	...	...	...	—	—	—	—	—
— Vancouver	NHL	11	0	1	1	33	0	0	0	—	—	—	—	—
95-96— Vancouver	NHL	63	4	8	12	137	-7	0	1	—	—	—	—	—
— Syracuse	AHL	15	3	12	15	52	...	...	...	16	9	8	17	39
96-97— Vancouver	NHL	64	3	15	18	132	2	0	0	—	—	—	—	—
NHL totals (3 years)		138	7	24	31	302	-5	0	1					

WALLIN, JESSE — D — RED WINGS

PERSONAL: Born March 10, 1978, in Saskatoon, Sask. ... 6-2/190. ... Shoots left. ... Name pronounced WAH-lihn.

TRANSACTIONS/CAREER NOTES: Selected by Detroit Red Wings in first round (first Red Wings pick, 26th overall) of NHL entry draft (June 22, 1996).

HONORS: Won Can.HL Humanitarian of the Year Award (1996-97). ... Won WHL Humanitarian Award (1996-97).

Season Team	League	REGULAR SEASON								PLAYOFFS				
		Gms.	G	A	Pts.	PIM	+/-	PP	SH	Gms.	G	A	Pts.	PIM
94-95— Red Deer	WHL	72	4	16	20	72	...	...	...	—	—	—	—	—
95-96— Red Deer	WHL	70	5	19	24	61	...	...	...	9	0	3	3	4
96-97— Red Deer	WHL	59	6	33	39	70	...	...	...	16	1	4	5	10

WALZ, WES — C

PERSONAL: Born May 15, 1970, in Calgary. ... 5-10/185. ... Shoots right.

TRANSACTIONS/CAREER NOTES: Selected by Boston Bruins in third round (third Bruins pick, 57th overall) of NHL entry draft (June 17, 1989). ... Traded by Bruins with D Garry Galley and future considerations to Philadelphia Flyers for D Gord Murphy, RW Brian Dobbin and third-round pick (LW Sergei Zholtok) in 1992 draft (January 2, 1992). ... Signed as free agent by Calgary Flames (August 31, 1993). ... Strained hip (February 26, 1995); missed one game. ... Signed as free agent by Detroit Red Wings (August 11, 1995).

HONORS: Won Jim Piggott Memorial Trophy (1988-89). ... Won WHL Player of the Year Award (1989-90). ... Named to WHL (East) All-Star first team (1989-90).

MISCELLANEOUS: Failed to score on a penalty shot (vs. Tim Cheveldae, November 2, 1991).

Season Team	League	REGULAR SEASON								PLAYOFFS				
		Gms.	G	A	Pts.	PIM	+/-	PP	SH	Gms.	G	A	Pts.	PIM
87-88— Prince Albert	WHL	1	1	1	2	0	...	...	...	—	—	—	—	—
88-89— Lethbridge	WHL	63	29	75	104	32	...	...	...	8	1	5	6	6
89-90— Boston	NHL	2	1	1	2	0	-1	1	0	—	—	—	—	—
— Lethbridge	WHL	56	54	86	140	69	...	...	...	19	13	*24	†37	33
90-91— Maine	AHL	20	8	12	20	19	...	...	...	2	0	0	0	21
— Boston	NHL	56	8	8	16	32	-14	1	0	2	0	0	0	0
91-92— Boston	NHL	15	0	3	3	12	-3	0	0	—	—	—	—	—
— Maine	AHL	21	13	11	24	38	...	...	...	—	—	—	—	—
— Hershey	AHL	41	13	28	41	37	...	...	...	6	1	2	3	0
— Philadelphia	NHL	2	1	0	1	0	1	0	0	—	—	—	—	—
92-93— Hershey	AHL	78	35	45	80	106	...	...	...	—	—	—	—	—
93-94— Calgary	NHL	53	11	27	38	16	20	1	0	6	3	0	3	2
— Saint John	AHL	15	6	6	12	14	...	...	...	—	—	—	—	—
94-95— Calgary	NHL	39	6	12	18	11	7	4	0	1	0	0	0	0
95-96— Adirondack	AHL	38	20	35	55	58	...	...	...	—	—	—	—	—
— Detroit	NHL	2	0	0	0	0	0	0	0	—	—	—	—	—
96-97—					Did not play.									
NHL totals (7 years)		169	27	51	78	71	10	7	0	9	3	0	3	2

WARD, AARON — D — RED WINGS

PERSONAL: Born January 17, 1973, in Windsor, Ont. ... 6-2/215. ... Shoots right. ... Full name: Aaron Christian Ward.

COLLEGE: Michigan.

TRANSACTIONS/CAREER NOTES: Selected by Winnipeg Jets in first round (first Jets pick, fifth overall) of NHL entry draft (June 22, 1991). ... Traded by Jets with fourth-round pick (D John Jakopin) in 1993 draft and future considerations to Detroit Red Wings for RW Paul Ysebaert (June 11, 1993); Jets sent RW Alan Kerr to Red Wings to complete deal (June 18, 1993). ... Suffered bronchitis (December 22, 1996); missed three games.

HONORS: Named to CCHA All-Rookie Team (1990-91).

MISCELLANEOUS: Member of Stanley Cup championship team (1997).

Season Team	League	REGULAR SEASON								PLAYOFFS				
		Gms.	G	A	Pts.	PIM	+/-	PP	SH	Gms.	G	A	Pts.	PIM
88-89— Nepean	COJHL	56	2	17	19	44	...	...	...	—	—	—	—	—
89-90— Nepean	COJHL	52	6	33	39	85	...	...	...	—	—	—	—	—
90-91— Univ. of Michigan	CCHA	46	8	11	19	126	...	...	...	—	—	—	—	—
91-92— Univ. of Michigan	CCHA	42	7	12	19	64	...	...	...	—	—	—	—	—
92-93— Univ. of Michigan	CCHA	30	5	8	13	73	...	...	...	—	—	—	—	—
— Canadian nat'l team	Int'l	4	0	0	0	8	...	...	...	—	—	—	—	—
93-94— Detroit	NHL	5	1	0	1	4	2	0	0	—	—	—	—	—
— Adirondack	AHL	58	4	12	16	87	...	...	...	9	2	6	8	6

Y

Season Team	League	Gms.	G	A	Pts.	PIM	+/-	PP	SH	Gms.	G	A	Pts.	PIM
		REGULAR SEASON								PLAYOFFS				
94-95 — Adirondack	AHL	76	11	24	35	87	...	...	...	4	0	1	1	0
— Detroit	NHL	1	0	1	1	2	1	0	0	—	—	—	—	—
95-96 — Adirondack	AHL	74	5	10	15	133	...	...	...	3	0	0	0	6
96-97 — Detroit	NHL	49	2	5	7	52	-9	0	0	19	0	0	0	17
NHL totals (3 years)		55	3	6	9	58	-6	0	0	19	0	0	0	17

WARD, DIXON — RW — SABRES

PERSONAL: Born September 23, 1968, in Edmonton. ... 6-0/200. ... Shoots right.
COLLEGE: North Dakota.
TRANSACTIONS/CAREER NOTES: Selected by Vancouver Canucks in seventh round (sixth Canucks pick, 128th overall) of NHL entry draft (June 11, 1988). ... Separated left shoulder (December 1990). ... Sprained ankle (March 14, 1993); missed four games. ... Suspended three games and fined $500 by NHL for checking from behind (October 15, 1993). ... Traded by Canucks with future considerations to Los Angeles Kings for C Jimmy Carson (January 8, 1994). ... Traded by Kings with C Guy Leveque, RW Shayne Toporowski and C Kelly Fairchild to Toronto Maple Leafs for LW Eric Lacroix, D Chris Snell and fourth-round pick (C Eric Belanger) in 1996 draft (October 3, 1994). ... Loaned by Maple Leafs to Chicago Wolves of IHL (March 16, 1995). ... Signed as free agent by Buffalo Sabres (August 24, 1995).
HONORS: Named to WCHA All-Star second team (1990-91 and 1991-92). ... Won Jack Butterfield Trophy (1995-96).

Season Team	League	Gms.	G	A	Pts.	PIM	+/-	PP	SH	Gms.	G	A	Pts.	PIM
		REGULAR SEASON								PLAYOFFS				
86-87 — Red Deer	AJHL	59	46	40	86	153	...	...	...	—	—	—	—	—
87-88 — Red Deer	AJHL	51	60	71	131	167	...	...	...	—	—	—	—	—
88-89 — North Dakota	WCHA	37	8	9	17	26	...	...	...	—	—	—	—	—
89-90 — North Dakota	WCHA	45	35	34	69	44	...	...	...	—	—	—	—	—
90-91 — North Dakota	WCHA	43	34	35	69	84	...	...	...	—	—	—	—	—
91-92 — North Dakota	WCHA	38	33	31	64	90	...	...	...	—	—	—	—	—
92-93 — Vancouver	NHL	70	22	30	52	82	34	4	1	9	2	3	5	0
93-94 — Vancouver	NHL	33	6	1	7	37	-14	2	0	—	—	—	—	—
— Los Angeles	NHL	34	6	2	8	45	-8	2	0	—	—	—	—	—
94-95 — Toronto	NHL	22	0	3	3	31	-4	0	0	—	—	—	—	—
— St. John's	AHL	6	3	3	6	19	...	...	...	—	—	—	—	—
— Detroit	IHL	7	3	6	9	7	...	...	...	5	3	0	3	7
95-96 — Rochester	AHL	71	38	56	94	74	...	...	...	19	11	*24	*35	8
— Buffalo	NHL	8	2	2	4	6	1	0	0	—	—	—	—	—
96-97 — Buffalo	NHL	79	13	32	45	36	17	1	2	12	2	3	5	6
NHL totals (5 years)		246	49	70	119	237	26	9	3	21	4	6	10	6

WARD, ED — RW — FLAMES

PERSONAL: Born November 10, 1969, in Edmonton. ... 6-3/205. ... Shoots right. ... Full name: Edward John Ward.
COLLEGE: Northern Michigan.
TRANSACTIONS/CAREER NOTES: Tore knee cartilage (August 1987). ... Selected by Quebec Nordiques in sixth round (seventh Nordiques pick, 108th overall) of NHL entry draft (June 11, 1988). ... Traded by Nordiques to Calgary Flames for D Francois Groleau (March 24, 1995). ... Bruised ribs (December 3, 1995); missed one game. ... Lacerated elbow (December 13, 1995); missed one game.

Season Team	League	Gms.	G	A	Pts.	PIM	+/-	PP	SH	Gms.	G	A	Pts.	PIM
		REGULAR SEASON								PLAYOFFS				
86-87 — Sherwood Park	AJHL	60	18	28	46	272	...	...	...	—	—	—	—	—
87-88 — Northern Michigan	WCHA	25	0	2	2	40	...	...	...	—	—	—	—	—
88-89 — Northern Michigan	WCHA	42	5	15	20	36	...	...	...	—	—	—	—	—
89-90 — Northern Michigan	WCHA	39	5	11	16	77	...	...	...	—	—	—	—	—
90-91 — Northern Michigan	WCHA	46	13	18	31	109	...	...	...	—	—	—	—	—
91-92 — Halifax	AHL	51	7	11	18	65	...	...	...	—	—	—	—	—
— Greensboro	ECHL	12	4	8	12	21	...	...	...	—	—	—	—	—
92-93 — Halifax	AHL	70	13	19	32	56	...	...	...	—	—	—	—	—
93-94 — Cornwall	AHL	60	12	30	42	65	...	...	...	12	1	3	4	14
— Quebec	NHL	7	1	0	1	5	0	0	0	—	—	—	—	—
94-95 — Cornwall	AHL	56	10	14	24	118	...	...	...	—	—	—	—	—
— Saint John	AHL	11	4	5	9	20	...	...	...	5	1	0	1	10
— Calgary	NHL	2	1	1	2	2	-2	0	0	—	—	—	—	—
95-96 — Saint John	AHL	12	1	2	3	45	...	...	...	16	4	4	8	27
— Calgary	NHL	41	3	5	8	44	-2	0	0	—	—	—	—	—
96-97 — Saint John	AHL	1	0	0	0	0	...	...	...	—	—	—	—	—
— Detroit	IHL	31	7	6	13	45	...	...	...	—	—	—	—	—
— Calgary	NHL	40	5	8	13	49	-3	0	0	—	—	—	—	—
NHL totals (4 years)		90	10	14	24	100	-7	0	0					

WARD, LANCE — D — DEVILS

PERSONAL: Born June 2, 1978, in Lloydminster, Alta. ... 6-3/195. ... Shoots left.
TRANSACTIONS/CAREER NOTES: Selected by New Jersey Devils in first round (first Devils pick, 10th overall) of NHL entry draft (June 22, 1996).

Season Team	League	Gms.	G	A	Pts.	PIM	+/-	PP	SH	Gms.	G	A	Pts.	PIM
		REGULAR SEASON								PLAYOFFS				
94-95 — Red Deer	WHL	28	0	0	0	57	...	...	...	—	—	—	—	—
95-96 — Red Deer	WHL	72	4	13	17	127	...	...	...	10	0	4	4	10
96-97 — Red Deer	WHL	70	5	34	39	229	...	...	...	16	0	3	3	36

W

WARE, JEFF   D   MAPLE LEAFS

PERSONAL: Born May 19, 1977, in Toronto. ... 6-4/220. ... Shoots left.
HIGH SCHOOL: Henry Street (Whitby, Ont.).
TRANSACTIONS/CAREER NOTES: Selected by Toronto Maple Leafs in first round (first Maple Leafs pick, 15th overall) of NHL entry draft (July 8, 1995).

				REGULAR SEASON								PLAYOFFS			
Season Team	League	Gms.	G	A	Pts.	PIM	+/-	PP	SH		Gms.	G	A	Pts.	PIM
93-94— Wexford	Tier II Jr. A	45	1	9	10	75	...	...	...		—	—	—	—	—
94-95— Oshawa	OHL	55	2	11	13	86	...	...	...		7	1	1	2	6
95-96— Oshawa	OHL	62	4	19	23	128	...	...	...		5	0	1	1	8
— St. John's	AHL	4	0	0	0	4	...	...	...		4	0	0	0	2
96-97— Toronto	NHL	13	0	0	0	6	2	0	0		—	—	—	—	—
— Oshawa	OHL	24	1	10	11	38	...	...	...		13	0	3	3	34
NHL totals (1 year)		13	0	0	0	6	2	0	0						

WARRENER, RHETT   D   PANTHERS

PERSONAL: Born January 27, 1976, in Shaunavon, Sask. ... 6-1/209. ... Shoots right. ... Name pronounced REHT WAHR-uh-nuhr.
TRANSACTIONS/CAREER NOTES: Selected by Florida Panthers in second round (second Panthers pick, 27th overall) of NHL entry draft (June 28, 1994). ... Strained groin (October 20, 1996); missed four games. ... Strained groin (November 11, 1996); missed two games. ... Strained groin (December 22, 1996); missed 10 games.

				REGULAR SEASON								PLAYOFFS			
Season Team	League	Gms.	G	A	Pts.	PIM	+/-	PP	SH		Gms.	G	A	Pts.	PIM
91-92— Saskatoon	WHL	2	0	0	0	0	...	...	...		—	—	—	—	—
92-93— Saskatoon	WHL	68	2	17	19	100	...	...	...		9	0	0	0	14
93-94— Saskatoon	WHL	61	7	19	26	131	...	...	...		16	0	5	5	33
94-95— Saskatoon	WHL	66	13	26	39	137	...	...	...		10	0	3	3	6
95-96— Carolina	AHL	9	0	0	0	4	...	...	...		—	—	—	—	—
— Florida	NHL	28	0	3	3	46	4	0	0		21	0	3	3	10
96-97— Florida	NHL	62	4	9	13	88	20	1	0		5	0	0	0	0
NHL totals (2 years)		90	4	12	16	134	24	1	0		26	0	3	3	10

WARRINER, TODD   LW/C   MAPLE LEAFS

PERSONAL: Born January 3, 1974, in Chatham, Ont. ... 6-1/188. ... Shoots left. ... Name pronounced WAHR-ih-nuhr.
HIGH SCHOOL: Herman E. Fawcett (Brantford, Ont.).
TRANSACTIONS/CAREER NOTES: Selected by Quebec Nordiques in first round (first Nordiques pick, fourth overall) of NHL entry draft (June 20, 1992). ... Traded by Nordiques with C Mats Sundin, D Garth Butcher and first-round pick (traded to Washington Capitals who selected D Nolan Baumgartner) in 1994 draft to Toronto Maple Leafs for LW Wendel Clark, D Sylvain Lefebvre, RW Landon Wilson and first-round pick (D Jeffrey Kealty) in 1994 draft (June 28, 1994). ... Suffered hip pointer (December 7, 1995); missed eight games. ... Injured hip flexor (October 3, 1996); missed one game. ... Injured hip flexor (November 19, 1996); missed four games. ... Suffered from the flu (April 2, 1997); missed one game.
HONORS: Won Can.HL Top Draft Prospect Award (1991-92). ... Won OHL Top Draft Prospect Award (1991-92). ... Named to Can.HL All-Star second team (1991-92). ... Named to OHL All-Star first team (1991-92).
MISCELLANEOUS: Member of silver-medal-winning Canadian Olympic team (1994).

				REGULAR SEASON								PLAYOFFS			
Season Team	League	Gms.	G	A	Pts.	PIM	+/-	PP	SH		Gms.	G	A	Pts.	PIM
88-89— Blenheim Jr. C	OHA	10	1	4	5	0	...	...	...		—	—	—	—	—
89-90— Chatham Jr. B	OHA	40	24	21	45	12	...	...	...		—	—	—	—	—
90-91— Windsor	OHL	57	36	28	64	26	...	...	...		11	5	6	11	12
91-92— Windsor	OHL	50	41	42	83	66	...	...	...		7	5	4	9	6
92-93— Windsor	OHL	23	13	21	34	29	...	...	...		—	—	—	—	—
— Kitchener	OHL	32	19	24	43	35	...	...	...		7	5	14	19	14
93-94— Canadian nat'l team	Int'l	50	11	20	31	33	...	...	...		—	—	—	—	—
— Can. Olympic team	Int'l	4	1	1	2	0	...	...	...		—	—	—	—	—
— Kitchener	OHL	—	—	—	—	—	...	...	...		1	0	1	1	0
— Cornwall	AHL	—	—	—	—	—	...	...	...		10	1	4	5	4
94-95— St. John's	AHL	46	8	10	18	22	...	...	...		4	1	0	1	2
— Toronto	NHL	5	0	0	0	0	-3	0	0		—	—	—	—	—
95-96— St. John's	AHL	11	5	6	11	16	...	...	...		—	—	—	—	—
— Toronto	NHL	57	7	8	15	26	-11	1	0		6	1	1	2	2
96-97— Toronto	NHL	75	12	21	33	41	-3	2	2		—	—	—	—	—
NHL totals (3 years)		137	19	29	48	67	-17	3	2		6	1	1	2	2

WASHBURN, STEVE   C   PANTHERS

PERSONAL: Born April 10, 1975, in Ottawa. ... 6-1/191. ... Shoots left.
TRANSACTIONS/CAREER NOTES: Selected by Florida Panthers in third round (fifth Panthers pick, 78th overall) of NHL entry draft (June 26, 1993). ... Sprained knee (April 11, 1997); missed remainder of season.

				REGULAR SEASON								PLAYOFFS			
Season Team	League	Gms.	G	A	Pts.	PIM	+/-	PP	SH		Gms.	G	A	Pts.	PIM
90-91— Gloucester	OPJHL	56	21	30	51	47	...	...	...		—	—	—	—	—
91-92— Ottawa	OHL	59	5	17	22	10	...	...	...		11	2	3	5	4

W

Season Team	League	REGULAR SEASON Gms.	G	A	Pts.	PIM	+/-	PP	SH	PLAYOFFS Gms.	G	A	Pts.	PIM
92-93— Ottawa	OHL	66	20	38	58	54	...	...	...	—	—	—	—	—
93-94— Ottawa	OHL	65	30	50	80	88	...	...	...	17	7	16	23	10
94-95— Ottawa	OHL	63	43	63	106	72	...	...	...	—	—	—	—	—
— Cincinnati	IHL	6	3	1	4	0	...	...	...	9	1	3	4	4
95-96— Carolina	AHL	78	29	54	83	45	...	...	...	—	—	—	—	—
— Florida....................	NHL	1	0	1	1	0	1	0	0	1	0	1	1	0
96-97— Carolina	AHL	60	23	40	63	66	...	...	...	—	—	—	—	—
— Florida....................	NHL	18	3	6	9	4	2	1	0	—	—	—	—	—
NHL totals (2 years)		19	3	7	10	4	3	1	0	1	0	1	1	0

WATT, MIKE   LW/C   OILERS

PERSONAL: Born March 31, 1976, in Seaforth, Ont. ... 6-1/218. ... Shoots left.
COLLEGE: Michigan State.
TRANSACTIONS/CAREER NOTES: Selected by Edmonton Oilers in second round (third Oilers pick, 32nd overall) of NHL entry draft (June 28, 1994).

Season Team	League	REGULAR SEASON Gms.	G	A	Pts.	PIM	+/-	PP	SH	PLAYOFFS Gms.	G	A	Pts.	PIM
91-92— Stratford Jr. B	OHA	46	5	26	31		...	...	...	—	—	—	—	—
92-93— Stratford Jr. B	OHA	45	20	35	55	100	...	...	...	—	—	—	—	—
93-94— Stratford Jr. B	OHA	48	34	34	68	165	...	...	...	—	—	—	—	—
94-95— Michigan State..........	CCHA	39	12	6	18	64	...	...	...	—	—	—	—	—
95-96— Michigan State..........	CCHA	37	17	22	39	60	...	...	...	—	—	—	—	—
96-97— Michigan State..........	CCHA	39	24	17	41	109	...	...	...	—	—	—	—	—

WEBB, STEVE   RW   ISLANDERS

PERSONAL: Born April 30, 1975, in Peterborough, Ont. ... 6-0/195. ... Shoots right.
TRANSACTIONS/CAREER NOTES: Selected by Buffalo Sabres in seventh round (eigth Sabres pick, 176th overall) of NHL entry draft (June 29, 1994). ... Signed as free agent by New York Islanders (October 14, 1996).

Season Team	League	REGULAR SEASON Gms.	G	A	Pts.	PIM	+/-	PP	SH	PLAYOFFS Gms.	G	A	Pts.	PIM
91-92— Peterborough............	Jr. B	37	9	9	18	195	...	...	...	—	—	—	—	—
92-93— Windsor....................	OHL	63	14	25	39	181	...	...	...	—	—	—	—	—
93-94— Windsor....................	OHL	33	6	15	21	117	...	...	...	—	—	—	—	—
— Peterborough............	OHL	2	0	1	1	9	...	...	...	—	—	—	—	—
94-95— Peterborough............	OHL	42	8	16	24	109	...	...	...	11	3	3	6	22
95-96— Detroit	IHL	4	0	0	0	24	...	...	...	—	—	—	—	—
— Muskegon................	Col.HL	58	18	24	42	263	...	...	...	5	1	2	3	22
96-97— Kentucky..................	AHL	25	6	6	12	103	...	...	...	2	0	0	0	19
— New York Islanders....	NHL	41	1	4	5	144	-10	1	0	—	—	—	—	—
NHL totals (1 year)		41	1	4	5	144	-10	1	0					

WEEKES, KEVIN   G   PANTHERS

PERSONAL: Born April 4, 1975, in Toronto. ... 6-0/158. ... Catches left. ... Name pronounced WEEKS.
HIGH SCHOOL: West Hill (Ont.) Secondary.
TRANSACTIONS/CAREER NOTES: Selected by Florida Panthers in second round (second Panthers pick, 41st overall) of NHL entry draft (June 26, 1993).

Season Team	League	REGULAR SEASON Gms.	Min	W	L	T	GA	SO	Avg.	PLAYOFFS Gms.	Min.	W	L	GA	SO	Avg.
91-92— St. Michaels Tier II	Jr. A	2	127	...	...	...	11	0	5.20	—	—	—	—	—	—	—
92-93— Owen Sound.................	OHL	29	1645	9	12	5	143	0	5.22	1	26	0	0	5	0	11.54
93-94— Owen Sound.................	OHL	34	1974	13	19	1	158	0	4.80	—	—	—	—	—	—	—
94-95— Ottawa	OHL	41	2266	13	23	4	154	1	4.08	—	—	—	—	—	—	—
95-96— Carolina	AHL	60	3403	24	25	8	229	2	4.04	—	—	—	—	—	—	—
96-97— Carolina	AHL	51	2899	17	†28	4	172	1	3.56	—	—	—	—	—	—	—

WEIBEL, LARS   G   BLACKHAWKS

PERSONAL: Born May 20, 1974, in Rapperswil, Switz. ... 6-0/178. ... Catches left.
TRANSACTIONS/CAREER NOTES: Selected by Chicago Blackhawks in 10th round (ninth Blackhawks pick, 248th overall) of NHL entry draft (June 29, 1994).

Season Team	League	REGULAR SEASON Gms.	Min	W	L	T	GA	SO	Avg.	PLAYOFFS Gms.	Min.	W	L	GA	SO	Avg.
92-93— Biel-Bienne	Switzerland	14	674	...	...	...	54	...	4.81	—	—	—	—	—	—	—
93-94—Lugano.......................	Switzerland	25	...	...	...	...	...	...	...	9	560	...	...	23	...	2.46
94-95—Lugano.......................	Switzerland	35	2076	...	...	...	95	...	2.75	—	—	—	—	—	—	—
95-96—Lugano.......................	Switzerland	36	2122	...	...	...	107	...	3.03	—	—	—	—	—	—	—
96-97—Lugano.......................	Switzerland	45	2667	...	...	...	144	...	3.24	8	513	...	...	24	...	2.81

W

WEIGHT, DOUG   C   OILERS

PERSONAL: Born January 21, 1971, in Warren, Mich. ... 5-11/200. ... Shoots left. ... Name pronounced WAYT.
COLLEGE: Lake Superior State (Mich.).
TRANSACTIONS/CAREER NOTES: Selected by New York Rangers in second round (second Rangers pick, 34th overall) of NHL entry draft (June 16, 1990). ... Sprained elbow (October 14, 1991); missed three games. ... Damaged ligaments (January 11, 1991). ... Suspended four off-days and fined $500 by NHL for cross-checking (November 5, 1992). ... Traded by Rangers to Edmonton Oilers for LW Esa Tikkanen (March 17, 1993). ... Played in Europe during 1994-95 NHL lockout. ... Sprained ankle (February 15, 1997); missed one game. ... Injured ankle (February 21, 1997); missed one game.
HONORS: Named to CCHA All-Rookie team (1989-90). ... Named to NCAA All-America West second team (1990-91). ... Named to CCHA All-Star first team (1990-91). ... Played in NHL All-Star Game (1996).
STATISTICAL PLATEAUS: Three-goal games: 1995-96 (1).
MISCELLANEOUS: Failed to score on a penalty shot (vs. Daren Puppa, January 3, 1996).

Season Team	League	REGULAR SEASON								PLAYOFFS				
		Gms.	G	A	Pts.	PIM	+/-	PP	SH	Gms.	G	A	Pts.	PIM
88-89— Bloomfield	NAJHL	34	26	53	79	105	...	...	...	—	—	—	—	—
89-90— Lake Superior State	CCHA	46	21	48	69	44	...	...	...	—	—	—	—	—
90-91— Lake Superior State	CCHA	42	29	46	75	86	...	...	...	—	—	—	—	—
— New York Rangers	NHL	—	—	—	—	—	—	—	—	1	0	0	0	0
91-92— New York Rangers	NHL	53	8	22	30	23	-3	0	0	7	2	2	4	0
— Binghamton	AHL	9	3	14	17	2	...	...	...	4	1	4	5	6
92-93— New York Rangers	NHL	65	15	25	40	55	4	3	0	—	—	—	—	—
— Edmonton	NHL	13	2	6	8	10	-2	0	0	—	—	—	—	—
93-94— Edmonton	NHL	84	24	50	74	47	-22	4	1	—	—	—	—	—
94-95— Rosenheim	Germany	8	2	3	5	18	...	...	...	—	—	—	—	—
— Edmonton	NHL	48	7	33	40	69	-17	1	0	—	—	—	—	—
95-96— Edmonton	NHL	82	25	79	104	95	-19	9	0	—	—	—	—	—
96-97— Edmonton	NHL	80	21	61	82	80	1	4	0	12	3	8	11	8
NHL totals (7 years)		425	102	276	378	379	-58	21	1	20	5	10	15	8

WEINRICH, ERIC   D   BLACKHAWKS

PERSONAL: Born December 19, 1966, in Roanoke, Va. ... 6-1/210. ... Shoots left. ... Full name: Eric John Weinrich. ... Name pronounced WIGHN-rihch.
HIGH SCHOOL: North Yarmouth (Maine) Academy.
COLLEGE: Maine.
TRANSACTIONS/CAREER NOTES: Dislocated shoulder (December 1984). ... Selected by New Jersey Devils in second round (third Devils pick, 32nd overall) of NHL entry draft (June 15, 1985). ... Traded by Devils with G Sean Burke to Hartford Whalers for RW Bobby Holik, second-round pick (LW Jay Pandolfo) in 1993 draft and future considerations (August 28, 1992). ... Suffered concussion (November 25, 1992); missed two games. ... Sprained knee (September 22, 1993); missed five games. ... Signed as free agent by Hartford Whalers (September 25, 1993). ... Injured right knee (October 5, 1993); missed five games. ... Traded with LW Patrick Poulin by Whalers to the Chicago Blackhawks for RW Steve Larmer and D Bryan Marchment (November 2, 1993). ... Broke jaw (February 24, 1994); missed 17 games. ... Cut eye (November 1, 1995); missed three games. ... Cut thigh (December 31, 1996); missed one game.
HONORS: Named to NCAA All-America East second team (1986-87). ... Named to Hockey East All-Star first team (1986-87). ... Won Eddie Shore Plaque (1989-90). ... Named to AHL All-Star first team (1989-90). ... Named to NHL All-Rookie team (1990-91).

Season Team	League	REGULAR SEASON								PLAYOFFS				
		Gms.	G	A	Pts.	PIM	+/-	PP	SH	Gms.	G	A	Pts.	PIM
83-84— N. Yarmouth Acad.	Maine H.S.	17	23	33	56	...	...	...	...	—	—	—	—	—
84-85— N. Yarmouth Acad.	Maine H.S.	20	6	21	27	...	...	...	...	—	—	—	—	—
85-86— University of Maine	Hockey East	34	0	15	15	26	...	...	...	—	—	—	—	—
86-87— University of Maine	Hockey East	41	12	32	44	59	...	...	...	—	—	—	—	—
87-88— University of Maine	Hockey East	8	4	7	11	22	...	...	...	—	—	—	—	—
— U.S. national team	Int'l	39	3	9	12	24	...	...	...	—	—	—	—	—
— U.S. Olympic team	Int'l	3	0	0	0	24	...	...	...	—	—	—	—	—
88-89— Utica	AHL	80	17	27	44	70	...	...	...	5	0	1	1	8
— New Jersey	NHL	2	0	0	0	0	-1	0	0	—	—	—	—	—
89-90— Utica	AHL	57	12	48	60	38	...	...	...	—	—	—	—	—
— New Jersey	NHL	19	2	7	9	11	1	1	0	6	1	3	4	17
90-91— New Jersey	NHL	76	4	34	38	48	10	1	0	7	1	2	3	6
91-92— New Jersey	NHL	76	7	25	32	55	10	5	0	7	0	2	2	4
92-93— Hartford	NHL	79	7	29	36	76	-11	0	2	—	—	—	—	—
93-94— Hartford	NHL	8	1	1	2	2	-5	1	0	—	—	—	—	—
— Chicago	NHL	54	3	23	26	31	6	1	0	6	0	2	2	6
94-95— Chicago	NHL	48	3	10	13	33	1	1	0	16	1	5	6	4
95-96— Chicago	NHL	77	5	10	15	65	14	0	0	10	1	4	5	10
96-97— Chicago	NHL	81	7	25	32	62	19	1	0	6	0	1	1	4
NHL totals (9 years)		520	39	164	203	383	44	11	2	58	4	19	23	51

WELLS, CHRIS   LW/C   PANTHERS

PERSONAL: Born November 12, 1975, in Calgary. ... 6-6/223. ... Shoots left.
HIGH SCHOOL: Meadowdale (Lynnwood, Wash.).
TRANSACTIONS/CAREER NOTES: Selected by Pittsburgh Penguins in first round (first Penguins pick, 24th overall) of NHL entry draft (June 28, 1994). ... Suffered tendinitis in knee (October 9, 1995); missed two games. ... Traded by Penguins to Florida Panthers for C Stu Barnes and D Jason Woolley (November 19, 1996).
HONORS: Named to WHL (West) All-Star first team (1994-95).

W

Season Team	League	REGULAR SEASON								PLAYOFFS				
		Gms.	G	A	Pts.	PIM	+/-	PP	SH	Gms.	G	A	Pts.	PIM
90-91 — Calgary Royals............	AJHL	35	13	14	27	33	...	...	...	—	—	—	—	—
91-92 — Seattle.......................	WHL	64	13	8	21	70	...	...	...	11	0	0	0	15
92-93 — Seattle.......................	WHL	63	18	37	55	111	...	...	...	5	2	3	5	4
93-94 — Seattle.......................	WHL	69	30	44	74	150	...	...	...	9	6	5	11	23
94-95 — Seattle.......................	WHL	69	45	63	108	148	...	...	...	3	0	1	1	4
— Cleveland	IHL	3	0	1	1	2	...	...	...	—	—	—	—	—
95-96 — Pittsburgh	NHL	54	2	2	4	59	-6	0	1	—	—	—	—	—
96-97 — Cleveland	IHL	15	4	6	10	9	...	...	...	—	—	—	—	—
— Florida.....................	NHL	47	2	6	8	42	5	0	0	3	0	0	0	0
NHL totals (2 years)		101	4	8	12	101	-1	0	1	3	0	0	0	0

WELLS, JAY   D   LIGHTNING

PERSONAL: Born May 18, 1959, in Paris, Ont. ... 6-1/210. ... Shoots left. ... Full name: Gordon Jay Wells.

TRANSACTIONS/CAREER NOTES: Selected by Los Angeles Kings in first round (first Kings pick, 16th overall) of NHL entry draft (August 9, 1979). ... Broke right hand in team practice (October 16, 1981). ... Tore medial collateral ligament in right knee (December 14, 1982). ... Sprained ankle (December 1983). ... Struck in eye during team practice (February 1987). ... Strained lower back (November 1987). ... Traded by Kings to Philadelphia Flyers for D Doug Crossman (September 29, 1988). ... Bruised right shoulder (October 1988). ... Broke knuckle on right hand (January 1989). ... Broke toe (November 1989). ... Traded by Flyers with fourth-round pick in 1991 draft to Buffalo Sabres for RW Kevin Maguire and second-round pick (RW Mikael Renberg) in 1990 draft (March 5, 1990). ... Fractured right ankle (March 6, 1990). ... Tore medial collateral ligament of right knee (October 13, 1990); missed 18 games. ... Traded by Sabres to New York Rangers for D Randy Moller (March 9, 1992). ... Sprained right knee (January 27, 1993); missed 27 games. ... Sprained wrist (March 25, 1994); missed one game. ... Suffered from the flu (April 2, 1994); missed one game. ... Traded by Rangers to St. Louis Blues for D Doug Lidster (July 31, 1995). ... Injured elbow (December 30, 1995); missed two games. ... Signed as free agent by Tampa Bay Lightning (July 29, 1996). ... Sprained knee (February 5, 1997); missed 17 games.

HONORS: Named to OMJHL All-Star first team (1978-79).

MISCELLANEOUS: Member of Stanley Cup championship team (1994).

Season Team	League	REGULAR SEASON								PLAYOFFS				
		Gms.	G	A	Pts.	PIM	+/-	PP	SH	Gms.	G	A	Pts.	PIM
76-77 — Kingston	OMJHL	59	4	7	11	90	...	...	...	—	—	—	—	—
77-78 — Kingston	OMJHL	68	9	13	22	195	...	...	...	5	1	2	3	6
78-79 — Kingston	OMJHL	48	6	21	27	100	...	...	...	11	2	7	9	29
79-80 — Los Angeles	NHL	43	0	0	0	113	...	0	0	4	0	0	0	11
— Binghamton	AHL	28	0	6	6	48	...	...	...	—	—	—	—	—
80-81 — Los Angeles	NHL	72	5	13	18	155	9	0	0	4	0	0	0	27
81-82 — Los Angeles	NHL	60	1	8	9	145	2	0	0	10	1	3	4	41
82-83 — Los Angeles	NHL	69	3	12	15	167	11	0	0	—	—	—	—	—
83-84 — Los Angeles	NHL	69	3	18	21	141	-10	0	0	—	—	—	—	—
84-85 — Los Angeles	NHL	77	2	9	11	185	4	0	0	3	0	1	1	0
85-86 — Los Angeles	NHL	79	11	31	42	226	7	4	0	—	—	—	—	—
86-87 — Los Angeles	NHL	77	7	29	36	155	-19	6	0	5	1	2	3	10
87-88 — Los Angeles	NHL	58	2	23	25	159	-3	1	0	5	1	2	3	21
88-89 — Philadelphia	NHL	67	2	19	21	184	-3	0	0	18	0	2	2	51
89-90 — Philadelphia	NHL	59	3	16	19	129	4	0	0	—	—	—	—	—
— Buffalo	NHL	1	0	1	1	0	1	0	0	6	0	0	0	12
90-91 — Buffalo	NHL	43	1	2	3	86	-18	0	0	1	0	1	1	0
91-92 — Buffalo	NHL	41	2	9	11	157	-3	0	0	—	—	—	—	—
— New York Rangers	NHL	11	0	0	0	24	2	0	0	13	0	2	2	10
92-93 — New York Rangers	NHL	53	1	9	10	107	-2	0	0	—	—	—	—	—
93-94 — New York Rangers	NHL	79	2	7	9	110	4	0	0	23	0	0	0	20
94-95 — New York Rangers	NHL	43	2	7	9	36	0	0	0	10	0	0	0	8
95-96 — St. Louis	NHL	76	0	3	3	67	-8	0	0	12	0	1	1	2
96-97 — Tampa Bay	NHL	21	0	0	0	13	-3	0	0	—	—	—	—	—
NHL totals (18 years)		1098	47	216	263	2359	...	11	0	114	3	14	17	213

WENINGER, DAVID   G   CAPITALS

PERSONAL: Born February 8, 1976, in Calgary. ... 6-1/160. ... Catches left.

COLLEGE: Michigan Tech.

TRANSACTIONS/CAREER NOTES: Selected by Washington Capitals in third round (sixth Capitals pick, 74th overall) of NHL entry draft (June 22, 1996).

Season Team	League	REGULAR SEASON							PLAYOFFS					
		Gms.	Min	W	L	T	GA	SO	Avg.	Gms.	Min.	W	L	GA	SO	Avg.
95-96 — Michigan Tech	WCHA	25	1209	11	7	2	67	0	3.33	—	—	—	—	—	—	—
96-97 — Michigan Tech	WCHA	18	855	1	13	0	59	1	4.14	—	—	—	—	—	—	—

WERENKA, BRAD   D   PENGUINS

PERSONAL: Born February 12, 1969, in Two Hills, Alta. ... 6-2/205. ... Shoots left. ... Full name: John Bradley Werenka. ... Name pronounced wuh-REHN-kuh.

HIGH SCHOOL: Fort Saskatchewan (Alta.).

COLLEGE: Northern Michigan.

TRANSACTIONS/CAREER NOTES: Selected by Edmonton Oilers as underage junior in second round (second Oilers pick, 42nd overall) of NHL entry draft (June 13, 1987). ... Tore stomach muscles (October 1988). ... Sprained right knee (November 3, 1989). ... Loaned by Oilers to Canadian Olympic team (February 10, 1994). ... Traded by Oilers to Quebec Nordiques for G Steve Passmore (March 21, 1994). ... Signed as free agent by Chicago Blackhawks (August 10, 1995). ... Signed as free agent by Pittsburgh Penguins (July 31, 1997).

W

HONORS: Named to NCAA All-America West first team (1990-91). ... Named to NCAA All-Tournament team (1990-91). ... Named to WCHA All-Star first team (1990-91). ... Won Governors Trophy (1996-97). ... Named to IHL All-Star first team (1996-97).
MISCELLANEOUS: Member of silver-medal-winning Canadian Olympic team (1994).

Season Team	League	REGULAR SEASON								PLAYOFFS				
		Gms.	G	A	Pts.	PIM	+/-	PP	SH	Gms.	G	A	Pts.	PIM
85-86— Fort Saskatchewan.....	AJHL	29	12	23	35	24	...	...	...	—	—	—	—	—
86-87— Northern Michigan.....	WCHA	30	4	4	8	35	...	...	...	—	—	—	—	—
87-88— Northern Michigan.....	WCHA	34	7	23	30	26	...	...	...	—	—	—	—	—
88-89— Northern Michigan.....	WCHA	28	7	13	20	16	...	...	...	—	—	—	—	—
89-90— Northern Michigan.....	WCHA	8	2	5	7	8	...	...	...	—	—	—	—	—
90-91— Northern Michigan.....	WCHA	47	20	43	63	36	...	...	...	—	—	—	—	—
91-92— Cape Breton	AHL	66	6	21	27	95	...	...	...	5	0	3	3	6
92-93— Canadian nat'l team ...	Int'l	18	3	7	10	10	...	...	...	—	—	—	—	—
— Edmonton	NHL	27	5	3	8	24	1	0	1	—	—	—	—	—
— Cape Breton	AHL	4	1	1	2	4	...	...	...	16	4	17	21	12
93-94— Cape Breton	AHL	25	6	17	23	19	...	...	...	—	—	—	—	—
— Edmonton	NHL	15	0	4	4	14	-1	0	0	—	—	—	—	—
— Can. Olympic team ...	Int'l	8	2	2	4	8	...	...	...	—	—	—	—	—
— Quebec......................	NHL	11	0	7	7	8	4	0	0	—	—	—	—	—
94-95— Milwaukee	IHL	80	8	45	53	161	...	...	...	15	3	10	13	36
95-96— Indianapolis	IHL	73	15	42	57	85	...	...	...	5	1	3	4	8
— Chicago	NHL	9	0	0	0	8	-2	0	0	—	—	—	—	—
96-97— Indianapolis	IHL	82	20	56	76	83	...	...	...	4	1	4	5	6
NHL totals (4 years)		62	5	14	19	54	2	0	1					

WESENBERG, BRIAN — RW — FLYERS

PERSONAL: Born May 9, 1977, in Peterborough, Ont. ... 6-3/173. ... Shoots right.
HIGH SCHOOL: Bishop MacDonnell (Guelph, Ont.).
TRANSACTIONS/CAREER NOTES: Selected by Mighty Ducks of Anaheim in second round (second Mighty Ducks pick, 29th overall) of NHL entry draft (July 8, 1995). ... Traded by Mighty Ducks to Philadelphia Flyers for C Anatoli Semenov and D Mike Crowley (March 19, 1996).

Season Team	League	REGULAR SEASON								PLAYOFFS				
		Gms.	G	A	Pts.	PIM	+/-	PP	SH	Gms.	G	A	Pts.	PIM
93-94— Cobourg	Tier II Jr. A	40	14	18	32	81	...	...	...	—	—	—	—	—
94-95— Guelph	OHL	66	17	27	44	81	...	...	...	14	2	3	5	18
95-96— Guelph	OHL	66	25	33	58	161	...	...	...	16	4	11	15	34
96-97— Guelph	OHL	64	37	43	80	186	...	...	...	18	4	9	13	59
— Philadelphia	AHL	—	—	—	—	—	...	...	...	3	0	0	0	7

WESLEY, GLEN — D — HURRICANES

PERSONAL: Born October 2, 1968, in Red Deer, Alta. ... 6-1/201. ... Shoots left.
TRANSACTIONS/CAREER NOTES: Selected by Boston Bruins as underage junior in first round (first Bruins pick, third overall) of NHL entry draft (June 13, 1987). ... Sprained left knee (October 1988). ... Broke foot (November 24, 1992); missed 14 games. ... Injured groin (February 1993); missed one game. ... Injured groin (March 1993); missed three games. ... Injured groin (April 1993); missed two games. ... Injured kidney (March 3, 1994); missed three games. ... Traded by Bruins to Hartford Whalers for first-round picks in 1995 (D Kyle McLaren), 1996 (D Johnathan Aitken) and 1997 (C Sergei Samsonov) drafts (August 26, 1994). ... Bruised shin (November 4, 1995); missed two games. ... Injured groin (December 28, 1995); missed three games. ... Sprained knee (January 6, 1996); missed three games. ... Injured groin (January 17, 1996); missed four games. ... Injured groin (January 25, 1996); missed three games. ... Injured hip flexor (November 4, 1996); missed one game. ... Broke foot (November 16, 1996); missed ten games. ... Suffered from the flu (February 5, 1997); missed one game. ... Whalers franchise moved to North Carolina and renamed Carolina Hurricanes for 1997-98 season; NHL approved move on June 25, 1997.
HONORS: Won WHL West Top Defenseman Trophy (1985-86 and 1986-87). ... Named to WHL (West) All-Star first team (1985-86 and 1986-87). ... Named to NHL All-Rookie team (1987-88). ... Played in NHL All-Star Game (1989).
STATISTICAL PLATEAUS: Three-goal games: 1993-94 (1).
MISCELLANEOUS: Captain of Hartford Whalers (1994-95).

Season Team	League	REGULAR SEASON								PLAYOFFS				
		Gms.	G	A	Pts.	PIM	+/-	PP	SH	Gms.	G	A	Pts.	PIM
83-84— Red Deer....................	AJHL	57	9	20	29	40	...	...	...	—	—	—	—	—
— Portland	WHL	3	1	2	3	0	...	...	...	—	—	—	—	—
84-85— Portland	WHL	67	16	52	68	76	...	...	...	6	1	6	7	8
85-86— Portland	WHL	69	16	75	91	96	...	...	...	15	3	11	14	29
86-87— Portland	WHL	63	16	46	62	72	...	...	...	20	8	18	26	27
87-88— Boston	NHL	79	7	30	37	69	21	1	2	23	6	8	14	22
88-89— Boston	NHL	77	19	35	54	61	23	8	1	10	0	2	2	4
89-90— Boston	NHL	78	9	27	36	48	6	5	0	21	2	6	8	36
90-91— Boston	NHL	80	11	32	43	78	0	5	1	19	2	9	11	19
91-92— Boston	NHL	78	9	37	46	54	-9	4	0	15	2	4	6	16
92-93— Boston	NHL	64	8	25	33	47	-2	4	1	4	0	0	0	0
93-94— Boston	NHL	81	14	44	58	64	1	6	1	13	3	3	6	12
94-95— Hartford	NHL	48	2	14	16	50	-6	1	0	—	—	—	—	—
95-96— Hartford	NHL	68	8	16	24	88	-9	6	0	—	—	—	—	—
96-97— Hartford	NHL	68	6	26	32	40	0	3	1	—	—	—	—	—
NHL totals (10 years)		721	93	286	379	599	25	43	7	105	15	32	47	109

WHITE, PETER — C — FLYERS

PERSONAL: Born March 15, 1969, in Montreal. ... 5-11/200. ... Shoots left. ... Full name: Peter Toby White.
COLLEGE: Michigan State.

W

TRANSACTIONS/CAREER NOTES: Selected by Edmonton Oilers in fifth round (fourth Oilers pick, 92nd overall) of NHL entry draft (June 17, 1989). ... Traded by Oilers with fourth-round pick (RW Jason Sessa) in 1996 draft to Toronto Maple Leafs for LW Kent Manderville (December 4, 1995). ... Signed as free agent by Philadelphia Flyers (July 17, 1996).
HONORS: Named to CCHA All-Rookie team (1988-89). ... Named CCHA Playoff Most Valuable Player (1989-90). ... Won John B. Sellenberger Trophy (1994-95 and 1996-97). ... Named to AHL All-Star second team (1994-95 and 1996-97).

Season Team	League	REGULAR SEASON								PLAYOFFS				
		Gms.	G	A	Pts.	PIM	+/-	PP	SH	Gms.	G	A	Pts.	PIM
87-88— Pembroke	COJHL	56	90	136	226	32	...	...	...	—	—	—	—	—
88-89— Michigan State	CCHA	46	20	33	53	17	...	...	...	—	—	—	—	—
89-90— Michigan State	CCHA	45	22	40	62	6	...	...	...	—	—	—	—	—
90-91— Michigan State	CCHA	37	7	31	38	28	...	...	...	—	—	—	—	—
91-92— Michigan State	CCHA	44	26	51	77	32	...	...	...	—	—	—	—	—
92-93— Cape Breton	AHL	64	12	28	40	10	...	...	...	16	3	3	6	12
93-94— Cape Breton	AHL	45	21	49	70	12	...	...	...	5	2	3	5	2
— Edmonton	NHL	26	3	5	8	2	1	0	0	—	—	—	—	—
94-95— Cape Breton	AHL	65	36	†69	*105	30	...	...	...	—	—	—	—	—
— Edmonton	NHL	9	2	4	6	0	1	2	0	—	—	—	—	—
95-96— Edmonton	NHL	26	5	3	8	0	-14	1	0	—	—	—	—	—
— Toronto	NHL	1	0	0	0	0	0	0	0	—	—	—	—	—
— St. John's	AHL	17	6	7	13	6	...	...	...	—	—	—	—	—
— Atlanta	IHL	36	21	20	41	4	...	...	...	3	0	3	3	2
96-97— Philadelphia	AHL	80	*44	61	*105	28	...	...	...	10	6	8	14	6
NHL totals (3 years)		62	10	12	22	2	-12	3	0					

WHITE, TOM   C   BLACKHAWKS

PERSONAL: Born August 25, 1975, in Chicago, Il. ... 6-1/185. ... Shoots left.
HIGH SCHOOL: Westminster School (Simsbury, Conn.).
COLLEGE: Miami of Ohio.
TRANSACTIONS/CAREER NOTES: Selected by Chicago Blackhawks in seventh round (eighth Blackhawks pick, 180th overall) of NHL entry draft (June 26, 1993).

Season Team	League	REGULAR SEASON								PLAYOFFS				
		Gms.	G	A	Pts.	PIM	+/-	PP	SH	Gms.	G	A	Pts.	PIM
90-91— Chicago	MNHL	68	41	47	88	26	...	...	...	—	—	—	—	—
91-92— Westminster School	Conn. H.S.	25	16	21	37	20	...	...	...	—	—	—	—	—
92-93— Westminster School	Conn. H.S.	22	14	13	27	22	...	...	...	—	—	—	—	—
93-94— Miami of Ohio	CCHA	31	1	6	7	26	...	...	...	—	—	—	—	—
94-95— Miami of Ohio	CCHA	35	2	5	7	24	...	...	...	—	—	—	—	—
95-96— Miami of Ohio	CCHA	36	7	4	11	56	...	...	...	—	—	—	—	—
96-97— Miami of Ohio	CCHA	40	7	8	15	42	...	...	...	—	—	—	—	—

WHITFIELD, TRENT   C   BRUINS

PERSONAL: Born June 17, 1977, in Alameda, Sask. ... 5-10/175. ... Shoots left.
TRANSACTIONS/CAREER NOTES: Selected by Boston Bruins in fourth round (fifth Bruins pick, 100th overall) of NHL entry draft (June 22, 1996).
HONORS: Named to WHL (West) All-Star first team (1996-97).

Season Team	League	REGULAR SEASON								PLAYOFFS				
		Gms.	G	A	Pts.	PIM	+/-	PP	SH	Gms.	G	A	Pts.	PIM
94-95— Spokane	WHL	48	8	17	25	26	...	...	...	11	7	6	13	5
95-96— Spokane	WHL	72	33	51	84	75	...	...	...	18	8	10	18	10
96-97— Spokane	WHL	58	34	42	76	74	...	...	...	9	5	7	12	10

WHITNEY, RAY   LW   SHARKS

PERSONAL: Born May 8, 1972, in Edmonton. ... 5-10/180. ... Shoots right.
TRANSACTIONS/CAREER NOTES: Selected by San Jose Sharks in second round (second Sharks pick, 23rd overall) of NHL entry draft (June 22, 1991). ... Sprained knee (October 30, 1993); missed 18 games. ... Suffered from the flu (December 15, 1993); missed one game. ... Injured ankle (February 20, 1995) and suffered eye infection (February 28, 1995); missed seven games. ... Suffered eye infection (March 21, 1995); missed one game. ... Suffered from the flu (April 9, 1995); missed one game. ... Injured groin (December 15, 1995); missed three games. ... Injured wrist (February 18, 1996); missed 17 games.
HONORS: Won Four Broncos Memorial Trophy (1990-91). ... Won Bob Clarke Trophy (1990-91). ... Won WHL (West) Player of the Year Award (1990-91). ... Won George Parsons Trophy (1990-91). ... Named to Memorial Cup All-Star team (1990-91). ... Named to WHL (West) All-Star first team (1990-91).

W

Season Team	League	REGULAR SEASON								PLAYOFFS				
		Gms.	G	A	Pts.	PIM	+/-	PP	SH	Gms.	G	A	Pts.	PIM
88-89— Spokane	WHL	71	17	33	50	16	...	...	...	—	—	—	—	—
89-90— Spokane	WHL	71	57	56	113	50	...	...	...	6	3	4	7	6
90-91— Spokane	WHL	72	67	118	*185	36	...	...	...	15	13	18	*31	12
91-92— San Diego	IHL	63	36	54	90	12	...	...	...	4	0	0	0	0
— San Jose	NHL	2	0	3	3	0	-1	0	0	—	—	—	—	—
— Koln	Germany	10	3	6	9	4	...	...	...	—	—	—	—	—
92-93— Kansas City	IHL	46	20	33	53	14	...	...	...	12	5	7	12	2
— San Jose	NHL	26	4	6	10	4	-14	1	0	—	—	—	—	—
93-94— San Jose	NHL	61	14	26	40	14	2	1	0	14	0	4	4	8
94-95— San Jose	NHL	39	13	12	25	14	-7	4	0	11	4	4	8	2

Season Team	League	Gms.	G	A	Pts.	PIM	+/-	PP	SH	Gms.	G	A	Pts.	PIM
				REGULAR SEASON								PLAYOFFS		
95-96— San Jose...............	NHL	60	17	24	41	16	-23	4	2	—	—	—	—	—
96-97— Kentucky...............	AHL	9	1	7	8	2	...	...	...	—	—	—	—	—
— Utah...................	IHL	43	13	35	48	34	...	...	...	7	3	1	4	6
— San Jose...............	NHL	12	0	2	2	4	-6	0	0	—	—	—	—	—
NHL totals (6 years)		200	48	73	121	52	-49	10	2	25	4	8	12	10

WICKENHEISER, CHRIS   G   OILERS

PERSONAL: Born January 4, 1972, in Lethbridge, Alta. ... 6-1/185. ... Catches left.
TRANSACTIONS/CAREER NOTES: Selected by Edmonton Oilers in seventh round (12th Oilers pick, 179th overall) of NHL entry draft (June 29, 1994).
HONORS: Named to WHL (West) All-Star second team (1996-97).

Season Team	League	Gms.	Min	W	L	T	GA	SO	Avg.	Gms.	Min.	W	L	GA	SO	Avg.
				REGULAR SEASON								PLAYOFFS				
92-93—Lethbridge	WCHL	44	2532	...	...	...	118	...	2.80	—	—	—	—	—	—	—
93-94—Red Deer	WHL	29	1356	11	13	0	114	0	5.04	—	—	—	—	—	—	—
94-95—Red Deer	WHL	47	2429	13	26	3	181	1	4.47	—	—	—	—	—	—	—
95-96—Red Deer	WHL	48	2666	17	27	2	183	1	4.12	10	550	3	†6	34	1	3.71
96-97—Red Deer	WHL	1	60	0	1	0	4	0	4.00	—	—	—	—	—	—	—
—Portland......................	WHL	40	2367	24	13	3	106	3	2.69	4	226	2	2	0	10	2.65

WIDMER, JASON   D   SHARKS

PERSONAL: Born August 1, 1973, in Calgary. ... 6-0/200. ... Shoots left. ... Name pronounced WIHD-muhr.
TRANSACTIONS/CAREER NOTES: Selected by New York Islanders in eighth round (eighth Islanders pick, 176th overall) of the NHL entry draft (June 20, 1992). ... Signed as free agent by San Jose Sharks (August 26, 1996).

Season Team	League	Gms.	G	A	Pts.	PIM	+/-	PP	SH	Gms.	G	A	Pts.	PIM
				REGULAR SEASON								PLAYOFFS		
89-90— Moose Jaw	WHL	58	1	8	9	33	...	...	...	—	—	—	—	—
90-91— Lethbridge	WHL	58	2	12	14	55	...	...	...	16	0	1	1	12
91-92— Lethbridge	WHL	40	2	19	21	181	...	...	...	5	0	4	4	9
92-93— Lethbridge	WHL	55	3	15	18	140	...	...	...	4	0	3	3	2
— Capital District	AHL	4	0	0	0	2	...	...	...	—	—	—	—	—
93-94— Lethbridge	WHL	64	11	31	42	191	...	...	...	9	3	5	8	34
94-95— Canadian nat'l team ...	Int'l	6	1	4	5	4	...	...	...	—	—	—	—	—
— Worcester	AHL	73	8	26	34	136	...	...	...	—	—	—	—	—
— New York Islanders....	NHL	1	0	0	0	0	-1	0	0	—	—	—	—	—
95-96— Worcester	AHL	76	6	21	27	129	...	...	...	4	2	0	2	9
— New York Islanders....	NHL	4	0	0	0	7	0	0	0	—	—	—	—	—
96-97— Kentucky................	AHL	76	4	24	28	105	...	...	...	4	0	0	0	8
— San Jose...................	NHL	2	0	1	1	0	1	0	0	—	—	—	—	—
NHL totals (3 years)		7	0	1	1	7	0	0	0					

WIEMER, JASON   LW   LIGHTNING

PERSONAL: Born April 14, 1976, in Kimberley, B.C. ... 6-1/215. ... Shoots left. ... Name pronounced WEE-muhr.
TRANSACTIONS/CAREER NOTES: Selected by Tampa Bay Lightning in first round (first Lightning pick, eighth overall) of NHL entry draft (June 28, 1994). ... Suffered from the flu (March 2, 1995); missed one game. ... Injured jaw (November 3, 1995); missed one game. ... Injured back (April 12, 1996); missed one game. ... Broke bursa sac in elbow (November 30, 1996); missed 14 games.
STATISTICAL PLATEAUS: Three-goal games: 1995-96 (1).

Season Team	League	Gms.	G	A	Pts.	PIM	+/-	PP	SH	Gms.	G	A	Pts.	PIM
				REGULAR SEASON								PLAYOFFS		
91-92— Portland.....................	WHL	2	0	1	1	0	...	...	...	—	—	—	—	—
— Kimberley..................	RMJHL	45	34	33	67	211	...	...	...	—	—	—	—	—
92-93— Portland.....................	WHL	68	18	34	52	159	...	...	...	16	7	3	10	27
93-94— Portland.....................	WHL	72	45	51	96	236	...	...	...	10	4	4	8	32
94-95— Portland.....................	WHL	16	10	14	24	63	...	...	...	—	—	—	—	—
— Tampa Bay	NHL	36	1	4	5	44	-2	0	0	—	—	—	—	—
95-96— Tampa Bay	NHL	66	9	9	18	81	-9	4	0	6	1	0	1	28
96-97— Tampa Bay	NHL	63	9	5	14	134	-13	2	0	—	—	—	—	—
— Adirondack.................	AHL	4	1	0	1	7	...	...	...	—	—	—	—	—
NHL totals (3 years)		165	19	18	37	259	-24	6	0	6	1	0	1	28

WIESEL, ADAM   D   CANADIENS

PERSONAL: Born January 25, 1975, in Holyoke, Mass. ... 6-3/211. ... Shoots right. ... Name pronounced WEE-sehl.
HIGH SCHOOL: South Hadley (Mass.).
COLLEGE: Clarkson (N.Y.).
TRANSACTIONS/CAREER NOTES: Selected by Montreal Canadiens in fourth round (fourth Canadiens pick, 85th overall) of NHL entry draft (June 26, 1993).

Season Team	League	Gms.	G	A	Pts.	PIM	+/-	PP	SH	Gms.	G	A	Pts.	PIM
				REGULAR SEASON								PLAYOFFS		
90-91— Springfield Jr. B.........	NEJHL	43	8	17	25	28	...	...	...	—	—	—	—	—
91-92— Springfield Jr. B.........	NEJHL	47	6	13	19	25	...	...	...	—	—	—	—	—

W

Season Team	League	REGULAR SEASON Gms.	G	A	Pts.	PIM	+/-	PP	SH	PLAYOFFS Gms.	G	A	Pts.	PIM
92-93 — Springfield Jr. B	NEJHL	41	11	20	31	34	...	...	...	—	—	—	—	—
93-94 — Clarkson	ECAC	33	3	7	10	28	...	...	...	—	—	—	—	—
94-95 — Clarkson	ECAC	36	6	13	19	28	...	...	...	—	—	—	—	—
95-96 — Fredericton	AHL	69	6	13	19	12	...	...	...	2	0	0	0	0
96-97 — Fredericton	AHL	65	4	7	11	14	...	...	...	—	—	—	—	—

WILFORD, MARTY — D — BLACKHAWKS

PERSONAL: Born April 17, 1977, in Cobourg, Ont. ... 6-0/207. ... Shoots left.
HIGH SCHOOL: Henry Street (Whitby, Ont.).
TRANSACTIONS/CAREER NOTES: Selected by Chicago Blackhawks in sixth round (seventh Blackhawks pick, 149th overall) of NHL entry draft (July 8, 1995).
HONORS: Named to OHL All-Star second team (1996-97).

Season Team	League	REGULAR SEASON Gms.	G	A	Pts.	PIM	+/-	PP	SH	PLAYOFFS Gms.	G	A	Pts.	PIM
93-94 — Peterborough	OHA Jr. A	40	3	19	22	107	...	...	...	—	—	—	—	—
94-95 — Oshawa	OHL	63	1	6	7	95	...	...	...	7	1	1	2	4
95-96 — Oshawa	OHL	65	3	24	27	107	...	...	...	5	0	1	1	4
96-97 — Oshawa	OHL	62	19	43	62	126	...	...	...	16	2	18	20	28

WILKIE, DAVID — D — CANADIENS

PERSONAL: Born May 30, 1974, in Ellensburg, Wash. ... 6-2/210. ... Shoots right.
COLLEGE: Cariboo (B.C.).
TRANSACTIONS/CAREER NOTES: Selected by Montreal Canadiens in first round (first Canadiens pick, 20th overall) of NHL entry draft (June 20, 1992). ... Injured right thigh (April 14, 1995); missed remainder of season. ... Injured groin (October 16, 1996); missed one game. ... Suffered concussion (February 1, 1997); missed four games.

Season Team	League	REGULAR SEASON Gms.	G	A	Pts.	PIM	+/-	PP	SH	PLAYOFFS Gms.	G	A	Pts.	PIM
89-90 — NW Americans	WCHL	41	21	27	48	59	...	...	...	—	—	—	—	—
90-91 — Seattle	WHL	25	1	1	2	22	...	...	...	—	—	—	—	—
91-92 — Kamloops	WHL	71	12	28	40	153	...	...	...	16	6	5	11	19
92-93 — Kamloops	WHL	53	11	26	37	109	...	...	...	6	4	2	6	2
93-94 — Kamloops	WHL	27	11	18	29	18	...	...	...	—	—	—	—	—
— Regina	WHL	29	27	21	48	16	...	...	...	4	1	4	5	4
94-95 — Fredericton	AHL	70	10	43	53	34	...	...	...	1	0	0	0	0
— Montreal	NHL	1	0	0	0	0	0	0	0	—	—	—	—	—
95-96 — Fredericton	AHL	23	5	12	17	20	...	...	...	—	—	—	—	—
— Montreal	NHL	24	1	5	6	10	-10	1	0	6	1	2	3	12
96-97 — Montreal	NHL	61	6	9	15	63	-9	3	0	2	0	0	0	2
NHL totals (3 years)		**86**	**7**	**14**	**21**	**73**	**-19**	**4**	**0**	**8**	**1**	**2**	**3**	**14**

WILKINSON, DEREK — G — LIGHTNING

PERSONAL: Born July 29, 1974, in Windsor, Ont. ... 6-0/160. ... Catches left.
TRANSACTIONS/CAREER NOTES: Selected by Tampa Bay Lightning in eighth round (eighth Lightning pick, 170th overall) of NHL entry draft (June 20, 1992). ... Broke right foot (November 13, 1995); missed 14 games.

Season Team	League	REGULAR SEASON Gms.	Min	W	L	T	GA	SO	Avg.	PLAYOFFS Gms.	Min.	W	L	GA	SO	Avg.
91-92 — Detroit	OHL	38	1943	16	17	1	138	1	4.26	7	313	3	2	28	0	5.37
92-93 — Detroit	OHL	4	245	1	2	1	18	0	4.41	—	—	—	—	—	—	—
— Belleville	OHL	59	3370	21	24	11	237	0	4.22	7	434	3	4	29	0	4.01
93-94 — Belleville	OHL	56	2860	24	16	4	179	2	3.76	12	700	6	†6	39	*1	3.34
94-95 — Atlanta	IHL	46	2415	22	17	‡2	121	1	3.01	4	197	2	1	8	0	2.44
95-96 — Atlanta	IHL	28	1433	11	11	‡2	98	1	4.10	—	—	—	—	—	—	—
— Tampa Bay	NHL	4	200	0	3	0	15	0	4.50	—	—	—	—	—	—	—
96-97 — Tampa Bay	NHL	5	169	0	2	1	12	0	4.26	—	—	—	—	—	—	—
— Cleveland	IHL	46	2595	20	17	‡6	138	1	3.19	14	893	8	*6	*44	0	2.96
NHL totals (2 years)		**9**	**369**	**0**	**5**	**1**	**27**	**0**	**4.39**							

WILKINSON, NEIL — D — PENGUINS

PERSONAL: Born August 15, 1967, in Selkirk, Man. ... 6-3/200. ... Shoots right. ... Full name: Neil John Wilkinson.
COLLEGE: Michigan State.
TRANSACTIONS/CAREER NOTES: Suffered concussion and broke nose (January 1986). ... Selected by Minnesota North Stars in second round (second North Stars pick, 30th overall) of NHL entry draft (June 21, 1986). ... Twisted knee ligaments during training camp (September 1988). ... Bruised left instep (November 9, 1989). ... Strained back (January 1990). ... Tore left thumb ligaments (March 6, 1991); missed five games. ... Selected by San Jose Sharks in NHL dispersal draft (May 30, 1991). ... Injured groin (December 16, 1991); missed four games. ... Injured eye (January 8, 1992); missed three games. ... Strained back (February 4, 1992); missed 13 games. ... Suffered facial contusions (October 28, 1992); missed two games. ... Strained back (November 10, 1992); missed 14 games. ... Injured hand (December 18, 1992); missed one game. ... Strained back (February 10, 1993); missed six games. ... Traded by Sharks to Chicago Blackhawks (July 9, 1993) to complete deal in which Blackhawks sent G Jimmy Waite to Sharks for future considerations (June 18, 1993). ... Traded by Blackhawks to

W

Winnipeg Jets for third-round pick in 1995 draft (June 3, 1994). ... Bruised back (April 7, 1995); missed six games. ... Broke foot (November 10, 1995); missed 14 games. ... Traded by Jets to Pittsburgh Penguins for D Norm Maciver (December 28, 1995). ... Bruised shoulder (January 31, 1996); missed three games. ... Bruised heel (February 14, 1996); missed two games. ... Underwent abdominal surgery (October 2, 1996); missed 38 games. ... Fractured cheekbone (January 15, 1997); missed nine games. ... Bruised shoulder (February 15, 1997); missed two games. ... Suffered abdominal pain (March 8, 1997); missed four games. ... Suffered recurring abdominal pain (April 5, 1997); missed five games.

				REGULAR SEASON								PLAYOFFS			
Season Team	League	Gms.	G	A	Pts.	PIM	+/-	PP	SH		Gms.	G	A	Pts.	PIM
85-86— Selkirk..............	MJHL	42	14	35	49	91	...	...	...		—	—	—	—	—
86-87— Michigan State.........	CCHA	19	3	4	7	18	...	...	...		—	—	—	—	—
87-88— Medicine Hat..............	WHL	55	11	21	32	157	...	...	...		5	1	0	1	2
88-89— Kalamazoo	IHL	39	5	15	20	96	...	...	...		—	—	—	—	—
89-90— Kalamazoo	IHL	20	6	7	13	62	...	...	...		—	—	—	—	—
— Minnesota..................	NHL	36	0	5	5	100	-1	0	0		7	0	2	2	11
90-91— Kalamazoo	IHL	10	0	3	3	38	...	...	...		—	—	—	—	—
— Minnesota..................	NHL	50	2	9	11	117	-5	0	0		22	3	3	6	12
91-92— San Jose..................	NHL	60	4	15	19	107	-11	1	0		—	—	—	—	—
92-93— San Jose..................	NHL	59	1	7	8	96	-50	0	1		—	—	—	—	—
93-94— Chicago..................	NHL	72	3	9	12	116	2	1	0		4	0	0	0	0
94-95— Winnipeg	NHL	40	1	4	5	75	-26	0	0		—	—	—	—	—
95-96— Winnipeg	NHL	21	1	4	5	33	0	0	1		—	—	—	—	—
— Pittsburgh................	NHL	41	2	10	12	87	12	0	0		15	0	1	1	14
96-97— Pittsburgh................	NHL	23	0	0	0	36	-12	0	0		5	0	0	0	4
— Cleveland	IHL	2	0	1	1	0	...	...	...		—	—	—	—	—
NHL totals (8 years)		402	14	63	77	767	-91	2	2		53	3	6	9	41

WILLIAMS, JEFF — C — DEVILS

PERSONAL: Born February 11, 1976, in Pointe-Claire, Que. ... 6-0/175. ... Shoots left.
HIGH SCHOOL: Bishop MacDonnell (Guelph, Ont.).
TRANSACTIONS/CAREER NOTES: Selected by New Jersey Devils in seventh round (eighth Devils pick, 181st overall) of NHL entry draft (June 29, 1994).
HONORS: Won William Hanley Trophy (1995-96).

				REGULAR SEASON								PLAYOFFS			
Season Team	League	Gms.	G	A	Pts.	PIM	+/-	PP	SH		Gms.	G	A	Pts.	PIM
91-92— Newmarket.................	Jr. B	4	1	1	2	4	...	...	...		—	—	—	—	—
92-93— Newmarket.................	Jr. B	45	28	35	63	18	...	...	...		—	—	—	—	—
93-94— Guelph	OHL	62	14	12	26	19	...	...	...		—	—	—	—	—
94-95— Guelph	OHL	52	15	32	47	21	...	...	...		14	5	5	10	0
95-96— Guelph	OHL	63	15	49	64	42	...	...	...		16	13	15	28	10
96-97— Albany	AHL	46	13	20	33	12	...	...	...		15	1	2	3	15
— Raleigh..............	ECHL	20	4	8	12	8	...	...	...		—	—	—	—	—

WILLIS, JORDAN — G — STARS

PERSONAL: Born February 28, 1975, in Kincardine, Ont. ... 5-9/155. ... Catches left.
TRANSACTIONS/CAREER NOTES: Selected by Dallas Stars in 10th round (eighth Stars pick, 243rd overall) of NHL entry draft (June 26, 1993).

				REGULAR SEASON								PLAYOFFS				
Season Team	League	Gms.	Min	W	L	T	GA	SO	Avg.		Gms.	Min.	W	L	GA	SO	Avg.
92-93—London	OHL	26	1428	13	6	3	101	1	4.24		—	—	—	—	—	—	—
93-94—London	OHL	44	2428	20	19	2	158	1	3.90		1	8	0	0	1	0	7.50
94-95—London	OHL	53	2824	16	29	3	202	0	4.29		3	165	0	3	15	0	5.45
95-96—Michigan.........	IHL	38	2184	17	9	‡9	118	1	3.24		4	237	1	3	17	0	4.30
—Dallas..............	NHL	1	19	0	1	0	1	0	3.16		—	—	—	—	—	—	—
96-97—Canadian nat'l team	Int'l	15	804	7	4	2	42	0	3.13		—	—	—	—	—	—	—
—Michigan.........	IHL	2	102	0	2	‡0	8	0	4.71		—	—	—	—	—	—	—
—Dayton	ECHL	8	429	4	4	‡0	25	0	3.50		—	—	—	—	—	—	—
NHL totals (1 year)		1	19	0	1	0	1	0	3.16								

WILM, CLARKE — C — FLAMES

PERSONAL: Born October 24, 1976, in Central Butte, Sask. ... 5-11/204. ... Shoots left. ... Name pronounced WIHLM.
TRANSACTIONS/CAREER NOTES: Selected by Calgary Flames in sixth round (fifth Flames pick, 150th overall) of NHL entry draft (July 8, 1995).

				REGULAR SEASON								PLAYOFFS			
Season Team	League	Gms.	G	A	Pts.	PIM	+/-	PP	SH		Gms.	G	A	Pts.	PIM
91-92— Saskatoon	WHL	—	—	—	—	—	...	...	...		1	0	0	0	0
92-93— Saskatoon	WHL	69	14	19	33	71	...	...	...		9	4	2	6	13
93-94— Saskatoon	WHL	70	18	32	50	181	...	...	...		16	0	9	9	19
94-95— Saskatoon	WHL	71	20	39	59	179	...	...	...		10	6	1	7	21
95-96— Saskatoon	WHL	72	49	61	110	83	...	...	...		4	1	1	2	4
96-97— Saint John	AHL	62	9	19	28	107	...	...	...		5	2	0	2	15

W

WILSON, LANDON   RW   BRUINS

PERSONAL: Born March 15, 1975, in St. Louis. ... 6-2/202. ... Shoots right. ... Son of Rick Wilson, defenseman, Montreal Canadiens, St. Louis Blues and Detroit Red Wings (1973-74 through 1976-77).
COLLEGE: North Dakota.
TRANSACTIONS/CAREER NOTES: Selected by Toronto Maple Leafs in first round (second Maple Leafs pick, 19th overall) of NHL entry draft (June 26, 1993). ... Traded by Maple Leafs with LW Wendel Clark, D Sylvain Lefebvre and first-round pick (D Jeffrey Kealty) in 1994 draft to Quebec Nordiques for C Mats Sundin, D Garth Butcher, LW Todd Warriner and first-round pick (traded to Washington Capitals who selected D Nolan Baumgartner) in 1994 draft (June 28, 1994). ... Nordiques franchise moved to Colorado and renamed Avalanche for 1995-96 season (June 21, 1995). ... Traded by Avalanche with D Anders Myrvold to Boston Bruins for first-round pick in 1998 draft (November 22, 1996). ... Sprained shoulder (December 12, 1996); missed 10 games. ... Suffered charley horse (January 7, 1997); missed 12 games.
HONORS: Named WCHA Rookie of the Year (1993-94). ... Named to WCHA All-Rookie team (1993-94).

		REGULAR SEASON								PLAYOFFS				
Season Team	League	Gms.	G	A	Pts.	PIM	+/-	PP	SH	Gms.	G	A	Pts.	PIM
92-93 — Dubuque	USHL	43	29	36	65	284	...	...	...	—	—	—	—	—
93-94 — North Dakota	WCHA	35	18	15	33	147	...	...	...	—	—	—	—	—
94-95 — North Dakota	WCHA	31	7	16	23	141	...	...	...	—	—	—	—	—
— Cornwall	AHL	8	4	4	8	25	...	...	...	13	3	4	7	68
95-96 — Cornwall	AHL	53	21	13	34	154	...	...	...	8	1	3	4	22
— Colorado	NHL	7	1	0	1	6	3	0	0	—	—	—	—	—
96-97 — Colorado	NHL	9	1	2	3	23	1	0	0	—	—	—	—	—
— Boston	NHL	40	7	10	17	49	-6	0	0	—	—	—	—	—
— Providence	AHL	2	2	1	3	2	...	...	...	10	3	4	7	16
NHL totals (2 years)		56	9	12	21	78	-2	0	0					

WILSON, MIKE   D   SABRES

PERSONAL: Born February 26, 1975, in Brampton, Ont. ... 6-6/212. ... Shoots left.
TRANSACTIONS/CAREER NOTES: Selected by Vancouver Canucks in first round (first Canucks pick, 20th overall) of NHL entry draft (June 26, 1993). ... Traded by Canucks with RW Mike Peca and first-round pick (D Jay McKee) in 1995 draft to Buffalo Sabres for RW Alexander Mogilny and fifth-round pick (LW Todd Norman) in 1995 draft (July 8, 1995). ... Suffered concussion (January 26, 1996); missed two games.
HONORS: Named to Can.HL All-Rookie team (1992-93). ... Named to OHL All-Rookie team (1992-93).

		REGULAR SEASON								PLAYOFFS				
Season Team	League	Gms.	G	A	Pts.	PIM	+/-	PP	SH	Gms.	G	A	Pts.	PIM
91-92 — Georgetown	OHA	41	9	13	22	65	...	...	...	—	—	—	—	—
92-93 — Sudbury	OHL	53	6	7	13	58	...	...	...	14	1	1	2	21
93-94 — Sudbury	OHL	60	4	22	26	62	...	...	...	9	1	3	4	8
94-95 — Sudbury	OHL	64	13	34	47	46	...	...	...	18	1	8	9	10
95-96 — Rochester	AHL	15	0	5	5	38	...	...	...	—	—	—	—	—
— Buffalo	NHL	58	4	8	12	41	13	1	0	—	—	—	—	—
96-97 — Buffalo	NHL	77	2	9	11	51	13	0	0	10	0	1	1	2
NHL totals (2 years)		135	6	17	23	92	26	1	0	10	0	1	1	2

WISEMAN, BRIAN   C   MAPLE LEAFS

PERSONAL: Born July 13, 1971, in Chatham, Ont. ... 5-8/175. ... Shoots left.
TRANSACTIONS/CAREER NOTES: Signed as free agent by Toronto Maple Leafs (August 14, 1996).

		REGULAR SEASON								PLAYOFFS				
Season Team	League	Gms.	G	A	Pts.	PIM	+/-	PP	SH	Gms.	G	A	Pts.	PIM
90-91 — Michigan	CCHA	47	25	33	58	58	...	...	...	—	—	—	—	—
91-92 — Michigan	CCHA	44	27	44	71	38	...	...	...	—	—	—	—	—
92-93 — Michigan	CCHA	35	13	37	50	40	...	...	...	—	—	—	—	—
93-94 — Michigan	CCHA	40	19	50	69	44	...	...	...	—	—	—	—	—
94-95 — Chicago	IHL	75	17	55	72	52	...	...	...	—	—	—	—	—
95-96 — Chicago	IHL	73	33	55	88	117	...	...	...	—	—	—	—	—
96-97 — St. John's	AHL	71	33	62	95	83	...	...	...	—	—	—	—	—
— Toronto	NHL	3	0	0	0	0	0	0	0	—	—	—	—	—
NHL totals (1 year)		3	0	0	0	0	0	0	0					

WITT, BRENDAN   D   CAPITALS

PERSONAL: Born February 20, 1975, in Humboldt, Sask. ... 6-1/205. ... Shoots left.
HIGH SCHOOL: Meadowdale (Lynnwood, Wash.).
TRANSACTIONS/CAREER NOTES: Selected by Washington Capitals in first round (first Capitals pick, 11th overall) of NHL entry draft (June 26, 1993). ... Broke wrist (January 28, 1996); missed 34 games. ... Suffered from the flu (November 15, 1996); missed five games.
HONORS: Named to WHL (West) All-Star first team (1992-93 and 1993-94). ... Won Bill Hunter Trophy (1993-94). ... Named to Can.HL All-Star first team (1993-94).

		REGULAR SEASON								PLAYOFFS				
Season Team	League	Gms.	G	A	Pts.	PIM	+/-	PP	SH	Gms.	G	A	Pts.	PIM
90-91 — Seattle	WHL	—	—	—	—	—	...	...	...	1	0	0	0	0
91-92 — Seattle	WHL	67	3	9	12	212	...	...	...	15	1	1	2	84
92-93 — Seattle	WHL	70	2	26	28	239	...	...	...	5	1	2	3	30
93-94 — Seattle	WHL	56	8	31	39	235	...	...	...	9	3	8	11	23
94-95 —								Did not play.						

W

Season Team	League	REGULAR SEASON								PLAYOFFS				
		Gms.	G	A	Pts.	PIM	+/-	PP	SH	Gms.	G	A	Pts.	PIM
95-96— Washington	NHL	48	2	3	5	85	-4	0	0	—	—	—	—	—
96-97— Washington	NHL	44	3	2	5	88	-20	0	0	—	—	—	—	—
— Portland	AHL	30	2	4	6	56	...	...	...	5	1	0	1	30
NHL totals (2 years)		92	5	5	10	173	-24	0	0					

WOLANIN, CRAIG D MAPLE LEAFS

PERSONAL: Born July 27, 1967, in Grosse Pointe, Mich. ... 6-3/205. ... Shoots left. ... Name pronounced woh-LAN-ihn.

TRANSACTIONS/CAREER NOTES: Selected by New Jersey Devils as underage junior in first round (first Devils pick, third overall) of NHL entry draft (June 15, 1985). ... Bruised left shoulder (October 31, 1985). ... Broke ring finger on left hand (February 1, 1986). ... Underwent surgery to finger (February 19, 1986). ... Suffered sore left hip (December 1987). ... Sprained right knee (November 15, 1988). ... Underwent surgery to right knee (December 1988). ... Injured finger (November 22, 1989). ... Traded by Devils with future considerations to Quebec Nordiques for C Peter Stastny (March 6, 1990); Devils sent D Randy Velischek to Nordiques to complete deal (August 13, 1990). ... Injured knee (April 1, 1990). ... Injured groin (October 17, 1991); missed three games. ... Injured knee (January 8, 1992); missed four games. ... Pulled muscle in right thigh (October 13, 1992); missed 24 games. ... Bruised ribs (December 20, 1992); missed six games. ... Injured groin (January 16, 1993); missed 28 games. ... Pulled groin (April 1, 1993); missed one game. ... Strained left groin (October 18, 1993); missed 11 games. ... Bruised right knee (November 27, 1993); missed one game. ... Strained left hip flexor (January 4, 1994); missed six games. ... Injured groin (January 21, 1995); missed four games. ... Bruised knee (February 25, 1995); missed four games. ... Nordiques franchise moved to Colorado and renamed Avalanche for 1995-96 season (June 21, 1995). ... Injured shoulder (December 18, 1995); missed five games. ... Traded by Avalanche to Tampa Bay Lightning for future considerations (July 29, 1996). ... Injured shoulder (October 5, 1996); missed 23 games. ... Traded by Lightning to Toronto Maple Leafs for third-round pick in 1998 draft (January 31, 1997). ... Sprained knee (March 26, 1997); missed seven games.

MISCELLANEOUS: Member of Stanley Cup championship team (1996).

Season Team	League	REGULAR SEASON								PLAYOFFS				
		Gms.	G	A	Pts.	PIM	+/-	PP	SH	Gms.	G	A	Pts.	PIM
84-85— Kitchener	OHL	60	5	16	21	95	...	...	...	4	1	1	2	2
85-86— New Jersey	NHL	44	2	16	18	74	-7	0	0	—	—	—	—	—
86-87— New Jersey	NHL	68	4	6	10	109	-31	0	0	—	—	—	—	—
87-88— New Jersey	NHL	78	6	25	31	170	0	1	1	18	2	5	7	51
88-89— New Jersey	NHL	56	3	8	11	69	-9	0	0	—	—	—	—	—
89-90— Utica	AHL	6	2	4	6	2	...	...	...	—	—	—	—	—
— New Jersey	NHL	37	1	7	8	47	-13	0	0	—	—	—	—	—
— Quebec	NHL	13	0	3	3	10	2	0	0	—	—	—	—	—
90-91— Quebec	NHL	80	5	13	18	89	-13	0	1	—	—	—	—	—
91-92— Quebec	NHL	69	2	11	13	80	-12	0	0	—	—	—	—	—
92-93— Quebec	NHL	24	1	4	5	49	9	0	0	4	0	0	0	4
93-94— Quebec	NHL	63	6	10	16	80	16	0	0	—	—	—	—	—
94-95— Quebec	NHL	40	3	6	9	40	12	0	0	6	1	1	2	4
95-96— Colorado	NHL	75	7	20	27	50	25	0	3	7	1	0	1	8
96-97— Tampa Bay	NHL	15	0	0	0	8	-9	0	0	—	—	—	—	—
— Toronto	NHL	23	0	4	4	13	3	0	0	—	—	—	—	—
NHL totals (12 years)		685	40	133	173	888	-27	1	5	35	4	6	10	67

WOOD, DODY C SHARKS

PERSONAL: Born May 8, 1972, in Chetywynd, B.C. ... 6-0/200. ... Shoots left.

TRANSACTIONS/CAREER NOTES: Selected by San Jose Sharks in third round (fourth Sharks pick, 45th overall) of NHL entry draft (June 22, 1991). ... Injured hand (November 29, 1995); missed two games. ... Injured back (February 10, 1996); missed seven games ... Injured back (March 5, 1996); missed 11 games. ... Sore foot (October 30, 1996); missed five games. ... Underwent wrist surgery (April 1, 1997); missed remainder of season.

Season Team	League	REGULAR SEASON								PLAYOFFS				
		Gms.	G	A	Pts.	PIM	+/-	PP	SH	Gms.	G	A	Pts.	PIM
89-90— Fort St. John.............	PCJHL	44	51	73	124	270	...	...	...	—	—	—	—	—
— Seattle........................	WHL	—	—	—	—	—	...	...	...	5	0	0	0	2
90-91— Seattle....................	WHL	69	28	37	65	272	...	...	...	6	0	1	1	2
91-92— Seattle....................	WHL	37	13	19	32	232	...	...	...	—	—	—	—	—
— Swift Current	WHL	3	0	2	2	14	...	...	...	7	2	1	3	37
92-93— Kansas City	IHL	36	3	2	5	216	...	...	...	6	0	1	1	15
— San Jose.....................	NHL	13	1	1	2	71	-5	0	0	—	—	—	—	—
93-94— Kansas City	IHL	48	5	15	20	320	...	...	...	—	—	—	—	—
94-95— Kansas City	IHL	44	5	13	18	255	...	...	...	21	7	10	17	87
— San Jose.....................	NHL	9	1	1	2	29	0	0	0	—	—	—	—	—
95-96— San Jose.................	NHL	32	3	6	9	138	0	0	1	—	—	—	—	—
96-97— San Jose.................	NHL	44	3	2	5	193	-3	0	0	—	—	—	—	—
— Kansas City...............	IHL	6	3	6	9	35	...	...	...	—	—	—	—	—
NHL totals (4 years)		98	8	10	18	431	-8	0	1					

WOOD, RANDY LW ISLANDERS

PERSONAL: Born October 12, 1963, in Princeton, N.J. ... 6-0/195. ... Shoots left.

COLLEGE: Yale.

TRANSACTIONS/CAREER NOTES: Signed as free agent by New York Islanders (August 1986). ... Suspended four games by NHL for stick-swinging incident (October 17, 1989). ... Strained right shoulder (March 17, 1990). ... Traded by Islanders with C Pat LaFontaine, D Randy Hillier and future considerations to Buffalo Sabres for C Pierre Turgeon, RW Benoit Hogue, D Uwe Krupp and C Dave McLlwain; Sabres later

W

received fourth-round pick (D Dean Melanson) in 1992 draft (October 25, 1991). ... Selected by Toronto Maple Leafs from Sabres in waiver draft for cash (January 18, 1995). ... Traded by Maple Leafs with LW Benoit Hogue to Dallas Stars for C Dave Gagner (January 28, 1996). ... Signed as free agent by New York Islanders prior to 1996-97 season. ... Separated shoulder (November 30, 1996); missed three games.
HONORS: Named to ECAC All-Star second team (1984-85). ... Named to ECAC All-Star first team (1985-86).
STATISTICAL PLATEAUS: Three-goal games: 1989-90 (1).
MISCELLANEOUS: Scored on a penalty shot (vs. Jeff Hackett, January 11, 1994).

		REGULAR SEASON								PLAYOFFS				
Season Team	League	Gms.	G	A	Pts.	PIM	+/-	PP	SH	Gms.	G	A	Pts.	PIM
82-83— Yale University	ECAC	26	5	14	19	10	...	...	...	—	—	—	—	—
83-84— Yale University	ECAC	18	7	7	14	10	...	...	...	—	—	—	—	—
84-85— Yale University	ECAC	32	25	28	53	23	...	...	...	—	—	—	—	—
85-86— Yale University	ECAC	31	25	30	55	26	...	...	...	—	—	—	—	—
86-87— Springfield	AHL	75	23	24	47	57	...	...	...	—	—	—	—	—
— New York Islanders	NHL	6	1	0	1	4	-1	0	0	13	1	3	4	14
87-88— New York Islanders	NHL	75	22	16	38	80	-2	0	1	5	1	0	1	6
— Springfield	AHL	1	0	1	1	0	...	...	...	—	—	—	—	—
88-89— Springfield	AHL	1	1	1	2	0	...	...	...	—	—	—	—	—
— New York Islanders	NHL	77	15	13	28	44	-18	0	0	—	—	—	—	—
89-90— New York Islanders	NHL	74	24	24	48	39	-10	6	1	5	1	1	2	4
90-91— New York Islanders	NHL	76	24	18	42	45	-12	6	1	—	—	—	—	—
91-92— New York Islanders	NHL	8	2	2	4	21	-3	0	0	—	—	—	—	—
— Buffalo	NHL	70	20	16	36	65	-9	7	1	7	2	1	3	6
92-93— Buffalo	NHL	82	18	25	43	77	6	3	2	8	1	4	5	4
93-94— Buffalo	NHL	84	22	16	38	71	11	2	2	6	0	0	0	0
94-95— Toronto	NHL	48	13	11	24	34	7	1	1	7	2	0	2	6
95-96— Toronto	NHL	46	7	9	16	36	-4	1	0	—	—	—	—	—
— Dallas	NHL	30	1	4	5	26	-11	0	0	—	—	—	—	—
96-97— New York Islanders	NHL	65	6	5	11	61	-7	0	1	—	—	—	—	—
NHL totals (11 years)		741	175	159	334	603	-53	26	10	51	8	9	17	40

WOOLLEY, JASON — D — PENGUINS

PERSONAL: Born July 27, 1969, in Toronto. ... 6-1/188. ... Shoots left. ... Full name: Jason Douglas Woolley.
COLLEGE: Michigan State.
TRANSACTIONS/CAREER NOTES: Selected by Washington Capitals in third round (fourth Capitals pick, 61st overall) of NHL entry draft (June 17, 1989). ... Broke wrist (October 12, 1992); missed 24 games. ... Tore abdominal muscle (January 2, 1994). ... Signed as free agent by Detroit Vipers (October 7, 1994). ... Contract sold by Vipers to Florida Panthers (February 14, 1995). ... Separated left shoulder (October 15, 1995); missed two games. ... Broke left thumb (November 18, 1995); missed 13 games. ... Traded by Panthers with C Stu Barnes to Pittsburgh Penguins for C Chris Wells (November 19, 1996). ... Injured groin (November 22, 1996); missed one game. ... Strained groin (February 27, 1997); missed one game. ... Strained groin (March 4, 1997); missed two games. ... Bruised wrist (March 18, 1997); missed two games.
HONORS: Named to CCHA All-Rookie team (1988-89). ... Named to NCAA All-America West first team (1990-91). ... Named to CCHA All-Star first team (1990-91).
MISCELLANEOUS: Member of silver-medal-winning Canadian Olympic team (1992).

		REGULAR SEASON								PLAYOFFS				
Season Team	League	Gms.	G	A	Pts.	PIM	+/-	PP	SH	Gms.	G	A	Pts.	PIM
87-88— St. Michael's	ODHA	31	19	37	56	22	...	...	...	—	—	—	—	—
88-89— Michigan State	CCHA	47	12	25	37	26	...	...	...	—	—	—	—	—
89-90— Michigan State	CCHA	45	10	38	48	26	...	...	...	—	—	—	—	—
90-91— Michigan State	CCHA	40	15	44	59	24	...	...	...	—	—	—	—	—
91-92— Canadian nat'l team	Int'l	60	14	30	44	36	...	...	...	—	—	—	—	—
— Can. Olympic team	Int'l	8	0	5	5	4	...	...	...	—	—	—	—	—
— Baltimore	AHL	15	1	10	11	6	...	...	...	—	—	—	—	—
— Washington	NHL	1	0	0	0	0	1	0	0	—	—	—	—	—
92-93— Baltimore	AHL	29	14	27	41	22	...	...	...	1	0	2	2	0
— Washington	NHL	26	0	2	2	10	3	0	0	—	—	—	—	—
93-94— Portland	AHL	41	12	29	41	14	...	...	...	9	2	2	4	4
— Washington	NHL	10	1	2	3	4	2	0	0	4	1	0	1	4
94-95— Detroit	IHL	48	8	28	36	38	...	...	...	—	—	—	—	—
— Florida	NHL	34	4	9	13	18	-1	1	0	—	—	—	—	—
95-96— Florida	NHL	52	6	28	34	32	-9	3	0	13	2	6	8	14
96-97— Florida	NHL	3	0	0	0	2	1	0	0	—	—	—	—	—
— Pittsburgh	NHL	57	6	30	36	28	3	2	0	5	0	3	3	0
NHL totals (6 years)		183	17	71	88	94	0	6	0	22	3	9	12	18

WORRELL, PETER — LW — PANTHERS

PERSONAL: Born August 18, 1977, in Pierre Fonds, Que. ... 6-6/225. ... Shoots left.
TRANSACTIONS/CAREER NOTES: Selected by Florida Panthers in seventh round (seventh Panthers pick, 166th overall) of NHL entry draft (July 8, 1995).

		REGULAR SEASON								PLAYOFFS				
Season Team	League	Gms.	G	A	Pts.	PIM	+/-	PP	SH	Gms.	G	A	Pts.	PIM
94-95— Hull	QMJHL	56	1	8	9	243	...	...	...	21	0	1	1	91
95-96— Hull	QMJHL	63	23	36	59	464	...	...	...	18	11	8	19	81
96-97— Hull	QMJHL	62	18	45	63	*495	...	...	...	14	3	13	16	83

W

WOTTON, MARK   D   CANUCKS

PERSONAL: Born November 16, 1973, in Foxwarren, Man. ... 6-0/190. ... Shoots left. ... Name pronounced WAH-tehn.
TRANSACTIONS/CAREER NOTES: Selected by Vancouver Canucks in 10th round (11th Canucks pick, 237th overall) of NHL entry draft (June 20, 1992). ... Suffered blood clot in eye (May 17, 1995); missed six playoff games.
HONORS: Named to WHL (East) All-Star second team (1993-94).

		REGULAR SEASON								PLAYOFFS				
Season Team	League	Gms.	G	A	Pts.	PIM	+/-	PP	SH	Gms.	G	A	Pts.	PIM
90-91 — Saskatoon	WHL	45	4	11	15	37	...	...	...	—	—	—	—	—
91-92 — Saskatoon	WHL	64	11	25	36	92	...	...	...	—	—	—	—	—
92-93 — Saskatoon	WHL	71	15	51	66	90	...	...	...	9	6	5	11	18
93-94 — Saskatoon	WHL	65	12	34	46	108	...	...	...	16	3	12	15	32
94-95 — Syracuse	AHL	75	12	29	41	50	...	...	...	—	—	—	—	—
— Vancouver	NHL	1	0	0	0	0	1	0	0	5	0	0	0	4
95-96 — Syracuse	AHL	80	10	35	45	96	...	...	...	15	1	12	13	20
96-97 — Syracuse	AHL	27	2	8	10	25	...	...	...	2	0	0	0	4
— Vancouver	NHL	36	3	6	9	19	8	0	1	—	—	—	—	—
NHL totals (2 years)		37	3	6	9	19	9	0	1	5	0	0	0	4

WREGGET, KEN   G   PENGUINS

PERSONAL: Born March 25, 1964, in Brandon, Man. ... 6-1/201. ... Catches left.
TRANSACTIONS/CAREER NOTES: Selected by Toronto Maple Leafs as underage junior in third round (fourth Maple Leafs pick, 45th overall) of NHL entry draft (June 9, 1982). ... Injured knee (December 26, 1985). ... Traded by Maple Leafs to Philadelphia Flyers for two first-round picks (RW Rob Pearson and D Steve Bancroft) in 1989 draft (March 6, 1989). ... Tore hamstring (November 1, 1989); missed seven games. ... Pulled hamstring (March 24, 1990). ... Strained right hip flexor (November 4, 1990); missed 15 games. ... Traded by Flyers with RW Rick Tocchet, D Kjell Samuelsson and conditional pick in 1992 draft to Pittsburgh Penguins for RW Mark Recchi, D Brian Benning and first-round pick (LW Jason Bowen) in 1992 draft (February 19, 1992). ... Bruised right knee (February 27, 1993); missed one game. ... Injured foot (April 4, 1994); missed five games. ... Strained ankle (March 24, 1995); missed two games. ... Strained ankle (April 5, 1995); missed four games. ... Pulled hamstring (December 26, 1996); missed 19 games. ... Reinjured hamstring (March 18, 1997); missed four games. ... Reinjured hamstring (April 5, 1997); missed three games.
HONORS: Won WHL Top Goaltender Trophy (1983-84). ... Named to WHL (East) All-Star first team (1983-84).
MISCELLANEOUS: Member of Stanley Cup championship team (1992). ... Stopped a penalty shot attempt (vs. Christian Ruuttu, November 15, 1987; vs. Lane Lambert, March 15, 1988; vs. Joe Nieuwendyk, January 23, 1993; vs. Scott Niedermayer, February 7, 1996). ... Allowed a penalty shot goal (vs. Rick Meagher, December 7, 1986; vs. Joe Sakic, December 9, 1989; vs. Doug Brown, November 23, 1991).

		REGULAR SEASON								PLAYOFFS						
Season Team	League	Gms.	Min	W	L	T	GA	SO	Avg.	Gms.	Min.	W	L	GA	SO	Avg.
81-82 — Lethbridge	WHL	36	1713	19	12	0	118	1	4.13	3	84	...	...	3	0	2.14
82-83 — Lethbridge	WHL	48	2696	26	17	1	157	1	3.49	*20	*1154	14	5	58	*1	*3.02
83-84 — Lethbridge	WHL	53	*3053	32	20	0	161	0	*3.16	4	210	1	3	18	0	5.14
— Toronto	NHL	3	165	1	1	0	14	0	5.09	—	—	—	—	—	—	—
84-85 — Toronto	NHL	23	1278	2	15	3	103	0	4.84	—	—	—	—	—	—	—
— St. Catharines	AHL	12	688	2	8	1	48	0	4.19	—	—	—	—	—	—	—
85-86 — St. Catharines	AHL	18	1058	8	9	0	78	1	4.42	—	—	—	—	—	—	—
— Toronto	NHL	30	1566	9	13	4	113	0	4.33	10	607	6	4	32	†1	3.16
86-87 — Toronto	NHL	56	3026	22	28	2	200	0	3.97	13	761	7	6	29	1	*2.29
87-88 — Toronto	NHL	56	3000	12	35	4	222	2	4.44	2	108	0	1	11	0	6.11
88-89 — Toronto	NHL	32	1888	9	20	2	139	0	4.42	—	—	—	—	—	—	—
— Philadelphia	NHL	3	130	1	1	0	13	0	6.00	5	268	2	2	10	0	2.24
89-90 — Philadelphia	NHL	51	2961	22	24	3	169	0	3.42	—	—	—	—	—	—	—
90-91 — Philadelphia	NHL	30	1484	10	14	3	88	0	3.56	—	—	—	—	—	—	—
91-92 — Philadelphia	NHL	23	1259	9	8	3	75	0	3.57	—	—	—	—	—	—	—
— Pittsburgh	NHL	9	448	5	3	0	31	0	4.15	1	40	0	0	4	0	6.00
92-93 — Pittsburgh	NHL	25	1368	13	7	2	78	0	3.42	—	—	—	—	—	—	—
93-94 — Pittsburgh	NHL	42	2456	21	12	7	138	1	3.37	—	—	—	—	—	—	—
94-95 — Pittsburgh	NHL	38	2208	*25	9	2	118	0	3.21	11	661	5	6	33	1	3.00
95-96 — Pittsburgh	NHL	37	2132	20	13	2	115	3	3.24	9	599	7	2	23	0	2.30
96-97 — Pittsburgh	NHL	46	2514	17	17	6	136	2	3.25	5	297	1	4	18	0	3.64
NHL totals (14 years)		504	27883	198	220	45	1752	8	3.77	56	3341	28	25	160	3	2.87

WREN, BOB   LW   MIGHTY DUCKS

PERSONAL: Born September 16, 1974, in Preston, Ont. ... 5-10/185. ... Shoots left.
TRANSACTIONS/CAREER NOTES: Selected by Los Angeles Kings in fourth round (third Kings pick, 94th overall) of NHL entry draft (June 26, 1993). ... Signed as free agent by Hartford Whalers (September 6, 1994). ... Signed as free agent by Mighty Ducks of Anaheim (October 17, 1996).
HONORS: Named to OHL All-Star second team (1992-93 and 1993-94).

		REGULAR SEASON								PLAYOFFS				
Season Team	League	Gms.	G	A	Pts.	PIM	+/-	PP	SH	Gms.	G	A	Pts.	PIM
89-90 — Guelph	Jr. B	48	24	36	60	12	...	...	...	—	—	—	—	—
90-91 — Kingston	Jr. B	32	27	28	55	85	...	...	...	—	—	—	—	—
91-92 — Detroit	OHL	62	13	36	49	58	...	...	...	7	3	4	7	19
92-93 — Detroit	OHL	63	57	88	145	91	...	...	...	15	4	11	15	20
93-94 — Detroit	OHL	57	45	64	109	81	...	...	...	17	12	18	30	20
94-95 — Springfield	AHL	61	16	15	31	118	...	...	...	—	—	—	—	—
— Richmond	ECHL	2	0	1	1	0	...	...	...	—	—	—	—	—
95-96 — Detroit	IHL	1	0	0	0	0	...	...	...	—	—	—	—	—
— Knoxville	ECHL	50	21	35	56	257	...	...	...	8	4	11	15	32
96-97 — Baltimore	AHL	72	23	36	59	97	...	...	...	3	1	1	2	0

W

WRIGHT, JAMIE — LW — STARS

PERSONAL: Born May 13, 1976, in Kitchener, Ont. ... 6-0/172. ... Shoots left.
HIGH SCHOOL: Bishop MacDonnell (Guelph, Ont.).
TRANSACTIONS/CAREER NOTES: Selected by Dallas Stars in fourth round (third Stars pick, 98th overall) of NHL entry draft (June 29, 1994).
HONORS: Won Bobby Smith Trophy (1994-95).

				REGULAR SEASON							PLAYOFFS			
Season Team	League	Gms.	G	A	Pts.	PIM	+/-	PP	SH	Gms.	G	A	Pts.	PIM
91-92— Elmira	OHA	44	17	11	28	46	...	...	...	—	—	—	—	—
92-93— Elmira	OHA	47	22	32	54	52	...	...	...	—	—	—	—	—
93-94— Guelph	OHL	65	17	15	32	34	...	...	...	8	2	1	3	10
94-95— Guelph	OHL	65	43	39	82	36	...	...	...	14	6	8	14	6
95-96— Guelph	OHL	55	30	36	66	45	...	...	...	16	10	12	22	35
96-97— Michigan	IHL	60	6	8	14	34	...	...	...	1	0	0	0	0

WRIGHT, TYLER — C — PENGUINS

PERSONAL: Born April 6, 1973, in Canora, Sask. ... 5-11/185. ... Shoots right.
TRANSACTIONS/CAREER NOTES: Selected by Edmonton Oilers in first round (first Oilers pick, 12th overall) of NHL entry draft (June 22, 1991). ... Traded by Oilers to Pittsburgh Penguins for seventh-round pick (RW Brandon LaFrance) in 1996 draft (June 22, 1996). ... Bruised ribs (December 13, 1996); missed one game.

				REGULAR SEASON							PLAYOFFS			
Season Team	League	Gms.	G	A	Pts.	PIM	+/-	PP	SH	Gms.	G	A	Pts.	PIM
89-90— Swift Current	WHL	67	14	18	32	119	...	...	...	4	0	0	0	12
90-91— Swift Current	WHL	66	41	51	92	157	...	...	...	3	0	0	0	6
91-92— Swift Current	WHL	63	36	46	82	295	...	...	...	8	2	5	7	16
92-93— Swift Current	WHL	37	24	41	65	76	...	...	...	17	9	17	26	49
— Edmonton	NHL	7	1	1	2	19	-4	0	0	—	—	—	—	—
93-94— Cape Breton	AHL	65	14	27	41	160	...	...	...	5	2	0	2	11
— Edmonton	NHL	5	0	0	0	4	-3	0	0	—	—	—	—	—
94-95— Cape Breton	AHL	70	16	15	31	184	...	...	...	—	—	—	—	—
— Edmonton	NHL	6	1	0	1	14	1	0	0	—	—	—	—	—
95-96— Edmonton	NHL	23	1	0	1	33	-7	0	0	—	—	—	—	—
— Cape Breton	AHL	31	6	12	18	158	...	...	...	—	—	—	—	—
96-97— Pittsburgh	NHL	45	2	2	4	70	-7	0	0	—	—	—	—	—
— Cleveland	IHL	10	4	3	7	34	...	...	...	14	4	2	6	44
NHL totals (5 years)		86	5	3	8	140	-20	0	0					

YACHMENEV, VITALI — RW — KINGS

PERSONAL: Born January 8, 1975, in Chelyabinsk, U.S.S.R. ... 5-9/180. ... Shoots left. ... Name pronounced vee-TAL-ee YAHCH-mih-nehf.
TRANSACTIONS/CAREER NOTES: Selected by Los Angeles Kings in third round (third Kings pick, 59th overall) of NHL entry draft (June 29, 1994). ... Sprained left shoulder (October 4, 1996); missed eight games. ... Sprained ankle (December 27, 1996); missed seven games. ... Suffered from the flu (February 11, 1997); missed one game.
HONORS: Named Can.HL Rookie of the Year (1993-94). ... Won Emms Family Award (1993-94). ... Named to Can.HL All-Rookie team (1993-94). ... Named to OHL All-Rookie team (1993-94). ... Won William Hanley Trophy (1994-95).
STATISTICAL PLATEAUS: Three-goal games: 1995-96 (1).

				REGULAR SEASON							PLAYOFFS			
Season Team	League	Gms.	G	A	Pts.	PIM	+/-	PP	SH	Gms.	G	A	Pts.	PIM
90-91— Traktor Chelyabinsk	USSR	80	88	60	148	72	...	..	...	—	—	—	—	—
91-92— Traktor Chelyabinsk	CIS	80	82	70	152	20	...	...	...	—	—	—	—	—
92-93— Mechel Chelyabinsk	CIS Div. II	51	23	20	43	12	...	...	...	—	—	—	—	—
93-94— North Bay	OHL	66	*61	52	113	18	...	...	...	18	13	19	32	12
94-95— North Bay	OHL	59	53	52	105	8	...	...	...	6	1	8	9	2
— Phoenix	IHL	—	—	—	—	—	...	...	...	4	1	0	1	0
95-96— Los Angeles	NHL	80	19	34	53	16	-3	6	1	—	—	—	—	—
96-97— Los Angeles	NHL	65	10	22	32	10	-9	2	0	—	—	—	—	—
NHL totals (2 years)		145	29	56	85	26	-12	8	1					

YAKE, TERRY — RW — SABRES

PERSONAL: Born October 22, 1968, in New Westminster, B.C. ... 5-11/175. ... Shoots right.
TRANSACTIONS/CAREER NOTES: Selected by Hartford Whalers in fourth round (third Whalers pick, 81st overall) of NHL entry draft (June 13, 1987). ... Selected by Mighty Ducks of Anaheim in NHL expansion draft (June 24, 1993). ... Traded by Mighty Ducks to Toronto Maple Leafs for RW David Sacco (September 28, 1994). ... Loaned by Maple Leafs to Denver Grizzlies of IHL (April 5, 1995). ... Signed as free agent by Buffalo Sabres (August 5, 1996).
STATISTICAL PLATEAUS: Three-goal games: 1993-94 (1).

				REGULAR SEASON							PLAYOFFS			
Season Team	League	Gms.	G	A	Pts.	PIM	+/-	PP	SH	Gms.	G	A	Pts.	PIM
84-85— Brandon	WHL	11	1	1	2	0	...	...	...	—	—	—	—	—
85-86— Brandon	WHL	72	26	26	52	49	...	...	...	—	—	—	—	—
86-87— Brandon	WHL	71	44	58	102	64	...	...	...	—	—	—	—	—
87-88— Brandon	WHL	72	55	85	140	59	...	...	...	3	4	2	6	7
88-89— Hartford	NHL	2	0	0	0	0	1	0	0	—	—	—	—	—
— Binghamton	AHL	75	39	56	95	57	...	...	...	—	—	—	—	—

Season Team	League	REGULAR SEASON Gms.	G	A	Pts.	PIM	+/-	PP	SH	PLAYOFFS Gms.	G	A	Pts.	PIM
89-90— Hartford	NHL	2	0	1	1	0	-1	0	0	—	—	—	—	—
— Binghamton	AHL	77	13	42	55	37	...	...	...	—	—	—	—	—
90-91— Hartford	NHL	19	1	4	5	10	-3	0	0	6	1	1	2	16
— Springfield	AHL	60	35	42	77	56	...	...	...	15	9	9	18	10
91-92— Hartford	NHL	15	1	1	2	4	-2	0	...	—	—	—	—	—
— Springfield	AHL	53	21	34	55	63	...	...	...	8	3	4	7	2
92-93— Springfield	AHL	16	8	14	22	27	...	...	...	—	—	—	—	—
— Hartford	NHL	66	22	31	53	46	3	4	1	—	—	—	—	—
93-94— Anaheim	NHL	82	21	31	52	44	2	5	0	—	—	—	—	—
94-95— Toronto	NHL	19	3	2	5	2	1	1	0	—	—	—	—	—
— Denver	IHL	2	0	3	3	2	...	...	...	17	4	11	15	16
95-96— Milwaukee	IHL	70	32	56	88	70	...	...	...	5	3	6	9	4
96-97— Rochester	AHL	78	34	*67	101	77	...	...	...	10	8	8	16	2
NHL totals (7 years)		205	48	70	118	106	1	10	1	6	1	1	2	16

YAKHANOV, ANDREI   D   BRUINS

PERSONAL: Born July 23, 1973, in Ufa, U.S.S.R. ... 5-11/187. ... Shoots right.
TRANSACTIONS/CAREER NOTES: Selected by Boston Bruins in 11th round (ninth Bruins pick, 281st overall) of NHL entry draft (June 29, 1994).

Season Team	League	REGULAR SEASON Gms.	G	A	Pts.	PIM	+/-	PP	SH	PLAYOFFS Gms.	G	A	Pts.	PIM
92-93— Salavat Yulayev Ufa ...	CIS	41	1	3	4	16	...	...	...	2	0	0	0	2
93-94— Salavat Yulayev Ufa ...	CIS	44	1	3	4	44	...	...	...	—	—	—	—	—
94-95— Salavat Yulayev Ufa ...	CIS	52	3	7	10	50	...	...	...	7	1	0	1	10
95-96— Salavat Yulayev Ufa ...	CIS	51	7	7	14	82	...	...	...	4	1	1	2	0
96-97— Salavat Yulayev Ufa ...	Russian	44	3	10	13	52	...	...	...	10	0	1	1	22

YASHIN, ALEXEI   C   SENATORS

PERSONAL: Born November 5, 1973, in Sverdlovsk, U.S.S.R. ... 6-3/216. ... Shoots right. ... Name pronounced uh-LEK-see YASH-ihn.
TRANSACTIONS/CAREER NOTES: Selected by Ottawa Senators in first round (first Senators pick, second overall) of NHL entry draft (June 20, 1992). ... Suffered strep throat (December 4, 1993); missed one game.
HONORS: Named to CIS All-Star team (1992-93). ... Played in NHL All-Star Game (1994).
STATISTICAL PLATEAUS: Three-goal games: 1993-94 (1), 1994-95 (1), 1995-96 (1). Total: 3.
MISCELLANEOUS: Holds Ottawa Senators all-time records for most goals (101), most assists (136) and most points (237).

Season Team	League	REGULAR SEASON Gms.	G	A	Pts.	PIM	+/-	PP	SH	PLAYOFFS Gms.	G	A	Pts.	PIM
90-91— Avtomo. Sverdlovsk	USSR	26	2	1	3	10	...	...	...	—	—	—	—	—
91-92— Dynamo Moscow	CIS	35	7	5	12	19	...	...	...	—	—	—	—	—
92-93— Dynamo Moscow	CIS	27	10	12	22	18	...	...	...	10	7	3	10	18
93-94— Ottawa	NHL	83	30	49	79	22	-49	11	2	—	—	—	—	—
94-95— Las Vegas	IHL	24	15	20	35	32	...	...	...	—	—	—	—	—
— Ottawa	NHL	47	21	23	44	20	-20	11	0	—	—	—	—	—
95-96— Ottawa	NHL	46	15	24	39	28	-15	8	0	—	—	—	—	—
96-97— Ottawa	NHL	82	35	40	75	44	-7	10	0	7	1	5	6	2
NHL totals (4 years)		258	101	136	237	114	-91	40	2	7	1	5	6	2

YAWNEY, TRENT   D

PERSONAL: Born September 29, 1965, in Hudson Bay, Sask. ... 6-3/195. ... Shoots left.
TRANSACTIONS/CAREER NOTES: Selected by Chicago Blackhawks as underage junior in third round (second Blackhawks pick, 45th overall) of NHL entry draft (June 9, 1984). ... Bruised left shoulder (March 1989). ... Strained right knee (April 24, 1989). ... Bruised kidney (November 11, 1989). ... Bruised thigh (January 1990). ... Strained knee (October 1990). ... Traded by Blackhawks to Calgary Flames for LW Stephane Matteau (December 16, 1991). ... Fractured right clavicle (September 26, 1992); missed first 20 games of season. ... Tore muscle in shoulder (September 9, 1993); missed 25 games. ... Strained left thumb ligaments (January 28, 1995); missed five games. ... Reinjured left thumb (February 11, 1995); missed two games. ... Strained right thumb ligaments (March 22, 1995); missed one game. ... Suffered from the flu (November 8, 1995); missed two games. ... Lacerated hand (January 5, 1996); missed one game. ... Injured knee (February 3, 1996); missed one game. ... Signed as free agent by St. Louis Blues (July 6, 1996).

Season Team	League	REGULAR SEASON Gms.	G	A	Pts.	PIM	+/-	PP	SH	PLAYOFFS Gms.	G	A	Pts.	PIM
81-82— Saskatoon	WHL	6	1	0	1	0	...	...	...	—	—	—	—	—
82-83— Saskatoon	WHL	59	6	31	37	44	...	...	...	6	0	2	2	0
83-84— Saskatoon	WHL	72	13	46	59	81	...	...	...	—	—	—	—	—
84-85— Saskatoon	WHL	72	16	51	67	158	...	...	...	3	1	6	7	7
85-86— Canadian nat'l team	Int'l	73	6	15	21	60	...	...	...	—	—	—	—	—
86-87— Canadian nat'l team	Int'l	51	4	15	19	37	...	...	...	—	—	—	—	—
87-88— Canadian nat'l team	Int'l	60	4	12	16	81	...	...	...	—	—	—	—	—
— Can. Olympic team	Int'l	8	1	1	2	6	...	...	...	—	—	—	—	—
— Chicago	NHL	15	2	8	10	15	1	2	0	5	0	4	4	8
88-89— Chicago	NHL	69	5	19	24	116	-5	3	1	15	3	6	9	20
89-90— Chicago	NHL	70	5	15	20	82	-6	1	0	20	3	5	8	27
90-91— Chicago	NHL	61	3	13	16	77	6	3	0	1	0	0	0	0
91-92— Indianapolis	IHL	9	2	3	5	12	...	...	...	—	—	—	—	—
— Calgary	NHL	47	4	9	13	45	-5	1	0	—	—	—	—	—

Y

Season Team	League	Gms.	G	A	Pts.	PIM	+/-	PP	SH	Gms.	G	A	Pts.	PIM
92-93—Calgary	NHL	63	1	16	17	67	9	0	0	6	3	2	5	6
93-94—Calgary	NHL	58	6	15	21	60	21	1	1	7	0	0	0	16
94-95—Calgary	NHL	37	0	2	2	108	-4	0	0	2	0	0	0	2
95-96—Calgary	NHL	69	0	3	3	88	-1	0	0	4	0	0	0	2
96-97—St. Louis	NHL	39	0	2	2	17	2	0	0	—	—	—	—	—
NHL totals (10 years)		528	26	102	128	675	18	11	2	60	9	17	26	81

YEGOROV, ALEXEI   LW   SHARKS

PERSONAL: Born May 21, 1975, in Leningrad, U.S.S.R. ... 5-11/185. ... Shoots left. ... Name pronounced yuh-GOHR-ahv.
TRANSACTIONS/CAREER NOTES: Selected by San Jose Sharks in third round (third Sharks pick, 66th overall) of NHL entry draft (June 29, 1994).
STATISTICAL PLATEAUS: Three-goal games: 1995-96 (1).

Season Team	League	Gms.	G	A	Pts.	PIM	+/-	PP	SH	Gms.	G	A	Pts.	PIM
92-93—SKA St. Petersburg	CIS	17	1	2	3	10	...	...	...	6	3	1	4	6
93-94—SKA St. Petersburg	CIS	23	5	3	8	18	...	...	...	6	0	0	0	4
94-95—SKA St. Petersburg	CIS	10	2	1	3	10	...	...	...	—	—	—	—	—
—Fort Worth	CHL	18	4	10	14	15	...	...	...	—	—	—	—	—
95-96—Kansas City	IHL	65	31	25	56	84	...	...	...	5	2	0	2	8
—San Jose	NHL	9	3	2	5	2	-5	2	0	—	—	—	—	—
96-97—Kentucky	AHL	75	26	32	58	59	...	...	...	4	0	1	1	2
—San Jose	NHL	2	0	1	1	0	1	0	0	—	—	—	—	—
NHL totals (2 years)		11	3	3	6	2	-4	2	0					

YELLE, STEPHANE   C   AVALANCHE

PERSONAL: Born May 9, 1974, in Ottawa. ... 6-1/187. ... Shoots left. ... Name pronounced YEHL.
TRANSACTIONS/CAREER NOTES: Selected by New Jersey Devils in eighth round (ninth Devils pick, 186th overall) of NHL entry draft (June 20, 1992). ... Traded by Devils with 11th-round pick (D Stephen Low) in 1994 draft to Quebec Nordiques for 11th-round pick (C Mike Hansen) in 1994 draft (June 1, 1994). ... Nordiques franchise moved to Colorado and renamed Avalanche for 1995-96 season (June 21, 1995). ... Pulled groin (February 15, 1996); missed nine games. ... Injured hip flexor (December 14, 1996); missed three games.
MISCELLANEOUS: Member of Stanley Cup championship team (1996).

Season Team	League	Gms.	G	A	Pts.	PIM	+/-	PP	SH	Gms.	G	A	Pts.	PIM
91-92—Oshawa	OHL	55	12	14	26	20	...	...	...	7	2	0	2	1
92-93—Oshawa	OHL	66	24	50	74	20	...	...	...	10	2	4	6	4
93-94—Oshawa	OHL	66	35	69	104	22	...	...	...	5	1	7	8	2
94-95—Cornwall	AHL	40	18	15	33	22	...	...	...	13	7	7	14	8
95-96—Colorado	NHL	71	13	14	27	30	15	0	2	22	1	4	5	8
96-97—Colorado	NHL	79	9	17	26	38	1	0	1	12	1	6	7	2
NHL totals (2 years)		150	22	31	53	68	16	0	3	34	2	10	12	10

YEPANCHINTSEV, VADIM   C   LIGHTNING

PERSONAL: Born March 16, 1976, in Spartak, U.S.S.R. ... 5-9/170. ... Shoots left.
TRANSACTIONS/CAREER NOTES: Selected by Tampa Bay Lightning in third round (third Lightning pick, 55th overall) of NHL entry draft (June 29, 1994).

Season Team	League	Gms.	G	A	Pts.	PIM	+/-	PP	SH	Gms.	G	A	Pts.	PIM
92-93—Yuzhny Ural Orsk	CIS	50	15	22	37	18	...	...	...	—	—	—	—	—
93-94—Spartak Moscow	CIS	46	6	5	11	12	...	...	...	—	—	—	—	—
94-95—Spartak Moscow	CIS	43	4	8	12	24	...	...	...	—	—	—	—	—
95-96—Spartak Moscow	CIS	51	20	12	32	28	...	...	...	—	—	—	—	—
96-97—Spartak Moscow	Russian	38	10	8	18	74	...	...	...	—	—	—	—	—

YLONEN, JUHA   C   COYOTES

PERSONAL: Born February 13, 1972, in Helsinki, Finland. ... 6-0/180. ... Shoots left. ... Name pronounced YOO-hah yee-LOH-nehn.
TRANSACTIONS/CAREER NOTES: Selected by Winnipeg Jets in fifth round (fifth Jets pick, 91st overall) of NHL entry draft (June 22, 1991). ... Jets franchise moved to Phoenix and renamed Coyotes for 1996-97 season; NHL approved move on January 18, 1996.

Season Team	League	Gms.	G	A	Pts.	PIM	+/-	PP	SH	Gms.	G	A	Pts.	PIM
90-91—Kiekko-Espoo	Finland Dv.II	40	12	21	33	4	...	...	...	—	—	—	—	—
91-92—HPK Hameenlinna	Finland	43	7	11	18	8	...	...	...	—	—	—	—	—
92-93—HPK Hameenlinna	Finland	48	8	18	26	22	...	...	...	12	3	5	8	2
93-94—Jokerit Helsinki	Finland	37	5	11	16	2	...	...	...	12	1	3	4	8
94-95—Jokerit Helsinki	Finland	50	13	15	28	10	...	...	...	11	3	2	5	0
95-96—Jokerit Helsinki	Finland	24	3	13	16	20	...	...	...	11	4	5	9	4
96-97—Springfield	AHL	70	20	41	61	6	...	...	...	17	5	†16	21	4
—Phoenix	NHL	2	0	0	0	0	0	0	0	—	—	—	—	—
NHL totals (1 year)		2	0	0	0	0	0	0	0					

YORK, HARRY   C   BLUES

PERSONAL: Born April 4, 1974, in Panoka, Alta. ... 6-2/215. ... Shoots left.
TRANSACTIONS/CAREER NOTES: Signed as free agent by St. Louis Blues (May 1, 1996).

		REGULAR SEASON								PLAYOFFS				
Season Team	League	Gms.	G	A	Pts.	PIM	+/-	PP	SH	Gms.	G	A	Pts.	PIM
95-96— Nashville	ECHL	64	33	50	83	122	...	...	...	—	—	—	—	—
— Worcester	AHL	13	8	5	13	2	...	...	...	4	0	4	4	4
96-97— St. Louis	NHL	74	14	18	32	24	1	3	1	5	0	0	0	2
NHL totals (1 year)		74	14	18	32	24	1	3	1	5	0	0	0	2

YORK, JASON   D   SENATORS

PERSONAL: Born May 20, 1970, in Nepean, Ont. ... 6-2/198. ... Shoots right.
TRANSACTIONS/CAREER NOTES: Selected by Detroit Red Wings in seventh round (sixth Red Wings pick, 129th overall) of NHL entry draft (June 16, 1990). ... Traded by Red Wings with C/RW Mike Sillinger to Mighty Ducks of Anaheim for LW Stu Grimson, D Mark Ferner and sixth-round pick (LW Magnus Nilsson) in 1996 draft (April 4, 1995). ... Sprained right ankle (December 1, 1995); missed two games. ... Traded by Mighty Ducks with C Shaun Van Allen to Ottawa Senators for C Ted Drury and rights to D Marc Moro (October 1, 1996). ... Strained groin (December 4, 1996); missed six games.
HONORS: Named to AHL All-Star first team (1993-94).

		REGULAR SEASON								PLAYOFFS				
Season Team	League	Gms.	G	A	Pts.	PIM	+/-	PP	SH	Gms.	G	A	Pts.	PIM
89-90— Windsor	OHL	39	9	30	39	38	...	...	...	—	—	—	—	—
— Kitchener	OHL	25	11	25	36	17	...	...	...	17	3	19	22	10
90-91— Windsor	OHL	66	13	80	93	40	...	...	...	11	3	10	13	12
91-92— Adirondack	AHL	49	4	20	24	32	...	...	...	5	0	1	1	0
92-93— Adirondack	AHL	77	15	40	55	86	...	...	...	11	0	3	3	18
— Detroit	NHL	2	0	0	0	0	0	0	0	—	—	—	—	—
93-94— Adirondack	AHL	74	10	56	66	98	...	...	...	12	3	11	14	22
— Detroit	NHL	7	1	2	3	2	0	0	0	—	—	—	—	—
94-95— Adirondack	AHL	5	1	3	4	4	...	...	...	—	—	—	—	—
— Detroit	NHL	10	1	2	3	2	0	0	0	—	—	—	—	—
— Anaheim	NHL	15	0	8	8	12	4	0	0	—	—	—	—	—
95-96— Anaheim	NHL	79	3	21	24	88	-7	0	0	—	—	—	—	—
96-97— Ottawa	NHL	75	4	17	21	67	-8	1	0	7	0	0	0	4
NHL totals (5 years)		188	9	50	59	171	-11	1	0	7	0	0	0	4

YOUNG, SCOTT   RW   AVALANCHE

PERSONAL: Born October 1, 1967, in Clinton, Mass. ... 6-0/190. ... Shoots right. ... Full name: Scott Allen Young.
HIGH SCHOOL: St. Mark's (Southborough, Mass.).
COLLEGE: Boston University.
TRANSACTIONS/CAREER NOTES: Selected by Hartford Whalers in first round (first Whalers pick, 11th overall) of NHL entry draft (June 21, 1986). ... Suffered lacerations above right eye (October 8, 1988). ... Lacerated face (February 18, 1990). ... Traded by Whalers to Pittsburgh Penguins for RW Rob Brown (December 21, 1990). ... Traded by Penguins to Quebec Nordiques for D Bryan Fogarty (March 10, 1992). ... Injured rib (February 14, 1993); missed one game. ... Bruised ribs (February 23, 1993); missed one game. ... Sprained right ankle (October 5, 1993); missed eight games. ... Played in Europe during 1994-95 NHL lockout. ... Nordiques franchise moved to Colorado and renamed Avalanche for 1995-96 season (June 21, 1995). ... Bruised right shoulder (December 23, 1996); missed five games.
HONORS: Named Hockey East Rookie of the Year (1985-86).
STATISTICAL PLATEAUS: Three-goal games: 1992-93 (1), 1993-94 (1), 1994-95 (1), 1996-97 (1). Total: 4.
MISCELLANEOUS: Member of Stanley Cup championship team (1991 and 1996).

		REGULAR SEASON								PLAYOFFS				
Season Team	League	Gms.	G	A	Pts.	PIM	+/-	PP	SH	Gms.	G	A	Pts.	PIM
84-85— St. Marks.	Mass. H.S.	23	28	41	69	...	...	...	...	—	—	—	—	—
85-86— Boston University	Hockey East	38	16	13	29	31	...	...	...	—	—	—	—	—
86-87— Boston University	Hockey East	33	15	21	36	24	...	...	...	—	—	—	—	—
87-88— U.S. Olympic team	Int'l	59	13	53	66	...	...	...	...	—	—	—	—	—
— Hartford	NHL	7	0	0	0	2	-6	0	0	4	1	0	1	0
88-89— Hartford	NHL	76	19	40	59	27	-21	6	0	4	2	0	2	4
89-90— Hartford	NHL	80	24	40	64	47	-24	10	2	7	2	0	2	2
90-91— Hartford	NHL	34	6	9	15	8	-9	3	1	—	—	—	—	—
— Pittsburgh	NHL	43	11	16	27	33	3	3	1	17	1	6	7	2
91-92— U.S. national team	Int'l	10	2	4	6	21	...	...	...	—	—	—	—	—
— U.S. Olympic team	Int'l	8	2	1	3	2	...	...	...	—	—	—	—	—
— Bolzano	Italy	18	22	17	39	6	...	...	...	—	—	—	—	—
92-93— Quebec	NHL	82	30	30	60	20	5	9	6	6	4	1	5	0
93-94— Quebec	NHL	76	26	25	51	14	-4	6	1	—	—	—	—	—
94-95— Frankfurt	Germany	1	1	0	1	0	...	...	...	—	—	—	—	—
— Landshut	Germany	4	6	1	7	6	...	...	...	—	—	—	—	—
— Quebec	NHL	48	18	21	39	14	9	3	3	6	3	3	6	2
95-96— Colorado	NHL	81	21	39	60	50	2	7	0	22	3	12	15	10
96-97— Colorado	NHL	72	18	19	37	14	-5	7	0	17	4	2	6	14
NHL totals (9 years)		599	173	239	412	229	-50	54	14	83	20	24	44	34

Y

YSEBAERT, PAUL   LW   LIGHTNING

PERSONAL: Born May 15, 1966, in Sarnia, Ont. ... 6-1/190. ... Shoots left. ... Full name: Paul Robert Ysebaert. ... Name pronounced IGHS-ih-bahrt.
COLLEGE: Bowling Green State.
TRANSACTIONS/CAREER NOTES: Selected by New Jersey Devils in fourth round (fourth Devils pick, 74th overall) of NHL entry draft (June 9, 1984). ... Pulled stomach and groin muscles (December 1988). ... Suffered contusion to left thigh (March 1989). ... Traded by New Jersey Devils to Detroit Red Wings for D Lee Norwood and future considerations; Devils later received fourth-round pick (D Scott McCabe) in 1992 draft to complete deal (November 27, 1990). ... Injured knee (December 1991); missed one game. ... Suffered from the flu (December 22, 1992); missed one game. ... Suffered from the flu (March 5, 1993); missed one game. ... Suffered from the flu (March 10, 1993); missed one game. ... Traded by Red Wings to Winnipeg Jets for D Aaron Ward, fourth-round pick (D John Jakopin) in 1993 draft and future considerations (June 11, 1993); Jets sent RW Alan Kerr to Red Wings to complete deal (June 18, 1993). ... Traded by Jets to Chicago Blackhawks for third-round pick (March 21, 1994). ... Traded by Blackhawks with RW Rich Sutter to Tampa Bay Lightning for RW Jim Cummins, D Jeff Buchanan and D Tom Tilley (February 22, 1995). ... Injured groin (March 24, 1995); missed two games. ... Strained groin (December 16, 1995); missed one game. ... Injured groin (January 6, 1996); missed 24 games. ... Strained groin (September 15, 1996); missed 34 games. ... Strained groin (February 15, 1997); missed nine games.
HONORS: Named CCHA Rookie of the Year (1984-85). ... Named to CCHA All-Star second team (1985-86 and 1986-87). ... Won Les Cunningham Plaque (1989-90). ... Won John B. Sollenberger Trophy (1989-90). ... Named to AHL All-Star first team (1989-90). ... Won Alka-Seltzer Plus Award (1991-92).
STATISTICAL PLATEAUS: Three-goal games: 1991-92 (1).
MISCELLANEOUS: Scored on a penalty shot (vs. Rob Stauber, November 27, 1992).

		REGULAR SEASON								PLAYOFFS				
Season Team	League	Gms.	G	A	Pts.	PIM	+/-	PP	SH	Gms.	G	A	Pts.	PIM
83-84 — Petrolia Jr. B	OHA	33	35	42	77	20	...	...	...	—	—	—	—	—
84-85 — Bowling Green	CCHA	42	23	32	55	54	...	...	...	—	—	—	—	—
85-86 — Bowling Green	CCHA	42	23	45	68	50	...	...	...	—	—	—	—	—
86-87 — Bowling Green	CCHA	45	27	58	85	44	...	...	...	—	—	—	—	—
— Canadian nat'l team	Int'l	5	1	0	1	4	...	...	...	—	—	—	—	—
87-88 — Utica	AHL	78	30	49	79	60	...	...	...	—	—	—	—	—
88-89 — Utica	AHL	56	36	44	80	22	...	...	...	5	0	1	1	4
— New Jersey	NHL	5	0	4	4	0	2	0	0	—	—	—	—	—
89-90 — New Jersey	NHL	5	1	2	3	0	0	0	0	—	—	—	—	—
— Utica	AHL	74	53	52	*105	61	...	...	...	5	2	4	6	0
90-91 — New Jersey	NHL	11	4	3	7	6	1	1	0	—	—	—	—	—
— Detroit	NHL	51	15	18	33	16	-8	5	0	2	0	2	2	0
91-92 — Detroit	NHL	79	35	40	75	55	*44	3	4	10	1	0	1	10
92-93 — Detroit	NHL	80	34	28	62	42	19	3	3	7	3	1	4	2
93-94 — Winnipeg	NHL	60	9	18	27	18	-8	1	0	—	—	—	—	—
— Chicago	NHL	11	5	3	8	8	1	2	0	6	0	0	0	8
94-95 — Chicago	NHL	15	4	5	9	6	4	0	0	—	—	—	—	—
— Tampa Bay	NHL	29	8	11	19	12	-1	0	0	—	—	—	—	—
95-96 — Tampa Bay	NHL	55	16	15	31	16	-19	4	1	5	0	0	0	0
96-97 — Tampa Bay	NHL	39	5	12	17	4	1	2	0	—	—	—	—	—
NHL totals (9 years)		440	136	159	295	183	36	21	8	30	4	3	7	20

YUSHKEVICH, DIMITRI   D   MAPLE LEAFS

PERSONAL: Born November 19, 1971, in Yaroslavl, U.S.S.R. ... 5-11/208. ... Shoots left. ... Name pronounced yoosh-KAY-vihch.
TRANSACTIONS/CAREER NOTES: Selected by Philadelphia Flyers in sixth round (sixth Flyers pick, 122nd overall) of NHL entry draft (June 22, 1991). ... Sprained wrist (January 28, 1993); missed two games. ... Strained groin (February 18, 1994); missed four games. ... Played in Europe during 1994-95 NHL lockout. ... Suffered from sore back (February 23, 1995); missed three games. ... Sprained left knee (April 16, 1995); missed five games. ... Traded by Flyers with second-round pick (G Francis Larivee) in 1996 draft to Toronto Maple Leafs for first-(RW Dainius Zubrus) and fourth-(traded to Los Angeles) round picks in 1996 draft and second-round pick (G Jean Marc Pelletier) in 1997 draft (August 30, 1995). ... Sprained knee (October 26, 1995); missed eight games. ... Bruised knee (December 30, 1995); missed two games. ... Pulled hamstring (December 14, 1996); missed four games. ... Injured knee (March 22, 1997); missed two games.

		REGULAR SEASON								PLAYOFFS				
Season Team	League	Gms.	G	A	Pts.	PIM	+/-	PP	SH	Gms.	G	A	Pts.	PIM
88-89 — Torpedo Yaroslavl	USSR	23	2	1	3	8	...	...	...	—	—	—	—	—
89-90 — Torpedo Yaroslavl	USSR	41	2	3	5	39	...	...	...	—	—	—	—	—
90-91 — Torpedo Yaroslavl	USSR	43	10	4	14	22	...	...	...	—	—	—	—	—
91-92 — Dynamo Moscow	CIS	41	6	7	13	14	...	...	...	—	—	—	—	—
— Unif. Olympic team	Int'l	8	1	2	3	4	...	...	...	—	—	—	—	—
92-93 — Philadelphia	NHL	82	5	27	32	71	12	1	0	—	—	—	—	—
93-94 — Philadelphia	NHL	75	5	25	30	86	-8	1	0	—	—	—	—	—
94-95 — Torpedo Yaroslavl	CIS	10	3	4	7	8	...	...	...	—	—	—	—	—
— Philadelphia	NHL	40	5	9	14	47	-4	3	1	15	1	5	6	12
95-96 — Toronto	NHL	69	1	10	11	54	-14	1	0	4	0	0	0	0
96-97 — Toronto	NHL	74	4	10	14	56	-24	1	1	—	—	—	—	—
NHL totals (5 years)		340	20	81	101	314	-38	7	2	19	1	5	6	12

YZERMAN, STEVE   C   RED WINGS

PERSONAL: Born May 9, 1965, in Cranbrook, B.C. ... 5-11/185. ... Shoots right. ... Name pronounced IGH-zuhr-muhn.
TRANSACTIONS/CAREER NOTES: Selected by Detroit Red Wings as underage junior in first round (first Red Wings pick, fourth overall) of NHL entry draft (June 8, 1983). ... Fractured collarbone (January 31, 1986). ... Injured ligaments of right knee and underwent surgery (March 1, 1988). ... Injured right knee in playoff game (April 8, 1991). ... Suffered herniated disc (October 21, 1993); missed 26 games. ... Sprained

Y

Y
Z

knee (May 27, 1995); missed three playoff games. ... Suffered from the flu (March 17, 1996); missed one game. ... Bruised ankle (April 9, 1997); missed one game.

HONORS: Named NHL Rookie of the Year by THE SPORTING NEWS (1983-84). ... Named to NHL All-Rookie team (1983-84). ... Played in NHL All-Star Game (1984, 1988-1993 and 1997). ... Won Lester B. Pearson Award (1988-89).

STATISTICAL PLATEAUS: Three-goal games: 1983-84 (1), 1984-85 (1), 1987-88 (2), 1988-89 (2), 1989-90 (2), 1990-91 (3), 1991-92 (3), 1992-93 (3). Total: 17. ... Four-goal games: 1989-90 (1). ... Total hat tricks: 18.

MISCELLANEOUS: Member of Stanley Cup championship team (1997). ... Captain of Detroit Red Wings (1986-87 through 1996-97). ... Scored on a penalty shot (vs. Bob Essensa, February 13, 1989; vs. Grant Fuhr, January 3, 1992; vs. Daren Puppa, January 29, 1992). ... Failed to score on a penalty shot (vs. Doug Keans, November 22, 1987; vs. Darcy Wakaluk, March 19, 1993; vs. Blaine Lacher, November 2, 1995). ... Became youngest player (18 years old) to play in NHL All-Star Game (January 31, 1984).

		REGULAR SEASON								PLAYOFFS				
Season Team	League	Gms.	G	A	Pts.	PIM	+/-	PP	SH	Gms.	G	A	Pts.	PIM
81-82— Peterborough	OHL	58	21	43	64	65	...	...	...	6	0	1	1	16
82-83— Peterborough	OHL	56	42	49	91	33	...	...	...	4	1	4	5	0
83-84— Detroit	NHL	80	39	48	87	33	-17	13	0	4	3	3	6	0
84-85— Detroit	NHL	80	30	59	89	58	-17	9	0	3	2	1	3	2
85-86— Detroit	NHL	51	14	28	42	16	-24	3	0	—	—	—	—	—
86-87— Detroit	NHL	80	31	59	90	43	-1	9	1	16	5	13	18	8
87-88— Detroit	NHL	64	50	52	102	44	30	10	6	3	1	3	4	6
88-89— Detroit	NHL	80	65	90	155	61	17	17	3	6	5	5	10	2
89-90— Detroit	NHL	79	62	65	127	79	-6	16	†7	—	—	—	—	—
90-91— Detroit	NHL	80	51	57	108	34	-2	12	6	7	3	3	6	4
91-92— Detroit	NHL	79	45	58	103	64	26	9	*8	11	3	5	8	12
92-93— Detroit	NHL	84	58	79	137	44	33	13	†7	7	4	3	7	4
93-94— Detroit	NHL	58	24	58	82	36	11	7	3	3	1	3	4	0
94-95— Detroit	NHL	47	12	26	38	40	6	4	0	15	4	8	12	0
95-96— Detroit	NHL	80	36	59	95	64	29	16	2	18	8	12	20	4
96-97— Detroit	NHL	81	22	63	85	78	22	8	0	20	7	6	13	4
NHL totals (14 years)		1023	539	801	1340	694	107	146	43	113	46	65	111	46

ZABRANSKY, LIBOR   D   BLUES

PERSONAL: Born November 25, 1973, in Budejovice, Czechoslovakia. ... 6-3/200. ... Shoots right.

TRANSACTIONS/CAREER NOTES: Selected by St. Louis Blues in ninth round (209th overall) of 1995 NHL entry draft.

		REGULAR SEASON								PLAYOFFS				
Season Team	League	Gms.	G	A	Pts.	PIM	+/-	PP	SH	Gms.	G	A	Pts.	PIM
94-95— Budejovice	Czech Rep.	44	2	6	8	54	...	...	...	9	0	4	4	6
95-96— Budejovice	Czech Rep.	40	4	7	11	...	...	...	...	10	0	1	1	0
96-97— St. Louis	NHL	34	1	5	6	44	-1	0	0	—	—	—	—	—
— Worcester	AHL	23	3	6	9	24	...	...	...	5	2	5	7	6
NHL totals (1 year)		34	1	5	6	44	-1	0	0					

ZALAPSKI, ZARLEY   D   FLAMES

PERSONAL: Born April 22, 1968, in Edmonton. ... 6-1/215. ... Shoots left. ... Name pronounced zuh-LAP-skee.

TRANSACTIONS/CAREER NOTES: Selected by Pittsburgh Penguins in first round (first Penguins pick, fourth overall) of NHL entry draft (June 21, 1986). ... Suffered from Spondylosis, deterioration of the structure of the spine (October 1987). ... Tore ligaments in right knee (December 29, 1988). ... Broke right collarbone (October 25, 1989). ... Sprained right knee (February 24, 1990); missed 13 games. ... Traded by Penguins with C John Cullen and RW Jeff Parker to Hartford Whalers for C Ron Francis, D Ulf Samuelsson and D Grant Jennings (March 4, 1991). ... Suffered from the flu (March 3, 1993); missed one game. ... Sprained knee (October 14, 1993); missed 10 games. ... Traded by Hartford Whalers with C Michael Nylander and D James Patrick to Calgary Flames for D Gary Suter, LW Paul Ranheim and C Ted Drury (March 10, 1994). ... Bruised thigh (February 16, 1994); missed one game. ... Suffered from the flu (November 8, 1995); missed two games. ... Tore knee ligament (October 6, 1996); underwent surgery (December 10, 1996) and missed remainder of season.

HONORS: Named to NHL All-Rookie team (1988-89). ... Played in NHL All-Star Game (1993).

		REGULAR SEASON								PLAYOFFS				
Season Team	League	Gms.	G	A	Pts.	PIM	+/-	PP	SH	Gms.	G	A	Pts.	PIM
84-85— Fort Saskatchewan	AJHL	23	17	30	47	14	...	...	...	—	—	—	—	—
85-86— Fort Saskatchewan	AJHL	27	20	33	53	46	...	...	...	—	—	—	—	—
— Canadian nat'l team	Int'l	32	2	4	6	10	...	...	...	—	—	—	—	—
86-87— Canadian nat'l team	Int'l	74	11	29	40	28	...	...	...	—	—	—	—	—
87-88— Canadian nat'l team	Int'l	47	3	13	16	32	...	...	...	—	—	—	—	—
— Can. Olympic team	Int'l	8	1	3	4	2	...	...	...	—	—	—	—	—
— Pittsburgh	NHL	15	3	8	11	7	10	0	0	—	—	—	—	—
88-89— Pittsburgh	NHL	58	12	33	45	57	9	5	1	11	1	8	9	13
89-90— Pittsburgh	NHL	51	6	25	31	37	-14	5	0	—	—	—	—	—
90-91— Pittsburgh	NHL	66	12	36	48	59	15	5	1	—	—	—	—	—
— Hartford	NHL	11	3	3	6	6	-7	3	0	6	1	3	4	8
91-92— Hartford	NHL	79	20	37	57	120	-7	4	0	7	2	3	5	6
92-93— Hartford	NHL	83	14	51	65	94	-34	8	1	—	—	—	—	—
93-94— Hartford	NHL	56	7	30	37	56	-6	0	0	—	—	—	—	—
— Calgary	NHL	13	3	7	10	18	0	1	0	7	0	3	3	2
94-95— Calgary	NHL	48	4	24	28	46	9	1	0	7	0	4	4	4
95-96— Calgary	NHL	80	12	17	29	115	11	5	0	4	0	1	1	10
96-97— Calgary	NHL	2	0	0	0	0	-1	0	0	—	—	—	—	—
NHL totals (10 years)		562	96	271	367	615	-15	37	3	42	4	22	26	43

ZAMUNER, ROB LW LIGHTNING

PERSONAL: Born September 17, 1969, in Oakville, Ont. ... 6-2/202. ... Shoots left. ... Name pronounced ZAM-ih-nuhr.
TRANSACTIONS/CAREER NOTES: Selected by New York Rangers in third round (third Rangers pick, 45th overall) of NHL entry draft (June 17, 1989). ... Signed as free agent by Tampa Bay Lightning (July 14, 1992); Rangers awarded third-round pick in 1993 draft as compensation (July 23, 1992). ... Hyperextended elbow (March 19, 1995); missed five games. ... Sprained knee (October 4, 1995); missed 10 games.
MISCELLANEOUS: Scored on a penalty shot (vs. Tommy Salo, January 11, 1997). ... Shares Tampa Bay Lightning all-time record for most games played (340).

		REGULAR SEASON							PLAYOFFS				
Season Team	League	Gms.	G	A	Pts.	PIM	+/-	PP	SH	Gms.	G	A	Pts.	PIM
86-87— Guelph	OHL	62	6	15	21	8	...	...	...	—	—	—	—	—
87-88— Guelph	OHL	58	20	41	61	18	...	...	...	—	—	—	—	—
88-89— Guelph	OHL	66	46	65	111	38	...	...	...	7	5	5	10	9
89-90— Flint	IHL	77	44	35	79	32	...	...	...	4	1	0	1	6
90-91— Binghamton	AHL	80	25	58	83	50	...	...	...	9	7	6	13	35
91-92— Binghamton	AHL	61	19	53	72	42	...	...	...	11	8	9	17	8
— New York Rangers	NHL	9	1	2	3	2	0	0	0	—	—	—	—	—
92-93— Tampa Bay	NHL	84	15	28	43	74	-25	1	0	—	—	—	—	—
93-94— Tampa Bay	NHL	59	6	6	12	42	-9	0	0	—	—	—	—	—
94-95— Tampa Bay	NHL	43	9	6	15	24	-3	0	3	—	—	—	—	—
95-96— Tampa Bay	NHL	72	15	20	35	62	11	0	3	6	2	3	5	10
96-97— Tampa Bay	NHL	82	17	33	50	56	3	0	4	—	—	—	—	—
NHL totals (6 years)		349	63	95	158	260	-23	1	10	6	2	3	5	10

ZEDNIK, RICHARD RW CAPITALS

PERSONAL: Born January 6, 1976, in Bystrica, Czechoslovakia. ... 5-10/172. ... Shoots left. ... Name pronounced ZEHD-nihk.
TRANSACTIONS/CAREER NOTES: Selected by Washington Capitals in 10th round (10th Capitals pick, 249th overall) of NHL entry draft (June 29, 1994). ... Suffered from the flu (November 6, 1996); missed two games.
HONORS: Named to WHL (West) All-Star second team (1995-96).

		REGULAR SEASON							PLAYOFFS				
Season Team	League	Gms.	G	A	Pts.	PIM	+/-	PP	SH	Gms.	G	A	Pts.	PIM
93-94— Banska Bystrica	Slovakia	25	3	6	9	...	...	...	...	—	—	—	—	—
94-95— Portland	WHL	65	35	51	86	89	...	...	...	9	5	5	10	20
95-96— Portland	WHL	61	44	37	81	154	...	...	...	7	8	4	12	23
— Portland	AHL	1	1	1	2	0	...	...	...	21	4	5	9	26
— Washington	NHL	1	0	0	0	0	0	0	0	—	—	—	—	—
96-97— Washington	NHL	11	2	1	3	4	-5	1	0	—	—	—	—	—
— Portland	AHL	56	15	20	35	70	...	...	...	5	1	0	1	6
NHL totals (2 years)		12	2	1	3	4	-5	1	0					

ZELEPUKIN, VALERI RW DEVILS

PERSONAL: Born September 17, 1968, in Voskresensk, U.S.S.R. ... 6-0/200. ... Shoots left. ... Name pronounced Vuh-LAIR-ee zehl-ih-POO-kihn.
TRANSACTIONS/CAREER NOTES: Selected by New Jersey Devils in 11th round (13th Devils pick, 221st overall) of NHL entry draft (June 22, 1990). ... Bruised shoulder (January 22, 1993); missed five games. ... Bruised left shoulder (December 22, 1993); missed one game. ... Injured chest (April 14, 1994); missed one game. ... Injured eye (January 24, 1995); missed first 42 games of season. ... Bruised finger (April 26, 1995); missed one game. ... Injured eye (October 7, 1995); missed first two games of season. ... Injured calf (November 27, 1995); missed two games. ... Injured foot (February 18, 1996); missed one game. ... Bruised right knee (March 23, 1996); missed six games. ... Suffered from the flu (November 14, 1996); missed three games. ... Suffered infected elbow (January 2, 1997); missed four games.
MISCELLANEOUS: Member of Stanley Cup championship team (1995).

		REGULAR SEASON							PLAYOFFS				
Season Team	League	Gms.	G	A	Pts.	PIM	+/-	PP	SH	Gms.	G	A	Pts.	PIM
84-85— Khimik	USSR	5	0	0	0	2	...	...	...	—	—	—	—	—
85-86— Khimik	USSR	33	2	2	4	10	...	...	...	—	—	—	—	—
86-87— Khimik	USSR	19	1	0	1	4	...	...	...	—	—	—	—	—
87-88— SKA Leningrad	USSR	18	18	6	24	...	...	...	...	—	—	—	—	—
— CSKA Moscow	USSR	19	3	1	4	8	...	...	...	—	—	—	—	—
88-89— CSKA Moscow	USSR	17	2	3	5	2	...	...	...	—	—	—	—	—
89-90— Khimik	USSR	46	17	14	31	26	...	...	...	—	—	—	—	—
90-91— Khimik	USSR	46	12	19	31	22	...	...	...	—	—	—	—	—
91-92— Utica	AHL	22	20	9	29	8	...	...	...	—	—	—	—	—
— New Jersey	NHL	44	13	18	31	28	11	3	0	4	1	1	2	2
92-93— New Jersey	NHL	78	23	41	64	70	19	5	1	5	0	2	2	0
93-94— New Jersey	NHL	82	26	31	57	70	36	8	0	20	5	2	7	14
94-95— New Jersey	NHL	4	1	2	3	6	3	0	0	18	1	2	3	12
95-96— New Jersey	NHL	61	6	9	15	107	-10	3	0	—	—	—	—	—
96-97— New Jersey	NHL	71	14	24	38	36	-10	3	0	8	3	2	5	2
NHL totals (6 years)		340	83	125	208	317	49	22	1	55	10	9	19	30

ZENT, JASON LW SENATORS

PERSONAL: Born April 15, 1971, in Buffalo. ... 5-11/204. ... Shoots left. ... Full name: Jason William Zent.
HIGH SCHOOL: Nichols School (Buffalo).

COLLEGE: Wisconsin.

TRANSACTIONS/CAREER NOTES: Selected by New York Islanders in third round (third Islanders pick, 44th overall) of NHL entry draft (June 17, 1989). ... Sprained ankle playing racquetball (January 1991). ... Traded by Islanders to Ottawa Senators for fifth-round pick (D Andy Berenzweig) in 1996 draft (October 15, 1994). ... Bruised thigh (February 16, 1997); missed seven games.

HONORS: Named to WCHA All-Rookie team (1990-91). ... Named to NCAA All-Tournament team (1991-92).

Season Team	League	REGULAR SEASON								PLAYOFFS				
		Gms.	G	A	Pts.	PIM	+/-	PP	SH	Gms.	G	A	Pts.	PIM
87-88 — Nichols School	N.Y. H.S.	21	20	16	36	28	...	...	...	—	—	—	—	—
88-89 — Nichols School	N.Y. H.S.	29	49	32	81	26	...	...	...	—	—	—	—	—
89-90 — Nichols School	N.Y. H.S.					Statistics unavailable.								
90-91 — Univ. of Wisconsin	WCHA	39	19	18	37	51	...	...	...	—	—	—	—	—
91-92 — Univ. of Wisconsin	WCHA	43	27	17	44	134	...	...	...	—	—	—	—	—
92-93 — Univ. of Wisconsin	WCHA	40	26	12	38	88	...	...	...	—	—	—	—	—
93-94 — Univ. of Wisconsin	WCHA	42	20	21	41	120	...	...	...	—	—	—	—	—
94-95 — Prin. Edward Island	AHL	55	15	11	26	46	...	...	...	9	6	1	7	6
95-96 — Prin. Edward Island	AHL	68	14	5	19	61	...	...	...	5	2	1	3	4
96-97 — Worcester	AHL	45	14	10	24	45	...	...	...	5	3	3	6	4
— Ottawa	NHL	22	3	3	6	9	5	0	0	—	—	—	—	—
NHL totals (1 year)		22	3	3	6	9	5	0	0					

ZETTLER, ROB   D   MAPLE LEAFS

PERSONAL: Born March 8, 1968, in Sept-Iles, Que. ... 6-3/200. ... Shoots left.

TRANSACTIONS/CAREER NOTES: Selected by Minnesota North Stars as underage junior in fifth round (fifth North Stars pick, 55th overall) of NHL entry draft (June 21, 1986). ... Tore hip flexor (January 21, 1991); missed 11 games. ... Selected by San Jose Sharks in NHL dispersal draft (May 30, 1991). ... Strained back (October 20, 1992); missed three games. ... Injured groin (April 8, 1993); missed one game. ... Traded by Sharks to Philadelphia Flyers for C Viacheslav Butsayev (February 1, 1994). ... Traded by Flyers to Toronto Maple Leafs for fifth-round pick (G Per-Ragna Bergqvist) in 1996 draft (July 8, 1995). ... Suspended two games by NHL for checking from behind (January 4, 1996). ... Strained groin (April 3, 1997); missed three games.

Season Team	League	REGULAR SEASON								PLAYOFFS				
		Gms.	G	A	Pts.	PIM	+/-	PP	SH	Gms.	G	A	Pts.	PIM
84-85 — Sault Ste. Marie	OHL	60	2	14	16	37	...	...	...	—	—	—	—	—
85-86 — Sault Ste. Marie	OHL	57	5	23	28	92	...	...	...	—	—	—	—	—
86-87 — Sault Ste. Marie	OHL	64	13	22	35	89	...	...	...	4	0	0	0	0
87-88 — Sault Ste. Marie	OHL	64	7	41	48	77	...	...	...	6	2	2	4	9
— Kalamazoo	IHL	2	0	1	1	0	...	...	...	7	0	2	2	2
88-89 — Minnesota	NHL	2	0	0	0	0	1	0	0	—	—	—	—	—
— Kalamazoo	IHL	80	5	21	26	79	...	...	...	6	0	1	1	26
89-90 — Minnesota	NHL	31	0	8	8	45	-7	0	0	—	—	—	—	—
— Kalamazoo	IHL	41	6	10	16	64	...	...	...	7	0	0	0	6
90-91 — Kalamazoo	IHL	1	0	0	0	2	...	...	...	—	—	—	—	—
— Minnesota	NHL	47	1	4	5	119	-10	0	0	—	—	—	—	—
91-92 — San Jose	NHL	74	1	8	9	99	-23	0	0	—	—	—	—	—
92-93 — San Jose	NHL	80	0	7	7	150	-50	0	0	—	—	—	—	—
93-94 — San Jose	NHL	42	0	3	3	65	-7	0	0	—	—	—	—	—
— Philadelphia	NHL	33	0	4	4	69	-19	0	0	—	—	—	—	—
94-95 — Philadelphia	NHL	32	0	1	1	34	-3	0	0	1	0	0	0	2
95-96 — Toronto	NHL	29	0	1	1	48	-1	0	0	2	0	0	0	0
96-97 — Utah	IHL	30	0	10	10	60	...	...	...	—	—	—	—	—
— Toronto	NHL	48	2	12	14	51	8	0	0	—	—	—	—	—
NHL totals (9 years)		418	4	48	52	680	-111	0	0	3	0	0	0	2

ZEZEL, PETER   C   DEVILS

PERSONAL: Born April 22, 1965, in Toronto. ... 5-11/200. ... Shoots left. ... Name pronounced ZEH-zuhl.

TRANSACTIONS/CAREER NOTES: Selected by Philadelphia Flyers as underage junior in second round (first Flyers pick, 41st overall) of NHL entry draft (June 8, 1983). ... Broke hand (November 1984). ... Tore medial cartilage in left knee (March 1987). ... Sprained right ankle (November 1987). ... Separated left shoulder (March 1988). ... Traded by Flyers to St. Louis Blues for C Mike Bullard (November 29, 1988). ... Pulled groin (December 1988). ... Bruised sternum (January 1989). ... Sprained right knee (March 5, 1989). ... Bruised right hip (March 11, 1990). ... Traded by Blues with D Mike Lalor to Washington Capitals for LW Geoff Courtnall (July 13, 1990). ... Sprained left ankle (October 23, 1990); missed 23 games. ... Reinjured ankle (December 28, 1990); missed two games. ... Traded by Capitals with D Bob Rouse to Toronto Maple Leafs for D Al Iafrate (January 16, 1991). ... Sprained knee (November 14, 1991); missed five games. ... Strained knee (March 5, 1992). ... Bruised knee (November 5, 1992); missed five games. ... Sprained wrist (January 6, 1993); missed three games. ... Sprained neck (March 25, 1993); missed five games. ... Injured back (October 16, 1993); missed 41 games. ... Suffered back spasms (January 30, 1994); missed one game. ... Awarded to Dallas Stars with RW Grant Marshall as compensation for Maple Leafs signing free-agent RW Mike Craig (August 10, 1994). ... Signed as free agent by Blues (October 19, 1995). ... Sprained wrist (January 4, 1996); missed 13 games. ... Sprained neck (February 20, 1996); missed two games. ... Sprained ankle during 1996-97 season; missed three games. ... Suffered back spasms (December 19, 1996); missed four games. ... Injured back (January 20, 1997); missed eight games. ... Traded by Blues to New Jersey Devils for D Chris McAlpine and ninth-round pick in 1999 draft (February 11, 1997). ... Stiff neck (March 15, 1997); missed one game. ... Suffered from the flu (April 1, 1997); missed three games. ... Bruised knee (April 9, 1997); missed final two games of regular season.

STATISTICAL PLATEAUS: Three-goal games: 1986-87 (1).

MISCELLANEOUS: Failed to score on a penalty shot (vs. Chris Osgood, March 4, 1994). ... Played three games as a striker for Toronto Blizzard in the North American Soccer League (1982).

Season Team	League	REGULAR SEASON								PLAYOFFS				
		Gms.	G	A	Pts.	PIM	+/-	PP	SH	Gms.	G	A	Pts.	PIM
81-82 — Don Mills Flyers	MTHL	40	43	51	94	36	...	...	...	—	—	—	—	—
82-83 — Toronto	OHL	66	35	39	74	28	...	...	...	4	2	4	6	0

Season Team	League	REGULAR SEASON Gms.	G	A	Pts.	PIM	+/-	PP	SH	PLAYOFFS Gms.	G	A	Pts.	PIM
83-84— Toronto	OHL	68	47	86	133	31	...	...	...	9	7	5	12	4
84-85— Philadelphia	NHL	65	15	46	61	26	22	8	0	19	1	8	9	28
85-86— Philadelphia	NHL	79	17	37	54	76	27	4	0	5	3	1	4	4
86-87— Philadelphia	NHL	71	33	39	72	71	21	6	2	25	3	10	13	10
87-88— Philadelphia	NHL	69	22	35	57	42	7	14	0	7	3	2	5	7
88-89— Philadelphia	NHL	26	4	13	17	15	13	0	0	—	—	—	—	—
— St. Louis	NHL	52	17	36	53	27	-1	5	1	10	6	6	12	4
89-90— St. Louis	NHL	73	25	47	72	30	-9	7	0	12	1	7	8	4
90-91— Washington	NHL	20	7	5	12	10	-13	6	0	—	—	—	—	—
— Toronto	NHL	32	14	14	28	4	-7	6	0	—	—	—	—	—
91-92— Toronto	NHL	64	16	33	49	26	-22	4	0	—	—	—	—	—
92-93— Toronto	NHL	70	12	23	35	24	0	0	0	20	2	1	3	6
93-94— Toronto	NHL	41	8	8	16	19	5	0	0	18	2	4	6	8
94-95— Dallas	NHL	30	6	5	11	19	-6	0	0	3	1	0	1	0
— Kalamazoo	IHL	2	0	0	0	0	...	...	...	—	—	—	—	—
95-96— St. Louis	NHL	57	8	13	21	12	-2	2	0	10	3	0	3	2
96-97— St. Louis	NHL	35	4	9	13	12	6	0	0	—	—	—	—	—
— New Jersey	NHL	18	0	3	3	4	4	0	0	2	0	0	0	10
NHL totals (13 years)		802	208	366	574	417	45	62	3	131	25	39	64	83

ZHAMNOV, ALEXEI   C   BLACKHAWKS

PERSONAL: Born October 1, 1970, in Moscow, U.S.S.R. ... 6-1/195. ... Shoots left. ... Name pronounced ZHAM-nahf.

TRANSACTIONS/CAREER NOTES: Selected by Winnipeg Jets in fourth round (fifth Jets pick, 77th overall) of NHL entry draft (June 16, 1990). ... Injured hip flexor (November 2, 1992); missed two games. ... Suffered back spasms (January 27, 1993); missed one game. ... Suffered back spasms (February 3, 1993); missed one game. ... Suffered back spasms (February 12, 1993); missed 12 games. ... Suffered left quad contusion (October 26, 1993); missed three games. ... Sprained back (December 27, 1993); missed eight games. ... Suffered back spasms (March 19, 1994); missed remainder of season .,. Suffered stress fracture in leg (October 12, 1995); missed eight games. ... Suffered from the flu (January 5, 1996); missed one game. ... Bruised back (March 7, 1996); missed four games. ... Injured back (March 16, 1996); missed remainder of regular season. ... Jets franchise moved to Phoenix and renamed Coyotes for 1996-97 season; NHL approved move on January 18, 1996. ... Traded by Coyotes with RW Craig Mills and first-round pick (RW Ty Jones) in 1997 draft to Chicago Blackhawks for C Jeremy Roenick (August 16, 1996).

HONORS: Named to NHL All-Star second team (1994-95).

STATISTICAL PLATEAUS: Three-goal games: 1993-94 (2), 1994-95 (1), 1995-96 (1), 1996-97 (1). Total: 5. ... Five-goal games: 1994-95 (1). ... Total hat tricks: 6.

MISCELLANEOUS: Member of gold-medal-winning Unified Olympic team (1992).

Season Team	League	REGULAR SEASON Gms.	G	A	Pts.	PIM	+/-	PP	SH	PLAYOFFS Gms.	G	A	Pts.	PIM
88-89— Dynamo Moscow.......	USSR	4	0	0	0	0	...	...	...	—	—	—	—	—
89-90— Dynamo Moscow.......	USSR	43	11	6	17	23	...	...	...	—	—	—	—	—
90-91— Dynamo Moscow.......	USSR	46	16	12	28	24	...	...	...	—	—	—	—	—
91-92— Dynamo Moscow.......	CIS	39	15	21	36	28	...	...	...	—	—	—	—	—
— Unif. Olympic team	Int'l	8	0	3	3	8	...	...	...	—	—	—	—	—
92-93— Winnipeg	NHL	68	25	47	72	58	7	6	1	6	0	2	2	2
93-94— Winnipeg .. ..,..........	NHL	61	26	45	71	62	-20	7	0	—	—	—	—	—
94-95— Winnipeg	NHL	48	30	35	65	20	5	9	0	—	—	—	—	—
95-96— Winnipeg	NHL	58	22	37	59	65	-4	5	0	6	2	1	3	8
96-97— Chicago.....................	NHL	74	20	42	62	56	18	6	1	—	—	—	—	—
NHL totals (5 years)		309	123	206	329	261	6	33	2	12	2	3	5	10

ZHITNIK, ALEXEI   D   SABRES

PERSONAL: Born October 10, 1972, in Kiev, U.S.S.R. ... 5-11/202. ... Shoots left. ... Name pronounced ZHIHT-nihk.

TRANSACTIONS/CAREER NOTES: Selected by Los Angeles Kings in fourth round (third Kings pick, 81st overall) of NHL entry draft (June 22, 1991). ... Suffered from the flu (January 12, 1993); missed five games. ... Suspended one game by NHL for cross-checking (November 30, 1993). ... Traded by Kings with D Charlie Huddy, G Robb Stauber and fifth-round pick (D Marian Menhart) in 1995 draft to Buffalo Sabres for G Grant Fuhr, D Philippe Boucher and D Denis Tsygurov (February 14, 1995). ... Broke thumb (February 19, 1995); missed three games. ... Reinjured thumb (March 8, 1995); missed one game. ... Ruptured calf muscle (March 19, 1995); missed 11 games. ... Suspended two games and fined $1,000 by NHL for high-sticking incident (November 1, 1996).

MISCELLANEOUS: Member of gold-medal-winning Unified Olympic team (1992).

Season Team	League	REGULAR SEASON Gms.	G	A	Pts.	PIM	+/-	PP	SH	PLAYOFFS Gms.	G	A	Pts.	PIM
90-91— Sokol Kiev..................	USSR	40	1	4	5	46	...	...	...	—	—	—	—	—
91-92— CSKA Moscow	CIS	36	2	7	9	48	...	...	...	—	—	—	—	—
— Unif. Olympic team	Int'l	8	1	0	1	0	...	...	...	—	—	—	—	—
92-93— Los Angeles	NHL	78	12	36	48	80	-3	5	0	24	3	9	12	26
93-94— Los Angeles	NHL	81	12	40	52	101	-11	11	0	—	—	—	—	—
94-95— Los Angeles	NHL	11	2	5	7	27	-3	2	0	—	—	—	—	—
— Buffalo	NHL	21	2	5	7	34	-3	1	0	5	0	1	1	14
95-96— Buffalo	NHL	80	6	30	36	58	-25	5	0	—	—	—	—	—
96-97— Buffalo	NHL	80	7	28	35	95	10	3	1	12	1	0	1	16
NHL totals (5 years)		351	41	144	185	395	-35	27	1	41	4	10	14	56

ZHOLTOK, SERGEI   C   SENATORS

PERSONAL: Born December 2, 1972, in Riga, U.S.S.R. ... 6-0/190. ... Shoots right. ... Name pronounced SAIR-gay ZHOHL-tahk.
TRANSACTIONS/CAREER NOTES: Selected by Boston Bruins in third round (second Bruins pick, 56th overall) of NHL entry draft (June 20, 1992). ... Signed as free agent by Las Vegas of IHL (August 8, 1995). ... Signed as free agent by Ottawa Senators (June 25, 1996).

		REGULAR SEASON								PLAYOFFS				
Season Team	League	Gms.	G	A	Pts.	PIM	+/-	PP	SH	Gms.	G	A	Pts.	PIM
90-91— Dynamo Riga	USSR	39	4	0	4	16	...	...	...	—	—	—	—	—
91-92— HC Riga	CIS	27	6	3	9	6	...	...	...	—	—	—	—	—
92-93— Providence	AHL	64	31	35	66	57	...	...	...	6	3	5	8	4
— Boston	NHL	1	0	1	1	0	1	0	0	—	—	—	—	—
93-94— Providence	AHL	54	29	33	62	16	...	...	...	—	—	—	—	—
— Boston	NHL	24	2	1	3	2	-7	1	0	—	—	—	—	—
94-95— Providence	AHL	78	23	35	58	42	...	...	...	13	8	5	13	6
95-96— Las Vegas	IHL	82	51	50	101	30	...	...	...	15	7	13	20	6
96-97— Las Vegas	IHL	19	13	14	27	20	...	...	...	—	—	—	—	—
— Ottawa	NHL	57	12	16	28	19	2	5	0	7	1	1	2	0
NHL totals (3 years)		82	14	18	32	21	-4	6	0	7	1	1	2	0

ZHURIK, ALEXANDER   D   OILERS

PERSONAL: Born May 29, 1975, in Minsk, U.S.S.R. ... 6-3/205. ... Shoots left. ... Name pronounced ZHOOR-ihk.
TRANSACTIONS/CAREER NOTES: Selected by Edmonton Oilers in seventh round (seventh Oilers pick, 163rd overall) of NHL entry draft (June 26, 1993).

		REGULAR SEASON								PLAYOFFS				
Season Team	League	Gms.	G	A	Pts.	PIM	+/-	PP	SH	Gms.	G	A	Pts.	PIM
92-93— Dynamo Minsk	CIS				Statistics unavailable.									
93-94— Kingston	OHL	59	7	23	30	92	...	...	...	6	0	0	0	4
94-95— Kingston	OHL	54	3	21	24	51	...	...	...	6	0	0	0	0
95-96— Cape Breton	AHL	80	5	36	41	85	...	...	...	—	—	—	—	—
96-97— Hamilton	AHL	72	5	16	21	49	...	...	...	22	2	11	13	14

ZMOLEK, DOUG   D   KINGS

PERSONAL: Born November 3, 1970, in Rochester, Minn. ... 6-2/220. ... Shoots left. ... Full name: Doug Allan Zmolek. ... Name pronounced zuh-MOH-lehk.
HIGH SCHOOL: John Marshall (Rochester, Minn.).
COLLEGE: Minnesota.
TRANSACTIONS/CAREER NOTES: Selected by Minnesota North Stars in first round (first North Stars pick, seventh overall) of NHL entry draft (June 17, 1989). ... Selected by San Jose Sharks in NHL dispersal draft (May 30, 1991). ... Traded by Sharks with D Mike Lalor to Dallas Stars for RW Ulf Dahlen and future considerations (March 19, 1994). ... Sprained thumb (March 12, 1994); missed one game. ... Separated shoulder (March 31, 1994); missed five games. ... Lacerated hand (March 6, 1995); missed no games. ... Bruised kneecap (April 7, 1995); missed six games. ... Injured shoulder (November 9, 1995); missed five games. ... Traded by Stars with RW Shane Churla to Los Angeles Kings for Darryl Sydor and seventh-round pick (G Eoin McInerney) in 1996 draft (February 17, 1996). ... Sprained left knee (March 23, 1996); missed last eight games of season. ... Bruised thigh (October 26, 1996); missed one game. ... Strained right shoulder (November 7, 1996); missed one game. ... Sprained right shoulder (December 9, 1996); missed six games. ... Bruised hand (January 14, 1997); missed one game. ... Suffered irregular heartbeat (February 17, 1997); missed five games.
HONORS: Named to NCAA All-America West second team (1991-92). ... Named to WCHA All-Star second team (1991-92).

		REGULAR SEASON								PLAYOFFS				
Season Team	League	Gms.	G	A	Pts.	PIM	+/-	PP	SH	Gms.	G	A	Pts.	PIM
87-88— John Marshall	Minn. H.S.	27	4	32	36	...	...	...	...	—	—	—	—	—
88-89— John Marshall	Minn. H.S.	29	17	41	58	...	...	...	...	—	—	—	—	—
89-90— Univ. of Minnesota	WCHA	40	1	10	11	52	...	...	...	—	—	—	—	—
90-91— Univ. of Minnesota	WCHA	42	3	15	18	94	...	...	...	—	—	—	—	—
91-92— Univ. of Minnesota	WCHA	44	6	21	27	88	...	...	...	—	—	—	—	—
92-93— San Jose	NHL	84	5	10	15	229	-50	2	0	—	—	—	—	—
93-94— San Jose	NHL	68	0	4	4	122	-9	0	0	—	—	—	—	—
— Dallas	NHL	7	1	0	1	11	1	0	0	7	0	1	1	4
94-95— Dallas	NHL	42	0	5	5	67	-6	0	0	5	0	0	0	10
95-96— Dallas	NHL	42	1	5	6	65	1	0	0	—	—	—	—	—
— Los Angeles	NHL	16	1	0	1	22	-6	0	0	—	—	—	—	—
96-97— Los Angeles	NHL	57	1	0	1	116	-22	0	0	—	—	—	—	—
NHL totals (5 years)		316	9	24	33	632	-91	2	0	12	0	1	1	14

ZUBOV, SERGEI   D   STARS

PERSONAL: Born July 22, 1970, in Moscow, U.S.S.R. ... 6-1/200. ... Shoots right. ... Name pronounced SAIR-gay ZOO-bahf.
TRANSACTIONS/CAREER NOTES: Selected by New York Rangers in fifth round (sixth Rangers pick, 85th overall) of NHL entry draft (June 16, 1990). ... Suffered concussion (February 26, 1993); missed one game. ... Suffered from the flu (February 4, 1995); missed one game. ... Underwent wrist surgery (February 27, 1995); missed nine games. ... Traded by Rangers with C Petr Nedved to Pittsburgh Penguins for LW Luc Robitaille and D Ulf Samuelsson (August 31, 1995). ... Broke finger (October 9, 1995); missed nine games. ... Reinjured finger (November 11, 1995); missed seven games. ... Bruised shoulder (March 31, 1996); missed one game. ... Traded by Penguins to Dallas Stars for D Kevin Hatcher (June 22, 1996). ... Suffered from the flu (November 20, 1996); missed one game. ... Suffered back spasms (January 24, 1997); missed two games.

MISCELLANEOUS: Member of Stanley Cup championship team (1994). ... Member of gold-medal-winning Unified Olympic team (1992).

			REGULAR SEASON								PLAYOFFS				
Season Team	League	Gms.	G	A	Pts.	PIM	+/-	PP	SH		Gms.	G	A	Pts.	PIM
88-89— CSKA Moscow..........	USSR	29	1	4	5	10	...	...	...		—	—	—	—	—
89-90— CSKA Moscow..........	USSR	48	6	2	8	16	...	...	...		—	—	—	—	—
90-91— CSKA Moscow..........	USSR	41	6	5	11	12	...	...	...		—	—	—	—	—
91-92— CSKA Moscow..........	CIS	36	4	7	11	6	...	...	...		—	—	—	—	—
—Unif. Olympic team....	Int'l	8	0	1	1	0	...	...	...		—	—	—	—	—
92-93— CSKA Moscow..........	CIS	1	0	1	1	0	...	...	...		—	—	—	—	—
— Binghamton	AHL	30	7	29	36	14	...	...	...		11	5	5	10	2
— New York Rangers.....	NHL	49	8	23	31	4	-1	3	0		—	—	—	—	—
93-94— New York Rangers.....	NHL	78	12	77	89	39	20	9	0		22	5	14	19	0
— Binghamton	AHL	2	1	2	3	0	...	...	...		—	—	—	—	—
94-95— New York Rangers.....	NHL	38	10	26	36	18	-2	6	0		10	3	8	11	2
95-96— Pittsburgh..................	NHL	64	11	55	66	22	28	3	2		18	1	14	15	26
96-97— Dallas........................	NHL	78	13	30	43	24	19	1	0		7	0	3	3	2
NHL totals (5 years)		307	54	211	265	107	64	22	2		57	9	39	48	30

ZUBRUS, DAINIUS   RW   FLYERS

PERSONAL: Born June 16, 1978, in Elektrenai, U.S.S.R. ... 6-3/215. ... Shoots left. ... Name pronounced DIGH-nuhz ZOO-bruhz.
TRANSACTIONS/CAREER NOTES: Selected by Philadelphia Flyers in first round (first Flyers pick, 15th overall) of NHL entry draft (June 22, 1996).

			REGULAR SEASON								PLAYOFFS				
Season Team	League	Gms.	G	A	Pts.	PIM	+/-	PP	SH		Gms.	G	A	Pts.	PIM
95-96— Pembroke	CJHL	28	19	13	32	73	...	...	...		—	—	—	—	—
— Caledon....................	Jr. A	7	3	7	10	2	...	...	...		17	11	12	23	4
96-97— Philadelphia	NHL	68	8	13	21	22	3	1	0		19	5	4	9	12
NHL totals (1 year)		68	8	13	21	22	3	1	0		19	5	4	9	12

ZUKIWSKY, JONATHAN   C   BLUES

PERSONAL: Born October 7, 1977, in St. Paul, Alta. ... 6-2/185. .. Shoots left. ... Name pronounced zuh-KYOO-skee.
TRANSACTIONS/CAREER NOTES: Selected by St. Louis Blues in fourth round (third Blues pick, 95th overall) of NHL entry draft (June 22, 1996).

			REGULAR SEASON								PLAYOFFS				
Season Team	League	Gms.	G	A	Pts.	PIM	+/-	PP	SH		Gms.	G	A	Pts.	PIM
93-94— Red Deer...................	WHL	59	12	15	27	38	...	...	...		4	0	2	2	0
94-95— Red Deer...................	WHL	71	19	24	43	45	...	...	...		—	—	—	—	—
95-96— Red Deer...................	WHL	72	20	28	48	38	...	...	...		10	5	2	7	6
96-97— Red Deer...................	WHL	66	27	26	53	41	...	...	...		16	6	5	11	10

ZYUZIN, ANDREI   D   SHARKS

PERSONAL: Born January 21, 1978, in Ufa, U.S.S.R. ... 6-1/187. ... Shoots left.
TRANSACTIONS/CAREER NOTES: Selected by San Jose Sharks in first round (first Sharks pick, second overall) of NHL entry draft (June 22, 1996).

			REGULAR SEASON								PLAYOFFS				
Season Team	League	Gms.	G	A	Pts.	PIM	+/-	PP	SH		Gms.	G	A	Pts.	PIM
94-95— Salavat Yulayev Ufa ...	CIS	30	3	0	3	16	...	...	...		—	—	—	—	—
95-96— Salavat Yulayev Ufa ...	CIS	41	6	3	9	24	...	...	...		2	0	0	0	4
96-97— Salavat Yulayev Ufa ...	Russian	32	7	10	17	28	...	...	...		7	1	1	2	4

1997 TOP DRAFT PICKS

AEBISCHER, DAVID   G   AVALANCHE

PERSONAL: Born February 7, 1978, in Fribourg, Switzerland. ... 6-1/185. ... Catches left.
TRANSACTIONS/CAREER NOTES: Selected by Colorado Avalanche in sixth round (seventh Avalanche pick, 161st overall) of NHL entry draft (June 21, 1997).

		REGULAR SEASON							PLAYOFFS					
Season Team	League	Gms.	Min	W	L	T	GA	SO	Avg.	Gms.	Min.	W	L	GA	SO	Avg.
96-97—Fribourg-Gotteron	Switzerland	10	577	...	...	...	34	...	3.54	3	184	...	...	13	...	4.24

AFINOGENOV, MAXIM   RW   SABRES

PERSONAL: Born September 4, 1979, in Moscow, U.S.S.R. ... 5-10/176. ... Shoots left.
TRANSACTIONS/CAREER NOTES: Selected by Buffalo Sabres in third round (third Sabres pick, 69th overall) of NHL entry draft (June 21, 1997).

		REGULAR SEASON					PLAYOFFS				
Season Team	League	Gms.	G	A	Pts.	PIM	Gms.	G	A	Pts.	PIM
95-96— Dynamo Moscow	CIS	1	0	0	0	0	—	—	—	—	—
96-97— Dynamo Moscow	Russian	29	6	5	11	10	4	0	2	2	0
— Dynamo-2 Moscow	Rus. Div. III	14	9	2	11	10	—	—	—	—	—

ANDERSSON, ERIK   RW   FLAMES

PERSONAL: Born August 19, 1971, in Stockholm, Sweden. ... 6-2/206. ... Shoots left. ... Full name: Erik Folke Andersson.
COLLEGE: Denver.
TRANSACTIONS/CAREER NOTES: Selected by Los Angeles Kings in sixth round (fifth Kings pick, 112th overall) of NHL entry draft (June 16, 1990). ... Returned to draft pool by Kings and selected by Calgary Flames in third round (sixth Flames pick, 70th overall) of NHL entry draft (June 21, 1997).

		REGULAR SEASON					PLAYOFFS				
Season Team	League	Gms.	G	A	Pts.	PIM	Gms.	G	A	Pts.	PIM
89-90— Danderyd	Swed. Dv.II	30	14	5	19	16	—	—	—	—	—
90-91— AIK Solna	Sweden	32	1	1	2	10	—	—	—	—	—
91-92— AIK Solna	Sweden	3	0	0	0	0	—	—	—	—	—
92-93—				Did not play.			—	—	—	—	—
93-94— University of Denver	WCHA	38	10	20	30	42	—	—	—	—	—
94-95— University of Denver	WCHA	42	12	19	31	42	—	—	—	—	—
95-96— University of Denver	WCHA	39	12	35	47	40	—	—	—	—	—
96-97— University of Denver	WCHA	39	17	17	34	42	—	—	—	—	—

ARVEDSON, MAGNUS   RW   SENATORS

PERSONAL: Born November 25, 1971, in Karlstad, Sweden. ... 6-2/198. ... Shoots left.
TRANSACTIONS/CAREER NOTES: Selected by Ottawa Senators in fifth round (fourth Senators pick, 119th overall) of NHL entry draft (June 21, 1997).

		REGULAR SEASON					PLAYOFFS				
Season Team	League	Gms.	G	A	Pts.	PIM	Gms.	G	A	Pts.	PIM
91-92— Orebro	Swed. Dv.II	32	12	21	33	30	7	4	4	8	4
92-93— Orebro	Swed. Dv.II	36	11	18	29	34	6	2	1	3	0
93-94— Farjestad Karlstad	Sweden	16	1	7	8	10	—	—	—	—	—
94-95— Farjestad Karlstad	Sweden	36	1	7	8	45	4	0	0	0	6
95-96— Farjestad Karlstad	Sweden	39	10	14	24	42	8	0	3	3	10
96-97— Farjestad Karlstad	Sweden	48	13	11	24	36	14	4	7	11	8

BALMOCHNYKH, MAXIM   LW   MIGHTY DUCKS

PERSONAL: Born March 7, 1979, in Lipetsk, U.S.S.R. ... 6-0/185. ... Shoots left.
TRANSACTIONS/CAREER NOTES: Selected by Mighty Ducks of Anaheim in second round (second Mighty Ducks pick, 45th overall) of NHL entry draft (June 21, 1997).

		REGULAR SEASON					PLAYOFFS				
Season Team	League	Gms.	G	A	Pts.	PIM	Gms.	G	A	Pts.	PIM
94-95— HC Lipetsk	CIS Div. II	3	0	1	1	4	—	—	—	—	—
95-96— HC Lipetsk	CIS Div. II	40	15	5	20	60	—	—	—	—	—
96-97— Lada Togliatti	USSR	18	6	1	7	22	—	—	—	—	—

BARNEY, SCOTT   C   KINGS

PERSONAL: Born March 27, 1979, in Oshawa, Ont. ... 6-4/198. ... Shoots right.
TRANSACTIONS/CAREER NOTES: Selected by Los Angeles Kings in second round (third Kings pick, 29th overall) of NHL entry draft (June 21, 1997).

Season Team	League	REGULAR SEASON Gms.	G	A	Pts.	PIM	PLAYOFFS Gms.	G	A	Pts.	PIM
94-95— North York	MTHL	41	16	19	35	88	—	—	—	—	—
95-96— Peterborough	OHL	60	22	24	46	52	24	6	8	14	38
96-97— Peterborough	OHL	64	21	33	54	110	9	0	3	3	16

BARTANUS, KAROL — RW — BRUINS

PERSONAL: Born June 9, 1978, in Liptovsky Mikulas, Czechoslovakia. ... 6-1/188. ... Shoots left.
TRANSACTIONS/CAREER NOTES: Selected by Boston Bruins in fourth round (sixth Bruins pick, 81st overall) of NHL entry draft (June 21, 1997).

Season Team	League	REGULAR SEASON Gms.	G	A	Pts.	PIM	PLAYOFFS Gms.	G	A	Pts.	PIM
94-95— Liptovsky Mikulas Jrs.	Slovakia	30	38	22	60	20	—	—	—	—	—
95-96— Liptovsky Mikulas Jrs.	Slovakia	35	46	24	70	...	—	—	—	—	—
— HK 32 Lip. Mikulas	Slovakia	15	2	1	3	0	—	—	—	—	—
96-97— Drummondville	QMJHL	61	40	44	84	115	8	1	2	3	20

BAUMGARTNER, GREGOR — C — CANADIENS

PERSONAL: Born July 13, 1979, in Leoben, Austria. ... 6-1/179. ... Shoots left.
COLLEGE: Clarkson.
TRANSACTIONS/CAREER NOTES: Selected by Montreal Canadiens in second round (second Canadiens pick, 37th overall) of NHL entry draft (June 21, 1997).
HONORS: Named to QMJHL All-Rookie team (1996-97).

Season Team	League	REGULAR SEASON Gms.	G	A	Pts.	PIM	PLAYOFFS Gms.	G	A	Pts.	PIM
95-96— Clarkson	ECAC	7	0	1	1	0	—	—	—	—	—
96-97— Laval	QMJHL	68	19	45	64	15	3	0	0	0	0

BELAK, GRAHAM — D — AVALANCHE

PERSONAL: Born August 1, 1979, in Battleford, Sask. ... 6-4/210. ... Shoots left. ... Brother of Wade Belak, defenseman in Colorado Avalanche system.
TRANSACTIONS/CAREER NOTES: Selected by Colorado Avalanche in second round (second Avalanche pick, 53rd overall) of NHL entry draft (June 21, 1997).

Season Team	League	REGULAR SEASON Gms.	G	A	Pts.	PIM	PLAYOFFS Gms.	G	A	Pts.	PIM
96-97— Edmonton	WHL	61	3	5	8	46	—	—	—	—	—

BERRY, RICK — D — AVALANCHE

PERSONAL: Born November 4, 1978, in Brandon, Manitoba. ... 6-1/192. ... Shoots left.
TRANSACTIONS/CAREER NOTES: Selected by Colorado Avalanche in third round (third Avalanche pick, 55th overall) of NHL entry draft (June 21, 1997).

Season Team	League	REGULAR SEASON Gms.	G	A	Pts.	PIM	PLAYOFFS Gms.	G	A	Pts.	PIM
95-96— Seattle	WHL	59	4	9	13	103	1	0	0	0	0
96-97— Seattle	WHL	72	12	21	33	125	15	3	7	10	23

BETIK, KAREL — D — LIGHTNING

PERSONAL: Born October 28, 1978, in Karvina, Czechoslovakia. ... 6-2/208. ... Shoots left.
TRANSACTIONS/CAREER NOTES: Selected by Tampa Bay Lightning in fifth round (sixth Lightning pick, 112th overall) of NHL entry draft (June 21, 1997).

Season Team	League	REGULAR SEASON Gms.	G	A	Pts.	PIM	PLAYOFFS Gms.	G	A	Pts.	PIM
95-96— HC Vitkovice Jrs.	Czech Rep.	48	3	12	15	88	—	—	—	—	—
96-97— Kelowna	WHL	56	3	10	13	76	6	1	1	2	2

BICEK, JIRI — LW — DEVILS

PERSONAL: Born December 3, 1978, in Kosice, Czechoslovakia. ... 5-11/183. ... Shoots left.
TRANSACTIONS/CAREER NOTES: Selected by New Jersey Devils in fifth round (fourth Devils pick, 131st overall) of NHL entry draft (June 21, 1997).

Season Team	League	REGULAR SEASON Gms.	G	A	Pts.	PIM	PLAYOFFS Gms.	G	A	Pts.	PIM
94-95— HC Kosice Jrs.	Slovakia	42	38	36	74	18	—	—	—	—	—
95-96— HC Kosice	Slovakia	30	10	15	25	16	9	2	4	6	0
96-97— HC Kosice	Slovakia	44	11	14	25	20	7	1	3	4	0

BILOTTO, NICHOLAS   D   BLUES

PERSONAL: Born February 24, 1979, in Montreal. ... 6-2/200. ... Shoots right.
TRANSACTIONS/CAREER NOTES: Selected by St. Louis Blues in sixth round (fifth Blues pick, 149th overall) of NHL entry draft (June 21, 1997).

		REGULAR SEASON					PLAYOFFS				
Season Team	League	Gms.	G	A	Pts.	PIM	Gms.	G	A	Pts.	PIM
96-97 — Beauport	QMJHL	29	3	2	5	30	4	0	1	1	2

BLANCHARD, SEAN   D   KINGS

PERSONAL: Born March 29, 1978, in Garson, Ont. ... 6-0/201. ... Shoots left.
TRANSACTIONS/CAREER NOTES: Selected by Los Angeles Kings in fourth round (fifth Kings pick, 99th overall) of NHL entry draft (June 21, 1997).
HONORS: Won Can.HL Defenseman of the Year Award (1996-97). ... Named to Can.HL All-Star first team (1996-97). ... Named to OHL All-Star first team (1996-97). ... Won Max Kaminsky Trophy (1996-97).

		REGULAR SEASON					PLAYOFFS				
Season Team	League	Gms.	G	A	Pts.	PIM	Gms.	G	A	Pts.	PIM
95-96 — Ottawa	OHL	64	7	29	36	49	—	—	—	—	—
96-97 — Ottawa	OHL	66	11	57	68	64	24	3	15	18	34

BONNI, RYAN   D   CANUCKS

PERSONAL: Born February 18, 1979, in Winnipeg. ... 6-3/187. ... Shoots left.
TRANSACTIONS/CAREER NOTES: Selected by Vancouver Canucks in second round (second Canucks pick, 34th overal) of NHL entry draft (June 21, 1997).

		REGULAR SEASON					PLAYOFFS				
Season Team	League	Gms.	G	A	Pts.	PIM	Gms.	G	A	Pts.	PIM
95-96 — Saskatoon	WHL	63	1	7	8	78	3	0	0	0	0
96-97 — Saskatoon	WHL	69	11	19	30	219	—	—	—	—	—

BOYNTON, NICHOLAS   D   CAPITALS

PERSONAL: Born January 14, 1979, in Toronto. ... 6-2/210. ... Shoots right.
TRANSACTIONS/CAREER NOTES: Selected by Washington Capitals in first round (first Capitals pick, ninth overall) of NHL entry draft (June 21, 1997).
HONORS: Named to OHL All-Rookie team (1995-96). ... Won Can.HL Plus/Minus Award (1996-97).

		REGULAR SEASON					PLAYOFFS				
Season Team	League	Gms.	G	A	Pts.	PIM	Gms.	G	A	Pts.	PIM
94-95 — Caledon	Jr. A	44	10	35	45	139	—	—	—	—	—
95-96 — Ottawa	OHL	64	10	14	24	90	4	0	3	3	10
96-97 — Ottawa	OHL	63	13	51	64	143	24	4	†24	28	38

BREWER, ERIC   D   ISLANDERS

PERSONAL: Born April 17, 1979, in Vernon, B.C. ... 6-3/195. ... Shoots left.
TRANSACTIONS/CAREER NOTES: Selected by New York Islanders in first round (second Islanders pick, fifth overall) of NHL entry draft (June 21, 1997).

		REGULAR SEASON					PLAYOFFS				
Season Team	League	Gms.	G	A	Pts.	PIM	Gms.	G	A	Pts.	PIM
95-96 — Prince George	WHL	63	4	10	14	25	—	—	—	—	—
96-97 — Prince George	WHL	71	5	24	29	81	15	2	4	6	16

BROWN, MIKE   C   PANTHERS

PERSONAL: Born April 27, 1979, in Surrey, B.C. ... 6-5/183. ... Shoots left.
TRANSACTIONS/CAREER NOTES: Selected by Florida Panthers in first round (first Panthers pick, 20th overall) of NHL entry draft (June 21, 1997).
HONORS: Won Jim Piggott Memorial Trophy (1995-96).

		REGULAR SEASON					PLAYOFFS				
Season Team	League	Gms.	G	A	Pts.	PIM	Gms.	G	A	Pts.	PIM
94-95 — Merritt	BCJHL	45	3	4	7	128	—	—	—	—	—
95-96 — Red Deer	WHL	62	4	5	9	125	10	0	0	0	18
96-97 — Red Deer	WHL	70	19	13	32	243	16	1	2	3	47

BUTSAYEV, YURI   C   RED WINGS

PERSONAL: Born October 11, 1978, in Togliatti, U.S.S.R. ... 6-1/183. ... Shoots left.
TRANSACTIONS/CAREER NOTES: Selected by Detroit Red Wings in second round (first Red Wings pick, 49th overall) of NHL entry draft (June 21, 1997).

Season Team	League	REGULAR SEASON					PLAYOFFS				
		Gms.	G	A	Pts.	PIM	Gms.	G	A	Pts.	PIM
95-96— Lada Togliatti	CIS	1	0	0	0	0	—	—	—	—	—
— Lada-2 Togliatti	CIS Div. II	...	19	7	26	...	—	—	—	—	—
96-97— Lada Togliatti	Russian	42	13	11	24	38	11	2	2	4	8

CALDER, KYLE C BLACKHAWKS

PERSONAL: Born January 5, 1979, in Mannville, Alta. ... 5-11/180. ... Shoots left.
TRANSACTIONS/CAREER NOTES: Selected by Chicago Blackhawks in fifth round (seventh Blackhawks pick, 130th overall) of NHL entry draft (June 21, 1997).

Season Team	League	REGULAR SEASON					PLAYOFFS				
		Gms.	G	A	Pts.	PIM	Gms.	G	A	Pts.	PIM
95-96— Regina	WHL	27	1	8	9	10	11	0	0	0	0
96-97— Regina	WHL	62	25	34	59	17	5	3	0	3	6

CAMPBELL, BRIAN D SABRES

PERSONAL: Born May 23, 1979, in Strathroy, Ont. ... 5-11/185. ... Shoots left.
TRANSACTIONS/CAREER NOTES: Selected by Buffalo Sabres in sixth round (seventh Sabres pick, 156th overall) of NHL entry draft (June 21, 1997).

Season Team	League	REGULAR SEASON					PLAYOFFS				
		Gms.	G	A	Pts.	PIM	Gms.	G	A	Pts.	PIM
94-95— Petrolia	Jr. B	50	1	2	3	...	—	—	—	—	—
95-96— Ottawa	OHL	66	5	22	27	22	4	0	1	1	2
96-97— Ottawa	OHL	66	7	36	43	12	24	2	11	13	8

CAULFIELD, KEVIN RW CAPITALS

PERSONAL: Born January 7, 1978, in Boston, Mass. ... 6-2/210. ... Shoots right.
HIGH SCHOOL: Thayer Academy (Braintree, Mass.).
COLLEGE: Boston College.
TRANSACTIONS/CAREER NOTES: Selected by Washington Capitals in fifth round (fourth Capitals pick, 116th overall) of NHL entry draft (June 21, 1997).

Season Team	League	REGULAR SEASON					PLAYOFFS				
		Gms.	G	A	Pts.	PIM	Gms.	G	A	Pts.	PIM
95-96— Thayer Academy	Mass. H.S.	31	12	23	35	45	—	—	—	—	—
96-97— Boston College	Hockey East	38	5	10	15	90	—	—	—	—	—

CECH, VRATISLAV D PANTHERS

PERSONAL: Born January 28, 1979, in Tabor, Czechoslovakia. ... 6-3/196. ... Shoots left.
TRANSACTIONS/CAREER NOTES: Selected by Florida Panthers in third round (third Panthers pick, 56th overall) of NHL entry draft (June 21, 1997).

Season Team	League	REGULAR SEASON					PLAYOFFS				
		Gms.	G	A	Pts.	PIM	Gms.	G	A	Pts.	PIM
95-96— Kometa Brno Jrs.	Czech Rep.	37	10	13	23	...	—	—	—	—	—
96-97— Kitchener	OHL	57	5	19	24	72	13	1	2	3	12

CHERNESKI, STEFAN RW RANGERS

PERSONAL: Born September 19, 1978, in Winnipeg. ... 6-0/185. ... Shoots left.
TRANSACTIONS/CAREER NOTES: Selected by New York Rangers in first round (first Rangers pick, 19th overall) of NHL entry draft (June 21, 1997).
HONORS: Won Can.HL Scholastic Player of the Year Award (1996-97).

Season Team	League	REGULAR SEASON					PLAYOFFS				
		Gms.	G	A	Pts.	PIM	Gms.	G	A	Pts.	PIM
95-96— Brandon	WHL	58	8	21	29	62	19	3	1	4	11
96-97— Brandon	WHL	56	39	29	68	83	—	—	—	—	—

CHERNOV, MIKHAIL D FLYERS

PERSONAL: Born November 11, 1978, in Prokopjevsk, U.S.S.R. ... 6-2/196. ... Shoots right.
TRANSACTIONS/CAREER NOTES: Selected by Philadelphia Flyers in fourth round (fourth Flyers pick, 103rd overall) of NHL entry draft (June 21, 1997).

Season Team	League	REGULAR SEASON					PLAYOFFS				
		Gms.	G	A	Pts.	PIM	Gms.	G	A	Pts.	PIM
94-95— Metal.-2 Novokuznetsk	CIS Div. II	12	0	3	3	0	—	—	—	—	—
95-96— Metal.-2 Novokuznetsk	CIS Div. II	40	2	7	9	10	—	—	—	—	—
96-97— Torpedo-2 Yaroslav	Rus. Div. III	33	4	2	6	40	—	—	—	—	—
— Torpedo Yaroslav	Russian	5	0	0	0	0	—	—	—	—	—

CHIMERA, JASON   C   OILERS

PERSONAL: Born May 2, 1979, in Edmonton. ... 6-0/160. ... Shoots left.
TRANSACTIONS/CAREER NOTES: Selected by Edmonton Oilers in fifth round (fifth Oilers pick, 121st overall) of NHL entry draft (June 21, 1997).

		REGULAR SEASON					PLAYOFFS				
Season Team	League	Gms.	G	A	Pts.	PIM	Gms.	G	A	Pts.	PIM
96-97 — Medicine Hat	WHL	71	16	23	39	64	4	0	1	1	4

CLEARY, DANIEL   LW   BLACKHAWKS

PERSONAL: Born December 18, 1978, in Carbonear, Nfld. ... 6-0/203. ... Shoots left.
TRANSACTIONS/CAREER NOTES: Selected by Chicago Blackhawks in first round (first Blackhawks pick, 13th overall) of NHL entry draft (June 21, 1997).
HONORS: Named to OHL All-Star first team (1995-96 and 1996-97).

		REGULAR SEASON					PLAYOFFS				
Season Team	League	Gms.	G	A	Pts.	PIM	Gms.	G	A	Pts.	PIM
93-94 — Kingston	Tier II Jr. A	41	18	28	46	33	—	—	—	—	—
94-95 — Belleville	OHL	62	26	55	81	62	16	7	10	17	23
95-96 — Belleville	OHL	64	53	62	115	74	14	10	17	27	40
96-97 — Belleville	OHL	64	32	48	80	88	6	3	4	7	6

CLYMER, BEN   D   BRUINS

PERSONAL: Born April 11, 1978, in Edina, Mass. ... 6-1/195. ... Shoots right.
HIGH SCHOOL: Jefferson Senior (Alexandria, Minn).
COLLEGE: Minnesota.
TRANSACTIONS/CAREER NOTES: Selected by Boston Bruins in second round (third Bruins pick, 27th overall) of NHL entry draft (June 21, 1997).
HONORS: Named to WCHA All-Rookie team (1996-97).

		REGULAR SEASON					PLAYOFFS				
Season Team	League	Gms.	G	A	Pts.	PIM	Gms.	G	A	Pts.	PIM
93-94 — Jefferson Senior	Minn. H.S.	23	3	7	10	6	—	—	—	—	—
94-95 — Jefferson Senior	Minn. H.S.	28	6	20	26	26	—	—	—	—	—
95-96 — Jefferson Senior	Minn. H.S.	19	12	28	40	38	—	—	—	—	—
96-97 — University of Minnesota	WCHA	29	7	13	20	64	—	—	—	—	—

COCKELL, MATT   G   CANUCKS

PERSONAL: Born May 4, 1979, in Calgary. ... 6-0/170. ... Catches left.
TRANSACTIONS/CAREER NOTES: Selected by Vancouver Canucks in fifth round (seventh Canucks pick, 117th overall) of NHL entry draft (June 21, 1997).

		REGULAR SEASON							PLAYOFFS					
Season Team	League	Gms.	Min	W	L	T	GA	SO	Avg.	Gms.	Min.	W	L	GA	SO	Avg.
95-96 — Winnipeg	MJHL	17	...	5	7	1	...	0	4.54	—	—	—	—	—	—	—
96-97 — Saskatoon	WHL	47	2609	14	26	4	175	0	4.02	—	—	—	—	—	—	—

COLAGIACOMO, ADAM   RW   SHARKS

PERSONAL: Born March 17, 1979, in Toronto. ... 6-2/206. ... Shoots right.
TRANSACTIONS/CAREER NOTES: Selected by San Jose Sharks in fourth round (third Sharks pick, 82nd overall) of NHL entry draft (June 21, 1997).

		REGULAR SEASON					PLAYOFFS				
Season Team	League	Gms.	G	A	Pts.	PIM	Gms.	G	A	Pts.	PIM
94-95 — Royal York Royals	OPJHL	33	39	20	59	48	—	—	—	—	—
95-96 — London	OHL	66	28	38	66	88	—	—	—	—	—
96-97 — Oshawa	OHL	49	25	21	46	69	13	1	5	6	4

COOKE, MATT   LW   CANUCKS

PERSONAL: Born September 7, 1978, in Belleville, Ont. ... 5-11/181. ... Shoots left.
TRANSACTIONS/CAREER NOTES: Selected by Vancouver Canucks in sixth round (eighth Canucks pick, 144th overall) of NHL entry draft (June 21, 1997).

		REGULAR SEASON					PLAYOFFS				
Season Team	League	Gms.	G	A	Pts.	PIM	Gms.	G	A	Pts.	PIM
95-96 — Windsor	OHL	61	8	11	19	102	7	1	3	4	6
96-97 — Windsor	OHL	65	45	50	95	146	5	5	5	10	4

CORVO, JOE — D — KINGS

PERSONAL: Born June 20, 1977, in Oak Park, Ill. ... 6-0/201. ... Shoots right.
COLLEGE: Western Michigan.
TRANSACTIONS/CAREER NOTES: Selected by Los Angeles Kings in fourth round (fourth Kings pick, 83rd overall) of NHL entry draft (June 21, 1997).
HONORS: Named to CCHA All-Rookie team (1995-96). ... Named to CCHA All-Star second team (1996-97).

Season Team	League	REGULAR SEASON					PLAYOFFS				
		Gms.	G	A	Pts.	PIM	Gms.	G	A	Pts.	PIM
95-96— Western Michigan Univ.	CCHA	41	5	25	30	38	—	—	—	—	—
96-97— Western Michigan Univ.	CCHA	32	12	21	33	85	—	—	—	—	—

CRUICKSHANK, CURTIS — G — CAPITALS

PERSONAL: Born March 21, 1979, in Ottawa. ... 6-2/209. ... Catches left.
TRANSACTIONS/CAREER NOTES: Selected by Washington Capitals in fourth round (third Capitals pick, 89th overall) of NHL entry draft (June 21, 1997).
HONORS: Named to OHL All-Rookie second team (1996-97).

Season Team	League	REGULAR SEASON							PLAYOFFS						
		Gms.	Min	W	L	T	GA	SO	Avg.	Gms.	Min.	W	L	GA	SO	Avg.
95-96—Ottawa	Tier II Jr. A	24	...	12	4	0	...	0	4.27	—	—	—	—	—	—	—
96-97—Kingston	OHL	35	1792	13	16	1	118	2	3.95	1	26	0	1	4	0	9.23

DAFOE, KYLE — D — HURRICANES

PERSONAL: Born January 11, 1979, in Charlottetown, P.E.I. ... 6-5/195. ... Shoots left.
TRANSACTIONS/CAREER NOTES: Selected by Carolina Hurricanes in sixth round (fifth Hurricanes pick, 142nd overall) of NHL entry draft (June 21, 1997).

Season Team	League	REGULAR SEASON					PLAYOFFS				
		Gms.	G	A	Pts.	PIM	Gms.	G	A	Pts.	PIM
96-97—Owen Sound	OHL	41	1	1	2	58	3	0	0	0	0

DAMPHOUSSE, JEAN-FRANCOIS — G — DEVILS

PERSONAL: Born July 21, 1979, in St. Alexis des Monts, Que. ... 6-0/146. ... Catches left.
TRANSACTIONS/CAREER NOTES: Selected by New Jersey Devils in first round (first Devils pick, 24th overall) of NHL entry draft (June 21, 1997).

Season Team	League	REGULAR SEASON							PLAYOFFS						
		Gms.	Min	W	L	T	GA	SO	Avg.	Gms.	Min.	W	L	GA	SO	Avg.
96-97—Moncton	QMJHL	39	2061	6	25	2	190	0	5.53	—	—	—	—	—	—	—

DARGUZAS, DAVE — C — CANUCKS

PERSONAL: Born January 20, 1979, in Maple Ridge, Alberta. ... 6-2/196. ... Shoots left.
TRANSACTIONS/CAREER NOTES: Selected by Vancouver Canucks in fifth round (sixth Canucks pick, 114th overall) of NHL entry draft (June 21, 1997).

Season Team	League	REGULAR SEASON					PLAYOFFS				
		Gms.	G	A	Pts.	PIM	Gms.	G	A	Pts.	PIM
95-96— Brandon	WHL	47	3	9	12	51	3	0	0	0	0
96-97— Edmonton	WHL	71	23	32	55	124	—	—	—	—	—

DEFAUW, BRAD — LW — HURRICANES

PERSONAL: Born November 10, 1977, in Edina, Minn. ... 6-2/210. ... Shoots left.
HIGH SCHOOL: Apple Valley (Minn.).
COLLEGE: North Dakota.
TRANSACTIONS/CAREER NOTES: Selected by Carolina Hurricanes in second round (second Hurricanes pick, 28th overall) of NHL entry draft (June 21, 1997).

Season Team	League	REGULAR SEASON					PLAYOFFS				
		Gms.	G	A	Pts.	PIM	Gms.	G	A	Pts.	PIM
95-96— Apple Valley	Minn. H.S.	28	21	34	55	14	—	—	—	—	—
96-97— Univ. of North Dakota	WCHA	37	7	6	13	39	—	—	—	—	—

DEGAGNE, SHAWN — G — RANGERS

PERSONAL: Born December 18, 1978, in North Bay, Ont. ... 5-11/164. ... Catches left.
TRANSACTIONS/CAREER NOTES: Selected by New York Rangers in sixth round (eighth Rangers pick, 154th overall) of NHL entry draft (June 21, 1997).

Season Team	League	REGULAR SEASON								PLAYOFFS						
		Gms.	Min	W	L	T	GA	SO	Avg.	Gms.	Min.	W	L	GA	SO	Avg.
95-96 — Kitchener	OHL	3	53	0	1	0	5	0	5.66	—	—	—	—	—	—	—
96-97 — Kitchener	OHL	25	1111	12	5	1	61	0	3.29	6	168	0	1	8	0	2.86

DELANEY, KEITH   C   PANTHERS

PERSONAL: Born May 7, 1979, in Labrador City, Nfld. ... 6-1/196. ... Shoots left.
TRANSACTIONS/CAREER NOTES: Selected by Florida Panthers in sixth round (seventh Panthers pick, 155th overall) of NHL entry draft (June 21, 1997).

Season Team	League	REGULAR SEASON					PLAYOFFS				
		Gms.	G	A	Pts.	PIM	Gms.	G	A	Pts.	PIM
96-97 — Barrie	OHL	64	5	5	10	19	9	0	1	1	0

DEMIDOV, ILJA   D   FLAMES

PERSONAL: Born April 14, 1979, in Moscow, U.S.S.R. ... 6-2/185. ... Shoots left.
TRANSACTIONS/CAREER NOTES: Selected by Calgary Flames in sixth round (10th Flames pick, 140th overall) of NHL entry draft (June 21, 1997).

Season Team	League	REGULAR SEASON					PLAYOFFS				
		Gms.	G	A	Pts.	PIM	Gms.	G	A	Pts.	PIM
95-96 — Dynamo-2 Moscow	CIS Div. II	10	0	14	14	...	—	—	—	—	—
96-97 — Dynamo-2 Moscow	Rus. Div. III	32	1	0	1	60	—	—	—	—	—

DESROSCHES, JONATHAN   D   CANADIENS

PERSONAL: Born May 23, 1979, in Granby, Que. ... 6-0/206. ... Shoots left.
TRANSACTIONS/CAREER NOTES: Selected by Montreal Canadiens in sixth round (seventh Canadiens pick, 145th overall) of NHL entry draft (June 21, 1997).

Season Team	League	REGULAR SEASON					PLAYOFFS				
		Gms.	G	A	Pts.	PIM	Gms.	G	A	Pts.	PIM
95-96 — Granby	QMJHL	44	1	6	7	38	11	0	0	0	2
96-97 — Granby ....,................	QMJHL	58	7	15	22	36	5	0	1	1	2

DIROBERTO, TORREY   C   SABRES

PERSONAL: Born April 17, 1978, in New York. ... 5-11/180. ... Shoots left.
TRANSACTIONS/CAREER NOTES: Selected by Buffalo Sabres in fifth round (sixth Sabres pick, 128th overall) of NHL entry draft (June 21, 1997).

Season Team	League	REGULAR SEASON					PLAYOFFS				
		Gms.	G	A	Pts.	PIM	Gms.	G	A	Pts.	PIM
95-96 — Seattle	WHL	70	16	19	35	118	5	0	2	2	8
96-97 — Seattle	WHL	72	37	44	81	91	9	9	5	14	8

DOME, ROBERT   RW   PENGUINS

PERSONAL: Born January 29, 1979, in Skalica, Czechoslovakia. ... 5-11/214. ... Shoots left.
TRANSACTIONS/CAREER NOTES: Selected by Pittsburgh Penguins in first round (first Penguins pick, 17th overall) of NHL entry draft (June 21, 1997).

Season Team	League	REGULAR SEASON					PLAYOFFS				
		Gms.	G	A	Pts.	PIM	Gms.	G	A	Pts.	PIM
95-96 — Utah	IHL	56	10	9	19	28	—	—	—	—	—
96-97 — Long Beach	IHL	13	4	6	10	14	—	—	—	—	—
— Las Vegas	IHL	43	10	7	17	22	—	—	—	—	—

DOVIGI, PATRICK   G   OILERS

PERSONAL: Born July 2, 1979, in Sault Ste. Marie, Ont. ... 6-0/180. ... Catches left.
TRANSACTIONS/CAREER NOTES: Selected by Edmonton Oilers in second round (second Oilers pick, 41st overall) of NHL entry draft (June 21, 1997).

Season Team	League	REGULAR SEASON								PLAYOFFS						
		Gms.	Min	W	L	T	GA	SO	Avg.	Gms.	Min.	W	L	GA	SO	Avg.
95-96 — Elmira	Jr. B	33	...	10	12	1	...	4	4.53	—	—	—	—	—	—	—
96-97 — Erie	OHL	36	1764	11	14	4	114	3	3.88	5	303	1	4	18	0	3.56

DRUKEN, HAROLD   LW/C   CANUCKS

PERSONAL: Born January 26, 1979, in St. John's, Nfld. ... 5-11/202. ... Shoots left.
HIGH SCHOOL: Noble & Greenough (Dedham, Mass.).
TRANSACTIONS/CAREER NOTES: Selected by Vancouver Canucks in second round (third Canucks pick, 36th overall) of NHL entry draft (June 21, 1997).

HONORS: Named to OHL All-Rookie team (1996-97).

Season Team	League	REGULAR SEASON					PLAYOFFS				
		Gms.	G	A	Pts.	PIM	Gms.	G	A	Pts.	PIM
95-96— Noble & Greenough..............	Mass. H.S.	30	37	28	65	28	—	—	—	—	—
96-97— Detroit....................	OHL	63	27	31	58	14	5	3	2	5	0

EDINGER, ADAM   C   ISLANDERS

PERSONAL: Born September 21, 1977, in Toledo, Ohio. ... 6-2/210. ... Shoots left.
COLLEGE: Bowling Green State.
TRANSACTIONS/CAREER NOTES: Selected by New York Islanders in fifth round (seventh Islanders pick, 115th overall) of NHL entry draft (June 21, 1997).

Season Team	League	REGULAR SEASON					PLAYOFFS				
		Gms.	G	A	Pts.	PIM	Gms.	G	A	Pts.	PIM
94-95— Learnington	Jr. B	38	19	62	81	100	—	—	—	—	—
95-96— Learnington	Jr. B	45	45	50	95	120	—	—	—	—	—
96-97— Bowling Green State	CCHA	34	11	17	28	42	—	—	—	—	—

ELICH, MATT   RW   LIGHTNING

PERSONAL: Born September 22, 1979, in Detroit. ... 6-3/187. ... Shoots right.
TRANSACTIONS/CAREER NOTES: Selected by Tampa Bay Lightning in third round (third Lightning pick, 61st overall) of NHL entry draft (June 21, 1997).

Season Team	League	REGULAR SEASON					PLAYOFFS				
		Gms.	G	A	Pts.	PIM	Gms.	G	A	Pts.	PIM
95-96— Windsor	OHL	52	10	2	12	17	5	1	0	1	2
96-97— Windsor	OHL	58	15	13	28	19	5	0	1	1	6

ELOFSSON, JONAS   D   OILERS

PERSONAL: Born January 31, 1979, in Ulricehamn, Sweden. ... 6-1/180. ... Shoots left.
TRANSACTIONS/CAREER NOTES: Selected by Edmonton Oilers in fourth round (fourth Oilers pick, 94th overall) of NHL entry draft (June 21, 1997).

Season Team	League	REGULAR SEASON					PLAYOFFS				
		Gms.	G	A	Pts.	PIM	Gms.	G	A	Pts.	PIM
95-96— Farjestad Karistad Jrs.	Sweden	26	6	11	17	18	—	—	—	—	—
96-97— Farjestad Karistad	Sweden	3	0	0	0	0	5	0	1	1	0

ELOMO, TEEMU   LW   STARS

PERSONAL: Born January 13, 1979, in Turku, Finland. ... 5-11/176. ... Shoots left.
TRANSACTIONS/CAREER NOTES: Selected by Dallas Stars in fifth round (fifth Stars pick, 132nd overall) of NHL entry draft (June 21, 1997).

Season Team	League	REGULAR SEASON					PLAYOFFS				
		Gms.	G	A	Pts.	PIM	Gms.	G	A	Pts.	PIM
95-96— Kiekko-67 Turku......................	Finland Dv.II	11	1	0	1	4	6	2	0	2	8
— TPS Turku Jrs........................	Finland	2	0	0	0	0	—	—	—	—	—
96-97— TPS Turku............................	Finland	6	0	1	1	0	3	0	0	0	2
— Kiekko-67 Turku....................	Finland Dv.II	15	4	3	7	24	—	—	—	—	—
— TPS Turku Jrs........................	Finland	9	6	2	8	16	—	—	—	—	—

FARKAS, JEFF   C   MAPLE LEAFS

PERSONAL: Born January 24, 1978, in Amherst, N.Y. ... 6-0/174. ... Shoots left.
COLLEGE: Boston College.
TRANSACTIONS/CAREER NOTES: Selected by Toronto Maple Leafs in third round (first Maple Leafs pick, 57th overall) of NHL entry draft (June 21, 1997).

Season Team	League	REGULAR SEASON					PLAYOFFS				
		Gms.	G	A	Pts.	PIM	Gms.	G	A	Pts.	PIM
94-95— Niagara	NAJHL	53	54	58	112	34	—	—	—	—	—
95-96— Niagara	NAJHL	74	64	107	171	95	—	—	—	—	—
96-97— Boston College	Hockey East	35	13	23	36	34	—	—	—	—	—

FERENCE, BRAD   D   CANUCKS

PERSONAL: Born April 2, 1979, in Calgary. ... 6-3/186. ... Shoots right.
TRANSACTIONS/CAREER NOTES: Selected by Vancouver Canucks in first round (first Canucks pick, 10th overall) of NHL entry draft (June 21, 1997).
HONORS: Named to Can.HL All-Rookie team (1996-97).

Season Team	League	REGULAR SEASON					PLAYOFFS				
		Gms.	G	A	Pts.	PIM	Gms.	G	A	Pts.	PIM
95-96— Spokane..............................	WHL	5	0	2	2	18	—	—	—	—	—
96-97— Spokane..............................	WHL	67	6	20	26	324	9	0	4	4	21

FLODELL, JORDON   D   FLYERS

PERSONAL: Born April 28, 1979, in Melfort, Sask. ... 6-2/198. ... Shoots right.
TRANSACTIONS/CAREER NOTES: Selected by Philadelphia Flyers in sixth round (fifth Flyers pick, 158th overall) of NHL entry draft (June 21, 1997).

		REGULAR SEASON					PLAYOFFS				
Season Team	League	Gms.	G	A	Pts.	PIM	Gms.	G	A	Pts.	PIM
95-96 — Moose Jaw	WHL	17	0	0	0	7	—	—	—	—	—
96-97 — Moose Jaw	WHL	39	0	3	3	48	12	0	3	3	8

FORTIN, JEAN-FRANCOIS   D   CAPITALS

PERSONAL: Born March 15, 1979, in Laval, Que. ... 6-2/190. ... Shoots right.
TRANSACTIONS/CAREER NOTES: Selected by Washington Capitals in second round (second Capitals pick, 35th overall) of NHL entry draft (June 21, 1997).

		REGULAR SEASON					PLAYOFFS				
Season Team	League	Gms.	G	A	Pts.	PIM	Gms.	G	A	Pts.	PIM
95-96 — Sherbrooke	QMJHL	69	7	15	22	40	7	2	6	8	2
96-97 — Sherbrooke	QMJHL	59	7	30	37	89	2	0	1	1	14

FRANCZ, ROBERT   LW   COYOTES

PERSONAL: Born March 30, 1978, in Bad Muskau, East Germany. ... 6-1/194. ... Shoots left.
TRANSACTIONS/CAREER NOTES: Selected by Phoenix Coyotes in sixth round (fourth Coyotes pick, 151st overall) of NHL entry draft (June 21, 1997).

		REGULAR SEASON					PLAYOFFS				
Season Team	League	Gms.	G	A	Pts.	PIM	Gms.	G	A	Pts.	PIM
94-95 — Rosenheim Jrs.	Germany	29	11	13	24	94	—	—	—	—	—
95-96 — Augsburg	Germany	36	0	1	1	43	6	0	0	0	0
— Augsburg Jrs.	Germany	7	1	1	2	62	—	—	—	—	—
96-97 — Peterborough	OHL	60	9	21	30	149	8	1	1	2	17

FREADRICH, KYLE   LW   CANUCKS

PERSONAL: Born December 28, 1978, in Edmonton. ... 6-5/230. ... Shoots left.
TRANSACTIONS/CAREER NOTES: Selected by Vancouver Canucks in third round (fourth Canucks pick, 64th overall) of NHL entry draft (June 21, 1997).

		REGULAR SEASON					PLAYOFFS				
Season Team	League	Gms.	G	A	Pts.	PIM	Gms.	G	A	Pts.	PIM
96-97 — Prince George	WHL	12	0	0	0	12	—	—	—	—	—
— Regina	WHL	50	1	3	4	152	4	0	0	0	8

GAFFANEY, BRIAN   D   PENGUINS

PERSONAL: Born October 4, 1977, in Alexandria, Minn. ... 6-5/205. ... Shoots left.
TRANSACTIONS/CAREER NOTES: Selected by Pittsburgh Penguins in second round (second Penguins pick, 44th overall) of NHL entry draft (June 21, 1997).

		REGULAR SEASON					PLAYOFFS				
Season Team	League	Gms.	G	A	Pts.	PIM	Gms.	G	A	Pts.	PIM
96-97 — North Iowa	Jr. A	48	8	13	21	49	—	—	—	—	—

GAINEY, STEVE   C   STARS

PERSONAL: Born January 26, 1979, in Montreal. ... 6-0/165. ... Shoots left.
TRANSACTIONS/CAREER NOTES: Selected by Dallas Stars in third round (third Stars pick, 77th overall) of NHL entry draft (June 21, 1997).

		REGULAR SEASON					PLAYOFFS				
Season Team	League	Gms.	G	A	Pts.	PIM	Gms.	G	A	Pts.	PIM
95-96 — Kamloops	WHL	49	1	4	5	40	3	0	0	0	0
96-97 — Kamloops	WHL	60	9	18	27	60	2	0	0	0	9

GARDINER, PETE   RW   BLACKHAWKS

PERSONAL: Born September 29, 1977, in Toronto. ... 6-5/220. ... Shoots right.
HIGH SCHOOL: Lawrence Park Collegiate Institute (Toronto).
COLLEGE: Rensselaer Polytechnic Institute.
TRANSACTIONS/CAREER NOTES: Selected by Chicago Blackhawks in fifth round (sixth Blackhawks pick, 120th overall) of NHL entry draft (June 21, 1997).
HONORS: Named to ECAC All-Rookie team (1996-97).

Season Team	League	REGULAR SEASON					PLAYOFFS				
		Gms.	G	A	Pts.	PIM	Gms.	G	A	Pts.	PIM
96-97 — R.P.I.	ECAC	36	10	21	31	47	—	—	—	—	—

GOC, SASCHA   D   DEVILS

PERSONAL: Born April 14, 1979, in Calw, West Germany. ... 6-2/196. ... Shoots right.
TRANSACTIONS/CAREER NOTES: Selected by New Jersey Devils in sixth round (fifth Devils pick, 159th overall) of NHL entry draft (June 21, 1997).

Season Team	League	REGULAR SEASON					PLAYOFFS				
		Gms.	G	A	Pts.	PIM	Gms.	G	A	Pts.	PIM
95-96 — Schwenningen Jrs.	Germany	11	3	6	9	77	—	—	—	—	—
— Schwenningen	Germany	1	0	0	0	0	—	—	—	—	—
96-97 — Schwenningen	Germany	41	3	1	4	28	5	0	0	0	0

GOOLDY, ERIC   LW   MAPLE LEAFS

PERSONAL: Born February 10, 1979, in Utica, N.Y. ... 6-2/200. ... Shoots left.
TRANSACTIONS/CAREER NOTES: Selected by Toronto Maple Leafs in sixth round (fourth Maple Leafs pick, 138th overall) of NHL entry draft (June 21, 1997).

Season Team	League	REGULAR SEASON					PLAYOFFS				
		Gms.	G	A	Pts.	PIM	Gms.	G	A	Pts.	PIM
96-97 — Detroit	OHL	66	7	11	18	131	5	0	1	1	15

GORDON, HEATH   RW   BLACKHAWKS

PERSONAL: Born May 28, 1978, in Boston. ... 6-1/192. ... Shoots left.
HIGH SCHOOL: Catholic Memorial (Boston), then Cushing Academy (Ashburnham, Mass.).
COLLEGE: Providence.
TRANSACTIONS/CAREER NOTES: Selected by Chicago Blackhawks in sixth round (eighth Blackhawks pick, 147th overall) of NHL entry draft (June 21, 1997).

Season Team	League	REGULAR SEASON					PLAYOFFS				
		Gms.	G	A	Pts.	PIM	Gms.	G	A	Pts.	PIM
93-94 — Catholic Memorial	Mass. H.S.	26	10	15	25	30	—	—	—	—	—
94-95 — Cushing Academy	Mass. H.S.	37	22	33	55	74	—	—	—	—	—
95-96 — Cushing Academy	Mass. H.S.	37	34	37	71	120	—	—	—	—	—
96-97 — Green Bay	USHL	52	16	28	44	71	—	—	—	—	—

GOREN, LEE   RW   BRUINS

PERSONAL: Born December 26, 1977, in Winnipeg. ... 6-3/190. ... Shoots right.
COLLEGE: North Dakota.
TRANSACTIONS/CAREER NOTES: Selected by Boston Bruins in third round (fifth Bruins pick, 63rd overall) of NHL entry draft (June 21, 1997).

GRIMES, KEVIN   D   AVALANCHE

PERSONAL: Born August 19, 1979, in Ottawa. ... 6-2/202. ... Shoots left. ... Related to Kris Draper, center, Detroit Red Wings.
TRANSACTIONS/CAREER NOTES: Selected by Colorado Avalanche in first round (first Avalanche pick, 26th overall) of NHL entry draft (June 21, 1997).
HONORS: Named to OHL All-Rookie second team (1996-97).

Season Team	League	REGULAR SEASON					PLAYOFFS				
		Gms.	G	A	Pts.	PIM	Gms.	G	A	Pts.	PIM
95-96 — Cumberland	CJHL	51	2	10	12	220	—	—	—	—	—
96-97 — Kingston	OHL	57	2	12	14	188	1	0	0	0	0

GRON, STANISLAV   C   DEVILS

PERSONAL: Born October 28, 1978, in Bratislava, Czechoslovakia. ... 6-1/189. ... Shoots left.
TRANSACTIONS/CAREER NOTES: Selected by New Jersey Devils in second round (second Devils pick, 38th overall) of NHL entry draft (June 21, 1997).

Season Team	League	REGULAR SEASON					PLAYOFFS				
		Gms.	G	A	Pts.	PIM	Gms.	G	A	Pts.	PIM
94-95 — Slovan Bratislava Jrs.	Slovakia	40	49	26	75	20	—	—	—	—	—
95-96 — Slovan Bratislava Jrs.	Slovakia	43	33	25	58	14	—	—	—	—	—
— Slovan Bratislava	Slovakia	—	—	—	—	—	1	0	0	0	0
96-97 — Slovan Bratislava Jrs.	Slovakia	22	20	16	36	...	—	—	—	—	—
— Slovan Bratislava	Slovakia	7	0	0	0	...	—	—	—	—	—

GUSTAFSSON, JUHA   D   COYOTES

PERSONAL: Born April 26, 1979, in Espoo, Finland. ... 6-3/200. ... Shoots left.

TRANSACTIONS/CAREER NOTES: Selected by Phoenix Coyotes in second round (first Coyotes pick, 43rd overall) of NHL entry draft (June 21, 1997).

Season Team	League	REGULAR SEASON					PLAYOFFS				
		Gms.	G	A	Pts.	PIM	Gms.	G	A	Pts.	PIM
95-96— Kiekko-Espoo Jrs..............	Finland	33	1	5	6	28	4	0	0	0	2
— Kiekko-Espoo.....................	Finland	1	0	0	0	0	—	—	—	—	—
96-97— Kiekko-Espoo Jrs..............	Finland	32	1	3	4	30	—	—	—	—	—
— Kiekko-Espoo.....................	Finland	3	0	0	0	0	3	0	0	0	0

HANNAN, SCOTT　　　　D　　　　SHARKS

PERSONAL: Born January 23, 1979, in Richmond, B.C. ... 6-1/210. ... Shoots left.
TRANSACTIONS/CAREER NOTES: Selected by San Jose Sharks in first round (second Sharks pick, 23rd overall) of NHL entry draft (June 21, 1997).

Season Team	League	REGULAR SEASON					PLAYOFFS				
		Gms.	G	A	Pts.	PIM	Gms.	G	A	Pts.	PIM
94-95— Tacoma	WHL	2	0	0	0	0	—	—	—	—	—
95-96— Kelowna	WHL	69	4	5	9	76	6	0	1	1	4
96-97— Kelowna	WHL	70	17	26	43	101	6	0	0	0	8

HAVELKA, PETR　　　　LW　　　　PENGUINS

PERSONAL: Born March 4, 1979, in Most, Czechoslovakia. ... 6-2/187. ... Shoots left.
TRANSACTIONS/CAREER NOTES: Selected by Pittsburgh Penguins in sixth round (sixth Penguins pick, 152nd overall) of NHL entry draft (June 21, 1997).

Season Team	League	REGULAR SEASON					PLAYOFFS				
		Gms.	G	A	Pts.	PIM	Gms.	G	A	Pts.	PIM
95-96 — Sparta Praha Jrs....................	Czech Rep.	40	15	10	25	...	—	—	—	—	—
96-97— Sparta Praha Jrs....................	Czech Rep.	23	14	13	27	...	—	—	—	—	—
— Sparta Praha........................	Czech Rep.	—	—	—	—	—	1	0	0	0	0

HENRY, BURKE　　　　D　　　　RANGERS

PERSONAL: Born January 21, 1979, in Ste. Rose, Manitoba. ... 6-2/190. ... Shoots left.
TRANSACTIONS/CAREER NOTES: Selected by New York Rangers in third round (third Rangers pick, 73rd overall) of NHL entry draft (June 21, 1997).

Season Team	League	REGULAR SEASON					PLAYOFFS				
		Gms.	G	A	Pts.	PIM	Gms.	G	A	Pts.	PIM
95-96— Brandon	WHL	50	6	11	17	58	19	0	4	4	19
96-97— Brandon	WHL	55	6	25	31	81	6	1	3	4	4

HOLMQVIST, MIKAEL　　　　C　　　　MIGHTY DUCKS

PERSONAL: Born June 8, 1979, in Stockholm, Sweden. ... 6-3/183. ... Shoots left.
TRANSACTIONS/CAREER NOTES: Selected by Mighty Ducks of Anaheim in first round (first Mighty Ducks pick, 18th overall) of NHL entry draft (June 21, 1997).

Season Team	League	REGULAR SEASON					PLAYOFFS				
		Gms.	G	A	Pts.	PIM	Gms.	G	A	Pts.	PIM
95-96— Djurgarden Stockholm Jrs......	Sweden	24	7	2	9	4	—	—	—	—	—
96-97— Djurgarden Stockholm Jrs......	Sweden	39	29	35	64	110	—	—	—	—	—
— Djurgarden Stockholm.........	Sweden	9	0	0	0	0	—	—	—	—	—

HORACEK, JAN　　　　D　　　　BLUES

PERSONAL: Born May 22, 1979, in Benesov, Czechoslovakia. ... 6-3/198. ... Shoots right.
TRANSACTIONS/CAREER NOTES: Selected by St. Louis Blues in fourth round (third Blues pick, 98th overall) of NHL entry draft (June 21, 1997).

Season Team	League	REGULAR SEASON					PLAYOFFS				
		Gms.	G	A	Pts.	PIM	Gms.	G	A	Pts.	PIM
95-96— Slavia Praha..........................	Czech Rep.	8	0	1	1	4	—	—	—	—	—
— Slavia Praha Jrs....................	Czech. Rep.	18	1	5	6	...	—	—	—	—	—
— HC Kralupy	Czech. II	11	0	0	0	...	—	—	—	—	—
96-97— Slavia Praha Jrs....................	Czech. Rep.	25	4	14	18	...	—	—	—	—	—
— Slavia Praha........................	Czech. Rep.	9	0	0	0	6	3	0	0	0	0
— HC Beroun	Czech. II	2	0	0	0	...	—	—	—	—	—

HOSSA, MARIAN　　　　RW　　　　SENATORS

PERSONAL: Born January 12, 1979, in Stara Lubovna, Czechoslovakia. ... 6-0/185. ... Shoots left.
TRANSACTIONS/CAREER NOTES: Selected by Ottawa Senators in first round (first Senators pick, 12th overall) of NHL entry draft (June 21, 1997).

Season Team	League	REGULAR SEASON Gms.	G	A	Pts.	PIM	PLAYOFFS Gms.	G	A	Pts.	PIM
95-96 — Dukla Trencin Jrs.	Slovakia Jrs.	53	42	49	91	26	—	—	—	—	—
96-97 — Dukla Trencin	Slovakia	46	25	19	44	33	7	5	5	10	0

HURME, JANI   G   SENATORS

PERSONAL: Born January 18, 1975, in Turku, Finland. ... 6-0/187. ... Catches left.
TRANSACTIONS/CAREER NOTES: Selected by Ottawa Senators in third round (second Senators pick, 58th overall) of NHL entry draft (June 21, 1997).

Season Team	League	REGULAR SEASON Gms.	Min	W	L	T	GA	SO	Avg.	PLAYOFFS Gms.	Min.	W	L	GA	SO	Avg.
92-93 — TPS Jr.	Finland	12	669	...	...	...	47	0	4.22	1	60	...	...	0	11	0.00
93-94 — TPS Turku	Finland	1	2	...	...	...	0	0	0.00	—	—	—	—	—	—	—
—Kiekko-67 Turku	Fin. Div.II	3	190	...	...	...	7	0	2.21	—	—	—	—	—	—	—
—Kiekko-67 Turku Jrs.	Finland	18	...	...	...	...	...	...	3.16	—	—	—	—	—	—	—
94-95 — Kiekko-67 Turku	Fin. Div.II	19	1049	...	...	...	53	...	3.03	3	180	...	...	6	...	2.00
—TPS Jr.	Finland	2	125	...	...	...	5	0	2.40	—	—	—	—	—	—	—
—Kiekko-67 Turku Jrs.	Finland	9	540	...	...	...	47	...	5.22	—	—	—	—	—	—	—
95-96 — TPS Turku	Finland	16	945	...	...	...	34	2	2.16	10	545	...	...	22	2	2.42
—Kiekko-67 Turku	Fin. Div.II	16	968	...	...	...	39	1	2.42	—	—	—	—	—	—	—
—TPS Jr.	Finland	13	777	...	...	...	34	1	2.63	—	—	—	—	—	—	—
96-97 — TPS Turku	Finland	48	2917	...	...	...	101	6	2.08	12	722	...	...	39	0	3.24

HUSELIUS, KRISTIAN   LW   PANTHERS

PERSONAL: Born November 10, 1978, in Stockholm, Sweden. ... 6-1/183. ... Shoots left.
TRANSACTIONS/CAREER NOTES: Selected by Florida Panthers in second round (second Panthers pick, 47th overall) of NHL entry draft (June 21, 1997).

Season Team	League	REGULAR SEASON Gms.	G	A	Pts.	PIM	PLAYOFFS Gms.	G	A	Pts.	PIM
94-95 — Hammarby Jrs.	Sweden	17	6	2	8	2	—	—	—	—	—
95-96 — Hammarby Jrs.	Sweden	25	13	8	21	14	—	—	—	—	—
— Hammarby	Swed. Div. II	6	1	0	1	0	—	—	—	—	—
96-97 — Farjestad Karistad	Sweden	13	2	0	2	4	5	1	0	1	0

JARVIS, WES   D   RANGERS

PERSONAL: Born April 16, 1979, in Toronto. ... 6-4/203. ... Shoots left.
TRANSACTIONS/CAREER NOTES: Selected by New York Rangers in second round (second Rangers pick, 46th overall) of NHL entry draft (June 21, 1997).

Season Team	League	REGULAR SEASON Gms.	G	A	Pts.	PIM	PLAYOFFS Gms.	G	A	Pts.	PIM
95-96 — Gloucester	Tier II Jr. A	43	3	6	9	73	—	—	—	—	—
96-97 — Kitchener	OHL	56	4	8	12	108	13	0	4	4	25

JOKINEN, OLLI   C   KINGS

PERSONAL: Born December 5, 1978, in Kuopio, Finland. ... 6-2/198. ... Shoots left.
TRANSACTIONS/CAREER NOTES: Selected by Los Angeles Kings in first round (first Kings pick, third overall) of NHL entry draft (June 21, 1997).

Season Team	League	REGULAR SEASON Gms.	G	A	Pts.	PIM	PLAYOFFS Gms.	G	A	Pts.	PIM
94-95 — KalPa Kuopio Jrs.	Finland	6	0	1	1	6	—	—	—	—	—
95-96 — KalPa Kuopio Jrs.	Finland	15	1	1	2	2	—	—	—	—	—
— KalPa Kuopio	Finland	15	1	1	2	2	—	—	—	—	—
96-97 — HIFK Helsinki	Finland	50	14	27	41	88	—	—	—	—	—

JONES, TY   RW   BLACKHAWKS

PERSONAL: Born February 22, 1979, in Richland, Wash. ... 6-3/210. ... Shoots right.
TRANSACTIONS/CAREER NOTES: Selected by Chicago Blackhawks in first round (second Blackhawks pick, 16th overall) of NHL entry draft (June 21, 1997).

Season Team	League	REGULAR SEASON Gms.	G	A	Pts.	PIM	PLAYOFFS Gms.	G	A	Pts.	PIM
95-96 — Spokane	WHL	34	1	0	1	77	3	0	0	0	6
96-97 — Spokane	WHL	67	20	34	54	202	9	2	4	6	0

KALLARSSON, TOMI   D   RANGERS

PERSONAL: Born March 15, 1979, in Lempaala, Finland. ... 6-3/194. ... Shoots left.
TRANSACTIONS/CAREER NOTES: Selected by New York Rangers in fourth round (fourth Rangers pick, 93rd overall) of NHL entry draft (June 21, 1997).

Season Team	League	REGULAR SEASON					PLAYOFFS				
		Gms.	G	A	Pts.	PIM	Gms.	G	A	Pts.	PIM
95-96 — Tappara Tampere Jrs.	Finland	31	3	5	8	24	6	0	3	3	0
96-97 — HPK Hameenlinna..................	Finland	31	1	3	4	26	—	—	—	—	—

KARLIN, MATTIAS   C   BRUINS

PERSONAL: Born July 4, 1979, in Ornskoldsvik, Sweden. ... 5-11/183. ... Shoots left.
TRANSACTIONS/CAREER NOTES: Selected by Boston Bruins in third round (fourth Bruins pick, 54th overall) of NHL entry draft (June 21, 1997).

Season Team	League	REGULAR SEASON					PLAYOFFS				
		Gms.	G	A	Pts.	PIM	Gms.	G	A	Pts.	PIM
95-96 — MoDo Ornskoldsvik Jrs.	Sweden	30	12	23	35	16	—	—	—	—	—
96-97 — MoDo Ornskoldvik..................	Sweden	6	0	0	0	0	—	—	—	—	—

KATCHER, JEFF   D   KINGS

PERSONAL: Born April 16, 1979, in Winnipeg. ... 6-3/178. ... Shoots right.
TRANSACTIONS/CAREER NOTES: Selected by Los Angeles Kings in sixth round (seventh Kings pick, 150th overall) of NHL entry draft (June 21, 1997).

Season Team	League	REGULAR SEASON					PLAYOFFS				
		Gms.	G	A	Pts.	PIM	Gms.	G	A	Pts.	PIM
96-97 — Brandon..................................	WHL	48	2	2	4	31	—	—	—	—	—

KAVANAGH, PAT   RW   FLYERS

PERSONAL: Born March 14, 1979, in Ottawa. ... 6-3/192. ... Shoots right.
TRANSACTIONS/CAREER NOTES: Selected by Philadelphia Flyers in second round (second Flyers pick, 50th overall) of NHL entry draft (June 21, 1997).

Season Team	League	REGULAR SEASON					PLAYOFFS				
		Gms.	G	A	Pts.	PIM	Gms.	G	A	Pts.	PIM
96-97 — Peterborough..........................	OHL	43	6	8	14	53	11	1	1	2	12

KOKOREV, DMITRI   D   FLAMES

PERSONAL: Born January 9, 1979, in Moscow, U.S.S.R. ... 6-3/198. ... Shoots left.
TRANSACTIONS/CAREER NOTES: Selected by Calgary Flames in second round (fourth Flames pick, 51st overall) of NHL entry draft (June 21, 1997).

Season Team	League	REGULAR SEASON					PLAYOFFS				
		Gms.	G	A	Pts.	PIM	Gms.	G	A	Pts.	PIM
94-95 — Dynamo Moscow....................	CIS Div. II	10	0	1	1	8	—	—	—	—	—
95-96 — Dynamo Moscow....................	CIS Div. II	4	0	4	4	...	—	—	—	—	—
96-97 — Dynamo-2 Moscow	Rus. Div. III	27	2	4	6	24	—	—	—	—	—
— Dynamo Moscow...................	Russian	1	0	0	0	0	—	—	—	—	—

KOS, KYLE   D   LIGHTNING

PERSONAL: Born May 25, 1979, in Hope, B.C. ... 6-3/184. ... Shoots left.
TRANSACTIONS/CAREER NOTES: Selected by Tampa Bay Lightning in second round (second Lightning pick, 33rd overall) of NHL entry draft (June 21, 1997).

Season Team	League	REGULAR SEASON					PLAYOFFS				
		Gms.	G	A	Pts.	PIM	Gms.	G	A	Pts.	PIM
96-97 — Red Deer................................	WHL	64	2	18	20	40	10	0	0	0	8

KRISTOFFERSON, MARCUS   RW   STARS

PERSONAL: Born January 22, 1979, in Ostersund, Sweden. ... 6-3/200. ... Shoots left.
TRANSACTIONS/CAREER NOTES: Selected by Dallas Stars in fourth round (fourth Stars pick, 105th overall) of NHL entry draft (June 21, 1997).

Season Team	League	REGULAR SEASON					PLAYOFFS				
		Gms.	G	A	Pts.	PIM	Gms.	G	A	Pts.	PIM
95-96 — Mora Jrs.	Sweden	16	2	2	4	28	—	—	—	—	—
— Mora......................................	Swed. Dv.II	26	1	0	1	20	5	0	0	0	2
96-97 — Mora......................................	Swed. Dv.II	33	1	5	6	26	—	—	—	—	—

LAING, QUINTIN   LW   RED WINGS

PERSONAL: Born June 8, 1979, in Rosetown, Sask. ... 6-2/175. ... Shoots left.
TRANSACTIONS/CAREER NOTES: Selected by Detroit Red Wings in fourth round (third Red Wings pick, 102nd overall) of NHL entry draft (June 21, 1997).

1997 TOP DRAFT PICKS

Season Team	League	REGULAR SEASON Gms.	G	A	Pts.	PIM	PLAYOFFS Gms.	G	A	Pts.	PIM
96-97 — Kelowna	WHL	63	13	24	37	54	1	0	0	0	0

LANGFELD, JOSH RW SENATORS

PERSONAL: Born July 17, 1977, in Fridley, Minn. ... 6-3/205. ... Shoots right.
TRANSACTIONS/CAREER NOTES: Selected by Ottawa Senators in third round (third Senators pick, 66th overall) of NHL entry draft (June 21, 1997).

Season Team	League	REGULAR SEASON Gms.	G	A	Pts.	PIM	PLAYOFFS Gms.	G	A	Pts.	PIM
96-97 — Lincoln	Jr. A	38	35	23	58	100	—	—	—	—	—

LARSEN, BRAD LW AVALANCHE

PERSONAL: Born June 28, 1977, in Nakusp, B.C. ... 6-0/196. ... Shoots left.
TRANSACTIONS/CAREER NOTES: Selected by Ottawa Senators in third round (third Senators pick, 53rd overall) of NHL entry draft (July 8, 1995). ... Traded by Senators to Colorado Avalanche for D Janne Laukkanen (January 25, 1996); did not sign. ... Selected by Avalanche in fourth round (fifth Avalanche pick, 87th overall) of NHL entry draft (June 21, 1997).
HONORS: Named to WHL (East) All-Star second team (1996-97).

Season Team	League	REGULAR SEASON Gms.	G	A	Pts.	PIM	PLAYOFFS Gms.	G	A	Pts.	PIM
92-93 — Nelson	Tier II Jr. A	42	31	37	68	164	—	—	—	—	—
93-94 — Swift Current	WHL	64	15	18	33	37	7	1	2	3	4
94-95 — Swift Current	WHL	62	24	33	57	73	6	0	1	1	2
95-96 — Swift Current	WHL	51	30	47	77	67	6	3	2	5	13
96-97 — Swift Current	WHL	61	36	46	82	61	0	0	0	0	0

LEAVINS, BOBBY LW ISLANDERS

PERSONAL: Born February 14, 1979, in Elrose, Sask. ... 6-1/190. ... Shoots left.
TRANSACTIONS/CAREER NOTES: Selected by New York Islanders in sixth round (eighth Islanders pick, 139th overall) of NHL entry draft (June 21, 1997).

Season Team	League	REGULAR SEASON Gms.	G	A	Pts.	PIM	PLAYOFFS Gms.	G	A	Pts.	PIM
95-96 — Brandon	WHL	1	0	0	0	0	—	—	—	—	—
96-97 — Brandon	WHL	59	5	6	11	42	3	0	0	0	2

LEGAULT, JAY LW MIGHTY DUCKS

PERSONAL: Born May 15, 1979, in Peterborough, Ont. ... 6-4/192. ... Shoots left.
TRANSACTIONS/CAREER NOTES: Selected by Mighty Ducks of Anaheim in third round (third Mighty Ducks pick, 72nd overall) of NHL entry draft (June 21, 1997).

Season Team	League	REGULAR SEASON Gms.	G	A	Pts.	PIM	PLAYOFFS Gms.	G	A	Pts.	PIM
95-96 — Oshawa	OHL	61	2	11	13	37	—	—	—	—	—
96-97 — London	OHL	67	19	39	58	87	—	—	—	—	—

LESSARD, FRANCIS D HURRICANES

PERSONAL: Born May 30, 1979, in Montreal. ... 6-2/184. ... Shoots right.
TRANSACTIONS/CAREER NOTES: Selected by Carolina Hurricanes in third round (third Hurricanes pick, 80th overall) of NHL entry draft (June 21, 1997).

Season Team	League	REGULAR SEASON Gms.	G	A	Pts.	PIM	PLAYOFFS Gms.	G	A	Pts.	PIM
96-97 — Val-d'Or	QMJHL	66	1	9	10	312	—	—	—	—	—

LINDBOM, JOHAN LW RANGERS

PERSONAL: Born July 8, 1971, in Alvesta, Sweden. ... 6-2/205. ... Shoots left.
TRANSACTIONS/CAREER NOTES: Selected by New York Rangers in fifth round (sixth Rangers pick, 134th overall) of NHL entry draft (June 21, 1997).

Season Team	League	REGULAR SEASON Gms.	G	A	Pts.	PIM	PLAYOFFS Gms.	G	A	Pts.	PIM
91-92 — Tyringe	Swed. Div. II	30	10	11	21	68	—	—	—	—	—
92-93 — Troja-Ljungby	Swed. Div. II	30	10	16	26	20	10	6	3	9	18
93-94 — Troja-Ljungby	Swed. Div. II	33	16	11	27	30	11	6	6	12	2
94-95 — HV 71 Jonkoping	Sweden	39	9	7	16	30	13	2	5	7	12
95-96 — HV 71 Jonkoping	Sweden	37	12	14	26	30	4	0	0	0	4
96-97 — HV 71 Jonkoping	Sweden	49	20	14	34	26	5	1	0	1	6

LINDSAY, EVAN   G   FLAMES

PERSONAL: Born May 15, 1979, in Calgary. ... 6-1/180. ... Catches left.
TRANSACTIONS/CAREER NOTES: Selected by Calgary Flames in second round (second Flames pick, 32nd overall) of NHL entry draft (June 21, 1997).

		REGULAR SEASON							PLAYOFFS					
Season Team	League	Gms.	Min	W	L	T	GA	SO	Avg.	Gms.	Min.	W	L	GA	SO	Avg.
95-96 — Olds	AJHL	11	...	4	5	...	0		3.64	—	—	—	—	—	—	—
96-97 — Prince Albert	WHL	44	2651	20	17	†6	153	1	3.46	4	240	0	4	16	0	4.00

LUONGO, ROBERTO   G   ISLANDERS

PERSONAL: Born April 4, 1979, in St. Leonard, Que. ... 6-2/176. ... Catches left. ... Name pronounced luh-WAHN-goh.
TRANSACTIONS/CAREER NOTES: Selected by New York Islanders in first round (Islanders first pick, fourth overall) of NHL entry draft (June 21, 1997).
HONORS: Won Michael Bossy Trophy (1996-97).

		REGULAR SEASON							PLAYOFFS					
Season Team	League	Gms.	Min	W	L	T	GA	SO	Avg.	Gms.	Min.	W	L	GA	SO	Avg.
95-96 — Val-d'Or	QMJHL	23	1199	6	11	4	74	0	3.70	3	68	0	1	5	0	4.41
96-97 — Val-d'Or	QMJHL	60	3305	32	21	2	171	2	3.10	13	777	8	5	44	0	3.40

LYASKENKO, ROMAN   C   STARS

PERSONAL: Born May 2, 1979, in Murmansk, U.S.S.R. ... 6-0/180. ... Shoots right.
TRANSACTIONS/CAREER NOTES: Selected by Dallas Stars in second round (second Stars pick, 52nd overall) of NHL entry draft (June 21, 1997).

		REGULAR SEASON				PLAYOFFS			
Season Team	League	Gms.	G	A	Pts.	PIM	Gms.	G	A	Pts.	PIM
95-96 — Torpedo-2 Yaroslavl	CIS Div. II	60	7	10	17	12	—	—	—	—	—
96-97 — Torpedo Yaroslav	Russian	42	5	7	12	16	9	3	0	3	6
— Torpedo-2 Yaroslav	Rus. Div. III	2	1	1	2	8	—	—	—	—	—

MAIR, ADAM   C   MAPLE LEAFS

PERSONAL: Born February 15, 1979, in Hamilton, Ont. ... 6-0/189. ... Shoots right.
TRANSACTIONS/CAREER NOTES: Selected by Toronto Maple Leafs in fourth round (second Maple Leafs pick, 84th overall) of NHL entry draft (June 21, 1997).

		REGULAR SEASON				PLAYOFFS			
Season Team	League	Gms.	G	A	Pts.	PIM	Gms.	G	A	Pts.	PIM
94-95 — Ohsweken	Jr. B	39	21	23	44	91	—	—	—	—	—
95-96 — Owen Sound	OHL	62	12	15	27	63	6	0	0	0	2
96-97 — Owen Sound	OHL	65	16	35	51	113	4	1	0	1	2

MALLETTE, KRIS   D   FLYERS

PERSONAL: Born January 19, 1979, in Lazo, B.C. ... 6-3/180. ... Shoots right.
TRANSACTIONS/CAREER NOTES: Selected by Philadelphia Flyers in third round (third Flyers pick, 62nd overall) of NHL entry draft (June 21, 1997).

		REGULAR SEASON				PLAYOFFS			
Season Team	League	Gms.	G	A	Pts.	PIM	Gms.	G	A	Pts.	PIM
95-96 — Parksville General	Jr. B	21	8	22	30	146	—	—	—	—	—
96-97 — Kelowna	WHL	67	0	3	3	206	6	0	0	0	8

MARA, PAUL   D   LIGHTNING

PERSONAL: Born September 7, 1979, in Ridgewood, N.J. ... 6-4/185. ... Shoots left.
HIGH SCHOOL: Belmont Hill (Mass.).
TRANSACTIONS/CAREER NOTES: Selected by Tampa Bay Lightning in first round (first Lightning pick, seventh overall) of NHL entry draft (June 21, 1997).
HONORS: Named to OHL All-Rookie team (1996-97).

		REGULAR SEASON				PLAYOFFS			
Season Team	League	Gms.	G	A	Pts.	PIM	Gms.	G	A	Pts.	PIM
94-95 — Belmont Hill	Mass. H.S.	29	19	24	43	24	—	—	—	—	—
95-96 — Belmont Hill	Mass. H.S.	28	18	20	38	40	—	—	—	—	—
96-97 — Sudbury	OHL	44	9	34	43	61	—	—	—	—	—

MARLEAU, PATRICK   C   SHARKS

PERSONAL: Born September 15, 1979, in Swift Current, Sask. ... 6-2/190. ... Shoots left.
TRANSACTIONS/CAREER NOTES: Selected by San Jose Sharks in first round (first Sharks pick, second overall) of NHL entry draft (June 21, 1997).
HONORS: Named to Can.HL All-Star second team (1996-97). ... Named to WHL (West) All-Star first team (1996-97).

Season Team	League	Gms.	G	A	Pts.	PIM	Gms.	G	A	Pts.	PIM
			REGULAR SEASON					PLAYOFFS			
94-95 — Swift Current	Jr. A	30	30	22	52	20	—	—	—	—	—
95-96 — Seattle	WHL	72	32	42	74	22	5	3	4	7	4
96-97 — Seattle	WHL	71	51	74	125	37	15	7	16	23	12

MARTIN, JEFF — C — SABRES

PERSONAL: Born April 26, 1979, in Stratford, Ont. ... 6-1/177. ... Shoots left.
TRANSACTIONS/CAREER NOTES: Selected by Buffalo Sabres in third round (fourth Sabres pick, 75th overall) of NHL entry draft (June 21, 1997).

Season Team	League	Gms.	G	A	Pts.	PIM	Gms.	G	A	Pts.	PIM
			REGULAR SEASON					PLAYOFFS			
95-96 — Windsor	OHL	63	9	5	14	8	7	1	1	2	4
96-97 — Windsor	OHL	65	24	23	47	37	5	2	0	2	2

MATHIEU, ALEXANDRE — C — PENGUINS

PERSONAL: Born February 12, 1979, in Repentigny, Que. ... 6-2/180. ... Shoots left.
TRANSACTIONS/CAREER NOTES: Selected by Pittsburgh Penguins in fourth round (fourth Penguins pick, 97th overall) of NHL entry draft (June 21, 1997).

Season Team	League	Gms.	G	A	Pts.	PIM	Gms.	G	A	Pts.	PIM
			REGULAR SEASON					PLAYOFFS			
96-97 — Halifax	QMJHL	70	12	22	34	18	18	2	5	7	2

McCALLUM, SCOTT — D — COYOTES

PERSONAL: Born February 15, 1979, in Dauphin, Manitoba. ... 6-3/218. ... Shoots left.
TRANSACTIONS/CAREER NOTES: Selected by Phoenix Coyotes in fourth round (second Coyotes pick, 96th overall) of NHL entry draft (June 21, 1997).

Season Team	League	Gms.	G	A	Pts.	PIM	Gms.	G	A	Pts.	PIM
			REGULAR SEASON					PLAYOFFS			
95-96 — Tri-City	WHL	45	1	1	2	28	6	0	0	0	0
96-97 — Tri-City	WHL	56	1	16	17	119	—	—	—	—	—

McCLEAN, JASON — G — RANGERS

PERSONAL: Born September 3, 1979, in Regina, Sask. ... 6-0/200. ... Catches left.
TRANSACTIONS/CAREER NOTES: Selected by New York Rangers in fifth round (fifth Rangers pick, 126th overall) of NHL entry draft (June 21, 1997).

Season Team	League	Gms.	Min	W	L	T	GA	SO	Avg.	Gms.	Min.	W	L	GA	SO	Avg.
			REGULAR SEASON								PLAYOFFS					
95-96 — Moose Jaw	WHL	11	544	1	7	1	38	0	4.19	—	—	—	—	—	—	—
96-97 — Moose Jaw	WHL	19	1014	7	7	2	60	0	3.55	—	—	—	—	—	—	—

MELICHAR, JOSEF — D — PENGUINS

PERSONAL: Born January 20, 1979, in Ceske Budejovice, Czechoslovakia. ... 6-3/198. ... Shoots left.
TRANSACTIONS/CAREER NOTES: Selected by Pittsburgh Penguins in third round (third Penguins pick, 71st overall) of NHL entry draft (June 21, 1997).

Season Team	League	Gms.	G	A	Pts.	PIM	Gms.	G	A	Pts.	PIM
			REGULAR SEASON					PLAYOFFS			
95-96 — HC Ceske Budejovice Jrs.	Czech Rep.	38	3	4	7	...	—	—	—	—	—
96-97 — HC Ceske Budejovice Jrs.	Czech Rep.	41	2	3	5	10	—	—	—	—	—

MIKA, PETR — LW — ISLANDERS

PERSONAL: Born February 12, 1979, in Prague, Czechoslovakia. ... 6-4/194. ... Shoots right.
TRANSACTIONS/CAREER NOTES: Selected by New York Islanders in fourth round (sixth Islanders pick, 85th overall) of NHL entry draft (June 21, 1997).

Season Team	League	Gms.	G	A	Pts.	PIM	Gms.	G	A	Pts.	PIM
			REGULAR SEASON					PLAYOFFS			
95-96 — Slavia Praha Jrs.	Czech Rep.	26	5	12	17	...	—	—	—	—	—
— Slavia Praha	Czech Rep.	1	0	0	0	0	—	—	—	—	—
96-97 — Slavia Praha Jrs.	Czech Rep.	15	8	0	8	...	—	—	—	—	—
— HC Beroun	Czech II	9	1	0	1	...	—	—	—	—	—
— Slavia Praha	Czech Rep.	20	1	2	3	6	—	—	—	—	—

MIKKOLA, ILKKA — D — CANADIENS

PERSONAL: Born January 18, 1979, in Oulu, Finland. ... 6-0/189. ... Shoots left.
TRANSACTIONS/CAREER NOTES: Selected by Montreal Canadiens in third round (third Canadiens pick, 65th overall) of NHL entry draft (June 21, 1997).

Season Team	League	REGULAR SEASON					PLAYOFFS				
		Gms.	G	A	Pts.	PIM	Gms.	G	A	Pts.	PIM
95-96 — Karpat Oulu	Finland Dv.II	10	0	4	4	29	2	0	0	0	2
— Karpat Oulu Jrs.	Finland	21	2	3	5	20	—	—	—	—	—
96-97 — Karpat Oulu	Finland Dv.II	40	7	12	19	32	6	0	0	0	4

MISKOVICH, AARON   C   AVALANCHE

PERSONAL: Born April 28, 1978, in Grand Rapids, Minn. ... 5-10/185. ... Shoots left.
TRANSACTIONS/CAREER NOTES: Selected by Colorado Avalanche in fifth round (sixth Avalanche pick, 133rd overall) of NHL entry draft (June 21, 1997).

Season Team	League	REGULAR SEASON					PLAYOFFS				
		Gms.	G	A	Pts.	PIM	Gms.	G	A	Pts.	PIM
96-97 — Green Bay	Jr. A	14	4	9	13	14	—	—	—	—	—

MOISE, MARTIN   LW   FLAMES

PERSONAL: Born January 18, 1979, in Valleyfield, Que. ... 6-0/197. ... Shoots left.
TRANSACTIONS/CAREER NOTES: Selected by Calgary Flames in fifth round (ninth Flames pick, 113th overall) of NHL entry draft (June 21, 1997).

Season Team	League	REGULAR SEASON					PLAYOFFS				
		Gms.	G	A	Pts.	PIM	Gms.	G	A	Pts.	PIM
96-97 — Beauport	QMJHL	70	21	23	44	23	4	4	1	5	0

MORROW, BRENDEN   LW   STARS

PERSONAL: Born January 16, 1979, in Carlyle, Sask. ... 5-11/195. ... Shoots left.
TRANSACTIONS/CAREER NOTES: Selected by Dallas Stars in first round (first Stars pick, 25th overall) of NHL entry draft (June 21, 1997).

Season Team	League	REGULAR SEASON					PLAYOFFS				
		Gms.	G	A	Pts.	PIM	Gms.	G	A	Pts.	PIM
95-96 — Portland	WHL	65	13	12	25	61	7	0	0	0	8
96-97 — Portland	WHL	71	39	49	88	178	6	2	1	3	4

MRAZEK, FRANTISEK   LW   MAPLE LEAFS

PERSONAL: Born May 16, 1979, in Ceske Budejovice, Czechoslovakia. ... 6-4/211. ... Shoots left.
TRANSACTIONS/CAREER NOTES: Selected by Toronto Maple Leafs in fifth round (third Maple Leafs pick, 111th overall) of NHL entry draft (June 21, 1997).

Season Team	League	REGULAR SEASON					PLAYOFFS				
		Gms.	G	A	Pts.	PIM	Gms.	G	A	Pts.	PIM
95-96 — Ceske Budejovice Jrs.	Czech Rep.	19	8	3	11	...	—	—	—	—	—
96-97 — Ceske Budejovice Jrs.	Czech Rep.	41	18	15	33	...	—	—	—	—	—

NEHRLING, LUCAS   D   DEVILS

PERSONAL: Born September 14, 1979, in Peterborough, Ont. ... 6-4/195. ... Shoots right.
TRANSACTIONS/CAREER NOTES: Selected by New Jersey Devils in fourth round (third Devils pick, 104th overall) of NHL entry draft (June 21, 1997).

Season Team	League	REGULAR SEASON					PLAYOFFS				
		Gms.	G	A	Pts.	PIM	Gms.	G	A	Pts.	PIM
96-97 — Sarnia	OHL	63	3	12	15	74	12	0	2	2	23

NIEMINEN, VILLE   RW   AVALANCHE

PERSONAL: Born April 6, 1977, in Tampere, Finland. ... 5-11/205. ... Shoots left.
TRANSACTIONS/CAREER NOTES: Selected by Colorado Avalanche in third round (fourth Avalanche pick, 78th overall) of NHL entry draft (June 21, 1997).

Season Team	League	REGULAR SEASON					PLAYOFFS				
		Gms.	G	A	Pts.	PIM	Gms.	G	A	Pts.	PIM
94-95 — Tappara Tampere Jrs.	Finland	16	11	21	32	47	—	—	—	—	—
— Tappara Tampere	Finland	16	0	0	0	0	—	—	—	—	—
95-96 — Tappara Tampere Jrs.	Finland	20	20	23	43	63	—	—	—	—	—
— Tappara Tampere	Finland	4	0	1	1	8	—	—	—	—	—
— KooVee Tampere	Finland	7	2	1	3	4	—	—	—	—	—
96-97 — Tappara Tampere	Finland	49	10	13	23	120	3	1	0	1	8

NITTEL, ADAM   RW   SHARKS

PERSONAL: Born July 17, 1978, in Kitchener, Ont. ... 6-1/206. ... Shoots right.
TRANSACTIONS/CAREER NOTES: Selected by San Jose Sharks in fifth round (fourth Sharks pick, 107th overall) of NHL entry draft (June 21, 1997).

Season Team	League	Gms.	G	A	Pts.	PIM	Gms.	G	A	Pts.	PIM
		REGULAR SEASON					PLAYOFFS				
95-96 — Niagara Falls	OHL	39	3	3	6	74	10	0	3	3	39
96-97 — Erie	OHL	46	8	11	19	194	—	—	—	—	—

NORONEN, MIKA — G — SABRES

PERSONAL: Born June 17, 1979, in Tampere, Finland. ... 6-1/191. ... Catches left.
TRANSACTIONS/CAREER NOTES: Selected by Buffalo Sabres in first round (first Sabres pick, 21st overall) of NHL entry draft (June 21, 1997).

Season Team	League	Gms.	Min	W	L	T	GA	SO	Avg.	Gms.	Min.	W	L	GA	SO	Avg.
		REGULAR SEASON								PLAYOFFS						
95-96 — Tappara Tampere Jrs.	Finland	16	962	...	...	...	37	2	2.31	—	—	—	—	—	—	—
96-97 — Tappara Tampere	Finland	5	215	...	...	...	17	0	4.74	—	—	—	—	—	—	—

NOVOSELTSEV, IVAN — RW — PANTHERS

PERSONAL: Born January 23, 1979, in Golitsino, U.S.S.R. ... 6-1/200. ... Shoots left.
TRANSACTIONS/CAREER NOTES: Selected by Florida Panthers in fourth round (fifth Panthers pick, 95th overall) of NHL entry draft (June 21, 1997).

Season Team	League	Gms.	G	A	Pts.	PIM	Gms.	G	A	Pts.	PIM
		REGULAR SEASON					PLAYOFFS				
95-96 — Krylja Sovetov Moscow	CIS	1	0	0	0	0	—	—	—	—	—
96-97 — Krylja Sovetov Moscow	Russian	30	0	3	3	18	2	0	0	0	4
— Krylja Sovetov-2 Moscow	Rus. Div. III	19	5	3	8	39	—	—	—	—	—

PARTHENAIS, PAT — D — PANTHERS

PERSONAL: Born July 17, 1979, in Rochester, N.Y. ... 6-3/212. ... Shoots left.
TRANSACTIONS/CAREER NOTES: Selected by Florida Panthers in fifth round (sixth Panthers pick, 127th overall) of NHL entry draft (June 21, 1997).

Season Team	League	Gms.	G	A	Pts.	PIM	Gms.	G	A	Pts.	PIM
		REGULAR SEASON					PLAYOFFS				
96-97 — Detroit	OHL	58	0	4	4	88	5	0	0	0	5

PELLETIER, JEAN-MARC — G — FLYERS

PERSONAL: Born March 4, 1978, in Atlanta. ... 6-3/195. ... Catches left.
COLLEGE: Cornell.
TRANSACTIONS/CAREER NOTES: Selected by Philadelphia Flyers in second round (first Flyers pick, 30th overall) of NHL entry draft (June 21, 1997).

Season Team	League	Gms.	Min	W	L	T	GA	SO	Avg.	Gms.	Min.	W	L	GA	SO	Avg.
		REGULAR SEASON								PLAYOFFS						
95-96 — Cornell	ECAC	5	179	1	2	0	15	0	5.03	—	—	—	—	—	—	—
96-97 — Cornell	ECAC	11	678	5	2	3	28	1	2.48	—	—	—	—	—	—	—

PETRE, HENRIK — D — CAPITALS

PERSONAL: Born April 9, 1979, in Stockholm, Sweden. ... 6-1/187. ... Shoots left.
TRANSACTIONS/CAREER NOTES: Selected by Washington Capitals in sixth round (fifth Capitals pick, 143rd overall) of NHL entry draft (June 21, 1997).

Season Team	League	Gms.	G	A	Pts.	PIM	Gms.	G	A	Pts.	PIM
		REGULAR SEASON					PLAYOFFS				
95-96 — Djurgarden Stockholm Jrs.	Sweden	32	8	6	14	16	—	—	—	—	—
96-97 — Djurgarden Stockholm Jrs.	Sweden				Statistics unavailable.						

POLLOCK, JAMIE — D — BLUES

PERSONAL: Born June 16, 1979, in Quebec City. ... 6-1/190. ... Shoots right.
TRANSACTIONS/CAREER NOTES: Selected by St. Louis Blues in fourth round (fourth Blues pick, 106th overall) of NHL entry draft (June 21, 1997).

Season Team	League	Gms.	G	A	Pts.	PIM	Gms.	G	A	Pts.	PIM
		REGULAR SEASON					PLAYOFFS				
95-96 — Seattle	WHL	32	0	1	1	15	—	—	—	—	—
96-97 — Seattle	WHL	66	15	19	34	94	15	3	5	8	16

PRATT, HARLAN — D — PENGUINS

PERSONAL: Born December 10, 1978, in Fort McMurray, Alberta. ... 6-1/202. ... Shoots right. ... Brother of Nolan Pratt, defenseman in Hartford Whalers system.
TRANSACTIONS/CAREER NOTES: Selected by Pittsburgh Penguins in fifth round (fifth Penguins pick, 124th overall) of NHL entry draft (June 21, 1997).

Season Team	League	REGULAR SEASON Gms.	G	A	Pts.	PIM	PLAYOFFS Gms.	G	A	Pts.	PIM
95-96 — Red Deer	WHL	60	2	3	5	22	10	0	0	0	4
96-97 — Red Deer	WHL	2	0	0	0	2	—	—	—	—	—
— Prince Albert	WHL	65	7	26	33	49	1	1	1	2	4

RAZIN, GENNADY   D   CANADIENS

PERSONAL: Born February 3, 1978, in Kharkov, U.S.S.R. ... 6-3/175. ... Shoots left.
TRANSACTIONS/CAREER NOTES: Selected by Montreal Canadiens in fifth round (sixth Canadiens pick, 122nd overall) of NHL entry draft (June 21, 1997).

Season Team	League	REGULAR SEASON Gms.	G	A	Pts.	PIM	PLAYOFFS Gms.	G	A	Pts.	PIM
95-96 — St. Albert	AJHL	52	3	16	19	113	18	1	10	11	8
96-97 — Kamloops	WHL	63	7	19	26	56	3	0	0	0	4

READY, RYAN   LW   FLAMES

PERSONAL: Born November 7, 1978, in Peterborough, Ont. ... 6-1/185. ... Shoots left.
TRANSACTIONS/CAREER NOTES: Selected by Calgary Flames in fourth round (eighth Flames pick, 100th overall) of NHL entry draft (June 21, 1997).

Season Team	League	REGULAR SEASON Gms.	G	A	Pts.	PIM	PLAYOFFS Gms.	G	A	Pts.	PIM
94-95 — Trentway	Jr. A	48	20	33	53	56	—	—	—	—	—
95-96 — Belleville	OHL	63	5	13	18	54	10	0	2	2	2
96-97 — Belleville	OHL	66	23	24	47	102	6	1	3	4	4

REICH, JEREMY   C   BLACKHAWKS

PERSONAL: Born February 11, 1979, in Craik, Sask. ... 6-1/188. ... Shoots left. ... Nephew of Jim Archibald, right winger, Minnesota North Stars (1984-85 through 1986-87).
TRANSACTIONS/CAREER NOTES: Selected by Chicago Blackhawks in second round (third Blackhawks pick, 39th overall) of NHL entry draft (June 21, 1997).

Season Team	League	REGULAR SEASON Gms.	G	A	Pts.	PIM	PLAYOFFS Gms.	G	A	Pts.	PIM
94-95 — Saskatoon	SJHL	35	13	20	33	81	—	—	—	—	—
95-96 — Seattle	WHL	65	11	11	22	88	5	0	1	1	10
96-97 — Seattle	WHL	62	19	31	50	134	15	2	5	7	36

RENNETTE, TYLER   C   BLUES

PERSONAL: Born April 16, 1979, in North Bay, Ont. ... 6-1/175. ... Shoots right.
TRANSACTIONS/CAREER NOTES: Selected by St. Louis Blues in second round (first Blues pick, 40th overall) of NHL entry draft (June 21, 1997).

Season Team	League	REGULAR SEASON Gms.	G	A	Pts.	PIM	PLAYOFFS Gms.	G	A	Pts.	PIM
95-96 — Waterloo Jr. B	OHA	45	27	47	74	64	—	—	—	—	—
96-97 — North Bay	OHL	63	24	34	58	42	—	—	—	—	—

RIESEN, MICHEL   LW   OILERS

PERSONAL: Born April 11, 1979, in Oberbalm, Switzerland. ... 6-2/183. ... Shoots right.
TRANSACTIONS/CAREER NOTES: Selected by Edmonton Oilers in first round (first Oilers pick, 14th overall) of NHL entry draft (June 21, 1997).

Season Team	League	REGULAR SEASON Gms.	G	A	Pts.	PIM	PLAYOFFS Gms.	G	A	Pts.	PIM
94-95 — Biel-Bienne	Switzerland	12	0	2	2	0	6	2	0	2	0
95-96 — Biel-Bienne	Switz. Div. II	34	9	6	15	2	3	1	0	1	0
96-97 — Biel-Bienne	Switz. Div. II	38	16	16	32	49	—	—	—	—	—

SAMSONOV, SERGEI   LW   BRUINS

PERSONAL: Born October 27, 1978, in Moscow, U.S.S.R. ... 5-8/184. ... Shoots right.
TRANSACTIONS/CAREER NOTES: Selected by Boston Bruins in first round (second Bruins pick, eighth overall) of NHL entry draft (June 21, 1997).
HONORS: Won Garry F. Longman Memorial Trophy (1996-97). ... Named to IHL All-Rookie team (1996-97).

Season Team	League	REGULAR SEASON Gms.	G	A	Pts.	PIM	PLAYOFFS Gms.	G	A	Pts.	PIM
94-95 — CSKA Moscow	CIS	13	2	2	4	14	2	0	0	0	0
95-96 — CSKA Moscow	CIS	51	21	17	38	12	3	1	1	2	4
96-97 — Detroit	IHL	73	29	35	64	18	19	8	4	12	12

SARNO, PETER   C   OILERS

PERSONAL: Born July 26, 1979, in Toronto. ... 5-11/180. ... Shoots left.
TRANSACTIONS/CAREER NOTES: Selected by Edmonton Oilers in sixth round (sixth Oilers pick, 141st overall) of NHL entry draft (June 21, 1997).
HONORS: Won Emms Family Award (1996-97). ... Named to OHL All-Rookie first team (1996-97).

		REGULAR SEASON					PLAYOFFS				
Season Team	League	Gms.	G	A	Pts.	PIM	Gms.	G	A	Pts.	PIM
95-96 — North York Flames	OPJHL	52	39	57	96	27	—	—	—	—	—
96-97 — Windsor	OHL	66	20	63	83	59	5	0	3	3	6

SCHNABEL, ROBERT   D   ISLANDERS

PERSONAL: Born November 10, 1978, in Prague, Czechoslovakia. ... 6-6/216. ... Shoots left.
TRANSACTIONS/CAREER NOTES: Selected by New York Islanders in third round (fifth Islanders pick, 79th overall) of NHL entry draft (June 21, 1997).

		REGULAR SEASON					PLAYOFFS				
Season Team	League	Gms.	G	A	Pts.	PIM	Gms.	G	A	Pts.	PIM
94-95 — Slavia Praha Jrs.	Czech. Rep.	35	11	6	17	14	—	—	—	—	—
95-96 — Slavia Praha Jrs.	Czech. Rep.	38	3	5	8	...	—	—	—	—	—
96-97 — Slavia Praha Jrs.	Czech. Rep.	36	5	2	7	...	—	—	—	—	—
— Slavia Praha	Czech. Rep.	4	0	0	0	4	1	0	0	0	0

SCHUTZ, DEREK   C   FLAMES

PERSONAL: Born March 5, 1979, in Yorkton, Sask. ... 6-2/185. ... Shoots right.
TRANSACTIONS/CAREER NOTES: Selected by Calgary Flames in third round (fifth Flames pick, 60th overall) of NHL entry draft (June 21, 1997).

		REGULAR SEASON					PLAYOFFS				
Season Team	League	Gms.	G	A	Pts.	PIM	Gms.	G	A	Pts.	PIM
94-95 — Spokane	WHL	2	0	0	0	2	—	—	—	—	—
95-96 — Spokane	WHL	70	10	7	17	121	18	1	4	5	37
96-97 — Spokane	WHL	61	20	21	41	126	9	1	3	4	9

SEELEY, RICHARD   D   KINGS

PERSONAL: Born April 30, 1979, in Powell River, B.C. ... 6-2/217. ... Shoots left.
TRANSACTIONS/CAREER NOTES: Selected by Los Angeles Kings in sixth round (sixth Kings pick, 137th overall) of NHL entry draft (June 21, 1997).

		REGULAR SEASON					PLAYOFFS				
Season Team	League	Gms.	G	A	Pts.	PIM	Gms.	G	A	Pts.	PIM
95-96 — Powell River	BCJHL	44	1	8	9	42	—	—	—	—	—
96-97 — Lethbridge	WHL	3	0	0	0	11	—	—	—	—	—
— Prince Albert	WHL	18	0	1	1	9	4	0	0	0	2

SHAPLEY, LARRY   D   CANUCKS

PERSONAL: Born February 6, 1978, in Dunnville, Ont. ... 6-6/215. ... Shoots right.
TRANSACTIONS/CAREER NOTES: Selected by Vancouver Canucks in sixth round (ninth Canucks pick, 148th overall) of NHL entry draft (June 21, 1997).

		REGULAR SEASON					PLAYOFFS				
Season Team	League	Gms.	G	A	Pts.	PIM	Gms.	G	A	Pts.	PIM
96-97 — Welland	Jr. B	35	3	10	13	27	—	—	—	—	—
— Peterborough	OHL	8	0	0	0	30	—	—	—	—	—

SIDULOV, KONSTANTIN   D   CANADIENS

PERSONAL: Born January 1, 1977, in Chelyabinsk, U.S.S.R. ... 6-1/185. ... Shoots left.
TRANSACTIONS/CAREER NOTES: Selected by Montreal Canadiens in fifth round (fifth Canadiens pick, 118th overall) of NHL entry draft (June 21, 1997).

		REGULAR SEASON					PLAYOFFS				
Season Team	League	Gms.	G	A	Pts.	PIM	Gms.	G	A	Pts.	PIM
94-95 — Traktor Chelyabinsk	CIS	2	0	0	0	0	—	—	—	—	—
95-96 — Traktor Chelyabinsk	CIS	52	1	0	1	58	—	—	—	—	—
96-97 — Traktor Chelyabinsk	Russian	42	0	0	0	28	—	—	—	—	—

SIMON, BEN   C   BLACKHAWKS

PERSONAL: Born June 14, 1978, in Cleveland. ... 5-11/178. ... Shoots left. ... Full name: Benjamin Clarke Simon.
HIGH SCHOOL: Shaker Heights (Cleveland).
COLLEGE: Notre Dame.

TRANSACTIONS/CAREER NOTES: Selected by Chicago Blackhawks in fifth round (fifth Blackhawks pick, 110th overall) of NHL entry draft (June 21, 1997).

		REGULAR SEASON					PLAYOFFS				
Season Team	League	Gms.	G	A	Pts.	PIM	Gms.	G	A	Pts.	PIM
92-93 — Shaker Heights	Ohio H.S.	...	15	21	36	...	—	—	—	—	—
93-94 — Shaker Heights	Ohio H.S.	...	45	41	86	...	—	—	—	—	—
94-95 — Shaker Heights	Ohio H.S.	...	61	68	129	...	—	—	—	—	—
95-96 — Cleveland	NAHL	50	45	46	91	...	—	—	—	—	—
96-97 — Notre Dame	CCHA	30	4	15	19	79	—	—	—	—	—

SKOPINTSEV, ANDREI   D   LIGHTNING

PERSONAL: Born September 28, 1971, in Elektrostal, U.S.S.R. ... 6-0/185. ... Shoots right.
TRANSACTIONS/CAREER NOTES: Selected by Tampa Bay Lightning in sixth round (seventh Lightning pick, 153rd overall) of NHL entry draft (June 21, 1997).

		REGULAR SEASON					PLAYOFFS				
Season Team	League	Gms.	G	A	Pts.	PIM	Gms.	G	A	Pts.	PIM
89-90 — Krylja Sovetov Moscow	USSR	20	0	0	0	10	—	—	—	—	—
90-91 — Krylja Sovetov Moscow	USSR	16	0	1	1	2	—	—	—	—	—
91-92 — Krylja Sovetov Moscow	CIS	36	1	1	2	14	—	—	—	—	—
92-93 — Krylja Sovetov Moscow	CIS	12	1	0	1	4	7	1	0	1	2
93-94 — Krylja Sovetov Moscow	CIS	43	4	8	12	14	3	1	0	1	0
94-95 — Krylja Sovetov Moscow	CIS	52	8	12	20	55	4	1	1	2	0
95-96 — Augsburg	Germany	46	10	20	30	32	7	3	2	5	22
96-97 — TPS Turku	Finland	46	3	6	9	80	10	1	1	2	4

SMITH, JARRETT   C   ISLANDERS

PERSONAL: Born June 15, 1979, in Edmonton ... 6-2/190. ... Shoots left.
TRANSACTIONS/CAREER NOTES: Selected by New York Islanders in third round (fourth Islanders pick, 59th overall) of NHL entry draft (June 21, 1997).

		REGULAR SEASON					PLAYOFFS				
Season Team	League	Gms.	G	A	Pts.	PIM	Gms.	G	A	Pts.	PIM
94-95 — Prince George	WHL	1	0	0	0	0	—	—	—	—	—
95-96 — Prince George	WHL	18	2	0	2	6	—	—	—	—	—
96-97 — Prince George	WHL	67	20	22	42	58	15	2	2	4	5

SMITH, NICK   C   PANTHERS

PERSONAL: Born March 23, 1979, in Hamilton, Ont. ... 6-1/165. ... Shoots left.
TRANSACTIONS/CAREER NOTES: Selected by Florida Panthers in third round (fourth Panthers pick, 74th overall) of NHL entry draft (June 21, 1997).

		REGULAR SEASON					PLAYOFFS				
Season Team	League	Gms.	G	A	Pts.	PIM	Gms.	G	A	Pts.	PIM
95-96 — Shelburne	Jr. A	42	13	18	31	12	—	—	—	—	—
96-97 — Barrie	OHL	63	10	18	28	15	9	3	8	11	13

SOUZA, MIKE   LW/C   BLACKHAWKS

PERSONAL: Born January 28, 1978, in Melrose, Mass. ... 6-1/190. ... Shoots left.
HIGH SCHOOL: Wakefield (Mass.).
COLLEGE: University of New Hampshire.
TRANSACTIONS/CAREER NOTES: Selected by Chicago Blackhawks in third round (fourth Blackhawks pick, 67th overall) of NHL entry draft (June 21, 1997).
HONORS: Named to the Hockey East All-Rookie team (1996-97).

		REGULAR SEASON					PLAYOFFS				
Season Team	League	Gms.	G	A	Pts.	PIM	Gms.	G	A	Pts.	PIM
95-96 — Wakefield	Mass. H.S.	21	25	31	56	22	—	—	—	—	—
96-97 — Univ. of New Hampshire	Hockey East	33	14	10	24	14	—	—	—	—	—

ST. CROIX, CHRIS   D   FLAMES

PERSONAL: Born May 2, 1979, in Voorhees, N.J. ... 6-1/186. ... Shoots right.
TRANSACTIONS/CAREER NOTES: Selected by Calgary Flames in fourth round (seventh Flames pick, 92nd overall) of NHL entry draft (June 21, 1997).

		REGULAR SEASON					PLAYOFFS				
Season Team	League	Gms.	G	A	Pts.	PIM	Gms.	G	A	Pts.	PIM
95-96 — Kamloops	WHL	61	4	6	10	27	13	0	2	2	4
96-97 — Kamloops	WHL	67	11	39	50	67	5	0	1	1	2

STANLEY, CHRIS   C   CANUCKS

PERSONAL: Born June 18, 1979, in Parry Sound, Ont. ... 6-0/187. ... Shoots left.

TRANSACTIONS/CAREER NOTES: Selected by Vancouver Canucks in fourth round (fifth Canucks pick, 90th overall) of NHL entry draft (June 21, 1997).

Season Team	League	REGULAR SEASON					PLAYOFFS				
		Gms.	G	A	Pts.	PIM	Gms.	G	A	Pts.	PIM
95-96 — OJHL	Tier II Jr. A	52	27	29	56	30	—	—	—	—	—
96-97 — Belleville	OHL	66	19	24	43	16	6	1	0	1	0

SULC, JAN — C — LIGHTNING

PERSONAL: Born February 17, 1979, in Litvinov, Czechoslovakia. ... 6-2/183. ... Shoots right.
TRANSACTIONS/CAREER NOTES: Selected by Tampa Bay Lightning in fifth round (fifth Lightning pick, 109th overall) of NHL entry draft (June 21, 1997).

Season Team	League	REGULAR SEASON					PLAYOFFS				
		Gms.	G	A	Pts.	PIM	Gms.	G	A	Pts.	PIM
95-96 — Chemopetrol Litvinov Jrs.	Czech Rep.	40	13	23	36	...	—	—	—	—	—
96-97 — Chemopetrol Litvinov Jrs.	Czech Rep.	37	14	17	31	...	—	—	—	—	—

SULLIVAN, JEFF — D — SENATORS

PERSONAL: Born September 18, 1978, in St. John's, Nfld. ... 6-1/185. ... Shoots left.
TRANSACTIONS/CAREER NOTES: Selected by Ottawa Senators in sixth round (fifth Senators pick, 146th overall) of NHL entry draft (June 21, 1997).

Season Team	League	REGULAR SEASON					PLAYOFFS				
		Gms.	G	A	Pts.	PIM	Gms.	G	A	Pts.	PIM
96-97 — Granby	QMJHL	25	4	8	12	47					
— Halifax	QMJHL	45	4	23	27	220	18	0	5	5	86

SUTER, CURTIS — D — COYOTES

PERSONAL: Born August 5, 1979, in Kerroberi, Sask. ... 6-4/220. ... Shoots left.
TRANSACTIONS/CAREER NOTES: Selected by Phoenix Coyotes in fifth round (third Coyotes pick, 123rd overall) of NHL entry draft (June 21, 1997).

Season Team	League	REGULAR SEASON					PLAYOFFS				
		Gms.	G	A	Pts.	PIM	Gms.	G	A	Pts.	PIM
96-97 — Spokane	WHL	56	2	2	4	133	2	0	0	0	0

SYKORA, PETR — C — RED WINGS

PERSONAL: Born December 21, 1978, in Pardubice, Czechoslovakia. ... 6-2/180. ... Shoots right.
TRANSACTIONS/CAREER NOTES: Selected by Detroit Red Wings in third round (second Red Wings pick, 76th overall) of NHL entry draft (June 21, 1997).

Season Team	League	REGULAR SEASON					PLAYOFFS				
		Gms.	G	A	Pts.	PIM	Gms.	G	A	Pts.	PIM
94-95 — HC Pardubice Jrs.	Czech Rep.	38	35	33	68	...	—	—	—	—	—
95-96 — HC Pardubice Jrs.	Czech Rep.	26	13	9	22	...	—	—	—	—	—
96-97 — Pojistovna Pardubice	Czech Rep.	29	1	3	4	4	—	—	—	—	—
— Poji. Pardubice Jrs.	Czech Rep.	12	14	4	18	...	—	—	—	—	—

TALLINDER, HENRIK — D — SABRES

PERSONAL: Born January 10, 1979, in Stockholm, Sweden. ... 6-3/194. ... Shoots left.
TRANSACTIONS/CAREER NOTES: Selected by Buffalo Sabres in second round (second Sabres pick, 48th overall) of NHL entry draft (June 21, 1997).

Season Team	League	REGULAR SEASON					PLAYOFFS				
		Gms.	G	A	Pts.	PIM	Gms.	G	A	Pts.	PIM
95-96 — AIK Solna Jrs.	Sweden	40	4	13	17	55	—	—	—	—	—
96-97 — AIK Solna	Sweden	1	0	0	0	0	—	—	—	—	—

TETRAULT, DANIEL — D — CANADIENS

PERSONAL: Born September 4, 1979, in St. Boniface, Manitoba. ... 6-0/198. ... Shoots right.
TRANSACTIONS/CAREER NOTES: Selected by Montreal Canadiens in fourth round (fourth Canadiens pick, 91st overall) of NHL entry draft (June 21, 1997).

Season Team	League	REGULAR SEASON					PLAYOFFS				
		Gms.	G	A	Pts.	PIM	Gms.	G	A	Pts.	PIM
95-96 — Brandon	WHL	72	6	13	19	91	19	1	1	2	25
96-97 — Brandon	WHL	64	5	24	29	136	6	0	0	0	14

THEORET, LUC — D — SABRES

PERSONAL: Born July 30, 1979, in Winnipeg. ... 6-1/197. ... Shoots left.
TRANSACTIONS/CAREER NOTES: Selected by Buffalo Sabres in fourth round (fifth Sabres pick, 101st overall) of NHL entry draft (June 21, 1997).

Season Team	League	REGULAR SEASON					PLAYOFFS				
		Gms.	G	A	Pts.	PIM	Gms.	G	A	Pts.	PIM
95-96 — Lethbridge	WHL	47	4	13	17	41	4	0	0	0	6
96-97 — Lethbridge	WHL	43	3	7	10	51	19	1	5	6	8

THOMPSON, MARK   D   LIGHTNING

PERSONAL: Born April 26, 1979, in St. Albert, Alta. ... 6-6/205. ... Shoots right.
TRANSACTIONS/CAREER NOTES: Selected by Tampa Bay Lightning in fifth round (fourth Lightning pick, 108th overall) of NHL entry draft (June 21, 1997).

Season Team	League	REGULAR SEASON					PLAYOFFS				
		Gms.	G	A	Pts.	PIM	Gms.	G	A	Pts.	PIM
96-97 — Regina	WHL	32	1	5	6	20	3	0	1	1	2

THORNTON, JOE   C   BRUINS

PERSONAL: Born July 2, 1979, in London, Ont. ... 6-4/198. ... Shoots left. ... Cousin of Scott Thornton, center, Montreal Canadiens.
TRANSACTIONS/CAREER NOTES: Selected by Boston Bruins in first round (first Bruins pick, first overall) of NHL entry draft (June 21, 1997).
HONORS: Won Can.HL Rookie of the Year Award (1995-96). ... Won Emms Family Trophy (1995-96). ... Won Can.HL Top Prospect Award (1996-97). ... Named to Can.HL All-Star second team (1996-97). ... Named to OHL All-Star second team (1996-97).

Season Team	League	REGULAR SEASON					PLAYOFFS				
		Gms.	G	A	Pts.	PIM	Gms.	G	A	Pts.	PIM
94-95 — St. Thomas	Jr. B	50	40	64	104	53	—	—	—	—	—
95-96 — Sault Ste. Marie	OHL	66	30	46	76	51	4	1	1	2	11
96-97 — Sault Ste. Marie	OHL	59	41	81	122	123	11	11	8	19	24

TIMKIN, ALEXEI   RW   STARS

PERSONAL: Born April 21, 1979, in Kirov, U.S.S.R. ... 6-2/184. ... Shoots left.
TRANSACTIONS/CAREER NOTES: Selected by Dallas Stars in sixth round (sixth Stars pick, 160th overall) of NHL entry draft (June 21, 1997).

Season Team	League	REGULAR SEASON					PLAYOFFS				
		Gms.	G	A	Pts.	PIM	Gms.	G	A	Pts.	PIM
95-96 — Torpedo-2 Yaroslavl	CIS Div. II	20	2	2	4	10	—	—	—	—	—
96-97 — Torpedo-2 Yaroslav	Rus. Div. III	47	16	6	22	54	—	—	—	—	—
— Torpedo Yaroslav	Russian	3	0	1	1	0	—	—	—	—	—

TIMOFEYEV, DENIS   D   BRUINS

PERSONAL: Born January 14, 1979, in Moscow, U.S.S.R. ... 6-5/198. ... Shoots left.
TRANSACTIONS/CAREER NOTES: Selected by Boston Bruins in sixth round (seventh Bruins pick, 135th overall) of NHL entry draft (June 21, 1997).

Season Team	League	REGULAR SEASON					PLAYOFFS				
		Gms.	G	A	Pts.	PIM	Gms.	G	A	Pts.	PIM
96-97 — CSKA-2 Moscow	Rus. Div. III	11	0	0	0	2	—	—	—	—	—

TKACZUK, DANIEL   C   FLAMES

PERSONAL: Born June 10, 1979, in Toronto. ... 6-0/190. ... Shoots left.
TRANSACTIONS/CAREER NOTES: Selected by Calgary Flames in first round (first Flames pick, sixth overall) of NHL entry draft (June 21, 1997).

Season Team	League	REGULAR SEASON					PLAYOFFS				
		Gms.	G	A	Pts.	PIM	Gms.	G	A	Pts.	PIM
95-96 — Barrie	OHL	61	22	39	61	38	7	1	2	3	8
96-97 — Barrie	OHL	62	45	48	93	49	9	7	2	9	2

TREMBLAY, DIDIER   D   BLUES

PERSONAL: Born May 4, 1979, in Laval, Que. ... 6-1/190. ... Shoots left.
TRANSACTIONS/CAREER NOTES: Selected by St. Louis Blues in fourth round (second Blues pick, 86th overall) of NHL entry draft (June 21, 1997).

Season Team	League	REGULAR SEASON					PLAYOFFS				
		Gms.	G	A	Pts.	PIM	Gms.	G	A	Pts.	PIM
95-96 — Halifax	QMJHL	56	4	10	14	80	6	0	3	3	4
96-97 — Halifax	QMJHL	68	11	26	37	79	12	3	1	4	6

TRIPP, JOHN   RW   FLAMES

PERSONAL: Born May 4, 1977, in Kingston, Ont. ... 6-2/208. ... Shoots right.
HIGH SCHOOL: Henry Street (Whitby, Ont.).
TRANSACTIONS/CAREER NOTES: Selected by Colorado Avalanche in third round (third Avalanche pick, 77th overall) of NHL entry draft (July 8, 1995). ... Returned to draft pool by Avalanche and selected by Calgary Flames in second round (third Flames pick, 42nd overall) of NHL entry draft (June 21, 1997).

Season Team	League	REGULAR SEASON					PLAYOFFS				
		Gms.	G	A	Pts.	PIM	Gms.	G	A	Pts.	PIM
93-94 — St. Mary's Jr. B	OHA	42	15	29	44	116	—	—	—	—	—
94-95 — Oshawa	OHL	58	6	11	17	53	7	0	1	1	4
95-96 — Oshawa	OHL	56	13	14	27	95	5	1	1	2	13
96-97 — Oshawa	OHL	59	28	20	48	126	18	*16	10	26	42

TSELIOS, NIKOS — D — HURRICANES

PERSONAL: Born January 20, 1979, in Oak Park, Ill. ... 6-4/187. ... Shoots left. ... Cousin of Chris Chelios, defenseman, Chicago Blackhawks.
TRANSACTIONS/CAREER NOTES: Selected by Carolina Hurricanes in first round (first Hurricanes pick, 22nd overall) of NHL entry draft (June 21, 1997).
HONORS: Named to Can.HL All-Rookie team (1996-97). ... Named to OHL All-Rookie first team (1996-97).

Season Team	League	REGULAR SEASON					PLAYOFFS				
		Gms.	G	A	Pts.	PIM	Gms.	G	A	Pts.	PIM
95-96 — Chicago	MNHL	27	5	8	13	40	—	—	—	—	—
96-97 — Belleville	OHL	64	9	37	46	61	—	—	—	—	—

VAILLANCOURT, LUC — G — MIGHTY DUCKS

PERSONAL: Born June 13, 1978, in Ferme-Neuve, Que. ... 6-1/189. ... Catches left.
TRANSACTIONS/CAREER NOTES: Selected by Mighty Ducks of Anaheim in fifth round (fourth Mighty Ducks pick, 125th overall) of NHL entry draft (June 21, 1997).
HONORS: Won Marcel Robert Trophy (1996-97).

Season Team	League	REGULAR SEASON							PLAYOFFS						
		Gms.	Min.	W	L	T	GA	SO	Avg.	Gms.	Min.	W	L	GA	SO	Avg.
95-96 — Beauport	QMJHL	22	882	7	8	0	71	0	4.83	2	80	1	0	3	0	2.25
96-97 — Beauport	QMJHL	51	2668	18	26	1	161	0	3.62	4	239	1	3	20	0	5.02

WARD, JASON — RW/C — CANADIENS

PERSONAL: Born January 16, 1979, in Chapleau, Ont. ... 6-2/184. ... Shoots right.
TRANSACTIONS/CAREER NOTES: Selected by Montreal Canadiens in first round (first Canadiens pick, 11th overall) of NHL entry draft (June 21, 1997).

Season Team	League	REGULAR SEASON					PLAYOFFS				
		Gms.	G	A	Pts.	PIM	Gms.	G	A	Pts.	PIM
94-95 — Oshawa	Tier II Jr. A	47	30	31	61	75	—	—	—	—	—
95-96 — Niagara Falls	OHL	64	15	35	50	139	10	6	4	10	23
96-97 — Erie	OHL	58	25	39	64	137	5	1	2	3	2

WIKSTROM, JOHN — D — RED WINGS

PERSONAL: Born January 30, 1979, in Lulea, Sweden. ... 6-3/200. ... Shoots left.
TRANSACTIONS/CAREER NOTES: Selected by Detroit Red Wings in fifth round (fourth Red Wings pick, 129th overall) of NHL entry draft (June 21, 1997).

Season Team	League	REGULAR SEASON					PLAYOFFS				
		Gms.	G	A	Pts.	PIM	Gms.	G	A	Pts.	PIM
95-96 — Lulea	Sweden	9	0	0	0	2	—	—	—	—	—
96-97 — Lulea	Sweden	9	0	0	0	0	3	0	0	0	0

WILLIS, SHANE — RW — HURRICANES

PERSONAL: Born June 13, 1977, in Edmonton. ... 6-0/170. ... Shoots right.
TRANSACTIONS/CAREER NOTES: Selected by Tampa Bay Lightning in third round (third Lightning pick, 56th overall) of NHL entry draft (July 8, 1995). ... Returned to draft pool by Lightning and selected by Carolina Hurricanes in fourth round (fourth Hurricanes pick, 88th overall) of NHL entry draft (June 21, 1997).
HONORS: Named to Can.HL All-Rookie team (1994-95). ... Named to WHL (East) All-Star first team (1996-97).

Season Team	League	REGULAR SEASON					PLAYOFFS				
		Gms.	G	A	Pts.	PIM	Gms.	G	A	Pts.	PIM
94-95 — Prince Albert	WHL	65	24	19	43	38	13	3	4	7	6
95-96 — Prince Albert	WHL	69	41	40	81	47	18	11	10	21	18
96-97 — Prince Albert	WHL	41	34	22	56	63	—	—	—	—	—
— Lethbridge	WHL	26	22	17	39	24	19	13	11	24	20

YERKOVICH, SERGEI — D — OILERS

PERSONAL: Born March 9, 1974, in Minsk, U.S.S.R. ... 6-3/210. ... Shoots left.
TRANSACTIONS/CAREER NOTES: Selected by Edmonton Oilers in third round (third Oilers pick, 68th overall) of NHL entry draft (June 21, 1997).

Season Team	League	REGULAR SEASON					PLAYOFFS				
		Gms.	G	A	Pts.	PIM	Gms.	G	A	Pts.	PIM
92-93 — Dynamo Minsk	CIS	1	0	0	0	0	—	—	—	—	—
93-94 — Tivali Minsk	CIS	39	2	1	3	34	—	—	—	—	—
94-95 — Tivali Minsk	CIS	45	3	1	4	52	—	—	—	—	—
95-96 — Tivali Minsk	CIS	41	5	3	8	30	—	—	—	—	—
96-97 — Las Vegas	IHL	76	6	19	25	167	—	—	—	—	—

YORK, MICHAEL   C   RANGERS

PERSONAL: Born January 3, 1978, in Pontiac, Mich. ... 5-9/179. ... Shoots right.
COLLEGE: Michigan State.
TRANSACTIONS/CAREER NOTES: Selected by New York Rangers in sixth round (seventh Rangers pick, 136th overall) of NHL entry draft (June 21, 1997).
HONORS: Named to CCHA All-Rookie team (1995-96).

Season Team	League	REGULAR SEASON					PLAYOFFS				
		Gms.	G	A	Pts.	PIM	Gms.	G	A	Pts.	PIM
95-96 — Michigan State	CCHA	39	12	27	39	20	—	—	—	—	—
96-97 — Michigan State	CCHA	37	18	29	47	42	—	—	—	—	—

YOUNG, B.J.   RW   RED WINGS

PERSONAL: Born July 23, 1977, in Anchorage, Alaska. ... 5-11/177. ... Shoots right.
TRANSACTIONS/CAREER NOTES: Selected by Detroit Red Wings in sixth round (fifth Red Wings pick, 157th overall) of NHL entry draft (June 21, 1997).
HONORS: Named to WHL (East) All-Star first team (1996-97).

Season Team	League	REGULAR SEASON					PLAYOFFS				
		Gms.	G	A	Pts.	PIM	Gms.	G	A	Pts.	PIM
93-94 — Tri-City	WHL	54	19	24	43	66	2	1	1	2	2
94-95 — Tri-City	WHL	30	6	3	9	39	—	—	—	—	—
— Red Deer	WHL	21	5	9	14	33	—	—	—	—	—
95-96 — Red Deer	WHL	67	49	45	94	144	8	4	9	13	12
96-97 — Red Deer	WHL	63	*58	56	114	97	16	8	14	22	26

ZEHR, JEFF   C/LW   ISLANDERS

PERSONAL: Born December 10, 1978, in Woodstock, Ont. ... 6-3/195. ... Shoots left.
TRANSACTIONS/CAREER NOTES: Selected by New York Islanders in second round (third Islanders pick, 31st overall) of NHL entry draft (June 21, 1997).

Season Team	League	REGULAR SEASON					PLAYOFFS				
		Gms.	G	A	Pts.	PIM	Gms.	G	A	Pts.	PIM
94-95 — Stratford	OPJHL	44	26	32	58	143	—	—	—	—	—
95-96 — Windsor	OHL	56	4	21	25	103	7	0	1	1	2
96-97 — Windsor	OHL	57	27	32	59	196	5	2	1	3	4

ZULTEK, MATT   LW   KINGS

PERSONAL: Born March 12, 1979, in Windsor, Ont. ... 6-4/218. ... Shoots left.
TRANSACTIONS/CAREER NOTES: Selected by Los Angeles Kings in first round (second Kings pick, 15th overall) of NHL entry draft (June 21, 1997).
HONORS: Named to OHL All-Rookie second team (1996-97).

Season Team	League	REGULAR SEASON					PLAYOFFS				
		Gms.	G	A	Pts.	PIM	Gms.	G	A	Pts.	PIM
95-96 — Caledon	Jr. A	50	19	14	33	40	—	—	—	—	—
96-97 — Ottawa	OHL	63	27	13	40	76	21	7	6	13	27

BOWMAN, SCOTTY   RED WINGS

PERSONAL: Born September 18, 1933, in Montreal. ... Full name: William Scott Bowman.
HONORS: Inducted into Hall of Fame (1991).

HEAD COACHING RECORD

BACKGROUND: Minor league hockey supervisor, Montreal Canadiens organization (1954-55 through 1956-57). ... Coach, Team Canada (1976 and 1981). ... Director of hockey operations/general manager, Buffalo Sabres (1979-80 through 1986-87). ... Director of player development, Pittsburgh Penguins (1990-91). ... Director of player personnel, Detroit Red Wings (1994-95 through present).
HONORS: Won Jack Adams Award (1976-77 and 1995-96). ... Named NHL Executive of the Year by THE SPORTING NEWS (1979-80). ... Named NHL Coach of the Year by THE SPORTING NEWS (1995-96).
RECORDS: Holds NHL career regular-season records for wins—1,013; and winning percentage—.659. ... Holds NHL career playoff records for wins—178; and games—283.

Season Team	League	\<REGULAR SEASON\> W	L	T	Pct.	Finish	\<PLAYOFFS\> W	L	Pct.
67-68—St. Louis	NHL	23	21	14	.517	3rd/Western Division	8	10	.444
68-69—St. Louis	NHL	37	25	14	.579	1st/Western Division	8	4	.667
69-70—St. Louis	NHL	37	27	12	.566	1st/Western Division	8	8	.500
70-71—St. Louis	NHL	13	10	5	.554	2nd/West Division	2	4	.333
71-72—Montreal	NHL	46	16	16	.692	3rd/Eastern Division	2	4	.333
72-73—Montreal	NHL	52	10	16	.769	1st/East Division	12	5	.706
73-74—Montreal	NHL	45	24	9	.635	2nd/East Division	2	4	.333
74-75—Montreal	NHL	47	14	19	.706	1st/Adams Division	6	5	.545
75-76—Montreal	NHL	58	11	11	.794	1st/Adams Division	12	1	.923
76-77—Montreal	NHL	60	8	12	.825	1st/Adams Division	12	2	.857
77-78—Montreal	NHL	59	10	11	.806	1st/Adams Division	12	3	.800
78-79—Montreal	NHL	52	17	11	.719	1st/Adams Division	12	4	.750
79-80—Buffalo	NHL	47	17	16	.688	1st/Adams Division	9	5	.643
81-82—Buffalo	NHL	18	10	7	.614	3rd/Adams Division	1	3	.250
82-83—Buffalo	NHL	38	29	13	.556	3rd/Adams Division	6	4	.600
83-84—Buffalo	NHL	48	25	7	.644	2nd/Adams Division	0	3	.000
84-85—Buffalo	NHL	38	28	14	.563	3rd/Adams Division	2	3	.400
85-86—Buffalo	NHL	18	18	1	.500	5th/Adams Division	—	—	—
86-87—Buffalo	NHL	3	7	2	.333	5th/Adams Division	—	—	—
91-92—Pittsburgh	NHL	39	32	9	.544	3rd/Adams Division	16	5	.762
92-93—Pittsburgh	NHL	56	21	7	.708	1st/Patrick Division	7	5	.583
93-94—Detroit	NHL	46	30	8	.595	1st/Central Division	3	4	.429
94-95—Detroit	NHL	33	11	4	.729	1st/Central Division	12	6	.667
95-96—Detroit	NHL	62	13	7	.799	1st/Central Division	10	9	.526
96-97—Detroit	NHL	38	26	18	.573	2nd/Central Division	16	4	.800
NHL totals (25 years)		**1013**	**460**	**263**	**.659**	**NHL totals (23 years)**	**178**	**105**	**.629**

NOTES:
1968—Defeated Philadelphia in Western Division finals; defeated Minnesota in Stanley Cup semifinals; lost to Montreal in Stanley Cup finals.
1969—Defeated Philadelphia in Stanley Cup quarterfinals; defeated Los Angeles in Stanley Cup semifinals; lost to Montreal in Stanley Cup finals.
1970—Defeated Minnesota in Stanley Cup quarterfinals; defeated Pittsburgh in Stanley Cup semifinals; lost to Boston in Stanley Cup finals.
1971—Lost to Minnesota in Stanley Cup quarterfinals.
1972—Lost to New York Rangers in Stanley Cup quarterfinals.
1973—Defeated Buffalo in Stanley Cup quarterfinals; defeated Philadelphia in Stanley Cup semifinals; defeated Chicago in Stanley Cup finals.
1974—Lost to New York Rangers in Stanley Cup quarterfinals.
1975—Defeated Vancouver in Stanley Cup quarterfinals; lost to Buffalo in Stanley Cup semifinals.
1976—Defeated Chicago in Stanley Cup quarterfinals; defeated New York Islanders in Stanley Cup semifinals; defeated Philadelphia in Stanley Cup finals.
1977—Defeated St. Louis in Stanley Cup quarterfinals; defeated New York Islanders in Stanley Cup semifinals; defeated Boston in Stanley Cup finals.
1978—Defeated Detroit in Stanley Cup quarterfinals; defeated Toronto in Stanley Cup semifinals; defeated Boston in Stanley Cup finals.
1979—Defeated Toronto in Stanley Cup quarterfinals; defeated Boston in Stanley Cup semifinals; defeated New York Rangers in Stanley Cup finals.
1980—Defeated Vancouver in Stanley Cup preliminary round; defeated Chicago in Stanley Cup quarterfinals; lost to New York Islanders in Stanley Cup semifinals.
1982—Lost to Boston in Stanley Cup preliminary round.
1983—Defeated Montreal in Adams Division semifinals; lost to Boston in Adams Division finals.
1984—Lost to Quebec in Adams Division semifinals.
1985—Lost to Quebec in Adams Division semifinals.
1992—Defeated Washington in Patrick Division semifinals; defeated New York Rangers in Patrick Division finals; defeated Boston in Wales Conference finals; defeated Chicago in Stanley Cup finals.
1993—Defeated New Jersey in Patrick Division semifinals; lost to New York Islanders in Patrick Division finals.
1994—Lost to San Jose in Western Conference quarterfinals.
1995—Defeated Dallas in Western Conference quarterfinals; defeated San Jose in Western Conference semifinals; defeated Chicago in Western Conference finals; lost to New Jersey in Stanley Cup finals.
1996—Defeated Winnipeg in Western Conference quarterfinals; defeated St. Louis in Western Conference semifinals; lost to Colorado in Western Conference finals.
1997—Defeated St. Louis in Western Conference quarterfinals; defeated Anaheim in Western Conference semifinals; defeated Colorado in Western Conference finals; defeated Philadelphia in Stanley Cup finals.

BOWNESS, RICK   ISLANDERS

PERSONAL: Born January 25, 1955, in Moncton, N.B. ... Played right wing. ... Shot right. ... Full name: Richard Gary Bowness. ... Name pronounced BOH-nihz.
HIGH SCHOOL: Halifax (Nova Scotia).

COLLEGE: St. Mary's (Nova Scotia).
TRANSACTIONS/CAREER NOTES: Selected by Atlanta Flames from Montreal Juniors in second round (second Flames pick, 26th overall) of NHL amateur draft (June 3, 1975). ... Sold by Atlanta Flames to Detroit Red Wings (September 1977). ... Sold by Red Wings to St. Louis Blues (September 1978). ... Traded by Blues to Winnipeg Jets for D Craig Norwich (June 19, 1980).

Season Team	League	|	REGULAR SEASON								|	PLAYOFFS				
			Gms.	G	A	Pts.	PIM	+/-	PP	SH		Gms.	G	A	Pts.	PIM
72-73— Quebec	QMJHL		30	2	7	9	2	...	...	...		—	—	—	—	—
73-74— Montreal	QMJHL		67	25	46	71	95	...	...	...		—	—	—	—	—
74-75— Montreal	QMJHL		71	24	76	100	130	...	...	...		—	—	—	—	—
75-76— Tulsa	CHL		64	25	38	63	160	...	...	...		9	4	3	7	12
— Nova Scotia	AHL		2	0	1	1	0	...	...	...		—	—	—	—	—
— Atlanta	NHL		5	0	0	0	0	...	...	...		—	—	—	—	—
76-77— Tulsa	CHL		39	15	15	30	72	...	...	...		8	0	1	1	20
— Atlanta	NHL		28	0	4	4	29	...	...	...		—	—	—	—	—
77-78— Detroit	NHL		61	8	11	19	76	...	...	...		4	0	0	0	2
78-79— St. Louis	NHL		24	1	3	4	30	...	...	...		—	—	—	—	—
— Salt Lake City	CHL		48	25	28	53	92	...	...	...		10	5	4	9	27
79-80— Salt Lake City	CHL		71	25	46	71	135	...	...	...		13	5	9	14	39
— St. Louis	NHL		10	1	2	3	11		0	0		—	—	—	—	—
80-81— Tulsa	CHL		35	12	20	32	82	...	...	...		—	—	—	—	—
— Winnipeg	NHL		45	8	17	25	45	-35	0	0		1	0	0	0	0
81-82— Tulsa	CHL		79	34	53	87	201	...	...	...		3	0	2	2	2
82-83— Sherbrooke	AHL		65	17	31	48	117	...	...	...		—	—	—	—	—
NHL totals (6 years)			**173**	**18**	**37**	**55**	**191**	...	...	...		**5**	**0**	**0**	**0**	**2**

HEAD COACHING RECORD

BACKGROUND: Player/assistant coach, Sherbrooke, Winnipeg Jets organization (1982-83). ... Assistant coach, Jets (1983-84 through 1986-87). ... General manager/coach, Moncton, Jets organization (1987-88). ... Associate coach, New York Islanders (xxxxx xxxxxx-January 24, 1997).

Season Team	League	|	REGULAR SEASON					|	PLAYOFFS		
			W	L	T	Pct.	Finish		W	L	Pct.
87-88— Moncton	AHL		27	45	8	.388	6th/North Division		—	—	—
88-89— Moncton	AHL		37	34	9	.519	3rd/North Division		—	—	—
— Winnipeg	NHL		8	17	3	.339	5th/Smythe Division		—	—	—
89-90— Maine	AHL		31	38	11	.456	5th/North Division		—	—	—
90-91— Maine	AHL		34	34	12	.500	5th/North Division		—	—	—
91-92— Boston	NHL		36	32	12	.525	2nd/Adams Division		8	7	.533
92-93— Ottawa	NHL		10	70	4	.143	6th/Adams Division		—	—	—
93-94— Ottawa	NHL		14	61	9	.220	7th/Northeast Division		—	—	—
94-95— Ottawa	NHL		9	34	5	.240	7th/Northeast Division		—	—	—
95-96— Ottawa	NHL		6	13	0	.316			—	—	—
96-97— New York Islanders	NHL		15	18	3	.458	7th/Atlantic Division		—	—	—
NHL totals (7 years)			**98**	**245**	**36**	**.306**	**NHL totals (1 year)**		**8**	**7**	**.533**

NOTES:
1992—Defeated Buffalo in Adams Division semifinals; defeated New York Rangers in Adams Division finals; lost to Pittsburgh in Wales Conference finals.
1996—Replaced as head coach by Jacques Martin (January 24) with club in sixth place.
1997—Replaced Mike Milbury as head coach (January 24) with club in seventh place.

BURNS, PAT — BRUINS

PERSONAL: Born April 4, 1952, in St.-Henri, Que.
MISCELLANEOUS: Served 17 years with the Gastineau (Quebec) and Ottawa Police Departments before assuming a professional hockey career.

HEAD COACHING RECORD

BACKGROUND: Assistant coach, Canadian national team (1986). ... Assistant coach, Canadian Jr. national team (1987).
HONORS: Named NHL Coach of the Year by THE SPORTING NEWS (1988-89 and 1992-93). ... Won Jack Adams Award (1988-89 and 1992-93).

Season Team	League	|	REGULAR SEASON					|	PLAYOFFS		
			W	L	T	Pct.	Finish		W	L	Pct.
83-84— Hull	QMJHL		25	45	0	.357	6th/LeBel Division		—	—	—
84-85— Hull	QMJHL		33	34	1	.493	2nd/LeBel Division		1	4	.200
85-86— Hull	QMJHL		54	18	0	.750	1st/LeBel Division		15	0	1.000
86-87— Hull	QMJHL		26	39	5	.407	4th/LeBel Division		4	4	.500
87-88— Sherbrooke	AHL		42	34	4	.550	3rd/North Division		2	4	.333
88-89— Montreal	NHL		53	18	9	.719	1st/Adams Division		14	7	.667
89-90— Montreal	NHL		41	28	11	.581	3rd/Adams Division		5	6	.455
90-91— Montreal	NHL		39	30	11	.556	2nd/Adams Division		7	6	.538
91-92— Montreal	NHL		41	28	11	.581	1st/Adams Division		4	7	.364
92-93— Toronto	NHL		44	29	11	.589	3rd/Norris Division		11	10	.524
93-94— Toronto	NHL		43	29	12	.583	2nd/Central Division		9	9	.500
94-95— Toronto	NHL		21	19	8	.521	4th/Central Division		3	4	.429
95-96— Toronto	NHL		25	30	10	.462	5th/Central Division		—	—	—
NHL totals (8 years)			**307**	**211**	**83**	**.580**	**NHL totals (7 years)**		**53**	**49**	**.520**

NOTES:
1985—Lost to Verdun in quarterfinals of President Cup playoffs.
1986—Defeated Shawinigan in quarterfinals of President Cup playoffs; defeated St. Jean in semifinals of President Cup playoffs; defeated Drummondville in President Cup finals.
1987—Eliminated in President Cup quarterfinal round-robin series.

1988—Lost to Fredericton in quarterfinals of Calder Cup playoffs.
1989—Defeated Hartford in Adams Division semifinals; defeated Boston in Adams Division finals; defeated Philadelphia in Wales Conference finals; lost to Calgary in Stanley Cup finals.
1990—Defeated Buffalo in Adams Division semifinals; lost to Boston in Adams Division finals.
1991—Defeated Buffalo in Adams Division semifinals; lost to Boston in Adams Division finals.
1992—Defeated Hartford in Adams Division semifinals; lost to Boston in Adams Division finals.
1993—Defeated Detroit in Norris Division semifinals; defeated St. Louis in Norris Division finals; lost to Los Angeles in Campbell Conference finals.
1994—Defeated Chicago in Western Conference quarterfinals; defeated San Jose in Western Conference semifinals; lost to Vancouver in Western Conference finals.
1995—Lost to Chicago in Western Conference quarterfinals.

CAMPBELL, COLIN   RANGERS

PERSONAL: Born January 28, 1953, in London, Ont. ... Played defense. ... Shot left. ... Full name: Colin John Campbell. ... Name pronounced KOH-lihn CAM-bihl.

TRANSACTIONS/CAREER NOTES: Selected by Pittsburgh Penguins in second round (third Penguins pick, 27th overall) of NHL amateur draft (May 15, 1973). ... Selected by Vancouver Blazers in WHA amateur draft (May 1973). ... Missed part of 1975-76 season due to elbow surgery. ... Rights transferred by Penguins to Colorado Rockies for 1976-77 season as part compensation for earlier deal in which Penguins received G Denis Herron from Rockies for RW Simon Nolet and G Michel Plasse (September 1, 1976). ... Loaned by Rockies to Oklahoma City Blazers (January 1977). ... Returned by Rockies to Penguins for future considerations (May 1977). ... Claimed by Edmonton Oilers from Penguins in NHL expansion draft (June 13, 1979). ... Claimed by Vancouver Canucks from Oilers in waiver draft (October 10, 1980). ... Broke wrist (December 10, 1980). ... Signed as free agent by Detroit Red Wings (July 26, 1982). ... Injured ribs (November 1982). ... Injured ribs (November 10, 1983). ... Underwent arthroscopic surgery to knee (March 1985). ... Announced retirement and named assistant coach of Red Wings (July 1985).

Season Team	League	REGULAR SEASON								PLAYOFFS				
		Gms.	G	A	Pts.	PIM	+/-	PP	SH	Gms.	G	A	Pts.	PIM
70-71— Peterborough	OHA Jr. A	59	5	18	23	160	...	...	...	—	—	—	—	—
71-72— Peterborough	OHA Jr. A	50	2	23	25	158	...	...	...	—	—	—	—	—
72-73— Peterborough	OHA Jr. A	60	7	40	47	189	...	...	...	—	—	—	—	—
73-74— Vancouver	WHA	78	3	20	23	191	...	...	...	—	—	—	—	—
74-75— Hershey	AHL	16	1	3	4	55	...	...	...	—	—	—	—	—
— Pittsburgh	NHL	59	4	15	19	172	...	...	...	9	1	3	4	21
75-76— Pittsburgh	NHL	64	7	10	17	105	...	...	...	3	0	0	0	0
76-77— Oklahoma City	CHL	7	1	2	3	9	...	...	...	—	—	—	—	—
— Colorado Rockies	NHL	54	3	8	11	67	...	...	...	—	—	—	—	—
77-78— Pittsburgh	NHL	55	1	9	10	103	...	...	...	—	—	—	—	—
78-79— Pittsburgh	NHL	65	2	18	20	137	...	...	...	7	1	4	5	30
79-80— Edmonton	NHL	72	2	11	13	196	...	0	0	3	0	0	0	11
80-81— Vancouver	NHL	42	1	8	9	75	10	0	0	3	0	1	1	9
81-82— Vancouver	NHL	47	0	8	8	131	4	0	0	16	2	2	4	89
82-83— Detroit	NHL	53	1	7	8	74	2	0	0	—	—	—	—	—
83-84— Detroit	NHL	68	3	4	7	108	0	0	0	4	0	0	0	21
84-85— Detroit	NHL	57	1	5	6	124	-14	0	0	—	—	—	—	—
WHA totals (1 year)		78	3	20	23	191				—	—	—	—	—
NHL totals (11 years)		636	25	103	128	1292	...	...	...	45	4	10	14	181

HEAD COACHING RECORD

BACKGROUND: Assistant coach, Detroit Red Wings (1985-86 through 1989-90). ... Assistant coach, New York Rangers (August 1990 through January 4, 1993 and 1993-94 season).

Season Team	League	REGULAR SEASON					PLAYOFFS		
		W	L	T	Pct.	Finish	W	L	Pct.
92-93— Binghamton	AHL	29	8	5	.750	1st/Southern Division	7	7	.500
94-95— New York Rangers	NHL	22	23	3	.490	4th/Atlantic Division	4	6	.400
95-96— New York Rangers	NHL	41	27	14	.585	2nd/Atlantic Division	5	6	.455
96-97— New York Rangers	NHL	38	34	10	.524	4th/Atlantic Division	9	6	.600
NHL totals (3 years)		101	84	27	.540	**NHL totals (3 years)**	18	18	.500

NOTES:
1995—Defeated Quebec in Eastern Conference quarterfinals; lost to Philadelphia in Eastern Conference semifinals.
1996—Defeated Montreal in Eastern Conference quarterfinals; lost to Pittsburgh in Eastern Conference semifinals.
1997—Defeated Florida in Eastern Conference quarterfinals; defeated New Jersey in Eastern Conference semifinals; lost to Philadelphia in Eastern Conference finals.

CASHMAN, WAYNE   FLYERS

PERSONAL: Born June 24, 1945, in Kingston, Ont. ... Played left wing. ... Shot right. ... Full name: Wayne John Cashman.
TRANSACTIONS/CAREER NOTES: Suffered injuries and broke ankle during 1967-68 season. ... Underwent surgery for ruptured spinal disc during 1974-75 season. ... Dislocated thumb during 1976-77 season. ... Sprained right knee during 1979-80 season. ... Stretched knee ligaments during 1979-80 season. ... Underwent offseason knee surgery prior to 1980-81 season. ... Suspended four games by NHL for throwing stick (December 20, 1981). ... Suffered charley horse (January 31, 1982); missed 10 games. ... Underwent offseason surgery to repair torn rotator cuff prior to 1982-83 season.
MISCELLANEOUS: Member of Stanley Cup championship team (1970 and 1972). ... Captain of Boston Bruins (1977-78 through 1982-83).

Season Team	League	REGULAR SEASON								PLAYOFFS				
		Gms.	G	A	Pts.	PIM	+/-	PP	SH	Gms.	G	A	Pts.	PIM
62-63— Oshawa Jr. A	OHA	1	0	1	1	...	...	...	...	—	—	—	—	—
63-64— Oshawa Jr. A	OHA	27	9	12	21	...	...	...	...	—	—	—	—	—
64-65— Oshawa Jr. A	OHA	55	27	46	73	...	...	...	...	—	—	—	—	—
— Boston	NHL	1	0	0	0	0	...	...	...	—	—	—	—	—

Season Team	League	REGULAR SEASON								PLAYOFFS				
		Gms.	G	A	Pts.	PIM	+/-	PP	SH	Gms.	G	A	Pts.	PIM
65-66— Oshawa Jr. A	OHA	48	26	44	70	98	...	...	...	—	—	—	—	—
66-67— Oklahoma City	CPHL	70	20	36	56	98	...	...	...	11	3	4	7	4
67-68— Oklahoma City	CPHL	42	21	30	51	66	...	...	...	—	—	—	—	—
— Boston	NHL	12	0	4	4	2	...	...	...	1	0	0	0	0
68-69— Hershey	AHL	21	6	9	15	30	...	...	...	—	—	—	—	—
— Boston	NHL	51	8	23	31	49	...	...	...	6	0	1	1	0
69-70— Boston	NHL	70	9	26	35	79	...	...	...	14	5	4	9	50
70-71— Boston	NHL	77	21	58	79	100	...	...	...	7	3	2	5	15
71-72— Boston	NHL	74	23	29	52	103	...	...	...	15	4	7	11	42
72-73— Boston	NHL	76	29	39	68	100	...	...	...	5	1	1	2	4
73-74— Boston	NHL	78	30	59	89	111	...	...	...	16	5	9	14	46
74-75— Boston	NHL	42	11	22	33	24	...	...	...	1	0	2	2	0
75-76— Boston	NHL	80	28	43	71	87	...	...	...	11	1	5	6	16
76-77— Boston	NHL	65	15	37	52	76	...	...	...	14	1	8	9	18
77-78— Boston	NHL	76	24	38	62	69	...	...	...	15	4	6	10	13
78-79— Boston	NHL	75	27	40	67	63	...	...	...	10	4	5	9	8
79-80— Boston	NHL	44	11	21	32	19	...	3	1	10	3	3	6	32
80-81— Boston	NHL	77	25	35	60	80	17	7	0	3	0	1	1	0
81-82— Boston	NHL	64	12	31	43	59	-17	3	0	9	0	2	2	6
82-83— Boston	NHL	65	4	11	15	20	2	1	0	8	0	1	1	0
NHL totals (17 years)		1027	277	516	793	1041	...	...	...	145	31	57	88	250

HEAD COACHING RECORD

BACKGROUND: Assistant coach, New York Rangers (1987-88 through 1991-92). ... Assistant coach, Tampa Bay Lightning (1992-93 through 1995-96). ... Assistant coach, San Jose Sharks (1996-97).

CONSTANTINE, KEVIN — PENGUINS

PERSONAL: Born December 27, 1958, in International Falls, Minn. ... Played goaltender. ... Caught left. ... Full name: Kevin Lars Constantine.
HIGH SCHOOL: International Falls (Minn.).
COLLEGE: Rensselaer Polytechnic Institute (N.Y.), then Nevada-Reno.
TRANSACTIONS/CAREER NOTES: Selected by Montreal Canadiens in ninth round (11th Canadiens pick, 154th overall) in NHL entry draft (June 15, 1978). ... Invited to Canadiens tryout camp (1980).

Season Team	League	REGULAR SEASON							PLAYOFFS					
		Gms.	Min	W	L	T	GA	SO	Avg.	Gms.	Min.	W	L	GA	SO	Avg.
77-78— R.P.I.	ECAC	6	229	2	2	0	13	0	3.41	—	—	—	—	—	—	—
78-79— R.P.I.	ECAC	5	233	3	2	0	15	0	3.86	—	—	—	—	—	—	—
79-80— R.P.I.	ECAC	24	1342	11	9	0	89	1	3.98	—	—	—	—	—	—	—

HEAD COACHING RECORD

BACKGROUND: Junior varsity coach, Northwood Prep School, Lake Placid, N.Y. (1986-87). ... Assistant coach, Kalamazoo, Minnesota North Stars organization (1988-89 through 1990-91). ... Assistant coach, Calgary Flames (1996-97).
HONORS: IHL Coach of the Year (1991-92). ... Won Commissioner's Trophy (1991-92).

Season Team	League	REGULAR SEASON					PLAYOFFS		
		W	L	T	Pct.	Finish	W	L	Pct.
85-86— North Iowa	USHL	17	31	0	.354	6th/USHL	2	3	.400
87-88— Rochester	USHL	39	7	2	.833	T1st/USHL	7	4	.636
91-92— Kansas City	IHL	56	22	4	.707	1st/West Division	12	3	.800
92-93— Kansas City	IHL	46	26	10	.622	2nd/Midwest Division	6	6	.500
93-94— San Jose	NHL	33	35	16	.488	3rd/Pacific Division	7	7	.500
94-95— San Jose	NHL	19	25	4	.438	3rd/Pacific Division	4	7	.364
95-96— San Jose	NHL	3	18	4	.200		—	—	—
NHL totals (3 years)		55	78	24	.427	NHL totals (2 years)	11	14	.440

NOTES:
1986—Lost to Sioux City in USHL quarterfinals.
1988—Defeated Sioux City in USHL quarterfinals; defeated St. Paul in USHL semifinals; lost to Thunder Bay in USHL finals. Finished first in USA Jr. A Championships.
1992—Defeated Salt Lake City in quarterfinals of Turner Cup playoffs; defeated Peoria in semifinals of Turner Cup playoffs; defeated Muskegon in Turner Cup finals.
1993—Defeated Milwaukee in quarterfinals of Turner Cup playoffs; lost to San Diego in semifinals of Turner Cup playoffs.
1994—Defeated Detroit in Western Conference quarterfinals; lost to Toronto in Western Conference semifinals.
1995—Defeated Calgary in Western Conference quarterfinals; lost to Detroit in Western Conference semifinals. Replaced as head coach by Jim Wiley (December 2) with club in seventh place.
1996—Replaced as head coach by Jacques Martin (January 24) with club in sixth place.

CRAWFORD, MARC — AVALANCHE

PERSONAL: Born February 13, 1961, in Belleville, Ont. ... Played left wing. ... Shot left. ... Full name: Marc Joseph John Crawford. ... Brother of Bob Crawford, right winger for four NHL teams (1979-80 through 1986-87).
TRANSACTIONS/CAREER NOTES: Selected by Vancouver Canucks in fourth round (third Canucks pick, 70th overall) of NHL entry draft (June 11, 1980). ... Suspended three games by NHL for leaving bench to fight (February 3, 1987).

Season Team	League	REGULAR SEASON								PLAYOFFS				
		Gms.	G	A	Pts.	PIM	+/-	PP	SH	Gms.	G	A	Pts.	PIM
79-80— Cornwall	OHL	54	27	36	63	127	...	...	...	18	8	20	28	48
80-81— Cornwall	OHL	63	42	57	99	242	...	...	...	19	20	15	35	27
81-82— Dallas	CHL	34	13	21	34	71	...	...	...	—	—	—	—	—
— Vancouver	NHL	40	4	8	12	29	0	0	0	14	1	0	1	11

Season Team	League	REGULAR SEASON								PLAYOFFS				
		Gms.	G	A	Pts.	PIM	+/-	PP	SH	Gms.	G	A	Pts.	PIM
82-83— Vancouver	NHL	41	4	5	9	28	-3	0	0	3	0	1	1	25
— Fredericton	AHL	30	15	9	24	59	...	...	...	9	1	3	4	10
83-84— Vancouver	NHL	19	0	1	1	9	0	0	0	—	—	—	—	—
— Fredericton	AHL	56	9	22	31	96	...	...	...	7	4	2	6	23
84-85— Vancouver	NHL	1	0	0	0	4	-4	0	0	—	—	—	—	—
85-86— Vancouver	NHL	54	11	14	25	92	-7	0	0	3	0	1	1	8
— Fredericton	AHL	26	10	14	24	55	...	...	...	—	—	—	—	—
86-87— Vancouver	NHL	21	0	3	3	67	-8	0	0	—	—	—	—	—
— Fredericton	AHL	25	8	11	19	21	...	...	...	—	—	—	—	—
87-88— Fredericton	AHL	43	5	13	18	90	...	...	...	2	0	0	0	14
88-89— Milwaukee	IHL	53	23	30	53	166	...	...	...	11	2	5	7	26
NHL totals (6 years)		176	19	31	50	229	-22	0	0	20	1	2	3	44

HEAD COACHING RECORD

BACKGROUND: Player/assistant coach, Fredericton Express of AHL (1987-88). ... Nordiques franchise moved to Denver for 1995-96 season and renamed Colorado Avalanche.

HONORS: Won Louis A.R. Pieri Memorial Award (1992-93). ... Named NHL Coach of the Year by THE SPORTING NEWS (1994-95). ... Won Jack Adams Award (1994-95).

Season Team	League	REGULAR SEASON					PLAYOFFS		
		W	L	T	Pct.	Finish	W	L	Pct.
89-90— Cornwall	OHL	24	38	4	.394	6th/Leyden Division	2	4	.333
90-91— Cornwall	OHL	23	42	1	.356	7th/Leyden Division	—	—	—
91-92— St. John's	AHL	39	29	12	.563	2nd/Atlantic Division	11	5	.688
92-93— St. John's	AHL	41	26	13	.594	1st/Atlantic Division	4	5	.444
93-94— St. John's	AHL	45	23	12	.638	1st/Atlantic Division	6	5	.545
94-95— Quebec	NHL	30	13	5	.677	1st/Northeast Division	2	4	.333
95-96— Colorado	NHL	47	25	10	.634	1st/Pacific Division	16	6	.727
96-97— Colorado	NHL	49	24	9	.652	1st/Pacific Division	10	7	.588
NHL totals (3 years)		126	62	24	.651	NHL totals (3 years)	28	17	.622

NOTES:

1990—Lost to Oshawa in Leyden Division quarterfinals.

1992—Defeated Cape Breton in first round of Calder Cup playoffs; defeated Moncton in second round of Calder Cup playoffs; lost to Adirondack in Calder Cup finals.

1993—Defeated Moncton in first round of Calder Cup playoffs; lost to Cape Breton in second round of Calder Cup playoffs.

1994—Defeated Cape Breton in first round of Calder Cup playoffs; lost to Moncton in second round of Calder Cup playoffs.

1995—Lost to New York Rangers in Eastern Conference quarterfinals.

1996—Defeated Vancouver in Western Conference quarterfinals; defeated Chicago in Western Conference semifinals; defeated Detroit in Western Conference finals; defeated Florida in Stanley Cup finals.

1997—Defeated Chicago in Western Conference quarterfinals; defeated Edmonton in Western Conference semifinals; lost to Detroit in Western Conference finals.

CRISP, TERRY   LIGHTNING

PERSONAL: Born May 28, 1943, in Parry Sound, Ont. ... Played center. ... Shot left. ... Full name: Terrance Arthur Crisp.

TRANSACTIONS/CAREER NOTES: Underwent appendectomy and hernia operation; missed part of 1963-64 season. ... Selected by St. Louis Blues from Boston Bruins in NHL expansion draft (June 6, 1967). ... Selected by New York Islanders from Blues in expansion draft (June 6, 1972). ... Traded by Islanders to Philadelphia Flyers for D Jean Potvin and future considerations (March 5, 1973); Islanders received D Glen Irwin to complete deal (May 18, 1973).

MISCELLANEOUS: Member of Stanley Cup championship team (1974 and 1975).

Season Team	League	REGULAR SEASON								PLAYOFFS				
		Gms.	G	A	Pts.	PIM	+/-	PP	SH	Gms.	G	A	Pts.	PIM
60-61— St. Mary's	OHA					Did not play.				—				
61-62— Niagara Falls	OHA	50	16	22	38	0	...	...	...	—				
62-63— Niagara Falls	OHA	50	39	35	74	0	...	...	...	—				
63-64— Minneapolis	CPHL	42	15	20	35	22	...	...	...	—				
64-65— Minneapolis	CPHL	70	28	34	62	22	...	...	...	5	0	2	2	0
65-66— Boston	NHL	3	0	0	0	0	...	...	...	—				
— Oklahoma City	CPHL	61	11	22	33	35	...	...	...	9	1	5	6	0
66-67— Oklahoma City	CPHL	69	31	42	73	37	...	...	...	11	3	7	10	0
67-68— St. Louis	NHL	73	9	20	29	10	...	...	...	18	1	5	6	6
68-69— Kansas City	CHL	4	1	1	2	4	...	...	...	—				
— St. Louis	NHL	57	6	9	15	14	...	...	...	12	3	4	7	20
69-70— St. Louis	NHL	26	5	6	11	2	...	...	...	16	2	3	5	2
— Buffalo	AHL	51	15	34	49	14	...	...	...	—				
70-71— St. Louis	NHL	54	5	11	16	13	...	...	...	6	1	0	1	2
71-72— St. Louis	NHL	75	13	18	31	12	...	...	...	11	1	3	4	2
72-73— New York	NHL	54	4	16	20	6	...	...	...	—				
— Philadelphia	NHL	12	1	5	6	2	...	...	...	11	3	2	5	2
73-74— Philadelphia	NHL	71	10	21	31	28	...	...	...	17	2	2	4	4
74-75— Philadelphia	NHL	71	8	19	27	20	...	...	...	9	2	4	6	0
75-76— Philadelphia	NHL	38	6	9	15	28	...	...	...	10	0	5	5	2
76-77— Philadelphia	NHL	2	0	0	0	0	...	...	...	—				
NHL totals (11 years)		536	67	134	201	135				110	15	28	43	40

HEAD COACHING RECORD

BACKGROUND: Assistant coach, Philadelphia Flyers (1977-78 and 1978-79). ... Assistant coach, Canadian national team (1990 through 1992).

HONORS: Won Matt Leyden Trophy (1982-83 and 1984-85). ... Named NHL Coach of the Year by THE SPORTING NEWS (1987-88).

Season Team	League	W	L	T	Pct.	Finish	W	L	Pct.
						REGULAR SEASON		PLAYOFFS	
79-80—Sault Ste. Marie	OHL	22	45	1	.331	6th/Leyden Division	—	—	—
80-81—Sault Ste. Marie	OHL	47	19	2	.706	1st/Leyden Division	8	7	.533
81-82—Sault Ste. Marie	OHL	40	25	3	.610	2nd/Emms Division	4	6	.400
82-83—Sault Ste. Marie	OHL	48	21	1	.693	1st/Emms Division	7	6	.538
83-84—Sault Ste. Marie	OHL	38	28	4	.571	3rd/Emms Division	8	4	.667
84-85—Sault Ste. Marie	OHL	54	11	1	.826	1st/Emms Division	12	2	.857
85-86—Moncton	AHL	34	34	12	.500	3rd/North Division	5	5	.500
86-87—Moncton	AHL	43	31	6	.575	3rd/North Division	2	4	.333
87-88—Calgary	NHL	48	23	9	.656	1st/Smythe Division	4	5	.444
88-89—Calgary	NHL	54	17	9	.731	1st/Smythe Division	16	6	.727
89-90—Calgary	NHL	42	23	15	.619	1st/Smythe Division	2	4	.333
92-93—Tampa Bay	NHL	23	54	7	.315	6th/Norris Division	—	—	—
93-94—Tampa Bay	NHL	30	43	11	.423	7th/Atlantic Division	—	—	—
94-95—Tampa Bay	NHL	17	28	3	.385	6th/Atlantic Division	—	—	—
95-96—Tampa Bay	NHL	38	32	12	.537	5th/Atlantic Division	2	4	.333
96-97—Tampa Bay	NHL	32	40	10	.451	6th/Atlantic Division	—	—	—
NHL totals (8 years)		284	260	76	.519	NHL totals (4 years)	24	19	.558

NOTES:

1981—Sault Ste. Marie had four playoff ties.

1982—Defeated Brantford in Emms Division semifinals; lost to Kitchener in Emms Division finals. Sault Ste. Marie had three playoff ties.

1983—Defeated Brantford in Emms Division semifinals; defeated Kitchener in Emms Division finals; lost to Oshawa in J. Ross Robertson Cup finals. Sault Ste. Marie had three playoff ties.

1984—Defeated Windsor in Emms Division quarterfinals; defeated Brantford in Emms Division semifinals; lost to Kitchener in Emms Division finals. Sault Ste. Marie had four playoff ties.

1985—Defeated Kitchener in Emms Division quarterfinals; defeated Hamilton in Emms Division semifinals; defeated Peterborough in J. Ross Robertson Cup finals. Sault Ste. Marie had two playoff ties.

1986—Defeated Maine in Calder Cup quarterfinals; lost to Adirondack in semifinals of Calder Cup playoffs.

1987—Lost to Adirondack in quarterfinals of Calder Cup playoffs.

1988—Defeated Los Angeles in Smythe Division semifinals; lost to Edmonton in Smythe Division finals.

1989—Defeated Vancouver in Smythe Division semifinals; defeated Los Angeles in Smythe Division finals; defeated Chicago in Campbell Conference finals; defeated Montreal in Stanley Cup finals.

1990—Lost to Los Angeles in Smythe Division semifinals.

1996—Lost to Philadelphia in Eastern Conference quarterfinals.

HARTSBURG, CRAIG — BLACKHAWKS

PERSONAL: Born June 29, 1959, in Stratford, Ont. ... Played defense. ... Shot left.

TRANSACTIONS/CAREER NOTES: Selected by Minnesota North Stars in first round (first North Stars pick, sixth overall) of NHL entry draft (August 9, 1979). ... Torn ligaments in left knee (September 1977). ... Separated shoulder (September 1980). ... Underwent surgery to remove bone spur on knee (October 10, 1983). ... Injured ligaments in left knee (January 10, 1984). ... Suffered hip pointer (October 1984). ... Suffered fractured femur (December 1984). ... Injured groin (January 16, 1986); missed four games. ... Suffered herniated disc (February 1987). ... Strained knee ligaments (March 1987). ... Suffered concussion (November 7, 1987). ... Injured left hip and separated shoulder (March 1988). ... Underwent shoulder surgery (March 1988). ... Suffered staph infection on right ankle and required hospitalization (October 11, 1988). ... Re-injured right ankle (January 2, 1989).

HONORS: Won Max Kaminsky Memorial Trophy (1976-77). ... Named to OHA All-Star second team (1976-77). ... Played in NHL All-Star game (1980, 1982 and 1983).

MISCELLANEOUS: Captain of Minnesota North Stars (1982-83 through 1987-88).

Season Team	League	Gms.	G	A	Pts.	PIM	+/-	PP	SH	Gms.	G	A	Pts.	PIM
		REGULAR SEASON								PLAYOFFS				
75-76—Sault Ste. Marie	OHA	64	9	19	28	65	...	...	...	—	—	—	—	—
76-77—Sault Ste. Marie	OHA	61	29	64	93	142	...	...	...	9	0	11	11	27
77-78—Sault Ste. Marie	OHA	36	15	42	57	101	...	...	...	13	4	8	12	24
78-79—Birmingham	WHA	77	9	40	49	73	...	...	...	—	—	—	—	—
79-80—Minnesota	NHL	79	14	30	44	81	...	7	0	15	3	1	4	17
80-81—Minnesota	NHL	74	13	30	43	124	-9	8	0	19	3	12	15	16
81-82—Minnesota	NHL	76	17	60	77	117	11	5	0	4	1	2	3	14
82-83—Minnesota	NHL	78	12	50	62	109	7	3	1	9	3	8	11	7
83-84—Minnesota	NHL	26	7	7	14	37	-2	5	0	—	—	—	—	—
84-85—Minnesota	NHL	32	7	11	18	54	-5	1	1	9	5	3	8	14
85-86—Minnesota	NHL	75	10	47	57	127	7	4	0	5	0	1	1	2
86-87—Minnesota	NHL	73	11	50	61	93	-2	4	0	—	—	—	—	—
87-88—Minnesota	NHL	27	3	16	19	29	-2	2	0	—	—	—	—	—
88-89—Minnesota	NHL	30	4	14	18	47	-8	1	0	—	—	—	—	—
WHA totals (1 year)		77	9	40	49	73	...	...	...					
NHL totals (10 years)		570	98	315	413	818	...	40	2	61	15	27	42	70

HEAD COACHING RECORD

BACKGROUND: Assistant coach, Minnesota North Stars (1989-90). ... Assistant coach, Philadelphia Flyers (1990-91 through 1993-94).

Season Team	League	W	L	T	Pct.	Finish	W	L	Pct.
						REGULAR SEASON		PLAYOFFS	
94-95—Guelph	OHL	47	14	5	.750	1st/Central Division	10	4	.714
95-96—Chicago	NHL	40	28	14	.573	2nd/Central Division	6	4	.600
96-97—Chicago	NHL	34	35	13	.494	5th/Central Division	2	4	.333
NHL totals (2 years)		74	63	27	.534	NHL totals (2 years)	8	8	.500

NOTES:
1995—Defeated Owen Sound in second round of OHL playoffs; defeated Belleville in third round of OHL playoffs; lost to Detroit in J. Ross Robertson Cup finals.
1996—Defeated Calgary in Western Conference quarterfinals; lost to Colorado in Western Conference semifinals.
1997—Lost to Colorado in Western Conference quarterfinals.

HITCHCOCK, KEN   STARS

PERSONAL: Born December 17, 1951, in Edmonton.
COLLEGE: University of Alberta.
HONORS: Named NHL Coach of the Year by THE SPORTING NEWS (1996-97).

HEAD COACHING RECORD
BACKGROUND: Assistant coach, Philadelphia Flyers (1990-93).

Season Team	League	W	L	T	Pct.	Finish	W	L	Pct.
							PLAYOFFS		
84-85—Kamloops	WHL	52	17	2	.746	1st/West Division	10	5	.667
85-86—Kamloops	WHL	49	19	4	.708	1st/West Division	14	2	.875
86-87—Kamloops	WHL	55	14	3	.785	1st/West Division	8	5	.615
87-88—Kamloops	WHL	45	26	1	.632	1st/West Division	12	6	.667
88-89—Kamloops	WHL	34	33	5	.507	3rd/West Division	8	8	.500
89-90—Kamloops	WHL	56	16	0	.778	1st/West Division	14	3	.824
93-94—Kalamazoo	IHL	48	26	7	.636	1st/Atlantic Division	1	4	.200
94-95—Kalamazoo	IHL	43	24	14	.617	2nd/Northern Division	10	6	.625
95-96—Dallas	NHL	15	23	5	.407	6th/Central Division	—	—	—
— Michigan	IHL	19	10	11	.613	2nd/Northern Division	—	—	—
96-97—Dallas	NHL	48	26	8	.634	1st/Central Division	2	4	.333
NHL totals (2 years)		63	49	13	.556	NHL totals (1 year)	2	4	.333

NOTES:
1985—Defeated Portland in West Division semifinals; defeated New Westminster in West Division finals; lost to Prince Albert in WHL finals.
1986—Defeated Seattle in West Division semifinals; defeated Portland in West Division finals; defeated Medicine Hat in WHL finals.
1987—Defeated Victoria in West Division semifinals; lost to Portland in West Division finals.
1988—Defeated New Westminster in West Division semifinals; defeated Spokane in West Division finals; lost to Medicine Hat in WHL finals.
1989—Defeated Victoria in West Division semifinals; lost to Portland in West Division finals.
1990—Defeated Spokane in West Division semifinals; defeated Seattle in West Division finals; defeated Lethbridge in WHL finals.
1994—Lost to Cincinnati in Eastern Conference quarterfinals.
1995—Defeated Chicago in Eastern Conference quarterfinals; defeated Cincinnati in Eastern Conference semifinals; lost to Kansas City in Eastern Conference finals.
1997—Lost to Edmonton in Western Conference quarterfinals.

LEMAIRE, JACQUES   DEVILS

PERSONAL: Born September 7, 1945, in Ville LaSalle, Que. ... Played center and left wing. ... Shot left. ... Full name: Jacques Gerard Lemaire. ... Name pronounced luh-MAIR.
HONORS: Inducted into Hall of Fame (1984).
MISCELLANEOUS: Member of Stanley Cup championship team (1968, 1969, 1971, 1973 and 1976-1979).

Season Team	League	Gms.	G	A	Pts.	PIM	+/-	PP	SH	Gms.	G	A	Pts.	PIM
		REGULAR SEASON								PLAYOFFS				
62-63— Lachine	QJHL	42	41	63	104	...		...	...	—	—	—	—	—
63-64— Montreal Jr. Canadiens	OHA Jr. A	42	25	30	55	...		...	...	—	—	—	—	—
64-65— Montreal Jr. Canadiens	OHA Jr. A	56	25	47	72	...		...	...	—	—	—	—	—
— Quebec	AHL	1	0	0	0	0		...	...	—	—	—	—	—
65-66— Montreal Jr. Canadiens	OHA Jr. A	48	41	52	93	69		...	...	—	—	—	—	—
66-67— Houston	CPHL	69	19	30	49	19		...	...	6	0	1	1	0
67-68— Montreal	NHL	69	22	20	42	16		...	...	13	7	6	13	6
68-69— Montreal	NHL	75	29	34	63	29		...	...	14	4	2	6	6
69-70— Montreal	NHL	69	32	28	60	16		...	...	—	—	—	—	—
70-71— Montreal	NHL	78	28	28	56	18		...	...	20	9	10	19	17
71-72— Montreal	NHL	77	32	49	81	26		...	...	6	2	1	3	2
72-73— Montreal	NHL	77	44	51	95	16		...	...	17	7	13	20	2
73-74— Montreal	NHL	66	29	38	67	10		...	...	6	0	4	4	2
74-75— Montreal	NHL	80	36	56	92	20		...	...	11	5	7	12	4
75-76— Montreal	NHL	61	20	32	52	20		...	...	13	3	3	6	2
76-77— Montreal	NHL	75	34	41	75	22		...	...	14	7	12	19	6
77-78— Montreal	NHL	75	36	61	97	14		...	...	15	6	8	14	10
78-79— Montreal	NHL	50	24	31	55	10		...	...	16	11	12	23	6
NHL totals (12 years)		852	366	469	835	217				145	61	78	139	63

HEAD COACHING RECORD
BACKGROUND: Assistant coach, University of Plattsburgh (1981-82). ... Assistant coach, Montreal Canadiens (October 1982-February 1983). ... Assistant to managing director/director of player personnel, Canadiens (1985-86 through 1987-88). ... Assistant to managing director of Verdun, Canadiens organization (1988-89). ... Assistant to managing director, Canadiens (1989-90 and 1990-91). ... Assistant to managing director of Fredericton, Canadiens organization (1991-92 and 1992-93). ... Served as interim coach of Montreal Canadiens while Jacques Demers was hospitalized with chest pains (March 10 and 11, 1993; team was 1-1 during that time).
HONORS: Named NHL Coach of the Year by THE SPORTING NEWS (1993-94). ... Won Jack Adams Award (1993-94).

Season Team	League	REGULAR SEASON					PLAYOFFS		
		W	L	T	Pct.	Finish	W	L	Pct.
79-80—Sierre	Swiss					Record unavailable.			
80-81—Sierre	Swiss					Record unavailable.			
82-83—Longueuil	QMJHL	37	29	4	.557	3rd/LeBel Division	8	7	.533
83-84—Montreal	NHL	7	10	0	.412	4th/Adams Division	9	6	.600
84-85—Montreal	NHL	41	27	12	.588	1st/Adams Division	6	6	.500
93-94—New Jersey	NHL	47	25	12	.631	2nd/Atlantic Division	11	9	.550
94-95—New Jersey	NHL	22	18	8	.542	2nd/Atlantic Division	16	4	.800
95-96—New Jersey	NHL	37	33	12	.524	5th/Atlantic Division	—	—	—
96-97—New Jersey	NHL	45	23	14	.634	1st/Atlantic Division	5	5	.500
NHL totals (6 years)		199	136	58	.580	NHL totals (5 years)	47	30	.610

NOTES:
1983—Defeated Chicoutimi in President Cup quarterfinals; defeated Laval in President Cup semifinals; lost to Verdun in President Cup finals.
1984—Defeated Boston in Adams Division semifinals; defeated Quebec in Adams Division finals; lost to New York Islanders in Wales Conference finals.
1985—Defeated Boston in Adams Division semifinals; lost to Quebec in Adams Division finals.
1994—Defeated Buffalo in Eastern Conference quarterfinals; defeated Boston in Eastern Confernce semifinals; lost to New York Rangers in Eastern Conference finals.
1995—Defeated Boston in Eastern Conference quarterfinals; defeated Pittsburgh in Eastern Conference semifinals; defeated Philadelphia in Eastern Conference finals; defeated Detroit in Stanley Cup finals.
1997—Defeated Montreal in Eastern Conference quarterfinals; lost to New York Rangers in Eastern Conference semifinals.

LOW, RON   OILERS

PERSONAL: Born June 21, 1950, in Birtle, Man. ... Played goaltender. ... Caught right. ... Full name: Ron Albert Low. ... Name pronounced LOH.
TRANSACTIONS/CAREER NOTES: Selected by Toronto Maple Leafs in eighth round (eighth Maple Leafs pick, 103rd overall) of NHL amateur draft (June 11, 1970). ... Claimed by Washington Capitals from Maple Leafs in expansion draft (June 12, 1974). ... Signed as free agent by Detroit Red Wings (August 17, 1977). ... Claimed by Quebec Nordiques from Red Wings in expansion draft (June 13, 1979). ... Traded by Nordiques to Edmonton Oilers for C Ron Chipperfield (March 11, 1980). ... Traded by Oilers to New Jersey Devils with D Jim McTaggart for G Lindsay Middlebrook and C Paul Miller (February 19, 1983).
HONORS: Named to CHL All-Star second team (1973-74). ... Won Tommy Ivan Trophy (1978-79). ... Named to CHL All-Star first team (1978-79).

Season Team	League	REGULAR SEASON							PLAYOFFS						
		Gms.	Min	W	L	T	GA	SO	Avg.	Gms.	Min.	W	L	GA	SO	Avg.
70-71—Jacksonville	EHL	49	2940	...	...	...	293	1	5.98	—	—	—	—	—	—	—
—Tulsa	CHL	4	192	...	...	...	11	0	3.44	—	—	—	—	—	—	—
71-72—Richmond	AHL	1	60	...	...	...	2	0	2.00	—	—	—	—	—	—	—
—Tulsa	CHL	43	2428	...	...	...	135	1	3.34	8	474	...	...	15	1	1.90
72-73—Toronto	NHL	42	2343	12	24	4	152	1	3.89	—	—	—	—	—	—	—
73-74—Tulsa	CHL	56	3213	...	...	...	169	1	3.16	—	—	—	—	—	—	—
74-75—Washington	NHL	48	2588	8	36	2	235	1	5.45	—	—	—	—	—	—	—
75-76—Washington	NHL	43	2289	6	31	2	208	0	5.45	—	—	—	—	—	—	—
76-77—Washington	NHL	54	2918	16	27	5	188	0	3.87	—	—	—	—	—	—	—
77-78—Detroit	NHL	32	1816	9	12	9	102	1	3.37	4	240	1	3	17	0	4.25
78-79—Kansas City	CHL	63	3795	...	...	...	244	0	3.86	4	237	...	...	15	...	3.80
79-80—Syracuse	AHL	15	905	5	9	1	70	0	4.64	—	—	—	—	—	—	—
—Quebec	NHL	15	828	5	7	2	51	0	3.70	—	—	—	—	—	—	—
—Edmonton	NHL	11	650	8	2	1	37	0	3.42	3	212	0	3	12	...	3.40
80-81—Edmonton	NHL	24	1260	5	13	3	93	0	4.43	—	—	—	—	—	—	—
—Wichita	CHL	2	120	0	2	0	10	0	5.00	—	—	—	—	—	—	—
81-82—Edmonton	NHL	29	1554	17	7	1	100	0	3.86	—	—	—	—	—	—	—
82-83—Edmonton	NHL	3	104	0	1	0	10	0	5.77	—	—	—	—	—	—	—
—New Jersey	NHL	11	608	2	7	1	41	0	4.05	—	—	—	—	—	—	—
83-84—New Jersey	NHL	44	2218	8	25	4	161	0	4.36	—	—	—	—	—	—	—
84-85—New Jersey	NHL	26	1326	6	11	4	85	1	3.85	—	—	—	—	—	—	—
NHL totals (11 year)		382	20502	102	203	38	1463	4	4.28	7	452	1	6	29	0	3.85

HEAD COACHING RECORD
BACKGROUND: Player/assistant coach, Nova Scotia Oilers (1985-86). ... Assistant coach, Nova Scotia Oilers (1986-87). ... Assistant coach, Edmonton Oilers (August 3, 1989 through 1994-95).

Season Team	League	REGULAR SEASON					PLAYOFFS		
		W	L	T	Pct.	Finish	W	L	Pct.
87-88—Nova Scotia	AHL	35	36	9	.494	4th/Northern Division	—	—	—
88-89—Cape Breton	AHL	27	47	6	.375	7th/Northern Division	—	—	—
94-95—Edmonton	NHL	5	7	1	.423	5th/Pacific Division	—	—	—
95-96—Edmonton	NHL	30	44	8	.415	5th/Pacific Division	—	—	—
96-97—Edmonton	NHL	36	37	9	.494	3rd/Pacific Division	5	6	.455
NHL totals (3 years)		71	88	18	.452	NHL totals (1 year)	5	6	.455

NOTES:
1997—Defeated Dallas in Western Conference quarterfinals; lost to Colorado in Western Conference semifinals.

MacLEAN, DOUG   PANTHERS

PERSONAL: Born April 12, 1954, in Summerside, P.E.I.
COLLEGE: Prince Edward Island, then Western Ontario (master's degree in educational psychology).

HEAD COACHING RECORD

BACKGROUND: Assistant coach, London Knights of OHL (1984-85). ... Assistant coach, St. Louis Blues (1986-87 and 1987-88). ... Assistant coach, Washington Capitals (1988-89 and 1989-1990). ... Assistant coach, Detroit Red Wings (1990-91 and 1991-92). ... Assistant general manager, Red Wings (1992-93 and 1993-94). ... General manager, Adirondack, Red Wings organization (1992-93 and 1993-94). ... Director of player development/scout, Florida Panthers (1994-95).

		REGULAR SEASON					PLAYOFFS		
Season Team	League	W	L	T	Pct.	Finish	W	L	Pct.
85-86—Univ. of New Brunswick	AUAA	33	46	5	.423	4th/Pacific Division	—	—	—
89-90—Baltimore	AHL	17	13	5	.557	3rd/Southern Division	6	6	.500
95-96—Florida	NHL	41	31	10	.561	3rd/Atlantic Division	12	10	.545
96-97—Florida	NHL	35	28	19	.543	3rd/Atlantic Division	1	4	.200
NHL totals (2 years)........................		76	59	29	.552	NHL totals (2 years)	13	14	.481

NOTES:

1990—Defeated Adirondack in quarterfinals of Calder Cup playoffs; lost to Rochester in semifinals of Calder Cup playoffs.

1996—Defeated Boston in Eastern Conference quarterfinals; defeated Philadelphia in Eastern Conference semifinals; defeated Pittsburgh in Eastern Conference finals; lost to Colorado in Stanley Cup finals.

1997—Lost to New York Rangers in Eastern Conference quarterfinals.

MARTIN, JACQUES   SENATORS

PERSONAL: Born October 1, 1952, in Rockland, Ont.

HEAD COACHING RECORD

BACKGROUND: Assistant coach, Chicago Blackhawks (1988-89 through 1989-90). ... Assistant coach, Quebec Nordiques (1990-91 through 1992-93 and 1994-95). ... Assistant coach, Colorado Avalanche (1995 through January 24, 1996).

		REGULAR SEASON					PLAYOFFS		
Season Team	League	W	L	T	Pct.	Finish	W	L	Pct.
85-86—Guelph	OHL	41	23	2	.636	2nd/Emms Division	15	3	.833
86-87—St. Louis	NHL	32	33	15	.494	1st/Norris Division	2	4	.333
87-88—St. Louis	NHL	34	38	8	.475	2nd/Norris Division	5	5	.500
93-94—Cornwall	AHL	33	36	11	.481	T3rd/Southern Division	4	2	.667
95-96—Ottawa	NHL	10	24	4	.316	6th/Northeast Division	—	—	—
96-97—Ottawa	NHL	31	36	15	.470	T3rd/Northeast Division	3	4	.429
NHL totals (4 years)........................		107	131	42	.457	NHL totals (3 years)	10	13	.435

NOTES:

1986—Defeated Sudbury in OHL quarterfinals; defeated Windsor in OHL semifinals; defeated Belleville in J. Ross Robertson Cup finals.

1987—Lost to Toronto in Norris Division semifinals.

1988—Defeated Chicago in Norris Division semifinals; lost to Detroit in Norris Division finals.

1994—Defeated Hamilton in quarterfinals of Calder Cup playoffs; defeated Hershey in division finals of Calder Cup playoffs; lost to Moncton in semifinals of Calder Cup playoffs.

1997—Lost to Buffalo in Eastern Conference quarterfinals.

MAURICE, PAUL   HURRICANES

PERSONAL: Born January 30, 1967, in Sault St. Marie, Ont.

HEAD COACHING RECORD

BACKGROUND: Assistant coach, Hartford Whalers (June 9-November 6, 1995). ... Whalers franchise moved to North Carolina and renamed Carolina Hurricanes for 1997-98 season; NHL approved move on June 25, 1997.

		REGULAR SEASON					PLAYOFFS		
Season Team	League	W	L	T	Pct.	Finish	W	L	Pct.
93-94—Detroit	OHL	42	20	4	.667	1st/West Division	11	6	.647
94-95—Detroit	OHL	44	18	4	.697	1st/West Division	16	5	.762
95-96—Hartford	NHL	29	33	8	.471	4th/Northeast Division	—	—	—
96-97—Hartford	NHL	32	39	11	.457	5th/Northeast Division	—	—	—
NHL totals (2 years)........................		61	72	19	.464				

NOTES:

1994—Defeated Owen Sound in quarterfinals of OHL playoffs; defeated Sault Ste. Marie in semifinals of OHL playoffs; lost to North Bay in OHL finals.

1995—Defeated London in first round of OHL playoffs; defeated Peterborough in second round of OHL playoffs; defeated Sudbury in third round of OHL playoffs; defeated Guelph in J. Ross Robertson Cup finals.

MURPHY, MIKE   MAPLE LEAFS

PERSONAL: Born September 12, 1950, in Toronto. ... Played right wing. ... Shot right.

COLLEGE: University of Toledo.

TRANSACTIONS/CAREER NOTES: Selected by New York Rangers in second round (25th overall) of 1970 NHL entry draft. ... Traded by Rangers with D Andre Dupont, LW Jack Egers and player to be named later to St. Louis Blues for RW Wayne Connelly, C Gene Carr and LW Jim Lorentz (November 1971). ... Traded by Blues to Rangers for D Ab DeMarco (March 1973). ... Traded by Rangers with C Tom Williams and D Sheldon Kannegiesser to Los Angeles Kings for D Giles Marotte and C Real Lemieux (November 1973).

HONORS: Named OHL Rookie of the Year (1970-71).

		REGULAR SEASON							PLAYOFFS				
Season Team	League	Gms.	G	A	Pts.	PIM	+/-	PP	SH	Gms.	G	A	Pts.	PIM
68-69 — Toronto........................	OHA M. Jr	44	16	23	39	53	...	...	...	—	—	—	—	—
69-70 — Toronto........................	OHA M. Jr.	54	23	27	50	68	...	...	...	—	—	—	—	—
70-71 — Omaha........................	CPHL	59	24	47	71	37	...	...	...	—	—	—	—	—
71-72 — Omaha........................	CPHL	8	1	4	5	12	...	...	...	—	—	—	—	—
— St. Louis........................	NHL	63	20	23	43	19	...	...	...	11	2	3	5	6

				REGULAR SEASON							PLAYOFFS			
Season Team	League	Gms.	G	A	Pts.	PIM	+/-	PP	SH		Gms.	G	A	Pts.	PIM
72-73— St. Louis	NHL	64	18	27	45	48	...	...	...		—	—	—	—	—
— New York	NHL	15	4	4	8	5	...	...	...		10	0	0	0	0
73-74— New York	NHL	16	2	1	3	0	...	...	...		—	—	—	—	—
— Los Angeles	NHL	53	13	16	29	38	...	...	...		5	0	4	4	0
74-75— Los Angeles	NHL	78	30	38	68	44	...	...	...		3	3	0	3	4
75-76— Los Angeles	NHL	80	26	42	68	61	...	...	...		9	1	4	5	6
76-77— Los Angeles	NHL	76	25	36	61	58	...	...	...		9	4	9	13	4
77-78— Los Angeles	NHL	72	20	36	56	48	...	...	...		2	0	0	0	0
78-79— Los Angeles	NHL	64	16	29	45	38	...	...	...		2	0	1	1	0
79-80— Los Angeles	NHL	80	27	22	49	29	...	7	3		4	1	0	1	2
80-81— Los Angeles	NHL	68	16	22	38	54	-7	2	1		1	0	1	1	0
81-82— Los Angeles	NHL	28	5	10	15	20	0	0	2		10	2	1	3	32
82-83— Los Angeles	NHL	74	16	11	27	52	-11	0	5		—	—	—	—	—
NHL totals (12 years)		831	238	317	555	514	...	...	...		66	13	23	36	54

HEAD COACHING RECORD

BACKGROUND: Assistant to general manager, Los Angeles Kings (1983 through January, 1984). ... Assistant coach, Kings (January 30, 1984 through January 10, 1987). ... Assistant coach, Vancouver Canucks (March 3, 1988 through 1989-90). ... Assistant coach, Toronto Maple Leafs (1991-92 through 1993-94). ... Assistant coach, New York Rangers (1994-95 through 1995-96).

		REGULAR SEASON					PLAYOFFS		
Season Team	League	W	L	T	Pct.	Finish	W	L	Pct.
86-87—Los Angeles	NHL	13	21	4	.395	4th/Smythe Division	1	4	.200
87-88—Los Angeles	NHL	7	17	7	.339		—	—	—
90-91—Milwaukee	IHL	36	43	3	.457	4th/West Division	2	4	.333
96-97—Toronto	NHL	30	44	8	.415	6th/Central Division	—	—	—
NHL totals (3 years)		50	82	19	.394	**NHL totals (1 year)**	1	4	.200

NOTES:
1987—Lost to Edmonton in Smythe Division semifinals.
1988—Replaced as head coach by Rogie Vachon (December 6), with club in fifth place.
1991—Lost to Peoria in quarterfinals of IHL playoffs.

PAGE, PIERRE   C   MIGHTY DUCKS

PERSONAL: Born April 30, 1948, in St. Hermas, Que. ... Played center. ... Shot left. ... Name pronounced PA-zhay.
COLLEGE: Rigaud College, then St. Francis-Xavier (N.S.), then Dalhousie (N.S.).

				REGULAR SEASON							PLAYOFFS			
Season Team	League	Gms.	G	A	Pts.	PIM	+/-	PP	SH		Gms.	G	A	Pts.	PIM
69-70— St. Francis-Xavier		22	16	33	49	...	...	...	...		—	—	—	—	—
70-71— St. Francis-Xavier		25	23	54	77	...	...	...	...		—	—	—	—	—

HEAD COACHING RECORD

BACKGROUND: Consultant, Nova Scotia, Montreal Canadiens organization (1973-74 through 1979-80). ... Assistant coach, Canadian Olympic team (1980). ... Assistant coach, Calgary Flames (1980-81 through 1981-82 and 1985-86 through 1987-88). ... General manager, Colorado Flames (1982-83 and 1983-84). ... General manager/coach, Moncton, Flames organization (1984-85). ... General manager, Quebec Nordiques (1990-91 through 1993-94).

		REGULAR SEASON					PLAYOFFS		
Season Team	League	W	L	T	Pct.	Finish	W	L	Pct.
71-72—Dalhousie University	AUAA	10	8	0	.556	3rd/AUAA	—	—	—
72-73—Dalhousie University	AUAA	7	14	0	.333	8th/AUAA	—	—	—
73-74—Dalhousie University	AUAA	6	11	4	.381	4th/Kelly Division	—	—	—
74-75—Dalhousie University	AUAA	12	6	0	.667	3rd/AUAA	—	—	—
75-76—Dalhousie University	AUAA	6	9	1	.406	6th/AUAA	—	—	—
76-77—Dalhousie University	AUAA	6	13	1	.325	6th/AUAA	—	—	—
77-78—Dalhousie University	AUAA	9	9	2	.500	5th/AUAA	—	—	—
78-79—Dalhousie University	AUAA	13	7	0	.650	2nd/AUAA	6	2	.750
79-80—Dalhousie University	AUAA	20	1	1	.932	1st/Kelly Division	2	3	.400
82-83—Colorado	CHL	41	36	3	.531	2nd/CHL	2	4	.333
83-84—Colorado	CHL	48	25	3	.651	1st/CHL	2	4	.333
84-85—Moncton	AHL	32	40	8	.450	6th/North Division	—	—	—
88-89—Minnesota	NHL	27	37	16	.438	4th/Norris Division	1	4	.200
89-90—Minnesota	NHL	36	40	4	.475	4th/Norris Division	3	4	.429
91-92—Quebec	NHL	17	34	11	.363	5th/Adams Division	—	—	—
92-93—Quebec	NHL	47	27	10	.619	2nd/Adams Division	2	4	.333
93-94—Quebec	NHL	34	42	8	.452	5th/Northeast Division	—	—	—
95-96—Calgary	NHL	34	37	11	.482	2nd/Pacific Division	0	4	.000
96-97—Calgary	NHL	32	41	9	.445	5th/Pacific Division	—	—	—
NHL totals (7 years)		227	258	69	.472	**NHL totals (3 years)**	6	16	.273

NOTES:
1979—Defeated Moncton in AUAA semifinals; defeated Saint Mary's in AUAA semifinals; defeated Guelph in CIAU Championship round; defeated Chicoutimi in CIAU Championship round; lost to Alberta in CIAU Championship finals.
1980—Defeated St. Francis-Xavier in AUAA semifinals; lost to Moncton in AUAA finals.
1983—Lost to Birmingham in Adams Cup semifinals.
1984—Lost to Indianapolis in Adams Cup semifinals.
1989—Lost to Chicago in Norris Division semifinals.
1990—Lost to St. Louis in Norris Division semifinals.
1993—Lost to Montreal in Adams Division semifinals.
1996—Lost to Chicago in Western Conference semifinals.

NHL HEAD COACHES

QUENNEVILLE, JOEL   BLUES

PERSONAL: Born September 15, 1958, in Windsor, Ont. ... Played defense. ... Shot left. ... Full name: Joel Norman Quenneville.
TRANSACTIONS/CAREER NOTES: Selected by Toronto Maple Leafs from Windsor Spitfires in second round (first Maple Leafs pick, 21st overall) of NHL amateur draft (June 15, 1978). ... Traded by Maple Leafs with RW Lanny McDonald to Colorado Rockies for RW Wilf Paiement and LW Pat Hickey (December 1979). ... Injured rib cage (March 1980). ... Underwent surgery to repair torn ligaments in ring finger of left hand (March 1980). ... Sprained ankle, twisted knee and suffered facial lacerations (January 4, 1982). ... Rockies franchise moved to New Jersey and became the Devils (June 30, 1982). ... Traded by Devils with C Steve Tambellini to Calgary Flames for C Mel Bridgman and D Phil Russell (July 1983). ... Traded by Flames with D Richie Dunn to Hartford Whalers for D Mickey Volcan and third-round pick in 1984 draft (August 1983). ... Broke right shoulder (December 18, 1986); missed 42 games. ... Separated left shoulder (January 19, 1989); missed nine games. ... Traded by Whalers to Washington Capitals for future considerations (October 3, 1990). ... Signed as free agent by Maple Leafs (July 30, 1991).
HONORS: Named to OMJHL All-Star second team (1977-78). ... Named to AHL All-Star second team (1991-92).

Season Team	League	REGULAR SEASON								PLAYOFFS				
		Gms.	G	A	Pts.	PIM	+/-	PP	SH	Gms.	G	A	Pts.	PIM
75-76— Windsor	OHA M. Jr.	66	15	33	48	61	...	...	...	—	—	—	—	—
76-77— Windsor	OMJHL	65	19	59	78	169	...	...	...	9	6	5	11	112
77-78— Windsor	OMJHL	66	27	76	103	114	...	...	...	6	2	3	5	17
78-79— Toronto	NHL	61	2	9	11	60	...	...	...	6	0	1	1	4
— New Brunswick	AHL	16	1	10	11	10	...	...	...	—	—	—	—	—
79-80— Toronto	NHL	32	1	4	5	24	...	1	0	—	—	—	—	—
— Colorado Rockies	NHL	35	5	7	12	26	...	1	0	—	—	—	—	—
80-81— Colorado Rockies	NHL	71	10	24	34	86	-24	3	0	—	—	—	—	—
81-82— Colorado Rockies	NHL	64	5	10	15	55	...	0	0	—	—	—	—	—
82-83— New Jersey	NHL	74	5	12	17	46	-13	0	1	—	—	—	—	—
83-84— Hartford	NHL	80	5	8	13	95	-11	0	2	—	—	—	—	—
84-85— Hartford	NHL	79	6	16	22	96	-15	0	0	—	—	—	—	—
85-86— Hartford	NHL	71	5	20	25	83	20	1	0	10	0	2	2	12
86-87— Hartford	NHL	37	3	7	10	24	8	0	1	6	0	0	0	0
87-88— Hartford	NHL	77	1	8	9	44	-13	0	0	6	0	2	2	2
88-89— Hartford	NHL	69	4	7	11	32	3	0	0	4	0	3	3	4
89-90— Hartford	NHL	44	1	4	5	34	9	0	0	—	—	—	—	—
90-91— Washington	NHL	9	1	0	1	0	-8	0	0	—	—	—	—	—
— Baltimore	AHL	59	6	13	19	58	...	...	...	6	1	1	2	6
91-92— St. John's	AHL	73	7	23	30	58	...	...	...	16	0	1	1	10
NHL totals (13 years)		803	54	136	190	705	...	...	...	32	0	8	8	22

HEAD COACHING RECORD

BACKGROUND: Player/coach, St. John's of the AHL (1991-92). ... Assistant coach, St. John's (1992-93). ... Assistant coach, Quebec Nordiques (1994-95). ... Quebec franchise moved to Denver and renamed Colorado Avalanche for 1995-96 season. ... Assistant coach, Colorado Avalanche (1995-96 through January 5, 1997).

Season Team	League	REGULAR SEASON					PLAYOFFS		
		W	L	T	Pct.	Finish	W	L	Pct.
93-94—Springfield	AHL	29	38	13	.444	4th/Northern Division	2	4	.333
96-97—St. Louis	NHL	18	15	7	.538	4th/Central Division	2	4	.333
NHL totals (1 year)		18	15	7	.538	**NHL totals (1 year)**	2	4	.333

NOTES:
1994—Lost to Adirondack in division semifinals of Calder Cup playoffs.
1997—Replaced Mike Keenan as coach (January 6). Lost to Detroit in Western Conference quarterfinals.

RENNEY, TOM   CANUCKS

PERSONAL: Born March 1, 1955, in Cranbrook, B.C.
COLLEGE: North Dakota (degree in physical education).

HEAD COACHING RECORD

BACKGROUND: Assistant coach, Canadian national team (1992). ... Coach, Canadian national team (1993-94 through 1995-96).
HONORS: Named WHL Coach of the Year (1990-91).

Season Team	League	REGULAR SEASON					PLAYOFFS		
		W	L	T	Pct.	Finish	W	L	Pct.
90-91—Kamloops	WHL	50	20	2	.708	1st/West Division	5	7	.417
91-92—Kamloops	WHL	51	17	4	.736	1st/West Division	12	5	.706
96-97—Vancouver	NHL	35	40	7	.470	4th/Pacific Division	—	—	—
NHL totals (1 year)		35	40	7	.470				

NOTES:
1991—Defeated Tri-City in West Division semifinals; lost to Spokane in West Division finals.
1992—Defeated Tacoma in West Division preliminary round; defeated Seattle in West Division finals; defeated Saskatoon in WHL finals.

ROBINSON, LARRY   KINGS

PERSONAL: Born June 2, 1951, in Winchester, Ont. ... Played defense. ... Shot left. ... Full name: Larry Clark Robinson. ... Brother of Moe Robinson, defenseman, Montreal Canadiens (1979-80).
TRANSACTIONS/CAREER NOTES: Selected by Montreal Canadiens from Kitchener Rangers in second round (fourth Canadiens pick, 20th overall) of NHL amateur draft (June 10, 1971). ... Injured knee; missed part of 1978-79 season. ... Separated right shoulder (March 6, 1980). ... Injured groin (October 1980). ... Separated left shoulder (November 14, 1980). ... Broke nose (January 8, 1981). ... Injured left shoulder (October 1982). ... Suffered skin infection behind right knee (October 1983). ... Hyperextended left elbow (March 1985). ... Strained ligaments in right ankle (March 9, 1987). ... Broke right leg (August 1987). ... Sprained right wrist (December 1987). ... Hyperextended knee (May 23,

1989). ... Signed as free agent by Los Angeles Kings (July 26, 1989). ... Suffered food poisoning (March 1990); missed games. ... Injured eye (November 26, 1991); missed two games.

HONORS: Named to COJHL All-Star first team (1969-70). ... Played in NHL All-Star Game (1974, 1976-1978, 1980, 1982, 1986, 1988, 1989 and 1992). ... Won James Norris Memorial Trophy (1976-77 and 1979-80). ... Named to THE SPORTING NEWS All-Star first team (1976-77 through 1979-80). ... Named to NHL All-Star first team (1976-77, 1978-79 and 1979-80). ... Won Conn Smythe Trophy (1977-78). ... Named to NHL All-Star second team (1977-78, 1980-81 and 1985-86). ... Named to THE SPORTING NEWS All-Star second team (1980-81, 1981-82 and 1985-86).

RECORDS: Holds NHL career playoff records for most games—227; and most consecutive years in playoffs—20 (1972-73 through 1991-92). ... Shares NHL career playoff record for most years in playoffs—20 (1972-73 through 1991-92).

MISCELLANEOUS: Member of Stanley Cup championship team (1973, 1976-1979 and 1986).

			REGULAR SEASON								PLAYOFFS				
Season Team	League	Gms.	G	A	Pts.	PIM	+/-	PP	SH		Gms.	G	A	Pts.	PIM
68-69— Brockville	COJHL				Statistics unavailable.										
69-70— Brockville	COJHL	40	22	29	51	74	...	...	...		—	—	—	—	—
70-71— Kitchener	OHA Jr. A	61	12	39	51	65	...	...	...		—	—	—	—	—
71-72— Nova Scotia	AHL	74	10	14	24	54	...	...	...		15	2	10	12	31
72-73— Nova Scotia	AHL	38	6	33	39	33	...	...	...		—	—	—	—	—
— Montreal	NHL	36	2	4	6	20	...	...	...		11	1	4	5	9
73-74— Montreal	NHL	78	6	20	26	66	...	...	...		6	0	1	1	26
74-75— Montreal	NHL	80	14	47	61	76	...	...	...		11	0	4	4	27
75-76— Montreal	NHL	80	10	30	40	59	...	...	...		13	3	3	6	10
76-77— Montreal	NHL	77	19	66	85	45	...	...	...		14	2	10	12	12
77-78— Montreal	NHL	80	13	52	65	39	...	...	...		15	4	*17	/d21	6
78-79— Montreal	NHL	67	16	45	61	33	...	...	...		16	6	9	15	8
79-80— Montreal	NHL	72	14	61	75	39	...	6	0		10	0	4	4	2
80-81— Montreal	NHL	65	12	38	50	37	46	7	0		3	0	1	1	2
81-82— Montreal	NHL	71	12	47	59	41	57	5	1		5	0	1	1	8
82-83— Montreal	NHL	71	14	49	63	33	33	6	0		3	0	0	0	2
83-84— Montreal	NHL	74	9	34	43	39	4	4	0		15	0	5	5	22
84-85— Montreal	NHL	76	14	33	47	44	32	6	0		12	3	8	11	8
85-86— Montreal	NHL	78	19	63	82	39	29	10	0		20	0	13	13	22
86-87— Montreal	NHL	70	13	37	50	44	24	6	0		17	3	17	20	6
87-88— Montreal	NHL	53	6	34	40	30	26	2	0		11	1	4	5	4
88-89— Montreal	NHL	74	4	26	30	22	23	0	0		21	2	8	10	12
89-90— Los Angeles	NHL	64	7	32	39	34	7	1	0		10	2	3	5	10
90-91— Los Angeles	NHL	62	1	22	23	16	22	0	0		12	1	4	5	15
91-92— Los Angeles	NHL	56	3	10	13	37	1	0	0		2	0	0	0	0
NHL totals (20 years)		1384	208	750	958	793	...	...	...		227	28	116	144	211

HEAD COACHING RECORD

BACKGROUND: Assistant coach, New Jersey Devils (1993-94 and 1994-95).

		REGULAR SEASON					PLAYOFFS		
Season Team	League	W	L	T	Pct.	Finish	W	L	Pct.
95-96—Los Angeles	NHL	24	40	18	.402	6th/Pacific Division	—	—	—
96-97—Los Angeles	NHL	28	43	11	.409	6th/Pacific Division	—	—	—
NHL totals (2 years)		52	83	29	.405				

RUFF, LINDY · SABRES

PERSONAL: Born February 17, 1960, in Warburg, Alta. ... Played defense. ... Shot left. ... Full name: Lindy Cameron Ruff.

TRANSACTIONS/CAREER NOTES: Selected by Buffalo Sabres as underage junior in second round (second Sabres pick, 32nd overall) of NHL entry draft (August 9, 1979). ... Fractured ankle (December 1980). ... Broke hand (March 1983). ... Injured shoulder (January 14, 1984). ... Separated shoulder (October 26, 1984). ... Broke left clavicle (March 5, 1986). ... Sprained shoulder (November 1988). ... Traded by Sabres to New York Rangers for fifth-round pick (D Richard Smehlik) in 1990 draft (March 7, 1989). ... Fractured rib (January 23, 1990); missed seven games. ... Broke nose (March 21, 1990). ... Bruised left thigh (April 1990). ... Signed as free agent by Sabres (September 1991). ... Signed as free agent by San Diego Gulls (August 24, 1992).

HONORS: Named to IHL All-Star team (1992-93).

MISCELLANEOUS: Captain of Buffalo Sabres (1986-87 through 1988-89). ... Scored on a penalty shot (vs. Mario Brunetta, November 26, 1989).

			REGULAR SEASON								PLAYOFFS				
Season Team	League	Gms.	G	A	Pts.	PIM	+/-	PP	SH		Gms.	G	A	Pts.	PIM
76-77— Taber	AJHL	60	13	33	46	112	...	...	...		—	—	—	—	—
— Lethbridge	WCHL	2	0	2	2	0	...	...	...		—	—	—	—	—
77-78— Lethbridge	WCHL	66	9	24	33	219	...	...	...		8	2	8	10	4
78-79— Lethbridge	WHL	24	9	18	27	108	...	...	...		6	0	1	1	0
79-80— Buffalo	NHL	63	5	14	19	38	...	1	0		8	1	1	2	19
80-81— Buffalo	NHL	65	8	18	26	121	3	1	0		6	3	1	4	23
81-82— Buffalo	NHL	79	16	32	48	194	1	3	0		4	0	0	0	28
82-83— Buffalo	NHL	60	12	17	29	130	14	2	0		10	4	2	6	47
83-84— Buffalo	NHL	58	14	31	45	101	15	3	0		3	1	0	1	9
84-85— Buffalo	NHL	39	13	11	24	45	-1	2	0		5	2	4	6	15
85-86— Buffalo	NHL	54	20	12	32	158	8	5	1		—	—	—	—	—
86-87— Buffalo	NHL	50	6	14	20	74	-12	0	0		—	—	—	—	—
87-88— Buffalo	NHL	77	2	23	25	179	-9	0	0		6	0	2	2	23
88-89— Buffalo	NHL	63	6	11	17	86	-17	0	0		—	—	—	—	—
— New York Rangers	NHL	13	0	5	5	31	-6	0	0		2	0	0	0	17
89-90— New York Rangers	NHL	56	3	6	9	80	-10	0	0		8	0	3	3	12
90-91— New York Rangers	NHL	14	0	1	1	27	-2	0	0		—	—	—	—	—
91-92— Rochester	AHL	62	10	24	34	110	...	...	...		13	0	4	4	16
92-93— San Diego	IHL	81	10	32	42	100	...	...	...		14	1	6	7	26
NHL totals (12 years)		691	105	195	300	1264	...	1	1		52	11	13	24	193

SCHOENFELD, JIM   COYOTES

PERSONAL: Born September 4, 1952, in Galt, Ont. ... Played defense. ... Shot left. ... Full name: James Grant Schoenfeld. ... Name pronounced SHAHN-fehld.

TRANSACTIONS/CAREER NOTES: Traded by London Knights with D Ken Southwick and RW Rick Kehoe to Hamilton Red Wings for D Gary Geldhart, RW Gordon Brooks, LW Dave Gilmour and Mike Craig (December 1969). ... Traded by Red Wings to Niagara Falls Flyers for C Russ Friesen and D Mike Healey (January 1971). ... Selected by New York Raiders in WHA player selection draft (February 1972). ... Selected by Buffalo Sabres in first round (first Sabres pick, fifth overall) of NHL amateur draft (June 8, 1972). ... Damaged nerve in leg (1972); underwent corrective surgery following season. ... Ruptured spinal disc (1973); missed most of season. ... Underwent back surgery (1973). ... Broke left foot (1974). ... Suffered from mononucleosis (1975). ... Suffered from viral pneumonia (1976). ... Broke right foot (1978). ... Separated shoulder (1978). ... Strained knee (1978). ... Injured hand and suffered from the flu (December 1980); missed nine games. ... Broke left little finger (September 1981). ... Broke metatarsal bone in right foot (October 18, 1981). ... Traded by Sabres with RW Danny Gare, G Bob Sauve and C Derek Smith to Detroit Red Wings for C Dale McCourt, RW Mike Foligno, C Brent Peterson and future considerations (December 1981). ... Separated ribs (October 1982). ... Released by Red Wings (June 1983). ... Signed as free agent by Boston Bruins (August 1983). ... Fractured and separated left shoulder (November 11, 1983); underwent surgery. ... Injured shoulder (February 27, 1984). ... Announced retirement (September 1984). ... Recalled to active player status by Sabres (December 19, 1984). ... Suffered stress fracture in right foot (January, 1985); missed 13 games. ... Announced retirement (June 1985).

HONORS: Named to the NHL All-Star second team (1979-80). ... Played in NHL All-Star Game (1976-77 and 1979-80).

MISCELLANEOUS: Captain of Buffalo Sabres (1974-75 through 1976-77).

		REGULAR SEASON								PLAYOFFS				
Season Team	League	Gms.	G	A	Pts.	PIM	+/-	PP	SH	Gms.	G	A	Pts.	PIM
69-70— London	OHA Jr.	16	1	4	5	81	...	...		—	—	—	—	—
— Hamilton Jr. A.	OHA	32	2	12	14	54	...	...		—	—	—	—	—
70-71— Hamilton Jr. A.	OHA	25	3	19	22	120	...	...		—	—	—	—	—
— Niagara Falls	OHA	30	3	9	12	85	...	...		—	—	—	—	—
71-72— Niagara Falls	OHA	40	6	46	52	*225	...	...		—	—	—	—	—
72-73— Buffalo	NHL	66	4	15	19	178	...	...		6	2	1	3	4
73-74— Cincinnati	AHL	2	0	2	2	4	...	...		—	—	—	—	—
— Buffalo	NHL	28	1	8	9	56	...	...		—	—	—	—	—
74-75— Buffalo	NHL	68	1	19	20	184	...	...		17	1	4	5	38
75-76— Buffalo	NHL	56	2	22	24	114	...	...		8	0	3	3	33
76-77— Buffalo	NHL	65	7	25	32	97	...	...		6	0	0	0	12
77-78— Buffalo	NHL	60	2	20	22	89	...	...		8	0	1	1	28
78-79— Buffalo	NHL	46	8	17	25	67	...	...		3	0	1	1	0
79-80— Buffalo	NHL	77	9	27	36	72	...	4	0	14	0	3	3	18
80-81— Buffalo	NHL	71	8	25	33	110	28	3	0	8	0	0	0	14
81-82— Buffalo	NHL	13	3	2	5	30	5	0	0	—	—	—	—	—
— Detroit	NHL	39	5	9	14	69	2	0	0	—	—	—	—	—
82-83— Detroit	NHL	57	1	10	11	18	-14	0	0	—	—	—	—	—
83-84— Boston	NHL	39	0	2	2	20	18	0	0	—	—	—	—	—
84-85— Buffalo	NHL	34	0	3	3	28	0	0	0	5	0	0	0	4
NHL totals (13 years)		719	51	204	255	1132	...	...	...	75	3	13	16	151

HEAD COACHING RECORD

		REGULAR SEASON					PLAYOFFS		
Season Team	League	W	L	T	Pct.	Finish	W	L	Pct.
84-85— Rochester	AHL	17	6	2	.720	3rd/South Division	—	—	—
85-86— Buffalo	NHL	19	19	5	.500	5th/Adams Division	—	—	—
87-88— New Jersey	NHL	17	12	1	.583	6th/Patrick Division	11	9	.550
88-89— New Jersey	NHL	27	41	12	.413	5th/Patrick Division	—	—	—
89-90— New Jersey	NHL	6	6	2	.500		—	—	—
93-94— Washington	NHL	19	12	6	.595	3rd/Atlantic Division	5	6	.455
94-95— Washington	NHL	22	18	8	.542	3rd/Atlantic Division	3	4	.429
95-96— Washington	NHL	39	32	11	.543	4th/Atlantic Division	2	4	.333
96-97— Washington	NHL	33	40	9	.457	5th/Atlantic Division	—	—	—
NHL totals (8 years)		182	180	54	.502	**NHL totals (4 years)**	21	23	.477

NOTES:
1988—Defeated New York Islanders in Patrick Division semifinals; defeated Washington in Patrick Division final; lost to Boston in Campbell Conference finals.
1994—Defeated Pittsburgh Penguins in Eastern Conference quarterfinals; lost to New York Ranges in Eastern Conference semifinals.
1995—Lost to Pittsburgh in Eastern Conference quarterfinals.
1996—Lost to Pittsburgh in Eastern Conference quarterfinals.

SUTTER, BRIAN   FLAMES

PERSONAL: Born October 7, 1956, in Viking, Alta. ... Played left wing. ... Shot left. ... Full name: Brian Louis Allen Sutter. ... Name pronounced SUH-tuhr. ... Brother of Darryl Sutter, head coach, San Jose Sharks and left winger, Chicago Blackhawks (1979-80 through 1986-87); brother of Brent Sutter, center, Blackhawks; brother of Ron Sutter, center, San Jose Sharks; brother of Rich Sutter, right winger, Chicago Blackhawks; and brother of Duane Sutter, right winger, New York Islanders and Blackhawks (1979-80 through 1989-90) and current head coach, Indianapolis Ice of IHL.

TRANSACTIONS/CAREER NOTES: Selected by St. Louis Blues from Lethbridge Broncos in second round (second Blues pick, 20th overall) of NHL amateur draft (June 1, 1976). ... Suffered hairline fracture of pelvis (November 3, 1983). ... Broke left shoulder (January 16, 1986). ... Re-injured left shoulder (March 8, 1986). ... Damaged left shoulder muscle (November 1986). ... Sprained ankle (November 1987). ... Retired as player and signed as head coach of Blues (June 1988).

HONORS: Played in NHL All-Star Game (1982, 1983 and 1985).

MISCELLANEOUS: Captain of St. Louis Blues (1979-80).

		REGULAR SEASON								PLAYOFFS				
Season Team	League	Gms.	G	A	Pts.	PIM	+/-	PP	SH	Gms.	G	A	Pts.	PIM
72-73— Red Deer	AJHL	51	27	40	67	54	...	...	...	—	—	—	—	—
73-74— Red Deer	AJHL	59	42	54	96	139	...	...	...	—	—	—	—	—
74-75— Lethbridge	WCHL	53	34	47	81	134	...	...	...	6	0	1	1	39
75-76— Lethbridge	WCHL	72	36	56	92	233	...	...	...	7	3	4	7	45
76-77— Kansas City	CHL	38	15	23	38	47	...	...	...	—	—	—	—	—
— St. Louis	NHL	35	4	10	14	82	...	...	...	4	1	0	1	14
77-78— St. Louis	NHL	78	9	13	22	123	...	...	...	—	—	—	—	—
78-79— St. Louis	NHL	77	41	39	80	165	...	...	...	—	—	—	—	—
79-80— St. Louis	NHL	71	23	35	58	156	...	6	0	3	0	0	0	4
80-81— St. Louis	NHL	78	35	34	69	232	12	17	0	11	6	3	9	77
81-82— St. Louis	NHL	74	39	36	75	239	-2	14	0	10	8	6	14	49
82-83— St. Louis	NHL	79	46	30	76	254	-1	11	0	4	2	1	3	10
83-84— St. Louis	NHL	76	32	51	83	162	-6	14	2	11	1	5	6	22
84-85— St. Louis	NHL	77	37	37	74	121	11	14	0	3	2	1	3	2
85-86— St. Louis	NHL	44	19	23	42	87	-12	8	0	9	1	2	3	22
86-87— St. Louis	NHL	14	3	3	6	18	-5	3	0	—	—	—	—	—
87-88— St. Louis	NHL	76	15	22	37	147	-16	4	1	10	0	3	3	49
NHL totals (12 years)		779	303	333	636	1786	...	...	...	65	21	21	42	249

HEAD COACHING RECORD

BACKGROUND: Assistant coach, Team Canada (1991).
HONORS: Won Jack Adams Award (1990-91).

		REGULAR SEASON					PLAYOFFS		
Season Team	League	W	L	T	Pct.	Finish	W	L	Pct.
88-89— St. Louis	NHL	33	35	12	.488	2nd/Norris Division	5	5	.500
89-90— St. Louis	NHL	37	34	9	.519	2nd/Norris Division	7	5	.583
90-91— St. Louis	NHL	47	22	11	.656	2nd/Norris Division	6	7	.462
91-92— St. Louis	NHL	36	33	11	.519	3rd/Norris Division	2	4	.333
92-93— Boston	NHL	51	26	7	.649	1st/Adams Division	0	4	.000
93-94— Boston	NHL	42	29	13	.577	2nd/Northeast Division	6	7	.462
94-95— Boston	NHL	27	18	3	.594	3rd/Northeast Division	1	4	.200
NHL totals (7 years)		273	197	66	.571	NHL totals (7 years)	27	36	.429

NOTES:
1989—Defeated Minnesota in Norris Division semifinals; lost to Chicago in Norris Division finals.
1990—Defeated Toronto in Norris Division semifinals; lost to Chicago in Norris Division finals.
1991—Defeated Detroit in Norris Division semifinals; lost to Minnesota in Norris Division finals.
1992—Lost to Chicago in Norris Division semifinals.
1993—Lost to Buffalo in Adams Division semifinals.
1994—Defeated Montreal in Eastern Conference quarterfinals; lost to New Jersey in Eastern Conference semifinals.
1995—Lost to New Jersey in Eastern Conference quarterfinals.

SUTTER, DARRYL — SHARKS

PERSONAL: Born August 19, 1958, in Viking, Alta. ... Played left wing. ... Shot left. ... Name pronounced SUH-tuhr. ... Brother of Brian Sutter, head coach, Calgary Flames and left winger, St. Louis Blues (1976-77 through 1987-88); brother of Duane Sutter, right winger, New York Islanders and Chicago Blackhawks (1979-80 through 1989-90) and current head coach, Indianapolis Ice of IHL; brother of Rich Sutter, right winger, Blackhawks; brother of Ron Sutter, center, San Jose Sharks; and brother of Brent Sutter, center, Blackhawks.
TRANSACTIONS/CAREER NOTES: Selected by Chicago Blackhawks in 11th round (11th Blackhawks pick, 179th overall) of NHL amateur draft (June 1978). ... Lacerated left elbow, developed infection and underwent surgery (November 27, 1981). ... Broke nose (November 7, 1982). ... Broke ribs (November 1983). ... Fracture left cheekbone and injured left eye (January 2, 1984). ... Underwent arthroscopic surgery to right knee (September 1984). ... Bruised ribs (October 1984). ... Broke left ankle (December 26, 1984). ... Separated right shoulder and underwent surgery (November 13, 1985); missed 30 games. ... Injured knee (February 1987). ... Retired as player and signed as assistant coach of Blackhawks (June 1987).
HONORS: Named top rookie of Japan National League (1978-79). ... Won Dudley (Red) Garrett Memorial Trophy (1979-80). ... Named to AHL All-Star second team (1979-80).
MISCELLANEOUS: Captain of Chicago Blackhawks (1982-83 through 1986-87).

		REGULAR SEASON								PLAYOFFS				
Season Team	League	Gms.	G	A	Pts.	PIM	+/-	PP	SH	Gms.	G	A	Pts.	PIM
74-75— Red Deer	AJHL	60	16	20	36	43	...	...	...	—	—	—	—	—
75-76— Red Deer	AJHL	60	43	93	136	82	...	...	...	—	—	—	—	—
76-77— Red Deer	AJHL	56	55	78	133	131	...	...	...	—	—	—	—	—
— Lethbridge	WCHL	1	1	0	1	0	...	...	...	15	3	7	10	13
77-78— Lethbridge	WCHL	68	33	48	81	119	...	...	...	8	4	9	13	2
78-79— New Brunswick	AHL	19	7	6	13	6	...	...	...	5	1	2	3	0
— Iwakura	Japan	20	28	13	41	0	...	...	...	—	—	—	—	—
79-80— New Brunswick	AHL	69	35	31	66	69	...	...	...	12	6	6	12	8
— Chicago	NHL	8	2	0	2	2	...	0	0	7	3	1	4	2
80-81— Chicago	NHL	76	40	22	62	86	-1	14	0	3	3	1	4	2
81-82— Chicago	NHL	40	23	12	35	31	0	4	3	3	0	1	1	2
82-83— Chicago	NHL	80	31	30	61	53	18	10	0	13	4	6	10	8
83-84— Chicago	NHL	59	20	20	40	44	-18	8	0	5	1	1	2	0
84-85— Chicago	NHL	49	20	18	38	12	8	2	0	15	12	7	19	12
85-86— Chicago	NHL	50	17	10	27	44	-15	3	0	3	1	2	3	0
86-87— Chicago	NHL	44	8	6	14	16	-3	1	0	2	0	0	0	0
NHL totals (8 years)		406	161	118	279	288	...	42	3	51	24	19	43	26

HEAD COACHING RECORD

BACKGROUND: Assistant coach, Chicago Blackhawks (1987-88). ... Associate coach, Blackhwaks (1991-92). ... Special assistant to general manager, Blackhawks (1995-96 and 1996-97).

Season Team	League	REGULAR SEASON						PLAYOFFS		
		W	L	T	Pct.	Finish		W	L	Pct.
88-89—Saginaw	IHL	46	26	10	.622	2nd/East Division		2	4	.333
89-90—Indianapolis	IHL	53	21	8	.695	1st/West Division		12	2	.857
90-91—Indianapolis	IHL	48	29	5	.616	2nd/East Division		3	4	.429
92-93—Chicago	NHL	47	25	12	.631	1st/Norris Division		0	4	.000
93-94—Chicago	NHL	39	36	9	.518	5th/Central Division		2	4	.333
94-95—Chicago	NHL	24	19	5	.552	3rd/Central Division		9	7	.563
NHL totals (3 years)		110	80	26	.569	NHL totals (3 years)		11	15	.423

NOTES:

1989—Lost to Fort Wayne in quarterfinals of Turner Cup playoffs.
1990—Defeated Peoria in quarterfinals of Turner Cup playoffs; defeated Salt Lake City in semifinals of Turner Cup playoffs; defeated Muskegon in Turner Cup finals.
1991—Lost to Fort Wayne in quarterfinals of Turner Cup playoffs.
1993—Lost to St. Louis in Norris Division semifinals.
1994—Lost to Toronto in Western Conference quarterfinals.
1995—Defeated Toronto in Western Conference quarterfinals; defeated Vancouver in Western Conference semifinals; lost to Detroit in Western Conference finals.

VIGNEAULT, ALAIN   CANADIENS

PERSONAL: Born May 14, 1961, in Quebec City, Quebec. ... Played defense. ... Shot right.
TRANSACTIONS/CAREER NOTES: Selected by St. Louis Blues in eighth round (seventh Blues pick, 167th overall) of NHL entry draft (June 1981).

Season Team	League	REGULAR SEASON								PLAYOFFS				
		Gms.	G	A	Pts.	PIM	+/-	PP	SH	Gms.	G	A	Pts.	PIM
79-80— Hull	QJHL	35	5	34	39	82	...	...	...	—	—	—	—	—
— Trois Rivieres Flam.	QJHL	28	6	19	25	93	...	...	...	—	—	—	—	—
80-81— Trois Rivieres Flam.	QJHL	67	7	55	62	181	...	...	...	—	—	—	—	—
81-82— Salt Lake City	CHL	64	2	10	12	266	...	...	...	—	—	—	—	—
— St. Louis	NHL	14	1	2	3	43	-1	0	0	—	—	—	—	—
82-83— Salt Lake City	CHL	33	1	4	5	189	...	...	...	—	—	—	—	—
— St. Louis	NHL	28	1	3	4	39	-4	0	0	—	—	—	—	—
83-84— Montana	CHL	47	2	14	16	139	...	...	...	—	—	—	—	—
— Maine	AHL	11	0	1	1	46	...	...	...	—	—	—	—	—
NHL totals (2 years)		42	2	5	7	82	-5	0	0					

HEAD COACHING RECORD

BACKGROUND: Assistant coach, Canadian junior team (1989 and 1991). ... Assistant coach, Ottawa Senators (1992-93 through November 20, 1995).
HONORS: Canadian Coach of the Year (1987-99).

Season Team	League	REGULAR SEASON						PLAYOFFS		
		W	L	T	Pct.	Finish		W	L	Pct.
86-87—Trois-Rivieres	QMJHL	26	37	2	.415	5th/Frank Dilio Division		—	—	—
87-88—Hull	QMJHL	43	23	4	.643	1st Robert Le Bel Division		12	7	.632
88-89—Hull	QMJHL	40	25	5	.607	3rd		5	4	.556
89-90—Hull	QMJHL	36	29	5	.550	T6th		4	7	.364
90-91—Hull	QMJHL	33	25	7	.562	2nd/Robert Le Bel Division		2	4	.333
91-92—Hull	QMJHL	40	23	5	.625	2nd/Robert Le Bel Division		2	4	.333
95-96—Beauport	QMJHL	19	7	5	.694	1st/Frank Dilio Division		13	7	.650
96-97—Beauport	QMJHL	24	44	2	.357	6th/Frank Dilio Division		1	3	.250

NOTES:

1988—Defeated Granby in quarterfinals of President Cup playoffs; defeated Laval in semifinals of President Cup playoffs; defeated Drummondville in President Cup finals
1989—Defeated St. Jean in quarterfinals of President Cup playoffs; lost to Victoriaville in semifinals of President Cup playoffs.
1990—Defeated Longueuil in quarterfinals of President Cup playoffs; lost to Laval in semifinals of President Cup playoffs.
1991—Lost to Laval in quarterfinals of President Cup playoffs.
1992—Lost to Laval in quarterfinals of President Cup playoffs.

WILSON, RON   CAPITALS

PERSONAL: Born May 28, 1955, in Windsor, Ont. ... Played defense. ... Shot right. ... Full name: Ronald Lawrence Wilson. ... Son of Larry Wilson, center, Detroit Red Wings and Chicago Blackhawks (1949-50 through 1955-56) and coach, Red Wings (1976-77); and nephew of Johnny Wilson, left winger with four NHL teams (1949-50 through 1961-62) and coach with four NHL teams and two WHA teams (1969-70 through 1979-80).
COLLEGE: Providence (bachelor of arts degree in economics).
TRANSACTIONS/CAREER NOTES: Selected by Toronto Maple Leafs in seventh round (seventh Maple Leafs pick, 132nd overall) in NHL entry draft (June 3, 1975). ... Loaned by Davos club to Minnesota North Stars for remainder of NHL season and playoffs (March 1985). ... Loaned by Davos club to Minnesota North Stars for remainder of NHL season and playoffs (March 1986). ... Traded by Davos to Minnesota North Stars for D Craig Levie (May 1986). ... Separated shoulder (March 9, 1987).
HONORS: Named to NCAA All-America East first team (1974-75 and 1975-76). ... Named to ECAC All-Star team (1973-74 through 1976-77). ... Named ECAC Player of the Year (1974-75).

Season Team	League	REGULAR SEASON								PLAYOFFS				
		Gms.	G	A	Pts.	PIM	+/-	PP	SH	Gms.	G	A	Pts.	PIM
73-74 — Providence College.........	ECAC	26	16	22	38	...	...	...	...	—	—	—	—	—
74-75 — Providence College.........	ECAC	27	26	61	87	12	...	...	...	—	—	—	—	—
— U.S. national team..........	Int'l	27	5	32	37	42	...	...	...	—	—	—	—	—
75-76 — Providence College.........	ECAC	28	19	47	66	44	...	...	...	—	—	—	—	—
76-77 — Providence College.........	ECAC	30	17	42	59	62	...	...	...	—	—	—	—	—
— Dallas	CHL	4	1	0	1	2	...	...	...	—	—	—	—	—
77-78 — Dallas	CHL	67	31	38	69	18	...	...	...	—	—	—	—	—
— Toronto..........................	NHL	13	2	1	3	0	...	...	...	—	—	—	—	—
78-79 — New Brunswick	AHL	31	11	20	31	13	...	...	...	—	—	—	—	—
— Toronto..........................	NHL	46	5	12	17	4	...	...	...	3	0	1	1	0
79-80 — New Brunswick	AHL	43	20	43	63	10	...	...	...	—	—	—	—	—
— Toronto..........................	NHL	5	0	2	2	0	...	0	0	3	1	2	3	2
80-81 — Davos HC	Switz.	Statistics unavailable.												
81-82 — Davos HC	Switz.	Statistics unavailable.												
82-83 — Davos HC	Switz.	Statistics unavailable.												
83-84 — Davos HC	Switz.	Statistics unavailable.												
84-85 — Davos HC	Switz.	Statistics unavailable.												
— Minnesota	NHL	13	4	8	12	2	-1	0	0	9	1	6	7	2
85-86 — Davos HC	Switz.	Statistics unavailable.												
— Minnesota	NHL	11	1	3	4	8	-2	1	0	5	2	4	6	4
86-87 — Minnesota	NHL	65	12	29	41	36	-9	6	0	—	—	—	—	—
87-88 — Minnesota	NHL	24	2	12	14	16	-4	1	0	—	—	—	—	—
NHL totals (7 years).................		177	26	67	93	66	...	...	...	20	4	13	17	8

HEAD COACHING RECORD

BACKGROUND: Assistant coach, Milwaukee, Vancouver Canucks organization (1989-90). ... Served as interim coach of Milwaukee while Ron Lapointe was hospitalized for cancer treatments (February and March 1990; team went 9-10). ... Assistant coach, Canucks (1990-91 through 1992-93).

Season Team	League	REGULAR SEASON					PLAYOFFS		
		W	L	T	Pct.	Finish	W	L	Pct.
93-94 — Anaheim	NHL	33	46	5	.423	4th/Pacific Division	—	—	—
94-95 — Anaheim	NHL	16	27	5	.385	6th/Pacific Division	—	—	—
95-96 — Anaheim	NHL	35	39	8	.476	4th/Pacific Division	—	—	—
96-97 — Anaheim	NHL	36	33	13	.518	2nd/Pacific Division	4	7	.364
NHL totals (4 years)............................		120	145	31	.458	NHL totals (1 year)	4	7	.364

NOTES:

1997—Defeated Phoenix in Western Conference quarterfinals; lost to Detroit in Western Conference semifinals.

Super Mario

He was Magnifique

He lived up to every expectation.
He single-handedly rescued a franchise. He turned hockey into art.
There will never be another like Mario Lemieux.

By Larry Wigge

October 11, 1984. Boston Garden.

First impressions are not misleading. Not when you are talking about Mario Lemieux, anyway. Few players have broken into the NHL with the kind of accolades as this lanky, 19-year-old French-Canadian with a tenuous command of English. It wasn't long before he showed us that was no exaggeration.

I remember watching on TV Lemieux's first game in a Penguins uniform. With the great ones, you don't have to wait long to see magic.

First shot in the NHL. Goal.

Like a shot, Lemieux bolted out of his zone. He was one-on-one with future Hall of Famer Ray Bourque. What I saw at that moment was the size of a giant, the speed of a thoroughbred and the board-inghouse reach of a talent that would go unmatched for the next 13 years. No one turns Bourque around like Lemieux did on that night.

One year earlier, I had seen Lemieux play one night for the Laval Voisins of the Quebec Major Junior Hockey League. A writer friend of mine rented a car in Montreal, and we traveled to Verdun to see him play. After two periods, my friend wanted to leave. Lemieux had disappointed him. No goals, no assists.

We went to the parking lot but found we were blocked from leaving. So, we went back into the arena. And Lemieux made the night unforgettable for us, getting three goals and two assists in the third period.

His fans in Quebec called him Magnifique. The name was and still is perfect.

There is no mistaking the long arms and gangly legs, that bent-over style as he surveys the defense. He is the quintessential package—a sharpshooter and precision passer who works magic with the puck. He's Michael Jordan on skates.

In his first few years in the league, skeptics said he was a floater. But two Stanley Cups, three MVP awards and six scoring championships have changed that. He's an unparalleled leader.

Two of those scoring titles have come in the past two years. Those accomplishments are even more remarkable considering they came after he missed a year because of Hodgkin's disease. But all of that is just a memory now. Super Mario has retired on his terms—on top.

Few athletes willingly quit when they're in that position. Jim Brown walked away from football at 30. Ken Dryden left hockey at 31—just like Mario.

Mario Lemieux is a quiet giant in his field. Because he lets few people get close to him, some consider him standoffish and uncaring; they say he is retiring because he's not as passionate about the game as Wayne Gretzky or Mark Messier or Gordie Howe, that he doesn't have the same fire the greats have had.

That perception is totally off-base.

While in Pittsburgh in the fall of 1995 to do a story on Lemieux's comeback, I was treated like a king by Mario. He gave me and our photographer access to the team's weight room and training table. He even offered me a chance to play a round of golf with him. He is a friend of mine, a friend of the game, not a quitter. He tried to set commissioner Gary Bettman straight last summer on the hooking and holding that has cut down the effectiveness of the game's stars. Unfortunately, he didn't listen.

Super Mario is going out because he is frustrated at the state of the league, he is frustrated that he can no longer do the things he did five or six years ago. He lapped the field in scoring the past two seasons, but he couldn't beat a defenseman one-on-one the way he once did. His standards are obviously greater than any of us could ever imagine.

He is going out with a two-points-per-game-average in his career—613 goals and 881 assists in 744 regular-season games. Only Gretzky can say that.

"One thing Mario did that few players have done is save a franchise for a city," Gretzky says. "The Penguins were dead in the water in Pittsburgh when he got there, drawing 6,000 people on good nights. He put people in all the seats and created great interest in hockey in the United States."

He not only beat Ray Bourque, he also beat the reputation as a selfish player without heart. He beat Hodgkin's disease and he beat the clock that runs out on so many of us. And he leaves the game without any regrets.

The day I talked to Lemieux, the Orioles' Cal Ripken had just broken Lou Gehrig's record of 2,130 consecutive games. I asked Mario if he ever dreamed of trading his body for, say Ripken's, so he could have played every day.

"No second guesses, whatsoever," he said. "Sometimes it's difficult to accept that you have so much to offer and it's taken away from you in a sense. It's frustrating, but you go on.

"Sure, I would have liked to have been in the lineup every night like Cal Ripken, but you go on in life with what God gave you—and I was blessed with a great deal of talent that I am proud of. I can't ask for more than that."

Larry Wigge has covered hockey for The Sporting News since 1969.

This article originally appeared in the May 5, 1997 issue of The Sporting News.

Career retrospective

Regular season records

Most goals, period...*4
Most shorthanded goals, season 13
Most overtime goals, career....................................9
Most overtime points, career 19
Highest goals-per-game average, career..............823

Playoff records

Most goals, game...*5
Most points, game *8
Most goals, period..*4
Most points, period *4
Highest goals-per-game average, career..............787
Most Conn Smythe Trophies won *2

All-Star game records

Most goals, game..*4
Most points, game 6
Most points, career *20

Notes on Lemieux's 613 goals

Of Lemieux's 613 regular season goals:
- 330 goals were scored at home
- 280 were scored on the road
- 3 were scored in neutral-site games
- 53 were unassisted
- 6 were scored on penalty shots (in eight attempts)
- 201 came on the power play
- 47 were shorthanded

- 65 were game-winning goals
- 186 were scored in the first period (30.3%)
- 201 were scored in the second period (32.8%)
- 217 were scored in the third period (35.4%)
- 9 were scored in overtime (1.5%)
- Lemieux scored on 114 different goaltenders and added 29 into an empty net.
- 110 different players were credited with assists on Lemieux's goals, led by Paul Coffey's 72.

Multiple-goal games:
- Lemieux recorded two-or-more goals in 140 of his 745 regular-season games (18.8%)
- 101 were two-goal games
- Of his 39 hat tricks (tied for second-most in NHL history with Mike Bossy and second to Wayne Gretzky's 49), 26 were three-goal games, 10 were four-goal games and three were five-goal games.

Pittsburgh Penguins records

Career
Most goals 613
Most assists 881
Most points 1,494
Most game-winning goals 65
Most shorthanded goals...47
Most hat tricks 39

Season
Most goals 85 (1988-89)
Most assists 114 (1988-89)
Most points 199 (1988-89)
Most power-play goals 31 (1995-96)
Most hat tricks 9 (1988-89)

Game
Most goals ....5 (three times)
Most assists ....*6 (three times)
Most points ....8 (twice)

Regular season scoring against goaltenders

Name, teams, goals
1. John Vanbiesbrouck, NYR-Fla............................30
2. Empty net goal 29
3. Ron Hextall, Phi.-Que. 19
4. Don Beaupre, Min.-Was.-Ott. 15
5. Pete Peters, Bos.-Was.-Phi. 14
   Kelly Hrudey, NYI-L.A. 14
   Bill Ranford, Bos.-Edm. 14
   Glenn Healy, L.A.-NYI-NYR 14
9. Sean Burke, N.J.-Har. 13
10. Alain Chevrier, N.J.-Chi. 11
    Bob Froese, Phi-NYR 11
    Mario Gosselin, Que.-Har. 11
    Mike Liut, Har. 11
    Clint Malarchuk, Que.-Was.-Buf. 11
    Ken Wregget, Tor.-Phi. 11
16. Jon Casey, Min.-Bos.-StL 10
    Mark Fitzpatrick, L.A.-NYI-Fla. 10
    Glen Hanlon, NYR-Det.......................................10
    Mike Richter, NYR 10
    Tommy Soderstrom, Phi.-NYI 10

Players assisting on regular season goals

Player, # of assists
1. Paul Coffey...72
2. Jaromir Jagr..68

3. Kevin Stevens..64
4. Ron Francis 60
5. Bob Errey...51
6. Rob Brown..39
7. Doug Bodger 31
8. Rick Tocchet...30
9. Moe Mantha..27
10. Terry Ruskowski...25
11. Larry Murphy 23
    Dan Quinn 23
13. Randy Cunneyworth...22
    Tomas Sandstrom 22
15. Zarley Zalapski 18
16. Craig Simpson 17
    Warren Young 17
18. Mike Bullard 14
    John Cullen 14
    Joe Muller 14
21. Randy Hillier 13
    Mark Recchi 13
23. Phil Bourque...12
    Rod Buskas 12
    Markus Naslund 12
    Doug Shedden 12
27. Petr Nedved 11
    Ville Siren..11
    Sergei Zubov 11
30. Wayne Babych 10
    Kevin Hatcher...10
    Jim Johnson..10

Statistical information compiled by Steve Bovino and Brian Coe of the Pittsburgh Penguins media relations.

* Shares record.

THE SPORTING NEWS

1996-97 NATIONAL HOCKEY LEAGUE LEADERS

Points
Mario Lemieux, Pittsburgh 122
Teemu Selanne, Anaheim...............................109
Paul Kariya, Anaheim.......................................99
Wayne Gretzky, N.Y. Rangers 97
John LeClair, Philadelphia................................97
Jaromir Jagr, Pittsburgh 95
Mats Sundin, Toronto 94
Ron Francis, Pittsburgh 90
Zigmund Palffy, N.Y. Islanders 90
Brendan Shanahan, Har.-Det............................88
Many tied with 82

Points by a defenseman
Brian Leetch, N.Y. Rangers 78
Sandis Ozolinsh, Colorado................................68
Niklas Lidstrom, Detroit.....................................57
Oleg Tverdovsky, Phoenix.................................55
Kevin Hatcher, Pittsburgh 54

Goals
Keith Tkachuk, Phoenix......................................52
Teemu Selanne, Anaheim..................................51
John LeClair, Philadelphia.................................50
Mario Lemieux, Pittsburgh 50
Zigmund Palffy, N.Y. Islanders 48
Jaromir Jagr, Pittsburgh 47
Brendan Shanahan, Har.-Det............................47
Peter Bondra, Washington.................................46
Paul Kariya, Anaheim.......................................44
Brett Hull, St. Louis 42

Assists
Wayne Gretzky, N.Y. Rangers 72
Mario Lemieux, Pittsburgh 72
Ron Francis, Pittsburgh 63
Steve Yzerman, Detroit 63
Doug Weight, Edmonton....................................61
Doug Gilmour, Tor.-N.J......................................60
Adam Oates, Bos.-Was.....................................60
Pierre Turgeon, Mon.-St.L.................................59
Peter Forsberg, Colorado..................................58
Brian Leetch, N.Y. Rangers 58
Teemu Selanne, Anaheim..................................58

Power-play goals
Brendan Shanahan, Har.-Det............................20
Ryan Smyth, Edmonton.....................................20
Paul Kariya, Anaheim.......................................15
Mario Lemieux, Pittsburgh 15
Keith Jones, Was.-Col.......................................14
Andrei Kovalenko, Edmonton............................14

Shorthanded goals
Michael Peca, Buffalo 6
Trent Klatt, Philadelphia 5
Mark Messier, N.Y. Rangers 5
Mike Modano, Dallas 5
Many tied with 4

Game-winning goals
Paul Kariya, Anaheim.......................................10
Mark Messier, N.Y. Rangers..............................9
Mike Modano, Dallas 9
Bill Guerin, New Jersey.....................................9

Teemu Selanne, Anaheim.................................8
Mats Sundin, Toronto 8

Game-tying goals
Adam Graves, N.Y. Rangers..............................5
Stu Barnes, Fla.-Pit..3
Theoren Fleury, Calgary 3
Many tied with 2

Shots
Paul Kariya, Anaheim......................................340
Theoren Fleury, Calgary 336
Brendan Shanahan, Har.-Det...........................336
Mario Lemieux, Pittsburgh 327
John LeClair, Philadelphia...............................324

Shooting percentage
(82 shots minimum)
Miroslav Satan, Edm.-Buf................................21.0
Jaromir Jagr, Pittsburgh 20.1
Martin Gelinas, Vancouver..............................19.8
Andrei Kovalenko, Edmonton...........................19.6
Teemu Selanne, Anaheim................................18.7

Plus/minus
John LeClair, Philadelphia...............................44
Mike Modano, Dallas 43
Dave Andreychuk, New Jersey.........................38
Vladimir Konstantinov, Detroit..........................38
Darryl Sydor, Dallas 37

Penalty minutes
Gino Odjick, Vancouver....................................371
Bob Probert, Chicago.......................................326
Paul Laus, Florida 313
Rob Ray, Buffalo 286
Tie Domi, Toronto 275
Matthew Barnaby, Buffalo 249
Donald Brashear, Mon.-Van.............................245
Scott Daniels, Philadelphia 237
Enrico Ciccone, Chicago 233
Keith Tkachuk, Phoenix....................................228

Consecutive-game point streaks
Adam Oates, Boston 20
Eric Lindros, Philadelphia.................................17
Wayne Gretzky, N.Y. Rangers 15
Mario Lemieux, Pittsburgh 15
Brian Leetch, N.Y. Rangers 14

Consecutive-game goal streaks
Jaromir Jagr, Pittsburgh 9
Mario Lemieux, Pittsburgh 7
Peter Bondra, Washington 6
Peter Forsberg, Colorado 6
Brett Hull, St. Louis 6
Jaromir Jagr, Pittsburgh 6
Mike Modano, Dallas 6

Consecutive-game assist streaks
Adam Oates, Boston 14
Vincent Damphousse, Montreal..........................8
Kevin Hatcher, Pittsburgh 8
Bernie Nicholls, San Jose 8
Doug Weight, Edmonton (twice)..........................8
Steve Yzerman, Detroit 8

Most games scoring three or more goals

Brendan Shanahan, Detroit 3
Ray Sheppard, Florida 3
Many tied with 2

Points by a rookie

Jarome Iginla, Calgary 50
Bryan Berard, N.Y. Islanders 48
Janne Niinimaa, Philadelphia 44
Jim Campbell, St. Louis 43
Sergei Berezin, Toronto 41

Goals by a rookie

Sergei Berezin, Toronto 25
Jim Campbell, St. Louis 23
Jarome Iginla, Calgary 21
Jonas Hoglund, Calgary 19
Mike Grier, Edmonton 15
Daymond Langkow, Tampa Bay 15
Ethan Moreau, Chicago 15

Assists by a rookie

Bryan Berard, N.Y. Islanders 40
Janne Niinimaa, Philadelphia 40
Jarome Iginla, Calgary 29
Jamie Langenbrunner, Dallas 26
Steve Sullivan, N.J.-Tor. 25

GOALTENDING

Games

Felix Potvin, Toronto 74
Grant Fuhr, St. Louis 73
Curtis Joseph, Edmonton 72
Nikolai Khabibulin, Phoenix 72
Martin Brodeur, New Jersey 67
Dominik Hasek, Buffalo 67
Guy Hebert, Anaheim 67

Minutes

Felix Potvin, Toronto 4271
Grant Fuhr, St. Louis 4261
Curtis Joseph, Edmonton 4100
Nikolai Khabibulin, Phoenix 4091
Dominik Hasek, Buffalo 4037

Goals allowed

Felix Potvin, Toronto 224
Curtis Joseph, Edmonton 200
Grant Fuhr, St. Louis 193
Nikolai Khabibulin, Phoenix 193
Guy Hebert, Anaheim 172

Shutouts

Martin Brodeur, New Jersey 10
Nikolai Khabibulin, Phoenix 7
Patrick Roy, Colorado 7
Curtis Joseph, Edmonton 6
Chris Osgood, Detroit 6

Lowest goals-against average
(25 games played minimum)

Martin Brodeur, New Jersey 1.88
Andy Moog, Dallas 2.15
Jeff Hackett, Chicago 2.16
Dominik Hasek, Buffalo 2.27
John Vanbiesbrouck, Florida 2.29

Highest goals-against average
(25 games played minimum)

Jason Muzzatti, Hartford 3.43
Robbie Tallas, Boston 3.33
Corey Hirsch, Vancouver 3.27
Bill Ranford, Bos.-Was. 3.250
Ken Wreggett, Pittsburgh 3.246

Games won

Patrick Roy, Colorado 38
Martin Brodeur, New Jersey 37
Dominik Hasek, Buffalo 37
Grant Fuhr, St. Louis 33
Mike Richter, N.Y. Rangers 33

Best winning percentage
(25 games played minimum)

Patrick Roy, Col. (38-15-7) .... .692
Martin Brodeur, N.J. (37-14-13) .... .680
Andy Moog, Dal. (28-13-5) .... .663
Ron Hextall, Phi. (31-16-5) .... .644
Patrick Lalime, Pit. (21-12-2) .... .629

Worst winning percentage
(25 games played minimum)

Stephane Fiset, L.A. (13-24-5) .... .3690
Olaf Kolzig, Was. (8-15-4) .... .3704
Ed Belfour, Chi.-S.J. (14-24-6) .... .386
Corey Hirsch, Van. (12-20-4) .... .389
Dwayne Roloson, Cal. (9-14-3) .... .404

Games lost

Felix Potvin, Toronto 36
Nikolai Khabibulin, Phoenix 33
Jim Carey, Was.-Bos. 31
Curtis Joseph, Edmonton 29
Rick Tabaracci, Cal.-T.B. 29

Shots against

Felix Potvin, Toronto 2438
Dominik Hasek, Buffalo 2177
Curtis Joseph, Edmonton 2144
Guy Hebert, Anaheim 2133
Nikolai Khabibulin, Phoenix 2094

Saves

Felix Potvin, Toronto 2214
Dominik Hasek, Buffalo 2024
Guy Hebert, Anaheim 1961
Curtis Joseph, Edmonton 1944
Nikolai Khabibulin, Phoenix 1901

Highest save percentage
(25 games played minimum)

Dominik Hasek, Buffalo .... .930
Jeff Hackett, Chicago .... .92657
Martin Brodeur, New Jersey .... .92657
Patrick Roy, Colorado .... .923
Guy Hebert, Anaheim .... .9194
John Vanbiesbrouck, Florida .... .9191

Lowest save percentage
(25 games played minimum)

Robbie Tallas, Boston .... .882
Jim Carey, Was.-Bos. .... .886
Bill Ranford, Bos.-Was. .... .887
Pat Jablonski, Mon.-Pho. .... .8875
Jason Muzzatti, Hartford .... .8883

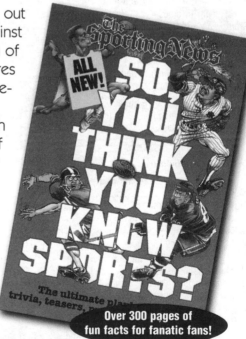
– 480 –